OUT OF MANY

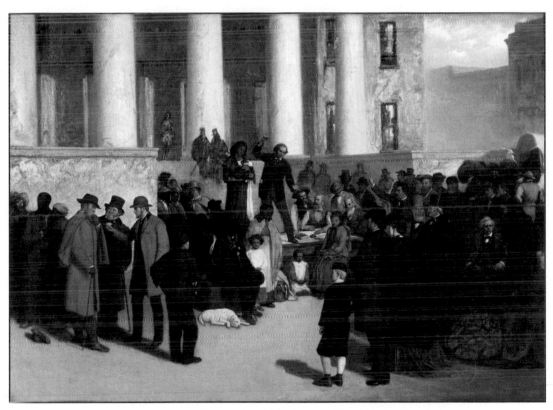

Thomas Satterwhite Noble, *Last Sale of Slaves on the Courthouse Steps*, 1860, oil on canvas, Missouri Historical Society.

OUT OF MANY

A History of the American People

Media Research Update

Fourth Edition

John Mack Faragher
YALE UNIVERSITY

Mari Jo Buhle
BROWN UNIVERSITY

Daniel Czitrom
MOUNT HOLYOKE COLLEGE

Susan H. Armitage
WASHINGTON STATE UNIVERSITY

Prentice Hall

Upper Saddle River, New Jersey 07458

Editorial Director: Charlyce Jones Owen
Senior Acquisitions Editor: Charles Cavaliere
Senior Media Editor: Deborah O'Connell
VP, Editor-in-Chief of Development: Rochelle Diogenes
Production Editor: Jean Lapidus, Jan Schwartz
Creative Director: Leslie Osher
Art Director: Ximena Tamvakopoulos
Marketing Managers: Claire Rehwinkel, Heather Shelstad
Interior and Cover Designer: C2K, Inc.
Scanning: Central Scanning Services
Cover Image Specialist: Karen Sanatar
AVP, Director of Production and Manufacturing: Barbara Kittle
Manufacturing Manager: Nick Sklitsis

Manufacturing Buyer: Sherry Lewis, Tricia Kenny
Photo Researcher: Linda Sykes
Director, Image Resource Center: Melinda Reo
Copy Editor: Stephen C. Hopkins
Line Art Manager: Guy Ruggiero
Artist: Mirella Signoretto
Photo Permissions Coordinator: Carolyn Gauntt
Editorial Assistant: Shannon Corliss
Indexer: Murray Fisher
Text Permissions: The Permissions Group
Cartographers: Alice and William Thiede/CARTO-GRAPHICS;
Mirella Signoretto

Cover Art: Thomas Satterwhite Noble, *Last Sale of Slaves on the
Courthouse Steps*, 1860, oil on canvas, Missouri
Historical Society

Credits and acknowledgments for materials borrowed from
other sources and reproduced, with permission, in this textbook
appear on page C-1.

This book was set in 11/12 Weiss by the TSI Graphics
And was printed and bound by RR Donnelley & Sons Company.
The cover was printed by Phoenix Color Corp.

Printed in the United States of America
10 9 8 7 6 5 4 3 2 1

ISBN 0-13-150259-X

Pearson Education LTD.
Pearson Education Australia PTY, Limited
Pearson Education Singapore, Pte. Ltd.
Pearson Education North Asia Ltd.
Pearson Education Canada, Ltd.
Pearson Educación de Mexico, S.A. de C.V.
Pearson Education—Japan
Pearson Education Malaysia, Pte. Ltd.

TO OUR STUDENTS,

OUR SISTERS,

AND OUR BROTHERS

BRIEF CONTENTS

CONTENTS

1 A Continent of Villages, to 1500 1

> **Community & Memory:
> The Battle Over Burials 26**
>
>
>
> **Researching the Past 27**

2 When Worlds Collide, 1492–1590 28

3 Planting Colonies in North America, 1588–1701 52

Community & Memory: The Invention of the Liberty Bell 174

Researching the Past 175

8 The United States of North America, 1787–1800 206

9 An Agrarian Republic, 1790–1824 236

Community & Memory: In the Footsteps of Lewis and Clark 271

Researching the Past 272

10 The Growth of Democracy, 1824–1840 273

11 The South and Slavery, 1790s–1850s 307

12 Industry and the North, 1790s–1840s 339

13 Coming to Terms with the New Age, 1820s–1850s 367

Community & Memory: Remembering the Alamo 432

Researching the Past 433

16 The Civil War, 1861–1865 465

19 The Incorporation of America, 1865–1900   564

Community & Memory: Representing Chicago's History   595

20 Commonwealth and Empire, 1870–1900   597

Community & Memory:
Battle for the Lower East Side 663

Researching the Past 664

23 The Twenties, 1920–1929   696

24 The Great Depression and the New Deal, 1929–1940   732

25 World War II, 1941–1945 768

Community & Memory: Exhibiting the *Enola Gay* 805

Researching the Past 806

26 The Cold War, 1945–1952 807

**Community & Memory:
Flying the "Stars and Bars"   900**

Researching the Past   901

29 War at Home, War Abroad, 1965–1974 902

30 The Conservative Ascendancy, 1974–1987 938

31 Toward a Transnational America, since 1988 974

**Community & Memory:
The World Trade Center and Ways
of Remembering 1006**

Researching the Past 1007

MAPS

U.S. HISTORY DOCUMENTS CD-ROM

Over 300 Primary Source Documents

PREFACE

*O*ut of Many: A History of the American People, fourth edition, offers a distinctive and timely approach to American history, highlighting the experiences of diverse communities of Americans in the unfolding story of our country. The stories of these communities offer a way of examining the complex historical forces shaping people's lives at various moments in our past. The debates and conflicts surrounding the most momentous issues in our national life—independence, emerging democracy, slavery, westward settlement, imperial expansion, economic depression, war, technological change—were largely worked out in the context of local communities. Through communities we focus on the persistent tensions between everyday life and those larger decisions and events that continually reshape the circumstances of local life. Each chapter opens with a description of a representative community. Some of these portraits feature American communities struggling with one another: African slaves and English masters on the rice plantations of colonial Georgia, or *Tejanos* and Americans during the Texas war of independence. Other chapters feature portraits of communities facing social change: the feminists of Seneca Falls, New York, in 1848, or the African Americans of Montgomery, Alabama, in 1955. As the story unfolds we find communities growing to include ever larger groups of Americans: the soldiers from every colony who forged the Continental Army into a patriotic national force at Valley Forge during the American Revolution, or the moviegoers who aspired to a collective dream of material prosperity and upward mobility during the 1920s.

Out of Many is also the only American history text with a truly continental perspective. With community vignettes from New England to the South, the Midwest to the far West, we encourage students to appreciate the great expanse of our nation. For example, a vignette of seventeenth-century Sante Fé , New Mexico, illustrates the founding of the first European settlements in the New World. We present territorial expansion into the American West from the viewpoint of the Mandan villagers of the upper Missouri River of North Dakota. We introduce the policies of the Reconstruction era through the experience of African Americans in Hale County, Alabama. A continental perspective drives home to students that American history has never been the preserve of any particular region.

In these ways *Out of Many* breaks new ground, but without compromising its coverage of the traditional turning points that we believe are critically important to an understanding of the American past. Among these watershed events are the Revolution and the struggle over the Constitution, the Civil War and Reconstruction, and the Great Depression and World War II. In *Out of Many*, however, we seek to integrate the narrative of national history with the story of the nation's many diverse communities. The Revolutionary and Constitutional period tested the ability of local communities to forge a new unity, and success depended on their ability to build a nation without compromising local identity. The Civil War and Reconstruction formed a second great test of the balance between the national ideas of the Revolution and the power of local and sectional communities. The Depression and the New Deal demonstrated the importance of local communities and the growing power of national institutions during the greatest economic challenge in our history. *Out of Many* also looks back in a new and comprehensive way—from the vantage point of the beginning of a new century and the end of the cold war—at the salient events of the last fifty years and their impact on American communities. The community focus of *Out of Many* weaves the stories of the people and the nation into a single compelling narrative.

Out of Many, fourth edition; includes expanded coverage of our diverse heritage. Our country is appropriately known as "a nation of immigrants," and the history of immigration to America, from the seventeenth to the twenty-first centuries, is fully integrated into the text. There is sustained and close attention to our place in the world, with special emphasis on our relations with the nations of the Western Hemisphere, especially our near neighbors, Canada and Mexico. In a completely new final chapter we consider the promises and the risks of American diversity in the new century. The statistical data has been completely updated with the results of the 2000 census. We have also incorporated new scholarship on the South, popular culture, science and technology, and the Cold War.

The fourth edition also includes an important new feature, Community & Memory, in which we examine the way American communities have attempted to commemorate and memorialize the past. Communities sometimes come to blows over different ways of looking at history. Arguments over the meaning of the past are not confined to the classroom.

SPECIAL FEATURES

With each edition of *Out of Many* we have sought to strengthen its unique integration of the best of traditional American history with its innovative community-based focus and strong continental perspective. A wealth of special features and pedagogical aids reinforces our narrative and helps students grasp key issues.

■ **Community and Diversity.** *Out of Many*, fourth edition, opens with an introduction, titled "Community and Diversity," that acquaints students with the major themes of the book, providing them with a framework for understanding American history.

■ **Community & Memory.** New to the fourth edition, this special illustrated feature, located at the end of Chapters 1, 4, 6, 9, 14, 19, 21, 25, 28, and 31, examines the ways in which American communities have attempted to commemorate the past and the conflicts that arise when the meaning of the past divides the members of a community. New **Researching the Past** sections at the end of each Community and Memory essay guide students through the many resources available on Research Navigator™ (see p. xxxvii).

■ **Maps.** *Out of Many*, fourth edition, has more maps than any other American history textbook. Most maps include topographical detail that helps students appreciate the impact of geography on history. Many maps have been redrawn to better reflect a hemispheric perspective.

■ **Web Explorations.** New to the fourth edition, Web explorations are tied directly to two maps in each chapter and provide interactive exploration of key geographical, chronological, and thematic concepts. Each Web Exploration is found on the Companion Website™ for *Out of Many*. Additional interactive maps are listed in the Media Resources section at the end of each chapter.

■ **Overview tables.** Overview tables provide students with a summary of complex issues.

■ **Graphs, charts, and tables.** Every chapter includes one or more graphs, charts, or tables that help students understand important events and trends.

■ **Photos and Illustrations.** The abundant illustrations in *Out of Many*, 30 percent of them new to the fourth edition, include many that have never before been used in an American history

text. None of the images is anachronistic—each one dates from the historical period under discussion. Extensive captions treat the images as visual primary source documents from the American past, describing their source and explaining their significance.

■ **Chapter-opening outlines and key topics lists.** These pedagogical aids provide students with a succinct preview of the material covered in each chapter.

■ **Chronologies.** A chronology at the end of each chapter helps students build a framework of key events.

■ **Review Questions.** Review questions helps students review, reinforce, and retain the material in each chapter and encourage them to relate the material to broader issues in American history.

■ **Recommended Reading and Additional Bibliography.** The works in the short, annotated Recommended Reading list at the end of each chapter have been selected with the interested introductory student in mind. The extensive Additional Bibliography provides a comprehensive overview of current scholarship on the subject of the chapter.

■ **Exploring America** sections in each chapter explore key episodes and developments in American history. These media-rich activities, located on the Companion Website™ for *Out of Many*, combine primary sources, illustrations, graphs, audio clips, interactive maps, and video to explore important topics indepth.

PRINT SUPPLEMENTS

Instructor's Resource Manual

A true time-saver in developing and preparing lecture presentations, the *Instructor's Resource Manual* contains chapter outlines, detailed chapter overviews, lecture topics, discussion questions, readings, and information about audio-visual resources.

Test Item File

The *Test Item File* offers a menu of more than 1,500 multiple-choice, identification, matching, true-false, and essay test questions and 10–15 questions per chapter on the maps found in each chapter. The guide includes a collection of blank maps that can be photocopied and used for map testing purposes or for other class exercises.

Prentice Hall Custom Test

This commercial-quality computerized test management program, available for Windows and Macintosh environments, allows instructors to select items from the *Test Item File* and design their own exams.

Transparency Pack

This collection of more than 160 full-color transparency acetates provides instructors with all the maps, charts, and graphs in the text for use in the classroom. Each transparency is accompanied by a page of descriptive material and discussion questions.

Study Guide, Volumes I and II

Each chapter in the *Study Guide* includes a chapter commentary and outline, identification terms, multiple-choice questions, short essay questions, map questions, and questions based on primary source extracts.

Documents Set, Volumes I and II

In revising the documents set for the fourth edition, the authors have selected and carefully edited more than 300 documents that relate directly to the themes and content of the text and organized them into five general categories: community, social history, government, culture, and politics. Each document is approximately two pages long and includes a brief introduction and study questions intended to encourage students to analyze the document critically and relate it to the content of the text. The *Documents Set* is available at a substantial discount when packaged with *Out of Many*.

Retrieving the American Past, 2003 Edition

Written and developed by leading historians and educators, this reader is an on-demand history database that offers 300 primary source documents (eight new to the 2003 edition) on key topics in American History, such as: Women on the Frontier, The Salem Witchcraft Scare, The Age of Industrial Violence, and Native American Societies, 1870–1995. Each module includes an introduction, several primary documents and secondary sources, follow-up questions, and recommendations for further reading. By deciding which modules to include and the order in which they will appear, instructors can compile a custom reader to fit their needs. Contact your local Prentice Hall representative for more information about this exciting custom publishing option.

Many Lives, Many Stories: Biographies in American History

New to the fourth edition, this two-volume collection of sixty-two biographies in American history was written specifically to match the chapter sequence and themes of *Out of Many*.

Introductions, prereading questions, suggested readings, and a special prologue about the role of biography in the study of American history enrich this important new supplement. Available free when packaged with *Out of Many*. Annotated links to relevant Websites for each biography can be found on the *Companion Website* for *Out of Many*.

Understanding and Answering Essay Questions

This brief guide suggests helpful study techniques as well as specific analytical tools for understanding different types of essay questions and provides precise guidelines for preparing well-crafted essay answers. The guide is available free to students when packaged with *Out of Many*.

Reading Critically about History

This brief guide provides students with helpful strategies for reading a history textbook. It is available free when packaged with *Out of Many*.

 ## Prentice Hall and Penguin Bundle Program

Prentice Hall and Penguin are pleased to provide adopters of *Out of Many* with an opportunity to receive significant discounts when orders for *Out of Many* are bundled together with Penguin titles in American history. Please contact your local Prentice Hall representative for details.

MULTIMEDIA SUPPLEMENTS

 ## U.S. History Documents CD-ROM

Bound with every new copy of *Out of Many, Media and Research Update*, the *U.S. History Documents CD-ROM* contains over 300 primary sources in an easily-navigable PDF file. Linked to a Companion Website™, each document is accompanied by essay questions that allow students to read important sources in American history and respond online.

 ## Out of Many Companion Website™

http://www.prenhall.com/faragher

With the *Out of Many* Companion Website™ students can take full advantage of the Web and use it in tandem with the text to enrich their study of American history. The Companion Website™ ties the text to related material available on the Internet. Its many instructional features include learning objectives and study questions organized by the primary subtopics of each chapter, map labeling exercises, annotated links, document questions, Community & Memory resources, and eThemes of *The New York Times*.

Evaluating Online Resources with Research Navigator

This brief guide introduces students to the origin and innovations behind the Internet and provides clear strategies for navigating the Web to find historical materials. Exercises in each chapter help students practice searching the wealth of resources available on Research Navigator, a powerful study tool. This 48-page supplementary book is bound with all new copies of *Out of Many, Media and Research Update.*

 OneKey

OneKey lets you in to the best teaching and learning resources all in one place. OneKey for *Out of Many* is all your students need for out-of-class work conveniently organized by chapter to reinforce and apply what they've learned in class and from the text. Among the resources available for each chapter are: a complete media-rich, interactive ebook version of *Out of Many*, quizzes organized by the main topics of each chapter, primary source documents, map labeling and interactive map quizzes. OneKey is all you need to plan and administer your course. All your instructor resources are in one place to maximize your effectiveness and minimize your time and effort. Instructor material includes: select images and maps from *Out of Many*, hundreds of documents, video and audio clips, interactive learning activities, and PowerPoint presentations.

 Instructor CD-ROM for *Out of Many*

The Instructor's Resource Center on the CD-ROM features many of the OneKey resources.

 The Prentice Hall History Resource Center

This site offers a rich array of hundreds of historical sources in textual, visual, or audio-visual format. All were carefully selected by history professors as particularly relevant to the United States survey course. Interactive maps present historical transformations in a clear and compelling way. Learning activities offer indepth explorations of important topics. The Prentice Hall History Resource Center also includes a comprehensive glossary of terms and Best of the Web links for additional study.

 Mapping American History CD-ROM

This innovative electronic supplement takes advantage of the interactive capabilities of multimedia technology to enrich students' understanding of the geographic dimensions of history with animated maps, timelines, and related on-screen activities tied directly to key issues in each chapter of *Out of Many.*

ACKNOWLEDGMENTS

In the years it has taken to bring *Out of Many* from idea to reality and to improve it in successive editions, we have often been reminded that although writing history sometimes feels like isolated work, it actually involves a collective effort. We want to thank the dozens of people whose efforts have made the publication of this book possible.

At Prentice Hall, Charles Cavaliere, Senior Acquisitions Editor, gave us his full support and oversaw the entire publication process. Susanna Lesan, Editor-in-Chief of Development, edited the first and fourth editions of the book; without her efforts this book would never have been published. Jean Lapidus, Production Editor, oversaw the entire complicated production process in an exemplary fashion. Linda Sykes, our photo researcher, expertly tracked down the many pertinent new images that appear in this edition.

Among our many other friends at Prentice Hall we also want to thank Yolanda de Rooy, President; Charlyce Jones Owen, Editorial Director; Deborah O'Connell, Senior Media Editor; Claire Rehwinkel, Heather Shelstad, Marketing Managers; Leslie Osher, Creative Design Director; Ximena Tamvakopoulos, Art Director; Jan Schwartz, Production Editor; Stephen Hopkins, Copy Editor; and Shannon Corliss, Editorial Assistant.

Although we share joint responsibility for the entire book, the chapters were individually authored: John Mack Faragher wrote chapters 1–8; Susan Armitage wrote chapters 9–16; Mari Jo Buhle wrote chapters 18–20, 25–26, 29; and Daniel Czitrom wrote chapters 17, 21–24, 27–28. (For this edition Buhle and Czitrom co-authored Chapters 30–31.)

Historians around the country greatly assisted us by reading and commenting on our chapters for this and previous editions. We thank them for the commitment of their valuable time.

Each of us depended on a great deal of support and assistance with the research and writing that went into this book. We want to thank: Kathryn Abbott, Nan Boyd, Krista Comer, Jennifer Cote, Crista DeLuzio, Keith Edgerton, Carol Frost, Jesse Hoffnung Garskof, Pailin Gaither, Jane Gerhard, Todd Gernes, Mark Krasovic, Melani McAlister, Cristiane Mitchell, J. C. Mutchler, Keith Peterson, Alan Pinkham, Tricia Rose, Gina Rourke, Jessica Shubow, Gordon P. Utz, Jr., and Maura Young.

Our families and close friends have been supportive and ever so patient over the many years we have devoted to this project. But we want especially to thank Paul Buhle, Meryl Fingrutd, Bob Greene, and Michele Hoffnung.

The *Out of Many Media and Research Update* provides a variety of integrated media assets:

The **History Resource Center** includes additional primary source documents and images; each chapter of the text provides the reader with a correlation.

Listing of documents found on the **U.S. History Documents CD-ROM** that pertain to each chapter.

Listing of Web Explorations and interactive maps for each chapter, with URLs for direct access.

▶ **MEDIA RESOURCES**

U.S. HISTORY DOCUMENTS CD-ROM
Colonizing the New World
2-2 Samuel de Champlain's Battle with the Iroquois, July 1609
2-3 An Act Concerning Servants and Slaves
2-4 Reasons for the Plantation in New England (1629)
2-11 Onandogas and Cayugas: Iroquois Chiefs Address the Governors of New York and Virginia (1684)
2-12 James Oglethorpe: The Stono Rebellion (1739)
2-13 Gottlieb Mittelberger, The Passage of Indentured Servants (1750)

COMPANION WEBSITE HIGHLIGHTS
To view an exploration, enter one of the URLs below in your browser.

Web Explorations
The African Slave Trade
http://www.prenhall.com/faragher/map 4.1
Triangular Trade across the Atlantic
http://www.prenhall.com/faragher/map 4.2

Additional Interactive Maps
To access the maps, go to this chapter's resources at http://www.prenhall.com/faragher/.
Slave Colonies of the Seventeenth and Eighteenth Centuries, page 84

HISTORY RESOURCE CENTER
To find the resources listed below, go to http://www.prenhall.com/historyresourcecenter.

Documents
Don Juan de Oñate, Plaus: A Settlement in New Mexico (1599)
John White, The Lost Colony (1590)
Jose de Acosta, A Spanish Priest Speculates on the Origins of the Indians (1590)
The Cambridge Agreement (1629)
Wessell Webling, A Free Man Signs an Indenture (1622)
Alexander Falconbridge, The African Slave Trade (1788)
Bacon's Rebellion: The Declaration (1676)
Olaudah Equiano, The Middle Passage (1788)
Petition of "A Grate Number of Blackes of the Province" to Governor Thomas Gage and the Members of the Massachusetts General Court (1774)

Images
"To be sold. . .a cargo of 170 prime young likely healthy Guinea slaves. Savannah, July 25, 1774."
Olaudah Equiano
Phillis Wheatley
Slave Sale Notice

---

soldiers. Although the Nez Perce and other Indians have strong oral traditions about their encounters with Lewis and Clark, most people don't know about them because until recently historians regarded them only as "legend," and therefore not as reliable as written evidence. As a result, most Americans have only heard one version of a series many-sided encounters that occurred as Lewis and Clark found themselves in Indian country.

To insure that the Indian view is heard, the National Park Service has appointed Otis Halfmoon, a Nez Perce, as tribal liaison for the planning of the NPS traveling exhibit, *Corps of Discovery II: 200 Years to the Future*. In another Park service effort, Gerard Baker, a Mandan-Hidatsa, has been chosen as superintendent of the Lewis and Clark National Historic Trail as well as serving as superintendent of the *Corps of Discovery II* exhibit.

Alan Pinkham and others have worked with the National Council for the Bicentennial to set the proper context for the observation of the bicentnnial. One of the first steps was to refer to the bicentennial as a commemoration, rather than a celebration, thus acknowledging the high price that all Indians paid for discovery. From the Indian point of view, Lewis and Clark brought disaster in their wake: like the Mandans in the chapter opener, every western tribe experienced disease, warfare, and the destruction of their way of life at the hands of white American pioneers. Indian peoples felt betrayed by the same hand that the peace medal promised would clasp forever in friendship.

Yet rather than recrimination, Pinkham sees the bicentennial as a unique opportunity to tell the remarkable story of Indian survival and adaptation. After all, says Pinkham, "After 200 years we're still here. We weren't killed off by disease and warfare." The bicentennial can serve to inform the public about modern Indian life and accomplishments. As the Nez Perce and other western Indians seize the occasion of the bicentennial to tell their own story, they hope to give a new and modern meaning to the two hands clasped together on the Jefferson medal. ■

 www.researchnavigator.com

The Community and Memory essay for this chapter deals with reflections on the journey of Lewis and Clark on the occasion of the bicentennial of their expedition. For further research on the Lewis and Clark expedition, use the tools available to you in Research Navigator.

As you investigate this topic, consider this question: "Why do American Indians believe their contribution to the expedition has been undervalued?"

ContentSelect: Search in the History database using the search term *Lewis and Clark*.

Links Library: Access the History: U.S. History database and explore the links for *Lewis and Clark Expedition*.

New York Times on the Web: To find more information on the bicentennial of the expedition, search using the term *Lewis and Clark*.

RESEARCHING THE PAST

An embedded **Research Navigator** activity is found at the end of each **Community Memory** essay. Key questions and search terms help guide students.

Each **Exploring America** activity contains a variety of integrated media elements.

EXPLORING AMERICA
THE DUST BOWL
http://www.prenhall.com/faragher/dustbowl

Audio Clip | Chronology | Documents | Images | Interactive Map | Video Clip

A brief overview provides students with a glimpse of what they will be exploring indepth in each online **Exploring America** Activity.

bowl? How did it change the lives of the people affected by it? How did the New Deal government programs respond to this crisis? How did the government programs help to record the human drama resulting from the dust storms? This module examines the one devastating episodes of the already disastic depression of the 1930s. *The Dust Bowl* causes of the dust storms that swept ins in the mid-1930s and chronicles the he people affected by these storms. The other resources show that both the dust bowl phenomenon and the reactions to it caused long-term, deep-rooted changes in American agriculture and society.

The Dust Bowl provides several methods to examine the impact of this tragic chapter in American history, showing that a combination of natural and human factors triggered the dust storms. The module relates the story of the Dust Bowl and its aftermath, stressing the human aspect by including numerous photographs taken by Farm Security Administration photographers employed by the federal government to visually chronicle the Great Depression. Magazine articles and other print sources enhance the photos, while the interactive map and chronology provide an important time and space contexts to the discussion.

The Dust Bowl

Farmer and sons walking into a dust storm. Cimarron County, Oklahoma, photographed by Arthur Rothstein, April, 1936 for the Farm Security Administration.
Click anywhere to go to the previous page

Reflect and Respond
1. "Documentary" photography recorded carefully chosen and composed "slices of life." The "art" of a

photographer such Rothstein was to create images that appeared "artless," that is, they appeared to be candid snapshots. Analyzing such photographs therefore requires the historian to look carefully at what the photographer decided to include, and to exclude, from the pictures, and at how he or she composed the image. Composition deals with such matters as lighting, the angle from which the photograph was taken, and the relative size of the objects within the picture. Choose three of the Rothstein photographs of the Visalia camp. What was he seeking to achieve in each? How did he seek to convey certain ideas and/or sentiments in each?

2. The Visalia photographs stand in stark contrast to the earlier pictures taken by Lange and Rothstein of migrant laborers and of the impact of the dust storms. Create two contrasting pairs of images. Explain what an analysis of each pair tells us about the experience of the Great Depression.

✓ Check it out
Dust storm approaches town

This photograph provides a striking picture of the power of a dust storm. The photo stands as one of many taken by government photographers hired specifically to chronicle on film the devastation caused by the Great Depression. One of the most compelling and serious issue was the creation of the Dust Bowl in the mid-1930s and the havoc it wreaked on the people living in that section of the Great Plains.

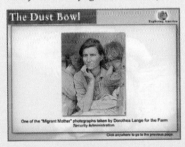

The Dust Bowl

One of the "Migrant Mother" photographs taken by Dorothea Lange for the Farm Security Administration
Click anywhere to go to the previous page

This Exploration is also available on the *Exploring America* CD-ROM.

ABOUT THE AUTHORS

Chris Freitag

JOHN MACK FARAGHER

John Mack Faragher is Arthur Unobskey Professor of American History and Director of the Howard R. Lamar Center for the Study of Frontiers and Borders at Yale University. Born in Arizona and raised in southern California, he received his B.A. at the University of California, Riverside, and his Ph.D. at Yale University. He is the author of *Women and Men on the Overland Trail* (1979), which won the Frederick Jackson Turner Award of the Organization of American Historians, *Sugar Creek: Life on the Illinois Prairie* (1986), *Daniel Boone: The Life and Legend of an American Pioneer* (1992), and (with Robert V. Hine) *The American West: A New Interpretive History* (2000).

MARI JO BUHLE

Mari Jo Buhle is William R. Kenan Jr. University Professor and Professor of American Civilization and History at Brown University, specializing in American women's history. She received her B.A. from the University of Illinois, Urbana–Champaign, and her Ph.D. from the University of Wisconsin, Madison. She is the author of *Women and American Socialism, 1870–1920* (1981) and *Feminism and Its Discontents: A Century of Struggle with Psychoanalysis* (1998). She is also coeditor of *Encyclopedia of the American Left*, second edition (1998). Professor Buhle held a fellowship (1991–1996) from the John D. and Catherine T. MacArthur Foundation.

DANIEL CZITROM

Daniel Czitrom is Professor of History at Mount Holyoke College. Born and raised in New York City, he received his B.A. from the State University of New York at Binghamton and his M.A. and Ph.D. from the University of Wisconsin, Madison. He is the author of *Media and the American Mind: From Morse to McLuhan* (1982), which won the First Books Award of the American Historical Association and has been translated into Spanish and Chinese. He has served as a historical consultant and a featured on-camera commentator for several documentary film projects, including two recent PBS series, *New York: A Documentary Film* and *American Photography: A Century of Images*.

SUSAN H. ARMITAGE

Susan H. Armitage is Claudius O. and Mary R. Johnson Distinguished Professor of History at Washington State University. She earned her Ph.D. from the London School of Economics and Political Science. Among her many publications on western women's history are three coedited books, *The Women's West* (1987), *So Much To Be Done: Women on the Mining and Ranching Frontier* (1991), and *Writing the Range: Race, Class, and Culture in the Women's West* (1997). She currently serves as an editor of a series of books on women and American history for the University of Illinois Press. She is the editor of *Frontiers: A Journal of Women's Studies*.

One of the most characteristic features of our country has always been its astounding variety. The American people include the descendants of native Indians, colonial Europeans, Africans, and migrants from virtually every country and continent. Indeed, as we enter a new century the United States is absorbing a flood of immigrants from Latin America and Asia that rivals the great tide of people from eastern and southern Europe one hundred years ago. What's more, our country is one of the world's most spacious, incorporating more than 3.6 million square miles of territory. The struggle to meld a single nation out of our many far-flung communities is what much of American history is all about. That is the story told in this book.

Every human society is made up of communities. A community is a set of relationships linking men, women, and their families to a coherent social whole that is more than the sum of its parts. In a community people develop the capacity for unified action. In a community people learn, often through trial and error, how to transform and adapt to their environment. The sentiment that binds the members of a community together is the mother of group identity and ethnic pride. In the making of history, communities are far more important than even the greatest of leaders, for the community is the institution most capable of passing a distinctive historical tradition to future generations.

Communities bind people together in multiple ways. They can be as small as local neighborhoods, in which people maintain face-to-face relations, or as large as the nation itself. This book examines American history from the perspective of community life—an

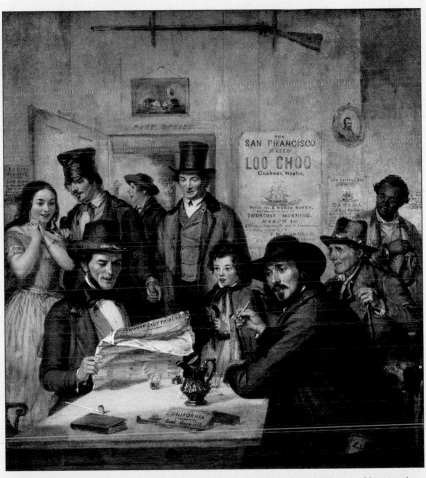

William Sidney Mount (1807–1868) *California News* 1850. Oil on canvas. The Long Island Museum of American Art, History and Carriages. Gift of Mr. and Mrs. Ward Melville, 1955.

Harvey Dinnerstein, *Underground, Together* 1996, oil on canvas, 90" × 107". Photograph courtesy of Gerold Wunderlich & Co., New York, NY.

ever-widening frame that has included larger and larger groups of Americans.

Networks of kinship and friendship, and connections across generations and among families, establish the bonds essential to community life. Shared feelings about values and history establish the basis for common identity. In communities, people find the power to act collectively in their own interest. But American communities frequently took shape as a result of serious conflicts among groups, and within communities there has often been significant fighting among competing groups or classes. Thus the term *community*, as we use it here, includes tension and discord as well as harmony and agreement.

For years there have been persistent laments about the "loss of community" in modern America. But community has not disappeared—it is continually being reinvented. Until the late eighteenth century, community was defined primarily by space and local geography. But in the nineteenth century communities began to be reshaped by new and powerful historical forces such as the marketplace, industrialization, the corporation, mass immigration, mass media, and the growth of the nation-state. In the twentieth century, Americans have struggled to balance commitments to several communities simultaneously. These were defined not simply by local spatial arrangements, but by categories as varied as racial and ethnic groups, occupations, political affiliations, and consumer preferences.

The "American Communities" vignettes that open each chapter reflect this shift. Most of the vignettes in the pre–Civil War chapters focus on geographically defined communities, such as the ancient Indian city at Cahokia, or the experiment in industrial urban planning in early nineteenth-century Lowell, Massachusetts. In the post–Civil War chapters different and more modern kinds of communities make their appearance. In the 1920s, movies and radio offered a new kind of community—a community of identification with dreams of freedom, material success, upward mobility, youth and beauty. In the 1950s, rock 'n' roll music helped germinate a new national community of teenagers, with profound effects on the culture of the entire country in the second half of the twentieth century. In the late 1970s, fear of nuclear accidents like the one at Three Mile Island brought concerned citizens together in communities around the country and produced a national movement opposing nuclear power.

The title for our book was suggested by the Latin phrase selected by John Adams, Benjamin Franklin, and Thomas Jefferson for the Great Seal of the United States: *E Pluribus Unum*—"Out of Many Comes Unity." These men understood that unity could not be imposed by a powerful central authority but had to develop out of mutual respect among Americans of different backgrounds. The revolutionary leadership expressed the hope that such respect could grow on the basis of a remarkable proposition: "We hold these truths to be self-evident, that all men are created equal; that they are endowed by their Creator with certain unalienable rights; that among these are life, liberty, and the pursuit of happiness." The national government of the United States would preserve local and state authority but would guarantee individual rights. The nation would be strengthened by guarantees of difference.

"Out of Many"—that is the promise of America, and the premise of this book. The underlying dialectic of American history, we believe, is that as a people we need to locate our national unity in the celebration of the differences that exist among us; these differences can be our strength, as long as we affirm the promise of the Declaration. Protecting the "right to be different," in other words, is absolutely fundamental to the continued existence of democracy, and that right is best protected by the existence of strong and vital communities. We are bound together as a nation by the ideal of local and cultural differences protected by our common commitment to the values of our Revolution.

Today those values are endangered by terrorists using the tactics of mass terror. In the wake of the September 11, 2001, attack on the United States, and with the continuing threat of biological, chemical, or

Thomas Satterwhite Noble, *Last Sale of Slaves on the Courthouse Steps*, 1860, oil on canvas, Missouri Historical Society.

even nuclear assaults, Americans can not afford to lose faith in our historic vision. The United States is a multicultural and transnational society. The thousands of victims buried in the smoking ruins of the World Trade Center included people from dozens of different ethnic and national groups. We must fight to protect and defend the promise of our diverse nation

Our history shows that the promise of American unity has always been problematic. Centrifugal forces have been powerful in the American past, and at times the country has seemed about to fracture into its component parts. Our transformation from a collection of groups and regions into a nation has been marked by painful and often violent struggles. Our past is filled with conflicts between Indians and colonists, masters and slaves, Patriots and Loyalists, Northerners and Southerners, Easterners and Westerners, capitalists and workers, and sometimes the government and the people. War can bring out our best, but it can also bring out our worst. During World War II thousands of Japanese American citizens were deprived of their rights and locked up in isolated detention centers simply because of their ethnic background. Americans often appear to be little more than a contentious collection of peoples with conflicting interests, divided by region and background, race and class.

Our most influential leaders have also sometimes suffered a crisis of faith in the American project of "liberty and justice for all." Thomas Jefferson not only believed in the inferiority of African Americans, but he feared that immigrants from outside the Anglo-American tradition might "warp and bias" the development of the nation "and render it a heterogeneous, incoherent, distracted mass." We have not always lived up to the American promise, and there is a dark side to our history. It took the bloodiest war in American history to secure the human rights of African Americans, and the struggle for full equality for all our citizens has yet to be won. During the great influx of immigrants in the early twentieth century, fears much like Jefferson's led to movements to Americanize the foreign born by forcing them, in the words of one leader, "to give up the languages, customs, and methods of life which they have brought with them across the ocean, and adopt instead the language, habits, and customs of this country, and the general standards and ways of American living." Similar thinking motivated Congress at various times to bar the immigration of Africans, Asians, and other ethnic groups and people of color

into the country, and to force assimilation on American Indians by denying them the freedom to practice their religion or even to speak their own language. Such calls for restrictive unity still resound in our own day.

But other Americans have argued for a more fulsome version of Americanization. "What is the American, this new man?" asked the French immigrant Michel Crévecoeur in 1782. "A strange mixture of blood which you will find in no other country." In America, he wrote, "individuals of all nations are melted into a new race of men." A century later Crévecoeur was echoed by historian Frederick Jackson Turner, who believed that "in the crucible of the frontier, the immigrants were Americanized, liberated, and fused into a mixed race, English in neither nationality nor characteristics. The process has gone on from the early days to our own."

The process by which diverse communities have come to share a set of common American values is one of the most fundamental aspects of our history. It did not occur, however, because of compulsory Americanization programs, but because of free public education, popular participation in democratic politics, and the impact of popular culture. Contemporary America does have a common culture: We share a commitment to freedom of thought and expression, we join in the aspirations to own our own homes and send our children to college, we laugh at the same television programs.

To a degree that too few Americans appreciate, this common culture resulted from a complicated process of mutual discovery that took place when different ethnic and regional groups encountered one another. Consider just one small and unique aspect of our culture: the barbecue. Americans have been barbecuing since before the beginning of written history. Early settlers adopted this technique of cooking from the Indians—the word itself comes from a native term for a framework of sticks over a fire on which meat was slowly cooked. Colonists typically barbecued pork, fed on Indian corn. African slaves lent their own touch by introducing the use of hot sauces. The ritual that is a part of nearly every American family's Fourth of July silently celebrates the heritage of diversity that went into making our common culture.

The American educator John Dewey recognized this diversity early in the last century. "The genuine American, the typical American, is himself a hyphenated character," he declared, "international and interracial in his make-up." The point about our "hyphenated character," Dewey believed, "is to see to it that the hyphen connects instead of separates." We, the authors of *Out of Many*, share Dewey's perspective on American history. "Creation comes from the impact of diversity," wrote the American philosopher Horace Kallen. We also endorse Kallen's vision of the American promise: "A democracy of nationalities, cooperating voluntarily and autonomously through common institutions, . . . a multiplicity in a unity, an orchestration of mankind." And now, let the music begin

Painting by Michael Hampshire. *Community Life at Cahokia.* Cahokia Mounds State Historic Site.

Cahokia: Thirteenth-Century Life
on the Mississippi

AS THE SUN ROSE OVER THE RICH FLOODPLAIN, THE PEOPLE of the riverbank city set about their daily tasks. Some went to shops where they manufactured tools, crafted pottery, worked metal, or fashioned ornamental jewelry—goods destined to be exchanged in the far corners of the continent. Others left their densely populated neighborhoods for the outlying countryside, where in the summer heat they worked the seemingly endless fields that fed the city. From almost any point people could see the great temple that rose from the center of their city—the temple where priests in splendid costumes acted out public rituals of death and renewal.

This thirteenth-century city was not in preindustrial Europe but in North America. Its residents lived and worked on the banks of the Mississippi River, across from present-day St. Louis, at a place archaeologists have named Cahokia. In the mid-1200s, Cahokia was an urban cluster of perhaps 30,000 people. Its farm fields were abundant with corn, beans, and pumpkins. The temple, a huge earthwork pyramid, covered fifteen acres at its base and rose as high as a ten-story building. On top were the sacred residences of chiefs and priests, who dressed in elaborate headdresses made from the plumage of American birds.

By the fourteenth century, Cahokia had been abandoned, but its great central temple mound and dozens of smaller ones in the surrounding area, as well as hundreds more throughout the Mississippi Valley, remained to puzzle the European immigrants who resettled the valley in the eighteenth and nineteenth centuries. Treasure seekers plundered the mounds, most of which were eventually dynamited and plowed under for farmland. Only a few were saved, inside parks and estates. Cahokia's central mound survived because in the nineteenth century its summit became the site of a monastery, now long gone.

The Europeans who first explored and excavated these mounds were convinced that they were the ruins of a vanished civilization, but could not believe they were the work of Indians. The first comprehensive study of Cahokia, published in 1848 under the sponsorship of the Smithsonian Institution, noted that "the mound-builders were an agricultural people, considerably advanced in arts, manners, habits, and religion." But because "Indians were hunters averse to labor, and not known to have constructed any works approaching [the] skillfulness of design or [the] magnitude" of Cahokia, surely those wonders were constructed by a "lost race."

The Smithsonian scientists were wrong. Historians now know that the ancestors of contemporary Native Americans constructed massive earthworks in the Mississippi Valley. The vast urban complex of Cahokia flourished from the tenth to the fourteenth century, and at its height stretched six miles along the Mississippi River. Its residents were not nomadic hunters but farmers, members of an agricultural society—which archaeologists call the Mississippian—with highly productive techniques of cultivation. Hundreds of acres of crops fed the people of Cahokia, the most populated urban community north of the complex civilization of the Aztecs in Mexico. Mississippian farmers constructed ingenious raised plots of land on which they heaped compost in wide ridges for improved drainage and protection against unseasonable frosts. To their square houses of wood and mud they attached pens in which they kept flocks of domesticated turkeys and, perhaps, small herds of young deer, which they slaughtered for meat and hides. Cahokia was at the center of a long-distance trading system that linked it to other Indian communities over a vast area. Copper came from Lake Superior, mica from the southern Appalachians, conch shells from the Atlantic coast, and Cahokia's specialized artisans were renowned for the manufacture of high-quality flint hoes, exported throughout the Mississippi Valley.

The archaeological evidence suggests that Cahokia was a city-state supported by tribute and taxation. Like the awe-inspiring public works of early urban societies in other parts of the world—the pyramids of ancient Egypt, the acropolis of Athens—the great temple mound

Cahokia

of Cahokia was intended to reflect the city's wealth and power. The mounds and other colossal public works at Cahokia were the monuments of a society ruled by an elite. From their residences atop the mound, priests and governors looked down upon their subjects.

The 1848 Smithsonian report on Cahokia reflected the stereotypical American view that all Indian people lived in hunting bands. But the history of North America before European colonization demonstrates that the native inhabitants of the continent lived in strong vibrant communities that ranged from small hunting bands to large agricultural cities like Cahokia and splendid imperial capitals like those of the Aztecs of Mexico or the Mayans of Central America. North America before colonization was, as one historian phrases it, "a continent of villages," a land with thousands of local communities. Over many centuries the Indian peoples of North America developed a variety of community types, each with its own system of family and social organization, each integrated with its natural surroundings. The wonders of Cahokia are but one aspect of the little-understood history of the Indians of the Americas. ■

KEY TOPICS

- The peopling of the Americas by migrants from Asia

- The adaptation of native cultures to the regions of North America

- The increase in complexity of many native societies following the development of farming

- The nature of Indian cultures in the three major regions of European invasion and settlement

---

SETTLING THE CONTINENT

"Why do you call us Indians?" a Massachusetts native complained to Puritan missionary John Eliot in 1646. Christopher Columbus, who mistook the Taino people of the Caribbean for the people of the East Indies, called them *Indios*. By the middle of the sixteenth century this Spanish word had passed into English as "Indians," and was commonly used to refer to all the native peoples of the Americas. Today anthropologists often use the term "Amerindians," and many people prefer "Native Americans." But most indigenous Americans call themselves "Indian people."

Who Are the Indian People?

At the time of their first contacts with Europeans at the beginning of the sixteenth century, the native inhabitants of the Western Hemisphere represented over 2,000 cultures, spoke hundreds of different languages, and made their livings in scores of fundamentally different environments. Just as the term "European" includes the English, French, and Spanish, so "Indian" covers an enormous diversity among the peoples of the Americas. Natives, of course, referred to themselves by their own names. For example, the people of the mid-Atlantic coast called themselves *Lenni Lenape*, meaning "true men"; a large group of natives in the western Great Lakes country called themselves *Lakota*, or "the allies"; and the nomadic hunters of the desert Southwest used the name *Dine* (pronounced "dee-nay"), meaning simply "the people." Europeans came to know these three groups by rather different names: the *Delawares* (from the principal river of the mid-Atlantic region), the *Sioux*, and the *Apaches* (both of which meant "enemy" in the language of neighboring tribes).

No single physical type characterized all the native peoples of the Americas. Although most had straight, black hair and dark, almond-shaped eyes, their skincolor ranged from mahogany to light brown and few fit the "redskin" descriptions used by North American colonists of the eighteenth and nineteenth centuries. Indeed, it was only when Europeans had compared Indian peoples with natives of other continents, such as Africans, that they seemed similar enough to be classified as a group.

Once Europeans realized that the Americas were in fact a "New World," rather than part of the Asian continent, a debate began over how people might have moved there from Europe and Asia, where the Judeo-Christian Bible indicated God had created the first man and woman. Writers proposed elaborate theories of transoceanic migrations linking Native Americans variously to ancient Greeks, Carthaginians, Tartars, Chinese, or Welsh, one even proposing that they were the survivors of mythical Atlantis. Common to all these theories was a belief that the Americas had been populated for a few thousand years at most, and that native societies were the degenerate offspring of a far superior Old World culture. A number of Spanish scholars thought more deeply about the question of Indian origins. In 1590, Joseph de Acosta reasoned that because Old World animals were present in the Americas, they must have crossed by a land bridge that could have been used by humans as well.

Migration from Asia

Acosta was the first to propose the Asian migration hypothesis that is today supported by most of the scientific evidence. The first "hard" data linking American Indians with Asians appeared in the 1980s with the finding that Indians and northeast Asians share a common and distinctive pattern in the arrangement of the teeth. But perhaps the most compelling support for the hypothesis comes from genetic research. Studies comparing the DNA variation of populations around the world consistently demonstrate the close genetic relationship of the

OVERVIEW

ORIGINS OF SOME INDIAN TRIBAL NAMES

Cherokee	A corruption of the Choctaw *chiluk-ki*, meaning "cave people," an allusion to the many caves in the Cherokee homeland. The Cherokees called themselves *Ani-Yun-Wiya*, or "real people."
Cheyenne	From the Sioux *Sha-hiyena*, "people of strange speech." The Cheyennes called themselves *Dzi-tsistas*, meaning "our people."
Hopi	A shortening of the Hopis' own name for themselves, *Hópitu*, which means "peaceful ones."
Mohawk	From the Algonquian *Mohawaúuck*, meaning "man-eaters." The Mohawks called themselves *Kaniengehaga*, "people of the place of the flint."
Pawnee	From the Pawnee term *paríki*, which describes a distinctive style of dressing the hair with paint and fat to make it stand erect like a horn. The Pawnees called themselves *Chahiksichahiks*, "men of men."

two populations, and recently geneticists studying a virus sequestered in the kidneys of all humans found that the strain of virus carried by Navajos and Japanese is nearly identical, while that carried by Europeans and Africans is quite different.

The migration could have begun over a land bridge connecting the continents. During the last Ice Age (the Wisconsinan Glaciation, from 70,000 to 10,000 years ago, the final act in the geologic epoch known as the Pleistocene), huge glaciers locked up massive volumes of water, and sea levels were as much as 300 feet lower than today. Asia and North America were joined by a huge subcontinent of ice-free, treeless grassland, 750 miles wide from north to south. Geologists have named this area Beringia, from the Bering Straits. Summers there were warm, winters were cold, dry, and almost snow-free. This was a perfect environment for large mammals—mammoth and mastodon, bison, horse, reindeer, camel, and saiga (a goatlike antelope). Small bands of Stone Age hunter-gatherers were attracted by these animal populations, which provided them not only with food but with hides for clothing and shelter, dung for fuel, and bones for tools and weapons. Accompanied by a husky-like species of dog, hunting bands gradually moved as far east as the Yukon River basin of northern Canada, where field excavations have uncovered the fossilized jawbones of several dogs and bone tools estimated to be about 27,000 years old.

Other evidence suggests that the migration from Asia began about 30,000 years ago—around the same time that Japan and Scandinavia were being settled. This evidence is based on blood type. The vast majority of modern Native Americans have type O blood and a few have type A, but almost none have type B.

Because modern Asian populations include all three blood types, however, the migrations must have begun before the evolution of type B, which geneticists believe occurred about 30,000 years ago. The study of the evolution of language offers another kind of evidence. Linguists argue that it would require at least 35,000 years to develop, from a single common base, the nearly 500 distinct languages of the Americas.

By 25,000 years ago human communities were established in western Beringia, which is present-day Alaska. But access to the south was blocked by a huge glacial sheet covering much of what is today Canada. How did the hunters get over those 2,000 miles of deep ice? The argument is that the climate began to warm with the passing of the Ice Age, and about 13,000 B.C.E. (before the Common Era, which began 2,000 years ago) glacial melting created an ice-free corridor—the original "Pan-American Highway"—along the eastern front range of the Rocky Mountains. Soon hunters of big game had reached the Great Plains.

In the past several years, however, new archaeological finds along the Pacific coast of North and South America have thrown this theory into question. Newly excavated early human sites in Washington state, California, and Peru have been radiocarbon dated to be 11,000 to 12,000 years old. The most spectacular find, at Monte Verde in southern Chile, produced striking evidence of tool making, house building, rock painting, and human footprints conservatively dated at 12,500 years ago, long before the highway had been cleared of ice. Many archaeologists now believe that migrants moved south in boats along a coastal route rather than overland—an ancient "Pacific Coast Highway." These people were probably gatherers and fishers rather than hunters of big game.

There were two later migrations into North America. About 5000 B.C.E. the Athapascan or Na-Dene people began to settle the forests in the northwestern area of the continent. Although they eventually adopted a technology similar to that of neighboring peoples, the Na-Dene maintained a separate cultural and linguistic identity. Eventually Athapascan speakers, the ancestors of the Navajos and Apaches, migrated across the Great Plains to the Southwest. The final migration began about 3000 B.C.E., after Beringia had been submerged, when a maritime hunting people crossed the Bering Straits in small boats. The Inuits (also known as the Eskimos) colonized the polar coasts of the Arctic, the Yupiks the coast of southwestern Alaska, and the Aleuts the Aleutian Islands (which are named for them).

While scientists debate the timing and mapping of these migrations, many Indian people hold to their oral traditions that say they have always lived in North America. Every culture has its origin stories, offering explanations of the customs and beliefs of the group. Yet a number of anthropologists argue that these origin stories may shed light on ancient history. The Haida people of the Northwest Pacific coast tell of a time, long ago, when the islands were much larger; but then the oceans rose, they say, and "flood tide woman" forced them to move to higher ground. Could these stories preserve a memory of the changes at the end of the Ice Age? It is notable that many Indian traditions include a long journey from a distant place of origin to a new homeland. The Pima people of the Southwest once sang an "Emergence Song":

> This is the White Land; we arrive singing,
> Headdresses waving in the breeze.
> We have come! We have come!
> The land trembles with our dancing and singing.

Clovis: The First American Technology

The earliest tools found at North American archaeological sites, crude stone or bone choppers and scrapers, are similar to artifacts from the same period found in Europe or Asia. About 10,000 B.C.E. however, ancient Americans developed a much more sophisticated style of tool making, named after the site of its first discovery near Clovis, New Mexico. The Clovis tradition was a powerful new and sophisticated technology, unlike anything found in the Old World. In the years since the initial discovery, archaeologists have unearthed Clovis artifacts at sites ranging from Montana to Mexico, Nova Scotia

reconstruction

A forensic artist reconstructed this bust from the skull of "Spirit Cave Man," whose mummified remains, taken from a desert cave in Nevada, scientists dated to 7420 B.C.E, making it the oldest human skeleton found in North America. About forty-five years old at the time of his death, Spirit Cave Man suffered blows to the head, possibly delivered by other individuals. He was buried in a fur robe and a shroud of woven tule reeds, with well-worn and patched leather moccasins on his feet.

SOURCE: Nevada State Museum, Carson City, NV

These Clovis points are typical of thousands that archaeologists have found at sites all over the continent, dating from a period about 12,000 years ago. When inserted in a spear shaft, these three- to six-inch fluted points made effective weapons for hunting mammoth and other big game. The ancient craftsmen who made these points often took advantage of the unique qualities of the stone they were working to enhance their aesthetic beauty.

SOURCE: Photograph by Warren Morgan. ©Warren Morgan/CORBIS

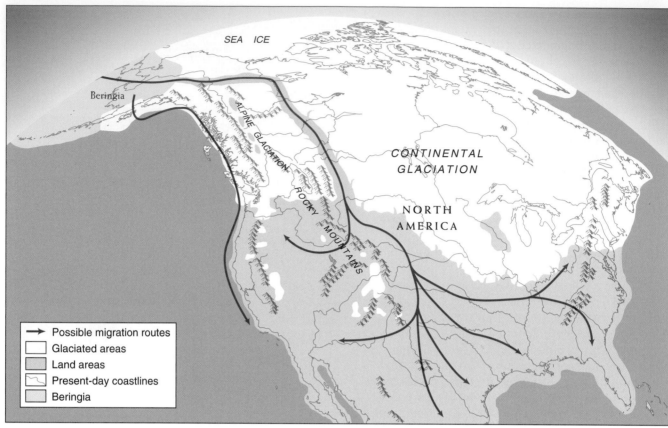

Migration Routes from Asia to America During the Ice Age, Asia and North America were joined where the Bering Straits are today, forming a migration route for hunting peoples. Either by boat along the coast, or through a narrow corridor between the huge northern glaciers, these migrants began making their way to the heartland of the continent as much as 30,000 years ago.

to Arizona, all of them dating back to within 1,000 or 2,000 years of one another, suggesting that the Clovis technology spread quickly throughout the continent. It may be that the initial settlement of North America was entering its final phase, as the continent filled with people. Scientists theorize that it was to feed their expanding populations that communities were driven to find a more efficient way to hunt and therefore developed this greatly improved Clovis technology.

The evidence suggests that Clovis bands were mobile communities of foragers numbering perhaps thirty to fifty individuals from several interrelated families. They returned to the same hunting camps year after year, migrating seasonally within territories of several hundred square miles. Near Delbert, Nova Scotia, archaeologists discovered the floors of ten tents arranged in a semicircle, their doors opening south to avoid the prevailing northerly winds. Both this camp and others found throughout the continent overlooked watering places that would attract game. Clovis blades have been excavated amid the remains

of mammoth, camel, horse, giant armadillo, and sloth. Hunters apparently drove these animals into shallow bogs, killed them with spears, and butchered them on the spot.

NEW WAYS OF LIVING ON THE LAND

About 13,000 B.C.E., a global warming trend began to alter the North American climate. As the giant continental glaciers began to melt, the northern latitudes were colonized by plants, animals, and humans. Meltwater created the lake and river systems of today and raised the level of the surrounding seas, flooding Beringia as well as vast stretches of the Atlantic and Gulf coasts and creating fertile tidal pools and offshore fishing banks. These huge transformations produced new patterns of wind, rainfall, and temperature, reshaping the ecology of the entire continent and gradually producing the distinct North American regions of today. The great integrating force of a single continental climate faded, and with its passing the continental Clovis culture fragmented into many different regional patterns.

Hunting Traditions

One of the most important effects of this massive climatic shift was the stress it placed on the big game animals best suited to an Ice Age environment. The archaeological record shows the extinction of thirty-two classes of large New World animals, including not only the mammoth and mastodon but the horse and camel, both of which evolved in America and then migrated to Asia across Beringia. Lowered reproduction and survival rates of large animals may have forced hunting bands to intensify their efforts, leading to what some archaeologists have called the "Pleistocene Overkill."

As the other large-mammal populations declined, hunters on the Great Plains concentrated on the herds of American bison, or buffalo. To hunt these animals people needed a weapon they could throw quickly with great accuracy and speed at fast-moving targets over distances of as much as a hundred yards. In archaeological sites dating from about 8000 B.C.E., a new style of tool is found mingled with animal remains. This technology, named "Folsom" after the site of the first major excavation in New Mexico, was a refinement of the Clovis tradition, featuring more delicate but deadlier spear points. In one dramatic find, a Folsom point was discovered between the fossilized ribs of an ancient species of bison. Hunters probably hurled the lances to which these points were attached with wooden spear-throwers, with far greater speed than they could achieve with their arms alone. By 7000 B.C.E., Folsom evolved into a tradition that archaeologists call "Plano"; the points are found with grinding tools for vegetable foods, demonstrating the development of a varied diet on the Great Plains.

These archaeological finds suggest the growing complexity of early Indian communities. Hunters frequently stampeded herds of bison into canyon traps or over cliffs. At one such kill site in southeastern Colorado, dated at about 6500 B.C.E., archaeologists uncovered the remains of nearly 200 bison that had been slaughtered and then systematically butchered on a single occasion. Such tasks required a sophisticated division of labor among dozens of men and women and the cooperation of a number of communities. Taking food in such great quantities also suggests a knowledge of basic preservation techniques. These people must have been among the first to make jerky (dried strips of meat) and pemmican (a mixture of dried meat, animal fat, and berries that can keep into

When in 1927 archaeologists at Folsom, New Mexico, uncovered this dramatic example of a projectile point embedded in the ribs of a long-extinct species of bison, it was the first proof that Indians had been in North America for many thousands of years.

SOURCE: Courtesy of the Denver Museum of Nature and Science.

the winter when stored in hide containers). These characteristic products of the Great Plains later became the staple foods of European fur traders in the North American West.

Desert Culture

The retreat of the glaciers led to new ways of finding food in other regions: hunting in the arctic, foraging in the arid deserts, fishing along the coasts, hunting and gathering in the forests. These developments took place roughly 10,000 to 2,500 years ago, during what archaeologists call the Archaic period (corresponding to the late phases of the Stone Age in Eurasia and Africa).

In the Great Basin of present-day Utah and Nevada the warming trend associated with the end of the Ice Age created a desert where once there had been enormous inland seas. Here Indian people developed Desert Culture, a way of life based on the pursuit of small game and the intensified foraging of plant foods. Small communities or bands of desert foragers migrated seasonally within a small range. They collected

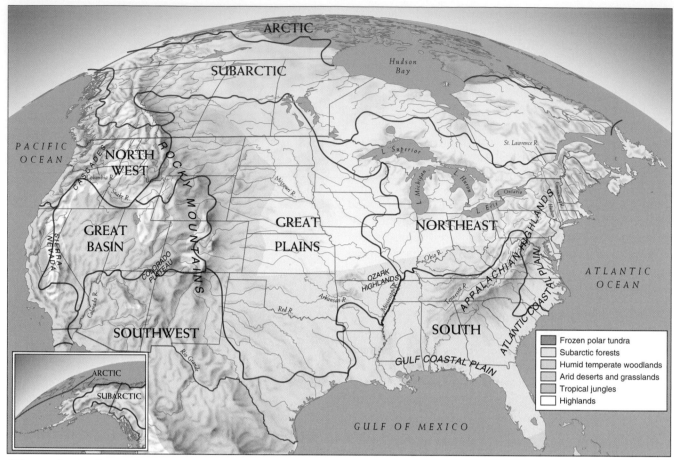

Climatological and Culture Regions of North America   Occupying more than a third of the continent, the United States is alone among the world's nations in encompassing all five general classes of global climate: tropical jungles, arid deserts and grasslands, temperate woodlands, subarctic forests, and frozen polar tundra. All peoples must adjust their diet, shelter, and other material aspects of their lives to the physical conditions of the world around them. By considering the ways in which Indian peoples developed distinct cultures adapted to their environments, anthropologists developed the concept of "culture areas." They divide the continent into nine fundamental regions that have greatly influenced the history of North America over the past 10,000 years. Just as regions shaped the lifeways and history of Indian peoples, after the coming of the Europeans they nurtured the development of regional American cultures.

seeds, fiber, and prickly pear from the yucca one season, then moved to highland mesas or plateaus to gather grass seed, acorns, juniper berries, and piñon nuts, and next to mountain streams to spear and net fish. This strategy required considerable skill in handicrafts and the production of fiber baskets for collecting, pitch-lined baskets for cooking, nets and traps, and stones shaped to grind seeds and nuts, as well as stone knives, hammers, and clubs.

Archaeologists today find the artifacts of desert foragers in the caves and rock shelters in which they lived. In addition to stone tools, there are objects of wood, hide, and fiber, wonderfully preserved for thousands of years in the dry climate. Desert Culture persisted into

the nineteenth century among modern Shoshone and Ute communities. Although these people were once scornfully labeled "Diggers" because of their practice of gathering edible roots and were ridiculed for their "primitive" life ways, they actually made very sophisticated adjustments to a harsh environment.

Descriptions of the culture of the modern Shoshones suggest that their emphasis on sharing and gift giving, their condemnation of hoarding, and their limitations on the accumulation of material goods, fostered by a nomadic lifestyle, prevented individuals or families from acquiring excessive wealth and forged a strong sense of community among these people of the desert. Desert communities were characterized by a kind of social equality in which decisions were made by consensus among the adults and leadership tended to be informal, based on achievement and reputation. Men of one band generally married women from another, and wives came to live with the people of their husband's families, creating important linkages between groups that contributed to the sense of shared ethnic identity.

The innovative practices of the Desert Culture gradually spread from the Great Basin to the Great Plains and the Southwest, where foraging for plant foods began to supplement hunting. Archaeologists estimate that about 6,000 years ago, Indians carried Desert Culture to California, where, in the natural abundance of the valleys and coasts, they developed an economy capable of supporting some of the densest populations and the first permanently settled communities in North America. Another dynamic center in the West developed along the Northwest Pacific coast, where Indian communities developed a way of life based on the use of abundant fish and sea mammals. Here, densely populated, permanently settled communities were also possible.

Forest Efficiency

There were similar trends east of the Mississippi. Before European settlers destroyed countless acres of woodland in the eighteenth and nineteenth centuries, the whole of eastern North America was a vast forest. Hardwoods grew in the north, southern pine in the south. The Winnebagos of the Great Lakes region sang of these forests:

> Pleasant it looked,
> this newly created world.
> Along the entire length and breadth
> of the earth, our grandmother
> extended the green reflection
> of her covering
> and the escaping odors
> were pleasant to inhale.

During the Archaic period, forest communities achieved a comfortable and secure life based on their sophisticated knowledge of the rich and diverse available resources, a principle that archaeologists call "forest efficiency." Indian communities of the forest hunted small game and gathered seeds, nuts, roots, and other wild plant foods. They also developed the practice of burning the woodlands and prairies to stimulate the growth of berries, fruits, and edible roots. These burns created meadows and edge environments that provided harvestable food and attracted grazing animals, which were hunted for their meat and hides. Another important resource was the abundant fish of the rivers.

Archaeological sites in the East suggest that during the late Archaic period community populations grew and settlements became increasingly permanent, providing convincing evidence of the viability of forest efficiency. The artifacts these people buried with their dead—axes, fishhooks, and animal bones with males, nut-cracking stones, beads, and pestles with females—reflect the different roles of men and women in their society.

THE DEVELOPMENT OF FARMING

The use of a wide variety of food sources during the Archaic period eventually led many Indian people to develop and adopt the practice of farming. The dynamic center of this development in North America was in the highlands of Mexico, from which the new technology spread north and east.

Mexico

At the end of the Stone Age ("Stone Age" is generic for all the world, while "Archaic" is specific to the New World and is the equivalent of "mesolithic" for Europe), people in four different parts of the world developed farming systems, each based on a different crop: rice in Southeast Asia, wheat in West Asia, maize (or Indian corn) in Mexico, and potatoes in the Andean highlands of South America. In Mexico a great variety of other crops—most importantly beans and squash, but also tomatoes, peppers, avocados, cocoa (chocolate), and vanilla—supplemented maize. Today, maize and potatoes, the two American crops, contribute more to the world's food supply than do wheat and rice. These "miracle crops" fueled the expansion of European human and livestock populations in the three centuries after 1650. Without these and other New World crops, such as tobacco, American cotton, and rubber, each crop being the basis of important new industries and markets, the history of the modern world would have been far different.

Archaeological evidence suggests that plant cultivation in the highlands of central Mexico began about 5,000 years ago. Ancient Mexicans developed crops that responded well to human care and produced larger quantities of food in a limited space than did plants growing in the wild. Maize was particularly productive; over time it was adapted to a wide range of American climates, and farming spread throughout the temperate regions of North America, those characterized by relatively mild climates.

As farming became increasingly important, it radically reshaped social life. Where a foraging society might require 100 square miles to support 100 people,

Mesoamerican maize cultivation, as illustrated by an Aztec artist for the *Florentine Codex*, a book prepared a few years after the Spanish conquest. The peoples of Mesoamerica developed a greater variety of cultivated crops than those found in any other region in the world, and their agricultural productivity helped sustain one of the world's great civilizations.

SOURCE: American Museum of Natural History.

a farming society required only one square mile. Population growth and the need for people to remain near their fields throughout the year led to the appearance of villages and permanent architecture and eventually to the emergence of large, densely settled communities like Cahokia. Autumn harvests had to be stored during winter months, and the storage and distribution of food had to be managed. The division of labor increased with the appearance of specialists like toolmakers, crafts workers, administrators, priests, and rulers as well as farmers and food processors. Ultimately, unequal access to wealth and power resulted in the emergence of classes.

By 1000 B.C.E. urban communities governed by permanent bureaucracies had begun to form in Mesoamerica, the region stretching from central Mexico to Central America. By the beginning of the first millennium C.E. (Common Era), highly productive farming was supporting complex urban civilizations in the Valley of Mexico (the location of present-day Mexico City), the Yucatan Peninsula, and other parts of Mesoamerica. Like many of the an-

cient civilizations of Asia and the Mediterranean, these Mesoamerican civilizations were characterized by the concentration of wealth and power in the hands of an elite class of priests and rulers, the construction of impressive temples and other public structures, and the development of systems of mathematics and astronomy and several forms of hieroglyphic writing. These civilizations also engaged in warfare between states and held terrifying public rituals of human sacrifice.

The great city of Teotihuacan in the Valley of Mexico, which emerged about 100 B.C.E., had a population of as many as 200,000 at the height of its power around C.E. 500. Teotihuacan's elite class of religious and political leaders controlled an elaborate state-sponsored trading system that stretched from present-day Arizona to Central America and may have included coastal shipping connections with the civilizations of Peru. The city had a highly specialized division of labor. Artisans manufactured tools and produced textiles, stoneware, pottery, and obsidian blades. The bureaucratic elite collected taxes and tribute. Farmers worked the fields, and armies of workers constructed such monumental edifices as the Pyramids of the Sun and Moon, which still dominate the site's ruins.

Teotihuacan began to decline in the sixth century, and by the eighth century it was mostly abandoned. A new empire, that of the Toltecs, dominated central Mexico from the tenth to the twelfth century. By the fourteenth century a people known as the Aztecs, migrants from the north, had settled in the Valley of Mexico and begun a dramatic expansion into a formidable imperial power (see Chapter 2).

The Mayan peoples of the Yucatan peninsula developed a group of competing city-states that flourished from about 300 B.C.E. until C.E. 900. Their achievements included advanced writing and calendar systems and a sophisticated knowledge of mathematics.

The Resisted Revolution

Historians once described the development of farming as a revolution. They believed that agricultural communities offered such obvious advantages that their neighbors must have rushed to adopt this way of life. Societies that remained without a farming tradition must simply have been too "primitive" to achieve this breakthrough; vulnerability to fickle nature was the penalty for their ignorance. This interpretation was based on a scheme of social evolution whose proponents viewed human history as the story of technological progress, with hunters gradually developing into civilized farmers.

But there is very little evidence to support this notion of a "revolution" occurring during a short, critical period. The adoption of farming was a gradual process, one that required hundreds, even thousands of years. Moreover, ignorance of cultivation was never the reason that cultures failed to take up farming, for all hunter-gatherer peoples understand a great deal about plant reproduction. The Menominee Indians of the northern forests of Wisconsin, for example, when gathering wild rice, purposely allowed some of it to fall back into the water to ensure a crop for the next season, and Paiutes of the Great Basin systematically irrigated stands of their favorite wild food sources.

The way today's remaining hunter-gatherers view the farming way of life is instructive. Foragers generally look upon their own method of getting food as vastly superior to any other. The food sources of desert gatherers, for example, are considerably more varied and higher in protein than those of desert farmers, whose diets concentrate almost exclusively on grains. Because foragers take advantage of natural diversity, they are also less vulnerable to climatological stress; although gathering communities frequently experience periods of scarcity and hunger, unlike farming societies they are rarely devastated by famine. Foragers also point out that farming requires much more work. Why sweat all day in the fields producing tasteless corn, they argue, when in an hour or two one can gather enough sweet prickly pear to last a week? Indeed, rather than freeing men and women from the tyranny of nature, farming has tied people to a work discipline unlike anything previously known in human history. Finally, foragers consider their migratory ways far more interesting than village life, which they claim is dull and monotonous, preferred only by those whose possessions are too cumbersome to move.

As this new farming technology became available, cultures in different regions assessed its advantages and limitations. In California and the Pacific Northwest, acorn gathering or salmon fishing made the cultivation of food crops seem a waste of time. In the Great Basin, several peoples attempted to farm, but without success. Before the invention of modern irrigation systems, which require sophisticated engineering, only the Archaic Desert Culture could prevail in this harsh environment. In the neighboring Southwest, however, farming resolved certain ecological dilemmas and transformed the way of life. Like the development of more sophisticated traditions of tool manufacture, farming represented another stage in economic intensifications (like the advance in tool making represented by Clovis technology) that kept populations and available resources in balance. It seems that where the climate favored it, people tended to adopt farming as a way of increasing the production of food, thus continuing the Archaic tradition of squeezing as much productivity as they could from their environment. In a few areas, however, farming truly did result in a revolutionary transformation, creating urban civilizations like the one in central Mexico or at Cahokia, on the banks of the Mississippi.

Increasing Social Complexity

Farming created the basis for much greater social complexity within Indian communities. There were significantly more elaborate systems of kinship. Greater population density prompted families to group themselves into clans. Often different clans became responsible for different social, political, or ritual functions. Clans became an important mechanism for binding together the people of several communities into a tribe. Tribes, based on ethnic, linguistic, and territorial unity, were led by leaders or chiefs from honored clans, who were often advised by councils of elders. These councils sometimes arbitrated disputes between individuals or families, but most crimes—theft, adultery, rape, murder—were avenged by the aggrieved kinship group itself. In all likelihood, the city of Cahokia was governed by such a system.

The primary function of chiefs was the supervision of the economy, the collection and storage of the harvest, and the distribution of food to the clans. Differences in wealth, though small by the standards of modern societies, might develop between the families of a farming tribe. These inequalities were kept in check by redistribution according to principles of sharing similar to those operating in foraging communities. Nowhere in North America did Indian cultures develop a concept of the private ownership of land or other resources, which were usually considered the common resource of the people and were worked collectively.

Indian communities practiced a rather strict division of labor according to gender, which in its details varied tremendously from culture to culture. Among foraging peoples, hunting was generally assigned to men, and the gathering of food and the maintenance of home-base camps were the responsibility of women. This pattern probably originated during the Archaic period. But the development of farming called these patterns into question. In Mexico, where communities became almost totally dependent on crops, both men and women worked in the fields. Where hunting remained important, the older division of labor remained, with women responsible for fieldwork. In general, however, Indian patterns contrasted in important ways with the norms of colonizing Europeans, prompting much misunderstanding. When English colonists saw Indian women working in the cornfields, for example, they thought them greatly oppressed; Indians, on the other hand, thought colonial men who labored in the fields were performing "women's work."

The creation of man and woman depicted on a pot (dated about C.E. 1000) from the ancient villages of the Mimbres River of southwestern New Mexico, the area of Mogollon culture. Mimbres pottery is renowned for its spirited artistry. Such artifacts were usually intended as grave goods, to honor the dead.

SOURCE: National Museum of the American Indian/Smithsonian Institution.

Human figures dance on this characteristic piece of red-on-buff pottery of the Hohokams (dated about C.E. 1000). The Hohokams, located on the floodplain of the Gila River near present-day Phoenix, Arizona, were the first irrigation farmers of North America. The Pima and Tohono O'Odham people of Arizona may be descended from them.

SOURCE: Arizona State Museum, University of Arizona. Photo by Helga Teiwes.

In most North American Indian farming communities, women and men belonged to separate social groupings, each with its own rituals and lore. Membership in these societies was one of the most important elements of a person's identity. Marriage ties, on the other hand, were relatively weak, and in most Indian communities divorce was usually simple. The couple separated without a great deal of ceremony, the children almost always remaining with the mother. All Indian women controlled their own bodies, were free to determine the timing of reproduction, and were free to use secret herbs to prevent pregnancy, induce abortion, or ease the pains of childbirth. All this was strikingly different from European patterns, in which the rule of men over women and fathers over households was thought to be the social ideal.

Farming communities were far more complex than foraging communities, but they were also less stable. Growing populations demanded increasingly large surpluses of food, and this need often led to social conflict and warfare. Moreover, farming systems were especially vulnerable to changes in climate, such as drought, as well as to crises of their own making, such as soil depletion or erosion.

The Religions of Foragers and Farmers

The religions of Indian peoples were shaped primarily by the two great traditions of foraging and farming. The first, rooted deep in the Archaic past, is sometimes called the Hunting Tradition. This complex of beliefs centered in the relationship of hunters to prey, and celebrated the existence of a "Master of Animals," often portrayed as the Sacred Bear. Associated with this tradition was the vision quest, a practice in which young men and women sought out personal protective spirits by going into the wilderness alone, exposing themselves to the elements, fasting, and inducing hallucinations and dreams. An individual who developed a special sensitivity to spiritual forces might become a shaman, a "medicine" man or woman of the community. The Hunting Tradition was important throughout the continent but was strongest in the northern latitudes, where hunting played a prominent role in the economy.

With the northward spread of maize farming came a second religious complex, known as the Agrarian Tradition, which emphasized and celebrated the notion of fertility in ritual festivals marking the annual change of seasons. At Cahokia, archaeological evidence of posts used to mark the summer and winter solstices suggests that the Agrarian Tradition was honored there. Because this tradition was associated with the greater social complexity of the farming way of life, it was generally characterized by organized cults and priesthoods rather than by individualistic shamans. At its most elaborate, it featured a war-sacrifice-cannibalism ideology that glorified violence and included the ritual consumption of enemy flesh, a tradition whose origins may be related to those of the awe-inspiring sacrificial rituals performed by the priests and leaders of the Mesoamerican city-states.

Although religious beliefs were probably as distinctive as the local communities that held them, some combination of the hunting and agrarian traditions characterized most of the Indian cultures of North America. Natural and supernatural forces were thought to be inseparable, a system of belief called "pantheism"; people were thought to share a basic kinship with animals, plants, inanimate objects, and natural forces. Although many native religions recognized the existence of a paramount spiritual force, they were also generally polytheistic, with numerous lesser gods and spirits.

Farmers of the Southwest

Farming communities began to emerge in the arid Southwest during the first millennium B.C.E. Among the first to develop a settled farming way of life were the Mogollon people, who lived from around 250 B.C.E. to C.E. 1450 along what is today the southern Arizona–New Mexico border. Living along mountain ridges and near streams in permanent villages of ingenious pit houses well suited to the region's temperature extremes, these people used digging sticks to cultivate maize, beans, and squash. Some of the Mogollon pit structures may have been what Southwestern peoples today call *kivas*, which are used for community religious rituals.

From about C.E. 300 to 1500 the people of the Hohokam ("those who are gone," in the language of the modern tribes of the area) culture flourished in the region along the floodplain of the Salt and Gila rivers in southern Arizona. The Hohokams, who lived in agricultural villages, built and maintained the first irrigation system in America north of Mexico, channeling river water many miles to desert fields of maize, beans, squash, tobacco, and cotton. They made jewelry from shells and developed a process for etching shells with animal designs. They shared many traits with Mesoamerican civilization to the south, including platform mounds for religious ceremonies and large courts for ball playing. At a site near present-day Phoenix called Snaketown by the Pima Indians, archaeologists have recovered a variety of goods from central America—rubber balls, mirrors of pyrite mosaics, copper bells, and fashionable ear ornaments—suggesting that Snaketown may have housed a community of merchants who traded Mesoamerican manufactured goods for locally mined turquoise.

In Chaco Canyon, in northern New Mexico, lie the ruins of Pueblo Bonito, built in the twelfth century C.E. during the golden age of the Anasazis, an agricultural people who created a complex urban civilization amid the arid landscape of the Colorado Plateau. Until the invention of the modern construction techniques, Pueblo Bonito held the record as the world's largest apartment house.

SOURCE: Photo by David Hiser.

The Anasazis

The best-known farming culture of the Southwest is that of the Anasazis, which developed around the first century C.E. several hundred miles to the north of the Hohokam communities in the Four Corners area, where today Arizona, New Mexico, Utah, and Colorado meet on the great plateau of the Colorado River. Around 750, possibly in response to population pressure and an increasingly dry climate, the Anasazis began a shift from pit-house villages to densely populated, multistoried apartment complexes that the Spanish invaders called *pueblos*. These clustered around central complexes with circular underground *kivas*. The Anasazis grew high-yield varieties of maize in terraced fields irrigated by canals flowing from mountain catchment basins. To supplement this vegetable diet, they hunted animals for their meat, using the bow and arrow that first appeared in the region about C.E. 500.

Anasazi culture extended over an area larger than California. The sites of more than 25,000 Anasazi communities are known in New Mexico alone. Only a few have been excavated, so there is much that archaeologists do not yet understand. The most prominent of the Anasazi centers was Pueblo Bonito in Chaco Canyon. Completed in the twelfth century, this complex of 650 interconnected rooms is a monument to the golden age of the Anasazis. Hundreds of miles of arrow-straight roads and an interpueblo communication system consisting of mountaintop signaling stations connect Chaco Canyon to outlying sites, making it the center of a food distribution, trading, and ceremonial network.

The Anasazis faced a major crisis in the thirteenth century. The arid climate became even dryer, and growing Anasazi populations had to redouble their efforts to improve food production, building increasingly complex irrigation canals, dams, and terraced fields. A devastating drought from 1276 to 1293 (precisely dated with the aid of tree-ring analysis) resulted in repeated crop failures and eventual famine. This was accompanied by the arrival of Athapascan migrants who for a thousand years or more had been moving south from subarctic regions. These people were the immediate ancestors of the Navajos and the Apaches, and judging by their descendants, they must have been fierce fighters. By the fourteenth and fifteenth centuries, the Athapascans were raiding Anasazi farming communities, taking food, goods, and possibly slaves. (Indeed, the name *Anasazi* means "the place where they fought us" in Athapascan.) The dramatic Anasazi cliff dwellings at Mesa Verde, Colorado, constructed about this time, may have been built as a defense against these raiders. Gradually the Anasazis abandoned the Four Corners area altogether. Their movements have not yet been fully traced, but most seem to have resettled in communities along the Rio Grande, joining with local residents to form the Pueblo people of modern times.

Farmers of the Eastern Woodlands

Archaeologists date the beginning of the farming culture of eastern North America, known as Woodland culture, from the first appearances of pottery in the region about 3,000 years ago. The Woodland culture was based on a sophisticated way of life that combined gathering and hunting with the cultivation of a few crops. Sunflowers provided seeds and cooking oil. The presence of pipes in archaeological digs indicates that these farmers grew tobacco, which had spread north from the Caribbean, where it was first domesticated. These eastern peoples lived most of the year in permanent community sites, but moved seasonally to take advantage of the resources such as fishing, hunting, and the gathering of wild plants at different locations.

Woodlands people began cultivating maize during the first millennium C.E., but even before had begun to adopt an increasingly settled existence and a more complex social organization. Between 1700 and 700 B.C.E., the people of the Poverty Point culture in the lower Mississippi Valley erected a remarkable site consisting of a series of concentric semicircular earthen mounds, covering an area about a mile square. The people of the Adena culture occupied the Ohio River basin from present-day Indiana to Pennsylvania from before 1000 B.C.E. to about C.E. 250. They lived in permanent or semipermanent villages and built large burial mounds.

Between about 200 B.C.E. and fifth century C.E., the Hopewell people settled in the Mississippi-Ohio Valley. Hopewell communities were devoted to mortuary

The Great Serpent Mound in southern Ohio, the shape of an uncoiling snake more than 1,300 feet long, is the largest effigy earthwork in the world. Monumental public works like these suggest the high degree of social organization of the Mississippian people.

SOURCE: Photo by George Gerster. Comstock Images.

cults, in which the dead were honored through ceremony, display, and the construction of enormous and elaborate burial mounds. Hopewell chiefs mobilized an elaborate trade network that acquired obsidian from the Rocky Mountains, copper from the Great Lakes, mica from the Appalachians, and shells from the Gulf coast. Hopewell artisans converted these materials into goods that played an important role in Hopewell trade and were buried with their dead in Hopewell graves.

Mississippian Society

The Hopewell culture collapsed in the fifth century, perhaps as a result of shifting climate patterns. Local communities continued to practice their late Archaic subsistence strategies, but abandoned the expensive cultural displays demanded by the Hopewell mortuary cult. Following the collapse of Hopewell, however, several important innovations were introduced in the East. The bow and arrow, developed on the Great Plains, appeared east of the Mississippi about the seventh century, greatly increasing the efficiency of hunting. Also between 450 and 800, maize farming spread widely in the East. Indian farmers had developed a new variety of maize called Northern Flint, with large cobs and plentiful kernels that matured in a short enough time to make it suitable for cultivation in temperate northern latitudes. A shift from digging sticks to flint hoes also took place about this time, further increasing the productive potential of maize farming.

It was on the basis of these innovations that the powerful new Mississippian culture arose in the seventh or eighth century. The Mississippians were master maize farmers who lived in permanent villages along the floodplain of the Mississippi River. Cahokia, the most important of these, was the urban heart of Mississippian America. Cahokia's dense urban center with its monumental temple, its residential neighborhoods, and its surrounding farmlands were mirrored in many other regional centers, each with thousands of residents. There were cities on the Arkansas River near Spiro, Oklahoma; on the Black Warrior River at Moundville, Alabama; at Hiawassee Island on the Tennessee River; and along the Etowah and Okmulgee rivers in Georgia. The Great Serpent Mound, the largest effigy earthwork in the world, was constructed by Mississippian peoples in southern Ohio. Like Cahokia, these cities probably had a sophisticated division of labor that included artisans, priests, and an elite class of rulers.

These centers, linked by the vast river transportation system of the Mississippi and its many tributaries, became the earliest city-states north of Mexico, hierarchical chiefdoms that extended political control over the farmers of the surrounding countryside. With con-

This bottle in the shape of a nursing mother (dated about 1300 B.C.E.) was found at a Mississippian site. Historians can only speculate about the thoughts and feelings of the Mississippians, but such works of art are testimonials to the universal human emotion of maternal affection.

SOURCE: St. Louis Science Center.

tinued population growth, these cities engaged in vigorous and probably violent competition for the limited space along the rivers. It may have been the need for more orderly ways of allocating territories that stimulated the evolution of political hierarchies. The tasks of preventing local conflict, storing large food surpluses, and redistributing foodstuffs from farmers to artisans and elites required a leadership class with the power to command. Mound building and the use of tribute labor in the construction of other public works testified to the power of chiefs, who lived in sumptuous quarters atop the mounds. If politics is defined as the organized contest for power among people and groups, then the Mississippians and the Anasazis were the first truly political societies north of Mexico.

Mississippian culture reached its height between the eleventh and thirteenth centuries C.E., the same period in which the Anasazis constructed their desert

Web Exploration   Explore the impact of the environment on Indian trade networks. How does the environment influence the relationship between trade and culture? www.prenhall.com/faragher/map 1.1

- ● Regional centers
- • Local centers
- → Customary trading connections

Native North American Trade Networks, ca. C.E. 1400   By determining the origin of artifacts found at ancient sites, historians have devised a conjectural map of Indian trade networks. Among large regional centers and smaller local ones, trade connected Indian peoples of many different communities and regions.

cities. Both groups adapted to their own environment the technology that was spreading northward from Mexico. Both developed impressive artistic traditions, and their feats of engineering reflect the beginnings of science and technology. They were complex societies characterized by urbanism, social stratification, craft specialization, and regional trade—except for the absence of a writing system, all the traits of European civilization.

The Politics of Warfare and Violence

The late thirteenth century marked the end of several hundred years of weather very favorable to maize farming and the beginning of a century and a half of

cool, dry conditions. Although the changes in climate in the Mississippi Valley were not as severe as those that devastated the Anasazis of the Southwest, over the long term they significantly lowered the potential of farming to support growing urban populations. Some archaeologists have suggested that one consequence of this extended drought may have been greatly increased violence and social disorder.

Warfare among Indian peoples certainly predated the colonial era. Organized violence was probably rare among hunting bands, who seldom could manage more than a small raid against an enemy. Certain hunting peoples, though, such as the southward-moving Athapascans, must have engaged in systematic raiding of settled farming communities. Warfare was also common among farming confederacies fighting to gain additional lands for cultivation. The first Europeans to arrive in the southeastern part of the continent described highly organized combat among large tribal armies. The bow and arrow was a deadly weapon of war, and the practice of scalping seems to have originated among warring tribes, who believed one could capture a warrior's spirit by taking his scalp lock. (During the colonial period, Europeans warring with Indians placed bounties on scalps, encouraging an increase in the practice, and it spread widely among the tribes of other regions.) Sculpted images of human sacrifice found at Mississippian sites suggest that the inhabitants practiced a war-sacrifice-cannibalism complex similar to that of Mexico.

The archaeological remains of Cahokia reveal that during the thirteenth and fourteenth centuries the residents surrounded the central sections of their city with a heavy log stockade. There must have been a great deal of violent warfare with other nearby communities. Also during this period, numerous towns were formed throughout the river valleys of the Mississippi, each based on the domination of farming countrysides by metropolitan centers. Eventually conditions in the upper Mississippi Valley deteriorated so badly that Cahokia and many other sites were abandoned altogether, and as the cities collapsed, people relocated in smaller, decentralized communities. Among the peoples of the South, however, Mississippian patterns continued into the period of colonization.

CULTURAL REGIONS OF NORTH AMERICA ON THE EVE OF COLONIZATION

The United States is unique among the world's nations in encompassing all five general classes of global climate: subtropical jungles, arid deserts and grasslands, temperate woodlands, subarctic boreal forests, and frozen polar tundra. The country also contains some of the world's largest lakes, mightiest rivers, and most extensive forests and prairies. Indian peoples developed widely divergent ways of life in these different environments. An appreciation of the ways human cultures adapted to geography and climate is fundamental to an understanding of American history, for just as regions shaped the development of Indian cultures in the centuries before the arrival of Europeans, so they continued to influence the character of American life in the centuries thereafter.

In order to understand the impact of regions on Indian cultures, anthropologists divide North America into several distinct "culture areas" within which groups shared a significant number of cultural traits: Arctic, Subarctic, Great Basin, Great Plains, California, Northwest, Plateau, Southwest, South, and Northeast.

The Population of Indian America

In determining the precolonial population of the Americas, historical demographers consider a number of factors—the population densities that different technological and economic systems could support, the archaeological evidence, the very earliest European accounts, and the estimated impact of epidemic diseases. (For a discussion of epidemics among Indian peoples, see Chapter 2.) Although estimates vary, there is general agreement among historians that in the fifteenth century the population of America north of Mexico was between 7 and 10 million. Perhaps as many as 25 million people lived in the complex societies of Mesoamerica. Thus at the time of their first contact with European explorers and settlers, the peoples of the Western Hemisphere numbered 60 to 70 million, about the same as Europe's population at the time.

But population density varied widely by region. Although the Arctic, Subarctic, Great Basin, and Great Plains together make up more than half the continent's area, they were inhabited by only a small fraction of the population. These regions were inhabited by scattered bands who practiced the Archaic economy of hunting and gathering. That way of life continued in California as well, although the population there was large and dense because of the natural abundance of the region. In the Northwest, the narrow coastal strip running 2,000 miles from northern California to southern Alaska, abundant salmon fisheries supported large populations concentrated in permanent villages. The Indian societies of the Northwest coast were characterized by an elaborate material culture—notable especially for their wood carvings—and by their "potlatch" ceremonies, where prestige and rank was accumulated by those people who could give away the most goods. The people of the Plateau also made their living by fishing, but their communities were not as large nor as concentrated.

The largest populations of the continent were in the Southwest, South, and Northeast. Since it was in these culture areas that European explorers, conquerors, and colonists first concentrated their efforts, they deserve more detailed examination.

The Southwest

The single overwhelming fact of life in the Southwest is aridity. Summer rains average only ten to twenty inches annually, and on much of the dry desert cultivation is

WebExploration

Examine the population densities of various North American regions on the eve of European contact. Why were some regions more populated than others? **www.prenhal.com/faragher/map 1.2**

Number of people per square mile
- 4 or more
- 1 – 4
- 0 – 1

Indian Settlement before European Colonization   Based on what is called the "carrying capacity" of different subsistence strategies—the population density they could support—historical demographers have mapped the hypothetical population density of Indian societies in the fifteenth century, before the era of European colonization. Populations were most dense in farming societies or in coastal areas with marine resources and least dense in extreme environments like the Great Basin.

impossible. A number of rivers, however, flow out of the pine-covered mountain plateaus. Flowing south to the Gulf of Mexico or the Gulf of California, these narrow bands of green winding through parched browns and reds have made possible irrigation farming along their courses.

On the eve of European colonization, Indian farmers had been cultivating their Southwest fields for nearly 3,000 years. In the floodplain of the Gila and Salt rivers lived the Pimas and Tohono O'Odhams, descendants of the ancient Hohokams. Working small irrigated fields along the Colorado River, even on the floor of the Grand Canyon, were the Yuman peoples. In their oasis communities, desert farmers cultivated corn, beans, squash, sunflowers, and cot-

ton, which they traded throughout the Southwest. Often described as individualists, desert farmers lived in dispersed settlements that the Spanish called *rancherias*, their dwellings separated by as much as a mile. That way, say the Pimas, people avoid getting on each other's nerves. Rancherias were governed by councils of adult men whose decisions required unanimous consent, although a headman was chosen to manage the irrigation works. Ceremonies focused, appropriately, on rainmaking; one ritual required everyone to drink cactus wine until thoroughly drunk, a state of purification that was thought to bring rain.

East of the Grand Canyon lived the Pueblo peoples, named by the Spanish for their unique dwellings

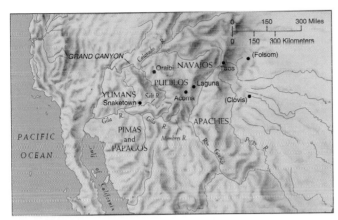

Southwestern Indian Groups on the Eve of Colonization   The Southwest was populated by desert farmers like the Pimas, Tohono O'Odhams, Yumans, and Pueblos, as well as by nomadic hunters and raiders like the Apaches and Navajos.

Southern Indian Groups on the Eve of Colonization   On the eve of colonization the Indian societies of the South shared many traits of the complex Mississippian farming culture.

of stacked, interconnected apartments. This building style originated with the Anasazis, who during the great population relocations of the fourteenth century joined with other indigenous groups to form the numerous Pueblo villages. Although speaking several languages, the Pueblos had a great deal in common, most notably their commitment to communal village life. A strict communal code of behavior that regulated personal conduct was enforced by a maze of matrilineal clans and secret religious societies; unique combinations of these clans and societies formed the governing systems of different Pueblo villages. Seasonal public ceremonies in the village squares included singing and chanting, dancing, colorful impersonations of the ancestral spirits called *kachinas*, and the comic antics of clowns who mocked in slapstick style those who did not conform to the communal ideal (pretending to drink urine or eat dirt, for example, in front of the home of a person who kept an unclean house).

The Pueblos inhabit the oldest continuously occupied towns in the United States. The village of Oraibi, Arizona, dates from the twelfth century, when the Hopis ("peaceful ones") founded it in the isolated central mesas of the Colorado Plateau. Using dry-farming methods and drought-resistant plants, these western Pueblo Indians produced rich harvests of corn and squash amid shifting sand dunes. On a mesa top about fifty miles southwest of present-day Albuquerque, New Mexico, Anasazi immigrants from Mesa Verde built Acoma, the "sky city," in the late thirteenth century. The Pueblo people established approximately seventy other villages during the next 200 years; fifty of these were still in existence in the seventeenth century when

the Spanish founded Santa Fé, and two dozen survive today, including the large Indian towns of Laguna, Isleta, Santo Domingo, Jémez, San Felipe, and Taos.

The Athapascans, more recent immigrants, also lived in the arid deserts and mountains. They hunted and foraged, traded meat and medicinal herbs with farmers, and often raided and plundered these same villages and rancherias. Gradually, some of the Athapascan people adopted the farming and handicraft skills of their Pueblo neighbors; they became known as the Navajos. Others, more heavily influenced by the hunting and gathering traditions of the Great Basin and Great Plains, remained nomadic and became known as the Apaches.

The South

The South enjoys a mild, moist climate with short winters and long summers, ideal for farming. From the Atlantic and Gulf coasts, a broad fertile plain extends inland to the Piedmont, a plateau separating the coastal plains from the Appalachian Mountains. The transition between plateau and coastal plain is marked by the Fall Line, an area of rapids and waterfalls on the descending rivers. The upper courses of the waterways originating in the Appalachian highlands offered ample rich bottom land for farming. The extensive forests, mostly of yellow pine, offered abundant animal resources. In the sixteenth century, large populations of Indian peoples farmed this rich land, fishing or hunting local fauna to supplement their diets. They lived in communities ranging from villages of twenty or so dwellings to large towns of a thousand or more inhabitants.

"The New Queen Being Taken to the King," engraved by Theodor de Bry in the sixteenth century from a drawing by Jacques le Moyne, an early French colonist of Florida. the communities of Florida were hierarchical, with classes and hereditary chiefs, some of whom were women. Here le Moyne depicted a "queen" being carried on an ornamental litter by men of rank.

SOURCE: Neg. No. 324281, photographed by Rota, engraving by de Bry. Courtesy Department Library Services, American Museum of Natural History.

Mississippian cultural patterns continued among many of the peoples of the South. Along the waterways many farming towns were organized into chiefdoms. Because most of these groups were decimated by disease in the first years of colonization, they are poorly documented. We know most about the Natchez, farmers of the rich floodplains of the lower Mississippi Delta, who survived into the eighteenth century before being destroyed in a war with the French. Overseeing the Natchez was a ruler known as the Great Sun, who lived in royal splendor on a ceremonial mound in the capital. When out among his subjects he was carried on a litter, the path before him swept by his retinue of servants and wives.

Natchez was a class society. Noble families ruled the majority, whom they called the "stinkards." Persistent territorial conflict with other confederacies elevated warriors to an honored status among the Natchez. Public torture and human sacrifice of enemies were common. The Natchez give us our best glimpse at what life would have been like in the community of Cahokia.

These chiefdoms were rather unstable. Under the pressure of climate change, population growth, and warfare many were weakened and others collapsed. As a result thousands of people left behind the grand mounds and earthworks to migrate to the woodlands and hill country where they took up hunting and foraging, returning to the tried and true methods of forest efficiency. They formed communities and ethnic confederacies that were less centralized and more egalitarian than the Mississippian chiefdoms, and would prove considerably more resilient to conquest.

Among the most prominent of these new ethnic groups were a people in present-day Mississippi and Alabama who came to be known as the Choctaws. Another group in western Tennessee became known as the Chickasaws, and another people in Georgia were known as the Creeks. On the mountain plateaus lived the Cherokees, the single largest confederacy, which included more than sixty towns. For these groups farming was somewhat less important, hunting somewhat more so. There were no ruling classes or kings, and leaders included women as well as men. Most peoples reckoned their descent matrilineally (back through generations of mothers), and after marriage husbands left the homes of their mothers to reside with the families of their wives. Women controlled household and village life, and were influential in the matrilineal clans that linked communities together. Councils of elderly men governed the confederacies, but were joined by clan matrons for annual meetings at the central council house. These gatherings could last days or even weeks because everyone, male or female, was given the opportunity to speak.

The peoples of the South celebrated a common round of agricultural festivals that brought clans together from surrounding communities. At the harvest festival, for example, people thoroughly cleaned their homes and villages. They fasted and purified themselves by consuming the "black drink," which induced visions. They extinguished the old fires and lit new ones, then celebrated the new crop of sweet corn with dancing and other festivities. During the days that followed, villages, clans, and groups of men and women competed against one another in the ancient stick-and-ball game that the French named lacrosse; in the evenings men and women played chunkey, a gambling game.

The Northeast

The Northeast, the colder sector of the eastern woodlands, has a varied geography of coastal plains and mountain highlands, great rivers, lakes, and valleys. After C.E. 500, cultivation became the main support of the Indian economy in those places where the growing season was long enough to bring a crop of corn to maturity. In such areas of the Northeast, along the coasts and in the river valleys, Indian populations were large and dense.

The Iroquois of present-day Ontario and upstate New York have lived in the region for at least 4,500 years. They were among the first northeastern peoples to adopt cultivation. The archaeological evidence suggests that as they shifted from primary reliance on fishing and hunting to maize farming, they relocated their villages from river bottoms to hilltops. There Iroquois women produced crops of corn, beans, squash, and sunflowers sufficient to support up to fifty longhouses, each occupied by a large matrilineal extended family. Some of those houses were truly long; archaeologists have excavated the foundations of some that extended 400 feet and would have housed dozens of families. Typically, these villages were surrounded by substantial wooden walls or palisades, clear evidence of intergroup conflict and warfare.

Population growth and the resulting intensification of farming in Iroquoia stimulated the development of chiefdoms there as elsewhere. By the fifteenth century several centers of population, each in a separate watershed, had coalesced from east to west across upstate New York. These were the five Iroquois chiefdoms or nations: the Mohawks, Oneidas, Onondagas, Cayugas, and Senecas. Iroquois oral histories collected during the nineteenth century recall this as a period of persistent violence, possibly the consequence of conflicts over territory.

Historians believe that the Iroquois founded a confederacy to control this violence. The confederacy outlawed warfare among the member nations and established regulated forms of gift exchange and

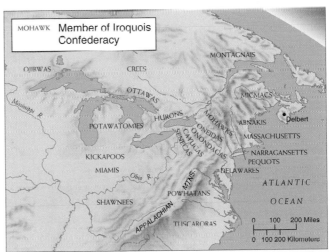

Northeastern Indian Groups on the Eve of Colonization   The Indians of the Northeast were mostly village peoples. In the fifteenth century five Iroquois groups—the Mohawks, Oneidas, Onondagas, Cayugas, and Senecas—joined together to form the Iroquois Five Nation Confederacy.

CHRONOLOGY

30,000–15,000 B.C.E.	First humans in the Americas		250 B.C.E.	Beginning of Mogollon culture in the Southwest
13,000 B.C.E.	Global warming trend begins		200 B.C.E.–C.E. 400	Hopewell culture flourishes
10,000 B.C.E.	Clovis technology		650	Bow and arrow, flint hoes, and Northern Flint corn in the Northeast
9000 B.C.E.	Extinction of big-game animals		775–1150	Hohokam site of Snaketown reaches its greatest extent
8000 B.C.E.	Beginning of the Archaic period		1000	Tobacco in use throughout North America
7000 B.C.E.	First cultivation of plants in the Mexican highlands		1150	Founding of Hopi village of Oraibi, oldest continuously occupied town in the United States
5000 B.C.E.	Athapascan migrations to America begin		1200	High point of Mississippian and Anasazi cultures
4000 B.C.E.	First settled communities along the Pacific coast		1276	Severe drought begins in the Southwest
3000 B.C.E.	Inupiat and Aleut migrations begin		1300	Arrival of Athapascans in the Southwest
1500–1000 B.C.E.	Maize and other Mexican crops introduced into the Southwest		1451	Founding of Iroquois Confederacy
1000 B.C.E.	Beginning of Adena culture First urban communities in Mexico			

payment to replace revenge. Iroquois oral history refers to the founder of the confederacy, Chief Deganawida the Lawgiver, as "blocking out the sun" as a demonstration of his powers, suggesting that these events might have taken place during a full solar eclipse, such as the one in the Northeast in 1451. Deganawida's message was proclaimed by his supporter, Hiawatha, a great orator, who convinced all the five Iroquois nations to join in confederacy. As a model of their government, the confederacy used the metaphor of the longhouse; each nation, it was said, occupied a separate hearth but acknowledged a common mother. As in the longhouse, women played important roles in the confederacy, choosing male leaders who would represent their lineages and chiefdom on the Iroquois council. The confederacy suppressed violence among its members, but did not

hesitate to encourage war against neighboring Iroquoian speakers, such as the Hurons or the Eries, who constructed defensive confederacies of their own at about the same time. The Iroquois Confederacy would become one of the most powerful forces during the colonial period.

The other major language group of the Northeast was Algonquian, whose speakers belonged to at least fifty distinct cultures. The Algonquian peoples north of the Great Lakes and in northern New England were hunters and foragers, organized into bands with loose ethnic affiliations. Several of these peoples, including the Micmacs, Crees, Montagnais, and Ojibwas (also known as the Chippewas), were the first to become involved in the fur trade with European newcomers. Among the Algonquians of the Atlantic coast from present-day Massachusetts south to Virginia, as well as among those in the Ohio Valley, farming led to the development of settlements as densely populated as those of the Iroquois.

In contrast to the Iroquois, most Algonquian peoples were patrilineal. In general, they lived in less extensive dwellings and in smaller villages, often without palisade fortifications. Although Algonquian communities were relatively autonomous, they began to form confederacies during the fifteenth and sixteenth centuries. Among these groupings were those of the Massachusetts, Narragansetts, and Pequots of New England; the Delawares and the peoples of Powhatan's confederacy on the mid-Atlantic coast; and the Shawnees, Miamis, Kickapoos, and Potawatomis of the Ohio Valley.

CONCLUSION

Over the thousands of years that elapsed between the settlement of North America and the invasion of Europeans at the end of the fifteenth century, Indian peoples developed hundreds of distinctive cultures that were fine-tuned to the geographic and climatic possibilities and limitations of their homelands. In the northern forests, they hunted game and perfected the art of processing furs and hides. Along the coasts and rivers they harvested the abundant runs of fish and learned to navigate the waters with sleek and graceful boats. In the arid Southwest, they mastered irrigation farming and made the deserts bloom, while in the humid Southeast, they mastered the large-scale production of crops that could sustain large cities with sophisticated political systems. North America was not a "virgin" continent, as so many of the Europeans believed. Indians had transformed the natural world, making it over into a human landscape.

"Columbus did not discover a new world," wrote historian J. H. Perry. "He established contact between two worlds, both already old." North America had a rich history, one that Europeans did not understand and later generations of Americans have too frequently ignored. The European colonists who came to settle encountered thousands of Indian communities with deep roots and vibrant traditions. In the confrontation that followed, Indian communities viewed the colonists as invaders and called upon their traditions and their gods to help them defend their homelands.

REVIEW QUESTIONS

1. List the evidence for the hypothesis that the Americas were settled by migrants from Asia.
2. Discuss the impact of environmental change and human hunting on the big-game populations of North America.
3. Review the principal regions of the North American continent and the human adaptations that made social life possible in each of them.
4. Define the concept of "forest efficiency." How does it help to illuminate the major development of the Archaic period?
5. Why did the development of farming lead to increasing social complexity? Discuss the reasons why organized political activity began in farming societies.
6. What were the Hunting and Agrarian Traditions? In what ways did the religious beliefs of Indian peoples reflect their environmental adaptations?
7. What factors led to the organization of the Iroquois Confederacy?

RECOMMENDED READING

Tom D. Dillehay, *The Settling of the Americas: A New Prehistory* (2000). A summary of the most recent archaeological findings, suggesting a much earlier migration to the Americas. For the newest discoveries, see the recent issues and websites of *National Geographic* and *Scientific American*.

Roger C. Echo-Hawk and Walter R. Echo-Hawk, *Battlefields and Burial Grounds: The Indian Struggle to Protect Ancestral Graves in the United States* (1994). A passionate discussion by a Pawnee lawyer and historian of the double standard that allows Indian graves to be ransacked while white graves are held sacred.

Thomas E. Emerson, *Cahokia and the Archaeology of Power* (1997). The fascinating story of North America's first metropolis.

Patricia Galloway, *Choctaw Genesis, 1500–1700* (1995). A path-breaking work that uses both archaeological and written evidence to tie together the precolonial and colonial periods of a tribal people of the South.

Alvin M. Josephy Jr., ed., *America in 1492* (1992). Important essays by leading scholars of the North American Indian experience. Includes beautiful illustrations and maps as well as an excellent bibliography.

Alice B. Kehoe, *North American Indians: A Comprehensive Account* (1992). The best general anthropological survey of the history and culture of the Indians of North America. Organized by culture areas, it covers all the peoples of the continent.

Stephen Plog, *Ancient Peoples of the American Southwest* (1998). Covers the shift to agriculture with a focus on both the costs and the benefits. An accessible text with wonderful photographs.

Robert Silverberg, *Mound Builders of Ancient America: The Archaeology of a Myth* (1968). A history of opinion and theory about the mound builders.

William C. Sturtevant, general ed., *Handbook of North American Indians*, 20 vols. proposed (1978–). The most comprehensive collection of the best current scholarship. The completed series will include a volume for each of the culture regions of North America; volumes on origins, Indian-white relations, languages, and art; a biographical dictionary; and a general index.

David Hurst Thomas, *Skull Wars: Kennewick Man, Archaeology, and the Battle for Native American Identity* (2000). A readable account of the controversy over Kennewick Man and the changing ideas about ancient North American history. When scholars, bureaucrats, and Indians go to court over these issues, he argues, everyone loses.

Russell Thornton, *American Indian Holocaust and Survival: A Population History since 1492* (1987). The best introduction to the historical demography of North America. Provides a judicious review of all the evidence in a field of considerable controversy.

▶ MEDIA RESOURCES

COMPANION WEBSITE HIGHLIGHTS
To view an exploration, enter one of the URLs below in your browser.

Web Explorations
Native North American Trade Networks, ca. C.E. 1400 and North American Elevation Regions
http://www.prenhall.com/faragher/map1.1
Indian Settlement before European Colonization
http://www.prenhall.com/faragher/map1.2

Additional Interactive Maps
To access the maps, go to this chapter's resources at
http://www.prenhall.com/faragher
Migration Routes from Asia to America, page 6
Climatological and Culture Regions of Native North America, page 8

Southwestern, Southern, and Northeastern Indian Groups on the Eve of Colonization, pages 19, 21

HISTORY RESOURCE CENTER
To find the resources listed below, go to
http://www.prenhall.com/historyresourcecenter

Images
Anasazi Cliff Palace
Aztec Rain God, Tlaloc
Clovis Points
Native American Agriculture
Powhatan In Longhouse
Pueblo Bonito

EXPLORING AMERICA

AMERICA AND THE HORSE

http://www.prenhall.com/faragher/thehorse

Why did a Spanish conquistador claim that after God, the horse was most responsible for his conquest of the Aztec empire in Mexico? Why did William Penn see horses as nuisances in colonial Pennsylvania? Where did the horse originate? How did the horse affect Navajo women? These questions and others are answered in the *America and the Horse* module of the Exploring America CD-ROM. The module explores the importance of the horse in North American history in narrative, primary source documents, pictures, a chronology, and an interactive map.

America and the Horse provides a variety of methods to examine the role this animal played in American history, showing that more than people contributed to the changes caused by the European intrusion into the Americas. Punctuated by important primary source excerpts, the narrative provides a tight storyline that describes the role of the horse in the development of Indian and European American cultures. The quotes by historical figures and the visual images illustrate the various ways the horse influenced Spanish conquest and Indian culture. The chronology and the interactive map provide important time and space contexts to the topic.

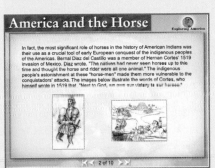

America and the Horse

In fact, the most significant role of horses in the history of American Indians was their use as a crucial tool of early European conquest of the indigenous peoples of the Americas. Bernal Diaz del Castillo was a member of Hernan Cortes' 1519 invasion of Mexico. Diaz wrote, "The natives had never seen horses up to this time and thought the horse and rider were all one animal." The indigenous people's astonishment at these "horse-men" made them more vulnerable to the conquistadors' attacks. The images below illustrate the words of Cortes, who himself wrote in 1519 that "Next to God, we owe our victory to our horses."

2 of 10

Reflect and Respond

1.   An old saying begins, "For want of a nail, the [horse] shoe was lost. For want of a shoe, the horse was lost. For want of a horse, the soldier was lost... "and so on until the kingdom is lost—"all for the want of a horseshoe nail." This is one example of what is called the ripple effect. If the horse was so important in commerce, war, postal service, information exchange, and industry, what effects rippled out from its presence in North America after the European conquest?

2.   What did it mean for the environment that populations of hundreds of horses had grown to millions? What did they eat? Where were they stabled or roaming? What effect might their

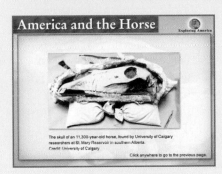

America and the Horse

The skull of an 11,300-year-old horse, found by University of Calgary researchers at St. Mary Reservoir in southern Alberta.
Credit: University of Calgary

Click anywhere to go to the previous page.

presence have had on other forms of animal and plant life? What ramifications were there for various American Indian lifestyles?

✓ Check it out

Growing Use of the Horse among Indians

This interactive map traces the spread of the horse from Mexico, north into the present-day United States. The map provides a good example of the Spanish influence on the development of Native American and European American cultures. Equally important, the spread of the horse indicates that tribes often associated with the animal, such as the Plains Indians, were rather late in encountering the animal that helped transform their way of life.

This exploration is also available on the *Exploring America* CD-ROM.

▶ The Battle Over Burials

There are thousands of ancient Indian burial mounds in the Midwest and South, dozens of them at Cahokia, maintained as a historical site by the state of Illinois. The people of the Adena, Hopewell, and Mississippian cultures built these mounds as memorials to commemorate their ancestors.

How should Americans manage the care of those mounds today? Should they be excavated for scientific study, exploited as tourist attractions, or treated as sacred sites? In 1990 such a dispute between American Indian activists and local residents wracked the small town of Lewiston, Illinois, about a hundred miles from Cahokia. Often communities come to blows over different ways of looking at history. Arguments over the meaning of the past are not confined to the classroom.

The controversy focused on the Dickson Mounds Museum, built on the site of several impressive mounds constructed by Mississippians around 1000 B.C.E. The museum's central attraction was an exhibit featuring the exposed graves of 237 individuals in one of the mounds. First opened in 1927 by Don Dickson, a local farmer who owned the land on which the mounds were located, the private exhibit attracted thousands of spectators. In the 1940s the state bought the site, constructed a large structure over the excavations, and installed a light and sound system. By the 1980s more than 80,000 visitors were coming each year to see the exposed graves.

As the site became more widely known it also became more controversial. Many Indians found the exhibit disrespectful and activists mounted strong pressure on the state to have the bodies reburied. How would Lewiston residents feel if their own cemeteries were excavated and exposed to public view? "It is my inherited responsibility to see the dead who were buried are responsibly reburied," said one Indian woman. Local residents, however, argued that reburial would deprive them of a valuable part of their heritage. For as long as people could remember, the town had boasted the "World's Greatest Display" of prehistoric Indian skeletons. The protesters were outsiders, and didn't have the community's best interests at heart. The exhibit displayed artifacts that local residents had discovered through hard work and persistence. It was "not a desecration but celebration of those who lived on and worked the land," in the words of one local politican. "Those Indians lived and died in our area, they're a part of our history," declared the town's mayor. The two groups interpreted the same site very differently. For one it was a buried treasure, an inheritance that had become a vital part of the life of the community. For the other it was a memorial to a great and departed culture.

While state officials worried over what to do, Indian activists took matters into their own hands. In April 1991 a group of several dozen protestors entered the museum, and using smuggled-in tools, began covering the graves with dirt before being stopped by museum guards. The protest got national attention. "What we did today was call the attention of this country's leaders to the last open burial exhibit in the country," said Charlene Teters, a member of the Spokane Nation and a graduate student at the University of Illinois. "The exhibit is a desecration of these ancients and should be closed."

The Lewistown dispute was part of a contentious national debate over the appropriate ways to memorialize the Indian past. Hundreds of museums around the country held extensive collections of Indian remains and sacred objects. There were, for example, thousands of Indian skulls at the Smithsonian Institution, many of them collected from nineteenth-century battle sites. "It wasn't enough that unarmed Cheyenne people were mowed down by the cavalry at the infamous Sand Creek massacre," wrote Suzan Shown Harjo, executive director of the National Congress of American Indians, "many were decapitated and their heads shipped to Washington." In 1989, after a long review of the question, the Smithsonian agreed to return the human remains in their collections to Indian tribes for reburial. The next year Congress passed the Native American Graves Protection and Repatriation Act (NAGPRA), which gave Indian communities the right to reclaim human remains and sacred objects to which they could establish historical linkage.

Despite fears that the law would result in the wholesale loss of valuable museum collections, for the most part curators, government officials, and Indians have found ways to work together. The return of Mississippian remains by the Missouri Historical Society in St. Louis, across the Mississippi from Cahokia, helped to build a relationship of trust with regional Indian

Lynn Kussman and Evelyn Voelker of the American Indian Center in St. Louis conduct a purification ceremony for Indian remains returned by the Missouri Historical Society. Although press reports have often focused on conflicts over remains, for the most part curators, government officials, and Indians have found ways to work together.

leaders. When the Society acquired a painted rawhide Comanche shield, tribal elders advised curators on how to properly handle it, enabling it to be displayed in a manner that Indians feel honors the spirit of the warrior who carried it.

At Lewistown the state of Illinois arranged a compromise designed to satisfy both Indian activists and local residents. The display was closed and the bones reburied, but the museum got a $4 million renovation. The new Dickson Mounds Museum, which reopened in 1994, is designed to be a site of memory for both Indians and local residents. Instead of gawking at skeletons, visitors watched multimedia presentations on local Indian history prepared in cooperation with Indian scholars and elders. There are also exhibits that interpret the history of the museum itself, with a special display honoring Don Dickson.

This flexible approach works in what cultural critic James E. Young calls the best tradition of memorials—suggesting to people different *ways* to remember, not precisely *what* to remember. Some local residents are still bitter about lost business. But others disagree. "In the past we had a display of bones," one said. "Now we have a museum. Our views and ideas of what is going on have changed." ■

www.researchnavigator.com

The Community and Memory essay for this chapter deals with questions surrounding the battle for control of ancient Indian burial sites at Cahokia in Illinois. For further research on the life and society of the peoples who built the mounds, use the tools available to you in Research Navigator.

As you investigate this topic, consider this question: "Why is there so much controversy surrounding the control of Indian burial sites?"

ContentSelect: Search in the anthropology and history databases using the search terms *Mississippian, Adena,* and *Hopewell.*

Links Library: Access the History: U.S. History and Anthropology databases.

New York Times on the Web: To find more information on recent American Indian issues, search using the term *National Congress of American Indians.*

The French, under the command of Jean Ribault, discover the River of May (St. Johns River) in Florida on May 1, 1562. Colored engraving, 1591, by Theodor de Bry after a now lost drawing by Jacques Le Moyne de Morgues; the Granger Collection.

The English and the Algonquians at Roanoke

IT WAS LATE AUGUST 1590 WHEN ENGLISH SHIPS SAILED through Hatteras Inlet into Pamlico Sound, off the coast of present-day North Carolina, and made their way north through rough seas to Roanoke Island, where Governor John White had left the first English community in North America three years before. Anxiously, White went ashore in search of the 115 colonists—mostly single men, but also twenty families, including his own daughter, son-in-law, and granddaughter Virginia Dare, the first English baby born in America. Finding the houses "taken down" and possessions "spoiled and scattered about," White suddenly noticed some writing on a tree trunk: "in fair capital letters was graven CROATOAN." Because this was the name of a friendly Indian village fifty miles south and because White found no sign of a cross, which he had instructed the colonists to leave if they were in trouble, he felt sure that his people awaited him at Croatoan, and he returned to his ship, anxious to speed to their rescue.

The Roanoke settlement had been sponsored by Walter Raleigh, a wealthy adventurer who sought profit and prestige by organizing an English colony to compete with the Spanish, who after the voyage of Columbus had founded a powerful empire in the New World. When his men returned from a reconnoitering expedition to the area in 1584, they reported that the coastal region was densely populated by a "very handsome and goodly people." These Indians, the most southerly of the Algonquian coastal peoples, enjoyed a prosperous livelihood farming, fishing, and hunting from their small villages of one or two dozen communal houses. At an island the Indians called Roanoke, the English had been "entertained with all love and kindness" by a chief named Wingina. The leader of several surrounding villages, Wingina welcomed the English as potential allies in his struggle to extend his authority over still others. So when Raleigh's adventurers asked the chief's permission to establish a settlement on the island, he readily granted it, even sending two of his men back to England to assist in preparations for the enterprise. Manteo and Wanchese, the Indian emissaries, worked with Thomas Harriot, an Oxford scholar, and John White, an artist. The four men learned one another's language, and there seems to have been a good deal of mutual respect among them.

But when an all-male force of Englishmen returned in 1585 to establish the colony of Virginia (christened in honor of England's virgin queen, Elizabeth I), the two Indian emissaries offered Chief Wingina conflicting reports. Although Manteo, from the village of Croatoan, argued that their technology would make the English powerful allies, Wanchese described the disturbing inequalities of English society and warned of potential brutality. Wanchese was right to suspect English intentions, for Raleigh's plans were based not on respect for the Indians but on the expectation of exploiting them. He warned of their treachery. Indeed, Raleigh had directed the mission's commander to "proceed with extremity" should the Indians prove difficult and "bring them all in subjection to civility," meaning that they should be made serfs to English colonial masters. Raleigh anticipated that his colony would return profits through the lucrative trade in furs, a flourishing plantation agriculture, or gold and silver mines. In any case, the Indians would supply the labor.

The English colony was incapable of supporting itself. After building a rough fort on the island, the colonists turned to Wingina for supplies. With the harvest in the storage pits, with fish running in the streams and fat game in the woods, Wingina did the hospitable thing. It was the duty of a chief to distribute presents and thus to create obligations on the part of the recipients. But as fall turned to winter and the stores declined, constant English demands threatened the Indians' resources. Wingina's people were also stunned by the new diseases that came with the intruders. "The people began to die very fast, and many in [a] short space," Harriot wrote. The "disease was so strange that they neither knew what it was, nor how to cure it." In the spring Wingina and his people ran out of patience. But before the Indians could act, the English caught wind of the rising hostility, and in May 1586 they surprised the villagers, killing several of the leading men and beheading Wingina. With the plan of using Indian labor now clearly impossible, the colonists returned to England.

John White and Thomas Harriot, who had spent their time exploring the physical and human world of the coast and recording their findings in notes and sketches, were appalled by this turn of events. Back in England, Harriot insisted to Raleigh that the attack on the villagers came "upon causes that on our part might easily enough have been borne" and argued that "through discreet dealing" the Indians might "honor, obey, fear and love us." White proposed a new plan for a colony of real settlers, a community of English families who might live in harmony with the Indians. Harriot and White clearly considered English civilization superior to Indian society, but their vision of colonization was considerably different from that of the plunderers.

In 1587, Raleigh arranged for John White to return to America as governor of a new civilian colony composed of English families. The party was supposed to land on Chesapeake Bay, but their captain dumped them instead at Roanoke so he could get on with the profitable activity of plundering the Spanish. Thus the colonists found themselves amid natives who were alienated by the bad treatment of the previous expedition. Within a month one of White's colonists had been shot full of arrows

by attackers under the leadership of Wanchese, who after Wingina's death became the most millitant opponent of the English among the Roanoke Indians. White retaliated with a counterattack that increased the hostility of the Indians. Knowing that their entire mission hung in the balance but lacking a vessel large enough to carry them all back to England, the colonists begged White to return home in their only seaworthy ship and to press Raleigh for support. Reluctantly, White set sail but arrived just as a war began between England and Spain. Three anxious years passed before White was able to return to Roanoke, only to find the settlement destroyed and the colonists gone.

As White and his crew set their sights for Croatoan that August morning in 1590, a great storm blew up. "We drove fast into the shore," White wrote, and all hands feared imminent shipwreck. Several times they dropped anchor, but each time the cable broke. Finally, White and the ship's captain agreed that they would have to leave the sound for deeper waters. It proved to be White's last glimpse of America. Tossed home on a stormy sea, he never returned. The English settlers of Roanoke became known as the Lost Colony, their disappearance and ultimate fate one of the enduring mysteries of colonial history.

The Roanoke experience is a reminder of the underlying assumptions of New World colonization. "The English would act just as the Spanish had done in creating their empire," writes the historian and geographer Carl Sauer. They had "naked imperial objectives." It also suggests the wasted opportunity of the Indians' initial welcome. But in an unexpected way, the Roanoke story also emphasizes the importance of community. There is evidence that the lost colonists lived out the rest of their lives with the Algonquians. In 1609 the English at Jamestown learned from local Indians that "some of our nation planted by Sir Walter Raleigh [are] yet alive," and many years later an English surveyor at Croatoan Island was greeted by natives who told him that "several of their Ancestors were white People," that "the English were forced to cohabit with them for Relief and Conversation, and that in the process of Time, they conformed themselves to the Manners of their Indian Relations." It may be that Virginia Dare and the other children married into Indian families, creating the first mixed community of English and Indians in North America. ■

Roanoke

KEY TOPICS

- The European background of American colonization

- Creation of the Spanish New World empire and its first extensions to North America

- The large-scale intercontinental exchange of peoples, crops, animals, and diseases

- The French role in the beginnings of the North American fur trade

- England's first overseas colonies in Ireland and America

THE EXPANSION OF EUROPE

Roanoke and other European colonial settlements of the sixteenth century came in the wake of Christopher Columbus's voyage of 1492. There may have been many unrecorded contacts between the peoples of America and the Old World before Columbus. Archaeological excavations at L'Anse aux Meadows on the fogbound Newfoundland coast provide evidence for a Norse landing in North America in the tenth or eleventh century. Norse sagas recounted the exploits of their pioneer heroes, yet they were forgotten within a century. But the contact with the Americas established by Columbus had earthshaking consequences. Within a generation of his voyage, continental exchanges of peoples, crops, animals, and germs had reshaped the Atlantic world. The key to understanding these remarkable events is the transformation of Europe during the several centuries preceding the world of Columbus.

European Communities

Western Europe was an agricultural society, the majority of its people peasant farmers. Farming and livestock raising had been practiced in Europe for thousands of years, but great advances in farming technology took place during the late Middle Ages. Water mills, iron plows, improved devices for harnessing ox and horse power, and systems of crop rotation greatly increased productivity. Over several centuries farmers more than doubled the quantity of European land in cultivation. The increased supply of food helped the population of western Europe nearly triple between the eleventh and fourteenth centuries.

Most Europeans were village people, living in family households. Men performed the basic field work; women were responsible for child care, livestock, and food preparation. In the European pattern, daughters usually left the home and village of their families to live among their husband's people. Women were furnished with dowries, but generally excluded from inheritance. Divorce was almost unknown.

Europe was a world of social contrasts. Europe was characterized by a social system historians have called "feudalism." The land was divided into hundreds of small territories, each ruled by a family of lords who claimed a disproportionate share of wealth and power. Feudal lords commanded labor service from peasants and tribute in the form of crops. They were the main beneficiaries of medieval economic expansion, accumulating great estates and building castles. The majority of peasants, however, experienced little improvement in their standard of living over time.

Most Europeans were Christians, united under the authority of the Roman Catholic Church, whose complex organization spanned thousands of local communities with a hierarchy that extended from parish priests all the way to the pope in Rome. At the core of Christian belief was a set of communal values: love of God the father, loving treatment of neighbors, and the fellowship of all believers. Yet the Catholic Church itself was one of the most powerful landowners in Europe, and it devoted most of its considerable resources to awe-inspiring display rather than the relief of poverty and suffering. It insisted on its dogmas and actively persecuted heretics, nonbelievers, and believers in older "pagan" religions, who were branded "witches." The church legitimized the power relationships of Europe and counseled the poor and downtrodden to place their hopes in heavenly rewards.

Europe was also home to numerous communities of Jews, who had fled from their their homeland in Palestine after a series of unsuccessful revolts against Roman rule in the first century C.E. Both church and civic authorities subjected the Jews to discriminatory treatment. Restricted to ghettos and forbidden from owning land, many Jews turned adversity to advantage, becoming merchants who specialized in long-distance trade. But Jewish success only seemed to stimulate

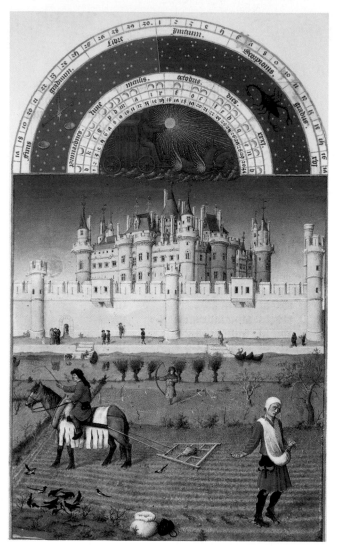

A French peasant labors in the field before a spectacular castle in a page taken from the illuminated manuscript *Tres Riches Heures,* made in the fifteenth century for the duc de Berry. In 1580 the essayist Montaigne talked with several American Indians at the French court who "noticed among us some men gorged to the full with things of every sort while their other halves were beggars at their doors, emaciated with hunger and poverty" and "found it strange that these poverty-stricken halves should suffer such injustice, and that they did not take the others by the throat or set fire to their houses."

SOURCE: Photograph by GIRAUDON, Art Resource, N.Y.

Christian hostility. Thus, in the thirteenth and fourteenth centuries the Jews were forced out of England, France, and Spain.

For the great majority of Europeans, living conditions were harsh. Most rural people survived on bread and porridge, supplemented with seasonal vegetables and an occasional piece of meat or fish. Infectious diseases abounded; perhaps a third of all children died

before their fifth birthday, and only half the population reached adulthood. Famines periodically ravaged the countryside. A widespread epidemic of bubonic plague, known as the "Black Death," swept in from Asia and wiped out a third of Europe's population between 1347 and 1353. Disease led to famine and violence, as groups fought for shares of a shrinking economy. In Flanders during the 1320s, peasants rose against both nobility and church, beginning a series of rebellions that culminated in the great English Peasants' Revolt of 1381. "We are made men in the likeness of Christ," one rebel declared, "but you treat us like savage beasts!"

The Merchant Class and the New Monarchies

Strengthened by the technological breakthroughs of the late Middle Ages, the European economy proved it had a great capacity for recovery. During the fourteenth century disease and famine did not reappear in the same calamatious pattern, and there was an expansion of commerce, especially trade in basic goods, such as cereals and timber, minerals and salt, wine, fish, and wool. Commercial expansion stimulated the growth of markets and towns. By 1500, Europe had recovered from the shock of the Black Death and the population had nearly returned to its former peak of about 62 million.

During this revival the monarchs of Western Europe emerged as the new centers of power, building legitimacy by promising internal order as they unifed their realms. In the fifteenth century they began the construction of royal bureaucracies and standing armies and navies. In many cases, these new monarchs found support among the rising merchant class, which in return sought lucrative royal contracts and trading monopolies. The alliance between commercial interests and the new states was an important development that prepared the way for European expansion.

The Renaissance

The heart of this dynamic European commercialism lay in the city-states of Italy. During the late Middle Ages, the cities of Venice, Genoa, and Pisa launched armed, commercial fleets that seized control of trade in the Mediterranean. Their merchants became the principal outfitters of the Crusades, a series of great military expeditions promoted by the Catholic Church to recover Palestine from the Muslims. The conquest of the Holy Land by Crusaders at the end of the eleventh century delivered the silk and spice trades of Asia into the hands of the Italian merchants. Tropical spices—cloves, cinnamon, nutmeg, and pepper from the Indies (now known as Indonesia)—were in great demand, for they made the European diet far less monotonous for the aristocrats who could afford the new products from East. Asian civilization also supplied a number of technical innovations that further propelled European economic growth, including the compass, gunpowder, and the art of printing with movable type—"the three greatest inventions known to man," according to English philosopher Francis Bacon.

Contact with Muslim civilization provided Western scholars with access to important ancient Greek and Roman texts that had been lost to them during the Middle Ages but preserved in the great Muslim libraries. The revival of interest in classical antiquity sparked the period of intellectual and artistic flowering in Europe during the fourteenth, fifteenth, and sixteenth centuries known as the Renaissance. The revolution in publishing (made possible by the perfection of the printing press and moveable type), the beginning of regular postal service, and the growth of universities helped spread this revival throughout the elite circles of Europe.

The Renaissance celebrated human possibility. "The nature of all other beings is limited," the Italian intellectual Pico della Mirandola wrote in 1486, "but you, constrained by no limits, in accordance with your own free will, shall ordain for yourself the limits of your nature." This human-centered perspective was evident in many endeavors. The Gothic style of medieval cathedrals, whose soaring forms were intended to take human thoughts heavenward, gradually gave way to the use of measured classical styles, thought to encourage rational reflection. In painting and sculpture there was a new focus on the human body. Artists modeled muscles with light and shadow to produce heroic images of men and women. These were aspects of a movement that became known as "humanism," a revolt against religious authority in which the secular took precedence over the purely religious. This Renaissance outlook was a critical component of the spirit that motivated the exploration of the Americas.

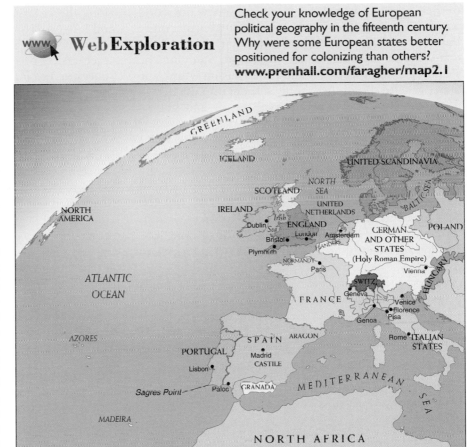

WebExploration   Check your knowledge of European political geography in the fifteenth century. Why were some European states better positioned for colonizing than others?
www.prenhall.com/faragher/map2.1

Western Europe in the Fifteenth Century   By the middle of the century, the monarchs of western Europe had unified their realms and begun to build royal bureaucracies and standing armies and navies. These states, all with extensive Atlantic coastlines, sponsored the voyages that inaugurated the era of European colonization.

Portuguese Explorations

Portugal, a narrow land along the western coast of the Iberian Peninsula with a long tradition of seafaring, became the first of the new Renaissance kingdoms to explore distant lands. Lisbon, the principal port on the sea route between the Mediterranean and northwestern Europe, was a bustling, cosmopolitan city with large enclaves of Italian merchants. By 1385 local merchants had grown powerful enough to place their own favorite, João I, on the throne, and he had ambitious plans to establish a Portugese trading empire.

A central figure in this development was the son of the king, Prince Henry, known to later generations as "the Navigator." In the spirit of Renaissance learning, Henry established an academy of eminent geographers, instrument makers, shipbuilders, and seamen at his institute on the southwestern tip of Portugal at Sagres Point. By the mid-fifteenth century, as a result of their efforts, all educated Europeans knew the world was a spherical globe. The idea that fifteenth-century Europeans believed the world to be "flat" is one of the many myths about Columbus's voyage. Studying the seafaring traditions of Asia and the Muslim world, the men of Sagres Point incorporated them into the design of a new ship called the caravel, faster and better-handling than any ship previously known in Europe.

Using caravels, the Portuguese explored the Atlantic coast of northwestern Africa for direct access to the lucrative gold and slave trades of that continent. By the time of Prince Henry's death in 1460, they had colonized the Atlantic islands of the Azores and the Madeiras and founded bases along the western African "Gold Coast." The Italian merchants of Lisbon were also interested in finding a way to sail around Africa to the Indies, because in 1453 the Ottoman Turks had captured Constantinople and prohibited Christians from using the overland trade routes to the Far East. In 1488 Portuguese captain Bartholomew Días rounded the southern tip of Africa, and ten years later Vasco da Gama, with the aid of Arab pilots, reached India. The Portuguese eventually erected strategic trading forts along the coasts of Africa, India, and China, the first and longest-lasting outposts of European world colonization, and gained control of much of the Asian spice trade. Most important for the history of the Americas, the Portuese established the Atlantic slave trade. (For a full discussion of slavery, see Chapter 4.)

Columbus Reaches the Americas

In 1476, Christopher Columbus, a young Genoan sailor, joined his brother in Lisbon, where he became a seafaring merchant for Italian traders. Over the next ten years he traveled widely—to the Madeira Islands, to Ireland and England, to the African Gold Coast. Gradually he developed the simple idea of opening a new route to the Indies by sailing west across the Atlantic Ocean, known at that time as the "Western Sea." Such a venture would require royal backing, but when he approached the various monarchs of Europe with his idea, their advisers laughed at his geographic ignorance, pointing out that his calculation of the distance to Asia was much too short. They were right, Columbus was wrong. But it turned out to be an error of monumental good fortune.

Columbus finally sold the plan to the monarchs of Castile and Aragon, Isabel and Ferdinand. These two had just completed the *Reconquista*, a centuries-long struggle between Catholics and Muslims that finally ended Muslim rule in Spain. Through these many generations of warfare, the Spanish had developed a military tradition that thrived on conquest and plunder. Military service was a popular means by which ordinary men could enrich themselves and rise into the ranks of the noble class. The Catholic monarchs of Spain were eager for new lands to conquer, and observing the successful Portuguese push to the south along the west coast of Africa, they became interested in opening lucrative trade routes of their own to the Indies. Columbus called his undertaking "the Enterprise of the Indies," suggesting his commercial intentions. But his mission was more than commercial. His expedition included men and supplies for founding a settlement, for one of his prime goals was to "occupy" the islands he found, establishing title for Spain

This ship, thought to be similar to Columbus's Niña, is a caravel, a type of vessel developed by the naval experts at Henry the Navigator's institute at Sagres Point in Portugal. To the traditional square-rigged Mediterranean ship, they added the "lateen" sail of the Arabs, which permitted much greater maneuverability. Other Asian improvements, such as the stern-post rudder and multiple masting, allowed caravels to travel farther and faster than any earlier ships, and made possible the invasion of America.

SOURCE: Drawing by BJORN LANDSTROM from *The Ship.* Dell Publishing.

by the right of occupancy. Like the adventurers who later established the first English colony at Roanoke, Columbus's objectives were starkly imperial.

Among the many Columbus myths is the story that Queen Isabel pawned her jewels to finance the voyage. In fact, the monarchs financed his expedition with funds confiscated from the Spanish Jews, hundreds of thousands of whom were expelled from the kingdom by royal decree in 1492. Columbus himself made the connection in a letter he later wrote to the monarchs. "After having driven out all the Jews from your realms, . . . Your Highnesses commanded me that, with a sufficient fleet, I should go to the said parts of India." It was an ominous sign of things to come.

Columbus's ships left the port of Palos, Spain, in August 1492, pushed west across the Atlantic by the prevailing trade winds. By October, flocks of birds and bits of driftwood announced the ships' approach to land. The first men to sight land were Luis Torres and Rodrigo de Triana. It was Friday night and the two men—both of them secret Jews—were sitting on deck quietly chanting Sabbath psalms. "We who had been awake all night were the first to see land," Torres later wrote. It turned out to be a small, flat island somewhere in the Bahamas, now thought by many to be Samana Cay. But Columbus believed he was in the Indies, somewhere near the Asian mainland.

He explored the northern island coasts of Cuba and Hispaniola before heading home, fortuitously catching the westerly winds that blow from the American coast toward Europe north of the tropics. One of Columbus's most important contributions was the discovery of the clockwise circulation of the Atlantic winds and currents that would carry thousands of European ships back and forth to the Americas.

Leading Columbus's triumphal procession to the royal court were half a dozen kidnapped Taino Indians from the Bahamas, dressed in bright feathers with ornaments of gold. The natives, Columbus noted, were "of a very acute intelligence," but had "no iron or steel

This image accompanied Columbus's account of his voyage, which was published in Latin and reissued in many other languages and editions that circulated throughout Europe before 1500. The Spanish King Ferdinand is shown directing the voyage to a tropical island, where the natives flee in terror. Columbus's impression of Native Americans as a people vulnerable to conquest shows clearly in this image.

SOURCE: The Granger Collection.

weapons." A conflict between the Tainos and several armed Spaniards had ended quickly with the deaths of two natives. "Should your majesties command it," Columbus announced to Ferdinand and Isabel, "all the inhabitants could be made slaves." Moreover he reported that "there are many spices and great mines of gold and of other metals." In fact, none of the spices familiar to Europeans grew in the Caribbean and there were only small quantities of precious metal in the riverbeds of the islands. But the sight of the little gold ornaments worn by the Indians infected Columbus with gold fever. He left a small force behind in a rough fort on Hispaniola—the first European foothold in the Americas.

The monarchs, enthusiastic about Columbus's report, financed a convoy of seventeen ships and 1,500 men that left in late 1493 to begin the colonization of the islands. Like the later English colonists at

Roanoke, Columbus expected that Indians would provide the labor. But at Hispaniola Columbus found his fort in ruins and his men killed by Indians who, like the Algonquians at Roanoke, had lost patience with continuing European demands. The Spanish destroyed the nearby native villages, enslaving the Tainos and demanding tribute in gold. Columbus sent boatloads of slaves back to Spain, but most soon sickened and died, and the supply of gold quickly ran out. By the time of Columbus's third voyage in 1500, the Spanish monarchs had become so dissatisfied with these results that they ordered Columbus home in leg irons.

Columbus made two additional trips to the Caribbean, both characterized by the same violent raiding for slaves and obsessive searching for gold. He died in Spain in 1506, still convinced that he had opened the way to the Indies. This belief persisted among many Europeans well into the sixteenth century. But others had already begun to see the discoveries from a different perspective. Amerigo Vespucci of Florence, who voyaged to the Caribbean in 1499, was the first to describe Columbus's Indies as *Mundus Novus*, a "New World." When European geographers finally named this continent in the sixteenth century, they honored Vespucci's insight by calling it America.

THE SPANISH IN THE AMERICAS

A century after Columbus's death, before the English had planted a single successful New World colony of their own, the Spanish had created a huge and wealthy empire in the Americas. In theory, all law and policy for the empire came from Spain; in practice, the isolation of the settlements led to a good deal of local autonomy. The Spanish created a caste system, in which a small minority of settlers and their offspring controlled the lives and labor of millions of Indian and African workers. But it was also a society in which colonists, Indians, and Africans mixed to form a new people.

The Invasion of America

The first stages of the Spanish invasion of America included frightful violence. Armies marched across the Caribbean islands, plundering villages, slaughtering men, and capturing women. Columbus and his successors established an institution known as the *encomienda*, in which Indians were compelled to labor in the service of Spanish lords. The relationship was supposed to be reciprocal, with lords protecting Indians in exchange for service, but in practice it amounted to slavery. Rather than work, one Spanish observer noted, many Indians took poison, "and others hanged themselves." Faced with labor shortages, slavers raided the Bahamas and soon had entirely depopulated them. The depletion of gold on Hispaniola led to the invasion of the islands of Puerto Rico and Jamaica in 1508, then Cuba in 1511. Meanwhile, rumors of wealthy societies to the west led to scores of probing expeditions. The Spanish invasion of Central America began in 1511,

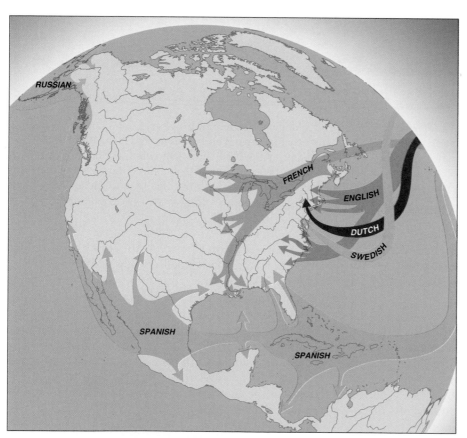

The Invasion of America   In the sixteenth century the Spanish first invaded the Caribbean and used it to stage their successive wars of conquest in North and South America. In the seventeenth century, the French, English, and Dutch invaded the Atlantic coast. The Russians, sailing across the northern Pacific, mounted the last of the colonial invasions in the eighteenth century.

The Cruelties used by the Spaniards on the Indians, from a 1599 English edition of *The Destruction of the Indies* by Bartolomé de las Casas. These scenes were copied from a series of engravings produced by Theodore de Bry that accompanied an earlier edition. SOURCE: British Library.

and two years later Vasco Núñez de Balboa crossed the Isthmus of Panama to the Pacific Ocean. In 1517 Spaniards landed on the coast of Mexico, and within a year they made contact with the Aztec empire.

The Aztecs had migrated to the highland valley of Mexico from the deserts of the American Southwest in the thirteenth century, in the wake of the collapse of the Toltec empire (see Chapter 1). The warlike Aztecs settled a marshy lake district and built the city of Tenochtitlán. By the early fifteenth century they dominated the peoples of the highlands, in the process building a powerful state. Tribute flowed into Tenochtitlán from all over Mexico and Central America. In public rituals designed to appease their gods, Aztec priests brutally sacrificed captives atop the grand pyramids. By 1519, the population of the Aztec capital numbered approximately 300,000, five times the size of the largest city in Spain.

Hernán Cortés, a veteran of the conquest of Cuba, landed on the Mexican coast with armed troops in 1519. Within two years he overthrew the Aztec empire, a spectacular military accomplishment that has no parallel in the annals of conquest. The Spanish had superior arms and rode horses, which the Indians found terrifying. But these were not the principal causes of the Spanish success. Cortés skillfully exploited the resentment of the many native peoples who lived under Aztec domination, forging Spanish-Indian alliances that became a model for the subsequent European colonization of the Americas. Here, as at Roanoke and

dozens of other sites of European invasion, colonists found Indians eager for allies to support them in their conflicts with their neighbors. Still, the Aztecs were militarily powerful, successfully drove the Spaniards from Tenochtitlán, and put up a bitter and prolonged defense of their besieged capital. But in the meantime the Aztecs suffered a devastating smallpox epidemic that killed thousands and undermined their ability to resist. In the aftermath of conquest, the Spanish unmercifully plundered Aztec society, providing the Catholic monarchs with wealth beyond their wildest imagining. Later, the discovery of rich silver mines and the exploitation of Mexican labor through the encomienda system turned Spain into the mightiest state in Europe.

The Destruction of the Indies

The Indian peoples of the Americas resisted Spanish conquest, but most proved a poor match for mounted warriors with steel swords and man-eating dogs. The record of the conquest, however, includes many brave Indian leaders and thousands of martyrs. The Carib people (from whom the Caribbean takes its name) successfully defended the outermost islands until the end of the sixteenth century, and in the arid lands of northern Mexico the nomadic tribes known collectively as the Chichimecs proved equally difficult to subdue.

Some Europeans protested the horrors of the conquest. Principal among them was Bartolomé de las

Casas, a Spanish Catholic priest who had participated in the plunder of Cuba in 1511, but who several years later suffered a crisis of conscience and began to denounce the Spanish conquerors. The Christian mission in the New World was to convert the Indians to Christianity, he argued, and "the means to effect this end are not to rob, to scandalize, to capture or destroy them, or to lay waste their lands." Long before the world recognized the concept of universal human rights, las Casas was proclaiming that "the entire human race is one," which earned him a reputation as one of the towering moral figures in the early history of the Americas. Las Casas had powerful supporters at court who made repeated but unsuccessful attempts to reform the treatment of Indians.

In his brilliant history of the conquest, *The Destruction of the Indies* (1552), las Casas blamed the Spanish for cruelties that resulted in millions of Indian deaths—in effect, genocide. Translated into several languages and widely circulated throughout Europe, las Casas's book was used by other European powers to condemn Spain, thereby covering up their own dismal colonial records—creating a "Black Legend" of Spanish colonization. Although later scholars disputed las Casas's

estimates of huge population losses, recent demographic studies suggest that the native people of Hispaniola numbered in the hundreds of thousands when Columbus arrived, and fifty years later they had been reduced to a few hundred. In Mexico, the 1519 population of 25 million plummeted to only a million a century later.

Las Casas was incorrect, however, in attributing most of these losses to warfare. To be sure, thousands of lives were lost in battle, but these deaths accounted for but a small proportion of the overall population decline. Thousands more starved because their economies were destroyed or their food stores taken by conquering armies. Even more important, native birthrates fell drastically after the conquest. Indian women were so "worn out with work," one Spaniard wrote, that they avoided conception, induced abortion, and even "killed their children with their own hands so that they shall not have to endure the same hardships."

Epidemic diseases—influenza, plague, smallpox, measles, typhus—were the primary cause of the drastic reduction of native populations. The Caribbean and Central America were home to many tropical diseases—most of them parasitic disorders such as typhus and spotted fever transmitted by insect bites. But preconquest America had no virulent epidemic diseases, which meant that Indian peoples lacked the antibodies necessary to protect them from European germs and viruses. Las Casas himself described the effects of epidemic disease on the Tainos: "There came among them such illness, death, and misery, that of fathers, mothers, and children an infinite number sadly died." Smallpox first came from Spain in 1518, exploding in an epidemic so virulent that, in the words of an early Spanish historian, "it left Hispaniola, Puerto Rico, Jamaica, and Cuba desolated of Indians." The epidemic crossed into Mexico in 1520, destroying the Aztecs, then spread along the existing Indian trade network, in 1524 strategically weakening the Inca empire eight years before it was conquered by Spanish conquistador Francisco Pizarro. Spanish chroniclers

This drawing of victims of the smallpox epidemic that struck the Aztec capital of Tenochtitlán in 1520 is taken from the *Florentine Codex*, a postconquest history written and illustrated by Aztec scribes. "There came amongst us a great sickness, a general plague," reads the account, "killing vast numbers of people. It covered many all over with sores: on the face, on the head, on the chest, everywhere. . . . The sores were so terrible that the victims could not lie face down, nor on their backs, nor move from one side to the other. And when they tried to move even a little, they cried out in agony."

SOURCE: The Granger Collection.

wrote that this single epidemic killed half the native Americans it touched. Disease was the secret weapon of the Spanish, and it helps explain their extraordinary success in the conquest.

Such devastating outbreaks of disease, striking for the first time against a completely unprotected population, are known as "virgin soil epidemics." After the conquest, Mexicans sang of an earlier time.

There was then no sickness.
They had then no aching bones.
They had then no high fever.
They had then no smallpox.
They had then no burning chest.
They had then no abdominal pains.
They had then no consumption.
They had then no headache.
At that time the course of humanity was orderly.
The foreigners made it otherwise when they arrived here.

Warfare, famine, lower birthrates, and epidemic disease knocked the population of Indian America into a downward spiral that did not swing upward until the beginning of the twentieth century. By that time the native population had fallen by 90 percent. It was the greatest demographic disaster in world history. The outstanding difference between the European colonial experience in the Americas and Africa or Asia was this radical reduction in the native population.

It is possible that the New World sent one disease, venereal syphilis, back across the Atlantic. The first recorded epidemic of syphilis in Europe took place in Spain in 1493, and many historians think it may have been carried home by the sailors on Columbus's ships. By 1495 the disease was spreading rapidly among Europe's armies, and by the sixteenth century it had found its way to Asia and Africa.

Intercontinental Exchange

The passage of diseases between the Old and New Worlds was one part of the large-scale continental exchange that marks the beginning of the modern era of world history. The most obvious exchange was the vast influx into Europe of the precious metals plundered from the Aztec and Incan empires of the New World. "The best thing in the world is gold," Columbus wrote, and Cortés remarked that "we Spaniards suffer from a disease of the heart, the specific remedy for which is gold." Most of the golden booty was melted down, destroying forever thousands of priceless Indian artifacts. Silver from mines the Spanish discovered and operated in Mexico and Peru tripled the amount of silver coin circulating in Europe between 1500 and 1550, then tripled it again before 1600. The result was runaway inflation, which stimulated com-

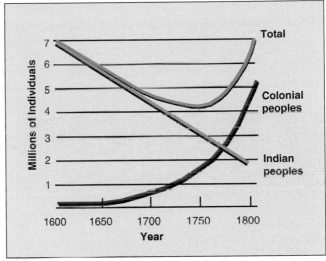

North America's Indian and Colonial Populations in the Seventeenth and Eighteenth Centuries

The primary factor in the decimation of native peoples was epidemic disease, brought to the New World from the Old. In the eighteenth century the colonial population overtook North America's Indian populations.

SOURCE: Historical Statistics of the United States (Washington, DC: Government Printing Office, 1976), 8, 1168; Russell Thornton, *American Indian Holocaust and Survival* (Norman: University of Oklahoma Press, 1987), 32.

merce and raised profits but lowered the standard of living for most people.

But of even greater long-term importance were the New World crops brought to Europe. Maize (Indian corn) from Mexico, the staff of life for most North Americans, became a staple crop in Mediterranean countries, the dominant feed for livestock elsewhere in Europe, and the primary provision for the slave ships of Africa. Over the next few centuries, potatoes from Peru provided the margin between famine and subsistence for the peasant peoples of northern Europe and Ireland. These "miracle crops" provided abundant food sources that went a long way toward ending the persistent problem of famine in Europe.

Although the Spanish failed to locate valuable spices such as black pepper or cloves in the New World, new tropical crops more than compensated. Tobacco was first introduced to Europe about 1550 as an antidote against disease, but was soon in wide use as a stimulant. American vanilla and chocolate both became highly valued. American cotton proved superior to Asian varieties for the production of cheap textiles. Each of these native plants, along with tropical transplants from the Old World to the New—sugar, rice, and coffee were among the most important—supplied the basis for important new industries and markets that altered the course of world history.

Columbus introduced domesticated animals into Hispaniola and Cuba, and livestock were later transported to Mexico. The movement of Spanish settlement into northern Mexico was greatly aided by an advancing wave of livestock, for grazing animals seriously disrupted native fields and forests. Horses, used by Spanish stockmen to tend their cattle, also spread northward. In the seventeenth century they reached the Great Plains of North America, where they eventually transformed the lives of the nomadic hunting Indians (see Chapter 5).

The First Europeans in North America

Ponce de León, governor of Puerto Rico, was the first conquistador to attempt to extend the Spanish conquest to North America. In 1513 he landed on the southern Atlantic coast, which he named in honor of the Easter season—*pascua florida*. Florida thus became the oldest European place name in the United States. Warriors from the powerful Indian chiefdoms there beat back Ponce de Leon's attempts to take slaves and finally suceeded in killing him in 1521. Seven years later another Spanish attempt to colonize Florida, under the command of Pánfilo de Narváez, also ended in disaster. Most of Narváez's men were lost in a shipwreck, but a small group of them survived, living and wandering for several years among the Indian peoples of the Gulf coast and the Southwest until they were finally rescued in 1536 by Spanish slave hunters in northern Mexico. One of these castaways, Alvar Núñez Cabeza de Vaca, published an account of his adventures in which he told of a North American empire known as Cíbola, with golden cities "larger than the city of Mexico."

Cabeza de Vaca's report inspired two Spanish expeditions. The first attempt to penetrate the mystery of North America was mounted by Hernán de Soto, a veteran of the conquest of Peru. After landing in Florida in 1539 with a Cuban army of over 700 men, he pushed hundreds of miles through the heavily populated South, commandeering food and slaves from the Mississippian Indian towns in his path. But de Soto failed to locate another Aztec empire. In present-day Alabama, thousands of warriors besieged his army, and a few months later the ancestors of the modern Chickasaws chewed the Spaniards apart. His army depleted by half, de Soto desperately drove his men westward, crossing the Mississippi and marching deep into present-day Arkansas before returning to the banks of the great river, where he died in 1542. Some 300 of de Soto's dispirited survivors eventually reached Mexico on rafts in 1543. They told of the great farming fields of the Mississippians but also emphasized the ferocity of the warriors. The native peoples of the South had successfully turned back Spanish invasion. But de Soto also introduced epidemic diseases that drastically depopulated and undermined the Mississippian chiefdoms of the South. When Europeans eventually returned to colonize the region they found native people living in decentralized confederacies.

In the year of the de Soto expedition, 1539, Spanish officials in Mexico launched a second attempt to conquer North America, this one aimed at the Southwest. Francisco Vásquez de Coronado led 300 mounted men and infantry and 800 Indian porters north along well-marked Indian trading paths, passing through the settlements of Piman Indians near the present border of the United States and Mexico and finally reaching the Pueblo villages along the Rio Grande. The initial resistance of the Pueblo people was quickly quashed. But Coronado was deeply disappointed by these towns "of stone and mud, rudely fashioned," and sent out expeditions in all directions in search of the legendary golden cities of Cíbola. He led his army as far north as the Great Plains, where they observed great herds of "shaggy cows" (buffalo) and made contact with nomadic hunting peoples, but returned without gold. For the next fifty years Spain lost all interest in the Southwest.

The Spanish New World Empire

By the late sixteenth century the Spanish had control of a powerful empire in the Americas. A century after Columbus, some 200,000 European immigrants, most of them Spaniards, had settled in the Americas. Another 125,000 Africans had been forcibly resettled as slaves on the Spanish plantations of the Caribbean, as well as on the Portuguese plantations of Brazil. (The Portuguese colonized Brazil under the terms of the Treaty of Tordesillas, a 1494 agreement dividing the Americas between Spain and Portugal. See Chapter 4.) Most of the Spanish settlers lived in the more than 200 urban communities founded during the conquest, including cities such as Santo Domingo in Hispaniola; Havana in Cuba; Mexico City, built atop the ruins of Tenochtitlán; and Quito and Lima in the conquered empire of the Incas. Only a small number of Spaniards and their offspring lived in the countryside. There they supervised Indian or African workers in mining, ranching, or agriculture.

Spanish women came to America as early as Columbus's second expedition, but over the course of the sixteenth century they made up only about 10 percent of the immigrants. Thus from the beginning male colonists married or cohabited with Indian or African women. The result was the growth of large mixed-ancestry groups known respectively as *mestizos* and *mulattoes*. The Spanish established a frontier of inclusion, their communities characterized by a great deal of marriage and sexual mixing between male colonists

Analyze the environmental factors that influenced French, Spanish, and English explorations. What were the reasons behind the different experiences of each of these countries?
www.prenhall.com/faragher/map2.2

Web Exploration

European Exploration, 1492–1591 By the mid-sixteenth century Europeans had explored most of the Atlantic coast of North America and penetrated into the interior in the disastrous expeditions of de Soto and Coronado.

and native women. Hundreds of thousands of Indians died, but Indian genes were passed on to generations of mixed ancestry people, who became the majority population in the mainland Spanish American empire.

Populated by Indians, Africans, Spanish colonists, and their mixed offspring, the New World colonies of Spain made up one of the largest empires in the history of the world. The empire operated, in theory, as a highly centralized and bureaucratic system. But the Council of the Indies, composed of advisers of the Spanish king who made all the laws and regulations for the empire, was located in Spain. Thus, what looked in the abstract like a centrally administered empire tolerated a great deal of local decision making. Passive resistance and sometimes outright defiance of central authority were common in this system.

NORTHERN EXPLORATIONS AND ENCOUNTERS

When the Spanish empire was at the height of its power in the sixteenth century, the merchants and monarchs of other European seafaring states looked across the Atlantic for opportunities of their own. France was first to sponsor expeditions to the New World in the early sixteenth century. At first the French attempted to plant settlements on the coasts of Brazil and Florida, but Spanish opposition ultimately persuaded them to concentrate on the North Atlantic. England did not develop its own plans to colonize North America until the second half of the sixteenth century, concentrating on the middle latitudes, between the Spanish in Florida and the French in the high latitudes of the north Atlantic coast.

Fish and Furs

Long before France and England made attempts to found colonies, however, European fishermen were exploring the coastal North American waters of the North Atlantic. The Grand Banks, off the coast of Newfoundland, had abundant cod. The waters teemed with "so great multitudes of certain big fishes," in the words of one early English seaman, "that they sometimes stayed my ships." It is possible that European fishermen were working those waters before Columbus's voyages. Certainly by 1500 hundreds of ships and thousands of sailors were sailing annually to the Grand Banks.

The first official voyages of exploration in the North Atlantic used the talents of experienced European sailors and fishermen. With a crew from Bristol, England, Genovese captain John Cabot reached Labrador in 1497, but the English did little to follow up on his voyage. In 1524, Tuscan captain Giovanni da Verrazano, sailing for the French, explored the North American coast from Cape Fear (North Carolina) to the Penobscot River (Maine). Encouraged by his report, the French king commissioned experienced captain Jacques Cartier to locate a "Northwest Passage" to the Indies. Although in his voyages of 1534, 1535, and 1541 Cartier failed to find a Northwest Passage, he reconnoitered the St. Lawrence River, which led deep into the continental interior to the Great Lakes, with easy access to the Ohio and Mississippi rivers, giving France an incomparable geographic edge over other colonial powers. Cartier's attempts to plant settlements on the St. Lawrence failed, but he established France's imperial claim to the lands of Canada.

The French and other northern Europeans thus discovered the Indian people of the northern woodlands, and the Indians in turn discovered them. Native tales told of seeing the approach of floating islands (ships) with many tall trees (masts) and hairy bears (sailors) running about in the branches. The contacts between Europeans and natives here took a different form than in the tropics, based on commerce rather

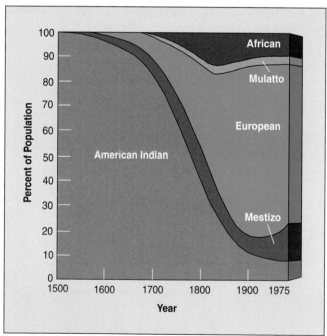

The African, Indian, and European Population of the Americas   In the 500 years since the European invasion of the Americas, the population has included varying proportions of Native American, European, and African peoples, as well as large numbers of persons of mixed ancestry.

SOURCE: Colin McEvedy and Richard Jones, *Atlas of World Population History* (New York: Penguin, 1978), 280.

This watercolor of Jacques le Moyne, painted in 1564, depicts the friendly relations between the Timucuas of coastal Florida and the colonists of the short-lived French colony of Fort Caroline. The Timucuas hoped that the French would help defend them against the Spanish, who plundered the coast in pursuit of Indian slaves.

SOURCE: Jacques Le Moyne, *Rene de Loudonniere and Chief Athore*, 1564 (watercolor), The New York Public Library, NY

than conquest. The Indians immediately appreciated the usefulness of textiles, glass, copper, and ironware. Seeing Cartier's approach, the Micmacs waved him ashore. "The savages showed marvelous great pleasure in possessing and obtaining iron wares and other commodities," he noted in his report. For his part, Cartier was interested in the fur coats of the Indians. Europeans, like Indians, used furs for winter clothing. But the growing population of the late Middle Ages had so depleted the wild game of Europe that the price of furs had risen beyond the reach of most people. The North American fur trade thus filled an important demand and produced high profits.

Beginning in the sixteenth century, the fur trade would continue to play an important role in the Atlantic economy for three centuries. By no means were Indians simply the victims of European traders. They had a sharp eye for quality, and cut-throat competition among traders provided them with the opportu-

nity to hold out for what they considered good prices. But the fur trade was essentially an unequal exchange, with furs selling in Europe for ten or twenty times what Indians received for them. The trade also had negative consequences. European epidemic disease followed in the wake of the traders, and violent warfare broke out between tribes over access to hunting grounds. By the end of the sixteenth century disease and violence had turned the valley of the St. Lawrence River into a virtual no-man's land. Moreover, as European manufactured goods, such as metal knives, kettles, and firearms, became essential to their way of life, Indians became dependent upon European suppliers. Ultimately, the fur trade was stacked in favor of Europeans.

By 1600, over a thousand European ships were trading for furs each year along the northern coast. The village of Tadoussac on the St. Lawrence, where a wide bay offered Europeans safe anchorage, became

In his sketch of this "Capitaine" of the Illinois nation (drawn about 1700), the French artist Charles Becard de Granville carefully noted the tattooing of the warrior's face and body, his distinctive costume and feather headdress, his spear and tobacco pipe.

SOURCE: Louis Nicholas, Northern Indian, *Capitaine de la Nation*, from the Codex Canadensis, 1701, by Charles Becard. National Archives of Canada/The Thomas Gilcrease Institute of American History and Art, Tulsa, Oklahoma

the customary place for several weeks of trading each summer, a forerunner of the western fur-trade rendezvous of the nineteenth century. Early in the seventeenth century the French would move to monopolize the trade there by planting colonies along the coast and on the St. Lawrence.

The Protestant Reformation and the First French Colonies

The first French colonies in North America, however, were planted further south by a group of religious dissenters known as the Huguenots. The Protestant Reformation—the religious revolt against the Roman Catholic Church—had begun in 1517 when German priest Martin Luther publicized his differences with Rome. Luther declared that eternal salvation was a gift from God and not related to works or service to the Catholic Church. His protests—Protestantism—fit into a climate of widespread dissatisfaction with the power and prosperity of the Catholic Church. Luther attracted followers all over northwestern Europe, including France, where they were persecuted by Catholic authorities. Converted to Luther's teachings in 1533, Frenchman John Calvin fled to Switzerland, where he developed a radical theology. His doctrine of predestination declared that God had chosen a small number of men and women for "election," or salvation, while condemning the vast majority to eternal damnation. Calvinists were instructed to cultivate the virtues of thrift, industry, sobriety, and personal responsibility, which Calvin argued were signs of election and essential to the Christian life. Calvinism was thus an important stimulant in the transition from a medieval agrarian economy to a commercial and industrial era.

Calvin's followers in France—the Huguenots—were concentrated among merchants and the middle class, but also included a portion of the nobility opposed to the central authority of the Catholic monarch. In 1560 the French monarchy defeated the attempt of a group of Huguenot nobles to seize power, which inagurated nearly forty years of violent religious struggle. In an attempt to establish a religious refuge in the New World, Huguenot leaders were behind the first French attempts to establish colonies in North America. In 1562, Jean Ribault and 150 Protestants from Normandy landed on Parris Island, near present-day Beaufort, South Carolina, and began the construction of a fort and crude mud huts. Ribault soon returned to France for supplies, where he was caught up in the religious wars. The colonists nearly starved and were finally forced to resort to cannibalism before being rescued by a passing British ship. In 1564, Ribault established another Huguenot colony, Fort Caroline on the St. Johns River of Florida, south of present-day Jacksonville. The native Timucuas, he reported, were friendly and hospitable, welcoming the colonists into their homes and honoring them with food and drink. At Fort Caroline the Huguenots seemed to enjoy the kind of relations with the Indians that John White hoped for at Roanoke.

The Spanish were alarmed by these moves. They had shown no interest in colonizing Florida, but worried about protecting their ships, riding home to Spain loaded with gold and silver on the offshore Gulf Stream. Not only was Fort Caroline manned by Frenchmen, but by Protestants—deadly enemies of the

Catholic monarchs of Spain. "We are compelled to pass in front of their port," wrote one official, "and with the greatest ease they can sally out with their armadas to seek us." In 1565 the Spanish crown sent Don Pedro Menéndez de Avilés, captain general of the Indies, to crush the Huguenots. After establishing a settlement south of the French at a place called St. Augustine, he marched his men overland through the swamps to surprise the Huguenots from the rear. "I put Jean Ribault and all the rest of them to the knife," Menéndez wrote triumphantly to the king, "judging it to be necessary to the service of the Lord Our God and of Your Majesty." More than 500 Frenchmen lay dead on the Florida beach, a disastrous end to Huguenot attempts to plant a colony in America. The Spanish built a fort and established a garrison at St. Augustine, which thus became the oldest continuously occupied European city in North America.

The Huguenots fared no better back in France. In 1572 the French crown directed the slaughter of more than 3,000 French Protestants in Paris, and many more throughout the country. This attack, known as the St. Bartholomew's Day Massacre, made France infamous as the enemy of Protestantism. In 1589 the Huguenot Henry IV became king, but he found it impossible to govern until he converted to Catholicism. In 1598 his Edict of Nantes declared the right of Huguenots to their views, but established Roman Catholicism as the official religion of France.

Sixteenth-Century England

The English movement across the Atlantic, like the French, was tied to social change at home. Perhaps most important were changes in the economy. As the prices of goods rose steeply—the result of New World inflation—English landlords, their rents fixed by custom, sought ways to increase their incomes. Seeking profits in the woolen trade, many converted the common pasturage used by tenants into grazing land for sheep, dislocating large numbers of farmers. Between 1500 and 1650 a third of all the common lands in England were "enclosed" in this way. Deprived of their livelihoods, thousands of families left their traditional rural homes and sought employment in English cities, crowding the roads with homeless people.

Sixteenth-century England also became deeply involved in the struggles of the Reformation. At first, King Henry VIII of England (reigned 1509–47) supported the Catholic Church and opposed the Protestants. But there was great public resentment in England over the vast properties owned by the Church and the loss of revenue to Rome. When the pope refused to grant Henry an annulment of his marriage to Catherine of Aragon, daughter of Ferdinand and Isabel of Spain, the king exploited this popular mood. Taking up the cause of reform in 1534, he declared himself head of a separate Church of England. He later took over the English estates of the Catholic Church—about a quarter of the country's land—and used their revenues to begin constructing a powerful English state system, including a standing army and navy. Working through Parliament, Henry carefully enlisted the support of the merchants and landed gentry for his program, parceling out a measure of royal prosperity in the form of titles, offices, lands, and commercial favors. By 1547, when Henry died, he had forged a solid alliance with the wealthy merchant class.

Henry was succeeded by his young and sickly son Edward VI, who soon died. Next in succession was Edward's half-sister Mary, who attempted to reverse her father's Reformation from the top by martyring hundreds of English Protestants, gaining herself the title of "Bloody Mary." But upon her death in 1558, her half-sister Elizabeth I (reigned 1558–1603) came to the throne. Elizabeth sought to end the religious turmoil by tolerating a variety of views within the English church. Criticized by radical Protestants for not going far enough, and condemned by Catholics for her "pretended title to the kingdom," Elizabeth nevertheless gained popularity among her subjects because of her moderate approach. The Spanish monarch, head of the most powerful empire in the world, declared himself the defender of the Catholic faith and vowed to overthrow her. England and Spain now became the two principal rivals in the Catholic-Protestant confrontation.

Fearing Spanish subversion on the neighboring Catholic island of Ireland, Elizabeth urged enterprising supporters such as Walter Raleigh and his half-brother Humphrey Gilbert to subdue the Irish Catholics and settle homeless English families on their land. During the 1560s, Raleigh, Humphrey, and many other commanders invaded the island and viciously attacked the Irish, forcing them to retreat beyond a frontier line of English settlement along the coast. So ferociously did the Irish resist the conquest that an image of the "wild Irish" became fixed in the English mind. Gilbert retaliated with even greater brutality, decapitating captured Irish men and women and using their head as paving stones, "so that none should come into his tent for any cause but commonly he must pass through a lane of heads." Such barbarism did not prevent the English from considering the Irish an inferior race, and the notion that civilized people could not mix with such "savages" was an assumption English colonists would carry with them to the Americas.

The Armada Portrait of Elizabeth I, painted by an unknown artist in 1648. The queen places her hand on the globe, symbolizing the rising seapower of England. Through the open windows we see the battle against the Spanish Armada in 1588 and the destruction of the Spanish ships in a providential storm, interpreted by the queen as an act of divine intervention.

SOURCE: *Elizabeth I,* Armada portrait, c. 1588 (oil on panel), by English School. Private collection/The Bridgeman Art Library International, Ltd.

Early English Efforts in the Americas

England's first ventures in the New World were made against the backdrop of its conflict with Spain. In 1562 John Hawkins violated Spanish regulations by transporting a load of African slaves to the Caribbean, bringing back valuable tropical goods. Thus the English began their participation in the slave trade. (For a full discussion see Chapter 4.) The Spanish attacked Hawkins on another of his voyages

in 1567, an event English privateers such as Francis Drake used as an excuse for launching a series of devastating and lucrative raids against Spanish New World ports and fleets. The goal was to punish the Spanish and in the process steal as much wealth as possible. "He that commands the sea commands the trade," declared Walter Raleigh, "and he that is lord of the trade of the world is lord of the wealth." The voyages of these English "Sea Dogs" greatly enriched their investors, including Elizabeth herself. The English thus began their American adventures by slaving and plundering.

A consensus soon developed among Elizabeth's closest advisers that the time had come to enter the competition for America. In a state paper written for the queen, Richard Hakluyt summarized the advantages that would come from colonies: they could provide bases from which to raid the Spanish in the Caribbean, outposts for an Indian market for English goods, and plantations for growing tropical products, freeing the nation from a reliance on the long-distance trade with Asia. Moreover, by populating them with the "multitudes of loiterers and idle vagabonds" of England, colonies offered a solution to the problem of social dislocation and homelessness. He urged Elizabeth to establish such colonies "upon the mouths of the great navigable rivers" from Florida to the St. Lawrence.

Although Elizabeth declined to commit the state to Hakluyt's plan, she authorized and invested in several private attempts at exploration and colonization. In the late 1570s, Martin Frobisher conducted three voyages of exploration in the North Atlantic. Fresh from the Irish wars, Raleigh and Gilbert planned the first true colonizing ventures. In 1583 Gilbert sailed with a flotilla of ships from Plymouth and landed at St. John's Bay, Newfoundland. He encountered fishermen from several other nations but nevertheless claimed the territory for his queen. But Gilbert's ship was lost on the return voyage.

Following his brother's death, Raleigh decided to establish a colony southward, in the more hospitable climate of the mid-Atlantic coast. Although the Roanoke enterprise of 1584–87 seemed far more promising than Gilbert's, it too eventually failed (as described in the opening of the chapter). In contrast to the French, who concentrated on commerce, the English drew on their Irish experience, attempting to dominate and conquer natives. The greatest legacy of the expedition was the work of Thomas Harriot and John White, who mapped the area, surveyed its commercial potential, and studied the Indian residents. Harriot's *A Briefe and True Report of the Newfound Land of Virginia* (1588), illustrated by engravings of White's watercolors, provided the single most accurate description of North American Indians at the moment of their contact with Europeans. Harriot's work was also addressed to the practical problem of identifying the "merchantable commodities" that might support a settlement, for without products—precious metals, furs, or tropical commodities—a colonial system was pointless.

King Philip II of Spain was outraged at the English incursions into territory reserved by the pope for Catholics. He had authorized the destruction of the

The care that John White brought to his painting is evident in this watercolor of an Algonquian mother and daughter (1585). The woman's fringed deerskin skirt is edged with white beads, and the decoration on her face and upper arms seems to be tatooed. The little wooden doll in the girl's hand was a gift from White. All the Indian girls, wrote Thomas Harriot, "are greatly dellighted with puppetts and babes which were brought out of England."

SOURCE: John White (1570–93), "Woman and Child of Pomeiooc." Watercolor. British Museum, London. The Bridgeman Art Library International Ltd.

French colony in Florida, and now he committed himself to smashing England. In 1588 he sent a fleet of 130 ships carrying 30,000 men to invade the British Isles. Countered by captains such as Drake and Hawkins, who commanded smaller and more maneuverable ships, and frustrated by an ill-timed storm that the English chose to interpret as an act of divine intervention, the Spanish Armada foundered. Half the ships were destroyed, their crews killed or captured. The war continued until 1604, but the Spanish monopoly of the New World had been broken in the English Channel.

CHRONOLOGY

1000	Norse settlement at L'Anse aux Meadows
1347–53	Black Death in Europe
1381	English Peasants' Revolt
1488	Bartolomeu Días sails around the African continent
1492	Christopher Columbus first arrives in the Caribbean
1494	Treaty of Tordesillas
1497	John Cabot explores Newfoundland
1500	High point of the Renaissance
1508	Spanish invade Puerto Rico
1513	Juan Ponce de León lands in Florida
1514	Bartolomé de las Casas begins preaching against the conquest
1516	Smallpox introduced to the New World
1517	Martin Luther breaks with the Roman Catholic Church
1519	Hernán Cortés lands in Mexico
1534	Jacques Cartier first explores the St. Lawrence River
1539–40	Hernán de Soto and Francisco Vásquez de Coronado expeditions
1550	Tobacco introduced to Europe
1552	Bartolomé de Las Casas's Destruction of the Indies published
1558	Elizabeth I of England begins her reign
1562	Huguenot colony planted along the mid-Atlantic coast
1565	St. Augustine founded
1572	St. Bartholomew's Day Massacre in France
1583	Humphrey Gilbert attempts to plant a colony in Newfoundland
1584–87	Walter Raleigh's colony on Roanoke Island
1588	English defeat the Spanish Armada
1590	John White returns to find Roanoke colony abandoned

CONCLUSION

The Spanish opened the era of European colonization in the Americas with Columbus's voyage in 1492. The consequences for the Indian peoples of the Americas were disastrous. The Spanish succeeded in constructing the world's most powerful empire on the backs of Indian and African labor. Inspired by the Spanish success, the French and the English attempted to colonize the coast of North America. By the end of the sixteenth century, however, they had not succeeded in establishing any lasting colonial communities. Instead, a very different kind of colonial encounter, based on commerce rather than conquest, was taking place in northeastern North America. In the next century the French would turn this development to their advantage. Along the mid-Atlantic coast in Virginia, however, the English would put their Irish experience to use, pioneering an altogether new kind of American colonialism.

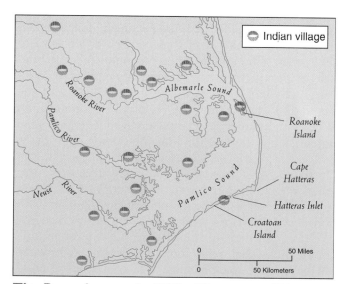

The Roanoke area in 1585   The surveys of Thomas Harriot and John White revealed that the Roanoke area was densely settled with Indian villages. The information on this map is taken from their report.

REVIEW QUESTIONS

1. Discuss the roles played by the rising merchant class, the new monarchies, Renaissance humanism, and the Reformation in the development of European colonialism.
2. Define a "frontier of inclusion." In what ways does this description apply to the Spanish empire in the Americas?
3. Make a list of the major exchanges that took place between the Old World and the New World in the centuries following the European invasion of America. Discuss some of the effects these exchanges had on the course of modern history.
4. In what ways did colonial contact in the Northeast differ from contacts in the Caribbean and Mexico?
5. In what ways might the English experience in Ireland have shaped expectations about American colonization?

RECOMMENDED READING

David Noble Cook, *Born to Die: Disease and New World Conquest, 1492–1650* (1998). A synthetic history of the impact of disease, including Indian and European views.

Cyclone Covey, trans. and ed., *Cabeza de Vaca's Adventures in the Unknown Interior of America* (1983). The captivity narrative that lured the Spanish into North America. An eye-opening story of the peoples and places of the preconquest Southwest.

Alfred W. Crosby Jr., *The Columbian Exchange: Biological and Cultural Consequences of 1492* (1972). Pathbreaking account of the intersection of the biospheres of the Old and New Worlds.

Richard Flint, *Great Cruelties Have Been Reported: The 1544 Investigation of the Coronado Expedition* (2001). Testimony regarding the treatment of Indians and subsequent human rights debates in Spain.

Charles Gibson, *Spain in America* (1966). Still the best introductory history of Spain's American empire.

Lewis Hanke, *The Spanish Struggle for Justice in the Conquest of America* (1949; reprint, 1965). The classic account of las Casas's attempts to rectify the wrongs committed by the Spanish against the Indians.

Charles M. Hudson, *Knights of Spain, Warriors of the Sun: Hernando de Soto and the South's Ancient Chiefdoms* (1997). A very readable history of the de Soto expedition, told from the viewpoint of the Indians.

Miguel Leon-Portilla, *The Broken Spears: The Aztec Account of the Conquest of Mexico* (1962; expanded ed., 1992). The history of the Spanish conquest as told by the Aztecs, drawn from manuscripts dating as early as 1528, only seven years after the fall of Tenochtitlán.

Samuel Eliot Morison, *The European Discovery of America: The Northern Voyages, A.D. 500–1600* (1971) and *The Southern Voyages, A.D. 1492–1616* (1974). The most detailed treatment of all the important European explorations of the Americas.

David Beers Quinn, *Set Fair for Roanoke: Voyages and Colonies, 1584–1606* (1985). The story of Roanoke—the Indian village, the English settlement, and the Lost Colony.

Kirkpatrick Sale, *The Conquest of Paradise: Christopher Columbus and the Columbian Legacy* (1990). A harsh view of Columbus, but important information on the world of the Caribbean and the disastrous effects of the encounter with Europeans.

Carl Ortwin Sauer, *Sixteenth Century North America: The Land and the People as Seen by the Europeans* (1971). An excellent source for the explorations of the continent, providing abundant descriptions of the Indians.

Hugh Thomas, *Conquest: Montezuma, Cortés, and the Fall of Old Mexico* (1993). A fascinating account, written by a master of historical style, that incorporates the Aztec view as well as the words of the conquerors.

Gustavo Verdesio, *Forgotten Conquests: Rereading New World History from the Margins* (2001). An argument that the old master historical narrative represents only one of many possible histories, and a suggestion for finding the colonial subjects who did not produce documents.

▶ MEDIA RESOURCES

 U.S. HISTORY DOCUMENTS CD-ROM

Meeting of Three Cultures

1-2   Christopher Columbus, Letter to Ferdinand and Isabella of Spain (1494)

1-3   Alvar Núñez Cabeza de Vaca, "Indians of the Rio Grande" (1528–1536)

1-4   Jacques Cartier: First Contact with the Indians (1534)

1-5   Bartolomé de Las Casas, "Of the Island of Hispaniola" (1542)

1-8   The Founding of St. Augustine, 1565

1-9   The Columbian Exchange (1590)

1-10 Thomas Harriot, The Algonquian Peoples of the Atlantic Coast (1588)

1-11 Jose de Acosta, A Spanish Priest Speculates on the Origins of the Indians (1590)

 COMPANION WEBSITE HIGHLIGHTS

To view an exploration, enter one of the URLs below in your browser.

 Web Explorations

Western Europe in the Fifteenth Century
http://www.prenhall.com/faragher/map2.1

European Exploration, 1492–1591
http://www.prenhall.com/faragher/map2.2

 Additional Interactive Maps

To access the maps, go to this chapter's resources at
http://www.prenhall.com/faragher
The Invasion of America, page 36

 HISTORY RESOURCE CENTER

To find the resources listed below, go to
http://www.prenhall.com/historyresourcecenter

Documents

Christopher Columbus, Letter to Luis de Sant Angel (1493)

Henry VII, First Letters Patent Granted to John Cabot and His Sons (1496)

Images

Columbus Taking Possession of a New Country

Cruel Conquistadors Torture Native Amerindians

Petri de Calyce's Cruelty to the Indians

Raleigh's Expedition at Roanoke

EXPLORING AMERICA

EXPLOITATION OF THE AMERICAS

http://www.prenhall.com/faragher/exploitation

Why did Christopher Columbus get his geography wrong in 1492? What motivated the Spanish to expand into the Americas? How did the Spanish and the Aztec perceive each other? Between 1492 and 1591, Spain created a vast overseas empire in North and South America. How and why the Spanish came to America and conquered the Aztecs is examined in the *Exploitation of the Americas* module of the Exploring America CD-ROM. Visual images, primary source documents, interactive maps, and a chronology, tied together by a narrative, tell the story of the first encounters between Europeans and Native Americans.

Exploitation of the Americas provides a variety of methods to explore the Spanish conquest and colonization of the Americas. The module demonstrates that the indigenous Americans possessed diverse cultures and, in the case of the Aztecs, a society as advanced as any in Europe. Using a combination of narrative and primary source excerpts, the module provides intriguing insight into how and why the Spanish were able to conquer and colonize the Native American

Exploitation of the Americas

First modern atlas: Abraham Ortelius. *Americae sive Novi Orbis, Nova Descripto*. In *Theatrum Orbis Terrarum*. Antwerp, 1570.

Click anywhere to go to the previous page.

cultures they encountered. The primary source excerpts also indicate that the Spanish triumph was not a foregone conclusion. The chronology and maps help place the content of the module into its proper historical and geographic contexts.

Reflect and Respond

1. Who paid for the European accumulation of wealth?
2. How long did the scramble for North America last?

✓ Check it out

Spanish Discussion of Tenochtitlán

This primary source document offers important information on the Aztec Empire and society. The Spanish had never seen a city as large as the Aztec capital. The document is important because it shows the high level of civilization achieved by the Aztecs. The Spanish marvel at the city's size, wealth, urban design, and architecture. The document also offers excellent detail on the abundant goods available in the marketplace.

Exploitation of the Americas

Route followed by Cortés from Veracruz, which he founded and where he burned his ships to force his men to stay with him. The goal of his journey was Tenochtitlán, present-day Mexico City.

Click anywhere to go to the previous page.

This exploration is also available on the *Exploring America* CD-ROM.

PLANTING COLONIES IN NORTH AMERICA

▶ 1588–1701

Theodore De Bry, *Crudelitas Petride Calyceerga Indos*, 1590. The New York Public Library Photographic Services.

Communities Struggle with Diversity in Seventeenth-Century Santa Fé

IT WAS A HOT AUGUST DAY IN 1680 WHEN THE FRANTIC MESsengers rode into the small mission outpost of El Paso with the news that the Pueblo Indians to the north had risen in revolt. The corpses of more than 400 colonists lay bleeding in the dust. Two thousand Spanish survivors huddled inside the Palace of Governors in Santa Fé, surrounded by 3,000 angry warriors. The Pueblo leaders had sent two crosses into the palace—white for surrender, red for death. Which would the Spaniards choose?

Spanish colonists had been in New Mexico for nearly a century. Franciscan priests came first, followed by a military expedition from Mexico in search of precious metals. In 1609, high in the picturesque foothills of the Sangre de Cristo Mountains, the colonial authorities founded La Villa Real de la Santa Fé de San Francisco—"the royal town of the holy faith of St. Francis"—soon known simply as Santa Fé. Colonization efforts included the conversion of the Pueblo Indians to Christianity, making them subjects of the king of Spain, and forcing them to work for the colonial elite who lived in the town.

In the face of overwhelming Spanish power, the Pueblos adopted a flexible attitude. Twenty thousand of them converted to Christianity, but most of these thought of the new religion as simply an appendage to their complex culture. The Christian God was but a minor addition to their numerous deities; church holidays were included in their own religious calendar and celebrated with native dances and rituals.

Most anthropologists agree that the Pueblos were a spirited people. Many of their public dances included erotic displays and sometimes ended in spectacles of mock public intercourse, symbolizing the powerful force that brought the separate worlds of men and women together, and also created community. The celibacy of the Franciscan priests not only astounded the Pueblos but horrified them, for it marked the priests as only half-persons. The Pueblos also found the Franciscan practice of subjecting themselves to prolonged fasts and tortures, such as self-flagellation, inexplicable. "You Christians are crazy," one Pueblo chief told a priest. "You go through the streets in groups, flagellating yourselves, and it is not well that the people of this pueblo should be encouraged to commit such madness."

The missionaries, outraged by what they considered Pueblo sacrileges, invaded underground kivas, destroyed sacred Indian artifacts, publicly humiliated holy men, and compelled whole villages to perform penance by working in irrigation ditches and fields. Such violations of the deepest traditions of Pueblo community life eventually led to the revolt of 1680. In New Mexico, several years before, the Spanish governor had executed three Pueblo religious leaders and publicly whipped dozens more for secretly practicing their religion. One of those leaders, Popé of San Juan Pueblo, vowed to overthrow the regime. During the next several years he carefully organized a conspiracy among more than twenty Indian towns.

Popé's job was not difficult, for there were plenty of local grievances. The Hopis of northern Arizona, for example, still tell of a missionary who capped his ever-escalating demands on them with the order that all the young women of the village be brought to live with him. When the revolt began, the Hopis surrounded the missionary's house. "I have come to kill you," the chief announced. "You can't kill me," the priest cried from behind his locked door. "I will come [back] to life and wipe out your whole tribe." But the chief shouted back, "my gods have more power than you have." He and his men broke down the door, hung the missionary from the beams, and lit a fire beneath his feet.

When the Indians demanded the surrender of the Spanish inside Santa Fé's Palace of Governors, the besieged colonists sent back the red cross, signaling defiance. But after a siege lasting five days, the Pueblos agreed to allow most of them to flee south to El Paso, "the poor women and children on foot and unshod," in the words of one Spaniard's account, and "of such a hue that they looked like dead people." The Indians then ransacked the missions and churches, desecrating the holy furnishings with human excrement and leaving the mutilated bodies of priests lying on their altars. They transformed the governor's chapel into a traditional kiva, his palace into a communal dwelling. On the elegant inlaid stone floors where the governor had held court, Pueblo women now ground their corn.

Santa Fé became the capital of a Pueblo confederacy led by Popé. He forced Christian Indians to the river to scrub away the taint of baptism. Then he ordered the destruction of everything Spanish. But this the Pueblos could not do. The colonists had introduced horses and sheep, fruit trees and wheat, new tools and new crafts, all of which the Indians found useful. Moreover, the Pueblos sorely missed the support of the Spanish in their struggle against their traditional enemies, the nomadic Navajos and Apaches. Equipped with stolen horses and weapons, these nomadic peoples had become considerably more dangerous, and their raids on the unprotected Pueblo villages became much more destructive after the colonists fled. With chaos mounting, Popé was deposed in 1690, and many of the Indians found themselves thinking the unthinkable: if only the Spanish would come back!

Come back they did, beginning in 1692, and after six years of fighting they succeeded in reestablishing Spanish authority. But both sides had learned a lesson, and over the next generation the colonists and the Indians reached an implicit understanding. Pueblos dutifully observed Catholicism in the missionary chapels, while missionaries tolerated the practice of traditional religion in the Indians' underground kivas. Royal officials guaranteed the inviolability of Indian lands, and Pueblos pledged loyalty to the Spanish monarch. Pueblos turned out for service on colonial lands, and colonists abandoned the system of forced labor. Together the Spanish and the Pueblos held off the nomadic tribes for the next 150 years. Colonist and Indian communities remained autonomous, but they learned to live with one another. ■

Santa Fé

KEY TOPICS

- A comparison of the European colonies established in North America in the seventeenth century

- The English and Algonquian colonial encounter in the Chesapeake

- The role of religious dissent in the planting of the New England colonies

- The restoration of the Stuart monarchy and the creation of new proprietary colonies

- Indian warfare and internal conflict at the end of the seventeenth century

SPAIN AND ITS COMPETITORS IN NORTH AMERICA

At the beginning of the seventeenth century the Spanish controlled the only colonial outposts on the mainland, a series of forts along the Florida coast to protect the Gulf Stream sea lanes used by the convoys carrying wealth from their New World colonies to Spain. During the first two decades of the new century, however, the Spanish, French, Dutch, and English were all drawn into planting far more substantial colonies in North America.

Because neither France nor Spain proved willing or able to transport large numbers of their subjects to populate these colonies, both relied on a policy of converting Indians into subjects, and in New Spain and New France there was a good deal of cultural and sexual mixing between colonists and natives. These areas became frontiers of inclusion, where native peoples were part of colonial society. The Dutch at first followed the French model when they established their colony on the Hudson River. But soon they changed course, fearing the great success of the English, who from the beginning adopted a different model of colonization, in which settlers and Indians lived in separate societies. The "frontiers of exclusion" in Virginia, New England, and New Netherlands offered a dramatic contrast to the situation in New Spain and New France.

New Mexico in the Seventeenth Century   By the end of the seventeenth century, New Mexico contained 3,000 colonial settlers in several towns, surrounded by an estimated 50,000 Pueblo Indians living in some fifty farming villages. The isolation and sense of danger among the Hispanic settlers are evident in their name for the road linking the colony with New Spain, *Jornada del Muerto,* "the Road of Death."

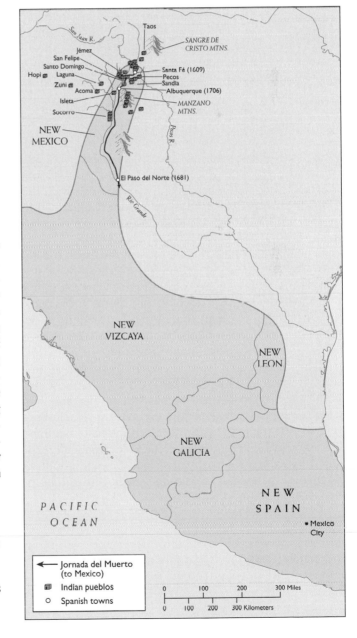

New Mexico

After the 1539 expedition of Francisco Vásquez de Coronado failed to turn up vast Indian empires to conquer in the northern Mexican deserts, the Spanish interest in the Southwest faded. The densely settled farming communities of the Pueblos did offer a harvest of converts for Christianity, however, and by the 1580s Franciscan missionaries were at work in the Southwest. Soon rumors drifted back to Mexico City of rich mines along the Rio Grande, raising the hopes of Spanish officials that they might find another Aztec empire. In 1598, Juan de Oñate, the son of a wealthy mining family of New Spain, financed a colonizing expedition made up of Indian and mestizo soldiers with the purpose of mining both gold and souls.

Moving north into the upper Rio Grande Valley, Oñate encountered varying degrees of resistance. He lay siege at Acoma, set high atop a great outcropping of desert rock. Indian warriors killed dozens of Spaniards with their arrows, and women and children bombarded them with stones. But in the end, the attackers succeeded in climbing the rock walls and laying waste to the town, killing 800 men, women, and children. All surviving warriors had one of their feet severed, and more than 500 people were enslaved. "If you who are Christians cause so much harm and violence," a Pueblo asked one of the priests, "why should we become Christians?" In 1606 Spanish authorities in Mexico recalled Oñate, not for his violence, but for his failure to locate the fabled gold mines.

The Spanish empire was based on the use of Indian labor to produce valuable commodities—precious metals, tobacco, or sugar. Without mines to exploit, interest in New Mexico waned. But the church convinced the Spanish monarchy to subsidize New Mexico as a special missionary colony. In 1609, a new governor founded the capital of Santa Fé, and from this base the Franciscan missionaries penetrated all the surrounding Indian villages. The Pueblos who most resisted Christianity—the Acomas, the Zunis, and the isolated Hopis—retained their old customs, including their way of tracing kinship through the maternal line. But many other communities were dramatically affected by contact with Spanish culture, and adopted the Spanish pattern of reckoning descent through both the father and mother's ancestors.

The colonial economy of New Mexico, based on small-scale agriculture and sheep raising, was never very prosperous. Indians labored for both colonists and priests. As one Spanish official put it, "one comes to the Indies not to plow and sow, but only to eat and loaf." After the initial conquest, few new colonists came up the dusty road from Mexico. Population growth was almost entirely the result of mar-

This drawing, by Samuel de Champlain, shows how Huron men funneled deer into enclosures, where they could be trapped and easily killed. SOURCE: Library of Congress.

riages between colonial men and Indian women. By the late seventeenth century this northernmost outpost of the far-flung Spanish empire in America contained some 3,000 mestizos (of mixed Indian and European ancestry) in a few towns along the Rio Grande, surrounded by an estimated 50,000 Pueblos in some fifty villages. New Mexico was a "frontier of inclusion."

New France

In the early seventeenth century the French devised a strategy to monopolize the northern fur trade. In 1605 Samuel de Champlain, acting as the agent of a royal monopoly, helped establish the outpost of Port Royal on the Bay of Fundy. It proved impossible, however, to control the coastal trade from that location. In 1608 he founded the settlement of Quebec on the St. Lawrence River at a site where he could intercept the traffic in furs to the Atlantic. He forged an alliance with the Huron Indians, who controlled access to the rich fur grounds of the Great Lakes, and in 1609 and 1610 joined them in making war on their traditional enemies, the Five Nation Iroquois Confederacy. In his diplomacy, Champlain relied on the tradition of commercial relations that had developed between Europeans and Indians during the sixteenth century. He sent agents and traders to live among native peoples, where they learned native languages and customs, and directed the flow of furs to Quebec.

The St. Lawrence was like a great roadway leading directly into the heart of the continent, and it provided the French with enormous geographic and political advantage. But the river froze during the winter, isolating the colonists, and the short growing season limited agricultural productivity in the region. Many

This illustration, taken from Samuel de Champlain's 1613 account of the founding of New France, depicts him joining the Huron attack on the Iroquois in 1609. The French and their Huron allies controlled access to the great fur grounds of the West. The Iroquois then formed an alliance of their own with the Dutch, who had founded a trading colony on the Hudson River. The palm trees in the background of this drawing suggest that it was not executed by an eyewitness but rather by an illustrator more familiar with South American scenes. SOURCE: Samuel de Champlain, *Les Voyages . . .*, Paris, 1613. Illus. opp. p. 322. Early battle with the Iroquois. Rare Books Div., The N.Y. Public Library, Astor, Lenox, and Tilden Foundations.

Frenchmen went to Canada and Acadia as *engagés* ("hired men") in the fur trade or the fishery, as craftsmen or as farmers, but nine out of ten of them returned to France. Huguenot dissenters would have been willing colonists, but French authorities refused to let them emigrate, declaring that New France would be an exclusively Catholic colony. It was the most serious mistake France made, for by closing Canada to Huguenot refugees they destroyed their only hope for mass emigration. As a result the population of Acadia on the Bay of Fundy and Canada on the St. Lawrence grew slowly in the seventeenth century, reaching a total of only about 15,000 by 1700. Quebec City, the administrative capital, was small by Spanish colonial standards, and Montreal, founded in 1642 as a missionary and trading center, remained little more than a frontier outpost. Small clusters of riverbank farmers known as *habitants* lived on the lands of *seigneurs*, or landlords. These communities, with their manor houses, Catholic churches, and perhaps a public building or two, resembled the towns of northern France. By using Indian farming techniques, habitants were able to produce subsistence crops, and eventually they developed a modest export economy.

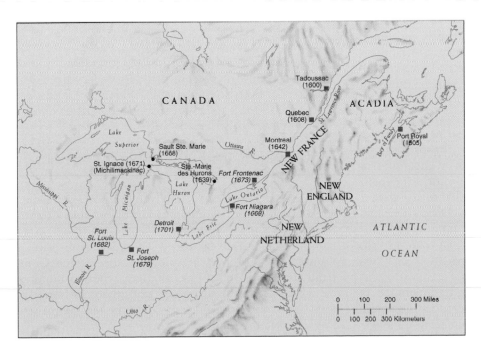

New France in the Seventeenth Century By the late seventeenth century, French settlements were spread from the town of Port Royal in Acadia to the post and mission at Sault Ste. Marie on the Great Lakes. But the heart of New France comprised the communities stretching along the St. Lawrence River between the towns of Quebec and Montreal.

The communities of Canada looked west toward the continental interior rather than toward the Atlantic. It was typical for the sons of habitants to take to the woods in their youth, working as independent traders or as as *coureurs de bois*, paid agents of the fur companies. Most eventually returned to take up farming, but others remained in Indian villages, where they married Indian women and raised families. Such French traders were living on the Great Lakes as early as the 1620s, and from the late 1660s to the 1680s the French established outposts at each of the strategic points on the lakes. By the 1670s, French fur traders and missionaries were exploring the reaches of the upper Mississippi River. In 1681–82, fur-trade commandant Robert Sieur de La Salle navigated the mighty river to its mouth on the Gulf of Mexico and claimed its entire watershed for France.

Both the French and Spanish established societies of inclusion, in which settlers intermarried with native peoples, but in other ways the two systems differed. The Spanish conquered native societies and organized Indians as a labor force for mines, plantations, and ranches. The French attempted to build an empire by allying themselves with independent Indian nations and establishing commercial relations with them. There were also important differences between Spanish and French missionary efforts. The Franciscans of New Mexico insisted that Indian people accept European cultural norms, while the Jesuits in New France introduced Christianity as a supplement to the existing Indian way of life.

New Netherland

The United Provinces of the Netherlands, commonly known as Holland, was only a fraction the size of France, but it was the center of Europe's economic transformation in the sixteenth century. On land reclaimed from the sea by an elaborate system of dikes, Dutch farmers used new methods of crop rotation and deep tilling that dramatically increased their yields, producing large surpluses that supported the growth of the world's most urban and commercial nation. After a century of rule by the Hapsburgs, the prosperous Dutch rose up against their Spanish masters and in 1581 suceeded in establishing their political independence. Amsterdam became the site of the world's first stock exchange and investment banks. Dutch investors built the largest commercial fleet in Europe and captured the lucrative Baltic and North Sea trade in fish, lumber, iron, and grain. It was said that the North Sea was Holland's "America."

Soon the Dutch were establishing trading outposts in America itself. Early in the seventeenth century the United Netherlands organized two great monopolies, the Dutch East India Company and the Dutch West India Company, combining naval military might and commercial strength in campaigns to seize the maritime trade of Asia and the Atlantic. Backed by powerfully armed men-of-war ships, during the first half of the seventeenth century Dutch traders built a series of trading posts in China, Indonesia, India, Africa, Brazil, the Caribbean, and North America, and Holland became the greatest commercial power in the world. The Dutch first appeared in North America in 1609 with the explorations of Henry Hudson, and within a few years they had founded settlements on the Hudson River at Fort Orange (today's Albany) and at New Amsterdam, on Manhattan Island, at the river's mouth. Seeking to match French success, they negotiated a commercial alliance with the Iroquois Confederacy to obtain furs. Access to superior Dutch products, including metal tools and firearms, greatly increased the power of the Iroquois, who embarked on a series of military expeditions against their neighbors, known as the Beaver Wars, which made them the strategic middlemen of the Dutch. In the late 1640s, the Iroquois attacked and dispersed the Hurons, who had long controlled the flow of furs from the Great Lakes to their allies the French. The Dutch also succeeded in overwhelming a small colony of Swedes on the lower Delaware River, incorporating that region into their sphere of influence in the 1640s. As a result of these conflicts, the Dutch were able to greatly extend their commercial reach, by 1650 surpassing the French as the continent's greatest fur traders.

ENGLAND IN THE CHESAPEAKE

England first attempted to plant colonies in North America during the 1580s, in Newfoundland and at Roanoke Island in present-day North Carolina (see Chapter 2). Both attempts were failures. England's war with Spain (1588 to 1604) suspended further efforts, but thereafter the English once again turned to the Americas.

Jamestown and the Powhatan Confederacy

Early in his reign, King James I (reigned 1603–25) issued royal charters for the colonization of the mid-Atlantic region, known as Virginia to English joint-stock companies, which raised capital by selling shares. In 1607, a London group of investors known as the Virginia Company sent ships to Chesapeake Bay, where a hundred men built a fort they named Jamestown, in honor of the king. It was destined to become the first permanent English settlement in North America.

The Chesapeake was already home to an estimated 24,000 Algonquian people. The English colonists were immediately confronted by Powhatan, the powerful *weroinance* (leader) of a confederacy of Algonquian tribes. Powhatan had mixed feelings about the English. The Spanish had already attempted to plant a base nearby, bringing conflict and disease to the region. But he looked forward to valuable trade with the English, as well as their support for his struggle to extend his confederacy over outlying tribes. As was the case in Mexico and along the St. Lawrence, Indians tried to use Europeans to pursue ends of their own.

The English saw themselves as conquistadors, and like the first Roanoke colonists, they proved unable to support themselves. Hating the idea of physical labor, they survived the first year only with Powhatan's mater-

ial assistance. "In our extremity the Indians brought us corn," wrote John Smith, the colony's military leader, "when we rather expected they would destroy us." Jamestown grew so dependent on Algonquian stores that Smith and his men plundered food from surrounding tribes. In retaliation, Powhatan decided to starve the colonists out. He now realized that the English had come "not for trade, but to invade my people and possess my country." During the terrible winter of 1609–10 hundreds of colonists starved and a number resorted to cannibalism. Of the 500 colonists at Jamestown in the fall, only sixty remained alive by the spring.

Determined to prevail, the Virginia Company sent out a large additional force of men, women, and livestock, committing themselves to a protracted war against the Indians. The grim fighting persisted until

The illustration on the left is a detail of John Smith's map of Virginia. It includes the names of many Indian villages, suggesting how densely settled was the Indian population of the coast of Chesapeake Bay. For the inset of Powhatan and his court in the upper left, the engraver borrowed images from John White's drawings of the Indians of the Roanoke area. The illustration on the right, from John Smith's memoirs (1624), was engraved by the artist Robert Vaughn. Seizing Chief Opechancanough, Powhatan's brother, by the scalplock, Smith attempts to obtain needed supplies from the Indians. Opechancanough later succeeded Powhatan and ruled the Chesapeake Algonquian Confederacy for a quarter century.

SOURCE: (a) Princeton University Library (b) Library of Congress.

1613, when the English captured Powhatan's favorite daughter, teenaged Pocahontas. Worn down by war and disease, and eager to see his child again, Powhatan accepted a treaty of peace in 1614. "I am old and ere long must die," he declared. "I know it is better to eat good meat, lie well, and sleep with my women and children, laugh and be merry, than to be forced to flee and be hunted." Pocahontas adopted English ways and married John Rolfe, one of the leading settlers. But she fell sick and died on a visit to England in 1617. Crushed by the news, Powhatan abdicated in favor of his brother Opechancanough before dying of despair.

Tobacco, Expansion, and Warfare

Tobacco provided the Virginia colonists with the "merchantable commodity" for which Thomas Harriot, the scientist who accompanied the Roanoke expedition, had searched (see Chapter 2). Tobacco had been introduced to the English by Francis Drake in the 1580s, and by the 1610s the smoking craze created strong demand for the product. Pocahontas's husband John Rolfe developed a mild hybrid variety with considerable appeal, and soon the first commercial shipments of cured Virginia leaf reached England. Tobacco provided the Virginia Company with the first returns on its investment. Its cultivation quickly exhausted the soil, however, creating pressures for further expansion into Indian territory.

Because tobacco also required a great deal of hand labor, the company instituted what were called "headright grants"—awards of large plantations to Englishmen on the condition that they transport workers from England at their own cost. Because at home in England thousands of families were being thrown off the land (see Chapter 2), they were attracted by the prospect of work in Virginia. Between 1619 and 1624 more than 4,500 English settlers arrived, many with families, although high mortality rates, probably the result of epidemics of typhoid fever, kept the total population at just over a thousand. England's ability to export people gave it an enormous advantage in the competition to found colonies in North America. Massive immigration was the key to English success in the New World. In populating their colony with families, the English chose a policy quite different from the Spanish practice of sending only male settlers. Moreover, the English emphasis on agriculture and lack of interest in trade with Indian peoples contrasted significantly with the French approach. With no need to incorporate Indians into the population, the English pushed Indian peoples to the periphery rather than incorporating them within colonial communities. Virginia was a "frontier of exclusion."

The settlers pressed the Indians for additional lands. Outraged, Opechancanough prepared the Chesapeake Algonquians for a final assault. He encouraged a cultural revival under the guidance of the shaman Nemattanew, who instructed his followers to reject the English and their ways but to learn the use of firearms. This was the first of many Indian resistance movements led jointly by strong political and religious figures. The uprising, which began on Good Friday, March 22, 1622, completely surprised the English. Nearly a third of the settlers, 347 people, were killed. Yet the colony managed to hang on. The attack stretched into a ten-year war of attrition in which both sides committed horrors. Yet English officials saw advantages in open warfare. As one wrote, "We may now by right of war, and law of nations, invade the country and destroy them who sought to destroy us, whereby we shall enjoy their cultivated places."

The Indians finally sued for peace in 1632, but in the meantime the war had bankrupted the Virginia Company. In 1624 the king converted Virginia into a royal colony with civil

In this eighteenth-century engraving, used to promote the sale of tobacco, slaves pack tobacco leaves into "hogsheads" for shipment to England, overseen by a Virginia planter and his clerk. Note the incorporation of the Indian motif.

SOURCE: The Granger Collection.

authorities appointed by the crown, although the colony's House of Burgesses, created in 1619, continued to include representatives of Virginia's boroughs. Although disease, famine, and warfare took a heavy toll, continual emigration from England allowed the colonial population to double every five years from 1625 to 1640, by which time it numbered approximately 10,000. Meanwhile, decimated by violence and disease, the Algonquians shrank to about the same number.

Numerical strength soon shifted in favor of the English. In 1644 Opechancanough organized a final desperate revolt in which more than 500 colonists were killed. But the next year the Virginians crushed the Algonquians, capturing and executing their leader. A formal treaty granted the Indians a number of small reserved territories. By 1670 the Indian population had fallen to just 2,000, overwhelmed by the 40,000 English colonists.

Maryland

In 1632, King Charles I (reigned 1625–49) granted 10 million acres at the northern end of Chesapeake Bay to the Calvert family, the Lords Baltimore, important supporters of the monarchy. The Calverts named their colony Maryland, in honor of the king's wife. The first party of colonists founded the settlement of St. Marys near the mouth of the Potomac River in 1634. Two features distinguished Maryland from Virginia. First, it was a "proprietary" colony. The Calverts were sole owners of all the land, which they planned to carve into feudal manors that would provide them with annual rents, and they appointed all the civil officers. Second, because the proprietors were Catholics, they encouraged settlement by their coreligionists, a persecuted minority in seventeenth-century England. In fact, Maryland became the only English colony in North America with a substantial Catholic minority. Wealthy Catholic landlords were appointed to the governing council, and they came to dominate Maryland's House of Delegates, founded in 1635.

Despite these differences, Maryland quickly assumed the character of neighboring Virginia. Its tobacco plantation economy created pressures for labor and expansion that could not be met under the Calverts' original feudal plans. In 1640, the colony adopted the system of headright grants previously developed in Virginia, and settlements of independent planters quickly spread out on both sides of the bay. By the 1670s Maryland's English population numbered more than 15,000.

Indentured Servants

At least three-quarters of the English migrants to the Chesapeake came as indentured servants. In exchange for the cost of their transportation to the New World,

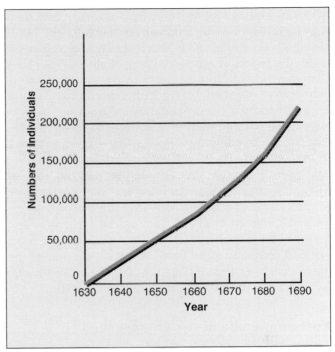

Population Growth of the British Colonies in the Seventeenth Century   The British colonial population grew steadily through the century, then increased sharply in the closing decade as a result of the new settlements of the Restoration colonies.

men and women contracted to labor for a master for a fixed term. Most indentured servants were young, unskilled males, who served for two to seven years; but some were skilled craftsmen, women, or even children (the latter were expected to serve a master until they reached the age of twenty-one). A minority were convicts or vagabonds bound into service by English courts for as long as fourteen years.

Masters were obliged to feed, clothe, and house these servants adequately. But work in the tobacco fields was backbreaking, and records include complaints of inadequate care. One Virginia ballad chronicled these complaints:

> Come all you young fellows wherever you be,
> Come listen awhile and I will tell thee,
> Concerning the hardships that we undergo,
> When we get lagg'd to Virginia.
> Now in Virginia I lay like a hog,
> Our pillow at night is a brick or a log,
> We dress and undress like some other sea dog,
> How hard is my fate in Virginia.

Many servants tried to escape, although capture could mean a doubling of their terms of service.

African slaves were first introduced to the Chesapeake in 1619, but slaves were more expensive than servants, and as late as 1680 they made up less than 7 percent of the Chesapeake population. In the hard-driving economy of the Chesapeake, however, masters treated servants as cruelly as they treated slaves. After arriving, bound laborers were inspected by planters who poked muscles, peered into open mouths, and pinched women. Approximately two out of five servants died during indenture. Those who survived were eligible for "freedom dues"—clothing, tools, a gun, or a spinning wheel, help getting started on their own—and many former servants headed west in the hope of cutting a farm from the wilderness. But most former servants who were able to raise the price of passage returned home to England. Indentured labor may not have been slavery, but the distinction may have seemed academic to servants. (Chapter 4 discusses the slave system and its implications for American society, as well as for the slaves and masters themselves.)

Community Life in the Chesapeake

Because most emigrants were men, whether free or indentured, free unmarried women often married as soon as they arrived in the Chesapeake. Moreover, in the disease-ridden environment of the early Chesapeake, English men seemed to suffer a higher rate of mortality than women, and widows remarried quickly, sometimes within days. Their scarcity provided women with certain advantages. Shrewd widows bargained for a remarriage agreement that gave them a larger share of the estate than those set by common law upon the death of their husband. So notable was the concentration of wealth in the hands of these widows that one historian has suggested that early Virginia was a "matriarchy." One seventeenth-century commentator declared, "rich widows [are] the Best Commodity this Country Affords." But because of high mortality rates, family size was smaller and kinship bonds—one of the most important components of community—were weaker than in England.

Visitors from England often remarked on the crude conditions of community life. Prosperous planters, investing everything in tobacco production, lived in rough wooden dwellings. On the western edge of the settlements, freed servants lived with their families in shacks, huts, or even caves. Colonists spread across the countryside in search of new tobacco lands, creating dispersed settlements and few towns. Before 1650 there were few community institutions such as schools and churches. Meanwhile, the Spanish in the Caribbean and Mexico were building communities that would grow into great cities with permanent institutions.

In contrast to the colonist of New France, who were developing a distinctive American identity because of their commercial connections with Native Americans, the population of the Chesapeake maintained close emotional ties to England. Colonial politics were shaped less by local developments than by a continuing relationship with the mother country. There was little movement toward a distinctively American point of view in the seventeenth-century Chesapeake.

THE NEW ENGLAND COLONIES

Both in climate and in geography, the northern coast of North America was far different from the Chesapeake. "Merchantable commodities" such as tobacco could not be produced there, and thus it was a far less favored for investment and settlement. Instead, the region became a haven for Protestant dissenters from England, who gave the colonies of the north a distinctive character.

The Social and Political Values of Puritanism

Most English men and women continued to practice a Christianity little different from traditional Catholicism. But the English followers of John Calvin, known as Puritans because they wished to purify and reform the English church from within, grew increasingly influential during the last years of Elizabeth's reign at the end of the sixteenth century. The Calvinist emphasis on enterprise meant that Puritanism appealed to merchants, entrepreneurs, and commercial farmers, those most responsible for the rapid economic and social transformation of England. But the Puritans were also the most vocal critics of the disruptive effects of that change, condemning the decline of the traditional rural community and the growing number of "idle and masterlessmen" produced by the enclosure of common lands. They argued for reviving communities by placing reformed Christian congregations at their core to monitor the behavior of individuals. Puritanism was as much a set of social and political values as religious ones, a way of managing change in troubling times. By the early seventeenth century Puritans controlled many congregations and had become an influential force at the universities in Oxford and Cambridge, training centers for the future political and religious leaders of England. (For a review of the Protestant Reformation and the enclosure movement in England, see Chapter 2.)

King James I, who assumed the throne after Elizabeth's death, abandoned her policy of religious tolerance. His persecution of the Puritans, however, merely stiffened their resolve and turned them toward open political opposition. An increasingly vocal Puritan minority in Parliament criticized King Charles I (reigned 1625–49), James's son and successor, for supporting "High Church" (of England) policies—which emphasized the authority of the church and its traditional forms of worship—as well as for marrying a Roman Catholic princess. In 1629, determined to rule without these troublesome opponents, Charles dismissed Parliament and launched a campaign of repression against the Puritans. "I am verily persuaded God will bring some heavy affliction upon this land," the Puritan leader John Winthrop despaired. This political turmoil provided the context for the migration of thousands of English Protestants to New England.

Early Contacts in New England

The northern Atlantic coast seemed an unlikely spot for English colonies, for the region was dominated by French and Dutch traders. In the early seventeenth century Samuel de Champlain had established trading contacts with coastal Algonquians as far south as Cape Cod. The Dutch had founded a trading post on the Connecticut River (near present-day Hartford) and established an alliance with the Pequot tribe, who lived along the lower reaches of the river. In 1613, desperate to keep their colonial options open, the English had dispatched a fleet from Jamestown that destroyed the French post on the Bay of Fundy and harassed the Dutch on the Hudson. The following year Captain John Smith of Virginia explored the northern coastline and christened the region "New England." The land was "so planted with Gardens and Corne fields," he wrote, that "I would rather live here than any where." But Smith's plans for a New England colony were aborted when he was captured by the French.

Then a twist of fate transformed English fortunes. From 1616 to 1618 an epidemic ravaged the native peoples of the northern Atlantic coast. Whole villages disappeared, and the trade of the French and the Dutch was seriously disrupted. Indians perished so quickly and in such numbers that few remained to bury the dead. Modern estimates confirm the testimony of a surviving Indian that his people were "melted down by this disease, whereof nine-tenths of them have died." The native population of New England as a whole dropped from an estimated 120,000 to less than 70,000. So crippled were the surviving coastal societies that they could not provide effective resistance to the planting of English colonies.

Plymouth Colony and the Mayflower Compact

The first English colony in New England was founded by a group of religious dissenters known to later generations as the Pilgrims. They were called Separatists because rather than reform the English church from within they believed it to be so corrupt that they had to establish their own independent congregations. One group moved to Holland in 1609, but fearful that tolerant Dutch society was seducing their children, they decided on emigration to North America. Backed by the Virginia Company of London and led by tradesman William Bradford, 102 people sailed from Plymouth, England, on the *Mayflower* in September 1620.

The little group, mostly families but including a substantial number of single men hired by the investors, arrived in Massachusetts Bay at the site of the former Indian village of Patuxet, which the English then named Plymouth. Soon the hired men began to grumble about Pilgrim authority, and to reassure them Bradford drafted an agreement by which the male members of the expedition did "covenant and combine [themselves] together into a civil body politic." The Mayflower Compact was the first document of self-government in North America.

Weakened by scurvy and malnutrition, nearly half the Pilgrims perished over the first winter. Like the earlier settlers of Roanoke and Jamestown, however, they were rescued by Indians. Massasoit, the sachem (leader) of the Pokanokets (also known as the Wampanoags), offered the newcomers food and advice in return for an alliance against his enemies, the Narragansets. It was the familiar pattern of Indians attempting to incorporate European colonists into their world.

The interpreter in these negotiations was an Indian named Squanto. He had learned to speak English when he was kidnapped by the captain of an English trading vessel in 1614. Then he had returned to New England as guide on another vessel five years later. He had arrived at his village of Patuxet to find that plague had wiped out his family and neighbors, and, knowledgeable in the ways of the Europeans, he then became an adviser to Massasoit. With the arrival of the Pilgrims, this last survivor of the Patuxets reestablished himself at the site of his old village, but now as interpreter and negotiator for the English. Squanto secured seed corn for the colonists and taught them how to sow and cultivate it.

Deeply in debt to its investors, always struggling to meet its payments through the Indian trade, fishing, and lumbering, the Plymouth colony was never a financial success. Most families raised their own crops and kept their own livestock, but produced little for export. Nevertheless, the Pilgrims succeeded during the first two or three decades in establishing the self-sufficient community they desired. So strong was their communal agreement that the annual meeting of property-owning men reelected William Bradford to thirty consecutive terms as governor. By midcentury, however, the Plymouth population had dispersed into eleven separate communities, and the growth of diverse local interests had begun to disrupt this Separatist retreat.

The Massachusetts Bay Colony

In England, the political climate of the late 1620s convinced a number of influential Puritans that the only way to protect their congregations was by emigration. In 1629 a royal charter was by granted to a group of wealthy Puritans who called their enterprise the Massachusetts Bay Company, and an advance force of 200 settlers left for the fishing settlement of Naumkeag on Massachusetts Bay, which they renamed Salem. They hoped to establish what John Winthrop, their leader and first governor, called "a city on a hill," a New England model of reform for old England. The Puritan emigration became known as the Great Migration, a phrase that would be repeated many times in American history. Between 1629 and 1643 some 20,000 people relocated to Massachusetts. They built the town of Boston in 1630 and within five years ringed it with towns as far as thirty miles inland. By 1640 their settlements had spread seventy-five miles west to the Connecticut River Valley.

Governor John Winthrop, c. 1640, a portrait by an unknown artist.

SOURCE: American Antiquarian Society.

Most colonists arrived in groups from long-established communities in the east of England and were often led by men with extensive experience in local English government. Taking advantage of a loophole in their charter, the Puritan leaders transferred company operations to America in 1629, and within a few years had transformed the company into a civil government. The original charter established a General Court composed of a governor and his deputy, a board of magistrates (or advisers), and the members of the corporation, known as freemen. In 1632 Governor Winthrop and his advisers declared all the male heads of households in Massachusetts, who were also church members, to be freemen. Two years later the freemen secured their right to select delegates to represent the towns in drafting the laws of the colony. These delegates and the magistrates later separated into two legislative houses. Thus the procedures of a joint-stock company provided the origins for democratic suffrage and the bicameral division of legislative authority in America.

Indians and Puritans

The Algonquian Indians of southern New England found the English very different from the French and Dutch traders who had preceded them. The principal concern of the English was not commerce, although the fur trade remained an important part of their economy, but the acquisition of Indian land for their growing settlements. Massasoit, leader of the Pokanokets, attempted to use the colonists to his own advantage. But he soon found that when the English attacked his enemies, their true motive was expansion.

In 1623, on Massasoit's urging, the Pilgrim military commander Miles Standish attacked a group of Massachusetts Indians north of Plymouth. When Standish brought back the sachem's head and placed it on a pike outside the settlement's gates, the meaning of the gesture was not lost on the Pokanokets. If we are allies, one Indian asked, "how cometh it to pass that when we come to Patuxet you stand upon your guard, with the mouths of your pieces [guns] presented to us?" Even the Pokanokets were soon calling their English allies *wotowquenange*, meaning "cutthroats" in Algonquian.

Ravaged by disease, the Pokanokets' northern neighbors, the Massachusetts, were ill-prepared for the Puritan landings that took place after 1629. The English believed they had the right to take what they thought of as "unused" lands—lands not being used, that is, in the "Englishway"—and depopulated Massachusetts villages became prime targets for expansion. As one colonist wrote, "Their land is spacious and void, and there are few and [they] do but run over the grass, as do also the foxes and wild beasts." The Indians did not consider that land could be privately owned, but understood it as a community resource. Conflicts between settlers over title, however, made it necessary to obtain original deeds from Indians, and the English used a variety of tactics to pressure them into signing "quitclaims," or documents in which the signers relinquished all claim to specified properties. The English allowed their livestock to graze native fields, making them useless for cultivation. They fined Indians for violations of English law, such as working on the Sabbath, and then demanded land as payment. In addition, they made deals with dishonest sachems. For giving up the land that became Charlestown, for example, the "Squaw Sachem" of the Pawtuckets, one of a number of women Algonquian leaders, received twenty-one coats, nineteen fathoms of wampum, and three bushels of corn. Disorganized and demoralized, many coastal Algonquians soon placed themselves under the protection of the English.

Indian peoples to the west, however, remained a formidable presence. They blocked Puritan expansion until they were devastated in 1633–34 by an epidemic of smallpox that spread from the St. Lawrence south to Long Island Sound. This epidemic took place just as hundreds of English migrants were crowding into coastal towns. "Without this remarkable and terrible stroke of God upon the natives," recorded a town scribe, "we would with much more difficulty have found room, and at far greater charge have obtained and purchased land." In the aftermath of the epidemic, Puritans established many new inland towns.

By the late 1630s the most powerful tribes in the vicinity of the Puritans were the Narragansets of present-day Rhode Island and their traditional enemies the Pequots, principal trading partners of the Dutch. The Pequots lived on Long Island Sound near the mouth of the Connecticut River, where they controlled the production of wampum, woven belts of sea shells used as a medium of exchange in the Indian trade. In 1637 the Narragansets, in alliance with the English, who were looking for an excuse to smash the Dutch, went to war against the Pequots. Narraganset warriors and English troops attacked the main Pequot village, killing most

The first map printed in the English colonies, this view of New England was published in Boston in 1677. With north oriented to the right, it looks west from Massachusetts Bay, the two vertical black lines indicating the approximate boundaries of the Commonwealth of Massachusetts. The territory west of Rhode Island is noted as an Indian stronghold, the homelands of the Narraganset, Pequot, and Nipmuck peoples.

SOURCE: John Foster, White Hills Map, 1677, woodcut. The John Carter Brown Library at Brown University.

of its slumbering residents, including women and children. Unaccustomed to such tactics, the shocked Narragansets cried out to the English: "It is too furious, it slays too many."

The New England Merchants

In England, the conflict between King Charles I and the Puritans in Parliament broke into armed conflict in 1642. Several years of violent confrontation led to the execution of the king in 1649 and the proclamation of an English Commonwealth, headed by the Puritan leader Oliver Cromwell. Because the Puritans were on the victorious side in the English Civil War, they no longer had the same incentive to migrate to New England. A number of settlers even returned to England.

New England's economy had depended on the sale of supplies and land to arriving immigrants, but as the Great Migration ended the importance of this "newcomer market" declined. Lacking a single exportable commodity, New England traders developed a diversified trade with a variety of commodities, including oak barrel staves, pine ship's masts, salted cod fish, and farm products. By the 1660s the New England merchants had a commercial fleet that was the envy of other colonies: 300 trading and fishing vessels that voyaged throughout the Atlantic—to the fishing grounds of the North Atlantic, to the sugar-producing colonies of the West Indies, to the wine-producing islands of the Atlantic, and to Africa and England. The development of a diversified economy provided New England with considerable long-term strength, and offered a striking contrast with the specialized fur-trade economy of New France.

Community and Family in Massachusetts

The Puritans stressed the importance of well-ordered communities. The Massachusetts General Court, the governing body of the colony, granted townships to a group of proprietors, the leaders of a congregation wishing to settle new lands. These men then distributed fields, pasture, and woodlands in quantities proportional to the social status of the recipient, with wealthy families receiving more than others. The Puritans believed that social hierarchy was ordained by God and made for well-ordered communities. Settlers typically clustered their dwellings in a central village, near the meetinghouse that served as both church and civic center. Some towns, particularly those along the coast such as Boston, soon became centers of shipping.

The Mason Children, by an unknown Boston artist, c. 1670. These Puritan children—David, Joanna, and Abigail Mason—are dressed in finery, an indication of the wealth and prominence of their family. The cane in young David's hand indicates his position as the male heir, while the rose held by Abigail is a symbol of childhood innocence.

SOURCE: Attributed to the Freake-Gibbs Painter, American, active Boston, MA., c. 1670. *The Mason Children: David, Joanna, and Abigail*, 1670. Oil on canvas, 39 x 421½ in. The Fine Arts Museum of San Francisco, Gift of Mr. and Mrs. John D. Rockefeller 3rd, 1979,7.3.

These clustered settlements and strong, vital communities made seventeenth-century New England quite different from Chesapeake society.

The ideal Puritan family was also well-ordered. "Surely there is in all children a stubbornness, and stoutness of mind arising from natural pride, which must be broken and beaten down," one Puritan declared. Parents often participated in the choice of mates for their offspring, and children typically married in the order of their births, younger siblings waiting until arrangements had been made for their elders. But well-disciplined children also needed education. Another source of New England's strength was the impressive system the Puritans built to educate their young. In 1647 Massachusetts required that towns with 50 families or more support a public school; those with 100 families were to establish a grammar school that taught Latin, knowledge of which was required for admission to Harvard College, founded in 1636. The colony of Connecticut enacted similar requirements. Literacy was higher in New England than elsewhere in North America, and even in most of Europe. But because girls were excluded from grammar schools, far fewer New England women than men could read and write. By 1639 the first printing press in the English colonies was in operation in Boston, and the following year it brought out the first American English publication, *The Bay Psalm Book.*

It is a mistake to regard the Puritans as "puritanical." Although adultery was a capital crime in New England, Puritans celebrated sexual expression within marriage. Men and women were expected to be in love when they married. Courting couples were even allowed to lie in bed together, with their lower bodies wrapped in an apron and separated by a board—a practice called bundling. In the words of an old New England ballad:

> *She is modest, also chaste*
> *While only bare from neck to waist,*
> *And he of boasted freedom sings,*
> *Of all above her apron strings.*

There were certainly many loving Puritan households with contented husbands and wives. Anne Bradstreet, a Massachusetts wife and mother and the first published poet of New England, wrote about her husband and marriage:

> *If ever two are one, then surely we.*
> *If ever man were lov'd by wife, then thee;*
> *If ever wife was happy in a man,*
> *Compare with me ye women if you can.*

The family economy operated through the combined efforts of husband and wife. Men were generally responsible for fieldwork, women for the work of the household, which included gardening, tending to the dairy and henhouse, and providing fuel and water. Women managed a rich array of tasks, and some independently traded garden products, milk, and eggs. "I meddle not with the geese nor turkeys," one New England husband declared, referring to his wife's domestic management, "for they are hers for she hath been and is a good wife to me." Indeed, women traders helped to create and sustain many of the bonds of New England communities.

Still, the cultural ideal was the subordination of women to men. "I am but a wife, and therefore it is sufficient for me to follow my husband," wrote Lucy Winthrop Downing, and her brother John Winthrop declared that "a true wife accounts her subjection her honor and freedom." Married women could not make contracts, own property, vote, or hold office. A typical woman, marrying in her early twenties and surviving through her forties, could expect to bear eight children and devote herself to husband and family. Aside from abstinence, there was no form of birth control. Wives who failed to have children, or widows who were economically independent, aroused significant suspicion among their neighbors. One Boston resident wrote that to be an "old maid . . . is thought such a curse as nothing can exceed it, and look'd on as a dismal Spectacle."

The mistrust of women came to the surface most notably in periodic witchcraft scares. During the course of the seventeenth century, according to one historian, 342 New England women were accused by their neighbors of witchcraft. The majority of them were unmarried, or childless, or widowed, or had reputations among their neighbors for assertiveness and independence. In the vast majority of cases these accusations were dismissed by authorities. In Salem, Massachusetts, in 1692, however, when a group of girls claimed that they had been bewitched by a number of old men and women, the whole community was thrown into a panic of accusations. Before the colonial governor finally called a halt to the persecutions in 1693, twenty people had been tried, condemned, and executed.

The Salem accusations of witchcraft may have reflected social tensions that found their outlet through an attack on people perceived as outsiders. Salem was a booming port, but although some residents were prospering, others were not. Most of the victims came from the commercial eastern end of town, the majority of their accusers from the economically stagnant western side. Most of the accused also came from families with religious affiliations with Anglicans, Quakers, or Baptists, not with the Puritans. Finally, a majority of the victims were old women, suspect because they lived alone, without men. The Salem witchcraft trials exposed the dark side of Puritan ideas about women.

Dissent and New Communities

The Puritans emigrated in order to practice their variety of Christianity, but they had little tolerance for other religious points of view. Religious disagreement among the colonists soon provoked the founding of new colonies. Thomas Hooker, minister of the congregation at Cambridge, disagreed with the policy of restricting suffrage to male church members. In 1636 he led his followers west to the Connecticut River, where they founded the town of Hartford near the site of the

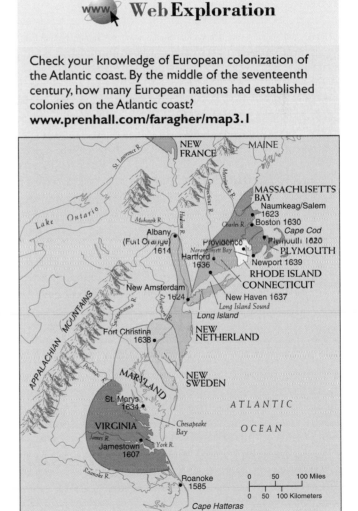

Web Exploration

Check your knowledge of European colonization of the Atlantic coast. By the middle of the seventeenth century, how many European nations had established colonies on the Atlantic coast?
www.prenhall.com/faragher/map3.1

European Colonies of the Atlantic Coast, 1607–39 Virginia on Chesapeake Bay was the first English colony in North America, but by the mid-seventeenth century Virginia was joined by settlements of Scandinavians on the Delaware River, and Dutch on the Hudson River, as well as English religious dissenters in New England. The territories indicated here reflect the vague boundaries of the early colonies.

trading post abandoned by the Dutch after epidemic disease had destroyed nearby Indian communities in 1634. Hooker helped write the Fundamental Orders that marked the beginning of the colony of Connecticut.

Another dissenter was the minister Roger Williams, who came to New England in 1631 to take up duties for the congregation in Salem. Williams believed in religious tolerance and the separation of church and state (discussed in Chapter 5). He also preached that the colonists had no absolute right to Indian land but must bargain for it in good faith. These were dangerous ideas, and Williams was banished from the colony in 1636. With a group of his followers, he emigrated to the Narraganset country, where he purchased land from the Indians and founded the town of Providence.

The next year Boston shook with another religious controversy. Anne Hutchinson, the wife of a Puritan merchant who had arrived in New England in 1634, was a brilliant woman who led religious discussion groups that criticized various Boston ministers for a lack of piety. The concentration of attention on good works, she argued, led people to believe that they could earn their way to heaven, a "popish" or Catholic heresy in the eyes of Calvinists. Hutchinson was called before the General Court, where the Puritan leaders made it clear that they would not tolerate a woman who publicly criticized men, and she was excommunicated and banished. She and her followers moved to Roger Williams's settlement, where they established another community in 1638.

In 1644 Roger Williams received a royal charter creating the colony of Rhode Island, named for the principal island in Narraganset Bay, as a protection for these dissenting communities. A new royal charter of 1663 guaranteed self-government and complete religious liberty.

By the 1670s Massachusetts's population had grown to more than 40,000, most of it concentrated in and around Boston, although there were communities as far west as the Connecticut River valley and as far north as the region known as Maine (not separated from Massachusetts until 1820), as well as in New Hampshire, which had been set off as a royal colony in 1680. Next in size after Massachusetts was Connecticut, its population numbering about 17,000. Plymouth's 6,000 inhabitants were absorbed by Massachusetts in 1691.

THE RESTORATION COLONIES

The Puritan Commonwealth established in England after the execution of King Charles attempted to provide a measure of central control over the colonies

WebExploration

Examine the processes underlying the founding of the Restoration Colonies. Compared to Map 3.1, how has the political landscape changed?
www.prenhall.com/faragher/map3.2

The Restoration Colonies   After the restoration of the Stuart monarchy in 1660, King Charles II of England created the new proprietary colonies of Carolina, New York, Pennsylvania, and New Jersey. New Hampshire was set off as a royal colony in 1680, and in 1704 the lower counties of Pennsylvania became the colony of Delaware.

with the passage in 1651 of an Act of Trade and Navigation, which was intended to keep Dutch ships out of England's overseas possessions. But the regime was preoccupied with English domestic affairs and left the colonies largely to their own devices. Cromwell ruled as Lord Protector of the Commonwealth, but the new order failed to survive his death in 1658. While wishing to reserve for itself certain significant powers of state, Parliament was desperate for political stability after nearly two decades of civil war. In 1660 it restored the Stuart monarchy, placing Charles II, son of the former king, on the throne. One of Charles's most

important acts was the establishment of several new proprietary colonies, known as the
Restoration Colonies.

Early Carolina

In 1663 the king issued his first
charters, calling for the establishment of a new colony called
Carolina, which stretched from
Virginia south to Spanish
Florida. Virginians had already
begun moving into the northern parts of this territory, and
in 1664 the Carolina proprietors appointed a governor for
the settlements in the area of
Albermarle Sound and created
a popularly elected assembly.
By 1675 North Carolina, as it
became known, was home to
5,000 small farmers and large
tobacco planters.

This is the earliest known view of New Amsterdam, printed in 1651. Indian traders are
shown arriving with their goods in a dugout canoe of distinctive design known to have
been produced by the native people of Long Island Sound. Twenty-five years after its
founding, the Dutch settlement still occupies only the lower tip of Manhattan Island.

SOURCE: New Amsterdam, 1650–53. The Hague Facsimile. Museum of the City of New York.
The J. Clarence Davies Collection 34.100.29.

Settlement farther south began in 1670 with the
founding of coastal Charles Town (Charleston today).
Most South Carolina settlers came from Barbados, a
Caribbean colony the English had founded in 1627,
which had grown rich from the production of sugar. By
the 1670s the island had become overpopulated with
English settlers and Africans. The latter, imported as
slaves to work the plantations, made up a majority of
the population. Hundreds of Barbadians, both masters
and their slaves, relocated to South Carolina, lending a
distinctly West Indian character to the colony. By the
end of the seventeenth century South Carolina's population included 6,000 settlers, some 2,500 of them enslaved Africans. (For a further discussion of slavery in
South Carolina, see Chapter 4.)

From New Netherland to New York

King Charles II also coveted the lucrative Dutch colony
of New Netherland. In response to the growth of New
England's population and its merchant economy, in the
1640s the Dutch West India Company began to sponsor
the emigration of European settlers to its colony in the
Hudson River valley, seeking to convert New Netherland from a specialized fur-trade economy to a diversified supply center for the West Indies. The result was
rising conflict with local Indian communities, pressed by
the Dutch to cede their lands for agriculture. The British
Navigation Act of 1651 was in part a response to what
the English viewed as the Dutch threat to the English
trade monopoly they sought to establish along the Atlantic coast. England's attempt to control Dutch shipping

led to an inconclusive naval war with Holland from 1652
to 1654, and a decade later the two powers clashed again
along the West African coast. Finally, in 1664, an English
fleet sailed into Manhattan harbor and forced the surrender of New Amsterdam without firing a shot, inagurating
a second full-fledged Anglo-Dutch war, which ended
with an inconclusive peace in 1667. A third and final
conflict from 1672 to 1674 resulted in the bankruptcy of
the Dutch West India Company and marked the ascension of the English to dominance in the Atlantic. Holland remained supreme in the Baltic and the East Indies.

Charles II granted the newly acquired Dutch colony
to his brother James, the Duke of York, renaming it New
York in his honor. Otherwise the English government
did little to disturb the existing order, preferring simply
to reap the benefits of acquiring this profitable and dynamic colony. Ethnically and linguistically diversified,
accommodating a wide range of religious sects, New
York boasted the most heterogeneous society in North
America. In 1665, the communities of the Delaware Valley were split off as the proprietary colony of New Jersey, although it continued to be governed by New York
until the 1680s. By the 1670s, the combined population
of these settlements numbered over 10,000, with more
than 1,500 people clustered in the governmental and
commercial center of New York City.

The Founding of Pennsylvania

In 1676 proprietary rights to the western portion of
New Jersey were sold to a group of English Quakers
that included William Penn, who intended to make the

The Delawares presented William Penn with this wampum belt after the Shackamaxon Treaty of 1682. In friendship, a Quaker in distinctive hat clasps the hand of an Indian. The diagonal stripes on either side of the figures convey information about the territorial terms of the agreement. Wampum belts like this one, made from strings of white and purple shells, were used to commemorate treaties throughout the colonial period and were the most widely accepted form of money in the northeastern colonies during the seventeenth century.

SOURCE: Photograph by Gavin Ashworth. The Historical Society of Pennsylvania.

area a religious haven for members of the Society of Friends, or Quakers. A dissenting sect, the Quakers were committed to religious toleration and pacifism. Penn himself had been imprisoned four times for publicly expressing these views. But he was the son of the wealthy and influential English admiral Sir William Penn, a close adviser to the king. In 1681, to settle a large debt owed to Sir William, King Charles granted the younger Penn a huge territory west of the Delaware River. The next year Penn supervised the laying out of his capital of Philadelphia on the Delaware.

Penn wanted this colony to be a "holy experiment." In his first Frame of Government, drafted in 1682, he included guarantees of religious freedom, civil liberties, and elected representation. He also attempted to deal fairly with the Algonquian Indians, not permitting colonization until settlement rights were negotiated and lands purchased. In 1682 and 1683, he made an agreement with the sachem Tammany of the Delaware tribe. In subsequent years Chief Tammany appeared in many popular stories and myths among the peoples of the mid-Atlantic region, and by the time of the Revolution his name had become emblematic of the American spirit of independence and was adpoted as the name of a New York political club, Tammany Hall. Although Pennsylvania's relations with the Indians later soured, during Penn's lifetime his reputation for fair dealing led a number of Indian groups to resettle in the Quaker colony.

During the first decade of Pennsylvania's settlement, over 10,000 colonists arrived from England, and agricultural communities were soon spreading from the Delaware into the fertile interior valleys. In 1704 Penn approved the creation of a separate government for the area formerly controlled by the Scandinavians and Dutch. This area became the colony of Delaware. In the eighteenth century Pennsylvania became known as America's breadbasket, and Philadelphia became the most important colonial port in North America.

CONFLICT AND WAR

Pennsylvania's ability to maintain peaceful relations with the Indians proved the great exception, for the last quarter of the seventeenth century was a time of great violence throughout the colonial regions of the continent. Much of this warfare was between colonists and Indians, but intertribal warfare and intercolonial rivalry greatly contributed to the violence. It extended from Santa Fé—where the

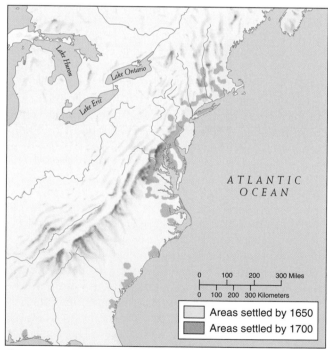

Spread of Settlement: British Colonies, 1650–1700 The spread of settlement in the English colonies in the late seventeenth century created the conditions for a number of violent conflicts, including King Philip's War, Bacon's Rebellion, the Wars in the South Wars, and King William's War.

OVERVIEW

CONFLICT AND WAR

The Beaver Wars	1640s–80s	The Iroquois extend their authority as middlemen in the Dutch and English trade system by attacking neighbors as far west as Illinois
King Philip's War	1675–76	The Indian peoples of southern New England and the Puritan colonies fight for control of land
Bacon's Rebellion	1675–76	Backcountry settlers attack Indians, and colonial authorities try to suppress these attacks
Wars in the South	1670s–1720s	British colonists in the Carolinas incite Creeks, Cherokees, and other Indian tribes to attack and enslave the mission Indians of Spanish Florida
The Glorious Revolution in America	1689	Colonists in Massachusetts, New York, and Maryland rise up against the colonial governments of King James II
King William's War	1689–97	The first of a series of colonial struggles between England and France, these conflicts occur principally on the frontiers of northern New England and New York

revolt of the Pueblos was the single most effective instance of Indian resistance to colonization—to the shores of Hudson's Bay, where French and English traders fought for access to the rich fur-producing region of the north.

King Philip's War

During the nearly forty years of peace that followed the Pequot War of 1637, the Algonquian and English peoples of New England lived in close, if tense, contact. Several Puritan ministers, including John Eliot and Thomas Mayhew, began to preach to the Indians, and several hundred Algonquian converts eventually relocated in Christian Indian communities called "praying towns." Outside the colonial boundaries, however, there remained a number of independent Indian tribes, including the Pokanokets and the Narragansets of Rhode Island and the Abenakis of northern New England. The extraordinary expansion of the Puritan population, and their hunger for land, created pressures for further expansion into those territories.

In 1671 the colonial authorities at Plymouth forced the Pokanokets to concede authority over their home territory. This humiliation convinced the sachem Metacomet (called King Philip by the English), son of Massasoit, that his people must break their half-century alliance with Plymouth and take up armed resistance. Meanwhile, the Puritan colonies prepared for a war of conquest.

In the spring of 1675 Plymouth magistrates arrested and executed three Pokanoket men for the murder of a Christian Indian. Fearing that the moment of confrontation had arrived, Metacomet appealed to the Narragansets for a defensive alliance. The United Colonies (the New England colonies led by Massachusetts Bay) and New York, hoping for territorial gain, took this as the moment to send armed forces into Narraganset country, attacking and burning a number of villages. What became known as King Philip's War soon engulfed all of New England.

At first things went well for the Indians. They forced the abandonment of English settlements on the Connecticut River and torched several towns less than twenty miles from Boston. By the beginning of 1676, however, their campaign was collapsing. A combined colonial army invaded Narraganset country, burning villages, killing women and children, and defeating a large Indian force in a battle known as the Great Swamp Fight. In western New England, Metacomet appealed to the Iroquois for supplies and support, but instead they attacked and defeated his forces. Metacomet retreated back to his homeland, where the colonists annihilated his army in August 1676. The victors killed Metacomet and triumphantly marched his head on a pike through their towns. The colonists sold his wife and son, among hundreds of other captives, into West Indian slavery.

In their attack on Metacomet's army, the Iroquois were motivated by interests of their own. Continuing the role they had played in the Dutch trading system, they now cast themselves in the role of powerful intermediaries between other tribes and the English. By attacking Metacomet they demonstrated where they stood. In a series of negotiations conducted at Albany in 1677, the Iroquois Confederacy and the colony of New York created an alliance known as the Covenant Chain, which sought to establish Iroquois dominance over all other tribes and thus put New York in an economically and politically dominant position among the other colonies. During the 1680s the Iroquois pressed their claims as far west as the Illinois country, fighting western Algonquian tribes allied with the French trading system.

At the end of King Philip's War, some 4,000 Algonquians and 2,000 English colonists were dead, and dozens of native and colonial towns lay in ruins. Fearing attack from Indians close at hand, colonists destroyed most of the Christian Indian praying towns, killing many of the residents. Measured against the size of the population, King Philip's War was one of the most destructive wars in American history.

Bacon's Rebellion

At the same time as King Philip's War, another English-Indian confrontation took place in the Chesapeake. In the 1670s the Susquehannock people of the upper Potomac River came into conflict with the tobacco planters expanding northward from Virginia. Violent raids in 1675, led by wealthy backcountry settler Nathaniel Bacon, included the indiscriminate murder of Indians. The efforts of Virginia governor William Berkeley to suppress these unauthorized military expeditions so infuriated Bacon and his followers—many of them former indentured servants—that in the spring of 1676 they turned their fury against the colonial capital of Jamestown itself. Berkeley fled across the Chesapeake while Bacon pillaged and burned the capital. Soon thereafter Bacon died of dysentery, a common fate of the day, and his rebellion collapsed. The next year Virginia signed a treaty ending hostilities with the Indians, but most of the Susquehannocks had already migrated to New York, where they became joined the Covenant Chain of the Iroquois.

This brief but violent clash marked an important change of direction for Virginia. Bacon had issued a manifesto demanding not only the death or removal of all Indians from the colony but also an end to the rule of aristocratic "grandees" and "parasites." The rebellion thus signaled a developing conflict between frontier districts such as Bacon's and the more established coastal region where the "Indian problem" had long since been settled. In 1677, in a replay of Virginia events known as Culpeper's Rebellion, backcountry men in the Albermarle region of North Carolina suceeded in overthrowing the established government, before being suppressed by English authorities. In the aftermath of these rebellions, colonial authorities in Virginia and North Carolina began to favor armed expansion into Indian territory, hoping to gain the support of backcountry men by enlarging the stock of available colonial land. Moreover, planters' fears of disorder among former indentured servants encouraged them to accelerate the transition to slave labor (see Chapter 4).

Indians and New Englanders skirmish during King Philip's War in a detail from John Seller's "A Mapp of New England," published immediately after the war.

SOURCE: John Seller Map of New England, 1675. Courtesy of the John Carter Brown Library at Brown University.

Wars in the South

There was also massive violence in South Carolina during the 1670s, as colonists there began the operation of a large-scale Indian slave trade. Charleston merchants encouraged Yamasees, Creeks, Cherokees, and Chickasaws to wage war on Indian tribes allied to rival colonial powers: the mission Indians of Spanish Florida, the Choctaw allies of the French, and the Tuscaroras, trading partners of the Virginians. The mission Indians of Florida were hit so hard that by 1710 more than 12,000 of them had been captured and sold, thousands of others had been killed or dispersed, and the Spanish mission system, in operation for more than a century, lay in ruins.

This vicious Indian slave trade extended well into the eighteenth century, and thousands of southern Indians were sold into captivity. Most of the Indian men were shipped from Charleston to Caribbean or northern colonies; the Indian women remained in South Carolina, where many eventually formed relationships and had children with male African slaves, forming a racial-ethnic group known as the "mustees."

The Glorious Revolution in America

Dynastic change in England was another factor that precipitated violence in North America. Upon Charles II's death in 1685, his brother and successor, James II, began a concerted effort to strengthen royal control over the colonies. During the preceding forty years colonial assemblies had grown powerful and independent, and King James was determined to reign them in. He abolished the New York assembly, which had been particularly troublesome, and placed all power in the hands of the royal governor. Colonial assemblies continued to operate in the other colonies, but many became involved in bitter disputes with their governors. In his most dramatic action, the king abolished the charter governments of the New England, New York, and New Jersey colonies, combining them into what was called the Dominion of New England. Edmund Andros, the new royal governor, imposed Anglican forms of worship in Puritan areas and violated traditions of local autonomy.

In England, the same imperious style on the part of the king alienated Parliament, and in a bloodless transition, afterward known as the Glorious Revolution, Parliament deposed James II in 1688 and replaced him with his daughter and Dutch son-in-law, Mary and William of Orange. The new monarchs agreed to a Bill of Rights, promising to respect traditional civil liberties, to summon and consult with Parliament annually, and to enforce and administer parliamentary legislation. These were significant concessions with profound implications for the future of English politics. England now had a "constitutional monarchy."

When news of the Glorious Revolution reached North America, colonists rose in a series of rebellions against the authorities set in place by James II. In the spring of 1689, Governor Andros was attacked by an angry Boston mob, inflamed by rumors that he was a secret Catholic. He was able to escape their wrath but was arrested and deported by the local militia. When news of the Boston revolt arrived in New York, it inspired another uprising there. A group led by German merchant Jacob Leisler, and including many prominent Dutch residents, seized control of the city and called for the formation of a new legislature. In Maryland, rumors of a Catholic plot led to the overthrow of the proprietary rule of the Calvert family by an insurgent group called the Protestant Association.

The new monarchs carefully measured their response to these uprisings. When Jacob Leisler attempted to prevent the landing of the king's troops in New York, he was arrested, tried, and executed. But the monarchs consented to the dismantling of the Dominion of New England and the end of proprietary rule in Maryland. The outcome of the Glorious Revolution in America was mixed. All the affected English colonies quickly revived their assemblies and returned to their tradition of self-government. The government of England did not fully reestablish its authority in these colonies until 1692 when Massachusetts, New York, and Maryland all were declared royal colonies.

King William's War

The year 1689 also marked the beginning of nearly seventy-five years of armed conflict between English and French forces for control of the North American interior. The Iroquois-English Covenant Chain challenged New France's fur-trade empire, and in response the French pressed further west in search of commercial opportunities. In the far north, the English countered French dominance with the establishment of Hudson's Bay Company, a royal fur-trade monopoly that sought to exploit the watershed of the great northern bay.

Hostilities began with English Iroquois attacks on Montreal and violence between rival French and English traders on Hudson's Bay. These skirmishes were part of a larger conflict between England and France called the War of the League of Augsburg in Europe. In the North American colonies the conflict was known as King William's War. In 1690, the French and their Algonquian allies counterattacked,

CHRONOLOGY

1598	Juan de Oñate leads Spanish into New Mexico
1607	English found Jamestown
1608	French found Quebec
1609	Spanish found Santa Fé
1620	Pilgrim emigration
1622	Indian uprising in Virginia
1625	Jesuit missionaries arrive in New France
1629	Puritans begin settlement of Massachusetts Bay
1637	Pequot War
1649	Charles I executed
1660	Stuart monarchy restored, Charles II becomes king
1675	King Philip's War
1676	Bacon's Rebellion
1680	Pueblo Revolt
1681–82	Robert Sieur de La Salle explores the Mississippi
1688	The Glorious Revolution
1689	King William's War
1698	Spanish reconquest of the Pueblos completed
1701	English impose royal governments on all colonies but Massachusetts, Connecticut, and Pennsylvania

burning frontier settlements in New York, New Hampshire, and Maine, and pressing their attacks against the towns of the Iroquois. The same year, a Massachusetts fleet captured and briefly held the strategic French harbor at Port Royal, on the Bay of Fundy in Acadia, but a combined English and colonial force failed in its attempt to conquer the French settlements along the St. Lawrence. This inconclusive war was ended by the Treaty of Ryswick of 1697, which established an equally inconclusive peace. War between England and France resumed only five years later.

The persistent violence of the last quarter of the seventeenth century greatly concerned English authorities, who began to fear the loss of their North American possessions either from outside attack or from internal disorder. To shore up central control, in 1701 the English Board of Trade recommended making all charter and proprietary governments into royal colonies. After a brief period under royal rule, William Penn regained private control of his domain, but Pennsylvania was the only remaining proprietary colony. Among the royal charter colonies, only Rhode Island and Connecticut retained their original governments. The result of this quarter-century of violence was the tightening of the imperial reins over its North American possessions.

CONCLUSION

At the beginning of the seventeenth century the European presence north of Mexico was extremely limited: Spanish bases in Florida, a few Franciscan missionaries among the Pueblos, and fishermen along the North Atlantic coast. By 1700 the human landscape of the Southwest, the South, and the Northeast had been transformed. More than a quarter million migrants from the Old World had moved into these regions, the vast majority to the British colonies. Indian societies had been disrupted, depopulated, and in some cases destroyed. The Spanish and French colonies were characterized by the inclusion of Indians in the social and economic life of the community. But along the Atlantic coast, the English and eventually the Dutch established communities of exclusion, with resulting implications for the future of relations between colonists and Indians that were ominous.

During the long civil war at home the English colonies had been left to run their own affairs. But with the Restoration in 1660 and the establishment of the constitutional monarchy in 1689, the English state began to supervise its troublesome colonists more closely, beginning a long struggle over the limits of self-government. The violence and warfare of the last decades of the century suggested that conflict would continue to play a significant role in the future of colonial America.

REVIEW QUESTIONS

1. Using examples drawn from this chapter, discuss the differences between colonizing "frontiers of inclusion" and "exclusion."
2. What factors turned England's Chesapeake colony of Virginia from stark failure to brilliant success?
3. Discuss the role of religious dissent in the founding of the first New England colonies and in stimulating the creation of others.
4. Compare and contrast William Penn's policy with respect to Indian tribes with the policies of other English settlers, in the Chesapeake and New England, and with the policies of the Spanish, the French, and the Dutch.
5. What were the principal causes of colonial violence and warfare of the late seventeenth century?

RECOMMENDED READING

James Axtell, *The European and the Indian: Essays in the Ethnohistory of Colonial America* (1981). A readable introduction to the dynamics of mutual discovery between natives and colonizers.

Leslie Choquette, *Frenchmen into Peasants: Modernity and Tradition in the Peopling of French Canada* (1997). A history of French immigrants to Canada and Acadia, based on a comprehensive database of hundreds of individuals. The most detailed study of French mobility to date.

Frederic W. Gleach, *Powhatan's World and Colonial Virginia: A Conflict of Cultures* (1997). Reconstructing the worldview of the Chesapeake Algonquians as they attempted to maintain control of their homeland.

Harold Adams Innis, *The Fur Trade in Canada: An Introduction to Canadian Economic History* (1999). A new edition of a classic that remains the definitive history of the fur trade.

Andrew L. Knaut, *The Pueblo Revolt of 1680* (1995). The most complete and sophisticated account of the revolt.

Edmund S. Morgan, *American Slavery, American Freedom* (1975). A classic interpretation of early Virginia.

Morgan argues that early American ideas of freedom for some were based on the reality of slavery for others.

Diana Newton, *Papists, Protestants, and Puritans, 1559–1714* (1998). The best survey of religious change during the Protestant Reformation, with a focus on the turmoil in England.

Neal Salisbury, *Manitou and Providence: Indians, Europeans, and the Making of New England* (1982). One of the best examples of the new ethnohistory of Indians; a provocative intercultural approach to the history of the Northeast.

Susan Sleeper-Smith, *Native Women and French Men: Rethinking Cultural Encounter in the Western Great Lakes* (2001). A study of Indian women who married French traders and became cultural brokers and creators of a middle ground.

David J. Weber, *The Spanish Frontier in North America* (1992). A powerful overview that includes the history of New Mexico and Florida.

▶ MEDIA RESOURCES

U.S. HISTORY DOCUMENTS CD-ROM

Meeting of Three Cultures

1-6   Thomas Mun, from England's Treasure by Foreign Trade (1664)

1-7   Don Juan de Oñate, Plaus: A Settlement in New Mexico (1599)

Colonizing the New World

2-1   John White, The Lost Colony (1590)

2-6   The Taking of the Fort at Mystic: A Brief History of the Pequot War

2-7   The Trial of Anne Hutchinson (1638)

2-8   A Jesuit Priest Describes New Amsterdam (1642)

2-9   George Alsop, The Importance of Tobacco (1660)

2-10   The Examination and Confession of Ann Foster at Salem Village (1692)

Colonial America

3-1   Navigation Act of September 13, 1660

3-2   Nathaniel Bacon's Challenge to William Berkeley and the Governor's Response (1676)

3-3   Early French Explorations of the Mississippi River (1673)

3-4   Edward Randolph Describes King Philip's War (1685)

3-6   William Penn's Charter of Privileges (1701)

 ### COMPANION WEBSITE HIGHLIGHTS

To view an exploration, enter one of the URLs below in your browser.

 ### Web Explorations

European Colonies of the Atlantic Coast, 1607–1639
http://www.prenhall.com/faragher/map3.1

The Restoration Colonies
http://www.prenhall.com/faragher/map3.2

 ### Additional Interactive Maps

To access the maps, go to this chapter's resources at
http://www.prenhall.com/faragher
New France in the Seventeenth Century, page 57
Spread of Settlement: British Colonies, 1650–1700, page 70

 ### HISTORY RESOURCE CENTER

To find the resources listed below, go to
http://www.prenhall.com/historyresourcecenter

Documents

Anne Bradstreet, Before the Birth of One of Her Children (ca. 1650)

John Smith, "The Starving Time" (1624)

John Winthrop, "A Model of Christian Charity" (1630)

Richard Frethorne, Letter to His Parents (1623)

The Charter of Maryland (1632)

The Laws of Virginia (1610–1611)

The Laws of Virginia (1662, 1691, 1705)

The Mayflower Compact (1620)

The Third Charter of Virginia (1612)

William Bradford, History of Plymouth Plantation (1630–1650)

William Penn, from "Model of Government" (1681)

Images

A Letter Written by William Penn

Captain John Smith fights with the Native American "King of Pamaunkee"

Champlain's Conference with the Indians

Events of John Smith's Life

Iroquois Fort

Pocahontas Pleading For John Smith's Life

Thanksgiving Proclamation, Connecticut, 1721

William Penn's Treaty with the Indians

EXPLORING AMERICA

JAMESTOWN

http://www.prenhall.com/faragher/jamestown

What motivated the English to found a colony at Jamestown? How did this original purpose change over time and why? How does the figure of Pocahontas symbolize the Native American experience with the English? The *Jamestown* module examines the origins and the travails of development experienced by the first, permanent English settlement in North America. Using a variety of images, an interactive map, a chronology, and primary source document excerpts, the module offers insight into the perils of colonization and also into the interaction of the English and the Native Americans they encountered.

Jamestown focuses on important individuals who contributed to the colony's development, including John Smith, John Rolfe, and Pocahontas. Primary

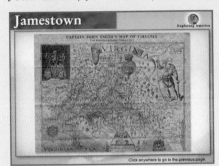

source documents, visual images, and the narrative bring the historical figures to life, especially the Native American princess who has become an icon of American folklore. The story of Pocahontas offers insight into the relations between the English and the indigenous people they met in Virginia. It also serves as a metaphor for the Native American experience during the age of European colonization. The chronology and interactive map provide context for this drama of early American history.

Reflect and Respond

1. What attributes of life at Jamestown might be construed as lasting in the pioneer heritage of the United States?

2. Of the actual events that happened at Jamestown, pick some that you would change. What would they be? Would you avoid expansion? Would you insist that all settlers be married couples? Would you separate exploration from settlement, so each task could be focused on separately? What other changes would you make?

✓ Check it out

Chronology

The up-and-down fortunes of the early years of the Jamestown colony are presented in the Chronology. The various dates and commentary trace the origins and development of Jamestown, highlighting the impor-

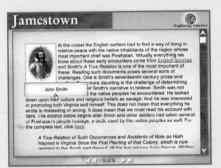

tance of relations with Native Americans and other factors that contributed to its survival, eventual success, and ultimate demise. Against this backdrop of general colonial development, important events in the lives of Pocahontas and John Rolfe provide a personal touch to the story.

This exploration is also available on the *Exploring America* CD-ROM. For another *Exploring America* activity related to this chapter, go to "Witches in the American Imagination," found on both the Companion Website™ and the CD-ROM.

FOUR
SLAVERY AND EMPIRE

▶ 1 4 4 1 – 1 7 7 0

Painting of slaves in Antigua. From William Clark's *Ten Views Found in the Island of Antigua*, early 19th century. The British Library.

African Slaves Build Their Own Community in Coastal Georgia

AFRICANS LABORED IN THE STEAMY HEAT OF THE COASTAL Georgia rice fields, the breeches of the men rolled up over their knees, the sack skirts of the women gathered and tied about their hips, leaving them, in the words of one shocked observer, "two thirds naked." Standing on the banks of canals that channeled water to the fields, African slave drivers, whips at the ready, supervised the work. Upriver, groups cut away cypress and gum trees and cleared the swampland's jungle maze of undergrowth; others constructed levees, preparing to bring more land under cultivation. An English overseer or plantation master could be seen here and there, but overwhelmingly it was a country populated by Africans.

These plantations were southern extensions of the South Carolina rice belt. Although slavery had been prohibited by Georgia's original charter of 1732, the restriction was lifted when Georgia became a royal colony two decades later. By 1770, 15,000 African Americans (80 percent of the region's population) lived on several hundred coastal rice plantations owned by a small elite of white people.

Rice was one of the most valuable commodities produced in mainland North America, surpassed in value only by tobacco and wheat. The growth of rice production in the lower South was matched by an enormous expansion in the Atlantic slave trade, and during the eighteenth century rice planters engaged in what one historian calls a "veritable orgy" of slave trading. Although the number of North American black people who were "country born" (native to America, and thus born into slavery) grew steadily over the century, before the American Revolution the majority of black people on the rice plantations were what were known as "saltwater" Africans. These people had endured the shock of enslavement. Ripped from their homeland communities in West Africa by slave raiders, they were brutally marched to coastal forts. There, they were imprisoned, subjected to humiliating inspections of their bodies, and branded on the buttocks like animals. Packed into the stinking holds of ships, they were forced into a nightmarish passage across the Atlantic Ocean. When finally unloaded on a strange continent, they were sold at dockside auctions, then once again marched overland to their destinations on New World plantations. On the rice plantations of isolated coastal Georgia, enslaved Africans suffered from overwork and numerous physical ailments, the results of poor diet, minimal and inappropriate clothing, and inadequate housing. Mortality rates were exceptionally high, especially for infants. Colonial laws permitted masters to discipline and punish slaves indiscriminately. They were whipped, confined in irons, castrated, or sold away, with little regard for their relations with family or friends.

Africans struggled to make a place for themselves in this inhospitable world. They had little power, but bargained with their masters to win acceptance of the familiar work routines of West Africa. Thus low-country plantations operated according to the task system: once slaves finished their specific jobs, they could use their remaining time to hunt, fish, or cultivate family gardens. Masters often complained that "tasking" did not produce the same level of profit as the gang labor system of the sugar plantations, but African rice hands refused to work any other way. "Although it is not fixed by law," one planter wrote in 1767, the tasking system was "so well settled by long usage," that any master who tried to increase the work load was faced with "such discontent amongst his slaves as to make them of but little use to him."

Still, many slaves ran away, like slaves everywhere in the Americas. Readers of Savannah newspapers were urged to look out for fugitives: Statira, a woman of the "Gold Coast Country" with tribal markings on her temples, or "a negro fellow named Mingo, about 40 years old, and his wife Quante, a sensible wench about 20 with her child, a boy about 3 years old, all this country born." Some fled in groups, heading for the Creek Indian settlements in northern Florida, or toward St. Augustine, where the Spanish, in an attempt to undermine the English colonies of the Lower South, promised them safe haven. Some struck out violently at their masters: a group of nine Africans from a Savannah plantation killed their master and stole a boat, planning to head upriver, but were apprehended as they lay in wait to murder their hated overseers.

So slaves resisted. But like slaves throughout the New World, the majority of Africans and African Americans of the Georgia coast remained and built communities of their own within the heartless world of slavery. Plantation slaves married, raised children, and over time constructed kinship networks. They passed on African names and traditions and created new ones. These links between individuals and families formed the basis for reestablished communities. Slave communities combined elements of African languages and English to form dialects that allowed newly arrived people from many different African ethnic groups as well as American-born slaves to communicate with one another. Neither individuals nor families alone can make a language; that is something only a community can do. Common African heritage and common slave status were the foundations of the African American community.

African Americans reworked traditional African dance, song, and story to fit New World circumstances, just as they reestablished traditional arts, such as woodworking, iron making, and weaving. Through their culture, the slaves shared a powerful awareness of their common oppression. They told or sang dialect tales of mistreatment, as in this song of Quow, the punished slave:

> Was matter Buddy Quow?
> I ble Obesha bang you . . . .
> Dah Backrow Man go wrong you, Buddy Quow,
> Dah Backrow Man go wrong you, Buddy Quow.
>
> [What's the matter Brother Quow?
> I believe the overseer's beat you . . . .
> The white man's wronged you, Brother Quow,
> The white man's wronged you, Brother Quow.]

Just as European settlers planted colonial communities, so Africans, who made up the largest ethnic group to come to North America during the colonial era, constructed distinctive communities of their own. The history of African Americans includes the story of the Atlantic slave trade, the plunder of Africa, and the profits of empire. But it is also a story of achievement under the most difficult circumstances, and of the making of families, kin networks, and communities. They "labor together and converse almost wholly among themselves," a minister wrote of low-country slaves. "They are, as 'twere, a nation within a nation." ∎

Georgia
Sea
Islands

= KEY TOPICS =

- The development of the slavery system

- The history of the slave trade and the Middle Passage

- Community development among African Americans in the eighteenth century

- The connections between the institution of slavery and the imperial system of the eighteenth century

- The early history of racism in America

THE BEGINNINGS OF AFRICAN SLAVERY

Household slaves had long been a part of the world of Mediterranean Europe. War captives were sold to wealthy families, who put them to work as servants or artisans. In the fifteenth century, Venetian and Genoese merchants led the traffic in captured Slavic peoples—the word "slave" derives from the name "Slav"—as well as Muslims and Africans. Many Europeans were disturbed, however, by the moral implications of enslaving Christians, and in the early fifteenth century the pope excommunicated a number of merchants engaged in selling such captives. Africans and Muslims, however, were sufficiently different in religion to quiet those concerns.

One of the goals of Portuguese expansion in the fifteenth century was access to the lucrative West African trade in gold, wrought iron, ivory, tortoiseshell, textiles, and slaves that had previously been dominated by the Moors of northern Africa. The first African slaves to arrive in Lisbon were kidnapped by a Portuguese captain in 1441. But European traders found it more efficient to leave the capture of men and women for slavery to Africans, who were willing to exchange the captured slaves for European commodities. By the mid-fifteenth century, the Portugese were shipping a thousand or more slaves per year from Africa.

Sugar and Slavery

The greatest market for these slaves was the large sugar plantations the Portuguese had established on their island colony of Madeira, off the coast of northern Africa. Sugar and slaves had gone together since Italian merchants of the fourteenth century had imported the first cane sugar from the Middle East and set up the first modern sugar plantations on the islands of the Mediterranean. Thus the use of Africans as slaves came to the Americas along with the spread of sugar production. One of the first products Columbus introduced to the New World was sugar cane. Sugar plantations were soon operating on the island of Hispaniola. At first the Spanish tried to use the native Indian people as a slave labor force, but because disease and warfare had so reduced the indigenous population, colonists soon turned to African slaves who were already working in Spain. Meanwhile, the Portuguese, aided by Dutch financiers, created a center of sugar production in northeast Brazil that became a model of the efficient and brutal exploitation of African labor. By 1600, some 25,000 enslaved Africans labored on the plantations of Hispaniola and Brazil.

The Dutch, using their experience in Brazil, became responsible for the next extension of slavery in the Americas. In 1630 they seized Brazil and for over twenty years they controlled this lucrative colony. Skilled at finance and commerce, they greatly expanded the European market for sugar, converting it from a luxury item for the rich to a staple for European workers. Along with addictive tropical commodities such as tobacco, coffee, and tea, sugar became what one historian calls a "proletarian hunger-killer," helping to sustain people through increasingly long working days. It was the Dutch who introduced sugar cultivation in the tropics. As a result, Barbados became the most valuable of England's colonies. Once the profitability of sugar had been demonstrated, the English sought to expand their Caribbean holdings by seizing the island of Jamaica from the Spanish in 1655 and making it over in the image of Barbados. Jamaica became the crown jewel of Britain's eighteenth-century empire.

The French repeated the process. They first developed sugar plantations on the small island of Martinique, then seized the eastern half of Hispaniola from

This image of Mansa Musa (1312–37), the ruler of the Muslim kingdom of Mali in West Africa, is taken from the *Catalan Atlas*, a magnificent map presented to the king of France in 1381 by his cousin, the king of Aragon. In the words of the Catalan inscription, Musa was "the richest, the most noble lord in all this region on account of the abundance of gold that is gathered in his land." He holds what was thought to be the world's largest gold nugget. Under Musa's reign, Timbuktu became a capital of world renown. SOURCE: Courtesy of Library of Congress.

the Spanish and created a sugar colony called St. Domingue (present-day Haiti). Caribbean sugar and slaves had become the centerpiece of the European colonial system.

West Africans

The men and women whose labor made these tropical colonies so profitable came from the long-established societies and local communities of West Africa. In the sixteenth century more than a hundred different peoples lived along the coast of West Africa, from Cape Verde south to Angola. In the north were the Wolofs, Mandingos, Hausas, Ashantis, and Yorubas; to the south the Ibos, Sekes, Bakongos, and Mbundus.

In all these societies the most important institution was the local community, which was organized by kinship. Decisions about production, storage, and distribution of goods were generally made by clan leaders and village chiefs; local courts arbitrated disputes. Men often took a second or third wife. This marriage system, known as polygyny, produced very large composite families with complex internal relationships.

Because of cultural restrictions on sexual relations, however, West African women bore fewer children than the typical European woman, and many enjoyed considerable social and economic independence as tradeswomen.

West African societies were based on sophisticated farming systems many thousands of years old. Africans practiced shifting cultivation: they cleared land by burning, used hoes or digging sticks to cultivate fields, and after several years moved on to other plots while the cleared land lay fallow. Men worked at clearing the land, women at cultivation and the sale of surpluses in the lively West African markets. The West African familiarity with regular agricultural labor was important in the history of slavery, because it proved to be practically impossible to convert large numbers of foraging or nomadic peoples into efficient plantation workers.

Farming sustained large populations and thriving networks of commerce, and in some areas kingdoms and states developed. Along the upper Niger River, where the grassland gradually turns to desert, towns such as Timbuktu developed into trading centers. West African goods made their way from these towns to the Mediterranean on trans-Saharan caravans organized by Moors and other Muslim traders. The attempt to control the wealth of this trade led to the rise and fall of a succession of military empires. The most extensive of these was Mali, whose greatest ruler, Mansa Musa, made Timbuktu a leading intellectual as well as commercial center. There were also a number of lesser states and kingdoms along the coast, and it was with these that the Portuguese first bargained for Africans who could be sold as slaves.

Varieties of household slavery were common in West African societies, although slaves there were often treated more as members of the family than as mere possessions. They were allowed to marry, and their children were born free. "With us they did no more work than other members of the community, even their master," remembered Olaudah Equiano, an Ibo captured and shipped to America as a slave in 1756, when he was a boy of eleven. "Their food, clothing, and lodging were nearly the same as [the others], except that they were not permitted to eat with those who were born free." When African merchants sold the first slaves to the Portuguese, they must have thought that European slavery would be similar. But as Equiano declared: "How different was their condition from that of the slaves in the West Indies!" Yet the West African familiarity with "unfree" labor made it possible for African and European traders to begin the trade in human merchandise.

Through a series of animated maps, analyze the role of geography and economics in the African slave trade. How and why were the people of Africa enslaved and brought to America?
www.prenhall.com/faragher/map4.1

The African Slave Trade   The enslaved men, women, and children transported to the Americas came from West Africa, the majority from the lower Niger River (called the Slave Coast) and the region of the Congo and Angola.

THE AFRICAN SLAVE TRADE

The movement of Africans across the Atlantic to the Americas was the largest forced migration in world history. Moreover, Africans made up the largest group of people to come to the Americas before the nineteenth century, outnumbering European immigrants by the astounding ratio of six to one. The Atlantic slave trade, which began with the Portuguese in the fifteenth century and did not end in the United States until 1807 (and continued elsewhere in the Americas until the 1870s), is a brutal chapter in the making of America.

The Demography of the Slave Trade

Scholars today estimate that slave ships transported 10 to 11 million Africans to the Americas during the four-century history of the trade. Seventy-six percent arrived from 1701 to 1810—the peak period of colonial demand for labor, when tens of thousands of people were shipped from Africa each year. Of this vast multitude, about half were delivered to Dutch, French, or British sugar plantations in the Caribbean, a third to Portuguese Brazil, and 10 percent to Spanish America. A much smaller proportion—about one in twenty, or an estimated 600,000 men, women, and children—were transported to the British colonies of North

America. With the exception of the 1750s, when the British colonies were engulfed by the Seven Years' War, the slave trade continued to rise in importance in the decades before the Revolution.

Among the Africans brought to the Americas, men generally outnumbered women two to one. Because most Africans were destined for fieldwork, this ratio probably reflected the preferences of plantation owners. The majority of captured and transported Africans were young people, between the ages of fifteen and thirty. Nearly every ethnic group in West Africa was represented among them.

Slavers of All Nations

All the nations of Western Europe participated in the slave trade. Dutch slavers began challenging Portuguese control of the trade at the end of the sixteenth century, and Holland became the most prominent slave-trading nation during the sugar boom of the seventeenth century. The English also entered the trade in

Slave Colonies of the Seventeenth and Eighteenth Centuries By the eighteenth century the system of slavery had created societies with large African populations throughout the Caribbean and along the southern coast of North America.

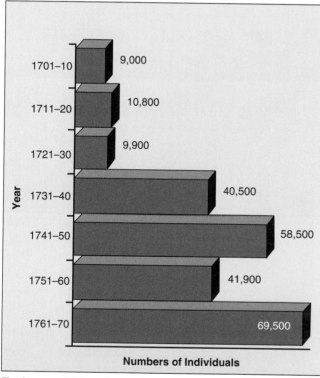

Estimated Number of Africans Imported to British North America, 1701–75 These official British statistics include only slaves imported legally and consequently undercount the total number who arrived on American shores. But the trend over time is clear. With the exception of the 1750s, when the British colonies were engulfed by the Seven Years War, the slave trade continued to rise in importance in the decades before the Revolution.

SOURCE: R. C. Simmons, *The American Colonies: From Settlement to Independence* (London: Longman, 1976), 186.

the sixteenth century with the African voyages of John Hawkins. The Royal African Company, a slave-trading monopoly based in London, was chartered in 1672, but in 1698 England threw open the trade to independent merchants. Soon hundreds of ships from Bristol and Liverpool were competing with those from London. As a result, the number of slaves shipped to North America skyrocketed. The Dutch and Portuguese, however, continued to play important roles, alongside slave traders from France, Sweden, and several German duchies.

Although the Portugese established a colony in Angloa, for the most part the European presence in Africa was confined to coastal outposts. Well-organized West African societies fiercely resisted any further encroachment. By the early eighteenth century, more than two dozen trading forts dotted the 220 miles of the Gold Coast alone. These forts became economic centers, developing large populations of European traders, Africans, and their mixed-ancestry offspring. By 1682 the Portugese headquarters at Elmina, for example, was surrounded by a town of 20,000 inhabitants, and fifty years later it was considerably larger than Charleston, South Carolina. As the slave trade peaked in the middle of the eighteenth century, however, the forts of trading companies gave way to independent European and American traders who set up operations with the cooperation of local headmen or chiefs. This informal manner of trading offered opportunities for small operators, such as the New England slavers who entered the trade in the early eighteenth century. Many great New England fortunes were built from profits in the slave trade.

The Shock of Enslavement

The slave trade was a collaboration between European or American and African traders. Dependent on the favor of local rulers, many colonial slave traders lived permanently in coastal forts and married African women, reinforcing their commercial ties with family relations. In many areas a mixed-ancestry group became prominent in the coastal slave trade. Continuing the practice of the Portuguese, the grim business of slave raiding was left to the Africans themselves. Slaves were not at all reticent about condemning the participation of their fellow Africans. "I must own to the shame of my own countrymen," wrote Ottobah Cugoano, who was sold into slavery in the mid-eighteenth century, "that I was first kidnapped and betrayed by those of my own complexion."

Most Africans were enslaved through warfare. Sometimes large armies launched massive attacks, burning whole towns and taking hundreds of prisoners. More common were smaller raids in which a group of armed men attacked at nightfall, seized everyone within reach, then escaped with their captives. Kidnapping, called "panyaring" in the jargon of the slave trade, was also common. One seaman, ashore while his slave ship awaited its cargo, amused himself by peeking at a young African woman bathing. Suddenly two raiders jumped from the bushes and dragged her off. He later saw them carry her on board and sell her to the captain, no questions asked.

As the demand for slaves increased in the eighteenth century with the expansion of the plantation system in the Americas, these raids extended deeper and deeper into the African interior. The march to the coast was filled with terrors. One account describes a two-month trip in which many captives died of hunger, thirst, or exhaustion, several attempted suicide, and the whole party was forced to hide to avoid being seized by a rival band of raiders. The captives finally arrived on the coast, where they were sold to an American vessel bound for South Carolina.

Enslavement was an unparalleled shock. Venture Smith, an African born in Guinea in 1729, was eight years old when he was captured. After many years in North American slavery, he still vividly recalled the attack on his village, the torture and murder of his father, and the long march of his people to the coast. "The shocking scene is to this day fresh in my mind," he wrote, "and I have often been overcome while thinking on it." The horror was captured in a song of captives marching to the Slave Coast from the interior kingdom of Bornu, imploring the assistance of one of their gods, a song long remembered by African Americans, and published by abolitionists in the nineteenth century:

> *Bornu-land was rich and good,*
> *Wells of water, fields of food;*
> *Bornu-land we see no longer,*
> *Here we thirst, and here we hunger,*
> *Here the Moor man smiles in anger;*
> *Where are we going, Rubee?*
> *Where are we going? Where are we going?*
> *Hear us, save us, Rubee!*
> *Moons of marches from our eyes,*
> *Bornu-land behind us lies;*
> *Hot the desert wind is blowing,*
> *Wild the waves of sand are flowing!*
> *Hear us! Tell us, where are we going?*
> *Where are we going, Rubee?*

Portrait of Olaudah Equiano, by an unknown English artist, ca. 1780. Captured in Nigeria in 1756 when he was eleven years old, Equiano was transported to America and was eventually purchased by an English sea captain. After ten years as a slave, he succeeded in buying his own freedom and dedicated himself to the antislavery cause. His book *The Interesting Narrative of the Life of Olaudah Equiano* (1789) was published in numerous editions, translated into several languages, and became the prototype for dozens of other slave narratives in the nineteenth century.

SOURCE: *Portrait of a Negro Man, Olaudah Equiano*, ca. 1780, (previously attributed to Joshua Reynolds) by English School. Royal Albert Memorial Museum, Exeter, Devon, UK/Bridgeman Art Library, London/New York.

A slave coffle in an eighteenth-century print. As the demand for slaves increased, raids extended deeper and deeper into the African interior. Tied together with forked logs or bark rope, men, women, and children were marched hundreds of miles toward the coast, where their African captors traded them to Europeans.

SOURCE: North Wind Picture Archives

On the coast, European traders and African raiders assembled their captives. Prisoners waited in dark dungeons or in open pens called "barracoons." To lessen the possibility of collective resistance, traders split up families and ethnic groups. Captains carefully inspected each man and woman, and those selected for transport were branded on the back or buttocks with the mark of the buyer. Olaudah Equiano remembered that "those white men with horrible looks, red faces, and long hair, looked and acted . . . in so savage a manner; . . . I had never seen among any people such instances of brutal cruelty." Equiano's narrative, written during the 1780s, after he had secured his freedom, is one of the few that provide an African account of enslavement. He and his fellow captives became convinced that they "had got into a world of bad spirits" and were about to be eaten by cannibals. A French trader wrote that many prisoners were "positively prepossessed with the opinion that we transport them into our country in order to kill and eat them."

The Middle Passage

In the eighteenth century, English sailors christened the voyage of slave ships as the "Middle Passage," the middle part of a trading triangle from England to Africa to America and back to England. From coastal forts and barra-coons, crews rowed small groups of slaves out to the waiting ships and packed them into shelves below deck only six feet long by two and a half feet high. "Rammed like herring in a barrel," wrote one observer, slaves were "chained to each other hand and foot, and stowed so close, that they were not allowed above a foot and a half for each in breadth." People were forced to sleep "spoon fashion," and the tossing of the ship knocked them about so violently that the skin over their elbows sometimes was worn to the bone from scraping on the planks. "It was more than a week after I left the ship before I could straighten my limbs," one former slave later remembered. One ship designed to carry 450 slaves regularly crossed the Atlantic tightly packed with more than 600.

Their holds filled with human cargo, the ships headed toward Cape Verde to catch the trade winds blowing toward America. A favorable voyage from Senegambia to Barbados might be accomplished in as little as three weeks, but a ship from Guinea or Angola becalmed in the doldrums or driven back by storms might take as much as three months.

The voyage was marked by a daily routine. In the morning the crew opened the hatch and brought the captives on deck, attaching their leg irons to a great chain running the length of the bulwarks. After a breakfast of beans came a ritual known as "dancing the slave." While an African thumped an upturned kettle or plucked a banjo, the crew commanded men and women to jump up and down in a bizarre session of exercise. A day spent chained on deck was concluded by a second bland meal and then the stowing away. During the night, according to one seaman, there issued from below "a howling melancholy noise, expressive of extreme anguish." Down in the hold, the groans of the dying, the shrieks of women and children, and the suffocating heat and stench were, in the words of Olaudah Equiano, "a scene of horror almost inconceivable."

Among the worst of the horrors was the absence of adequate sanitation. There were "necessary tubs" set below deck, but Africans, "endeavoring to get to them, tumble over their companions," as one eighteenth-century ship's surgeon wrote. "And as the necessities of nature are not to be resisted, they ease themselves as they lie." Efficient captains ordered crews to scrape and swab the holds daily, but so sickening was the task that on many ships it was rarely performed and Africans were left to wallow in their urine and feces. When first taken below deck, the boy Equiano remembered, "I received such a salutation in my nostrils as I had never experienced in my life," and "became so sick and low that I was not able to eat." Atlantic sailors said you could "smell a slaver five miles down wind." Many captives sickened and died in these conditions. Many others contracted dysentery, known as the "flux." Frequent shipboard epidemics of smallpox, measles, and yellow fever added to the misery. The dying continued even as the ships anchored at their destinations. Historians estimate that during the Middle Passage of the eighteenth century one in every six Africans perished.

The unwilling voyagers offered plenty of resistance. As long as ships were still within sight of the African coast, hope remained alive and the danger of revolt was great. One historian has found references to fifty-five slave revolts on British and American ships from 1699 to 1845. Once on the open sea, however, the captives' resistance took more desperate form. The sight of the disappearing coast of Africa "left me abandoned to despair," wrote Equiano. "I now saw myself deprived of all chance of returning to my native country, or even the least glimpse of hope of gaining the shore." He witnessed several Africans jump overboard and drown, "and I believe many more would very soon have done the same if they had not been prevented by the ship's crew." Captains took the precaution of spreading netting along the sides of their ships. "Could I have got over the nettings," Equiano declared, "I would have jumped over the side."

Arrival in the New World

As the ship approached its destination the crew prepared the human cargo for market. All but the most rebellious were freed from their chains and allowed to wash themselves and move about the deck. Captains did what they could to get their Africans into presentable condition. To impress buyers, slavers might parade Africans off the ship to the tune of an accordion or the beat of a drum. But the toll of the Middle Passage was difficult to disguise. One observer described a disembarking group as "walking skeletons covered over with a piece of tanned leather."

Slaves below deck on a Spanish slaver, a sketch made when the vessel was captured by a British warship in the early nineteenth century. Slaves were "stowed so close, that they were not allowed above a foot and a half for each in breadth," wrote one observer. The close quarters and unsanitary conditions created a stench so bad that Atlantic sailors said you could "smell a slaver five miles down wind."

SOURCE: The Granger Collection

Some cargoes were destined for a single wealthy planter, or consigned to a merchant who sold the captives in return for a commission; in other cases the captain himself was responsible. Buyers painstakingly examined the Africans, who once again suffered the indignity of probing eyes and poking fingers. This caused "much dread and trembling among us," wrote Equiano, and "bitter cries." In ports such as Charleston, sales were generally made by auction, or by a cruel method known as the scramble—fixed prices set in advance, the Africans driven into a corral, and on cue the buyers rushing among them, grabbing their pick. The noise, clamor, and eagerness of the buyers, Equiano remembered, renewed all the terrible apprehensions of the Africans. "In this manner, without scruple, are relations and friends separated, most of them never to see each other again." Bought by a Virginian, Equiano was taken to an isolated tobacco plantation where he found himself unable to communicate with any of his fellow slaves, who came from other ethnic groups.

Political and Economic Effects on Africa

Africa began the sixteenth century with genuine independence. But as surely as Europe and America grew stronger as a result of the trade and the labor of slaves, so Africa grew weaker by their loss. In the short term, slave-trading kingdoms on the coast increased their

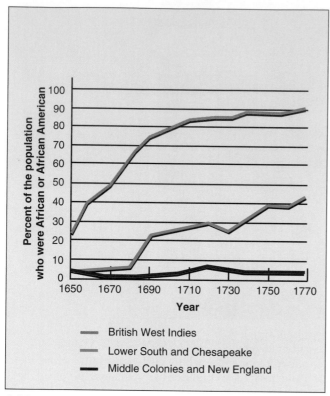

Africans as a Percentage of Total Population of the British Colonies, 1650–1770 Although the proportion of Africans and African Americans was never as high in the South as in the Caribbean, the ethnic structure of the South diverged radically from that of the North during the eighteenth century.

SOURCE: Robert W. Fogel and Stanley L. Engerman, *Time on the Cross* (Boston: Little, Brown, 1974), 21.

power at the expense of interior states. Thus the interior empire of Mali gave way to the Gold Coast state of Akwamu. In the Niger Delta the slaving states of Nembe, Bonny, and Kalabari arose, and to the south the kingdom of Imbangala drew slaves from central Africa. But these coastal states found that the slave trade was a viper that could easily strike back at them. "Merchants daily seize our own subjects, sons of the land and sons of our noblemen, they grab them and cause them to be sold," King Dom Affonso of the Kongo wrote to the Portuguese monarch in the sixteenth century. "And so great, Sir, is their corruption and licentiousness that our country is being utterly depopulated."

More serious still, however, than the loss of millions of men and women over the centuries was the long-term stagnation of the West African economy. Labor was drawn away from farming and other productive activities, and imported consumer goods such as textiles and metal wares stifled local manufacturing. African traders were expert at driving a hard bargain

for slaves, and over several centuries they gained an increasing price for slaves, the result of rising demand and increased competition among European slavers. But even when they appeared to get the best of the exchange, the ultimate advantage lay with the Europeans, who received wealth-producing workers in return for mere consumer goods.

For every man or woman taken captive, at least another died in the chronic slave raiding. Many of the new West African states became little more than machines for supplying captives to European traders, and a "gun-slave cycle" pushed neighboring kingdoms into a destructive arms race. The resulting political and cultural demoralization prepared the way for the European conquest of Africa in the nineteenth century. The leaders of West Africa during the centuries of slave trading, writes the Nigerian poet Chinweizu, "had been too busy organizing our continent for the exploitative advantage of Europe, had been too busy with slaving raids upon one another, too busy decorating themselves with trinkets imported from Europe, too busy impoverishing and disorganizing the land, to take thought and long-range action to protect our sovereignty."

THE DEVELOPMENT OF NORTH AMERICAN SLAVE SOCIETIES

New World slavery was nearly two centuries old before it became an important system of labor in North America. There were slaves in each of the British colonies during the seventeenth century, but in 1700 slaves accounted for only 11 percent of the colonial population. During the eighteenth century slavery greatly expanded, and by 1770 Africans and African Americans in British North America numbered 460,000, or more than 20 percent of the colonial population.

Slavery Comes to North America

The first Africans in Virginia arrived in 1619 when a Dutch slave trader exchanged "20 and odd Negars" for badly needed provisions with planter John Rolfe. But because slaves generally cost twice as much as indentured servants, yet had the same appallingly short life expectancy, they offered planters little economic benefit. Consequently, over the next several decades planters in the Chesapeake region employed far more indentured servants than slaves. Until the 1670s servants and slaves on Virginia plantations worked together, ate and slept in common quarters, and often developed intimate relationships. The Chesapeake was what historians term a *society with slaves*, a society in which slavery was one form of labor among several.

Under these circumstances the status of black Virginians could be ambiguous. An interesting case illustrates the point. In 1654, the African John Castor told a local court that "he came unto Virginia for seven or eight years of indenture, yet Anthony Johnson his Master had kept him his servant seven years longer than he should or ought." Johnson claimed that "he had the Negro for his life." The court decided in the master's favor. But strange to say, Johnson himself was of African descent. He had arrived in 1621 as a slave but by hiring himself out during his free time had earned enough to gain freedom for himself and his family. Eventually he suceeded in becoming a landowner. "I know myne owne ground and I will worke when I please and play when I please," Johnson declared. Property records reveal that other Africans acquired farms and servants or slaves of their own. Many slaves were baptised, and since religious difference had traditionally been a justification for slavery, their new status as Christians raised doubts about whether or not they could be kept as slaves. Moreover, sexual relations among Africans, Indians, and Europeans produced a sizable group of free people of mixed ancestry known as *mulattoes*. It was only later that dark skin came automatically to mean slavery, segregation, and a lack of rights.

In the last quarter of the seventeenth century, however, a number of developments encouraged the transformation of the Chesapeake from a society with slaves into a *slave society*, a society in which slavery was the dominant form of labor. In the aftermath of Bacon's Rebellion, planters consolidated their control of the Virginia colony. They were concerned about future rebellions among former indentured servants. Because people were living longer, possibly the result of being better fed and more resistant to disease, more servants were surviving their indentures, and such a population could be troublesome. But these improvements in living conditions also affected Africans, increasing their rates of survival and allowing planters to amortize the purchase price of slaves over a considerably longer span. Also contributing to the transition was the development of better opportunities for European immigrants in colonies such as Pennsylvania, and the beginning of direct shipments of slaves from West Africa to the North American mainland by the English Royal African Company. As a result of these developments, during the last twenty years of the seventeenth century the emigration of servants from the British Isles practically ceased, but Chesapeake planters imported more than 10,000 African slaves.

Thus the workforce of indentured servants was replaced by a workforce of slaves. In 1670 servants greatly outnumbered slaves in the Chesapeake, but by 1700 slaves outnumbered servants. People of African descent made up 22 percent of the population of Maryland and Virginia. In South Carolina indentured servants were never an important part of the labor force, and by the end of the century Africans made up over 40 percent of the population.

As the proportions of slaves in the colonial population rose, colonists wrote slavery into law, a process best observed in the case of Virginia. In 1662 colonial officials declared that children inherited the status of their slave mothers; five years later they added that baptism as a Christian could no longer alter conditions of servitude. Two important avenues to freedom were thus closed. The colony then placed life-threatening violence in the hands of masters, declaring in 1669 that the death of a slave during punishment "shall not be accounted felony." Such regulations accumulated piecemeal until 1705, when Virginia gathered them into a comprehensive slave code that became a model for other colonies.

Thus the institution of slavery was strengthened just as the Atlantic slave trade reached flood tide in the eighteenth century. During that century's first decade, more Africans were imported into North America than the total number for the previous century. The English colonies were primed for an unprecedented growth of plantation slavery.

The Tobacco Colonies

Slave societies were characterized by the production of some commodity that could command an international market. In the Chesapeake that commodity was tobacco. Over the eighteenth century the European demand for tobacco increased more than tenfold, and it was supplied largely by increased production in the Chesapeake. Tobacco plantations spread through all sections of the sea-level coastal region known as the Tidewater, extending from the colony of Delaware south through Maryland and Virginia into the Albemarle Sound region of North Carolina. Planters eventually extended their operations above the "fall line," where waterfalls or rapids mark the end of the Tidewater and the beginning of the foothill region known as the Piedmont. Tobacco was far and away the single most important commodity produced in eighteenth-century North America, accounting for more than a quarter of the value of all colonial exports.

The expansion of tobacco production could not have taken place without a corresponding growth in the size of the slave labor force. Unlike sugar, tobacco

An Overseer Doing His Duty, a watercolor sketch made by Benjamin Henry Latrobe during a trip to Virginia in 1798. The majority of masters in the tobacco region owned only one or two slaves and worked with them in the fields. In his portrayal of this overseer, relaxing as he supervises his workers, Latrobe clearly expressed his disgust for slavery.

SOURCE: Benjamin Henry Latrobe, *An Overseer Doing His Duty*. Watercolor on paper. Collection of the Maryland Historical Society, Baltimore.

profit caused tobacco planters to pay more attention to the health of their labor force, establishing work routines that were not quite so deadly. Moreover, food supplies were more plentiful in North America, which made the Chesapeake populations of Africans more resistant to disease. By the 1730s the slave population of the Chesapeake had become the first in the Western Hemisphere to achieve self-sustained population growth. Natural increase gradually put the ratio of slave men and women in better balance, further encouraging population growth. Planters came to recognize that they stood to benefit from the fertility of their slaves. "A woman who brings a child every two years [is] more valuable than the best man on the farm," wrote Virginia planter Thomas Jefferson, "for what she produces is an addition to the capital." By the 1750s, about 80 percent of Chesapeake slaves were "country-born."

did not require large plantations and could be produced successfully on small farms. But it was a crop that demanded a great deal of hand labor and close attention. As tobacco farming grew, slaveholding became widespread. By the mid-eighteenth century slaves were included in a majority of Piedmont households and as many as three-quarters of the households in the Tidewater. Tobacco farms varied in size, from small establishments where farmers worked side by side with one or two slaves, to large, self-sufficient plantations with dozens of slaves. By 1770 more than a quarter million slaves labored in the colonies of the Upper South (Maryland, Virginia, and North Carolina), and because of the exploding market for tobacco, their numbers were expanding at about double the rate of the general population.

Shipments from Africa accounted for part of the growth of the slave population. From 1700 to 1770 a total of perhaps 80,000 Africans were imported into these colonies. But in this region natural increase was much more important. In the Caribbean and Brazil, where profits from sugar were high, many sugar planters chose to work their slaves to death, replenishing them with a constant stream of new arrivals, mostly men, from Africa. In Virginia, however, lower rates of

The Lower South

The Chesapeake did not become a slave society until almost a century after its founding. But in South Carolina settlement and slavery went hand in hand, and the colony was a slave society from the beginning. The most valuable part of the early Carolina economy was the Indian slave trade. Practicing a strategy of divide and conquer, using Indian tribes to fight one another, Carolinians enslaved tens of thousands of Indians before the 1730s, shipping many to slave markets in the Caribbean, employing others raising cattle or felling timber. In 1713 colonists attacked the Tuscarora tribe, killing at least a thousand warriors and enslaving a thousand women and children. In retaliation, the Yamasee tribe staged a general uprising in 1715 that nearly defeated colonial forces. Only by enlisting the aid of the Cherokees was South Carolina able to turn the tide.

By the time of the Yamasee War, however, planter preference had turned toward African rather than Indian slaves. Rice production was rapidly becoming the most dynamic sector of the South Carolina economy, and with their experience in agriculture West Africans made much better rice workers than Indians. Another important crop was added in the 1740s, when a young South Carolina woman named Elizabeth Lucas Pinck-

TOBACCO AND RICE EXPORTS TO ENGLAND (in thousands of pounds)		
	Tobacco	Rice
1700	37,840	304
1725	21,046	5,367
1750	51,339	16,667
1775	55,968	57,692

ney successfully adapted West Indian indigo to the low-country climate. The indigo plant, native to India, produced a deep blue dye important in textile manufacture. Rice grew in the lowlands, but indigo could be cultivated on high ground, and with different seasonal growing patterns, planters were able to harmonize their production. Rice and indigo were two of the most valuable commodities exported from the mainland colonies of North America. The boom in these two crops depended on the growth of African slavery.

In good years, rice planters expected rates of return in excess of 20 percent; these were fabulous profits, far exceeding the 5 or 10 percent of tobacco planters. And profits climbed over the century, so that the time it took for field slaves to produce the equivalent of their purchase price dropped from four years to two years from the 1720s to the 1770s. Such proceeds stimulated a huge flow of African slaves. Before the international slave trade to the United States was ended in 1808, at least 100,000 had arrived in South Carolina. It is estimated that one of every five ancestors of today's African Americans passed through Charleston on the way to the rice fields.

By the 1740s, many of the arriving Africans were being taken to Georgia, a colony created by an act of the English Parliament in 1732. Its leader, James Edward Oglethorpe, hoped to establish a buffer against Spanish invasion from Florida and make it a haven for poor British farmers who could then sell their products in the markets of South Carolina. Under Oglethorpe's influence, Parliament agreed to prohibit slavery in Georgia. Soon, however, Georgia's coastal regions were being colonized by South Carolina planters with their slaves. In 1752, Oglethorpe and Georgia's trustees abandoned their experiment, and the colony was opened to slavery under royal authority. The Georgia coast had already become an extension of the Carolina low-country slave system.

Tobacco plantations in the Chesapeake were often small affairs, but rice plantations required a minimum of thirty slaves and more commonly had fifty to seventy-five, which meant large black majorities in the colonies of the Lower South. By 1770 there were nearly 90,000 African Americans in the Lower South, about 80 percent of the coastal population of South Carolina and Georgia. In the words of one eighteenth-century observer, "Carolina looks more like a negro country than like a country settled by white people." The African American communities of the Lower South achieved self-sustained growth in the middle of the eighteenth century, a generation later than those in the Chesapeake.

Slavery in the Spanish Colonies

Slavery was basic to the Spanish colonial labor system, yet doubts about the enslavement of Africans were raised by both church and crown. The papacy denounced slavery many times as a violation of Christian principles. But the institution of slavery remained intact, and later in the eighteenth century, when sugar production expanded in Cuba, the slave system there was as brutal as any in the history of the Americas.

The character of slavery varied with local conditions. One of the most benign forms operated in Florida. Slaves could be found in many Florida settlements, but the conditions of their servitude resembled the household slavery common in Mediterranean and African communities more than the plantation slavery of the British colonies. In 1699, in an attempt to undermine the English colonies of the Lower South, the Spanish declared Florida a refuge for escaped slaves from the British colonies, offering free land to fugitives who would help defend their colony. Over the next half-century, refugee Indians and fugitive Africans established many communities in the countryside surrounding St. Augustine. North of the city, Fort Mose was manned by Negro troops commanded by their own officers. By 1763, 3,000 African Americans, a quarter of them free, made up 25 percent of St. Augustine's population.

In New Mexico, the Spanish depended on Indian slavery. In the sixteenth century the colonial governor sent Indian slaves to the mines of Mexico. The enslavement of Indians was one of the causes of the Pueblo Revolt (see Chapter 3). During the eighteenth century, the Spanish were much more cautious in their treatment of the Pueblos, who were officially considered Catholics. But they captured and enslaved "infidel Indians" such as the Apaches or nomads from the Great Plains, using them as house servants and fieldworkers.

French Louisiana

Slavery was also important in Louisiana, the colony founded by the French in the lower Mississippi Valley in the early eighteenth century. After Robert

Residence and Slave Quarters of Mulberry Plantation, by Thomas Coram, ca. 1770. The slave quarters are on the left in this painting of a rice plantation near Charleston, South Carolina. The steep roofs of the slave cabins, an African architectural feature introduced in America by slave builders, kept living quarters cool by allowing the heat to rise and dissipate in the rafters.

SOURCE: Thomas Coram, *Residence and Slave Quarters of Mulberry Plantation*, ca. 1770. Oil on paper, 10 × 17.6 cm. Gibbes Museum of Art, Carolina Art Association.

Sieur de La Salle's voyage down the Mississippi River in 1681–82, the French planned colonies to anchor their New World empire. In the early eighteenth century French Canadians established bases at Biloxi and Mobile on the Gulf of Mexico, but it was not until 1718 that they laid out the city of New Orleans on the Mississippi Delta. The French Company of the Indies imported some 6,000 African slaves, and planters invested in tobacco and indigo plantations on the Mississippi River in the country of the Natchez Indians. But in 1629, the Natchez and the slaves together rose in an armed uprising, the Natchez Rebellion, that took the lives of more than 200 French settlers, 10 percent of the population. Although colonial authorities were able to put down the rebellion—crushing and dispersing the Natchez people—the Louisiana French pulled back from a total commitment to slavery. Although the French planned to make Louisiana a slave society, it instead became a society with slaves.

After the Natchez Rebellion, Louisiana's economy grew more diversified. Several thousand French colonists established farms and plantations on the Gulf Coast and in a narrow strip of settlement along the Mississippi River. Although there were tobacco, indigo, and rice plantations, there were also small subsistence farms. Lumbering, fishing, and fur trading were important features of the economy. African slaves amounted to no more than a third of the colonial population of 10,000. It was not until the end of the eighteenth century that the colony of Louisiana became an important North American slave society.

Slavery in the North

Slavery was a fundamental, acceptable, thoroughly American institution. Although none of the northern colonies could be characterized as a slave society, slavery was an important form of labor in many areas. Over the course of the eighteenth century it

London Coffee House.

The London Coffee House, near the docks of Philadelphia, was the center of the city's business and political life in the mid-eighteenth century. Sea captains and merchants congregated here to do business, and as this contemporary print illustrates, it was the site of many slave auctions. Slavery was a vital part of the economy of northern cities.

SOURCE: The Library Company of Philadelphia.

grew increasingly significant in the commercial farming regions of southeast Pennsylvania, central New Jersey, and Long Island, where slaves made up about 10 percent of the rural residents. In the vicinity of Newport, Rhode Island, the proportion of slaves in the population reached nearly 25 percent, a concentration resulting from that port's dominance in the midcentury slave trade. The area was unique for the large slave gangs used in cattle and dairy operations in the Narragansett country, some of which were as large as Virginia plantations. Elsewhere in the New England countryside slavery was relatively uncommon.

It was widespread in all the port cities, however, including Boston. There was "not a house" that "has not one or two," a visitor to that city wrote in the 1680s, and a visitor to Philadelphia about the same time noted that slaves were bought "by almost everyone who could afford [them]." Slave ownership was nearly universal among the wealthy and ordinary among craftsmen and professionals. By 1750 slaves and small free black populations made up 15 to 20 percent of the residents of Boston, New York City, and Philadelphia.

The Quakers of Pennsylvania and New Jersey, many of whom kept slaves, were the first colonists to voice antislavery sentiment. In 1715 John Hepburn of New Jersey published the first North American critique of slavery, but his was a lonely voice. By midcentury, however, there was a significant antislavery movement among the Quakers. In *Considerations on the Keeping of Negroes* (1754), John Woolman urged his readers to imagine themselves in the place of the African people. Suppose, he wrote,

> that our ancestors and we had been exposed to constant servitude in the more servile and inferior employments of life; that we had been destitute of the help of reading and good company; that amongst ourselves we had had few wise and pious instructors; that the religious amongst our superiors seldom took notice of us; that while others in ease had plentifully heaped up the fruit of our labour, we had received barely enough to relieve nature, and being wholly at the command of others had generally been treated as a contemptible, ignorant part of mankind. Should we, in that case, be less abject than they now are?

In 1758 the Philadelphia Friends Meeting voted to condemn slavery and urged masters to voluntarily free their slaves. It was not until the Revolution, however, that antislavery attitudes became more widespread in the colonies.

AFRICAN TO AFRICAN AMERICAN

In 1774 a group of enslaved Massachusetts Africans spoke for tens of thousands of others when they petitioned the British authorities for their freedom. "We were unjustly dragged by the cruel hand of power from our dearest friends," they wrote, "and some of us stolen from the bosoms of our tender parents and from a populous, pleasant and plentiful country, and brought hither to be made slaves for life in a Christian land." Men and women from dozens of ethnic groups, representing many different languages, religions, and customs, had been transported across the Atlantic without any of their cultural possessions. In America they were subjected to the control of masters intent on maximizing their work and minimizing their liberty. Yet African Americans carved out lives of their own with a degree of independence. Their African heritage was not erased; it provided them with a fundamental outlook, the basis for a common identity.

The majority of Africans transported to North America arrived during the eighteenth century. They were met by a rapidly growing population of country-born slaves, or "creoles," (from the French *créole* and Spanish *criollo*, meaning "born" or "raised"), a term first used by slaves in Brazil to distinguish their children, born in the New World, from newly arrived Africans. The perspective of creoles was shaped by their having grown up under slavery, and that perspective helped them to determine which elements of African culture they would incorporate into the emerging culture of the African American community. That community was formed out of the relationship between creoles and Africans, and between slaves and their European masters.

The Daily Life of Slaves

Because slaves formed the overwhelming majority of the labor force that made the plantation colonies so profitable, it is fair to say that Africans built the South. As an agricultural people, Africans, both women and men, were accustomed to the routines of rural labor, and this was put to use on the plantations. Most Africans were field hands, and even domestic servants labored in the fields when necessary.

Masters provided their workers with rude clothing, sufficient in the summer but nearly always inadequate in the winter. Increasingly the plantations were supplied by cheap goods from the new industrial looms of England. Stiff shoes were a necessity in the cold months, but they so cramped the feet that everyone looked forward to shedding them in the spring and going barefoot all summer and fall. Hand-me-down clothes from the master's family offered slaves an opportunity to brighten their costumes, and many of them dressed in a variety of styles and colors. Similarly, they relieved the monotony of their rations of corn and pork with vegetables from their small gardens, game and fish from field and stream, and wild plant foods from the forests.

On small plantations and farms, which were typical in the tobacco country of the Chesapeake, Africans might work side by side with their owners and, depending on the character of the master, might enjoy a standard of living not too different from those of other family members. The work was more demanding and living conditions less sustaining on the great rice and indigo plantations of the Lower South, where slaves usually lived separately from the master in their own quarters. But large plantations, with large numbers of slaves, created the concentration of population necessary for the emergence of African American communities and African American culture. This was one of the profound ironies of American slavery. On the great plantations life was much harder, but slaves had more opportunity for some autonomy.

Families and Communities

The family was the most important institution for the development of African American community and culture, but slave codes did not provide for legal slave marriages, for that would have contradicted the master's freedom to dispose of his property as he saw fit. "The endearing ties of husband and wife are strangers to us," declared the Massachusetts slaves who petitioned for their freedom in 1774, "for we are no longer man and wife than our masters or mistresses think proper." How, they asked, "can a slave perform the duties of a husband to a wife or parent to his child? How can a husband leave master to work and cleave to his wife? How can [wives] submit themselves to their husbands in all things? How can [children] obey their parents in all things?"

Planters commonly separated families by sale or bequest, dividing husbands and wives and even separating mothers from their children. Charles Ball was sold away from his wife and children when his master sold him to a rice planter in Georgia. "My heart died away within me," Ball remembered vividly, "I felt incapable of weeping or speaking, and in my despair I laughed loudly." With his hands bound, he was sent away the same day he learned of his fate, and on his journey he dreamed he could see his wife and children "beseeching and imploring my master on their knees." He never saw them again. Another planter sold the children of a slave mother, allowing only that her infant could "suck its mother till twelve months old," but then was also to be sold.

Despite these barriers, however, during the eighteenth century slaves in both the Chesapeake and the Lower South created the families that were essential for the development of African American culture. On large plantations throughout the southern colonies, travelers found Africans living in family households. In the Lower South, where there were greater concentrations of slaves on the great rice plantations, husbands and

Buddy Qua of St. Vincent. African names for weekdays, such as "Qua" or "Quow" (Tuesday), were common among the slaves of the Caribbean and the Lower South. This sketch comes from an eighteenth-century series showing slaves going about their daily tasks. SOURCE: National Library of Jamaica.

wives often lived together in the slave quarters, and this was clearly the ideal. On the smaller plantations of the Upper South, men often married women from neighboring farms, and with the permission of both owners visited their families in the evenings or on Sundays.

Generally, slave couples married when the woman became pregnant. "Their marriages are generally performed amongst themselves," one visitor to North Carolina wrote of the Africans he observed in the 1730s. "The man makes the woman a present, such as a brass ring or some other toy, which she accepts of, [and] becomes his wife." Common throughout the South was the postnuptial ritual in which the couple jumped over a broomstick together, declaring their relationship to the rest of the community. This custom may have originated in Africa, although versions of it were practiced in medieval Europe as well.

Recent studies of naming practices among eighteenth-century African Americans illustrate their commitment to establishing a system of kinship. Frequently sons were named for their fathers, perhaps a way of strengthening the paternal bonds of men forced to live away from their families. Children of both sexes were named for grandparents and other kin. African names were common; names such as Cudjo (Monday),

Quow (Thursday), or Coffee (Friday) continued the African tradition of "weekday" names. Later in the century Anglo names became more general. Margery and Moody, slaves of Francis Jerdone of Louisa County, Virginia, named their six children Sam, Rose, Sukey, Mingo, Maria, and Comba, mixing both African and English traditions. Many Africans carried names known only within their community, and these were often African. In the sea island region of the Lower South, such names were common until the twentieth century.

Emotional ties to particular places, connections between the generations, and relations of kinship and friendship linking neighboring plantations and farms were the foundation stones of African American community life. Kinship was especially important. African American parents encouraged their children to use family terms in addressing unrelated persons: "auntie" or "uncle" became a respectful way of addressing older men and women, "brother" and "sister" affectionate terms for agemates. Fictive kinship may have been one of the first devices enslaved Africans used to humanize the world of slavery. During the Middle Passage, it was common for children to call their elders "aunt" and "uncle," for adults to address all children as "son" or "daughter."

African American Culture

The eighteenth century was the formative period in the development of the African American community, for it was then that the high birthrate and the growing numbers of country-born provided the necessary stability for the evolution of culture. During this period, men and women from dozens of African ethnic groups molded themselves into a new people. Distinctive patterns in music and dance, religion, and oral tradition illustrate the resilience of the human spirit under bondage as well as the successful struggle of African Americans to create a spiritually sustaining culture of their own.

Eighteenth-century masters were reluctant to allow their slaves to become Christians, fearing that baptism would open the way to claims of freedom or give Africans dangerous notions of universal brotherhood and equality with masters. One frustrated missionary was told by a planter that a slave was "ten times worse when a Christian than in his state of paganism." Because of this attitude, a Protestant minister wrote from South Carolina in the 1770s that most slaves "are to this day as great strangers to Christianity, and as much under the influence of pagan darkness, idolatry and superstition, as they were at their first arrival from Africa." The majority of black southerners before the American Revolution practiced some form of African religion. Large numbers of African Americans were not converted to Christianity until the Great Awakening, which swept across the South after the 1760s (see Chapter 5).

This eighteenth-century painting depicts a celebration in the slave quarters on a South Carolina plantation. One planter's description of a slave dance seems to fit this scene: the men leading the women in "a slow shuffling gait, edging along by some unseen exertion of the feet, from one side to the other— sometimes courtesying down and remaining in that posture while the edging motion from one side to the other continued." The women, he wrote, "always carried a handkerchief held at arm's length, which was waved in a graceful motion to and fro as she moved."

SOURCE: Abby Aldrich Rockefeller Folk Art Center, Williamsburg, Virginia.

One of the most crucial areas of religious practice concerned the rituals of death and burial. In their separate graveyards, African Americans often decorated graves with shells and pottery, an old African custom. African Americans generally believed that the spirits of their dead would return to Africa. The burial ceremony was often held at night to keep it secret from masters, who objected to the continuation of African traditions. The deceased was laid out, and around the body men and women would move counterclockwise in a slow dance step while singing ancestral songs. The pace gradually increased, finally reaching a frenzied but joyful conclusion. Dance was a form of worship, a kind of prayer, a means of achieving union with the ancestors and the gods. The circle dance was a widespread custom in West Africa, and in America it became known as the "ring shout." As slaves from different backgrounds joined together in the circle, they were beginning the process of cultural unification.

Music and dance may have formed the foundation of African American culture, coming even before a common language. Many eighteenth-century observers commented on the musical and rhythmic gifts of Africans. Olaudah Equiano remembered his people,

the Ibos, as "a nation of dancers, musicians, and poets." Thomas Jefferson, raised on a Virginia plantation, wrote that blacks "are more generally gifted than the whites, with accurate ears for tune and time." Many Africans were accomplished players of stringed instruments and drums, and their style featured improvisation and rhythmic complexity, elements that would become prominent in African American music. In America, slaves recreated African instruments, as in the case of the banjo, and mastered the art of the European violin and guitar. Fearing that slaves might communicate by code, authorities often outlawed drums. But using bones, spoons, or sticks, or simply "patting juba" (slapping their thighs), slaves produced elaborate multi-rhythmic patterns.

One of the most important developments of the eighteenth century was the invention of an African American language. An English traveler during the 1770s complained he could not understand Virginia slaves, who spoke "a mixed dialect between the Guinea and English." But such a language made it possible for country-born and "saltwater" Africans to communicate. The two most important dialects were Gullah and Geechee, named after two of the African peoples most prominent in the Carolina and Georgia low country, the Golas and Gizzis of the Windward Coast. These creole languages were a transitional phenomenon, gradually giving way to distinctive forms of black English, although in certain isolated areas, such as the sea islands of the Carolinas and Georgia, they persisted into the twentieth century.

The Africanization of the South

The African American community often looked to recently arrived Africans for religious leadership and medical magic. Throughout the South, many whites had as much faith in slave conjurers and herb doctors as the slaves themselves did, and slaves won fame for their healing powers. This was one of many ways in which white and black Southerners came to share a common culture. Acculturation was by no means a one-way street; English men and women in the South were also being Africanized.

Slaves worked in the kitchens of their masters, and thus introduced an African style of cooking into colonial diets already transformed by the addition of Indian crops. African American culinary arts are responsible for such southern culinary specialties perennials as barbecue, fried chicken, black-eyed peas, and collard greens. And the liberal African use of red pepper, sesame seeds, and other sharp flavors established the southern preference for highly spiced foods. In Louisiana a combination of African, French, and Indian elements produced a distinguished American regional cuisine, exemplified by gumbos (soups) and jambalayas (stews).

Mutual acculturation is also evident in many aspects of material culture. Southern basket weaving used Indian techniques and African designs. Woodcarving often featured African motifs. African architectural designs featuring high, peaked roofs (to drain off the heat) and broad, shady porches gradually became part of a distinctive southern style. The West African iron-working tradition was evident throughout the South, especially in the ornamentation of the homes of Charleston and New Orleans.

Even more important were less tangible aspects of culture. Slave mothers nursed white children as well as their own. As one English observer wrote, "each child has its [black] Momma, whose gestures and accent it will necessarily copy, for children, we all know, are imitative beings." In this way many Africanisms passed into the English language of the South: goober (peanut), yam, banjo, okay, tote, buddy. Some linguists have argued that the southern "drawl," evident among both black and white speakers, derived from the incorporation of African intonations of words and syllables.

African American music and dance also deeply affected white culture. These art forms offer a good example of mutual acculturation. At eighteenth-century plantation dances, the music was usually provided by Africans playing European instruments and their own, such as the banjo. African American fiddlers were common throughout the South by the time of the Revolution, but the banjo also became the characteristic folk instrument of the white South. Toward the end of the evening, the musicians were often told to play some "Negro jigs," and slaves were asked to demonstrate the African manner of dancing. Dancing provided slaves with a unique opportunity to express themselves. "Us slaves watched white folks' parties where the guests danced a minuet," an old South Carolina slave woman recalled, "then we'd do it too, but we used to mock 'em, every step." Whites in turn attempted to imitate African rhythmic dance styles. A slave named Dick related how his master loved to listen to him play the banjo and watch the slave women dance on moonlit nights. The master himself "could shake a desperate foot at the fiddle," said Dick, attempting to outperform the slaves at the "Congo minuet." In such a back-and-forth fashion the traditions of both groups were gradually transformed.

Violence and Resistance

Slavery was a system based on the use of force and violence. Fear underlay the daily life of both masters and slaves. Owners could be humane, but slaves had no guarantees of benevolent treatment, and the kindest master could turn cruel. Even the most cultured plantation owners of the eighteenth century thought nothing

Fugitive slaves flee through the swamps in Thomas Moran's *Slave Hunt* (1862). Many slaves ran away from their masters, and colonial newspapers included notices urging readers to be on the lookout for them. Some fled in groups or collected together in isolated communities called "maroon" colonies, located in inaccessible swamps and woods.

SOURCE: Thomas Moran, *The Slave Hunt*, 1862, oil on canvas, 86.4 x 111.8 cm. Gift of Laura A. Clubb, The Philbrook Museum of Art, Tulsa, Oklahoma.

about floggings of fifty or seventy-five lashes. "Der prayer was answered," sang the Africans of South Carolina, "wid de song of a whip." Although the typical planter punished slaves with extra work, public humiliation, or solitary confinement, the threat of the lash was omnipresent. There were sadistic masters who stabbed, burned, maimed, mutilated, raped, or castrated their slaves.

Former slave David George, who was born and raised on a Virginia plantation, wrote a searing account of plantation violence. "My oldest sister was called Patty. I have seen her several times so whipped that her back has been all corruption, as though it would rot. My brother Dick ran away, but they caught him. . . . After he had received 500 lashes, or more, they washed his back with salt water and whipped it in, as well as rubbed it in with a rag. . . . I also have been whipped many a time on my naked skin, and sometimes till the blood has run down over my waist band. But the greatest grief I then had was to see them whip my mother, and to hear her, on her knees, begging for mercy."

Yet African Americans demonstrated a resisting spirit. In their day-to-day existence they often refused to cooperate: they malingered, they mistreated tools and animals, they destroyed the master's property. "Let an hundred men shew him how to hoe, or drive a wheelbarrow," wrote a frustrated planter, "he'll still take the one by the bottom, and the other by the wheel." Flight was also an option, and judging from the advertisements placed by masters in colonial newspapers, even the most trusted Africans ran away. "That this slave should run away and attempt getting his liberty, is very alarming," read the notice of one Maryland master in 1755. "He has always been too kindly used" and was "one in whom his master has put great confidence, and depended on him to overlook the rest of the slaves, and he had no kind of provocation to go off." An analysis of hundreds of eighteenth-century advertisements for runaways reveals that 80 percent of them were men, most in their twenties, suggesting that flight was an option primarily for young, unattached men.

Runaways sometimes collected together in communities called "maroons," from the Spanish *cimarron*, meaning "wild and untamed." The African communities in Spanish Florida were often called maroons. Indeed, as a whole these mixed African and Creek Indian peoples in Florida called themselves Seminoles, a name deriving from their pronunciation of cimarron. Maroons were also found in the backcountry of the Lower South. In 1771, Georgia's governor warned that north of Savannah "a great number of fugitive Negroes had committed many robberies and insults," and he sent a detachment of militia to destroy their camps. The "black Indian" violence continued, however, and reached catastrophic proportions during the Revolu-

tion. Although maroons were less common in the Upper South, a number of fugitive communities existed in the Great Dismal Swamp between Virginia and North Carolina. In the 1730s, a group of escaped Africans built a community of grass houses and set up a tribal government there, but they were soon dispersed by the authorities.

The most direct form of resistance was revolt. The first notable slave uprising of the colonial era occurred in New York City in 1712. Taking an oath of secrecy, twenty-three Africans vowed revenge for what they called the "hard usage" of their masters. They armed themselves with guns, swords, daggers, and hatchets, killed nine colonists, and burned several buildings before being surrounded by the militia. Six of the conspirators committed suicide rather than surrender. Those captured were hanged, burned at the stake, or broken on the wheel. In 1741 New York authorities uncovered what they thought was another conspiracy. Thirteen black leaders were burned alive, eighteen hanged, and eighty sold and shipped off to the West Indies. A family of colonists and a Catholic priest, accused of providing weapons, were also executed.

There were also isolated but violent uprisings in the Lower South, where slaves were a majority of the population, in 1704, 1720, and 1730. In 1738 a series of violent revolts broke out throughout South Carolina and Georgia. Then in 1739, the largest slave rebellion of the colonial period took place when a group of twenty recently arrived Angolans sacked the armory in Stono, South Carolina. They armed themselves and began a march toward Florida and freedom. Beating drums to attract other slaves to their cause, they grew to nearly one hundred. They plundered a number of planters' homes along the way and killed some thirty colonists. Pausing in a field to celebrate their victory with dance and song, they were overtaken by the militia and destroyed in a pitched battle. That same year there was an uprising in Georgia. Another took place in South Carolina the following year. Attributing these revolts to the influence of newly arrived Africans, colonial officials shut off the slave trade through Charleston for the next ten years.

Wherever masters held slaves, fears of uprisings persisted. But compared with such slave colonies as Jamaica, Guiana, or Brazil, there were few slave revolts in North America. The conditions favoring revolt— large African majorities, brutal exploitation with correspondingly low survival rates, little acculturation, and geographic isolation—prevailed only in some areas of the Lower South. Indeed, the very success of African Americans in British North America at establishing families, communities, and a culture of their own inevitably made them less likely to take the risks that rebellions required.

SLAVERY AND THE ECONOMICS OF EMPIRE

Slavery contributed enormously to the economic growth and development of Europe during the colonial era, and it was an important factor in Great Britain, just before the Industrial Revolution of the eighteenth century. Slavery was the most dynamic force in the Atlantic economy during that century, creating the conditions for industrialization. But because slave-owning colonists single-mindedly committed their resources to the expansion and extension of the plantation system, they derived very little benefit from the economic diversification that characterized industrialization.

Slavery the Mainspring

The slave colonies—the sugar islands of the West Indies and the colonies of the South—accounted for 95 percent of exports from the Americas to Great Britain from 1714 to 1773. Although approximately half of all Great Britain's American colonists lived in New England and the mid-Atlantic, the colonies in those regions contributed less than 5 percent of total exports during this period. Moreover, there was the prime economic importance of the slave trade itself, which one economist of the day described as the "foundation" of the British economy, "the mainspring of the machine which sets every wheel in motion." According to another English writer, slavery was "the strength and sinews of this western world." The

 Web Exploration

In this activity, examine the dynamics that fueled the "Triangular Trade." How were Europe, Africa, and America linked together by commerce?
www.prenhall.com/faragher/map4.2

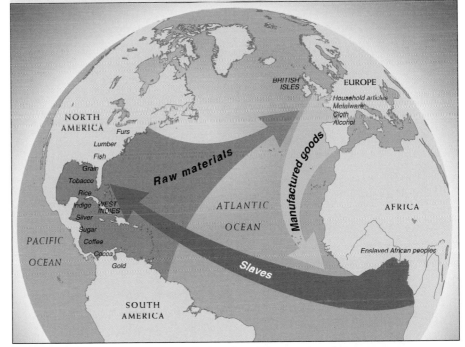

Triangular Trade across the Atlantic The pattern of commerce among Europe, Africa, and the Americas became known as the "Triangular Trade." Sailors called the voyage of slave ships from Africa to America the "Middle Passage" because it formed the crucial middle section of this trading triangle.

labor of African slaves was largely responsible for the economic success of the British Empire in the Americas.

Slavery greatly contributed to the economic development of Great Britain in three principal ways. First, slavery provided an enormous stimulus to the growth of manufacturing by creating a huge colonial market for exports. From 1700 to 1740 the growth in American and African demand for manufactured goods (principally textiles, metal products, and ship's wares)

BRITISH COLONIAL TRADE IN THE AMERICAS, 1714–73 (in thousands of British pounds sterling)				
	Exports to Britain		Imports from Britain	
	£	%	£	%
British West Indies	96,808	64.0	41,653	38.8
Lower South and Chesapeake	47,192	31.2	27,561	25.7
Middle Colonies and New England	7,160	4.7	37,939	35.4
Total	151,160	99.9	107,153	99.9

SOURCE: Eric Williams, *Capitalism and Slavery* (Chapel Hill: University of North Carolina Press, 1944), 225–26.

Eighteenth-century ships being unloaded of their colonial cargoes on London's Old Custom House Quay. Most of the goods imported into England from the American colonies were produced by slave labor.

SOURCE: Samuel Scott, *Old Custom House Quay* Collection. By courtesy of the Board of Trustees of the Victoria and Albert Museum.

The profits of the slave trade and slave production contributed greatly to the accumulation of capital. Although economic historians differ in their estimates, profits derived from the triangular trade in slaves, plantation products, and manufactured goods furnished from 21 to 35 percent of Great Britain's fixed capital formation in the eighteenth century. This capital funded the first modern banks and insurance companies, and eventually found its way into a wide range of economic activities. Merchant capitalists were prominent investors in the expansion of the merchant marine, the improvement of harbors, the construction of canals.

The multiplier effects of these activities are best seen in the growth of English ports such as Liverpool and Bristol. There, the African and American trades provided employment for ships' crews, dockmen, construction workers, traders, shopkeepers, lawyers, clerks, factory workers, and officials of all ranks down to the humblest employees of the custom house. It was said of Bristol that "there is not a brick in the city but what is cemented with the blood of a slave." In the countryside surrounding Liverpool and elsewhere, capital acquired through slavery was invested in the new industrial methods of producing cotton textiles, the beginning of the Industrial Revolution.

accounted for nearly 70 percent of the expansion of British exports.

Second, slavery generated enormous profits that became a source of investment in the economy. The profits of individual investors in the slave system varied widely. But as the British economist Adam Smith wrote, "the profits of a sugar plantation in any of our West Indian colonies are generally much greater than those of any other cultivation that is known either in Europe or America." Economic historians estimate that annual profits during the eighteenth century averaged 15 percent of invested capital in the slave trade, 10 percent in plantation agriculture. Some of the first of England's great modern fortunes were made out of slavery's miseries.

Third, and finally, slavery contributed to the economic development of Great Britain by supplying the raw cotton essential to the Industrial Revolution. In 1787 slave plantations in the Caribbean supplied 69 percent of the raw cotton for British mills. The insatiable demand for cotton led to the development of the cotton gin and the rise of cotton plantations in the United States (see Chapter 11). The connections between slavery and the growth of industry were clear and dramatic.

The Politics of Mercantilism

When imperial officials argued that colonies existed solely for the benefit of the mother country, they had in mind principally the great wealth produced by slavery.

To ensure that this wealth benefited their states, European imperial powers created a system of regulations that became known as "mercantilism." The essence of mercantilist policy was the political control of the economy by the state. First advanced in France in the seventeenth century under the empire of Louis XIV, in the eighteenth century mercantilist politics were most successfully applied by Great Britain. The monarchy and Parliament established a uniform national monetary system, regulated wages, encouraged agriculture and manufacturing, and erected tariff barriers to protect themselves from foreign competition. England also sought to organize and control colonial trade to the maximum advantage of its own shippers, merchants, manufacturers, and bureaucrats.

The mercantilists viewed the economy as a "zero-sum" game, in which total economic gains were equal to total losses. As an English mercantilist put it, "there is but a certain proportion of trade in the world." Profits were thought to result from successful speculation, crafty dealing, or simple plunder—all forms of stealing wealth. The institution of slavery confirmed the theory, for slavery was nothing more than a highly developed system by which some people stole the labor of others. The essence of the competition between states, the mercantilists argued, was the struggle to acquire and hoard the fixed amount of wealth that existed in the world. The nation that accumulated the largest treasure of gold and silver specie would be the most powerful.

Wars for Empire

The mercantilist era was thus a period of intense and violent competition among European states. Wars usually arose out of Old World issues, spilling over into the New World, but they also originated in conflicts over the colonies themselves. In the Anglo-Dutch Wars of the 1650s through the 1670s, England successfully overtook Holland as the dominant Atlantic power. Then, beginning with King William's War (1689–97), England and France (generally allied with Spain) opened a long struggle for colonial supremacy in North America. (For discussion of these conflicts, see Chapter 3.) The fighting took place mainly at the edges of the empire, on the frontiers separating Spanish Florida from British Georgia and New France from New England.

Colonial wars in the southern region had everything to do with slavery. The first fighting of the eighteenth century took place during Queen Anne's War (known in Europe as the War of the Spanish Succession), a conflict that pitted Great Britain and its allies against France and Spain. In 1702 troops from South Carolina invaded Florida, plundering and burning St. Augustine in an attempt to destroy the refuge for fugitive slaves there. A combined French and Spanish fleet took revenge in 1706 by bombarding Charleston. The British finally prevailed, and in 1713, as part of the Peace of Utrecht, Spain ceded to the English the exclusive lucrative right to supply slaves to its American colonies.

The entrance of British slavers into Spanish ports also provided an opportunity for illicit trade, and sporadic fighting between the two empires broke out over this issue a number of times during the next two decades. Robert Walpole, British prime minister from 1721 to 1748, wished to avoid the outbreak of full-scale war, but a faction in the House of Commons that wanted to bring even more slave colonies into the British orbit looked forward to smashing the Spanish in the Caribbean. In 1739, at the urging of this faction, a one-eared sea captain by the name of Jenkins testified before Parliament about the indignities suffered by British merchant sailors at the hands of the Spanish. In a dramatic flourish he produced a dried and withered ear, which he claimed they had cut from his head. A public outrage followed, finally forcing Walpole to agree to a war of Caribbean conquest that the British called the War of Jenkins's Ear.

English troops allied with Creek Indians invaded Florida once again, laying waste the last of the old mission stations but failing to capture St. Augustine. In response, Spanish troops, including several companies of African Americans, invaded Georgia. Although the Spanish were defeated seventy-five miles south of Savannah, the campaign produced an agreement on the boundary between British Georgia and Spanish Florida that today still separates those states. Elsewhere the British were not so lucky: in the Caribbean the imperial fleet suffered disaster at the hands of the Spanish navy.

In the northern region, the principal focus of this imperial struggle was control of the Indian trade. In 1704, during Queen Anne's War, the French and their Algonquian Indian allies raided New England frontier towns, such as Deerfield, Massachusetts, dragging men, women, and children into captivity in Canada. In turn, the English mounted a series of expeditions against the strategic French fortress of Port Royal in Acadia, which they captured in 1710. At the war's conclusion in 1713, France was forced to cede Acadia, Newfoundland, and Hudson's Bay to Great Britain in exchange for guarantees of security for the French-speaking residents of those provinces. Nearly thirty years of peace followed, but from 1744 to 1748 England again battled France in King George's War (known in Europe as the War of the Austrian Succession). The French attacked the British in Nova Scotia. Indian and Canadian raids again devastated the border towns of New England and New York, and hundreds of British subjects were killed or captured.

The French, allied with the Spanish and Prussians, were equally successful in Europe. What finally turned the tide of this war was the capture in 1745 of the

OVERVIEW

THE COLONIAL WARS

King William's War	1689–97	France and England battle on the northern frontiers of New England and New York.
Queen Anne's War	1702–13	England fights France and Spain in the Caribbean and on the northern frontier of New France. Part of the European conflict known as the War of the Spanish Succession.
War of Jenkins's Ear	1739–43	Great Britain versus Spain in the Caribbean and Georgia. Part of the European conflict known as the War of the Austrian Succession.
King George's War	1744–48	Great Britain and France fight in Acadia and Nova Scotia; the second American round of the War of the Austrian Succession.
French and Indian War	1754–63	Last of the great colonial wars pitting Great Britain against France and Spain. Known in Europe as the Seven Years War.

French fortress of Louisburg on Cape Breton Island by an expedition of Massachusetts troops in conjunction with the royal navy. Deprived of the most strategic of their American ports, and fearful of losing the wealth of their sugar islands, the French agreed to a negotiated settlement in 1748. But despite the capture of Louisburg, the war had been fought elsewhere to a stalemate, so the treaty restored the prewar status quo, returning Louisburg to France. This disgusted the merchants of New England, who wanted to expand their commercial influence in the maritime colonies, and left the North American conflict between France and Britain still simmering. Significantly, however, this was the first time that the concluding battle of a European war had been fought on North American soil, and it was a harbinger of things to come: the next war was destined to start as a conflict between French and British colonists before engulfing Europe (see Chapter 6).

British Colonial Regulation

Mercantilists used means other than war to win the wealth of the world. In the sixteenth century the Spanish monarchy created the first state trading monopoly—the Casa de Contratación—to manage the commerce of its empire. It was widely emulated by others: the Dutch East Indies Company, the French Company of the Indies, the English East India Company, Hudson's Bay Company, and Royal African Company.

English manufacturers complained that merchant-dominated trading monopolies too frequently carried foreign (particularly Dutch) products to colonial markets, ignoring English domestic industry. Reacting to these charges, between 1651 and 1696 Parliament passed the Navigation Acts, which created the legal and institutional structure of Britain's eighteenth-century colonial system. The acts defined the colonies as both suppliers of raw materials and as markets for English manufactured goods. Merchants from other nations were expressly forbidden to trade in the colonies, and all trade had to be conducted in ships built in England or the British colonies themselves.

The regulations specified a list of colonial products that could be shipped only to England. These included the products of the southern slave colonies (sugar, molasses, rum, tobacco, rice, and indigo), those of the northern Indian trade (furs and skins), and those essential for supplying the shipping industry (pine masts, tar, pitch, resin, and turpentine). The bulk of these products were not destined for English consumption; at great profit they were reexported elsewhere.

England also placed limitations on colonial enterprises that might compete with those at home. A series of enactments—including the Wool Act of 1699, the Hat Act of 1732, and the Iron Act of 1750—forbade the manufacture of those products. Moreover, colonial assemblies were forbidden to impose tariffs on English imports as a way to protect colonial industries. Banking was disallowed, local coinage prohibited, and the export of coin from England forbidden. Badly in need of a circulating monetary medium, Massachusetts illegally minted copper coin, and several colonies issued paper currency, forcing Parliament to explicitly legislate against the practice. The colonists depended mostly on "commodity money" (furs, skins, or hogsheads of tobacco) and the circulation of foreign currency, the most common being the Spanish silver *peso* and the German silver *thaler*, which Americans

The New England artist John Greenwood painted this amusing view of New England sea captains in Surinam in 1757. By the early eighteenth century, New England merchant traders like these had become important participants in the traffic in slaves and sugar to and from the West Indies. Northern ports thus became important pivots in the expanding commercial network linking slave plantations with Atlantic markets.

SOURCE: John Greenwood, *Sea Captains Carousing in Surinam*, 1757. Oil on bed ticking, 95.9 × 191.2 cm. The Saint Louis Art Museum, Museum Purchase.

pronounced "dollar." Official rates of exchange between commodity money, colonial paper, foreign currency, and English pounds allowed this chaotic system to operate without too much difficulty.

As the trade in colonial products increased, the British came to agree that it made little sense to tamper with such a prosperous system. Prime Minister Robert Walpole pursued a policy later characterized as one of "salutory neglect." Any colonial rules and regulations deemed contrary to good business practice were simply ignored and not enforced. Between 1700 and 1760 the quantity of goods exported from the colonies to the mother country rose 165 percent, while imports from Britain to North America increased by more than 400 percent. In part because of the lax enforcement, but mostly because the system operated to the profit of colonial merchants, colonists complained very little about the operation of the mercantilist system before the 1760s.

The Colonial Economy

Despite the seemingly harsh mercantilist regulations, the economic system operated to the benefit of planters, merchants, and white colonists in general. Southern slave owners made healthy profits on the sale of their commodities. They enjoyed a protected market in

which competing goods from outside the empire were heavily taxed. Planters found themselves with steadily increasing purchasing power. Pennsylvania, New York, and New England, and increasingly the Chesapeake as well, produced grain, flour, meat, and dairy products. None of these were included in the list of enumerated goods, and thus they could be sold freely abroad. They found their most ready market in the British West Indies and the Lower South, where food production was slighted in favor of sugar and rice. Most of this trade was carried in New England ships. Indeed, the New England shipbuilding industry was greatly stimulated by the allowance under the Navigation Acts for ships built and manned in the colonies. So many ships were built for English buyers that by midcentury nearly a third of all British tonnage was American made.

The greatest benefits for the port cities of the North came from their commercial relationship to the slave colonies. New England merchants had become important players in the slave trade by the early eighteenth century, and soon thereafter they began to make inroads into the export trade of the West Indian colonies. It was in the Caribbean that northern merchants most blatantly ignored mercantilist regulations. In violation of Spanish, French, and Dutch regulations prohibiting foreign trade, New Englanders traded

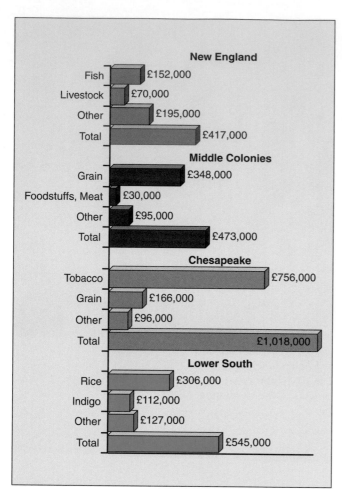

Value of Colonial Exports by Region, Annual Average, 1768–72 With tobacco, rice, grain, and indigo, the Chesapeake and Lower South accounted for nearly two-thirds of colonial exports in the late eighteenth century. The Middle Colonies, however, were also becoming major exporters of grain.

SOURCE: James F. Shepherd and Gary M. Walton, *Shipping, Maritime Trade and the Economic Development of Colonial America* (Cambridge: Cambridge University Press, 1972), 211–27.

foodstuffs for sugar in foreign colonies. They illegally sent the sugar to New England. By 1750 more than sixty distilleries in Massachusetts Bay were exporting more than 2 million gallons of rum, most of it produced from sugar obtained illegally. Because the restrictive rules and regulations enacted by Britain for its colonies were not enforced, such growth and prosperity among the merchants and manufacturers of the port cities of the North prospered.

By the mid-eighteenth century, the Chesapeake and Lower South regions were major exporters of tobacco, rice, and indigo, and the middle colonies major exporters of grain to Europe. The carrying trade in the products of slave labor made it possible for the northern and middle colonies to earn the income necessary to purchase British imports despite the lack of valuable products from their own regions. Gradually, the commercial economies of the Northeast and the South were becoming integrated. From the 1730s to the 1770s, for example, while the volume of trade between Great Britain and Charleston doubled, the trade between Charleston and northern ports grew sevenfold. The same relationship was developing between the Chesapeake and the North. Merchants in Boston, Newport, New York, and Philadelphia increasingly provided southern planters not only with shipping services but also with credit and insurance. Like London, Liverpool, and Bristol—though on a smaller scale—the port cities of the North became pivots in the expanding trade network linking slave plantations with Atlantic markets. This trade provided northern merchants with the capital that financed commercial growth and development in their cities and the surrounding countryside. Slavery thus contributed to the growth of a score of northern port cities, forming an indirect but essential part of their economies.

SLAVERY AND FREEDOM

The prosperity of the eighteenth-century plantation economy thus improved the living conditions for the residents of northern cities as well as for a large segment of the population of the South, providing them with the opportunity for a kind of freedom unknown in the previous century. The price of prosperity and freedom was the oppression and exploitation of millions of Africans and African Americans. Freedom for white men based on the slavery of African Americans is the most important contradiction of American history.

The Social Structure of the Slave Colonies

At the summit of southern colonial society stood a small elite of wealthy planters, in contrast with the mass of slave men and women who formed the working population. Slavery had produced a society in which property was concentrated in the hands of a wealthy few. The richest 10 percent of colonists owned more than half the cultivated land and over 60 percent of the wealth. Although there was no colonial aristocracy— no nobility or royal appointments—the landed elite of the slave colonies came very close to constituting one. Bound together through strategic marriages, carefully crafted business dealings, and elaborate rituals designed to awe common folk and slaves, they constituted what one historian calls an "interlocking directorate."

The typical wealthy Virginia planter lived in a Tidewater county; owned several thousand acres of prime farmland and more than a hundred slaves; resided in a luxurious plantation mansion, built perhaps in the fashionable Georgian style; and had an estate valued at more than £10,000. Elected to the House of Burgesses and forming the group from which the magistrates and counselors of the colony were chosen, these "first families of Virginia"—the Carters, Harrisons, Lees, Fitzhughs, Washingtons, Randolphs, and others—were a self-perpetuating governing class. A similar elite ruled the Lower South, although wealthy landowners spent little time on their plantations. They lived instead in fashionable Charleston, where they made up a close-knit group who controlled the colonial government. "They live in as high a style here, I believe, as any part of the world," a visitor wrote.

A considerable distance separated this slave-owning elite from typical southern landowners. About half the adult white males were small planters and farmers. But while the gap between rich and middling colonists grew larger during the eighteenth century, the prosperity of the plantation economy created generally favorable conditions for landowning class as a whole. Slave ownership, for example, became widespread among this group during the eighteenth century. In Virginia at midcentury, 45 percent of heads of household held one to four slaves and even poorer farmers kept one or two.

Despite the prosperity that accompanied slavery in the eighteenth century, however, a substantial portion of colonists owned no land or slaves at all. Some rented land or worked as tenant farmers, some hired out as overseers or farm workers, and still others were indentured servants. Throughout the plantation region, landless men constituted about 40 percent of the population. A New England visitor found a "much greater disparity between the rich and poor in Virginia" than at home.

White Skin Privilege

But all the white colonists of eighteenth-century North America shared the privileged status of their skin color. In the early seventeenth century there had been more diversity in views about race. For some, black skin was thought to be a sign of God's curse. "The blackness of the Negroes," one Englishman argued, "proceedeth of some natural infection." But not everyone shared those views. "I can't think there is any intrinsic value in one colour more than another," a second Englishman remarked, "nor that white is better than black, only we think it so because we are so."

As slavery became increasingly important, however, Virginia officials took considerable care to create legal distinctions between the status of colonists and that of Africans. Beginning in 1670, free Africans were prohibited from owning Christian servants. Ten years later, another law declared that any African, free or slave, who struck a Christian would receive thirty lashes on his bare

back. One of the most important measures was designed to suppress intimate interracial contacts between white servants and enslaved Africans. A 1691 act "for prevention of that abominable mixture and spurious issue which hereafter may encrease in this dominion" established severe penalties for interracial sexual relationships.

Such penalties were rarely applied to masters, who frequently forced themselves on African women. But some slave women may have willingly established intimate relations with masters to better their condition or the opportunities for their children. After the death of his wife, Thomas Jefferson's father-in-law took a slave woman as his concubine. They had six children. After Jefferson's wife died, it was rumored that he established a sexual relationship with Sally Hemings, the youngest of those children, and his late wife's half-sister. Recent scientific tests have confirmed that Jefferson was likely the father of Sally's children, who enjoyed a privileged position in the household and were freed in Jefferson's will. The Jefferson household was one in which interracial sex was commonplace.

Relationships between white masters or indentured servants and African slaves produced a rather large group of mulattoes. Because by law children inherited the bondage or free status of their mothers, the majority of those of mixed ancestry were slaves; a minority, the children of European women and African men, were free. According to a Maryland census of 1755, more than 60 percent of mulattoes were slaves. But Maryland mulattoes also made up three-quarters of a small free African American population. This group, numbering about 4,000 in the 1770s, was denied the right to vote, to hold office, or to testify in court— all on the basis of racial background. Denied the status of

RUN away from the subscriber in *Albemarle*, a Mulatto slave called *Sandy*, about 35 years of age, his stature is rather low, inclining to corpulence, and his complexion light; he is a shoemaker by trade, in which he uses his left hand principally, can do coarse carpenters work, and is something of a horse jockey; he is greatly addicted to drink, and when drunk is insolent and disorderly, in his conversation he swears much, and in his behaviour is artful and knavish. He took with him a white horse, much scarred with traces, of which it is expected he will endeavour to dispose; he also carried his shoemakers tools, and will probably endeavour to get employment that way. Whoever conveys the said slave to me, in *Albemarle*, shall have 40 s. reward, if taken up within the county, 4 l. if elsewhere within the colony, and 10 l. if in any other colony, from
THOMAS JEFFERSON.

Thomas Jefferson placed this advertisement in the *Virginia Gazette* on September 14, 1769. Americans need to seriously consider the historical relationship between the prosperity and freedom of white people and the oppression and exploitation of Africans and African Americans.

SOURCE: Virginia Historical Society.

CHRONOLOGY

1441	African slaves first brought to Portugal
1518	Spain grants official license to Portuguese slavers
1535	Africans constitute a majority on Hispaniola
1619	First Africans brought to Virginia
1655	English seize Jamaica
1662	Virginia law makes slavery hereditary
1670	South Carolina founded
1672	Royal African Company organized
1691	Virginia prohibits interracial sexual contact
1698	Britain opens the slave trade to all its merchants
1699	Spanish declare Florida a refuge for escaped slaves
1702	South Carolinians burn St. Augustine
1705	Virginia Slave Code established
1706	French and Spanish navies bombard Charleston
1710	English capture Port Royal in Acadia
1712	Slave uprising in New York City
1713	Peace of Utrecht
1721–48	Robert Walpole leads British cabinet
1729	Natchez Rebellion in French Louisiana
1733	Molasses Act
1739	Stono Rebellion in South Carolina
1739–43	War of Jenkins's Ear
1740–48	King George's War
1741	Africans executed in New York for conspiracy
1752	Georgia officially opened to slavery
1770s	Peak period of the English colonies' slave trade
1808	Importation of slaves into the United States ends

citizenship enjoyed by even the poorest white men, free blacks were an outcast group who raised the status of white colonials by contrast. Racial distinctions were a constant reminder of the freedom of white colonists and the debasement of all blacks, slave or free.

Racism set up a wall of contempt between colonists and African Americans. Jefferson wrote of "the real distinctions which nature has made" between the races. "In memory they are equal to the whites," he wrote of the slaves, but "in reason much inferior." He gave no consideration to the argument of freed slave Olaudah Equiano that "slavery debases the mind." Jefferson was on firmer ground when he argued that the two peoples were divided by "deep rooted prejudices entertained by the whites" and "ten thousand recollections, by the blacks, of the injuries they have sustained." Perhaps he knew of these feelings from his long relationship with Sally Hemings. "I tremble for my country when I reflect that God is just," Jefferson concluded in a deservedly famous passage, and remember "that his justice cannot sleep forever."

CONCLUSION

During the eighteenth century nearly half a million Africans were kidnapped from their homes, marched to the African coast, and packed into ships for up to three months before arriving in British North America. They provided the labor that made colonialism pay. Southern planters, northern merchants, and especially British traders and capitalists benefited greatly from the commerce in slave-produced crops, and that prosperity filtered down to affect many of the colonists of British North America. Slavery was fundamental to the operation of the British empire in North America. Mercantilism was a system designed to channel colonial wealth produced by slaves to the nation-state, but as long as profits were high, the British tended to wink at colonists' violations of mercantilist regulations.

Although African Americans received little in return, their labor helped build the greatest accumulation of capital that Europe had ever seen. But despite enormous hardship and suffering, African Americans survived by forming new communities in the colonies, rebuilding families, restructuring language, and reforming culture. African American culture added important components of African knowledge and experience to colonial agriculture, art, music, and cuisine. The African Americans of the English colonies lived better lives than the slaves worked to death on Caribbean sugar plantations, but lives of misery compared with the men they were forced to serve. As the slaves sang on the Georgia coast, "Dah Backrow Man go wrong you, Buddy Quow."

REVIEW QUESTIONS

1. Trace the development of the system of slavery, and discuss the way it became entrenched in the Americas.
2. Describe the effects of the slave trade both on enslaved Africans and on the economic and political life of Africa.
3. Describe the process of acculturation involved in becoming an African American. In what ways did slaves "Africanize" the South?
4. Explain the connection between the institution of slavery and the building of a commercial empire.
5. In what ways did colonial policy encourage the growth of racism?

RECOMMENDED READING

Ira Berlin, *Many Thousands Gone: The First Two Centuries of Slavery in North America* (1998). A history of colonial slavery with attention to the differences between the regions of the Chesapeake, the Lower South, Louisiana, and the North. Emphases the distinction between slave societies and societies with slaves.

Michael Craton, *Sinews of Empire: A Short History of British Slavery* (1974). An introduction to the British mercantilist system that emphasizes the importance of slavery. Includes a comparison of the mainland colonies with the Caribbean.

Philip D. Curtin, *The African Slave Trade: A Census* (1969). The pioneer work in the quantitative history of the slave trade. All subsequent histories of the slave trade are indebted to Curtin.

Winthrop D. Jordan, *White over Black: American Attitudes Toward the Negro, 1550–1812* (1968). Remains the best and most comprehensive history of racial attitudes. A searching examination of British and American literature, folklore, and history.

Herbert S. Klein, *The Atlantic Slave Trade* (1999). A new and important synthesis of the most recent studies of the slave trade, covering the social and cultural effects of the trade, especially for Africans.

Peter Kolchin, *American Slavery, 1619–1877* (1993). This survey features comparisons with slavery in Brazil and the Caribbean and serfdom in Russia. Includes a comprehensive bibliographic essay.

Philip D. Morgan, *Slave Counterpoint: Black Culture in the Eighteenth-Century Chesapeake and Low-country* (1998). A comprehensive and detailed examination of cultural forms and ways of life in the two regions that leaves hardly a stone unturned.

Walter Rodney, *How Europe Underdeveloped Africa* (1974). This highly influential book traces the relationship between Europe and Africa from the fifteenth to the twentieth century, and demonstrates how Europe's industrialization became Africa's impoverishment.

Mechal Sobel, *The World They Made Together: Black and White Values in Eighteenth-Century Virginia* (1987). Demonstrates the ways in which both Africans and Europeans shaped the formation of American values, perceptions, and identities.

Ian K. Steele, *Warpaths: Invasions of North America* (1994). A new synthesis of the colonial wars from the sixteenth to the eighteenth century that places Indians as well as empires at the center of the action.

▶ MEDIA RESOURCES

 U.S. HISTORY DOCUMENTS CD-ROM

Colonizing the New World

2-2   Samuel de Champlain's Battle with the Iroquois, July 1609

2-3   An Act Concerning Servants and Slaves

2-4   Reasons for the Plantation in New England (1629)

2-11   Onandogas and Cayugas: Iroquois Chiefs Address the Governors of New York and Virginia (1684)

2-12   James Oglethorpe: The Stono Rebellion (1739)

2-13   Gottlieb Mittelberger, The Passage of Indentured Servants (1750)

 COMPANION WEBSITE HIGHLIGHTS

To view an exploration, enter one of the URLs below in your browser.

 Web Explorations

The African Slave Trade
http://www.prenhall.com/faragher/map4.1
Triangular Trade across the Atlantic
http://www.prenhall.com/faragher/map4.2

 Additional Interactive Maps

To access the map, go to this chapter's resources at
http://www.prenhall.com/faragher
Slave Colonies of the Seventeenth and Eighteenth Centuries, page 84

HISTORY RESOURCE CENTER

To find the resources listed below, go to
http://www.prenhall.com/historyresourcecenter

Documents

Don Juan de Oñate, Plaus: A Settlement in New Mexico (1599)

John White, The Lost Colony (1590)

Jose de Acosta, A Spanish Priest Speculates on the Origins of the Indians (1590)

The Cambridge Agreement (1629)

Wessell Webling, A Free Man Signs an Indenture (1622)

Alexander Falconbridge, The African Slave Trade (1788)

Bacon's Rebellion: The Declaration (1676)

Olaudah Equiano, The Middle Passage (1788)

Petition of "A Grate Number of Blackes of the Province" to Governor Thomas Gage and the Members of the Massachusetts General Court (1774)

Images

"To be sold . . . a cargo of 170 prime young likely healthy Guinea slaves. Savannah, July 25, 1774."

Olaudah Equiano

Phillis Wheatley

Slave Sale Notice

EXPLORING AMERICA
RACISM IN AMERICAN HISTORY
http://www.prenhall.com/faragher/racism

How were slavery and racism connected? How was skin color used to rationalize notions of racial superiority? How did racism provide a justification for the brutal treatment of Africans in the slave trade? What impact did the American Revolution have on slavery? On racism? Race is a central feature in the world today and a basic theme of American history. This module explores racism in the colonial and early national period from several perspectives. It shows that slavery in the seventeenth and eighteenth centuries was connected to European perceptions of Africans. It also illustrates how the American Revolution altered attitudes toward slavery but not necessarily race.

Racism in American History uses a variety of methods to examine the connection between slavery and race. Contemporary accounts, including one by an ex-slave, depict the brutal treatment Africans received in the slave trade. Visual images portray the ways in which slaves were treated as commodities in a marketplace while print documents illuminate the issues over racism that emerged during the revolutionary period. The module also shows the accomplishments of

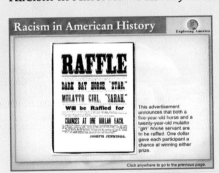

This advertisement announces that both a five-year-old horse and a twenty-year-old mulatto "girl" house servant are to be raffled. One dollar gave each participant a chance at winning either prize.

African Americans such as Phyllis Wheatley and Benjamin Banneker. Interactive maps and the chronology provide space and time contexts.

Reflect and Respond

1. Racism helped justify the institution of slavery. It also provided an excuse for the brutal treatment of Africans. Based on the writings of Equiano and Fitzhugh, what does the treatment of Africans suggest about the humanity of Europeans?

2. How did the American Revolution affect attitudes toward slavery? How did they affect racist beliefs?

3. How did African Americans try to use the rhetoric of the American Revolution to secure equal rights?

✓ Check it out

Olaudah Equiano, The Middle Passage

This primary source document offers a first-hand account of the treatment of Africans in the slave trade. It provides insight into the thoughts and feelings of Africans who were caught in the slave trade.

Olaudah Equiano

The document also describes the process by which Africans were loaded onto slave ships.

This exploration is only available on the *Out of Many*, Fourth Edition Companion Website™.

▶ The Living History of Slavery

The 1,268 acres of freshwater marsh at the Howfyl-Broadfield Plantation State Historic Site, located on the Altamaha River delta of the Georgia sea coast, is maintained by a private trust as a nature center. But historically it was a large rice plantation, its ditches, dikes, and fields arduously cleared, constructed, and cultivated by large numbers of enslaved Africans and African Americans. The plantation supported five generations of owners until the last descendant willed the property to the state of Georgia in the early 1970s. There is a plantation house with period furnishings, and along several miles of trails visitors can observe the relict fields, now gradually returning to salt marsh. This place was once a prime example of the slave society of the Lower South, but until recently slavery wasn't much mentioned at How-fyl-Broadfield Plantation. Huge live oaks festooned with Spanish moss provided a romantic backdrop for the annual "old-fashioned Christmas" observance of the Glynn County Garden Club. Candles lit the way to the plantation house, decorated with greenery and bows, where guests were greeted by actors portraying Scarlet O'Hara and Robert E. Lee. Around back they were served wassail, heated in a 150-year-old black kettle. Howfyl-Broadfield is one of hundreds of historic slave plantations where slavery was a repressed memory, while people memorialized the "moonlight and magnolias" version of Old South history.

But those days are now behind us. During the past quarter-century there has been a growing interest in the history of slavery, in part prompted by the confirmation through DNA testing of Thomas Jefferson's relationship with Sally Hemmings (see discussion in this chapter). Hollywood told a version of that story in "Jefferson in Paris," and attempted to seriously dramatize slavery itself in the films "Beloved," "Amistad," and "Glory." The United States Congress entered the action, mandating that the National Park Service address the history of slavery at its Civil War sites. President Bill Clinton went to Africa and issued a

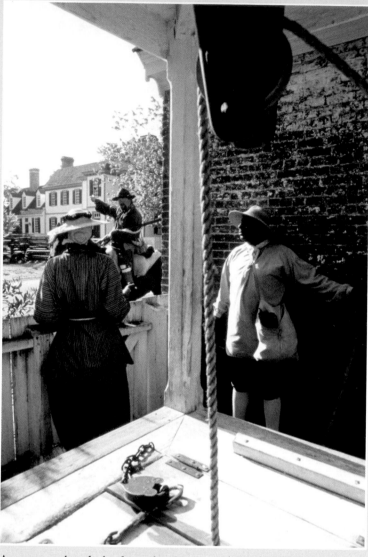

A runaway slave hides from the slave patrol, a re-enactment at Carter's Grove plantation. Many visitors are caught up in these dramas, some offering to help slaves escape, others turning on the owners. Slavery is the most painful topic in American history.

SOURCE: Colonial Williamsburg Foundation, Williamsburg, VA.

statement of regret over the historic role of the United States in the slave trade. What accounts for this national attention? According to distinguished historian of slavery Ira Berlin, behind the interest in slavery is the crisis of race in America. In a society in which blacks and whites hardly talk to each other, slavery is a way to discuss race, a way of addressing some of the deepest hurts that Americans feel.

Incorporating slavery into the interpretation of historic slave plantations has proved controversial.

The issue arouses deep anger and bitterness for many African Americans, embarrassment and shame for many white people. According to Rex Ellis, a director of interpretation at Colonial Williamsburg, the historical park where he works "was never a place for blacks to come to." Although he grew up in the area, neither his African American family nor any of his neighbors would visit. "That place points to slavery," his father would say, "and that's something we don't want to talk about." But in the mid-1980s Colonial Williamsburg made the decision it was something that had to be talked about, and in 1989 the institution opened a reconstruction of the slave quarters at nearby Carter's Grove plantation, staffed by interpreters portraying slaves and masters. For the first time African Americans began to come. Many visitors — white as well as black — found themselves caught up in the re-enactments. Some offered to help the slaves escape, while others turned on the slave owners and had to be physically restrained. On the other hand, some of the African-American actors reported feeling that they were being treated like slaves, not only by visitors but by those playing roles as masters.

Slavery remains the most painful topic in American history. For years "there was an unwritten rule not to be controversial," says Dwight T. Pitcaithley, chief historian for the National Park Service, but "it didn't make for good history." Pitcaithley oversees the program to include the history of slavery at the nation's Civil War battlefield sites. The idea is to make slavery as vivid in the public imagination as the bloody war it precipitated. Some parts of the slave past, however, may be too sensitive for the medium of living history. When the interpretive staff at Colonial Williamsburg staged a slave auction, civil rights groups picketed and sang "We Shall Overcome." At another living history program in Georgia, middle school students who witnessed a re-enactment of a slave auction were asked to imagine what it would feel like to be a slave. "There I was on the auction block," one African American student wrote. "I had to take off my clothes in front of all those white people. I forgot to be proud and I was ashamed."

So far the movement to incorporate slavery into the interpretation at historic sites has not changed things very much at Howfyl-Broadfield Plantation. An archaeological investigation of the site in the mid-1990s did reveal traces of the old slave quarters out

back, not far from the Christmas wassail kettle. Archaeologist Kay Wood would like to do more excavation and create an interpretive exhibit featuring the history of slavery on the rice coast of Georgia, but funds are short. "There really hasn't been a lot done on rice plantations in Georgia," she told a reporter. "This is where history begins on this coast. This is where Georgia begins." But meanwhile the old-fashioned Christmas celebrations continue, perpetuating a different memory of the rice coast, a memory in which slaves are invisible. ■

www.researchnavigator.com

The Community and Memory essay for this chapter deals with the effort to recover, preserve, and discuss the painful history of slavery in the United States. For further research on the history of slavery, use the tools available to you in Research Navigator.

As you investigate this topic, consider this question: "Why was the history of slavery repressed for so long? Why has interest in the subject grown in the past quarter of a century?"

ContentSelect: Search in the Anthropology, Sociology, and History databases using the search terms *slavery, plantation,* and *Sally Hemmings.*

Links Library: Access the History: U.S. History, Sociology, and Anthropology databases.

New York Times on the Web: To find more information on the decision to include slaves as part of the living history of Colonial Williamsburg, search using the term *Colonial Williamsburg.*

RESEARCHING THE PAST

FIVE

THE CULTURES OF COLONIAL NORTH AMERICA

▶ 1700–1780

Peter Cooper, *The South East Prospect of the City of Philadelphia*, ca. 1720. The Library Company of Philadelphia.

From Deerfield to Kahnawake: Crossing Cultural Boundaries

TWO HOURS BEFORE DAYLIGHT ON FEBRUARY 29, 1704, Reverend John Williams and his wife, Eunice, of Deerfield, Massachusetts, awoke to "horrid shouting and yelling" and the crash of axes and hatchets breaking open the doors and windows of their house. Leaping out of bed they knew immediately that the town was under attack by Indians and their French allies; this frontier settlement on the northwestern fringe of New England had already been attacked six times in the perennial fighting with New France. Never before, however, had the enemy penetrated the town's stockade. Suddenly the door burst open and "with painted faces and hideous exclamations" Indians began pushing inside. "I reached up my hands for my pistol," Williams remembered, "cocked it, and put it to the breast of the first Indian that came up." It misfired, and as the couple stood trembling in their night-clothes, they were bound and dragged into the central hall with their seven children. In horror they were forced to watch the invaders club and kill their resisting six-year-old son, their screaming newborn infant daughter, and their black nursemaid. The family was hustled out into the frigid dawn and, with more than a hundred other captives, marched north through snow and ice toward Canada, leaving the frightful sight of the burning town behind.

This raid was one of the most infamous events in a long series of attacks and counterattacks between English and French colonists. At Deerfield, one hundred and forty residents of the town managed to hold off the invasion and survive, but fifty others died in the attack. Among the captives, twenty-one were murdered along the way, in most cases because they were too weak to travel; those murdered included Mrs. Williams, who had not yet recovered from a difficult childbirth just six weeks before. The governor of Massachusetts ordered a day of fasting and prayed that "the Designs of the barbarous Salvages against us be defeated; our exposed Plantations preserved; and the poor Christian Captives in their hands returned." Authorities raised the bounty on Indian scalps from £10 to £100 and organized bloody raids of their own on the French and Indian settlements to the north.

Most of the Deerfield captives were delivered to the French authorities in Montreal. Within two years, fifty-nine of them had been ransomed and returned home to Deerfield, the Reverend Williams and four of his surviving children among them. Williams soon published an account of his captivity, *The Redeemed Captive Returning to Zion*. In colonial America, with its many peoples and cultures, readers were fascinated by the problems and dilemmas of crossing the frontiers between colonial and Indian societies, as well as the borders between the English, French, and Spanish empires. What was life like for you, people wanted to know, on the other side of the frontier? How were you changed by your experience? Did you remain loyal to your community? Can you still be trusted?

Questions of this sort were vitally important to the colonists, for over the years hundreds of Europeans who had been captured by Indians had chosen to remain with their captors rather than return home. Among the Deerfield captives, thirty-one—including ten-year-old Eunice Williams, her mother's namesake—remained in Canada. Eunice and many of the other Deerfield captives lived at Kahnawake, a community of Catholic Indians near Montreal. Like Deerfield, Kahnawake was a farming town of fifty or sixty homes clustered around a central church and surrounded by a stockade to protect it from enemy raiders. The differences between the two communities, however, were more striking than the similarities.

Founded in the seventeenth century by Jesuit missionaries as a refuge for Iroquois converts, Kahnawake not only became home to a great variety of Native American Catholics but also welcomed people of mixed Indian and European ancestry. The "great mixture of the blood of whites with that of aborigines is observable in the persons of the inhabitants," wrote one visitor, struck by the appearance of people who seemed to be Indians in all respects except their blue eyes. Such mixing was also evident in the community's culture, the exotic combination of European and Indian clothing, the use of both Indian and French names, and the special ways the community bent Catholic ritual to fit traditional Iroquois practices. Community members crossed boundaries in other ways, too: many residents were smugglers who engaged in the illegal trade of furs and other Indian products across the frontier into New York. According to the frustrated authorities in Montreal, Kahnawake operated as "a sort of republic," insisting on its freedom and independence.

As the historian John Demos writes, Kahnawake was "a unique experiment in bicultural living." Its residents were skilled at offering sympathetic

sanctuary to traumatized captive children, and by the time Eunice Williams's father and siblings were ransomed, she told the man who had come to fetch her that she was "unwilling to return." Soon she converted to Catholicism. Over the years the father sent several emissaries to retrieve her, but all she would say were two words of Iroquois: *jaghte oghte*, meaning "maybe not." She refused to acknowledge her English name, having taken another: *A'ongonte*, which in Iroquois means "she has been planted as a person." In 1713, at the age of sixteen, she married a Kahnawake Mohawk. Father and daughter would meet only once more, the following year, when he went to Kahnawake a final time to beg her to return. But she would "not so much as give me one pleasant look," Williams wrote mournfully. "She is yet obstinatly resolved to live and dye here."

And that is what happened. A'ongonte and her husband remained good Catholics, raising a family and working as traders. John Williams died in 1729, surrounded by his children and grandchildren but longing for his "unredeemed" daughter. It was not until 1739 that A'ongonte found the courage to bring her family south for a visit, for she feared being held in New England against her will. Her brother Stephen wrote in his diary that at long last "we had ye joyfull, Sorrowfull meeting of our poor Sister that we had been Sepratd from fer above 36 years." After that A'ongonte visited only rarely because of the continuing warfare. "We have a great desire of going down to see you," she wrote to her brother through an interpreter near the end of their lives in the 1770s, "but do not know when an oppertunity may offer. . . . I pray the Lord that he may give us grace so to Live in this as to be prepared for a happey meeting in the worled to Come." And, perhaps as a sign of reconciliation, she signed the letter, "Loving Sister until death, Eunice Williams." ■

Deerfield

NORTH AMERICAN REGIONS

American colonial history too often is written as if only the British colonists along the Atlantic coast really mattered. But as the experience of the Deerfield community and the Williams family suggests, this is a mistake eighteenth-century colonists could not afford to make. In the first place, Indian America was a critically important part of the eighteenth-century world. From the fringes of colonial societies into the native heart of the continent, from the eastern foothills of the Appalachians to the western flank of the Sierra Nevada in California, hundreds of Indian cultures—despite being deeply affected by the spread of colonial culture—remained firmly in control of their homelands. And in addition to the British provinces stretching along the Atlantic coast, there were Hispanic colonists who defended the northern borderlands of the Spanish Caribbean and Mexican empire in isolated communities from Florida to California, and French communities that occupied the valley of the St. Lawrence River and scattered down the Mississippi Valley from the Great Lakes to the Gulf of Mexico. There were impressive similarities among these colonial societies, representing a continuation in the New World of traditional Old World beliefs, customs, and institutions, as well as a general pattern of European adaptation to American conditions.

Indian America

As the native peoples of the Atlantic coastal plain lost their lands to colonists through battles or treaties and moved into or beyond the Appalachian Mountains, they became active in the fur trade. Indians demonstrated a remarkable capacity for change and adaptation. They began participating in a commercial economy, using metal tools, building their homes of logs as frontier set-tlers did, but in the process they also became dependent on firearms, metal tools, and other manufactured goods they had no capacity to produce themselves. Yet, until

A portrait of the Delaware chief Tishcohan by Gustavus Hesselius, painted in 1732. In his purse of chipmunk hide is a clay pipe, a common item of the Indian trade. Tishcohan was one of the Delaware leaders forced by Pennsylvania authorities into signing a fraudulent land deal that reversed that colony's history of fair dealing with Indians over land. He moved west to the Ohio River as settlers poured into his former homeland. SOURCE: The Historical Society of Pennsylvania.

Consider the environmental factors surrounding the spread of the horse in North America. Why did the Indians of the Great Plains exploit the potential of the horse more fully than others?
www.prenhall.com/faragher/map5.1

Growing Use of the Horse by Plains Indians   In the seventeenth and eighteenth centuries, Spanish settlers introduced horses into their New Mexican colony. Through trading and raiding, horses spread northward in streams both west and east of the Rocky Mountains. The horse, whose genetic ancestor had been native to the American continent in pre-Archaic times, offered the Indian peoples of the Great Plains the opportunity to create a distinctive hunting and warrior culture.

field raid, but they also traded with the English. In the Lower South, the Creeks similarly traded with both the French and the English as a means of maintaining their autonomy.

In general, the French had significantly better relations with native peoples than the English, but inevitably as they pursued their expansionist plans they came into conflict with Indian groups, and when opposed they could be just as cruel and violent as any other European power. In the early eighteenth century the Fox Indians blocked French passage between the Great Lakes and the upper Mississippi, attempting to make themselves into middlemen in the fur trade. Sporadic fighting continued until the French defeated the tribe in 1716. But Fox warriors rose again in 1726, and it took massive violence before the French were able to force the tribe into signing a treaty in 1738. On the lower Mississippi, the Natchez and Chickasaw tribes opposed the arrival of the French, engaging them in a series of bloody conflicts during the 1720s, which concluded only when the French decimated the Natchez in 1731.

The preeminent concern of the Indians of the eastern half of the continent was the tremendous growth of colonial population in the British Atlantic coastal colonies, especially the movement of settlers westward. In the 1730s and 1740s Pennsylvania perpetrated a series of fraudulent seizures of western lands from the Delawares. Particularly in the light of Pennsylvania's previous history of fair dealing with Indian peoples, these acts were another disturbing sign of things to come. Thus Indian alliances with the French resulted not from any great affection but from their great fear of British expansion.

Meanwhile, a long-term population decline continued among the Indian peoples of North America. Indian America continued to take a terrific beating from epidemics of European disease. There was no

the American Revolution, they continued to assert a proud independence and gained considerable skill at playing colonial powers off against one another. The Iroquois Five Nations battled the French and their Indian allies in King William's War, but in 1701 they signed a treaty of neutrality with France that kept them out of harm's way during the next round of conflicts. The Catholic Iroquois of Kahnawake sometimes supported the French, as they did by mounting the Deer-

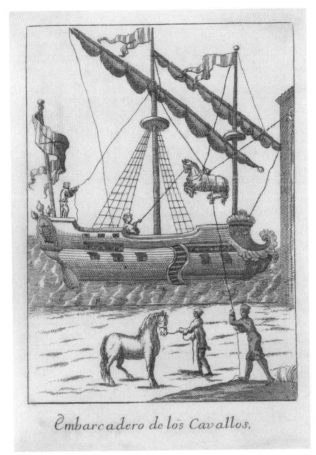

Spanish horses being unloaded in Mexico, from a sixteenth-century print by Manuel Osserio y Vega.

SOURCE: Courtesy of the Bancroft Library, University of California, Berkeley

systematic census of North American Indians before the nineteenth century, but historians estimate that from a high of 7 to 10 million Native Americans north of Mexico in 1500, the population had probably fallen to around a million by 1800. Thus, during the eighteenth century colonial population overtook and began to overwhelm the native population of the continent. Population loss did not affect all Indian tribes equally, however. Native peoples with a century or more of colonial contact and interaction had lost 50 percent or more of their numbers, but most Indian societies in the interior had yet to be struck by the horrible epidemics.

Colonization introduced other, less distressing changes in Indian cultures. By the early eighteenth century, Indians on the southern fringe of the Great Plains were using horses stolen from the Spanish in New Mexico. Horses enabled Indian hunters to exploit the buffalo herds much more efficiently, and on the base of this more productive economy a number of groups built a distinctive and elaborate nomadic culture. Great numbers of Indian peoples moved onto the plains during the eighteenth century, pulled by this new way of life, pushed by colonial invasions and disruptions radiating southwest from Canada and north from the Spanish borderlands. The invention of nomadic Plains Indian culture was another of the dramatic cultural innovations of the eighteenth century. The mounted Plains Indian, so often used as a symbol of native America, was actually a product of the colonial era.

The Spanish Borderlands

In the mid-eighteenth century what is today the Sunbelt of the United States formed the periphery of the largest and most prosperous European colony on the North American continent—the viceroyalty of New Spain, which included approximately 1 million Spanish colonists and mestizos and at least 2 million Indians. Mexico City, the administrative capital of New Spain, was the most sophisticated urban area in the Western Hemisphere, the site of one of the world's great universities, with broad avenues and spectacular architecture. New Spain's northern borderland provinces of Florida, Texas, New Mexico, and California, however, were far removed from this sophistication. Officials of the viceroyalty of New Spain, who oversaw these colonies, thought of them as buffer zones, protecting New Spain from the expanding colonial empires of Spain's New World rivals. Compared to the dynamic changes going on in the English colonies, society in the Spanish borderland was relatively static.

In Florida, the oldest of European colonies in North America, fierce fighting among the Spanish, the British, and the Indians had by the early eighteenth century reduced the colonial presence to little more than the forts of St. Augustine on the Atlantic and Pensacola on the Gulf of Mexico, each surrounded by small colonized territories populated with the families of Spanish troops. In their weakened condition, the Spanish had no choice but to establish cooperative relations with the Creek and Seminole Indians who dominated the region, as well as the hundreds of African American runaways who considered St. Augustine a refuge from the cruel slave regimes in Georgia and Carolina. Like the community of Kahnawake, eighteenth-century Florida included a growing mestizo population and a considerable number of free African Americans and Hispanicized Indians from the old missions.

Nearly 2,000 miles to the west, New Mexico was similarly isolated from the mainstream of New Spain. One Spanish observer characterized the province as "little populated and poverty-stricken, although

Regions in Eighteenth-Century North America   By the middle of the eighteenth century, European colonists had established a number of distinctive colonial regions in North America. The northern periphery of New Spain, the oldest and most prosperous European colony, stretched from Baja California to eastern Texas, then jumped to the settlements on the northern end of the Florida peninsula; cattle ranching was the dominant way of life in this thinly populated region. New France was like a great crescent, extending from the plantation communities along the Mississippi near New Orleans to the French colonial communities along the St. Lawrence; in between were isolated settlements and forts, connected only by the extensive French trading network.

endowed with natural resources." At midcentury New Mexico included some 20,000 Pueblo Indians (their numbers greatly reduced by disease since their first contact with Europeans) and perhaps 10,000 mestizo colonists. The prosperity of these colonists, who supported themselves with subsistence agriculture, was severely limited by a restrictive colonial economic policy that forced them to exchange their wool, pottery, buffalo hides, and buckskin for imported goods at unfavorable rates. Unlike the colonial population of Florida, however, the settlements of New Mexicans were gradually expanding, following the valleys and streams that led east and north from the original colonial outposts scattered along the upper Rio Grande.

The Spanish also founded new northern outposts during the eighteenth century. Concerned about French colonization of the Mississippi Valley, they established a number of military posts or *presidios* on the

fringes of the colony of Louisiana and in 1716 began the construction of a string of Franciscan missions among the Indian peoples of Texas. By 1750 the settlement of San Antonio had become the center of a

Region	Population
New France	70,000
New England	400,000
New York	100,000
Pennsylvania	230,000
Chesapeake	390,000
Lower South	100,000
Backcountry	100,000
Northern New Spain	20,000
Indian America	1,500,000

The church of San Xavier del Bac, constructed in the late eighteenth century, is located a few miles south of the city of Tucson, where Jesuit Father Eusebio Kino founded a mission among the Pima Indians in 1700. Known as the White Dove of the Desert, it is acclaimed as the most striking example of Spanish colonial architecture in the United States.

SOURCE: Photograph by Jack W. Dykinga.

developing frontier province. The Spanish also established new colonial outposts west of New Mexico, in what is today southern Arizona. In the 1690s, Jesuit missionaries, led by Father Eusebio Kino, founded missions among the desert Indians of the lower Colorado River and Gila River valleys. Mission San Xavier del Bac near Tucson is acclaimed the most striking example of Spanish colonial architecture in the United States. Cattle ranching, introduced by the Jesuits, and farming spread along the lower Rio Grande Valley; in fact, ranching continued to define the region's economy for the next 200 years.

Midcentury also found the Spanish considering new settlements along the California coast. Juan Cabrillo, an associate of Hernán Cortés, had first explored the coastal waters in 1542 and was the first European to sail into the fine harbor at San Diego. In 1603 explorer Sebastián Vizcaíno had come upon Monterey Bay. The Spanish did little to follow up on these finds, but in 1769, acting on rumors of Russian expansion along the northern Pacific coast (for a discussion of Russian America, see Chapter 9), officials in Mexico City ordered Gaspar de Portolá, governor of what is now Baja California, to establish a Spanish presence in the north. With him were Franciscan missionaries led by Junípero Serra, president of the missions in Baja. At the harbor of San Diego, Portolá and Serra founded the first mission and pueblo complex in present-day California. Portolá then proceeded overland, becoming the first European to explore the interior valleys and mountains, and in 1770 he and Serra established their headquarters at Monterey Bay on the central coast. Two years later Juan Bautista de Anza established an overland route across the blistering deserts connecting Arizona and California, and in 1776 he led a colonizing expedition that founded the pueblo of San Francisco. Over the next fifty years the number of California settlements grew to include twenty-one missions and a half-dozen presidios and pueblos, including the town of Los Angeles. Founded in 1781 by a group of mestizo settlers from Sinaloa, Mexico, by the end of the century Los Angeles, with a population of only 300, was California's largest town.

For the Spanish, conquest demanded conversion to Catholicism, which, according to theory, would lead Indians toward "civilization." Like the efforts of the Jesuits at Kahnawake and elsewhere in New France, the Spanish experiment in cultural transformation was designed to make Indians into Catholics and loyal Spanish subjects by educating them and putting them to work raising cattle and crops. The most extensive mission project took place in California, where under the direction of priests thousands of Indian laborers produced a flourishing local economy based on irrigated farming as well as horse, cattle, and sheep ranching. San Gabriel, near the pueblo of Los Angeles, was one of the most prosperous missions, where large vineyards and orchards produced fine wines and brandies. Indian people also constructed the adobe and stone churches, built on Spanish and Moorish patterns, whose ruins symbolize California's colonial society. To keep the system functioning, the Franciscan missionaries resorted to cruel and sometimes violent means of controlling their Indian subjects: shackles, solitary confinement, and whipping posts. Indians resisted from the very beginning. In 1775 the villagers around San Diego rose up and killed several priests. The history of many missions was punctuated by revolts, but the arms and organization of Spanish soldiers were usually sufficient to suppress the uprisings. Another form of protest was flight: whole villages sometimes fled. Aggressive tribes in the hills and deserts, however, often proved even more threatening than the Spanish, so many mission Indians remained despite the harsh discipline.

Foreign observers noted the despondency of California's mission Indians. "I have never seen any of them laugh," one European visitor wrote. "I have never seen a single one look anyone in the face. They have the air of taking no interest in anything." Overwork, inadequate nutrition, overcrowding, poor sanitation, and epidemic disease contributed to death rates that exceeded birthrates. During the period of the mission system the native population of California fell by at least 25 percent.

As the prominence of mission settlements in California, Texas, and New Mexico suggests, the Catholic Church played a dominant role in the community life of the borderlands. In the eighteenth century, religion was no private affair. It was a deadly serious business dividing nations into warring camps, and the Spanish considered themselves the special protectors of the traditions of Rome. The object of colonization, one colonial promoter wrote in 1584, was "enlarging the glorious gospel of Christ, and leading the infinite multitudes of these simple people that are in error into the right and perfect way of salvation." Although these are the words of the English imperialist Richard Hakluyt, they could as easily have come from the Spanish padres Kino or Serra or the Jesuit missionaries at Kahnawake. There was no tradition of religious dissent. Certain of the truth of their "right and perfect way," the Spanish could see no reason for tolerating the errors of others.

The French Crescent

In France, as in Spain, church and state were closely interwoven. During the seventeenth century the French prime ministers, Cardinal Richelieu and Cardinal Mazarin, laid out a fundamentally Catholic imperial policy, and under their guidance colonists constructed a second Catholic empire in North America. In 1674 church and state collaborated in establishing the bishopric of Quebec, which founded local seminaries, oversaw the appointment and review of priests, and laid the foundation of the resolutely Catholic culture of New France. Meanwhile, Jesuit missionaries continued to carry Catholicism deep into the continent.

The number of French colonists rose from fewer than 15,000 in 1700 to more than 70,000 at midcentury. During the eighteenth century the French

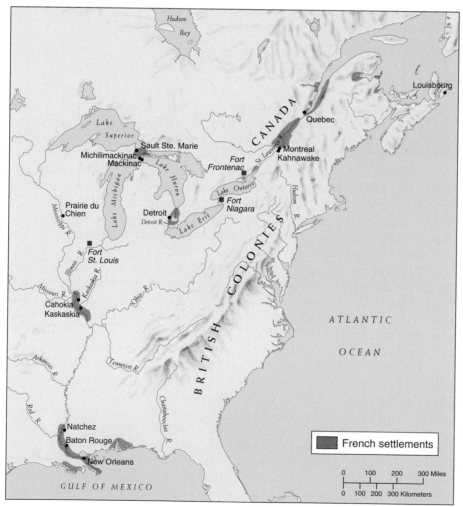

The French Crescent   The French empire in North America was based on a series of alliances and trade relations with Indian nations linking a great crescent of colonies, settlements, and outposts that extended from the mouth of the St. Lawrence River, through the Great Lakes, and down the Mississippi River to the Gulf of Mexico. In 1713 Acadia was ceded to the British, but the French established the fortress of Louisbourg to anchor the eastern end of the crescent.

used their trade network and alliances with the Indians to establish a great crescent of colonies, military posts, and settlements that extended from the mouth of the St. Lawrence River southwest through the Great Lakes, then down the Mississippi River to the Gulf of Mexico. Although the maritime colony of Acadia was ceded to the British in 1713 (see Chapter 4), the French anchored the crescent on the northeast by founding the fortress of Louisbourg on Ile Royale (Cape Breton Island), which soon became the most important French port in the North Atlantic. The colony of Louisiana formed the other end of the crescent at the mouth of the Mississippi. Over this vast territory the French laid a thin colonial veneer, the beginning of what they planned as a great continental empire that would limit the Protestant British to a narrow strip of Atlantic coastline. By the middle of the century, the French were moving into trans-Mississippi country, ascending the Missouri and Arkansas rivers and planting traders within Indian communities deep in the interior. French colonial society was more dynamic than the Spanish, although less transformative than the English along the Atlantic coast.

At the heart of the French empire in North America were the farming communities of the colony of Canada along the banks of the St. Lawrence, including the towns of Montreal and Quebec. There were also farming communities in the Illinois country, which shipped wheat down the Mississippi to supply the booming sugar plantations of Louisiana. By the mid-eighteenth century, those plantations, extending along the river from Natchez and Baton Rouge to New Orleans, had become the most profitable French enterprise in North America.

One of the most distinctive French stamps on the North American landscape were the "long lots" stretching back from the rivers that provided each settler family a share of good bottomland to farm as well as frontage on the waterways, the "interstate highway system" of the French Crescent. Long lots were laid out along the lower Mississippi River in Louisiana and at sites on the upper Mississippi such as Kaskaskia and Prairie du Chien, as well as at the strategic passages of the Great Lakes, the communities of Mackinac, Sault Ste. Marie, and Detroit. In 1750, Detroit was a stockaded town with a military garrison, a small administrative center, several stores, a Catholic church, and 100 households of *métis* (French for mestizo) families. French and métis farmers worked the land along the Detroit River, not far from communities inhabited by more than 6,000 Ottawa, Potawatomi, and Huron Indians.

Communities of this sort that combined both French and Indian elements were in the tradition of the inclusive frontier, supported by a commercial economy in furs, maple sugar, timber, and some mining, in which Indians, French, and métis all participated. Detroit

The persistence of French colonial long lots in the pattern of modern landholding is clear in this enhanced satellite photograph of the Mississippi River near New Orleans. Long lots, the characteristic form of property holding in New France, were designed to offer as many settlers as possible a share of good bottomland as well as a frontage on the waterways, which served as the basic transportation network.

SOURCE: EROS Data Center, U.S. Geological Survey.

looked like "an old French village," said one observer, except that its houses were "mostly covered with bark," in Indian style. "It is not uncommon to see a Frenchman with Indian shoes and stockings, without breeches, wearing a strip of woolen cloth to cover what decency requires him to conceal," wrote another. "Yet at the same time he wears a fine ruffled shirt and a laced waistcoat, with a fine handkerchief on his head." Detroit had much of the character of the mixed community of Kahnawake on the St. Lawrence.

Family and kinship in these interior communities were also cast in the Indian pattern. Households often consisted of several related families, but wives limited their births, having on average only two or three children. There were arranged marriages and occasional polygamy, but women had easy access to divorce and enjoyed property rights. Yet the people focused their activities on commerce and identified themselves overwhelmingly as Catholic. More often than not choosing a path of mutual accommodation, the French and Indians established some of the most interesting and distinct of North American communities.

New England

Just as New Spain and New France had their official church, so did the people of New England: local communities in all the New England colonies but Rhode Island were governed by Puritan congregations. Under the plan established in Massachusetts, the local church of a community was free to run its own affairs under the guidance of the General Court (the governor and the representatives selected by the towns). The Puritan colonies allotted each congregation a tract of communal land. Church members divided this land among themselves on the basis of status and seniority, laying out central villages such as Deerfield and building churches (called meetinghouses) that were maintained through taxation. Adult male church members constituted the freemen of the town, and thus there was very little distinction between religious and secular authority. At the town meeting the freemen chose their minister, voted on his salary and support, and elected local men to offices ranging from town clerk to fence viewer.

The Puritan tradition was a curious mix of freedom and repression. Although local communities had considerable autonomy, they were tightly bound by the restrictions of the Puritan faith and the General Court. Contrary to widespread beliefs, the Puritans did not come to America to create a society where religion could be freely practiced. Rather, they sought to establish their own version of the "right and perfect way," which placed severe restraints on individuals. Not only did the Puritans exile dissidents such as Roger Williams and Anne Hutchinson who threatened the religious orthodoxy of Massachusetts (see Chapter 3), they banned Anglicans and Baptists and exiled, jailed, whipped, and even executed members of the Society of Friends, who came repeatedly among them to preach the tenets of the Quaker faith.

One of the first formal arguments for religious toleration was made by New Englander Roger Williams, leader of dissenting Rhode Island. "Forced worship," he wrote, "stinks in God's nostrils." After the religious excesses of the English civil war, this argument began to have an appeal. In 1661, King Charles II ordered a stop to religious persecution in Massachusetts. The new climate of opinion was best expressed by the English philosopher John Locke in his *Letter on Tolerance* (1688). Churches were voluntary societies, he argued, and could work only through persuasion. That a religion was sanctioned by the state was no evidence of its truth, because different nations had different official religions. Consequently, the state had no legitimate concern with religious belief. The Toleration Act, passed by Parliament in 1689, was at first resisted by the Puritans. Under pressure from English authorities, however, Massachusetts and Connecticut reluctantly allowed other Protestant denominations to begin practicing their religions openly in 1700, although Congregationalism (as the Puritan Church had become because the congregations governed themselves) continued to be supported officially through taxation. By the 1730s there were Anglican, Baptist, and Presbyterian congregations in many New England towns.

As towns grew too large for the available land, groups of residents left together, "hiving off" to form new churches and towns elsewhere. The region was knit together by an intricate network of roads and rivers. Seventy-five years after the Indians of southern New England suffered their final defeat in King Philip's War (see Chapter 3), Puritan farm communities had taken up most of the available land of Massachusetts, Connecticut, and Rhode Island, leaving only a few communities of Pequots, Narragansets, and Wampanoags on restricted reservations. Northern Algonquians and Catholic Iroquois allied with the French in Quebec, however, maintained a defensive barrier that prevented New Englanders from expanding northward into Maine, New Hampshire, and the region later called Vermont. Deerfield represented the far northern limit of safe settlement. By midcentury, then, as the result of growing population, New England was reaching the limit of its land supply.

The Middle Colonies

The colony of New York had one of the most ethnically diverse populations on the continent, in striking contrast to the ethnically homogeneous neighboring New England colonies of Connecticut and Massachusetts. At midcentury, society along the lower Hudson River, including the counties in northern New Jersey, was a veritable mosaic of ethnic communities: the Dutch of Flatbush, the Huguenots of New Rochelle, the Flemish of Bergen County, and the Scots of Perth Amboy were but a few. African Americans, both slave and free, made up more than 15 percent of the lower Hudson population. Congregations of Puritans, Baptists, Quakers, and Catholics worshiped without legal hindrance. New York City was also home to the first Jewish community in the country, established in 1654. Several hundred Jewish families attended services in North America's first synagogue, built in 1730. There was a great deal of intermingling (as there was at places such as Kahnawake), but these different communities would long retain their ethnic and religious distinctions, which made New York something of a cultural "salad bowl" rather than a "melting pot."

New York City grew by leaps and bounds in the eighteenth century, but because the elite who had inherited the rich lands and great manors along the

The Turner House (immortalized by Nathaniel Hawthorne in his novel *The House of the Seven Gables*) in Salem, Massachusetts, was constructed in the seventeenth century. In this style of architecture, function prevailed over form as structures grew to accommodate their residents; rooms were added where and when they were needed. In England, wood for building was scarce, but the abundance of forests in North America created the conditions for a golden age of wood construction.

SOURCE: Photograph courtesy Peabody Essex Museum.

yet made a good Christian," he argued. Indeed, the Quakers were opposed to all signs of rank, refusing to doff their hats to superiors but greeting all comers, whatever their station, with the extended handshake of brotherhood. To a remarkable extent, these attitudes extended to relations between the sexes as well. English founder George Fox had proclaimed that "in souls there is no sex," and among American Friends, women preached equally with men.

These Quaker attitudes were well suited to the ethnically and religiously diverse population of Pennsylvania. Although the Society of Friends remained the affiliation of the governing elite, it never became an established church. Most German immigrants were Lutherans or Calvinists, most North Britons were Presbyterians, and there were plenty of Anglicans and Baptists as well.

upper Hudson chose to rent to tenants rather than to sell, this region was much less attractive to immigrants. By contrast, Pennsylvania was what one German immigrant called "heaven for farmers." The colony's Quaker proprietors were willing to sell land to anyone who could pay the modest prices. Thus as the region around New York City filled up, immigrants by the thousand made the decision to land at Philadelphia, Pennsylvania's growing port on the Delaware River. During the eighteenth century the population of this region and an extended area that encompassed portions of New Jersey, Delaware, and Maryland grew more dramatically than any other in North America. Here, immigration played the dominant role in achieving the astonishing annual growth rate of nearly 4 percent. Boasting some of the best farmland in North America, the region was soon exporting abundant produce through Philadelphia.

The Quakers who had founded Pennsylvania quickly became a minority, but, unlike the Puritans, they were generally comfortable with religious and ethnic pluralism. Many of the founders of the Society of Friends had been imprisoned for their beliefs in pre-Restoration England, and they were determined to prevent a repetition of this injustice in their own province. William Penn himself had been prominent in the struggle for religious toleration "Force never

The institutions of government were another pillar of community organization. Colonial officials appointed justices of the peace from among the leading local men, and these justices provided judicial authority for the countryside. Property-owning farmers chose their own local officials. Country communities were tied together by kinship bonds and by bartering and trading among neighbors. The substantial stone houses and great barns of the Pennsylvania countryside testified to the social stability and prosperity of this system. The communities of the middle colonies, however, were more loosely bound than those of New England. Rates of mobility were considerably higher, with about half the population moving in any given decade. Because land was sold in individual lots rather than in communal parcels, farmers tended to disperse themselves at will over the open countryside. Villages gradually developed at crossroads and ferries but with little forethought or planning. It was Pennsylvania, which emphasized individual settlement, that provided the basic model for American expansion.

The Backcountry

By 1750 Pennsylvania's exploding population had pushed beyond the first range of the Appalachian highlands. Settlers occupied the northern reaches of the Great Valley, which extended southwest from

This two-story log house, built in Pennsylvania in the early eighteenth century, is one of the oldest surviving examples of the method and style of log construction introduced in America by the Scandinavian colonists on the lower Delaware River. Learning New World farming and woodland hunting techniques from the Indians, these settlers forged a tradition of settlement that proved enormously successful for pioneers. SOURCE: Courtesy Henry Glassie.

Pennsylvania into Virginia. Although they hoped to become commercial farmers, these settlers began more modestly, planting Indian corn and raising hogs, hunting in the woods for meat and furs, and building log cabins. This strategy had originated with the settlers of the New Sweden colony on the lower Delaware River. Scandinavian immigrants brought their hunting traditions and introduced log cabin construction to North America. From the Delaware Indians they incorporated the methods of New World farming and woodland hunting, just as the Indians took from them the use of firearms and metal tools and began to build log structures of their own. These were some of the most successful cross-cultural adaptations of the eighteenth century. The movement into the Pennsylvania and Virginia backcountry that began during the 1720s was the first of the great pioneer treks that would take Americans into the continental interior. Many, perhaps most, of these pioneers held no legal title to the lands they occupied; they simply hacked out and defended their squatters' claims from Indian tribes and all other comers. Many of these settlers came from the northern borders of England and Ireland, where there was considerable clan and ethnic violence, so they adapted well to the violence of the backcountry. To the Delawares and Shawnees, who had been pushed into the interior, or the Cherokees, who occupied the Appalachian highlands to the south, these pioneers presented a new and deadly threat. Rising fears and resentments over this expanding population triggered much eighteenth-century warfare.

Through a series of interactive maps, look at the spread of English settlement in the eighteenth century. How did the movement into the backcountry affect the relations among colonists, Indians, and English authorities?
www.prenhall.com/faragher/map5.2

Spread of Settlement: Movement into the Backcountry, 1720–1760   The spread of settlement from 1720 to 1760 shows the movement of population into the backcountry during the midcentury.

One of the distinctive characteristics of the backcountry was the settlers' disdain for rank. "The rain don't know broadcloth from bluejeans," they said. But the myth of frontier equality was simply that. Most pioneers owned little or no land, whereas "big men" held great tracts and dominated local communities with their bombastic style of personal leadership. Here the men were warriors, the women workers. The story was told of one pioneer whose wife began to "jaw at" him. "He pulled off his breeches and threw them down to her, telling her to 'put them on and wear them.'"

The South

The Chesapeake and the Lower South were triracial societies, with intermingled communities of white colonists and black slaves, along with substantial Indian communities living on the fringes of colonial settlement. Much of the population growth of the region resulted from the forced migration of enslaved Africans, who by 1750 made up 40 percent of the population. Colonial settlement had filled not only the Tidewater area of the southern Atlantic coast but a good deal of the Piedmont as well. Specializing in rice, tobacco, and other commercial crops, these colonies were overwhelmingly rural. Farms and plantations were dispersed across the countryside, and villages or towns were few.

English authorities made the Church of England the state religion in the Chesapeake colonies. Residents paid taxes to support the Church and were required to attend services. No other churches were allowed into Virginia and Maryland, (despite its being founded by Catholics) and dissenters were excluded or exiled. Before the 1750s, the Toleration Act was little enforced in the South; at the same time, the Anglican establishment was internally weak. It maintained neither a colonial bishop nor local institutions for training clergy.

Along the rice coast, the dominant institution of social life was the large plantation. Transforming the tangle of woods and swamps along the region's rivers into an ordered pattern of dams, dikes, and flooded fields required a heavy capital investment. Consequently, only men of means could undertake rice cultivation. By midcentury, established rice plantations typically were dominated by a large main house, generally located on a spot of high ground overlooking the fields. Drayton Hall near Charleston, a mansion of the period that still survives, was built of pink brick in classically symmetrical style, with hand-carved interior moldings of imported Caribbean mahogany. Nearby, but a world apart, were the slave quarters, rough wooden cabins lining two sides of a muddy pathway near the outbuildings and barns. In this contrast between "big house" and "quarters," the Lower South was the closest thing in North America to the societies of the Caribbean sugar islands.

Because tobacco, unlike rice, could be grown profitably in small plots, the Chesapeake included a greater variety of farmers and a correspondingly diverse landscape. Tobacco quickly drained the soil of its nutrients, and plantings had to be shifted to fresh ground every few years. Former tobacco land could be planted with corn for several years but then required twenty years or more of rest before reuse. The landscape was thus a patchwork of fields, many in various stages of ragged second growth. The poorest farmers lived in wooden cabins little better than the shacks of the slaves. More prosperous farm families lived with two or three slaves in houses that nevertheless were considerably smaller than the substantial homes of New England.

In the Lower South, where the plantations were little worlds unto themselves, there was little community life outside the plantation. But by midcentury the Chesapeake had given rise to well-developed neighborhoods based on kinship networks and economic connections. Encouraging the developing sense of community more than any other institution was the county court, which held both executive and judicial power. On court day, white people of all ranks held a great gathering that included public business, horse racing, and perhaps a barbecue. The gentleman justices of the county, appointed by the governor, included the heads of the leading planter families. These men in turn selected the grand jury, composed of substantial freeholders. One of the most significant bonding forces in this free white population was a growing sense of racial solidarity in response to the increasing proportion of African slaves dispersed throughout the neighborhoods.

Traditional Culture in the New World

In each of these North American colonial societies the family and kinship, the church, and the local community were the most significant factors in everyday life. Throughout the continent, colonists tended to live much as they had in their European homelands at the time their colonies were settled. Thus, the residents of New Mexico, Quebec, and New England continued to be attached to the religious passions of the seventeenth century long after their mother countries had put those religious controversies aside in favor of imperial geopolitics. Nostalgia for Europe helped to fix a conservative colonial attitude toward culture.

These were oral cultures, depending on the transmission of information by the spoken word rather than through print, on the passage of traditions through storytelling, song, music, and crafts. North American colonial folk cultures, traditional and suspicious of change, preserved an essentially medieval worldview. The rhythms of life were regulated by the hours of sunlight and the seasons of the year. People rose with the sun and went to bed soon after it went down. The demands of the season determined their working routines. They farmed with simple tools and were subject to the whims of nature, for drought, flood, or pestilence might quickly sweep away their efforts. Experience told them that the natural world imposed limitations within which men and women had to learn to live. Even patterns of reproduction conformed to nature's cycle: in nearly every European colonial community of North America the number of births peaked in late winter, then fell to a low point during the summer. For African

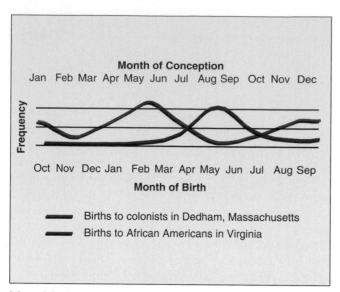

Monthly Frequency of Successful Conceptions
Human reproduction in colonial America corresponded to cycles. But European colonists and African American slaves had different patterns, with white births peaking in March, black births peaking in May and June. Historians do not yet know the cause of this variation, but it is probably tied to old English and African traditions.

SOURCE: James A. Henretta and Gregory H. Nobles, *Evolution and Revolution: American Society, 1600–1820* (Lexington, MA.: Heath, 1987), 37; Mechal Sobel, *The World They Made Together: Black and White Values in Eighteenth-Century Virginia* (Princeton, NJ: Princeton University Press, 1987), 67.

Americans, by contrast, births peaked in early summer. Historians have not yet accounted for this intriguing pattern or provided an explanation for the differences between white and black families, but apparently there was some "inner" seasonal clock tied to old European and African patterns. Human sexual activity itself seemed to fluctuate with the rural working demands created by the seasons.

These were also communal cultures. In Quebec, villagers worked side by side to repair the roads; in New Mexico they collectively maintained the irrigation canals; and in New England they gathered in town meetings to decide the dates when common fields were to be plowed, sowed, and harvested. When in 1620 the Pilgrims and the other *Mayflower* passengers signed their compact, promising "due submission" to "the general good," they explicitly set down principles with which most North American colonists could agree. Even the artifacts of everyday life reveal this collective emphasis. Houses offered little privacy, with families often sleeping together in the same chamber, sitting together on benches rather than in chairs, and taking their supper from a common bowl or trencher. For most North American colonists of the mid-eighteenth century, the community was more important than the individual.

Throughout North America, most colonists continued the traditional European occupation of working the land. Plantation agriculture was designed to be a commercial system, in which crops were commodities for sale. Commercial farming also developed in some particularly fertile areas, notably southeastern Pennsylvania, which became known as the breadbasket of North America, as well as in the country surrounding colonial cities such as New York, Boston, and Quebec. The majority of the farmers of eighteenth-century North America, however, grew crops and raised livestock for their own needs or for local barter, and communities were largely self-sufficient. Most farmers attempted to produce small surpluses as well, which they sold to pay their taxes and buy some manufactured goods. But rather than specializing in the production of one or two crops for sale, they attempted to remain as independent of the market as possible, diversifying their activities. The primary goal was ownership of land and the assurance that children and descendants would be able to settle within the community on lands nearby.

Rural households often practiced crafts or trades as a sideline. Farm men were also blacksmiths, coopers, weavers, or carpenters. Some farm women were independent traders in dairy products or eggs. Others served the community as midwives and medicinal experts. In one Maine community, for example, the midwife Martha Ballard delivered 797 babies over twenty-seven years, and both male and female patients came to her for salves, pills, syrups, ointments, or advice.

In colonial cities, artisans and craftsmen worked at their trades full time, organizing themselves according to the European craft system. In the colonial cities of the Atlantic coast, carpenters, ironmakers, blacksmiths, shipwrights, and scores of other tradesmen had their own self-governing associations. Young men who wished to pursue a trade served several years as apprentices, working in exchange for learning the skills and secrets of the craft. After completing their apprenticeships they sought employment in a shop. Their search often required them to migrate to some other area, thus becoming "journeymen." Most craftsmen remained at the journeyman level for their whole careers. But by building a good name and carefully saving, journeymen hoped to become master craftsmen, opening shops and employing journeymen and apprentices of their own. As in farming, the ultimate goal was independence.

With the exception of midwifery, there were few opportunities for women outside the household. By law, husbands held managerial rights over family property, but widows received support in the form of a one-third lifetime interest, known as "dower," in a deceased husband's real estate (the rest of the estate being divided among the heirs). And in certain occupations, such as printing (which had a tradition of employing women), widows succeeded their husbands in business. As a result, some colonial women played active roles in eighteenth-century journalism. Ann Smith Franklin, Benjamin Franklin's sister-in-law, took over the operation of her husband's Rhode Island shop after his death. Widow Cornelia Smith Bradford continued to publish her deceased husband's Philadelphia paper and was an important force in publishing throughout the 1750s.

The Frontier Heritage

The colonial societies of eighteenth-century North America also shared perspectives unique to their common frontier heritage. European colonists came from Old World societies in which land was scarce and monopolized by property-owning elites. They settled in a continent where, for the most part, land was abundant and cheap. This was probably the most important distinction between North America and Europe. American historians once tied the existence of this "free land" directly to the development of democracy. But the colonial experience encouraged assumptions that were anything but democratic.

One of the most important of those colonial assumptions was the popular acceptance of forced labor. A woman of eighteenth-century South Carolina once offered advice on how to achieve a good living. "Get a few slaves," she declared, and "beat them well to make them work hard." There was a labor shortage

A spinner and carpenter from *The Book of Trades*, an eighteenth-century British survey of the crafts practiced in colonial America. In colonial cities artisans organized themselves into the traditional European craft system, with apprentices, journeymen, and masters. There were few opportunities for the employment of women outside the household, but women sometimes earned income by establishing sidelines as midwives or spinners.

SOURCE: The Granger Collection.

throughout all the colonies. In a land where free men and women could work for themselves on their own plot of ground, there was little incentive to work for wages. Thus the use of forced labor was one of the few ways a landowner could secure an agricultural workforce. In the Spanish borderlands, captured Apache children were made lifetime servants, and an Indian slave trade flourished through the eighteenth century. In Quebec one could see African American slaves from the French Caribbean working side-by-side with enslaved Indians captured by other tribes in the West and sold to French traders. In Philadelphia, according to Benjamin Franklin, wages for free workers were so high that most of the unskilled labor was "performed chiefly by indentured servants." All the colonists came from European cultures that believed in social hierarchy and subordination, and involuntary servitude was easily incorporated into their worldview.

At least half the immigrants to eighteenth-century British America arrived as indentured servants. This system allowed poor immigrants to arrange passage across the Atlantic in exchange for four or five years of service in America. Usually indentured servants were single men, often skilled artisans. Sometimes families without means emigrated as "redemptioners." Under this system, they arranged with the ship's owner to pay their passage upon arrival in North America. If no one in the colonies stepped forth to pay, they sold themselves into service for the payment. Family members were sometimes separated. In addition, during the eighteenth century the British sent over, mostly to the Chesapeake, some 50,000 convicts sentenced to seven or fourteen years at hard labor. One historian, accounting for the cost of passage and upkeep, estimates that indentured servants earned their masters, on average, about fifty pounds sterling over their terms of service, the equivalent of something like four or five thousand dollars in today's values. But at the conclusion of their terms of service, eighteenth-century servants enjoyed more opportunity than their seventeenth-century counterparts, probably because of the rise in overall prosperity in the British colonies. Over the course of the century the chance of former servants achieving positions of moderate comfort rose from one in five in 1700 to better than fifty-fifty by 1750. The majority of redemptioners, for example, appear to have become small farmers.

The expectation of property ownership was a second important assumption that flowed from the frontier heritage and abundance of land in colonial America. This expectation led to rising popular demands in all regions that more and more land be taken from the Indian inhabitants and opened to white settlement. Some colonists justified such wars of dispossession by arguing, as Puritans did, that Indians deserved to lose their lands because they had failed to use their lands to the utmost capacity. Others simply maintained that Indians should be dispossessed because they were "savages." But whatever their specific justifications, the majority of colonists, whether British, Spanish, or French, accepted the violence and brutality directed against Indians tribes as an essential aspect of colonial life. This attitude was as true of inclusive as exclusive societies—with the difference that in the former, native peoples were incorporated into colonial society, while in the latter, tribes were pushed from the frontier. Thus did the Puritan minister Cotton Mather praise Hannah Dustin, a New England woman who escaped her captors during King William's War by killing and scalping nine sleeping Indians, including two women and six children. With this as the prevailing attitude, one can understand why Eunice Williams was hesitant to return to Deerfield after she had married an Indian.

DIVERGING SOCIAL AND POLITICAL PATTERNS

Despite these important similarities among the colonial regions of North America, in the eighteenth century the experience of the British colonies began to diverge sharply from that of the French and Spanish. Immigration, economic growth, and provincial political struggles all pushed British colonists in a radically new direction.

Population Growth and Immigration

All the colonial regions of North America experienced unprecedented growth in the eighteenth century. "Our people must at least be doubled every twenty years," wrote Benjamin Franklin in a remarkable 1751 essay on population, and he was nearly right. In 1700 there were 290,000 colonists north of Mexico; fifty years later they had grown to approximately 1.3 million, an average annual growth rate of about 3 percent. Typical preindustrial societies grow at rates of less than 1 percent per year, approximately the pace of Europe's expansion in the eighteenth century. But the colonial societies of North America experienced what English economist Thomas Malthus, writing at the end of the century, described as "a rapidity of increase probably without parallel in history."

High fertility played an important role in this extraordinary growth. It was common for women in the British colonies to bear seven or more children during their childbearing years, and colonial women in the French villages along the St. Lawrence or the towns of New Mexico were equally fertile. In addition, mortality rates were low: in most colonial areas there were fewer

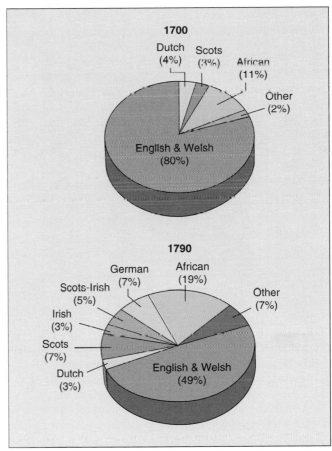

The Ancestry of the British Colonial Population
The legacy of eighteenth-century immigration to the British colonies was a population of unprecedented ethnic diversity.

SOURCE: Thomas L. Purvis, "The European Ancestry of the United States Population," *William and Mary Quarterly* 61 (1984): 85–101.

Ethnic Groups in Eighteenth-Century British North America The first federal census, taken in 1790, revealed remarkable ethnic diversity. New England was filled with people from the British Isles, but the rest of the colonies were a patchwork. Most states had at least three different ethnic groups within their borders, and although the English and Scots-Irish were heavily represented in all colonies, in some they had strong competition from Germans (eastern and southern Pennsylvania) and from African peoples (Virginia and South Carolina).

than 30 deaths for every 1,000 persons, a death rate 15 or 20 percent lower than rates in Europe. Moreover, levels of infant mortality were low. Blessed with fertile lands and the effectiveness of Indian agricultural techniques, North America had no famines. For the colonists, North America was a remarkably healthy environment.

Yet, although all North American colonial societies had high fertility rates, the British colonies grew far more rapidly than did those of other nations. The difference is explained by immigration. The Spanish,

fearful of depleting their population at home, severely limited the migration of their own subjects to their colonies, and absolutely forbade the immigration of foreigners. The French, dedicated to keeping their North American colonies exclusively Catholic, ignored the desire of Protestant Huguenots to emigrate. Instead they sent thousands of Catholic *engagés* to Canada, but most returned, discouraged by the climate and the lack of commercial opportunity. The English, however, sent an estimated 400,000 of their own countrymen to populate their North American colonies during the seventeenth and eighteenth centuries. Moreover, the British were the only colonial power to encourage the immigration of foreign nationals. William Penn was the first colonial official to promote the immigration of western Europeans, sending agents to recruit settlers in Holland, France, and the German principalities along the Rhine River in the 1680s. His

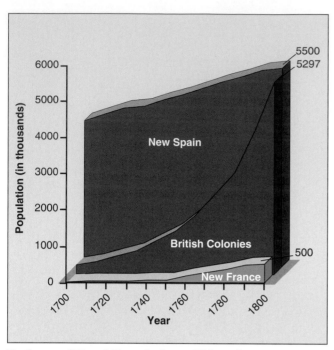

Estimated Total Population of New Spain, New France, and the British North American Colonies, 1700–1780 Although the populations of all three North American colonial empires grew in the eighteenth century, the explosive growth of the British colonies was unmatched.

SOURCE: *Historical Statistics of the United States* (Washington, D.C.: Government Printing Office, 1976), 1168.

experiment proved so successful that the leaders of other British colonies soon were sending recruiting agents of their own to Europe. By the second quarter of the eighteenth century, shippers had developed a system that contemporaries called the "trade in strangers." Carrying migrants provided English and Dutch merchants with a way of making a profit on the westbound voyages of vessels sent to North America to bring back tobacco, rice, indigo, timber, and flour. The eighteenth-century trade in strangers was the prototype for the great movements of European immigrants in the nineteenth century.

Further encouraging this development, most of the British colonies enacted liberal naturalization laws in the early eighteenth century, allowing immigrants who professed Protestantism and swore allegiance to the British crown to become free "denizens" with all the privileges of natural-born subjects. In 1740, Parliament passed a general naturalization law that extended that policy to all the British colonies. The new legislation continued to prohibit the naturalization of Catholic and Jewish immigrants, however, and these groups remained tiny minorities in the British

colonies. Still, immigration to what would become the United States was characterized by extraordinary diversity. First there were the Africans, the largest group to come to North America in the colonial period, larger even than the English. Forced relocation brought an estimated 600,000 to the colonies before the official end of the slave trade to the United States in 1807. Then there was the massive emigration from the northern British Isles. Squeezed by economic hardship, an estimated 150,000 Highland Scots and Protestant Irish from the Ulster region (known as the "Scots-Irish") emigrated to North America in the eighteenth century. German-speakers were next in importance; at least 125,000 of them settled in the colonies, where they became known as the "Dutch" (from *Deutsch*, the German-language term for "German"). It is worth noting again that a majority of these European immigrants came as bonded servants.

The European crossing of the Atlantic was nowhere near as tramatic as the African Middle Passage, but it was harrowing. One immigrant described a voyage to Philadelphia in which several hundred people were packed like sardines in the ship's hold. "The ship is filled with pitiful signs of distress," he wrote, "smells, fumes, horrors, vomiting, various kinds of sea sickness, fever, dysentery, headaches, heat, constipation, boils, scurvy, cancer, mouth-rot, and similar afflictions. In such misery all the people on board pray and cry pitifully together." In 1750, Pennsylvania was finally compelled to pass a law to prevent the overcrowding of ships filled with indentured passengers.

The results of the first federal census of the United States in 1790 provide a summary of this significant eighteenth-century experiment in ethnic diversity and cultural encounter. Less than 50 percent of the population was English in origin, and nearly 20 percent was African; 15 percent were Irish, Scots-Irish, or Scots and 7 percent German, with other ethnic backgrounds making up the remainder. There were significant differences by region. New England remained more than three-quarters English, but Pennsylvania was nearly 40 percent German. The backcountry was populated largely by Scots-Irish. The population of the coastal South was nearly half African. The legacy of eighteenth-century immigration to the British colonies was thus a population of unprecedented diversity.

Social Class

Although traditional working roles were transferred to North America, attempts to transplant the European class system by creating land monopolies were far less successful. In New France the landowning seigneurs claimed privileges similar to those enjoyed by their

Espanol con India.
Mestizo.

Mestizo con Espanola.
Castiza.

Castizo con Espanola.
Espanol.

Espanol con Mora.
Mulato.

5

6

Mulato con Espanola.
Morisco.

Morisco con Espanola.
Chino.

7

Chino con India.
Salta atras.

Salta atras con Mulata.
Tinoo.

An eighteenth-century genre painting from New Spain showing various racial *castas*, the result of ethnic mixing.

SOURCE: Photograph by SCHALKWIJK. Art Resource, New York.

aristocratic counterparts at home; the Spanish system of encomienda and the great manors created by the Dutch and continued by the English along the Hudson River also represented attempts to bring the essence of European feudalism to North America. But in most areas, because settlers had free access to land, these monopolies proved difficult or impossible to maintain. There was a system of economic rank and an unequal distribution of wealth, prestige, and power. North American society was not aristocratic, but neither was it without social hierarchy.

In New Spain the official criterion for status was racial purity. *Españoles* (Spaniards) or *gente de razon* (literally, "people of reason") occupied the top rung of the social ladder, with *mestizos*, mulattoes, and others on descending levels. African slaves and Indians were at the bottom. In the isolated northern borderlands, however, these distinctions tended to disappear, with *castas* (persons of mixed background) enjoying considerably more opportunity. Mestizos who acquired land might suddenly be reclassified as españoles. "The only two castas we know of here are the gente de razón and Indians," observed a missionary in California, "and all the former are considered Spaniards." Similarly, census takers in eighteenth-century Texas listed everyone but Indians as españoles, producing curious listings such as "Spaniard from Canada" or "Spaniard from France." Even so, Spanish and French colonial societies were cut in the style of the Old World, with its hereditary ranks and titles. The landlords of New France and the Spanish borderlands may have lacked the means to accumulate real wealth, but they lived lives of elegance compared to the hard toil of the people who owed them labor service or rent.

The upper class of British colonial society—the wealthiest 10 percent of all whites—was made up of large landowners, merchants, and prosperous professionals. In the eighteenth century, property valued at £2,000 marked a family as well-to-do, and £5,000 was real wealth. Leading merchants, with annual incomes in excess of £500, lived in opulence. Despite their lack of titles, the wealthy planters and merchants in the British colonies lived far more extravagantly than the seigneurs of New France or the dons of the Spanish borderlands. What separated the culture of class in the British colonies from that of New France or New Mexico was not so much the material conditions of life as the prevailing attitude toward social rank. In the Catholic cultures, the upper class attempted to obscure its origins, claiming descent from European nobility. But in British North America people celebrated social mobility. The class system was remarkably open, and the entrance of newly successful planters, commercial farmers, and merchants into the upper ranks was not only possible but common, although by midcentury most upper-class families had inherited, not earned, their wealth.

To be sure, there was a large lower class in the British colonies. Slaves, bound servants, and poor laboring families made up at least 40 percent of the population. For them, the standard of living did not rise above bare subsistence. Most lived from hand to mouth, often suffering through seasons of severe privation. A small proportion of poor whites could expect their condition to improve during their lifetimes, but slaves were a permanently servile population. Enslaved African Americans stood apart from the gains in the standard of living enjoyed by immigrants from Europe. Their lives had been degraded beyond measure from the conditions prevailing in their native lands.

The feature of the class system most often commented on by eighteenth-century observers was not the character or composition of the lower ranks but rather the size and strength of the middle class, a rank entirely absent in the colonies of France and Spain. As one Pennsylvanian wrote at midcentury, "The people of this province are generally of the middling sort." More than half the population of the British colonies, and nearly 70 percent of all white settlers, might be so classified. Most were families of landowning farmers of small to moderate means, but the group also included artisans, craftsmen, and small shopkeepers.

At the low end, the colonial middle class included families whose standard of living was barely above subsistence; at the high end were those whose holdings approached real wealth. Households solidly in the center of this broad ranking owned land or other property worth approximately £500 and earned the equivalent of about £100 per year. They enjoyed a standard of living higher than that of the great majority of people in England and Europe. The low mortality of British Americans was important testimony to generally better living conditions. Touring the British Isles at midcentury, Benjamin Franklin was shocked at the squalid conditions of farmers and workers, and he wrote of his renewed appreciation of America, where everyone "lives in a tidy, warm house, has plenty of good food and fuel, with whole cloths from head to foot, the manufacture perhaps of his own family." For the majority of British colonists in North America it was possible to achieve "roast beef and apple pie" comfort.

Economic Growth and Increasing Inequality

One of the most important differences among North American colonial regions in the eighteenth century was the economic stagnation in New France and New Spain compared with the impressive economic growth

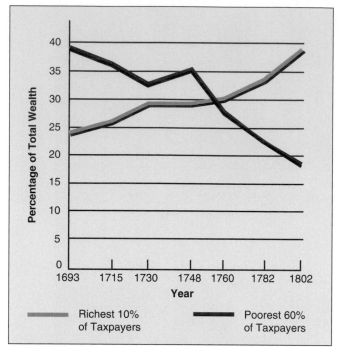

Distribution of Assessed Taxable Wealth in Eighteenth-Century Chester County This graph charts the concentration of assets in the hands of wealthy families. From 1693 to 1802 the percentage of total wealth held by the richest 10 percent of taxpayers rose from 24 to 38 percent, while the percentage held by the poorest 60 percent of taxpayers fell from 39 to 18 percent. This pattern was typical for regions dominated by commerce.

SOURCE: James Lemon and Gary Nash, "The Distribution of Wealth in Eighteenth-Century America," *Journal of Social History* 2 (1968):1–24.

of the British colonies. Weighed down by royal bureaucracies and overbearing regulations, neither the French Crescent nor New Spain evidenced much prosperity. In British North America, however, per capita production grew at an annual rate of 0.5 percent. Granted, this was considerably less than the average annual growth rate of 1.5 percent that prevailed during the era of industrialization, from the early nineteenth through the mid-twentieth century. But as economic growth steadily increased the size of the economic pie, most middle- and upper-class British Americans began to enjoy improved living conditions, better than those of any people in Europe. Improving standards of living and open access to land encouraged British colonists to see theirs as a society where hard work and savings could translate into prosperity, thus producing an upward spiral of economic growth.

At the same time, this growth produced increasing social inequality. In the commercial cities, for example, prosperity was accompanied by a concentration

WEALTH HELD BY RICHEST 10 PERCENT OF THE POPULATION: NORTHERN AND SOUTHERN BRITISH COLONIES COMPARED, 1770		
	North	South
Frontier	33	40
Rural subsistence farming	35	45
Rural commercial farming	45	65
Cities	60	65
Overall	45	55

SOURCE: Jackson Turner Main, *The Social Structure of Revolutionary America* (Princeton, NJ: Princeton University Press, 1965), 276n.

of assets in the hands of wealthy families. In Boston and Philadelphia at the beginning of the century, the wealthiest 10 percent of households owned about half of the taxable property; by about midcentury this small group owned 65 percent or more. In the commercial farming region of Chester County in southeastern Pennsylvania, the holdings of the wealthiest 10 percent of households increased more modestly, from 24 to 30 percent of taxable property during the first half of the century. But at the same time the share of taxable property owned by the poorest third fell from 17 to 6 percent. The general standard of living may have been rising, but the rich were getting richer and the poor poorer. The greatest concentrations of wealth occurred in the cities and in regions dominated by commercial farming, whether slave or free, while the greatest economic equality continued to be found in areas of self-sufficient farming such as the backcountry.

Another eighteenth-century trend worked against the hope of social mobility in the countryside. As population grew and as generations succeeded one another in older settlements, all the available land in the towns was taken up. Under the pressure of increased demand, land prices rose almost beyond the reach of families of modest means. As a family's land was divided among the heirs of the second and third generations, parcels became ever smaller and thus more intensively farmed. Eventually the soil was exhausted.

By the eighteenth century, many farm communities did not have sufficient land to provide those of the emerging generation with farms of their own. This problem was particularly acute in New England, where colonists were hemmed in by the French and Indians on the north and the great landed estates of the Hudson Valley on the west. There were notable increases in the number of landless poor in the towns of New England as well as the disturbing appearance of the

"strolling poor," homeless people who traveled from town to town looking for work or a handout. Destitute families crowded into Boston, which by midcentury was spending more than £5,000 annually on relief for the poor, who were required to wear a large red P on their clothing. In other regions, land shortages in the older settlements almost inevitably prompted people to leave in search of cheap or free land. In New England, young men unable to obtain land in hometowns often moved to the towns and cities of the seaboard, for New England enjoyed a strong seafaring tradition. Fishing and shipping had first become important during the late seventeenth century, as merchants struggled to find a successful method of earning foreign exchange. The expanding slave market in the South opened new opportunities, prompting the growth of thriving coastal ports such as New Haven, Newport, Salem, and Boston. By midcentury New England had become the most urban of all North America's regions. Boston, the largest city in the British colonies, was the metropolis of a region that included not only New England but also the maritime settlements of Nova Scotia and Newfoundland, where New England merchants dominated commerce and recruited seamen for their fishing and shipping fleets.

Contrasts in Colonial Politics

The administration of the Spanish and French colonies was highly centralized. French Canada was ruled by a superior council including the royal governor (in charge of military affairs), the intendant (responsible for civil administration), and the bishop of Quebec. New Spain was governed by the Council of the Indies, which sat in Spain, and direct executive authority over all political affairs was exercised by the viceroy in Mexico City. Although local communities had informal independence, the highly bureaucratized and centralized governments of the French Crescent and the Spanish borderlands left little room for the development of vigorous traditions of self-government.

The situation in the British colonies was quite different. During the early eighteenth century the British government of Prime Minister Robert Walpole assumed that a decentralized administration would best accomplish the nation's economic goals. Contented colonies, Walpole argued, would present far fewer problems. "One would not strain any point where it can be of no service to our King or country," a British official advised the governor of South Carolina in 1722. "The government should be as easy and mild as possible." Each of the colonies was administered by royally appointed governors, its taxes and finances set by constituent assemblies. Those who owned property could vote for representatives to the assembly. Because many people—mostly white males—owned property, the proportion of adult white men able to vote was 50 percent or higher in all the British colonies. Proportionally, the electorate of the British colonies was the largest in the world.

That did not mean, however, that the British colonies were democratic. The basic principle of order in eighteenth-century British culture was the ideal of deference to natural hierarchies. The well-ordered family, in which children were to be strictly governed by their parents, and wives by their husbands, was the common metaphor for civil order. Members of subordinate groups, such as women, the non-English, African American slaves, servants, and Indians—who in some colonies constituted nine of every ten adults in the population—could not vote or hold public office. Moreover, for the most part the men who did vote chose wealthy landowners, planters, or merchants to serve as their leaders. Thus, provincial assemblies were controlled by colonial elites.

The important political developments in eighteenth-century British North America, then, had nothing to do with what we commonly call democracy. To educated British colonists, the word "democracy" implied rule by the mob, the normal order of things turned upside-down. Over the century there was, however, an important trend toward stronger institutions of representative government. By midcentury most colonial assemblies in British North America had achieved considerable power over provincial affairs and shared authority with governors and other imperial officials. They collected local revenues and allocated funds for government programs, asserted the right to audit the accounts of public officers, and in some cases even acquired the power to approve the appointment of provincial officials. Because the assemblies controlled the finances of government—the "purse strings"—most royal governors were unable to resist this trend. The royal governors who were most successful at realizing their agendas were those who became adept at playing one provincial faction off against another. All this conflict had the important effect of schooling the colonial elite in the art of politics. It was not democratic politics, but schooling in the ways of patronage, coalition-building, and behind-the-scenes intrigue that would have important implications for the development of American institutions.

THE CULTURAL TRANSFORMATION OF BRITISH NORTH AMERICA

Despite broad similarities, the colonial regions of North America developed along divergent lines during the eighteenth century. The British colonies were marked by increasing ethnic diversity, economic growth, social tensions, and conflictual politics that proved to be training for self-government. In the middle decades of the eighteenth century, significant cultural transformation began to take place. New ideas and writings associated with the Enlightenment made their way across the Atlantic on the same ships that transported European immigrants and European goods. In New Spain and New France, by contrast, colonial officials worked diligently to suppress these challenging new ideas and writings. The Catholic Church effectively banned the works of hundreds of authors. In Mexico, officials of the Inquisition conducted house-to-house searches in pursuit of prohibited texts that they feared had been smuggled into the country.

The Enlightenment Challenge

Drawing from the discoveries of Galileo, Copernicus, and the seventeenth-century scientists René Descartes and Sir Isaac Newton, Enlightenment thinkers in Britain and on the Continent argued that the universe was governed by natural laws that people could understand and apply to their own advantage. John Locke, for example, articulated a philosophy of reason in proposing that the state existed to provide for the happiness and security of individuals, who were endowed with inalienable rights to life, liberty, and property. Enlightenment writers emphasized rationality, harmony, and order, themes that stood in stark contrast to folk culture's traditional emphasis on the unfathomable mysteries of God and nature and the inevitability of human failure and disorder.

Enlightenment thinking undoubtedly appealed most to those whose ordered lives had improved their lot. The colonial elite had good reason to believe in progress. They sent their sons to college, where the texts of the new thinkers were promoted. Harvard, established in 1636, remained the only institution of higher education in British America until 1693, when Anglicans established the College of William and Mary at Williamsburg, soon to become the new capital of Virginia. Puritans in Connecticut, believing that Harvard was too liberal, founded Yale College in 1701. The curricula of these colleges, modeled on those of Oxford and Cambridge in England, were designed to train ministers, but gradually each institution intro-

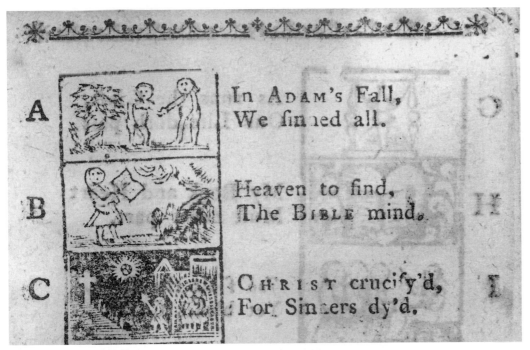

The first page of the *New England Primer* (1689), published in Boston, which in its various editions sold more than five million copies. In addition to the letters of the alphabet, illustrated by crude but charming woodcuts and couplets, the book contained simple moral texts based on Biblical history and wisdom.

SOURCE: Courtesy American Antiquarian Society.

duced courses and professors influenced by the Enlightenment. In the 1730s Harvard endowed a chair of mathematics and natural philosophy, and appointed John Winthrop, grandson of the Puritan leader and a disciple of Isac Newton, to fill it.

A mixture of traditional and Enlightenment views characterized the colonial colleges, as it did the thought of men like Cotton Mather. A conservative defender of the old order, Mather wrote a book supporting the existence of witches. On the other hand, he was also a member of the Royal Society, an early supporter of inoculation against smallpox, and a defender of the Copernican sun-centered model of the universe. On hearing a scientific lecture of Mather's that could have been construed as raising conflicts with a literal reading of the Bible, one old Boston minister noted in his diary, "I think it inconvenient to assert such problems."

This clergyman's views probably characterized a majority of the reading public. About half the adult men and a quarter of the adult women of the British colonies could read, a literacy rate that was comparable to those of England and Scandinavia. In striking contrast, in the French and Spanish colonies reading was a skill confined to a tiny minority of upper-class men. In New England, where the Puritans were committed to Bible reading and developed a system of public education, literacy rates were 85 percent among men and approximately 50 percent among women—the highest in the entire Atlantic world. The famous *New England Primer* (1689), one of the more influential books ever printed in America, was part of the most successful literacy campaign in history.

But the tastes of ordinary readers ran to traditional rather than Enlightenment fare. Benjamin Harris, the Boston publisher and perhaps the author of the *New England Primer*, was also the publisher of the laws of Massachusetts, religious works by Cotton Mather, broadsides, ballads, and in 1690 the first newspaper in the colonies, *Public Occurrences both Foreign and Domestick*, which the authorities suppressed after just one issue. In 1704, under a friendlier administration, however, the Boston *News-Letter* became the first continuously published newspaper. By midcentury there were more than twenty newspapers in the British colonies. These papers did not use reporters, but depended on letters, official government announcements, and travelers' and correspondents' reports for news. The Pennsylvania *Chronicle* summed up its coverage in this description: "Containing the freshest Advices, both Foreign and Domestic; with a Variety of other Matters, useful, instructive, and entertaining." Readership was sizable. By the mid-eighteenth century most literate people had access to newspapers, and they were read aloud in taverns, making their information available to all within hearing.

Another popular literary form was the almanac, a combination calendar, astrological guide, and source-book of medical advice and farming tips reflecting the concerns of traditional folk culture. The best remembered is *Poor Richard's Almanac* (1732–57), published by Philadelphia newspaper publisher Benjamin Franklin, although it was preceded and outlived by a great many others. What was so innovative about Franklin's almanac, and what made it so important, was the manner in which the author used this traditional literary form to promote the new Enlightenment emphasis on useful and practical knowledge. Posing as the simple bump-kin Poor Richard, the highly sophisticated Franklin was one of the first Americans to bring Enlightenment thought to ordinary folk.

Not surprisingly, the best-selling book of the colonial era was the Bible. In second place was that unique American literary form, the captivity narrative. The first publication of that genre was *Sovereignty and Goodness of God* (1682), Mary Rowlandson's story of her captivity among the Indians during King Philip's War, a kind of "pilgrim's progress" through the American wilderness. "It is good for me that I have been afflicted," she wrote, for "I have learned to look beyond present and smaller troubles, and to be quieted under them." Appearing in fifteen editions during the colonial period, Rowlandson's account stimulated the publication of at least 500 other such narratives (including the Reverend John Williams's *The Redeemed Captive Returning to Zion*, cited in the beginning of this chapter), most with a lot less religion and a great deal more gore.

The growth of the economy in the British colonies and the development of a colonial upper class stimulated the emergence of a more cosmopolitan Anglican culture, particularly in the cities of the Atlantic coast. "The culture of minds by the finer arts and sciences," Franklin wrote in 1749, "was necessarily postponed to times of more wealth and leisure." And now, he added, "these times are come." A rising demand for drama, poetry, essays, novels, and history was met by urban booksellers who imported British publications. In Boston bookshops at midcentury one could buy the works of William Shakespeare and John Milton, the essays of Joseph Addison, Richard Steele, Jonathan Swift, and Samuel Johnson, and editions of the classics. In shops elsewhere around the colonies one might also find editions of novels such as *Moll Flanders* by Daniel Defoe and *Tom Jones* by Henry Fielding—but not in New England, where such works were considered indecent. Many of these works were exerpted and reprinted in colonial newspapers.

A Decline in Religious Devotion

At the same time that these new ideas were flourishing, religion seemed in decline. South of New England, the Anglican Church was weak, its ministers uninspiring, and many families remained "unchurched." A historian of religion has estimated that only one adult in fifteen was a member of a congregation. Although this figure may understate the impact of religion on community life, it helps keep things in perspective. The Puritan churches of New England also suffered declining membership and falling attendance at services, and many ministers began to warn of Puritanism's "declension," pointing to the "dangerous" trend toward the "evil of toleration." By the second decade of the eighteenth century only one in five New Englanders belonged to an established congregation. When Puritanism had been a sect, membership in the church was voluntary and leaders could demand that followers testify to their religious conversion. But when Puritanism became an established church, attendance was expected of all townspeople, and conflicts inevitably arose over the requirement of a conversion experience. An agreement of 1662, known as the Half-Way Covenant, offered a practical solution: members' children who had not experienced conversion themselves could join as "half-way" members, restricted only from participation in communion. Thus the Puritans chose to manage rather than to resolve the conflicts involved in becoming an established religion. Tensions also developed between congregational autonomy and the central control that traditionally accompanied the establishment of a state church. In 1708 the churches of Connecticut agreed to the Saybrook Platform, which enacted a system of governance by councils of ministers and elders rather than by congregations. This reform also had the effect of weakening the passion and commitment of church members.

In addition, an increasing number of Congregationalists began to question the strict Calvinist theology of predestination—the belief that God had predetermined the few men and women who would be saved in the Second Coming. In the eighteenth century many Puritans turned to the much more comforting idea that God had given people the freedom to choose salvation by developing their faith and by doing good works. This belief, known as Arminianism, was in harmony with the Enlightenment view that men and women were not helpless pawns but rational beings who could actively shape their own destinies. Also implicit in these new views was an image of God as a loving rather than a punishing father. Arminianism became a force at Harvard in the early eighteenth century, and soon a new generation of

Arminian ministers began to assume leadership in New England's churches. These liberal ideas appealed to groups experiencing economic and social improvement, especially commercial farmers, merchants, and the comfortable middle class with its rising expectations. But among ordinary people, especially those in the countryside where traditional patterns lingered, there was a good deal of opposition to these unorthodox new ideas.

The Great Awakening

The first stirrings of a movement challenging this rationalist approach to religion occurred during the 1730s, most notably in the movement sparked by Reverend Jonathan Edwards in the community of Northampton, in western Massachusetts. As the leaders of the community increasingly devoted their energies to the pursuit of wealth, the enthusiasm seemed to go out of religion. The congregation adopted rules allowing church membership without evidence of a conversion experience and adopted a seating plan for the church that placed wealthy families in the prominent pews, front and center. But the same economic forces that made the "River Gods"—as the wealthy landowners of the Connecticut Valley were known—also impoverished others. Young people from the community's poorer families grew disaffected as they were forced to postpone marriage because of the scarcity and expense of the land needed to set up a farm household. Increasingly they refused to attend church meetings, instead gathering together at night for "frolics" that only seemed to increase their discontent. Reverend Edwards made this group of young people his special concern. Believing that they needed to "have their hearts touched," he preached to them in a style that appealed to their emotions. For the first time in a generation, the meetinghouse shook with the fire and passion of Puritan religion. "Before the sermon was done," one Northampton parishioner remembered about one notable occasion, "there was a great moaning and crying through the whole house—What shall I do to be saved?—Oh I am going to Hell!—Oh what shall I do for Christ?" Religious fervor swept through the community, and church membership began to grow. There was more to this than the power of one preacher, for similar revivals were soon breaking out in other New England communities, as well as among German pietists and Scots–Irish Presbyterians in Pennsylvania. Complaining of "spiritual coldness," people abandoned ministers whose sermons read like rational dissertations for those whose preaching was more emotional. These local revivals became an intercolonial phenomenon thanks to the preaching of George Whitefield, an evangelical Anglican minister from England, who in 1738 made the first of several tours of the colonies. By all accounts, his preaching had a powerful effect. Even Benjamin Franklin, a religious skeptic, wrote of the "extraordinary influence of [Whitefield's] oratory" after attending an outdoor service in Philadelphia where 30,000 people crowded the streets to hear him. Whitefield began as Edwards did, chastising his listeners as "half animals and half devils," but he left them with the hope that God would be responsive to their desire for salvation. "The word was sharper than a two-edged sword," Whitefield wrote after one of his sermons. "The bitter cries and groans were enough to pierce the hardest heart. Some of the people were as pale as death; others were wringing their hands; others lying on the ground; others sinking into the arms of their friends; and most lifting their eyes to heaven and crying to God for mercy. They seemed like persons awakened by the last trumpet, and coming out of their graves to judgement." Whitefield avoided sectarian differences. "God help us to forget party names and become Christians in deed and truth," he declared.

Historians of religion consider this widespread colonial revival of religion, which later generations called the Great Awakening, to be an American version of the second phase of the Protestant Reformation (see Chapter 2). Religious leaders condemned the laxity, decadence, and officalism of established Protestantism and reinvigorated it with calls for piety and purity. People undergoing the economic and social stresses of the age, unsure about their ability to find land, marry, and participate in the promise of a growing economy, found relief in religious enthusiasm.

In Pennsylvania, two important leaders were William Tennent and his son Gilbert. An Irish-born Presbyterian, the elder Tennent was an evangelical preacher who established a school in Pennsylvania to train like-minded men for the ministry. His lampooned "Log College," as it was called, ultimately evolved into the College of New Jersey—later Princeton University—founded in 1746. In the early 1740s, disturbed by what he called the "presumptuous security" of the colonial church, Tennent toured with Whitefield and delivered the famous sermon "The Dangers of an Unconverted Ministry," in which he called upon Protestants to examine the religious convictions of their own ministers.

Among Presbyterians, open conflict broke out between the revivalists and the old guard, and in some regions the church hierarchy divided into separate organizations. In New England, similar factions, known as the New Lights and the Old Lights, accused each other of heresy. The New Lights railed against Arminianism as a rationalist heresy and called for a revival of Calvinism. The Old Lights condemned emotional enthusiasm as part of the heresy of believing in a personal

Baptism by full immersion in the Schuylkill River of Pennsylvania, an engraving by Henry Dawkins illustrating events in the history of American Baptists, was published in Philadelphia in 1770. With calls for renewed piety and purity, the Great Awakening reinvigorated American Protestantism. The Baptists preached an egalitarian message, and their congregations in the South often included both white and black Protestants.

SOURCE: John Carter Brown Library at Brown University.

and direct relationship with God outside the order of the church. Itinerant preachers appeared in the countryside, stirring up trouble. The followers of one traveling revivalist burned their wigs, jewelry, and fine clothes in a bonfire, then marched around the conflagration, chanting curses at their opponents, whose religious writings they also consigned to the flames. Many congregations split into feuding factions, and ministers found themselves challenged by their newly awakened parishioners. In one town, members of the congregation voted to dismiss their minister, who lacked the emotional fire they wanted in a preacher. When he refused to vacate his pulpit, they pulled him down, roughed him up, and threw him out the church door. Never had there been such turmoil in New England churches.

Although some historians have raised questions about how cohesive these revivals were, they were so widespread and were typical of so many communities that they might be seen as one of the first national events in American history. They began somewhat later in the South, developing first in the mid-1740s among Scots–Irish Presbyterians, then achieved full impact with the organizational work of Methodists and particularly Baptists in the 1760s and early 1770s. These revivals not only affected white Southerners but also introduced many slaves to Christianity for the first time. Local awak-

enings were often a phenomenon shared by both whites and blacks. The Baptist churches of the South in the era of the American Revolution included members of both races and featured spontaneous preaching by slaves as well as masters. In the nineteenth century white and black Christians would go their separate ways, but the joint experience of the eighteenth-century Awakening shaped the religious cultures of both groups.

Many other "unchurched" colonists were brought back to Protestantism by eighteenth-century revivalism. But a careful examination of statistics suggests that the proportion of church members in the general population probably did not increase during the middle decades of the century. While the number of churches more than doubled from 1740 to 1780, the colonial population grew even faster, increasing threefold. The greatest impact was on families already associated with the churches. Before the Awakening, attendance at church had been mostly an adult affair, but throughout the colonies the revival of religion had its deepest effects on young people, who flocked to church in greater numbers than ever before. For years the number of people experiencing conversion had been steadily falling, but now full membership surged. Church membership previously had been concentrated among women, leading Cot-

CHRONOLOGY

1636	Harvard College founded
1644	Roger Williams's *Bloudy Tenent of Persecution*
1662	Half-Way Covenant in New England
1674	Bishopric of Quebec established
1680s	William Penn begins recruiting settlers from the European Continent
1682	Mary Rowlandson's *Sovereignty and Goodness of God*
1689	Toleration Act passed by Parliament
1690s	Beginnings of Jesuit missions in Arizona
1693	College of William and Mary is founded
1700s	Plains Indians begin adoption of the horse
1701	Yale College founded Iroquois sign treaty of neutrality with France
1704	Deerfield raid
1708	Saybrook Platform in Connecticut
1716	Spanish begin construction of Texas missions

1730s	French decimate the Natchez and defeat the Fox Indians
1732	Franklin begins publishing *Poor Richard's Almanac*
1738	George Whitefield first tours the colonies
1740s	Great Awakening gets under way in the Northeast
1740	Parliament passes a naturalization law for the colonies
1746	College of New Jersey (Princeton) founded
1760s	Great Awakening achieves full impact in the South
1769	Spanish colonization of California begins
1775	Indian revolt at San Diego
1776	San Francisco founded
1781	Los Angeles founded

ton Mather, for one, to speculate that perhaps women were indeed more godly. But men were particularly affected by the revival of religion, and their attendance and membership rose. "God has surprisingly seized and subdued the hardest men, and more males have been added here than the tenderer sex," wrote one Massachusetts minister.

The Politics of Revivalism

Revivalism appealed most of all to groups who felt bypassed by the economic and cultural development of the British colonies during the first half of the eighteenth century. The New Lights tended to draw their greatest strength from small farmers and less prosperous craftsmen. Many members of the upper class and the comfortable "middling sort" viewed the excesses of revivalism as indications of anarchy, and they became even more committed to rational religion.

Some historians have argued for important political implications of revivalism. In Connecticut, for example, Old Lights politicized the religious dispute by passing a series of laws in the General Assembly designed to suppress revivalism. In one town, separatists refused to pay taxes that supported the established church and were jailed. New Light judges were thrown off the bench, and others were denied their elected seats in the assembly. The arrogance of these actions was met with popular outrage: by the 1760s the Connecticut New Lights had organized themselves politically and, in what amounted to a political rebellion, succeeded in turning the Old Lights out of office. These New Light politicians would provide the leadership for the American Revolution in Connecticut.

Such direct connections between religion and politics were rare. There can be little doubt, however, that for many people revivalism offered the first opportunity to participate actively in public debate and public action that affected the direction of their lives. Choices about religious styles, ministers, and doctrine were thrown open for public discourse, and ordinary people began to believe that their opinions actually counted for something. Underlying the debate over these issues were insecurities about warfare, economic growth, and the development of colonial society. Revivalism empowered ordinary people to question their leaders, an experience that would prove critical in the political struggles to come.

CONCLUSION

By the middle of the eighteenth century a number of distinct colonial regions had emerged in North America, all of them with rising populations who demanded that more land be seized from the Indians. Some colonies attempted to ensure homogeneity, whereas others embraced diversity. Within the British colonies, New England in particular seemed bound to the past, whereas the Middle Colonies and the backcountry pointed the way toward pluralism and expansion. These developments placed them in direct competition with the expansionist plans of the French and at odds with Indian peoples committed to the defense of their homelands.

The economic development of the British colonies introduced new social and cultural tensions that led to the Great Awakening, a massive revival of religion that was the first transcolonial event in American history. Thousands of people experienced a renewal of religious passions, but rather than resuscitating old traditions, the Awakening pointed people toward a more active role in their own political futures. These transformations added to the differences between the British colonies, on the one hand, and New Spain and the French Crescent, on the other.

REVIEW QUESTIONS

1. What were the principal colonial regions of North America? Discuss their similarities and their differences. Contrast the development of their political systems.

2. Why did the Spanish and the French close their colonies to immigration? Why did the British open theirs? How do you explain the ethnic homogeneity of New England and the ethnic pluralism of New York and Pennsylvania?

3. What were the principal trends in the history of Indian America in the eighteenth century?

4. Discuss the development of class differences in the Spanish, French, and British colonies in the eighteenth century.

5. Discuss the effects of the Great Awakening on the subsequent history of the British colonies.

RECOMMENDED READING

Jon Butler, *Becoming America: The Revolution Before 1776* (2000). A history that emphases the diversity, economic prosperity, participatory politics, and religious pluralism of the eighteenth-century British colonies.

Edward Countryman, *Americans: A Collision of Histories* (1996). An important new synthesis that includes the many peoples and cultures of North America.

John Demos, *The Unredeemed Captive: A Family Story from Early America* (1994). A moving history of the Deerfield captives, focusing on the experience of Eunice Williams, the unredeemed captive.

W. J. Eccles, *The Canadian Frontier, 1534–1760* (1983). An introduction to the history of French America by a leading scholar on colonial Canada.

David Hackett Fischer, *Albion's Seed: Four British Folkways in America* (1990). An engaging history with fascinating details on the regions of New England, Pennsylvania, Virginia, and the backcountry.

Jack P. Greene, *Pursuits of Happiness: The Social Development of Early Modern British Colonies and the Formation of American Culture* (1986). A distillation of a tremendous amount of historical material on community life in British North America.

Frank Lambert, *Inventing the "Great Awakening"* (1999). Argues that the revivialists themselves created the idea of the Great Awakening to further their evangelical work.

Jackson Turner Main, *The Social Structure of Revolutionary America* (1965). A detailed treatment of colonial social structure, with statistics, tables, and enlightening interpretations.

D. W. Meinig, *The Shaping of America: Atlantic America, 1492–1800* (1986). A geographer's overview of the historical development of the North American continent in the era of European colonialism. Provides a survey of the British and French colonies.

Lucy Eldersveld Murphy, *A Gathering of Rivers: Indians, Métis, and Mining in the Western Great Lakes, 1737–1832* (2000). Demonstrates the success of Indian communities in adapting to colonialism through the diversification of their economies, intermarriage, and constructing multiethnic communities.

David J. Weber, *The Spanish Frontier in North America* (1992). A magnificent treatment of the entire Spanish borderlands, from Florida to California. Includes important chapters on colonial government and social life.

Marianne S. Wokeck, *Trade in Strangers: The Beginning of Mass Migration to North America* (1999). The first important study of immigration in the eighteenth century, arguing that these migrations served as models for European mass migration in the next century.

▶ MEDIA RESOURCES

U.S. HISTORY DOCUMENTS CD-ROM

Colonizing the New World
2-5   John Winthrop, "A Model of Christian Charity" (1630)

Colonial America
3-5   Excerpt from Cotton Mather's "Memorable Providences, Relating to Witchcrafts and Possessions" (1689)

3-7   William Byrd II, Diary (1709)

3-8   Manners and Etiquette in the Eighteenth Century

Prelude to Revolution
4-1   John Peter Zenger and the Responsibility of the Press (1734)

The American Revolution
5-1   Benjamin Franklin, "Observations Concerning the Increase of Mankind, Peopling of Countries, etc." (1751)

COMPANION WEBSITE HIGHLIGHTS

To view an exploration, enter one of the URLs below in your browser.

Web Explorations
Growing Use of the Horse by Plains Indians
http://www.prenhall.com/faragher/map5.1
Spread of Settlement: Movement into the Backcountry, 1720–1760
http://www.prenhall.com/faragher/map5.2

Additional Interactive Maps
To access the maps, go to this chapter's resources at
http://www.prenhall.com/faragher

Regions in Eighteenth-Century North America, page 118
The French Crescent, page 120

 HISTORY RESOURCE CENTER

To find the resources listed below, go to
http://www.prenhall.com/historyresourcecenter

Documents
Elizabeth Sprigs, Letter to Her Father (1756)
James Oglethorpe: The Stono Rebellion (1739)
John Hammond, "Leah and Rachel, or the Two Fruitfull Sisters, Virginia and Mary-Land" (1656)
Jonathan Edwards, from "Sinners in the Hands of an Angry God" (1741)
Jonathan Edwards, from "Some Thoughts Concerning the Present Revival of Religion in New England" (1742)
Michel-Guillaume-Jean de Crèvecoeur, from Letters from an American Farmer (1782)
James Oglethorpe, "Some Account of the Designs of the Trustees for Establishing the Colony of Georgia" (1733)

Images
Cotton Mather's "Late Memorable Providences Relating to Witchcrafts and Possessions" Clearly Manifesting
Cotton Mather's "The Wonders of the Invisible World"
Jonathan Edwards
San Xavier del Bac
The Old Tun Tavern, Philadelphia

Turn to the next page for the *Exploring America* activity for this chapter.

EXPLORING AMERICA
THE GREAT AWAKENING
http://www.prenhall.com/faragher/awakening

How does religion affect the development of society? What was happening in colonial British North America in the seventeenth century that stimulated such a massive religious revival? How did Benjamin Franklin characterize the Great Awakening? How did colonists from different backgrounds respond to the revival and the religious sentiment it engendered? These questions and others are examined in *The Great Awakening* module. Primary source documents, visual images, and an interactive map supplement a strong narrative to assess this important event in American history.

The Great Awakening stresses first-hand accounts with supplementary commentary to examine the first major religious revival in America. The comments by

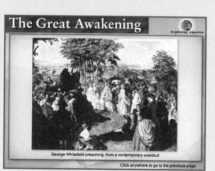

George Whitefield preaching, from a contemporary woodcut

Click anywhere to go to the previous page

such figures as Benjamin Franklin offer insight into both the revivals themselves and the responses of people from various backgrounds. The excerpts act as a debate over the Great Awakening and the style of religion that resulted from it. The interactive map illuminates the geographic aspects of the revival movement. The Great Awakening was a pivotal event in American history that's influence extended beyond religion to the political sphere.

Reflect and Respond

1. How did the Rev. Mr. William Shurtleff, Pastor of the 2nd Church in Portsmouth, interpret the circum-

stance of "the Chimney of an House that stood near to it [the church] happening to take Fire and blaze out to an uncommon Degree"?

2. He realized that, in telling of the fire, "with how much Derision such a Relation as this is likely to be entertained by a great many of the Humourists of the Age." Why then did he include this "small and inconsiderable circumstance"?

3. According to the sources here, what were the signs of a genuine conversion?

4. What dangers did those seeking salvation face, according to these sources?

✓ Check it out

Settlement Populations in British Mainland Colonies in the Eighteenth Century

This map traces the settlement patterns of the ethnic and racial groups comprising the colonial population. It

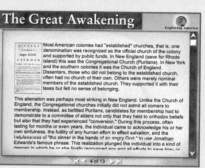

shows how various groups tended to settle in certain areas offering insight into which groups were most supportive of the Great Awakening. It also raises questions about the role conditions in the backcountry frontier may have played in religious revivals.

This exploration is also available on the *Exploring America* CD-ROM.

SIX

FROM EMPIRE TO INDEPENDENCE

▶ 1750–1776

William Walcutt, *Pulling Down the Statue of George III at Bowling Green*, 1857. Oil on canvas, 51 5/8″ × 77 5/8″ Lafayette College Art Collection, Easton, Pennsylvania.

The First Continental Congress Shapes a National Political Community

BRITAIN'S NORTH AMERICAN COLONIES HAD ENJOYED considerable prosperity during the late seventeenth and early eighteenth centuries. Beginning with the Stamp Act in 1765, however, the British government began to apply pressure, largely in the form of taxes and new trade restrictions, that drew increasing resistance from the colonies. In convening the First Continental Congress in September 1774, the colonies made clear their displeasure with the government's actions. Fifty-six elected delegates from twelve of the colonies met at Philadelphia to draft a common response to what they called the Intolerable Acts—the closing of the port of Boston, the suspension of Massachusetts government, and several other measures of British repression—that were the latest attempt to force the colonies to accept the power of Parliament to make laws binding them "in all cases whatsoever." This was the first meeting of the colonies since the Stamp Act Congress of 1765 (discussed later in this chapter). If the colonies now failed to act together, they would be "attacked and destroyed by piecemeal," declared Arthur Lee of Virginia. "Every part will in its turn feel the vengeance which it would not unite to repel." Abigail Adams, the politically astute wife of John Adams of Massachusetts, agreed. "You have before you," she wrote to her husband, "the greatest national concerns that ever came before any people."

The opening minutes of the first session on September 5 did not bode well. One delegate moved that they begin with prayer; another responded that they were "so divided in religious sentiments, some Episcopalians, some Quakers, some Anabaptists, some Presbyterians and some Congregationalists, so that we could not join in the same act of worship." Were the delegates to be stymied from the very beginning by things that separated rather than united them? John Adams's cousin, fellow Massachusetts delegate Samuel Adams, jumped to his feet. He was no bigot, he said, "and could hear a prayer from any gentleman of piety and virtue who was at the same time a friend to his country." The delegates finally agreed to ask a local clergyman, a supporter of the American cause, to officiate. The minister took for his text the Thirty-fifth Psalm: "Plead my cause, O Lord, with them that strive with me; fight against them that fight against me." John Adams was delighted. The minister "prayed with such fervor, such Ardor, such Earnestness and Pathos, and in Language so elegant and sublime," he wrote home, that "it has had an excellent Effect upon every Body here."

This incident highlighted the most important task confronting the Continental Congress: they had to develop trust in one another, for what they were doing was considered treason by the British authorities. They had to find a way to support the common cause without compromising their local identities. At first it was as if the delegates were "ambassadors from a dozen belligerent powers of Europe," wrote John Adams. The delegates represented different colonies, whose traditions and histories were as different as those of separate countries. Moreover, these lawyers, merchants, and planters, who were leaders in their respective colonies, were strangers to one another. Their political opinions ranged from loyalty to the British crown and empire to a belief in the necessity of violent revolution. "Every man," Adams wrote, "is a great man, an orator, a critic, a statesman, and therefore every man, upon every question, must show his oratory, his criticism, and his political abilities." As a result, he continued, "business is drawn and spun out to an immeasurable length. I believe that if it was moved and seconded that we should come to a resolution that three and two make five, we should be entertained with logic and rhetorick, law, history, politicks and mathematics concerning the subject for two whole days."

During seven weeks of deliberations, the men of the Continental Congress succeeded in forging an agreement on the principles and policies they would have to follow in addressing the most serious crisis in the history of Britain's North American colonies. Equally important, the delegates found ways to work together and harmonize their interests. They immediately resolved that each colony would have one vote, thereby committing themselves to preserving provincial autonomy. They sent their most vexing problems to committees, whose members could sound each other out on the issues without speaking for the public record, and they added to their daily routine a round of dinners, parties, and late-night drinking. The greatest single accomplishment of the Continental Congress was the creation of a community of leadership for the united colonies. "It has taken us much time to get acquainted," John Adams wrote to Abigail, but he left Philadelphia thinking of his fellow representatives as "a collection of the greatest men upon this continent."

The First Continental Congress thus took the first steps toward the creation of a national political community. The bonds of community can be local, regional, national, or international. In a town or village the feel-

ing of association comes from daily, face-to-face contact, but for larger groups these feelings must be created, or "imagined," as the historian Benedict Anderson puts it. The delegates took some of the first steps in this direction. In their final declaration they pledged to "firmly agree and associate, under the sacred ties of virtue, honor and love of our "country." They urged their fellow Americans to "encourage frugality, economy, and industry, and promote agriculture, arts and the manufactures of this country," to "discountenance and discourage every species of extravagance and dissipation, especially all horse-racing, and all kinds of gaming, cock fighting, exhibitions of shows, plays, and other expensive diversions and entertainments." In other words, they called upon the common religious and cultural traditions of British Americans. They asked their countrymen to remember "the poorer sort" among them during the coming economic troubles. And in demanding that their fellow Americans "break off all dealings" and treat with contempt anyone violating the compact, the delegates were declaring who was "inside" and who was "outside" their community. Drawing boundaries is the essential first act in the construction of a new community.

Patrick Henry of Virginia, one of the delegates already committed to independence, was exuberant when the First Continental Congress adjourned in late October. "The distinctions between Virginians, Pennsylvanians, New Yorkers, and New Englanders, are no more. I am not a Virginian, but an American," he declared. Henry voiced an important truth. Great Britain had forced the colonists to recognize that they shared a community of interest distinct from that of the mother country. Theirs was a first attempt to overcome local diversity and difference in pursuit of a common national goal. In the months and years to come the strength of local community would sometimes threaten to pull them apart, and the "imagined community" of America would be sorely tested as the colonies cautiously moved toward independence. ■

KEY TOPICS

- The final struggle among Great Britain, France, and American Indian tribes for control of eastern North America

- American nationalism in the aftermath of the French and Indian War

- Great Britain's changing policy toward its North American colonies

- The political assumptions of American republicanism

- The colonies' efforts to achieve unity in their confrontation with Great Britain

---

THE SEVEN YEARS' WAR IN AMERICA

The first attempt at cooperation among the leaders of the British colonies occurred in 1754, when representatives from New England, New York, Pennsylvania, and Maryland met to consider a joint approach to the French and Indian challenge. Even as the delegates met, fighting between French Canadians and Virginians began on the Ohio River, the first shots in a great global war for empire, known in Europe as the Seven Years' War, that pitted Britain (allied with Prussia) against the combined might of France, Austria, and Spain. In North America this would be the final and most destructive armed conflict between the British and the French before the French Revolution. Ultimately it decided the future of the vast region between the Appalachian Mountains and the Mississippi River, and lay the ground for the conflict between the British and the colonists that led to the American Revolution.

The Albany Conference of 1754

The 1754 meeting, which included an official delegation from the Iroquois Confederacy, took place in the New York town of Albany on the Hudson River, convened by the British Board of Trade. British officials wanted the colonies to consider a collective response to the continuing conflict with New France and the Indians of the interior. High on the agenda was the negotiation of a settlement with the leaders of the Iroquois Confederacy, who had grown impatient with colonial land grabbing. Because the powerful Iroquois Confederacy, with its Covenant Chain of alliances with other Indian tribes, occupied such a strategic location between New France and the British colonies, the British could ill afford Iroquois discontent. But the

official Iroquois delegation walked out of the conference, refusing all offers to join a British alliance.

The Albany Conference did adopt Benjamin Franklin's Plan of Union, which proposed that Indian affairs, western settlement, and other items of mutual interest be placed under the authority of a grand council made up of representatives elected by the colonial assemblies and led by a royally appointed president. Franklin, who had been appointed by the British government as deputy postmaster general for all of British North America and charged with improving intercolonial communication and commerce, had become extremely sensitive to the need for cooperation among the colonies. Indeed, referring to the Iroquois Confederacy, he declared, "It would be a very strange thing if ignorant savages should be capable of forming a scheme for such a union, and yet a like union should be impracticable for ten or a dozen English colonies." But the colonial assemblies rejected the Albany Plan of Union. As one British official noted, each colony had "a distinct government, wholly independent of the rest, pursuing its own interest and subject to no general command."

Colonial Aims and Indian Interests

The absence of cooperation among the colonies in North America would prove to be one of the greatest weaknesses of the British Empire, because the ensuing war would be fought at a number of widespread locations and required the coordination of command. There were three principal flash points of conflict in North America. The first was along the northern Atlantic coast. In 1713 France had ceded to Britain its colony of Acadia (which the British renamed Nova Scotia), but France then built the fortress of Louisburg, from which it guarded its fishing grounds and the St. Lawrence approach to New France. New Englanders had captured this prize in 1745 during King George's War, but the French then reclaimed it upon the settlement of that conflict in 1748. They subsequently reinforced Louisburg to such an extent that it became known as the Gibraltar of the New World.

A second zone of conflict was the border region between New France and New York, from Niagara Falls to Lake Champlain, where Canadians and New Yorkers were in furious competition for the Indian trade. Unable to compete effectively against superior English goods, the French resorted to armed might, constructing fortifications on Lake George and reinforcing their base at Niagara. In this zone the strategic advantage was held by the Iroquois Confederacy.

It was the Ohio country—the trans-Appalachian region along the Ohio River—that became the primary focus of British and French attention. This rich land was a prime target of British backcountry settlers and frontier land speculators. The French worried that their isolated settlements would be overrun by the expanding British population and that the loss of the Ohio River would threaten their entire Mississippi trading empire. To reinforce their claims, in 1749 the French sent a heavily armed force down the Ohio River to ward off the British,

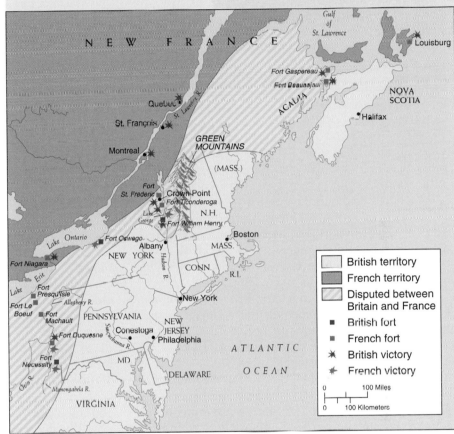

In this exploration, consider the principal military engagements of the Seven Years' War. How did the Indian trade affect the war? Which military defeats dealt the worst blows to the French?
www.prenhall.com/faragher/map6.1

WebExploration

Map legend:
- British territory
- French territory
- Disputed between Britain and France
- ■ British fort
- ■ French fort
- ✳ British victory
- ✳ French victory

0 — 100 Miles
0 — 100 Kilometers

The War for Empire in North America, 1754–1763   The Seven Years' War in America (also known as the French and Indian War) was fought in three principal areas: Nova Scotia and what was then Acadia, the frontier between New France and New York, and the upper Ohio River—gateway to the Old Northwest

and in 1752, supported by their northern Indian allies, they expelled a large number of British traders from the region. To prevent the British from returning to the west, they began the next year to construct a series of forts running south from Lake Erie to the junction of the Allegheny and Monongahela rivers, the site known as the Forks of the Ohio River.

The French "have stripped us of more than nine parts in ten of North America," one British official cried, "and left us only a skirt of coast along the Atlantic shore." In preparation for a general war, the British established the port of Halifax in Nova Scotia as a counter to Louisbourg. In northern New York, they strengthened existing forts and constructed new ones. Finally, the British king decided to directly chal-

lenge the French claim to the upper Ohio Valley. He conferred an enormous grant of land on the Ohio Company, organized by Virginia and London capitalists, and the company made plans to build a fort at the Forks of the Ohio River.

The impending conflict did not involve only the competing colonial powers, however, for the Indian peoples of the interior had interests of their own. In addition to its native inhabitants, the Ohio country had become a refuge for Indian peoples who had fled the Northeast—Delawares, Shawnees, Hurons, and Iroquois among them. Most of the Ohio Indians opposed the British and were anxious to preserve the Appalachians as a barrier to westward expansion. They were also disturbed by the French movement into their country. The French outposts, however, unlike those of the British, did not become centers of expanding agricultural settlements.

The Iroquois Confederacy as a whole sought to play off one European power against the other, to its own advantage. In the South the Creeks carved out a similar role for themselves among the British, the French in Louisiana, and the Spanish in Florida. The Cherokees and Choctaws attempted, less successfully, to do the same. It was in the interests of these Indian tribes, in other words, to perpetuate the existing colonial stalemate. Their position would be greatly undermined by an overwhelming victory for either side.

Frontier Warfare

At the Albany Congress the delegates received news that Colonel George Washington, a young militia officer sent by the governor of Virginia to expel the French from the region granted to the Ohio Company, had been forced to surrender his troops to a French force near the headwaters of the Monongahela River. The Canadians now commanded the interior country from their base at Fort Duquesne, which they had built at the Forks of the Ohio and named for the governor of French Canada.

Taking up the challenge, the British government dispatched two Irish regiments under General Edward Braddock across the Atlantic in 1755 to attack and destroy Fort Duquesne. Meanwhile, colonial militias (the equivalent of today's National Guard) commanded by colonial officers were to strike at the New York frontier and the North Atlantic coast. An army of New England militiamen succeeded in capturing two important French forts on the border of Nova Scotia, but the other two prongs of the campaign were failures. The offensive in New York was repulsed. And in the worst defeat of a British army during the eighteenth century, Braddock's force was destroyed by a smaller number of French and Indians on the upper Ohio, and Braddock himself was killed.

Braddock's defeat was followed by the outbreak of full-scale warfare between Britain and France in 1756. Known as the Seven Years' War in Europe, in North America it came to be called the French and Indian War. The fighting of 1756 and 1757 was a near catastrophe for Great Britain. Canadians captured the British forts in northern New York. Indians pounded backcountry settlements, killed thousands of settlers, and raided deep into the coastal colonies, throwing British colonists into panic. "There is no surer way to sicken the people of the English colonies," a Canadian commander mused, "and to make them desire the return of peace." The absence of colonial cooperation greatly hampered the British attempt to mount a counterattack. When British commanders tried to exert direct control over provincial troops, in order to coordinate their strategy, they succeeded only in angering local authorities.

In this climate of defeat, the British adopted a harsh policy of retribution against the French-speaking farmers of Acadia, who had lived peacefully under British rule for over forty years. The Acadians' refusal to swear allegiance to the crown was now used as an excuse for their expulsion. In the fall of 1755, New England troops began the forcible removal of approximately 10,000 Acadians, selling their farms at bargain prices to immigrants from New England. Suffering terrible hardship and heartbreak, the Acadians were dispersed throughout the Atlantic world, a substantial number of them ending up in Louisiana, then under Spanish control, where they became known as "Cajuns." The Acadian expulsion is one of the most infamous chapters in the British imperial record in North America.

The Conquest of Canada

In the darkest days of 1757, William Pitt, an enthusiastic advocate of British expansion, became prime minister of Great Britain. "I know that I can save this country," Pitt declared, "and that no one else can." Deciding that the global war could be won in North America, he subsidized the Prussians to fight the war in Europe, and reserved his own forces and resources for naval and colonial operations. Pitt committed the British to the conquest of Canada and the elimination of all French competition in North America. Such a goal could be achieved only with a tremendous outpouring of men and money. By promising that the war would be fought "at His Majesty's expense," Pitt was able to buy colonial cooperation. A massive infusion of British currency and credit greatly stimulated the North American economy. Pitt dispatched over 20,000 regular British troops across the Atlantic. Combining them with colonial forces, he massed over 50,000 armed men against Canada.

The British attracted Indian support for their plans by "redressing the grievances complained of by the Indians, with respect to the lands which have been fraudulently taken from them," in the words of a British official. In 1758 officials promised the Iroquois Confederacy and the Ohio Indians that the crown would "agree upon clear and fixed boundaries between our settlements and their hunting grounds, so that each party may know their own and be a mutual protection to each other of their respective possessions."

Thus did Pitt succeed in reversing the course of the war. Regular and provincial forces captured Louisburg in July 1758, setting the stage for the penetration of the St. Lawrence Valley. A month later a force of New Englanders captured the strategic French fort of Oswego

The death of General James Wolfe, at the conclusion of the battle in which the British captured Quebec in 1759, became the subject of American artist Benjamin West's most famous painting, which was exhibited to tremendous acclaim in London in 1770.

SOURCE: Benjamin West (1738–1820), *The Death of General Wolfe*, 1770. Oil on canvas, 152.6 x 214.5 cm. Transfer from the Canadian War Memorials, 1921. (Gift of the 2nd Duke of Westminster, Eaton Hall, Cheshire, 1918.) National Gallery of Canada, Ottawa, Ontario.

on Lake Ontario, thereby preventing the Canadians from resupplying their western posts. Encouraged by British promises, many Indian tribes abandoned the French alliance. The French were forced to give up Fort Duquesne, and a large British force soon took control of this French fort at the Forks of the Ohio, renaming the post Fort Pitt (Pittsburgh today) in honor of the prime minister. "Blessed be God," wrote a Boston editor. "The long looked for day is arrived that has now fixed us on the banks of the Ohio." The last of the French forts on the New York frontier fell in 1759. In the South, regular and provincial British troops invaded the homeland of the Cherokees and crushed them.

British forces now converged on Quebec, the heart of French Canada. In the summer of 1759 British troops, responding to General James Wolfe's order to "burn and lay waste the country," plundered farms and shelled the city of Quebec. Finally, in an epic battle fought on the Plains of Abraham before the city walls, more than 2,000 British, French, American, and Canadian men lost their lives, including both Wolfe and the French commander, the Marquis de Montcalm. The British army prevailed, and Quebec fell. Finally, the conquest of Montreal in 1760 marked the destruction of the French empire in America. "The great day is now come," declared the editor of the *Boston News-Letter*, "the fall of the American Carthage."

In the final two years of the war the British swept French ships from the seas, invaded Havana and conquered Cuba, took possession of several other important Spanish and French colonies in the Caribbean, achieved dominance in India, and even captured the Spanish Philippines. In the Treaty of Paris, signed in 1763, France lost all its possessions on the North

American mainland. It ceded its claims east of the Mississippi to Great Britain, with the exception of New Orleans. That town, along with the other French trans-Mississippi claims, passed to Spain. For its part, in exchange for the return of all its Caribbean and Pacific colonies, Spain ceded Florida to Britain. The imperial rivalry in eastern North America that had begun in the sixteenth century now came to an end with complete victory for the British Empire.

The Struggle for the West

When the Ohio Indians heard of the French cession of the western country to Britain, they were shocked. "The French had no right to give away [our] country," they told a British trader. "They were never conquered by any nation." A new set of British policies soon shocked them all the more. Both the French and the British had long used gift-giving as a way of gaining favor with Indians. The Spanish officials who replaced the French in Louisiana made an effort to continue the old policy. But the British military governor of the western region, General Jeffery Amherst, in one of his

first official actions, banned presents to Indian chiefs and tribes, demanding that they learn to live without "charity." Not only were Indians angered by Amherst's reversal of custom, but they were also frustrated by his refusal to supply them with the ammunition they required for hunting. Many were left starving.

In this climate, hundreds of Ohio Indians became disciples of an Indian visionary named Neolin ("The Enlightened One" in Algonquian), known to the English as the Delaware Prophet. The core of Neolin's teaching was that Indians had been corrupted by European ways and needed to purify themselves by returning to their traditions and preparing for a holy war. "Drive them out," he declared of the settlers. A confederacy of tribes organized by a group of chiefs who had gained influence by adopting Neolin's ideas laid plans for a coordinated attack against the British in the spring of 1763. The principal figure among them was the Ottawa chief Pontiac, renowned as an orator and political leader. This combination of inspirational religious and political leadership was a pattern in the long history of Indian resistance to colonial expansion in North America. The first instance of this approach on

European Claims in North America, 1750 and 1763   As a result of the British victory in the Seven Years' War, the map of colonial claims in North America was fundamentally transformed.

the part of Indian tribes had taken place among the Algonquians of the Chesapeake in the early seventeenth century (see Chapter 3).

In May 1763, the Indian confederacy simultaneously attacked all the British forts in the West. Warriors in a suprise attack overran Fort Michilimackinac, at the narrows between Lakes Michigan and Huron, by scrambling through the gates supposedly in pursuit of a lacrosse ball, cheered on by unsuspecting soldiers. In raids throughout the backcountry, Indians killed more than 2,000 settlers. At Fort Pitt, General Amherst proposed that his officers "send the smallpox among the disaffected tribes" by distributing infected blankets from the fort's hospital. This early instance of germ warfare resulted in an epidemic that spread from the Delawares and Shawnees to the southern Creeks, Choctaws, and Chickasaws, killing hundreds of people. Although they sacked and burned eight British posts, the Indians failed to take the key forts of Niagara, Detroit, and Pitt. Pontiac fought on for another year, but most of the Indians sued for peace, fearing the destruction of their villages. The British came to terms because they knew they could not overwhelm the Indian peoples. The war thus ended in stalemate.

Even before the uprising, the British had been at work on a policy they hoped would help to resolve frontier tensions. In the Royal Proclamation of 1763, the British government set aside the region west of the crest of the Appalachian Mountains as "Indian Country," and required the specific authorization of the crown for any purchase of these protected Indian lands. Indians were pleased with the proclamation, but land speculators and backcountry British Americans were outraged.

Colonists had expected that the removal of the French threat would allow them to move unencumbered into the West, regardless of the wishes of the Indian inhabitants. They could not understand why the British would award territory to Indian enemies who had slaughtered more than 4,000 settlers during the previous war. In an act emblematic of the anger backcountry settlers felt about these restrictions, a mob of Pennsylvanians known as the Paxton Boys butchered twenty Indian men, women, and children at the small village of Conestoga on the Susquehanna River in December 1763. When colonial authorities moved to arrest them, 600 frontiersmen marched into Philadelphia in protest. Negotiations led by Benjamin Franklin helped to prevent a bloody confrontation.

In fact, the British proved unable and ultimately unwilling to prevent the westward migration that was to be a dynamic part of the colonization of British North America. Within a few years of the war, New Englanders by the thousands were moving into the northern Green Mountain district, known as Vermont. In the middle colonies, New York settlers pushed ever closer to the

A treaty between the Delaware, Shawnee, and Mingo (western Iroquois) Indians and Great Britain, July 13, 1765, at the conclusion of the Indian uprising. The Indian chiefs signed with pictographs symbolizing their clans, each notarized with an official wax seal.

SOURCE: Photo by Carmelo Guadagno. Photograph Courtesy of National Museum of the American Indian, Smithsonian Institution.

homeland of the Iroquois, while others settled within the protective radius of Fort Pitt in western Pennsylvania. Hunters, stock herders, and farmers crossed over the first range of the Appalachians in Virginia and North Carolina, planting pioneer communities in what are now West Virginia and eastern Tennessee.

Moreover, the press of population growth and economic development turned the attention of investors and land speculators to the area west of the Appalachians. George Washington, now a prominent investor in western lands, believed that the Royal Proclamation of 1763 declaring an Appalachian boundary to western expansion was merely "a temporary expedient." In 1768, the Ohio Company sent surveyors to mark out their grant in the upper Ohio Valley. In response to demands by settlers and speculators, British authorities were soon pressing the Iroquois and Cherokees for cessions of land in Indian Country. No longer able to play off rival colonial powers, Indians were reduced to a choice between compliance and resistance. Weakened by the recent war, they chose to sign away lands. In the Treaty of Hard Labor in 1768, the Cherokees ceded a vast tract on the waters of the upper Tennessee River, where British settlers had already planted communities. In the Treaty of Fort Stanwix of the same year, the Iroquois gave up their claim to the Ohio Valley, hoping thereby to deflect English settlement away from their own homeland.

The individual colonies were even more aggressive. Locked in a dispute with Pennsylvania about jurisdiction in the Ohio country, in 1773 Virginia governor John Murray, Earl of Dunmore, sent a force to occupy

Fort Pitt. In 1774, in an attempt to gain legitimacy for his dispute with Pennsylvania, Dunmore provoked a frontier war with the Shawnees. After defeating them he forced their cession of the upper Ohio River Valley to Virginia. The Iroquois and Ohio Indians angrily complained about the outcome of what came to be known as Dunmore's War. The English king, they argued, had guaranteed that the boundary between colonial and Indian land "should forever after be looked upon as a barrier between us." But the Americans "entirely disregard, and despise the settlement agreed upon by their superiors and us." They "are come in vast numbers to the Ohio, and [give] our people to understand that they would settle wherever they pleased. If this is the case, we must look upon every engagement you made with us as void and of no effect." This continuing struggle for the West would be an important issue in the coming American Revolution.

THE IMPERIAL CRISIS IN BRITISH NORTH AMERICA

No colonial power of the mid-eighteenth century could match Britain in projecting imperial power over the face of the globe. During the years following its victory in the Seven Years' War, Britain turned confidently to the reorganization of its North American empire. This new colonial policy plunged British authorities into a new and ultimately more threatening conflict with the colonists, who had begun to develop a sense of a separate identity.

The Emergence of American Nationalism

Despite the anger of frontier settlers over the Proclamation of 1763, the conclusion of the Seven Years' War had left most colonists proud of their place in the British empire. But during the war many had begun to note important contrasts between themselves and the mother country. The soldiers of the British army, for example, shocked Americans with their profane, lewd, and violent behavior. But the colonists were equally shocked by the swift and terrible punishment that aristocratic officers used to keep these soldiers in line. David Perry of Massachusetts witnessed the punishment of two soldiers sentenced to 800 lashes apiece. "The flesh appeared to be entirely whipped from their shoulders," he wrote, "and they hung as mute and motionless as though they had long since been deprived of life." A military doctor stood nearby with a vial of smelling salts, periodically reviving the men and taunting them: "Damn you, you can bear it yet!" It was, Perry concluded, "a specimen of British cruelty." Those who had witnessed such savage

punishments found it easy to believe in the threat of Britain enslaving American colonists.

Colonial forces, by contrast, were composed of volunteer companies. Officers tempered their administration of punishment, knowing they had to maintain the enthusiasm of their troops. Discipline thus fell considerably below the standards to which British officers were accustomed. "Riff-raff," one British general said of the colonials, "the lowest dregs of the people, both officers and men." The British made no secret of their poor opinion of colonial fighting men. "The Americans are in general the dirtiest, most contemptible, cowardly dogs that you can conceive," wrote General Wolfe. For their part, many colonial officers believed that the British ignored the important role the Americans had played in the Seven Years' War. Massachusetts, for example, lost between 1,500 and 2,000 fighting men. This mutual suspicion and hostility was often expressed in name calling: British soldiers called New Englanders "Yankees," while colonists heckled the red-coated British with taunts of "Lobster." It was during the war that many colonists began to see themselves as distinct from the British.

The Seven Years' War also strengthened a sense of identity among the colonies. Farmers who never before had ventured outside the communities of their birth fought in distant regions with men like themselves from other colonies. Such experiences reinforced a developing nationalist perspective. From 1735 to 1775, while trade with Britain doubled, commerce among the colonies increased by a factor of four. People and ideas moved along with goods. The first stage lines linking seaboard cities began operation in the 1750s. Spurred by Postmaster Benjamin Franklin, many colonies built or improved post roads for transporting the mails.

The Press, Politics, and Republicanism

One of the most important means of intercolonial communication was the weekly newspaper. Early in the eighteenth century the colonial press functioned as a mouthpiece for the government. Editors who criticized public officials could land in jail. In 1735, New York City editor John Peter Zenger was indicted for seditious libel after printing antigovernment articles. But as it turned out, the case provided the precedent for greater freedom of the press. "Shall the press be silenced that evil governors may have their way?" Zenger's attorney asked the jury. "The question before the court is not the cause of a poor printer," he declared, but the cause "of every free man that lives under a British government on the main of America." Zenger was acquitted. By 1760, more than twenty highly opinionated weekly newspapers circulated in the British colonies, and according to one estimate, a quarter of all male colonists were regular readers.

The midcentury American press focused increasingly on intercolonial affairs. One study of colonial newspapers indicates that intercolonial coverage increased sixfold over the four decades preceding the Revolution. Editors of local papers increasingly looked at events from what they called a "continental" perspective. This trend accelerated during the Seven Years' War, when communities demanded coverage of events in distant colonies where their men might be fighting. During these years the British colonists of North America first began to use the term "American" to denote their common identity. More than any previous event, the Seven Years' War promoted a new spirit of nationalism and a wider notion of community. This was the social base of the political community later forged at the First Continental Congress.

The pages of the colonial press reveal the political assumptions held by informed colonists. For decades governors had struggled with colonial assemblies over their respective powers. As commentary on the meaning of these struggles, colonial editors often reprinted the writings of the radical Whigs of eighteenth-century England, pamphleteers such as John Trenchard and Thomas Gordon, political theorists such as John Locke, and essayists such as Alexander Pope and Jonathan Swift. They warned of the growing threat to liberty posed by the unchecked exercise of power. In their more emotional writings they argued that a conspiracy existed among the powerful—kings, aristocrats, and Catholics—to quash liberty and institute tyranny. Their political principles included extension of the ballot to greater numbers of men, apportionment of legislative representation on the basis of population, and responsiveness by representatives to their constituents. The only effective counterweight to the abuse of power, they argued, was the constant vigilance of the people and their exercise of public virtue, that is, the sacrifice of self-interest for the public good. Outside the mainstream of British political opinion, these ideas came to define the political consensus in the British colonies, a point of view called "republicanism."

Republicanism declared that the truly just society provided the greatest possible liberty to individuals. As the power of the state, by its very nature, was antithetical to liberty, it had to be limited. John Locke argued that the authority of a ruler should be conditional rather than absolute and that the people had the inherent right to select their own form of governance and to withdraw their support if the government did not fulfill its trust. The best guarantee of good government, then, was the broad distribution of power to the people, who would not only select their own leaders but vote them out as well. In this view, republican government depended on the virtue of the people, their willingness to make the health and sta-

James Franklin began publishing the *New-England Courant* in Boston in 1721. When Franklin criticized the government, he was jailed, and the paper continued under the editorship of his brother Benjamin. The *Courant* ceased publication in 1726, and the Franklin brothers went on to other papers— James to the *Rhode Island State Gazette*, Benjamin to the *Pennsylvania Gazette* in Philadelphia. Before the *Zenger case* in 1735, few editors dared to challenge the government.

SOURCE: Massachusetts Historical Society.

bility of the political community their first priority, and was possible only for an "independent" population that controlled its own affairs. As Thomas Jefferson once wrote, ". . . dependence begets subservience and venality, suffocates the germ of virtue, and prepares fit tools for the designs of ambition." Individual ownership of property, especially land, he argued, was the foundation of an independent and virtuous people.

This was a political theory that fit the circumstances of American life, with its wide base of property ownership, its tradition of representative assemblies, and its history of struggle with royal authority. Contrast the assumptions of republicans with those of British monarchists, who argued that the good society was one in which a strong state, controlled by a hereditary elite, kept a vicious and unruly people in line.

The Sugar and Stamp Acts

The emerging sense of American political identity was soon tested by British measures designed to raise revenues in the colonies. To quell Indian uprisings and stifle discontent among the French and Spanish populations of Quebec and Florida, 10,000 British troops remained stationed in North America at the conclusion of the Seven Years' War. The cost of maintaining this force added to the enormous debt Britain had run up during the fighting and created a desperate need for additional revenues. Increased excise taxes at home, however, resulted in disruptive demonstrations in the South of England, and Parliament was flooded by petitions from landlords and merchants protesting any attempt to raise revenues at their expense. In 1764, the Chancellor of the Exchequer, George Grenville, deciding to obtain the needed revenue from America, pushed through Parliament a measure known as the Sugar Act.

The Sugar Act placed a duty on sugar imported into the colonies and revitalized the customs service, introducing stricter registration procedures for ships and adding more officers. In fact, the duty was significantly less than the one that had been on the books and ignored for years, but the difference was that the British now intended to enforce it. In anticipation of American resistance, the legislation increased the jurisdiction of the vice-admiralty court at Halifax, where customs cases were heard. These courts were hated because there was no presumption of innocence and the accused had no right to a jury trial. These new regulations promised not only to squeeze the incomes of American merchants but also to cut off their lucrative smuggling operations. Moreover, colonial taxes, which had been raised during the war, remained at an all-time high. In many cities, merchants as well as artisans protested loudly. Boston was especially vocal: in response to the sugar tax, the town meeting proposed a boycott of certain English imports. This movement for nonimportation soon spread to other port towns.

James Otis, Jr., a Massachusetts lawyer fond of grand oratory, was one of the first Americans to strike a number of themes that would become familiar over the next fifteen years. A man's "right to his life, his liberty, his property" was "written on the heart, and revealed to him by his maker," he argued in language echoing the rhetoric of the Great Awakening. It was "inherent, inalienable, and indefeasible by any laws, pacts, contracts, covenants, or stipulations which man could devise." He declared that "an act against the Constitution is void." There could be "no taxation without representation."

But it was only fair, Grenville argued in return, that the colonists help pay the costs of the empire, and what better way to do so than by a tax? Taxes in the colonies were much lower than taxes at home. In early 1765, unswayed by American protests, he followed the Sugar Act with a second and considerably more sweeping revenue measure, the Stamp Act. This tax required the purchase of specially embossed paper for all newspapers, legal documents, licenses, insurance policies, ship's papers, and even dice and playing cards.

The Stamp Act Crisis

During the summer and autumn of 1765 the American reaction to the Stamp Act created a crisis of unprecedented proportions. The stamp tax had to be paid in hard money, and it came during a period of economic stagnation. Many colonists complained of being "miserably burdened and oppressed with taxes."

Of more importance for the longer term, however, were the constitutional implications. Although colonial male property owners elected their own assemblies, they could not vote in British elections. But the British argued that Americans were subject to the acts of Parliament because of virtual representation. That is, members of Parliament were thought to represent not just their districts, but all citizens of the empire. As one British writer put it, the colonists were "represented in Parliament in the same manner as those inhabitants of Britain are who have not voices in elections." But in an influential pamphlet of 1765, *Considerations on the Propriety of Imposing Taxes*, Maryland lawyer Daniel Dulany rejected this theory. Because Americans were members of a separate political community, he insisted, Parliament could impose no tax on them. Instead, he argued for "actual representation," emphasizing the direct relationship that must exist between the people and their political representatives.

It was just such constitutional issues that were emphasized in the Virginia Stamp Act Resolutions, pushed through the Virginia assembly by the passionate young lawyer Patrick Henry in May 1765. Although the Virginia House of Burgesses rejected the most radical of Henry's resolutions, they were all reprinted throughout the colonies. By the end of 1765 the assemblies of eight other colonies had approved similar measures denouncing the Stamp Act and proclaiming their support of "no taxation without representation."

In Massachusetts the leaders of the opposition to the Stamp Act came from a group of upper- and middle-class men who had long opposed the conservative leaders of the colony. These men had worked years to establish a political alliance with Boston craftsmen and workers who met at taverns, in volunteer fire companies, or at social clubs. One of these clubs, known as the Loyall Nine, included a member named Samuel Adams, an associate and friend of James Otis, who had made his career in local politics. Using his contacts with professionals, craftsmen, and laboring men, Adams helped put together an anti-British alliance that spanned Boston's social classes. "If our trade may be taxed," he reasoned with working men, "why not our lands? Why not the produce of our lands and everything we possess or make use of?" In August 1765 Adams and the Loyall Nine were instrumental in organizing a protest of Boston working-men against the Stamp Act.

Whereas Boston's elite had prospered during the eighteenth century, the conditions for workers and the poor had worsened. Unemployment, inflation, and high taxes had greatly increased the level of poverty during the depression that followed the Seven Years' War, and many were resentful. Concerted action by crowds, as when people took to the streets to demand fair prices for bread, or when posses formed to capture criminals, were commonplace in eighteenth-century communities throughout Europe and the colonies. It was therefore not suprising when a large Boston crowd assembled on August 14, 1765, in the shade of an old elm tree—which became known as the "Liberty Tree"—and strung up effigies of several British officials, including Boston's stamp distributor, Andrew Oliver. The restless crowd then vandalized Oliver's office and home. At the order of Oliver's brother-in-law, Lieutenant Governor Thomas Hutchinson, leader of the Massachusetts conservatives, the town sheriff tried to break up the crowd, but he was pelted with paving stones and bricks. Soon thereafter, Oliver resigned his commission. The unified action of Boston's social groups had had its intended effect.

Twelve days later, however, a similar crowd gathered at the aristocratic home of Hutchinson himself. As the family fled through the back door, the crowd smashed through the front with axes. Inside they demolished furniture, chopped down the interior walls, consumed the contents of the wine cellar, and looted everything of value, leaving the house a mere shell. As these events demonstrated, it was not always possible to keep popular protests within bounds. During the fall and winter, urban crowds in commercial towns from Halifax in the North to Savannah in the South forced the resignation of many British tax officials.

In many colonial cities and towns, groups of merchants, lawyers, and craftsmen sought to moderate the

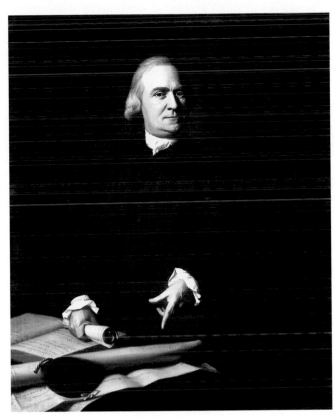

Samuel Adams, a second cousin of John Adams, was a leader of the Boston radicals and an organizer of the Sons of Liberty. The artist of this portrait, John Singleton Copley, was known for setting his subjects in the midst of everyday objects; here he portrays Adams in a middle-class suit with the charter guaranteeing the liberties of Boston's freemen.

SOURCE: John Singleton Copley (1738–1815), *Samuel Adams*, 1772. Oil on canvas, 127 cm × 102.2 cm. Deposited by the City of Boston. Courtesy, Museum of Fine Arts, Boston.

resistance movement by seizing control of it. Calling themselves the Sons of Liberty, these groups encouraged moderate forms of protest. They circulated petitions, published pamphlets, and encouraged crowd actions only as a last resort; always they emphasized limited political goals. Then in October 1765, delegations from nine colonies (New Hampshire and Georgia declined the invitation to attend, and the governors of Virginia and North Carolina prevented their delegates from accepting) met at what has been called the Stamp Act Congress in New York City, where they passed a set of resolutions denying Parliament's right to tax the colonists, since taxation depended on representation. But the delegates also agreed that Parliament had the authority to pass laws regulating colonial trade. These moderate efforts defused the radicals, and there were few repetitions of mob attacks, but by the end of 1765 almost all the stamp distributors had resigned or fled, making it impossible for Britain to enforce the Stamp Act.

Repeal of the Stamp Act

In the fall of 1765, British merchants, worried about the effects of the growing nonimportation movement among the colonists, began petitioning Parliament to repeal the Stamp Act. About 40 percent of England's exports went to the British colonies in North America. "I rejoice that America has resisted," said William Pitt, who was no longer prime minister but spoke for the merchant interests in Parliament. "It is my opinion that this kingdom has no right to lay a tax upon the colonies." Grenville demanded that the British army be used to enforce the act. "Tell me," he demanded of Pitt, "when the Americans were emancipated." Pitt's response was memorable: "I desire to know when they were made slaves." Parliament heard the testimony of several interested parties, including Benjamin Franklin, who warned that Grenville's proposal to use troops could bring on a rebellion.

However, it was not until March 1766 that a bill for repeal passed the House of Commons. This news was greeted with celebrations throughout the America colonies, and the nonimportation associations were disbanded. Overlooked in the mood of optimism was Parliament's assertion in this Declaratory Act of its full authority to make laws binding the colonies "in all cases whatsoever." The notion of absolute parliamentary supremacy over colonial matters was basic to the British theory of empire. Even Pitt, friend of America that he was, asserted "the authority of this kingdom over the colonies to be sovereign and supreme, in every circumstance of government and legislation whatsoever." The Declaratory Act signaled that the conflict had not been resolved, but merely postponed.

"SAVE YOUR MONEY AND SAVE YOUR COUNTRY"

Colonial resistance to the Stamp Act was stronger in urban than in rural communities, stronger among merchants, craftsmen, and planters than among farmers and frontiersmen. When Parliament next moved to impose its will, as it had promised to do in the Declaratory Act, imposing new duties on imported goods, the American opposition again adopted the tactic of nonimportation. But this time resistance spread from the cities and towns into the countryside. As the editor of the *Boston Gazette* phrased the issue, "Save your money and you save your country." It became the slogan of the movement.

The Townshend Revenue Acts

During the 1760s there was a rapid turnover of government leaders that made it difficult for Britain to form a consistent and even-handed policy toward the colonies. In 1767, after several failed governments, King George III asked William Pitt to again become prime minister. Pitt enjoyed enormous good will in America, and a government under his leadership stood a good chance of reclaiming colonial credibility. But, suffering from a prolonged illness, he was soon forced to retire, and his place as head of the cabinet was assumed by Charles Townshend, Chancellor of the Exchequer.

One of the first problems facing the new government was the national debt. At home there were massive unemployment, riots over high prices, and tax protests. The large landowners forced a bill through Parliament slashing their taxes by 25 percent. The government feared continued opposition at home far more than opposition in America. So as part of his plan to close the

Demonstrations against the Stamp Act, 1765
From Halifax in the North to Savannah in the South, popular demonstrations against the Stamp Act forced the resignation of British tax officials. The propaganda of 1765 even reached the breakfast table, emblazoned on teapots.

SOURCE: *No Stamp Act* teapot, Colonial Williamsburg Foundation.

budget gap, Townshend proposed a new revenue measure for the colonies that placed import duties on commodities such as lead, glass, paint, paper, and tea. By means of these new Revenue Acts, enacted in 1767, Townshend hoped to redress colonial grievances against internal taxes such as those imposed by the Stamp Act. For most colonists, however, it proved to be a distinction without a difference.

The most influential response to these Revenue Acts came in a series of articles by John Dickinson, *Letters from a Farmer in Pennsylvania*, that were reprinted in nearly every colonial newspaper. Dickinson was a wealthy Philadelphia lawyer, but in this work he posed as a humble farmer. Parliament had the right to regulate trade through the use of duties, he conceded. It could place prohibitive tariffs, for example, on foreign products. But it had no constitutional authority to tax goods in order to raise revenues in America. As the preface to the Revenue Acts made clear, the income they produced would be used to pay the salaries of royal officials in America. Thus, Dickinson pointed out, since colonial assemblies were no longer paying their salaries, colonial administrators would not be subject to the financial oversight of elected representatives.

Other Americans warned that this was part of the British conspiracy to suppress American liberties. Their fears were reinforced by Townshend's stringent enforcement of the Revenue Acts. He created a new and strengthened Board of Commissioners of the Customs, and established a series of vice-admiralty courts at Boston, Philadelphia, and Charleston to prosecute violators of the duties—the first time these hated institutions had appeared in the most important American port cities. To demonstrate his power, he also suspended New York's assembly. That body had refused to vote public funds to support the British troops garrisoned in the colony. Until the citizens of New York relented, Townshend declared, they would no longer be represented.

In response to these measures, some men argued for violent resistance. But it was Dickinson's essays that had the greatest effect on the public debate, not only because of their convincing arguments, but because of their mild and reasonable tone. "Let us behave like dutiful children," Dickinson urged, "who have received unmerited blows from a beloved parent." As yet, no sentiment for independence existed in America.

The Repeal or the Funeral Procession of Miss Americ-Stamp, a British cartoon engraving of 1766. The repeal of the Stamp Tax was supported by English exporters, whose trade with the colonies dropped precipitously as a result. The warehouses in the background symbolize the revival of trade with America.

SOURCE: The Granger Collection.

Nonimportation: An Early Political Boycott

Associations of nonimportation and nonconsumption, revived in October 1767 when the Boston town meeting drew up a long list of British products to boycott, became the main weapon of the resistance movement. Over the next few months other port cities, including Providence, Newport, and New York, set up nonimportation associations of their own. Towns such as Philadelphia, however, were unable to overcome conflicts between merchants and artisans. The economy had begun to improve since the earlier boycott, and many merchants saw little advantage in curtailing imports. Craftsmen, on the other hand, supported nonimportation with enthusiasm, because it meant that consumers would buy their products rather than foreign ones. Supported by workers, artisans took to the streets in towns and cities throughout the colonies to force merchants to stop importing British goods. The associations published the names of uncooperative importers and retailers. These people then became the object of protesters, who sometimes resorted to violence. Coercion was very much a part of the movement.

Adopting the language of Protestant ethics, nonimportation associations pledged to curtail luxuries and stimulate local industry. These aims had great appeal in small towns and rural districts, which

This British cartoon, *A Society of Patriotic Ladies*, ridiculed the efforts of American women to support the Patriot cause by boycotting tea. The moderator of the meeting appears coarse and masculine, while an attractive scribe is swayed by the amorous attention of a gentleman. The activities under the table suggest that these women are neglecting their true duty.

SOURCE: Library of Congress.

previously had been uninvolved in the anti-British struggle. In 1768 and 1769 colonial newspapers paid a great deal of attention to women's support for the boycott. Groups of women, some calling themselves Daughters of Liberty, organized spinning and weaving bees to produce homespun for local consumption. The actual work performed at these bees was less important than the symbolic message. "The industry and frugality of American ladies," wrote the editor of the *Boston Evening Post*, "are contributing to bring about the political salvation of a whole continent." Other women renounced silks and satins and pledged to stop serving tea to their husbands. Women sang:

> *Throw aside your topknots of pride,*
> *Wear none but your own country linen.*
> *Of economy boast, let your pride be the most,*
> *To show clothes of your own make and spinning.*

The poet Milcah Martha Moore urged American women to

> *Stand firmly resolv'd, and bid Grenville to see,*
> *That rather than freedom we part with our tea,*
> *And well as we love the dear draught when a-dry,*
> *As American patriots our taste we deny.*

Nonimportation appealed to the traditional values of rural communities—self-sufficiency and independence—and for the first time brought country people into the growing community of resistance.

Nonimportation was greatly strengthened in May 1769 when the Virginia House of Burgesses enacted the first provincial legislation banning the importation of goods enumerated in the Townshend Acts, and slaves and luxury commodities as well. Over the next few months all the colonies but New Hampshire enacted similar associations. Because of these efforts, the value of colonial imports from Britain declined by 41 percent.

The Massachusetts Circular Letter

Boston and Massachusetts were at the center of the agitation over the Townshend Revenue Acts. In February 1768, the Massachusetts House of Representatives approved a letter, drawn up by Samuel Adams, addressed to the speakers of the other provincial assemblies. Designed largely as a propaganda device and having little practical significance, the letter denounced the Townshend Revenue Acts, attacked the British plan to make royal officials independent of colonial assemblies, and urged the colonies to find a way to "harmonize with each other." Massachusetts governor Francis Bernard condemned the document for stirring up rebellion and dissolved the legislature. In Britain, Lord Hillsborough, secretary of state for the colonies, ordered each royal governor in America to likewise dissolve his colony's assembly if it should endorse the letter. Before this demand reached America, the assemblies of New Hampshire, New Jersey, and Connecticut had commended Massachusetts. Virginia, moreover, had issued a circular letter encouraging a "hearty union" among the colonies and urging common action against the British measures that "have an immediate tendency to enslave us."

Hillsborough now ordered Massachusetts Governor Bernard to force the newly elected House of Representatives to rescind Adams's letter and delete all mention of it from its journal. The radicals could have asked for nothing better; resistance to the Townshend duties had been flagging, but there was great support for the prerogative and independence of the assembly. After protracted debate in June 1768, the representatives voted ninety-two to seventeen to defy Bernard, who immediately shut them down. The "Glorious Ninety-two" became heroes of the hour, and men in taverns throughout the colonies drank "ninety-two toasts" to the brave men of Massachusetts. The "rescinders," meanwhile, were condemned by public and press, in local elections the next year, seven of them lost their seats.

Throughout this crisis there were rumors and threats of mob rule in Boston. "I am no friend to riots, tumult, and unlawful assemblies," Samuel Adams declared, "but when the people are oppressed . . . they are not to be blamed." Because customs agents enforced the law against smugglers and honest traders alike, they enraged merchants, seamen, and dockworkers. In June 1768, a crowd assaulted customs officials who had seized John Hancock's sloop *Liberty* for nonpayment of duties. So frightened were the officials that they fled the city. Hancock, reportedly the wealthiest merchant in the colonies and a vocal opponent of the British measures, had become a principal target of the customs officers. In September the Boston town meeting called on the people to arm themselves, and in the absence of an elected assembly it invited all the other towns to send delegates to a provincial convention. There were threats of armed resistance, but little support for it in the convention, which broke up in chaos. Nevertheless the British, fearing insurrection, occupied Boston with infantry and artillery regiments on October 1, 1768. With this action, they sacrificed a great deal of good will and respect and added greatly to the growing tensions.

The Politics of Revolt and the Boston Massacre

The British troops stationed in the colonies were the object of scorn and hostility over the next two years. There were regular conflicts between soldiers and radicals in New York City, often focusing on the Sons of Liberty. These men would erect "liberty poles"—in emulation of Boston's Liberty Tree, where resistance was said to have begun—festooned with banners and flags proclaiming their cause, and the British troops would promptly destroy them. When the New York assembly finally bowed to Townshend in December 1769 and voted an appropriation to support the troops, the New York City Sons of Liberty organized a demonstration and erected a large liberty pole. The soldiers chopped it down, sawed it into pieces, and left the wood on the steps of a tavern frequented by the Sons. This led to a riot in which British troops used their bayonets against several thousand New Yorkers armed with cutlasses and clubs. Several men were wounded.

Confrontations also took place in Boston. Sam Adams played up reports and rumors of soldiers harassing women, picking fights, or simply taunting residents with versions of "Yankee Doodle." Soldiers were often hauled into Boston's courts, and local judges adopted a completely unfriendly attitude toward these members of the occupying army. In February 1770, an eleven-year-old boy was killed when a customs officer opened fire on a rock-throwing crowd. Although no soldiers

Paul Revere, *British Landing Troops in Boston, 1768*. Colored engraving. British troops, charged with protecting custom officials, disembark from a ship at the end of Long Wharf in Boston in 1768, in an engraving published by Paul Revere.

SOURCE: Photograph by Will Brown. Rare Book Department, The Free Library of Philadelphia.

were involved, this incident heightened the tensions between citizens and troops.

A persistent source of conflict was the competition between troops and townsmen over jobs. Soldiers were permitted to work when off duty, putting them in competition with day laborers. In early March 1770, an off-duty soldier walked into a ropewalk (a long narrow building in which ropes are made) in search of a job. "You can clean my shithouse," he was told. The soldier left but returned with his friends, and a small riot ensued. Fighting continued over the next few days in the streets between the wharf and the Common, where the soldiers were encamped. On the evening of March 5, 1770, a crowd gathered at the Customs House and began taunting a guard, calling him a "damned rascally scoundrel lobster" and worse. A captain and seven soldiers went to his rescue, only to be pelted with snowballs and stones. Suddenly, without orders, the frightened soldiers began to fire. Five of the crowd fell dead, and six more were wounded, two of these dying later. The first blood shed was that of Crispus Attucks, whose mother was Indian and father was African American. The soldiers escaped to their barracks, but a mob numbering in the hundreds rampaged through the streets demanding vengeance. Fearing for the safety of his men and the security of the state, Thomas Hutchinson, now governor of Massachusetts, ordered British troops out of Boston and arrested the soldiers who had fired the shots. The soldiers were tried later that year. Defending them were John Adams and Josiah Quincy, Jr., two leaders of the radicals. Adams and Quincy established a reputation for fairness and statesmanship by convincing a jury of Bostonians that the soldiers had fired in fear of their lives. The Boston Massacre became infamous throughout the colonies, in part because of the circulation of an inflammatory print produced by the Boston engraver Paul Revere, which depicted the British as firing on a crowd of unresisting civilians. But for many colonists, the incident was a disturbing reminder of the extent to which relations with the mother country had deteriorated. During the next two years, many people found themselves pulling back from the brink. "There seems," one Bostonian wrote, "to be a pause in politics."

The growth of American resistance was slowed as well by the news that Parliament had repealed most of the Townshend Revenue Acts on March 5, 1770—the same day as the Boston Massacre. In the climate of apprehension and confusion, there were few celebrations of the repeal, and the nonimportation associations almost immediately collapsed. Over the next three years, the value of British imports rose by 80 percent. The parliamentary retreat on the question of duties, like the earlier repeal of the Stamp Act, was accompanied by a face-saving measure—retention of the tax on tea "as a mark of the supremacy of Parliament," in the words of Frederick Lord North, the new prime minister.

FROM RESISTANCE TO REBELLION

The tax revolt in America was not an isolated incident, but the largest of numerous resistance movements to taxation—in Russa, the Netherlands, Corsica, Ireland, and Great Britain itself. There was a lull in the American controversy during the early 1770s, but the situation turned violent in 1773, when Parliament again infuriated the Americans. This time it was an ill-advised Tea Act, and it propelled the colonists onto a swift track from resistance to outright rebellion.

Intercolonial Cooperation

In June 1772, Governor Hutchinson inaugurated another controversy by announcing that henceforth his salary and those of other royally appointed Massachusetts officials would be paid by the crown. In effect, this made the executive and judiciary branches

In Paul Revere's version of the Boston Massacre, issued three weeks after the incident, the British fire an organized volley into a defenseless crowd. Revere's print—which he plagiarized from another Boston engraver—may have been inaccurate, but it was enormously effective propaganda. It hung in so many Patriot homes that the judge hearing the murder trial of these British soldiers warned the jury not to be swayed by "the prints exhibited in our houses."

SOURCE: The Library of Congress.

of the colony's government independent of elected representatives. In October, the Boston town meeting appointed a Committee of Correspondence to communicate with other towns regarding this challenge. The next month the meeting issued what became known as the Boston Pamphlet, a series of declarations written by Samuel Adams and other radicals, concluding that British encroachments on colonial rights pointed to a plot to enslave Americans.

In March 1773, the Virginia House of Burgesses appointed a standing committee for correspondence among the colonies "to obtain the most early and authentic intelligence" of British actions affecting America, "and to keep up and maintain a correspondence and communication with our sister colonies." The Virginia committee, including Patrick Henry, Richard Henry Lee, and young Thomas Jefferson, served as a model, and within a year all the colonies except Pennsylvania, where conservatives controlled the legislature, had created committees of their own. These committees became the principal channel for sharing information, shaping public opinion, and building cooperation among the colonies before the Continental Congress of 1774.

The information most damaging to British influence came from the radicals in Boston. Governor Hutchinson put himself at the center of controversy by declaring early in 1773 that the colonists were mistaken if they thought they enjoyed all the rights of Englishmen. Furthermore, even though they had removed themselves across the Atlantic, he argued, they were still subordinate to Parliament. "I know of no line that can be drawn," he asserted, "between the supreme authority of Parliament and the total independence of the colonies." This bold declaration outraged colonists, who during the years of agitation against taxes and duties had convinced themselves of the case against parliamentary supremacy.

In June 1773, the Boston committee circulated a set of confidential letters from Hutchinson to the ministry in Britain, obtained in London by Benjamin Franklin from friends within the British government. Because Franklin had pledged to keep the letters to himself, he became the center of a scandal in London, and was dismissed from his position as postmaster general. But the British cause in the colonies suffered much more than Franklin's reputation. The letters revealed Hutchinson's call for "an abridgement of what are called English liberties" in the colonies. "I wish to see some further restraint of liberty," he had written, "rather than the connection with the parent state should be broken." This statement seemed to be the "smoking gun" of the conspiracy theory, and it created a torrent of anger against the British and their officials in the colonies.

A British tax man is tarred and feathered and forced to drink tea, while the Boston Tea Party takes place in the background, in this image of 1774. SOURCE: Christie's Images, Inc.

The Boston Tea Party

It was in this context that the colonists received the news that Parliament had passed a Tea Act. Colonists were major consumers of tea, but because of the tax on it that remained from the Townshend duties, the market for colonial tea had collapsed, bringing the East India Company to the brink of bankruptcy. This company was the sole agent of British power in India, and Parliament could not allow it to fail. The British therefore devised a scheme in which they offered tea to Americans at prices that would tempt the most patriotic tea drinker. The radicals argued that this was merely a device to make palatable the payment of unconstitutional taxes—further evidence of the British effort to corrupt the colonists.

In October a mass meeting in Philadelphia denounced anyone importing the tea as "an enemy of his country." A group calling itself the Committee for Tarring and Feathering plastered posters all over the city asking if the pilots of ships carrying the tea might like "ten gallons of liquid tar decanted on your pate—with the feathers of a dozen wild geese laid over that to enliven your appearance?" The Philadelphia merchants scheduled to accept the tea backed out in terror. Similar protests in New York City forced withdrawals there as well. The town meeting in Boston passed resolutions patterned on those of Philadelphia, but the tea agents there, including two of Governor Hutchinson's sons, resisted the call to refuse the shipments.

The first of the tea ships arrived in Boston Harbor late in November. Mass meetings in Old South Church, which included many country people drawn to the scene of the crisis, resolved to keep the tea from being unloaded. Governor Hutchinson was equally firm in refusing to allow the ship to leave the harbor. Five thousand people on December 16, 1773, crowded into the church to hear the captain of the tea ship report to Samuel Adams that he could not move his ship. "This meeting can do nothing more to save the country," Adams declared. This was the signal for a disciplined group of fifty or sixty men, including farmers, artisans, merchants, professionals, and apprentices, to march to the wharf disguised as Indians. There they boarded the ship and dumped into the harbor 45 tons of tea, valued at £18,000, all the while cheered on by Boston's citizens. "Boston Harbor's a tea-pot tonight," the crowd chanted.

Boston's was the first tea party. Other incidents of property destruction soon followed. When the Sons of Liberty learned that a cargo of tea had landed secretly in New York, they dressed themselves as Indians and dumped the tea chests into the harbor. At Annapolis a ship loaded with tea was destroyed by fire, and arson also consumed a shipment stored at a warehouse in New Jersey. But it was the action in Boston at which the British railed. The government became convinced that something had to be done about the rebellious colony of Massachusetts. Strong measures were required, King George wrote to Lord North, for "we are now to dispute whether we have, or have not, any authority in that country."

OVERVIEW

ELEVEN BRITISH MEASURES THAT LED TO REVOLUTION

Legislation	Year	
Sugar Act	1764	Placed prohibitive duty on imported sugar; provided for greater regulation of American shipping to suppress smuggling
Stamp Act	1765	Required the purchase of specially embossed paper for newspapers, legal documents, licenses, insurance policies, ships' papers, and playing cards; struck at printers, lawyers, tavern owners, and other influential colonists. Repealed in 1766
Declaratory Act	1766	Asserted the authority of Parliament to make laws binding the colonies "in all cases whatsoever"
Townshend Revenue Acts	1767	Placed import duties, collectible before goods entered colonial markets, on many commodities including lead, glass, paper, and tea. Repealed in 1770
Tea Act	1773	Gave the British East India Company a monopoly on all tea imports to America, hitting at American merchants
Coercive or Intolerable Acts	1774	
Boston Port Bill		Closed Boston harbor
Massachusetts Government Act		Annulled the Massachusetts colonial charter
Administration of Justice Act		Protected British officials from colonial courts by sending them home for trial if arrested
Quartering Act		Legalized the housing of British troops in private homes
Quebec Act		Created a highly centralized government for Canada

The Intolerable Acts

During the spring of 1774 an angry Parliament passed a series of acts—called the Coercive Acts, but known by Americans as the Intolerable Acts—that were calculated to punish Massachusetts and strengthen the British hand. The Boston Port Bill prohibited the loading or unloading of ships in any part of Boston Harbor until the town fully compensated the East India Company and the customs service for the destroyed tea. The Massachusetts Government Act annulled the colonial charter: delegates to the upper house would no longer be elected by the assembly, but henceforth were to be appointed by the king. Civil officers throughout the province were placed under the authority of the royal governor, and the selection of juries was given over to governor-appointed sheriffs. Town meetings, an important institution of the resistance movement, were prohibited from convening more than once a year except with the approval of the governor, who was to control their agendas. With these Acts the British terminated the long history of self-rule by communities in the colony of Massachusetts. The Administration of Justice Act protected British officials from colonial courts, thereby encouraging them to vigorously pursue the work of suppression. Those accused of committing capital crimes while putting down riots or collecting revenue, such as the soldiers involved in the Boston Massacre, were now to be sent to England for trial.

Additional measures affected the other colonies and encouraged them to see themselves in league with suffering Massachusetts. The Quartering Act legalized the housing of troops at public expense, not only in taverns and abandoned buildings, but in occupied dwellings and private homes as well. Finally, in the Quebec Act, the British authorized a permanent government for the territory taken from France during the Seven Years' War. This government was both authoritarian and antirepublican, with a royal government and an appointed council. Furthermore, the act confirmed the feudal system of land tenure along the St. Lawrence. It also granted religious toleration to the Roman Catholic Church and upheld the church's traditional right to collect tithes, thus, in effect, establishing Catholicism as the state religion in Quebec.

To the American colonists, the Quebec Act was a frightening preview of what imperial authorities might have in store for them, and it confirmed the prediction of the Committees of Correspondence that there was a British plot to destroy American liberty. The argument was made for them in Parliament by the radical Whig Charles James Fox: "To establish a perfectly despotic government, contrary to the genius and spirit of the

Web Exploration

Examine the boundaries set by the Quebec Act of 1774. How did they contribute to rising tensions between the colonists and imperial authorities?
www.prenhall.com/faragher/map6.2

The Quebec Act of 1774   With the Quebec Act, Britain created a centralized colonial government for Canada and extended that colony's administrative control southwest to the Ohio River, invalidating the sea-to-sea boundaries of many colonial charters.

British constitution," he warned his colleagues, "carries with it the appearance of a love of despotism, and a settled design to enslave the people of America." Moreover, the act extended Quebec's jurisdiction to the Ohio Valley, thus violating the "sea-to-sea" provisions of many of the colonies' charters. The British appeared to be giving the Old Northwest back to the very people from whom it had been won.

In May, General Thomas Gage arrived in Boston to replace Hutchinson as governor. The same day, the Boston town meeting called for a revival of nonimportation measures against Britain. In Virginia the Burgesses declared that Boston was enduring a "hostile invasion"

PREMIÈRE ASSEMBLÉE DU CONGRÈS.

The engraving of the first session of the Continental Congress, published in France in 1782, is the only contemporary illustration of the meeting. Peyton Randolph of Virginia presides from the elevated chair, but otherwise there are no recognizable individuals. The Congress had to find a way to form a community among the leaders from each of the colonies without compromising their local identities.

SOURCE: Library of Congress.

and made provision for a "day of fasting, humiliation, and prayer, devoutly to implore the divine interposition for averting the heavy calamity, which threatens destruction to our civil rights and the evils of civil war." For this expression of sympathy, Governor Dunmore suspended the legislature. Nevertheless, throughout the colony on the first of June, funeral bells tolled, flags flew at half mast, and people flocked to the churches.

The First Continental Congress

It was amid this crisis that town meetings and colonial assemblies alike chose representatives for the Continental Congress. The delegates who arrived in Philadelphia in September 1774 included the most im-

portant leaders of the American cause. Cousins Samuel and John Adams, the radicals from Massachusetts, were joined by Patrick Henry and George Washington from Virginia and Christopher Gadsden of South Carolina. Many of the delegates were conservatives: John Dickinson and Joseph Galloway of Philadelphia and John Jay and James Duane from New York. With the exception of Gadsden, a hothead who proposed an attack on British forces in Boston, the delegates wished to avoid war and favored a policy of economic coercion.

After one of their first debates, the delegates passed a Declaration and Resolves, in which they asserted that all the colonists sprang from a common tradition and enjoyed rights guaranteed "by the immutable laws of nature, the principles of the English constitution, and the several charters or compacts" of their provinces. Thirteen acts of Parliament, passed since 1763, were declared in violation of these rights. Until these acts were repealed, the delegates pledged, they would impose a set of sanctions against the British. These would include not only the nonimportation and nonconsumption of British goods, but a prohibition on the export of colonial commodities to Britain or its other colonies.

To enforce these sanctions, the Continental Congress urged that "a committee be chosen in every county, city, and town, by those who are qualified to vote for representatives in the legislature, whose business it shall be attentively to observe the conduct of all persons." This call for democratically elected local committees in each community had important political ramifications. The following year, these groups, known as Committees of Observation and Safety, took over the functions of local government throughout the colonies. They organized militia companies, called extralegal courts, and combined to form colonywide congresses or conventions. By dissolving the colonial legislatures, royal governors unwittingly aided the work of these committees. The committees also scrutinized the activities of fellow citizens, suppressed the expression of Loyalist opinion from pulpit or press, and practiced other forms of coercion. Throughout most of the colonies the committees formed a bridge between the old colonial administrations and the revolutionary governments organized over the next few years. Committees began to link localities together in the cause of a wider American community. It was at this point that people began to refer to the colonies as the American "states."

Lexington and Concord

On September 1, 1774, General Gage sent troops from Boston to seize the stores of cannon and ammunition the Massachusetts militia had stored at armories in Charlestown and Cambridge. In response, the Massachusetts House of Representatives, calling itself the

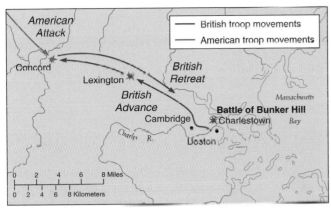

The First Engagements of the Revolution

The first military engagements of the American Revolution took place in the spring of 1775 in the countryside surrounding Boston.

Provincial Congress, created a Committee of Safety empowered to call up the militia. On October 15 the committee authorized the creation of special units, to be known as "minutemen," who stood ready to be called at a moment's notice. The armed militia of the towns and communities surrounding Boston faced the British army, quartered in the city.

It was no rabble he was up against, Gage wrote to his superiors, but "the freeholders and farmers" of New England who believed they were defending their communities. Worrying that his forces were insufficient to suppress the rebellion, he requested reinforcements. The stalemate continued through the fall and winter. To raise their spirits, the New England militia ridiculed the British army:

> And what have you got now with all your designing,
> But a town without victuals to sit down and dine in;
> And to look on the ground like a parcel of noodles,
> And sing, how the Yankees have beaten the Doodles.
> I'm sure if you're wise you'll make peace for a dinner,
> For fighting and fasting will soon make ye thinner.

But King George was convinced that the time had come for war. "The New England governments are in a state of rebellion," he wrote privately. "Blows must decide whether they are to be subject to this country or independent." In Parliament, Pitt proposed withdrawing troops from Boston, but was overruled by a large margin. Attempting to find a balance between hardliners and advocates of conciliation, Lord North organized majority support in the House of Commons for a plan in which Parliament would "forbear" to levy taxes for purposes of revenue once the colonies had agreed to tax themselves for the common defense. But simultaneously Parliament passed legislation severely restraining colonial commerce. "A great empire and little

minds go ill together," Edmund Burke quipped in March 1775 in a brilliant speech in Parliament opposing this bill. "Let it be once understood that your government may be one thing and their privileges another, that these two things may exist without any mutual relation." Then he declared in prophetic words, "The cement is gone, the cohesion is loosened, and everything hastens to decay and dissolution."

In Virginia, at almost the same moment, Patrick Henry predicted that hostilities would soon begin in New England. "Gentlemen may cry peace, peace!—but there is no peace," he thundered in prose later memorized by millions of American schoolchildren. "Is life so dear, or peace so sweet, as to be purchased at the price of chains and slavery? Forbid it, Almighty God! I know not what course others may take, but as for me, give me liberty or give me death!" Three weeks later, on April 14, General Gage received orders to strike at once against the Massachusetts militia. "It will surely be better," read his instructions, "that the conflict should be brought on upon such ground than in a riper state of rebellion."

On the evening of April 18, 1775, Gage ordered 700 men to capture the store of American ammunition at the town of Concord. Learning of the operation, the Boston committee dispatched two men, Paul Revere and William Dawes, to alert the militia of the countryside. By the time the British forces had reached Lexington, midway to their destination, some seventy armed minutemen had assembled on the green in the center of town, but they were disorganized and confused. "Lay down your arms, you damned rebels, and disperse!" cried one of the British officers. The Americans began to withdraw in the face of overwhelming opposition, but they took their arms with them. "Damn you, why don't you lay down your arms!" someone shouted from the British lines. "Damn them! We will have them!" No order to fire was given, but shots rang out, killing eight Americans and wounding ten others.

The British marched on to Concord, where they burned a small quantity of supplies and cut down a liberty pole. Meanwhile, news of the skirmish at Lexington had spread through the country, and the militia companies of communities from miles around converged on the town. Seeing smoke, they mistakenly concluded that the troops were burning homes. "Will you let them burn the town!" one man cried, and the Americans moved to the Concord bridge. There they attacked a British company, killing three soldiers—the first British casualties of the Revolution. The British immediately turned back for Boston but were attacked by Americans at many points along the way. Reinforcements met them at Lexington, preventing a complete disaster, but by the time they finally marched into Boston, 73 were dead and 202 wounded or missing.

Soon after the fighting at Lexington and Concord, the artist Ralph Earl and the engraver Amos Doolittle visited the location and interviewed participants. They produced a series of four engravings of the incident, the first popular prints of the battles of the Revolutionary War. This view shows the British soldiers marching back to Boston through the hail of sniper fire from colonial militiamen.

SOURCE: Connecticut Historical Society.

The British troops were vastly outnumbered by the approximately 4,000 Massachusetts militiamen, who suffered 95 casualties. The engagement forecast what would be a central problem for the British: they would be forced to fight an armed population defending their own communities against outsiders.

DECIDING FOR INDEPENDENCE

"We send you momentous intelligence," read the letter received by the Charleston, South Carolina, Committee of Correspondence on May 8, reporting the violence in Massachusetts. Community militia companies mobilized throughout the colonies. At Boston, thousands of militiamen from Massachusetts and the surrounding provinces besieged the city, leaving the British no escape but by sea; their siege would last for nearly a year. Meanwhile, delegates from twelve colonies reconverged on Philadelphia.

The Second Continental Congress

The members of the Second Continental Congress, which opened on May 10, 1775, represented twelve of the British colonies on the mainland of North America. From New Hampshire to South Carolina, Committees of Observation and Safety had elected colonywide conventions, and these extralegal bodies in turn had chosen delegates. Consequently, few conservatives or Loyalists

were among them. Georgia, unrepresented at the first session of the Continental Congress, remained absent at the opening of the second. The newest mainland colony, it depended heavily on British subsidies, and its leaders were cautious, fearing both slave and Indian uprisings. But in 1775 the political balance in Georgia shifted in favor of the radicals, and by the end of the summer the colony had delegates in Philadelphia.

Among the delegates at the Continental Congress were many familiar faces and a few new ones, including Thomas Jefferson, a plantation owner and lawyer from Virginia, gifted with one of the most imaginative and analytical minds of his time. All the delegates carried news of the enthusiasm for war that raged in their home provinces. "A frenzy of revenge seems to have seized all ranks of people," said Jefferson. George Washington attended all the sessions in uniform. "Oh that I was a soldier," an envious John Adams wrote to his wife, Abigail. The delegates agreed that defense was the first issue on their agenda.

On May 15, the Second Continental Congress resolved to put the colonies in a state of defense, but the delegates were divided on how best to do it. They lacked the power and the funds to immediately raise and supply an army. After debate and deliberation, John Adams made the practical proposal that the delegates simply designate as a Continental Army the militia forces besieging Boston. On June 14, the Congress resolved to supplement the New England militiamen with six companies of expert riflemen raised in Pennsylvania, Maryland, and Virginia. The delegates agreed that in order to emphasize their national aspirations, they had to select a man from the South to command these New England forces. All eyes turned to George Washington. Although Washington had suffered defeat at the beginning of the Seven Years' War, he had subsequently compiled a distinguished record. On June 15, Jefferson and Adams nominated Washington to be commander-in-chief of all Continental forces, and he was elected by a unanimous vote. He served without salary. The Continental Congress soon appointed a staff of major generals to support him. On June 22, in a highly significant move, the Congress voted to finance the army with an issue of $2 million in bills of credit, backed by the good faith of the Confederated Colonies. Thus began the long and complicated process of financing the Revolution.

During its first session in the spring of 1775, the Continental Congress had begun to move cautiously down the path toward independence. Few would admit, even to themselves, however, that this was their goal. John Adams, who was close to advocating independence, wrote that he was "as fond of reconciliation as any man" but found the hope of peaceful resolution unreasonable. "The cancer is too deeply rooted," he thought, "and too far spread to be cured by anything short of cutting it out entire." Still, on July 5, 1775, the delegates passed the so-called Olive Branch Petition, written by John Dickinson of Pennsylvania, in which they professed their attachment to King George and begged him to prevent further hostilities so that there might be an accommodation. The next day they approved a Declaration of the Causes and Necessities of Taking Up Arms, written by Jefferson and Dickinson. Here the delegates adopted a harder tone, resolving "to die freemen rather than to live slaves." Before the Second Continental Congress adjourned at the beginning of August, the delegates appointed commissioners to negotiate with the Indian nations in an attempt to keep them out of the conflict. They also reinstated Benjamin Franklin as postmaster general in order to keep the mails moving and protect communication among the colonies.

The Connecticut artist John Trumbull painted *The Battle of Bunker Hill* in 1785, the first of a series that earned him the informal title of "the Painter of the Revolution." Trumbull was careful to research the details of his paintings but composed them in the grand style of historical romance. In the early nineteenth century he repainted this work, and three other Revolutionary scenes, for the rotunda of the Capitol in Washington, D.C.

SOURCE: The Granger Collection.

Canada, the Spanish Borderlands, and the Revolution

How did the rest of North America react to the coming conflict? The Continental Congress contacted many of the other British colonies. In one of their first acts, delegates called on "the oppressed inhabitants of Canada" to join in the struggle for "common liberty." After the Seven Years' War, the British treated Quebec as a conquered province, and French Canadians felt little sympathy for the empire. On the other hand, the Americans were traditional enemies, much feared because of their aggressive expansionism. Indeed, when the Canadians failed to respond positively and immediately, the Congress reversed itself and voted to authorize a military expedition against Quebec to eliminate any possibility of a British invasion from that quarter, thus killing any chance of the Canadians' joining the anti-British cause. This set a course toward the development of the separate nations of the United States and Canada.

There was some sympathy at first for the American struggle in the British island colonies. The legislative assemblies of Jamaica, Grenada, and Barbados declared themselves in accord with the Continental Congress, but the British navy prevented them from sending representatives. A delegation from Bermuda succeeded in getting to Philadelphia, but the Americans were so preoccupied with more pressing matters they were unable to provide any assistance, and the spark of resistance on the island sputtered out. The island colonies would remain aloof from the imperial crisis, largely because the colonists there were dependent on a British military presence to guard against slave revolts. Things at first seemed more promising in Nova Scotia (not then a part of Canada), where many New Englanders had relocated after the expulsion of the Acadians. There had been Stamp Act demonstrations in Halifax, and when the British attempted to recruit among the Nova Scotians for soldiers to serve in Boston, one community responded that since "almost all of us [were] born in New England, [we are] divided betwixt natural affection to our nearest relations and good faith and friendship to our king and country." The British naval stronghold at Halifax, however, secured the province for the empire. Large contingents of British troops also kept Florida (which Britain had divided into the two colonies of East and West Florida) solidly in the empire.

In Cuba, some 3,000 exiled Spanish Floridians, who had fled rather than live under British rule in 1763, clamored for Spain to retake their homeland. Many of them were active supporters of American independence. (Two centuries later there would be thousands of Cuban exiles in Florida.) Spanish authorities in Cuba, who also administered the newly acquired colony of Louisiana, were somewhat torn in their sympathies. They certainly felt no solidarity with the cause of rebellion, which they understood posed a great danger to monarchy and empire. But with painful memories of the British invasion of Havana in 1763, they passionately looked forward to working revenge on their traditional enemy, as well as to regaining control of the Floridas and eliminating the British threat to their Mexican and Caribbean colonies. In 1775, Spain adopted the recommendation of the Havana authorities and declared a policy of neutrality in the looming independence struggle.

Secretly, however, Spain looked for an opportunity to support the Americans. That presented itself in the late spring of 1776, when a contingent of Americans arrived in Spanish New Orleans via the Mississippi River bearing a proposal from patriot forces in Virginia. British naval supremacy was making it impossible to obtain supplies from overseas. Would the Spanish be willing to quietly sell guns, ammunition, and other provisions to the Americans in New Orleans and allow them to be shipped by way of the Mississippi and Ohio Rivers? If they were cooperative, the Americans might be willing to see the Spanish retake possession of the Floridas and administer them as a "protectorate" for the duration of the independence struggle. Authorities forwarded the proposal to Spain, where a few months later the Spanish king and his ministers approved the plan. Havana and New Orleans became important supply centers for the patriots.

Fighting in the North and South

Both North and South saw fighting in 1775 and early 1776. In May 1775, a small force of armed New Englanders under the command of Ethan Allen of Vermont surprised the British garrison at Fort Ticonderoga on Lake Champlain, demanding—"in the name of Great Jehovah and the Continental Congress"—that the commander surrender. The Continental Congress, in fact, knew nothing of this campaign, and when news of it arrived, members of the New York delegation were distressed at this New England violation of their territorial sovereignty. With great effort, the Americans transported the fort's cannon overland to be used in the siege of Boston.

At Boston, the British hastened to reinforce Gage's forces and by the middle of June 1775 had approximately 6,500 soldiers in the city. By that time the American forces had increased to nearly 10,000. Fearing Gage would occupy the heights south of town, the Americans countered by occupying the Charlestown peninsula to the north. On June 17, British ships in the harbor began to fire on the American positions, and Gage decided on a frontal assault to dislodge them. In bloody fighting that, although it occurred at Breed's Hill, has since been known as the Battle of Bunker Hill, the British finally succeeded in routing the Americans, killing 140 men, but not before suffering over a thousand casualties of their own, including 226 dead. The fierce reaction in England to this enormous loss ended all possibility of any last-minute reconciliation. In August 1775, King George rejected the Olive Branch Petition and issued a royal proclamation declaring the colonists to be in "open and avowed rebellion." "Divers wicked and desperate persons" were the cause of the problem, said the king, and he called on his loyal subjects in America to "bring the traitors to justice."

In June 1775, the Continental Congress assembled an expeditionary force against Canada. One thousand Americans moved north up the Hudson River corridor, and in November General Richard Montgomery forced the capitulation of Montreal. Meanwhile, Benedict Arnold set out from Massachusetts with another American army, and after a torturous march through the forests and mountains of Maine, he joined Montgomery outside the walls of Quebec. Unlike the assault of British General Wolfe in 1759, however, the American assault failed to take the city. Montgomery and 100 Americans were killed, and another 300 were taken prisoner. Although Arnold held his position, the American siege was broken the following spring by British reinforcements who had come down the St. Lawrence. By the summer of 1776 the Americans had been forced back from Canada.

Elsewhere there were successes. Washington installed artillery on the heights south of Boston, placing the city and harbor within cannon range. General William Howe, who had replaced Gage, had little choice but to evacuate the city. In March the British sailed out of Boston harbor for the last time, heading north to Halifax with at least 1,000 American Loyalists. In the South, American militia rose against the Loyalist forces of Virginia's Governor Dunmore, who had alienated the planter class by promising freedom to any slave who would fight with the British. After a decisive defeat of his forces, Dunmore retreated to British naval vessels, from which he shelled and destroyed much of the city of Norfolk, Virginia, on January 1, 1776. In North Carolina, the rebel militia crushed a Loyalist force at the Battle of Moore's Creek Bridge near Wilmington in February, ending British plans for an invasion of that province. The British decided to attack Charleston, but at Fort Moultrie in Charleston harbor an American force turned back the assault. It would be more than two years before the British would try to invade the South again.

No Turning Back

Hopes of reconciliation died with the mounting casualties. The Second Continental Congress, which was rapidly assuming the role of a new government for all the provinces, reconvened in September 1775 and received news of the king's proclamation that the colonies were in formal rebellion. Although the delegates disclaimed any intention of denying the sovereignty of the king, they now moved to organize an American navy. They declared British vessels open to capture and authorized privateering. The Congress took further steps toward de facto independence when it authorized contacts with foreign powers through its agents in Europe. In the spring of 1776, France, hoping that the creation of a new American nation might provide the opportunity of gaining a larger share of the colonial trade while also diminishing British power, joined Spain in approving the shipping of supplies to the rebellious provinces. The Continental Congress then declared colonial ports open to the trade of all nations but Britain.

The emotional ties to Britain proved difficult to break. But in 1776 help arrived in the form of a pamphlet written by Thomas Paine, a radical Englishman recently arrived in Philadelphia. In *Common Sense*, Paine proposed to offer "simple fact, plain argument, and common sense" on the crisis. For years Americans had defended their actions by wrapping themselves in the mantle of British traditions. But Paine argued that the British system rested on "the base remains of two ancient tyrannies," aristocracy and monarchy, neither of which was appropriate for America. Paine placed the blame for the oppression of the colonists on the shoulders of King George, whom he labeled the "royal Brute." Appealing to the millennial spirit of American Protestant culture, Paine wrote: "We have it in our power to begin the world over again. A situation, similar to the present, hath not happened since the days of Noah until now." *Common Sense* was the single most important piece of writing during the Revolutionary era, selling more than 100,000 copies within a few months of its publication in January 1776. It reshaped popular thinking and put independence squarely on the agenda.

In April, the North Carolina convention, which operated as the revolutionary replacement for the old colonial assembly, became the first to empower its delegates to vote for a declaration of independence. News that the British were recruiting a force of German mercenaries to use against the Americans provided an additional push toward what now began to seem inevitable. In May the Continental Congress voted to recommend that the individual states move as quickly as possible toward the adoption of state constitutions. When John Adams wrote, in the preamble

The Manner in which the American Colonies Declared themselves INDEPENDENT of the King of ENGLAND, a 1783 English print. Understanding that the coming struggle would require the steady support of ordinary people, in the Declaration of Independence the upper-class men of the Continental Congress asserted the right of popular revolution and the great principle of human equality.

SOURCE: The Granger Collection.

to this statement, that "the exercise of every kind of authority under the said crown should be totally suppressed," he sent a strong signal that the delegates were on the verge of approving a momentous declaration.

The Declaration of Independence

On June 7, 1776, Richard Henry Lee of Virginia offered a motion to the Continental Congress: "That these united colonies are, and of right ought to be, free and independent states, that they are absolved from all allegiance to the British crown, and that all political connection between them and the state of Great Britain is, and ought to be, totally dissolved." After some debate, a vote was postponed until July, but a committee composed of John Adams, Thomas Jefferson, Benjamin Franklin, Roger Sherman of Connecticut, and Robert Livingston of New York was asked to prepare a draft declaration of American independence. The committee assigned the writing to Jefferson.

The intervening month allowed the delegates to sample the public discussion and debate and receive instructions from their state conventions. By the end of the month, all the states but New York had authorized a vote for independence. When the question came up for debate again on July 1, a large majority in the Continental Congress supported independence. The final vote, taken on July 2, was twelve in favor of independence, none against, with New York abstaining. The delegates then turned to the declaration itself and made a number of changes in Jefferson's draft, striking out, for example, a long passage condemning slavery. In this and a number of other ways the final version was somewhat more cautious than the draft, but it was still a stirring document.

Its central section reiterated the "long train of abuses and usurpations" on the part of King George that had led the Americans to their drastic course; there was no mention of Parliament, the principal opponent since 1764. But it was the first section that expressed the highest ideals of the delegates:

> We hold these truths to be self-evident, that all men are created equal, that they are endowed by their creator with certain unalienable rights, that among these are life, liberty, and the pursuit of happiness. That to secure these rights, governments are instituted among men, deriving their just powers from the consent of the governed. That whenever any form of government becomes destructive of these ends, it is the right of the people to alter or to abolish it, and to institute a new government, laying its foundation on such principles, and organizing its powers in such form, as to them shall seem most likely to effect their safety and happiness.

There was very little debate in the Continental Congress about these principles. The delegates, mostly men of wealth and position, realized that the coming struggle for independence would require the steady support of ordinary people, so they asserted this great principle of equality and the right of revolution. There was little debate about the implications or potential consequences. Surely no statement would reverberate more through American history; the idea of equality inspired the poor as well as the wealthy, women as well as men, blacks as well as whites.

But it was the third and final section that may have contained the most meaning for the delegates: "For the support of this declaration, with a firm reliance on the protection of divine providence, we mutually pledge to each other our lives, our fortunes, and our sacred

CHRONOLOGY

1713	France cedes Acadia to Britain	1764	Sugar Act
1745	New Englanders capture Louisburg	1765	Stamp Act and Stamp Act Congress
1749	French send an expeditionary force down the Ohio River	1766	Declaratory Act
		1767	Townshend Revenue Acts
1753	French begin building forts from Lake Erie to the Ohio	1768	Treaties of Hard Labor and Fort Stanwix
1754	Albany Congress	1770	Boston Massacre
1755	British General Edward Braddock defeated by a combined force of French and Indians	1772	First Committee of Correspondence organized in Boston
	Britain expels Acadians from Nova Scotia	1773	Tea Act
1756	Seven Years' War begins in Europe		Boston Tea Party
1757	William Pitt becomes prime minister	1774	Intolerable Acts
1758	Louisburg captured by the British for the second time		First Continental Congress
			Dunmore's War
1759	British capture Quebec	1775	Fighting begins at Lexington and Concord
1763	Treaty of Paris		Second Continental Congress
	Pontiac's uprising	1776	Americans invade Canada
	Proclamation of 1763 creates "Indian Country"		Thomas Paine's *Common Sense*
	Paxton Boys massacre		Declaration of Independence

honor." In voting for independence, the delegates proclaimed their community, but they also committed treason against their king and empire. They could be condemned as traitors, hunted as criminals, and stand on the scaffold to pay for their sentiments. On July 4, 1776, these men approved the text of the Declaration of Independence without dissent.

CONCLUSION

Great Britain emerged from the Seven Years' War as the dominant power in North America. Yet despite its attempts at strict regulation and determination of the course of events in its colonies, it faced consistent resistance and often complete failure. Perhaps British leaders felt as John Adams had when he attended the first session of the Continental Congress in 1774: how could a motley collection of "ambassadors from a dozen belligerent powers" effectively organize as a single, independent, and defiant body? The British underestimated the political consensus that existed among the colonists about the importance of "republican" government. They also underestimated the ability of the colonists to inform one another, to work together, to build a sentiment of nationalism that cut across the

boundaries of ethnicity, region, and economic status. Through newspapers, pamphlets, Committees of Correspondence, community organizations, and group protest, the colonists discovered the concerns they shared, and in so doing they fostered a new, American identity. Without that identity it would have been difficult for them to consent to the treasonous act of declaring independence, especially when the independence they sought was from an international power that dominated much of the globe.

REVIEW QUESTIONS

1. How did overwhelming British success in the Seven Years' War lead to an imperial crisis in British North America?
2. Outline the changes in British policy toward the colonies from 1750 to 1776.
3. Trace the developing sense of an American national community over this same period.
4. What were the principal events leading to the beginning of armed conflict at Lexington and Concord?
5. How were the ideals of American republicanism expressed in the Declaration of Independence?

RECOMMENDED READING

Benedict Anderson, *Imagined Communities: Reflections on the Origin and Spread of Nationalism*, rev. ed. (1991).

Fred Anderson, *The Crucible of War: The Seven Years' War and the Fate of Empire in British North America, 1754–1766* (2000).

Bernard Bailyn, *The Ideological Origins of the American Revolution* (1967).

David A. Copeland, *Debating the Issues in Colonial Newspapers: Primary Documents on Events of the Period* (2000).

Eric Foner, *Tom Paine and Revolutionary America* (1976).

William H. Hallahan, *The Day the Revolution Began: 19 April 1775* (2000).

Francis Jennings, *Empire of Fortune: Crowns, Colonies, and Tribes in the Seven Years' War in America* (1988).

Pauline Maier, *American Scripture: Making the Declaration of Independence* (1997).

Richard L. Merritt, *Symbols of American Community, 1735–1775* (1966).

William R. Nester, *"Haughty Conquerors": Amherst and the Great Indian Uprising of 1763* (2000).

▶ MEDIA RESOURCES

U.S. HISTORY DOCUMENTS CD-ROM

Colonial America

3-9   "The Storm Arising in the West," George Washington Delivers a Warning to the French (1753)

3-10   The Closing of the Frontier (1763)

3-11   The Adventures of Daniel Boone (1769)

Prelude to Revolution

4-2   Declaration of the Injured Frontier Inhabitants [of Pennsylvania] (1764)

4-3   Benjamin Franklin, Testimony Against the Stamp Act (1766)

4-4   "Letters From a Farmer in Pennsylvania" (1767)

4-5   John Dickinson, from Letters from a Farmer in Pennsylvania (1768)

4-6   The Boston "Massacre" or Victims of Circumstance? (1770)

4-7   John Andrews to William Barrell, Letter Regarding the Boston Tea Party (1773)

4-8   Address of the Inhabitants of Anson County to Governor Martin (1774)

The American Revolution

5-2   James Otis, The Rights of the British Colonies Asserted and Proved (1763)

5-3   The Crisis Comes to a Head: April 19, 1775

5-6   Petition of "A Grate Number of Blackes of the Province" to Governor Thomas Gage and the Members of the Massachusetts General Court (1774)

5-7   Joseph Warren, "Account of the Battle of Lexington" (1775)

5-9   Rights of Women in an Independent Republic

COMPANION WEBSITE HIGHLIGHTS

To view an exploration, enter one of the URLs below in your browser.

Web Explorations

The War for Empire in North America, 1754–1763
http://www.prenhall.com/faragher/map6.1
The Quebec Act of 1774
http://www.prenhall.com/faragher/map6.2

Additional Interactive Maps

To access the maps, go to this chapter's resources at
http://www.prenhall.com/faragher
European Claims in North America, 1750 and 1763, page 150
The First Engagements of the Revolution, page 165

HISTORY RESOURCE CENTER

To find the resources listed below, go to
http://www.prenhall.com/historyresourcecenter

Documents

"Virginia Nonimportation Resolutions" (1769)

Abigail Adams and John Adams Letters; Abigail Adams Letter to Mercy Otis Warren

Benjamin Franklin, "Observations Concerning the Increase of Mankind, Peopling of Countries, etc." (1751)

George Robert Twelves Hewes, A Retrospect of the Boston Tea-Party (1834)

Patrick Henry, "Give Me Liberty or Give Me Death" (1775)

Peter Oliver, Origin and Progress of the American Rebellion (1781)

Thomas Jefferson, "Original Rough Draught" of the Declaration of Independence (1776)

Images

"Patrick Henry Addressing the Virginia Assembly, 1765"

A View of the Taking of Quebec

Benjamin Franklin at the Court of France

Boston Tea Party

(Continued)

(Continued)

EXPLORING AMERICA

THE STAMP ACT

http://www.prenhall.com/faragher/stampact

The colonial protest against the Stamp Act was a turning point in American history. Why did the colonists react so strongly to the tax on stamps? How had the past British administration of the colonies pave the way for the protest? How did the colonists view their rights and representation? How did the British view the colonies and the protests? *The Stamp Act* module answers these questions.

The Stamp Act presents a wide variety of sources to explore this important event in American history.

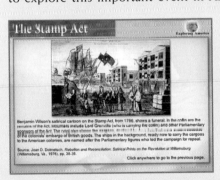

Benjamin Wilson's satirical cartoon on the Stamp Act, from 1766, shows a funeral. In the coffin are the remains of the Act. Mourners include Lord Grenville (who is carrying the coffin) and other Parliamentary supporters of the Act. The print also shows the wagons, docks and the warehouses of the colonists' embargo of British goods. The ships in the background, ready now to carry the cargoes to the American colonies, are named after the Parliamentary figures who led the campaign for repeal.

Source: Joan D. Dolmetsch, *Rebellion and Reconciliation: Satirical Prints on the Revolution at Williamsburg* (Williamsburg, Va.: 1976), pp. 38-39.

Click anywhere to go to the previous page.

The primary sources show the emotions the Stamp Act stimulated on both sides of the Atlantic Ocean. The quotes offer impassioned yet rational arguments that illuminate both sides of the taxation issue, presaging later debates that culminated in the American Revolution. The interactive map graphically demonstrates the economic power of the colonists while the chronology supplies an important time context to the unfolding events.

Reflect and Respond

1.   What did Whately mean when he claimed "every Member of Parliament sits in the House, not as Representative of his own Constituents, but as one of that august Assembly by which all the Commons of Great Britain are represented"?

2.   What specific experiences of American colonists in their battles with royal governors underlay their insistence on "actual representation"?

3.   William Pitt proposed that "the sovereign authority of this country [Great Britain] over the colonies be asserted in as strong terms as can be devised, and be made to extend every point of legislation whatsoever: that we may bind their trade, confine their manufactures, and exercise every power whatsoever—except that of taking money out of their pockets without their consent." Would Patrick Henry or the delegates to the Stamp Act Congress have accepted his formulation? Support your answer.

4.   How consistent was Pitt's claim of Parliamentary authority, other than with regard to revenues, in reference to his argument over "virtual" representation? Would not binding trade or confining (limiting or prohibiting) manufactures also constitute ways "of taking money out of their pockets without their consent"?

✓ Check it out

Stamp Act resolutions

This document presents the resolutions of the Stamp Act Congress to Great Britain. It offers colonial arguments against the Act and also depicts the attitudes of the colonists toward Great Britain. Equally important, the resolutions offer insight into the idea of rights during the early years of colonial protest against Great Britain.

This exploration is also available on the *Exploring America* CD-ROM

▶ The Invention of the Liberty Bell

The First Continental Congress of 1774 met in Carpenters' Hall, the downtown headquarters of one of Philadelphia's guilds. When the Congress reassembled in 1775 it moved to the more commodious State House two blocks away. It was there that the delegates adopted the Declaration of Independence in 1776 and the Articles of Confederation in 1777. Those occasions were commemorated by the tolling of a large bell in the building's steeple. In 1787 the nation's leaders drafted the United States Constitution in the same building, and later that year the State House bell rang upon its ratification by the states.

The State House (today more commonly known as Independence Hall) and the Liberty Bell are two of the most famous symbols of the nation's struggle for independence. Yet in the decades following the Revolution few Americans knew or cared about their existence. Just as Patriot leaders had to imagine and construct the idea of a national community, so these historical memorials had to be deliberately created and invented.

When the state of Pennsylvania moved its capital out of Philadelphia in 1799 it abandoned the State House and the bell. No one gave any thought to preserving them as relics of the nation's founding. The building, dating from the 1740s, was a beautiful Georgian structure, but by the turn of the century it was falling apart. The bell, cast by order of the Pennsylvania Assembly in 1752 to mark the fiftieth anniversary of representative government in the province, was inscribed with a Biblical passage: "PROCLAIM LIBERTY THROUGHOUT ALL THE LAND UNTO ALL THE INHABITANTS THEREOF." But Philadelphians were not particularly sentimental about it. Early in its history the bell developed hairline fractures, resulting in a harsh and shrill tone. By the early nineteenth century the bell was mostly forgotten. Misuse and vandalism caused the fractures in its surface to grow worse, and on one occasion, when rung to celebrate Washington's birthday, it cracked so badly it was rendered completely useless. Authorities made arrangements to scrap it.

But the bell was rescued in the 1830s by the emerging anti-slavery movement, which adopted it as a symbol of the uncompleted promise of American liberty. In

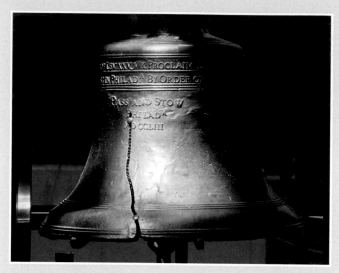

Today the Liberty Bell is displayed in a special pavilion on the mall in front of Independence Hall in Philadelphia.

SOURCE: Photograph by Richard Cummins. © Richard Cummins/CORBIS.

1837 a poem entitled "The Liberty Bell" appeared in the national abolitionist newspaper, *The Liberator*:

> *Our Liberty Bell! let its startling tone*
> *Abroad o'er a slavish land be thrown! . . .*

Anti-slavery advocates began publication of a series known as The Liberty Bell, annual volumes of stories, poems, and essays devoted to the cause of emancipation. Thus the bell was named and made famous by a movement directed against the power of slavery. By 1852 so many visitors to the Philadelphia State House were asking to see the bell, it was placed on public display.

Thus did the cracked Liberty Bell became a symbol of a divided rather than a united national community. Abolitionists used it to criticize the South. In one anti-slavery story a slave owner visits Independence Hall and ridicules the inscription he reads on the bell. Those sentiments are wrong, he says, the few should rule the many. "That is the way we do in the South. We have outgrown not only the sentiment inscribed on the bell, but the Declaration of Independence also." The bell cracked, he says, "because the doctrine is false." Suddenly a sad, ghostly voice

Philadelphia adopted the bell as its most prominent icon. A huge illuminated replica that stood at the entrance became one of the most popular attractions. The bell was promoted as a symbol of the unity of the nation at the moment of its creation, a reminder to Americans of their joint effort in the cause of independence, and a call to Americans from South and North to reunite in the aftermath of the Civil War. The bell was shipped to numerous expositions around the country — in New Orleans, Chicago, Atlanta, Boston, St. Louis, and finally to San Francisco as part of a triumphant railroad tour of much of the country. By World War I, when the Liberty Bell played a prominent role in the campaign to sell war bonds ("Liberty Bonds"), the use of the bell in the campaign against slavery had been suppressed and forgotten. Historical memorials are what we make of them. ■

Visitors to the 1876 Centennial Exhibition in Philadelphia were offered a wide assortment of souvenirs featuring the Liberty Bell. The token is marked "1776" and "1876" and "Liberty Bell," and the silk bookmark features a portrait of George Washington along with the bell. In the aftermath of the Civil War the Liberty Bell was used as a symbol of national unity.

SOURCE: Liberty Bell Museum.

issues from the bell. "The Lord, seeing that I should speak ever after to a nation of hypocrites," it says, "inflicted upon me this hideous crack, that whenever I did speak, there should issue from me nothing but a miserable clatter. . . . Nor shall I ever speak again in clear and ringing tones, till Liberty has been proclaimed to all the land, to all the inhabitants thereof." During the Civil War the Liberty Bell became one of the most prominent representations of the Union cause, and by war's end it was beloved in the North and loathed in the South.

In the aftermath of the war, the Liberty Bell was reinvented once again as a symbol of the national community. In 1876 the Centennial Exposition in

 www.researchnavigator.com

The Community and Memory essay for this chapter deals with the history of the Liberty Bell as a symbol of American values and the state of the American nation. For further research on the history of the Liberty Bell, use the tools available to you in Research Navigator.

As you investigate this topic, consider this question: "What did abolitionists find so appealing about the Liberty Bell as a symbol of their cause?"

ContentSelect: Search in the History database using the search terms *antislavery*, *Liberty Bell*, and *Liberator*.

Links Library: Access the History: U.S. History database and explore the links for *abolitionism* and *Liberator*.

New York Times on the Web: To find more information on the connection between the Liberty Bell and the antislavery movement, search using the term *Liberty Bell*.

THE CREATION OF THE UNITED STATES

▶ 1776–1786

William Ranney, *The Battle of Cowpens*. Oil on canvas. Photo by Sam Holland. Courtesy South Carolina State House.

AMERICAN COMMUNITIES

A National Community Evolves at Valley Forge

A DRUM ROLL USHERED IN A JANUARY MORNING IN 1778, summoning the Continental Army to roll call. Along a two-mile line of log cabins, doors slowly opened and ragged men stepped out onto the frozen ground of Valley Forge. "There comes a soldier," wrote army surgeon Albigense Waldo. "His bare feet are seen through his worn-out shoes, his legs nearly naked from the tattered remains of an only pair of stockings, his breeches not sufficient to cover his nakedness, his shirt hanging in strings, his hair disheveled, his face meagre." The reek of foul straw and unwashed bodies filled the air. "No bread, no soldier!" The chant began as a barely audible murmur, then was picked up by men all along the line. "No bread, no soldier! No bread, no soldier!" At last the chanting grew so loud it could be heard at General Washington's headquarters, a mile away. The 11,000 men of the American army were surviving on little more than "firecake," a mixture of flour and water baked hard before the fire that, according to Waldo, turned "guts to pasteboard." Two thousand men were without shoes; others were without blankets and had to sit up all night about the fires to keep from freezing. Addressing the Continental Congress, Washington wrote, "Three or four days of bad weather would prove our destruction."

Valley Forge was to become a national symbol of endurance. After marching hundreds of weary miles and suffering a series of terrible defeats at the hands of a British force nearly twice their number, the soldiers of the Continental Army had retreated to this winter headquarters only to find themselves at the mercy of indifferent local suppliers. Contractors demanded exorbitant rates for food and clothing, rates the Congress had refused to pay, and as a result local farmers preferred to deal with the British, who paid in pounds sterling, not depreciated Continental currency.

The 11,000 men of the Continental Army, who had not been paid for nearly six months, were divided into sixteen brigades composed of regiments from nine states. An unsympathetic observer described them as "a vagabond army of ragamuffins," and indeed many of the men were drawn from the ranks of the poor and disadvantaged: indentured servants, landless farmers, and nearly a thousand African Americans, both slave and free. Most of the men came from thinly settled farm districts or small towns where precautions regarding sanitation had been unnecessary. Every thaw revealed ground covered with "much filth and nastiness," and officers ordered sentinels to fire on any man "easing himself elsewhere than at ye vaults." Typhoid fever and other infectious diseases spread quickly. Along with dysentery, malnutrition, and exposure, these diseases claimed as many as 2,500 lives that winter. More than 700 women—wives, lovers, cooks, laundresses, and prostitutes—lived at Valley Forge that winter, and they were kept busy nursing the sick and burying the dead.

"What then is to become of this army?" Washington worried during the depth of the winter. But six months later the force he marched out of Valley Forge was considerably stronger for its experience there. Most important were the strong relationships that formed among the men, twelve of whom bunked together in each cabin, grouped by state regiments and brigade. In these units they fashioned "a band of brotherhood" and "shared with each other their hardships, dangers, and sufferings," wrote common soldier Joseph Plumb Martin. And they "sympathized with each other in trouble and sickness, assisted in bearing each other's burdens, [and] endeavored to conceal each other's faults." During the coming trials of battle, Washington, who referred to his staff as "family," would rely greatly on the bonds of affection his men had developed during that hard winter. As psychologists know today, it is this sense of community that contributes most to success in warfare.

To some American Patriots—as the supporters of the Revolution called themselves—the European-style Continental Army betrayed the ideals of the citizen-soldier and the autonomy of local communities that were central

tenets of the Revolution. Washington argued strongly, however, that the Revolution could not be won without a national army insulated from politics and able to withstand the shifting popular mood. Moreover, through the developing sense of community among these men—who came from hundreds of localities and a variety of ethnic backgrounds—the Continental soldiers became living examples of the egalitarian ideals of the Revolution. They were a popular democratic force that counterbalanced the conservatism of the new republic's elite leadership. The national spirit they built at Valley Forge would sustain them through four more years of war and provide momentum for the long process of forging a national political system out of the persistent localism of American politics. "I admire them tremendously!" wrote one European officer serving with Washington. "It is incredible that soldiers composed of men of every age, even children of fifteen, of whites and blacks, almost naked, unpaid, and rather poorly fed, can march so well and withstand fire so steadfastly." Asked to explain why his men served, another officer declared: "Nothing but virtue and that great principle, the love of our country." ■

Valley Forge

KEY TOPICS

- The major alignments and divisions among Americans during the American Revolution

- Major military campaigns of the Revolution

- The Articles of Confederation and the role of the Confederation Congress during the Revolutionary War

- The states as the setting for significant political change

- The economic crisis in the aftermath of the American Revolution

THE WAR FOR INDEPENDENCE

At the beginning of the Revolution, the British had the world's best-equipped and most disciplined army, as well as a navy that was unopposed in American waters. But they greatly underestimated the American capacity to fight. With a native officer corps and considerable experience in the colonial wars of the eighteenth century, the Patriot forces proved formidable. The British also misperceived the sources of the conflict. Seeing the rebellion as the work of a small group of disgruntled conspirators, initially they defined their objective as defeating this Patriot opposition. In the wake of a military victory, they believed, they could easily reassert political control. But the geography of eastern North America offered no single vital center whose conquest would end the war. The Patriots had the advantage of fighting on their own ground and among a population thinly spread over a territory stretching along 1,500 miles of coastline and extending 100 miles or more into the interior. When the British succeeded in defeating the Patriots in one area, resistance would spring up in another. The key factor in the outcome of the war for independence, then, was the popular support for the American cause.

The Patriot Forces

Most American men of fighting age had to face the call to arms. From a population of approximately 350,000 eligible men, more than 200,000 saw action, though no more than 25,000 were engaged at any one time. More than 100,000 served in the Continental Army, under Washington's command and the authority of the Continental Congress; the other soldiers served in Patriot militia companies.

These militias—armed bodies of men drawn from local communities—proved important in the defense of their own areas, for they had homes as well as local reputations to protect. But the Revolutionary War was not won by citizen-soldiers who exchanged plows for guns, or backcountry riflemen who picked off British soldiers from behind trees. In the exuberant days of 1776, many Patriots did believe that militias alone could win the war against the British. As one observer wrote, "The *Rage Militaire*, as the French call a passion for arms, has taken possession of the whole Continent." But because men preferred to serve with their neighbors in local companies rather than subject themselves to the discipline of the regular service, the states failed to meet their quotas for regiments in the Continental Army. Serving short terms of enlistment, often with officers of their own choosing, militiamen resisted discipline. Washington's deputy, General Nathanael Greene, declared that they lacked the fortitude "to stand the shocking scenes of war," having never been "steeled by habit or fortified by military pride." Indeed, in the face of battle, militia companies demonstrated appalling rates of desertion.

The final victory, rather, resulted primarily from the steady struggle of the Continental Army. The American Revolution had little in common with modern national liberation movements in which armed populations engage in guerrilla warfare. Washington and his officers required a force that could directly engage the British, and from the beginning of the war he argued with a skeptical Congress that victory could be won only with a full commitment to a truly national army. His views conflicted with popular fears of a standing army. Congress initially refused to invoke a draft or mandate army enlistments exceeding one year.

The failings of the militias in the early battles of the war sobered Congress, and it both greatly enlarged state quotas for the army and extended the term of service to

Jean Baptiste Antoine de Verger, a French officer serving with the Continental Army, made these watercolors of American soldiers during the Revolution. Some 200,000 men saw action, including at least 5,000 African Americans; more than half of these troops served with the Continental Army. SOURCE: Anne S.K. Brown Military Collection, John Hay Library, Brown University.

three years or the war's duration. To spur enlistment Congress offered bounties, regular wages, and promises of free land after victory. By the spring of 1777 Washington's army had grown to nearly 9,000 men.

Discipline was essential in a conflict in which men fired at close range, charged each other with bayonets, and engaged in hand-to-hand combat. One Connecticut man wrote of the effects of cannon on his regiment: "The ball first cut off the head of Smith, a stout heavy man, and dashed it open, then took Taylor across the bowels; it then struck Sergeant Garret of our company on the hip, took off the point of the hip bone." "Oh! What a sight that was," he concluded, "to see within a distance of six rods those men with their legs and arms and guns and packs all in a heap." In New Jersey, a sergeant in the Continental Army witnessed British troops slaughtering wounded Americans lying on the field: "The men that was wounded in the thigh or leg, they dashed out their brains with their muskets and run them through with their bayonets, made them like sieves. This was barbarity to the utmost."

According to the best estimates, a total of 25,674 American men died in the Revolution, approximately 6,000 from wounds suffered in battle, 10,000 from the effects of disease, the rest as prisoners of war or missing in action. Regiments of the Continental Army experienced the highest casualty rates, sometimes 30 or 40 percent. Indeed, the casualty rate overall was higher than in any other American conflict except the Civil War. In most areas the war claimed few civilian lives, for it was confined largely to direct engagements between the armies. In the backcountry and in regions of the South, however, where Patriot and Loyalist militias waged vicious campaigns, noncombatant casualties were considerable.

Both the Continentals and the militias played important political roles as well. At a time when Americans identified most strongly with their local communities or their states, the Continental Army, through experiences like the Valley Forge winter, evolved into a powerful force for nationalist sentiment. But shortages of food and pay led to many army mutinies. In the most serious incident, among the Pennsylvania Line in January 1781, enlisted men killed one officer, wounded two others, and set off from their winter quarters in New Jersey for Philadelphia to ask Congress to uphold its commitments. As they marched they were joined by British agents who encouraged them to go over to the king. Enraged at this attempt at subversion, the mutineers hanged the agents and gave up their resistance. Angry as they were at Congress, they were Americans first and hated the British. Over 100,000 men from every state served in the Continental Army, contributing mightily to the unity of purpose—the formation of a national community—that was essential to the process of nation making.

In most communities Patriots had seized control of local government during the period of committee organizing in 1774 and 1775 (see Chapter 6), and with war imminent they pressed the obligation to serve in a Patriot militia upon most eligible men. In Farmington, Connecticut, in 1776, eighteen men were imprisoned "on suspicion of their being inimical to America" when they failed to join the muster of the local militia. After individual grilling by the authorities, they petitioned for pardon. "They appeared to be penitent of their former conduct," it was reported, and understood "that there was no such thing" as remaining neutral. Probably the most important role of the Patriot militias was to force even the most apathetic of Americans to think seriously about the Revolution, and to choose sides under the scrutiny of their neighbors.

As men marched off to war, many women assumed the management of family farms and businesses. Abigail Adams, for example, ran the Adams family's farm at Quincy for years. She wrote eloquently and often to her husband, John, on issues surrounding the American struggle for independence and, later, on the structure of the new republic. Some women participated even more directly in patriotic politics. The Boston home of Mercy Otis Warren, daughter of James Otis, was a center of Patriot political activity, and this dedicated revolutionary woman published a series of satires supporting the American cause and scorning the Loyalists. When the fighting shifted to their locales, women volunteered as seamstresses, cooks, nurses, and even spies.

When the months of fighting lengthened into years, many women left their homes to join husbands and lovers, fathers and brothers, in army encampments. Some were officially employed, but most voluntarily took care of their own men, and many fought with them side by side. Best known among the women who stayed by their husbands' sides even in camp were Martha Washington and Catherine Greene, wives of the two most important American generals of the war. But less socially prominent women were remembered as well. Mary Ludwig Hays (later McCauley) earned the name "Molly Pitcher" for her courage in bringing water to the Patriots during the Battle of Monmouth in June 1778. When her husband was overcome by heat, Mary Hays took his place at the cannon. In another instance, when Margaret Corbin's husband died in battle she stepped into his position. Other women, such as Deborah Sampson of Massachusetts, disguised themselves as men and enlisted.

The Loyalists

Not all Americans were Patriots. Many sat on the fence, confused by the conflict and waiting for a clear turn in the tide of the struggle before declaring their allegiance. About a fifth of the population, perhaps as many as half a million people, remained loyal to the British crown. They called themselves Loyalists, but were known to Patriots as Tories, the popular name for the conservative party in England, which traditionally supported the authority of the king over Parliament. Loyalism was strongest in the Lower South, weakest in New England. British colonial officials were almost always Loyalists, as were most Anglican clergymen and many lawyers who had worked with colonial administrators. Other Loyalists were conservatives, fearful of political or social upheaval, or were temperamentally opposed to resistance to established authority. The Loyalists included members of ethnic minorities who had been persecuted by the dominant majority, such as the Highland Scots of the Carolinas and western New York, and southern tenant farmers who had Patriot landlords. Moreover, many slaves and most Indians, the latter fearing aggressive expansion by independent American states, identified with the Loyalists. Patriots passed state treason acts that prohibited speaking or

John Singleton Copley's portrait of Mercy Otis Warren captured her at the age of thirty-six, in 1765. During the Revolution her home in Boston was a center of patriotic political activity.

SOURCE: John Singleton Copley, U.S., 1738–1815 *Mrs. James Warren (Mercy Otis),* ca. 1763. Oil on canvas. 51¼ × 41 in. (130.1 × 104.1 cm). Bequest of Winslow Warren. Courtesy of Museum of Fine Art, Boston.

writing against the Revolution. They also punished Loyalists by issuing bills of attainder, a legal process (later made illegal by the United States Constitution) by which Loyalists lost their civil rights and their property. In some areas, notably New York, South Carolina, Massachusetts, and Pennsylvania, Loyalists faced mob violence. One favorite punishment was the "grand Tory ride," in which a crowd hauled the victim through the streets astride a sharp fence rail. Another was tarring and feathering, in which men were stripped to "buff and breeches" and their naked flesh coated liberally with heated tar and then feathers. One broadside recommended that Patriots "then hold a lighted Candle to the feathers, and try to set it all on fire." The torment rarely went that far, but it was brutally painful nonetheless.

The most infamous American supporter of the British cause was Benedict Arnold, whose name has become synonymous, in the United States, with treason. Arnold was a hero of the early battles of the Revolution on the American side. But in 1779, angry and resentful about what he perceived to be assignments and rank below his station, he became a paid informer of General Henry Clinton, head of the British army in New York City. In 1780 Patriots uncovered Arnold's plot to betray the strategic post of West Point, which he commanded. After fleeing to the British, who paid him a handsome stipend and pension, he became a brigadier general in the British army. Arnold became the most hated man in America. In his hometown of Norwich, Connecticut, a crowd destroyed the gravestones of his family, and in cities and towns throughout America thousands burned his effigy. During the last two years of the war he led British raids against his home state as well as against Virginia, and after the Revolution he lived in England until his death in 1801.

The TORY's Day of JUDGMENT.

A Patriot mob torments Loyalists in this print published during the Revolution. One favorite punishment was the "grand Tory ride," in which a crowd hauled the victim through the streets astride a fence rail. In another men were stripped to "buff and breeches" and their naked flesh coated liberally with heated tar and feathers.

SOURCE: The Granger Collection.

The British strategy for suppressing the Revolution depended on mobilizing the Loyalists, but in most areas this proved impossible, since they were not a monolithic group but were divided in their opinions. As many as 50,000 Loyalists, however, fought for the king during the Revolution. Many joined Loyalist militias or engaged in irregular warfare, especially in the Lower South. In 1780, when Washington's Continentals numbered about 9,000, there were 8,000 American Loyalists serving in the British army in America.

As many as 80,000 Loyalists fled the country during and after the Revolution. Many went to England or the British West Indies, but the largest number settled in Canada; the Canadian provinces of Ontario, Nova Scotia, and New Brunswick honor the Loyalist refugees as founders. Loyalist property was confiscated by the states and sold at public auction. Although the British government compensated many for their losses, most Loyalists were unhappy exiles. "I earnestly wish to spend the remainder of my days in America," wrote William Pepperell, formerly of Maine, from London in 1778. "I love the country, I love the people." Former governor Thomas Hutchinson of Massachusetts wrote that he "had rather die in a little country farm-house in New England than in the best nobleman's seat in old England." Despite their disagreement with the Patriots on essential political questions, they remained Americans, and they mourned the loss of their country.

The Campaign for New York and New Jersey

During the winter of 1775–76 the British developed a strategic plan for the war. From his base at Halifax, Nova Scotia, Sir William Howe was to take his army to New York City, which the British navy would make impregnable. From there Howe was to drive north along the Hudson, while another British army marched south from Canada to Albany. The two armies would converge, cutting New England off from the rest of the colonies, then turn eastward to reduce the rebellious Yankees into submission. Washington, who had arrived at Boston to take command of the militia forces there in the summer of 1775, anticipated this strategy, and in the spring of 1776 he shifted his forces southward toward New York.

In early July, as Congress was taking its final vote on the Declaration of Independence, the British began their operation at New York City, landing 32,000 men, a third of them Hessian mercenaries (from the German state of Hesse), on Staten Island. The Americans, meanwhile, set up fortified positions across the harbor in Brooklyn. Attacking in late August, the British inflicted heavy casualties on the Americans, and the militia forces under Washington's command proved unreliable under fire. The Battle of Long Island ended

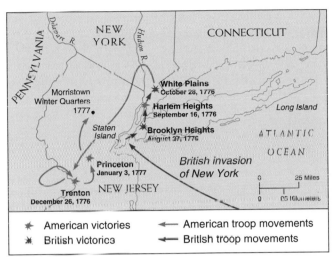

Campaign for New York and New Jersey, 1775–1777

in disaster for the Patriots, and they were forced to withdraw across the East River to Manhattan.

The British now offered Congress an opportunity to negotiate, and on September 6, Benjamin Franklin, John Adams, and Edward Rutledge sat down with General Howe and his brother, Admiral Richard Howe, on Staten Island. But the meeting broke up when the Howes demanded repeal of the Declaration of Independence. The stage was set for another round of fighting. Six days later the British invaded Manhattan island, and only an American stand at Harlem Heights prevented the destruction of a large portion of the Patriot army. Enjoying naval control of the harbor, the British quickly outflanked the American positions. In a series of battles over the next few months, they forced Washington back at White Plains and overran the American posts of Fort Washington and Fort Lee, on either side of the Hudson River. By November the Americans were fleeing south across New Jersey in a frantic attempt to avoid the British under General Charles Cornwallis.

With morale desperately low, whole militia companies deserted; others, announcing the end of their terms of enlistment, left for home. American resistance seemed to be collapsing all around Washington. "Our troops will not do their duty," he wrote painfully to Congress as he crossed the Delaware River into Pennsylvania. Upon receiving his message, the delegates in Philadelphia fled to Baltimore. "I think the game is pretty near up," Washington admitted to his brother. But rather than fall back further, which would surely have meant the dissolution of his entire force, he decided to risk a counterattack. On Christmas night 1776, he led 2,400 troops back across the Delaware, and the next morning defeated the Hessian forces in a

surprise attack on their headquarters at Trenton, New Jersey. The Americans inflicted further heavy losses on the British at Princeton, then drove them all the way back to the environs of New York City.

Although these small victories had little strategic importance, they salvaged American morale. As Washington settled into winter headquarters at Morristown, he realized he had to pursue a defensive strategy, avoiding direct confrontations with the British while checking their advances and hurting them wherever possible. "We cannot conquer the British force at once," wrote General Greene, "but they cannot conquer us at all." This last sentiment was more a hope than a conviction, but it defined the essentially defensive American strategy of the Revolution. Most important to that strategy was the survival of the Continental Army.

The Northern Campaigns of 1777

The fighting with the American forces had prevented Howe from moving north up the Hudson River, and the British advance southward from Canada had been stalled by American resistance at Lake Champlain. In 1777, however, the British decided to replay their strategy. From Canada they dispatched General John Burgoyne with nearly 8,000 British and German troops. Howe was to move his force from New York, first taking the city of Philadelphia, the seat of the Continental Congress, and then moving north to meet Burgoyne.

Fort Ticonderoga fell to Burgoyne on July 6, but by August the general found himself bogged down and harassed by Patriot militias in the rough country south of Lake George. After several defeats in September at the hands of an American army commanded by General Horatio Gates, Burgoyne retreated to Saratoga. There his army was surrounded by a considerably larger force of Americans, and on October 19, lacking alternatives, he surrendered his nearly 6,000 men. It would be the biggest British defeat until Yorktown, decisive because it forced the nations of Europe to recognize that the Americans had a fighting chance to win their Revolution.

The Americans were less successful against Howe. A force of 15,000 British troops left New York in July, landing a month later, at the northern end of Chesapeake Bay. At Brandywine Creek the British outflanked the Americans, inflicting heavy casualties and forcing a retreat. Ten days later, the British routed the Americans a second time with a frightful bayonet charge at Paoli that left many Patriots dead. When British troops occupied Philadelphia on September 26, Congress had already fled. Washington attempted a valiant counterattack at Germantown on October 4, but initial success was followed by miscoordination that eventually doomed the operation.

American victories

British victories

← American troop movements

← British troop movements

Northern Campaigns, 1777–1778

After this campaign the Continentals headed for winter quarters at Valley Forge, a few dozen miles from Philadelphia, the bitterness of their defeats muted somewhat by news of the surrender at Saratoga. In taking Philadelphia, the British had

gained the most important city in North America, but it proved to have little strategic value. Central government was virtually nonexistent, and so the unified effort suffered little disruption. At the end of two years of fighting, the British strategy for winning the war had to be judged a failure.

The French Alliance and the Spanish Borderlands

During these first two years of fighting, the Americans were sustained by loans from France and Spain, allies against Britain. Both saw an opportunity to win back North American territories lost to Great Britain in the Seven Years' War. The Continental Congress maintained a diplomatic delegation in Paris headed by Benjamin Franklin. The urbane and cosmopolitan Franklin, who captured French hearts by dressing in homespun and wearing a "frontiersman" fur cap, maintained excellent relations with Comte de Vergennes, the French foreign minister. Franklin negotiated with Vergennes for recognition of American independence and a Franco-American alliance against the British, in addition to loans from the French to finance the Revolution. But was unable to convince him. France wanted to weaken the British empire any way it could, and was inclined to support the Americans, but was reluctant to encourage a republican revolution against monarchy and colonialism.

In England, meanwhile, the Whig opposition argued strongly against the war. "The measures toward America are erroneous," declared Lord Rockingham, "the adherence to them is destruction." William Pitt warned his countrymen to "beware the gathering storm" if and when France decided to support the Americans actively. When, in December 1777, British Prime Minister Lord North received the news of Burgoyne's surrender, he dispatched agents to begin peace discussions with Franklin in Paris. Fears of British conciliation with the revolutionaries, as well as the victory at Saratoga, finally persuaded French Foreign Minister Vergennes to tie France to the United States. In mid-December he informed Franklin that the king's council had decided to recognize American independence.

In February 1778, the American delegation submitted to Congress a treaty of commerce and alliance it had negotiated with the French. In the treaty, to take effect upon a declaration of war between France and Britain, the French pledged to "maintain effectually the liberty, sovereignty, and independence" of the United States. "Neither of the two parties," the document read, "shall conclude either truce or peace with Great Britain, without the formal consent of the other." France agreed to guarantee to the United States all the "northern parts of America" as well as other "conquests" made in the war, while the United States promised to recognize French acquisitions of British islands in the West Indies. Warfare between France and Britain broke out in June.

A year later Spain also entered the war. Spanish officials in New Orleans were already providing substantial ammunition and provisions for American forts in the West, including supplies of beef from herds of cattle driven to New Orleans by *vaqueros* (cowboys) from Texas. In New Spain the viceroy levied a special tax to pay for these supplies, and borderland colonists in Sonora, Texas, New Mexico, and California contributed their share. Father Junípero Serra, president of the California missions, prescribed a weekly prayer for American victory, and the scene of California Indian converts praying for the freedom of European colonists on the other coast is surely one of the more ironic of the era. But American attempts to establish a formal Spanish alliance met with failure. The Spanish saw the Revolution as an opportunity to regain Florida from the British and extend their control of the Mississippi Valley, but they feared the threat the Americans would pose to New Spain. "Its people are active, industrious, and aggressive," one Mexican official wrote of the United States, and "it would be culpable negligence on our part not to thwart their schemes for conquest."

Thus the Spanish pursued an independent strategy against the British, taking the weakly defended Mississippi River towns of Natchez and Baton Rouge from the British in 1779, and winning the important Gulf ports of Mobile and Pensacola in 1780 and 1781 respectively. The victory at Pensacola was achieved with the help of several companies of Florida exiles, many of them African Americans. Alarmed by the quick spread of American settlements west of the Appalachians, the Spanish attempted to establish a claim of their own to the British territory north of the Ohio by sending an expedition into the Northwest, which in 1781 succeeded in taking the minor British post of St. Joseph, in present-day Michigan.

The first French ambassador to the United States arrived with instructions to do everything he could to prevent the Americans from enlarging their territory at the expense of the Spanish borderland colonies. Like the Spanish, the French also feared the potential power of an independent United States. Several years before, Vergennes had warned the British that if the American gained their independence they "would immediately set about forming a great marine [naval armed force] ," and use it in the Caribbean to "conquer both your islands and ours." Eventually they would sweep south and "not leave a foot of that hemisphere in the possession of any European power." Many American leaders did indeed have expansionist aspirations, and understood that the wartime alliance with France and tacit support of Spain were expedients.

Worried over the consequences of French involvement, in the spring of 1778 Lord North sent a peace commission to America with promises to repeal the parliamentary legislation that had provoked the crisis in the first place and pledging never again to impose revenue taxes on the colonies. Three years earlier such a pledge would surely have forestalled the movement toward independence. But the Continental Congress now declared that any person coming to terms with the peace commission would be labeled a traitor; the only possible topics of negotiation were the withdrawal of British forces and the recognition of American independence.

When France entered the war, the British were forced to rethink their military strategy. With the West Indies at risk, they shipped 5,000 troops from New York to the Caribbean, and succeded in beating back a French attack. Fearing the arrival of the French fleet along the North American coast, the new British commander in America, General Henry Clinton, evacuated Philadelphia in June 1778. In hot pursuit were Washington's Continentals, fresh out of Valley Forge. At the Battle of Monmouth on June 28, the British blunted the American drive and retreated to New York. The Americans, centered at West Point, took up defensive positions surrounding the lower Hudson. Confidence in an impending victory now spread through the Patriot forces. But after a failed American-French joint campaign against British forces at Newport, Rhode Island, General Washington settled for a defensive strategy. Although the Americans enjoyed several small successes in the Northeast over the next two years, the war there went into a stall.

At sea the fighting mostly involved the British and the French, but Continental, state, and private vessels raided British merchant ships and conducted isolated naval patrols. The foremost American naval hero of the war was John Paul Jones, who raided the coast of Scotland in 1777. In 1779, while commanding the French ship *Bonhomme Richard* (named in honor of Franklin's "Poor Richard"), Jones engaged in a celebrated battle with the British warship *Serapis*. When the two ships locked together, the British captain hailed Jones, asking if he were ready to surrender. Jones's reply—"I have not yet begun to fight"— became one of the most quoted lines of the Revolution. Jones won his battle, though it had little military consequence. After the war Congress decommissioned the small American navy and dismissed its officers, including Jones, who went on to serve in the imperial Russian navy.

Joseph Brant, the brilliant chief of the Mohawks who sided with Great Britain during the Revolution, in a 1786 painting by the American artist Gilbert Stuart. After the Treaty of Paris, Brant led a large faction of Iroquois people north into British Canada, where they established a separate Iroquois Confederacy.

SOURCE: Gilbert Stuart. *Joseph Brant*, 1786. Oil on canvas, 30″ × 25″. New York State Historical Association, Cooperstown.

Indian Peoples and the Revolution in the West

At the beginning of the conflict both sides solicited the support of the Indians. A committee of the Continental Congress reported that "securing and preserving the friendship of Indian nations appears to be a subject of the utmost moment to these colonies." Most concerned about the stance of the Iroquois Confederacy—long one of the most potent political forces in colonial North America—a delegation from Congress told the Iroquois that the conflict was a "family quarrel" and urged them to keep out of it. British agents, on the other hand, pressed the Iroquois to unite against the Americans. Many Indian people were reluctant to get involved: "We are unwilling to join on either side of such a contest," an Oneida chief responded. "Let us Indians be all of one mind, and live with one another, and you white people settle your own disputes between yourselves."

Ultimately, however, the British were more persuasive. It became clear to Indians that a Patriot victory would mean the extension of American settlements into their homelands. Native peoples fought in the Revolution for some of the same reasons Patriots did—for political independence, cultural integrity, and the protection of their land and property—but Indian fears of American expansion led them to oppose the Patriot rhetoric of natural rights and the equality of all men. Almost all the tribes that engaged in the fighting did so on the side of the British.

British officials marshaled the support of Cherokees, Creeks, Choctaws, and Chickasaws in the South, supplying them with arms from the British arsenal at Pensacola until it was taken by the Spanish in 1781. The consequence was a ferocious Indian war in the southern backcountry. In the summer of 1776, a large number of Cherokees, led by the warrior chief Dragging Canoe (*Tsiyu-Gunsini*), attacked dozens of American settlements. It took hard fighting before Patriot militia companies managed to drive the Cherokees into the mountains, destroying many of their towns. Although the Cherokees even-

This American cartoon, published during the Revolution, depicts "the Scalp Buyer," Colonel Henry Hamilton, paying bounties to Indians. In fact, Indian warriors were not simply pawns of the British but fought for the same reasons the Patriots did—for political independence, cultural integrity, and protection of land and property.

SOURCE: The Bostonian Society/Old State House.

Fighting in the West, 1778–1779

tually made an official peace, sporadic violence between Patriots and Indians continued along the southern frontier.

Among the Iroquois of New York, the Mohawk leader Joseph Brant (*Thayendanegea*) succeeded in bringing most Iroquois warriors into the British camp, although he was opposed by the chiefs of the Oneidas and Tuscaroras, who supported the Patriots. In 1777 and 1778, Iroquois and Loyalist forces raided the northern frontiers of New York and Pennsylvania. In retaliation an American army invaded the Iroquois homelands in 1779. Supported by Oneida and Tuscarora warriors, the Americans destroyed dozens of western villages and thousands of acres of crops. For the first time since the birth of their confederacy in the fifteenth century, the Iroquois were fighting each other.

Across the mountains, the Ohio Indians formed an effective alliance under the British at Detroit, and in 1777 and 1778 they sent warriors south against pioneer communities in western Virginia and Kentucky that had been founded in defiance of the Proclamation of 1763. Boonesborough, Kentucky, was nearly destroyed by repeated attacks, and the Americans barely held out. Virginian George Rogers Clark countered by organizing an expedition of Kentucky militia against the old French settlements in the Illinois country, which were controlled by the British. They succeeded in taking the British post at Kaskaskia in the summer of 1778, and in early 1779, in a daring winter raid on Vincennes, they captured Colonel Henry Hamilton, British commander in the West, infamously known as "the Scalp Buyer" because of the bounty he had placed on Patriots' lives.

But Clark lacked the strength to attack the strategic British garrison at Detroit. Coordinating his Iroquois forces with those in Ohio, Brant mounted a new set of offensives that cast a shadow over Clark's successes. Raids back and forth across the Ohio River by Indians and Americans claimed hundreds of lives over the next three years. The war in the West would not end with the conclusion of hostilities in the East. With barely a pause, the fighting in the trans-Appalachian West between Americans and Indians would continue for another two decades.

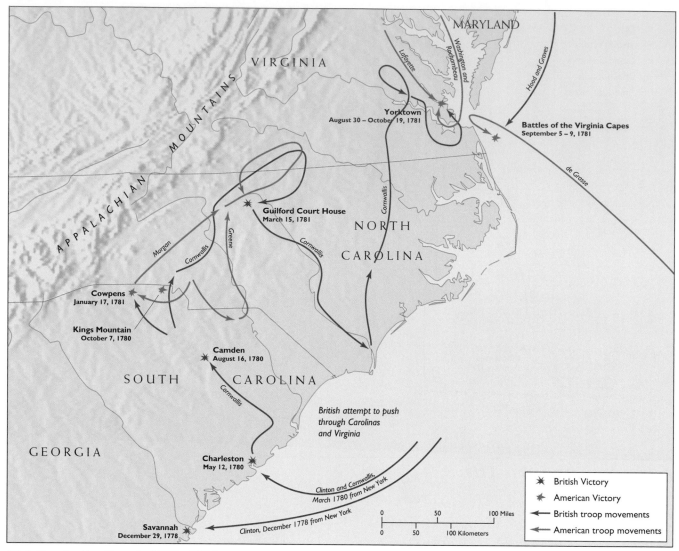

Fighting in the South, 1778–1781

The War in the South

The most important fighting of the Revolution took place in the South. There the war had begun with a slave uprising. In late 1775 Lord Dunmore, the last royal governor of Virginia, issued a proclamation calling on slaves to desert their masters and take up arms with the British. More than 800 slaves responded to his call, terrifying Chesapeake planters. When Patriot forces effectively routed Dunmore's army in July 1776, they fought a large number of African-American troops wearing sashes emblazoned with the words "Liberty to Slaves." Many of these black soldiers succumbed to smallpox, but at least 300 sailed with Dunmore when he departed.

General Clinton regained the initiative for Britain in December 1778 by sending a force from New York against Georgia, the weakest of the colonies. The British crushed the Patriot militia at Savannah and began to organize the Loyalists in an effort to reclaim the colony. Several American counterattacks failed, including one in which the French fleet bombarded Savannah. Encouraged by their success in Georgia, the British decided to apply the lessons learned there throughout the South. This involved a fundamental change from a strategy of military conquest to one of pacification. Territory would be retaken step by step, then handed over to Loyalists who would reassert colonial authority loyal to the crown. In October 1779, Clinton evacuated Rhode Island, the last British stronghold in New England, and proceeded with 8,000 troops for a campaign against Charleston. Outflanking the American defenders, Clinton forced the surrender of more than 5,000 troops in May—the most significant American defeat of the war. Horatio Gates, the hero of Saratoga, led a detachment of Continentals southward, but in August they were defeated by General Cornwallis at Camden, South Carolina. Patriot resistance collapsed in the Lower South, and American fortunes were suddenly at their lowest ebb since the beginning of the war.

During the British campaign through the South, thousands of slaves responded to General Clinton's promise of liberty to those who would fight. In response, Maryland, Virginia, and North Carolina grudgingly attempted to recruit free persons of color and even slaves into their armed forces. Northern states, led by New England, had already solicited African-American recruits, and Rhode Island had placed an African-American regiment in the field. Some of these men served in the infantry, many more were commissary workers or teamsters. By war's end at least 5,000 African Americans had served in Patriot militias or the Continental Army, and in the Upper South some slaves won their freedom through military service. In the Lower South, however, where the numerical superiority of slaves bred fears of rebellion among white people, there was no similar movement.

The southern campaign was marked by vicious violence between partisan militias of Patriots and Loyalists. "The Whigs and Tories persecute each other with little less than savage fury," wrote General Greene, appointed to succeed Gates after the disaster at Camden. "There is nothing but murders and devastations in every quarter." The violence peaked in September 1780 with Cornwallis's invasion of North Carolina, where the Patriots were stronger and better organized. There the British found their southern strategy untenable: plundering towns and farms in order to feed the army in the interior had the effect of producing angry support for the Patriots. The Patriots won two important battles at Kings Mountain in October 1780 and the Cowpens in January 1781.

Into 1781 the Continentals and Patriot militias waged what General Greene called a fugitive war of hit and run against the British. "I am quite tired of marching about the country in quest of adventures," Cornwallis wrote; he declared himself "totally in the dark" about what to do next. He won a victory over the Patriots at Guilford Court House in March, but, finally deciding he would not be able to hold the Carolinas as long as Virginia remained a base of support and supply for the Americans, he led his army north in the summer of 1781. After marauding through the Virginia countryside he reached the Chesapeake, where he expected reinforcements from New York. The British withdrawal from North Carolina allowed Greene to reestablish Patriot control of the Lower South.

Yorktown

While the British raged through the South, the stalemate continued in the Northeast. In the summer of 1780, taking advantage of the British evacuation of Rhode Island, the French landed 5,000 troops at Newport under the command of General Rochambeau. But it was not until the spring of 1781 that the general risked joining his force to Washington's Continentals north of New York. They planned a campaign against the city, but in August Washington learned that the French Caribbean fleet was headed for the Chesapeake. Washington saw the opportunity for a decisive turn if only he and Rochambeau could move their troops south in coordination with the French naval operation, locking Cornwallis into his camp at Yorktown. Leaving a small force behind as a decoy, Washington and Rochambeau moved quickly down the coast to the Virginia shore.

More than 16,000 American and French troops had converged on the almost 8,000-man British garrison at Yorktown by mid-September. "If you cannot relieve me very soon," Cornwallis wrote to Clinton in New York, "you must expect to hear the worst." French and American heavy artillery hammered the British unmercifully until the middle of October. Cornwallis found it impossible to break the siege, and after the failure of a planned retreat across the York River, he opened negotiations for the surrender of his army. Two days later, on October 19, 1781, between lines of victorious American and French soldiers, the British troops came out from their trenches to surrender, marching to the melancholy tune of "The World Turned Upside Down":

> If buttercups buzzed after the bee,
> If boats were on land, churches on sea,
> If summer were spring and t'other way round,
> Then all the world would be upside down.

It must have seemed that way to Cornwallis, who, pleading illness, sent his second-in-command, General Charles O'Hara, to surrender. O'Hara first approached General Rochambeau, but the Frenchman waved him toward Washington. It was almost incomprehensible to the British that they would be surrendering to former subordinates. Everyone knew this was an event of incalculable importance, but few guessed it was the end of the war, for the British still controlled New York.

In London, at the end of November, Lord North received the news "as he would have taken a ball in the breast," reported the colonial secretary. "Oh God!" he moaned, "it is all over!" British fortunes were at low ebb in India, the West Indies, Florida, and the Mediterranean; the cost of the war was enormous; and there was little support among the public and members of Parliament for it. King George III wished to press on, but North submitted his resignation, and in March 1782 the king was forced to accept the counsel of Lord Rockingham, who favored granting Americans their independence.

THE UNITED STATES IN CONGRESS ASSEMBLED

The motion for independence, offered to the Continental Congress by Richard Henry Lee on June 7, 1776, called for a confederation of the states. The Articles of Confederation, the first written constitution of the United States, created a national government of sharply limited powers. This arrangement reflected the concerns of people fighting to free themselves from a coercive central government. The weak Confederation government found it difficult to forge the unity and assemble the resources necessary to fight the war and win the peace.

The Articles of Confederation

The debate over confederation that took place in the Continental Congress following the Declaration of Independence made it clear that the delegates favoring a loose union of autonomous states outnumbered those who wanted a strong central government. The following year a consensus finally emerged. In November 1777, the Articles of Confederation were formally adopted by the Continental Congress and sent to the states for ratification. The Articles created a national assembly, called the Congress, in which each state had a single vote. Delegates, selected annually in a manner determined by the individual state legislatures, could serve no more than three years out of six. A presiding president elected annually by Congress was eligible no more than one year out of three. Votes would be decided by a simple majority of the states, except for major questions, which would require the agreement of nine states.

Congress was granted national authority in the conduct of foreign affairs, matters of war and peace, and maintenance of the armed forces. It could raise loans, issue bills of credit, establish a coinage, and regulate trade with Indian peoples, and it was to be the final authority in jurisdictional disputes between states.

The Continental Congress printed currency to finance the Revolution. Because of widespread counterfeiting, engravers attempted to incorporate complex designs, like the unique vein structure in the leaf on this eighteen-pence note. In case that wasn't enough, the engraver of this note also included the warning: "To counterfeit is Death."

SOURCE: Library of Congress.

It was charged with establishing a national postal system as well as a common standard of weights and measures. Lacking the power to tax citizens directly, however, the national government was to apportion its financial burdens among the states according to the extent of their surveyed land. The Articles explicitly guaranteed the sovereignty of the individual states, reserving to them all powers not expressly delegated to Congress. Ratification or amendment required the agreement of all thirteen states. This constitution thus created a national government of specific yet sharply circumscribed powers.

The legislatures of twelve states soon voted in favor of the Articles, but final ratification was held up for more than three years by the state of Maryland. Representing the interests of states without claims to lands west of the Appalachians, Maryland demanded that states cede to Congress their western claims, the new nation's most valuable resource, for "the good of the whole." The colonial grants made to land companies, however, would be considered an exception. The eight states with western claims were reluctant to give them up, and the remaining states included powerful land speculators among their most influential citizens. While the stalemate over western lands continued, Congress remained an extralegal body, but it agreed to work under the terms of the unratified document. It was 1781 before Virginia, the state with the largest western claims, broke the log-jam by promising to cede its lands. Maryland then agreed to ratification, and in March the Articles of Confederation took effect.

Financing the War

Congress financed the Revolution through grants and loans from friendly foreign powers and by issuing paper currency. The total foreign subsidy by the end of the war approached $9 million, but this was insufficient to back the circulating Continental currency that Congress had authorized, the face value of which had risen to $200 million. Congress called on the states to raise taxes, payable in Continental dollars, so that this currency could be retired. But most of the states were unwilling to do this. In fact, the states resorted to printing currency of their own, which totaled another $200 million by the end of the war. The results of this growth in the money supply were the rapid depreciation of Continental currency and runaway inflation. People who received fixed incomes for services—Continental soldiers, for example, as well as merchants, landlords, and other creditors—were devastated. When Robert Morris, one of the wealthiest merchants in the country, became secretary of finance in May 1781, Continental currency had ceased to circulate; things of no value were said to be "not worth a Continental."

Morris persuaded Congress to charter the Bank of North America in Philadelphia, the first private commercial bank in the United States. There he deposited large quantities of gold and silver coin and bills of exchange obtained through loans from Holland and France. He then issued new paper currency backed by this supply. Once confidence in the bank had developed, Morris was able to begin supplying the Conti-

nental Army through private contracts. He was also able to meet the interest payments on the debt, which in 1783 he estimated to be about $30 million.

Negotiating Independence

Peace talks between the United States and Great Britain opened in July 1782, when Benjamin Franklin sat down with the British emissary in Paris. Congress had issued its first set of war aims in 1779. The fundamental demands were recognition of American independence and withdrawal of British forces. The American negotiators were to press for as much territory as possible, including Canada, and guarantees of the American right to fish the North Atlantic. As for its French ally, Congress instructed the commissioners to be guided by friendly advice, but also by "knowledge of our interests, and by your own discretion, in which we repose the fullest confidence." But as the British pushed through the South over the next two years, in 1780–81, and as the Americans grew increasingly dependent on French loans and military might, the French ambassador in Philadelphia worked to limit potential American power. In June 1781, partly as a result of French pressure, Congress issued a new set of instructions: the commissioners were to settle merely for a grant of independence and withdrawal of troops, and to be subject to the guidance and control of the French in the negotiations.

Franklin, John Jay, and John Adams, the peace commissioners in Paris, were aware of French attempts to manipulate the outcome of negotiations and to limit potential American power. In violation of instructions and treaty obligations, and without consulting the French, they signed a preliminary treaty with Britain in November 1782. The British were delighted at the thought of separating the wartime allies. In the treaty, Britain acknowledged the United States as "free, sovereign & independent" and agreed to withdraw its troops from all forts within American territory "with all convenient speed." They guaranteed Americans "the right to take fish" in northern waters. The American commissioners pressed the British for Canada, but settled for western territorial boundaries extending to the Mississippi. Britain received American promises to erect "no lawful impediments" to the recovery of debts, to cease confiscating Loyalist property, and to try to persuade the states to fairly compensate Loyalist exiles. Finally, the two nations agreed to unencumbered navigation of the Mississippi. The American commissioners had accomplished an astounding coup. The peace terms, they wrote to Congress, "appear to leave us little to complain of and not much to desire."

France was thus confronted with an accomplished fact. When the French criticized the commissioners, the Americans responded by hinting that resistance to the treaty provisions could result in a British–American alliance. France thereupon quickly made an agreement of its own with the British.

Though left out of the negotiations, Spain claimed sovereignty over much of the trans-Appalachian territory granted to the United States as a result of its successful campaign against the British on the Mississippi and the Gulf Coast. The most important issue here was American use of the Mississippi, which depended on access to the Spanish-controlled port of New Orleans. Refusing to deal directly with the Americans, the

Spanish arranged a separate peace with Great Britain, in which it won the return of Florida. The final Treaty of Paris—actually a series of separate agreements among the United States, Great Britain, France, and Spain—was signed at Versailles on September 3, 1783.

The Crisis of Demobilization

During the two years between the surrender at Yorktown and the signing of the Treaty of Paris, the British continued to occupy New York City, Charleston, and a

 Web Exploration   Examine the impact of the Treaty of Paris on North America's geopolitical landscape. How did the treaty alter the balance of power in North America?
www.prenhall.com/faragher/map7.1

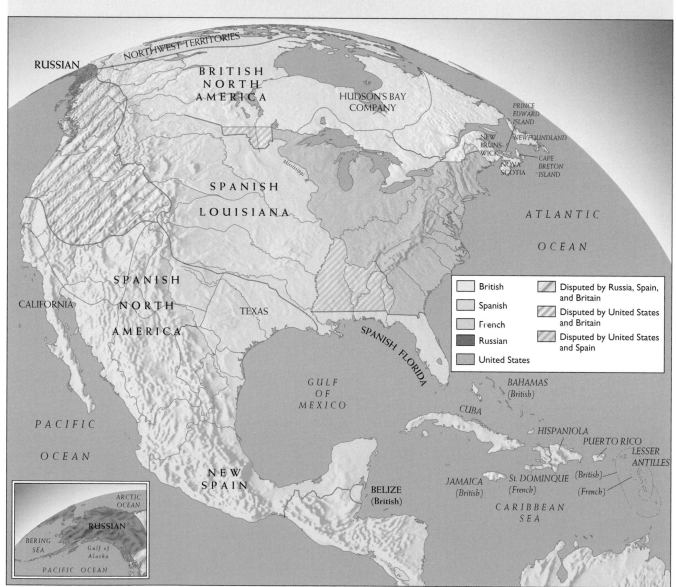

North America after the Treaty of Paris, 1783   The map of European and American claims to North America was radically altered by the results of the American Revolution.

series of western posts. The Continental Army remained on wartime alert, with some 10,000 men and an estimated 1,000 women encamped at Newburgh, New York, north of West Point. The soldiers had long been awaiting their pay, and were very concerned about the postwar bounties and land warrants promised them. The most serious problem, however, lay not among the enlisted men but in the officer corps.

Continental officers had extracted a promise from Congress of life pensions at half pay in exchange for enlistment for the duration of the war. By 1783, however, Congress had still not made specific provisions for veteran's pensions. With peace at hand, officers began to fear that the army would be disbanded before the problem was resolved, and they would lose whatever power they had to pressure Congress. In January 1783, a group of prominent senior officers petitioned Congress, demanding that pensions be converted to a bonus equal to five years of full pay. "Any further experiments on their patience," they warned, "may have fatal effects." Despite this barely veiled threat of military intervention, Congress rejected their petition.

With the backing of congressional nationalists, a group of army officers associated with General Horatio Gates called an extraordinary meeting of the officer corps at Newburgh. But General Washington, on whom the officers counted for support, condemned the meeting as "disorderly" and called an official meeting of his own. There was enormous tension as the officers assembled on March 15; at stake was nothing less than the possibility of a military coup at the very moment of American victory. The American Revolution was the first of many successful colonial revolutions, and in hindsight it is clear that post-independence military rule was a common outcome. Washington strode into the room and mounted the platform. Turning his back in disdain on General Gates, he told the assembly that he wished to read a statement, and then pulled a pair of glasses from his pocket. None of his officers had seen their leader wearing glasses before. "Gentlemen, you must pardon me,"

State Claims to Western Lands   The ratification of the Articles of Confederation in 1781 awaited settlement of the western claims of eight states. Vermont, claimed by New Hampshire and New York, was not made a state until 1791, after disputes were settled the previous year. The territory north of the Ohio River was claimed in whole or in part by Virginia, New York, Connecticut, and Massachusetts. All of them had ceded their claims by 1786, except for Connecticut, which had claimed an area just south of Lake Erie, known as the Western Reserve; Connecticut ceded this land in 1800. The territory south of the Ohio was claimed by Virginia, North Carolina, South Carolina, and Georgia; in 1802 the latter became the last state to cede its claims.

said Washington when he noticed their surprise. "I have grown gray in your service and now find myself growing blind." He then went on to denounce any resort to force, but it was his offhand remark about growing gray that made the greatest impact. Who had sacrificed more than their commander in chief? After he left, the officers adopted resolutions rejecting intervention, and a week later, on Washington's urging, Congress decided to convert the pensions to bonuses after all.

Washington's role in this crisis was one of his greatest contributions to the nation. In December 1783 he resigned his commission as general of the army despite calls for him to remain. There is little doubt that he could have assumed the role of American dictator. Instead, by his actions and example, the principle of military subordination to civil authority was firmly established.

WebExploration

Through a series of animated maps, consider the ways in which the Northwest Ordinance affected the admission of new states into the Union. What were the consequences for western lands?
www.prenhall.com/faragher/map7.2

Legend:
- Northwest Territory
- – – – Disputed boundaries
- ■ British forts

Map labels:
BRITISH NORTH AMERICA (CANADA)
Lake of the Woods
Lake Superior
Fort Michilimackinac
MICHIGAN (1837)
WISCONSIN (1848)
Mississippi R.
Lake Michigan
Lake Huron
St. Lawrence R.
MAINE (Mass.)
Point-au-Fer
Dutchman's Point
NEW HAMPSHIRE
Lake Ontario
Oswego
Fort Niagara
NEW YORK
Hudson R.
MASSACHUSETTS
RHODE ISLAND
CONNECTICUT
Fort Detroit
Lake Erie
PENNSYLVANIA
NEW JERSEY
Wabash R.
OHIO (1803)
Scioto R.
DELAWARE
MARYLAND
ILLINOIS (1818)
INDIANA (1816)
Illinois R.
Ohio R.
VIRGINIA
ATLANTIC OCEAN
SPANISH LOUISIANA
KENTUCKY (1792)
TENNESSEE (1796)
NORTH CAROLINA

Scale: 0   50   100   150 Miles
0   50 100 150 Kilometers

The Northwest Territory and the Land Survey System of the United States

As for the common soldiers, they wanted simply to be discharged. In May 1783, Congress voted the soldiers three months' pay as a bonus and instructed Washington to begin dismissing them. Some troops remained at Newburgh until the British had evacuated New York in November, but by the beginning of 1784 the Continental Army had shrunk to no more than a few hundred men.

The Problem of the West

After Yorktown, the British abandoned their Indian allies in the West. When the Indians learned of the armistice, according to one British officer, they were "thunderstruck." Neither the Iroquois nor the Ohio tribes, who had fought with the British, considered

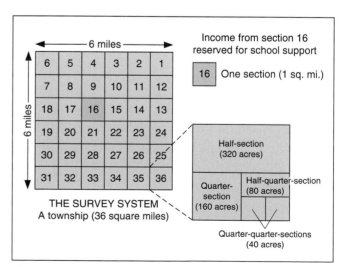

Income from section 16 reserved for school support

16 One section (1 sq. mi.)

THE SURVEY SYSTEM
A township (36 square miles)

6	5	4	3	2	1
7	8	9	10	11	12
18	17	16	15	14	13
19	20	21	22	23	24
30	29	28	27	26	25
31	32	33	34	35	36

6 miles

Half-section (320 acres)
Quarter-section (160 acres)
Half-quarter-section (80 acres)
Quarter-quarter-sections (40 acres)

The Land Ordinance of 1785 created an ordered system of survey (revised by the Northwest Ordinance of 1787), dividing the land into townships and sections.

themselves defeated, but the United States claimed that its victory over Great Britain was a victory over the Indians as well. A heavily armed American nation now pressed for large grants of territory according to the right of conquest. Even Patriot allies were not exempt. The Oneidas, for example, who had supported the Americans, suffered territorial demands along with the other Iroquois.

Even during the Revolution thousands of Americans migrated west, and after the war settlers poured over the mountains and down the Ohio River. The population of Kentucky (still a part of Virginia until admitted as a state in 1792) grew to more than 30,000 by 1785. Five years later at the first census of 1790 its population count was 74,000, while the area that would become Tennessee counted another 36,000. Thousands of Americans pressed against the Indian country north of the Ohio River, and destructive violence continued along the frontier. British troops continued to occupy posts in the Northwest and encouraged Indian attacks on vulnerable settlements. Spain refused to accept the territorial settlement of the Treaty of Paris, and they closed the port of New Orleans to Americans, effectively blockading the Mississippi River. Westerners who saw that route as their primary access to markets were outraged.

The American leadership saw the West as the common inheritance of the entire nation and critical to the continued development of the national community. John Jay, appointed secretary for foreign affairs by the Confederation Congress in 1784, attempted to negotiate with the British for withdrawal from the Northwest, but was told that was not possible until all outstanding debts from before the war were settled. Jay also negotiated with the Spanish for guarantees of territorial sovereignty and commercial relations, but they insisted that the Americans relinquish free navigation of the Mississippi. Congress would approve no treaty under those conditions, and under these frustrating circumstances, some Westerners considered leaving the Confederation. There were prominent Kentuckians who advocated rejoing the British, while others, including George Rogers Clark and General James Wilkinson, secretly worked for the Spanish as informants and spies. The people of the West "stand as it were upon a pivot," wrote Washington in 1784 after a trip down the Ohio. "The touch of a feather would turn them any way." In the West, local community interest continued to override the fragile development of national community sentiment.

In 1784, Congress took up the problem of extending national authority over the West. Legislation was drafted, principally by Thomas Jefferson, providing for "Government for the Western Territory." All territory outside the original thirteen states could presumably have been treated as a colonial domain, but impressed with the necessity of including Westerners in the national community, the legislation instead proposed a remarkably democratic colonial policy. The western public domain would eventually be divided into states, fully the equal of the original thirteen, with guarantees of self-government and republican institutions. Once the population of a territory numbered 20,000, the residents could call a convention and establish a constitution and government of their own choosing. And once the population grew to equal that of the smallest of the original thirteen states, the territory could petition for statehood, provided it agreed to remain forever a member of the Confederation. Congress accepted these proposals, but rejected by a vote of seven to six Jefferson's clause forever prohibiting slavery in the West.

Passed the following year, the Land Ordinance of 1785 provided for the survey and sale of western lands. To avoid the chaos of overlapping surveys and land claims that had characterized Kentucky, the authors of the ordinance created an ordered system of survey, dividing the land into townships composed of thirty-six sections of one square mile (640 acres) each. This measure would have an enormous impact on the North American landscape, as can be seen by anyone who has flown over the United States and looked down at the patchwork pattern. Jefferson argued that land ought to be given away to actual settlers. But, eager to establish a revenue base for the government, Congress provided for the auction of public lands for not less than one dollar per acre. In the treaties of Fort Stanwix in 1784 and Fort McIntosh in 1785, congressional commissioners forced the Iroquois and some of the Ohio Indians to cede a portion of their territory in what is now eastern Ohio, and surveyors were immediately sent there to divide up the land. These treaties were not the result of negotiation; the commissioners dictated the terms by seizing hostages and forcing compliance. The first surveyed lands were not available for sale until the fall of 1788. In the meantime, Congress, desperate for revenue, sold a tract of more than 1.5 million acres to a new land company, the Ohio Company, for a million dollars.

Thousands of Westerners chose not to wait for the official opening of the public land north of the Ohio River, but settled illegally. In 1785 Congress raised troops and evicted many of them, but once the troops left the squatters returned. The persistence of this problem convinced many congressmen to revise Jefferson's democratic territorial plan. It was necessary, explained Richard Henry Lee of Virginia, "for the security of property among uninformed and perhaps licentious people, as the greater part of those who go there are, that a strong toned government should exist."

In the Northwest Ordinance of 1787, Congress established a system of government for the territory north of the Ohio. Three to five states were to be carved out of the giant Northwest Territory and admitted "on an equal footing with the original states in all respects whatsoever." Slavery was prohibited. But the initial guarantee of self-government in Jefferson's plan was replaced by the rule of a congressionally appointed court of judges and governor. Once the free white male population of the territory had grown to 5,000, these citizens would be permitted to choose an assembly, but the governor was given the power of absolute veto on all territorial legislation. National interest would be imposed on the localistic western communities. The Northwest Territory was a huge region that included the future states of Ohio, Indiana, Illinois, Michigan, and Wisconsin. In an early instance of government in the hands of developers, Congress chose Arthur St. Clair, president of the Ohio Company, as the first governor of the Northwest Territory.

The creation of the land system of the United States was the major achievement of the Confederation government. But there were other important accomplishments. Under the Articles of Confederation, Congress led the country through the Revolution and its commissioners negotiated the terms of a comprehensive peace treaty. In organizing the departments of war, foreign affairs, the post office, and finance, the Confederation government created the beginnings of a national bureaucracy.

REVOLUTIONARY POLITICS IN THE STATES

Despite these accomplishments, most Americans focused not on the Confederation government in Philadelphia, but on the governments of their own states. During the revolutionary era, most Americans identified politically and socially with their local communities and states rather than with the American nation. People spoke of "these United States," emphasizing the plural. The single national community feeling of the Revolution was overwhelmed by persistent localism. The states were the setting for the most important political struggles of the Confederation period and for long afterwards.

The Broadened Base of Politics

The political mobilization that took place in 1774 and 1775 greatly broadened political participation. Mass meetings in which ordinary people expressed their opinions, voted, and gained political experience were common, not only in the cities but in small towns and rural communities as well. During these years, a greater proportion of the population began to participate in elections. South Carolina, for example, employed a system of universal white manhood suffrage for the selection of delegates to the Continental Congress, and many other states relaxed property qualifications. Compared with the colonial assemblies, the new state legislatures included more men from rural and western districts—farmers and artisans as well as lawyers, merchants, and large landowners. For example, many delegates to the Massachusetts provincial congress of 1774 were men from small farming communities who lacked formal education and owned little property.

This transformation was accompanied by a dramatic shift in the political debate. During the colonial period, when only the upper crust of society had been truly engaged in the political process, the principal argument took place between the Tory and Whig positions. The Tory position, argued by royal officials, was that colonial governments were simply convenient instruments of the king's prerogative, serving at his pleasure. Colonial elites, seeking to preserve and increase their own power, had argued for stronger assemblies. They used traditional Whig arguments about the need for a balanced government, represented by the governor, the upper house, and the assembly. This debate was ended by the Revolution. The Tory position lost all legitimacy. For the first time in American history, democracy became a term of approval. Patriots who took a Whig position on balanced government found themselves challenged by farmers, artisans, and other ordinary people armed with a new and radical democratic ideology.

One of the first post-Revolution debates focused on the appropriate governmental structure for the new states. The thinking of democrats was indicated by the title of a New England pamphlet of 1776: *The People the Best Governors*. Power, the anonymous author argued, should be vested in a single, popularly elected assembly. There should be no property qualifications for either voting or holding office. The governor should simply execute the wishes of the people as voiced by their representatives in the assembly. Judges, too, should be popularly elected, and their decisions reviewed by the assembly. The people, the pamphlet said, "best know their wants and necessities, and therefore are best able to govern themselves." The ideal form of government, according to democrats, was the community or town meeting, in which the people set their own tax rates, created a militia, controlled their own schools and churches, and regulated the local economy. State government was necessary only for coordination among communities.

Conservative Americans took up the Whig argument on the need for a balanced government. The "unthinking many," wrote another pamphleteer, should be checked by a strong executive and an upper house. Both of these would be insulated from popular control by property qualifications and long terms in office, the latter designed to draw forth the wisdom and talent of the country's wealthiest and most accomplished men. The greatest danger, according to conservatives, was the possibility of majority tyranny, which might lead to the violation of property rights and to dictatorship. "We must take mankind as they are," one conservative wrote, "and not as we could wish them to be."

The First State Constitutions

Fourteen states—the original thirteen plus Vermont—adopted constitutions between 1776 and 1780. Each of these documents was shaped by debate between radicals and conservatives, democrats and Whigs, and reflected a political balance of power. The constitutions of Pennsylvania, Maryland, and New York typified the political range of the times. Pennsylvania instituted a radical democracy, Maryland created a conservative set of institutions designed to keep citizens and rulers as far apart as possible, and New York adopted a system somewhere in the middle.

In Pennsylvania, a majority of the political conservatives had become Loyalists, allowing the democrats to seize power in 1776. The election of delegates to the constitutional convention was open to every man in the militia, an arrangement that further strengthened the advocates of democracy. The document this convention adopted clearly reflected a democratic agenda. It created a unicameral assembly elected annually by all free male taxpayers. So that delegates would be responsive to their constituents, sessions of the assembly were open to the public and included roll-call votes—the latter somewhat rare in colonial assemblies. There was no governor, but rather an elected executive committee. Judges were removable by the assembly.

By contrast, the Maryland constitution, adopted the same year, was written by conservative planters. It created property requirements for officeholding that left only about 10 percent of Maryland men eligible to serve in the assembly, 7 percent in the senate. A powerful governor, elected by large property owners, controlled a highly centralized government. Judges and other high executive officers served for life. These two states, Maryland and Pennsylvania, represented the political extremes. Georgia, Vermont, and North Car-

olina followed Pennsylvania's example; South Carolina's constitution was much like Maryland's.

In New York, the constitutional convention of 1777 included a large democratic faction. But conservatives such as John Jay, Gouverneur Morris, and Robert R. Livingston, managing the convention with great skill, helped produce a document that reflected Whiggish principles while still appealing to the people. There would be a bicameral legislature, each house having equal powers. The lower house, or assembly, was democratically elected, but there were stiff property qualifications for election to the upper house, or senate, and senators represented districts apportioned by wealth, not population. The governor, also elected by property owners, had the power of veto, which could be overridden only by a two-thirds vote of both houses. Ultraconservatives wanted a constitution more like Maryland's, but Jay argued that "another turn of the winch would have cracked the cord"; conservatives, in other words, had gotten about as much as they could without alienating the mass of voters. Other states whose constitutions blended democratic and conservative elements were New Hampshire, New Jersey, and Massachusetts.

Declarations of Rights

One of the most important innovations of the state constitutions was a guarantee of rights patterned on the Virginia Declaration of Rights of June 1776. Written by George Mason—a wealthy planter, democrat, and brilliant political philosopher—the Virginia declaration set a distinct tone in its very first article: "That all men are by nature equally free and independent, and have certain inherent rights, . . . namely, the enjoyment of life and liberty, with the means of acquiring and possessing property and pursuing and obtaining happiness and safety." The fifteen articles declared, among other things, that sovereignty resided in the people, that government was the servant of the people, and that the people had the "right to reform, alter, or abolish" that government. There were guarantees of due process and trial by jury in criminal prosecutions, and prohibitions of excessive bail and "cruel and unusual punishments." Freedom of the press was guaranteed as "one of the great bulwarks of liberty," and the people were assured of "the free exercise of religion, according to the dictates of conscience."

Eight state constitutions included a general declaration of rights similar to the first article of the Virginia declaration; others incorporated specific guarantees. A number of states proclaimed the right of the people to engage in free speech and free assembly, to instruct their representatives, and to petition for the redress of

By giving the vote to "all free inhabitants," the 1776 constitution of New Jersey enfranchised women as well as men who met the property requirements. The number of women voters eventually led to male protests. Wrote one: "What tho' we read, in days of yore, / The woman's occupation / Was to direct the wheel and loom, / Not to direct the nation." In 1807 a new state law explicitly limited the right of franchise to "free white male citizens."

SOURCE: CORBIS.

grievances—rights either inadvertently or deliberately omitted from Virginia's declaration. These declarations were important precedents for the Bill of Rights, the first ten amendments to the federal Constitution. Indeed, George Mason of Virginia was a leader of the democrats who insisted that the Constitution stipulate such rights.

A Spirit of Reform

The political upheaval of the Revolution raised the possibility of other reforms in American society. The 1776 Constitution of New Jersey, by granting the vote to "all free inhabitants" who met the property requirements, enfranchised women as well as men. The number of women voters eventually led to male protests and a new state law explicitly limiting the right to vote to "free white male citizens."

The New Jersey controversy may have been an anomaly, but women's participation in the Revolution wrought subtle but important changes. In 1776 Abigail Adams wrote to her husband John Adams, away at the Continental Congress, "In the new code of laws which I suppose it will be necessary for you to make I desire you would remember the ladies, and be more generous and favourable to them than your ancestors." In the aftermath of the Revolution, there was evidence of increasing sympathy in the courts for women's property

rights and fairer treatment of women's petitions for divorce. And the postwar years witnessed an increase in opportunities for women seeking an education. From a strictly legal and political point of view, the Revolution may have done little to change women's role in society, but it did seem to help change expectations. Abigail Adams's request to her husband was directed less toward the shape of the new republic than toward the structure of family life. "Do not put such unlimited powers into the hands of husbands," she wrote, "for all men would be tyrants if they could." She had in mind a new, companionate ideal of marriage that contrasted with older notions of patriarchy. Men and women ought to be more like partners, less like master and servant. This new ideal took root in America during the era of the Revolution.

The most steadfast reformer of the day was Thomas Jefferson, who after completing work on the Declaration of Independence returned to Virginia to take a seat in its House of Delegates. In 1776 he introduced a bill that abolished the law of entails, which had confined inheritance to particular heirs in order that landed property remain undivided. Jefferson believed that "entail" and "primogeniture" (inheritance of all the family property by the firstborn son)—legal customs long in effect in aristocratic England—had no place in a republican society. The legislation had little practical effect because few estates were entailed, but the repeal was symbolically important, for it repudiated an ancient aristocratic custom. By 1790, every state but one had followed Virginia's lead (Rhode Island finally acted in 1798).

Jefferson's other notable success was his Bill for Establishing Religious Freedom. Indeed, he considered this document one of his greatest accomplishments. At the beginning of the Revolution, there were established churches—denominations officially supported and funded by the government—in nine of the thirteen colonies: the Congregationalists in Massachusetts, New Hampshire, and Connecticut and the Anglicans in New York and in the South. (See also Chapter 5 for a discussion of colonial religion.) Established religion was increasingly opposed in the eighteenth century, in part because of Enlightenment criticism of the power it had over free and open inquiry, but, more important, because of the growing sectarian diversity produced by the religious revival of the Great Awakening. Many Anglican clergymen harbored Loyalist sympathies, and as part of an anti-Loyalist backlash New York, Maryland, the Carolinas, and Georgia had little difficulty passing acts that disestablished the Anglican Church. In Virginia, however, many planters viewed Anglicanism as a bulwark against Baptist and Methodist democratic thinkers, resulting in bitter and protracted opposition to Jefferson's bill. Patrick Henry, grown conservative, defended state support for the church, and it was not until 1786 that the bill passed.

New England Congregationalists proved even more resistant to change. Although Massachusetts, New Hampshire, and Connecticut allowed dissenters to receive tax support, they maintained the official relationship between church and state well into the nineteenth century. Other states, despite disestablishment, retained religious tests in their legal codes. Georgia, the Carolinas, and New Jersey limited officeholding to Protestants; New York required legislators to renounce allegiance to the pope; and even Pennsylvania, where religious freedom had a long history, required officials to swear to a belief in the divine inspiration of the Old and New Testaments.

Jefferson proposed several more reforms of Virginia law, all of which failed to pass. He would have created a system of public education, revised the penal code to restrict capital punishment to the crimes of murder and treason, and established the gradual emancipation of slaves by law. (This, by the way, marked the third time Jefferson had tried to encourage an end to slavery; the first time was in his antislavery clause in the Declaration of Independence, the second was his proposed "Government for the Western Territory" of 1784.) Other states witnessed more progress, but on the whole, the Revolutionary generation, like Jefferson, were more successful in raising these issues than in accomplishing reforms. The problems of penal reform, public education, and slavery remained for later generations of Americans to resolve.

African Americans and the Revolution

For most African Americans there was little to celebrate in the American victory, for it perpetuated the institution of slavery. Few people were surprised when thousands of black fighters and their families departed with the Loyalists and the British at the end of the war, settling in the West Indies, Canada, and Africa. Most of these refugees were fugitive slaves rather than committed Loyalists. Virginia and South Carolina were said to have lost 30,000 and 25,000 slaves as a result of the war.

To many white Americans there was an obvious contradiction in waging a war for liberty while continuing to support the institution of slavery. Slavery was

This portrait of the African American poet Phillis Wheatley was included in the collection of her work published in London in 1773, when she was only twenty. Kidnapped in Africa when a girl, then purchased off the Boston docks, she was more like a daughter than a slave to the Wheatley family, and later married and lived as a free woman of color before her untimely death in 1784.

SOURCE: Bettman/CORBIS.

first abolished in the state constitution of Vermont in 1777, and in Massachusetts and New Hampshire in 1780 and 1784 respectively. Pennsylvania, Connecticut, and Rhode Island adopted systems of gradual emancipation during these years, freeing the children of slaves at birth. By 1804 every northern state had provided for abolition or gradual emancipation, although as late as 1810, 30,000 African Americans remained enslaved in the North.

In the Upper South, revolutionary idealism, the Christian egalitarianism of Methodists and Baptists, and a shift from tobacco farming to the cultivation of cereal grains such as wheat and corn combined to weaken the commitment of many planters to the slave system. There was a great increase in "manumissions," grants of freedom to slaves by individual masters. In the Upper South there was a small but important movement to encourage gradual emancipation by convincing masters to free their slaves in their wills. George Washington not only freed several hundred of his slaves upon his death but developed an elaborate plan for apprenticeship and tenancy for the able-bodied, and lodging and pensions for the aged. Planters in the Lower South, however, heavily dependent as they were on slave labor, resisted the growing calls for an end to slavery. Between 1776 and 1786 all the states but South Carolina and Georgia prohibited or heavily taxed the international slave trade, and this issue became an important point of conflict at the Constitutional Convention in 1787 (see Chapter 8).

Perhaps the most important result of these developments was the growth of the free African-American population; from a few thousand in 1750, this population grew to more than 200,000 by the end of the century. The increase was most notable in the Upper South. The free black population of Virginia, for example, grew from less than 2,000 in 1780 to approximately 20,000 in 1800. Largely excluded from the institutions of white Americans, the African-American community now had enough strength to establish schools, churches, and other institutions of its own. At first this development was opposed. In Williamsburg, Virginia, for instance, the leader of a black congregation was seized and whipped when he attempted to gain recognition from the Baptist Association. But by the 1790s, the Williamsburg African Church had grown to over 500 members, and the Baptist Association reluctantly recognized it. In Philadelphia, Reverend Absalom Jones established St. Thomas's African Episcopal Church. The incorporation of the word "African" in the names of churches, schools, and mutual benefit societies reflected the pride African Americans took in their heritage. New York's African Marine Fund, to take one example, described itself as an organization for assisting "our African brethren and the descendants of our mother country."

A small group of African-American writers rose to prominence in the revolutionary era. Benjamin Banneker, born free in Maryland, where he received an education, was one of the most accomplished mathematicians and astronomers of late eighteenth-century America. In the 1790s he published a popular almanac that both white and black Americans consulted. Jupiter Hammon, a Long Island slave, took up contemporary issues in his poems and essays, one of the most important of which was his "Address to the Negroes of the State of New York," published in 1787. The most famous African-American writer, however, was Phyllis Wheatley, who came to public attention when her *Poems on Various Subjects, Religious and Moral* appeared in London in 1773, while she was still a domestic slave in Boston. Kidnapped in Africa as a young girl and converted to Christianity during the Great Awakening, Wheatley wrote poems that combined her piety and a concern for her people. "On Being Brought from Africa to America" is a good example:

'Twas mercy brought me from my pagan land,
Taught my benighted soul to understand
That there's a God, that there's a Saviour too;
Once I redemption neither sought nor knew.
Some view our sable race with scornful eye,
"Their colour is a diabolic dye."
Remember, Christians, Negros, black as Cain,
May be refin'd, and join th'angelic train.

"In every human breast God has implanted a principle, which we call love of freedom; it is impatient of oppression, and pants for deliverance," Wheatley wrote in a letter. "The same principle lives in us."

Economic Problems

During the Revolution, the shortage of goods resulting from the British blockade, the demand for supplies by the army and the militias, and the flood of paper currency issued by the Congress and the states combined to create the worst inflation that Americans have ever

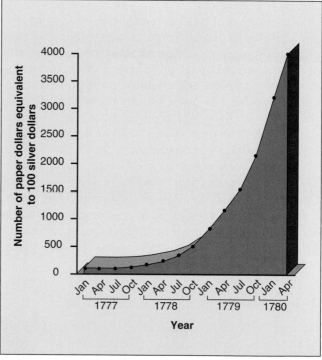

Postwar Inflation, 1777–1780: The Depreciation of Continental Currency (Number of paper dollars equal to 100 silver dollars) The flood of Continental currency issued by Congress, combined with the shortage of goods resulting from the British blockade, combined to create the worst inflation Americans have ever experienced. Things of no value were said to be "not worth a Continental."

SOURCE: John McCusker, "How Much Is That in Real Money?" *Proceedings of the American Antiquarian Society*, N.S. 102 (1992): 297–359.

experienced. Continental dollars traded against Spanish dollars at the rate of 3 to 1 in 1777, 40 to 1 in 1779, and 146 to 1 in 1781, by which time Congress had issued more than $190 million in Continentals. Most of this paper money ended up in the hands of merchants, who paid only a fraction of its face value. There was a popular outcry at the incredible increase in prices, and communities and states in the North responded with laws regulating wages and prices.

The sponsors of wage and price schedules often blamed high prices on hoarding and profiteering. Although it is doubtful that such practices caused the inflation, many merchants did gouge their customers. Many communities experienced demonstrations and food riots; men and women demanded fair prices, and when they did not receive them, they broke into storehouses and took what they needed. People organized local committees to monitor economic activity and punish wrongdoers. Abigail Adams told of a Boston merchant who refused to sell coffee for the price demanded by the committee. "A number of females, some say a hundred, some say more," she wrote, "seized him by his neck and tossed him into the cart. Upon his finding no quarter he delivered the keys," and the women opened his warehouse and took the coffee. "A large concourse of men stood amazed, silent spectators of the whole transaction."

After the war, inflation was suddenly replaced by depression. Political revolution could not alter economic realities: the independent United States continued to be a supplier of raw materials and an importer of manufactured products, and Great Britain remained its most important trading partner. After the Treaty of Paris was signed in 1783, British merchants dumped their unsold goods on the American market, offering easy terms of credit. The production of exportable goods, however, had been drastically reduced by the fighting. With few exports to offset all the imports, the trade deficit with Britain for the period 1784–86 rose to approximately £5 million. The deficit acted like a magnet, drawing hard currency from American accounts. Short of hard currency, the commercial banks in the United States insisted on immediate repayment of old loans and refused to issue new ones. The country was left with very little coin in circulation. It added up to a serious depression, lasting from 1784 to 1788. At their lowest level, in 1786, prices had fallen by 25 percent.

The depression struck while the country was burdened with the huge debt incurred during the Revolution. The total debt owed by the national and state governments amounted to more than $50 million in 1785. Not allowed to raise taxes on its own, the Confederation Congress requisitioned the states for the funds necessary for debt repayment. The states in turn taxed their residents. At a time when there was almost no

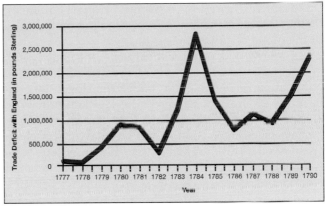

The Trade Deficit with Great Britain   The American trade deficit with Great Britain rose dramatically with the conclusion of the Revolution.

SOURCE: *Historical Statistics of the United States* (Washington, D.C.: Government Printing Office, 1976), 1176.

money in circulation, people rightly feared being crushed by the burden of private debt and public taxes. Thus the economic problem became a political problem.

State Remedies

Where there were manufacturing interests, as in the Northeast, states erected high tariffs to curb imports and protect infant industries. But shippers could avoid these duties simply by unloading their cargo in neighboring seaboard states that lacked tariffs; domestic merchants then distributed the products overland. To be effective, commercial regulation had to be national. Local sentiment had to give way to the unity of a national community. The "means of preserving ourselves," wrote John Adams, will "never be secured entirely, until Congress shall be made supreme in foreign commerce, and shall have digested a plan for all the states."

The most controversial economic remedies were those designed to relieve the burden on debtors and ordinary taxpayers. In some areas, farmers called for laws permitting payment of taxes or debts in goods and commodities, a kind of institutionalized barter. More commonly, farmers and debtors pressed their state governments for legal tender laws, which would require creditors to accept at specified rates of exchange a state's paper currency—regardless of its worth—for all debts public and private.

Understandably, creditors opposed such a plan. But farmers were strong enough to enact currency laws in seven states during the depression. For the most part, these were modest programs that worked rather well, caused little depreciation, and did not result in the problems feared by creditors. In most instances, the notes were loaned to farmers, who put up the value of their land as collateral.

It was the radical plan of the state of Rhode Island, however, that received most of the attention. A rural political party campaigning under the slogan "To Relieve the Distressed" captured the legislature in 1786 and enacted a currency law. The supply of paper money issued in relation to the population was much greater under this program than in any other state. The law declared the currency legal tender for all debts. If creditors refused to accept it, people could satisfy their obligations by depositing the money with a county judge, who would then advertise the debt as paid. "In the state of Rogue Island," wrote a shocked merchant, "fraud and injustice" had been "enjoined by solemn law." Conservatives pointed to Rhode Island as an example of the evils that could accompany unchecked democracy. But such programs were perhaps the only alternative without effective national legislation, which required the development of national community sentiment and national political authority.

Shays' Rebellion

The combination of political uncertainty and economic instability developed into a crisis in a rural uprising of Massachusetts communities that shook the nation in 1786. Farmers in the western part of the state

A mocking pamphlet of 1787 pictured Daniel Shays and Job Shattuck, two leaders of Shays' Rebellion. The artist gives them uniforms, a flag, and artillery, but the rebels were actually an unorganized group of farmers armed only with clubs and simple muskets. When the rebellion was crushed, Shattuck was wounded and jailed, and Shays, along with many others left Massachusetts. He fled to a remote region of Vermont and then settled in New York.

SOURCE: National Portrait Gallery, Smithsonian Institution/Art Resource, NY

had been hit particularly hard during the depression, when country merchants pressed them to pay their debts in hard currency they didn't have. About a third of all male heads of household were sued for debt during the 1780s, and the county jails were filled with debtors who couldn't pay. Dozens of towns petitioned the state government for relief, but the legislature, dominated by urban and merchant interests, rejected legal tender and paper currency laws. During the spring and summer of 1786, farmers throughout the rural parts of the state mustered their community militia companies and closed the courts—precisely what they had done during the Revolution. "Whenever any encroachments are made either upon the liberties or properties of the people," declared one rebel, "if redress cannot be had without, it is virtue in them to disturb government."

This uprising quickly became known as Shays' Rebellion, after Daniel Shays, one of the leaders of the "committee of the people" who had also been a leader in the Revolution. Although the rebellion was most widespread in Massachusetts, similar disorders occurred in every other New England state except Rhode Island, where the farmers had already taken power. There were incidents outside New England as well. A "tumultuary assemblage of the people" closed the court of one Maryland county, and in York, Pennsylvania, 200 armed men stopped a farm auction whose proceeds were marked for debt payment. "Following the example of the insurgents in Massachusetts," a conservative wrote, debtor associations in Virginia prevented auctions and, according to James Madison, officials throughout the state watched "prisons and courthouses and clerks' offices willfully burnt."

The crisis ended in Massachusetts when a militia force raised in communities from the eastern part of the state marched west and crushed the Shaysites in January 1787 as they marched on the armory in Springfield. Fifteen of the leaders were subsequently sentenced to death; two were hanged before the remainder were pardoned, and several hundred farmers had to swear an oath of allegiance to the state. In fact, these men had wanted little more than temporary relief from their indebtedness, and rural discontent quickly disappeared once the depression began to lift in 1788. Daniel Shays himself fled to Vermont under sentence of death, but after his pardon in 1788 moved to New York, where he farmed until his death in 1825.

The most important consequence of Shays' Rebellion was its effect on conservative nationalists unhappy with the distribution of power between the states and national government under the Articles of Confederation. The uprising "wrought prodigious changes in the minds of men respecting the powers of government," wrote the Secretary of War Henry Knox. "Everybody

CHRONOLOGY

1775	Lord Dunmore, royal governor of Virginia, appeals to slaves to support Britain
1776	July: Declaration of Independence August: Battle of Long Island initiates retreat of Continental Army September: British land on Manhattan Island December: George Washington counterattacks at Trenton
1777	Slavery abolished in Vermont September: British General William Howe captures Philadelphia October: British General John Burgoyne surrenders at Saratoga November: Continentals settle into winter quarters at Valley Forge December: France recognizes American independence
1778	June: France enters the war June: Battle of Monmouth hastens British retreat to New York July: George Rogers Clark captures Kaskaskia December: British capture Savannah
1779	Spain enters the war
1780	February: British land at Charleston July: French land at Newport September: British General Charles Cornwallis invades North Carolina
1781	February: Robert Morris appointed superintendent of finance March: Articles of Confederation ratified October: Cornwallis surrenders at Yorktown
1782	Peace talks begin
1783	March: Washington mediates issue of officer pensions September: Treaty of Paris signed November: British evacuate New York
1784	Treaty of Fort Stanwix Postwar depression begins
1785	Land Ordinance of 1785 Treaty of Fort McIntosh
1786	Jefferson's Bill for Establishing Religious Freedom Rhode Island currency law Shays' Rebellion

says they must be strengthened and that unless this shall be effected, there is no security for liberty and property." It was time, he declared, "to clip the wings of a mad democracy."

CONCLUSION

The Revolution was a tumultuous era, marked by violent conflict between Patriots and Loyalists, masters and slaves, settlers and Indian peoples. The advocates of independence emerged successful, largely because of their ability to pull together and to begin to define their national community. But fearful of the power of central authority, Americans created a relatively weak national government. People identified strongly with their local and state communities, and these governments became the site for most of the struggles over political direction that characterized the Revolution and its immediate aftermath.

By the mid-1780s, however, many nationalists were paraphrasing Washington's question of 1777: "What then is to become of this nation?" The economic crisis that followed the Revolution sorely tested the resources of local communities, and increasingly people found that local problems were really national problems. Conservative and moderate Patriots, who had been thrown on the defensive by the radical shift of the political debate to the left, saw this as their opportunity to successfully reenter the fray. Led by their Whiggish arguments, increasing numbers of Americans would seek to answer Washington's question by attempting to reform the national government and build a strong new national community.

REVIEW QUESTIONS

1. Assess the relative strengths of the Patriots and the Loyalists in the American Revolution.
2. What roles did Indian peoples and African Americans play in the Revolution?
3. Describe the structure of the Articles of Confederation. What were its strengths and weaknesses?
4. How did the Revolution affect state politics?
5. What were the issues in Shays' Rebellion? How do they help to illustrate the political conflict in the nation during the 1780s?

RECOMMENDED READING

Thomas Fleming, *Liberty! The American Revolution* (1997)

Merrill Jensen, *The New Nation: A History of the United States during the Confederation, 1781–1789* (1950).

Max M. Mintz, *Seeds of Empire: The American Revolutionary Conquest of the Iroquois* (1999).

Charles Patrick Neimeyer, *America Goes to War: A Social History of the Continental Army* (1996).

Mary Beth Norton, *Liberty's Daughters: The Revolutionary Experience of American Women, 1750–1800* (1980).

John W. Pulis, *Moving On: Black Loyalists in the Afro-Atlantic World* (1999).

Ray Raphael, *A People's History of the American Revolution: How Common People Shaped the Fight for Independence* (2001).

Charles Royster, *A Revolutionary People at War* (1979).

David P. Szatmary, *Shays' Rebellion: The Making of an Agrarian Insurrection* (1980).

▶ MEDIA RESOURCES

U.S. HISTORY DOCUMENTS CD-ROM

Prelude to Revolution

4-9   J. Hector St. John Crèvecoeur, "What Is an American?" (1782)

The American Revolution

5-4   A Freelance Writer Urges His Readers To Use Common Sense (1776)

5-5   Abigail Adams and John Adams Letters; Abigail Adams Letter to Mercy Otis Warren

5-8   Thomas Jefferson, "Original Rough Draught" of the Declaration of Independence (1776)

5-10   The Rise of Partisan Warfare in the South (1778)

Forging a Constitution

6-1   Constitution of Pennsylvania (1776)

6-2   A Declaration of the Rights of the Inhabitants of the Commonwealth of Massachusetts (1780)

6-3   George Washington, The Newburgh Address (1783)

6-4   Henry Knox, Letter to George Washington (1786)

6-5   Marquis de Chastellux, Travels in North America (1786)

COMPANION WEBSITE HIGHLIGHTS

To view an exploration, enter one of the URLs below in your browser.

Web Explorations

North America after the Treaty of Paris, 1783
http://www.prenhall.com/faragher/map7.1

The Northwest Territory and the Land Survey System of the United States
http://www.prenhall.com/faragher/map7.2

Additional Interactive Maps

To access the maps, go to this chapter's resources at
http://www.prenhall.com/faragher

Campaign for New York and New Jersey, 1775–1777, page 183

Northern Campaigns, 1777–1778, page 184

Fighting in the West, 1778–1779, page 187

Fighting in the South, 1778–1781, page 188

HISTORY RESOURCE CENTER

To find the resources listed below, go to
http://www.prenhall.com/historyresourcecenter

Documents

John Adams to Abigail Adams (July 3, 1776)

Rights of Women in an Independent Republic

Royal Proclamation of Rebellion (1775)

Shays' Rebellion (1787)

Joseph Warren, "Account of the Battle of Lexington" (1775)

The New Jersey Constitution of 1776

The New Jersey Plan (1787)

Images

Abigail Adams

Articles of Confederation (1, 2)

Joseph Brant, Tayandanegea, the Great Captain of the Six Nations

Phillis Wheatley

Valley Forge, 1777

EXPLORING AMERICA

EXPLORING THE GEOGRAPHY OF THE AMERICAN REVOLUTION

http://www.prenhall.com/faragher/revolution

Geography played an important role in the rise and development of the United States. How did the shifting fortunes of European powers influence the movement toward independence? What role did assemblies play in the creation and development of the United States? How did the experiences at Valley Forge help develop a national identity and consciousness? What provisions did the United States take to ensure the peaceful expansion of the Union? These questions and others are addressed in the *Exploring the Geography of the American Revolution* module.

Exploring the Geography of the American Revolution stresses the assembly and war experiences as the mechanisms to create national bonds and methods of governance. It uses the perceptions of a foreign visitor to depict the incredible diversity and local character of the United States in the 1780s. Interactive maps illustrate the deep-rooted changes that occurred in eastern North America as a result of warfare. The narrative and chronology provide historical contexts to the discussion.

Reflect and Respond

1.   History is often a study of "what ifs." The decisions made guide events down certain paths. But what if different decisions had been made? Reflect on the likely consequences if the Treaty of Paris of 1763 had not led to the French removal from North America. Would the British colonists still have followed a path to independence?

2.   How did the experience at Valley Forge strengthen the United States?

3.   What role did the assembly tradition of colonial, and later state, cooperation play in the origins and development of the United States?

✓ Check it out

Northwest Territory and the Land Survey System

This interactive map addresses a vexing issue for the new nation: How to accommodate the reality of achieving nationhood and empire status at the same time. The ability to develop a plan for peaceful settlement and the incorporation of new states into the Union that guided the expansion of the United States across the continent played a strong role in the short and long term success of the United States.

This exploration is only available on the *Out of Many*, Fourth Edition Companion Website™.

South East Corner of 3rd and Market Streets, Philadelphia, 1799. Photograph by Will Brown. Rare Book Department, The Free Library of Philadelphia.

Mingo Creek Settlers Refuse to Pay the Whiskey Tax

IT WAS A HOT JULY AFTERNOON IN 1794 WHEN THE FEDERAL marshal and the tax collector arrived at the backcountry farm of William Miller in Mingo Creek, a community south of Pittsburgh. Like most of his neighbors, Miller had failed to pay the federal excise tax on his homemade whiskey still, and these authorities had come to serve him with a notice to appear in federal court in Philadelphia. "I felt myself mad with passion," said the farmer, knowing that the fine and the cost of the trip back east would ruin him. As the men argued, thirty or forty of Miller's neighbors suddenly appeared, armed with muskets and pitchforks. Members of the Mingo Creek Democratic Society, they had come to fight off this infringement on their liberty. There was an angry confrontation, and someone fired a gun into the air. No one was hit, and after a heated verbal confrontation, the two officials rode off. But the farmers were fuming, and decided to make a "citizen's arrest" of the officials the next day.

At Mingo Creek, poverty was the outstanding fact of life. A third of the farm families owned no land, but rented or simply squatted on the acres of others. The tax collector or "exciseman" was one of the great landlords of Mingo Creek, not only controlling most of the local wealth but monopolizing political office as well. Other landlords lived outside the community, the most powerful being President George Washington himself, who owned thousands of acres in the West, much of it in the vicinity of Mingo Creek. The president had evicted so many squatters from his land that local people considered him a grasping speculator. Washington returned the compliment by describing these frontier settlers as "a parcel of barbarians" who lived little better than "dogs or cats."

In the Ohio region farm families lived in miserable mud-floored log huts scattered along the creeks of the Monongahela Valley. But despite appearances, the farmers of Mingo Creek were bound together in networks of family and clan, work and barter, religion and politics. The militiamen had acted together in what they perceived to be the interests of their community.

Like all the western territories, this was a violent place in a violent time. No-holds-barred fights at local taverns were common, and travelers remarked on the presence of one-eyed men, the victims of brutal gougings. Everyone knew of men or women lost in the continuing Indian wars. In 1782 militia companies from the area had taken their revenge by massacring ninety-six unresisting Christian Indians at Gnadenhutten, north of the Ohio River, hacking their bodies and bringing home their scalps as trophies. The new federal government had committed over 80 percent of its operating budget to defeating the Indians, but the failure of its campaigns had left backcountry families resentful.

It was to help pay the costs of these campaigns that Congress had placed the tax on whiskey in 1791. The tax applied to the owners of stills, whether they produced commercially or simply for family and neighbors. Corn was not worth the cost of shipping it east, but whiskey made from corn was another matter, and many a farm family depended on the income from their stills. Farmers throughout America protested that the excise ran counter to the principles of the Revolution. "Internal taxes upon consumption," declared the citizens of Mingo Creek, are "most dangerous to the civil rights of freemen, and must in the end destroy the liberties of every country in which they are introduced." Hugh Henry Brackenridge, editor of the *Pittsburgh Gazette*, argued for a tax on the "unsettled lands which all around us have been purchased by speculating men, who keep them up in large bodies and obstruct the population of the country." In other words, Congress should tax land speculators, like President Washington, instead of backcountry squatters.

Protest followed the course familiar from the Revolution. At first citizens gathered peacefully and petitioned their representatives, but when the tax collectors appeared, there was vigilante action. Faces blackened or covered with handkerchiefs, farmers tarred and feathered the tax men. Although the immediate issue was taxation, larger matters were at stake. The Mingo Creek Democratic Society was part of Thomas Jefferson's political movement that supported republicanism and the French Revolution, in opposition to the conservative principles of the Washington administration. The tax protesters made this linkage explicit when they raised banners proclaiming the French slogan of "Liberty, Equality, Fraternity" and then adding their own phrase, "and No Excise!" In North Carolina the rebels sang:

> *Some chaps whom freedom's spirit warms*
> *Are threatening hard to take up arms,*
> *And headstrong in rebellion rise*
> *'Fore they'll submit to that excise:*
> *Their liberty they will maintain,*
> *They fought for't, and they'll fight again.*

But it was only in western Pennsylvania that the protests turned to riot. When the Mingo Creek militia went to arrest the tax collector, several of their number were killed in the confrontation. The tax collector and his family escaped from their house as it was consumed by a fire set by the farmers. In a community meeting afterward, the protesters resolved to attack and destroy Pittsburgh, where the wealthy and powerful local landlords resided. Terrified residents of the town saved the day by welcoming the rebels with free food and drink. "It cost me four barrels of whiskey that day," declared one man, but "I would rather spare that than a single quart of blood." Destruction was averted, but an angry farmer rode through the street waving a tomahawk and warning, "It is not the excise law only that must go down. A great deal more is to be done. I am but beginning yet."

Declaring the Whiskey Rebellion "the first ripe fruit" of the democratic sentiment sweeping the country, President George Washington organized a federal army of 13,000 men, larger than the one he had commanded during the Revolution, and ordered the occupation of western Pennsylvania. Federal soldiers dragged half-naked men from their beds and forced them into open pens, where they remained for days in the freezing rain. Authorities arrested twenty people, and a judge convicted two of treason. The protest gradually died down. Washington pardoned the felons, sparing their lives.

Federal power had prevailed over the local community. In his Farewell Address to the nation the following year Washington warned of an excessive spirit of localism that "agitates the community with ill-founded jealousies and false alarms; kindles the animosity of one part against another; foments occasionally riot and insurrection." But resistance to the excise remained widespread, and no substantial revenue was ever collected from the tax on whiskey.

More important, the whiskey rebels had raised some of the most important issues of the day: the power and authority of the new federal government, the relationship of the West to the rest of the nation, the nature of political dissent, and the meaning of the Revolution. ■

Mingo Creek

FORMING A NEW GOVERNMENT

Eight years before the Whiskey Rebellion a similar rural uprising, Shays' Rebellion (see Chapter 7), had solidified beliefs that the powers of the federal government must be increased lest the budding nation wither. The action at Mingo Creek was the first test of the sovereignty of the newly formed central government, whose strength grew out of the Constitution forged in 1787 by delegates from all the colonies. In putting down the Whiskey Rebellion, federal forces exercised powers that the delegates to the Constitutional Convention agonized over but ultimately granted to the national community they wanted to build.

Nationalist Sentiment

Nationalists had long argued for a strengthened union of the states. Even before ratification of the Articles of Confederation, Alexander Hamilton, a New York lawyer and close associate of George Washington who had served during the Revolution as his aide, was advocating a "solid, coercive union" having "complete sovereignty" over the civil, military, and economic life of the states, along with permanent revenues from taxes and duties. But after emerging victorious from the Revolutionary War, most Americans turned their attention back to the states.

In general, the nationalists were drawn from the elite circles of American life. "Although there are no nobles in America, there is a class of men denominated 'gentlemen,'" the French ambassador to America wrote home in 1786. "They are creditors, and therefore interested in strengthening the government, and watching over the execution of the law. The majority of them being merchants, it is for their interest to establish the credit of the United States in Europe on a solid foundation by the exact payment of debts, and to grant to Congress powers extensive enough to compel the people to contribute for this purpose." In addition to merchants, the ambassador identified others who leaned toward national government: former officers in the Continental Army whose experience with the Continental Congress had made them firm believers in a stronger central government, and conservatives who wanted to restrain what they considered the excessive democracy of the states.

The economic crisis that followed the Revolutionary War (see Chapter 7) provided the nationalists with their most important opportunity to organize. In March 1785, a group of men from Virginia and Maryland, including James Madison, George Mason, and George Washington, drafted an agreement to present to legislatures recommending uniform commercial regulations, duties, and currency laws. Early the next year, at Madison's urging, the Virginia legislature invited all the states to send representatives to a commercial conference to be held at Annapolis in the fall.

Only five states sent strong nationalist delegates to the Annapolis Convention in September 1786. Hamilton, who played a leading role at the meeting, drew up a report calling on Congress to endorse a new convention to be held in Philadelphia to discuss all matters necessary "to render the constitution of the federal government adequate to the exigencies of the union." By this time, although there were still serious disagreements between localists and nationalists about the powers of the national government, most Americans agreed that the Articles needed strengthening, especially in regard to commercial regulation and the generation of revenue. Early in 1787 the Confederation Congress cautiously endorsed the plan for a convention "for the sole and express purpose of revising the Articles of Confederation."

The Constitutional Convention

Fifty-five men from twelve states assembled at the Pennsylvania State House in Philadelphia in late May 1787. Rhode Island, where radical localists held power (see Chapter 7), refused to send a delegation. A number of prominent men were missing. Thomas Jefferson and John Adams were serving as ambassadors in Europe, and crusty localist Patrick Henry declared that he "smelt a rat." But most of America's best-known leaders were present: George Washington, Benjamin Franklin, Alexander Hamilton, James Madison, George Mason, Robert Morris. Twenty-nine of them were college educated, thirty-four were lawyers, twenty-four had served in Congress, and twenty-one were veteran officers of the Revolution. At least nineteen owned slaves, and there were also land speculators and merchants. But there were no ordinary farmers or artisans present, and of course no women, African Americans, or Indians. The Constitution was framed by white men who represented America's social and economic elite.

On their first day of work, the delegates agreed to vote by states, as was the custom of Congress. They chose Washington to chair the meeting, and to ensure candid debate they decided to keep their sessions secret. James Madison, a young, conservative Virginian with a profound knowledge of history and political philosophy, took voluminous daily minutes of the entire convention. Madison and his fellow Virginians had arrived early and drafted what became known as the Virginia Plan. Presented by Governor Edmund Randolph of Virginia on May 29, it set the convention's agenda.

The authors of the Virginia Plan proposed scrapping the Articles of Confederation in favor of a "consolidated government" having the power to tax and to enforce its laws directly rather than through the states. "A spirit of locality," Madison declared, was destroying "the aggregate interests of the community," by which he meant the great community of the nation. The Virginia Plan would have reduced the states to little more than administrative districts. Representation in the bicameral national legislature was to be based on population districts, the members of the House of Representatives elected by popular vote, but senators chosen indirectly by state legislators so that they might be insulated from democratic pressure. The Senate would lead, controlling foreign affairs and the appointment of officials. An appointed chief executive and a national judiciary would together form a Council of Revision having the power to veto both national and state legislation.

The main opposition to these proposals came from the delegates from small states, who feared being swallowed up by the large ones. After two weeks of debate, William Paterson of New Jersey introduced

George Washington presides over a session of the Constitutional Convention, meeting in Philadelphia's State House (now known as Independence Hall), in an engraving of 1799. SOURCE: Free Library of Philadelphia.

an alternative, a set of "purely federal" principles known since as the New Jersey Plan. He proposed increasing the powers of the central government but retaining a single-house Congress in which the states were equally represented. After much debate, and a series of votes that split the convention down the middle, the delegates finally agreed to what has been called the Great Compromise: proportional representation in the House, representation by states in the Senate. The compromise allowed the creation of a strong national government while still providing an important role for the states.

Part of this agreement was a second, fundamental compromise that brought together the delegates from North and South. To boost their power in the new government, the southern delegates wanted to include slaves in the population for the purpose of determining state proportional representation, but to exclude them when it came to apportioning taxes. Ultimately it was agreed that five slaves would be counted as equivalent to three freemen—the "three-fifths rule." Furthermore, the representatives of South Carolina and Georgia demanded protection for the slave trade, and after bitter debate the delegates included a provision preventing any federal restriction on the importation of slaves for twenty years. Another article legitimized the return of fugitive slaves from free states. The word "slave" was nowhere used in the text of the Constitution (it was avoided by using such phrases as "other persons" and "persons held to labor"), but these provisions amounted to national guarantees for southern slavery. Although many delegates were opposed to slavery, and regretted having to give in on this issue, they agreed with Madison, who wrote that "great as the evil is, a dismemberment of the union would be worse."

There was still much to decide regarding the other branches of government. Madison's Council of Revision was scratched in favor of a strong federal judiciary with the implicit power to declare acts of Congress unconstitutional. Demands for a powerful chief executive raised fears that the office might prove to be, in the words of Edmund Randolph of Virginia, "the fetus of monarchy." But there was considerable support for a president with veto power to check the legislature. In fact, according to James McHenry, a delegate from Maryland, twenty-one delegates favored some form of monarchy, and Alexander Hamilton went on record supporting the creation of a constitutional monarch. To keep the president independent of Congress, the delegates decided he should be elected; but fearing that ordinary voters could never "be sufficiently informed" to select wisely, they insulated the process from popular choice by creating the Electoral College. Voters in the states would not actually vote for president. Rather, in a manner to be determined by its legislature, each state would select a slate of "electors" equal

in number to the state's total representation in the House and Senate. Following the general election, the electors in each state would meet to cast their ballots and elect the president.

In early September, the delegates turned their rough draft of the Constitution over to a Committee of Style, which shaped it into an elegant and concise document providing the general principles and basic framework of government. But Madison, known to later generations as "the Father of the Constitution," was gloomy, believing that the revisions of his original plan doomed the Union to the kind of inaction that had characterized government under the Articles of Confederation. It was left for Franklin to make the final speech to the convention. "Can a perfect production be expected?" he asked. "I consent, Sir, to this Constitution, because I expect no better, and because I am not sure that it is not the best." The delegates voted their approval on September 17, 1787, and transmitted the document to Congress, agreeing that it would become operative after ratification by nine states. Despite some congressmen who were outraged that the convention had exceeded its charge of simply modifying the Articles of Confederation, Congress called for a special ratifying convention in each of the states.

Ratifying the New Constitution

The supporters of the new Constitution immediately adopted the name Federalists to describe themselves. Their outraged opponents objected that the existing Confederation already provided for a "federal" government of balanced power between the states and the Union, and that the Constitution would replace it with a "national" government. But in this, as in much of the subsequent process of ratification, the Federalists (or nationalists) grabbed the initiative, and their opponents had to content themselves with the label Anti-Federalists. Mercy Otis Warren, a leading critic of the Constitution, commented on the dilemma in which the Anti-Federalists found themselves. "On the one hand," she wrote, "we stand in need of a strong federal government, founded on principles that will support the prosperity and union of the colonies. On the other, we have struggled for liberty and made costly sacrifices at her shrine and there are still many among us who revere her name too much to relinquish, beyond a certain medium, the rights of man for the dignity of government."

These critics of the Constitution were by no means a unified group. Because most of them were localists, they represented a variety of social and regional interests. But most believed the Constitution granted far too much power to the central government, weakening the autonomy of communities and states. As

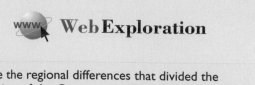

Web Exploration

Explore the regional differences that divided the ratification of the Constitution. Why did some regions support the Constitution and others did not?
www.prenhall.com/faragher/map8.1

The Ratification of the Constitution, 1787–1790
The distribution of the vote for the ratification of the Constitution demonstrated its wide support in sections of the country linked to the commercial economy and its disapproval in more remote and backcountry sections. (Note that Maine remained a part of Massachusetts until admitted as a separate state in 1820.)

local governments "will always possess a better representation of the feelings and interests of the people at large," one critic wrote, "it is obvious that these powers can be deposited with much greater safety with the state than the general government."

All the great political thinkers of the eighteenth century had argued that a republican form of government could work only for small countries. As French philosopher Montesquieu had observed, "In an extensive republic, the public good is sacrificed to a thou-

sand private views." But in *The Federalist*, a brilliant series of essays in defense of the Constitution written in 1787 and 1788 by James Madison, Alexander Hamilton, and John Jay, Madison stood Montesquieu's assumption on its head. Rhode Island had demonstrated that the rights of property might not be protected in even the smallest of states. Asserting that "the most common and durable source of factions has been the various and unequal distribution of property," Madison concluded that the best way to control such factions was to "extend the sphere" of government. That way, he continued, "you take in a greater variety of parties and interests; you make it less probable that a majority of the whole will have a common motive to invade the rights of other citizens; or, if such a common motive exists, it will be more difficult for all who feel it to discover their own strength and to act in unison with each other." Rather than a disability, Madison argued, great size is an advantage: interests are so diverse that no single faction is able to gain control of the state, threatening the freedoms of others.

It is doubtful whether Madison's sophisticated argument, or the arguments of the Anti-Federalists for that matter, made much of a difference in the popular voting in the states to select delegates for the state ratification conventions. The alignment of forces generally followed the lines laid down during the fights over economic issues in the years since the Revolution. For example, in Pennsylvania—the first state to convene a ratification convention, in November 1787—48 percent of the Anti-Federalist delegates to the convention were farmers. By contrast, 54 percent of the Federalists were merchants, manufacturers, large landowners, or professionals. What tipped the Pennsylvania convention in favor of the Constitution was the wide support the document enjoyed among artisans and commercial farmers, who saw their interests tied to the growth of a commercial society. As one observer pointed out, "The counties nearest [navigable waters] were in favor of it generally, those more remote, in opposition."

Similar agrarian-localist and commercial-cosmopolitan alignments characterized most of the states. The most critical convention took place in Massachusetts in early 1788. Five states—Delaware, Pennsylvania, New Jersey, Georgia, and Connecticut—had already voted to ratify, but the states with the strongest Anti-Federalist movements had yet to convene. If the Constitution lost in Massachusetts, its fate would be in great danger. At the convention, Massachusetts opponents of ratification enjoyed a small majority. But several important Anti-Federalist leaders, including Samuel Adams, were swayed by the enthusiastic support for the Constitution among Boston's townspeople, and on February 16 the convention voted narrowly in favor of ratification. To no one's surprise, Rhode Island rejected

A cartoon published in July 1788 when New York became the eleventh state to ratify the Constitution. After initially voting to reject, North Carolina soon reconsidered, but radical and still reluctant Rhode Island did not join the Union until 1790.

SOURCE: Collection of The New York Historical Society.

the Constitution in March, but Maryland and South Carolina approved it in April and May. On June 21 New Hampshire became the ninth state to ratify.

New York, Virginia, and North Carolina were left with the decision of whether to join the new Union. Anti-Federalist support was strong in each of these states. North Carolina voted to reject. (It did not join the Union until the next year, followed by a still reluctant Rhode Island in 1790.) In New York the delegates were moved to vote their support by a threat from New York City to secede from the state and join the Union separately if the state convention failed to ratify. The Virginia convention was almost evenly divided, but promises to amend the Constitution to protect the people from the potential abuses of the federal government persuaded enough delegates to produce a victory for the Constitution. The promise of a Bill of Rights was important in the ratification vote of five of the states.

The Bill of Rights

Although the Bill of Rights—the first ten amendments to the Constitution—was adopted during the first session of the new federal Congress, it was first proposed during the debates over ratification. The Constitutional Convention had considered a Bill of Rights patterned on the declarations of rights in the state constitutions (see Chapter 7) but then rejected it as superfluous, agreeing with Madison that the federal government would exercise only those powers expressly delegated to it. However, George Mason, author of Virginia's Declaration of Rights, refused to sign the Constitution because it failed to contain similar provisions. He played an important role in getting the Virginia ratifying convention to endorse a set of constitutional amendments. Campaigning for a seat in the new Congress, Madison was pressed to affirm his willingness to propose and support a set of amendments guaranteeing "essential rights."

The various state ratification conventions had proposed a grab bag of over 200 potential amendments. Madison set about transforming these into a series of proposals that he introduced into the new Congress in June 1789. Congress passed twelve and sent them to the states, and ten survived the ratification process to become the Bill of Rights in 1791. (In 1992, more than 200 years after being proposed, one of those two failed amendments—providing that a law raising the salaries of senators and representatives could not take effect until after the next election—was ratified by two-thirds of the states.)

The First Amendment prohibits Congress from establishing an official religion and provides for the freedom of assembly. It also ensures freedom of speech, a free press, and the right of petition. The other amendments guarantee the right to bear arms, limit the government's power to quarter troops in private homes, and restrain the government from unreasonable searches or seizures; they assure the people their legal rights under the common law, including the prohibition of double jeopardy, the right not to be compelled to testify against oneself, and due process of law before life, liberty, or property can be taken away. Finally, the unenumerated rights of the people are protected, and the powers not delegated to the federal government are reserved to the states.

The first ten amendments to the Constitution have been a restraining influence on the growth of government power over American citizens. Their provisions have become an admired aspect of the American political tradition throughout the world. The Bill of Rights is the most important constitutional legacy of the Anti-Federalists.

THE NEW NATION

Ratification of the Constitution was followed by the first federal elections—for the Congress and the presidency—and in the spring of 1789 the new federal government assumed power in the temporary capital of New York City. The inauguration of George Washington as the first president of the United States took place on April 30, 1789, on the balcony of Federal Hall, at the corner of Wall and Broad Streets. Re-elected without opposition in 1792, Washington served until 1797.

The activities of the first federal government were far removed from the everyday lives of most Americans, but as the Whiskey Rebellion demonstrated, there were moments when the two intersected dramatically. Moreover, the first years under the new federal Constitution were especially important for the future, because they shaped the structure of the American nation-state in ways that would be enormously significant for later generations.

The Washington Presidency

During its first month, the Congress debated what to call the president of the United States. Believing that no government could long endure without the awe and veneration of its citizens, Vice President John Adams, sitting as the president of the Senate, proposed "His Highness the President of the United States." But a majority of the House of Representatives saw this title as a dangerous flirtation with "the trappings and splendor of royalty." The ensuing controversy was finally resolved by Washington himself, who declared that the whole topic had been raised "without any privity of knowledge of it on my part." By custom he came to be addressed simply as "Mr. President." This issue encapsulated an important conflict of these early years—the desire of some nationalists to add to the power of executive authority versus the faith of localists in a strong Congress, independent of the executive.

Although he dressed in plain American broadcloth at his inauguration and claimed to be content with a plain republican title, Washington was counted among the nationalists. He was anything but a man of the people. By nature reserved and solemn, he chose to ride about town in a grand carriage drawn by six horses and escorted by uniformed liverymen. At receptions held in his house each Tuesday afternoon, Washington would formally bow to each visitor, a gesture that enabled him to avoid the egalitarian custom of shaking hands. In the tradition of British royalty, he delivered his addresses personally to Congress and received from both houses an official reply. These customs were continued by John Adams, Washington's successor, but ended by Thomas Jefferson, who denounced them as "rags of royalty." He began the practice, continued throughout the nineteenth century, of sending written presidential messages to Congress. On the other hand, Washington worked hard to adhere to the letter of the Constitution, refusing, for example, to use the veto power except where he thought the Congress had acted unconstitutionally, and personally seeking the "advice and consent" of the Senate.

Congress quickly moved to establish departments to run the executive affairs of state, and Washington soon appointed Thomas Jefferson his secretary of state, Alexander Hamilton to run the Treasury, Henry Knox the War Department, and Edmund Randolph the Justice Department, as attorney general. The president consulted each of these men regularly, and during his first term met with them as a group to discuss matters of policy. By the end of Washington's presidency the secretaries had coalesced in what came to be known as the cabinet, an institution that has survived to the present despite the absence of constitutional authority or enabling legislation. Washington was a powerful and commanding personality, but he understood the importance of national unity, and in his style of leadership, his consultations, and his appointments he sought to achieve a balance of conflicting political perspectives and sectional interests. These intentions would be sorely tested during the eight years of his administration.

Two coins from the first decade of the federal republic illustrate political controversies of the period. The Washington cent was proposed by Treasury Secretary Alexander Hamilton in 1792 in the hope of enhancing popular respect for the new government by having the president's bust impressed on coins in the manner of European kings. But after long debate Congress defeated the plan, the opponents claiming it smacked of monarchy. The Liberty coin, issued by the Mint of the United States in 1795, when under the authority of Secretary of State Thomas Jefferson, features Liberty wearing a liberty cap and bearing a marked resemblance to the French Revolutionary icon Marianne. SOURCE: Smithsonian Institution, NNC, Douglas Mudd.

An Active Federal Judiciary

The most important piece of legislation to emerge from the first session of Congress was the Judiciary Act of 1789, which implemented the judicial clause of the Constitution, which impowered Congress to determine the number of justices on the Supreme Court and create a system of federal courts. Congress established a high court of six justices (in 1869 this was increased to nine) and established three circuit and thirteen district courts. Strong nationalists argued for a powerful federal legal system that would provide a uniform code of civil and criminal justice throughout the country. But the localists in Congress fought successfully to retain the various bodies of law that had developed in the states. They wanted to preserve local community autonomy. The act gave federal courts limited original jurisdiction, restricting them mostly to appeals from state courts. But it thereby established the principle of federal judicial review of state legislation, despite the silence of the Constitution on this point.

Under the leadership of Chief Justice John Jay, the Supreme Court heard relatively few cases during its first decade. Still, it managed to raise considerable political controversy. In *Chisholm v. Georgia* (1793) it ruled in favor of two South Carolina residents who had sued the state of Georgia for the recovery of confiscated property. Thus did the Court overthrow the common law principle that a sovereignty could not be sued without its consent, and it supported the Constitution's grant of federal jurisdiction over disputes "between a state and citizens of another state." Many localists feared that this nationalist ruling threatened the integrity of the states. In response, they proposed the Eleventh Amendment to the Constitution, ratified in 1798, which declared that no state could be sued by citizens from another state. The Supreme Court nevertheless established itself as the final authority on questions of law when it invalidated a Virginia statute in *Ware v. Hylton* (1796) and upheld the constitutionality of an act of Congress in *Hylton v. United States* (1796).

Hamilton's Controversial Fiscal Program

Fiscal and economic affairs pressed upon the new government. Lacking revenues, and faced with the massive national debt contracted during the Revolution, the government took power in a condition of virtual bankruptcy. Congress passed the Tariff of 1789, a compromise between advocates of protective tariffs (with duties so high that they made foreign products prohibitively expensive, thus "protecting" American products) and those who wanted moderate tariffs that produced income for the federal government. Duties on imported goods, rather than direct taxes on property or incomes, would constitute the bulk of federal revenues until the twentieth century.

In 1790 Treasury Secretary Hamilton submitted a series of reports on the nation's economic future. The leader of the nationalists, he brilliantly constructed his proposals so that their fiscal advantages could not be achieved without accepting his political objectives — the marriage of the nation's financial leaders to the government and enhanced federal power in institutions such as the national bank. In his "Report on the Public Credit" he recommended that the federal government assume the obligations accumulated by the states during the previous fifteen years and redeem the national debt—owed to both domestic and foreign leaders—by agreeing to a new issue of interest-bearing bonds. To raise the revenue required to retire the debt, Hamilton recommended an excise tax on the manufacture of distilled liquor.

By this means, Hamilton sought to inspire the confidence of domestic and foreign investors in the public credit of the new nation. Congress endorsed his plan to pay off the $11 million owed to foreign creditors but balked at funding the domestic debt of $27 million and assuming the state debts of $25 million. Necessity had forced many individuals to sell off at deep discounts the notes, warrants, and securities the government had issued them during the Revolution. Yet Hamilton now advocated paying these obligations at face value, providing any speculator who held them with fabulous profits. An even greater debate took place over the assumption of the state debts, for some states, mostly those in the South, had already arranged to liquidate them, whereas others had left theirs unpaid. Congress remained deadlocked on these issues for six months, until congressmen from Pennsylvania and Virginia arranged a compromise.

Final agreement, however, was stalled by a sectional dispute over the location of the new national capital. Southerners supported Washington's desire to plant it on the Potomac River, but northerners argued for Philadelphia. In return for Madison's pledge to obtain enough southern votes to pass Hamilton's debt assumption plan—which Madison had earlier opposed as a "radically immoral" windfall for speculators—northern congressmen agreed to a location for the new federal district on the boundary of Virginia and Maryland. In July 1790, Congress passed legislation moving the temporary capital from New York to Philadelphia until the expected completion of the federal city in the District of Columbia in 1800. Two weeks later it adopted Hamilton's credit program. This was the first of many sectional compromises.

Hamilton now proposed the second component of his fiscal program, the establishment of a Bank of the United States. The bank, a public corporation funded by private capital, would serve as the depository of government funds and the fiscal agent of the Treasury. Congress narrowly approved it, but Madison's opposition raised doubts in the president's mind about the constitutionality of the measure, and Washington solicited the opinion of his cabinet. Here for the first time were articulated the classic interpretations of constitutional authority. Jefferson took a "strict constructionist" position, arguing that the powers of the federal government must be limited to those specifically enumerated in the Constitution. This position came closest to the basic agreement of the men who had drafted the document. Hamilton, on the other hand, reasoned that the Constitution "implied" the power to use whatever means were "necessary and proper" to carry out its enumerated powers—a loose constructionist position. Persuaded by Hamilton's opinion, Washington signed the bill, and the bank went into operation in 1791. Hamilton and Jefferson thus came to represent two opposing political tendencies. Their dispute is illustrated by a small but interesting dispute over the question of coinage. Hamilton proposed a design that featured President Washington's head and name. This caused a furor in Congress, where democrats pointed out that this followed monarchical practice. They argued instead that American coins should feature the head of Liberty. Since the federal mint was under the direction of the State Department, headed by Jefferson, he followed congressional advice.

The final component of Hamilton's fiscal program, outlined in his famous "Report on Manufactures," was an ambitious plan, involving the use of government securities as investment capital for "infant industries," and high protective tariffs to encourage the development of an industrial economy. Congressmen from farming areas, who objected to Hamilton's preference for the "monied interests," were able to block this proposal. Hamilton's views, they argued, would limit them to roles exactly like those they had played within the British empire; in effect they would be exchanging British for Boston and New York masters. Of equal importance, the plan failed to inspire American capitalists, who continued to be more interested in investments in shipping or in land speculation than in industrial production.

Many of Hamilton's specific proposals for increased tariff protection, however, became part of a revision of duties that took place in 1792. Moreover, his fiscal program as a whole dramatically restored the financial health of the United States. Foreign investment in government securities increased and, along with domestic capital, provided the Bank of the United States with enormous reserves. Its bank notes became the most important circulating medium of the North American commercial economy, and their wide acceptance greatly stimulated business enterprise. "Our public credit," Washington declared toward the end of his first term, "stands on that ground which three years ago it would have been considered as a species of madness to have foretold."

The Beginnings of Foreign Policy

The Federalist political coalition, forged during the ratification of the Constitution, was sorely strained by these debates over fiscal policy. By the middle of 1792, Jefferson, representing the southern agrarians, and Hamilton, speaking for northern capitalists, were locked in a full-scale feud within the Washington administration. Hamilton conducted himself more like a prime minister than a cabinet secretary, greatly offending Jefferson, who considered himself the president's heir apparent. But the dispute went deeper than a mere conflict of personalities. Hamilton stated the difference clearly when he wrote that "one side appears to believe that there is a serious plot to overturn the State governments, and substitute a monarchy to the present republican system," while "the other side firmly believes that there is a serious plot to overturn the general government and elevate the separate powers of the States upon its ruins." The conflict between Hamilton and Jefferson was to grow even more bitter over the issue of American foreign policy.

The commanding event of the Atlantic world during the 1790s was the French Revolution, which had begun in 1789. Most Americans enthusiastically welcomed the fall of the French monarchy. After the people of Paris stormed the Bastille, Lafayette sent Washington the key to its doors as a symbol of the relationship between the two revolutions. But with the beginning of the Reign of Terror in 1793, which claimed upon the guillotine the lives of hundreds of aristocrats, American conservatives began to voice their opposition. The execution of King Louis XVI, and especially the onset of war between revolutionary France and monarchical Great Britain in 1793, firmly divided American opinion.

Most at issue was whether the Franco-American alliance of 1778 required the United States to support France in its war with Britain. All of Washington's cabinet agreed on the importance of American neutrality. With France and Britain prowling for each other's vessels on the high seas, the vast colonial trade of Europe was delivered up to neutral powers, the United States prominent among them. In other words, neutrality meant windfall profits. Jefferson believed it highly unlikely that the French would call upon the Americans to honor the 1778 treaty; the administration should simply wait and see. But Hamilton argued that so great was the danger of American involvement in the war that Washington should immediately declare the treaty "temporarily and provisionally suspended."

These disagreements revealed two contrasting perspectives on the course the United States should chart in international waters. Hamilton and the nationalists believed in the necessity of an accommodation with Great Britain, the most important trading partner of the United States and the world's greatest naval power. Jefferson, Madison, and the democrats, on the other hand, looked for more international independence, less connection with the British, and thus closer relations with Britain's traditional rival, France. They pinned their hopes on the future of American western expansion, an expression of not only independence but isolation from Europe's troubles. There was room for compromise between these two points of view, but in the debate over the French Revolution the positions were polarized.

The debate in the United States grew hotter with the arrival in early 1793 of French ambassador Edmond Genêt. Large crowds of supporters greeted him throughout the nation, and among them he solicited contributions and distributed commissions authorizing American privateering raids against the British. Understandably, a majority of Americans still nursed a hatred of imperial Britain, and these people expressed a great deal of sympathy for republican France. Conservatives such as Hamilton, however, favored a continuation of traditional commercial relations with Britain and feared the antiaristocratic violence of the French. Washington sympathized with Hamilton's position, but most of all he wished to preserve American independence and neutrality. Knowing he must act before "Citizen" Genêt (as the ambassador was popularly known) compromised American sovereignty and involved the United States in a war with Britain, the president issued a proclamation of neutrality on April 22, 1793. In it he assured the world that the United States intended to pursue "a conduct friendly and impartial towards the belligerent powers," while continuing to do business with all sides.

Hamilton's supporters applauded the president, but Jefferson's friends were outraged. "The cause of France is the cause of man," declared Hugh Henry Brackenridge of Pittsburgh, "and neutrality is desertion." Throughout the country those sympathetic to France organized Democratic Societies, political clubs modeled after the Sons of Liberty. Society members corresponded with each other, campaigned on behalf of candidates, and lobbied with congressmen. Conceiving themseves radical democrats, they addressed each other as "citizen," and scorned all titles and rank.

People interpreted the international question in the light of issues of local importance. Thus the members of the Mingo Creek Democratic Society used enthusiasm for the French Revolution as a way of organizing political opposition to the Washington administration. Brackenridge described the society's Mingo Creek chapter as "an engine of election," in other words, a political machine. In a speech to Congress, President Washington denounced what he called these "self-created societies," declaring them "the most diabolical attempt to destroy the best fabric of human government and happiness."

Web Exploration

Investigate settlement patterns west of the Appalachians between 1770 and 1790. Why did tensions between Indians and settlers increase during this period?
www.prenhall.com/faragher/map8.2

Areas settled by 1770
Areas settled by 1780
Areas settled by 1790

Spread of Settlement: The Backcountry Expands, 1770–1790   From 1770 to 1790 American settlement moved across the Appalachians for the first time. The Ohio Valley became the focus of bitter warfare between Indians and settlers.

Citizen Genêt miscalculated, however, alienating even his supporters, when he demanded that Washington call Congress into special session to debate neutrality. Jefferson, previously a confidant of the ambassador, now denounced Genêt as "hot-headed" and "indecent towards the President." But these words came too late to save his reputation in the eyes of Washington, and at the end of 1793 Jefferson left the administration. The continuing upheaval in France soon swept Genêt's party from power and he was recalled, but fearing the guillotine, he claimed sanctuary and remained in the United States. During his time in the limelight, however, he furthered the division of the Federalist coalition into a faction identifying with Washington, Hamilton, and conservative principles and a faction supporting Jefferson, Madison, democracy, and the French Revolution.

The United States and the Indian Peoples

Among the many problems of the Washington presidency, one of the most pressing concerned the West. The American attempt to treat the western tribes as conquered peoples after the Revolution had resulted only in further violence and warfare. In the Northwest Ordinance of 1787 (see Chapter 7), the Confederation Congress abandoned that premise for a new approach. "The utmost good faith shall always be observed towards the Indians," the Ordinance read. "Their lands and property shall never be taken from them without their consent." Yet the Ordinance was premised on the opening of Indian land north of the Ohio River to American settlement, its survey and sale, and the creation of new state governments. The Ordinance pointed in wildly contradictory directions.

The Constitution was silent regarding Indian policy, but the new federal government continued to pursue this inconsistent policy. In 1790 Congress passed the Intercourse Act, the basic law by which the United States would "regulate trade and intercourse with the Indian tribes." To eliminate the abuses of unscrupulous traders, the act created a federal licensing system; subsequent legislation authorized the creation of subsidized trading houses, or "factories," where Indians could obtain goods at reasonable prices. Trade abuses continued unabated for lack of adequate policing power, but these provisions indicated the best intentions of the Washington administration.

To clarify the question of Indian sovereignty, the act declared public treaties between the United States and the Indian nations to be the only legal means of obtaining Indian land. Treaty making thus became the procedure for establishing and maintaining relations. In the twentieth century, a number of Indian tribes have successfully appealed for the return of lands obtained by states or individuals in violation of this provision of the Intercourse Act.

On the other hand, one of the federal government's highest pri-

Little Turtle, a war chief of the Miami tribe of the Ohio valley, led a large pan-Indian army to victory over the Americans in 1790 and 1791. After his forces were defeated at the Battle of Fallen Timbers in 1794, he became a friend of the United States. This lithograph is a copy of an oil portrait, which no longer survives, by the artist Gilbert Stuart.

SOURCE: Indiana Historical Society Library.

orities was the acquisition of western Indian land to supply a growing population of farmers. The federal government, in fact, was unable to control the flood of settlers coming down the Ohio River. As one army officer wrote, "they carry on private expeditions against the Indians and kill them whenever they meet them," adding that there was not a jury in the West that would dare to punish a man for such crimes. An American expeditionary force was sent to evict the settlers, but inevitably they ended up fighting the Indians. In defense of their homelands, villages of Shawnees, Delawares, and other Indian peoples confederated with the Miamis under their war chief Little Turtle. In the fall of 1790 Little Turtle lured federal forces led by General Josiah Harmar into the confederacy's stronghold in Ohio and badly mauled them. In November 1791 the confederation inflicted an even more disastrous defeat on a large American force under General Arthur St. Clair, governor of the Northwest Territory. More than 900 Americans were killed or wounded, making this the worst defeat of an army by Indians in North American history.

In the aftermath of this defeat the House of Representatives launched the first formal investigation of the executive branch undertaken by the Congress. They found St. Clair's leadership "incompetent," and he soon resigned. Yet few Americans were willint to admit to the contradiction at the heart of American policy. "We acknowledge the Indians as brothers," yet we "seize their lands," Senator Benjamin Hawkins of North Carolina wrote to President Washington. "This doctrine it might be expected would be disliked by the independent Tribes. . . . It is the source of their hostility."

Spanish Florida and British Canada

The position of the United States in the West was made even more precarious by the hostility of Spain and Great Britain, who controlled the adjoining territories. Under the dynamic leadership of King Carlos III and his able ministers, Spain introduced liberal reforms to revitalize the rule-bound economy of its American empire; as a result the economy of New Spain grew rapidly in the 1780s. Moreover, Spain had reasserted itself in North America, acquiring the French claims to Louisiana before the end of the Seven Years' War, expanding into California, seizing the Gulf Coast during the American Revolution, and regaining Florida from Britain in the Treaty of Paris in 1783. The Spanish were deeply suspicious of the Americans. The settlers, the Spanish governor of Florida declared, "were nomadic like Arabs,...distinguished from savages only in their color, language, and the superiority of their depraved cunning and untrustworthiness." Spain claimed for itself most of

the territory south of the Ohio River and pursued a policy designed to block the expansion of the new republic.

Spain's anti-American policy in the West had several facets. Controlling both sides of the lower Mississippi, they closed the river to American shipping, making it impossible for western American farmers to market their crops through the port of New Orleans. They also sought to create a barrier to American settlement by promoting immigration to Louisiana and Florida. They succeeded in attracting several thousand of the Acadians whom the British had deported during the Seven Years' War. Reassembling their distinctive communities in the bayou country of Louisiana, these tough emigrants became known as the Cajuns. But otherwise the Spanish had little success with immigration and relied mostly on creating a barrier of pro-Spanish Indian nations in the lower Mississippi Valley. In exchange for supplies and Spanish recognition of them as "free and independent nations," the tribes of the South pledged themselves to "the preservation of the Dominion" of Spain in Louisiana and Florida. To consolidate these gains, in the early 1790s the Spanish constructed two new Mississippi River forts at sites that would later become the cities of Vicksburg and Memphis.

North of the Ohio River the situation was much the same. Thousands of Loyalists had fled the United States in the aftermath of the Revolution and settled in the country north of lakes Ontario and Erie. They were understandably hostile to the new republic. In 1791 the British Parliament passed the Canada Act, creating the province of Upper Canada (later renamed Ontario) and granting the Loyalists limited self-government. To protect this province, British troops remained at a number of posts within American territory at places such as Detroit, where they supplied the Indian nations with arms and ammunition, hoping to create a buffer to American expansion. In early 1794 the governor general of Canada told an assembly of Indian leaders from the Ohio country that war between Britain and the United States was almost certain, and that when it broke out, "a line must then be drawn by the warriors." British soldiers began constructing Fort Miami in the Maumee Valley, west of Lake Erie, well within American territory.

Domestic and International Crises

Washington faced the gravest crisis of his presidency in 1794. In the West, the inability of the federal government to subdue the Indians, eliminate the British from the northern fur trade, or arrange with the Spanish for unencumbered use of the Mississippi River stirred frontiersmen to loud protests. There were rumblings of rebellion and secession from western

In this 1794 painting, President George Washington reviews some 13,000 troops at Fort Cumberland on the Potomac before dispatching them to suppress the Whiskey Rebellion. Washington's mobilization of federal military power dramatically demonstrated the federal commitment to the preservation of the Union and the protection of the western boundary.

SOURCE: Francis Kemmelmeyer, "General George Washington Reviewing the Western Army at Fort Cumberland the 18th of October 1794," after 1794. Oil on paper backed with linen. Dimensions: 18-1/8 × 23-1/8. Courtesy of Winterthur Museum.

communities. As the opening to this chapter illustrates, this discontent was strengthened by Hamilton's federal excise tax on whiskey, which hit backcountry farmers hardest. "The people of the western counties," wrote an English commentator, find "themselves grievously taxed for the support of the government without enjoying the blessings of it." In the Old Northwest and Old Southwest, English and Spanish secret agents gave liberal bribes to entice American settlers to quit the Union and join themselves to Canada or Florida. In the Atlantic, Great Britain declared a blockade of France and seized vessels trading with the French West Indies. From 1793 to the beginning of 1794 the British confiscated the cargoes of more than 250 American ships, threatening hundreds of merchants with ruin. The United States was being "kicked, cuffed, and plundered all over the ocean," declared Madison, and in Congress he introduced legislation imposing retaliatory duties on British ships and merchandise.

The Whiskey Rebellion, which broke out in the summer of 1794, thus came at a time when President Washington considered the nation to be under siege. The combination of Indian attack, international intrigue, and domestic insurrection, he believed, created the greatest threat to the nation since the Revolution. In April the president had dispatched Chief Justice

John Jay to London to arrange a settlement with the British. At the same time, war seemed increasingly likely, and Washington feared that any sign of federal weakness in the face of western rebellion would invite British or Spanish intervention. With Hamilton's urging he took the decisive course described in the opening of this chapter: he raised a large militia even as he pursued halfhearted negotiations with local authorities and made preparations to occupy the area around Pittsburgh, including Mingo Creek. It is clear now that the president overreacted, for although there was riot and violence in western Pennsylvania, there was no organized insurrection. Nevertheless, his mobilization of federal military power dramatically demonstrated the federal commitment to the preservation of the Union, the protection of the western boundary, and the supremacy of the national over the local community.

This action was reinforced by an impressive American victory against the Indian confederacy. Following the disastrous defeat of St. Clair by Little Turtle, Washington appointed General Anthony Wayne to lead a greatly strengthened American force to subdue the Indian confederacy and secure the Old Northwest. At the battle of Fallen Timbers, fought in the Maumee country of northern Ohio on August 20, 1794, Wayne crushed the Indians. Retreating, the warriors found the gates of Fort Miami closed and barred, the British inside unprepared to engage the powerful American force. The victory set the stage for the Treaty of Greenville in 1795, in which the representatives of twelve Indian nations ceded a huge territory encompassing most of present-day Ohio, much of Indiana, and other enclaves in the Northwest, including the town of Detroit and the tiny village of Chicago.

Jay's and Pinckney's Treaties

The strengthened American position in the West encouraged the British to settle their dispute with the United States so that they might concentrate on defeating republican France. In November 1794, Jay and the British signed an agreement providing for British withdrawal from American soil by 1796, limited American trade with the British East and West Indies, and "most-favored-nation" status for both countries (meaning that each nation would enjoy trade benefits equal to those the other accorded any other nation-state). The treaty represented a solid gain for the young republic. With only a small army and no navy to speak of, the United States was in no position to wage war. Details of Jay's Treaty leaked out in a piecemeal fashion that inflamed public debate. The treaty represented a victory for Hamilton's conception of American neutrality. The Jeffersonians, on the other hand, were enraged over this accommodation with Great Britain at France's expense. The absence in the treaty of any mention of compensation for the slaves who had fled to the British side during the Revolution alienated Southerners. Throughout the country Democratic Societies and Jeffersonian partisans organized protests and demonstrations. Upon his return to the United States, Jay joked, he could find his way across the country by the light of his burning effigies. Despite these protests, the Senate, dominated by supporters of Hamilton, ratified the agreement in June 1795. In the House, a coalition of Southerners, Westerners, and friends of France attempted to stall the treaty by threatening to withhold the appropriations necessary for its implementation. They demanded that they be allowed to examine the diplomatic correspondence regarding the whole affair, but the president refused, establishing the precedent of "executive privilege" in matters of state.

The deadlock continued until late in the year, when word arrived in Philadelphia that the Spanish had abandoned their claims to the territory south of the Ohio River. Having declared war on revolutionary France, Spain had suffered a humiliating defeat. Fearing the loss of its American empire, the Spanish had suddenly found it expedient to mollify the quarrelsome Americans. In 1795 American envoy Thomas Pinckney negotiated a treaty in which Spain agreed to a boundary with the United States at the 31st parallel and opened the Mississippi to American shipping. This treaty fit the Jeffersonian conception of empire, and congressmen from the West and South were delighted with its terms. But administration supporters demanded their acquiescence in Jay's Treaty before the approval of Pinckney's Treaty.

These two important treaties finally established American sovereignty over the land west of the Appalachians and opened to American commerce a vast market extending from Atlantic ports to the Mississippi Valley. From a political standpoint, however, the events of 1794 and 1795 brought Washington down from his pedestal. Vilified by the opposition press, sick of politics, and longing to return to private life, Washington rejected the offer of a third term.

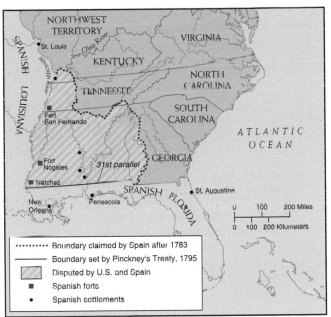

Spanish Claims to American Territory, 1783–1795   Before 1795 the Spanish claimed the American territory of the Old Southwest and barred Americans from access to the port of New Orleans, effectively closing the Mississippi River. This dispute was settled by Pinckney's Treaty in 1795.

Washington's Farewell Address

During the last months of his term, Washington published his Farewell Address to the nation, an appeal for national unity. "With slight shades of difference," Washington said to his countrymen, "you have the same religion, manners, habits, and political principles," and "union ought to be considered as a main prop of your liberty." He warned against sectional loyalty and "the baneful effects of the spirit of party." In the increasingly polarized political debate, however, this appeal fell on deaf ears.

The second part of the address was considerably more influential. "Our detached and distant situation," Washington explained, invited the nation to "defy material injury from external annoyance." He argued not for American isolation, but rather for American disinterest in the affairs of Europe. "The great rule of conduct for us in regard to foreign nations is, in extending our commercial relations to have with them as little political connection as possible." Why, he asked "entangle our peace and prosperity in the toils of European ambition, rivalship, interest, humor, or caprice?" Thomas Jefferson, in his Inaugural Address of 1801, paraphrased this first principle of American foreign policy as "peace, commerce, and honest friendship with all nations, entangling alliances with none." Jefferson's statement underscored the extent to which Washington articulated principles agreed to by all the major political figures of his day.

FEDERALISTS AND JEFFERSONIAN REPUBLICANS

The framers of the Constitution envisioned a one-party state in which partisan distinctions would be muted by patriotism and public virtue. "Among the numerous advantages promised by a well constructed Union," Madison had written in *The Federalist*, is "its tendency to break and control the violence of faction." Not only did he fail to anticipate the rise of political parties or factions, but he saw them as potentially harmful to the new nation. It is thus ironic that when Madison broke with the Washington administration on questions of fiscal policy, he took steps toward organizing a political opposition, a group that became known as the Republicans. At the height of the agitation of the Democratic Societies in 1794, Hamilton cried that "unless soon checked," the "spirit of faction" would "involve the country in all the horrors of anarchy." Yet in acting as Washington's political lieutenant, he did more than anyone else to solidify the "Friends of Order," as his supporters were first known, into a disciplined political party known as the Federalists. Despite the framers' intentions, in the twelve years between the ratification of the Constitution and the federal election of 1800 political parties became a fundamental part of the American system of government.

The Rise of Political Parties

Evident in the debates and votes of Congress from 1789 to 1795 were a series of shifting coalitions that pitted commercial against agrarian interests, representatives from the Atlantic seaboard against those from the frontier, Anglophiles against Francophiles. The potential division of Northerners versus Southerners inspired the greatest fears, and politicians worked hard to achieve sectional compromise by agreeing to avoid the troublesome issue of slavery. Antislavery petitions submitted to Congress were dismissed by nearly unanimous votes, and a law for the apprehension of fugitive slaves by federal officers anywhere in the Union was approved by a large majority in 1793.

These shifting coalitions first began to polarize into political factions during the debate over Jay's Treaty in 1795, when agrarians, Westerners, Southerners, and supporters of France came together in opposition to the treaty. In the House, Madison acted as a leader of this coalition when it met for the first time and attempted to implement a collective strategy. By the elections of 1796, people had begun to give names to the two factions. The supporters of Hamilton claimed the mantle of Federalism. "I am what the phraseology of politicians has denominated a FEDERALIST," declared one North Carolina candidate for office, "the friend of order, of government, and of the present administration." Forced to find another term, the Jeffersonian opposition became known as the Republicans, meant to imply that the Federalists were really monarchists at heart. "There are two parties at present in the United States," wrote a New York editor sympathetic to Jefferson, "aristocrats, endeavoring to lay the foundations of monarchical government, and Republicans, the real supports of independence, friends to equal rights, and warm advocates of free elective government." Hamilton insisted on labeling his opponents the Anti-Federalists, while others scorned them as anarchists, Jacobins, or *sans-culottes*— all labels from the French Revolution. Historians often call this coalition the Jeffersonian Republicans.

These two political coalitions played a fitful role in the presidential election of 1796, which pitted John

OVERVIEW

THE FIRST AMERICAN PARTY SYSTEM

Federalist Party	Organized by figures in the Washington administration who were in favor of a strong federal government, friendship with the British, and opposition to the French Revolution; its power base was among merchants, property owners, and urban workers tied to the commercial economy. A minority party after 1800, it was regionally strong only in New England.
Democratic Republican Party	Arose as the opposition to the Federalists; its adherents were in favor of limiting federal power; they were sympathetic to the French Revolution, and hostile to Great Britain; the party drew strength from southern planters and northern farmers. The majority party after 1800.

Adams, Washington's vice president, against Thomas Jefferson. Partisan organization was strongest in the Middle States, where there was a real contest of political forces, weakest in New England and the South, where sectional loyalty prevailed and organized opposition was weaker. The absence of party discipline was demonstrated when the ballots of the presidential electors, cast in their respective state capitals, were counted in the Senate. Adams was victorious, but the electors chose Jefferson rather than a Federalist for vice president. Thus the new administration was born divided.

The Adams Presidency

Adams was put in the difficult situation of facing a political opposition led by his own vice president. He nevertheless attempted to conduct his presidency along the lines laid down by Washington, and retained most of the former president's appointees. This arrangement presented Adams with another problem. Although Hamilton had retired the year before, the cabinet remained committed to his advice, actively seeking his opinion and following it. As a result, Adams's authority was further undercut.

On the other hand, Adams benefited from the rising tensions between the United States and France. Angered by Jay's Treaty, the French suspended diplomatic relations at the end of 1796 and inaugurated a tough new policy toward American shipping. During the next two years they seized more than 300 American vessels and confiscated cargoes valued at an estimated $20 million. Hoping to resolve the crisis, Adams sent an American delegation to France. But in dispatches sent back to the United States the American envoys reported that agents of the French foreign ministry had demanded a bribe before any negotiations could be undertaken. Pressed for copies of these dispatches by suspicious Jeffersonian Republicans in Congress, in 1798 Adams released them after substituting the letters X, Y, and Z for the names of the French agents. The documents proved a major liability for the Jeffersonian Republicans, sparking powerful anti-French sentiment throughout the country. To the demand for a bribe, the American delegates had actually answered "Not a sixpence," but in the inflated rhetoric of the day the response became the infinitely more memorable: "Millions for defense, but not one cent for tribute!" The XYZ Affair, as it became known, sent Adams's popularity soaring.

Adams and the Federalists prepared the country for war during the spring of 1798. Congress authorized tripling the size of the army, and Washington came out of retirement to command the force. Fears of a French invasion declined after word arrived of the British naval victory over the French in August 1798 at Aboukir Bay in Egypt, but the "Quasi-War" between France and the United States continued.

The Alien and Sedition Acts

In the summer of 1798 the Federalist majority in Congress, with the acquiescence of President Adams, passed four acts severely limiting both freedom of speech and the freedom of the press and threatening the liberty of foreigners in the United States. Embodying the fear that immigrants, in the words of one Massachusetts Federalist, "contaminate the purity and simplicity of the American character" by introducing dangerous democratic and republican ideas, the Naturalization Act extended the period of residence required for citizenship from five to fourteen years. The Alien Act and the Alien Enemies Act authorized the

In this contemporary cartoon, "Congressional Pugilists, Congress Hall in Philadelphia, February 15, 1798," Roger Griswold, a Connecticut Federalist, uses his cane to attack Matthew Lyon, a Vermont Democratic Republican, who retaliates with fire tongs. During the first years of the American republic there was little understanding of the concept of a "loyal opposition," and disagreement with the policy of the Federalist administration was misconstrued as disloyalty.

SOURCE: Collection of The New York Historical Society.

president to order the imprisonment or deportation of suspected aliens during wartime. Finally, the Sedition Act provided heavy fines and imprisonment for anyone convicted of writing, publishing, or speaking anything of "a false, scandalous and malicious" nature against the government or any of its officers.

The Federalists intended these repressive laws as weapons to defeat the Jeffersonian Republicans. Led by Albert Gallatin, a Swiss immigrant and congressman from Pennsylvania (replacing Madison, who had retired from politics to devote his time to his plantation), the Jeffersonian Republicans contested all the Federalist war measures and acted as a genuine opposition party, complete with caucuses, floor leaders, and partisan discipline. For the first time, the two parties contested the election of Speaker of the House of Representatives, which became a partisan office. The more effective the Jeffersonian Republicans became, the more treasonous they appeared in the eyes of the Federalists. On at least one occasion acrimonious debate in the House gave way to fisticuffs. Matthew Lyon, a Jeffersonian Congressman from Vermont, spit in the eye of Connecticut Federalist Roger Griswold. Griswold responded by attacking Lyon with a cane. Lyon defended himself with a pair of fire tongs, and the two had to be pulled apart. With the Revolution still fresh in memory, Americans had only a weak understanding of the concept of a loyal opposition. Disagreement with the administration was misconstrued by the Federalists as opposition to the state itself.

The Federalists thus pursued the prosecution of dissent, indicting leading Jeffersonian Republican newspaper editors and writers, fining and imprisoning at least twenty-five of them. The most vilified was Congressman Lyon, scorned by Federalists as "Ragged Matt the Democrat." Lyon was convicted in July 1798 of publishing libelous statements about President Adams and thrown into a Vermont prison. Later that year, however, he conducted a campaign from his cell and was reelected to Congress.

From Virginia, Madison wrote that the Sedition Act "ought to produce universal alarm, because it is levelled against the right of freely examining public characters and measures, and of free communication among the people thereon, which has ever been deemed the only effectual guardian of every other right." He and Jefferson anonymously authored resolutions, passed by the Virginia and Kentucky legislatures, that declared the Constitution to be nothing more than a compact between the sovereign states, and which advocated the power of those states to "nullify" unconstitutional laws. When threatened with overbearing central authority, the Jeffersonian Republicans argued, the states had the right to go their own way. The Virginia and Kentucky Resolves, as they were

known, had grave implications for the future of the Union, for they stamped the notion of secession with the approval of two of the founding fathers. The resolutions would later be used to justify the secession of the southern states at the beginning of the Civil War.

The Revolution of 1800

The Alien and Sedition Acts were overthrown by the Jeffersonian Republican victory in the national elections of 1800. As the term of President Adams drew to a close, Federalists found themselves seriously divided. In 1799, by releasing seized American ships and requesting negotiations, the French convinced Adams that they were ready to settle their dispute with the United States. The president also sensed the public mood running toward peace. But the Hamiltonian wing of the party, always scornful of public sentiment, continued to beat the drums of war. When Federalists in Congress tried to block the president's attempt to negotiate, Adams threatened to resign and turn the government over to Vice President Jefferson. In the Convention of 1800, the United States abandoned its demand of compensation for seized cargoes in exchange for French abrogation of its 1778 alliance with the American colonies. "The end of war is peace," Adams declared, "and peace was offered me." Adams considered the settlement of this conflict with France to be one of the

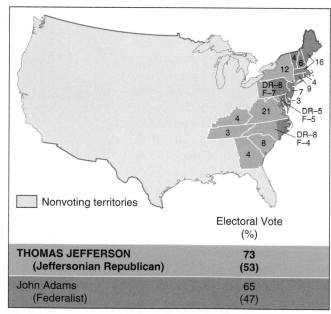

Electoral Vote
(%)

THOMAS JEFFERSON **(Jeffersonian Republican)**	**73** **(53)**
John Adams (Federalist)	65 (47)

The Election of 1800   In the presidential election of 1800, Democratic Republican victories in New York and the divided vote in Pennsylvania threw the election to Jefferson. The combination of the South and these crucial Middle States would keep the Democratic Republicans in control of the federal government for the next generation.

greatest accomplishments of his career, but it earned him the scorn of conservative Federalists, including Hamilton.

The Federalists also divided over a domestic controversy. Under their leadership Congress had enacted a direct tax on houses, similar to the earlier tax on whiskey. In eastern Pennsylvania in 1799 several dozen farmers, displaying symbols of the French Revolution, routed the tax collectors and freed from jail a tax resister, one John Fries, who had been involved in the Whiskey Rebellion. Adams sent federal troops to restore order, and for leading Fries's Rebellion, a court issued death sentences for three men, including Fries. The president's cabinet demanded that Adams enforce "exemplary rigor" by allowing the sentence to be carried out, but in 1800 Adams responded to popular pressure and pardoned the three. To the jeers of conservative Federalists, Adams now dumped the Hamiltonians

The presidential election of 1800 was the first to feature campaign advertising. "T. Jefferson, President of the United States of America; John Adams—no more," reads the streamer on this election banner, illustrated with an American eagle and a portrait of Jefferson. This was mild rhetoric in a campaign characterized by wild charges. The Republicans labeled Adams a warmonger and a monarchist, while the Federalists denounced Jefferson as an atheist, Jacobin, and sexual libertine.

SOURCE: The Granger Collection.

from his cabinet. During the war scare with France, Washington had insisted that Hamilton be appointed as second in command of the enlarged army. "You crammed him down my throat!" Adams cried. Now he denounced Hamilton as "a bastard, and as much an alien as Gallatin." Hamilton responded by circulating a private letter in which he condemned Adams for his "disgusting egotism," "distempered jealousy," and "vanity without bounds." This letter fell into the hands of Aaron Burr, leader of the New York Jeffersonian Republicans, and he published it, to the consternation of the Federalists.

The Federalists divided at precisely the time when unity was necessary, allowing the Jeffersonian Republicans to capture the state governments of Pennsylvania and New York in 1799, the first important inroads of the party in the North. These states had been taken over, cried a shocked Federalist, by "the most God-provoking Democrats on this side of Hell." From Virginia, Jefferson proclaimed his hope that "with Pennsylvania we can defy the universe!" The presidential campaign of 1800 was the first in which Jeffersonian Republicans and Federalists operated as two national political parties. Caucuses of congressmen nominated respective slates: Adams and Charles Cotesworth Pinckney of South Carolina for the Federalists, Jefferson and Aaron Burr of New York for the Jeffersonian Republicans. Both tickets thus represented

attempts at sectional balance. The Jeffersonian Republicans presented themselves as the party of traditional agrarian purity, of liberty and states' rights, of "government rigorously frugal and simple," in the words of Jefferson. They were optimistic, convinced that they were riding the wave of the future. Divided and embittered, the Federalists waged a defensive struggle for strong central government and public order, and often resorted to negative campaigning. They denounced Jefferson as an atheist, a Jacobin, and the father of mulatto children. (The first two charges were without foundation, but the last was apparently true, according to the results of recent DNA matching tests. See Chapter 4.) One campaign placard put the issue succinctly: "GOD—AND A RELIGIOUS PRESIDENT" or "JEFFERSON—AND NO GOD!"

The balloting for presidential electors took place between October and December 1800. Adams took all the New England states while Jefferson captured the South and West. Jefferson called it "the Revolution of 1800." Party discipline was so effective that one of the provisions of the Constitution was shown to be badly outmoded. By this clause, the candidate receiving a majority of electoral votes became president and the runner-up became vice president. But by casting all their ballots for Jefferson and Burr, Jeffersonian Republican electors unintentionally created a tie and forced the election into the House of Representatives. Because the new Jeffersonian Republican–controlled Congress would not convene until March 1801, the Federalist majority was given a last chance to decide the election. They attempted to make a deal with Burr, who refused but who also would not withdraw his name from consideration. Finally, on the thirty-fifth ballot the Federalists gave up and arranged with their opponents to elect Jefferson without any of them having to cast a single vote in his favor. Congressman Matthew Lyon cast the symbolic final vote in a gesture of sweet revenge. The Twelfth Amendment, creating separate ballots for president and vice president, was ratified in time for the next presidential election.

Democratic Political Culture

Accompanying the rise of partisan politics was a transformation in popular political participation. Consider the custom of celebrating Independence Day. At the beginning of the 1790s, in many communities, the day featured demonstrations of military prowess by veteran officers, followed by banquets for leaders. Relatively few Americans played a direct role. But during the political controversies of the decade a tradition of popular celebration developed. People took to the streets, set off fireworks, erected liberty poles, and listened to readings of the preamble of the Declaration of Independence, which more than any other document encapsulated and symbolized republican ideology. The first of these celebrations took place in Philadelphia, then other large cities, and eventually spread throughout the country. By 1800 the Fourth of July had become the nation's most important holiday.

There was a corresponding increase in the suffrage. In 1789 state regulations limited the franchise to a small percentage of the adult population. Women, African Americans, and Indians could not vote, but neither could a third to a half of all free adult males, who were excluded by tax-paying or property-owning requirements. Moreover, even among the eligible, the turnout was generally low. The traditional manner of voting was *viva voce*, by voice. At the polling place in each community individuals announced their selections aloud to the clerk of elections, who wrote them down. Not surprisingly, this system allowed wealthy men, landlords, and employers of the community to pressure poorer voters.

These practices changed with the increasing competition between Jeffersonian Republicans and Federalists. Popular pressure resulted in the introduction of universal white manhood suffrage in four states by 1800 and the reduction of property requirements in others. Thus was inaugurated a movement that would sweep the nation over the next quarter century. As a consequence voter turnout increased in all the states. The growth of popular interest in politics was a transformation as important as the peaceful transition from Federalists to Jeffersonian Republicans in national government.

"THE RISING GLORY OF AMERICA"

In 1771, Philip Freneau and Hugh Henry Brackenridge addressed their graduating class at Princeton on "The Rising Glory of America." Thus far American contributions to learning and the arts had been slim, they admitted. But they were boundlessly optimistic about the potential of their country. "This is the land of every joyous sound," they proclaimed, "where the arts shall rise and grow." Indeed, judged against the literary and artistic work of individuals in the colonial period, artists and others of the Revolutionary generation accomplished a great deal in their effort to build a national culture.

Art and Architecture

The first American to achieve prominence in the artistic world of Europe was Benjamin West, who painted portraits in his native Pennsylvania before leaving for the Continent and England, where he became popular as a painter of historical scenes. His *Death of General Wolfe* (1770) was one of the more acclaimed paintings of its day and the first to elevate an American scene to the high status of monumental historical painting. In 1774 West was joined in London by John Singleton Copley, a Boston portraitist who left America because of his Loyalist sentiments. Copley's work is renowned for the truth and straightforwardness of his depictions, as in his famous portrait of Samuel Adams (1772). Both West and Copley remained in England after the Revolution. Their most promising student was Gilbert Stuart, whose work in the fashionable style of the day included a portrait of Mohawk leader Joseph Brant. Stuart returned to the United States in 1792 to paint what became the most famous portrait of President Washington.

The preeminent painter of the Revolution was Charles Willson Peale, who studied for a time with Benjamin West in London. He returned to America, however, and during the Revolution turned his talents to producing wartime propaganda. Although the almond eyes and bloated torsos of his figures suggest his technical limitations, Peale's work has a naive charm. His paintings of Washington, for example, seem more revealing of character than Stuart's placid portrait. In-

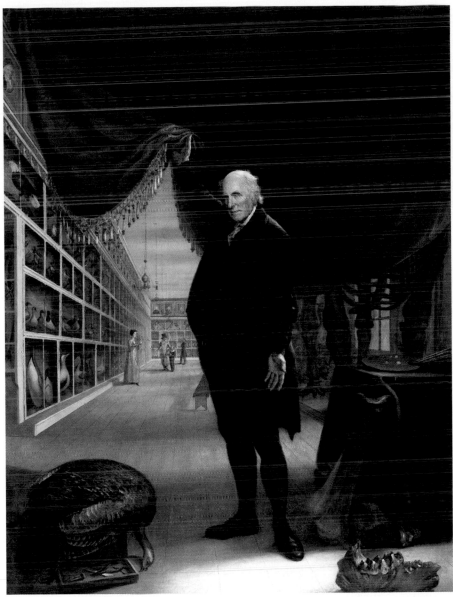

In this self-portrait, American artist Charles Willson Peale dramatically lifts the curtain on his Philadelphia Museum. Peale's three sons—whom he named after the artists Raphael, Rembrandt, and Titian—and two of his nieces—Anna and Sarah—also became noted painters, constituting something of a first family of American art in the early years of the new republic.

SOURCE: Charles Willson Peale, *The Artist in His Museum*, 1822. Oil on canvas, 103¾" × 79⅞". Courtesy of the Pennsylvania Academy of the Fine Arts, Philadelphia. Gift of Mrs. Sarah Harrison. (The Joseph Harrison, Jr. Collection.)

John Trumbull of Connecticut, who had predicted America's rise to his Yale classmates, served as a soldier during the Revolution, then went to London to study with West. There he painted *The Battle of Bunker's Hill* (1785), the first of a series of Revolutionary scenes, four of which he repainted in the Capitol rotunda in the early nineteenth century. Influenced by the grand style of eighteenth-century historical painting, Trumbull was concerned above all else with documentary detail in his scenes of the birth of America.

Nationalism was also evident in architecture. The greatest architectural project of the day was the new federal capital city, named for President Washington. In 1790, after Congress had agreed on the site, Washington retained Pierre Charles L'Enfant, a French engineer who had served as an officer during the Revolution, to lay out the city. The survey was conducted by Andrew Ellicott, assisted by the African American mathematician Benjamin Banneker. L'Enfant took full advantage of the lay of the land and the Potomac River, placing the Capitol building on a hill "which stands as a pedestal waiting for a monument." He linked public buildings such as the president's house and the Capitol with radial avenues, allowing for what he called "a reciprocity of sight." And he planned a grand mall from the Capitol to the river, along which there would be public museums, academies, and assembly halls. Development during the nineteenth century obscured L'Enfant's original design, but it was revived in 1901. Jefferson recommended "the models of antiquity" for the public buildings of the federal city, a suggestion carried out in William Thornton's original design for the Capitol.

"Architecture is worth great attention," declared Jefferson, for "as we double our numbers every twenty years, we must double our houses. It is, then, among the most important arts; and it is desirable to introduce taste

spired by nationalist zeal, Peale planned a public gallery of heroes in Philadelphia that eventually grew into a famous museum of curios, reflecting his interest in natural history, archaeology, and exotic cultures. Federalists joked that its chaotic arrangement of exhibits mirrored Peale's Jeffersonian politics. Part science, part circus, the collection was purchased after Peale's death by the pioneer American entertainer P. T. Barnum.

George Town and Federal City, or City of Washington, a colored aquatint of 1801 by T. Cartwright. When President John Adams first occupied the White House in 1800, Washington was still a small village, its streets merely muddy pathways.

SOURCE: Courtesy of The Library of Congress.

into an art which shows so much." In New England, architect Asher Benjamin popularized an American variant of the Georgian style, emphasizing economy of decoration and recommending the use of indigenous materials when writing handbooks such as *The Country Builder's Assistant* (1797). A great deal of the urban building undertaken in coastal cities during the shipping boom of the 1790s was characterized by this restrained classicism, which was known as the Federal style.

But the majority of Americans lived in small, bare, even squalid conditions. A nationwide tax on houses produced the first comprehensive survey of the nation's housing in 1798. There was tremendous variation in living conditions. The wealthiest 10 percent lived in dwellings estimated to be worth more than half the total value of all houses. By contrast, the value of housing owned by the wealthiest tenth of Americans today is only 30 percent of the total. Forty percent of American houses in 1798 were valued at $99 or less (the

equivalent of about $1,500 today), and were little more than shacks. In the expanding cities, many residents lived along dingy back alleys and in damp basements. In the country, the typical house was a one-story structure of two or three rooms. As the population continued to grow, and Americans continued to move west, many more people would be found in log hovels like those in the community along Mingo Creek.

The Liberty of the Press

At the beginning of the Revolution in 1775 there were thirty-seven weekly or semiweekly newspapers in the thirteen colonies, only seven of which were Loyalist in sentiment. By 1789 the number of papers in the United States had grown to ninety-two, including eight dailies; three papers were being published west of the Appalachians. Relative to population, there were more newspapers in the United States than in any other

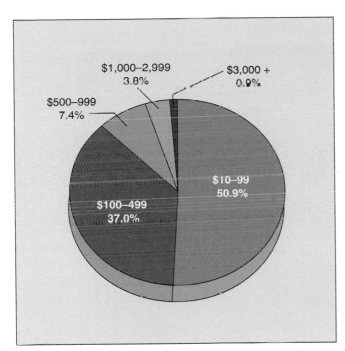

Housing Values, 1798   In 1798 Congress enacted a direct tax on buildings, resulting in an inventory of American housing that has never been equaled. The data revealed an enormous gap between rich and poor. The majority lived in squalid cabins valued at $99 or less, while the wealthiest 10 percent of Americans lived in dwellings that, taken together, were worth just over half the total value of all the nation's houses.

SOURCE: Lee Soltow, "Egalitarian America and Its Inegalitarian Housing in the Federal Period," *Social Science History* 9 (1985): 199–213.

country in the world—a reflection of the remarkably high literacy rate of the American people (see Chapter 5). In New England almost 90 percent of the population could read, and even on the frontier, where Brackenridge edited the *Pittsburgh Gazette*, about two-thirds of the males were literate.

During the political controversy of the 1790s, the press became the principal medium of Federalist and Jeffersonian Republican opinion, and papers came to be identified by their politics. In 1789, John Fenno, aided by Alexander Hamilton, began publication of the *Federalist Gazette of the United States*, and in 1791 Jefferson encouraged Philip Freneau to establish the competing *National Gazette*. The columns of these papers broadcast the feud between the two cabinet secretaries.

The prosecutions under the Sedition Act, however, threatened to curb the further development of the media, and in their opposition to these measures Jeffersonian Republicans played an important role in establishing the principle of a free press. In *An Essay on Liberty of the Press* (1799), the Virginia lawyer George Hay, later appointed to the federal bench by President Jefferson, wrote that "a man may say everything which

his passions suggest." Were this not true, he argued, the First Amendment would have been "the grossest absurdity that was ever conceived by the human mind." In his first Inaugural Address, Jefferson echoed this early champion of the freedom of expression. "Error of opinion may be tolerated," he declared, "where reason is left free to combat it."

The Birth of American Literature

During the post-Revolutionary years there was an enormous outpouring of American publications. In the cities the number of bookstores grew in response to the demand for reading matter. Perhaps even more significant was the appearance in the countryside of numerous book peddlers who supplied farm households with Bibles, gazettes, almanacs, sermons, and political pamphlets. One such peddler was Mason Locke Weems, a man trained as a doctor and ordained an Anglican minister, who gave up these careers in the early 1790s for book-selling. Parson Weems, as he was known, wrote that he found his southern backcountry customers "uninformed, their minds bitter, and their manners savage," but that they cried out for "books, books, books!"

The literature of the Revolution understandably reflected the dominating political concerns of the times. Mercy Otis Warren and Hugh Henry Brackenridge wrote propagandistic dramas, and the poet Joel Barlow composed a nationalist epic, *The Vision of Columbus* (1787). *M'Fingal* (1782), a mock epic satirizing the British, was written by John Trumbull (a cousin of the painter), a leader of the literary group known as the Connecticut Wits. It sold enough copies to be considered the best-selling fictional work of the war. But the majority of "best-sellers" during the Revolutionary era were political. The most important were Thomas Paine's *Common Sense* (1776) and his series of stirring pamphlets, published under the running title *The American Crisis* (1776–83), the first of which began with the memorable phrase "These are the times that try men's souls."

In the cause of reform, Paine later returned to England and published *The Rights of Man* (1791), a defense of the French Revolution. Banished from Britain for this expression of radical politics, he went to France, jumped into politics, and, in one of the periodic political turns of the revolution, found himself imprisoned for a time. From his jail cell Paine wrote *The Age of Reason* (1795), a powerful attack on organized religion that became one of the most popular American books of its day, loved by Jeffersonians and loathed by Federalists. Book-selling Parson Weems, for example, made a steady profit from the sale of Paine's work, though he offered pious sermons and religious tracts to placate those objecting to Paine's politics.

Pages from Noah Webster's famous *American Spelling Book,* the largest seller of all American books during the nineteenth century. Believing that "the King's English" reflected aristocratic standards, Webster argued for spelling reform to create "the American language."

SOURCE: Courtesy of American Antiquarian Society.

Some of the most interesting American books of the postwar years examined the developing American character. The French immigrant Michel-Guillaume Jean de Crèvecoeur, in *Letters from an American Farmer* (1782), proposed that the American, a product of many cultures, was a "new man" with ideas new to the world. John Filson, the author of the *Discovery, Settlement, and Present State of Kentucke* (1784), presented the narrative of one such new man, the Kentucky pioneer Daniel Boone. In doing so, he took an important step toward the creation of that most American of literary genres, the western. In a satirical novel entitled *Modern Chivalry* (1792), featuring incidents from the Whiskey Rebellion, Pittsburgh editor Brackenridge dipped his pen "in the inkstand of human nature" and produced one of the first dialect portraits of "dat son o'd a whore," the American frontiersman. Brackenridge wrote with an appreciation for his crude characters but expressed frustration that the Revolution had failed to elevate the culture of ordinary people. By shunning simple celebration, however, he was one of the first to take a critical look at the American character.

The single best-selling book of the Revolutionary era was Noah Webster's *American Spelling Book* (1783), the famous "Blue-Backed Speller," which soon after its publication was selling 200,000 copies annually. It became the largest-selling of all American books, a good indicator of the remarkable literacy of the American people. With it, Webster launched a lifelong campaign for a distinctive American form of English, which culminated in his *American Dictionary of the English Language* (1828). In a belief that "the King's English" reflected aristocratic standards, Webster argued for a time that "the American language" must be guided by "republican principles," for example, spelling words as they sounded. "Ther iz no alternativ," he wrote. Eventually he abandoned the most radical of his suggestions, although many of his reforms stuck, dropping the "u" from the English spelling of "colour," for example, in favor of "color." The speller was the first in a graded series of textbooks that included a grammar and a reader designed to "diffuse the principles of virtue and patriotism." These texts included standard selections from not only British but also American writers. Webster compiled a list of important dates beginning with Columbus's voyage and ending with the British surrender at Yorktown—the first attempt at a distinctively American historical chronology. Other writers produced more formal histories. Not surprisingly, Jeffersonian authors stressed the tradition of resistance to authority, whereas Federalists emphasized the importance, particularly during wartime, of central direction and unity. Fearing criticism by Federalist writers, Jeffersonian Republican Mercy Otis Warren delayed publishing her *History of the Rise, Progress, and Termination of the American Revolution* (1805) until after Jefferson's victory in 1800.

Parson Weems found readers fascinated by the historical heroes of the Revolution, so he drew up plans for a series of "quarter of dollar books on subjects calculated to strike the popular curiosity, printed in very large numbers and properly distributed." When Washington died in December 1799, Weems was already at work on a short biography of the first president. "Washington, you know, is gone!" he wrote to his publisher. "Millions are gaping to read something about him. I am very nearly primed and cocked for 'em." His *Life of Washington* (1800, enlarged edition 1806), became the most popular history of the Revolution and introduced a series of popular and completely fabricated anecdotes, including the story of young George Washington and the cherry tree. The book was a pioneering effort in mass culture, and Weems, as one historian puts it, was "the father of the Father of his Country."

Condemned by serious writers and scholars, even at the time of its publication, Weems's biography was loved by ordinary Americans of all political persuasions. In the mid-nineteenth century, Abraham Lincoln recalled that he had read Weems "away back in my childhood, the earliest days of my being able to read," and had been profoundly impressed by "the struggles for the liberties of the country." In praise of Washington, Weems wrote, "all parties join with equal alacrity and earnestness." Although Washington had in fact become a partisan leader of the Federalists during his second term, Weems presented him as a unifying figure for the political culture of the new nation, and this was the way he would be remembered. Jefferson echoed these sentiments in his Inaugural Address in 1801, when as a gesture of conciliation to his opponents he declared, "We have called by different names brethren of the same principle. We are all Republicans, we are all Federalists."

Women on the Intellectual Scene

One of the most interesting literary trends of the 1790s was the growing demand for books that appealed to women readers. Susanna Haswell Rowson's *Charlotte Temple* (1791), a tale of seduction and abandonment, ran up tremendous sales and remained in print for more than a century. Other romantic works of fiction included *The Power of Sympathy* (1789) by William Hill Brown, sometimes called the first American novel; the gothic novels of Charles Brockden Brown, such as *Arthur Mervyn* (1799); and *The Coquette* (1797) by Hannah Webster Foster. The young republic thus marked the first dramatic appearance of women writers and women readers. Although women's literacy rates continued to be lower than men's, they rose steadily as girls joined boys in common schools. This increase was one of the most important social legacies of the democratic struggles of the Revolutionary era.

Some writers argued that the new republican order ought to provide new roles for women as well as for men. The first avowed feminist in American history

In this 1792 cartoon from the *Lady's Magazine*, the allegorical figure of "Columbia" receives a petition for the "Rights of Woman." In the aftermath of the Revolution, Americans debated the issue of an expanded role for women in the new republic. Many Federalists condemned "women of masculine minds," but there was general agreement among both conservatives and democrats that the time had come for better education for American women.

SOURCE: The Library Company of Philadelphia.

was Judith Sargent Murray, who publicly stated her belief that women "should be taught to depend on their own efforts, for the procurement of an establishment in life." She was greatly influenced by the English feminist Mary Wollstonecraft, but developed her line of thinking independently, as demonstrated by her essay "On the Equality of the Sexes," written in 1779 and finally published in 1790 in a Massachusetts magazine. "I expect to see our young women forming a new era in female history," Murray predicted. Federalists listened to such opinions with horror. "Women of masculine minds," one Boston minister sneered, "have generally masculine manners."

CHRONOLOGY

1786	Annapolis Convention
1787	Constitutional Convention
1787–88	*The Federalist* published
1788	Constitution ratified
	First federal elections
1789	President George Washington inaugurated in New York City
	Judiciary Act
	French Revolution begins
1790	Agreement on site on the Potomac River for the nation's capital
	Indian Intercourse Act
	Judith Sargent Murray publishes "On the Equality of the Sexes"
1791	Bill of Rights ratified
	Bank of the United States chartered
	Alexander Hamilton's "Report on Manufactures"
	Ohio Indians defeat General Arthur St. Clair's army
1793	England and France at war; America reaps trade windfall
	Citizen Genêt affair
	President Washington proclaims American neutrality in Europe
	British confiscate American vessels
	Supreme Court asserts itself as final authority in *Chisholm* v. *Georgia*
1794	Whiskey Rebellion
	Battle of Fallen Timbers
	Jay's Treaty with the British concluded
1795	Pinckney's Treaty negotiated with the Spanish
	Treaty of Greenville
	Thomas Paine publishes *The Age of Reason*
1796	President Washington's Farewell Address
	John Adams elected president
1797–98	French seize American ships
1798	XYZ Affair
	"Quasi-war" with France
	Alien and Sedition Acts
	Kentucky and Virginia Resolves
1799	Fries's Rebellion
1800	Convention of 1800
	Thomas Jefferson elected president
	Mason Locke Weems publishes *Life of Washington*

There seemed to be general agreement among all parties, however, that the time had come for better-educated and better-informed women. Republican institutions of self-government were widely thought to depend on the wisdom and self-discipline of the American people. Civic virtue, so indispensable for the republic, must be taught at home. The share that every male citizen had in the government of the country, Benjamin Rush said in 1787, required that women have "suitable education, to concur in instructing their sons in the principles of liberty and government." By placing her learning at the service of her family, the "republican mother" was spared the criticism leveled at independent-minded women such as Murray. "A woman will have more commendation in being the mother of heroes," said a Federalist, "than in setting up, Amazon-like, for a heroine herself." Thus were women provided the opportunity to be not simply "helpmates," but people "learned and wise." But they were also expected to be content with a narrow role, not to wish for fuller participation in American democracy.

CONCLUSION

In 1800, the population of Canada numbered about 500,000. Those of European background in New Mexico and the other Spanish North American colonies numbered approximately 25,000. And the Indian people of the continent numbered anywhere from 500,000 to a million. Overwhelming all these groups was the population of the United States, which stood at 5.3 million and was growing at the astounding annual rate of 3 percent.

During the last years of the eighteenth century the United States had adopted a new constitution and established a new national government. It had largely repaid the debt run up during the Revolution and made peace with adversaries abroad and Indian peoples at home. Americans had begun to learn how to channel their disagreements into political struggle. The nation had withstood a first decade of stress, but tensions continued to divide the people. As some of the rebel supporters had promised at the beginning of the Whiskey Rebellion, "their liberty they will maintain, / They fought for't, and they'll fight again." At the beginning of the new century it remained uncertain whether the new nation would find a way to control and channel the energies of an expanding people.

REVIEW QUESTIONS

1. Discuss the conflicting ideals of local and national authority in the debate over the Constitution.
2. What were the major crises faced by the Washington and Adams administrations?
3. Describe the roles of Madison and Hamilton in the formation of the first American political parties.
4. What did Jefferson mean when he talked of "the Revolution of 1800"?
5. Discuss the contributions of the Revolutionary generation to the construction of a national culture.

RECOMMENDED READING

Akhil Reed Amar, *The Bill of Rights: Creation and Reconstruction* (1998). A legal analysis arguing that the first ten Amendments were meant to protect the majority from the potential tyranny of the federal government.

William N. Chambers, *Political Parties in a New Nation: The American Experience, 1776–1809* (1963). An introduction to the formation of the American party system. Though several decades old, it remains essential.

Stanley Elkins and Eric McKitrick, *The Age of Federalism* (1993). A massive and informative account of the politics of the 1790s, from the ratification of the Constitution to the election of Jefferson.

Joanne B. Freeman, *Affairs of Honor: National Politics in the New Republic* (2001). A major reassessment of political culture in the new republic, stressing the importance of the culture of honor.

Reginald Horsman, *The Frontier in the Formative Years, 1783–1815* (1970). A sensitive survey of developments in the West, emphasizing that the "western question" was one of the most important facing the young republic.

Jackson Turner Main, *The Antifederalists: Critics of the Constitution, 1781–1788* (1961). A detailed examination of the localist tradition in early American politics. Includes a discussion of the ratification of the Constitution from the point of view of its opponents.

Simon P. Newman, *Parades and the Politics of the Street: Festive Culture in the Early American Republic* (1997). The participation of ordinary Americans in the political culture of the new republic.

Willard Sterne Randall, *George Washington: A Life* (1997). The best one-volume biography of "the Father of his Country."

Thomas P. Slaughter, *The Whiskey Rebellion: Frontier Epilogue to the American Revolution* (1986). A detailed history of the rebellion in western Pennsylvania during the 1790s. Includes a thorough examination of the politics and culture of both the (Jeffersonian) backcountry and the federal government at a moment of crisis.

James M. Smith, *Freedom's Fetters: The Alien and Sedition Laws and American Civil Liberties* (1966). Remains the best overview of the Federalist threat to liberty, as well as the Democratic Republican (Jeffersonian) counterattack.

Bernard A. Weisberger, *American Afire: Jefferson, Adams, and the Revolutionary Election of 1800* (2000). Shows that the election and the transfer of power were victories for popular self-government and that they set a major precedent for all other elections.

Gordon Wood, *The Creation of the American Republic, 1776–1787* (1969). This general survey provides the best overview of the Constitutional Convention.

▶ MEDIA RESOURCES

 U.S. HISTORY DOCUMENTS CD-ROM

Colonial America

3-12 Alexander Falconbridge, The African Slave Trade (1788)

3-13 Olaudah Equiano, The Middle Passage (1788)

Forging a Constitution

6-6 Shays' Rebellion: Letters of Generals William Shepard and Benjamin Lincoln to Governor James Bowdoin of Massachusetts (1787)

6-7 Divergent Reactions to Shays' Rebellion

6-8 The "Distracting Question" in Philadelphia (1787)

6-9 Patrick Henry Speaks Against Ratification of the Constitution (1788)

6-10 Benjamin Banneker, Letter to Thomas Jefferson (1791)

6-11 James Wilson, An Introductory Lecture To a Course of Law Lectures (1791)

6-12 Molly Wallace, Valedictory Oration (1792)

The Federalist Era

7-1 James Madison Defends the Constitution (1788)

7-2 [William Maclay], "For the Independent Gazetteer" (1790)

7-3 Alexander Hamilton, Final Version of "An Opinion on the Constitutionality of an Act to Establish a Bank" (1791)

7-4 Questions Concerning the Constitutionality of the National Bank (1791)

7-5 Opposing Visions for the New Nation (1791)

7-8 George Washington, Farewell Address (1796)

7-10 Questions of Constitutionality and the Roots of Nullification (1798)

 COMPANION WEBSITE HIGHLIGHTS

To view an exploration, enter one of the URLs below in your browser.

 Web Explorations

The Ratification of the Constitution, 1787–1790
http://www.prenhall.com/faragher/map8.1
Spread of Settlement: The Backcountry Expands, 1770–1790
http://www.prenhall.com/faragher/map8.2

 Additional Interactive Maps

To access the map, go to this chapter's resources at
http://www.prenhall.com/faragher
Spanish Claims to American Territory, 1783–1795, page 221

 HISTORY RESOURCE CENTER

To find the resources listed below, go to
http://www.prenhall.com/historyresourcecenter

Documents

A Declaration of the Rights of the Inhabitants of the Commonwealth of Massachusetts (1780)

George Washington, Sixth Annual Address to Congress (1794)

Publius (James Madison), Federalist Paper #10 (1788)

The Alien and Sedition Acts (1798)

The Virginia, or Randolph, Plan (1787)

Thomas Jefferson, Notes on the State of Virginia (1787)

Thomas Jefferson, "The Kentucky Resolutions" (1798)

Images

George Washington's Arrival in New York City, 1789
Painting in General by James L. Walker
Robert Owen's Harmony Community
Take Notice!
The Anatomy of Man's Body . . .
Title page from "Benjamin Banneker's Pennsylvania . . ."
Washington Taking the Oath of Office
Washington's First Cabinet

EXPLORING AMERICA

RATIFICATION OF THE CONSTITUTION

http://www.prenhall.com/faragher/constitution

What event precipitated the call for a constitutional convention? What arguments did proponents and opponents of the Constitution present? How did the debate in Pennsylvania reflect those going on in other states? What roles did Benjamin Franklin and James Madison play in the ratification campaign? How long did it take for all the states to ratify the Constitution? The *Ratification of the Constitution* module examines the process by which the United States adopted the Constitution, which has been the law of the land for over 200 years, showing that its passage was not a foregone conclusion.

The Ratification of the Constitution offers

both a general discussion and a case study of the debate over the Constitution, indicating that ratification was an arduous struggle. The narrative provides a structure for the extensive primary source excerpts that set the positions for and against the Constitution. It also offers the philosophy of such pivotal founding fathers as James Madison regarding government, politics in a republic, and other important concerns.

Reflect and Respond

1. When Madison sought an example to illustrate his argument that "different classes of legislators" were "advocates and parties to the causes which they determine," he first turned to "private debts." How much credit does Daniel Shays deserve for persuading Madison and the other framers of the need for a stronger central government?

2. Antifederalists saw a thinly disguised attack upon popular rule in the renewed emphasis upon "balance." Here is how "Aristocrotis" sarcastically put it:

> In article first, section first, of the new plan, it is declared that "all legislative powers herein granted shall be vested in a Congress of the United States which shall consist of a Senate"—very right, quite agreeable to nature and House of Representatives. . . . This is a palpable [obvious] compliance with the humors and corrupt practices of the times. But what follows in section 2 is still worse: "The House of Representatives shall be composed of members chosen every second year by the people of the several states." This is a most dangerous power, and must soon produce fatal and pernicious consequences, were it not circumscribed and poised by proper checks and balances... There is a small thrust given to it in the body of the conveyance itself. The term of holding elections is every two years; this is much better than the detestable mode of annual elections, so fatal to energy.

3. How did Madison answer in Federalist 51?

✓ Check it out

Ratification of the Constitution, 1787-1790

This map depicts the ratification of the Constitution over time and space. It shows that the Constitution's passage was not a foregone conclusion and that attitudes for and against crossed regional boundaries. The map is also important for stressing the importance of the larger states in ratification.

This exploration is also available on the *Exploring America* CD-ROM. For another *Exploring America* activity related to this chapter, go to "The Partisan Press" found on both the Companion Website™ and the CD-ROM.

AN AGRARIAN REPUBLIC

▶ 1790–1824

George Catlin (1796–1892). *Bull Dance, Mandan-o-kee-pa Ceremony,* 1832. Copyright Smithsonian American Art Museum, Washington, D.C./Art Resource, NY.

AMERICAN COMMUNITIES

Expansion Touches Mandan Villages on the Upper Missouri

IN MID-OCTOBER 1804, NEWS ARRIVED AT THE MANDAN VILlages, prominently situated on bluffs overlooking the upper Missouri River, that an American expedition led by Meriwether Lewis and William Clark was coming up the river. The principal chiefs, hoping for expanded trade and support against their enemies the Sioux, welcomed these first American visitors. As the expedition's three boats and forty-three men approached the village, Clark wrote, "great numbers on both sides flocked down to the bank to view us." That evening the Mandans welcomed the Americans with an enthusiastic dance and gifts of food.

Since the fourteenth century, when they had migrated from the East, the Mandans had lived along the Missouri, on the edge of the Great Plains in what is now North Dakota. They believed their homeland was "the very center of the world," and indeed it is in the heart of the North American continent. Mandan men hunted buffalo and Mandan women kept storage pits full with abundant crops of corn, beans, squash, sunflowers, and tobacco grown on the fertile soil of the river bottomlands. The Mandan villages were also the central marketplace of the northern Plains; at trading time in late summer they filled with Crows, Assiniboins, Cheyennes, Kiowas, and Arapahoes. Well before any of these people, or those of other tribes, had met a European, they were trading in kettles, knives, and guns acquired from the French and English to the east and leatherwork, glassware, and horses acquired from the Spanish in the Southwest.

The eighteenth century had been a golden age for the Mandan, who with their closely related Hidatsa neighbors numbered about 3,000 in 1804. In each of their five villages, earth lodges surrounded a central plaza. One large ceremonial lodge was used for community gatherings, and each of the other earth lodges was home to a senior woman, her husband, her sisters (perhaps married to the same man as she, for the Mandans practiced polygamy), their daughters and their unmarried sons, along with numerous grandchildren. Matrilineal clans, the principal institution of the community, distributed food to the sick, adopted orphans, cared for the dependent elderly, and punished wrongdoers. A village council of male clan leaders selected chiefs who led by consensus and lost power when people no longer accepted their opinions.

Lewis and Clark had been sent by President Thomas Jefferson to survey the Louisiana Purchase and to find an overland route to the Pacific Ocean. They were also instructed to inform the Indians that they now owed loyalty—and trade—to the American government, thereby challenging British economic control over the lucrative North American fur trade. Meeting with the village chiefs, the Americans offered the Mandans a military and economic alliance. His people would like nothing better, responded Chief Black Cat, for the Mandans had fallen on hard times over the past decade. [Some twenty years earlier], "the smallpox destroyed the greater part of the nation," the chief said. "All the nations before this malady [were] afraid of them, [but] after they were reduced, the Sioux and other Indians waged war, and killed a great many." Black Cat was skeptical that the Americans would deter the Sioux, but Clark reassured him. "We were ready to protect them," Clark reported in his journal, "and kill those who would not listen to our good talk."

The Americans spent the winter with the Mandans, joining in their communal life and establishing firm and friendly relations with them. There were dances and joint hunting parties, frequent visits to the earth lodges, long talks around the fire, and, for many of the men, pleasant nights in the company of Mandan women. Lewis and Clark spent many hours acquiring important geographic information from the Mandans, who drew charts and maps showing the course of the Missouri, the ranges of the Rocky Mountains, and places where one could cross the Continental Divide. The information provided by the Mandans and other Indian peoples to the west was vital to the success of the expedition. Lewis and Clark's "voyage of discovery" depended largely on the willingness of Indian peoples to share their knowledge of the land with the Americans.

Also in need of interpreters who could help them communicate with other Indian communities on their way, the Americans hired several multilingual Frenchmen who lived with the Mandans. They also acquired the services of Sacajawea, the fifteen-year-old Lemhi wife of one of the Frenchmen, who became the only woman to join the westward journey. The presence of Sacajawea and her baby son was a signal, as Clark noted, to "all the Indians as to our friendly intentions"; everyone knew that women and children did not go on war parties.

When the party left the Mandan villages in March, Clark wrote, his men were "generally healthy, except venereal complaints which is very common amongst the natives and the men catch it from them." After an arduous journey across the Rockies, the party reached the Pa-

cific Ocean at the mouth of the Columbia River, where they spent the winter. Overdue and feared lost, they returned in triumph to St. Louis in September 1806. Before long the Americans had established Fort Clark at the Mandan villages, giving American traders a base for challenging British dominance of the western fur trade. The permanent American presence brought increased contact, and with it much more disease. In 1837 a terrible smallpox epidemic carried away the vast majority of the Mandans, reducing the population to fewer than 150. Four Bears, a Mandan chief who had been a child at the time of the Lewis and Clark visit, spoke these last words to the remnants of his people:

"I have loved the whites," he declared. "I have lived with them ever since I was a boy." But in return for the kindness of the Mandans, the Americans had brought this plague. "I do not fear death, my friends," he said, "but to die with my face rotten, that even the wolves will shrink with horror at seeing me, and say to themselves, that is Four Bears, the friend of the whites." "They have deceived me," he pronounced with his last breath. "Those that I always considered as brothers turned out to be my worst enemies."

In sending Lewis and Clark on their "voyage of discovery" to claim the land and the loyalty of the Mandans and other western Indian communities, President Jefferson was motivated by his vision of an expanding American republic of self-sufficient farmers. During his and succeeding presidencies, expansion became a key element of national policy and pride. Yet, as the experience of the Mandans showed, what Jefferson viewed as enlargement of "the empire for liberty" had a dark side—the destruction, from disease and coerced displacement, of the communities created by America's first peoples. The effects—economic, political, and social—of continental expansion dominate the history of American communities in the first half of the nineteenth century. ■

Mandan Villages

KEY TOPICS

- The development of America's economy in a world of warring great powers

- The role of Jefferson's presidency and his agrarian republicanism in forging a national identity

- The ending of colonial dependency by the divisive War of 1812

- Westward expansion becomes a nationalizing force

NORTH AMERICAN COMMUNITIES FROM COAST TO COAST

At first glance, the United States of America in 1800 was little different from the scattered colonies of the pre-Revolution era. Two-thirds of the young nation's people still lived in a long thin line of settlement within fifty miles of the Atlantic coast. From New Hampshire to Georgia, most people lived on farms or in small towns. Travel from home was slow and difficult, for the roads were poor, and a horse and carriage could go no more than three or four miles an hour. It took two days to travel from New York to Philadelphia, four days to Boston. Because they rarely traveled far from home, people's horizons were limited and local. Nevertheless, the new nation was already transforming itself: between 1790 and 1800, according to the first and second federal censuses, the American population grew from 3.9 million to 5.3 million. Growth by migration was greatest in the trans-Appalachian West, a region that was already home to approximately 100,000 Indians. From 1800 to 1850, in an extraordinary burst of territorial expansion, Americans surged westward all the way to the Pacific. In 1880 few people would have predicted that within fifty years the nation would encompass the entire continent. Then, the United States of America was a new and weak nation sharing a continent with many of the world's greater powers.

New Spain

On paper, Spain possessed most of North America, but in fact Spanish control crumbled rapidly in the 1790s as Spain became involved in the wars of the French Revolution and the Napoleonic Wars that followed. This decline in control was readily apparent in New Spain, the richest colony in Spanish America. The wealth derived more from agriculture (tobacco espe-

cially), ranching, and domestic commerce than from the famous silver mines of northern Mexico, which supplied a mere 15 percent of New Spain's annual production. Reflecting the flourishing economy, Mexico City, with a population of 200,000, was by far the largest and most elegant city on the continent. But there were smoldering problems. Spain's firm mercantilist grip assured that much more wealth was exported to Spain than remained in the New World. Tensions mounted between the Spanish-born *peninsulares*, high officials and bureaucrats, and the native-born *criollos* of Spanish descent, who chafed at their subordination, especially after the success of the American Revolution. In the 1790s there were two abortive criollo conspiracies on behalf of independence in Mexico City alone. Furthermore, none of New Spain's northern provinces, created to protect the approaches to Mexico's fabulously wealthy silver mines, thrived. In all of the older settlements—San Antonio, Santa Fe, and Tucson—only a handful of persons of Spanish descent lived among a preponderantly native population. This was true even in the most recently founded northern province, Alta (Upper) California.

Spain had always sought to control all of the Pacific Coast of North America and by the 1770s had explored and made claim to the mouth of the Columbia River, Nootka Sound (on Vancouver Island), and the coast of southeastern Alaska. But Spanish attempts to seal off the rich seaborne fur trade from other nations failed. The Russians were a strong presence in Alaska, and the British, already the major power in the land-based fur trade, built a trading post for sea otter furs at Nootka Sound in 1789 in spite of Spanish protests. Americans, who soon dominated the sea otter trade, made their first voyage to the Pacific Northwest in 1787.

In another effort to protect their rich colony of Mexico, the Spanish pushed north into Alta California, establishing a chain of twenty-one missions that stretched north from San Diego (1769) to Sonoma (1823). The largest of these missions was Los Angeles, which in 1800 had a largely mestizo population of 300.

The town, which was the social center for the vast countryside surrounding it, functioned chiefly as a center of governmental authority (see Chapter 5). Despite Spain's desire to seal its territory from commerce with other nations, a brisk but illegal trade in otter skins, hides, and tallow developed between the United States and California after the first American ship, the *Lelia Bird*, arrived in 1803.

A French Legacy: New Orleans and Louisiana

Spain acquired New Orleans from France at the end of the Seven Years' War in 1763. But the city, founded by Jean Baptiste le Moyne, Sieur de Bienville, in 1718, was undeniably still French. Originally little more than a small port at the mouth of the Mississippi River, its location gave it access to the vast and vaguely defined continental interior that the French called Louisiana. By 1800, New Orleans had a population of about 8,000, half white and half black. Two-thirds of the black population were slaves; the remainder were "free persons of color," who under French law enjoyed legal rights equal to those of white people. The white population was a mixture of French people of European and West Indian origin. Among them were French-speaking exiles from Acadia, who became known in New Orleans as Cajuns (see Chapters 6 and 8). But there were also Spanish, Germans, English, Irish, Americans, and native-born creoles (persons of French descent), causing one observer to call the community "a veritable tower of Babel." All these people were there because New Orleans was becoming a thriving international port. In 1801, it shipped more than $3 million worth of tobacco, sugar, rice, cotton, fruits, and vegetables to Europe. Every year, a greater proportion of products for the New Orleans trade was supplied by Americans living some distance up the Mississippi River. In 1801 alone, an observer in Natchez counted nearly 600 flatboats on their way to New Orleans from American settlements upriver. Pinckney's 1795 treaty with Spain guaranteed Americans free navigation of the Mississippi River and the right to deposit goods at the port of New Orleans. Nevertheless, Americans were uncomfortably aware that the city's crucial location at the mouth of the Mississippi meant that whatever foreign nation possessed New Orleans had the power to choke off the flourishing trade in the vast Mississippi Valley river system.

More than 600 miles north was the small trading town of St. Louis, founded by the New Orleans trader Pierre Laclède in 1763. By 1800, the town had fewer than a thousand residents, three-quarters of whom were involved in the Indian trade of the Missouri River. Spanish officials tried to supervise that trade from their offices in the town, but real control rested in the hands of the Laclèdes and other French traders. Americans visiting this shabby little place laughed at Pierre Laclède's prediction that St. Louis would become "one of the finest cities in America," but he was right.

The Floridas and the Caribbean

Both East and West Florida were important to Spain because they dominated the Gulf of Mexico. East Florida controlled access to the Atlantic sea lanes and Cuba, the great Spanish sugar-producing colony in the Caribbean. But Spanish settlements, even the long-established fortress city of St. Augustine, were small islands in what remained predominantly Indian territories (Seminoles in East Florida, and Creeks, Choctaws, and Chickasaws in West Florida). Desperate for more population and unable to stop the relentless pressure on their northern borders from restless American frontiersmen, in the 1780s Spain began to accept immigrant Americans but required them to take an oath of allegiance. In reality, they opened the Floridas to Americanization long before the territories became officially part of the United States.

The Caribbean posed other challenges. The rich sugar-producing islands, variously colonies of Spain (Cuba, Puerto Rico, Santo Domingo), France (Martinique, Guadaloupe, and Saint-Domingue), and Britian (Barbados, Jamaica, and a number of smaller islands) provided 80 to 90 percent of the European supply of sugar. They were all slave societies, with enslaved Africans as the labor force. Thus they shared with the slaveholding American South a distinctive Afro-North American society that cut across national boundaries. This world was jolted by the 1791 revolt of black slaves in Saint-Domingue, France's richest colony. In 1804, under the leadership of Toussaint L'Ouverture, the former colony, renamed Haiti, became North America's first independent black nation. Its existence struck fear into the hearts of white slave-owners at the same time that it served as a beacon of hope to the enslaved.

British North America

British North America had been wrested from the French in the Seven Years' War (see Chapter 6). In 1800, its heart remained the former French colony of Quebec (at that time called the province of Lower Canada), with a predominantly French population of about 160,000. Most of the rest of the settlers elsewhere were American, either Loyalists driven out at the time of the Revolution or simply farmers in search of better land. British authorities, fearing civil disturbances, discouraged American immigrants from settling among the French, directing them instead either to the Maritime Provinces, dominated by Nova Scotia's great port, Halifax, or to Upper Canada, the first inland colony north of the Great Lakes, established in 1791. Further west (and closed to settlement) lay Rupertsland, the great stretch of the Canadian North and West that was administered by the Hudson's Bay Company. To allay popular demands stimulated by the American Revolution, Britain established legislative assemblies in Upper and Lower Canada and in the Maritimes in 1791, but, learning from their American fiasco, Britain kept the legislatures under strong executive control. British North America dominated the continental fur trade and the great succession of waterways—the St. Lawrence River, the Great Lakes, and the rivers beyond—that made it possible. Britain was on friendly terms with many of the native peoples who were part of the trade. This economic grip was a challenge and frustration to many westward-moving Americans. At the same time, the dispersed nature of the Canadian colonies made them, at least in the eyes of some Americans, ripe for conquest.

This view shows Sitka, the center of Russian activities in Alaska, in 1827. Russian architectural styles and building techniques are apparent in the Church of St. Michael the Archangel in the right background, contrasting with the Asian and Indian origins of most of Sitka's inhabitants.

From an engraving by Freidrich H. von Kittlitz, 1827. Elmer E. Rosmusen Library Rare Books, University of Alaska, Fairbanks.

Russian America: Sitka

Russian settlement of what is now Alaska was an extension of its conquest of Siberia, which was driven by the fur trade. In 1741, commissioned by Tsar Peter the Great, the Danish-born naval officer Vitus Bering sailed east from Kamchatka across the sea that now bears his name, explored the Aleutian Islands, and made landfall on the southern coast of Alaska. In the aftermath of his voyages, Russian and Siberian fur trappers, known as *promyshleniki*, became regular visitors to the Aleutian Islands and the Alaskan coast. By the late 1750s, they were shipping a steady supply of furs from Russian America.

The Russians sometimes took furs by force, holding whole villages hostage and brutalizing the native Inuit and Aleut peoples. After the Aleut Revolt of 1766, the Russian authorities promised to end the abuse, but by 1800 the precontact population of 25,000 Aleuts had been greatly reduced. At the same time, sexual relations and intermarriage between fur trappers and Aleut women created a large group of Russian creoles who assumed an increasingly promi-

nent position in the Alaskan fur trade as navigators, explorers, clerks, and traders as the fur trade became permanent.

The Russian-American Company, chartered by the Tsar in 1799, first set up American headquarters at Kodiak. When overhunting caused a scarcity of furs, the Russians moved their headquarters south to Sitka, in what is now the southeastern panhandle of Alaska. This was the homeland of the Tlingits, a warrior society, who destroyed the Russians' first fortress in the Tlingit Revolt of 1802. The Russians reestablished Sitka by force in 1804, and over the next generation established Russian settlements along the Pacific coast as far south as Fort Ross, which was just north of San Francisco Bay and well within Spanish territory. The Russian presence in North America was rapidly expanding even as Spain's faltered. In 1800, however, this imperial duel was far from the consciousness of most Americans, who were more concerned about the continuing presence of the British to the north in Canada and the nearby racial powder keg in the Caribbean.

Trans-Appalachia: Cincinnati

Within the United States itself, the region of greatest growth was territory west of the Appalachian Mountains, and it was this area that was most affected by fears of continuing British influence on regional

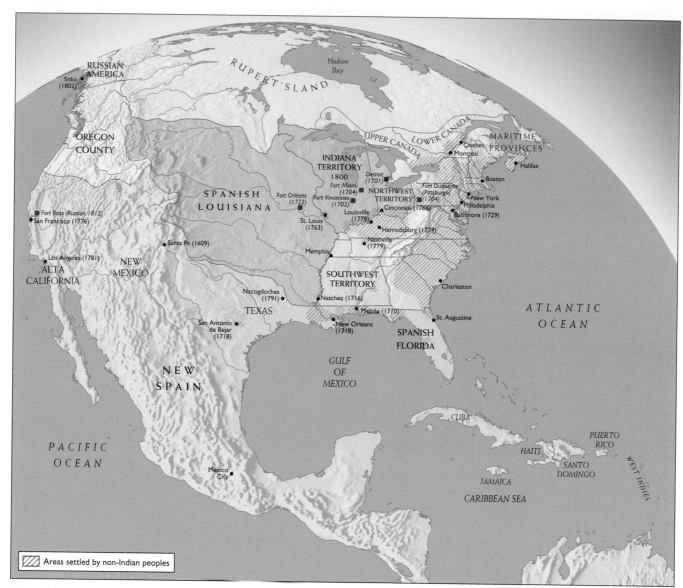

America in 1800 In 1800, the new United States of America was surrounded by territories held by the European powers: British Canada, French Louisiana (secretly ceded that year to France by Spain), Spanish Florida, Spanish Mexico, and Russian Alaska expanding southward along the Pacific coast. Few people could have imagined that by 1850 the United States would span the continent. But the American settlers who had crossed the Appalachians to the Ohio River valley were already convinced that opportunity lay in the West.

Indian peoples. By 1800, about 500,000 people (the vast majority from Virginia and North Carolina) had found rich and fertile land along the splendid rivers of the interior—the Tennessee, the Cumberland, and the Ohio, all draining into the Mississippi River, which marked the western boundary of the United States. Soon there was enough population for statehood. Kentucky (1792) and Tennessee (1796) were the first trans-Appalachian states admitted to the Union.

Migration was a principal feature of American life. Probably 5 to 10 percent of all American households moved each year. In the rural areas of the Atlantic seaboard, a third of the households counted in the 1790 census had moved by 1800; in cities, the proportion was closer to half. Migration to the West was generally a family affair, with groups of kin moving together to a new area. One observer wrote of a caravan moving across the mountains: "They had prepared baskets made of fine hickory withe or splints, and fastening two of them together with ropes they put a child in each basket and put it across a pack saddle." Once pioneers had managed to struggle by road over the Appalachians, they gladly took to the rivers, especially the Ohio, to move farther west.

Cincinnati, strategically situated 450 miles downstream from Pittsburgh, was a particularly dramatic example of the rapid community growth and development that characterized the trans-Appalachian region. Founded in 1788, Cincinnati began life as a military fort, defending settlers in the fertile Miami River valley of Ohio from resistance by Shawnee and Miami Indians. Conflict between these Indian peoples and the new settlers was so fierce that the district was grimly referred to as "the slaughterhouse." As fear of attack led the white settlers to group together for protection, the basic form of settlement in early Kentucky was the "station," or fort; north of the Ohio River, compact settlements on the New England model were favored. After the battle of Fallen Timbers broke Indian resistance in 1794, Cincinnati became the point of departure for immigrants arriving by the Ohio River on their way to settle the interior of the Old Northwest: Ohio, Indiana, and Illinois. In the boom years of settlement, the number of people passing through was so great that the entire town seemed to consist of hotels and eating places. In 1800, Cincinnati had a population of about 750 people. By 1810, it had tripled in size, confirming its boast to be "the Queen City of the West."

Cincinnati merchants were soon shipping farm goods from the fertile Miami Valley down the Ohio-Mississippi river system to New Orleans, 1,500 miles away. River hazards like snags and sandbars made the downriver trip by barge or keelboat hazardous, and the return trip upriver was slow, more than three months from New Orleans to Cincinnati. Frequently rivermen simply abandoned their flatboats in New Orleans and traveled home overland, on foot or horseback, by the long and dangerous Natchez Trace, an old Indian trail that linked Natchez on the Mississippi with Nashville, Tennessee. Nevertheless, river traffic increased yearly, and the control of New Orleans became a key concern of western farmers and merchants. If New Orleans refused to accept American goods, Cincinnati merchants and many thousands of trans-Appalachian farmers would be ruined.

Atlantic Ports: From Charleston to Boston

Although only 3 percent of the nation's population lived in cities, the Atlantic ports continued, as in the colonial era, to dominate the nation economically and politically. Seaports benefited from the advantage of relatively quick waterborne trade and communication over much slower land travel. Merchants in the

seaboard cities found it easier to cross the Atlantic than to venture into their own backcountry in search of trade. In 1800, the nation's most important urban centers were all Atlantic seaports: Charleston (which had a population of 20,000), Baltimore (26,000), Philadelphia (70,000), New York (60,000), and Boston (25,000). Each had a distinctive regional identity.

Charleston, South Carolina, was the South's premier port. In colonial days, Charleston had grown rich on its links with the British West Indies and on trade with England in rice, long-staple cotton, and indigo. The social center for the great low-country plantation owners, Charleston was a multiracial city of whites, African Americans (2,000 of them free), Indian peoples, and the mixed-race offspring of the these three groups. One was as likely to hear French, Spanish, or Gullah and Geeche (African-based dialects of low-country slaves) as English. This graceful, elegant city was a center for the slave trade until 1808.

Baltimore was the major port for the tobacco of the Chesapeake Bay region and thus was connected with the slave-owning aristocracy of the Upper South. But proximity to the wheat-growing regions of the Pennsylvania backcountry increasingly inclined the city's merchants to look westward and to consider ways to tap the trade of the burgeoning Ohio country.

Philadelphia, William Penn's "City of Brotherly Love," was distinguished by the commercial and banking skills of Quaker merchants. These merchants had built international trade networks for shipping the farm produce of Pennsylvania's German farmers. Philadelphia served as the nation's capital in the 1790s and was acknowledged as its cultural and intellectual leader as well.

New York, still faintly Dutch in architecture and social customs, was soon to outgrow all the other cities. New York merchants were exceptionally aggressive in their pursuit of trade. Unlike their counterparts in Philadelphia and Boston, New Yorkers accepted the British auction system, which cut out the middleman and offered goods in large lots at wholesale prices at open auctions. Increasingly, British imports entered America through the port of New York. New York's shipping, banking, insurance, and supporting industries boomed, and as early as 1800 a quarter of all American shipping was owned by New York merchants.

Boston, the cockpit of the American Revolution, was also the capital of Massachusetts. The handsome State House, built on Beacon Hill, reflected the origins of Boston's merchant wealth: a carved wooden codfish occupied a place of honor in the new building. By the late eighteenth century, however, Boston's commercial wealth had diversified into shipbuilding, shipping, banking, and insurance.

Though small in population, these Atlantic cities led the nation socially, politically, and above all economically. In 1800, the merchants in these seaports still primarily looked across the Atlantic to Europe. In the coming half-century, however, it was the cities that developed the strongest ties with the trans-Appalachian West that were to thrive.

A NATIONAL ECONOMY

In 1800, the United States was a producer of raw materials. The new nation faced the same challenge that developing nations confront today. At the mercy of fluctuating world commodity prices they cannot control, such countries have great difficulty protecting themselves from economic dominance by stronger, more established nations. In 1800, America was in just such a situation.

The Economy of the Young Republic

In 1800 the United States was predominantly rural and agricultural. In 1800, according to the census, 94 of 100 Americans lived in communities of fewer than 2,500 people, and four of five families farmed the land, either for themselves or for others. Farming families followed centuries-old traditions of working with hand tools and draft animals, producing most of their own food and fiber, and most Americans dressed in cloth that had been spun, woven, and tailored by women in their own families. Seaboard farmers of the Middle States and those near urban centers engaged in some commercial farming, but for most, crops were grown for home use rather than for sale. Production of a "surplus" to sell was a small sideline. Commodities such as whiskey and hogs (both easy to transport) provided small and irregular cash incomes or items for barter. As late as 1820, only 20 percent of the produce of American farms was consumed outside the local community.

In contrast to this pattern, the plantation agriculture of the South was wholly commercial and international. Slave owners, however, faced a growing dilemma: their heavy capital investment in African American slave labor was not matched by a growth in the demand for tobacco and rice, the traditional export crops. The tobacco trade, which accounted for about a third of the value of all colonial exports, remained at or below pre-Revolutionary levels, and the demand for rice had actually declined. The demand for a third crop, cotton, was growing rapidly in response to the boom in the industrial production of textiles in England and Europe, but extracting the seeds from the fibers of the variety of cotton that grew best in the southern interior required an enormous investment of labor. The cotton gin, which mechanized this process, was invented in 1793, but not until the nineteenth century did cotton assume a commanding place in the foreign trade of the United States.

In 1790, increasing foreign demand for American goods and services hardly seemed likely. Trade with Britain, still the biggest customer for American raw materials, was considerably less than it had been before the Revolution. As an independent nation, the United States no longer benefited from British mercantilist trade privileges. Britain and France both excluded Americans from their lucrative West Indian trade and taxed American ships with discriminatory duties. It was difficult to be independent in a world dominated by great powers.

Shipping and the Economic Boom

Despite these restrictions on American commerce, the strong shipping trade begun during the colonial era and centered in the Atlantic ports became a major asset in the 1790s, when events in Europe provided America with extraordinary opportunities.

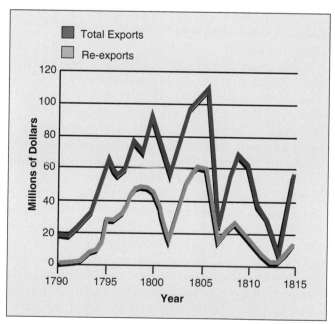

American Export Trade, 1790–1815   This graph shows how completely the American shipping boom was tied to European events. Exports, half of which were reexports, surged when Britain and France were at war and America could take advantage of its status as neutral. Exports slumped in the brief period of European peace in 1803–1805 and plunged following the Embargo Act of 1807 and the outbreak of the War of 1812.

SOURCE: Douglass C. North, *The Economic Growth of the United States, 1790–1860* (New York: Norton, 1966), p. 26.

The French Revolution, which began in 1789, soon initiated nearly twenty-five years of warfare between Britain and France. As the European powers converted their ships from international trade to military purposes, American vessels were ready to replace them. All along the Atlantic seaboard, urban centers thrived as American ships carried European goods that could no longer be transported on British ships without danger of French attack (and vice versa). Because America was neutral, its merchants had the legal right to import European goods and promptly reexport them to other European countries. In spite of British and French efforts to prevent the practice (see Chapter 8), reexports amounted to half of the profits in the booming shipping trade.

The vigorous international shipping trade had dramatic effects within the United States. The coastal cities all grew substantially from 1790 to 1820. In 1790, only twelve cities in the United States held more than 5,000 people and only 3 percent of the population was urban; by 1820 city dwellers made up 7 percent of the population and thirty-five cities had a population exceeding 5,000. This rapid urbanization was a sign of vigorous economic growth (rather than a sign that poverty was pushing rural workers off the farms, as occurs in some developing countries today), for it reflected expanding opportunities in the cities. In fact, the rapid growth of cities stimulated farmers to produce the food to feed the new urban dwellers. The long series of European wars also allowed enterprising Americans to seize such lucrative international opportunities as the China trade. In 1784 the *Empress of China* set sail from New York for Canton with forty tons of ginseng. When it returned in 1785 with a cargo of teas, silks, and chinaware, the sponsors of the voyage, Philadelphia financier Robert Morris and his partners, made a 30 percent profit. Other merchants were quick to follow Morris's example, and to improve on it. In 1787 Robert Gray left Boston in the *Columbia*, sailing south around Cape Horn, then north to Nootka Sound in the Pacific Northwest, where he bought sea otter skins cheaply from the coastal Indians. Then, in 1789, Gray sailed west across the Pacific to China, where he sold the furs at fabulous profits before rounding the Cape of Good Hope and returning to Boston laden with tea. In his second voyage in 1792, Gray discovered the mouth of a major Northwest river, which he named for his ship. (When Lewis and Clark ventured west in 1804, part of their task was to chart the exact path of Gray's "Columbia's River.") Soon New England so dominated the seaborne trade in furs to China that the Pacific Northwest Indians called all Americans "Bostons."

Built for speed, the narrow beamed, many-sailed American clipper ships were the technological marvel of their age. In 1854, the most famous clipper ship, *Flying Cloud,* shown here, made the voyage from New York to San Francisco in 89 days.

SOURCE: Museum of the City of New York/CORBIS.

The active American participation in international trade fostered a strong and diversified shipbuilding industry. All the major Atlantic ports boasted expanding shipbuilding enterprises. The average size of full-rigged ships built in one shipyard in Portsmouth, New Hampshire, increased from 361 tons in 1825 to 2,145 tons in 1855. Demands for speed increased as well, resulting in what many people have regarded as the flower of American shipbuilding, the clipper ship. The narrow-hulled, many-sailed clipper ships of the 1840s and 1850s set records for ships of their size. In 1854, *Flying Cloud*, built in the Boston shipyards of Donald McKay, sailed from New York to San Francisco—a 16,000-mile trip that usually took 150 to 200 days—in a mere 89 days. The clipper ships' average speed of 300 miles a day made them competitive with steamships through the 1850s.

In every seaport, this booming trade stimulated the development of financial services, such as insurance companies, banks, and brokers, geared more to international than to local concerns. By 1820, the United States was well on its way to building a strong and diversified national economy. At the same time, the wealth, confidence, and power of the merchants in the seacoast cities greatly increased.

THE JEFFERSON PRESIDENCY

Thomas Jefferson began his presidency with a symbolic action worthy of a twenty-first—century media-wise politician. At noon on March 4, 1801, he walked from his modest boardinghouse through the swampy streets of the new federal city of Washington to the unfinished Capitol. George Washington and John Adams had ridden in elaborate carriages to their inaugurals. Jefferson, although accepting a military honor guard, demonstrated by his actions that he rejected the elaborate, quasi-monarchical style of the two Federalist presidents, and their (to his mind) autocratic style of government as well.

For all its lack of pretension, Jefferson's inauguration as the third president of the United States was a momentous occasion in American history, for it marked the peaceful transition from one political party, the Federalists, to their hated rivals, the Jeffersonian

Tall, ungainly, and diffident in manner, Thomas Jefferson was nonetheless a man of genius. Jefferson designed and supervised every aspect of the building and furnishing of Monticello, his classical home atop a hill near Charlottesville, Virginia. The process took almost forty years (from 1770 to 1809), for Jefferson constantly changed and refined his design, subjecting both himself and his family to years of uncomfortable living in the partially completed structure. The result, however, was one of the most civilized—and most autobiographical— houses ever built.

SOURCE: Courtesy of the Library of Congress.

Republicans. Beginning in an atmosphere of exceptional political bitterness, Jefferson's presidency was to demonstrate that a strongly led party system could shape national policy without leading either to dictatorship or to revolt. It was a great achievement.

Republican Agrarianism

Jefferson brought to the presidency a clearly defined political philosophy. Behind all the events of his administration (1801–09) and those of his successors in what became known as the Virginia Dynasty (James Madison, 1809–17; James Monroe, 1817–25) was a clear set of beliefs that embodied Jefferson's interpretation of the meaning of republicanism for Americans.

Jefferson's years as ambassador to France in the 1780s were particularly important in shaping his political thinking. Recoiling from the extremes of wealth and poverty he saw there, he came to believe that it was impossible for Europe to achieve a just society that could guarantee to most of its members the "life, liberty and . . . pursuit of happiness" of which he had written in the Declaration of Independence.

The growth of the factory system in England horrified Jefferson, who deplored the squalor of teeming new factory towns such as Manchester in the north of England. He opposed industrialization in America: in the 1790s, when Alexander Hamilton and the Federalists had proposed fostering manufacturing in the United States, Jefferson had responded with outrage (see Chapter 8). He was convinced that the Federalist program would create precisely the same extremes of wealth and the same sort of unjust government that prevailed in Europe.

Jefferson believed that only America provided fertile earth for the true citizenship necessary to a republican form of government. What America had, and Europe lacked, was room to grow. Jefferson envisaged a nation of small family farms clustered together in rural communities—an agrarian republic. He believed that only a nation of roughly equal yeoman farmers, each secure in his own possessions and not dependent on someone else for his livelihood, would exhibit the concern for the community good that was essential in a republic. More romantically, Jefferson also believed that rural contact with the cycles and rhythms of nature was essential to the republican character. Indeed, Jefferson said that "those who labor in the earth are the chosen people of God," and so he viewed himself, though his "farm" was the large slave-owning plantation of Monticello.

Yet another European event influenced Jefferson's thinking. In 1798, the Englishman Thomas Malthus had published the deeply pessimistic and widely influential *Essay on the Principle of Population*. Warning of an impending population explosion, Malthus predicted that the British population would soon outstrip the country's food supply. Unless this population growth was checked, misery and poverty would soon be widespread throughout Europe and even, Malthus warned, in America. Malthus's prediction alarmed many Americans, who had taken pride in having one of the fastest rates of population growth in the world, close to 40

This symbol of the Philadelphia Society for Promoting Agriculture illustrates the principles of republican agrarianism. The yeoman farmer is ploughing his field under the approving gaze of the female figure of Columbia. His activity expresses the values of the American republic that she represents and in which Thomas Jefferson so strongly believed. As he said, "those who labor in the earth are the chosen people of God."

SOURCE: Library of Congress.

percent per decade. Thomas Jefferson was not worried. He used Malthus to underline the opportunity created by America's vast land resources. The Malthusian prediction need not trouble the United States, Jefferson said, as long as the country kept expanding.

Jefferson's vision of an expanding agrarian republic remains to this day one of our most compelling ideas about America's uniqueness and special destiny. But expansionism contained some negative aspects. The lure of the western lands fostered constant mobility and dissatisfaction rather than the stable, settled communities of yeoman farmers that Jefferson envisaged. Expansionism caused environmental damage, in particular soil exhaustion—a consequence of abandoning old lands, rather than conserving them, and moving on to new ones. Finally, expansionism bred a ruthlessness toward Indian peoples, who were pushed out of the way for white settlement or who, like the Mandans, were devastated by the diseases that accompanied European trade and contact. Jefferson's agrarianism thus bred some of the best and some of the worst traits of the developing nation.

Jefferson's Government

Thomas Jefferson came to office determined to reverse the Federalist policies of the 1790s and to ensure an agrarian "republic of virtue." Accordingly, he proposed a program of "simplicity and frugality," promising to cut all internal taxes, to reduce the size of the army (from 4,000 to 2,500 men), the navy (from twenty-five ships to seven), and the government staff, and to eliminate the entire national debt inherited from the Federalists. He kept all of these promises, even the last, although the Louisiana Purchase of 1803 cost the Treasury $15 million. This diminishment of government was a key matter of republican principle to Jefferson. If his ideal yeoman farmer was to be a truly self-governing citizen, the federal government must not, Jefferson believed, be either large or powerful. His cost-cutting measures simply carried out the pledge he had made in his inaugural address for "a wise and frugal government, which shall restrain men from injuring one another, [and] shall leave them otherwise free to regulate their own pursuits."

Perhaps one reason for Jefferson's success was that the federal government he headed was small and unimportant by today's standards. For instance, Jefferson found only 130 federal officials in Washington (a grand total of nine in the State Department, including the secretary of state). The national government's main service to ordinary people was mail delivery, and already in 1800 there were persistent complaints about slowness, unreliability, and expense in the Postal Service! Everything else—law and order, education, welfare, road maintenance, economic control—rested with state or local governments. Power and political loyalty were still local, not national.

This small national government also explains why for years the nation's capital was so unimpressive. The French designer Pierre L'Enfant had laid out a magnificent plan of broad streets and sweeping vistas reminiscent of Paris. Congress had planned to pay for the grand buildings with money from land sales in the new city, but few people besides politicians and boardinghouse keepers (a largely female occupation) chose to live in Washington. Construction lagged: the President's House lacked a staircase to the second floor until 1808, and although the House and Senate chambers were soon completed, the central portion of the Capitol was missing. Instead of the imposing dome we know so well today, the early Capitol consisted of two white marble boxes connected by a boardwalk. It is a telling indicator of the true location of national power that a people who had no trouble building new local communities across the continent should have had such difficulty establishing their federal city.

An Independent Judiciary

Although determined to reverse Federalist fiscal policies, Jefferson was much more moderate concerning Federalist officeholders. He resisted demands by other Jeffersonian Republicans that "the board should be swept" and all Federalist officeholders replaced with party loyalists. During his term of office, Jefferson allowed 132 Federalists to remain at their posts, while placing Jeffersonian Republicans in 158 other posts. This restrained use of patronage did much to attract moderate Federalists to the Jeffersonian Republican party. Jefferson's restraint, however, did not extend to the most notorious Federalist appointees, the so-called midnight judges. In the last days of the Adams administration, the Federalist-dominated Congress passed several acts that created new judgeships and other positions within the federal judiciary. In one of his last acts in office, President Adams appointed Federalists—quickly dubbed the "midnight judges"—to these new positions. William Marbury, whom President Adams had appointed Justice of the Peace for Washington, D.C., and three other appointees sued James Madison, Jefferson's secretary of state, to receive their commissions for their offices. Before the case came to trial, however, Congress, controlled by Jeffersonian Republicans who feared that the losing Federalist Party was trying to use the judiciary to increase the power of the federal government over the states, repealed the acts. This case, *Marbury* v. *Madison*, provoked a landmark decision from the Supreme Court, head of the federal judiciary.

At issue was a fundamental constitutional point: Was the federal judiciary an independent and final authority on questions of constitutional law, as Supreme Court decisions during the Federalist administrations of the 1790s had asserted, or did the election of a Jeffersonian

Republican administration that favored states' rights curtail the powers of federal courts as well? In his celebrated 1803 decision in *Marbury v. Madison*, Chief Justice John Marshall, himself a strong Federalist and an Adams appointee, managed to find a way to please both parties. On the one hand, Marshall proclaimed that the courts had a duty "to say what the law is," thus unequivocally defending the independence of the judiciary and the principle of judicial review. On the other hand, Marshall conceded that the Supreme Court was not empowered by the Constitution to force the executive branch to give Marbury his commission. At first glance, Jefferson's government appeared to have won the battle over Adams's last-minute appointees. But in the long run, Marshall established the principle that only the federal judiciary could decide what was constitutional. This was a vital

step in realizing the three-way balance of power among the branches of the federal government—executive (president), legislative (Congress), and judiciary (courts)—envisaged in the Constitution. Equally important, during his long tenure in office (1801–35), Chief Justice Marshall consistently led the Supreme Court in a series of decisions that favored the federal government over state governments. Under Marshall's direction, the Supreme Court became a powerful nationalizing force, often to the dismay of defenders of states' rights.

Opportunity: The Louisiana Purchase

In 1800 the United States was a new and fragile democracy in a world dominated by two contending great powers: Britain and France. If France sought to

WebExploration Follow the path of the Lewis and Clark expedition. How did the terrain influence the routes of the journey?
www.prenhall.com/faragher/Map9.1

Louisiana Purchase The Louisiana Purchase of 1803, the largest peaceful acquisition of territory in United States history, more than doubled the size of the nation. The Lewis and Clark expedition (1804–06) was the first to survey and document the natural and human richness of the area. The American sense of expansiveness and continental destiny owes more to the extraordinary opportunity provided by the Louisiana Purchase than to anything else.

regain territory that it had once held in North America, this would pose a threat to both American commerce and national security. In 1799, the young general Napoleon Bonaparte seized control of France and began a career of military conquests. Four years later, Great Britain went to war against him. Following one year of peace, Britain and France were again at war in 1803, beginning a twelve-year duel that ended only with Napoleon's defeat at the battle of Waterloo in 1815. As had his predecessors, Napoleon looked at North America as a potential battleground on which to fight the British. In 1800, in a secret treaty, France reacquired the Louisiana Territory, the vast western drainage of the Mississippi and Missouri rivers, from Spain, which had held the region since 1763. From Louisiana, if he chose, Napoleon could launch an attack to regain Canada from the British. As a springboard to a new French North American empire, in 1802 Napoleon sent an army of 30,000 to reconquer Haiti (the former Saint-Domingue) and thereby crush Afro-Caribbean dreams of independence.

When President Jefferson learned of the secret agreement in 1801, he was alarmed. He feared that French control would threaten the growing American trade on the Mississippi River and force the young nation to take military action. In fact, in 1802 the Spanish commander at New Orleans (the French had not yet taken formal control) closed the port to American shippers, thus disrupting commerce as far away as Cincinnati. As Jefferson feared, Federalists in Congress clamored for military action to reopen the port, and Jefferson was determined to end this threat to American commerce.

Initially, Jefferson offered to buy New Orleans and the surrounding area for $2 million (or up to $10 million, if necessary). As it happened, Napoleon was eager to sell. His army of 30,000 men had just withdrawn from Haiti, defeated by yellow fever as well as by an army of former slaves led by Toussaint L'Ouverture. In the wake of the French defeat, and in need of money for European military campaigns, Napoleon offered the entire Louisiana Territory, including the crucial port of New Orleans, to the Americans for $15 million. Exceeding his instructions, special American envoy James Monroe seized the opportunity and bought the entire Louisiana Territory from Napoleon in Paris in April 1803. Overnight, the size of the United States more than doubled. It was the largest peaceful acquisition of territory in United States history.

At home, Jefferson suffered brief qualms. The Constitution did not authorize the president to purchase territory, and Jefferson had always rigidly insisted on a limited interpretation of executive rights. But he had also long held a sense of destiny about the West and had planned the Lewis and Clark expedition

before the Louisiana Purchase was a reality. In any case, the prize was too rich to pass up. Jefferson now argued that Louisiana was vital to the nation's republican future. "By enlarging the empire of liberty," Jefferson wrote, "we . . . provide new sources of renovation, should its principles, at any time, degenerate, in those portions of our country which gave them birth." In other words, expansion was essential to liberty. Congress and the general public joined Jefferson in welcoming the purchase. Of course, the support was not unanimous. Some Federalists disputed Jefferson's claim that expansion would foster liberty and predicted that it would doom the republican form of government. As Federalist Fisher Ames dramatically warned, "By adding an unmeasured world beyond [the Mississippi] . . . we rush like a comet into infinity."

Incorporating Louisiana

The immediate issue following the Louisiana Purchase was how to treat the French and Spanish inhabitants of the Louisiana Territory. Many people thought that the only way to deal with a population so "foreign" was to wipe out its customs and laws and to impose American ones as quickly as possible. But this did not happen. The incorporation of Louisiana into the American federal system was a remarkable story of adaptation between two different communities—American and French.

In 1803, when the region that is now the state of Louisiana became American property, it had a racially and ethnically diverse population of 43,000 people, of whom only 6,000 were American. French and French-speaking people were numerically and culturally dominant, especially in the city of New Orleans. There the French community effectively challenged the initial American plan of rapidly supplanting French culture and institutions with American ones. At a public ball held in New Orleans in January 1804, for example, American and French military officers almost came to blows over whether an English country dance or a French waltz would be played first.

Officials in Washington dismissed the reported conflict as mere frivolity, but the U.S. representative in New Orleans and governor of Lower Louisiana Territory, William Claiborne, did not. Over the next four years Claiborne came to accept the value of French institutions to the region. As a result, with Claiborne's full support, Louisiana adopted a legal code in 1808 that was based on French civil law rather than English common law. This was not a small concession. French law differed from English law in many fundamental respects, such as in family property (communal versus male ownership), in inheritance (forced heirship versus free disposal), and even in contracts, which were much more strictly regulated in the French system. Remnants of the French legal system remain part of Louisiana state law to this day. In 1812, with the required 60,000 free inhabitants, Louisiana was admitted to the Union. New Orleans remained for years a distinctively French city, illustrating the flexibility possible under a federal system.

Texas and the Struggle for Mexican Independence

Spain objected, in vain, to Napoleon's 1803 sale of Louisiana to America. For years Spain had attempted to seal off its rich colony of Mexico from commerce with other nations. Now, American Louisiana shared one vague and disputed boundary with Mexico's northern province of Texas (a parcel of land already coveted by some Americans) and, on the east, a similarly uncertain boundary with Spanish Florida.

Soon Napoleon brought turmoil to all of Mexico. In 1808, having invaded Spain, he installed his brother Joseph Bonaparte as king, forcing Spain's king, Charles IV, to renounce his throne. For the next six years, as warfare convulsed Spain, the country's long-prized New World empire slipped away. Mexico, divided between royalists loyal to Spain and populists seeking social and economic justice for mestizos and Indians, edged bloodily toward independence. Two populist revolts—one in 1810 led by Father Miguel Hidalgo and the other in 1813 led by Father José María Morelos—were suppressed by the royalists, who executed both revolutionary leaders. In 1812 a small force, led by Mexican republican Bernardo Gutiérrez but composed mostly of American adventurers, invaded Texas, captured San Antonio, assassinated the provincial governor Manuel Salcedo, and declared Texas independent. A year later, however, the Mexican republicans were defeated by a royalist army, which then killed suspected collaborators and pillaged the province so thoroughly that the local economy was devastated. The Mexican population declined to fewer than 2,000. Under these circumstances, Mexico's difficult path toward independence seemed, at least to some Americans, to offer yet another opportunity for expansion.

RENEWED IMPERIAL RIVALRY IN NORTH AMERICA

Fresh from the triumph of the Louisiana Purchase, Jefferson scored a major victory over the Federalist Charles Cotesworth Pinckney in the presidential election of 1804, garnering 162 electoral votes to Pinckney's 14. Jefferson's shrewd wooing of moderate Federalists had been so successful that the remaining Federalists dwindled to a highly principled but sectional group, unable to attract voters outside of its home base in New England.

Jefferson's Louisiana success was not repeated, however, and few other consequences of the ongoing struggle between Britain and France were so easy to solve. Their rivalry caused problems for America both on the high seas and on the nation's western borders.

Problems with Neutral Rights

In his first inaugural address in 1801, Jefferson had announced a foreign policy of "peace, commerce, and honest friendship with all nations, entangling alliances with none." This was a difficult policy to pursue after 1803, when the Napoleonic Wars resumed. By 1805 Napoleon had conquered most of Europe, but Britain, the victor at the great naval battle of Trafalgar, controlled the seas. The United States, trying to profit from trade with both countries, was caught in the middle. The British did not look kindly as their former colonists tried to evade their blockade of the French by claiming neutrality. Beginning in 1805, the British targeted the American reexport trade between the French West Indies and France by seizing American ships that were bringing French West Indian goods to Europe. Angry Americans viewed these seizures as violations of their rights as shippers of a neutral nation.

An even more contentious issue arose from the substantial desertion rate of British sailors. Many deserters promptly signed up on American ships, where they drew better pay and sometimes obtained false naturalization papers as well. The numbers involved were large: as many as a quarter of the 100,000 seamen on American ships were British. Soon the British were stopping American merchant vessels and removing any man they believed to be British, regardless of his papers. The British refusal to recognize genuine naturalization papers (on the principle "once a British subject, always a British subject") was particularly insulting to the new American sense of nationhood.

At least 6,000 innocent American citizens suffered forced impressment into the British navy from 1803 to 1812. In 1807 impressment turned bloody when the British ship *Leopard* stopped the American ship *Chesapeake* in American territorial waters and demanded to search for deserters. When the American captain refused, the *Leopard* opened fire, killing three men, wounding eighteen, and removing four deserters (three with American naturalization papers) from the damaged ship. An indignant public protested British interference and the death of innocent sailors. Had Congress been in session and the country militarily strong, public pressure might very well have forced a declaration of war against Britain.

The Embargo Act

Fully aware that commerce was essential to the new nation, Jefferson was determined to insist on America's right as a neutral nation to ship goods to Europe. But Britain possessed the world's largest and strongest navy, one the small American navy could not effectively challenge. Jefferson first tried diplomatic protests, then negotiations, and finally threats, all to no avail. In 1806 Congress passed the Non-Importation Act, hoping that a boycott of British goods, which had worked so well during the Revolutionary War, would be effective once again. It was not. The boycott was suspended late in 1806 while the Jefferson administration tried to negotiate with the British; when that effort failed, the boycott was resumed. Finally, in desperation, Jefferson imposed the Embargo Act in December 1807. This act forbade American ships from sailing to any foreign port, thereby cutting off all exports as well as imports. The intent of the act was to force both Britian and France to recognize neutral rights by depriving them of American-shipped raw materials. Jefferson hoped especially for a speedy change of British policy, because Britain's large navy caused much more harm to American shipping than did the smaller French navy.

But the results were a disaster for American trade. The commerce of the new nation, which Jefferson himself had done so much to promote, came to a standstill. Exports fell from $108 million in 1807 to $22 million in 1808, and the nation was driven into a deep depression. There was widespread evasion of the embargo. A remarkable number of ships in the coastal trade found themselves "blown off course" to the West Indies or Canada. Other ships simply left port illegally. Smuggling flourished. Pointing out that the American navy's weakness was due largely to the deep cuts Jefferson had inflicted on it, the Federalists sprang to life with a campaign of outspoken opposition to Jefferson's policy, and they found a ready audience in New England, the area hardest hit by the embargo.

Madison and the Failure of "Peaceable Coercion"

In this troubled atmosphere, Thomas Jefferson despondently ended his second term, acknowl-edging the failure of what he called "peaceable coercion." He was followed in office by his friend and colleague James Madison of Virginia. Although Madison defeated the Federalist candidate—again Charles Cotesworth Pinkney—by 122 electoral votes to 47, Pinckney's share of the votes was three times what it had been in 1804, a reflection of the resentment New Englanders felt to the disproportionate hardships they suffered from the Embargo Act.

Ironically, the Embargo Act had almost no effect on its intended victims. The French used the embargo as a pretext for seizing American ships, claiming they must be British ships in disguise. The British, in the absence of American competition, developed new markets for their goods in South America. And at home, as John Randolph sarcastically remarked, the embargo was attempting "to cure corns by cutting off the toes." In March 1809, Congress admitted failure and the Embargo Act was repealed. But the struggle to remain neutral in the confrontation between the European giants continued. The next two years saw passage of several acts—among them the Non-Intercourse Act of 1809 and Macon's Bill Number 2 in 1810—that unsuccessfully attempted to prohibit trade with Britain and France unless they ceased their hostile treatment of U.S. shipping. Frustration with the ineffectiveness of government policy mounted.

This double portrait of two Sac Indians by John Wesley Jarvis, painted in 1833, symbolized the hopes of official American Indian policy. The traditional Indian ways represented by Whirling Thunder's attire would be superseded by the "civilized" attitude represented by his father Black Hawk's European dress.

SOURCE: John Wesley Jarvis, *Black Hawk and His Son, Whirling Thunder,* 1833. Oil on canvas. 23" x 30". (60.3 x 76 cm.) Gilcrease Museum, Tulsa, Oklahoma.

A Contradictory Indian Policy

The United States also faced other conflicts besides those with Britain and France over neutral shipping rights. In the West, the powerful Indian nations of the Ohio Valley were determined to resist the wave of expansion that had carried thousands of white settlers onto their lands. North of the Ohio River lived the Northwest Confederation of the Shawnees, Delawares, Miamis, Potawatomis, and several smaller tribes. To the south of the Ohio were the so-called "Five Civilized Tribes," the Cherokees, Chickasaws, Choctaws, Creeks, and (in Florida) the Seminoles.

According to the Indian Intercourse Act of 1790, the United States could not simply seize Indian land; it could only acquire it when the Indians ceded it by treaty. But this policy conflicted with the harsh reality of westward expansion. Commonly, settlers pushed ahead of treaty boundaries. When Indian peoples re- sisted the invasion of their lands, the pioneers fought back and called for military protection. Defeat of an Indian people led to further land cessions. The result for the Indians was a relentless cycle of invasion, resistance, and defeat.

Thomas Jefferson was deeply concerned with the fate of the western Indian peoples. Unlike most of the pioneers, who saw them simply as dangerous obstacles to be removed, Jefferson believed in coexistence and acculturation. His Indian policy was designed to solve the fundamental dilemma of expansion—the conflicting needs of white and Indian peoples. The Indians would cede the lands the pioneers craved, and in return white people would teach them how to farm and live like whites on their new, compressed reservations. Convinced that Indians had to give up hunting in favor of the yeoman-farmer lifestyle he so favored for all Americans, Jefferson

Tecumseh, a Shawnee military leader, and his brother Tenskwatawa, a religious leader called The Prophet, led a pan-Indian revitalization and resistance movement that posed a serious threat to American westward expansion. Tecumseh traveled widely, attempting to build a military alliance on his brother's spiritual message. He achieved considerable success in the Old Northwest, but less in the Old Southwest, where many Indian peoples put their faith in accommodation. Tecumseh's death at the Battle of the Thames (1813) and British abandonment of their Shawnee allies at the end of the War of 1812 brought an end to organized Indian resistance in the Old Northwest.

SOURCE: The Field Museum of Natural History; Library of Congress.

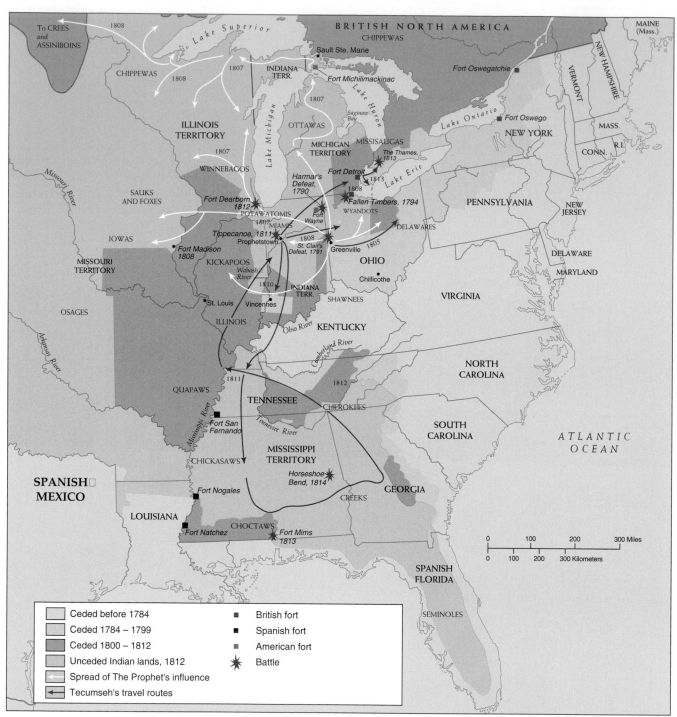

Indian Resistance, 1790–1816   American westward expansion put relentless pressure on the Indian nations in the Trans-Appalachian South and West. The Trans-Appalachian region was marked by constant warfare from the time of the earliest settlements in Kentucky in the 1780s to the War of 1812. Tecumseh's Alliance in the Old Northwest (1809–11) and the Creek Rebellion in the Old Southwest (1813–14) were the culminating struggles in Indian resistance to the American invasion of the Trans-Appalachian region.

directed the governors of the Northwest Territories to "promote energetically" his vision for civilizing the Indians.

Although he was notoriously indifferent to organized religion, Jefferson strongly supported efforts to

Christianize Indian peoples and educate them in white ways. A number of denominations, among them the Moravians, Quakers, and Baptists, sent missionaries to the western Indians. Others formed special missionary societies, such as the Society for Propagating the

Gospel among Indians (1797) and the American Board of Commissioners for Foreign Missions (1810). The latter was a joint effort of the Congregationalist, Presbyterian, and Dutch Reformed churches. Jefferson's Indian civilization plan was never adequately funded by Congress or supported by territorial governors and settlers. Although missionaries promoted literacy and a knowledge of white ways, they were generally disdainful of Indian culture. This created deep divisions within Indian tribes between those who converted to Christianity and those who actively resisted conversion and were unwilling to give up traditional ways, especially their hunting culture. Thus missionary efforts unwittingly weakened tribes already disoriented by the loss of their lands and lifeways.

After the Louisiana Purchase, Jefferson offered traditionalist Indian groups new lands west of the Mississippi River, claiming that they would be able to live there undisturbed by white settlers for centuries. But he failed to consider the pace of westward expansion. Less than twenty years later, Missouri, the first trans-Mississippi state, was admitted to the Union. The Indians living in Missouri, some of whom had been removed from the Old Northwest in accord with Jefferson's plan, were forced to move again to lands farther west. Western Indians like the Mandans, who had seemed so remote when Lewis and Clark wintered with them in 1804–05, were now threatened by further westward expansion.

In fact, Jefferson's Indian policy, because it did nothing to slow down the ever-accelerating westward expansion, offered little hope to Indian peoples. The alternatives they faced were stark: acculturation, removal, or extinction. Deprived of hunting lands, decimated by disease, increasingly dependent on the white economy for trade goods and annuity payments in exchange for land cessions, many Indian peoples despaired. Like the Mandans after Lewis and Clark's visit, they came to dread the effects of white contact. Nearly every tribe found itself bitterly split between accommodationists and traditionalists. Some, like groups of Cherokees and associated tribes in the South, advocated adapting their traditional agricultural lifestyles and pursuing a pattern of peaceful accommodation. In the Northwest Territory, however, many Indians chose the path of armed resistance.

Indian Resistance

The Shawnees, a seminomadic hunting and farming tribe (the men hunted, the women farmed) of the Ohio Valley, had resisted white settlement in Kentucky and Ohio since the 1750s. The decisive defeat of the Indian Confederacy led by Little Turtle, a Miami Indian, at Fallen Timbers (1794) and the continuing pressure of American settlement, however, had left the

Shawnees divided. One group, led by Black Hoof, accepted acculturation. Soon Quaker and Moravian missionaries were converting Black Hoof's band, teaching them farming. The rest of the tribe tried to maintain traditional ways. Most broke into small bands and tried to eke out a living by hunting, but their numbers were reduced by disease and the survivors were further demoralized by the alcohol offered them illegally by private traders. One group of traditional Shawnees, however, led by the warrior Tecumseh, sought refuge farther west.

But there was no escape from white encroachment. Between 1801 and 1809, William Henry Harrison, governor of Indiana Territory, concluded fifteen treaties with the Delawares, Potawatomis, Miamis, and other tribes. These treaties opened eastern Michigan, southern Indiana, and most of Illinois to white settlement and forced the Indians into ever-smaller reservations. Many of these treaties were obtained by coercion, bribery, and outright trickery, and most Indians did not accept them.

In 1805 Tecumseh's brother, Tenskwatawa, known as The Prophet, began preaching a message of Indian revitalization: a rejection of all contact with the Americans, including the use of American alcohol, clothing, and trade goods, and a return to traditional practices of hunting and farming. He preached an end to quarreling, violence, and sexual promiscuity and to the accumulation of private property. Wealth was valuable only if it was given away, he said. If the Northwest Indians returned to traditional ways, Tenskwatawa promised, "the land will be overturned so that all the white people will be covered and you alone shall inhabit the land."

This was a powerful message, but it was not new. Just six years earlier, Handsome Lake had led the Seneca people of upstate New York in a similar revitalization movement. Tecumseh, however, succeeded in molding his brother's religious following into a powerful pan-Indian military resistance movement. With each new treaty that Harrison concluded, Tecumseh gained new followers among the Northwest Confederation tribes. Significantly, he also had the support of the British, who, after 1807, began sending food and guns to him from Canada.

The pan-Indian strategy was at first primarily defensive, aimed at preventing further westward expansion. But the Treaty of Fort Wayne in 1809, in which the United States gained 3 million acres of Delaware and Potawatomi land in Indiana, led to active resistance. Confronting Harrison directly, Tecumseh argued that the land belonged to the larger community of all the Indian peoples; no one tribe could give away the common property of all. He then warned that any surveyors or settlers who ventured into the 3 million acres would risk their lives.

Tecumseh took his message of common land ownership and military resistance to all the Indian peoples of the Northwest Confederacy. He was not uniformly successful, even among the Shawnees. Black Hoof, for example, refused to join. Tecumseh also recruited, with mixed success, among the tribes south of the Ohio River. In councils with Choctaws, Chickasaws, Creeks, and Cherokees, he promoted active resistance:

> The white race is a wicked race. Since the days when the white race first came in contact with the red men, there has been a continual series of aggressions. The hunting grounds are fast disappearing, and they are driving the red man farther and farther to the west. Such has been the fate of the Shawnees, and surely will be the fate of all tribes if the power of the whites is not forever crushed. The mere presence of the white man is a source of evil to the red men. His whiskey destroys the bravery of our warriors, and his lust corrupts the virtue of our women. The only hope for the red man is a war of extermination against the paleface.

In November 1811, while Tecumseh was still recruiting among the southern tribes, Harrison marched to the pan-Indian village of Tippecanoe with 1,000 soldiers. The 600 to 700 Indian warriors at the town, urged on by Tenskwatawa, attacked Harrison's forces before dawn on November 7, hoping to surprise them. The attack failed, and in the battle that followed the Americans inflicted about 150 Indian casualties, while sustaining about as many themselves. Although Harrison claimed victory, the truth was far different. Dispersed from Tippecanoe, Tecumseh's angry followers fell on American settlements in Indiana and southern Michigan, killing many pioneers and forcing the rest to flee to fortified towns. Tecumseh himself entered into a formal alliance with the British. For western settlers, the Indian threat was greater than ever.

THE WAR OF 1812

Many westerners blamed the British for Tecumseh's attacks on pioneer settlements in the Northwest. British support of western Indians and the long-standing difficulties over neutral shipping rights were the two grievances cited by President Madison when he asked Congress for a declaration of war against Britain on June 1, 1812. Congress obliged him on June 18. But the war had other, more general causes as well.

The War of 1812 On land, the War of 1812 was fought to define the nation's boundaries. In the North, American armies attacked British forts in the Great Lakes region with little success, and the invasion of Canada was a failure. In the South, the Battle of New Orleans made a national hero of Andrew Jackson, but it occurred after the peace treaty had been signed. On the sea, with the exception of Oliver Perry's victory in the Great Lakes, Britain's dominance was so complete and its blockade so effective that British troops were able to invade the Chesapeake and burn the capital of the United States.

The War Hawks

A rising young generation of political leaders, first elected to Congress in 1810, strongly resented the continuing influence of Britain, the former mother country, on American affairs. These War Hawks, who included such future leaders as Henry Clay of Kentucky and John C. Calhoun of South Carolina, were young Jeffersonian Republicans from the West and South. They found all aspects of British interference, such as impressment of sailors and support for western Indians, intolerable. Eager to assert independence from England once and for all, these young men saw themselves finishing the job begun by the aging revolutionary generation.

The War Hawks were vehemently expansionist, and their dreams of expansion entailed control of peoples of other races—resistant Indians and rebellious African Americans—at the edges of the national boundaries. Southerners wanted to occupy Florida to prevent runaway slaves from seeking refuge with the Seminole Indians. Westerners wanted to invade Canada, hoping thereby to end threats from British-backed Indians in the Northwest, such as Tecumseh and his followers. As resentments against England and frustrations over border issues merged, the pressure for war—always a strong force for national unity—mounted.

Unaware that the British, seriously hurt by the American trade embargo, were about to adopt a more conciliatory policy, President James Madison yielded to the War Hawks' clamor for action in June 1812, and his declaration of war passed the U.S. Senate by the close vote of 19 to 13, the House by 79 to 49. All the Federalists voted against the war. (The division along party lines continued in the 1812 presidential election, in which Madison garnered 128 electoral votes to 89 for his Federalist opponent, DeWitt Clinton.) The vote was sectional, with New England and the Middle States in opposition and the West and South strongly prowar. Thus the United States entered the War of 1812 more deeply divided along sectional lines than during any other foreign war in American history. Nor was that the end of the difficulties. As a result of Jefferson's economizing, the American army and navy were small and weak. In contrast, the British, after almost ten years' entanglement in the Napoleonic Wars, were in fighting trim. As a result, although the War of 1812 brought Americans a few moments of glory, it was on the whole an ignominious struggle that gained them little.

The Campaign against Canada

The American goal of expansion fared badly. Americans envisaged a quick victory over sparsely populated British Canada that would destroy British support for Tecumseh and his Northwest Indian allies, but instead the British-Indian alliance defeated them. In July 1812, a foray into western Canada by General William Hull of Michigan Territory was repulsed by a joint British and Indian force, which went on, in August, to capture Detroit, Fort Dearborn (site of Chicago), and Hull's army of 2,000 men. The American burning of York (now Toronto) in April 1813 achieved little, but in September, at the battle of Put-in-Bay, Captain Oliver H. Perry defeated a British naval squadron on Lake Erie, sending out the famous message, "We have met the enemy and they are ours." Without control of Lake Erie, the British could no longer assure their hold on Detroit. In October, William Henry Harrison retook Detroit and followed its retreating British and Indian defenders. Assisted by naval forces commanded by Perry, Harrison defeated them in the battle of the Thames. Among those slain in the battle was Tecumseh. Later attempts by the United States to invade Canada in the Niagara area failed, but so too did British attempts to invade the United States in the same area.

One reason for the abortive Canadian invasion, aside from failure to appreciate the strength of the British-Indian forces, was that the New England states actively opposed the war. Massachusetts, Rhode Island, and Connecticut refused to provide militia or supplies, and other New England governors turned a blind eye to the flourishing illegal trade across the U.S.–Canadian border. Another reason was the reaction of Canadians themselves, the majority of whom were former Americans. Ironically, the most decisive effect of the American attacks was the formation of a Canadian sense of national identity and a determination never to be invaded or absorbed by the United States.

War in the South

In the South, warfare similar to that waged against Tecumseh's pan-Indian resistance movement in the Northwest dramatically affected the southern Indian peoples. The first of the southern Indian peoples to battle the Americans were the Creeks, a trading nation with a long history of contacts with the Spanish and French. When white settlers began to occupy Indian lands in northwestern Georgia and central Alabama early in the nineteenth century, the Creeks, like the Shawnees in the Northwest, were divided in their response. Although many Creek bands argued for accommodation, a group known as the Red Sticks were determined to fight. During the War of 1812 the Red Sticks, allied with the British and Spanish, fought not only the Americans but other Indian groups.

In August 1813, the Red Sticks attacked Fort Mims on the Alabama River, killing more than 500 Americans and mixed-race Creeks who had gathered there for safety. Led by Andrew Jackson, troops from the

Tennessee and Kentucky militias combined with the Creeks' traditional foes—the Cherokees, Choctaws, and Chickasaws—and some opposing bands of Creeks to exact revenge. Jackson's troops matched the Creeks in ferocity, shooting the Red Sticks "like dogs," one soldier reported. At the battle of Horseshoe Bend in March 1814, the Creeks were trapped between American cannon fire and their Indian enemies: more than 800 were killed, more than in any other battle in the history of Indian-white warfare. Jackson then marched on the remaining Red Stick villages, burning and killing as he went. Cornered, one remaining Red Stick leader, Red Eagle, personally confronted Jackson:

> General Jackson, I am not afraid of you. I fear no man, for I am a Creek warrior. I have nothing to request in behalf of myself. . . . But I come to beg you to send for the women and children of the war party, who are now starving in the woods. . . . If I could fight you any longer I would most heartily do so. Send for the women and children. They never did you any harm. But kill me, if the white people want it done.

At the end of the Creek War in 1814 Jackson demanded huge land concessions from the Creeks (including from some Creek bands that had fought on his side): 23 million acres, or more than half the Creek domain. The Treaty of Fort Jackson (1814) confirming these land concessions earned Jackson his Indian name, Sharp Knife.

The war failed to achieve another of its initial goals, that of capturing Florida from Spain. Mobile was captured in 1813, but although Jackson captured Pensacola in 1814, he was unable to hold it.

In early 1815 (after the peace treaty had been signed but before news of it arrived in America), Andrew Jackson achieved his best-known victory, an improbable win over veteran British troops in the battle of New Orleans.

The Naval War

At sea the British navy quickly established a strong blockade, harassing coastal shipping along the Atlantic seaboard and attacking coastal settlements at will. In the most humiliating attack, the British burned Washington in the summer of 1814, forcing the president and Congress to flee. Dolley Madison, the president's wife, achieved a permanent footnote in history by saving a portrait of George Washington from the White House as she fled. The indignity of the burning of Washington was somewhat assuaged in September, when Americans beat back a British attack on Baltimore and Fort

Most of the important battles of the War of 1812 were fought on the Canadian border, on water as well as on land. This picture celebrates a rare American naval triumph in the war, the victory of Captain Oliver T. Perry over a British naval squadron on Lake Erie in September 1813. SOURCE: Bettmann/CORBIS.

McHenry. Watching the "rockets' red glare" in the battle, onlooker Francis Scott Key was moved to write the words to the "Star-Spangled Banner." There were a few American naval successes. The American frigate *Constitution*, known as "Old Iron Sides," destroyed two British men-of-war, the *Guerrière* and the *Java*, in classic naval battles, but these failed to lift the British blockade.

The Hartford Convention

America's occasional successes failed to diminish the angry opposition of the New England Federalists to the War of 1812. In late 1814, Federalist representatives from the five New England states met in Hartford, Connecticut, to air their grievances. At first the air was full of talk of secession from the Union, but soon cooler heads prevailed. The Hartford Convention's final document contained a long list of grievances, but it did not mention secession. It did, however, insist that a state had the right "to interpose its authority" to protect its citizens against unconstitutional federal laws. This nullification doctrine was not new; Madison and Jefferson had proposed it in the Virginia and Kentucky Resolves opposing the Alien and Sedition Acts in 1798 (see Chapter 8). In any event, the nullification threat from Hartford was ignored, for peace with Britain was announced as delegates from the convention made their way to Washington to deliver their message to Congress. There, the convention's grievances were treated not as serious business but as an anticlimactic joke.

The Treaty of Ghent

In 1814, as the long Napoleonic Wars in Europe were drawing to a close, the British decided to end their minor war with the Americans. The peace treaty, after months of hard negotiation, was signed at Ghent, Belgium, on Christmas Eve in 1814. Like the war itself, the treaty was inconclusive. The major issues of impressment and neutral rights were not mentioned, but the British did agree to evacuate their western posts, and late in the negotiations they abandoned their insistence on a buffer state for neutral Indian peoples in the Northwest.

For all its international inconsequence, the war did have an important effect on national morale. As one historian has said, Americans had fought "for their chance to grow up." Andrew Jackson's victory at New Orleans allowed Americans to believe that they had defeated the British. It would be more accurate to say that by not losing the war the Americans had ended their own feelings of colonial dependency. Equally important, they convinced the British government to stop thinking of America as its colony. As it turned out, the War of 1812 was the last war the United States and Britain were to fight against each other.

At the same time, the war was a dangerous risk to new and fragile ideas of national unity. It was one of America's most divisive wars, and what made the opposition so serious was its sectional nature. Had the conflict continued, it might have led to the secession of New England. The only clear losers of the war were the Indian nations in the Northwest and their southern allies. With the death of Tecumseh in 1813 and the defeat of the southern Creeks in 1814, the last hope of a united Indian resistance to white expansion perished forever. Britain's abandonment of its Indian allies in the Treaty of Ghent sealed their fate. By 1815, American settlers were on their way west again.

DEFINING THE BOUNDARIES

With the War of 1812 behind them, Americans turned, more seriously than ever before, to the tasks of expansion and national development. The so-called Era of Good Feelings (1817–23) found politicians largely in agreement on a national agenda, and a string of diplomatic

Spread of Settlement: Westward Surge, 1800–1820   Within a period of twenty years, a quarter of the nation's population had moved west of the Appalachian Mountains. The westward surge was a dynamic source of American optimism.

achievements forged by John Quincy Adams gave the nation sharper definition. But the limits to expansion also became clear: the Panic of 1819 showed the dangers in economic growth, and the Missouri Crisis laid bare the sectional split that attended westward expansion.

Another Westward Surge

The end of the War of 1812 was followed by a westward surge to the Mississippi River that populated the Old Northwest (Ohio, Indiana, Illinois, Michigan, and Wisconsin) and the Old Southwest (western Georgia, Alabama, Mississippi, and Louisiana). The extent of the population redistribution was dramatic: in 1790, about 95 percent of the nation's population had lived in states bordering the Atlantic Ocean; by 1820 fully 25 percent of the population lived west of the Appalachians.

What accounted for the westward surge? There were both push and pull factors. Between 1800 and 1820, the nation's population almost doubled, increas-

ing from 5.3 million to 9.6 million. Although many easterners were attracted to the rapidly growing seacoast cities, 2.5 million, most of them farmers, chose to go westward. Overpopulated farmland in all of the seaboard states pushed farmers off the land, while new land pulled them westward. The defeat and removal of Indians in the War of 1812 was another important pull factor. In the Southwest, the Creeks ceded a huge tract of land amounting to three-fifths of Alabama and one-fifth of Georgia in the Treaty of Fort Jackson (1814); in the Northwest, the threat to settlers posed by Tecumseh's alliance had been removed.

The most important pull factor, however, was the attractive price of western land. The Land Ordinance of 1785 priced western lands too high for all but speculators and the wealthy (see Chapter 7), but subsequent realities had slowly forced Congress to enact land laws more favorable to the small farmer. The most sustained challenge came from "squatters," who repeatedly took up land before it was officially open for sale and then claimed a "preemption" right of purchase at a lower price that reflected the value of improvements they made to the land. Congress sought to suppress this illegal settlement and ordered the expulsion of squatters on several occasions, but to no avail. When federal lands were officially opened for sale in Illinois in 1814, for example, there were already 13,000 settlers, forcing Congress to reverse itself and grant them all preemption rights.

Settlement of the heavily forested Old Northwest and Old Southwest required much heavy labor to clear the land. One common laborsaving method settlers learned from Indians was to "girdle" the trees (cutting the bark all around), thereby killing them. Dead trees could be more easily chopped and burned. SOURCE: Library of Congress

Western Land Sales Surges in western land sales reflect surges in westward expansion. Western land sales following the War of 1812 reached an unprecedented 3.5 million acres, but that was small in comparison with what was to come in the 1830s and 1850s. Not all land sales reflected actual settlement, however, and speculation in western lands was rampant. Collapse of the postwar speculative boom contributed to the Panic of 1819, and the abrupt end to the boom of the 1830s led to the Panic of 1837.

SOURCE: Robert Riegel and Robert Athearn, *America Moves West* (New York: Holt, Rinehart, 1964).

Look at the different migration routes favored by Americans between 1800 and 1820. How did westward movement vary by region?
www.prenhall.com/faragher/Map9.2

Web Exploration

Major Migration Routes, 1800–1820   The barrier of the Appalachian Mountains permitted only a few routes to the west. Settlers from the northern states took the Genesee Turnpike, Middle States migrants favored the Philadelphia-Pittsburgh Turnpike and the National Road, and Southerners used the Wilderness and Federal Roads. Because most westward movement was lateral, regional mixing among western settlers was rare. New Englanders carried their attitudes West, and Southerners did the same.

SOURCE: Donald Meinig, *The Shaping of America*, vol. 2, Continental America (New Haven, CT: Yale University Press, 1994).

There were four major migration routes. In upstate New York, the Mohawk and Genesee Turnpike led New England migrants to Lake Erie, where they traveled by boat to northern Ohio. In the Middle States region, the turnpike from Philadelphia to Pittsburgh led to the Ohio River, as did the National Road that began in Baltimore and led to Wheeling. In the South, the Wilderness Road through the Cumberland Gap led to Kentucky, and passes in the mountains of North and South Carolina led to Tennessee. The Federal Road skirted the southern edge of the Appalachians and allowed farmers from South Carolina and eastern Georgia to move directly into Alabama and Mississippi. In this way, geography facilitated lateral westward movement (Northerners tended to migrate to the Old Northwest, Southerners to the Old Southwest). Except in southern Ohio and parts of Kentucky and Tennessee, there was very little contact between regional cultures. New Englanders carried their values and lifestyles directly west and settled largely with their own communities; Southerners did the same.

One section of northern Ohio along Lake Erie, for example, had been Connecticut's western land claim since the days of its colonial charter. Rather than give up the land when the Northwest Territory was established in 1787, Connecticut held onto the Western Reserve (as it was known) and encouraged its citizens to move there. Group settlement was common. General Moses Cleaveland of the Revolutionary War led one of the first groups of Yankees, fifty-two in all. In 1795 they settled the community that bears his name (though not his spelling of it). Many other groups followed, naming towns such as Norwalk after those they had left in Connecticut. These New Englanders brought to the

Finally, in the Land Act of 1820, Congress set the price of land at $1.25 an acre, the minimum purchase at eighty acres (in contrast to the 640-acre minimum in 1785), and a down payment of $100 in cash. This was the most liberal land law yet passed in American history, but the cash requirement still favored speculators, who had more cash than most small farmers.

Western Reserve their religion (Congregational), their love of learning (tiny Norwalk soon boasted a three-story academy), and their adamant opposition to slavery.

Western migration in the South was very different. Just as on other frontiers, pioneers hacked wagon roads through the wilderness, encountered resistance from Indian peoples, and cleared the land for settlements and farms. But on this frontier, the hands on the ax handle were likely to be black, the people clearing the land doing it not for themselves but to create plantations for slave owners. More than half of the migrants to the Old Southwest after 1812 were involuntary—enslaved African Americans.

Even before the war, plantation owners in the Natchez district of Mississippi had made fortunes growing cotton, which they shipped to Britain from New Orleans. After the war, as cotton growing expanded, hopeful slave owners from older parts of the South (Virginia, North and South Carolina, Georgia) flooded into the region. The movement was like a gold rush, characterized by high hopes, land speculation, and riches—for a few. Most of the settlers in the Old Southwest were small farm families living in forest clearings. Most did not own slaves, but they hoped to, for ownership of slaves was the means to wealth. The lifestyle and values of older southern states were quickly replicated on this new frontier.

The western transplantation of distinctive regional cultures explains why, although by 1820 western states accounted for more than a third of all states (eight out of twenty-three), the West did not form a third, unified political region. Although there were common western issues—in particular, the demand for better roads and other transportation routes—communities in the Old Northwest, in general, shared New England political attitudes, whereas those in the Old Southwest shared southern attitudes.

The Second Great Awakening on the Frontier

The religious movement known as the Second Great Awakening began quietly in the 1790s in New England, but by 1800 it had spread through the Protestant churches of the entire country. It was most dramatic on the frontier, where church organization was naturally weak. The great institution of western Protestantism became the "camp meeting," an outdoor gathering that included many sects and might go on for days. The greatest of the early camp meetings took place at Cane Ridge, Kentucky, in 1801, when an estimated 20,000 people came together for a week of preaching and singing. This was a remarkable assembly considering that the largest town in the West at the time had fewer than 2,000 inhabitants. Preachers shouted from the stand, and in the flickering firelight of evening hun-

dreds of people, overcome with religious enthusiasm, fell into speaking in tongues or jerking uncontrollably. "Many things transpired there," one observer wrote, "that had the same effects as miracles on infidels and unbelievers."

Organized religion became one of the most important institutions within the continuing westward migration. Camp meetings frequently provided the first occasion for the new settlers of an area to come together, and religious meetinghouses were often the first public buildings erected in a community. In the absence of resident ministers, preaching was provided by Methodist circuit riders or perhaps a Baptist farmer who heard "the call" and had himself licensed as a lay preacher. On the frontier as well as in the East, women were often in the majority among church members. They thus played an important role in an institution that was fundamental to the planting of new American communities.

The Election of 1816 and the Era of Good Feelings

In 1816 James Monroe, the last of the Virginia Dynasty, was easily elected president over his Federalist opponent Rufus King (183 to 34 electoral votes). This was the last election in which Federalists ran a candidate. Monroe had no opponent in 1820 and was re-elected nearly unanimously (231 to 1). The triumph of the Jeffersonian Republicans over the Federalists seemed complete. But although the Republicans kept their name, they had accepted so many Federalist political principles that it was not easy to tell which party had actually triumphed.

Tall, dignified, dressed in the old-fashioned style of knee breeches and white-topped boots that Washington had worn, Monroe looked like a traditional figure. But his politics reflected changing times. Soon after his inauguration, the president made a goodwill tour of the country, the first president since Washington to do so. Reflecting the new geography of the nation, he went the farthest west any president had yet traveled to visit the frontier post of Detroit. When he visited Boston, as recently as 1815 the heart of a secession-minded Federalist region, he received an enthusiastic welcome, prompting the Federalist *Columbian Centinel* to proclaim an "Era of Good Feelings." The phrase has been applied to Monroe's presidency (1817–25) ever since.

Monroe sought a government of national unity, and he chose men from North and South, Jeffersonian Republicans and Federalists, for his cabinet. He selected John Quincy Adams, a former Federalist, as his secretary of state, virtually assuring that Adams, like his father, would become president. To balance Adams,

The rural and community nature of the Second Great Awakening is captured in this illustration. The preacher exhorts the large audience, which responds with emotion. Many of the most enthusiastic converts were women, who gained a new feeling of moral and social consequence through their religious experience.

SOURCE: *Camp Meeting.* Color lithograph by Kennedy and Lucas, after a painting by A. Rider, ca. 1835, negative number 26275. Collection of the New York Historical Society, New York City.

Monroe picked John C. Calhoun of South Carolina, a prominent War Hawk, as secretary of war. And Monroe supported the American System, a program of national economic development that became identified with Westerner Henry Clay, Speaker of the House of Representatives.

In supporting the American System, Monroe was following President Madison, who had proposed the program in his message to Congress in December 1815. Madison and Monroe broke with Jefferson's agrarianism to embrace much of the Federalist program for economic development, including the chartering of a national bank, a tax on imported goods to protect American manufacturers, and a national system of roads and canals. All three of these had first been proposed by Alexander Hamilton in the 1790s (see Chapter 8). At the time these proposals had met with bitter Jeffersonian Republican opposition. The support that

Madison and Monroe gave to Hamilton's ideas following the War of 1812 was a crucial sign of the dynamism of the American commercial economy. Many Republicans now acknowledged that the federal government had a role to play in fostering the economic and commercial conditions in which both yeoman farmer and merchant could succeed. This active support for capitalist development explained why so many former Federalists were willing to join Monroe's party of national unity.

In 1816 Congress chartered the Second Bank of the United States for twenty years. Located in Philadelphia, the bank had a capital of $35 million, of which the government contributed $7 million. The bank was to provide the large-scale financing that the smaller state banks could not handle and to create a strong national currency. Because they feared concentrated economic power, Jeffersonian Republicans had allowed the charter of the original Bank of the United States, founded in 1791, to expire in 1811. The Republican about-face in 1816 was a sign that the strength of commercial interests had grown to rival that of farmers, whose distrust for central banks persisted.

The Tariff of 1816 was the first substantial protective tariff in American history. In 1815, British manufacturers, who had been excluded for eight years (from the Embargo Act of 1807 to the end of the War of 1812), flooded the United States market with their products. American manufacturers complained that the British were dumping goods below cost in order to prevent the growth of American industries. Congress responded with a tariff on imported woolens and cottons, on iron, leather, hats, paper, and sugar. The measure had southern as well as northern support, although in later years differences over the passage of higher tariffs would become one of the most persistent sources of sectional conflict.

The third item in the American System, funding for roads and canals—internal improvements, as they came to be known—was more controversial. Monroe and Madison both supported genuinely national (that is, interstate) projects such as the National Road from Cumberland, Maryland, to Vandalia, Illinois. Congressmen, however, aware of the urgent need to improve transportation in general and sensing the political advantages that could accrue to them from directing funds to their districts, proposed spending federal money on local projects. Both Madison and Monroe vetoed such local proposals, believing them to be unconstitutional. Thus it was that some of the most famous projects of the day, such as the Erie Canal, which lay wholly within New York state, and the early railroads, were financed by state or private money.

The support of Madison and Monroe for measures initially identified with their political opposition was an indicator of their realism. The three aspects of the American System—bank, tariff, roads—were all parts of the basic infrastructure that the American economy needed in order to develop. Briefly, during the Era of Good Feelings, politicians agreed about the need for all three. Later, each would be a source of heated partisan argument.

The Diplomacy of John Quincy Adams

The diplomatic achievements of the Era of Good Feelings were due almost entirely to the efforts of one man, John Quincy Adams, Monroe's secretary of state. Adams set himself the task of tidying up the borders of the United States. Two accords with Britain—the Rush-Bagot Treaty of 1817 and the Convention of 1818—fixed the border between the United States and Canada at the 49th parallel and resolved conflicting

U.S. and British claims to Oregon with an agreement to occupy it jointly for ten (eventually twenty) years. The American claim to Oregon (present-day British Columbia, Washington, Oregon, northern Idaho, and parts of Montana) was based on China trader Robert Gray's discovery of the Columbia River in 1792 and on the Lewis and Clark expedition of 1804–06. The British Hudson's Bay Company, however, had land-based fur-trading operations in the region, and established a major base at Fort Vancouver on the Columbia River in 1825. Adams's major diplomatic accomplishment was the Adams-Onís or Transcontinental Treaty of 1819, in which he skillfully wrested concessions from the faltering Spanish empire. In 1818, General Andrew Jackson led an American force on a mission purportedly to end raids on the Florida border by Seminole Indians against American settlements. Exceeding his orders, Jackson invaded Florida itself, and Spain, preoccupied with revolts throughout its Latin American empire, was unable to repulse him. Jackson's success made it clear that the United States could easily snatch Florida from Spain by force. Adams convinced Spain not only to cede Florida but also to drop all previous claims it had to the Louisiana Territory and Oregon. In return, the United States relinquished claims on Texas and assumed responsibility for the $5 million in claims that U.S. citizens had against Spain. Although many Westerners believed Adams should have been able to obtain Texas as well as Florida, the Transcontinental Treaty was hailed at the time as a success. It proved an important spur to American expansionism and highlighted Americans' growing confidence in foreign affairs.

That growing confidence was also apparent in Adams's culminating diplomatic success. In 1821, Mexico achieved its independence from Spain; by 1822, Argentina, Chile, and Colombia were independent as well. Adams picked his way through these remarkable changes in Latin America, developing the policy that bears his president's name, the Monroe Doctrine. The United States was the first country outside Latin America to recognize the independence of Spain's former colonies. Many Americans enthusiastically supported the Latin American revolutions and were proud to think that they were modeled on the American Revolution, as the Latin American liberator Simón Bolívar claimed.

But then the European powers (France, Austria, Russia, and Prussia) began talk of a plan to help Spain recover the lost colonies. What was the United States to do? The British, suspicious of the European powers, proposed a British-American declaration against European intervention in the hemisphere. Others might have been flattered by an approach from the British empire, but Adams would have none of it. Showing the national pride that was so characteristic of the era,

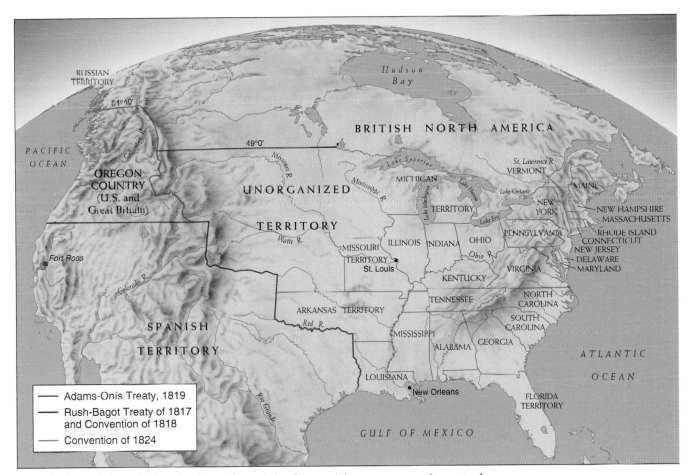

John Quincy Adams's Border Treaties   John Quincy Adams, secretary of state in the Monroe administration (1817–25), solidified the nation's boundaries in several treaties with Britain and Spain. The Rush-Bagot Treaty of 1817 and the Conventions of 1818 and 1824 settled the northern boundary with Canada and the terms of a joint occupancy of Oregon. The Adams-Onís Treaty of 1819 added Florida to the United States and settled the disputed border between the American Louisiana Territory and Spanish possessions in the West.

Adams insisted on an independent American policy. He therefore drafted for the president the hemispheric policy that the United States has followed ever since.

On December 2, 1823, the president presented the Monroe Doctrine to Congress and the world. He called for the end of colonization of the Western Hemisphere by European nations (this was aimed as much at Russia and its Pacific coast settlements as at other European powers). Intervention by European powers in the affairs of the independent New World nations would be considered by the United States a danger to its own peace and safety. Finally, Monroe pledged that the United States would not interfere in the affairs of European countries or in the affairs of their remaining New World colonies.

All of this was a very loud bark from a very small dog. In 1823, the United States lacked the military and economic force to back up its grand statement. In fact, what kept the European powers out of Latin America

was British opposition to European intervention, enforced by the Royal Navy. But the Monroe Doctrine was to take on quite another aspect at the end of the century, when the United States did have the power to enforce it. The Monroe Doctrine was more immediately useful in Adams's last diplomatic achievement, the Convention of 1824, in which Russia gave up its claim to the Oregon Territory and accepted 54° 40′ north latitude as the southern border of Russian America. Thus Adams had contained another possible threat to American continental expansion.

In the short space of twenty years, the position of the United States on the North American continent had been transformed. Not only was America a much larger nation, but the Spanish presence was much diminished, Russian expansion on the West Coast contained, and peace prevailed with Britain. This string of diplomatic achievements—the treaties with Russia, Britain, and Spain and the Monroe Doctrine—represented a great personal triumph for the stubborn, principled John Quincy Adams. A committed nationalist and expansionist, he showed that reason and diplomacy were in some circumstances more effective than force. Adams's diplomatic achievements were a fitting end to the period dominated by the Virginia Dynasty, the trio of enlightened revolutionaries who did so much to shape the new nation.

The Panic of 1819

Across this impressive record of political and economic nation building fell the shadow of the Panic of 1819. A delayed reaction to the end of the War of 1812 and the Napoleonic Wars, the panic forced Americans to come to terms with their economic place in a peaceful world. As British merchant ships resumed trade on routes they had abandoned during the wars, the American shipping boom ended. And as European farm production recovered from the wars, the international demand for American foodstuffs declined and American farmers and shippers suffered.

Domestic economic conditions made matters worse. The western land boom that began in 1815 turned into a speculative frenzy. Land sales, which had totaled 1 million acres in 1815, mushroomed to 3.5 million in 1818. Some lands in Mississippi and Alabama, made valuable by the international demand for cotton, were selling for $100 an acre. Many settlers bought on credit, aided by loans from small and irresponsible "wildcat" state banks. A number of speculators, carried away by the excitement of it all, also bought large tracts of land on credit and promoted them heavily. This was not the first—or the last—speculative boom in western lands. But it ended like all the rest—with a sharp contraction of credit, begun on this occasion by the Second Bank of the United States, which in 1819 forced state banks to foreclose on many bad loans. Many small farmers were ruined, and six years of depression followed.

In response to farmer protests, Congress passed a relief act in 1821 that extended the payment period for purchases of western lands, and some state legislatures passed "stay laws" that prevented banks from executing foreclosures. Nonetheless, many small banks failed, taking down their creditors with them. Many western farmers blamed the faraway Bank of the United States for their troubles. In the 1830s, Andrew Jackson would build a political movement on their resentment.

Urban workers suffered both from the decline in international trade and from manufacturing failures caused by competition from British imports. As urban workers lobbied for local relief (there was no federal welfare), they found themselves deeply involved in urban politics, where they could express their resent-ment against the merchants and owners who had laid them off. Thus developed another component of Andrew Jackson's new political coalition.

Another confrontation arose over the tariff. Southern planters, hurt by a decline in the price of cotton, began to actively protest the protective tariff, which kept the price of imported goods high even when cotton prices were low. Manufacturers, hurt by British competition, lobbied for even higher rates, which they achieved in 1824 over southern protests. Southerners then began to express doubts about the fairness of a political system in which they were always outvoted.

The Panic of 1819 was a symbol of this transitional time. It showed how far the country had moved since 1800, from Jefferson's republic of yeoman farmers toward a nation dominated by commerce. And the anger and resentment expressed by the groups harmed by the depression—farmers, urban workers, and southern planters—were portents of the politics of the upcoming Jackson era.

The Missouri Compromise

In the Missouri Crisis of 1819–21, the nation confronted the momentous issue that had been buried in the general enthusiasm for expansion: as America moved west, would the largely southern system of slavery expand as well? Until 1819, this question was decided regionally. As residents of the northern states moved west, the territory into which they expanded (the Old Northwest) was free of slavery. As southerners moved into Alabama, Mississippi, and Louisiana (the Old Southwest), they brought their slaves with them. This regional difference had been mandated by Congress in the Northwest Ordinance of 1787, which explicitly banned slavery in the northern section of trans-Appalachia but made no mention of it elsewhere. Because so much of the expansion into the Old Northwest and Southwest was lateral (Northerners stayed in the north, Southerners in the south), there was little conflict over sectional differences. In 1819, however, the sections collided—in Missouri.

In 1819, Missouri applied for admission to the Union as a slave state. To the slave-owning Kentuckians and Tennesseans who were the territory's major settlers, this extension of slavery seemed natural and inevitable. But Illinois, also an adjacent state, prohibited slavery. The northern states, all of which had abolished slavery by 1819, looked askance at the extension of slavery northward.

In addition to the moral issue of slavery, the Missouri question raised the political issue of sectional balance. Northern politicians did not want to admit another slave state. To do so would tip the balance of power in the Senate, where the 1819 count of slave

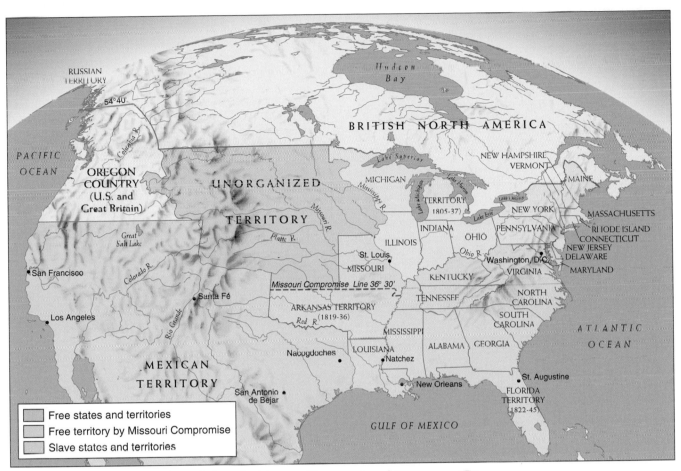

The Missouri Compromise   Before the Missouri Compromise of 1820, the Ohio River was the dividing line between the free states of the Old Northwest and the slaveholding states of the Old Southwest. The compromise stipulated that Missouri would enter the Union as a slave state (balanced by Maine, a free state), but slavery would be prohibited in the Louisiana Territory north of 36° 30' (Missouri's southern boundary). This awkward compromise lasted until 1846 when the Mexican-American War reopened the issue of the expansion of slavery.

and free states was eleven apiece. For their part, Southerners believed they needed an advantage in the Senate; because of faster population growth in the North, they were already outnumbered (105 to 81) in the House of Representatives. But above all, Southerners did not believe Congress had the power to limit the expansion of slavery. They were alarmed that Northerners were considering national legislation on the matter. Slavery, in southern eyes, was a question of property and therefore a matter for state rather than federal legislation. Thus, from the very beginning the expansion of slavery raised constitutional issues.

The urgency of these considerations among politicians in 1819 illustrates how delicate matters of sectional balance had already become. Indeed, the aging politician of Monticello, Thomas Jefferson, immediately grasped the seriousness of the question of the expansion of slavery. As he prophetically wrote to a friend, "This momentous question like a fire bell in the night, awakened and filled me with terror. I considered it at once the [death] knell of the Union."

In 1819, Representative James Tallmadge Jr. of New York began more than a year of congressional controversy when he demanded that Missouri agree to the gradual end of slavery as the price of entering the Union. At first, the general public paid little attention, but religious reformers (Quakers prominent among them) organized a number of antislavery rallies in northern cities that made politicians take notice. Former Federalists in the North who had seen their party destroyed by the achievements of Jefferson and his successors in the Virginia Dynasty eagerly seized on the Missouri issue. This was the first time that the growing northern reform impulse had intersected with sectional politics. It was also the first time that southern threats of secession were made openly in Congress.

CHRONOLOGY

1790s	Second Great Awakening begins
1800	Thomas Jefferson elected president
1802	Russian-American Company headquarters established at Sitka, Alaska
1803	Louisiana Purchase
	Marbury v. Madison
	Ohio admitted to the Union
1804	Lewis and Clark expedition leaves St. Louis
	Thomas Jefferson reelected president
	Russians reestablish Sitka following the Tlingit Revolt
	Haiti becomes independent
1807	*Chesapeake-Leopard* incident
	Embargo Act
1808	James Madison elected president
1809	Tecumseh forms military alliance among Northwest Confederacy peoples
1810	Mexican independence movement, led by Father Miguel Hidalgo, begins
1811	Battle of Tippecanoe
1812	War of 1812 begins
	James Madison reelected president

	Louisiana admitted to the Union
	Russians establish Fort Ross in Alta California
1814	Hartford Convention
	Treaty of Ghent
1815	Battle of New Orleans
1816	James Monroe elected president
	Congress charters Second Bank of the United States
	Indiana admitted to the Union
1817	Mississippi admitted to the Union
1818	Illinois admitted to the Union
	Andrew Jackson invades Florida
1819	Panic of 1819
	Adams-Onís Treaty
	Alabama admitted to the Union
1819–20	Missouri Crisis and Compromise
1820	James Monroe reelected president
	Maine admitted to the Union
1821	Missouri admitted to the Union as a slave state
1823	Monroe Doctrine

The Senate debate over the admission of Missouri, held in the early months of 1820, was the nation's first extended debate over slavery. Observers noted the high proportion of free African Americans among the listeners in the Senate gallery. They, like Thomas Jefferson, realized that the fate of the Union and the fate of the black race in America were inseparable. But the full realization that the future of slavery was central to the future of the nation would not become apparent to the general public until the 1850s.

In 1820, Congress achieved compromise over the sectional differences. Henry Clay forged the first of the many agreements that were to earn him the title of "the Great Pacificator" (peacemaker). A glance at the map shows the state of Missouri as an awkward intrusion into an otherwise slave-free area, a visual break in the smooth westward continuation of sectionalism. This visual impression is reflected in the Missouri Compromise itself, which was difficult to arrange and had an awkward air about it. The compromise maintained the balance between free and slave states: Maine (which had been part of Massachusetts) was admitted as a free state in 1820 and Missouri as a slave state in the following year. A policy was also enacted with respect to slavery in the rest of the Louisiana Purchase: slavery was prohibited north of 36° 30′ north latitude—the southern boundary of Missouri—and permitted south of that line. This meant that the vast majority of the Louisiana Territory would be free. In reality, then, the Missouri Compromise could be only a temporary solution, because it left open the question of how the balance between slave and free states would be maintained.

CONCLUSION

In complex ways a developing economy, geographical expansion, and even a minor war helped shape American unity. Local, small, settled, face-to-face communities in both the North and the South began to send their more mobile, expectant members to new occupations in urban centers or west to form new settlements, displacing Indian communities in the process. The westward movement was the novel element in the American national drama. Europeans believed that large size and a population in motion bred instability and political disintegration. Thomas Jefferson thought otherwise, and the Louisiana Purchase was the gamble that confirmed his guess. The westward population movement dramatically changed the political landscape and Americans' view of themselves. Few of those changes, though, were fully apparent in 1820.

Expansion would not create the settled communi-ties of yeoman farmers Jefferson had hoped for. Rather, it would breed a nation of restless and acquisi-tive people and a new kind of national democratic politics that reflected their search for broader defini-tions of community.

REVIEW QUESTIONS

1. What economic and political problems did the United States face as a new nation?
2. Jefferson's republican agrarianism made it appeal-ing to many Americans who wished to believe in their nation's uniqueness, but how realistic was it?
3. Some Federalists opposed the Louisiana Purchase, warning of the dangers of westward expansion.

What are arguments for and against expansion?
4. What contradictions in American Indian policy did the confrontations between Tecumseh's al-liance and soldiers and settlers in the Old North-west reveal? Can you suggest solutions to them?
5. What did the War of 1812 accomplish?
6. Why did the Era of Good Feelings come to an end?

RECOMMENDED READING

Catharine Allgor, *Parlor Politics: In Which the Ladies of Washington Help Build a City and a Government* (2000).

Stephen E. Ambrose, *Undaunted Courage: Meriweather Lewis, Thomas Jefferson, and the Opening of the American West* (1996).

Frank Bergon, ed., *The Journals of Lewis and Clark* (1989).

John Boles, *The Great Revival, 1787–1805* (1972).

R. David Edmunds, *Tecumseh and the Quest for Indian Lead-ership* (1984).

Joseph J. Ellis, *American Sphinx: The Character of Thomas Jefferson* (1998).

John Mack Faragher, *Sugar Creek* (1987).

Donald Hickey, *The War of 1812: A Forgotten Conflict* (1989).

Drew McCoy, *The Elusive Republic: Political Economy in Jef-fersonian America* (1980).

Peter S. Onuf, *Jefferson's Empire* (2000).

James Ronda, *Lewis and Clark among the Indians* (1984).

▶ MEDIA RESOURCES

U.S. HISTORY DOCUMENTS CD-ROM

The Federalist Era

7-7 Backcountry Turmoil Puts the New Govern-ment to the Test (1794)

7-9 The Alien and Sedition Acts (1798)

7-11 Reverend Peter Cartwright on Cane Ridge and the "New Lights" (1801)

7-12 Marbury v. Madison (1803)

Jefferson and the Republic

8-2 Thomas Jefferson, "First Inaugural Address" (1801)

8-3 Margaret Bayard Smith Meets Thomas Jeffer-son (1801)

8-4 Constitutionality of the Louisiana Purchase (1803)

8-5 The United States Navy and the Bombardment of Tripoli (1803)

8-6 A Matter of Honor or Vengeance? (1804)

8-7 Fisher Ames, "The Republican. No. II" (1804)

8-8 Sacagawea Interprets for Lewis and Clark (1804)

8-9 An "Uncommon Genius" Advocates Indian Unity (1809)

8-10 Indian Hostilities (1812)

8-11 The British Attack Baltimore (1814)

8-12 Report and Resolutions of the Hartford Con-vention (1814)

Economic and Social Change

9-1 The Western Country, "Extracts from Letters Published in Niles' Weekly Register" (1816)

9-2 The Cherokee Treaty of 1817

9-5 Thomas Jefferson Reacts to the "Missouri Question" (1820)

9-6 The Monroe Doctrine and a Reaction (1823)

 COMPANION WEBSITE HIGHLIGHTS

To view an exploration, enter one of the URLs below in your browser.

 Web Explorations

Louisiana Purchase
http://www.prenhall.com/faragher/map 9.1

Major Migration Routes, 1800–1820
http://www.prenhall.com/faragher/map 9.2

(Continued)

Additional Interactive Maps
To access the maps, go to this chapter's resources at
http://www.prenhall.com/faragher
Indian Resistance 1790–1816, page 254
The War of 1812, page 256
Spread of Settlement: Westward Surge, 1800–1820,
    page 259
The Missouri Compromise, page 267

HISTORY RESOURCE CENTER
To find the resources listed below, go to
http://www.prenhall.com/historyresourcecenter

Documents
Lewis and Clark Meet the Shoshone, 17 August 1805
Marbury v. Madison (1801)
Martin v. Hunter's Lessee (1816)
McCulloch v. Maryland (1819)
Missouri Enabling Act, 6 March 1820
Richard McNemar, The Kentucky Revival (1808)
Thomas Jefferson, "First Inaugural Address" (1801)
Thomas Jefferson, Letter to James Madison (1794)

Images
Albert Gallatin
Burning of the White House in 1814
Death of Captain Lawrence, Don't Give up the Ship
Decatur's Conflict with the Algerine at Tripoli.
Reuben James Interposing His Head . . .
Eli Whitney's Cotton Gin Patent Drawing
James Madison
Planning the Lewis and Clark Exploration . . .
The Battle of Tippecanoe
Thomas Jefferson

EXPLORING AMERICA
CONTINENTALISM
http://www.prenhall.com/faragher/continentalism

Why did the American colonists call their assembly the Continental Congress? What beliefs fueled western expansion? How were Native Americans affected by the settlement and expansion of the United States? The *Continentalism* module answers these and other questions.

Continentalism focuses on two important aspects of the westward expansion of the United States. Interactive maps, visual images, and print documents illuminate the issue of Native American removal. The role of the War of 1812 in Native American removal is discussed, as is the Cherokee resistance to removal. The other focus, on transportation advances, stresses the Erie Canal. A print docu-

Continentalism
Chronology

1784–1785	Treaties of Fort Stanwix and Fort McIntosh result in cession of Native American lands in Ohio
1800	Thomas Jefferson elected president
1803	United States purchases Louisiana from France
1804–1805	Lewis and Clark expedition surveys Louisiana Purchase
1808	National Road construction financed
1812–1815	War of 1812
1817–1825	Erie Canal constructed
1820	Missouri Compromise provides guide for admitting new states to the Union
1830	Congress passes Indian Removal Act
1838	Cherokee removal on "Trail of Tears"

2 of 8

ment explains the benefits of the Canal. Maps and the chronology provide historical perspective to the discussion.

Reflect and Respond
1. Referring to the comments of Black Hawk and on the Cherokee Memorial, assess the influence of treaties on Native Americans.
2. Why was the Erie Canal important to the westward expansion of the United States?
3. Was the expansion of the United States across the continent inevitable?

✓ Check it out
Indian Resistance, 1790–1816

This interactive map puts Native American resistance against United States intrusion into geographic and historical perspectives. The map illuminates the various aspects of Native American resistance and also the areas where western expansion exerted the greatest pressure on Indians.

This exploration is only available on the *Out of Many*, Fourth Edition Companion Website™.

In the Footsteps of Lewis and Clark

As we saw in the chapter opener, in March of 1805 the Lewis and Clark expedition left the hospitable Mandans and headed west, eager to face the unknown challenges that lay between them and the Pacific Ocean. Six months later, however, as the exhausted and starving members of the expedition struggled to find their way through the snow in the Bitterroot Mountains of present-day Montana and Idaho, it appeared that their luck had run out.

Instead, near the present-day town of Weippe, Idaho, the expedition was rescued by a small band of Nez Perce Indians. The Nez Perce fed the weakened party, gave

This shows the medal Lewis and Clark presented to the Nez Perce Indians in 1805. One side shows a profile of Thomas Jefferson, with the description "Th. Jefferson, President of the U.S. A.D. 1802," while the clasped hands on the other side promise Peace and Friendship.

SOURCE: Courtesy of the National Park Service/U.S. Department of the Interior. National Park Service photo.

them a chance to regain their strength and later helped them build canoes and served as guides for the final stage of their journey down the waters of the Columbia River drainage to the Pacific Ocean. When the expedition returned in the spring of 1806, they rested a month with the Nez Perce before recrossing the mountains into present-day Montana. As was their custom with other tribes, Lewis and Clark presented the Nez Perce with a Jefferson medal inscribed on one side with a picture of two clasped hands and the message "Peace and Friendship."

The bicentennial of the Lewis and Clark expedition from St. Louis to the Pacific Ocean occurs in 2003–06. Public interest is high, with millions of tourists expected to visit sites along the route during the bicentennial years. Many of them plan to relive the exploration by literally following in the footsteps of Lewis and Clark. Some of them will find themselves, as the explorers did 200 years ago, in Indian country. Or at least that is the hope of some western Indian tribes who see the bicentennial as a strategic opportunity to tell the Indian side of the expedition's history.

One of the American Indians holding that view is Alan Pinkham of the Nez Perce Tribe, who has been a member of the National Council of the Lewis and

Clark Bicentennial since its inception in the mid-1990s. Until recently, most white historians have believed that the hospitality that Indians showed to the expedition along its route was due to the exceptional persuasive power of Lewis and Clark. But Pinkham points out that the Nez Perce were hardly likely to have been persuaded by the group of weakened wanderers they met in the fall of 1805. Every Indian tribe had its own reasons for choosing to help—or not to help—the expedition. The Nez Perce and other Indian groups plan to use the bicentennial to tell their own stories about their encounters with Lewis and Clark.

There are formidable obstacles hindering the Indian effort to be heard. Western history has traditionally been told from the point of view of the white explorers and the settlers who followed them. Most people assume that *real* history didn't begin in the West until white people and written records arrived. The reliance on written material is an important reason for the heroic stature of Lewis and Clark, for historical accounts of the expedition have always relied for evidence on their own journals, supplemented by those of a few of the expedition's soldiers. Although the Nez Perce and other Indians have strong oral traditions about their encounters with Lewis and Clark, most people don't know about them because until recently historians regarded them only as "legend,"

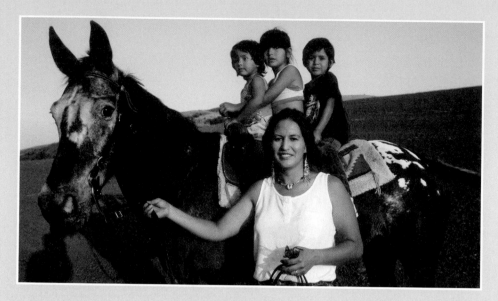

This contemporary photograph of Nez Perce tribal member Carla High Eagle leading her children home contains echoes of the past when the Nez Perce were famous for their large herds of spotted Appaloosa horses like the one shown here.

SOURCE: Carla High Eagle of the Lupwai Indian Reservation, Leviston, Idaho, June 1992. Photograph by David & Peter Turnley. Courtesy of CORBIS. © David & Peter Turnley/CORBIS.

and therefore not as reliable as written evidence. As a result, most Americans have only heard one version of a series many-sided encounters that occurred as Lewis and Clark found themselves in Indian country.

To insure that the Indian view is heard, the National Park Service has appointed Otis Halfmoon, a Nez Perce, as tribal liaison for the planning of the NPS traveling exhibit, *Corps of Discovery II: 200 Years to the Future*. In another Park service effort, Gerard Baker, a Mandan-Hidatsa, has been chosen as superintendent of the Lewis and Clark National Historic Trail as well as serving as superintendent of the *Corps of Discovery II* exhibit.

Alan Pinkham and others have worked with the National Council for the Bicentennial to set the proper context for the observation of the bincentnnial. One of the first steps was to refer to the bicentennial as a commemoration, rather than a celebration, thus acknowledging the high price that all Indians paid for discovery. From the Indian point of view, Lewis and Clark brought disaster in their wake: like the Mandans in the chapter opener, every western tribe experienced disease, warfare, and the destruction of their way of life at the hands of white American pioneers. Indian peoples felt betrayed by the same hand that the peace medal promised would clasp forever in friendship.

Yet rather than recrimination, Pinkham sees the bicentennial as a unique opportunity to tell the remarkable story of Indian survival and adaptation. After all, says Pinkham, "After 200 years we're still here. We weren't killed off by disease and warfare." The bicen-

tennial can serve to inform the public about modern Indian life and accomplishments. As the Nez Perce and other western Indians seize the occasion of the bicentennial to tell their own story, they hope to give a new and modern meaning to the two hands clasped together on the Jefferson medal. ■

  www.researchnavigator.com

The Community and Memory essay for this chapter deals with reflections on the journey of Lewis and Clark on the occasion of the bicentennial of their expedition. For further research on the Lewis and Clark expedition, use the tools available to you in Research Navigator.

As you investigate this topic, consider this question: "Why do American Indians believe their contribution to the expedition has been undervalued?"

ContentSelect: Search in the History database using the search term *Lewis and Clark*.

Links Library: Access the History: U.S. History database and explore the links for *Lewis and Clark Expedition*.

New York Times on the Web: To find more information on the bicentennial of the expedition, search using the term *Lewis and Clark*.

THE GROWTH OF DEMOCRACY

▶ 1824 – 1840

George Caleb Bingham (American, 1811–1879), *Stump Speaking*, 1853–1854. Oil on canvas, 42 ¹/₂ × 58 in. The Saint Louis Art Museum, Gift of Bank of America. Photo © The Saint Louis Art Museum.

Martin Van Buren Forges a New Kind of Political Community

W HEN MARTIN VAN BUREN LEFT ALBANY FOR WASHINGton in the fall of 1821 to take up his new position as junior senator from New York, he wrote complacently: "I left the service of the state [of New York] for that of the federal government with my friends in full and almost unquestioned possession of the state government in all its branches, at peace with each other and overflowing with kindly feelings towards myself." Thus did Van Buren sum up more than ten years of intense activity in New York State politics in which he and his allies, nicknamed the Bucktails (for the Indian-inspired insignia, the tail of a buck, that members wore on their hats), created one of the first modern democratic political parties. How could it be, Washington politicians asked, that this short, invariably pleasant but rather nondescript man had triumphed over the renowned DeWitt Clinton?

Tall, handsome, arrogant DeWitt Clinton, governor of New York from 1817 to 1823 (and again from 1825 until his death in 1828), had been swept into office on a tide of enthusiasm for his plan to build a canal the length of the state. Clinton soon gained legislative approval for the project—the Erie Canal—the most ambitious and most successful canal project in an era of canal building. An aristocrat in wealth, connections, and attitude, Clinton represented old-style politics. During his first terms as governor he ran the New York Jeffersonian Republican Party as though it were his personal property, dispensing patronage to relatives and friends (many of whom were Federalists) on the basis of their loyalty to him rather than their political principles.

Martin Van Buren was a new kind of politician. Born in the small, Dutch-dominated town of Kinderhook, New York, Van Buren was the son of a tavern keeper, not a member of the wealthy elite. He grew up with an enduring resentment of the aristocratic landowning families, such as the Van Schaacks and the Van Rensselaers (and, by extension, the Clintons), who disdained him when he was young. Masking his anger with charming manners, Van Buren took advantage of the growing strength of the Jeffersonian Republican Party in New York State to wrest control of the party from Clinton and forge it into a new kind of political organization. Clinton's use of patronage to reward friends at the expense of young party loyalists infuriated Van Buren and other rising politicians. Two years after Clinton became governor, Van Buren wrote bitterly to a friend: "A man to be a sound politician and in any degree useful to his country must be guided by higher and steadier considerations than those of personal sympathy and private regard. . . . In the name of all that is holy, where is the evidence of that towering mind and those superior talents which it has been the business of puffers and toad eaters to attribute to [Clinton]?"

By 1819, Van Buren had gathered together enough other disgruntled Jeffersonian Republicans to form the Bucktail faction and openly challenge Clinton. Two years later, at the state constitutional convention of 1821 (where they made up three-fourths of the delegates), the Bucktails sealed their victory. Meeting in Albany to revise the out-of-date constitution of 1777, the convention voted to streamline the organization of state government and sharply curtail the patronage powers of the governor. To cement these changes, delegates enacted nearly total manhood suffrage: all adult male citizens who paid state or local taxes, served in the militia, or worked on state roads—more than four-fifths of the adult male population—were now eligible to vote directly for state legislators, governor, and members of Congress.

This dramatic democratization of politics reflected the state's changing population. Already the bustling port of New York was the nation's largest city, and the state's commercial opportunities were attracting shrewd Yankee traders from New England, "whose laws, customs and usages," conservative senator Rufus King complained, "differ from those of New York." The old ruling families, failing to recognize the new commercial and social values of the newcomers, were losing their grip on politics. Rising politicians like Van Buren and other Bucktails, in contrast, found opportunity in these changing conditions. Attuned to popular feeling, they responded to the state's growing and increasingly diverse population by creating a new kind of political community. A political party, they maintained, should be a democratic organization expressing the will of all its members, not an organization dominated by an elite group like Clinton's and bound together only by family ties and political favors. All party members, including leaders, would have to abide by majority rule. Party loyalty, rather than personal opinion or friendship, would be the bond that kept the party together and, rather than aristocratic background, the principal requirement for party leadership. "The first man we see step to the rear," wrote Bucktail Silas Wright Jr., still smarting from the factionalism and favoritism of the Clinton years, "we cut down." In the new party system, there would be no tolerance for politicans who followed their own self-interest rather than the larger good of the party.

By the time he departed for Washington in the fall of 1821, Van Buren had established in Albany a closely knit group of friends and allies who practiced these new political principles. Party decisions, reached by discussion in legislative caucus and publicized by the party newspaper, the *Albany Argus*, were binding on all members and enforced by patronage decisions. The group, dubbed the "Albany Regency," ran New York State politics for twenty years. For all those years Martin Van Buren was in Washington, where he was a major architect of the new democratic politics of mass participation that has been called the Second American Party System. This new movement created, for the first time in American history, national communities of political partisans. Van Buren understood how to create these new communities. Van Buren believed that organization and discipline were essential not for their own sake but because they allowed democracy to flourish. He claimed that what made him different from DeWitt Clinton and earlier politicians was his "faith in the capacity of the masses of the people of our Country to govern themselves, and in their general integrity in the exercise of that function." This unprecedented confidence in popular opinion made American politics and politicians unique in the changing world of the early nineteenth century. ∎

Albany

THE NEW DEMOCRATIC POLITICS IN NORTH AMERICA

The early years of the nineteenth century were a time of extraordinary growth and change not only the United States but for all the countries of North America. Seen in continental perspective, the American embrace of popular democracy was unusual. Elsewhere, crises over popular rights dominated.

Continental Struggles Over Popular Rights

In 1821, after eleven years of revolts (see Chapter 9), Mexico achieved its independence from Spain.

Briefly united under the leadership of Colonel Agustin de Iturbide, Mexico declared itself a constitutional monarchy that promised equality for everyone—peninsulares, criollos, mestizos, and Indians alike. But because Spanish colonial rule had left a legacy of deep social divisions, the initial unity was short-lived. Iturbide reigned as Emperor of Mexico for little more than a year before he was overthrown by a military junta and later executed as a traitor. The Constitution of 1824, closely modeled on the U.S. Constitution, created a federal republic but continued a powerful political role for the Catholic Church and granted the president extraordinary powers in times of emergency. A series of weak presidents repeatedly invoked emergency powers and relied on the army as they attempted to revive a faltering economy and reconcile the differences between the centralists—the vested interests of clergy, large landowners, and the military—and the federalists, largely criollos and mestizos, who hoped to create a liberal republic modeled on the American one. The strongest of the early presidents was General Antonio Lopez de Santa Anna, who became a national hero by saving Mexico from a Spanish invasion in 1829 and overthrowing an unpopular dictatorship in 1832. Elected to the presidency for the first time in 1833, he dominated Mexican politics for the next twenty years, during which he assumed dictatorial, centralized power, surviv-

ing the loss of Texas in 1836 and the other northern provinces in 1848 to the United States (see Chapter 15). The unresolved issue of elite versus popular rule continued to undermine the hope for unity, popular rights, and stable government in an independent Mexico.

The independence of Haiti in 1804 (see Chapter 9) set the pattern for events in many other Caribbean islands in subsequent years. Independence destroyed the sugar industry, for freed slaves asserted their popular rights by refusing to perform the killing labor demanded of them on sugar plantations. The British Caribbean islands were racked with revolts, the largest occurring on Barbados in 1816 and on Jamaica in 1831. In response, and following years of humanitarian protests at home, the British Parliament abolished slavery in all British colonies in 1834. As in Haiti, sugar production then plunged. The only island where sugar production increased was Spanish Cuba, where slavery remained legal until 1880. Elsewhere, most of the 750,000 former British slaves became poor peasants struggling to stay out of debt. The economic collapse following emancipation also destroyed the political authority of local white elites, forcing the British government to impose direct rule. Most of the British possessions in the Caribbean remained Crown Colonies until the 1920s. This sequence of events—revolt, emancipation, economic collapse, loss of local political autonomy—was closely observed by slaveowners in the American South and made them fear for their own futures.

Still a third crisis of popular rights occurred in British North America. In 1837 both Upper and Lower Canada rebelled against the limited representative government that the British government had imposed in the Constitutional Act of 1791. By far the most serious revolt was in predominantly French Lower Canada, where armed uprisings were brutally suppressed by British troops. Fearing that the true aim of the rebels was independence or, worse, becoming a part of the United States, the British government refused to recognize the French Canadian demand for their own political voice. In 1840, Britain abolished the local government of

Lower Canada joined it to Upper Canada in a union that most French Canadians opposed and in which they were a minority. In his report to the British government, Lord Durham announced that the purpose of union was to end the ethnic enmity between British and French by forcing the latter to assimilate and "abandon their vain hopes of nationality." Lord Durham suggested increased colonial self-government, but the British government, fearing further trouble, refused to grant it.

In comparison to these experiences, the rapid spread of suffrage in the United States and the growth of a vibrant but stable democratic political culture seemed extraordinary. But after a brilliant start, in the 1850s the United States, like its neighbors, foundered on sectional differences that not even political democracy could reconcile. (See Chapter 15.)

The Expansion and Limits of Suffrage

Before 1800 most of the original thirteen states had limited the vote to property owners or taxpayers amounting to less than half the white male population. In DeWitt Clinton's New York and other states the wealthy held the reins of political power. In national politics as well, in spite of occasional revolts from below, such as the Whiskey Rebellion of 1794 (see Chapter 8), political control remained in the hands of the traditional elite until the end, in 1825, of the Virginia Dynasty of presidents—Jefferson, Madison, and Monroe. Westward expansion changed the nature of American politics. Mobility itself promoted change by undermining the traditional authority structures in the older states. "Old America seems to be breaking up and moving westward," an observer commented in 1817. Rapid westward expansion bolstered the national pride that Americans felt in their successful republican revolution and fostered a spirit of self-reliance. As Andrew Jackson, recruiting troops for the War of 1812, boasted, "We are the free born sons of America; the citizens of the only republic now existing in the world; and the only people

on earth who possess rights, liberties, and property which they dare call their own." Furthermore, the nine new states west of the Appalachians that entered the Union between 1800 and 1840—making up one third of the membership of the U.S. Senate—contributed their own regional perspective to national politics. Westerners as a whole shared common concerns and attitudes that national politicians from the two older areas could not ignore if they wished to build strong political allegiances in the new region.

The new western states extended the right to vote to all white males over the age of twenty-one. Kentucky entered the Union with universal manhood suffrage in 1792, and Tennessee (1796) and Ohio (1803) entered with low taxpayer qualifications that approached universal suffrage. Soon older states such as

Population Trends: Westward Expansion, 1830   Westward population movement, a trickle in 1800, had become a flood by 1830. Between 1800 and 1830 the U.S. white and African American population more than doubled (from 5.3 million to 12.9 million), but the trans-Appalachian population grew tenfold (from 370,000 to 3.7 million). By 1830 more than a third of the nation's inhabitants lived west of the original thirteen states.

New Jersey (1807) and Maryland (1810) dropped their property qualification for voting. By 1820, most of the older states had followed suit. In most states the driving force behind reform was not idealistic but very practical: competition for votes between parties or factions of parties (such as the Bucktails and the Clintonians in New York).

In Connecticut, the Jeffersonian Republicans, appealing to young, democratically minded but propertyless young men, first challenged the state's controlling Federalists in 1802 and finally in 1817 achieved suffrage for all men who paid taxes or served in the militia (that is, nearly everyone). In South Carolina, the rivalry was geographical, pitting the more numerous up-country residents who supported Jefferson's Republicans against the wealthy Federalist slaveowning political elite of the low country, who controlled the state legislature. A compromise agreement of 1808 allocated votes to the lower house by population (favoring the up-country citizens), and to the upper house by wealth (favoring the low country slaveowners). This redistribution of power led directly to a demand for universal white manhood suffrage, which became law (with a two-year residency requirement) in South Carolina in 1810. There were laggards—Rhode Island, Virginia, and Louisiana did not liberalize their voting qualifications until later—but by 1840 more than 90 percent of adult white males in the nation could vote. And they could vote for more officials: governors and (most important) presidential electors were now elected by direct vote, rather than chosen by small groups of state legislators.

Universal white manhood suffrage, of course, was far from true universal suffrage: the right to vote remained barred to most of the nation's free African American males and to women of any race. Only in five New England states (Maine, New Hampshire, Vermont, Massachusetts, and Rhode Island) could free African American men vote before 1865. In most of the other northern states, the right of free African American men to vote was limited, first by custom and later by law. In 1821 in New York, for example, the same Bucktail-dominated legislature that voted to extend the franchise to most white men also restricted it among African American men to those with property valued at $250 or more, a very high amount at the time. As a result, only 68 of the nearly 13,000 African Americans in New York City qualified to vote in 1825.

Free African American men were denied the vote in all southern states and, surprisingly, in the new western states as well. The Ohio constitution of 1802 denied African Americans the right to vote, to hold public office, and to testify against white men in court cases. Later restrictions barred black men from serving

Web Exploration

Analyze the changes in white male suffrage between 1800 and 1830. How were less wealthy white males, women, and African Americans excluded from voting? www.prenhall.com/faragher/map10.1

The Growth of Universal White Male Suffrage Kentucky was the first western state to enact white male suffrage without tax or property qualifications. Other western states followed, and by 1820 most of the older states had dropped their suffrage restrictions as well. By 1840, more than 90 percent of the nation's white males could vote. But although voting was democratized for white men, restrictions on free African American male voters grew tighter, and women were excluded completely.

in the state militia and on juries. The constitutions of other western states—Illinois, Indiana, Michigan, Iowa, Wisconsin, and (later) Oregon—attempted to solve the "problem" of free African Americans by simply denying them entry into the state at all.

The denial of suffrage to white women stemmed from the patriarchal belief that men headed households and represented the interests of all household members. Even wealthy single women who lived alone were considered subordinate to male relatives and denied the right to vote. (New Jersey had been an exception to this rule until it amended its constitution in 1807 to withdraw the franchise from propertied women.) Although unable to vote, women of the upper classes had long played important informal roles in national politics, and nowhere was that more true than in Washington, D.C. Presidents' wives like Abigail Adams and Dolley Madison were famous for their ability to provide the social settings in which their husbands could quietly conduct political business. Another unrecognized group of skilled politicians were the women who ran the Washington boardinghouses where most congressmen lived during the legislative term. These women, longtime Washington residents, often served as valuable sources of information and official contacts for their boarders. At the state and local level of politics as well, women—often the wives of politicians—engaged in political activities.

Although the extension of suffrage to all classes of white men seemed to indicate that women had no role in public affairs, in fact women's informal involvement in politics grew along with the increasing pace of political activity. At the same time, however, as "manhood" rather than property became the qualification for voting, men began to ignore women's customary political activity and to regard their participation as inappropriate, an attitude that politically active women increasingly resented.

Thus, in a period famous for democratization and "the rise of the common man," the exclusion of important groups—African American men and women of all races—marked the limits of liberalization. It is also true that nowhere else in the world was the right to vote so widespread as it was in the United States. The extension of suffrage to the common man marked a major step beyond the republicanism advocated by the Revolutionary generation. Thomas Jefferson had envisaged a republic of property-owning yeoman farmers. Now, however, propertyless farm workers and members of the laboring poor in the nation's cities could vote as well. European observers were curious about the democratization of voting: Could "mob rule" possibly succeed? And how would it affect traditional politics? The election of 1824 provided the first outline of the answer.

The Election of 1824

The 1824 election marked a dramatic end to the political truce that James Monroe had established in 1817. In that Era of Good Feelings, one big political party, the expanded Jeffersonian Republicans, had absorbed the remaining Federalists. This brief moment of unanimity did not survive the Panic of 1819 and the Missouri Crisis (see Chapter 9). Thus five candidates, all of them members of the Republican Party, ran for president in the elections of 1824. The candidate chosen by the usual method of congressional caucus was William H. Crawford of Georgia. The traditional stepping stone to the presidency, however, had been the office of secretary of state, giving a strong claim to John Quincy Adams of Massachusetts, who held that position in President Monroe's administration. Adams was nominated by his state legislature, as were two other candidates, Henry Clay of Kentucky and Andrew Jackson of Tennessee. The fifth candidate, John C. Calhoun of

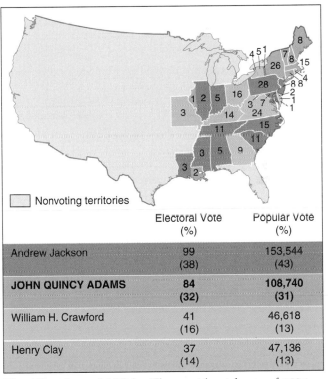

	Electoral Vote (%)	Popular Vote (%)
Andrew Jackson	99 (38)	153,544 (43)
JOHN QUINCY ADAMS	**84** (32)	**108,740** (31)
William H. Crawford	41 (16)	46,618 (13)
Henry Clay	37 (14)	47,136 (13)

The Election of 1824   The presidential vote of 1824 was clearly sectional. John Quincy Adams carried his native New England and little else, Henry Clay carried only his own state of Kentucky and two adjoining states, and Crawford's appeal was limited to Virginia and Georgia. Only Andrew Jackson moved beyond the regional support of the Old Southwest to wider appeal and the greatest number of electoral votes. Because no candidate had a majority, however, the election was thrown into the House of Representatives, which chose Adams.

South Carolina, Monroe's secretary of war, withdrew before the election to run for vice president. Each candidate was clearly identified with a region: Adams with New England, Crawford and Calhoun with the South, Clay and Jackson with the West. Jackson, a latecomer to the race, was at first not taken seriously because his record as a legislator was lackluster and his political views unknown. His reputation as a military hero, however, enabled him to run as a national candidate despite his regional identification. He won 43 percent of the popular vote and 99 electoral votes—more than any other candidate. The runner-up, John Quincy Adams, won 31 percent of the popular vote and 84 electoral votes. But neither had an electoral majority, leaving it up to the House of Representatives, as in the election of 1800, to pick the winner. After some political dealing, Henry Clay threw his support to Adams and the House elected Adams president. This was customary and proper: the Constitution gave the House the power to decide, and Clay had every right to advise his followers how to vote. But when Adams named Clay his secretary of state, the traditional stepping-stone to the highest office, Jackson's supporters promptly accused them of a "corrupt bargain." Popular opinion, the new element in politics, supported Jackson. John Quincy Adams served four miserable years as president, knowing that Jackson would challenge him, and win, in 1828.

The legislative accomplishments of Adams's presidency were scanty. Adams's ambitious proposals for internal improvements were rebuffed by a hostile Congress, although he did succeed in obtaining funding for an extension of the National Road west from Wheeling—an issue on which he could count on western votes. Congress stalled Adams's request to send American delegates to a conference in Panama called by the Latin American liberator Simón Bolívar, in part because Southerners feared attendance might lead to recognition of the revolutionary black republic of Haiti. Thus Adams's desire to lead the nation from a position above politics was frustrated by a political opposition that he thought illegitimate but that was in reality an early sign of the emerging two-party system.

The New Popular Democratic Culture

In 1834, the French visitor Michel Chevalier witnessed a mile-long nighttime parade in support of Andrew Jackson. Stunned by the orderly stream of banners lit by torchlight, the portraits of George Washington, Thomas Jefferson, and Jackson, and the enthusiastic cheering of the crowd, Chevalier wrote, "These scenes belong to history. They are the episodes of a wondrous epic which will bequeath a lasting memory to posterity, that of the coming of democracy." Mass campaigns—huge political rallies, parades, and candidates

with wide "name recognition," such as military heroes—were the hallmarks of the new popular democratic culture. So were less savory customs such as the distribution of lavish food and (especially) drink at polling places, which frequently turned elections into rowdy, brawling occasions. As Chevalier noted, the spirit that motivated the new mass politics was democratic pride in participation. And as the election of 1824 showed, along with the spread of universal male suffrage went a change in popular attitudes that spelled the end of the dominance of small political elites.

Besides wider suffrage, there were other causes for the exuberance of popular democratic culture. In the nation's cities, workers had always participated in the parades and celebrations that were a part of urban life. Marching with the symbols of their trades, artisans had not only demonstrated pride in their craft but had asserted their importance in an earlier political world ruled by elites (see Chapter 13). A print revolution had helped to democratize politics by spreading word far beyond the nation's cities about the parades, protests, and celebrations that became a basic part of popular democracy.

Politics, abetted by the publication of inexpensive party newspapers, was a great topic of conversation among men in early nineteenth-century America, as Richard Caton Woodville's 1845 painting *Politics in an Oyster House* suggests.

SOURCE: Richard Caton Woodville, *Politics in an Oyster House*, 1848. The Walters Art Museum.

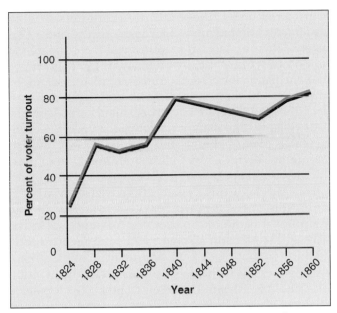

Pre–Civil War Voter Turnout   The turnout of voters in presidential elections more than doubled from 1824 to 1828, the year Andrew Jackson was first elected. Turnout surged to 80 percent in 1840, the year the Whigs triumphed. The extension of suffrage to all white men and heated competition between two political parties with nationwide membership turned presidential election campaigns into events with great popular appeal.

The Burgeoning of Newspapers   Newspapers have a long history in the United States. Even before the American Revolution the colonies boasted 37 newspapers (see Chapter 6), and within little more than a decade that number had nearly tripled. Toward the end of the century, however, the number of newspapers expanded rapidly, by 1835 numbering more than 30 times that of 1775.

The print revolution had begun in 1826 when a reform organization, the American Tract Society, installed the country's first steam-powered press. Three years later the new presses had turned out 300,000 Bibles and 6 million religious tracts, or pamphlets. The greatest growth, however, was in newspapers that reached a mass audience. The number of newspapers soared from 376 newspapers in 1810 to 1,200 in 1835. This rise paralleled the growth of interest in politics, for most newspapers were published by political parties and were openly partisan. Packed with articles that today would be considered libelous and scandalous, newspapers were entertaining and popular reading, and they rapidly became a key part of democratic popular culture.

Martin Van Buren was one of the first to realize the full potential of popular feeling, but politicians in other states shared Van Buren's vision of tightly organized, broad-based political groups. John C. Calhoun of South Carolina was first elected to his state legislature in 1808, the year that the iron-fisted grip of the low-country planters was weakened in South Carolina politics. Calhoun, who came from the up-country, depended throughout his political career on the up-country voters who achieved universal white manhood suffrage in 1810. In Virginia, a group known as the Richmond Junto had control of state politics by 1816, and in Tennessee the Nashville Junto, masterminded by John Overton, held sway by 1822. In New Hampshire, Isaac Hill's Concord Regency was firmly in control by 1825. Each of these organizations, to a greater or lesser extent, aspired to the same discipline and control as demonstrated by the Albany Regency, and each had wider aspirations. The Nashville Junto led the way by nominating Andrew Jackson for president in 1824.

The new politics placed great emphasis on participation and party loyalty. Just as professional politicians such as Van Buren were expected to be loyal, so the average voter was encouraged to make a permanent commitment to a political party. One way to show that loyalty was to turn out for parades. Political processions were huge affairs, marked by the often spontaneous participation of men carrying badges and party regalia, banners and placards, and portraits of the candidates, accompanied by bands, fireworks, and the shouting and singing of party slogans and songs. The political party provided some of the same satisfactions that popular sports offer today: excitement, entertainment, and a sense of belonging. In effect, political parties functioned as giant national men's clubs. They made politics an immediate and engrossing topic of conversation and argument for men of all walks of life. In this sense, the political party was the political manifestation of a wider social impulse toward community. But the glue that held political parties together went beyond the appeal of a particular leader or loyalty to one's friends. Political parties were based on genuine differences of political opinion. The task of politicians, as Van Buren recognized, was to emphasize those differences in ways that forged support not just for one election but for permanent, national communities of political interest.

The Election of 1828

The election of 1828 was the first to demonstrate the power and effectiveness of the new popular democratic culture and party system. With the help of Martin Van Buren, his campaign manager, Andrew Jackson rode the wave of the new democratic politics to the presidency. Voter turnout in 1828 was more than twice that of 1824. Jackson's party, the Democratic Republicans (they soon dropped "Republicans" and became simply the Democrats), spoke the language of democracy, and they opposed the special privilege personified for them by President John Quincy Adams and his National Republican (as distinguished from the earlier Jeffersonian Republican) Party. Neither Jackson nor Adams campaigned on his own—that was

considered undignified. But the supporters of both candidates campaigned vigorously, freely, and negatively. Jackson's supporters portrayed the campaign as a contest between "the democracy of the country, on the one hand, and a lordly purse-proud aristocracy on the other." In their turn, Adams's supporters depicted Jackson as an illiterate backwoodsman, a murderer (he had killed several men in duels), and an adulterer (apparently unwittingly, he had married Rachel Robards before her divorce was final). Jackson's running mate for vice president was John C. Calhoun of South Carolina. Although this choice assured Jackson of valuable southern support, it also illustrated the transitional nature of politics, for Calhoun was at the time of the election serving as vice president to John Quincy Adams, Jackson's opponent. That Calhoun was able easily to lend his support to a rival faction was a holdover from the old elite and personal politics that would soon be impossible in the new democratic political system.

Jackson won 56 percent of the popular vote (well over 80 percent in much of the South and West) and a decisive electoral majority of 178 votes to Adams's 83. The vote was interpreted as a victory for the common man. But the most important thing about Jackson's victory was the coalition that achieved it. The new democratically based political organizations—the Richmond and Nashville juntos, the Albany and Concord regencies, with help from Calhoun's organization in South Carolina—worked together to elect him. Popular appeal, which Jackson the military hero certainly possessed, was not enough to ensure victory. To be truly national, a party had to create and maintain a coalition of North, South, and West. The Democrats were the first to do this.

THE JACKSON PRESIDENCY

Andrew Jackson's election ushered in a new era in American politics, an era that historians have called the "Age of the Common Man." Jackson himself, however, was no common man: he was a military hero, a rich slave owner, and an imperious and decidedly undemocratic personality. "Old Hickory," as Jackson was affectionately called, was tough and unbending, just like hickory itself, one of the hardest of woods. Yet he had a mass appeal to ordinary people unmatched—and indeed unsought—by earlier presidents. The secret to Jackson's extraordinary appeal lies in the changing nature of American society. Jackson was the first to respond to the ways in which westward expansion and the extension of the suffrage were changing politics at the national as well as the local and state levels.

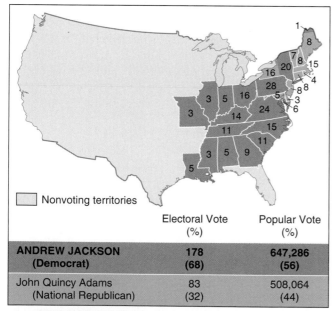

☐ Nonvoting territories

	Electoral Vote (%)	Popular Vote (%)
ANDREW JACKSON (Democrat)	**178 (68)**	**647,286 (56)**
John Quincy Adams (National Republican)	83 (32)	508,064 (44)

The Election of 1828   Andrew Jackson's victory in 1828 was the first success of the new national party system. The coalition of state parties that elected him was national, not regional. Although his support was strongest in the South and West, his ability to carry Pennsylvania and parts of New York demonstrated his national appeal.

A Popular Figure

Jackson was born in 1767 and raised in North Carolina. During the American Revolution he was captured and beaten by the British, an insult he never forgot. As a young man without wealth or family support, he moved west to the frontier station (fort) at Nashville, Tennessee, in 1788. There he made his career as a lawyer and his considerable wealth as a slave-owning planter. He had a touchy sense of pride and honor that led him into many duels. As he showed in his campaigns against the Five Civilized Tribes in the Old Southwest during the War of 1812, he was ruthless toward Indians. He first became a national hero with his underdog win against the British in the battle of New Orleans in 1815. In the popular mind, his fierce belligerence came to symbolize pioneer independence. The fact that he had little political experience, which would have made his nomination impossible under the traditional system of politics, was not a hindrance in the new age of popular politics.

On March 4, 1829, Andrew Jackson was inaugurated as president of the United States. Jackson himself was still in mourning for his beloved wife Rachel, whose recent death he attributed to the slanders of the campaign. But everyone else was celebrating. The small community of Washington was crowded with strangers, many of them Westerners and common people who had come especially for Jackson's inauguration. Jackson's brief inaugural address was almost drowned out by the cheering of the crowd, and after the ceremony the new president was mobbed by well-wishers. The same unrestrained enthusiasm was evident at a White House reception, where the crowd was large and disorderly. People stood on chairs and sofas to catch glimpses of Jackson and shoved and pushed to reach the food and drink, which was finally carried out to the lawn. In the rush to follow, some people exited through windows rather than the doors. This was the exuberance of democracy in action. It marked something new in American politics. Indeed, Jackson's administration was different from all those before it.

A Strong Executive

The mob scene that accompanied Jackson's inauguration was more than a reflection of the popular enthusiasm for Old Hickory. It also signaled a higher level of

Until 1829, presidential inaugurations had been small, polite, and ceremonial occasions. Andrew Jackson's popularity, however, brought a horde of well-wishers to Washington for his inaugural. Conservative critics, dismayed by the disorderly crowd at Jackson's frontier-style open house at the White House, feared "the reign of King Mob" had begun.

SOURCE: *All Creation Going to the White House*, by Robert Cruickshank. Library of Congress.

controversy in national politics. Jackson's personal style quickly stripped national politics of the polite and gentlemanly aura of cooperation it had acquired during the Era of Good Feelings and that Adams had vainly tried to maintain. Jackson had played rough all his life, and he relished controversy. His administration (1829–37) had plenty of it. Andrew Jackson dominated his administration. Except for Martin Van Buren, whom he appointed secretary of state, he mostly ignored the heads of government departments who made up his official cabinet. Instead he consulted with an informal group, dubbed the "Kitchen Cabinet," made up of Van Buren and old western friends. The Kitchen Cabinet did not include John C. Calhoun, the vice president, or either of the other two great sectional representatives, Henry Clay and Daniel Webster. Jackson never forgave Clay for his role in the "corrupt bargain" of 1825, and he saw Daniel Webster as a representative of his favorite political target, the privileged elite.

Jackson used social distance to separate himself from other politicians. When Jackson's secretary of war, John Henry Eaton, married a beautiful woman of flamboyant reputation, he transgressed the social code of the time. It was rumored that Peggy Eaton had been Eaton's mistress and that there were other men in her past. She was, in nineteenth-century thinking, a fallen woman and unfit for polite society. The respectable ladies of Washington shunned her. But Jackson, aroused by memories of the slanders against his own wife, defended Peggy Eaton and urged his cabinet members to force their wives to call on her. When, to a woman, they refused, Jackson called the husbands henpecked. This episode chilled the social life of cabinet members and their families and drove a wedge between Jackson and Calhoun, whose wife was a leader in the anti-Eaton group. Although Jackson claimed to be motivated only by chivalry, he wanted to change Washington politics, and this episode helped him do it. The important although quiet role that women had played since 1800 in Washington politics came to an abrupt end. Ironically, the Eaton episode might never have occurred had Jackson not been a widower. His wife Rachel would surely have sided with Mrs. Calhoun in upholding the moral code of the time.

Jackson freely used the tools of his office to strengthen the executive branch of government at the expense of the legislature and judiciary. By using the veto more frequently than all previous presidents combined (twelve vetoes compared with nine by the first six presidents), Jackson forced Congress to constantly consider his opinions. Even more important, Jackson's "negative activism" restricted federal activity, thereby allowing more power to remain in state hands.

In one of his most famous and unexpected actions, the veto of the Maysville Road Bill of 1830, Jackson refused to allow federal funding of a southern spur of the National Road in Kentucky, claiming such funding should be left to the state. Like Presidents James Madison and James Monroe before him, Jackson believed that federal funding for extensive and expensive transportation measures was unconstitutional because it infringed on the "reserved powers" the Constitution left to the states. The veto was unexpected because it disappointed Jackson's strongest supporters, Westerners who wanted better transportation. But by addressing his veto message to a popular audience, not just to Congress, and by dramatically portraying federal funding as a threat to the popular political principle of states' rights (and by making it clear that he was not opposed to federal funding of all internal improvements), Jackson actually gained political support. He also had the satisfaction of defeating a measure central to the American System proposed by his western rival, Henry Clay.

The Nation's Leader versus Sectional Spokesmen

Despite his western origins, Jackson was a genuinely national figure. He was more interested in asserting strong national leadership than in promoting sectional compromise. He believed that the president, who symbolized the popular will of the people, ought to dominate the government. As he put it in his first annual message, "the first principle of our system [is that] the majority is to govern." This was new. Voters were much more accustomed to thinking of politics in sectional terms. Jackson faced a Congress full of strong and immensely popular sectional figures. Three stood out: Southerner John C. Calhoun, Northerner Daniel Webster, and Westerner Henry Clay.

Intense, dogmatic, and uncompromising, John C. Calhoun of South Carolina had begun his political career as an ardent nationalist and expansionist in his early days as a War Hawk before the War of 1812. Since the debate over the Missouri Compromise in 1820, however, Calhoun had wholeheartedly identified with southern interests, first and foremost among which was the expansion and preservation of slavery. As the South's minority position in Congress became clear over the years, Calhoun's defense of southern economic interests and slavery became more and more rigid. Not for nothing did he earn his nickname the "Cast-Iron Man."

Senator Daniel Webster of Massachusetts was the outstanding orator of the age. Large, dark, and stern, Webster delivered his speeches in a deep, booming voice that, listeners said, "shook the world." He was capable of pathos as well, bringing tears to the eyes of those who heard him say, while defending Dartmouth College before the Supreme Court (in the case of the same name), "It is, Sir, a small college, and yet there are those who love it." Webster, a lawyer for business interests, became the main spokesman for the new northern commercial interests, supporting a high protective tariff, a national bank, and a strong federal government. Webster's fondness for comfortable living, and especially brandy, made him less effective as he grew older, but then, as a contemporary of his remarked, "No man could be as great as Daniel Webster looked."

In contrast with the other two, Henry Clay of Kentucky, spokesman of the West, was charming, witty, and always eager to forge political compromises. Clay held the powerful position of Speaker of the House of Representatives from 1811 to 1825 and later served several terms in the Senate. A spellbinding storyteller and well known for his ability to make a deal, Clay worked to incorporate western desires for cheap and good transportation into national politics. It was he who promoted the political agenda known as the American System: a national bank, a protective tariff, and the use of substantial federal funds for internal improvements such as roads, canals, and railroads (see Chapter 9). Clay might well have forged a political alliance between the North and the West if not for the policies of President Jackson, his fellow Westerner and greatest rival. Jackson's preeminence thwarted Clay's own ambition to be president.

The prominence and popularity of these three politicians show that sectional interests remained strong even under a president as determined as Jackson to override them and disrupt "politics as usual" by imposing his own personal style.

INTERNAL IMPROVEMENTS: BUILDING AN INFRASTRUCTURE

Despite the ongoing constitutional debate over who should fund internal improvements, no one argued that they should not be funded at all. On the contrary, ordinary people and politicians of all persuasions agreed that both federal and state governments had an important role in encouraging economic growth and in fostering the development of a national market. And that role included subsidizing the costs of the basic infrastructure—the canals and railroads—that would tie the national market together.

The Transportation Revolution

Between 1800 and 1840 the United States experienced truly revolutionary improvements in transportation. More than any other development, these improvements encouraged Americans to look beyond their local communities to broader ones and to foster the enterprising commercial spirit for which they became so widely known.

 Web Exploration

Through a series of interactive maps, look at the impact of canals, steamboats, and improved roads on travel time between 1800 and 1857. What effect did the transportation revolution have on national identity?
www.prenhall.com/faragher/map10.2

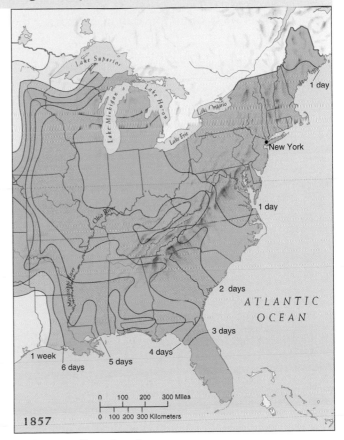

Travel Times, 1800 and 1857   The transportation revolution dramatically reduced travel times and vastly expanded everyone's horizons. Improved roads, canals, and the introduction of steamboats and railroads made it easier for Americans to move, and made even those who did not move less isolated. Better transportation linked the developing West to the eastern seaboard and fostered a national identity and pride.

Improved transportation had dramatic effects both on individual mobility and on the economy. By 1840 it was easier for people to move from one locale to another, but, even more remarkably, people now had easy access in their own cities and towns to commercial goods made in distant centers. Thus even for people who remained in one place, horizons were much broader in 1840 than they had been forty years before. The difference lay in better roads, in improvements in water transport, and in the invention and speedy development of railroads.

In 1800, travel by road was difficult for much of the year. Mud in the spring, dust in the summer, and snow in the winter all made travel by horseback or carriage uncomfortable, slow, and sometimes dangerous. Over the years, localities and states tried to improve local roads or contracted with private turnpike companies to build, maintain, and collect tolls on important stretches of road. In general, however, local roads remained poor. The federal government demonstrated its commitment to the improvement of interregional transportation by funding the National Road in 1808, at the time the greatest single federal transportation expense (its eventual cost was $7 million). Built of gravel on a stone foundation, it crossed the

Appalachian Mountains at Cumberland, Maryland, thereby opening up the West. Built in stages—to Wheeling, Virginia (now West Virginia), by 1818, to Columbus, Ohio, by 1833, to Vandalia, Illinois, almost at the Mississippi River, by 1850—the National Road tied the East and the West together, providing strong evidence of the nation's commitment to both expansion and cohesion and helping to foster a national community.

Although the federal commitment was great, the states actually spent more than the federal government on internal improvements—canals and railroads as well as roads. In the 1820s, state spending for internal improvements totaled $26 million. Half of this amount was incurred by two states, New York and Pennsylvania, but even smaller states such as South Carolina spent $2 million, largely on canals. In the next decade, state spending for canals, railroads, and turnpikes soared to $108 million. States and towns, especially in newly populated areas of the West, competed against one another in giving land, subsidies, and other forms of encouragement to road, canal, and railroad companies to provide transportation to their particular localities. Some of these commitments were overly generous and led to financial difficulty: by 1842,

This 1829 painting of Fairview Inn on the National Road just three miles west of Baltimore illustrates the importance of good transportation. The busy traffic attests to commercial activity and to confidence in westward expansion—the canvas-covered wagons were able to travel as far west as Ohio on the National Road at the time.

SOURCE: Thomas Coke Ruckle, *Fairview Inn or Three Mile House on Old Frederick Road*, c. 1829?, watercolor on paper. Collection of the Maryland Historical Society, Baltimore, Maryland.

nine states (Arkansas, Florida, Illinois, Indiana, Louisiana, Maryland, Michigan, Mississippi, and Pennsylvania) had defaulted on some of their transportation loans, and Ohio and New York were forced to suspend dividends to investors.

Canals and Steamboats

However much they helped the movement of people, the National Road and other roads were unsatisfactory in a commercial sense. Shipments of bulky goods like grain were too slow and expensive by road. Waterborne transportation was much cheaper and still the major commercial link among the Atlantic seaboard states and in the Mississippi-Ohio river system. But before the 1820s most water routes were north-south or coastal (Boston to Charleston, for example); east-west links were urgently needed. Canals turned out to be the answer.

The Erie Canal—the most famous canal of the era—was the brainchild of New York governor DeWitt Clinton, who envisioned a link between New York City and the Great Lakes through the Hudson River and a 364-mile-long canal stretching from Albany to Buffalo. When Clinton proposed the canal in 1817 it was derisively called "Clinton's Ditch"; the longest then existing American canal was only 27 miles long and had taken nine years to build. Nevertheless, Clinton convinced the New York legislature to approve a bond issue for the canal, and investors (New York and British merchants) subscribed to the tune of $7 million, an immense sum for the day. Building the canal—40 feet wide, 4 feet deep, 364 miles long, with 83 locks and more than 300 bridges along the way—was a vast engineering and construction challenge. What came to be called "Yankee ingenuity" showed at every step of the way, from the creation of stump pullers to remove trees from the route, to substitutes for cement (previously imported from England), to the widespread use of Dupont blasting powder, the forerunner of dynamite (which was not invented for another forty years).

Manpower was another concern. In the early stages nearby farmers worked for $8 a month, but when malaria hit the workforce in the summer of 1819, many

Governor DeWitt Clinton is shown pouring a keg of Lake Erie water into New York Harbor at the *Wedding of the Waters* ceremony on November 4, 1825, marking the official opening of his pet project, the Erie Canal. Initially derided as "Clinton's Ditch," the completion of the 364 mile canal opened America's heartland to settlement and international commerce.

SOURCE: C. Y. Turner, *The Marriage of the Waters*. Mural in DeWitt Clinton High School, New York City. Courtesy of Margaret Yardley Voelker and *American Heritage Magazine*.

went home. They were replaced by 3,000 Irish contract laborers, who were much more expensive—50 cents a day plus room and board—but more reliable (if they survived). Local people regarded the Irish workers as different and frightening, but the importation of foreign contract labor for this job was a portent of the future. Much of the heavy construction work on later canals and railroads was performed by immigrant labor.

DeWitt Clinton had promised, to general disbelief, that the Erie Canal would be completed in less than ten years, and he made good on his promise. The canal was the wonder of the age. On October 26, 1825, Clinton declared it open in Buffalo and sent the first boat, the *Seneca Chief*, on its way to New York at the incredible speed of four miles an hour. (Ironically, the Seneca Indians, for whom the boat was named, had been removed from the path of the canal and confined to a small reservation.) The boat reached New York City on November 4, where it was greeted with elaborate ceremonies, including one in which vials of water from the great rivers of the world—the Nile, Ganges, Mississippi, Rhine, and Danube—were emptied into New York harbor to symbolize the opening of commerce between the heart of America and the world.

This grand gesture was appropriate. The Erie Canal provided easy passage to and from the interior, both for people and for goods. It drew settlers like a magnet from the East and, increasingly, from overseas: by 1830, some 50,000 people a year were moving west on the canal to the rich farmland of Indiana, Illinois, and territory farther west. Earlier settlers now had a national, indeed an international, market for their produce. Moreover, farm families began purchasing household goods and cloth, formerly made at home. Indeed, one of the most dramatic illustrations of the canal's impact was a rapid decline in the production of homespun cloth in the towns and counties along its route. In 1825, the year the Erie Canal opened, New York homesteads produced 16.5 million yards of textiles. By 1835 this figure had shrunk by almost half—8.8 million yards—and by 1855 it had dropped to less than 1 million.

Towns along the canal—Utica, Rochester, Buffalo—became instant cities, each an important commercial center in its own right. Perhaps the greatest beneficiary was New York City, which quickly established a commercial and financial supremacy no American city could match. The Erie Canal decisively turned New York's merchants away from Europe and toward America's own heartland, building both interstate commerce and a feeling of community. As the famous song put it,

> You'll always know your neighbor,
> You'll always know your pal,
> If you've ever navigated
> On the Erie Canal.

The phenomenal success of the Erie Canal prompted other states to construct similar waterways to tap the rich interior market. Between 1820 and 1840, $200 million was invested in canal building, three-quarters of it provided by state governments. The Blackstone Canal linked Worcester, Massachusetts, with Providence, Rhode Island; the Pennsylvania Main Line Canal ran all the way from Philadelphia to Pittsburgh; and many other canals were built in Maine, Maryland, Ohio, Indiana, and Illinois. None of these waterways achieved the success of the Erie, which collected $8.5 million in tolls in its first nine years. And the port cities they were meant to benefit—Philadelphia and Baltimore, for example—never threatened New York's commercial supremacy. Nevertheless, the spurt of canal building ended the geographical isolation of much of the country. For example, Ohio's canal system opened up the American interior by linking the Ohio River to Lake Erie in the north and to the Pennsylvania canals to the east. An even more important improvement in water transportation, especially in the American interior, was the steamboat. Robert Fulton first demonstrated the commercial feasibility of steamboats in 1807, and they were soon operating in the East. Redesigned with more efficient engines and shallower, broader hulls, steamboats transformed commerce on the country's great inland river system: the Ohio, the Mississippi, the Missouri, and their tributaries. Steamboats were extremely dangerous, however; boiler explosions, fires, and sinkings were common. Public outrage at these conditions led to one of the first uses of federal regulatory power in the public interest. The first Steamboat Act, passed in 1838 and strengthened in 1852, set standards for the construction, equipment, and operation of steamboat boilers, required measures to prevent fire and collisions, and established an inspection system to make sure the new regulations were carried out. Although steamboats were privately owned and operated, the public that they served insisted on the need for safety standards to promote the wider community welfare.

Dangerous as they were, steamboats greatly stimulated trade in the nation's interior. There had long been downstream trade on flatboats along the Mississippi River system, but it was limited by the return trip overland on the arduous and dangerous Natchez Trace. For a time, steamboats actually increased the downriver flatboat trade, because boatmen could now make more round trips in the same amount of time, traveling home by steamboat in speed and comfort. The increased river- and canal-borne trade, like the New England shipping boom of a generation earlier, stimulated urban growth and all kinds of commerce. Cities such as Cincinnati, already notable for its rapid growth, experienced a new economic surge. A frontier outpost in 1790, Cincinnati was by the 1830s a center of steamboat manufacture and machine tool production as well as a central shipping point for food for the southern market.

Railroads

Remarkable as all these transportation changes were, the most remarkable was still to come. Railroads, new in 1830 (when the Baltimore and Ohio Railroad opened with 13 miles of track), grew to an astounding 31,000 miles by 1860. By that date, New England and the Old Northwest had laid a dense network of rails, and several lines had reached west beyond the Mississippi. The South, the least industrialized section of the nation, had fewer railroads. "Railroad mania" surpassed even canal mania as investors—as many as one-quarter of them British—rushed to profit from the new invention.

Early railroads, like the steamboat, had to overcome many technological and supply problems with far-reaching economic effects. For example, locomotives, to generate adequate power, had to be heavy. Heavy locomotives, in turn, required iron rather than wooden rails. The resulting increased demand forced America's iron industry to modernize (at first, railroad iron was imported from England). Heavy engines also required a solid gravel roadbed and strong wooden ties. Arranging steady supplies of both and the labor to lay them was a construction challenge on a new scale. The demand for locomotives and the need to service them fostered the development of a specialized industry, represented by Philadelphia's Baldwin Locomotive Works.

Finally, there were problems of standardization and production quality. Because so many early railroads were short and local, intended simply to connect nearby towns, builders used any gauge (track width) that served their purposes. Thus gauges varied from place to place, forcing long-haul passengers and freight to change trains frequently. For each change, commercial shippers were burdened with the cost of unloading goods from one train and loading them onto another. At one time, the trip from Philadelphia to Charleston involved eight gauge changes. Add to this that the early railroads—often hurriedly and poorly built by private companies trying to save money—were prone to frequent breakdowns and accidents, and it's not surprising to learn that traveling by ship between Philadelphia and Charleston long remained more pleasant than traveling by rail.

For some years after the introduction of the railroad, canal boats and coastal steamers carried more freight and at lower cost. It was not until the 1850s that consolidation of local railroads into larger systems began in earnest. But already it was clear that this youngest transportation innovation would have far-reaching social consequences.

The Legal Infrastructure

Accompanying the transportation revolution was a series of decisions by federal courts asserting broad federal powers over interstate commerce. The effect of these decisions was to vastly encourage commercial enterprise. By preventing states from interfering with interstate commerce, the government assured entrepreneurs the freedom and security to operate in the risky new national market. Two key decisions were handed down by Chief Justice John Marshall (who had been on the bench since 1801). In *Dartmouth College* v. *Woodward* (1819), the Supreme Court prevented states from interfering in contracts, and in *Gibbons* v. *Ogden* (1824), it enjoined the state of New York from giving a monopoly over a steamboat line to Robert Fulton, inventor of the vessel. Although Fulton's invention was protected by a federal patent, its commercial application was not. Patenting thus encouraged technology,

but not at the expense of competition. A decision handed down by Marshall's successor, Roger Taney, *Charles River Bridge* v. *Warren Bridge* (1837), again supported economic opportunity by denying a monopoly. All three cases involved federal reversal of decisions made at the state level, illustrating how the Supreme Court, under Marshall's leadership, strengthened the power of the federal government and thus fostered national policy rather than localism.

At the state level, another crucial commercial protection was the passage of laws concerning incorporation of businesses that had grown too large for individual proprietorship, family ownership, or limited partnership. Businesses that needed to raise large amounts of capital by attracting many investors found the contractual protections provided by incorporation to be essential. The protection investors wanted most was limited liability—the assurance that they would lose no more than what they had invested in a corporation if it were sued or went bankrupt. Initially transportation companies and banks benefited the most from state charters of incorporation. They were less commonly used by merchants and manufacturers until later in the century. Incorporation increased the powers of government, for it made businesses subject to state regulation. Nevertheless, the net effect of state incorporation laws was to encourage large-scale economic activity and to hasten the commercialization of rural areas.

Commercial Agriculture in the Old Northwest

The impact of the transportation revolution and of technological innovation on rural people (who in spite of the growth of cities still constituted more than two-thirds of the American population) went far beyond the breaking down of rural isolation. Every advance in transportation—better roads, canals, steamboats, railroads—made it easier for farmers to get their produce to market. Improvements in agricultural machinery increased the amount of acreage a farmer could cultivate. These two developments, added to the availability of rich, inexpensive land in the heartland, moved American farmers permanently away from subsistence agriculture and into production for sale.

The impact of the transportation revolution on the Old Northwest was particularly marked. Settlement of the region, ongoing since the 1790s, accelerated. In the 1830s, after the opening of the Erie Canal, migrants from New England streamed into northern Ohio, Illinois, Indiana, southern Wisconsin, and Michigan and began to reach into Iowa.

Government policy strongly encouraged western settlement. The easy terms of federal land sales were an important inducement: terms eased from an initial rate of $2.00 per acre for a minimum of 320 acres in 1800, to $1.25 an acre for 80 acres in 1820. Still, this was too much for most settlers to pay all at once. Some people simply squatted, taking their chances that they could make enough money to buy the land before someone else bought it. Less daring settlers relied on credit, which was extended by banks, storekeepers, speculators, promoters, and, somewhat later, railroads, which received large grants of federal lands.

The very need for cash to purchase land involved western settlers in commercial agriculture from the beginning. Farmers, and the towns and cities that grew up to supply them, needed access to markets for their crops. Canals, steamboats, and railroads ensured that access, immediately tying the individual farm into national and international commercial networks. The long period of subsistence farming that had characterized colonial New England and the early Ohio Valley frontier was superseded by commercial agriculture stimulated by the transportation revolution.

Commercial agriculture in turn encouraged regional specialization. Ohioans shipped corn and hogs first by flatboat and later by steamboat to New Orleans. Cincinnati, the center of the Ohio trade, earned the nickname "Porkopolis" because of the importance of its slaughterhouses. By 1840, the national center of wheat production had moved west of the Appalachians to Ohio. Wheat flowed from the upper Midwest along the Erie Canal to eastern cities and increasingly to Europe. Because in each new western area wheat yields were higher than in earlier ones, farmers in older re-

gions were forced to shift away from wheat to other crops. The constant opening of new farmland encouraged mobility and wasteful soil practices. Many farmers did not wish to make a permanent commitment to their land, but rather counted on rising land prices and short-term crop profits to improve their financial situation. Prepared to move on when the price was right, they regarded their farmland not as a permanent investment but as a speculation.

At the same time, farmers who grew wheat or any other cash crop found themselves at the mercy of far-off markets, which established crop prices; distant canal or railroad companies, which set transportation rates; and the state of the national economy, which determined the availability of local credit. This direct dependence on economic forces outside the control of the local community was something new. So, too, was the dependence on technology, embodied in expensive new machines that farmers often bought on credit.

New tools made western farmers unusually productive. John Deere's steel plow (invented in 1837) cut plowing time in half, making cultivation of larger acreages possible. Seed drills were another important advance. But the most remarkable innovation was Cyrus McCormick's reaper, patented in 1834. Earlier, harvesting had depended on manpower alone. A man could cut two or three acres of wheat a day with a cradle scythe, but with the horse-drawn reaper he could cut twelve acres. Impressed by these figures, western farmers rushed to buy the new machines, confident that increased production would rapidly pay for them.

In most years, their confidence was justified. But in bad years, farmers found that their new levels of debt could mean failure and foreclosure. They were richer but more economically vulnerable than they had been before.

Effects of the Transportation Revolution

The effects of the transportation revolution were many. The new ease of transportation fueled economic growth by making distant markets accessible. The startling successes of innovations such as canals and railroads attracted large capital investments, including significant amounts from foreign investors ($500 million between 1790 and 1861), which fueled further growth. In turn, the transportation revolution fostered

Cyrus McCormick is shown demonstrating his reaper to skeptical farmers. When they saw that the machine cut four times as much wheat a day as a hand-held scythe, farmers flocked to buy McCormick's invention. Agricultural practices, little changed for centuries, were revolutionized by machines like this.

SOURCE: *The Testing of the First Reaping Machine*, lithograph, 1831. Courtesy of the Chicago Historical Society.

Commercial Links: Rivers, Canals, Roads, 1830, and Rail Lines, 1850   By 1830, the United States was tied together by a network of roads, canals, and rivers. This "transportation revolution" fostered a great burst of commercial activity and economic growth. Transportation improvements accelerated the commercialization of agriculture by getting farmers' products to wider, nonlocal markets. Access to wider markets likewise encouraged new textile and other manufacturers to increase their scale of production. By 1850, another revolutionary mode of transportation, the railroad, had emerged as a vital link to the transportation infrastructure.

an optimistic, risk-taking mentality in the United States that stimulated invention and innovation. More than anything, the transportation revolution allowed people to move with unaccustomed ease. Already a restless people compared with Europeans, Americans took advantage of new transport to move even more often—and farther away—than they had before. Disease moved with them. Epidemics that once were localized in the nation's seaports spread as travel expanded. In 1832 and 1849 cholera epidemics devastated New York City (see Chapter 13). Because of the Erie Canal and other westward travel routes, the effect of cholera was equally devastating in growing inland cities, among them St. Louis and Cincinnati, each of which lost 10 percent of their population. Cholera even stalked the Overland Trails, striking down eager goldseekers long before they reached California (see Chapter 14).

There were other, less directly economic effects. Every east-west road, canal, and railroad helped to reorient Americans away from the Atlantic and toward the heartland. This new focus was decisive in the creation of national pride and identity. Transportation improvements such as the Erie Canal and the National Road linked Americans in larger communities of interest beyond the local community in which they lived. Other results were less positive. The technological triumphs of canal building and rail laying fostered a brash spirit of conquest over nature that was to become part of the American myth of the frontier. Furthermore, although every new transportation or communication link broke down local and regional isolation and helped to build a spirit of pride in the nation, it also refocused attention on questions of national politics. The new transportation system caused a subtle political shift, for it strengthened the influence of the North by improving the North's ties with the West more than its ties with the South. In this way, the new modes of communication and transportation served to heat up the politics of the era.

JACKSON AND HIS OPPONENTS: THE RISE OF THE WHIGS

As transportation improvements, increased commercialization, and the new democratic politics drew the people of the United States out of localism into larger networks, fundamental questions about national unity arose. What was the correct balance between local interests—the rights of the states—and the powers of the central government? The men who wrote the federal Constitution in Philadelphia in 1787 had not been able to reach agreement on this question. Because the

Constitution deliberately left the federal structure ambiguous, all sectional disagreements automatically became constitutional issues that carried a threat to national unity. The great issues of Jackson's presidency expressed this continuing tension between nationalism and sectionalism. Jackson's responses to them created such controversy that a permanent opposition—another political party, known as the Whigs—was born.

The Nullification Crisis

The political issue that came to symbolize the divergent sectional interests of North and South, pitting the rights of individual states against the claims of a federal majority, was the protective tariff that placed a duty (or surcharge) on imported goods. The first substantial tariff was enacted in 1816 after northern manufacturing interests clamored for protection from the ruthless British competition that followed the War of 1812 (see Chapter 9). As a group, wealthy southern planters were opposed to tariffs, both because duties raised the cost of the luxury goods they imported from Europe and because they believed in the principle of free trade, fearing that American tariffs would cause other countries to retaliate with tariffs against southern cotton. Most southern congressmen, assured that the 1816 tariff was a temporary postwar recovery measure, voted for it. But it was not temporary. As the North industrialized and new industries demanded protection, tariff bills in 1824 and 1828 raised rates still higher and protected more items. Southerners protested, but they were outvoted in Congress by northern and western representatives, who agreed both on the need to protect industry and on the tariff as a way to raise federal revenue. The 1828 tariff, nicknamed the "Tariff of Abominations," was a special target of southern anger, because Jackson's supporters in Congress had passed it in order to increase northern support for him in the presidential campaign of that year. It imposed especially high tariffs on imported textiles and iron, the tariffs ranged from a third to a half of the total value of those products. Southerners in Congress lacked the votes to block the tariff and faced the bleak prospect that their economic interests would always be ignored by the majority. Southern opponents of the tariff insisted that it was not a truly national measure but a sectional one that helped only some groups while harming others. Thus, they claimed, it was unconstitutional because it violated the rights of some of the states.

South Carolina, Calhoun's home state, reacted the most forcefully to the Tariff of 1828. Of the older southern states, South Carolina had been the hardest hit by the opening of the new cotton lands in the Old Southwest, which had drained both population and commerce from the state. One index of South Carolina's changed status was the declining position of Charleston. In 1800 it was still as important a seaport as New York and Boston, but by the 1820s it had been eclipsed by all the major northern ports as well as by Mobile and New Orleans, then the major ports for exporting cotton. To these economic woes were added the first real fears about national attitudes toward slavery. South Carolinians, who had always had close personal ties with slave owners in the Caribbean islands, were shaken by the news that the British Parliament, bowing to popular pressure at home, was planning to emancipate all the slaves in the British West Indies. If Congress had the power to impose tariffs that were harmful to some states, South Carolinians asked, what would prevent it from enacting legislation like Britain's, depriving Southerners of their slaves and, thus, of their livelihood? The result of these fears was a renewed interest in the doctrine of nullification, a topic that became the subject of widespread discussion in South Carolina in 1828. The doctrine upheld the right of a state to declare a federal law null and void and to refuse to enforce it within the state. This was not a new argument. Thomas Jefferson and James Madison had used it in the Kentucky and Virginia Resolves of 1798, which they had written in opposing the Alien and Sedition Acts (see Chapter 8). The Hartford Convention of 1814–15, at which Federalists protested grievances related to the War of 1812, had adopted the same position (see Chapter 9). At issue in each case was the power of the state against that of the federal government. Now the same constitutional issue emerged again, this time linked to the most intractable sectional issue, the South's determination to protect the institution of slavery.

South Carolina had an important supporter of nullification in the person of John C. Calhoun, who wrote a widely circulated defense of the doctrine, the *Exposition and Protest*, in 1828. Because Calhoun was soon to serve as Andrew Jackson's vice president, he wrote the *Exposition* anonymously. He hoped to use his influence with Jackson to gain support for nullification, but he was disappointed.

Where Calhoun saw nullification as a safeguard of the rights of the minority, Jackson saw it as a threat to national unity. As the president said at a famous exchange of toasts at the annual Jefferson Day dinner in 1830, "Our Federal Union, it must be preserved." In response to Jackson, Calhoun offered his own toast: "The Union—next to our liberty most dear. May we always remember that it can only be preserved by distributing equally the benefits and burdens of the Union." The president and the vice president were thus in open disagreement on a matter of crucial national importance. The outcome was inevitable: Calhoun lost all influence with Jackson, and two years later he took the unusual step of resigning the vice presidency. Martin Van Buren was elected to the office for Jackson's second term. Calhoun, his presidential aspirations in ruins, became a senator from South Carolina, and in that capacity participated in the last act of the nullification drama.

In 1832 the nullification controversy became a full-blown crisis. In passing the Tariff of 1832, Congress (in spite of Jackson's disapproval) retained high taxes on woolens, iron, and hemp, although it reduced duties on other items. South Carolina responded with a special convention and an Ordinance of Nullification, in which it rejected the tariff and refused to collect the taxes it required. The state further issued a call for a volunteer militia and threatened to secede from the Union if Jackson used force against it. Jackson responded vehemently, denouncing the nullifiers— "Disunion by armed force is treason"—and obtaining from Congress a Force Bill authorizing the federal government to collect the tariff in South Carolina at gunpoint if necessary. Intimidated, the other southern states refused to follow South Carolina's lead. More quietly, Jackson also asked Congress to revise the tariff. Henry Clay, the Great Pacificator, swung into action and soon, with Calhoun's support, had crafted the Tariff Act of 1833. This measure appeared to meet southern demands by pledging a return to the tariff rate of 1816 (an average of 20 percent) by 1842 through a series of very small annual decreases for nine years, followed by a large cut in the final year. (In fact, in 1842 Congress quickly voted a return to higher tariff rates.) In 1833 the South Carolina legislature, unwilling to act without the support of other southern states, quickly accepted this face-saving compromise and repealed its nullification of the tariff of 1832. In a final burst of bravado, the legislature nullified the Force Bill, but Jackson defused the crisis by ignoring this second nullification.

The nullification crisis was the most serious threat to national unity that the United States had ever experienced. South Carolinians, by threatening to secede, had forced concessions on a matter they believed of vital economic importance. They—and a number of other Southerners—believed that the resolution of the crisis illustrated the success of their uncompromising tactics. Most of the rest of the nation simply breathed a sigh of relief, echoing Daniel Webster's sentiment, spoken in the heat of the debate over nullification, "Liberty and Union, now and forever, one and inseparable!" Most Americans firmly believed that although every effort should be made to address sectional concerns, national unity and majority rule came first. But another event of the Jackson years, Indian removal, clearly showed how unfair majority rule could be when the minority was not strong enough to force a compromise.

Indian Removal

The official policy of the United States government from the time of Jefferson's administration was to promote the assimilation of Indian peoples by encouraging them to adopt white ways. To Indian groups who resisted "civilization" or who needed more time to adapt, Jefferson offered the alternative of removal from settled areas in the East to the new Indian Territory west of the Mississippi River. Following this logic, at the end of the War of 1812, the federal government signed removal treaties with a number of Indian nations of the Old Northwest, thereby opening up large tracts of land for white settlement (see Chapter 9). In the Southwest, however, the Five Civilized Tribes—the Cherokees, Chickasaws, Choctaws, Creeks, and Seminoles—remained. By the 1830s, under constant pressure from settlers, each of the five tribes had ceded most of its lands, but sizable self-governing groups lived in Georgia, Alabama, Mississippi, and Florida. All of these (except the Seminoles) had moved far in the direction of coexistence with whites, and they resisted suggestions that they should voluntarily remove themselves.

The Cherokees took the most extensive steps to adopt white ways. Their tribal lands in northwestern Georgia boasted prosperous farms, businesses, grain and lumber mills, and even plantations with black slaves.

Intermarriage with whites and African Americans had produced an influential group of mixed bloods within the Cherokee nation, some of whom were eager to accept white ways. Schooled by Congregationalist, Presbyterian, and Moravian missionaries, the Cherokees were almost totally literate in English. They took special pride in the alphabet for their own language that was developed by the Cherokee scholar Sequoyah, and in 1828 they began publishing a tribal newspaper, the *Cherokee Phoenix*, in both Cherokee and English. A year earlier the tribe had abolished its traditional form of government and established a constitutional republic.

Despite the evidence of the Cherokees' successful adaptation to the dominant white culture, in the 1820s the legislatures of Georgia, Alabama, and Mississippi, responding to pressures from land-hungry whites, voted to invalidate federal treaties granting special self-governing status to Indian lands. Because the federal government, not the states, bore responsibility for Indian policy, these state actions constituted a sectional challenge to federal authority. In this instance, however, unlike the Nullification Crisis, the resisting states had presidential support. Living up to his reputation as a ruthless Indian fighter, Jackson determined on a federal policy of wholesale removal of the southern Indian tribes.

In 1830, at President Jackson's urging, the U.S. Congress passed the hotly debated Indian Removal Act, which appropriated funds for relocation, by force if necessary. When Jackson increased the pressure by sending federal officials to negotiate removal treaties with the southern tribes, most reluctantly signed and prepared to move. The Cherokees, however, fought their removal by using the white man's weapon—the law. At first they seemed to have won: in *Cherokee Nation* v. *Georgia* (1831) and *Worcester* v. *Georgia* (1832), Chief Justice John Marshall ruled that the Cherokees, though not a state or a foreign nation, were a "domestic dependent nation" that could not be forced by the state of Georgia to give up its land against its will. However, when President Jackson heard the Supreme Court's decision, he is reputed to have said, "John Marshall has made his decision. Now let him enforce it." Ignoring the decision, Jackson continued his support for removal.

Faced by the Cherokees' de facto defeat, what could the other

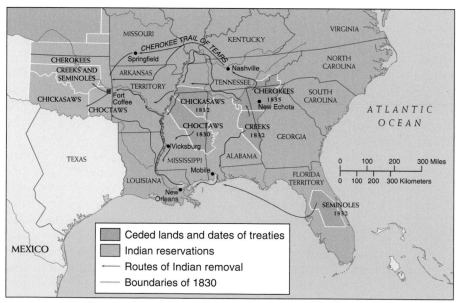

Southern Indian Cessions and Removals, 1830s   Pressure on the five major southern Indian peoples—the Cherokees, Chickasaws, Choctaws, Creeks, and Seminoles—that began during the War of 1812 culminated with their removal in the 1830s. Some groups from every tribe ceded their southern homelands peacefully and moved to the newly established Indian Territory west of Arkansas and Missouri. Some, like the Seminoles, resisted by force. Others, like the Cherokees, resisted in the courts but finally lost when President Andrew Jackson refused to enforce a Supreme Court decision in their favor. The Cherokees, the last to move, were forcibly removed by the U.S. Army along the "Trail of Tears" in 1838.

Indian tribes do? Some Seminoles of Florida chose to fight. Aided by runaway slaves and by their own unsurpassed knowledge of their homeland, the Florida Everglades, some Seminole bands fought a guerrilla war that lasted into the 1840s, before the U.S. military gave up and allowed them to remain. The majority of Seminoles and members of other tribes were much less fortunate; most of the Choctaws moved west in 1830; the last of the Creeks were forcibly moved by the military in 1836, and the Chickasaws a year later. And in 1838, in the last and most infamous removal, resisting Cherokees were driven west to Oklahoma along what came to be known as the "Trail of Tears." A 7,000-man army escorting them watched thousands (perhaps a quarter of the 16,000 Cherokees) die along the way. Another futile effort to resist removal, the Black Hawk "war," occurred in the Old Northwest. In 1832, Sac and Fox Indians, led by Black Hawk, attempted to move back to their old tribal grounds in Illinois following removal, but settlers saw the move as an invasion and demanded military protection. Federal troops chased the Black Hawk band to Wisconsin, where more than 300 Indians died in a final battle, and Black Hawk himself was taken prisoner. As in the South, the last of the remaining Indians east of the Mississippi were removed by the end of the 1830s.

Indian removal was a deeply divisive national issue. President Jackson's sweeping policy undoubtedly expressed the opinion of most Southerners and Westerners. But northern opinion, led by Protestant missionaries and reform groups, was so strongly opposed that the Indian Removal Act passed the House of Representatives by only 3 votes (out of 200). Jackson's presidential claim to speak for popular opinion was running into increasing opposition.

The Bank War

The last major event of Jackson's presidency, his refusal to renew the charter of the Second Bank of the United States, had lasting political consequences. Jackson's opponents, already angry about his earlier actions, were so infuriated by the bank episode that they formed the permanent opposition party known as the Whigs. It was from the heat of the Bank War that the now characteristic American two-party system emerged.

In 1816 Congress had granted a twenty-year charter to the Second Bank of the United States. The Bank played a powerful role in the expanding American economy, encouraging the growth of strong and stable financial interests and curbing less stable and irresponsible ones. The Bank was not a government agency but a private institution, the majority of whose directors were appointed by the government. Its stockholders were some of the nation's richest men (New York's John

This figurehead of Andrew Jackson, carved in 1834 for the navy frigate *Constitution*, captures the unmovable resolve that made Jackson so popular early in his presidency and so reviled during the Bank War.

SOURCE: Museum of the City of New York (M52.11)

Jacob Astor and Philadelphia's Stephen Girard among them). The Bank was directed by the erudite and aristocratic Nicholas Biddle of Philadelphia. Biddle, a friend of Thomas Jefferson and an avid amateur scientist, was the editor of the journals of Lewis and Clark.

The Bank, which with thirty branches was the nation's largest, performed a variety of functions: it held the government's money (about $10 million), sold government bonds, and made commercial loans. But its most important function was the control it exercised over state banks. At the time, America lacked a national currency. The money in circulation was a mixture of paper money (U.S. notes and the notes of state banks) and gold and silver coins (specie, or hard currency), many of them of foreign origin. Because state banks tended to issue more paper money than they could back with hard currency, the Bank always demanded repayment of its loans to them in coin. This policy forced state banks to maintain adequate reserves, curbed inflationary pressures (overprinting of their banknotes), and restricted speculative activities such as risky loans. In times of recession, the bank eased the pressure on state banks, demanding only partial payment in coin. Thus the Bank acted as a currency stabilizer by helping to control the money supply. It brought a semblance of order to what we today would consider a chaotic money system—coins of various weights and a multitude of state banknotes, many of which were discounted (not accepted at full face value) in other states.

The concept of a strong national bank was supported by the majority of the nation's merchants and businessmen and was a key element in Henry Clay's American System. Nevertheless, the Bank had many opponents. Western land speculators, and many western farmers, chafed at the Bank's tight control over the currency reserves of state banks, claiming it was harmful to western development. Both western farmers and urban workers had bitter memories of the Panic of 1819, which the Bank had caused (at least in part) by sharply cutting back on available credit. To some people, the economic power of the Bank was frightening; they feared that monied elites would use it to their own advantage. Although the rapid growth of the national economy made some sort of control necessary, many ordinary people were uneasy not only about the Bank but about banks of all kinds. They believed that a system based on paper currency would be manipulated by bankers in unpredictable and dangerous ways. Among those who held that opinion was Andrew Jackson, who had hated and feared banks ever since the 1790s, when he had lost a great deal of money in a speculative venture.

Early in his administration, Jackson hastened to tell Nicholas Biddle, "I do not dislike your Bank any more than all banks." By 1832, Jackson's opinion had changed and he and Biddle were locked in a personal conflict that harmed not only the national economy but the reputations of both men. Biddle, urged on by Henry Clay and Daniel Webster, precipitated the conflict by making early application for rechartering the Bank. Congress approved the application in July 1832. Clay and Webster, though well aware of Jackson's antibank feelings, believed the president would not risk a veto in an election year. They were wrong. Jackson immediately decided on a stinging veto, announcing to Van Buren, "The bank . . . is trying to kill me, but I will kill it!"

And kill it he did that same July, with one of the strongest veto messages in American history. Denouncing the Bank as unconstitutional, harmful to states' rights, and "dangerous to the liberties of the people," Jackson presented himself as the spokesman for the majority of ordinary people and the enemy of special privilege. Asserting that the Bank's "exclusive privileges" were benefiting only the rich, Jackson claimed to speak for the "humble members of society—the farmers, mechanics and laborers"—and to oppose injustice and inequality. These were the men who were the most eager participants in the new popular democratic culture. Nor did Jackson's veto message speak only of the sharp division between social classes. It also aroused sectional and national feelings by its allusions to the many British and eastern bank stockholders who were profiting from the debts of poor Southerners and Westerners. In short, the veto spoke directly to many of the hopes and fears that Americans felt at this time of exceptionally rapid economic and social change. Jackson's message was a campaign document, written to appeal to voters. Most of the financial community was appalled, believing both the veto and the accompanying message to be reckless demagoguery.

Jackson's Reelection in 1832

Nevertheless, Jackson's veto message was a great popular success, and it set the terms for the presidential election of 1832. Henry Clay, the nominee of the anti-Jackson forces, lost the battle for popular opinion. Democrats successfully painted Clay as the defender of the Bank and of privilege. His defeat was decisive: he drew only 49 electoral votes, to Jackson's 219. A handful of votes went to the first third party in American history, the short-lived Anti-Masonic Party. This party expressed the resentments that some new voters felt against the traditional political elite by targeting the secrecy of one fraternal group, the Masonic Order, to which many politicians (including both Jackson and Clay) belonged. The Anti-Masonic Party did make one lasting contribution to the political process. It was the first to hold a national nominating convention, an innovation quickly adopted by the other political parties.

Although the election was a triumph for Jackson, the Bank War continued. It was to have serious effects on the economy and on political principle. The Bank charter did not expire until 1836, but Jackson, declaring that "the hydra of corruption is only scotched, not dead," decided to kill the Bank by transferring its $10 million in government deposits to favored state banks ("pet banks," critics called them). Cabinet members objected, but Jackson ignored them. Two secretaries of the treasury refused to carry out Jackson's orders and were abruptly removed. Jackson then found a more pliant man, Roger Taney, to do the job. (Jackson later rewarded him with the post of chief justice of the Supreme Court.) Henry Clay led an unprecedented vote of censure of the president in the Senate, but in the House loyal Democrats prevented a censure vote. To all of these protests, Jackson responded that the election had given him a popular mandate to act against the Bank. The president was the direct representative of the people, he claimed, and could act upon the popular will, regardless of the opinion of Congress or even the cabinet. Short of impeachment, there was nothing Congress could do to prevent Jackson from acting on his expansive—and novel—interpretation of presidential powers.

Whigs, Van Buren, and the Election of 1836

But there was someone outside Congress with power to respond: the Bank's director, Nicholas Biddle. "This worthy President thinks that because he has scalped Indians...he is to have his way with the Bank," Biddle commented. "He is mistaken." As the government withdrew its deposits, Biddle abruptly called in the Bank's commercial loans, thereby causing a sharp panic and recession in the winter of 1833–34. Merchants, businessmen, and southern planters were all furious—at Jackson. His opponents, only a loose coalition up to this time, coalesced into a formal opposition party that called itself the Whigs. Evoking the memory of the Patriots who had resisted King George III in the American Revolution, the new party called on everyone to resist tyrannical "King Andrew." Just as Jackson's own calls for popular democracy had appealed to voters in all regions, so his opponents overcame their sectional differences to unite in opposition to his economic policies and arbitrary methods.

The Whigs first tested their strength against Vice President Martin Van Buren, Jackson's designated successor, in the presidential election of 1836. Still not completely free of the methods and attitudes of traditional politics, the Whigs ran four sectional candidates: William Henry Harrison of Ohio, Hugh Lawson White of Tennessee, W. P. Mangum of North Carolina, and Daniel Webster of Massachusetts. The Whigs hoped the combined votes for these regional candidates would deny Van Buren a majority and force the election into the House of Representatives, where they hoped to win. The strategy failed, but not by much: although Van Buren captured 170 electoral votes to the Whigs' 124, the popular vote was much closer, 50.9 percent to 49.1 percent. A shift of only 2,000 votes in Pennsylvania would have thrown the election into the House of Representatives, vindicating the Whig strategy. The Whig defeat drove home the weakness of the traditional sectional politics, but the closeness of the popular vote showed that the basis for a united national opposition did exist. In 1840, the Whigs would prove that they had learned this lesson.

The Panic of 1837

Meanwhile, the consequences of the Bank War continued. The recession of 1833–34 was followed by a wild speculative boom, caused as much by foreign investors as by the expiration of the Bank. Many new state banks were chartered that were eager to give loans, the price of cotton rose rapidly, and speculation in western lands was feverish (in Alabama and Mississippi, the mid-1830s were known as the "Flush Times"). A government surplus of $37 million distributed to the states in 1836 made the inflationary pressures worse. Jackson became alarmed at the widespread use of paper money (which

he blamed for the inflation), and in July 1836 he issued the Specie Circular, announcing that the government would accept payment for public lands only in hard currency. At the same time, foreign investors, especially British banks, affected by a world recession, called in their American loans. The sharp contraction of credit led to the Panic of 1837 and a six-year recession, the worst the American economy had yet known. Ironically, Andrew Jackson, whose bad experience with speculation had led him to destroy the Bank of the United States, set in motion the events that caused the boom and bust he so feared. And he left his successor, Martin Van Buren, an impossible political legacy.

In 1837, some 800 banks suspended business, refusing to pay out any of their $150 million in deposits. The collapse of the banking system led to business closures and outright failures. Nationwide, the unemployment rate is estimated to have reached more than 10 percent. In the winter of 1837–38 in New York City alone, one-third of all manual laborers were unemployed and an estimated 10,000 were living in abject poverty. New York laborers took to the streets. Four or five thousand protesters carrying signs reading "Bread, Meat, Rent, Fuel!" gathered at City Hall on February 10, 1838, then marched to the warehouse of a leading merchant, Eli Hart. Breaking down the door, they took possession of the thousands of barrels of flour Hart had stored there rather than sell at what the mob considered a fair price. Policemen and state militia who tried to prevent the break-in were beaten by the angry mob.

Nor were the working class and the poor the only victims. Among the many hurt by the panic was Philip Hone, former mayor of New York and once a man of considerable wealth. Hone lost two-thirds of his own fortune and was unable to help his three grown sons when they lost their jobs. "Business of all kinds [is] completely at a stand," Hone noted in 1840, wondering "how the poor man manages to get a dinner for his family." The Panic of 1837 lasted six long years, causing widespread misery. Not until 1843 did the economy show signs of recovery.

In neither 1837 nor 1819 did the federal government take any action to aid victims of economic recession. No banks were bailed out, no bank depositors were saved by federal insurance, no laid-off workers got unemployment payments. Nor did the government undertake any public works projects or pump money into the economy. All of these steps, today seen as essential to prevent economic collapse and to alleviate human suffering, were unheard of in 1819 and 1837. Soup kitchens and charities were mobilized in major cities, but only by private, volunteer groups, not by local or state governments. Panics and depressions were believed to be natural stages in the business cycle, and government intervention was considered unwarranted—although it was perfectly acceptable for government to intervene to

This contemporary cartoon bitterly depicts the terrible effects of the Panic of 1837 on ordinary people—bank failures, unemployment, drunkenness, and destitution—which the artist links to the insistence of the rich on payment in specie (as Jackson had required in the Species Circular of 1836). Over the scene waves the American flag, accompanied by the ironic message, "61st Anniversary of our Independence." SOURCE: Panic of 1837 cartoon, *The Times*. Courtesy of the Library of Congress.

promote growth. As a result, workers, farmers, and members of the new business middle class suddenly realized that participation in America's booming economy was very dangerous. The rewards could be great, but so could the penalties.

Martin Van Buren (quickly nicknamed "Van Ruin") spent a dismal four years in the White House presiding over bank failures, bankruptcies, and massive unemployment. Van Buren, who lacked Jackson's compelling personality, could find no remedies to the depression. His misfortune gave the opposition party, the newly formed Whigs, their opportunity.

THE SECOND AMERICAN PARTY SYSTEM

The First American Party System, the confrontation between the Federalists and the Jeffersonian Republicans that began in the 1790s, had been widely viewed at the time as an unfortunate factional squabble that

threatened the common good of the republic (see Chapter 8). By the 1830s, with the expansion of suffrage, the reality of continuing political disagreements had come to be taken as a fact of life. The political struggles of the Jackson era, coupled with the dramatic social changes caused by expansion and economic growth, created the basic pattern of American politics: two major parties, each with at least some appeal among voters of all social classes and in all sections of the country. That pattern, which we call the "Second American Party System," remains to this day.

Whigs and Democrats

There were genuine differences between the Whigs and the Democrats, but they were not sectional differences. Instead, the two parties reflected just-emerging class and cultural differences. The Democrats, as they themselves were quick to point out, had inherited Thomas Jefferson's belief in the democratic rights of the small, independent yeoman farmer. Because most of the country was rural, it is not surprising that the

OVERVIEW

THE SECOND AMERICAN PARTY SYSTEM

Democrats	First organized to elect Andrew Jackson to the presidency in 1828. The Democratic Party spoke for Jeffersonian democracy, expansion, and the freedom of the "common man" from interference from government or from financial monopolies like the Bank of the United States. It found its power base in the rural South and West and among some northern urban workers. The Democratic Party was the majority party from 1828 to 1860.
Whigs	Organized in opposition to Andrew Jackson in the early 1830s. Heir to Federalism, the Whig Party favored a strong role for the national government in the economy (for example, it promoted Henry Clay's American System) and supported active social reform. Its power base lay in the North and Old Northwest among voters who benefited from increased commercialization and among some southern planters and urban merchants. The Whigs won the elections of 1840 and 1848.

Democrats had nationwide appeal, especially in the South and West, the most rural regions. As a result of Jackson's presidency, Democrats came to be identified with independence and a distaste for interference, whether from the government or from economic monopolies such as the Bank of the United States. They favored expansion, Indian removal, and the freedom to do as they chose on the frontier. In the politics of the time, these were conservative values. They reflected the opposition of most Democratic voters to the rapid social and economic changes that accompanied the transportation revolution.

The Whigs were themselves often the initiators and beneficiaries of economic change and were more receptive to it. Heirs of the Federalist belief in the importance of a strong federal role in the national economy (see Chapter 8), they supported the elements of Henry Clay's American System: a strong central government, the Bank of the United States, a protective tariff, and internal improvements. In fact, when it came to improvements, the Whigs wanted to improve people as well as roads. Religion was an important element in political affiliation, and many Whigs were members of evangelical reforming denominations. Reformers believed that everyone, rich and poor, was capable of the self-discipline that would lead to a good life. Thus Whigs favored government intervention in both economic and social affairs, calling for education and social reforms, such as temperance, that aimed to improve the ordinary citizen. Many rich men were Whigs, but so were many poorer men who had a democratic faith in the perfectibility of all Americans. The Whigs' greatest strength was in New England and the northern part of the West (the Old Northwest), the areas most affected by commercial agriculture and factory work.

Yet neither party was monolithic. As has continued to be true of American political parties, both the Democrats and the Whigs were a coalition of interests affected by local and regional factors. The job of the party leader, as the Democrats' Martin Van Buren had been among the first to realize, was to forge the divergent local party interests into a winning national majority. Although Jackson's appeal was strongest in the rural South and West, the Democrats also appealed to some workers in northern cities. Reflecting the emerging issues of class and ethnicity, these Democrats, many of them immigrants, voted against the wealthier, native-born Americans, who were mostly Whigs. Urban workers cared little about rural issues, and they were less committed to the slave system than many Southerners, but they shared with Democrats from other regions a dislike of big business. On the other hand, a number of southern planters, who had close ties to merchant and banking interests, and residents of the South's commercial cities were attracted to the Whig policy of a strong federal role in economic development, though they were less active than many northern Whigs in advocating sweeping social reform.

The Campaign of 1840

In 1840, the Whigs set out to beat the Democrats at their own game. Passing over the ever-hopeful Henry Clay, the Whigs nominated a man as much like Andrew Jackson as possible, the aging Indian fighter William Henry Harrison, former governor of the Indiana Territory from 1801 to 1812. In an effort to duplicate Jackson's winning appeal to the South as well as the West, the Whigs balanced the ticket by nominating a Southerner, John Tyler, for vice president. The campaign slogan was "Tippecanoe and Tyler too" (Tippecanoe was the site of Harrison's famous victory over Tecumseh's Indian confederation in 1811). As if this were not enough, Whigs made Harrison out to be a humble man who would be happy to live in a log cabin, although he actually lived in a large and comfortable house. Thus began another long-lived political legend. The Whigs reached out to ordinary people with torchlight parades, barbecues, songs, coonskin caps, bottomless jugs of hard cider, and claims that Martin Van Buren, Harrison's hapless opponent, was a man of privilege and aristocratic tastes. Nothing could be further from the truth: Van Buren was the son of a tavern keeper. But Van Buren, a short man who lacked a commanding presence, had always dressed meticulously, and now even his taste in coats and ties was used against him.

The Whig campaign tactics, added to the popular anger at Van Buren because of the continuing depression, gave Harrison a sweeping electoral victory, 234 votes to 60. Even more remarkable, the campaign achieved the greatest voter turnout up to that time (and rarely equaled since), 80 percent.

The Whig Victory Turns to Loss: The Tyler Presidency

Although the Whig victory of 1840 was a milestone in American politics, the triumph of Whig principles was short-lived. William Henry Harrison, who was sixty-eight, died of pneumonia a month after his inauguration. For the first time in American history the vice president stepped up to the presidency. Not for the last time, important differences between the dead president and his successor reshaped the direction of American politics. John Tyler of Virginia was a former Democrat who had left the party because he disagreed with Jackson's autocratic style. The Whigs had sought him primarily for his sectional appeal and had not inquired too closely into his political opinions, which turned out to be anti-Whig as well as anti-Jackson. President Tyler vetoed a series of bills embodying all the elements of Henry Clay's American System: tariffs, internal improvements, a new Bank of the United States. In exasperation, congressional Whigs forced Tyler out of the party, and his entire cabinet of Whigs resigned. To replace them, Tyler appointed former Democrats like himself. Thus the Whig triumph of 1840, one of the clearest victories in American electoral politics, was negated by the stalemate between Tyler and the Whig majority in Congress. The Whigs were to win only one more election, that of 1848.

Although the circumstances that robbed the Whigs of their victory were accidental, the Tyler debacle laid bare the great division that the two-party system was intended to hide: the sectional difference between the North and the South. The Whigs were a

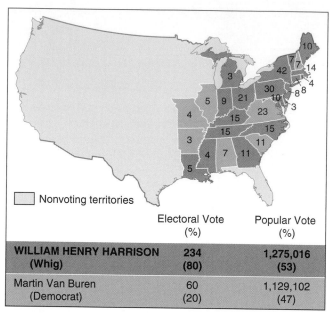

	Electoral Vote (%)	Popular Vote (%)
WILLIAM HENRY HARRISON (Whig)	**234 (80)**	**1,275,016 (53)**
Martin Van Buren (Democrat)	60 (20)	1,129,102 (47)

The Election of 1840   The Whigs triumphed in the election of 1840 by beating the Democrats at their own game. Whigs could expect to do well in the commercializing areas of New England and the Old Northwest, but their adopted strategy of popular campaigning worked well in the largely rural South and West as well, contributing to Harrison's victory. The Whigs' choice of John Tyler as vice presidential candidate, another strategy designed to appeal to southern voters, backfired when Harrison died and Tyler, who did not share Whig principles, became America's first vice president to succeed to the presidency.

short-lived national party because they could not bridge that gap. And by the 1850s not even the Democrats could remain united.

AMERICAN ARTS AND LETTERS

Jackson's presidency was a defining moment in the development of an American identity. His combination of western belligerency and combative individualism was the strongest statement of American distinctiveness since Thomas Jefferson's agrarianism. Did Jackson speak for all of America? The Whigs did not think so. And the definitions of American identity that were beginning to emerge in popular culture and in intellectual circles were more complex than the message coming from the White House. Throughout the nation, however, there was a widespread interest in information and literature of all kinds. The Age of the Common Man would prove to be the period when American writers and painters found the national themes that allowed them to produce the first distinctively American literature and art.

Popular Cultures and the Spread of the Written Word

The print revolution, described earlier in connection with political parties, had effects far beyond politics. Newspapers and pamphlets fostered a variety of popular cultures. For western readers, the Crockett almanacs offered a mix of humorous stories and tall tales attributed to Davy Crockett (the boisterous Tennessee "roarer" who died defending the Alamo in 1836) along with meteorological and climate information. In New York City the immensely popular "penny papers" (so called from their price), the *New York Morning Post* and the *New York Sun*, that began appearing in 1833 fostered a distinctive urban culture. These papers, with lurid headlines such as "Double Suicide," and "Secret Tryst," fed the same popular appetite for scandal as did other popular publications. The *Police Gazette* magazine; pamphlets about murder trials, swindlers, and pirates; and temperance dime novels such as *The Inebriate*, written in 1842 by a struggling young newspaperman named Walter (later Walt) Whitman, were read by many. Throughout the country, religious literature was still most widely read, but a small middle-class audience existed for literary magazines and, among women especially, for sentimental magazines and novels.

Accompanying all these changes in print communication was an invention that outsped them all: the telegraph, so innovative that its inventor spent years fruitlessly seeking private funds to back its application. Finally, with financing from the federal government, Samuel F. B. Morse sent his first message from Washington to Baltimore in 1844. Soon messages in Morse code would be transmitted instantaneously across the continent. The impact of this revolutionary invention, the first to separate the message from the speed at which a human messenger could travel, was immediate. The timeliness of information available to the individual, from important national news to the next train's arrival time, vastly increased. Distant events gained new and exciting immediacy. Everyone's horizon and sense of community was widened.

Creating a National American Culture

For all the improvements in communication, the United States was a provincial culture, still looking to Britain for values, standards, and literary offerings, and still mocked by the British. In a famous essay in the *Edinburgh Review* in 1820, Sidney Smith bitingly inquired, "In the four quarters of the globe, who reads an American book? or goes to an American play? or looks at an American picture or statue? What does the world yet owe to American physicians or surgeons? What new substances have their chemists discovered?" The answer was nothing—yet.

In the early years of the nineteenth century, eastern seaboard cities actively built the cultural foundation that would nurture American art and literature. Philadelphia's American Philosophical Society, founded by Benjamin Franklin in 1743, boasted a distinguished roster of scientists, including Thomas Jefferson—concurrently its president and president of the United States—and Nicholas Biddle, Jackson's opponent in the Bank War. Culturally, Boston ran a close second to Philadelphia, founding the Massachusetts General Hospital (1811) and the Boston Athenaeum (1807), a gentlemen's library and reading room containing "the works of learning and science in all languages; particularly such rare and expensive publications as are not generally to be obtained in this country." The *North American Review*, published in Boston, emerged as the country's most important and long-lasting intellectual magazine. Devoted to keeping its readers in touch with European intellectual developments, the *Review* had a circulation of 3,000 in 1826, about the same as similar British journals. Southern cities were much less successful in supporting culture.

A Regular Row in the Backwoods. The 1841 issue of the *Crockett Almanac*, named after the Tennessee backwoodsman made famous by his self-serving tall tales, portrayed a rough rural "sport." Inexpensive comic almanacs combined illustrated jokes on topical subjects with astrological and weather predictions.

SOURCE. *Crockett Almanac* (1841)—Prints and Photographs Division, Library of Congress.

Charleston had a Literary and Philosophical Society (founded in 1814), but the widely dispersed residences of the southern elite made urban cultural institutions difficult to sustain. Thus, unwittingly, the South ceded cultural leadership to the North.

The cultural picture was much spottier in the West. A few cities, such as Lexington, Kentucky, and Cincinnati, Ohio, had civic cultural institutions, and some transplanted New Englanders maintained connections with New England culture. A group of pioneers in Ames, Ohio, for example, founded a "coonskin library" composed of books purchased from Boston and paid for in coonskins. But most pioneers were at best uninterested and at worst actively hostile to traditional literary culture. This was neither from lack of literacy nor from a failure to read. Newspaper and religious journals both had large readerships in the West: The *Methodist Christian Advocate*, for example, reached 25,000 people yearly (compared with the *North American Review*'s 3,000). The frontier emphasis on the practical was hard to distinguish from antiintellec-

tualism. As writer Hugh Henry Brackenridge lamented from Pittsburgh, it was not "the want of learning I consider as a defect, but the contempt of it."

Thus in the early part of the nineteenth century, the gap between the intellectual and cultural horizons of a wealthy Bostonian and a frontier farmer in Michigan widened. Part of the unfinished task of building a national society was the creation of a national culture that could fill this gap. For writers and artists, the challenge was to find distinctively American themes.

Of the eastern cities, New York produced the first widely recognized American writers. In 1819, Washington Irving published *The Sketch Book*, thus immortalizing Rip Van Winkle and the Headless Horseman. Within a few years James Fenimore Cooper's Leatherstocking novels (of which *The Last of the Mohicans*, published in 1826, is the best known) achieved wide success in both America and Europe. Cooper's novels featured a heroic frontiersman, Natty Bumppo (modeled on Daniel Boone), who observes favorably the nobility of the Indians even as he participates in their

The Boston Athenaeum was one of Boston's leading cultural institutions. The library, shown in this engraving, was probably the finest in the country in the early nineteenth century.

SOURCE: Library of the Athenaeum. Wood engraving, 1855. *Collection of the Boston Athenaeum.*

defeat by the forces of civilization. Cooper's novels established the long American experience of westward expansion, of which the conquest of the Indians was a vital part, as a serious and distinctive American literary theme. It was New England, however, that claimed to be the forge of American cultural independence from Europe. As Ralph Waldo Emerson proclaimed in "The American Scholar," a lecture he delivered in 1837 to the Harvard faculty, "Our day of dependence, our long apprenticeship to the learning of other lands, draws to a close." He went on to encourage American writers to find inspiration in the ordinary details of daily life. The stuff of literature, he declared, was to be found in "the familiar, the low . . . the milk in the pan; the ballad in the street; the news of the boat." Immensely popular, Emerson was the star of the lyceum circuit, a lecture network that sent speakers on cultural subjects to all parts of the country. He gave more than 1,500 lectures in twenty states between 1833 and 1860. "The American Scholar," his most famous lecture, carried a message of cultural self-sufficiency that Americans were eager to hear.

Artists and Builders

Artists were as successful as novelists in finding American themes. Thomas Cole, who came to America from England in 1818, found great inspiration in the American landscape, painting scenes of New York State's Catskill and Adirondack Mountains that reflect the influence of the British romantic school of landscape painting. With these works, Cole founded the Hudson River school of American painting. The frankly nationalistic style and subject matter of this school are reflected in the comment of New Yorker Philip Hone: "Every American is bound to prove his love of country by admiring Cole."

The western painters—realists such as Karl Bodmer and George Catlin as well as the romantics who followed them, like Albert Bierstadt and Thomas Moran—drew on the dramatic western landscape and its peoples. Their art was an important contribution to the American sense of the land and to the nation's identity. Catlin, driven by a need to document Indian life before it disappeared, spent eight years among the tribes of the upper Missouri River. Then he assembled his collection—more than 500 paintings in all—and toured the country from 1837 to 1851 in an unsuccessful attempt to arouse public indignation about the plight of the western Indian nations. Another unusual western painter, John James Audubon, could at first find no publisher in this country for his striking and sometimes grotesque etchings of American birds. George Caleb Bingham, an accomplished genre painter, produced somewhat tidied-up scenes of real-life American workers, such as flatboatmen on the Missouri

River. All these painters found much to record and to celebrate in American life. Ironically, the inspiration for the most prevalent theme, the American wilderness, was profoundly endangered by the rapid western settlement of which the nation was so proud.

The haste and transiency of American life are nowhere so obvious as in the architectural record of this era, which is sparse. The monumental neoclassical style (complete with columns) that Jefferson had recommended for official buildings in Washington continued to be favored for public buildings elsewhere and by private concerns trying to project an imposing image, such as banks. A few southern planters built impressive mansions, and there were odd experiments such as the prison built in Philadelphia in the 1820s that was designed to look like a medieval castle. The effect of this building on the imagination, one admiring commentator remarked, was "peculiarly impressive, solemn and instructive."

But in general Americans were in too much of a hurry to build for the future, and in balloon-frame construction they found the perfect technique for the present. Balloon-frame structures—which consist of a

Asher Durand, a member of the Hudson River School of landscape painting, produced this work, *Kindred Spirits*, in 1849 as a tribute to Thomas Cole, the school's leader. Cole is one of the figures depicted standing in a romantic wilderness. SOURCE: Courtesy of The New York Public Library.

CHRONOLOGY

1817	Erie Canal construction begins
1818	National Road completed to Wheeling, Virginia (now West Virginia)
1819	*Dartmouth College* v. *Woodward*
1821	Martin Van Buren's Bucktails defeat DeWitt Clinton in New York Mexican independence from Spain
1824	*Gibbons* v. *Ogden* John Quincy Adams elected president by the House of Representatives
1825	Erie Canal opens
1826	First American use of the steam-powered printing press
1828	Congress passes "Tariff of Abominations" Andrew Jackson elected president John C. Calhoun publishes *Exposition and Protest* anonymously
1830	Jackson vetoes Maysville Road Bill Congress passes Indian Removal Act Baltimore and Ohio Railroad opens
1832	Nullification Crisis begins Jackson vetoes renewal of Bank of the United States charter Jackson reelected president

1833	National Road completed to Columbus, Ohio General Antonio Lopez de Santa Anna elected president of Mexico
1834	Cyrus McCormick patents the McCormick reaper Whig party organized British abolish slavery in their Caribbean colonies
1836	Jackson issues Specie Circular Martin Van Buren elected president
1837	*Charles River Bridge* v. *Warren Bridge* John Deere invents steel plow Revolts against Britain in Upper and Lower Canada Ralph Waldo Emerson first presents "The American Scholar" Panic of 1837
1838	Cherokee removal along the "Trail of Tears"
1840	Whig William Henry Harrison elected president Act of Union merges Upper and Lower Canada
1841	John Tyler assumes presidency at the death of President Harrison
1844	Samuel F. B. Morse operates first telegraph

basic frame of wooden studs fastened with cross-pieces top and bottom—could be put up quickly, cheaply, and without the help of a skilled carpenter. Covering the frame with wooden siding was equally simple, and the resultant dwelling was as strong, although not as well insulated, as a house of solid timber or logs. Balloon-frame construction was first used in Chicago in the 1830s, where it created the city almost instantly. The four-room balloon-frame house, affordable to many who could not have paid for a traditionally built dwelling, became standard in that decade. This was indeed housing for the common man and his family.

CONCLUSION

Andrew Jackson's presidency witnessed the building of a strong national party system based on nearly universal white manhood suffrage. At the same time that the nation expanded politically (nine new western states were admitted between 1800 and 1840), construction of new roads, canals, and railroads, and other improvements in transportation and communication, created the infrastructure that united the nation physically. Sectionalism and localism seemed to have been replaced by a more national consciousness that was clearly expressed in the two national political parties, the Whigs and the Democrats. The Second American Party System created new democratic political communities united by common political opinions.

Culturally, American writers and artists began to establish a distinctive American identity in the arts. But as the key battles of the Jackson presidency—the Nullification Crisis, Indian removal, the Bank War—showed, the forces of sectionalism resisted the strong nationalizing tendencies of the era. As the next two chapters will show, economic and social forces continued to force the South and the North apart.

REVIEW QUESTIONS

1. What reasons might a person of the 1820s and 1830s give for opposing universal white manhood suffrage? Suffrage for free African American men? For women of all races?
2. Andrew Jackson's presidency is considered one of the most influential in American history. Explain the changes in political organization and attitude that made his election possible.
3. Both the Nullification Crisis and Indian removal raised the constitutional issue of the rights of a mi

nority in a nation governed by majority rule. What rights does a minority have, and what kinds of laws are necessary to defend those rights?

4. Why was the issue of government support for internal improvements so controversial?
5. What were the key differences between Whigs and Democrats? What did each party stand for?
6. What distinctive American themes did the writers, artists, and builders of the 1820s and 1830s express in their works?

RECOMMENDED READING

Donald B. Cole, *The Presidency of Andrew Jackson* (1993).

Ronald P. Formisano, *The Transformation of Political Culture: Massachusetts Parties, 1790s–1840s* (1983).

William W. Freehling, *Prelude to Civil War* (1966).

Michael Holt, *The Rise and Fall of the American Whig Party* (1999).

Reeve Huston, *Land and Freedom: Rural Society, Popular Protest, and Party Politics in Antebellus New York* (2000).

John Lauritz Larson, *Internal Improvement: National Public Works and the Promise of Popular Government in the Early United States* (2001).

Jean V. Matthews, *Toward a New Society: American Thought and Culture, 1800–1830* (1991).

Simon Newman, *Parades and the Politics of the Street* (1997).

Robert Remini, *Andrew Jackson and the Course of American Freedom* (1981).

Carol Sheriff, *The Artificial River: The Erie Canal and the Paradox of Progress, 1817–1862* (1996).

Alan Taylor, *William Cooper's Town: Power and Persuasion on the Frontier of the Early American Republic* (1995).

Harry L. Watson, *Liberty and Power: The Politics of Jacksonian America* (1990).

▶ MEDIA RESOURCES

U.S. HISTORY DOCUMENTS CD-ROM

Jefferson and the Republic

8-13   Davy Crockett, Advice to Politicians (1833)

Economic and Social Change

9-4   John Marshall Affirms the Power of the Federal Government

9-8   Imminent Dangers to the Free Institutions of the United States through Foreign Immigration (1835)

9-10   James F. Cooper, Notions of the Americans (1840)

Jacksonian Democracy

10-1   Joseph Smith and the Beginnings of Mormonism (1823)

10-4   The "Commoner" Takes Office (1828)

10-5   Andrew Jackson, First Annual Message to Congress (1829)

10-6   "Memorial of the Cherokee Nation" (1830)

10-7   Andrew Jackson, Veto of the Bank Bill (1832)

10-8   President Andrew Jackson's Proclamation Regarding Nullification (1832)

10-9   The Force Bill (1833)

10-11   A French Traveler Reports on American Society (1835)

COMPANION WEBSITE HIGHLIGHTS

To view an exploration, enter one of the URLs below in your browser.

Web Explorations

The Growth of Universal White Manhood Suffrage
http://www.prenhall.com/faragher/map10.1

Travel Times, 1800 and 1857
http://www.prenhall.com/faragher/map10.2

Additional Interactive Maps

To access the maps, go to this chapter's resources at
http://www.prenhall.com/faragher

Population Trends: Westward Expansion, 1830, page 277

Commercial Links: Rivers, Canals, Roads, 1830, and Rail Lines, 1850, page 291

Southern Indian Cessions and Removals, 1830s, page 294

(Continued)

(Continued)

HISTORY RESOURCE CENTER

To find the resources listed below, go to
http://www.prenhall.com/historyresourcecenter

Documents

Charles Finney, Religious Revival (1835)

Michel Chevalier, Society, Manners and Politics in
the United States (1834)

Nicholas Biddle, Commencement Address (1835)

South Carolina's Ordinance of Nullification (1832)

Images

Erie Canal

Fort Pierre [South Dakota] and the Adjacent Prairie,
1832

Antirailroad poster

Teton Sioux Horse Races in Front of Fort Pierre,
South Dakota, 1833

William Henry Harrison Campaign Poster

EXPLORING AMERICA

AMERICAN ART

http://www.prenhall.com/faragher/americanart

In the period between 1800 and 1860, several important American literary figures called for a distinctive American art. Walt Whitman, Ralph Emerson, and Herman Melville, among others, championed the idea of an American culture. What characterized American art during this period? Where were American painters trained and who provided them with the recognition needed to succeed? What types of art appealed to American audiences? The *American Art* module uses visual images, letters, and other writings to explore the rise of a uniquely American art and culture before 1860.

American Art examines European influence on American art and the attempts to gain artistic independence from this influence. The quotes by literary figures frame the argument for an American art while the discussion of the popularity of sculpture shows the endurance of European ideals.

Reflect and Respond

1. Emerson addressed himself to the potential "American Scholar" of whom he demanded great things. Melville addressed the American reader and critic. What did he demand of them?

2. Emerson claimed universality for his own experience. Whitman, in contrast, pointed to specific features of American life of which he claimed "Here at last is something in the doings of man that corresponds with the broadcast doings of the day and night." What made the United States so unique for Whitman?

3. Does Whitman's formulation correspond to William Cullen Bryant's "earlier, wilder image" of America?

✓ Check it out

Thomas Cole, "The Course of Empire"

This series of paintings by American artist Thomas Cole depicts the rise, development, and decline of empires. The paintings follow the course of the nations described in Thomas Gibbons' book, *The Rise and Fall of the Roman Empire*. It also reflects a general belief in the cycle nations follow, a chilling prediction for a fledgling republic.

This exploration is also available on the *Exploring America* CD-ROM.

Taylor, *An American Slave Market*, 1852. Oil on canvas. Chicago Historical Society.

Natchez-under-the-Hill

THE WHARFMASTER HAD JUST OPENED THE PUBLIC AUCTION of confiscated cargoes in the center of Natchez when a great cry was heard. An angry crowd of flatboatmen, Bowie knives in hand, was storming up the bluffs from the Mississippi shouting, as the local newspaper reported, "threats of violence and death upon all who attempted to sell and buy their property." It was November 1837, and the town council had just enacted a restrictive tax of $10 per flatboat, a measure designed to rid the wharf district known as Natchez-under-the-Hill of the most impoverished and disreputable of the flatboatmen. The council had made its first confiscation of cargo after nine captains refused to pay this tax. As the boatmen approached, merchants and onlookers shrank back in fear. But the local authorities had called out the militia, and a company of farmers and planters now came marching into the square with their rifles primed and lowered. "The cold and sullen bayonets of the Guards were too hard meat for the Arkansas toothpicks," reported the local press, and "there was no fight." The boatmen sullenly turned and went back down the bluffs. It was the first confrontation in the "Flatboat Wars" that erupted as Mississippi ports tried to bring their troublesome riverfronts under regulation.

The first European to take notice of this "land abundant in subsistence" was a member of Hernando de Soto's expedition in the sixteenth century. The area was "thickly peopled" by the Natchez Indians, he wrote. It was not until the French established the port of Fort Rosalie in the 1720s, however, that Europeans settled in the area. The French destroyed the highly organized society of the Natchez Indians in the 1730s and the port became a major Mississippi River trading center. From Fort Rosalie, the French conducted an extensive frontier trade that brought peoples of different races together, leading to intermarriage and the growth of a mixed-race population. French traders bought deerskins, for which there was a large export market, from Choctaw, Chickasaw, and Creek hunters. During the same period, some Africans who had been imported by the French to work as slaves on plantations found roles in the French-Indian trade as boatmen, hunters, soldiers, and interpreters.

When the Spanish took control of the territory in 1763 they laid out the new town of Natchez high on the bluffs, safe from Mississippi flooding. Fort Rosalie, rechristened Natchez-under-the-Hill, continued to flourish as the produce grown by American farmers in Kentucky and Tennessee moved downriver on flatboats. Thus Americans became the newest additions to the ethnic diversity of this well-established trading center. When Americans took possession of Mississippi in 1798, the district surrounding the port became the most important center of settlement in the Old Southwest. Once again this abundant land of rich, black soil became thickly peopled, but this time with cotton planters and their African American slaves.

Under-the-Hill gained renown as the last stop for boatmen before New Orleans. Minstrel performers sang of their exploits:

Den dance de boatmen dance,
O dance de boatmen dance,
O dance all night till broad daylight,
An go home wid de gals in de morning.

According to one traveler, "They feel the same inclination to dissipation as sailors who have long been out of port." There were often as many as 150 boats drawn up at the wharves. The crowds along the riverfront, noted John James Audubon, who visited in the 1820s, "formed a medley which it is beyond my power to describe." Mingling among American rivermen of all descriptions were trappers and hunters in fur caps, Spanish shopkeepers in bright smocks, French gentlemen from New Orleans in velvet coats, Indians wrapped in their trade blankets, African Americans both free and slave—a pageant of nations and races. Clapboard shacks and flatboats dragged on shore and converted into storefronts served as grog shops, card rooms, dance halls, and hotels. Whorehouses with women of every age and color abounded.

On the bluffs, meanwhile, the town of Natchez had become the winter home to the southwestern planter elite. They built their mansions with commanding views of the river. A visitor attending a ball at one of these homes was dazzled by the display: "Myriads of wax candles burning in wall sconces, sparkling chandeliers, entrancing music, the scent of jasmine, rose and sweet olive, the sparkle of wine mellowed by age, the flow of wit and brilliant repartee, all were there." Sustaining this American aristocracy was the labor of thousands of enslaved men and women, who lived in the squalid quarters behind the great house and worked the endless fields of cotton. It was they who made possible the greatest accumulations of wealth in early nineteenth-century America.

The Natchez planters, their wealth and confidence growing with cotton's growing dominance of the local economy, found Under-the-Hill an increasing irritant. "A gentleman may game with a gambler by the hour," one resident remembered, "and yet despise him and refuse to recognize him afterward." The Under-the-Hill elite, however—gamblers, saloon keepers, and pimps—disturbed this social boundary when they began staying at hotels and even building town houses in Natchez town. And in the wake of the slave revolt led by Nat Turner in Virginia in 1831, in which

fifty-five white people were killed, the planters began to feel increasingly threatened by the racial mingling of the riverfront.

In the late 1830s the Natchez elite was jolted by rumors that their slaves were conspiring to murder them during Fourth of July celebrations while Under-the-Hill desperadoes looted their mansions. The rumors reinforced the growing conviction among planters that they could no longer tolerate the polyglot community of the riverfront. The measures that ultimately provoked the flatboatmen's threats in November 1837 soon followed.

In response to these threats, the planters issued an extralegal order giving all the gamblers, pimps, and whores of Under-the-Hill twenty-four hours to evacuate the district. As the Mississippi militia sharpened their bayonets, panic swept the wharves, and that night dozens of flatboats loaded with a motley human cargo headed for the more tolerant community of New Orleans. Other river ports issued similar orders of expulsion. "The towns on the river," one resident remembered, "became purified from a moral pestilence which the law could not cure." Three years later a great tornado hit Under-the-Hill, leveling the shacks that had served so long as a rendezvous for the rivermen, and gradually the Mississippi reclaimed the old river bottom.

These two communities—Natchez, home to the rich slave-owning elite, and Natchez-under-the-Hill, the bustling polyglot trading community—epitomize the paradox of the American South in the early nineteenth century. Enslaved African Americans grew the region's most lucrative crop, cotton. On the resulting profits, aristocratic Southerners built a sumptuous and distinctive lifestyle for themselves. The boatmen and traders of Natchez-under-the-Hill who brought the cotton and other products to market were vital to the planters' prosperity. But the polyglot racial and social mixing of Natchez-under-the-Hill threatened the system of control, built on a rigid distinction between free white people and enslaved black people by which the planters maintained slavery. Because the slave owners could not control the boatmen, they expelled them. This defensive reaction—to seal off the world of slavery from the wider commercial world—exposed the vulnerability of the slave system at the very moment of its greatest commercial success. ∎

Natchez

KEY TOPICS

- The domination of southern life by the slave system

- The economic implications of "King Cotton"

- The creation of African American communities under slavery

- The social structure of the white South and its increasing defensivenesss

---

KING COTTON AND SOUTHERN EXPANSION

Slavery had long dominated southern life. African American slaves grew the great export crops of the colonial period—tobacco, rice, and indigo—on which slave owners' fortunes were made, and their presence shaped southern society and culture (see Chapter 4). Briefly, in the early days of American independence, the slave system waned, only to be revived by the immense profitability of cotton in a newly industrializing world. Cotton became the dominant crop in a rapidly expanding South that included not only the original states of Maryland, Delaware, Virginia, North and South Carolina, and Georgia, but also Kentucky, Tennessee, Missouri, Alabama, Mississippi, Louisiana, Arkansas, Florida, and Texas. The overwhelming economic success of cotton and of the slave system on which it depended created a distinctive regional culture quite different from that developing in the North.

The Cotton Gin and Expansion into the Old Southwest

Short-staple cotton had long been recognized as a crop ideally suited to southern soils and growing conditions. But it had one major drawback: the seeds were so difficult to remove from the lint that it took an entire day to hand-clean a single pound of cotton. The invention in 1793 that made cotton growing profitable was the result of collaboration between a young Northerner named Eli Whitney,

recently graduated from Yale College, and Catherine Greene, a South Carolina plantation owner and widow of Revolutionary War General Nathanael Greene, who had hired Whitney to tutor her children. Whitney built a prototype cotton engine, dubbed "gin" for short, a simple device consisting of a hand-cranked cylinder with teeth that tore the lint away from the seeds. At Greene's suggestion, the teeth were made of wire. With the cotton gin it was possible to clean more than fifty pounds of cotton a day. Soon large and small

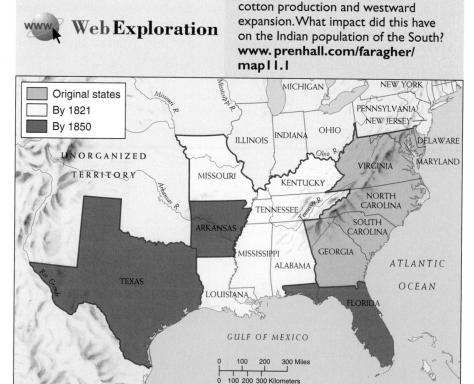

Consider the relationship between cotton production and westward expansion. What impact did this have on the Indian population of the South? www. prenhall.com/faragher/map11.1

WebExploration

Legend:
- Original states
- By 1821
- By 1850

The South Expands, 1790–1850 This map shows the dramatic effect cotton production had on southern expansion. From the original six states of 1790, westward expansion, fueled by the search for new cotton lands, added another six states by 1821, and three more by 1850.

planters in the inland regions of Georgia and South Carolina had begun to grow cotton. By 1811, this area was producing 60 million pounds of cotton a year, and exporting most of it to England.

Other areas of the South quickly followed South Carolina and Georgia into cotton production. New land was wanted because cotton growing rapidly depleted the soil. The profits to be made from cotton growing drew a rush of southern farmers into the so-called black belt—an area stretching through western Georgia, Alabama, and Mississippi that was blessed with exceptionally fertile soil. Following the War of 1812, Southerners were seized by "Alabama Fever." In one of the swiftest migrations in American history, white Southerners and their slaves flooded into western Georgia and the areas that would become Alabama and Mississippi (the Old Southwest). On this frontier, African American pioneers (albeit involuntary ones) cleared the forests, drained the swamps, broke the ground, built houses and barns, and planted the first crops.

This migration caused the population of Mississippi to double (from 31,306 to 74,448) and that of Alabama to grow sixteenfold (from 9,046 to 144,317) between 1810 and 1820. This and subsequent western land booms dramatically changed the population of the original southern states as well. Nearly half of all white South Carolinians born after 1800 eventually left the state, usually to move west. By 1850 there were more than 50,000 South Carolina natives living in Georgia, almost as many in Alabama, and 26,000 in Mississippi.

Southerners had historically taken the lead in westward expansion. Backcountry residents of Virginia and North Carolina were the first to venture over the Appalachians, and Virginians and Carolinians were the major settlers of the first two trans-Appalachian states, Kentucky (1792) and Tennessee (1796). John C. Calhoun of South Carolina and Henry Clay of Kentucky had been two of the most prominent expansionist War Hawks in Congress before the War of 1812. Like the simultaneous expansion into the Old Northwest, settlement of the Old Southwest took place at the expense of the region's Indian population (see Chapter 9). Beginning with the defeat of the Creeks at Horseshoe Bend in 1814 and ending with the Cherokee forced migration along the "Trail of Tears" in 1838, the Five Civilized Tribes—the Cherokees, Chickasaws, Choctaws, Creeks, and Seminoles—were forced to give up their lands and move to Indian Territory (see Chapter 10).

On the southern frontier, as on the northern frontier, the killing, confinement, and removal of Indian peoples was the result of white expansion and settlement motivated by the hunger for land and profit. In the South, however, there was an additional motivation, rooted in slavery, for Indian removal: there was simply no room in the southern social order for any-

Steamboats at New Orleans await loads of cotton, the nation's major export. Just as the giant bales crowd the wharf, so too the culture created by "King Cotton" dominated southern life.

SOURCE: Courtesy of the Library of Congress.

thing other than white and black, master and slave. Literate, slave-owning "redskins" confused this simple picture: they were too "civilized" to be like slaves, but the wrong color to be masters. Thus southern Indian removal, like southern expansion, was dictated by the needs of the slave system.

Following the "Alabama Fever" of 1816–20, several later surges of southern expansion (1832–38, and again in the mid-1850s) carried cotton planting over the Mississippi River into Louisiana and deep into Texas. Each surge ignited feverish speculative frenzies, remembered in terms like the "Flush Times" for the heated rush of the 1830s. In the minds of the mobile, enterprising Southerners who sought their fortunes in the West, cotton profits and expansion went hand in hand. But the expansion of cotton meant the expansion of slavery.

Changing Attitudes toward Slavery

In the flush of freedom following the American Revolution, all the northern states abolished slavery or passed laws for gradual emancipation and a number of slave owners in the Upper South freed their slaves (see Chapter 7). Thomas Jefferson, ever the optimist, claimed that "a total emancipation with the consent of the masters" could not be too far in the future. Nevertheless, southern legislatures were unwilling to write steps toward emancipation into law, preferring to depend on the charity of individual slave owners. Between 1776 and 1786 all the states except South Carolina and Georgia either banned or heavily taxed the international slave trade. Following the successful slave revolt in Haiti in 1791 all the southern states banned the importation of foreign slaves, fearing that Caribbean revolutionaries might incite their own slaves to rebellion.

But attitudes rapidly changed in the South following the invention of the cotton gin in 1793 and the realization of the riches to be made from cotton. White Southerners believed that only African slaves could be forced to work day after day, year after year, at the rapid and brutal pace required in the cotton fields of large plantations in the steamy southern summer. As the production of cotton climbed higher every year in response to a seemingly inexhaustible international demand, so too did the demand for slaves and the conviction of Southerners that slavery was an economic necessity.

Slave smuggling became so rampant that South Carolina officially reopened the trade in 1804. For the next four years, Charleston boomed as one of the world's largest slaving ports: at least 40,000 Africans were imported. It was clear, however, that national opinion found the international slave trade abhorrent, and on January 1, 1808, the earliest date permitted by the Constitution, a bill to abolish the importation of slaves became law. Although a small number of slaves continued to be smuggled from Africa, the growth of the slave labor force after 1808 depended primarily on natural increase. And the ban on foreign importations vastly increased the importance of the internal slave trade.

The Internal Slave Trade

The cotton boom caused a huge increase in the domestic slave trade. Plantation owners in the Upper South (Delaware, Kentucky, Maryland, Virginia, and Tennessee) sold their slaves to meet the demand for labor in the new and expanding cotton-growing regions of the Old Southwest. In every decade after 1820 at least

150,000 slaves were uprooted either by slave trading or planter migration to the new areas, and in the expansions of the 1830s and the 1850s, the number reached a quarter of a million. Cumulatively, between 1820 and 1860 nearly 50 percent of the slave population of the Upper South took part against their will in southern expansion. More slaves—an estimated 1 million—were uprooted by this internal slave trade and enforced migration in the early nineteenth century than were brought to North America during the entire time the international slave trade was legal (see Chapter 4).

Purchased by slave traders from owners in the Upper South, slaves were gathered together in notorious "slave pens" in places like Richmond and Charleston and then moved south by train or boat. In the interior, they were carried as cargo on steamboats on the Mississippi River, hence the dreaded phrase "sold down the river." Often slaves moved on foot, chained together in groups of fifty or more known as "coffles." Chained slaves in coffles were a common sight on southern roads, and one difficult to reconcile with the notion of slavery as a benevolent institution. Arriving at a central market in the Lower South like Natchez, New Orleans, or Mobile, the slaves, after being carefully inspected by potential buyers, were sold at auction to the highest bidder.

Although popular stereotype portrayed slave traders as unscrupulous outsiders who persuaded kind and reluctant masters to sell their slaves, the historical truth is much harsher. Traders, far from being shunned by slave-owning society, were often respected community members. One Charleston trader, Alexander McDonald, served as both an alderman and a bank president and was described as "a man of large means and responsible for all his engagements" who had "the confidence of the public." Similarly, the sheer scale of the slave trade makes it impossible to believe that slave owners only reluctantly parted with their slaves at times of economic distress. Instead, it is clear that many owners sold slaves and separated slave families not out of necessity but to increase their profits. The sheer size and profitability of the internal slave trade made a mockery of Southern claims for the benevolence of the slave system.

The immense size of the internal slave trade made sights like this commonplace on southern roads. Groups of slaves, chained together in gangs called coffles, were marched from their homes in the Upper South to cities in the Lower South, where they were auctioned to new owners.

SOURCE: Library of Congress.

The Economics of Slavery

The rapid growth of cotton production was an international phenomenon, prompted by events occurring far from the American

South. The insatiable demand for cotton was a result of the technological and social changes that we know today as the Industrial Revolution. Beginning early in the eighteenth century, a series of inventions resulted in the mechanized spinning and weaving of cloth in the world's first factories in the north of England. The ability of these factories to produce unprecedented amounts of cotton cloth revolutionized the world economy. The invention of the cotton gin came at just the right time. British textile manufacturers were eager to buy all the cotton that the South could produce. Was the southern plantation system profitable? Clearly, in the years before 1860, southern farmers believed so. The figures for cotton production support this conclusion: from 720,000 bales in 1830, to 2.85 million bales in 1850, to nearly 5 million in 1860. By the time of the Civil War, cotton accounted for almost 60 percent of American exports, representing a total value of nearly $200 million a year. Cotton's central place in the national economy and its international importance led Senator James Henry Hammond of South Carolina to make a famous boast in 1858:

> Without firing a gun, without drawing a sword, should they make war on us, we could bring the whole world to our feet. What would happen if no cotton was furnished for three years? . . . England would topple headlong and carry the whole civilized world with her save the South. No, you dare not to make war on cotton. No power on the earth dares to make war upon it. Cotton is King.

Indeed, the export of cotton from the South was the dynamic force in the developing American economy in the period 1790–1840. Just as the international slave trade had been the dynamic force in the Atlantic economy of the eighteenth century (see Chapter 4), southern slavery financed northern industrial development in the nineteenth century.

The connection between southern slavery and northern industry was very direct. Most mercantile services associated with the cotton trade (insurance, for example) were in northern hands and, significantly, so was shipping. This economic structure was not new. In colonial times, New England ships dominated the African slave trade. Some New England families—like the Browns of Providence who made fortunes in the slave trade—invested some of their profits in the new technology of textile manufacturing in the 1790s. Other merchants—such as the Boston Associates who financed the cotton textile mills at Lowell—made their money from cotton shipping and brokerage. Thus as cotton boomed, it provided capital for the new factories of the North.

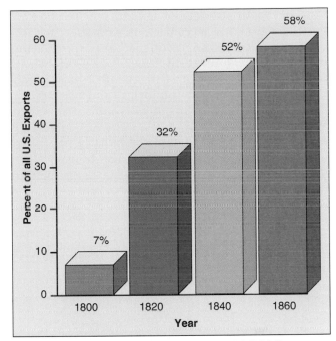

Cotton Exports as a Percentage of All U.S. Exports, 1800–1860   One consequence of the growth of cotton production was its importance in international trade. The growing share of the export market, and the great value (nearly $200 million in 1860) led southern slave owners to believe that "Cotton Is King." The importance of cotton to the national economy entitled the South to a commanding voice in national policy, many Southerners believed.

Cotton Culture

Cotton cultivation created a different kind of society in the South than in the North. At a time when the North was experiencing the greatest spurt of urban growth in the nation's history, southern cities did not keep pace. Charleston, for example, one of America's five largest cities in 1800, had a population of only 41,000 in 1860, compared with Boston's 177,840 and Baltimore's 212,418. The one exception was New Orleans, the great port at the mouth of the extensive Mississippi River transportation system. In 1860 New Orleans was the nation's fifth largest city, with a population of 169,000. The nine other leading cities were all northern or western. Most of the South remained rural: less than 3 percent of Mississippi's population lived in cities of more than 2,500 residents, and only 10 percent of Virginia's did. There was no question that concentration on plantation agriculture diverted energy and resources from the South's cities. The agrarian ideal, bolstered by the cotton boom, encouraged the antiurban and anticommercial sentiments of many white Southerners.

The South also lagged behind the North in industrialization and in canals and railroads. In 1860, only 15 percent of the nation's factories were located in the South. (Noteworthy exceptions were the iron industry near Richmond, which in 1860 boasted four rolling mills, fourteen foundries, and various machine shops employing 1,600 mechanics, and William Gregg's cotton textile mills in Graniteville, just east of Augusta, Georgia.) Similarly, the South was also initially left behind by the transportation revolution. In 1850, only 26 percent of the nation's railroads were in the South, increasing to still only 35 percent by 1860.

The failure of the South to industrialize at the northern rate was not a matter of ignorance but of choice. Southern capital was tied up in land and slaves, and Southerners, buoyed by the world's insatiable demand for cotton, saw no reason to invest in economically risky railroads, canals, and factories. Nor were they eager to introduce the disruptive factor of free wage labor into the tightly controlled slave system. Cotton was safer. Cotton was King.

Thus the cotton boom created a distinctive regional culture. Although cotton was far from being the only crop (the South actually devoted more acreage to corn than to cotton in 1860), its vast profitability affected all aspects of society. In the first half of the nineteenth century, King Cotton reigned supreme over an expanding domain as Southerners increasingly tied their fortunes to the slave system of cotton production. As a British tourist to Mobile wryly noted in the 1850s, the South was a place where "people live in cotton houses and ride in cotton carriages. They buy cotton, sell cotton, think cotton, eat cotton, drink cotton, and dream cotton. They marry cotton wives, and unto them are born cotton children." The South was truly in thrall to King Cotton.

TO BE A SLAVE

Slavery had become distinctively southern: by 1820, as a result of laws passed after the Revolution, all of the northern states had abolished slaveholding. The slave population, estimated at 700,000 in 1790, grew to more than 4 million in 1860. After 1808 (when official American participation in the international slave trade ceased) the growth occurred because of natural increase—that is, through births within the slave population. A distinctive African American slave community,

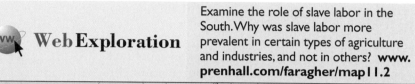

Examine the role of slave labor in the South. Why was slave labor more prevalent in certain types of agriculture and industries, and not in others? **www. prenhall.com/faragher/map11.2**

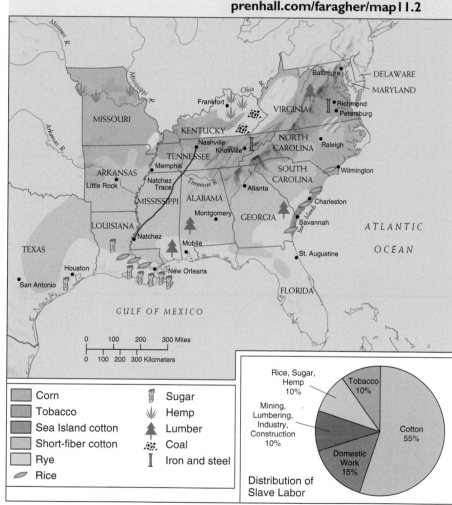

Agriculture, Industry, and Slavery, 1850   The distribution of the slave population in the South was determined by agricultural and industrial patterns. In 1850, 55 percent of all slaves worked in cotton, 10 percent in tobacco, and another 10 percent in rice, sugar, and hemp. Ten percent worked in mining, lumbering, industry, and construction, and 15 percent worked as domestic servants. Slaves were not generally used to grow corn, the staple crop of the yeoman farmer.

which had first emerged in the eighteenth century (see Chapter 4), matured in the early years of the nineteenth century. This community was as much shaped by King Cotton as was the white South.

The Maturing of the American Slave System

The explosive growth of cotton plantations changed the nature of southern slave labor. In 1850, 55 percent of all slaves were engaged in cotton growing. Another 20 percent labored to produce other crops: tobacco (10 percent), rice, sugar, and hemp. About 15 percent of all slaves were domestic servants, and the remaining 10 percent worked in mining, lumbering, industry, and construction.

Cotton growing concentrated slaves on plantations, in contrast to the more dispersed distribution on smaller farms in earlier generations. Although more than half of all slave owners owned five slaves or fewer, 75 percent of all slaves now lived in groups of ten or more. This disproportionate distribution could have a major impact on a slave's life, for it was a very different matter to be the single slave of a small farmer as opposed to being a member of a 100-person black community on a large plantation. The size of cotton plantations fostered the growth of African-American slave communities.

On the other hand, the westward expansion of cotton undermined the stability of these communities. As expansion to the Southwest accelerated, so did the demand for slaves in the newly settled regions, thus fueling the internal slave trade. Slaves were increasingly clustered in the Lower South, as Upper South slave owners sold slaves "down the river" or migrated westward with their entire households. An estimated 1 million slaves migrated involuntarily to the Lower South between 1820 and 1860. Finally, of all the New World slave societies, the one that existed in the American South was the only one that grew by natural increase rather than through the constant importation of captured Africans. This fact alone made the African-American community of the South different from the slave societies of Cuba, the Caribbean islands, and Brazil. The first thing to understand, then, are the circumstances of survival and growth.

The Challenge to Survive

Slave owners thought of the health of their slaves in several ways. First and foremost, they demanded labor from their slaves, and they provided the food, housing, and clothing to keep them healthy enough to work. They also wanted them to be healthy enough to reproduce, for every slave baby increased the wealth of the owner. These sometimes contradictory demands were played out in the lives of slave women.

Mortality rates for slave children under five were twice those for their white counterparts. Historians now say that mortality was high because pregnant black women were inadequately nourished, worked too hard, or were too frequently pregnant, giving birth to six to eight children at year-and-a-half intervals. At the time, owners often accused women of smothering their infants by rolling over them when asleep. When the British actress Fanny Kemble came to live on her husband's Georgia plantation in 1837, what shocked her more deeply than any other aspect of the slave system was the treatment of pregnant black women. Sensing her sympathy, pregnant slave women came to Kemble to plead for relief from field work, only to be brusquely ordered back to the fields by the overseer and Kemble's husband.

Health remained a lifelong issue for slaves. Malaria and infectious diseases such as yellow fever and cholera were endemic in the South. White people as well as black died, as the life expectancy figures for 1850 show: 40–43 years for white people and 30–33 years for African Americans. Slaves were more at risk because of the circumstances of slave life: poor housing, poor diet, and constant, usually heavy work. Sickness was chronic: 20 percent or more of the slave labor force on most plantations were sick at any one time. Many owners believed sick slaves were only "malingering." Because of the poor medical knowledge of the time, they failed to realize that adequate diet, warm housing, and basic sanitation might have prevented the pneumonia and dysentery that killed or weakened many slaves, and that exacted an especially high toll on very young children.

From Cradle to Grave

Slavery was a lifelong labor system, and the constant and inescapable issue between master and slave was how much work the slave would—or could be forced—to do. Southern white slave owners claimed that by housing, feeding, and clothing their slaves from infancy to death they were acting more humanely than northern industrialists who employed people only during their working years. But in spite of occasional instances of manumission—the freeing of a slave—the child born of a slave was destined to remain a slave.

Children lived with their parents (or with their mother if the father was a slave on another farm or plantation) in housing provided by the owner. Slaves owned by small farmers usually had only a bed or mattress to sleep on in the attic or a back room. Larger slave owners housed slaves in one-room cabins with dirt floors and few furnishings (a table, stools, a cooking pot and a few dishes, a bed, or corn-shuck

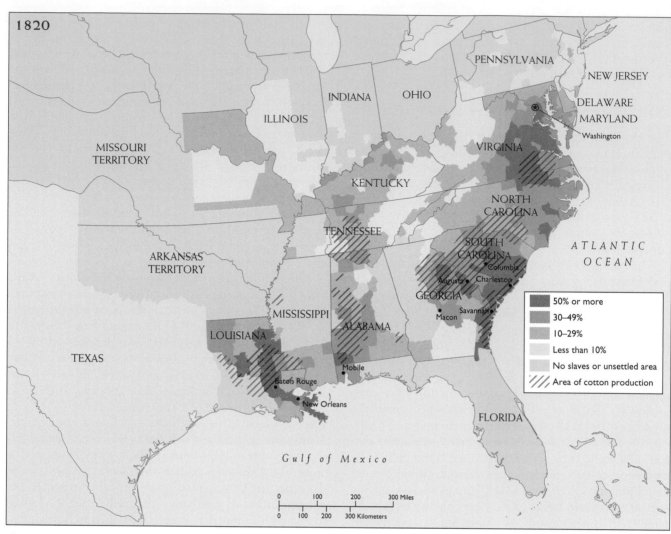

1820

Cotton Production, 1820–1860 In the forty-year period from 1820 to 1860, cotton production grew dramatically both in quantity and in extent. The westward expansion that cotton production encouraged in the 1830s and 1850s is reflected in the symbols for 1840 and 1860, and the growing concentration of cotton production in the black belt (so-called for its rich soils) of the Lower South is clearly evident.

SOURCE: Sam Bowers Hilliard, *Atlas of Antebellum Southern Agriculture* (Baton Rouge: Louisiana State University Press, 1984), pp. 67–71.

mattresses). Fanny Kemble described, with some horror, the one-room slave cabins she found on her husband's plantation:

> These cabins consist of one room, about twelve feet by fifteen, with a couple of closets smaller and closer than the state-rooms of a ship, divided off from the main room and each other by rough wooden partitions, in which the inhabitants sleep. They have almost all of them a rude bedstead, with the gray moss of the forests for mattress, and filthy, pestilential-looking blankets for covering. Two families (sometimes eight and ten in number) reside in one of these huts, which are mere wooden frames pinned, as it were, to the earth by a brick chimney outside.

Masters supplied food to their slaves. One common ration for a week was three pounds of meat, four quarts of corn meal, and some molasses for each person. Often slaves were encouraged to supplement their diet by keeping their own gardens, and by hunting—though not, of course, with guns. The opportunity to garden and to hunt, in other words not to be completely dependent on their masters, was one slaves cherished. Slaves were also provided with clothes, usually of rough homespun cloth: two shirts, two pairs of

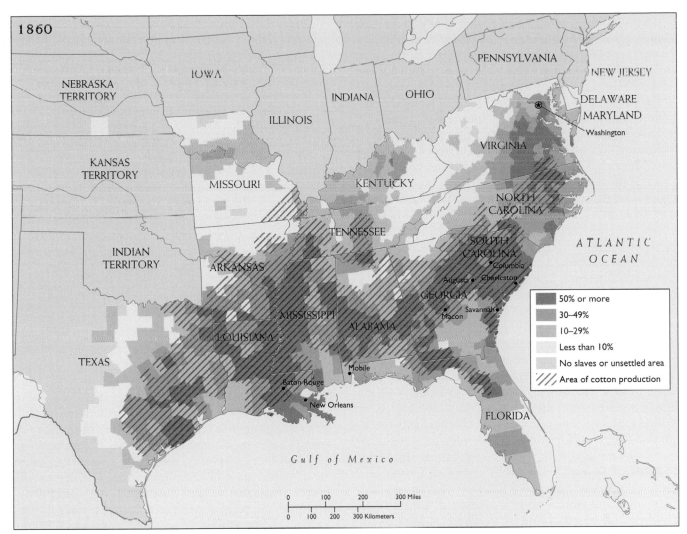

Slave Population, 1820–1860 The growth of cotton production caused a redistribution of the enslaved African American population in the South. Although slaves were still used to grow tobacco in Virginia and rice in coastal South Carolina, after 1830 an increasing number were sold "down the river" to work new cotton plantations in the Lower South. Thus although U.S. participation in the international slave trade was outlawed in 1808, the domestic trade in slaves flourished.

SOURCE: Sam Bowers Hilliard, *Atlas of Antebellum Southern Agriculture* (Baton Rouge: Louisiana State University Press, 1984), pp. 29–34.

pants, and a pair of shoes a year for men, and enough cloth for women to make an equal number of smocks for themselves and their children yearly. This clothing was barely adequate, and in severe winters slaves suffered badly.

From birth to about age seven, slave children played with one another and with white children, observing and learning how to survive. They saw the penalties: black adults, perhaps their own parents, whipped for disobedience; black women, perhaps their own sisters, violated by white men. And they might see one or both parents sold away as punishment or for fi-

nancial gain. They would also see signs of white benevolence: special treats for children at holidays, appeals to loyalty from the master or mistress, perhaps friendship with a white child. One former slave recalled:

> Yessum, when they used to have company in the big house, Miss Ross would bring them to the door to show them us children. And, my blessed, the yard would be black with us children, all string up there next the doorstep looking up in they eyes. Old Missus would say, "Ain't I got a pretty crop of little niggers coming on?"

The children would learn slave ways of getting along: apparent acquiescence in white demands; pilfering, malingering, sabotage, and other methods of slowing the relentless work pace. Fanny Kemble, an accomplished actress, was quick to note the pretense in the "outrageous flattery" she received from her husband's slaves. But many white Southerners genuinely believed that their slaves were both less intelligent and more loyal than they really were. An escaped slave, Jermain Loguen, recalled with some distaste the charade of "servile bows and counterfeit smiles . . . and other false expressions of gladness" with which he placated his master and mistress. Frederick Douglass, whose fearless leadership of the abolitionist movement made him the most famous African American of his time, wryly noted, "As the master studies to keep the slave ignorant, the slave is cunning enough to make the master think he succeeds."

Most slaves spent their lives as field hands, working in gangs with other slaves under a white overseer, who was usually quick to use his whip to keep up the work pace. But there were other occupations. In the "big house" there were jobs for women as cooks, maids, seamstresses, laundresses, weavers, and nurses. Black men became coachmen, valets, and gardeners, or skilled craftsmen—carpenters, mechanics, and blacksmiths. Some children began learning these occupations at age seven or eight, often in an informal apprentice system. Other children, both boys and girls, were expected to take full care of younger children while the parents were working. Of course black children had no schooling of any kind: in most of the southern states, it was against the law to teach a slave to read, although indulgent owners often rewarded their "pet" slaves by teaching them in spite of the law. At age twelve, slaves were considered full grown and put to work in the fields or in their designated occupation. As Mary Raines, a former slave in South Carolina, recalled, "I was a strong gal, went to de field when I's twelve years old, hoe my acre of cotton, 'long wid de grown ones, and pick my 150 pounds of cotton."

House Servants

At first glance, working in the big house might seem to have been preferable to working in the fields. Physically it was much less demanding, and house slaves were often better fed and clothed. They also had much more access to information, for white people, accustomed to servants and generally confident of their loyalty, often forgot their presence and spoke among themselves about matters of interest to the slaves: local gossip, changes in laws or attitudes, policies toward disobedient or rebellious slaves. As Benjamin Russel, a former slave in South Carolina, recalled:

How did we get the news? Many plantations were strict about this, but the greater the precaution, the alerter became the slave, the wider they opened their ears and the more eager they became for outside information. The sources were: girls that waited on the tables, the ladies' maids and the drivers; they would pick up everything they heard and pass it on to the other slaves.

For many white people, one of the worst surprises of the Civil War was the eagerness of their house slaves to flee. Considered by their masters the best treated and the most loyal, these slaves were commonly the first to leave or to organize mass desertions. Even the Confederacy's first family, President Jefferson Davis and his wife Varina, were chagrined by the desertion of their house servants in 1864.

From the point of view of the slave, the most unpleasant thing about being a house servant (or the single slave of a small owner) was the constant presence of white people. There was no escape from white supervision. Many slaves who were personal maids and children's nurses were required to live in the big house and rarely saw their own families. Cooks and other house servants were exposed to the tempers and whims of all members of the white family, including the children, who prepared themselves for lives of mastery by practicing giving orders to slaves many times their own age. And house servants, more than any others, were forced to act grateful and ingratiating. The demeaning images of Uncle Tom and the ever-smiling mammy derive from the roles slaves learned as the price of survival. At the same time, genuine intimacy was possible, especially between black nurses and white children. But these were bonds that the white children were ultimately forced to reject as the price of joining the master class.

Artisans and Skilled Workers

A small number of slaves were skilled workers: weavers, seamstresses, carpenters, blacksmiths, mechanics. More slave men than women achieved skilled status (partly because many jobs considered appropriate for women, like cooking, were not thought of as skilled). Solomon Northup, a northern free African American kidnapped into slavery, explained in his 1853 narrative, *Twelve Years a Slave*, that he had been forced to do a variety of work. He had had three owners and had been hired out repeatedly as a carpenter and as a driver of other slaves in a sugar mill; he had also been hired out to clear land for a new Louisiana plantation and to cut sugar cane. Black people worked as lumberjacks (of the 16,000 lumber workers in the South, almost all were slaves), as miners, as deckhands and stokers on Mississippi riverboats, as stevedores loading cotton on the docks of Charleston, Savannah, and New Orleans, and sometimes as workers in the handful of southern factories. Because slaves were their masters' property, the wages of the slave belonged to the owner, not the slave.

The extent to which slaves made up the laboring class was most apparent in cities. A British visitor to Natchez in 1835 noted slave "mechanics, draymen, hostelers, labourers, hucksters and washwomen and the heterogeneous multitude of every other occupation." In the North, all these jobs were performed by white workers. In part, because the South failed to attract as much immigrant labor as the North, southern cities offered both enslaved and free black people opportunities in skilled occupations such as blacksmithing and carpentering that free African Americans in the North were denied.

Field Work and the Gang System of Labor

A full 75 percent of all slaves were field workers, and it was these workers who were most directly affected by the labor system employed on cotton plantations. Cotton was a crop that demanded nearly year-round labor: from planting in April to constant hoeing and cultivation through June to a picking season that began in August and lasted until December. The work was less skilled than on tobacco or sugar plantations, but more constant. Owners divided their slaves into gangs of twenty to twenty-five, a communal labor pattern reminiscent of parts of Africa, but with a crucial difference—these workers were supervised by overseers with whips. Field hands, both men and women, worked from "can see to can't see" (sunup to sundown) summer and winter, and frequently longer at harvest, when eighteen-hour days were common. On most plantations, the bell sounded an hour before sunup, and slaves were expected to be on their way to the fields as soon as it was light. Work continued till noon, and after an hour or so for lunch and rest the slaves worked nearly until dark. In the evening the women prepared dinner at the cabins and everyone snatched a few hours of unsupervised socializing before bedtime. Work days were shorter in the winter, perhaps only ten hours.

Work was tedious in the hot and humid southern fields, and the overseer's whip was never far away. Cotton growing was hard work: plowing and planting, chopping weeds with a heavy hoe, and picking the ripe cotton from the stiff and scratchy bolls at the rate of 150 pounds a day. A strong, hardworking slave—a "prime field hand"—was valuable property, worth at least $1,000 to the master. Slaves justifiably took pride in their strength, as observed by a white Northerner

traveling in Mississippi in 1854 who came across a work gang happy to be going home early because of rain:

> First came, led by an old driver carrying a whip, forty of the largest and strongest women I ever saw together . . . they carried themselves loftily, each having a hoe over the shoulder, and walking with a free, powerful stride. Behind them came the . . . [plowhands and their mules], thirty strong, mostly men, but a few of them women. . . . A lean and vigilant white overseer, on a brisk pony, brought up the rear.

That, of course, is only one side of the story. Compare Solomon Northup's memory of cotton picking:

> It was rarely that a day passed by without one or more whippings. The delinquent [who had not picked enough cotton] was taken out, stripped, made to lie upon the ground, face downwards, when he received a punishment proportioned to his offence. It is the literal, unvarnished truth, that the crack of the lash, and the shrieking of the slaves, can be heard from dark till bed time, on [this] plantation, any day almost during the entire period of the cotton-picking season.

Slaves aged fast in this regime. Poor diet and heavy labor undermined health. When they were too old to work, they took on other tasks within the black community, such as caring for young children. Honored by the slave community, the elderly were tolerated by white owners, who continued to feed and clothe them until their deaths. Few actions show the hypocrisy of southern paternalism more clearly than the speed with which white owners evicted their elderly slaves in the 1860s when the end of the slave system was in sight.

Sold "Down the River"

The experience of slaves who were sold or forced by their owners to migrate to the newly opened cotton lands of the Southwest (western Georgia, Alabama, Mississippi, Arkansas, and Texas) sheds light on the dynamics and tensions underlying the South's cotton-induced prosperity. Although some owners brought existing slave communities with them, the most common experience was that of the individual slave, forcibly separated from family and kin and sent alone with other strangers to a new life far away. Owners had good reason to fear the resentment of slaves who were forced into these new circumstances. For the individual slave, migration to the Southwest was a long ordeal.

Upper South slaveowners sold slaves to large trading firms, who collected them during the summer in slave

This engraving from *Harpers Weekly* shows slaves, dressed in their best clothing, lined up outside a New Orleans slave pen for inspection by potential buyers before the actual auction began. They were often threatened with punishment if they did not present a good appearance and manner that would fetch a high price.

SOURCE: U.S. slave market, ca. 1863, in New Orleans. Courtesy of Culver Pictures, Inc.

pens in Baltimore, Richmond, Nashville, and other northern cities. When the weather cooled, slaves were sent south in chains on foot in coffles, by sailing ship, or by steamboat on the Mississippi to be sold in New Orleans. There, in the streets outside of large slave pens near the French Quarter, thousands of slaves were displayed and sold each year. Dressed in new clothes provided by the traders and exhorted by the traders to walk, run, and otherwise show their stamina, slaves were presented to buyers. For their part, suspicious buyers, unsure that traders and slaves themselves were truthful, poked, prodded, and frequently stripped male and female slaves to be sure they were as healthy as the traders claimed. Aside from obvious signs of illness, buyers often looked for scars on a slave's back: too many scars were a sign of the frequent whippings that a rebellious or "uppity" slave had provoked. Most slaves were sold as individuals: with their own needs in mind, buyers rarely responded to pleas to buy an "extra" slave to keep a family together.

Once sold, slaves could face a variety of conditions. A number, especially in the early years of settlement in the Old Southwest, found themselves in frontier circumstances. Young male slaves were chosen for the back-breaking work of cutting trees and clearing land for cultivation. Some worked side by side with their owners to clear the land for small farms devoted to raising food for immediate consumption. In these circumstances slaves were often highly self-reliant and expected by owners to hunt and fish to supplement the basic diet. This relatively cooperative and permissive attitude was also evident on larger farms engaged in the variety of tasks required in mixed farming. But uniformity and strict discipline were the rule on cotton plantations. Owners eager to clear land rapidly so as to make quick profits often drove the clearing crews at an unmerciful pace. And they attempted to impose strict discipline and a rapid pace on the work gangs that planted, hoed, and harvested cotton. Slaves from other parts of the South, used to more individual and less intense work, hated the cotton regime and most of all hated the overseers who enforced it. They also fought to retain their rights to supplement the owner-supplied diet with their own garden produce and by hunting.

Thus the new land in the Old Southwest that appeared to offer so much opportunity for owners bred tensions caused by forcible sale and migration, by the organization and pace of cotton cultivation, and by the owners' efforts to abrogate what slaves saw as traditional rights. Behind the owners' interest in "scientific management" in cotton must have lurked constant fear of what resentful gangs of slaves might do if freed from watchful supervision.

THE AFRICAN AMERICAN COMMUNITY

Surely no group in American history has faced a harder job of community building than the black people of the antebellum South. Living in intimate, daily contact with their oppressors, African Americans nevertheless created an enduring culture of their own, a culture that had far-reaching and lasting influence on all of southern life and American society as a whole (see Chapter 4). Within their own communities, African-American values and attitudes, and especially their own forms of Christianity, played a vital part in shaping a culture of endurance and resistance.

Few African Americans were unfortunate enough to live their lives alone among white people. Over half of all slaves lived on plantations with twenty or more other slaves, and others, on smaller farms, had links with slaves on nearby properties. Urban slaves were able to make and sustain so many secret contacts with other African Americans in cities or towns that slave owners wondered whether slave discipline could be maintained in urban settings. There can be no question that the bonds among African Americans were what sustained them during the years of slavery.

In law, slaves were property, to be bought, sold, rented, worked, and otherwise used (but not abused or killed) as the owner saw fit. But slaves were also human beings, with feelings, needs, and hopes. Even though most white Southerners believed black people to be members of an inferior, childish race, all but the most brutal masters acknowledged the humanity of their slaves. Furthermore, as a practical matter, white owners had long since learned that unhappy or rebellious slaves were poor workers. White masters learned to live with the two key institutions of African-American community life: the family and the African American church.

Five generations of one family on a South Carolina plantation are gathered together for this 1862 picture, providing evidence of the importance of kinship in the building of African American communities.

SOURCE: *Remains of Slave Quarters, Fort George Island, Florida*, ca. 1865. Stereograph. (c) Collection of the New York Historical Society.

Slave Families

As had been true in the eighteenth century, families remained essential to African-American culture (see Chapter 4). No southern state recognized slave marriages in law. Most owners, though, not only recognized but encouraged them, sometimes even performing a kind of wedding ceremony for the couple. James Henry Hammond conducted a special ceremony for his slaves, to whom he gave $5.00 for a first marriage and $3.50 for a second marriage. Masters sometimes tried to arrange marriages, but slaves usually found their own mates, sometimes on their own plantation, sometimes elsewhere. Masters encouraged marriage among their slaves, believing it made the men less rebellious, and for economic reasons they were eager for the slave women to have children. Whatever marriages meant to the masters, to slaves they were a haven of love and intimacy in a cruel world and the basis of the African-American community. Husbands and wives had a chance, in their own cabins, to live their own lives among loved ones. The relationship between slave husband and wife was different from that of the white husband and wife. The patriarchal system dictated that the white marriage be unequal, for the man had to be dominant and the woman dependent and submissive. Slave marriages were more equal, for husband and wife were both powerless within the slave system. Both knew that neither could protect the other from abuse at the hands of white people.

Husband and wife cooperated in loving and sheltering their children and teaching them survival skills. Above all, family meant continuity. Parents made great efforts to teach their children the family history and to surround them with a supportive and protective kinship network.

The strength of these ties is shown by the many husbands, wives, children, and parents who searched for each other after the Civil War when slavery came to an end. Observing African Americans' postwar migrations, a Freedmen's Bureau agent commented that "every mother's son among them seemed to be in search of his mother; every mother in search of her children." As the ads in black newspapers indicate, some family searches went on into the 1870s and 1880s, and many ended in failure.

Given the vast size of the internal slave trade, fear of separation was constant—and real. Far from being a rare event prompted only by financial necessity, separations of slave families were common. One in every five slave marriages was broken, and one in every three children sold away from their families. These figures clearly show that slave owners' support for slave marriages was secondary to their desire for profits. The scale of the trade was a strong indication of the economic reality that underlay their protestations of paternalism.

In the face of constant separation, slave communities attempted to act like larger families. Following practices developed early in slavery, children were taught to respect and learn from all the elders, to call all adults of a certain age "aunt" or "uncle," and to call children of their own age "brother" or "sister" (see Chapter 4). Thus, in the absence of their own family, separated children could quickly find a place and a source of comfort in the slave community to which they had been sold.

This emphasis on family and on kinship networks had an even more fundamental purpose. The kinship of the entire community, where old people were respected and young ones cared for, represented a conscious rejection of white paternalism. The slaves' ability, in the most difficult of situations, to structure a community that expressed their values, not those of their masters, was extraordinary. Equally remarkable was the way in which African Americans reshaped Christianity to serve their needs.

African American Religion

Slaves brought religions from Africa but were not allowed to practice them, for white people feared religion would create a bond among slaves that might lead to rebellion. African religions managed to survive in the slave community in forms that white people considered as "superstition" or "folk belief," such as the medicinal use of roots by conjurers. Religious ceremonies survived, too, in late-night gatherings deep in the woods where the sound of drumming, singing, and dancing could not reach white ears (see Chapter 4). In the nineteenth century, these African traditions allowed African Americans to reshape white Christianity into their own distinctive faith.

Most masters of the eighteenth century made little effort to Christianize their slaves, afraid they might take the promises of universal brotherhood and equality too literally. The Great Awakening, which swept the South after the 1760s, introduced many slaves to

Christianity, often in mixed congregations with white people (see Chapter 5). The transformation was completed by the Second Great Awakening, which took root among black and white Southerners in the 1790s. The number of African-American converts, preachers, and lay teachers grew rapidly, and a distinctive form of Christianity took shape. Free African Americans founded their own independent churches and denominations. The first African-American Baptist and Methodist churches were founded in Philadelphia in 1794 by the Reverend Absalom Jones and the Reverend Richard Allen. In 1816, the Reverend Allen joined with African-American ministers from other cities to form the African Methodist Episcopal (AME) denomination. By the 1830s, free African-American ministers like Andrew Marshall of Savannah and many more enslaved black preachers and lay ministers preached, sometimes secretly, to slaves. Their message was one of faith and love, of deliverance, of the coming of the promised land.

African Americans found in Christianity a powerful vehicle to express their longings for freedom and justice. But why did their white masters allow it? Some white people, themselves converted by the revivals, doubtless believed that they should not deny their slaves the same religious experience. But the evangelical religion of the early nineteenth century was also a powerful form of social control. Southern slave owners, seeking to counteract the appeal of African-American religion, expected their Christianity to make their slaves obedient and peaceful. Forbidding their slaves to hold their own religious gatherings, owners insisted that their slaves attend white church services. Slaves were quick to realize the owners' purpose. As a former Texas slave recalled: "We went to church on the place and you ought to heard that preachin'. Obey your massa and missy, don't steal chickens and eggs and meat, but nary a word 'bout havin' a soul to save." On many plantations, slaves attended religious services with their masters every Sunday, sitting quietly in the back of the church or in the balcony as the minister preached messages justifying slavery and urging obedience. But at night, away from white eyes, they held their own prayer meetings. Another former Texas slave recalled:

> [We] used to have a prayin' ground down in the hollow and sometimes we come out of the field, between eleven and twelve at night, scorchin' and burnin' up with nothin' to eat, and we wants to ask the good Lawd to have mercy. We put grease in a snuff pan or bottle and make a lamp. We takes a pine torch, too, and goes down to the hollow to pray. Some gits so joyous they starts to holler loud and we has to stop up they mouth [so the whites won't hear].

African cultural patterns persisted in the preference for night funerals and for solemn pageantry and song, as depicted in British artist John Antrobus's *Plantation Burial*, ca. 1860. Like other African American customs, the community care of the dead contained an implied rebuke to the masters' care of the living slaves.

SOURCE: John Antrobus, *Negro Burial*. The Historic New Orleans Collection.

In churches and in spontaneous religious expressions, the black community made Christianity its own. Fusing Christian texts with African elements of group activity, such as the circle dance, the call-and-response pattern, and, above all, group singing, black people created a unique community religion full of emotion, enthusiasm, and protest. Nowhere is this spirit more compelling than in the famous spirituals: "Go Down Moses," with its mournful refrain "Let my people go"; the rousing "Didn't My Lord Deliver Daniel . . . and why not every man"; the haunting "Steal Away." Some of these spirituals became as well known to white people as to black people, but only African Americans seem to have appreciated the full meaning of their subversive messages.

Nevertheless, this was not a religion of rebellion, for that was unrealistic for most slaves. Black Christianity was an enabling religion: it helped slaves to survive, not as passive victims of white tyranny but as active opponents of an oppressive system that they daily protested in small but meaningful ways. In their faith, African Americans expressed a spiritual freedom that white people could not destroy.

Freedom and Resistance

The rapid geographical spread of cotton itself introduced a new source of tension and resistance into the slave-master relationship. Whatever their dreams, most slaves knew they would never escape. Freedom was too far away. Almost all successful escapes in the nineteenth century (approximately 1,000 a year) were from the Upper South (Delaware, Maryland, Virginia, Kentucky, and Missouri). A slave in the Lower South or the Southwest simply had too far to go to reach freedom. In addition, white Southerners were determined to prevent escapes. Slave patrols were a common sight on southern roads. Any black person without a pass from his or her master was captured (usually roughly) and returned home to certain punishment. But despite almost certain recapture, slaves continued to flee and to help others do so. Escaped slave Harriet Tubman of Maryland, who made nineteen rescue missions freeing 300 slaves in all, had extraordinary determination and skill. As a female runaway, she was unusual, too: most escapees were young men, for women often had small children they were unable to take and unwilling to leave behind.

Much more common was the practice of "running away nearby." Slaves who knew they could not reach freedom still frequently demonstrated their desire for liberty or their discontent over mistreatment by taking unauthorized leave from their plantation. Hidden in nearby forests or swamps, provided with food smuggled by other slaves from the plantation, the runaway might return home after a week or so, often to rather mild punishment. Although in reality most slaves could have little hope of gaining freedom, even failed attempts at rebellion shook the foundations of the slave system and thus temporary flight by any slave was a warning sign of discontent that a wise master did not ignore.

Slave Revolts

The ultimate resistance, however, was the slave revolt. Southern history was dotted with stories of former slave conspiracies and rumors of current plots (see Chapter 4). Every white Southerner knew about the last-minute failure of Gabriel Prosser's insurrection in Richmond in 1800 and the chance discovery of Denmark Vesey's plot in Charleston in 1822. But when in 1831, Nat Turner actually started a rebellion in which a number of white people were killed, southern fears were greatly magnified. Gabriel Prosser, a literate blacksmith, had gathered more than a thousand slaves

Harriet Tubman escaped in 1849 from slavery in Maryland, and returned nineteen times to free almost 300 other slaves. Here Tubman (at left), the most famous "conductor" on the Underground Railroad, is shown with some of those she led to freedom.

SOURCE: Courtesy of Sophia Smith Collection, Smith College.

for an assault on Richmond. Although the attempt was aborted at the last minute and Prosser and thirty-five others were caught and hanged, white people were especially frightened to learn that Prosser had organized under a banner proclaiming "Death or Liberty" and had hoped for help from the independent black people of Haiti. The notion of an international force of revolutionary slaves demanding their freedom was a fundamental challenge to slave owners' assumptions about their own liberty and power.

Denmark Vesey was a former seaman who lived in Charleston and worked as a carpenter. Free, well-read, and eloquent, he was a lay preacher at Charleston's African Methodist Episcopal Church. His co-conspirator, Gullah Jack, was a "conjure-man" who drew on the African religious traditions that flourished among the slaves in the South Carolina low country. In 1822, the year after the Missouri Compromise, Vesey and Gullah Jack drew up a plan to seize Charleston and ultimately to sail to the free black Caribbean nation of Haiti.

Vesey and Gullah Jack recruited at least eighty country and city slaves into the conspiracy, including several trusted house slaves of South Carolina governor Thomas Bennett. Betrayed at the last moment, thirty-five black rebels were hanged (Vesey among them) and thirty-seven others sold down the river. But some rebels were not caught because their fellow conspirators died without naming them. Charlestonians had to live with the knowledge that some of their city's most trusted black servants had conspired to kill their masters—and might still plan to do so.

In the wake of the Vesey conspiracy, Charlestonians turned their fear and anger outward. Planter Robert J. Turnbull wrote bitterly, "By the Missouri question, our slaves thought, there was a charter of liberties granted them by Congress. . . . [The Vesey conspiracy] will long be remembered, as amongst the choicest fruits of that question in Congress." White people attempted to seal off the city from dangerous outside influences. The AME Church (where radical ideas such as the Missouri question had been discussed) was destroyed, and in December 1822 the South Carolina legislature passed a bill requiring that all black seamen be seized and jailed while their ships were in Charleston harbor. Initially most alarmed about free black people from Haiti, Charlestonians soon came to believe that northern free black seamen were spreading antislavery ideas among their slaves.

The most famous slave revolt—Nat Turner's revolt in Southampton County, Virginia—was a partial success. A literate man, Nat Turner was, like Denmark Vesey, a lay preacher, but unlike Vesey he was also a slave. It was Turner's intelligence and strong religious commitment that made him a leader in the slave community and, interestingly, these very same qualities led his master, Joseph Travis, to treat him with kindness even though Turner had once run away for a month after being mistreated by an overseer. Turner began plotting his revolt after a religious vision in which he saw "white spirits and black spirits engaged in battle"; "the sun was darkened—the thunder rolled in the Heavens, and blood flowed in streams." Turner and five other slaves struck on the night of August 20, 1831, first killing Travis, who, Turner said, "was to me a kind master, and placed the greatest confidence in me; in fact, I had no cause to complain of his treatment of me."

Moving from plantation to plantation and killing a total of fifty-five white people, the rebels numbered sixty by the next morning, when they fled from a group of armed white men. More than forty blacks were executed after the revolt, including Turner, who was captured accidentally after he had hidden for two months in the woods. Thomas R. Gray, a white lawyer to whom Turner dictated a lengthy confession before his death, was impressed by Turner's composure. "I looked on him," Gray said, "and my blood curdled in my veins." If intelligent, well-treated slaves such as Turner could plot revolts, how could white Southerners ever feel safe?

Gabriel's Rebellion, the Denmark Vesey plot, and Nat Turner's Revolt were the most prominent examples of organized slave resistance, but they were far from

This drawing shows the moment, almost two months after the failure of his famous and bloody slave revolt, when Nat Turner was accidentally discovered in the woods near his home plantation. Turner's cool murder of his owner and methodical organization of his revolt deeply frightened many white Southerners.

SOURCE: Courtesy of the Library of Congress.

the only ones. Conspiracies and actual or rumored slave resistance began in colonial times (see Chapter 4) and never ceased. These plots exposed the truth white Southerners preferred to ignore: Only force kept Africans and African Americans enslaved, and because no system of control could ever be total, white Southerners could never be completely safe from the possibility of revolt. Nat Turner brought white Southerners' fears to the surface. After 1831, the possibility of slave insurrection was never far from their minds.

Free African Americans

Another source of white disquiet was the growing number of free African Americans. By 1860, nearly 250,000 free black people lived in the South. For most, freedom dated from before 1800, when antislavery feeling among slave owners in the Upper South was widespread and cotton cultivation had yet to boom. In Virginia, for example, the number of manumitted (freed) slaves jumped tenfold in twenty years (see Chapter 7). But a new mood became apparent in 1806 when Virginia tightened its lenient manumission law: now the freed person was required to leave the state within a year or be sold back into slavery. After 1830 manumission was virtually impossible throughout the South. Most free black people lived in the countryside of the Upper South, where they worked as tenant farmers or farm laborers. Urban African Americans were much more visible. Life was especially difficult for female-headed families because

only the most menial work—street peddling and laundry work, for example—was available to free black women. The situation for African-American males was somewhat better. Although they were discriminated against in employment and in social life, there were opportunities for skilled black craftsmen in trades such as blacksmithing and carpentry.

Cities such as Charleston, Savannah, and Natchez were home to flourishing free African-American communities that formed their own churches and fraternal orders. In Natchez, a free black barber, William Johnson, owned several barber shops, a small farm, and an estate valued at $25,000 in 1851 that included fifteen slaves. Johnson had a white attorney and friends among the city's leading politicians, and he lived in a white neighborhood. Half a dozen other free African Americans in Natchez were similarly prosperous, and they, too, were slave owners. This tiny elite kept a careful social distance from most of Natchez's approximately 1,000 free black people (one-quarter of all free African Americans in Mississippi in 1840), who were miserably poor. This free black elite treated white people with great tact and deference.

Free African Americans had reason to be careful, for their position was increasingly precarious. Throughout the South in the 1830s, state legislatures tightened black codes—laws concerning free black people. Free African Americans could not carry firearms, could not purchase slaves (unless they were members of their own family), and were liable to the criminal penalties meted out to slaves (that is, whippings and summary judgments without a jury trial). They could not testify against whites, hold office, vote, or serve in the militia. In other words, except for the right to own property, free blacks had no civil rights. Following the cleanup of the alarming race mixing in Natchez-under-the-Hill, the Natchez elite focused on free African Americans. In 1841, whites

One of the ways Charleston attempted to control its African American population was to require all slaves to wear badges showing their occupation. After 1848, free black people also had to wear badges, which were decorated, ironically, with a liberty cap.

SOURCE: Courtesy of the American Numismatic Society of New York.

mounted a campaign to deport from the state any free black person who adopted "the practices of the rogue, the incendiary, and the abolitionist." Many poor free African Americans were deported from Natchez that summer and in the following years. William Johnson, whose own security was not threatened, aided some poor black people by quietly helping them obtain attestations of good character from white planters. For all of his (comparative) wealth, as a black man he could do nothing openly to help his own people.

As this episode shows, white people increasingly feared the influence free black people might have on slaves, for free African Americans were a living challenge to the slave system. Their very existence disproved the basic southern equations of white equals free, and black equals slave. No one believed more fervently in those equations than the South's largest population group, white people who did not own slaves.

THE WHITE MAJORITY

The pervasive influence of the slave system in the South is reflected in the startling contrast of two facts: two-thirds of all Southerners did not own slaves, yet slave owners dominated the social and political life of the region. Who were the two-thirds of white Southerners who did not own slaves, and how did they live? Throughout the South, slave owners occupied the most productive land: tobacco-producing areas in Virginia and Tennessee, coastal areas of South Carolina and Georgia where rice and cotton grew, sugar lands in Louisiana, and large sections of the cotton-producing black belt, which stretched westward from South Carolina to Texas. Small farmers, usually without slaves, occupied the rest of the rural land and a small middle class lived in the cities of the South.

The Middle Class

In the predominantly rural South, cities provided a home for a commercial middle class of merchants, bankers, factors (agents), and lawyers on whom the agricultural economy depended to sell its produce to a world market. Urban growth lagged far behind the North. The cities that grew were major shipping centers for agricultural goods: the river cities of Louisville, St. Louis, Memphis, and New Orleans, and the cotton ports of Mobile and Savannah. Formal educational institutions, libraries, and cultural activities were located in cities, and so were the beginnings of the same kind of entreprenurial and commercial spirit so evident in the North. As in the North, small industrial cities often including textile mills and heavier industry, clustered along the fall line, where the rivers dropped down

from the highlands to the coastal plains. Columbus, Georgia, located at the falls of the Chattahoochee River, was an example of such a small city.

The effort of William Gregg of South Carolina to establish the cotton textile industry illustrates some of the problems facing southern entrepreneurs. Gregg, a successful jeweler from Columbia, South Carolina, became convinced that textile factories were a good way to diversify the southern economy and to provide a living for poor whites who could not find work in the slave-dominated employment system. He enthusiastically publicized the findings of his tour of northern textile mills, but found a cool reception. His request to the planter-dominated South Carolina legislature for a charter of incorporation for a textile mill passed by only one vote. In 1846 he built a model mill and a company town in Graniteville, South Carolina, that attracted poor white families as employees. Gregg adapted southern paternalism to industry, providing a school and churches and prohibiting alcohol and dancing, yet paying his workers twenty percent less than northern wages. His experience in the competitive textile industry led him to favor the protective tariff, thus putting him at odds with the general attitude in South Carolina that had solidified at the time of the Nullification Crisis (see Chapter 10).

John Letcher, a lawyer and politician in Lexington, Virginia, had typical moderate, urban, middle-class attitudes. A Democrat, he participated in the Virginia Constitutional Convention of 1850–51, and in accord with his politics pushed for the democratizing of the vote and of political office. He served four terms in the U.S. Congress in the 1850s, where he acquired a reputation as a moderate in favor of limited government, earning the nickname "Honest John Letcher, Watchdog of the Treasury." Elected governor of Virginia in 1860, he led his state out of the Union once the Civil War began and devoted his efforts to unity in pursuit of Confederate war aims. Like some other members of the urban middle class, he owned only enough slaves (a family with children) to do the domestic work for his own family and at one time, early in his career, he had favored gradual emancipation.

Many southern planters scorned members of the commercial middle class like Letcher and Gregg because they had to please their suppliers and customers, and thus lacked, in their eyes, true independence. No one cherished his independence more than the yeoman farmer.

Yeomen

The word "yeoman," originally a British term for a farmer who works his own land, is often applied to independent farmers of the South, most of whom lived on family-sized farms. Although yeoman farmers sometimes owned a few slaves, in general they and their families worked their land by themselves. This land ranged from adequate to poor, from depleted, once-rich regions in Virginia to the Carolina hill country and the pine barrens of Mississippi. Typical of the yeoman-farmer community was northwestern Georgia, once home to the Creeks and Cherokees, but now populated by communities of small farmers who grew enough vegetables to feed their families, including corn, which they either ate themselves or fed to hogs. In addition, these farmers raised enough cotton every year (usually no more than one or two bales) to bring in a little cash. At least 60 percent owned their own farms, but some were wealthier than others. Isaac Cobb of Carroll County owned 700 acres of land on which he grazed cattle, sheep, and hogs. On 200 of these acres, twelve slaves helped him produce 2,000 bushels

The goal of yeoman farm families was economic independence. Their mixed farming and grazing enterprises, supported by kinship and community ties, afforded them a self-sufficiency epitomized by Carl G. von Iwonski's painting of this rough but comfortable log cabin in New Braunfels, Texas.

SOURCE: Daughters of the Republic of Texas Library. Yanaguana Society Collection.

of grain and twelve bales of cotton. In contrast, Richard White, of the same county, used only family labor to farm fifty acres devoted to food and grains and the grazing of a few cattle, sheep, and hogs. These two men, and thousands like them, were the yeomen Thomas Jefferson celebrated—economically independent yet intimately tied to a larger but still very local group.

The local community was paramount. Farm men and women depended on their relatives and neighbors for assistance in large farm tasks such as planting, harvesting, and construction. Projects requiring lots of hands like logrollings, corn shuckings, and quilting bees were community events. Farmers repaid this help, and obtained needed goods, through complex systems of barter with other members of the community. In their organization, southern farm communities were no different from northern ones, with one major exception—slavery. In the South, one of the key items in the community barter system was the labor of slaves, who were frequently loaned out to neighbors by small slave owners such as Isaac Cobb to fulfill an obligation to another farmer.

Where yeomen and large slave owners lived side by side, as in the Georgia black belt where cotton was the major crop, slavery again provided a link between the rich and middle class. Large plantation owners often bought food for their slaves from small local farmers, ground the latter's corn in the plantation mill, ginned their cotton, and transported and marketed it as well. But although planters and much smaller yeomen were part of a larger community network, in the black belt the large slave owners were clearly dominant. Only in their own up-country communities did yeomen feel truly independent.

Poor White People

Not all small farmers were on an equal footing. One-third of the farmers in the Georgia up-country were tenant farmers. Some were farmers' sons, striking out on their own while waiting to inherit their fathers' land. But others were poor whites with little hope of improving their condition. From 30 to 50 percent of all southern white people were landless, a proportion similar to that in the North. But the existence of slavery affected the opportunities for southern poor white people. Slaves made up the permanent, stable workforce in agriculture and in many skilled trades. Many poor white people led highly transient lives in search of work, such as doing farm labor at harvest time, which was only temporary. Others were tenant farmers working under share-tenancy arrangements that kept them in debt to the landowner. Although they farmed poorer land with less equipment than landowning farmers, most tenant farmers grew enough food to sustain their families. Like the yeomen, but with more difficulty, tenant farmers aspired to independence.

Relationships between poor whites and black slaves were complex. White men and women often worked side by side with black slaves in the fields and were socially and sexually intimate with enslaved and free African Americans. White people engaged in clandestine trade to supply slaves with items like liquor that slave owners prohibited, helped slaves to escape, and even (in an 1835 Mississippi case) were executed for their participation in planning a slave revolt. At the same time, the majority of poor white people insisted, sometimes violently, on their racial superiority over blacks. For their part, many African American slaves, better dressed, better nourished, and healthier, dismissed them as "poor white trash." But the fact was that the difficult lives of poor whites, whom one contemporary described as "a third class of white people," served to blur the crucial racial distinction between independent whites and supposedly inferior, dependent black people on which the system of slavery rested. Like the boatmen whom the Natchez slave owners viewed with such alarm, poor white people posed a potential threat to the slave system.

Yeoman Values

In 1828 and 1832, southern yeomen and poor white men voted overwhelmingly for Andrew Jackson. They were drawn variously to his outspoken policy of ruthless expansionism, his appeals to the common man, and his rags-to-riches ascent from poor boy to rich slave owner. It was a career many hoped to emulate. The dominance of the large planters was due at least in part to the ambition of many yeomen, especially those with two or three slaves, to expand their holdings and become rich. These farmers, enthusiastic members of the lively democratic politics of the South, supported the leaders they hoped to join.

But for a larger group of yeomen, independence and not wealth was most important. Many southern yeomen lived apart from large slaveholders, in the up-country regions where plantation agriculture was unsuitable. The very high value southern yeomen placed on freedom grew directly from their own experience as self-sufficient property-owning farmers in small, family-based communities and from the absolute, patriarchal control they exercised over their own wives and children. This was a way of life that southern "plain folk" were determined to preserve. It made them resistant to the economic opportunities and challenges that capitalism and industrialization posed for northern farmers, which southern yeomen perceived as encroachments on their freedom.

The irony was that the freedom yeomen so prized rested on slavery. White people could count on slaves to perform the hardest and worst labor, and the degradation of slave life was a daily reminder of the freedom they enjoyed in comparison. Slavery meant that all

white people, rich and poor, were equal in the sense that they were all free. This assumption of white skin privilege had formed in the eighteenth century as slavery became the answer to the South's labor problem (see Chapter 4). The democratization of politics in the early nineteenth century and the enactment of nearly universal white manhood suffrage perpetuated the belief in white skin privilege, even though the gap between rich and poor white people was widening.

Southern yeomen did not blindly follow the rich slave owners who were their political leaders. Rather, they supported a freedom they believed they would not have under any other system. But southern unanimity on this point, which looked so strong, was actually very fragile. Anything that appeared to threaten slavery threatened the entire southern social structure, trapping Southerners in ever more rigid and defensive positions.

PLANTERS

Remarkably few slave owners fit the popular stereotype of the rich and leisured plantation owner with hundreds of acres of land and hundreds of slaves. Only 36 percent of southern white people owned slaves in 1830, and only 2.5 percent owned fifty slaves or more. Just as yeomen and poor whites were diverse, so, too, were southern slave owners.

Small Slave Owners

The largest group of slave owners were small yeomen taking the step from subsistence agriculture to commercial production. To do this in the South's agricultural economy, they had to own slaves. But upward mobility was difficult. Owning one or two slaves increased farm production only slightly, and it was hard to accumulate the capital to buy more. One common pattern was for a slave owner to leave one or two slaves to farm while he worked another job (this arrangement usually meant that his wife had assumed responsibility for their supervision). In other cases, small farmers worked side by side with their slaves in the fields. In still other cases, owners hired out their slaves to larger slave owners.

In every case, the owner was economically vulnerable: a poor crop or a downturn in cotton prices could wipe out his gains and force him to sell his slaves. When times improved, he might buy a new slave or two and try again, but getting a secure footing on the bottom rung of the slave-owner ladder was very difficult. The roller-coaster economy of the early nineteenth century did not help matters, and the Panic of 1837 was a serious setback to many small farmers.

John Flintoff was an aspiring slave owner who moved from North Carolina to Mississippi in 1841,

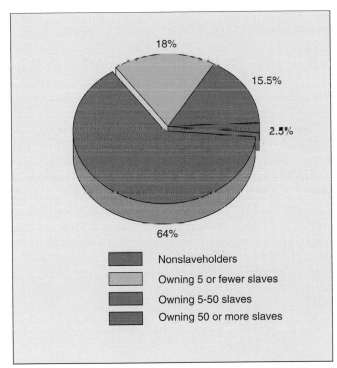

18%

15.5%

2.5%

64%

- Nonslaveholders
- Owning 5 or fewer slaves
- Owning 5-50 slaves
- Owning 50 or more slaves

Slaveholding and Class Structure in the South, 1830   The great mass of the southern white population were yeoman farmers. In 1830, slave owners made up only 36 percent of the southern white population; owners of more than fifty slaves constituted a tiny 2.5 percent. Yet they and the others who were middling planters dominated politics, retaining the support of yeomen who prized their freedom as white men above class-based politics

SOURCE: U.S. Bureau of the Census.

hoping to make his fortune. Working as an overseer on his uncle's land, Flintoff began his career as a slave owner by buying three slave children (one was seven years old), the cheapest slaves available. Over the years he bought nine in all. While an overseer, Flintoff married and began a family. But he was unsuccessful as an overseer. As he confessed in his diary, "managing negroes and large farms is soul destroying." In 1853 his uncle fired him. Flintoff was forced to sell his slaves and return to North Carolina, where, with the help of his in-laws, he bought 124 acres of land. Assisted by several slaves he grew corn, wheat, and tobacco—not the wonderfully profitable cotton of which he had dreamed. By 1860, Flintoff was modestly successful; wealthy enough to send his son to college and to free his wife from routine farm chores. As he boasted, his wife "has lived a Lady."

For a smaller group of slave owners, the economic struggle was not so hard. Middle-class professional men—lawyers, doctors, and merchants—frequently managed to become large slave owners because they already had capital (the pay from their professions) to

invest in land and slaves. Sometimes they received payment for their services not in money but in slaves. These owners were the most likely to own skilled slaves—carpenters, blacksmiths, and other artisans—and to rent them out for profit. By steady accumulation, the most successful members of this middle class were able to buy their way into the slave-owning elite and to confirm that position by marrying their sons or daughters into the aristocracy. Here the career of Andrew Jackson of Tennessee is instructive. Jackson, an orphan, had no family money. He began a profitable career as a prosecutor in Nashville in the 1790s, frequently taking small plots of land as payment for his services. In 1796, the year he was elected Tennessee's delegate to the U.S. House of Representatives, he owned ten slaves. In 1798 Jackson owned fifteen slaves. He widened his economic activities, buying land, partnership in a store, a plantation for himself (the Hermitage), and a racetrack. Then came some bad years—the mercantile business failed, and debts on land came due—and Jackson was soon preoccupied with military matters. But he continued to accumulate slaves: 44 by 1820, 95 by 1828 (the year he was elected president), 150 a few years later, and almost 200 by the time of his death in 1845.

The Old Planter Elite

The slave-owning elite, those 2.5 percent who owned fifty slaves or more, enjoyed the prestige, the political leadership, and the lifestyle to which many white Southerners aspired. Almost all great slave owners inherited their wealth. They were rarely self-made men, although most tried to add to the land and slaves they had inherited. Men of wealth and property had led southern politics since colonial times, but increasingly after 1820 it was men from the middle classes who were most often elected to political office. As the nation moved toward universal manhood suffrage, planters tried to learn how to appeal to the popular vote, but most never acquired "the common touch." It was the smaller slave owners who formed a clear majority in every southern state legislature before 1860.

The eastern seaboard had first given rise to a class of rich planters in the colonial period, as attested by the plantations of William Byrd and Robert "King" Carter of Virginia and the cultured life of the planter elite, centered in Charleston, that had established itself in the South Carolina low country and Sea Islands.

One such planter was Thomas Chaplin, descended from an indentured servant who arrived in 1672 from the British sugar-producing island of Barbados. In 1839 he married Mary McDowell, granddaughter of a rich Charleston merchant, and in 1840 they moved into the old family house on the 376-acre Tombee Plantation on St. Helena Island near Beaufort, South Carolina. Master of sixty to seventy slaves, Chaplin grew sea-island cotton (a long-staple variety), potatoes, and corn, and raised beef and mutton. Although St. Helena land was rich and fertile, the climate bred mosquito-borne malaria, epidemic from mid-May until November. Most planters and their families lived in Charleston or in the healthier up country during the "sickly season," and few poorer white people lived on St. Helena at all. As a consequence, by 1845 black people outnumbered white people eight to one on the island (2,000 African Americans to 250 whites). As a result, St. Helena and the other Sea Islands of South Carolina were unique in the relative autonomy of their black population and the persistence of African customs and language.

Soon after he took possession of Tombee Plantation, Chaplin was forced to sell off more than half his slaves to settle family debts and lawsuits. Land rich but labor poor, like many members of the old planter class, Chaplin fretted in 1850: "So many mouths to feed & so few to work that it is impossible for me to get along." Unlike many planters, Chaplin refused to attend slave weddings, dismissing them as "tomfoolery," and only grudgingly did he permit his slaves to choose husbands and wives from other plantations. He complained unceasingly about the high rate of infant mortality among slaves, going so far as to accuse mothers of killing their own babies. He failed to realize that overwork and poor nutrition (counteracted only in part by the constant pilfering from his storehouses and barns) were to blame. Unlike most planters, Chaplin never hired an overseer for the work in his fields, but after 1852 he increasingly left the details of management to a black slave driver.

The Natchez "Nabobs"

As Southerners and slave owning spread westward, membership in the elite broadened to include the new wealth of Alabama, Mississippi, Louisiana, and Texas. The rich planters of the Natchez community were popularly called "nabobs" (from a Hindi word for Europeans who had amassed fabulous wealth in India). Frederick Stanton, owner of Stanton Hall in Natchez, was a physician who had immigrated from Northern Ireland. The source of his wealth was not medicine but the cotton commission (brokerage) business. At the time of his death he owned 444 slaves and 15,109 acres of land on six Louisiana and Mississippi plantations that produced more than 3,000 bales of cotton a year. Another great Natchez family, the Surgets, of French origin, traced their wealth further back, to a Spanish land grant of 2,500 acres to Pierre Surget. In the 1850s his grandsons Frank and James Surget controlled some 93,000 acres in Mississippi, Arkansas, and Louisiana (half of it plantation land and half bought on speculation, for resale). Each brother sold 4,000 bales of cotton a year, and between them they owned upwards of 1,000 slaves. Each also owned palatial mansions in Natchez—Cherry Hill and Clifton.

The extraordinary concentration of wealth in Natchez—in 1850 it was the richest county in the nation—fostered a self-consciously elite lifestyle that derived not from long tradition but from suddenly acquired riches. Fastidious Northerners such as Thomas Taylor, a Pennsylvania Quaker who visited Natchez in 1847, noted: "Many of the chivalric gentry whom I have been permitted to see dashing about here on highbred horses, seem to find their greatest enjoyment in recounting their bear hunts, 'great fights,' and occasional exploits with revolvers and Bowie knives—swearing 'terribly' and sucking mint juleps & cherry cobblers with straws."

Plantation Life

The urban life of the Natchez planters was unusual. Many wealthy planters, especially those on new lands in the Old Southwest, lived in isolation on their plantations with their families and slaves. Through family networks, common boarding school experience, political activity, and frequent visiting, the small new planter elite consciously worked to create and maintain a distinctive lifestyle that was modeled on that of the English aristocracy, as Southerners understood it. This entailed a large estate, a spacious, elegant mansion, and lavish hospitality. For men, the gentlemanly lifestyle meant immersion in masculine activities such as hunting, soldiering, or politics, and a touchy concern with "honor" that could lead to duels and other acts of bravado. Women of the slave-owning elite, in contrast, were expected to be gentle, charming, and always welcoming of relatives, friends, and other guests.

But this gracious image was at odds with the economic reality. Large numbers of black slaves had to be forced to work to produce the wealth of the large plantations. Each plantation, like the yeoman farm but on a larger scale, aimed to be self-sufficient, producing not only the cash crop but most of the food and clothing for both slaves and family. There were stables full of horses for plowing, transportation, and show. There were livestock and vegetable gardens to be tended, and carpentry, blacksmithing, weaving, and sewing to be done. A large plantation was an enterprise that required many hands, many skills, and a lot of management. Large plantation owners might have overseers or black drivers to supervise field work, but frequently they themselves had direct financial control of daily

This scene is part of a larger mural, created by artist William Henry Brown in 1842, which depicts everyday life at Nitta Yuma, a Mississippi cotton plantation. The elegant white woman, here seen elaborately dressed to go riding, depended for her leisure status on the work of African American slaves, such as this one feeding her horse.

SOURCE: William H. Brown, *Hauling the Whole Week's Picking* (detail), 1842. Watercolor. The Historic New Orleans Collection.

operations. Even if they were absentee landlords (like, for example, Thomas Chaplin in South Carolina and the richest of the Natchez elite), planters usually required careful accounts from their overseers and often exercised the right to overrule their decisions.

A paternalistic ideology infused the life of large plantations that permitted the planter elite to rationalize their use of slaves and the submissiveness they demanded of wives. According to this ideology, each plantation was a family composed of both black and white. The master, as head of the plantation, was head of the family, and the mistress was his "helpmate." The master was obligated to provide for all of his family, both black and white, and to treat them with humanity. In return, slaves were to work properly and do as they were told, as children would. Most elite slave owners spoke of their position of privilege as a duty and a burden. (Their wives were even more outspoken about the burdensome aspects of supervising slave labor, which they bore more directly than their husbands.) John C. Calhoun spoke for many slave owners when he described the plantation as "a little community" in which the master directed all operations so that the abilities and needs of every member, black and white, were "perfectly harmonized." Convinced of their own benevolence, slave owners expected not only obedience but gratitude from all members of their great "families."

The Plantation Mistress

Southern paternalism not only laid special burdens on plantation mistresses but put restrictions on their lives and activities not experienced by northern women of the same social rank. For example, although northern women like southern women were barred from public life and taught that their proper role was domestic and family-based, in the North, women came clearly to control the domestic "sphere" and to carry domestic concerns outside the family and into a wide range of activities that addressed various social reforms. Such autonomous behavior was out of the question for plantation mistresses, who were locked by the paternalistic model into positions that bore heavy responsibility but carried no real authority. The difficulties experienced by these in some ways quite privileged women illustrate the way the slave system affected every aspect of the personal life of slave owners.

Plantation mistresses spent most of their lives tending "family" members—including slaves—in illness and in childbirth, and supervising their slaves' performance of such daily tasks as cooking, housecleaning, weaving, and sewing. In addition, the plantation mistress often had to spend hours, even days, of behind-the-scenes preparation for the crowds of guests she was expected to welcome in her role as elegant and gracious hostess.

Despite the reality of the plantation mistress's daily supervision of an often extensive household, she did not rule it: her husband did. The plantation master was the source of authority to whom wife, children, and slaves were expected to look for both rewards and punishments. A wife who challenged her husband or sought more independence from him threatened the entire paternalistic system of control. After all, if she were not dependent and obedient, why should slaves be? In addition, although many southern women were deeply affected by evangelical religion and exhortations to care for those in need, their response was personal rather than social. Enlisting in reform movements like their northern counterparts would have been far too threatening to the system of slave control to be tolerated in the South, for it might have led slaves to believe that their lives, too, could be improved.

In addition to their strictly defined family roles, many southern women also suffered deeply from their isolation from friends and kin. Sometimes the isolation of life on rural plantations could be overcome by long visits, but women with many small children and extensive responsibilities found it difficult to leave. Plantation masters, on the other hand, often traveled widely for political and business reasons. John C. Calhoun, for example, who spoke so earnestly about the plantation community, spent much less time than his wife on the family plantation, Fort Hill. He spent years in Washington as a politician while Floride Calhoun, who had accompanied him in his early career, remained at Fort Hill after the first five of their ten children were born.

Plantation women in the Old Southwest, many of whom had moved unwillingly and now were far from their families on the eastern seaboard, were particularly lonely. "I seldom see any person aside from our own family, and those employed upon the plantation," Mary Kendall wrote. "For about three weeks I did not have the pleasure of seeing one white female face, there being no white family except our own upon the plantation." The irony is that she was surrounded by women, but the gap between the white mistress and her black slaves was generally unbridgeable.

Although on every plantation black women served as nursemaids to young white children and as lifelong maids to white women, usually accompanying them when they moved as brides into their own homes, there are few historical examples of genuine sympathy and understanding of black women by white women of the slave-owning class. Few of the latter seemed to understand the sadness, frustration, and despair often experienced by their lifelong maids, who were forced to leave their own husbands and children to serve in their mistresses' new homes. A number of southern women did rail against "the curse of slavery," but few meant the inhumanity of the system; most were actually complaining about the extra work entailed by housekeeping with slaves. As one plantation mistress explained, "Slaves are a continual source of more trouble to housekeepers than all other things, vexing them, and causing much sin. We are compelled to keep them in ignorance and much responsibility rests on us." Years later many former slaves remembered their mistresses as being kinder than their masters, but fully a third of such accounts mention cruel whippings and other punishments by white women.

Coercion and Violence

There were generous and benevolent masters, but most large slave owners believed that constant discipline and coercion were necessary to make slaves work hard. Some slave owners used their slaves with great brutality. Owners who killed slaves were occasionally brought to trial (and usually acquitted), but no legal action was taken in the much more frequent cases of excessive punishment, general abuse, and rape. All southern slave owners, not just those who experienced the special tensions of new and isolated plantations in the Old Southwest, were engaged in a constant battle of wills with their slaves that owners frequently resolved by violence.

One of the most common violations of the paternalistic code of behavior (and of southern law) was the sexual abuse of female slaves by their masters. Usually,

This Louisiana slave named Gordon was photographed in 1863 after he had escaped to Union lines during the Civil War. He bears the permanent scars of the violence that lay at the heart of the slave system. Few slaves were so brutally marked, but all lived with the threat of beatings if they failed to obey.

SOURCE: National Archives and Records Administration.

masters forcibly raped their women slaves at will, and slave women had little hope of defending themselves from these attacks. Sometimes, however, long-term intimate relationships between masters and slaves developed. James Henry Hammond kept two slave mistresses, Sally Johnson and her daughter Louisa, for twenty years and fathered several children by each of them. Hammond's instructions to his (white) son Harry, written in 1856, about the future of his mistresses and slave children tell us much about the boundaries of the slave system: "In the last will I made I left to you . . . Sally Johnson the mother of Louisa & all the children of both. . . . I cannot free these people & send them North. It would be cruelty to them. . . . Do not let Louisa or any of my children . . . be the slaves of strangers. Slavery in the family will be their happiest earthly condition."

It was rare for slave owners to publicly acknowledge fathering slave children or to free these children, and black women and their families were helpless to protest their treatment. Equally silenced was the master's wife, who for reasons of modesty as well as her subordinate position was not supposed to notice either her husband's infidelity or his flagrant crossing of the color lines. As Mary Boykin Chesnut, wife of a South Carolina slave owner, vehemently confided to her diary: "God forgive us, but ours is a monstrous system. . . . Like the patriarchs of old, our men live all in one house with their wives and their concubines, and the mulattoes one sees in every family partly resemble the white children. Any lady is ready to tell you who is the father of all the mulatto children in everybody's household but her own. Those, she seems to think, drop from the clouds."

An owner could do what he chose on his plantation, and his sons grew up expecting to do likewise. Unchecked power is always dangerous, and it is not surprising that it was sometimes misused. Perhaps the most surprising thing about the southern slave system is how much humanity survived despite the intolerable conditions. For that, most of the credit goes not to white paternalism but to African Americans and the communities they created under slavery.

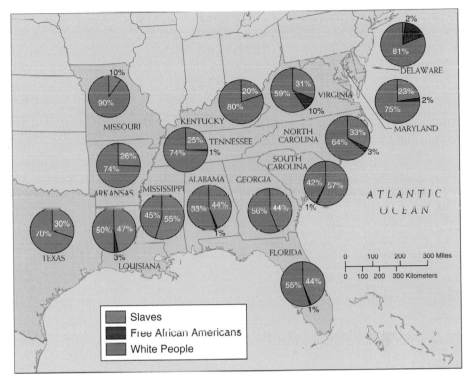

Population Patterns in the South, 1850 In South Carolina and Mississippi the enslaved African American population outnumbered the white population; in four other Lower South states the percentage was above 40 percent. These ratios frightened many white Southerners. White people also feared the free black population, though only three states in the Upper South and Louisiana had free black populations of over 3 percent. Six states had free black populations that were so small (less than 1 percent) as to be statistically insignificant.

THE DEFENSE OF SLAVERY

"Slavery informs all our modes of life, all our habits of thought, lies at the basis of our social existence, and of our political faith," announced South Carolina planter William Henry Trescot in 1850, explaining why the South would secede from the Union before giving up slavery. Slavery bound white and black Southerners together in tortuous ways that eventually led, as Trescot had warned, to the Civil War. Population figures tell much of the story of the complex relationship between whites and blacks: of the 12 million people who lived in the South in 1860, 4 million were slaves. Indeed, in the richest agricultural regions, such as the Sea Islands of South Carolina and Georgia and parts of the black belt, black people outnumbered whites. These sheer numbers of African Americans reinforced white peo-

ple's perpetual fears of black retaliation for the violence exercised by the slave master. Every rumor of slave revolts, real or imagined, kept those fears alive. The basic question was this. What might slaves do if they were not controlled? Thomas Jefferson summed up this dilemma: "We have the wolf by the ears; and we can neither hold him nor safely let him go. Justice is in one scale, and self-preservation in the other."

Developing Proslavery Arguments

Once the cotton boom began in the 1790s, Southerners increasingly sought to justify slavery. They found justifications for slavery in the Bible and in the histories of Greece and Rome, both slave-owning societies. The strongest defense was a legal one: the Constitution allowed slavery. Though never specifically mentioned in the final document, slavery had been a major issue between North and South at the Constitutional Convention in 1787. In the end, the delegates agreed that seats in the House of Representatives would be apportioned by counting all of the white population and three-fifths of the black people (Article I, Section 2, Paragraph 3); they included a clause requiring the return of runaway slaves who had crossed state lines (Article IV, Section 2,

Paragraph 3); and they agreed that Congress could not abolish the international slave trade for twenty years (Article I, Section 9, Paragraph 1). There was absolutely no question: the Constitution did recognize slavery.

The Missouri Crisis of 1819–20 alarmed most Southerners, who were shocked by the evidence of widespread antislavery feeling in the North. South Carolinians viewed Denmark Vesey's conspiracy, occurring only two years after the Missouri debate, as an example of the harm that irresponsible northern antislavery talk could cause. After Nat Turner's revolt in 1831, Governor John Floyd of Virginia blamed the uprising on "Yankee peddlers and traders" who supposedly told slaves that "all men were born free and equal." Thus northern antislavery opinion and the fear of slave uprisings were firmly linked in southern minds.

After Nat Turner

In 1831 the South began to close ranks in defense of slavery. Several factors contributed to this regional solidarity. Nat Turner's revolt was important, linked as it was in the minds of many Southerners with antislavery agitation from the North. Militant abolitionist William Lloyd Garrison began publishing the *Liberator*, the newspaper that was to become the leading antislavery organ, in 1831. The British gave notice that they would soon abolish slavery on the sugar plantations of the West Indies, an action that seemed to many Southerners much too close to home. Emancipation for West Indian slaves came in

1834. Finally, 1831 was the year before the Nullification Crisis (see Chapter 10) was resolved. Although the other southern states did not support the hotheaded South Carolinians who called for secession, they did sympathize with the argument that the federal government had no right to interfere with a state's special interest (namely, slavery). Following the crisis, other southern states joined with South Carolina in the belief that the only effective way to prevent other federal encroachment was through the militant and vehement defense of slavery.

In the 1830s, southern states began to barricade themselves against "outside" antislavery propaganda. In 1835, a crowd broke into a Charleston post office, made off with bundles of antislavery literature, and set an enormous bonfire, to fervent state and regional acclaim. By 1835, every southern legislature had tightened its laws concerning control of slaves. For example, they tried to blunt the effect of abolitionist literature by passing laws forbidding slaves to learn how to read. In only three border states—Kentucky, Tennessee, and Maryland—did slave literacy remain legal. By 1860, it is estimated, only 5 percent of all slaves could read. Slaves were forbidden to gather for dances, religious services, or any kind of organized social activity without a white person present. They were forbidden to have whiskey because it might encourage them toward revolt. The penalty for plotting insurrection was death. Other laws made manumission illegal and placed even more restrictions on the lives of free black people (as in Natchez). In many areas slave patrols were augmented and became more vigilant in restricting African American movement and communication between plantations.

In 1836, Southerners introduced a "gag rule" in Washington to prevent congressional consideration of abolitionist petitions. Attempts were made to stifle all open debate about slavery within the South; dissenters were pressured to remain silent or to leave. A few, such as James G. Birney and Sarah and Angelina Grimké of South Carolina, left for the North to act on their antislavery convictions, but most chose silence. Among those under the greatest pressure to conform were Christian ministers, many of whom professed to believe that preaching obedience to slaves was a vital part of making slavery a humane system.

In addition to fueling fears of slave rebellions, the growing abo-

This 1841 proslavery cartoon contrasts healthy, well-cared-for African American slaves with unemployed British factory workers living in desperate poverty. The comparison between contented southern slaves and miserable northern "wage slaves" was frequently made by proslavery advocates.

SOURCE: Library of Congress.

litionist sentiment of the 1830s raised the worry that southern opportunities for expansion would be cut off. Southern politicians painted melodramatic pictures of a beleaguered white South hemmed in on all sides by "fanatic" antislavery states, while at home Southerners were forced to contemplate what might happen when they had "to let loose among them, freed from the wholesome restraints of patriarchal authority . . . an idle, worthless, profligate set of free negroes" whom they feared would "prowl the . . . streets at night and [haunt] the woods during the day armed with whatever weapons they could lay their hands on."

Finally, southern apologists moved beyond defensiveness to develop proslavery arguments. One of the first to do this was James Henry Hammond, elected a South Carolina congressman in 1834. In 1836 Hammond delivered a major address to Congress in which he denied that slavery was evil. Rather, he claimed, it had produced "the highest toned, the purest, best organization of society that has ever existed on the face of the earth."

In 1854 another southern spokesman, George Fitzhugh, asserted that "the negro slaves of the South are the happiest, and, in some sense, the freest people in the world" because all the responsibility for their care was borne by concerned white masters. Fitzhugh contrasted southern paternalism with the heartless individualism that ruled the lives of northern "wage slaves." Northern employers did not take care of their workers, Fitzhugh claimed, because "selfishness is almost the only motive of human conduct in free society, where every man is taught that it is his first duty to change and better his pecuniary situation." In contrast, Fitzhugh argued, southern masters and their slaves were bound together by a "community of interests."

Changes in the South

In spite of these defensive and repressive proslavery measures, which made the South seem monolithic in northern eyes, there were some surprising indicators of dissent. Most came from up-country nonslaveholders. One protest occurred in the Virginia state legislature in 1832, when nonslave-holding delegates, alarmed by the Nat Turner rebellion, forced a two-week debate on the merits of gradual abolition. In the final vote, abolition was defeated 73 to 58. Although the subject was never raised again, this debate was a startling indicator of frequently unvoiced doubts about slavery that existed in the South.

But slavery was not a static system. From the 1830s on, financial changes increasingly underlined class differences between southern whites. It was harder to become a slaveholder: from 1830 to 1860 slave owners declined from 36 to 25 percent of the population. In 1860 the average slaveholder was ten times as wealthy as the average nonslaveholder. A major reason for the shrinking number of slave owners and their increased wealth was the rapidly increasing price of slaves: a "prime field hand" was worth more than $1,500 in 1855. Such prices caused the internal slave trade to flourish: during the 1850s slave owners from the Upper South sold some 250,000 slaves to the Lower South for handsome profits. Such a difference in the extent of slaveholding between Upper and Lower South threatened regional political unity and provoked concern. One remedy suggested in South Carolina was to reopen the international slave trade!

An even more alarming trend was evident in southern cities, where the slave system was disintegrating. The number of urban slaves had greatly decreased because plantation owners deeply distrusted the effect of cities on the institution of slavery. Urban slaves led much more informed lives than rural ones and were often in daily contact with free black and urban poor whites. Many slaves were hired out and a number even hired out their own time, making them nearly indistinguishable from northern "free labor." Other urban slaves worked in commercial and industrial enterprises in jobs that were nearly indistinguishable from those of whites. Planters viewed all of these changes with suspicion, yet they also had to acknowledge that southern cities were successful and bustling centers of commerce.

Economic changes adversely affected poor whites and yeomen as well. Increased commercialization of agriculture (other than cotton) led to higher land prices that made it harder for poor whites to buy or rent land. Extensive railroad building in up-country regions during the boom of the 1850s ended the isolation of many yeomen, exposing them for the first time to the temptations and dangers of the market economy. While slave owners grew increasingly worried about threats from the abolitionist and capitalist North, yeomen worried about local threats to their independence from banks, railroads, and activist state governments. In North Carolina, disputes between slave owners and nonslaveholders erupted in print in 1857, when Hinton Helper published an attack on slavery in a book titled *The Impending Crisis*. His protest was an indicator of the growing tensions between the haves and the have-nots in the South. Equally significant, though, Helper's book was published in New York, where he was forced to move once his views became known.

In spite of these signs of tension and dissent, the main lines of the southern argument were drawn in the 1830s and remained fixed thereafter. The defense of slavery stifled debate within the South, prevented a search for alternative labor systems, and narrowed the possibility of cooperation in national politics. In time, it made compromise impossible.

CHRONOLOGY

1790s	Second Great Awakening Black Baptist and African Methodist Episcopal churches founded
1793	Cotton gin invented
1800	Gabriel Prosser's revolt discovered in Virginia
1806	Virginia tightens law on manumission of slaves
1808	Congress prohibits U.S. participation in the international slave trade
1816–20	"Alabama Fever": migration to the Old Southwest
1819–20	Missouri Crisis
1822	Denmark Vesey's conspiracy in Charleston
1831	Nat Turner's revolt in Virginia William Lloyd Garrison begins publishing antislavery newspaper, the *Liberator*
1832	Nullification Crisis
1832–38	"Flush Times": second wave of westward expansion

1832	Virginia legislature debates and defeats a measure for gradual emancipation
1834	Britain frees slaves throughout the empire, including in its Caribbean colonies
1835	Charleston crowd burns abolitionist literature Tightening of black codes completed by southern legislatures
1836	Congress passes "gag rule" to prevent discussion of antislavery petitions James Henry Hammond announces to Congress that slavery is not evil
1846	William Gregg opens model textile mill at Graniteville, South Carolina
1854	George Fitzhugh publishes *Sociology for the South*, a defense of slavery
1857	Hinton Helper publishes *The Impending Crisis*, an attack on slavery
1858	James Henry Hammond's "King Cotton" speech

CONCLUSION

The amazing growth of cotton production after 1793 transformed the South and the nation. Physically, the South expanded explosively westward: in all, seven southern states were admitted to the Union between 1800 and 1845. Cotton production fastened the slave system of labor upon the region. Although the international slave trade was abolished in 1808, the internal slave trade flourished, with devastating effects on African American families. Nationally, the profitable cotton trade fueled economic development and provided much of the original capital for the infant factory system of the North. Cotton production was based on the labor of African American slaves, who built strong communities under extremely difficult circumstances. The cohesion of African American families and the powerful faith of African American Christianity were the key community elements that bred a spirit of endurance and resistance. White Southerners, two-thirds of whom did not own slaves, denied their real dependence on slave labor by claiming equality in white skin privi-

lege, while slave owners boasted of their own paternalism. But the extreme fear generated by a handful of slave revolts, the exaggerated reaction to the race mixing of Natchez-under-the Hill, and the growing number of free African Americans in many areas gave the lie to white claims of benevolence. In the 1830s, the South defensively closed ranks against real and perceived threats to the slave system. In this sense, the white South was nearly as trapped as the African American slaves they claimed to control. And in defending the slave system, the South was increasingly different from the dynamic capitalist free-labor system that was gaining strength in the North.

REVIEW QUESTIONS

1. How did cotton production after 1793 transform the social and political history of the South? How did the rest of the nation benefit? In what way was it an "international phenomenon"?
2. What were the two key institutions of the African American slave community? How did they function, and what beliefs did they express?

3. The circumstances of three very different groups—poor whites, educated and property-owning American Indians, and free African Americans—put them outside the dominant southern equations of white equals free and black equals slave. Analyze the difficulty each group encountered in the slave-owning South.

4. Who were the yeoman farmers? What was their interest in slavery?

5. Southern slaveholders claimed that their paternalism justified their ownership of slaves, but paternalism implied obligations as well as privileges. How well do you think slaveholders lived up to their paternalistic obligations?

6. How did slaveowners justify slavery? How did their defense change over time?

RECOMMENDED READING

Ira Berlin, *Slaves without Masters* (1974).

Charles C. Bolton, *Poor Whites of the Antebellum South: Tenants and Laborers in Central North and Northeast Mississippi* (1994).

Orville Vernon Burton, *In My Father's House Are Many Mansions: Family and Community in Edgefield, South Carolina* (1985).

Thomas D. Clark and John D. W. Guice, *Frontiers in Conflict: The Old Southwest, 1795–1830* (1989).

Catherine Clinton, *The Plantation Mistress: Woman's World in the Old South* (1982).

Drew Gilpin Faust, *James Henry Hammond and the Old South* (1982).

Lacy K. Ford Jr., *Origins of Southern Radicalism: The South Carolina Upcountry, 1800–1860* (1988).

Eugene Genovese, *Roll, Jordan, Roll: The World the Slaves Made* (1974)

Steven Hahn, *The Roots of Southern Populism: Yeoman Farmers and the Transformation of the Georgia Upcountry, 1850–1890* (1983).

Walter Johnson, *Soul by Soul: Life Inside the Antebellum Slave Market* (1999).

Peter Kolchin, *American Slavery 1619–1877* (1993).

Bruce Levine, *Half Slave and Half Free: The Roots of Civil War* (1992).

Stephanie McCurry, *Masters of Small Worlds: Yeoman Households, Gender Relations, and the Political Culture of the Antebellum South Carolina Low Country* (1995).

Donald P. McNeilly, *The Old South Frontier: Cotton Plantations and the Formation of Arkansas Society, 1819–1861* (2000).

James Oakes, *The Ruling Race: A History of American Slaveholders* (1982).

Brenda Stevenson, *Life in Black and White: Family and Community in the Slave South* (1996).

Michael Tadman, *Speculators and Slaves: Masters, Traders, and Slaves in the Old South* (1989).

▶ MEDIA RESOURCES

💿 U.S. HISTORY DOCUMENTS CD-ROM

The Federalist Era

7-6   An African American Calls for an End to Slavery (1791)

Jefferson and the Republic

8-1   Memoirs of a Monticello Slave, as Dictated to Charles Campbell by Isaac (1847)

Economic and Social Change

9-12   The Trials of a Slave Girl

Antebellum South

13-1   State v. Boon (1801)

13-2   A Black Abolitionist Speaks Out (1829)

13-3   Nat Turner, Confession (1831)

13-4   An Abolitionist Defends the Amistad Mutineers (1839)

The Sectional Crisis

14-1   William Lloyd Garrison, from The Liberator (1831)

14-2   Harriet Beecher Stowe, from Uncle Tom's Cabin

14-3   National Convention of Colored People, Report on Abolition (1847)

COMPANION WEBSITE HIGHLIGHTS

To view an exploration, enter one of the URLs below in your browser.

Web Explorations

The South Expands, 1790–1850

http://www.prenhall.com/faragher/map11.1

Agriculture, Industry, and Slavery, 1850

http://www.prenhall.com/faragher/map11.2

Additional Interactive Maps

To access the maps, go to this chapter's resources at

http://www.prenhall.com/faragher

Cotton Production, 1820–1860, page 316

Slave Population, 1820–1860, page 317

Population Patterns in the South, 1850, page 333

HISTORY RESOURCE CENTER

To find the resources listed below, go to

http://www.prenhall.com/historyresourcecenter

(Continued)

(Continued)

Images

Cotton Fields of Mississippi

Five Generations of an African-American Family

Harriet Tubman

The Scars from a Whipping on a Slave's Back

EXPLORING AMERICA

ALEXIS DE TOCQUEVILLE

http://www.prenhall.com/faragher/tocqueville

Democracy in America by Alexis de Tocqueville is considered a seminal study of the early American republic and a classic work on the United States. In the 1830s, de Tocqueville traveled around the United States observing the nation and its people, and conducting interviews. How did he perceive the diverse society and peoples of the United States? What issues did he believe posed a danger to the republic? What trends were influencing the development of the nation? These questions and others are answered in the aptly named module, *de Tocqueville*.

The excerpts from *Democracy in America* provide much insight into the developing American society, especially the development of northern and southern communities and regional economies. The interactive maps supply an important geographic context to the discussion not only by illustrating economic, demographic, and political ways the United States was expanding, but also by highlighting the nation's diversity.

The Nullification Crisis provides a potent example supporting de Tocqueville's ideas. The excerpts include a discussion of the differences seen on either side of the

Ohio River between free Ohio and slave Kentucky. Alexis de Tocqueville sees northerners engaged in a heroic pursuit of gain but suggests this quest was missing in the South. He suggests power is shifting to the northwest, which was experiencing substantial growth in the 1830s.

Reflect and Respond

Alexis de Tocqueville argued that southern states, including South Carolina, had more to gain from the Union than did northern states such as New York. Nonetheless, southern states were more likely to seek to break the Union up. He argued that they "are more

New England manufacturing town, ca. 1830's

Click anywhere to go to the previous page.

hurt in their feelings and their passions than in their interests. But this is amply sufficient to endanger the maintenance of the Union. If kings and peoples had only had their true interests in view ever since the beginning of the world, war would scarcely be known among mankind."

1. What contributed to the different rates of growth in the North and the South?

2. How did de Tocqueville distinguish between "feelings" and "passions" on the one hand and "interests" on the other?

3. On what basis did he criticize Congress's response to the Nullification Crisis?

✓ Check it out

Population Trends

This map depicts the growth of the American population and the various trends that characterized this growth.

This exploration is also available on the *Exploring America* CD-ROM.

Unidentified artist, *Middlesex Company Woolen Mills of Lowell, Mass.*, ca. 1848. Oil on canvas. Museum of
American Textile History, North Andover, Mass.

Women Factory Workers Form a Community in Lowell, Massachusetts

IN THE 1820s AND 1830s, YOUNG FARM WOMEN FROM ALL OVER New England flocked to Lowell to work a twelve-hour day in one of the first cotton textile factories in America. Living six to eight to a room in nearby boardinghouses, the women of Lowell earned an average of $3 a week. Some also attended inexpensive nighttime lectures or classes. Lowell, considered a model factory town, drew worldwide attention. As one admirer of its educated workers said, Lowell was less a factory than a "philanthropic manufacturing college."

The Boston investors who financed Lowell were businessmen, not philanthropists, but they wanted to keep Lowell free of the dirt, poverty, and social disorder that made English factory towns notorious. Built in 1823, Lowell boasted six neat factory buildings grouped around a central clock tower, the area pleasantly landscaped with flowers, shrubs, and trees. Housing was similarly well ordered: a Georgian mansion for the company agent; trim houses for the overseers; row houses for the mechanics and their families; and boardinghouses, each supervised by a responsible matron, for the workforce that made Lowell famous—young New England farm women.

The choice of young women as factory workers seemed shockingly unconventional. In the 1820s and 1830s, young unmarried women simply did not live alone; they lived and worked with their parents until they married. In these years of growth and westward expansion, however, America was chronically short of labor, and the Lowell manufacturers were shrewd enough to realize that young farm women were an untapped labor force. For farmers' sons, the lure of acquiring their own farms in the West was much stronger than factory wages, but for their sisters, escaping from rural isolation and earning a little money was an appealing way to spend a few years before marriage. To attract respectable young women, Lowell offered supervision both on the job and at home, with strict rules of conduct, compulsory religious services, cultural opportunities such as concerts and lectures, and cash wages.

When they first arrived in Lowell, the young women were often bewildered by the large numbers of townspeople and embarrassed by their own rural clothing and ways of speech. The air of the mill was hot, humid, and full of cotton lint, and the noise of the machinery—"The buzzing and hissing and whizzing of pulleys and rollers and spindles and flyers"—was constant. Very quickly, however, other women workers—often their own sisters or neighbors who had preceded them to the mill—helped them adjust. It was company policy for senior women to train the newcomers. The work itself was simple, consisting largely of knotting broken threads on spinning machines and power looms. Most women enjoyed the work. They were not bothered by the long hours; farm people were accustomed to long days. One woman wrote home. "The work is not disagreeable. It tried my patience sadly at first, but in general I like it very much. It is easy to do, and does not require very violent exertion, as much of our farm work does."

The most novel aspect of textile mills was a rigid work schedule. Power-driven machinery operated at a sustained, uniform pace throughout every mill; human workers had to learn to do the same. Each mill published elaborate schedules and imposed fines and penalties on latecomers. It was this kind of precise work schedule that represented the single largest change from preindustrial work habits; it was the hardest for workers to adjust to. Moreover, each mill positioned one or two overseers on every floor to make sure the pace was maintained. Men held these positions, and they earned more than the women who made up most of the workforce; this arrangement was unquestioned.

Why did young women come to Lowell? Some worked out of need and some to add to their family's income, but most regarded Lowell as an opportunity. It was escape from rural isolation and from parental supervision, a chance to buy the latest fashions and learn "city ways," to attend lectures and concerts, to save for a dowry or to pay for an education. As writer Lucy Larcom, one of the most famous workers, said, the young farm women who came to Lowell sought "an opening into freer life." Working side by side and living in company boardinghouses with six to twelve other women, some of whom might be relatives or friends from home, the Low-

Lowell

ell women built a close, supportive community for themselves.

The owners of Lowell made large profits. They also drew praise for their carefully managed community with its intelligent and independent workforce. But their success was short-lived. In the 1830s, because of competition and poor economic conditions, the owners imposed wage cuts and work speedups that their model workforce did not take lightly. Although the Lowell women had been brought together under a system of paternalistic control, the close bonds they forged in the boardinghouses gave them the courage and solidarity to "turn out" in spontaneous protests, which were, however, unsuccessful in reversing the wage cuts. By 1850 the "philanthropic manufacturing college" was no more. The original Lowell workforce of New England farm girls had been replaced by poor Irish immigrants of both sexes, who tended more machines for much less pay than their predecessors. Now Lowell was simply another mill town.

The history of Lowell epitomizes the process by which the North (both the New England and the Middle Atlantic states) began to change from a society composed largely of self-sufficient farm families (Jefferson's "yeoman farmers") to one of urban wageworkers in an industrial economy. Industrialization did not occur overnight. Large factories were not common until the 1880s, but by that decade most workers had already experienced a fundamental change in their working patterns. Once under way, the market revolution changed the very basis of community: how people worked, how they thought, how they lived. In the early years of the nineteenth century, northern communities led this transformation, fostering attitudes far different from those prevalent in the South. ■

KEY TOPICS

- Preindustrial ways of working and living

- The nature of the market revolution

- The effects of industrialization on workers in early factories

- Ways the market revolution changed the lives of ordinary people

- The emergence of the middle classs

PREINDUSTRIAL WAYS OF WORKING

The Lowell mill was a dramatic example of the changes factories imposed on people's accustomed ways of working and interacting with each other. To fully understand the novelty of these changes in long-established patterns of work, it is important to understand traditional ways of working on farms—where 97 percent of all Americans lived in 1800—and in cities.

Rural Life: The Springer Family

The young family of Thomas and Elizabeth Springer began farming near the city of Wilmington in Mill Creek, Delaware, in the 1790s. Although no single family can represent all of the nation's farmers, a close look at the Springers can help to identify traditional patterns and the seeds of commercial change. The Springers, who had two infant daughters, owned 129 acres of farmland, 104 of which Thomas Springer had bought from his father for less than the market price. At twenty-nine, Springer, to whom family wealth had given a substantial advantage, owned four African American slaves: Ace, a young man; Sara and Amelia, young girls; and Will, aged sixty. Ace was in the process of buying his freedom, something he could not have done further south.

Although Delaware remained a slave state until the Civil War, as the case of Ace suggests, it developed differently from states further south. By 1861, only 2 percent of the state's population was still enslaved. In part, this decline reflected the strong antislavery feeling that many residents of Delaware shared with people in the neighboring free state of Pennsylvania. But it was primarily because farmers like Thomas Springer found their soil was not suitable for growing cotton, the crop that fastened slavery on the states of the Deep South (see Chapter 11).

The Springers had access to a commercial market for their crops. From their herd of thirty or forty sheep and at least fifteen milking cows, the Springers provided Wilmington butchers with some livestock, and they sold wool, milk, and butter in local markets. They also raised oats, hay, and Indian corn to feed the livestock, as well as wheat and vegetables for both family use and commercial sale. They may have sold some of the wheat to Wilmington merchants for transshipment to Philadelphia and then Europe, but in general the Springers, like most preindustrial farm families, planted and produced a diverse range of crops for their own use. Only after their own needs were met did they sell their surplus on the commercial market.

It was Elizabeth Springer who, with the help of the female slaves and perhaps female relatives, was in charge of spinning the wool and collecting the dairy cows' milk that was intended for sale, and she was also responsible for preparing all the farm meals and preserving the vegetables and fruits grown for the family. Both the Springers, who had family living nearby, and all the neighboring farmers who made up the larger community shared their labor with each other in a barter system. They helped each other construct houses and barns, pick apples, thresh wheat, cut firewood, and prune trees. Neighbor women assisted one another in childbirth. Thus the Springers, like their neighbors, produced goods for their own use, for a community network, and for a larger, cash market, in that order. This kind of community network of barter and mutual obligation characterized traditional farming families throughout the nation. But because of the thriving cash market in nearby Wilmington, the Springers already, in a small way, had begun the transition from traditional to commercial agriculture.

The Family Labor System

In the traditional, preindustrial economy, people like the Springers did most of their work at or near their homes. One kind of traditional work was the labor of caring for the home itself and for its members, including spinning, weaving, and sewing clothes for everyone. These jobs, which fell to the women of the family,

In the 1840s Edward Hicks painted his childhood home, rendering an idealized image of rural harmony that owes more to faith in republican agrarianism than to the artist's accurate memory. The prosperous preindustrial farm depicted was similar to the Springers' farm described in the text in its mixed yield—sheep, cattle, dairy products, and field crops—and in its employment of an African American farm worker, shown plowing.

SOURCE: *Residence of David Twinning*, 1787. Abby Aldrich Rockefeller Folk Art Museum.

Two other notable characteristics of rural home production were slated soon to disappear. First, things had no fixed prices, and money rarely exchanged hands. People usually paid for a home-crafted item or a neighbor's help with a particular task in foodstuffs or a piece of clothing or by helping the neighbor with a job he needed to have done. Thus goods and services originating in the home were part of the complicated reciprocal arrangements among community residents who knew each other well. The "just price" for an item was set by agreement among neighbors, not by some impersonal market. Another characteristic of traditional rural work was its relatively slow, unscheduled, task-oriented pace. There was no fixed production schedule or specified period of time for task completion. People did their jobs as they needed to be done, along with the daily household routine. "Home" and "work" were not separate locations or activities, but intermixed.

were time-consuming, multistage activities that occupied much of the year. Mothers introduced their daughters to the easiest tasks, such as carding wool, at a young age, and taught them the more difficult skills of spinning and weaving as they grew older. This informal family apprenticeship system was echoed in the barn and field tasks sons learned from their fathers. In this way, one generation passed along essential skills to the next generation.

On the rocky farms of New England, where farm surpluses were rare and a home-produced item was cheaper and easier to obtain than an item from Britain or even Boston, many farmers worked off the farm at some other job. Sometimes an entire family developed a skill such as shoemaking that they could practice over the long New England winters. Much of what families crafted was for local and immediate use, not for a distant market. Among New England farmers, the need to find several jobs bred ingenuity and flexibility. As Noah Webster observed in 1785, "Every man is in some measure an artist—he makes a variety of utensils, rough indeed, but such as will answer his purpose—he is a husbandman [farmer] in summer and mechanic in winter."

Urban Artisans and Workers

In urban areas, skilled craftsmen had controlled preindustrial production since the early colonial period. Trades were perpetuated through a formal system of apprenticeship in which a boy went to work in the shop of a master, usually at the age of twelve or fourteen. Over the next three to seven years the young apprentice learned all aspects of the craft, gaining increasing responsibility and status as the day approached when he could strike out on his own. During that time, the master not only taught the apprentice his trade but housed, fed, and clothed him. Usually the apprentice lived with the master craftsman and was treated more like a member of the family than an employee. Thus the family-learning model used on farms was formalized in the urban apprenticeship system. At the end of the contract period, the apprentice became a journeyman craftsman. Journeymen worked for wages in the shop of a master craftsman until they had enough capital to set up shop for themselves. Generally, they could not afford to marry until they achieved master status.

Every small community had artisans such as blacksmiths and wheelwrights who did such essential work as shoeing horses and mending wagons for local farmers. Artist John Neagle's heroic image of the blacksmith Pat Lyon presents him as the very model of honest industry.

SOURCE: John Neagle, *Pat Lyon at the Forge*. Museum of Fine Arts Boston.

Like farmers, urban artisans usually kept long hours—sunup to sundown was common—but the pace of work varied enormously with the time of year and the number of orders. And work was frequently interrupted by family activities and neighborliness. Most cities were densely settled, and one bumped into one's neighbors all the time. Sales, business contracts, meals, and other occasions were often accompanied by a friendly drink of rum or other spirits. There was no clear separation between work and leisure.

Although women as well as men did task-oriented skilled work, the formal apprenticeship system was exclusively for men. Because it was assumed that women would marry, most people thought that all girls needed to learn were domestic skills. Women who needed or wanted work, however, found a small niche of respectable occupations as domestic servants, laundresses, or seamstresses, often in the homes of the wealthy, or as cooks in small restaurants or as food vendors on the street. Some owned and managed

boardinghouses. Prostitution, another common female occupation (especially in seaport cities), was not respectable.

Patriarchy in Family, Work, and Society

Like the farm family, an entire urban household was commonly organized around one kind of work. Usually the family lived at the shop or store, and all family members worked with the craftsman at his trade. A printer's wife, for example, would be capable of keeping most of the shop's functions going in the printer's absence and of supervising the work of apprentices and her children. Some artisans, like blacksmiths, needed shops separate from their homes but probably relied on their children to fetch and carry and to help with some of the work. Others, like bakers, who generally had to get up in the middle of the night to perform their work, relied on their wives to sell their products during the day.

In both rural and urban settings, working families were organized along strictly patriarchal lines. The man had unquestioned authority to direct the lives and work of family members and apprentices and to decide on occupations for his sons and marriages for his daughters. His wife had many crucial responsibilities—feeding, clothing, child rearing, taking care of apprentices, and all the other domestic affairs of the household—but in all these duties she was subject to the direction of her husband. Men were heads of families and bosses of artisanal shops; although entire families were engaged in the enterprise, the husband and father was the trained craftsman, and assistance by the family was informal and generally unrecognized.

The patriarchal organization of the family was reflected in society as a whole. Legally, men had all the power: neither women nor children had property or legal rights. For example, a married woman's property belonged to her husband, a woman could not testify on her own behalf in court, and in the rare cases of divorce the husband kept the children, for they were considered his property. When a man died, his son or sons inherited his property. It was customary to allow widows the use of one-third of the property, but unfilial sons could deprive their mothers of support if they chose. Some widows successfully continued a family business, and some single daughters received inheritances from rich fathers, but these were exceptions. The basic principle was that the man, as head of the household, represented the common interests of everyone for whom he was responsible—women, children, servants, apprentices. He thus controlled everything of value, and he alone could vote for political office.

The Social Order

In this preindustrial society everyone, from the smallest yeoman farmer to the largest urban merchant, had a fixed place in the social order. The social status of artisans was below that of wealthy merchants but decidedly above that of common laborers. Yeoman farmers, less grand than large landowners, ranked above tenant farmers and farm laborers. Although men of all social ranks mingled in their daily work, they did not mingle as equals, for great importance was placed on rank and status, which were distinguished by dress and manner. Although by the 1790s many artisans who owned property were voters and vocal participants in urban politics, few directly challenged the traditional authority of the rich and powerful to run civic affairs. The rapid spread of universal white manhood suffrage after 1800 democratized politics (see Chapter 10). At the same time, economic changes undermined the preindustrial social order.

Beginning to upset this social order were a few wealthy artisans in seacoast cities like New York. Cabinetmaker Duncan Phyfe, who gave his name to a distinctive style of furniture, is one example. Phyfe, immigrating from Scotland, opened his first shop in 1792. By 1815 he had an elegant salesroom, three workshops employing up to 100 journeymen, and a fortune of $500,000, much of it from real estate investments. Another successful New York artisan, Stephen Allen, began as an apprentice sailmaker. Allen made his fortune when he arranged to bypass the traditional middlemen and buy his materials directly from wholesalers. His sailmaking operation made a profit of $100,000 between 1802 and 1825, and when he retired he was elected mayor of New York, customarily a position reserved for gentlemen. These New York artisans, and others like them in other cities, owed much of their success to the ever-expanding effects of the economic upheaval known as the market revolution.

THE MARKET REVOLUTION

The market revolution, the most fundamental change American communities ever experienced, was the outcome of three interrelated developments: rapid improvements in transportation (see Chapter 10), commercialization, and industrialization. Improved transportation allowed both people and goods to move

WEALTH IN BOSTON, 1687–1848				
Percent of the Population	**Percent of Wealth Held**			
	1687	1771	1833	1848
Top 1 percent	10%	16%	33%	37%
Top 10 percent	42	65	75	82
Lowest 80 percent	39	29	14	4

This table tracing the distribution of wealth in Boston reflects the gains made by merchants during the international shipping boom of 1790–1807 and the way in which intermarriage between wealthy families consolidated these gains.

with new ease and speed. Commercialization involved the replacement of household self-sufficiency and barter with the production of goods for a cash market. And industrialization involved the use of power-driven machinery to produce goods once made by hand. Taken together, these three developments rapidly joined most ordinary Americans into a commercial market that supplied them with abundant quantities of inexpensive manufactured goods.

The Accumulation of Capital

In the northern states, the business community was composed largely of merchants in the seaboard cities: Boston, Providence, New York, Philadelphia, and Baltimore. Many had made substantial profits in the international shipping boom of the period 1790–1807 (as discussed in Chapter 9). During those years, the proportion of American trade carried in American ships jumped from 59 to 92 percent, and earnings to American merchants rose from $5.9 million to $42.1 million.

Such extraordinary opportunities attracted enterprising people. Established merchants like Philadelphia's Robert Morris opened up new markets such as the China trade, but there was room for newcomers as well. John Jacob Astor, who had arrived penniless from Germany in 1784, made his first fortune in the Pacific Northwest fur trade with China and eventually dominated the fur trade in the United States through his American Fur Company. Astor made a second fortune in New York real estate, and when he retired in 1834 with $25 million he was reputed to be the wealthiest man in America. Many similar stories of success, though not so fabulous as Astor's, demonstrated that risk-takers might reap rich rewards in international trade.

But the early years of the nineteenth century posed difficulties for international trade. Following the 1807 Embargo Act only the most daring American merchants were willing to risk restrictions and the chance of capture to reap exceptional profits. More cautious men perceived opportunity in the potentially huge domestic American market, deprived of cheap British goods by war in Europe (and later, by the War of 1812) and underserved by the traditional family-centered, slow-paced, and localized system of skilled craftsmanship. Mobilizing the capital available within the business community, merchants began to control, transform, and increase American home-based production.

Some of the nation's wealthiest men turned to local investments. In Providence, Rhode Island, Moses Brown and his son-in-law William Almy began to invest some of the profits the Brown family had reaped from a worldwide trade in iron, candles, rum, and African slaves in the new manufacture of cotton textiles. Philadelphia merchant and banker Stephen Girard, who had made his fortune in the West Indies trade, invested in the Lehigh Valley coalfields and in the canals and railroads that linked the coalfields to Philadelphia. Cincinnati merchants banded together to finance the building of the first steamboats to operate on the Ohio River. And even in rural towns, local merchants and shopkeepers invested in the work of local craftsmen.

Much of the capital for the new investments came from banks, both those in seaport cities that had been established for the international trade and those, like the Lynn, Massachusetts, Mechanics Bank, founded in 1814 by a group of Lynn's Quaker merchants, that served local clients. An astonishing amount of capital, however, was raised through family connections. In the late eighteenth century, members of the business communities in the seaboard cities had begun to consolidate their position and property by intermarriage. In Boston, such a strong community developed that when Francis Cabot Lowell needed $300,000 in 1813 to build the world's first automated cotton mill in Waltham, Massachusetts (the prototype of the Lowell mills), he had only to turn to his family network.

Although much of the original capital for American manufacturing, such as Almy and Brown's collaboration with Samuel Slater, came from the shipping boom of 1790–1807, southern cotton provided the capital for continuing development. Because Northerners built the nation's ships, controlled the shipping trade, and provided the nation's banking, insurance, and financial services, the astounding growth in southern cotton exports enriched northern merchants almost as much as southern planters. In 1825, for example, of the 204,000 bales of cotton shipped from New Orleans, about one-third (69,000) were transshipped through the northern ports of New York, Philadelphia, and Boston. Southerners complained that their combined financial and shipping costs diverted forty cents of every dollar paid for their cotton to Northerners. Profits from cotton shipping provided some of the funds the Boston Associates made available to Francis Cabot Lowell. In another example, New

York merchant Anson Phelps invested the profits he made from cotton shipping in iron mines in Pennsylvania and metalworks in Connecticut. Although imperfectly understood at the time, the truth is that the development of northern industry was paid for by southern cotton produced by enslaved African American labor. The surprising wealth that cotton brought to southern planters fostered the market revolution in another way as well, by providing large and predictable consumer markets for cheap clothing for slaves and luxury items such as furniture for their masters. Northern merchants soon realized that both ends of this consumer market could be profitably supplied by the new methods of production that replaced artisanal labor.

Finally, the willingness of American merchants to "think big" and risk their money in the development of a large domestic market was caused in part by American nationalism. This confidence in a future that did not yet exist was not simply a sober economic calculation but an assertion of pride in the potential of this new and exapanding nation.

The Putting-Out System

Initially, the American business community invested not in machinery and factories but in the "putting-out system" of home manufacture, thereby expanding and transforming it. In this significant departure from preindustrial work, people still produced goods at home but under the direction of a merchant, who "put out" the raw materials to them, paid them a certain sum per finished piece, and sold the completed item to a distant market.

A crucial aspect of the new putting-out system was the division of labor. In the preindustrial system, an individual worker or his household made an entire item—a shoe, for example. Now an unskilled worker often made only a part of the finished product in large quantities for low per-piece wages.

The change in the shoe industry in Lynn, Massachusetts, shows how the putting-out system transformed American manufacturing. Long a major center of the shoe industry, Lynn, in 1800, produced 400,000 pairs of shoes—enough for every fifth person in the country. The town's 200 master artisans and their families, including journeymen and apprentices, worked together in hundreds of small home workshops called "ten-footers" (from their size, about ten feet square). The artisans and journeymen cut the leather, the artisans' wives and daughters did the binding of the upper parts of the shoe, the men stitched the shoe together, and children and apprentices helped where needed. In the early days, the artisan commonly bartered his shoes for needed products. For example, in 1773, a Lynn shopkeeper wrote to Providence merchant Nicholas Brown (Moses Brown's brother) offering to

This carved and painted figure, designed as a whirligig and trade sign, shows a woman at a spinning wheel. Until cotton textile mills industrialized this work, spinning was one of the most time-consuming tasks that women and young girls did at home.

SOURCE: *Woman at Spinning Wheel*, ca. 1850–70. Carved and painted wood and iron. Photographed by Ken Burris. Shelburne Museum, Shelburne, Vermont.

trade 100 pairs of shoes for 100 pounds of tea! Sometimes an artisan sold his shoes to a larger retailer in Boston or Salem, and sometimes a sea captain arranged to lend an artisan money for the raw materials and then sold the finished shoes at every port his ship visited. Although production of shoes in Lynn increased yearly from 1780 to 1810 as markets widened, shoes continued to be manufactured in traditional artisanal ways.

The investment of merchant capital in the shoe business changed everything. In Lynn, a small group of Quaker shopkeepers and merchants, connected by family, religious, and business ties, took the lead in reorganizing the trade. Financed by the bank they founded in 1814, Lynn capitalists like Micajah Pratt built large, two-story central workshops to replace the scattered ten-footers. Pratt employed a few skilled craftsmen to cut leather for shoes, but he put out the rest of the shoemaking to less-skilled workers who were no longer connected by family ties. Individual farm women and children sewed the uppers, which, when completed, were soled by farm men and boys. Putting-out workers were paid on a piecework basis;

the men and boys earned more than the women and children but much less than a master craftsman or a journeyman. This arrangement allowed the capitalist to employ much more labor for the same investment than with the traditional artisan workshop. Shoe production increased enormously: the largest central shop in 1832 turned out ten times more shoes than the largest shopkeeper had sold in 1789. Gradually the putting-out system and central workshops replaced artisan's shops. Some artisans became wealthy owners of workshops, but most became wage earners, and the apprenticeship system eventually disappeared.

The putting-out system moved the control of production from the individual artisan households to the merchant capitalists, who could now control labor costs, production goals, and shoe styles to fit certain markets. For example, the Lynn trade quickly monopolized the market for cheap boots for southern slaves and western farmers, leaving workshops in other cities to produce shoes for wealthier customers. This specialization of the national market—indeed, even thinking in terms of a national market—was new. Additionally, and most important from the capitalist's point of view, the owner of the business controlled the workers and could cut back or expand the labor force as economic and marketplace conditions warranted. The unaccustomed severity of economic slumps like the Panics of 1819 and 1837 made this flexibility especially desirable.

While the central workshop system prevailed in Lynn and in urban centers like New York City, the putting-out system also fostered a more dispersed form of home production. By 1810 there were an estimated 2,500 so-called outwork weavers in New England, operating handlooms in their own homes. Other crafts that rapidly became organized according to the putting-out system were flax and wool spinning, straw braiding, glove making, and the knitting of stockings. For example, the palm-leaf hat industry that supplied farm laborers and slaves in the South and West relied completely on women and children, who braided the straw for the hats at home part-time. Absorbed into families' overall domestic routines, the outwork activity seemed small, but the size of the industry itself was surprising: in 1837, 33,000 Massachusetts women braided palm-leaf hats, whereas only 20,000 worked in the state's cotton textile mills. They were producing for a large national market, made possible by the dramatic improvements in transportation that occurred between 1820 and 1840.

The Spread of Commercial Markets

Although the putting-out system meant a loss of independence for artisans such as those in Lynn, Massachusetts, New England farm families liked it. From their point of view, the work could easily be combined with domestic work, and the pay was a new source of income that they could use to purchase mass-produced goods—among them shoes, boots, hats, buttons, stockings, suspenders, horsewhips, machine-made textiles, and men's work clothes—rather than spend the time required to make these things themselves. It was in this way that farm families moved away from the local barter system and into a larger market economy.

Commercialization, or the replacement of barter by a cash economy, did not happen immediately or uniformly throughout the nation. Fixed prices for goods produced by the new principles of specialization and division of labor appeared first along established trade routes, such as the Connecticut River Valley stretching from Long Island Sound to Vermont, the Erie Canal, and the expanding commercial networks around great cities like Philadelphia and New Orleans. Rural areas in established sections of the country that were remote from trade routes continued in the old ways. Strikingly, however, western farming frontiers were commercial from the very start (see Chapter 10). The existence of a cash market was an important spur to westward expansion.

British Technology and American Industrialization

Important as were the transportation revolution and the commercialization made possible by the putting-out system, the third component of the market revolution, industrialization, brought the greatest changes to personal lives. Begun in Britain in the eighteenth century, industrialization was the result of a series of technological changes in the textile trade. Mechanization moved the production of cotton and woolen yarn out of the home to the "manufactory" ("factory" for short), where power-driven machines did the work. In marked contrast to the putting-out system, in which capitalists had dispersed work into many individual households, industrialization required workers to concentrate in factories and pace themselves to the rhythms of power-driven machinery.

Many British people, especially the elite, looked on factories with horror. In England, the first factory workers were orphaned children, women, and poor Irish immigrants. These people flooded into ill-prepared rural factory towns. Horrified at the dirt and squalor of these towns, and by the relentless pace of the machinery, British poet William Blake condemned the entire concept of industrialization, writing ominously of "dark, satanic mills." If this was progress, he wanted no part of it.

Some Americans, most notably Thomas Jefferson, shared these sentiments, basing their dream of American development on the independent yeoman farmer rather than on industrialization. But no businessman could overlook the fact that industrialization quickly made Britain the wealthiest country in the world. Moveover, conditions in New England favored rapid industrialization. New England had swift rivers that could power factory machinery, and it had wealthy merchants looking for new ways to invest their capital.

Some of these merchants, whose fortunes derived from shipping southern cotton to textile factories in England, quickly realized that the manufacturing could be done in New England—if Americans could learn the secrets of British industrial technology.

Slater's Mill

The simplest and quickest way for America to industrialize was to copy the British, but the British, well aware of the value of their machinery, enacted laws forbidding its export and even the emigration of skilled workers. Over the years, however, Americans managed to lure a number of British artisans to the United States.

In 1789 Samuel Slater, who had just finished an apprenticeship in the most up-to-date cotton spinning factory in England, disguised himself as a farm laborer

This early nineteenth-century watercolor shows Slater's mill, the first cotton textile mill in the United States, which depended on the waterpower of Pawtucket Falls for its energy. New England was rich in swiftly flowing streams that could provide power to spinning machines and power looms. SOURCE: "Pawtucket Bridge and Falls." Rhode Island Historical Society.

and slipped out of England without even telling his mother good-bye. In Providence, Rhode Island, he met Moses Brown and William Almy, who had been trying without success to duplicate British industrial technology. Having carefully committed the designs to memory before leaving England, Slater promptly built copies of the latest British machinery for Brown and Almy. Slater's mill, as it became known, began operation in 1790. It was the most advanced cotton mill in America. Although Slater was a skilled mechanic and improved on the original British machines, it is nonetheless true that American industrialization owed its start to technology that the British had not wished to share.

Following British practice, Slater drew his workforce primarily from among young children (ages seven to twelve) and women, whom he paid much less than the handful of skilled male workers he hired to keep the machines working. The yarn spun at Slater's mill was then put out to local home weavers, who turned it into cloth on handlooms. As a result, home weaving flourished in areas near the mill, giving families a new opportunity to make money at a task with which they were already familiar. In 1790, home weavers had no way of knowing that their profitable occupation would soon be challenged by power looms in factories.

Many others followed Slater's lead, and the rivers of New England were soon dotted with mills wherever waterpower could be tapped. Embargo and war sheltered American factories from British competition from 1807 to 1815, but when the War of 1812 ended, the British cut prices ruthlessly in an effort to drive the newcomers out of business. In 1816 Congress passed the first tariff, aimed largely against British cotton textiles, in response to the clamor by New England manufacturers for protection for their young industry. Interestingly, the issue of tariff protection, usually regarded as a sectional issue between North and South

(see Chapter 10) initially aroused controversy in New England, where many seaport merchants opposed it because they saw it as a threat to the international free trade from which they had so richly profited

The Lowell Mills

Another way to deal with British competition was to beat the British at their own game. With the intention of designing better machinery, a young Bostonian, Francis Cabot Lowell, made an apparently casual tour of British textile mills in 1810. Lowell, the founder of the Lowell mills described in the opening of this chapter, made a good impression on his English hosts, who were pleased by his interest and his intelligent questions. They did not know that each night, in his hotel room, Lowell made sketches from memory of the machines he had inspected during the day.

Lowell was more than an industrial spy, however. When he returned to the United States, he went to work with a Boston mechanic, Paul Moody, to improve on the British models. Lowell and Moody not only made the machinery for spinning cotton more efficient, but they also invented a power loom. This was a great advance, for now all aspects of textile manufacture, from the initial cleaning and carding (combing) to the production of finished lengths of cloth, could be gathered together in the same factory. Such a mill required a much larger capital investment than a small spinning mill such as Slater's, but Lowell's family network gave him access to the needed funds. In 1814 he opened the world's first integrated cotton mill in Waltham, near Boston. It was a great success: in 1815, the Boston Associates (Lowell's partners) made profits of 25 percent, and their efficiency allowed them to survive the intense British competition following the War of 1812 (see Chapter 9). Many smaller New England

This 1850 engraving by the American Banknote company shows women tending looms at Lowell. The contrast between this industrial activity and the picture of a woman spinning at home (p. 347) illustrates one of the most important effects of industrialization: Now machines, not individuals, determined the pace of production.

SOURCE: Print Collection, Miriam and Ira D. Wallach Division of Art, Prints and Photographs, The New York Public Library, Astor, Lenox and Tilden Foundations.

Lowell, Massachusetts, 1832 This town plan of Lowell, Massachusetts, in 1832 illustrates the comprehensive relationship the owners envisaged between the factories and the workforce. The mills are located on the Merrimack River, while nearby are the boardinghouses for the single young female workers, row houses for the male mechanics and their families, and houses for the overseers. Somewhat farther away is the mansion of the company agent.

mills did not survive, even with the tariff protection approved by Congress in 1816. The lesson was clear: size mattered.

The Boston Associates took the lesson to heart, and when they moved their enterprise to a new location in 1823, they thought big. They built an entire town at the junction of the Concord and Merrimack Rivers where the village of East Chelmsford stood, renaming it Lowell in memory of Francis, who had died, still a young man, in 1817. As the opening of this chapter describes, the new industrial community boasted six mills and company

housing for all the workers. In 1826 the town had 2,500 inhabitants; ten years later the population was 17,000.

Family Mills

Lowell was unique. No other textile mill was ever such a showplace. None was as large, integrated so many tasks, or relied on such a homogeneous workforce. Its location in a new town was also unusual. Much more common in the early days of industrialization were small rural spinning mills, on the model of Slater's first

Use these interactive maps to look at the growth of cotton textile manufacturing between 1810 and 1840. How did this growth transform the way people lived and worked?
www.prenhall.com/faragher/map12.2

The Growth of Cotton Textile Manufacturing, 1810–1840   Although cotton textile manufacturing spread to other parts of the country after 1810, New England never lost its early lead. By 1839, the extent of industrialization in New England far outstripped that of other regions. Although much of New England was still rural, more and more residents were drawn into the market economy. Nationally, the proportion of wage laborers rose from 12 percent in 1800 to 40 percent in 1860. The majority of them were New Englanders who had made the transition from artisan to worker.

mill, built on swiftly running streams near existing farm communities. Although the economic benefits to local residents were considerable, the presence of the mills and mill workers brought rural communities troubling new issues of authority and diversity.

Because the owners of smaller mills often hired entire families, their operations came to be called family mills. The employment pattern at these mills followed that established by Slater at his first mill in 1790. Children aged eight to twelve, whose customary job was "doffing" (changing) bobbins on the spinning machines, made up 50 percent of the workforce. Women and men each made up about 25 percent of the workforce, but men had the most skilled and best-paid jobs.

The engagement of an entire family in a particular line of work was hardly new; both farm and artisan families were accustomed to working at a family enterprise. And unless a family member was very highly skilled, more than one worker per family was a necessity. To take one example, in the Rockdale mills, located on Chester Creek in Delaware, wages in the 1840s ranged from $1 a week for unskilled children to $12 a week for skilled workers. Unskilled adult laborers earned between $2.50 and $3.50 a week, or between $110 and $150 a year, allowing for sickness and temporary layoffs. Wages of $300 a year were necessary to keep a family safely above the poverty line. Single workers, who had to pay $70 to

$100 a year for room and board, were at a disadvantage compared with a family, who could rent a house for $25 a year and survive on an estimated $200 a year for food.

Relations between these small rural mill communities and the surrounding farming communities were often difficult, as the history of the towns of Dudley and Oxford, Massachusetts, shows. Samuel Slater, now a millionaire, built three small mill communities near these towns in the early years of the nineteenth century. Each consisted of a small factory, a store, and cottages and a boardinghouse for workers. Slater or one of his sons ran the mills personally; they were not absentee owners. Most of Slater's workers came from outside the Dudley-Oxford area. They were a mixed group—single young farm women of the kind Lowell attracted, the poor and destitute, and workers from other factories looking for better conditions. They rarely stayed long: almost 50 percent of the workforce left every year.

Slater's mills provided a substantial amount of work for local people, putting out to them both the initial cleaning of the raw cotton and the much more lucrative weaving of the spun yarn. But in spite of this economic link, relations between Slater and his workers on one side and the farmers and shopkeepers of the Dudley and Oxford communities on the other were stormy. They disagreed over the building of mill dams (essential for the mill power supply, these dams sometimes flooded local fields), over taxes, over the upkeep of local roads, and over schools. Slater, hoping to save money and exercise more control over his mill workers' time, wanted to set up his own school for factory children. The debates were so constant, and so heated, that in 1831 Slater petitioned the Massachusetts General Court to create a separate town, Webster, that would encompass his three mill communities. For their part, the residents of Dudley and Oxford became increasingly hostile to Slater's authoritarian control, which they regarded as undemocratic. Their dislike carried over to the workers as well. Disdaining the mill workers for their poverty and transiency, people in the rural communities began referring to them as "operatives," making them somehow different in their work roles from themselves. Industrial work thus led to new social distinctions. Even though the people of Dudley and Oxford benefited from the mills, they did not fully accept the social organization on which their new prosperity rested, nor did they feel a sense of community with those who did the work that led to their increased well-being.

"The American System of Manufactures"

Not all American industrial technology was copied from British inventions, for there were many home-grown inventors. Indeed, calling Americans "mechanic[s] by nature," one Frenchman observed that "in Massachusetts and Connecticut there is not a labourer who had not invented a machine or tool." By the 1840s, to take but one example, small towns like St. Johnsbury, Vermont, boasted many small industries based on local inventions, such as those by Erastus Fairbanks in scales and plows, Lemuel Hubbard in pumps, and Nicanor Kendall in guns. But perhaps most important was the pioneering American role in the development of standardized parts.

The concept of interchangeable parts, realized first in gun manufacturing, was so unusual that the British soon dubbed it "the American system of manufactures." In this system, a product such as a gun was broken down into its component parts and an exact mold was made for each. All pieces made from the same mold (after being hand filed by inexpensive unskilled laborers) matched a uniform standard. As a result, repairing a gun that malfunctioned required only installing a replacement for the defective part rather than laboriously making a new part or perhaps an entirely new gun.

Eli Whitney, the co-inventor of the cotton gin, was the first to take up the challenge of interchangeable parts, and in 1798 he contracted with the government to make 10,000 rifles in twenty-eight months, an incredibly short period had he been planning to produce each rifle by hand in the traditional way. Whitney's ideas far outran his performance. It took him ten years to fulfill his contract, and even then he had not managed to perfect the production of all the rifle parts. Two other New Englanders, Simeon North and John Hall, created milling machines that could grind parts to the required specifications and brought the concept to fruition, North in 1816 and Hall in 1824. Subsidized by the government to make rifles for the national armory at Harpers Ferry, Virginia, Hall wrote triumphantly to the secretary of war, "I have succeeded in an object which has hitherto baffled . . . all the endeavors of those who have heretofore attempted it—I have succeeded in establishing methods of fabricating arms exactly alike." When the system of interchangeable machine-made parts was adopted by the other national armory, at Springfield, Massachusetts, the Springfield rifle got its name.

America's early lead in interchangeable parts was a substantial source of national pride. As American gunmaker Samuel Colt boasted, "There is nothing that cannot be made by machine." Standardized production quickly revolutionized the manufacture of items as simple as nails and as complicated as clocks. By 1810, a machine had been developed that could produce 100 nails a minute, cutting the cost of nail making by two-thirds. Finely made wooden and brass clocks, previously made (expensively) by hand, were replaced by mass-produced versions turned out in the Connecticut factories of Eli Terry, Seth Thomas, and Chauncey Jerome and sold nationwide by Yankee peddlers. Now

In 1816 Connecticut gunsmith Simeon North did what Eli Whitney had only hoped to do. North produced the first gun with interchangeable parts. North's invention, taken up and improved by the national armories at Springfield and Harpers Ferry, formed the basis of the American system of manufactures.

SOURCE: (top) Photograph by James L. Amos, (bottom) John H. Hall's patent for a breech loading rifle, 1811. Both, National Geographic Society.

ordinary people could keep precise time rather than estimate time by the sun, and factories could require workers to come to work on time. The need of railroads for precise timekeeping gave further support to the new system of manufacture.

Like the factory system itself, the American system spread slowly. For example, Isaac Singer's sewing machine, first patented in 1851, was not made with fully interchangeable parts until 1873, when the company was already selling 230,000 machines a year. The sewing machine revolutionized the manufacture of clothing, which up to this time had been made by women for their families at home and by hand.

American businesses mass-produced high-quality goods for ordinary people earlier than manufacturers in Britain or any other European country were able to do. The availability of these goods was a practical demonstration of American beliefs in democracy and equality. As historian David Potter has perceptively remarked: "European radical thought is prone to demand that the man of property be stripped of his carriage and his fine clothes. But American radical thought is likely to insist, instead, that the ordinary man is entitled to mass-produced copies, indistinguishable from the originals."

Other Factories

Although cotton textile mills were the first and best known of the early factories, some factories produced other items, among them metal and iron. Like the textile mills, many of these factories were rural because they depended on natural water sources for power or because they needed to be near their raw materials, such as iron ore. And like the early textile mills, these first heavy industries initially coexisted with the traditional artisanal system.

The rapid development of the steamship industry in Cincinnati illustrates both the role of merchant capital and the coexistence of old and new production methods. The first steamboat appeared on the Ohio River in 1811, and Cincinnati's merchants, who had heretofore invested their profits in land and real estate speculation, were quick to see its advantages. Cincinnati's first steamboat, financed by local merchant capital, was commissioned in 1816. It proved so successful that by 1819 one-quarter of all western steamboats were being built in Cincinnati. By 1826, Cincinnati's steamship industry had grown to include four iron foundries employing 54 men, five steam engine and finishing factories employing 126 people, and three boat yards with 200 workers. At the same time, much of the detail work on the steamboat was performed by traditional artisans such as cabinetmakers, upholsterers, tinsmiths, and blacksmiths, who did record-breaking amounts of work in their small, independent shops. In this way, new factory methods and industrial techniques were often coupled with old craft techniques.

The new concepts of specialization and standardization and the increased production they brought about were basic to the system of industrial capitalism. In turn, the system led to vast increases in wealth and in living standards for many—eventually most—of the inhabitants of industrial nations. But for many workers in early nineteenth-century America, the transition from the old method of production to the new one did not come without a price.

FROM ARTISAN TO WORKER

The changes wrought by the market revolution had major and lasting effects on ordinary Americans. The proportion of wage laborers in the nation's labor force rose from 12 percent in 1800 to 40 percent by 1860. Most of these workers were employed in the North, and almost half were women, performing outwork in their homes. The young farm woman who worked at Lowell for a year or two, then returned home; the master craftsman in Lynn who expanded his shop with the aid of merchant capital; the home weaver who prospered on outwork from Slater's mill—all were participating, often unknowingly, in fundamental personal and social changes.

Personal Relationships

The immense increase in productivity made possible by the principles of division of labor and specialization effectively destroyed artisan production and the apprenticeship system. For example, in New York by the mid-1820s, tailors and shoemakers were teaching apprentices only a few simple operations, in effect using them as helpers. Printers undercut the system by hiring partly trained apprentices as journeymen. In almost every trade, apprentices no longer lived with the master's family, and their parents received cash payment for the child's work.

Thus, in effect, the apprenticeship system was replaced by child labor.

Artisans who helped to destroy the older system did so unwillingly, in response to harsh new competition caused by improvements in transportation. For example, in the 1850s Philadelphia's 7,000 shoemakers, shut out of the cheap shoe market by the success of the shoe manufacturers of Lynn, turned to the specialty markets of ladies' shoes and expensive men's shoes and boots. But even in this luxury market, the pressure of cheaper competition forced them to accept the central shop and the putting-out system rather than the individual artisanal shop. To compete, they had to change and adopt the same new labor organization as their rivals.

Although the breakdown of the family work system undoubtedly harmed independent urban artisans, it may have had a liberating effect on the women and children of farm families. About a third of the Lowell women workers did not return to their farm homes, instead remaining in town and marrying urban men or continuing to work. And of the women who did return home, fewer than half married farmers. There is no doubt that working at Lowell provided these women with new options. Women and children who earned wages by doing outwork at home may have found their voices strengthened by this evidence of their power and worth. Patriarchal control over family members was no longer absolute.

The breakdown of the patriarchal relationship between the master craftsman and his workers became an issue in the growing political battle between the North and the South over slavery. Southern defenders of slavery compared their cradle-to-grave responsibility to their slaves with northern employers' "heartless" treatment of their "wage slaves." Certainly the new northern employer assumed less responsibility for individual workers than had the traditional artisan. Although the earliest textile manufacturers, like those at Lowell, provided housing for their workers, workers soon became responsible for their own food and housing. Moreover, northern employers felt no obligation to help or care for old or disabled workers. Southerners were right: this was a

This illustration of seamstresses at work from *Sartain's Union Magazine,* January 1851, shows an early abuse created by the market revolution. Women workers were crowded into just a few occupations, thereby allowing owners to offer very low wages for very long hours of work. The women in this illustration appear to be gathered together in a central workshop where they had each other for company. Many other women sewed alone at home, often for even lower wages. SOURCE: Illustration from *Sartain's Union Magazine,* January 1851. Courtesy American Antiquarian Society.

heartless system. But Northerners were also right: industrialization was certainly freer than the slave system, freer even than the hierarchical craft system, although it sometimes offered only the freedom to starve.

Mechanization and Women's Work

Industrialization posed a major threat to the status and independence of skilled male workers. In trade after trade, mechanization meant that most tasks could be performed by unskilled labor. For example, the textile mills at Lowell and elsewhere hired a mere handful of skilled mechanics; most of the rest of the workers were unskilled and lower paid. In fact, the work in the textile mills was so simple that children came to form a large part of the workforce. By 1850, in New York City, many formerly skilled trades, including shoemaking, weaving, silversmithing, pottery making, and cabinet-making, were filled with unskilled, low-paid workers who did one specialized operation or tended machinery. Many former artisans were reduced to performing wage labor for others. Because women were so frequently hired in the putting-out system, male workers began to oppose female participation in the workforce, fearing that it would lower their own wages.

Mechanization changed the nature of women's work in other ways as well. The industrialization of textiles—first in spinning, then in weaving—relieved women of a time-consuming home occupation. To supplement family income, women now had the choice of following textile work into the factory or finding other kinds of home work. At first, these were attractive options, but negative aspects soon developed, especially in the nation's cities.

The 1820s saw the birth of the garment industry. In New York City, employers began hiring women to sew ready-made clothing, at first rough, unfitted clothing for sailors and southern slaves, but later overalls and shirts for Westerners and finer items, such as men's shirts. Most women performed this work at low piecework rates in their homes. Although by 1860 Brooks Brothers, the famous men's clothing firm, had 70 "inside" workers in a model central workshop, the firm relied primarily on putting out sewing to 3,000 women who worked at home.

Soon the low pay and seasonal nature of the industry became notorious. Two basic problems were overcrowding of the market and low wages. Women were pushed into the garment trade because they were barred from many occupations considered inappropriate for them, and the oversupply of workers led to wage cutting. To make matters worse, most people believed that "respectable" women did not do factory work (Lowell in its "model" years was the exception that proved the rule), and this disparagement fostered low pay and poor working conditions.

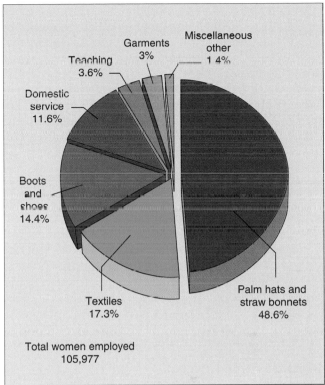

Occupations of Women Wage Earners in Massachusetts, 1837   This chart shows how important outwork was for women workers. Textile work in factories occupied less than 20 percent of women, while outwork in palm leaf hats, straw bonnets, and boots and shoes accounted for over half of the total workforce. Teaching was a new occupation for women in 1837. The small percentage of 3.6 would grow in the future.

SOURCE: Based on Thomas Dublin, *Transforming Women's Work* (Ithaca, NY: Cornell University Press, 1991), table 1.1, p. 20.

Manufacturers in the garment trade made their profits not from efficient production but by obtaining intensive labor for very low wages. The lower the piece rate, the more each woman, sewing at home, had to produce to earn enough to live. The invention of the sewing machine only made matters worse. Manufacturers dropped their piecework rates still lower, and some women found themselves working fifteen to eighteen hours a day, producing more than they ever had, but earning the same pay.

Time, Work, and Leisure

Preindustrial work had a flexibility that factory work did not, and it took factory workers a while to get accustomed to the constant pace of work. Long hours did not bother them, for they were accustomed to twelve-hour workdays and six-day weeks on the farm and in the shop. But in the early days of Slater's mill in Rhode Island, workers sometimes took a few hours off to go berry picking or to attend to other business. And when Slater insisted on a twelve-hour day that required candles for night work, one upset father demanded that his children be sent home at sunset, the traditional end of the workday.

Factory workers gradually adjusted to having their lives regulated by the sound of the factory bell, but they did not necessarily become the docile "hands" the owners wanted. Absenteeism was common, accounting for about 15 percent of working hours, and there was much pilfering. Workers were beginning to think of themselves as a separate community whose interests differed from those of owners, and the tyranny of time over their work was certainly one reason for this.

Another adjustment required by the constant pace was that time now had to be divided into two separate activities—work and leisure. In preindustrial times work and leisure were blended for farmers and artisans. The place of work—often the home—and the pace made it possible to stop and have a chat or a friendly drink with a visitor. Now, however, the separation of home and workplace and the pace of production not

only squeezed the fun out of the long workday but left a smaller proportion of time for leisure activities.

For many workingmen, the favored spot for after-hours and Sunday leisure became the local tavern. Community-wide celebrations and casual sociability, still common in rural areas, began to be replaced in cities by spectator sports—horse racing, boxing, and (beginning in the 1850s) baseball—and by popular entertainments, such as plays, operas, minstrel shows, concerts, and circuses. Some of these diversions, such as plays and horse racing, appealed to all social classes, but others, like parades, rowdy dance halls, and tavern games like quoits and ninepins were favored working-class amusements. The effect of these changes was to make working-class amusements more distinct, and visible, than they had been before.

The Cash Economy

Another effect of the market revolution was the transformation of a largely barter system into a cash economy. For example, a farm woman might pay in butter and eggs for a pair of shoes handmade for her by the local shoemaker. A few years later that same woman, now part of the vast New England outwork industry, might buy new footwear with the cash she had earned from braiding straw for hats, making gloves, or sewing shirts at home. Moreover, the shoes would have been commercially manufactured, perhaps in Lynn. In this way, in hundreds of thousands of small transactions, community economic ties were replaced by distant, sometimes national ones.

The rise of the cash economy also changed the relationships between workers and their employers. In some cases the pay envelope was the only direct contact between factory worker and (often absentee) owner. For workers, this change was both unsettling and liberating. On the minus side, workers were no longer part of a settled, orderly, and familiar community. On the plus side, they were now free to labor wherever they could, at whatever wages their skills or their bargaining power could command. That workers took their freedom seriously is evidenced by the very high rate of turnover in the New England textile mills. By the 1830s, at both the small family mills and the model mills at Lowell, almost half the workforce left every year.

But if moving on was a sign of increased freedom of opportunity for some workers, for others it was an unwanted consequence of the market revolution. In New England, for example, many quite prosperous artisans and farmers faced disruptive competition from factory goods and western commercial agriculture. They could remain where they were only if they were willing to become factory workers or commercial farmers. Often the more conservative choice was to move west and try to reestablish one's traditional lifestyle on the frontier.

TIME TABLE OF THE LOWELL MILLS,

To take effect on and after Oct. 21st, 1851.

The Standard time being that of the meridian of Lowell, as shown by the regulator clock of JOSEPH RAYNES, 43 Central Street.

	From 1st to 10th inclusive.				From 11th to 20th inclusive.				From 21st to last day of month.			
	1st Bell	2d Bell	3d Bell	Eve.Bell	1st Bell	2d Bell	3d Bell	Eve.Bell	1st Bell	2d Bell	3d Bell	Eve.Bell
January,	5.00	6.00	6.50	*7.30	5.00	6 00	6.50	*7.30	5.00	6.00	6.50	*7.30
February,	4.30	5.30	6.40	*7.30	4.30	5.30	6.25	*7.30	4.30	5.30	6.15	*7.30
March,	5.40	6.00		*7.30	5.20	5.40		*7.30	5.05	5.25		6.35
April,	4.45	5.05		6.45	4.30	4.50		6.55	4.30	4.50		7.00
May,	4 30	4.50		7·00	4.30	4.50		7.00	4.30	4.50		7 00
June,	"	"		"	"	"		"	"	"		"
July,	"	"		"	"	"		"	"	"		"
August,	"	"		"	"	"		"	"	"		"
September,	4.40	5.00		6.45	4.50	5.10		6.30	5.00	5.20		*7.30
October,	5.10	5.30		*7.30	5.20	5.40		*7.30	5.35	5.55		*7.30
November,	4.30	5.30	6.10	*7.30	4.30	5.30	6.20	*7.30	5.00	6.00	6.35	*7.30
December,	5.00	6.00	6.45	*7.30	5.00	6.00	6.50	*7.30	5.00	6·00	6.50	*7.30

* Excepting on Saturdays from Sept. 21st to March 20th inclusive, when it is rung at 20 minutes after sunset.

YARD GATES,
Will be opened at ringing of last morning bell, of meal bells, and of evening bells; and kept open Ten minutes.

MILL GATES.
Commence hoisting Mill Gates, Two minutes before commencing work.

WORK COMMENCES,
At Ten minutes after last morning bell, and at Ten minutes after bell which "rings in" from Meals.

BREAKFAST BELLS.
During March "Ring out".........at....7.30 a. m........."Ring in" at 8.05 a. m.
April 1st to Sept. 20th inclusive.....at....7 00 " " .... " " at 7.35 " "
Sept. 21st to Oct. 31st inclusive.....at....7.30 " " .... " " at 8.05 " "
Remainder of year work commences after Breakfast.

DINNER BELLS.
" Ring out"...... ....12.30 p. m........."Ring in".... 1.05 p. m.

In all cases, the *first* stroke of the bell is considered as marking the time.

This timetable from the Lowell Mills illustrates the elaborate time schedules that the cotton textile mills expected their employees to meet. For workers, it was difficult to adjust to the regimentation imposed by clock time, in contrast to the approximate times common to preindustrial work. SOURCE: Baker Library, Graduate School of Business Administration, Harvard University.

Free Labor

At the heart of the industrializing economy was the notion of free labor. Originally, "free" referred to individual economic choice—that is, to the right of workers to move to another job rather than be held to a position by customary obligation or the formal contract of apprenticeship or journeyman labor. But "free labor" soon came to encompass as well the range of attitudes—hard work, self-discipline, and a striving for economic independence—that were necessary for success in a competitive, industrializing economy. These were profoundly individualistic attitudes, and owners cited them in opposing labor unions and the use of strikes to achieve wage goals. As the *Cincinnati Gazette* put it in 1857: "We are not speaking of leaving work—that all men have the right to do; but of combining to interrupt and arrest the machinery. The first is a plain, individual right. The last is a conspiracy against the interest, and even the safety of the public." Owners opposed government action, such as proposals for legislation mandating a ten-hour day, on the same grounds: it denied workers wishing to work a twelve-hour day the opportunity to do so!

For their part, many workers were inclined to define freedom more collectively, arguing that their just grievances as free American citizens were not being heard. As a group of New Hampshire female workers rhetorically asked, "Why [is] there . . . so much want, dependence and misery among us, if forsooth, we are freemen and freewomen?" Or, as the Lowell strikers of 1836 sang as they paraded through the streets:

> *Oh! Isn't it a pity, such a pretty girl as I,*
> *Should be sent to the factory to pine away and die?*
> *Oh! I cannot be a slave,*
> *I will not be a slave,*
> *For I'm so fond of liberty*
> *That I cannot be a slave.*

Early Strikes

Rural women workers led some of the first strikes in American labor history. Because young women formed the majority of the workforce in early textile mills like Lowell, their participation in spontaneous protests is not surprising. What was surprising was that women, whose public role and activities were limited at the time, were the ones who led these protests. In 1824, in one of the first of these actions, women workers at a Pawtucket, Rhode Island, textile mill led their coworkers, female and male, out on strike to protest wage cuts and longer hours.

More famous were the strikes that the women at the model mill at Lowell led. The first serious trouble came in 1834, when 800 women participated in a spontaneous turnout to protest a wage cut of 25 percent. The owners were shocked and outraged by the strike, considering it both unfeminine and ungrateful. The workers, however, were bound together by a sense of sisterhood and were protesting not just the attack on their economic independence but the blow to their position as "daughters of freemen still." Nevertheless the wage cuts were enforced, as were more cuts in 1836, again in the face of a turnout. Many women simply packed their clothes in disgust and returned home to the family farm.

Like these strikes, most turnouts by factory workers in the 1830s—male or female—were unsuccessful. Owners, claiming that increasing competition made wage cuts inevitable, were always able to find new workers—Irish immigrants or, after the failed 1837 revolt, French-Canadians for example—who would work at lower wages. The preindustrial notion of a community of interest between owner and workers had broken down.

Collective labor action by the women workers of Lowell underlined that point. In 1845 they formed the first chapter of the New England Female Labor Reform Association. The chapter soon had over 400 members, and other chapters sprang up in mill towns such as Fall River, Dover, Nashua, and Manchester. The Lowell chapter, led by Sarah Bagley, submitted a petition to the Massachusetts legislature demanding a law limiting the workday to ten hours, which the Lowell owners were unwilling to consider. The ten-hour day, a major labor goal throughout the nation, had first been demanded by skilled male workers in Boston in 1825. When the Massachusetts legislature ignored the Lowell petition on the grounds that many of the signers were nonvoters (because they were women), Bagley broke with customary notions of female propriety and challenged the legislature in a formal address: "For the last half century, it has been deemed a violation of woman's sphere to appear before the public as a speaker; but when our rights are trampled upon and we appeal in vain to our legislator, what are we to do? . . . Shall not our voice be heard . . . shall it be [said] to the daughters of New England that they have not political rights?"

The answer seemed at first to be yes. The Massachusetts legislature continued adamantly to ignore the ten-hour-day proposal even when presented with another petition in 1846 that had 10,000 signatures, 4,000 from Lowell women. But in 1847, legislators in New Hampshire, responding to a petition from women workers in Nashua who had refused to work after "lighting up" (after dark), made theirs the first state to enact a ten-hour-day law. Maine followed in 1848 and Pennsylvania in 1849. For the first time, thanks to women's pioneering role in factory protests, a group of workers had obtained state legislation improving their working conditions.

A NEW SOCIAL ORDER

The market revolution reached into every aspect of life, down to the most personal family decisions. It also fundamentally changed the social order, creating a new middle class with distinctive habits and beliefs.

Wealth and Class

There had always been social classes in America. Since the early colonial period planters in the South and merchants in the North had comprised a wealthy elite. Somewhere below the elite but above the mass of people were the "middling sort": a small professional group that included lawyers, ministers, schoolteachers, doctors, public officials, some prosperous farmers, prosperous urban shopkeepers and innkeepers, and a few wealthy artisans such as Boston silversmith Paul Revere. "Mechanics and farmers"—artisans and yeoman farmers—made up another large group, and the laboring poor, consisting of ordinary laborers, servants, and marginal farmers were below them. At the very bottom were the paupers—those dependent on public charity—and the enslaved. This was the "natural" social order that fixed most people in the social rank to which they were born. Although many a male servant in early America aspired to become a small farmer or artisan, he did not usually aspire to become a member of the wealthy elite, nor did serving maids often marry rich men.

The market revolution ended this stable and hierarchical social order, creating the dynamic and unstable one we recognize today: upper, middle, and working classes, whose members all share the hope of climbing as far up the social ladder as they can. This social mobility was new, and it fascinated French observer Alexis de Tocqueville: "The first thing that strikes one in the United States is the innumerable crowd of those striving to escape from their original social condition." In the early nineteenth century the upper class remained about the same in size and composition. In the seacoast cities, as the example of Francis Cabot Lowell showed, the elite was a small, intermarried group, so distinctive in its superior cultural style that in Boston its members were nicknamed "Brahmins" (after the highest caste in India). The expanding opportunities of the market revolution enriched this already rich class: by the 1840s, the top 1 percent of the population owned about 40 percent of the nation's wealth. At the other extreme, fully one-third of the population possessed little more than the clothes they wore and some loose change.

The major transformation came in the lives of the "middling sort." As discussed earlier, the market revolution downgraded many independent artisans but elevated others, like Duncan Phyfe and Stephen Allen of New York, who became wealthy businessmen and

WEALTH IN NEW YORK CITY, 1828–1845		
Percent of the Population	Percent of Wealth Held	
	1828	1845
Top 1 percent	40%	50%
Top 4 percent	63	80

The impact of the market revolution on New York City, the nation's largest seaport, is shown by the dramatic increase in wealth of the already wealthy elite in a period of less than 20 years.

manufacturers. Other formerly independent artisans or farmers (or more frequently, their children) joined the rapidly growing ranks of managers and white-collar workers such as accountants, bank tellers, clerks, bookkeepers, and insurance agents. Occupational opportunities shifted dramatically in just one generation. In Utica, New York, for example, 16 percent of the city's young men held white-collar jobs in 1855, compared with only 6 percent of their fathers. At the same time, 15 percent fewer younger men filled artisanal occupations than older men.

These new white-collar workers owed not only their jobs but their lifestyles to the new structure and organization of industry. The new economic order demanded certain habits and attitudes of workers: sobriety, responsibility, steadiness, and hard work. Employers, for their part, were expected to maintain both physical and psychological distance from their workers and to rein in employees' traditional spontaneity and boisterous sociability. Historian Paul Johnson has sketched this change in lifestyle in his study of the city of Rochester: "In 1825 a northern businessman dominated his wife and children, worked irregular hours, consumed enormous amounts of alcohol, and seldom voted or went to church. Ten years later the same man went to church twice a week, treated his family with gentleness and love, drank nothing but water, worked steady hours and forced his employees to do the same." Rochester, a town transformed by the opening of the Erie Canal in 1825, grew from 300 in 1815 to 10,000 in 1830. In this pressure-cooker environment, new middle-class attitudes like that of Johnson's businessman were formed.

Religion and Personal Life

Religion, which had undergone dramatic changes since the 1790s, played a key role in the emergence of the new attitudes. The Second Great Awakening (see Chapter 9) had supplanted the orderly and intellectual Puritan religion of early New England. The new evangelistic religious spirit, which stressed the achievement of salvation through personal faith, was more democratic and more enthusiastic than the earlier faith. The old concern with sin survived in dramatic sermons that vividly portrayed hellfire and damnation, but the way to salvation was broader. The concept of original sin, the cornerstone of Puritan belief, was replaced by the optimistic belief that a willingness to be saved was enough to ensure salvation. Conversion and repentance were now community experiences, often taking place in huge revival meetings in which an entire congregation focused on the sinners about to be saved. But although continued support from the community was important, the converted bore a heavy personal responsibility to demonstrate their faith in their own daily lives through morally respectable behavior. In this way the new religious feeling fostered individualism and self-discipline.

The Second Great Awakening had its greatest initial success on the western frontier in the 1790s, but by the 1820s evangelical religion was reaching a new audience: the people whose lives were being changed by the market revolution and who needed help in adjusting to the demands made by the new economic conditions. In 1825, in Utica, New York, and other towns along the recently opened Erie Canal, evangelist Charles G. Finney began a series of dramatic revival meetings. His spellbinding message reached both rich and poor, converting members of all classes to the new evangelistic religion. In 1830, made famous by these gatherings, Finney was invited by businessmen to preach in Rochester. Finney preached every day for six months—three times on Sundays—and his wife, Lydia, made home visits to the unconverted and mobilized the women of Rochester for the cause. Under the Finneys' guidance and example, prayer meetings were held in schools and businesses, and impromptu religious services were held in people's homes. As one person recalled, "You could not go upon the streets and hear any conversation, except upon religion."

Evangelism rapidly became the religion of the new middle class. Men, like the Rochester businessman discussed earlier, soon found that evangelism's stress on self-discipline and individual achievement helped them adjust to new business conditions. The enthusiasm and optimism of evangelism aided what was often a profound personal transformation in the face of the market's stringent new demands. Moreover, it gave businessmen a basis for demanding the same behavior from their workers. Businessmen now argued that traditional paternalism had no role in the new business world. Because achievement depended on individual character, each worker was responsible for making his own way.

Master artisans, themselves successful businessmen, often took the lead in reforming the habits of younger workers. Stephen Allen, the New York sailmaker who became mayor, attributed his success to long workdays, avoidance of debt, and "employing the utmost economy in all my concerns." Another New York artisan, master baker Thomas Mercein, took advantage of the opening of the Apprentices' Library, founded by the General Society of Mechanics and Tradesmen in 1820, to preach a similar message. "Cherish, I beseech you, a deep-rooted abhorrence of the alluring but fatal paths of vice and dissipation," Mercein told the apprentices. "Industry, ardour, sobriety, and perseverance in your different pursuits will lead to a successful competition in the world."

The New Middle-Class Family

The economic changes of the market revolution reshaped family roles, first in the middle class and eventually throughout the entire society. As men increasingly concentrated their energies on their careers and occupations, women assumed major new responsibilities for rearing the children and inculcating in them the new attitudes necessary for success in the business world. The division of labor that occurred in industry was reflected in the middle-class home: father the breadwinner, mother the nurturer.

As the work roles of middle-class men and women diverged, so did social attitudes about appropriate male and female characteristics and behavior. Men were expected to be steady, industrious, responsible, and painstakingly attentive to their business. They had little choice: in the competitive, uncertain, and rapidly changing business conditions of the early nineteenth century, these qualities were essential for men who hoped to hold their existing positions or to get ahead. In contrast, women were expected to be nurturing, gentle, kind, moral, and selflessly devoted to their families. They were expected to operate within the "woman's sphere"—the home. Neither this division of responsibilities nor the distinction between men's and women's desirable characteristics and behavior was completely new; they were implicit in much earlier thinking about appropriate gender roles. But now clearly defined gender roles became a matter of social importance.

The unsettling demands of the market revolution forced a dramatic change in family life. When the master craftsman became a small manufacturer, or the small subsistence farmer began to manage a large-scale commercial operation, production moved away from both the family home and its members. Husbands and fathers became managers of paid workers—or workers themselves—and although they were still considered the heads of their households, they spent most of the day away from their homes and families. The husband was no longer the undisputed head of a family unit that combined work and personal life. Their wives, on the other hand, remained at home, where they were still responsible for cooking, cleaning, and other domestic tasks but no longer contributed directly to what had previously been the family enterprise. Instead, women took on a new responsibility, that of providing a quiet, well-ordered, and relaxing refuge from the pressures of the industrial world. As Utica author John Mather Austin advised in his manual *A Voice to the Married*, the husband should regard his home as "an elysium to which he can flee and find rest from the stormy strife of a selfish world."

Women's magazines like Sarah Josepha Hale's *Ladies' Magazine* gave homemakers some help in creating this refuge for their husbands and families, describing "patterns of virtue, of piety, of intelligence and usefulness in private life." By 1850 this magazine, which Hale merged in 1837 with Godey's *Lady's Book*—a magazine that concentrated on fashion—offered 70,000 readers a popular mixture of advice, recipes, and patterns for everything from simple embroidery to ballgowns to "model cottages," as the new suburban ideal middle-class homes were called.

The invention of photography made possible family portraits that earlier were too expensive for all but the wealthiest. This portrait of the Edward Miner Gallaudet family, photographed by Mathew Brady in the 1860s, exhibits the gender differences expected in the middle-class family: strong, self-reliant men and softer, more clinging women.

SOURCE: Brown Brothers.

A sure sign that traditional methods were inadequate for new needs was the appearance of housekeeping guides such as Catharine Beecher's book *Treatise on Domestic Economy*. First published in 1841, this book became the standard guide for a generation of middle-class American women. In it, Beecher combined innovative ideas for household design—she introduced important principles of organization for the kitchen in particular—with medical information, child-rearing advice, recipes, and much discussion of the mother's moral role in the family. Beecher's attempt to help women modernize their traditional housekeeping tasks within the context of their newly defined family role clearly filled a need: her book and the Bible were the only books that many pioneer women carried west.

The maintenance or achievement of a middle-class lifestyle required the joint efforts of husband and wife. More cooperation between them was called for than in the preindustrial, patriarchal family. The nature of the new, companionate marriage that evolved in response to the market revolution was reflected most clearly in decisions concerning children.

Family Limitation

Middle-class couples chose to have fewer children than their predecessors. Children who were being raised to succeed in the middle class placed considerable demands on family resources: They required more care, training, and education than children who could be put to work at traditional tasks at an early age. The dramatic fall in the birthrate during the nineteenth century (from an average of seven children per woman in 1800 to five in 1860) is evidence of conscious decisions about family limitation, first by members of the new middle class and later by working-class families. Few couples used mechanical methods of contraception such as the condom, partly because these were difficult to obtain and partly because most people associated their use with prostitution and the prevention of venereal disease rather than with family planning. Instead, people used birth control methods that relied on mutual consent: coitus interruptus (withdrawal before climax), the rhythm method (intercourse only during the woman's infertile period), and, most often, abstinence or infrequent intercourse. Medical manuals suggested that couples consider ending their sex life after they had reached the desired number of children.

When mutual efforts at birth control failed, married women often sought a surgical abortion, a new technique that was much more reliable than the folk remedies women had always shared among themselves. Surgical abortions were widely advertised after 1830, and widely used, especially by middle-class married women seeking to limit family size. Some historians estimate that one out of every four pregnancies was aborted in the years 1840–60 (about the same rate as in 1990). The rising rate of abortion by married women (in other words, its use as birth control) prompted the first legal bans; by 1860, twenty states had outlawed the practice. Even in the absence of accurate statistics, it is clear that dangerous illegal abortions continued, especially among unmarried women who believed they lacked alternatives.

Accompanying the interest in family limitation was a redefinition of sexuality. Doctors generally recommended that sexual urges be controlled, but they believed that men would have much more difficulty exercising such control than women, partly because, they also believed, women were uninterested in sex. (Women who were visibly interested ran the risk of being considered immoral or "fallen," and thereupon shunned by the middle class.) Medical manuals of the period suggested that it was the task of middle-class women to help their husbands and sons restrain their sexuality by appealing to their higher, moral natures. Although it is always difficult to measure the extent to which the suggestions in advice books were applied in actual practice, it seems that many middle-class women accepted this new and limited definition of their sexuality because of their desire to limit the number of their pregnancies.

Many women of the late eighteenth century wanted to be free of the medical risks and physical debility that too-frequent childbearing brought, but they had little chance of achieving that goal until men became equally interested in family limitation. The rapid change in attitudes toward family size that occurred in the early nineteenth century has been repeated around the world as other societies undergo the dramatic experience of industrialization. It is a striking example of the ways economic changes affect our most private and personal decisions.

Middle-Class Children

Child rearing had been shared in the preindustrial household, boys learning farming or craft skills from their fathers while girls learned domestic skills from their mothers. The children of the new middle class, however, needed a new kind of upbringing, one that involved a long period of nurturing in the beliefs and personal habits necessary for success. Mothers assumed primary responsibility for this training, in part because fathers were too busy but also because people believed that women's superior qualities of gentleness, morality, and loving watchfulness were essential to the task. Fathers, away from the household all day at their places of work, inevitably lost the closeness to their children that had occurred when they worked side-by-

side in the preindustrial household. Now the father's primary contribution to his children was financial. To be a good provider meant to earn a good income. This division of labor between wives and husbands was a characteristic of middle-class childrearing.

Fathers retained a strong role in major decisions concerning children, but mothers commonly turned to other women for advice on daily matters. Through their churches, women formed maternal associations for help in raising their children to be religious and responsible. In Utica, New York, for example, these extremely popular organizations enabled women to form strong networks sustained by mutual advice and by publications such as *Mother's Magazine*, issued by the Presbyterian Church, and *Mother's Monthly Journal*, put out by the Baptists.

Middle-class status required another sharp break with tradition. As late as 1855, artisanal families expected all children over fifteen to work. Middle-class families, on the other hand, sacrificed to keep their sons in school or in training for their chosen professions, and they often housed and fed their sons until the young men had "established" themselves financially and could marry, often as late as age thirty.

Mothers continued to be concerned about their children's character and morality, as women's activities in the great religious revivals of the 1830s showed. They also took the lead in an important informal activity: making sure their children had friends and contacts that would be useful when they were old enough to consider careers and marriage. Matters such as these, rarely considered by earlier generations living in small communities, now became important in the new middle-class communities of America's towns and cities.

Contrary to the growing myth of the self-made man, middle-class success was not a matter of individual achievement. Instead it was usually based on a family strategy in which fathers provided the money and mothers the nurturance. The reorganization of the family described in this section was successful: from its shelter and support emerged generations of ambitious, responsible, and individualistic middle-class men. But although boys were trained for success, this was not an acceptable goal for their sisters. Women were trained to be the nurturing, silent "support system" that undergirded male success. And women were also expected to ease the tensions of the transition to new middle-class behavior by acting as models and monitors of traditional values.

Sentimentalism

The individualistic competitiveness engendered by the market revolution caused members of the new middle class to place extraordinary emphasis on sincerity and feeling. So-called sentimentalism sprang from nostalgia for the imagined trust and security of the familiar, face-to-face life of the preindustrial village. Sermons, advice manuals, and articles now thundered warnings to young men of the dangers and deceits of urban life, and especially of fraudulent "confidence men and painted ladies" who were not what they seemed. Middle-class women were expected to counteract the impersonality and hypocrisy of the business world by the example of their own morality and sincere feeling.

For guidance in this new role women turned to a new literary form, the sentimental novel. In contrast to older forms like sermons and learned essays, the novel was popular, accessible, and emotionally engrossing. Although denounced by ministers and scholars as frivolous, immoral, and subversive of authority, the novel found a ready audience among American women. Publishers of novels found a lucrative market, one that increased from $2.5 million in 1820 to $12.5 million in 1850. By 1850, *Harper's Magazine* estimated, four-fifths of the reading public were women, and they were reading novels written by women.

To be a "lady novelist" was a new and rather uncomfortably public occupation for women. Several authors, such as Susan Warner, were driven to novel writing when their fathers lost their fortunes in the Panic of 1837. Novel writing could be very profitable:

Warner's 1850 novel *The Wide Wide World* went through fourteen editions in two years, and works by other authors such as Lydia Maria Child, Catherine Sedgwick, and E. D. E. N. Southworth sold in the thousands of copies. Sentimental novels concentrated on private life. Religious feeling, antipathy toward the dog-eat-dog world of the commercial economy, and the need to be prepared for unforeseen troubles were common themes. Although the heroines usually married happily at the end of the story, few novels concentrated on romantic love. Most of these domestic novels, as they were known, presented readers with a vision of responsibility and community based on moral and caring family life.

Although sentimentalism originally sprang from genuine fear of the dangers individualism posed to community trust, it rapidly hardened into a rigid code of etiquette for all occasions. Moments of genuine and deep feeling, such as death, were smothered in elaborate rules concerning condolences, expressions of grief, and appropriate clothing. A widow, for example, was expected to wear "deep mourning" for a year—dresses of dull black fabrics and black bonnets covered with long, thick black veils—and in the following year "half mourning"—shiny black silk dresses, perhaps with trim of gray, violet, or white, and hats without veils. Thus sentimentalism rapidly became concerned not with

In a time before ready-made clothing was available, middle class women used *Godey's Ladies Book* as a pattern book, taking elaborate fashion illustrations such as this one from 1856 to local seamstresses, or remaking older dresses to fit the current trends. SOURCE: CORBIS ©Bettmann/CORBIS.

feelings but social codes. Transformed into a set of rules about genteel manners to cover all occasions, sentimentalism itself became a mark of middle-class status. And it became one of the tasks of the middle-class woman to make sure her family conformed to the social code and associated only with other respectable families. In this way, women forged and enforced the distinctive social behavior of the new middle class.

Transcendentalism and Self-Reliance

As the new middle class conformed to the rules of sentimental behavior, it also sought a more general intellectual reassurance. Middle-class men, in particular, needed to feel comfortable about their public assertions of individualism and self-interest. One source of reassurance was the philosophy of transcendentalism and its well-known spokesman, Ralph Waldo Emerson. Originally a Unitarian minister, Emerson quit the pulpit in 1832 and became what one might call a secular minister. Famous as a writer and lecturer, he popularized transcendentalism, a romantic philosophical theory claiming that there was an ideal, intuitive reality transcending ordinary life. The best place to achieve that individual intuition of the Universal Being, Emerson suggested, was not in church or in society but alone in the natural world. As he wrote in "Nature" (1836),

Emerson's romantic glorification of nature included the notion of himself as a "transparent eyeball," as he wrote in "Nature" in 1836. This caricature of Emerson is from "Illustrations of the New Philosophy" by Christopher Pearce Cranch. SOURCE: Library of Congress.

"Standing on the bare ground—my head bathed by the blithe air, and uplifted into infinite space—all mean egotism vanishes. I become a transparent Eyeball; I am nothing; I see all; the currents of the Universal Being circulate through me; I am part and parcel of God." The same assertion of individualism rang through Emerson's stirring polemic "Self-Reliance" (1841). Announcing "Whoso would be a man, must be a nonconformist," Emerson urged that "Nothing is at last sacred but the integrity of your own mind." Inspirational but down-to-earth, Emerson was just the philosopher to inspire young businessmen of the 1830s and 1840s to achieve success in a responsible manner.

Emerson's younger friend, Henry David Thoreau, pushed the implications of individualism further than the more conventional Emerson. Determined to live the transcendental ideal of association with nature, Thoreau lived in solitude in a primitive cabin for two years at Walden Pond, near Concord, Massachusetts, confronting "the essential facts of life." His experience was the basis for *Walden* (1854), a penetrating criticism of the spiritual cost of the market revolution. Denouncing the materialism that led "the mass of men [to] lead lives of quiet desperation," Thoreau recommended a simple life of subsistence living that left time for spiritual thought. Margaret Fuller, perhaps the most intellectually gifted of the transcendental circle, was patronized by Emerson because she was a woman. She expressed her sense of women's wasted potential in her pathbreaking work *Woman in the Nineteenth Century* (1845) Intellectually and emotionally, however, Fuller achieved liberation only when she moved to Europe and participated in the liberal Italian revolution of 1848. The romantic destiny she sought was tragically fulfilled when she, her Italian husband, and their child died in a shipwreck off the New York coast as they returned to America in 1850.

Although Thoreau and Fuller were too radical for many readers, Emerson's version of the romantic philosophy of transcendentalism, seemingly so at odds with the competitive and impersonal spirit of the market revolution, was in fact an essential component of it. Individualism, or, as Emerson called it, self-reliance, was at the heart of the personal transformation required by the market revolution. Sentimentalism, transcendentalism, and evangelical religion all helped the new middle class to forge values and beliefs that were appropriate to their social roles.

CONCLUSION

The market revolution involved three transformations: improvements in transportation, commercialization, and industrialization. Each began at different times.

CHRONOLOGY

1790	Samuel Slater's first mill opens in Rhode Island
1793	Cotton gin invented
1798	Eli Whitney contracts with the federal government for 10,000 rifles, which he undertakes to produce with interchangeable parts
1807	Embargo Act excludes British manufactures
1810	Francis Cabot Lowell tours British textile factories First steamboat on the Ohio River
1812	Micajah Pratt begins his own shoe business in Lynn, Massachusetts
1813	Francis Cabot Lowell raises $300,000 to build his first cotton textile factory at Waltham, Massachusetts
1815	War of 1812 ends; British competition in manufactures resumes
1816	First protective tariff
1820s	Large-scale outwork networks develop in New England
1823	Lowell mills open
1824	John Hall successfully achieves interchangeable parts at Harpers Ferry armory Women lead strike at Pawtucket textile mill
1825	Erie Canal opens
1830	Charles G. Finney's Rochester revivals
1834	First strike at Lowell mills
1836	Ralph Waldo Emerson lecture "Nature" published
1841	Catharine Beecher's *Treatise on Domestic Economy* published
1845	New England Female Labor Reform Association formed
1847	New Hampshire passes first ten-hour-day laws

The transportation revolution (discussed in Chapter 10), usually dated from 1825 (the year of the opening of the Erie Canal), accelerated with the building of railroads in the 1830s and 1840s. Commercialization began earlier, around 1805, as a consequence of the reorganization of manufacturing through the putting-out system by northern entrepreneurs. After 1805, the cash purchase of items manufactured elsewhere slowly eroded local barter arrangements. American industrialization began with Samuel Slater's small cotton spinning mill in Rhode Island in 1790, but the most famous early example was the mill town of Lowell, Massachusetts, whose factories opened in 1823. These three transformations, taken together, constituted the market revolution that, by changing the ways people worked, changed how they thought.

For most people the changes were gradual. Until midcentury, the lives of rural people were still determined largely by community events, although the spread of democratic politics and the availability of newspapers and other printed material increased their connection to a larger world. Wage earners made up only 40 percent of the working population in 1860, and factory workers made up an even smaller percentage.

The new middle class was most dramatically affected by the market revolution. All aspects of life, in-

cluding intimate matters of family organization, gender roles, and the number and raising of children, changed. New values—evangelical religion, sentimentalism, and transcendentalism—helped the members of the new middle class in their adjustment. As the next chapter describes, the nation's cities were the first arena where old and new values collided.

REVIEW QUESTIONS

1. What changes in preindustrial life and work were caused by the market revolution?
2. This chapter argues that when people begin doing new kinds of work, their beliefs and attitudes change. Give three examples of such changes described in the chapter. Can you think of other examples?
3. Discuss the opinion offered by historian David Potter that mass production has been an important democratizing force in American politics. Do you agree? Why or why not?
4. Consider the portrait of the nineteenth-century middle-class family offered in this chapter and imagine yourself as a member of such a family. What new aspects of family relations would you welcome? Which would be difficult? Why?

RECOMMENDED READING

Christopher Clark, *The Roots of Rural Capitalism: Western Massachusetts, 1780–1860* (1990).

Alan Dawley, *Class and Community: The Industrial Revolution in Lynn* (1976).

Thomas Dublin, *Women at Work: The Transformation of Work and Community in Lowell, Massachusetts, 1826–1860* (1979).

Thomas Dublin, *Transforming Women's Work: New England Lives in the Industrial Revolution* (1994).

Karen Halttunen, *Confidence Men and Painted Women: A Study of Middle-Class Culture in America* (1982).

David Houndshell, *From the American System to Mass Production, 1800–1932* (1984).

Shawn Johansen, *Family Men: Middle-Class Fatherhood in Early Industrializing America* (2001).

Paul Johnson, *A Shopkeeper's Millennium: Society and Revivals in Rochester, New York, 1815–1837* (1978).

Bruce Laurie, *Artisans into Workers: Labor in Nineteenth-Century America* (1989).

Jonathan Prude, *The Coming of Industrial Order: Town and Factory Life in Rural Massachusetts, 1810–1860* (1983).

Steven J. Ross, *Workers on the Edge: Work, Leisure and Politics in Industrializing Cincinnati, 1788–1890* (1985).

Mary Ryan, *The Making of the Middle Class* (1981).

Charles Sellers, *The Market Revolution: Jacksonian America, 1815–1846* (1991).

Christine Stansell, *City of Women: Sex and Class in New York, 1789–1860* (1983).

▶ MEDIA RESOURCES

 U.S. HISTORY DOCUMENTS CD-ROM

Economic and Social Change

9-3   The Case for the Erie Canal

9-7   Henry Clay, "Defense of the American System" (1832)

9-9   The Harbinger, Female Workers of Lowell (1836)

9-11   Resolutions of the Boston Carpenters' Strike (1845)

Jacksonian Democracy

10-12   Female Industry Association, from the New York Herald (1845)

Reforming the Nation

11-6   A Lowell Mill Girl Tells Her Story (1836)

COMPANION WEBSITE HIGHLIGHTS

 To view an exploration, enter one of the URLs below in your browser.

Web Explorations

 Lowell, Massachusetts, 1832
http://www.prenhall.com/faragher/map12.1
The Growth of Cotton Textile Manufacturing, 1810–1840
http://www.prenhall.com/faragher/map12.2

 Additional Interactive Maps

To access the map, go to this chapter's resources at
http://www.prenhall.com/faragher
Occupations of Women Wage Earners in Massachusetts, 1837, page 355

HISTORY RESOURCE CENTER

To find the resources listed below, go to
http://www.prenhall.com/historyresourcecenter

Documents

"Petition of the Catholics of New York" (1840)

Jacob Bigelow, "Inaugural Address" (1816)

James F. Cooper, Notions of the Americans (1840)

Letters of John and Elizabeth Hodgdon (1840)

Images

Calico Printing

Cotton Mills

Mississippi River Steamer

Occupational Portraits—Pre–Civil War Daguerreotypes

Salt Lake City in 1850

Wall Street, New York City, 1850s

Woman at Spinning Wheel

Turn to the next page for the *Exploring America* activity for this chapter. ☞

EXPLORING AMERICA

MACHINERY

http://www.prenhall.com/faragher/machinery

What defines progress? Between 1800 and 1860 approximately, technological advances connected to industrialization transformed the United States. What advances occurred and where did they exert the most influences? How did life change for an American who lived between the early 1800s and 1860 approximately? How did attitudes on the stages of civilization development apply to the rapidly industrializing United States? How did machinery help define this period of American history? Video clips, prints and drawings, documents, and interactive maps help answer these and other questions.

Machinery uses a variety of sources to demonstrate

the diverse and expansive influences industrialization exerted on American development. Paintings by Thomas Cole that depict stages of civilization development provide an interesting context to the discussion of technology and change. The interactive maps show how transportation developments reduced travel times, an important consideration in the far-flung, fledgling American republic. Video clips explore the impact of railroads and factories. The comments by historical figures offer interesting insight into technology and change, while the narrative supplies a tight story line for the expansive technological advances and their impact.

Reflect and Respond

1. How well might Currier and Ives's *Progress* illustrate Ichabod Washburn's account of his life as a "mechanic"? Choose specific images from the lithograph you think are relevant.

2. Contrast the drawing of Washburn's *Worcester Wire Works* with Cole's *Consummation*. Cole imagined the United States recapitulating the fate of the Roman Empire. Growth and prosperity would reach a peak, a consummation, which would lead to a period of destruction. Washburn's account imagines no such prospect. How did he imagine the future course of American history?

✓ Check it out

Commercial Links: Rivers, Canals, Roads, 1830, Rail Lines, 1850

This interactive map depicts the growth of various transportation systems in the United States. The map

shows not only what types of systems developed and when but also the general direction they followed. It also indicates which sections of the country were most involved in developing canals, roads, and rail lines as well which type predominated.

This exploration is also available on the *Exploring America* CD-ROM.

Johann Caspar Wild, *View of Cincinnati*, 1830–40. The Cincinnati Historical Society.

Seneca Falls: Women Reformers Respond to the Market Revolution

IN THE SUMMER OF 1848, A SMALL ADVERTISEMENT APPEARED in an upstate New York newspaper announcing a "convention to discuss the social, civil, and religious condition and rights of woman," to be held at Seneca Falls on July 19 and 20.

Charlotte Woodward, a nineteen-year-old glove maker who did outwork in her rural home, saw the advertisement and persuaded six friends to join her in the forty-mile journey to the convention. "At first we travelled quite alone," she recalled. "But before we had gone many miles we came on other wagon-loads of women, bound in the same direction. As we reached different crossroads we saw wagons coming from every part of the country, and long before we reached Seneca Falls we were a procession."

To the surprise of the convention organizers, almost 300 people—men as well as women—attended the two-day meeting. The focus of their discussions was the Declaration of Sentiments, a petition for women's rights modeled on the Declaration of Independence. "We hold these truths to be self-evident," it announced: "That all men and women are created equal." As the Declaration of Independence detailed the oppressions King George III had imposed on the colonists, the Declaration of Sentiments detailed, in a series of resolutions, the oppressions men had imposed on women. Men had deprived women of legal rights, of the right to own their own property, of custody of their children in cases of divorce, of the right to higher education (at that time only Oberlin College and Mount Holyoke Female Seminary admitted women), of full participation in religious worship and activity, and of the right to vote. After discussion, the attendees approved all the resolutions, and all but the last of them, which a minority found too radical, unanimously. "Why Lizzie, thee will make us ridiculous!" Quaker Lucretia Mott had exclaimed when Elizabeth Cady Stanton proposed the voting rights measure. Indeed the newspapers reporting on the convention thought the demand for the vote was ridiculously unfeminine. But the group that assembled in Seneca Falls was undeterred. Buoyed by the success of this first women's rights convention, they promptly planned another one three weeks later in New York's largest upstate city, Rochester, to reach new supporters and to develop strategies to implement their resolutions.

The fight for women's rights was only one of many reform movements that emerged in the United States in the wake of the economic and social disruptions of the market revolution. The Seneca Falls region was itself deeply affected by that revolution. A farming frontier in 1800, it had been drawn into national commerce in 1828 when it was reached by an offshoot of the Erie Canal. It was drawn even further into the modern age when the railroad arrived in 1841. A village of 200 in 1824, Seneca Falls had grown to a town of over 4,000 by 1842. It was now a center for flour milling (in 1845, the nine mills in the town produced a total of 2,000 barrels of flour a day) and manufacturing, and a hub of the outwork network of which Charlotte Woodward was a part. Swamped by newcomers (among them a growing number of poor Irish

Catholics), the inhabitants of Seneca Falls struggled to maintain a sense of community. They formed volunteer organizations of all kinds—religious, civic, social, educational, recreational. And they became active participants in reform movements seeking to counteract the effects of industrialization, rapid growth, and the influx of newcomers.

Many reformers belonged to liberal religious groups with wide social perspectives. Perhaps a third of those attending the women's rights convention, for example, were members of the Wesleyan Methodist Society of Seneca Falls, which had broken with the national Methodist organization because it would not take a strong stand against slavery. Another quarter were Progressive Quakers of the nearby town of Waterloo, who had broken with their national organization for the same reason. Both groups were outspoken in their belief in the moral equality of all humankind and in their commitment to social activism. The Wesleyans, for example, resolved in 1847 that "we cannot identify our Christian and moral character with societies where women and colored persons are excluded." Seneca Falls had been the site of a "Temperance Reformation" in the early 1840s, and many attendees at the Women's Rights convention were also active in the temperance movement, a more limited but extremely popular reform cause dedicated to promoting abstinence from alcohol.

The idea for the Women's Rights convention emerged during a meeting in early July 1848, between Lucretia Mott—a Philadelphia Quaker and the nation's best-known woman reformer—and Elizabeth Cady Stanton of Seneca Falls, wife of a well-known antislavery orator and niece of a leading reform philanthropist. Reflecting her many concerns, Mott had just finished a tour of the new penitentiary at Auburn and a nearby Indian reservation and was visiting her sister in Waterloo. Stanton called for tea to renew her acquaintance with Mott, and it was in this context of friendship and shared concern for reform that the two began planning the convention that was held two weeks later.

Stanton and her family had moved from Boston, where, she remembered, they had "near neighbors, a new home with all the modern conveniences, and well-trained servants." Living in a house on the outskirts of Seneca Falls,

her three children suffering from malaria, she had none of those things. "I now fully understood," she mused,

> the practical difficulties most women had to contend with. . . . The general discontent I felt with woman's portion as wife, mother, housekeeper, physician and spiritual guide, the chaotic conditions into which everything fell without her constant supervision, and the wearied anxious look of the majority of women impressed me with a strong feeling that some active measures should be taken to remedy the wrongs of society in general, and of women in particular.

As she and Mott spoke of the changes that would be necessary to allow women to care for their families but have energy left over to reform "the wrongs of society," the idea of a women's rights convention was born. The women's rights movement that took shape from this convention proved exceptionally long-lasting. Stanton, soon to form a working partnership with former temperance worker Susan B. Anthony, devoted the rest of her life to women's rights.

But what of Charlotte Woodward, a local farm girl, unaware of the national reform community? Why was she there? In this age of hopefulness and change she wanted a better life for herself. She was motivated, she said, by "all the hours that I sat and sewed gloves for a miserable pittance, which, after it was earned, could never be mine." By law and custom her father, as head of the household, was entitled to her wages. "I wanted to work," she explained, "but I wanted to choose my task and I wanted to collect my wages." The reforming women of Seneca Falls, grouped together on behalf of social improvement, had found in the first women's rights convention a way to speak for the needs of working women such as Charlotte Woodward.

All over the North, in communities like Seneca Falls as well as in cities like New York, Americans gathered together in reform organizations to try to solve the problems that the market revolution posed for work, family life, personal and social values, and urban growth. Through these organizations local women and men became participants in wider communities of concern. ■

Seneca Falls

KEY TOPICS

- The new social problems that accompanied urbanization and immigration

- The responses of reformers

- The origins and political effects of the abolitionist movement

- The involvement of women in reform efforts

URBAN AMERICA

Although the market revolution affected all aspects of American life, nowhere was its impact so noticeable as in the cities. It was within the urban environment, with its stimulating, frightening confusion of rapid physical growth, occupational and ethnic change, and economic competition, that new American political and social forms began to emerge.

The Growth of Cities

The market revolution dramatically increased the size of America's cities, with the great seaports leading the way. The proportion of America's population living in cities increased from only 7 percent in 1820 to almost 20 percent in 1860, a rate of growth greater than at any other time in the country's history. This rapid growth fundamentally changed the small and compact nature of urban life. The preindustrial cities of eighteenth-century America had been "walking cities," in which people, rich and poor, lived near their work in a dense, small-scale housing pattern that fostered neighborliness and the mingling of social classes.

The nation's five largest cities in 1850 were the same as in 1800, with one exception. New York, Philadelphia, Baltimore, and Boston still topped the list, but New Orleans had edged out Charleston (see Chapters 9 and 11). The rate of urban growth was extraordinary. All four Atlantic seaports grew at least 25 percent each decade between 1800 and 1860, and often much more. New York, which grew from 60,000 in 1800 to 202,600 in 1830 and to more than 1 million in 1860, emerged as the nation's most populous city, its largest port, and its financial center. Between 1820 and 1830, the decade in which the Erie Canal added commerce with the American interior to the city's long-standing international trade, New York's population grew 64 percent.

Philadelphia, which had been the nation's largest city in 1800, was half the size of New York in 1850.

Nevertheless, its growth was substantial—from 70,000 in 1800 to 389,000 in 1850 and to 565,529 in 1860. Philadelphia became as much an industrial as a commercial city. Old artisanal industries such as handloom weaving, tailoring, and shoe manufacture coexisted with new industries such as the huge Baldwin locomotive works, foundries, and chemical companies.

Baltimore, with 212,418 residents in 1860 was about half the size of Philadelphia. The city's merchants, hoping to counter the threat posed by the Erie Canal to their trade links with the trans-Appalachian West, financed the nation's first important railroad, the Baltimore and Ohio, which began operation in 1830. Although Baltimore remained the east coast center of the tobacco trade with Europe, by 1850 its major partner in foreign trade was Brazil, to which it shipped flour and from which it imported coffee.

Boston, in colonial times, had dominated the triangular trade linking Britain and the West Indies. By 1860, with a population of 177,840, the city had emerged as the center of a new triangular trade: the ships of Boston merchants carried New England cotton cloth, shoes, and other manufactured goods to the South, delivered southern cotton to British and European ports, and returned to Boston with European manufactured goods. Boston still dominated the China trade as well.

New Orleans, fed by the expansion of cotton throughout the South and commercial agriculture in the Mississippi Valley, had a population of 168,675 in 1860, and this population, as had been true in 1800, was the most racially diverse of any large city. In the 1850s, New Orleans handled about half the nation's cotton exports and by 1860, its exports—$5 million in 1815—had risen to $107 million.

The market revolution oriented the attention of each of these major seaports away from the oceans and toward trade with the nation's interior. Prosperous merchants in these cities now depended on American exports rather than European imports for their profits.

Another result of the market revolution was the appearance of "instant" cities at critical points on the new transportation network. Utica, New York, once a frontier trading post, was transformed by the opening of the Erie Canal into a commercial and manufacturing center. By 1850 the city's population had reached 22,000. Chicago, on the shores of Lake Michigan, was transformed by the coming of the railroad into a major junction for water and rail transport. The city, which emerged as a fur trading center around Fort Dearborn, an army post built in 1803, had become, by the 1850s, a hub of trade boasting grain storage facilities, slaughterhouses, and warehouses of all kinds. Farm implement manufacturers such as Cyrus McCormick built manufacturing plants there to serve the needs of Midwest farmers. By 1860 Chicago had a population of 100,000, making it the nation's eighth largest city (after Cincinnati and St. Louis).

Patterns of Immigration

One of the key aspects of urban growth was a surge in immigration to the United States that began in the 1820s and accelerated dramatically after 1830. From an annual figure of about 20,000 in 1831, immigration ballooned to a record 430,000 in 1854 before declining in the years prior to the Civil War. The proportion of immigrants in the population jumped from 1.6 percent in the 1820s to 11.2 percent in 1860. In the nation's cities, the proportion was vastly larger: by 1860, nearly half of New York's population (48 percent) was foreign-born.

Most of the immigrants to the United States during this period came from Ireland and Germany. Political unrest and poor economic conditions in Germany and the catastrophic Potato Famine of 1845–1850 in Ireland was responsible for an enormous surge in immigration from those countries between 1845 and 1854. The starving, desperate "Famine Irish" who crowded into eastern seaports were America's first large refugee group. Between them, the Germans and the Irish represented the largest influx of non-English immigrants the country had known (many Americans found the Irish dialect as strange as a foreign language). They were also the poorest, most of the Irish arrived destitute. In addition, most of the Irish and half of the Germans were Catholics, an unwelcome novelty to many Protestant Americans.

The influx of mostly poor, mostly Catholic foreigners provoked nativist hostility among many Protestant, native-born Americans, including many leaders of the major reform movements (see Chapter 15). It would be a mistake, however, to think that immigration was unwelcome to everyone. Industries needed willing workers, and western states were eager for settlers. In 1852 Wisconsin appointed a commissioner of emigration with responsibility for attracting Europeans to the state. Soon Iowa and Minnesota joined Wisconsin in advertising widely in Europe for settlers.

Immigrant labor fueled the nation's expanding economy and helped turn wilderness into farmland. Many of the changes in industry and transportation

Wright's Grove, shown here in an 1868 illustration, was the popular picnic grounds and beer garden for the large German community on Chicago's North Side. Establishments such as this horrified American temperance advocates, who warned about the dangerous foreign notion of mixing alcohol with family fun. SOURCE: Chicago Historical Society.

that accompanied the market revolution would have been impossible without immigrants. Irish contract workers, for example, were essential to the completion of the Erie Canal in 1825. And Irish women and men kept the mills at Lowell operating when the mill operators, facing increasing competition, sought cheaper labor to replace their original labor force of farm women.

Few immigrants found life in the United States pleasant or easy. In addition to the psychological difficulties of leaving a home and familiar ways behind, most immigrants endured harsh living and working conditions. America's cities were unprepared for the social problems posed by large numbers of immigrants. Until the 1880s, the task of receiving immigrants fell completely on cities and states, not the federal government. New York City, by far the largest port of entry, did not even establish an official reception center until 1855, when Castle Garden, at the bottom of Manhattan Island (near present-day Battery Park), was so designated.

Irish Immigration

The first major immigrant wave to test American cities was caused by the catastrophic Irish Potato Famine of 1845–49. The Irish, held in unwilling colonial status by the British, subsisted poorly on small plots of farmland on which they grew grain for British landlords and potatoes for their own food. Irish emigration to the United States dated from colonial times; young people who knew they could not hope to own land in Ireland had long looked to America for better opportunities. Indeed, from 1818 to 1845, at least 10,000 Irish emigrated yearly. But in the latter year Ireland's green fields of potato plants turned black with blight. The British government could not cope with the scale of the disaster. The Irish had two choices: starve or leave. One million people died, and another 1.5 million emigrated, the majority to the United States. Starving, diseased (thousands died of typhus during the voyage), and destitute, hundreds of thousands (250,000 in 1851 alone) disembarked in the east coast ports of New York, Philadelphia, Boston, and Baltimore. Lacking the money to go inland and begin farming, they remained in the cities. Crowded together in miserable housing, desperate for work at any wages, foreign in their religion and pastimes (drinking and fighting, their critics said), tenaciously nationalistic and bitterly anti-British, they created ethnic enclaves of a kind new to American cities.

The largest numbers of Irish came to New York, which managed to absorb them. But Boston, a much smaller and more homogeneous city, was overwhelmed by the Irish influx. By 1850, a quarter of Boston's population was Irish, most of them recent immigrants. Boston, the home of Puritanism and the center of American intellectualism, did not welcome illiterate

Irish Catholic peasants. All over the city in places of business and in homes normally eager for domestic servants the signs went up: "No Irish Need Apply." The Irish were able to get only the worst and poorest-paying jobs and could afford housing only in an area of East Boston that was described by a Boston health committee in 1849 as "a perfect hive of human beings, without comforts and mostly without common necessaries; in many cases, huddled together like brutes, without regard to sex or age or sense of decency." Yet what critics regarded with horror was in fact a remarkable achievement of community building.

German Immigration

Germans, like the Irish, had a long history of emigration to America. William Penn, impressed by the industriousness of Germans, had taken pains to invite them to immigrate to the colony he founded, and by 1790 they made up one-third of Pennsylvania's population. The nineteenth-century immigration of Germans began somewhat later and more slowly than that of the Irish, but by 1854 it had surpassed the Irish influx. Some German peasants, like the Irish, were driven from their homeland by potato blight in the mid-1840s. But the typical German immigrant was a small farmer or artisan dislodged by the same market forces at work in America: the industrialization of production and consolidation and the commercialization of farming. There was also a small group of middle-class liberal intellectuals who left the German states (Germany was not yet a unified nation) after 1848 when attempts at revolution had failed. Among these individuals was Carl Schurz, who rose to become a general in the Union Army, a senator from Missouri, and secretary of the interior in the administration of Rutherford B. Hayes. On the whole, German migrants were not as poor as the Irish, and they could afford to move out of the east coast seaports to other locations. Nevertheless, like the Irish, they formed their own communities and initially encountered American hostility for their "foreign" ways.

The first two major ports of embarkation for the Germans were Bremen (in northern Germany) and Le Havre (in northern France), which were also the main ports for the importation of American tobacco and cotton. The tobacco boats bore the Bremen passengers to Baltimore, and the cotton ships took them to New Orleans, a major entry point for European immigrants until the Civil War. From these ports, many Germans made their way up the Mississippi and Ohio valleys, where they settled in Pittsburgh, Cincinnati, and St. Louis and on farms in Ohio, Indiana, Missouri, and Texas. In Texas, the nucleus of a German community began with a Mexican land grant in the

Distribution of Foreign-Born Residents of the United States in 1860.   The ethnic composition of the American population was increased by Irish and German immigration in the 1840s and 1850s, Chinese attraction to the California gold rush, Mormon recruitment of Scottish and English followers to Utah, and the reclassification of Mexicans after the Mexican-American War as foreigners in what had been their own lands.

1830s. Few Germans settled either in northeastern cities or in the South.

German agricultural communities took a distinctive form that fostered cultural continuity. Immigrants formed predominantly German towns by clustering, or taking up adjoining land. A small cluster could support German churches, German-language schools, and German customs and thereby attract other Germans, some directly from Europe and some from other parts of the United States. Such communities reinforced the traditional values of German farmers, such as persistence, hard work, and thrift. Non-German neighbors often sold out and moved on, but the Germans stayed and improved the land so they could pass it on to the next generation. They used soil conservation practices that were unusual for the time. Persistence paid: German cluster communities exist to this day in Texas, the Midwest, and the Pacific Northwest, and families of German origin are still the single largest ethnic group in agriculture.

Another area attracting immigrants in the early nineteenth century was Gold Rush California, which drew, among others, numbers of Chinese (see Chapter 14). The Chinese who came to California worked in the mines, most as independent prospectors. Other miners disliked their industriousness and their clannishness. One reporter noted groups of twenty or thirty "Chinamen, stools, tables, cooking utensils, bunks, etc., all huddled up together in indiscriminate confusion, and enwreathed with dense smoke, inhabiting close cabins, so small that one would not be of sufficient size to allow a couple of Americans to breathe in it." By the mid-1860s, Chinese workers made up 90 percent of the laborers building the Central Pacific Railroad, replacing more expensive white laborers and sowing the seeds of the long-lasting hostility of American workers toward Chinese. In the meantime, however, San Francisco's Chinatown, the oldest Chinese ethnic enclave in America, became a well established, thriving community.

In the years to come, as hostility against the Chinese broke into violence, Chinatowns in San Francisco and elsewhere served a vital function as safe refuges for the Chinese who remained in the United States.

Class Structure and Living Patterns in the Cities

Immigration not only contributed to urban growth. It also changed the character of urban life by sharpening class differences.

Although per capita income in America is estimated to have doubled between 1800 and 1850, the gap between rich and poor increased and became glaringly apparent in the nation's cities. The benefits of the market revolution were unequally distributed: by the 1840s the top 1 percent of the population owned about 40 percent of the nation's wealth, while, at the other extreme, one-third of the population owned virtually nothing. In the cities, then, there was a very small group of wealthy people with a net worth of more than $5,000 (about 3 percent of the population), a very large group of poor people with a net worth of $100 or less (nearly 70 percent), and a middle class with incomes in between (25–30 percent).

Differences in income affected every aspect of urban life. Very poor families, including almost all new immigrants, performed unskilled labor in jobs where the future was uncertain at best, lived in cheap rented housing, moved frequently, and depended on more than one income to survive. Artisans and skilled workers with incomes of $500 or more could live adequately, though often in cramped quarters that also served as their shops. A middle-class family with an income of more than $1,000 a year could live comfortably in a house of four to six rooms complete with carpeting, wallpaper, and good furniture. The very rich built mansions and large town houses and staffed them with many servants. In the summer they left the cities for country estates or homes at seaside resorts such as Newport, Rhode Island, which attracted wealthy families from all over the country.

Early nineteenth-century cities lacked municipal water supplies, sewers, and garbage collection. People drank water from wells, used outdoor privies that often contaminated the water supply, and threw garbage and slop out the door to be foraged by roaming herds of pigs. Clearly, this was a recipe for disease, and every American city suffered epidemics of sanitation-related diseases such as yellow fever, cholera, and typhus. Philadelphia's yellow fever epidemic of 1793 caused 4,000 deaths and

American Cities, 1820

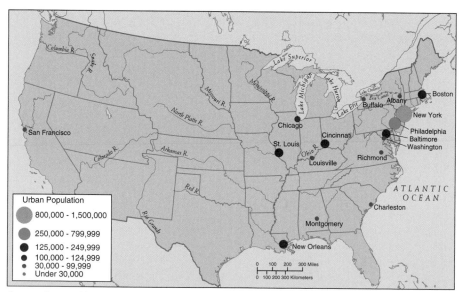

American Cities, 1860   The cities of North America grew more rapidly between 1820 and 1860 than at any other time in the nation's history. Eastern seaport cities remained the largest, but New York grew to twice the size of the second largest city, Philadelphia. New York's growth, due in large part to the increase in trade following the opening of the Erie Canal, illustrates the importance of trade between port cities and the nation's interior. Inland river cities like Cincinnati and St. Louis and the great Mississippi seaport of New Orleans grew rapidly. San Francisco, Louisville, and Buffalo—still villages in 1820—grew also, but Chicago, which rapidly emerged as a hub for both water and rail transport, surpassed them all.

SOURCE: Statistical Abstract of the United States

stopped all business with the outside world for more than a month. Major cholera epidemics ravaged New York in 1832 and 1849, and New Orleans suffered repeated attacks of cholera and yellow fever.

Yet the cities were slow to take action. In part this was due to poor medical understanding of disease but at least equally to expense. In response to the yellow fever epidemic, Philadelphia completed a city water system in 1801, but users had to pay a fee, and only the richest subscribed in the early days. Neither New York nor Boston had a public water system until the 1840s. Garbage collection remained a private service, and cities charged property owners for the costs of sewers, water mains, and street paving. Poorer areas of the cities could not afford the costs. When disease struck, wealthier people simply left the cities, leaving the poor to suffer the brunt of disease.

Provision of municipal services forced residential segregation. Richer people clustered in neighborhoods that had the new amenities. One of New York's first wealthy areas, Gramercy Park, was developed in 1831 by a speculator who transformed what had been Gramercy Farm into "an ornamental private square or park, with carriageways and footwalks." Only purchasers of the surrounding lots had keys to the park; everyone else was excluded. By the 1850s, the middle class began to escape cities completely by moving to the new "streetcar suburbs," named for the new mode of urban transportation that connected these nearby areas to the city itself.

As the middle class left the city, the poor clustered in bad neighborhoods that became known as slums. The worst New York slum in the nineteenth century was Five Points, a stone's throw from city hall. There, immigrants, free black people, and criminals were crammed into rundown buildings known in the slang of the time as "rookeries." Notorious gangs of thieves and pickpockets with names such as the Plug Uglies and the Shirt Tails dominated the district. Starvation and murder were commonplace.

Five Points was grim even in comparison with the notorious slums of London. As knowledgeable an Englishman as the author Charles Dickens exclaimed on a visit to the district in 1842, "All that is loathsome, drooping and decayed is here . . . Where dogs would howl to lie, women, and men and boys slink

The Five Points neighborhood in lower Manhattan illustrates the segregated housing patterns that emerged as New York City experienced rapid growth. Immigrants, free African Americans, the poor and criminals were crowded together in New York's most notorious slum, while wealthier people moved to more prosperous neighborhoods.

SOURCE: 1859 lithograph; The Granger Collection.

off to sleep, forcing the dislodged rats to move away in quest of better lodgings." With the influx of European immigrants after 1830, middle-class Americans increasingly saw slums as the home of strange and foreign people, who deserved less than American-born citizens. In this way, residential patterns came to embody larger issues of class and citizenship. Even disease itself was blamed on immigrants. When cholera epidemics, for example, disproportionately struck slum dwellers, well-to-do New Yorkers assumed that it must be the fault of the people in the slums. As banker John Pintard reasoned in 1832, the cholera epidemic must be God's judgment on "the lower classes of intemperate dissolute and filthy people huddled together like swine in their polluted habitations."

Ethnic Neighborhoods

To poverty-stricken Irish immigrants, these same slums represented not only family ties and familiar ways but community support as they learned how to survive in new surroundings. Isolated partly by their own beliefs (for Catholics fully reciprocated the hatred and fear that Protestants had showed them), Irish immigrants created their own communities in Boston and New York, their major destinations. They raised the money to erect Catholic churches with Irish priests. They established parochial schools with Irish nuns as teachers and sent their children to them in preference to the openly anti-Catholic public schools. They formed mutual aid societies based on kinship or town of origin in Ireland. Men and women formed religious and social clubs, lodges, and brotherhoods and their female auxiliaries. Irishmen manned fire and militia companies as well. This dense network of associations served the same purpose that social welfare organizations do today: providing help in time of need and offering companionship in a hostile environment.

Germans who settled in urban areas also built their own ethnic enclaves—"Little Germanies"—in which they sought to duplicate the rich cultural life of German cities. In general, German immigrants were skilled workers and not as poor as the Irish. Like the Irish, however, the Germans formed church societies, mutual benefit societies, and fire and militia companies to provide mutual support. Partly because their communities were more prosperous than those of the Irish, the Germans also formed a network of leisure organizations: singing societies, debating and political clubs, concert halls like New York's Beethoven Hall, theaters, turnvereins (gymnastics associations), and beer gardens. They published German-language newspapers as well.

Ethnic clustering, then, allowed new immigrants to hold onto aspects of their culture that they valued and to transplant them to American soil. Many native-born Americans, however, viewed ethnic neighborhoods with deep suspicion. The *Boston American* expressed the sentiments of many in 1837 when it remarked:

> our foreign population are too much in the habit of retaining their own national usages, of associating too exclusively with each other, and living in groups together. It would be the part of wisdom, to ABANDON AT ONCE ALL USAGES AND ASSOCIATIONS WHICH MARK THEM AS FOREIGNERS, and to become in feeling and custom, as well as in privileges and rights, citizens of the United States.

Urban Popular Culture

The size, diversity, and changing working conditions in American cities bred a new urban popular culture with New York, the largest city, leading the way. In the period 1820–60, urban workers experienced the replacement of artisanal labor by wagework, two serious depressions (1837–43 and 1857), and vastly increased competition from immigrant labor. In response to these pressures, working-class amusements became rougher and rowdier. Taverns that served as neighborhood centers of drink and sociability were also frequent centers of brawls and riots. Community groups such as fire engine companies that had once included men of all social classes now attracted rough young laborers who formed their own youth gangs and defended "their" turf against other gangs. Some trades, such as that of butcher, became notorious for starting fights in taverns and grog shops.

Theaters, which had been frequented by men of all social classes, provided another setting for violence. Few women, except for the prostitutes who met their customers in the third tier of the balcony, attended. In the 1820s, a long-standing tradition of small-scale rioting by poorer patrons against unpopular actors began to change into more serious violence. The Astor Place Riot of 1849 began as a theater riot against a British actor but escalated into a pitched battle between the mob and the militia that left twenty-two dead.

By the 1830s, middle-class and upper-class men withdrew to more respectable theaters to which they could bring their wives and daughters. Workers found new amusements in theaters such as the Lafayette Circus, which featured dancing girls and horseback riders as well as theatrical acts. Another popular urban working-class amusement was the blackface minstrel show. White actors (often Irish) blacked their faces and entertained audiences with songs (including the famous "Dixie," written by an Irishman as

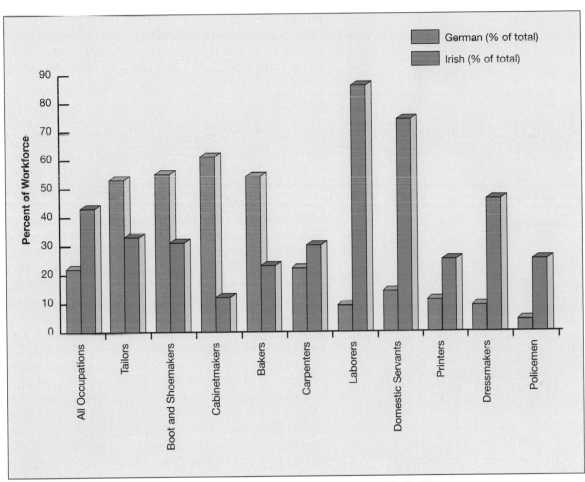

Participation of Irish and German Immigrants in the New York City Workforce for Selected Occupations, 1855

SOURCE: Robert Ernst, *Immigrant Life in New York City 1825-1863* (Syracuse: Syracuse University Press, 1994).

a blackface song), dances, theatrical skits, and anti-black political jokes. Cruel stereotypes such as Zip Coon, an irresponsible free black man, and Jim Crow, a slow-witted slave, entertained white audiences. Historians have speculated that the popularity of blackface expressed not only white racism but also nostalgia for the freer behavior of preindustrial life that was now impossible for white workers but that they imagined African American slaves continued to enjoy in carefree dependency.

The new working-class culture flourished especially on the Bowery, a New York City street filled with artisanal workshops, small factories, shops with cheap goods, dance halls, theaters, ice cream parlors, and oyster bars. Here working-class youth, the "Bowery b'hoys" (slang pronunciation of "boys") and "gals," found Saturday night amusements and provided it for themselves with outrageous clothing and behavior. The deliberately provocative way they dressed was in effect a way of thumbing their noses at the more re-

spectable classes. The costumes worn by the characters in one long-running series of melodramas staged by the Bowery Theater imitated this style. Mose, the hero of the series, dressed more like a pirate captain than a worker, and his gal Lise wore a bright-colored, body-hugging dress that challenged the discreet, sober fashions worn by middle-class women.

These challenges to middle-class respectability were fostered and publicized by the immensely popular "penny papers," which began publication in 1833, and by the rapidly-growing number of political papers (see Chapter 10). This exhuberant urban popular culture was unquestionably a part of the same new democratic political spirit that led to the great upsurge in political participation discussed in Chapter 10. And it was the inspiration for some of America's most innovative writers, foremost among them urban journalist, Democratic Party activist, and poet Walt Whitman, who distilled his passionate love for the variety and commonness of the American people in

This 1848 playbill promotes *A Glance at New York,* which featured two well-known working-class figures, Mose, the Bowery B'hoy, and his gal, Lise. His exaggerated clothing and hairstyle and her flashy colors were deliberate parodies aimed at New York's respectable middle class for the benefit of the rowdy working-class culture that grew up in the Bowery district of the city in the 1830s. SOURCE: Library of Congress.

Leaves of Grass, a book of free-verse poems published in 1855. Regarded at the time as scandalous because of its frank language, Whitman's poetry nevertheless captured the driving energy and democratic spirit of the new urban popular culture. In a rather more sinister way, so did the writings of Edgar Allan Poe, who found the inspiration for his gothic horror stories such as "The Murders in the Rue Morgue" (1841) and "The Mystery of Marie Roget" (1842) not in Europe (as his titles might suggest) but in contemporary American crimes.

This fascination with urban violence led one observer to comment cynically in 1859 that "No narrative of human depravity or crime can shock or horrify an American reader." But Alexis de Tocqueville, the fa-mous French observer who visited the United States in 1831–32 wrote with foreboding, "I look upon the size of certain American cities, and especially on the nature of their population, as a real danger." Here was an expression of a new fear in American urban life—concern about civic order.

Civic Order

Alexis de Tocqueville's fears for civic order echoed that of the urban middle class, who now found menacing even traditions of lower-class amusement that dated back to colonial times. New York City's tradition of New Year's Eve "frolics," in which laborers, apprentices, and other members of the lower classes paraded through the streets playing drums, trumpets, whistles, and other noisemakers, was an example. By the 1820s the revelry had been taken over by gangs of young workers from the lower classes who called themselves the Callithumpian Band. On New Year's Eve 1828, the band, 4,000 strong and equipped with drums, tin kettles, rattles, horns, and whistles, marched through the city. On their way they overturned carts and broke windows in the commercial district, in some wealthy homes near Battery Park, and in an African American church. They then marched to the City Hotel, where middle-class couples were just leaving a ball, and obstructed traffic. The indignant couples watched helplessly as several hundred watchmen called to disperse the mob cautiously declined to do so. In the following year, the traditional New Year's Eve parade was banned by the city government.

Working class use of the streets for parades, celebrations, and marches was an established aspect of urban life, and perhaps nowhere so much a part of the city as in New Orleans. There, African American bands played in funeral processions, and dances drawing hundreds of slaves were regularly held in Congo Square, while elsewhere Choctaw Indians drummed and respectable middle-class men rang cowbells as they took part in rowdy street serenades in response to unpopular events.

In New York the prosperous classes were frightened by the urban poor and by working-class rowdyism. They resented having to avoid many parts of the city that were unsafe for them, and they disliked even more the disturbances in "their" parts of the city, as this irritable notation in the diary of merchant Philip Hone indicates: "Riot, disorder, and violence increase in our city; every night is marked by some outrage committed by gangs of young ruffians who prowl the streets insulting females, breaking into the houses of unoffending publicans [tavern keepers], making night hideous by yells of disgusting inebriety, and—unchecked by the city authorities—committing every sort of enormity with apparent impunity."

In colonial days, civic disturbances had been handled informally: members of the city watch asked onlookers for such assistance as was necessary to keep the peace. New York City's first response in the 1820s and 1830s to increasing civic disorder was to hire more city watchmen and to augment them with constables and marshals. When riots occurred, the militia were called, and deaths were increasingly common as they forcibly restrained mobs. Finally, in 1845, the city created a permanent police force with a mandate to keep the poor in order. There had been substantial opposition to the idea of a professional police force in the United States on the grounds that it infringed personal liberty, but as middle-class fear of what became known as "the dangerous classes" grew, police protection came to seem necessary. Here was an indication that the harmonious preindustrial urban community no longer existed. It should be noted that because of fear of slave disorder, southern cities had felt the need for policing as early as 1790s. By the 1820s New Orleans, Charleston, and Savannah had moved beyond informal militia activity to armed and uniformed city guards who patrolled in military fashion.

But even with police forces in place, the pressures of rapid urbanization, immigration, and the market revolution proved to be more than America's cities could contain. The violence was more than just rowdyism and socially disapproved behavior. Beginning in the 1830s, a series of urban riots broke out against the two poorest urban groups: Catholics and free black people. As if their miserable living conditions were not enough, Irish immigrants were met with virulent anti-Catholicism. In 1834 rioters burned an Ursuline convent in Charlestown, Massachusetts; in 1844 a Philadelphia mob attacked priests and nuns and vandalized Catholic churches; in 1854 a mob destroyed an Irish neighborhood in Lawrence, Massachusetts. Often the Irish replied in kind—for example, in the 1806 riot in New York when they counterattacked a mob that disrupted their Christmas Eve mass in a Catholic church on Augustus Street. But the most common targets of urban violence were free African Americans.

Urban Life of Free African Americans

By 1860, there were nearly half a million free African Americans in the United States, constituting about 11 percent of the country's total black population. More than half of all free African Americans lived in the North, mostly in cities, where they competed with immigrants and native-born poor white people for jobs as day laborers and domestic servants. Their relative social position is reflected in statistics on per capita annual income in Boston in the 1850s: $91 for black people and $131 for Irish immigrants compared to

Free African Americans suffered many forms of discrimination, but as this 1850 daguerreotype of an unknown woman shows, they sought to achieve the same levels of education and economic comfort as other Americans. SOURCE: Zelsa P. Mackay Collection. Courtesy George Eastman House.

$872 for the population at large. Philadelphia and New York had the largest black communities: 22,000 African Americans in Philadelphia and 12,500 in New York (another 4,313 lived just across the East River in Brooklyn). There were much smaller but still significant black communities in the New England cities of Boston, Providence, and New Haven and in Ohio cities like Cincinnati.

Free African Americans in northern cities faced residential segregation (except for the domestic servants who lived in with white families), pervasive job discrimination, segregated public schools, and severe limitations on their civil rights. In addition to these legal restrictions there were matters of custom: African Americans of all economic classes endured daily affronts, such as exclusion from public concerts, lectures, and libraries, and segregation or exclusion from public transportation. For example, in Massachusetts—which had the reputation of being more hospitable to black people than any other northern state—the famed African American abolitionist Frederick Douglass was denied admission to a zoo on Boston Common, a public lecture and revival meeting, a restaurant, and a public omnibus, all within the space of a few days.

In common with Irish and German immigrants, African Americans created defenses against the larger hostile society by building their own community structures. They formed associations for aiding the poorest members of the community, for self-improvement, and for socializing. Tired of being insulted by the white press, African American communities supported their own newspapers. The major community organization was the black Baptist or African Methodist Episcopal (AME) church, which served, as one historian put it, as "a place of worship, a social and cultural center, a political meetingplace, a hiding place for fugitives, a training ground for potential community leaders, and one of the few places where blacks could express their true feelings."

Employment prospects for black men deteriorated from 1820 to 1850. Those who had held jobs as skilled artisans were forced from their positions, and their sons denied apprenticeships, by white mechanics and craftsmen who were themselves suffering from the effects of the market revolution. Limited to day labor, African Americans found themselves in direct competition with the new immigrants, especially the Irish, for jobs. On the waterfront, black men lost their jobs as carters and longshoremen to the Irish. One of the few occupations to remain open to them was that of seaman. More than 20 percent of all American sailors in 1850 were black, and over the years their ranks included an increasing number of runaway slaves. The pay was poor and the conditions miserable, but many black men found more equality aboard ship than they did ashore. Mothers, wives, and daughters were left ashore to work as domestic servants (in competition with Irishwomen), washerwomen, and seamstresses.

Free African Americans remained committed to their enslaved brethren in the South. In New York, for example, black communities rioted four times—in 1801, 1819, 1826, and 1832—against slave catchers taking escaped slaves back to slavery. But even more frequently, free African Americans were themselves targets of urban violence. An 1829 riot in Cincinnati sent a thousand black people fleeing to Canada in fear for their lives; a three-day riot in Providence in 1831 destroyed an African American district; and an 1834 New York riot destroyed a black church, a school, and a dozen homes. Philadelphia, "the City of Brotherly Love," had the worst record. Home to the largest free African American community in the North, Philadelphia was repeatedly rocked by antiblack riots in the period between 1820 and 1859. A riot in 1834 destroyed two churches and thirty-one homes and left one African American dead and many injured. In 1842, a predominantly Irish mob attacked black marchers celebrating Jamaican Emancipation Day. The marchers counterattacked, wounding three Irish boys and provoking widespread arson, which firemen refused to put out for fear of the mob. The disturbance ended only when the mayor called out seven companies of the militia. Other cities had similar stories. Urban riots of all kinds had cost 125 lives by 1840, and more than 1,000 by 1860.

THE LABOR MOVEMENT AND URBAN POLITICS

Universal white manhood suffrage and the development of mass politics (see Chapter 10), coupled with the rapid growth of cities, changed urban politics. The traditional leadership role of the wealthy elite waned, and members of the wealthiest class gradually withdrew from direct participation in urban politics. In New York City, elite political leaders had disappeared by 1845. In their place were professional politicians whose job it was to make party politics work. In New York and in other large cities, this change in politics was spurred by working-class activism.

The Tradition of Artisanal Politics

The nation's urban centers had long been strongholds of craft associations for artisans and skilled workers. These organizations, and their parades and celebrations, were recognized parts of the urban community. Groups of master craftsmen marching in community parades with signs such as "By Hammer and Hand All Arts Do Stand" were visible symbols of the strength and solidarity of workers' organizations.

Also traditional were riots and demonstrations by workers (usually journeymen or apprentices, not the master artisans themselves) over matters as political and far-reaching as the American Revolution or as practical and immediate as the price of bread. In fact, protests by urban workers had been an integral part of the older social order controlled by the wealthy elite. In the eighteenth century, when only men of property could vote, such demonstrations usually indicated widespread discontent or economic difficulty among workers. They served as a warning signal that the political elite rarely ignored.

By the 1830s the status of artisans and independent craftsmen in the nation's cities had changed. As discussed in Chapter 12, the artisanal system was crumbling, undercut by competition between cities (the result of the transportation revolution) and by the growth of the putting-out system. Furthermore, the rapid influx of immigrants changed the character of the labor force. New York provides a particularly dramatic example. The city's rapid growth as a manufacturing center was based on the labor of Irish and German immigrant workers, who made up 65 percent of the workforce by 1855. Germans clustered primarily in the skilled trades, while the Irish performed most of the low-paid labor. Indeed, 86 percent of day laborers were Irishmen, while Irishwomen made up 74 percent of the domestic servants.

There was no safety net for workers who lost their jobs—no unemployment insurance or welfare—and no public regulation of wages and conditions of work. The first protests against these harsh conditions came from the women workers at the new cotton textile factories in Lowell and elsewhere. The members of urban workers' associations, increasingly angry over their declining status in the economic and social order, also became—tentatively at first, but then with growing conviction—active defenders of working-class interests.

What was new was the open antagonism between workers and employers. The community of interest between masters and workers in preindustrial times broke down. Workers realized they had to depend on other workers, not employers, for support. In turn, employers and members of the middle class began to take urban disorders much more seriously than their grandfathers might have done.

The Union Movement

Urban worker protest against changing conditions quickly took the form of party politics. The Workingmen's Party was founded in Philadelphia in 1827, and chapters quickly formed in New York and Boston as well. Using the language of class warfare—"two distinct classes . . . those that live by their own labor and they that live upon the labor of others"—the "Workies" campaigned for the ten-hour day and the preservation of the small artisanal shop. They also called for the end of government-chartered monopolies—banks were high on the list. And they were in favor of a public school system and cheap land in the West. Although the Workies themselves did not survive as a party, Jacksonian Democrats were quick to pick up on some of their themes. The Democrats attracted many Workingmen's votes in 1832, the year Andrew Jackson campaigned against the "monster" Bank of the United States.

Both major parties competed for the votes of urban workers. In

New York City in 1835 a radical antimonopoly branch of the Democratic Party, known officially as the Equal Rights Party, attracted some worker support. For their part, the Whigs wooed workers by assuring them that Henry Clay's American System, and tariff protection in particular, would be good for the economy and for workers' jobs. Nevertheless, neither major political party really spoke to the primary need of workers—for well-paid, stable jobs that assured them independence and respect. Unsatisfied with the response of political parties, workers turned to labor organization to achieve their goals.

Between 1833 and 1837 a wave of strikes in New York City cut the remaining ties between master craftsmen and the journeymen who worked for them. In 1833, journeymen carpenters struck for higher wages. Workers in fifteen other trades came to their support, and within a month the strike was won. The lesson was obvious: if skilled workers banded together across craft lines, they could improve their conditions. The same year, representatives from nine different craft groups formed the General Trades Union (GTU) of New York. By 1834 similar groups had sprung up in over a dozen cities—Boston, Louisville, and Cincinnati among them. In New York alone, the GTU helped organize almost forty strikes between 1833 and 1837, and it encouraged the formation of more than fifty unions. In 1834 also, representatives of several local

This seal of the General Society of Mechanics and Tradesmen illustrates in its motto—"By Hammer and Hand All Arts Do Stand"—the personal and community pride artisans took in their work. SOURCE: Abraham Godwin, print. Courtesy, Winterthur Museum.

GTUs met in Baltimore and organized the National Trades Union (NTU). In its founding statement the NTU criticized the "unjustifiable distribution of the wealth of society in the hands of a few individuals," which had created for working people "a humiliating, servile dependency, incompatible with . . . natural equality."

Naturally, employers disagreed with the NTU's criticism of the economic system. In Cincinnati and elsewhere, employers prevailed upon police to arrest strikers even when no violence had occurred. In another case, New York employers took striking journeymen tailors to court in 1836. Judge Ogden Edwards pronounced the strikers guilty of conspiracy and declared unions un-American. He assured the strikers that "the road of advancement is open to all" and that they would do better to strive to be masters themselves rather than "conspire" with their fellow workers. The GTU responded with a mass rally at which Judge Edwards was burned in effigy. A year later, stunned by the effects of the Panic of 1837, the GTU collapsed. The founding of these general unions, a visible sign of a class-based community of interest among workers, is generally considered to mark the beginning of the American labor movement. However, these early unions included only white men in skilled trades who made up only a small percentage of all workers. The majority of workers—men in unskilled occupations, all free African Americans, and all women—were excluded.

Big-City Machines

Although workers were unable to create strong unions or stable political parties that spoke for their economic interests, they were able to shape urban politics. As America's cities experienced unprecedented growth, the electorate mushroomed. In New York, for example, the number of voters grew from 20,000 in 1825 to 88,900 in 1855. Furthermore, by 1855 half of the voters were foreign-born. At the time, America was the only country in the world where propertyless white men had the vote. The job of serving this largely working-class electorate and making the new mass political party work at the urban level fell to a new kind of career politician—the boss—and a new kind of political organization—the machine.

Just as the old system of elite leadership had mirrored the social unity of eighteenth-century cities, so the new system of machine politics reflected the class structure of the rapidly growing nineteenth-century cities. Feelings of community, which had arisen naturally out of the personal contact that characterized neighborhoods in earlier, smaller cities, now were cultivated politically. The existence of distinct ethnic neighborhoods fostered political organization. Because immigrants clustered in neighborhoods, their impact on politics could be concentrated and manipulated. Legally, three years' residence in the United States was required before one could apply for citizenship, but there was clear evidence of swifter naturalization in large cities with effective political organizations. In New York, for example, the Irish-dominated districts quickly became Democratic Party strongholds. Germans, who were less active politically than the Irish, nevertheless voted heavily for the new Republican Party in the 1850s. Between them, these two new blocs of immigrant voters destroyed the Whig Party that had controlled New York politics before the immigrants arrived.

In New York City, the Tammany Society, begun in the 1780s as a fraternal organization of artisans, slowly evolved into the key organization of the new mass politics. (Named after the Delaware chief mentioned in Chapter 3, the society met in a hall called the Wigwam and elected "sachems" as their officers.) Tammany, which was affiliated with the national Democratic Party, reached voters by using many of the techniques of mass appeal made popular earlier by craft organizations—parades, rallies, current songs, and party newspapers.

Along with these new techniques of mass appeal went new methods of organization: a tight system of political control beginning at the neighborhood level with ward committees and topped by a chairman of a citywide general committee. At the citywide level, ward leaders—bosses—bartered the loyalty and votes of their followers for positions on the city payroll for party members and community services for their neighborhood. This was machine politics. Through it workers, although they lacked the political or organizational strength to challenge the harmful effects of the market revolution, could use their numbers to ameliorate some of its effects at the local level. Machine politics served to mediate increasing class divisions and ethnic diversity as well. The machines themselves offered personal ties and loyalties—community feeling—to recent arrivals in the big cities (increasingly, immigrants from Europe) and help in hard times to workers who cast their votes correctly.

In America's big cities the result was apparent by midcentury: the political "machine" controlled by the "boss"—the politician who represented the interests of his group and delivered their votes in exchange for patronage and favors.

Critics said that big-city machines were corrupt, and indeed they often were. Antagonism between reformers, who were usually members of the upper and middle classes, and machine politicians, who spoke for the working class, was evident by the 1850s. This an-

By 1855, half the voters in New York City were foreign-born. This 1858 engraving of an Irish bar in the Five Points area appeared in the influential *Harper's Weekly*. It expressed the dislike of temperance reformers for immigrants and their drinking habits and the dismay of political reformers that immigrant saloons and taverns were such effective organizing centers for urban political machines. SOURCE: Frank and Marie-Therese Wood Print Collections, The Picture Bank.

tagonism was to become chronic in American urban politics. One result of the market revolution was the political expression, in a democratic society, of the conflict of interests between owners and workers.

SOCIAL REFORM MOVEMENTS

The passion for reform that had become such an important part of the new middle-class thinking was focused on the problems of the nation's cities. As the opening of this chapter describes, the earliest response to the dislocations caused by the market revolution was community-based and voluntary. Middle-class people tried to deal with social changes in their communities by joining organizations devoted to reforms. The temperance movement and reforms involving education, prisons and asylums, women's rights, abolitionism, and, above all, the spread of evangelical religion were all concerns of the middle class. The reform message was vastly amplified by inventions such as the steam printing press, which made it possible to publish

reform literature in great volume. Soon there were national networks of reform groups.

Alexis de Tocqueville commented on the vast extent of American voluntary associations and their many purposes. "In no country in the world," he noted, "has the principle of association been more successfully used, or more unsparingly applied to a multitude of different objects, than in America." The widespread reform movements of the era depended on the energy and hope of communities of like-minded people.

Evangelism, Reform, and Social Control

Evangelical religion was fundamental to social reform. Men and women who had been converted to the enthusiastic new faith assumed personal responsibility for making changes in their own lives. Personal reform quickly led to social reform; recall, for example, the northern businessman described in Chapter 12 who gave up drinking alcohol and insisted that his employees do the same. Religious converts were encouraged in their social activism by such leading revivalists as

Charles G. Finney, who preached a doctrine of "perfectionism," claiming it was possible for all Christians to personally understand and live by God's will and thereby become "as perfect as God." Furthermore, Finney predicted, "the complete reformation of the whole world" could be achieved if only enough converts put their efforts into moral reform. This new religious feeling was intensely hopeful: members of evangelistic religions really did expect to convert the world and create the perfect moral and religious community on earth.

Much of America was swept by the fervor of moralistic reform, and it was the new middle class, who applied new notions of morality to the movement, that set the agenda for reform. Reform efforts arose from the recognition that the traditional methods of small-scale local relief were no longer adequate. In colonial times, families (sometimes at the request of local government) had housed and cared for the ill or incapacitated. Small local almshouses and prisons had housed the poor and the criminal. Reformers now realized that large cities had to make large-scale provisions for social misfits and that institutional rather than private efforts were needed. This thinking was especially true of the institutional reform movements that began in the 1830s, such as the push for insane asylums. At this time, of course, the federal government provided no such relief.

A second characteristic of the reform movements was a belief in the basic goodness of human nature. All reformers believed that the condition of the unfortunate—the poor, the insane, the criminal—would improve in a wholesome environment. Thus insane asylums were built in rural areas, away from the noise and stress of the cities, and orphanages had strict rules that were meant to encourage discipline and self-reliance. Prison reform carried this sentiment to the extreme. On the theory that bad social influences were largely responsible for crime, some "model" prisons completely isolated prisoners from one another, making them eat, sleep, work, and do required Bible reading in their own cells. The failure of these prisons to achieve dramatic changes for the better in their inmates (a number of isolated prisoners went mad, and some committed suicide) or to reduce crime was one of the first indications that reform was not a simple task.

A third characteristic of the reform movements was their moralistic dogmatism. Reformers were certain they knew what was right and were determined to see their improvements enacted. It was a short step from developing individual self-discipline to imposing discipline on others. The reforms that were proposed thus took the form of social controls. Lazy, sinful, intemperate, or unfit members of society were to be reformed for their own good, whether they wanted to be or not. This attitude was bound to cause controversy; by no means did all Americans share the reformers' beliefs, nor did those for whom it was intended always take kindly to being the targets of the reformers' concern.

Indeed, some aspects of the social reform movements were harmful. The evangelical Protestantism of the reformers promoted a dangerous hostility to Catholic immigrants from Ireland and Germany that, as noted earlier, repeatedly led to urban riots. The temperance movement, in particular, targeted immigrants for their free drinking habits. Seeking uniformity of behavior rather than tolerance, the reformers thus helped to promote the virulent nativism that infected American politics between 1840 and 1860 (see Chapter 15).

Regional and national reform organizations quickly grew from local projects to deal with social problems such as drinking, prostitution, mental illness, and crime. In 1828, for example, Congregationalist minister Lyman Beecher joined other ministers in forming a General Union for Promoting the Observance of the Christian Sabbath; the aim was to prevent business on Sundays. To achieve its goals, the General Union adopted the same methods used by political parties: lobbying, petition drives, fundraising, and special publications. These and other efforts, Beecher said, were all for the purpose of establishing "the moral government of God." Beecher was also a leader of the anti-Catholic and antiimmigrant movement, warning in 1835 of a "terrific inundation" of Catholics in the West (he meant the Ohio Valley) that threatened American democracy. His vehement sermons warning of the danger contributed to the popular anger that led to the burning of the Charlestown convent in 1834.

In effect, Beecher and similar reformers engaged in political action but remained aloof from direct electoral politics, stressing their religious mission. In any case, sabbatarianism was controversial. Workingmen (who usually worked six days a week) were angered when the General Union forced the Sunday closure of their favorite taverns and were quick to vote against the Whigs, the party perceived to be most sympathetic to reform thinking. But in many new western cities, sabbatariansim divided the business class itself. In Rochester, a city created by the Erie Canal, businessmen who wished to observe Sunday only in religious ways were completely unable to stop the traffic of passenger and freight boats owned by other businessmen. Other reforms likewise muddied the distinction between political and social activity. It is not surprising that women, who were barred from electoral politics but not from moral and social activism, were major supporters of reform.

Education and Women Teachers

Women became deeply involved in reform movements through their churches. It was they who did most of the fundraising for the home missionary societies that were beginning to send the evangelical message worldwide—at first by ministers alone, later by married couples. Nearly every church had a maternal association, where mothers gathered to discuss ways to raise their children as true Christians. These associations reflected a new and more positive definition of childhood. The Puritans had believed that children were born sinful and that their wills had to be broken before they could become godly. Early schools reflected these beliefs: teaching was by rote, and punishment was harsh and physical. Educational reformers, however, tended to believe that children were born innocent and needed gentle nurturing and encouragement if they were to flourish. At home, mothers began to play the central role in child rearing. Outside the home, women helped spread the new public education pioneered by Horace Mann, secretary of the Massachusetts State Board of Education.

Although literacy had long been valued, especially in New England, schooling since colonial times had been a private enterprise and a personal expense. Town grammar schools, required in Massachusetts since 1647, had been supported primarily by parents' payments, with some help from local property taxes. In 1827, Massachusetts pioneered compulsory education by legislating that public schools be supported by public taxes. Soon schooling for white children between the ages of five and nineteen was common, although, especially in rural schools, the term might be only a month or so long. Uniformity in curriculum and teacher training, and the grading of classes by ability—measures pioneered by Horace Mann in the 1830s—quickly caught on in other states. In the North and West (the South lagged far behind), more and more children went to school, and more and more teachers, usually young single women, were hired to teach them.

The spread of public education created the first real career opportunity for women. Horace Mann insisted that to learn well, children needed schools with a pleasant and friendly atmosphere. One important way to achieve that atmosphere, Mann recommended, was to group children by ages rather than combining everyone in the traditional ungraded classroom and to pay special attention to the needs of the youngest pupils. Who could better create the friendly atmosphere of the new classroom than women? The great champion of teacher training for women was Catharine Beecher, daughter of Lyman, who clearly

Catharine E. Beecher. SOURCE: The Schlesinger Library, Radcliffe College.

saw her efforts as part of the larger work of establishing "the moral government of God." Arguing that women's moral and nurturing nature ideally suited them to be teachers, Beecher campaigned tirelessly on their behalf. Since "the mind is to be guided chiefly by means of the affections," she argued, "is not woman best fitted to accomplish these important objects?"

By 1850 women were dominant in primary school teaching, which had come to be regarded as an acceptable occupation for educated young women during the few years between their own schooling and marriage. For some women, teaching was a great adventure; they enthusiastically volunteered to be "schoolmarms" on the distant western frontiers of Wisconsin and Iowa. Still others thought globally. The young women who attended Mary Lyon's Mount Holyoke Female Seminary in Massachusetts, founded in 1837, hoped to be missionary teachers in distant lands. For others, a few years of teaching was quite enough. Low pay (half of what male schoolteachers earned) and community supervision (women teachers had to board with families in the community) were probably sufficient to make almost any marriage proposal look appealing.

Temperance

Reformers believed not only that children could be molded but that adults could change. The largest reform organization of the period, the American Society for the Promotion of Temperance, founded in 1826, boasted more than 200,000 members by the mid-1830s.

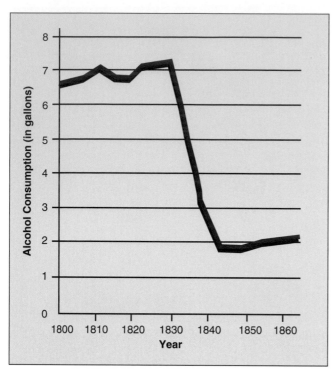

Per Capita Consumption of Alcohol, 1800–1860
The underlying cause for the dramatic fall in alcohol consumption during the 1830s was the changing nature of work brought about by the market revolution. Contributing factors were the shock of the Panic of 1837 and the untiring efforts of temperance reformers.

SOURCE: W. J. Rorabaugh, *The Alcoholic Republic: An American Tradition* (New York: Oxford University Press, 1979).

Dominated by evangelicals, local chapters used revival methods—lurid temperance tracts detailing the evils of alcohol, large prayer and song meetings, and heavy group pressure—to encourage young men to stand up, confess their bad habits, and "take the pledge" not to drink. Here again, women played an important role.

Excessive drinking was a national problem, and it appears to have been mostly a masculine one, for respectable women did not drink in public. (Many did, however, drink alcohol-based patent medicines. Lydia Pinkham's Vegetable Compound, marketed for "female complaints," was 19 percent alcohol.) Men drank hard cider and liquor—whiskey, rum—in abundance. Traditionally, drinking had been a basic part of men's working lives. It concluded occasions as formal as the signing of a contract and accompanied such informal activities as card games. Drink was a staple offering at political speeches, rallies, and elections. In the old artisanal workshops, drinking had been a customary pastime. Much of the drinking was well within the bounds of sociability, but the widespread use (more than seven gallons of hard liquor per capita in 1830—more than twice as much as today's rate) must have encouraged drunkenness.

There were many reasons to support temperance. Heavy-drinking men hurt their families economically by spending their wages on drink. Women had no recourse: the laws of the time gave men complete financial control of the household, and divorce was difficult as well as socially unacceptable. Excessive drinking also led to violence and crime, both within the family and in the larger society.

But there were other reasons as well. The new middle class, preoccupied with respectability, morality, and efficiency, found the old easygoing drinking ways unacceptable. Much of the new industrial machinery was dangerous and workers needed sobriety to be safe. As work patterns changed, employers banned alcohol at work and increasingly considered drinking men not only unreliable but immoral. Temperance became a social and political issue. Whigs, who embraced the new morality, favored it; Democrats, who in northern cities consisted increasingly of immigrant workers, were opposed. Both German and Irish immigrants valued the social drinking that occurred in beer gardens and saloons and were hostile to temperance reform.

The Panic of 1837 affected the temperance movement. Whereas most temperance crusaders in the 1820s had been members of the middle class, the long depression of 1837–43 prompted artisans and skilled workers to give up or at least cut down substantially on drinking. Forming associations known as Washington Temperance Societies, these workers spread the word that temperance was the workingman's best chance to survive economically and to maintain his independence. Their wives, gathered together in Martha Washington Societies, were frequently even more committed to temperance than their husbands. While the men's temperance groups were often deeply involved in working-class politics, the women's groups stressed the harm that alcoholism could do to homes and families and provided financial help to distressed women and children.

Campaigns against alcohol were frequent and successful. By the mid-1840s alcohol consumption had been more than halved, to less than two gallons per capita, about the level of today. Concern over drinking would remain constant throughout the nineteenth century and into the twentieth.

Moral Reform, Asylums, and Prisons

Alcohol was not the only "social evil" that reform groups attacked. Another was prostitution, which was common in the nation's port cities. The customary approach of evangelical reformers was to "rescue" prostitutes, offering them the salvation of religion, prayer, and temporary shelter. The success rate was not very high. As an alternative to prostitution, reformers usu-

Temperance tracts, produced in the hundreds of thousands, painted lurid pictures of the perils of alcohol. Both melodramatic stories of ruin and cartoons like this 1826 tract, "The Drunkard's Progress," spread the temperance message in popular, easily understood forms.

SOURCE: Library of Congress.

ally offered domestic work, a low-paying and restrictive occupation that many women scorned. Nevertheless, campaigns against prostitution, generally organized by women, continued throughout the nineteenth century.

One of the earliest and most effective antiprostitution groups was the Female Moral Reform Society. Founded by evangelical women in New York in 1834 (the first president was Lydia Finney), it boasted 555 affiliates throughout the country by 1840. It was surprising that so many respectable women were willing to acknowledge the existence of something so disreputable as prostitution. Even more surprising was the speed with which the societies realized that prostitution was not so much a moral as an economic issue. The societies rapidly moved to organize charity and work for poor women and orphans. They also took direct action against the patrons of prostitutes by printing their names in local papers, and they successfully lobbied the New York state legislature for criminal penalties against the male clients as well as the women themselves.

Another dramatic example of reform was the asylum movement, spearheaded by the woman evangelist Dorothea Dix. In 1843, Dix horrified the Massachusetts state legislature with the results of her several years of study into the conditions to which insane women were subjected. She described in graphic detail how the women were incarcerated with ordinary criminals, locked up in "cages, closets, stalls, pens! Chained, naked, beaten with rods, and lashed into obedience!" Dix's efforts led to the establishment of a state asylum for the insane in Massachusetts and to similar institutions in other states. Between 1843 and 1854 Dix traveled more than 30,000 miles to publicize the movement for humane treatment of the insane. By 1860 twenty-eight states had public institutions for the insane.

Other reformers were active in related causes, such as prison reform and the establishment of orphanages, homes of refuge, and hospitals. Model penitentiaries were built in Auburn and Ossining (known as "Sing Sing"), New York, and in Philadelphia and Pittsburgh. Characterized by strict order and discipline, these prisons were supposed to reform rather than simply incarcerate their inmates, but their regimes of silence and isolation caused despair more often than rehabilitation.

Utopianism and Mormonism

Amid all the political activism and reform fervor of the 1830s, a few people chose escape into utopian communities and new religions. The upstate New York area along the Erie Canal was the seedbed for this movement, just as it was for evangelical revivals and reform movements like the Seneca Falls convention. The area was so notable for its reform enthusiasms that it has been termed "the Burned-Over District," a reference to the waves of reform that swept through like forest fires.

Apocalyptic religions tend to spring up in places experiencing rapid social change. The Erie Canal region, which experienced the full impact of the market revolution in the early nineteenth century, was such a place. A second catalyst is hard times, and the prolonged depression that began with the Panic of 1837 led some people to embrace a belief in imminent catastrophe. The Millerites (named for their founder, William Miller) believed that the Second Coming of Christ would occur on October 22, 1843. In anticipation, members of the church sold their belongings and bought white robes for their ascension to heaven. When the Day of Judgment did not take place as expected, most of Miller's followers drifted away. But a small group persisted. Revising their expectations, they formed the core of the Seventh-Day Adventist faith, which is still active today.

The Shakers, founded by "Mother" Ann Lee in 1774, were the oldest utopian group. An offshoot of the Quakers, the Shakers espoused a radical social philosophy that called for the abolishment of the tradi-tional family in favor of a family of brothers and sisters joined in equal fellowship. Despite its insistence on celibacy, the Shaker movement grew between 1820 and 1830, eventually reaching twenty settlements in eight states with a total membership of 6,000. The Shaker's simple and highly structured lifestyle, their isolation from the changing world, and their belief in equality drew new followers, especially among women. In contrast, another utopian community, the Oneida Community, became notorious for its sexual freedom. Founded by John Humphrey Noyes in 1848, the Oneida community, like the Shaker community, viewed itself as one family. But rather than celibacy, members practiced "complex marriage," a system of highly regulated group sexual activity. Only "spiritually advanced" males (Noyes himself and a few others) could father children, who were raised communally. These practices gave the sect a notorious reputation as a den of "free love" and "socialism," preventing Noyes from increasing its membership beyond 200.

Still other forthrightly socialist communities flourished briefly. New Harmony, Indiana, founded by the famous Scottish industrialist Robert Owen in 1825, was to be a manufacturing community without poverty and unemployment. The community survived only three years. Faring little better were the "phalanxes," huge communal buildings structured on the socialist theories of the French thinker Charles Fourier. Based on his belief that there was a rational way to divide work, Fourier suggested, for example, that children would make the best garbage collectors because they didn't mind dirt! And Louisa May Alcott (who later wrote *Little Women* and many other novels and stories) lived with her family at Fruitlands in Massachusetts, which had begun as a rural community of transcendentalists. The rapid failure of these socialist communities was due largely to inadequate planning and organization. Another reason may have been, as Alcott suggested in her satirical reminiscence, *Transcendental Wild Oats*, that the women were left to do all the work while the men philosophized. Nevertheless, it is striking that at a time when so many voluntary associations successfully organized the activities of their members, so few cooperative communities succeeded.

Shaker Hannah Cohoon's 1845 painting of the *Tree of Life*—her effort to reproduce a vision she had seen while in a religious trance—communicates the intense spirituality of Shaker life.

SOURCE: Hannah Harrison Cohoon, *Tree of Life*, 1845, tempera on paper. From the collection of Hancock Shaker Village, Pittsfield, Mass.

Explore the many religious revivals and reform movements in the Burned-Over District in the 1830s and 1840s. Why were they strongest in this region of the country?
www.prenhall.com/faragher/map13.1

Reform Movements in the Burned-Over District
The so-called Burned-Over District, the region of New York State most changed by the opening of the Erie Canal, was a seedbed of religious and reform movements. The Mormon Church originated there and Utopian groups and sects like the Millerites and the Fourierists thrived. Charles G. Finney held some of his most successful evangelical revivals in the district. Antislavery feeling was common in the region, and the women's rights movement began at Seneca Falls.

SOURCE: Whitney Cross, *The Burned-Over District* (1950; reprint, New York: Hippocrene Books, 1981).

The most successful of the nineteenth-century communitarian movements was also a product of the Burned-Over District. In 1830, a young man named Joseph Smith founded the Church of Jesus Christ of Latter-Day Saints, based on the teachings of the Book of Mormon, which he claimed to have received from an angel in a vision.

Initially, Mormonism, as the new religion became known, seemed little different from the many other new religious groups and utopian communities of the time. But under the benevolent but absolute authority of its patriarch, Joseph Smith, it rapidly gained distinction for its extraordinary communitarianism. Close cooperation and hard work made the Mormon community successful, attracting both new followers and the animosity of neighbors, who resented Mormon exclusiveness and economic success. The Mormons were harassed in New York and driven west to Ohio and then Missouri. Finally they seemed to find an ideal home in Nauvoo, Illinois, where in 1839 they built a model community, achieving almost complete self-government and isolation from non-Mormon neighbors. But in 1844, dissension within the community over Joseph Smith's new doctrine of polygamy (marriage between one man and more than one woman, simultaneously) gave outsiders a chance to intervene. Smith and his brother were arrested peacefully but were killed by a mob from which their jailers failed to protect them.

The beleaguered Mormon community decided to move beyond reach of harm. Led by Brigham Young, the Mormons migrated in 1846 to the Great Salt Lake in present-day Utah. After several lean years (once, a grasshopper plague was stopped by the providential arrival of sea gulls, who ate the insects), the Mormon method of communal settlement proved successful. Their hopes of isolation were dashed, however, by the California Gold Rush of 1849.

ANTISLAVERY AND ABOLITIONISM

The antislavery feeling that was to play such an important role in the politics of the 1840s and 1850s also had its roots in the religious reform movements that began in the 1820s and 1830s. Three groups—free African Americans, Quakers, and militant white reformers—worked to bring an end to slavery, but each in different ways. Their efforts eventually turned a minor reform movement into the dominant political issue of the day.

Antislavery activity was not new. For free African Americans the freedom of other black people had always been a major goal, but in order to achieve legal change they needed white allies. In 1787 antislavery advocates had secured in the Constitution a clause specifying a date after which American participation in the international slave trade could be made illegal, and Congress outlawed it in 1808. By 1800 slavery had been abolished or gradual emancipation enacted in most northern states. In 1820 the Missouri Compromise prohibited slavery in most of the Louisiana Purchase lands. None of these measures, however, addressed the continuing reality of slavery in the South.

The American Colonization Society

The first attempt to "solve" the problem of slavery was a plan for gradual emancipation of slaves (with compensation to their owners) and their resettlement in Africa. This plan was the work of the American Colonization

WebExploration

Through a series of interactive maps, follow the progress of the Mormon community westward. Why did the Mormons settle near the Great Salt Lake?
www.prenhall.com/faragher/map13.2

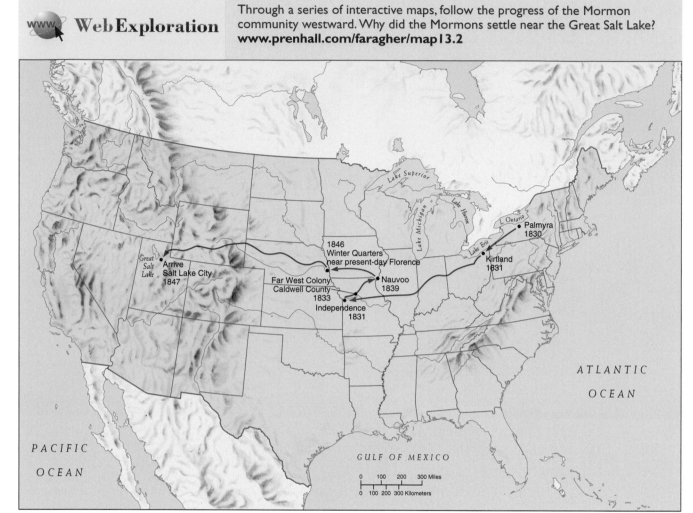

The Mormon Migration, 1830–1847 The Mormon church and community, founded by Joseph Smith of Palmyra, New York, in 1830, aroused intense opposition. Two early settlements, one in Kirtland, Ohio, and another near Independence, Missouri, were driven out in 1838. The Mormons regrouped and prospered in Nauvoo, Illinois, until the mob murder of Joseph Smith in 1844. Their escape to the West began in 1846, first to Winter Quarters, Nebraska, and finally to the desolate Great Salt Lake region of Utah, where the Mormons hoped to be free of outside interference.

Society, formed in 1817 by northern religious reformers (Quakers prominent among them) and a number of southern slave owners, most from the Upper South and the border states (Kentuckian Henry Clay was a supporter). Northerners were especially eager to send the North's 250,000 free black people back to Africa, describing them, in the words of the society's 1829 report, as "notoriously ignorant, degraded and miserable, mentally diseased, [and] broken-spirited," a characterization that completely ignored the legal and social discrimination they faced. Some northern members of the society also supported laws disenfranchising and restricting the rights of free African Americans. The American Colo-

nization Society was remarkably ineffective; by 1830, it had managed to send only 1,400 black people to a colony in Liberia, West Africa. Critics pointed out that more slaves were born in a week than the society sent back to Africa in a year.

African Americans' Fight against Slavery

Most free African Americans rejected colonization, insisting instead on a commitment to the immediate end of slavery and the equal treatment of black people in America. "We are natives of this country," an African American minister in New York pointed out. Then he

THE

PENITENTIAL TYRANT;

OR,

Slave Trader Reformed:

A

PATHETIC POEM,

IN FOUR CANTOS.

———

BY THOMAS BRANAGAN.

———

THE SECOND EDITION, ENLARGED.

———

" AM I NOT A MAN, AND A BROTHER?"

New-York:

PRINTED AND SOLD BY SAMUEL WOOD,

NO. 362, PEARL-STREET

1807

The different dates on these two widely used antislavery images are important. The title page of Thomas Branagan's 1807 book includes a then already commonly used image of a male slave. The engraving of a chained female slave was made by Patrick Reason, a black artist, in 1835. The accompanying message, "Am I Not a Woman and a Sister?" spoke particularly to white female abolitionists in the North, who were just becoming active in antislavery movements in the 1830s.

SOURCE: Library of Congress.

added bitterly, "We only ask that we be treated as well as foreigners." By 1830 there were at least fifty black abolitionist societies in the North. These organizations held yearly national conventions, where famous African American abolitionists like Frederick Douglass, Harriet Tubman, and Sojourner Truth spoke. The first African American newspaper, founded in 1827 by John Russwurm and Samuel Cornish, announced its antislavery position in its title, *Freedom's Journal*.

In 1829 David Walker, a free African American in Boston, wrote a widely distributed pamphlet, *Appeal to the Colored Citizens of the World*, that encouraged slave rebellion. "We must and shall be free . . . in spite of you," Walker warned whites. "And woe, woe will be it to you if we have to obtain our freedom by fighting." White Southerners blamed pamphlets such as these and the militant articles of African American journalists for stirring up trouble among southern slaves, and in particular for Nat Turner's revolt in 1831. The vehe-

mence of white southern reaction testifies to the courage of that handful of determined free African Americans who persisted in speaking for their enslaved brothers and sisters long before most white Northerners even noticed.

Abolitionists

The third and best-known group of antislavery reformers was headed by William Lloyd Garrison. In 1831 Garrison broke with the gradualist persuaders of the American Colonization Society and began publishing his own paper, the *Liberator*. In the first issue Garrison declared, "I am in earnest—I will not equivocate—I will not excuse—I will not retreat a single inch—AND I WILL BE HEARD." Garrison, the embodiment of moral indignation, was totally incapable of compromise. His approach was to mount a sweeping crusade condemning slavery as sinful and demanding its immediate

In 1837 white abolitionist Elijah P. Lovejoy had placed the press he used to print his antislavery newspaper in an Alton, Illinois warehouse in order to protect the press against a mob. This contemporary woodcut depicts the mob's attack on the warehouse. Lovejoy died defending it. SOURCE: The Granger Collection.

Slavery As It Is (based in part on the recollections of Angelina Grimké, whom Weld had married) that provided graphic details of abuse under slavery. Lyman Beecher's daughter, Harriet Beecher Stowe, was to draw on the Grimké-Weld book for her immensely popular antislavery novel *Uncle Tom's Cabin*, published in 1852.

The style of abolitionist writings and speeches was similar to the oratorical style of the religious revivalists. Northern abolitionists believed that a full description of the evils of slavery would force southern slave owners to confront their wrongdoing and lead to a true act of repentance—freeing their slaves. They were confrontational, denunciatory, and personal in their message, much like the evangelical preachers. Southerners, however, regarded abolitionist attacks as libelous and abusive.

Abolitionists adopted another tactic of revivalists and temperance workers when, to enhance their powers of persuasion, they began to publish great numbers of antislavery tracts. In 1835 alone they mailed more than a million pieces of antislavery literature to southern states. This tactic also drew a backlash: southern legislatures banned abolitionist literature, encouraged the harassment and abuse of anyone distributing it, and looked the other way when (as in South Carolina) proslavery mobs seized and burned it. The Georgia legislature even offered a $5,000 reward to anyone who would kidnap William Lloyd Garrison and bring him to the South to stand trial for inciting rebellion. Most serious, the majority of southern states reacted by toughening laws concerning emancipation, freedom of movement, and all aspects of slave behavior. Hoping to prevent the spread of the abolitionist message, most southern states reinforced laws making it a crime to teach a slave how to read. Ironically, then, the immediate impact of abolitionism in the South was to stifle dissent and make the lives of slaves harder (see Chapter 11).

Even in the North, controversy over abolitionism was common. Some places were prone to antiabolitionist violence. The Ohio Valley, settled largely by Southerners, was one such place, as were northern cities experiencing the strains of rapid growth, such as Philadelphia. Immigrant Irish, who found themselves pitted against free black people for jobs, were often violently antiabolitionist. A tactic that abolitionists borrowed from revivalists—holding large and emotional

abolishment. Garrison's crusade, like evangelical religion, was personal and moral. In reality, Garrison did not expect that all slaves would be freed immediately, but he did want and expect everyone to acknowledge the immorality of slavery. On the other hand, Garrison took the truly radical step of demanding full social equality for African Americans, referring to them individually as "a man and a brother" and "a woman and a sister." Garrison's determination electrified the antislavery movement, but his inability to compromise limited his effectiveness as a leader.

Garrison's moral vehemence radicalized northern antislavery religious groups. Theodore Weld, an evangelical minister, joined Garrison in 1833 in forming the American Anti-Slavery Society. The following year, Weld encouraged a group of students at Lane Theological Seminary in Cincinnati to form an antislavery society. When the seminary's president, Lyman Beecher, sought to suppress it, the students moved en masse to Oberlin College in northern Ohio, where they were joined by revivalist Charles Finney, who became president of the college. Oberlin soon became known as the most liberal college in the country, not only for its antislavery stance but for its acceptance of African American students and of women students as well.

Moral horror over slavery engaged many Northerners deeply in the abolitionist movement. They flocked to hear firsthand accounts of slavery by Frederick Douglass and Sojourner Truth, and by the white sisters from South Carolina, Angelina and Sarah Grimké. Northerners eagerly read slave narratives and books such as Theodore Weld's 1839 treatise *American* meetings—opened the door to mob action. Crowds of people often disrupted such meetings, especially those addressed by Theodore Weld, whose oratorical style earned him the title of "the Most Mobbed Man in the United States." William Lloyd Garrison was stoned, dragged through the streets, and on one occasion almost hanged by a Boston mob. In the three-day New York riot of 1834, abolitionist Arthur Tappan's home and store were sacked at the same time that black churches and homes were damaged and free blacks attacked. In 1837, antislavery editor Elijah P. Lovejoy of Alton, Illinois, was killed and his press destroyed. In 1838, a mob threatened a meeting of the Philadelphia Female Anti-Slavery Society one night and, the next night, burned down the hall in which they had met.

Abolitionism and Politics

Abolitionism began as a social movement but soon intersected with sectional interests and became a national political issue. In the 1830s, massive abolitionist petition drives gathered a total of nearly 700,000 petitions requesting the abolition of slavery and the slave trade in the District of Columbia but were rebuffed by Congress. At southern insistence and with President Andrew Jackson's approval, Congress passed a "gag rule" in 1836 that prohibited discussion of antislavery petitions.

Many Northerners viewed the gag rule and censorship of the mails, which Southerners saw as necessary defenses against abolitionist frenzy, as alarming threats to free speech. First among them was Massachusetts representative John Quincy Adams, the only former president ever to serve in Congress after leaving the executive branch. Adams so publicly and persistently denounced the gag rule as a violation of the constitutional right to petition that it was repealed in 1844. Less well-known Northerners like the thousands of women who canvassed their neighborhoods with petitions made personal commitments to abolitionism that they did not intend to abandon.

John Quincy Adams was also a key figure in the abolitionists' one undoubted victory, the fight to free the fifty-three slaves on the Spanish ship *Amistad* and return them to Africa. Although the Africans successfully mutinied against the *Amistad's* crew in 1839, when the ship was found in American waters a legal battle over their "ownership" ensued, during which the Africans themselves were held in jail. Prominent abolitionists, most notably Lewis Tappan, financed the legal fight which went all the way to the Supreme Court, where Adams won the case for the *Amistad* defendants against the American government, which supported the Spanish claim.

Although abolitionist groups raised the nation's emotional temperature, they failed to achieve the moral unity they had hoped for, and they began to

splinter. One perhaps inevitable but nonetheless distressing split was between white and black abolitionists. Frederick Douglass and William Lloyd Garrison parted ways when Douglass, refusing to be limited to a simple recital of his life as a slave, began to make specific suggestions for improvements in the lives of free African Americans. When Douglass chose the path of political action, Garrison denounced him as "ungrateful." Douglass and other free African Americans worked under persistent discrimination, even from antislavery whites; some of the latter refused to hire black people or to meet with them as equals. For example, some Philadelphia Quaker meetings, though devoted to the antislavery cause, maintained segregated seating for black people in their churches. While many white reformers eagerly pressed for civil equality for African Americans, they did not accept the idea of social equality. On the other hand, black and white "stations" worked closely in the risky enterprise of passing fugitive slaves north over the famous Underground Railroad, as the various routes by which slaves made their way to freedom were called. Contrary to abolitionist legend, however, it was free African Americans, rather than white people, who played the major part in helping the fugitives.

Among white abolitionists, William Lloyd Garrison remained controversial, especially after 1837, when he espoused a radical program that included women's rights, pacifism, and the abolition of the prisons and asylums that other reformers were working to establish. In 1840 the abolitionist movement formally split. The majority moved toward party politics (which Garrison abhorred), founding the Liberty Party and choosing James G. Birney (whom Theodore Weld had converted to abolitionism) as their presidential candidate. Thus the abolitionist movement, which began as an effort at moral reform, took its first major step into politics, and this step in turn led to the formation of the Republican Party in the 1850s and to the Civil War.

For one particular group of antislavery reformers, the abolitionist movement opened up new possibilities for action. Through their participation in antislavery activity, some women came to a vivid realization of the social constraints on their activism.

THE WOMEN'S RIGHTS MOVEMENT

American women, without the vote or a role in party politics, found a field of activity in social reform movements. There was scarcely a reform movement in which women were not actively involved. Often men were the official leaders of such movements, and some women—especially those in the temperance, moral reform, and abolitionist movements—formed all-female chapters to define and implement their own policies and programs.

The majority of women did not participate in these activities, for they were fully occupied with housekeeping and child rearing (families with five children were the average). A few women—mostly members of the new middle class, who could afford servants—had the time and energy to look beyond their immediate tasks. Touched by the religious revival, these women enthusiastically joined reform movements. Led thereby to challenge social restrictions, some, like the Grimké sisters, found that their commitment carried them beyond the limits of what was considered acceptable activity for women.

The Grimké Sisters

Sarah and Angelina Grimké, members of a prominent South Carolina slaveholding family, rejected slavery out of religious conviction and moved north to join a Quaker community near Philadelphia. In the 1830s, these two sisters found themselves drawn into the growing antislavery agitation in the North. Because they knew about slavery firsthand, they were in great demand as speakers. At first they spoke to "parlor meetings" of women only, as was considered proper. But interested men kept sneaking into the talks, and soon the sisters found themselves speaking to mixed gatherings. The meetings got larger and larger, and soon the sisters realized that they had become the first female public speakers in America. In 1837 Angelina Grimké became the first woman to address a meeting of the Massachusetts state legislature (Sarah Bagley, the Lowell worker, was the second).

The sisters challenged social norms on two grounds. There was widespread disapproval of the antislavery movement, and many famous male orators were criticized by the press and mobbed at meetings. The Grimké sisters were criticized for speaking because they were women. A letter from a group of ministers cited the Bible in reprimanding the sisters for stepping out of "woman's proper sphere" of silence and subordination. Sarah Grimké answered the ministers in her 1838 *Letters on the Equality of the Sexes and the Condition of Women*, claiming that "men and women were CREATED EQUAL. . . . Whatever is right for a man to do, is right for woman." She followed with this ringing assertion: "I seek no favors for my sex. I surrender not our claim to equality. All I ask of our brethren is, that they will take their feet from off our necks and permit us to stand upright on that ground which God designed us to occupy."

Not all female assertiveness was as dramatic as Sarah Grimké's, but women in the antislavery movement found it a constant struggle to be heard. Some solved the problem of male dominance by forming their own groups, like the Philadelphia Female Anti-Slavery Society. In the antislavery movement and other reform groups as well, men accorded women a secondary role, even when—as was frequently the case—women constituted a majority of the members.

Women's Rights

The Seneca Falls Convention of 1848, the first women's rights convention in American history, was an outgrowth of almost twenty years of female activity in social reform. Every year after 1848 women gathered to hold women's rights conventions and to work for political, legal, and social equality. Over the years, in response to persistent lobbying, states passed property laws more favorable to women and altered divorce laws to allow women to retain custody of children. Teaching positions in

Women's gatherings, like the first women's rights convention in Seneca Falls in 1848 and this meeting of strikers in Lynn in 1860, were indicators of widespread female activism. SOURCE: Lynn Museum.

CHRONOLOGY

1817	American Colonization Society founded
1820s	Shaker colonies grow
1825	New Harmony founded, fails three years later
1826	American Society for the Promotion of Temperance founded
1827	Workingmen's Party founded in Philadelphia
	Freedom's Journal begins publication
	Public school movement begins in Massachusetts
1829	David Walker's *Appeal to the Colored Citizens of the World* is published
1830	Joseph Smith founds Church of Jesus Christ of Latter-Day Saints (Mormon Church)
	Charles G. Finney's revivals in Rochester
1831	William Lloyd Garrison begins publishing antislavery newspaper, the *Liberator*
1832	Immigration begins to increase
1833	American Anti-Slavery Society founded by William Lloyd Garrison and Theodore Weld
1834	First Female Moral Reform Society founded in New York
	National Trades Union formed
1836	Congress passes "gag rule" to prevent discussion of antislavery petitions
1837	Antislavery editor Elijah P. Lovejoy killed
	Angelina Grimké addresses Massachusetts legislature
	Sarah Grimké, *Letters on the Equality of the Sexes and the Condition of Women*
	Panic begins seven-year depression
1839	Theodore Weld publishes *American Slavery As It Is*
1840s	New York and Boston complete public water systems
1840	Liberty Party founded
1843	Millerites await the end of the world
	Dorothea Dix spearheads asylum reform movement
1844	Mormon leader Joseph Smith killed by mob
	New York creates city police force
1845	Beginning of Irish Potato Famine and mass Irish immigration into the United States
1846	Mormons begin migration to the Great Salt Lake
1848	Women's Rights Convention at Seneca Falls
	John Noyes founds Oneida Community

higher education opened up to women, as did jobs in some other occupations, and women gained the vote in some states, beginning with Wyoming Territory in 1869. In 1920, seventy-two years after universal woman suffrage was first proposed at Seneca Falls, a woman's right to vote was at last guaranteed in the Nineteenth Amendment to the Constitution.

Historians have only recently realized how much the reform movements of this "Age of the Common Man" were due to the efforts of the "common woman." Women played a vital role in all the social movements of the day. In doing so they implicitly challenged the popular notion of separate spheres for men and women—the public world for him, home and family for her. The separate spheres argument, although it heaped praise on women for their allegedly superior moral qualities, was meant to exclude them from political life. The reforms discussed in this chapter show clearly that women reformers believed they had a right and a duty to propose solutions for the moral and social problems of the day. Empowered by their own religious beliefs and activism, the Seneca Falls reformers spoke for all American women when they demanded an end to the unfair restrictions they suffered as women.

CONCLUSION

Beginning in the 1820s, the market revolution changed the size and social order of America's preindustrial cities and towns. Immigration, dramatically rapid population growth, and changes in working life and class structure created a host of new urban problems ranging from sanitation to civic order. These changes occurred so rapidly that they seemed overwhelming. Older, face-to-face methods of social control no longer worked. To fill the gap, new kinds of associations—the political party, the religious crusade, the reform cause, the union movement—sprang up. These associations were new manifestations of the deep human desire for social connection, for continuity, and—especially in the growing cities—for social order. A striking aspect of these associations was the uncompromising nature of the attitudes and beliefs on which they were based. Most groups were formed of like-minded people who wanted to impose their will on others. Such intolerance boded ill for the future. If political parties, religious bodies, and reform groups were to splinter along sectional lines (as happened in the 1850s), political compromise would be very difficult. In the meantime, however, Americans came to terms with the market revolution by engaging in a passion for improvement. As a perceptive foreign observer, Francis Grund, noted, "Americans love their country not as it is but as it will be."

REVIEW QUESTIONS

1. What impact did the new immigration of the 1840s and 1850s have on American cities?
2. Why did urbanization produce so many problems?
3. What motivated the social reformers of the period? Were they benevolent helpers or dictatorial social controllers? Study several reform causes and discuss similarities and differences among them.
4. Abolitionism differed little from other reforms in its tactics, but the effects of antislavery activism were politically explosive. Why was this so?

RECOMMENDED READING

Tyler Anbinder, *Five Points* (2001).

Paul Boyer, *Urban Masses and Moral Order in America, 1820–1920* (1978).

Amy Bridges, *A City in the Republic: Antebellum New York and the Origins of Machine Politics* (1984).

David Grimsted, *American Mobbing, 1828–1865: Toward Civil War* (1998).

James Oliver Horton and Lois E. Horton, *In Hope of Liberty: Culture, Community and Protest Among Northern Free Black, 1700–1860* (1997).

Eric Lott, *Love and Theft: Blackface Minstrelsy and the American Working Class* (1993).

Steven Mintz, *Moralists and Modernizers: America's Pre–Civil War Reformers* (1995).

David Roediger, *The Wages of Whiteness* (1991).

David Rothman, *The Discovery of the Asylum: Social Order and Disorder in the New Republic* (1971).

Mary Ryan, *Civic Wars: Democracy and Public Life in the American City During the Nineteenth Century* (1997).

Kathryn Sklar, *Catharine Beecher: A Study in American Domesticity* (1973).

Sean Wilentz, *Chants Democratic: New York City and the Rise of the American Working Class, 1788–1850* (1983).

▶ MEDIA RESOURCES

 ### U.S. HISTORY DOCUMENTS CD-ROM

Jacksonian Democracy

10-2   A "Corrupt Bargain" or Politics as Usual? (1824)

10-3   A Disaffected Mason Speaks Out Against the Order (1826)

10-10   Black Hawk, "Life of Black Hawk" (1833)

Reforming the Nation

11-1   Joshua and Sally Wilson, Letters to George Wilson (1823)

11-2   Lyman Beecher, Six Sermons on Intemperance (1828)

11-3   "Early Habits of Industry," The Mother's Magazine (1834)

11-4   Charles Finney, "What a Revival of Religion Is" (1835)

11-5   Temperance and the Washingtonians (1836)

11-7   "Petition of the Catholics of New York" (1840)

11-8   Ralph Waldo Emerson, "Self-Reliance" (1841)

11-9   Ja Norcom, Letter to Mary Matilda Norcom (1846)

11-10   Declaration of Sentiments and Resolutions, Woman's Rights Convention, Seneca Falls, New York (1848)

11-11   Horace Mann on Education and National Welfare

11-12   John Humphrey Noyes and Bible Communism (1845 and 1849)

11-13   Sojourner Truth, Address to the Woman's Rights Convention, Akron, Ohio (1851)

 ### COMPANION WEBSITE HIGHLIGHTS

To view an exploration, enter one of the URLs below in your browser.

 ### Web Explorations

Reform Movements in the Burned-Over District
http://www.prenhall.com/faragher/map13.1
The Mormon Migration, 1830–1847
http://www.prenhall.com/faragher/map13.2

 ### Additional Interactive Maps

To access the maps, go to this chapter's resources at
http://www.prenhall.com/faragher
The Distribution of Foreign-born Residents of the United States in 1860, page 373
American Cities, 1820 and American Cities, 1860, page 374

 ### HISTORY RESOURCE CENTER

To find the resources listed below, go to
http://www.prenhall.com/historyresourcecenter

(Continued)

(Continued)

Documents

"... The Representation of the [Canal] Commissioners of the State of New York" (1817)

Elizabeth Cady Stanton, Declaration of Sentiments (1848)

Extract from the Albany Daily Advertiser (1819)

Henry Clay, "Defense of the American System" (1832)

Horace Mann, from Report of the Massachusetts Board of Education (1848)

Nathaniel Hawthorne, A Letter from Brook Farm (1841)

Images

A Glance at New York

American Songsheets

The American Antislavery Society

The Drunkard's Progress from the Glass to the Grave

EXPLORING AMERICA

ANGELINA GRIMKÉ

http://www.prenhall.com/faragher/angelinagrimke

Why did the appearance of Angelina Grimké before a mixed audience of men and women create an uproar? Why did a similar speaking appearance by Maria Stewart, a free African American woman, go unnoticed? What prompted Grimké to speak against slavery? How did her speech affect other women? What was the role of women in public affairs? The module *Angelina Grimké* connects the growing antislavery reform movement to the increasing activism of women in public affairs.

Angelina Grimké effectively employs print and visual documents in the discussion of women and antislavery. The speeches by Grimké and Maria Stewart tie the antislavery reform effort to the increasing presence of women in the public sphere. The primary source documents focus on both subjects and include transcripts of speeches and political broadsides. The module explores the hostility to Grimké's speech and antislavery activism, offering insight into public attitudes toward change. It also shows the important role women played in reform movements. The interactive map provides historical context for the discussion.

This image from a broadside of the American Anti-Slavery Society shows the battle between the "Eagle of Liberty" and the "Serpent of Slavery" (1838).

Reflect and Respond

1. If Grimké emphasized the role of women in ending slavery, Whittier did not. What about his poem suggests who he thought his readers were?

2. Grimké grounded her arguments against slavery in religion and the Bible. Whittier also made a religious appeal in the latter stanzas of his poem, but most of his references were to American history and to contemporary political events in Europe. Why did he believe Americans should end slavery?

3. Stewart based her arguments on religion and history. On what basis did she claim that the condition of free blacks was virtually as bad as that of slaves?

✓ Check it out

The Conflict Over

This poster shows the vision of late 1830s antislavery advocates. "The Conflict Over" is important because it illuminates the ideas of antislavery reformers regarding how their crusade would ultimately end. It also shows that the antislavery campaign was tied to patriotic themes.

This exploration is also available on the *Exploring America* CD-ROM.

FOURTEEN

THE TERRITORIAL EXPANSION OF THE UNITED STATES

▶ 1830s–1850s

Alfred Jacob Miller (American, 1810–1874), *Fort Laramie*, 1851. Oil on canvas, 18 x 27 in. (0126.727) SOURCE: © Gilcrease Museum, Tulsa

Texans and Tejanos "Remember the Alamo!"

FOR THIRTEEN DAYS IN FEBRUARY AND MARCH 1836, A FORCE of 187 Texans held the mission fortress known as the Alamo against a siege by 5,000 Mexican troops under General Antonio López de Santa Anna, president of Mexico. Santa Anna had come north to subdue rebellious Texas, the northernmost part of the Mexican province of Coahuila y Tejas, and to place it under central authority. On March 6 he ordered a final assault, and in brutal fighting that claimed over 1,500 Mexican lives, his army took the mission. All the defenders were killed, including Commander William Travis and the well-known frontiersmen Jim Bowie and Davy Crockett. It was a crushing defeat for the Texans, but the cry "Remember the Alamo!" rallied their remaining forces, which, less than two months later, routed the Mexican army and forced Santa Anna to grant Texas independence from Mexico. Today the Alamo, in San Antonio, is one of the most cherished historic shrines in the United States.

But memory is selective: some things tend to be forgotten. Within a generation of the uprising few remembered that many Tejanos, Spanish-speaking people born in Texas, had joined with American settlers fighting for Texas independence. The Americans were concentrated in the central and eastern portions of the huge Texas territory, where during the 1820s the Mexican government had authorized several colonies managed by *empresarios* (land agents) like Stephen F. Austin. These settler communities consisted mostly of farmers from the Mississippi Valley, who introduced slavery and cotton growing to the rich lands of coastal and upland Texas.

The Tejano community, descended from eighteenth-century Spanish and Mexican settlers, included wealthy rancheros who raised cattle on the shortgrass prairies of south Texas, as well as the cowboys known as *vaqueros* and the *peónes*, or poor tenant farmers. Although there was relatively little contact between the Americans and Tejanos, their leaders interacted in San Antonio, the center of regional government. The Tejano elite welcomed the American immigrants and were enthusiastic about their plans for the economic development of Texas. Many Americans married into elite Tejano families, who hoped that by thus assimilating and sharing power with the Americans they could not only maintain but strengthen their community.

The Mexican state, however, was politically and socially unstable during these first years after its successful revolt against Spain in 1821. Liberals favored a loose federal union, conservatives a strong central state. As a northern frontier province, Texas did not have the benefits of statehood; as a result most Tejanos found themselves taking the liberal side in the struggle, opting for more local control over government activities. When, in 1828, the conservative centralists came to power in Mexico City and decided the Americans had too much influence in Texas, many Tejanos rose up with the Americans in opposition. In 1832, the Tejano elite of San Antonio and many prominent rancheros went on record in favor of provincial autonomy and a strong role for the Americans.

One of the leaders of the San Antonio community was the wealthy ranchero Juan Nepomuceno Seguín. As Santa Anna's army approached from the south, Seguín recruited a company of Tejano volunteers and joined the American force inside the walls of the Alamo. During the siege, Commander Travis sent Seguín and some of his men for reinforcements. Stopped by Mexican troops on his way across the lines, Seguín called out, "¡Somos paisanos!" (We are countrymen!), confusing the guards just long enough for Seguín and his men to make their escape despite the hail of gunfire that quickly ensued. Seguín returned from his unsuccessful mission to find the burned bodies of the Alamo defenders, including seven San Antonio Tejanos. "Texas será libre!" (Texas shall be free!) Seguín called out as he directed the burial of the Alamo defenders. In April, Seguín led a regiment of Tejanos in the decisive battle of San Jacinto that won independence for Texas.

At first Tejanos were pleased with independence and played an important political role in the new Republic of Texas. The liberal Lorenzo de Zavala was chosen vice president, and Seguín became the mayor of San Antonio. But soon things began to change, illustrating a recurring pattern in the American occupation of new lands—a striking shift in the relations between different cultures in frontier areas. Most commonly, in the initial stage newcomers blended with native peoples, creating a "frontier of inclusion." The first hunters, trappers, and traders on every American frontier—west of the Appalachians, in the Southwest, and in the Far West—married into the local community and tried to learn native ways. Outnumbered Americans adapted to local societies as a matter of simple survival.

A second, unstable stage occurred when the number of Americans increased and they began occupying more and more land or, as in California, "rushing" in great numbers to mine gold, overrunning native communities. The usual result was warfare and the rapid growth of hostility and racial prejudice—all of which was largely absent in earlier days.

A third stage—that of stable settlement—occurred when the native community had been completely "removed" or isolated. In this "frontier of exclusion," racial mixing was rare. Generally, when Europeans pushed American Indians onto reservations they cut themselves off from sources of human history that could have helped them more fully understand the country into which they had moved. And in Texas, American settlers—initially invited in by Mexicans and Tejanos—developed an anti-Mexican passion, regarding all Spanish-speakers as their Mexican enemies rather than their Tejano allies.

Unscrupulous Americans exploited these prejudices to acquire Tejano property. If the rancheros were "sufficiently scared," one wrote, they would "make an advantageous sale of their lands," and if "two or three hundred of our troops should be stationed here, I have no doubt but a man could make some good speculations." Tejanos were attacked and forced from their homes; some of their villages were burned to the ground. "On the pretext that they were Mexicans," Seguín wrote, Americans treated Tejanos "worse than brutes . . . My countrymen ran to me for protection against the assaults or exactions of these adventurers." But even in his capacity as mayor Seguín could do little, and in 1842 he and his family, like hundreds of other Tejano families, fled south to Mexico in fear for their lives.

Thus the Tejanos became symbols of a romanticized past rather than full participants in the building of western communities. Spanish-speaking communities in Texas, and later in New Mexico and California, like the communities of Indians throughout the West, became conquered peoples. "White folks and Mexicans were never made to live together," a Texas woman told a traveler a few years after the revolution. "The Mexicans had no business here," she said, and the Americans might "just have to get together and drive them all out of the country." The descendants of the first European settlers of the American Southwest had become foreigners in the land their people had lived in for two centuries. ∎

San Antonio

KEY TOPICS

- Continental expansion and the concept of Manifest Destiny

- The contrasting examples of frontier development in Oregon, Texas, and California

- How the political effects of expansion heightened sectional tensions

EXPLORING THE WEST

There seemed to be no stopping the expansion of the American people. By 1840 they had occupied all of the land east of the Mississippi River and had organized all of it (except for Florida and Wisconsin) into states. Of the ten states admitted to the Union between 1800 and 1840, all but one were west of the Appalachian Mountains. Less than sixty years after the United States gained its independence, the majority of its population lived west of the original thirteen states. This rapid expansion was caused by the market revolution, and especially the extraordinary expansion of transportation and commerce (see Chapter 12).

The speed and success of this expansion were a source of deep national pride that whetted appetites for further expansion. Many Americans looked eagerly westward to the vast unsettled reaches of the Louisiana Purchase: to Texas, Santa Fé, and trade with Mexico, and even to the Far West, where New England sea captains had been trading for furs since the 1790s. By 1848 the United States had gained all of these coveted western lands. This chapter examines the way the United States became a continental nation, forming many frontier communities in the process. Exploring the vast continent of North America and gaining an understanding of its geography took several centuries and the efforts of many people.

The Fur Trade

The fur trade, which flourished from the 1670s to the 1840s, was an important spur to exploration on the North American continent. In the 1670s, the British Hudson's Bay Company and its French Canadian rival, Montreal's North West Company, began exploring beyond the Great Lakes in the Canadian West in search of beaver pelts. Traders and trappers for both companies depended on the goodwill and cooperation of the native peoples of the region, in particular the Assiniboins,

Crees, Gros Ventres, and Blackfeet, all of whom moved freely across what later became the U.S.–Canadian border. From the marriages of European men with native women arose a distinctive mixed-race group, the "métis" (see Chapter 5). In 1821, the Hudson's Bay Company absorbed its Montreal rival and ran the fur trade from trading posts in the far Canadian North, such as Norway House, Cumberland House, and Fort George. British, French Canadian, and métis employees of the Hudson's Bay Company also trapped and explored throughout the Canadian West and in the Oregon Country, then jointly occupied by the British and Americans. This British-dominated fur trade was an important aspect of international commerce. Americans had long coveted a part of it. Indeed, Thomas Jefferson had sent Lewis and Clark west in 1803 in part to challenge British dominance of the fur trade with western Indian peoples (see Chapter 9).

Not until the 1820s were American companies able to challenge British dominance of the trans-Mississippi fur trade. In 1824, William Henry Ashley of the Rocky Mountain Fur Company instituted the "rendezvous" system. This was a yearly trade fair, held deep in the Rocky Mountains (Green River and Jackson Hole were favored locations), to which trappers brought their catch of furs. There they traded them for goods transported by the fur companies from St. Louis: traps, guns, ammunition, tobacco, beads and fabrics (for later trade with Indian peoples), and alcohol. These yearly fur rendezvous were modeled on traditional Indian trade gatherings such as the one at the Mandan villages on the upper Missouri River and the huge gathering that took place every year at Celilo Falls on the Columbia River during the annual salmon run. Like its Indian model, the fur rendezvous was a boisterous, polyglot, many-day affair at which trappers of many nationalities—Americans and Indian peoples, French Canadians, and métis, as well as Mexicans from Santa Fé and Taos—gathered to trade, drink, and gamble.

The artist Alfred Jacob Miller, a careful observer of the western fur trade, shows us a mountain man and his Indian wife in his 1837 *Bourgeois Walker & His Wife*. Both Walker and his wife worked together to trap and prepare beaver pelts for market.

SOURCE: The Walters Art Museum, Baltimore (37.1940.78).

For the "mountain men" employed by the American fur companies, the rendezvous was their only contact with American society. The rest of the year they spent deep in the mountains trapping beaver and living in some sort of relationship with local Indian peoples. Some lived in a constant state of danger, always alert to the possibility of attack by parties of local people. But most trappers sought accommodation and friendship: nearly half of them contracted long-lasting marriages with Indian women, who not only helped in the trapping and curing of furs but also acted as vital diplomatic links between the white and Indian worlds. Contemporaries often viewed the mountain men— tough, bearded, leather-clad, fluent in Indian tongues—as half-savage, but we should perhaps see them as the advance guard of the market revolution, adapting the ways of native peoples so as to trade with them. One legendary trapper adapted so well that he became a Crow chief: the African American Jim Beckwourth, who married a Crow woman and was accepted into her tribe.

For all its adventure, the American fur trade was short-lived. By the 1840s, the population of beaver in western streams was virtually destroyed, and the day of the mountain man was over. But with daring journeys like that of Jedediah Smith, the first American to enter

California over the Sierra Nevada mountains, the mountain men had helped forge a clear picture of western geography. Soon permanent settlers would follow the trails they had blazed.

Government-Sponsored Exploration

The federal government played a major role in the exploration and development of the West. Thomas Jefferson decisively influenced American westward expansion with the Louisiana Purchase of 1803. When he dispatched the Lewis and Clark expedition the next year, it may have been largely to satisfy his own intense scientific and geographic curiosity about the West, but he also instructed Meriwether Lewis and William Clark to draw the western Indians into the American trading network, away from the British.

The exploratory and scientific aspects of the Lewis and Clark expedition set a precedent for many government-financed quasi-military expeditions. In 1806 and 1807, Lieutenant Zebulon Pike led an expedition to the Rocky Mountains in Colorado. Major Stephen Long's exploration and mapping of the Great Plains in the years 1819–20 was part of a show of force meant to frighten British fur trappers out of the West. Then, in 1843 and 1844, another military explorer, John C. Frémont, mapped the overland trails to Oregon and California. In the 1850s, the Pacific Railroad surveys explored possible transcontinental railroad routes. The tradition of government-sponsored western exploration continued after the Civil War in the famous geological surveys, the best known of which is the 1869 Grand Canyon exploration by Major John Wesley Powell.

Beginning with Long's expedition, the results of these surveys were published by the government, complete with maps, illustrations, and, after the Civil War, photographs. These publications fed a strong popular appetite for pictures of the breathtaking scenery of the Far West and information about its inhabitants. Artists like Karl Bodmer, who accompanied a private expedition by the scientifically inclined German prince Maximilian in the years 1833–34, produced stunning portraits of American Indians. Over

Web Exploration   Examine the routes taken by major expeditions westward between 1804 and 1830. What role did they play in shaping United States policy in the West?
www.prenhall.com/faragher/map14.1

Exploration of the Continent, 1804–1830   Lewis and Clark's "voyage of discovery" of 1804–06 was the first of many government-sponsored western military expeditions. Crossing the Great Plains in 1806, Lieutenant Zebulon Pike was captured by the Spanish in their territory and taken to Mexico but returned in 1807 via Texas. Major Stephen Long, who crossed the Plains in 1819–20, found them "arid and forbidding." Meanwhile fur trappers, among them the much-traveled Jedediah Smith, became well acquainted with the West as they hunted beaver for their pelts.

the next three decades Thomas Moran, Albert Bierstadt, and other landscape artists traveled west with government expeditions and came home to paint grand (and sometimes fanciful) pictures of Yosemite Valley and the Yellowstone River region (later designated among the first national parks). All these images of the American West made a powerful contribution to the emerging American self-image. American pride in the land—the biggest of this, the longest of that, the most spectacular of something else—was founded on the images brought home by government surveyors and explorers.

In the wake of the pathfinders came hundreds of government geologists and botanists as well as the surveyors who mapped and plotted the West for settlement according to the Land Ordinance of 1785. The basic pattern of land survey and sale established by these measures (see Chapter 7) was followed all the way to the Pacific Ocean. The federal government sold the western public lands at low prices and, to veterans of the War of 1812, gave away land in the Old Northwest. And following policies established in the Old Northwest (see Chapter 9), the federal government also shouldered the expense of Indian removal, paying the soldiers or the officials who fought or talked Indian peoples into giving up their lands. The federal government also made long-term commitments to compensate the Indian people themselves. The government also supported the forts and soldiers whose task was to maintain peace between settlers and Indian peoples in newly opened areas.

Expansion and Indian Policy

While American artists were painting the way of life of western Indian peoples, eastern Indian tribes were being removed from their homelands to Indian Territory (present-day Oklahoma, Kansas, and Nebraska), a region west of Arkansas, Missouri, and Iowa on the eastern edge of the Great Plains, widely regarded as unfarmable and popularly known as the Great American Desert. The justification for this western removal, as Thomas Jefferson had explained early in the century, was the creation of a space where Indian people could live undisturbed by white people while they slowly adjusted to "civilized" ways. But the government officials who negotiated the removals failed to predict the tremendous speed at which white people would settle the West.

As a result, encroachment on Indian Territory was not long in coming. The territory was crossed by the Santa Fé Trail, established in 1821; in the 1840s the northern part was crossed by the heavily traveled Overland Trails to California, Oregon, and the Mormon community in Utah. In 1854, the government abolished the northern half of Indian Territory, establishing the Kansas and Nebraska Territories in its place and opening them to immediate white settlement. The tribes of the area—the Potawatomis, Wyandots, Kickapoos, Sauks, Foxes, Delawares, Shawnees, Kaskaskias, Peorias, Piankashaws, Weas, Miamis, Omahas, Otos, and Missouris—signed treaties accepting either vastly reduced reservations or allotments. Those who accepted allotments—sections of private land—often sold them, under pressure, to white people. Thus many of the Indian people who had hoped for independence and escape from white pressures in Indian Territory lost both their autonomy and their tribal identity.

The people in the southern part of Indian Territory, in what is now Oklahoma, fared somewhat better. Those members of the southern tribes—the Cherokees, Chickasaws, Choctaws, Creeks, and Seminoles—who had survived the trauma of forcible removal from the Southeast in the 1830s quickly created impressive new communities. The five tribes divided up the territory and established self-governing nations with their own schools and churches. The societies they created were not so different from the American societies from which they had been expelled. The five tribes even carried slavery west with them: an elite economic group established plantations and shipped their cotton to New Orleans like other Southerners. Until after the Civil War, these southern tribes were able to withstand outside pressures and remain the self-governing communities that treaties had assured them they would be.

The removal of the eastern tribes did not solve "the Indian Problem," the term many Americans used to describe their relationship with the first occupants of the land. West of Indian Territory were the nomadic and warlike Indians of the Great Plains: the Sioux, Cheyennes, Arapahoes, Comanches, and Kiowas. Beyond them were the seminomadic tribes of the Rocky Mountains—the Blackfeet, Crows, Utes, Shoshonis, Nez Percé, and Salish peoples—and, in the Southwest, the farming cultures of the Pueblos, Hopis, Acomas, Zunis, Pimas, and Papagos and the migratory Apaches and Navajos. Even farther west were hundreds of small tribes in California and the Pacific Northwest. Clearly, all of these people could not be "removed," for where could they go? The first western pioneers ignored the issue. Beginning in the 1840s, they simply passed through the far western tribal lands on their way to establish new frontiers of settlement in California and Oregon. Later, after the Civil War, the government would undertake a series of Indian wars that ultimately left the remaining Indian peoples penned up on small reservations.

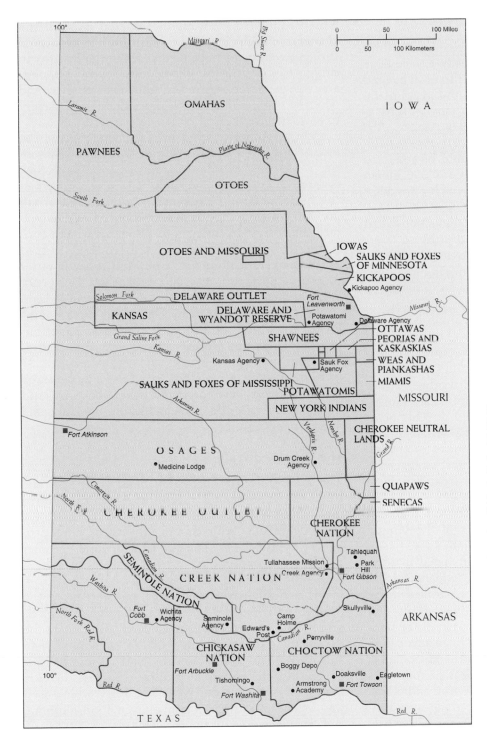

Indian Territory before the Kansas-Nebraska Act of 1854
Indian Territory lay west of Arkansas, Missouri, and Iowa and east of Spanish Territory. Most of the Indian peoples who lived there in the 1830s and the 1840s had been "removed" from east of the Mississippi River. The southern part (now Oklahoma) was inhabited by peoples from the Old Southwest: the Cherokees, Chickasaws, Choctaws, Creeks, and Seminoles. North of that (in what is now Kansas and Nebraska) lived peoples who had been removed from the Old Northwest. All these Indian peoples had trouble adjusting not only to a new climate and a new way of life but to the close proximity of some Indian tribes who were their traditional enemies.

THE POLITICS OF EXPANSION

America's rapid expansion had many consequences, but perhaps the most significant was that it reinforced Americans' sense of themselves as pioneering people. In the 1890s Frederick Jackson Turner, America's most famous historian, observed that the repeated experience of settling new frontiers across the continent had shaped Americans into a uniquely adventurous, optimistic, and democratic people. Other historians have disagreed with Turner, but there is no question that his view of the frontier long ago won the battle for popular opinion. Ever since the time of Daniel Boone, venturing into the wilderness has held a special place in the American imagination, seen almost as an American right.

Manifest Destiny, an Expansionist Ideology

How did Americans justify their restless expansionism? After all, the United States was already a very large country with much undeveloped land. To push beyond existing boundaries was to risk war with Great Britain, which claimed the Pacific Northwest, and with Mexico, which held what is now Texas, New Mexico, Arizona, Utah, Nevada, California, and part of Colorado. If the United States prevailed it would be reducing 75,000 Spanish-speaking people and 150,000 Indian people to subject status. Undertaking such a conquest required a rationale.

In 1845 newspaperman John O'Sullivan provided it. It was, he wrote, "our manifest destiny to overspread the continent allotted by Providence for the free development of our yearly multiplying millions." Sullivan argued that Americans had a God-given right to bring the benefits of American democracy to other, more backward peoples—meaning Mexicans and Indians—by force, if necessary. The notion of manifest destiny summed up the powerful combination of pride in what America had achieved and missionary zeal and racist attitudes toward other peoples that lay behind the thinking of many expansionists. Americans were proud of their rapid development: the surge in population, the remarkable canals and railroads, the grand scale of the American enterprise. Why shouldn't it be even bigger? Almost swaggering, Americans dared other countries—Great Britain in particular—to stop them.

Behind the bravado was some new international thinking about the economic future of the United States. After the devastating Panic of 1837 (see Chapter 10), many politicians became convinced that the nation's prosperity depended on vastly expanded trade with Asia. The China trade had accustomed many New Englanders to trade across the Pacific, and greater markets beckoned (see Chapter 9). Senator Thomas Hart Benton of Missouri had been advocating trade with India by way of the Missouri and Columbia rivers since the 1820s (not the easiest of routes, as Lewis and Clark had shown). Soon Benton and others were pointing out how much Pacific trade would increase if the United States held the magnificent harbors of the west coast, among them Puget Sound in the Oregon Country, held jointly with Britain, and the bays of San Francisco and San Diego, both in Mexican-held California.

Expansionism was deeply tied to national politics. O'Sullivan, whose "manifest destiny" became the expansionist watchword, was not a neutral observer: he was the editor of the *Democratic Review*, a party newspaper. Most Democrats were wholehearted supporters of expansion, whereas many Whigs (especially in the North) opposed it. Whigs welcomed most of the changes wrought by industrialization but advocated strong government policies that would guide growth and development within the country's existing boundaries; they feared (correctly) that expansion would raise the contentious issue of the extension of slavery to new territories.

On the other hand, many Democrats feared the industrialization that the Whigs welcomed. Where the Whigs saw economic progress, Democrats saw economic depression (the Panic of 1837 was the worst the nation had experienced), uncontrolled urban growth, and growing social unrest. For many Democrats, the answer to the nation's social ills was to continue to follow Thomas Jefferson's vision of establishing agriculture in the new territories in order to counterbalance industrialization (see Chapter 9). Another factor in the political struggle over expansion in the 1840s was that many Democrats were Southerners, for whom the continual expansion of cotton-growing lands was a matter of social faith as well as economic necessity.

These were politicians' reasons. The average farmer moved west for many other reasons: land hunger, national pride, plain and simple curiosity, and a sense of adventure.

The Overland Trails

The 2,000-mile trip on the Overland Trails from the banks of the Missouri River to Oregon and California usually took seven months, sometimes more. Travel was slow, dangerous, tedious, and exhausting. Forced to lighten their loads as animals died and winter weather threatened, pioneers often arrived at their destination with little food and few belongings. Uprooted from family and familiar surroundings, pioneers faced the prospect of being, in the poignant and much-used biblical phrase, "strangers in a strange land." Yet despite the risks, settlers streamed west: 5,000 to Oregon by 1845 and about 3,000 to California by 1848 (before the discovery of gold). Some arrived by ship, but this was more expensive than the overland journey, which itself was not cheap: a wagon, a team of oxen, food, clothing, and essential tools cost between $500 and $1,000.

Pioneers had many motives for making the trip. Glowing reports from Oregon's Willamette Valley, for example, seemed to promise economic opportunity and healthy surroundings, an alluring combination to farmers in the malaria-prone Midwest who had been hard hit by the Panic of 1837. But rational motives do not tell the whole story. Many men were motivated by a sense of adventure, by a desire to experience the unknown, or, as they put it, to "see the elephant." Women were more likely to think of the trip as *A Pioneer's Search*

The Overland Trails, 1840

All the great trails west started at the Missouri River. The Oregon, California, and Mormon Trails followed the Platte River into Wyoming, crossed South Pass, and divided in western Wyoming. The much harsher Santa Fé Trail stretched 900 miles southwest across the Great Plains. All of the trails crossed Indian Territory and, to greater or lesser extent, Mexican possessions as well.

for an Ideal Home, the title that Phoebe Judson chose for her account of her family's 1852 trip to Oregon.

Few pioneers traveled alone, partly because they feared Indian attack (which was rare) but largely because they needed help fording rivers or crossing mountains with heavy wagons. Most Oregon pioneers traveled with their families but usually also joined a larger group, forming a "train." In the earliest years, when the route was still uncertain, trains hired a "pilot," generally a former fur trapper. Often the men of the wagon train drew up semimilitary constitutions, electing a leader. Democratic as this process appeared, not everyone was willing to obey the leader, and many trains experienced dissension and breakups along the trail. But in essence all pioneers—men, women, and children—were part of a new, westward-moving community in which they had to accept both the advantages and disadvantages of community membership.

Wagon trains started westward as soon as the prairies were green (thus ensuring feed for the livestock). The daily routine was soon established. Men took care of the moving equipment and the animals, while the women cooked and kept track of the children. Slowly, at a rate of about fifteen miles a day, the wagon trains moved west along the Platte River, cross-

ing the Continental Divide at South Pass in present-day Wyoming. West of the Rockies the climate was much drier. The long, dusty stretch along the Snake River in present-day southern Idaho finally gave way to Oregon's steep and difficult Blue Mountains and to the dangerous rafting down the Columbia River, in which many drowned and all were drenched by the cold winter rains of the Pacific Northwest. California-bound migrants faced even worse hazards: the complete lack of water in the Humbolt Sink region of northern Nevada and the looming Sierra Nevadas, which had to be crossed before the winter snows came. (Members of the ill-fated Donner party, snowbound on the Nevada side of that range in 1846–47, resorted to cannibalism before they were rescued.)

In addition to the ever-present tedium and exhaustion, wagon trains were beset by such trail hazards as illness and accident. Danger from Indian attack, which all pioneers feared, was actually very small. Before the 1849 California Gold Rush, conflicts between wagon trains and Indians claimed the lives of only thirty-four white people (twenty-four in one wagon train) and twenty-five Indians. In subsequent years, as thousands of gold rushers flocked west, the deaths increased, but, significantly, more Indians than white people died. It

J. Goldsborough Bruff, one of thousands who rushed to California for gold in 1849, sketched many events in his Overland Trail journey. Here he depicts several wagons being ferried over the Platte River. The need for individuals to cooperate is obvious. Less obvious in this sketch is the danger: most river crossing points lacked ferries, and both people and livestock often drowned trying to ford them.

SOURCE: Joseph Goldsborough Bruff, *Ferriage of the Platte above the Mouth of Deer Creek, July 20, 1849.* The Henry E. Huntington Library and Art Gallery, San Marino, Calif. (HM 8044, #50).

appears that unprovoked white attacks on Indians were more common than the reverse.

In contrast, cholera killed at least a thousand people a year in 1849 and in the early 1850s when it was common along sections of the trail along the Platte River. Spread by contaminated water, cholera caused vomiting and diarrhea, which in turn led to extreme dehydration and death, often in one night. In the afflicted regions, trailside graves were a frequent and grim sight. Drownings were not uncommon, nor were accidental ax wounds or shootings, and children sometimes fell out of wagons and were run over. The members of the wagon train community did what they could to arrange decent burials, and they provided support for survivors: men helped widows drive their wagons onward, women nursed and tended babies whose mothers were dead, and at least one parentless family, the seven Sager children, were brought to Oregon in safety.

By 1860 almost 300,000 people had traveled the Overland Trails to Oregon or California. Ruts from the wagon wheels can be seen in a number of places along the route even today. In 1869, the completion of the transcontinental railroad marked the end of the wagon train era (although many people made shorter trips to other western locations by wagon). In retrospect, the pioneers remembered their journey as more dangerous and less tedious than it actually was. The stories that came down to their grandchildren told of a heroic adventure. These "pioneers' tales" were not the truth as it had really happened but an effort to find the true heroism in an important episode by making a good story out of it.

Oregon

The American settlement of Oregon provides a capsule example of the stages of frontier development. The first contacts between the region's Indian peoples and Europeans were commercial. Spanish, British, Russian, and American ships traded for sea otter skins from the 1780s to about 1810. Subsequently land-based groups scoured the region for beaver skins as well. In this first "frontier of inclusion" there were frequent, often sexual contacts between Indians and Europeans.

Both Great Britain and the United States claimed the Oregon Country by right of discovery, but in the Convention of 1818 the two nations agreed to occupy it jointly, postponing a final decision on its disposition. In reality, the British clearly dominated the region. In 1824 the Hudson's Bay Company consolidated Britain's position by establishing a major fur trading post at Fort Vancouver, on the banks of the Columbia River. Like all fur-trading ventures, the post exemplified the racial mixing of a "frontier of inclusion." Fort Vancouver housed a polyglot population of eastern Indians (Delawares and Iroquois), local Chinook Indians, French and métis from Canada, British traders, and Hawaiians. But the effect of the fur trade on native tribes in Oregon was catastrophic; suffering the fate of all Indian peoples after their initial contact with Europeans, they were decimated by European diseases.

Discovered by British Captain James Cook in 1778, Hawaii was visited by the first American ship in 1790. The island kingdom quickly became a favorite stop for American and British traders in sea otter furs destined for China and later for New England whaling ships. Hawaiian men, famous for their sailing skills, often joined the crews of American and British ships and served, as at Fort Vancouver, as workers in the fur trade.

The first permanent European settlers in Oregon were retired fur trappers and their Indian wives and families. They favored a spot in the lush and temperate Willamette Valley that became known as French Prairie, although the inhabitants were a mixed group of Americans, British, French Canadians, Indian peoples, and métis. The next to arrive were Protestant and Catholic missionaries, among them Methodist Jason Lee in 1834, Congregationalists Marcus and Narcissa Whitman in 1837, Franciscan priests Frances Blanchet

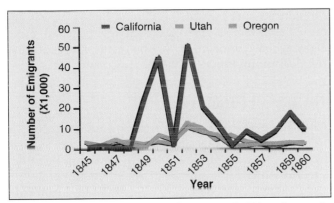

Overland Emigration to Oregon, California, and Utah, 1840–1860 Before 1849 the westward migration consisted primarily of family groups going to Oregon or Utah. The discovery of gold in California dramatically changed the migration: through 1854 most migrants were single men "rushing" to California, which remained the favored destination up until 1860. Over the twenty-year period from 1840 to 1860 the Overland Trails were transformed from difficult and dangerous routes to well-marked and well-served thoroughfares.

SOURCE: John Unruh Jr., *The Plains Across* (Champaign-Urbana: University of Illinois Press, 1979), pp. 119–20.

and Modeste Demers in 1838, and Jesuit Pierre-Jean De Smet in 1840. None of these missionaries was very successful. Epidemics had taken the lives of many of the region's peoples, and those who were left were disinclined to give up their nomadic life and settle down as the missionaries wanted them to do.

Finally, in the 1840s, came the Midwest farmers who would make up the majority of Oregon's permanent settlers, carried on the wave of enthusiasm known as "Oregon fever" and lured by free land and patriotism. By 1845 Oregon boasted 5,000 American settlers, most of them living in the Willamette Valley and laying claim to lands to which they had as yet no legal right because neither Britain nor the United States had concluded land treaties with Oregon's Indian peoples. Their arrival signaled Oregon's shift from a "frontier of inclusion" to a "frontier of exclusion."

For these early settlers, life was at first very difficult. Most arrived in late autumn, exhausted from the strenuous overland journey. They could not begin to farm until the spring, and so they depended on the earlier settlers for their survival over the winter. In the earliest years American settlers got vital help from the Hudson's Bay Company, even though its director, John McLoughlin, had been ordered by the British government not to encourage American settlement. McLoughlin disregarded his orders, motivated both by sympathy for the plight of the newcomers and by a keen sense of the dangers his enterprise would face if he were outnumbered by angry Americans.

The handful of American settlers in Oregon found themselves in possession of a remote frontier. One of the first things they did was to draw up their own constitution. When the first Oregon settlers (including a number of former mountain men) met in the summer of 1843 to draft a constitution, they prohibited African Americans (both free and enslaved) from settling in the territory. By avoiding the divisive issue of slavery, they

This watercolor of tiny Oregon City in 1846 suggests how small the American population of the Oregon Territory was when its status was being decided in America's favor. With just 953 inhabitants in 1850, Oregon City was the largest city in the territory.

SOURCE: Henry James Warre, *American Settlement of Oregon City, 1846.* Watercolor. Courtesy American Antiquarian Society (#33).

hoped to build community feeling between white settlers from the North and the South. In spite of the law, some Southerners did bring their slaves to Oregon with them, but when an early free African American pioneer, George Bush, came to Oregon, he deliberately settled north of the Columbia River, in what later became Washington Territory. Thus, Oregon got African American slaves that it did not want and lost a free man, who became renowned for his willingness to cooperate with others and his community spirit.

The influx of American settlers and their efforts to establish their own government created strains between the United States and Britain. In 1845, President James K. Polk, who was deeply anti-British, coined the belligerent slogan "Fifty-four Forty or Fight," suggesting that the United States would go to war if it didn't get control of all the territory south of 54°40′ north latitude, the border between Russian Alaska and British Canada. In office, however, Polk was willing to compromise. In June 1846, Britain and the United States concluded a treaty establishing the 49th parallel as the U.S.–Canada border but leaving the island of Vancouver in British hands. The British then quietly wound up their declining fur trade in the region. In 1849 the Hudson's Bay Company closed Fort Vancouver and moved its operations to Victoria, thus ending the Pacific Northwest's largely successful experience with joint occupancy. Oregon's Donation Land Claim Act of 1850 codified the practice of giving 320 acres to each white male age eighteen or over and 640 acres to each married couple to settle in the territory (African Americans, Hawaiians, and American Indians were excluded).

The white settlers realized that they had to forge strong community bonds if they hoped to survive on their distant frontier. Cooperation and mutual aid were the rule. Until well into the 1850s, residents organized yearly parties that traveled back along the last stretches of the Oregon Trail to help straggling parties making their way to the territory. Kinship networks were strong and vital: many pioneers came to join family who had migrated before them. Although most settlers lived on their own land claims rather than in towns, neighborly cooperation was crucial. Food sharing and mutual labor were essential in the early years, when crop and livestock loss to weather or natural predators was common. Help, even to total strangers, was customary in times of illness or death.

Although this community feeling did not extend to Indian groups as a whole, relations with the small and unthreatening disease-thinned local Indian tribes were generally peaceful until 1847, when Cayuse Indians killed the missionaries Marcus and Narcissa Whitman. Their deaths triggered a series of "wars" against the remaining native people. A "frontier of exclusion" had been achieved. Nonetheless the process by which

Oregon became part of the United States (it was admitted as a state in 1859) was relatively peaceful, especially when compared with American expansion into the Spanish provinces of New Mexico and Texas.

The Santa Fé Trade

Commerce with Santa Fé, first settled by colonists from Mexico in 1609 and the center of the Spanish frontier province of New Mexico, had long been desired by American traders. But Spain had forcefully resisted American penetration. For example, Lieutenant Zebulon Pike's Great Plains and Rocky Mountain exploration of 1806–07 ended ignominiously with his capture by Spanish soldiers.

When Mexico gained its independence from Spain in 1821, this exclusionary policy changed. American traders were now welcome in Santa Fé, but the trip over the legendary Santa Fé Trail from Independence, Missouri, was a forbidding 900 miles of arid plains, deserts, and mountains. On the Santa Fé trail, unlike the Oregon Trail, there was serious danger of Indian attack, for neither the Comanches nor the Apaches of the southern high plains tolerated trespassers. In 1825, at the urging of Senator Benton and others, Congress voted federal protection for the Santa Fé Trail, even though much of it lay in Mexican territory. The number of people venturing west in the trading caravans increased yearly because the profits were so great (the first American trader to reach Santa Fé, William Becknell, realized a thousand percent profit). By the 1840s, a few hundred American trappers and traders (called *extranjeros*, or "foreigners") lived permanently in New Mexico. In Santa Fé, some American merchants married daughters of important local families, suggesting the start of the inclusive stage of frontier contact.

Settlements and trading posts soon grew up along the long Santa Fé Trail. One of the most famous was Bent's Fort, on the Arkansas River in what is now eastern Colorado, which did a brisk trade in beaver skins and buffalo robes. Like most trading posts, it had a multiethnic population. In the 1840s the occupants included housekeeper Josefa Tafoya of Taos, whose husband was a carpenter from Pennsylvania; an African American cook; a French tailor from New Orleans; Mexican muleteers; and a number of Indian women, including the two Cheyenne women who were the (successive) wives of William Bent, cofounder of the fort. The three small communities of Pueblo, Hardscrabble, and Greenhorn, spinoffs of Bent's Fort, were populated by men of all nationalities and their Mexican and Indian wives. All three communities lived by trapping, hunting, and a little farming. This racially and economically mixed existence was characteristic of all

Alfred Jacob Miller painted the busy life of Fort Laramie, a multiracial trading fort, in 1837. Bent's Fort, another multiracial trading center, would have looked much like this.

SOURCE: *The Interior of Fort Laramie*, 1858–1860. The Walters Art Museum, Baltimore (37.1940.1).

early trading frontiers, but another western frontier, the American agricultural settlement in Texas, was different from the start.

Mexican Texas

In 1821, when Mexico gained its independence from Spain, there were 2,240 Tejano (Spanish-speaking) residents of Texas. Established in 1716 as a buffer against possible French attack on New Spain, the main Texas settlements of Nacogdoches, Goliad, and San Antonio remained small, far-flung frontier outposts (see Chapter 5). As was customary throughout New Spain, communities were organized around three centers: missions and *presidios* (forts), which formed the nucleus of towns, and the large cattle-raising ranchos on which rural living depended. As elsewhere in New Spain, society was divided into two classes: the *ricos* (rich), who claimed Spanish descent, and the mixed-blood *pobres* (poor). Tejano town life was traditionally hierarchical, dominated by the ricos, who were connected by blood or marriage with the great ranching families. The most colorful figures on the ranchos were *mestizo* (mixed-blood) *vaqueros*, renowned for their horsemanship; Americanization of their name made "buckaroos" of the American cowboys to whom they later taught their

skills. Most Tejanos were neither ricos nor vaqueros but small farmers or common laborers who led hardscrabble frontier lives. But all Tejanos, rich and poor, faced the constant threat of raids by Comanche Indians.

The Comanches exemplified the revolutionary changes brought about in the lives of Plains Indians by the reintroduction of horses into the American continent (see Chapter 5). "A Comanche on his feet is out of his element . . . but the moment he lays his hands upon his horse," said artist George Catlin, "I doubt very much whether any people in the world can surpass [him]." Legendary warriors, the Comanches raided the small Texas settlements at will and even struck deep into Mexico itself. Once they raided so far south that they saw brightly plumed birds (parrots) and "tiny men with tails" (monkeys); apparently they had reached the tropical Yucatán. The nomadic Comanches followed the immense buffalo herds on which they depended for food and clothing. Their relentless raids on the Texas settlements rose from a determination to hold onto this rich buffalo territory, for the buffalo provided all that they wanted. They had no interest in being converted by mission priests or incorporated into mixed-race trading communities.

Americans in Texas

In 1821, seeking to increase the strength of its buffer zone between the heart of Mexico and the marauding Comanches, the Mexican government granted Moses Austin of Missouri an area of 18,000 square miles within the territory of Texas. Moses died shortly thereafter, and the grant was taken up by his son Stephen F. Austin, who became the first American *empresario* (land agent). From the beginning, the American settlement of Texas differed markedly from that of other frontiers. Elsewhere, Americans frequently settled on land to which Indian peoples still held title, or, as in the case of Oregon, they occupied lands to which other countries also made claim. In contrast, the Texas settlement was fully legal: Austin and other empresarios owned their lands as a result of formal contracts with the Mexican government. In exchange, Austin agreed that he and his colonists would become Mexican citizens and would adopt the Catholic religion. It is difficult to say which of these two provisions was the more remarkable, for most nineteenth-century Americans defined their Americanness in terms of citizenship and the Protestant religion.

Additionally, in startling contrast with the usual frontier free-for-all, Austin's community was populated with handpicked settlers, Austin insisting that "no frontiersman who has no other occupation than that of hunter will be received—no drunkard, no gambler, no profane swearer, no idler." Austin chose instead prosperous southern slaveowners eager to expand the lands devoted to cotton. Soon Americans (including African American slaves, to whose presence the Mexican government turned a blind eye) outnumbered Tejanos by nearly two to one: in 1830 there were an estimated 7,000 Americans and 4,000 Tejanos living in Texas.

The Austin settlement of 1821 was followed by others, twenty-six in all, concentrating in the fertile river bottoms of east Texas (along the Sabine River) and south central Texas (the Brazos and the Colorado rivers). These large settlements were highly organized farming enterprises whose principal crop was cotton, grown by African American slave labor and sold in the international market. By the early 1830s, Americans in Texas, ignoring the border between Mexican Texas and the United States, were sending an estimated $500,000 worth of goods (mostly cotton) yearly to New Orleans for export.

Austin's colonists and those who settled later were predominantly Southerners who viewed Texas as a nat-

ural extension of the cotton frontier in Mississippi and Louisiana (see Chapter 11). These settlers created "enclaves" (self-contained communities) that had little contact with Tejanos or Indian peoples. In fact, although they lived in Mexican territory, most Americans never bothered to learn Spanish. Nor, in spite of Austin's promises, did they become Mexican citizens or adopt the Catholic religion. Yet because of the nature of agreements made by the empresarios, the Americans could not set up local American-style governments like the one created by settlers in Oregon. Like the immigrants who flooded into east coast cities (see Chapter 13) the Americans in Texas were immigrants to another country—but one they did not intend to adapt to.

The one exception to American exclusiveness occurred in San Antonio, the provincial government center. There, just as in Santa Fé, a handful of wealthy Americans married into the Tejano elite with ease. One such marriage in San Antonio linked wealthy Louisianan James Bowie, the legendary fighter for whom the Bowie knife is named, and Ursula Veramendi, daughter of the vice governor of Texas. With the marriage, Bowie became a wealthy, honored, and well-connected Mexican merchant. Only after the death of his wife and children in a cholera epidemic in 1833 did Bowie support the cause of Anglo-Texan independence, going on to fight—and die—at the Alamo.

The great ranchos excited the admiration of many Americans, who later made cattle raising a major western industry. In these early days in Texas, Americans watched and learned as Tejanos rounded up range cattle, branded them, and drove more than 20,000 each year to Nacogdoches for the U.S. market. Praise for Tejano horsemanship was unstinting: they are "not surpassed perhaps by any other people in the Globe," enthused one American immigrant. Tejano customs, especially multiday celebrations that mixed religious ceremonies, feasting, horse racing, and elaborate *fandangos* (dances), offered striking evidence of the richly textured community life created by Tejanos of all social classes.

For a brief period Texas was big enough to hold three communities: Comanche, Tejano, and American. The nomadic Comanches rode the high plains of northern and western Texas, raiding settlements, primarily for

Painted by George Catlin about 1834, this scene, *Comanche Village Life,* shows how the everyday life of the Comanches was tied to buffalo. The women in the foreground are scraping buffalo hide, and buffalo meat can be seen drying on racks. The men and boys may be planning their next buffalo hunt.

SOURCE: Art Resource, N.Y.

horses. The Tejanos maintained their ranchos and missions mostly in the South, while American farmers occupied the eastern and south central sections. Each group would fight to hold its land: the Comanches, their rich hunting grounds; the Mexicans, their towns and ranchos; and the newcomers, the Americans, their rich land grants.

The Texas Revolt

The balance between the three communities in Texas was broken in 1828, when centrists gained control of the government in Mexico City and, in a dramatic shift of policy, decided to exercise firm control over the northern province. As the Mexican government restricted American immigration, outlawed slavery, levied customs duties and taxes, and planned other measures, Americans seethed and talked of rebellion. Bolstering their cause were as many as 20,000 additional Americans, many of them openly expansionist, who flooded into Texas after 1830. These most recent settlers did not intend to become Mexican citizens. Instead, they planned to take over Texas. What ensued was reminiscent of the American Revolution, at least in the eyes of some Americans. But for all the invocations of the Revolution, the real issue in Texas was conquest.

Whereas many of the older American settlers in Texas found much that was admirable, or at least understandable, in Spanish-Mexican culture, many of the post-1830 immigrants were vehemently anti-Mexican. Many had grievances: failure to obtain a land grant, restrictions on trade because of Mexican customs regulations, difficulties in understanding Hispanic law, which differed markedly from the Anglo-American legal tradition. Above all, in the eyes of many Americans, there was the matter of race. Statements of racial superiority were commonplace, and even Stephen Austin wrote in 1836 that he saw the Texas conflict as one of barbarism on the part of "a mongrel Spanish-Indian and negro race, against civilization and the Anglo-American race." Most recent American migrants to Texas had come from the South, and racist statements of this sort made political compromise with the Mexican government, a step favored by many of the older American settlers, impossible.

Between 1830 and 1836, in spite of the mediation efforts of Austin (who was imprisoned for eighteen months by the Mexican government for his pains), the mood on both the Mexican and the American-Texan sides became more belligerent. In the fall of 1835 war finally broke out, and a volunteer American Texan and Tejano army seized Goliad and San Antonio, in the heart of Mexican Texas, from the small Mexican army that was sent to quell them. Believing they had won, the Americans were caught off guard by a major

counterattack led by the Mexican general and president Antonio López de Santa Anna. As described in the opening of this chapter, on March 6, 1836, Santa Anna and his forces overwhelmed the 187 men who refused to surrender—or to escape from—the Alamo, a mission building, in San Antonio. At Santa Anna's orders, the women at the Alamo—one American woman and several Tejanas—and an African American slave named Joe were spared so that Texans could hear their eyewitness accounts. From those accounts the legend of the Alamo was born.

From San Antonio, Santa Anna divided his army and led part of it in pursuit of the remaining army of American and Tejano volunteers commanded by General Sam Houston. On April 21, 1836, at the San Jacinto River in eastern Texas, Santa Anna thought he had Houston trapped at last. Confident of victory against the exhausted Texans, Santa Anna's army rested in the afternoon, failing even to post sentries. Although Houston advised against it, Houston's men voted to attack immediately rather than wait till the next morning. Shouting "Remember the Alamo!" for the first time, the Texans completely surprised their opponents and won an overwhelming victory. On May 14, 1836, Santa Anna signed a treaty fixing the southern boundary of the newly independent Republic of Texas at the Rio Grande. The Mexican Congress, however, repudiated the treaty and refused to recognize Texan independence. It also rejected the offer by President Andrew Jackson to solve the matter through purchase.

The Republic of Texas

Despite the military triumph of the Americans who had proclaimed the Republic of Texas, the land between the Rio Grande and the Nueces River remained disputed territory. In the eyes of the Mexicans, the American insistence on the Rio Grande boundary was little more than a blatant effort to stake a claim to New Mexico, an older and completely separate Spanish settlement. An effort by the Republic of Texas in 1841 to capture Santa Fé was easily repulsed.

The Republic of Texas was unexpectedly rebuffed in another quarter as well. The U.S. Congress refused to grant it statehood when, in 1837, Texas applied for admission to the Union. Petitions opposing the admission of a fourteenth slave state (there were then thirteen free states) poured into Congress. Congressman (and former president) John Quincy Adams of Massachusetts led the opposition to the admission of Texas. Congress debated and ultimately dropped the Texas application. Although President Jackson was sympathetic to the Texan cause, he knew that he did not have the power to quell the controversy that the admission of Texas would arouse. But he did manage to extend diplomatic recognition to

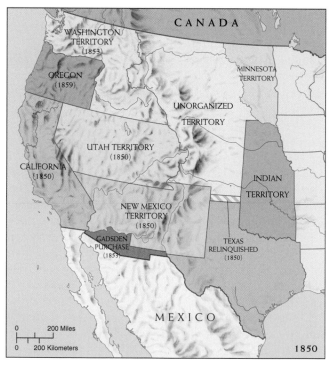

Texas: From Mexican Province to U.S. State

In the space of twenty years, Texas changed shape three times. Initially part of the Mexican province of Coahuila y Tejas, it became the Republic of Texas in 1836, following the Texas Revolt, and was annexed to the United States in that form in 1845. Finally, in the Compromise of 1850 following the Mexican-American War, it took its present shape.

the Republic of Texas, on March 3, 1837, less than twenty-four hours before he left office. Breaking the good news to Texas agents at the White House, Jackson offered toasts to the Republic of Texas and to its president, his old friend Sam Houston.

Sam Houston must often have wondered whether the presidency of the Republic of Texas was an honor worth having. The unresolved conflict with Mexico put heavy stress on American-Tejano relations. Immediately after the revolt, many Tejano residents fled to Mexico, and American squatters moved in to claim their lands. In some regions, vigilantes forced Tejanos to leave. San Antonio, however, the most important city of Mexican Texas, saw an accommodation between the old elite and the new American authorities. Although they slowly lost political power, members of the Tejano elite were not immediately dispossessed of their property. As before, ambitious Anglos married into the Tejano elite. The intermarriages made it easier for the Tejano elite to adjust to the changes in law and commerce that the Americans quickly enacted. But following a temporary recapture of San Antonio by Mexican forces in 1842, positions hardened. Many more of the Tejano elite fled to Mexico, and Americans discussed banishing or imprisoning all Tejanos until the border issue was settled. This was, of course, impossible. Culturally, San Antonio remained a Mexican city long after the Americans had declared independence. The Americans in the Republic of Texas were struggling to reconcile American ideals of democracy with the reality of subordinating those with a prior claim, the Tejanos, to the status of a conquered people.

Ethnocentric attitudes quickly triumphed. Tejanos and other Mexicans were soon being blamed by Americans for their own subordination. Senator Edward Hannegan of Indiana was one of the most outspoken: "Mexico and the United States are peopled by two distinct and utterly unhomogeneous races," he announced in 1847. "In no reasonable period could we amalgamate." In the same year, the *Democratic Review*, completely ignoring the Spanish discovery and conquest of the Americas, offered the following rationalization: "Had Mexico been settled by a vigorous race of Europeans . . . that would have turned its advantages to account, developed its wealth, increased its commerce and multiplied its settlements, she would not now be in danger of losing her lands by emigration from the North."

American control over the other Texas residents, the Indians, was also slow in coming. Although the coastal Indian peoples were soon killed or removed, the Comanches still rode the high plains of northern and western Texas. West of the Rio Grande, equally fierce Apache bands were in control. Both groups soon learned to distrust American promises to stay out of their territory, and they did not hesitate to raid settlements and to kill trespassers. Not until after the Civil War and major campaigns by the U.S. Army were these fierce Indian tribes conquered.

Texas Annexation and the Election of 1844

Martin Van Buren, who succeeded Andrew Jackson as president in 1837, was too cautious to raise the Texas issue during his term of office. But Texans themselves continued to press for annexation to the United States, while at the same time seeking recognition and support from Great Britain. The idea of an independent and expansionist republic on its southern border that might gain the support of America's traditional enemy alarmed many Americans. Annexation thus became an urgent matter of national politics. This issue also added to the troubles of a governing Whig Party that was already deeply divided by the policies of John Tyler, who had become president by default when William Harrison died in office (see Chapter 10). Tyler raised the issue of annexation in 1844, hoping thereby to ensure his reelection, but the strategy backfired. Presenting the annexation treaty to Congress, Secretary of State John Calhoun awakened sectional fears by connecting Texas with the urgent need of southern slave owners to extend slavery.

In a storm of antislavery protest, Whigs rejected the treaty proposed by their own president and ejected Tyler himself from the party. In his place, they chose Henry Clay, the party's longtime standard-bearer, as their presidential candidate. Clay took a noncommittal stance on Texas, favoring annexation, but only if Mexico approved. Since Mexico's emphatic disapproval was well known, Clay's position was widely interpreted as a politician's effort not to alienate voters on either side of the fence.

In contrast, in the Democratic Party wholehearted and outspoken expansionists seized control. Sweeping aside their own senior politician, Van Buren, who like Clay tried to remain uncommitted, the Democrats nominated their first "dark horse" candidate, James K. Polk of Tennessee. Southerners and Westerners among the Democrats—including such notables as Robert Walker of Mississippi, Stephen Douglas of Illinois, and Lewis Cass of Michigan—beat the drum of manifest destiny, promising that expansion meant a glorious extension of democracy. They enthusiastically endorsed Polk's platform, which called for "the re-occupation of Oregon and the re-annexation of Texas at the earliest practicable period."

Polk won the 1844 election by the narrow margin of 40,000 popular votes (although he gained 170 electoral votes to Clay's 105). An ominous portent for the Whigs was the showing of James G. Birney of the Liberty Party, who polled 62,000 votes, largely from northern antislavery Whigs. Birney's third-party campaign was the first political sign of the growing strength of antislavery opinion. Nevertheless, the 1844 election was widely interpreted as a mandate for expansion. Thereupon John Tyler, in one of his last actions as president, pushed through Congress a joint resolution (which did not require the two-thirds approval by the Senate necessary for treaties) for the annexation of Texas. Three months later the Texas congress approved annexation, and thus nine years after its founding the Republic of Texas disappeared. Florida had just been approved for statehood as well, and when Texas entered the Union in December 1845 it was the twenty-eighth state and the fifteenth slave state.

WebExploration   Consider the strategies of each side in the Mexican–American War. Why was the United States more successful than Mexico in achieving its goals?
www.prenhall.com/faragher/map14.2

The Mexican-American War, 1846–1848   The Mexican-American War began with an advance by U.S. forces into the disputed area between the Nueces River and the Rio Grande in Texas. The war's major battles were fought by General Zachary Taylor in northern Mexico and General Winfield Scott in Vera Cruz and Mexico City. Meanwhile Colonel Stephen Kearny secured New Mexico and, with the help of the U.S. Navy and John C. Frémont's troops, California.

THE MEXICAN–AMERICAN WAR

James K. Polk lived up to his campaign promises. In 1846 he peacefully added Oregon south of the 49th parallel to the United States; in 1848, following the Mexican-American War, he acquired Mexico's northern provinces of California and New Mexico as well. Thus, with the annexation of Texas, the United States, in the short space of three years, had added 1.5 million square miles of territory, an increase of nearly 70 percent. Polk was indeed the "manifest destiny" president.

Origins of the War

In the spring of 1846, just as the controversy over Oregon was drawing to a peaceful conclusion, tensions with Mexico grew more serious. As soon as Texas was granted statehood in 1845, the Mexican government broke diplomatic relations with the United States. In addition, because the United States accepted the Texas claim of all land north of the Rio Grande, it found itself embroiled in a border dispute with Mexico. In June 1845, Polk sent General Zachary Taylor to Texas, and by October a force of 3,500 Americans were on the Nueces River with orders to defend Texas in the event of a Mexican invasion.

Polk had something bigger than border protection in mind. He coveted the continent clear to the Pacific Ocean. At the same time that he sent Taylor to Texas, Polk secretly instructed the Pacific naval squadron to seize the California ports if Mexico declared war. He also wrote the American consul in Monterey, Thomas Larkin, that a peaceful takeover of California by its residents—Spanish Mexicans and Americans alike—would not be unwelcome. When, in addition, the federally commissioned explorer John C. Frémont and a band of armed men appeared in California in the winter of 1845–46, Mexican authorities became alarmed and ordered him to leave. After withdrawing briefly to Oregon, Frémont returned to California and was on hand in Sonoma in June to assist in the Bear Flag Revolt, in which a handful of American settlers, declaring that they were playing "the Texas game," announced California's independence from Mexico.

Meanwhile, in November 1845, Polk followed up his warlike gestures by sending a secret envoy, John Slidell, to Mexico with an offer of $30 million or more for the Rio Grande border in Texas and Mexico's provinces of New Mexico and California. When the Mexican government refused even to receive Slidell, an angry Polk ordered General Taylor and his forces south to the Rio Grande, into the territory that Mexicans considered their soil. In April 1846 a brief skirmish between American and Mexican soldiers broke out in the disputed zone. Polk seized on the event, sending a war message to Congress: "Mexico has passed the boundary of the United States, has invaded our territory and shed American blood upon American soil. . . . War exists, and, notwithstanding all our efforts to avoid it, exists by the act of Mexico herself." This last claim of President Polk's was, of course, contrary to fact. On May 13, 1846, Congress declared war on Mexico.

Mr. Polk's War

From the beginning, the Mexican-American War was politically divisive. Whig critics in Congress, among them a gawky young congressman from Illinois named Abraham Lincoln, questioned Polk's account of the border incident. They accused the president of misleading Congress and of maneuvering the country into an unnecessary war. It is with these suspicions that the history of congressional concern over the way presidents have exercised their war powers begins. The issue would again be prominent, for example, more than a hundred years later during the Vietnam War and in the Reagan years. As the Mexican-American War dragged on and casualties and costs mounted—13,000 Americans and 50,000 Mexicans died and the United States spent $97 million—opposition increased, especially among northern antislavery Whigs. More and more people came to the opinion that the war was nothing more than a plot by Southerners to expand slavery. Many Northerners asked why Polk had been willing to settle for only a part of Oregon but was so eager to pursue a war for slave territory. Thus expansionist dreams served to fuel sectional antagonisms.

The northern states witnessed both mass and individual protests against the war. In Massachusetts, the legislature passed a resolution condemning Polk's declaration of war as unconstitutional, and philosopher-writer Henry David Thoreau went to jail rather than pay the taxes he believed would support the war effort. Thoreau's dramatic gesture was undercut by his aunt, who paid his fine after he had spent only one night in jail. Thoreau then returned to his cabin on Walden Pond, where he wrote his classic essay "Civil Disobedience," justifying the individual's moral right to oppose an immoral government. In the early twentieth century, the Indian nationalist

General Winfield Scott's amphibious attack on the Mexican coastal city of Vera Cruz in March 1847 was a considerable military feat that was greeted with wide popular acclaim in the United States. Popular interest in the battles of the Mexican-American War was fed by illustrations such as this in newspapers and magazines.

SOURCE: Nathaniel Currier, *General Winfield Scott at the Siege of Vera Cruz, March 1847*. Lithograph. The Granger Collection (4GCR 295).

Mohandas Gandhi used Thoreau's essay to justify his campaign of "passive resistance" against British imperial rule in India. In turn, Martin Luther King and others used Gandhi's model of civil disobedience as a basis for their activities in the American civil rights movement of the 1950s and 1960s.

Whigs termed the war with Mexico "Mr. Polk's War," but the charge was not just a Whig jibe. Although he lacked a military background, Polk assumed the overall planning of the war's strategy (a practice that the critical Mr. Lincoln was to follow in the Civil War). By his personal attention to the coordination of civilian political goals and military requirements, Polk gave a new and expanded definition to the role of the president as commander-in-chief during wartime. In 1846 Polk sent General Taylor south into northeastern Mexico and Colonel Stephen Kearny to New Mexico and California. Taylor captured the northern Mexico cities of Palo Alto in May and Monterrey in September 1846. Meanwhile, Kearny marched his men 900 miles to Santa Fé, which surrendered peacefully. Another march of roughly the same distance brought him by fall to southern California, which he took with the help of naval forces and Frémont's irregular troops.

The northern provinces that Polk had coveted were now secured, but contrary to his expectations, Mexico refused to negotiate. In February 1847, General Santa Anna of Alamo fame attacked the American troops led by General Taylor at Buena Vista, but was repulsed by Taylor's small force. A month later, in March 1847, General Winfield Scott launched an amphibious attack on the coastal city of Veracruz and rapidly captured it. Americans celebrated these twin victories joyously, but they were to be the last easy victories of the war. It took Scott six months of brutal fighting against stubborn Mexican resistance on the battlefield and harassing guerrilla raids to force his way to Mexico City. American troops reacted bitterly to their high casualty rates, retaliating against Mexican citizens with acts of murder, robbery, and rape. Even General Scott himself admitted that his troops had "committed atrocities to make Heaven weep and every American of Christian morals blush for his country." In September Scott took Mexico City, and Mexican resistance came to an end.

With the American army went a special envoy, Nicholas Trist, who delivered Polk's terms for peace. In the Treaty of Guadalupe Hidalgo, signed February 2, 1848, Mexico ceded its northern provinces of California and New Mexico (which included present-day Arizona, Utah, Nevada, and part of Colorado) and accepted the Rio Grande as the boundary of Texas. The United States agreed to pay Mexico $15 million and assume about $2 million in individual claims against that nation.

When Trist returned to Washington with the treaty, however, Polk was furious. He had actually recalled Trist after Scott's sweeping victory, intending to send a new envoy with greater demands, but Trist had ignored the recall order. "All Mexico!" had become the phrase widely used by those in favor of further expansion, Polk among them. But two very different groups opposed further expansion. The first group, composed of northern Whigs, included such notables as Ralph Waldo Emerson, who grimly warned, "The United States will conquer Mexico, but it will be as the man swallows arsenic, which brings him down in turn. Mexico will poison us." The second group was composed of Southerners who realized that Mexicans could not be kept as conquered people but would have to be offered territorial government as Louisiana had been offered in 1804. Senator John C. Calhoun of South Carolina, leading the opposition, warned against admitting "colored and mixed-breed" Mexicans "on an equality with people of the United States." "We make a great mistake, sir," he argued on the floor of the Senate, "when we suppose that all people are capable of self-government." Bowing to these political protests, Polk reluctantly accepted the treaty. A later addition, the $10 million Gadsden Purchase of parts of present-day New Mexico and Arizona,

Territory Added, 1845–1853 James K. Polk was elected president in 1844 on an expansionist platform. He lived up to most of his campaign rhetoric by gaining the Oregon Country (to the forty-ninth parallel) peacefully from the British, Texas by the presidential action of his predecessor John Tyler, and present-day California, Arizona, Nevada, Utah, New Mexico, and part of Colorado by war with Mexico. In the short space of three years, the size of the United States grew by 70 percent. In 1853, the Gadsden Purchase added another 30,000 square miles.

added another 30,000 square miles to the United States in 1853. This purchase, made to facilitate a southern transcontinental railroad route through arid borderland, was a far cry from the rich heartland of Mexico that Polk had hoped to annex.

The Press and Popular War Enthusiasm

The Mexican-American War was the first war in which regular, on-the-scene reporting by representatives of the press caught the mass of ordinary citizens up in the war's daily events. Thanks to the recently invented telegraph, newspapers could get the latest news from their reporters, who were among the world's first war correspondents. The "penny press," with more than a decade's experience of reporting urban crime and scandals, was quick to realize that the public's appetite for sensational war news was apparently insatiable. For the first time in American history, accounts by journalists, and not the opinions of politicians, became the major shapers of popular attitudes toward a war. From beginning to end, news of the war stirred unprecedented popular excitement.

The reports from the battlefield united Americans in a new way: they became part of a temporary but highly emotional community linked by newsprint and

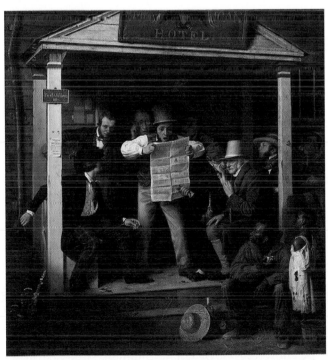

The unprecedented immediacy of the news reporting of the Mexican-American War, transmitted for the first time by telegraph, is captured here by Richard Caton Woodville in *War News from Mexico* (1848). By including an African American man and child, the artist is also voicing a political concern about the effect of the war on slavery.

SOURCE: Richard Caton Woodville, *War News from Mexico*, oil on canvas. Manovgian Foundation on loan to the National Gallery of Art, Washington, DC.

buttressed by public gatherings. In the spring of 1846, news of Zachary Taylor's victory at Palo Alto prompted the largest meeting ever held in the cotton textile town of Lowell, Massachusetts. In May 1847, New York City celebrated the twin victories at Veracruz and Buena Vista with fireworks, illuminations, and a "grand procession" estimated at 400,000 people. Generals Taylor and Scott became overnight heroes, and in time both became presidential candidates. Exciting, sobering, and terrible, war news had a deep hold on the popular imagination. It was a lesson newspaper publishers never forgot.

CALIFORNIA AND THE GOLD RUSH

In the early 1840s California was inhabited by many seminomadic Indian tribes whose people numbered approximately 50,000. There were also some 7,000 *Californios*, descendants of the Spanish Mexican pioneers who had begun to settle in 1769. The American presence in California at first consisted of a few traders and settlers who often intermarried with Californios. Even American annexation at the end of the Mexican-American War changed little for the handful of Americans on this remote frontier. But then came the Gold Rush of 1849, which changed California permanently.

Russian-Californio Trade

The first outsiders to penetrate the isolation of Spanish California were not Americans but Russians. Because the distance between California and Mexico City was so great, the Spanish had found it difficult to maintain the elaborate system of twenty-one missions first established in the eighteenth century (see Chapter 5). Nevertheless, Spanish officials in Mexico insisted on isolation, forbidding the colonists to trade with other nations. Evading Spanish regulations, Californios conducted a small illegal trade in cattle hides with American merchant ships (for the shoes made in the workshops of Massachusetts), and a much larger trade with the Russian American Fur Company in Sitka, Alaska. A mutually beneficial barter of California food for iron tools and woven cloth from Russia was established in 1806. This arrangement became even brisker after the Russians settled Fort Ross (near present-day Mendocino) in 1812, and led in time to regular trade with Mission San Rafael and Mission Sonoma. That the Russians in Alaska, so far from their own capital, were better supplied with manufactured goods than the Californios is an index of the latter's isolation.

When Mexico became independent in 1821, the California trade was thrown open to ships of all nations. Nevertheless, Californios continued their special relationship with the Russians, exempting them from the taxes and inspections that they required of Americans. However, agricultural productivity declined after 1832, when the Mexican government ordered the secularization of the California missions, and the Russians regretfully turned to the rich farms of the Hudson's Bay Company in the Pacific Northwest for their food supply. In 1841, they sold Fort Ross, and the Russian-Californio connection came to an end.

Early American Settlement

It was Johann Augustus Sutter, a Swiss who had settled in California in 1839, becoming a Mexican citizen, who served as a focal point for American settlement in the 1840s. Sutter held a magnificent land grant in the Sacramento Valley. At the center of his holdings was Sutter's Fort, a walled compound that was part living quarters and part supply shop for his vast cattle ranch, which was run largely on forced Indian labor. In the 1840s, Sutter offered valuable support to the handful of American overlanders who chose California over Oregon, the destination preferred by most pioneers. Most of these Americans, keenly aware that they were interlopers in Mexican territory, settled near Sutter in California's Central Valley, away from the Californios clustered along the coast.

The 1840s immigrants made no effort to intermarry with the Californios or to conform to Spanish ways. They were bent on taking over the territory. In June 1846 these Americans banded together at Sonoma in the Bear Flag Revolt (so called because their flag bore a bear emblem), declaring independence from Mexico. The American takeover of California was not confirmed until the Treaty of Guadalupe Hidalgo in 1848. In the meantime, California was regarded by most Americans merely as a remote, sparsely populated frontier, albeit one with splendid potential. Polk and other expansionists coveted the magnificent harbors in San Diego and San Francisco as the basis for Pacific trade with Asia, but in 1848 this prospect was still only a dream.

Gold!

In January 1848 carpenter James Marshall noticed small flakes of gold in the millrace at Sutter's Mill (present-day Coloma). Soon he and all the rest of John Sutter's employees were panning for gold in California's streams. The news, which they had hoped to keep secret, spread, and before long it seemed that all the men in California were at the mines. When explorer John Frémont returned to San Francisco in June 1848, he found it almost deserted because of the "gold fever."

In the autumn of 1848, the east coast heard the first rumors about the discovery of gold in California. The reports were confirmed in mid-November when an

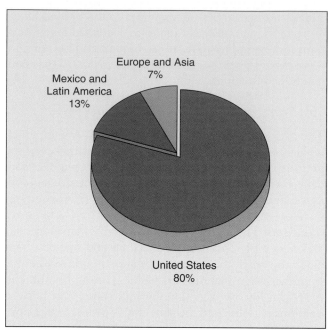

Where the Forty-Niners Came From   Americans drawn to the California Gold Rush of 1849 encountered a more diverse population than most had previously known. Nearly as novel to them as the 20 percent from foreign countries was the regional variety from within the United States itself.

army courier arrived in Washington carrying a tea caddy full of gold dust and nuggets. The spirit of excitement and adventure so recently aroused by the Mexican-American War was now directed toward California, the new El Dorado. Thousands left farms and jobs and headed west, by land and by sea, to make their fortune. Later known as "forty-niners" for the year the gold rush began in earnest, these people came from all parts of the United States—and indeed, from all over the world. They transformed what had been a quiet ranching paradise into a teeming and tumultuous community in search of wealth in California's rivers and streams.

Eighty percent of the forty-niners were Americans. They came from every state. The Gold Rush was an eye-opening expansion of their horizons for the many who had known only their hometown folks before. The second largest group of migrants were from nearby Mexico and the west coast of Latin America (13 percent). The remainder came from Europe and Asia.

The presence of Chinese miners surprised many Americans. Several hundred Chinese arrived in California in 1849 and 1850, and in 1852 more than 20,000 landed in San Francisco hoping to share in the wealth of "Gum Sam" (Golden Mountain). Most came, like the Americans, as temporary sojourners, intending to return home as soon as they made some money. Again, like most of the American miners, the majority of Chinese were men who left their wives at home. Dressed in their distinctive blue cotton shirts, baggy pants, and broad-brimmed hats, and with long queues hanging down their backs, hardworking Chinese miners soon became a familiar sight in the gold fields, as did the presence of "Chinatowns." The distinctive appearance of the Chinese, added to the threat of economic competition that they posed, quickly aroused American hostility. A special tax was imposed on foreign miners in 1852, and in the 1870s, Chinese immigration was sharply curtailed.

In 1849, as the gold rush began in earnest, San Francisco, the major entry port and supply point, sprang to life. From a settlement of 1,000 in 1848 it grew to a city of 35,000 in 1850. This surge suggested that the real money to be made in California was not in panning for gold but from feeding, clothing, housing, provisioning, and entertaining the miners. Among the first to learn that lesson was the German Jewish immigrant Levi Strauss, who sold so many tough work pants to miners that his name became synonymous with his product. And Jerusha Marshall, who opened a twenty-room boardinghouse in the city, candidly wrote to her eastern relatives: "Never was there a better field for making money than now presents itself in this place. . . . We are satisfied to dig our gold in San Francisco." From these "instant" beginnings San Francisco stabilized to become a major American city. Meanwhile, the white population of California had jumped from an estimated pre–Gold Rush figure of 11,000 to more than 100,000 by 1852. California was admitted into the Union as a state in 1850.

Mining Camps

As had occured in San Francisco, most mining camps boomed almost instantly to life, but unlike San Francisco, they were empty again within a few years. In spite of the aura of glamour that surrounds the names of the famous camps—Poker Flat, Angels Camp, Whiskey Bar, Placerville, Mariposa—they were generally dirty and dreary places. Most miners lived in tents or hovels, unwilling to take time from mining to build themselves decent quarters. They cooked monotonous meals of beans, bread, and bacon, or, if they had money, bought meals at expensive restaurants and boardinghouses (where the table might be no more than a plank over two flour barrels). Many migrants traveled to the mines with relatives or fellow townspeople. But often they split up in California—each man with his own idea of where he could find gold the easiest—and ended up on their own. They led a cheerless, uncomfortable, and unhealthy existence, especially during the long, rainy winter months, with few distractions apart from the saloon, the gambling hall, and the prostitute's crib.

California in the Gold Rush   This map shows the major gold camps along the Mother Lode in the western foothills of the Sierra Nevada mountains. Gold seekers reached the camps by crossing the Sierra Nevadas near Placerville on the Overland Trail or by sea via San Francisco. The main area of Spanish-Mexican settlement, the coastal region between Monterey and Los Angeles, was remote from the gold fields.

SOURCE: Warren A. Beck and Ynez D. Haase, *Historical Atlas of California* (Norman: University of Oklahoma Press, 1974), map 50.

Most miners were young, unmarried, and unsuccessful. Only a small percentage ever struck it rich in California. Gold deposits that were accessible with pick and shovel were soon exhausted, and the deeper deposits required capital and machinery. Some of the workings at the Comstock Lode in Virginia City, Nevada, a later mining center, were half a mile deep. But many men were ashamed to come home until they had "made their pile." Increasingly, as they stayed on in California, they had to give up the status of independent miners and become wage earners for large mining concerns.

As in San Francisco, a more reliable way to earn money in the camps was to supply the miners. Every mining community had its saloonkeepers, gamblers,

This drawing of the bar of a gambling saloon in San Francisco in 1855 shows the effects of the Gold Rush on California. Men from all parts of the world are gathered at this elegant bar in the large cosmopolitan city of San Francisco, which had been only a small trading post before gold was discovered in 1849.

SOURCE: Frank Marryat, *The Bar of a Gambling Saloon*, published 1855. Lithograph. Collection of the New–York Historical Society, New York City (48381).

spectably, but most died young of drugs, venereal disease, or violence. Most of the other women were hardworking wives of miners, and in this predominantly male society they made good money doing domestic work: keeping boardinghouses, cooking, doing laundry. Even the wives of professional men who in the East might have been restrained by propriety succumbed to the monetary opportunities and kept boardinghouses.

Partly because few people put any effort into building communities—they were too busy seeking gold—violence was endemic in mining areas, and much of it was racial. Discrimination, especially against Chinese, Mexicans, and African Americans, was common. Frequently miners' claims were "jumped": thieves would rob them of the gold they had accumulated, kill them, or chase them away, and then file their own claim for the victims' strike. Or unscrupulous miners might use the law to their advantage to secure the claims of others without violence—for example by taking advantage of the prohibitively high mining tax on foreigners.

prostitutes, merchants, and restauranteurs. Like the miners themselves, these people were transients, always ready to pick up and move at the word of a new gold strike. The majority of women in the early mining camps were prostitutes. Some grew rich or married re-

Chinese first came to California in 1849 attracted by the Gold Rush. Frequently, however, they were forced off their claims by intolerant whites. Rather than enjoy an equal chance in the gold fields they were often forced to work as servants or in other menial occupations.

SOURCE: Head of Auburn Ravine, 1852, Gold miners with Chinese laborers, California State Library (912).

In the end, most mining camps were at best temporary communities. The gold "played out" and people moved on, leaving ghost towns behind. By the mid-1850s, the immediate effects of the Gold Rush had passed. California had a booming population, a thriving agriculture, and a corporate mining industry. The Gold Rush also left California with a population that was larger, more affluent, and (in urban San Francisco) more culturally sophisticated than that in other newly settled territories. It was also significantly more multicultural than the rest of the nation, for many of the Chinese and Mexicans, as well as immigrants from many European countries, remained in California after the Gold Rush subsided. But the rough equality of the early days was gone, and peoples of what were considered "lesser races" were kept in subordination.

The Gold Rush left some permanent scars, and not just on the foothills landscape: the virtual extermination of the California Indian peoples, the dispossession of many Californios who were legally deprived of their land grants, and the growth of racial animosity toward the Chinese in particular. The major characteristics of the mining frontier, evident first in the California Gold Rush and repeated many times thereafter in similar "rushes" in Colorado, Montana, Idaho, South Dakota, Arizona, and Alaska were a lack of stable communities and a worsening of racial tensions. The lesson seemed to be that when Americans arrived in great numbers, as in the Gold Rush in California, the possibility of an inclusive frontier vanished and American dominance was complete.

THE POLITICS OF MANIFEST DESTINY

In three short years, from 1845 to 1848, the territory of the United States grew an incredible 70 percent, and a continental nation took shape. This expansion, pushed by economic desires and feelings of American cultural superiority, led directly to the emergence of the divisive issue of slavery as the dominant issue in national politics.

The "Young America" Movement

One source of the belief in manifest destiny was national pride—the conviction that American democracy was so superior it would lead inevitably to the expansion of the nation. The swift victory in the Mexican-American War and the "prize" of California gold seemed to confirm that conviction. European events in 1848 also served to foster American pride. In that year a series of democratic revolutions—in Italy,

This Japanese painting shows Commodore Matthew Perry landing in Japan in 1854. The commercial treaty Perry signed with the Japanese government, which opened a formerly closed country to American trade, was viewed in the United States as another fruit of manifest destiny.

SOURCE: *The Landing of Commodore Perry in Japan* in 1853. Perry's ship and procession (Ukiyo-e School). Bigelow Collection, The Museum of Fine Arts Boston (11.6054).

France, Germany, Hungary, and parts of the Austrian Empire—swept the Continent. Expansionists assumed that American democracy and manifest destiny were the models for these liberal revolutions. When Lajos Kossuth, the famed Hungarian revolutionary, visited the United States in 1851, he was given a hero's welcome, and Daniel Webster complacently assured him that "we shall rejoice to see our American model upon the lower Danube."

In an even more confident gesture, President Franklin Pierce dispatched Commodore Matthew Perry across the Pacific to Japan, a nation famous for its insularity and hostility to outsiders. The mission resulted in 1854 in a commercial treaty that opened Japan to American trade. Perry's feat caused a newspaper in tiny Olympia, Washington, to boast, "We shall have the boundless Pacific for a market in manifest destiny. We were born to command it."

But efforts closer to home by the Young America movement, as expansionist Democrats styled themselves, were more controversial. Victory in the Mexican-American War and the evident weakness of the Mexican government whetted the appetite of some southern expansionists for more territory. But most American politicians were cautious about further gains. When in the spring of 1848 Polk recommended American intervention in the civil war in the Mexican province of Yucatán, Congress rebuffed him. Senator John C. Calhoun, harking back to Polk's manipulation of Congress in 1846, cautioned, "I did hope that the experience of the Mexican War—that precipitate and

rash measure which has cost the country so dearly in blood and treasure—would have taught the administration moderation and caution." In the winter of 1848, rumors swept Washington that Polk had offered Spain up to $100 million for Cuba (compared with the $15 million paid for Mexico's provinces of California and New Mexico). The nation was spared a raging political battle when Spain spurned all offers.

Thus the Mexican-American War was divisive even after it was won. A small group of expansionists, most from the South, wanted more, in spite of clear evidence that most Americans had had enough. Throughout the 1850s, these expansionists continued to covet Mexico, Central America, and Cuba. Adventures in these directions, all organized by Southerners intent on acquiring new lands for cotton, further inflamed the festering sectional differences of the 1850s (which will be discussed further in Chapter 15).

The Wilmot Proviso

In 1846, almost all the northern members of the Whig Party opposed Democratic president James Polk's belligerent expansionism on antislavery grounds. Northern Whigs correctly feared that expansion would reopen the issue of slavery in the territories. "We appear . . . to be rushing upon perils headlong, and with our eyes all open," Daniel Webster warned in 1847. His remedy? "We want no extension of territory; we want no accession of new states. The country is already large enough." But the outpouring of popular enthusiasm for the

---

OVERVIEW

EXPANSION CAUSES THE FIRST SPLITS IN THE SECOND AMERICAN PARTY SYSTEM

1844	Whigs reject President John Tyler's move to annex Texas and expel him from the Whig Party. Southern Democrats choose expansionist James K. Polk as their presidential candidate, passing over Martin Van Buren, who is against expansion.
	Liberty Party runs abolitionist James Birney for president, attracting northern antislavery Whigs.
1846	The Wilmot Proviso, proposing to ban slavery in the territories that might be gained in the Mexican-American War, splits both parties: southern Whigs and Democrats oppose the measure; northern Whigs and Democrats support it.
1848	The new Free-Soil Party runs northern Democrat Martin Van Buren for president, gaining 10 percent of the vote from abolitionists, antislavery Whigs, and some northern Democrats. This strong showing by a third party causes Democrat Lewis Cass to lose the electoral votes of New York and Pennsylvania, allowing the Whig Zachary Taylor to win.

Mexican-American War drowned Webster's words and convinced most Whig congressmen that they needed to vote military appropriations for the war in spite of their misgivings.

Ironically it was not the Whigs but a freshman Democratic congressman from Pennsylvania, David Wilmot, who opened the door to sectional controversy over expansion. In August 1846, only a few short months after the beginning of the Mexican-American War, Wilmot proposed, in an amendment to a military appropriations bill, that slavery be banned in all the territories acquired from Mexico. He was ready, Wilmot said, to "sustain the institutions of the South as they exist. But sir, the issue now presented is not whether slavery shall exist unmolested where it is now, but whether it shall be carried to new and distant regions, now free, where the footprint of a slave cannot be found." In the debate and voting that followed, something new and ominous occurred: southern Whigs joined southern Democrats to vote against the measure, while Northerners of both parties supported it. Sectional interest had triumphed over party loyalty. Wilmot's Proviso triggered the first breakdown of the national party system and reopened the debate about the place of slavery in the future of the nation.

The Wilmot Proviso was so controversial that it was deleted from the necessary military appropriations bills during the Mexican-American War. But in 1848, following the Treaty of Guadalupe Hidalgo, the question of the expansion of slavery could no longer be avoided or postponed. Antislavery advocates from the North argued with proslavery Southerners in a debate that was much more prolonged and more bitter than in the Missouri Crisis debate of 1819. Civility quickly wore thin: threats were uttered and fistfights broke out on the floor of the House of Representatives. The Wilmot Proviso posed a fundamental challenge to both parties. Neither the Democrats nor the Whigs could take a strong stand on the amendment because neither party could get its northern and southern wings to agree. Decisive action, for or against, was a serious threat to party unity. Webster's fear that expansion would lead to sectional conflict had become a reality.

The Free-Soil Movement

Why did David Wilmot propose this controversial measure? Wilmot, a northern Democrat, was propelled not by ideology but by the pressure of practical politics. The dramatic rise of the Liberty Party, founded in 1840 by abolitionists, threatened to take votes away from both the Whig and the Democratic parties. The Liberty Party won 62,000 votes in the 1844 presidential election, all in the North. This was more than enough to deny victory to the Whig candidate, Henry Clay. Neither party could afford to ignore the strength of this third party.

The Liberty Party took an uncompromising stance against slavery. As articulated by Ohio's Salmon P. Chase, the party platform called for the "divorce of the federal government from slavery." The party proposed to prohibit the admission of slave states to the Union, end slavery in the District of Columbia, and abolish the interstate slave trade that was vital to the expansion of cotton growing into the Old Southwest (see Chapter 11). Liberty Party members also favored denying office to all slaveholders (a proposal that would have robbed all the southern states of their senators) and forbidding the use of slave labor on federal construction projects. In short, the party proposed to quickly strangle slavery. The popularity of this radical program among northern voters in 1844 was an indication of the moral fervor of abolitionism (see Chapter 13).

But Liberty Party doctrine was too uncompromising for the mass of northern voters, who immediately realized that the southern states would leave the Union before accepting it. Still, as the 1844 vote indicated, many Northerners opposed slavery. From this sentiment the Free-Soil Party was born. The free-soil argument was a calculated adjustment of abolitionist principles to practical politics. It shifted the focus from the question of the morality of slavery to the ways in which slavery posed a threat to northern expansion. The free-soil doctrine thus established a direct link between expansion, which most Americans supported, and sectional politics.

Free-soilers were willing to allow slavery to continue in the existing slave states because they supported the Union, not because they approved of slavery. They were unwilling, however, to allow the extension of slavery to new and unorganized territory. If the South were successful in extending slavery, they argued, northern farmers who moved west would find themselves competing at an economic disadvantage with large planters using slave labor. Free-soilers also insisted that the northern values of freedom and individualism would be destroyed if the slave-based southern labor system were allowed to spread. To free-soilers, the South was composed of little more than corrupt aristocrats, degraded slaves, and a large class of poor whites who were deprived of opportunity because they did not understand the value of honest labor.

Many free-soilers really meant "antiblack" when they said "antislavery." They proposed to ban all

African American people from the new territories (a step that four states—Indiana, Illinois, Iowa, and Oregon—took but did not always enforce). William Lloyd Garrison promptly denounced the free-soil doctrine as "whitemanism," a racist effort to make the territories white. There was much truth to his charge, but there was no denying that the free-soil doctrine was popular. Although abolitionists were making headway in their claim for moral equality regardless of skin color, most Northerners were unwilling to consider social equality for African Americans, free or slave. Banning all black people from the western territories seemed a simple solution.

Finally, the free-soil movement was a repudiation of the sectional compromise of 1820. If the Missouri Compromise line were carried westward to the Pacific Ocean, as Secretary of State James Buchanan proposed in 1848, much of present-day New Mexico and Arizona and the southern half of California would have been admitted as slave states, and everything to the north would have been free. Free-soilers opposed this arrangement. Their opposition in 1848 to the Missouri Compromise line indicated how influential antislavery feeling was becoming in the North.

The Election of 1848

A swirl of emotions—pride, expansionism, sectionalism, abolitionism, free-soil sentiment—surrounded the election of 1848. The Treaty of Guadalupe Hidalgo had been signed earlier in the year, and the vast northern Mexican provinces of New Mexico and California and the former Republic of Texas had been incorporated into the United States. But the issues raised by the Wilmot Proviso remained to be resolved, and every candidate had to have an answer to the question of whether slavery should be admitted in the new territories.

Lewis Cass of Michigan, the Democratic nominee for president (Polk, in poor health, declined to run for

In 1848, the Whigs again adopted the campaign strategy that had worked so well for them in the presidential election of 1840. They nominated a hero of the Mexican-American War, General Zachary Taylor, who ran on his military exploits. This kerchief, printed for the campaign, shows Taylor at the center, surrounded by scenes from the battles of Buena Vista, Monterrey, Resaca de la Palma, and Palo Alto.

SOURCE: *Zachary Taylor Kerchief depicting Battles of the Mexican War*, 1848. Cotton, 26 3/8 × 29 3/4 in. © Collection of The New York Historical Society. Acc. No. 1941.129.

CHRONOLOGY

1609	First Spanish settlement in New Mexico
1670s	British and French Canadians begin fur trade in western Canada
1716	First Spanish settlements in Texas
1769	First Spanish settlement in California
1780s	New England ships begin sea otter trade in Pacific Northwest
1790	First American ship visits Hawaii
1803	Louisiana Purchase
1804–06	Lewis and Clark expedition
1806	Russian-Californio trade begins
1806–07	Zebulon Pike's expedition across the Great Plains to the Rocky Mountains
1819–20	Stephen Long's expedition across the Great Plains
1821	Hudson's Bay Company gains dominance of western fur trade
	Mexico seizes independence from Spain
	Santa Fé Trail opens, soon protected by U.S. military
	Stephen F. Austin becomes first American empresario in Texas
1824	First fur rendezvous sponsored by Rocky Mountain Fur Company
	Hudson's Bay Company establishes Fort Vancouver in Oregon Country
1830	Indian Removal Act moves eastern Indians to Indian Territory

1833–34	Prince Maximilian and Karl Bodmer visit Plains Indians
1834	Jason Lee establishes first mission in Oregon Country
1835	Texas revolts against Mexico
1836	Battles of the Alamo and San Jacinto Republic of Texas formed
1843–44	John C. Frémont maps trails to Oregon and California
1844	Democrat James K. Polk elected president on an expansionist platform
1845	Texas annexed to the United States as a slave state
	John O'Sullivan coins the phrase "manifest destiny"
1846	Oregon question settled peacefully with Britain
	Mexican-American War begins
	Bear Flag Revolt in California
	Wilmot Proviso
1847	Cayuse Wars begin in Oregon
	Americans win battles of Buena Vista, Veracruz, and Mexico City
1848	Treaty of Guadalupe Hidalgo
	Free-Soil Party captures 10 percent of the popular vote in the North
	General Zachary Taylor, a Whig, elected president
1849	California Gold Rush

a second term), proposed to apply the doctrine of popular sovereignty to the crucial slave–free issue. This democratic-sounding notion of leaving the decision to the citizens of each territory was based on the Jeffersonian faith in the common man's ability to vote both his own self-interest and the common good.

Popular sovereignty was based on the accepted constitutional principle that decisions about slavery (like, for example, rules about suffrage) should be made at the state rather than the national level. In reality, popular sovereignty was an admission of the nation's failure to resolve sectional differences. It simply shifted

428 Chapter 14 The Territorial Expansion of the United States 1830s–1850s

decision making on the crucial issue of the expansion of slavery from national politicians to the members of territorial and state legislatures, who, belonging to different parties, were in as much disagreement as members of Congress and just as unable to resolve it.

As Cass stated it, the doctrine of popular sovereignty was deliberately vague about when a territory would choose its status. Would it do so during the territorial stage? at the point of applying for statehood? Clearly, this question was crucial, for no slave owner would invest in new land if the territory could later be declared free, and no abolitionist would move to a territory that was destined to become a slave state. Cass hoped his ambiguity on this point would win him votes in both North and South. Even so, sectional differences ran so deep that the Democrats found it necessary to print two campaign biographies of Cass. The biography circulated in the North touted Cass's doctrine of popular sovereignty as the best way to keep slavery out of the territories; the biography in the South implied the opposite.

For their part, the Whigs passed over perennial candidate Henry Clay and turned once again to a war hero, General Zachary Taylor. Taylor, a Louisiana slaveholder, refused to take a position on the Wilmot Proviso, allowing both northern and southern voters to hope that he agreed with them. Privately, Taylor opposed the expansion of slavery. In public, he evaded the issue by running as a war hero and a national leader who was above sectional politics.

The deliberate vagueness of the two major candidates displeased many northern voters. An uneasy mixture of disaffected Democrats (among them David Wilmot) and Whigs joined former Liberty Party voters to support the candidate of the Free-Soil Party, former president Martin Van Buren. Van Buren, angry at the Democratic Party for passing him over in 1844 and displeased with the growing southern dominance of the Democratic Party, ran as a spoiler. He knew he could not win the election, but he could divide the Democrats. In the end, Van Buren garnered 10 percent of the vote (all in the North). The vote for the Free-Soil Party cost Cass the electoral votes of New York and Pennsylvania, and General Zachary Taylor won the election with only 47 percent of the popular vote. This was the second election after 1840 that the Whigs had won by

running a war hero who could duck hard questions by claiming to be above politics. Uncannily, history was to repeat itself: Taylor, like William Henry Harrison, died before his term was completed, and the chance he offered to maintain national unity—if ever it existed—was lost.

CONCLUSION

In the decade of the 1840s, westward expansion took many forms, from relatively peaceful settlement in Oregon, to war with Mexico over Texas, to the overwhelming numbers of gold rushers who changed California forever. Most of these frontiers—in Oregon, New Mexico, and California—began as frontiers of inclusion in which a small number of Americans were eager for trade, accommodation, and intermarriage with the original inhabitants. Texas, with its agricultural enclaves, was the exception to this pattern. Yet on every frontier, as the number of American settlers increased, so did the sentiment for exclusion, so that by 1850, whatever their origins, the far-flung American continental settlements were more similar than different and the success of manifest destiny seemed overwhelming.

The election of 1848, virtually a referendum on manifest destiny, yielded ironic results. James K. Polk, who presided over the unprecedented expansion, did not run for a second term, and thus the Democratic Party gained no electoral victory to match the military one. The electorate that had been so thrilled by the war news voted for a war hero—who led the anti-expansionist Whig Party. The election was decided by Martin Van Buren, the Free-Soil candidate who voiced the sentiments of the abolitionists, a reform group that had been insignificant just a few years before. The amazing expansion achieved by the Mexican-American War—America's manifest destiny—made the United States a continental nation but stirred up the issue that was to tear it apart. Sectional rivalries and fears now dominated every aspect of politics. Expansion, once a force for unity, now divided the nation into Northerners and Southerners, who could not agree on the community they shared—the federal Union.

REVIEW QUESTIONS

1. Define and discuss the concept of manifest destiny.
2. Trace the different ways in which the frontiers in Oregon, Texas, and California moved from frontiers of inclusion to frontiers of exclusion.
3. Take different sides (Whig and Democrat) and debate the issues raised by the Mexican-American War.
4. Referring back to Chapter 13, compare the positions of the Liberty Party and the Free-Soil Party. Examine the factors that made the free-soil doctrine politically acceptable to many, and abolitionism so controversial.

RECOMMENDED READING

Arnoldo De Leon, *The Tejano Community, 1836–1900* (1982). Traces the changing status of Tejanos after Texas came under the control of American Texans.

John Mack Faragher, *Women and Men on the Overland Trail* (1979). One of the first books to consider the experience of women on the journey west.

William Goetzman, *Exploration and Empire: The Explorer and the Scientist in the Winning of the American West* (1966). Considers the many government-sponsored explorations of the West.

Julie Roy Jeffrey, *Converting the West: A Biography of Narcissa Whitman* (1991). Makes a clear connection between the missionary Whitman's evangelical upbringing and her failure to understand the culture of Oregon's Cayuse Indians.

Robert W. Johannsen, *To the Halls of the Montezumas: The Mexican War in the American Imagination* (1985). A lively book that explores the impact of the Mexican-American War on public opinion.

Susan Johnson, *Roaring Camp: The Social World of the California Gold Rush* (2000). A beautifully written study of the varieties of mining camp experience.

Paul D. Lack, *The Texas Revolutionary Experience: A Political and Social History, 1835–1836* (1992). A political and social history that stresses the chaotic and discordant nature of the Texas Revolt.

Janet Lecompte, *Pueblo, Hardscrabble, Greenhorn: The Upper Arkansas, 1832–1856* (1978). A social history that portrays the racial and ethnic diversity of the trading frontier.

Michael Morrison, *Slavery and the American West: The Eclipse of Manifest Destiny and the Coming of the Civil War* (1997). In a study of competing ideas over the future of the West, the author stresses the links between expansion and sectional disagreements.

Malcolm Rohrbough, *Days of Gold: The California Gold Rush and the American Nation* (1997). A lively history that emphasizes the effects of this "great American epic" on the national self-image.

David J. Weber, *The Mexican Frontier, 1821–1846: The American Southwest under Mexico* (1982). A fine study of the history of the Southwest before American conquest. The author is a leading borderlands historian.

Richard White, *"It's Your Misfortune and None of My Own": A History of the American West* (1991). A major reinterpretation that focuses on the history of the region itself rather than on the westward expansion of Americans. Pays much more attention to Spanish Mexicans and Indian peoples than earlier texts.

▶ MEDIA RESOURCES

 U.S. HISTORY DOCUMENTS CD-ROM

Manifest Destiny

12-1 The Treaties of Velasco (May 14, 1836)

12-2 The Aroostook War (1839)

12-3 Across the Plains with Catherine Sager Pringle in 1844

12-4 John L. O'Sullivan, "The Great Nation of Futurity" (1845)

12-5 Thomas Corwin, Against the Mexican War (1847)

12-6 Chief Seattle, Oration (1854)

New South, Expanding West

17-1 Edward Gould Buffum, Six Months in the Gold Mines (1850)

17-2 Lydia Allen Rudd, Diary of Westward Travel (1852)

 COMPANION WEBSITE HIGHLIGHTS

To view an exploration, enter one of the URLs below in your browser.

 Web Explorations

Exploration of the Continent, 1804–1830
http://www.prenhall.com/faragher/map14.1

The Mexican-American War, 1846–1848
http://www.prenhall.com/faragher/map14.2

 Additional Interactive Maps

To access the maps, go to this chapter's resources at
http://www.prenhall.com/faragher

The Overland Trails, 1840, page 407

Texas: From Mexican Province to U.S. State, page 414

Territory Added, 1845–1853, page 418

California in the Gold Rush, page 421

 HISTORY RESOURCE CENTER

To find the resources listed below, go to
http://www.prenhall.com/historyresourcecenter

Documents

"Memorial of the Cherokee Nation" (1830)

Andrew Jackson, First Annual Message to Congress (1829)

Black Hawk, "Life of Black Hawk" (1833)

Walt Whitman, Preface to Leaves of Grass (1855)

Images

A Forty-Niner's Covered Wagon

Austin, Texas 1840

Galveston, Texas 1844

General Winfield Scott in Mexico City

Houston, Texas 1845

The Storming of Chapultepec

EXPLORING AMERICA
THE UNWELCOME MAT

http://www.prenhall.com/faragher/unwelcomemat

A major theme of United States history is immigration. A corollary theme is nativism, or the opposition to immigration and immigrants by native-born citizens. Why did nativism become so prevalent in the 1840s and 1850s? Who were the targets of this anti-immigrant campaign? What methods were used against immigrants? Why did these people come to America? Why were they not welcomed into the country? How does the idea of nativism and anti-immigration sentiment fit within the democratic ideals of the United States? *The Unwelcome Mat* module explores immigration and nativism focusing on the experiences of the Irish and Chinese.

Continued

Continued

The Unwelcome Mat comprehensively examines the issue of immigration and responses to the immigrants in the decade prior to the Civil War. The narrative punctuated by primary source documents, an interactive map, a chronology, and audio clips shows

that in the 1840s and 1850s, immigration and the response it elicited was a complex phenomenon that set the stage for later controversies involving different peoples who sought to settle in the United States.

The module explores the idea of America as a chosen land by examining the experiences of the newly arrived Irish and Chinese in the United States. It also offers details on conditions in Ireland that prompted

the large exodus and places emigration in global perspective showing that while the United States was the favored destination, many also went to other places, especially Australia and New Zealand. The module includes discussion of a court ruling that lumped Chinese with African Americans, reducing their status, and of negative media portrayals of Irish by Republican journals. The primary source documents and other features illuminate this important topic. An audio clip explains the unique holiday status

of St. Patrick's Day. Showing the distribution of foreign born Americans, a map places the Irish and Chinese migration into a larger perspective while the chronology supplies a time context and a chart traces Irish emigrant destinations. An 1847 news article with sketches offers insight into conditions in Ireland.

Was the United States the chosen land for immigrants? Was the unwelcome mat the reality? Using the module and perhaps expanding to research other works, these questions provide a good topic for a short paper, classroom discussion, or even role-playing where students portray Irish and Chinese immigrants, Americans tied to the Democratic or Republican Party, and perhaps African Americans.

Reflect and Respond

1. What might the Census Commissioners have possibly meant by "the general advancement of the country"?
2. Use the morality and emigration data to calculate the "remarkable" decline in the population of Ireland in the wake of the famine.
3. How did the reporter for the *Illustrated London News* seek to make the suffering of the Irish vivid for his readers? Which details did he emphasize? Which stories did he tell?
4. The *Illustrated London News* was a new type of publication, one later copied by magazines such as *Harper's Weekly*. How did the use of "sketches" convey the conditions in Ireland? Choose two sketches. What details did the artist use to get across the horror of the situation? What portions of the text did the sketches illustrate?

✓ Check it out

Distribution of Foreign Born

This map depicts the settlement patterns of foreign immigrants in the United States. It shows which regions and types of communities attracted immigrants from which countries. It is also important because it illustrates the ways that immigration influenced the development of the United States.

This exploration is also available on the *Exploring America* CD-ROM.

▶ Remembering the Alamo

The Alamo is the number one tourist attraction in the state of Texas. Located in a small but tranquil park, remote from the noise and traffic of surrounding downtown San Antonio, the site evokes feelings of hushed reverence and respect for the famous Anglo American heroes—William Barret Travis, Jim Bowie, and Davy Crockett—of the gallant but futile 1836 defense described in the chapter opener.

Today, only the chapel remains from the much larger Mission San Antonio de Valero established in 1718. Only the popular nickname—the Alamo—remains from the first soldiers, a troop of Spanish cavalry who came from the Mexican town of El Alamo in 1801 when the mission became a military fort. There are no signs of the 1836 battle itself aside from a few relics preserved inside the chapel. A brass plaque affixed to the wall of the chapel notes this varied history from mission to fort to finally, in defeat, into the "Cradle of Texas Liberty." What remains of the Alamo today and what is commemorated serves as an example of how long-ago choices about what to preserve continue to shape our present-day understanding of our historic past.

In the aftermath of the 1836 battle the legend of the famous defeat at the Alamo grew and was used by some people, as the chapter opener shows, to consolidate American control by fostering antiMexican sentiment. But until 1883 the Alamo itself was used for a variety of practical purposes by the U. S. Army and commercial interests. By 1883, when the Catholic Church sold the chapel to the State of Texas for $20,000, very little remained of the original grounds. A growing San Antonio encroached on all sides: the convent adjacent to the chapel, a remnant of the original mission, was used as a store and commercial museum. There was a livery stable and blacksmith shop behind the chapel, a public meat market and several saloons across the way. At this point, local boosters alert to its tourist potential joined with Texas patriots to limit the commercialism and demand that the Alamo be preserved as a memorial to the 1836 battle.

The preservation of the Alamo was entrusted by the Texas State Legislature to the San Antonio Chapter of the Daughters of the Republic of Texas. The custodianship of historic sites by exclusive women's groups

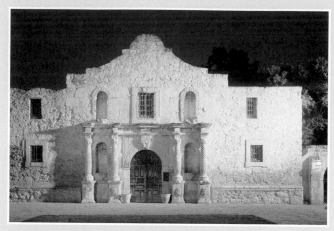

This modern photograph of the Alamo chapel by the well-known landscape photographer David Muench conveys the romantic and rather nostalgic atmosphere of the site that describes itself as "the Cradle of Texas liberty."

SOURCE: © David Muench/CORBIS.

such as the Daughters of the American Revolution and the Mount Vernon Ladies Association was common throughout the United States at the time. Usually this meant that control over historic sites was kept firmly in the hands of wealthy Anglo women. But membership in the Daughters of the Republic of Texas was open to *all* women who could trace their ancestry to persons who settled in Texas before 1846. In the 1890s the president of the San Antonio chapter of the DRT was Adina De Zavala, granddaughter of the Tejano patriot who became the first Vice-President of Texas, Lorenzo de Zavala. Adina De Zavala, with the help of her sister DRT member, the wealthy Clara Driscoll, led the effort to raise money to preserve the Alamo site.

No sooner had the DRT obtained control of the Alamo than disagreement arose. In a bitter controversy sometimes called the "Second Battle of the Alamo" De Zavala and Driscoll disagreed about the relative importance of the buildings. De Zavala wanted to retain the full history of the site as a mission and fort while Driscoll, in common with most Anglo-Americans of her time, preferred to emphasize only the chapel as a shrine to the well-known Anglo heroes of the 1836 battle. Driscoll won: the convent was partially demolished, De Zavala and her supporters were legally barred from more than sixty percent of the city's occupants are Mexican American. As at other historic sites around the country, this ongoing struggle reflects deeper social changes: Mexican-Americans see changes in the Alamo as a matter of equity and historical accuracy, while many Anglo-Texans oppose change in the name of tradition. This unresolved controversy reminds us that there is more than one version of the past, thus making the question of who interprets history much more than an academic matter. ■

This sculpture is part of the Alamo Cenotaph, a memorial to the slain defenders of the Alamo that was erected in Alamo Plaza in 1940. The two prominent figures are the famous defenders William B. Travis (in uniform) and Davy Crockett. Photograph by Lee Snider.

SOURCE: CORBIS. ©Lee Snider/CORBIS.

custodianship, and the Alamo chapel, surrounded by a memorial park and wall, assumed its present day form.

Today, nearly a century after its preservation as a historic site, the Battle of the Alamo has flared anew. The state-appointed guardians of the Alamo, the Daughters of the Republic of Texas, are under attack for their lack of historical professionalism. Although custodianship of historic sites by elite women's groups was common a century ago, today professionals trained to consider the full historic record are much more likely to administer and preserve such sites. The most sustained protest, however, has come from the Texans of Mexican heritage who feel that the Tejano role in defense of the Alamo (as described in the chapter opener) has not received enough attention, and that the Spanish colonial history of the site has been ignored. In part, these protests reflect the growing political power of Mexican Americans in Texas, which in turn is based on population. In San Antonio itself,

 www.researchnavigator.com

The Community and Memory essay for this chapter deals with the battle to preserve and present the history of the Alamo. For further research on the history of the Alamo, use the tools available to you in Research Navigator.

As you investigate this topic, consider this question: "Why did the Alamo become such a potent symbol of the history of Texas?"

ContentSelect: Search in the History database using the search term *Alamo*.

Links Library: Access the History: U.S. History database and explore the links for *Annexation of Texas*.

New York Times on the Web: To find more about the contentious history of the battle, search using the term *Alamo*.

FIFTEEN
THE COMING CRISIS

▶ The 1850s

SOURCE: Robert Marshall Root, *Lincoln–Douglas Debate at Charleston, Illinois*. Henry Horner Lincoln Collection. Courtesy of the Illinois State Historical Library.

Illinois Communities Debate Slavery

ON SEVEN OCCASIONS THROUGH THE LATE SUMMER AND autumn of 1858, in each of the seven small Illinois towns of Ottawa, Freeport, Jonesboro, Charleston, Galesburg, Quincy, and Alton, thousands of Illinois farmers and townspeople put aside their daily routines and customary chores; climbed into carriages, farm wagons, carts, and conveyances of all sorts; and converged on their local town green. Entertained by brass bands, pageantry, and vast quantities of food and local gossip, they waited impatiently for the main event, the chance to take part in the debate on the most urgent question of the day—slavery. Two Illinois politicians—Democratic Senator Stephen A. Douglas and his Republican challenger, Springfield lawyer Abraham Lincoln, the principal figures in the debates—presented their views in three hours of closely reasoned argument. But they did not speak alone. Cheers, boos, groans, and shouted questions from active, engaged listeners punctuated all seven of the now famous confrontations between the two men. Although commonly referred to as the Lincoln-Douglas debates, these were really community events in which Illinois citizens—who, as did Americans everywhere, held varying political beliefs—took part. Some individuals were proslavery, some antislavery, and many were undecided, but all were agreed that democratic politics gave them the means to air their opinions and resolve their differences.

"The prairies are on fire," announced the *New York Evening Post* correspondent who covered the debates. "It is astonishing how deep an interest in politics this people take." The reason was clear: by 1858, the American nation was in deep political crisis. The decade-long effort to solve the problem of the future of slavery had failed. For most of this time Washington politicians trying to build broad national parties with policies acceptable to voters in both the North and the South had done their best not to talk about slavery. Thus, that the Lincoln-Douglas debates were devoted to one issue alone—slavery and the future of the Union—showed how serious matters had become.

Democrat Stephen Douglas was the leading Democratic contender for the 1860 presidential nomination, but before he could mount a campaign for national office he had first to win reelection to the Illinois seat he had held in the U.S. Senate for twelve years. His vote against allowing slavery in Kansas had alienated him from the strong southern wing of his own party and had put him in direct conflict with its top leader, President James Buchanan. Because the crisis of the Union was so severe and Douglas's role so pivotal, his reelection campaign clearly previewed the 1860 presidential election. For the sake of its future, the Republican Party had to field a strong opponent: it found its candidate in Abraham Lincoln.

Lincoln had represented Illinois in the House of Representatives in the 1840s but had lost political support in 1848 because he had opposed the Mexican-American War. Developing a prosperous Springfield law practice, he had been an influential member of the Illinois Republican Party since its founding in 1856. Although he had entered political life as a Whig, Lincoln was radicalized by the issue of the extension of slavery. Even though his wife's family were Kentucky slave owners, Lincoln's commitment to freedom and his resistance to the spread of slavery had now become absolute: for him, freedom and Union were inseparable.

Much less well known than Douglas, Lincoln was the underdog in the 1858 Senate race, and thus it was he who challenged Douglas to debate. As they squared off in each of the seven Illinois towns, Douglas and Lincoln were an amusing sight. Douglas was short (5 feet, 4 inches) and his build was very square; his nickname was the "Little Giant." Lincoln, on the other hand, was very tall (6 feet, 4 inches) and very thin. Both were eloquent and powerful speakers—and they had to be. The three-hour debates were held without amplification of any kind. Nevertheless, in every town, audiences of 10,000 to 15,000 listened attentively and responded vocally to each speaker's long and thought-packed arguments.

Douglas had many strengths going into the debates. He spoke for the Union, he claimed, pointing out that the Democratic Party was a national party whereas the Republican Party was only sectional. He repeatedly appealed to the racism of much of his audience with declarations such as, "I would not blot out the great inalienable rights of the white men for all the negroes that ever existed!" He repeatedly called his opponent a "Black Republican," implying that Lincoln and his party favored the social equality of whites and blacks, even race mixing.

Lincoln did not believe in the social equality of the races, but he did believe wholeheartedly that slavery was a moral wrong. Pledging the Republican Party to the "ultimate extinction" of slavery, Lincoln continually warned that Douglas's position would lead to the opposite result: the spread of slavery everywhere. Although in this argument Lincoln was addressing the northern fear of an expansionist "slave power," he strove at the same time to present himself as a moderate. He did not favor the breakup of the Union, but he never wavered from his antislavery stance.

The first of the seven debates, held in Ottawa on Saturday, August 21, 1858, showed not only the serious-

ness but the exuberance of the democratic politics of the time. By early morning the town was jammed with people. The clouds of dust raised by carriages driving to Ottawa, one observer complained, turned the town into "a vast smoke house." By one o'clock the town square was filled to overflowing. At two o'clock, just as the debate was about to begin, the wooden awning over the speakers' platform collapsed under the weight of those sitting on it, delaying the start for half an hour. But then the debate got under way, enthralling an estimated 12,000 people. Ottawa, in northern Illinois, was pro-Republican, and the audience heckled Douglas unmercifully. At the second debate, a week later in Freeport, Douglas's use of the phrase "Black Republicans" drew angry shouts of "White, white" from the crowd. But as the debates moved south in the state, where Democrats predominated, the tables were turned, and Lincoln sometimes had to plead for a chance to be heard.

Although Douglas won the 1858 senatorial election in Illinois, the acclaim that Lincoln gained in the famous debates helped establish the Republicans' claim to be the only party capable of stopping the spread of slavery and made Lincoln himself a strong contender for the Republican presidential nomination in 1860. But the true winners of the Lincoln-Douglas debates were the people of Illinois who gathered peacefully to discuss the most serious issue of their time. The young German immigrant Carl Schurz, who attended the Quincy debate, was deeply impressed by its democratic character. He noted, "There was no end of cheering and shouting and jostling on the streets of Quincy that day. But in spite of the excitement created by the political contest, the crowds remained very good-natured, and the occasional jibes flung from one side to the other were uniformly received with a laugh." The Illinois people who participated in the community debates of 1858 showed the strong faith Americans held in their democratic institutions and the hope—finally shattered in the election of 1860—that a lasting political solution to the problem of slavery could be found. ■

Illinois

AMERICA IN 1850

In 1850, after half a century of rapid growth and change, America was a very different nation from the republic of 1800. Geographic expansion, population increase, economic development, and the changes wrought by the market revolution had transformed the struggling new nation. Economically, culturally, and politically Americans had forged a strong sense of national identity.

Expansion and Growth

America was now a much larger nation than it had been in 1800. Through war and diplomacy, the country had grown to continental dimensions, more than tripling in size from 890,000 to 3 million square miles. Its population had increased enormously: from 5.3 million in 1800 to more than 23 million, 4 million of whom were African American slaves and 2 million new immigrants, largely from Germany and Ireland. Comprising just sixteen states in 1800, America in 1850 had thirty-one, and more than half of the population lived west of the Appalachians. America's cities had undergone the most rapid half-century of growth they were ever to experience.

America was also much richer: it is estimated that real per capita income doubled between 1800 and 1850, moving the nation decisively out of the "developing" category. Southern cotton, which had contributed so much to American economic growth, continued to be the nation's principal export, but it was no longer the major influence on the domestic economy. The growth of manufacturing in the Northeast and the rapid opening up of rich farmlands in the Midwest fostered the interdependence of these two regions, which was aided by the rapid growth and consolidation of railway links between them in the 1850s. The future of the United States as a manufacturing nation, second only to Britain, and as a major exporter of agricultural products was assured. Nevertheless, the development of manufacturing in the Northeast and the increased economic importance of the Midwest had serious domestic political

implications. As the South's share of responsibility for economic growth waned, so did its political importance—at least in the eyes of many Northerners. Thus the very success of the United States both in geographic expansion and economic development served to undermine the role of the slave South in national politics and to hasten the day of open conflict between it and the free-labor North and Midwest.

Cultural Life and Social Issues

By 1850, the first shocks of the far-reaching social changes caused by the market revolution had been absorbed. The conflicting social impulses played out in the politics and reform movements of the Jacksonian period were gradually giving way to new middle-class values, institutions, and ideas. Newspapers, magazines, and communication improvements of all kinds created a national audience for American scholars and writers. Since the turn of the century, American writers had struggled to find distinctive American themes, and these efforts bore fruit in the 1850s in the burst of creative activity termed the "American Renaissance." During this decade, Henry Thoreau, Nathaniel Hawthorne, Walt Whitman, Herman Melville, Emily Dickinson, Frederick Douglass, and others wrote works of fiction and nonfiction that are considered American classics.

During the American Renaissance, American writers pioneered new literary forms. Nathaniel Hawthorne, in works like "Young Goodman Brown" (1835), raised the short story to a distinctive American literary form. Poets like Walt Whitman and Emily Dickinson experimented with unrhymed and "off-rhyme" verse, Whitman (in *Leaves of Grass*, published in 1855) to celebrate the boisterous pleasures of everyday life in New York City, Dickinson (who lived as a recluse in Amherst, Massachusetts) to catch her every fleeting thought and feeling in scraps of poetry that were not published until after her death. Another recluse, Henry David Thoreau, published *Walden* in 1854. A pastoral celebration of his life at Walden Pond, in Concord, Massachusetts, the essay was also a searching meditation on the cost to the individual of the loss of contact with nature that was a consequence of the market revolution.

Indeed, most of the writers of the American Renaissance were social critics. In *The Scarlet Letter* (1850) and *The House of the Seven Gables* (1851), both set in Puritan New England in the colonial period, Nathaniel Hawthorne brilliantly explored the moral choices faced by individuals as they try to reconcile repressive social expectations with private desires. Hawthorne's friend Herman Melville, in his great work *Moby Dick* (1851), drew on his own personal experience to write about the lives of ordinary sailors on a whaling voyage. But the story had deeper meanings: Melville's novel of Captain Ahab's obsessive search for the white whale is a profound study of the nature of good and evil and a critique

of American society in the 1850s. The strongest social critique, however, was Frederick Douglass's starkly simple autobiography, *Narrative of the Life of Frederick Douglass* (1845), which told of his brutal life as a slave.

The most successful American novel of the mid-nineteenth century was about the great issue of the day, slavery. In writing *Uncle Tom's Cabin*, Harriet Beecher Stowe combined the literary style of the then-popular women's domestic novels (discussed in Chapter 12) with vivid details of slavery culled from firsthand accounts by northern abolitionists and escaped slaves. Stowe, the daughter of the reforming clergyman Lyman Beecher, had married a Congregational minister and was herself a member of the evangelical movement. She had long been active in antislavery work, and a new Fugitive Slave Law passed

Web Exploration Think about the differences in population density in the United States at this time. What were the reasons behind these growth patterns?
www.prenhall.com/faragher/Map15.1

U.S. Population and Settlement, 1850 By 1850, the United States was a continental nation. Its people, whom Thomas Jefferson had once thought would not reach the Mississippi River for forty generations, had not only passed the river but leapfrogged to the west coast. In comparison to the America of 1800 (see the map on p. 242) the growth was astounding.

in 1850 impelled her to write a novel that would persuade everyone of the evils of slavery. She wrote every night at her kitchen table after putting her six children to bed, and, as she said later, the events of the novel came to her "with a vividness that could not be denied," making her feel like "an instrument of God."

Stowe's famous novel told a poignant story of the Christ-like slave Uncle Tom, who patiently endured the cruel treatment of an evil white overseer, Simon Legree. Published in 1851, it was a runaway best seller. More than 300,000 copies were sold in the first year, and within ten years the book had sold more than 2 million copies, becoming the all-time American best-seller in proportion to population. Turned into a play that remained popular throughout the nineteenth century, *Uncle Tom's Cabin* reached an even wider audience. Scenes from the novel such as that of Eliza carrying her son across the ice-choked Ohio River to freedom, Tom weeping for his children as he was sold south, and the death of little Eva are among the best-known passages in all of American literature. *Uncle Tom's Cabin* was more than a heart-tugging story: it was a call to action. In 1863, when Harriet Beecher Stowe was introduced to Abraham Lincoln, the president remarked, "So you're the little woman who wrote the book that made this great war!"

Political Parties and Slavery

Stowe's novel clearly spoke to the growing concern of the American people. Slavery had long been a divisive issue in national politics. Until the 1840s, compromises had always been found, most notably in the Constitution itself (see Chapter 8) and in the Missouri Crisis of 1820 (see Chapter 9). But the struggle over the place of slavery in the vast new territories gained in the Mexican-American War gave rise to intractable new sectional arguments. The year 1850 opened to the most serious political crisis the United States had ever known. The struggle over the issue of slavery in the territories had begun in 1846 with the Wilmot Proviso and was still unresolved. Increasingly, both politicians and ordinary people began to consider the almost unthinkable possibility of disunion. As politician James Buchanan wrote to a friend early in the year, "The blessed Union of these states is now in greater danger than it has ever been since the adoption of the federal Constitution." He feared that the two great national parties, the Whigs and the Democrats, would not be able to find a solu-

tion to the increasingly sectional division between North and South over slavery.

The Second American Party System forged in the great controversies of Andrew Jackson's presidency (see Chapter 10) was a national party system. In their need to mobilize great masses of recently enfranchised voters to elect a president every four years, politicians created organized party structures that overrode deeply rooted sectional differences. Politicians from all sections of the country cooperated because they knew their party could not succeed without national appeal. At a time when the ordinary person still had very strong sectional loyalties, the mass political party created a national community of like-minded voters. Yet, by the election of 1848 sectional interests were eroding the political "glue" in both parties. Although each party still appeared united, sectional fissures already ran deep.

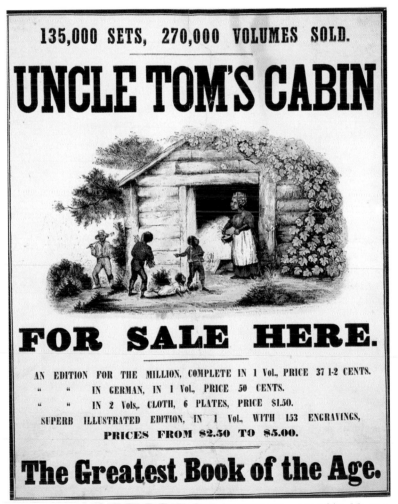

This poster advertises *Uncle Tom's Cabin*, the bestselling novel by Harriet Beecher Stowe. This poignant story of long-suffering African American slaves had an immense impact on Northern popular opinion, swaying it decisively against slavery. In that respect, the poster's boast, "the greatest book of the age" was correct.

Political splits were preceded by divisions in other social institutions. Disagreements about slavery had already split the country's great religious organizations into northern and southern groups, the Presbyterians in 1837, the Methodists in 1844, and the Baptists in 1845. (Some of these splits turned out to be permanent. The Southern Baptist Convention, for example, is still a separate body.) Theodore Weld, the abolitionist leader, saw these splits as inevitable: "Events . . . have for years been silently but without a moment's pause, settling the basis of two great parties, the nucleus of one slavery, of the other, freedom." Indeed, the abolitionists had been posing this simple yet uncompromising choice between slavery or freedom since the 1830s. Moreover, they had been insisting on a compelling distinction: as Liberty Party spokesman Salmon P. Chase said, "Freedom is national; slavery only is local and sectional."

States' Rights and Slavery

But was freedom national and slavery sectional, or was it the other way around? Southern politicians took the latter view, as their foremost spokesman, South Carolina's John C. Calhoun, made ringingly clear throughout his long career.

In 1828 Calhoun had begun the protracted Nullification Crisis by asserting the constitutional right of states to "nullify" national laws that were harmful to their interests (see Chapter 10). Calhoun argued, as others have since, that the states' rights doctrine protected the legitimate rights of a minority in a democratic system governed by majority rule.

In 1847, Calhoun responded to the 1846 Wilmot Proviso with an elaboration of the states' rights argument. In spite of the apparent precedents of the Northwest Ordinance of 1787 and the Missouri Compromise, Calhoun argued that Congress did not have a constitutional right to prohibit slavery in the territories. The territories, he said, were the common property of all the states, north and south, and Congress could not discriminate against slave owners as they moved west. On the contrary, Calhoun argued, slave owners had a constitutional right to the protection of their property wherever they moved. Of course, Calhoun's legally correct description of African American slaves as property enraged abolitionists. But on behalf of the South, Calhoun was expressing the belief—and the fear—that his interpretation of the Constitution was the only protection for slave owners, whose right to own slaves (a fundamental right in southern eyes) was being attacked. Calhoun's position on the territories quickly became southern dogma: anything less than full access to the territories was unconstitutional. Slavery, Calhoun and other Southerners insisted, had to be national.

As Congressman Robert Toombs of Georgia put the case in 1850, there was very little room for compromise:

> I stand upon the great principle that the South has the right to an equal participation in the territories of the United States. . . . She will divide with you if you wish it, but the right to enter all or divide I shall never surrender. . . . Deprive us of this right and appropriate the common property to yourselves, it is then your government, not mine. Then I am its enemy. . . . Give us our just rights, and we are ready . . . to stand by the Union. . . . Refuse [them], and for one, I will strike for independence.

Northern Fears of "The Slave Power"

The words of Southerners like Calhoun and Toombs confirmed for many Northerners the warnings of antislavery leaders that they were endangered by a menacing "slave power." Liberty Party leader James Birney, in a speech in 1844, was the first to add this phrase to the nation's political vocabulary. "The slave power," Birney explained, was a group of aristocratic slave owners who not only dominated the political and social life of the South but conspired to control the federal government as well, posing a danger to free speech and free institutions throughout the nation.

Birney's "slave power" was a caricature of the influence slave owners wielded over southern politics and of the increasingly defensive and monolithic response of southern representatives in national politics after 1830 (see Chapter 11). The proslavery strategy of maintaining supremacy in the Senate by having at least as many slave as free states admitted to the Union (a plan that required slavery expansion) and of maintaining control, or at least veto power, over presidential nominees seemed, in southern eyes, to be nothing less than ordinary self-defense. But to antislavery advocates, these actions looked like a conspiracy by sectional interests to control national politics. Birney's warnings about "the slave power" seemed in 1844 merely the overheated rhetoric of an extremist group of abolitionists. But the defensive southern political strategies of the 1850s were to convince an increasing number of northern voters that "the slave power" did in fact exist. Thus in northern eyes the South became a demonic monolith that threatened the national government.

Two Communities, Two Perspectives

Ironically, it was a common belief in expansion that made the arguments between Northerners and Southerners so irreconcilable. Southerners had been the strongest supporters of the Mexican-American War, and they still hoped to expand into Cuba, believing that the slave system must grow or wither. On the other hand, although many northern Whigs had opposed the Mexican-American War, most did so for antislavery reasons, not because they opposed expansion. The strong showing of the Free-Soil Party (which evolved out of the Liberty Party) in the election of 1848 (getting 10 percent of the popular vote) was proof of that. Basically, both North and South believed in manifest destiny, but each on its own terms.

Similarly, both North and South used the language of basic rights and liberties in the debate over expansion. But free-soilers were speaking of personal liberty, whereas Southerners meant their right to own a particular kind of property (slaves) and to maintain a way of life based on the possession of that property. In defending its own rights, each side had taken measures that infringed on the rights of the other. Southerners pointed out that abolitionists had libeled slave owners as a class and that they had bombarded the South with unwanted literature, abused the right of petition to Congress, incited slaves to rebellion, and actively helped slaves to escape. For their part, Northerners accused slave owners of censorship of the mails; imposition of the "gag rule" (repealed in 1844), which prohibited any petition against slavery from being read to or discussed by Congress; suppression of free speech in the South; and, of course, commission of the moral wrong of enslaving others in the first place.

By 1850, North and South had created fixed stereotypes of the other. To antislavery Northerners, the South was an economic backwater dominated by a small slave-owning aristocracy that lived off the profits of forced labor and deprived poor whites of their democratic rights and the fruits of honest work. The slave system was not only immoral but a drag on the entire nation, for, in the words of Senator William Seward of New York, it subverted the "intelligence, vigor and energy" that were essential for national growth. In contrast, the dynamic and enterprising commercial North boasted a free labor ideology that offered economic opportunity to the common man and ensured his democratic rights (see Chapter 12).

Things looked very different through southern eyes. Far from being economically backward, the

South, through its export of cotton, was, according to Southerners, the great engine of national economic growth from which the North benefited. Slavery was not only a blessing to an inferior race but the cornerstone of democracy, for it ensured the freedom and independence of all white men without entailing the bitter class divisions that marked the North. Slave owners accused northern manufacturers of hypocrisy for practicing "wage slavery" without the paternal benevolence they claimed to bestow on their slaves. The North, James Henry Hammond of South Carolina charged, had eliminated the "name [of slavery], but not the thing," for "your whole hireling class of manual laborers and 'operatives' . . . are essentially slaves."

By the early 1850s, these vastly different visions of the North and the South—the result of many years of political controversy—had become fixed, and the chances of national reconciliation increasingly slim. Over the course of the decade, many Americans came to believe that the place of slavery in the nation's life had to be permanently settled. And they increasingly wondered whether their two sectional communities—one slave, one free—could continue to be part of a unitary national one.

In 1850, the three men who had long represented America's three major regions attempted to resolve the political crisis brought on by the applications of California and Utah for statehood. Henry Clay is speaking; John C. Calhoun stands third from right; and Daniel Webster is seated at the left with his head in his hand. Both Clay and Webster were ill, and Calhoun died before the Compromise of 1850 was arranged by a younger group of politicians led by Stephen A. Douglas.

SOURCE: Library of Congress.

THE COMPROMISE OF 1850

By 1850 the issue raised by the Wilmot Proviso—whether slavery should be extended to the new territories—could no longer be ignored. Overnight, the California Gold Rush had turned a remote frontier into a territory with a booming population. In 1849 both California and Utah applied for statehood. Should these territories be admitted as slave or free states? A simmering border war between Texas, a slave state, and New Mexico, which seemed likely to be a free state, had to be settled, as did the issue of the debts Texas had incurred as an independent republic. Closer to home, antislavery forces demanded the end of slavery in the District of Columbia, while slave owners complained that Northerners were refusing to return escaped slaves, as federal law mandated.

Debate and Compromise

The Compromise of 1850 was the final act in the political careers of the three aging men who in the public mind best represented America's sections: Westerner Henry Clay; Southerner John C. Calhoun; and Daniel Webster, spokesman for the North. It was sadly appropriate to the bitter sectional argument of 1850 that the three men contributed great words to the debate but that the compromise itself was enacted by younger men. Calhoun brought an aura of death with him to the Senate as he sat, shrouded in flannels, listening to the speech that he was too ill to read for himself. He died less than a month later, still insisting on the right of the South to secede if necessary to preserve its way of life. Daniel Webster claimed to speak "not as a Massachusetts man, nor as a Northern man, but as an American. . . . I speak today for the preservation of the Union." He rejected southern claims that peaceable secession was possible or desirable and pleaded with abolitionists to compromise enough to keep the South in the Union. Clay, claiming he had "never before risen to address any assemblage so oppressed, so appalled, and so anxious," argued eloquently for compromise, but left the Senate in ill health before his plea was answered.

On July 9, 1850, in the midst of the debate, President Zachary Taylor died of acute gastroenteritis, caused by a hasty snack of fruit and cold milk at a Fourth of July celebration. A bluff military man, Taylor had been prepared to follow Andrew Jackson's precedent during the Nullification Crisis of 1832 and simply demand that southern dissidents compromise. When Vice President Millard Fillmore assumed the presidency, however, he helped adjust the Compromise of 1850 to southern liking. Fillmore was a moderate northern Whig and more prosouthern than the southern-born Taylor had been. Moreover, although Clay had

assembled all the necessary parts of the bargain, it was not he but members of a younger political generation, and in particular the rising young Democrat from Illinois, Stephen Douglas, who drove the Compromise of 1850 through Congress. The final product consisted of five separate bills (it had been impossible to obtain a majority for a comprehensive measure), embodying three separate compromises.

First, California was admitted as a free state, but the status of the remaining former Mexican possessions was left to be decided by popular sovereignty (a vote of the territory's inhabitants) when they applied for statehood. (Utah's application for statehood was not accepted until 1896 because of controversy over the Mormon practice of polygamy.) The result was, for the time being, fifteen slave states and sixteen free states. Second, Texas (a slave state) was required to cede land to New Mexico Territory (free or slave status undecided). In return, the federal government assumed $10 million of debts Texas had incurred before it became a state. Finally, the slave trade, but not slavery itself, was ended in the District of Columbia, but a stronger fugitive slave law was enacted.

Jubilation and relief greeted the news that compromise had been achieved. In Washington, where the anxiety and concern had been greatest, drunken crowds serenaded Congress, shouting, "The Union is saved!" That was certainly true for the moment, but analysis of the votes on the five bills that made up the compromise revealed no consistent majority. The sectional splits within each party that had existed before the compromise remained. Antislavery northern Whigs and proslavery southern Democrats, each the larger wing of their party, were the least willing to compromise. Southern Whigs and northern Democrats were the forces for moderation, but each group was dwindling in popular appeal as sectional animosities grew.

In the country as a whole, the feeling was that the problem of slavery in the territories had been solved. The *Philadelphia Pennsylvanian* was confident that "peace and tranquillity" had been ensured, and the *Louisville Journal* said that a weight seemed to have been lifted from the heart of America. But as former Liberty Party spokesman Salmon P. Chase, now a senator from Ohio, soberly noted, "The question of slavery in the territories has been avoided. It has not been settled." And many Southerners felt that their only real gain in the contested compromise was the Fugitive Slave Law, which quickly turned out to be an inflammatory measure.

The Fugitive Slave Act

From the early days of their movement, northern abolitionists had urged slaves to escape, promising assistance and support when they reached the North. Some

OVERVIEW

THE GREAT SECTIONAL COMPROMISES

Missouri Compromise	1820	Admits Missouri to the Union as a slave state and Maine as a free state; prohibits slavery in the rest of the Louisiana Purchase Territory north of 36°30'.
		Territory Covered: The entire territory of the Louisiana Purchase, exclusive of the state of Louisiana, which had been admitted to the Union in 1812.
Compromise of 1850	1850	Admits California to the Union as a free state, settles the borders of Texas (a slave state); sets no conditions concerning slavery for the rest of the territory acquired from Mexico.
		Territory Covered: The territory that had been part of Mexico before the end of the Mexican-American War and the Treaty of Guadalupe Hidalgo (1848): part of Texas, California, Utah Territory (now Utah, Nevada, and part of Colorado), and New Mexico Territory (now New Mexico and Arizona).

free African Americans had offered far more than verbal support. At great risk to themselves, they consistently offered refuge and assistance to escaped slaves. In spite of the renown of the organized network of whites and blacks known as the Underground Railroad, it rescued only a few slaves. Most escaped slaves found their most reliable help within northern free black communities. Northerners had long been appalled by professional slave catchers, who zealously seized African Americans in the North and took them south into slavery again. Most abhorrent in northern eyes was that captured black people were at the mercy of slave catchers because they had no legal right to defend themselves. In more than one case, a northern free African American was captured in his own community and helplessly shipped into slavery.

Solomon Northup was one such person. In his widely sold account *Twelve Years a Slave*, published in 1853, he told a harrowing tale of being kidnapped in Washington, the nation's capital, and shipped south. Northup spent twelve years as a slave before he was able to send a message to northern friends to bring the legal proof to free him. As a result of stories like Northup's and the very effective publicity generated by abolitionists, nine northern states passed personal liberty laws between 1842 and 1850, serving notice that they would not cooperate with federal recapture efforts. These northern laws enraged Southerners, who had long been convinced that all Northerners, not just abolitionists, were actively hindering efforts to reclaim

their escaped slaves. At issue were two distinct definitions of "rights": Northerners were upset at the denial of legal and personal rights to escaped slaves; Southerners saw illegal infringement of their property rights. Southerners insisted that a strong federal law be part of the Compromise of 1850.

The Fugitive Slave Law, enacted in 1850, dramatically increased the power of slave owners to capture escaped slaves. The full authority of the federal government now supported slave owners, and although fugitives were guaranteed a hearing before a federal commissioner, they were not allowed to testify on their own behalf. Furthermore, the new law imposed federal penalties on citizens who protected or assisted fugitives, or who did not cooperate in their return. A number of free northern blacks, afraid that they might share Solomon Northup's fate, emigrated to Canada. Soon 30,000 to 40,000 African Americans, some formerly slave, some free, lived in Upper Canada, with the reluctant acquiescence of local authorities. Like many Americans, most Canadians were unwilling to accept black people as social equals, but they also were unwilling to force African Americans to risk recapture and return to slavery. In Boston, the center of the American abolitionist movement, reaction to the Fugitive Slave Law was fierce. When an escaped slave named Shadrach Minkins was seized in February 1851, a group of African American men broke into the courtroom, overwhelmed the federal marshals, seized Minkins, and sent him safely to Canada. Although the

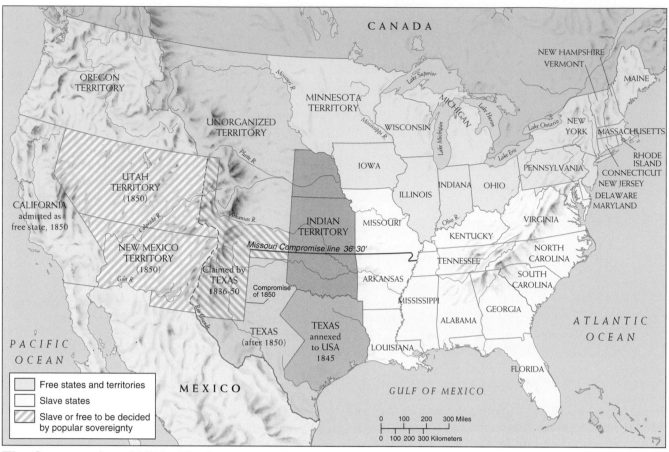

The Compromise of 1850 The Compromise of 1850 reflected heightened sectional tensions by being even messier and more awkward than the Missouri Compromise of 1820. California was admitted as a free state, the borders of Texas were settled, and the status of the rest of the former Mexican territory was left to be decided later by popular sovereignty. No consistent majority voted for the five separate bills that made up the compromise.

action had community support—a Massachusetts jury defiantly refused to convict the perpetrators—many people, including Daniel Webster and President Fillmore, condemned it as "mob rule."

The federal government responded with overwhelming force. In April 1851, 300 armed soldiers were mobilized to prevent the rescue of Thomas Sims, who was being shipped back into slavery. In the most famous case in Boston, a biracial group of armed abolitionists led by Unitarian clergyman Thomas Wentworth Higginson stormed the federal courthouse in 1854 in an attempt to save escaped slave Anthony Burns. The rescue effort failed, and a federal deputy marshal was killed. President Pierce sent marines, cavalry, and artillery to Boston to reinforce the guard over Burns and ordered a federal ship to be ready to deliver the fugitive back into slavery. When the effort by defense lawyers to argue for Burns's freedom failed, Bostonians raised money to buy his freedom. But the U.S. attorney, ordered by the president to enforce

the Fugitive Slave Law in all circumstances, blocked the purchase. The case was lost, and Burns was marched to the docks through streets lined with sorrowing abolitionists. Buildings were shrouded in black and draped with American flags hanging upside down, while bells tolled as if for a funeral.

The Burns case radicalized many Northerners. Conservative Whig George Hilliard wrote to a friend, "When it was all over, and I was left alone in my office, I put my face in my hands and wept. I could do nothing less." During the 1850s, 322 black fugitives were sent back into slavery; only 11 were declared free. Northern popular sentiment and the Fugitive Slave Law, rigorously enforced by the federal government, were increasingly at odds. The northern abolitionists who used force to rescue captured slaves were breaking the law, but they were winning the battle for public opinion.

In this volatile atmosphere, escaped African Americans wrote and lectured bravely on behalf of freedom. Frederick Douglass, the most famous and eloquent of the fugitive slaves, spoke out fearlessly in support of armed resistance. "The only way to make the Fugitive Slave Law a dead letter," he said in 1853, "is to make a half dozen or more dead kidnappers." Openly active in the underground network that helped slaves reach safety in Canada, Douglass himself had been constantly in danger of capture until his friends bought his freedom in 1847. Harriet Jacobs, who escaped to the North after seven years in hiding in the South, wrote bitterly in her *Incidents in the Life of a Slave Girl* (1861) that the Fugitive Slave Law made her feel that "I was, in fact, a slave in New York, as subject to slave laws as I had been in a slave state. . . . I had been chased during half my life, and it seemed as if the chase was never to end." Threatened by owners who came north for her, Jacobs went into hiding again, until she was informed that friends had arranged her purchase: "A gentleman near me said, 'It's true; I have seen the bill of sale.' 'The bill of sale!' Those words struck me like a blow. So I was sold at last! A human being sold in the free city of New York!"

The Fugitive Slave Law brought home the reality of slavery to residents of the free states. In effect, this law made slavery national and forced northern communities to confront what that meant. Although most people were still unwilling to grant social equality to the free African Americans who lived in the northern states, more and more had come to believe that the institution of slavery was wrong. The strong northern reaction against the Fugitive Slave Law also had consequences in the South. As Democrat Cave Johnson of Tennessee warned, "If the fugitive slave bill is not enforced in the North, the moderate men of the South . . . will be overwhelmed by the 'fire-eaters,'" the extremists who favored immediate secession. Northern protests against the Fugitive Slave Law bred suspicion in the South and encouraged secessionist thinking. These new currents of public opinion were reflected in the election of 1852.

The Election of 1852

The first sign of the weakening of the national party system in 1852 was the difficulty both parties experienced at their nominating conventions. With long-time Whig party leader Henry Clay now dead, William Seward of New York became the unofficial party head, much to the displeasure of southern Whigs. Seward preferred General Winfield Scott (a military hero like the party's previous two candidates) to the prosouthern Fillmore, and after fifty-two ballots, managed to get him nominated. Many southern Whigs were angered and alienated by the choice and either abstained during the voting, like Georgia's Alexander

Stephens, or, like Robert Toombs, cast a protest vote for the Democratic candidate. Although southern Whigs were still elected to Congress, their loyalty to the national party was strained to the breaking point. The Whigs never again fielded a presidential candidate.

The Democrats had a wider variety of candidates: Lewis Cass of popular sovereignty fame; Stephen Douglas, architect of the Compromise of 1850; and James Buchanan, described as a "Northern man with Southern principles." Cass, Douglas, and Buchanan competed for forty-nine ballots, each strong enough to block the others but not strong enough to win. Finally the party turned to a handsome, affable nonentity, Franklin Pierce of New Hampshire, who was thought to have southern sympathies. Uniting on a platform pledging "faithful execution" of all parts of the Compromise of 1850, including the Fugitive Slave Law, Democrats polled well in the South and in the North. Most Democrats who had voted for the Free-Soil Party in 1848 voted for Pierce. So, in record numbers, did immigrant Irish and German voters, who were eligible for citizenship after three years' residence. The strong immigrant vote for Pierce was a sign of the strength of the Democratic machines in northern cities (see Chapter 13), and reformers complained, not for the last time, about widespread corruption and "vote buying" by urban ward bosses. Overall, however, "Genl. Apathy is the strongest candidate out here," as one Ohioan reported. Pierce easily won the 1852 election, 254 electoral votes to 42. Voter turnout was below 70 percent, lower than it had been since 1836.

"Young America": The Politics of Expansion

Pierce entered the White House in 1853 on a wave of good feeling. Massachusetts Whig Amos Lawrence reported, "Never since Washington has an administration commenced with the hearty [good] will of so large a portion of the country." This goodwill was soon strained by Pierce's support for the expansionist adventures of the "Young America" movement.

The "Young America" movement began as a group of writers and politicans in the New York Democratic Party who believed in the democratic and nationalistic promise of "manifest destiny" (a term coined by one of their members, John Sullivan). By the 1850s, however, their lofty goals had shrunk to a desire to conquer Central America and Cuba. Young America expansionists had glanced covetously southward since the end of the Mexican-American War. President Polk himself had wanted to buy Cuba and to intervene in Mexican politics but was rebuffed by Congress (see Chapter 14). When in 1858 the perennial conflict between centrists and liberals in Mexico broke into civil war, the fighting served to convince some southerners that Mexico was ripe for expansion, but ironically, before they could act, America's own Civil War intervened.

During the Pierce administration, several private "filibusters" (from the Spanish *filibustero*, meaning an "adventurer" or "pirate") invaded Caribbean and Central American countries, usually with the declared intention of extending slave territory. The best-known of the filibusters, William Walker, was also the most improbable. Short, slight, and soft-spoken, Walker led not one but three invasions of Nicaragua. After the first invasion in 1855, Walker became ruler of the country and encouraged settlement by southern slave owners, but he was unseated by a regional revolt in 1857. His subsequent efforts to regain control of the country failed, and in his last attempt he was captured and executed by firing squad in Honduras.

The Pierce administration, not directly involved in the filibustering, was deeply involved in an effort to obtain Cuba. In part, the effort was prompted by abortive slave revolts in Cuba in 1843–44, which led some Cuban slave owners to want annexation to the United States so that slavery could continue. In 1854, Pierce authorized his minister to Spain, Pierre Soulé, to try to force the unwilling Spanish to sell Cuba for $130 million. Soulé met in Ostend, Belgium, with the American ministers to France and England, John Mason and James Buchanan, to compose the offer, which was a mixture of cajolements and threats. At first appealing to Spain to recognize the deep affinities between the Cubans and American Southerners that made them "one people with one destiny," the document went on to threaten to "wrest" Cuba from Spain if necessary. This amazing document, which became known as the Ostend Manifesto, was supposed to be secret but was soon leaked to the press. Deeply embarrassed, the Pierce administration was forced to repudiate it.

The complicity between the Pierce administration and proslavery expansionists was foolhardy and lost it the northern goodwill with which it had begun. The sectional crisis that preceded the Compromise of 1850 had made obvious the danger of reopening the territorial issue. Ironically, it was not the Young America expansionists but the prime mover of the Compromise of 1850, Stephen A. Douglas, who reignited the sectional struggle over slavery expansion.

THE CRISIS OF THE NATIONAL PARTY SYSTEM

In 1854, Douglas introduced the Kansas-Nebraska Act, proposing to open those lands that had been the northern part of Indian Territory to American settlers under the principle of popular sovereignty. He thereby reopened the question of slavery in the territories. Douglas knew he was taking a political risk, but he believed he could satisfy both his expansionist aims and his presidential ambitions. He was wrong. Instead, he pushed the national party system into crisis, first killing the Whigs and then destroying the Democrats.

The Kansas-Nebraska Act

Until 1854, white Americans thought of Kansas only as a passageway to other places farther west. A part of Indian Territory, Kansas was peopled largely by tribes who had been moved from their original homes in the East. In the great Indian removals of the 1830s, these tribes had been promised the Kansas lands "as long as grass grows and water flows." The promise was broken in 1854, when prior treaties were ignored and the northern part of Indian Territory was thrown open to white settlement.

In a stunning example of the expansionist pressures generated by the market revolution, Stephen Douglas introduced the Kansas-Nebraska Act to further the construction of a transcontinental railroad across what was still considered the "Great American Desert" to California. Douglas wanted the rail line to terminate in Chicago, in his own state of Illinois, rather than in the rival St. Louis, but for that to happen, the land west of Iowa and Missouri had to be organized into territories (the first step toward statehood). To get Congress to agree to the organization of the territories, however, Douglas needed the votes of southern Democrats, who were unwilling to support him unless the territories were open to slavery. Douglas also coveted his party's nomination for the presidency in 1856, and needed the continuing support of southern Democrats to secure it.

Douglas thought he was solving his problem by proposing that the status of slavery in the new territories be governed by the principle of popular sovereignty. Democratic politicians had favored this democratic-sounding slogan, vague enough to appeal to both proslavery and antislavery voters, ever since 1848. Douglas thought Southerners would support his bill because of its popular sovereignty provision, and Northerners because it favored a northern route for the transcontinental railroad. Privately, Douglas believed that the topography of the Kansas-Nebraska region was unsuitable for slave agriculture and that the region's inhabitants would decide to enter the Union as free states. Douglas chose also to downplay the price he had to pay for southern support—by allowing the possibility of slavery in the new territories his bill in effect repealed the Missouri Compromise of 1820, which barred slavery north of latitude 36°30'.

The Kansas-Nebraska Act, 1854   The Kansas-Nebraska Act, proposed by Steven A. Douglas in 1854, opened the central and northern Great Plains to settlement. The act had two major faults: it robbed Indian peoples of half the territory guaranteed to them by treaty, and, because it repealed the Missouri Compromise Line, it opened up the lands to warring proslavery and antislavery factions.

The Kansas-Nebraska bill passed, but it badly strained the major political parties. Southern Whigs voted with southern Democrats in favor of the measure, northern Whigs rejected it absolutely, creating an irreconcilable split that left Whigs unable to field a presidential candidate in 1856. The damage to the Democratic Party was almost as great. In the congressional elections of 1854, northern Democrats lost two-thirds of their seats (a drop from ninety-one to twenty-five), giving the southern Democrats (who were solidly in favor of slavery extension) the dominant voice both in Congress and within the party.

Douglas had committed one of the greatest miscalculations in American political history. A storm of protest arose throughout the North. More than 300 large anti-Nebraska rallies occurred during congressional consideration of the bill, and the anger did not subside. Douglas, who confidently believed that "the people of the North will sustain the measure when they come to understand it," found himself shouted down more than once at public rallies when he tried to explain the bill.

The Kansas-Nebraska bill shifted a crucial sector of northern opinion: the wealthy merchants, bankers, and manufacturers, called the "Cotton Whigs," who had economic ties with southern slave owners and had always disapproved of abolitionist activity. Convinced that the bill would encourage antislavery feeling in the North, Cotton Whigs urged southern politicians to vote against it, only to be ignored. Passage of the Kansas-Nebraska Act convinced many northern Whigs that compromise with the South was impossible. Even as sober a newspaper as the *New York Times* regarded the act as "part of this great scheme for extending and perpetuating the supremacy of the Slave Power." Joining the antislavery cause were some Cotton Whigs like manufacturer Amos Lawrence of Massachusetts, who had so warmly welcomed the prospect of sectional peace at the beginning of the Pierce administration. Lawrence provided the financial backing for the first group of antislavery New

Englanders who settled Kansas in 1854, and in gratitude they named their town for him.

In Kansas in 1854, hasty treaties were concluded with the Indian tribes who owned the land. Some, such as the Kickapoos, Shawnees, Sauks, and Foxes, agreed to relocate to small reservations. Others, like the Delawares, Weas, and Iowas, agreed to sell their lands to whites. Still others, such as the Cheyennes and Sioux, kept the western part of Kansas Territory (now Colorado)—until gold was discovered there in 1859. Once the treaties were signed, both proslavery and antislavery white settlers began to pour in, and the battle was on.

"Bleeding Kansas"

The first to claim land in Kansas were residents of nearby Missouri, itself a slave state. Egged on by Democratic Senator David Atchison of Missouri (who took a leave of absence from Congress to lead them), Missourians took up land claims, established proslavery strongholds such as the towns of Leavenworth, Kickapoo, and Atchison, and repeatedly and blatantly swamped Kansas elections with Missouri votes. In 1855,

VOTING IN KICKAPOO.

This engraving shows "Border Ruffians" from Missouri lining up to vote for slavery in the Kickapoo, Kansas Territory election of 1855. The widespread practice of illegal voting and of open violence earned Kansas the dreadful nickname of "Bleeding Kansas."

SOURCE: The Granger Collection (4E1041/36).

in the second of several notoriously fraudulent elections, 6,307 ballots were cast in a territory that had fewer than 3,000 eligible voters. The rest of the votes—all proslavery—were cast by "border ruffians," as they proudly called themselves, from Missouri. These were frontiersmen, fond of boasting that they could "scream louder, jump higher, shoot closer, get drunker at night and wake up soberer in the morning than any man this side of the Rocky Mountains."

Northerners quickly responded, with the encouragement of sympathetic politicians. Free-Soil (antislavery) New Englanders were recruited to Kansas by the New England Emigrant Aid Society, founded by abolitionist Eli Thayer of Massachusetts. The first party of New Englanders arrived in the summer of 1854 and established the free-soil town of Lawrence. More than a thousand others had joined them by the following summer. Lawrence quickly blossomed from a town of tent homes to one of solid log cabins, a church, a sawmill, stores, and a stone foundation for what became the Free State Hotel, sponsored by the Emigrant Aid Society. These migrants were all free-soilers, and many were religious reformers as well. The contrast of values between them and the border ruffians was almost total. When nondrinking William Phillips stiffly refused a friendly offer of a drink from a Missourian, the border ruffian burst out, "That's just it! This thing of temperance and abolitionism and the Emigrant Aid Society are all the same kind of thing."

Kansas soon became a bloody battleground as the two factions struggled to secure the mandate of "popular sovereignty." Free-soilers in Lawrence received shipments of heavy crates, innocuously marked "BOOKS" but actually containing Sharps repeating rifles, sent by eastern supporters. For their part, the border ruffians—already heavily armed, with Bowie knives in their boots, revolvers at their waists, rifles slung from their shoulders, and swords at their sides—called for reinforcements. David Atchison exhorted Alabamans: "Let your young men come forth to Missouri and Kansas! Let them come well armed!"

In the summer of 1856, these lethal preparations exploded into open warfare. First, proslavery forces burned and looted the town of Lawrence. The Free State Hotel, among other buildings, was burned to the ground. In retaliation, a grim old man named John Brown led his sons in a raid on the proslavery settlers of Pottawatomie Creek, killing five unarmed people. A wave of violence ensued. Armed bands roamed the countryside, and burnings and killings became commonplace. John Brown and his followers were just one of many bands of marauding murderers who were never arrested, never brought to trial, and never stopped from committing further violence. Peaceful residents of large sections of rural Kansas were repeatedly forced to flee to the safety of military forts when rumors of one or another armed band reached them.

The rest of the nation watched in horror as the residents of Kansas slaughtered each other in the pursuit of sectional goals. Americans' pride in their nation's great achievements was threatened by the endless violence in one small part—but a part that increasingly seemed to represent the divisions of the whole.

The Politics of Nativism

The violence in Kansas was echoed by increasing violence in the nation's cities. In New York, the violence of the 1850s was presaged by the Astor Place riot of 1849. What began as a rather commonplace protest against an aristocratic British actor escalated into a pitched battle between thousands of workingmen (many of them Irish) and the city's most elite militia, the Seventh Regiment. In the end, twenty-two were dead, 150 wounded, and 117 arrested. Serious violence marred the elections of 1854 and 1856 in New York. In 1857, popular rage focused on the state militia who were called in to suppress a Fourth of July fight between two rival political gangs, the Bowery Boys and the Dead Rabbits. Widespread rioting, involving women and children as well as workingmen spread far beyond the slum area of Five Points into middle class areas of the city. In New Orleans, anger over corrupt elections caused a self-appointed vigilance committee to attempt a takeover of the city government. The vigilantes recruited several hundred men to erect barricades in Jackson Square in the heart of the city, where they skirmished for five days with an opposing force composed largely of Catholics and immigrants. In Chicago, riots started in 1855 when the mayor attempted to close the saloons on Sunday. German workingmen joined by Irishmen and Swedes paraded in protest and were met by 200 men of the National Guard, militia and special police. The ensuing "Lager Beer Riots" ended with the imposition of martial law on the entire city.

This urban violence, like that in Kansas, was caused by the breakdown of the two party system. The breakup of the Whig Party left a political vacuum that was filled with one of the strongest bursts of nativism, or anti-immigrant feeling, in American history and by the rapid growth of the new American Party, which formed in 1850 to give political expression to nativism. The new party was in part a reaction to the Democratic Party's success in capturing the support of the rapidly growing population of mostly Catholic foreign-born voters. Irish immigrants in particular voted Democratic, both in reaction to Whig hostility (as in Boston) and because of their own antiblack prejudices. Frequently in competition with free African Americans for low-paying jobs, Irish immigrants were more likely to share the attitudes of Southerners than those of abolitionists.

The reformist and individualistic attitudes of many Whigs inclined them toward nativism. Many Whigs disapproved of the new immigrants because they were poor, Catholic, and often disdainful of the temperance movement. The Catholic Church's opposition to the liberal European revolutions of 1848 also fueled anti-Catholic fears. If America's new Catholic immigrants opposed the revolutions in which other Americans took such pride (believing them to be modeled on the American example), how could the future of America's own democracy be ensured? Finally, nativist Whigs held immigration to be solely responsible for the increases in crime and the rising cost of relief for the poor that accompanied the astoundingly rapid urban growth of the 1830s and 1840s (see Chapter 13).

Women reformers were as prone to nativism as men. As early as 1838, the influential Lydia Sigourney wrote in alarm in her *Letters to Mothers* about the "influx of untutored foreigners" that had made the United States "a repository for the waste and refuse of other nations." Sigourney urged women to organize an internal missionary movement that would carry the principles of middle-class American domesticity to the unenlightened foreigners.

Nativism drew former Whigs, especially young men in white-collar and skilled blue-collar occupations, to the new American Party. At the core of the party were several secret fraternal societies open only to native-born Protestants who pledged never to vote for a Catholic, on the grounds that all Catholics took their orders straight from the pope in Rome. When questioned about their beliefs, party members maintained secrecy by answering, "I know nothing"—hence the popular name for American Party members, the Know-Nothings. Few Know-Nothings were wealthy: most were workers or small farmers whose jobs or ways of life were threatened by the cheap labor and unfamiliar culture of the new immigrants. But the secretiveness and intolerance of the Know-Northings were new to American political culture, provoking the urban violence described above.

Know-Nothings scored startling victories in northern state elections in 1854, winning control of the legislature in Massachusetts and polling 40 percent of the vote in Pennsylvania. No wonder one Pennsylvania Democrat reported, "Nearly everybody seems to have gone altogether deranged on Nativism." Although most of the new immigrants lived in the North, resentment and anger against them was national, and the American Party initially polled well in the South, attracting the votes of many former southern Whigs. But in the 1850s, no party could ignore slavery, and in 1855 the American Party split into northern (antislavery) and southern (proslavery) wings. Soon after this split, many people who had voted for the Know-Nothings shifted their support to another new party, one that combined many characteristics of the Whigs with a westward-looking, expansionist, free-soil policy. This was the Republican Party, founded in 1854.

The Republican Party and the Election of 1856

In 1854 a Massachusetts voter described the elections in his state in terms of "freedom, temperance, and Protestantism against slavery, rum, and Romanism," linking nativism with sectional politics. "Slavery, rum, and Romanism" were supposed to describe the national Democratic Party, whose supporters included southern slave owners and northern immigrant Catholics. "Freedom, temperance, and Protestantism," were meant to characterize the Republican Party. Many constituencies, however, found room in the new party. Its supporters included many former northern Whigs who opposed slavery absolutely, many Free-Soil Party supporters who opposed the expansion of slavery but were willing to tolerate it in the South, and many northern reformers concerned about temperance and Catholicism. The Republicans also attracted the economic core of the old Whig Party—the merchants and industrialists who wanted a strong national government to promote economic growth by supporting a protective tariff, transportation improvements, and cheap land for western farmers. In quieter times it would have taken this party a while to sort out all its differences and become a true political community. But because of the sectional crisis, the fledgling party nearly won its very first presidential election.

The immediate question facing the nation in 1856 was which new party, the Know-Nothings or the Republicans, would emerge the stronger. But the more important question was whether the Democratic Party could hold together. The two strongest contenders for the Democratic nomination were President Pierce and Stephen A. Douglas. Douglas had proposed the Kansas-Nebraska Act and Pierce had actively supported it. Both men therefore had the support of the southern wing of the party. But it was precisely their support of this act that made Northerners oppose both of them. The Kansas-Nebraska Act's divisive effect on the Democratic Party now became clear: no one who had voted on the bill, either for

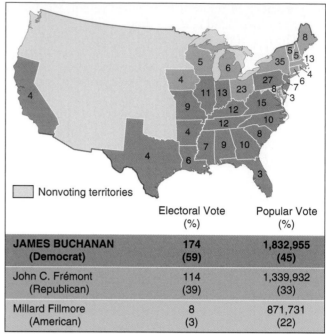

	Electoral Vote (%)	Popular Vote (%)
JAMES BUCHANAN (Democrat)	**174** **(59)**	**1,832,955** **(45)**
John C. Frémont (Republican)	114 (39)	1,339,932 (33)
Millard Fillmore (American)	8 (3)	871,731 (22)

Legend: ☐ Nonvoting territories

The Election of 1856 Because three parties contested the 1856 election, Democrat James Buchanan was a minority president. Although Buchanan alone had national support, Republican John Frémont won most of the free states, and Millard Fillmore of the American Party gained 40 percent of the vote in most of the slave states.

This 1855 cartoon by Nathaniel Currier illustrates the Know Nothings' fear of an antidemocratic Catholic "invasion" of America. As the shamrock caught by the boathook is meant to indicate, Irish Catholics were a special target of Know Nothing suspicion.

SOURCE: *The Propagation Society—More Free Than Welcome.* Courtesy of the Library of Congress (LC-US762/30815).

OVERVIEW

POLITICAL PARTIES SPLIT AND REALIGN

Whig Party	Ran its last presidential candidate in 1852. The candidate, General Winfield Scott, alienated many southern Whigs, and the party was so split it could not field a candidate in 1856.
Democratic Party	Remained a national party through 1856, but Buchanan's actions as president made southern domination of the party so clear that many northern Democrats were alienated. Stephen Douglas, running as a northern Democrat in 1860, won 29 percent of the popular vote; John Breckinridge, running as a southern Democrat, won 18 percent.
Liberty Party	Antislavery party; ran James G. Birney for president in 1844. He won 62,000 votes, largely from northern antislavery Whigs.
Free-Soil Party	Ran Martin Van Buren, former Democratic president, in 1848. Gained 10 percent of the popular vote, largely from Whigs but also from some northern Democrats.
American (Know-Nothing) Party	Nativist party made striking gains in 1854 congressional elections, attracting both northern and southern Whigs. In 1856, its presidential candidate Millard Fillmore won 21 percent of the popular vote.
Republican Party	Founded in 1854. Attracted many northern Whigs and northern Democrats. Presidential candidate John C. Frémont won 33 percent of the popular vote in 1856; in 1860 Abraham Lincoln won 40 percent and was elected in a four-way race.

or against, could satisfy both wings of the party. A compromise candidate was found in James Buchanan of Pennsylvania, the "Northern man with Southern principles." Luckily for him, he had been ambassador to Great Britain at the time of the Kansas-Nebraska Act and thus had not had to commit himself.

The election of 1856 appeared to be a three-way contest that pitted Buchanan against explorer John C. Frémont of the Republican Party and the American (Know-Nothing) Party's candidate, former president Millard Fillmore. In fact, the election was two separate contests, one in the North and one in the South. The southern race was between Buchanan and Fillmore. Frémont's name appeared on the ballot in only four southern states, all in the Upper South, and even there he polled almost no votes. Fillmore received strong support from many former southern Whigs. Although he carried only the state of Maryland, he attracted more than 40 percent of the vote in ten other slave states. Buchanan, though, won the electoral votes in all those states.

Frémont decisively defeated Buchanan in the North, winning eleven of sixteen free states. Nationwide he garnered 1.3 million votes to Buchanan's 1.8 million. Buchanan won the election with only 45 percent of the popular vote because he was the only national candidate. His southern support, plus the electoral votes of Pennsylvania, New Jersey, Illinois, Indiana, and California

gave him the victory. But the Republicans, after studying the election returns, claimed "victorious defeat," for they realized that in 1860 the addition of just two more northern states to their total would mean victory. Furthermore, the Republican Party had clearly defeated the American Party in the battle to win designation as a major party. These were grounds for great optimism— and for great concern, for the Republican Party was a sectional rather than a national party; it drew almost all its support from the North. Southerners viewed its very existence as an attack on their vital interests. Thus the rapid rise of the Republicans posed a growing threat to national unity.

The election of 1856 attracted one of the highest voter turnouts in American history—79 percent. Ordinary people had come to share the politicians' concern about the growing sectional rift. The combined popular vote for Buchanan and Fillmore (67 percent) showed that most voters, north and south, favored politicians who at least claimed to speak for national rather than sectional interests. The northern returns also showed something else. Northerners had decided that the threat posed by the expansion of slavery was greater than that posed by the new immigrants; although it never disappeared, nativism subsided. The Buchanan administration, however, proved unequal to the task of resolving the free versus slave issue, and the nation began an inexorable slide into civil war.

THE DIFFERENCES DEEPEN

In one dreadful week in 1856 the people of the United States heard, in quick succession, about the looting and burning of Lawrence, Kansas, about John Brown's retaliatory massacre at Pottawatomie, and about unprecedented violence on the Senate floor. In the last of these incidents, Senator Charles Sumner of Massachusetts suffered permanent injury in a vicious attack by Congressman Preston Brooks of South Carolina. Trapped at his desk, Sumner was helpless as Brooks beat him so hard with his cane that it broke. Blood streaming from his head, Sumner escaped only by wrenching loose his desk from the screws that held it to the floor. A few days earlier, Sumner had given an insulting antislavery speech entitled "The Crime against Kansas." Using the abusive, accusatory style favored by abolitionists, he had singled out for ridicule Senator Andrew Butler of South Carolina, charging him with choosing "the harlot, slavery" as his mistress. Senator Butler was Preston Brooks's uncle; in Brooks's mind, he was simply avenging an intolerable affront to his uncle's honor. So far had the behavioral codes of North and South diverged that each man found his own action perfectly justifiable and the action of the other outrageous. Their attitudes were mirrored in their respective sections.

The Dred Scott Decision

Although James Buchanan firmly believed that he alone could hold together the nation so riven by hatred and violence, his self-confidence outran his abilities. When he entered the White House in March 1857, Buchanan was the oldest president (sixty-five) ever elected and a veteran of forty years of politics. Unfortunately, despite his experience, he was indecisive at moments that called for firm leadership. He was also so deeply indebted to the strong southern wing of the Democratic Party that he could not take the impartial actions necessary to heal "Bleeding Kansas." And his support for a momentous prosouthern decision by the Supreme Court further aggravated sectional differences.

In *Dred Scott* v. *Sandford*, decided on March 6, 1857, two days after James Buchanan was sworn in, a southern-dominated Supreme Court attempted—and failed—to solve the political controversy over slavery. Dred Scott had been a slave all his life. His owner, army surgeon John Emerson, had taken Scott on his military assignments during the 1830s to Illinois (a free state) and Wisconsin Territory (a free territory, north of the Missouri Compromise line). During that time Scott married another slave, Harriet, and their daughter Eliza was born in free territory. Emerson and the Scotts then returned to Missouri (a slave state) and there, in 1846, Dred Scott sued for his freedom and that of his wife and his daughter born in Wisconsin Territory (who as women had no legal standing of their own) on the grounds that residence in free lands had made them free. It took eleven years for the case to reach the Supreme Court, and by then its importance was obvious to everyone.

Chief Justice Roger B. Taney, of Maryland, seventy-nine years old, hard of hearing and failing of sight, insisted on reading his majority opinion in its entirety, a process that took four excruciating hours. Declaring the Missouri Compromise unconstitutional, Taney asserted that the federal government had no right to interfere with the free movement of property throughout the territories. Taney was in effect making John C. Calhoun's states' rights position, always con-

This political cartoon shows the devastating impact of the Supreme Court's 1857 *Dred Scott* decision on politics and the election of 1860. Dred Scott, shown with a fiddle in the middle, plays for (clockwise from upper right): Republican Abraham Lincoln and an African American woman; John Bell with an Indian; Northern Democrat Stephen A. Douglas with an Irishman; and Southern Democrat John Breckinridge with President James Buchanan, the "Northern Democrat with Southern sympathies."

SOURCE: Courtesy of the Library of Congress (301318/LCUSZ62/14827).

sidered an extremist southern position, the law of the land. He then dismissed the *Dred Scott* case on the grounds that only citizens could bring suits before federal courts and that black people—slave or free—were not citizens. With this bold judicial intervention into the most heated issue of the day, Taney intended to settle the controversy over the expansion of slavery once and for all. Instead, he enflamed the conflict.

The five southern members of the Supreme Court concurred in Taney's decision, as did one Northerner, Robert C. Grier. Historians have found that President-elect Buchanan had pressured Grier, a fellow Pennsylvanian, to support the majority. Two of the three other Northerners vigorously dissented, and the last voiced other objections. This was clearly a sectional decision, and the response to it was sectional. Southerners expressed great satisfaction and strong support for the Court. The *Louisville Democrat* said, "The decision is right . . . but whether or not [it is right], what this tribunal decides the Constitution to be, that it is; and all patriotic men will acquiesce." More bluntly, the *Georgia Constitutionalist* announced, "Southern opinion upon the subject of southern slavery . . . is now the supreme law of the land . . . and opposition to southern opinion upon this subject is now opposition to the Constitution, and morally treason against the Government."

Northerners disagreed. Few were quite so contemptuous as the *New York Tribune*, which declared that the decision was "entitled to just as much moral weight as would be the judgment of a majority of those congregated in any Washington barroom." Still, many were so troubled by the *Dred Scott* decision that for the first time they found themselves seriously questioning the power of the Supreme Court to establish the "law of the land." Many northern legislatures denounced the decision. New York passed a resolution declaring that the Supreme Court had lost the confidence and respect of the people of that state and another resolution refusing to allow slavery within its borders "in any form or under any pretense, or for any time, however short." New York Republicans also proposed an equal suffrage amendment for free African Americans, who were largely disenfranchised by a stringent property qualification for voting. But this was too liberal for the state's voters, who defeated it. This racist attitude was a bitter blow to free African Americans in the North. Frederick Douglass was so disheartened that he seriously considered emigrating to Haiti.

For the Republican Party, the *Dred Scott* decision represented a formidable challenge. By invalidating the Missouri Compromise, the decision swept away the free-soil foundation of the party. But to directly challenge a Supreme Court decision was a weighty matter. The most sensational Republican counterattack—made by both Abraham Lincoln and William

Seward—was the accusation that President Buchanan had conspired with the southern Supreme Court justices to subvert the American political system by withholding the decision until after the presidential election. Lincoln also raised the frightening possibility that "the next *Dred Scott* decision" would legalize slavery even in free states that abhorred it. And, in his 1858 debate at Freeport, Illinois, with Stephen A. Douglas, Lincoln attempted to drive Douglas, a believer in popular sovereignty, into an impossible choice. Was there any way, Lincoln asked Douglas, that a territory could exclude slavery if its people wished to do so? If Douglas said yes and supported popular sovreignty, he alienated the South, while if he said no and fully accepted the *Dred Scott* decision, he would lose support in the North.

In his answer, the so-called Freeport doctrine, Douglas made the common-sense point that no matter what the Supreme Court said, obviously slavery could not exist in a territory unless the people supported it. Popular sovereignty appeared to be vindicated, a position that further diminished Douglas's popularity among southern slave owners.

The Lecompton Constitution

In Kansas the doctrine of popular sovereignty led to continuing civil strife and the political travesty of two territorial governments. The first election of officers to a territorial government in 1855 produced a lop-sided proslavery outcome that was clearly the result of illegal voting by Missouri border ruffians. Free-soilers protested by forming their own government, giving Kansas both a proslavery territorial legislature in Lecompton and a free-soil government in Topeka. Because free-soil voters boycotted a June 1857 election for a convention to write a constitution for the territory once it reached statehood, the convention had a proslavery majority that wrote the proslavery Lecompton constitution and then applied to Congress for admission to the Union under its terms. In the meantime, in October free-soil voters had participated in relatively honest elections for the territorial legislature, elections that returned a clear free-soil majority. Nevertheless, Buchanan, in the single most disastrous mistake of his administration, endorsed the proslavery constitution because he feared the loss of the support of southern Democrats. It seemed that Kansas would enter the Union as a sixteenth slave state, making the number of slave and free states equal.

Unexpected congressional opposition came from none other than Stephen Douglas, author of the legislation that had begun the Kansas troubles in 1854. Now, in 1857, in what was surely the bravest step of his political career, Douglas opposed the Lecompton constitution on the grounds that it violated the principle of popular sovereignty. He insisted that the Lecompton constitution must be voted upon by Kansas voters in honest elections (as indeed Buchanan had initially promised). Douglas's decision was one of principle, but it was also motivated by the realization that a proslavery vote would never be accepted by the northern wing of the Democratic Party. Defying James Buchanan, his own president, Douglas voted with the majority in Congress in April 1858 to refuse admission to Kansas under the Lecompton constitution. In a new referendum, the people of Kansas also rejected the Lecompton constitution, 11,300 to 1,788. In 1859 Kansas held another constitutional convention, this one dominated by delegates from the new Republican Party. Kansas was finally admitted as a free state in January 1861.

The defeat of the Lecompton constitution did not come easily. There was more bloodshed in Kansas: sporadic ambushes and killings, including a mass shooting of nine free-soilers. And there was more violence in Congress: a free-for-all involving almost thirty congressmen broke out in the House late one night after an exchange of insults between Republicans and southern Democrats. There was conflict on still another level—the Democratic Party was breaking apart. Douglas had intended to preserve the Democrats as a national party, but instead he lost the support of the southern wing. Southerners reviled him, one claiming that Douglas was "stained with the dishonor of treachery without a parallel." Summing up these events, Congressman Alexander Stephens of Georgia wrote glumly to his brother: "All things here are tending my mind to the conclusion that the Union cannot and will not last long."

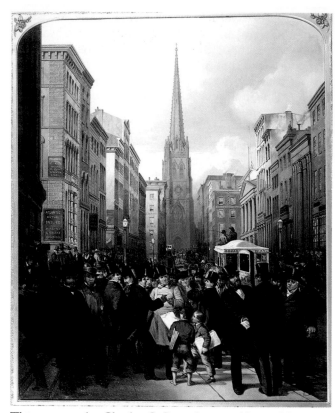

This painting by Charles G. Rosenberg and James H. Cafferty shows a worried crowd exchanging the latest news on Wall Street during the Panic of 1857. This was the first economic depression in which the telegraph played a part by carrying bad financial news in the West to New York much more rapidly than in the past.

SOURCE: Photograph by J. Cafferty & C. Rosenberg. Courtesy of the Museum of the City of New York (40.54).

The Panic of 1857

Adding to the growing political tensions was the short but sharp depression of 1857 and 1858. Technology played a part. In August 1857, the failure of an Ohio investment house—the kind of event that had formerly taken weeks to be widely known—was the subject of a news story flashed immediately over telegraph wires to Wall Street and other financial markets. A wave of panic selling ensued, leading to business failures and slowdowns that threw thousands out of work. The major cause of the panic was a sharp but temporary downturn in agricultural exports to Britain, and recovery was well under way by early 1859. In the meantime, Republicans and some northern Democrats in Congress proposed to raise tariffs to help industries hurt by the depression but were outvoted by about half of northern Democrats and almost all southern representatives. The South had resisted protective tariffs since the 1820s (see Chapter 10), but now the opposition was regarded,

in the bitter words of one Republican, as yet another example of a Congress "shamelessly prostituted, in a base subserviency to the Slave Power."

Because it affected cotton exports less than northern exports, the Panic of 1857 was less harmful to the South than to the North. Southerners took this as proof of the superiority of their economic system to the free-labor system of the North, and some could not resist the chance to gloat. Senator James Henry Hammond of South Carolina drove home the point in his celebrated "King Cotton" speech of March 1858:

When the abuse of credit had destroyed credit and annihilated confidence; when thousands of the strongest commercial houses in the world were coming down . . . when you came to a deadlock, and revolutions were threatened, what brought you up? . . . We have poured in upon you one million six hundred thousand bales of cotton just at the moment to save you from destruction. . . . We have sold it for $65,000,000, and saved you.

It seemed that all matters of political discussion were being drawn into the sectional dispute. The next step toward disunion was an act of violence perpetrated by the grim abolitionist from Kansas, John Brown.

John Brown's Raid

In the heated political mood of the late 1850s, some improbable people became heroes. None was more improbable than John Brown, the self-appointed avenger who had slaughtered unarmed proslavery men in Kansas in 1856. In 1859, Brown proposed a wild scheme to raid the South and start a general slave uprising. He believed, as did most northern abolitionists, that discontent among southern slaves was so great that such an uprising needed only a spark to get going. Significantly, free African Americans—among them Frederick Douglass—did not support Brown, thinking his plan to raid the federal arsenal at Harpers Ferry, Virginia, was doomed to failure. They were right. On October 16, 1859, Brown led a group of twenty-two white and African American men against the arsenal. However, he had made no provision for escape. Even more incredible, he had not notified the Virginia slaves whose uprising it was supposed to initiate. In less than a day the raid was over. Eight of Brown's men (including two of his sons) were dead, no slaves had joined the fight, and Brown himself was captured. Moving quickly to prevent a lynching by local mobs, the state of Virginia tried and convicted Brown (while he was still weak from the wounds of battle) of treason, murder, and fomenting insurrection.

Ludicrous in life, possibly insane, Brown was nevertheless a noble martyr. In his closing speech prior to sentencing, Brown was magnificently eloquent: "Now, if it is deemed necessary that I should forfeit my life for the furtherance of the end of justice, and mingle my blood further with the blood of my children and with the blood of millions in this slave country whose rights are disregarded by wicked, cruel, and unjust enactments, I say, let it be done."

Brown's death by hanging on December 2, 1859, was marked throughout northern communities with public rites of mourning not seen since the death of George Washington. Church bells tolled, buildings were draped in black, ministers preached sermons, prayer meetings were held, abolitionists issued eulogies. Ralph Waldo Emerson said that Brown would "make the gallows as glorious as the cross," and Henry David Thoreau called him "an angel of light." In a more militant frame of mind, abolitionist Wendell Phillips announced, "The lesson of the hour is insurrection." Naturally, not all Northerners supported Brown's action. Northern Democrats and conservative opinion generally repudiated him. In New York, for example, 20,000

merchants signed a petition for a public meeting designed to reassure the South of northern good intentions. But many people, while rejecting Brown's raid, did support the antislavery cause that he represented.

Brown's raid shocked the South because it aroused the greatest fear, that of slave rebellion. Southerners believed that northern abolitionists were provoking slave revolts, a suspicion apparently confirmed when documents captured at Harpers Ferry revealed that Brown had the financial support of half a dozen members of the northern elite. These "Secret Six"—Gerrit Smith, George Stearns, Franklin Sanborn, Thomas Wentworth Higginson, Theodore Parker, and Samuel Gridley Howe—had been willing to finance armed attacks on the slave system.

Even more shocking to Southerners than the raid itself was the extent of northern mourning for Brown's death. Although the Republican Party disavowed Brown's actions, Southerners simply did not believe the party's statements. Southerners wondered how they could stay in the Union in the face of "Northern insolence." The *Richmond Enquirer* reported, "The Harpers Ferry invasion has advanced the cause of disunion more than any other event that has happened since the formation of [the] government." The alarm in up-country South Carolina was so great that vigilance committees

JOHN BROWN AT HARPER'S FERRY.

In a contemporary engraving, John Brown and his followers are shown trapped inside the armory at Harper's Ferry in October 1859. Captured, tried, and executed, Brown was regarded as a martyr in the North and a terrorist in the South.

SOURCE: The Granger Collection (4E950/14).

were formed in every district. Throughout the next year, these committees remained armed and ready to deal with strangers (they might be abolitionists) and any hint of slave revolt. This extreme defensiveness was not a good portent for the election year of 1860. Looking to the presidential race, Senator Robert Toombs of Georgia warned that the South would "never permit this Federal government to pass into the traitorous hands of the Black Republican party."

Talk of secession as the only possible response to the northern "insults" of the 1850s—the armed protests against the Fugitive Slave Law, the rejection of the Lecompton constitution, and now the support for John Brown's raid—was common throughout the South. Although the majority of Southerners probably rejected secession, the political passions of the election year fostered secessionist thinking.

THE SOUTH SECEDES

By 1860, sectional differences had caused one national party, the Whigs, to collapse. The second national party, the Democrats, stood on the brink of dissolution. Not only the politicians but ordinary people in both the North and the South were coming to believe there was no way to avoid what in 1858 William Seward (once a Whig, now a Republican) had called an "irrepressible conflict."

The Election of 1860

The split of the Democratic Party into northern and southern wings that had occurred during President Buchanan's tenure became official at the Democratic nominating conventions in 1860. The party convened first in Charleston, South Carolina, the center of secessionist agitation. It was the worst possible location in which to attempt to reach unity. Although Stephen Douglas had the support of the plurality of delegates, he did not have the two-thirds majority necessary for nomination. As the price of their support, Southerners insisted that Douglas support a federal slave code—a guarantee that slavery would be protected in the territories. Douglas could not agree without violating his own belief in popular sovereignty and losing his northern support. After ten days, fifty-nine ballots, and two southern walkouts, the convention ended where it had begun: deadlocked. Northern supporters of Douglas were angry and bitter: "I never heard Abolitionists talk more uncharitably and rancorously of the people of the South than the Douglas men," one reporter wrote. "They say they do not care a damn where the South goes."

In June, the Democrats met again in Baltimore. The Douglasites, recognizing the need for a united

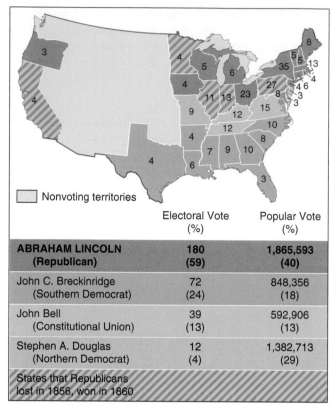

	Electoral Vote (%)	Popular Vote (%)
ABRAHAM LINCOLN (Republican)	**180 (59)**	**1,865,593 (40)**
John C. Breckinridge (Southern Democrat)	72 (24)	848,356 (18)
John Bell (Constitutional Union)	39 (13)	592,906 (13)
Stephen A. Douglas (Northern Democrat)	12 (4)	1,382,713 (29)

Nonvoting territories

States that Republicans lost in 1856, won in 1860

The Election of 1860   The election of 1860 was a sectional election. Lincoln won no votes in the South, Breckinridge none in the North. The contest in the North was between Lincoln and Douglas, and although Lincoln swept the electoral vote, Douglas's popular vote was uncomfortably close. The large number of northern Democratic voters opposed to Lincoln was a source of political trouble for him during the Civil War.

party, were eager to compromise wherever they could, but most southern Democrats were not. More than a third of the delegates bolted. Later, holding a convention of their own, they nominated Buchanan's vice president John C. Breckinridge of Kentucky. The remaining two-thirds of the Democrats nominated Douglas, but everyone knew that a Republican victory was inevitable. To make matters worse, some southern Whigs joined with some border-state nativists to form the Constitutional Union Party, which nominated John Bell of Tennessee.

Republican strategy was built on the lessons of the 1856 "victorious defeat." The Republicans planned to carry all the states Frémont had won, plus Pennsylvania, Illinois, and Indiana. The two leading Republican contenders were Senator William H. Seward of New York and Abraham Lincoln of Illinois. Seward, the party's best-known figure, had enemies among party moderates, who thought he was too radical, and among nativists with whom he had clashed in the New York Whig Party. Lincoln, on the other hand, appeared new, impressive, more moderate than Seward, and certain to carry Illinois. Lincoln won the nomination on the third ballot.

The election of 1860 presented voters with one of the clearest choices in American history. On the key issue of slavery, Breckinridge supported its extension to the territories; Lincoln stood firmly for its exclusion. Douglas attempted to hold the middle ground with his principle of popular sovereignty; Bell vaguely favored compromise as well. The Republicans offered other platform planks designed to appeal to northern voters: support for a homestead act (free western lands), for a transcontinental railroad, for other internal improvements, and for a higher tariff. Although they spoke clearly against the extension of slavery, Republicans sought to dispel their radical abolitionist image. The Republican platform condemned John Brown's raid as "the gravest of crimes," repeatedly denied that Republicans favored the social equality of black people, and strenuously affirmed that they sought to preserve the Union. In reality, Republicans simply did not believe the South would secede if Lincoln won. In this the Republicans were not alone; few Northerners believed southern threats—Southerners had threatened too many times before.

Breckinridge insisted that he and his supporters were loyal to the Union—as long as their needs concerning slavery were met. The only candidate who spoke urgently and openly about the impending threat of secession was Douglas. Breaking with convention, Douglas campaigned personally, in both the North and, bravely, in the hostile South, warning of the danger of dissolution and presenting himself as the only truly national candidate. Realizing his own chances for election were slight, he told his private secretary, "Mr. Lincoln is the next President. We must try to save the Union. I will go South."

In accordance with tradition, Lincoln did not campaign for himself, but many other Republicans spoke for him. In an estimated 50,000 campaign speeches, they built the image of "Honest Abe," the candidate who really had been born in a log cabin. The Republicans made a special effort, headed by Carl Schurz, to attract the German immigrant vote. They were successful with German Protestants but less so with Catholics, who were put off by the Republicans' lingering reputation for nativism. The general mood among the northern electorate was one of excitement and optimism. The Republicans were almost certain to win and to bring, because of their uncompromising opposition to the expansion of slavery, an end to the long sectional crisis. "I will vote the Republican ticket next Tuesday," wrote New York businessman and former Whig George Templeton Strong. "The only alternative is everlasting submission to the South." The Republicans did not campaign in the South; Breckinridge did not campaign in the North. Each side was therefore free to believe the worst about

the other. All parties, North and South, campaigned with oratory, parades and rallies, free food and drink. Even in the face of looming crisis, this presidential campaign was the best entertainment of the day.

In spite of Breckinridge's protestations of loyalty to the Union, the mood in the Deep South was close to mass hysteria. Rumors of slave revolts—in Texas, Alabama, and South Carolina—swept the region, and vigilance committees sprang up to counter the supposed threat. Responding to the rumors, Alabaman Sarah R. Espy wrote in her diary, "The country is getting in a deplorable state owing to the depredations committed by the Abolitionist[s] especially in Texas; and the safety of the country depend[s] on who is elected to the presidency." Apparently, southern voters talked of little else, as another Alabaman, Benjamin F. Riley, recalled: "Little else was done this year, than discuss politics. Vast crowds would daily assemble at the places of popular resort, to canvass the questions at issue. Stump speaking was a daily occurrence. Men were swayed more by passion than by calm judgment."

In the South Carolina upcountry, the question of secession dominated races for the state legislature. Candidates such as A. S. Wallace of York, who advocated "patriotic forbearance" if Lincoln won, were soundly defeated. The very passion and excitement of the election campaign moved Southerners toward extremism. Even the weather—the worst drought and heat wave the South had known for years—contributed to the tension.

The election of 1860 produced the second highest voter turnout in U.S. history (81.2 percent, topped only by 81.8 percent in 1876). The election turned out to be two regional contests: Breckinridge versus Bell in the South, Lincoln versus Douglas in the North. Breckinridge carried eleven slave states with 18 percent of the popular vote; Bell carried Virginia, Tennessee, and Kentucky with 13 percent of the popular vote. Lincoln won all eighteen of the free states (he split New Jersey with Douglas) and almost 40 percent of the popular vote. Douglas carried only Missouri, but gained nearly 30 percent of the popular vote. Lincoln's electoral vote total was overwhelming: 180 to a combined 123 for the other three candidates. But although Lincoln had won 54 percent of the vote in the northern states, his name had not even appeared on the ballot in ten southern states. The true winner of the 1860 election was sectionalism.

The South Leaves the Union

Charles Francis Adams, son and grandson of presidents, wrote in his diary on the day Lincoln was elected, "The great revolution has actually taken place. . . . The country has once and for all thrown off

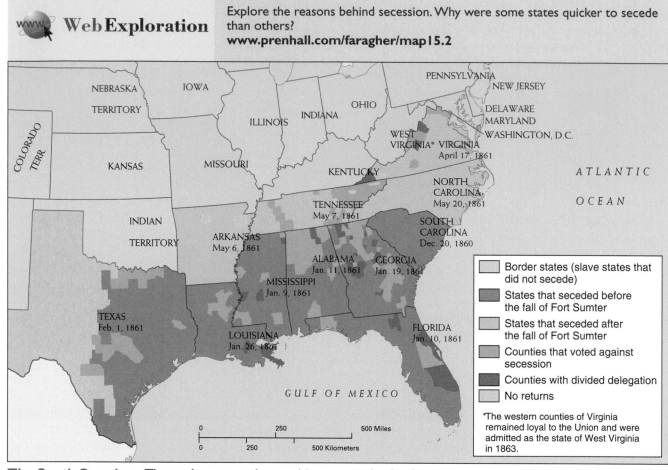

WebExploration

Explore the reasons behind secession. Why were some states quicker to secede than others?
www.prenhall.com/faragher/map15.2

The South Secedes   The southern states that would constitute the Confederacy seceded in two stages. The states of the Lower South seceded before Lincoln took office. Arkansas and three states of the Upper South—Virginia, North Carolina, and Tennessee— waited until after the South fired on Fort Sumter. And four border slave states—Delaware, Maryland, Kentucky and Missouri—chose not to secede. Every southern state (except South Carolina) was divided on the issue of secession, generally along up-country— low-country lines. In Virginia, this division was so extreme that West Virginia split off to become a separate nonslave state and was admitted to the Union in 1863.

the domination of the Slaveholders." That was precisely what the South feared.

The results of the election shocked Southerners. They were humiliated and frightened by the prospect of becoming a permanent minority in a political system dominated by a party pledged to the elimination of slavery. In southern eyes the Republican triumph meant they would become unequal partners in the federal enterprise, their way of life (the slave system) existing on borrowed time. As a Georgia newspaper said ten days after Lincoln's election, "African slavery, though panoplied by the Federal Constitution, is doomed to a war of extermination. All the powers of a Government which has so long sheltered it will be turned to its destruction. The only hope for its preser-

vation, therefore, is out of the Union." And Mary Boykin Chesnut, member of a well-connected South Carolina family, confided to her diary, "The die is cast—no more vain regrets—sad forebodings are useless. The stake is life or death."

The governors of South Carolina, Alabama, and Mississippi, each of whom had committed his state to secession if Lincoln were elected, immediately issued calls for special state conventions. At the same time, calls went out to southern communities to form vigilance committees and volunteer militia companies. A visiting Northerner, Sereno Watson, wrote to his brother in amazement: "This people is apparently gone crazy. I do not know how to account for it & have no idea what might be the end of it. Union men,

OVERVIEW

THE IRREPRESSIBLE CONFLICT

Declaration of Independence	1776	Thomas Jefferson's denunciation of slavery deleted from the final version
Northwest Ordinance	1787	Slavery prohibited in the Northwest Territory (north of the Ohio River).
Constitution	1787	Slavery unmentioned but acknowledged in Article I, Section 2, counting three-fifths of all African Americans, slave and free, in a state's population; and in Article I, Section 9, which barred Congress from prohibiting the international slave trade for twenty years.
Louisiana Purchase	1803	Louisiana admitted as a slave state in 1812; no decision about the rest of Louisiana Purchase.
Missouri Compromise	1820	Missouri admitted as a slave state, but slavery prohibited in Louisiana Purchase north of 36°30'.
Wilmot Proviso	1846	Proposal to prohibit slavery in territory that might be gained in Mexican-American War causes splits in national parties.
Compromise of 1850	1850	California admitted as free state; Texas (already admitted in 1845) is a slave state; the rest of Mexican Cession to be decided by popular sovereignty. Ends the slave trade in the District of Columbia, but a stronger Fugitive Slave Law, leading to a number of violent recaptures, arouses northern antislavery opinion.
Kansas-Nebraska Act	1854	At the urging of Stephen A. Douglas, Congress opens Kansas and Nebraska Territories for settlement under popular sovereignty. Open warfare between proslavery and antislavery factions breaks out in Kansas.
Lecompton Constitution	1857	President James Buchanan's decision to admit Kansas to the Union with a proslavery constitution is defeated in Congress.
***Dred Scott* Decision**	1857	The Supreme Court's denial of Dred Scott's case for freedom is welcomed in the South, condemned in the North.
John Brown's Raid and Execution	1859	Northern support for John Brown shocks the South.
Democratic Party Nominating Conventions	1860	The Democrats are unable to agree on a candidate; two candidates, one northern (Stephen A. Douglas) and one southern (John C. Breckinridge) split the party and the vote, thus allowing Republican Abraham Lincoln to win.

Douglas men, Breckinridge men are alike in their loud denunciation of submission to Lincoln's administration. There are of course those who think differently but they scarcely dare or are suffered to open their mouths." In the face of this frenzy, cooperationists (the term used for those opposed to immediate secession) were either intimidated into silence or simply left behind by the speed of events.

On December 20, 1860, a state convention in South Carolina, accompanied by all the hoopla and excitement of bands, fireworks displays, and huge rallies, voted unanimously to secede from the Union. In the weeks that followed, conventions in six other southern states (Mississippi, Florida, Alabama, Georgia, Louisiana, and Texas) followed suit, with the support, on average, of 80 percent of their delegates.

The succession of rapid, state by state conventions was a deliberate strategy developed by secessionists, who feared that a single convention of all the southern states would move too slowly, allowing co-operationists time to organize. There was genuine division of opinion in the Deep South, especially in Georgia and Alabama, along customary up-country–low-country lines. Yeoman farmers who did not own slaves and workers in the cities of the South were most likely to favor compromise with the North. But secessionists constantly reminded both groups that the Republican victory would lead to the emancipation of the slaves and the end of white privilege (see Chapter 11). And all Southerners, most of whom were deeply loyal to their state and region, believed that Northerners threatened their way of life. In reality, although class divisions among them were very real, none of the Deep South states held anywhere near the number of Unionists that Republicans had hoped. Throughout the South, secession occurred because Southerners no longer believed they had a choice. "Secession is a desperate remedy," acknowledged South Carolina's David Harris, "but of the two evils I do think it is the lesser."

In every state that seceded, the joyous scenes of South Carolina were repeated as the decisiveness of action replaced the long years of anxiety and tension. People danced in the streets, most believing the North had no choice but to accept secession peacefully. They ignored the fact that eight other slave states—Delaware, Maryland, Kentucky, Missouri, Virginia, North Carolina, Tennessee, and Arkansas—had not acted—though the latter four states would secede after war broke out. Just as Republicans had miscalculated in thinking southern threats a mere bluff, so secessionists now miscalculated in believing they would be able to leave the Union in peace.

The North's Political Options

What should the North do? Buchanan, indecisive as always, did nothing. The decision thus rested with Abraham Lincoln, even before he officially became president. One possibility was compromise, and many proposals were suggested, ranging from full adoption of the Breckinridge campaign platform to reinstatement of the Missouri Compromise line. Lincoln cautiously refused them all, making it clear that he would not compromise on the extension of slavery, which was the South's key demand. He hoped, by appearing firm but moderate, to discourage additional southern states from seceding while giving pro-Union Southerners time to organize. He succeeded in his first aim, but not

in the second. Lincoln and most of the Republican Party had seriously overestimated the strength of pro-Union sentiment in the South.

A second possibility, suggested by Horace Greeley of the *New York Tribune*, was to let the seven seceding states "go in peace." This is what many secessionists expected, but too many Northerners—including Lincoln himself—believed in the Union for this to happen. As Lincoln said, what was at stake was "the necessity of proving that popular government is not an absurdity. We must settle this question now, whether in a free government the minority have the right to break up the government whenever they choose." At stake was all the accumulated American pride in the federal government as a model for democracies the world over.

The third possibility was force, and this was the crux of the dilemma. Although he believed their action was wrong, Lincoln was loath to go to war to force the seceding states back into the Union. On the other hand, he refused to give up federal powers over military forts and customs posts in the South. These were precisely the powers the seceding states had to command if they were to function as an independent nation. A confrontation was bound to come. Abraham Lincoln, not for the last time, was prepared to wait for the other side to strike the first blow.

Establishment of the Confederacy

In February, delegates from the seven seceding states met in Montgomery, Alabama, and created the Confederate States of America. They wrote a constitution that was identical to the Constitution of the United States, with a few crucial exceptions: it strongly supported states' rights and made the abolition of slavery practically impossible. These two clauses did much to define the Confederate enterprise. It was difficult to avoid the conclusion that the structure of the new Confederacy had been decided by the southern dependence on slave labor. L. W. Spratt of South Carolina confessed as much in 1859: "We stand committed to the South, but we stand more vitally committed to the cause of slavery. It is, indeed, to be doubted whether the South [has] any cause apart from the institution which affects her." The South's entire defense of slavery was built on a commitment to individualism and decentralization: the rights of the slave owner over his slaves; the right of freedom claimed by all white men; and the rights of individual states versus the federal government. The military defense of the South, however, would require a strong central government. This was to be the South's basic dilemma throughout the Civil War.

The Montgomery convention passed over the fire-eaters—the men who had been the first to urge secession—and chose Jefferson Davis of Mississippi as president and Alexander Stephens of Georgia as vice president of the new nation. Both men were known as moderates. Davis, a slave owner who had been a general in the Mexican-American War and secretary of war in the Pierce administration, and who was currently a senator from Mississippi, had expressed his own uncertainties by retaining his Senate seat for two weeks after Mississippi seceded. Stephens, a former leader in the Whig Party, had been a cooperationist delegate to Georgia's convention, where he urged that secession not be undertaken hastily.

The choice of moderates was deliberate, for the strategy of the new Confederate state was to argue that secession was a normal, responsible, and expectable course of action, and nothing for the North to get upset about. This was the theme that President Jefferson Davis of the Confederate States of America struck in his Inaugural Address, delivered to a crowd of 10,000 from the steps of the State Capitol at Montgomery, Alabama, on February 18, 1861. "We have changed the constituent parts," Davis said, "but not the system of our Government." Secession was a legal and peaceful step that, Davis said, quoting from the Declaration of Independence, "illustrates the American idea that governments rest on the consent of the governed . . . and that it is the right of the people to alter or abolish them at will whenever they become destructive of the ends for which they were established." After insisting that "a just perception of mutual interest [should] permit us peaceably to pursue our separate political [course]," Davis concluded, "Obstacles may retard, but they cannot long prevent, the progress of a movement sanctified by its justice and sustained by a virtuous people." This impressive inaugural prompted a deeply moved correspondent for the *New York Herald* to report, "God does not permit evil to be done with such earnest solemnity, such all-pervading trust in His Providence, as was exhibited by the whole people on that day."

Lincoln's Inauguration

The country as a whole waited to see what Abraham Lincoln would do, which at first appeared to be very little. In Springfield, Lincoln refused to issue public statements before his inaugural (although he sent many private messages to Congress and to key military officers), for fear of making a delicate situation worse. Similarly, during a twelve-day whistle-stopping rail-road trip east from Springfield, he was careful to say nothing controversial. Eastern intellectuals, already suspicious of a mere "prairie lawyer," were not impressed. Finally, hard evidence of an assassination plot forced Lincoln to abandon his whistle-stops at Harrisburg and, protected by Pinkerton detectives, he traveled incognito into Washington, "like a thief in the night," as he complained. These signs of moderation and caution did not appeal to an American public with a penchant for electing military heroes. Americans wanted leadership and action.

Lincoln continued, however, to offer nonbelligerent firmness and moderation. And at the end of his Inaugural Address on March 4, 1861, as he stood ringed by federal troops called out in case of a Confederate attack, the new president offered unexpected eloquence:

> I am loath to close. We are not enemies, but friends. We must not be enemies. Though passion may have strained, it must not break our bonds of affection. The mystic chords of memory, stretching from every battlefield, and patriot grave, to every living heart and hearthstone, all over this broad land, will yet swell the chorus of the Union, when again touched, as surely they will be, by the better angels of our nature.

CONCLUSION

Americans had much to boast about in 1850. Their nation was vastly larger, richer, and more powerful than it had been in 1800. But the issue of slavery was slowly dividing the North and the South, two communities with similar origins and many common bonds. The following decade was marked by frantic efforts at political compromise, beginning with the Compromise of 1850, continuing with the Kansas-Nebraska Act of 1854, and culminating in the Supreme Court's 1859 decision in the *Dred Scott* case. Increasingly, the ordinary people of the two regions demanded resolution of the crisis. The two great parties of the Second American Party System, the Democrats and the Whigs, unable to find a solution, were destroyed. Two new sectional parties—the Republican Party and a southern party devoted to the defense of slavery—fought the 1860 election, but Southerners refused to accept the national verdict. Politics had failed: the issue of slavery was irreconcilable. The only remaining recourse was war. But although Americans were divided, they were still one people. That made the war, when it came, all the more terrible.

CHRONOLOGY

1820	Missouri Compromise
1828–32	Nullification Crisis
1846	Wilmot Proviso
1848	Treaty of Guadalupe Hidalgo ends Mexican-American War
	Zachary Taylor elected president
	Free-Soil Party formed
1849	California and Utah seek admission to the Union as free states
1850	Compromise of 1850
	California admitted as a free state
	American (Know-Nothing) Party formed
	Zachary Taylor dies, Millard Fillmore becomes president
1851	North reacts to Fugitive Slave Law
	Harriet Beecher Stowe's *Uncle Tom's Cabin* published
1852	Franklin Pierce elected president
1854	Ostend Manifesto
	Kansas-Nebraska Act
	Treaties with Indians in northern part of Indian Territory renegotiated
	Republican Party formed as Whig Party dissolves

1855	William Walker leads first filibustering expedition to Nicaragua
1856	Burning and looting of Lawrence, Kansas
	John Brown leads Pottawatomie massacre
	Attack on Senator Charles Sumner
	James Buchanan elected president
1857	*Dred Scott* decision
	President Buchanan accepts proslavery Lecompton constitution in Kansas
	Panic of 1857
1858	Congress rejects Lecompton constitution
	Lincoln-Douglas debates
1859	John Brown's raid on Harpers Ferry
1860	Four parties run presidential candidates
	Abraham Lincoln elected president
	South Carolina secedes from Union
1861	Six other Deep South states secede
	Confederate States of America formed
	Lincoln takes office

REVIEW QUESTIONS

1. What aspects of the remarkable economic development of the United States in the first half of the nineteenth century contributed to the sectional crisis of the 1850s?

2. How might the violent efforts by abolitionists to free escaped slaves who had been recaptured and the federal armed enforcement of the Fugitive Slave Act have been viewed differently by Northern merchants (the so-called Cotton Whigs), Irish immigrants, and abolitionists?

3. Consider the course of events in "Bloody Kansas" from Douglas's Kansas-Nebraska Act to the congressional rejection of the Lecompton constitution. Were these events the inevitable result of the political impasse in Washington, or could other decisions have been taken that would have changed the outcome?

4. The nativism of the 1850s that surfaced so strongly in the Know-Nothing Party was eclipsed by the crisis over slavery. But nativist sentiment has been a recurring theme in American politics. Discuss why it was strong in the 1850s and why it has emerged periodically since then.

5. Evaluate the character and actions of John Brown. Was he the hero proclaimed by northern supporters or the terrorist condemned by the South?

6. Imagine that you lived in Illinois, home state to both Douglas and Lincoln, in 1860. How would you have voted in the presidential election, and why?

RECOMMENDED READING

William L. Barney, *The Secessionist Impulse: Alabama and Mississippi in 1860* (1974). Covers the election of 1860.

Don E. Fehrenbacher, *The Dred Scott Case: Its Significance in American Law and Politics* (1978). A major study.

Eric Foner, *Free Soil, Free Labor, Free Men: The Ideology of the Republican Party before the Civil War* (1970). A landmark work.

Lacey K. Ford Jr., *Origins of Southern Radicalism: The South Carolina Upcountry, 1800–1860* (1988). Examines the attitudes of up-country farmers in South Carolina.

Homan Hamilton, *Prologue to Conflict: The Crisis and Compromise of 1850* (1964). The standard treatment.

Bruce Levine, *Half Slave and Half Free: The Roots of the Civil War* (1992). Good survey of the contrasting attitudes of North and South.

Alice Nichols, *Bleeding Kansas* (1954). The standard source on the battles over Kansas.

David M. Potter, *The Impending Crisis, 1848–1861* (1976). A comprehensive account of the politics leading up to the Civil War.

Anne C. Rose, *Voices of the Marketplace: American Thought and Culture, 1830–1860* (1995). A new study that considers the effects of the concepts of Christianity, democracy, and capitalism on American cultural life.

Kenneth M. Stampp, *America in 1857: A Nation on the Brink* (1990). A study of the "crucial" year.

Albert J. Von Frank, *The Trials of Anthony Burns: Freedom and Slavery in Emerson's Boston* (1998). An eloquent study of the trial and the links between transcendentalist and abolitionist opinion.

Edward L. Widmer, *Young America: The Flowering of Democracy in New York City* (1999). Recovers the idealism of the early years of this literary/political movement and traces its decline.

▶ MEDIA RESOURCES

U.S. HISTORY DOCUMENTS CD-ROM

Antebellum South

13-5   De Bow's Review, "The Stability of the Union" (1850)

13-6   Benjamin Drew, Narratives of Escaped Slaves (1855)

13-7   George Fitzhugh, "The Blessings of Slavery" (1857)

The Sectional Crisis

14-4   A Dying Statesman Speaks Out against the Compromise of 1850

14-5   Frederick Douglass, Independence Day Speech (1852)

14-6   Kansas Begins to Bleed (1856)

14-7   A White Southerner Speaks Out against Slavery (1857)

14-8   Dred Scott v. Sanford (1857)

14-9   Abraham Lincoln, "A House Divided" (1858)

COMPANION WEBSITE HIGHLIGHTS

To view an exploration, enter one of the URLs below in your browser.

Web Explorations

U.S. Population and Settlement, 1850
http://www.prenhall.com/faragher/map15.1

The South Secedes
http://www.prenhall.com/faragher/map15.2

Additional Interactive Maps

To access the maps, go to this chapter's resources at
http://www.prenhall.com/faragher
The Compromise of 1850, page 444
The Kansas-Nebraska Act, 1854, page 447
The Election of 1860, page 456

HISTORY RESOURCE CENTER

To find the resources listed below, go to
http://www.prenhall.com/historyresourcecenter

Documents

Abraham Lincoln, Debate at Gatesburg, Illinois (1858)

Harriet Beecher Stowe, from Uncle Tom's Cabin

John C. Calhoun, Proposal to Preserve the Union (1850)

Roger B. Taney, The Dred Scott Decision (1857)

Images

Abraham Lincoln, February 27, 1860

Frederick Douglass

Harriet Tubman

Raffling Off a Slave

Stephen Douglas

Turn to the next page for the *Exploring America* activity for this chapter.

EXPLORING AMERICA

ANTHONY BURNS

http://www.prenhall.com/faragher/anthonyburns

Was kidnapping legal in 1854? What protected African Americans who escaped from slavery from the clutches of those seeking to return them to bondage—even if they resided in free states? How could antislavery reformers help African Americans such as *Anthony Burns* from being returned to slavery? Anthony Burns tells the story of one escaped African American slave caught in the legal snares of the Fugitive Slave Law. First-hand accounts combined with letters, visual images, a chronology, and interactive maps provide a very personal perspective to the impact of the Fugitive Slave Law on African Americans in the 1850s. These sources combined with the narrative offer insight into the unchanging status of the runaway slaves no matter how far north they escaped.

Anthony Burns offers a straightforward account of his plight, the actions taken on his behalf, and the eventual solution to the problem caused by the Fugitive Slave Law. The rationale behind the passage of the law in the increasingly tense 1850s is discussed. Despite the attempt by politicians to avert conflict, as the module shows, applying the law in the North only raised tensions, exacerbating the situation. The chronology and the maps help put the Anthony Burns incident into historical perspective.

Reflect and Respond

1. Might Phillips' plan for rescuing Burns have succeeded? What would have had to happen for it to have worked?

2. Historians have noted the ironic outcome of the Burns' "kidnapping." Had the antislavery activists succeeded in rescuing him and sending him on to Canada, the event would have sharpened sectional animosities but done comparatively little to strengthen the antislavery cause. Failure to rescue Burns, on the other hand, made him a household word throughout the North. What specific features of his story strike you as providing ammunition for the abolitionists?

3. What personal characteristics of Burns made him such an appealing figure to antislavery activists? Use the poster depicting his life to illustrate your answer.

✓ Check it out

Slave Market of America

This poster graphically depicts the treatment African Americans experienced in the slave trade. The posters illustrate the different aspects of slavery in a series of graphic images. It shows not only the brutality of the slave trade but also how this brutality was used to protest against slavery providing a poignant addition to the story of Anthony Burns.

Anthony Burns

The middle panel shows the use of publicly financed prisons in the slave trade. Again, one reads from the center image outward. In the middle is an auction. A male to be sold stands on a platform. To the right, the auctioneer extols his value. Two small white children in the left foreground walk past. The intent is to show how the buying and selling of human beings coarsens the children, who paid no heed to the auction. Slaves, awaiting sale, this time a mother and child, are examined by prospective buyers in a cell in the image to the right. The prison itself is sketched in the image to the left.

Click anywhere to go to the previous page.

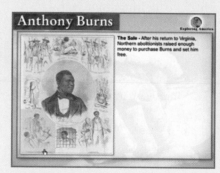

Anthony Burns

The Sale - After his return to Virginia, Northern abolitionists raised enough money to purchase Burns and set him free.

This exploration is also available on the *Exploring America* CD-ROM.

▷ 1 8 6 1 – 1 8 6 5

Winslow Homer, *Near Andersonville*, 1865. Oil on canvas. Photograph by Armen Shamalian Photographers. The Newark Museum, Gift of the Corbin family in memory of their parents Hannah Stockton Corbin and Horace Kellogg Corbin.

Mother Bickerdyke Connects Northern Communities to Their Boys at War

IN MAY 1861 THE REVEREND EDWARD BEECHER INTERRUPTED his customary Sunday service at Brick Congregational Church in Galesburg, Illinois, to read a disturbing letter to the congregation. Two months earlier, Galesburg had proudly sent 500 of its young men off to join the Union army. They had not yet been in battle. Yet, the letter reported, an alarming number were dying of diseases caused by inadequate food, medical care, and sanitation at the crowded military camp in Cairo, Illinois. Most army doctors were surgeons, trained to operate and amputate on the battlefield. They were not prepared to treat soldiers sick with dysentery, pneumonia, typhoid, measles—all serious, frequently fatal diseases that could often be cured with careful nursing. The letter writer, appalled by the squalor and misery he saw around him, complained of abuses by the army. The Union army, however, was overwhelmed with the task of readying recruits for battle and had made few provisions for their health when they were not in combat.

The shocked and grieving members of Beecher's congregation quickly decided to send not only supplies but one of their number to inspect the conditions at the Cairo camp and to take action. In spite of warnings from a veteran of the War of 1812 that army regulations excluded women from encampments, the congregation voted to send their most qualified member, Mary Ann Bickerdyke, a middle-aged widow who made her living as a "botanic physician." This simple gesture of community concern launched the remarkable Civil War career of "the Cyclone in Calico," who defied medical officers and generals alike in her unceasing efforts on behalf of ill, wounded, and convalescent Union soldiers.

"Mother" Bickerdyke, as she was called, let nothing stand in the way of helping her "boys." When she arrived in Cairo, she immediately set to work cleaning the hospital tents and the soldiers themselves, and finding and cooking nourishing food for them. Ordered to leave by the hospital director, who resented her interference, she blandly continued her work. When he reported her to the commanding officer, General Benjamin Prentiss, she quickly convinced the general to let her stay. "I talked sense to him," she later said.

From a peacetime point of view, what Mother Bickerdyke was doing was not unusual. Every civilian hospital had a matron who made sure patients were supplied with clean bed linen and bandages and were fed the proper convalescent diet. But in the context of the war—the sheer number of soldiers, the constant need to set up new field hospitals and commandeer scarce food for an army on the move—it was unusual indeed and required an unusual person. A plain spoken, hardworking woman, totally unfazed by rank or tender masculine egos, Mother Bickerdyke single-mindedly devoted herself to what she called "the Lord's work." The ordinary soldiers loved her; wise generals supported her. Once, when an indignant officer's wife complained about Bickerdyke's rudeness, General William Tecumseh Sherman joked, "You've picked the one person around here who outranks me. If you want to lodge a complaint against her, you'll have to take it to President Lincoln."

By their actions, Mother Bickerdyke and others like her exposed the War Department's inability to meet the needs of the nation's first mass army. And like the Galesburg congregation, other communities all over the North rallied to make up for the department's shortcomings with supplies and assistance. The efforts of women on the local level—for example, to make clothing for men from their communities who had gone off to the war—quickly took on national dimensions. The Women's Central Association of Relief (WCAR), whose organizers were mostly reformers experienced in the abolitionist, temperance, and education movements, eventually had 7,000 chapters throughout the North. Its volunteers raised funds, made and collected a variety of items—food, clothes, medicine, bandages, and more than 250,000 quilts and comforters—and sent them to army camps and hospitals. Volunteers also provided meals, housing, and transportation to soldiers on furlough. All told, association chapters supplied an estimated $15 million worth of goods to the Union troops.

In June 1861, responding to requests by officials of the WCAR for formal recognition of the organization, President Abraham Lincoln created the United States Sanitary Commission and gave it the power to investigate and advise the Medical Bureau. Henry Bellows, a Unitarian clergyman, became president of the organization, and Frederick Law Olmsted, the author of influential books about the slaveholding South and later the designer of New York's Central Park, was named its executive secretary. The commission's more than 500 "sanitary inspectors" (usually men) instructed soldiers in such matters as water supply, placement of latrines, and safe cooking.

Although at first she worked independently and remained suspicious of all organizations (and even of many other relief workers), in 1862 Mother Bickerdyke was persuaded to become an official agent of "the Sanitary," as it was known. The advantage to her was access to the commission's warehouses and the ability to order from them precisely what she needed. The advantage to the Sanitary was that Mother Bickerdyke was an unequaled fundraiser. In speaking tours throughout Illinois, she touched her female listeners with moving stories of wounded boys whom she had cared for as if they were her own sons. Her words to men were more forceful. It was a man's business to fight, she said. If he was too old or ill to fight with a gun, he should fight with his dollars. With the help of Bickerdyke's blunt appeals, the Sanitary raised $50 million for the Union war effort.

As the Civil War continued, Mother Bickerdyke became a key figure in the medical support for General Ulysses S. Grant's campaigns along the Mississippi River. She was with the army at Shiloh, and as Grant slowly fought his way to Vicksburg, she set up convalescent hospitals in Memphis. Grant authorized her to commandeer any army wagons she needed to transport supplies. Between fifty and seventy "contrabands" (escaped former slaves) worked on her laundry crew. On the civilian side, the Sanitary Commission authorized her to draw on its supply depots in Memphis, Cairo, Chicago, and elsewhere. She was thus in a practical sense a vital "middlewoman" between the home front and the battlefield—and in a symbolic and emotional sense too, as a stand-in for all mothers who had sent their sons to war.

The Civil War was a community tragedy, ripping apart the nation's political fabric and producing more casualties than any other war in the nation's history. Yet in another sense, it was a community triumph. Local communities directly supported and sustained their soldiers on a massive scale in unprecedented ways. As national unity failed, the strength of local communities, symbolized by Mother Bickerdyke, endured. ■

Memphis

COMMUNITIES MOBILIZE FOR WAR

A neutral observer in March 1861 might have seen ominous similarities. Two nations—the United States of America (shorn of seven states in the Deep South) and the Confederate States of America—each blamed the other for the breakup of the Union. Two new presidents—Abraham Lincoln and Jefferson Davis—each faced the challenging task of building and maintaining national unity. Two regions—North and South—scorned each other and boasted of their own superiority. But the most basic similarity was not yet apparent: both sides were unprepared for the ordeal that lay ahead.

Fort Sumter: The War Begins

In their Inaugural Addresses, both Abraham Lincoln and Jefferson Davis prayed for peace but positioned themselves for war. Careful listeners to both addresses realized that the two men were on a collision course.

Jefferson Davis claimed that the Confederacy would be forced to "appeal to arms . . . if . . . the integrity of our territory and jurisdiction [is] assailed." Lincoln said, "The power confided to me will be used to hold, occupy, and possess the property and places belonging to the government." One of those places, Fort Sumter, in South Carolina, was claimed by both sides.

Fort Sumter, a major federal military installation, sat on a granite island at the entrance to Charleston harbor. So long as it remained in Union hands, Charleston, the center of secessionist sentiment, would be immobilized. Realizing its military and symbolic importance, South Carolinians had begun demanding that the fort be turned over to them even before they seceded. Thus it was hardly surprising that Fort Sumter would provide President Lincoln with his first crisis.

With the fort dangerously low on supplies, Lincoln had to decide whether to abandon it or risk the fight that might ensue if he ordered it resupplied. In a process he would follow on many other occasions, Lincoln first hesitated, canvassed opinions of all kinds, and then took

This Currier and Ives lithograph shows the opening moment of the Civil War. On April 12, 1861, Confederate General P. G. T. Beauregard ordered the shelling of Fort Sumter in Charleston harbor. Two days later, Union Major Robert Anderson surrendered and mobilization began for what turned out to be the most devastating war in American history.

SOURCE: The Granger Collection, New York (0011697/4GCR303).

cautious and careful action (even as some of his cabinet urged more decisive steps). On April 6, Lincoln notified the governor of South Carolina that he was sending a relief force to the fort carrying only food and no military supplies. Now the decision rested with Jefferson Davis. Like Lincoln, Davis faced a divided cabinet; unlike Lincoln, however, he opted for decisive action. On April 10 he ordered General P. G. T. Beauregard to demand the surrender of Fort Sumter and to attack it if the garrison did not comply. On April 12, as Lincoln's relief force neared Charleston harbor, Beauregard opened fire. Two days later, the defenders surrendered and the Confederate Stars and Bars rose over Fort Sumter. The people of Charleston celebrated wildly. "I did not know," wrote Mary Boykin Chesnut in her diary, "that one could live such days of excitement."

The Call to Arms

Even before the attack on Fort Sumter, the Confederate Congress had authorized a volunteer army of 100,000 men to serve for twelve months. There was no difficulty finding volunteers. Men flocked to enlist, and their communities sent them off in ceremonies featuring bands, bonfires, and belligerent oratory. Most of that oratory, like Jefferson Davis's Inaugural Address (see Chapter 15), evoked the Revolutionary War and the right of free people to resist tyranny. In many places, the response to the hostilities at Fort Sumter was even more visceral. The first war circular, printed in Hickman County, Tennessee, trumpeted, "To Arms! Our Southern soil must be defended. We must not stop to ask who brought about war, who is at fault, but let us go and do battle . . . and then settle the question of who is to blame." Exhilarated by their own rapid mobilization, most Southerners believed that Unionists were cowards who would not be able to face up to southern bravery. "Just throw three or four shells among those blue-bellied Yankees," one North Carolinian boasted, "and they'll scatter like sheep." The cry of "On to Washington!" was raised throughout the South, and orators confidently predicted that the city would be captured and the war concluded within sixty days. For the early recruits, war was a patriotic adventure.

The "thunderclap of Sumter" startled the North into an angry response. The apathy and uncertainty that had prevailed since Lincoln's election disappeared, to be replaced by strong feelings of patriotism. On April 15, Lincoln issued a proclamation calling for 75,000 state militiamen to serve in the federal army for ninety days. Enlistment offices were swamped with so many enthusiastic volunteers that many men were sent home. Free African Americans, among the most eager to serve, were turned away: this was not yet a war for or by black people.

Public outpourings of patriotism were common. New Yorker George Templeton Strong recorded one example on April 18: "Went to the [City] Hall. The [Sixth] Massachusetts Regiment, which arrived here last night, was marching down on its way to Washington. Immense crowd; immense cheering. My eyes filled with tears, and I was half choked in sympathy with the contagious excitement. God be praised for the unity of feeling here! It is beyond, very far beyond, anything I hoped for."

The mobilization in Chester, Pennsylvania, was typical of the northern response to the outbreak of war. A patriotic rally was held at which a company of volunteers (the first of many from the region) calling themselves the "Union Blues" were mustered into the Ninth Regiment of Pennsylvania Volunteers amid cheers and band music. As they marched off to Washington (the gathering place for the Union army), companies of home guards were organized by the men who remained behind. Within a month, the women of Chester had organized a countywide system of war relief that sent a stream of clothing, blankets, bandages, and other supplies to the local troops and provided assistance to their families at home. Such relief organizations, some formally organized, some informal, emerged in every community, North and South, that sent soldiers off to the Civil War. These organizations not only played a vital role in supplying the troops but maintained the human, local link on which so many soldiers depended. In this sense, every American community accompanied its young men to war. And every American community stood to suffer terrible losses when its young men went into battle.

The Border States

The first secession, between December 20, 1860, and February 1, 1861, had taken seven Deep South states out of the Union. Now, in April, the firing on Fort Sumter and Lincoln's call for state militias forced the other southern states to take sides. Courted—and pressured—by both North and South, four states of the Upper South (Virginia, Arkansas, Tennessee, and North Carolina) joined the original seven in April and May 1861. Virginia's secession tipped the other three toward the Confederacy. The capital of the Confederacy was now moved to Richmond. This meant that the two capitals—Richmond and Washington—were less than 100 miles apart.

Still undecided was the loyalty of the northernmost tier of slave-owning states: Missouri, Kentucky, Maryland, and Delaware. Each controlled vital strategic assets. Missouri not only bordered the Mississippi River but controlled the routes to the west. Kentucky controlled the Ohio River. The main railroad link with the West ran through Maryland and the hill region of western Virginia (which split from Virginia to become the free state of West Virginia in 1863). Delaware controlled access to

Philadelphia. Finally, were Maryland to secede, the nation's capital would be completely surrounded by Confederate territory.

Delaware was loyal to the Union (less than 2 percent of its population were slaves), but Maryland's loyalty was divided, as an ugly incident on April 19 showed. When the Sixth Massachusetts Regiment (the one George Templeton Strong had cheered in New York) marched through Baltimore, a hostile crowd of 10,000 southern sympathizers, carrying Confederate flags, pelted the troops with bricks, paving stones, and bullets. Finally, in desperation the troops fired on the crowd, killing twelve people and wounding others. In retaliation, southern sympathizers burned the railroad bridges to the North and destroyed the telegraph line to Washington, cutting off communication between the capital and the rest of the Union for six days.

Lincoln's response was swift and stern. He stationed Union troops along Maryland's crucial railroads, declared martial law in Baltimore, and arrested the suspected ringleaders of the pro-Confederate mob and held them without trial. In July, he ordered the detention of thirty-two secessionist legislators and many sympathizers. Thus was Maryland's loyalty to the Union ensured.

In detaining the Baltimore agitators, Lincoln suspended the writ of habeas corpus, the constitutional requirement that authorities explain to a court their reasons for arresting someone. Chief Justice Roger B. Taney of the Supreme Court ruled that the president had no right to do this, but Lincoln at first ignored him. Later Lincoln argued that the suspension of certain civil rights might be necessary to suppress rebellion. The arrests in Maryland were the first of a number of violations of basic civil rights during the war, all of which the president justified on the basis of national security.

As in Maryland, the loyalties of the other border states were also divided. Missouri was plagued by guerrilla battles (reminiscent of the prewar "Bleeding Kansas") throughout the war. In Kentucky, division took the form of a huge illegal trade with the Confederacy through neighboring Tennessee, to which Lincoln, determined to keep Kentucky in the Union, turned a blind eye. The conflicting loyalties of the border states were often mirrored within families. Kentucky Senator John J. Crittenden had two sons who were major generals, one in the Union army and the other in the Confederate army. Such family divisions reached all the way to the White House: three brothers of Kentucky-born Mary Todd Lincoln, the president's wife, died fighting for the Confederacy.

That Delaware, Maryland, Missouri, and Kentucky chose to stay in the Union was a severe blow to the Confederacy. Among them, the four states could have added 45 percent to the white population and military manpower of the Confederacy and 80 percent to its manufacturing capacity. Almost as damaging, the decision of four slave states to stay in the Union punched a huge hole in the Confederate argument that the southern states were forced to secede to protect the right to own slaves.

The Battle of Bull Run

Once sides had been chosen and the initial flush of enthusiasm had passed, the nature of the war, and the mistaken notions about it, soon became clear. The event that shattered the illusions was the First Battle of Bull Run, at Manassas Creek in Virginia in July 1861. Confident of a quick victory, a Union army of 35,000 men marched south, crying "On to Richmond!" So lighthearted and unprepared was the Washington community that the troops were accompanied not only by journalists but by a crowd of politicians and sightseers. At first the Union troops held their ground against the 25,000 Confederate troops commanded by General P. G. T. Beauregard (of Fort Sumter fame). But when 2,300 fresh Confederate troops arrived as reinforcements, the untrained northern troops broke ranks in an uncontrolled retreat that swept up the frightened sightseers as well. Soldiers and civilians alike retreated in disarray to Washington. Confederate Mary Boykin Chesnut recorded in her diary, "We might have walked into Washington any day for a week after Manassas, such was the consternation and confusion there." But the Confederates lacked the organization and the strength to follow the retreating Union troops and capture the capital.

Bull Run was sobering—and prophetic. The Civil War was the most lethal military conflict in American history, leaving a legacy of devastation on the battlefield and desolation at home. It claimed the lives of nearly 620,000 soldiers, more than the the First and Second World Wars combined. One out of every four soldiers who fought in the war never returned home.

The Relative Strengths of North and South

Overall, in terms of both population and productive capacity, the Union seemed to have a commanding edge over the Confederacy. The North had two and a half times the South's population (22 million to 9 million, of whom 3.5 million were slaves) and enjoyed an even greater advantage in industrial capacity (nine times that of the South). The North produced almost all of the nation's firearms (97 percent), had 71 percent of its railroad mileage, and produced 94 percent of its cloth and 90 percent of its footwear. The North seemed able to feed, clothe, arm, and transport all the soldiers it chose. The North's wholehearted commitment to the market revolution, shown in particular in its superior ability to organize its economic advantage, was ultimately to prove decisive: by the end of the war the Union had managed to field and equip more than 2 million soldiers as compared to the Confederacy's 800,000. But in the short term the South had important assets to counter the advantage of the North.

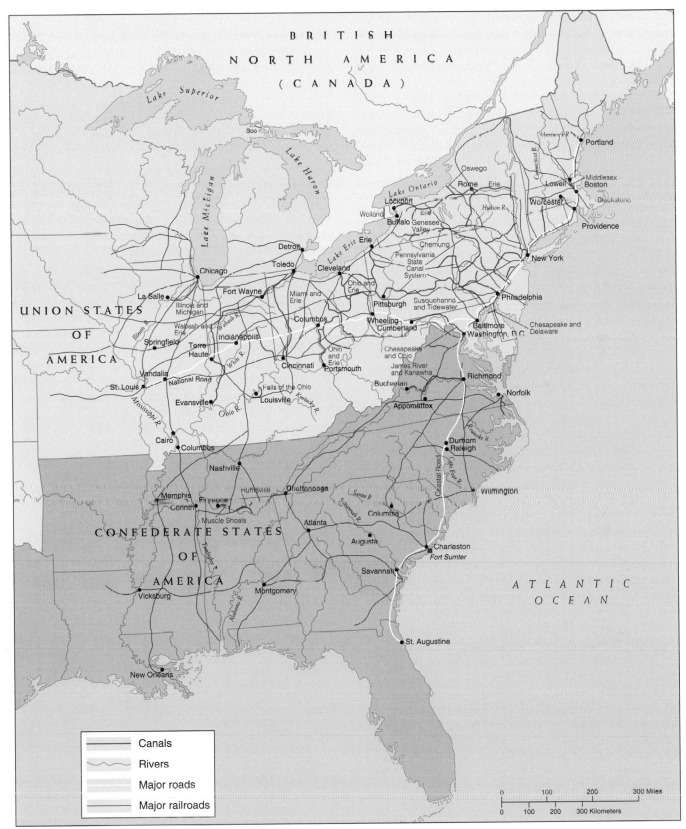

Comparative Transportation Systems, 1860   Transportation systems were an important index of comparative strength: the North had almost three times the railroad mileage of the South. The relative lack of transportation hurt the Confederacy by hindering its ability to move troops and to distribute military and medical supplies.

The first was the nature of the struggle. For the South, this was a defensive war in which, as the early volunteers showed, the most basic principle of the defense of home and community united almost all white citizens, regardless of their views about slavery. The North would have to invade the South and then control it against guerrilla opposition in order to win. The parallels with the Revolutionary War were unmistakable. Most white Southerners were confident that the North, like Great Britain in its attempt to subdue the rebellious colonies, would turn out to be a lumbering giant against whom they could secure their independence.

Second, the military disparity was less extreme than it appeared. Although the North had manpower, its troops were mostly untrained. The professional federal army numbered only 16,000, and most of its experience had been gained in small Indian wars. Moreover, the South, because of its tradition of honor and belligerence (see Chapter 11), appeared to have an advantage in military leadership. More than a quarter of all the regular army officers chose to side with the South. The most notable was Robert E. Lee. Offered command of the Union army by President Lincoln, Lee hesitated but finally decided to follow his native state, Virginia, into the Confederacy, saying, "I have been unable to make up my mind to raise my hand against my native state, my relatives, my children, and my home."

Finally, the North's economic advantages, which were eventually decisive, initially seemed unimportant. The South could feed itself, and many soldiers brought their own weapons, uniforms, horses, and sometimes slaves when they enlisted. It was widely believed that slavery would work to the South's advantage, for slaves could continue to do the vital plantation work while their masters went off to war. But above all, the South had the weapon of cotton. "Cotton is King," James Henry Hammond had announced in 1858, at the height of the cotton boom that made the 1850s the most profitable decade in southern history. Because of the crucial role of southern cotton in industrialization, Hammond had declared, "The slaveholding South is now the controlling power of the world." Southerners were confident that the British and French need for southern cotton would soon bring those countries to recognize the Confederacy as a separate nation.

GOVERNMENTS ORGANIZE FOR WAR

The Civil War forced the federal government to assume powers unimaginable just a few years before. Abraham Lincoln took as his primary task

to lead and unify the nation in his responsibility as commander in chief. He found the challenge almost insurmountable. Jefferson Davis's challenge was even greater. He had to create a Confederate nation out of a loose grouping of eleven states, each believing strongly in states' rights. Yet in the Confederacy, as in the Union, the conduct of the war required central direction.

Lincoln as War President

Lincoln's first task as president was to assert control over his own cabinet. Because he had few national contacts outside the Republican Party, Lincoln chose to staff his cabinet with other Republicans, including, most unusually, several who had been his rivals for the presidential nomination. Secretary of State William Seward, widely regarded as the leader of the Republican Party, at first expected to "manage" Lincoln as he had Zachary Taylor in 1848, but he soon became the president's willing partner. On the other hand, Treasury Secretary Salmon P. Chase, a staunch abolitionist, adamantly opposed concessions to the South and considered Lincoln too conciliatory. Chase, a key member of a group known as the Radical Republicans, remained a vocal and dangerous critic. That the Republican Party was a not-quite-jelled mix of former Whigs, abolitionists, moderate Free-Soilers, and even some prowar Democrats made Lincoln's task as party leader much more difficult than it might otherwise have been.

After the fall of Fort Sumter, military necessity prompted Lincoln to call up the state militias, order a

This aerial view of Washington shows the nation's capital during the Civil War as it underwent an abrupt transition from a small slave-owning community to the busy hub of the Union's war effort. Throughout the Civil War, the unfinished dome of the Capitol Building loomed over the city, its incompleteness symbolizing the divided state of the nation.

SOURCE: In the summer of 1861, from *Harper's Weekly*. The Picture Bank.

naval blockade of the South, and vastly expand the military budget. Breaking with precedent, he took these actions without congressional sanction because Congress was not in session. Military necessity—the need to hold the border states—likewise prompted other early actions, such as the suspension of habeas corpus and the acceptance of Kentucky's ambiguous neutrality. Over howls of protest from abolitionists, the president also repudiated an unauthorized declaration issued by General John C. Frémont, military commander in Missouri, in August 1861 that would have freed Missouri's slaves. Lincoln feared that such an action would lead to the secession of Kentucky and Maryland.

Although James K. Polk had assumed responsibility for overall American military strategy during the Mexican-American War (see Chapter 14), Lincoln was the first president to act as commander-in-chief in both a practical and a symbolic way. He actively directed military policy, although he sometimes wondered whether he would ever find generals capable of carrying out his orders. Lincoln's involvement in military strategy sprang from his realization that a civil war presented problems different from those of a foreign war of conquest. Lincoln wanted above all to persuade the South to rejoin the Union, and his every military move was dictated by the hope of eventual reconciliation—hence his cautiousness, and his acute sense of the role of public opinion. Today we recognize Lincoln's exceptional abilities and eloquent language, but in his own time some of his most moving statements fell on deaf ears. Not all of Lincoln's problems came from the South. His first priority had to be to keep the Union unified. He always had to step carefully as he tried to find common ground across a wide spectrum of opinions from militant abolitionist to southern sympathizer. At the same time, he presided over a vast expansion of the powers of the federal government.

Expanding the Power of the Federal Government

The greatest expansion in government power during the war was in the War Department, which by early 1862 was faced with the unprecedented challenge of feeding, clothing, and arming 700,000 Union soldiers. Initially the government relied on the individual states to equip and supply their vastly expanded militias. States often contracted directly with textile mills and shoe factories to clothe their troops. In many northern cities, volunteer groups sprang up to recruit regiments, buy them weapons, and send them to Washington. Other such community groups, like the one in Chester, Pennsylvania, focused on clothing and providing medical care to soldiers. By January 1862 the War Department, under the able direction of Edwin M. Stanton, a former Democrat from Ohio, was able to perform many basic functions of procurement and supply without too much

delay or corruption. But the size of the Union army and the complexity of fully supplying it demanded constant efforts at all levels—government, state, and community—throughout the war. Thus, in the matter of procurement and supply, as in mobilization, the battlefront was related to the home front on a scale that Americans had not previously experienced.

The need for money for the vast war effort was pressing. Treasury Secretary Chase worked closely with Congress to develop ways to finance the war. They naturally turned to the nation's economic experts—private bankers, merchants, and managers of large businesses. With the help of Philadelphia financier Jay Cooke, the Treasury used patriotic appeals to sell war bonds to ordinary people in amounts as small as $50. Cooke sold $400 million in bonds, taking for himself what he considered a "fair commission." By the war's end, the United States had borrowed $2.6 billion for the war effort, the first example in American history of the mass financing of war. Additional sources of revenue were sales taxes and the first federal income tax (of 3 percent). Imposed in August 1861, the income tax affected only the affluent: anyone with an annual income under $800 was exempt.

Most radical of all was Chase's decision—which was authorized only after a bitter congressional fight—to print and distribute Treasury notes (paper money). Until then, the money in circulation had been a mixture of coins and state bank notes issued by 1,500 different state banks. The Legal Tender Act of February 1862 created a national currency. Because of its color, the paper bank notes were popularly known as "greenbacks." In 1863, Congress passed the National Bank Act, which prohibited state banks from issuing their own notes and forced them to apply for federal charters. Thus was the first uniform national currency created, at the expense of the independence that many state banks had prized. "These are extraordinary times, and extraordinary measures must be resorted to in order to save our Government and preserve our nationality," pleaded Congressman Elbridge G. Spaulding, sponsor of the legislation. Only through this appeal to wartime necessity were Spaulding and his allies able to overcome the opposition, for the switch to a national currency was widely recognized as a major step toward centralization of economic power in the hands of the federal government. Such a measure would have been unthinkable if southern Democrats had still been part of the national government. The absence of southern Democrats also made possible passage of a number of Republican economic measures not directly related to the war.

Although the outbreak of war overshadowed everything else, the Republican Party in Congress was determined to fulfill its campaign pledge of a comprehensive program of economic development. Republicans quickly passed the Morrill Tariff Act (1861), by 1864, this and subsequent measures had raised tariffs to more than double their prewar rate. In 1862 and 1864, Congress created two federally chartered corporations to build a transcontinental railroad—the Union Pacific Railroad Company, to lay track westward from Omaha, and the Central Pacific, to lay track eastward from California—thus fulfilling the dreams of the many expansionists who believed America's economic future lay in trade with Asia across the Pacific Ocean. Two other measures, both passed in 1862, had long been sought by Westerners. The Homestead Act gave 160 acres of public land to any citizen who agreed to live on the land for five years, improve it by building a house and cultivating some of the land, and pay a small fee. The Morrill Land Grant Act gave states public land that would allow them to finance land-grant colleges offering education to ordinary citizens in practical skills such as agriculture, engineering, and military science. Coupled with this act, the establishment of a federal Department of Agriculture in 1862 gave American farmers a big push toward modern commercial agriculture.

This package revealed the Whig origins of many Republicans, for in essence the measures amounted to an updated version of Henry Clay's American System of national economic development, illustrating yet again the unstoppable nature of the market revolution. They were to have a powerful nationalizing effect, connecting ordinary people to the federal government in new ways. As much as the extraordinary war measures, the enactment of the Republican program increased the role of the federal government in national life. Although many of the executive war powers lapsed when the battles ended, the accumulation of strength by the federal government, which southern Democrats would have opposed had they been in Congress, was never reversed.

Diplomatic Objectives

To Secretary of State William Seward fell the job of making sure that Britain and France did not extend diplomatic recognition to the Confederacy. Although Southerners had been certain that King Cotton would gain them European support, they were wrong. British public opinion, which had strongly supported the abolition of slavery within the British Empire in the 1830s, would not now countenance the recognition of a new nation based on slavery. British cotton manufacturers found economic alternatives, first using up their backlog of southern cotton and then turning to Egypt and India for new supplies. In spite of Union protests, however, both Britain and France did allow Confederate vessels to use their ports, and British shipyards sold six ships to the Confederacy. But in 1863, when the Confederacy commissioned Britain's Laird shipyard to

build two ironclad ships with pointed prows for ramming Union ships, the Union threatened war and the British government made sure that the Laird ironclads were never delivered. Seward had wanted to threaten Britain with war earlier, in 1861, when the prospect of diplomatic recognition for the Confederacy seemed most likely, but Lincoln had overruled him, cautioning, "One war at a time."

Nonbelligerence was also the Union response in 1861, when a bankrupt Mexico suffered the ignominy of a joint invasion by British, Spanish, and French troops determined to collect the substantial debts owed by Mexico to their nations. This was a serious violation of Mexican independence, just the kind of European intervention that the Monroe Doctrine had been formulated to prevent (see Chapter 9). When it became clear that France was bent on conquest, Britain and Spain withdrew, and Mexican forces repelled the French troops on May 5, 1862. Ever since, Mexico has celebrated *El Cinco de Mayo*. France eventually prevailed and installed the Austrian archduke Maximilian as emperor. In normal times, the French conquest could have led to war, but fearing that France might recognize the Confederacy or invade Texas, Seward had to content himself with refusing to recognize the new Mexican government. In the meantime, he directed Union troops to gain a stronghold in Texas as soon as possible. In November, five months after the French marched into Mexico City, Union troops seized Brownsville, a town on the Texas-Mexico border, sending a clear signal to the French to go no further. In 1866, after the Civil War, strong diplomatic pressure from Seward convinced the French to withdraw from Mexico. The following year, the hapless Maximilian was captured and shot during a revolt led by a future Mexican president, Benito Juárez. To him fell the task of reviving Mexico after a disastrous decade that included civil war (see Chapter 14), and economic collapse, as well as foreign invasion.

Although the goal of Seward's diplomacy—preventing recognition of the Confederacy by the European powers—was always clear, its achievement was uncertain for more than two years. Northern fears and southern hopes seesawed with the fortunes of battle. Not until the victories at Vicksburg and Gettysburg in July 1863 could Seward be reasonably confident of success.

Jefferson Davis as Confederate President

Although Jefferson Davis had held national cabinet rank (as secretary of war under President Franklin Pierce), had experience as an administrator, and was a former military man (none of which was true of Abraham Lincoln), he was unable to hold the Confederacy together. Perhaps no one could have. Born, like Lincoln, in Kentucky,

Davis ultimately settled in Mississippi, where he became a rich planter. Davis was thus a "cotton nabob" (one of the newly rich class of slave owners), and as such was as scorned by some members of the old southern aristocracy (as was Abraham Lincoln by some members of the northern elite). Davis's problems, however, were as much structural as they were personal.

Davis's first cabinet of six men, appointed in February 1861, included a representative from each of the states of the first secession except Mississippi, which was represented by Davis himself. This careful attention to the equality of the states pointed to the fundamental problem that Davis was unable to overcome. For all of its drama, secession was a conservative strategy for preserving the slavery-based social and political structure that existed in every southern state. A shared belief in states' rights—that is, in their own autonomy—was a poor basis on which to build a unified nation. Davis, who would have preferred to be a general rather than a president, lacked Lincoln's persuasive skills and political astuteness. Although he saw the need for unity, he was unable to impose it. Soon his autonomous style of leadership—he wanted to decide every detail himself—angered his generals, alienated cabinet members, and gave southern governors reason to resist his orders. By the second year of the war, when rich slave owners were refusing to give up their privileges for the war effort, Davis no longer had the public confidence and support he needed to coerce them. After the first flush of patriotism had passed, the Confederacy never lived up to its hope of becoming a unified nation.

Confederate Disappointments in Diplomacy and the Economy

The failure of "cotton diplomacy" was a crushing blow. White Southerners were stunned that Britain and France would not recognize their claim to independence. Well into 1863, the South hoped that a decisive battlefield victory would change the minds of cautious Europeans. In the meantime, plantations continued to grow cotton, but the Confederacy withheld it from market, hoping that lack of raw material for their textile mills would lead the British and French to recognize the Confederacy. The British reacted indignantly, claiming that the withholding of cotton was economic blackmail and that to yield "would be ignominious beyond measure," as Lord Russell put it. Because British textile manufacturers had found new sources of cotton, when the Confederacy ended the embargo in 1862 and began to ship its great surplus, the world price of cotton plunged.

Then too, the Union naval blockade, weak at first, began to take effect. Cotton turned out to be not so powerful a diplomatic weapon after all.

Perhaps the greatest southern failure was in the area of finances. At first the Confederate government tried to raise money from the states, but governors refused to impose new taxes. By the time uniform taxes were levied in 1863, it was too late. Heavy borrowing and the printing of great sums of paper money produced runaway inflation (a ruinous rate of 9,000 percent per annum by 1865, compared with 80 percent in the North). Inflation, in turn, caused incalculable damage to morale and prospects for unity.

After the initial surge of volunteers, enlistment in the military fell off, as it did in the North also. In April 1862, the Confederate Congress passed the first draft law in American history, and the Union Congress followed suit in March 1863. The southern law declared that all able-bodied men between eighteen and thirty-five were eligible

This painting by William C. Washington, *Jackson Entering the City of Winchester,* shows the dashing Confederate General "Stonewall" Jackson saving the Virginia town from Union capture in 1862. Jackson and other Confederate generals evoked fierce loyalty to the Confederacy. Unfortunately, by the time this victory was commemorated, Jackson himself was dead, killed by friendly fire at the Battle of Chancellorsville in May of 1863. SOURCE: 1863–1865, 48⅛ × 60⅛ in. (120.3 × 150.3 cm.) Valentine Museum Library, Richmond, Virginia (31726).

for three years of military service. Purchase of substitutes was allowed, as in the North, but in the South the price was uncontrolled, rising eventually to $10,000 in Confederate money. The most disliked part of the draft law was a provision exempting one white man on each plantation with twenty or more slaves. This provision not only seemed to disprove the earlier claim that slavery freed white men to fight, but it aroused class resentments. A bitter phrase of the time complained, "It's a rich man's war but a poor man's fight."

Contradictions of Southern Nationalism

In the early days of the war, Jefferson Davis successfully mobilized feelings of regional identity and patriotism. Many Southerners felt part of a beleaguered region that had been forced to resist northern tyranny. But most Southerners felt loyalty to their own state and local communities, not to a Confederate nation. The strong belief in states' rights and aristocratic privilege undermined the Confederate cause. Some Southern governors resisted potentially unifying actions such as moving militias outside their home states. Broader

measures, such as general taxation, were widely evaded by rich and poor alike. The inequitable draft was only one of many things that convinced the ordinary people of the South that this was a war for privileged slave owners, not for them. With its leaders and citizens fearing (perhaps correctly) that centralization would destroy what was distinctively southern, the Confederacy was unable to mobilize the resources—financial, human, and otherwise—that might have prevented its destruction by northern armies.

THE FIGHTING THROUGH 1862

Just as political decisions were often driven by military necessity, the basic northern and southern military strategies were affected by political considerations as much as by military ones. The initial policy of limited war, thought to be the best route to ultimate reconciliation, ran into difficulties because of the public's impatience for victories. But victories, as the mounting slaughter made clear, were not easy to achieve.

The contrast between the hope and valor of these young southern volunteer soldiers, photographed shortly before the first battle of Bull Run, and the later advertisements for substitutes is marked. Southern exemptions for slave owners and lavish payment for substitutes increasingly bred resentment among the ordinary people of the South. SOURCE: (a) First Virginia Regiment, Cook Collection. Valentine Museum Library/ Richmond History Center; (b) *Richmond Dispatch*, Library of Congress.

SUBSTITUTE NOTICES.

WANTED—A SUBSTITUTE for a conscript, to serve during the war. Any good man over the age of 35 years, not a resident of Virginia, or a foreigner, may hear of a good situation by calling at Mr. GEORGE BAGBY'S office, Shockoe Slip, to-day, between the hours of 9 and 11 A. M.   [jy 9—1t*]   A COUNTRYMAN.

WANTED—Two SUBSTITUTES—one for artillery, the other for infantry or cavalry service. Also, to sell, a trained, thoroughbred cavalry HORSE. Apply to   DR. BROOCKS, Corner Main and 12th streets, or to
jy 9—3t*   T. T. BROOCKS, Petersburg, Va.

WANTED—Immediately, a SUBSTITUTE. A man over 35 years old, or under 18, can get a good price by making immediate application to Room No. 50, Monument Hotel, or by addressing "J. W.," through Richmond P. O.   jy 9—1t*

WANTED—A SUBSTITUTE, to go into the 24th North Carolina State troops, for which a liberal price will be paid. Apply to me at Dispatch office this evening at 4 o'clock P. M.
jy 9---1t*   R. R. MOORE.

WANTED—A SUBSTITUTE, to go in a first-rate Georgia company of infantry, under the heroic Jackson. A gentleman whose health is impaired, will give a fair price for a substitute. Apply immediately at ROOM, No. 13, Post-Office Department, third story, between the hours of 10 and 3 o'clock.   jy 9—6t*

WANTED—Two SUBSTITUTES for the war. A good bonus will be given. None need apply except those exempt from Conscript. Apply to-day at   GEORGE I. HERRING'S,
jy 9—1t*   Grocery store, No. 56 Main st.

The War in Northern Virginia

The initial northern strategy, dubbed by critics the Anaconda Plan (after the constrictor snake), envisaged slowly squeezing the South with a blockade at sea and on the Mississippi River. Proposed by the general in chief, Winfield Scott, a native of Virginia, it avoided invasion and conquest in the hope that a strained South would recognize the inevitability of defeat and thus surrender. Lincoln accepted the basics of the plan, but public clamor for a fight pushed him to agree to the disastrous Battle of Bull Run and then to a major buildup of Union troops in northern Virginia under General George B. McClellan.

Dashing in appearance, McClellan was extremely cautious in battle. In March 1862, after almost a year spent drilling the raw Union recruits and after repeated exhortations by an impatient Lincoln, McClellan committed 120,000 troops to what became known as the Peninsular campaign. The objective was to capture Richmond, the Confederate capital. McClellan had his troops and their supplies ferried in 400 ships from Washington to Fortress Monroe, near the mouth of the James River, an effort that took three weeks. Inching up the James Peninsula toward Richmond, he tried to avoid battle, hoping his overwhelming numbers would convince the South to surrender. By June, McClellan's troops were close enough

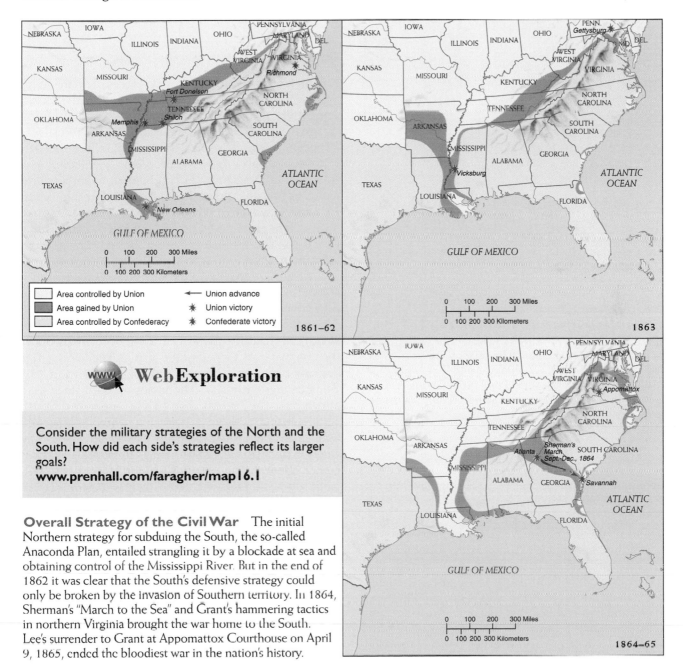

WebExploration

Consider the military strategies of the North and the South. How did each side's strategies reflect its larger goals?
www.prenhall.com/faragher/map16.1

Overall Strategy of the Civil War   The initial Northern strategy for subduing the South, the so-called Anaconda Plan, entailed strangling it by a blockade at sea and obtaining control of the Mississippi River. But in the end of 1862 it was clear that the South's defensive strategy could only be broken by the invasion of Southern territory. In 1864, Sherman's "March to the Sea" and Grant's hammering tactics in northern Virginia brought the war home to the South. Lee's surrender to Grant at Appomattox Courthouse on April 9, 1865, ended the bloodiest war in the nation's history.

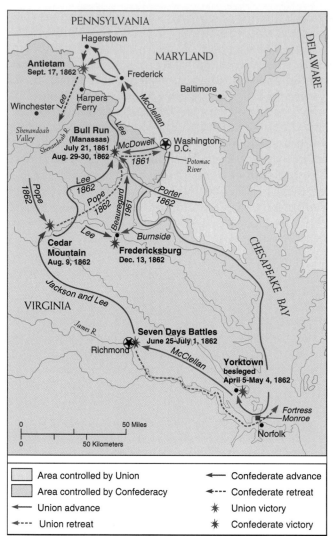

Major Battles in the East, 1861–1862
Northern Virginia was the most crucial and the
most constant theater of battle. The prizes were
the two opposing capitals, Washington and Richmond,
only 70 miles apart. By the summer of 1862, George B.
McClellan, famously cautious, had achieved only stalemate
in the Peninsular campaign. He did, however, turn back
Robert E. Lee at Antietam in September.

to Richmond to hear the church bells ringing—but not
close enough for victory. In a series of battles known as
the Seven Days, Robert E. Lee (who had just assumed
command of the Confederacy's Army of Northern Virginia) boldly counterattacked, repeatedly catching Mc-
Clellan off guard. Taking heavy losses as well as inflicting
them, Lee drove McClellan back. In August, Lee routed
another Union army, commanded by General John Pope,
at the Second Battle of Bull Rull (Second Manassas). Lincoln, alarmed at the threat to Washington and disappointed by McClellan's inaction, ordered him to abandon
the Peninsular campaign and return to the capital.

Jefferson Davis, like Abraham Lincoln, was an active
commander-in-chief. And like Lincoln, he responded to
a public that clamored for more action than a strictly
defensive war entailed. After the Seven Days victories,
Davis supported a Confederate attack on Maryland. At
the same time, he issued a proclamation urging the people of Maryland to make a separate peace. But in the
brutal battle of Antietam on September 17, 1862, which
claimed more than 5,000 dead and 19,000 wounded,
McClellan's army checked Lee's advance. Lee retreated
to Virginia, inflicting terrible losses on northern troops
at Fredericksburg when they again made a thrust toward
Richmond in December 1862. The war in northern Virginia was stalemated: neither side was strong enough to
win, but each was too strong to be defeated.

Shiloh and the War for the Mississippi

Although most public attention was focused on the fighting in Virginia, battles in Tennessee and along the Mississippi River proved to be the key to eventual Union
victory. The rising military figure in the West was
Ulysses S. Grant, who had once resigned from the service because of a drinking problem. Reenlisting as a
colonel after the capture of Fort Sumter, Grant was promoted to brigadier general within two months. In February 1862, Grant captured Fort Henry and Fort Donelson,
on the Tennessee and Cumberland rivers, establishing
Union control of much of Tennessee and forcing Confederate troops to retreat into northern Mississippi.

Moving south with 28,000 men, Grant met a
40,000-man Confederate force commanded by General
Albert Sidney Johnston at Shiloh Church in April 1862.
Seriously outnumbered on the first day, Grant's forces
were reinforced by the arrival of 35,000 troops under
the command of General Don Carlos Buell. After two
days of bitter and bloody fighting in the rain, the
Confederates withdrew. The losses on both sides were
enormous: the North lost 13,000 men, the South
11,000, including General Johnston, who bled to death.
McClellan's Peninsular campaign was already under way
when Grant won at Shiloh, and Jefferson Davis, concerned about the defense of Richmond, refused to reinforce the generals who were trying to stop Grant.
Consequently, Union forces kept moving, capturing
Memphis in June and beginning a campaign to eventually capture Vicksburg, "the Gibraltar of the Mississippi." Grant and other Union generals faced strong
Confederate resistance, and progress was slow. Earlier
that year, naval forces under Admiral David Farragut had
captured New Orleans and then continued up the
Mississippi River. By the end of 1862 it was clearly only
a matter of time before the entire river would be in
Union hands. Arkansas, Louisiana, and Texas would
then be cut off from the rest of the Confederacy.

The War in the Trans-Mississippi West

Although only one western state, Texas, seceded from the Union, the Civil War was fought in small ways in many parts of the West. Southern hopes for the extension of slavery into the Southwest were reignited by the war, and the just-announced discovery of gold in Colorado impelled the Confederacy to attempt to capture it. Texans mounted an attack on New Mexico, which they had long coveted, and kept their eyes on the larger prizes of Arizona and California. A Confederate force led by General Henry H. Sibley occupied Santa Fé and Albuquerque early in 1862 without resistance, thus posing a serious Confederate threat to the entire Southwest. Confederate hopes were dashed, however, by a ragtag group of 950 miners and adventurers organized

Major Battles in the West, 1862–1863
Ulysses S. Grant waged a mobile war, winning at Fort Henry and Fort Donelson in Tennessee in February 1862 and at Shiloh in April, and capturing Memphis in June. He then laid siege to Vicksburg, as Admiral David Farragut captured New Orleans and began to advance up the Mississippi River.

into the first Colorado Volunteer Infantry Regiment. After an epic march of 400 miles from Denver, which was completed in thirteen days despite snow and high winds, the Colorado militia stopped the unsuspecting Confederate troops in the Battle of Glorieta Pass on March 26–28, 1862. This dashing action, coupled with the efforts of California militias to safeguard Arizona and Utah from seizure by Confederate sympathizers, secured the Far West for the Union.

Other military action in the West was less decisive. The chronic fighting along the Kansas-Missouri border set a record for brutality when Confederate William Quantrill's Raiders made a predawn attack on Lawrence, Kansas, in August 1863, massacring 150 inhabitants and burning the town. Another civil war took place in Indian Territory, south of Kansas. The southern Indian tribes who had been removed there from the Old Southwest in the 1830s included many who were still bitter over the horrors of their removal by federal troops, and they sympathized with the Confederacy. John Ross, leader of the majority pro-Union Cherokee fullbloods, at first tried to assure the safety of his people by proclaiming their neutrality, but later in 1861, bordered by Confederate states and lacking support from Washington, he signed a treaty of alliance with the Confederates. The Confederacy actively sought Indian support by offering Indian people representation in the Confederate Congress. Consequently, many Indians fought for the South, among them Stand Watie, who became a Confederate military officer. Union victories at Pea Ridge (in northwestern Arkansas) in 1862 and near Fort Gibson (in Indian Territory) in 1863 secured the area for the Union but did little to stop dissension among the Indian groups themselves. Ross, captured in 1862 and held at Fort Leavenworth in Kansas, never returned to his tribe, which factionalized badly after his departure. After the Civil War the victorious federal government used the tribes' wartime support for the Confederacy as a justification for demanding further land cessions.

Elsewhere in the West, other groups of Indians found themselves caught up in the wider war. An uprising by the Santee Sioux in Minnesota occurred in August 1862, just as McClellan conceded defeat in the Peninsular campaign in Virginia. Alarmed whites, certain that the uprising was a Confederate plot, ignored legitimate Sioux grievances and responded in kind to Sioux ferocity. In little more than a month, 500 to 800 white settlers and an even greater number of Sioux were killed. Thirty-eight Indians were hanged in a mass execution in Mankato on December 26, 1862, and subsequently all Sioux were expelled from Minnesota. In 1863, U.S. Army Colonel Kit Carson invaded Navajo country in Arizona in retaliation for Indian raids on U.S. troops. Eight thousand Navajos were forced on the brutal "Long Walk" to Bosque

Redondo on the Pecos River in New Mexico, where they were held prisoner until a treaty between the United States and the Navajos was signed in 1868.

The hostilities in the West showed that no part of the country, and none of its inhabitants, could remain untouched by the Civil War.

The Naval War

The Union's naval blockade of the South, intended to cut off commerce between the Confederacy and the rest of the world, was initially unsuccessful. The U.S. Navy had only thirty-three ships with which to blockade 189 ports along 3,500 miles of coastline. Southern blockade runners evaded Union ships with ease: only an estimated one-eighth of all Confederate shipping was stopped in 1862. Moreover, the Confederacy licensed British-made privateers to strike at northern shipping. In a two-year period one such Confederate raider, the *Alabama*, destroyed sixty-nine Union ships with cargoes valued at $6 million. Beginning in 1863, however, as the Union navy became larger, the blockade began to take effect. In 1864 a third of the blockade runners were captured, and in 1865 half of them. As a result, fewer and fewer supplies reached the South.

North and South also engaged in a brief duel featuring the revolutionary new technology of ironcladding. The Confederacy refitted a scuttled Union vessel, the *Merrimac*, with iron plating and renamed it the *Virginia*. On March 8, 1862, as McClellan began his Peninsular campaign, the *Virginia* steamed out of Norfolk harbor to challenge the Union blockade. The iron plating protected the *Virginia* from the fire of the Union ships, which found themselves defenseless against its ram and its powerful guns. Two Union ships went down, and the blockade seemed about to be broken. But the North had an experimental ironclad of its own, the *Monitor*, which was waiting for the *Virginia* when it emerged from port on March 9. The *Monitor*, which looked like "an immense shingle floating on the water, with a gigantic cheese box rising from its center," was the ship of the future, for the "cheese box" was a revolving turret, a basic component of battleships to come. The historic duel between these first two ironclads was inconclusive, and primitive technology together with limited resources made them of little consequence for the rest of the war. But this brief duel prefigured the naval and land battles of the world wars of the twentieth century as much as did the massing of huge armies on the battlefield.

For the Union, the most successful naval operation in the first two years of the war was not the blockade but the seizing of exposed coastal areas. The Sea Islands of South Carolina were taken, as were some of the North Carolina islands and Fort Pulaski, which commanded the harbor of Savannah, Georgia. Most damaging to the South was the capture of New Orleans.

The Black Response

The capture of Port Royal in the South Carolina Sea Islands in 1861 was important for another reason. Whites fled at the Union advance, but 10,000 slaves greeted the troops with jubilation and shouts of gratitude. Union troops had unwittingly freed these slaves in advance of any official Union policy on the status of slaves in captured territory.

Early in the war, an irate Southerner who saw three of his slaves disappear behind Union lines at Fortress Monroe, Virginia, demanded the return of his property, citing the Fugitive Slave Law. The Union commander, Benjamin Butler, replied that the Fugitive Slave Law no longer applied and that the escaped slaves were "contraband of war." News of Butler's decision spread rapidly among the slaves in the region of Fortress Monroe. Two days later, eight runaway slaves appeared; the next day, fifty-nine black men and women arrived at the fort. Union commanders had found an effective way to rob the South of its basic workforce. The "contrabands," as they were known, were put to work building fortifications and doing other useful work in northern camps. Washington, D.C., became a refuge for contraband blacks, who crowded into the capital to join the free black people who lived there (at 9,000 people, they were one of the largest urban black populations outside the Confederacy). Many destitute contrabands received help from the Contraband Relief Association. Modeled on the Sanitary Commission, the association was founded by former slave Elizabeth Keckley, seamstress to Mary Todd Lincoln, the president's wife.

As Union troops drove deeper into the South, the black response grew. When Union General William Tecumseh Sherman marched his army through Georgia in 1864, 18,000 slaves—entire families, people of all ages—flocked to the Union lines. By the war's end, nearly a million black people, fully a quarter of all the slaves in the South, had "voted with their feet" for the Union.

THE DEATH OF SLAVERY

The overwhelming response of black slaves to the Union advance changed the nature of the war. As increasing numbers of slaves flocked to Union lines, the conclusion was unmistakable: the southern war to defend the slave system did not have the support of slaves themselves. Any northern policy that ignored the issue of slavery and the wishes of the slaves was unrealistic.

The Politics of Emancipation

In 1862, as the issue of slavery loomed ever larger, Abraham Lincoln, acutely aware of divided northern opinion, inched his way toward a declaration of emancipation.

Lincoln was correct to be worried about the unity of opinion in the North. Before the war, within the Republican Party, only a small group of abolitionists had favored freeing the slaves. Most Republicans were more concerned about the expansion of slavery than they were about the lives of slaves themselves. They did not favor the social equality of black people, whom they considered inferior. The free-soil movement, for example, was as often antiblack as it was antislave. For their part, most northern Democrats were openly antiblack. Irish workers in northern cities had rioted against free African Americans, with whom they often competed for jobs. There was also the question of what would become of slaves who were freed. Even the most fervent abolitionists had refused to face up to this issue. Northern Democrats effectively played on racial fears in the 1862 congressional elections, warning that freed slaves would pour into northern cities and take jobs from white laborers.

Nevertheless, the necessities of war edged Lincoln toward a new position. In March 1862 he proposed that every state undertake gradual, compensated emancipation, after which former slaves would be resettled in Haiti and Panama (neither of which was under U.S. control). This unrealistic colonization scheme, as well as the reluctance of politicians in the border states to consider emancipation, doomed the proposal.

Radical Republicans chafed at Lincoln's conservative stance. In August 1862, Horace Greeley, editor of the *New York Tribune*, pressed the point in an open letter to the president. "On the face of this wide earth, Mr. President, there is not one disinterested, determined, intelligent champion of the Union cause who does not feel that all attempts to put down the Rebellion and at the same time uphold its inciting cause are preposterous and futile." Greeley's statement was incorrect, for many Northerners did not care what happened to the slaves but did care what happened to the Union. Lincoln's famous answer implicitly acknowledged the many shades of public opinion and cast his decision in terms of military necessity: "If I could save the Union without freeing any slave, I would do it; and if I could save it by freeing all the slaves, I would do it; and if I could do it by freeing some and leaving others alone, I would also do that. What I do about Slavery and the colored race, I do because I believe it helps to save this Union."

In fact, Lincoln had already made up his mind to issue the Emancipation Proclamation, and was simply waiting for the right moment. Following the Union victory at Antietam in September 1862, Lincoln issued a preliminary decree: unless the rebellious states returned to the Union by January 1, 1863, he would declare their slaves "forever free." Although Lincoln did not expect the Confederate states to surrender because of his proclamation, the decree increased the pressure on the South by directly linking the slave system to the war effort. Thus the freedom of black people became part of the struggle. Frederick Douglass, the voice of black America, wrote, "We shout for joy that we live to record this righteous decree."

On January 1, 1863, Lincoln duly issued the final Emancipation Proclamation, which turned out to be just as tortuous as his response to Greeley in August. The proclamation freed the slaves in the areas of rebellion—the areas the Union did not control—but specifically exempted slaves in the border states and in former Confederate areas conquered by the Union. Lincoln's purpose was to meet the abolitionist demand for a war against slavery while not losing the support of conservatives, especially in the border states. But the proclamation was so equivocal that Lincoln's own secretary of state, William Seward, remarked sarcastically, "We show our sympathy with slavery by emancipating slaves where we cannot reach them and holding them in bondage where we can set them free." And in Britain, where Lincoln had hoped to make a favorable impression on the public, government officials were more puzzled than impressed by the proclamation.

One group greeted the Emancipation Proclamation with open celebration. On New Year's Day, hundreds of African Americans gathered outside the White House and cheered the president. They called to him, as pastor Henry M. Turner recalled, that "if he would come out of that palace, they would hug him to death." Realizing the symbolic importance of the proclamation, free African Americans predicted that the news would encourage southern slaves either to flee to Union lines or refuse to work for their masters. Both of these things were already happening as African Americans seized on wartime changes to reshape white-black relations in the South. In one sense, then, the Emancipation Proclamation simply gave a name to a process already in motion.

Abolitionists set about moving Lincoln beyond his careful stance in the Emancipation Proclamation. Reformers such as Elizabeth Cady Stanton and Susan B. Anthony lobbied and petitioned for a constitutional amendment outlawing slavery. Lincoln agreed with them, and encouraged the Republican Party to support such an amendment in its 1864 election platform. Congress, at Lincoln's urging, approved and sent to the states a statement banning slavery throughout the United States. Quickly ratified by the Union states in 1865, the statement became the Thirteenth Amendment to the Constitution. (The southern states, being in a state of rebellion, could not vote.) Lincoln's firm support for this amendment is a good indicator of his true feelings about slavery when he was freed of the kinds of military and political considerations necessarily taken into account in the Emancipation Proclamation.

Black Fighting Men

As part of the Emancipation Proclamation, Lincoln gave his support for the first time to the recruitment of black soldiers. Early in the war, eager black volunteers had been bitterly disappointed at being turned away. Many, like Robert Fitzgerald, a free African American from Pennsylvania, found other ways to serve the Union cause. Fitzgerald first drove a wagon and mule for the Quartermaster Corps, and later, in spite of persistent seasickness, he served in the Union navy. After the Emancipation Proclamation, however, Fitzgerald was able to do what he had wanted to do all along: be a soldier. He enlisted in the Fifth Massachusetts Cavalry, a regiment that, like all the units in which black soldiers served, was 100 percent African American but commanded by white officers. The most famous black regiment, the Fifty-fourth Massachusetts Colored Infantry, was commanded by abolitionist Robert Gould Shaw of Boston, who was killed in action along with half of his troops in a fruitless attack on Fort Wagner, South Carolina, in 1863. Thomas Wentworth Higginson, the Unitarian minister who had supported John Brown, led another of the first black regiments, the First South Carolina Volunteers.

In Fitzgerald's company of eighty-three men, half came from slave states and had run away to enlist; the other half came mostly from the North but also from Canada, the West Indies, and France. Other regiments had volunteers from Africa. The proportion of volunteers from the loyal border states (where slavery was still legal) was upwards of 25 percent—a lethal blow to the slave system in those states.

After a scant two months of training, Fitzgerald's company was sent on to Washington and thence to battle in northern Virginia. Uncertain of the reception they would receive in northern cities with their history of antiblack riots, Fitzgerald and his comrades were pleasantly surprised. "We are cheered in every town we pass through," he wrote in his diary. "I was surprised to see a great many white people weeping as the train moved South." White people had reason to cheer: black volunteers, eager and willing to fight, made up 10 percent of the Union army. Nearly 200,000 African Americans (one out of every five black males in the nation) served in the Union army or navy. A fifth of them— 37,000—died defending their own freedom and the Union.

Military service was something no black man could take lightly. He faced prejudice of several kinds. In the North, most white people believed that black people were inferior both in intelligence and in courage. Most army officers shared these opinions— but usually not those who had volunteered to lead black troops. Thus African-American soldiers had to prove themselves in battle. The performance of black soldiers at Fort Wagner and in battles near Vicksburg, Mississippi, in 1863 helped to change the minds of the Union army command. In the battle of Milliken's Bend, untrained and poorly armed former slaves fought desperately—and successfully. "The bravery of the blacks . . . completely revolutionized the sentiment of the army with regard to the employment of negro troops," wrote Charles Dana, assistant secretary of war. "I heard prominent officers who formerly in private had sneered at the idea of negroes fighting express themselves after that as heartily in favor of it."

Among the Confederates, however, the feeling was very different. They hated and feared African American troops and threatened to treat any captured black soldier as an escaped slave subject to execution. On at least one occasion, the threats were carried out. In 1864 Confederate soldiers massacred 262 black soldiers at Fort Pillow, Tennessee, after they had surrendered. Although large-scale episodes such as this were rare (especially after President Lincoln threatened retaliation), smaller ones were not. On duty near Petersburg, Virginia, Robert Fitzgerald's company lost a picket to Con-

This painting, *The Storming of Fort Wagner*, shows the attack on the fort near Charleston, South Carolina, by the 54th Massachusetts African American Regiment on July 18, 1863. The attack failed, and more than half the members of this first Union all-black regiment and their white commanding officer, Robert Gould Shaw, were killed.

SOURCE: Kurtz and Allison. Courtesy of the Library of Congress.

federate hatred: wounded in the leg, he was unable to escape from Confederate soldiers, who smashed his skull with their musket butts. Fitzgerald wrote in his diary, "Can such men eventually triumph? God forbid!"

Another extraordinary part of the story of the African American soldiers was their reception by black people in the South, who were overjoyed at the sight of armed black men, many of them former slaves themselves, wearing the uniform of the Union army. As his regiment entered Wilmington, North Carolina, one soldier wrote, "Men and women, old and young, were running throughout the streets, shouting and praising God. We could then truly see what we have been fighting for."

Robert Fitzgerald's own army career was brief. Just five months after he enlisted, he caught typhoid fever. Hearing of his illness, Fitzgerald's mother traveled from Pennsylvania and nursed him, probably saving his life. Eventually, 117 members of his regiment died of disease—and only 7 in battle. Eight months after he had enlisted, Fitzgerald was discharged for poor eyesight. His short military career nevertheless gave him, in the words of a granddaughter, the distinguished lawyer Pauli Murray, "a pride which would be felt throughout his family for the next century."

African American soldiers were not treated equally by the Union army. They were segregated in camp, given the worst jobs, and paid less than white soldiers ($10 a month rather than $13). Although they might not be able to do much about the other kinds of discrimination, the men of the Fifty-fourth Massachusetts found an unusual way to protest their unequal pay: they refused to accept it, preferring to serve the army for free until it decided to treat them as free men. The protest was effective; in June 1864 the War Department equalized the wages of black and white soldiers.

In other ways the army service of black men made a dent in northern white racism. Massachusetts, the state where abolitionist feeling was the strongest, went the furthest by enacting the first law forbidding discrimination against African Americans in public facilities. Some major cities, among them San Francisco, Cincinnati, Cleveland, and New York, desegregated their streetcars. Some states—Ohio, California, Illinois—repealed statutes that had barred black people from testifying in court or serving on juries. But above all, as Frederick Douglass acutely saw, military service permanently changed the status of African Americans. "Once let the black man get upon his person the brass letters, U.S., let him get an eagle on his button and a musket on his shoulder and bullets in his pocket," Douglass said, and "there is no power on earth that can deny that he has earned the right to citizenship."

THE FRONT LINES AND THE HOME FRONT

Civil War soldiers wrote millions of letters home, more proportionately than in any American war. Their letters and the ones they received in return were links between the front lines and the home front, between the soldiers and their home communities. They are a testament to the patriotism of both Union and Confederate troops, for the story they tell is frequently one of slaughter and horror.

The Toll of War

In spite of early hopes for what one might call a "brotherly" war, one that avoided excessive brutality, Civil War battles were appallingly deadly. One reason was technology: improved weapons, particularly modern rifles, had much greater range and accuracy than the muskets they replaced. The Mexican-American War had been fought with smooth-bore muskets, which were slow to reload and accurate only at short distances. As Ulysses Grant said, "At a distance of a few hundred yards, a man could fire at you all day [with a musket] without your finding out." The new Springfield and Enfield rifles were accurate for a quarter of a mile or more.

Civil War generals, however, were slow to adjust to this new reality. Almost all Union and Confederate generals remained committed to the conventional military doctrine of massed infantry offensives—the "Jomini doctrine"—that they had learned in their military classes at West Point. Part of this strategy had been to "soften up" a defensive line with artillery before an infantry assault, but now the range of the new rifles made artillery itself vulnerable to attack. As a result, generals relied less on "softening up" than on immense numbers of infantrymen, hoping that enough of them would survive the withering rifle fire to overwhelm the enemy line. Enormous casualties were a consequence of this basic strategy.

Medical ignorance was another factor in the casualty rate. Because the use of antiseptic procedures was in its infancy, men often died because minor wounds became infected. Gangrene was a common cause of death. Disease was an even more frequent killer, taking twice as many men as were lost in battle. The overcrowded and unsanitary conditions of many camps were breeding grounds for smallpox, dysentery, typhoid, pneumonia, and, in the summer, malaria. The devastating effect of disease was apparent, for example, in McClellan's Peninsular campaign. Among his 130,000 men, nearly a quarter of the unwounded were ill in July 1862. The knowledge that this situation could only deteriorate during August and September—the most disease-ridden months—was one of the reasons Lincoln decided to recall McClellan and his army.

Both North and South were completely unprepared to handle the supply and health needs of their large armies. Twenty-four hours after the battle of Shiloh, most of the wounded still lay on the field in the rain. Many died of exposure; some, unable to help themselves, drowned. Nor were the combatants prepared to deal with masses of war prisoners, as the shocking example of the Confederate prison camp at Andersonville in northern Georgia demonstrated. Andersonville was an open stockade with no shade or shelter, erected early in 1864 to hold 10,000 northern prisoners. But by midsummer, it held 33,000. During the worst weeks of that summer, 100 prisoners died of disease, exposure, or malnutrition each day.

Army Nurses

Many medical supplies that the armies were unable to provide were donated by the United States Sanitary Commission in the North, as described in the opening of this chapter, and by women's volunteer groups in the South. But in addition to supplies, there was also an urgent need for skilled nurses to care for wounded and convalescent soldiers. Nursing within a family context was widely considered to be women's work. Caring for sick family members was a key domestic responsibility for women, and most had considerable experience with it. But taking care of strange men in hospitals was another thing. There were strong objections that such work was "unseemly" for respectable women.

Under the pressure of wartime necessity, and over the objections of most army doctors—who resented the challenge to their authority from people no different than their daughters or wives—women became army nurses. Hospital nursing, previously considered a job only disreputable women would undertake, now became a suitable vocation for middle-class women. Under the leadership of veteran reformer Dorothea Dix of the asylum movement (see Chapter 13), and in cooperation with the Sanitary Commission (and with the vocal support of Mother Bickerdyke), by the war's end more than 3,000 northern women had worked as paid army nurses and many more as volunteers.

One of the volunteers was Ellen Ruggles Strong of New York, who, over her husband's objections, insisted on nursing in the Peninsular campaign of 1862. "The little woman has come out amazingly strong during these two months," George Templeton Strong wrote in his diary with a mixture of pride and condescension. "Have never given her credit for a tithe of the enterprise, pluck, discretion, and force of character that she has shown. God bless her." Other women organized other volunteer efforts outside the Sanitary Commission umbrella. Perhaps the best known was Clara Barton, who had been a government clerk before the war and consequently knew a number of influential members of Congress. Barton organized nursing and the distribution of medical supplies; she also used her congressional contacts to force reforms in army medical practice, of which she was very critical.

Southern women were also active in nursing and otherwise aiding soldiers, though the South never boasted a single large-scale organization like the Sanitary Commission. The women of Richmond volunteered when they found the war on their doorstep in the summer of 1862. During the Seven Days Battles, thousands of wounded poured into Richmond; many died in the streets because there was no room for them in hospitals. Richmond women first established informal "roadside hospitals" to meet the need, and their activities expanded from there. As in the North, middle-class women at first faced strong resistance from army doctors and even their

Nurse Ann Bell shown preparing medicine for a wounded soldier. Prompted by the medical crisis of the war, women such as Bell and "Mother" Bickerdyke actively participated in the war effort as nurses.

SOURCE: Union hospital. Center of Military History, U.S. Army.

own families, who believed that a field hospital was "no place for a refined lady." Kate Cumming of Mobile, who nursed in Corinth, Mississippi, after the Battle of Shiloh, faced down such reproofs, though she confided to her diary that nursing wounded men was very difficult: "Nothing that I had ever heard or read had given me the faintest idea of the horrors witnessed here." She and her companion nurses persisted and became an important part of the Confederate medical services. For southern women, who had been much less active in the public life of their communities than their northern reforming sisters, this Civil War activity marked an important break with prewar tradition.

Although women had made important advances, most army nurses and medical support staff were men. One volunteer nurse was the poet Walt Whitman, who visited wounded soldiers in the hospital in Washington, D.C. Horrified at the suffering he saw, Whitman also formed a deep admiration for the "incredible dauntlessness" of the common soldier in the face of slaughter and privation. While never denying the senselessness of the slaughter, Whitman nevertheless found hope in the determined spirit of the common man and woman.

The Life of the Common Soldier

The conditions experienced by the eager young volunteers of the Union and Confederate armies included massive, terrifying, and bloody battles, apparently unending, with no sign of victory in sight. Soldiers suffered from the uncertainty of supply, which left troops, especially in the South, without uniforms, tents, and sometimes even food. They endured long marches over muddy, rutted roads while carrying packs weighing fifty or sixty pounds. Disease was rampant in their dirty, verminous, and unsanitary camps, and hospitals were so dreadful that more men left them dead than alive. Many soldiers had entered military service with unrealistic, even romantic ideas about warfare. The Mexican-American War had been short and glorious (or at least far enough away to seem so), and the Revolutionary War was even more shrouded in myth. Reality was thus a rude shock, and not all soldiers reacted as nobly as those glorified by Walt Whitman. Desertion was common: an estimated one of every nine Confederate soldiers and one of every seven Union soldiers deserted. Unauthorized absence was another problem. At Antietam, Robert E. Lee estimated that unauthorized absence reduced his strength by a third to a half.

Another widespread phenomenon was fraternization between the two sides. A southern private, for example, wrote about how he celebrated the Fourth of July after the Seven Days Battles in 1862: "There are blackberries in the fields so our boys and the Yanks made a bargain not to fire at each other, and went out in the field, leaving one man on each post with the arms, and gathered berries together and talked over the fight, and traded tobacco and coffee and newspapers as peacefully and kindly as if they had not been engaged for . . . seven days in butchering one another." In October 1861 a Louisiana man wrote to his brother-in-law: "You spoke as if you had some notion of volunteering. I advise you to stay at home." Once the initial patriotic fervor had waned, attitudes such as his were increasingly common, both on the battlefield and at home.

Wartime Politics

In the earliest days of the war, Northerners had joined together in support of the war effort. Democrat Stephen A. Douglas, Lincoln's defeated rival, paid a visit to the White House to offer Lincoln his support, then traveled home to Illinois, where he addressed a huge rally of Democrats in Chicago: "There can be no neutrals in this war, only patriots—or traitors!" Within a month, Douglas was dead at age forty-eight. The Democrats had lost the leadership of a broad-minded man who might have done much on behalf of northern unity. By 1862 Democrats had split into two factions: the War Democrats and the Peace Democrats, derogatorily called "Copperheads" (from the poisonous snake).

Despite the split in the party in 1860 and the secession of the South, the Democratic Party remained a powerful force in northern politics. It had received 44 percent of the popular vote in the North in the 1860 election and its united opposition to the emancipation of slaves explains much of Lincoln's equivocal action on this issue. But the Peace Democrats went far beyond opposition to emancipation, denouncing the draft, martial law, and the high-handed actions of "King Abraham." Echoing old complaints against the Whigs, Peace Democrats appealed to the sympathies of western farmers by warning that agriculture was being hurt by the Republican Party's tariff and industrial policies. At the same time, they appealed to urban workers and immigrants with racist warnings that Republican policies would bring a flood of black workers into northern cities.

The leader of the Copperheads, Clement Vallandigham, a former Ohio congressman, advocated an armistice and a negotiated peace that would "look only to the welfare, peace and safety of the white race, without reference to the effect that settlement may have on the African." Western Democrats, he threatened, might form their own union with the South, excluding New England with its radical abolitionists and high-tariff industrialists.

At the time, long before Grant captured Vicksburg and gained control of the Mississippi River, Lincoln could not afford to take Vallandigham's threats lightly. Besides, he was convinced that some Peace Democrats were members of secret societies—the Knights of the Golden Circle and the Sons of Liberty—that had been conspiring with the Confederacy. In 1862, Lincoln proclaimed that all people who discouraged enlistments in the army or otherwise engaged in disloyal practices would be subject to martial law. In all, 13,000 people were arrested and imprisoned, including Vallandigham, who was exiled to the Confederacy. Lincoln rejected all protests, claiming that his arbitrary actions were necessary for national security.

Lincoln also faced challenges from the radical faction of his own party. As the war continued, the Radicals gained strength: it was they who pushed for emancipation in the early days of the war and for harsh treatment of the defeated South after it ended. The most troublesome Radical was Salmon P. Chase, who in December 1862 caused a cabinet crisis when he encouraged Senate Republicans to complain that Secretary of State William Seward was "lukewarm" in his support for emancipation. This Radical challenge was a portent of the party's difficulties after the war, which Lincoln did not live to see—or prevent.

Economic and Social Strains on the North

Wartime needs caused a surge in northern economic growth, but the gains were unequally distributed. Early in the war, some industries suffered: textile manufacturers could not get cotton, and shoe factories that had made cheap shoes for slaves were without a market. But other industries boomed—boot making, shipbuilding, and the manufacture of woolen goods such as blankets and uniforms, to give just three examples. Coal mining expanded, as did ironmaking, especially the manufacture of iron rails for railroads. Agricultural goods were in great demand, promoting further mechanization of farming. The McCormick brothers grew rich from sales of their reapers. Once scorned as a "metal grasshopper," the ungainly-looking McCormick reaper made hand harvesting of grain a thing of the past and led to great savings in manpower. Women, left to tend the family farm while the men went to war, found that with mechanized equipment they could manage the demanding task of harvesting.

Meeting wartime needs enriched some people honestly, but speculators and profiteers also flourished, as they have in every war. By the end of the war, government contracts had exceeded $1 billion. Not all of this business was free from corruption. New wealth was evident in every northern city. *Harper's Monthly* reported that "the suddenly enriched contractors, speculators, and stock-jobbers . . . are spending money with a profusion never before witnessed in our country." Some peo-

ple were appalled at the spectacle of wealth in the midst of wartime suffering. Still, some of the new wealth went to good causes. Of the more than $3 million raised by the female volunteers of the United States Sanitary Commission, some came from gala Sanitary Fairs designed to attract those with money to spend.

For most people, however, the war brought the day-to-day hardship of inflation. During the four years of the war, the North suffered an inflation rate of 80 percent, or nearly 15 percent a year. This annual rate, three times what is generally considered tolerable, did much to inflame social tensions. Wages rose only half as much as prices, and workers responded by joining unions and striking. Thirteen occupational groups, among them tailors, coal miners, and railroad engineers, formed unions during the Civil War. Manufacturers, bitterly opposed to unions, freely hired strikebreakers (many of whom were African Americans, women, or immigrants) and formed organizations of their own to prevent further unionization and to blacklist union organizers. Thus both capital and labor moved far beyond the small, localized confrontations of the early industrial period. The formation of large-scale organizations, fostered by wartime demand, laid the groundwork for the national battle between workers and manufacturers that would dominate the last part of the nineteenth century.

Another major source of social tension was conscription. The Union draft, introduced in March 1863, was based on the theory that the very threat of coercion would stimulate reenlistments and encourage volunteering. It soon became clear, however, that coercion, backed by federal marshals, was necessary to fill the ranks. Especially unpopular was a provision in the draft law that allowed the hiring of substitutes or the payment of a commutation fee of $300. Substitutes were mostly recent immigrants who had not yet filed for citizenship and were thus not yet eligible to be drafted. It is estimated that immigrants (some of whom were citizens) made up 20 percent of the Union army. Substitution had been accepted in all previous European and American wars. It was so common that President Lincoln, though overage, tried to set an example by paying for a substitute himself. The Democratic Party, however, made substitution an inflammatory issue. Pointing out that $300 was almost a year's wages for an unskilled laborer, they denounced the draft law (88 percent of Democratic congressmen had voted against it). They appealed to popular resentment by calling it "aristocratic legislation" and to fear by running headlines such as "Three Hundred Dollars or Your Life."

As practiced in the local communities, conscription was indeed often marred by favoritism and prejudice. Local officials called up many more poor than rich men and selected a higher proportion of immigrants than nonimmigrants. In reality, however, only 7

A black man is lynched during the New York City Draft Riots in July 1863. Free black people and their institutions were major victims of the worst rioting in American history until then. The riots were less a protest against the draft than an outburst of frustration over urban problems that had been festering for decades.

SOURCE: Culver Pictures, Inc.

percent of all men called to serve actually did so. About 25 percent hired a substitute, another 15 percent were exempted for "cause" (usually health reasons), and another 20–25 percent simply failed to report to the community draft office. Nevertheless, by 1863 many northern urban workers believed that the slogan "a rich man's war but a poor man's fight," though coined in the South, applied to them as well.

The New York City Draft Riots

In the spring of 1863 there were protests against the draft throughout the North. Riots and disturbances broke out in many cities, and several federal enrollment officers were killed. The greatest trouble occurred in New York City between July 13 and July 16, 1863, where a wave of working-class looting, fighting, and lynching claimed the lives of 105 people, many of them African American. The rioting, the worst up to that time in American history, was quelled only when five units of the U.S. Army were rushed from the battlefield at Gettysburg, where they had been fighting Confederates the week before.

The riots had several causes. Anger at the draft and racial prejudice were what most contemporaries saw. George Templeton Strong, a staunch Republican, believed that the "brutal, cowardly ruffianism and plunder"

was instigated by Confederate agents stirring up "the rabble" of "the lowest Irish day laborers." From a historical perspective, however, the riots had less to do with the war than with the urban growth and tensions described in Chapter 13. The Civil War made urban problems worse and heightened the visible contrast between the lives of the rich and those of the poor. These tensions exploded, but were not solved, during those hot days in the summer of 1863.

Ironically, African American men, a favorite target of the rioters' anger, were a major force in easing the national crisis over the draft. Though they had been barred from service until 1863, in the later stages of the war African American volunteers filled much of the manpower gap that the controversial draft was meant to address.

The Failure of Southern Nationalism

The war brought even greater changes to the South. As in the North, war needs led to expansion and centralization of government control over the economy. In many cases, Jefferson Davis himself initiated government control (over railroads, shipping, and war production, for example), often in the face of protest or inaction by governors who favored states' rights. The expansion of government brought sudden urbanization, a new experience for the predominantly rural South. The population of Richmond, the Confederate capital, almost tripled, in large part because the Confederate bureaucracy grew to 70,000 people. Because of the need for military manpower, a good part of the Confederate bureaucracy consisted of women, who were referred to as "government girls." All of this—government control, urban growth, women in the paid workforce—was new to Southerners, and not all of it was welcomed.

Even more than in the North, the voracious need for soldiers fostered class antagonisms. When small yeoman farmers went off to war, their wives and families struggled to farm on their own, without the help of mechanization, which they could not afford, and without the help of slaves, which they had never owned. But wealthy men could be exempted from the draft if they had more than twenty slaves. Furthermore, many upper-class Southerners—at least 50,000—avoided military service by paying liberally ($5,000 and more) for substitutes. In the face of these inequities, desertions from the Confederate army soared. One Mississippi soldier spoke for many when he said that "he did not propose to fight for the rich men while they were at home having a good time." But the rich men, the South's traditional ruling class, paid little attention to such complaints.

Worst of all was the starvation. The North's blockade and the breakdown of the South's transportation system restricted the availability of food in the South, and these problems were vastly magnified by runaway inflation. Prices in the South rose by an unbelievable 9,000 percent. Speculation and hoarding by the rich made matters even worse. Women and children were left destitute, and a government-sponsored civilian relief program was soon diverted to meet the pressing needs of the military. Ordinary people suffered. "It is folly for a poor mother to call on the rich people about here," one woman wrote bitterly. "Their hearts are of steel; they would sooner throw what they have to spare to the dogs than give it to a starving child."

In the spring of 1863 food riots broke out in four Georgia cities (Atlanta among them) and in North Carolina. In Richmond, more than a thousand people, mostly women, broke into bakeries and snatched loaves of bread, crying "Bread! Bread! Our children are starving while the rich roll in wealth!" When the bread riot threatened to turn into general looting, Jefferson Davis himself appealed to the crowd to disperse—but found he had to threaten the rioters with gunfire before they would leave. A year later, Richmond stores sold eggs for $6 a dozen and butter for $25 a pound. One woman wept, "My God! How can I pay such prices? I have seven children; what shall I do?"

Increasingly, the ordinary people of the South, preoccupied with staying alive, refused to pay taxes, to provide food, or to serve in the army. Soldiers were drawn home by the desperation of their families as well as the discouraging course of the war. By January 1865 the desertion rate had climbed to 8 percent a month.

At the same time, the life of the southern ruling class was irrevocably altered by the changing nature of slavery. By the end of the war, one-quarter of all slaves had fled to the Union lines, and those who remained often stood in a different relationship to their owners. As white masters and overseers left to join the army, white women were left behind on the plantation to cope with shortages, grow crops, and manage the labor of slaves. Lacking the patriarchal authority of their husbands, white women found that white-black relationships shifted, sometimes drastically (as when slaves fled) and sometimes more subtly. Slaves increasingly made their own decisions about when and how they would work, and they refused to accept the punishments that would have accompanied this insubordination in prewar years. One black woman, implored by her mistress not to reveal the location of a trunk of money and silver plate when the invading Yankees arrived, looked her in the eye and said, "Mistress, I can't lie over that; you bought that silver plate when you sold my three children."

Peace movements in the South were motivated by a confused mixture of realism, war weariness, and the animosity of those who supported states' rights and opposed Jefferson Davis. The anti-Davis faction was led by his own vice president, Alexander Stephens, who early in 1864 suggested a negotiated peace. Peace sentiment was especially strong in North Carolina, where more than a hundred public meetings in support of negotiations were held in the summer of 1863. Davis would have none of it, and he commanded enough votes in the Confederate Congress to enforce his will and to suggest that peace sentiment was traitorous. The Confederacy, which lacked a two-party system, had no official way to consider alternatives. Thus the peace sentiment, which grew throughout 1864, flourished outside the political system in secret societies such as the Heroes of America and the Red Strings. As hopes of Confederate victory slipped away, conflict expanded beyond the battlefield to include the political struggles that southern civilians were fighting among themselves.

THE TIDE TURNS

As Lincoln's timing of the Emancipation Proclamation showed, by 1863 the nature of the war was changing. The proclamation freeing the slaves struck directly at the southern home front and the civilian workforce. That same year, the nature of the battlefield war changed as well. McClellan's notion of a limited war with modest battlefield casualties was gone forever. The Civil War became the first total war.

The Turning Point of 1863

In the summer of 1863 the moment finally arrived when the North could begin to hope for victory. But for the Union army the year opened with stalemate in the East and slow and costly progress in the West. For the South, 1863 represented its highest hopes for military success and for diplomatic recognition by Britain or France.

Attempting to break the stalemate in northern Virginia, General Joseph "Fighting Joe" Hooker and a Union army of 130,000 men attacked a Confederate army half that size at Chancellorsville in May. In response, Robert E. Lee daringly divided his forces, sending General Thomas "Stonewall" Jackson and 30,000 men on a day-long flanking movement that caught the Union troops by surprise. Although Jackson was killed (shot by his own men by mistake), Chancellorsville was a great Confederate victory; there were 17,000 Union losses. However, Confederate losses were also great: 13,000 men, representing more than 20 percent of Lee's army.

Though weakened, Lee moved to the attack. In June, in his second and most dangerous single thrust into Union territory, he moved north into Maryland and Pennsylvania. His purpose was as much political as military: he hoped that a great Confederate victory would lead Britain and France to intervene in the war and demand a negotiated peace. The ensuing Battle of Gettysburg, July 1–3, 1863, was another horrible slaughter. On the last day, Lee sent 15,000 men, commanded by George Pickett, to attack the heavily defended Union center. The charge was suicidal. When the Union forces opened fire at 700 yards, one southern officer reported, "Pickett's division just seemed to melt away. . . . Nothing but stragglers came back." The next day a Union officer reported, "I tried to ride over the field but could not, for dead and wounded lay too thick to guide a horse through them."

Pickett's Charge, one historian has written, was the perfect symbol of the entire Confederate war effort: "matchless valor, apparent initial success, and ultimate disaster." Lee retreated from the field, leaving more than one-third of his army behind—28,000 men killed, wounded, or missing. Union general George Meade elected not to pursue with his battered Union army (23,000 casualties). "We had them in our grasp," Lincoln said in bitter frustration. "We had only to stretch forth our arms and they were ours. And nothing I could say or do could make the Army move." Nevertheless, Lee's great gamble had failed; he never again mounted a major offensive.

The next day, July 4, 1863, Ulysses S. Grant took Vicksburg, Mississippi, after a costly siege. The combined news of Gettysburg and Vicksburg dissuaded Britain and France from recognizing the Confederacy and checked the northern peace movement. It also tightened the North's grip on the South, for the Union now controlled the entire Mississippi River. In November, Generals Grant and Sherman broke the Confederate hold on Chattanooga, Tennessee, thereby opening the way to Atlanta.

Grant and Sherman

In March 1864, President Lincoln called Grant east and appointed him general in chief of all the Union forces. Lincoln's critics were appalled. Grant was an uncouth Westerner (like the president) and (unlike the president) was rumored to have a drinking problem. Lincoln replied that if he knew the general's brand of whiskey, he would send a barrel of it to every commander in the Union army.

Grant devised a plan of strangulation and annihilation. While he took on Lee in northern Virginia, he sent General William Tecumseh Sherman to defeat Confed-

Follow Lee's campaign northward. What was he hoping to achieve and why was his defeat at Gettysburg the war's turning point?
www.prenhall.com/faragher/map16.2

The Turning Point: 1863   In June, Lee boldly struck north into Maryland and Pennsylvania, hoping for a victory that would cause Britain and France to demand a negotiated peace on Confederate terms. Instead, he lost the hard-fought battle of Gettysburg, July 1–3. The very next day, Grant's long siege of Vicksburg succeeded. These two great Fourth of July victories turned the tide in favor of the Union. The Confederates never again mounted a major offensive. Total Union control of the Mississippi now exposed the Lower South to attack.

erate general Joe Johnston's Army of Tennessee, which was defending the approach to Atlanta. Both Grant and Sherman exemplified the new kind of warfare. They aimed to inflict maximum damage on the fabric of southern life, hoping that the South would choose to surrender rather than face total destruction. This decision to broaden the war so that it directly affected civilians was new in American military history and prefigured the total wars of the twentieth century.

In northern Virginia, Grant pursued a policy of destroying civilian supplies. He said he "regarded it as humane to both sides to protect the persons of those found at their homes, but to consume everything that could be used to support or supply armies." One of those supports was slaves. Grant welcomed fleeing slaves to Union lines and encouraged army efforts to put them to work or enlist them as soldiers. He also cooperated with the efforts of groups like the New England Freedmen's Aid Society, which sent northern volunteers (many of them women) into Union-occupied parts of the South to educate former slaves. (The Freedmen's Bureau, authorized by Congress in March 1865, continued this work into Reconstruction. One of the northern teachers who went south in 1866 to work for the bureau was Robert Fitzgerald, the former soldier.)

The most famous example of the new strategy of total war was General Sherman's 1864 march through Georgia. Sherman captured Atlanta on September 2, 1864, after outmaneuvering and outfighting Johnson and his successor, John Bell Hood. Atlanta lay in ruins as Sherman and his troops entered the city. With the rest of Georgia now vulnerable, gloom enveloped the South. "Since Atlanta I have felt as if all were dead within me, forever," Mary Boykin Chesnut wrote in her diary. "We are going to be wiped off the earth."

In November, Sherman set out to march the 285 miles to the coastal city of Savannah, living off the land and destroying everything in his path. His military purpose was to tighten the noose around Robert E. Lee's army in northern Virginia by cutting off Mississippi, Alabama, and Georgia from the rest of the Confederacy. But his second purpose, openly stated, was to "make war so terrible" to the people of the South, to "make them so sick of war that generations would pass away before they would again appeal to it." Accordingly, he told his men to seize, burn, or destroy everything in their path (but, significantly, not to harm civilians).

One Union soldier wrote to his father, "You can form no idea of the amount of property destroyed by us on this raid. . . . A tornado 60 miles in width from Chattanooga to this place 290 miles away could not have done half the damage we did." A southern woman supplied the details: "The fields were trampled down and the road was lined with carcasses of horses, hogs and cattle that the invaders, unable either to consume or to carry with them, had wantonly shot down to starve our people and prevent them from making their crops. The stench in some places was unbearable." It was estimated

that Sherman's army did $100 million worth of damage. "They say no living thing is found in Sherman's track," Mary Boykin Chesnut wrote, "only chimneys, like telegraph poles, to carry the news of [his] attack backwards."

Terrifying to white southern civilians, Sherman was initially hostile to black Southerners as well. In the interests of speed and efficiency, his army turned away many of the 18,000 slaves who flocked to it in Georgia, causing a number to be recaptured and reenslaved. This callous action caused such a scandal in Washington that Secretary of War Edwin Stanton arranged a special meeting in Georgia with Sherman and twenty African American ministers who spoke for the freed slaves. This meeting in itself was extraordinary: no one had ever before asked slaves what they wanted. Equally extraordinary was Sherman's response in Special Field Order 15, issued in January 1865: he set aside more than 400,000 acres of Confederate land to be given to the freed slaves in forty-acre parcels. This was war of a kind that white Southerners had never imagined.

Far to the North, a much smaller unimaginable event occurred in October, when twenty-six Confederate sympathiers invaded St. Albans Vermont, robbing three banks, setting fires, killing a man—and then escaping over the border into Canada. When a Montreal magistrate released the men on a technicality, American military authorities threatened retaliation if Canadian authorities ever again allowed such an event. Canada was not unprepared for an American attack, but the defenders were British troops: the uncertain diplomatic and naval issues between the Union and Britain had led to the stationing of 14,000 troops to Canada, the largest number of British troops in North America since the War of 1812. The St. Albans incident, minor in itself, caused both the British government and Canadian officials to think seriously about how to defend against the possibility of future American invasions. The answer was obvious: the Canadian provinces, which by 1860 stretched from one coast to the other, would need to be united. In 1867, all of the Canadian provinces joined in confederation and henceforth were known as the Dominion of Canada. In this way, a small Confederate pinprick helped to foster the unity of America's large northern neighbor.

The 1864 Election

The war complicated the 1864 presidential election, aggravating the usual political factionalism. Public opinion about Lincoln and the conduct of the war had been on a roller coaster, soaring to great heights with news of Union victories and plunging during long periods of stalemate. Just as in the Mexican-American War, the "instant news" provided by the telegraph and special correspondents pulled people out of their daily

Sherman's Campaign in Georgia, 1864

Ulysses S. Grant and William Tecumseh Sherman, two like-minded generals, commanded the Union's armies in the final push to victory. While Grant hammered away at Lee in northern Virginia, Sherman captured Atlanta in September (a victory that may have been vital to Lincoln's reelection) and began his March to the Sea in November 1864.

The Final Battles in Virginia, 1864–1865

In the war's final phase early in 1865, Sherman closed one arm of a pincers by marching north from Savannah while Grant attacked Lee's last defensive positions in Petersburg and Richmond. Lee retreated from them on April 2 and surrendered at Appomattox Court House on April 9, 1865.

lives and fixed their attention on the war. But the Civil War was much larger and much nearer. Almost everyone had a son or father or brother at the front, or knew someone in their community who did. The war news was personal.

Lincoln was renominated during a low period. Opposed by the Radicals, who thought he was too conciliatory toward the South, and by Republican conservatives, who disapproved of the Emancipation Proclamation, Lincoln had little support within his own party. Secretary of the Treasury Salmon P. Chase, a man of immense ego, went so far as to encourage his supporters to propose him, rather than Lincoln, as the party's nominee.

The Democrats had an appealing candidate: General George McClellan, a war hero (always a favorite with American voters) who was known to be sympathetic to the South, although he was unwilling to endorse the plank of the Democratic Party platform that proclaimed the war a failure and proposed an armistice to end it. Other Democrats played shamelessly on the racist fears of the urban working class, accusing Republicans of being "negro-lovers" and warning that racial mixing lay ahead.

A deeply depressed Lincoln fully expected to lose the election. "I am going to be beaten," he told an army officer in August 1864, "and unless some great change takes place badly beaten." A great change did take place: Sherman captured Atlanta on September 2. Jubilation swept the North: some cities celebrated with 100-gun salutes. Lincoln won the election with 55 percent of the popular vote. Seventy-eight percent of the soldiers voted for him rather than for their former commander. The vote probably saved the Republican Party from extinction. Furthermore, the election was important evidence of northern support for Lincoln's policy of unconditional surrender for the South. There would be no negotiated peace; the war would continue.

In many ways, Lincoln's reelection was extraordinary. Ordinary people and war-weary soldiers had voted to continue a difficult and divisive conflict. This was the first time in American history that the people had been able to vote on whether they were willing to continue wartime hardships, and that 45 percent of the electorate voted against Lincoln suggests how severe those hardships were.

Nearing the End

As Sherman devastated the lower South, Grant was locked in struggle with Lee in northern Virginia. Grant did not favor subtle strategies. He bluntly said, "The art of war is simple enough. Find out where your enemy is. Get at him as soon as you can. Strike at him as hard as you can, and keep moving on." Following this plan, Grant eventually hammered Lee into submission, but at enormous cost. Lee had learned the art of defensive warfare (his troops called him "the King of Spades" because he made them dig trenches so often), and he inflicted heavy losses on the Union army in a succession of bloody encounters in the spring and summer of 1864: almost 18,000 at the battle of the Wilderness, more than 8,000 at Spotsylvania, and 12,000 at Cold Harbor. At Cold Harbor, Union troops wrote their names and addresses on scraps of paper and pinned them to their backs, so certain were they of being killed or wounded in battle. Grim and terrible as Grant's strategy was, it proved effective. Rather than pulling back after his failed assaults, he kept moving South, finally settling in for a prolonged siege of Lee's forces at Petersburg. The North's great advantage in population finally began to tell. There were more Union soldiers to replace those lost in battle, but there were no more white Confederates.

In desperation, the South turned to what had hitherto been unthinkable: arming slaves to serve as soldiers in the Confederate army. As Jefferson Davis said in February 1865, "We are reduced to choosing whether the negroes shall fight for or against us." But—and this was the bitter irony—the African American soldiers and their families would have to be promised freedom or they would desert to the Union at the first chance they had. Even though Davis's proposal had the support of General Robert E. Lee, the Confederate Congress balked at first. As one member said, the idea was "revolting to Southern sentiment,

This striking photograph by Thomas C. Roche shows a dead Confederate soldier, killed at Petersburg on April 3, 1865, only six days before the surrender at Appomattox. The new medium of photography conveyed the horror of the war with a gruesome reality to the American public.

SOURCE: Library of Congress.

Southern pride, and Southern honor." Another candidly admitted, "If slaves make good soldiers our whole theory of slavery is wrong." Finally, on March 13, the Confederate Congress authorized a draft of black soldiers—without mentioning freedom. Although two regiments of African American soldiers were immediately organized in Richmond, it was too late. The South never had to publicly acknowledge the paradox of having to offer slaves freedom so that they would fight to defend slavery.

By the spring of 1865, public support for the war simply disintegrated in the South. Starvation, inflation, dissension, and the prospect of military defeat were too much. In February, Jefferson Davis sent his vice president, Alexander Stephens, to negotiate terms at a peace conference at Hampton Roads. Lincoln would not countenance anything less than full surrender, although he did offer gradual emancipation with compensation for slave owners. Davis, however, insisted on southern independence at all costs. Consequently, the Hampton Roads conference failed and southern resistance faded away. In March 1865, Mary Boykin Chesnut recorded in her diary: "I am sure our army is silently dispersing. Men are going the wrong way all the time. They slip by now with no songs nor shouts. They have given the thing up."

Abraham Lincoln toured Richmond, the Confederate capital, just hours after Jefferson Davis had fled. This photograph, taken April 4, 1865, shows Yankee cavalry horses in the foreground and the smoldering city in the background. It gives a sense of the devastation suffered by the South and the immense task of rebuilding and reconciliation that Lincoln would not live to accomplish.

SOURCE: Library of Congress.

Appomattox

Grant's hammering tactics worked—slowly. In the spring of 1865 Lee and his remaining troops, outnumbered two to one, still held Petersburg and Richmond. Starving, short of ammunition, and losing men in battle or to desertion every day, Lee retreated from Petersburg on April 2. The Confederate government fled Richmond, stripping and burning the city. Seven days later, Lee and his 25,000 troops surrendered to Grant at Appomattox Court House. Grant treated Lee with great respect and set a historic precedent by giving the Confederate troops parole. This meant they could not subsequently be prosecuted for treason. Grant then sent the starving army on its way with three days' rations for every man. Jefferson Davis, who had hoped to set up a new government in Texas, was captured in Georgia on May 10. The war was finally over.

Death of a President

Sensing that the war was near its end, Abraham Lincoln visited Grant's troops when Lee withdrew from Petersburg on April 2. Thus it was that Lincoln came to visit Richmond, and to sit briefly in Jefferson Davis's presidential office, soon after Davis had left it. As Lincoln walked the streets of the burned and pillaged city, black people poured out to see him and surround him, shouting "Glory to God! Glory! Glory! Glory!" Lincoln in turn said to Admiral David Porter: "Thank God I have lived to see this. It seems to me that I have been dreaming a horrid dream for four years, and now the nightmare is gone." Lincoln had only the briefest time to savor the victory. On the night of April 14, President and Mrs. Lincoln went to Ford's Theater in Washington. There Lincoln was shot at point-blank range by John Wilkes Booth, a Confederate sympathizer. He died the next day. For the people of the Union, the joy of victory was muted by mourning for their great leader. After a week of observances in Washington, Lincoln's coffin was loaded on a funeral train that slowly carried him back to Springfield. All along the railroad route, day and night, in small towns and large, people gathered to see the train pass and to pay their last respects. At that moment, the Washington community and the larger Union community were one and the same.

The nation as a whole was left with Lincoln's vision for the coming peace, expressed in the unforgettable words of his Second Inaugural Address:

> With malice toward none, with charity for all, with firmness in the right as God gives us to see the right, let us strive on to finish the work we are in, to bind up the nation's wounds, to care for him who shall have borne the battle and for his widow and his orphan, to do all which may achieve and cherish a just and lasting peace among ourselves and with all nations.

CONCLUSION

In 1865, a divided people had been forcibly reunited by battle. Their nation, the United States of America, had been permanently changed by civil war. Devastating losses among the young men of the country—the greatest such losses the nation was ever to suffer—would affect not only their families but all of postwar

CHRONOLOGY

1861   March: Morrill Tariff Act

April: Fort Sumter falls; war begins

April: Mobilization begins

April–May: Virginia, Arkansas, Tennessee, and North Carolina secede

June: United States Sanitary Commission established

July: First Battle of Bull Run

December: French troops arrive in Mexico, followed by British and Spanish forces in January.

1862   February: Legal Tender Act

February: Battles of Fort Henry and Fort Donelson

March: Battle of Pea Ridge

March: Battle of the *Monitor* and the *Merrimack* (renamed the *Virginia*)

March–August: George B. McClellan's Peninsular campaign

March: Battle of Glorieta Pass

April: Battle of Shiloh

April: Confederate Conscription Act

April: David Farragut captures New Orleans

May: *Cinqo de Mayo*: Mexican troops repel Franch invaders

May: Homestead Act

June–July: Seven Days Battles

July: Pacific Railway Act

July: Morrill Land Grant Act

August: Santee Sioux Uprising, Minnesota

September: Battle of Antietam

December: Battle of Fredericksburg

1863   January: Emancipation Proclamation

February: National Bank Act

March: Draft introduced in the North

March: Colonel Kit Carson sends 8,000 Navajos on the "Long Walk" to Bosque Redondo, New Mexico Territory

April: Richmond bread riot

May: Battle of Chancellorsville

June: French occupy Mexico City

July: Battle of Gettysburg

July: Surrender of Vicksburg

July: New York City Draft Riots

November: Battle of Chattanooga

November: Union troops capture Brownsville, Texas

1864   March: Ulysses S. Grant becomes general in chief of Union forces

April: Fort Pillow massacre

May: Battle of the Wilderness

May: Battle of Spotsylvania

June: Battle of Cold Harbor

June: Maximillian becomes Emperor of Mexico

September: Atlanta falls

October: St. Albans incident

November: Abraham Lincoln reelected president

November–December: William Tecumseh Sherman's March to the Sea

1865   April: Richmond falls

April: Robert E. Lee surrenders at Appomattox

April: Lincoln assassinated

December: Thirteenth Amendment to the Constitution becomes law

society. Politically, the deepest irony of the Civil War was that only by fighting it had America become completely a nation. For it was the war that broke down local isolation. Ordinary citizens in local communities, North and South, developed a national perspective as they sent their sons and brothers to be soldiers, their daughters to be nurses and teachers. Then, too, the federal government, vastly strengthened by wartime necessity, reached the lives of ordinary citizens more than ever before. The question now was whether this strengthened but divided national community, forged in battle, could create a just peace.

REVIEW QUESTIONS

1. At the outset of the Civil War, what were the relative advantages of the North and the South, and how did they affect the final outcome?
2. In the absence of the southern Democrats, in the early 1860s the new Republican Congress was able to pass a number of party measures with little opposition. What do these measures tell you about the historical roots of the Republican Party? More generally, how do you think we should view legislation passed in the absence of the customary opposition, debate, and compromise?
3. The greatest problem facing Jefferson Davis and the Confederacy was the need to develop a true feeling of nationalism. Can the failure of this effort be blamed on Davis's weakness as a leader alone, or are there other causes?
4. In what ways can it be said that the actions of African Americans, both slave and free, came to determine the course of the Civil War?
5. Wars always have unexpected consequences. List some of these consequences both for soldiers and for civilians in the North and in the South.
6. Today, Abraham Lincoln is considered one of our greatest presidents, but he did not enjoy such approval at the time. List some of the contemporary criticisms of Lincoln, and evaluate them.

RECOMMENDED READING

Jeanie Attie, *Patriotic Toil: Northern Women and the American Civil War* (1998).

Iver Bernstein, *The New York City Draft Riots* (1990).

David J. Eocher, *The Longest Night* (2001).

Drew Gilpin Faust, *Mothers of Invention: Women of the Slaveholding South in the American Civil War* (1996).

Alvin Josephy, *The Civil War in the West* (1992).

Bryan and Nelson Langford, eds. *Eye of the Storm: A Civil War Odyssey* (2000).

James M. McPherson, *The Negro's Civil War: How American Negroes Felt and Acted during the War for the Union* (1965).

———, *Battle Cry of Freedom: The Civil War Era* (1988).

Phillip Shaw Paludan, *"A People's Contest": The Union at War, 1861–1865* (1988).

▶ MEDIA RESOURCES

U.S. HISTORY DOCUMENTS CD-ROM

The Civil War

15-1   Jefferson Davis, Address to the Provisional Congress of the Confederate States of America (1861)

15-2   The "Cornerstone Speech" (1861)

15-3   Mary Boykin Chesnut, A Confederate Lady's Diary (1861)

15-4   Why They Fought (1861)

15-5   A Confederate General Assesses First Bull Run (1861)

15-6   Charles Harvey Brewster, Three Letters from the Civil War Front (1862)

15-7   Clara Barton, Medical Life at the Battlefield (1862)

15-8   James Henry Gooding, Letter to President Lincoln (1863)

15-9   Abraham Lincoln, Gettysburg Address (1863)

15-10 John Dooley, Passages from a Journal (1863)

15-11 A Firsthand Account of the New York Draft Riots (1863)

15-12 Susie King Taylor, Reminiscences of an Army Laundress (1902)

15-13 General William Tecumseh Sherman on War (1864)

COMPANION WEBSITE HIGHLIGHTS

To view an exploration, enter one of the URLs below in your browser.

Web Explorations

Overall Strategy of the Civil War
http://www.prenhall.com/faragher/map16.1

The Turning Point: 1863
http://www.prenhall.com/faragher/map16.2

Additional Interactive Maps

To access the maps, go to this chapter's resources at
http://www.prenhall.com/faragher

Major Battles in the East, 1861–1862, page 478

Major Battles in the West, 1862–1863, page 479

Sherman's Campaign in Georgia, 1864, page 491

The Final Battles in Virginia, 1864–1865, page 491

HISTORY RESOURCE CENTER

To find the resources listed below, go to
http://www.prenhall.com/historyresourcecenter

(Continued)

(Continued)

EXPLORING AMERICA

FORT PILLOW MASSACRE

http://www.prenhall.com/faragher/fortpillow

Did a massacre occur at Fort Pillow? How do the accounts of the battle by Union and Confederate sources compare? What role did the press play in the growing controversy? Did the presence of large numbers of African American troops influence the Confederate military strategy? The *Fort Pillow Massacre* module examines one of the most sordid and tragic episodes in the history of the Civil War. Press reports including illustrations, first-hand accounts by military personnel, official reports, and other documents provide answers to these questions.

The Fort Pillow Massacre touches on important themes regarding war, the role of the press in society, and race in America. The narrative provides a story line for the print and visual source documents, and an audio clip illuminating the various aspects of this important incident. The accounts by the military personnel on both sides also show the circuitous route taken to discover what really happened at Fort Pillow, while the chronology places the incident in historical context.

Reflect and Respond

On June 28, 1864, Forrest's superior, Lieutenant General S. D. Lee, offered an explanation of what happened at Fort Pillow in a letter to Union General Washburn. After you read the letter, consider these questions:

1. Did General Lee, in effect, concede that troops under Major General Forrest slaughtered Union troops after the fall of Fort Pillow?

2. Lee cited the presence of "a servile race, armed against their masters" as a circumstance that made it more difficult for Confederate officers to control their troops. Was the fact that Forrest's troops did take "both white and colored prisoners" evidence that "our officers . . . endeavored to prevent the effusion of blood"?

3. With the two-page illustration from *Harper's Weekly* from 1864 as your guide, describe how ardent Unionists regarded Confederate policy toward black troops.

✓ Check it out

Report of Acting Master William Ferguson, U.S. Navy, of the capture of Fort Pillow, Memphis, TN, April 14, 1864

This report describes the aftermath of the battle of Fort Pillow and the alleged massacre of African American Union troops. Ferguson's eyewitness account presents the Union side of this event that is countered by Confederate accounts presented in the module.

This exploration is also available on the *Exploring America* CD-ROM.

Theo Kaufmann, *On to Liberty*, 1867. Oil on canvas, 36″ × 56″. The Metropolitan Museum of Art, Gift of Erving and Joyce Wolf, 1982. (1982.443.3). Photograph © 1982 The Metropolitan Museum of Art.

Hale County, Alabama: From Slavery to Freedom in a Black Belt Community

ON A BRIGHT SATURDAY MORNING IN MAY 1867, 4,000 FORMER slaves eagerly streamed into the town of Greensboro, bustling seat of Hale County in west-central Alabama. They came to hear speeches from two delegates to a recent freedmen's convention in Mobile and to find out about the political status of black people under the Reconstruction Act just passed by Congress. Tensions mounted in the days following this unprecedented gathering as military authorities began supervising voter registration for elections to the upcoming constitutional convention that would rewrite the laws of Alabama. On June 13, John Orrick, a local white, confronted Alex Webb, a politically active freedman, on the streets of Greensboro. Webb had recently been appointed a voter registrar for the district. Orrick swore he would never be registered by a black man, and shot Webb dead. Hundreds of armed and angry freedmen formed a posse to search for Orrick, but failed to find him. Galvanized by Webb's murder, 500 local freedmen formed a chapter of the Union League, the Republican Party's organizational arm in the South. The chapter functioned as both a militia company and a forum to agitate for political rights.

Violent political encounters between black people and white people were common in southern communities in the wake of the Civil War. The war had destroyed slavery and the Confederacy, but left the political and economic status of newly emancipated African Americans unresolved. Communities throughout the South struggled over the meaning of freedom in ways that reflected their particular circumstances. The 4 million freed people constituted roughly one-third of the total southern population, but the black–white ratio in individual communities varied enormously. In some places the Union army had been a strong presence during the war, hastening the collapse of the slave system and encouraging experiments in free labor. Other areas had remained relatively untouched by the fighting. In some areas small farms prevailed; in others, including Hale County, large plantations dominated economic and political life.

West-central Alabama had emerged as a fertile center of cotton production just two decades before the Civil War. There, African Americans, as throughout the South's black belt, constituted more than three-quarters of the population. The region was virtually untouched by fighting until the very end of the Civil War. But with the arrival of federal troops in the spring of 1865, African Americans in Hale County, like their counterparts elsewhere, began to challenge the traditional organization of plantation labor.

One owner, Henry Watson, found that his entire workforce had deserted him at the end of 1865. "I am in the midst of a large and fertile cotton growing country," Watson wrote to a partner. "Many plantations are entirely without labor, many plantations have insufficient labor, and upon none are the laborers doing their former accustomed work." Black women refused to work in the fields, preferring to stay home with their children and tend garden plots. Nor would male field hands do any work, such as caring for hogs, that did not directly increase their share of the cotton crop.

Above all, freed people wanted more autonomy. Overseers and owners thus grudgingly allowed them to work the land "in families," letting them choose their own supervisors and find their own provisions. The result was a shift from the gang labor characteristic of the antebellum period, in which large groups of slaves worked under the harsh and constant supervision of white overseers, to the sharecropping system, in which African American families worked small plots of land in exchange for a small share of the crop. This shift represented less of a victory for newly freed African Americans than a defeat for plantation owners, who resented even the limited economic independence it forced them to concede to their black workforce.

Only a small fraction—perhaps 15 percent—of African American families were fortunate enough to be able to buy land. The majority settled for some version of sharecropping, while others managed to rent land from owners, becoming tenant farmers. Still, planters throughout Hale County had to change the old routines of plantation labor. Local African Americans also organized politically. In 1866 Congress had passed the Civil Rights Act and sent the Fourteenth Amendment to the Constitution to the states for ratification; both promised full citizenship rights to former slaves. Hale County freedmen joined the Republican Party and local Union League chapters. They used their new political power to press for better labor contracts, demand greater autonomy for the black workforce, and agitate for the more radical goal of land confiscation and redistribution. "The colored people are very anxious to get land of their own to live upon independently; and they want money to buy stock to make crops,"

reported one black Union League organizer. "The only way to get these necessaries is to give our votes to the [Republican] party . . . making every effort possible to bring these blessings about by reconstructing the State." Two Hale County former slaves, Brister Reese and James K. Green, won election to the Alabama state legislature in 1869.

It was not long before these economic and political gains prompted a white counterattack. In the spring of 1868, the Ku Klux Klan—a secret organization devoted to terrorizing and intimidating African Americans and their white Republican allies—came to Hale County. Disguised in white sheets, armed with guns and whips, and making nighttime raids on horseback, Klansmen flogged, beat, and murdered freed people. They intimidated voters and silenced political activists. Planters used Klan terror to dissuade former slaves from leaving plantations or organizing for higher wages.

With the passage of the Ku Klux Klan Act in 1871, the federal government cracked down on the Klan, breaking its power temporarily in parts of the former Confederacy. But no serious effort was made to stop Klan terror in the west Alabama black belt, and planters there succeeded in reestablishing much of their social and political control.

The events in Hale County illustrate the struggles that beset communities throughout the South during the Reconstruction era after the Civil War. The destruction of slavery and the Confederacy forced African Americans and white people to renegotiate their old economic and political roles. These community battles both shaped and were shaped by the victorious and newly expansive federal government in Washington. In the end, Reconstruction was only partially successful. Not until the "Second Reconstruction" of the twentieth-century civil rights movement would the descendants of Hale County's African Americans begin to enjoy the full fruits of freedom—and even then not without challenge. ■

Greensboro

KEY TOPICS

- Competing political plans for reconstructing the defeated Confederacy

- Difficult transition from slavery to freedom for African Americans

- The political and social legacy of Reconstruction in the southern states

- Post–Civil War transformations in the economic and political life of the North

---

THE POLITICS OF RECONSTRUCTION

When General Robert E. Lee's men stacked their guns at Appomattox, the bloodiest war in American history ended. More than 600,000 soldiers had died during the four years of fighting, 360,000 Union and 260,000 Confederate. Another 275,000 Union and 190,000 Confederate troops had been wounded. Although President Abraham Lincoln insisted early on that the purpose of the war was to preserve the Union, by 1863 it had evolved as well into a struggle for African American liberation. Indeed, the political, economic, and moral issues posed by slavery were the root cause of the Civil War, and the war ultimately destroyed slavery, although not racism, once and for all.

The Civil War also settled the Constitutional crisis provoked by the secession of the Confederacy and its justification in appeals to states' rights. The name "United States" would from now on be understood as a singular rather than a plural noun, signaling an important change in the meaning of American nationality. The old notion of the United States as a voluntary union of sovereign states gave way to the new reality of a single nation in which the federal government took precedence over the individual states. The key historical developments of the Reconstruction era revolved around precisely how the newly strengthened national government would define its relationship with the defeated Confederate states and the 4 million newly freed slaves.

The Defeated South

The white South paid an extremely high price for secession, war, and defeat. In addition to the battlefield casualties, the Confederate states sustained deep material and psychological wounds. Much of the best agricultural land lay waste, including the rich fields of northern Virginia, the Shenandoah Valley, and large sections of Tennessee, Mississippi, Georgia, and South Carolina. Many towns and cities—including Richmond, Atlanta, and Columbia, South Carolina—were in ruins. By 1865, the South's most precious commodities, cotton and African American slaves, no longer were measures of wealth and prestige. Retreating Confederates destroyed most of the South's cotton to prevent its capture by federal troops. What remained was confiscated by Union agents as contraband of war. The former slaves, many of whom had fled to Union lines during the latter stages of the war, were determined to chart their own course in the reconstructed South as free men and women.

It would take the South's economy a generation to overcome the severe blows dealt by the war. In 1860 the South held roughly 25 percent of the nation's wealth; a decade later it controlled only 12 percent. Many white Southerners resented their conquered status, and white notions of race, class, and "honor" died hard. A white North Carolinian, for example, who had lost almost everything dear to him in the war—his sons, home, and slaves—recalled in 1865 that in spite of all his tragedy he still retained one thing. "They've left me one inestimable privilege—to hate 'em. I git up at half-past four in the morning, and sit up till twelve at night, to hate 'em." As late as 1870 the Reverend Robert Lewis Dabney of Virginia wrote: "I do not forgive. I try not to forgive. What! forgive those people, who have invaded our country, burned our cities, destroyed our homes, slain our young men, and spread desolation and ruin over our land! No, I do not forgive them."

Emancipation proved the most bitter pill for white Southerners to swallow, especially the planter elite. Conquered and degraded, and in their view robbed of their slave property, white people responded by regarding African Americans more than ever as inferior to themselves. In the antebellum South, white skin had defined a social bond that transcended economic class. It gave even the lowliest poor white a badge of superiority over even the most skilled slave or prosperous free African American. Emancipation, however, forced

Decorating the Graves of Rebel Soldiers, *Harper's Weekly*, August 17, 1867. After the Civil War, both Southerners and Northerners created public mourning ceremonies honoring fallen soldiers. Women led the memorial movement in the South which, by establishing cemeteries and erecting monuments, offered the first cultural expression of the Confederate tradition. This engraving depicts citizens of Richmond, Virginia decorating thousands of Confederate graves with flowers at the Hollywood Memorial Cemetery on the James River. A local women's group raised enough funds to transfer over 16,000 Confederate dead from Northern cemeteries for reburial in Richmond.

SOURCE: The Granger Collection (4E1090.99).

ing slaves, to white Southerners willing to swear an oath of allegiance to the United States and its laws, including the Emancipation Proclamation. Prominent Confederate military and civil leaders were excluded from Lincoln's offer, though he indicated that he would freely pardon them.

The president also proposed that when the number of any Confederate state's voters who took the oath of allegiance reached 10 percent of the number who had voted in the election of 1860, this group could establish a state government that Lincoln would recognize as legitimate. Fundamental to this Ten Percent Plan was acceptance by the reconstructed governments of the abolition of slavery. Lincoln's plan was designed less as a blueprint for Reconstruction than as a way to shorten the war and gain white people's support for emancipation. It angered those Republicans—known as Radical Republicans—who advocated not only equal rights for the freedmen but a tougher stance toward the white South. As a result, when Arkansas and Louisiana met the president's requirements for reentry into the Union, Congress refused to seat their representatives.

white people to redefine their world. Many believed that without white direction, the freed people would languish, become wards of the state, or die off. Most white people believed that African Americans were too lazy to take care of themselves and survive. At the very least, whites reasoned, the South's agricultural economy would suffer at the hands of allegedly undisciplined and inefficient African Americans. The specter of political power and social equality for African Americans made racial order the consuming passion of most white Southerners during the Reconstruction years. In fact, racism can be seen as one of the major forces driving Reconstruction and, ultimately, undermining it.

Abraham Lincoln's Plan

By late 1863, Union military victories had convinced President Lincoln of the need to fashion a plan for the reconstruction of the South (see Chapter 16). Lincoln based his reconstruction program on bringing the seceded states back into the Union as quickly as possible. He was determined to respect private property (except in the case of slave property), and he opposed imposing harsh punishments for rebellion. His Proclamation of Amnesty and Reconstruction of December 1863 offered "full pardon" and the restoration of property, not includ-

In July 1864, Senator Benjamin F. Wade of Ohio and Congressman Henry W. Davis of Maryland, both Radicals, proposed a harsher alternative to the Ten Percent Plan. The Wade-Davis bill required 50 percent of a seceding state's white male citizens to take a loyalty oath before elections could be held for a convention to rewrite the state's constitution. The bill also guaranteed equality before the law (although not suffrage) for former slaves. Unlike the president, the Radical Republicans saw Reconstruction as a chance to effect a fundamental transformation of southern society. They thus wanted to delay the process until war's end and to limit participation to a small number of southern Unionists. Lincoln viewed Reconstruction as part of the larger effort to win the war and abolish slavery. He wanted to weaken the Confederacy by creating new state governments that could win broad support from southern white people. The Wade-Davis bill threatened his efforts to build political consensus within the southern states, and Lincoln therefore pocket-vetoed it, by refusing to sign it within ten days of the adjournment of Congress.

Redistribution of southern land among former slaves posed another thorny issue for Lincoln, Congress, and federal military officers. As Union armies occupied parts of the South, commanders had improvised a variety of arrangements involving confiscated plantations and the African American labor force. For example, in 1862 General Benjamin F. Butler began a policy of transforming slaves on Louisiana sugar plantations into wage laborers under the close supervision of occupying federal troops. Butler's policy required slaves to remain on the estates of loyal planters, where they would receive wages according to a fixed schedule, as well as food and medical care for the aged and sick. Abandoned plantations would be leased to northern investors. Butler's successor, General Nathaniel P. Banks, extended this system throughout occupied Louisiana. By 1864, some 50,000 African American laborers on nearly 1,500 Louisiana estates worked either directly for the government or for individual planters under contracts supervised by the army.

In January 1865, General William T. Sherman issued Special Field Order 15, setting aside the Sea Islands off the Georgia coast and a portion of the South Carolina low-country rice fields for the exclusive settlement of freed people. Each family would receive forty acres of land and the loan of mules from the army—the origin, perhaps, of the famous call for "forty acres and a mule" that would soon capture the imagination of African Americans throughout the South. Sherman's intent was not to revolutionize southern society but to relieve the demands placed on his army by the thousands of impoverished African Americans who followed his march to the sea. By the summer of 1865 some 40,000 freed people, eager to take advantage of the general's order, had been settled on 400,000 acres of "Sherman land."

Conflicts within the Republican Party prevented the development of a systematic land distribution program. Still, Lincoln and the Republican Congress supported other measures to aid the emancipated slaves. In March 1865 Congress established the Freedmen's Bureau. Along with providing food, clothing, and fuel to destitute former slaves, the bureau was charged with supervising and managing "all the abandoned lands in the South and the control of all subjects relating to refugees and freedmen." The act that established the bureau also stated that forty acres of abandoned or confiscated land could be leased to freed slaves or white Unionists, who would have an option to purchase after three years and "such title thereto as the United States can convey." To guarantee the end of slavery once the war ended, Republicans drafted the Thirteenth Amendment, declaring that "neither slavery nor involuntary servitude, except as a punishment for crime . . . , shall exist within the United States." This amendment passed both houses of Congress by January 1865 and was ratified by the necessary three-fourths of the states on December 18, 1865—eight months after Lee's surrender.

At the time of Lincoln's assassination, his Reconstruction policy remained unsettled and incomplete. In its broad outlines the president's plans had seemed to favor a speedy restoration of the southern states to the Union and a minimum of federal intervention in their affairs. But with his death the specifics of postwar Reconstruction had to be hammered out by a new president, Andrew Johnson of Tennessee, a man whose personality, political background, and racist leanings put him at odds with the Republican-controlled Congress.

Andrew Johnson and Presidential Reconstruction

Andrew Johnson, a Democrat and former slaveholder, was a most unlikely successor to the martyred Lincoln. By trade a tailor, educated by his wife, Johnson overcame his impoverished background and served as state legislator, governor, and U.S. senator. Throughout his career Johnson had championed yeoman farmers and viewed the South's plantation aristocrats with contempt. He was the only southern member of the U.S. Senate to remain loyal to the Union, and he held the planter elite responsible for secession and defeat. In 1862 Lincoln appointed Johnson to the difficult post of military governor of Tennessee. There he successfully began wartime Reconstruction and cultivated Unionist support in the mountainous eastern districts of that state.

In 1864 the Republicans, in an appeal to northern and border state "War Democrats," nominated Johnson for vice president. But despite Johnson's success in Tennessee and in the 1864 campaign, many Radical Republicans distrusted him, and the hardscrabble Tennessean remained a political outsider in Republican circles. In the immediate aftermath of Lincoln's murder, however, Johnson appeared to side with those Radical Republicans who sought to treat the South as a conquered province. "Treason is a crime and must be made odious," Johnson declared. "Traitors must be impoverished. . . . They must not only be punished, but their social power must be destroyed." The new president also hinted at indicting prominent Confederate officials for treason, disfranchising them, and confiscating their property. Such tough talk appealed to Radical Republicans. But support for Johnson quickly faded as the new president's policies unfolded. Johnson defined Reconstruction as the province of the executive, not the legislative branch, and he planned to restore the Union as quickly as possible. He blamed individual Southerners—the planter elite—rather than entire states for leading the South down the disastrous road to secession. In line with this philosophy, Johnson outlined mild terms for reentry to the Union.

In the spring of 1865 Johnson granted amnesty and pardon, including restoration of property rights except slaves, to all Confederates who pledged loyalty to the Union and support for emancipation. Fourteen classes of Southerners, mostly major Confederate officials and wealthy landowners, were excluded. But these men could apply individually for presidential pardons. The power to pardon his former enemies—the Old South's planter elite—gratified Johnson and reinforced his class bias. It also helped win southern support for his lenient policies, for Johnson pardoned former Confederates liberally. In September 1865 Johnson granted an average of a hundred pardons a day, and during his tenure he pardoned roughly 90 percent of those who applied. Significantly, Johnson instituted this plan while Congress was not in session.

Johnson also appointed provisional governors for seven of the former Confederate states, requiring them to hold elections for state constitutional conventions. Participation in this political process was limited to white people who had been pardoned or who had taken a loyalty oath. Johnson also called on state conventions to repudiate secession, acknowledge the abolition of slavery, and void state debts incurred during the war. By the fall of 1865 ten of the eleven Confederate states claimed to have met Johnson's requirements to re-enter the Union. On December 6, 1865, in his first annual message to Congress, the president declared the "restoration" of the Union virtually complete. But a serious division within the federal government was taking shape, for the Congress was not about to allow the president free rein in determining the conditions of southern readmission.

Andrew Johnson used the term "restoration" rather than "reconstruction." A lifelong Democrat with ambitions to be elected president on his own in 1868, Johnson hoped to build a new political coalition composed of northern Democrats, conservative Republicans, and southern Unionists. Firmly committed to white supremacy, he opposed political rights for the freedmen. In 1866, after Frederick Douglass and other black leaders had met with him to discuss black suffrage, Johnson told an aide: "Those damned sons of bitches thought they had me in a trap! I know that damned Douglass; he's just like any nigger, and he would sooner cut a white man's throat than not." Johnson's open sympathy for his fellow white Southerners, his antiblack bias, and his

determination to control the course of Reconstruction placed him on a collision course with the powerful Radical wing of the Republican Party.

The Radical Republican Vision

Most Radicals were men whose careers had been shaped by the slavery controversy. At the core of their thinking lay a deep belief in equal political rights and equal economic opportunity, both guaranteed by a powerful national government. They argued that once free labor, universal education, and equal rights were implanted in the South, that region would be able to share in the North's material wealth, progress, and fluid social mobility. Representative George W. Julian of Indiana typified the Radical vision for the South. He called for elimination of the region's "large estates, widely scattered settlements, wasteful agriculture, popular ignorance, social degradation, the decline of manufactures, contempt for honest labor, and a pampered oligarchy." This process would allow Republicans to develop "small farms, thrifty tillage, free schools, social independence, flourishing manufactures and the arts, respect for honest labor, and equality of political rights."

The Fifteenth Amendment, 1870. The Fifteenth Amendment, ratified in 1870, stipulated that the right to vote could not be denied "on account of race, color, or previous condition of servitude." This illustration expressed the optimism and hopes of African Americans generated by this Constitutional landmark aimed at protecting black political rights. Note the various political figures (Abraham Lincoln, John Brown, Frederick Douglass) and movements (abolitionism, black education) invoked here, providing a sense of how the amendment culminated a long historical struggle.

SOURCE: Courtesy of the Library of Congress.

In the Radicals' view, the power of the federal government would be central to the remaking of southern society, especially in guaranteeing civil rights and suffrage for freedmen. In the most far-reaching proposal, Representative Thaddeus Stevens of Pennsylvania called for the confiscation of 400 million acres belonging to the wealthiest 10 percent of Southerners, to be redistributed to black and white yeomen and northern land buyers. "The whole fabric of southern society must be changed," Stevens told Pennsylvania Republicans in September 1865, "and never can it be done if this opportunity is lost. How can republican institutions, free schools, free churches, free social intercourse exist in a mingled community of nabobs and serfs? If the South is ever to be made a safe republic let her lands be cultivated by the toil of the owners."

Northern Republicans were especially outraged by the stringent "black codes" passed by South Carolina, Mississippi, Louisiana, and other states. These were designed to restrict the freedom of the black labor force and keep freed people as close to slave status as possible. Laborers who left their jobs before contracts expired would forfeit wages already earned and be subject to arrest by any white citizen. Vagrancy, very broadly defined, was punishable by fines and involuntary plantation labor. Apprenticeship clauses obliged black children to work without pay for employers. Some states attempted to bar African Americans from land ownership. Other laws specifically denied African Americans equality with white people in civil rights, excluding them from juries and prohibiting interracial marriages.

The black codes underscored the unwillingness of white Southerners to accept the full meaning of freedom for African Americans. Mississippi's version contained a catchall section levying fines and possible imprisonment for any former slaves "committing riots, routs, affrays, trespasses, malicious mischief, cruel treatment to animals, seditious speeches, insulting gestures, language, or acts, or assaults on any person, disturbance of the peace, exercising the function of a minister of the Gospel without a license . . . vending spiritous or intoxicating liquors, or committing any other misdemeanor, the punishment of which is not specifically provided for by law."

The Radicals, although not a majority of their party, were joined by moderate Republicans as growing numbers of Northerners grew suspicious of white southern intransigence and the denial of political rights to freedmen. When the Thirty-ninth Congress convened in December 1865, the large Republican majority prevented the seating of the white Southerners elected to Congress under President Johnson's provisional state governments. Republicans also established the Joint Committee on Reconstruction. After hearing extensive testimony from a broad range of witnesses, it concluded that not only were old Confederates back in power in the South but that black codes and racial violence required increased protection for African Americans.

As a result, in the spring of 1866, Congress passed two important bills designed to aid African Americans. The landmark Civil Rights bill, which bestowed full citizenship on African Americans, overturned the 1857 *Dred Scott* decision and the black codes. It defined all persons born in the United States (except Indian peoples) as national citizens, and it enumerated various rights, including the rights to make and enforce contracts, to sue, to give evidence, and to buy and sell property. Under this bill, African Americans

Office of the Freedmen's Bureau, Memphis, Tennessee, *Harper's Weekly,* June 2, 1866. Established by Congress in 1865, the Freedmen's Bureau provided economic, educational, and legal assistance to former slaves in the post-Civil War years. Bureau agents were often called upon to settle disputes between black and white Southerners over wages, labor contracts, political rights, and violence. While most Southern whites only grudgingly acknowledged the Bureau's legitimacy, freed people gained important legal and psychological support through testimony at public hearings like this one.

SOURCE: Library of Congress.

acquired "full and equal benefit of all laws and proceedings for the security of person and property as is enjoyed by white citizens."

Congress also voted to enlarge the scope of the Freedmen's Bureau, empowering it to build schools and pay teachers, and also to establish courts to prosecute those charged with depriving African Americans of their civil rights. The bureau achieved important, if limited, success in aiding African Americans. Bureau-run schools helped lay the foundation for southern public education. The bureau's network of courts allowed freed people to bring suits against white people in disputes involving violence, nonpayment of wages, or unfair division of crops. The very existence of courts hearing public testimony by African Americans provided an important psychological challenge to traditional notions of white racial domination.

But an angry President Johnson vetoed both of these bills. In opposing the Civil Rights bill, Johnson denounced the assertion of national power to protect African American civil rights, claiming it was a "stride toward centralization, and the concentration of all legislative powers in the national Government." In the case of the Freedmen's Bureau, Johnson argued that Congress lacked jurisdiction over the eleven unrepresented southern states. But Johnson's intemperate attacks on the Radicals—he damned them as traitors unwilling to restore the Union—united moderate and Radical Republicans and they succeeded in overriding the vetoes. Congressional Republicans, led by the Radical faction, were now unified in challenging the president's power to direct Reconstruction and in using national authority to define and protect the rights of citizens.

In June 1866, fearful that the Civil Rights Act might be declared unconstitutional and eager to settle the basis for the seating of southern representatives, Congress passed the Fourteenth Amendment. The amendment defined national citizenship to include former slaves ("all persons born or naturalized in the United States") and prohibited the states from violating the privileges of citizens without due process of law. It also empowered Congress to reduce the representation of any state that denied the suffrage to males over twenty-one. Republicans adopted the Fourteenth Amendment as their platform for the 1866 congressional elections and suggested that southern states would have to ratify it as a condition of readmission. President Johnson, meanwhile, took to the stump in August to support conservative Democratic and Republican candidates. His unrestrained speeches often degenerated into harangues, alienating many voters and aiding the Republican cause.

For their part, the Republicans skillfully portrayed Johnson and northern Democrats as disloyal and white Southerners as unregenerate. Republicans began an effective campaign tradition known as "waving the bloody shirt"—reminding northern voters of the hundreds of thousands of Yankee soldiers left dead or maimed by the war. In the November 1866 elections, the Republicans increased their majority in both the House and the Senate and gained control of all the northern states. The stage was now set for a battle between the president and Congress. Was it to be Johnson's "restoration" or Congressional Reconstruction?

Congressional Reconstruction and the Impeachment Crisis

United against Johnson, Radical and moderate Republicans took control of Reconstruction early in 1867. In March, Congress passed the First Reconstruction Act over Johnson's veto. This act divided the South into five military districts subject to martial law. To achieve restoration, southern states were first required to call new constitutional conventions, elected by universal manhood suffrage. Once these states had drafted new

Web Exploration

In these interactive maps, consider the politics of Reconstruction in the South. What were the competing plans for reconstructing the southern states?
www.prenhall.com/faragher/map17.1

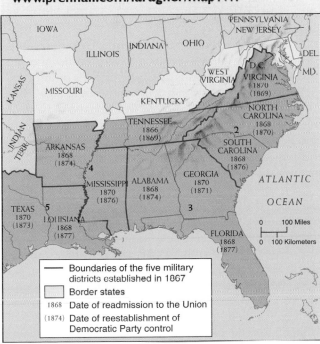

Reconstruction of the South, 1866–1877 Dates for the readmission of former Confederate states to the Union and the return of Democrats to power varied according to the specific political situations in those states.

constitutions, guaranteed African American voting rights, and ratified the Fourteenth Amendment, they were eligible for readmission to the Union. Supplementary legislation, also passed over the president's veto, invalidated the provisional governments established by Johnson, empowered the military to administer voter registration, and required an oath of loyalty to the United States.

Congress also passed several laws aimed at limiting Johnson's power. One of these, the Tenure of Office Act, stipulated that any officeholder appointed by the president with the Senate's advice and consent could not be removed until the Senate had approved a successor. In this way, congressional leaders could protect Republicans, such as Secretary of War Edwin M. Stanton, entrusted with implementing Congressional Reconstruction. In August 1867, with Congress adjourned, Johnson suspended Stanton and appointed General Ulysses S. Grant interim secretary of war. This move enabled the president to remove generals in the field that he judged to be too radical and replace them with men who were sympathetic to his own views. It also served as a challenge to the Tenure of Office Act. In January 1868, when the Senate overruled Stanton's suspension, Grant broke openly with Johnson and vacated the office. Stanton resumed his position and barricaded himself in his office when Johnson attempted to remove him once again.

Outraged by Johnson's relentless obstructionism, and seizing upon his violation of the Tenure of Office Act as a pretext, Radical and moderate Republicans in the House of Representatives again joined forces and voted to impeach the president by a vote of 126 to 47 on February 24, 1868, charging him with eleven counts of high crimes and misdemeanors. To ensure the support of moderate Republicans, the articles of impeachment focused on violations of the Tenure of Office Act. The case against Johnson would have to be made on the basis of willful violation of the law. Left unstated were the Republicans' real reasons for wanting the president removed: Johnson's political views and his opposition to the Reconstruction Acts.

An influential group of moderate Senate Republicans feared the damage a conviction might do to the constitutional separation of powers. They also worried about the political and economic policies that might be pursued by Benjamin Wade, the president pro tem of the Senate and a leader of the Radical Republicans, who, because there was no vice president, would succeed to the presidency if Johnson were removed from office. Behind the scenes during his Senate trial, Johnson agreed to abide by the Reconstruction Acts. In May, the Senate voted 35 for conviction, 19 for acquittal—one vote shy of the two-thirds necessary for removal from office. Johnson's narrow acquittal established the precedent that only criminal actions by a president—not political disagreements—warranted removal from office.

The Election of 1868

By the summer of 1868, seven former Confederate states (Alabama, Arkansas, Florida, Louisiana, North Carolina, South Carolina, and Tennessee) had ratified the revised constitutions, elected Republican governments, and ratified the Fourteenth Amendment. They had thereby earned readmission to the Union. Though Georgia, Mississippi, Texas, and Virginia still awaited readmission, the presidential election of 1868 offered some hope that the Civil War's legacy of sectional hate and racial tension might finally ease.

Republicans nominated Ulysses S. Grant, the North's foremost military hero. An Ohio native, Grant had graduated from West Point in 1843, served in the Mexican War, and resigned from the army in 1854. Unhappy in civilian life, Grant received a second chance during the Civil War. He rose quickly to become commander in the western theater, and he later destroyed Lee's army in Virginia. Although his armies suffered terrible losses, Grant enjoyed tremendous popularity after the war, especially when he broke with Johnson. Totally lacking in political experience, Grant admitted after receiving the nomination that he had been forced into it in spite of himself: "I could not back down without leaving the contest for power for the next four years between mere trading politicians, the elevation of whom, no matter which party won, would lose to us, largely, the results of the costly war which we have gone through."

Significantly, at the very moment that the South was being forced to enfranchise former slaves as a prerequisite for readmission to the Union, the Republicans rejected a campaign plank endorsing black suffrage in the North. Their platform left "the question of suffrage in all the loyal States . . . to the people of those States." State referendums calling for black suffrage failed in eight northern states between 1865 and 1868, succeeding only in Iowa and Minnesota. The Democrats, determined to reverse Congressional Reconstruction, nominated Horatio Seymour, former governor of New York and a long-time foe of emancipation and supporter of states' rights. Democrats North and South exploited the race question to garner votes. Their platform blasted the Republicans for subjecting the nation "in time of profound peace, to military despotism and negro supremacy." The party sought "the abolition of the Freedmen's Bureau; and all political instrumentalities designed to secure negro supremacy." Throughout the South, violence marked the electoral process. The Ku Klux Klan, founded as a Tennessee social club in 1866, emerged as a potent instrument of terror (see the opening of this chapter). In Louisiana, Arkansas, Georgia, and South Carolina the Klan threatened, whipped, and murdered black and white Republicans to prevent them from voting. This terrorism enabled the Democrats to carry Georgia and Louisiana, but it ultimately cost the Democrats votes in the North. In the final tally, Grant carried twenty-six of the thirty-four states for an electoral college victory of 214 to 80. But he received a popular majority of less than 53 percent, beating Seymour by only 306,000 votes. Significantly, more than 500,000 African American voters cast their ballots for Grant, demonstrating their overwhelming support for the Republican Party. The Republicans also retained large majorities in both houses of Congress.

In February 1869, Congress passed the Fifteenth Amendment, providing that "the right of citizens of the United States to vote shall not be denied or abridged . . . on account of race, color, or previous condition of servitude." Noticeably absent was language prohibiting the states from imposing educational, residential, or other qualifications for voting. Moderate Republicans feared that filling these discriminatory loopholes might make it difficult to obtain ratification for the amendment by the required three-quarters of

the states. To enhance the chances of ratification, Congress required the three remaining unreconstructed states—Mississippi, Texas, and Virginia—to ratify both the Fourteenth and Fifteenth Amendments before readmission. They did so and rejoined the Union in early 1870. The Fifteenth Amendment was ratified in February 1870. In the narrow sense of simply readmitting the former Confederate states to the Union, Reconstruction was complete.

Woman Suffrage and Reconstruction

The battles over the political status of African Americans proved an important turning point for women as well. The Fourteenth and Fifteenth Amendments, which granted citizenship and the vote to freedmen, both inspired and frustrated women's rights activists. Many of these women had long been active in the abolitionist movement. During the war, they had actively supported the Union cause through their work in the National Woman's Loyal League and the United States Sanitary Commission. Elizabeth Cady Stanton and Susan B. Anthony, two leaders with long involvement in both the antislavery and feminist movements, objected to the inclusion of the word "male" in the Fourteenth Amendment. "If that word 'male' be inserted," Stanton predicted

OVERVIEW

RECONSTRUCTION AMENDMENTS TO THE CONSTITUTION, 1865–1870

Amendment and Date Passed by Congress	Main Provisions	Ratification Process (3/4 of all states including ex-Confederate states required)
13 (January 1865)	Prohibited slavery in the United States)	December 1865 (27 states, including 8 southern states
14 (June 1866)	• Conferred national citizenship on all persons born or naturalized in the United States • Reduced state representation in Congress proportionally for any state disfranchising male citizens • Denied former Confederates the right to hold state or national office • Repudiated Confederate debt	July 1868 (after Congress makes ratification a prerequisite for readmission of ex-Confederate states to the Union)
15 (February 1869)	Prohibited denial of suffrage because of race, color, or previous condition of servitude	March 1870 (ratification required for readmission of Virginia, Texas, Mississippi, and Georgia)

in 1866, "it will take us a century at least to get it out." Insisting that the causes of the African American vote and the women's vote were linked, Stanton, Anthony, and Lucy Stone founded the American Equal Rights Association in 1866. The group launched a series of lobbying and petition campaigns to remove racial and sexual restrictions on voting from state constitutions. In Kansas, for example, an old antislavery battlefield, the association vigorously supported two 1867 referendums that would have removed the words "male" and "white" from the state's constitution. But Kansas voters rejected both woman suffrage and black suffrage. Throughout the nation, the old abolitionist organizations and the Republican Party emphasized passage of the Fourteenth and Fifteenth Amendments and withdrew funds and support from the cause of woman suffrage. Disagreements over these amendments divided suffragists for decades.

The radical wing, led by Stanton and Anthony, opposed the Fifteenth Amendment, arguing that ratification would establish an "aristocracy of sex," enfranchising all men while leaving women without political privileges. In arguing for a Sixteenth Amendment that would secure the vote for women, they used racist and elitist appeals. They urged "American women of wealth, education, virtue, and refinement" to support the vote for women and oppose the Fifteenth Amendment "if you do not wish the lower orders of Chinese, Africans, Germans, and Irish, with their low ideas of womanhood to make laws for you and your daughters." Other women's rights activists, including Lucy Stone and Frederick Douglass, asserted that "this hour belongs to the Negro." They feared a debate over woman suffrage at the national level would jeopardize passage of the two amendments.

By 1869 woman suffragists had split into two competing organizations. The moderate American Woman Suffrage Association (AWSA), led by Lucy Stone, Julia Ward Howe, and Henry Blackwell, focused on achieving woman suffrage at the state level. It maintained close ties with the Republican Party and the old abolitionist networks, worked for the Fifteenth Amendment, and actively sought the support of men. The more radical wing founded the all-female National Woman Suffrage Association (NWSA). For the NWSA, the vote represented only one part of a broad spectrum of goals inherited from the Declaration of Sentiments manifesto adopted at the first women's rights convention held in 1848 at Seneca Falls, New York (see Chapter 13).

Although women did not win the vote in this period, they did establish an independent suffrage movement that eventually drew millions of women into political life. The NWSA in particular demonstrated that self-government and democratic participation in

Susan B. Anthony (1820–1906) and Elizabeth Cady Stanton (1815–1902), the two most influential leaders of the woman suffrage movement, ca. 1892. Anthony and Stanton broke with their longtime abolitionist allies after the Civil War when they opposed the Fifteenth Amendment. They argued that the doctrine of universal manhood suffrage it embodied would give constitutional authority to the claim that men were the social and political superiors of women. As founders of the militant National Woman Suffrage Association, Stanton and Anthony established an independent woman suffrage movement with a broader spectrum of goals for women's rights and drew millions of women into public life during the late nineteenth century.

SOURCE: The Susan B. Anthony House, Rochester, NY.

the public sphere were crucial for women's emancipation. Stanton and Anthony toured the country, speaking to women's audiences and inspiring the formation of suffrage societies. The NWSA's weekly magazine, *Revolution*, became a forum for feminist ideas on divorce laws, unequal pay, women's property rights, and marriage. The failure of woman suffrage after the Civil War was less a result of factional fighting than of the larger defeat of Radical Reconstruction and the ideal of expanded citizenship.

THE MEANING OF FREEDOM

For 4 million slaves, freedom arrived in various ways in different parts of the South. In many areas, slavery had collapsed long before Lee's surrender at Appomattox. In regions far removed from the presence of federal troops, African Americans did not learn of slavery's end until the spring of 1865. There were thousands of sharply contrasting stories, many of which revealed the need for freed slaves to confront their owners. One Virginia slave, hired out to another family during the war, had been working in the fields when a friend told her she was now free. "Is dat so?" she exclaimed. Dropping her hoe, she ran the seven miles to her old place, confronted her former mistress, and shouted, "I'se free! Yes, I'se free! Ain't got to work fo' you no mo'. You can't put me in yo' pocket now!" Her mistress burst into tears and ran into the house. That was all the former slave needed to see. But regardless of specific regional circumstances, the meaning of "freedom" would be contested for years to come. The deep desire for independence from white control formed the underlying aspiration of newly freed slaves. For their part, most southern white people sought to restrict the boundaries of that independence. As individuals and as members of communities transformed by emancipation, former slaves struggled to establish economic, political, and cultural autonomy. They built on the twin pillars of slave culture—the family and the church—to consolidate and expand African American institutions and thereby laid the foundation for the modern African American community.

Emancipation greatly expanded the choices available to African Americans. It helped build confidence in their ability to effect change without deferring to white people. Freedom also meant greater uncertainty and risk. But the vast majority of African Americans were more than willing to take their chances. Many years later, one former Texas slave pondered the question "What I likes bes, to be slave or free?" She answered: "Well, it's dis way. In slavery I owns nothin' and never owns nothin'. In freedom I's own de home and raise de family. All dat cause me worryment and in slavery I has no worryment, but I takes de freedom."

Moving About

The first impulse of many emancipated slaves was to test their freedom. The simplest, most obvious way to do this involved leaving home. By walking off a plantation, coming and going without restraint or fear of punishment, African Americans could savor freedom. Throughout the summer and fall of 1865, observers in the South noted enormous numbers of freed people on the move. One former slave squatting in an abandoned tent outside Selma, Alabama, explained his feeling to a northern journalist: "I's want to be free man, cum when I please, and nobody say nuttin to me, nor order me roun'." When urged to stay on with the South Carolina family she had served for years as a cook, a slave woman replied firmly: "No, Miss, I must go. If I stay here I'll never know I am free."

Yet many who left their old neighborhoods returned soon afterward to seek work in the general vicinity, or even on the plantation they had left. Many wanted to separate themselves from former owners, but not from familial ties and friendships. Others moved away altogether, seeking jobs in nearby towns and cities. Many former slaves left predominantly white counties, where they felt more vulnerable and isolated, for new lives in the relative comfort of predominantly black communities. In most southern states, there was a significant population shift toward black belt plantation counties and towns after the war. Many African Americans, attracted by schools, churches, and fraternal societies as well as the army, preferred the city. Between 1865 and 1870, the African American population of the South's ten largest cities doubled, while the white population increased by only 10 percent.

Disgruntled planters had difficulty accepting African American independence. During slavery, they had expected obedience, submission, and loyalty from African Americans. Now many could not understand why so many former slaves wanted to leave despite urgent pleas to continue working at the old place. The deference and humility white people expected from African Americans could no longer be taken for granted. Indeed, many freed people went out of their way to reject the old subservience. Moving about freely was one way of doing this, as was refusing to tip one's hat to white people, ignoring former masters or mistresses in the streets, and refusing to step aside on sidewalks. After encountering an African American who would not step aside, Eliza Andrews, a Georgia plantation mistress, complained, "It is the first time in my life that I have ever had to give up the sidewalk to a man, much less to negroes!" When freed people staged parades, dances, and picnics to celebrate their new freedom, as they did, for example, when commemorating the Emancipation Proclamation, white people invariably condemned them angrily for "insolence," "outrageous spectacles," or "putting on airs."

The African American Family

Emancipation allowed freed people to strengthen family ties. For many former slaves, freedom meant the opportunity to reunite with long-lost family members. To track down relatives, freed people trekked to faraway places, put ads in newspapers, sought the help of Freedmen's

Bureau agents, and questioned anyone who might have information about loved ones. Many thousands of family reunions, each with its own story, took place after the war. To William Curtis of Georgia, whose father had been sold to a Virginia planter, "that was the best thing about the war setting us free, he could come back to us." One North Carolina slave, who had seen his parents separated by sale, recalled many years later what for him had been the most significant aspect of freedom. "I has got thirteen great-gran' chilluns an' I know whar dey ever'one am. In slavery times dey'd have been on de block long time ago."

Thousands of African American couples who had lived together under slavery streamed to military and civilian authorities and demanded to be legally married. By 1870, the two-parent household was the norm for a large majority of African Americans. "In their eyes," a Freedmen's Bureau agent reported, "the work of emancipation was incomplete until the families which had been dispersed by slavery were reunited." For many freed people the attempt to find lost relatives dragged on for years. Searches often proved frustrating, exhausting, and ultimately disappointing. Some "reunions" ended painfully with the discovery that spouses had found new partners and started new families.

Emancipation brought changes to gender roles within the African American family as well. By serving in the Union army, African American men played a more direct role than women in the fight for freedom. In the political sphere, black men could now serve on juries, vote, and hold office; black women, like their white counterparts, could not. Freedmen's Bureau agents designated the husband as household head and established lower wage scales for women laborers. African American editors, preachers, and politicians regularly quoted the biblical injunction that wives submit to their husbands. African American men asserted their male authority, denied under slavery, by insisting their wives work at home instead of in the fields.

For years after 1865, southern planters complained about the scarcity of women and children available for fieldwork. African American women generally wanted to devote more time than they had under slavery to caring for their children and to performing such domestic chores as cooking, sewing, gardening, and laundering. Yet African American women continued to work outside the home, engaging in seasonal field labor for wages or working a family's rented plot. Most rural black families barely eked out a living, and thus the labor of every family member was essential to survival. The key difference from slave times was that African American families themselves, not white masters and overseers, decided when and where women and children worked.

African American Churches and Schools

The creation of separate African American churches proved the most lasting and important element of the energetic institution building that went on in postemancipation years. Before the Civil War, southern Protestant churches had relegated slaves and free African Americans to second-class membership. Black worshipers were required to sit in the back during services, they were denied any role in church governance, and they were excluded from Sunday schools. Even in larger cities, where all-black congregations sometimes built their own churches, the law required white pastors. In rural areas, slaves preferred their own preachers to the sermons of local white ministers who quoted Scripture to justify slavery and white supremacy. "That old white preachin' wasn't

An overflow congregation crowds into Richmond's First African Baptist Church in 1874. Despite their poverty, freed people struggled to save, buy land, and erect new buildings as they organized hundreds of new black churches during Reconstruction. As the most important African American institution outside the family, the black church, in addition to tending to spiritual needs, played a key role in the educational and political life of the community.

SOURCE: Wood engraving. The Granger Collection (4E1090.98).

nothin'," former slave Nancy Williams recalled. "Old white preachers used to talk with their tongues without sayin' nothin', but Jesus told us slaves to talk with our hearts."

In communities around the South, African Americans now pooled their resources to buy land and build their own churches. Before these structures were completed, they might hold services in a railroad boxcar, where Atlanta's First Baptist Church began, or in an outdoor arbor, the original site of the First Baptist Church of Memphis. By late 1866 Charleston's African American community could boast of eleven churches in the city—five Methodist, two Presbyterian, two Episcopalian, one Baptist, and one Congregational. In rural areas, different denominations frequently shared the same church building. Churches became the center not only for religious life but for many other activities that defined the African American community: schools, picnics, festivals, and political meetings. They also helped spawn a host of organizations devoted to benevolence and mutual aid, such as burial societies, Masonic lodges, temperance clubs, and trade associations.

The church became the first social institution fully controlled by African Americans. In nearly every community ministers, respected for their speaking and organizational skills, were among the most influential leaders. By 1877 the great majority of black Southerners had withdrawn from white-dominated churches. In South Carolina, for example, only a few hundred black Methodists attended biracial churches, down from over 40,000 in 1865. The various Protestant denominations competed for the allegiance of African American worshipers. Among Methodists, the African Methodist Episcopal Church, originally founded in 1816, gained ascendancy over white-dominated rivals. Black Baptist churches, with their decentralized and democratic structure and more emotional services, attracted the greatest number of freed people. By the end of Reconstruction the vast majority of African American Christians belonged to black Baptist or Methodist churches.

The rapid spread of schools reflected African Americans' thirst for self-improvement. Southern states had prohibited education for slaves. But many free black people managed to attend school, and a few slaves had been able to educate themselves. Still, over 90 percent of the South's adult African American population was illiterate in 1860. Access to education thus became a central part of the meaning of freedom. Freedmen's Bureau agents repeatedly expressed amazement at the number of makeshift classrooms organized by African Americans in rural areas. A bureau officer described these "wayside schools": "A negro riding on a loaded wagon, or sitting on a hack waiting for a train, or by the cabin door, is often seen, book in hand delving after the rudiments of knowledge. A group on the platform of a depot, after carefully conning an old spelling book, resolves itself into a class."

African American communities received important educational aid from outside organizations. By 1869 the Freedmen's Bureau was supervising nearly 3,000 schools serving over 150,000 students throughout the South. Over half the roughly 3,300 teachers in these schools were African Americans, many of whom had been free before the Civil War. Other teachers included dedicated northern white women, volunteers sponsored by the American Missionary Association (AMA). The bureau and the AMA also assisted in the founding of several black colleges, including Tougaloo, Hampton, and Fisk, designed to train black teachers. Black self-help proved crucial to the education effort. Throughout the South in 1865 and 1866, African Americans raised money to build schoolhouses, buy supplies, and pay teachers. Black artisans donated labor for construction, and black families offered room and board to teachers.

Land and Labor after Slavery

Most newly emancipated African Americans aspired to quit the plantations and to make new lives for themselves. Leaving the plantation was not as simple as walking off. Some freed people did find jobs in railroad building, mining, ranching, or construction work. Others raised subsistence crops and tended vegetable gardens as squatters. White planters, however, tried to retain African Americans as permanent agricultural laborers. Restricting the employment of former slaves was an important goal of the black codes. For example, South Carolina legislation in 1865 provided that "no person of color shall pursue or practice the art, trade, or business of an artisan, mechanic, or shopkeeper, or any other trade, employment, or business, besides that of husbandry, or that of a servant under contract for service or labor" without a special and costly permit.

The majority of African Americans hoped to become self-sufficient farmers. As *DeBow's Review* observed in 1869, the freedman showed "great anxiety to have his little home, with his horse, cow, and hogs, separate and apart from others." Many former slaves believed they were entitled to the land they had worked throughout their lives. General Oliver O. Howard, chief commissioner of the Freedmen's Bureau, observed that many "supposed that the Government [would] divide among them the lands of the conquered owners, and furnish them with all that might be necessary to begin life as an independent farmer." This perception was not merely a wishful fantasy. The Freedmen's Bureau Act of 1865 specifically required that abandoned land be leased for three years in forty-acre lots, with an option to buy. Frequent reference in the Congress and the press to the question of land distribution made the idea of "forty acres and a mule" not just a pipe dream but a matter of serious public debate.

Above all, African Americans sought economic autonomy, and ownership of land promised the most independence. "Give us our own land and we take care of ourselves," was how one former slave saw it. "But widout land, de ole massas can hire us or starve us, as dey please." At the Colored Convention in Montgomery, Alabama, in May 1867, delegates argued that the property now owned by planters had been "nearly all earned by the sweat of our brows, not theirs. It has been forfeited to the government by the treason of its owners, and is liable to be confiscated whenever the Republican Party demands it." But by 1866 the federal government had already pulled back from the various wartime experiments involving the breaking up of large plantations and the leasing of small plots to individual families. President Johnson directed General Howard of the Freedmen's Bureau to evict tens of thousands of freed people settled on confiscated and abandoned land in southeastern Virginia, southern Louisiana, and the Georgia and South Carolina low country. These evictions created a deep sense of betrayal among African Americans. A former Mississippi slave, Merrimon Howard, bitterly noted that African Americans had been left with "no land, no house, not so much as a place to lay our head. . . . We were friends on the march, brothers on the battlefield, but in the peaceful pursuits of life it seems that we are strangers."

A variety of labor arrangements could be found in southern agriculture in the immediate postwar years. Each featured both advantages and disadvantages for planters and freed people. Writing in 1866, white planter Percy Roberts identified three distinct "systems of hire" for working the land: money wages, share wages, and sharecropping. Under both the money wage and share wage systems, planters contracted former slaves to work in large gangs, paying them either in cash (money wage) or with a share of the crop that the workers divided among themselves (share wage). Freedmen's Bureau agents, who generally advocated the money wage arrangement, would often help freedmen negotiate labor contracts with planters. Planters tended to prefer the money wage system because it clearly defined laborers as hirelings and gave planters more direct control over the labor force—for example, by enabling them to discharge the hands they thought inefficient. Yet most planters were forced to adopt share wages at the insistence of black laborers who were adamantly opposed to serving as mere hirelings.

But both the money wage and share wage systems were unsatisfactory from the perspective of freed people. Both systems relied on the gang labor approach so reminiscent of slavery. And both systems often left African Americans at the mercy of unscrupulous planters who cheated them of their wages or fair shares.

Above all, the deep desire for economic improvement and greater autonomy led many African Americans to press for an alternative. By the late 1860s, black people's resistance to working in gangs and their desire to establish independent homesteads forced planters into the compromise system of sharecropping, which emerged as the dominant form of working the land.

Under sharecropping arrangements, individual families contracted with landowners to be responsible for a specific plot. Large plantations were thus broken into family-sized farms. Generally, sharecropper families received one-third of the year's crop if the owner furnished implements, seed, and draft animals, or one-half if they provided their own supplies. African Americans preferred sharecropping to gang labor, as it allowed families to set their own hours and tasks and offered freedom from white supervision and control. For planters, the system stabilized the workforce by requiring sharecroppers to remain until the harvest and to employ all family members. It also offered a way around the chronic shortage of cash and credit that plagued the postwar South. But as the *Southern Argus* of Selma, Alabama, editorialized, sharecropping was "an unwilling concession to the freedmen's desire to become a proprietor. . . . It is not a voluntary association from similarity of aims and interests." Freed people did not aspire to sharecropping. Owning land outright or tenant farming (renting land) were both more desirable. But though black sharecroppers clearly enjoyed more autonomy than in the past, the vast majority never achieved economic independence or land ownership. They remained a largely subordinate agricultural labor force.

Sharecropping came to dominate the southern agricultural economy and African American life in particular. By 1880 about 80 percent of the land in the black belt states—Mississippi, Alabama, and Georgia—had been divided into family-sized farms. Nearly three-quarters of black Southerners were sharecroppers. Through much of the black belt, family and community were one. Often several families worked adjoining parcels of land in common, pooling their labor in order to get by. Men usually oversaw crop production. Women went to the fields seasonally during planting or harvesting, but they mainly tended to household chores and child care. In addition, women frequently held jobs that might bring in cash, such as raising chickens or taking in laundry. The cotton harvest engaged all members of the community, from the oldest to the youngest. Cotton picking remained a difficult, labor-intensive task that took priority over all other work.

The Origins of African American Politics

Although the desire for autonomy had led African Americans to pursue their economic and religious goals largely apart from white people, inclusion rather than

The Barrow Plantation, Oglethorpe County, Georgia, 1860 and 1881 (approx. 2,000 acres) These two maps, based on drawings from *Scribner's Monthly*, April 1881, show some of the changes brought by emancipation. In 1860 the plantation's entire black population lived in the communal slave quarters, right next to the white master's house. In 1881 black sharecropper and tenant families lived on individual plots, spread out across the land. The former slaves had also built their own school and church.

separation was the objective of early African American political activity. The greatest political activity by African Americans occurred in areas occupied by Union forces during the war. In 1865 and 1866, African Americans throughout the South organized scores of mass meetings, parades, and petitions that demanded civil equality and the right to vote. In the cities, the growing web of churches and fraternal societies helped bolster early efforts at political organization.

Hundreds of African American delegates, selected by local meetings or churches, attended statewide political conventions held throughout the South in 1865 and 1866. Previously free African Americans, as well as black ministers, artisans, and veterans of the Union army, tended to dominate these proceedings, setting a pattern that would hold throughout Reconstruction. Convention debates sometimes reflected the tensions within African American communities, such as friction between poorer former slaves and better-off free black people, or between lighter- and darker-skinned African Americans. But most of these state gatherings concentrated on passing resolutions on issues that united all African Americans. The central concerns were suffrage and equality before the law. Black Southerners firmly proclaimed their identification with the nation's history and republican traditions. The 1865 North Carolina freedmen's convention was typical in describing universal manhood suffrage as "an essential and inseparable element of self-government." It also praised the Declaration of Independence as "the broadest, the deepest, the most comprehensive and truthful definition of human freedom that was ever given to the world."

The passage of the First Reconstruction Act in 1867 encouraged even more political activity among African Americans. The military started registering the South's electorate, ultimately enrolling approximately 735,000 black and 635,000 white voters in the ten unreconstructed states. Five states—Alabama, Florida, Louisiana, Mississippi, and South Carolina—had black electoral majorities. Fewer than half the registered white voters participated in the elections for state constitutional conventions in 1867 and 1868. In contrast, four-fifths of the registered black voters cast ballots in these elections. Much of this new African American political activism was channeled through local Union League chapters throughout the South. However, as the fate of Alex Webb in Hale County, Alabama, again makes clear, few whites welcomed this activism.

Begun during the war as a northern, largely white middle-class patriotic club, the Union League now be-

came the political voice of the former slaves. Union League chapters brought together local African Americans, soldiers, and Freedmen's Bureau agents to demand the vote and an end to legal discrimination against African Americans. It brought out African American voters, instructed freedmen in the rights and duties of citizenship, and promoted Republican candidates. Not surprisingly, newly enfranchised freedmen voted Republican and formed the core of the Republican Party in the South. In 1867 and 1868, the promise of Radical Reconstruction enlarged the scope of African American political participation and brought new leaders to the fore. Many were teachers, preachers, or others with useful skills, such as literacy. For most ordinary African Americans, politics was inseparable from economic issues, especially the land question. Grass-roots political organizations frequently intervened in local disputes with planters over the terms of labor contracts. African American political groups closely followed the congressional debates over Reconstruction policy and agitated for land confiscation and distribution. Perhaps most important, politics was the only arena where black and white Southerners might engage each other on an equal basis. As the delegates to an Alabama convention asserted in 1867: "We claim exactly the same rights, privileges and immunities as are enjoyed by white men—we ask nothing more and will be content with nothing less. . . . The law no longer knows white nor black, but simply men, and consequently we are entitled to ride in public conveyances, hold office, sit on juries and do everything else which we have in the past been prevented from doing solely on the ground of color."

SOUTHERN POLITICS AND SOCIETY

By the summer of 1868, when the South had returned to the Union, the majority of Republicans believed the task of Reconstruction to be finished. Ultimately, they put their faith in a political solution to the problems facing the vanquished South. That meant nurturing a viable two-party system in the southern states, where no Republican Party had ever existed. If that could be accomplished, Republicans and Democrats would compete for votes, offices, and influence, just as they did in northern states. Most Republican congressmen were moderates, conceiving Reconstruction in limited terms. They rejected radical calls for confiscation and redistribution of land, as well as permanent military rule of the South. The Reconstruction Acts of 1867 and 1868 laid out the requirements for the readmission of southern states, along with the procedures for forming and electing new governments.

W. L. Sheppard, "Electioneering at the South," *Harper's Weekly*, July 25, 1868. Throughout the Reconstruction-era South, newly freed slaves took a keen interest in both local and national political affairs. The presence of women and children at these campaign gatherings illustrates the importance of contemporary political issues to the entire African American community.

SOURCE: Library of Congress.

Yet over the next decade the political structure created in the southern states proved too restricted and fragile to sustain itself. Republicans had to employ radical means to protect their essentially conservative goals. To most southern whites the active participation of African Americans in politics seemed extremely dangerous. Federal troops were needed to protect Republican governments and their supporters from violent opposition. Congressional action to monitor southern elections and protect black voting rights became routine. Despite initial successes, southern Republicanism proved an unstable coalition of often conflicting elements, unable to sustain effective power for very long. By 1877, Democrats had regained political control of all the former Confederate states.

Southern Republicans

Three major groups composed the fledgling Republican coalition in the postwar South. African American voters made up a large majority of southern Republicans throughout the Reconstruction era. Yet African Americans outnumbered whites in only three southern states—South Carolina, Mississippi, and Louisiana. They made up roughly one-quarter of the population in Texas, Tennessee, and Arkansas, and between 40 and 50 percent in Virginia, North Carolina, Alabama, Florida, and Georgia. Thus, Republicans would have to attract white support to win elections and sustain power.

A second group consisted of white Northerners, derisively called "carpetbaggers" by native white Southerners. One Democratic congressman in 1871 said the term "applied to the office seeker from the North who came here seeking office by the negroes, by arraying their political passions and prejudices against the white people of the community." In fact, most carpetbaggers combined a desire for personal gain with a commitment to reform the "unprogressive" South by developing its material resources and introducing Yankee institutions such as free labor and free public schools. Most were veterans of the Union army who stayed in the South after the war. Others included Freedmen's Bureau agents and businessmen who had invested capital in cotton plantations and other enterprises.

Carpetbaggers tended to be well educated and from the middle class. Albert Morgan, for example, was an army veteran from Ohio who settled in Mississippi after the war. When he and his brother failed at running a cotton plantation and sawmill, Morgan became active in Republican politics as a way to earn a living. He won election to the state constitutional convention, became a power in the state legislature, and risked his life to keep the Republican organization alive in the Mississippi Delta region. Although they made up a tiny percentage of the population, carpetbaggers played a disproportionately large role in southern politics. They won a large share of Reconstruction offices, particularly in Florida, South Carolina, and Louisiana and in areas with large African American constituencies.

The third major group of southern Republicans were the native whites pejoratively termed "scalawags." They had even more diverse backgrounds and motives than the northern-born Republicans. Some were prominent prewar Whigs who saw the Republican Party as their best chance to regain political influence. Others viewed the party as an agent of modernization and economic expansion. "Yankees and Yankee notions are just what we want in this country," argued Thomas Settle of North Carolina. "We want their capital to build factories and workshops. We want their intelligence, their energy and enterprise." Their greatest influence lay in the up-country strongholds of southern Unionism, such as eastern Tennessee, western North Carolina, and northern Alabama. Loyalists during the war and traditional enemies of the planter elite (most were small farmers), these white Southerners looked to the Republican Party for help in settling old scores and relief from debt and wartime devastation.

Deep contradictions strained the alliance of these three groups. Southern Republicans touted themselves as the "party of progress and civilization" and promised a new era of material progress for the region. Republican state conventions in 1867 and 1868 voiced support for internal improvements, public schools, debt relief, and railroad building. Yet few white Southerners identified with the political and economic aspirations of African Americans. Nearly every party convention split between "confiscation radicals" (generally African Americans) and moderate elements committed to white control of the party and to economic development that offered more to outside investors than to impoverished African Americans and poor whites.

Reconstructing the States: A Mixed Record

With the old Confederate leaders barred from political participation, and with carpetbaggers and newly enfranchised African Americans representing many of the plantation districts, Republicans managed to dominate the ten southern constitutional conventions of 1867–69. Well-educated carpetbaggers usually chaired the important committees and drafted key provisions of the new constitutions. Most of the delegates were southern white Republicans. African Americans formed a majority of the conventions in Louisiana and South Carolina, but they were generally underrepresented. In all, there were 258 African Americans among the 1,027 convention delegates at the ten conventions.

Most of the conventions produced constitutions that expanded democracy and the public role of the state. The new documents guaranteed the political and civil rights of African Americans, and they abolished property qualifications for officeholding and jury service, as well as imprisonment for debt. They created the first state-funded systems of education in the South, to be administered by state commissioners. The new constitutions also mandated establishment of orphanages, penitentiaries, and homes for the insane. The changes wrought in the South's political landscape seemed quite radical to many. In 1868, only three years after the end of the war, Republicans came to power in most of the southern states. By 1869, new constitutions had been ratified in all the old Confederate states. "These constitutions and governments," one South Carolina Democratic newspaper vowed bitterly, "will last just as long as the bayonets which ushered them into being, shall keep them in existence, and not one day longer."

Republican governments in the South faced a continual crisis of legitimacy that limited their ability to legislate change. They had to balance reform against the need to gain acceptance, especially by white Southerners. Their achievements were thus mixed. In the realm of race relations there was a clear thrust toward equal rights and against discrimination. Republican legislatures followed up the federal Civil Rights Act of 1866 with various antidiscrimination clauses in new constitutions and laws prescribing harsh penalties for civil rights violations. While most African Americans supported autonomous African American churches, fraternal societies, and schools, they insisted that the state be "color-blind." African Americans could now be employed in police forces and fire departments, serve on juries, school boards, and city councils, and they could hold public office at all levels of government.

Segregation, though, became the norm in public school systems. African American leaders often accepted segregation because they feared that insistence on integrated education would jeopardize funding for the new school systems. They generally agreed with Frederick Douglass that separate schools were "infinitely superior" to no schools at all. So while they opposed constitutional language requiring racial segregation in schools, most African Americans were less interested in the abstract ideal of integrated education than in ensuring educational opportunities for their children and employment for African American teachers. Many, in fact, believed all-black schools offered a better chance of securing these goals.

Patterns of discrimination persisted. Demands by African Americans to prohibit segregation in railroad cars, steamboats, theaters, and other public spaces revealed and heightened the divisions within the Republican Party. Moderate white Republicans feared such laws would only further alienate potential white supporters. But by the early 1870s, as black influence and assertiveness grew, laws guaranteeing equal access to transportation and public accommodation were passed in many states. By and large, though, such civil rights laws were difficult to enforce in local communities.

In economic matters, Republican governments failed to fulfill African Americans' hopes of obtaining land. Few former slaves possessed the cash to buy land in the open market, and they looked to the state for help. Republicans tried to weaken the plantation system and promote black ownership by raising taxes on land. Yet even when state governments seized land for nonpayment of taxes, the property was never used to help create black homesteads. In Mississippi, for example, 6 million acres, or about 20 percent of the land, had been forfeited by 1875. Yet virtually all of it found its way back to the original owners after they paid minimal penalties.

Republican leaders emphasized the "gospel of prosperity" as the key to improving the economic fortunes of all Southerners, black and white. Essentially, they envisioned promoting northern-style capitalist development—factories, large towns, and diversified agriculture—through state aid. Much Republican state lawmaking was devoted to encouraging railroad construction. Between 1868 and 1873 state legislatures passed hundreds of bills promoting railroads. Most of the government aid consisted not of direct cash subsidies but of official endorsements of a company's bonds. This government backing gave railroad companies credibility and helped them raise capital. In exchange, states received liens on railroads as security against defaults on payments to bondholders.

Between 1868 and 1872 the southern railroad system was rebuilt and over 3,000 new miles of track added, an increase of almost 40 percent. But in spite of all the new laws, it proved impossible to attract significant amounts of northern and European investment capital. The obsession with railroads withdrew resources from education and other programs. As in the North, it also opened the doors to widespread corruption and bribery of public officials. Finally, the frenzy of railroad promotion soon led to an overextension of credit and to many bankruptcies, saddling Republican governments with enormous debts. Railroad failures eroded public confidence in the Republicans' ability to govern. The "gospel of prosperity" ultimately failed to modernize the economy or solidify the Republican Party in the South.

White Resistance and "Redemption"

The emergence of a Republican Party in the reconstructed South brought two parties but not a two-party system to the region. The opponents of Reconstruction, the Democrats, refused to acknowledge Republicans' right to participate in southern political life. In their view, the Republican Party, supported primarily by the votes of former slaves, was the partisan instrument of the northern Congress. Since Republicans controlled state governments, this denial of legitimacy meant, in effect, a rejection of state authority itself. In each state, Republicans were split between those who urged conciliation in an effort to gain white acceptance and those who emphasized consolidating the party under the protection of the military.

From 1870 to 1872 the Ku Klux Klan fought an ongoing terrorist campaign against Reconstruction governments and local leaders. Although not centrally organized, the Klan was a powerful presence in nearly every southern state. It acted as a kind of guerrilla military force in the service of the Democratic Party, the planter class, and all those who sought the restoration of white supremacy. Klansmen employed violence to intimidate African Americans and white Republicans, murdering innocent people, driving them from their homes, and destroying their property. Planters sometimes employed Klansmen to enforce labor discipline by driving African Americans off plantations to deprive them of their harvest share.

In October 1870, after Republicans carried Laurens County in South Carolina, bands of white people drove 150 African Americans from their homes and murdered 13 black and white Republican activists. In March 1871, three African Americans were arrested in Meridian, Mississippi, for giving "incendiary" speeches. At their court hearing, Klansmen killed two of the defendants and the Republican judge, and thirty more African Americans were murdered in a day of rioting. The single bloodiest episode of Reconstruction era violence took place in Colfax, Louisiana, on Easter Sunday 1873. Nearly 100 African Americans were murdered after they failed to hold a besieged courthouse during a contested election. One former Confederate officer observed that the Klan's goal was "to defy the reconstructed State Governments, to treat them with contempt, and show that they have no real existence."

The Ku Klux Klan emerged as a potent political and social force during Reconstruction, terrorizing freed people and their white allies. An 1868 Klan warning threatens Louisiana governor Henry C. Warmoth with death. Warmoth, an Illinois-born "carpetbagger," was the state's first Republican governor. Two Alabama Klansmen, photographed in 1868, wear white hoods to hide their identities.

SOURCE: (a) University of North Carolina Southern Historical Collection; (b) Rutherford B. Hayes Presidential Center.

Southern Republicans looked to Washington for help. In 1870 and 1871 Congress passed three Enforcement Acts designed to counter racial terrorism. These declared that interference with voting was a federal offense. The acts provided for federal supervision of voting, and authorized the president to send the army and to suspend the writ of habeas corpus in districts declared to be in a state of insurrection. The most sweeping measure was the Ku Klux Klan Act of April 1871, which made the violent infringement of civil and political rights a federal crime punishable by the national government. Attorney General Amos T. Akerman prosecuted hundreds of Klansmen in North Carolina and Mississippi. In October 1871 President Grant sent federal troops to occupy nine South Carolina counties and rounded up thousands of Klan members. By the election of 1872, the federal government's intervention had helped break the Klan and restore a semblance of law and order.

The Civil Rights Act of 1875 outlawed racial discrimination in theaters, hotels, railroads, and other public places. But the law proved more an assertion of principle than a direct federal intervention in southern affairs. Enforcement required African Americans to take their cases to the federal courts, a costly and time-consuming procedure.

As wartime idealism faded, northern Republicans became less inclined toward direct intervention in southern affairs. They had enough trouble retaining political control in the North. In 1874 the Democrats gained a majority in the House of Representatives for the first time since 1856. Key northern states also began to fall to the Democrats. Northern Republicans slowly abandoned the freedmen and their white allies in the South. Southern Democrats were also able to exploit a deepening fiscal crisis by blaming Republicans for excessive extension of public credit and the sharp increase in tax rates. Republican governments had indeed spent public money for new state school systems, orphanages, roads, and other internal improvements.

Gradually, conservative Democrats "redeemed" one state after another. Virginia and Tennessee led the way in 1869, North Carolina in 1870, Georgia in 1871, Texas in 1873, and Alabama and Arkansas in 1874. In Mississippi, white conservatives employed violence and intimidation to wrest control in 1875 and "redeemed" the state the following year. Republican infighting in Louisiana in 1873 and 1874 led to a series of contested election results, including bloody clashes between black militia and armed whites, and finally to "redemption" by the Democrats in 1877. Once these states returned to Democratic rule, African Americans faced obstacles to voting, more stringent controls on plantation labor, and deep cuts in social services.

Several Supreme Court rulings involving the Fourteenth and Fifteenth Amendments effectively constrained federal protection of African American civil rights. In the so-called Slaughterhouse cases of 1873, the Court issued its first ruling on the Fourteenth Amendment. The cases involved a Louisiana charter that gave a New Orleans meat-packing company a monopoly over the city's butchering business on the grounds of protecting public health. A rival group of butchers had sued, claiming the law violated the Fourteenth Amendment, which prohibited states from depriving any person of life, liberty, or property without due process of law. The Court held that the Fourteenth Amendment protected only the former slaves, not butchers, and that it protected only national citizenship rights, not the regulatory powers of states. The ruling in effect denied the original intent of the Fourteenth Amendment—to protect against state infringement of national citizenship rights as spelled out in the Bill of Rights.

Three other decisions curtailed federal protection of black civil rights. In *United States* v. *Reese* (1876) and *United States* v. *Cruikshank* (1876), the Court restricted congressional power to enforce the Ku Klux Klan Act. Future prosecution would depend on the states rather than on federal authorities. In these rulings the Court held that the Fourteenth Amendment extended the federal power to protect civil rights only in cases involving discrimination by states; discrimination by individuals or groups was not covered. The Court also ruled that the Fifteenth Amendment did not guarantee a citizen's right to vote; it only barred certain specific grounds for denying suffrage—"race, color, or previous condition of servitude." This interpretation opened the door for southern states to disfranchise African Americans for allegedly nonracial reasons. States back under Democratic control began to limit African American voting by passing laws restricting voter eligibility through poll taxes and property requirements.

Finally, in the 1883 Civil Rights Cases decision, the Court declared the Civil Rights Act of 1875 unconstitutional, holding that the Fourteenth Amendment gave Congress the power to outlaw discrimination by states, but not by private individuals. The majority opinion held that black people must no longer "be the special favorite of the laws." Together, these Supreme Court decisions marked the end of federal attempts to protect African American rights until well into the next century.

White Yeomen, White Merchants, and "King Cotton"

The Republicans' vision of a "New South" remade along the lines of the northern economy failed to materialize. Instead, the South declined into the country's poorest agricultural region. Unlike midwestern and western farm towns burgeoning from trade in wheat, corn, and livestock, southern communities found themselves almost entirely dependent on the price of one commodity. Cotton growing had defined the economic life of large plantations in the coastal regions and black belt communities of the antebellum South. In the post–Civil War years "King Cotton" expanded its realm, as greater numbers of small white farmers found themselves forced to switch from subsistence crops to growing cotton for the market.

The triumph of "King Cotton" reflected the chronic shortage of capital and banking throughout the region. Large planters and town merchants were often the only sources of credit. They advanced loans and supplies to small owners, tenant farmers, and sharecroppers in exchange for a lien, or claim, on the year's cotton crop. The spread of the "crop lien" system as the South's main form of agricultural credit forced more and more farmers into cotton growing. "Cotton is the thing to get credit on in this country," one small farmer explained to a federal commission investigating commodity prices. "You can always sell cotton. You leave home with a wagon load of cotton and you will go home at night with money in your pocket."

The transition to cotton dependency developed unevenly, at different speeds in different parts of the South. Penetration by railroads, the availability of commercial fertilizers, and the opening up of new lands to

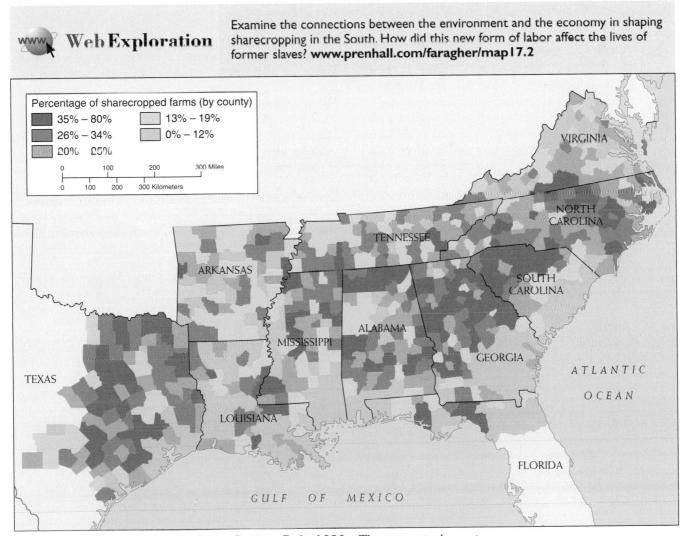

Web Exploration   Examine the connections between the environment and the economy in shaping sharecropping in the South. How did this new form of labor affect the lives of former slaves? **www.prenhall.com/faragher/map17.2**

Percentage of sharecropped farms (by county)

- 35% – 80%
- 26% – 34%
- 20% – 25%
- 13% – 19%
- 0% – 12%

Southern Sharecropping and the Cotton Belt, 1880   The economic depression of the 1870s forced increasing numbers of southern farmers, both white and black, into sharecropping arrangements. Sharecropping was most pervasive in the cotton belt regions of South Carolina, Georgia, Alabama, Mississippi, and east Texas.

cultivation were key factors in transforming communities from diversified, locally oriented farming to the market-oriented production of cotton. In the South Carolina upcountry, for example, cotton farmers had produced 170,000 bales in 1860; the ravages of war and its aftermath had reduced that figure to 99,000 in 1870. But by 1880 the figure had jumped to 284,000, and by 1890 to 387,000. In the South overall, white farmers had grown only 10 percent of the cotton in 1860; by the mid-1870s they were growing 40 percent of the total, much of it on small farms of 200 acres or less.

The pent-up demand for cotton following the war brought high prices (as much as 43 cents per pound) through the late 1860s. But as the "crop lien" system spread, and as more and more farmers turned to cotton growing as the only way to obtain credit, expanding production depressed prices. Competition from new cotton centers in the world market, such as Egypt and India, accelerated the downward spiral. As cotton prices declined alarmingly, to roughly 11 cents per pound in 1875 to 5 cents by the early 1890s, per capita wealth in the South fell steadily, equaling only one-third that of the East, Midwest, or West by the 1890s. Merchants and planters frequently charged exorbitant interest rates on advances, as well as marking up the prices of the goods they sold in their stores. Taking advantage of the high illiteracy rates among poor Southerners, landlords and merchants easily altered their books to inflate the figures. At the end of the year, sharecroppers and tenants found themselves deep in debt to stores for seed, supplies, and clothing. Despite hard work and even bountiful harvests, few small farmers could escape from heavy debt. Small farmers caught up in a vicious cycle of low cotton prices, debt, and dwindling food crops found their old ideal of independence sacrificed to the cruel logic of the cotton market. When asked how he had fallen into this trap, cotton farmer J. Pope Brown impatiently testified to investigators: "We were poor, had nothing to go on, had no collateral, and we just had to plant the crop that would bring money right away. We did not have time to wait."

By 1880, nearly 40 percent of all Southern farms were operated by tenants and sharecroppers. About one-third of the white farmers and nearly three-quarters of the African American farmers in the cotton states were sharecroppers or tenants. To obtain precious credit, most found themselves forced to produce cotton for market and thus became enmeshed in the debt-ridden crop lien system. In traditional cotton producing areas, especially the black belt, landless farmers growing cotton had replaced slaves growing cotton. In the upcountry and newer areas of cultivation, cotton-dominated commercial agriculture, with landless tenants and sharecroppers as the main workforce, had replaced the more diversified subsistence economy of the antebellum era.

One class of white Southerners benefiting from these arrangements were local merchants. As hundreds of new villages (communities of less than 2,500 people) sprang up in every corner of the South, especially in the new upcountry and Piedmont settlements, local merchants provided both goods and credit for local farmers. In 1866, for example, the mercantile firm of Smith and Melton opened for business in the up-country town of Chester, South Carolina. By 1869 it was advancing some $20,000 per year in credit and supplies to Chester farmers, and could boast over $100,000 in financial backing. By marketing local cotton crops, merchants also served as middlemen between small towns and the larger national economy.

With their power based on control of credit and marketing, merchants emerged as a new economic elite unconnected to the antebellum planters whose power had rested on the ownership of land and slaves. But within both the new towns and the old planter elite, white families increasingly defined their social position by celebrating a certain type of ideal household. Women found meaning in their role as upholders of domestic virtue by creating a comfortable home environment and tending to the needs of children and husbands. Men were to be of strong moral fiber and to provide material support for the family. These elite ideals, articulated in magazines, schools, sermons, and other public discourse, rested on a belief that one's ability to reach the standards of womanhood and manhood rested solely upon moral character and individual choice.

RECONSTRUCTING THE NORTH

Abraham Lincoln liked to cite his own rise as proof of the superiority of the northern system of "free labor" over slavery. "There is no permanent class of hired laborers amongst us," Lincoln asserted. "Twenty-five years ago, I was a hired laborer. The hired laborer of yesterday, labors on his own account today; and will hire others to labor for him tomorrow. Advancement—improvement in condition—is the order of things in a society of equals." But the triumph of the North brought with it fundamental changes in the economy, labor relations, and politics that brought Lincoln's ideal vision into question. The spread of the factory system, the growth of large and powerful corporations, and the rapid expansion of capitalist enterprise all hastened the development of a large unskilled and routinized workforce. Rather than becoming independent producers, more and more workers found themselves consigned permanently to wage labor.

The old Republican ideal of a society bound by a harmony of interests had become overshadowed by a grimmer reality of class conflict. A violent national railroad strike in 1877 was broken only with the direct intervention of federal troops. That conflict struck many Americans as a turning point. Northern society, like the society of the South, appeared more hierarchical than equal. That same year the last federal troops withdrew from their southern posts, marking the end of the Reconstruction era. By then, the North had undergone its own "reconstruction" as well.

The Age of Capital

In the decade following Appomattox, the North's economy continued the industrial boom begun during the Civil War. By 1873, America's industrial production had grown 75 percent over the 1865 level. By that time, too, the number of nonagricultural workers in the North had surpassed the number of farmers. Between 1860 and 1880 the number of wage earners in manufacturing and construction more than doubled, from 2 million to over 4 million. Only Great Britain boasted a larger manufacturing economy than the United States. During the same period, nearly 3 million immigrants arrived in America, almost all of whom settled in the North and West.

The railroad business both symbolized and advanced the new industrial order. Shortly before the Civil War, enthusiasm mounted for a transcontinental line. Private companies took on the huge and expensive job of construction, but the federal government funded the project, providing the largest subsidy in American history. The Pacific Railway Act of 1862 granted the Union Pacific and the Central Pacific rights to a broad swath of land extending from Omaha, Nebraska, to Sacramento, California. An 1864 act bestowed a subsidy of $15,000 per mile of track laid over smooth plains country and varying larger amounts up to $48,000 per mile in the foothills and mountains of the Far West. The Union Pacific employed gangs of Irish American and African American workers to lay track heading west from Omaha, while the Central

Pacific brought in more than 10,000 men from China to handle the difficult work in the Sierra Nevada mountain region.

On May 10, 1869, Leland Stanford, the former governor of California and president of the Central Pacific Railroad, traveled to Promontory Point in Utah Territory to hammer a ceremonial golden spike, marking the finish of the first transcontinental line. Other railroads went up with less fanfare. The Southern Pacific, chartered by the state of California, stretched from San Francisco to Los Angeles, and on through Arizona and New Mexico to connections with New Orleans. The Atchison, Topeka, and Santa Fe reached the Pacific in 1887 by way of a southerly route across the Rocky Mountains. The Great Northern, one of the few lines financed by private capital, extended west from St. Paul, Minnesota, to Washington's Puget Sound.

Railroads paved the way for the rapid settlement of the West, and both rural and urban areas grew dramatically over the next several decades. The combined population of Minnesota, the Dakotas, Nebraska, and Kansas, for example, jumped from 300,000 in 1860 to over 2 million in 1880. In the fifty years after 1870, the nation's railroad system expanded to more than a quarter million miles—more than all the rest of the world's railroad track combined.

Completion of the transcontinental railroad, May 10, 1869, as building crews for the Union Pacific and Central Pacific meet at Promontory Point, Utah. The two locomotive engineers salute each other, while the chief engineers for the two railroads shake hands. Construction had begun simultaneously from Omaha and Sacramento in 1863, with the help of generous subsidies from Congress. Work crews, consisting of thousands of ex-soldiers, Irish immigrants, and imported Chinese laborers, laid nearly 1,800 miles of new track.

SOURCE: The Granger Collection, New York (4E377.23).

Railroad corporations became America's first big businesses. Railroads required huge outlays of investment capital, and their growth increased the economic power of banks and investment houses centered in Wall Street. Bankers often gained seats on the boards of directors of these railroad companies, and their access to capital sometimes gave them the real control of railways. By the early 1870s the Pennsylvania Railroad stood as the nation's largest single company, with more than 20,000 employees. A new breed of aggressive entrepreneur sought to ease cutthroat competition by absorbing smaller companies and forming "pools" that set rates and divided the market. A small group of railroad executives, including Cornelius Vanderbilt, Jay Gould, Collis P. Huntington, and James J. Hill, amassed unheard-of fortunes. When he died in 1877, Vanderbilt left his son $100 million. By comparison, a decent annual wage for working a six-day week was around $350.

A growing number of Republican politicians maintained close connections with railroad interests. Railroad promoters, lawyers, and lobbyists became ubiquitous figures in Washington and state capitals, wielding enormous influence among lawmakers. "The galleries and lobbies of every legislature," one Republican leader noted, "are thronged with men seeking . . . an advantage." Railroads benefited enormously from government subsidies. Between 1862 and 1872, Congress alone awarded more than 100 million acres of public lands to railroad companies and provided them over $64 million in loans and tax incentives.

Some of the nation's most prominent politicians routinely accepted railroad largesse. Republican senator William M. Stewart of Nevada, a member of the Committee on Pacific Railroads, received a gift of 50,000 acres of land from the Central Pacific for his services. Senator Lyman Trumbull of Illinois took an annual retainer from the Illinois Central. The worst scandal of the Grant administration grew out of corruption involving railroad promotion. As a way of diverting funds for the building of the Union Pacific Railroad, an inner circle of Union Pacific stockholders created the dummy Crédit Mobilier construction company. In return for political favors, a group of prominent Republicans received stock in the company. When the scandal broke in 1872, it politically ruined Vice President Schuyler Colfax and led to the censure of two congressmen.

Other industries also boomed in this period, especially those engaged in extracting minerals and processing natural resources. Railroad growth stimulated expansion in the production of coal, iron, stone, and lumber, and these also received significant government aid. For example, under the National Mineral Act of 1866, mining companies received millions of acres of free public land. Oil refining enjoyed a huge expansion in the 1860s and 1870s. As with railroads, an early pe-

riod of fierce competition soon gave way to concentration. By the late 1870s, John D. Rockefeller's Standard Oil Company controlled almost 90 percent of the nation's oil-refining capacity. The production of pig iron tripled from 1 million tons in 1865 to 3 million tons in 1873. Between 1869 and 1879 both the capital investment and the number of workers in iron nearly doubled. Coal production shot up from 17 million tons in 1861 to 72 million tons in 1880. The size of individual ironworks and coal mines—measured by the number of employees and capital invested—also grew in these years, reflecting the expanding scale of industrial enterprise as a whole.

Liberal Republicans and the Election of 1872

With the rapid growth of large-scale, capital-intensive enterprises, Republicans increasingly identified with the interests of business rather than the rights of freedmen or the antebellum ideology of "free labor." The old Civil War–era Radical Republicans had declined in influence. State Republican parties now organized themselves around the spoils of federal patronage rather than grand causes such as preserving the Union or ending slavery. Despite the Crédit Mobilier affair, Republicans had no monopoly on political scandal. In 1871 New York City newspapers reported the shocking story of how Democratic Party boss William M. Tweed and his friends had systematically stolen tens of millions from the city treasury. The "Tweed Ring" had received enormous bribes and kickbacks from city contractors and businessmen. Grotesquely caricatured by Thomas Nast's cartoons in *Harper's Weekly*, Tweed emerged as the preeminent national symbol of increasingly degraded and dishonest urban politics. But to many, the scandal represented only the most extreme case of the routine corruption that now plagued American political life.

By the end of President Grant's first term, a large number of disaffected Republicans sought an alternative. They were led by a small but influential number of intellectuals, professionals, businessmen, and reformers who articulated an ideology that helped reshape late nineteenth-century politics. The Liberal Republicans, as they called themselves, shared several core values. First, they emphasized the doctrines of classical economics, stressing the law of supply and demand, free trade, defense of property rights, and individualism. They called for a return to limited government, arguing that bribery, scandal, and high taxes all flowed from excessive state interference in the economy.

Liberal Republicans were also suspicious of expanding democracy. "Universal suffrage," Charles Francis Adams Jr. wrote in 1869, "can only mean in plain English the government of ignorance and vice—it means a European, and especially Celtic, proletariat on the Atlantic coast, an African proletariat on the shores of the Gulf, and a Chinese proletariat on the Pacific." Liberal Republicans believed that politics ought to be the province of "the best men"—educated and well-to-do men like themselves, devoted to the "science of government." They proposed civil service reform as the best way to break the hold of party machines on patronage. Competitive examinations, they argued, were the best way to choose employees for government posts. At a time when only a very small fraction of Americans attended college, this requirement would severely restrict the pool of government workers.

Although most Liberal Republicans had enthusiastically supported abolition, the Union cause, and equal rights for freedmen, they now opposed continued federal intervention in the South. The national government had done all it could for the former slaves; they must now take care of themselves. "Root, Hog, or Die" was the harsh advice offered by Horace Greeley, editor of the *New York Tribune*. In the spring of 1872 a diverse collection of Liberal Republicans nominated Greeley to run for president. A longtime foe of the Democratic Party, Greeley nonetheless won that party's presidential nomination as well. He made a new policy for the South the center of his campaign against Grant. The "best men" of both sections, he argued, should support a more generous Reconstruction policy based on "universal amnesty and impartial suffrage." All Americans, Greeley urged, must put the Civil War behind them and "clasp hands across the bloody chasm."

Grant easily defeated Greeley, carrying every state in the North and winning 56 percent of the popular vote. Most Republicans were not willing to abandon the regular party organization, and "waving the bloody shirt" was still a potent vote-getter. But the 1872 election accelerated the trend toward federal abandonment of African American citizenship rights. The Liberal Republicans quickly faded as an organized political force. But their ideas helped define a growing conservative consciousness among the northern public. For the rest of the century, their political and economic views attracted a growing number of middle-class professionals and businessmen. This agenda included retreat from the ideal of racial justice, hostility toward trade unions, suspicion of working-class and immigrant political power,

celebration of competitive individualism, and opposition to government intervention in economic affairs.

The Depression of 1873

In the fall of 1873 the postwar boom came to an abrupt halt as a severe financial panic triggered a deep economic depression. The collapse resulted from commercial overexpansion, especially speculative investing in the nation's railroad system. The investment banking house of Jay Cooke and Company failed in September 1873 when it found itself unable to market millions of dollars in Northern Pacific Railroad bonds. Soon other banks and brokerage houses, especially those dealing in railroad securities, caved in as well, and the New York Stock Exchange suspended operations. By 1876 half the nation's railroads had defaulted on their bonds. Over the next two years more than 100 banks folded and 18,000 businesses shut their doors. The depression that began in 1873 lasted sixty-five months—the longest economic contraction in the nation's history until then.

The human toll of the depression was enormous. As factories began to close across the nation, the unemployment rate soared to about 15 percent. In many cities the jobless rate was much higher; roughly one-quarter of New York City workers were unemployed in 1874. Many thousands of men took to the road in search of work, and the "tramp" emerged as a new and

"The Tramp," *Harper's Weekly*, September 2, 1876. The depression that began in 1873 forced many thousands of unemployed workers to go "on the tramp" in search of jobs. Men wandered from town to town, walking or riding railroad cars, desperate for a chance to work for wages or simply for room and board. The "tramp" became a powerful symbol of the misery caused by industrial depression and, as in this drawing, an image that evoked fear and nervousness among the nation's middle class.

SOURCE: The Picture Bank, Frank & Marie Therese Wood Print Collection.

menacing figure on the social landscape. The Pennsylvania Bureau of Labor Statistics noted that never before had "so many of the working classes, skilled and unskilled . . . been moving from place to place seeking employment that was not to be had." Farmers were also hard hit by the depression. Agricultural output continued to grow, but prices and land values fell sharply. As prices for their crops fell, farmers had a more difficult time repaying their fixed loan obligations; many sank deeper into debt.

During the winter of 1873, New York labor leaders demanded to know what measures would be taken "to relieve the necessities of the 10,000 homeless and hungry men and women of our city whose urgent appeals have apparently been disregarded by our public servants." Mass meetings of workers in New York and other cities issued calls to government officials to create jobs through public works. But these appeals were rejected. Indeed, many business leaders and political figures denounced even meager efforts at charity. E. L. Godkin wrote in the Christmas 1875 issue of *The Nation* that "free soup must be prohibited, and all classes must learn that soup of any kind, beef or turtle, can be had only by being paid for." Men such as Godkin saw the depression as a natural, if painful, part of the business cycle, one that would allow only the strongest enterprises (and workers) to survive. They dismissed any attempts at government interference, in the form of either job creation or relief for the poor.

Increased tensions, sometimes violent, between labor and capital reinforced the feeling of many Americans that the nation was no longer immune from European-style class conflict. The depression of the 1870s prompted workers and farmers to question the old free-labor ideology that celebrated a harmony of interests in northern society. More people voiced anger at and distrust of large corporations that exercised great economic power from outside their communities. Businessmen and merchants, meanwhile, especially in large cities, became more conscious of their own class interests. New political organizations such as Chicago's Citizens' Association united businessmen in campaigns for fiscal conservatism and defense of property rights. In national politics, the persistent depression made the Republican Party, north and south, more vulnerable than ever.

The Electoral Crisis of 1876

With the economy mired in depression, Democrats looked forward to capturing the White House in 1876. New scandals plaguing the Grant administration also weakened the Republican Party. In 1875, a conspiracy surfaced between distillers and U.S. revenue agents to cheat the government out of millions in tax revenues. The government secured indictments against more than 200 members of this "Whiskey Ring," including Orville E. Babcock, Grant's private secretary. Though acquitted, thanks to Grant's intervention, Babcock resigned in disgrace. In 1876, Secretary of War William W. Belknap was impeached for receiving bribes for the sale of trading posts in Indian Territory, and he resigned to avoid conviction.

Though Grant himself was never implicated in any wrongdoing, Democrats hammered away at his administration's low standard of honesty in government. For president they nominated Governor Samuel J. Tilden of New York, who brought impeccable reform credentials to his candidacy. In 1871 he had helped expose and prosecute the "Tweed Ring" in New York City. As governor he had toppled the "Canal Ring," a graft-ridden scheme involving inflated contracts for repairs on the Erie Canal. In their platform, the Democrats linked the issue of corruption to an attack on Reconstruction policies. They blamed the Republicans for instituting "a corrupt centralism" that subjected southern states to "the rapacity of carpetbag tyrannies," riddled the national government "with incapacity, waste, and fraud," and "locked fast the prosperity of an industrious people in the paralysis of hard times."

Republican nominee Rutherford B. Hayes, governor of Ohio, also sought the high ground. As a lawyer in Cincinnati he had defended runaway slaves. Later he had distinguished himself as a general in the Union

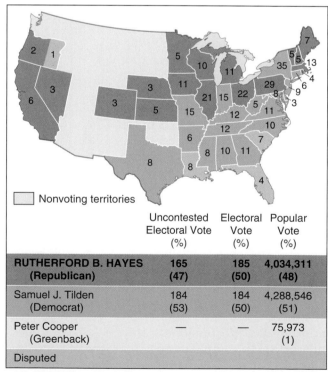

	Uncontested Electoral Vote (%)	Electoral Vote (%)	Popular Vote (%)
RUTHERFORD B. HAYES (Republican)	**165 (47)**	**185 (50)**	**4,034,311 (48)**
Samuel J. Tilden (Democrat)	184 (53)	184 (50)	4,288,546 (51)
Peter Cooper (Greenback)	—	—	75,973 (1)
Disputed			

Nonvoting territories

The Election of 1876 The presidential election of 1876 left the nation without a clear-cut winner.

CHRONOLOGY

1865 Freedmen's Bureau established

Abraham Lincoln assassinated

Andrew Johnson begins Presidential Reconstruction

Black codes begin to be enacted in southern states

Thirteenth Amendment ratified

1866 Civil Rights Act passed

Congress approves Fourteenth Amendment

Ku Klux Klan founded

1867 Reconstruction Acts, passed over President Johnson's veto, begin Congressional Reconstruction

Tenure of Office Act

Southern states call constitutional conventions

1868 President Johnson impeached by the House, but acquitted in Senate trial

Fourteenth Amendment ratified

Most southern states readmitted to Union

Ulysses S. Grant elected president

1869 Congress approves Fifteenth Amendment

Union Pacific and Central Pacific tracks meet at Promontory Point in Utah Territory

Suffragists split into National Woman Suffrage Association and American Woman Suffrage Association

1870 Fifteenth Amendment ratified

1871 Ku Klux Klan Act passed

"Tweed Ring" in New York City exposed

1872 Liberal Republicans break with Grant and Radicals, nominate Horace Greeley for president

Crédit Mobilier scandal

Grant reelected president

1873 Financial panic and beginning of economic depression

Slaughterhouse cases

1874 Democrats gain control of House for first time since 1856

1875 Civil Rights Act

1876 Disputed election between Samuel Tilden and Rutherford B. Hayes

1877 Electoral Commission elects Hayes president

President Hayes dispatches federal troops to break Great Railroad Strike and withdraws last remaining federal troops from the South

---

army. Republicans charged Tilden with disloyalty during the war, income tax evasion, and close relations with powerful railroad interests. Hayes promised, if elected, to support an efficient civil service system, to vigorously prosecute officials who betrayed the public trust, and to introduce a system of free universal education.

On an election day marred by widespread vote fraud and violent intimidation, Tilden received 250,000 more popular votes than Hayes. But Republicans refused to concede victory, challenging the vote totals in the electoral college. Tilden garnered 184 uncontested electoral votes, one shy of the majority required to win, while Hayes received 165. The problem centered in 20 disputed votes from Florida, Louisiana, South Carolina,

and Oregon. In each of the three southern states two sets of electoral votes were returned. In Oregon, which Hayes had unquestionably carried, the Democratic governor nevertheless replaced a disputed Republican elector with a Democrat.

The crisis was unprecedented. In January 1877 Congress moved to settle the deadlock, establishing an Electoral Commission composed of five senators, five representatives, and five Supreme Court justices; eight were Republicans and seven were Democrats. The commission voted along strict partisan lines to award all the contested electoral votes to Hayes. Outraged by this decision, Democratic congressmen threatened a filibuster to block Hayes's inauguration. Violence and stalemate were avoided when Democrats and Republicans struck a compromise in February. In return for Hayes's ascendance to the presidency, the Republicans promised to appropriate more money for southern internal improvements, to appoint a Southerner to Hayes's cabinet, and to pursue a policy of noninterference ("home rule") in southern affairs.

Shortly after assuming office, Hayes ordered removal of the remaining federal troops in Louisiana and South Carolina. Without this military presence to sustain them, the Republican governors of those two states quickly lost power to Democrats. "Home rule" meant Republican abandonment of freed people, Radicals, carpetbaggers, and scalawags. It also effectively nullified the Fourteenth and Fifteenth Amendments and the Civil Rights Act of 1866. The "Compromise of 1877" completed repudiation of the idea, born during the Civil War and pursued during Congressional Reconstruction, of a powerful federal government protecting the rights of all American citizens. As one black Louisianan lamented, "The whole South—every state in the South—had got into the hands of the very men that held us slaves." Other voices hailed this turning point in policy. "The negro," declared *The Nation*, "will disappear from the field of national politics. Henceforth, the nation, as a nation, will have nothing more to do with him."

CONCLUSION

Reconstruction succeeded in the limited political sense of reuniting a nation torn apart by the Civil War. The Radical Republican vision, emphasizing racial justice, equal civil and political rights guaranteed by the Four-teenth and Fifteenth Amendments, and a new southern economy organized around independent small farmers, never enjoyed the support of the majority of its party or the northern public. By 1877 the political force of these ideals was spent and the national retreat from them nearly complete.

The end of Reconstruction left the way open for the return of white domination in the South. The freed people's political and civil equality proved only temporary. It would take a "Second Reconstruction," the civil rights movement of the next century, to establish full black citizenship rights once and for all. The federal government's failure to pursue land reform left former slaves without the economic independence needed for full emancipation. Yet the newly autonomous black family, along with black-controlled churches, schools, and other social institutions, provided the foundations for the modern African American community. If the federal government was not yet fully committed to protecting equal rights in local communities, the Reconstruction era at least pointed to how that goal might be achieved. Even as the federal government retreated from the defense of equal rights for black people, it took a more aggressive stance as the protector of business interests. The Hayes administration responded decisively to one of the worst outbreaks of class violence in American history by dispatching federal troops to several northern cities to break the Great Railroad Strike of 1877. In the aftermath of Reconstruction, the struggle between capital and labor had clearly replaced "the southern question" as the number one political issue of the day. "The overwhelming labor question has dwarfed all other questions into nothing," wrote an Ohio Republican. "We have home questions enough to occupy attention now."

REVIEW QUESTIONS

1. How did various visions of a "reconstructed" South differ? How did these visions reflect the old political and social divisions that had led to the Civil War?
2. What key changes did emancipation make in the political and economic status of African Americans? Discuss the expansion of citizenship rights in the post–Civil War years. To what extent did women share in the gains made by African Americans?
3. What role did such institutions as the family, the church, the schools, and the political parties play in the African American transition to freedom?
4. How did white Southerners attempt to limit the freedom of former slaves? How did these efforts succeed, and how did they fail?
5. Evaluate the achievements and failures of Reconstruction governments in the southern states.
6. What were the crucial economic changes occurring in the North and South during the Reconstruction era?

RECOMMENDED READING

Paul A. Cimbala and Randall M. Miller, eds., *The Freedmen's Bureau and Reconstruction* (1999). Pays special attention to recapturing the historical voices of freed people.

Jane Dailey, *Before Jim Crow: The Politics of Race in Post Emancipation Virginia* (2000). Focuses on the tension between the drive to establish white supremacy and the struggle for biracial coalitions.

Laura F. Edwards, *Gendered Strife & Confusion: The Political Culture of Reconstruction* (1997). Analyzes how gender ideologies played a role in shaping party politics and social relations.

Michael W. Fitzgerald, *The Union League Movement in the Deep South* (1989). Examines race relations and the close connections between politics and economic change in the post–Civil War South.

Eric Foner, *Reconstruction: America's Unfinished Revolution, 1863–1877* (1988). Comprehensive and thoroughly researched overview of the Reconstruction era.

William Gillette, *Retreat from Reconstruction: A Political History, 1867–1878* (1979). Covers the national political scene.

Jacqueline Jones, *Labor of Love, Labor of Sorrow* (1985). Excellent material on the work and family lives of African American women.

Leon Litwack, *Been in the Storm So Long: The Aftermath of Slavery* (1979). A detailed analysis of the transition from slavery to freedom.

Scott Reynolds Nelson, *Iron Confederacies: Southern Railways, Klan Violence, and Reconstruction* (1999). Analysis of how conservative southern and northern business interests rebuilt the South's railroad system.

Edward Royce, *The Origins of Southern Sharecropping* (1993). Explains how sharecropping emerged as the dominant form of agricultural labor in the post–Civil War South.

▶ MEDIA RESOURCES

U.S. HISTORY DOCUMENTS CD-ROM

Reconstruction

16-1 "Address from the Colored Citizens of Norfolk, Virginia, to the People of the United States" (1865)

16-2 Carl Schurz, Report on the Condition of the South (1865)

16-3 Clinton B. Fisk, Plain Counsels for Freedmen (1865)

16-4 Mississippi Black Code (1865)

16-5 James C. Beecher, Report on Land Reform in the South Carolina Islands (1865, 1866)

16-6 The Memphis Riot (1866)

16-7 The Fourteenth Amendment (1868)

16-8 Albion W. Tourgee, Letter on Ku Klux Klan Activities (1870)

16-9 The Nation, "The State of the South" (1872)

16-10 Susan B. Anthony and the "New Departure" for Women (1873)

COMPANION WEBSITE HIGHLIGHTS

To view an exploration, enter one of the URLs below in your browser.

Web Explorations

Reconstruction of the South, 1866–1877
http://www.prenhall.com/faragher/map17.1

Southern Sharecropping and the Cotton Belt, 1880
http://www.prenhall.com/faragher/map17.2

Additional Interactive Maps

To access the maps, go to this chapter's resources at
http://www.prenhall.com/faragher

The Barrow Plantation, Oglethorpe County, Georgia, 1860 and 1881, page 513

The Election of 1876, page 524

HISTORY RESOURCE CENTER

To find the resources listed below, go to
http://www.prenhall.com/historyresourcecenter

Documents

A Sharecrop Contract (1882)

James T. Rapier, Testimony before U.S. Senate Regarding the Agricultural Labor Force in the South (1880)

The Fourteenth Amendment (1868)

Images

"From The Plantation to the Senate"

"The Shackle Broken"

1868 Democratic National Convention in New York City

Massacre at New Orleans

Thaddeus Stevens

Turn to the next page for the *Exploring America* activity for this chapter.

EXPLORING AMERICA

DID RECONSTRUCTION WORK FOR THE FREED PEOPLE?

http://www.prenhall.com/faragher/reconstruction

The emancipation of African Americans during the Civil War raised issues regarding what would happen to the freed people after the return of peace. How would African Americans cope with freedom? How would southerners respond? What role should the federal government play in reconstructing the South and helping African Americans? How should the South be reconstructed and what role should African Americans play in this process? *Did Reconstruction Work for the Freed People?* seeks to answer this important question and many others raised by the consequences of the Civil War. The module uses the Freedmen's Bureau to relate the complex, often violent story of the African American experience during Reconstruction against the backdrop of the political struggles that characterized this pivotal period in U.S. history.

Did Reconstruction Work for the Freed People?

approaches the issue of African American freedom from various perspectives, indicating the politics that influenced the answering of this question. The visual, print, and video sources are tied together by the narrative and focus on the Freedmen's Bureau, but they also

show that the end of the Civil War did not mean the return of peace or the changing of attitudes and practices regarding race and African Americans. Equally important, the module indicates that the process of Reconstruction in its several manifestations still had a long road to travel when it ended in 1877.

Reflect and Respond

In 1880, three years after the withdrawal of federal troops from the former Confederacy, Frederick Dou-

glass assessed the situation of freed men and women.

Douglass had escaped from slavery in the early 1840s, had become a noted abolitionist and newspaper editor, and had campaigned vigorously for both emancipation and the use of black troops. His dismay is palpable:

> *Today, in most of the Southern States, the fourteenth and fifteenth amendments are virtually nullified....*
>
> *In the hurry and confusion of the hour, and the eager desire to have the Union restored, there was more care for the sublime superstructure of the republic than for the solid foundation upon which it could alone be upheld. . . . He who can say to his fellow-man, "You shall serve me or starve," is a master and his subject is a slave. . . .*

Use the first-hand accounts and other materials here to assess Douglas' analysis.

1. Was the "former slave completely in the power of the old master"? If so, how did this happen?
2. What "solid foundation" might have enabled the freed men and women and the "honorable" statesmen who wished to help them to achieve the rights promised them in the fourteenth and fifteenth amendments?

✓ Check it out

Petition, {CityPoint? Virginia, May or June 1865}

This petition by discharged African American Union soldiers presents their view of what was promised them for fighting in the Civil War. It provides a window into the hopes and dreams of African Americans facing the prospect of freedom.

This exploration is also available on the *Exploring America* CD-ROM.

EIGHTEEN
CONQUEST AND SURVIVAL

▶ The Trans-Mississippi West, 1860-1900

Emigrants to the American West. Colored engraving, 19th century. John Gast, *American Progress.*
SOURCE: The Granger Collection, New York (009675/4E645.28).

The Oklahoma Land Rush

DECADES AFTER THE EVENT, COWBOY EVAN G. BARNARD VIVIDLY recalled the preparations made by settlers when Oklahoma territorial officials announced the opening of No Man's Land to the biggest "land rush" in American history. "Thousands of people gathered along the border. . . . As the day for the race drew near, the settlers practiced running their horses and driving carts." Finally the morning of April 22, 1889, arrived. "At ten o'clock people lined up . . . ready for the great race of their lives." Like many others, Barnard displayed his guns prominently on his hips, determined to discourage competitors from claiming the 160 acres of prime land that he intended to grab for himself.

Evan Barnard's story was one strand in the larger tale of the destruction and creation of communities in the trans-Mississippi West. In the 1830s, the federal government designated what was to become the state of Oklahoma as Indian Territory, reserved for the Five Civilized Tribes (Cherokees, Chickasaws, Choctaws, Creeks, and Seminoles) that had been forcibly removed from their eastern lands. All five tribes had reestablished themselves as sovereign republics in Indian Territory. The Cherokees and Chocktaws became prosperous cotton growers. The Creeks managed large herds of hogs and cattle, and the Chickasaws grazed not only cattle but sheep and goats on their open fields. The Five Tribes also ran sawmills, gristmills, and cotton gins. Indian merchants were soon dealing with other tribespeople as well as licensed white traders and even contracting with the federal government.

The Civil War, however, took a heavy toll on their success. Some tribes, slaveholders themselves, sided with the Confederacy; others with the Union. When the war ended, more than 10,000 people—nearly one-fifth of the population of Indian Territory—had died. To make matters worse, new treaties required the Five Civilized Tribes to cede the entire western half of the territory, including the former northern Indian territory of Nebraska and Kansas, for the resettlement of tribes from other regions.

Western Oklahoma thereby became home to thousands of newly displaced peoples, including the Pawnees, Peorias, Ottawas, Wyandots, and Miamis. Many small tribes readily took to farming and rebuilt their communities. But the nomadic, buffalo-hunting Kiowas, Cheyennes, Comanches, and Arapahoes did not settle so peacefully. They continued to traverse the plains until the U.S. Army finally forced them onto reservations. Eventually, more than 80,000 tribespeople were living on twenty-one separate reservations in western Oklahoma, all governed by agents appointed by the federal government.

The opening of the unassigned far western district of Oklahoma known as No Man's Land to non-Indian homesteading, however, signaled the impending end of Indian sovereignty. Many non-Indians saw this almost 2 million acre strip as a Promised Land, perfect for dividing into thousands of small farms. African Americans, many of whom were former slaves of Indian planters, appealed to the federal government for the right to stake claims there. Another group of would-be homesteaders, known as "Boomers," quickly tired of petitioning and invaded the district in 1880, only to be booted out by the Tenth Cavalry. Meanwhile, the railroads, seeing the potential for lucrative commerce, put constant pressure on the federal government to open No Man's Land for settlement. In 1889 the U.S. Congress finally gave in.

Cowboy Barnard was just one of thousands to pour into No Man's Land on April 22, 1889. Many homesteaders simply crossed the border from Kansas. Southerners, dispossessed by warfare and economic ruin in their own region, were also well represented. Market-minded settlers claimed the land nearest the railroads, and by nightfall of April 22 they had set up tent cities along the tracks. In a little over two months, after 6,000 homestead claims had been filed, the first sod houses appeared, sheltering growing communities of non-Indian farmers, ranchers, and other entrepreneurs.

Dramatic as it was, the land rush of 1889 was only one in a series of events that soon dispossessed Oklahoma's Indians of their remaining lands. First, the federal government broke up the estates held collectively by various tribes in western Oklahoma, assigning to individuals the standard 160-acre allotment and allowing non-Indian homesteaders to claim the rest. Then, in 1898, Congress passed the Curtis Act, formally dissolving Indian Territory and dispossessing the Five Tribes. Members of the former Indian nations were directed to dismantle their governments, abandon their estates, and join the ranks of other homesteaders. They nevertheless retained many of their tribal customs and managed to regain their sovereign status in 1977.

Later generations of Oklahomans often celebrated their his-

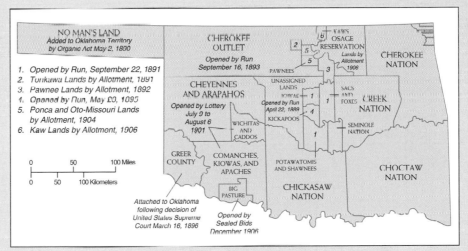

Oklahoma Territory Land openings to settlers came at different times, making new land available through various means.

toric ties to the Indian nations. At formal ceremonies marking statehood, just before the newly elected governor took the oath of office, a mock wedding ceremony united a tough and virile cowboy with a demure and submissive Indian maiden. By this time, in 1907, tribespeople were outnumbered in Oklahoma by ten to one.

By this time also, nearly one-quarter of the entire population of the United States lived west of the Mississippi River. Hundreds of new communities, supported primarily by cattle ranching, agriculture, mining, or other industries, had not only grown with the emerging national economy but helped to shape it in the process. The newcomers displaced communities that had formed centuries earlier. They also drastically transformed the physical landscape. Through their activities and the support of Easterners, the United States realized an ambition that John L. O'Sullivan had described in 1845 as the nation's "manifest destiny to overspread the continent" and remake it in a new image. ∎

KEY TOPICS

- The impact of western expansion on Indian societies

- The West as an "internal empire" and the development of new technologies and new industries

- The creation of new communities and the displacement of old communities

- The West as myth and legend

INDIAN PEOPLES UNDER SIEGE

The tribespeople living west of the Mississippi River keenly felt the pressure of the gradual incorporation of the West into the nation. The Oregon Trail opened the Northwest to large numbers of non-Indian settlers, and by 1845 nearly 5,000 people had braved the six-to-eight-month journey by wagon to reach present-day Oregon and Washington. The following year, the United States reached an agreement with Great Britain for the division of the Oregon Country. Then came the addition of the vast territories taken from Mexico following the Mexican-American War. California quickly became a state in 1850, Oregon in 1859. Congress consolidated the national domain in the next decades by granting territorial status to Utah, New Mexico, Washington, Dakota, Colorado, Nevada, Arizona, Idaho, Montana, and Wyoming. The purchase of Alaska in 1867 added an area twice the size of Texas and extended the nation beyond its contiguous borders so that it reached almost to Russia and the North Pole. The federal government made itself the custodian of all these thinly settled regions, permitting limited self-rule, with appointed governors supervising the transition from territorial status to statehood.

Competition for the land and its resources was central to this encounter. Unlike the settlers wedded to the principles of private property, the tribespeople mainly believed that the land belongs to those who revere it across many generations. Their prospects to preserve their ways of life amid this contest dimmed considerably following the discovery of gold in California in 1848, the opening of western lands to homesteaders in 1862, and the completion of the transcontinental railroad in 1869. White settlers, hoping to build a new life for themselves, rushed into these new territories and repeatedly invaded Indian lands west of the Mississippi. Violent outbreaks between white emigrants and Indian peoples became increasingly commonplace. Since the Jefferson administration, federal officials had promoted the assimilation of Indian peoples; they now became even more determined to break up their tribal councils and to bring them into the American mainstream.

On the Eve of Conquest

Before the European colonists reached the New World, tribespeople of the Great Plains, Southwest, and Far West had occupied the lands for more than 20,000 years. Hundreds of tribes, totaling perhaps a million members, had adapted to such extreme climates as the desert aridity of present-day Utah and Nevada, the bitter cold of the northern Great Plains, and the seasonally heavy rain of the Pacific Northwest. Many cultivated maize (corn), foraged for wild plants, fished, or hunted game. Several tribes built cities with several thousand inhabitants and traded across thousands of miles of western territory.

Invasion by the English, Spanish, and other Europeans brought disease, religious conversion, and new patterns of commerce. But geographic isolation still gave many tribes a margin of survival unknown in the East. At the close of the Civil War, approximately 360,000 Indian people still lived in the trans-Mississippi West, the majority of them in the Great Plains.

The surviving tribes adapted to changing conditions. The Plains Indians learned to ride the horses and shoot the guns introduced by Spanish and British traders. The Pawnees migrated farther westward to evade encroaching non-Indian settlers, while the Sioux and the Comanches fought neighboring tribes to gain control of large stretches of the Great Plains. The southwestern Hopis and Zunis, conquered earlier by the Spanish, continued to trade extensively with the Mexicans who lived near them. Some tribes took dramatic steps toward accommodation with white ways. Even before they were uprooted and moved across the Mississippi River, the Cherokees had learned English, converted to Christianity, established a constitutional republic, and become a nation of farmers.

Web Exploration
Explore the conflicts between Indians and white settlers from 1860 to 1900.
Why were the Indians forcibly removed to reservations?
www.prenhall.com/faragher/map18.1

Major Indian Battles and Indian Reservations, 1860–1900   As commercial routes and white populations passed through and occupied Indian lands, warfare inevitably erupted. The displacement of Indians to reservations opened access by farmers, ranchers, and investors to natural resources and to markets.

Legally, the federal government had long regarded Indian tribes as autonomous nations residing within American boundaries and had negotiated numerous treaties with them over land rights and commerce. But pressured by land-hungry whites, several states had violated these federal treaties so often that the U.S. Congress passed the Indian Removal Act of 1830 (see Chapter 10), which provided funds to relocate all eastern tribes by force if necessary. The Cherokees challenged this legislation, and the Supreme Court ruled in their favor in *Cherokee Nation* v. *Georgia* (1831). Ignoring

the Court's decision, President Andrew Jackson, known as a hardened Indian fighter, forced many tribes to cede their land and remove to Indian Territory. There, it was believed, they might live undisturbed by whites and gradually adjust to "civilized" ways. But soon, the onslaught of white settlers, railroad entrepreneurs, and prospectors rushing for gold pressured tribes to cede millions of their acres to the United States. In 1854, to open the Kansas and Nebraska Territories for white settlement, the federal government simply abolished the northern half of Indian Territory.

As demand for resources and land accelerated, the entire plan for a permanent Indian Territory fell apart.

Reservations and the Slaughter of the Buffalo

As early as the 1840s, highly placed officials had outlined a plan to subdue the intensifying rivalry over natural resources and land. Under the terms of their proposal, individual tribes would agree to live within clearly defined zones—reservations—and, in exchange, the Bureau of Indian Affairs would provide guidance while U.S. military forces ensured protection. This reservation policy also reflected the vision of many "Friends of the Indian," educators and Protestant missionaries who aspired to "civilize the savages." By the end of the 1850s eight western reservations had been established where Indian peoples were induced to speak English, take up farming, and convert to Christianity. The U.S. Commissioner of Indian affairs Luke Lea predicted that reservations would speed the "ultimate incorporation" of the Indians "into the great body of our citizen population."

Several tribes did sign treaties, although often under duress. High-handed officials, such as governor Isaac Stevens of Washington Territory, made no attempt at legitimate negotiations, choosing instead to intimidate or deceive Indian peoples into signing away their lands. Most of the tribes in Washington responded by remaining in their old villages. But Stevens finally had his way. State officials moved the Indians onto three reservations after their leaders signed away 45,000 square miles of tribal land. The Suquamish leader Seattle admitted defeat but warned the governor: "Your time of decay may be distant, but it will surely come."

Those tribes that moved to reservations often found federal policies inadequate to their needs. The federal government repeatedly reduced the size of land allotments, forcing tribes to compete with each other for increasingly scarce resources and making subsistence farming on the reservation virtually impossible. The Medicine Lodge Treaty of 1867 assigned reservations in existing Indian Territory to Comanches, Plains (Kiowa) Apaches, Kiowas, Cheyennes, and Arapahoes, bringing these tribes together with Sioux, Shoshones, and Bannocks. All told, more than 100,000 people found themselves competing intensely for survival. Over the next decade, a group of Quakers appointed by President Ulysses S. Grant attempted to mediate differences among the tribes and to supply the starving peoples

Chief Red Cloud in an 1868 photograph. The Oglala Sioux spiritual leader is seen with Red Dog, Little Wound, interpreter John Bridgeman (on his right), American Horse, and Red Shirt (on his left). He ventured to Washington with his delegation to discuss with President Ulysses S. Grant the various provisions of the peace treaty, just signed, to end the violent conflict over the Bozeman Trail.

SOURCE: National Anthropological Archives/Smithsonian Institution (3238/E).

with food and seed. At the same time, white prospectors and miners continued to flood the Dakota Territory. "They crowded in," Iron Teeth recalled bitterly, "so we had to move out." Moreover, corrupt officials of the Bureau of Indian Affairs routinely diverted funds for their own use and reduced food supplies, a policy promoting malnutrition, demoralization, and desperation.

The nomadic tribes that traditionally hunted and gathered over large territories saw their freedom sharply curtailed. The Lakotas, or Western Sioux, a loose confederation of bands scattered across the northern Great Plains, were one of the largest and most adaptive of all Indian nations. Seizing buffalo-hunting territory from their rivals, the Pawnees and the Crows, the Sioux had learned to follow the herds on horseback. Buffalo meat and hides fed and clothed the Sioux and satisfied many of their other needs as well. Images of buffalo appeared in their religious symbols and ceremonial dress. The Sioux were also vision seekers. Young men and women pursued dreams that would provide them guidance for a lifetime; elders themselves followed dreams that might guide the destiny of the entire tribe or nation.

The mass slaughter of the buffalo brought the crisis provoked by the increasing restriction of the nomadic Plains peoples to a peak. In earlier eras, vast herds of buffalo had literally darkened the western horizon. Buffalo grazed over distances of several hundred miles, searching for water and wallowing in mud to fend off insects. The expansion of trade in buffalo robes, involving both tribespeople and Europeans and Americans, proved devastating for the herds and the populations who had come to depend on them. By midcentury, non-Indian traders avidly sought fur for coats, hide for leather, bones for fertilizer, and heads for trophies. As gunpowder and the railroad came to the range, the number of buffalo fell rapidly. New rifles, like the .50 caliber Sharps, could kill at 600 feet; one sharpshooter bragged of killing 3,000 buffalo. Army commanders encouraged the slaughter, accurately predicting that starvation would break tribal resistance to the reservation system. With their food sources practically destroyed, diseases such as smallpox and cholera (brought by fur traders) sweeping through their

villages, and their way of life undermined, many Great Plains tribes, including many Sioux, concluded that they could only fight or die.

The Indian Wars

Under these pressures, a handful of tribes organized themselves and their allies to resist both federal policies and the growing wave of white settlers. The overwhelming majority of tribespeople did not take up arms. But settlers, thousands of them Civil War veterans with weapons close at hand, responded to real or imaginary threats with their own brands of violence.

Large-scale war erupted in 1864. Having decided to terminate all treaties with tribes in eastern Colorado, territorial governor John Evans encouraged a group of white civilians, the Colorado Volunteers, to stage raids through Cheyenne campgrounds. Seeking protection, Chief Black Kettle brought a band of 800 Cheyennes to a U.S. fort and received orders to set up camp at Sand Creek. Feeling secure in this arrangement, Black Kettle sent out most of his men to hunt. Several weeks later, on November 29, 1864, the Colorado Volunteers and soldiers attacked. While Black Kettle held up a U.S. flag and a white truce banner, a disorderly group of 700 men, many of them drunk, slaughtered 105 Cheyenne women and children and 28 men. They

Preparing for a War Expedition, ca. 1887. This sketch on paper was made by an Indian artist, Silverhorn, who had himself taken part in the final revolt of the Kiowas in 1874. He later became a medicine man, and then served as a private in the U.S. Cavalry at Fort Sill, Oklahoma Territory.

SOURCE: Silverhorn, Native American, *Kiowa Preparing for a War Expedition*. From *Sketchbook*, 1887. Graphite ink and crayon. Gift of Mrs. Terrell Bartlett. Collection of the McNay Art Museum.

mutilated the corpses and took scalps back to Denver to exhibit as trophies. Iron Teeth, a Cheyenne woman who survived, remembered seeing a woman "crawling along on the ground, shot, scalped, crazy, but not yet dead." Months after the Sand Creek Massacre, bands of Cheyennes, Sioux, and Arapahoes were still retaliating, burning civilian outposts and sometimes killing whole families.

The Sioux played the most dramatic roles in the Indian Wars. In 1851, believing the U.S. government would recognize their own rights of conquest over other Indian tribes, the Sioux relinquished large tracts of land as a demonstration of good faith. But within a decade, a mass invasion of miners and the construction of military forts along the Bozeman Trail in Wyoming, the Sioux's principal buffalo range, threw the tribe's future into doubt. During the Great Sioux War of 1865–67, the Oglala Sioux warrior Red Cloud fought the U.S. Army to a stalemate and forced the government to abandon its forts, which the Sioux then burned to the ground. The Treaty of Fort Laramie, signed in 1868, created the Great Sioux Reservation, which included the present state of South Dakota west of the Missouri River, but restored only a temporary peace to the region.

The Treaty of Fort Laramie granted the Sioux the right to occupy the Black Hills, or Paha Sapa, their sacred land, "as long as the grass shall grow," but the discovery of gold soon undermined this guarantee. White prospectors hurriedly invaded the territory. Directed to quash rumors of fabulous deposits of the precious metal, Lieutenant Colonel George Armstrong Custer organized a surveying expedition to the Black Hills during the summer of 1874, but, contrary to plan, the Civil War hero described rich veins of ore that could be cheaply extracted. The U.S. Congress then pushed to acquire the territory for Americans. To protect their land, Sioux, Cheyenne, and Arapaho warriors, ranging between 2,000 and 9,000 in number, moved into war camps during the summer of 1876 and prepared for battle.

After several months of skirmishes and battles between the U.S. Army and Sioux warriors, Lieutenant Colonel Custer, the most flamboyant of calvary commanders (and in the eyes of many of his own troops, the most irresponsible) was ordered to move the Seventh Calvary into position to meet another infantry division. Custer abandoned the plan and decided to rush ahead to a site in Montana that was known to white soldiers as Little Bighorn and to Lakotas as Greasy Grass. This foolhardy move offered the allied Cheyenne and Sioux warriors a perfect opportunity to cut off Custer's logistical and military support. On June 25, 1876, Custer and his troops were wiped out by one of the largest Indian contingents ever assembled, an estimated 2,000 to 4,000 warriors.

"Custer's Last Stand" gave Indian-haters the emotional ammunition to whip up public excitement. After Custer's defeat, spiritual leader Sitting Bull reportedly said, "Now they will never let us rest." The U.S. Army tracked down the disbanded Indian contingents one by one and forced them to surrender. In February, 1877, the U.S. government formally took possession of the Black Hills. After the defiant warrior Crazy Horse was fatally stabbed while under arrest at a U.S. Army camp, Sioux leadership in the Indian Wars came to an end.

Among the last to hold out against the reservation system were the Apaches in the Southwest. Most Apache bands had abided by the Medicine Lodge Treaty of 1867, and in 1872 Cochise, one of the ablest Apache chiefs, agreed to live with his people on a reservation on a portion of the tribe's ancestral land. Cochise died two years later, and some of the Apache bands, unable to tolerate the harsh conditions on the reservation, returned to their old ways of seizing territory and stealing cattle. For the next ten years, Cochise's successor Geronimo led intermittent raids against white outposts in the rough Arizona terrain.

Pursued by the U.S. Army, the Apaches earned a reputation as intrepid warriors. Their brilliant strategists and horse-riding braves became legendary for lightning-swift raids followed by quick disappearances. The Kiowas and the Comanches, both powerful tribes, joined the Apaches in one of the bloodiest conflicts, the Red River War of 1874–75. The U.S. Army ultimately prevailed less by military might than by denying Indians access to food. Even after the Red River War, small-scale warfare sputtered on. Not until September 1886, his band reduced to only thirty people, did Geronimo finally surrender, ending the Indian Wars.

The Nez Percé

In crushing the Plains tribes, the U.S. government had conquered those peoples who had most actively resisted the advance of non-Indians into the West. But even tribes that had long tried to cooperate found themselves embattled. The Nez Percé (meaning "pierced nose") had been given their name by French Canadian fur trappers, who thought they had seen members of the tribe wearing shells in their septums. For generations the Nez Percé had regarded themselves as good friends to white traders and settlers. Living in the plateau where Idaho, Washington, and Oregon now meet, they had saved the Lewis and Clark expedition from starvation in 1803. The Nez Percé had occasionally assisted American armies against hostile tribes, and many of them were converts to Christianity.

But the discovery of gold on Nez Percé territory in 1860 changed their relations with whites for the worse. Pressed by prospectors and mining companies, government commissioners, in the treaty of 1863, demanded the Nez Percé cede 6 million acres, nine-tenths of their land, at less than ten cents per acre. Some of the Nez Percé leaders agreed to the terms of the treaty, which had been fraudulently signed on behalf of the entire tribe, but others refused. Old Chief Tuekekas, one of the first to convert to Christianity, threw away his Bible and returned to his old religion. His son and successor, Chief Joseph, swore to protect the peoples of the Wallowa Valley in present-day Oregon. At first, federal officials listened to Nez Percé complaints against the treaty and decided to allow them to remain on their land. But responding to pressure from settlers and politicians, however, they almost immediately reversed their decision, ordering the Nez Percé, including Chief Joseph and his followers, to sell their land and to move onto a reservation.

Intending to comply, Chief Joseph's band set out from the Wallowa Valley with their livestock and all the possessions they could carry. Along the way, some young members of another Indian band traveling with them rode away from camp to avenge the death of one of their own by killing several white settlers. Hoping to explain the situation, a Nez Percé truce team approached U.S. troops. The troops opened fire, and the Indian riders fired back, killing one-third of the soldiers. Chief Joseph and his people then undertook a monumental journey in search of sanctuary in Canada. Brilliantly outmaneuvering vengeful U.S. troops sent to intercept them, the 750 Nez Percé—including women, children, and the elderly—retreated for some 1,400 miles into Montana and Wyoming through mountains and prairies, and across the Bitterroot Range. Along the way, they unintentionally terrified tourists at the newly created Yellowstone National Park. Over the three and a half months of their journey, Nez Percé braves fought 2,000 regular U.S. troops and eighteen Indian auxiliary detachments in eighteen separate engagements and two major battles. U.S. troops finally trapped the Nez Percé in the Bear Paw Mountains of northern Montana, just 30 miles from the Canadian border. Suffering from hunger and cold, they surrendered.

General Sherman remarked admiringly at the Nez Percé's ingenious tactics, courage, and avoidance of cruelty. Newspapers described Chief Joseph as a "Red Napoleon" defying overwhelming odds. (Actually, Joseph did not plan military strategy but mainly attended to the needs of dependent tribal members.)

Promised they would be returned to Oregon, the Nez Percé were sent instead to disease-ridden bottomland near Fort Leavenworth in Kansas, and then to Oklahoma. Arguing for the right of his people to return to their Oregon reservation, Joseph spoke eloquently, through an interpreter, to Congress in 1879. "Treat all men alike. Give them all the same law. Give them all an

even chance to live and grow. All men were made by the same Great Spirit Chief," Joseph pleaded. The last remnant of Joseph's band were deported under guard to a non Nez Percé reservation in Washington, where Chief Joseph died in 1904 "of a broken heart," and where his descendants continue to live in exile to this day.

THE INTERNAL EMPIRE

Since the time of Christopher Columbus, the Americas had inspired in Europeans visions of a land of incredible wealth, free for the taking. In the nineteenth century, the North American continent, stretching across scarcely populated territories toward the Pacific Ocean, revived this fantasy, especially as early reports conjured dreams of mountains of gold and silver. Determined to make their fortunes, be it from copper in Arizona, wheat in Montana, or oranges in California, numerous adventurers traveled west. As a group they carried out the largest migration and greatest commercial expansion in American history.

But the settlers themselves also became the subjects of a huge "internal empire" whose financial, political, and industrial centers of power remained in the East. A vast system of international markets also shaped the development of mines, farms, and new communities, even as Americans romantically imagined the West to be the last frontier of individual freedom and wide open spaces. Only a small number of settlers actually struck it rich in the great extractive industries—mining, lumbering, ranching, and farming—that ruled the western economy. Meanwhile, older populations—Indian peoples, Hispanic peoples, and more recently settled communities like the Mormons—struggled to create places for themselves in this new order.

Mining Towns

The discovery of gold in California in 1848 roused fortune seekers from across the United States, Europe, and as far away as Chile and China. Just ten years later, approximately 35,000 Chinese men were working in mines, some having taken over the camps abandoned by American miners. Meanwhile, prospecting parties overran the western territories, setting a pattern for intermittent rushes for gold, silver, and copper that extended from the Colorado mountains to the Arizona deserts, from California to Oregon and Washington, and from Alaska to the Black Hills of South Dakota. Mining camps and boomtowns soon dotted what had once been thinly settled regions. The population of California alone jumped from 14,000 in 1848 to 223,856 just four years later. More than any other industry or commercial enterprise, mining fostered western expansion.

Pan across a map of the West during the period 1860–1900. How did the growth of railroads and mining impact the environment and the lives of native peoples?
www.prenhall.com/faragher/map18.2

Railroad Routes, Cattle Trails, Gold and Silver Rushes, 1860–1900   By the end of the nineteenth century, the vast region of the West was crosscut by hundreds of lines of transportation and communication. The trade in precious metals and in cattle helped build a population almost constantly on the move, following the rushes for gold or the herds of cattle.

SOURCE: Encyclopedia of American Social History.

The first miners required little preparation to stake their claims. The miner needs nothing, the military governor of California announced, "but his pick and shovel and tin pan with which to dig and wash the gravel." A handful of individual prospectors did strike it rich. Many more found themselves employees of the so-called bonanza kings, the owners or operators of the most lucrative enterprises. Only in 1896–97, with

A "hard rock" miner demonstrates the tiring and often dangerous task of hammering a drill into a rock to prepare a blasting hole. New technologies, such as diamond-headed drills, quickly revolutionized the extractive process, but potentially lethal hazards, including cave-ins and poisonous gases, remained great.

SOURCE: Artist unknown, *Miners Underground*, 1897. Glass plate negative. Photograph by Timothy O'Sullivan. Courtesy Colorado Historical Society.

news of "gold on the Klondike" in Alaska, did prospectors again hit on a vein worth millions of dollars.

The mining industry quickly grew from its treasure-hunt origins into a grand corporate enterprise. The Comstock Lode of silver, discovered by Henry Comstock along the Carson River in Nevada in 1859, sent about 10,000 miners across the Sierra Nevada from California, but few individuals came out wealthy. Comstock himself eventually sold his claims for a mere $11,000 and two mules. Those reaping the huge profits were the entrepreneurs who could afford to invest in the heavy—and expensive—equipment necessary to drill more than 3,000 feet deep and to hire engineers with the technical knowledge to manage the operations. Having secured a capital investment of nearly $900,000, the owners of the Gould and Curry mill, built on the Comstock Lode, did very well.

The most successful mineowners bought out the smaller claims and built an entire industry around their stakes. They found investors to finance their expansion and used the borrowed capital to purchase the latest in extractive technology, such as new explosives, compressed-air or diamond-headed rotary drills, and wire cable. They gained access to timber to fortify their underground structures and water to feed the hydraulic pumps that washed down mountains. They built smelters to refine the crude ore into ingots and often financed railroads to transport the product to distant markets. By the end of the century, the Anaconda Copper Mining Company, which had mining interests throughout the West, had expanded into hydroelectricity to become one of the most powerful corporations in the nation.

The mining corporations laid the basis for a new economy as well as an interim government and established many of the region's first white settlements. Before the advent of railroads, ore had to be brought out of, and supplies brought into, mining areas by boats, wagons, and mules traveling hundreds of miles over rough territory. The railroad made transportation of supplies and products easier and faster. The shipping trade meanwhile grew into an important industry of its own, employing thousands of merchants, peddlers, and sailors. Dance halls, saloons, theaters, hospitals, and newspapers followed. Gold Hill and nearby Virginia City, Nevada, began as a cluster of small mining camps and by the early 1860s became a thriving urban community of nearly 6,000 people. A decade later, the population had quadrupled, but it subsequently fell sharply as the mines gave out. Occasionally, ore veins lasted long enough—as in Butte, Montana, center of the copper-mining district—to create permanent cities.

Many short-lived boomtowns were known as "Helldorados." Men outnumbered women by as much as ten to one, and very few lived with families or stayed very long. They often bunked with male kin and worked alongside friends or acquaintances from their hometown or, in the case of Butte, with fellow immigrants from Ireland. Some lived unusually well, feasting on oysters trucked in at great expense. Amateur sporting events, public lectures, and large numbers of magazines and books filled many of their leisure hours. But the town center was usually the saloon, where, as one observer complained, men "without the restraint of law, indifferent to public opinion, and unburdened by families, drink whenever they feel like it, whenever they have the money to pay for it, and whenever there is nothing else to do."

The western labor movement began in these camps, partly as a response to dangerous working conditions. In the hardrock mines of the 1870s, one of every thirty workers was disabled, one of eighty killed. Balladeers back in Ireland sang of Butte as the town "where the streets were paved with Irish bones," and departing emigrants promised their mothers that they would never go underground in Montana. Miners began to organize in the 1860s, demanding good pay for dangerous and life-shortening work. In 1892, miners in the Coeur d'Alene region of Idaho, in the aftermath of a bitter and violent strike, formed the Western Federation of Miners. With organizers traveling to mining towns and camps throughout the West, they established by the end of the century one of the strongest unions in the nation.

Violence on both sides characterized western labor relations. When mineowners' private armies "arrested" strikers or fought their unions with rifle fire, miners burned down the campsites, seized trains loaded with ore, and sabotaged company property. The miners' unions also helped to secure legislation mandating a maximum eight-hour day for certain jobs and workmen's compensation for injuries. Such laws were enacted in Idaho, Arizona, and New Mexico by the 1910s, long before similar laws in most eastern states.

The unions fought hard, but they did so exclusively for the benefit of white workers. The native-born and the Irish and Cornish immigrants (from Cornwall, England) far outnumbered other groups before the turn of the century, when Italians, Slavs, and Greeks began to replace them. Labor unions eventually admitted these new immigrants, but refused Chinese, Mexican, and Indian workers. In 1869 white miners at the Comstock Lode rioted to protest the employment of Chinese miners. In Arizona, Mexican Americans had secured jobs in the copper and silver mines, but they usually received less pay and worked under worse conditions than white workers.

When prices and ore production fell sharply, not even unions could stop the owners from shutting down the mines and leaving ghost towns in their wake. Often they also left behind an environmental disaster. Hydraulic mining, which used water cannons to blast hillsides and expose gold deposits, drove tons of rock and earth into the rivers and canyons. By the late 1860s southern California's rivers were clogged, producing floods that wiped out towns and farms. In 1893, Congress finally passed the Caminetti Act, giving the state the power to regulate the mines. (The act also created the Sacramento River Commission, which began to replace free-flowing rivers with canals and dams.) Underground mining continued unregulated, using up whole forests for timbers and filling the air with dangerous, sulfurous smoke.

Mormon Settlements

While western expansion fostered the growth of new commercial cities such as the numerous if unstable mining towns, it simultaneously placed new restrictions on established communities. The Mormons (members of

the Church of Jesus Christ of Latter-Day Saints) had fled western New York in the 1830s for Illinois and Missouri, only to face greater persecution in the Midwest. When their founder, Joseph Smith, was murdered after proclaiming the doctrine of polygamy (the taking of more than one wife), the community sought refuge in the West. Led by their new prophet, Brigham Young, the Mormons migrated in 1846–47 to the Great Basin in present-day Utah and formed an independent theocratic state called Deseret. However, their dream was cut short in 1850 when Congress set up Utah Territory. In 1857 President James Buchanan declared the Mormons to be in "a state of substantial rebellion" (for being

Mormon Cultural Diffusion, ca. 1883
Mormon settlements permeated many sparsely populated sections of Idaho, Nevada, Arizona, Wyoming, Colorado, and New Mexico. Built with church backing and the strong commitment of community members, they survived and even prospered in adverse climates.

an independent state within U.S. territory) and sent the U.S. Army to occupy the territory.

Although federal troops remained until the outbreak of the Civil War in 1861, the Mormon population continued to grow. By 1870, more than 87,000 Mormons lived in Utah Territory, creating relatively stable communities that were unique in the West for their religious and ethnic homogeneity. Contrary to federal law, church officials forbade the selling of land. Mormons instead held property in common. They created sizable settlements complemented by satellite villages joined to communal farmlands and a common pasture. Relying on agricultural techniques learned from local Indian tribes, the Mormons built dams for irrigation and harvested a variety of crops from desert soil. Eventually nearly 500 Mormon communities spread from Oregon to Idaho to northern Mexico.

But as territorial rule tightened, the Mormons saw their unique way of life once again threatened. The newspapers and the courts repeatedly assailed the Mormons for the supposed sexual excesses of their system of "plural marriage," condemning them as heathens and savages. "There is an irrepressible conflict," one journalist wrote, "between the Mormon power and the principles upon which our free institutions are established, and one or the other must succumb." Preceded by prohibitory federal laws enacted in 1862 and 1874, the Supreme Court finally ruled against polygamy in the 1879 case of *United States* v. *Reynolds*, which granted the freedom of belief but not the freedom of practice. In 1882, Congress passed the Edmunds Act, which effectively disfranchised those who believed in or practiced polygamy and threatened them with fines and imprisonment. Equally devastating was the Edmunds-Tucker Act, passed five years later, which destroyed the temporal power of the Mormon Church by confiscating all assets over $50,000 and establishing a federal commission to oversee all elections in the territory. By the early 1890s, Mormon leaders officially renounced the practice of plural marriage.

Polygamy had actually been practiced by no more than 15 to 20 percent of Mormon families, but it had been important to their sense of messianic mission. Forced to abandon the practice, they gave up most other aspects of their distinctive communal life, including the common ownership of land. By the time Utah became a state in 1896, Mormon communities resembled in some ways the society that the original settlers had sought to escape. Nevertheless, they combined their religious cohesion with leadership in the expanding regional economy to become a major political force in the West.

Borderland Communities

American expansionism transformed deserts and grasslands that had been contested for centuries among world powers. In 1845, Texas was annexed as a state,

and the following year President James K. Polk whipped up a border dispute with Mexico into a war. The one-sided conflict ended in 1848 with the United States taking fully half of all Mexican territory—the future states of Arizona, California, Nevada, and Utah, most of New Mexico, and parts of Wyoming, and Colorado. The Gadsden Purchase of 1853 rounded off this prize, giving the United States a strip of land from El Paso west to the Colorado River—in short, all the land north of the Rio Grande River.

The Treaty of Guadalupe Hidalgo, which ended the Mexican-American War, allowed the Hispanic people north of the Rio Grande to choose between immigrating to Mexico or staying in what was now the United States. But the new Mexican-American border, one of the longest unguarded boundaries in the world, could not successfully sever communities that had been connected for centuries. Despite the change in sovereignty, elites and common folk alike continued to travel back and forth between the two nations, and the majority of people who became U.S. citizens retained their identity as Mexicans. Even those who migrated farther north, a process that accelerated after the discovery of gold in California and the silver strikes in Nevada, kept their ties with friends and family in Mexico. What gradually emerged was an economically and socially interdependent zone, the Anglo-Hispanic borderlands linking the United States and Mexico.

Equality, however, did not provide the basis for relationships between the two nations and their peoples. Although under the treaty all Hispanics were formally guaranteed citizenship and the "free enjoyment of their liberty and property," local "Anglos" (as the Mexicans called white Americans) often violated these provisions and, through fraud or coercion, took control of the land. The Sante Fe Ring, a group of lawyers, politicians, and land speculators, stole millions of acres from the public domain and grabbed over 80 percent of the Mexicano landholdings in New Mexico alone. More often, Anglos used new federal laws to their own benefit.

For a time, Arizona and New Mexico seemed to hold out hope for a mutually beneficial interaction between Mexicanos and Anglos. A prosperous class of Hispanic landowners, with long-standing ties to Anglos through marriage, had established itself in cities like Albuquerque and Tucson, old Spanish towns that had been founded in the seventeenth and eighteenth centuries. Estevan Ochoa, merchant, philanthropist, and the only Mexican to serve as mayor of Tucson following the Gadsden Purchase, managed to build one of the largest business empires in the West. In Las Cruces, New Mexico, an exceptional family such as the wealthy Amadors could shop by mail from Bloomingdales, travel to the World's Fair in Chicago, and send their children to English-language Catholic schools. Even the small and struggling Mexicano middle class could afford such

Mexican Americans in San Antonio continued to conduct their traditional market bazaar well after the incorporation of this region into the United States. Forced off the land and excluded from the better-paying jobs in the emerging regional economy, many Mexicanos and especially women sought to sell the products of their own handiwork for cash or for bartered food and clothing.

SOURCE: Thomas Allen, *Market Plaza*, 1878–1879. Oil on canvas, 26" × 39½". Witte Museum, San Antonio, Texas (36-65/8P).

modern conveniences as kitchen stoves and sewing machines. These Mexican elites, well integrated into the emerging national economy, continued to wield political power as ranchers, landlords, and real estate developers until the end of the century. They secured passage of bills for education in their regions and often served as superintendents of local schools. Several prominent merchants became territorial delegates to Congress.

But the majority of Mexicans who had lived in the mountains and deserts of the Southwest for well over two centuries were less prepared for these changes. Most had worked outside the commercial economy, farming and herding sheep for their own subsistence. Before 1848 they had few contacts with the outside world. With the Anglos came land closures as well as commercial expansion prompted by railroad, mining, and timber industries. Many poor families found themselves crowded onto plots too small for subsistence farming. Many turned to seasonal labor on the new Anglo-owned commercial farms, where they became the first of many generations of poorly paid migratory workers. Other Mexicanos adapted by taking jobs on the railroad or in the mines. Meanwhile their wives and daughters moved to the new towns and cities in such numbers that by the end of the century Mexicanos had become a predominantly urban population, dependent on wages for survival.

Women were quickly drawn into the expanding network of market and wage relations. They tried to make ends meet by selling produce from their backyard gardens; more often they worked as seamstresses

or laundresses. Formerly at the center of a communal society, Mexicanas found themselves with fewer options in the cash economy. What wages they could now earn fell below even the low sums paid to their husbands, and women lost status within both the family and community.

Occasionally, Mexicanos organized to reverse these trends or at least to limit the damage done to their communities. In the border town of Brownsville, Texas, in 1859, Juan Nepomuceno Cortina, known as the Red Robber of the Rio Grande, and sixty of his followers pillaged white-owned stores and killed four Anglos who had gone unpunished for murdering several Mexicans. "Cortina's War" marked the first of several sporadic rebellions. As late as the 1880s, Las Gorras Blancas, a band of agrarian rebels in New Mexico, were destroying railroad ties and farm machinery and posting demands for justice on fences of the new Anglo farms and ranches. In 1890 Las Gorras turned from social banditry to political organization, forming *El Partido del Pueblo Unido* (The People's Party). Organized along similar lines, *El Alianzo Hispano-Americano* (The Hispanic-American Alliance) was formed "to protect and fight for the rights of Spanish Americans" through political action. *Mutualistes* (mutual aid societies) provided sickness and death benefits to Mexican families.

Despite many pressures, Mexicanos preserved much of their cultural heritage. Many persisted in older ways simply because they had few choices. In addition, the influx of new immigrants from Mexico helped to reinforce traditional cultural norms. Beginning in the late 1870s, the modernizing policies of Porfirio Díaz, the president of Mexico from 1876 to 1911, brought deteriorating living conditions to the masses of poor people and prompted a migration northward that accelerated through the first decades of the twentieth century. These newcomers revitalized old customs and rituals associated with family and religion. The Roman Catholic Church retained its influence in the community, and most Mexicans continued to turn to the church to baptize infants, to celebrate the feast day of their patron saints, to marry, and to bury the dead. Special saints like the Virgin of Guadalupe and distinctive holy days like the Day of the Dead survived along with fiestas celebrating the change of seasons. Many communities continued to commemorate Mexican national holidays, such as *Cinco de Mayo* (the Fifth of May), marking the Mexican victory over French invaders in the battle of Puebla in 1862. Spanish language and Spanish place names continued to distinguish the Southwest.

But for the encroaching Anglo majority, large regions in the West had been "won" from the populations who had previously settled the region. Americans had brought in commercial capitalism, their political and legal systems, as well as many of their social and cultural institutions. Ironically, though, even after statehood, white settlers would still be only distant representatives of an empire whose financial, political, and industrial centers remained in the Northeast. In return for raw produce or ore drawn out of soil or rock, they received washtubs, clothes, and whiskey; model legal statutes; and doctors, lawyers, and teachers. But they were often frustrated by their continued isolation, and they were enraged at the federal regulations that governed them, and at the eastern investors and lawyers who seemed poised on all sides to rob them of the fruits of their labor. Embittered Westerners, along with Southerners, would form the core of a nationwide discontent that would soon threaten to uproot the American political system.

THE CATTLE INDUSTRY

The slaughter of the buffalo made way for the cattle industry, one of the most profitable businesses in the West. Texas longhorns, introduced by the Spanish, numbered over 5 million at the close of the Civil War and represented a potentially plentiful supply of beef for eastern consumers. In the spring of 1866, entrepreneurs such as Joseph G. McCoy began to build a spectacular cattle market in the eastern part of Kansas, where the Kansas Pacific Railroad provided crucial transportation links to slaughtering and packing houses and commercial distributors in Kansas City, St. Louis, and Chicago.

In 1867 only 35,000 head of cattle reached McCoy's new stockyards in Abilene, but 1868 proved the first of many banner years. Drovers pushed herd after herd north from Texas through Oklahoma on the trail marked out by part-Cherokee trader Jesse Chisholm. Great profits were made on Texas steers bought for $7–$9 a head and sold in Kansas for upward of $30. In 1880 nearly 2 million cattle were slaughtered in Chicago alone. For two decades, cattle represented the West's bonanza industry.

Cowboys

The great cattle drives depended on the cowboy, a seasonal or migrant worker. After the Civil War, cowboys—one for every 300–500 head of cattle on the trail—rounded up herds of Texas cattle and drove them as much as 1,500 miles north to grazing ranches or to the stockyards where they were readied for shipping by rail to eastern markets. The boss supplied the horses, the cowboy his own bedroll, saddle, and spurs. The workday lasted from sunup to sundown, with short night shifts for guarding the cattle. Scurvy, a widespread ailment, could be traced to the basic chuckwagon menu of sowbelly, beans, and coffee, a diet bereft of fruits and vegetables. The cowboy worked without protection from rain or hail, and severe dust storms could cause temporary blindness. As late as 1920, veterans of the range complained that no company would sell life insurance to a cowboy.

In return for his labor, the cowboy received at the best of times about $30 per month. Wages were usually paid in one lump sum at the end of a drive, a policy that encouraged cowboys to spend their money quickly and recklessly in the booming cattle towns of Dodge City, Kansas, or Cheyenne, Wyoming. In the 1880s, when wages began to fall along with the price of beef, cowboys fought back by stealing cattle or by forming unions. In 1883 many Texas cowboys struck for higher wages; nearly all Wyoming cowboys struck in 1886. Aided by the legendary camaraderie fostered in the otherwise desolate conditions of the long drive, cowboys, along with miners, were among the first western workers to organize against employers.

Like other parts of the West, the cattle range was ethnically diverse. Between one-fifth and one-third of all workers were Indian, Mexican, or African American. Indian cowboys worked mainly on the northern plains and in Indian Territory; the *vaqueros*, who had previously worked on the Mexican cattle *haciendas*, or huge estates, predominated in South Texas and California. African American cowboys worked primarily in Texas, where the range cattle industry was founded.

Like the vaqueros, African American cowboys were highly skilled managers of cattle. Some were sons of former slaves who had been captured from the African territory of Gambia, where cattle raising was an age-old art. Unlike Mexicans, they earned wages comparable to those paid to Anglos and especially during the early years worked in integrated drover parties. By the 1880s, as the center of the cattle industry shifted to the more settled regions around the northern ranches, African Americans were forced out, and they turned to other kinds of work. Although the majority of Anglo cowboys also came from the South and shared with former slaves the hope of escaping the postwar economic devastation of their region, they usually remained loyal to the racial hierarchy of the Confederacy.

Cowgirls and Prostitutes

Sally Redus, wife of an early Texas cattleman, once accompanied her husband on the long drive from Texas to Kansas. Carrying her baby on her lap, she most likely rode the enormous distance "sidesaddle," with both legs on one side of the horse. Although few women worked as trail hands, they did find jobs on the ranches, usually in the kitchen or laundry. Occasionally a husband and wife worked as partners, sharing even the labor of wrangling cattle, and following her

husband's death, a woman might take over altogether. Elizabeth Collins, for example, turned her husband's large ranch into an extraordinarily prosperous business, earning for herself the title "Cattle Queen of Montana." The majority of women attended to domestic chores, caring for children and maintaining the household. Their daughters, however, enjoyed better prospects. By the end of the century, women, who as girls had accompanied their fathers in outside chores, were riding astride, "clothespin style," roping calves, branding cattle or cutting their ears to mark them, and castrating bulls. But not until 1901 did a woman dare to enter an official rodeo contest.

In cattle towns as well as mining camps, many women worked as prostitutes. During the first cattle drive to Abilene in 1867, a few women were so engaged; but by the following spring, McCoy's assistant recalled, "they came in swarms, & as the weather was warm 4 or 5 girls could huddle together in a tent very comfortably." Although some women worked in trailside "hoghouses," the best-paid prostitutes congregated in "brothel districts" or "tenderloins." Most cattle towns boasted at least one dance hall where prostitutes plied their trade. Dodge city had two: one with white prostitutes for white patrons; another with black prostitutes for both white and black men. Although prostitution was illegal in most towns, the laws were rarely enforced until the end of the century, when reformers led campaigns to shut down the red-light districts.

Perhaps 50,000 women engaged in prostitution west of the Mississippi during the second half of the nineteenth century. Like most cowboys, most prostitutes were unmarried and in their teens or twenties. Often fed up with underpaid jobs in dressmaking or domestic service, they found few alternatives to prostitution in the cattle towns, where the cost of food and lodging was notoriously high. Still, earnings in prostitution were slim, except during the cattle-shipping season when young men outnumbered women by as much as three to one. In the best of times, a fully employed Wichita prostitute might earn $30 per week, nearly two-thirds of which would go for room and board. Injury or even death from violent clients, addiction to narcotics such as cocaine or morphine, and venereal disease were workaday dangers.

Curly Wolves Howled on Saturday Night, a commercial woodcut from the 1870s. The artist, recording this scene at a tavern near Billings, Montana, captured what he called a "Dude and a Waitress" dancing the "Bull Calves' Medley on the Grand Piano." Illustrations depicting a wild and lively West appeared prominently in magazines like *Harper's Weekly,* which circulated mainly among readers east of the Mississippi.

SOURCE: Horace Bradley. Courtesy of the Library of Congress.

Community and Conflict on the Range

The combination of prostitution, gambling, and drinking discouraged the formation of stable communities. According to a Kansas proverb, "There's no Sunday west of Junction City and no god west of Salina." Personal violence was notoriously commonplace on the streets and in the barrooms of cattle towns and mining camps populated mainly by young, single men. Many western towns such as Wichita outlawed the carrying of handguns, but enforcement usually lagged. Local specialty shops and mail-order catalogues continued to sell weapons with little regulation. But contrary to popular belief, gunfights were relatively rare. Local police officers, such as Wyatt Earp and James "Wild Bill" Hickok, worked mainly to keep order among drunken cowboys.

After the Civil War, violent crime, assault, and robbery rose sharply throughout the United States. In the West, the most prevalent crimes were horse theft and cattle rustling, which peaked during the height of the open range period and then fell back by the 1890s. Death by legal hanging or illegal lynching—at "necktie parties" in which the victims were "jerked to Jesus"—was the usual sentence. In the last half of the century, vigilantes acting outside the law mobilized more than 200 times, claiming altogether more than 500 victims.

The "range wars" of the 1870s produced violent conflicts. By this time, both farmers and sheep herders were encroaching on the fields where cattle had once grazed freely. Sheep chew grass down to its roots, making it practically impossible to raise cattle on land they have grazed. Farmers meanwhile set about building fences to protect their domestic livestock and property. Great cattle barons fought back against farmers by ordering cowboys to cut the new barbed-wire fences. Rivalry among the owners of livestock was even more vicious, particularly in the Southwest and Pacific Northwest. In these areas, Mexicano shepherds and Anglo cattlemen often fought each other for land. In Lincoln County, New Mexico, the feuds grew so intense in 1878 that one faction hired gunman Billy the Kid to protect its interests. President Rutherford B. Hayes finally sent troops to halt the bloodshed.

The cattle barons helped to bring about their own demise, but they did not go down quietly. Ranchers eager for greater profits, and often backed by foreign capital, overstocked their herds, and eventually the cattle began to deplete the limited supply of grass. Finally, during 1885–87, a combination of summer drought and winter blizzards killed 90 percent of the cattle in the northern Plains. Prices also declined sharply. Many big ranchers fell into bankruptcy. Along the way, they often took out their grievances against the former cowboys who had gathered small herds for

themselves. They charged these small ranchers with cattle rustling, taking them to court or, in some cases, rounding up lynching parties. As one historian has written, violence was "not a mere sideshow" but "an intrinsic part of western society."

FARMING COMMUNITIES ON THE PLAINS

The vision of a huge fertile garden extending from the Appalachians to the Pacific Ocean had inspired Americans since the early days of the republic. But the first explorers who actually traveled through the Great Plains quashed this dream. "The Great Desert" was the name they gave to the region stretching west from Kansas and Nebraska, north to Montana and the Dakotas, and south again to Oklahoma and Texas. Few trees fended off the blazing sun of summer or promised a supply of lumber for homes and fences. The occasional river or stream flowed with "muddy gruel" rather than pure, sweet water. Economically, the entire region appeared as hopelessly barren as it was vast. It took massive improvements in both transportation and farm technology—as well as unrelenting advertising and promotional campaigns—to open the Great Plains to widescale agriculture.

The Homestead Act

The Homestead Act of 1862 offered the first incentive to prospective white farmers. This act granted a quarter section (160 acres) of the public domain free to any settler who lived on the land for at least five years and improved it; or a settler could buy the land for $1.25 per acre after only six months' residence. Restricting its provisions to unmarried women, the Homestead Act encouraged adventurous and hard-working women to file between 5 and 15 percent of the claims, which allowed approximately 400,000 households to build farms for themselves.

Homesteaders achieved their greatest success in the central and upper Midwest where the soil was rich and weather relatively moderate. But those settlers lured to the Great Plains by descriptions of land "carpeted with soft grass—a sylvan paradise" found themselves locked in a fierce struggle with the harsh climate and arid soil. The average holding could rarely furnish a livelihood, even with hard work. Nearly half of all homesteaders failed to improve the land and therefore lost their claims.

Rather than filing a homestead claim with the federal government, most settlers acquired their land outright. State governments and land companies usually held the most valuable land near transportation and markets, and the majority of farmers were willing to pay a hefty price for these benefits. A few women speculators did very well, particularly in the Dakotas, where they acquired acreage under the generous terms of the Homestead Act, not to farm but to sell when prices for land increased. The big-time land speculators gained even more, plucking choice locations at bargain prices. And the railorads, which received land grants from the federal government, did best, selling off the holding near their routes at top dollar. By the end of the century, farm acreage west of the Mississippi had tripled, but perhaps only 10 percent of all farmers got their start under Homestead Act provisions.

The dream of a homestead nevertheless died hard. Five years after the passage of the Homestead Act, *New York Tribune* editor Horace Greeley still advised his readers to strike off "into the broad, free West" and "make yourself a farm from Uncle Sam's generous domain, you will crowd nobody, starve nobody, and . . . neither you nor your children need evermore beg for Something to Do." He was wrong. Although the Homestead Act did spark the largest migration in American history, it did not lay the foundation for a nation of prosperous family farms.

Populating the Plains

The rapid settlement of the West could not have taken place without the railroad. Although the Homestead Act offered prospective farmers free land, it was the railroad that promoted settlement, brought people to their new homes, and carried crops and cattle to eastern markets. The railroads therefore wielded tremendous economic and political power throughout the West. Their agents—reputed to know every cow in the district—made major decisions regarding territorial welfare. In designing routes and locating depots, railroad companies put whole communities "on the map," or left them behind.

Along with providing transportation links between the East and the West and potential markets as distant as China, the western railroads directly encouraged settlement. Unlike the railroads built before the Civil War, which followed the path of villages and towns, the western lines preceded settlement. Bringing people west became their top priority, and the railroad companies conducted aggressive promotional and marketing campaigns. Agents enticed Easterners and Europeans alike with long-term loans and free transportation by rail to distant points in the West. The railroads also sponsored land companies to sell parcels of their own huge allotments from the federal government. The National Land Company, founded in Chicago in 1869, alone organized sixteen colonies of mainly European

immigrants in parts of Kansas and Colorado. The Santa Fe Railroad sent agent C. B. Schmidt to Germany, where he managed to entice nearly 60,000 Germans to settle along the rail line.

More than 2 million Europeans, many recruited by professional promoters, settled the Great Plains between 1870 and 1900. Some districts in Minnesota seemed to be virtual colonies of Sweden; others housed the largest number of Finns in the New World. In sparsely settled North Dakota, Scandinavians constituted 30 percent of the population, with Norwegians the largest group. Nebraska, whose population as early as 1870 was 25 percent foreign-born, concentrated Germans, Swedes, Danes, and Czechs. Amid this diverse population, Germans outnumbered all other immigrants by far. A smaller portion of European immigrants reached Kansas, still fewer the territories to the south where Indian and Hispanic peoples and African Americans remained the major ethnic populations. By the end of the century, the West was second only to New England in the proportion of foreign-born persons in its regional population.

Many immigrants found life on the Great Plains difficult but endurable. "Living in Nebraska," the locals joked, "is a lot like being hanged; the initial shock is a bit abrupt, but once you hang there for awhile you sort of get used to it." The German-speaking Russians who settled the Dakotas discovered soil similar to that of their homeland but weather that was even more severe. Having earlier fled religious persecution in Germany for Russia, they brought with them heavy coats and the technique of using sun-dried bricks to build houses in areas where lumber was scarce. These immigrants often provided examples for other settlers less familiar with such harsh terrain.

Having traveled the huge distance with kin or members of their Old World villages, immigrants tended to form tight-knit communities on the Great Plains. Often they advised others still at home to join them and thereby gradually enlarged their distinctive settlements. Many married only within their own group. For example, only 3 percent of Norwegian men married women of a different ethnic background. Like many Mexicanos in the Southwest, several immigrant groups retained their languages well into the twentieth century, usually by sponsoring parochial school systems and publishing their own newspapers. A few groups closed their communities to outsiders. The Poles who migrated to central Nebraska in the 1880s, for example, formed an exclusive settlement; and the German Hutterites, who disavowed private property, lived as much as possible in seclusion in the Bon Homme colony of South Dakota, established in 1874.

Among the native-born settlers of the Great Plains, the largest number had migrated from states bordering the Mississippi River. Settling as individual families rather than as whole communities, they faced an exceptionally solitary life on the Great Plains. The usual rectangular homestead of 160 acres placed farm families at least a half-mile and often much farther from each other. To stave off isolation, homesteaders sometimes built their homes on the adjoining corners of their plots. Still, the prospect of doing better, which brought most homesteaders to the Great Plains in the first place, caused many families to keep seeking greener pastures. Mobility was so high that between one-third and one-half of all households pulled up stakes within a decade.

Communities eventually flourished in prosperous towns, like Grand Island, Nebraska; Coffeyville, Kansas; and Fargo, North Dakota, that served the larger agricultural region. Built alongside the railroad, they grew into commercial centers, home to banking, medical, legal, and retail services. Town life fostered a special intimacy; even in the county graveyard, it was said, a town resident remained among neighbors. But closeness did not necessarily promote social equality or even friendship. A social hierarchy based on education (for the handful of doctors and lawyers) and, more important, investment property (held mainly by railroad agents and bankers) governed relationships between individuals and families. Religion also played a large part in defining these differences. Upwards of 70 percent of town residents were church-affiliated, the largest group being Roman Catholics, followed by Methodists, Lutherans, Baptists, and Presbyterians. Reinforced by family ties and ethnic affiliation, religious allegiances just as often provided a basis for conflict as for community.

Work, Dawn to Dusk

By the 1870s the Great Plains, once the home of buffalo and Indian hunters, was becoming a vast farming region populated mainly by immigrants from Europe and white Americans from east of the Mississippi. In place of the first one-room shanties, sod houses, and log cabins stood substantial frame farmhouses, along with a variety of other buildings like barns, smokehouses, and stables. But the built environment took nothing away from the predominating vista—the expansive fields of grain. "You have no idea, Beulah," wrote a Dakota farmer to his wife, "of what [the wheat farms] are like until you see them. For mile after mile there is not a sign of a tree or stone and just as level as the floor of your house. . . . Wheat never looked better and it is nothing but wheat, wheat, wheat."

Most farm families survived, and prospered if they could, through hard work, often from dawn to dusk. Men's activities in the fields tended to be seasonal,

with heavy work during planting and harvest; at other times, their labor centered on construction or repair of buildings and on taking care of livestock. Women's activities were usually far more routine, week in and week out: cooking and canning of seasonal fruit and vegetables, washing, ironing, churning cream for butter, and keeping chickens for their eggs. Women might occasionally take in boarders, usually young men working temporarily in railroad construction, and they tended to the young children. Many women complained about the ceaseless drudgery, especially when they watched their husbands invest in farm equipment rather than in domestic appliances. The majority felt, as one farm woman put it, "quite lonesome & solitary. . . . I have very little female society." Some, however, relished the challenge. An Iowa woman, for example, liked "to have whole control of my house; can say I am monarch of all I survey and none to dispute my right."

Children also joined in the family's labors. Milking the cows, hauling water, and running errands to neighboring farms could be done by the children, once they had reached the age of nine or so. The "one-room school," where all grades learned together, taught the basics of literacy and arithmetic that a future farmer or commercial employee would require. Sons might be expected to work for ten to twenty years on the family farm, generally for their subsistence alone. Older sons and daughters alike might move to the nearest town to find wagework and contribute their earnings to the family coffer.

The harsh climate and unyielding soil nevertheless forced all but the most reclusive families to seek out friends and neighbors. Many hands were needed to clear the land for cultivation or for roadbeds, to raise houses and barns, or to bring in a harvest before a threatening storm. Neighbors might agree to work together haying, harvesting, and threshing grain. They also traded their labor, calculated by the hour, for use of equipment or for special assistance. A well-to-do farmer might "rent" his threshing machine in exchange for a small cash fee and, for instance, three days' labor. His wife might barter her garden produce for her neighbor's bread and milk or for help during childbirth or disability. Women often combined work and leisure in quilting bees and sewing circles, where they made friends while sharing scraps of material and technical information. Whole communities turned out for special events, such as the seasonal husking bees and apple bees, which were organized mainly by women.

Much of this informal barter, however, resulted from lack of cash rather than a lasting desire to cooperate. When annual harvests were bountiful, even the farm woman's practice of bartering goods with neighbors and local merchants—butter and eggs in return for yard

These homesteaders in Nebraska, 1886, confronted the typically harsh conditions of treeless plains by erecting sod huts. They often brought with them an assortment of seeds and seedlings for spring plantings and a small number of livestock. A good fall harvest would provide the cash for building more substantial frame houses and outbuildings and encourage other homesteaders to settle near them. Communities eventually grew from these crude beginnings.

SOURCE: Sylvester Rawding Family sod house, 1884. Nebraska State Historical Society, Solomon D. Butcher Collection (RG2608–1784).

goods or seed—diminished sharply, replaced by cash transactions. Still, wheat production proved unsteady in the last half of the nineteenth century, and few farm families could remain reliant wholly on themselves.

For many farmers, the soil simply would not yield a livelihood, and they often owed more money than they took in. Start-up costs, including the purchase of land and equipment, put many farmers deep in debt to local creditors. Some lost their land altogether. By 1880, when the Bureau of the Census began to compile statistics on tenant-operated farms, nearly 18 percent of the farms in Nebraska were worked by tenants; a decade later the portion had risen to nearly one-quarter. By the turn of the century, more than one-third of all farmers in the United States were tenants on someone else's land.

The Garden of Eden was not to be found on the prairies or on the plains, no matter how hard the average farm family worked. Again and again foreclosures wiped out the small landowner through dips in commodity prices, bad decisions, natural disasters, or illness. In one especially bad year, 1881, a group of farmers in western Iowa chose to burn off rather than harvest their wheat because the yield promised to be so small. Many farmers stood only a step away from financial disaster, wondering if they had chosen the best life for themselves and their families. The swift growth of rural population soon ended. Although writers and orators alike continued to celebrate the family farm as the source of virtue and economic well-being, the hard reality of big money and political power told a far different story.

THE WORLD'S BREADBASKET

During the second half of the nineteenth century commercial farms employed the most intensive and extensive methods of agricultural production in the world. Hard-working farmers brought huge numbers of acres under cultivation, while new technologies allowed them to achieve unprecedented levels of efficiency in the planting and harvesting of crops. As a result, western agriculture became increasingly tied to international trade, and modern capitalism soon ruled western agriculture, as it did the mining and cattle industries.

New Production Technologies

Only after the trees had been cleared and grasslands cut free of roots could the soil be prepared for planting. But as farmers on the Great Plains knew so well, the sod west of the Mississippi did not yield readily to cultivation and often broke the cast-iron plows typically used by eastern farmers. Farther west, some farmers resorted to drills to plant seeds for crops such as wheat and oats. Even in the best locations, where loamy, fertile ground had built up over centuries into eight or more inches of decayed vegetation, the preliminary breaking, or "busting," of the sod required hard labor. One man would guide a team of five or six oxen pulling a plow through the soil, while another regulated the depth of the cut, or furrow. But, as a North Dakota settler wrote to his wife back in Michigan, after the first crop the soil became as "soft as can be, any team [of men and animals] can work it."

This "thirty-three horse team harvester" was photographed at the turn of the century in Walla Walla, Washington. Binding the grain into sheaves before it could hit the ground, the "harvester" cut, threshed, and sacked wheat in one single motion.

SOURCE: ca. 1902. Library of Congress.

Agricultural productivity depended as much on new technology as on the farmers' hard labor. In 1837 John Deere had designed his famous "singing plow" that easily turned prairie grasses under and turned up even highly compacted soils. Around the same time, Cyrus McCormick's reaper began to be used for cutting grain; by the 1850s his factories were turning out reapers in mass quantities. McCormick's design featured ridges of triangular knives, like sharks' teeth, that mechanically sliced through the stalks as the reaper moved forward pulled by horses or, later, by steam- or gasoline-powered engines. The harvester, invented in the 1870s, drew the cut stalks upward to a platform where two men could bind them into sheaves; by the 1880s an automatic knotter tied them together. Drastically reducing the number of people traditionally required for this work, the harvester increased the pace many times over.

Improvements were not limited to the reaper and harvester, although these machines underwent continuous redesign and were enhanced first by steam and eventually gasoline power. From the 1840s on, the U.S. Patent Office recorded an astonishing number of agricultural inventions. The introduction of mechanized corn planters and mowing or raking machines for hay all but completed the technological arsenal.

In the 1890s, the U.S. commissioner of labor measured the impact of technology on farm productivity. Before the introduction of the wire binder in 1875, he reported, a farmer could not plant more than 8 acres of wheat if he were to harvest it successfully without help; by 1890 the same farmer could rely on his new machine to handle 135 acres with relative ease and without risk of spoilage. The improvements in the last half of the century allowed an average farmer to produce up to ten times more than was possible with the old implements.

Scientific study of soil, grain, and climatic conditions was another factor in the record output. Heretofore, farmers relied on tradition or experimented with whatever the grain merchants had to offer. Beginning in the mid-nineteenth century, federal and state governments added inducements to the growing body of expertise, scientific information, and hands-on advice. Through the Morrill Act of 1862, "land-grant" colleges acquired space for campuses in return for promising to institute agricultural programs. The Department of Agriculture, which attained cabinet level status in 1889, and the Weather Bureau (transferred from the War Department in 1891) also made considerable contributions to farmers' knowledge. The federal Hatch Act of 1887, which created a series of state experimental stations, provided for basic agricultural research, especially in the areas of soil minerals and plant growth. Many states added their own agricultural stations, usually connected with state colleges and universities.

Nature nevertheless often reigned over technological innovation and seemed in places to take revenge against these early successes. West of the 98th meridian—a north-south line extending through western Oklahoma, central Kansas and Nebraska, and eastern Dakota—perennial dryness due to an annual rainfall of less than 20 inches constantly threatened to turn soil into dust and to break plows on the hardened ground. Summer heat burned out crops and ignited grass fires. Mountains of winter snows turned rivers into spring torrents that flooded fields; heavy fall rains washed crops away. Even good weather invited worms and flying insects to infest the crops. During the 1870s grasshoppers in clouds a mile long ate everything organic, including tree bark and clothes. Mormons erected a statue to the

HAND V. MACHINE LABOR ON THE FARM, CA. 1880				
	Time Worked		Labor Cost	
Crop	Hand	Machine	Hand	Machine
Wheat	61 hours	3 hours	$3.55	$0.66
Corn	39 hours	15 hours	3.62	1.51
Oats	66 hours	7 hours	3.73	1.07
Loose Hay	21 hours	4 hours	1.75	0.42
Baled Hay	35 hours	12 hours	3.06	1.29

gulls who made a surprise appearance in Utah to eat the "hoppers"; however, most farmers were not as lucky as the Mormons.

Producing for the Market

From the Midwest to the far reaches of the Great Plains, farming changed in important ways during the last third of the nineteenth century. Although the family remained the primary source of labor, farmers tended to put more emphasis on production for exchange rather than for home use. They continued to plant vegetable gardens and often kept fowl or livestock for the family's consumption, but farmers raised crops mainly for the market and measured their own success or failure in terms of cash products.

Most large-scale or "bonanza" farmers specialized in one or two crops, such as corn, rye, or barley, and sent their goods by railroad to eastern distributors and thence to national and international markets. Wheat farmers in particular prospered. With the world population increasing at a rapid rate, the international demand for wheat was enormous, and American farmers made huge profits from the sale of this crop. Wheat production ultimately served as a barometer of the agricultural economy in the West. Farmers in all corners of the region, from Nebraska to California, expanded or contracted their holdings and planned their crops according to the price of wheat.

The new machines and expanding market did not necessarily guarantee success. Land, draft animals, and equipment remained very expensive, and start-up costs could keep a family in debt for decades. A year of good returns often preceded a year of financial disaster. Weather conditions, international markets, and railroad and steamship shipping prices all proved equally unpredictable and heartless.

Farmers who settled on good lands in the 1860s and 1870s were more fortunate than those to follow. These pioneers, who began with only a little capital and worked twenty or thirty years to build up livestock and crops, frequently reached old age knowing that they could leave productive farmland to their sons or daughters. Latecomers found most of the good land already locked up in production or too expensive to acquire.

The new technology and scientific expertise favored the large, well-capitalized farmer over the small one. Such is the story of the large-scale wheat operations in the great Red River Valley of North Dakota. Here a shrewd worker such as Oliver Dalrymple could take advantage of a spectacular bonanza. When Dalrymple started out in 1875, he managed a farm owned by two officials of the Northern Pacific Railroad. He cleared their land, planted wheat, and yielded a sizable harvest the first year. He did much better the second year and

began to invest in his own farm. A decade later his operations included 32,000 acres in wheat and 2,000 in oats. Dalrymple now had the financial resources to use the latest technology to harvest these crops and to employ up to 1,000 seasonal laborers at a time. The majority of farmers with fewer resources expanded at more modest rates. Between 1880 and 1900, average farm size in the seven leading grain-growing states increased from 64.4 acres to more than 100 acres.

California Agribusiness

The trend toward big farms reached an apex in California, where farming as a business surpassed farming as a way of life. The conclusion of the Mexican-American War in 1848 coincided with the beginning of the Gold Rush, and the Anglos flooding the new territory wanted the land that had been held for centuries by the Spanish-speaking peoples, the Californios. The U.S. Congress created the Lands Claims Commission in 1851 to examine the great land-grant system that had been introduced by the Spaniards. Although the Supreme Court ultimately validated many of their holdings, the cost of litigation and steep land taxes forced many Californios into debt. Bankers, railroad magnates, and other Anglos made rich by the Gold Rush took possession of the best farming land in the state. The new owners introduced the latest technologies, built dams and canals, and invested huge amounts of capital, setting the pattern for the state's prosperous agribusiness. Farms of nearly 500 acres dominated the California landscape in 1870; by the turn of the century, two-thirds of the state's arable land was in 1,000-acre farms. As land reformer and social commentator Henry George noted, California was "not a country of farms but a country of plantations and estates."

This scale of production made California the national leader in wheat production by the mid-1880s. But it also succeeded dramatically with fruit and vegetables. Large- and medium-sized growers, shrewdly combined in cooperative marketing associations during the 1870s and 1880s, used the new refrigerator cars to ship their produce in large quantities to the East and even to Europe. By 1890, cherries, apricots, and oranges, packed with mountains of ice, made their way into homes across the United States.

California growers learned quickly that they could satisfy consumer appetites and even create new ones. Orange producers packed their products individually in tissue paper, a technique designed to convince eastern consumers that they were about to eat a luxury fruit. By the turn of the century, advertisers for the California Citrus Growers' Association described oranges as a necessity for good health, inventing the trademark "Sunkist" to be stamped on each orange. Meanwhile

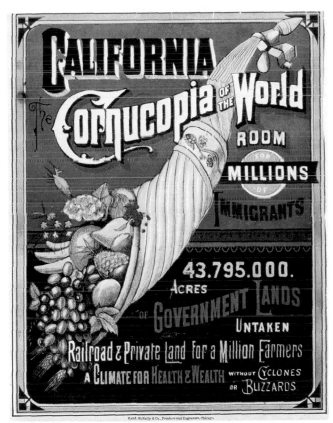

In the decades after the Civil War, agricultural production expanded at a fast pace as farmers migrated farther westward. California farmers, who enjoyed the benefits of a temperate climate, produced a great variety of crops, including wheat, vegetables, fruits, and nuts. Railroad advertisers, hoping to attract prospective farmers to the region, commonly relied on this popular image of California as a region overflowing in fresh produce.

SOURCE: *California, Cornucopia of the World,* ca. 1880. Lithograph poster from the Bella C. Landauer Collection. © Collection of The New York Historical Society. Negative no. 41800.

California's grape growing grew into a big business, led by promoter and winemaker Paul Masson. Long considered inferior to French wines, California wines found a ready market at lower prices. Other grape growers made their fortunes in raisins. By the early twentieth century, one association trademarked its raisins as "Sun Maid" and packaged them for schoolchildren in the famous "nickel" box.

By 1900, California had become the model for American agribusiness, not the home of self-sufficient homesteaders but the showcase of heavily capitalized farm factories. Machines soon displaced animals and even many people. Many Californios tried to hold onto their traditional forms of labor if not their land, only to join the Chinese workers who by 1870 had become the backbone of the state's migrant workforce. Intense

battles in the state legislature over land and irrigation rights underscored the message that powerful forces had gathered in California to promote large-scale agricultural production.

The Toll on the Land

The delicate ecologies of the West perished more quickly under human pressure than those prevailing anywhere else on the continent. Viewing the land as a resource to command, the new inhabitants often looked past the existing flora and fauna toward a landscape remade strictly for commercial purposes. The changes they produced in some areas were nearly as cataclysmic as those that occurred during the Ice Age.

Banishing many existing species, farmers "improved" the land by introducing exotic plants and animals— that is, biological colonies indigenous to other regions and continents. Some of the new plants and animals flourished in alien surroundings; many did not. Farmers also unintentionally introduced new varieties of weeds, insect pests, and rats. Surviving portions of older grasslands and meadows eventually could be found only alongside railroad tracks, in graveyards, or inside national parks.

Numerous species disappeared altogether or suffered drastic reduction. The grizzly bear, for example, an animal exclusive to the West, could once be found in large numbers from the Great Plains to California and throughout much of Alaska; by the early decades of the twentieth century, one nature writer estimated that only 800 survived, mostly in Yellowstone National Park. At the same time the number of wolves declined from perhaps as many as 2 million to just 200,000. "If you count the buffalo for hides and the antelope for backstraps and the passenger pigeons for target practice and the Indian ponies (killed by whites, to keep the Indian poor)," one scholar estimates, "it is conceivable that 500 million creatures died" on the Great Plains alone. By the mid-1880s, no more than 5,000 buffalo survived in the entire United States, and little remained of the once vast herds but great heaps of bones sold for $7.50 per ton.

The slaughter of the buffalo had a dramatic impact, not only on the fate of the species but also on the grasslands of the Great Plains. Overall, the biological diversity of the region had been drastically reduced. Unlike the grizzly and wolf, buffalo had not been exclusively Western animals. Before European colonization they had grazed over an area of 3 million square miles, nearly to the east coast; as the wide-ranging herds moved on, the grasslands were replenished. Having killed off the giant herds, ranchers and farmers quickly shifted to cattle and sheep production. Unlike the roaming buffalo, these livestock did not range widely and soon devoured the native grasses down to their roots. With the ground cover destroyed, the soil eroded and became barren. By the end of the century, huge dust storms formed across the windswept plains.

New forests, many settlers hoped, would improve the weather, restore the soil, and also provide a source for fencing and fuel. In 1873 the U.S. Congress passed the Timber Culture Act, which allotted homesteaders an additional 160 acres of land in return for planting and cultivating forty acres of trees. Because residence was not required, and because tree planting could not be assessed for at least thirteen years, speculators filed for several claims at once, then turned around and sold the land without having planted a single tree. Although some forests were restored, neither the weather nor the soil improved.

Large-scale commercial agriculture also took a heavy toll on inland waters. Before white settlement, rainfall had drained naturally into lakes and underground aquifers, and watering spots were abundant throughout the Great Plains. Farmers mechanically

rerouted and dammed water to irrigate their crops, causing many bodies of water to disappear and the water table to drop significantly. Successful farmers pressed for ever greater supplies of water. In 1887 the state of California formed irrigation districts, securing bond issues for the construction of canals, and other western states followed. But by the 1890s, irrigation had seemed to reach its limit without federal support. The Newlands or National Reclamation Act of 1902 added 1 million acres of irrigated land, and state irrigation districts added more than 10 million acres. Expensive to taxpayers, and ultimately benefiting corporate farmers rather than small landowners, these projects further diverted water and totally transformed the landscape.

Although western state politicians and federal officials debated water rights for decades, they rarely considered the impact of water policies on the environment. Lake Tulare in California's Central Valley, for example, had occupied up to 760 square miles. After farmers began to irrigate their land by tapping the rivers that fed

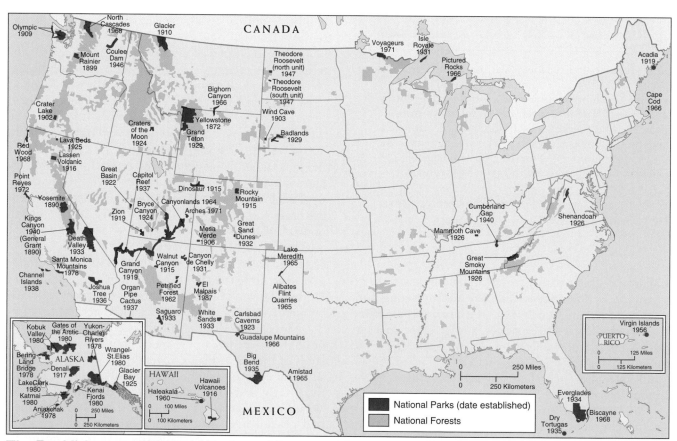

The Establishment of National Parks and Forests The setting aside of land for national parks saved large districts of the West from early commercial development and industrial degradation, setting a precedent for the later establishment of additional parks in economically marginal but scenic territory. The West, home to the vast majority of park space, became a principal site of tourism by the end of the nineteenth century.

Tulare, the lake shrank dramatically, covering a mere 36 square miles by the early twentieth century. Finally the lake, which had supported rich aquatic and avian life for thousands of years, disappeared entirely. The land left behind, now wholly dependent on irrigation, grew so alkaline in spots that it could no longer be used for agricultural purposes.

The need to maintain the water supply indirectly led to the creation of national forests and the Forest Service. Western farmers supported the General Land Revision Act of 1891, which gave the president the power to establish forest reserves to protect watersheds against the threats posed by lumbering, overgrazing, and forest fires. In the years that followed, President Benjamin Harrison established fifteen forest reserves exceeding 16 million acres, and President Grover Cleveland added more than 21 million acres. But only in 1897 did the secretary of the interior finally gain the authority to regulate the use of these reserves.

The Forest Management Act of 1897 and the National Reclamation Act of 1902 set the federal government on the path of large-scale regulatory activities. The Forest Service was established in 1905, and in 1907 forest reserves were transferred from the Department of the Interior to the Department of Agriculture. The federal government would now play an even larger role in economic development of the West, dealing mainly with corporate farmers and ranchers eager for improvements.

THE WESTERN LANDSCAPE

Throughout the nineteenth century, many Americans viewed western expansion as the nation's "manifest destiny," and just as many marveled at the region's natural and cultural wonders. Their fascination grew with the proliferation of printed literature, "Wild West" entertainments, sideshows, and traveling exhibits featuring western themes. The public east of the Mississippi craved stories about the West and visual images of its sweeping vistas. Artists and photographers built their reputations in what they saw and imagined. Scholars, from geologists and botanists to historians and anthropologists, toured the trans-Mississippi West in pursuit of new data. The region and its peoples came to represent what was both unique and magnificent about the American landscape.

Nature's Majesty

Alexis de Tocqueville, the famed commentator on American society, found little beauty in the land west of the Mississippi. Writing in the 1830s, he described the landscape as "more and more uneven and sterile," the soil "punctured in a thousand places by primitive rocks

sticking out here and there like the bones of a skeleton when sinews of flesh have perished." By the end of the century, scores of writers had provided an entirely different image of the American West. They described spectacular, breathtaking natural sites like the Grand Tetons and High Sierras, vast meadows of waving grasses and beautiful flowers, expansive canyons and rushing white rivers, and exquisite deserts covered with sagebrush or dotted with flowering cactus and enticing precisely for their stark qualities. A traveler through Yellowstone country recalled "the varied scenery" of the West and its "stupendous & remarkable manifestations of nature's forces," an impression destined to stay with him "as long as memory lasts."

Landscape painters, particularly the group that became known as the Rocky Mountain School, also piqued the public's interest in western scenery. Exhibited in galleries and museums and reproduced in popular magazines, their sketches and paintings circulated western imagery throughout the country and through much of Europe. In the 1860s, German-born Albert Bierstadt, equipped with a camera, traveled the Oregon Trail. Using his photographs as inspiration, Bierstadt painted mountains so wondrous that they seemed nearly surreal, projecting a divine aura behind the majesty of nature. His "earthscapes"—huge canvases with exacting details of animals and plants—thrilled viewers and sold for tens of thousands of dollars.

Moved by such evidence, the federal government began to set aside huge tracts of land as nature reserves. In 1864 Congress passed the Yosemite Act, which placed the spectacular cliffs and giant sequoias under the management of the state of California. Meanwhile, explorers returned to the East awestruck by the varied terrain of the Rocky Mountains, the largest mountain chain in North America. These early visitors described huge sky-high lakes, boiling mud, and spectacular waterfalls. Finally, in 1871, the federal government funded a major undertaking by a team of researchers from the Geological and Geographical Survey of the Territories, which included the early landscape photographer William H. Jackson and the painter Thomas Moran. These researchers brought back to Congress visual proof of the monumental scenery of the West, including the Grand Canyon. In 1872 Congress named Yellowstone the first national park. Yosemite and Sequoia in California, Crater Lake in Oregon, Mount Ranier in Washington, and Glacier in Montana all became national parks between 1890 and 1910.

Many of the wilderness enthusiasts, however, worked to set aside these territories at the expense of the Indian peoples who occupied them. Aware that tourists fearing Indian presence would avoid national parks, federal officials attempted to fortify the territories. In 1886, the U.S. Army took over the job of protecting

Albert Bierstadt became one of the first artists to capture on enormous canvases the vastness and rugged terrain of mountains and western wilderness. Many other artists joined Bierstadt to form the Rocky Mountain School. In time, the camera largely replaced the paintbrush, and most Americans formed an image of these majestic peaks from postcards and magazine illustrations.

SOURCE: Albert Bierstadt. *Merced River, Yosemite Valley, 1866.* Oil on canvas, 4.36′ × 50″. The Metropolitan Museum of Art. Gift of the Sons of William Paton, 1909 (09.214.1). Photograph © 1982 The Metropolitan Museum of Art.

Yellowstone from the bands of Crow, Shoshone, and Bannock that, by treaty rights, customarily used the park for hunting game. Ten years later, the U. S. Supreme Court ruled that Wyoming, on becoming a state, gained the right to regulate hunting, thus in effect nullifying the preexisting treaties. *Ward* v. *Racehorse*, the deciding court case, significantly diminished the presence of Indian bands in Yellowstone and, as other states followed suit, in all public lands, and it restricted them to reservations except during open hunting seasons.

The Legendary Wild West

Legends of the Wild West grew into a staple of popular culture just as the actual work of cowboys became more routine. By the end of the century, many Americans, rich and poor alike, imagined the West as a land of promise and opportunity and, above all, of excitement and adventure. Future president Theodore Roosevelt helped to promote this view. Soon after his election to the New York State Assembly in 1882, Roosevelt was horrified to see himself lampooned in the newspapers as a dandy and weakling. A year later, after buying a ranch in South Dakota, he began to reconstruct his public image. He wrote three books recounting his adventures in the West, claiming that they had not only instilled in him

personal bravery and "hardihood" but self-reliance. In 1886 he was back in New York, running for mayor as the "Cowboy of the Dakotas." In April 1899, he addressed the members of Chicago's elite Hamilton Club, inviting them to join him in "the strenuous life" as exemplified by their Indian-fighter ancestors. Indeed, by this time many Americans had joined Roosevelt in imagining the West as a source of rejuvenation and virility. Young men at Harvard and Yale universities, for example, had named their hunting clubs after Daniel Boone and Davy Crockett. The West, as Roosevelt insisted, meant "vigorous manhood."

The first "westerns," the "dime novels" that sold in the 1860s in editions of 50,000 or more, reflected these myths. Competing against stories about pirates, wars, crime, and sea adventures, westerns outsold the others. Edward Zane Carroll Judson's *Buffalo Bill, the King of the Border Men,* first published in 1869, spawned hundreds of other novels, thousands of stories, and an entire magazine devoted to Buffalo Bill. Even before farmers had successfully halted the free-grazing of cattle, writers made tough cowboys and high-spirited women into legends of the Wild West. Real-life African American cowboy Nat Love lived on in the imaginations of many generations as Edward L. Wheeler's dime novel hero "Deadwood Dick," who rode the range as a white cowboy in black clothes in over thirty stories. His girlfriend "Calamity Jane"—"the most reckless buchario in ther Hills"—also took on mythic qualities.

Railroad promoters and herd owners actively promoted these romantic and heroic images. Cowman Joseph McCoy staged Wild West shows in St. Louis and Chicago, where Texas cowboys entertained prospective buyers by roping calves and breaking horses. Many cowboys played up this imaginary role, dressing and talking to match the stories told about them. "The drovers of the seventies were a wild and reckless bunch," recalled cowboy Teddy Blue. Typically, they had worn a "wide brimmed beaver hat, black or brown with a low crown, fancy shirts, high heeled boots, and sometimes a vest." In the 1880s cowboys adopted the high-crowned Stetson hat, ornately detailed shirts with pockets, and striped or checked pants. The first professional photographers often made their living touring the West, setting

Buffalo Bill's "Wild West Show" poster from 1899. William Cody's theatrical company toured the United States and Europe for decades, reenacting various battles and occasionally switching to football (cowboys versus Indians). Cody's style set the pace for both rodeos and Western silent films.

SOURCE: Library of Congress.

up studios where cowboys and prostitutes posed in elaborate costumes.

For thirty years, Wild West shows toured the United States and Europe. The former Pony Express rider, army scout, and famed buffalo hunter William F. Cody hit upon the idea of an extravaganza that would bring the legendary West to those who could never experience it in person. "Buffalo Bill" Cody made sharpshooter Annie Oakley a star performer. Entrancing crowds with her stunning accuracy with pistol or rifle, Oakley shot dimes in midair and cigarettes from her husband's mouth. Cody also hired Sioux Indians and hundreds of cowboys to perform in mock stagecoach robberies and battles. Shows like Custer's Last Stand thrilled crowds, including Britain's Queen Victoria. Revamped as the rodeo, the Wild West show long outlasted Buffalo Bill, who died in 1917.

With far less fanfare, many veteran cowboys enlisted themselves on "dude ranches" for tourists or performed as rope twirlers or yodeling singers in theaters across the United States. In 1902 Owen Wister's novel *The Virginian* fixed in the popular imagination the scene of the cowboy facing down the villain and saying, "When you call me that, *smile!*"

The "American Primitive"

New technologies of graphic reproduction encouraged painters and photographers to provide new images of the West, authentic as well as fabricated. A young German

American artist, Charles Schreyvogel, saw Buffalo Bill's tent show in Buffalo and decided to make the West his life's work. His canvases depicted Indian warriors and U.S. cavalry fighting furiously but without blood and gore. Charles Russell, a genuine cowboy, painted the life he knew, but also indulged in imaginary scenarios, producing paintings of buffalo hunts and first encounters between Indian peoples and white explorers.

Frederic Remington, the most famous of all the western artists, left Yale Art School to visit Montana in 1881, became a Kansas sheep herder and tavern owner, and then returned to painting. Inspired by newspaper stories of the army's campaign against the Apaches, he made himself into a war correspondent and captured vivid scenes of battle in his sketches. Painstakingly accurate in physical details, especially of horses, his paintings celebrated the "winning of the West" from the Indian peoples. By the turn of the century, Remington was the chief magazine illustrator of western history.

Remington joined hundreds of other painters and engravers in reproducing the most popular historic event: Custer's Last Stand. Totally fictionalized by white artists to show a heroic General Custer personally holding off advancing Indian warriors, these renditions dramatized the romance and tragedy of conquest. Indian artists recorded Custer's defeat in far less noble fashion.

Photographers often produced highly nuanced portraits of Indian peoples. Dozens of early photographers from the Bureau of American Ethnology captured the gaze of noble tribespeople or showed them hard at work digging clams or grinding corn. President Theodore Roosevelt praised Edward Sheriff Curtis for vividly conveying tribal virtue. Generations later, in the 1960s and 1970s, Curtis's photographs again captured the imagination of western enthusiasts, who were unaware or unconcerned that this sympathetic artist had often posed his subjects or retouched his photos to blur out any artifacts of white society.

Painters and photographers led the way for scholarly research on the various Indian societies. The early ethnographer and pioneer of fieldwork in anthropology Lewis Henry Morgan devoted his life to the study of Indian family or kinship patterns, mostly of eastern tribes such as the Iroquois, who adopted him into their Hawk Clan. In 1851 he published *League of the Ho-de-no-sau-nee, or*

Iroquois, considered the first scientific account of an Indian tribe. A decade later Morgan ventured into Cheyenne country to examine the naming patterns of this tribe. In his major work, *Ancient Society*, published in 1877, he posited a universal process of social evolution leading from savagery to barbarism to civilization.

One of the most influential interpreters of the cultures of living tribespeople was the pioneering ethnographer Alice Cunningham Fletcher. In 1879, Fletcher met Suzette (Bright Eyes) La Flesche of the Omaha tribe, who was on a speaking tour to gain support for her people, primarily to prevent their removal from tribal lands. Fletcher, then forty-two years old, accompanied La Flesche to Nebraska, telling the Omahas that she had come "to learn, if you will let me, something about your tribal organization, social customs, tribal rites, traditions and songs. Also to see if I can help you in any way." After transcribing hundreds of songs, Fletcher became well known as an expert on Omaha music. She also supported the Omahas' campaign to gain individual title to tribal lands, eventually drafting legislation that was enacted by Congress as the Omaha Act of 1882. In 1885, Fletcher produced for the U.S. Senate a report titled *Indian Education and Civilization*, one of the first general statements on the status of Indian peoples. As a founder of the American Anthropological Society and president of the American Folk-Lore Society, she encouraged further study of Indian societies.

While white settlers and the federal government continued to threaten the survival of tribal life, Indian lore became a major pursuit of scholars and amateurs alike. Adults and children delighted in turning up arrowheads. Fraternal organizations such as the Elks and Eagles borrowed tribal terminology. The Boy Scouts and Girl Scouts, the nation's premier youth organizations, used tribal lore to instill strength of character. And the U.S. Treasury stamped images of tribal chiefs and buffalo on the nation's most frequently used coins.

THE TRANSFORMATION OF INDIAN SOCIETIES

In 1871, the U.S. government formally ended the treaty system, eclipsing without completely abolishing the sovereignty of Indian nations. Still, the tribes persisted. Using a mixture of survival strategies from farming and trade to the leasing of reservation lands, they both adapted to changing conditions and maintained old traditions.

Reform Policy and Politics

By 1880, many Indian tribes had been forcibly resettled on reservations, but very few had adapted to white ways. For decades, reformers, mainly from the Protestant churches, had lobbied Congress for a program of salvation through assimilation, and they looked to the Board of Indian Commissioners, created in 1869, to carry out this mission. The board often succeeded in

OVERVIEW

MAJOR INDIAN TREATIES AND LEGISLATION OF THE LATE NINETEENTH CENTURY

1863	Nez Percé Treaty	Signed illegally on behalf of the entire tribe in which the Nez Percé abandoned 6 million acres of land in return for a small reservation in northeastern Oregon. Led to Nez Percé wars, which ended in 1877 with the surrender of Chief Joseph.
1867	Medicine Lodge Treaty	Assigned reservations in existing Indian Territory to Comanches, Plains (Kiowa), Appaches, Kiowas, Cheyennes, and Arapahoes, bringing these tribes together with Sioux, Shoshones, Bannocks, and Navajos.
1868	Treaty of Fort Laramie	Successfully ended Red Cloud's war by evacuating federal troops from Sioux Territory along the Bozeman Trail; additionally granted Sioux ownership of the western half of South Dakota and rights to use Powder River county in Wyoming and Montana.
1871		Congress declares end to treaty system.
1887	Dawes Severalty Act	Divided communal tribal land, granting the right to petition for citizenship to those Indians who accepted the individual land allotment of 160 acres. Successfully undermined sovereignty.

mediating conflicts among the various tribes crowded onto reservations but made far less headway in converting them to Christianity or transforming them into prosperous farming communities. The majority of Indian peoples lived in poverty and misery, deprived of their traditional means of survival and more often than not subjected to fraud by corrupt government officials and private suppliers. Reformers who observed these conditions firsthand nevertheless remained unshaken in their belief that tribespeople must be raised out of the darkness of ignorance into the light of civilization. Some conceded, however, that the reservation system might not be the best means to this end.

Unlike most Americans, who saw the conquest of the West as a means to national glory, some reformers were genuinely outraged by the government's continuous violation of treaty obligations and the military enforcement of the reservation policy. One of the most influential was Helen Hunt Jackson, a noted poet and author of children's stories. In 1879 Jackson had attended a lecture in Hartford, Connecticut, by a chief of the Ponca tribe whose destitute people had been forced from their Dakota homeland. Heartstruck, Jackson lobbied former abolitionists such as Wendell Phillips to work for Indians' rights and herself began to write against government policy. Her book-length exposé, *A Century of Dishonor*, published in 1881, detailed the plight of Indian peoples.

Jackson threw herself into the Indian Rights Association, an offshoot of the Women's National Indian Association (WNIA), which had been formed in 1874 to rally public support for a program of assimilation. The two organizations helped to place Protestant missionaries in the West to work to eradicate tribal customs as well as to convert Indian peoples to Christianity. According to the reformers' plans, men would now farm as well as hunt, while women would leave the fields to take care of home and children. Likewise, all communal practices would be abandoned in favor of individually owned homesteads, where families could develop in the "American" manner and even celebrate proper holidays such as the Fourth of July. Children, hair trimmed short, would be placed in boarding schools where, removed from their parents' influence, they

would shed traditional values and cultural practices. By 1882 the WNIA had gathered 100,000 signatures on petitions urging Congress to phase out the reservation system, to establish universal education for Indian children, and to award title to 160 acres to any Indian individual willing to work the land.

The Dawes Severalty Act, passed by Congress in 1887, incorporated many of these measures and established federal Indian policy for decades to come. The act allowed the president to distribute land not to tribes but to individuals legally "severed" from their tribes. The commissioner of Indian affairs rendered the popular interpretation that "tribal relations should be broken up, socialism destroyed and the family and autonomy of the individual substituted. The allotment of land in severalty, the establishment of local courts and police, the development of a personal sense of independence and the universal adoption of the English language are means to this end."

Those individuals who accepted the land allotment of 160 acres and agreed to allow the government to sell unallotted tribal lands (with some funds set aside for education) could petition to become citizens of the United States. A little over a decade after its enactment,

In 1890, the celebrated artist Frederic Remington (1861–1909) produced this color sketch of Oglala Sioux at the Pine Ridge Indian Reservation in South Dakota. By this time, Remington had established himself as a leading illustrator of western themes, including the Indian Wars. He had traveled extensively in the West, gathering information, making sketches, and taking photographs, which he later used at his studio in New Rochelle, New York. Remington sold his illustrations to major magazines, including *Harper's Weekly*.

The ghost dance of 1890, pictured here, provided artists like Remington with vivid imagery. The dancers wore brightly patterned robes and shirts, some decorated with stars symbolizing the coming of a new age for the Indians

SOURCE: Frederic Remington, *Oglala Sioux performing the Ghost Dance at the Pine Ridge Indian Agency, South Dakota, 1890*/The Granger Collection, New York (4E400.03).

many reformers believed that the Dawes Act had resolved the basis of the "Indian problem." Hollow Horn Bear, a Sioux chief, offered a different opinion, judging the Dawes Act to be "only another trick of the whites."

The Dawes Act successfully undermined tribal sovereignty but offered little compensation. Indian religions and sacred ceremonies were banned, the telling of legends and myths forbidden, and shaman and medicine men imprisoned or exiled for continuing their traditional practices. "Indian schools" forbade Indian languages, clothing styles, and even hair fashions in order to "kill the Indian . . . and save the man," as one schoolmaster put it.

These and other measures did little to integrate Indians into white society. Treated as savages, Indian children fled most white schools. Nor did adults receive much encouragement to become property holders. Government agencies allotted them inferior farmland, inadequate tools, and little training for agricultural self-sufficiency. Seeing scant advantage in assimilating, only a minority of adults dropped their tribal religion for Christianity or their communal ways for the accumulation of private property. Within the next forty years, the Indian peoples lost 60 percent of the reservation land remaining in 1887 and 66 percent of the land allotted to them as homesteaders. The tenets of the Dawes Act were not reversed until 1934. In that year, Congress passed the Indian Reorganization Act, which affirmed the integrity of Indian cultural institutions and returned some land to tribal ownership (see Chapter 24).

The Ghost Dance

After the passage of the Dawes Severalty Act, one more cycle of rebellion remained for the Sioux. In 1888, the Paiute prophet Wovoka, ill with scarlet fever, had a vision during a total eclipse of the sun. In his vision, the Creator told him that if the Indian peoples learned to love each other, they would be granted a special place in the afterlife. The Creator also gave him the Ghost Dance, which the prophet performed for others and soon spread throughout the tribe. The Sioux came to believe that when the day of judgment came, all Indian peoples who had ever lived would return to their lost world and white peoples would vanish from the earth. The chant sounded:

> The whole world is coming.
> A nation is coming, a nation is coming.
> The Eagle has brought the message to the tribe.
> The father says so, the father says so.
> Over the whole earth they are coming.
> The buffalo are coming, the buffalo are coming.
> The Crow has brought the message to the tribe,
> The Father says so, the Father says so.

Many white settlers and federal officials feared the Ghost Dancers, even though belief in a sudden divine judgment was common among Christians and Jews. Before the Civil War, Protestant groups such as the Millerites, who had renounced personal property and prepared themselves for the millennium, were tolerated by other Americans. But after decades of Indian warfare, white Americans took the Ghost Dance as a warning of tribal retribution rather than a religious ceremony. As thousands of Sioux danced to exhaustion, local whites intolerantly demanded the practice be stopped. The U.S. Seventh Cavalry, led in part by survivors of the Battle of Little Bighorn, rushed to the Pine Ridge Reservation, and a group of the Sioux led by Big Foot, now fearing mass murder, moved into hiding in the Bad Lands of South Dakota. After a skirmish, the great leader Sitting Bull and his young son lay dead.

The Seventh Calvary pursued the Sioux Ghost Dancers and 300 undernourished Sioux, freezing and without horses, to Wounded Knee Creek on the Pine Ridge Reservation. There, on December 29, 1890, while the peace-seeking Big Foot, who had personally raised a white flag of surrender, lay dying of pneumonia, they were surrounded by soldiers armed with automatic guns. The U.S. troops expected the Sioux to surrender their few remaining weapons, but an accidental gunshot from one deaf brave who misunderstood the command caused panic on both sides.

Within minutes, 200 Sioux had been cut down and dozens of soldiers wounded, mostly by their own cross fire. For two hours soldiers continued to shoot at anything that moved—mostly women and children straggling away. Many of the injured froze to death in the snow; others were transported in open wagons and finally laid out on beds of hay under Christmas decorations at the Pine Ridge Episcopal church. The massacre, which took place almost exactly 400 years after Columbus "discovered" the New World for Christian civilization, seemed to mark the final conquest of the continent's indigenous peoples.

Black Elk later recalled, "I can see that something else died there in the bloody mud, and was buried in the blizzard. A people's dream died there. It was a beautiful dream. . . . The nation's hoop is broken and scattered. There is no center any longer, and the sacred tree is dead."

Endurance and Rejuvenation

The most tenacious tribes were those occupying land rejected by white settlers or those distant from their new communities. Still, not even an insular, peaceful agricultural existence on semiarid, treeless terrain necessarily provided protection. Nor did a total willingness to peacefully accept white offers prevent attack.

The Pimas of Arizona, for instance, had a well-developed agricultural system adapted to a scarce supply of water, and they rarely warred with other tribes. After the arrival of white settlers, they integrated Christian symbolism into their religion, learned to speak English, and even fought with the U.S. cavalry against the Apaches. Still, the Pimas saw their lands stolen, their precious waterways diverted, and their families impoverished.

The similarly peaceful Yana tribes of California, hunters and gatherers rather than farmers, were even less fortunate. Suffering enslavement, prostitution, and multiple new diseases from white settlers, they faced near extinction within a generation. One Yana tribe, the Yahi, chose simply to disappear. For more than a decade, they lived in caves and avoided all contact with white settlers.

Many tribes found it difficult to survive in the proximity of white settlers. The Flatheads, for example, seemed to Indian commissioners in the Bitterroot region of Montana to be destined for quick assimilation. They had refused to join the Ghost Dance and had agreed to sell their rich tribal land and move to a new reservation. But while waiting to be moved, the dispossessed Flatheads nearly starved. When they finally reached the new reservation in October 1891, the remaining 250 Flatheads put on their finest war paint and whooped and galloped their horses, firing guns in the air in celebration. But disappointment and tragedy lay ahead. The federal government drastically reduced the size of the reservation, using a large part of it to provide a national reserve for buffalo. Only handfuls of Flatheads, mostly elderly, continued to live together in pockets of rural poverty.

A majority of tribes, especially smaller ones, sooner or later reached numbers too low to maintain their collective existence. Intermarriage, although widely condemned by the white community, drew many young people outside their Indian communities. Some tribal leaders also deliberately chose a path toward assimilation. The Quapaws, for example, formally disbanded in the aftermath of the Dawes Severalty Act. The minority that managed to prosper in white society as tradespeople or farmers abandoned their language, religious customs, and traditional ways of life. Later generations petitioned the federal government and regained tribal status, established ceremonial grounds and cultural centers (or bingo halls), and built up one of the most durable powwows in the state. Even so, much of the tribal lore that had underpinned distinct identity had simply vanished.

For those tribes who remained on reservations, the aggressively assimilationist policies of the Office of Indian Affairs (OIA) challenged their traditional ways. The Southern Ute, for example, at one time hunted, fished, and gathered throughout a huge region spanning the Rocky Mountains and the Great Basin. In 1848 they began to sign a series of treaties in accord with the reservation policy of the U.S. government. Twenty years later their territory had been reduced to approximately one-quarter of Colorado Territory, and in 1873, they had further relinquished about one-quarter of this land. After the passage of the Dawes Act, the U.S. government, pressured by white settlers, gave the tribe two choices: they could break up their communal land holdings and accept the 160 acres granted to the male heads of families or they could maintain their tribal status and move to a reservation in Utah. The Utes divided over the issue, but a considerable number chose to live on reservations under the administration of the OIA.

Under the terms of the Dawes Act, Southern Ute men and women endured continuous challenges to their egalitarian practices. The OIA assumed, for example, that Ute men would represent the tribe in all official matters, a policy that forced Ute women to petition the U.S. government to recognize their rights and concerns. Similarly, Ute women struggled to hold on to their roles as producers within the subsistence family economy against the efforts of the OIA agents to train them for homemaking alone. In the 1880s, the OIA established a matrons program to teach Ute women to create a "civilizing" home, which included new lessons about sanitation, home furnishings, and health care. But even fifty years later, some Ute preferred to live at least part of the year in a teepee in a multigenerational family rather than in a private residence designed for a single married couple and their children.

A small minority of tribes, grown skillful in adapting to dramatically changing circumstances, managed to persist and even grow. Never numbering more than a few thousand people, during the late eighteenth century the Cheyennes had found themselves caught geographically between aggressive tribes in the Great Lakes region and had migrated into the Missouri area, where they split into small village-sized communities. By the mid-nineteenth century they had become expert horse traders on the Great Plains, well prepared to meet the massive influx of white settlers by shifting their location frequently. They avoided the worst of the pestilence that spread from the diseases white people carried, and likewise survived widespread intermarriage with the Sioux in the 1860s and 1870s. Instructed to settle, many Cheyenne took up elements of the Christian religion and became farmers, also without losing their tribal identity. Punished by revenge-hungry soldiers after the battle of Little Bighorn, their lands repeatedly taken away, they still held on. The Cheyennes were survivors.

The Navajos experienced an extraordinary renewal, largely because they built a life in territory considered worthless by whites. Having migrated to the Southwest from the northwestern part of the continent perhaps 700 years ago, the Diné ("the People") as they called themselves had already survived earlier invasions by the

CHRONOLOGY

1848	Treaty of Guadalupe Hidalgo
1849–60s	California Gold Rush
1853	Gadsden Purchase
1858	Comstock Lode discovered
1859	Cortina's War in South Texas
1862	Homestead Act makes free land available
	Morrill Act authorizes "land-grant" colleges
1865–67	Great Sioux War
1866	Texas cattle drives begin
	Medicine Lodge Treaty established reservation system
	Alaska purchased
1869	Board of Indian Commissioners created
	Buffalo Bill, the King of the Border Men, sets off "Wild West" publishing craze
1870s	Grasshopper attacks on the Great Plains

1872	Yellowstone National Park created
1873	Timber Culture Act
	Red River War
1874–75	Sioux battles in Black Hills of Dakotas
1876	Custer's Last Stand
1877	Defeat of the Nez Percé
1881	Helen Hunt Jackson, *A Century of Dishonor*
1882	Edmunds Act outlaws polygamy
1885–87	Droughts and severe winters cause the collapse of the cattle boom
1887	Dawes Severalty Act
1890	Sioux Ghost Dance movement
	Massacre of Lakota Sioux at Wounded Knee
	Census Bureau announces the end of the frontier line
1887	Forest Management Act gives the federal government authority over forest reserves

Spanish. In 1863 they had been conquered again through the cooperation of hostile tribes led by the famous Colonel Kit Carson. Their crops burned, their fruit trees destroyed, 8,000 Navajo were forced in the 300-mile "Long Walk" to the desolate Bosque Redondo reservation, where they nearly starved. Four years later, the Indian Bureau allowed the severely reduced tribe to return to a fraction of its former lands.

By 1880 the Navajos' population had returned to nearly what it had been before their conquest by white Americans. Quickly depleting the deer and antelope on their hemmed-in reservation, they had to rely on sheep alone as a food reserve during years of bad crops. With their wool rugs and blankets much in demand in the East, the Navajos increasingly turned to crafts, including eventually silver jewelry as well as weaving, to survive. Although living on the economic margin, they persevered to become the largest Indian nation in the United States.

The nearby Hopis, like the Navajos, survived by stubbornly clinging to lands unwanted by white settlers and by adapting to drastically changing conditions. A famous tribe of "desert people," the Hopis had lived for centuries in their cliff cities. Their highly developed theological beliefs, peaceful social system, sand paintings, and kachina dolls interested many educated and influential whites. The resulting publicity helped them gather the public supporters and financial resources needed to fend off further threats to their reservations.

Fortunate northwestern tribes remained relatively isolated from white settlers until the early twentieth century, although they had begun trading with white visitors centuries earlier. Northwestern peoples relied largely on salmon and other resources of the region's rivers and bays. In potlatch ceremonies, leaders redistributed tribal wealth and maintained their personal status and the status of their tribe by giving lavish gifts to invited guests. Northwest peoples also made intricate wood carvings, including commemorative "totem" poles, that recorded their history and identified their regional status. Northwestern peoples maintained their cultural integrity in part through connections with kin in Canada, as did southern tribes with kin in Mexico. In Canada and Mexico, native populations suffered less pressure from new populations and retained more tribal authority than in the United States.

Indian nations approached their nadir as the nineteenth century came to a close. The descendants of the great pre-Columbian civilizations had been conquered by foreigners, their population reduced to fewer than 250,000. Under the pressure of assimilation, the remaining tribespeople became known to non-Indians as "the vanishing Americans." It would take several generations before Indian sovereignty experienced a resurgence.

CONCLUSION

The transformation of the trans-Mississippi West pointed up the larger meaning of expansion. Almost overnight, mines opened, cities grew, and farms and cattle ranches spread out across the vast countryside. New communities formed rapidly and often displaced old ones. In 1890 the director of the U.S. Census announced that the nation's "unsettled area has been so broken into by isolated bodies of settlement that there can hardly be said to be a frontier line."

The development of the West met the nation's demands for mineral resources for its expanding industries and agricultural products for the people of the growing cities. Envisioning the West as a cornucopia whose boundless treasures would offer themselves to the willing pioneer, most of the new residents failed to calculate the odds against their making a prosperous livelihood as miners, farmers, or petty merchants. Nor could they appreciate the long term consequences of the violence they brought with them from the battlefields of the Civil War to the far reaches of the West.

REVIEW QUESTIONS

1. Discuss the role of federal legislation in accelerating and shaping the course of westward expansion.
2. How did the incorporation of western territories into the United States affect Indian nations such as the Sioux or the Nez Percé? Discuss the causes and consequences of the Indian Wars. Discuss the significance of reservation policy and the Dawes Severalty Act for tribal life.
3. What were some of the major technological advances in mining and in agriculture that promoted the development of the western economy?
4. Describe the unique features of Mexicano communities in the Southwest before and after the mass immigration of Anglos. How did changes in the economy affect the patterns of labor and the status of women in these communities?
5. What role did the Homestead Act play in western expansion? How did farm families on the Great Plains divide chores among their members? What factors determined the likelihood of economic success or failure?
6. Describe the responses of artists, naturalists, and conservationists to the western landscape. How did their photographs, paintings, and stories shape perceptions of the West in the East?

RECOMMENDED READING

William Cronon, George Miles, and Jay Gitlin, eds., *Under an Open Sky: Rethinking America's Western Past* (1992). A useful collection of essays. Reinterpreting older evidence and adding new data, these essays stress the bitter conflicts over territory, the racial and gender barriers against democratic community models, and the tragic elements of western history.

Jon Gjerde, *The Minds of the West: Ethnocultural Evolution in the Rural Middle West, 1830–1914* (1997). A combination cultural and economic history that weighs the importance of ethnicity in the shaping of American identities in the farming regions of the Middle West. Gjerde pays close attention to the religious institutions and systems of belief of European immigrants as the basis of community formation.

Lisbeth Haas, *Conquests and Historical Identities in California, 1769–1936* (1995). A multiethnic history, centered in San Juan Capistrano, that examines the political intersection of geography and community formation. The author studies the processes of Americanization among the Spanish and Indian populations who settled this land.

Robert V. Hine and John Mack Faragher, *The American West: A New Interpretive History* (2000). A sweeping, amply illustrated survey of western history with reference to recent scholarship. The authors emphasize Native Americans and include rich material on ethnicity, the environment, and the role of women.

John C. Hudson, *Making the Corn Belt: A Geographical History of Middle-Western Agriculture* (1994). An ecologically oriented study of corn growing that traces its development from Indians to Southerners moving westward.

Andrew C. Isenberg, *The Destruction of the Bison: An Environmental History, 1750–1920* (2000). A rich study of the forces behind the near-extinction of the bison.

Karl Jacoby, *Crimes Against Nature: Squatters, Poachers, Thieves, and the Hidden History of American Conservation* (2001). A complex analysis of the origins of national parks in the Adirondacks, Yellowstone, and the Grand Canyon. Rather than focusing on the individuals and groups that led the conservation of vast public lands, Jacoby switches perspective to focus on those who were dispossessed by the process.

Elizabeth Jameson and Susan Armitage, eds., *Writing the Range* (1997). A collection of essays on women in the West that presents an inclusive historical narrative based on the experiences of women of differing backgrounds, races, and ethnic groups.

Katherine M. B. Osburn, *Southern Ute Women: Autonomy and Assimilation on the Reservation, 1887–1934* (1998). Presents a careful analysis of the impact of the Dawes Act on the role and status of women among the Southern Ute.

Glenda Riley, *Building and Breaking Families in the American West* (1996). Essays covering the variety of cultures in the American West.

Thomas E. Sheridan, *Los Tucsonenses: The Mexican Community in Tucson, 1854–1941* (1986). A highly readable account of Mexican-American communities in the Southwest. Sheridan shows how a midcentury accommodation of Anglos and Mexicanos faded with the absorption of the region into the national economy and with the steady displacement of Mexicano community from its agricultural landholdings.

Liping Zhu, *A Chinaman's Chance: The Chinese on the Rocky Mountain Mining Frontier* (1997). Studies the mining communities of Chinese in the Boise Basin of Idaho. Zhu emphasizes the success the Chinese enjoyed not only as miners but as merchants in the face of discriminatory practices and laws.

▶ MEDIA RESOURCES

U.S. HISTORY DOCUMENTS CD-ROM

Reconstruction

16-11 James T. Rapier, Testimony before U.S. Senate Regarding the Agricultural Labor Force in the South (1880)

16-12 A Sharecrop Contract (1882)

New South, Expanding West

17-3 Horace Greeley, an Overland Journey (1860)

17-4 Joseph G. McCoy, Historic Sketches of the Cattle Trade of the West and Southwest (1874)

17-5 Helen Hunt Jackson, from a Century of Dishonor (1881)

17-6 Congressional Report on Indian Affairs (1887)

17-7 Tragedy at Wounded Knee (1890)

17-8 Benjamin Harrison, Report on Wounded Knee Massacre and the Decrease in Indian Land Acreage (1891)

17-9 The Omaha Platform of the Populist Party (1892)

17-10 From Plessy v. Ferguson (1896)

COMPANION WEBSITE HIGHLIGHTS

To view an exploration, enter one of the URLs below in your browser.

Web Explorations

Major Indian Battles and Indian Reservations, 1860–1900

http://www.prenhall.com/faragher/map18.1
Railroad Routes, Cattle Trails, Gold and Silver Rushes, 1860–1900
http://www.prenhall.com/faragher/map18.2

Additional Interactive Maps

To access the maps, go to this chapter's resources at
http://www.prenhall.com/faragher
Mormon Cultural Diffusion, ca. 1883, page 540
The Establishment of National Parks and Forests, page 552

HISTORY RESOURCE CENTER

To find the resources listed below, go to
http://www.prenhall.com/historyresourcecenter

Documents

Edward Gould Buffum, Six Months in the Gold Mines (1850)

Lydia Allen Rudd, Diary of Westward Travel (1852)

Proceedings of the Thirteenth Session of the National Grange of the Patrons of Husbandry (1879)

Images

California Gold Diggers

Mining on the Comstock

New Orleans, Louisiana, 1881

Phoenix, Arizona, 1888

EXPLORING AMERICA
DAKOTA SIOUX CONFLICT
http://www.prenhall.com/faragher/dakotasioux

When did the largest mass public execution occur? Who was executed and for what reasons? How did this execution and the events that led up to it offer a preview of the next 25 years of Native American-United States relations? The *Dakota Sioux Conflict* module explores a violent clash that occurred in Minnesota during the Civil War. The module explores the conflict and its aftermath from the perspectives of both the Sioux and the white settlers, offering insight into this pivotal five weeks in American history. It also touches on the role of race in the United States. Using a variety of print and visual primary sources, maps, and a chronology wrapped around a narrative, the *Dakota Sioux Conflict* probes one example of a central issue in U.S. history.

Drawing upon a history of the events by a white observer, transcripts of testimony by a Sioux chief, a mulatto who lived with the Indians, and a bishop, the story of origins, development, and eventual conclusion of the Dakota Sioux Conflict unfolds. The sources

Battle of Birch Coulee, September 2, 1862

Click anywhere to go to the previous page.

and narrative demonstrate that each side had a different interpretation of the conflict and its causes. They also illustrate the role the U.S. government played in precipitating the conflict and bringing it to a violent conclusion. The chronology and the maps provide important historical and geographic contexts.

Reflect and Respond
1.   Bishop Whipple was far more sympathetic to the Dakota than Isaac Heard. Choose two or three phrases Whipple used that, in your view, best reveal his view of "Indians."

2.   Given Whipple's view, how reliable do you find his account of the causes of the conflict? What is Whipple's explanation for why the conflict started?
3.   Given the central role Godfrey played in the military tribunal, it is especially important to assess his reliability. Why did Heard and the members of the tribunal decide to rely on him in interrogating other accused?
4.   How credible do you find Godfrey's account of his own behavior? Cite specific portions of his testimony to support your answer.
5.   Who among the following, in your estimation, bears some measure of responsibility for the conflict: The four young men described by Big Eagle? The Indian agents and traders? Little Crow? The white settlers? The federal government? Others?
6.   How would you distribute that responsibility?
7.   How "just" was the military tribunal?

✓ Check it out
Chronology

The chronology traces the course of events of the Dakota Sioux Conflict providing an essential time context to the events. It shows how the relationships between the Sioux, the white settlers, and the

government changed over time, leading to the outbreak of violence. The chronology also depicts the aftermath of the conflict. Equally important, the ways in which the United States used the law to maintain its domination of Native American tribes is highlighted.

This exploration is also available on the *Exploring America* CD-ROM.

NINETEEN

THE INCORPORATION OF AMERICA

▶ 1865–1900

Bessemer steel manufacture at Andrew Carnegie's Pittsburgh steel works in 1886. Contemporary colored engraving.
SOURCE: The Granger Collection, New York (0009141/4E452.14).

AMERICAN COMMUNITIES

Packingtown, Chicago, Illinois

APPROACHING PACKINGTOWN, THE NEIGHBORHOOD ADJOINING the Union Stockyards, the center of Chicago's great meatpacking industry, one noticed first the pungent odor, a mixture of smoke, fertilizer, and putrid flesh, blood, and hair from the slaughtered animals. A little closer, the stench of the uncovered garbage dump blended in. Finally one crossed "Bubbly Creek," a lifeless offshoot of the Chicago River, aptly named for the effect of the carbolic acid gas that formed from the decaying refuse poured in by the meatpacking plants. Railroads crisscrossed the entire area, bringing in thousands of animals each day and carrying out meat for sale in markets across the country.

Packingtown occupied about one square mile of land bounded by stockyards, packing plants, and freight yards. With a population of 30,000 to 40,000 at the end of the nineteenth century, it was a rapidly growing community of old and new immigrants who depended on the meatpacking industry for their livelihood. An average household included six or seven people—parents, two or three children, and two or three boarders. They lived typically in wooden houses divided into four or more flats. Although Irish, Germans, Bohemians, Poles, Lithuanians, and Slovaks were squeezed together in this solidly working-class neighborhood, strong ethnic identities persisted. Few households included residents of more than one nationality, and interethnic marriages were rare. Nearly everyone professed the Roman Catholic faith, yet each ethnic group maintained its own church and often its own parochial school, where children were taught in their parents' language. Political organizations, fraternal societies, and even gymnastic clubs and drama groups reflected these ethnic divisions.

The one local institution that bridged the different groups was the saloon. Located on virtually every street corner, saloons offered important services to the community, hosting weddings and dances, providing meeting places for trade unions and fraternal societies, and cashing paychecks. During the frequent seasons of unemployment, Packingtown workers spent a lot of time in saloons. Here they often made friends across ethnic divisions, an extension of their common work experience in the nearby stockyard and packinghouses.

Most of the meatpacking industry's first "knife men"—the skilled workers in the "killing gangs" that managed the actual slaughtering and cutting operations—were German and Irish. Many had learned their butcher's craft in the Old Country. Below them were the common laborers, mainly recent immigrants from eastern Europe. Having no previous experience in meatpacking, these workers found themselves in the lowest paid jobs, such as the by-product manufacturing of glue and oleo. A sizable portion had never before earned wages. They soon discovered, as one Lithuanian laborer put it, that "money was everything and a man without money must die." But the money available—a daily wage of $2 (or less)—was often not enough. The death rate from tuberculosis in Packingtown was thought to be the highest in Chicago and among the highest in the nation.

The Packingtown community, small and insular as it seemed to the residents, was bound into an elaborate economic network that reached distant parts of the United States, transforming the way farmers raised livestock and grains, railroads operated, and consumers ate their meals. These workers helped make Chicago a gateway city, a destination point for raw materials coming in from the West as well as a point of export for products of all kinds.

Chicago meatpackers, led by the "big five" of Armour, Cudahy, Morris, Schwarzschild and Sulzberger, and Swift, expanded more than 900 percent between 1870 and 1890, dominating the national market for meat and establishing a standard for monopoly capitalism in the late nineteenth century. In the process, they also became the city's largest manufacturing employer. They built huge, specialized factories during the 1860s and 1870s that speeded the killing process and—thanks to mountains of ice brought by rail from ponds and lakes—operated year round. The introduction of an efficiently refrigerated railroad car in the 1880s made it possible to ship meat nationwide. Consumers had long believed that only meat butchered locally was safe to eat, but now cheap Chicago-packed beef and pork began to appear on every meateater's table. Local packinghouses throughout the Midwest succumbed to the ruthless competition from Chicago.

Chicago's control of the mass market for meat affected all aspects of the industry. Midwestern farmers practically abandoned raising calves on open pastures. Instead, they bought two-year-old steers from the West and fattened them on homegrown corn in feedlots, making sure that bulk went into edible parts rather than muscle and bone. The feedlot—a kind of rural factory—replaced pasture just as pasture had earlier supplanted prairie grasslands.

Few of the workers in Chicago's stockyards had seen a farm since they left their homelands. But as the working hands of what poet Carl Sandburg would later call the "Hog butcher for the world, . . . City of the big shoulders," they played their part, along with the farmer, the grain dealer, the ironworker, the teamster, and many others in bringing together the neighboring countryside, distant regions, and the city in a common endeavor. ■

Chicago

KEY TOPICS

- The rise of big business and the formation of the national labor movement
- The transformation of southern society
- The growth of cities

- The Gilded Age
- Changes in education
- Commercial amusements and organized sports

THE RISE OF INDUSTRY, THE TRIUMPH OF BUSINESS

At the time of the Civil War, the typical American business firm was a small enterprise, owned and managed by a single family, and producing goods for a local or regional market. By the turn of the century, businesses depending on large-scale investments had organized as corporations and grown to unforeseen size. These mammoth firms could afford to mass-produce goods for national and even international markets. At the helm stood unimaginably wealthy men such as Andrew Carnegie, Philip Danforth Armour, Jay Gould, and John D. Rockefeller, all powerful leaders of a new national business community.

A Revolution in Technology

In the decades after the Civil War, American industry transformed itself into a new wonder of the world. The Centennial Exposition of 1876, held in Philadelphia, celebrated not so much the American Revolution 100 years earlier as the industrial and technological promise of the century to come. Its central theme was power. In the main building—at the time the largest on earth—the visiting emperor of Brazil marked the opening day by throwing a switch on a giant steam engine. Examining the telephone, which he had never before seen in operation, he gasped, "My God, it talks!" Patented that year by Alexander Graham Bell, the telephone signaled the rise of the United States to world leadership in industrial technology.

The year 1876 also marked the opening of Thomas Alva Edison's laboratory in Menlo Park, New Jersey, one of the first devoted to industrial research. Not yet thirty years old, Edison could already claim credit for the mimeograph, the multiplex telegraph, and the stock ticker. In October 1879 his research team hit upon its most marketable invention, an incandescent lamp that burned for more than thirteen hours. On December 31 Edison brought 3,000 people by a special train to witness the sight of hundreds of electric lights illuminating his shop and neighborhood streets. By 1882 the Edison Electric Light Company had launched its service in New York City's financial district. A wondrous source of light and power, electricity revolutionized both industry and urban life.

A whimsical rendition of Thomas Edison's laboratories in Menlo Park, New Jersey, ca. 1880. The commercial artist imagined a giant electric light illuminating the entire region. Six weeks after Edison announced the invention of the electric light in 1879, the stock market turned jittery and gas company shares fell sharply: investors feared his "magic."

SOURCE: Hebert Orth, *Edison's Menlo Park Laboratories*, a fanciful painting. U.S. Department of the Interior, National Park Service, Edison National Historic Site

By this time American inventors, who had filed nearly half a million patents since the close of the Civil War, were previewing the marvels of the next century. Henry Ford, working as an electrical engineer for the Detroit Edison Company, was already experimenting with the gasoline-burning internal combustion engine and designing his own automobile. By 1900 American companies had produced more than 4,000 automobiles. The prospect of commercial aviation emerged in 1903 when Wilbur and Orville Wright staged the first airplane flight near Kitty Hawk, North Carolina.

A major force behind economic growth was the vast transcontinental railroad, completed in 1869. The addition of three more major rail lines (the Southern Pacific; the Northern Pacific; and the Atchison, Topeka, and Santa Fe) in the early 1880s, and the Great Northern a decade later, completed the most extensive transportation network in the world. As the nation's first big business, railroads linked cities in every state and served a nationwide market for goods. Freight trains carried the bountiful natural resources, such as iron, coal, and minerals that supplied the raw materials for industry, as well as food for the growing urban populations.

The monumental advances in transportation and communication facilitated the progressively westward relocation of industry. The geographic center of manufacturing (as computed by the gross value of products) was near the middle of Pennsylvania in 1850, in western Pennsylvania by 1880, and near Mansfield, Ohio, in 1900. The geographic center of flour milling moved from the East Coast to Rochester, New York, then to Ohio, and finally to Minneapolis and Kansas City. Similarly, the centers for the manufacture of agricultural equipment moved from central New York to Illinois and Wisconsin, while the production of wire moved from Massachusetts to Illinois.

Web Exploration Explore patterns of industry in each region of the United States in 1900. Why did industrial patterns differ from region to region? www.prenhall.com/faragher/map19.1

Patterns of Industry, 1900 Industrial manufacturing concentrated in the Northeast and Midwest, while the raw materials for production came mostly from other parts of the nation.

Industry grew at a pace that was not only unprecedented but previously unimaginable. In 1865 the annual production of goods was estimated at $2 billion; by 1900 it stood at $13 billion, transforming the United States from fourth to first in the world in terms of productivity. By the early twentieth century, American industry manufactured one-third of the world's goods.

Mechanization Takes Command

This second industrial revolution depended on many factors, but none was more important than the application of new technologies to increase the productivity of labor and the volume of goods. Machines, factory managers, and workers together created a system of continuous production by which more could be made, and faster, than anywhere else on earth. Higher productivity depended not only on machinery and technology but on economies of scale and speed, reorganization of factory labor and business management, and the unparalleled growth of a market for goods of all kinds.

All these changes depended in turn on anthracite coal, a new source of fuel, which was widely used after 1850. Reliable and inexpensive sources of energy made possible dramatic changes in the industrial uses of light, heat, and motion. Equally important, coal fueled the great open-hearth furnaces and mills of the iron and steel industry. By the end of the century, the U.S. steel industry was the world's largest, churning out rails to carry trains and parts to make more machines to produce yet more goods.

New systems of mass production replaced wasteful and often chaotic practices and speeded up the delivery of finished goods. In the 1860s meatpackers set up one of the earliest production lines. The process of converting livestock into meat began with a live animal. A chain around the hind leg whirled the body to an overhead rail, which carried it to slaughter—all in barely half a minute's time. Then hair and bristles were removed by a scraping machine, the carcass shifted to a conveyer belt where the chest was split and the organs removed, and the body placed in a cooler. This "disassembly line" displaced patterns of hand labor that were centuries old. The production line became standard in most areas of manufacturing.

Sometimes the invention of a single machine could instantly transform production, mechanizing every stage from processing the raw material to packaging the product. The cigarette-making machine, patented in 1881, shaped the tobacco, encased it in an endless paper tube, and snipped off the tube at cigarette-length intervals. This machine could produce more than 7,000 cigarettes per hour, replacing the worker who at best made 3,000 per day. After a few more improvements, fifteen machines could meet the total demand for American cigarettes. Within a generation, continuous production also revolutionized the making of furniture, cloth, grain products, soap, and canned goods; the refining, distilling, and processing of animal and vegetable fats; and eventually the manufacture of automobiles.

The Expanding Market for Goods

To distribute the growing volume of goods, businesses demanded new techniques of marketing and merchandising. For generations, legions of sellers, or "drummers," had worked their routes, pushing goods, especially hardware and patent medicines, to individual buyers and retail stores. The appearance of mail-order houses after the Civil War accompanied the consolidation of the railroad lines and the expansion of the postal system. Rates were lowered for freight and postage alike, and railroad stations opened post offices and sold money orders. By 1896 rural free delivery had reached distant communities.

Growing directly out of these services, the successful Chicago-based mail-order houses drew rural and urban consumers into a common marketplace. Sears, Roebuck and Company and Montgomery Ward offered an enormous variety of goods, from shoes to buggies to gasoline stoves and cream separators. The Montgomery Ward catalogue provided "a real link between us and civilization," a Nebraska farmwoman wrote. The mail-order catalogue also returned to rural folks the fruits of their own labor, now processed and packaged for easy use. The Sears catalogue offered Armour's summer sausage as well as Aunt Jemima's Pancake Flour and Queen Mary Scotch Oatmeal, both made of grains that came from the agricultural heartland. In turn, the purchases made by farm families through the Sears catalogue sent cash flowing into Chicago.

The chain store achieved similar economies of scale. By 1900, a half-dozen grocery chains had sprung up. The largest was A&P, originally named the Great Atlantic and Pacific Tea Company to celebrate the completion of the transcontinental railroad. Frank and Charles Woolworth offered inexpensive variety goods in five-and-ten-cent stores, of which more than 1,000 were established in the United States and Great Britain by 1919. Other chains selling drugs, costume jewelry, shoes, cigars, and furniture soon appeared, offering a greater selection of goods and lower prices than the small, independent stores. Hurt financially by this competition, community-based retailers headed the lobby for antichain legislation.

The department stores reigned over the urban market. These palaces of merchandise, with their attractive displays and convenient arrangements of goods, enticed

John D. Rockefeller, who formed the Standard Oil Company in 1870, sought to control all aspects of the industry, from the transportation of crude oil to the marketing and distribution of the final products. By the end of the decade, after making shrewd deals with the railroads and underselling his rivals, he managed to control 90 percent of the oil-refining industry. To further consolidate his interests, in 1882 Rockefeller created the Standard Oil Trust, which, by integrating both vertically and horizontally, became a model for other corporations and an inspiration for critical commentary and antitrust legislation.

This cartoon, published in *Puck* in 1904, shows the stranglehold Standard Oil had on government and industry alike. In 1911, in response to an antitrust suit, the Supreme Court ordered the company to break up.

SOURCE: Courtesy of the Library of Congress (LCUS264-435).

buyers and browsers alike. Opening shortly after the Civil War, department stores began to take up much of the business formerly enjoyed by specialty shops, offering a spectrum of services that included restaurants, rest rooms, ticket agencies, nurseries, reading rooms, and post offices. Elegantly appointed with imported carpets, sweeping marble staircases, and crystal chandeliers, the department store raised retailing to new heights. By the close of the century, the names of Marshall Field of Chicago, Filene's of Boston, The Emporium of San Francisco, Wanamaker's of Philadelphia, and Macy's of New York had come to represent the splendors of those great cities as well as the apex of mass retailing.

Advertising lured customers to the department stores, the chains, and the independent neighborhood shops. The advertising revolution began in 1869, when Francis Wayland Ayer founded the earliest advertising agency, but the firm did not hire its first full-time copy writers until 1891. Ayer's handled the accounts of such companies as Montgomery Ward, Procter & Gamble,

and the National Biscuit Company. With the help of this new sales tool, gross revenues of retailers raced upward from $8 million in 1860 to $102 million in 1900.

Integration, Combination, and Merger

The business community aspired to exercise greater control of the economy and to enlarge the commercial empire. From the source of raw materials to the organization of production, from the conditions of labor to the climate of public opinion, business leaders acted shrewdly. Economic cycles alternating between rapid growth and sharp decline also promoted the rise of big business. Major economic setbacks in 1873 and 1893 wiped out weaker competitors, allowing the strongest firms to rebound swiftly and to expand their sales and scale of operation during the recovery period.

Businesses grew in two distinct, if overlapping, ways. Through *vertical integration* a firm gained control of production at every step of the way—from raw materials through processing to transport and merchandising of the finished items. In 1899 the United Fruit Company began to build a network of wholesale houses, and within two years it had opened distribution centers in twenty-one major cities. Eventually it controlled an elaborate system of Central American plantations and temperature-controlled shipping and storage facilities for its highly perishable bananas. The firm became one of the nation's largest corporations, its "empire in bananas" dominating the economic and political life of whole nations in Central America.

The second means of growth, *horizontal combination,* entailed gaining control of the market for a single product. The most famous case was the Standard Oil Company, founded by John D. Rockefeller in 1870. Operating out of Cleveland in a highly competitive but lucrative field, Rockefeller first secured preferential rates from railroads eager to ensure a steady supply of oil. He then convinced or coerced other local oil operators to sell their stock to him. The Standard Oil Trust, established in 1882, controlled over 90 percent of the nation's oil-refining industry. Rockefeller understood the larger implications of his success, writing that he had "revolutionized the way of doing business all over the world. . . . The day of combination is here to stay."

In 1890 Congress passed the Sherman Antitrust Act to restore competition by encouraging small business and outlawing "every . . . combination . . . in restraint of trade." Ironically, the courts interpreted the law in ways that inhibited the organization of trade unions (on the ground that they restricted the free flow of labor) and actually helped the consolidation of business. More than 2,600 firms vanished between 1898 and 1902 alone. By 1910 the industrial giants that would dominate the American economy until the last half of the twentieth century—U.S. Rubber, Goodyear, American Smelting and Refining, Anaconda Copper, General Electric, Westinghouse, Nabisco, Swift and Company, Armour, International Harvester, Eastman Kodak, and American Can—had already formed.

The Gospel of Wealth

The preeminent financiers and corporation magnates not only took pride in the collective triumph of the business community but felt spiritually fulfilled by the accumulation of wealth. Ninety percent of the nation's business leaders were Protestant, and the majority attended church services regularly. They attributed their personal achievement to hard work and perseverance and made these the principal tenets of a new faith that imbued the pursuit of wealth with old-time religious zeal. "God gave me my money," declared John D. Rockefeller. Baptist minister Russell Conwell's pamphlet *Acres of Diamonds,* which sold more than 1 million copies,

argued that to build a fortune was a profound Christian duty. "To make money honestly," he preached, "is to preach the gospel."

One version of this "gospel of wealth" justified the ruthless behavior of entrepreneurs who accumulated unprecedented wealth and power through shady deals and conspiracies. Speculator Jay Gould, known in the popular press as the "Worst Man in the World," wrung his fortune, it was widely believed, from the labor of others. Through a series of financial maneuvers (one of which allegedly drove a partner to suicide) and such high-handed measures as sending armed employees to seize a factory, he rose quickly from his modest origins in western New York state. After abandoning his tanning business, he turned to stock trading and became a major player on Wall Street.

Speculation in railroads proved to be Gould's forte. He took over the Erie Railroad, paying off New York legislators to get the state to finance its expansion, and he acquired the U.S. Express Company by pressuring and tricking its stockholders. When threatened with arrest, Gould sold off his shares for $9 million and moved on to the Union Pacific, where he cut wages, precipitated strikes, and manipulated elections in the western and Plains states. Tired of being caricatured in the press as a great swindler, he bought the leading newspapers. At his death, one obituary described Jay Gould as "an incarnation of cupidity and sordidness" whose life symbolized "idolatrous homage [to] the golden calf."

Andrew Carnegie—the "Richest Man in the World"—offered a strikingly different model. He represented the "captain of industry" who had risen from the ranks through diligence and who refused to worship wealth for its own sake. Late in his life, he outlined his personal philosophy in a popular essay, *The Gospel of Wealth* (1889), explaining that "there is no genuine, praiseworthy success in life if you are not honest, truthful, and fair-dealing."

A poor immigrant from Scotland, Carnegie spent his boyhood studying bookkeeping at night while working days in a textile mill. At age thirteen he had become a messenger for Western Union, and by age seventeen he was the fastest telegraph key operator in Pittsburgh. In 1852 he became the personal secretary of the superintendent of the Pennsylvania Railroad's western division. Well placed to learn the principles of the business, Carnegie stepped into the superintendent's job seven years later. While improving passenger train service, he invested brilliantly to build funds for his next venture.

Carnegie built an empire in steel. A genius at vertical integration, he undercut his competitors by using the latest technology and designing his own system of cost analysis. By 1900 Carnegie managed the most efficient steel mills in the world, which accounted for one-third of the nation's output. When he sold out to J. P. Morgan's

The Two Philanthropists by Joseph Keppler, from *Puck Magazine*, February 23, 1888. This famous artist of the late nineteenth century drew caricatures of magnates Jay Gould and Cornelius Vanderbilt, stressing not their "good works" but their less than beneficent control of the nation's railroads and telegraph systems. Illustrated magazines, such as *Puck*, reproduced such drawings in quantity, due in part to technological advances in the lithographic process.

SOURCE: Color engraving by J. Keppler (1838–94) from *Puck*, February 23, 1881, Collection of the New-York Historical Society, New York City (#48872).

new United States Steel Corporation in 1901, his personal share of the proceeds came to $225 million.

Carnegie was well known as a civic leader. From one point of view, he was a factory despot who underpaid his employees and ruthlessly managed their working conditions. But to the patrons of the public libraries, art museums, concert halls, colleges, and universities that he funded, Carnegie appeared to be the single greatest philanthropist of the age. By the time he died, he had given away his massive personal fortune.

Whether following the rough road of Gould or the smooth path of Carnegie, the business community worked together to fashion the new conservative ideology of social Darwinism, which purportedly explained, and justified, why some Americans grew rich while others remained poor. Derived from the famed British naturalist Charles Darwin's scientific theories of evolution presented in *On the Origin of Species* (1859), social Darwinism superimposed the brutal struggle for existence that supposedly dominated nature onto modern society and underscored the principle of "survival of the fittest." The Yale professor William Graham Sumner gave this idea an economic spin. In an essay published in 1883 entitled *What Social Classes Owe to Each Other*, he argued that only a few individuals were capable of putting aside selfish pleasures to produce the capital needed to drive the emerging industrial economy and, moreover, they were fully deserving of their great fortunes. In contrast, the vast majority, too lazy or profligate to rise above poverty, deserved their own miserable fates. To tamper with this "natural" order by establishing welfare programs to help the poor or redistributing wealth in any way would be hazardous to society. Meanwhile, the popular writer Horatio Alger produced a more temperate version of this credo. Publishing more than 100 rags-to-riches novels, he created heroes who manage to rise out of poverty by both hard work and luck and ultimately acquire, if not vast wealth, middle-class respectability and comfort.

LABOR IN THE AGE OF BIG BUSINESS

It was a common item of faith among most working people that, as labor reformer George E. McNeill put it in 1877, "labor produces all the wealth of the world. . . . [The laborer] makes civilization possible." Like the gospel of wealth, the "gospel of work" affirmed the dignity of hard work, the virtue of thrift, and the importance of individual initiative. Both doctrines elaborated the simple phrase adorning many needlework samplers, "Work Is Prayer." But unlike business leaders, the philosophers of American working people did not believe in riches as the proof of work well done, or in the lust for power as the driving force of progress. On the contrary, they contended that honesty and competence should become the cornerstones of a society "so improved that labor shall become a blessing instead of a curse," recognized by all as the badge of the morally responsible citizen.

This faith inspired a slender minority, less than 3 percent of the workforce, to form unions in various trades and industries. Despite its small size, the labor movement represented the most significant and lasting response of workers to the rise of big business and the consolidation of corporate power.

The Wage System

The accelerating growth of industry, especially the steady mechanization of production, dramatically changed employer-employee relations and created new categories of workers. Self-employment became less common. The 1870 census revealed that the number of people working for wages already totaled almost 5 million (3.5 million in industry) of the nearly 13 million people who were gainfully employed. Farmers still accounted for 3 million or so, agricultural laborers for nearly 4 million. But by the end of the century, two-thirds of all Americans were working not for themselves but for wages. Many of these workers were also employed by large firms. For example, just sixty-six companies of Chicago's 3,000 largest firms employed nearly one-fifth of the city's entire wage-earning population in 1890.

For most craft workers, the new system destroyed long-standing practices, chipped away at their customary autonomy, and placed them in competition with other, mainly unskilled workers. Frederick Winslow Taylor, the pioneer of scientific management, explained that managers must "take all the important decisions . . . out of the hands of workmen." Teams of ironworkers, for example, had previously set the rules of production as well as their wages while the company supplied equipment and raw materials. Once steel replaced iron, most companies gradually introduced a new system. Managers now constantly supervised workers, set the pace of production and rate of payment, and introduced new, faster machinery that made many skills obsolete. In the woodworking trades, highly skilled cabinetmakers, who for generations had brought their own tools to the factory, were largely replaced with "green hands"—immigrants, including many women—who with only minimal training and close supervision could operate new woodworking machines at cheaper rates of pay.

Not all trades conformed to this pattern. The garment industry, for example, grew at a very fast pace in New York, Boston, Chicago, Philadelphia, Cleveland, and St. Louis but retained older systems of labor along with the new. The highly mechanized factories that employed hundreds of thousands of young immigrant women, while the outwork system, established well before the Civil War, contracted ever-larger numbers of families to work in their homes on sewing machines or by hand. However, companies fostered extreme competition between these two groups of workers by continually increasing daily production quotas. Paid by the piece—a seam stitched, a collar turned, a button attached—workers labored faster and longer at home

or in the factory to forestall a dip in wages. Meanwhile, in some older trades such as machine tooling and textiles, the surviving craft jobs continued to pass from fathers to sons, nephews, or family friends.

The new system of production required a vast number of people. Lured by the promise of a paying job in industry, many young men and women fled the family farm for the factory. A smaller number escaped the peonage system of agricultural labor in the South. By far the largest proportion came from Europe or Asia. Between 1860 and 1890, 10 million people immigrated to the United States. A 1910 report on twenty-one industries estimated that nearly 53 percent of all wage workers were foreign-born, with two-thirds coming from southern and eastern Europe. In many occupations—meat processing, clothing and textile manufacturing, cigar making, and mining, for example—immigrants predominated.

Industrial expansion also offered new opportunities for women to work outside the home. African American and immigrant women found employment in trades least affected by technological advances, such as domestic service. In contrast, English-speaking white women moved into the better-paying clerical and sales positions in the rapidly expanding business sector. After the typewriter and telephone came into widespread use in the 1890s, the number of women employed in office work rose even faster. At the turn of the century, 8.6 million women worked outside their homes—nearly triple the number in 1870.

By contrast, African American men found themselves excluded from many fields. In Cleveland, for example, the number of black carpenters declined after 1870, just as the volume of construction was rapidly increasing. African American men were also systematically driven from restaurant service and barred from newer trades such as boilermaking, plumbing, electrical work, and paperhanging, which European immigrants secured for themselves.

Discriminatory or exclusionary practices fell hardest on workers recruited earlier from China. Driven by severe famine and political turmoil in their homeland and drawn by news of jobs in the California Gold Rush and railroad construction, young men mostly between the ages of sixteen and twenty-four immigrated to the United States. They worked in the mines, in the construction of the railroads, and in market gardening. From the 1860s on, many Chinese established laundries and restaurants in west coast cities where they were viewed as potential competitors by white workers and proprietors of small businesses. A potent and racist anti-Chinese movement organized to protest "cheap Chinese labor" and to demand a halt to Chinese immigration. By the late 1870s white rioters were insistently calling for deportation measures and razing Chinese neighborhoods. In 1882 Congress passed the Chinese

Between 1852 and the Chinese Exclusion Act of 1882, approximately 322,000 Chinese immigrated to the United States. Many helped to build the Central Pacific Railroad and, after fulfilling their labor contracts, moved on to work as cooks or laundry workers in mining and timber camps. Nearly 90 percent of all American Chinese settled in the West. This family, celebrating a wedding, posed for a photographer in Idaho City, Idaho, their new hometown.

SOURCE: The Denver Public Library—Western History Collection.

Exclusion Act, which suspended Chinese immigration, limited the civil rights of resident Chinese, and forbade their naturalization.

For even the best-placed wage earners, the new workplace could be unhealthy, even dangerous. Meatpacking produced its own hazards—the dampness of the pickling room, the sharp blade of the slaughtering knife, and the noxious odors of the fertilizer department. Factory owners often failed to mark high-voltage wires, locked fire doors, and allowed the emission of toxic fumes. Extractive workers, such as coal and copper miners, labored in mineshafts where the air could suddenly turn poisonous and where cave-ins were possible and deadly. Moreover, machines ran faster in American factories than anywhere else in the world, and workers who could not keep up or suffered serious injury found themselves without a job.

Even under less hazardous conditions, workers complained about the tedium of performing repetitive tasks for many hours each day. Although federal employees had been granted the eight-hour day in 1868, most workers still toiled upward of ten or twelve hours. "Life in a factory," one textile operative grumbled, "is perhaps, with the exception of prison life, the most monotonous life a human being can live." Nor could glamour be found in the work of saleswomen in the elegant department stores. Clerks could not sit down, despite workdays as long as sixteen hours in the busy

season, or hold "unnecessary conversations" with customers or other clerks. Despite these disadvantages, most women preferred sales and manufacturing jobs to domestic service, which required live-in servants to be on call seven days a week, enjoying at best an occasional afternoon off.

Moreover, steady employment was rare. Between 1866 and 1897, fourteen years of prosperity stood against seventeen of hard times. The major depressions of 1873–79 and 1893–97 were the worst in the nation's history up to that time. Three "minor" recessions (1866–67, 1883–85, and 1890–91) did not seem insignificant to the millions who lost their jobs during those periods. "At one time they drive us like slaves," a labor official complained in 1883, "and at other times we have to beg for work." During that year, 40 percent of all industrial workers lived below the poverty line ($500 per year). Whereas a highly skilled worker who earned between $800 and $1,000 per year might be able to save for a "rainy day," a common laborer who received only $1.50 for a day's work could not.

The Knights of Labor

The Noble and Holy Order of the Knights of Labor, founded by a group of Philadelphia garment cutters in 1869, grew to become the largest labor organization in the nineteenth century. Led by Grand Master Workman Terence V. Powderly, the order sought to bring together all wage earners regardless of skill. Only by organizing widely, one member insisted, would workers be able to achieve their "emancipation" from wage slavery.

The Knights endorsed a variety of reform measures—child labor reform, a graduated income tax, more land set aside for homesteading, the abolition of contract labor, and monetary reform—to offset the power of the industrialists. They believed that the "producing classes," once freed from the grip of corporate monopoly and the curses of ignorance and alcohol, would transform the United States into a genuinely democratic society.

The Knights promoted economic cooperation as the alternative to the wage system and advocated a system of producers' cooperatives. In these factories workers collectively made all decisions on prices and wages and shared all the profits. Local assemblies launched thousands of these small co-ops, such as the Our Girls Co-operative Manufacturing Company, which was established by Chicago seamstresses in the 1880s. The Knights also ran small cooperative cigar shops and grocery stores, often housed in their own assembly buildings. Successful for a time, most cooperatives could not complete against the heavily capitalized enterprises and ultimately failed.

The Knights reached their peak during the great campaign for a shorter workday. The Eight-Hour League, led by Ira Steward, advocated a "natural" rhythm of eight hours for work, eight hours for sleep, and eight hours for leisure. After staging petition campaigns, marches, and a massive strike in New York City, the movement collapsed during the economic recession of the 1870s. The Knights helped revive it in the next decade, and their newspapers ran advertisements promoting "eight-hour" shoes, "eight-hour" romance novels, and "eight-hour" picnics and concerts sponsored by groups eager for the reform. This time the campaign aroused widespread support from consumers, who boycotted brands of beer, bread, and other products made in longer-hour shops.

During the first weeks of May 1886, more than a third of a million workers walked off their jobs. Approximately 200,000 of them won shorter hours, including Packingtown's workers, who joined the Knights of Labor en masse. To celebrate, the community staged a huge parade of twelve marching bands and twenty-eight decorated wagons.

The eight-hour campaign swelled the ranks of the Knights of Labor. The organization grew from a few thousand in 1880 to nearly three-quarters of a million six years later. Nearly 3,000 women formed their own "ladies assemblies" or joined mixed locals. The organization was already committed to securing "for both sexes equal pay for equal work," but Leonora Barry, who was now appointed to organize women, helped to increase their share of membership to 10 percent. African Americans also joined the Knights—20,000 to 30,000 nationally—mainly in separate assemblies within the organization.

In Chicago, the shorter-hours campaign ended in tragedy. On May 4, 1886, following a series of confrontations between strikers and authorities, a protest against police violence at Haymarket Square seemed to be ending quietly until someone threw a bomb that killed one policeman and left seven others fatally wounded. Police responded by firing wildly into the crowd, killing an equal number. After Chicago authorities arrested anarchist leaders, a sensational trial ended in death sentences, although no evidence linked

THE GOSPEL OF THE KNIGHTS OF LABOR.
"We work not selfishly for ourselves alone, but extend the hand of fellowship to all mankind."—*Mr. Powderly, at Richmond.*

This anti-labor cartoon was published in the satirical magazine *Puck*, October 13, 1886, shortly after the national convention of the Knights of Labor in Richmond, Virginia, which attracted attention for the prominent role played by African American delegates. At this meeting, Grand Master Terence Powderly had declared, "We work not selfishly for ourselves alone but extend the hand of fellowship to all mankind." Joseph Keppler, *Puck* editor and artist, parodies Powderly's pronouncement by depicting him as belligerent in his defense of unionized workers.

SOURCE: The Granger Collection, New York (0008409).

the accused to the bombing. Four of the convicted were hanged, one committed suicide, and three other "Haymarket Martyrs," as they were called, remained jailed until pardoned in 1893 by Illinois governor John Peter Altgeld.

The Knights of Labor had suffered an irreparable setback. Employers' associations successfully pooled funds to rid their factories of troublesome organizers and announced that companies would no longer bargain with unions. In Packingtown, the Big Five firms drew up a blacklist to get rid of labor organizers and quickly reinstituted the ten-hour day. The Knights' membership dropped precipitously. The wage system had triumphed.

The American Federation of Labor

The events of 1886 also signaled the rise of a very different kind of organization, the American Federation of Labor (AFL). Unlike the Knights, the AFL accepted the wage system. Following a strategy of "pure and simple unionism," the AFL sought to gain recognition of its union status to bargain with employers for better working conditions, higher wages, and shorter hours. In return, it offered compliant firms the benefit of amenable day-to-day relations with the most highly skilled wage earners. Only if companies refused to bargain in good faith would union members strike.

The new federation, with twelve national unions and 140,000 affiliated members, declared war on the Knights of Labor. In the wake of the Haymarket tragedy and the collapse of the eight-hour movement, the AFL pushed ahead of its rival by organizing craft workers. AFL president Samuel Gompers refused to include unskilled workers, racial minorities, women, and immigrants, believing they were impossible to organize and even unworthy of equal status. Under his leadership, the AFL member became the "aristocrat of labor," the best-paid worker in the world.

Far from the national leadership of Gompers, who served as president until 1924, local AFL members recuperated some of the best qualities of the Knights of Labor and establish a firm basis for the survival of the labor movement. Across the country, Central Federations of Labor formed in cities and small industrial towns. Often they published their own weekly newspaper. Always they sought to coordinate the activities of affiliated locals, from providing support to strikers, to gathering votes for prolabor political candidates, to conducting mass social gatherings in the warm summer months.

Chicago's Central Labor Federation embodied the new spirit of the AFL. After the Haymarket tragedy, labor activists worked more closely with urban reformers. Finding allies among women's clubs and church groups, within the state legislature and even among some socially minded members of the business community, unionists cultivated an atmosphere of civic responsibility. The Illinois Factory Investigation Act of 1893 offered evidence of their hard work and patience, securing funds from the state legislature to monitor working conditions and particularly to improve the woeful situation of the many women and children who worked in sweatshops. Although craft unionism represented only a small minority of working Americans—about 10 percent at the end of the century—local federations of skilled workers often played important roles in their communities. They may not have been able to slow the steady advance of mechanization, which diminished the craft worker's autonomy and eliminated some of the most desirable jobs, but AFL members managed to make their presence felt. Local politicians courted their votes, and Labor Day, first celebrated in the 1880s, became a national holiday in 1894.

THE NEW SOUTH

"Fifteen years have gone over" since the Civil War, journalist Whitelaw Reid complained, yet the South "still sits crushed, wretched, busy displaying and bemoaning her wounds." Physically and financially devastated by the war, the South had little investment capital and relatively few banks to manage it. The area was economically stagnant, its per capita wealth only 27 percent of that of the northeastern states. The South's remote countryside receded into greater isolation, while its few urban regions moved very slowly into the era of modern industry and technology. As late as 1880 mining and manufacturing employed only 5 percent of Alabama's workforce. At the turn of the century southern industries lagged far behind enterprises in other regions of the country. Their progress was held back by dependence on northern finance capital, continued reliance on cotton production, and the legacy of slavery.

An Internal Colony

In the 1870s a vocal and powerful new group of Southerners headed by Henry Woodfin Grady, editor of the *Atlanta Constitution*, insisted that the region enjoyed a great potential in its abundant natural resources of coal, iron, turpentine, tobacco, and lumber. Grady and his peers envisioned a "New South" where modern textile mills operated efficiently and profitably, close to the sources of raw goods, the expansive fields of cotton, and a plentiful and cheap supply of labor, unrestricted by unions or by legal limitations on the employment of children. Arguing against those planters who aspired to rejuvenate the agricultural economy based on the cultivation of a few staple crops, this group forcefully promoted industrial development and welcomed northern investors.

Northern investors secured huge concessions from southern state legislatures, including land, forest, and mineral rights and large tax exemptions. Exploiting the incentives, railroad companies laid over 22,000 miles of new track, connecting the region to national markets and creating new cities. By 1890 a score of large railroad companies, centered mainly in New York, held more than half of all the track in the South. Northern-owned lumber companies meanwhile stripped southern forests.

Northerners also employed various means to protect their investments from southern competition. By the late 1870s, southern merchants, with help from foreign investors, had begun to run iron factories around Birmingham, Alabama. Southern iron production was soon encroaching on the northeastern market. Andrew Carnegie toured the city's iron mills and then declared, "The South is Pennsylvania's most formidable industrial enemy." To stave off this competition, Carnegie ordered the railroads to charge higher freight fees to Birmingham's iron producers. New York bankers later succeeded in expatriating Birmingham's profits through stock ownership in southern firms. After the turn of the century, U.S. Steel simply bought out the local merchants and took over much of Birmingham's production.

The production of cotton textiles followed a similar course. Powerful merchants and large landowners, realizing that they could make high profits by controlling the cotton crop from field to factory, promoted the vertical integration of the cotton industry. The Mississippi Valley Cotton Planters' Association, for example, advised planters to "set up spindles in the cotton fields"—that is, to build mills on their land. Meanwhile, New South promoters in Atlanta hosted the International Cotton Exposition of 1881 in a bold public relations campaign to attract investors. The number of mills in the South grew from 161 in 1880 to 400 in 1900. Southern investors supplied large amounts of the capital for the industrial expansion and technological improvements. The latest machines ran the new mills, and the South boasted the first factory fully equipped with electricity. Production in the four leading cotton-manufacturing states—North Carolina, South Carolina, Georgia, and Alabama—skyrocketed, far outpacing the New England mills.

Recognizing the potential for great profit in these new factories with their cheap labor, northern manufacturers, including many New England mill owners, shifted their investments to the South. By the 1920s, northern investors held much of the South's wealth, including the major textile mills, but returned through employment or social services only a small share of the profits to the region's people.

Beyond iron or steel and textiles, southern industry remained largely extractive and, like the South itself, rural. Turpentine and lumbering businesses pushed ever farther into diminishing pine forests, the sawmills and distilleries moving with them. Toward the end of the century, fruit canning and sugar refining flourished. For the most part, southern enterprises mainly produced raw materials for consumption or use in the North, thereby perpetuating the economic imbalance between the sections.

The governing role of capital investments from outside the region reinforced long-standing relationships. Even rapid industrialization—in iron, railroads, and textiles—did not carry the same consequences achieved in the North. The rise of the New South reinforced, rather than diminished, the region's status as the nation's internal colony.

Southern Labor

The advance of southern industry did little to improve the working lives of most African Americans. The majority of African Americans lived in the southern states,

making up 35 percent of the region's population as late as 1910. In several states, such as Mississippi and South Carolina, they represented the majority. Although black workers continued to prevail in the agricultural economy, large numbers were moving to the new manufacturing centers and growing cities in search of better-paying jobs. African American men did find work with the railroads; in booming cities like Atlanta they even gained skilled positions in the construction trades and worked as bricklayers, carpenters, and painters. For the most part, however, African Americans were limited to unskilled, low-paying jobs. In the textile mills and cigarette factories, which employed both black and white workers, the workforce was rigidly segregated. African Americans were assigned mainly to janitorial jobs and rarely worked alongside the white workers who tended the machines. Nearly all African American women who earned wages did so as household workers. By 1880 Atlanta's washerwomen outnumbered the African American men who worked as common laborers. While the vast majority of adult women did laundry, girls as young as ten years worked as domestics or as nurses for white children.

In general, white workers fiercely protected their relatively privileged positions. Locals of the all-white carpenters' union maintained a segregation policy so absolute that if too few members were available for a job, the union would send for out-of-town white workers rather than employ local members of the black carpenters' union. In an Atlanta mill in 1897, 1,400 white women operatives went on strike when the company proposed to hire two black spinners.

Only at rare moments did southern workers unite across racial lines. In the 1880s, the Knights of Labor briefly organized both black and white workers. At its high point, the Knights' local union, District Assembly 92, enrolled two-thirds of Richmond's 5,000 tobacco operatives and made significant inroads among quarry workers, coopers, typographers, iron molders, and builders. But when white politicians and local newspapers began to raise the specter of black domination, the Knights were forced to retreat. Across the region their assemblies collapsed. Other unions remained the exclusive preserve of white skilled workers.

With few of the new immigrant groups that had found work in northern industries, the South depended on its own regional labor market and therefore maintained low wages for both black and white workers. In 1890, white skilled workers in Richmond's iron trades, including plumbers, carpenters, and gas fitters, made 10 to 30 percent less in 1890 than comparable workers elsewhere in the United States. Southern textile workers' wages were barely half those of New Englanders. In the 1880s, when investors enjoyed profits ranging from 30 percent to 75 percent, southern mill workers earned as little as 12 cents per hour. Black men earned at or below the poverty line of $300 per year, while black women rarely earned more than $120, and white women about $220, annually. The poorest paid workers were children, the mainstay of southern mill labor.

As industry expanded throughout the nation, so too did the number of children earning wages. This was especially so in the South. In 1896 only one in twenty Massachusetts mill workers was younger than sixteen, but one in four North Carolina cotton mill operatives was that age or younger. Traditions rooted in the agricultural economy reinforced the practice of using the labor of all family members, even the very young. In oyster-canning factories, for example, even five-year-olds joined their parents in work. Seasonal labor, such as picking crops or grinding sugarcane, put families on the move, making formal education all but impossible. Not until well into the twentieth century did compulsory school attendance laws effectively restrict child labor in the South.

The processing of raw tobacco employed thousands of African American women, who sorted, stripped, stemmed, and hung tobacco leaves as part of the redrying process. After mechanization was introduced, white women took jobs as cigarette rollers, but black women kept the worst, most monotonous jobs in the tobacco factories. The women shown in this photograph are stemming tobacco in a Virginia factory while their white male supervisor oversees their labor.

SOURCE: Cook Collection, Valentine Museum/Richmond History Center.

A system of convict labor also thrived in the South. Bituminous coal mines and public work projects of all kinds, especially in remote areas, employed disciplinary methods and created living and working conditions reminiscent of slavery. With African Americans constituting up to 90 percent of the convict workforce, public officials felt little need to justify the occasional practice of capturing unsuspecting black strangers and placing them alongside criminals in labor gangs. Transported and housed like animals—chained together by day and confined in portable cages at night—these workers suffered high mortality rates. Southern leaders took pride in what they called the "good roads movement"—the chief use of convict labor—as proof of regional progress.

The Transformation of Piedmont Communities

The impact of the New South was nowhere greater than in the Piedmont, the region extending from southern Virginia and the central Carolinas into northern Alabama and Georgia. After 1870, long-established farms and plantations gave way to railroad tracks, textile factories, numerous mill villages, and a few sizable cities. By the turn of the century, five Piedmont towns had populations over 10,000. Even more dramatic was the swelling number of small towns with populations between 1,000 and 5,000—from fourteen in 1870 to fifty-two in 1900. Once the South's backcountry, the Piedmont now surpassed New England in the production of yarn and cloth to stand first in the world.

Rural poverty and the appeal of a new life encouraged many farm families to strike out for a mill town. As prices of cotton or tobacco fell and farmers' debts to the merchants rose, many families turned to tenant farming and its life of hopeless indebtedness. Those with the least access to land and credit—mainly widows and their children and single women—were the first to go into the mills. Then families sent their children. Some families worked in the mills on a seasonal basis, between planting and harvesting. But as the agricultural crisis deepened, more and more people abandoned the countryside entirely for what they called "public work." Hoping to do better, the majority of these families soon found themselves residents of a company town, owned "lock, stock and barrel" by the manufacturers who employed them.

A mill community typically comprised rows of single-family houses, a small school, several churches, a company-owned store, and the home of the superintendent who governed everyone's affairs. The manager of the King Cotton Mill in Burlington, North Carolina, not only kept the company's accounts in order, purchased raw material, and sold the finished yarn, but even bought Christmas presents for the workers' children. It was not unknown for a superintendent to prowl the neighborhood to see which families burned their lanterns past nine o'clock at night and, finding a violator, to knock on the door and tell the offenders to go to bed. Millworkers frequently complained that they had no private life at all. A federal report published shortly after the turn of the century concluded that "all the affairs of the village and the conditions of living of all the people are regulated entirely by the mill company. Practically speaking, the company owns everything and controls everything, and to a large extent controls everybody in the mill village."

Mill superintendents also relied on schoolteachers and clergy to set the tone of community life. They hired and paid the salaries of Baptist and Methodist ministers to preach a faith encouraging workers to be thrifty, orderly, temperate, and hardworking. Ministers conducted evening prayer services, brought men and women into the choir, and sponsored Bible classes and missionary societies. The schools, similarly subsidized by the company, reinforced the lesson of moral and social discipline required of industrial life and encouraged students to follow their parents into the mill. But it was mainly young children between six and eight years old who attended school. When more hands were needed in the mill, superintendents plucked out these youngsters and sent them to join their older brothers and sisters who were already at work.

Piedmont mill villages like Greenville, South Carolina, and Burlington, Charlotte, and Franklinville, North Carolina, nevertheless developed a cohesive character typical of isolated rural communities. The new residents maintained many aspects of their agricultural pasts, tilling small gardens and keeping chickens, pigs, and cows in their yards. Factory owners rarely paved roads or sidewalks or provided adequate sanitation. Mud, flies, and diseases such as typhoid fever flourished. Millworkers endured poverty and health hazards by strengthening community ties through intermarriage. Within a few generations, most of the village residents had, according to one study, "some connection to each other, however distant, by marriage," blood, or both. Even the men and women without families boarded in households where privacy was scarce and collective meals created a familylike atmosphere. Historians have called this complex of intimate economic, family, and community ties the customs of incorporation.

THE INDUSTRIAL CITY

Before the Civil War, manufacturing had centered in the countryside, in burgeoning factory towns such as Lowell, Massachusetts, and Troy, New York. The expanding rail system of the postwar decades promoted new growth in the older commercial cities of Boston, Philadelphia, and New York and created urban outposts like Minneapolis, Kansas City, and Denver. By the end of the nineteenth century, 90 percent of all manufacturing took place in cities. The metropolis stood at the center of the growing industrial economy, a magnet drawing raw material, capital, and labor, and a key distribution point for manufactured goods.

The industrial city inspired both great hope and great trepidation. Civic leaders often bragged about its size and rate of growth; immigrants wrote to their countryfolk of its pace, both exciting and exhausting. Philosopher Josiah Strong described the city as the nation's "storm center." "Here luxuries are gathered—everything that dazzles the eye, or tempts the appetite" as well as, he pointedly added, "the desperation of starvation." Whatever the assessment, the city dominated the nation's economic, social, and cultural life.

Populating the City

The United States was on its way to becoming an urban nation. The population of cities grew at double the rate of the nation's population as a whole. In 1860 only sixteen cities had more than 50,000 residents. By 1890 one-third of all Americans were city dwellers. Eleven cities claimed more than 250,000 people. Both Chicago and Philadelphia had 1 million inhabitants. But although New York City in 1900 was home to almost 3.5 million people, the West had become the nation's most urbanized region in terms of both the proportion of people living in cities and the concentration of wealth in urban areas. In California, for example, 40 percent of the state's population lived in the two urban areas of San Francisco–Oakland and Los Angeles.

The growth of cities in the western and southern states reflected the expansion of the nation's railroads in those regions and the efficient transportation of goods and people that expansion made possible. The growth of Atlanta, for example, was tied to the expansion of the southern rail system. Like Chicago in the Midwest and Los Angeles in the West, Atlanta became a hub and distribution center for regionally produced goods.

The nation's largest cities—New York, Chicago, Philadelphia, St. Louis, Boston, and Baltimore—achieved international fame for the size and diversity of their populations. Many of their new residents had migrated from rural communities within the United States. Between 1870 and 1910, an average of nearly 7,000 African Americans moved north each year, hoping to escape the poverty and oppression prevailing in the South and to find better-paying jobs. By the end of the century, nearly 80 percent of African Americans in the North lived in urban areas. Among those aged sixteen to thirty-five in all native-born groups, urban women outnumbered men. Whereas young white men in particular aspired to inherit the family farm or seek a fortune in the West, their sisters sought jobs in urban manufacturing, commercial trades, and housekeeping.

Immigrants and their children were the major source of urban population growth in the late nineteenth century. Most of those in the first wave of immigration, before the Civil War, had settled in the countryside. In contrast, after the war it was the industrial city that drew the so-called new immigrants, who came primarily from eastern and southern Europe. In 1880 San Francisco claimed the highest proportion of foreign born (45 percent), although not the largest number. By the turn of the century Chicago had more Germans than all but a few German cities and more Poles than most Polish cities; New York had more Italians than a handful of the largest Italian cities, and Boston had nearly as many Irish as Dublin. In almost every group except the Irish, men outnumbered women.

Like rural migrants, immigrants came to the American city to take advantage of the expanding opportunities for employment. While many hoped to build a new home in the land of plenty, many others intended to work hard, save money, and return to their families in the Old Country. In the 1880s, for example, nearly half of all Italian, Greek, and Serbian men returned to their native lands. Others could not return to their homelands or did not wish to. Jews, for instance, had emigrated to escape persecution in Russia and Russian-dominated Polish and Romanian lands. A Yiddish writer later called this generation the "Jews without Jewish memories. . . . They shook them off in the boat when they came across the seas. They emptied out their memories." Those Chinese immigrants who could not return home during their lifetime often requested that their bodies or ashes be sent back to China.

Of all groups, Jews had the most experience with urban life. Forbidden to own land in most parts of Europe and boxed into *shtetls* (villages), Jews had also formed thriving urban communities in Vilna, Berlin, London, and Vienna. Many had worked in garment manufacturing, in London's East End, for example, and followed a path to American cities like New York, Rochester, Philadelphia, or Chicago where the needle trades flourished.

Other groups, the majority coming from rural parts of Europe, sought out their kinfolk in American cities, where they could most easily find housing and employment. Bohemians settled largely in Chicago, Pittsburgh, and Cleveland. They often lived and worked near German immigrants, although in poorer housing and in less-skilled jobs as lumberyard workers, cigar rollers, and garment workers. French Canadians, a relatively small group of a few hundred thousand, emi-grated from Quebec and settled almost exclusively in New England and upper New York State. Finding work mainly in textile mills, they transformed smaller industrial cities like Woonsocket, Rhode Island, into French-speaking communities. Cubans, themselves often first- or second-generation immigrants from Spain, moved to Ybor City, a section of Tampa, Florida, to work in cigar factories. Still other groups tended toward cities dominated by fishing, shoemaking, or even glassblowing, a craft carried directly from the Old Country. Italians, the most numerous among the new immigrants, settled mainly in northeastern cities. With few skills and little education, they often became laborers, laying railroad track, excavating subways, and erecting buildings.

Resettlement in an American city did not necessarily mark the end of the immigrants' travels. Newcomers, both native-born and immigrant, moved frequently from one neighborhood to another and from one city to another. As manufacturing advanced outward from the city center, working populations followed. American cities experienced a total population turnover three or four times during each decade of the last half of the century.

The American city was transformed under the pressure of these various groups. In 1882, when 1.2 million people immigrated to the United States, the novelist Henry James described what he called a "sharp sense of dispossession." To the immigrants, the scene was also disquieting. Before he left his village, Allesandro DeLuca remembered hearing that New York was not only bigger but better than any city in Italy. After he arrived, he felt disillusioned and doubted that he would ever "find here my idea."

The Urban Landscape

Faced with a population explosion and an unprecedented building boom, the cities encouraged the creation of many beautiful and useful structures, including commercial offices, sumptuous homes, and efficient public services—but at a cost. Builders and city planners often disregarded the natural beauty and the architectural landmarks of earlier generations. Laid out in a simple geometric gridiron pattern, streets and housing ran over the sites of hills that had been leveled, ponds that had been filled, farmlands and farm houses that had been eradicated. Factories often occupied the best sites, near waterways where goods could be easily transported and wastes dumped.

In New York City, the majority of the population who worked in dingy factories lived in crowded tenements designed to maximize the use of space by impoverished families. Built by the thousands after the Civil War, the typical "dumbbell" model sat on a lot 25 by 100 feet and rose to five stories. Each floor was subdivided

Web Exploration

Consider the percentages of foreign-born residents in the different regions of the United States in 1900. Why did immigrants tend to settle in some regions and not in others?
www.prenhall.com/faragher/map19.2

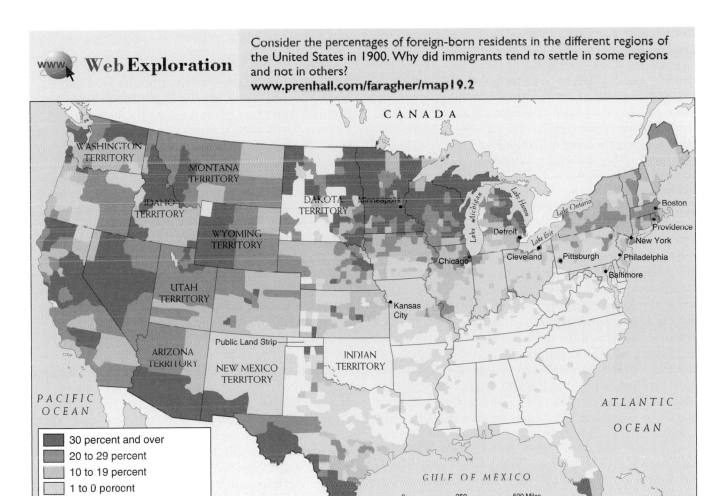

Population of Foreign Birth by Region, 1880   European immigrants after the Civil War settled primarily in the industrial districts of the northern Midwest and parts of the Northeast. French Canadians continued to settle in Maine, Cubans in Florida, and Mexicans in the Southwest, where earlier immigrants had established thriving communities.

SOURCE: Clifford L. Lord and Elizabeth H. Lord, *Lord & Lord Historical Atlas of the United States* (New York: Holt, 1953).

into four family units of no more than three rooms each. One room served as a combined cooking and living room, the remaining two as bedrooms. By 1890 New York's Lower East Side packed more than 700 people per acre into back-to-back buildings, producing one of the highest population densities in the world.

At the other end of the urban social scale, New York's Fifth Avenue, St. Paul's Summit Avenue, Chicago's Michigan Avenue, and San Francisco's Nob Hill fairly gleamed with new mansions and town houses. Commonwealth Avenue marked Boston's fashionable Back Bay district, built on a filled-in 450-acre tidal flat. State engineers planned this community, with its magnificent boulevard, uniform five-story brownstones, and back

alleys designed for deliveries. Like wealthy neighborhoods in other cities, Back Bay also provided space for the city's magnificent public architecture, its stately public library, fine arts and science museums, and orchestra hall. Back Bay opened onto the Fenway Park system designed by the nation's premier landscape architect, Frederick Law Olmsted.

Cities such as Boston, Chicago, Baltimore, and San Francisco managed to rebuild after major fires, employing the latest technological and architectural innovations. The Chicago Fire broke out in October 1871—though not, as legend had it, because "Mrs. O'Leary's cow" had kicked over a lantern—and swept through the ramshackle wooden houses that had been thrown up for workers. By the time it was doused, the fire had destroyed more than 60,000 buildings within four square miles, including much of the commercial district, and had left nearly 100,000 people homeless. Louis H. Sullivan, recently schooled in Europe, eagerly surveyed the newly cleared sites in the aftermath of the conflagration. Although he did little to improve residential living, he came up with a plan for a new type of commercial building, the skyscraper, a "proud and soaring thing, rising in [such] sheer exultation that from bottom to top it is a unit without a single dissenting line." Emphasizing vertical grandeur rising as high as twenty stories, and using iron, steel, and masonry to deter fires, Sullivan made the skyscraper the symbol of the modern city.

Architects played a key role in what is sometimes called the American Renaissance or City Beautiful movement. Grand concrete boulevards were constructed at enormous public cost. New sports amphitheaters dazzled the public and evoked pride in the city's accomplishments. New schools, courthouses, capitols, hospitals, museums, and department stores arose. Influenced by the Parisian Beaux-Arts style, architects regularly replaced the simple Greek Revival buildings constructed earlier in the century with domed palaces. These massive, often highly ornate structures expressed the city's pride in its commercial success. The city center also became more congested and noisy, making it a more desirable place to visit than to live.

The city also inspired other architectural marvels. Opened in 1883, the Brooklyn Bridge won wide acclaim from engineers, journalists, and poets as the most original American construction. Designed by John Roebling, who died from an accident early in its construction, and by his son Washington Roebling, who became an invalid during its construction, the bridge was considered an aesthetic and practical wonder. Its soaring piers, elegant arches, and intricate steel cables convey an image of strength and elasticity, inspiring a belief among artists and writers in the potential of technology to unite function and beauty. The Brooklyn Bridge also helped to speed the transformation of rural townships into suburban communities.

The emergence of inexpensive, rapid mass transportation systems also altered the spatial design of cities. Like the railroad but on a smaller scale, streetcars and elevated railroads changed business dramatically because they moved traffic of many different kinds—information, people, and goods—faster and farther than before. Although San Francisco introduced the first mechanically driven cable car in 1873, within a decade Chicago would claim the most extensive cable car system in the world. The first electrified street railway was tested in Richmond, Virginia in 1888, and by 1895 more than 800 communities operated systems of electrically powered cars or trolleys on track totaling 10,000 miles. Two years later Boston rerouted a mile and a half of track underground, establishing the nation's first subway trolley. In 1902 New York opened its subway system, which would grow to become the largest in the nation.

Mass transit, by bringing so many people into the heart of the city, played a large part in boosting the value of real estate and promoting the development of central business districts. The value of property in Chicago's "Loop" district, for example, increased by 700 percent between 1877 and 1991. Soon financial, commercial, and cultural institutions replaced small factories and private residences, which moved to neighborhoods where property and rent were less expensive. In turn, the new structures made fuller use of the land, rising high to maximize the space available to tenants.

In his watercolor *The Bowery at Night,* painted in 1885, W. Louis Sonntag, Jr. shows a New York City scene transformed by electric light. Electricity transformed the city in other ways as well, as seen in the electric streetcars and elevated railroad.

SOURCE: *The Bowery at Night,* 1885. Watercolor. Museum of the City of New York.

At the same time, by making it possible for a great number of workers to live in communities distant from their place of employment, mass transportation also allowed the metropolitan region to grow dramatically. By the end of the nineteenth century, suburban trains were bringing nearly 100,000 riders daily into the city of Chicago. Outside Boston, suburbs like Dorchester and Brookline sprang up, offering many professional workers quiet residential retreats from the city's busy downtown. New retail and service businesses followed as the dynamism of the great city radiated outward while the bulk of industry and pollution remained behind.

The City and the Environment

Electric trolleys eliminated the tons of waste from horsecars that had for decades fouled city streets. But the new rail systems also increased congestion and created new safety hazards for pedestrians. During the 1890s, 600 people were killed each year by Chicago's trains. To relieve congestion, Chicago as well as New York and Boston elevated portions of their rapid transit systems and in the process placed entire communities under the shadow of noisy and rickety wooden platforms. Despite many technological advances, the quality of life in the nation's cities did not necessarily improve.

In the half-century after the Civil War, efforts to improve sanitary conditions absorbed many urban tax dollars. Although cast iron pipes and steam pumps had delivered water into cities since the early part of the century, the filtration systems introduced in the 1890s greatly improved water quality and, by providing cleaner water, played an important role in reducing the incidence of typhoid. By the 1880s, bathrooms with showers and flush toilets had become standard features in hospitals and in many middle-class homes. In turn, the greater quantity of water as well as waste required larger and better drainage and sewer systems. Modern water and sewer systems now constituted a hidden city of pipes and wires mirroring the growth of the visible city above ground.

These advances did not in themselves eradicate serious environmental or health problems. Most cities continued to dump sewage into nearby bodies of water. Moreover, rather than outlawing upriver dumping by factories, municipal governments usually moved to establish separate clean-water systems through the use of reservoirs. Meanwhile the filthy rivers, such as the Providence and Woonasquatucket Rivers in Providence, Rhode Island, were paved over as they passed through downtown. The Chicago River was reversed through an engineering feat so as to transport sewage away from Lake Michigan, the city's source of drinking water. Chicago's residents enjoyed cleaner tap water, but downriver communities began to complain about the unendurable stench from the diverted flow.

The unrestricted burning of coal to fuel the railroads and to heat factories and homes after 1880 greatly intensified urban air pollution. Noise levels continued to rise in the most compacted living and industrial areas. Overcrowded conditions and inadequate sanitary facilities bred tuberculosis, smallpox, and scarlet fever, among other contagious diseases. Children's diseases like whooping cough and measles spread rapidly through poor neighborhoods such as Packingtown. A major yellow fever epidemic in 1878 prompted the creation of the National Board of Health, which in turn began to advise state and city officials and provide emergency assistance. However, in several states, local health officials refused to cooperate with the new national board and directed their representatives in Congress to reduce its appropriations and, finally, to abolish the national board in 1893. Meanwhile, scientific advances in the field of bacteriology prompted local hospital administrators and physicians to supplement public health measures, such as improved sanitation, with efforts to control disease. By the 1890s many urban school systems employed doctors and nurses to screen children for common contagious diseases. But only after the turn of the century, amid an intensive campaign against municipal corruption, did laws and administrative practices address the serious problems of public health (see Chapter 21).

Meanwhile the distance between the city and the countryside narrowed. Naturalists had hoped for large open spaces—a buffer zone—to preserve farmland and wild areas, protect future water supplies, and diminish regional air pollution. But soon the industrial landscape invaded the countryside. Nearby rural lands not destined for private housing or commercial development became sites for water treatment and sewage plants, garbage dumps, and graveyards—services essential to the city's growing population.

CULTURE AND SOCIETY IN THE GILDED AGE

The growth of industry and spread of cities had a profound impact on all regions of the United States. During the final third of the nineteenth century the standard of living climbed, although unevenly and erratically. Real wages (pay in relation to the cost of living) rose, fostering improvements in nutrition, clothing, and housing. More and cheaper products were within the reach of all but the very poor. Food from the farms became more abundant and varied—grains for bread or beer; poultry, pork, and beef; fresh fruits and vegetables from California. Although many

Americans continued to acknowledge the moral value of hard work, thrift, and self-sacrifice, the explosion of consumer goods and services promoted sweeping changes in behavior and beliefs. Leisure, play, and consumption became part of a new ideal and measure of success. Nearly everyone felt the impact of the transformation from an economy grounded in production toward one based on consumption, although in vastly and increasingly different ways.

"Conspicuous Consumption"

Labeled the "Gilded Age" by humorist and social critic Mark Twain, the era following the Civil War favored the growth of a new class united in its pursuit of money and leisure. The well-to-do enjoyed great status throughout the nineteenth century, but only after the war did upper-class Americans form national networks to consolidate their power. Business leaders built diverse stock portfolios and often served simultaneously on the boards of several corporations. Similarly, they intertwined their interests by joining the same religious, charitable, athletic, and professional societies. They sent their sons to private boarding schools such as St. Paul's, then on to Harvard, Yale, or Princeton. During the summer months, their wives and children vacationed together in the sumptuous new seashore and mountain resorts, while they themselves made deals at their leisure in new downtown social clubs and on the golf links of suburban country clubs. During the winter, high society regrouped in Palm Beach, Florida, linked by rail to points north and lined with fine, warm-weather resorts. Just as Dun and Bradstreet ranked the leading corporations, the Social Register identified the 500 families that controlled most of the nation's wealth.

According to economist and social critic Thorstein Veblen, the rich had created a new style of "conspicuous consumption." The Chicago mansion of real estate tycoon Potter Palmer, for example, was constructed in 1885 without exterior doorknobs. Not only could no one enter uninvited, but a visitor's calling card supposedly passed through the hands of twenty-seven servants before admittance was allowed. At the nearby McCormick mansion, dinner guests chose from a menu printed in French. A vice president of the Chicago & Northwestern Railroad, Perry H. Smith, built his marble palace in the style of the Greek Renaissance. Its ebony staircase was trimmed in gold, its butler's pantry equipped with faucets not only for hot and cold water but for iced champagne. The women who oversaw these elaborate households themselves served as measures of their husbands' status, according to Veblen, by adorning themselves in jewels, furs, and dresses of the latest Paris design.

Conspicuous consumption reached toward new heights of extravagance. In New York, wealthy families hosted dinner parties for their dogs or pet monkeys, dressing the animals in fancy outfits for the occasion. Railroad magnate "Diamond Jim" Brady commonly enjoyed after-theater snacks at the city's "lobster palaces," where he consumed vast quantities of food—oysters for an appetizer, two soups, fish, a main dinner of beef and vegetables, punches and sherbet on the side, dessert, coffee, and quarts of orange juice.

Perhaps no display of wealth matched the ostentation of the "cottages" of Newport, Rhode Island, where the rich created a summer community centering on consumption. Architect H. H. Richardson and his protégés built manor houses more magnificent than the English homes they mimicked. Here wealthy young men and women engaged in new amateur sports such as polo, rowing, and lawn tennis. Young and old alike joined in yachting and golf tournaments.

Toward the end of the century, the wealthy added a dramatic public dimension to the "high life." New York's Waldorf-Astoria hotel, which opened in 1897, incorporated the grandeur of European royalty but with an important difference. Because rich Americans wanted to be watched, the elegantly appointed corridors and restaurants were visible to the public through huge windows, and floor-to-ceiling mirrors allowed diners to observe one another. The New York rich also established a unique custom to welcome the New Year: they opened wide the curtains of their Fifth Avenue mansions so that passersby could marvel at the elegant decor.

The wealthy also became the leading patrons of the arts as well as the chief importers of art treasures from Europe and Asia. They provided the bulk of funds for the new symphonies, operas, and ballet companies, which soon rivaled those of Continental Europe. Nearly all major museums and art galleries, including the Boston Museum of Fine Arts, the Philadelphia Museum of Art, the Art Institute of Chicago, and the Metropolitan Museum of Art in New York, were founded during the last decades of the nineteenth century. Many were the gifts of individual donors, such as the libraries, museums, and galleries in Pittsburgh that all bore the name "Carnegie."

Gentility and the Middle Class

A new middle class, very different from its predecessor, formed during the last half of the century. The older middle class comprised the owners or superintendents of small businesses, doctors, lawyers, teachers, and ministers and their families. The new middle class included these professionals but also the growing number of salaried employees—the managers, technicians, clerks, and engineers who worked in the complex web of corporations and government. Long hours of labor earned their families a modest status and sufficient income to live securely in style and comfort and, equally important, to separate work and home.

Most middle-class American families valued their home not simply as a sign of their social station but as a haven from the tumultuous society outside. For as little as $10 a month, a family could finance the construction of a suburban retreat from the noise, filth, and dangers of the city. This peaceful domestic setting, with its manicured lawns and well-placed shrubs, afforded family members both privacy and rejuvenation. But to accomplish this goal, middle-class families had to separate business activities from leisure, and the breadwinner from his family for most of the day. Assisted by modern transportation systems, men often traveled one to two hours each day, five or six days a week, to their city offices and back again. Women and children stayed behind.

The interior design of middle-class homes reflected a desire for refinement. A rush of new magazines and volumes on homemaking, like Harriet Spofford's *Art Decoration* (1879), set the standards, including elaborate front entryways, wallpapers stenciled by housewives themselves, stained-glass windows, and solid furniture. Reserved for visitors, the parlor featured upholstered furniture, inexpensive prints of famous paintings, and framed photographs of family members. Outside, the fenced-in yard served as a safe playground for small children and their pets.

Middle-class women found themselves devoting a large part of their day to housework. They frequently employed one or two servants but relied increasingly on the many new household appliances to get their work done. Improvements in the kitchen stove, such as the conversion from wood fuel to gas, saved a lot of time. Yet, simultaneously, with the widespread circulation of cookbooks and recipes in newspapers and magazines, as well as the availability of new foods, the preparation of meals became more complex and time-consuming. New devices such as the eggbeater speeded some familiar tasks, but the era's fancy culinary practices offset any gains in saving time. Similarly, the new carpet sweepers surpassed the broom in efficiency, but the fashionable high-napped carpeting demanded more care. The foot-powered treadle sewing machine, a staple of the middle-class home, encouraged the fashion-conscious housewife to produce fancier clothing for herself and her family. Thus, rather than diminishing with technological innovation, household work expanded to fill the time available.

Almost exclusively white, Anglo-Saxon, and Protestant, the new middle class embraced "culture" not for purposes of conspicuous consumption but as a means of self-improvement and moral uplift. Whole families

visited the new museums and art galleries. One of the most cherished institutions, the annual season of lectures at the Chautauqua campgrounds in upstate New York, brought thousands of families together in pursuit of knowledge of literature and the fine arts. The middle class also provided the bulk of patrons for the new public libraries.

Middle-class families applied the same standards to their leisure activities. What one sporting-goods entrepreneur rightly called the "gospel of EXERCISE" involved men and women in calisthenics and outdoor activities, not so much for pleasure as for physical and mental discipline. Hiking was a favorite among both men and women and required entirely new outfits: for women, loose upper garments and skirts short enough to prevent dragging; for men, rugged outer wear and jaunty hats. Soon men and women began camping out, with almost enough amenities to re-create a middle-class home in the woods. Roller skating and ice skating, which became crazes shortly after the Civil War, took place in specially designed rinks in almost every major town. By the 1890s, the "safety" bicycle had also been marketed. It replaced the large-wheel variety, which was difficult to keep upright. A good-quality "bike" cost $100 and, like the piano, was a symbol of middle-class status. In 1995 Chicago hosted thirty-three cycle clubs comprising nearly 10,000 members.

Leisure became the special province of middle-class childhood. Removed from factories and shops and freed from many domestic chores, children enjoyed creative play and physical activity. Summer camps, offering several weeks of sports and handicrafts, attracted many children to New England during this period. The toy market boomed, and lower printing prices helped children's literature flourish. The *Brownie Book* (1898), about imaginary elflike beings, was tremendously popular. Children's magazines such as *St. Nicholas* and *Youth's Companion* were filled with stories, poems, and pictures. Slightly older children read westerns, sports novels of many kinds, and such perennial and uplifting classics as *Little Women* and *Black Beauty.*

Life in the Streets

Immigrants often weighed the material abundance they found in the United States against their memories of the Old Country. One could "live better" here, but only by working much harder. In letters home, immigrants described the riches of the new country but warned friends and relatives not to send weaklings, who would surely die of stress and strain. Even if their bodies thrived, their spirits might sink amid the alien and intense commercialism of American society. In many immigrant communities, alcoholism and suicide rates did soar above contemporary European standards. Germans in

Chicago, it was said half jokingly, drank more beer and whiskey than all the Germans in Germany. Each group had its own phrase to express its feelings of disenchantment. Embittered German immigrants called their new land *Malhuerica*, "misfortune"; Jews called it *Ama Reka*, Hebrew for "without soul"; and Slavs referred to it as *Dollerica*.

To alleviate the stress of adjustment to life in an unfamiliar city, newcomers often established close-knit ethnic communities. European immigrants usually preferred to live together with people from their own country of origin, if possible from their home district. The poorest of new immigrants, like the Italians of Providence, Rhode Island, or the Slavs of Homestead, Pennsylvania, made special sacrifices to resettle with people who would be familiar to them. Aunts and uncles became almost as dear as parents, cousins as close as brothers and sisters. Young adults married within their communities, often setting up households within a few blocks of their parents and not infrequently within the same "triple-decker" or tenement.

Many newcomers, having little choice about their place of residence, concentrated in districts marked off by racial or ethnic lines. In San Francisco, city ordi-

The intersection of Orchard and Hester Streets on New York's Lower East Side, photographed ca. 1905. Unlike the middle classes, who worked and played hidden away in offices and private homes, the Jewish lower-class immigrants who lived and worked in this neighborhood spent the greater parts of their lives on the streets.

SOURCE: Oil over a photograph. The Granger Collection (4E534.23).

nances prevented Chinese from operating laundries in most of the city's neighborhoods, and the city's schools excluded their children. In the 1880s, Chinese San Franciscans, representing 10 percent of the city's population, were crowded into a dozen blocks of restaurants, shops, and small factories known as Chinatown. In Los Angeles and San Antonio, Mexicans lived in distinctive barrios. In most cities, African American families were similarly compelled to remain in the dingiest, most crime-ridden, and dangerous sections of town.

Young people who had left their families behind, whether in Europe or in the American countryside, usually took rooms in small residential hotels or boardinghouses. The Young Men's Christian Association (YMCA), established in the 1850s, and the Young Women's Christian Association (YWCA), organized a decade later, provided temporary residences mainly to native-born, white, self-supporting men and women. The most successful "women adrift," such as clerical workers and retail clerks, lived in the new furnished-room districts bordering the city's business center. The least prosperous landed on "skid row," where homeless people spent time in the rough taverns, eating free lunches in return for purchased beer, waiting for casual labor, and sometimes trading sexual favors for money.

The working-class home did not necessarily ensure privacy or offer protection from the dangers of the outside world. In the tenements, families often shared their rooms with other families or paying boarders. During the summer heat, adults, children, and boarders alike competed for a sleeping place on the fire escape or roof, and all year round noise resounded through paper-thin walls. But so complex and varied were income levels and social customs that no single pattern emerged. Packingtown's Slovaks, Lithuanians, and Poles, for example, frequently took in boarders, yet Bohemians rarely did. Neither did the skilled iron rollers who worked at the Carnegie Steel Company in Homestead, Pennsylvania. These well-paid craft workers often owned their own homes, boasting parlors and even imported Belgian carpets. At the other extreme, Italian immigrants, who considered themselves fortunate to get work with a shovel, usually lived in overcrowded rented apartments, just a paycheck away from eviction.

Whether it was a small cottage or a tenement flat, the working-class home involved women and children in routines of household labor without the aid of the new mechanical devices. In addition to cooking and cleaning, women used their cramped domestic space for work that provided a small income. They gathered their children—and their husbands after a hard day's labor—to sew garments, wrap cigars, string beads, or paint vases for a contractor who paid them by the piece. And they cooked and cleaned for the boarders whose rent supplemented the family income. In short, the home was a second work place, usually involving the entire family.

Despite working people's slim resources, their combined buying power created new and important markets for consumer goods. Often they bought shoddy replicas of products sold to the middle class: cheaper canned goods, inferior cuts of meat, and partially spoiled fruit. Several leading clothing manufacturers specialized in inexpensive ready-to-wear items, usually copied from patterns designed for wealthier consumers but constructed hastily from flimsy materials. Patent medicines for ailments caused by working long periods in cramped conditions sold well in working-class communities, where money for doctors was scarce. These nostrums failed to restore health, except perhaps through the power of suggestion. On the other hand, their high alcohol content might lift a person's spirits, if only temporarily.

The close quarters of the urban neighborhood allowed immigrants to preserve many Old World customs. In immigrant communities such as Chicago's Packingtown, Pittsburgh's Poletown, New York's Lower East Side, or San Francisco's Chinatown, people usually spoke their native language while visiting their friends and relatives. The men might play cards while women and children gathered in the stairwell or on the front stoop to trade stories. In good weather they walked and talked, an inexpensive pastime common in European cities. No organization was as important as the fraternal society, which sponsored social clubs and provided insurance benefits. Social organizations, known as *huiguan*, were especially important in preserving clan and dialect among the largely male unmarried population of Chinese San Francisco. Immigrants also re-created Old World religious institutions such as the temple, church, or synagogue, or secular institutions such as German family-style taverns or Russian Jewish tearooms. Chinese theaters, in inexpensive daily and nightly performances, presented dramas depicting historical events or explicating moral teachings and thereby preserved much of Chinese native culture. Immigrants also replicated their native cuisine (as much as available foods allowed) and sang their own songs, accompanied by the polka, mazurka, or tamburitza, according to tradition. They married, baptized children, and buried their dead according to Old World customs.

In the cosmopolitan cities, immigrants, by being innovative entrepreneurs as well as the best customers, helped to shape the emerging popular culture. German immigrants, for example, created Tin Pan Alley, the center of the popular music industry, and wrote such well liked ballads as "Down by the Old Mill Stream." They also became the first promoters of ragtime, which found its way north from Storyville, the red-light district of New Orleans. Created by African American and creole bands, ragtime captivated those teenage off-spring of immigrants who rushed to the new dance halls. Disdaining their parents' sentimental favorites, such as "Beautiful Dreamer," the youngsters seemed to associate the new syncopated sounds with the pulse of urban life. They also gave ragtime musicians paying work and budding musical entrepreneurs the idea that music with African American roots could become the biggest commercial entertainment of all.

In the same years, the first great amusement parks began to enthrall masses of immigrants and other city dwellers. The most spectacular was Coney Island, at the southern edge of Brooklyn, New York, which grew out of a series of fancy hotels and gambling (and prostitution) parlors. When developers realized that "wholesome fun" for the masses could pay better than upper-class leisure or lower-class vice, they decided to transform Coney Island into a magnificent seaside park filled with ingenious amusements such as water slides, mechanized horse races, carousels, roller coasters, and fun houses. Three amusement parks opened between 1895 and 1903. On the rides or at the nearby beach, young men and women could easily meet apart from their parents, cast off their inhibitions, and enjoy a hug or kiss. Or they could simply stroll through the grounds, looking at exotic performers, enjoying make-believe trips to the Far East or even the moon, entranced by fantastic towers, columns, minarets, and lagoons lit up at night to resemble dreams rather than reality. At Coney Island or at Riverview, Chicago's oldest amusement park located on the city's North Side, millions of working-class people enjoyed cheap thrills that offset the hardships of their working lives.

CULTURES IN CONFLICT, CULTURE IN COMMON

The new commercial entertainments gave Americans from various backgrounds more in common than they would otherwise have had. On New York's Lower East Side, for instance, theater blossomed with dramas that Broadway would adopt years later, while children dreamed of going "uptown" where the popular songs they heard on the streets were transcribed onto sheet music and sold in stores throughout the city. Even so, nothing could smooth the tensions caused by conflicting claims to the same resources, such as public schools and urban parks.

Education

As industries grew and cities expanded, so did the nation's public school system. Business and civic leaders realized that the welfare of society now depended on an educated population, one possessing the skills and knowledge required to keep both industry and government running. In the last three decades of the nineteenth century, the idea of universal free schooling, at least for white children, took hold. Kindergartens in particular flourished. St. Louis, Missouri, opened the first public school kindergarten in 1873, and by the turn of the century more than 4,000 similar programs throughout the country enrolled children between the ages of three and seven.

The number of public high schools, which were rare before the Civil War, also increased, from 160 in 1870 to 6,000 by the end of the century. In Chicago alone, average daily attendance increased sixfold. Despite this spectacular growth, which was concentrated in urban industrial areas, as late as 1890 only 4 percent of children between the ages of fourteen and seventeen were enrolled in school, the majority of them girls planning to become teachers or office workers. Most high schools continued to serve mainly the middle class. In 1893 the National Education Association reaffirmed the major purpose of the nation's high schools as preparation for college, rather than for work in trades or industry, and endorsed a curriculum of rigorous training in the classics, such as Latin, Greek, and ancient history. The expected benefits of this kind of education rarely outweighed the immediate needs of families who depended on their children's wages. At the end of the century, 50 percent of the children in Chicago between the ages of ten and twelve were working for wages.

Higher education also expanded along several lines. Agricultural colleges formed earlier in the century developed into institutes of technology and took their places alongside the prestigious liberal arts colleges. To extend learning to the "industrial classes," Representative Justin Morrill of Vermont sponsored the Morrill Federal Land Grant Act of 1862, which funded a system of state colleges and universities for teaching agriculture and mechanics "without excluding other scientific and classic studies." Meanwhile, established private institutions like Harvard, Yale, Princeton, and Columbia grew, with the help of huge endowments from business leaders such as Rockefeller and Carnegie. By 1900, sixty-three Catholic colleges were serving mainly the children of immigrants from Ireland and eastern and southern Europe. Still, as the overall number of colleges and universities grew from 563 in 1870 to nearly 1,000 by 1910, only 3 percent of the college-age population took advantage of these new opportunities.

One of the most important developments occurred in the area of professional training. Although medical and law schools dated from the mid-eighteenth century, their numbers grew rapidly after the Civil War. Younger professions, such as engineering, pharmacy, and journalism, also established specialized training institutions. In 1876 the Johns Hopkins University pioneered a program of research and graduate studies, and by the end of the century several American universities, including Stanford University and the University of Chicago, offered advanced degrees in the arts and sciences.

This expansion benefited women, who previously had had little access to higher education. After the Civil War, a number of women's colleges were founded, beginning in 1865 with Vassar, which set the academic standard for the remainder of the century. Smith and Wellesley followed in 1875, Bryn Mawr in 1885. By the end of the century, 125 women's colleges offered a first-rate education comparable to that given to men at Harvard, Yale, or Princeton. Meanwhile, coeducation grew at an even faster rate; by 1890, 47 percent of the nation's colleges and universities admitted women. The proportion of women college students changed dramatically. Women constituted 21 percent of undergraduate enrollments in 1870, 32 percent in 1880, and 40 percent in 1910. Despite these gains, many professions remained closed to women.

An even greater number of women enrolled in vocational courses. Normal schools, which offered one- or two-year programs for women who planned to become elementary school teachers, developed a collegiate character after the Civil War and had become accredited state teachers' colleges by the end of the century. Normal schools enrolled many women from rural areas, particularly from poor families. Upon graduation, these women filled the personnel ranks of the rapidly expanding system of public education. Other institutions, many founded by middle-class philanthropists, also prepared women for vocations. For example, the first training school for nurses opened in Boston in 1873, followed in 1879 by a diet kitchen that taught women to become cooks in the city's hospitals. Founded in 1877, the Women's Educational and Industrial Union offered a multitude of classes to Boston's wage-earning women, ranging from elementary French and German, to drawing, watercoloring, and oil and china painting, to dressmaking and millinery, stenography and typing, as well as crafts less familiar to women, such as upholstering, cabinetmaking, and carpentry. In the early 1890s, when the entering class at a large women's college like Vassar still averaged under 100, the Boston Women's Educational and Industrial Union reported that its staff of 83 served an estimated 1,500 clients per day. By that time, one of its most well-funded programs was a training school for domestic servants.

The leaders of the business community had also begun to promote manual training for working-class and immigrant boys. One leading San Francisco merchant described the philosophy behind this movement as a desire to train boys "to earn a living with little study and plenty of work." Craft unionists in several cities actively opposed this development, preferring their own methods of apprenticeship to training programs they could not control. But local associations of merchants and manufacturers lobbied hard for "industrial education" and raised funds to supplement the public school budget. In 1884 the Chicago Manual Training School opened, teaching "shop work" along with a few academic subjects, and by 1895 all elementary and high schools in the city offered courses that trained working-class boys for future jobs in industry and business.

The expansion of education did not benefit all Americans or benefit them all in the same way. Because African Americans were prohibited from enrolling in colleges attended by white students, special colleges were founded in the southern states shortly after the Civil War. All-black Atlanta and Fisk universities both soon offered a rigorous curriculum in the liberal arts. Other institutions, such as Hampton, founded in 1868, specialized in vocational training, mainly in manual trades. Educator Booker T. Washington encouraged African Americans to resist "the craze for Greek and

George Washington Carver (1864–1943), who had been born in slavery, had been invited by Booker T. Washington to direct agricultural research at the Tuskegee Institute in Alabama. A leader in development of agriculture in the New South, Carver promoted crop diversification to rejuvenate soil that was depleted by the continuous planting of cotton and encouraged the cultivation of alternative, high-protein crops such as peanuts and soybeans. He designed his programs in sustainable agriculture mainly for African American farmers and sharecroppers rather than for commercial purposes.

SOURCE: ca. 1900. The Granger Collection, New York (0002916).

Latin learning" and to strive for practical instruction. In 1881 he founded the Tuskegee Institute in Alabama to provide industrial education and moral uplift. By the turn of the century, Tuskegee enrolled 1,400 men and women in more than thirty different vocational courses, including special cooking classes for homemakers and domestic servants. Black colleges, including Tuskegee, trained so many teachers that by the century's end the majority of black schools were staffed by African Americans.

The nation's educational system was becoming more inclusive and yet more differentiated. The majority of children attended school for several years or more. At the same time, students were tracked—by race, gender, and class—to fill particular roles in an industrial society.

Leisure and Public Space

Most large cities set aside open land for leisure-time use by residents. New York's Central Park opened for ice skating in 1858, providing a model for urban park systems across the United States. In 1869, planners in Chicago secured funds to create a citywide system comprising six interconnected large parks, and within a few years, Lincoln Park, on the city's north side, was attracting crowds of nearly 30,000 on Sundays. These parks were rolling expanses, cut across by streams and pathways and footbridges and set off by groves of trees, ornamental shrubs, and neat flower gardens. According to the designers' vision, the urban middle class might find here a respite from the stresses of modern life. To ensure this possibility, posted regulations forbade many activities, ranging from walking on the grass to gambling, picnicking, or ball playing without permission, to speeding in carriages.

The working classes had their own ideas about the use of parks and open land. Trapped in overcrowded tenements or congested neighborhoods, they wanted space for sports, picnics, and lovers' trysts. Young people openly defied ordinances that prohibited play on the grassy knolls, while their elders routinely voted against municipal bonds that did not include funds for more recreational space in their communities. Immigrant ward representatives on the Pittsburgh city council, for instance, argued that band shells for classical music meant little to their constituents, while spaces suitable for sports meant much.

Eventually, most park administrators set aside some sections for playgrounds and athletic fields and others for public gardens and band shells. Yet intermittent conflicts erupted. The Worcester, Massachusetts, park system, for example, allowed sports leagues to schedule events but prohibited pickup games. This policy gave city officials more control over the use of the park for outdoor recreation but at the same time forced many ball-playing boys into the streets. When working-class parents protested, city officials responded by instituting programs of supervised play, to the further dismay of the children.

Public drinking of alcoholic beverages, especially on Sunday, provoked similar disputes. Pittsburgh's "blue laws," forbidding businesses to open on Sunday, were rigidly enforced when it came to neighborhood taverns, while large firms like the railroads enjoyed exemptions. Although the Carnegie Institute hoped to discourage Sunday drinking by sponsoring alternative events, such as free organ recitals and other concerts, many working people, especially beer-loving German immigrants, continued to treat Sunday as their one day of relaxation. In Chicago, when not riding the streetcars to the many beer gardens and taverns that thrived on the outskirts, Germans gathered in large numbers for picnics in the city's parks.

Toward the end of the century, many park administrators relaxed the rules and expanded the range of permitted activities. By this time, large numbers of the middle class had become sports enthusiasts and pressured municipal governments to turn meadowlands into tennis courts and golfing greens. In the 1890s bicycling brought many women into the parks. Still, not all city residents enjoyed these facilities. Officials in St. Louis, for example, barred African Americans from the city's grand Forest Park and set aside the smaller Tandy Park for their use. After challenging this policy in court, African Americans won a few concessions, such as the right to picnic at any time in Forest Park and to use the golf course on Monday mornings.

National Pastimes

Toward the end of the century, the younger members of the urban middle class had begun to find common ground in lower-class pastimes, especially ragtime music. Introduced to many Northerners by the African American composer Scott Joplin at the Chicago World's Fair of 1893, "rag" quickly became the staple of entertainment in the new cabarets and nightclubs. Middle-class urban dwellers began to seek out ragtime bands and congregated in nightclubs and even on the rooftops of posh hotels to listen and dance and even to drink.

Vaudeville, the most popular form of commercial entertainment since the 1880s, also bridged middle- and working-class tastes. Drawing on a variety-show tradition of singers, dancers, comedians, jugglers, and acrobats, who had entertained Americans since colonial days, "vaude" became a big business that made ethnic and racial stereotypes and the daily frustrations of city life into major topics of amusement. Vaudeville palaces—ten in New York, six in Philadelphia, five in Chicago, and at least one in every other large city—attracted huge, "respectable" crowds that sampled between twenty and thirty dramatic, musical, and comedy acts averaging fifteen minutes each. One study estimated that before vaudeville gave way to movie theaters in the 1920s, between 14 and 16 percent of all city dwellers attended shows at least once a week. Sunday matinees were especially popular with women and children.

Sports, however, outdistanced all other commercial entertainments in appealing to all kinds of fans and managing to create a sense of national identity. No doubt the most popular parks in the United States were the expanses of green surrounded by grandstands and marked by their unique diamond shape—the baseball field. During the last quarter of the nineteenth century the amateur sport of gentlemen and Union soldiers suddenly became the "national pastime." Both American and English children had for years been playing a form of baseball, known mainly as "rounders," when a group of young men in Manhattan formed the Knickerbocker Base Ball Club in 1845 and proceeded to set down the game's rules in

One of the finest American painters of the period, known for realistic depictions of physical exertion in amateur athletics, Thomas Eakins here turned his attention to the commercial baseball park. The batter and catcher appear as well-poised athletes, dignified in their dress and manner—everything that the baseball player of the late nineteenth century was not very likely to be.

SOURCE: Thomas Eakins, *Baseball Players*, 1875. Watercolor. The Rhode Island School of Design Museum of Art (36.172).

CHRONOLOGY

1862	Morrill Act authorizes "land-grant" colleges
1869	Knights of Labor founded
1870	Standard Oil founded
1871	Chicago Fire
1873	Financial panic brings severe depression
1876	Baseball's National League founded
	Alexander Graham Bell patents the telephone
1879	Thomas Edison invents the incandescent bulb
	Depression ends
1881	Tuskegee Institute founded
1882	Peak of immigration to the United States (1.2 million) in the nineteenth century
	Chinese Exclusion Act passed
	Standard Oil Trust founded
1883	William Graham Sumner published the social Darwinist classic *What Social Classes Owe to Each Other*
1886	Campaigns for eight-hour workday peak
	Haymarket riot and massacre discredit the Knights of Labor
	American Federation of Labor founded
1890	Sherman Antitrust Act passed
1893	Stock market panic precipitates severe depression
1895	Coney Island opens
1896	Rural free delivery begins
1900	Andrew Carnegie's *Gospel of Wealth* recommends honesty and fair dealing
1901	U.S. Steel Corporation formed

writing. Baseball clubs soon formed in many cities, and shortly after the Civil War traveling teams with regular schedules made baseball a professional sport. The formation of the National League in 1876 encouraged other spectator sports, but for generations baseball remained the most popular.

Rowdy behavior gave the game a working-class ambience. Well-loved players known for their saloon brawls occasionally disappeared for a few days on "benders." Team owners, themselves often proprietors of local breweries, counted heavily on beer sales in the parks. Having to contend with hundreds of drunken fans, officials maintained order only with great difficulty. Outfielders occasionally leaped into the grandstand to punch spectators who had heckled them. To attract more subdued middle-class fans, the National League raised admission prices, banned the sale of alcohol, and observed Sunday blue laws. Catering to a working-class audience, the American Association kept the price of admission low, sold liquor, and played ball on Sunday.

Baseball, like many other sports, soon became tied to the larger business economy. In Chicago, for example, the first baseball clubs organized in the 1850s. After the Civil War local merchants, such as Marshall Field, began to support teams and by the end of the decade there were more than fifty company-sponsored teams playing the local leagues. By 1870, a Chicago Board of Trade team emerged as the city's first professional club, the White Stockings. Capitalized as a joint stock company, the White Stockings soon succeeded in recruiting a star pitcher from the Boston Red Stockings, Albert Spalding, who eventually became manager and then president of the team. Spalding also came to see baseball as a source of multiple profits. He procured the exclusive rights to manufacture the official ball and the rule book, while producing large varieties of other sporting equipment. Meanwhile, he built impressive baseball parks in Chicago with seating for 10,000 and special private boxes above the grandstands for the wealthy. He easily became the foremost figure in the National League.

Spalding also succeeded in tightening the rules of participation in the sport. In 1879 he dictated the "reserve clause," which prevented players from negotiating a better deal and leaving the team that originally signed them. He encouraged his player manager "Cap" Anson to forbid the White Stockings from playing against any team with an African American member. The firing of Moses "Fleet" Walker, an African-American, from the Cincinnati team in 1884 marked the first time the color line had been drawn in a major professional sport.

Effectively excluded, African Americans organized their own traveling teams. In the 1920s they formed the Negro Leagues, which produced some of the nation's finest ballplayers.

Players occasionally organized to regain control over their sport. They frequently complained about low wages and arbitrary rules, and like factory workers in the 1880s they formed their own league, the Brotherhood of Professional Base Ball Players, with profits divided between participants and investors. This effort failed, partly because fans would not desert the established leagues, but mostly because successful baseball franchises demanded large quantities of capital. American sports had become big business.

As attendance continued to grow, the enthusiasm for baseball straddled major social divisions, bringing together Americans of many backgrounds, if only on a limited basis. By the end of the century, no section of the daily newspaper drew more readers than the sports pages. Although it interested relatively few women, sports news riveted the attention of men from all social classes. Loyalty to the "home team" helped to create an urban identity, while individual players became national heroes.

CONCLUSION

By the end of the nineteenth century, industry and the growing cities had opened a new world for Americans. Fresh from Europe or from the native countryside, ordinary urban dwellers struggled to form communities of fellow newcomers through work and leisure, in the factory, the neighborhood, the ballpark, and the public school. Meanwhile, their "betters," the wealthy and the new middle class, made and executed the decisions of industry and marketing, established the era's grand civic institutions, and set the tone for high fashion and art.

Rich and poor alike shared many aspects of the new order. Yet inequality persisted and increased, as much a part of the new order as the Brooklyn Bridge or advertising. During the mostly prosperous 1880s, optimists believed that unfair treatment based on region, on class, and perhaps even on race and gender might ease in time. By the depressed 1890s, however, these hopes had worn thin, and the lure of overseas empire appeared as one of the few goals that held together a suffering and divided nation.

REVIEW QUESTIONS

1. Discuss the sources of economic growth in the decades after the Civil War. Historians often refer to this period as the era of the "second industrial revolution." Do you agree with this description?

2. Describe the impact of new technologies and new forms of production on the routines of industrial workers. How did these changes affect African American and women workers in particular? What role did trade unions play in this process?

3. Choose one major city, such as Boston, New York, Chicago, Birmingham, or San Francisco, and discuss changes in its economy, population, and urban space in the decades after the Civil War.

4. Discuss the role of northern capital in the development of the New South. How did the rise of indus-

try affect the lives of rural Southerners? Analyze these changes from the point of view of African Americans.

5. How did urban life change during the Gilded Age? How did economic development affect residential patterns? How did the middle class aspire to live during the Gilded Age? How did their lifestyles compare with those of working-class urbanites?

6. How did the American educational system change to prepare children for their adult roles in the new industrial economy?

7. How did the rise of organized sports and commercial amusements reflect and shape social divisions at the end of the century? Which groups were affected most (or least) by new leisure activities?

RECOMMENDED READING

Cindy S. Aron, *Working at Play: A History of Vacations in the United States* (1999).

James R. Barrett, *Work and Community in the Jungle* (1987).

Alfred D. Chandler Jr., *The Visible Hand: The Managerial Revolution in American Business* (1977).

William Cronon, *Nature's Metropolis* (1991).

Herbert G. Gutman, *Work, Culture and Society in Industrializing America: Essays in American Working-Class and Social History* (1977).

Alice Kessler-Harris, *Out to Work: A History of Wage-Earning Women in the United States* (1982).

Kenneth L. Kusmer, *A Ghetto Takes Shape, Black Cleveland, 1870–1930* (1976).

Lawrence H. Larsen, *The Rise of the Urban South* (1985).

David F. Noble, *America by Design: Science, Technology and the Rise of Corporate Capitalism* (1977).

Dave Roediger and Franklin Rosemont, eds., *Haymarket Scrapbook* (1986).

Roy Rosenzweig, *Eight Hours for What We Will: Workers and Leisure in an Industrial City, 1870–1920* (1983).

Alan Trachtenberg, *The Incorporation of America: Culture and Society in the Gilded Age* (1982).

▶ MEDIA RESOURCES

 U.S. HISTORY DOCUMENTS CD-ROM

Industrializing America

18-1   Charles Loring Brace, "The Life of the Street Rats" (1872)

18-2   Progress and Poverty (1879)

18-3   The Gilded Age (1880)

18-4   Richard K. Fox, from Coney Island Frolics (1883)

18-5   Address by George Engel, Condemned Haymarket Anarchist (1886)

18-6   Edward Bellamy, from Looking Backward (1888)

18-7   The Assassination of President Garfield (1889)

18-8   Ida B. Wells-Barnett, from a Red Record (1895)

18-9   Booker T. Washington, Atlanta Exposition Address (1895)

18-10 United States Sanitary Commission, Sketch of Its Purposes (1864)

Immigrant and Urban Nation

19-1   Memorial of the Chinese Six Companies to U.S. Grant, President of the United States (1876)

19-2   Plain Facts for Old and Young (1884)

19-3   Anglo-Saxon Culture Under Siege (1885)

19-4   How the Other Half Lives (1890)

19-5   The People's Party Platform (1892)

19-6   The Secret Oath of the American Protective Association (1893)

America Around the Globe

20-1   Josiah Strong, from Our Country (1885)

The Progressive Era

21-1   Frederick Winslow Taylor, "A Piece-Rate System" (1896)

 ### Companion Website Highlights

To view an exploration, enter one of the URLs below in your browser.

 ### Web Explorations

Patterns of Industry, 1900
http://wwwprenhall.com/faragher/map19.1

Population of Foreign Birth by Region, 1880
http://www.prenhall.com/faragher/map19.2

HISTORY RESOURCE CENTER

To find the resources listed below, go to
http://www.prenhall.com/historyresourcecenter

Documents

Andrew Carnegie, from The Gospel of Wealth (1889)

From Plessy v. Ferguson (1896)

Images

Booker T. Washington

The New Fad, 1886

William Jennings Bryan

Grover Cleveland

Rutherford B. Hayes

Turn to the next page for the *Exploring America* activity for this chapter. ☞

EXPLORING AMERICA
FRENCH CANADIAN CONTROVERSY
http://www.prenhall.com/faragher/frenchcanadian

How pervasive was white supremacy among northerners in the late 1800s? How did this status affect immigration? What does the concept of supremacy based on skin color suggest about ideas and attitudes toward race? Why did Mark Twain defend the Chinese? What politician tried to gain the White House by playing on antiChinese sentiment? What do the Chinese and French-Canadians in the United States have in common? The module answers these and other questions regarding immigration and race, exploring antiChinese sentiment and its political manifestations. It also offers an interesting corollary to the white supremacy argument by discussing the situation of the French-Canadian community in Massachusetts.

The French Canadian Controversy uses various methods to examine race, antiChinese sentiment, and white supremacy in the late nineteenth century. It

highlights the strength and pervasiveness of the white supremacist position as it affected Chinese immigration and the presidential aspirations of a noted Republican politician. Cartoons and documents from Chinese political parties and candidates, the U.S. government, literary figures, and others debate the issue of Chinese exclusion and later the controversy over the status of French-Canadians. The narrative, interactive map, and chronology provide a strong structure to this expansive topic demonstrating its longevity.

Reflect and Respond

1. What threats, according to James G. Blaine, did the "cooly" pose to the free Anglo-Saxon laborer?
2. How similar is Blaine's view to that espoused by Denis Kearney?

3. On what basis did Thomas Nast oppose Blaine? In answering, make explicit reference to Nast's infamous antiCatholic (and antiIrish) 1875 cartoon, "The American River Ganges." It portrays the defenders of the public schools valiantly seeking to prevent Catholic bishops from devouring innocent children.
4. What "Chinese" traits did Carroll D. Wright attribute to French-Canadian immigrants?
5. How could Americans simultaneously view the Chinese as "coolies" and also as criminal geniuses such as the fictitious Fu Manchu?
6. How do you see the debate over Chinese exclusion as illuminating, and as complicating the American conversation about the meaning of equality?

✓ Check it out

A Memorial from Representative Chinamen in America to His Excellency U. S. Grant, President of the United States

This memorial written by leaders of the San Francisco Chinese community presents their views on the positive attributes of Chinese immigrants and the constructive ways the Chinese had

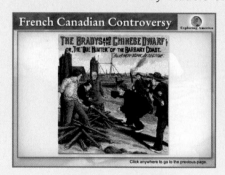

contributed to the betterment of the United States. It also addresses the U.S. policy of welcoming immigrants from all countries as well as the peaceful relations between China and the United States. From the Chinese-American perspective, the Memorial refutes the contentions made by antiChinese proponents and offers a glimpse into the ideas and actions taken by those attacked by nativists seeking to limit immigration.

This exploration is also available on the *Exploring America* CD-ROM.

Representing Chicago's History

Packingtown occupies a unique niche in Chicago's historical memory in that it came to represent the very essence of the city. As the poet Carl Sandburg wrote, Chicago was "the city of big shoulders," "hog butcher to the world." There was a certain grittiness and muscularity about the Midwestern metropolis that for generations delighted residents and intrigued visitors.

This image of Chicago began to circulate widely after the publication of Upton Sinclair's muckraking novel, *The Jungle*. Commissioned by a socialist newspaper to write a novel about immigrant workers in the meat packing houses, Sinclair collected a $500 advance and spent nearly two months researching the working and living conditions of Packingtown. In *The Jungle*, which was published in 1905, he described in vivid detail the blood and guts of the killing floors and the squalid neighborhood that adjoined the stock yards. His story revolved around a family of recent immigrants from Lithuania, and he provided close descriptions of their everyday life, down to the clothes they wore. Sinclair, a socialist himself, hoped to mobilize his readers to overthrow the system that created the grave social injustices that put so much strain on the immigrant community, but he succeeded mainly in buttressing a campaign for the regulation of the food industry. "I aimed at the public's heart," he lamented, "and by accident hit it in the stomach." Partly in a response to his best-selling novel, Congress passed the Pure Food and Drug Act and the Meat Inspection Act in 1906. But *The Jungle*, which within a few years sold more than 150,000 copies and was published in 17 languages, also enhanced Packingtown's reputation as symbol of the industrial city at its prime.

Despite Sinclair's intention, *The Jungle* helped to make Packingtown the focal point of Chicago history. By the time of its publication, the Union Stock Yards were already attracting tourists from all over the world. In 1893, more people went to see the killing floors than the famed world's fair, the Columbian Exposition. Ironically, Sinclair's vivid descriptions of the gore further piqued their curiosity about work and life in Packingtown. Well into the 1940s, the big packinghouses like Armour and Swift's maintained a special visitors entrance for tourists who continued to come by the trainload to see the way meat was mass produced.

Established in 1865, Chicago's Union Stockyards was processing more than 9 million livestock by the turn of the century. "The Yards" covered more than a square mile of land on the city's South Side. The livestock, brought in by trainloads, were held in pens until moved to the "killing floors" for slaughter. It wasn't a "pretty sight," as one Chicagoan remarked, but the meatpacking industry "put Chicago into contention as a world-class city." SOURCE: © CORBIS.

Chicagoans themselves nurtured this aspect of their history. They took pride in being the center of the meat packing industry, which, after steel, reigned for nearly a century as the city's largest industry. They described the Union Stockyards as one of the wonders of the world. They even bragged about the notorious stench of the neighborhood. As one long-time member of the community noted, "the first memory" of anybody from Packingtown was "the overpowering smell from the packing houses and the fertilizer plants." Scratch any Chicagoan, a popular saying went, and some stockyard smell would come out. Contrary to Sinclair's intention to expose the degradation of Packingtown's residents, Chicagoans took pride in themselves as survivors of harsh conditions. However, by end of the twentieth century, few Chicagoans could nurture this memory.

Since its origin as a primarily German and Irish neighborhood in the 1860s and transformation into a community of Eastern European immigrants when the stockyards were at their peak, slaughtering 15 million livestock a year and employing 44,000 people, Packingtown underwent a series of dramatic changes. After

World War II, as a consequence of the decentralization of the meat packing industry, the stock yards began a period of sharp decline. By the late 1950s, when some of the biggest firms closed their doors, new populations moved in. Meanwhile, postwar prosperity had encouraged the majority of Poles and Lithuanians to find cleaner jobs in other industries and to flee to the suburbs. Mexicans and African Americans took their place and stayed. At one time there were a dozen Polish-American Catholic parishes; after 1971, when the Union Stock Yards finally shut down, the parishes that remained were Mexican. In the 1980s, the City of Chicago, partnering with the Back of the Yards Council, a community organization founded in the late 1930s, launched a redevelopment plan that laid the foundation for the Stockyards Industrial Park. The new complex of small businesses and retail stores employed about one-third the number of workers as the packing houses and retained a link to the past in name only. All that remained of the scenes made famous by Upton Sinclair and celebrated by Chicagoans themselves was the limestone arch that marks the entryway to the old stockyards complex. By the time Chicago designated the old stone gate as an official landmark in 1972, only the memories of old-timers kept this chapter of Chicago's history alive.

By the end of the twentieth century, a new generation of Chicagoans were poised to celebrate not the city's gritty past but its future in finance, service, and tourist industries. In 1999, the city sponsored "Cows on Parade," a public art project that brought to downtown sidewalks more than 200 "cows" made of a fiberglass-polyester mixture and painted in a rainbow of colors and a variety of styles. One cow perched atop a skateboard, for example, another was on skis. The cows had cute names, such as Rhinestone Cowgirl, Cowbelle de Fruits, and Wow Cow. Local businesses and art patrons vied to purchase a cow of their own for a standard fee of $3,500, and at the end of the summer they could either take home their trophy or donate it to a public auction for charity. "Cows on Parade" enchanted children, tourists, and the thousands of office workers who filled the downtown skyscrapers—including the Sears Tower, which, since 1974, stood as the city's new source of pride as the tallest building in the nation.

A few Chicagoans, however, complained that "Cows on Parade" had supplanted the stockyards as the city's chief symbol and, in the process, obliterated much of its history. "Chicago seems to be erasing its gritty, less-glitzy past," one local critic observed. "The hog (and cattle) butcher to the world," he added, "has become a Technicolor, DisneyQuest, chrome-and-glass kinda town." Another detractor refused to relinquish the time-tested symbol, insisting that the "true monument to Chicago's past" was not the whimsical cows currently on display but "a bull named Sherman." Named after one of the founders of the Union Stockyard, John B. Sherman, this rugged bust of the prize-winning steer still tops the old stone gate.

But what remains of the historical memory of Chicago as the nation's premier industrial city and community of hard-working Eastern European immigrants?

During the summer of 1999, while upscale Chicago basked in the publicity garnered from "Cows on Parade," the new residents of what had once been Packingtown displayed their own cows, a trio of colorfully painted figures contributed not by the big-name artists who crafted the downtown versions but by local schoolchildren and community groups. Few Chicagoans from other parts of the city bothered to visit them. "And there they sit," as one nostalgic observer recorded at the time: "No tourists or cameras. Just three forgotten cows marking Chicago's forgotten past." ■

 www.researchnavigator.com

The Community and Memory essay for this chapter deals with the changing ways the residents of Chicago have seen themselves and their city. For further research on the history of the image of Chicago, use the tools available to you in Research Navigator.

As you investigate this topic, consider this question: "Why has Packingtown played such an important role in Chicagoans vision of themselves and their city?"

ContentSelect: Search in the History and Sociology databases using the search term *Chicago*.

Links Library: Access the History: U.S. History database and explore the links for *muckraking*.

New York Times on the Web: To find more about the stockyards place in Chicago's history, use the search term *Chicago stockyards*.

THE PAST

COMMONWEALTH AND EMPIRE

▶ 1870–1900

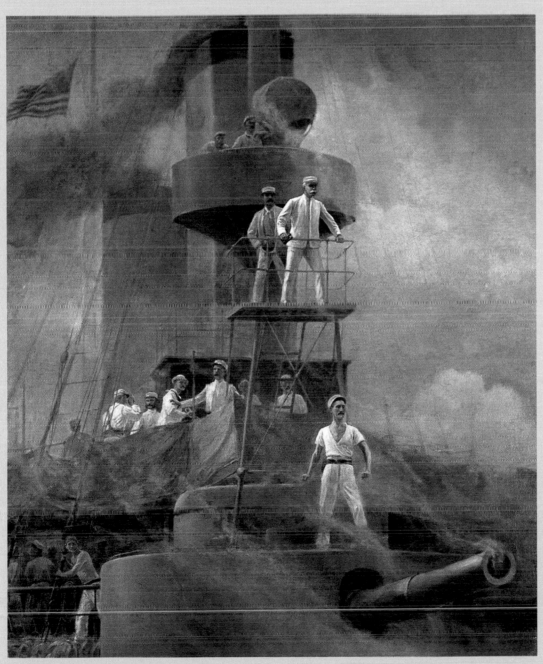

Fred Pansing, *Simpson and Schley Leading the Fleet into New York Harbor, August 20, 1898.*
SOURCE: © Museum of the City of New York/CORBIS (NY001109).

AMERICAN COMMUNITIES

The Cooperative Commonwealth

EDWARD BELLAMY'S *LOOKING BACKWARD* (1888), THE CENTURY'S best-selling novel after Harriet Beecher Stowe's *Uncle Tom's Cabin*, tells the story of a young man who awakens in the year 2000 after a sleep lasting more than 100 years. He is surprised to learn that Americans had solved their major problems. Poverty, crime, war, taxes, air pollution—even housework—no longer exist. Nor are there politicians, capitalists, bankers, or lawyers. Most amazing, gone is the great social division between the powerful rich and the suffering poor. In the year 2000 everyone lives in material comfort, happily and harmoniously. No wonder Bellamy's hero shudders at the thought of returning to the late nineteenth century, a time of "worldwide bloodshed, greed and tyranny."

Community and cooperation are the key concepts in Bellamy's utopian tale. The nation's businesses, including farms and factories, have been given over to the collective ownership of the people. Elected officials now plan the production and distribution of goods for the common well-being. With great efficiency, they even manage huge department stores and warehouses full of marvelous manufactured goods and oversee majestic apartment complexes with modern facilities for cooking, dining, and laundering. To get the necessary work done, an industrial army enlists all adult men and women, but automated machinery has eliminated most menial tasks. The workday is only four hours; vacations extend to six months of each year. At forty-five everyone retires to pursue hobbies, sports, and culture.

Bellamy envisioned his technological utopia as promoting the "highest possible physical, as well as mental, development for everyone." There was nothing fantastic in this plan, the author insisted. It simply required Americans to share equally the abundant resources of their land. If the nation's citizens actually lived up to their democratic ideals, Bellamy declared, the United States would become a "cooperative commonwealth," that is, a nation governed by the people for their common welfare.

Bellamy, a journalist and writer of historical fiction from Chicopee Falls, Massachusetts, moved thousands of his readers to action. His most ardent fans endorsed his program for a "new nation" and formed the Nationalist movement, which by the early 1890s reached an apex of 165 clubs. Terence V. Powderly of the Knights of Labor declared himself a Nationalist. Many leaders of the woman suffrage movement also threw in their support. They endorsed *Looking Backward*'s depiction of marriage as a union of "perfect equals" and admired Bellamy's sequel, *Equality* (1897), which showed how women might become "absolutely free agents" by ending their financial dependence on men.

During the 1890s Bellamy's disciples actually attempted to create new communities along the lines set forth in *Looking Backward*. The best known and longest lasting of these settlements was established in Point Loma, California, in 1897. Situated on 330 acres, with avenues winding through gardens and orchards newly planted with groves of eucalyptus trees, Point Loma was known for its physical beauty. Many young married couples chose to live in small bungalows, which were scattered throughout the colony's grounds, others opted for private rooms in a large communal building. Either way, they all met twice daily to share meals and usually spent their leisure hours together. On the ocean's edge the residents constructed an outdoor amphitheater and staged plays and concerts.

The colony's founder, Katherine Tingley, described Point Loma as "a practical illustration of the possibility of developing a higher type of humanity." No one earned wages, but all 500 residents lived comfortably. They dressed simply in clothes manufactured by the community's women. The majority of the men worked in agriculture. They conducted horticultural experiments that yielded new types of avocados and tropical fruits and eventually produced over half of the community's food supply. Children, who slept in a special dormitory from the time they reached school age, enjoyed an outstanding education. They excelled in the fine arts, including music and drama, and often demonstrated their talents to audiences in nearby San Diego.

The Point Loma community never met all its expenses, but with the help of donations from admirers across the country it remained solvent for decades. Baseball entrepreneur Albert Spalding, who lived there during his retirement,

Point Loma

helped make up the financial deficit. As late as the 1950s the community still had some seventy-five members living on about 100 acres of land.

Even relatively successful cooperative communities such as Point Loma, however, could not bring about the changes that Bellamy hoped to see, and he knew it. Only a mobilization of citizens nationwide could overturn the existing hierarchies and usher in the egalitarian order depicted in *Looking Backward*. Without such a rigorous challenge, the economic and political leadership that had been emerging since the Civil War would continue to consolidate its power and become even further removed from popular control.

The last quarter of the nineteenth century saw just such a challenge, producing what one historian calls "a moment of democratic promise." Ordinary citizens sought to renew the older values of community through farm and labor organizations as well as philanthropic and charitable societies. They could not clearly see, however, that the fate of the nation depended increasingly on events beyond its territorial boundaries. Business leaders and politicians had proposed their own vision of the future: an American empire extending to far distant lands.

TOWARD A NATIONAL GOVERNING CLASS

The basic structure of government changed dramatically in the last quarter of the nineteenth century. Mirroring the fast-growing economy, public administration expanded at all levels—municipal, county, state, and federal—and took on greater responsibility for regulating society, especially market and property relations. Whereas most political theorists continued to advise that the best government is the one that governs least, governments began to do much more than simply maintain order.

This expansion offered ample opportunities for politicians who were eager to compete against one another for control of the new mechanisms of power. Political campaigns, especially those staged for the presidential elections, became mass spectacles, and votes became precious commodities. The most farsighted politicians attempted to rein in the growing corruption and to promote both efficiency and professionalism in the expanding structures of government.

The Growth of Government

Before the Civil War, local governments attended mainly to the promotion and regulation of trade and relied on private enterprise to supply vital services such as fire protection and water supply. As cities became more responsible for their residents' well-being, they introduced professional police and firefighting forces and began to finance school systems, public libraries, and parks. Municipal ownership and administration of basic services became so common that by the end of the century only nine of the nation's fifty largest cities still depended on private corporations for their water supplies.

This expansion demanded huge increases in local taxation. Boston, for example, spent five times more per resident in 1875 than it had just thirty years earlier, and

its municipal debt rose from $784,000 to more than $27 million. The city now paid the salaries of many civil servants, including a growing class of sanitary engineers. By 1880 one of every eight New York voters appeared on a government payroll.

At the national level, mobilization for the Civil War and Reconstruction had demanded an unprecedented degree of coordination, and the federal government continued to expand under the weight of new tasks and responsibilities. Federal revenues also skyrocketed, from $257 million in 1878 to $567 million in 1900. The administrative bureaucracy also grew dramatically, from 50,000 employees in 1871 to 100,000 only a decade later.

The modern apparatus of departments, bureaus, and cabinets took shape amid this upswing. The Department of Agriculture was established in 1862 to provide information to farmers and to consumers of farm products. The Department of the Interior, which had been created in 1849, grew into the largest and most important federal department after the Post Office. It came to comprise more than twenty agencies, including the Bureau of Indian Affairs, the U.S. Geological Survey, and the Bureau of Territorial and International Affairs. The Department of the Treasury, responsible for collecting federal taxes and customs as well as printing money and stamps, grew from 4,000 employees in 1873 to nearly 25,000 in 1900. The Pension Act of 1890 made virtually every Union army veteran and his dependents eligible for benefits; within a decade the Veterans Bureau became known as "the largest executive bureau in the world," employing nearly 60,000 men and women.

The nation's first independent regulatory agency took charge of the nation's most important industry. The Interstate Commerce Commission (ICC) was created in 1887 to bring order to the growing patchwork of state laws concerning railroads. The five-member commission appointed by the president approved freight and passenger rates set by the railroads. The ICC could take public testimony on possible violations, examine company records, and generally oversee enforcement of the law.

This first regulatory agency set a precedent for future regulation of trade as well as for positive government—that is, for the intervention of the government into the affairs of private enterprise. It also marked a shift in the balance of power from the states to the federal government.

The Machinery of Politics

Only gradually did Republicans and Democrats adapt to the demands of governmental expansion. The Republican Party continued to run on its Civil War record, pointing to its achievements in reuniting the nation and in passing new reform legislation. Democrats, by contrast, sought to reduce the influence of the federal government, slash expenditures, repeal legislation, and protect states' rights. While Republicans held on to their long-time constituencies, Democrats gathered support from southern white voters and immigrants newly naturalized in the North. But neither party commanded a clear majority of votes until the century drew to a close.

Presidents in the last quarter of the century— Rutherford B. Hayes (1877–81), James A. Garfield (1881), Chester A. Arthur (1881–85), Grover Cleveland (1885–89), Benjamin Harrison (1889–93), and Cleveland again (1893–97)—did not espouse a clear philosophy of government. They willingly yielded power to Congress and the state legislatures. Only 1 percent of the popular vote separated the presidential candidates in three of five elections between 1876 and 1892. Congressional races were equally tight, less than 2 percentage points separating total votes for Democratic and Republican candidates in all but one election in the decade before 1888. Democrats usually held a majority in the House and Republicans a majority in the Senate, but neither party had sufficient strength to govern effectively. One result was that Congress passed little legislation before 1890.

One major political issue of the late nineteenth century was the tariff. First instituted in 1789 to raise revenue for the young republic, the tariff imposed a fee on imported goods, especially manufactured commodities. Soon its major purpose became the protection of the nation's "infant industries" from foreign competition. Manufacturing regions, especially the Northeast, favored a protective policy, while agricultural regions like the South opposed high tariffs as unfair to farmers who had to pay the steep fees on imported necessities. Democrats, with a stronghold among southern voters, argued for sharp reductions in the tariff as a way to save the rural economy and to give a boost to workers. Republicans, who represented mainly business interests, raised tariffs to new levels on a wide array of goods during the Civil War and retained high tariffs as long as they held power.

Although their platforms encompassed broad national issues, none more important than the tariff, both political parties operated essentially as state or local organizations. Successful politicians responded primarily to the particular concerns of their constituents. To please local voters, Democrats and Republicans repeatedly crosscut each other by taking identical positions on controversial issues.

Political campaigns were great spectacles in the late nineteenth century. Candidates of both parties pursued swing voters furiously. "We work through one campaign," quipped one candidate, "take a bath and start in on the next." Election paraphernalia—leaflets or pamphlets, banners, hats, flags, buttons, inscribed playing cards, or clay pipes featuring a likeness of a candidate's face or the party symbol—became a major expense for both parties. Partisans embraced the Democratic donkey or the Republican elephant as symbols of party fidelity. And voters did turn out. During the last quarter of the century, participation in presidential elections peaked at nearly 80 percent of those eligible to vote. Thousands, in fact, voted several times on any given election day; voters who had died, or had never lived, also miraculously cast ballots.

The rising costs of maintaining local organizations and orchestrating mammoth campaigns drove party leaders to seek ever-larger sources of revenue. Winners often seized and added to the "spoils" of office through an elaborate system of payoffs. Legislators who supported government subsidies for railroad corporations, for instance, commonly received stock in return and sometimes cash bribes. At the time, few politicians or business leaders regarded these practices as unethical.

At the local level, powerful bosses and political machines dominated both parties. Democrats William Marcy Tweed of New York's powerful political organization, Tammany Hall, and Michael "Hinky Dink" Kenna of Chicago specialized in giving municipal jobs to loyal voters and holiday food baskets to their families. Tweed's machine wooed working-class voters by expanding city services in their neighborhoods and even by staging major sporting events or entertainments for the Irish Americans and German Americans who made up over half of New York City's population. Hundreds of smaller political machines ruled cities and rural courthouses through a combination of "boodle" (bribe money) and personal favors.

A large number of federal jobs, meanwhile, changed hands each time the presidency passed from one party to another. More than 50 percent of all federal jobs were

This wooden noisemaker was designed for Grover Cleveland's presidential campaign in 1892. Pursuing the voters, political campaigners devised ingenious signs, buttons, and other miscellaneous novelties for supporters to display, especially at public demonstrations. When shaken vigorously, noisemakers literally demanded the attention of bystanders.

SOURCE: Cleveland campaign noisemaker, 1892. Museum of American Political Life, University of Hartford. Photo by Sally Andersen-Bruce.

patronage positions—nearly 56,000 in 1881—jobs that could be awarded to loyal supporters as part of the "spoils" of the winner. Observers estimated that decisions about congressional patronage filled one-third of all legislators' time. No wonder Bellamy's utopian community operated without politicians and political parties.

One Politician's Story

A typical politician of the age was James Garfield, the nation's twentieth president. Born in a frontier Ohio log cabin in 1831, Garfield briefly worked as a canal boat driver, an experience he later exploited as proof of his humble origins. A Civil War hero—he fought at Shiloh, was honored for gallantry at Chickamauga, and was a major general when he took a seat in Congress in 1863—the Ohio legislator carefully prepared his move into the national political arena.

While serving in Congress, Garfield seemed at first committed to social reform. He introduced a bill to cre-

ate a Department of Education, arguing that public education would prove the best stepping-stone to equality. He denounced his own Republican Party for allowing corruption to flourish during Ulysses S. Grant's administration. The nation's "next great fight," he insisted, would pit the people against the corporations.

With the failure of Reconstruction, Garfield shifted his stance and began to espouse more conservative views. Nearly defeated in a Democratic congressional landslide in 1874, he concluded that "the intelligence of the average American citizen" fell short of the demands of the democratic system. As a result, he came out against universal suffrage. Garfield now looked to the probusiness faction of the Republican Party as a vehicle for realizing his personal ambition. After six years of shrewd maneuvering, trading votes and favors to build his reputation, Garfield became the party's candidate for the 1880 presidential election. In a mediocre race with no outstanding issues, Garfield won by less than 40,000 popular votes out of 9 million cast.

Garfield the idealist had grown into Garfield the machine politician and lackluster president. He had already shown himself indecisive and even indifferent to governing when a frustrated patronage seeker shot him just 200 days after his inauguration. Like other presidents of his era, Garfield assumed that the nation's chief executive served as his party's titular leader and played mainly a ceremonial role in office.

The Spoils System and Civil Service Reform

As early as 1865, Republican representative Thomas A. Jenckes of Rhode Island proposed a bill for civil service reform. Congress feared that such a measure would hamper candidates in their relentless pursuit of votes. President Hayes took up the cause, introducing a few reforms in the New York Customhouse and federal post offices, but Congress again refused to join in a major reform effort. Finally, a group consisting of mainly professors, newspaper editors, lawyers, and ministers organized the Civil Service Reform Association and enlisted Democratic senator George H. Pendleton to sponsor reform legislation.

In January 1883, a bipartisan congressional majority passed the Pendleton Civil Service Reform Act. This measure allowed the president to create, with Senate approval, a three-person commission to draw up a set of guidelines for executive and legislative appointments. The commission established a system of standards for various federal jobs and instituted "open, competitive examinations for testing the fitness of applicants for public service." The Pendleton Act also barred political candidates from soliciting campaign contributions from government workers. Patronage did not disappear, but public service did improve.

Many departments of the federal government took on a professional character similar to that which doctors, lawyers, and scholars were imposing on their fields through regulatory societies such as the American Medical Association and the American Historical Association. At the same time, the federal judiciary began to act more aggressively to establish the parameters of government. With the Circuit Courts of Appeals Act of 1891, Congress granted the U.S. Supreme Court the right to review all cases at will.

Despite these reforms, many observers still viewed government as a reign of outsiders, people pulling the levers of the party machinery or spending money to influence important decisions. Edward Bellamy agreed. He advised Americans to organize their communities for the specific purpose of wresting control of government from the hands of politicians.

FARMERS AND WORKERS ORGANIZE THEIR COMMUNITIES

Farmers and workers began to organize in the late 1860s and succeeded in building powerful national organizations to oppose, as a Nebraska newspaper put it, "the wealthy and powerful classes who want the control of government to plunder the people." It was clear by that time that the nation's political agenda was shifting from the issues raised by the Civil War and Reconstruction to the increasingly tense relationship between capital and labor as well as between work and wages. This relationship became increasingly strained as industrial employers, responding to a series of business downturns, not only increased their scale of production and formed cartels but moved aggressively to cut labor costs. In the process, many of the agreements made with the craft unions fell by the wayside. Meanwhile, farmers in the West and South saw prices for their crops drop while rates for credit and transportation rose.

The railroad, as the most important industry in the nineteenth century and at the peak of its own "system building" into a national network, played a large part in generating protest from workers and farmers. By the end of the century the communities whose livelihoods depended directly or indirectly on the railroads presented the most significant challenge to the political system since the Civil War—the Populist movement.

The Grange

In 1867 farmers on the Great Plains formed the Patrons of Husbandry for their own "social, intellectual, and moral improvement." Led by Oliver H. Kelley, an em-

ployee of the Department of Agriculture, this fraternal society resembled the secretive Masonic order. Whole families staffed a complex array of offices engaged in mysterious rituals involving passwords, flags, songs, and costumes. In many farming communities, the headquarters of the local chapter, known as the Grange (a word for "farm"), became the center of social activity, the site of summer dinners and winter dances.

The Grange movement spread rapidly, especially in areas where farmers were experiencing their greatest hardships. Great Plains farmers barely survived the blizzards, grasshopper infestations, and droughts of the early 1870s. Meanwhile, farmers throughout the trans-Mississippi West and the South watched the prices for grains and cotton fall year by year in the face of growing competition from producers in Canada, Australia, Argentina, Russia, and India. In the hope of improving their condition through collective action, many farmers joined their local Grange. The Patrons of Husbandry soon swelled to more than 1.5 million members.

Grangers blamed hard times on a band of "thieves in the night"—especially railroads and banks—that

The symbols chosen by Grange artists represented their faith that all social value could be traced to honest labor and most of all to the work of the entire farm family. The hardworking American required only the enlightenment offered by the Grange to build a better community

SOURCE: *Kingfisher Reformer*, May 3, 1894, Library of Congress.

charged exorbitant fees for service. They fumed at American farm equipment manufacturers, such as Cyrus McCormick, who sold farm equipment more cheaply in Europe than in the United States. To purchase equipment and raw materials, farmers borrowed money and accrued debts averaging twice that of Americans not engaged in business.

Grangers mounted their greatest assault on the railroad corporations. By bribing state legislators, railroads enjoyed a highly discriminatory rate policy, commonly charging farmers more to ship their crops short distances than over long hauls. In 1874 several midwestern states responded to pressure and passed a series of so-called Granger laws establishing maximum shipping rates. Grangers also complained to their lawmakers about the price-fixing policies of grain wholesalers, warehousers, and operators of grain elevators. In 1873 the Illinois legislature passed a Warehouse Act establishing maximum rates for storing grains. Chicago firms challenged the legality of this measure, but in *Munn* v. *Illinois* (1877) the Supreme Court upheld the law, ruling that states had the power to regulate private property in the public interest.

Determined to buy less and produce more, Grangers created a vast array of cooperative enterprises for both the purchase of supplies and the marketing of crops. They established local grain elevators, set up retail stores, and even manufactured some of their own farm machinery. As early as 1872, the Iowa Grange claimed to control one-third of the grain elevators and warehouses in the state. In other states Grangers ran banks as well as fraternal life and fire insurance companies.

The deepening depression of the late 1870s wiped out most of these cooperative programs. By 1880 Grange membership had fallen to 100,000. Meanwhile, the Supreme Court overturned most of the key legislation regulating railroads. Despite these setbacks, the Patrons of Husbandry had nonetheless promoted a model of cooperation that would remain at the heart of agrarian protest movements until the end of the century.

The Farmers' Alliance

Agrarian unrest did not end with the downward turn of the Grange but instead moved south. In the 1880s farmers organized in communities where both poverty and the crop-lien system prevailed (see Chapter 17). New South newspaper writers and politicians advised farmers to trim expenditures and to diversify out of cotton into other crops. But with household budgets falling from $50 to as low as $10 a year, southern farmers had no leeway to cut expenses. And the cost of shipping perishable crops made diversification untenable despite the low price of cotton. In response to these conditions, Texas farmers—proclaiming "Equal Rights to All, Special Privileges to None"—began to organize.

In 1889, several regional organizations joined forces to create the National Farmers' Alliance and Industrial Union. Within a year the combined movement claimed 3 million white members. Separately, the Colored Farmers' Alliance and Cooperative Union grew from its beginnings in Texas and Arkansas in 1888 and quickly spread across the South to claim more than a million members of its own. These parallel organizations reflected both increasing racial segregation and the racism of white farmers.

In the South, the falling price of cotton underscored the need for action, and farmers readily translated their anger into intense loyalty to the one organization pledged to improve their lot. With more than 500 chapters in Texas alone, and cooperative stores complemented by the cooperative merchandising of crops, the Southern Farmers' Alliance became a viable alternative to the capitalist marketplace—if only temporarily.

The Northern Farmers' Alliance took shape in the Great Plains states, drawing upon larger organizations in Minnesota, Nebraska, Iowa, Kansas, and the Dakota Territory. During 1886 and 1887, summer drought followed winter blizzards and ice storms, reducing wheat harvests by one-third on the Plains. Locusts and cinch bugs ate much of the rest. As if this were not enough, prices on the world market fell sharply for what little remained. Many farmers left the land; western Kansas lost nearly half its population by the early 1890s. Skilled agitators played upon these hardships—especially the overpowering influence of railroads over the farmers' lives—boosting the alliance movement. By 1890 the Kansas Alliance alone claimed 130,000 members.

Grangers had pushed legislation that would limit the salaries of public officials, provide public school students with books at little or no cost, establish a program of teacher certification, and widen the admissions policies of the new state colleges. But only rarely did they put up candidates for office. In comparison, the Farmers' Alliance had few reservations about taking political stands or entering electoral races. At the end of the 1880s, regional alliances drafted campaign platforms demanding state ownership of the railroads, a graduated income tax, lower tariffs, restriction of land ownership to citizens, and easier access to money through "the free and unlimited coinage of silver." In several states, alliance candidates for local and state office won elections. By 1890 the alliances had gained control of the Nebraska legislature and held the balance of power in Minnesota and South Dakota.

Workers Search for Power

The depression following the Panic of 1873, which produced 25 percent unemployment in many cities, served as a catalyst for workers to organize their communities. In New York City, a group marched to City Hall to present a petition on behalf of 10,000 workers who were without jobs or homes. Turned back repeatedly by the police, the organizers decided to stage a rally to advertise their demand for a steady job at a living wage. City officials refused to grant a permit. When 7,000 working-class men and women showed up on January 13, 1874, a battalion of 1,600 police—nearly two-thirds of the city's force—rushed into the crowd and began striking out indiscriminately with their clubs. This incident, known as the Tompkins Square Riot, inaugurated an era of unprecedented labor conflict and violence.

The railroad, which played a key role in the industrial and urban transformations following the Civil War, became the focus of protests by workers and farmers alike. Within the few months after the Panic of 1873, workers struck so many times that the *New York Railroad Gazette* complained, "Strikes are . . . as much a disease of the body politic as the measles or indigestion are of our physical organization." Although most of these strikes ended in failure, they revealed the readiness of workers to spell out their grievances in a direct and dramatic manner. They also suggested how strongly many townspeople, including merchants who depended on workers' wages, would support local strikes and turn them into community uprisings.

Despite these warnings, the railroad corporations were unprepared for the Great Uprising of 1877, the first nationwide strike. The strike began in Martinsburg, West Virginia, where workers protesting a 10 percent wage cut uncoupled all engines. No trains would run, they promised, until wages were restored. Within a few days, the strike had spread along the railroad routes to New York, Buffalo, Pittsburgh, Chicago, Kansas

City, and San Francisco. In all these cities, workers in various industries and masses of the unemployed formed angry crowds, defying armed militia ordered to disperse them by any means. Young men and boys gathered at railroad crossings to throw stones at the trains that ran right through the heart of their neighborhoods. Angry at these ironhorse intruders, the crowds halted train traffic, sometimes pulling up entire rails and seizing carloads of food for hungry families. Energized by the activity, workers in St. Louis even took over the city's administration.

The rioting persisted for nearly a week, spurring business leaders to call for the deportation, arrest, or execution of strike leaders. Law and Order Leagues swept through working-class neighborhoods and broke up union meetings. Fearing a "national insurrection," President Hayes set a precedent by calling in the U.S. Army to suppress the strike. In Pittsburgh, federal troops equipped with semiautomatic machine guns fired into a crowd and killed more than twenty people. By the time the strike finally ended, more than 100 people were dead.

Memories of the Uprising of 1877 haunted business and government officials for decades, prompting the creation of the National Guard and the construction of armories in working-class neighborhoods. Workers also drew lessons from the events. Before the end of the century, more than 6 million workers would strike in industries ranging from New England textiles to southern tobacco factories to western mines. The labor movement also expanded its sphere of influence to the halls of city government. While the Farmers' Alliance put up candidates in the South and Plains states, workers

The Great Uprising of 1877, which began as a strike of railroad workers, spread rapidly to communities along the railroad routes. Angry crowds defied the armed militia and the vigilantes hired to disperse them. In Philadelphia, for example, strikers set fire to the downtown, destroying many buildings before federal troops were brought in to stop them. More than a hundred people died before the strike ended, and the railroad corporations suffered about $10 million loss in property.

SOURCE: Contemporary engraving. The Granger Collection, New York (0008654).

launched labor parties in dozens of industrial towns and cities.

In New York City, popular economist and land reformer Henry George, with the ardent support of the city's Central Labor Council and the Knights of Labor, put himself forward in 1886 as candidate for mayor on the United Labor Party ticket. His best-selling book *Progress and Poverty* (1879), advocated a sweeping tax on all property to generate enough revenue to allow all Americans to live in comfort. Especially popular among Irish Americans, who had seen their homeland swallowed up by British landlords, George's ideas also appealed to German Americans, who, with the Irish, made up the heart of the city's labor movement. George called upon "all honest citizens" to join in independent political action as "the only hope of exposing and breaking up the extortion and speculation by which a standing army of professional politicians corrupt the people whom they plunder."

Tammany Hall delivered many thousands of the ballots cast for George straight into the Hudson River. Nevertheless, George managed to finish a respectable second with 31 percent of the vote, running ahead of young patrician Theodore Roosevelt. Although his campaign ended in defeat, George had issued a stern warning to the entrenched politicians. Equally important, his impressive showing encouraged labor groups in other cities to form parties calling for the defeat of the "power of aggregated wealth." The results, in local elections around the country, stunned Republicans and Democrats alike.

In the late 1880s labor parties won seats on many city councils and state legislatures. The Milwaukee People's Party elected the mayor, a state senator, six assemblymen, and one member of Congress. In smaller industrial towns where workers outnumbered the middle classes, labor parties did especially well. In Rochester, New Hampshire, with a population of only 7,000, workers, mainly shoemakers, elected a majority slate, from city council to mayor.

Women Build Alliances

Women helped build both the labor and agrarian protest movements while campaigning for their own rights as citizens. Like woman suffrage leader Elizabeth Cady Stanton, many women believed that "government based on caste and class privilege cannot stand." In its place, as Bellamy predicted in *Equality*, would arise a new cooperative order in which women would be "absolutely free agents in the disposition of themselves."

Women in the Knights of Labor endorsed the order's political planks while putting forth their own set of demands. In 1886 sixteen women attending the national convention lobbied for the creation of a special department "to investigate the abuses of which our sex is subjected by unscrupulous employers, to agitate the principles which our Order teaches of equal pay for equal work and the abolition of child labor." The delegates accepted the plan with little dissent and appointed knit-goods worker Leonora M. Barry general investigator. With perhaps 65,000 women members at its peak, the Knights ran day-care centers for the children of wage-earning mothers and occasionally even set up bakery cooperatives to reduce the drudgery of cooking.

Women made a similar mark on farmers' organizations. The Patrons of Husbandry issued a charter to a local chapter only when women were well represented on its rolls, and in the 1870s delegates to its conventions routinely gave speeches endorsing woman suffrage and even dress reform. The Farmers' Alliance continued this policy, enjoining women to assist their fathers, husbands, or sons in agitation efforts. Whole families shared in social programs, such as songfests on Sunday afternoons, lecture series, and contests featuring antimonopoly games. In both the Northern and Southern Alliances, women made up perhaps one-quarter of the membership, and several advanced through the ranks to become leading speakers and organizers. Mary E. Lease, who achieved lasting fame for advising farmers to raise less corn and more hell, vividly expressed their sense of purpose. "Ours is a grand, a holy mission," she proclaimed, "to drive from our land and forever abolish the triune monopoly of land, money, and transportation."

Women in both the Knights of Labor and the Farmers' Alliance found their greatest leader in Frances E. Willard, the most famous woman of the nineteenth century. Willard assumed that women, who guarded their families' physical and spiritual welfare, would, if granted the right to vote, extend their influence throughout the

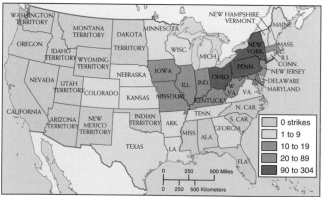

Strikes by State, 1880   Most strikes after the Uprising of 1877 could be traced to organized trades, concentrated in the manufacturing districts of the Northeast and Midwest.

SOURCE: Carville Earle, *Geographical Inquiry and American Historical Problems* (Stanford, CA: Stanford University Press, 1992).

Susan B. Anthony and Elizabeth Cady Stanton, on the platform, founded the National Woman Suffrage Association in 1869. They found many supporters for their cause among the Knights of Labor, the Farmers' Alliance, and the Woman's Christian Temperance Union.

SOURCE: Contemporary colored engraving. The Granger Collection, New York (4E26.32).

whole society. From 1878 until her death in 1897, Willard presided over the Woman's Christian Temperance Union (WCTU), at the time the largest organization of women in the world, and encouraged her numerous followers to "do everything." She mobilized nearly 1 million women to, in her words, "make the whole world HOMELIKE." WCTU members preached total abstinence from the consumption of alcohol, but they also worked to reform the prison system, eradicate prostitution, and eliminate the wage system. Willard went so far as to draw up plans for a new system of government whereby all offices, right up to the presidency, would be shared jointly by men and women. She also became a member of the Knights of Labor and endorsed the platform of the Farmers' Alliance.

Under Willard's leadership, the WCTU grew into the major force behind the campaign for woman suffrage, far surpassing the American Woman Suffrage Association and the National Woman Suffrage Association. By 1890, when the two rival suffrage associations merged to form the National American Woman Suffrage Association, the WCTU had already pushed the heart of the suffrage campaign into the Great Plains states and the West. In Iowa, Nebraska, Colorado, and especially Kansas, agitation for the right to vote provided a political bridge among women organized in the WCTU, Farmers' Alliance, Knights of Labor, and various local suffrage societies.

In 1891 representatives from various women's organizations formed the National Women's Alliance. The founding convention called for "full equality of the sexes," "harmony and unity of action among the Sisterhood" of the nation, "prevention of war," and the rejection of alcohol, tobacco, and narcotics as injurious to health. The organization's newspaper, the *Farmer's Wife*, spelled out basic principles in epigrams like "Give our women encouragement and victory is yours" and "Put 1,000 women lecturers in the field and the revolution is here."

Although women lecturers such as Kansas's Annie Diggs were outstanding crowd pleasers, women in the Knights of Labor and the Farmers' Alliance failed to gain equality within the protest movements. Most political parties endorsed by these organizations included planks calling for equal wages for equal work but refused to endorse woman suffrage. Only in Colorado did local third-party candidates support the 1893 campaign that secured women's right to vote in that state. In the Southern Alliance, women themselves opposed women's enfranchisement. It was, however, an increasing emphasis on electoral politics that effectively placed voteless women on the sidelines.

Farmer-Labor Unity

In December 1890 the Farmers' Alliance called a meeting at Ocala, Florida, to press for a national third-party movement. This was a risky proposition because the Southern Alliance hoped to capture control of the Democratic Party, whereas many farmers in the Plains states voted Republican. In some areas, however, the Farmers' Alliance established its own parties, put up full slates of candidates for local elections, won majorities in state legislatures, and even sent a representative to Congress. Reviewing these successes, delegates at Ocala decided to push ahead and form a national party, and they appealed to other farm, labor, and reform organizations to join them. Edward Bellamy advised his followers to take advantage of "the largest opportunity yet presented in the history of our movement" and support the third-party effort.

The time had come, the Alliance announced, "to establish the moral solidarity of the farmer and toiler societies." In February 1892, representatives from the Farmers' Alliance, the Knights of Labor, and the National Colored Farmers' Alliance, among others, met in St. Louis under a broad banner that read: "We do not ask for sympathy or pity. We ask for justice." The 1,300 delegates adopted a platform for the new People's Party. It called for government ownership of railroads, banks, and telegraph lines, prohibition of large land-holding companies, a graduated income tax, an eight-hour workday, and restriction of immigration. The People's Party convened again in Omaha in July 1892 and nominated James Baird Weaver of Iowa for president and, to please the South, the Confederate veteran James Field from Virginia for vice president.

The Populists, as supporters of the People's Party styled themselves, quickly became a major factor in American politics. In some southern states, Populists cooperated with local Republicans in sponsoring "pepper and salt" state and local tickets that put black and white candidates on a single slate. To hold their voters, some Democrats adopted the Populist platform wholesale; others resorted to massive voter fraud and intimidation. In the West, Democrats threw their weight behind the Populist ticket mainly to defeat the ruling Republicans.

Although Democrat Grover Cleveland regained the presidency in 1892 (he had previously served from 1885 to 1889), Populists scored a string of local victories. In Idaho, Nevada, Colorado, Kansas, and North Dakota, they won 50 percent or more of the vote. Nationwide, they elected three governors, ten representatives to Congress, and five senators. The national ticket received more than 1 million votes (8.5 percent of the total) and 22 electoral college votes—the only time since the Civil War that a third party had received any electoral votes. Despite poor showings among urban workers east of the Mississippi, Populists looked forward to the next round of state elections in 1894. But the great test would come with the presidential election in 1896.

THE CRISIS OF THE 1890s

Populist Ignatius Donnelly wrote in the preface to his pessimistic novel *Caesar's Column* (1891) that industrial society appears to be a "wretched failure" to "the great mass of mankind." On the road to disaster rather than to the egalitarian community that Bellamy had envisioned, "the rich, as a rule, hate the poor; and the poor are coming to hate the rich . . . society divides itself into two hostile camps. . . . They wait only for the drum beat and the trumpet to summon them to armed conflict."

A series of events in the 1890s shook the confidence of many citizens in the reigning political system. But nothing was more unsettling than the severe economic depression that consumed the nation and lasted for five years. Many feared—while others hoped—that the entire political system would topple.

Financial Collapse and Depression

Railroads were at the center of the economic growth of the late nineteenth century. By the early 1890s they represented capital totaling $2.5 billion. As a result,

when the nation's major rail lines went bankrupt in 1893, the business boom of nearly two decades ended and the entire economy ground to a halt. The depression that followed made the hard times of the 1870s appear a mere rehearsal for worse misery to come.

Although the economic downturn began in agriculture and mining, the crisis came when the railroads registered the impact of the loss of income from these principal shippers. In March 1883, the collapse of the Philadelphia and Reading Railroad, followed by the downfall of the National Cordage Company, precipitated a crash in the stock market and sent waves of panic splashing over banks across the country. In a few months, more than 150 banks went into receivership and hundreds more closed; nearly 200 railroads and more than 15,000 businesses also slipped into bankruptcy. In the steel industry alone thirty companies collapsed within six months of the panic. Agricultural prices meanwhile continued to plummet until they reached new lows. The economy slowly began to pick up again in 1897, but new century arrived before prosperity returned.

In many cities, unemployment rates reached 25 percent; Samuel Gompers, head of the American Federation of Labor (AFL), estimated nationwide unemployment at 3 million. "I have seen more misery in this last week than I ever saw in my life before," wrote a young reporter from Chicago. Few people starved, but millions suffered. Inadequate diets prompted a rise in communicable diseases, such as tuberculosis and pellagra. Unable to buy food, clothes, or household items, families learned to survive with the barest minimum.

Tens of thousands "rode the rails" or went "on the tramp" to look for work, hoping that their luck might change in a new city or town. Some panhandled for the nickel that could buy a mug of beer and a free lunch at a saloon. By night they slept in parks or, in the colder months, flocked to the "bum tanks" of the city jail or to fleabag hotels. Vagrancy laws (enacted during the 1870s) forced many into prison. In New York City alone, with more than 20,000 homeless people, thousands ended up in jail. Newspapers warned against this "menace" and blamed the growing crime rates on the "dangerous classes."

Another Populist, Jacob Sechler Coxey, decided to gather the masses of unemployed into a huge army and then to march to Washington, D.C., to demand from Congress a public works program. On Easter Sunday, 1894, Coxey left Massillon, Ohio, with several hundred followers. Meanwhile, brigades from Boston, Los Angeles, San Francisco, Tacoma, Denver, Salt Lake City, Reno, Butte, and Omaha joined his "petition in boots." Communities across the country welcomed the marchers, but U.S. attorney general Richard C. Olney, a former lawyer for the railroad companies, conspired with state and local officials to halt them. Only 600 men and women reached the nation's capital,

Jacob Coxey's "Commonwealth of Christ Army," April 1894. Attracting the sympathetic attention of working people and the hostility of most of the wealthier classes, "Industrial Armies" marched through U.S. cities en route to the nation's capital.

SOURCE: Library of Congress.

where the police first clubbed and then arrested the leaders for trespassing on the grass. "Coxey's Army" quickly disbanded, but not before voicing the public's growing impatience with government apathy toward the unemployed.

Strikes and Labor Solidarity

Meanwhile, in several locations the conflict between labor and capital had escalated to the brink of civil war. Wage cuts in the silver and lead mines of northern Idaho led to one of the bitterest conflicts of the decade. To put a brake on organized labor, mineowners had formed a "protective association," and in March 1892 they announced a lower wage scale throughout the Coeur d'Alene district. After the miners' union refused to accept the cut, the owners locked out all union members and brought in strikebreakers by the train-load. Unionists tried peaceful methods of protest. But after three months of stalemate, they loaded a railcar with explosives and blew up a mine. Strikebreakers fled while mineowners appealed to the Idaho governor for assistance. A force of 1,500 state and federal troops occupied the district, and more than 300 union members were herded into bullpens, where they were kept under unsanitary conditions for several weeks before their

trial. Ore production meanwhile resumed with "scab" labor, and by November, when the troops were withdrawn, the mineowners declared a victory. But the miners' union survived, and most members eventually regained their jobs. "We have made a fight that we are proud of and propose to continue it to the end," one striker declared. The following spring, Coeur d'Alene miners sent delegates to Butte, Montana, where they helped form the Western Federation of Miners, which soon became one of the strongest labor organizations in the nation.

Coeur d'Alene strikers had been buoyed by the news that steelworkers at Homestead, Pennsylvania, had likewise taken guns in hand to defend their union. Members of the Amalgamated Iron, Steel and Tin Workers, the most powerful union of the AFL, had carved out an admirable position for themselves in the Carnegie Steel Company. Well paid, proud of their skills, the unionists customarily directed their unskilled helpers without undue influence of company supervisors. But, determined to gain control over every stage of production, Carnegie and his chairman, Henry C. Frick, decided not only to lower wages but to break the union.

In 1892, when the Amalgamated's contract expired, Frick announced a drastic wage cut. He also ordered a wooden stockade built around the factory, with grooves for rifles and barbed wire on top. When Homestead's city government refused to assign police to disperse the strikers, Frick dispatched a barge carrying a private army armed to the teeth. Gunfire broke out and continued throughout the day. After the governor sent the Pennsylvania National Guard to restore order, Carnegie's factory reopened, with strikebreakers doing the work.

After four months, the union was forced to concede a crushing defeat, not only for itself but, in effect, for all steelworkers. The Carnegie company reduced its workforce by 25 percent, lengthened the workday, and cut wages 25 percent for those who remained on the job. If the Amalgamated Iron, Steel and Tin Workers, known throughout the industry as the "aristocrats of labor," could be brought down, less-skilled workers could expect little from the corporate giants. Within a decade, every major steel company operated without union interference.

But the spirit of labor solidarity did not die. Just two years after the strikes at Coeur d'Alene and Homestead, the greatest railway strike since 1877 again dramatized the importance of the railroad as well as the extent of collusion between the government and corporations to crush the labor movement.

Unlike Packingtown, Pullman, Illinois, just south of Chicago, had been constructed as a model industrial community. Its creator and proprietor, George M. Pullman, had manufactured luxurious "sleeping cars" for railroads since 1881. He built his company as a self-contained community, with the factory at the center, surrounded by modern cottages, a library, churches, parks, an independent water supply, even its own cemetery, but no saloons. The Pullman Palace Car Company deducted rent, library fees, and grocery bills from each worker's weekly wages. In good times workers enjoyed a decent livelihood, although many resented Pullman's autocratic control of their daily affairs.

When times grew hard, the company cut wages by as much as one-half, in some cases down to less than $1 a day. Charges for food and rent remained unchanged. Furthermore, factory supervisors sought to make up for declining profits by driving workers to produce more. In May 1894, after Pullman fired members of a committee that had drawn up a list of grievances, workers voted to strike.

Pullman workers found their champion in Eugene V. Debs, who had recently formed the American Railway Union (ARU) in order to bring railroad workers across the vast continent into one organization. Debs, the architect of the ARU's victory over the Great Northern rail line just one month earlier, advised caution, but delegates to an ARU convention voted to support a nationwide boycott of all Pullman cars. This action soon turned into a sympathy strike by railroad workers across the country. Support for the strike was especially strong in the western states.

Compared to the Uprising of 1877, the orderly Pullman strike at first produced little violence. ARU officials urged strikers to ignore all police provocations and hold their ground peacefully. But Attorney General Richard C. Olney, claiming that the ARU was disrupting mail shipments (actually Debs had banned such interference), issued a blanket injunction against the strike. On July 4, President Cleveland sent federal troops to Chicago, over Illinois governor John Peter Altgeld's objections. After a bitter confrontation that left thirteen people dead and more than fifty wounded, the army dispersed the strikers. For the next week, railroad workers in twenty-six other states resisted federal troops, and a dozen more people were killed. On July 17, the strike finally ended when federal marshals arrested Debs and other leaders.

"The Debs of fable," wrote the editor of a Unitarian weekly, "lighted a fire in the car yards of Chicago. The Debs of fact lighted an idea in the dangerous shadows of the Republic." Assailing the arrogance of class privilege that encouraged the government to use brute force against its citizens, Debs concluded that the labor movement could not regain its dignity under the present system. An avid fan of Bellamy's *Looking Backward*, he came out of jail committed to the ideals of socialism and in 1898 helped to form a political party dedicated to its principles.

Across the industrial belt and in the West and Southwest, in railroad towns, factory villages, and farms, tens of thousands of people supported Debs. Declining nomination on the Populist ticket in 1896, he ran for president as a socialist in 1900 and in four subsequent elections. The odds against him grew with the scale of the

In 1894, to protest a cut in wages, the workers of the Pullman Palace Car Company struck. Eugene V. Debs, president of the American Railway Union, ordered a nationwide boycott against the Pullman Company. The United States Cavalry was brought in to escort the trains run by "scab" laborers.

SOURCE: Library of Congress (49255/3526).

booming economy, but Debs made his point on moral grounds. His friend James Whitcomb Riley, the nation's most admired sentimental poet, wrote in rural dialect that Debs had "the kindest heart that ever beat/betwixt here and the jedgment [judgment] seat."

The Social Gospel

Like Edward Bellamy, a growing number of Protestant and Catholic clergy and lay theologians noted a discrepancy between the ideals of Christianity and prevailing attitudes toward the poor. Like Bellamy, they could no longer sanction an economic system that allowed so many to toil long hours under unhealthy conditions and for subsistence wages. They demanded that the church lead the way to a new cooperative order. In 1889 Episcopalian clergyman W. D. P. Bliss, a charter member of Boston's Bellamy Nationalist club, began to publish a monthly magazine, *The Dawn*, whose motto was "He works for God who works for man."

Coinciding with an upswing in religious revivals in the nation's cities, some liberal congregations broke away from established churches to side with the working class and the immigrant poor. Ministers called for civil service reform and the end of child labor. Supporting labor's right to organize and, if necessary, to strike, they petitioned government officials to regulate corporations and place a limit on profits. Washington Gladden, a Congregationalist minister, warned that if churches continued to ignore pressing social problems they would devolve into institutions whose sole purpose was to preserve obscure rituals and superstitions. In the wake of the Great Uprising of 1877, he had called upon his congregation in Columbus, Ohio, to take an active part in the fight against social injustice. Gladden's *Applied Christianity* (1886) appealed to the nation's business leaders to return to Christ's teachings.

Less famous but more numerous, local Protestant ministers and community leaders likewise sought to restore what they considered the true spirit of Christianity. As labor reformer George McNeill wrote in 1890, some ministers might be the servants of wealth, but in the long run "the influence of the teachings of the Carpenter's Son" will "counteract the influence of Mammon," the biblical embodiment of greed. McNeill looked forward to the day when "every man shall have according to his needs." Although the social gospel spread most rapidly through the northern industrial cities, southern African Americans espoused their own version. They reinterpreted the Gospel as Jesus' promise to emancipate their race from satanic white power brokers. The biblical republic of "Beulahland" became their model of redemption.

The depression of the 1890s produced an outpouring of social gospel treatises. The very popular *If Christ Came to Chicago* (1894), by British journalist W. T. Stead, forced readers to confront the "ugly sight" of a city with 200 millionaires and 200,000 unemployed men. It inspired Edward Everett Hale's *If Jesus Came to Boston* (1894), which similarly questioned social inequalities. The most famous tract, *In His Steps* (1896), by Methodist minister Charles M. Sheldon of Topeka, Kansas, urged readers to rethink their actions in the light of the simple question "What would Jesus do?" By 1933 Sheldon's book had sold more than 23 million copies.

Catholics, doctrinally more inclined than Protestants to accept poverty as a natural condition, joined the social gospel movement in smaller numbers. In the early 1880s Polish Americans broke away from the Roman Catholic Church to form the Polish National Church, which was committed to the concerns of working people. Irish Americans, especially prominent in the Knights of Labor, encouraged priests to ally themselves with the labor movement. Pope Leo XIII's encyclical *Rerum Novarum* (1891) endorsed the right of workers to form trade unions.

Women guided the social gospel movement in their communities. In nearly every city, groups of women affiliated with various evangelical Protestant sects raised money to establish small, inexpensive residential hotels for working women, whose low wages rarely covered the price of safe, comfortable shelter. Many of these groups joined to form the Young Women's Christian Association (YWCA), which by 1900 had more than 600 local chapters. The "Y" sponsored a range of services for needy Christian women, ranging from homes for the elderly and for unmarried mothers to elaborate programs of vocational instruction and physical fitness. The Girls Friendly Societies, an organization of young women affiliated with Episcopal churches, sponsored similar programs. Meanwhile Catholic lay women and nuns served the poor women of their faith, operating numerous schools, hospitals, and orphanages.

Although centered in the cities, the social gospel rallied many small-town and rural women, especially ardent admirers of Frances Willard. "The time will come," Willard insisted, "when the human heart will be so much alive that no one could sleep in any given community, if any of that group of human beings were cold, hungry, or miserable."

POLITICS OF REFORM, POLITICS OF ORDER

The severe hardships of the 1890s, following a quarter of a century of popular unrest and economic uncertainty, led to a crisis in the two-party system, making the presidential election of 1896 a turning point in

American politics. Republicans and Democrats continued to enjoy long-standing voter loyalties among specific groups or regions. Particularly in the South, the Democrats could generally depend on the masses of white voters to unite against any movement threatening to compromise the "color line." But Populists were tenacious contenders.

The election of 1896, however, indicated not merely the regrouping of American voters. It also revealed the power of the conservative ascendancy. By the 1890s, the reform movements were losing ground while nativist and racist sentiments were consolidating, even within the reform movements themselves.

The Free Silver Issue

Grover Cleveland owed his victory in 1892 over Republican incumbent Benjamin Harrison to the predictable votes of the Democratic "solid South" and to the unanticipated support of such northern states as Illinois and Wisconsin, whose German-born voters turned against the increasingly nativist Republicans. But when the economy collapsed the following year, Cleveland and the Democrats who controlled Congress faced a public eager for action. Convinced that the economic crisis was "largely the result of financial policy . . . embodied in unwise laws," the president called a special session of Congress to reform the nation's currency.

For generations, reformers had advocated "soft" currency—that is, an increase in the money supply that would loosen credit. During the Civil War the federal government took decisive action, replacing state bank notes with a national paper currency popularly called "greenbacks" (from the color of the bills). Then, in 1873 the Coinage Act tightened the money supply by eliminating silver from circulation, prompting farmers who depended on credit to call it "the Crime of '73." This measure actually had little real impact on the economy but opened the door to yet more tinkering and, especially during hard times, the currency question simmered. For the most part, the business community consistently advocated the gold-standard. A compromise was reached with the passage of the Sherman Silver Purchase Act of 1890. The act directed the Treasury to increase the amount of currency coined from silver mined in the West and also permitted the U.S. government to print paper currency backed by the silver. In turn, Westerners who stood to benefit most from this reform, agreed to support the McKinley Tariff of 1890 that, in establishing the highest import duties yet on foreign goods, pleased the business community.

Following the crash of 1893, as the economy fell into ruins, a desperate President Cleveland demanded the repeal of the Sherman Act, insisting that only the gold standard could pull the nation out of depression. By exerting intense pressure on congressional Democrats, Cleveland succeeded in October 1893, but not without ruining his chances for renomination. The midterm elections in 1894 brought the largest shift in congressional power in American history: the Republicans gained 117 seats, while the Democrats lost 113. The "Silver Democrats" of Cleveland's own party vowed revenge and began to look to the Populists, mainly Westerners and farmers who favored "free silver"—that is, the unlimited coinage of silver. Republicans confidently began to prepare for the presidential election of 1896, known as the "battle of the standards."

Populism's Last Campaigns

Populists had been buoyed by the 1894 election, which delivered to their candidates nearly 1.5 million votes, a gain of 42 percent over their 1892 totals. They made impressive inroads into several southern states. West of the Mississippi, political excitement steadily increased. David Waite, the Populist governor of Colorado, talked of a coming revolution and declared, "It is better, infinitely better, that blood should flow [up] to the horses' bridles rather than our national liberties should be destroyed." Still, even in the Midwest where Populists doubled their vote, they managed to win less than 7 percent of the total.

As Populists prepared for the 1896 election, they found themselves at a crossroad: What were they to do with the growing popularity of Democrat William Jennings Bryan? Son of an Illinois judge who had run unsuccessfully for Congress, Bryan had relocated to Nebraska, where he practiced law. A spellbinding orator, he won a congressional seat in 1890. After seizing the Populist slogan "Equal Rights to All, Special Privilege to None," Bryan became a major contender for president of the United States.

Noting the surging interest in free silver, Bryan became its champion. "I don't know anything about free silver," he once admitted, but "the people of Nebraska are for free silver and I am for free silver. I will look up the arguments later." For two years before the 1896 election, Bryan wooed potential voters in a speaking tour that took him to every state in the nation. Pouring new life into his divided party, Bryan pushed Silver Democrats to the forefront.

At the 1896 party convention, the thirty-six-year-old orator thrilled delegates with his evocation of agrarian ideals. "Burn down your cities and leave our farms," Bryan preached, "and your cities will spring up again as if by magic; but destroy our farms and the grass will grow in the streets of every city in the country." What became one of the most famous speeches in American political history closed on a yet more dramatic note. Spreading his arms to suggest the crucified Christ figure,

Bryan pledged to answer all demands for a gold standard by saying, "You shall not press down upon the brow of labor this crown of thorns, you shall not crucify mankind upon a cross of gold." The next day, Bryan won the Democratic presidential nomination.

The Populists knew that the Democrats, in nominating Bryan, had stolen their thunder. Although many feared that the growing emphasis on currency would overshadow their more important planks calling for government ownership of the nation's railroads and communications systems, few Populists had expected either major party to come out for free silver. As the date of their own convention approached, delegates divided over strategy: they could endorse Bryan and give up their independent status; or they could run an independent campaign and risk splitting the silver vote. Neither

choice was good. "If we fuse," one Populist explained, "we are sunk; if we don't fuse, all the silver men we have will leave us for the more powerful Democrats."

In the end, the Populists nominated Bryan for president and chose one of their own ranks, the popular Georgian Tom Watson, for the vice presidential candidate. Most of the state Democratic Party organizations, however, refused to put the "fusion" ticket on the ballot, and Bryan and his Democratic running mate Arthur Sewall simply ignored the Populist campaign.

The Republican Triumph

After Cleveland's blunders, Republicans anticipated an easy victory in 1896, but Bryan's nomination, as party stalwart Mark Hanna warned, "changed everything." Luckily, they had their own handsome, knowledgeable, courteous, and ruthless candidate, Civil War veteran William McKinley.

The Republican campaign in terms of sheer expense and skill of coordination outdid all previous campaigns and established a precedent for future presidential elections. Hanna guided a strategy that raised up to $7 million and outspent Bryan more than ten to one. Using innumerable pamphlets, placards, hats, and parades, Republicans advertised their promise to "rebuild out of the ruins of the last four years the stately mansions of national happiness, prosperity and self-respect." McKinley even invited voters to his home, managing to attract as many as 750,000 people to his famous "Front Porch." In the campaign's final two weeks, organizers dispatched 1,400 speakers to spread the word. Fearful that the silver issue could divide their own ranks, Republicans stepped around it while emphasizing the tariff. Delivering a hard-hitting negative campaign, they consistently cast adversary Bryan as a dangerous naysayer willing to risk the nation's well-being and cost voters their jobs or worse.

McKinley triumphed in the most important presidential election since Reconstruction. Bryan managed to win 46 percent of the popular vote but failed to carry the Midwest, West Coast, or Upper South. Moreover, the free silver campaign rebuffed traditionally Democratic urban voters who feared that soft money would bring higher prices. Many Catholics uncomfortable with Bryan's Protestant moral piety also deserted the Democrats. Finally, neither the reform-minded middle classes nor impoverished blue-collar workers were convinced that Bryan's grand reform vision really included them. The Populist following, disappointed and disillusioned, dwindled away, and for the next sixteen years, Democrats dominated no region but the South. Voter apathy set in, and participation began to spiral downward from its 1896 peak, when upwards of 80 percent of the electorate turned out.

This Republican campaign poster of 1896 depicts William McKinley standing on sound money and promising a revival of prosperity. The depression of the 1890s shifted the electorate into the Republican column.

SOURCE: The Granger Collection, New York (4E 1033 90)

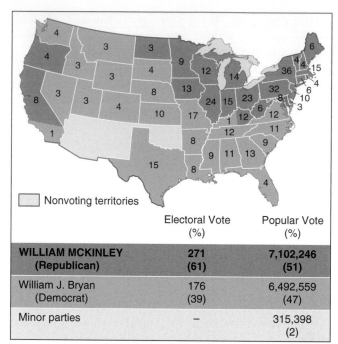

	Electoral Vote (%)	Popular Vote (%)
WILLIAM MCKINLEY (Republican)	**271 (61)**	**7,102,246 (51)**
William J. Bryan (Democrat)	176 (39)	6,492,559 (47)
Minor parties	–	315,398 (2)

Election of 1896 Democratic candidate William Jennings Bryan carried most of rural America but could not overcome Republican William McKinley's stronghold in the populous industrial states.

Once in office, McKinley promoted a mixture of probusiness and expansionist measures. He supported the Dingley Tariff of 1897, which raised import duties to an all-time high. In 1897 McKinley also encouraged Congress to create the United States Industrial Commission, which would plan business regulation; in 1898 he promoted a bankruptcy act that eased the financial situation of small businesses; and he proposed the Erdman Act of the same year, which established a system of arbitration to avoid rail strikes. The Supreme Court ruled in concert with the president, finding eighteen railways in violation of antitrust laws and granting states the right to regulate hours of labor under certain circumstances. In 1900 he oversaw the passage of the Gold Standard Act.

McKinley's triumph ended the popular challenge to the nation's governing system. With prosperity returning by 1898 and nationalism rising swiftly, McKinley encouraged Americans to go for "a full dinner pail," the winning Republican slogan of the 1900 presidential election. With news of his second triumph, stock prices on Wall Street skyrocketed.

Nativism and Jim Crow

Campaign rhetoric aside, McKinley and Bryan differed only slightly on the major problems facing the nation in 1896. Neither Bryan the reformer nor McKinley the

prophet of prosperity addressed the escalation of racism and nativism (antiimmigrant feeling) throughout the nation. After the election, McKinley made white supremacy a major tenet of his foreign policy; Bryan, twice more a presidential contender, championed the white race and deemed "social equality" impossible.

Toward the end of the century, many political observers noted, the nation's patriotic fervor took on a strongly nationalistic and antiforeign tone. Striking workers and their employers alike tended to blame "foreigners" for the hard times. AFL leader Samuel Gompers, himself a Jewish immigrant from Europe, lobbied Congress to restrict immigration from eastern and southern Europe, and even the sons and daughters of earlier immigrants attacked the newcomers as unfit for democracy. Imagining a Catholic conspiracy directed by the pope, semisecret organizations such as the American Protective Association sprang up to defend American institutions. Fourth of July orators continued to celebrate freedom and liberty but more often boasted about the might and power of their nation.

In the South, white racism tightened its grip on the region. Local and state governments codified racist ideology by passing discriminatory and segregationist legislation, which became known as Jim Crow laws. The phrase, dating from the early decades of the nineteenth century, was made popular by a white minstrel in black face who used the name "Jim Crow" to characterize all African Americans. Before the Civil War, abolitionists described segregated railroad cars as "Jim Crow." By the end of the century, "Jim Crow" referred to the customs of segregation that were becoming codified by law and practice throughout the South. With nine of every ten black Americans living in this region, the significance of this development was sweeping.

"The supremacy of the white race of the South," New South promoter Henry W. Grady declared in 1887, "must be maintained forever . . . because the white race is the superior race." To secure their privileges, Grady and other white Southerners acted directly to impose firm standards of segregation and domination and to forestall any appearance of social equality. State after state in the South enacted new legislation to cover facilities such as restaurants, public transportation, and even drinking fountains. Signs "White Only" and "Colored" appeared over theaters, parks, rooming houses, and toilets. In banks, post offices, and stores, blacks were required to wait until all whites had been served, and special rules prohibited such common practices as trying on shoes or hats before purchasing them.

The United States Supreme Court upheld the new discriminatory legislation. Its decisions in the *Civil Rights Cases* (1883) overturned the Civil Rights Act of

1875, and in *Plessy v. Ferguson* (1896) the Court upheld a Louisiana state law formally segregating railroad cars on the basis of the "separate but equal" doctrine. In *Cumming v. Richmond County Board of Education* (1899), the Court allowed separate schools for blacks and whites, even where facilities for African American children did not exist.

The new restrictions struck especially hard at the voting rights of African Americans. Southern states enacted new literacy tests and property qualifications for voting, demanding proof of $300 to $500 in property and the ability to read and write. Loopholes permitted poor whites to vote even under these conditions, except where they threatened the Democratic Party's rule. "Grandfather clauses," invented in Louisiana, exempted from all restrictions those who had been entitled to vote on January 1, 1867, together with their sons and grandsons, a measure that effectively enfranchised whites while barring African Americans. In 1898, the Supreme Court ruled that poll taxes and literacy requirements enacted in order to prevent blacks (and some poor whites) from voting were a proper means of restricting the ballot to "qualified" voters. By this time, only 5 percent of the southern black electorate voted, and African Americans were barred from public office and jury service. Supreme Court Justice John Marshall Harlan, the lone dissenter in *Plessy v. Ferguson*, lamented that the Court's majority rulings gave power to the states "to place in a condition of legal inferiority a large body of American citizens." Depriving African Americans of equal rights and protection under the law, Jim Crow legislation encouraged states outside the South to pass similar measures.

THE SPREAD OF DISFRANCHISEMENT

1889	Florida	Poll tax
	Tennessee	Poll tax
1890	Mississippi	Poll tax, literacy test, understanding clause
1891	Arkansas	Poll tax
1893, 1901	Alabama	Poll tax, literacy test, grandfather clause
1894, 1895	South Carolina	Poll tax, literacy test, understanding clause
1894, 1902	Virginia	Poll tax, literacy test, understanding clause
1897, 1898	Louisana	Poll tax, literacy test, grandfather clause
1899, 1900	North Carolina	Poll tax, literacy test, grandfather clause
1902	Texas	Poll tax
1908	Georgia	Poll tax, literacy test, understanding clause, grandfather clause

Racial violence in turn escalated. Not only race riots but thousands of lynchings took place. Between 1882 and the turn of the century, the number of lynchings usually exceeded 100 each year; 1892 produced a record 230 deaths (161 black, 69 white). Mobs often burned or dismembered victims in order to drag out their agony and entertain the crowd of onlookers. Announced in local newspapers, lynchings became public spectacles for entire white families, and railroads sometimes offered special excursion rates for travel to these events.

Antilynching became the one-woman crusade of Ida B. Wells, young editor of a black newspaper in Memphis. After three local black businessmen were lynched in 1892, Wells vigorously denounced the outrage, blaming the white business competitors of the victims. Her stand fanned the tempers of local whites, who destroyed her press and forced the outspoken editor to leave the city.

Wells set out to investigate lynching in a systematic fashion. She paid special attention to the common defense of lynching—that it was a necessary response to attempts by black men to rape white women. Her 1895 pamphlet *A Red Record* showed that the vast majority of black lynching victims had not even been accused of rape. In fact, Wells showed, lynching was primarily a brutal device to eliminate African Americans who

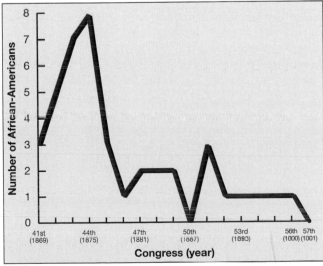

African-American Representation in Congress, 1867–1900   Black men served in the U.S. Congress from 1870 until 1900. All were Republicans.

had become too prosperous or competed with white businesses.

Wells launched an international movement against lynching, lecturing across the country and in Europe, demanding an end to the silence about this barbaric crime. Her work also inspired the growth of a black women's club movement. The National Association of Colored Women, founded in 1896, provided a home for black women activists who had been excluded from white women's clubs. United by a growing sense of racial pride, black women's clubs took up the antilynching cause and also fought to protect black women from exploitation by white men and from charges of sexual depravity.

Tom Watson

Few white reformers rallied to defend African Americans. At its 1899 convention, the National American Woman Suffrage Association appeased new southern white members by voting down a resolution condemning racial segregation in public facilities. A far greater tragedy was a racist turn in the Populist movement, whose leaders even in the South had at times challenged white supremacy. The story of Thomas E. Watson, briefly a champion of interracial unity, illustrates the rise and fall of hopes for an egalitarian South.

Son of a prosperous cotton farmer who had been driven into bankruptcy during the depression of the 1870s, Tom Watson had once campaigned to restore the civil rights of southern African Americans. "Why is not the colored tenant [farmer] open to the conviction that he is in the same boat as the white tenant; the colored laborer with the white laborer?" he asked. Watson planned to overturn Democratic rule by capturing and building up the black vote for the People's Party.

Watson's followers in Georgia were jailed, shot at, denied the protection of the courts, and driven from their churches. Yet tens of thousands regarded him as a savior. Flowers decorated the bridges along his speaking routes, crowds standing in pouring rain begged him to continue speaking, and wagons of loyalists carried Winchester rifles to defend him from armed attack. Preaching government ownership of railroads and banks and political equality for both races, Watson stirred the only truly grass-roots interracial movement the South had yet seen.

By early 1896, however, Watson perceived that the increasing ardor for free silver and the move toward cooperation with Democrats would doom the Populist movement. He nevertheless accepted the nomination for vice president on the "fusion" ticket and campaigned in several states. After McKinley's triumph, Watson withdrew from politics, returning to his Georgia farm to write popular histories of the United States and to plot his future.

Watson returned to public life after the turn of the century but with a totally different approach to race relations. He still bitterly attacked the wealthy classes but now blamed black citizens for conspiring against poor whites. Political salvation now hinged, he concluded, on accommodation to white supremacy. Watson expressed a southern variation of the new national creed that prepared Americans to view the luckless inhabitants of distant lands as ripe for colonization by the United States.

"IMPERIALISM OF RIGHTEOUSNESS"

Many Americans attributed the crisis of 1893–97 not simply to the collapse of the railroads and the stock market but to basic structural problems: an overbuilt economy and an insufficient market for goods. Profits from total sales of manufactured and agricultural products had grown substantially over the level achieved in the 1880s, but output increased even more rapidly. While the number of millionaires shot up from 500 in 1860 to more than 4,000 in 1892, the majority of working people lacked enough income to buy back a significant portion of what they produced. As Republican Senator Albert J. Beveridge of Indiana put it, "We are raising more than we can consume . . . making more than we can use. Therefore, we must find new markets for our produce, new occupation for our capital, new work for our labor."

In 1893 Frederick Jackson Turner reminded Americans that the continent had now been settled. Having passed "from the task of filling up the vacant spaces of the continent," the nation is now "thrown back upon itself," the young historian concluded. Obviously, Americans required a new "frontier" if democracy were to survive.

The White Man's Burden

Turner read his famous essay, "The Significance of the Frontier in American History," at the meeting of the American Historical Association, which was held in Chicago at the time of the World's Fair, less than two months after the nation's economy had collapsed. On May Day 1893, crowds flocked to the fair—"a little ideal world, a realization of Utopia . . . [foreshadowing] some far away time when the earth should be as pure, as beautiful, and as joyous as the White City itself." A complex of more than 400 buildings, newly constructed in beaux arts design, commemorated the four hundredth anniversary of Columbus's landing. Such expositions, President McKinley explained, served as "timekeepers of progress."

The captains of Chicago's industry—Armour, Swift, McCormick, Field, and Pullman—had campaigned hard to bring the fair to Chicago and delighted in its triumphant display of American business ingenuity. Agriculture Hall showcased the production of corn, wheat, and other crops and featured a gigantic globe encircled by samples of American-manufactured farm machinery. The symbolism was evident: all eyes were on worldwide markets for American products. Another building housed a model of a canal cut across Nicaragua, suggesting the ease with which American traders might reach Asian markets if transport ships could travel directly from the Caribbean to the Pacific. One of the most popular exhibits, attracting 20,000 people a day, featured a mock ocean liner built to scale by the International Navigation Company, where fairgoers could imagine themselves as "tourists," sailing in luxury to distant parts of the world.

The World's Fair also "displayed" representatives of the people who populated foreign lands. The Midway Plaisance, a strip nearly a mile long and more than 600 feet wide, was an enormous sideshow of re-created Turkish bazaars and South Sea island huts. There were Javanese carpenters, Dahomean drummers, Egyptian swordsmen, and Hungarian Gypsies as well as Eskimos, Syrians, Samoans, and Chinese. Very popular was the World Congress of Beauty, parading "40 Ladies from 40 Nations" dressed in native costume. Another favorite attraction was "Little Egypt," who performed at the Persian Palace of Eros; her *danse du ventre* became better known as the hootchy-kootchy. According to the guidebook, all these peoples had come "from the nightsome North and the splendid South, from the wasty West and the effete East, bringing their manners, customs, dress, religions, legends, amusements, that we might know them better." One of the exposition's directors, Frederick Ward Putnam, head of Harvard's Peabody Museum of American Archeology and Ethnology, explained more fully that the gathering gave fairgoers "a grand opportunity to see . . . the material advantages which civilization brings to mankind."

By celebrating the brilliance of American industry and simultaneously presenting the rest of the world's people as a source of exotic entertainment, the planners of the fair delivered a powerful message. Former abolitionist Frederick Douglass, who attended the fair on "Colored People's Day," recognized it immediately. He noted that the physical layout of the fair, by carefully grouping exhibits, sharply divided the United States and Europe from the rest of the world, namely from the nations of Africa, Asia, and the Middle East. Douglass objected to the stark contrast setting off Anglo-Saxons from people of color, an opposition between "civiliza-

tion" and "savagery." Douglass and Ida B. Wells jointly wrote a pamphlet that referred to the famed exposition as "a whited sepulcher." Wells advised African Americans to boycott the fair, but Douglass chose to attend. He used the occasion to deliver a speech upbraiding those white Americans who labeled the African American "a moral monster."

The Chicago World's Fair gave material shape to prevalent ideas about the superiority of American civilization and its racial order. At the same time, by showcasing American industries, it made a strong case for commercial expansion abroad. Social gospeler Josiah Strong, a Congregational minister who had begun his career trying to convert Indians to Christianity, provided a timely synthesis. He argued that the United States, as the most economically advanced and most Christian nation in the world, commanded a providential role. Thus linking economic and spiritual expansion, Strong advocated an "imperialism of righteousness." The rest of the world "is to be Christianized and civilized," Strong insisted, by the white Americans, who were best suited to this greatest task of all time. "Pure spiritual Christianity" and a "genius for colonizing" compelled Americans to move beyond their own national interests to consider the needs of the people of Africa and the Pacific and beyond. It was the white American, Strong argued, who had been "divinely commissioned to be, in a peculiar sense, his brother's keeper."

Senator Beveridge faithfully carried this message to Congress, insisting that God "has made us [white, English-speaking people] adept in government that we may administer governments among savages and senile peoples. . . . He has marked the American people as His chosen nation to finally lead in the regeneration of the world." According to many newspaper reporters and editorialists, it would be morally wrong for Americans to shirk what the British poet Rudyard Kipling called the "White Man's Burden."

Foreign Missions

The push for overseas expansion coincided with a major wave of religious evangelism and foreign missions. Early in the nineteenth century, Protestant missionaries, hoping to fulfill what they believed to be a divine command to carry God's message to all peoples and to win converts for their church, had focused on North America. Many disciples, like Josiah Strong himself, headed west and stationed themselves on Indian reservations. Others worked among the immigrant populations of the nation's growing cities. As early as the 1820s, however, a few missionaries had traveled to the Sandwich Islands (Hawai'i) in an effort to supplant the indigenous religion with Christianity. After the Civil War, following the formation of the Women's Union Missionary Society of

American Protestant missionaries opened refuge homes for Chinese women, many brought to the United States as prostitutes or under contracts resembling indentured servitude, and offered shelter, vocational training, and religious instruction. The Chinese women pictured here, all with bound feet, are studying with the matron.

SOURCE: Harvard University.

Americans for Heathen Lands, the major evangelical Protestant denominations all sponsored missions directed at foreign lands.

Funded by wealthy men and the vigorous campaigns of female church members, these societies soon attracted a large membership. By the 1890s, college campuses blazed with missionary excitement, and the intercollegiate Student Volunteers for Foreign Missions spread rapidly under the slogan "The Evangelicization of the World in This Generation." Magazines bristled with essays such as "The Anglo-Saxon and the World's Redemption." Young Protestant women rushed to join foreign missionary societies. In 1863 there had been only 94 Methodist women missionaries in China; by 1902 the number had jumped to 783. In all, some twenty-three American Protestant churches had established missions in China by the turn of the century, the majority staffed by women. By 1915, more than 3 million women had enrolled in forty denominational missionary societies, surpassing in size all other women's organizations in the United States. Their foreign missions ranged from India and Africa to Syria, the Pacific Islands, and nearby Latin America.

With so many agents in the field, missionaries scored numerous successes. They recruited many "natives," including the "rice-Christians" who feigned conversion in order to be fed by the missions. By 1898 Protestants claimed to have made Christians of more than 80,000

Chinese, a tiny portion of the population but a significant stronghold for American interests in their nation. The missionaries did more than spread the gospel. They taught school, provided rudimentary medical care, offered vocational training programs, and sometimes encouraged young men and women to pursue a college education in preparation for careers in their homelands. Such work depended on, and in turn inspired, enthusiastic church members in the United States.

Outside the churches proper, the YMCA and YWCA, which had set up nondenominational missions for the working poor in many American cities, also embarked on a worldwide crusade to reach non-Christians. By the turn of the century, the YWCA had foreign branches in Ceylon (present-day Sri Lanka) and China. After foreign branches multiplied in the next decade, a close observer ironically suggested that the United States had three great occupying forces: the army, the navy, and the "Y." He was not far wrong.

Missionaries played an important role both in generating public interest in foreign lands and in preparing the way for American economic expansion. As Josiah Strong aptly put it, "Commerce follows the missionary."

An Overseas Empire

Not only missionaries but business and political leaders had set their sights on distant lands, which, in turn, meant new markets. In the 1860s, Secretary of State William Henry Seward, under Abraham Lincoln and then under Andrew Johnson, encouraged Americans to defer to "a political law—and when I say political law, I mean higher law, a law of Providence—that empire has [had], for the last three thousand years." Seward correctly predicted that foreign trade would play an increasingly important part in the American economy. Between 1870 and 1900 exports more than tripled, from about $400 million to over $1.5 billion, with textiles and agricultural products leading the way. But as European markets for American goods began to contract, business and political leaders of necessity looked more eagerly to Asia as well as to lands closer by.

Since the American Revolution, many Americans had regarded all nearby nations as falling naturally within their own territorial realm, destined to be acquired when opportunity allowed. Seward advanced these imperialist principles in 1867 by negotiating the purchase of Alaska (known at the time as Seward's Icebox) from Russia for $7.2 million, and he hoped someday to see the American flag flying over Canada and Mexico. Meanwhile, with European nations launched on their own imperialist missions in Asia and Africa, the United States increasingly viewed the Caribbean as an "American lake" and all of Latin America as a vast potential market for U.S. goods. The crisis of the 1890s transformed this long-standing desire into a perceived economic necessity. Large-scale conquest, however, appeared to American leaders more expensive and less appealing than economic domination and selective colonization. Unlike European imperialists, powerful Americans dreamed of empire without large-scale permanent military occupation and costly colonial administration.

Americans focused their expansionist plans on the Western Hemisphere, determined to dislodge the dominant power, Great Britain. In 1867, when Canada became a self-governing dominion, American diplomats hoped to annex their northern neighbor, believing that

Great Britain would gladly accede in order to concentrate its imperial interests in Asia. But Great Britain refused to give up Canada, and the United States backed away. Central and South America proved more accommodating to American designs.

Republican stalwart James G. Blaine, secretary of state under presidents Garfield and Harrison, determined to work out a Good Neighbor policy (a phrase coined by Henry Clay in 1820). "What we want," he explained, "are the markets of these neighbors of ours that lie to the south of us. We want the $400,000,000 annually which to-day go to England, France, Germany and other countries. With these markets secured new life would be given to our manufactures, the product of the Western farmer would be in demand, the reasons for and inducements to strikers, with all their attendant evils,

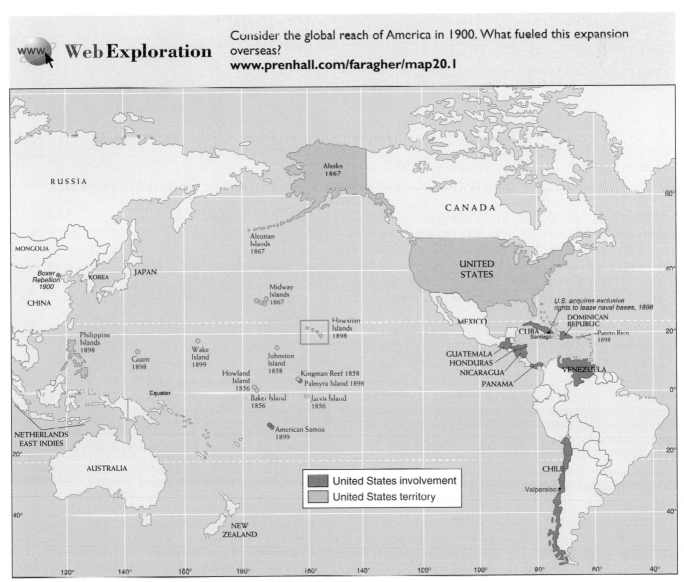

WebExploration

Consider the global reach of America in 1900. What fueled this expansion overseas?
www.prenhall.com/faragher/map20.1

The American Domain, ca. 1900 The United States claimed numerous islands in the South Pacific and intervened repeatedly in Latin America to secure its economic interests.

would cease." Bilateral treaties with Mexico, Colombia, the British West Indies, El Salvador, and the Dominican Republic allowed American business to dominate local economies, importing their raw materials at low prices and flooding their local markets with goods manufactured in the United States. Often American investors simply took over the principal industries of these small nations, undercutting national business classes. The first Pan-American Conference, held in 1889–90, marked a turning point in hemispheric relations.

The Good Neighbor policy depended, Blaine knew, on peace and order in the Latin American states. As early as 1875, when revolt shook Venezuela, the Department of State warned European powers not to meddle. If popular uprisings proved too much for local officials, the U.S. Navy would intervene and return American allies to power.

In 1883, wishing to enforce treaties and protect overseas investments, Congress appropriated funds to build up American seapower. Beginning with ninety small ships, over one-third of them wooden, the navy grew quickly to include modern steel fighting ships. The hulls of these ships were painted a gleaming white, and the armada was known as the Great White Fleet. One of the most popular exhibits at the Chicago World's Fair featured full-sized models of the new armor-plated steel battleships. Congress also established the Naval War College in Newport, Rhode Island, in 1884 to train the officer corps. One of its first presidents, Captain Alfred Thayer Mahan, prescribed an imperialist strategy based on command of the seas. His book, *The Influence of Sea Power upon American History, 1660–1873* (1890), helped to define American foreign policy at the time. Mahan insisted that international strength rested not only on open markets but on the control of colonies. He advocated the annexation of bases in the Caribbean and the Pacific to enhance the navy's ability to threaten or wage warfare.

The annexation of Hawai'i on July 7, 1898, followed nearly a century of economic penetration and diplomatic maneuver. American missionaries, who had arrived in the 1820s to convert Hawai'ians to Christianity, began to buy up huge parcels of land and to subvert the existing feudal system of landholding. They also encouraged American businesses to buy into sugar plantations, and by 1875 U.S. corporations dominated the sugar trade. They tripled the number of plantations by 1880 and sent Hawai'ian sugar duty-free to the United States. By this time Hawai'i appeared, in Blaine's opinion, to be "an outlying district of the state of California," and he began to push for annexation. In 1887 a new treaty allowed the United States to build a naval base at Pearl Harbor on the island of Oahu.

The next year, American planters took a step further, arranging the overthrow of the weak king Kalakaua

and securing a new government allied to their economic interests. In 1891, the new ruler, Queen Liliuokalani, struck back by issuing a constitution granting her more discretionary power. The U.S. minister, prompted by the pineapple magnate Sanford B. Dole, responded by calling for military assistance. On January 16, 1893, U.S. sailors landed on Hawai'i to protect American property. Liliuokalani was deposed, a new provisional government was installed, and Hawai'i was proclaimed an American protectorate (a territory protected and partly controlled by the United States). The American diplomat John L. Stevens, stationed in Hawai'i, eagerly wired Washington that the "Hawai'ian pear is now fully ripe, and this is the golden hour for the United States to pluck it." President Cleveland refused to consider annexation, but five years later McKinley affirmed a joint congressional resolution under which Hawai'i would

Brought to power with the assistance of American businessmen, Queen Liliuokalani nevertheless sought to limit the outsiders' influence. American marines, Christian missionaries, and sugar planters joined in 1893 to drive her from her throne. A century later, the U.S. government apologized to native Hawai'ians for this illegal act.

SOURCE: Library of Congress.

become an American territory in 1900. The residents of Hawai'i were not consulted about this momentous change in their national identity.

Hawai'i was often viewed as a steppingstone to the vast Asian markets. A U.S. admiral envisioned the happy future: "The Pacific is the ocean bride of America—China, Japan and Korea—and their innumerable islands, hanging like necklaces about them, are the bridesmaids. . . . Let us as Americans . . . determine while yet in our power, that no commercial rival or hostile flag can float with impunity over the long swell of the Pacific sea."

To accelerate railroad investment and trade, a consortium of New York bankers created the American China Development Company in 1896. They feared, however, that the tottering Manchu dynasty would fall to European, Russian, and Japanese colonial powers, which would then prohibit trade with the United States. Secretary of State John Hay responded in 1899 by proclaiming the Open Door policy. According to this doctrine, outlined in notes to six major powers, the United States enjoyed the right to advance its commercial interests anywhere in the world, at least on terms equal to those of the other imperialist nations. The Chinese marketplace was too important to lose.

Chinese nationalist rebellion, however, threatened to overwhelm all the outsiders' plans for China. An antiforeign secret society known as the Harmonious Righteous Fists (dubbed "Boxers" by the Western press) rioted repeatedly in 1898 and 1899, actually occupying the capital city of Beijing and surrounding the foreign embassies. Shocked by the deaths of thousands, including many Chinese converts to Christianity, and determined to maintain American economic interests, President McKinley, not bothering to request congressional approval, contributed 5,000 U.S. troops to an international army that put down the Boxer uprising. The Boxer Rebellion dramatized the Manchu regime's inability to control its own subjects and strengthened John Hay's determination to preserve the economic status quo. A second series of Open Door notes by the secretary of state restated the intention of the United States to trade in China and laid the basis for twentieth century foreign policy.

THE SPANISH–AMERICAN WAR

During his 1896 campaign, William McKinley firmly committed himself to the principle of economic expansion. It was for him the proper alternative to Edward Bellamy's program for a cooperative commonwealth. Indeed, he once described his "greatest ambition" as achieving American supremacy in world markets. As president, McKinley not only reached out for markets

but took his nation into war while proclaiming its humanitarian and democratic goals.

The Spanish-American War was the most popular war since the American war for independence from Great Britain. It was short, lasting only sixteen weeks. It claimed relatively few lives—about 2,500 men died from diseases, mainly yellow fever, typhoid, or malaria—ten times the number killed in combat. And the war cost the government only $250 million. When it ended, the United States waged another war and annexed the Philippines. By the end of the century, the nation had joined Europe and Japan in the quest for empire and had become a formidable world power with territories spread out across the Carribean Sea and Pacific Ocean.

A "Splendid Little War" in Cuba

"I have ever looked on Cuba," Thomas Jefferson wrote, "as the most interesting addition which could ever be made to our system of States." Before the Civil War, Southerners hoped to acquire Cuba, still owned by Spain, for the expansion of slavery in its sugar mills, tobacco plantations, and mines. After attempting several times to buy the island outright, the United States settled for the continuation of the status quo, reaffirming Jefferson's conclusion that preserving Cuba's "independence against all the world, *except* Spain . . . would be nearly as valuable to us as if it were our own." Throughout the nineteenth century, the United States resolved to protect Spain's sovereignty over Cuba against the encroachment of other powers, including Cuba itself.

In Cuba, a movement for independence began in the mid-1860s when Spain, its empire in ruins, began to impose stiff taxes on the island. After defeat during the Ten Years War of 1868–78 and yet another series of setbacks, the insurgents rallied under the nationalist leadership of José Martí. In May 1895 Spanish troops ambushed and killed Martí, turning him into a martyr and fanning the flames of rebellion. By July, the rebels declared Cuba a republic and established a rudimentary government. Meanwhile, the war for independence moved closer to Havana, the island's seat of power.

Many Americans, invoking the legacy of their own war for independence, supported the movement for *Cuba Libre*. Grisly stories of Spain's treatment of captured insurrectionists circulated in American newspapers and aroused popular sympathy for the Cuban cause. In 1896 both the Democratic and Republican parties adopted planks supporting Cuba's freedom. President Cleveland refused to back the Cuban revolutionaries and instead urged Spain to grant the island a limited autonomy. Even when Congress passed a resolution in 1896 welcoming the future independence of Cuba, Cleveland and his advisers demurred.

Look at both theaters of action in the Spanish-American War. What did the United States gain from victories in each of these conflicts?
www.prenhall.com/faragher/map20.2

The Spanish-American War   In two theaters of action, the United States used its naval power adeptly against a weak foe.

After he took over the office, President McKinley also drew back. In his Inaugural Address he declared, "We want no wars of conquest; we must avoid the temptation of territorial aggression." The tide turned, however, when Spain appeared unable to maintain order. In early 1898 public indignation, whipped up by tabloid press headlines and sensational stories, turned into frenzy on February 15, when an explosion ripped through the battleship USS *Maine,* stationed in Havana harbor ostensibly to rescue American citizens.

McKinley, suspecting war was close, had already begun to prepare for intervention. Newspapers ran banner headlines charging a Spanish conspiracy, although there was no proof. The impatient public meanwhile demanded revenge for the death of 266 American sailors. Within days a new slogan appeared: "Remember the Maine! To Hell with Spain!"

Finally, on April 11, McKinley asked Congress for a declaration of war against Spain. Yet Congress barely passed the war resolution on April 25, and only with the inclusion of an amendment by Senator Henry Teller of Colorado that disclaimed "any disposition or intention to exercise sovereignty, jurisdiction or control over said island, except for the pacification thereof." McKinley called for 125,000 volunteers, and men seeking to enlist nearly overwhelmed the administration. For the first time, former Confederates served in the higher ranks of the U.S. Army, symbolically uniting North and South in this patriotic endeavor. African Americans volunteered in great numbers, in a display of patriotism and also in sympathy with Cubans who were, like themselves, a generation or less away from slavery. By the end of April, the fighting had begun.

Charles Post, *Spanish Civil War*. Badly supplied Cuban insurrectos had practiced guerrilla warfare against the Spanish colonizers since the mid-1890s, but after the explosion on the USS *Maine*, American forces took over the war and abandoned the cause of Cuban self-determination. This picture, by the young U.S. volunteer, was one of a series of sketches later transformed into watercolor and oil paintings.

SOURCE: Library of Congress. Courtesy of Mrs. Charles Johnson Post and Miss Phyllis B. Post

An outpouring of patriotic joy inspired massive parades, topical songs, and an overpowering enthusiasm. "Populists, Democrats, and Republicans are we," went one jingle, "But we are all Americans to make Cuba free." Just as the Civil War inspired masses of women to form relief societies so, too, did the Spanish–American war. The Women's Relief Corps and women's clubs across the country raised money and sent food and medical supplies to U.S. military camps.

Ten weeks later the war was all but over. On land, Lieutenant Colonel Theodore Roosevelt—who boasted of killing Spaniards "like jackrabbits"—led his Rough Riders to victory. On July 3, the main Spanish fleet near Santiago Bay was destroyed; two weeks later Santiago itself surrendered, and the war drew to a close. Although fewer than 400 Americans died in battle, disease and the inept treatment of the wounded created a medical disaster, spreading sickness and disease to more than 20,000 in the regiments. Roosevelt nevertheless felt invigorated by the conflict, agreeing with John Hay that it had been a "splendid little war."

On August 12, at a small ceremony in McKinley's office marking Spain's surrender, the United States secured Cuba's independence from Spain but not its own sovereignty. One member of Congress thus announced the unanticipated outcome of the war from Cuba's point of view: "What greater liberty, freedom, and independence can be obtained than that enjoyed under the protection of our flag?" On January 1, 1899, at ceremonies in Havana marked the end of four hundred years of Spanish rule and the passage of sovereignty over the island to the United States. The Cubans who waged the struggle for independence for nearly forty years sat on the sidelines, the words of José Martí—"Cuba must be free from Spain and the United States"—receding into the distant past.

American businesses proceeded to tighten their hold on Cuban sugar plantations, while U.S. military forces oversaw the formation of a constitutional convention that made Cuba a protectorate of the United States. Under the Platt Amendment, sponsored by Republican senator Orville H. Platt of Connecticut in 1901, Cuba was required to provide land for American bases; to devote national revenues to pay back debts to the United States; to sign no treaty that would be detrimental to American interests; and to acknowledge the right of the United States to intervene at any time to protect its interests in Cuba. During the occupation, which lasted until 1902, there were more U.S. troops in Cuba than during the war. After the U.S. withdrawal, the terms of the Platt amendment were incorporated into the Cuban-American Treaty of 1903. This treaty, which remained in place until 1934, paved the way for American domination of the island's sugar industry and contributed to anti–American sentiment among Cuban nationalists.

War in the Philippines

The Philippines, another of Spain's colonies, seemed an especially attractive prospect, its 7,000 islands a natural way station to the markets of mainland Asia. In 1897 Assistant Secretary of the Navy Theodore Roosevelt and President McKinley had discussed the merits of taking the Pacific colony in the event of war with Spain. At the first opportunity, McKinley acted to bring these islands into the U.S. strategic orbit. Shortly after Congress declared war on Spain, on May 4, the president dispatched 5,000 troops to occupy the Philippines. George Dewey, a Civil War veteran who commanded the American Asiatic Squadron, was ordered to "start offensive action." During the first week of the conflict, he demolished the Spanish fleet in Manila Bay through seven hours of unimpeded target practice. Once the war ended, McKinley refused to sign the armistice unless Spain relinquished all claims to its Pacific islands. When Spain conceded, McKinley quickly drew up plans for colonial administration. He pledged "to educate the Filipinos, and to uplift and civilize and Christianize them." But after centuries of Spanish rule, the majority of islanders—already Christians—were eager to create their own nation.

The Filipino rebels, like the Cubans, at first welcomed American troops and fought with them against Spain. But when the Spanish-American War ended and they perceived that American troops were not preparing to leave, the rebels, led by Emilio Aguinaldo, turned against their former allies and attacked the American base of operations in Manila in February 1899. Predicting a brief skirmish, American commanders seriously underestimated the population's capacity to endure great suffering for the sake of independence.

U.S. troops had provoked this conflict in various ways. Military leaders, the majority veterans of the Indian Wars, commonly described the natives as "gugus," and reported themselves, as one said, as "just itching to get at the niggers." While awaiting action, American soldiers repeatedly insulted or physically abused civilians, raped Filipino women, and otherwise whipped up resentment.

The resulting conflict took the form of modern guerrilla warfare, with brutalities on both sides. By the time the fighting slowed down in 1902, 4,300 American lives had been lost, and one of every five Filipinos had died in battle or from starvation or disease. On some of the Philippine islands, intermittent fighting lasted until 1935.

The United States nevertheless refused to pull out. In 1901 William Howard Taft headed a commission that established a government controlled by Americans; after 1905, the president appointed a Filipino governor general to maintain the provincial government. Meanwhile, Americans bought up the best land and invested heavily in the island's sugar economy.

The conquest of the Philippines, which remained a U.S. territory until 1946, evoked for its defenders the vision of empire. At the very least, the Philippines joined Hawai'i as yet another steppingstone for U.S. merchants en route to China. At the end of the Spanish-American War, the United States advanced its interests in the Caribbean to include Puerto Rico, ceded by Spain, and eventually the Virgin Islands of St. Thomas, St. John, and St. Croix, purchased from Denmark in 1917. The acquisition of Pacific territories, including Guam, marked the emergence of the United States as a global colonial power.

Once again, Josiah Strong proclaimed judgment over an era. His famous treatise *Expansion* (1900) roundly defended American overseas involvements by carefully distinguishing between freedom and independence. People could achieve freedom, he argued, only under the rule of law. And because white Americans had proven themselves superior in the realm of

government, they could best bring "freedom" to nonwhite peoples by setting aside the ideal of national independence for a period of enforced guidance. Many began to wonder, however, whether the United States could become an empire without sacrificing its democratic spirit, and to ask whether the subjugated people were really so fortunate under the rule of the United States.

Critics of Empire

No mass movement formed to forestall U.S. expansion, but distinguished figures like Mark Twain, Andrew Carnegie, William Jennings Bryan, and Harvard philosopher William James voiced their opposition strongly. Dissent followed two broad lines of argument. In 1870, when President Grant urged the annexation of Santo Domingo, the nation-state occupying half of the island of Hispaniola (Haiti occupying the other half), opponents countered by insisting that the

"Uncle Sam Teaches the Art of Self-Government," editorial cartoon, 1898. Expressing a popular sentiment of the time, a newspaper cartoonist shows the rebels as raucous children who constantly fight among themselves and need to be brought into line by Uncle Sam. The Filipino leader, Emilio Aguinaldo, appears as a dunce for failing to learn properly from the teacher. The two major islands where no uprising took place, Puerto Rico and Hawai'i, appear as passive but exotically dressed women, ready to learn their lessons.

SOURCE: Library of Congress.

CHRONOLOGY

1867	Grange founded
	Secretary of State Seward negotiates the purchase of Alaska
1874	Tompkins Square Riot
	Granger laws begin to regulate railroad shipping rates
1877	Rutherford B. Hayes elected president
	Great Uprising of 1877
1879	Henry George publishes *Progress and Poverty*
1881	President James A. Garfield assassinated; Chester A. Arthur becomes president
1883	Pendleton Act passed
1884	Grover Cleveland elected president
1887	Interstate Commerce Act creates the Interstate Commerce Commission
1888	Edward Bellamy publishes *Looking Backward*
	National Colored Farmers' Alliance and Cooperative Union formed
	Benjamin Harrison elected president
1889	National Farmers' Alliance and Industrial Union formed
1890	Sherman Silver Purchase Act
	McKinley tariff enacted
	National American Woman Suffrage Association formed
1891	National Women's Alliance formed
	Populist (People's) Party formed

1892	Coeur d'Alene miners' strike
	Homestead strike
	Ida B. Wells begins crusade against lynching
1893	Western Federation of Miners formed
	Financial panic and depression
	World's Columbian Exhibition opens in Chicago
1894	"Coxey's Army" marches on Washington, D.C.
	Pullman strike and boycott
1896	*Plessy v. Ferguson* upholds segregation
	William McKinley defeats William Jennings Bryan for president
1897	Dingley tariff again raises import duties to an all-time high
1898	Eugene V. Debs helps found Social Democratic Party
	Hawai'i is annexed
	Spanish-American War begins
	Anti-Imperialist League formed
1899	*Cumming v. Richmond County Board of Education* sanctions segregated education
	Secretary of State John Hay announces Open Door policy
	Guerrilla war begins in the Philippines
1900	Gold Standard Act
	Josiah Strong publishes *Expansion*

United States stood unequivocally for the right of national self-determination and the consent of the governed. Others opposed annexation on the ground that dark-skinned and "ignorant" Santo Domingans were unworthy of American citizenship. These two contrary arguments, democratic and racist, were sounded repeatedly as the United States joined other nations in the armed struggle for empire.

Organized protest to military action, especially against the widely reported atrocities in the Philippines, owed much to the Anti-Imperialist League, which was founded by a small group of prominent Bostonians. In historic Faneuil Hall, which had witnessed the birth of both the American Revolution and the antislavery movement, a mass meeting was convened in June 1898 to protest the "insane and wicked ambition which is driving the nation to ruin." Within a few months, the league reported 25,000 members. Most supported American economic expansion but advocated free trade rather than political domination as the means to reach this goal. All strongly opposed the annexation of new territories. The league drew followers from every walk of life, including such famous writers as Charles Francis Adams and Mark Twain, *Nation* editor E. L. Godkin, African American scholar W. E. B. Du Bois, and Civil War veteran Thomas Wentworth Higginson.

The Anti-Imperialist League brought together like-minded societies from across the country, encouraged mass meetings, and published pamphlets, poems, and broadsides. The *National Labor Standard* expressed the common hope that all those "who believe in the Republic against Empire should join." By 1899, the league claimed a half-million members. A few outspoken anti-imperialists, such as former Illinois governor John Peter Altgeld, openly toasted Filipino rebels as heroes. Morrison Swift, leader of the Coxey's Army contingent from Massachusetts, formed a Filipino Liberation Society and sent antiwar materials to American troops. Others, such as Samuel Gompers, a league vice president, felt no sympathy for conquered peoples, describing Filipinos as "perhaps nearer the condition of savages and barbarians than any island possessed by any other civilized nation on earth." Gompers simply wanted to prevent colonized nonwhites from immigrating into the United States and "inundating" American labor.

Military leaders and staunch imperialists did not distinguish between racist and nonracist antiimperialists. They called all dissenters "unhung traitors" and demanded their arrest. Newspaper editors accused universities of harboring antiwar professors, although college students as a group were enthusiastic supporters of the war.

Within the press, which overwhelmingly supported the Spanish-American War, the voices of opposition appeared primarily in African American and labor papers. The *Indianapolis Recorder* asked rhetorically in 1899, "Are the tender-hearted expansionists in the United States Congress really actuated by the desire to save the Filipinos from self-destruction or is it the worldly greed for gain?" The *Railroad Telegrapher* similarly commented, "The wonder of it all is that the working people are willing to lose blood and treasure in fighting another man's battle."

Most Americans put aside their doubts and welcomed the new era of imperialism. Untouched by the private tragedies of dead or wounded American soldiers and the mass destruction of civilian society in the Philippines, the vast majority could approve Theodore Roosevelt's defense of armed conflict: "No triumph of peace is quite so great as the supreme triumphs of war."

CONCLUSION

The conflicts marking the last quarter of the nineteenth century that pitted farmers, workers, and the proprietors of small businesses against powerful outside interests had offered Americans an important moment of democratic promise. By the end of the century, however, the rural and working-class campaigns to retain a large degree of self-government in their communities had been defeated, their organizations destroyed, their autonomy eroded. The rise of a national governing class and its counterpart, the large bureaucratic state, established new rules of behavior, new sources of prestige, and new rewards for the most successful citizens.

But the nation would pay a steep price, in the next era, for the failure of democratic reform. Regional antagonisms, nativist movements against the foreign-born, and above all deepening racial tensions blighted American society. As the new century opened, progressive reformers moved to correct flaws in government while accepting the framework of a corporate society and its overseas empire. But they found the widening divisions in American society difficult—if not impossible—to overcome.

REVIEW QUESTIONS

1. Discuss some of the problems accompanying the expansion of government during the late nineteenth century. What role did political parties play in this process? Explain how a prominent reformer such as James Garfield might become a leading "machine" politician?

2. What were the major causes and consequences of the Populist movement of the 1880s and 1890s? Why did the election of 1896 prove so important to the future of American politics?

3. Discuss the role of women in both the Grange and the People's Party. What were their specific goals?

4. Discuss the causes and consequences of the financial crisis of the 1890s. How did various reformers and politicians respond to the event? What kinds of programs did they offer to restore the economy or reduce poverty?

5. How did the exclusion of African Americans affect the outcome of populism? Explain the rise of Jim Crow legislation in the South, and discuss its impact on the status of African Americans.

6. Describe American foreign policy during the 1890s. Why did the United States intervene in Cuba and the Philippines? What were some of the leading arguments for and against overseas expansion?

RECOMMENDED READING

Ruth Bordin, *Woman and Temperance: The Quest for Power and Liberty, 1873–1900* (1981).

Matthew Frye Jacobson, *Barbarian Virtues: The United States Encounters Foreign Peoples at Home and Abroad, 1876–1917* (2000).

Michael Kazin, *The Populist Persuasion: An American History* (1995, rev. ed., 1998).

Walter LaFeber, *The New Empire: An Interpretation of American Expansion, 1860–1898* (1963, 1998).

Leon F. Litwack, *Trouble in Mind: Black Southerners in the Age of Jim Crow* (1998).

Nell Irvin Painter, *Standing at Armageddon: The United States, 1877–1919* (1987).

Emily S. Rosenberg, *Spreading the American Dream: American Economic and Cultural Expansion, 1890–1945* (1982).

Elizabeth Sanders, *Roots of Reform: Farmers, Workers, and the American State, 1877–1917* (1999).

David O. Stowell, *Streets, Railroads, and the Great Strike of 1877* (1999).

William Appleman Williams, *Empire as a Way of Life: An Essay on the Causes and Character of America's Present Predicament* (1982).

▶ MEDIA RESOURCES

U.S. HISTORY DOCUMENTS CD-ROM

America Around the Globe

20-2 Henry Cabot Lodge, "The Business World v. the Politicians" (1895)

20-3 Albert Beveridge, "The March of the Flag" (1898)

20-4 The Spanish-American War (1898)

20-5 William McKinley, "Decision on the Philippines" (1900)

20-6 The Boxer Rebellion (1900)

20-7 Theodore Roosevelt, Third Annual Message to Congress (1903)

The Progressive Era

21-2 William Graham Sumner, What the Social Classes Owe to Each Other (1883)

COMPANION WEBSITE HIGHLIGHTS

To view an exploration, enter one of the URLs below in your browser.

Web Explorations

The American Domain ca. 1900
http://www.prenhall.com/faragher/map20.1
The Spanish-American War
http://www.prenhall.com/faragher/map20.2

Additional Interactive Maps

To access the maps, go to this chapter's resources at
http://www.prenhall.com/taragher
Strikes by State, 1880, page 606
The Election of 1896, by States, page 614

HISTORY RESOURCE CENTER

To find the resources listed below, go to
http://www.prenhall.com/historyresourcecenter

Documents

Josiah Strong, from *Our Country* (1885)

Mark Twain, "Incident in the Philippines" (1924)

W.E.B. Du Bois, from "Of Mr. Booker T. Washington and Others" (1903)

William T. Riordon, from *Plunkitt of Tammany Hall* (1905)

William Graham Sumner, from "On Empire and the Philippines" (1898)

Images

Building The Panama Canal
Emilio Aguinaldo
Explosion on the Maine
Filipino Guerillas
Irish Immigrants in Boston, 1882
Italian Immigrants in San Francisco, 1891
U.S. Soldiers in the Philippines, 1899

Turn to the next page for the *Exploring America* activity for this chapter.

EXPLORING AMERICA
WHITE MAN'S BURDEN
http://www.prenhall.com/faragher/whiteman

The Spanish-American War signaled a change in United States foreign policy and its role in the world. It also sparked a strong debate over these changes. Why did the United States embrace imperialism? What was the "white man's burden" and what was its impact on other nations? How did racism affect U.S. imperialism? Why did the Philippines become the focus of the debate over imperialism? The *White Man's Burden* module answers these and other questions. It examines the issue of imperialism from varying perspective to identify its origins and also the ideas behind those supported overseas expansion and those opposing it.

The White Man's Burden uses the Rudyard Kipling

poem of the same name as the focus to examine why the United States sought to expand overseas and to explore the various reactions to this expansionist thrust. In addition to Kipling's poem, congressional testimony, the 1901 Republican Party platform, a letter from Mark Twain, and visual images illustrate the complex issues raised by this important topic. Interactive maps and an audio clip help expand the coverage and provide new insights into the causes of expansion and its later consequences.

Reflect and Respond

1. Tillman claimed that, as a white Southerner, he knew all about the "white man's burden." What did he mean by the phrase?
2. How similar were Tillman's racial ideas to Kipling's? Cite specific images and passages.

3. How does Tillman's description of the Filipinos compare with Kipling's?
4. Kipling insisted that the "white man" acquired imperial possessions to "serve" his "captive's needs." Twain referred to this as "the Blessings of Civilization trust." The supposed "Blessings of Civilization" were "an outside cover, gay and pretty and attractive, displaying the special patterns of our Civilization which we reserve for Home Consumption, while inside the bale is the Actual Thing that the Customer Sitting in Darkness buys with his blood and tears and land and liberty. That Actual Thing is, indeed, Civilization, but it is only for Export. Is there a difference between the two brands? In some of the details, yes." What details did Twain have in mind?
5. Twain contrasted the "European" and the "American" game. What did he mean by each?
6. Kipling described the Filipinos as childlike and at best semicivilized. Tillman offered his own description. What was Twain's?

✓ Check it out
The United States in the Pacific

This map shows the course of imperialism in Asia. It depicts the intrusion of European nations, Japan, and the

United States offering a geographic context to the rise of an American overseas empire in the Pacific. The map also indicates that as had been true throughout history, the roads to trade led to China. But, in the age of imperialism, foreign powers desired much more than a trading relationship among nations.

This exploration is also available on the *Exploring America* CD-ROM. For another *Exploring America* activity related to this chapter, go to "Homestead Strike of 1892" found on both the Companion Website™ and the CD-ROM.

John Sloan (1871–1951), *Italian Procession, New York*, 1913–1925. Oil on canvas, 24″ × 28″. SOURCE: San Diego Museum of Art, gift of Mr. and Mrs. Appleton S. Bridges.

AMERICAN COMMUNITIES

The Henry Street Settlement House: Women Settlement House Workers Create a Community of Reform

ASHY AND FRIGHTENED YOUNG GIRL APPEARED IN THE DOORWAY OF A weekly home-nursing class for women on Manhattan's Lower East Side. The teacher beckoned her to come forward. Tugging on the teacher's skirt, the girl pleaded in broken English for the teacher to come home with her. "Mother," "baby," "blood," she kept repeating. The teacher gathered up the sheets that were part of the interrupted lesson in bed making. The two hurried through narrow, garbage-strewn, foul-smelling streets, then groped their way up a pitch-dark, rickety staircase. They reached a cramped, two-room apartment, home to an immigrant family of seven and several boarders. There, in a vermin-infested bed, encrusted with dried blood, lay a mother and her newborn baby. The mother had been abandoned by a doctor because she could not afford his fee.

The teacher, Lillian Wald, was a twenty-five-year-old nurse at New York Hospital. Years later she recalled this scene as her baptism by fire and the turning point in her life. Born in 1867, Wald had enjoyed a comfortable upbringing in a middle-class German Jewish family in Rochester. Despite her parents' objections, she had moved to New York City to become a professional nurse. Resentful of the disdainful treatment nurses received from doctors and horrified by the inhumane conditions at a juvenile asylum she worked in, Wald determined to find a way of caring for the sick in their neighborhoods and homes. With nursing school classmate Mary Brewster, Wald rented a fifth-floor walk-up apartment on the Lower East Side and established a visiting nurse service. The two provided professional care in the home to hundreds of families for a nominal fee of 10 to 25 cents. They also offered each family they visited information on basic health care, sanitation, and disease prevention. In 1895, philanthropist Jacob Schiff generously donated a red brick Georgian house on Henry Street as a new base of operation.

The Henry Street Settlement stood in the center of perhaps the most overcrowded neighborhood in the world, New York's Lower East Side. Roughly 500,000 people were packed into an area only as large as a midsized Kansas farm. Population density was about 500 per acre, roughly four times the figure for the rest of New York City and far more concentrated than even the worst slums of London or Calcutta. A single city block might have as many as 3,000 residents. Home for most Lower East Siders was a small tenement apartment that might include paying boarders squeezed in alongside the immediate family. Residents were mostly recent immigrants from southern and eastern Europe: Jews, Italians, Germans, Greeks, Hungarians, Slavs. Men, women, and children toiled in the garment shops, small factories, retail stores, breweries, and warehouses to be found on nearly every street. An Irish-dominated machine controlled local political affairs.

The Henry Street Settlement became a model for a new kind of reform community composed essentially of college-educated women who encouraged and supported one another in a wide variety of humanitarian, civic, political, and cultural activities. Settlement house living arrangements closely resembled those in the dormitories of such new women's colleges as Smith, Wellesley, and Vassar. Like these colleges, the settlement house was an "experiment," but one designed, in settlement house pioneer Jane Addams's words, "to aid in the solution of the social and industrial problems which are engendered by the modern conditions of urban life." Unlike earlier moral reformers who tried to impose their ideas from outside, settlement house residents lived in poor communities and worked for immediate improvements in the health and welfare of those communities. Yet, as Addams and others repeatedly stressed, the college-educated women were beneficiaries as well. The settlement house allowed them to preserve a collegial spirit, satisfy the desire for service, and apply their academic training.

With its combined moral and social appeal, the settlement house movement attracted many educated young women and grew rapidly. There were six settlement houses in the United States in 1891, some 74 in 1897, more than 200 by 1900, and more than 400 by 1910. Few women made settlement work a career. The average stay was less than five years. Roughly half of those who worked in the movement eventually married. Those who did make a career of settlement house work, however, typically chose not to marry, and most lived together with female companions. As the movement flourished, settlement house residents called attention to the plight of the poor and fostered respect for different cultural heritages in countless articles and lectures. Leaders of the

movement, including Jane Addams, Lillian Wald, and Florence Kelley, emerged as influential political figures during the progressive era.

Wald attracted a dedicated group of nurses, educators, and reformers to live at the Henry Street Settlement. By 1909 Henry Street had more than forty residents, supported by the donations of well-to-do New Yorkers. Wald and her allies convinced the New York Board of Health to assign a nurse to every public school in the city. They lobbied the Board of Education to create the first school lunch programs. They persuaded the city to set up municipal milk stations to ensure the purity of milk. Henry Street also pioneered tuberculosis treatment and prevention. Its leaders became powerful advocates for playground construction, improved street cleaning, and tougher housing inspection. The settlement's Neighborhood Playhouse became an internationally acclaimed center for innovative theater, music, and dance.

As settlement house workers expanded their influence from local neighborhoods to larger political and social circles, they became, in the phrase of one historian, "spearheads for reform." Lillian Wald became a national figure—an outspoken advocate of child labor legislation and woman suffrage and a vigorous opponent of American involvement in World War I. She offered Henry Street as a meeting place to the National Negro Conference in 1909, out of which emerged the National Association for the Advancement of Colored People. It was no cliché for Wald to say, as she did on many occasions, "The whole world is my neighborhood." ■

New York City

KEY TOPICS

- The political, social, and intellectual roots of progressive reform

- Tensions between social justice and social control

- The urban scene and the impact of new immigration

- Political activism by the working class, women, and African Americans

- Progressivism in national politics

THE CURRENTS OF PROGRESSIVISM

Between the 1890s and World War I, a large and diverse number of Americans claimed the political label "progressive." Progressives could be found in all classes, regions, and races. They shared a fundamental ethos, or belief, that America needed a new social consciousness to cope with the problems brought on by the enormous rush of economic and social change in the post–Civil War decades. Yet progressivism was no unified movement with a single set of principles. It is best understood as a varied collection of reform communities, often fleeting, uniting citizens in a host of political, professional, and religious organizations, some of which were national in scope.

Progressivism drew from deep roots in hundreds of local American communities. At the state level it flowered in the soil of several key issues: ending political corruption, bringing more businesslike methods to governing, and offering a more compassionate legislative response to the excesses of industrialism. As a national movement, progressivism reached its peak in 1912, when the four major presidential candidates all ran on some version of a progressive platform. This last development was an important measure of the extent to which local reform movements, like the Henry Street Settlement, and new intellectual currents had captured the political imagination of the nation.

The many contradictions and disagreements surrounding the meaning of progressivism have led some historians to dismiss the term as hopelessly vague. Some progressives focused on expanding state and federal regulation of private interests for the public welfare. Others viewed the rapid influx of new immigrants and the explosive growth of large cities as requiring more stringent social controls. Another variant emphasized eliminating corruption in the political system as

the key to righting society's wrongs. In the South, progressivism was for white people only. Progressives could be forward looking in their vision or nostalgic for a nineteenth-century world rapidly disappearing. Self-styled progressives often found themselves facing each other from opposite sides of an issue.

Yet at the local, state, and finally national levels, reform rhetoric and energy shaped most of the political and cultural debates of the era. Understanding progressivism in all its complexity thus requires examining what key reform groups, thinkers, and political figures actually did and said under its ambiguous banner.

Unifying Themes

Three basic attitudes underlay the various crusades and movements that emerged in response to the fears gnawing at large segments of the population. The first was anger over the excesses of industrial capitalism and urban growth. At the same time, progressives shared an essential optimism about the ability of citizens to improve social and economic conditions. They were reformers, not revolutionaries. Second, progressives emphasized social cohesion and common bonds as a way of understanding how modern society and economics actually worked. They largely rejected the ideal of individualism that had informed nineteenth-century economic and political theory. For progressives, poverty and success hinged on more than simply individual character; the economy was more than merely a sum of individual calculations. Progressives thus opposed social Darwinism, with its claim that any effort to improve social conditions would prove fruitless because society is like a jungle in which only the "fittest" survive. Third, progressives believed in the need for citizens to intervene actively, both politically and morally, to improve social conditions. They pushed for a stronger government role in regulating the economy and solving the nation's social problems.

OVERVIEW

CURRENTS OF PROGRESSIVISM

	Key Figures	Issues	Institutions/Achievements
Local Communities	Jane Addams, Lillian Wald, Florence Kelley, Frederic C. Howe, Samuel Jones	■ Improving health, education, welfare in urban immigrant neighborhoods ■ Child labor, eight-hour day ■ Celebrating immigrant cultures ■ Reforming urban politics ■ Municipal ownership/regulation of utilities	■ Hull House Settlement ■ Henry Street Settlement ■ National Consumers League ■ New York Child Labor Committee ■ Bureau of Municipal Research
State	Robert M. LaFollette, Hiram Johnson, Al Smith	■ Limiting power of railroads, other corporations ■ Improving civil service ■ Direct democracy ■ Applying academic scholarship to human needs	■ "Wisconsin Idea" ■ State Workmen's Compensation ■ Unemployment Insurance ■ Public utility regulation
	James K. Vardaman, Hoke Smith	■ Disfranchisement of African Americans	■ Legalized segregation
National	Theodore Roosevelt	■ Trustbusting ■ Conservation and Western development ■ National regulation of corporate and financial excesses	■ Reclamation Bureau (1902) ■ U.S. Forest Service (1905) ■ Food and Drug Administration (1906) ■ Meat Inspection Act (1906) ■ Hepburn Act–ICC (1906)
	Woodrow Wilson	■ National regulation of corporate and financial excesses ■ Reform of national banking	■ Graduated Income Tax (1913) ■ Federal Reserve Act (1913) ■ Clayton Antitrust Act (1914) ■ Federal Trade Commission (1914)
Intellectual/ Cultural	Jacob Riis	■ Muckraking	■ *How the Other Half Lives* (1890)
	Lincoln Steffens, Ida Tarbell, Upton Sinclair, S. S. McClure		■ *Shame of the Cities* (1902) ■ *History of Standard Oil* (1904) ■ *The Jungle* (1906) ■ *McClure's Magazine*
	John Dewey	■ Education reform	■ *Democracy and Education* (1916)
	Louis Brandeis	■ Sociological jurisprudence	■ *Muller v. Oregon* (1908)
	Edwin A. Ross	■ Empowering "ethical elite"	■ *Social Control* (1901)

Progressive rhetoric and methods drew on two distinct sources of inspiration. One was evangelical Protestantism, particularly the late nineteenth-century social gospel movement. Social gospelers rejected the idea of original sin as the cause of human suffering. They emphasized both the capacity and the duty of Christians to purge the world of poverty, inequality, and economic greed. A second strain of progressive thought looked to natural and social scientists to develop rational measures for improving the human condition, believing that experts trained in statistical analysis and engineering could make government and industry more efficient. Progressivism thus offered an uneasy combination of social justice and social control, a tension that would characterize American reform for the rest of the twentieth century.

Women Spearhead Reform

In the 1890s the settlement house movement had begun to provide an alternative to traditional concepts of private charity and humanitarian reform. Settlement workers found they could not transform their neighborhoods without confronting a host of broad social questions: chronic poverty, overcrowded tenement houses, child labor, industrial accidents, public health. As on Henry Street, college-educated, middle-class women constituted a key vanguard in the crusade for social justice. As reform communities, settlement houses soon discovered the need to engage the political and cultural life of the larger communities that surrounded them.

Photographer Lewis Hine, one of the pioneers of social documentary photography, made this evocative 1908 portrait of "Mamie," a typical young spinner working at a cotton mill in Lancaster, South Carolina. The National Child Labor Committee hired Hine to help document, publicize, and curb the widespread employment of children in industrial occupations. "These pictures," Hine wrote, "speak for themselves and prove that the law is being violated."

SOURCE: Lewis Hine (American, 1874–1940), *A Carolina Spinner*, 1908. Gelatin silver print, 4 3/4 × 7 in. Milwaukee Art Museum, Gift of the Sheldon M. Barnett Family. (M1973.83).

Jane Addams founded one of the first settlement houses, Hull House, in Chicago in 1889 after years of struggling to find work and a social identity equal to her talents. A member of one of the first generation of American women to attend college, Addams was a graduate of Rockford College. Many educated women were dissatisfied with the life choices conventionally available to them: early marriage or the traditional female professions of teaching, nursing, and library work. Settlement work provided these women with an attractive alternative. Hull House was located in a run-down slum area of Chicago. It had a day nursery, a dispensary for medicines and medical advice, a boardinghouse, an art gallery, and a music school. Addams often spoke of the "subjective necessity" of settlement houses. By this she meant that they gave young, educated women a way to satisfy their powerful desire to connect with the real world. "There is nothing after disease, indigence and guilt," she wrote, "so fatal to life itself as the want of a proper outlet for active faculties."

Social reformer Florence Kelley helped direct the support of the settlement house movement behind groundbreaking state and federal labor legislation. Arriving at Hull House in 1891, Kelley found what she described as a "colony of efficient and intelligent women." In 1893, she wrote a report detailing the dismal conditions in sweatshops and the effects of long hours on the women and children who worked in them. This report became the basis for landmark legislation in Illinois that limited women to an eight-hour workday, barred children under fourteen from working, and abolished tenement labor. Illinois governor John Peter Altgeld appointed Kelley as chief inspector for the new law. In 1895 Kelley published *Hull House Maps and Papers*, the first scientific study of urban poverty in America. Moving to Henry Street Settlement in 1898, Kelley served as general secretary of the new National Consumers' League. With Lillian Wald she established the New York Child Labor Committee and pushed for the creation of the U.S. Children's Bureau, established in 1912.

Kelley, Addams, Wald, and their circle consciously used their power as women to reshape politics in the progressive era. Electoral politics and the state were historically male preserves, but female social progressives turned their gender into an advantage. They built upon the tradition of female moral reform, where women had long operated outside male-dominated political institutions to agitate and organize. Activists like Kelley used their influence in civil society to create new state powers in the service of social justice. They left a legacy that simultaneously expanded the social welfare function of the state and increased women's public authority and influence.

The young Jane Addams, founder of the Hull House settlement in south Chicago, and a leading voice for a variety Progressive era reform campaigns. Addams inspired thousands of educated, middle class American women to put their intelligence, energy, and moral passion into serving the needs of the urban poor.

SOURCE: Jane Addams Memorial Collection (JAMC neg.21), The University Library, University of Illinois at Chicago.

The Urban Machine

Women had to work outside existing political institutions not just because they could not vote, but also because city politics had become a closed and often corrupt system. By the turn of the century Democratic Party machines, usually dominated by first- and second-generation Irish, controlled the political life of most large American cities. The keys to machine strength were disciplined organization and the delivery of essential services to both immigrant communities and business elites. The successful machine politician viewed his work as a business, and he accumulated his capital by serving people who needed assistance. For most urban dwellers, the city was a place of economic and social insecurity. Recent immigrants in particular faced frequent unemployment, sickness, and discrimination. In exchange for votes, machine politicians offered their constituents a variety of services. These included municipal jobs in the police and

fire departments, work at city construction sites, intervention with legal problems, and food and coal during hard times.

For those who did business with the city—construction companies, road builders, realtors—staying on the machine's good side was simply another business expense. In exchange for valuable franchises and city contracts, businessmen routinely bribed machine politicians and contributed liberally to their campaign funds. George Washington Plunkitt, a stalwart of New York's Tammany Hall machine, good-naturedly defended what he called "honest graft": making money from inside information on public improvements. "It's just like lookin' ahead in Wall Street or in the coffee or cotton market. . . . I seen my opportunities and I took 'em."

The machines usually had close ties to a city's vice economy and commercial entertainments. Organized prostitution and gambling, patronized largely by visitors to the city, could flourish only when "protected" by politicians who shared in the profits. Many machine figures began as saloonkeepers, and liquor dealers and beer brewers provided important financial support for "the organization." Vaudeville and burlesque theater, boxing, horse racing, and professional baseball were other urban enterprises with economic and political links to machines. Entertainment and spectacle made up a central element in the machine political style as well. Constituents looked forward to the colorful torchlight parades, free summer picnics, and riverboat excursions regularly sponsored by the machines.

On New York City's Lower East Side, where the Henry Street Settlement was located, Timothy D. "Big Tim" Sullivan embodied the popular machine style. Big Tim, who had risen from desperate poverty, remained enormously popular with his constituents until his death in 1913. "I believe in liberality," he declared. "I am a thorough New Yorker and have no narrow prejudices. I never ask a hungry man about his past; I feed him, not because he is good, but because he needs food. Help your neighbor but keep your nose out of his affairs." Critics charged that Sullivan controlled the city's gambling and made money from prostitution. But his real fortune came through his investments in vaudeville and the early movie business. Sullivan, whose district included the largest number of immigrants and transients in the city, provided shoe giveaways and free Christmas dinners to thousands every winter. To help pay for these and other charitable activities, he informally taxed the saloons, theaters, and restaurants in the district.

Progressive critics of machine politics routinely exaggerated the machine's power and influence. State legislatures, controlled by Republican rural and small-town elements, proved a formidable check on what city-based machines could accomplish. Reform campaigns that publicized excessive graft and corruption sometimes led voters to throw machine-backed mayors and aldermen out of office. And there were never enough patronage jobs for all the people clamoring for appointments. In the early twentieth century, to expand their base of support, political machines in the Northeast began concentrating more on passing welfare legislation beneficial to working-class and immigrant constituencies. In this way machine politicians often allied themselves with progressive reformers in state legislatures. In New York, for example, Tammany Hall figures such as Robert Wagner, Al Smith, and Big Tim Sullivan worked with middle-class progressive groups to pass child labor laws, factory safety regulations, worker compensation plans, and other efforts to make government more responsive to social needs. As Jewish and Catholic immigrants expanded in number and proportion in the city population, urban machines also began to champion cultural pluralism, opposing prohibition and immigration restrictions and defending the contributions made by new ethnic groups in the cities.

Political Progressives and Urban Reform

Political progressivism originated in the cities. It was both a challenge to the power of machine politics and a response to deteriorating urban conditions. City governments, especially in the Northeast and industrial Midwest, seemed hardly capable of providing the basic services needed to sustain large populations. For example, an impure water supply left Pittsburgh with one of the world's highest rates of death from typhoid, dysentery, and cholera. Most New York City neighborhoods rarely enjoyed street cleaning, and playgrounds were nonexistent. "The challenge of the city," Cleveland progressive Frederic C. Howe said in 1906, "has become one of decent human existence."

Reformers placed much of the blame for urban ills on the machines and looked for ways to restructure city government. The "good government" movement, led by the National Municipal League, fought to make city management a nonpartisan, even nonpolitical, process by bringing the administrative techniques of large corporations to cities. Reformers revised city charters in favor of stronger mayoral power and expanded use of appointed administrators and career civil servants. The New York Bureau of Municipal Research, founded in 1906, became a prototype for similar bureaus around the country. It drew up blueprints for model charters, ordinances, and zoning plans designed by experts trained in public administration.

Business and professional elites became the biggest boosters of structural reforms in urban government. In the summer of 1900 a hurricane in the Gulf of Mexico unleashed a tidal wave on Galveston, Texas. To cope with this disaster, leading businessmen convinced the state legislature to replace the mayor-council government with a small board of commissioners. Each commissioner was elected at large, and each was responsible for a different city department. Under this plan voters could more easily identify and hold accountable those responsible for city services. The city commission, enjoying both policy-making and administrative powers, proved very effective in rebuilding Galveston. By 1917 nearly 500 cities, including Houston, Oakland, Kansas City, Denver, and Buffalo, had adopted the commission form of government. Another approach, the city manager plan, gained popularity in small and midsized cities. In this system, a city council appointed a professional, nonpartisan city manager to handle the day-to-day operations of the community.

Progressive politicians who focused on the human problems of the industrial city championed a different kind of reform, one based on changing policies rather than the political structure. In Toledo, Samuel "Golden Rule" Jones served as mayor from 1897 to 1904. A capitalist who had made a fortune manufacturing oil well machinery, Jones created a strong base of working-class and ethnic voters around his reform program. He advocated municipal ownership of utilities, built new parks and schools, and established an eight-hour day and a minimum wage for city employees. In Cleveland, wealthy businessman Thomas L. Johnson served as mayor from 1901 to 1909. He emphasized both efficiency and social welfare. His popular program included lower streetcar fares, public baths, milk and meat inspection, and an expanded park and playground system.

Progressivism in the Statehouse: West and South

Their motives and achievements were mixed, but progressive politicians became a powerful force in many state capitals. In Wisconsin, Republican dissident Robert M. La Follette forged a coalition of angry farmers, small businessmen, and workers with his fiery attacks on railroads and other large corporations. Leader of the progressive faction of the state Republicans, "Fighting Bob" won three terms as governor (1900–06), then served as a U.S. senator until his death in 1925. As governor he pushed through tougher corporate tax rates, a direct primary, an improved civil service code, and a railroad commission designed to regulate freight charges. La Follette used faculty experts at the University of Wisconsin to help research and write his bills. Other states began copying the "Wisconsin Idea"—the application of academic scholarship and theory to the needs of the people.

La Follette railed against "the interests" and invoked the power of the ordinary citizen. In practice, however, his railroad commission accomplished far less than progressive rhetoric claimed. It essentially represented special interests—commercial farmers and businessmen seeking reduced shipping rates. Ordinary consumers did not see lower passenger fares or reduced food prices. And as commissioners began to realize, the national reach of the railroads limited the effectiveness of state regulation. Although La Follette championed a more open political system, he also enrolled state employees in a tight political machine of his own. The La Follette family would dominate Wisconsin politics for forty years.

Western progressives displayed the greatest enthusiasm for institutional political reform. In the early 1900s, Oregon voters approved a series of constitutional amendments designed to strengthen direct democracy. The two most important were the *initiative*, which allowed a direct vote on specific measures put on the state ballot by petition, and the *referendum*, which allowed voters to decide on bills referred to them by the legislature. Other reforms included the direct *primary*, which allowed voters to cross party lines, and the *recall*, which gave voters the right to remove elected officials by popular vote. Widely copied throughout the West, all these measures intentionally weakened political parties.

Western progressives also targeted railroads, mining and timber companies, and public utilities for reform. Large corporations such as Pacific Gas and Electric and the Southern Pacific Railroad had amassed enormous wealth and political influence. They were able to corrupt state legislatures and charge consumers exorbitant rates. An alliance between middle class progressives and working-class voters reflected growing disillusionment with the ideology of individualism that had helped pave the way for the rise of the big corporation. In California, attorney Hiram Johnson won a 1910 progressive campaign for governor on the slogan "Kick the Southern Pacific Railroad Out of Politics." In addition to winning political reforms, Johnson also put through laws regulating utilities and child labor, mandating an eight-hour day for working women, and providing a state-worker compensation plan.

In the South, the populist tradition of the 1880s and 1890s had been based in part on a biracial politics of protest. But southern progressivism was for white people only. Indeed, southern progressives believed that the disfranchisement of black voters and the creation of a legally segregated public sphere were necessary preconditions for political and social reform. Reform governors, such as James Vardaman of Mississippi and Hoke Smith of Georgia, made strident racism a key element in their campaigns against entrenched conservative Democratic machines. With African Americans removed from political life, white southern progressives argued, the direct primary system of nominating candidates would give white voters more influence. Between 1890 and 1910 southern states passed a welter of statutes specifying poll taxes, literacy tests, and property qualifications with the explicit goal of preventing voting by blacks. This systematic disfranchisement of African American voters stripped black communities of any political power. To prevent the disfranchisement of poor white voters under these laws, states established so-called understanding and grandfather clauses. Election officials had discretionary power to decide whether an illiterate person could understand and reasonably interpret the Constitution when read to him. Unqualified white men were also registered if they could show that their grandfathers had voted.

Southern progressives also supported the push toward a fully segregated public sphere. Between 1900 and 1910 southern states strengthened "Jim Crow" laws requiring separation of races in restaurants, streetcars, beaches, and theaters. Schools were separate but hardly equal. A 1916 Bureau of Education study found that per capita expenditures for education in southern states averaged $10.32 a year for white children and $2.89 for black children. And African American teachers received far lower salaries than their white counterparts. Black taxpayers, in effect, subsidized improved schools for whites, even as they saw their own children's educational opportunities deteriorate. The legacy of southern progressivism was thus closely linked to the strengthening of the legal and institutional guarantees of white supremacy.

Based mostly in New South towns and cities, and with growing strength among educated professionals, small businessmen, and women's benevolent societies, southern progressives organized to control both greedy corporations and "unruly" citizens. Citizens groups, city boards of trade, and newspapers pressed reluctant legislators to use state power to regulate big business. Between 1905 and 1909 nearly every southern state moved to regulate railroads by mandating lower passenger and freight rates. Prohibition enjoyed wide appeal in the South, as progressives active in the Anti-Saloon League argued that banning the alcohol trade would protect the family structure and victimized women, as well as reducing crime among African Americans. Employing aggressive lobbying, petitions, and massive parades, prohibition forces succeeded in pushing six southern states to ban the manufacture and sale of alcoholic beverages by 1909. Southern progressives also directed their energies at the related problems of child labor and educational reform. In 1900, at least one-quarter of all southern cotton mill workers were between the ages of ten and sixteen, many of whom worked over sixty hours per week. Led by reform minded ministers Edgar Gardner Murphy and Alexander McKelway, and drawing upon the activism of white club women, reformers attacked child labor by focusing on the welfare of children and their mothers and emphasizing the degradation of "Anglo Saxons." In 1903 Alabama and North Carolina enacted the first state child labor laws, setting twelve as a minimum age for employment. But the laws were weakened by many exemptions and no provisions for enforcement, as lawmakers also heard the loud complaints from parents and mill owners who resented the efforts of reformers to limit their choices. Progressives also mounted related state campaigns for compulsory education, as the South lagged behind the rest of the nation in literacy rates, school attendance, and overall spending. In 1906 the General Education Board, funded by John D. Rockefeller, Jr., began working with southern state boards of education and local officials to build high schools, lengthen the school year, and improve teachers' salaries. By 1920 only half as many southern children were illiterate as in 1900, and thousands of new school buildings had been constructed throughout the region.

New Journalism: Muckraking

Changes in journalism helped fuel a new reform consciousness by drawing the attention of millions to urban poverty, political corruption, the plight of industrial workers, and immoral business practices. As early as 1890, journalist Jacob Riis had shocked the nation with his landmark book *How the Other Half Lives*, a portrait of New York City's poor. A Danish immigrant who arrived in New York City in 1871, Riis became a newspaper reporter, covering the police beat and learning about the city's desperate underside. Riis's book included a remarkable series of photographs he had taken in tenements, lodging houses, sweatshops, and saloons. These striking pictures, combined with Riis's analysis of slum housing patterns, had a powerful impact on a whole generation of urban reformers.

Within a few years, magazine journalists had turned to uncovering the seamier side of American life. The key innovator was S. S. McClure, a young Midwestern editor who in 1893 started America's first large-circulation magazine, *McClure's*. Charging only a dime for his monthly, McClure effectively combined popular fiction with articles on science, technology, travel, and recent history. He attracted a new readership among the urban middle class through aggressive subscription and promotional campaigns, as well as newsstand sales. By the turn of the century *McClure's* and several imitators—*Munsey's*, *Cosmopolitan*, *Collier's*, *Everybody's*, and the *Saturday Evening Post*—had circulations in the hundreds of thousands. Making extensive use of photographs and illustrations, these cheap upstarts soon far surpassed older, more staid and expensive magazines such as the *Atlantic Monthly* and *Harper's* in circulation.

In 1902 McClure began hiring talented reporters to write detailed accounts of the nation's social problems. Lincoln Steffens's series *The Shame of the Cities* (1902) revealed the widespread graft at the center of American urban politics. He showed how big-city bosses routinely worked hand in glove with businessmen seeking lucrative municipal contracts for gas, water, electricity, and mass transit. Ida Tarbell, in her *History of the Standard Oil Company* (1904), thoroughly documented how John D. Rockefeller ruthlessly squeezed out competitors with unfair business practices. Ray Stannard Baker wrote detailed portraits of life and labor in Pennsylvania coal towns.

McClure's and other magazines discovered that "exposure journalism" paid off handsomely in terms of increased circulation. The middle-class public responded to this new combination of factual reporting and moral exhortation. A series such as Steffens's fueled reform campaigns that swept individual communities. Between 1902 and 1908, magazines were full of articles exposing insurance scandals, patent medicine frauds, and stock market swindles. Upton

This picture of Bohemian immigrant cigar makers at work in a New York City tenement first appeared in Jacob Riis's How the Other Half Lives (1890), a pathbreaking work of "exposure journalism." Apartments like these, owned and rented out by cigar manufacturers, served as both living quarters and workshops, leading to filthy and unhealthy conditions. Note how the entire family works together to roll as many cigars as possible.

SOURCE: Bohemian Cigar Makers at Work in Their Tenement, ca. 1890. Museum of the City of New York, The Jacob A. Riis Collection, (#147.90.13.1.150).

Sinclair's 1906 novel *The Jungle*, a socialist tract set among Chicago packinghouse workers, exposed the filthy sanitation and abysmal working conditions in the stockyards and the meatpacking industry. In an effort to boost sales, Sinclair's publisher devoted an entire issue of a monthly magazine it owned, *World's Work*, to articles and photographs that substantiated Sinclair's devastating portrait.

In 1906, David Graham Phillips, in a series for *Cosmopolitan* called "The Treason of the Senate," argued that many conservative U.S. senators were no more than mouthpieces for big business. President Theodore Roosevelt, upset by Phillips's attack on several of his friends and supporters, coined a new term when he angrily denounced Phillips and his colleagues as "muckrakers" who "raked the mud of society and never looked up." Partly due to Roosevelt's outburst, the muckraking vogue began to wane. By 1907, S. S. McClure's original team of reporters had broken up. But muckraking had demonstrated the powerful potential for mobilizing public opinion on a national scale. Reform campaigns need not be limited to the local community. Ultimately, they could engage a national community of informed citizens.

Intellectual Trends Promoting Reform

On a deeper level than muckraking, a host of early twentieth-century thinkers challenged several of the core ideas in American intellectual life. Their new theories of education, law, economics, and society provided effective tools for reformers. The emergent fields of the social sciences—sociology, psychology, anthropology, and economics—emphasized empirical observation of how people actually lived and behaved in their communities. Progressive reformers linked the systematic analysis of society and the individual characteristic of these new fields of inquiry to the project of improving the material conditions of American society. In doing so, they called on the academy for something it had never before been asked to provide—practical help in facing the unprecedented challenges of rapid industrialization and urbanization.

Sociologist Lester Frank Ward, in his pioneering work *Dynamic Sociology* (1883), offered an important critique of social Darwinism, the then orthodox theory that attributed social inequality to natural selection and the "survival of the fittest." Ward argued that the conservative social theorists responsible for social Darwinism, such as Herbert Spencer and William Graham Sumner, had wrongly applied evolutionary theory to human affairs. They had confused organic evolution with social evolution. Nature's method was genetic: unplanned, involuntary, automatic, and me-

chanical. An octopus had to lay 50,000 eggs to maintain itself; a codfish hatched a million young fish a year in order that two might survive. By contrast, civilization had been built on successful human intervention in the natural processes of organic evolution. The human method was telic: planned, voluntary, rational, dynamic. "Every implement or utensil," Ward argued, "every mechanical device, every object of design, skill, and labor, every artificial thing that serves a human purpose, is a triumph of mind over the physical forces of nature in ceaseless and aimless competition."

Philosopher John Dewey criticized the excessively rigid and formal approach to education found in most American schools. In books such as *The School and Society* (1899) and *Democracy and Education* (1916), Dewey advocated developing what he called "creative intelligence" in students, which could then be put to use in improving society. Schools ought to be "embryonic communities," miniatures of society, where children were encouraged to participate actively in different types of experiences. By cultivating imagination and openness to new experiences, schools could develop creativity and the habits required for systematic inquiry. Dewey placed excessive faith in the power of schools to promote community spirit and democratic values. But his belief that education was the "fundamental method of social progress and reform" inspired generations of progressive educators.

At the University of Wisconsin, John R. Commons founded the new field of industrial relations and organized a state industrial commission that became a model for other states. Working closely with Governor Robert M. La Follette, Commons and his students helped draft pioneering laws in worker compensation and public utility regulation. Another Wisconsin faculty member, economist Richard Ely, argued that the state was "an educational and ethical agency whose positive aim is an indispensable condition of human progress." Ely believed the state must directly intervene to help solve public problems. He rejected the doctrine of laissez faire as merely "a tool in the hands of the greedy." Like Commons, Ely worked with Wisconsin lawmakers, applying his expertise in economics to reforming the state's labor laws.

Progressive legal theorists began challenging the conservative view of constitutional law that had dominated American courts. Since the 1870s, the Supreme Court had interpreted the Fourteenth Amendment (1868) as a guarantee of broad rights for corporations. That amendment, which prevented states from depriving "any person of life, liberty, or property, without due process of law," had been designed to protect the civil rights of African Americans against violations by the states. But the Court, led by Justice Stephen J. Field, used the due process clause to strike down state laws regulating business and labor conditions. The Supreme Court and state courts had thus made the Fourteenth Amendment a bulwark for big business and a foe of social welfare measures.

The most important dissenter from this view was Oliver Wendell Holmes Jr. A scholar and Massachusetts judge, Holmes believed the law had to take into account changing social conditions. And courts should take care not to invalidate social legislation enacted democratically. After his appointment to the Supreme Court in 1902, Holmes authored a number of notable dissents to conservative court decisions overturning progressive legislation. Criticizing the majority opinion in *Lochner* v. *New York* (1905), in which the Court struck down a state law setting a ten-hour day for bakers, Holmes insisted that the Constitution "is not intended to embody a particular theory."

Holmes's pragmatic views of the law seldom convinced a majority of the Supreme Court before the late 1930s. But his views influenced a generation of lawyers who began practicing what came to be called sociological jurisprudence. In *Muller* v. *Oregon* (1908), the Court upheld an Oregon law limiting the maximum hours for working women, finding that the liberty of contract "is not absolute." Noting that "woman's physical structure and the performance of maternal functions place her at a disadvantage," the Court found that "the physical well-being of woman becomes an object of public interest and care." Louis Brandeis, the state's attorney, amassed statistical, sociological, and economic data, rather than traditional legal arguments, to support his arguments. The "Brandeis Brief" became a common strategy for lawyers defending the constitutionality of progressive legislation.

The new field of American sociology concentrated on the rapidly changing nature of community. German social theorist Ferdinand Tönnies developed an extremely influential model for describing the recent evolution of Western society from *Gemeinschaft* to *Gesellschaft*: from a static, close-knit, morally unified community to a dynamic, impersonal, morally fragmented society. If the new urban-industrial order had weakened traditional sources of morality and values—the family, the church, the small community—then where would the mass of people now learn these values?

This question provided the focus for Edward A. Ross's landmark work *Social Control* (1901), a book whose title became a key phrase in progressive thought. Ross argued that society needed an "ethical elite" of citizens "who have at heart the general welfare and know what kinds of conduct will promote this welfare." The "surplus moral energy" of this elite—ministers, educators, professionals—would have to guide the new mechanisms of social control needed in America's *Gesellschaft* communities.

SOCIAL CONTROL AND ITS LIMITS

Many middle- and upper-class Protestant progressives feared that immigrants and large cities threatened the stability of American democracy. They worried that alien cultural practices were disrupting what they viewed as traditional American morality. Viewing themselves as part of what sociologist Edward Ross called the "ethical elite," progressives often believed they had a mission to frame laws and regulations for the social control of immigrants, industrial workers, and African Americans. This was the moralistic and frequently xenophobic side of progressivism, and it provided a powerful source of support for the regulation of drinking, prostitution, leisure activities, and schooling. Organizations devoted to social control constituted other versions of reform communities. But these attempts at moral reform met with mixed success amid the extraordinary cultural and ethnic diversity of America's cities.

The more extreme proponents of these views also embraced the new pseudoscience of eugenics, based on the biological theories of the English scientist Francis Galton. Eugenicists stressed the primacy of inherited traits over environmental conditions for understanding human abilities and deficiencies. They argued that human society could be bettered only by breeding from the best stock and limiting the offspring of the worst. By the 1920s, these theories had gained enough influence to contribute to the drastic curtailing of immigration to America (see Chapter 23).

The Prohibition Movement

During the last two decades of the nineteenth century, the Woman's Christian Temperance Union had grown into a powerful mass organization. The WCTU appealed especially to women angered by men who used alcohol and then abused their wives and children. It directed most of its work toward ending the production, sale, and consumption of alcohol. But local WCTU chapters put their energy into nontemperance activities as well, including homeless shelters, Sunday schools, prison reform, child nurseries, and woman suffrage. The WCTU thus provided women with a political forum in which they could fuse their traditional moral posture as guardians of the home with broader public concerns. By 1911 the WCTU, with a quarter million members, was the largest women's organization in American history.

Other temperance groups had a narrower focus. The Anti-Saloon League, founded in 1893, began by organizing local-option campaigns in which rural counties and small towns banned liquor within their geographical limits. It drew much of its financial support from local businessmen, who saw a link between closing a community's saloons and increasing the productivity of workers. The league was a one-issue pressure group that played effectively on antiurban and antiimmigrant prejudice. League lobbyists targeted state legislatures, where big cities were usually underrepresented. They hammered away at the close connections among saloon culture, liquor dealers, brewers, and big city political machines.

The prohibition movement found its core strength among Protestant, native-born, small-town, and rural Americans. But prohibition found support as well in the cities, where the battle to ban alcohol revealed deep ethnic and cultural divides within America's urban communities. Opponents of alcohol were generally "pietists," who viewed the world from a position of moral absolutism. These included native-born, middle-class Protestants associated with evangelical churches along with some old-stock Protestant immigrant denominations. Opponents of prohibition were generally "ritualists" with less arbitrary notions of personal morality. These were largely new-stock, working-class Catholic and Jewish immigrants, along with some Protestants, such as German Lutherans.

The Social Evil

Many of the same reformers who battled the saloon and drinking also engaged in efforts to eradicate prostitution. Crusades against "the social evil" had appeared at intervals throughout the nineteenth century. But they reached a new level of intensity between 1895 and 1920. In part, this new sense of urgency stemmed from the sheer growth of cities and the greater visibility of prostitution in red-light districts and neighborhoods. Antiprostitution campaigns epitomized the diverse makeup and mixed motives of so much progressive reform. Male business and civic leaders joined forces with feminists, social workers, and clergy to eradicate "commercialized vice."

Between 1908 and 1914 exposés of the "white slave traffic" became a national sensation. Dozens of books, articles, and motion pictures alleged an international conspiracy to seduce and sell girls into prostitution. Most of these materials exaggerated the practices they attacked. They also made foreigners, especially Jews and southern Europeans, scapegoats for the sexual anxieties of native-born whites. In 1910 Congress passed legislation that permitted the deportation of foreign-born prostitutes or any foreigner convicted of procuring or employing them. That same year, the Mann Act made it a federal offense to transport women across state lines for "immoral purposes."

But most antiprostitution activity took place at the local level. Between 1910 and 1915, thirty-five cities and states conducted thorough investigations of prostitution. The progressive bent for defining social problems through statistics was nowhere more evident than in these reports. Vice commission investigators combed red-light districts, tenement houses, hotels, and dance halls, drawing up detailed lists of places where prostitution took place. They interviewed prostitutes, pimps, and customers. These reports agreed that commercialized sex was a business run by and for the profit and pleasure of men. They also documented the dangers of venereal disease to the larger community. The highly publicized vice reports were effective in forcing police crackdowns in urban red-light districts.

Reformers had trouble believing that any woman would freely choose to be a prostitute; such a choice was antithetical to conventional notions of female purity and sexuality. But for wage-earning women, prostitution was a rational choice in a world of limited opportunities. Maimie Pinzer, a prostitute, summed up her feelings in a letter to a wealthy female reformer: "I don't propose to get up at 6:30 to be at work at 8 and work in a close, stuffy room with people I despise, until dark, for $6 or $7 a week! When I could, just by phoning, spend an afternoon with some congenial person and in the end have more than a week's work could pay me." The antivice crusades succeeded in closing down many urban red-light districts and larger brothels, but these were replaced by the streetwalker and call girl, who were more vulnerable to harassment and control by policemen and pimps. Rather than eliminating prostitution, reform efforts transformed the organization of the sex trade.

The Redemption of Leisure

Progressives faced a thorny issue in the growing popularity of commercial entertainment. For large numbers of working-class adults and children, leisure meant time and money spent at vaudeville and burlesque theaters, amusement parks, dance halls, and motion picture houses. These competed with municipal parks, libraries, museums, YMCAs, and school recreation centers. For many cultural traditionalists, the flood of new urban commercial amusements posed a grave threat. As with prostitution, urban progressives sponsored a host of recreation and amusement surveys detailing the situation in their individual cities. "Commercialized leisure," warned Frederic C. Howe in 1914, "must be controlled by the community, if it is to become an agency of civilization rather than the reverse."

By 1908 movies had become the most popular form of cheap entertainment in America. One survey estimated that 11,500 movie theaters attracted 5 million patrons each day. For 5 or 10 cents "nickelodeon" theaters offered programs that might include a slapstick

Movies, by John Sloan, 1913, the most talented artist among the so-called Ashcan realist school of painting. Active in socialist and bohemian circles, Sloan served as art editor for *The Masses* magazine for several years. His work celebrated the vitality and diversity of urban working-class life and leisure, including the new commercial culture represented by the motion picture.

SOURCE: John Sloan, *Movies*, 1913. Oil painting. The Toledo Museum of Art.

comedy, a Western, a travelogue, and a melodrama. Early movies were most popular in the tenement and immigrant districts of big cities, and with children. As the films themselves became more sophisticated and as "movie palaces" began to replace cheap storefront theaters, the new medium attracted a large middle-class clientele as well.

Progressive reformers seized the chance to help regulate the new medium as a way of improving the commercial recreation of the urban poor. Movies held out the promise of an alternative to the older entertain-

ment traditions, such as concert saloons and burlesque theater, that had been closely allied with machine politics and the vice economy. In 1909, New York City movie producers and exhibitors joined with the reform-minded People's Institute to establish the voluntary National Board of Censorship (NBC). Movie entrepreneurs, most of whom were themselves immigrants, sought to shed the stigma of the slums, attract more middle-class patronage, and increase profits. A revolving group of civic activists reviewed new movies, passing them, suggesting changes, or condemning them. Local censoring committees all over the nation subscribed to the board's weekly bulletin. They aimed at achieving what John Collier of the NBC called "the redemption of leisure." By 1914 the NBC was reviewing 95 percent of the nation's film output.

Standardizing Education

Along with reading, writing, and mathematics, schools inculcated patriotism, piety, and respect for authority. Progressive educators looked to the public school primarily as an agent of "Americanization." Elwood Cubberley, a leading educational reformer, expressed the view that schools could be the vehicle by which immigrant children could break free of the parochial ethnic neighborhood. "Our task," he argued in *Changing Conceptions of Education* (1909), "is to break up these groups or settlements, to assimilate and amalgamate these people as a part of our American race, and to implant in their children, so far as can be done, the Anglo-Saxon conception of righteousness, law and order, and popular government."

The most important educational trends in these years were the expansion and bureaucratization of the nation's public school systems. In most cities, centralization served to consolidate the power of older urban elites who felt threatened by the large influx of immigrants. Children began school earlier and stayed there longer. Kindergartens spread rapidly in large cities. They presented, as one writer put it in 1903, "the earliest opportunity to catch the little Russian, the little Italian, the little German, Pole, Syrian, and the rest and begin to make good American citizens of them." By 1918 every state had some form of compulsory school attendance. High schools also multiplied, extending the school's influence beyond the traditional grammar school curriculum. In 1890 only 4 percent of the nation's youth between fourteen and seventeen were enrolled in school; by 1930 the figure was 47 percent.

High schools reflected a growing belief that schools be comprehensive, multifunctional institutions. In 1918 the National Education Association offered a report defining Cardinal Principles of Secondary Education. These included instruction in health, family life, citizenship, and ethical character. Academic programs prepared a small number of students for college. Vocational programs trained boys and girls for a niche in the new industrial order. Boys took shop courses in metal trades, carpentry, and machine tools. Girls learned typing, bookkeeping, sewing, cooking, and home economics. The Smith-Hughes Act of 1917 provided federal grants to support these programs and set up a Federal Board for Vocational Education.

Educational reformers also established national testing organizations such as the College Entrance Examination Board (founded in 1900) and helped standardize agencies for curriculum development and teacher training. In 1903, E. L. Thorndike published *Educational Psychology*, which laid the groundwork for education research based on experimental and statistical investigations. Progressives led in the development of specialized fields such as educational psychology, guidance counseling, and educational administration.

WORKING-CLASS COMMUNITIES AND PROTEST

The Industrial Revolution, which had begun transforming American life and labor in the nineteenth century, reached maturity in the early twentieth. In 1900, out of a total labor force of 28.5 million, 16 million people worked at industrial occupations and 11 million on farms. By 1920, in a labor force of nearly 42 million, almost 29 million were in industry, but farm labor had declined to 10.4 million. The world of the industrial worker included large manufacturing towns in New England; barren mining settlements in the West; primitive lumber and turpentine camps in the South; steelmaking and coal-mining cities in Pennsylvania and Ohio; and densely packed immigrant ghettos from New York to San Francisco, where workers toiled in garment trade sweatshops.

All these industrial workers shared the need to sell their labor for wages in order to survive. At the same time, differences in skill, ethnicity, and race proved powerful barriers to efforts at organizing trade unions that could bargain for improved wages and working conditions. So, too, did the economic and political power of the large corporations that dominated much of American industry. Yet there were also small, closely knit groups of skilled workers, such as printers and brewers, who exercised real control over their lives and labors. And these years saw many labor struggles that created effective trade unions or laid the groundwork for others. Industrial workers also became a force in local and national politics, adding a chorus of insistent voices to the calls for social justice.

New Immigrants from Two Hemispheres

On the eve of World War I, close to 60 percent of the industrial labor force was foreign-born. Most of these workers were among the roughly 9 million new immigrants from southern and eastern Europe who arrived in the United States between 1900 and 1914. In the nineteenth century, much of the overseas migration had come from the industrial districts of northern and western Europe. English, Welsh, and German artisans had brought with them skills critical for emerging

IMMIGRATION TO THE UNITED STATES (1901–1920)

Total: 14,532,000		% of Total
Italy	3,157,000	22%
Austria-Hungary	3,047,000	21
Russia and Poland	2,524,000	17
Canada	922,000	6
Great Britain	867,000	6
Scandinavia	709,000	5
Ireland	487,000	3
Germany	486,000	3
France and Low Countries (Belgium, Netherlands, Switz.)	361,000	2
Mexico	268,000	2
West Indies	231,000	2
Japan	213,000	2
China	41,000	*
Australia and New Zealand	23,000	*

*Less than 1% of total

SOURCE: U.S. Bureau of the Census, *Historical Statistics of the United States from Colonial Times to 1970*, Washington, DC, 1975.

industries such as steelmaking and coal mining. Unlike their predecessors, nearly all the new Italian, Polish, Hungarian, Jewish, and Greek immigrants lacked industrial skills. They thus entered the bottom ranks of factories, mines, mills, and sweatshops.

These new immigrants had been driven from their European farms and towns by several forces, including the undermining of subsistence farming by commercial agriculture; a falling death rate that brought a shortage of land; and religious and political persecution. American corporations also sent agents to recruit cheap labor. Except for Jewish immigrants, a majority of whom fled virulent anti-Semitism in Russia and Russian Poland, most newcomers planned on earning a stake and then returning home. Hard times in America forced many back to Europe. In the depression year of 1908, for example, more Austro-Hungarians and Italians left than entered the United States.

The decision to migrate usually occurred through social networks—people linked by kinship, personal acquaintance, and work experience. These "chains," extending from places of origin to specific destinations in the United States, helped migrants cope with the considerable risks entailed by the long and difficult journey. A study conducted by the U.S. Immigration Commission in 1909 found that about 60 percent of the new immigrants had their passage arranged by

In 1892 the federal government opened the immigration station on Ellis Island, located in New York City's harbor, where about 80 percent of the immigrants to the United States landed. As many as 5,000 passengers per day reported to federal immigration officers for questions about their background and for physical examinations, such as this eye exam. Only about 1 percent were quarantined or turned away for health problems.

SOURCE: Brown Brothers.

immigrants already in America. An Italian who joined his grandfather and cousins in Buffalo in 1906 recalled, "In western New York most of the first immigrants from Sicily went to Buffalo, so that, from 1900 on, the thousands who followed them to this part of the state also landed in Buffalo."

Immigrant communities used ethnicity as a collective resource for gaining employment in factories, mills, and mines. One Polish steelworker recalled how the process operated in the Pittsburgh mills: "Now if a Russian got his job in a shear department, he's looking for a buddy, a Russian buddy. He's not going to look for a Croatian buddy. And if he sees the boss looking for a man he says, 'Look, I have a good man,' and he's picking out his friends. A Ukrainian department, a Russian department, a Polish department. And it was a beautiful thing in a way." Such specialization of work by ethnic origin was quite common throughout America's industrial communities.

The low-paid, backbreaking work in basic industry became nearly the exclusive preserve of the new immigrants. In 1907, of the 14,359 common laborers employed at Pittsburgh's U.S. Steel mills, 11,694 were eastern Europeans. For twelve-hour days and seven-day weeks, two-thirds of these workers made less than $12.50 a week, one-third less than $10.00. This was far less than the $15.00 that the Pittsburgh Associated Charities had estimated as the minimum for providing necessities for a family of five. Small wonder that the new immigration was disproportionately male. One-third of the immigrant steelworkers were single, and among married men who had been in the country less than five years, about two-thirds reported that their wives were still in Europe. Workers with families generally supplemented their incomes by taking in single men as boarders.

Not all the new immigrants came from Europe, as hemispheric migration increased sharply as well. Over 300,000 French Canadians arrived in the U.S. between 1900 and 1930, settling mostly in New England. But the maturing continental railroad system had widened the choice of destinations to communities in upstate New York and Detroit, which had the largest number of French Canadian migrants outside New England. The pull of jobs in New England's textile industry, along with its physical proximity, attracted male farmers and laborers unable to make a living in the rural districts of Quebec. Roughly one-third of female migrants were domestic servants looking for the higher pay and greater independence associated with factory labor. The significant French Canadian presence in communities such as Lowell, Holyoke, Manchester, Nashua, and Waterville often made them the largest single ethnic group. By 1918, for example, one quarter of the Fall River, Massa-

chusetts, population of 28,000 was French Canadian. French language churches, newspapers, private schools, and mutual benefit societies reinforced the distinctive cultural milieu, and the presence of kin or fellow villagers facilitated the arrival of largely rural migrants into these new, highly industrialized, and urbanized settings. As Bruno Noury, a single eighteen-year-old farm laborer who emigrated from Quebec to Mainville, Rhode Island, recalled: "When I left, I wasn't sure whether it was temporary or to stay. I had two of my older brothers there, so I said, 'I'll do like them.' I wanted to try what they had done."

Mexican immigration also grew in these years, providing a critical source of labor for the West's farms, railroads, and mines. Between 1900 and 1914, the number of people of Mexican descent living and working in the United States tripled, from roughly 100,000 to 300,000. Economic and political crises spurred tens of thousands of Mexico's rural and urban poor to emigrate north. Large numbers of seasonal agricultural workers regularly came up from Mexico to work in the expanding sugar beet industry, and then returned. But a number of substantial resident Mexican communities also emerged in the early twentieth century.

Throughout Texas, California, New Mexico, Arizona, and Colorado, western cities developed *barrios*, distinct communities of Mexicans. Mexican immigrants attracted by jobs in the smelting industry made El Paso the most thoroughly Mexican city in the United States. In San Antonio, Mexicans worked at shelling pecans, becoming perhaps the most underpaid and exploited group of workers in the country. By 1910, San Antonio contained the largest number of Mexican immigrants of any city. In southern California, labor agents for railroads recruited Mexicans to work on building new interurban lines around Los Angeles. Overcrowding, poor sanitation, and deficient public services made many of these enclaves unhealthy places to live. Mexican barrios suffered much higher rates of disease and infant mortality than surrounding Anglo communities.

Between 1898 and 1907 more than 80,000 Japanese entered the United States. The vast majority were young men working as contract laborers in the West, mainly in California. American law prevented Japanese immigrants (the *Issei*) from obtaining American citizenship, because they were not white. This legal discrimination, along with informal exclusion from many occupations, forced the Japanese to create niches for themselves within local economies. Most Japanese settled near Los Angeles, where they established small communities centered around fishing, truck farming, and the flower and nursery business. In 1920 Japanese farmers produced 10 percent of the dollar volume of

California agriculture on 1 percent of the farm acreage. By 1930 over 35,000 Issei and their children (the *Nisei*) lived in Los Angeles.

Urban Ghettos

In large cities, new immigrant communities took the form of densely packed ghettos. By 1920, immigrants and their children constituted almost 60 percent of the population of cities over 100,000. They were an even larger percentage in major industrial centers such as Chicago, Pittsburgh, Philadelphia, and New York. The sheer size and dynamism of these cities made the immigrant experience more complex than in smaller cities and more isolated communities. Workers in the urban garment trades toiled for low wages and suffered layoffs, unemployment, and poor health. But conditions in the small, labor-intensive shops of the clothing industry differed significantly from those in the large-scale, capital-intensive industries like steel.

New York City had become the center of both Jewish immigration and America's huge ready-to-wear clothing industry. The city's Jewish population was 1.4 million in 1915, almost 30 percent of its inhabitants. New York produced 70 percent of all women's clothing and 40 percent of all men's clothing made in the country. In small factories, lofts, and tenement apartments some 200,000 people, most of them Jews, some of them Italians, worked in the clothing trades. Most of the industry operated on the grueling piece-rate, or task, system, in which manufacturers and subcontractors paid individuals or teams of workers to complete a certain quota of labor within a specific time.

The garment industry was highly seasonal. A typical work week was sixty hours, with seventy common during busy season. But there were long stretches of unemployment in slack times. Even skilled cutters, all men, earned an average of only $16 per week. Unskilled workers, nearly all of them young single women, made only $6 or $7 a week. Perhaps a quarter of the workforce, classified as "learners," earned only $3 to $6 a week. Often forced to work in cramped, dirty, and badly lit rooms, garment workers strained under a system in which time equaled money. Morris Rosenfeld, a presser of men's clothing who wrote Yiddish poetry, captured the feeling:

> *The tick of the clock is the boss in his anger*
> *The face of the clock has the eye of a foe*
> *The clock—I shudder—Dost hear how it draws me?*
> *It calls me "Machine" and it cries to me "Sew!"*

In November 1909 two New York garment manufacturers responded to strikes by unskilled women workers by hiring thugs and prostitutes to beat up pickets. The strikers won the support of the Women's Trade Union League, a group of sympathetic female reformers

that included Lillian Wald, Mary Dreier, and prominent society figures. At a dramatic mass meeting in Cooper Union Hall, Clara Lemlich, a teenage working girl speaking in Yiddish, made an emotional plea for a general strike. She called for everyone in the crowd to take an old Jewish oath: "If I turn traitor to the cause I now pledge, may this hand wither from the arm I now raise." The Uprising of the 20,000, as it became known, swept through the city's garment district.

The strikers demanded union recognition, better wages, and safer and more sanitary conditions. They drew support from thousands of suffragists, trade unionists, and sympathetic middle-class women as well. Hundreds of strikers were arrested, and many were beaten by police. After three cold months on the picket line, the strikers returned to work without union recognition. But the International Ladies Garment Workers Union (ILGWU), founded in 1900, did gain strength and negotiated contracts with some of the city's shirtwaist makers. The strike was an important breakthrough in the drive to organize unskilled workers into industrial unions. It opened the doors to women's involvement in the labor movement and created new leaders, such as Clara Lemlich, Pauline Newman, and Rose Schneiderman.

On March 25, 1911, the issues raised by the strike took on new urgency when a fire raced through three

New York City Police set up this makeshift morgue to help identify victims of the disastrous Triangle Shirtwaist Company fire, March 25, 1911. Unable to open the locked doors of the sweatshop and desperate to escape from smoke and flames, many of the 146 who died had leaped eight stories to their death.

SOURCE: UPI/CORBIS.

floors of the Triangle Shirtwaist Company. As the flames spread, workers found themselves trapped by exit doors that had been locked from the outside. Fire escapes were nonexistent. Within half an hour, 146 people, mostly young Jewish women, had been killed by smoke or had leaped to their death. In the bitter aftermath, women progressives led by Florence Kelley and Frances Perkins of the National Consumers' League joined with Tammany Hall leaders Al Smith, Robert Wagner, and Big Tim Sullivan to create a New York State Factory Investigation Commission. Under Perkins's vigorous leadership, the commission conducted an unprecedented round of public hearings and on-site inspections, leading to a series of state laws that dramatically improved safety conditions and limited the hours for working women and children.

Company Towns

Immigrant industrial workers and their families often established their communities in a company town, where a single large corporation was dominant. Cities such as Lawrence, Massachusetts; Gary, Indiana; and Butte, Montana, revolved around the industrial enterprises of Pacific Woolen, U.S. Steel, and Anaconda Copper. Workers had little or no influence over the economic and political institutions of these cities. In the more isolated company towns, residents often had no alternative but to buy their food, clothing, and supplies at company stores, usually for exorbitantly high prices. But they did maintain some community control in other ways. Family and kin networks, ethnic lodges, saloons, benefit societies, churches and synagogues, and musical groups affirmed traditional forms of community in a setting governed by individualism and private capital.

On the job, modern machinery and industrial discipline meant high rates of injury and death. In Gary, non–English speaking immigrant steelworkers suffered twice the accident rate of English-speaking employees, who could better understand safety instructions and warnings. A 1910 study of work accidents revealed that nearly a fourth of all new steelworkers were killed or injured each year. As one Polish worker described the immigrant's lot to his wife: "If he comes home sick then it is trouble, because everybody is looking only for money to get some of it, and during the sickness most will be spent." Mutual aid associations, organized around ethnic groups, offered some protection through cheap insurance and death benefits.

In steel and coal towns, women not only maintained the household and raised the children, they also boosted the family income by taking in boarders, sewing, and laundry. Many women also tended gardens and raised chickens, rabbits, and goats. Their produce and income helped reduce dependence on the company store.

Working-class women felt the burdens of housework more heavily than their middle-class sisters. Pump water, indoor plumbing, and sewage disposal were often available only on a pay-as-you-go basis. The daily drudgery endured by working-class women far outlasted the "man-killing" shift worked by the husband. Many women struggled with the effects of their husbands' excessive drinking and faced early widowhood.

The adjustment for immigrant workers was not so much a process of assimilation as adaptation and resistance. Efficiency experts, such as Frederick Taylor (see Chapter 19), carefully observed and analyzed the time and energy needed for each job, then set standard methods for each worker. In theory, these standards would increase efficiency and give managers more control over their workers. But work habits and Old World cultural traditions did not always mesh with factory discipline or Taylor's "scientific management." A Polish wedding celebration might last three or four days. A drinking bout following a Sunday funeral might cause workers to celebrate "St. Monday" and not show up for work. Employers made much of the few Slavs allowed to work their way up into the ranks of skilled workers and foremen. But most immigrants were far more concerned with job security than with upward mobility. The newcomers learned from more skilled and experienced British and American workers that "slowing down" or "soldiering" spread out the work. As new immigrants became less transient and more permanently settled in company towns, they increased their involvement in local politics and union activity.

The power of large corporations in the life of company towns was most evident among the mining communities of the West, as was violent labor conflict. The Colorado Fuel and Iron Company (CFI) employed roughly half of the 8,000 coal miners who labored in that state's mines. In mining towns such as Ludlow and Trinidad, the CFI thoroughly dominated the lives of miners and their families. "The miner," one union official observed, "is in this land owned by the corporation that owns the homes, that owns the boarding houses, that owns every single thing there is there . . . not only the mines, but all the grounds, all the buildings, all the places of recreation, as well as the school and church buildings." By the early twentieth century, new immigrants, such as Italians, Greeks, Slavs, and Mexicans, composed a majority of the population in these western mining communities. About one-fifth of CFI miners spoke no English.

In September 1913, the United Mine Workers led a strike in the Colorado coalfields, calling for improved safety, higher wages, and recognition of the union. Thousands of miners' families moved out of company housing and into makeshift tent colonies provided by the union. In October, Governor Elias Ammons ordered the Colorado National Guard into the tense strike region to keep order. The troops, supposedly neutral, proceeded to ally themselves with the mine operators. By spring the strike had bankrupt the state, forcing the governor to remove most of the troops. The coal companies then brought in large numbers of private mine guards who were extremely hostile toward the strikers. On April 20, 1914, a combination of guardsmen and private guards surrounded the largest of the tent colonies at Ludlow, where more than a thousand mine families lived. A shot rang out (each side accused the other of firing), and a pitched battle ensued that lasted until the poorly armed miners ran out of ammunition. At dusk, the troops burned the tent village to the ground, routing the families and killing fourteen, eleven of them children. Enraged strikers attacked mines throughout southern Colorado in an armed rebellion that lasted ten days, until President Woodrow Wilson ordered the U.S. Army into the region. News of the Ludlow Massacre shocked millions and aroused widespread protests and demonstrations against the policies of Colorado Fuel and Iron and its owner, John D. Rockefeller Jr.

The AFL: "Unions, Pure and Simple"

Following the depression of the 1890s, the American Federation of Labor (AFL) emerged as the strongest and most stable organization of workers. Samuel Gompers's strategy of recruiting skilled labor into unions organized by craft had paid off. Union membership climbed from under 500,000 in 1897 to 1.7 million by 1904. Most of this growth took place in AFL affiliates in coal mining, the building trades, transportation, and machine shops. The national unions—the United Mine Workers of America, the Brotherhood of Carpenters and Joiners, the International Association of Machinists—represented workers of specific occupations in collective bargaining. Trade autonomy and exclusive jurisdiction were the ruling principles within the AFL.

But the strength of craft organization also gave rise to weakness. In 1905 Gompers told a union gathering in Minneapolis that "caucasians" would not "let their standard of living be destroyed by negroes, Chinamen, Japs, or any others." Those "others" included the new immigrants from eastern and southern Europe, men and women, who labored in the steel mills and garment trades. Each trade looked mainly to the welfare of its own. Many explicitly barred women and African Americans from membership. There were some important exceptions. The United Mine Workers of America (UMWA) followed a more inclusive policy, recruiting both skilled underground pitmen and the unskilled aboveground workers. The UMWA even tried to recruit strikebreakers brought in by coal operators. With

260,000 members in 1904, the UMWA became the largest AFL affiliate.

AFL unions had a difficult time holding on to their gains. Economic slumps, technological changes, and aggressive counterattacks by employer organizations could be devastating. Trade associations using management-controlled efficiency drives fought union efforts to regulate output and shop practices. The National Association of Manufacturers (NAM), a group of smaller industrialists founded in 1903, launched an "open shop" campaign to eradicate unions altogether. "Open shop" was simply a new name for a workplace where unions were not allowed. The NAM supplied strikebreakers, private guards, and labor spies to employers. It also formed antiboycott associations to prevent unions in one trade from supporting walkouts in another.

Unfriendly judicial decisions also hurt organizing efforts. In 1906 a federal judge issued a permanent injunction against an iron molders strike at the Allis Chalmers Company of Milwaukee. In the so-called Danbury Hatters' Case (*Loewe* v. *Lawler*, 1908), a federal court ruled that secondary boycotts, aimed by strikers at other companies doing business with their employer, such as suppliers of materials, were illegal under the Sherman Antitrust Act. Long an effective labor tactic, secondary boycotts were now declared a conspiracy in restraint of trade. Not until the 1930s would unions be able to count on legal support for collective bargaining and the right to strike.

The IWW: "One Big Union"

Some workers developed more radical visions of labor organizing. In the harsh and isolated company towns of Idaho, Montana, and Colorado, miners suffered from low wages, poor food, and primitive sanitation, as well as injuries and death from frequent cave-ins and explosions. The Western Federation of Miners (WFM) had gained strength in the metal mining regions of the West by leading several strikes marred by violence. In 1899, during a strike in the silver mining district of Coeur d'Alene, Idaho, the Bunker Hill and Sullivan Mining Company had enraged the miners by hiring armed detectives and firing all union members. Desperate miners retaliated by destroying a company mill with dynamite. Idaho's governor declared martial law and obtained federal troops to enforce it. In a pattern that would become familiar in western labor relations, the soldiers served as strikebreakers, rounding up hundreds of miners and imprisoning them for months in makeshift bullpens.

In response to the brutal realities of labor organizing in the West, most WFM leaders embraced socialism and industrial unionism. In 1905, leaders of the WFM, the Socialist Party, and various radical groups gathered in Chicago to found the Industrial Workers of the World (IWW). The IWW charter proclaimed bluntly, "The working class and the employing class have nothing in common. . . . Between these two classes a struggle must go on until the workers of the world unite as a class, take possession of the earth and the machinery of production, and abolish the wage system."

William D. "Big Bill" Haywood, an imposing, one-eyed, hard-rock miner, emerged as the most influential and flamboyant spokesman for the IWW, or Wobblies, as they were called. Haywood, a charismatic speaker and effective organizer, regularly denounced the AFL for its conservative emphasis on organizing skilled workers by trade. He insisted that the IWW would exclude no one from its ranks. The Wobblies concentrated their efforts on miners, lumberjacks, sailors, "harvest stiffs," and other casual laborers. They glorified transient and unskilled workers in speeches and songs, aiming to counter their hopelessness and degradation. Openly contemptuous of bourgeois respectability, the IWW stressed the power of collective direct action on the job—strikes and, occasionally, sabotage.

The IWW briefly became a force among eastern industrial workers, tapping the rage and growing militance of the immigrants and unskilled. In 1909, an IWW-led steel strike at McKees Rocks, Pennsylvania, challenged the power of U.S. Steel. In the 1912 "Bread and Roses" strike in Lawrence, Massachusetts, IWW organizers turned a spontaneous walkout of textile workers into a successful struggle for union recognition. Wobbly leaders such as Haywood, Elizabeth Gurley Flynn, and Joseph Ettor used class-conscious rhetoric and multilingual appeals to forge unity among the ethnically diverse Lawrence workforce of 25,000.

These battles gained the IWW a great deal of sympathy from radical intellectuals, along with public scorn from the AFL and employers' groups. The IWW failed to establish permanent organizations in the eastern cities, but it remained a force in the lumber camps, mines, and wheat fields of the West. In spite of its militant rhetoric, the IWW concerned itself with practical gains. "The final aim is revolution," said one Wobbly organizer, "but for the present let's see if we can get a bed to sleep in, water enough to take a bath in and decent food to eat."

The occasional use of violence by union organizers sometimes backfired against the labor movement. On October 1, 1910, two explosions destroyed the printing plant of the *Los Angeles Times*, killing twenty-one workmen. When John and James McNamara, two brothers active in the ironworkers' union, were charged with the bombing and indicted for murder, unionists of all political persuasions rallied to their defense. Leaders of the AFL, IWW, and Socialist Party joined in a massive campaign that stressed the labor-

versus-capital aspects of the case. The *Los Angeles Times* and its influential owner Harrison Gray Otis, they noted, were strongly antiunion and had helped keep Los Angeles a largely nonunion city. Some even suggested that Otis himself, looking to give labor a black eye, was responsible for the bombs. On Labor Day 1911, as the trial approached, huge crowds in America's largest cities gathered to proclaim the McNamara brothers innocent. But they were guilty. In the middle of the trial, the McNamaras confessed to the dynamiting, shocking their many supporters. A Socialist candidate for mayor of Los Angeles, favored to win the election, was decisively defeated, and the city remained a nonunion stronghold.

Rebels In Bohemia

During the 1910s, a small but influential community of painters, journalists, poets, social workers, lawyers, and political activists coalesced in the New York City neighborhood of Greenwich Village. These cultural radicals, nearly all of middle-class background and hailing from provincial American towns, shared a deep sympathy toward the struggles of labor, a passion for modern art, and an openness to socialism and anarchism. "Village bohemians," especially the women among them, challenged the double standard of Victorian sexual morality, rejected traditional marriage and sex roles, advocated birth control, and experimented with homosexual relations. They became a powerful national symbol for rebellion and the merger of political and cultural radicalism.

The term "bohemian" referred to anyone who had artistic or intellectual aspirations and who lived with disregard for conventional rules of behavior. Other American cities, notably Chicago at the turn of the century, had supported bohemian communities. But the Village scene was unique, if fleeting. The neighborhood offered cheap rents, studio space, and good ethnic restaurants, and it was close to the exciting political and labor activism of Manhattan's Lower East Side. The worldview of the Village's bohemian community found expression in *The Masses*, a monthly magazine founded in 1911 by socialist critic Max Eastman, who was also its editor. "The broad purpose of *The Masses*," wrote John Reed, one of its leading writers, "is a social one—to everlastingly attack old systems, old morals, old prejudices—the whole weight of outworn thought that dead men have saddled upon us." Regular contributors included radical labor journalist Mary Heaton Vorse, artists John Sloan and George Bellows, and writers Floyd Dell and Sherwood Anderson.

At private parties and public events, the Village brought together a wide variety of men and women looking to combine politics, art, and support for the labor movement. Birth control activist Margaret Sanger found a sympathetic audience, as did IWW leader Big Bill Haywood. Journalist Walter Lippmann lectured on the new psychological theory of Sigmund Freud. Anarchist and feminist Emma Goldman wooed financial supporters for her magazine *Mother Earth.* Photographer Alfred Stieglitz welcomed artists to his gallery-studio "291."

For some, Greenwich Village offered a chance to experiment with sexual relationships or work arrangements. For others, it was an escape from small-town conformity or a haven for like-minded artists and activists. Yet the Village bohemians were united in their search for a new sense of community. Mary Heaton

Publicity poster for the 1913 pageant, organized by John Reed and other Greenwich Village radicals, supporting the cause of striking silk workers in Paterson, New Jersey. This poster drew on aesthetic styles associated with the Industrial Workers of the World, typically including a heroic, larger than life image of a factory laborer.

SOURCE: The original Paterson Pageant Program, on which this drawing appeared, is part of the collection of the American Labor Museum/Botto House National Landmark. The poster is a copy of the program cover.

Vorse expressed their deeply pessimistic conviction that modern American society could no longer satisfy the elemental needs of community. "This is our weakness," she wrote. "Our strength does not multiply in our daily lives. There is a creative force in people doing things together." Intellectuals and artists, as well as workers, feeling alienated from the rest of society, sought shelter in the collective life and close-knit social relations of the Village community.

The Paterson, New Jersey, silk workers' strike of 1913 provided the most memorable fusion of bohemian sensibility and radical activism. After hearing Haywood speak about the strike at Mabel Dodge's apartment, John Reed offered to organize a pageant on the strikers' behalf at Madison Square Garden. The idea was to publicize the strike to the world and also raise money. The Villagers helped write a script, designed sets and scenery, and took care of publicity. A huge crowd watched more than a thousand workers reenact the silk workers' strike, complete with picket line songs, a funeral, and speeches by IWW organizers.

The spectacular production was an artistic triumph. One critic described the pageant as "a new art form, a form in which the workers would present their own story without artifice or theatricality, and therefore with a new kind of dramatic power." But the pageant was also a financial disaster. The Village bohemia lasted only a few years, a flame snuffed out by the chill political winds accompanying America's entry into World War I. Yet for decades Greenwich Village remained a mecca for young men and women searching for alternatives to conventional ways of living.

WOMEN'S MOVEMENTS AND BLACK AWAKENING

Progressive era women were at the forefront of several reform campaigns, such as the settlement house movement, prohibition, suffrage, and birth control. Millions of others took an active role in new women's associations that combined self-help and social mission. These organizations gave women a place in public life, increased their influence in civic affairs, and nurtured a new generation of female leaders.

In fighting racial discrimination, African Americans had a more difficult task. As racism gained ground in the political and cultural spheres, black progressives fought defensively to prevent the rights they had secured during Reconstruction from being further undermined. Still, they managed to produce leaders, ideas, and organizations that would have a long-range impact on American race relations.

The New Woman

The settlement house movement discussed in the opening of this chapter was just one of the new avenues of opportunity that opened to progressive era women. A steady proliferation of women's organizations attracted growing numbers of educated, middle-class women in the early twentieth century. With more men working in offices, more children attending school, and family size declining, the middle-class home was emptier. At the same time, more middle-class women were graduating from high school and college. In 1900, only 7 percent of Americans went to high school, but 60 percent of those who graduated were women. Moreover, in 1870, only 1 percent of college-age Americans had attended college, about 20 percent of them women; by 1910 about 5 percent of college-age Americans attended college, but the proportion of women among them had doubled to 40 percent.

Single-sex clubs brought middle-class women into the public sphere by celebrating the distinctive strengths associated with women's culture: cooperation, uplift, service. The formation of the General Federation of Women's Clubs in 1890 brought together 200 local clubs representing 20,000 women. By 1900 the federation boasted 150,000 members, and by World War I it claimed to represent over a million women. The women's club movement combined an earlier focus on self-improvement and intellectual pursuits with newer benevolent efforts on behalf of working women and children. The Buffalo Union, for example, sponsored art lectures for housewives and classes in typing, stenography, and bookkeeping for young working women. It also maintained a library, set up a "noon rest" downtown where women could eat lunch, and ran a school for training domestics. In Chicago the Women's Club became a powerful ally for reformers, and club member Louise Bowen, a Hull House trustee, gave the settlement three-quarters of a million dollars.

For many middle-class women the club movement provided a new kind of female-centered community. As one member put it: "What college life is to the young woman, club life is to the woman of riper years, who amidst the responsibilities and cares of home life still wishes to keep abreast of the time, still longs for the companionship of those who, like herself, do not wish to cease to be students because they have left school." Club activity often led members to participate in other civic ventures, particularly "child-saving" reforms, such as child labor laws and mothers' pensions. Some took up the cause of working-class women, fighting for protective legislation and offering aid to trade unions. As wives and daughters of influential and well-off men in their communities, clubwomen had access to funds and could generate support for projects they undertook.

Other women's associations made even more explicit efforts to bridge class lines between middle-class homemakers and working-class women. The National Consumers' League (NCL), started in 1898 by Maud Nathan and Josephine Lowell, sponsored a "white label" campaign in which manufacturers who met safety and sanitary standards could put NCL labels on their food and clothing. Under the dynamic leadership of Florence Kelley, the NCL took an even more aggressive stance by publicizing labor abuses in department stores and lobbying for maximum-hour and minimum-wage laws in state legislatures. In its efforts to protect home and housewife, worker and consumer, the NCL embodied the ideal of "social housekeeping." "The home does not stop at the street door," said Marion Talbot, dean of women at the University of Chicago in 1911. "It is as wide as the world into which the individual steps forth."

Birth Control

The phrase "birth control," coined by Margaret Sanger around 1913, described her campaign to provide contraceptive information and devices for women. Sanger had seen her own mother die at age forty-nine after bearing eleven children. In 1910, Sanger was a thirty-year-old nurse and housewife living with her husband and three children in a New York City suburb. Excited by a socialist lecture she had attended, she convinced her husband to move to the city, where she threw herself into the bohemian milieu. She became an organizer for the IWW, and in 1912 she wrote a series of articles on female sexuality for a socialist newspaper.

When postal officials confiscated the paper for violating obscenity laws, Sanger left for Europe to learn more about contraception. She returned to New York determined to challenge the obscenity statutes with her own magazine, the *Woman Rebel.* Sanger's journal celebrated female autonomy, including the right to sexual expression and control over one's body. When she distributed her pamphlet *Family Limitation,* postal inspectors confiscated copies and she found herself facing forty-five years in prison. In October 1914 she fled to Europe again. In her absence, anarchist agitator Emma Goldman and many women in the Socialist Party took up the cause.

An older generation of feminists had advocated "voluntary motherhood," or the right to say no to a husband's sexual demands. The new birth control advocates embraced contraception as a way of advancing sexual freedom for middle-class women as well as responding to the misery of those working-class women who bore numerous children while living in poverty. Sanger returned to the United States in October 1915. After the government dropped the obscenity charges, she embarked on a national speaking tour. In 1916 she again defied the law by opening a birth control clinic in a working-class neighborhood in Brooklyn and offering birth control information without a physician present. Arrested and jailed, she gained more publicity for her crusade. Within a few years, birth control leagues and clinics could be found in every major city and most large towns in the country.

Racism and Accommodation

At the turn of the century, four-fifths of the nation's 10 million African Americans still lived in the South, where most eked out a living working in agriculture. In the cities, most blacks were relegated to menial jobs, but a small African American middle class of entrepreneurs and professionals gained a foothold by selling services and products to the black community. They all confronted a racism that was growing in both intensity and influence in American politics and culture. White racism came in many variants and had evolved significantly since slavery days. The more virulent strains, influenced by Darwin's evolutionary theory, held that blacks were a "degenerate" race, genetically predisposed to vice, crime, and disease and destined to lose the struggle for existence with whites. By portraying blacks as incapable of improvement, racial Darwinism justified a policy of repression and neglect toward African Americans.

Southern progressives articulated a more moderate racial philosophy. They also assumed the innate inferiority of blacks, but they believed that black progress was necessary to achieve the economic and political progress associated with a vision of the New South. Their solution to the "race problem" stressed paternalist uplift. Edgar Gardner Murphy, an Episcopal clergyman and leading Alabama progressive, held that African Americans need not be terrorized. The black man, Murphy asserted, "will accept in the white man's country the place assigned him by the white man, will do his work, not by stress of rivalry, but by genial cooperation with the white man's interests."

African Americans also endured a deeply racist popular culture that made hateful stereotypes of black people a normal feature of political debate and everyday life. Benjamin Tillman, a U.S. senator from South Carolina, denounced the African American as "a fiend, a wild beast, seeking whom he may devour." Thomas Dixon's popular novel *The Clansman* (1905) described the typical African American as "half child, half animal, the sport of impulse, whim, and conceit . . . a being who, left to his will, roams at night and sleeps in the day, whose speech knows no word of love, whose passions, once aroused, are as the fury of a tiger." In northern cities "coon songs," based on gross caricatures

of black life, were extremely popular in theaters and as sheet music. As in the antebellum minstrel shows, these songs reduced African Americans to creatures of pure appetite—for food, sex, alcohol, and violence. The minstrel tradition of white entertainers "blacking up"—using burnt cork makeup to pretend they were black—was still a widely accepted convention in American show business.

Amid this political and cultural climate, Booker T. Washington won recognition as the most influential black leader of the day. Born a slave in 1856, Washington was educated at Hampton Institute in Virginia, one of the first freedmen's schools devoted to industrial education. In 1881 he founded Tuskegee Institute, a black school in Alabama devoted to industrial and moral education. He became the leading spokesman for racial accommodation, urging blacks to focus on economic improvement and self-reliance, as opposed to political and civil rights. In an 1895 speech delivered at the Cotton States Exposition in Atlanta, Washington outlined the key themes of accommodationist philosophy. "Cast down your buckets where you are," Washington told black people, meaning they should focus on improving their vocational skills as industrial workers and farmers. "In all things that are purely social," he told attentive whites, "we can be as separate as the fingers, yet one as the hand in all things essential to mutual progress."

Washington's message won him the financial backing of leading white philanthropists and the respect of progressive whites. His widely read autobiography, *Up from Slavery* (1901), stands as a classic narrative of an American self-made man. Written with a shrewd eye toward cementing his support among white Americans, it stressed the importance of learning values such as frugality, cleanliness, and personal morality. But Washington also gained a large following among African Americans, especially those who aspired to business success. With the help of Andrew Carnegie he founded the National Negro Business League to preach the virtue of black business development in black communities.

Presidents Theodore Roosevelt and William Howard Taft consulted Washington on the few political patronage appointments given to African Americans. Washington also had a decisive influence on the flow of private funds to black schools in the South. Publicly he insisted that "agitation of questions of social equality is the extremest folly." But privately Washington also spent money and worked behind the scenes trying to halt disfranchisement and segregation. He offered secret financial support, for example, for court cases that challenged Louisiana's grandfather clause, the exclusion of blacks from Alabama juries, and railroad segregation in Tennessee and Georgia.

Racial Justice, the NAACP, Black Women's Activism

Washington's focus on economic self-help remained deeply influential in African American communities long after his death in 1915. But alternative black voices challenged his racial philosophy while he lived. In the early 1900s, scholar and activist W. E. B. Du Bois created a significant alternative to Washington's leadership. A product of the black middle class, Du Bois had been educated at Fisk University and Harvard, where in 1895 he became the first African American to receive a Ph.D. His book *The Philadelphia Negro* (1899) was a pioneering work of social science that refuted racist stereotypes by, for example, discussing black contributions to that city's political life and describing the wide range of black business activity. In *The Souls of Black Folk* (1903), Du Bois declared prophetically that "the problem of the twenti-

eth century is the problem of the color line." Through essays on black history, culture, education, and politics, Du Bois explored the concept of "double consciousness." Black people, he argued, would always feel the tension between an African heritage and their desire to assimilate as Americans.

Unlike Booker T. Washington, Du Bois did not fully accept the values of the dominant white society. He worried that "our material wants had developed much faster than our social and moral standards." *Souls* represented the first effort to embrace African American culture as a source of collective black strength and something worth preserving. Spiritual striving, rooted in black folklore, religion, music, and history, were just as important as industrial education.

Du Bois criticized Booker T. Washington's philosophy for its acceptance of "the alleged inferiority of the Negro." The black community, he argued, must fight for the right to vote, for civic equality, and for higher education for the "talented tenth" of their youth. In 1905 Du Bois and editor William Monroe Trotter brought together a group of educated black men to oppose Washington's conciliatory views. Discrimination they encountered in Buffalo, New York, prompted the men to move their meeting to Niagara Falls, Ontario. "Any discrimination based simply on race or color is barbarous," they declared. "Persistent manly agitation is the way to liberty." The Niagara movement protested legal segregation, the exclusion of blacks from labor unions, and the curtailment of voting and other civil rights.

The Niagara movement failed to generate much change. But in 1909 many of its members, led by Du Bois, attended a National Negro Conference held at the Henry Street Settlement in New York. The group included a number of white progressives sympathetic to the idea of challenging Washington's philosophy. A new, interracial organization emerged from this conference, the National Association for the Advancement of Colored People. Du Bois, the only black officer of the original NAACP, founded and edited the *Crisis*, the influential NAACP monthly journal. For the next several decades the NAACP would lead struggles to overturn legal and economic barriers to equal opportunity.

The disfranchisement of black voters in the South severely curtailed African American political influence. In response, African American women created new strategies to challenge white supremacy and improve life in their communities. As Sallie Mial, a North Carolina Baptist home missionary told her male brethren, "We have a peculiar work to do. We can go where you cannot afford to go." Founded in 1900, the Women's Convention of the National Baptist Convention, the largest black denomination in the United States, offered African American women a new public space to pursue reform work and "racial uplift." They organized

In July 1905, a group of African American leaders met in Niagara Falls, Ontario, to protest legal segregation and the denial of civil rights to the nation's black population. This portrait was taken against a studio backdrop of the falls. In 1909, the leader of the Niagara movement, W. E. B. Du Bois (second from right, middle row) founded and edited *The Crisis*, the influential monthly journal of the National Association for the Advancement of Colored People.

settlement houses and built playgrounds; they created day-care facilities and kindergartens; they campaigned for women's suffrage, temperance, and advances in public health. In effect, they transformed church missionary societies into quasi social service agencies. In close alliance with the Women's Convention, the National Association of Black Women's Clubs provided a secular umbrella for African American women's activism. Using the motto "Lifting as We Climb," the NACW by 1914 boasted 50,000 members in 1,000 clubs nationwide.

NATIONAL PROGRESSIVISM

The progressive impulse had begun at local levels and percolated up. Progressive forces in both major political parties pushed older, entrenched elements to take a more aggressive stance on the reform issues of the day. Both Republican Theodore Roosevelt and Democrat Woodrow Wilson laid claim to the progressive mantle during their presidencies—a good example of how on the national level progressivism animated many perspectives. In their pursuit of reform agendas, both significantly reshaped the office of the president. As progressivism moved to Washington, nationally organized interest groups and public opinion began to rival the influence of the old political parties in shaping the political landscape.

Theodore Roosevelt and Presidential Activism

The assassination of William McKinley in 1901 made forty-two-year-old Theodore Roosevelt the youngest man to ever hold the office of president. Born to a wealthy New York family in 1858, Roosevelt overcame a sickly childhood through strenuous physical exercise and rugged outdoor living. After graduating from Harvard he immediately threw himself into a career in the rough and tumble of New York politics. He won election to the state assembly, ran an unsuccessful campaign for mayor of New York, served as president of the New York City Board of Police Commissioners, and went to Washington as assistant secretary of the navy. During the Spanish-American War, he won national fame as leader of the Rough Rider regiment in Cuba. Upon his return, he was elected governor of New York and then in 1900 vice president. Roosevelt viewed the presidency as a "bully pulpit"—a platform from which he could exhort Americans to reform their society—and he aimed to make the most of it.

Roosevelt was a uniquely colorful figure, a shrewd publicist, and a creative politician. His three-year stint as a rancher in the Dakota Territory; his fondness for hunting and nature study; his passion for scholarship, which resulted in ten books before he became president—all these set "T. R." apart from most of his upper-class peers. Roosevelt preached the virtues of "the strenuous life," and he believed that educated and wealthy Americans had a special responsibility to serve, guide, and inspire those less fortunate.

In style, Roosevelt made key contributions to national progressivism. He knew how to inspire and guide public opinion. He stimulated discussion and aroused curiosity like no one before him. In 1902 Roosevelt demonstrated his unique style of activism when he personally intervened in a bitter strike by anthracite coal miners. Using public calls for conciliation, a series of White House bargaining sessions, and private pressure on the mine owners, Roosevelt secured a settlement that won better pay and working conditions for the miners, but without recognition of their union. Roosevelt also pushed for efficient government as the solution to social problems. Unlike most nineteenth-century Republicans, who had largely ignored economic and social inequalities, Roosevelt frankly acknowledged them. Administrative agencies run by experts, he believed, could find rational solutions that could satisfy everyone.

Trustbusting and Regulation

One of the first issues Roosevelt faced was growing public concern with the rapid business consolidations taking place in the American economy. In 1902 he directed the Justice Department to begin a series of prosecutions under the Sherman Antitrust Act. The first target was the Northern Securities Company, a huge merger of transcontinental railroads brought about by financier J. P. Morgan. The deal would have created a giant holding company controlling nearly all the long-distance rail lines from Chicago to California. The Justice Department fought the case all the way through a hearing before the Supreme Court. In *Northern Securities* v. *United States* (1904), the Court held that the stock transactions constituted an illegal combination in restraint of interstate commerce.

This case established Roosevelt's reputation as a "trustbuster." During his two terms, the Justice Department filed forty-three cases under the Sherman Antitrust Act to restrain or dissolve business monopolies. These included actions against the so-called tobacco and beef trusts and the Standard Oil Company. Roosevelt viewed these suits as necessary to publicize the issue and assert the federal government's ultimate authority over big business. But he did not really believe in the need to break up large corporations. Unlike many progressives, who were nostalgic for smaller companies and freer competition, Roosevelt accepted centralization as a fact of modern economic life.

Roosevelt considered government regulation the best way to deal with big business. After easily defeating Democrat Alton B. Parker in the 1904 election, Roosevelt felt more secure in pushing for regulatory legislation. In 1906 Roosevelt responded to public pressure for greater government intervention and, overcoming objections from a conservative Congress, signed three important measures into law. The Hepburn Act strengthened the Interstate Commerce Commission (ICC), established in 1887 as the first independent regulatory agency, by authorizing it to set maximum railroad rates and inspect financial records.

Two other laws passed in 1906 also expanded the regulatory power of the federal government. The battles surrounding these reforms demonstrate how progressive measures often attracted supporters with competing motives. The Pure Food and Drug Act established the Food and Drug Administration (FDA), which tested and approved drugs before they went on the market. The Meat Inspection Act empowered the Department of Agriculture to inspect and label meat products. In both cases, supporters hailed the new laws as providing consumer protection against adulterated or fraudulently labeled food and drugs. Sensational exposés by muckrakers, documenting the greed, corruption, and unhealthy practices in the meatpacking and patent medicine industries, contributed to public support for the measures. Upton Sinclair's best-selling novel *The Jungle*, depicting the horrible conditions in Chicago's packinghouses, was the most sensational and influential of these.

But regulatory legislation found advocates among American big business as well. Large meatpackers such as Swift and Armour strongly supported stricter federal regulation as a way to drive out smaller companies that could not meet tougher standards. The new laws also helped American packers compete more profitably in the European export market by giving their meat the official seal of federal inspectors. Large pharmaceutical manufacturers similarly supported new regulations that would eliminate competitors and patent medicine suppliers. Thus these reforms won support from large corporate interests that viewed stronger federal regulation as a strategy for consolidating their economic power. Progressive era expansion of the nation-state had its champions among—and benefits for—big business as well as American consumers.

Conservation, Preservation, and the Environment

As a naturalist and outdoorsman, Theodore Roosevelt also believed in the need for government regulation of the natural environment. He worried about the destruction of forests, prairies, streams, and the wilderness. The conservation of forest and water resources, he argued, was a national problem of vital import. In 1905 he created the U.S. Forest Service and named conservationist Gifford Pinchot to head it. Pinchot recruited a force of forest rangers to manage the reserves. By 1909 total timber and forest reserves had increased from 45 to 195 million acres, and more than 80 million acres of mineral lands had been withdrawn from public sale. Roosevelt also sponsored a National Conservation Commission, which produced the first comprehensive study of the nation's mineral, water, forest, and soil resources.

On the broad issue of managing America's natural resources, the Roosevelt administration took the middle ground between preservation and unrestricted commercial development. Pinchot established the basic pattern of federal regulation based on a philosophy of what he called the "wise use" of forest reserves. "Wilderness is waste," Pinchot was fond of saying, reflecting an essentially utilitarian vision that balanced the demands of business with wilderness conservation. But other voices championed a more radical vision of conservation, emphasizing the preservation of wilderness lands against the encroachment of commercial exploitation.

The most influential and committed of these was John Muir, an essayist and founder of the modern environmentalist movement. Muir made a passionate and spiritual defense of the inherent value of the American wilderness. Wild country, he argued, had a mystical power to inspire and refresh. "Climb the mountains and get their good tidings," he advised. "Nature's peace will flow into you as the sunshine into the trees. The winds will blow their freshness into you, and the storms their energy, while cares will drop off like autumn leaves."

Muir had been a driving force behind the Yosemite Act of 1890. Yosemite Park, located in a valley amid California's majestic Sierra Nevada range, became the nation's first preserve consciously designed to protect wilderness. Muir served as first president of the Sierra Club, founded in 1892 to preserve and protect the mountain regions of the west coast as well as Yellowstone National Park in Wyoming, Montana, and Idaho. Muir was a tireless publicist, and his writings won wide popularity among Americans, who were increasingly drawn to explore and enjoy the outdoors. By the turn of the century, misgivings about the effects of "overcivilization" and the association of untamed lands with the nation's frontier and pioneer past had attracted many to his thinking.

A bitter, drawn-out struggle over new water sources for San Francisco revealed the deep conflicts between conservationists, represented by Pinchot, and preservationists, represented by Muir. After a devastating earthquake in 1906, San Francisco sought federal approval to

William Hahn, *Yosemite Valley from Glacier Point* (1874). Congress established Yosemite as a national park in 1890. Paintings like this one, along with contemporary photographs, helped convince Congress of the uniqueness of Yosemite's natural beauty.

SOURCE: William Hahn (1829–1887), *Yosemite Valley from Glacier Point*, 1874, 271/4″ × 461/4″. California Historical Society, gift of Albert M. Bender.

dam and flood the spectacular Hetch Hetchy Valley, located 150 miles from the city in Yosemite National Park. The project promised to ease the city's chronic freshwater shortage and to generate hydroelectric power. Conservationists and their urban progressive allies argued that developing Hetch Hetchy would be a victory for the public good over greedy private developers, since the plan called for municipal control of the water supply. To John Muir and the Sierra Club, Hetch Hetchy was a "temple" threatened with destruction by the "devotees of ravaging commercialism."

Both sides lobbied furiously in Congress and wrote scores of articles in newspapers and magazines. Congress finally approved the reservoir plan in 1913; utility and public development triumphed over the preservation of nature. Although they lost the battle for Hetch Hetchy, the preservationists gained much ground in the larger campaign of alerting the nation to the dangers of a vanishing wilderness. A disappointed John Muir took some consolation from the fact that "the conscience of the whole country has been aroused from sleep." Defenders of national parks now realized that they could not make their case simply on scenic merit alone. They began to use their own utilitarian rationales, arguing that national parks would encourage economic growth through tourism and provide Americans with a healthy escape from urban and industrial areas. In 1916 the preservationists obtained their own bureaucracy in Washington with the creation of the National Park Service.

The Newlands Reclamation Act of 1902 represented another important victory for the conservation strategy of Roosevelt and Pinchot. With the goal of turning arid land into productive family farms through irrigation, the act established the Reclamation Bureau within the Department of the Interior and provided federal funding for dam and canal projects. But in practice, the bureau did more to encourage the growth of large-scale agribusiness and western cities than small farming. The Roosevelt Dam on Arizona's Salt River, along with the forty-mile Arizona Canal, helped develop the Phoenix area. The Imperial Dam on the Colorado River diverted water to California's Imperial and Coachella Valleys. The bureau soon became a key player in western life and politics, with large federally funded water projects providing flood control and the generation of electricity, as well as water for irrigation. The Newlands Act thus established a growing federal presence in managing water resources, the critical issue in twentieth-century western development.

Republican Split

When he won reelection in 1904, Roosevelt proclaimed his support for a "Square Deal" for all people. He was still essentially a conservative who supported progressive reform as the best way to head off the potential of class war. By the end of his second term, Roosevelt had moved beyond the idea of regulation to push for the most far-reaching federal economic and social programs ever proposed. He saw the central problem as "how to exercise . . . responsible control over the business use of vast wealth." To that end, he proposed restrictions on the use of court injunctions against labor strikes, as well as an eight-hour day for federal employees, a worker compensation law, and federal income and inheritance taxes.

In 1908, Roosevelt kept his promise to retire after a second term. He chose Secretary of War William Howard Taft as his successor. Taft easily defeated Democrat William Jennings Bryan in the 1908 election. During Taft's presidency, the gulf between "insurgent" progressives and the "stand pat" wing split the Republican Party wide open. To some degree, the battles were as much over style as substance. Compared with Roosevelt, the reflective and judicious Taft brought a much more restrained concept of the presidency to the White House. He supported some progressive measures, including the constitutional amendment legalizing a graduated income tax (ratified in 1913), safety codes for mines and railroads, and the creation of a federal Children's Bureau (1912). But in a series of bitter political fights involving tariff, antitrust, and conservation policies, Taft alienated Roosevelt and many other progressives.

After returning from an African safari and a triumphant European tour in 1910, Roosevelt threw himself back into national politics. He directly challenged Taft for the Republican Party leadership. In a dozen bitter state presidential primaries (the first ever held), Taft and Roosevelt fought for the nomination. Although Roosevelt won most of these contests, the old guard still controlled the national convention and renominated Taft in June 1912. Roosevelt's supporters stormed out, and in August the new Progressive Party nominated Roosevelt and Hiram Johnson of California as its presidential ticket. Roosevelt's "New Nationalism" presented a vision of a strong federal government, led by an activist president, regulating and protecting the various interests in American society. The platform called for woman suffrage, the eight-hour day, prohibition of child labor, minimum-wage standards for working women, and stricter regulation of large corporations.

The Election of 1912: A Four-Way Race

With the Republicans so badly divided, the Democrats sensed a chance for their first presidential victory in twenty years. They chose Governor Woodrow Wilson

This political cartoon, drawn by Charles Jay Budd, appeared on the cover of *Harper's Weekly*, September 28, 1912. It employed the imagery of autumn county fairs to depict voters as unhappy with their three choices for president. Note that the artist did not include the fourth candidate, Socialist Eugene V. Debs, who was often ignored by more conservative publications such as *Harper's*.

SOURCE: Theodore Roosevelt Collection, Harvard College Library.

of New Jersey as their candidate. Although not nearly as well known nationally as Taft and Roosevelt, Wilson had built a strong reputation as a reformer. The son of a Virginia Presbyterian minister, Wilson spent most of his early career in academia. He studied law at the University of Virginia and then earned a Ph.D. in political science from Johns Hopkins. After teaching history and political science at several schools, he became president of Princeton University in 1902. In 1910, he won election as New Jersey's governor, running against the state Democratic machine. He won the Democratic nomination for president with the support of many of the party's progressives, including William Jennings Bryan.

Wilson declared himself and the Democratic Party to be the true progressives. Viewing Roosevelt rather than Taft as his main rival, Wilson contrasted his New Freedom campaign with Roosevelt's New Nationalism.

Crafted largely by progressive lawyer Louis Brandeis, Wilson's platform was far more ambiguous than Roosevelt's. The New Freedom emphasized restoring conditions of free competition and equality of economic opportunity. Wilson did favor a variety of progressive reforms for workers, farmers, and consumers. But in sounding older, nineteenth-century Democratic themes of states' rights and small government, Wilson argued against allowing the federal government to become as large and paternalistic as Roosevelt advocated. "What this country needs above everything else," Wilson argued, "is a body of laws which will look after the men who are on the make rather than the men who are already made."

Socialist party nominee Eugene V. Debs offered the fourth and most radical choice to voters. The Socialists had more than doubled their membership since 1908, to more than 100,000. On election days Socialist strength was far greater than that, as the party's candidates attracted increasing numbers of voters. By 1912 more than a thousand Socialists held elective office in thirty-three states and 160 cities. Geographically, Socialist strength had shifted to the trans-Mississippi South and West.

Debs had been a national figure in American politics since the 1890s, and he had already run for president three times. An inspiring orator who drew large and sympathetic crowds wherever he spoke, Debs proved especially popular in areas with strong labor movements and populist traditions. He wrapped his socialist message in an apocalyptic vision. Socialists would "abolish this monstrous system and the misery and crime which flow from it." His movement would "tear up all privilege by the roots, and consecrate the earth and all its fullness to the joy and service of all humanity." Debs and the Socialists also took credit for pushing both Roosevelt and Wilson further toward the left. Both the Democratic and Progressive Party platforms contained proposals that had been considered extremely radical only ten years earlier.

In the end, the divisions in the Republican Party gave the election to Wilson. He won easily, polling 6.3 million votes to Roosevelt's 4.1 million. Taft came in third with 3.5 million. Eugene Debs won 900,000 votes, 6 percent of the total, for the strongest Socialist showing in American history. Even though he won with only 42 percent of the popular vote, Wilson swept the electoral college with 435 votes to Roosevelt's 88 and Taft's 8, giving him the largest electoral majority up to that time. In several respects, the election of 1912 was the first "modern" presidential race. It featured the first direct primaries, challenges to traditional party loyalties, an issue-oriented campaign, and a high degree of interest group activity.

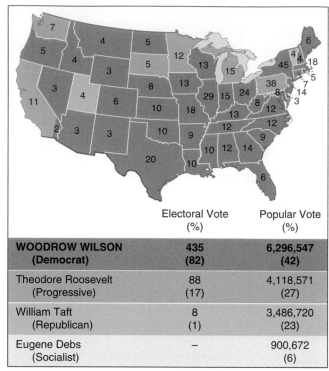

	Electoral Vote (%)	Popular Vote (%)
WOODROW WILSON (Democrat)	**435 (82)**	**6,296,547 (42)**
Theodore Roosevelt (Progressive)	88 (17)	4,118,571 (27)
William Taft (Republican)	8 (1)	3,486,720 (23)
Eugene Debs (Socialist)	–	900,672 (6)

The Election of 1912 The split within the Republican Party allowed Woodrow Wilson to become only the second Democrat since the Civil War to be elected president. Eugene Debs's vote was the highest ever polled by a Socialist candidate.

Woodrow Wilson's First Term

As president, Wilson followed Roosevelt's lead in expanding the activist dimensions of the office. He became more responsive to pressure for a greater federal role in regulating business and the economy. This increase in direct lobbying—from hundreds of local and national reform groups, Washington-based organizations, and the new Progressive Party—was itself a new and defining feature of the era's political life. With the help of a Democratic-controlled Congress, Wilson pushed through a significant battery of reform proposals. By 1916 his reform program looked more like the New Nationalism that Theodore Roosevelt had run on in 1912 than Wilson's own New Freedom platform. Four legislative achievements in Wilson's first term stand out.

The Underwood-Simmons Act of 1913 substantially reduced tariff duties on a variety of raw materials and manufactured goods, including wool, sugar, agricultural machinery, shoes, iron, and steel. Taking advantage of the newly ratified Sixteenth Amendment, which gave Congress the power to levy taxes on income, it also imposed the first graduated tax (up to 6 percent) on personal incomes. The Federal Reserve Act that same year restructured the nation's banking and currency system. It created twelve Federal Reserve Banks, regulated by a central board in Washington. Member banks were required to keep a portion of their cash reserves in the Federal Reserve Bank of their district. By raising or lowering the percentage of reserves required, "the Fed" could either discourage or encourage credit expansion by member banks. Varying the interest rate charged on loans and advances by federal reserve banks to member banks also helped regulate both the quantity and cost of money circulating in the national economy. By giving central direction to banking and monetary policy, the Federal Reserve Board diminished the power of large private banks.

Wilson also supported the Clayton Antitrust Act of 1914, which replaced the old Sherman Act of 1890 as the nation's basic antitrust law. The Clayton Act reflected the growing political clout of the American Federation of Labor. It exempted unions from being construed as illegal combinations in restraint of trade, and it forbade federal courts from issuing injunctions against strikers. But Wilson adopted the view that permanent federal regulation was necessary for checking the abuses of big business. The Federal Trade Commission (FTC), established in 1914, sought to give the federal government the same sort of regulatory control over corporations that the ICC had over railroads. Wilson believed a permanent federal body like the FTC would provide a method for corporate oversight superior to the erratic and time-consuming process of legal trustbusting. Wilson's hope that the FTC would usher in an era of harmony between government and business recalled the aims of Roosevelt and his big business backers in 1912.

On social issues, Wilson proved more cautious in his first two years. His initial failure to support federal child labor legislation and rural credits to farmers angered many progressives. A Southerner, Wilson also sanctioned the spread of racial segregation in federal offices. "I would say," he explained in 1913, "that I do approve of the segregation that is being attempted in several of the departments." As the reelection campaign of 1916 approached, Wilson worried about defections from the labor and social justice wings of his party. He proceeded to support a rural credits act providing government capital to federal farm banks, as well as federal aid to agricultural extension programs in schools. He also came out in favor of a worker compensation bill for federal employees, and he signed the landmark Keating-Owen Act, which banned children under fourteen from working in enterprises engaged in interstate commerce. Although it covered less than 10 percent of the nation's 2 million working children, the new law established a minimum standard of protection and put the power of federal authority behind the prin-

ciple of regulating child labor. But by 1916 the dark cloud of war in Europe had already begun to cast its long shadow over progressive reform.

CONCLUSION

The American political and social landscape was significantly altered by progressivism, but these shifts reflected the tensions and ambiguities of progressivism itself. A review of changes in election laws offers a good perspective on the inconsistencies that characterized progressivism. Nearly every new election law had the effect of excluding some people from voting while including others. For African Americans, progressivism largely meant disfranchisement from voting altogether. Direct primary laws eliminated some of the most blatant abuses of big-city machines, but in cities and states dominated by one party, the majority party's primary effectively decided the general election. Stricter election laws made it more difficult for third parties to get on the ballot, another instance in which progressive reform had the effect of reducing political options available to voters. Voting itself steadily declined in these years.

Overall, party voting became a less important form of political participation. Interest group activity, congressional and statehouse lobbying, and direct appeals to public opinion gained currency as ways of influencing government. Business groups such as the National Association of Manufacturers and individual trade associations were among the most active groups pressing their demands on government. Political action often shifted from legislatures to the new administrative agencies and commissions created to deal with social and economic problems. Popular magazines and journals grew significantly in both number and circulation, becoming more influential in shaping and appealing to national public opinion.

Social progressives and their allies could point to significant improvements in the everyday lives of ordinary Americans. On the state level, real advances had been made through a range of social legislation covering working conditions, child labor, minimum wages, and worker compensation. Social progressives, too, had discovered the power of organizing into extraparty lobbying groups such as the National Consumers' League and the National American Woman Suffrage Association. Yet the tensions between fighting for social justice and the urge toward social control remained unresolved. The emphasis on efficiency, uplift, and rational administration often collided with humane impulses to aid the poor, the immigrant, the slum dweller. The

CHRONOLOGY

1889	Jane Addams founds Hull House in Chicago
1890	Jacob Riis, *How the Other Half Lives*
1895	Booker T. Washington addresses Cotton States Exposition in Atlanta
	Lillian Wald establishes Henry Street Settlement in New York
1898	Florence Kelley becomes general secretary of the new National Consumers' League
1900	Robert M. La Follette elected governor of Wisconsin
1901	Theodore Roosevelt succeeds the assassinated William McKinley as president
1904	Lincoln Steffens publishes *The Shame of the Cities*
1905	President Roosevelt creates U.S. Forest Service
	Industrial Workers of the World is founded in Chicago
1906	Upton Sinclair, *The Jungle*
	Congress establishes Food and Drug Administration
1908	In *Muller v. Oregon* the Supreme Court upholds a state law limiting maximum hours for working women
1909	Uprising of 20,000 garment workers in New York City's garment industries
	National Association for the Advancement of Colored People (NAACP) is founded
1911	Triangle Shirtwaist Company fire kills 146 garment workers in New York City
	Socialist critic Max Eastman begins publishing *The Masses*
1912	Democrat Woodrow Wilson wins presidency
	Bread and Roses strike involves 25,000 textile workers in Lawrence, Massachusetts
	Margaret Sanger begins writing and speaking in support of birth control for women
1913	Sixteenth Amendment, legalizing a graduated income tax, is ratified
1914	Clayton Antitrust Act exempts unions from being construed as illegal combinations in restraint of trade
	Federal Trade Commission is established
	Ludlow Massacre occurs
1916	National Park Service is established

large majority of African Americans, blue-collar workers, and urban poor remained untouched by federal assistance programs.

Progressives had tried to confront the new realities of urban and industrial society. What had begun as a discrete collection of local and state struggles had by 1912 come to reshape state and national politics. Politics itself had been transformed by the calls for social justice. Federal and state power would now play a more decisive role than ever in shaping work, play, and social life in local communities. That there was so much contention over the "true meaning" of progressivism is but one measure of its defining role in shaping early twentieth-century America.

REVIEW QUESTIONS

1. Discuss the tensions within progressivism between the ideals of social justice and the urge for social control.
2. To what extent did progressives redefine the role of the state in American politics?
3. What gains were made by working-class communities in the progressive era? What barriers did they face?
4. How did the era's new immigration reshape America's cities and workplaces?
5. Analyze the progressive era from the perspective of African Americans. What political and social developments were most crucial, and what legacies did they leave?
6. Evaluate the lasting impact of progressive reform. How do the goals, methods, and language of progressives still find voice in contemporary America?

RECOMMENDED READING

Robert M. Crunden, *Ministers of Reform: The Progressives' Achievement in American Civilization, 1889–1920* (1982).
Alan Dawley, *Struggles for Justice: Social Responsibility and the Liberal State* (1991).
Susan A. Glenn, *Daughters of the Shtetl: Life and Labor in the Immigrant Generation* (1990).
Dewey Grantham, *Southern Progressivism: The Reconciliation of Progress and Tradition* (1982).

Morton Keller, *Regulating A New Society: Public Policy and Social Change in America, 1900–1930* (1994).

Arthur Link and Richard L. McCormick, *Progressivism* (1983).

Daniel T. Rodgers, *Atlantic Crossings: Social Politics in A Progressive Age* (1998).

Elizabeth Sanders, *Roots of Reform. Farmers, Workers, and the American State, 1877–1917* (1999).

Kathryn Kish Sklar, *Florence Kelley and the Nation's Work* (1995).

Christine Stansell, *American Moderns: Bohemian New York and the Creation of A New Century* (2000).

▶ MEDIA RESOURCES

U.S. HISTORY DOCUMENTS CD-ROM

New South, Expanding West

17-11 W. E. B. Du Bois, from "Of Mr. Booker T. Washington and Others" (1903)

Industrializing America

18-11 Lincoln Steffens, from The Shame of the Cities (1904)

18-12 Etiquette for the Upper Classes (1919)

18-13 Scientific Management   (1919)

Immigrant and Urban Nation

19-7 Adna Weber, The Growth of Cities in the Nineteenth Century (1899)

19-8 Lee Chew, Life of a Chinese Immigrant (1903)

19-9 Lincoln Steffens, from The Shame of the Cities (1904)

19-10 William T. Riordon, from Plunkitt of Tammany Hall (1905)

19-11 John Spargo, from The Bitter Cry of Children (1906)

19-12 Mary Antin, The Promised Land (1912)

The Progressive Era

21-3 Eugene v. Debs, "The Outlook for Socialism in the United States" (1900)

21-4 Platform Adopted by the National Negro Committee (1909)

21-5 James H. Patten, Chairman of the National Legislative Committee of the American Purity Federation, Testimony Before Congress (1910)

21-6 Jane Addams, Twenty Years at Hull House (1910)

21-7 Theodore Roosevelt, from The New Nationalism (1910)

21-8 Walker Percy, "Birmingham under the Commission Plan" (1911)

21-9 Helen M. Todd, "Getting Out the Vote" (1911)

21-10 Louis Brandeis, Other People's Money and How the Bankers Use It (1913)

21-11 Woodrow Wilson, from The New Freedom (1913)

21-12 Herbert Croly, Progressive Democracy (1914)

COMPANION WEBSITE HIGHLIGHTS

To view an exploration, enter one of the URLs below in your browser.

Additional Interactive Maps

To access the map, go to this chapter's resources at http://www.prenhall.com/faragher

Immigration to the United States, 1901–1920, page 644

The Election of 1912, page 658

HISTORY RESOURCE CENTER

To find the resources listed below, go to http://www.prenhall.com/historyresourcecenter

Documents

Caroline Manning, The Immigrant Woman and Her Job (1930)

Charles Loring Brace, "Life of the Street Rats" (1872)

Charlotte Perkins Gilman, "If I Were a Man" (1914)

Edward Bellamy, from Looking Backward (1888)

George Waring, Sanitary Conditions in N.Y. (1897)

Interstate Commerce Act (1887)

Lee Chew, Life of a Chinese Immigrant (1903)

Letters from The Great Migration (1917)

Mark Twain, from The Gilded Age (1873)

Proposal to Buffalo, N.Y., Park Commission (1888)

Richard K. Fox, from Coney Island Frolics (1883)

Suit by the United States Against the Workingman's Amalgamated Council of New Orleans (1893)

The Omaha Platform of the Populist Party (1892)

Theodore Roosevelt, Message to Congress (1903)

William Jennings Bryan, Cross of Gold Speech (1896)

Jane Addams, "Ballot Necessary for Women" (1906)

National American Woman Suffrage Association, Mother's Day Letter (1912)

Images

"The Life of A Fireman"

"The Role of Immigrants in America"

A tenement room, 1900

Brooklyn Bridge

Chemistry Lab at the Tuskegee Institute

Chicago Steelworks

Chinese Americans in San Francisco, 1897

(Continued)

(Continued)

EXPLORING AMERICA

HETCH HETCHY

http://www.prenhall.com/faragher/hetchhetchy

How did the Louisiana Purchase and the Mexican War affect the settlement of western lands? Why did the conservation movement emerge in the late 1800s? What divided conservation advocates John Muir and Gifford Pinchot? What was Hetch Hetchy and why did it create such a controversy? *Hetch Hetchy* examines the importance of the conservation movement in the United States and also illuminates the differences that existed between conservationists over strategies on how to best protect the environment. The module uses a tight narrative, photographs, a painting, and a variety of other resources to examine this early chapter in the history of the conservation movement.

Hetch Hetchy uses several methods to examine the issue of land use and environmental conservation. It explains the historical conditions that placed the federal government at the center of the controversy. Visual images, including a painting by artist Alfred Bierstedt, illustrate the unique, natural beauty of the Hetch Hetchy valley, while and a magazine and congressional testimony discuss the opposing viewpoints on conservation. The sources and the narrative related the twist and turns of the public debate over Hetch Hetchy while the interactive map and the chronology place the incident in perspective of time and space.

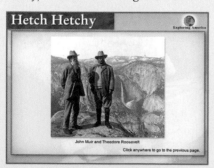

Reflect and Respond

1. Does it make sense to you that Pinchot should insist on an amendment to the Raker Bill to protect trees, even dead and fallen trees?

2. Could his arguments have been used by Muir to apply to the Hetch Hetchy Valley?

3. Does Muir's argument that "everybody needs beauty as well as bread, places to play in and pray in, where Nature may heal and cheer and give strength to body and soul" apply to Hetch Hetchy given its virtual inaccessibility?

4. Secretary Lane conceded that his sense of beauty might differ from that of others. Might a dam actually add beauty to a landscape, as he suggested it would in the case of Hetch Hetchy?

✓ Check it out

The Establishment of National Parks and Forests

This map traces the establishment of national parks and forests in the United States, showing that this movement is a post–Civil War phenomenon and that it has a definite regional bias. The map illustrates that the conservation movement goal of preserving the natural environment has remained a priority in recent decades.

This exploration is also available on the *Exploring America* CD-ROM.

▶ Battle for the Lower East Side

When Lillian Wald opened the doors of the Henry Street Settlement House in 1893, the surrounding Lower East Side of New York was the poorest and most polyglot neighborhood in the city, as well as the most overcrowded quarter in the world. Settlement house workers dedicated themselves to helping recent immigrants and the working poor cope with lives scarred by poverty, disease, poor food, and dank tenements. Henry Street Settlement offered a variety of programs, including a free visiting nurse service, advice on cooking and child rearing, art classes, a theater, and a music school. Wald and other settlement house leaders soon saw that, in order to improve the miserable conditions they observed in their communities, they needed to get involved in larger political struggles to improve sanitation, health care, housing, and education. Henry Street Settlement often made common cause in these battles with some of the other political activists who flourished in the Lower East Side community, including socialists, anarchists, trade unionists, woman suffragists, socially conscious artists, and public health reformers.

Over most of the twentieth century the character of the Lower East Side remained fairly stable, though its dominant ethnic groups changed. By the 1950s the Italian, German, and Eastern European Jewish immigrants had largely moved away, while Puerto Ricans, Ukranians, and Asians poured in. But regardless of ethnicity, the neighborhood was still one of the city's poorest, and decent affordable housing remained difficult to get. Tens of thousands of poor working class people still lived in old, dilapidated nineteenth century tenements. The neighborhood's historic reputation as a center for political and cultural radicalism also attracted newcomers. Many Beat poets and jazz musicians settled there in the 1950s, and during the 1960s and 1970s the area became a magnet for hippies, rock bands, and young runaways. Local concert halls like the Fillmore East and C.B.G.B.'s, cheap ethnic restaurants, funky clothing shops, and a flourishing drug culture also made the area something of a tourist attraction for young people from around the country and the world. Tompkins Square, a ten-acre park that provided the only swatch of green in the neighborhood, became a popular rallying point for antiVietnam War protest, the Black Panther Party, and other political causes.

But by the late 1980s two new groups appeared on the scene and their presence sparked tense debate over

Uniformed young women, part of the Visiting Nurse Service founded by Lillian Wald, leave the Henry Street Settlement for their rounds among tenement families of New York's Lower East Side. By the early 1900s the service was sending scores of trained nurses on tens of thousands of visits every year to provide health care for the poor. SOURCE: ©Bettman/CORBIS.

the historical legacy of the Lower East Side. Hundreds of homeless people began living in Tompkins Square Park, and hundreds of "squatters" occupied abandoned buildings in the surrounding blocks. The area's homeless represent only a small fraction of New York's total, estimated to be in the tens of thousands. At the same time, a wave of young urban professionals arrived, attracted by the downtown Manhattan location and old apartments newly renovated by real estate developers. Young couples expecting to enjoy the grassy park were afraid to walk near the grungy shantytown that had sprung up. "We've had an ongoing battle," said the Rev. George Kuhn of nearby St. Brigid's Church, "between the people who believe they are going to be displaced here and the people who are moving into the area." A loose coalition of neighborhood squatters, young radicals, artists, and punk rockers took up the cause of the homeless, defending their right to live in the park and attacking the influx of "yuppies." These protesters invoked the Lower East Side's historic traditions of tolerance and sympathy for the down and out. In the summer of 1988 the city announced it would enforce a 1 a.m. curfew in Tompkins Square Park, setting the stage for a violent confrontation. On August 7 over 400 riot equipped police swept through the park, forcibly removing the homeless colony, and clashing with hundreds of demonstrators. Throughout the night, angry protesters hurled bottles, fireworks, and insults as squads of policemen on horseback charged into crowds on nearby streets.

In the bitter aftermath of the riot, deep disagreements over the meaning of the neighborhood's history emerged. "We've always had a fairly diverse, progressive tradition," said Barbara Ingram who ran Children's Liberation daycare center and expressed support for the homeless. "It's something that everyone has tried to protect, because this community *is* different. In this neighborhood, people try to show concern for one another." Tom Calley, a 24-year-old artist and self-described anarchist, thought "this trouble in the park has been great. It's been a rallying point for people who once fought, like blacks and whites." "We can't ignore this problem any longer," argued another young political organizer. "The homeless shouldn't have been carted off, and a lot of activists are going to be demonstrating here this summer." But Maryann Williams, who with her husband and young daughter had just moved to the neighborhood, spoke for many newcomers: "I sympathize with the homeless. I consider myself pro-homeless. But people don't have a right to live in the park. Isn't it supposed to be for everyone? Or am I crazy?" Some, like the neighborhood's City Councilman Antonio Pagan, denounced the protesters for "living out their revolutionary fantasies. They are white, middle class young people from the suburbs hiding behind the banner of helping the homeless." He noted that "poor and working people have not had access to that park," and he asked, "why should a poor, working class neighborhood serve as the burning torch of homelessness for the city of New York?" Edgy conflict continued for years. The city closed the park for renovations in 1991, once again removing hundreds of homeless. Mass evictions of squatters also continued, as did raucous, sometimes violent protests against these police actions.

Henry Street Settlement celebrated its centennial anniversary in 1993 with a giant street festival and parade. Its current community service programs include a battered women's shelter, a day-care facility, art education, and feeding the homeless. Like Lillian Wald and other settlement house pioneers, today's advocates for the poor insist on connecting their plight to policies made far away from the neighborhood. "The community is overwhelmed by the terrible problems of homelessness and drug abuse," declared the Lower East Side Planning Council, a coalition of churches and synagogues. "The lack of affordable housing is the major reason for this situation." Gentrification has meant skyrocketing rents for apartment dwellers and small businesses. A recent survey showed more than half the area's families pay over 30% of their income for housing, and two-thirds reported their apartments had some vital malfunction—no heat, hot water, or electricity. Grinding poverty remains a grim fact of life for much of the Lower East Side, where the median family income is only one-third the city average. The 1997 Broadway musical "Rent" became a smash hit by glamorizing the Lower East Side's roiling world of poverty, struggling artists, yuppie ambition, and escalating housing costs. But as one late 90s protester and longtime resident ironically noted, "Now, for the first time in the Lower East Side's history, the poor can't afford to live here." ■

 www.researchnavigator.com

The Community and Memory essay for this chapter deals with changing demographics of New York's Lower East Side. For further research on the history of this neighborhood, use the tools available to you in Research Navigator.

As you investigate this topic, consider this question: "Why did the Lower East Side serve as a center for political and cultural radicalism for so long?"

ContentSelect: Search in the History and Sociology databases using the search term *immigration history*.

Links Library: Access the History: U.S. History database and explore the links for *new left movement* and *progressive era*.

New York Times on the Web: To find more about the fight for control of the Lower East Side, use the search term *Lower East Side homeless*.

THE PAST

TWENTY-TWO

WORLD WAR I

▶ 1914–1920

Dodge Macknight (American, 1860–1950), *Flags, Mills Street,* 1918. Watercolor, 60.32 × 42.71 cm (23¾ × 16¹³/₁₆″).
Bequest of Mrs. Stephen S. Fitzgerald. SOURCE: Museum of Fine Arts, Boston. Reproduced with permission. © 2000
Museum of Fine Arts, Boston. All Rights Reserved (64.1907).

Vigilante Justice in Bisbee, Arizona

EARLY IN THE MORNING OF JULY 12, 1917, 2,000 ARMED VIGILANTES swept through Bisbee, Arizona, acting on behalf of the Phelps-Dodge mining company and Bisbee's leading businessmen to break a bitter strike that had crippled Bisbee's booming copper industry. The vigilantes seized miners in their homes, on the street, and in restaurants and stores. Any miner who wasn't working or willing to work was herded into Bisbee's downtown plaza, where two machine guns commanded the scene. From the Plaza more than 2,000 were marched to the local baseball park. There, mine managers gave them a last chance to return to work. Hundreds accepted and were released. The remaining 1,400 were forced at gunpoint onto a freight train, which took them 173 miles east to Columbus, New Mexico, where they were dumped in the desert.

The Bisbee deportation occurred against a complex backdrop. America had just entered World War I, corporations were seeking higher profits, and labor militancy was on the rise. Bisbee was only one of many American communities to suffer vigilantism during the war. Any number of offenses—not displaying a flag, failing to buy war bonds, criticizing the draft, alleged spying, any apparently "disloyal" behavior—could trigger vigilante action. In western communities like Bisbee, vigilantes used the superpatriotic mood to settle scores with labor organizers and radicals.

Arizona was the leading producer of copper in the United States. With a population of 8,000, Bisbee lay in the heart of the state's richest mining district. The giant Phelps-Dodge Company dominated Bisbee's political and social life. It owned the town's hospital, department store, newspaper, library, and largest hotel. With the introduction of new technology and open pit mining after 1900, unskilled laborers—most of them Slavic, Italian, Czech, and Mexican immigrants—had increasingly replaced skilled American and English-born miners in Bisbee's workforce.

America's entry into the war pushed the price of copper to an all-time high, prompting Phelps-Dodge to increase production. Miners viewed the increased demand for labor as an opportunity to flex their own muscle and improve wages and working conditions. Two rival union locals, one affiliated with the American Federation of Labor (AFL), the other with the more radical Industrial Workers of the World (IWW), or "Wobblies," sought to organize Bisbee's workers. On June 26, 1917, Bisbee's Wobblies went on strike. They demanded better mine safety, an end to discrimination against union workers, and a substantial pay increase. The IWW, making special efforts to attract lower-paid, foreign-born workers to their cause, even hired two Mexican organizers. Although the IWW had only 300 or 400 members in Bisbee, more than half the town's 4,700 miners supported the strike.

The walkout was peaceful, but Walter Douglas, district manager for Phelps-Dodge, was unmoved. "There will be no compromise," he declared, "because you cannot compromise with a rattlesnake." Douglas, Cochise County Sheriff Harry Wheeler, and Bisbee's leading businessmen met secretly to plan the July 12 deportation. The approximately 2,000 men they deputized to carry it out were members of Bisbee's Citizens' Protective League and the Workers Loyalty League. These vigilantes included company officials, small businessmen, professionals, and antiunion workers. Local telephone and telegraph offices agreed to isolate Bisbee by censoring outgoing messages. The El Paso and Southwestern Railroad, a subsidiary of Phelps-Dodge, provided the waiting boxcars.

The participants in this illegal conspiracy defended themselves by exaggerating the threat of organized labor. They also appealed to patriotism and played on racial fears. The IWW opposed American involvement in the war, making it vulnerable to charges of disloyalty. A proclamation, posted in Bisbee the day of the deportation, claimed, "There is no labor trouble—we are sure of that—but a direct attempt to embarrass and injure the government of the United States." Sheriff Wheeler told a visiting journalist he worried that Mexicans "would take advantage of the disturbed conditions of the strike and start an uprising, destroying the mines and murdering American women and children."

An army census of the deportees, who had found temporary refuge at an army camp in Columbus, New Mexico, offered quite a different picture. Of the 1,400 men, 520 owned property in Bisbee. Nearly 500 had already registered for the draft, and more than 200 had purchased Liberty Bonds. More than 400 were married with children; only 400 were members of the IWW. Eighty percent were immigrants, including nearly 400 Mexicans. A presidential mediation committee concluded that "conditions in Bisbee were in fact peaceful and free from manifestations of disorder or violence." The deported miners nonetheless found it difficult to shake the accusations that their strike was anti-American and foreign inspired.

At their camp, the miners organized their own police force and elected an executive committee to seek relief. In a letter to President Wilson, they claimed "Common American citizens here are now convinced that they have no constitutional rights." They promised to return to digging copper if the federal government operated the

nation's mines and smelters. IWW leader William D. "Big Bill" Haywood threatened a general strike of metal miners and harvest workers if the government did not return the deportees to their homes. The presidential mediation committee criticized the mine companies and declared the deportation illegal. But it also denied that the federal government had any jurisdiction in the matter. Arizona's attorney general refused to offer protection for a return to Bisbee.

In September, the men began gradually to drift away from Columbus. Only a few ever returned to Bisbee. The events convinced President Wilson that the IWW was a subversive organization and a threat to national security. The Justice Department began planning an all-out legal assault that would soon cripple the Wobblies. But Wilson could not ignore protests against the Bisbee outrage from such prominent and patriotic Americans as Samuel Gompers, head of the American Federation of Labor. To demonstrate his administration's commitment to harmonious industrial relations, the president appointed a special commission to investigate and mediate wartime labor conflicts. But Arizona's mines would remain union free until the New Deal era of the 1930s.

America's entry into the war created a national sense of purpose and an unprecedented mobilization of resources. Unifying the country and winning the war now took precedence over progressive reforms. The war also aroused powerful political emotions and provided an excuse for some citizens to try to cleanse their communities of anyone who did not conform. In a 1918 speech, Arizona State Senator Fred Sutter hailed the benefits of vigilante justice. "And what are the results in Bisbee since the deportation?" he asked. "They are, sir, a practically 100 percent American camp; a foreigner to get a job there today had to give a pretty good account of himself. The mines are today producing more copper than ever before and we are a quiet, peaceful, law-abiding community and will continue so, so long as the IWWs or other enemies of the government let us alone." ■

Bisbee

KEY TOPICS

- America's expanding international role

- From neutrality to participation in the Great War

- Mobilizing the society and the economy for war

- Dissent and its repression

- Woodrow Wilson's failure to win the peace

BECOMING A WORLD POWER

In the first years of the new century the United States pursued a more vigorous and aggressive foreign policy than it had in the past. Presidents Theodore Roosevelt, William Howard Taft, and Woodrow Wilson all contributed to "progressive diplomacy," in which commercial expansion was backed by a growing military presence in the Caribbean, Asia, and Mexico. This policy reflected a view of world affairs that stressed moralism, order, and a special, even God-given, role for the United States. By 1917, when the United States entered the Great War, this policy had already secured the country a place as a new world power.

Roosevelt: The Big Stick

Theodore Roosevelt left a strong imprint on the nation's foreign policy. Like many of his class and background, "T.R." took for granted the superiority of Protestant Anglo-American culture and the goal of spreading its values and influence. He believed that to maintain and increase its economic and political stature, America must be militarily strong. In 1900 Roosevelt summarized his activist views, declaring, "I have always been fond of the West African proverb, 'Speak softly and carry a big stick, you will go far.'"

Roosevelt brought the "big stick" approach to several disputes in the Caribbean region. Since the 1880s, several British, French, and American companies had pursued various plans for building a canal across the Isthmus of Panama, thereby connecting the Atlantic and Pacific Oceans. The canal was a top priority for Roosevelt, and he tried to negotiate a leasing agreement with Colombia, of which Panama was a province. But when the Colombian Senate rejected a final American offer in the fall of 1903, Roosevelt invented a new strategy. A combination of native forces and foreign promoters associated with the canal project plotted a revolt against Colombia. Roosevelt kept in touch with at least one leader of the revolt, Philippe Bunau-Varilla, an engineer and agent for the New Panama Canal Company, and the president let him know that U.S. warships were steaming toward Panama.

On November 3, 1903, just as the USS *Nashville* arrived in Colón harbor, the province of Panama declared itself independent of Colombia. The United States immediately recognized the new Republic of Panama. Less than two weeks later, Bunau-Varilla, serving as a minister from Panama, signed a treaty granting the United States full sovereignty in perpetuity over a ten-mile-wide canal zone. America guaranteed Panama's independence and agreed to pay it $10 million initially and an additional $250,000 a year for the canal zone. Years after the canal was completed, the U.S. Senate voted another $25 million to Colombia as compensation.

The Panama Canal was a triumph of modern engineering and gave the United States a tremendous strategic and commercial advantage in the Western Hemisphere. It took eight years to build and cost hundreds of poorly paid manual workers their lives. Several earlier attempts to build a canal in the region had failed. But with better equipment and a vigorous campaign against disease, the United States succeeded. In 1914, after $720 million in construction costs, the first merchant ships sailed through the canal.

"The inevitable effect of our building the Canal," wrote Secretary of State Elihu Root in 1905, "must be to require us to police the surrounding premises." Roosevelt agreed. He was especially concerned that European powers might step in if America did not. In 1903 Great Britain, Germany, and Italy had imposed a blockade on Venezuela in a dispute over debt payments owed to private investors. To prevent armed intervention by the Europeans, Roosevelt in 1904 proclaimed what became known as the Roosevelt Corollary to the Monroe Doctrine. "Chronic wrongdoing, or an impotence which results in a general loosening of the ties of civilized society," the statement read, justified "the exercise

THE WORLD'S CONSTABLE.

This 1905 cartoon portraying President Theodore Roosevelt, "The World's Constable," appeared in *Judge* magazine. In depicting the president as a strong but benevolent policeman bringing order in a contentious world, the artist Louis Dalrymple drew on familiar imagery from Roosevelt's earlier days as a New York City police commissioner.

SOURCE: The Granger Collection (4E218.07).

of an international police power" anywhere in the hemisphere. Roosevelt invoked the corollary to justify U.S. intervention in the region, beginning with the Dominican Republic in 1905. To counter the protests of European creditors (and the implied threat of armed intervention), Washington assumed management of the Dominican debt and customs services. Roosevelt and later presidents cited the corollary to justify armed intervention in the internal affairs of Cuba, Haiti, Nicaragua, and Mexico.

American diplomacy in Asia reflected the Open Door policy formulated by Secretary of State John Hay in 1899. Japan and the western European powers had carved key areas of China into spheres of influence, in which individual nations enjoyed economic dominance. The United States was a relative latecomer to the potentially lucrative China market, and Hay sought guarantees of equal opportunity for its commercial interests there. In a series of diplomatic notes, Hay won approval for the so-called Open Door approach, giving all nations equal access to trading and development rights in China. The outbreak of war between Japan and Russia in 1905 threatened this policy. Roosevelt worried that a total victory by Russia or Japan could upset the balance of power in East Asia and threaten American business enterprises there. He became especially concerned after the Japanese scored a series of military victories over Russia and began to loom as a dominant power in East Asia.

Roosevelt mediated a settlement of the Russo-Japanese War at Portsmouth, New Hampshire, in 1905 (for which he was awarded the 1906 Nobel Peace Prize). In this settlement, Japan won recognition of its dominant position in Korea and consolidated its economic control over Manchuria. Yet repeated incidents of anti-Japanese racism in California kept American-Japanese relations strained. In 1906, for example, the San Francisco school board, responding to nativist fears of a "yellow peril," ordered the segregation of Japanese, Chinese, and Korean students. Japan angrily protested. In 1907, in the so-called gentlemen's agreement, Japan agreed not to issue passports to Japanese male laborers looking to emigrate to the United States and Roosevelt promised to fight anti-Japanese discrimination. He then persuaded the San Francisco school board to exempt Japanese students from the segregation ordinance.

But Roosevelt did not want these conciliatory moves to be interpreted as weakness. He thus built up American naval strength in the Pacific, and in 1908 he sent battleships to visit Japan in a muscle flexing display of sea power. In that same year, the two burgeoning Pacific powers reached a reconciliation. The Root-Takahira Agreement affirmed the "existing status quo" in Asia, mutual respect for territorial possessions in the Pacific, and the Open Door trade policy in China. From the Japanese perspective, the agreement recognized Japan's colonial dominance in Korea and southern Manchuria.

Taft: Dollar Diplomacy

Roosevelt's successor, William Howard Taft, believed he could replace the militarism of the big stick with the more subtle and effective weapon of business investment. Taft and his secretary of state, corporate lawyer Philander C. Knox, followed a strategy (called "dollar diplomacy" by critics) in which they assumed that political influence would follow increased U.S. trade and investment. As Taft explained in 1910, he advocated "active intervention to secure for our merchandise and our capitalists opportunity for profitable investment." He hoped to substitute "dollars for bullets," but he was to discover limits to this approach in both the Caribbean and Asia.

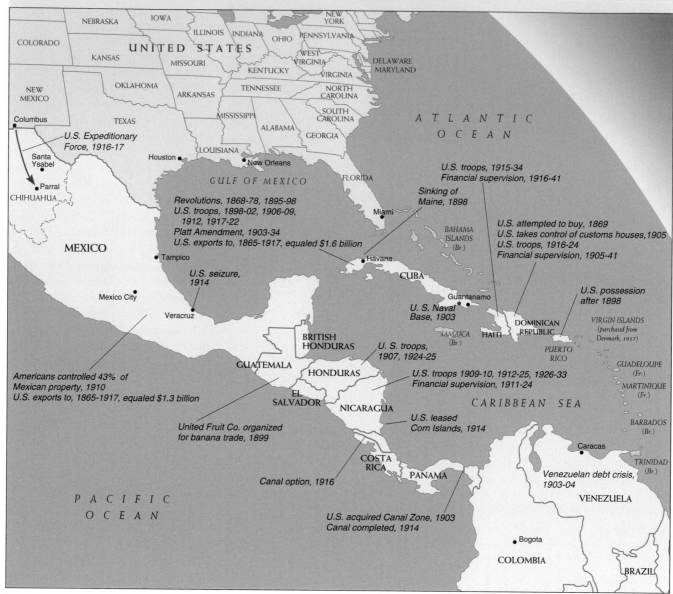

The United States in the Caribbean, 1865–1933 An overview of U.S. economic and military involvement in the Caribbean during the late nineteenth and early twentieth centuries. Victory in the Spanish-American War, the Panama Canal project, and rapid economic investment in Mexico and Cuba all contributed to a permanent and growing U.S. military presence in the region.

Overall American investment in Central America grew rapidly, from $41 million in 1908 to $93 million by 1914. Most of this money went into railroad construction, mining, and plantations. The United Fruit Company alone owned about 160,000 acres of land in the Caribbean by 1913. But dollar diplomacy ended up requiring military support. The Taft administration sent the navy and the marines to intervene in political disputes in Honduras and Nicaragua, propping up factions pledged to protect American business interests. A contingent of U.S. Marines remained in Nicaragua until 1933. The economic and political structures of Honduras and Nicaragua were controlled by both the dollar and the bullet.

In China, Taft and Knox pressed for a greater share of the pie for U.S. investors. They gained a place for

U.S. bankers in the European consortium building the massive new Hu-kuang Railway in southern and central China. But Knox blundered by attempting to "neutralize" the existing railroads in China. He tried to secure a huge international loan for the Chinese government that would allow it to buy up all the foreign railways and develop new ones. Both Russia and Japan, which had fought wars over their railroad interests in Manchuria, resisted this plan as a threat to the arrangements hammered out at Portsmouth with the help of Theodore Roosevelt. Knox's "neutralization" scheme, combined with U.S. support for the Chinese Nationalists in their 1911 revolt against the ruling Manchu dynasty, prompted Japan to sign a new friendship treaty with Russia. The Open Door to China was now effectively closed, and American relations with Japan began a slow deterioration that ended in war thirty years later.

Wilson: Moralism and Realism in Mexico

Right after he took office in 1913, President Woodrow Wilson observed that "it would be the irony of fate if my administration had to deal chiefly with foreign affairs." His political life up to then had centered on achieving progressive reforms in the domestic arena. As it turned out, Wilson had to face international crises from his first day in office. These were of a scope and complexity unprecedented in U.S. history. Wilson had no experience in diplomacy, but he brought to foreign affairs a set of fundamental principles that combined a moralist's faith in American democracy with a realist's understanding of the power of international commerce. He believed that American economic expansion, accompanied by democratic principles and Christianity, was a civilizing force in the world. "Our industries," he told the Democratic National Convention in 1912, "have expanded to such a point that they will burst their jackets if they cannot find a free outlet to the markets of the world. . . . Our domestic markets no longer suffice. We need foreign markets."

Wilson, like most corporate and political leaders of the day, emphasized foreign investments and industrial exports as the keys to the nation's prosperity. He believed that the United States, with its superior industrial efficiency, could achieve supremacy in world commerce if artificial barriers to free trade were removed. He championed and extended the Open Door principles of John Hay, advocating strong diplomatic and military measures "for making ourselves supreme in the world from an economic point of view." Wilson often couched his vision of a dynamic, expansive American capitalism in terms of a moral crusade. As he put it in a speech to a congress of salesmen, "[Since] you are Americans and are meant to carry liberty and justice and the principles of humanity wherever you go, go out and sell goods that will make the world more comfortable and more happy,

and convert them to the principles of America." Yet he quickly found that the complex realities of power politics could interfere with moral vision.

Wilson's policies toward Mexico, which foreshadowed the problems he would encounter in World War I, best illustrate his difficulties. The 1911 Mexican Revolution had overthrown the brutally corrupt dictatorship of Porfirio Díaz, and popular leader Francisco Madero had won wide support by promising democracy and economic reform for millions of landless peasants. U.S. businessmen, however, were nervous about the future of their investments, which totaled over $1 billion, an amount greater than Mexico's own investment and more than all other foreign investment in that country combined. Wilson at first gave his blessing to the revolutionary movement, expressed regret over the Mexican-American War of 1846–48, and disavowed any interest in another war. "I have constantly to remind myself," he told a friend, "that I am not the servant of those who wish to enhance the value of their Mexican investments."

But right before he took office, Wilson was stunned by the ousting and murder of Madero by his chief lieutenant, General Victoriano Huerta. Other nations, including Great Britain and Japan, recognized the Huerta regime, but Wilson refused. He announced that the United States would support only governments that rested on the rule of law. An armed faction opposed to Huerta, known as the Constitutionalists and led by Venustiano Carranza, emerged in northern Mexico. Both sides rejected an effort by Wilson to broker a compromise between them. Carranza, an ardent nationalist, pressed for the right to buy U.S. arms, which he won in 1914. Wilson also isolated Huerta diplomatically by persuading the British to withdraw their support in exchange for American guarantees of English property interests in Mexico.

But Huerta stubbornly remained in power. In April 1914 Wilson used a minor insult to U.S. sailors in Tampico as an excuse to invade. American naval forces bombarded and then occupied Veracruz, the main port through which Huerta received arms shipments. Nineteen Americans and 126 Mexicans died in the battle, which brought the United States and Mexico close to war and provoked anti-American demonstrations in Mexico and throughout Latin America. Wilson accepted the offer of the ABC Powers—Argentina, Brazil, and Chile—to mediate the dispute. Huerta rejected a plan for him to step aside in favor of a provisional government. But then in August, Carranza managed to overthrow Huerta. Playing to nationalist sentiment, Carranza too denounced Wilson for his intervention.

As war loomed in Europe, Mexico's revolutionary politics continued to frustrate Wilson. For a brief period Wilson threw his support behind Francisco "Pancho" Villa, Carranza's former ally who now led a rebel army of his own in northern Mexico. But Carranza's

Mexican revolutionary leaders and sometime allies Francisco "Pancho" Villa (center) and Emiliano Zapata (right) are shown at the National Palace in Mexico City, ca. 1916. Zapata's army operated out of a base in the southern agricultural state of Morelos, while Villa's army controlled large portions of Mexico's north. In 1914 Villa captured the imagination of American reformers, journalists, and moviemakers with his military exploits against the oppressive Huerta regime. But in 1916, after several border clashes between his forces and U.S. military units, President Wilson dispatched a punitive expedition in pursuit of Villa.

SOURCE: Culver Pictures, Inc. (PE0151CP007023)

forces dealt Villa a major setback in April 1915. In October, its attention focused on the war in Europe, the Wilson administration recognized Carranza as Mexico's de facto president. Meanwhile Pancho Villa, feeling betrayed, turned on the United States and tried to provoke a crisis that might draw Washington into war with Mexico. In 1916, Villa led several raids in Mexico and across the border into the United States that killed a few dozen Americans. The man once viewed by Wilson as a fighter for democracy was now dismissed as a dangerous bandit.

In March 1916, enraged by Villa's defiance, Wilson dispatched General John J. Pershing and an army that eventually numbered 15,000 to capture him. For a year, Pershing's troops chased Villa in vain, penetrating 300 miles into Mexico. The invasion made Villa a symbol of national resistance in Mexico, and his army grew from 500 men to 10,000 by the end of 1916. Villa's effective hit-and-run guerrilla tactics kept the U.S. forces at bay. A frustrated General Pershing complained that he felt "just a little bit like a man looking for a needle in a haystack." He urged the U.S. government to occupy the northern Mexican state of Chihuahua and later called for the occupation of the entire country.

Pershing's invasion angered the Carranza government and the Mexican public. Skirmishes between

American forces and Carranza's army brought the two nations to the brink of war again in June 1916. Wilson prepared a message to Congress asking permission for American troops to occupy all of northern Mexico. But he never delivered it. There was fierce opposition to war with Mexico throughout the country. Perhaps more important, mounting tensions with Germany caused Wilson to hesitate. He told an aide that "Germany is anxious to have us at war with Mexico, so that our minds and our energies will be taken off the great war across the sea." Wilson thus accepted negotiations by a face-saving international commission. In early 1917, with America moving toward direct involvement in the European war, Wilson began withdrawing American troops. Just a month before the United States entered World War I, Wilson officially recognized the Carranza regime.

Wilson's attempt to guide the course of Mexico's revolution and protect U.S. interests left a bitter legacy of suspicion and distrust in Mexico. It also suggested the limits of a foreign policy tied to a moral vision rooted in the idea of American exceptionalism. Militarism and imperialism, Wilson had believed, were hallmarks of the old European way. American liberal values—rooted in capitalist development, democracy, and free trade—were the wave of the future. Wilson believed the United States could lead the world in establishing a new international system based on peaceful commerce and political stability. In both the 1914 invasion and the 1916 punitive expedition, Wilson declared that he had no desire to interfere with Mexican sovereignty. But in both cases that is exactly what he did. The United States, he argued, must actively use its enormous moral and material power to create the new order. That principle would soon engage America in Europe's bloodiest war and its most momentous revolution.

THE GREAT WAR

World War I, or the Great War, as it was originally called, took an enormous human toll on an entire generation of Europeans. The unprecedented slaughter on the battlefields of Verdun, Ypres, Gallipoli, and scores of other places appalled the combatant nations. At the war's start in August 1914, both sides had confidently predicted a quick victory. Instead, the killing dragged on for more than four years and in the end transformed the old power relations and political map of Europe. The United States entered the war reluctantly, and American forces played a supportive rather than a central role in the military outcome. Yet the wartime experience left a sharp imprint on the nation's economy, politics, and cultural life—one that would last into the next decades.

The Guns of August

In August 1914 a relatively minor incident plunged the European continent into the most destructive war in its history until then. The last decades of the nineteenth century had seen the major European nations, especially Germany, enjoy a great rush of industrial development. During the same period, these nations acquired extensive colonial empires in Africa, Asia, and the Middle East. Only a complex and fragile system of alliances had kept the European powers at peace with each other since 1871. Two great competing camps had evolved by 1907: the Triple Alliance (also known as the Central Powers), which included Germany, Austria-Hungary, and Italy; and the Triple Entente (also known as the Allies), which included Great Britain, France, and Russia. At the heart of this division was the competition between Great Britain, long the world's dominant colonial and commercial power, and Germany, which had powerful aspirations for an empire of its own.

The alliance system managed to keep small conflicts from escalating into larger ones for most of the late nineteenth and early twentieth centuries. But its inclusiveness was also its weakness: the alliance system threatened to entangle many nations in any war that did erupt. On June 28, 1914, Archduke Franz Ferdinand, heir to the throne of the unstable Austro-Hungarian Empire, was assassinated in Sarajevo, Bosnia. The archduke's killer was a Serbian nationalist who believed the Austro-Hungarian province of Bosnia ought to be annexed to neighboring Serbia. Germany pushed Austria-Hungary to retaliate against Serbia, and the Serbians in turn asked Russia for help.

By early August both sides had exchanged declarations of war and begun mobilizing their forces. Germany invaded Belgium and prepared to move across the French border. But after the German armies were stopped at the River Marne in September, the war settled into a long, bloody stalemate. New and grimly efficient weapons, such as the machine gun and the tank, and the horrors of trench warfare meant unprecedented casualties for all involved. Centered in northern France, the fighting killed 5 million people over the next two and a half years.

American Neutrality

The outbreak of war in Europe shocked Americans. President Wilson issued a formal proclamation of neutrality and urged citizens to be "impartial in thought as well as in action." Most of the country shared the editorial view expressed that August in the *New York Sun*: "There is nothing reasonable in such a war, and it would be folly for the country to sacrifice itself to the frenzy of dynastic policies and the clash of ancient hatreds which is urging the Old World to destruction."

In practice, powerful cultural, political, and economic factors made the impartiality advocated by Wilson impossible. The U.S. population included many ethnic groups with close emotional ties to the Old World. Out of a total population of 92 million in 1914, about one-third were "hyphenated" Americans, either foreign-born or having one or both parents who were immigrants. Strong support for the Central Powers could be found among the 8 million German Americans, as well as the 4 million Irish Americans, who shared their ancestral homeland's historical hatred of English rule. On the other side, many Americans were at least mildly pro-Allies due to cultural and language bonds with Great Britain and the tradition of Franco-American friendship.

Both sides bombarded the United States with vigorous propaganda campaigns. The British effectively exploited their bonds of language and heritage with Americans. Reports of looting, raping, and the killing of innocent civilians by German troops circulated widely in the press. Many of these atrocity stories were exaggerated, but verified German actions—the invasion of neutral Belgium, submarine attacks on merchant ships, and the razing of towns—lent them credibility. German propagandists blamed the war on Russian expansionism and France's desire to avenge its defeat by Germany in 1870–71. It is difficult to measure the impact of war propaganda on American public opinion. As a whole, though, it highlighted the terrible human costs of the war and thus strengthened the conviction that America should stay out of it.

Economic ties between the United States and the Allies were perhaps the greatest barrier to true neutrality. Early in the war Britain imposed a blockade on all shipping to Germany. The United States, as a neutral country, might have insisted on the right of nonbelligerents to trade with both sides, as required by international law. But in practice, although Wilson protested the blockade, he wanted to avoid antagonizing Britain and disrupting trade between the United States and the Allies. Trade with Germany all but ended while trade with the Allies increased dramatically. As war orders poured in from Britain and France, the value of American trade with the Allies shot up from $824 million in 1914 to $3.2 billion in 1916. By 1917 loans to the Allies exceeded $2.5 billion compared to loans to the Central Powers of only $27 million. Through exclusive contracts with the British government, J. P. Morgan and Company emerged as the world's single largest purchaser of goods. It brokered more than than 4,000 contracts between the Allies and U.S. companies that sold munitions, chemicals, cotton, machine tools, and foodstuffs. As America's annual export trade jumped from $2 billion in 1913 to nearly $6 billion in 1916, the nation enjoyed a great economic boom—transforming the economy in places like Bisbee, Arizona—and the United States became neutral in name only.

Preparedness and Peace

In February 1915, Germany declared the waters around the British Isles to be a war zone, a policy that it would enforce with unrestricted submarine warfare. All enemy shipping, despite the requirements of international law to the contrary, would be subject to surprise submarine attack. Neutral powers were warned that the problems of identification at sea put their ships at risk. The United States issued a sharp protest to this policy, calling it "an indefensible violation of neutral rights," and threatened to hold Germany accountable.

On May 7, 1915, a German U-boat sank the British liner *Lusitania* off the coast of Ireland. Among the 1,198 people who died were 128 American citizens. The *Lusitania* was in fact secretly carrying war materials, and passengers had been warned about a possible attack. Wilson nevertheless denounced the sinking as illegal and inhuman, and the American press loudly condemned the act as barbaric. An angry exchange of diplomatic notes led Secretary of State William Jennings Bryan to resign in protest against a policy he thought too warlike.

Tensions heated up again in March 1916 when a German U-boat torpedoed the *Sussex*, an unarmed French passenger ship, injuring four Americans. President Wilson threatened to break off diplomatic relations with Germany unless it abandoned its methods of submarine warfare. He won a temporary diplomatic victory when Germany promised that all vessels would be visited prior to attack. But the crisis also prompted

The *New York Times* printed a special Extra edition announcing that a German submarine had torpedoed the British passenger liner Lusitania on May 7, 1915, off the Irish coast. The ship's manifest later revealed that the *Lusitania* carried a shipment of arms along with its passengers. The 1,198 lives lost included 128 Americans, and the incident helped push the United States toward "preparedness" for war.

SOURCE: ©Bettmann/CORBIS (PG3064A).

Wilson to begin preparing for war. The National Security League, active in large eastern cities and bankrolled by conservative banking and commercial interests, helped push for a bigger army and navy and, most important, a system of universal military training. In June 1916, Congress passed the National Defense Act, which more than doubled the size of the regular army to 220,000 and integrated the state National Guards under federal control. In August, Congress passed a bill that dramatically increased spending for new battleships, cruisers, and destroyers.

Not all Americans supported these preparations for battle, and opposition to military buildup found expression in scores of American communities. As early as August 29, 1914, 1,500 women clad in black had marched down New York's Fifth Avenue in the Woman's Peace Parade. Out of this gathering evolved the American Union against Militarism, which lobbied against the preparedness campaign and against intervention in Mexico. Antiwar feeling was especially strong in the South and Midwest. Except for its vitally important cotton exports, the South generally had weaker economic ties to the Allies than other parts of the nation, as well as a historical suspicion of military power concentrated in Washington. The Midwest included communities with large German and socialist influences, both of which opposed U.S. aid to the Allies.

A group of thirty to fifty House Democrats, led by majority leader Claude Kitchin of North Carolina, stubbornly opposed Wilson's military buildup. Jane Addams, Lillian D. Wald, and many other prominent progressive reformers spoke out for peace. A large reservoir of popular antiwar sentiment flowed through the culture in various ways. Movie director Thomas Ince won a huge audience for his 1916 film *Civilization*, which depicted Christ returning to reveal the horrors of war to world leaders. Two of the most popular songs of 1915 were "Don't Take My Darling Boy Away" and "I Didn't Raise My Boy to Be a Soldier."

To win reelection in 1916, Wilson had to acknowledge the active opposition to involvement in the war. In the presidential campaign, Democrats adopted the winning slogan "He Kept Us Out of War." Wilson made a strong showing in the West, where antiwar sentiment was vigorous, and he managed to draw hundreds of thousands of votes away from the anti-war Socialist Party as well. Wilson made a point of appealing to progressives of all kinds, stressing his support for the eight-hour day and his administration's efforts on behalf of farmers. The war-induced prosperity no doubt helped him to defeat conservative Republican Charles Evans Hughes in a very close election. But Wilson knew that the peace was as fragile as his victory.

Safe for Democracy

By the end of January 1917, Germany's leaders had decided against a negotiated peace settlement, placing their hopes instead in a final decisive offensive against the Allies. On February 1, 1917, with the aim of breaking the British blockade, Germany declared unlimited submarine warfare, with no warnings, against all neutral and belligerent shipping. This strategy went far beyond the earlier, more limited use of the U-boat. The decision was made with full knowledge that it might bring America into the conflict. In effect, German leaders were gambling that they could destroy the ability of the Allies to fight before the United States would be able to effectively mobilize manpower and resources.

Wilson was indignant and disappointed. He still hoped for peace, but Germany had made it impossible for him to preserve his twin goals of U.S. neutrality and freedom of the seas. Reluctantly, Wilson broke off diplomatic relations with Germany and called on Congress to approve the arming of U.S. merchant ships. On March 1, the White House shocked the country when it made public a recently intercepted coded message, sent by German foreign secretary Arthur Zimmermann to the German ambassador in Mexico. The Zimmer-

mann note proposed that an alliance be made between Germany and Mexico if the United States entered the war. Zimmermann suggested that Mexico take up arms against the United States and receive in return the "lost territory in New Mexico, Texas, and Arizona." The note caused a sensation and became a very effective propaganda tool for those who favored U.S. entry into the war. "As soon as I saw it," wrote Republican senator Henry Cabot Lodge of Massachusetts, an interventionist, "I knew it would arouse the country more than any other event." The specter of a German-Mexican alliance helped turn the tide of public opinion in the Southwest, where opposition to U.S. involvement in the war had been strong.

Revelation of the Zimmermann note stiffened Wilson's resolve. He issued an executive order in mid-March authorizing the arming of all merchant ships and allowing them to shoot at submarines. In that month, German U-boats sank seven U.S. merchant ships, leaving a heavy death toll. Anti-German feeling increased, and thousands took part in prowar demonstrations in New York, Boston, Philadelphia, and other cities. Wilson finally called a special session of Congress to ask for a declaration of war.

On April 2, on a rainy night before a packed and very quiet assembly, Wilson made his case. He reviewed the escalation of submarine warfare, which he called "warfare against mankind," and said that neutrality was no longer feasible or desirable. But the conflict was not merely about U.S. shipping rights, Wilson argued. He employed highly idealistic language to make the case for war, reflecting his deeply held belief that America had a special mission as mankind's most enlightened and advanced nation:

> It is a fearful thing to lead this great peaceful people into war, into the most terrible and disastrous of all wars, civilization itself seeming to be in the balance. But the right is more precious than peace, and we shall fight for the things which we have always carried nearest to our hearts—for democracy, for the right of those who submit to authority to have a voice in their own governments, for the rights and liberties of small nations, for a universal dominion of right by such a concert of free peoples as shall bring peace and safety to all nations and make the world itself at last free.

This was a bold bid to give the United States a new role in international affairs. It asserted not just the right to protect U.S. interests but called also for change in basic international structures. Wilson's eloquent speech won over the Congress, most of the press, and even his bitterest political critics, such as Theodore Roosevelt. The Senate adopted the war resolution 82 to 6, the House 373 to 50. On April 6, President Wilson signed

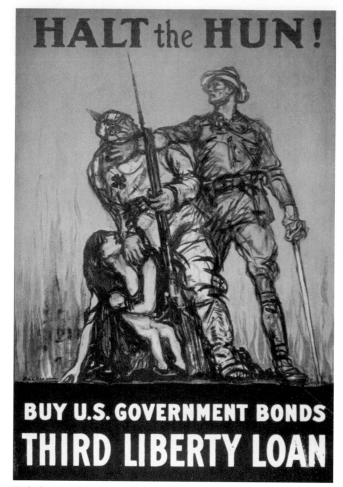

Halt the Hun. This 1918 Liberty Loan poster used anti-German sentiment to encourage the purchase of war bonds. Its depiction of an American soldier as the protector of an innocent mother and child implied that the Germans were guilty of unspeakable war crimes.

SOURCE: Howard Chandler Christy, *Hold the Hun! Fight or Buy Bonds,* poster, 1917. Museum of the City of New York, gift of John Campbell. The Granger Collection (4E695.09).

the declaration of war. All that remained was to win over the American public.

AMERICAN MOBILIZATION

The overall public response to Wilson's war message was enthusiastic. Most newspapers, religious leaders, state legislatures, and prominent public figures endorsed the call to arms. But the Wilson administration was less certain about the feelings of ordinary Americans and their willingness to fight in Europe. It therefore took immediate steps to win over public support for the war effort, to place a legal muzzle on antiwar dissenters, and to establish a universal military draft. War mobilization was above all a campaign to unify the country.

Selling the War

Just a week after signing the war declaration, Wilson created the Committee on Public Information (CPI) to organize public opinion. It was dominated by its civilian chairman, the journalist and reformer George Creel. He had become a personal friend of Wilson's while handling publicity for the 1916 Democratic campaign. Creel quickly transformed the CPI from its original function as coordinator of government news into a sophisticated and aggressive agency for promoting the war. Creel remarked that his aim was to mold Americans into "one white-hot mass . . . with fraternity, devotion, courage, and deathless determination."

To sell the war, Creel raised the art of public relations to new heights. He enlisted more than 150,000 people to work on a score of CPI committees. They produced more than 100 million pieces of literature—pamphlets, articles, books—that explained the causes and meaning of the war. The CPI also created posters, slides, newspaper advertising, and films to promote the war. It called upon movie stars such as Charlie Chaplin, Mary Pickford, and Douglas Fairbanks to help sell war bonds at huge rallies. Famous journalists like the muckraker Ida Tarbell and well-known artists like Charles Dana Gibson were recruited. Across the nation, a volunteer army of 75,000 "Four Minute Men" gave brief patriotic speeches before stage and movie shows.

Three major themes dominated the materials disseminated by the CPI: America as a unified moral community; the war as an idealistic crusade for peace and freedom; and the enemy as a despicable foe. The last of these featured an aggressively negative campaign against all things German. Posters and advertisements depicted the Germans as Huns, bestial monsters outside the civilized world. The CPI supported films such as *The Kaiser: The Beast of Berlin* and *The Prussian Cur.* German music and literature, indeed the German language itself, were suspect, and were banished from the concert halls, schools, and libraries of many communities. The CPI also urged ethnic Americans to abandon their Old World ties, to become "unhyphenated Americans." The CPI's push for conformity would soon encourage thousands of local, sometimes violent, campaigns of harassment against German Americans, radicals, and peace activists.

Fading Opposition to War

By defining the call to war as a great moral crusade, President Wilson was able to win over many Americans who had been reluctant to go to war. In particular, many liberals and progressives were attracted to the possibilities of war as a positive force for social change. Many progressives identified with President Wilson's definition of the war as an idealistic crusade to defend democracy, spread liberal principles, and redeem European decadence and militarism. John Dewey, the influ-

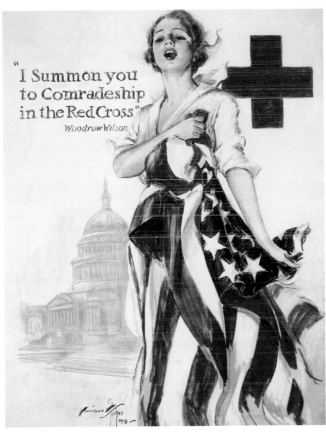

"I Summon you to Comradeship in the Red Cross"
Woodrow Wilson

Founded by Clara Barton after the Civil War, the American Red Cross grew in both size and importance during World War I. Female volunteers, responding to humanitarian and patriotic appeals combined in posters like this one, provided most of the health and sanitary services to military and civilian casualties of the war.

SOURCE: Library of Congress.

ential philosopher, believed the war offered great "social possibilities" for developing the public good through science and greater efficiency.

Social welfare advocates, suffragists, tax reformers, even many socialists, now viewed war as a unique opportunity. War would require greater direct and coordinated involvement by the government in nearly every phase of American life. A group of prominent progressives quickly issued a statement of support for Wilson's war policy. They argued that "out of the sacrifice of war we may achieve broader democracy in Government, more equitable distribution of wealth, and greater national efficiency in raising the level of the general welfare."

The writer and cultural critic Randolph Bourne was an important, if lonely, voice of dissent among intellectuals. A former student of Dewey's at Columbia University, Bourne wrote a series of antiwar essays warning of the disastrous consequences for reform movements of all kinds. He was particularly critical of "war intellectuals" such as Dewey who were so eager to shift their energies to serving the war effort. "War is essentially the health of the State," Bourne wrote, and he accurately predicted sharp infringements on political and intellectual freedoms.

The Woman's Peace Party, founded in 1915 by feminists opposed to the preparedness campaign, dissolved. Most of its leading lights—Florence Kelley, Lillian D. Wald, and Carrie Chapman Catt—threw themselves into volunteer war work. Catt, leader of the huge National American Woman Suffrage Association (NAWSA), believed that supporting the war might help women win the right to vote. She joined the Women's Committee of the Council of National Defense and encouraged suffragists to mobilize women for war service of various kinds. A few lonely feminist voices, such as Jane Addams, continued steadfastly to oppose the war effort. But war work proved very popular among activist middle-class women. It gave them a leading role in their communities—selling bonds, coordinating food conservation drives, and working for hospitals and the Red Cross.

"You're in the Army Now"

The central military issue facing the administration was how to raise and deploy U.S. armed forces. When war was declared, there were only about 200,000 men in the army. Traditionally, the United States had relied on volunteer forces organized at the state level. But volunteer rates after April 6 were less than they had been for the Civil War or the Spanish-American War, reflecting the softness of prowar sentiment. The administration thus introduced the Selective Service Act, which provided for the registration and classification for military service of all men between ages twenty-one and thirty-five. Secretary of War Newton D. Baker was anxious to prevent the widespread, even violent, opposition to the draft that had occurred during the Civil War. Much of the anger over the Civil War draft stemmed from the unpopular provision that allowed draftees to buy their way out by paying $300 for a substitute. The new draft made no such allowances. Baker stressed the democratic procedures for registration and the active role of local draft boards in administering the process.

On June 5, 1917, nearly 10 million men registered for the draft. There was scattered organized resistance, but overall, registration records offered evidence of national support. A supplemental registration in August 1918 extended the age limits to eighteen and forty-five. By the end of the war some 24 million men had registered. Of the 2.8 million men eventually called up for service, about 340,000, or 12 percent, failed to show up. Another 2 million Americans volunteered for the various armed services.

The vast, polyglot army posed unprecedented challenges of organization and control. But progressive elements within the administration also saw opportunities for pressing reform measures involving education, alcohol, and sex. Army psychologists gave the new Stanford-Binet intelligence test to all recruits and were shocked to find illiteracy rates as high as 25 percent. The low test scores among recent immigrants and rural African Americans undoubtedly reflected the cultural biases embedded in the tests and a lack of proficiency in English for many test takers. Most psychologists at the time, however, interpreted low scores in terms of racial theories of innate differences in intelligence. After the war, intelligence testing became a standard feature of America's educational system.

Ideally, the army provided a field for social reform and education, especially for the one-fifth of U.S. soldiers born in another country. "The military tent where they all sleep side by side," Theodore Roosevelt predicted, "will rank next to the public schools among the great agents of democratization." The recruits themselves took a more lighthearted view, while singing the army's praises:

> *Oh, the army, the army, the democratic army,*
> *They clothe you and feed you because the army needs you*
> *Hash for breakfast, beans for dinner, stew for suppertime,*
> *Thirty dollars every month, deducting twenty-nine.*
> *Oh, the army, the army, the democratic army,*
> *The Jews, the Wops, and the Dutch and Irish Cops,*
> *They're all in the army now!*

U.S. soldiers leaving training camp, on their way to the European front, 1918. In just over a year national mobilization expanded the armed forces twentyfold, to nearly 5 million men and women. By November 1918, when the fighting ended, more than 2 million American troops were in Europe.

SOURCE: 69th New York City Infantry going off to WWI. National Archives and Records Administration.

Racism in the Military

But African Americans who served found severe limitations in the U.S. military. They were organized into totally segregated units, barred entirely from the marines and the Coast Guard, and largely relegated to working as cooks, laundrymen, stevedores, and the like in the army and navy. Thousands of black soldiers endured humiliating, sometimes violent treatment, particularly from southern white officers. African American servicemen faced hostility from white civilians as well, North and South, often being denied service in restaurants and admission to theaters near training camps. The ugliest incident occurred in Houston, Texas, in August 1917. Black infantrymen, incensed over continual insults and harassment by local whites, seized weapons from an armory and killed seventeen civilians. The army executed thirty black soldiers and imprisoned forty-one others for life, denying any of them a chance for appeal.

More than 200,000 African Americans eventually served in France, but only about one in five saw combat, as opposed to two out of three white soldiers. Black combat units served with distinction in various divisions of the French army. The all-black 369th U.S. Infantry, for example, saw the first and longest service of any American regiment deployed in a foreign army, serving in the trenches for 191 days. The French government awarded the Croix de Guerre to the entire regiment, and 171 officers and enlisted men were cited individually for exceptional bravery in action. African American soldiers by and large enjoyed a friendly reception from French civilians as well. The contrast with their treatment at home would remain a sore point with these troops upon their return to the United States.

Americans in Battle

Naively, many Americans had assumed that the nation's participation in the war could be limited to supplying economic aid and military hardware. At first, the main contribution came on the sea. German U-boats were sinking Allied ships at a rate of 900,000 tons each month; one of four British ships never returned to port. The United States began sending warships and destroyers to protect large convoys of merchant ships and to aid the British navy in assaulting U-boats. Within a year,

African American troops advance toward the sound of gunfire in northern France, 1918. Nearly 400,000 black men served in World War I, but due to the racist beliefs held by most military and political leaders, only 42,000 went into combat. "Many of the white field officers," wrote black Lieutenant Howard H. Long, "seemed far more concerned with reminding their Negro subordinates that they were Negroes than they were in having an effective unit that would perform well in combat."

SOURCE: Brown Brothers (F149).

shipping tonnage lost each month to submarine warfare had been reduced to 200,000; the flow of weapons, supplies, and troops continued. No American soldiers were lost on the way to Europe.

President Wilson appointed General John J. Pershing, recently returned from pursuing Pancho Villa in Mexico, as commander of the American Expeditionary Force (AEF). Pershing insisted that the AEF maintain its own identity, distinct from that of the French and British armies. He was also reluctant to send American troops into battle before they had received at least six months' training. The AEF's combat role would be brief but intense: not until early 1918 did AEF units reach the front in large numbers; eight months later the war was over.

Like Ulysses S. Grant, Pershing believed the object of war to be total destruction of the enemy's military power. He expressed contempt for the essentially defensive tactics of trench warfare pursued by both sides. But the brutal power of modern military technology had made trench warfare inevitable from 1914 to 1917. The awesome firepower of the machine gun and long-range artillery made the massed frontal confrontations of the Civil War era obsolete. The grim reality of life in the trenches—cold, wet, lice-ridden, with long periods of boredom and sleeplessness—also made a mockery of older notions about the glory of combat.

In the early spring of 1918 the Germans launched a major offensive that brought them within fifty miles of Paris. In early June about 70,000 AEF soldiers helped the French stop the Germans in the battles of Château-Thierry and Belleau Wood. In July, Allied forces led by Marshal Ferdinand Foch of France, began a counter-offensive designed to defeat Germany once and for all. American reinforcements began flooding the ports of Liverpool in England and Brest and Saint-Nazaire in France. The "doughboys" (a nickname for soldiers dating back to Civil War–era recruits who joined the army for the money) streamed in at a rate of over 250,000 a month. By September, General Pershing had more than a million Americans in his army.

In late September 1918, the AEF took over the southern part of a 200-mile front in the Meuse-Argonne offensive. In seven weeks of fighting, most through terrible mud and rain, U.S. soldiers used more ammunition than the entire Union army had in the four years of the Civil War. The Germans, exhausted and badly outnumbered, began to fall back and look for a cease-fire. On November 11, 1918, the war ended with the signing of an armistice.

The massive influx of American troops and supplies no doubt hastened the end of the war. About two-thirds of the U.S. soldiers saw at least some fighting, but even they managed to avoid the horrors of the sustained trench warfare that had marked the earlier years of the war. For most Americans at the front, the war experience was a mixture of fear, exhaustion, and fatigue. Their time in France would remain a decisive moment in their lives. In all, more than 52,000 Americans died in battle. Another 60,000 died from influenza and pneumonia, half of these while still in training camp. More than 200,000 Americans were wounded in the war. These figures, awful as they were, paled against the estimated casualties (killed and wounded) suffered by the European nations: 9 million for Russia, more than 6 million for Germany, nearly 5 million for France, and over 2 million each for Great Britain and Italy.

The Western Front, 1918   American units saw their first substantial action in
late May, helping to stop the German offensive at the Battle of Cantigny. By
September, more than 1 million American troops were fighting in a counteroffensive
campaign at St. Mihiel, the largest single American engagement of the war.

OVER HERE

In one sense, World War I can be understood as the ultimate progressive crusade, a reform movement of its own. Nearly all the reform energy of the previous two decades was turned toward the central goal of winning the war. The federal government would play a larger role than ever in managing and regulating the wartime economy. Planning, efficiency, scientific analysis, and cooperation were key principles for government agencies and large volunteer organizations. Although much of the regulatory spirit was temporary, the war experience started some important and lasting organizational trends in American life.

Organizing the Economy

In the summer of 1917 President Wilson established the War Industries Board (WIB) as a clearinghouse for industrial mobilization to support the war effort. Led by the successful Wall Street speculator Bernard M. Baruch, the WIB proved a major innovation in expanding the regulatory power of the federal government. It was given broad

authority over the conversion of industrial plants to wartime needs, the manufacture of war materials, and the purchase of supplies for the United States and the Allies. The WIB had to balance price controls against war profits. Only by ensuring a fair rate of return on investment could it encourage stepped-up production.

The WIB eventually handled 3,000 contracts worth $14.5 billion with various businesses. Standardization of goods brought large savings and streamlined production. Baruch continually negotiated with business leaders, describing the system as "voluntary cooperation with the big stick in the cupboard." At first Elbert Gary of U.S. Steel refused to accept the government's price for steel and Henry Ford balked at limiting private car production. But when Baruch warned that he would instruct the military to take over their plants, both industrialists backed down.

In August 1917, Congress passed the Food and Fuel Act, authorizing the president to regulate the production and distribution of the food and fuel necessary for the war effort. To lead the Food Administration (FA), Wilson appointed Herbert Hoover, a millionaire engineer who had already won fame for directing a program of war relief for Belgium. He became one of the best-known figures of the war administration. Hoover imposed price controls on certain agricultural commodities, such as sugar, pork, and wheat. These were purchased by the government and then sold to the public through licensed dealers. The FA also raised the purchase price of grain so that farmers would increase production. But Hoover stopped short of imposing mandatory food rationing, preferring to rely on persuasion, high prices, and voluntary controls.

Hoover's success, like George Creel's at the CPI, depended on motivating hundreds of thousands of volunteers in thousands of American communities. The FA coordinated the work of local committees that distributed posters and leaflets urging people to save food, recycle scraps, and substitute for scarce produce. The FA directed patriotic appeals for "Wheatless Mondays, Meatless Tuesdays, and Porkless Thursdays." Hoover exhorted Americans to "go back to simple food, simple clothes, simple pleasures." He urged them to grow their own vegetables. These efforts resulted in a sharp cut back in the consumption of sugar and wheat as well as a boost in the supply of livestock. The resultant increase in food exports helped sustain the Allied war effort.

The enormous cost of fighting the war, about $33 billion, required unprecedentedly large expenditures for the federal government. The tax structure shifted dramatically as a result. Taxes on incomes and profits replaced excise and customs levies as the major source of revenue. The minimum income subject to the graduated federal income tax, in effect only since 1913, was lowered to $1,000 from $3,000, increasing the number of Americans who paid income tax from 437,000 in 1916 to 4,425,000 in 1918. Tax rates were as steep as 70 percent in the highest brackets.

The bulk of war financing came from government borrowing, especially in the form of the popular Liberty Bonds sold to the American public. Bond drives became highly organized patriotic campaigns that ultimately raised a total of $23 billion for the war effort. The administration also used the new Federal Reserve Banks to expand the money supply, making borrowing easier. The federal debt jumped from $1 billion in 1915 to $20 billion in 1920.

The Business of War

Overall, the war meant expansion and high profits for American business. Between 1916 and 1918, Ford Motor Company increased its workforce from 32,000 to 48,000, General Motors from 10,000 to 50,000. Total capital expenditure in U.S. manufacturing jumped from $600 million in 1915 to $2.5 billion in 1918. Corporate profits as a whole nearly tripled between 1914 and 1919, and many large businesses did much better than that.

Annual prewar profits for United States Steel had averaged $76 million; in 1917 they were $478 million. The Bethlehem Shipbuilding Company increased its annual profits from $6 million in peacetime to $49 million in wartime. Du Pont quadrupled its assets. The demand for foodstuffs led to a boom in agriculture as well. The total value of farm produce rose from $9.8 billion in 1914 to $21.3 billion by 1918. Expanded farm acreage and increased investment in farm machinery led to a jump of 20–30 percent in overall farm production.

The most important and long-lasting economic legacy of the war was the organizational shift toward corporatism in American business. The wartime need for efficient management, manufacturing, and distribution could be met only by a greater reliance on the productive and marketing power of large corporations. Never before had business and the federal government cooperated so closely. Under war administrators like Baruch and Hoover, entire industries (such as radio manufacturing) and economic sectors (such as agriculture and energy) were organized, regulated, and subsidized. War agencies used both public and private power—legal authority and voluntarism—to hammer out and enforce agreements. Here was the genesis of the modern bureaucratic state.

Some Americans worried about the wartime trend toward a greater federal presence in their lives. As *The Saturday Evening Post* noted, "All this government activity will be called to account and re-examined in due time." Although many aspects of the government–business partnership proved temporary, some institutions and practices grew stronger in the postwar years. Among these were the Federal Reserve Board, the income tax system, the Chamber of Commerce, the Farm Bureau, and the growing horde of lobbying groups that pressed Washington for special interest legislation.

One key example of the long-range impact of the government–business partnership was the infant radio industry. Wireless communication technology found many uses among naval and ground forces in wartime. As in most industries, the Justice Department guaranteed radio manufacturers protection against patent infringement and antitrust suits. These guarantees helped stimulate research and the mass production of radios for airplanes, ships, and infantry. In 1919 the government helped create the Radio Corporation of America (RCA), which bought out a British company that had dominated America's wireless system. As part of the deal, the U.S. military was allowed a permanent representative on the RCA board of directors. The creation of RCA, jointly owned by General Electric, American Telephone and Telegraph, and Westinghouse, assured the United States a powerful position in the new age of global communications. It also set the stage for the new radio broadcasting industry of the 1920s.

Labor and the War

Organized labor's power and prestige, though by no means equal to those of business or government, clearly grew during the war. The expansion of the economy, combined with army mobilization and a decline in immigration from Europe, caused a growing wartime labor shortage. As the demand for workers intensified, the federal government was forced to recognize that labor, like any other resource or commodity, would have to be more carefully tended to than in peacetime. For the war's duration, working people generally enjoyed higher wages and a better standard of living. Trade unions, especially those affiliated with the American Federation of Labor (AFL), experienced a sharp rise in membership. In effect, the government took in labor as a junior partner in the mobilization of the economy.

Samuel Gompers, president of the AFL, emerged as the leading spokesman for the nation's trade union movement. An English immigrant and cigar maker by trade, Gompers had rejected the socialism of his youth for a philosophy of "business unionism." By stressing the concrete gains that workers could win through collective bargaining with employers, the AFL had reached a total membership of about 2 million in 1914. Virtually all its members were skilled white males, organized in highly selective crafts in the building trades, railroads, and coal mines.

Gompers pledged the AFL's patriotic support for the war effort, and in April 1918 President Wilson appointed him to the National War Labor Board (NWLB). During 1917 the nation had seen thousands of strikes involving more than a million workers. Wages were usually at issue, reflecting workers' concerns with spiraling inflation and higher prices. The NWLB, co-chaired by labor attorney Frank Walsh and former president William H. Taft, acted as a kind of supreme court for labor, arbitrating disputes and working to prevent disruptions in production. The great majority of these interventions resulted in improved wages and reduced hours of work.

Most important, the NWLB supported the right of workers to organize unions and furthered the acceptance of the eight-hour day for war workers—central aims of the labor movement. It also backed time-and-a-half pay for overtime, as well as the principle of equal pay for women workers. AFL unions gained more than a million new members during the war, and overall union membership rose from 2.7 million in 1914 to more than 5 million by 1920. The NWLB established important precedents for government intervention on behalf of labor.

Wartime conditions often meant severe disruptions and discomfort for America's workers. Overcrowding, rapid workforce turnover, and high inflation rates were typical in war-boom communities. In Bridgeport, Connecticut, a center for small-arms manufacturing, the population grew by 50,000 in less than a year. In 1917 the number of families grew by 12,000, but available housing stock increased by only 6,000 units. Chronic congestion became common in many cities; Philadelphia reported the worst housing shortage in its history.

In the Southwest, the demand for wartime labor temporarily eased restrictions against the movement of Mexicans into the United States. The Immigration Act of 1917, requiring a literacy test and an $8 head tax, had cut Mexican immigration nearly in half, down to about 25,000 per year. But employers complained of severe shortages of workers. Farmers in Arizona's Salt River Valley and southern California needed hands to harvest grain, alfalfa, cotton, and fruit. El Paso's mining and smelting industries, Texas's border ranches, and southern Arizona's railroads and copper mines insisted they depended on unskilled Mexican labor as well.

Responding to these protests, in June 1917, the Department of Labor suspended the immigration law for the duration of the war and negotiated an agreement with the Mexican government permitting some 35,000 Mexican contract laborers to enter the United States. Mexicans let in through this program had to demonstrate they had a job waiting before they could cross the border. They received identification cards and transportation to their place of work from American labor contractors. Pressure from southwestern employers kept the exemptions in force until 1921, well after the end of the war, demonstrating the growing importance of cheap Mexican labor to the region's economy.

If the war boosted the fortunes of the AFL, it also spelled the end for more radical elements of the U.S. labor movement. The Industrial Workers of the World (IWW) had followed a different path from the "pure and simple" trade unionism of Gompers. Unlike the AFL, the IWW concentrated on organizing unskilled workers into all-inclusive industrial unions. The Wobblies denounced capitalism as an unreformable system based on exploitation, and they opposed U.S. entry into the war. IWW leaders advised their members to refuse induction for "the capitalists' war."

With vigorous organizing, especially in the West, the IWW had grown in 1916 and 1917. It gained strength among workers in several areas crucial to the war effort: copper mining, lumbering, and wheat harvesting. In September 1917, just after the vigilante attack in Bisbee and the IWW's efforts to expose it, the Wilson administration responded to appeals from western business leaders for a crackdown on the Wobblies. Justice Department agents, acting under the broad authority of the recently passed Espionage Act, swooped down on IWW offices in more than sixty towns and cities, arresting more than 300 people and confiscating files. The mass trials and convictions that followed broke the back of America's radical labor movement and marked the beginning of a powerful wave of political repression.

Women at Work

World War I marked the first time that women were mobilized directly into the armed forces. Over 16,000 women served overseas with the AEF in France, where most worked as nurses, clerical workers, telephone operators, and canteen operators. Another 12,000 women served stateside in the navy and U.S. Marine Corps, and tens of thousands of civilian women were employed in army offices and hospitals. But the war's impact on women was greatest in the broader civilian economy. For many of the 8 million women already in the labor force, the war meant a chance to switch from low-paying jobs, such as domestic service, to higher-paying industrial employment. About a million women workers joined the labor force for the first time. Of the estimated 9.4 million workers directly engaged in war work, some 2.25 million were women. Of these, 1.25 million worked in manufacturing. Female munitions plant workers, train engineers, drill press operators, street-car conductors, and mail carriers became a common sight around the country.

Women workers at the Midvale Steel and Ordinance Company in Pennsylvania, 1918. Wartime labor shortages created new opportunities for over one million women to take high wage manufacturing jobs like these. The opening proved temporary, however, and with the war's end nearly all of these women lost their jobs. By 1920 the number of women employed in manufacturing was lower than it had been in 1910.

SOURCE: National Archives and Records Administration (1-SC-31731).

In response to the widened range of female employment, the Labor Department created the Women in Industry Service (WIS). Directed by Mary Van Kleeck, the service advised employers on using female labor and formulated general standards for the treatment of women workers. The WIS represented the first attempt by the federal government to take a practical stand on improving working conditions for women. Its standards included the eight-hour day, equal pay for equal work, a minimum wage, the prohibition of night work, and the provision of rest periods, meal breaks, and restroom facilities. These standards had no legal force, however, and WIS inspectors found that employers often flouted them. They were accepted nonetheless as goals by nearly every group concerned with improving the conditions of working women.

Many women resented the restrictiveness of the WIS guidelines. Myrtle Altenburg, a Wisconsin widow, complained of being prevented from working on a local railroad. "It is my belief," she wrote the state railway commission, "that a woman can do everything that a man can do that is within her strength. Hundreds and hundreds of women might work and release men for war or war work, could they, the women, be employed on the railroads." Even when hired, women suffered discrimination over pay. Government surveys found that women's average earnings were roughly half of men's in the same industries.

At war's end, women lost nearly all their defense-related jobs. Wartime women railroad workers, for example, were replaced by returning servicemen through the application of laws meant to protect women from hazardous conditions. But the war accelerated female employment in fields already dominated by women. By 1920, more women who worked outside the home did so in white-collar occupations—as telephone operators, secretaries, and clerks, for example—than in manufacturing or domestic service. The new awareness of women's work led Congress to create the Women's Bureau in the Labor Department, which continued the WIS wartime program of education and investigation through the postwar years.

Woman Suffrage

The presence of so many new women wageworkers, combined with the highly visible volunteer work of millions of middle-class women, helped finally to secure the vote for women. Volunteer war work—selling bonds, saving food, organizing benefits—was very popular among housewives and clubwomen. These women played a key role in the success of the Food Administration, and the Women's Committee of the Council of National Defense included a variety of women's organizations.

Until World War I, the fight for woman suffrage had been waged largely within individual states. Western states and territories had led the way. Various forms of woman suffrage had become law in Wyoming in 1869, followed by Utah (1870), Colorado (1893), Idaho (1896), Washington (1910), California (1911), Arizona and Oregon (1912), and Montana and Nevada (1914). The reasons for this regional pattern had less to do with dramatically different notions of gender roles in the West than with the distinctiveness of western politics and society. Rocky Mountain and Pacific coast states did not have the sharp ethnocultural divisions between Catholics and Protestants that hindered suffrage efforts in the East. The close identification in the East between the suffrage and prohibition movements led many Catholic immigrants and German Lutherans to oppose the vote for women because they feared it would lead to prohibition. Mormons in Utah supported woman suffrage as a way to preserve polygamy and defend their distinctive social order from attack.

The U.S. entry into the war provided a unique opportunity for suffrage groups to shift their strategy to a national campaign for a constitutional amendment granting the vote to women. The most important of these groups was the National American Woman Suffrage Association. Before 1917, most American suffragists had opposed the war. Under the leadership of Carrie Chapman Catt, the NAWSA threw its support behind the war effort and doubled its membership to 2 million. Catt gambled that a strong show of patriotism would help clinch the century-old fight to win the vote for women. The NAWSA pursued a moderate policy of lobbying Congress for a constitutional amendment and calling for state referendums on woman suffrage.

At the same time, more militant suffragists led by the young Quaker activist Alice Paul, injected new energy and more radical tactics into the movement. Paul had spent several years in England working with militant suffragists there, and in 1913 she returned to the United States to form the Congressional Union within the NAWSA to lobby for a federal amendment. Dissatisfied with the NAWSA's conservative strategy of quiet lobbying and orderly demonstrations, Paul left the organization in 1916. She joined forces with western women voters to form the National Woman's Party. Borrowing from English suffragists, this party pursued a more aggressive and dramatic strategy of agitation. Paul and her supporters picketed the White House, publicly burned President Wilson's speeches, and condemned the presi-

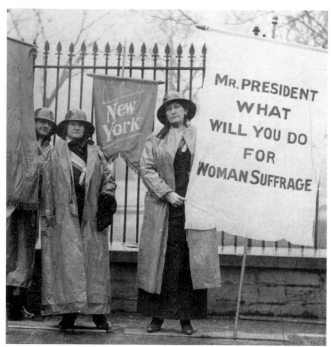

Members of the National Woman's Party picketed President Wilson at the White House in 1917. Their militant action in the midst of the war crisis aroused both anger and sympathy. The NWP campaign helped push the president and the Congress to accept woman suffrage as a "war measure."

SOURCE: Library of Congress.

dent and the Democrats for failing to produce an amendment. In one demonstration they chained themselves to the White House fence and after their arrest went on a hunger strike in jail. The militants generated a great deal of publicity and sympathy.

Although some in the NAWSA objected to these tactics, Paul's radical approach helped make the NAWSA position more acceptable to Wilson. Carrie Chapman Catt used the president's war rhetoric as an argument for granting the vote to women. The fight for democracy, she argued, must begin at home, and she urged passage of the woman suffrage amendment as a "war measure." She won Wilson's support, and in 1917 the president urged Congress to pass a woman suffrage amendment as "vital to the winning of the war." The House did so in January 1918 and a more reluctant Senate approved it in June 1919. Another year of hard work was spent convincing the state legislatures. In August 1920, Tennessee gave the final vote needed to ratify the Nineteenth Amendment to the Constitution, finally making woman suffrage legal nationwide.

Prohibition

Significantly, another reform effort closely associated with women's groups triumphed at the same time. The movement to eliminate alcohol from American life

Chart the progress of the women's suffrage movement. What were the reasons behind the regional differences in support of women's suffrage?
www.prenhall.com/faragher/map22.2

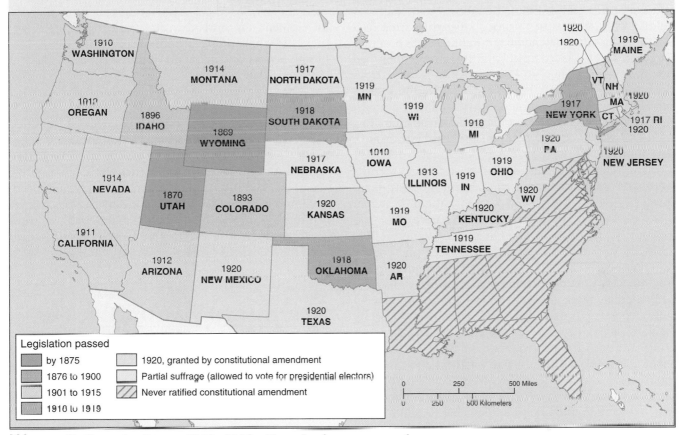

Woman Suffrage by State, 1869–1919   Dates for the enactment of woman suffrage in the individual states. Years before ratification of the Nineteenth Amendment in 1920, a number of western states had legislated full or partial voting rights for women. In 1917 Montana suffragist Jeannette Rankin became the first woman elected to Congress.

SOURCE: Barbara G. Shortridge, *Atlas of American Women* (New York: Macmillan, 1987)

had attracted many Americans, especially women, since before the Civil War. Temperance advocates saw drinking as the source of many of the worst problems faced by the working class, including family violence, unemployment, and poverty. By the early twentieth century the Woman's Christian Temperance Union, with a quarter-million members, had become the single largest women's organization in American history.

The moral fervor that accompanied America's entry into the war provided a crucial boost to the cause. With so many breweries bearing German names, the movement benefited as well from the strong anti-German feeling of the war years. Outlawing beer and whiskey would also help to conserve precious grain, prohibitionists argued.

In 1917, a coalition of progressives and rural fundamentalists in Congress pushed through a constitutional amendment providing for a national ban on alcoholic

drinks. The Eighteenth Amendment was ratified by the states in January 1919 and became the law of the land one year later. Although Prohibition would create a host of problems in the postwar years, especially as a stimulus for the growth of organized crime, many Americans, particularly native Protestants, considered it a worthy moral reform.

Public Health

Wartime mobilization brought deeper government involvement with public health issues, especially in the realm of sex hygiene, child welfare, and disease prevention. The rate of venereal disease among draftees was as high as 6 percent in some states, presenting a potential manpower problem for the army. In April 1917, the War Department mounted a vigorous campaign against venereal disease, which attracted the energies of progressive era sex reformers—social hygienists and antivice crusaders. Under the direction of Raymond Fosdick and the Commission on Training Camp Activities, the military educated troops on the dangers of contracting syphilis and gonorrhea and distributed condoms to soldiers. "A Soldier who gets a dose," warned a typical poster, "is a Traitor." More than a hundred red-light districts near military bases were closed down, and the army established five-mile "pure zones" to keep prostitutes away from the camps. Yet the sexual double standard still operated. Female activists angrily protested when military authorities, while refusing to arrest soldiers for patronizing prostitutes, arrested the women en masse and held them in detention centers.

The scientific discussions of sex to which recruits were subjected in lectures, pamphlets, and films were surely a first for the vast majority of them. Venereal disease rates for soldiers declined by more than 300 percent during the war. The Division of Venereal Diseases, created in the summer of 1918 as a branch of the U.S. Public Health Service, established clinics offering free medical treatment to infected persons. It also coordinated an aggressive educational campaign through state departments of health.

The wartime boost to government health work continued into the postwar years. The Children's Bureau, created in 1912 as a part of the Labor Department, undertook a series of reports on special problems growing out of the war: the increase in employment of married women, the finding of day care for children of working mothers, and the growth of both child labor and delinquency. In 1918 Julia C. Lathrop, chief of the bureau, organized a "Children's Year" campaign designed to promote public protection of expectant mothers and infants and to enforce child labor laws. Millions of health education pamphlets were distributed nationwide, and mothers were encouraged to have their infants and children weighed and measured. Thousands of community-based committees enrolled some 11 million women in the drive.

In 1917, Lathrop, who had come to the Children's Bureau from the settlement house movement, proposed a plan to institutionalize federal aid to the states for protection of mothers and children. Congress finally passed the Maternity and Infancy Act in 1921, appropriating over $1 million a year to be administered to the states by the Children's Bureau. In the postwar years, clinics for prenatal and obstetrical care grew out of these efforts and greatly reduced the rate of infant and maternal mortality and disease.

The disastrous influenza epidemic of 1918–19 offered the most serious challenge to national public health during the war years. Part of a worldwide pandemic that claimed as many as 20 million lives, few Americans paid attention to the disease until it swept through military camps and eastern cities in September 1918. A lethal combination of the "flu" and respiratory complications (mainly pneumonia) killed roughly 550,000 Americans in ten months. Most victims were young adults between the ages of twenty and forty. Professional groups such as the American Medical Association called for massive government appropriations to search for a cure. Congress did appropriate a million dollars to the Public Health Service to combat and suppress the epidemic, but it offered no money for research.

The Public Health Service found itself overwhelmed by calls for doctors, nurses, and treatment facilities. Much of the care for the sick and dying came from Red Cross nurses and volunteers working in local communities across the nation. With a war on, and the nation focused on reports from the battlefront, even a public health crisis of this magnitude went relatively unnoticed. Although funding for the Public Health Service continued to grow in the 1920s, public and private expenditures on medical research were barely one-fiftieth of what they would become after World War II.

REPRESSION AND REACTION

World War I exposed and intensified many of the deepest social tensions in American life. On the local level, as exemplified by the Bisbee deportations, vigilantes increasingly took the law into their own hands to punish those suspected of disloyalty. The push for national unity led the federal government to crack down on a wide spectrum of dissenters from its war policies. The war inflamed racial hatred, and the worst race riots in the nation's history exploded in several cities. At war's end, a newly militant labor movement briefly asserted itself in mass strikes around the nation. Over all these developments loomed the 1917 Bolshevik Revolution in Russia. Radicals around the world had drawn inspiration from what looked like the first successful revolution against a capitalist state. Many conservatives worried that similar revolutions were imminent. From 1918 through 1920 the federal government directed a repressive antiradical campaign that had crucial implications for the nation's future.

Muzzling Dissent: The Espionage and Sedition Acts

The Espionage Act of June 1917 became the government's key tool for the suppression of antiwar sentiment. It set severe penalties (up to twenty years' imprisonment and a $10,000 fine) for anyone found guilty of aiding the enemy, obstructing recruitment, or causing insubordination in the armed forces. The act also empowered the postmaster general to exclude from the mails any newspapers or magazines he thought treasonous. Within a year the mailing rights of forty-five newpapers had been revoked. These included several anti-British and pro-Irish publications, as well as such leading journals of American socialism as the Kansas-based *Appeal to Reason*, which had enjoyed a prewar circulation of half a million, and *The Masses*.

To enforce the Espionage Act, the government had to increase its overall police and surveillance machinery. Civilian intelligence was coordinated by the newly created Bureau of Investigation in the Justice Department. This agency was reorganized after the war as the Federal Bureau of Investigation (FBI). In May 1918 the Sedition Act, an amendment to the Espionage Act, outlawed "any disloyal, profane, scurrilous, or abusive language intended to cause contempt, scorn, contumely, or disrepute" to the government, Constitution, or flag.

In all, more than 2,100 cases were brought to trial under these acts. They became a convenient vehicle for striking out at socialists, pacifists, radical labor activists, and others who resisted the patriotic tide. The most celebrated prosecution came in June 1918 when federal agents arrested Eugene V. Debs in Canton, Ohio, after he gave a speech defending antiwar protesters. Sentenced to ten years in prison, Debs defiantly told the court: "I have been accused of having obstructed the war. I admit it. Gentlemen, I abhor war. I would oppose the war if I stood alone." Debs served thirty-two months in federal prison before being pardoned by President Warren G. Harding on Christmas Day 1921.

The Supreme Court upheld the constitutionality of the acts in several 1919 decisions. In *Schenck v. United States* the Court unanimously agreed with Justice Oliver Wendell Holmes's claim that Congress could restrict speech if the words "are used in such circumstances and are of such a nature as to create a clear and present danger." The decision upheld the conviction of Charles Schenck for having mailed pamphlets urging potential army inductees to resist conscription. In *Debs v. United States*, the Court affirmed the guilt of Eugene V. Debs for his antiwar speech in Canton, even though he had not explicitly urged violation of the draft laws. Finally, in *Abrams v. United States*, the Court upheld Sedition Act convictions of four Russian immigrants who had printed pamphlets denouncing American military intervention in the Russian Revolution. The nation's highest court thus endorsed the severe wartime restrictions on free speech.

The deportation of striking miners in Bisbee offered an extreme case of vigilante activity. Thousands of other instances took place as government repression and local vigilantes reinforced each other. The American Protective League, founded with the blessing of the Justice Department, mobilized 250,000 self-appointed "operatives" in more than 600 towns and cities. Members of the league, mostly businessmen, bankers, and former policemen, spied on their neighbors and staged a series of well-publicized "slacker" raids on antiwar protesters and draft evaders. Many communities, inspired by Committee on Public Information campaigns, sought to ban the teaching of the German language in their schools or the performance of German music in concert halls.

The Great Migration and Racial Tensions

Economic opportunity brought on by war prosperity triggered a massive migration of rural black Southerners to northern cities. From 1914 to 1920, somewhere between 300,000 and 500,000 African Americans left the rural South for the North. Chicago's black population increased by 65,000, or 150 percent; Detroit's by 35,000, or 600 percent. Acute labor shortages led northern factory managers to recruit black migrants to the expanding industrial centers. The Pennsylvania Railroad alone drew 10,000 black workers from Florida and

THE GREAT MIGRATION: BLACK POPULATION GROWTH IN SELECTED NORTHERN CITIES, 1910–1920					
	1910		**1920**		
City	No.	Percent	No.	Percent	Percent Increase
New York	91,709	1.9%	152,467	2.7%	66.3%
Chicago	44,103	2.0	109,458	4.1	148.2
Philadelphia	84,459	5.5	134,229	7.4	58.9
Detroit	5,741	1.2	40,838	4.1	611.3
St. Louis	43,960	6.4	69,854	9.0	58.9
Cleveland	8,448	1.5	34,451	4.3	307.8
Pittsburgh	25,623	4.8	37,725	6.4	47.2
Cincinnati	19,739	5.4	30,079	7.5	53.2

SOURCE: U.S. Department of Commerce.

south Georgia. Black workers eagerly left low-paying jobs as field hands and domestic servants for the chance at relatively high-paying work in meatpacking plants, shipyards, and steel mills.

Kinship and community networks were crucial in shaping what came to be called the Great Migration. They spread news about job openings, urban residential districts, and boardinghouses in northern cities. Black clubs, churches, and fraternal lodges in southern communities frequently sponsored the migration of their members, as well as return trips to the South. Single African American women often made the trip first because they could more easily obtain steady work as maids, cooks, and laundresses. One recalled that "if [white employers] liked the way the women would work in their homes or did ironing, they might throw some work to your husband or son." Relatively few African American men actually secured high-paying skilled jobs in industry or manufacturing. Most had to settle for work as construction laborers, teamsters, janitors, porters, or other low-paying jobs.

The persistence of lynching and other racial violence in the South no doubt contributed to the Great Migration. But racial violence was not limited to the South. Two of the worst race riots in American history occurred as a result of tensions brought on by wartime migration. On July 2, 1917, in East St. Louis, Illinois, a

This southern African American family is shown arriving in Chicago around 1910. Black migrants to northern cities often faced overcrowding, inferior housing, and a high death rate from disease. But the chance to earn daily wages of $6 to $8 (the equivalent of a week's wages in much of the South), as well as the desire to escape persistent racial violence, kept the migrants coming.

SOURCE: Stock Montage, Inc./Historical Pictures Collection.

ferocious mob of whites attacked African Americans, killing at least 200. Before this riot, some of the city's manufacturers had been steadily recruiting black labor as a way to keep local union demands down. Unions had refused to allow black workers as members, and politicians had cynically exploited white racism in appealing for votes. In Chicago, on July 27, 1919, antiblack rioting broke out on a Lake Michigan beach. For two weeks white gangs hunted African Americans in the streets and burned hundreds out of their homes. Twenty-three African Americans and fifteen whites died, and more than 500 were injured.

In both East St. Louis and Chicago, local authorities held African Americans responsible for the violence. President Wilson refused requests for federal intervention or investigation. A young black veteran who had been chased by a mob in the Chicago riot asked: "Had the ten months I spent in France been all in vain? Were all those white crosses over dead bodies of those dark skinned boys lying in Flanders field for naught? Was democracy a hollow sentiment?"

In terms of service in the armed forces, compliance with the draft, and involvement in volunteer work, African Americans had supported the war effort as faithfully as any group. In 1917, despite a segregated army and discrimination in defense industries, most African Americans thought the war might improve their lot. "If we again demonstrate our loyalty and devotion to our country," advised the *Chicago Defender*, "those injustices will disappear and the grounds for complaint will no longer exist." By the fall of 1919, writing in *The Crisis*, the journal of the National Association for the Advancement of Colored People (NAACP), black author James Weldon Johnson gloomily concluded that "an increased hatred of race was an integral part of wartime intolerance."

Black disillusionment about the war grew quickly. So did a newly militant spirit. A heightened sense of race consciousness and activism was evident among black veterans and the growing black communities of northern cities. Taking the lead in the fight against bigotry and injustice, the NAACP held a national conference in 1919 on lynching. It pledged to defend persecuted African Americans, publicize the horrors of lynch law, and seek federal legislation against "Judge Lynch." By 1919 membership in the NAACP had reached 60,000 and the circulation of its journal exceeded half a million.

Labor Strife

The relative labor peace of 1917 and 1918 dissolved after the armistice. More than 4 million American workers were involved in some 3,600 strikes in 1919 alone. This unprecedented strike wave had several causes. Most of the modest wartime wage gains were wiped out by spiraling inflation and high prices for food, fuel, and housing. With the end of government controls on industry, many employers withdrew their recognition of unions. Difficult working conditions, such as the twelve-hour day in steel mills, were still routine in some industries.

Several of the postwar strikes received widespread national attention. They seemed to be more than simple economic conflicts, and they provoked deep fears about the larger social order. In February 1919, a strike in the shipyards of Seattle, Washington, over wages escalated into a general citywide strike involving 60,000 workers. The local press and Mayor Ole Hanson denounced the strikers as revolutionaries. Hanson effectively ended the strike by requesting federal troops to occupy the city.

In September, Boston policemen went out on strike when the police commissioner rejected a citizens' commission study that recommended a pay raise. Massachusetts governor Calvin Coolidge called in the National Guard to restore order and won a national reputation by crushing the strike. The entire police force was fired. Coolidge declared, "There is no right to strike against the public safety by anybody, anywhere, any time."

The biggest strike took place in the steel industry, involving some 350,000 steelworkers. Centered in several midwestern cities, this epic struggle lasted from September 1919 to January 1920. The AFL had hoped to build on wartime gains in an industry that had successfully resisted unionization before the war. The major demands were union recognition, the eight-hour day, and wage increases. The steel companies used black strikebreakers and armed guards to keep the mills running. Elbert Gary, president of U.S. Steel, directed a sophisticated propaganda campaign that branded the strikers as revolutionaries. Public opinion turned against the strike and condoned the use of state and federal troops to break it. The failed steel strike proved to be the era's most bitter and devastating defeat for organized labor.

AN UNEASY PEACE

The armistice of November 1918 ended the fighting on the battlefield, but the war continued at the peace conference. In the old royal palace of Versailles near Paris, delegates from twenty-seven countries spent five months hammering out a settlement. Yet neither Germany nor Russia was represented. The proceedings were dominated by leaders of the "Big Four": David Lloyd George (Great Britain), Georges Clemenceau (France), Vittorio Orlando (Italy), and Woodrow Wilson (United States). President Wilson saw the peace conference as a historic opportunity to project his domestic liberalism onto the world stage. But the stubborn realities of power politics would frustrate Wilson at Versailles and lead to his most crushing defeat at home.

The Fourteen Points

Wilson arrived in Paris with the United States delegation in January 1919. He believed the Great War revealed the bankruptcy of diplomacy based on alliances and the "balance of power." Peacemaking, he thought, meant an opportunity for America to lead the rest of the world toward a new vision of international relations. He brought with him a plan for peace that he had outlined a year earlier in a speech to Congress on U.S. war aims. The Fourteen Points, as they were called, had originally served wartime purposes: to appeal to antiwar factions in Austria-Hungary and Germany, to convince Russia to stay in the war, and to help sustain Allied morale. As a blueprint for peace, they contained three main elements. First, Wilson offered a series of specific proposals for setting postwar boundaries in Europe and creating new countries out of the collapsed Austro-Hungarian and Ottoman empires. The key idea here was the right of all peoples to "national self-determination." Second, Wilson listed general principles for governing international conduct, including freedom of the seas, free trade, open covenants instead of secret treaties, reduced armaments, and mediation for competing colonial claims. Third, and most important, Wilson called for a League of Nations to help implement these principles and resolve future disputes.

The Fourteen Points offered a plan for world order deeply rooted in the liberal progressivism long associated with Wilson. The plan reflected a faith in efficient government and the rule of law as means for solving international problems. It advocated a dynamic democratic capitalism as a middle ground between Old World autocracy and revolutionary socialism. Wilson's vision was a profoundly moral one, and he was certain it was the only road to a lasting and humane peace.

The most controversial element, both at home and abroad, would prove to be the League of Nations. The heart of the League covenant, Article X, called for collective security as the ultimate method of keeping the peace: "The members of the League undertake to respect and preserve as against external aggression the territorial integrity and existing political independence of all Members." In the United States, Wilson's critics would focus on this provision as an unacceptable surrender of the nation's sovereignty and independence in foreign affairs. They also raised constitutional objections, arguing that the American system vested the power to declare war with the Congress. Would membership in the League violate this basic principle of the Constitution?

Wilson in Paris

The president was pleased when the conference at first accepted his plan as the basis for discussions. He also enjoyed wildly enthusiastic receptions from the public in Paris and several other European capitals he visited.

Woodrow Wilson, Georges Clemenceau, and David Lloyd George are among the central figures depicted in John Christen Johansen's *Signing of the Treaty of Versailles*. But all the gathered statesmen appear dwarfed by their surroundings.

SOURCE: John Christen Johansen, *Signing of the Treaty of Versailles*, 1919. National Portrait Gallery, Smithsonian Institution, Washington, D.C./Art Resource, New York (S0022240).

France's Clemenceau was less enamored. He sarcastically observed, "God gave us the Ten Commandments, and we broke them. Wilson gave us the Fourteen Points. We shall see." Wilson's plan could not survive the hostile atmosphere at Versailles.

Much of the negotiating at Versailles was in fact done in secret among the Big Four. The ideal of self-determination found limited expression. The independent states of Austria, Hungary, Poland, Yugoslavia, and Czechoslovakia were carved out of the homelands of the beaten Central Powers. But the Allies resisted Wilson's call for independence for the colonies of the defeated nations. A compromise mandate system of protectorates gave the French and British control of parts of the old German and Turkish empires in Africa and West Asia. Japan won control of former German colonies in China. Among those trying, but failing, to influence the treaty negotiations were the sixty-odd delegates to the first Pan African Congress, held in Paris at the same time as the peace talks. The group included Americans W. E. B. Du Bois and William Monroe Trotter as well as representatives from Africa and the West Indies. All were disappointed with the failure of the peace conference to grant self-determination to thousands of Africans living in former German colonies.

Another disappointment for Wilson came with the issue of war guilt. He had strongly opposed the extraction of harsh economic reparations from the Central Powers. But the French and British, with their awful war losses fresh in mind, insisted on making Germany pay. The final treaty contained a clause attributing the war to "the aggression of Germany," and a commission later set German war reparations at $33 billion. Bitter resentment in Germany over the punitive treaty helped sow the seeds for the Nazi rise to power in the 1930s.

The final treaty was signed on June 28, 1919, in the Hall of Mirrors at the Versailles palace. The Germans had no choice but to accept its harsh terms. President Wilson had been disappointed by the secret deals and the endless compromising of his ideals, no doubt underestimating the stubborn reality of power politics in the wake of Europe's most devastating war. He had nonetheless won a commitment to the League of Nations, the centerpiece of his plan, and he was confident that the American people would accept the treaty. The tougher fight would be with the Senate, where a two-thirds vote was needed for ratification.

The Treaty Fight

Preoccupied with peace conference politics in Paris, Wilson had neglected politics at home. His troubles had actually started earlier. Republicans had captured both the House and the Senate in the 1918 elections. Wilson had then made a tactical error by including no prominent Republicans in the U.S. peace delegation. He therefore faced a variety of tough opponents to the treaty he brought home.

Wilson's most extreme enemies in the Senate were a group of about sixteen "irreconcilables," opposed to a treaty in any form. Some were isolationist progressives, such as Republicans Robert M. La Follette of Wisconsin and William Borah of Idaho, who opposed the League of Nations as steadfastly as they opposed American entry into the war. Others were racist xenophobes like Democrat James Reed of Missouri. He objected, he said, to submitting questions to a tribunal "on which a nigger from Liberia, a nigger from Honduras, a nigger from India, and an unlettered gentleman from Siam, each have votes equal to the great United States of America."

The less dogmatic but more influential opponents were led by Republican Henry Cabot Lodge of Massachusetts, powerful majority leader of the Senate. They had strong reservations about the League of Nations, especially the provisions for collective security in the event of a member nation's being attacked. Lodge argued that this provision impinged on congressional authority to declare war and placed unacceptable restraints on the nation's ability to pursue an independent foreign policy. Lodge proposed a series of amendments that would have weakened the League. But Wilson refused to compromise, motivated in part by the long-standing hatred he and Lodge felt toward each other.

In September, Wilson set out on a speaking tour across the country to drum up support for the League and the treaty. His train traveled 8,000 miles—through the Midwest, to the Pacific, and then back East. The crowds were large and responsive, but they did not change any votes in the Senate. The strain took its toll. On September 25, after speaking in Pueblo, Colorado, the sixty-three-year-old Wilson collapsed from exhaustion. His doctor canceled the rest of the trip. A week later, back in Washington, the president suffered a stroke that left him partially paralyzed. In November, Lodge brought the treaty out of committee for a vote, having appended to it fourteen reservations—that is, recommended changes. A bedridden Wilson stubbornly refused to compromise and instructed Democrats to vote against the Lodge version of the treaty. On November 19, Democrats joined with the "irreconcilables" to defeat the amended treaty, 39 to 55.

Wilson refused to budge. In January, he urged Democrats to either stand by the original treaty or vote it down. The 1920 election, he warned, would be "a great and solemn referendum" on the whole issue. In the final vote, on March 19, 1920, twenty-one Democrats broke with the president and voted for the Lodge version, giving it a majority of 49 to 35. But this was seven votes short of the two-thirds needed for ratification. As a result, the United States never signed the Versailles Treaty, nor did it join the League of Nations. The absence of the United States weakened the League and made it more difficult for the organization to realize Wilson's dream of a peaceful community of nations.

The Russian Revolution and America's Response

Since early 1917, the turmoil of the Russian Revolution had changed the climate of both foreign affairs and domestic politics. The repressive and corrupt regime of Czar Nicholas II had been overthrown in March 1917 by a coalition of forces demanding change. The new provisional government, headed by Alexander Kerensky, vowed to keep Russia in the fight against Germany. But the war had taken a terrible toll on Russian soldiers and civilians, and had become very unpopular. The radical Bolsheviks, led by V. I. Lenin, gained a large following by promising "peace, land, and bread," and they began plotting to seize power. The Bolsheviks followed the teachings of German revolutionary Karl Marx, emphasizing the inevitability of class struggle and the replacement of capitalism by communism.

In November 1917 the Bolsheviks took control of the Russian government. In March 1918, to the dismay of the Allies, the new Bolshevik government negotiated a separate peace with Germany, the Treaty of Brest-Litovsk. Russia was now lost as a military ally, and her

defection made possible a massive shift of German troops to the Western Front. As civil war raged within Russia, British and French leaders wanted to help counterrevolutionary forces overthrow the new Bolshevik regime, as well as reclaim military supplies originally sent for use against the Germans.

Although sympathetic to the March revolution overthrowing the czar, President Wilson refused to recognize the authority of the Bolshevik regime. Bolshevism represented a threat to the liberal-capitalist values that Wilson believed to be the foundation of America's moral and material power and that provided the basis for the Fourteen Points. At the same time, however, Wilson at first resisted British and French pressure to intervene in Russia, citing his commitment to national self-determination and noninterference in other countries' internal affairs. "I believe in letting them work out their own salvation, even though they wallow in anarchy for a while," he wrote to one Allied diplomat.

By August 1918, as the Russian political and military situation became increasingly chaotic, Wilson agreed to British and French plans for sending troops to Siberia and northern Russia. Meanwhile, Japan poured troops into Siberia and northern Manchuria in a bid to control the commercially important Chinese Eastern and Trans-Siberian railways. After the Wilson administration negotiated an agreement that placed these strategic railways under international control, the restoration and protection of the railways became the primary concern of American military forces in Russia. Wilson justified the intervention on trade and commercial grounds, telling Congress, "It is essential that we maintain the policy of the Open Door." But, however reluctantly, the United States had in fact become an active, anti-Bolshevik participant in the Russian civil war.

Wilson's idealistic support for self-determination had succumbed to the demands of international power politics. Eventually, some 15,000 American troops served in northern and eastern Russia, with some remaining until 1920. They stayed for two reasons: to counter Japanese influence, and because Wilson did not want to risk alienating the British and French, who opposed withdrawal. The Allied armed intervention widened the gulf between Russia and the West. In March 1919, Russian Communists established the Third International, or Comintern. Their call for a worldwide revolution deepened Allied mistrust, and the Paris Peace Conference essentially ignored the new political reality posed by the Russian Revolution.

The Red Scare

In the United States, strikes, antiwar agitation, even racial disturbances were increasingly blamed on foreign radicals and alien ideologies. Pro-German sentiment, socialism, the IWW, and trade unionism in general—all were conveniently lumped together. The accusation of Bolshevism became a powerful weapon for turning public opinion against strikers and political dissenters of all kinds. In the 1919 Seattle general strike, for example, Mayor Ole Hanson claimed, contrary to all evidence, that the strikers "want to take possession of our American Government and try to duplicate the anarchy of Russia." In truth, by 1919 the American radicals were already weakened and badly split. The Socialist Party had around 40,000 members. Two small Communist Parties, made up largely of immigrants, had a total of perhaps 70,000. In the spring of 1919, a few extremists mailed bombs to prominent business and political leaders. That June, simultaneous bombings in eight cities killed two people and damaged the residence of Attorney General A. Mitchell Palmer. With public alarm growing, state and federal officials began a coordinated campaign to root out subversives and their alleged Russian connections.

Palmer used the broad authority of the 1918 Alien Act, which enabled the government to deport any immigrant found to be a member of a revolutionary organization prior to or after coming to the United States. In a series of raids in late 1919, Justice Department agents in eleven cities arrested and roughed up several hundred members of the IWW and the Union of Russian Workers. Little evidence of revolutionary intent was found, but 249 people were deported, including prominent anarchists Emma Goldman and Alexander Berkman. In early 1920, some 6,000 people in thirty-three cities, including many U.S. citizens and noncommunists, were arrested and herded into prisons and bullpens. Again, no evidence of a grand plot was found, but another 600 aliens were deported. The Palmer raids had a ripple effect around the nation, encouraging other repressive measures against radicals. In New York, the state assembly refused to seat five duly elected Socialist Party members.

A report prepared by a group of distinguished lawyers questioned the legality of the attorney general's tactics. Palmer's popularity had waned by the spring of 1920, when it became clear that his predictions of revolutionary uprisings were wildly exaggerated. But the Red Scare left an ugly legacy: wholesale violations of constitutional rights, deportations of hundreds of innocent people, fuel for the fires of nativism and intolerance. Business groups, such as the National Association of Manufacturers, found "Red-baiting" to be an effective tool in postwar efforts to keep unions out of their factories. Indeed, the government-sanctioned Red Scare reemerged later in the century as a powerful political force.

The Red Scare took its toll on the women's movement as well. Before the war, many suffragists and feminists had maintained ties and shared platforms with socialist and labor groups. The suffrage movement in particular had brought together women from very different class backgrounds and political perspectives. But the calls for "100 percent Americanism" during and after the war destroyed the fragile alliances that had made a group such as the National American Woman Suffrage Association so powerful. After the war, many women's organizations that had been divided over American involvement in the war reunited under the umbrella of the National Council for Prevention of War. But when military spokesmen in the early 1920s attacked the group for advocating communism, two of its largest affiliates—the General Federation of Women's Clubs and the Parent-Teacher Association—withdrew in fear. Hostility to radicalism marked the political climate of the 1920s, and this atmosphere narrowed the political spectrum for women activists.

The Election of 1920

The presidential contest of 1920 suggested that Americans wanted to retreat from the internationalism, reform fervor, and social tensions associated with the war. Woodrow Wilson had wanted the 1920 election to be a "solemn referendum" on the League of Nations and his conduct of the war. Ill and exhausted, Wilson did not run for reelection. A badly divided Democratic Party compromised on Governor James M. Cox of Ohio as its candidate. A proven vote-getter, Cox distanced himself from Wilson's policies, which had come under withering attack from many quarters.

The Republicans nominated Senator Warren G. Harding of Ohio. A political hack, the handsome and genial Harding had virtually no qualifications to be president, except that he looked like one. Harding's campaign was vague and ambiguous about the Versailles Treaty and almost everything else. He struck a chord with the electorate in calling for a retreat from Wilsonian idealism. "America's present need," he said, "is not heroics but healing; not nostrums but normalcy; not revolution but restoration."

The notion of a "return to normalcy" proved very attractive to voters exhausted by the war, inflation, big government, and social dislocation. Harding won the greatest landslide in history to that date, carrying every state outside the South and taking the popular vote by 16 million to 9 million. Republicans retained their majorities in the House and Senate as well. Socialist Eugene V. Debs, still a powerful symbol of the dream of radical social change, managed to poll 900,000 votes from jail. But the overall vote repudiated Wilson and the progressive movement. Americans seemed eager to pull back from moralism in public and international controversies. Yet many of the economic,

CHRONOLOGY

1903	U.S. obtains Panama canal rights
1905	President Theodore Roosevelt mediates peace treaty between Japan and Russia at Portsmouth Conference
1908	Root-Takahira Agreement with Japan affirms status quo in Asia and Open Door policy in China
1911	Mexican Revolution begins
1914	U.S. forces invade Mexico Panama Canal opens World War I begins in Europe President Woodrow Wilson issues proclamation of neutrality
1915	Germany declares war zone around Great Britain German U-boat sinks *Lusitania*
1916	Pancho Villa raids New Mexico, is pursued by General Pershing Wilson is reelected National Defense Act establishes preparedness program
1917	February: Germany resumes unrestricted submarine warfare March: Zimmermann Note, suggesting a German-Mexican alliance, shocks Americans

	April: U.S. declares war on the Central Powers May: Selective Service Act is passed June: Espionage Act is passed November: Bolshevik Revolution begins in Russia
1918	January: Wilson unveils Fourteen Points May: Sedition Act is passed June: U.S. troops begin to see action in France November: Armistice ends war
1919	January: Eighteenth Amendment (Prohibition) is ratified Wilson serves as Chief U.S. negotiator at Paris Peace Conference June: Versailles Treaty is signed in Paris July: Race riot breaks out in Chicago Steel strike begins in several mid-western cities November: Palmer raids begin
1920	March: Senate finally votes down Versailles Treaty and League of Nations August: Nineteenth Amendment (woman suffrage) is ratified November: Warren G. Harding is elected president

social, and cultural changes wrought by the war would accelerate during the 1920s. In truth, there could never be a "return to normalcy."

CONCLUSION

Compared to the casualties and social upheavals endured by the European powers, the Great War's impact on American life might appear slight. Yet the war created economic, social, and political dislocations that helped reshape American life long after Armistice Day. Republican administrations invoked the wartime partnership between government and industry to justify an aggressive peacetime policy fostering cooperation between the state and business. Wartime production needs contributed to what economists later called "the second industrial revolution." Patriotic fervor and the exaggerated specter of Bolshevism were used to repress radicalism, organized labor, feminism, and the entire legacy of progressive reform.

The wartime measure of national prohibition evolved into perhaps the most contentious social issue of peacetime. Sophisticated use of sales techniques, psychology, and propaganda during the war helped define the newly powerful advertising and public relations industries of the 1920s. The growing visibility of immigrants and African Americans, especially in the nation's cities, provoked a xenophobic and racist backlash in the politics of the 1920s. More than anything else, the desire for "normalcy" reflected the deep anxieties evoked by America's wartime experience.

REVIEW QUESTIONS

1. What central issues drew the United States deeper into international politics in the early years of the century? How did American presidents justify a more expansive role? What diplomatic and military policies did they exploit for these ends?
2. Compare the arguments for and against American participation in the Great War. Which Americans were most likely to support entry? Which were more likely to oppose it?
3. How did mobilizing for war change the economy and its relationship to government? Which of these changes, if any, spilled over to the postwar years?
4. How did the war affect political life in the United States? What techniques were used to stifle dissent? What was the war's political legacy?
5. To what extent was the war an extension of progressivism?
6. Analyze the impact of the war on American workers. How did the conflict affect the lives of African Americans and women?
7. What principles guided Woodrow Wilson's Fourteen Points? How would you explain the United States' failure to ratify the Treaty of Versailles?

RECOMMENDED READING

Marc Allen Eisner, *From Warfare State to Welfare State: World War I, Compensatory State Building, and the Limits of the Modern Order* (2000). Examines policymakers and business organizations.

Kathleen Kennedy, *Disloyal Mothers and Scurrilous Citizens: Women and Subversion During World War I* (1999). Analyzes the Federal government's campaign against antiwar women activists.

Thomas J. Knock, *To End All Wars: Woodrow Wilson and the Quest for a New World Order* (1992). A persuasive analysis of Wilson's internationalism.

Walter LaFeber, *The American Age* (1989). A fine survey of the history of U.S. foreign policy.

Paul L. Murphy, *World War I and the Origin of Civil Liberties* (1979). A good overview.

Ronald Schaffer, *America in the Great War: The Rise of the War Welfare State* (1991). Excellent material on how the war transformed the relationship between business and government.

Joe William Trotter Jr., ed., *The Great Migration in Historical Perspective* (1991). An excellent collection of essays examining the Great Migration.

Neil A. Wynn, *From Progressivism to Prosperity: World War I and American Society* (1986). An illuminating account of the social impact of the war on American life.

Robert H. Zieger, *America's Great War: World War I and the American Experience* (2000). The best one volume synthesis on how the war transformed the U. S.

Susan Zeiger, *In Uncle Sam's Service: Women Workers With the American Expeditionary Force, 1917–1919* (1999). Indepth study of women's experiences in the armed forces.

▶ MEDIA RESOURCES

U.S. HISTORY DOCUMENTS CD-ROM

World War One

22-1 The Great War
22-2 Boy Scouts of America from, "Boy Scouts Support the War Effort" (1917)
22-3 Letters from the Great Migration (1917)
22-4 American Troops in the Trenches (1918)
22-5 Eugene Kennedy, A "Doughboy" Describes the Fighting Front (1918)
22-6 Newton D. Baker, "The Treatment of German Americans" (1918)
22-7 An Official Report
22-8 Woodrow Wilson, The Fourteen Points (1918)

COMPANION WEBSITE HIGHLIGHTS

To view an exploration, enter one of the URLs below in your browser.

Web Explorations

The United States in the Caribbean, 1865–1933
http://www.prenhall.com/faragher/map22.1
Woman Suffrage by State, 1869–1919
http://www.prenhall.com/faragher/map22.2

Additional Interactive Maps

To access the map, go to this chapter's resources at
http://www.prenhall.com/faragher
The Western Front, 1918, page 680

HISTORY RESOURCE CENTER

To find the resources listed below, go to
http://www.prenhall.com/historyresourcecenter

Documents

Report of the Vice Commission, Louisville, Kentucky (1915)
Woodrow Wilson, from The New Freedom (1913)

(Continued)

(Continued)

Images

"Buy War Bonds" Poster
"Gee!! I Wish I Were a Man" Poster
"The Navy Needs You" Poster
African American Recruiting Poster
American Troops on the Road in Esnes, France
French Couple Welcomes Two American Soldiers

Life in the Trenches
Mrs. Hearst Reviews a Liberty Loan Parade
Saying Goodbye
Temporary Shelter for American Wounded
Trench Warfare
World War I Recruiting Poster

EXPLORING AMERICA
BECOMING "AMERICAN"

http://www.prenhall.com/faragher/becomingamerican

The late nineteenth and early twentieth centuries witnessed an abrupt change in immigration policy. What caused this change and how is it connected to the idea of being an American? How did fear of alien radicals influence supporters of excluding immigrants? What role did contemporary concepts of race play in the debate over immigration? What impact did World War I and the initial transition to peace play in the movement to change immigration policy? The *Becoming 'American'* module explores the longstanding issue of immigration and the pivotal events leading to substantial changes in U.S. immigration policy in the 1920s.

Becoming "American" shows that race and ethnicity strongly influenced the immigration restriction movement as did the rise of radicalism in the late 1800s. It also illustrates the important role played by World War I in defining who was an American and who should be allowed to immigrate to the United States. The narrative is supplement by visual images, print primary source documents, graphs, interactive maps, and audio clips to explore a topic that remains an issue today. The chronology provides an important time frame for the discussion.

Reflect and Respond

1. In the 1920s, a new Ku Klux Klan attracted millions of members and exercised significant political clout, not simply in the South, but in the Northeast, Northwest, and Midwest as well. At the heart of their appeal was their fierce antiCatholicism and opposition to immigration. Use the cartoons and other materials in the Web Connection to analyze the excerpts from Imperial Wizard Hiram Wesley Evans' 1923 address. In what ways was he drawing upon the stereotypes and images connected with the Great Red Scare and the Americanization movement? In what ways did he diverge from those images?

✓ **Check it out**
Immigration to the United States, 1901–1920

This map depicts the worldwide immigration to the United States in the first two decades of the twentieth century. It shows nation by nation the number of immigrants coming to the United States, offering an important global perspective to this movement. Equally important, while the statistics presented help identify where the largest number of immigrants where coming from, they also presage future trends in immigration.

This exploration is also available on the *Exploring America* CD-ROM.

▶ 1920–1929

SOURCE: Thomas Hart Benton, *City Activities with Dance Hall* from America Today, 1930. Distemper and egg tempera with oil glaze on gessoed linen, 92″ × 134 1/2″. Collection, The Equitable Life Assurance Society of the U.S. © T. H. Benton and R. P. Benton Testamentary Trusts/Licensed by VAGA, New York, N.Y.

The Movie Audience and Hollywood: Mass Culture Creates a New National Community

INSIDE MIDTOWN MANHATTAN'S MAGNIFICENT NEW ROXY THEATER, A sellout crowd eagerly settled in for opening night. Outside, thousands of fans cheered wildly at the arrival of movie stars such as Charlie Chaplin, Gloria Swanson, and Harold Lloyd. A squadron of smartly uniformed ushers guided patrons under a five-story-tall rotunda to some 6,200 velvet-covered seats. The audience marveled at the huge gold and rose-colored murals, classical statuary, plush carpeting, and Gothic-style windows. It was easy to believe newspaper reports that the theater had cost $10 million to build. Suddenly, light flooded the orchestra pit and 110 musicians began playing "The Star Spangled Banner." A troupe of 100 performers took the stage, dancing ballet numbers and singing old southern melodies such as "My Old Kentucky Home" and "Swanee River." Congratulatory telegrams from President Calvin Coolidge and other dignitaries flashed on the screen. Finally, the evening's feature presentation, *The Love of Sunya,* starring Gloria Swanson, began. Samuel L. "Roxy" Rothapfel, the theater's designer, had realized his grand dream—to build "the cathedral of the motion picture."

When Roxy's opened in March 1927, nearly 60 million Americans "worshiped" each week at movie theaters across the nation. The "movie palaces" of the 1920s were designed to transport patrons to exotic places and different times. As film pioneer Marcus Loew put it, "We sell tickets to theaters, not movies." Every large community boasted at least one opulent movie theater. Houston's Majestic was built to represent an ancient Italian garden; it had a ceiling made to look like an open sky, complete with stars and cloud formations. The Tivoli in Chicago featured opulent French Renaissance decor; Grauman's Egyptian in Los Angeles re-created the look of a pharaoh's tomb; and Albuquerque's Kimo drew inspiration from Navajo art and religion.

The remarkable popularity of motion pictures, and later radio, forged a new kind of community. A huge national audience regularly went to the movies, and the same entertainment could be enjoyed virtually anywhere in the country by just about everyone. Movies emerged as the most popular form in the new mass culture, with an appeal that extended far beyond the films themselves, or even the theaters. Americans embraced the cult of celebrity, voraciously consuming fan magazines, gossip columns, and news of the stars. By the 1920s, the production center for this dream world was Hollywood, California, a suburb of Los Angeles that had barely existed in 1890.

Motion picture companies found Hollywood an alluring alternative to the east coast cities where they had been born. Its reliably sunny and dry climate was ideal for year-round filming. Its unique surroundings offered a perfect variety of scenic locations—mountains, desert, ocean—and downtown Los Angeles was only an hour away. Land was cheap and plentiful. And because Los Angeles was the leading nonunion, open-shop city in the country, so was labor. By the early 1920s Hollywood produced more than 80 percent of the nation's motion pictures and was assuming mythical status. The isolation of the town, its great distance from the eastern cities, its lack of traditional sources of culture and learning—all contributed to movie folk looking at life in a self-consciously "Hollywood" way.

With its feel of a modern frontier boomtown, Hollywood was a new kind of American community. It lured the young and cosmopolitan with the promise of upward mobility and a new way of life. Most of the top studio executives were Jewish immigrants from eastern and central Europe. In contrast to most Americans, who hailed from rural areas or small towns, more than half of Hollywood's writers, directors, editors, and actors were born in cities of over 100,000. Two-thirds of its performers were under thirty-five, and three-fourths of its actresses were under twenty-five. More than 90 percent of its writers (women made up one-third to one-half of this key group) had attended college or worked in journalism. The movies this untypical community created evoked the pleasures of leisure, consumption, and personal freedom, redefining the nation's cultural values in the 1920s.

Movie stars dominated Hollywood. Charlie Chaplin, Mary Pickford, Rudolph Valentino, Gloria Swanson, and Douglas Fairbanks became popular idols as much for their highly publicized private lives as for their roles on screen. Many accumulated great wealth, becoming the nation's experts on how to live well. Movie folk built luxurious mansions in a variety of architectural styles and outfitted them with swimming pools, tennis courts, golf courses, and lavish gardens.

Visitors often noted that Hollywood had no museums, art galleries, live theater, or other traditional institutions of high culture. How would the town's wealthy movie elite spend their time and money? By 1916 Charlie Chaplin, a working-class immigrant from the London slums, was earning $10,000 a week for the comedies that made his the most famous face in the world. He recalled trying to figure out what to do with his new wealth. "The money I earned was legendary, a symbol in figures, for I had never actually seen it. I therefore had to do something to prove I had it. So I procured a secretary, a valet, a car, a chauffeur."

Ordinary Americans found it easy to identify with movie stars despite their wealth and status. Unlike industrialists or politicians, stars had no social authority over large groups of employees or voters. They, too, had to answer to a boss, and most had risen from humble beginnings. But above all, Hollywood, like the movies it churned out, represented for millions of Americans new possibilities: freedom, material success, upward mobility, and the chance to remake one's very identity. By the end of the decade the Hollywood "dream factory" had helped forge a national community whose collective aspirations and desires were increasingly defined by those possibilities, even if relatively few Americans realized them during the 1920s. ■

Hollywood

KEY TOPICS

- A second industrial revolution that transforms the economy

- The promise and limits of prosperity in the 1920s

- New mass media and the culture of consumption

- Republican Party dominance

- Political and cultural opposition to modern trends

POSTWAR PROSPERITY AND ITS PRICE

Republican Warren G. Harding won the presidency in 1920, largely thanks to his nostalgic call for a "return to normalcy." But in the decade following the end of World War I, the American economy underwent profound structural changes that guaranteed life would never be "normal" again. The 1920s saw an enormous increase in the efficiency of production, a steady climb in real wages, a decline in the length of the average employee's work week, and a boom in consumer goods industries. Americans shared unevenly in the postwar prosperity, and by the end of the decade certain basic weaknesses in the economy helped to bring on the worst depression in American history. Yet overall, the nation experienced crucial transformations in how it organized its business, earned its living, and enjoyed its leisure time.

The Second Industrial Revolution

The prosperity of the 1920s rested on what historians have called the "second industrial revolution" in American manufacturing, in which technological innovations made it possible to increase industrial output without expanding the labor force. Electricity replaced steam as the main power source for industry in these years, making possible the replacement of older machinery with more efficient and flexible electric machinery. In 1914 only 30 percent of the nation's factories were electrified; by 1929, 70 percent relied on the electric motor rather than the steam engine.

Much of the newer, automatic machinery could be operated by unskilled and semiskilled workers, and it boosted the overall efficiency of American industry. Thus in 1929 the average worker in manufacturing produced roughly three-quarters more per hour than he or she had in 1919. The machine industry itself, particularly the manufacture of electrical machinery, led in productivity gains, enjoying one of the fastest rates of expansion. It employed more workers than any other manufacturing sector—some 1.1 million in 1929—supplying not only a growing home market but 35 percent of the world market as well.

During the late nineteenth century, heavy industries such as machine tools, railroads, iron, and steel had pioneered mass-production techniques. These industries manufactured what economists call producer-durable goods. In the 1920s, modern mass-production techniques were increasingly applied as well to newer consumer-durable goods—automobiles, radios, washing machines, and telephones—permitting firms to make large profits while keeping prices affordable. Other consumer-based industries, such as canning, chemicals, synthetics, and plastics, began to change the everyday lives of millions of Americans. With more efficient management, greater mechanization, intensive product research, and ingenious sales and advertising methods, the consumer-based industries helped to nearly double industrial production in the 1920s.

America experienced a building boom during the 1920s, and its construction industry played a large role in the new prosperity. Expenditures for residential housing, nonresidential building, and public construction projects all showed steady growth after 1921. The demand for new housing was unprecedented, particularly with the backlog created during World War I, when little new construction took place. The growth in automobile ownership, as well as improvements in public mass transit, made suburban living more attractive to families and suburban construction more profitable for developers. Commercial banks, savings and loan associations, and insurance companies provided greatly expanded credit for home buying. America's residential mortgage debt jumped from about $8 billion in 1919 to $27 billion in 1929.

The Modern Corporation

The organization and techniques of American business underwent crucial changes during the postwar decade. In the late nineteenth century, individual entrepreneurs such as John D. Rockefeller in oil and Andrew Carnegie in steel had provided a model for success. They maintained both corporate control (ownership) and business leadership (management) in their enterprises. In the 1920s, a managerial revolution increasingly divorced ownership of corporate stock from the everyday control of businesses. The new corporate ideal was to be found in men such as Alfred P. Sloan of General Motors and Owen D. Young of the Radio Corporation of America. A growing class of salaried executives, plant managers, and engineers formed a new elite who made corporate policy without themselves having a controlling interest in the companies they worked for. They stressed scientific management and the latest theories of behavioral psychology in their effort to make their workplaces more productive, stable, and profitable.

During the 1920s, the most successful corporations were those that led in three key areas: the integration of production and distribution, product diversification, and the expansion of industrial research. Until the end of World War I, for example, the chemical manufacturer Du Pont had specialized in explosives such as gunpowder. After the war, Du Pont moved aggressively into the consumer market with a diverse array of products. The company created separate but integrated divisions that produced and distributed new fabrics (such as rayon),

paints, dyes, and celluloid products (such as artificial sponges). The great electrical manufacturers—General Electric and Westinghouse—similarly transformed themselves after the war. Previously concentrating on lighting and power equipment, they now diversified into household appliances like radios, washing machines, and refrigerators. The chemical and electrical industries also led the way in industrial research, hiring personnel to develop new products and test their commercial viability.

By 1929 the 200 largest corporations owned nearly half the nation's corporate wealth—that is, physical plant, stock, and property. Half the total industrial income—revenue from sales of goods—was concentrated in 100 corporations. Oligopoly—the control of a market by a few large producers—became the norm. Four companies packed almost three-quarters of all American meat. Another four rolled nine out of every ten cigarettes. National chain grocery stores, clothing shops, and pharmacies began squeezing out local neighborhood businesses. One grocery chain alone, the Great Atlantic and Pacific Tea Company (A&P), accounted for 10 percent of all retail food sales in America. Its 15,000 stores sold a greater volume of goods than Ford Motor Company at its peak. These changes meant that Americans were increasingly members of national consumer communities, buying the same brands all over the country, as opposed to locally produced goods.

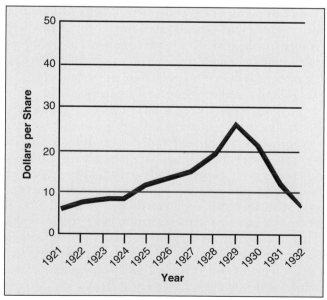

Stock Market Prices, 1921–1932 Common stock prices rose steeply during the 1920s. Although only about 4 million Americans owned stocks during the period, "stock watching" became something of a national sport.

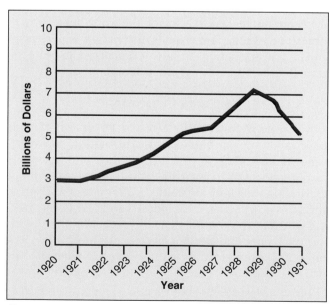

Consumer Debt, 1920–1931 The expansion of consumer borrowing was a key component of the era's prosperity. These figures do not include mortgages or money borrowed to purchase stocks. They reveal the great increase in "installment buying" for such consumer durable goods as automobiles and household appliances.

The A&P grocery chain expanded from 400 stores in 1912 to more than 15,000 by the end of the 1920s, making it a familiar sight in communities across America. A&P advertisements, like this one from 1927, emphasized cleanliness, order, and the availability of name brand goods at discount prices.

SOURCE: From Ladies Home Journal. A&P Food Stores LTD.

Welfare Capitalism

The wartime gains made by organized labor and the active sympathy shown to trade unions by government agencies such as the National War Labor Board troubled most corporate leaders. To challenge the power and appeal of trade unions and collective bargaining, large employers aggressively promoted a variety of new programs designed to improve worker well-being and morale. These schemes, collectively known as welfare capitalism, became a key part of corporate strategy in the 1920s.

One approach was to encourage workers to acquire property through stock-purchase plans or, less frequently, home ownership plans. By 1927, 800,000 employees had more than $1 billion invested in more than 300 companies. Other programs offered workers insurance policies covering accidents, illness, old age, and death. By 1928 some 6 million workers had group insurance coverage valued at $7.5 billion. Many plant managers and personnel departments consciously worked to improve safety conditions, provide medical

services, and establish sports and recreation programs for workers. Employers hoped such measures would encourage workers to identify personally with the company and discourage complaints on the job. To some extent they succeeded. But welfare capitalism could not solve the most chronic problems faced by industrial workers: seasonal unemployment, low wages, long hours, and unhealthy factory conditions.

Large corporations also mounted an effective antiunion campaign in the early 1920s called "the American plan," a name meant to associate unionism with foreign and un-American ideas. Backed by powerful business lobbies such as the National Association of Manufacturers and the Chamber of Commerce, campaign leaders called for the open shop, in which no employee would be compelled to join a union. If a union existed, nonmembers would still get whatever wages and rights the union had won—a policy that put organizers at a disadvantage in signing up new members.

The open shop undercut the gains won in a union shop, where new employees had to join an existing union, or a closed shop, where employers agreed to hire only union members. As alternatives, large employers such as U.S. Steel and International Harvester began setting up company unions. Their intent was to substitute largely symbolic employee representation in management conferences for the more confrontational process of collective bargaining. Company unions were often established simultaneously with antiunion campaigns in specific industries or communities.

These management strategies contributed to a sharp decline in the ranks of organized labor. Total union membership dropped from about 5 million in 1920 to 3.5 million in 1926. A large proportion of the remaining union members were concentrated in the skilled crafts of the building and printing trades. A conservative and timid union leadership was also responsible for the trend. William Green, who became president of the American Federation of Labor after the death of Samuel Gompers in 1924, showed no real interest in getting unorganized workers, such as those in the growing mass-production industries of automobiles, steel, and electrical goods, into unions. The federal government, which had provided limited wartime support for unions, now reverted to a more probusiness posture. The Supreme Court in particular was unsympathetic toward unions, consistently upholding the use of injunctions to prevent strikes, picketing, and other union activities.

The Auto Age

In their classic community study *Middletown* (1929), sociologists Robert and Helen Lynd noted the dramatic impact of the car on the social life of Muncie, Indiana. "Why on earth do you need to study what's changing this country?" asked one lifelong Muncie resident in 1924. "I can tell you what's happening in just four letters: A-U-T-O!" This remark hardly seems much of an exaggeration today. No other single development could match the impact of the postwar automobile explosion on the way Americans worked, lived, and played. The auto industry offered the clearest example of the rise to prominence of consumer durables. During the 1920s, America made approximately 85 percent of all the world's passenger cars. By 1929 the motor vehicle industry was the most productive in the United States in terms of value. In that year the industry added 4.8 million new cars to the more than 26 million—roughly one for every five people—already on American roads.

This extraordinary new industry had mushroomed in less than a generation. Its great pioneer, Henry Ford, had shown how the use of a continuous assembly line could drastically reduce the number of worker hours required to produce a single vehicle. Ford revolutionized the factory shop floor with new, custom-built machinery, such as the engine-boring drill press and the pneumatic wrench, and a more efficient layout. "Every piece of work in the shop moves," Ford boasted. "It may move on hooks or overhead chains, going to assembly in the exact order in which the parts are required; it may travel on a moving platform, or it may go by gravity, but the point is that there is no lifting or trucking of anything other than materials." In 1913 it took thirteen hours to produce one automobile. In 1914, at his sprawling new Highland Park assembly plant just outside Detroit, Ford's system finished one car every ninety minutes. By 1925, cars were rolling off his assembly line at the rate of one every ten seconds.

In 1914 Ford startled American industry by inaugurating a new wage scale: $5 for an eight-hour day. This was roughly double the going pay rate for industrial labor, along with a shorter workday as well. But in defying the conventional economic wisdom of the day, Ford acted less out of benevolence than out of shrewdness. He understood that workers were consumers as well as producers, and the new wage scale helped boost sales of Ford cars. It also reduced the high turnover rate in his

Finished automobiles roll off the moving assembly line at the Ford Motor Company, Highland Park, Michigan, ca. 1920. During the 1920s Henry Ford achieved the status of folk hero, as his name became synonymous with the techniques of mass production. Ford cultivated a public image of himself as the heroic genius of the auto industry, greatly exaggerating his personal achievements.

SOURCE: Brown Brothers.

labor force and increased worker efficiency. Roughly two-thirds of the labor force at Ford consisted of immigrants from southern and eastern Europe. By the early 1920s Ford also employed about 5,000 African Americans, more than any other large American corporation. Ford's mass-production system and economies of scale permitted him to progressively reduce the price of his cars, bringing them within the reach of millions of Americans. The famous Model T, thoroughly standardized and available only in black, cost just under $300 in 1924—about three months' wages for the best-paid factory workers.

By 1927 Ford had produced 15 million Model Ts. But by then the company faced stiff competition from General Motors, which had developed an effective new marketing strategy. Under the guidance of Alfred P. Sloan, GM organized into separate divisions, each of which appealed to a different market segment. Cadillac, for example, produced GM's most expensive car, which was targeted at the wealthy buyer; Chevrolet produced its least expensive model, which was targeted at working-class and lower middle-class buyers. The GM business structure, along with its attempts to match production with demand through sophisticated market research and sales forecasting, became a widely copied model for other large American corporations.

The auto industry provided a large market for makers of steel, rubber, glass, and petroleum products. It stimulated public spending for good roads and extended the housing boom to new suburbs. Showrooms, repair shops, and gas stations appeared in thousands of communities. New small enterprises, from motels to billboard advertising to roadside diners, sprang up as motorists took to the highway. The rapid development of Florida and California, in particular, was partly a response to the growing influence of the automobile and the new possibilities it presented for seeing far-off places.

Automobiles widened the experience of millions of Americans. They made the exploration of the world outside the local community easier and more attractive. For some the car merely reinforced old social patterns, making it easier for them to get to church on Sunday, for example, or visit neighbors. Others used their cars to go to new places, shop in nearby cities, or take vacations. The automobile made leisure, in the sense of getting away from the routines of work and school, a more regular part of everyday life. It undoubtedly also changed the courtship practices of America's youth. Young people took advantage of the car to gain privacy and distance from their parents. "What on earth do you want me to do?" complained one "Middletown" high school girl to her anxious father. "Just sit around home all evening?" Many had their first sexual experiences in a car.

Cities and Suburbs

Cars also promoted urban and suburban growth. The federal census for 1920 was the first in American history in which the proportion of the population that lived in urban places (those with 2,500 or more people) exceeded the proportion of the population living in rural areas. More revealing of urban growth was the steady increase in the number of big cities. In 1910 there were sixty cities with more than 100,000 inhabitants; in 1920 there were sixty-eight; and by 1930 there were ninety-two. During the 1920s New York grew by 20 percent to nearly 7 million, whereas Detroit, home of the auto industry, doubled its population, to nearly 2 million.

Cities promised business opportunity, good jobs, cultural richness, and personal freedom. They attracted millions of Americans, white and black, from small towns and farms, as well as immigrants from abroad. Im-

migrants were drawn to cities by the presence there of family and people of like background in already established ethnic communities. In a continuation of the Great Migration that began during World War I, roughly 1.5 million African Americans from the rural South migrated to cities in search of economic opportunities during the 1920s, doubling the black populations of New York, Chicago, Detroit, and Houston.

Cities grew both vertically and horizontally in these years. Skylines around the country were remade as architects took advantage of steel-skeleton construction technology to build skyscrapers. By 1930, American cities boasted nearly 400 buildings more than twenty stories tall. New York's Empire State Building, completed in 1931, was the tallest building in the world, rising 1,250 feet into the sky. It had room for 25,000 commercial and residential tenants in its 102 stories.

Houston offers a good example of how the automobile shaped an urban community. In 1910 it was a sleepy railroad town with a population of about 75,000 that served the Texas Gulf coast and interior. The enormous demand for gasoline and other petroleum products

Cancel distance & conquer weather

The woman who drives her own Ford Closed Car is completely independent of road and weather conditions in any season.

It enables her to carry on all those activities of the winter months that necessitate travel to and fro—in

or out of town. Her time and energy are conserved; her health is protected, no matter how bitterly cold the day, or how wet and slushy it is underfoot.

A Ford Sedan is always comfortable—warm and snug in winter, and in summer with ventilator and windows open wide, as cool and airy as an open car.

This seasonal comfort is combined with fine looks and Ford dependability; no wonder there is for this car so wide and ever-growing a demand.

FORD MOTOR COMPANY, DETROIT, MICHIGAN

TUDOR SEDAN, $580 .·. FORDOR SEDAN, $660
COUPE, $530 .·. ALL PRICES F. O. B. DETROIT

Ford

CLOSED CARS

Until 1924 Henry Ford had disdained national advertising for his cars. But as General Motors gained a competitive edge by making yearly changes in style and technology, Ford was forced to pay more attention to advertising. This ad was directed at "Mrs. Consumer," combining appeals to both female independence and motherly duties.

helped transform the city into a busy center for oil refining. Its population soared to 300,000 by the end of the 1920s. Abundant cheap land and the absence of zoning ordinances, combined with the availability of the automobile, pushed Houston to expand horizontally rather than vertically. It became the archetypal decentralized, low-density city, sprawling miles in each direction from downtown, and thoroughly dependent upon automobiles and roads for its sense of community. Other Sunbelt cities, such as Los Angeles, Miami, and San Diego, experienced similar land-use patterns and sharp population growth during the decade.

Suburban communities grew at twice the rate of their core cities, also thanks largely to the automobile boom. Undeveloped land on the fringes of cities became valuable real estate. Grosse Pointe, near Detroit, and Elmwood Park, near Chicago, grew more than 700 percent in ten years. Long Island's Nassau County, just east of New York City, tripled in population. All the new "automobile suburbs" differed in important ways from earlier suburbs built along mass transit lines. The car allowed for a larger average lot size, and in turn lower residential density. It also became essential for commuting to work and encouraged the movement of workplaces out of the central city. The suburbs would increasingly become not only places to live but centers for working and shopping as well.

Exceptions: Agriculture, Ailing Industries

Amid prosperity and progress, there were large pockets of the country that lagged behind. Advances in real income and improvements in the standard of living for workers and farmers were uneven at best. During the 1920s, one-quarter of all American workers were employed in agriculture, yet the farm sector failed to share in the general prosperity. The years 1914–19 had been a kind of golden age for the nation's farmers. Increased wartime demand, along with the devastation of much of European agriculture, had led to record-high prices for many crops. In addition, the wartime Food Administration had encouraged a great increase in agricultural production. But with the war's end, American farmers began to suffer from a chronic worldwide surplus of such farm staples as cotton, hogs, and corn.

Prices began to drop sharply in 1920. Cotton, which sold at 37 cents a pound in mid-1920, fell to 14 cents by year's end. Hog and cattle prices declined nearly 50 percent. By 1921 net farm income was down more than half from the year before. Land values also dropped, wiping out billions in capital investment. Behind these aggregate statistics were hundreds of thousands of individual human tragedies on the nation's 6 million farms. A 1928 song, "Eleven Cent Cotton," expressed the farmer's lament:

'Leven cent cotton, forty cent meat,
How in the world can a poor man eat?
Pray for the sunshine, 'cause it will rain,
Things gettin' worse, drivin' us insane.

During the war many farmers had gone heavily into debt to buy land and expand operations with new machinery. Farm mortgages doubled between 1910 and 1920, from $3.3 billion to $6.7 billion, and another $2.7 billion was added to the total by 1925. These debts saddled farmers with fixed expenses that grew crushingly burdensome as commodity prices spiraled downward. American farm products, moreover, faced stiffer competition abroad from reviving European agriculture and the expanding output from Canada, Argentina, and Australia. Efforts to ease the farmer's plight through governmental reform were largely unsuccessful. Individual farmers, traditionally independent, could not influence the price of commodities they sold or bought. It was extremely difficult for farmers to act collectively.

In the South, farmers dependency on "King Cotton" deepened, as the region lagged farther behind the rest of the nation in both agricultural diversity and standard of living. Cotton acreage expanded as large and heavily mechanized farms opened up new land in Oklahoma, west Texas, and the Mississippi-Yazoo delta. But in most of the South, from North Carolina to east Texas, small one- and two-mule cotton farms, most under 50 acres, still dominated the countryside. While editors, state officials, and reformers preached the need for greater variety of crops, southern farmers actually raised less corn and livestock by the end of the decade. With few large urban centers and inadequate transportation, even those southern farmers who had access to capital found it extremely difficult to find reliable markets for vegetables, fruit, poultry, or dairy products. The average southern farm had land and buildings worth $3,525; for northern farms, the figure was $11,029. The number of white tenant farmers increased by 200,000 during the 1920s, while black tenantry declined slightly as a result of the Great Migration. Some 700,000 southern farmers, roughly half white and half black, still labored as sharecroppers. Modern conveniences such as electricity, indoor plumbing, automobiles, and phonographs remained far beyond the reach of the great majority of southern farmers. Widespread rural poverty, poor diet, little access to capital—the world of southern agriculture had changed very little since the days of Populist revolt in the 1890s.

To be sure, some farmers thrived. Wheat production jumped more than 300 percent during the 1920s. Across the plains of Kansas, Nebraska, Colorado, Oklahoma, and Texas, wheat farmers brought the methods of industrial capitalism to the land. They hitched disc plows and combined harvester-threshers to gasoline-powered tractors, tearing up millions of acres of grassland to create a vast wheat factory. With prices averaging above $1 per bushel over the decade, mechanized farming created a new class of large-scale wheat entrepreneurs on the plains. Ida Watkins, "the Wheat Queen" of Haskell County, Kansas, made a profit of $75,000 from her 2,000 acres in 1926. Hickman Price needed twenty-five combines to harvest the wheat on his Plainview, Texas, farm—34,500 acres stretching over fifty-four square miles. When the disastrous dust storms of the 1930s rolled across the grassless plains, the long range ecological impact of destroying so much native vegetation became evident.

Improved transportation and chain supermarkets allowed for a wider and more regular distribution of such foods as oranges, lemons, and fresh green vegetables. Citrus, dairy, and truck farmers in particular profited from the growing importance of national markets. But per capita farm income remained well below what it had been in 1919, and the gap between farm and nonfarm income widened. By 1929 the average income per person on farms was $223, compared with $870 for nonfarm workers. By the end of the decade, hundreds of thousands had quit farming altogether for jobs in mills and factories. And fewer farmers owned their land. In 1930, 42 percent of all farmers were tenants, compared with 37 percent in 1919.

The most important initiatives for federal farm relief were the McNary-Haugen bills, a series of complicated measures designed to prop up and stabilize farm prices. The basic idea, borrowed from the old Populist proposals of the 1890s, was for the government to purchase farm surpluses and either store them until prices rose or sell them on the world market. The result was supposed to be higher domestic prices for farm products. But President Calvin Coolidge viewed these measures as unwarranted federal interference in the economy and vetoed the McNary-Haugen Farm Relief bill of 1927 when it finally passed Congress. Hard-pressed farmers would not benefit from government relief until the New Deal programs implemented in response to the Great Depression in the 1930s.

Other large sectors of American industry also failed to share in the decade's general prosperity. As oil and natural gas gained in importance, America's coal mines became a less important source of energy. A combination of shrinking demand, new mining technology, and a series of losing strikes reduced the coal labor force by one-quarter. The United Mine Workers, perhaps the strongest AFL union in 1920 with 500,000 members, had shrunk to 75,000 by 1928. Economic hardship was widespread in many mining communities dependent on coal, particularly in Appalachia and the southern Midwest. And those miners who did work earned lower hourly wages.

The number of miles of railroad track actually decreased after 1920 as automobiles and trucks began to displace trains. In textiles, shrinking demand and overcapacity (too many factories) were chronic problems. The women's fashions of the 1920s generally required less material than had earlier fashions, and competition from synthetic fibers such as rayon depressed demand for cotton textiles. To improve profit margins, textile manufacturers in New England and other parts of the Northeast began a long-range shift of operations to the South, where nonunion shops and substandard wages became the rule. Between 1923 and 1933, 40 percent of New England's textile factories closed and nearly 100,000 of the 190,000 workers employed there lost their jobs. Older New England manufacturing centers such as Lawrence, Lowell, Nashua, Manchester, and Fall River were hard hit by this shift.

The center of the American textile industry shifted permanently to the Piedmont region of North and South Carolina. Southern mills increased their work force from 220,000 to 257,000 between 1923 and 1933. By 1933 they employed nearly 70 percent of the workers in the industry. One of the biggest new textile communities was Gastonia, North Carolina, which proudly called itself the "South's City of Spindles." As the dominant employers and overall economic powers in southern textile communities, manufacturers aggressively tried to improve productivity and cut costs. Southern mills generally operated night and day, used the newest labor-saving machinery, and cut back on the wage gains of the World War I years. Southern mill hands paid the price for what they called "stretch-out"—a catchall term describing the changes that had them tending more and more machines, receiving lower wages, working nights, and losing nearly all control over the pace and method of production.

THE NEW MASS CULTURE

New communications media reshaped American culture in the 1920s. The phrase "Roaring Twenties" captures the explosion of image- and sound-making machinery that came to dominate so much of American life. Movies, radio, new kinds of journalism, the recording industry, and a more sophisticated advertising industry were deeply connected with the new culture of consumption. They also encouraged the parallel emergence of celebrity as a defining element in modern life. As technologies of mass impression, the media established national standards and norms for much of our culture— habit, dress, language, sounds, social behavior. For millions of Americans, the new media radically altered the rhythms of everyday life and redefined what it meant to be "normal." To be sure, most working-class families had only limited access to the world of mass consumption—and many had only limited interest in it. But the new mass culture helped redefine the ideal of "the good life" and made the images, if not the substance, of it available to a national community.

Movie-Made America

The early movie industry, centered in New York and a few other big cities, had made moviegoing a regular habit for millions of Americans, especially immigrants and the working class. They flocked to cheap, storefront theaters, called nickelodeons, to watch short Westerns, slapstick comedies, melodramas, and travelogues. By 1914 there were about 18,000 "movie houses" showing motion pictures, with more than 7 million daily admissions and $300 million in annual receipts. With the shift of the industry westward to Hollywood, movies entered a new phase of business expansion.

Large studios such as Paramount, Fox, Metro-Goldwyn-Mayer (M-G-M), Universal, and Warner Brothers dominated the business with longer and more expensively produced movies—feature films. These

Mary Pickford, one of the most popular movie stars of the 1910s and 1920s, shown here reading a feminist newspaper in a publicity photo ca. 1917. Pickford frequently portrayed young women struggling for economic freedom from men. She wrote weekly columns for women in which she backed suffrage and urged her female readers to be more self-sufficient. Pickford embodied the new, mass media-based "celebrity" of the 1920s.

SOURCE: Culver Pictures, Inc.

companies were founded and controlled by immigrants from Europe, all of whom had a talent for discovering and exploiting changes in popular tastes. Adolph Zukor, the Hungarian-born head of Paramount, had been a furrier in New York City. Warsaw-born Samuel Goldwyn, a founder of M-G-M, had been a glove salesman. William Fox, of Fox Pictures, began as a garment cutter in Brooklyn. Most of the immigrant moguls had started in the business by buying or managing small movie theaters before beginning to produce films.

The studio system, which came to dominate moviemaking, was based on industrial principles. Each studio combined the three functions of production, distribution, and exhibition, and each controlled hundreds of movie theaters around the country. The era of silent films ended when Warner Brothers scored a huge hit in 1927 with *The Jazz Singer*, starring Al Jolson, which successfully introduced sound. New genres—musicals, gangster films, and screwball comedies—soon became popular. The higher costs associated with "talkies" also increased the studios' reliance on Wall Street investors and banks for working capital.

At the heart of Hollywood's success was the star system and the accompanying cult of celebrity. Stars became vital to the fantasy lives of millions of fans. For many in the audience, there was only a vague line separating the on-screen and off-screen adventures of the stars. Studio publicity, fan magazines, and gossip columns reinforced this ambiguity. Film idols, with their mansions, cars, parties, and private escapades, became the national experts on leisure and consumption. Their movies generally emphasized sexual themes and celebrated youth, athleticism, and the liberating power of consumer goods. Young Americans in particular looked to movies to learn how to dress, wear their hair, talk, or kiss. One researcher looking into the impact of moviegoing on young people asked several to keep "motion picture diaries." "Upon going to my first dance I asked the hairdresser to fix my hair like Greta Garbo's," wrote one eighteen-year-old college student. "In speaking on graduation day I did my best to finish with the swaying-like curtsy which Pola Negri taught me from the screen."

Moviemakers attracted new fans by producing more spectacular movies and by building elegant "movie palaces," like the Roxy Theater described in the opening of this chapter, in which to watch them. But many Americans, particularly in rural areas and small towns, worried about Hollywood's impact on traditional sexual morality. They attacked the permissiveness associated with Hollywood life, and many states created censorship boards to screen movies before allowing them to be shown in theaters. In 1921, the popular comedian Roscoe "Fatty" Arbuckle became embroiled in a highly publicized sex scandal when he was accused of raping and murdering actress Virginia Rappe. Although Arbuckle was acquitted, the sensational atmosphere surrounding the case badly frightened studio heads. They resolved to improve their public image.

To counter growing calls for government censorship, Hollywood's studios came up with a plan to censor themselves. In 1922 they hired Will Hays to head the Motion Picture Producers and Distributors of America. Hays was just what the immigrant moguls needed. An Indiana Republican, elder in the Presbyterian Church, and former postmaster general under President Harding, he personified midwestern Protestant respectability. As the movie industry's czar, Hays lobbied against censorship laws, wrote pamphlets defending the movie business, and began setting guidelines for what could and could not be depicted on the screen. He insisted that movies be treated like any other industrial enterprise, for he understood the relationship between Hollywood's success and the growth of the nation's consumer culture. "More and more," Hays argued in 1926, "is the motion picture being recognized as a stimulant to trade. No longer does the girl in Sullivan, Indiana, guess what the styles are going to be in three months. She knows because she sees them on the screen."

Radio Broadcasting

In the fall of 1920, Westinghouse executive Harry P. Davis noticed that amateur broadcasts from the garage of an employee had attracted attention in the local Pittsburgh press. A department store advertised radio sets capable of picking up these "wireless concerts." Davis converted this amateur station to a stronger one at the Westinghouse main plant. Beginning with the presidential election returns that November, station KDKA offered regular nightly broadcasts that were probably heard by only a few hundred people. Radio broadcasting, begun as a service for selling cheap radio sets left over from World War I, would soon sweep the nation.

Before KDKA, wireless technology had been of interest only to the military, the telephone industry, and a few thousand "ham" (amateur) operators who enjoyed communicating with each other. The "radio mania" of the early 1920s was a response to the new possibilities offered by broadcasting. By 1923 nearly 600 stations had been licensed by the Department of Commerce, and about 600,000 Americans had bought radios. Early programs included live popular music, the playing of phonograph records, talks by college professors, church services, and news and weather reports. For millions of Americans, especially in rural areas and small towns, radio provided a new and exciting link to the larger national community of consumption.

Who would pay for radio programs? In the early 1920s, owners and operators of radio stations included radio equipment manufacturers, newspapers, department stores, state universities, cities, ethnic societies, labor unions, and churches. But by the end of the decade commercial (or "toll") broadcasting emerged as the answer. The dominant corporations in the industry—General Electric, Westinghouse, Radio Corporation of America (RCA), and American Telephone and Telegraph (AT&T)—settled on the idea that advertisers would foot the bill for radio. Millions of listeners might be the consumers of radio shows, but sponsors were to be the customers. Only the sponsors and their advertising agencies enjoyed a direct relationship with broadcasters. Sponsors advertised directly or indirectly to the mass audience through such shows as the *Eveready Hour*, the *Ipana Troubadors*, and the *Taystee Loafers*. AT&T leased its nationwide system of telephone wires to allow the linking of many stations into powerful radio networks, such as the National Broadcasting Company (1926) and the Columbia Broadcasting System (1928).

Radio broadcasting created a national community of listeners, just as motion pictures created one of viewers. NBC and CBS led the way in creating popular radio programs that relied heavily on older cultural forms. The variety show, hosted by vaudeville comedians, became network radio's first important format. Radio's first truly national hit, The *Amos 'n' Andy Show* (1928), was a direct descendant of nineteenth-century "blackface" minstrel entertainment. Radio did more than any previous medium to publicize and commercialize previously isolated forms of American music such as country-and-western, blues, and jazz. Broadcasts of baseball and college football games proved especially popular. In 1930, some 600 stations were broadcasting to more than 12 million homes with radios, or roughly 40 percent of American families. By that time all the elements that characterize the present American system of broadcasting—regular daily programming paid for and produced by commercial advertisers, national networks carrying shows across the nation, and mass ownership of receiver sets in American homes—were in place.

Since it transcended national boundaries, broadcasting had a powerful hemispheric impact as well. In Canada, American manufacturers supplied most of the radio receivers and the larger U.S. stations in cities such as Detroit and Buffalo could easily be heard in Toronto and Montreal. American signals thus interfered with Canadian ones. In response, the 1929 Royal Commission on Radio Broadcasting created a national Canadian broadcasting system, establishing a public network (run by the Canadian Broadcasting Corporation), but also allowing private stations to operate. In a bid to counter American influence, both the public and private elements of the system were charged with providing Canadian programing for their audiences. Yet despite these efforts to "Canadianize" broadcasting, American shows—and advertising—continued to dominate Canadian airwaves. Similarly, U.S. broadcasting interests helped shape early Mexican radio. The 1926 Law of Electric Communications declared the radio spectrum a national resource and created a system combining government-owned stations with private commercial broadcasters licensed by the state. Large private Mexican radio stations were often started in partnership with American corporations such as RCA, as a way to create demand for receiving sets. Language barriers limited the direct impact of U.S. broadcasts, but American advertisers became the backbone of commercial radio in Mexico. They encouraged Mexican broadcasters to adapt successful U.S.-radio formulas, as when Colgate Palmolive pioneered the *radionovela* format similar to the North American soap opera. In both Canada and Mexico, then, governments established national broadcasting systems to bolster cultural and political nationalism. But radio broadcasting significantly amplified the influence of American commercialism throughout the hemisphere.

New Forms of Journalism

A new kind of newspaper, the tabloid, became popular in the postwar years. The *New York Daily News*, founded in 1919 by Joseph M. Patterson, was the first to develop the tabloid style. Its folded-in-half page size made it convenient to read on buses or subways. The *Daily News* devoted much of its space to photographs and other illustrations. With a terse, lively reporting style that emphasized sex, scandal, and sports, *Daily News* circulation reached 400,000 in 1922 and 1.3 million by 1929.

This success spawned a host of imitators in New York and elsewhere. New papers like the *Chicago Times* and the *Los Angeles Daily News* brought the tabloid style to cities across America, while some older papers, such as the *Denver Rocky Mountain News*, adopted the new format. The circulation of existing dailies was little affected. Tabloids had instead discovered an audience of millions who had never read newspapers before. Most of these new readers were poorly educated working-class city dwellers, many of whom were immigrants or children of immigrants.

The tabloid's most popular new feature was the gossip column, invented by Walter Winchell, an obscure former vaudevillian who began writing his column "Your Broadway and Mine" for the *New York Daily Graphic* in 1924. Winchell described the secret lives of public figures with a distinctive, rapid-fire, slangy style that made the reader feel like an insider. He chronicled the connections among high society, show business

stars, powerful politicians, and the underworld. By the end of the decade, scores of newspapers "syndicated" Winchell's column, making him the most widely read—and imitated—journalist in America.

Many critics dismissed the tabloids for being, as one put it, "synonomous with bad taste, vulgarity, and a degenerate sensationalism." But the popularity of the tabloids forced advertising agencies to expand their definition of the consumer market to include working-class and immigrant readers. And advertisers borrowed freely from tabloid techniques—"true confession" stories, racy headlines, shocking photos, sexually charged images—to reach that market.

Journalism followed the larger economic trend toward consolidation and merger. Newspaper chains like Hearst, Gannett, and Scripps-Howard flourished during the 1920s. There was a sizable increase in the number of these chains and in the percentage of total daily circulation that was chain-owned. By the early 1930s, the Hearst organization alone controlled twenty-six dailies in eighteen cities, accounting for 14 percent of the nation's newspaper circulation. One of every four Sunday papers sold in America was owned by the Hearst group. One journalist lamented this standardization in 1930: "When one travels through the country on a Sunday on a fast train and buys Sunday papers, one finds the same 'comics,' the same Sunday magazines, the same special 'features' in almost all of them and, of course, in most of them precisely the same Associated Press news." New forms of journalism, like radio and the movies, contributed to the growth of a national consumer community.

Advertising Modernity

A thriving advertising industry both reflected and encouraged the growing importance of consumer goods in American life. Previously, advertising had been confined mostly to staid newspapers and magazines and offered little more than basic product information. The most creative advertising was usually for dubious products, such as patent medicines. The successful efforts of the government's Committee on Public Information, set up to "sell" World War I to Americans, suggested that new techniques using modern communication media could convince people to buy a wide range of goods and services. As a profession, advertising reached a higher level of respectability, sophistication, and economic power in American life during the 1920s. Total advertising volume in all media—newspapers, magazines, radio, billboards—jumped from $1.4 billion in 1919 to $3 billion in 1929.

The larger ad agencies moved toward a more scientific approach by sponsoring market research and welcoming the language of psychology to their profession.

Cigarette smoking increased enormously in the 1920s among both men and women, and tobacco companies were among the largest national advertisers. This ad linked smoking to male sexual prowess.

SOURCE: 1918 Murad ad showing men and women at the beach. Gaslight Advertising Archives, Commack, N.Y.

Advertisers began focusing on the needs, desires, and anxieties of the consumer rather than on the qualities of the product. "There are certain things that most people believe," noted one ad agency executive in 1927. "The moment your copy is linked to one of those beliefs, more than half your battle is won." Ad agencies and their clients invested extraordinary amounts of time, energy, and money trying to discover and, to some extent, shape those beliefs. Leading agencies such as Lord and Thomas in Chicago and J. Walter Thompson in New York combined knowledge gained from market research and consumer surveys with carefully prepared ad copy and graphics to sell their clients' wares.

High-powered ad campaigns made new products like Fleischmann's Yeast and Kleenex household words across the country. One of the more spectacular examples of advertising effectiveness involved an old product, Listerine, which had been marketed as a general antiseptic for years by Lambert Pharmaceutical Com-

pany. A new ad campaign touting Listerine as a cure for halitosis—a scientific-sounding term for bad breath—boosted Lambert's profits from $100,000 in 1922 to more than $4 million in 1927.

Above all, advertising celebrated consumption itself as a positive good. In this sense the new advertising ethic was a therapeutic one, promising that products would contribute to the buyer's physical, psychic, or emotional well-being. Certain strategies, such as appeals to nature, medical authority, or personal freedom, were used with great success. Many of these themes and techniques are still familiar today. Well-financed ad campaigns were especially crucial for marketing newer consumer goods such as cars, electrical appliances, and personal hygiene products.

The Phonograph and the Recording Industry

Like radio and movies, the phonograph came into its own in the 1920s as a popular entertainment medium. Originally marketed in the 1890s, early phonographs used wax cylinders that could both record and replay. But the sound quality was poor, and the cylinders were difficult to handle. The convenient permanently grooved disc recordings introduced around World War I were eagerly snapped up by the public, even though the discs could not be used to make recordings at home. The success of records transformed the popular music business, displacing both cylinders and sheet music as the major source of music in the home.

Dance crazes such as the fox trot, tango, and grizzly bear, done to complex ragtime and Latin rhythms, boosted the record business tremendously. Dixieland jazz, which recorded well, also captured the public's fancy in the early 1920s, and records provided the music for new popular dances like the Charleston and the black bottom. In 1921 more than 200 companies produced some 2 million records and annual record sales exceeded 100 million.

Record sales declined toward the end of the decade due to competition from radio. But in a broader cultural sense, records continued to transform American popular culture. Record companies discovered lucrative regional and ethnic markets for country music, which appealed primarily to white Southerners, and blues and jazz, which appealed primarily to African Americans. Country musicians like the Carter Family and Jimmie Rodgers, and blues singers like Blind Lemon Jefferson and Ma Rainey, had their performances put on records for the first time. Their records sold mainly in specialized "hillbilly" and "race" markets. Yet they were also played over the radio, and millions of Americans began to hear musical styles and performers who had previously been isolated from the general population. Blues great Bessie Smith sold hundreds of thousands of records and single-handedly kept the fledgling Columbia Record Company profitable. The combination of records and radio started an extraordinary cross-fertilization of American musical styles that continues to this day.

Sports and Celebrity

During the 1920s, spectator sports enjoyed an unprecedented growth in popularity and profitability. As radio, newspapers, magazines, and newsreels exhaustively documented their exploits, athletes took their place alongside movie stars in defining a new culture of celebrity. Big-time sports, like the movies, entered a new corporate phase. Yet it was the athletes themselves, performing extraordinary feats on the field and transcending their often humble origins, who attracted millions of new fans. The image of the modern athlete—rich, famous, glamorous, and often a rebel against social convention—came into its own during the decade.

Major league baseball had more fans than any other sport, and its greatest star, George Herman "Babe" Ruth, embodied the new celebrity athlete. In 1920 the game had suffered a serious public relations disaster with the unfolding of the "Black Sox" scandal. The previous year, eight members of the poorly paid Chicago White Sox had become involved in a scheme to "throw" the World Series in exchange for large sums of money from gamblers. Although they were acquitted in the courts, baseball commissioner Judge Kenesaw Mountain Landis, looking to remove any taint of gambling from the sport, banned the accused players for life. Landis's actions won universal acclaim, but doubts about the integrity of the "national pastime" lingered.

Ruth did more than anyone to repair the damage and make baseball more popular than ever. Born in 1895, he was a product of Baltimore's rough waterfront district. After spending most of his youth in an orphanage for delinquent boys, he broke into baseball as a pitcher for the Boston Red Sox. Traded to the New York Yankees in 1920, he switched to the outfield and began attracting enormous attention with the length and frequency of his home runs. He hit fifty-four in his first year in New York, eclipsing the old record by twenty-nine. The next year he hit fifty-nine. "The Sultan

of Swat," as one sportswriter dubbed him, transformed the game. Before Ruth, the "homer" was an infrequent event in a game built around pitching, defense, and speed. Fans now flocked to games in record numbers to see the new, more offensive-oriented baseball.

Ruth was a larger-than-life character off the field as well as on. In New York, media capital of the nation, newspapers and magazines chronicled his enormous appetites—for food, whiskey, expensive cars, and big-city nightlife. He hobnobbed with politicians, movie stars, and gangsters, and he regularly visited sick children in hospitals. Ruth became the first athlete avidly sought after by manufacturers for celebrity endorsement of their products. As one of the most photographed individuals of the era, Ruth's round, beaming face became a familiar image around the world. In 1930, at the onset of the Great Depression, when a reporter told him that his $80,000 salary was more than President Herbert Hoover's, the Babe replied good naturedly, "Well, I had a better year than he did."

Baseball attendance exploded during the 1920s, reaching a one-year total of 10 million in 1929. The attendance boom prompted urban newspapers to increase their baseball coverage, and the larger dailies featured separate sports sections. The best sportswriters, such as Grantland Rice, Heywood Broun, and Ring

The Pittsburgh Crawfords, one of the most popular and successful baseball teams in the Negro National League, organized in 1920. Excluded from major league baseball by a "whites only" policy, black ballplayers played to enthusiastic crowds of African Americans from the 1920s through the 1940s. The "Negro leagues" declined after major league baseball finally integrated in 1947. SOURCE: 1935 Pittsburgh Crawfords, champion Negro National League. National Baseball Hall of Fame Library, Cooperstown, N.Y.

Lardner, brought a poetic sensibility to descriptions of the games and their stars. William K. Wrigley, owner of the Chicago Cubs, discovered that by letting local radio stations broadcast his team's games, the club could win new fans, especially among housewives.

Baseball owners solidified their monopolistic control of the game in 1922 when the Supreme Court, ruling in an antitrust suit, declared that baseball, while obviously a business, was not "trade or commerce in the commonly accepted use of those words." By exempting baseball from antitrust prosecution, the Court gave the game a uniquely favored legal status and also ensured the absolute control of owners over their players. Among those excluded from major league baseball were African Americans, who had been banned from the game by an 1890s' "gentleman's agreement" among owners.

During the 1920s black baseball players and entrepreneurs developed a world of their own, with several professional and semiprofessional leagues catering to expanding African American communities in cities. The largest of these was the Negro National League, organized in 1920 by Andrew "Rube" Foster. Black ballclubs also played exhibitions against, and frequently defeated, teams of white major leaguers. African Americans had their own baseball heroes, such as Josh Gibson and Satchel Paige, who no doubt would have been stars in the major leagues if not for racial exclusion.

The new media configuration of the 1920s created heroes in other sports as well. Radio broadcasts and increased journalistic coverage made college football a big-time sport, as millions followed the exploits of star players such as Illinois's Harold E. "Red" Grange and Stanford's Ernie Nevers. Teams like Notre Dame, located in sleepy South Bend, Indiana, but coached by the colorful Knute Rockne, could gain a wide national following. Sportswriter Grantland Rice contributed to the school's mystique when he dubbed its backfield the "Four Horsemen of Notre Dame." The earnings potential of big-time athletics was not lost on college administrators, and it blurred the old lines separating amateur and professional sports. The center of college football shifted from the old elite schools of the Ivy League to the big universities of the Midwest and Pacific coast, where most of the players were now second-generation Irish, Italians, and Slavs. Athletes like boxers Jack Dempsey and Gene Tunney, tennis players Bill Tilden and Helen Wills, and swimmers Gertrude Ederle and Johnny Weissmuller became household names who brought legions of new fans to their sports.

A New Morality?

Movie stars, radio personalities, sports heroes, and popular musicians became the elite figures in a new culture of celebrity defined by the mass media. They were the model for achievement in the new age. Great events and abstract issues were made real through movie close-ups, radio interviews, and tabloid photos. The new media relentlessly created and disseminated images that are still familiar today: Babe Ruth trotting around the bases after hitting a home run; the wild celebrations that greeted Charles Lindbergh after he completed the first solo transatlantic airplane flight in 1927; the smiling gangster Al Capone, bantering with reporters who transformed his criminal exploits into important news events.

But images do not tell the whole story. Consider one of the most enduring images of the "Roaring Twenties," the flapper. She was usually portrayed on screen, in novels, and in the press as a young, sexually aggressive woman with bobbed hair, rouged cheeks, and short skirt. She loved to dance to jazz music, enjoyed smoking cigarettes, and drank bootleg liquor in cabarets and dance halls. She could also be competitive, assertive, and a good pal. As writer Zelda Fitzgerald put it in 1924: "I think a woman gets more happiness out of being gay, light-hearted, unconventional, mistress of her own fate. . . . I want [my daughter] to be a flapper, because flappers are brave and gay and beautiful."

This 1925 *Judge* cartoon, "Sheik with Sheba," drawn by John Held, Jr., offered one view of contemporary culture. The flashy new automobile, the hip flask with illegal liquor, the cigarettes, and the stylish "new woman" were all part of the "Roaring Twenties" image.

SOURCE: The Granger Collection (4E746.21).

712   Chapter 23   The Twenties, 1920–1929

Was the flapper a genuine representative of the 1920s? Did she embody the "new morality" that was so widely discussed and chronicled in the media of the day? The flapper certainly did exist, but she was neither as new nor as widespread a phenomenon as the image would suggest. The delight in sensuality, personal pleasure, and rhythmically complex dance and music had long been key elements of subcultures on the fringes of middle-class society: bohemian enclaves, communities of political radicals, African American ghettos, working-class dance halls. In the 1920s, these activities became normative for a growing number of white middle-class Americans, including women. Jazz, sexual experimentation, heavy makeup, and cigarette smoking spread to college campuses.

Several sources, most of them rooted in earlier years, can be found for the increased sexual openness of the 1920s. Troops in the armed forces during World War I had been exposed to government-sponsored sex education. New psychological and social theories like those of Havelock Ellis, Ellen Key, and Sigmund Freud stressed the central role of sexuality in human experience, maintaining that sex is a positive, healthy impulse that, if repressed, could damage mental and emotional health. The pioneering efforts of Margaret Sanger in educating women about birth control had begun before World War I (see Chapter 21). In the 1920s, Sanger campaigned vigorously—through her journal *Birth Control Review,* in books, on speaking tours—to make contraception freely available to all women.

Advertisers routinely used sex appeal to sell products. Tabloid newspapers exploited sex with "cheesecake" photos, but they also provided features giving advice on sex hygiene and venereal disease. And movies, of course, featured powerful sex symbols such as Rudolph Valentino, Gloria Swanson, John Gilbert, and Clara Bow. Movies also taught young people an etiquette of sex. One typical eighteen-year-old college student wrote in the motion picture diary she kept for a sociological study: "These passionate pictures stir such longings, desires, and urges as I never expected any person to possess. Just the way the passionate lover held his sweetheart suggests so many beautiful and intimate relations, which even my reenacting a scene does not satisfy any more."

Sociological surveys also suggested that genuine changes in sexual behavior began in the prewar years among both married and single women. Katherine Bement Davis's pioneering study of 2,200 middle-class women, carried out in 1918 and published in 1929, revealed that most used contraceptives and described sexual relations in positive terms. A 1938 survey of 777 middle-class females found that among those born between 1890 and 1900, 74 percent were virgins before marriage; for those born after 1910 the figure dropped

to 32 percent. Women born after the turn of the century were twice as likely to have had premarital sex as those born before 1900. The critical change took place in the generation that came of age in the late teens and early twenties. By the 1920s, male and female "morals" were becoming more alike.

THE STATE, THE ECONOMY, AND BUSINESS

Throughout the 1920s, a confident Republican Party dominated national politics, certain that it had ushered in a "new era" in American life. A new and closer relationship between the federal government and American business became the hallmark of Republican policy in both domestic and foreign affairs during the administrations of three successive Republican presidents: Warren Harding (1921–23), Calvin Coolidge (1923–29), and Herbert Hoover (1929–33). And Republicans never tired of claiming that the business-government partnership their policies promoted was responsible for the nation's economic prosperity.

Harding and Coolidge

Handsome, genial, and well-spoken, Warren Harding may have looked the part of a president—but acting like one was another matter. Harding was a product of small-town Marion, Ohio, and the machine politics in his native state. Republican Party officials had made a point of keeping Senator Harding, a compromise choice, as removed from the public eye as possible in the 1920 election. They correctly saw that active campaigning could only hurt their candidate by exposing his shallowness and intellectual weakness. Harding understood his own limitations. He sadly told one visitor to the White House shortly after taking office, "I knew that this job would be too much for me."

Harding surrounded himself with a close circle of friends, the "Ohio gang," delegating to them a great deal of administrative power. The president often conducted business as if he were in the relaxed, convivial, and masculine confines of a small-town saloon. Alice Roosevelt Longworth, Theodore Roosevelt's daughter, described the scene she encountered in Harding's crony-filled study when she tagged along with her husband, Congressman Nicholas Longworth, to a card game: "The air heavy with tobacco smoke, trays with bottles containing every imaginable brand of whiskey [standing] about, cards and poker chips ready at hand—a general atmosphere of waistcoat unbuttoned, feet on the desk, and spitoons alongside." In the summer of 1923 Harding began to get wind of the scandals for which his administration is best remembered. He wearily told his friend Kansas journalist William Allen White: "This is a hell of a job! I have no trouble with my enemies. . . . But my damned friends, . . . White, they're the ones that keep me walking the floor nights."

A series of congressional investigations soon revealed a deep pattern of corruption. Attorney General Harry M. Daugherty had received bribes from violators of the Prohibition statutes. He had also failed to investigate graft in the Veterans Bureau, where Charles R. Forbes had pocketed a large chunk of the $250 million spent on hospitals and supplies. The worst affair was the Teapot Dome scandal involving Interior Secretary Albert Fall. Fall received hundreds of thousands of dollars in payoffs when he secretly leased navy oil reserves in Teapot Dome, Wyoming, and Elk Hills, California, to two private oil developers. He eventually became the first cabinet officer ever to go to jail.

But the Harding administration's legacy was not all scandal. Andrew Mellon, an influential Pittsburgh banker, served as secretary of the treasury under all three Republican presidents of the 1920s. One of the richest men in America, and a leading investor in the Aluminum Corporation of America and Gulf Oil, Mellon believed government ought to be run on the same conservative principles as a corporation. He was a leading voice for trimming the federal budget and cutting taxes on incomes, corporate profits, and inheritances. These cuts, he argued, would free up capital for new investment and thus promote general economic growth. Mellon's program sharply cut taxes for both higher-income brackets and for businesses. By 1926, a person with an income of a million a year paid less than a third of the income tax he or she had paid in 1921. Overall, Mellon's policies succeeded in rolling back much of the progressive taxation associated with Woodrow Wilson.

When Harding died in office of a heart attack in August 1923, Calvin Coolidge succeeded to the presidency. Coolidge seemed to most people the temperamental opposite of Harding. Born and raised in rural Vermont, elected governor of Massachusetts, and coming to national prominence only through the 1919 Boston police strike (see Chapter 22), "Silent Cal" was the quintessential New England Yankee. Taciturn, genteel, and completely honest, Coolidge believed in the least amount of government possible. He spent only four hours a day at the office. His famous aphorism, "The business of America is business," perfectly captured the core philosophy of the Republican new era. He was in awe of wealthy men such as Andrew Mellon, and he thought them best suited to make society's key decisions.

Coolidge easily won election on his own in 1924. He benefited from the general prosperity and the contrast he provided with the disgraced Harding. Coolidge

Calvin Coolidge combined a spare, laconic political style with a flair for publicity. He frequently posed in the dress of a cowboy, farmer, or Indian chief.

SOURCE: Calvin Coolidge in headdress and robes after joining Sioux Indians as Chief Leading Eagle, c. 1928. CORBIS.

defeated little-known Democrat John W. Davis, the compromise choice of a party badly divided between its rural and urban wings. Also running was Progressive Party candidate Robert M. La Follette of Wisconsin, who mounted a reform campaign that attacked economic monopolies and called for government ownership of utilities.

In his full term, Coolidge showed most interest in reducing federal spending, lowering taxes, and blocking congressional initiatives. He saw his primary function as clearing the way for American businessmen. They, after all, were the agents of the era's unprecedented prosperity.

Herbert Hoover and the "Associative State"

The most influential figure of the Republican new era was Herbert Hoover, who as secretary of commerce dominated the cabinets of Harding and Coolidge before becoming president himself in 1929. A successful engineer, administrator, and politician, Hoover effectively embodied the belief that enlightened business, encouraged and informed by the government, would act in the public interest. In the modern industrial age, Hoover believed, the government needed only to advise private citizens' groups about what national or international polices to pursue. "Reactionaries and radicals," he wrote in *American Individualism* (1922), "would assume that all reform and human advance must come through government. They have forgotten that progress must come from the steady lift of the individual and that the measure of national idealism and progress is the quality of idealism in the individual."

Hoover thus fused a faith in old-fashioned individualism with a strong commitment to the progressive possibilities offered by efficiency and rationality. Unlike an earlier generation of Republicans, Hoover wanted not just to create a favorable climate for business but to actively assist the business community. He spoke of creating an "associative state," in which the government would encourage voluntary cooperation among corporations, consumers, workers, farmers, and small businessmen. This became the central occupation of the Department of Commerce under Hoover's leadership. Under Hoover, the Bureau of Standards became one of the nation's leading research centers, setting engineering standards for key American industries such as machine tools and automobiles. The bureau also helped standardize the styles, sizes, and designs of many consumer products such as canned goods and refrigerators.

Hoover actively encouraged the creation and expansion of national trade associations. By 1929 there were about 2,000 of them. At industrial conferences called by the Commerce Department, government officials explained the advantages of mutual cooperation in figuring prices and costs and then publishing the information. The idea was to improve efficiency by reducing competition. To some this practice violated the spirit of antitrust laws, but in the 1920s the Justice Department's Antitrust Division took a very lax view of its responsibility. In addition, the Supreme Court consistently upheld the legality of trade associations. Hoover also had a strong influence on presidential appointments to regulatory commissions; most of these went to men who had worked for the very firms the commissions had been designed to supervise. Regulatory commissions thus benefited from the technical expertise brought by industry leaders, but they in turn tended to remain uncritical of the industries they oversaw.

The government thus provided an ideal climate for the concentration of corporate wealth and power. The trend toward large corporate trusts and holding companies had been well under way since the late nineteenth century, but it accelerated in the 1920s. By 1929, the 200 largest American corporations owned almost half the total corporate wealth and about a fifth of the total national wealth. Concentration was particularly strong in manufacturing, retailing, mining, banking, and utilities. The number of vertical combinations—large, integrated firms that controlled the raw materials, manufacturing processes, and distribution networks for their products—also increased. Vertical inegration became common not only in older industries but also in the automobile, electrical, radio, motion picture, and other new industries as well.

War Debts, Reparations, Keeping the Peace

The United States emerged from World War I the strongest economic power in the world. The war transformed it from the world's leading debtor nation to its most important creditor. European governments owed the U.S. government about $10 billion in 1919. In the private sector, the war ushered in an era of expanding American investment abroad. As late as 1914 foreign investments in the United States were about $3 billion more than the total of American capital invested abroad. By 1919 that situation was reversed: America had $3 billion more invested abroad than foreigners had invested in the United States. By 1929 the surplus was $8 billion. New York replaced London as the center of international finance and capital markets.

During the 1920s, war debts and reparations were the single most divisive issue in international economics. In France and Great Britain, which both owed the United States large amounts in war loans, many concluded that the Uncle Sam who had offered assistance during wartime was really a loan shark in disguise. In turn, many Americans viewed Europeans as ungrateful debtors. As President Coolidge acidly remarked, "They hired the money, didn't they?" In 1922 the U.S. Foreign Debt Commission negotiated an agreement with the debtor nations that called for them to repay $11.5 billion over a sixty-two-year period. But by the late 1920s, the European financial situation had become so desperate that the United States agreed to cancel a large part of these debts. Continued insistence by the United States that the Europeans pay at least a portion of the debt fed anti-American feeling in Europe and isolationism at home.

The Germans believed that war reparations, set at $33 billion by the Treaty of Versailles, not only unfairly punished the losers of the conflict but, by saddling their civilian economies with such massive debt, also deprived them of the very means to repay. In 1924 Herbert Hoover and Chicago banker Charles Dawes worked out a plan to aid the recovery of the German economy. The Dawes Plan reduced Germany's debt, stretched out the repayment period, and arranged for American bankers to lend funds to Germany. These measures helped stabilize Germany's currency and allowed it to make reparations payments to France and

Great Britain. The Allies, in turn, were better able to pay their war debts to the United States.

The horrors of the Great War led millions of citizens, as well as government officials, to advocate curbs on the world's armed forces. In 1921 Secretary of State Charles Evans Hughes took the initiative on arms limitations by inviting representatives from Great Britain, Japan, Italy, France, and China to meet in Washington to discuss reductions in military budgets. Hughes offered to scrap thirty major American ships and asked for comparable actions by the British and Japanese. He asked for a ten-year moratorium on the construction of new battleships and cruisers and proposed limiting naval tonnage. The following year the Five-Power Treaty agreed to this scaling down of navies and also pledged to respect the territorial integrity of China. But the Italians and Japanese soon complained about the treaty's restraints, and ultimately the limits placed on navy construction were abandoned.

The United States never joined the League of Nations, but it maintained an active, if selective, involvement in world affairs. In addition to the Dawes Plan and the American role in naval disarmament, the United States joined the league-sponsored World Court in 1926 and was represented at numerous league conferences. In 1928, with great fanfare, the United States and sixty-two other nations signed the Pact of Paris (better known as the Kellogg-Briand Pact for the U.S. Secretary of State Frank B. Kellogg and French Foreign Minister Aristide Briand who initiated it), which grandly and naively renounced war in principle. Peace groups, such as the Woman's Peace Party and the Quaker-based Fellowship of Reconciliation, hailed the pact for formally outlawing war. But critics charged that the Kellogg-Briand Pact was essentially meaningless since it lacked powers of enforcement and relied solely on the moral force of world opinion. Within weeks of its ratification, the U.S. Congress had appropriated $250 million for new battleships.

Commerce and Foreign Policy

Secretary of State Charles Evans Hughes, a former governor of New York and the Republican candidate for president in 1916, played a leading role in shaping America's postwar foreign policy. Hughes argued that the United States must seek "to establish a Pax Americana maintained not by arms but by mutual respect and good will and the tranquilizing processes of reason." Hughes's push for the arms reduction agreements of 1921 went hand in hand with his deep belief that America's economic wealth—not military or political power—could help create a new and prosperous international system free of the rivalries that had led to the disastrous Great War.

Throughout the 1920s, Hughes and other Republican leaders pursued policies designed to expand American economic activity abroad. They understood that capitalist economies must be dynamic; they must expand their markets if they were to thrive. The focus must be on friendly nations and investments that would help foreign citizens to buy American goods. Toward this end, Republican leaders urged close cooperation between bankers and the government as a strategy for expanding American investment and economic influence abroad. They insisted that investment capital not be spent on U.S. enemies, such as the new Soviet Union, or on nonproductive enterprises such as munitions and weapons. Throughout the 1920s, investment bankers routinely submitted loan projects to Hughes and Secretary of Commerce Hoover for informal approval, thus reinforcing the close ties between business investment and foreign policy.

Foreign policymakers were not shy about brandishing America's postwar economic power to gain advantage. In 1926, the British tried to drive up the world price of rubber, a crucial product for the burgeoning automobile industry. Hoover retaliated by threatening a less friendly U.S. attitude toward British loans and war debts and by encouraging American investors to enlarge their rubber plantations in Southeast Asia and Liberia. Within three months, Hoover had succeeded in driving down the price of rubber from $1.21 a pound to 40 cents. For Hoover and other policymakers, American business abroad was simply rugged individualism at work around the globe.

American oil, autos, farm machinery, and electrical equipment supplied a growing world market. Much of this expansion took place through the establishment of branch plants overseas by American companies. America's overall direct investment abroad increased from $3.8 billion in 1919 to $7.5 billion in 1929. Leading the American domination of the world market were General Electric, Ford, and Monsanto Chemical. American oil companies, with the support of the State Department, also challenged Great Britain's dominance in the oil fields of the Middle East and Latin America, forming powerful cartels with English firms.

The strategy of maximum freedom for private enterprise, backed by limited government advice and assistance, significantly boosted the power and profits of American overseas investors. But in Latin America, in particular, aggressive U.S. investment also fostered chronically underdeveloped economies, dependent on a few staple crops (sugar, coffee, cocoa, bananas) grown for export. American investments in Latin America more than doubled between 1924 and 1929, from $1.5 billion to over $3.5 billion. A large part of this money went to taking over vital mineral resources, such as Chile's copper and Venezuela's oil. The growing wealth and power of

U.S. companies made it more difficult for these nations to grow their own food or diversify their economies. U.S. economic dominance in the hemisphere also hampered the growth of democratic politics by favoring autocratic, military regimes that could be counted on to protect U.S. investments.

During the 1920s, U.S. negotiators peacefully resolved long-simmering disputes with Mexico over oil and mineral holdings of American companies. The United States withdrew its marines from the Dominican Republic in 1924, after many years of direct military intervention. But in Nicaragua, American troops continued to prop up the conservative government of Adolfo Díaz, who had worked closely with the State Department since the first U.S. intervention in 1911. When a popular revolt led by General Augusto Sandino broke out in 1927, American marines landed and wound up supervising Nicaraguan elections over the next five years. They were not finally withdrawn until 1933, leaving a bitter legacy that would lead to crisis once again in the 1980s.

RESISTANCE TO MODERNITY

One measure of the profound cultural changes of the 1920s was the hostility and opposition expressed toward them by large sectors of the American public. Deep and persistent tensions, with ethnic, racial, and geographical overtones, characterized much of the decade's politics. The postwar Red Scare had given strength to the forces of antiradicalism in politics and traditionalism in culture. Resentments over the growing power of urban culture were very strong in rural and small-town America. The big city, in this view, stood for all that was alien, corrupt, and immoral in the country's life. Several trends and mass movements reflected this anger and the longing for a less complicated past.

Prohibition

The Eighteenth Amendment, banning the manufacture, sale, and transportation of alcoholic beverages, took effect in January 1920. Prohibition was the culmination of a long campaign that associated drinking with the degradation of working-class family life and the worst evils of urban politics. Supporters, a coalition of women's temperance groups, middle-class progressives, and rural Protestants, hailed the new law as "a noble experiment." But it became clear rather quickly that enforcing the new law would be extremely difficult. The Volstead Act of 1919 established a federal Prohibition Bureau to enforce the Eighteenth Amendment. Yet the bureau was severely understaffed, with only about 1,500 agents to police the entire country.

The public demand for alcohol, especially in the big cities, led to widespread lawbreaking. Drinking was such a routine part of life for so many Americans that bootlegging quickly became a big business. Illegal stills and breweries, as well as liquor smuggled in from Canada, supplied the needs of those Americans who continued to drink. Nearly every town and city had at least one "speakeasy," where people could drink and enjoy music and other entertainment. Local law enforcement personnel, especially in the cities, were easily bribed to overlook these illegal establishments. By the early 1920s many eastern states no longer made even a token effort at enforcing the law.

But because liquor continued to be illegal, Prohibition gave an enormous boost to violent organized crime. The profits to be made in the illegal liquor trade dwarfed the traditional sources of criminal income—gambling, prostitution, and robbery. The pattern of organized crime in the 1920s closely resembled the larger trends in American business: smaller operations gave way to larger and more complex combinations. Successful organized crime figures, like Chicago's Al "Scarface" Capone, became celebrities in their own right and received heavy coverage in the mass media. Capone himself shrewdly used the rhetoric of the Republican new era to defend himself: "Everybody calls me a racketeer. I call myself a businessman. When I sell liquor it's bootlegging. When my patrons serve it on a silver tray on Lake Shore Drive, it's hospitality."

Organized crime, based on its huge profits from liquor, also made significant inroads into legitimate businesses, labor unions, and city government. By the time Congress and the states ratified the Twenty-first Amendment in 1933, repealing Prohibition, organized crime was a permanent feature of American life. Politically, Prohibition continued to be a controversial issue in national politics, as "wets" and "drys" debated the merits of the law. Prohibition did, in fact, significantly reduce per capita consumption of alcohol. In 1910, annual per capita consumption stood at 2.6 gallons; in 1934 the figure was less than a gallon. Many drinkers—especially wage earners—probably consumed less because of the higher price of bootleg beer and spirits. Yet among young people, especially college students, the excitement associated with speakeasies and lawbreaking contributed to increased drinking during Prohibition.

Immigration Restriction

Sentiment for restricting immigration, growing since the late nineteenth century, reached its peak immediately after World War I. Antiimmigrant feeling reflected the growing preponderance after 1890 of "new immigrants"—those from southern and eastern

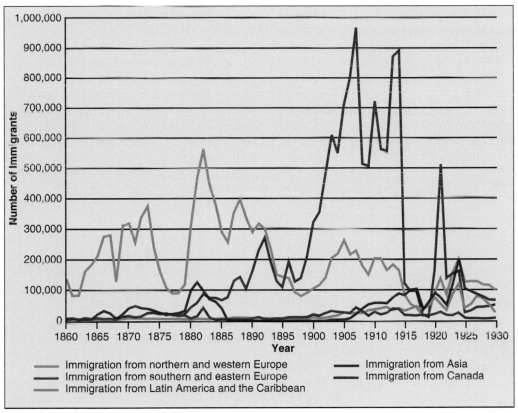

Annual Immigration to the United States, 1860–1930

Europe—over the immigrants from northern and western Europe who had predominated before 1890. Between 1891 and 1920, roughly 10.5 million immigrants arrived from southern and eastern Europe. This was nearly twice as many as arrived during the same years from northern and western Europe.

The "new immigrants" were mostly Catholic and Jewish, and they were darker-skinned than the "old immigrants." To many Americans they seemed more exotic, more foreign, and less willing and able to assimilate the nation's political and cultural values. They were also relatively poorer, more physically isolated in the nation's cities, and less politically strong than earlier immigrants. In the 1890s, the anti-Catholic American Protective Association called for a curb on immigration, and by exploiting the economic depression of that decade it reached a membership of 2.5 million. In 1894 a group of prominent Harvard graduates, including Henry Cabot Lodge and John Fiske, founded the Immigration Restriction League, providing an influential forum for the fears of the nation's elite. The league used newer scientific arguments, based on a flawed application of Darwinian evolutionary theory and genetics, to support its call for immigration restriction.

Theories of scientific racism, which had become more popular in the early 1900s, reinforced antiimmigrant bias. The most influential statement of racial hierarchy was Madison Grant's *The Passing of the Great Race* (1916), which distorted genetic theory to argue that America was committing "race suicide." According to Grant, inferior Alpine, Mediterranean, and Jewish stock threatened to extinguish the superior Nordic race that had made America great. Eugenicists, who enjoyed considerable vogue in these years, held that heredity determined almost all of a person's capacities and that genetic inferiority predisposed people to crime and poverty. Such pseudoscientific thinking sought to explain historical and social development solely as a function of "racial" differences.

Against this background, the war and its aftermath provided the final push for immigration restriction. The "100 percent American" fervor of the war years fueled nativist passions. So did the Red Scare of 1919–20, which linked foreigners with Bolshevism and radicalism of all kinds in the popular mind. The postwar depression coincided with the resumption of massive immigration, bringing much hostile comment on the relationship between rising unemployment and the new influx of foreigners. The American Federation of Labor proposed stopping all immigration for two years. Sensational press coverage of organized crime figures, many of them Italian or Jewish, also played a part.

In 1921 Congress passed the Immigration Act, setting a maximum of 357,000 new immigrants each year. Quotas limited annual immigration from any European country to 3 percent of the number of its natives counted in the 1910 U.S. census. But restrictionists complained that the new law still allowed too many southern and eastern Europeans in, especially since the northern and western Europeans did not fill their quotas. The Johnson-Reed Immigration Act of 1924 revised the quotas to 2 percent of the number of foreign-born counted for each nationality in the census for 1890, when far fewer southern or eastern Europeans were present in the United States. The maximum total allowed each year was also cut, to 164,000. The quota laws did not apply to Canada, Mexico, or any other nation in the western hemisphere.

The immigration restriction laws reversed earlier practices and became a permanent feature of national policy. Republican congressman Albert Johnson of Washington, coauthor of the 1924 act, defended it by claiming that "our capacity to maintain our cherished institutions stands diluted by a stream of alien blood, with all its inherited misconceptions respecting the relationships of the governing power to the governed. . . . The day of unalloyed welcome to all peoples, the day of indiscriminate acceptance of all races, has definitely ended." In effect, Congress had accepted the racial assumptions of such popular, pseudoscientific writers as Madison Grant, basing immigration restriction on a presumed hierarchy of superior and inferior "races."

The Ku Klux Klan

If immigration restriction was resurgent nativism's most significant legislative expression, a revived Ku Klux Klan was its most effective mass movement. The original Klan had been formed in the Reconstruction South as an instrument of white racial terror against newly freed slaves (see Chapter 17). It had died out in the 1870s. The new Klan, born in Stone Mountain, Georgia, in 1915, was inspired by D. W. Griffith's racist spectacle *The Birth of a Nation*, a film released in that year depicting the original KKK as a heroic organization. The new Klan patterned itself on the secret rituals and antiblack hostility of its predecessor, and until 1920 it was limited to a few local chapters in Georgia and Alabama.

When Hiram W. Evans, a dentist from Dallas, became imperial wizard of the Klan in 1922, he transformed the organization. Evans hired professional fundraisers and publicists and directed an effective recruiting scheme that paid a commission to sponsors of new members. The Klan advocated "100 percent Americanism" and "the faithful maintenance of White Supremacy." The Klan also staunchly supported the

enforcement of Prohibition, and it attacked birth control and Darwinism. The new Klan made a special target of the Roman Catholic Church, labeling it a hostile and dangerous alien power. In a 1926 magazine piece titled "The Klan's Fight for Americanism," Evans alleged that the Church's "theocratic autocracy and its claim to full authority in temporal as well as spiritual matters, all make it impossible for it as a church, or for its members if they obey it, to cooperate in a free democracy in which Church and State have been separated."

The new Klan presented itself as the righteous defender of the embattled traditional values of small-town Protestant America. But ironically, to build its membership rolls, it relied heavily on the publicity, public relations, and business techniques associated with modern urban culture. By 1924 the new Klan counted more than 3 million members across the country. President Harding had joined in a special White House ceremony. Its slogan, "Native, White, Protestant Supremacy," proved especially attractive in the Midwest and South, including many cities. Klansmen boycotted businesses, threatened families, and sometimes resorted to violence—public whippings, arson, and lynching—against their chosen enemies. The Klan's targets sometimes included white Protestants accused of sexual promiscuity, blasphemy, or drunkenness, but most victims were African Americans, Catholics, and Jews. Support for Prohibition enforcement probably united Klansmen more than any single issue.

On another level, the Klan was a popular social movement. Many members were more attracted by the Klan's spectacular social events and its efforts to reinvigorate community life than by its attacks on those considered outsiders. Perhaps a half million women joined the Women of the Ku Klux Klan, and women constituted nearly half of the Klan membership in some states. Klanswomen drew on family and community traditions, such as church suppers, kin reunions, and gossip campaigns, to defend themselves and their families against what they saw as corruption and immorality. One northern Indiana Klanswoman recalled, "Store owners, teachers, farmers . . . the good people, all belonged to the Klan. They were going to clean up the government, and they were going to improve the school books that were loaded with Catholicism." The Klan's power was strong in many communities precisely because it fit so comfortably into the everyday life of white Protestants.

Studies of Klan units suggest that the appeal and activities of the organization varied greatly from community to community. Local conditions and circumstances often attracted followers more than the extremist and nativist appeals of the national office. In

Women members of the Ku Klux Klan in New Castle, Indiana, August 1, 1923. The revived Klan was a powerful presence in scores of American communities during the early 1920s, especially among native-born white Protestants who feared cultural and political change. In addition to preaching "100 percent Americanism," local Klan chapters also served as a social function for members and their families.

SOURCE: Ball State University Libraries, Archives & Special Collections, W.A. Swift Photo Collection.

Anaheim, California, for example, most Klansmen were migrants from midwestern states who attended mainstream Protestant churches. They focused their anger on the local economic elite, whom they held responsible for a failure to enforce Prohibition, a rising crime rate, and runaway economic growth. In Colorado, Prohibition and vice law violations appeared to be the main concern. Vigilante attacks on Catholic priests and Jewish synagogues were more prevalent in cities like Denver and Pueblo, which had small but visible nonwhite Protestant communities.

At its height, the Klan also became a powerful force in Democratic Party politics in Texas, Oklahoma, Indiana, Colorado, Oregon, and other states. It had a strong presence among delegates to the 1924 Democratic National Convention. The Klan began to fade in 1925 when its Indiana leader, Grand Dragon David C. Stephenson, became involved in a sordid personal affair. Stephenson had picked up a young secretary at a party, got her drunk on bootleg liquor, and then assaulted her on a train. After the woman took poison and died, Stephenson was convicted of manslaughter. With one of its most famous leaders disgraced and in

jail, the new Klan began to lose members and influence. The success of immigration restriction, the receding concern over Bolshevism, wrangling among Klan leaders, and the general economic prosperity also contributed to the movement's rapid decline by the late 1920s.

Religious Fundamentalism

Paralleling political nativism in the 1920s was the growth of religious fundamentalism. In many Protestant churches, congregations focused less on religious practice and worship than on social and reform activities in the larger community. By the early 1920s, a fundamentalist revival had developed in reaction to these tendencies. The fundamentalists emphasized a literal reading of the Bible, and they rejected the tenets of modern science as inconsistent with the revealed word of God. Fundamentalist publications and Bible colleges flourished, particularly among Southern Baptists.

One special target of the fundamentalists was the theory of evolution, first set forth by Charles Darwin in his landmark work *The Origin of Species* (1859). Using

Clarence Darrow (left) and William Jennings Bryan at the Scopes Trial in Dayton, Tennessee, in 1925. Their courtroom battle embodied the larger cultural conflict between religious fundamentalism and secular values. In the trial's most dramatic moment, Darrow called Bryan to the witness stand to testify as an expert on the Bible.

SOURCE: AP/Wide World Photos.

The Scopes "monkey trial"— so called because fundamentalists trivialized Darwin's theory into a claim that humans were descended from monkeys—became one of the most publicized and definitive moments of the decade. The real drama was the confrontation between Darrow and Bryan. Darrow, denied by the judge the right to call scientists to testify for the defense, put the "Great Commoner," Bryan, himself on the stand as an expert witness on the Bible. Bryan delighted his supporters with a staunch defense of biblical literalism. But he also drew scorn from many of the assembled journalists, including cosmopolitan types such as H. L. Mencken of the *Baltimore Sun*, who ridiculed Bryan's simplistic faith. Scopes's guilt was never in question. The jury convicted him quickly, although the verdict was later thrown out on a technicality. Bryan died a week after the trial; his epitaph read simply, "He kept the Faith." The struggle over the teaching of evolution continued in an uneasy stalemate; state statutes were not repealed, but prosecutions for teaching evolution ceased. Fundamentalism, a religious creed and a cultural defense against the uncertainties of modern life, continued to have a strong appeal for millions of Americans.

fossil evidence, evolutionary theory suggested that over time many species had become extinct and that new ones had emerged through the process of natural selection. These ideas directly contradicted the account of one, fixed creation in the Book of Genesis. Although most Protestant clergymen had long since found ways of blending the scientific theory with their theology, fundamentalists launched an attack on the teaching of Darwinism in schools and universities. By 1925 five southern state legislatures had passed laws restricting the teaching of evolution.

A young biology teacher, John T. Scopes, deliberately broke the Tennessee law prohibiting the teaching of Darwinism in 1925 in order to challenge it in court. The resulting trial that summer in Dayton, a small town near Chattanooga, drew international attention to the controversy. Scopes's defense team included attorneys from the American Civil Liberties Union and Clarence Darrow, the most famous trial lawyer in America. The prosecution was led by William Jennings Bryan, the old Democratic standard-bearer who had thrown himself into the fundamentalist and antievolutionist cause. Held in a circus atmosphere in sweltering heat, the trial attracted thousands of reporters and partisans to Dayton and was broadcast across the nation by the radio.

PROMISES POSTPONED

The prosperity of the 1920s was unevenly distributed and enjoyed across America. Older, progressive reform movements that had pointed out inequities faltered in the conservative political climate. But the Republican new era did inspire a range of critics deeply troubled by unfulfilled promises in American life. Feminists sought to redefine their movement in the wake of the suffrage victory. Mexican immigration to the United States shot up, and in the burgeoning Mexican American communities of the Southwest and Midwest, economic and social conditions were very difficult. African Americans, bitterly disappointed by their treatment during and after the Great War, turned to new political and cultural strategies. Many American intellectuals found themselves deeply alienated from the temper and direction of modern American society.

Feminism in Transition

The achievement of the suffrage removed the central issue that had given cohesion to the disparate forces of female reform activism. In addition, female activists of all persuasions found themselves swimming against a national tide of hostility to political idealism. During the 1920s, the women's movement split into two main wings over a fundamental disagreement about female identity. Should activists stress women's differences from men—their vulnerability and the double burden of work and family—and continue to press for protective legislation, such as laws that limited the length of the work week for women? Or should they emphasize the ways that women were like men—sharing similar aspirations—and push for full legal and civil equality?

In 1920, the National American Woman Suffrage Association reorganized itself as the League of Women Voters. The league represented the historical mainstream of the suffrage movement, those who believed that the vote for women would bring a nurturing sensibility and a reform vision to American politics. This view was rooted in politicized domesticity, the notion that women had a special role to play in bettering society: improving conditions for working women, abolishing child labor, humanizing prisons and mental hospitals, and serving the urban poor. Most league members continued working in a variety of reform organizations, and the league itself concentrated on educating the new female electorate, encouraging women to run for office, and supporting laws for the protection of women and children.

A newer, smaller, and more militant group was the National Woman's Party (NWP), founded in 1916 by militant suffragist Alice Paul. The NWP downplayed the significance of suffrage and argued that women were still subordinate to men in every facet of life. The NWP opposed protective legislation for women, claiming that such laws reinforced sex stereotyping and prevented women from competing with men in many fields. Largely representing the interests of professional and business women, the NWP focused on passage of a brief Equal Rights Amendment (ERA) to the Constitution, introduced in Congress in 1923: "Men and women shall have equal rights throughout the United States and every place subject to its jurisdiction."

Since the ERA would wipe out sex as a legal category, its opponents worried about the loss of hard-won protective legislation that benefited poor and working-class women. Many of the older generation of women reformers opposed the ERA as elitist, arguing that far more women benefited from protective laws than were injured by them. "So long as men cannot be mothers," Florence Kelley declared, "so long legislation adequate for them can never be adequate for wage-earning women; and the cry Equality, Equality, where nature has created inequality, is as stupid and as deadly as the cry of Peace, Peace, where there is no Peace." Mary Anderson, director of the Women's Bureau in the Department of Labor, argued that "women who are wage earners, with one job in the factory and another in the home, have little time and energy left to carry on the fight to better their economic status. They need the help of other women and they need labor laws."

ERA supporters countered that maximum hours laws or laws prohibiting women from night work prevented women from getting many lucrative jobs. According to Harriot Stanton Blatch, daughter of feminist pioneer Elizabeth Cady Stanton, "In many highly paid trades women have been pushed into the lower grades of work, limited in earning capacity, if not shut out of the trade entirely by these so-called protective laws." M. Carey Thomas, president of Bryn Mawr College, defended the ERA with language reminiscent of laissez faire: "How much better by one blow to do away with discriminating against women in work, salaries, promotion and opportunities to compete with men in a fair field with no favour on either side!"

But most women's groups did not think there was a "fair field." Positions solidified. The League of Women Voters, the National Consumers' League, and the Women's Trade Union League opposed the ERA. ERA supporters generally stressed individualism, competition, and the abstract language of "equality" and "rights." ERA opponents emphasized the grim reality of industrial exploitation and the concentration of women workers in low-paying jobs in which they did not compete directly with men. ERA advocates dreamed of a labor market that might be, one in which women might have the widest opportunity. Anti-ERA forces looked at the labor market as it was, insisting it was more important to protect women from existing exploitation. The NWP campaign failed to get the ERA passed by Congress, but the debates it sparked would be echoed during the feminist movement of the 1970s, when the ERA became a central political goal of a resurgent feminism.

A small number of professional women made real gains in the fields of real estate, banking, and journalism. The press regularly announced new "firsts" for women, such as Amelia Earhart's 1928 airplane flight across the Atlantic. Anne O'Hare McCormick won recognition as the "first lady of American journalism" for her reporting and editorial columns in the New York Times. As business expanded, a greater percentage of working women were employed in white-collar positions, as opposed to manufacturing and domestic service. In 1900 less than 18 percent of employed women worked in clerical, managerial, sales, and professional areas. By 1930 the number was 44 percent. But studies showed that most of these women were clustered in the low-paying areas of typing, stenography, bookkeeping, cashiering, and sales clerking. Men still dominated in the higher-paid and managerial white-collar occupations.

The most significant, if limited, victory for feminist reformers was the 1921 Sheppard-Towner Act, which established the first federally funded health-care program, providing matching funds for states to set up prenatal and child health care centers. These centers also provided public health nurses for house calls. Although hailed as a genuine reform breakthrough, especially for women in rural and isolated communities, the act aroused much opposition. The NWP disliked it for its assumption that all women were mothers. Birth control advocates such as Margaret Sanger complained that contraception was not part of the program. The American Medical Association (AMA) objected to government-sponsored health care and to nurses who functioned outside the supervision of physicians. By 1929, largely as a result of intense AMA lobbying, Congress cut off funds for the program.

Mexican Immigration

While immigration restriction sharply cut the flow of new arrivals from Europe, the 1920s also brought a dramatic influx of Mexicans to the United States. Mexican immigration, which was not included in the immigration laws of 1921 and 1924, had picked up substantially after the outbreak of the Mexican Revolution in 1911, when political instability and economic hardships provided incentives to cross the border to *El Norte*. According to the U.S. Immigration Service, an estimated 459,000 Mexicans entered the United States between 1921 and 1930, more than double the number for the previous decade. The official count no doubt underrepresented the true numbers of immigrants from Mexico. Many Mexicans shunned the main border crossings at El Paso, Texas; Nogales, Arizona; and Calexico, California, and thus avoided paying the $8 head tax and $10 visa fee.

The primary pull was the tremendous agricultural expansion occurring in the American Southwest. Irrigation and large-scale agribusiness had begun transforming California's Imperial and San Joaquin Valleys from arid desert into lucrative fruit and vegetable fields. Cotton pickers were needed in the vast plantations of Lower Rio Grande Valley in Texas and the Salt River Valley in Arizona. The sugar beet fields of Michigan, Minnesota, and Colorado also attracted many Mexican farm workers. American industry had also begun recruiting Mexican workers, first to fill wartime needs and later to fill the gap left by the decline in European immigration.

The new Mexican immigration appeared more permanent than previous waves—that is, more and more

newcomers stayed—and, like other immigrants, settled in cities. This was partly the unintended consequence of new policies designed to make immigration more difficult. As the Border Patrol (established in 1924) made border crossing more difficult (through head taxes, visa fees, literacy tests, and document checks), what had once been a two-way process for many Mexicans became a one-way migration. Permanent communities of Mexicans in the U.S. grew rapidly. By 1930, San Antonio's Mexican community accounted for roughly 80,000 people out of a total population of a quarter million. Around 100,000 Mexicans lived in central and east Los Angeles, including 55,000 who attended city schools. Substantial Mexican communities also flourished in midwestern cities such as Chicago, Detroit, Kansas City, and Gary. Many of the immigrants alternated between agricultural and factory jobs, depending on the seasonal availability of work. Mexican women often worked in the fields alongside their husbands. They also had jobs as domestics and seamstresses or took in laundry and boarders.

Racism and local patterns of residential segregation confined most Mexicans to barrios. Housing conditions were generally poor, particularly for recent arrivals, who were forced to live in rude shacks without running water or electricity. Disease and infant mortality rates were much higher than average, and most Mexicans

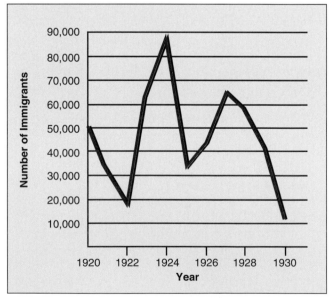

Mexican Immigration to the United States in the 1920s Many Mexican migrants avoided official border crossing stations so they would not have to pay visa fees. Thus these official figures probably underestimated the true size of the decade's Mexican migration. As the economy contracted with the onset of the Great Depression, immigration from Mexico dropped off sharply.

Mexican workers gathered outside a San Antonio labor bureau in 1924. These employment agencies contracted Mexicans to work for Texas farmers, railroads, and construction companies. Note the three Anglo men in front (wearing suits and ties), who probably owned and operated this agency. During the 1920s, San Antonio's Mexican population doubled from roughly 40,000 to over 80,000, making it the second largest *colonia* in *El Norte* after Los Angeles.

SOURCE: Goldbeck Collection, Harry Ransom Humanities Research Center, University of Texas at Austin. Photo by Summerville (46ND).

worked at low-paying, unskilled jobs and received inadequate health care. Legal restrictions passed by states and cities made it difficult for Mexicans to enter teaching, legal, and other professions. Mexicans were routinely banned from local public works projects as well. Many felt a deep ambivalence about applying for American citizenship. Loyalty to the Old Country was strong, and many cherished dreams of returning to live out their days in Mexico.

Ugly racist campaigns against Mexicans were common in the 1920s, especially when "cheap Mexican labor" was blamed for local unemployment or hard times. Stereotypes of Mexicans as "greasers" or "wetbacks" were prevalent in newspapers and movies of the day. Nativist efforts to limit Mexican immigration were thwarted by the lobbying of powerful agribusiness interests. The Los Angeles Chamber of Commerce typically employed racist stereotyping in arguing to keep the borders open. Mexicans, it claimed, were naturally suited for agriculture, "due to their crouching and bending habits. . . , while the white is physically unable to adapt himself to them."

Mutual aid societies—*mutualistas*—became key social and political institutions in the Mexican communities of the Southwest and Midwest. They provided death benefits and widows' pensions for members and also served as centers of resistance to civil rights violations and discrimination. In 1928, the Federation of Mexican Workers Unions formed in response to a large farm labor strike in the Imperial Valley of California. A group of middle-class Mexican professionals in Texas organized the League of United Latin American Citizens (LULAC) in 1929. The founding of these organizations marked only the beginnings of a long struggle to bring economic, social, and racial equality to Mexican Americans.

The "New Negro"

The Great Migration spurred by World War I showed no signs of letting up during the 1920s, and African American communities in northern cities grew rapidly. By far the largest and most influential of these communities was New York City's Harlem. Previously a

www.   **Web Exploration**   Examine the Great Migration in more detail. Why were African Americans drawn to northern cities?
www.prenhall.com/faragher/map23.1

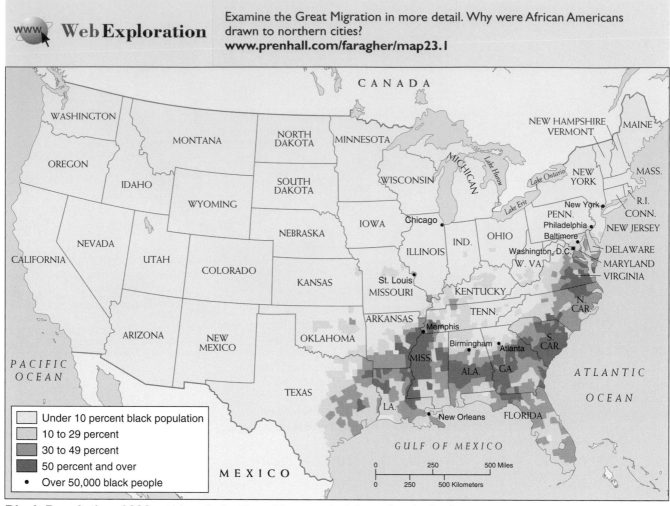

Black Population, 1920   Although the Great Migration had drawn hundreds of thousands of African Americans to the urban north, the southern states of the former Confederacy still remained the center of the African American population in 1920.

residential suburb, Harlem began attracting middle-class African Americans in the prewar years. After the war, heavy black migration from the South and the Caribbean encouraged real estate speculators and landlords to remake Harlem as an exclusively black neighborhood. Between 1920 and 1930 some 120,000 new black arrivals settled in Harlem, giving it a black population of roughly 200,000.

Harlem emerged as the demographic and cultural capital of black America, but its appeal transcended national borders as mass migration from the Caribbean helped reshape the community. Between 1900 and 1930 some 300,000 West Indians emigrated to the United States, roughly half of whom settled in New York City. By the late 1920s about one-quarter of Harlem's population had been born in Jamaica, Barbados, Trinidad, the Bahamas, and other parts of the Caribbean. Some of the leading cultural, business, and political figures of the

era—poet Claude McKay, newspaper publisher P. M. H. Savory, labor organizer Hubert Harrison, black nationalist Marcus Garvey—had roots in the West Indies. Most black Caribbean migrants came from societies where class differences mattered more than racial ones, and many refused to accept racial bigotry without protest. A large number also carried with them entrepreneurial experience that contributed to their success in running small businesses. Intraracial tensions and resentment between American-born blacks and an increasingly visible West Indian population was one reflection of Harlem's transformation into a hemispheric center for black people.

The demand for housing in this restricted geographical area led to skyrocketing rents, but most Harlemites held low-wage jobs. This combination produced extremely overcrowded apartments, unsanitary conditions, and the rapid deterioration of housing stock. Disease

A 1925 pensive portrait of Langston Hughes, one of the leading literary voices of the Harlem Renaissance. Winold Reiss's work suggested Hughes's determination to create poetry out of the everyday life experiences of Harlem's burgeoning African American population.

SOURCE: Winold Reiss, Portrait of Langston Hughes (1902–1967 Poet) © 1925. National Portrait Gallery, Washington, DC, USA. Art Resource, N.Y. (S0041021)

and death rates were abnormally high. Harlem was well on its way to becoming a slum. Yet Harlem also boasted a large middle-class population and supported a wide array of churches, theaters, newspapers and journals, and black-owned businesses. It became a magnet for African American intellectuals, artists, musicians, and writers from all over the world. Poet Langston Hughes expressed the excitement of arriving in the community in 1921: "I can never put on paper the thrill of the underground ride to Harlem. I went up the steps and out into the bright September sunlight. Harlem! I stood there, dropped my bags, took a deep breath and felt happy again."

Harlem became the political and intellectual center for what writer Alain Locke called the "New Negro." Locke was referring to a new spirit in the work of black writers and intellectuals, an optimistic faith that encour-

aged African Americans to develop and celebrate their distinctive culture, firmly rooted in the history, folk culture, and experiences of African American people. This faith was the common denominator uniting the disparate figures associated with the Harlem Renaissance. The assertion of cultural independence resonated in the poetry of Langston Hughes and Claude McKay, the novels of Zora Neale Hurston and Jessie Fauset, the essays of Countee Cullen and James Weldon Johnson, the acting of Paul Robeson, and the blues singing of Bessie Smith. Most would agree with Johnson when he wrote in 1927 that "nothing can go farther to destroy race prejudice than the recognition of the Negro as a creator and contributor to American civilization."

There was a political side to the "New Negro" as well. The newly militant spirit that black veterans had brought home from World War I matured and found a variety of expressions in the Harlem of the 1920s. New leaders and movements began to appear alongside established organizations like the National Association for the Advancement of Colored People. A. Philip Randolph began a long career as a labor leader, socialist, and civil rights activist in these years, editing the *Messenger* and organizing the Brotherhood of Sleeping Car Porters. Harlem was also headquarters to Marcus Garvey's Universal Negro Improvement Association. An ambitious Jamaican immigrant who had moved to Harlem in 1916, Garvey created a mass movement that stressed black economic self-determination and unity among the black communities of the United States, the Caribbean, and Africa. His newspaper, *Negro World*, spoke to black communities around the world, urging black businesses to trade among themselves. With colorful parades and rallies and a central message affirming pride in black identity, Garvey attracted as many as a million members worldwide.

Garvey's best-publicized project was the Black Star Line, a black-owned and -operated fleet of ships that would link people of African descent around the world. But insufficient capital and serious financial mismanagement resulted in the spectacular failure of the enterprise. In 1923, Garvey was found guilty of mail fraud in his fundraising efforts; he later went to jail and was subsequently deported to England. Despite the disgrace, Harlem's largest newspaper, the *Amsterdam News*, explained Garvey's continuing appeal to African Americans: "In a world where black is despised, he taught them that black is beautiful. He taught them to admire and praise black things and black people."

Harlem in the 1920s also became a popular tourist attraction for "slumming" whites. Nightclubs like the Cotton Club were often controlled by white organized crime figures. They featured bootleg liquor, floor shows, and the best jazz bands of the day, led by Duke Ellington, Fletcher Henderson, Cab Calloway, and

Louis Armstrong. Yet these clubs were rigidly segregated. Black dancers, singers, and musicians provided the entertainment, but no African Americans were allowed in the audience. Chronicled in novels and newspapers, Harlem became a potent symbol to white America of the ultimate good time. Yet the average Harlemite never saw the inside of a nightclub. For the vast majority of Harlem residents, working menial jobs for low wages and forced to pay high rents, the day-to-day reality was depressingly different.

Intellectuals and Alienation

War, Prohibition, growing corporate power, and the deep currents of cultural intolerance troubled many intellectuals in the 1920s. Some felt so alienated from the United States that they left to live abroad. In the early 1920s Gertrude Stein, an American expatriate writer living in Paris, told the young novelist Ernest Hemingway: "All of you young people who served in the war, you are a lost generation." The phrase "a lost generation" was widely adopted as a label for American writers, artists, and intellectuals of the postwar era. Yet it is difficult to generalize about so diverse a community. For one thing, living abroad attracted only a handful of American writers. Alienation and disillusion with American life were prominent subjects in the literature and thought of the 1920s, but artists and thinkers developed these themes in very different ways.

The mass slaughter of World War I provoked revulsion and a deep cynicism about the heroic and moralistic portrayal of war so popular in the nineteenth century. Novelists Hemingway and John Dos Passos, who both served at the front as ambulance drivers, depicted the war and its aftermath in world-weary and unsentimental tones. The search for personal moral codes that would allow one to endure life with dignity and authenticity was at the center of Hemingway's fiction. In the taut, spare language of *The Sun Also Rises* (1926) and *A Farewell to Arms* (1929), he questioned idealism, abstractions, and large meanings. As Jake Barnes, the wounded war hero of *The Sun Also Rises* explained, "I did not care what it was all about. All I wanted to know was how to live it."

Hemingway and F. Scott Fitzgerald were the most influential novelists of the era. Fitzgerald joined the army during World War I but did not serve overseas. His work celebrated the youthful vitality of the "Jazz Age" (a phrase he coined) but was also deeply distrustful of the promises of American prosperity and politics. His first novel, *This Side of Paradise* (1920), won a wide readership around the country with its exuberant portrait of a "new generation," "dedicated more than the last to the fear of poverty and the worship of success;

grown up to find all Gods dead, all wars fought, all faiths in man shaken." Fitzgerald's finest work, *The Great Gatsby* (1925), written in the south of France, depicted the glamorous parties of the wealthy while evoking the tragic limits of material success.

At home, many American writers engaged in sharp attacks on small-town America and what they viewed as its provincial values. Essayist H. L. Mencken, caustic editor of the *American Mercury*, heaped scorn on fundamentalists, Prohibition, and nativists, while ridiculing what he called the "American booboisie." Mencken understood the power of the small town and despaired of reforming politics. "Our laws," he wrote, "are invented, in the main, by frauds and fanatics, and put upon the statute books by poltroons and scoundrels." Fiction writers also skewered small-town America, achieving commercial and critical success in the process. Sherwood Anderson's *Winesburg, Ohio* (1919) offered a spare, laconic, pessimistic yet compassionate view of middle America. He had a lasting influence on younger novelists of the 1920s.

The most popular and acclaimed writer of the time was novelist Sinclair Lewis. In a series of novels satirizing small-town life, such as *Main Street* (1920) and especially *Babbitt* (1922), Lewis affectionately mocked his characters. His treatment of the central character in *Babbitt*—George Babbitt of Zenith—also had a strong element of self-mockery, for Lewis could offer no alternative set of values to Babbitt's crass self-promotion, hunger for success, and craving for social acceptance. In 1930 Lewis became the first American author to win the Nobel Prize for literature.

The playwright Eugene O'Neill revolutionized the American stage with his naturalistic and brooding dramas. O'Neill's depictions of the darker side of family life and his exploration of race relations helped push American theater past the melodramatic conventions of the late nineteenth century. Among his influential early plays were *Beyond the Horizon* (1920), *The Emperor Jones* (1921), and *The Great God Brown* (1926). Two expatriate poets, T. S. Eliot and Ezra Pound, were breaking Victorian conventions by pushing American verse in revolutionary new directions. Eliot's *The Waste Land* (1922), perhaps the most influential poem of the century, used the metaphor of impotence to comment on the postwar world.

In the aftermath of the postwar Red Scare, American radicalism found itself on the defensive throughout the 1920s. But one *cause celebre* did attract a great deal of support from intellectuals. In 1921 two Italian American immigrants, Nicola Sacco and Bartolomeo Vanzetti, were tried and convicted for murder in the course of robbing a shoe factory in South Braintree, Massachusetts. Neither Sacco, a shoemaker, nor Vanzetti, a fish peddler, had criminal records, but both had long been active in militant anarchist circles, labor organizing, and antiwar agitation. Their trial took place amidst an intense atmosphere of nativist and antiradical feeling, and both the judge and prosecuting attorney engaged in clearly prejudicial conduct toward the defendants. A six year struggle to save Sacco and Vanzetti following the trial failed, despite attracting support from a broad range of liberal intellectuals including Harvard law professor and future Supreme Court justice Felix Frankfurter. The two men were finally executed in 1927, and for many years their case would remain a powerful symbol of how the criminal justice system could be tainted by political bias and antiimmigrant fervor. Many intellectuals agreed with literary critic Edmund Wilson who wrote that the Sacco and Vanzetti case "revealed the whole anatomy of American life with all its classes, professions, and points of view and all their relations, and it raised almost every fundamental question of our political and social system."

Another side of intellectual alienation was expressed by writers critical of industrial progress and the new mass culture. The most important of these were a group of poets and scholars centered in Vanderbilt University in Nashville, Tennessee, collectively known as the Fugitives. They included Allen Tate, John Crowe Ransom, Donald Davidson, and Robert Penn Warren, all of whom invoked traditional authority, respect for the past, and older agrarian ways as ideals to live by. The Fugitives attacked industrialism and materialism as modern-day ills. Self-conscious Southerners, they looked to the antebellum plantation-based society as a model for a community based on benevolence toward dependents (such as black people and women) and respect for the land. Their book of essays, *I'll Take My Stand* (1930), was a collective manifesto of their ideas.

Not all intellectuals, of course, were critics of modern trends. Some, like the philosopher John Dewey, retained much of the prewar optimism and belief in progress. But many others, such as Walter Lippmann and Joseph Wood Krutch, articulated a profound uneasiness with the limits of material growth. In his 1929 book *A Preface to Morals*, the urbane and

sophisticated Lippmann expressed doubts about the moral health of the nation. Modern science and technological advances could not address more cosmic questions of belief. The erosion of old religious faiths and moral standards, along with the triumph of the new mass culture, had left many people with nothing to believe in. Lippmann called for a new "religion of the spirit" to offer a guide for living an ethical life. He was unclear as to just what the "religion of the spirit" might be. But he was certain that the moralist would have to persuade rather than command people to live the good life. His job would be "not to exhort men to be good but to elucidate what the good is."

The Election of 1928

The presidential election of 1928 served as a kind of national referendum on the Republican new era. It also revealed just how important ethnic and cultural differences had become in defining American politics. The contest reflected many of the deepest tensions and conflicts in American society in the 1920s: native-born versus immigrant; Protestant versus Catholic;

Clifford K. Berryman's 1928 political cartoon interpreted that year's presidential contest along sectional lines. It depicted the two major presidential contenders as each setting off to campaign in the regions where their support was weakest. For Democrat Al Smith, that meant the West, and for Republican Herbert Hoover, the East.

SOURCE: Copyright, 1928, *Los Angeles Times.* Reprinted by permission

Prohibition versus legal drinking; small-town life versus the cosmopolitan city; fundamentalism versus modernism; traditional sources of culture versus the new mass media.

The 1928 campaign featured two politicians who represented profoundly different sides of American life. Al Smith, the Democratic nominee for president, was a pure product of New York City's Lower East Side. Smith came from a background that included Irish, German, and Italian ancestry, and he was raised as a Roman Catholic. After attending parochial school and working in the Fulton Fish Market, he rose through the political ranks of New York's Tammany Hall machine. A personable man with a deep sympathy for poor and working-class people, Smith won a reputation as an effective state legislator in Albany. He served four terms as governor of New York, pushing through an array of laws reforming factory conditions, housing, and welfare programs. Two of his closest advisers were the progressives Frances Perkins and Belle Moskowitz. Smith thus fused older-style machine politics with the newer reform emphasis on state intervention to solve social problems.

Herbert Hoover easily won the Republican nomination after Calvin Coolidge announced he would not run for reelection. Hoover epitomized the successful and forward-looking American. An engineer and self-made millionaire, he offered a unique combination of experience in humanitarian war relief, administrative efficiency, and probusiness policies. Above all, Hoover stood for a commitment to voluntarism and individualism as the best method for advancing the public welfare. He was one of the best-known men in America and promised to continue the Republican control of national politics.

Smith himself quickly became the central issue of the campaign. His sharp New York accent, jarring to many Americans who heard it over the radio, marked him clearly as a man of the city. So did his brown derby and fashionable suits, as well as his promise to work for the repeal of Prohibition. As the first Roman Catholic nominee of a major party, Smith also drew a torrent of anti-Catholic bigotry, especially in the South and Midwest. Nativists and Ku Klux Klanners shamelessly exploited old anti-Catholic prejudices and intimidated participants in Democratic election rallies. But Smith was also attacked from more respectable quarters. Bishop James Cannon, head of the Southern Methodist Episcopal Church, insisted that "no subject of the Pope" should be permitted to occupy the White House. William Allen White, the old and influential progressive editor from Kansas, denounced Smith as the candidate of gambling, prostitution, and liquor interests.

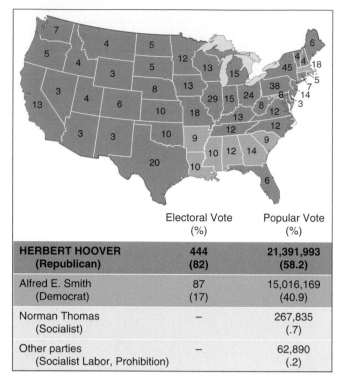

	Electoral Vote (%)	Popular Vote (%)
HERBERT HOOVER (Republican)	**444 (82)**	**21,391,993 (58.2)**
Alfred E. Smith (Democrat)	87 (17)	15,016,169 (40.9)
Norman Thomas (Socialist)	–	267,835 (.7)
Other parties (Socialist Labor, Prohibition)	–	62,890 (.2)

The Election of 1928 Although Al Smith managed to carry the nation's twelve largest cities, Herbert Hoover's victory in 1928 was one of the largest popular and electoral landslides in the nation's history.

For his part, Smith ran a largely conservative race. He appointed John Raskob, a Republican vice president of General Motors, to manage his campaign, and tried to outdo Hoover in his praise for business. He avoided economic issues such as the unevenness of the prosperity, the plight of farmers, or the growing unemployment. Democrats remained regionally divided over Prohibition, Smith's religion, and the widening split between rural and urban values. Hoover did not have to do much, other than take credit for the continued prosperity.

In retrospect, probably no Democrat could have won in 1928. The incumbent majority party would not lose during prosperous times. Hoover polled 21 million votes to Smith's 15 million, and swept the electoral college 444 to 87, including New York State. Even the Solid South, reliably Democratic since the Civil War, gave five states to Hoover—a clear reflection of the ethnocultural split in the party. Yet the election offered important clues to the future of the Democrats. Smith ran better in the big cities of the North and East than any Democrat in modern times. He outpolled Hoover in the aggregate vote of the nation's twelve largest cities

CHRONOLOGY

1920	Prohibition takes effect
	Warren G. Harding is elected president
	Station KDKA in Pittsburgh goes on the air
	Census reports that urban population is greater than rural population for the first time
1921	First immigration quotas are established by Congress
	Sheppard-Towner Act establishes first federally funded health-care program
1922	Washington conference produces Five-Power Treaty, scaling down navies
1923	Equal Rights Amendment is first introduced in Congress
	Harding dies in office; Calvin Coolidge becomes president
1924	Ku Klux Klan is at height of its influence
	Dawes Plan for war reparations stabilizes European economies
	Johnson-Reed Immigration Act tightens quotas established in 1921
1925	Scopes trial pits religious fundamentalism against modernity
	F. Scott Fitzgerald publishes *The Great Gatsby*
1926	National Broadcasting Company establishes first national radio network
1927	McNary-Haugen Farm Relief bill finally passed by Congress but is vetoed by President Coolidge as unwarranted federal interference in the economy
	Warner Brothers produces *The Jazz Singer*, the first feature-length motion picture with sound
	Charles Lindbergh makes first solo flight across the Atlantic Ocean
1928	Kellogg-Briand Pact renounces war
	Herbert Hoover defeats Al Smith for the presidency
1929	Robert and Helen Lynd publish their classic community study *Middletown*

and carried six of them, thus pointing the way to the Democrats' future dominance with urban, Northeastern, and ethnic voters.

CONCLUSION

America's big cities, if not dominant politically, now defined the nation's cultural and economic life as never before. The mass media of motion pictures, broadcasting, and chain newspapers brought cosmopolitan entertainments and values to the remotest small communities. The culture of celebrity knew no geographic boundaries. New consumer durable goods associated with mass-production techniques—automobiles, radios, telephones, household appliances—were manufactured largely in cities. The advertising and public relations companies that sang their praises were also distinctly urban enterprises. Even with the curtailing of European immigration, big cities attracted a kaleidoscopic variety of migrants: white people from small towns and farms, African Americans from the rural South, Mexicans from across the border, intellectuals and professionals looking to make their mark.

Many Americans, of course, remained deeply suspicious of postwar cultural and economic trends. Yet the partisans of Prohibition, members of the Ku Klux Klan, and religious fundamentalists usually found themselves on the defensive against what they viewed as alien cultural and economic forces centered in the metropolis. Large sectors of the population did not share in the era's prosperity. But the large numbers who did—or at least had a taste of good times—ensured Republican political dominance throughout the decade. Thus America in the 1920s balanced dizzying change in the cultural and economic realms with conservative politics. The reform crusades that attracted millions during the progressive era were a distant memory. Political activism was no match for the new pleasures promised by technology and prosperity.

REVIEW QUESTIONS

1. Describe the impact of the "second industrial revolution" on American business, workers, and consumers. Which technological and economic changes had the biggest impact on American society?
2. Analyze the uneven distribution of the 1920's economic prosperity. Which Americans gained the most, and which were largely left out?
3. How did an expanding mass culture change the contours of everyday life in the decade following World War I? What role did new technologies of mass communication play in shaping these changes?

What connections can you draw between the "culture of consumption," then and today?
4. What were the key policies and goals articulated by Republican political leaders of the 1920s? How did they apply these to both domestic and foreign affairs?
5. How did some Americans resist the rapid changes taking place in the post–World War I world? What cultural and political strategies did they employ?
6. Discuss the 1928 election as a mirror of the divisions in American society.

RECOMMENDED READING

Nancy F. Cott, *The Grounding of American Feminism* (1987).

Lynn Dumenil, *The Modern Temper: America in the 1920s* (1995).

James J. Flink, *The Car Culture* (1975).

David J. Goldberg, *Discontented America: The United States in the 1920s* (1999).

Ellis W. Hawley, *The Great War and the Search for Modern Order* (1979).

Desmond King, *Making Americans: Immigration, Race, and the Origins of Diverse Democracy* (2000).

Nancy Maclean, *Behind the Mask of Chivalry: The Making of the Second Ku Klux Klan* (1994).

Roland Marchand, *Advertising the American Dream: Making Way for Modernity, 1920–1940* (1985).

Emily S. Rosenberg, *Spreading the American Dream* (1982).

Susan Smulyan, *Selling Radio: The Commercialization of American Broadcasting, 1920–1934* (1994).

▶ MEDIA RESOURCES

 U.S. HISTORY DOCUMENTS CD-ROM

America Around the Globe

20-8   Mark Twain, "Incident in the Philippines" (1924)

World War One

22-9   Warren G. Harding, Campaign Speech at Boston (1920)

22-10   Edward Earle Purinton, "Big Ideas from Big Business" (1921)

The 1920s and Modern America

23-1   J. Grimke, "Address of Welcome to the Men Who Have Returned from the Battlefront" (1919)

23-2   The Sahara of the Bozart (1920)

23-3   National Origins Quota Act (1924)

23-4   Advertisements (1925, 1927)

23-5   Family Planning   (1926)

23-6   Bartolomeo Vanzetti, Court Statement (1927)

 COMPANION WEBSITE HIGHLIGHTS

To view an exploration, enter one of the URLs below in your browser.

 Web Explorations

Black Population, 1920

http://www.prenhall.com/faragher/map23.1

 Additional Interactive Maps

To access the map, go to this chapter's resources at

http://www.prenhall.com/faragher

The Election of 1928, page 728

 HISTORY RESOURCE CENTER

To find the resources listed below, go to

http://www.prenhall.com/historyresourcecenter

Documents

Comprehensive Immigration Law (1924)

Images

Charles Lindbergh

Ford Model T

Scopes Monkey Trial

Warren G. Harding

Warren G. Harding and Calvin Coolidge

EXPLORING AMERICA

HARLEM RENAISSANCE

http://www.prenhall.com/faragher/harlem

The Great Migration of African Americans to northern cities during and after World War I influenced the development of a cultural flowering in New York City known as the Harlem Renaissance. What forces stimulated this migration and the subsequent cultural renaissance in Harlem? Who was the New Negro? What role did jazz play? How did mainstream white Americans respond to the flowering of African American culture? The module examines the Harlem Renaissance phenomenon of the 1920s, answering these and other questions about one of the most important cultural movements of the twentieth century. The importance of the Harlem Renaissance is explored through diverse resources but especially through the jazz music of the twenties that helped defined that decade.

Harlem Renaissance examines how changes in racial consciousness and pride helped stimulate the rich cultural profusion that occurred in Harlem and elsewhere in the 1920s. While the narrative, interactive map, and chronology provide an important context to this topic, the stress is on presenting works of the poets and jazz musicians as representing the diverse group of artists, photographers, and musicians who defined the Harlem Renaissance and who have profoundly influenced American culture.

Reflect and Respond

1. Use various resources in the article and on the Internet to annotate Cullen's "Harlem Life" poems. Use the poems themselves, images, and the sound files to illustrate, comment upon, and complicate your understanding of Cullen's portraits of Harlem life. Can the posters for *The Jazz Singer* (Warner Brothers' "Supreme Triumph") help explain Cullen's insistence upon the physical beauty of his "brown girl" and "brown boy"?

2. Choose two poems from the Harlem Renaissance and discuss how you would use other materials presented here to illuminate their significance as historical evidence for understanding this time period.

✓ Check it out

Duke Ellington, Black and Tan Fantasy

This song by one of the foremost jazz artists of the 1920s epitomizes the music that defined the 1920s. Jazz represented an important African American achievement both in the African American, the mainstream, and other ethnic communities. The music also became popular and influential worldwide. Equally important, Ellington and other jazz musicians were accorded high status both in the United States and other countries.

This exploration is also available on the *Exploring America* CD-ROM.

TWENTY-FOUR
THE GREAT DEPRESSION AND THE NEW DEAL

▶ 1929–1940

Reginald Marsh (1898–1954), *The Park Bench*, 1933. Tempera on masonite on panel, 24 × 36 in. Sheldon Memorial Art Gallery, University of Nebraska–Lincoln, Nebraska Art Association Collection 1938.N–43.

Sit-Down Strike at Flint: Automobile Workers Organize a New Union

IN THE GLOOMY EVENING OF FEBRUARY 11, 1937, 400 TIRED, UNSHAVEN, but very happy strikers marched out of the sprawling automobile factory known as Fisher Body Number 1. Most carried American flags and small bundles of clothing. A makeshift banner on top of the plant announced "Victory Is Ours." A wildly cheering parade line of a thousand supporters greeted the strikers at the gates. Shouting with joy, honking horns, and singing songs, the celebrants marched to two other factories to greet other emerging strikers. After forty-four days, the great Flint sit-down strike was over.

Flint, Michigan, was the heart of production for General Motors, the largest corporation in the world. In 1936 GM's net profits had reached $285 million, and its total assets were $1.5 billion. Originally a center for lumbering and then carriage making, Flint had boomed with the auto industry during the 1920s. Thousands of migrants streamed into the city, attracted by assembly-line jobs averaging about $30 a week. By 1930 Flint's population had grown to about 150,000 people, 80 percent of whom depended on work at General Motors. A severe housing shortage made living conditions difficult. Tar-paper shacks, tents, even railroad cars were the only shelter available for many. Parts of the city resembled a mining camp.

The Great Depression hit Flint very hard. Employment at GM fell from a 1929 high of 56,000 to fewer than 17,000 in 1932. As late as 1938 close to half the city's families were receiving some kind of emergency relief. By that time, as in thousands of other American communities, Flint's private and county relief agencies had been overwhelmed by the needs of the unemployed and their families. Two new national agencies based in Washington, D.C., the Federal Emergency Relief Administration and the Works Progress Administration, had replaced local sources of aid during the economic crisis.

The United Automobile Workers (UAW) came to Flint in 1936 seeking to organize GM workers into one industrial union. The previous year, Congress had passed the National Labor Relations Act (also known as the Wagner Act), which made union organizing easier by guaranteeing the right of workers to join unions and to bargain collectively. The act established the National Labor Relations Board to oversee union elections and prohibit illegal antiunion activities by employers. But the obstacles to labor organizing were still enormous. Unemployment was high, and GM had maintained a vigorous antiunion policy for years. By the fall of 1936, the UAW had signed up only a thousand members. The key moment came with the seizure of two Flint GM plants by a few hundred auto workers on December 30, 1936. The idea was to stay in the factories until strikers could achieve a collective bargaining agreement with General Motors. "We don't aim to keep the plants or try to run them," explained one sit-downer to a reporter, "but we want to see that nobody takes our jobs. We don't think we're breaking the law, or at least we don't think we're doing anything really bad."

The sit-down strike was a new and daring tactic that gained popularity among American industrial workers during the 1930s. In 1936 there were forty-eight sit-downs involving nearly 90,000 workers, and in 1937 some 400,000 workers participated in 477 sit-down strikes. Sit-downs expressed the militant exuberance of the rank and file. As one union song of the day put it:

> When they tie the can to a union man,
> Sit down! Sit down!
> When they give him the sack they'll take him back,
> Sit down! Sit down!
> When the speed up comes, just twiddle your thumbs,
> Sit down! Sit down!
> When the boss won't talk don't take a walk,
> Sit down! Sit down!

The Flint strikers carefully organized themselves into what one historian called "the sit-down community." Each plant elected a strike committee and appointed its own police chief and sanitary engineer. Strikers were divided into "families" of fifteen, each with a captain. No alcohol was allowed, and strikers were careful not to destroy company property. Committees were organized for every conceivable purpose: food, recreation, sanitation, education, and contact with the outside. Sit-downers formed glee clubs and small orchestras to entertain themselves. Using loudspeakers, they broadcast concerts and speeches to their supporters outside the gates. A Women's Emergency Brigade—the strikers' wives, mothers, and daughters—provided crucial support preparing food and maintaining militant picket lines.

As the sit-down strike continued through January 1937, support in Flint and around the nation grew. Overall production in the GM empire dropped from 53,000 vehicles per week to 1,500. Reporters and union supporters flocked to the plants. On January 11, in the so-called Battle of Running Bulls, strikers and their supporters clashed violently with Flint police and private GM guards. Michigan governor Frank Murphy, sympathetic to the strikers, brought in the National Guard to protect them. He refused to enforce an injunction obtained by GM to evict the strikers.

In the face of determined unity by the sit-downers, GM gave in and recognized the UAW as the exclusive bargaining agent in all sixty of its factories. The strike was perhaps the most important in American labor history, sparking a huge growth in union membership in the automobile and other mass-production industries. Rose Pesotta, a textile union organizer, described the wild victory celebration in Flint's overflowing Pengelly Building: "People sang and joked and laughed and cried, deliriously joyful. Victory meant a freedom they had never known before. No longer would they be afraid to join unions."

Out of the tight-knit, temporary community of the sit-down strike emerged a looser yet more permanent kind of community: a powerful, nationwide trade union of automobile workers. The UAW struggled successfully to win recognition and collective bargaining rights from other carmakers, such as Chrysler and Ford. The national UAW, like other new unions in the mass-production industries, was composed of locals around the country. The permanent community of unionized auto workers won significant improvements in wages, working conditions, and benefits. Locals also became influential in the political and social lives of their larger communities—industrial cities such as Flint, Detroit, and Toledo. Nationally, organized labor became a crucial component of the New Deal political coalition and a key power broker in the Democratic Party. The new reality of a national community of organized labor would alter the national political and economic landscape for decades to come. ■

Flint

> ## KEY TOPICS
>
> - Causes and consequences of the Great Depression
> - The politics of hard times
> - Franklin D. Roosevelt and the two New Deals
> - The expanding federal sphere in the West
> - American cultural life during the 1930s
> - Legacies and limits of New Deal reform

HARD TIMES

No event of the twentieth century had a more profound impact on American life than the Great Depression of the 1930s. Statistics can document a slumping economy, mass unemployment, and swelling relief rolls—but these numbers tell only part of the story. The emotional and psychological toll of these years, what one writer called "the invisible scar," must also be considered in understanding the worst economic crisis in American history. Even today, Depression era experiences retain a central, even mythical, place in the lives and memories of millions of American families.

The Bull Market

Stock trading in the late 1920s captured the imagination of the broad American public. The stock market resembled a sporting arena, millions following stock prices as they did the exploits of Babe Ruth or Jack Dempsey. Many business leaders and economists as much as told Americans that it was their duty to buy stocks. John J. Raskob, chairman of the board of General Motors, wrote an article for the *Ladies' Home Journal* titled "Everybody Ought to Be Rich." A person who saved $15 each month and invested it in good common stocks would, he claimed, have $80,000 within twenty years. *The Saturday Evening Post* printed a poem that captured the fever:

> *Oh, hush thee, my babe, granny's bought some more shares*
> *Daddy's gone out to play with the bulls and the bears,*
> *Mother's buying on tips and she simply can't lose,*
> *And baby shall have some expensive new shoes!*

During the bull market of the 1920s, stock prices increased at roughly twice the rate of industrial production. Paper value far outran real value. By the end of the decade, stocks that had been bought mainly on the basis of their earning power, which was passed on to stockholders in the form of dividends, now came to be purchased only for the resale value after their prices rose. Anyone reading the financial pages of a newspaper would be amazed at the upward climb. In 1928 alone, for example, the price of Radio Corporation of America stock shot up from $85 to $420; Chrysler stock more than doubled, from $63 to $132.

Yet only about 4 million Americans owned any stocks at all, out of a total population of 120 million. Many of these stock buyers had been lured into the market through easy-credit, margin accounts. Margin accounts allowed investors to purchase stocks by making a small down payment (as low as 10 percent), borrowing the rest from a broker, and using the shares as collateral, or security, on the loan. Just as installment plans had stimulated the automobile and other industries, "buying on the margin" brought new customers to the stock market. Investment trusts, similar to today's mutual funds, attracted many new investors with promises of high returns based on their managers' expert knowledge of the market. Corporations with excess capital found that lending money to stockbrokers was more profitable than plowing it back into their own plants to develop new technologies. All these new approaches to buying stock contributed to an expansive and optimistic atmosphere on Wall Street.

The Crash

Although often portrayed as a one- or two-day catastrophe, the Wall Street crash of 1929 was in reality a steep downward slide. The bull market peaked in early September, and prices drifted downward. On October 23 the Dow Jones industrials lost 21 points in one hour, and many large investors concluded the boom was over. The boom itself rested on expectations of continually rising prices; once those expectations began to melt, the market had to decline. On Monday, October 28, the Dow lost 38 points, or 13 percent of its value. On October 29, "Black Tuesday," the bottom

Stockbrokers, their customers, and employees of the New York Stock Exchange gather nervously on Wall Street during the stock market crash of 1929. October 29 was the worst single day in the 112-year history of the exchange, as panic selling caused many stocks to lose half their value.

SOURCE: Brown Brothers (010634-1).

seemed to fall out. Over 16 million shares, more than double the previous record, were traded as panic selling took hold. For many stocks no buyers were available at any price.

The situation worsened. The market's fragile foundation of credit, based on the margin debt, quickly crumbled. Many investors with margin accounts had no choice but to sell when stock values fell. Since the shares themselves represented the security for their loans, more money had to be put up to cover the loans when prices declined. By mid-November about $30 billion in the market price of stocks had been wiped out. Half the value of the stocks listed in the *New York Times* index was lost in ten weeks.

The nation's political and economic leaders downplayed the impact of Wall Street's woes. "The fundamental business of the country," President Herbert Hoover told Americans in late October, "is on a sound and prosperous basis." Secretary of the Treasury Andrew Mellon spoke for many in the financial world when he described the benefits of the slump: "It will purge the rottenness out of the system. High costs of living and high living will come down. People will work harder, live a more moral life. Values will be adjusted, and enterprising people will pick up the wrecks from less competent people." At the end of 1929 hardly anyone was predicting that a depression would follow the stock market crash.

DISTRIBUTION OF TOTAL FAMILY INCOME AMONG VARIOUS SEGMENTS OF THE POPULATION, 1929–1944 (IN PERCENTAGES)

Year	Poorest Fifth	Second Poorest Fifth	Middle Fifth	Second Wealthiest Fifth	Wealthiest Fifth	Wealthiest 5 Percent
1929	12.5		13.8	19.3	54.4	30.0
1935–1936	4.1	9.2	14.1	20.9	51.7	26.5
1941	4.1	9.5	15.3	22.3	48.8	24.0
1944	4.9	10.9	16.2	22.2	45.8	20.7

SOURCE: Adapted from U.S. Bureau of the Census, *Historical Statistics of the United States, Colonial Times to 1970*, Bicentennial ed. (Washington, D.C.: U.S. Government Printing Office, 1975), p. 301.

Underlying Weaknesses

It would be oversimple to say that the stock market crash "caused" the Great Depression. But like a person who catches a chill, the economy after the crash became less resistant to existing sources of infection. The resulting sickness revealed underlying economic weaknesses left over from the previous decade. First, workers and consumers by and large received too small a share of the enormous increases in labor productivity. Better machinery and more efficient industrial organization had increased labor productivity enormously. But wages and salaries had not risen nearly as much.

In effect, the automobile of American capitalism had one foot pressed to the accelerator of production and another on the brake of consumption. Between 1923 and 1929 manufacturing output per worker-hour increased by 32 percent. But wages during the same period rose only 8 percent, or one-quarter the rise in productivity. Moreover, the rise in productivity itself had encouraged overproduction in many industries. The farm sector had never been able to regain its prosperity of the World War I years. Farmers suffered under a triple burden of declining prices for their crops, a drop in exports, and large debts incurred by wartime expansion (see Chapter 23).

The most important weakness in the economy was the extremely unequal distribution of income and wealth. In 1929, the top 0.1 percent of American families (24,000 families) had an aggregate income equal to that of the bottom 42 percent (11.5 million families). The top 5 percent of American families received 30 percent of the nation's income; the bottom 60 percent got only 26 percent. About 71 percent of American families had annual incomes below $2,500. Nearly 80 percent of the nation's families (21.5 million households) had no savings; the top 0.1 percent held 34 percent of all savings. The top 0.5 percent of Americans owned 32.4 percent of the net wealth of the entire population—the greatest such concentration of wealth in the nation's history.

The stock market crash undermined the confidence, investment, and spending of businesses and the well-to-do. Manufacturers decreased their production and began laying off workers, and layoffs brought further declines in consumer spending and another round of production cutbacks. A spurt of consumer spending might have checked this downward spiral, but consumers had less to spend as industries laid off workers and reduced work hours. With a shrinking market for products, businesses were hesitant to expand. A large proportion of the nation's banking funds were tied to the speculative bubble of Wall Street stock buying. Many banks began to fail as anxious depositors withdrew their funds, which were uninsured. Thousands of families lost their savings to these failures. An 86 percent plunge in agricultural prices between 1929 and 1933, compared to a decline in agricultural production of only 6 percent, brought suffering to America's farmers.

Mass Unemployment

At a time when unemployment insurance did not exist and public relief was completely inadequate, the loss of a job could mean economic catastrophe for workers and their families. Massive unemployment across America became the most powerful sign of a deepening depression. In 1930 the Department of Labor estimated that 4.2 million workers, or roughly 9 percent of the labor force, were out of work. These figures nearly doubled in 1931, and by 1933, 12.6 million workers—over one-quarter of the labor force—were without jobs. Other sources put the figure that year above 16 million, or nearly one out of every three workers. None of these statistics tells us how long people were unemployed or how many Americans found only part-time work.

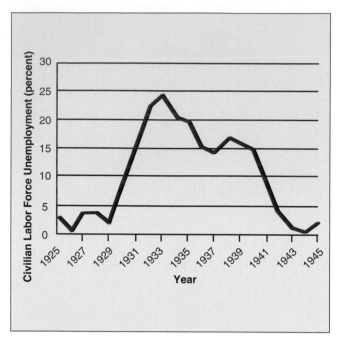

Unemployment, 1929–1945   In 1939, despite six years of New Deal programs, unemployment still hovered around 18 percent of the workforce. Only the onset of World War II ended the unemployment crisis.

SOURCE: U.S. Bureau of the Census, *Historical Statistics of the United States, Colonial Times to 1970*, Bicentennial ed. (Washington, D.C.: U.S. Government Printing Office, 1975), p. 135.

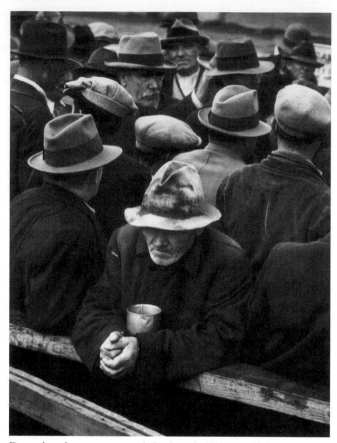

Dorothea Lange captured the lonely despair of unemployment in *White Angel Bread Line*, San Francisco, 1933. During the 1920s Lange had specialized in taking portraits of wealthy families, but by 1932 she could no longer stand the contradiction between her portrait business and "what was going on in the street." She said of this photograph: "There are moments such as these when time stands still and all you can do is hold your breath and hope it will wait for you."

SOURCE: Dorothea Lange, *White Angel Bread Line, San Francisco, 1933*. Copyright, the Dorothea Lange Collection, The Oakland Museum of California, City of Oakland. Gift of Paul S. Taylor.

What did it mean to be unemployed and without hope in the early 1930s? Figures give us only an outline of the grim reality. Many Americans, raised believing that they were responsible for their own fate, blamed themselves for their failure to find work. Contemporary journalists and social workers noted the common feelings of shame and guilt expressed by the unemployed. Even those who did not blame themselves struggled with feelings of inadequacy, uselessness, and despair. One unemployed Houston woman told a relief caseworker, "I'm just no good, I guess. I've given up ever amounting to anything. It's no use." "Drives a man crazy, or drives him to drink, hangin' around," said an out-of-work Connecticut knife maker. For many, nighttime was the worst. "What is going to become of us?" wondered an Arizona man. "I've lost twelve and a half pounds this month, just thinking. You can't sleep, you know. You wake up about 2 A.M., and you lie and think." A West Virginia man wrote his senator to complain, "My children have not got no shoes and clothing to go to school with, and we haven't got enough bed clothes to keep us warm." For the most desperate, contemplating suicide was not unusual. "Can you be so kind as to advise me as to which would

be the most humane way to dispose of my self and family, as this is about the only thing that I see left to do," one despondent Pennsylvania man inquired of a state relief agency.

Joblessness proved especially difficult for men between the ages of thirty-five and fifty-five, the period in their lives when family responsibilities were heaviest. Nathan Ackerman, a psychiatrist who went to Pennsylvania to observe the impact of prolonged unemployment on coal miners, found an enormous sense of "internal distress":

They hung around street corners and in groups. They gave each other solace. They were loath to go home because they were indicted, as if it were their fault for being unemployed. A jobless man was a lazy good-for-nothing. The women punished the men for not bringing home the bacon, by withholding themselves sexually. . . . These men suffered from depression. They felt despised, they were ashamed of themselves. They cringed, they comforted one another. They avoided home.

Unemployment upset the psychological balance in many families by undermining the traditional authority of the male breadwinner. Women, because their labor was cheaper than men's, found it easier to hold onto jobs. Female clerks, secretaries, maids, and waitresses earned much less than male factory workers, but their jobs were more likely to survive hard times. Men responded in a variety of ways to unemployment. Some withdrew emotionally; others became angry or took to drinking. A few committed suicide. One Chicago social worker, writing about unemployment in 1934, summed up the strains she found in families: "Fathers feel they have lost their prestige in the home; there is much nagging, mothers nag at the fathers, parents nag at the children. Children of working age who earn meager salaries find it hard to turn over all their earnings and deny themselves even the greatest necessities and as a result leave home."

Pressures on those lucky enough to have a job increased as well. Anna Novak, a Chicago meat packer, recalled the degrading harassment at the hands of foremen: "You could get along swell if you let the boss slap you on the behind and feel you up. God, I hate that stuff, you don't know!" Fear of unemployment and a deep desire for security marked the Depression generation. "I mean there's a conditioning here by the Depression," a sanitation worker told an interviewer many years later. "I'm what I call a security cat. I don't dare switch [jobs]. 'Cause I got too much whiskers on it, seniority."

Hoover's Failure

The enormity of the Great Depression overwhelmed traditional—and meager—sources of relief. In most communities across America these sources were a patchwork of private agencies and local government units, such as towns, cities, or counties. They simply lacked the money, resources, and staff to deal with the worsening situation. In large urban centers like Detroit and Chicago, unemployment approached 50 percent by 1932. Smaller communities could not cope either. One West Virginia coal-mining county with 1,500 unemployed miners had only $9,000 to meet relief needs for that year. Unemployed transients, attracted by warm weather, posed a special problem for communities in California and Florida. By the end of 1931, Los Angeles had 70,000 nonresident jobless and homeless men; new arrivals numbered about 1,200 a day.

There was great irony, even tragedy, in President Hoover's failure to respond to human suffering. He had administered large-scale humanitarian efforts during World War I with great efficiency. Yet he seemed to most people a man with little personal warmth. Hoover made his reputation as an engineer and as one who believed in the importance of objective studies of social and economic problems, yet he failed to face the facts of the Depression. He ignored all the mounting evidence to the contrary when he claimed in his 1931 State of the Union Address, "Our people are providing against distress from unemployment in true American

Isaac Soyer's *Employment Agency,* a 1937 oil painting, offered one of the decade's most sensitive efforts at depicting the anxiety and sense of isolation felt by millions of Depression-era job hunters.

SOURCE: Isaac Soyer, *Employment Agency,* 1937. Oil on canvas, 34½" × 45", (87 × 114.3 cm). Whitney Museum of American Art, New York.

fashion by magnificent response to public appeal and by action of the local governments."

Hoover resisted the growing calls from Congress and local communities for a greater federal role in relief efforts or public works projects. He worried, as he told Congress after vetoing one measure, about injuring "the initiative and enterprise of the American people." The President's Emergency Committee for Unemployment, established in 1930, and its successor, the President's Organization for Unemployment Relief (POUR), created in 1931, did little more than encourage local groups to raise money to help the unemployed. Walter S. Gifford, chairman of POUR and president of AT&T, insisted that local relief groups could handle the needs of Americans in distress. "My sober and considered judgement," he told Congress in early 1932, "is that at this stage Federal aid would be a disservice to the unemployed."

Hoover's plan for recovery centered on restoring business confidence. His administration's most important institutional response to the depression was the Reconstruction Finance Corporation (RFC), established in early 1932 and based on the War Finance Corporation of the World War I years. The RFC was designed to make government credit available to ailing banks, railroads, insurance companies, and other businesses, thereby stimulating economic activity. The key assumption here was that the credit problem was one of supply (for businesses) rather than demand (from consumers). But given the public's low purchasing power, most businesses were not interested in obtaining loans for expansion.

The RFC managed to save numerous banks and other businesses from going under, but its approach did not hasten recovery. And Hoover was loath to use the RFC to make direct grants to states, cities, or individuals. In July 1932, congressional Democrats pushed through the Emergency Relief Act, which authorized the RFC to lend $300 million to states that had exhausted their own relief funds. Hoover grudgingly signed the bill, but less than $30 million had actually been given out by the end of 1933. Although Congress authorized the RFC to spend money on public works, only a small fraction of its $2 billion budget went to such programs.

Protest and the Election of 1932

By 1932, the desperate mood of many Americans was finding expression in direct, sometimes violent protests that were widely covered in the press. On March 7, Communist organizers led a march of several thousand Detroit auto workers and unemployed to the Ford River Rouge factory in nearby Dearborn. When the demonstrators refused orders to turn back, Ford-controlled police fired tear gas and bullets, killing four and seriously wounding fifty others. Some 40,000 people attended a tense funeral service a few days later. Desperate farmers in Iowa organized the Farmers' Holiday Association, aimed at raising prices by refusing to sell produce. In August, some 1,500 farmers turned back cargo trucks outside Sioux City, Iowa, and made a point by dumping milk and other perishables into ditches.

The spring of 1932 also saw the "Bonus Army" begin descending on Washington, D.C. This protest took its name from a 1924 act of Congress that had promised a $1,000 bonus—in the form of a bond that would not mature until 1945—to every veteran of World War I. The veterans who were gathering in Washington demanded immediate payment of the bonus in cash. By summer they and their families numbered around 20,000 and were camped out all over the capital city. Their lobbying convinced the House to pass a bill for immediate payment, but the Senate rejected the bill and most of the veterans left. At the end of July, U.S. Army troops led by Chief of Staff General Douglas MacArthur forcibly evicted the remaining 2,000 veterans from their encampment. MacArthur exaggerated the menace of the peaceful demonstrators, insisting they were driven by "the essence of revolution." The spectacle of these unarmed and unemployed men, the heroes of 1918, being driven off by bayonets and bullets provided the most disturbing evidence yet of the failure of Hoover's administration.

The congressional elections of 1930 had already revealed a growing dissatisfaction with Hoover's approach. Democrats had won control of the House of Representatives for the first time since 1916 and gained eight seats in the Senate. In 1932, Democrats nominated Franklin D. Roosevelt, governor of New York, as their candidate. Roosevelt's acceptance speech stressed the need for reconstructing the nation's economy. "I pledge you, I pledge myself," he said, "to a new deal for the American people."

Roosevelt's plans for recovery were vague at best. He frequently attacked Hoover for reckless and extravagant spending and accused him of trying to center too much power in Washington. He also spoke of the need for government to meet "the problem of underconsumption" and to help in "distributing wealth and products more equitably." Hoover bitterly condemned Roosevelt's ideas as a "radical departure" from the American way of life. But with the Depression growing worse every day, probably any Democrat would have defeated Hoover. The Democratic victory was overwhelming. Roosevelt carried forty-two states, taking the electoral college 472 to 59 and the popular vote by about 23 million to 16 million. Democrats won big majorities in both the House and the Senate. The stage was set for FDR's "new deal."

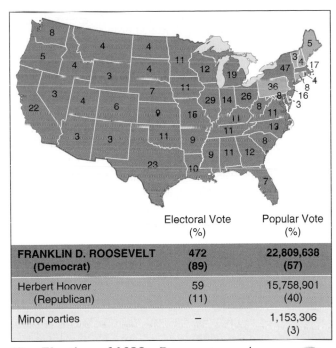

	Electoral Vote (%)	Popular Vote (%)
FRANKLIN D. ROOSEVELT (Democrat)	**472 (89)**	**22,809,638 (57)**
Herbert Hoover (Republican)	59 (11)	15,758,901 (40)
Minor parties	–	1,153,306 (3)

The Election of 1932   Democrats owed their overwhelming victory in 1932 to the popular identification of the Depression with the Hoover administration. Roosevelt's popular vote was about the same as Hoover's in 1928, and FDR's electoral college margin was even greater.

WWW.

FDR AND THE FIRST NEW DEAL

No president of this century had a greater impact on American life and politics than Franklin Delano Roosevelt. To a large degree, the New Deal was a product of his astute political skills and the sheer force of his personality. The only president ever elected to four terms, FDR would loom as the dominant personality in American political life through depression and war. Roosevelt's leadership also inaugurated a forty-year-long period during which the Democrats would be the nation's majority party.

FDR the Man

Franklin Delano Roosevelt was born in 1882 in Dutchess County, New York, where he grew up an only child, secure and confident, on his family's vast estate. Franklin's father, James, had made a fortune through railroad investments, but he was already in his fifties when Franklin was born, and it was his mother, Sara Delano, who was the dominant figure in his childhood. Roosevelt's education at Groton, Harvard, and Columbia Law School reinforced the aristocratic values of his family: a strong

sense of civic duty, the importance of competitive athletics, and a commitment to public service.

In 1905, Franklin married his distant cousin, Anna Eleanor Roosevelt, niece of President Theodore Roosevelt. Eleanor would later emerge as an influential adviser and political force on her own. Franklin turned to politics as a career early on. He was elected as a Democrat to the New York State Senate in 1910, served as assistant navy secretary from 1913 to 1920, and was nominated for vice president by the Democrats in the losing 1920 campaign.

In the summer of 1921 Roosevelt was stricken with polio at his summer home. He was never to walk again without support. The disease strengthened his relationship with Eleanor, who encouraged him not only to fight his handicap but to continue his political career. The disease and FDR's response to it proved a turning point. His patience and determination in fighting the illness transformed him. The wealthy aristocrat, for whom everything had come relatively easy, now personally understood the meaning of struggle and hardship. "Once I spent two years lying in bed trying to move my big toe," he recalled. "After that anything else seems easy."

Elected governor of New York in 1928, Roosevelt served two terms and won a national reputation for reform. As governor, his achievements included instituting unemployment insurance, strengthening child labor laws, providing tax relief for farmers, and providing pensions for the old. As the Depression hit the state, he slowly increased public works and set up a Temporary Emergency Relief Administration. With his eye on the White House, he began assembling a group of key advisers, the "brains trust," who would follow him to Washington. The central figures were Columbia Law School professor and progressive Raymond Moley; two economists, Rexford G. Tugwell and Adolf A. Berle; and attorneys Samuel Rosenman, Basil O'Connor, and Felix Frankfurter. The "brain trusters" shared a faith in the power of experts to set the economy right and a basic belief in government–business cooperation. They rejected the old progressive dream of re-creating an ideal society of small producers. Structural economic reform, they argued, must accept the modern reality of large corporate enterprise based on mass production and distribution.

Restoring Confidence

In the first days of his administration Roosevelt conveyed a sense of optimism and activism that helped restore the badly shaken confidence of the nation. "First of all," he told Americans in his Inaugural Address on March 4, 1933, "let me assert my firm belief that the only thing we have to fear is fear itself." The very next day he issued an executive order calling for a four-day "bank holiday" to shore up the country's ailing financial system. More than 1,300 banks failed in 1930, more than 2,000 in 1931. Contemporary investigations had revealed a disquieting pattern of stock manipulation, illegal loans to bank officials, and tax evasion that helped erode public confidence in the banking system. Between election day and the inauguration, the banking system had come alarmingly close to shutting down altogether due to widespread bank failures and the hoarding of currency.

Roosevelt therefore called for a special session of Congress to deal with the banking crisis as well as with unemployment aid and farm relief. On March 12 he broadcast his first "fireside chat" to explain the steps he had taken to meet the financial emergency. These radio broadcasts became a standard part of Roosevelt's political technique, and they proved enormously suc-

This *New Yorker* magazine cover depicted an ebullient Franklin D. Roosevelt riding to his 1933 inauguration in the company of a glum Herbert Hoover. This drawing typified many mass media images of the day contrasting the different moods and temperaments of the new President and the defeated incumbent. SOURCE: By Peter Arno, March 4, 1933. Franklin D. Roosevelt Library (CT65-521).

cessful. They gave courage to ordinary Americans and communicated a genuine sense of compassion from the White House.

Congress immediately passed the Emergency Banking Act, which gave the president broad discretionary powers over all banking transactions and foreign exchange. It authorized healthy banks to reopen only under licenses from the Treasury Department and provided for greater federal authority in managing the affairs of failed banks. By the middle of March about half the country's banks, holding about 90 percent of the nation's deposits, were open for business again. Banks began to attract new deposits from people who had been holding back their money. The bank crisis had passed.

The Hundred Days

From March to June of 1933—the "Hundred Days"—FDR pushed through Congress an extraordinary number of acts designed to combat various aspects of the Depression. What came to be called the New Deal was no unified program to end the Depression but rather an improvised series of reform and relief measures, some of which seemed to contradict each other. Roosevelt responded to pressures from Congress, from business, and from organized labor, but he also used his own considerable influence over public opinion to get his way. His program focused on reviving both the industrial and agricultural sectors of the economy along with providing emergency relief for the unemployed.

Five measures were particularly important and innovative. The Civilian Conservation Corps (CCC), established in March 1933 as an unemployment relief effort, provided work for jobless young men in protecting and conserving the nation's natural resources. Road construction, reforestation, flood control, and national park improvements were some of the major projects performed in work camps across the country. CCC workers received room and board and $30 each month, up to $25 of which had to be sent home to dependents. By the time the program was phased out in 1942, more than 2.5 million youths had worked in some 1,500 CCC camps.

In May, Congress authorized $500 million for the Federal Emergency Relief Administration (FERA). Half the money went as direct relief to the states; the rest was distributed on the basis of a dollar of federal aid for every three dollars of state and local funds spent for relief. This system of outright federal grants differed significantly from Hoover's approach, which provided only for loans. Establishment of work relief projects, however, was left to state and local governments.

The Agricultural Adjustment Administration (AAA) was set up to provide immediate relief to the nation's farmers. The AAA established a new federal role in agri-

OVERVIEW

KEY LEGISLATION OF THE FIRST NEW DEAL ("HUNDRED DAYS," MARCH 9–JUNE 16, 1933)

Legislation	Purpose
Emergency Banking Relief Act	Enlarged federal authority over private banks Government loans to private banks
Civilian Conservation Corps	Unemployment relief Conservation of natural resources
Federal Emergency Relief Administration	Direct federal money for relief, funneled through state and local governments
Agricultural Adjustment Administration	Federal farm-aid based on parity pricing and subsidy
Tennessee Valley Authority	Economic development and cheap electricity for Tennessee Valley
National Industrial Recovery Act	Self-regulating industrial codes to revive economic activity
Public Works Administration	Federal public works projects to increase employment and consumer spending

cultural planning and price setting. It established parity prices for basic farm commodities, including corn, wheat, hogs, cotton, rice, and dairy products. The concept of parity pricing was based on the purchasing power that farmers had enjoyed during the prosperous years of 1909 to 1914. That period now became the benchmark for setting the prices of farm commodities. The AAA also incorporated the principle of subsidy, whereby farmers received benefit payments in return for reducing acreage or otherwise cutting production where surpluses existed. The funds for these payments were to be raised from new taxes on food processing.

The AAA raised total farm income and was especially successful in pushing up the prices of wheat, cotton, and corn. But it had some troubling side effects as well. Landlords often failed to share their AAA payments with tenant farmers, and they frequently used benefits to buy tractors and other equipment that displaced sharecroppers. Many Americans were disturbed, too, by the sight of surplus crops, livestock, and milk being destroyed while millions went hungry. The Southern Tenant Farmers Union (STFU), founded in 1934, emerged as an important voice of protest against AAA policies. Active in six states and composed of about 30,000 tenant farmers (over half of whom were black), the STFU protested evictions, called strikes to raise farm labor wages, and challenged landlords to give tenants their fair share of subsidy payments. The STFU succeeded in drawing national attention to the plight of sharecroppers and tenant farmers, but it failed

to influence national farm policy. The 1937 Bankhead-Jones Tenancy Act offered a very limited program of loans to tenant farmers, and the AAA remained a boon to large landlords.

The Tennessee Valley Authority (TVA) proved to be one of the most unique and controversial projects of the New Deal era. It had its origins in the federal government's effort during World War I to build a large hydroelectric power complex and munitions plant on the Tennessee River at Muscle Shoals, Alabama. During the 1920s, Republican senator George W. Norris of Nebraska had led an unsuccessful fight to provide for permanent government operation of the Muscle Shoals facilities on behalf of the area's population. The TVA, an independent public corporation, built dams and power plants, produced cheap fertilizer for farmers, and, most significantly, brought cheap electricity for the first time to thousands of people in six southern states. Denounced by some as a dangerous step toward socialism, the TVA stood for decades as a model of how careful government planning could dramatically improve the social and economic welfare of an underdeveloped region.

On the very last of the Hundred Days, Congress passed the National Industrial Recovery Act, the closest attempt yet at a systematic plan for economic recovery. It had two main parts. The National Recovery Administration (NRA) sought to stimulate production and competition in business by means of industrial codes regulating prices, output, and trade practices. In theory,

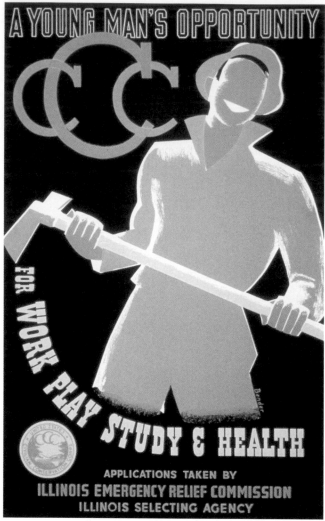

A recruitment poster represents the Civilian Conservation Corps as much more than simply an emergency relief measure, stressing character building and the opportunity for self-improvement. By the time the CCC expired in 1942 it had become one of the most popular of all the New Deal programs.

SOURCE: Albert M. Bender, *CCC—A Young Man's Opportunity for Work, Play, Study and Health*, 1941. © CORBIS (IH151596).

each industry would be self-governed by a code hammered out by representatives of business, labor, and the consuming public. Once approved by the NRA in Washington, led by General Hugh Johnson and symbolized by the distinctive Blue Eagle stamp, the codes would have the force of law. In practice, almost all the NRA codes were written by the largest firms in any given industry; labor and consumers got short shrift. The sheer administrative complexities involved with code writing and compliance made a great many people unhappy with the NRA's operation. Overall, the NRA looked to business and industry leaders to find a way to recovery.

The second component, the Public Works Administration (PWA), led by Secretary of the Interior Harold Ickes, authorized $3.3 billion for the construction of roads, public buildings, and other projects. The idea was to provide jobs and thus stimulate the economy through increased consumer spending. A favorite image for this kind of spending was "priming the pump." Just as a farmer had to prime a pump with water before it could draw more water from the well, the government had to prime the economy with jobs for the unemployed. Eventually the PWA spent over $4.2 billion building roads, schools, post offices, bridges, courthouses, and other public buildings around the country. In thousands of communities today, these structures remain the most tangible reminders of the New Deal era.

LEFT TURN AND THE SECOND NEW DEAL

The Hundred Days legislative package tried to offer something for everybody. Certainly the active, can-do spirit in Washington brought reassurance that the nation was back on track. Yet the Depression remained a stark reality for many millions. From the beginning, the New Deal had loud and powerful critics who complained bitterly that FDR had overstepped the traditional boundaries of government action. Others were angry that Roosevelt had not done nearly enough. These varied voices of protest helped shape the political debates of FDR's first term. Ultimately, they would push the New Deal in more radical directions.

Roosevelt's Critics

Criticism of the New Deal came from the right and the left. On the right, pro-Republican newspapers and the American Liberty League, a group of conservative businessmen organized in 1934, denounced Roosevelt and his advisers. They held the administration responsible for what they considered an attack on property rights, for the growing welfare state, and for the decline of personal liberty. Dominated by wealthy executives of Du Pont and General Motors, the league attracted support from a group of conservative Democrats, including Al Smith, the former presidential candidate, who declared the New Deal's laws "socialistic." The league supported anti-New Dealers for Congress, but in the 1934 election Democrats built up their majorities from 310 to 319 in the House and from 60 to 69 in the Senate—an unusually strong showing for the incumbent party in a midterm election.

Some of Roosevelt's staunchest early supporters turned critical. Father Charles E. Coughlin, a Catholic priest in suburban Detroit, attracted a huge national radio audience of 40 million listeners with passionate sermons attacking Wall Street, international bankers, and "plutocratic capitalism." Coughlin at first supported Roosevelt and the New Deal, and he tried to build a close personal relationship with the president. But by 1934 the ambitious Coughlin, frustrated by his limited influence on the administration, began attacking FDR. Roosevelt was a tool of special interests, he charged, who wanted dictatorial powers. New Deal policies were part of a Communist conspiracy, threatening community autonomy with centralized federal power. Coughlin finally broke with FDR and founded the National Union for Social Justice. In 1936 the Coughlin-dominated Union Party nominated William Lemke, an obscure North Dakota congressman, to run for president. Lemke polled only 900,000 votes, but Coughlin continued his biting attacks on Roosevelt through 1940.

More troublesome for Roosevelt and his allies were the vocal and popular movements on the left. These found the New Deal too timid in its measures. In California, well-known novelist and socialist Upton Sinclair entered the 1934 Democratic primary for governor by running on a program he called EPIC, for End Poverty in California. He proposed a $50 a month pension for all poor people over age sixty. His campaign also emphasized a government-run system of "production for use" (rather than profit) workshops for the unemployed. Sinclair shocked local and national Democrats by winning the primary easily. He lost a close general election only because the Republican candidate received heavy financial and tactical support from wealthy Hollywood studio executives and frightened regular Democrats.

Another Californian, Francis E. Townsend, a retired doctor, created a large following among senior citizens with his Old Age Revolving Pension plan. He called for payments of $200 per month to all people over sixty, provided the money was spent within thirty days. The pensions would be financed by a national 2 percent tax on all commercial transactions. This plan managed to attract a nationwide following of more than 3 million by 1936. But Townsend's plan was essentially regressive, since it proposed to tax all Americans equally, regardless of their income.

Huey Long, Louisiana's flamboyant backcountry orator, posed the greatest potential threat to Roosevelt's leadership. Long had captured Louisiana's governorship in 1928 by attacking the state's entrenched oil industry and calling for a radical redistribution of wealth. In office, he significantly improved public education, roads, medical care, and other public services, winning the loyalty of the state's poor farmers and industrial workers. Elected to the U.S. Senate in 1930, Long came to Washington with national ambitions. He at first supported Roosevelt, but in 1934 his own presidential ambitions and his impatience with the pace of New Deal measures led to a break with Roosevelt.

Long organized the Share Our Wealth Society. Its purpose, he thundered, "was to break up the swollen fortunes of America and to spread the wealth among all our people." Limiting the size of large fortunes, Long promised, would mean a homestead worth $5,000 and a $2,500 annual income for everyone. Although Long's economics were fuzzy at best, he undoubtedly touched a deep nerve with his "Every Man a King" slogan. The Democratic National Committee was shocked when a secret poll in the summer of 1935 revealed that Long might attract 3 or 4 million votes. Only his assassination that September by a disgruntled political enemy prevented Long's third-party candidacy, which might have proved disastrous for FDR.

In the nation's work places and streets, a rejuvenated and newly militant labor movement also loomed as a force to be reckoned with. In many industrial cities Unemployed Councils, organized largely by the Communist Party, held marches and rallies demanding public works projects and relief payments. Section 7a of the National Industrial Recovery Act required that workers be allowed to bargain collectively with employers, through representatives of their own choosing. Though this provision of the NIRA was not enforced, it did help raise expectations and spark union organizing. Almost 1.5 million workers took part in some 1,800 strikes in 1934. But employers resisted unionization nearly everywhere, often with violence and the help of local and state police.

In Minneapolis, a local of the International Brotherhood of Teamsters won a bloody strike against the combined opposition of the union's own national officials, vehemently antiunion employers, and a brutal city police force. Violence against strikers helped unite the city's working classes. The Minneapolis Central Labor Union was prepared to support a general strike, and the funeral of a striker shot by police drew 100,000 people. In San Francisco in 1934, a general strike in support of striking members of the International Longshoremen's Association (ILA) effectively shut down the city. Employer use of strikebreakers and violent intimidation prompted an outpouring of support for the ILA from the city's working class, as well as from many shopkeepers and middle-class professionals. When the ILA accepted government arbitration, it won on its main issue—control over the hiring halls on the waterfront. In both Minneapolis and San Francisco, workers had demonstrated the power of labor solidarity and mass protest.

The Second Hundred Days

The popularity of leaders like Sinclair, Townsend, and Long suggested Roosevelt might be losing electoral support among workers, farmers, the aged, and the

OVERVIEW

KEY LEGISLATION OF THE SECOND NEW DEAL (1935–1938)

Legislation	Purpose
Emergency Relief Appropriations Act (1935) (includes Works Progress Administration)	Large-scale public works program for the jobless
Social Security Act (1935)	Federal old-age pensions and unemployment insurance
National Labor Relations Act (1935)	Federal guarantee of right to organize trade unions and collective bargaining
Resettlement Administration (1935)	Relocation of poor rural families Reforestation and soil erosion projects
National Housing Act (1937)	Federal funding for public housing and slum clearance
Fair Labor Standards Act (1938)	Federal minimum wage and maximum hours

unemployed. In early 1935, Roosevelt and his closest advisers responded by turning left and concentrating on a new program of social reform. They had three major goals: strengthening the national commitment to creating jobs; providing security against old age, unemployment, and illness; and improving housing conditions and cleaning slums. What came to be called the "Second Hundred Days" marked the high point of progressive lawmaking in the New Deal.

In April the administration pushed through the Emergency Relief Appropriation Act, which allocated $5 billion for large-scale public works programs for the jobless. New Deal economists, following the theories of Britain's John Maynard Keynes, argued that each government dollar spent had a multiplier effect, pumping two or three dollars into the depressed gross national product. The major responsible agency here was the Works Progress Administration (WPA), led by Harry Hopkins. Born and raised in Iowa, Hopkins had pursued a social work career in New York City. Streetwise, driven by a deep moral passion to help the less fortunate, and impatient with bureaucracy, Hopkins emerged as the key figure in New Deal relief programs. People often referred to him as the "assistant president." Over the next seven years Hopkins oversaw the employment of more than 8 million Americans on a vast array of construction projects: roads, bridges, dams, airports, and sewers. Among the most innovative WPA programs were community service projects that employed thousands of jobless artists, musicians, actors, and writers.

The landmark Social Security Act of 1935 provided for old-age pensions and unemployment insurance. A payroll tax on workers and their employers created a fund from which retirees received monthly pensions after age sixty-five. Payment size depended upon how much employees and their employers had contributed over the years. The unemployment compensation plan established a minimum weekly payment and a minimum number of weeks during which those who lost jobs could collect. The Social Security Board administered this complex system of federal-state cooperation. The original law failed to cover domestics and farm workers, many of whom were Latinos and African Americans. It also made no provisions for casual laborers or public employees. The old-age pensions were quite small at first, as little as $10 a month. And to collect unemployment, one had to have first lost a job. But the law, which has since been amended many times, established the crucial principle of federal responsibility for America's most vulnerable citizens.

Roosevelt and congressional New Dealers called for new legislation to strengthen labor's right to organize after the Supreme Court, in May 1935, ruled the National Industrial Recovery Act unconstitutional, including its provisions protecting union organizing. In July 1935, Congress passed the National Labor Relations Act, often called the Wagner Act for its chief sponsor, Democratic senator Robert F. Wagner of New York. The new law had far-reaching implications for American politics and the economy. For the first time, the federal government guaranteed the right of American workers to join or form independent labor unions and bargain collectively for improved wages, benefits, and working conditions. The National Labor Relations Board would conduct secret-ballot elections in shops and factories to determine which union, if any, workers desired as their sole bargaining agent. The law also defined and prohibited unfair labor practices by employers, including firing workers for union activity. The Wagner Act, described as the "Magna Carta for labor," quickly proved a boon to union growth, especially in previously unorganized industries such as automobiles, steel, and textiles. It set the stage for the sit-down strike in Flint and for General Motors' eventual acceptance of union labor in its factories.

Finally, the Resettlement Administration (RA) produced one of the most utopian New Deal programs, one designed to create new kinds of model communities. Established by executive order and led by key brain truster Rexford G. Tugwell, the RA helped destitute farm families relocate to more productive areas. It granted loans for purchasing land and equipment, and it directed reforestation and soil erosion projects, particularly in the hard-hit Southwest. Due to lack of funds and poor administration, however, only about 1 percent of the projected 500,000 families were actually moved.

Tugwell, one of the New Deal's most ardent believers in planning, was more successful in his efforts at creating model greenbelt communities combining the best of urban and rural environments. "My idea," he wrote, "is to go just outside centers of population, pick up cheap land, build a whole community and entice people into it." Though his vision was only partially fulfilled, several of these communities, such as Greenhills, near Cincinnati, and Greendale, near Milwaukee, still thrive.

Labor's Upsurge: Rise of the CIO

In 1932 the American labor movement was nearly dead. Only 2.8 million workers were union members, a half-million fewer than in 1929 and more than 2 million fewer than in 1920. Yet by 1942, unions claimed more than 10.5 million members, nearly a third of the total nonagricultural workforce. This remarkable turnaround was one of the key events of the Depression era. The growth in the size and power of the labor movement permanently changed the work lives and economic status of millions, as well as the national and local political landscapes.

At the core of this growth was a series of dramatic successes in the organization of workers in large-scale, mass-production industries, such as those producing automobiles, steel, rubber, electrical goods, and textiles. Workers in these fields had largely been ignored by the conservative, craft-conscious unions that dominated the American Federation of Labor. At the 1935 AFL convention, a group of more militant union officials led by John L. Lewis (of the United Mine Workers) and Sidney Hillman (of the Amalgamated Clothing Workers) formed the Committee for Industrial Organization

(CIO). Their goal was to organize mass-production workers by industry rather than by craft. They emphasized the need for opening the new unions to all, regardless of a worker's level of skill. And they differed from nearly all old-line AFL unions by calling for the inclusion of black and women workers.

Lewis was the key figure in the CIO. The gruff son of a Welsh miner, Lewis was articulate, ruthless, and very ambitious. He saw the new legal protection given by the Wagner Act as a historic opportunity. But despite the Act—whose constitutionality was unclear until 1937—Lewis knew that establishing permanent unions in the mass-production industries would be a bruising battle. He committed the substantial resources of the United Mine Workers to a series of organizing drives, focusing first on the steel and auto industries. Many CIO organizers were Communists or radicals of other persuasions, and their dedication, commitment, and willingness to work within disciplined organizations proved invaluable in the often dangerous task of creating industrial unions. Of the roughly 200 full-time organizers on the payroll of the Steel Workers Organizing Committee in 1937, almost a third were members of the Communist Party.

Militant rank-and-file unionists were often ahead of Lewis and other CIO leaders. The sit-down strike—refusing to work but staying in the factory to prevent "scab" workers from taking over—emerged as a popular tactic among rubber and auto workers. After the dramatic breakthrough in the Flint sit-down strike at General Motors, membership in CIO unions grew rapidly. In eight months, membership in the United Automobile Workers alone soared from 88,000 to 400,000. CIO victories in the steel, rubber, and electrical industries followed, but often at a very high cost. One bloody example of the perils of union organizing was the 1937 Memorial Day Massacre in Chicago. In a field near the struck Republic Steel Mill in South Chicago, police fired into a crowd of union supporters, killing ten workers and wounding scores more.

Overall, the success of the CIO's organizing drives was remarkable. In 1938 CIO unions, now boasting nearly 4 million members, withdrew from the AFL and reorganized themselves as the Congress of Industrial Organizations. Ahead lay many hard battles organizing workers in such nonunion bastions as the Ford Motor Company and the textile plants of the South. But for the first time ever, the labor movement had gained a permanent place in the nation's mass-production industries. Organized labor took its place as a key power broker in Roosevelt's New Deal and the national Democratic Party. Frances Perkins, FDR's secretary of labor and the nation's first woman cabinet member, captured the close relationship between the new unionism and the New Deal: "Programs long thought of as merely

Philip Evergood, *American Tragedy* (1937). A classic example of the social realism characteristic of much Depression-era art, this painting depicts the police violence against strikers at the Republic Steel Mill. Evergood was one of many artists who found work in the Federal Art Project painting murals in public buildings.

SOURCE: Philip Evergood, *American Tragedy*, 1937. Oil on canvas, 29½″ × 39½″. Private Collection, Terry Dintenfass Gallery. Photo by Philip Evergood.

Roosevelt attacked the "economic royalists" who denied that government "could do anything to protect the citizen in his right to work and his right to live." At the same time, FDR was careful to distance himself from radicalism. "It was this administration," he declared, "which saved the system of private profit and free enterprise after it had been dragged to the brink of ruin." As Roosevelt's campaign crossed the country, his advisers were heartened by huge and enthusiastic crowds, especially in large cities like Chicago and Pittsburgh. Still, the vast majority of the nation's newspapers endorsed Landon. And a widely touted "scientific" poll by the *Literary Digest* forecast a Republican victory in November.

Election day erased all doubts. Roosevelt carried every state but Maine and Vermont, polling 61 percent of the popular vote. Democrats increased their substantial majorities in the House and Senate as well. The *Literary Digest*, it turned out, had drawn the sample for its poll from people whose addresses were listed in telephone directories and car registration records, thus omitting the poorer Americans who had no telephones or cars—and who supported Roosevelt. In 1936 the Democrats drew millions of new voters into the political process and at the same time forged a new coalition of voters that would dominate national politics for two generations.

This "New Deal coalition," as it came to be known, included traditional-minded white southern Democrats, big-city political machines, industrial workers of all races, trade unionists, and many Depression-hit farmers. The Democrats' strong showing in the ethnic wards of America's large urban centers amplified a trend that had begun with Al Smith's 1928 campaign. Organized labor put an unprecedented amount of money and people power into Roosevelt's reelection. Black voters in the North and West, long affiliated with the Republicans as the party of Abraham Lincoln, went Democratic in record numbers. The Great Depression was by no means over. But the New Deal's active response to the nation's misery, particularly the bold initiatives taken in 1935, had obviously struck a powerful chord with the American electorate.

Roosevelt was especially popular among first- and second-generation Catholics and Jews, and the New

labor welfare, such as shorter hours, higher wages, and a voice in the terms of conditions of work, are really essential economic factors for recovery."

The New Deal Coalition at High Tide

Did the American public support Roosevelt and his New Deal policies? Both major political parties looked forward to the 1936 elections as a national referendum, and the campaign itself was an exciting and hard-fought contest. Very few political observers predicted its lopsided result.

Republicans nominated Governor Alfred M. Landon of Kansas, who had gained attention by surviving the Democratic landslide of 1934. Landon, an easygoing, colorless man with little personal magnetism, emphasized a nostalgic appeal to traditional American values. His campaign served as a lightning rod for all those, including many conservative Democrats, who were dissatisfied with Roosevelt and the direction he had taken. Al Smith, the Democratic nominee in 1928, categorically denounced the New Deal as "socialistic" and supported Landon. Kansas Republican William Allen White, editor of the *Emporia Gazette*, attacked the New Deal for building up the federal government and creating "a great political machine centered in Washington."

Deal drew enthusiastic support from millions in the ethnic working class who had never bothered with politics. As one Slovak worker in Chicago's stock yards put it, "Our people did not know anything about the government until the Depression years. In my neighborhood, I don't remember anyone voting." The severity of the Great Depression had overwhelmed the ethnically based support networks—mutual benefit societies, immigrant banks, and religious charities—that had traditionally helped so many to survive hard times. Working-class voters in large cities like New York, Chicago, Detroit, and Philadelphia increasingly took credit for putting and keeping Democrats in power locally and nationally—and their attitudes toward politics changed. The federal government no longer seemed so remote or irrelevant to their lives. Popular federal programs like Social Security, the WPA, and Home Owners Loan Corporation mortgages changed the consciousness of a generation of the ethnic working class. In exchange for their votes, they now looked to the state—especially the federal government—for relief, protection, and help in achieving the American dream.

THE NEW DEAL AND THE WEST

The New Deal had a more profound impact on the West than on any other region in the nation. Western citizens received more from the federal government in per capita payments for welfare, work relief, and loans than the people of any other section. But perhaps more important, New Deal programs, based on a philosophy of rational planning of resource use, transformed western agriculture, water and energy sources, and Indian policy. From Great Plains farming communities in Kansas and Oklahoma to Pacific coast cities such as Los Angeles and Seattle, federal subsidy and management became an integral part of western life. In the process, the New Deal helped propel the West into the modern era. The region's economic development and politics would now be dominated by a combination of Washington-based bureaucracies, large-scale agriculture, and new industrial enterprises.

The Dust Bowl

An ecological and economic disaster of unprecedented proportions struck the southern Great Plains in the mid 1930s. The region had suffered several drought years in the early 1930s. Such dry spells occurred regularly in roughly twenty-year cycles. But this time the parched earth became swept up in violent dust storms the likes of

which had never been seen before. The dust storms were largely the consequence of years of stripping the landscape of its natural vegetation. During World War I, wheat fetched record-high prices on the world market, and for the next twenty years Great Plains farmers had turned the region into a vast wheat factory.

The wide flatlands of the Great Plains were especially suited to mechanized farming, and gasoline-powered tractors, disc plows, and harvester-thresher combines increased productivity enormously. Back in 1830 it had taken some fifty-eight hours of labor to bring an acre of wheat to the granary; in much of the Great Plains a hundred years later it required less than three hours. As wheat prices fell in the 1920s, farmers broke still more land to make up the difference with increased production. Great Plains farmers had

Web Exploration

Through a series of rollover maps, consider the extent of the Dust Bowl from 1935–1940. What were the reasons for this ecological disaster?
www.prenhall.com/faragher/map24.1

The Dust Bowl, 1935–1940   This map shows the extent of the Dust Bowl in the southern Great Plains. Federal programs designed to improve soil conservation, water management, and farming practices could not prevent a mass exodus of hundreds of thousands out of the Great Plains.

created an ecological time bomb that exploded when drought returned in the early 1930s. With native grasses destroyed for the sake of wheat growing, there was nothing left to prevent soil erosion. Dust storms blew away tens of millions of acres of rich topsoil, and thousands of farm families left the region. Those who stayed suffered deep economic and psychological losses from the calamity. The hardest-hit regions were western Kansas, eastern Colorado, western Oklahoma, the Texas Panhandle, and eastern New Mexico. It was the calamity in this southern part of the Great Plains that prompted a Denver journalist to coin the phrase "Dust Bowl."

Black blizzards of dust a mile and a half high rolled across the landscape, darkening the sky and whipping the earth into great drifts of dust that settled over hundreds of miles. Dust storms made it difficult for humans and livestock to breathe and destroyed crops and trees over vast areas. Dust storms turned day into night, terrifying those caught in them. "Dust pneumonia" and other respiratory infections afflicted thousands, and many travelers found themselves stranded in automobiles and trains unable to move. The worst storms occurred in the early spring of 1935. A Garden City, Kansas, woman gave an account of her experience for the *Kansas City Times:*

> All we could do about it was just sit in our dusty chairs, gaze at each other through the fog that filled the room and watch that fog settle slowly and silently, covering everything—including ourselves—in a thick, brownish gray blanket. When we opened the door swirling whirlwinds of soil beat against us unmercifully. The door and windows were all shut tightly, yet those tiny particles seemed to seep through the very walls. It got into cupboards and clothes closets; our faces were as dirty as if we had rolled in the dirt; our hair was gray and stiff and we ground dirt between our teeth.

Several federal agencies intervened directly to relieve the distress. Many thousands of Great Plains farm families were given direct emergency relief by the Resettlement Administration. Other federal assistance included crop and seed loans, moratoriums on loan payments, and temporary jobs with the Works Progress Administration. In most Great Plains counties, from one-fifth to one-third of the families applied for relief; in the hardest-hit communities, as many as 90 percent of the families received direct government aid. The Agricultural Adjustment Administration paid wheat farmers millions of dollars not to grow what they could not sell and encouraged the diversion of acreage from soil-depleting crops like wheat to soil-enriching crops such as sorghum.

Years of Dust. This 1936 poster by the artist and photographer Ben Shahn served to publicize the work of the Resettlement Administration, which offered aid to destitute farm families hit hard by the Dust Bowl. Shahn's stark imagery here was typical of the documentary aesthetic associated with Depression-era art and photography.

SOURCE: The Granger Collection (4EBU96).

To reduce the pressure from grazing cattle on the remaining grasslands, the Drought Relief Service of the Department of Agriculture purchased more than 8 million head of cattle in 1934 and 1935. For a brief time, the federal government was the largest cattle owner in the world. This agency also lent ranchers money to feed their remaining cattle. The Taylor Grazing Act of 1934 brought stock grazing on 8 million acres of public domain lands under federal management.

The federal government also pursued longer-range policies designed to alter land-use patterns, reverse soil erosion, and nourish the return of grasslands. The Department of Agriculture, under Secretary Henry A. Wallace, sought to change farming practices. The spearhead for this effort was the Soil Conservation Service (SCS), which conducted research into controlling wind and water erosion, set up demonstration projects, and offered technical assistance, supplies, and equipment to farmers engaged in conservation work on farms and ranches. The SCS pumped additional federal funds into the Great Plains and created a new rural organization, the soil conservation district, which administered conservation regulations locally.

By 1940 the acreage subject to blowing in the Dust Bowl area of the southern Plains had been reduced from roughly 50 million acres to less than 4 million acres. In the face of the Dust Bowl disaster, New Deal farm policies had restricted market forces in agriculture. But the return of regular rainfall and the outbreak of World War II led many farmers to abandon the techniques that the SCS had taught them to accept. Wheat farming expanded and farms grew as farmers once again pursued commercial agriculture with little concern for its long-term effects on the land.

While large landowners and ranchers reaped sizable benefits from AAA subsidies and other New Deal programs in the southern Plains, tenant farmers and sharecroppers received very little. In the cotton lands of Texas, Oklahoma, Missouri, and Arkansas, thousands of tenant and sharecropper families were forced off the land. They became part of a stream of roughly 300,000 people, disparagingly called "Okies," who migrated to California in the 1930s. California migrants included victims of the Dust Bowl, but the majority were blue-collar workers and small businessmen looking to improve their economic lot. California suffered from the Depression along with the rest of the nation, but it still offered more jobs, higher wages, and higher relief payments than the states of the southern Plains. Most Okies could find work only as poorly paid agricultural laborers in the fertile San Joaquin and Imperial Valley districts. There they faced discrimination and scorn as "poor white trash" while they struggled to create communities amid the squalor of migrant labor camps. Only with the outbreak of World War II and the pressing demand for labor were migrants able to significantly improve their situation.

Mexican farm laborers faced stiff competition from Dust Bowl refugees. By the mid-1930s they no longer dominated California's agricultural workforce. In 1936 an estimated 85 to 90 percent of the state's migratory workers were white Americans, as compared to less than 20 percent before the Depression. Mexican farm worker families who managed to stay employed in California, Texas, and Colorado saw their wages plummet. Southwestern communities, responding to racial hostility from unemployed whites and looking for ways to reduce their welfare burden, campaigned to deport Mexicans and Mexican Americans. Employers, private charities,

and the Immigration and Naturalization Service joined in this effort. Authorities made little effort to distinguish citizens from aliens; most of the children they deported had been born in the United States and were citizens. Los Angeles County had the most aggressive campaign, using boxcars to ship out more than 13,000 Mexicans between 1931 and 1934. The hostile climate convinced thousands more to leave voluntarily. Overall, over 400,000 left the United States during the decade. Some Mexican deportees crossed the border with a melancholy song on their lips:

> And so I take my leave,
> may you be happy.
> Here the song ends,
> but the Depression goes on forever.

Water Policy

The New Deal ushered in an era of large-scale water projects designed to provide irrigation and cheap power and to prevent floods. The long-range impact of these undertakings on western life was enormous. The key government agency in this realm was the Bureau of Reclamation of the Department of the Interior, established under the National Reclamation Act of 1902. The bureau's original responsibility had been to construct dams and irrigation works and thereby encourage the growth of small farms throughout the arid regions of the West. Until the late 1920s the bureau's efforts had been of little consequence, providing irrigation for only a very small portion of land. But its fortunes changed when its focus shifted to building huge multipurpose dams designed to control entire river systems.

The first of these projects was the Boulder Dam (later renamed the Hoover Dam). The dam, actually begun during the Hoover administration, was designed to harness the Colorado River, wildest and most isolated of the major western rivers. Its planned benefits included flood prevention, the irrigation of California's Imperial Valley, the supplying of domestic water for southern California, and the generation of cheap electricity for Los Angeles and southern Arizona. Hoover, however, had opposed the public power aspect of the project, arguing that the government ought not to compete with private utility companies. This position was contrary to that of most Westerners, who believed cheap public power was critical for development. Roosevelt's support for government-sponsored power projects was a significant factor in his winning the political backing of the West in 1932 and subsequent election years.

Boulder Dam was completed in 1935 with the help of funds from the Public Works Administration. Its total cost was $114 million, which was to be offset by the sale of the hydroelectric power it generated.

Web Exploration Consider the many water projects sponsored by federal agencies during the New Deal. Why were many of these projects located in the West?
www.prenhall.com/faragher/map24.2

The New Deal and Water This map illustrates U.S. drainage areas and the major large-scale water projects begun or completed by federal agencies during the New Deal. By providing irrigation, cheap power, flood control, and recreation areas, these public works had a historically unprecedented impact on America's western communities.

Los Angeles and neighboring cities built a 259-mile aqueduct, costing $220 million, to channel water to their growing populations. Lake Mead, created by construction of the dam, became the world's largest artificial lake, extending 115 miles up the canyon and providing a popular new recreation area. The dam's irrigation water helped make the Imperial Valley, covering over 500,000 acres, one of the most productive agricultural districts in the world.

The success of Boulder Dam transformed the Bureau of Reclamation into a major federal agency with huge resources at its disposal. In 1938 it completed the All-American Canal—an 80-mile channel connecting the Colorado River to the Imperial Valley, with a 130-mile branch to the Coachella Valley. The canal

cost $24 million to build and carried a flow of water equal to that of the Potomac River. More than a million acres of desert land were opened up to the cultivation of citrus fruits, melons, vegetables, and cotton. Irrigation districts receiving water promised to repay, without interest, the cost of the canal over a forty-year period. This interest-free loan was in effect a huge government subsidy to the private growers who benefited from the canal.

In 1935 the bureau began the giant Central Valley Project (CVP). The Central Valley, stretching through the California interior, is a 500-mile oblong watershed with an average width of 125 miles. The idea was to bring water from the Sacramento River in the north down to the arid lands of the larger San Joaquin Valley in the south. Completed in 1947, the project eventually cost $2.3 billion. The CVP stored water and transferred it to the drier southern regions of the state. It also provided electricity, flood control, and municipal water. The federal government, local municipalities, and buyers of electric power paid most of the cost, and the project proved a boon to large-scale farmers in the Sacramento and San Joaquin river valleys.

The largest power and irrigation project of all was the Grand Coulee Dam, northwest of Spokane, Washington. Completed in 1941, it was designed to convert the power of the Columbia River into cheap electricity and to irrigate previously uncultivated land, thereby stimulating the economic development of the Pacific Northwest. The construction of Grand Coulee employed tens of thousands of workers and pumped millions of dollars into the region's badly depressed economy. Between 1933 and 1940 Washington State ranked first in per capita federal expenditures. In the longer run, Grand Coulee provided the cheapest electricity in the United States and helped attract new manufacturing to a region previously dependent on the export of raw materials, such as lumber and metals.

These technological marvels and the new economic development they stimulated were not without an environmental and human cost. The Grand Coulee and smaller dams nearby reduced the Columbia River, long a potent symbol of the western wilderness, to a string of lakes. Spawning salmon could no longer run the river above the dam. In California, the federal guarantee of river water made a relative handful of large farmers fabulously wealthy. But tens of thousands of farm workers, mostly of Mexican descent, labored in the newly fertile fields for very low wages, and their health suffered from contact with pesticides. The Colorado River, no longer emptying into the Pacific, began to build up salt deposits, making its water increasingly unfit for drinking or irrigation. Water pollution in the form of high salinity continues to plague the 2,000-mile river to this day.

A New Deal for Indians

The New Deal brought important changes and some limited improvements to the lives of Indians. In 1933 some 320,000 Indian people, belonging to about 200 tribes, lived on reservations. Most were in Oklahoma, Arizona, New Mexico, and South Dakota. Indian people suffered from the worst poverty of any group in the nation and an infant mortality rate twice that of the white population. The incidence of alcoholism and other diseases, such as tuberculosis and measles, was much higher on the reservations than off. Half of all those on reservations were landless, forced to rent or live with relatives. The Bureau of Indian Affairs

(BIA), oldest of the federal bureaucracies in the West, had a long history of corruption and mismanagement. The BIA had for years tried to assimilate Indians through education and had routinely interfered with Indian religious affairs and tribal customs. In 1928 the Merriam Report, prepared by the Institute for Government Research, had offered a scathing and widely publicized critique of BIA mismanagement. But the Hoover administration made no effort to reform the agency.

In 1933 President Roosevelt appointed John Collier to bring change to the BIA. Collier had deep roots in progressive-era social work and community organizing in eastern big-city slums. During the 1920s he had become passionately interested in Indian affairs after spending time in Taos, New Mexico. He became involved with the struggle of the Pueblo Indians to hold onto their tribal lands, and he had served as executive secretary of the American Indian Defense Association. As the new BIA head, Collier pledged to "stop wronging the Indians and to rewrite the cruel and stupid laws that rob them and crush their family lives." Collier brought a reformer's zeal to his new job, and he quickly demonstrated his bureaucratic skills. He halted the sale of Indian lands, obtained emergency conservation work for 77,000 Indians under the CCC program, and secured millions of dollars in PWA funds to finance Indian day schools on the reservations. He also fired incompetent and corrupt BIA officials and insisted that those who remained respect tribal customs.

Most important, Collier became the driving force behind the Indian Reorganization Act (IRA) of 1934. The IRA reversed the allotment provisions of the Dawes Severalty Act of 1887, which had weakened tribal sovereignty by shifting the distribution of land from tribes to individuals (see Chapter 18). The new legislation permitted the restoration of surplus reservation lands to tribal ownership and allocated funds for the purchase of additional lands and for economic development. At its heart, the IRA sought to restore tribal structures by making the tribes instruments of the federal government. Any tribe that ratified the IRA could then elect a tribal council that would enjoy federal recognition as the legal tribal government. In this way, Collier argued, tribes would be "surrounded by the protective guardianship of the federal government and clothed with the authority of the federal government." He fought first to get the legislation through a reluctant Congress, which, uneasy with reversing the long-standing policy of Indian assimilation, insisted on many changes to Collier's original plan.

The more difficult battle involved winning approval by Indian peoples. Collier's efforts to win acceptance of the IRA met with mixed results on the reservations. Linguistic barriers made it nearly impossible for some tribes to fully assess the plan. The Papagos of southern Arizona, for example, had no words for "budget" and "representative." Their language made no distinction among the terms "law," "rule," "charter," and "constitution," and they used the same word for "president," "reservation agent," "king," and "Indian commissioner." In all, 181 tribes organized governments under the IRA, while seventy-seven tribes rejected it.

The Navajos, the nation's largest tribe with over 40,000 members, rejected the IRA, illustrating some of the contradictions embedded in federal policy. The Navajo refusal came as a protest against the BIA's forced reduction of their livestock, part of a soil conservation program. The government blamed Navajo sheep for the gullying and erosion that threatened to fill in Lake Mead and make Boulder Dam inoperable. But the hundreds of thousands of sheep in the Navajos' herds were central to their economy and society. They used sheep for barter, to pay religious leaders, and as their primary source of meat.

The Navajos believed the erosion stemmed not from overgrazing but from lack of sufficient water and inadequate acreage on the reservation. Howard Gorman, a Navajo political leader, angrily responded to Collier's last-minute personal appearance before the tribal council: "This thing, the thing you said that will make us strong, what do you mean by it? We have been told that not once but many times this same thing, and all it is is a bunch of lies. . . . You're wasting your time coming here and talking to us." Facing loss of half their sheep, Navajos took their anger out on Collier, rejecting the reorganization plan.

Under Collier's tenure, the BIA became much more sensitive to Indian cultural and religious freedom. The number of Indian people employed by the BIA itself increased from a few hundred in 1933 to more than 4,600 in 1940. Collier trumpeted the principle of Indian political autonomy, a radical idea for the day. But in practice, both the BIA and Congress regularly interfered with reservation governments, especially in money matters. Collier often dictated economic programs for tribes, which Congress usually underfunded. For the long run, Collier's most important legacy was the reassertion of the status of Indian tribes as semi-sovereign nations. In 1934 a Department of the Interior lawyer, Nathan Margold, wrote a legal opinion that tribal governments retained all their original powers— their "internal sovereignty"—except when these were specifically limited by acts of Congress. In later years U.S. courts would uphold the Margold Opinion, leading to a significant restoration of tribal rights and land to Indian peoples of the West.

DEPRESSION-ERA CULTURE

American culture in the 1930s, like all other aspects of national life, was profoundly shaped by the Great Depression. The themes and images in various cultural forms frequently reflected Depression-related problems. Yet contradictory messages coexisted, sometimes within the same novel or movie. With American capitalism facing its worst crisis, radical expressions of protest and revolution were more common than ever. But there were also strong celebrations of individualism, nostalgia for a simpler, rural past, and searches for core American virtues. The 1930s also saw important shifts in the organization and production of culture. For a brief but significant moment, the federal government offered substantial and unprecedented support to artists and writers. In the realm of popular culture, Hollywood movies, network radio broadcasting, and big-band jazz achieved a central place in the everyday lives of Americans.

A New Deal for the Arts

The Depression hit America's writers, artists, and teachers just as hard as blue-collar workers. In 1935, the WPA allocated $300 million for the unemployed in these fields. Over the next four years, Federal Project No. 1, an umbrella agency covering writing, theater, music, and the visual arts, proved to be one of the most innovative and successful New Deal programs. "Federal One," as it was called, offered work to desperate artists and intellectuals, enriched the cultural lives of millions, and left a substantial legacy of artistic and cultural production. Nearly all these works were informed by the spirit of the documentary impulse, a deep desire to record and communicate the experiences of ordinary Americans. Photographer Lewis Hine defined the documentary attitude simply and clearly: "I wanted to show the things that had to be corrected. I wanted to show the things that had to be appreciated."

At its height, the Federal Writers Project (FWP) employed 5,000 writers on a variety of programs. Most notably, it produced a popular series of state and city guidebooks, each combining history, folklore, and tourism. The 150-volume "Life in America" series included valuable oral histories of former slaves, studies of ethnic and Indian cultures, and pioneering collections of American songs and folk tales. Work on the Writers Project helped many American writers to survive, hone their craft, and go on to great achievement and prominence. These included Ralph Ellison, Richard Wright, Margaret Walker, John Cheever, Saul Bellow, and Zora Neale Hurston. Novelist Anzia Yezierska recalled a strong spirit of camaraderie among

Fletcher Martin painted *Mine Rescue* (1939) in the Kellogg, Idaho post office. The work was part of a Treasury Department program that employed unemployed artists to beautify government buildings. The mural was eventually removed under pressure from local citizens who worried that it might upset those who had lost loved ones in mine accidents.

SOURCE: Fletcher Martin (1904–1979), *Mine Rescue*, 1939. Copyright Smithsonian American Art Museum, Washington, DC/Art Resource, NY (SO137776).

the writers: "Each morning I walked to the Project as lighthearted as if I were going to a party." For poet Muriel Rukeyser, the FWP embodied an essential part of the era: "The key to the 30s was the joy to awake and see life entire and tell the stories of real people."

The Federal Theater Project (FTP), under the direction of the dynamic Hallie Flanagan of Vassar College, reached as many as 30 million Americans with its productions. The FTP sought to expand the audience for theater beyond the regular patrons of the commercial stage. Tickets for its productions were cheap, and it made variety of dramatic forms available. Among its most successful productions were the "Living Newspaper" plays based on contemporary controversies and current events. *Power* concerned the public ownership of utilities; *Triple A Plowed Under* dealt with farm problems; *Injunction Granted* documented unionizing struggles. Other FTP productions brought classics as well as new plays to communities. Among the most successful productions were T. S. Eliot's *Murder in the Cathedral*, Maxwell Anderson's *Valley Forge*, and Orson Welles's version of *Macbeth*, set in Haiti with an all-black cast.

The FTP often came under attack from congressional critics who found it too radical. But Flanagan defended her vision of a theater that confronted political issues. If the plays were mixed with politics, she wrote, "it was because life in our country was mixed with politics. These Arts projects were coming up,

through, and out of the people." The FTP supported scores of community-based theatrical units around the country, giving work and experience to actors, playwrights, directors, and set designers. It brought vital and exciting theater to millions who had never attended before.

Two smaller but similar programs were the Federal Music Project (FMP) and the Federal Art Project (FAP). The FMP, under Nikolai Sokoloff of the Cleveland Symphony Orchestra, employed 15,000 musicians and financed hundreds of thousands of low-priced public concerts by touring orchestras. The Composers' Forum Laboratory supported new works by American composers such as Aaron Copland and William Schuman.

Among the painters who received government assistance through the FAP were Willem de Kooning, Jackson Pollock, and Louise Nevelson. The FAP also employed painters and sculptors to teach studio skills and art history in schools, churches, and settlement houses. The Index of American Design was a comprehensive compilation of American folk art from colonial times. The FAP also commissioned artists to paint hundreds of murals on the walls of post offices, meeting halls, courthouses, and other government buildings. Many of these, done in the style of the revolutionary Mexican muralists Diego Rivera and José Clemente Orozco, emphasized political and social themes. All these projects, declared Holger Cahill, director of the FAP, were aimed at "raising a generation sensitive to their visual environment and capable of helping to improve it."

The Documentary Impulse

"You can right a lot of wrongs with 'pitiless publicity,'" Franklin Roosevelt once declared. Social change, he argued, "is a difficult thing in our civilization unless you have sentiment." During the 1930s an enormous number of artists, novelists, journalists, photographers, and filmmakers tried to document the devastation wrought by the Depression in American communities. They also depicted people's struggles to cope with and reverse hard times. Some of these efforts were consciously linked to promoting political action, often as part of a radical commitment to overthrowing capitalism. Others were interested less in fomenting social change than in recording vanishing ways of life. Mainstream mass media, such as the photo essays found in *Life* magazine or "March of Time" newsreels, also adapted this stance.

Regardless of political agendas or the medium employed, what one historian calls the "documentary impulse" became a prominent style in 1930s cultural expression. At its core, the documentary impulse directly influenced its audience's intellect and feelings through documentary "evidence" of social problems and human suffering. The most direct and influential expression of the documentary style was the photograph. In 1935 Roy Stryker, chief of the Historical Section of the Resettlement Administration (later part of the Farm Security Administration), gathered a remarkable group of photographers to help document the work of the agency. Stryker encouraged them to photograph whatever caught their interest, even if the pictures had no direct connection with RA projects. These photographers, including Dorothea Lange, Walker Evans, Arthur Rothstein, Russell Lee, Ben Shahn, and Marion Post Wolcott, left us the single most significant visual record of the Great Depression.

The photographers traveled through rural areas, small towns, and migrant labor camps, often not stopping even long enough to learn the names of their subjects. They produced powerful images of despair and resignation as well as hope and resilience. These photographs were reproduced in newspapers and magazines across America. Individual images could be interpreted in different ways, depending on context and captions. Stryker believed that the faces of the subjects were most memorable. "You could look at the people," he wrote, "and see fear and sadness and desperation. But you saw something else, too. A determination that not even the Depression could kill. The photographers saw it—documented it."

That double vision, combining a frank portrayal of pain and suffering with a faith in the possibility of overcoming disaster, could be found in many other cultural works of the period. John Steinbeck's *Grapes of Wrath* (1939) sympathetically portrayed the hardships of Oklahoma Dust Bowl migrants on their way to California. "We ain't gonna die out," Ma Joad asserts near the end of the book. "People is goin' on—changin' a

The Joad family prepares to leave the Dust Bowl in Oklahoma for a new life in California in this still-photo from the movie "The Grapes of Wrath" (1940). Director John Ford's adaptation of John Steinbeck's novel reflected the influence of the "documentary impulse" in Hollywood films and other forms of Depression-era popular culture.

SOURCE: The Museum of Modern Art/Film Stills Archive.

little, maybe, but goin' right on." A similar, if more personal, ending could be found in Margaret Mitchell's 1936 bestseller *Gone with the Wind*. Although this romantic novel was set in the Civil War–era South, many Americans identified with Scarlett O'Hara's determination to overcome the disaster of war and the loss of Rhett Butler. "With the spirit of her people who would not know defeat, even when it stared them in the face, she raised her chin. She could get Rhett back. She knew she could."

Many writers interrupted their work to travel around the country and discover the thoughts and feelings of ordinary people. "With real events looming larger than any imagined happenings," novelist Elizabeth Noble wrote, "documentary films and still photographs, reportage and the like have taken the place once held by the grand invention." Writers increasingly used documentary techniques to communicate the sense of upheaval around the nation. In *Puzzled America* (1935), Sherwood Anderson wrote of the psychological toll taken by unemployment. American men, especially, he wrote, were losing "that sense of being some part of the moving world of activity, so essential to an American man's sense of his manhood—the loss of this essential something in the joblessness can never be measured in dollars." Yet writers also found a remarkable absence of bitterness and a great deal of faith. James Rorty, in *Where Life Is Better* (1936), was actually encouraged by his cross-country trip. "I had rediscovered for myself a most beautiful land, and a most vital, creative, and spiritually unsubdued people."

Waiting for Lefty

For some, the capitalist system itself, with its enormous disparities of private wealth amid desperate poverty, was the culprit responsible for the Great Depression. Relatively few Americans became Communists or socialists in the 1930s (at its height, the Communist Party of the United States had perhaps 100,000 members), and many of these remained active for only a brief time. Yet Marxist analysis, with its emphasis on class conflict and the failures of capitalism, had a wide influence on the era's thought and writing.

Some writers joined the Communist Party believing it to be the best hope for political revolution. They saw in the Soviet Union an alternative to an American system that appeared mired in exploitation, racial inequality, and human misery. Communist writers, like the novelist Michael Gold and the poet Meridel LeSueur, sought to radicalize art and literature, and they celebrated collective struggle over individual achievement. Gold's *Jews without Money* (1930) was one of the more successful attempts at a proletarian novel. It dramatized the sense of being locked into a system

that could deliver only despair rather than prosperity. Granville Hicks, an editor of the Communist magazine the *New Masses*, flatly declared: "If there is any other working interpretation of the apparent chaos than that which presents itself in terms of the class struggle, it has not been revealed."

A more common pattern for intellectuals, especially when they were young, was brief flirtation with communism. Many African American writers, attracted by the Communist Party's militant opposition to lynching, job discrimination, and segregation, briefly joined the party or found their first supportive audiences there. These included Richard Wright, Ralph Ellison, and Langston Hughes. Many playwrights and actors associated with New York's influential Group Theater were part of the Communist Party orbit in those years. One production of the group, Clifford Odets's *Waiting for Lefty* (1935), depicted a union organizing drive among taxi drivers. At the play's climax, the audience was invited to join the actors in shouting "Strike!" A commercial and political success, it offered perhaps the most celebrated example of radical, politically engaged art.

Left-wing influence reached its height after 1935 during the "Popular Front" period. Alarmed by the rise of fascism in Europe, communists around the world followed the Soviet line of uniting with liberals and all other antifascists. The American Communist Party adopted the slogan "Communism is Twentieth-Century Americanism." Communists became strong supporters of Roosevelt's New Deal, and their influence was especially strong within the various WPA arts projects. Some 3,200 Americans volunteered for the Communist Party–organized Abraham Lincoln Brigade, which fought in the Spanish civil war on the republican side against the fascists led by Francisco Franco. The Lincoln Brigade's sense of commitment and sacrifice appealed to millions of Americans sympathetic to the republican cause. Communists and other radicals, known for their dedication and effectiveness, also played a leading role in the difficult CIO unionizing drives in the auto, steel, and electrical industries. The successful sit-down strike at General Motors in Flint benefited from the organizing efforts of Communist Party activists who lent their expertise and helped keep the strikers and their families focused and supplied with food.

Hollywood in the 1930s

Commercial popular culture also boomed in the Depression years. The coming of "talking pictures" toward the end of the 1920s helped make movies the most popular entertainment form of the day. More than 60 percent of Americans attended one of the nation's 20,000 movie

Reginald Marsh, *Twenty Cent Movie*, 1936. Marsh documented the urban landscape of the 1930s with great empathy, capturing the city's contradictory mix of commercialism, optimism, energy, and degradation. The popularity of Hollywood films and their stars reached new heights during the Great Depression.

SOURCE: Reginald Marsh, *Twenty Cent Movie*, 1936. Egg tempera on composition board, 40" × 40". Whitney Museum of American Art, New York.

houses each week. Through fan magazines and gossip columns they followed the lives and careers of movie stars more avidly than ever. With so many movies being churned out by Hollywood studios for so many fans, it is difficult to generalize about the cultural impact of individual films. Moviegoing itself, usually enjoyed with friends, family, or a date, was perhaps the most significant development of all.

It is too easy to dismiss movies as mere escapism. The more interesting question is, What were people escaping to? Several film genres proved enormously popular during the 1930s. Gangster films did very well in the early Depression years. *Little Caesar* (1930), starring Edward G. Robinson, and *Public Enemy* (1931), with James Cagney, set the standard. They all depicted violent criminals brought to justice by society—but along

the way they gave audiences a vicarious exposure to the pleasures of wealth, power, and lawbreaking. Social disorder could also be treated comically, as in such Marx Brothers films as *Duck Soup* (1933) and *A Night at the Opera* (1935). Mae West's popular comedies, such as *She Done Him Wrong* (1933) and *I'm No Angel* (1933), made people laugh by subverting expectations about sex roles. West was an independent woman, not afraid of pleasure. When Cary Grant asked her, "Haven't you ever met a man who could make you happy?" she replied, "Sure, lots of times."

Movie musicals offered audiences extravagant song-and-dance spectacles, as in Busby Berkeley's *Gold Diggers of 1933* and *42nd Street* (1933). "Screwball comedies" featured sophisticated, fast-paced humor and usually paired popular male and female stars: Clark

Gable and Claudette Colbert in *It Happened One Night* (1934), Katharine Hepburn and Cary Grant in *Bringing Up Baby* (1938). A few movies, notably from the Warner Brothers studio, tried to offer a more "socially conscious" view of Depression-era life. These included *I Am a Fugitive from a Chain Gang* (1932), *Wild Boys of the Road* (1933), and *Black Legion* (1936). By and large, however, Hollywood avoided confronting controversial social or political issues.

Some 1930s filmmakers expressed highly personal visions of core American values. Two who succeeded in capturing both popular and critical acclaim were Walt Disney and Frank Capra. By the mid-1930s, Disney's animated cartoons had become moral tales that stressed keeping order and following the rules. The Mickey Mouse cartoons and the full-length features, such as *Snow White and the Seven Dwarfs* (1937), pulled back from the fantastic stretching of time and space in earlier cartoons. Capra's comedies, such as *Mr. Deeds Goes to Town* (1936) and *You Can't Take It with You* (1938), idealized a small-town America with close families and comfortable homes. Although Capra's films dealt with contemporary problems more than most—unemployment, government corruption, economic monopoly—he made no critique of the social and economic system. Rather, he seemed to suggest that most of the country's ills could be solved if only its leaders learned the old-fashioned values of "common people"—kindness, loyalty, charity.

The Golden Age of Radio

Radio broadcasting emerged as the most powerful medium of communication in the home, profoundly changing the rhythms and routines of everyday life. In 1930 roughly 12 million American homes, 40 percent of the total, had a radio set. By the end of the decade radios could be found in 90 percent of the nation's homes. Advertisers dominated the structure and content of American radio, forming a powerful alliance with the two large networks, the National Broadcasting Company (NBC) and the Columbia Broadcasting System (CBS). The Federal Communications Commission (FCC), established in 1934, continued long-standing policies that favored commercial broadcasting over other arrangements, such as municipal or university programming. By 1937 NBC and CBS controlled about 90 percent of the wattage in the American broadcasting industry. Nearly all network shows were produced by advertising agencies.

The Depression actually helped radio expand. An influx of talent arrived from the weakened worlds of vaudeville, ethnic theater, and the recording industry. The well-financed networks offered an attractive outlet to advertisers seeking a national audience. Radio pro-

gramming achieved a regularity and professionalism absent in the 1920s, making it much easier for a listener to identify a show with its sponsor. Companies with national distribution paid thousands of dollars an hour to networks; by 1939 annual radio advertising revenues totaled $171 million.

Much of network radio was based on older cultural forms. The variety show, hosted by comedians and singers and based on the old vaudeville format, was the first important style. It featured stars like Eddie Cantor, Ed Wynn, Kate Smith, and Al Jolson, who constantly plugged the sponsor's product. The use of a studio audience re-created the human interaction so necessary in vaudeville. The popular comedy show *Amos 'n' Andy* adapted the minstrel "blackface" tradition to the new medium. White comedians Freeman Gosden and Charles Correll used only their two voices to invent a world of stereotyped African Americans for their millions of listeners.

The spectacular growth of the daytime serial, or soap opera, dominated radio drama. Aimed mainly at women working in the home, these serials alone constituted 60 percent of all daytime shows by 1940. Soaps such as *Ma Perkins*, *Helen Trent*, and *Clara Lou and Em* revolved around strong, warm female characters who provided advice and strength to weak, indecisive friends and relatives. Action counted very little; the development of character and relationships was all-important. Contemporary studies found that the average soap opera fan regularly tuned in to six or more different series. Evening radio dramas included thrillers such as *Inner Sanctum* and *The Shadow*, which emphasized crime and suspense. These shows made great use of music and sound effects to sharpen their impact.

In the late 1930s serious drama bloomed briefly, independent of commercial sponsorship, over CBS's Columbia Workshop. Archibald MacLeish's *Fall of the City*, a parable about fascism, and Orson Welles's *War of the Worlds*, a superrealistic adaptation of the H. G. Wells classic, proved the persuasive power of radio. Welles's show convinced many who tuned in that a Martian invasion was actually underway. Radio became a key factor in politics as well, as President Roosevelt showed early on with his popular "fireside" chats.

Finally, radio news arrived in the 1930s, showing the medium's potential for direct and immediate coverage of events. Network news and commentary shows multiplied rapidly over the decade. Complex political and economic issues and the impending European crisis fueled a news hunger among Americans. A 1939 survey found that 70 percent of Americans relied on the radio as their prime source of news. Yet commercial broadcasting, dominated by big sponsors and large radio manufacturers, failed to cover politically controversial events, such as labor struggles. The most powerful station in the country, WLW in Cincinnati, refused to even mention strikes on the air. NBC routinely canceled programs it feared might undermine "public confidence and faith."

The Swing Era

One measure of radio's cultural impact was its role in popularizing jazz. Before the 1930s, jazz was heard largely among African Americans and a small coterie of white fans and musicians. Regular broadcasts of live performances began to expose a broader public to the music. So did radio disc jockeys who played jazz records on their shows. Bands led by black artists such as Duke Ellington, Count Basie, and Benny Moten began to enjoy reputations outside of traditional jazz centers like Chicago, Kansas City, and New York.

Benny Goodman became the key figure in the "swing era," largely through radio exposure. Goodman, a white, classically trained clarinetist, had been inspired by African American band-

The Benny Goodman band at the Meadowbrook Lounge, Cedar Grove, New Jersey, September 1941. After his breakthrough into national prominence in 1935, Goodman became one of the first white bandleaders to hire and feature African American musicians. Although most in the audience were undoubtedly dancing to the "King of Swing," note the crowd of serious listeners gathered around the bandstand.

SOURCE: Frank Driggs Collection.

leaders Fletcher Henderson and Don Redman. These men created arrangements for big bands that combined harmonic call-and-response patterns with breaks for improvised solos. Goodman purchased a series of arrangements from Henderson, smoothing out the sound but keeping the strong dance beat. His band's late-Saturday-night broadcasts began to attract attention.

In 1935, at the Palomar Ballroom in Los Angeles, Goodman made the breakthrough that established his enormous popularity. When the band started playing the Henderson arrangements, the young crowd, primed by the radio broadcasts, roared its approval and began to dance wildly. Goodman's music was perfect for doing the jitterbug or lindy hop, dances borrowed from African American culture. As the "King of Swing," Goodman helped make big-band jazz a hit with millions of teenagers and young adults from all backgrounds. In the late 1930s, big-band music by the likes of Goodman, Basie, Jimmie Lunceford, and Artie Shaw accounted for the majority of million-selling records.

Despite the Depression, the mass culture industry expanded enormously during the 1930s. Millions of Americans no doubt used mass culture as a temporary escape from their problems, but the various meanings they drew from movies, radio, and popular music were by no means monolithic. In most communities, Americans, especially young people, identified more closely than ever with the national communities forged by modern media. If mass culture offered little in the way of direct responses to the economic and social problems of the day, it nonetheless played a more integral role than ever in shaping the rhythms and desires of the nation's everyday life.

THE LIMITS OF REFORM

In his second Inaugural Address Roosevelt emphasized that much remained to be done to remedy the effects of the Depression. Tens of millions of Americans were still denied the necessities for a decent life. "I see one-third of a nation ill-housed, ill-clad, ill-nourished," the president said. With his stunning electoral victory, the future for further social reform seemed bright. Yet by 1937 the New Deal was in retreat. A rapid political turnaround over the next two years put continuing social reform efforts on the defensive

Court Packing

FDR and his advisers were frustrated by several Supreme Court rulings declaring important New Deal legislation unconstitutional. In May 1935, in *Schecter v. United States*, the Court found the National Recovery Administration unconstitutional in its entirety. The grounds included excessive delegation of legislative power to the executive and the regulation of business that was intrastate, as opposed to interstate or national, in character. In early 1936, ruling in *Butler v. United States*, the Court invalidated the Agricultural Adjustment Administration, declaring it an unconstitutional attempt at regulating agriculture. The Court was composed mostly of Republican appointees, six of whom were over seventy. Roosevelt looked for a way to get more friendly judges on the high court.

In February 1937, FDR asked Congress for legislation that would expand the Supreme Court from nine to a maximum of fifteen justices. The president would be empowered to make a new appointment whenever an incumbent judge failed to retire upon reaching age seventy. Roosevelt argued that age prevented justices from keeping up with their workload, but few people believed this logic. Newspapers almost unanimously denounced FDR's "court-packing bill."

Even more damaging was the determined opposition from a coalition of conservatives and outraged New Dealers in the Congress, such as Democratic senator Burton K. Wheeler of Montana. The president gamely fought on, maintaining that his purpose was simply to restore the balance of power among the three branches of the federal government. As the battle dragged on through the spring and summer, FDR's claims weakened. Conservative justice Willis Van Devanter announced plans to retire, giving Roosevelt the chance to make his first Court appointment.

More important, the Court upheld the constitutionality of some key laws from the second New Deal, including the Social Security Act and the National Labor Relations Act. At the end of August, FDR backed off from his plan and accepted a compromise bill that reformed lower court procedures but left the Supreme Court untouched. FDR lost the battle for his judiciary proposal, but he may have won the war for a more responsive Court. Still, the political price was very high. The Court fight badly weakened Roosevelt's relations with Congress. Many more conservative Democrats now felt free to oppose further New Deal measures.

The Women's Network

The Great Depression and the New Deal brought some significant changes for women in American economics and politics. Most women continued to perform unpaid domestic labor within their homes, work that was not covered by the Social Security Act. A growing minority, however, also worked for wages and salaries outside the home. Women represented 24.3 percent of all workers in 1930; by 1940, 25.1 percent of the workforce was female. There was also an increase in married working women as a result of hard times. Between 1930 and 1940 the proportion of married women among the female workforce jumped from 28.8 percent to 35 percent. Jobs in which men predominated, such as construction and heavy industry, were hardest hit by the Depression. In contrast, secretarial, sales, and other areas long associated with women's labor were less affected. But sexual stereotyping still routinely forced women into low-paying and low-status jobs.

The New Deal brought a measurable, if temporary, increase in women's political influence. For those women associated with social reform, the New Deal opened up possibilities to effect change. A "women's network," linked by personal friendships and professional connections, made its presence felt in national politics and government. Most of the women in this network had long been active in movements promoting suffrage, labor law reform, and welfare programs.

Eleanor Roosevelt became a powerful political figure in her own right, actively using her prominence as First Lady to fight for the liberal causes she believed in. She revolutionized the role of the political wife by taking a position involving no institutional duties and turning it into a base for independent action. Privately, she enjoyed great influence with her husband, and her support for a cause could give it instant credibility. She worked behind the scenes with a wide network of women professionals and reformers whom she had come to know in the 1920s. She was a strong supporter of protective labor legislation for women, and her overall outlook owed much to the social reform tradition of the women's movement. "When all is said and done," she wrote in *It's Up to the Women* (1933), "women are different from men. They are equal in many ways, but they cannot refuse to acknowledge their differences. . . . Their physical functions in life are different and perhaps in the same way the contributions which they are to bring to the spiritual side of life are different."

One of Eleanor Roosevelt's first public acts as First Lady was to convene a White House Conference on the Emergency Needs of Women in November 1933. She helped Ellen Woodward, head of women's projects in the Federal Emergency Relief Administration, find

Eleanor Roosevelt on a campaign tour with her husband in Nebraska, 1935. Long active in women's organizations and Democratic Party circles, she used political activity both to maintain her independence and make herself a valuable ally to FDR. "The attitude of women toward change in society," she argued, "is going to determine to a great extent our future in this country."

SOURCE: UPI/CORBIS (UP11).

policies and candidates. Her success impressed the president, and he relied on her judgment in recommending political appointments. Dewson placed more than a hundred women in New Deal positions.

Perhaps Dewson's most important success came in persuading FDR to appoint Frances Perkins secretary of labor—the first woman cabinet member in U.S. history. A graduate of Mount Holyoke College and a veteran activist for social welfare and reform, Perkins had served as FDR's industrial commissioner in New York before coming to Washington. As labor secretary, Perkins embodied the gains made by women in appointive offices. Her department was responsible for creating the Social Security Act and the Fair Labor Standards Act of 1938, both of which incorporated protective measures long advocated by women reformers. Perkins defined feminism as "the movement of women to participate in service to society." Yet despite the best efforts of the "women's network," women never constituted more than 19 percent of those employed by work relief programs, even though they made up 37 percent of the unemployed.

New Deal agencies opened up spaces for scores of women in the federal bureaucracy. These women were concentrated in Perkins's Labor Department, the FERA and WPA, and the Social Security Board. In addition, the social work profession, which remained roughly two-thirds female in the 1930s, grew enormously in response to the massive relief and welfare programs. In sum, although the 1930s saw no radical challenges to existing male and female roles, working-class women and professional women held their own and managed to make some gains.

A New Deal for Minorities?

"The Negro was born in Depression," recalled Clifford Burke. "It only became official when it hit the white man." Long near the bottom of the American economic ladder, African Americans suffered disproportionately

jobs for 100,000 women, ranging from nursery school teaching to sewing. Roosevelt worked vigorously for antilynching legislation, compulsory health insurance, and child labor reform, and she fought racial discrimination in New Deal relief programs. She saw herself as the guardian of "human values" within the administration, a buffer between Depression victims and government bureaucracy. She frequently testified before legislative committees, lobbied her husband privately and the Congress publicly, and wrote a widely syndicated newspaper column.

Eleanor Roosevelt's closest political ally was Molly Dewson. A long-time social worker and suffragist, Dewson wielded a good deal of political clout as director of the Women's Division of the national Democratic Party. Under her leadership, women for the first time played a central role in shaping the party platform and running election campaigns. Dewson proved a tireless organizer, traveling to cities and towns around the country and educating women about Democratic through the difficult days of the 1930s. The old saying among black workers that they were "last hired, first fired" was never more true than during times of high unemployment. With jobs made scarce by the Depression, even traditional "Negro occupations"—domestic service, cooking, janitorial work, elevator operating— were coveted. One white clerk in Florida expressed a widely held view among white Southerners when he defended a lynch mob attack on a store with black employees: "A nigger hasn't got no right to have a job when there are white men who can do the work and are out of work."

Overall, the Roosevelt administration made little overt effort to combat the racism and segregation entrenched in American life. FDR was especially worried about offending the powerful southern Democratic congressmen who were a key element in his political coalition. And local administration of many federal programs meant that most early New Deal programs routinely accepted discrimination. The CCC established separate camps for African Americans. The NRA labor codes tolerated lower wages for black workers doing the same jobs as white workers. African Americans could not get jobs with the TVA. In Atlanta, relief payments for black clients averaged $19.29 per month, compared with $32.66 for white clients. When local AAA committees in the South reduced acreage and production to boost prices, thousands of black sharecroppers and farm laborers were forced off the land. Racism was also embedded in the entitlement provisions of the Social Security Act. The act excluded domestics and casual laborers—workers whose ranks were disproportionately African Americans—from old-age insurance.

Yet some limited gains were made. President Roosevelt issued an executive order in 1935 banning discrimination in WPA projects. In the cities, the WPA, paying minimum wages of $12 a week, enabled thousands of African Americans to survive. Between 15 and 20 percent of all WPA employees were black people, although African Americans made up less than 10 percent of the nation's population. The Public Works Administration, under Harold Ickes, constructed a number of integrated housing complexes and employed more than its fair share of black workers in construction.

FDR appointed several African Americans to second-level positions in his administration. This group became known as "the Black Cabinet." Mary McLeod Bethune, an educator who rose from a sharecropping background to found Bethune-Cookman College, proved a superb leader of the Office of Minority Affairs in the National Youth Administration. Her most successful programs substantially reduced black illiteracy.

Harvard-trained Robert Weaver advised the president on economic affairs and in 1966 became the first black cabinet member when he was appointed secretary of housing and urban development. Yet Roosevelt himself was diffident about advancing civil rights. Typically, he spoke out against lynching in the South, but unlike his wife, he refused to support legislation making it a federal crime. Nor would he risk alienating white Southerners by working for long-denied voting rights for African Americans in the South.

Hard times were especially trying for Mexican Americans as well. As the Great Depression drastically reduced the demand for their labor, they faced massive layoffs, deepening poverty, and deportation. During the 1930s over 400,000 Mexican nationals and their children returned to Mexico, often coerced by local officials unwilling to provide them with relief but happy to offer train fare to border towns. Many native-born Americans argued that deporting Mexicans could reduce unemployment for U.S. citizens. But these claims reflected deep racial prejudice inflamed by the economic crisis. In Detroit, deportations reduced the size of that city's thriving Mexican *colonia* from 15,000 to 3,000 by 1933. In Los Angeles, where 100,000 Mexicans constituted the largest *colonia* in the Unites States, fully one third became *repatriados*. For those who stayed, the New Deal programs did little to help. The AAA benefited large growers, not stoop laborers. Neither the National Labor Relations Act nor the Social Security Act made any provisions for farm laborers. The Federal Emergency Relief Administration and the Works Progress Administration did, at first, provide relief and jobs to the needy irrespective of citizenship status. But after 1937, the WPA eliminated aliens from eligibility, causing great hardship for thousands of Mexican families. Yet both mass repatriation and New Deal public works programs would have profound long-range implications for Mexican American communities. By World War II, colonias would be increasingly dominated by the American-born second generation, rather than those born in Mexico. And since only citizens or aliens who had begun the process of naturalization were eligible for public works jobs, these programs motivated more Mexican immigrants to become U.S. citizens.

The New Deal record for minorities was mixed at best. African Americans, especially in the cities, benefited from New Deal relief and work programs, though this assistance was not colorblind. Black industrial workers made inroads into labor unions affiliated with the CIO. The New Deal made no explicit attempt to attack the deeply rooted patterns of racism and discrimination in American life. The deteriorating economic and political conditions faced by Mexicans and Mexican Americans resulted in a mass reverse exodus.

Yet by 1936, for the first time ever, a majority of black voters had switched their political allegiance to the Democrats—concrete evidence that they supported the directions taken by FDR's New Deal.

The Roosevelt Recession

The nation's economy had improved significantly by 1937. Unemployment had declined to "only" 14 percent (9 million people), farm prices had improved to 1930 levels, and industrial production was slightly higher than the 1929 mark. Economic traditionalists, led by Secretary of the Treasury Henry Morgenthau, called for reducing the federal deficit, which had grown to more than $4 billion in fiscal year 1936. Roosevelt, always uneasy about the growing national debt, called for large reductions in federal spending, particularly in WPA and farm programs. Federal Reserve System officials, worried about inflation, tightened credit policies.

Rather than stimulating business, the retrenchment brought about a steep recession. The stock market collapsed in August 1937, and industrial output and farm prices plummeted. Most alarming was the big increase in unemployment. By March 1938, the jobless rate hovered around 20 percent, with more than 13 million people looking for work. As conditions worsened, Roosevelt began to blame the "new depression" on a "strike of capital," claiming businessmen had refused to invest because they wanted to hurt his prestige. In truth, the administration's own severe spending cutbacks were more responsible for the decline.

The blunt reality was that even after five years the New Deal had not brought about economic recovery. Throughout 1937 and 1938 the administration drifted. Roosevelt received conflicting advice on the economy. Some advisers, suspicious of the reluctance of business to make new investments, urged a massive antitrust campaign against monopolies. Others urged a return to the strategy of "priming the economic pump" with more federal spending. Emergency spending bills in the spring of 1938 pumped new life into the WPA and the PWA. But Republican gains in the 1938 congressional elections (eighty seats in the House, seven in the Senate) made it harder than ever to get new reform measures through.

There were a couple of important exceptions. The 1938 Fair Labor Standards Act established the first federal minimum wage (25 cents an hour) and set a maximum work week of forty-four hours for all employees engaged in interstate commerce. The National Housing Act of 1937, also known as the Wagner-Steagall Act, funded public housing construction and slum clearance and provided rent subsidies for low-income families. But by and large, by 1938 the reform whirlwind of the New Deal was over.

CONCLUSION

Although American capitalism and democracy survived the cataclysm of the Great Depression, the New Deal failed in its central mission. It was never able to bring full economic recovery or end the scourge of mass unemployment. Only the economic boom that accompanied World War II would do that. Far from being the radical program its conservative critics charged, the New Deal did little to alter fundamental property relations or the distribution of wealth. Indeed, most of its programs largely failed to help the most powerless groups in America—migrant workers, tenant farmers and sharecroppers, African Americans, and other minorities.

But the New Deal profoundly changed many areas of American life. Overall, it radically increased the role of the federal government in American lives and communities. Western and southern communities in particular were transformed through federal intervention in water, power, and agricultural policies. Relief programs and the Social Security system established at least the framework for a welfare state. For the first time in American history, the national government took responsibility for assisting its needy citizens. And also for the first time, the federal government guaranteed the right of workers to join trade unions, and it set standards for minimum wages and maximum hours. In politics, the New Deal established the Democrats as the majority party. Some version of the Roosevelt New Deal coalition would dominate the nation's political life for another three decades.

Compared to other hemispheric responses to the Great Depression, the New Deal looks even more sweeping in its innovations. In Canada, where the Great Depression brought massive industrial unemployment and extremely hard times for western farmers, the country's economic and political structure in 1939 remained essentially unchanged. Both the Conservative government led by Richard B. Bennett and the Liberal government of Mackenzie King largely avoided taking on new federal responsibility for unemployment, insisting that this was a provincial or local responsibility. They did little to promote farm relief, old-age insurance, or public works projects. The few new federal initiatives, such as the Bank of Canada and the Canadian Wheat Board, focused on regulating business, avoiding deficit spending, and maintaining high tariffs. In Mexico, fiscal and monetary responses also dominated. Hard times in the United States had triggered a steep decline in the demand for Mexican goods and services, producing widespread unemployment and sharp contraction in the money supply. The Bank of Mexico abandoned the gold standard in response, printing paper money that

CHRONOLOGY

1929	Stock market crash
1930	Democrats regain control of the House of Representatives
1932	Reconstruction Finance Corporation established to make government credit available
	Bonus Army marches on Washington
	Franklin D. Roosevelt elected president
1933	Roughly 13 million workers unemployed
	The "hundred days" legislation of the First New Deal
	Twenty-first Amendment repeals Prohibition (Eighteenth Amendment)
1934	Indian Reorganization Act repeals Dawes Severalty Act and reasserts the status of Indian tribes as semisovereign nations
	Growing popularity of Father Charles E. Coughlin and Huey Long, critics of Roosevelt
1935	Second New Deal

	Committee for Industrial Organization (CIO) established
	Dust storms turn the southern Great Plains into the Dust Bowl
	Boulder Dam completed
1936	Roosevelt defeats Alfred M. Landon in reelection landslide
	Sit-down strike begins at General Motors plants in Flint, Michigan
1937	General Motors recognizes United Automobile Workers
	Roosevelt's "Court-packing" plan causes controversy
	Memorial Day Massacre in Chicago demonstrates the perils of union organizing
	"Roosevelt recession" begins
1938	CIO unions withdraw from the American Federation of Labor to form the Congress of Industrial Organizations
	Fair Labor Standards Act establishes the first federal minimum wage

helped ease the crisis and permitted the government to engage in more public spending. The devaluation of the peso helped revive the export sector as well. Populist President Lázaro Cárdenas (1934–40) widened the power of the federal government by aggressively pushing land reform and nationalizing the oil business. He reorganized his party and named it the *Partido Revolucionario Mexicano* (Mexican Revolutionary Party), which would dominate Mexican political life for the rest of the century.

The New Deal's efforts to end racial and gender discrimination were modest at best. Some of the more ambitious programs, such as subsidizing the arts or building model communities, enjoyed only brief success. Other reform proposals, such as national health insurance, never got off the ground. Conservative counterpressures, especially after 1937, limited what could be changed.

Still, the New Deal did more than strengthen the presence of the national government in people's lives. It also fed expectations that the federal presence would intensify. Washington became a much greater center of economic regulation and political power, and the federal bureaucracy grew in size and influence. With the coming of World War II, the direct role of national government in shaping American communities would expand beyond the dreams of even the most ardent New Dealer.

REVIEW QUESTIONS

1. What were the underlying causes of the Great Depression? What consequences did it have for ordinary Americans, and how did the Hoover administration attempt to deal with the crisis?

2. Analyze the key elements of Franklin D. Roosevelt's first New Deal program. To what degree did these succeed in getting the economy back on track and in providing relief to suffering Americans?

3. How did the so-called Second New Deal differ from the first? What political pressures did Roosevelt face that contributed to the new policies?

4. How did the New Deal reshape western communities and politics? What specific programs had the greatest impact in the region? How are these changes still visible today?

5. Evaluate the impact of the labor movement and radicalism on the 1930s. How did they influence American political and cultural life?

6. To what extent were the grim realities of Depression reflected in popular culture? To what degree were they absent?

7. Discuss the long- and short-range effects of the New Deal on American political and economic life. What were its key successes and failures? What legacies of New Deal–era policies and political struggles can you find in contemporary America?

RECOMMENDED READING

Anthony J. Badger, *The New Deal: The Depression Years, 1933–1940* (1989).

Alan Brinkley, *The End of Reform: New Deal Liberalism in Recession and War* (1995).

Lizabeth Cohen, *Making a New Deal: Industrial Workers in Chicago, 1919–1939* (1990).

Michael Denning, *The Cultural Front: The Laboring of American Culture in the Twentieth Century* (1997).

Ronald Edsforth, *The New Deal: America's Response to the Great Depression* (2000).

David M. Kennedy, *Freedom From Fear: The American People in Depression and War* (1999).

Richard Lowitt, *The New Deal and the West* (1984).

Robert S. McElvaine, *The Great Depression: America, 1929–1941* (1984).

Lois Scharf, *To Work and to Wed* (1980).

Harvard Sitkoff, *A New Deal for Blacks* (1978).

 ## ► MEDIA RESOURCES

 ### U.S. HISTORY DOCUMENTS CD-ROM
Depression and the New Deal

24-1   Herbert Hoover, Speech at New York City (1932)

24-2   FDR's First Inauguration Speech (1932)

24-3   Franklin Delano Roosevelt, Speech at San Francisco (1932)

24-4   Share the Wealth

24-5   The Victims of the Ku Klux Klan (1935)

24-6   Father Charles E. Coughlin, "A Third Party" (1936)

24-7   Mrs. Henry Weddington, Letter to President Roosevelt (1938)

 ### COMPANION WEBSITE HIGHLIGHTS
To view an exploration, enter one of the URLs below in your browser.

 Web Explorations
The Dust Bowl, 1935–1940
http://www.prenhall.com/faragher/map24.1
The New Deal and Water
http://www.prenhall.com/faragher/map24.2

 Additional Interactive Maps
To access the map, go to this chapter's resources at
http://www.prenhall.com/faragher
The Election of 1932, page 741

HISTORY RESOURCE CENTER
To find the resources listed below, go to
http://www.prenhall.com/historyresourcecenter

Documents
Franklin D. Roosevelt, First Inaugural Address (1932)
Huey Long, "Share Our Wealth" (1935)

Images
"World's Highest Standard of Living" Billboard
Abandoned Oklahoma Farmstead, 1937
Agricultural Worker's Shack
Arkies on the Road
Bonus Expeditionary Force March on Washington
Despair in the Texas Panhandle
Family in a Dust Storm
From Texas Farmer to Migratory Worker
Index of American Design
Migrant Mother
The Caravan Theatre
WPA Project at Tonawanda Reservation
WPA's Federal Art Project

EXPLORING AMERICA

THE DUST BOWL

http://www.prenhall.com/faragher/dustbowl

What caused the Dust Bowl? Where was the Dust Bowl? How did it change the lives of the people affected by it? How did the New Deal government programs respond to this crisis? How did the government programs help to record the human drama resulting from the dust storms? This module examines the one of the most devastating episodes of the already disastrous economic depression of the 1930s. *The Dust Bowl* examines the causes of the dust storms that swept across the plains in the mid-1930s and chronicles the responses of the people affected by these storms. The narrative and other resources show that both the dust bowl phenomenon and the reactions to it caused long-term, deep-rooted changes in American agriculture and society.

The Dust Bowl provides several methods to examine the impact of this tragic chapter in American history, showing that a combination of natural and

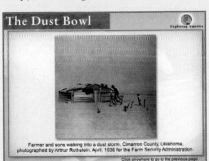

Farmer and sons walking into a dust storm, Cimarron County, Oklahoma, photographed by Arthur Rothstein, April, 1936 for the Farm Security Administration.
Click anywhere to go to the previous page.

human factors triggered the dust storms. The module relates the story of the Dust Bowl and its aftermath, stressing the human aspect by including numerous photographs taken by Farm Security Administration photographers employed by the federal government to visually chronicle the Great Depression. Magazine articles and other print sources enhance the photos, while the interactive map and chronology provide an important time and space contexts to the discussion.

Reflect and Respond

1. "Documentary" photography recorded carefully chosen and composed "slices of life." The "art" of a photographer such as Dorothea Lange or Arthur Rothstein was to create images that appeared "artless," that is, they appeared to be candid snapshots. Analyzing such photographs therefore requires the historian

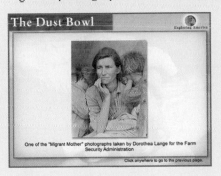

One of the "Migrant Mother" photographs taken by Dorothea Lange for the Farm Security Administration
Click anywhere to go to the previous page.

to look carefully at what the photographer decided to include, and to exclude, from the pictures, and at how he or she composed the image. Composition deals with such matters as lighting, the angle from which the photograph was taken, and the relative size of the objects within the picture. Choose three of the Rothstein photographs of the Visalia camp. What was he seeking to achieve in each? How did he seek to convey certain ideas and/or sentiments in each?

2. The Visalia photographs stand in stark contrast to the earlier pictures taken by Lange and Rothstein of migrant laborers and of the impact of the dust storms. Create two contrasting pairs of images. Explain what an analysis of each pair tells us about the experience of the Great Depression.

✓ Check it out

Dust Storm Approaches Town

This photograph provides a striking picture of the power of a dust storm. The photo stands as one of many taken by government photographers hired specifically to chronicle on film the devastation caused by the Great Depression. One of the most compelling and serious issue was the creation of the Dust Bowl in the mid-1930s and the havoc it wreaked on the people living in that section of the Great Plains.

This exploration is also available on the *Exploring America* CD-ROM.

TWENTY-FIVE

WORLD WAR II

▶ 1941–1945

SOURCE: Thomas Hart Benton, *Back Him Up*. Courtesy Christie's Images, Inc. (NYAMP 310585284)

AMERICAN COMMUNITIES

Los Alamos, New Mexico

O
N MONDAY, JULY 16, 1945, AT 5:29:45 A.M., MOUNTAIN WAR Time, the first atomic bomb exploded in a brilliant flash visible in three states. Within just seven minutes, a huge, multicolored, bell-shaped cloud soared 38,000 feet into the atmosphere and threw back a blanket of smoke and soot to the earth below. The heat generated by the blast was four times the temperature at the center of the sun, and the light produced rivaled that of nearly twenty suns. Even ten miles away people felt a strong surge of heat. The giant fireball ripped a crater a half-mile wide in the ground, fusing the desert sand into glass. The shock wave blew out windows in houses more than 200 miles away. The blast killed every living creature—squirrels, rabbits, snakes, plants, and insects—within a mile and the smells of death lingered for nearly a month.

Very early that morning, Ruby Wilkening had driven to a nearby mountain ridge, where she joined several other women waiting for the blast. Wilkening worried about her husband, a physicist, who was already at the test site. No one knew exactly what to expect, not even the scientists who developed the bomb.

The Wilkenings were part of a unique community of scientists who had been marshaled for war. President Franklin D. Roosevelt, convinced by Albert Einstein and other physicists that the Nazis might successfully develop an atomic bomb, had inaugurated a small nuclear research program in 1939. Soon after the United States entered World War II, the president released resources to create the Manhattan Project and placed it under the direction of the Army Corps of Engineers. By December 1942 a team headed by Italian-born Nobel Prize–winner Enrico Fermi had produced the first chain reaction in uranium under the University of Chicago's football stadium. Now the mission was to build a new, formidable weapon of war, the atomic bomb.

The government moved the key researchers and their families to Los Alamos, New Mexico, a remote and sparsely populated region of soaring peaks, ancient Indian ruins, modern Pueblos, and villages occupied by the descendents of the earliest Spanish settlers. The scientists and their families arrived in March 1943. They occupied a former boys' preparatory school until new houses could be built. Some families doubled up in rugged log cabins or nearby ranches. Telephone service to the outside world was poor, and the mountain roads were so rough that changing flat tires became a tiresome but familiar routine. Construction of new quarters proceeded slowly, causing nasty disputes between the "longhairs" (scientists) and the "plumbers" (army engineers) in charge of the grounds. Despite the chaos, outstanding American and European scientists eagerly signed up. Most were young, with an average age of twenty-seven, and quite a few were recently married. Many couples began their families at Los Alamos, producing a total of nearly a thousand babies between 1943 and 1949.

The scientists and their families formed an exceptionally close-knit community, united by the need for secrecy and their shared antagonism toward their army guardians. The military atmosphere was oppressive.

769

Homes and laboratories were cordoned off by barbed wire and guarded by military police. Everything, from linens to food packages, was stamped "Government Issue." The scientists were followed by security personnel whenever they left Los Alamos. Several scientists were reprimanded for discussing their work at home, although many of their wives worked forty-eight hours a week in the Technical Area. All outgoing mail was censored. Well-known scientists commonly worked under aliases—Fermi became "Eugene Farmer"—and code names were used for such terms as atom, bomb, and uranium fission. The birth certificates of babies born at Los Alamos listed their place of birth simply as rural Sandoval County, and children registered without surnames at nearby public schools. Even automobile accidents went unreported, and newspapers carried no wedding announcements or obituaries. Only a group thoroughly committed to the war effort could accept such restrictions on personal liberty.

A profound urgency motivated the research team, which included refugees from Nazi Germany and Fascist Italy and a large proportion of Jews. The director of the project, California physicist J. Robert Oppenheimer, promoted a scientific élan that offset the military style of commanding general Leslie Groves. Just thirty-eight, slightly built, and deeply emotional, "Oppie" personified the idealism that helped the community of scientists overcome whatever moral reservations they held about placing such a potentially ominous weapon in the hands of the government.

In the Technical Area of Los Alamos, Oppenheimer directed research from an office with a desk, long tables, and blackboard along the walls in a typical two-story army building. At seven o'clock each workday morning, the siren dubbed "Oppie's Whistle" called the other scientists to their laboratories to wrestle with the theoretical and practical problems of building an atomic device. Once a week Oppenheimer called together the heads of the various technical divisions to discuss their work in round-table conferences. From May to November 1944, after the bomb had been designed, the key issue was testing it. Many scientists feared a test might fail, scattering the precious plutonium at the bomb's core and discrediting the entire project. Finally, with plutonium production increasing, the Los Alamos team agreed to test "the gadget" at a site 160 miles away.

The unprecedented scientific mobilization at Los Alamos mirrored changes occurring throughout American society as the nation rallied behind the war effort. Sixteen million men and women left home for military service and nearly as many moved to take advantage of wartime jobs. Several states in the South and Southwest experienced huge surges in population. California alone grew by 2 million people, a large proportion from Mexico. Many broad social changes with roots in earlier times—the economic expansion of the West, the erosion of farm tenancy among black people in the South and white people in Appalachia, and the increasing employment of married women—accelerated during the war. The United States, initially reluctant to enter the war, emerged from it the world's leading superpower and free from the weight of the Great Depression. The events of the war eroded old communities, created new ones like Los Alamos, and transformed nearly all aspects of American society. ■

Los Alamos

KEY TOPICS

- The events leading to Pearl Harbor and the declaration of war

- The marshaling of national resources for war

- American society during wartime

- The mobilization of Americans into the armed forces

- The war in Europe and Asia

- Diplomacy and the atomic bomb

THE COMING OF WORLD WAR II

The Great Depression was not confined to the United States. It was a worldwide economic decline that further undermined a political order that had been shaky since World War I. Production declined by nearly 40 percent, international trade dropped by as much as two-thirds, and unemployment rose. While rivalries for markets and access to raw materials intensified, political unrest spread across Europe and Asia. Demagogues played upon nationalist hatreds, fueled by old resentments and current despair, and offered solutions in the form of territorial expansion by military conquest.

Preoccupied with restoring the domestic economy, President Franklin D. Roosevelt had no specific plan to deal with growing conflict elsewhere in the world. Moreover, the majority of Americans strongly opposed foreign entanglements. But as debate over diplomatic policy heated up, terrifying events overseas pulled the nation steadily toward war.

The Shadows of War

War spread first across Asia. Militarist-imperialist leaders in Japan, which suffered economically from loss of trade during the 1930s, determined to make their nation the richest in the world. The Japanese army seized control of Manchuria in 1931 and in 1932 installed a puppet government there. When reprimanded by the League of Nations, Japan simply withdrew from the organization. In 1937 Japan provoked full-scale war with an invasion of northern China. When it seized control of the capital city of Nanking, Japan's army murdered as many as 300,000 Chinese men, women, and children and destroyed much of the city. Within the year Japan controlled all but China's western interior and threatened all Asia and the Pacific.

Meanwhile, the rise of authoritarian nationalism in Italy and Germany cast a dark shadow over Europe. The economic hardships brought on by the Great Depression—and, in Germany, resentment over the harsh terms of the Treaty of Versailles, which ended World War I—fueled the rise of demagogic mass movements. Glorifying war as a test of national virility, the Italian Fascist dictator Benito Mussolini, who had seized power in 1922, declared, "We have buried the putrid corpse of liberty." In Germany, the National Socialists (Nazis), led by Adolf Hitler, combined militaristic rhetoric with a racist doctrine of Aryan (Nordic) supremacy that claimed biological superiority for the blond-haired and blue-eyed peoples of northern Europe and classified nonwhites, including Jews, as "degenerate races."

Hitler, who became chancellor of Germany in January 1933 with the backing of major industrialists and about a third of the electorate, prepared for war. With his brown-shirted storm troopers ruling the streets, he quickly destroyed opposition parties and effectively made himself dictator of the strongest nation in central Europe. Renouncing the disarmament provisions of the Versailles treaty, he began, with no effective protest from France and Britain, to rebuild Germany's armed forces. Intending to make Germany the center of a greater Reich that would last a millennium, the Nazi leader built up a vast industrial infrastructure for an army of a half-million men poised to conquer Europe.

The prospect of war grew as both Mussolini and Hitler began to act on their imperial visions. In 1935 Italy invaded Ethiopia and formally claimed the impoverished African kingdom as a colony. In 1936 Hitler sent 35,000 troops to occupy the Rhineland, a region demilitarized by the Versailles treaty. When the Spanish Civil War broke out later that year, Italy and Germany both supported the fascist insurrection of General Francisco Franco and then, in November, drew up a formal alliance to become the Rome-Berlin Axis. Hitler was now nearly ready to put into operation his plan to secure *Lebensraum*—living space for Germany's growing population—through further territorial expansion.

After annexing his native Austria, Hitler turned his attention to Czechoslovakia, a country which both Britain and France were pledged by treaty to assist. War seemed imminent. But Britain and France surprised

Hitler by agreeing, at a conference in Munich the last week of September 1938, to allow Germany to annex the Sudetenland, a part of Czechoslovakia bordering Germany. In return, Hitler pledged to stop his territorial advance. Less than six months later, in March 1939, Hitler seized the rest of Czechoslovakia.

By this time, much of the world was aware of the horror of Hitler's regime, especially its virulent racist doctrines. After 1935, when Hitler published the notorious Nuremberg Laws denying civil rights to Jews, the campaign against them became steadily more vicious. On the night of November 9, 1938, Nazi storm troopers rounded up Jews, beating them mercilessly and murdering an untold number. They smashed windows in Jewish shops, hospitals, and orphanages and burned synagogues to the ground. This attack came to be known as *Kristallnacht*, "the Night of Broken Glass." The Nazi government soon expropriated Jewish property and excluded Jews from all but the most menial forms of employment. Pressured by Hitler, Hungary and Italy also enacted laws against Jews.

Isolationism

World War I had left a legacy of strong isolationist sentiment in the United States. Senseless slaughter might be a centuries-old way of life in Europe, many Americans reasoned, but not for the United States, which, as Thomas Jefferson had advised, should stay clear of "entangling alliances." While Hollywood movies such as *All Quiet on the Western Front* (1930) graphically depicted the horrors of war, historians published scores of popular books criticizing the abandonment of America's isolationist policy during the Great War. As late as 1937, nearly 70 percent of Americans responding to a Gallup poll stated that U.S. involvement in World War I had been a mistake.

This sentiment won strong support in Congress. In 1934, a special committee headed by Republican senator Gerald P. Nye of North Dakota had charged weapons manufacturers with driving the United States into World War I in the hopes of windfall profits, which, in fact, many realized. In 1935, Congress passed the first of five Neutrality Acts to deter future entanglements, requiring the president to declare an embargo on the sale and shipment of munitions to all belligerent nations.

College students, seeing themselves as future cannon fodder, strongly opposed foreign entanglements. In 1933, 39 percent of those polled stated that they would refuse to fight in any war; 33 percent would fight only if the United States were attacked. Three years later, 500,000 boycotted classes in a nationwide "student strike" to demonstrate their opposition to any preparation for war.

Isolationism spanned the political spectrum. In 1938 socialist Norman Thomas gathered leading liberals and trade unionists into the Keep America Out of War Congress; the communist-influenced American League against War and Fascism claimed more than 1 million members. Meanwhile, Republican senator Robert A. Taft of Ohio, son of former president William Howard Taft, argued that a new war would harm American democracy by enlarging the federal government and tightening its grip on the citizenry.

In 1940 the arch-conservative America First Committee was formed to oppose U.S. intervention. The group was particularly strong in the Midwest. Some America Firsters championed the Nazis while others simply advocated American neutrality. Chaired by top Sears executive Robert E. Wood, the America First Committee quickly gained attention because its members included such well-known personalities as movie stars Robert Young and Lillian Gish, automobile manufacturer Henry Ford, and Charles A. Lindbergh, famous for his 1927 solo flight across the Atlantic. Within a year, America First had launched more than 450 chapters.

Roosevelt Readies for War

While Americans looked on anxiously, the twists and turns of world events prompted President Franklin D. Roosevelt to ready the nation for war. In October 1937 he had called for international cooperation to "quarantine the aggressors." "Let no one imagine that America will escape, that America may expect mercy, that this Western Hemisphere will not be attacked." But a poll of Congress revealed that a two-thirds majority opposed economic sanctions, calling any such plan a "back door to war." Forced to draw back, Roosevelt nevertheless won from Congress $1 billion in appropriations to enlarge the navy. But as late as January 1939, in his annual address to Congress, Roosevelt insisted that the United States must use all means "short of war" to deter aggression.

Everything changed on September 1, 1939, when Hitler invaded Poland. Committed by treaty to defend Poland against unprovoked attack, Great Britain and France issued a joint declaration of war against Germany two days later. After the fall of Warsaw at the end of the month, the fighting slowed to a near halt. Even along their border, French and German troops did not exchange fire. From the east, however, the invasion continued. Just two weeks before Hitler overran Poland, the Soviet Union had stunned the world by signing a nonaggression pact with its former enemy. The Red Army now entered Poland, and the two great powers proceeded to split the hapless nation between them. Soviet forces then headed north, invading Finland on November 30. The European war had begun.

Calculating that the United States would stay out of the war, Hitler began a crushing offensive against western Europe in April 1940. Using the technique of

Blitzkrieg (lightning war)—massed, fast-moving columns of tanks supported by air power—that had overwhelmed Poland, Nazi troops moved first against Germany's northern neighbors. After taking Denmark and Norway, the Nazi armored divisions swept over Holland, Belgium, and Luxembourg and sent more than 338,000 British troops into retreat across the English Channel from Dunkerque. Hitler's army, joined by the Italians, easily conquered France in June 1940. Hitler now turned toward England. In the Battle of Britain, Nazi bombers pounded population and industrial centers while U-boats cut off incoming supplies.

Even with Great Britain under attack, opinion polls indicated Americans' determination to stay out of the war. But most Americans, like Roosevelt himself, believed that the security of the United States depended on both a strong defense and the defeat of Germany. Invoking the Neutrality Act of 1939, which permitted the sale of arms to Britain, France, and China, the president clarified his position: "all aid to the Allies short of war." In May 1940 he began to transfer surplus U.S. planes and equipment to the Allies. In September the president secured the first peacetime military draft in American history, the Selective Service Act of 1940, which sent 1.4 million men to army training camps by July 1941. Yet even when he secured huge congressional appropriations for the production of airplanes and battleships, Roosevelt did so in the name of "hemispheric defense," not intervention. President Roosevelt could not yet admit the inevitability of U.S. involvement—especially during an election year. His popularity had dropped with the "Roosevelt recession" that began in 1937, raising doubts that he could win what would be an unprecedented third term. Waiting until July 1940, the eve of the Democratic Party convention, Roosevelt announced that world events compelled him to accept a party "draft" for renomination. In his campaign he promised voters not to "send your boys to any foreign wars." Roosevelt and his vice presidential candidate Henry Wallace won by a margin of 5 million popular votes over the Republican darkhorse candidate, Wendell L. Willkie of Indiana.

Roosevelt now moved more aggressively to aid the Allies in their struggle with the Axis powers. In his annual

Gallup Polls: European War and World War I, 1938–1940   These three polls conducted by the American Institute of Public Opinion indicate the persistence of isolationist sentiment and popular criticism of U.S. involvement in World War I. Many respondents believed the United States, despite its commitments to European allies, should stay out of war. After 1940, in the aftermath of Nazi military victories in Europe, many Americans reconsidered their opposition, fearing a threat to democracy in their own nation.

OCTOBER 2, 1938
EUROPEAN WAR

If England and France go to war against Germany do you think the United States can stay out?

Yes	57%
No	43

By Region

	Yes	No
New England	46%	54%
Middle Atlantic	61	39
East Central	60	40
West Central	57	43
South	60	40
West	51	49

Interviewing Date 9/15–20/1938, Survey #132, Question #4

FEBRUARY 21, 1940
EUROPEAN WAR

If it appears that Germany is defeating England and France, should the United States declare war on Germany and send our army and navy to Europe to fight?

Yes	23%
No	77

7 percent expressed no opinion.

Interviewing Date 2/2–7/1940, Survey #183-K, Question #6

DECEMBER 16, 1940
EUROPEAN WAR

Do you think it was a mistake for the United States to enter the last World War?

Yes	39%
No	42
No opinion	19

By Political Affiliation
Democrats

Yes	33%
No	46
No opinion	21

Republicans

Yes	46%
No	38
No opinion	16

Interviewing Date 11/21–30/1940, Survey #244-K, Question #6

message to Congress, he proposed a bill that would allow the president to sell, exchange, or lease arms to any country whose defense appeared vital to U.S. security. Passed by Congress in March, 1941, the Lend-Lease Act made Great Britain the first beneficiary of massive aid. Roosevelt also extended the U.S. "security zone" nearly halfway across the Atlantic Ocean and ordered the Coast Guard to seize any German-controlled or German ships that entered an American port. He directed Germany and Italy to close their U.S. consulates and ordered U.S. ships to shoot any Nazi vessel in U.S. "defensive waters" on sight. After Congress authorized the merchant marine

to sail fully armed while conveying lend-lease supplies directly to Britain, a formal declaration of war was only a matter of time.

In August 1941 Roosevelt met secretly at sea off Newfoundland with British prime minister Winston Churchill to map military strategy and declare common goals for the postwar world. Known as the Atlantic Charter, their proclamation specified the right of all peoples to live in freedom from fear, want, and tyranny. The Atlantic Charter also called for free trade among all nations, an end to territorial seizures, and disarmament. Eventually endorsed by the Soviet Union and

Japanese attack planes devastated the U.S. fleet stationed on the Hawaiian island of Oahu. Before December 7, 1941, few Americans had heard of Pearl Harbor, but the "sneak" attack became a symbol of Japanese treachery and the necessity for U.S. revenge.

SOURCE: National Archives and Records Administration.

fourteen other nations, the Atlantic Charter pledged to all nations—vanquished as well as victors—the right to self-determination.

By this time the European war had moved to a new stage. Hitler had conquered the Balkans and then set aside the expedient Nazi-Soviet Pact to resume his quest for the entire European continent. In June 1941 Hitler launched an invasion of the Soviet Union, promising its rich agricultural land to German farmers. Observing this dramatic escalation, the United States moved closer to intervention.

Pearl Harbor

Throughout 1940 and much of 1941 the United States focused on events in Europe, but the war in Asia went on. Roosevelt, anticipating danger to American interests in the Pacific, had directed the transfer of the Pacific Fleet from bases in California to Pearl Harbor, on the island of Oahu, Hawai'i, in May 1940. On September 27 Japan formally joined Germany and Italy as the Asian partner of the Axis alliance. Under the terms of the expanded alliance, Germany would support Japan's seizure of Dutch, British, and French colonial possessions as part of Japan's attempt to create a regional bloc under its rule.

The United States and Japan each played for time. Roosevelt wanted to save his resources to fight against Germany, while Japan's leaders gambled that America's preoccupation with Europe might allow them to conquer all of Southeast Asia, including the French colonies in Indochina (Vietnam, Cambodia, and Laos) and the British possessions of Burma and India. When Japan occupied Indochina in July 1941, however, Roosevelt responded by freezing Japanese assets in the United States and cutting off its oil supplies. Confrontation with Japan now looked likely. U.S. intelligence had broken the Japanese diplomatic code, and the president knew that Japan was preparing for war against the Western powers. Roosevelt's advisers expected an attack somewhere in the Pacific and by the end of November placed all American forces there on high alert.

Japan, however, intended to knock the United States out of the Pacific in a single blow. Early Sunday morning, December 7, 1941, Japanese carriers launched an attack on Pearl Harbor that caught American forces completely off guard. Sailors on the decks of American ships looked up to see Japanese dive-bombers in the sky above them. Loudspeakers warned: "Japs are coming! Japs attacking us! Go to your battle stations!" Within two hours, Japanese pilots had destroyed nearly 200 American planes and badly damaged the fleet; more than 2,400 Americans were killed and nearly 1,200 wounded. On the same day, Japan struck U.S. bases on the Philippines, Guam, and Wake Island.

On December 8, declaring the attack on Pearl Harbor a day that "will live in infamy," Roosevelt asked Congress for a declaration of war against Japan. With only one dissenting vote—by pacifist Jeannette Rankin of Montana, who had voted against U.S. entry into World War I in 1917—Congress acceded. The United States had not yet declared war on Japan's European allies, but Hitler made that unnecessary when he asked the *Reichstag* on December 11 to support war against the "half Judaized, and the other half Negrified" American nation. Mussolini joined him in the declaration, and the United States on the same day recognized that a state of war existed with Germany and Italy. World War II now began for Americans.

On the day after the attack on Pearl Harbor, President Franklin D. Roosevelt addressed a joint session of Congress and asked for an immediate declaration of war against Japan. The resolution passed with one dissenting vote, and the United States entered World War II.

SOURCE: AP/Wide World Photos.

ARSENAL OF DEMOCRACY

Late in 1940 President Roosevelt called upon all Americans to make the nation a "great arsenal of democracy." During the next three years, the economic machinery that had failed during the 1930s was swiftly retooled for military purposes, with dramatic results. The Great Depression suddenly ended. Never before had the federal government poured so much energy and money into production or assigned such a great army of experts to manage it. This marshaling of resources involved a concentration of power in the federal government that exceeded anything planned by the New Deal.

Mobilizing for War

A few days after the United States declared war on Germany, Congress passed the War Powers Act, which established a precedent for executive authority that would endure long after the war's end. The president gained the power to reorganize the federal government and create new agencies; to establish programs censoring all news and information and abridging civil liberties; to seize property owned by foreigners; and even to award government contracts without competitive bidding.

Roosevelt promptly created special wartime agencies. At the top of his agenda was a massive reorientation and management of the economy, and an alphabet soup of new agencies arose to fill any gaps in production. The Supply Priorities and Allocation Board (SPAB) oversaw the use of scarce materials and resources vital to the war, adjusting domestic consumption (even ending it for some products such as automobiles) to military needs. The Office of Price Administration (OPA) checked the threat of inflation from the government's sudden massive spending by imposing price controls. The National War Labor Board (NWLB) mediated disputes between labor and management, halting strikes and also controlling inflation by limiting wage increases. The War Manpower Commission (WMC) directed the mobilization of military and civilian services. And the Office of War Mobilization (OWM), headed by New Dealer James F. Byrnes, coordinated operations among all these agencies.

Several new agencies focused on domestic propaganda. The attack on Pearl Harbor evoked an outpouring of rage against Japan and effectively quashed much opposition to U.S. intervention. Still, for most Americans, World War II would remain a foreign war, and the government stepped in to fan the fires of patriotism and to shape public opinion. In June 1942 the president created the Office of War Information (OWI) to coordinate information from the multiplying federal agencies and to engage the press, radio, and film industry in an informational campaign—in short, to sell the war to the American people.

The OWI gathered data and controlled the release of news, emphasizing the need to make reports on the war both dramatic and encouraging. Like the Committee on Public Information during World War I, during the first twenty-one months of the war the new agency banned the publication of advertisements, photographs, and newsreels showing American dead, fearing that such images would demoralize the public. In 1943, worrying that Americans had become overconfident, officials changed their policy. A May issue of *Newsweek* featured graphic photographs of Americans wounded in battle, explaining that "to harden home-front morale, the military services have adopted a new policy of letting civilians see photographically what warfare does to men who fight." To spare families unnecessary grief, throughout the war the OWI prohibited the publication of any photograph revealing the identity of the American dead. The OWI also published leaflets and booklets for the armed services and flooded enemy ranks with subversive propaganda.

Propaganda also fueled the selling of war bonds. Secretary of the Treasury Henry Morgenthau, Jr. not only encouraged Americans to buy government bonds to finance the war but planned a campaign "to use bonds to sell the war, rather than vice versa." Bonds, the ads for them claimed, were a good investment that gave everyone an opportunity "to have a financial stake in American democracy." Buying them would "mean bullets in the bellies of Hitler's hordes!" Discovering through research that Americans felt more antagonism to Japan than Germany, Morgenthau directed his staff to use more negative stereotypes of the Japanese in their advertising copy. Polls showed, however, that most Depression-stung Americans bought war bonds—$185.7 billion by war's end—mainly to invest safely, to counter inflation, and to save for postwar purchases.

The federal government also sponsored various measures to prevent subversion of the war effort. Concerned about enemy propaganda, the Office of Facts and Figures hired political scientist Harold Lasswell of Yale University to devise a means to measure the patriotic content of magazines and newspapers. The Federal Bureau of Investigation (FBI) was kept busy, its appropriation rising from $6 million to $16 million in just two years. The attorney general authorized wiretapping in cases of espionage or sabotage, but the FBI used it extensively—and illegally—in domestic surveillance. The Joint Chiefs of Staff created the Office of Strategic Services (OSS) to assess the enemy's military strength, to gather intelligence information, and to oversee espionage activities. Its head, Colonel William Donovan, envisioned the OSS as an "adjunct to military strategy" and engaged leading social scientists to plot psychological warfare against the enemy.

One important outcome of these activities was to increase the size of the government many times over its New Deal level, which conservatives already considered far too large. It cost about $250 million a day to fight the war. As a result, the federal government spent twice as much during the war as it had during the nation's entire history up to then. The federal budget grew to ten times what it had been during the New Deal. Nearly half the revenue required to fight the war was produced by new rates of taxation. The number of Americans filing income tax returns jumped from 4 million before the war to 42.6 million at war's end. At the same time, the number of federal employees nearly quadrupled, from a little over 1 million in 1940 to nearly 4 million by the war's end.

Despite this pattern of expansion, however, the New Deal itself fell victim to the war. As President Roosevelt announced in 1942, "Dr. New Deal" had been replaced by "Dr. Win the War." No longer carrying the heavy responsibility of bringing the nation out of the Great Depression, his administration directed all its resources toward securing the planes, ships, guns, and food required for victory. Moreover, the 1942 elections weakened the New Deal coalition by unseating many liberal Democrats. The Republicans gained forty-six new members in the House of Representatives, nine in the Senate. Republicans now had greater opportunity to quash proposals to extend the social programs instituted during the 1930s. One by one, New Deal agencies vanished. One of the most popular programs, the Civilian Conservation Corps, secured funds from Congress, but only to cover its liquidation. In December 1942, the Works Progress Administration, which handled various forms of work relief, was given, in Roosevelt's words, a "wartime furlough"; a few months later Congress granted the agency an "honorable discharge." Major New Deal agencies, including the National Youth Administration and the Federal Writers Project, were dismantled by 1943.

Economic Conversion

The decisive factor for victory, even more than military prowess and superior strategy, would be, many observers agreed, the ability of the United States to outproduce its enemies. The country enjoyed many advantages to meet this challenge: a large industrial base, abundant natural resources (largely free from interference by the war), and a civilian population large enough to permit it to increase both its labor force and its armed forces. The war would lift the United States out of the Great Depression and create the biggest economic boom in the history of any nation. But first the entire civilian economy had to be both expanded and transformed for the production of arms and other military supplies.

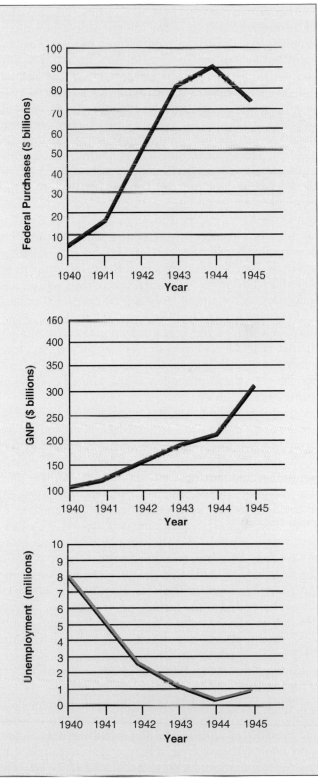

Effects of War Spending, 1940–1945   Wartime spending had a multiplier effect on the U.S. economy. Government contracts with industry rapidly increased the gross national product, and the sharp upswing in production utilized all available workers and sharply reduced unemployment.

SOURCE: Robert L. Heilbroner, *The Economic Transformation of America* (New York: Harcourt, Brace, 1977), p. 205.

Economic conversion resulted from a combination of government spending and foreign orders for military supplies. The American public firmly opposed rearmament until 1938, when expenditures for military purposes amounted to only 1.5 percent of the federal budget. The revision of neutrality legislation in 1939 eased previous restrictions on the sale of war materials to France and Great Britain, creating a huge market and boosting production significantly. By the summer of 1941 the federal government was pouring vast amounts into defense production. Six months after the attack on Pearl Harbor its allocations topped $100 billion for equipment and supplies, which exceeded what American firms had produced in any previous war. Facing war orders too large to fill, American industries were now primed for all-out production. Before the Japanese attack on Pearl Harbor, President Roosevelt counted on American businesses to manage their own war-related industries. After announcing a goal of 60,000 planes, 45,000 tanks, and 8 million tons of ships for 1942, Roosevelt formed the War Production Board in January of that year. He directed the new agency to "exercise general responsibility" for the economy. By June, nearly half of everything produced in the United States was war materiel.

Every economic indicator pointed upward. The gross national product (accounting for inflation) rose from $88.6 billion in 1939 to $198.7 billion in five years. Investment in new plants and equipment, including the manufacture of newly discovered synthetic rubber and fabrics, made possible an increase of 50 percent in the nation's productive capacity and the creation of 17 million jobs. Factories operated around-the-clock, seven days a week. With better equipment and more motivation, American workers proved twice as productive as the Germans, five times as productive as the Japanese. No wonder the actual volume of industrial output expanded at the fastest rate in American history. Military production alone grew from 2 percent of the 1939 total gross national product to 40 percent of the 1943 total. "Something is happening," announced *Time* magazine, "that Adolf Hitler does not understand . . . it is the miracle of production."

Businesses scored huge profits from military contracts. The government provided low-interest loans and even direct subsidies for the expansion of facilities, with generous tax write-offs for retooling. The 100 largest corporations, which manufactured 30 percent of all goods in 1940, garnered 70 percent of all war and civilian contracts and the bulk of the war profits. On the other hand, many small businesses closed, a half-million between 1941 and 1943 alone.

Defense production transformed entire regions. The impact was strongest in the West—the major staging area for the war in the Pacific—where the federal government spent nearly $40 billion for military and industrial expansion. California secured 10 percent of all federal funds, and by 1944 Los Angeles had become the nation's second largest manufacturing center, only slightly behind Detroit. The South also benefited from 60 of the army's 100 new camps. Its textile factories hummed: the army alone required nearly 520 million pairs of socks and 230 million pairs of pants. The southern branch of the Manhattan Project, the Oak Ridge, Tennessee, facility for the production of uranium, employed more than 80,000 workers during 1945, its peak year. The economic boom lifted entire populations out of sharecropping and tenancy into well-paid industrial jobs in the cities and pumped unprecedented profits into southern business. Across the country the rural population decreased by almost 20 percent.

Despite a "Food for Freedom" program, American farmers could not keep up with the rising international demand or even the domestic market for milk, potatoes, fruits, and sugar. The Department of Agriculture reached its goals only in areas such as livestock production, thanks to skyrocketing wholesale prices for meat. The war also speeded the development of large-scale, mechanized production of crops, including the first widespread use of chemical fertilizers and pesticides. By 1945 farm income had doubled, but thousands of small farms had disappeared, never to return.

New Workers

The wartime economy brought an unprecedented number of new workers into the labor force. The *bracero* program, negotiated by United States and Mexico in 1942, brought more than 200,000 Mexicans into the United States for short-term employment as mainly manual laborers and agricultural workers. The program also opened trades previously closed to them, such as shipbuilding on the Pacific coast. In 1944 a survey published by the Bureau of Indian Affairs reported that more than 46,000 Indian peoples were working in either agriculture or industry. The Sioux and Navajos, for example, were hired in large numbers to help build military depots and military training centers. African Americans found new opportunities in industry, in just four years securing a greater variety of jobs than in the seven decades since the outbreak of the Civil War. The number of black workers rose from 2,900,000 to 3,800,000.

The war most dramatically altered the wage-earning patterns of women. The female labor force grew by over 50 percent, reaching 19.5 million in 1945. The rate of growth proved especially high for white women over the age of thirty-five, and for the first time married women became the majority of female wage earners. The employment rate changed comparatively little for African

Facing a shortage of workers and increased production demands, the War Manpower Commission and the Office of War Information conducted a campaign to recruit women into the labor force. Women were encouraged to "take a job for your husband/son/brother" and to "keep the world safe for your children." Higher wages also enticed many women to take jobs in factories producing aircraft, ships, and ordnance. This photograph shows women working on the assembly line at Douglas Aircraft's plant in Long Beach, California, in 1944.

SOURCE: The Granger Collection (4E887.35).

Their skill with a vacuum cleaner easily translated into riveting on huge ships. "Instead of cutting a cake," one newsreel explained, "this woman [factory worker] cuts the pattern of aircraft parts. Instead of baking a cake, this woman is cooking gears to reduce the tension in the gears after use."

In practice, however, many stereotypes broke down. Women mined coal, repaired aircraft engines, cut and welded sheet metal, and operated forklifts and drill presses. On the Pacific coast, more than one-third of all workers in aircraft and shipbuilding were women. One female African American ship welder recalled: "There is nothing in the training to prepare you for the excruciating noise you get down in the ship. Any who were not heart-and-soul determined to stick it out would fade out right away. . . . And it isn't only your muscles that must harden. It's your nerve, too."

Compared to the Great Depression, when married women were barred from many jobs, World War II opened up new fields. The number of women automobile workers, for example, jumped from 29,000 to 200,000, that of women electrical workers from 100,000 to 374,000. Polled near the end of the war, the overwhelming majority—75 percent—of women workers expressed a desire to keep working, preferably at the same jobs. One woman spoke for many in describing her wartime work as "thrilling" and "exciting," adding that it was also "something women have never been allowed to do before." Many also candidly admitted that they most of all liked earning good money. One woman reported that her assembly-line job in the aircraft industry paid $1.15 per hour, a huge increase over the hourly wage she formerly earned as a waitress: 20 cents, with no tips allowed.

Although wartime employment changed the lives and raised the expectations of many new workers, the major advances proved short-lived. As early as 1943 some industries began planning to lay off women as war production wound down. With jobs reserved for returning veterans, women in industry saw their numbers diminish rapidly; as many as 4 million lost their jobs between 1944 and 1946. Although skyrocketing inflation propelled many married women back into the

American women; fully 90 percent had been in the labor force in 1940. However, many black women left domestic service for higher-paying jobs in manufacturing.

Despite this jump in employment rates, neither government nor industry rushed to recruit women. Well into the summer of 1942 the Department of War advised businesses to hold back from hiring women "until all available male labor in the area had first been employed." Likewise, neither government nor industry expected women to stay in their jobs when the war ended. Recruitment campaigns targeted "Mrs. Stay-at-Home" yet underscored the temporary aspect of her wartime service. "Rosie the Riveter" appeared in posters and advertisements as the model female citizen, but only "for the duration." In Washington, D.C., women bus drivers were given badges to wear on their uniforms that read: "I am taking the place of a man who went to war."

For the most part, advertisers used conventional gender stereotypes to make wartime jobs appealing to women. Recruitment posters and informational films depicted women's new industrial jobs as simple variations of domestic tasks. Where once housewives sewed curtains for their kitchens, they now produced silk parachutes.

labor force by the end of the decade, they did not pick up lucrative jobs in heavy industry.

Wartime Strikes

Although the wartime economy drained just about all pools of unemployed labor remaining from the Great Depression, the gains from the 17 million new jobs were not evenly distributed. Wages during wartime increased by as much as 50 percent but never as fast as profits or prices. This widely reported disparity produced one of the most turbulent periods in American labor history.

Labor strife began even before U.S. involvement in World War II. Only two weeks after the 1940 election, workers struck at the Vultee aircraft plant in Los Angeles. After the attorney general denounced the strikers as unpatriotic and the FBI began to harass participants, workers throughout the city walked off their jobs in sympathy with the aircraft workers. In April 1941 the president himself intervened in a large strike at Allis-Chalmers near Milwaukee, threatening seizure of the plant and forcing a settlement after seventy-five days of work stoppage. Later that year Roosevelt ordered troops to break the North American Aviation strike at Inglewood, California.

More workers went on strike in 1941, before the United States entered the war, than in any previous year except 1919. Rising production orders and tightening labor markets made strikes feasible: jobs were plentiful, and business leaders, anticipating hefty profits, had reason to settle quickly. This climate prompted a militant union drive at Ford Motor Company's enormous River Rouge plant, and the United Auto Workers (UAW) emerged as one of the most powerful labor organizations in the world.

Once the United States entered the war, the major unions dutifully agreed to no-strike pledges for its duration. The National War Labor Board, with representatives from business and labor, encouraged employers to allow unions in their plants, and unions secured contracts that included automatic dues checkoff, high wages, and new fringe benefits such as pension plans. Total union membership increased from 10.5 million to 14.7 million, with the women's share alone rising from 11 to 23 percent.

Unions also enrolled 1,250,000 African Americans, twice the prewar number. But many white workers resisted this change. "Hate strikes" broke out in plants across the country when African Americans were hired or promoted to jobs customarily held by white workers. For example, at a U.S. Rubber Company factory in Detroit, more than half the workers walked out in 1943 when African American women began to operate the machinery. Such strikes usually ended quickly because black workers refused to back down.

Rank-and-file union members staged other illegal "wildcat" strikes. The most dramatic, a walkout of more than a half-million coal miners in 1943 led by the rambunctious John L. Lewis, withstood the attacks of the government and the press. Roosevelt repeatedly ordered the mines seized, only to find, as Lewis retorted, that coal could not be mined with bayonets. The Democratic majority in Congress passed the first federal antistrike bill, giving the president power to penalize strikers, even to draft them. And yet the strikes grew in size and number, reaching a level greater than in any other four-year period in American history. Most, however, were of short duration and did not interrupt the war effort.

	STRIKES AND LOCKOUTS IN THE UNITED STATES, 1940–1945			
Year	Number of Strikes	Number of Workers Involved	Number of Man-Days Idle	Percent of Total Employed
1940	2,508	576,988	6,700,872	2.3
1941	4,288	2,362,620	23,047,556	8.4
1942	2,968	839,961	4,182,557	2.8
1943	3,752	1,981,279	13,500,529	6.9
1944	4,956	2,115,637	8,721,079	7.0
1945	4,750	3,467,000	38,025,000	12.2

Despite "no-strike" pledges, workers staged wildcat strikes in the war years. Union leaders negotiated shorter hours, higher wages, and seniority rules and helped to build union membership to a new height. When the war ended, nearly 30 percent of all nonagricultural workers were union members.

SOURCE: "Work Stoppages Caused by Labor-Management Disputes in 1945," *Monthly Labor Review,* May 1946, p. 720; and Martin Glaberman, *War Time Strikes* (Detroit: Bewick, 1980), p. 36.

THE HOME FRONT

Most Americans thoroughly appreciated the burst of prosperity brought on by wartime production. But they also experienced dramatic and unanticipated changes in the ways they worked and lived. Food rationing, long workdays, and separation from loved ones were just a few of the new conditions of daily life. Americans in communities across the country endured four intense years of adjustment.

Most Americans were happy and proud to make whatever sacrifices they could to help bring about the Allied victory. But alongside national unity ran deep conflicts on the home front. Racial and ethnic hostilities flared repeatedly and on several occasions erupted in violence.

Families in Wartime

Despite the uncertainties of wartime, or perhaps because of them, men and women rushed into marriage. The surge in personal income caused by the wartime economic boom meant that many young couples could afford to set up their own households—something their counterparts in the 1930s had not been able to do. As one social scientist remarked at the time, "Economic conditions were ripe for a rush to the altar." For other couples, the prospect of separation provided the incentive. The U.S. Census Bureau estimated that between 1940 and 1943 at least a million more people married than would have been expected had there been no war. The marriage rate skyrocketed, peaking in 1946. The median age for first marriage for women dropped to an unprecedented low of 20.3 years. But by 1946 the number of divorces also set records.

Housing shortages were acute, and rents were high. So scarce were apartments that taxi drivers became, for an extra fee, up-to-the-minute guides to vacancies. Able to set their own terms, landlords frequently discriminated against families with children and even more so against racial minorities. To ease these pressures, the National Housing Agency kicked off the "Share Your Home" campaign, which ultimately encouraged 1.5 million families to open their homes to friends, relatives, or

Students at Officers' Training School at Northwestern University, who were not allowed to marry until they were commissioned as ensigns, apply for marriage licenses in Chicago, August 20, 1943, shortly before graduation. These young couples helped the marriage rate skyrocket during World War II.

SOURCE: CORBIS (CS/695089).

strangers. The federal government also financed the construction of low-cost housing projects, which furnished approximately 2 million new residential units.

Supplying a household was scarcely less difficult. Although retailers extended their store hours into the evenings and weekends, shopping had to be squeezed in between long hours on the job. Extra planning was necessary for purchasing government-rationed staples such as meat, cheese, sugar, milk, coffee, gasoline, and even shoes. To free up commercially grown produce for the troops overseas, many families grew their own fruits and vegetables. In 1943, the peak year of Victory Gardens, three-fifths of the population were "growing their own," which amounted to a staggering 8 million tons of food that year.

Although the Office of Price Administration tried to prevent inflation and ensure an equitable distributions of foodstuffs, many women found it nearly impossible to manage both a demanding job and a household. This dual responsibility contributed to high turnover and absentee rates in factories. A 1943 survey reported that 40 percent of all women who left war plants did so for marital or household reasons rather than because of unsatisfactory wages or working conditions.

The care of small children became a major problem. Wartime employment or military service often separated husbands and wives, leaving children in the hands of only one parent. But even when families stayed together, both adults often worked long hours, sometimes on different shifts. Although the War Manpower Commission estimated that as many as 2 million children needed some form of child care, federally funded day-care centers served less than 10 percent of defense workers' children. Polls indicated that the majority of mothers would in any case refuse to send their youngsters to a public child-care center. In some communities, industries and municipal governments established limited facilities that could not keep up with the rapid increase in the number of "latchkey" children.

Juvenile delinquency rose during the war. With employers often relaxing minimum age requirements for employment, many teenagers quit school for the high wages of factory jobs. Between 1941 and 1944 high school enrollments decreased by 1.2 million. Runaways drifted from city to city, finding temporary work at wartime plants or at military installations. Gangs formed in major urban areas, leading to brawling, prostitution, or automobile thefts for joy rides. Overall, however, with so many young men either employed or serving in the armed forces, crime by juvenile as well as adult males declined. In contrast, complaints against girls, mainly for sexual offenses or for running away from home, increased significantly. In response, local officials created various youth agencies and charged them with developing more recreational and welfare programs.

In 1944 the U.S. Office of Education and the Children's Bureau inaugurated a back-to-school campaign. Local school boards appealed to employers to hire only older workers, and toward the end of the war the student dropout rate began to decline. The public schools, meanwhile, expanded their curriculums to include nutrition, hygiene, first aid, and the political context of the war itself. Although many teachers had quit to take better-paying jobs in industry, those who remained often organized scrap and salvage missions, war bond drives, Victory Gardens, and letter-writing campaigns. In many localities, the school stood at the center of community war efforts.

Public health improved greatly during the war. Forced to cut back on expenditures for medical care during the Great Depression, many Americans now spent large portions of their wartime paychecks on doctors, dentists, and prescription drugs. But even more important were the benefits provided to the more than 16 million men inducted into the armed forces and their dependents. The majority of young, well-trained physicians and dentists worked in uniform, providing their services at government expense. The number of doctors and dentists also increased dramatically: the graduating classes of 1944 were twice as large as those of any pre-war year. Nationally, incidences of such communicable diseases as typhoid fever, tuberculosis, and diphtheria dropped considerably, the infant death rate fell by more than a third, and life expectancy increased by three years. The death rate in 1942, excluding battle deaths, was the lowest in the nation's history. In the South and Southwest, however, racism and widespread poverty combined to halt or even reverse these trends. These regions continued to have the highest infant and maternal mortality rates in the nation.

The Internment of Japanese Americans

After the attack on Pearl Harbor, many Americans feared an invasion of the mainland and suspected Japanese Americans of secret loyalty to an enemy government. On December 8, 1941, the federal government froze the financial assets of those born in Japan, known as Issei, who had been barred from U.S. citizenship. Politicians, patriotic organizations, and military officials, meanwhile, called for the removal of all Americans of Japanese descent from Pacific coastal areas. Although a State Department intelligence report certified their loyalty, Japanese Americans—two-thirds of whom were American-born citizens—became the only ethnic group singled out for legal sanctions.

Charges of sedition masked long-standing racial prejudices. The press began to use the word "Jap" in headlines, while political cartoonists employed blatant racial stereotypes. Popular songs appeared with titles like

"You're a Sap, Mister Jap, to Make a Yankee Cranky." The head of the army's Western Defense Command, General John L. DeWitt, called the Japanese "an enemy race," bound by "racial affinities" to their homeland no matter how many generations removed. "The very fact that no sabotage has taken place to date," an army report suggested, with twisted logic, "is a disturbing and confirming indication that action will be taken."

On February 19, 1942, President Roosevelt signed Executive Order 9066, suspending the civil rights of Japanese Americans and authorizing the exclusion of more than 112,000 men, women, and children from designated military areas, mainly in California, but also in Oregon, Washington, and southern Arizona. At first, sectors of the small, insular communities voluntarily moved away from the Pacific coast, planning to resettle in the Midwest or East. When several governors objected to Japanese migration to their states, General DeWitt issued a "freeze order." The army prepared for forced evacuation, rounding up and removing

Byron Takashi Tsuzuki, *Forced Removal, Act II*, 1944. This Japanese American artist illustrates the forced relocation of Japanese Americans from their homes to one of ten inland camps in 1942. About 110,000 Japanese Americans were interned during World War II, some for up to four years. Beginning in January 1945, they were allowed to return to the Pacific coast.

SOURCE: Byron Takashi Tsuzuki, *Forced Removal, Act II*, 1944. Japanese American National Museum, Collection of August and MASKO (Kitty) Nakagawa.

Japanese Americans from the communities where they had lived and worked, sometimes for generations.

During the spring of 1942, Japanese American families received one week's notice to close up their businesses and homes before being transported to one of the ten internment camps managed by the War Relocation Authority. The guarded camps were located as far away as Arkansas, although the majority had been set up in isolated and arid districts of Utah, Colorado, Idaho, Arizona, Wyoming, and California. Karl G. Yoneda described his quarters at Manzanar in northern California:

> There were no lights, stoves, or window panes. My two cousins and I, together with seven others, were crowded into a 25 × 30 foot room. We slept on army cots with our clothes on. The next morning we discovered that there were no toilets or washrooms. . . . We saw GIs manning machine guns in the watchtowers. The barbed wire fence which surrounded the camp was visible against the background of the snow-covered Sierra mountain range. "So this is the American-style concentration camp," someone remarked.

By August, virtually every West Coast resident who had at least one Japanese grandparent had been interned. The majority in the camps were young, 75 percent under the age of twenty-five, and approximately 6,000 more were born there.

The Japanese American Citizens League charged that "racial animosity" rather than military necessity had dictated the internment policy. Despite the protest of the American Civil Liberties Union and several church groups against the abridgment of the civil rights of Japanese Americans, the Supreme Court in *Korematsu v. United States* (1944) upheld the constitutionality of relocation on grounds of national security. By this time a program of gradual release was in place, although the last center, at Tule Lake, California, did not close until March 1946. In protest, nearly 6,000 Japanese Americans renounced their U.S. citizenship. Japanese Americans had lost homes and businesses valued at $500 million in what many historians judge as being the worst violation of American civil liberties during the war. Not until 1988 did the U.S. Congress vote reparations of $20,000 and a public apology to each of the 60,000 surviving victims.

Civil Rights and Race Riots

Throughout the war, African American activists conducted a "Double V" campaign, mobilizing not only for Allied victory but for their own rights as citizens. "The army is about to take me to fight for democracy," one Detroit resident said, "but I would as leave fight for democracy right here." Black militants demanded, at a minimum, fair housing and equal employment opportunities. President Roosevelt responded in a lukewarm fashion, supporting advances in civil rights that would not, in his opinion, disrupt the war effort.

Before the United States entered the war, A. Philip Randolph, president of both the Brotherhood of Sleeping Car Porters and the National Negro Congress, had organized the March on Washington Movement. At a planning meeting in Chicago a black woman had proposed sending African Americans to Washington, D.C., "from all over the country, in jalopies, in trains, and any way they can get there until we get some action from the White House." Local rallies were held across the country in preparation for the "great rally" of no less than 100,000 people at the Lincoln Memorial on the Fourth of July.

Eager to stop the movement, President Roosevelt met with Randolph, who proposed an executive order "making it mandatory that Negroes be permitted to work." Randolph reviewed several drafts before approving the text that became, on June 25, 1941, Executive Order 8802, banning discrimination in defense industries and government. The president later appointed a Fair Employment Practices Committee to hear complaints and to take "appropriate steps to redress grievances." Randolph called off the march but did not disband his all-black March on Washington organization. He remained determined to "shake up white America."

Other civil rights organizations formed during wartime to fight both discrimination and Jim Crow practices, including segregation in the U.S. armed forces. The interracial Congress of Racial Equality (CORE), formed by pacifists in 1942, staged sit-ins at Chicago, Detroit, and Denver restaurants that refused to serve African Americans. In several cities, CORE used nonviolent means to challenge racial segregation in public facilities. Meanwhile, membership in the National Association for the Advancement of Colored People (NAACP), which took a strong stand against discrimination in the military, grew from 50,000 in 1940 to 450,000 in 1946.

The struggle for equality took shape within local communities. Approximately 1.2 million African Americans left the rural South to take jobs in wartime industries. They faced not only serious housing shortages but whites who were determined to keep them out of the best jobs and neighborhoods. In February 1942, when twenty black families attempted to move into new federally funded apartments adjacent to a Polish American community in Detroit, a mob of 700 white protesters halted the moving vans and burned a cross on the project's grounds. The police overlooked the white rioters but arrested black youths. Finally, two months later, 1,000 state troopers supervised the move of these families into the Sojourner Truth Homes, named after the famous abolitionist and former slave.

Racial violence reached its wartime peak during the summer of 1943, when 274 conflicts broke out in nearly fifty cities. In Detroit, where the black population had grown by more than a third since the beginning of the war, twenty-five blacks and nine whites were killed and more than 700 were injured. After the riot, one writer reported: "I thought that I had witnessed an experience

This painting is by Horace Pippin, a self-taught African American artist who began painting as therapy for an injury suffered while serving with the U.S. Army's 369th Colored Infantry Regiment during World War I. It is one of a series drawn during World War II illustrating the contradiction between the principles of liberty and justice, for which Americans were fighting abroad, and the reality of race prejudice at home.

SOURCE: Horace Pippin (1888–1946), *Mr. Prejudice,* 1943. Oil on canvas, 18″ × 14″. Philadelphia Museum of Art, Gift of Dr. and Mrs. Matthew T. Moore. Photo by Graydon Wood (1984–108–1).

peculiar to the Deep South. On the streets of Detroit I saw again the same horrible exhibition of uninhibited hate as they fought and killed one another—white against black—in a frenzy of homicidal mania, without rhyme or reason." The poet Langston Hughes, who supported U.S. involvement in the war, wrote:

> Looky here, America
> What you done done—
> Let things drift
> Until the riots come
>
> Yet you say we're fighting
> For democracy.
> Then why don't democracy
> Include me?
>
> I ask you this question
> Cause I want to know
> How long I got to fight
> BOTH HITLER—AND JIM CROW.

The poet and educator Pauli Murray summed up the situation in a letter sent to President Roosevelt: "It is my conviction . . . that the problem of race, intensified by economic conflict and war nerves . . . will eventually . . . occupy a dominant position as a national domestic problem." Her words proved prescient.

Zoot-suit Riots

On the night of June 4, 1943, sailors poured into nearly 200 cars and taxis to drive through the streets of East Los Angeles in search of Mexican Americans dressed in zoot suits. The sailors assaulted their victims at random, even chasing one youth into a movie theater and stripping him of his clothes while the audience cheered. Riots broke out and continued for five days.

Two communities had collided, with tragic results. The sailors had only recently been uprooted from their hometowns and regrouped under the strict discipline of boot camp. Now stationed in southern California while awaiting departure overseas, they came face-to-face with Mexican American teenagers wearing long-draped coats, pegged pants, pocket watches with oversized chains, and big floppy hats. To the sailors, the zoot suit was not just a flamboyant fashion. Unlike the uniform the young sailors wore, the zoot suit signaled a lack of patriotism.

The zoot-suiters, however, represented less than 10 percent of their community's youth. More than 300,000 Mexican Americans were serving in the armed forces (a number representing a greater proportion of their draft-age population than other Americans), and they served in the most hazardous branches, the paratrooper and marine corps. Many others were employed in war industries in Los Angeles, which had become home to the largest community of Mexican Americans in the nation. For the first time Mexican Americans were finding well-paying jobs, and, like African Americans, they expected their government to protect them from discrimination.

There were several advances during the war. The Fair Employment Practices Committee fostered a limited expansion of civil rights. The Spanish-Speaking People's Division in the Office of Inter-American Affairs established centers in Denver, Salt Lake City, and Los Angeles to bring together community, business, and educational leaders in programs on Latin American culture. The office also developed programs to instill cultural pride and self-esteem among Mexican American children. School districts in California and throughout the Southwest introduced lessons on the Mexican heritage and encouraged bilingual education. Many schools also added vocational training classes to channel graduates into wartime industry.

But these new programs did little to ease the bitter racial and cultural conflict that on occasion became vicious. In Los Angeles, military and civilian authorities eventually contained the zoot-suit riots by ruling several sections of the city off limits to military personnel. The Los Angeles City Council passed legislation making the wearing of a zoot suit in public a criminal offense. Later, the Joint Finding Committee on Un-American Activities in California conducted hearings to determine whether foreign enemy agents had plotted the unrest. Nevertheless, many Mexican Americans expressed concern about their personal safety; some feared that, after the government rounded up the Japanese, they would be the next group sent to internment camps.

Popular Culture and "The Good War"

Global events shaped the lives of American civilians but appeared to touch them only indirectly in their everyday activities. Food shortages, long hours in the factories, and even fears for loved ones abroad did not take away all the pleasures of full employment and prosperity. With money in their pockets, Americans spent freely at vacation resorts, country clubs, race-tracks, nightclubs, dance halls, and movie theaters. Sales of books skyrocketed, and spectator sports attracted huge audiences.

Popular culture, especially music, seemed to bridge the growing racial divisions of the neighborhood and the work place. Transplanted southern musicians, black and white, brought their regional styles to northern cities and adapted them quickly to the electric amplification of nightclubs and recording studios. "They'd made them steel guitars cry and whine," Ray Charles later remembered. Played on jukeboxes in bars, bus stations, and cafes, "country" and "rhythm & blues" not only won over new audiences but also inspired musicians themselves to crisscross old boundaries. The International Sweethearts of Rhythm, a group of black and white women singers, started in the Mississippi Delta but soon pleased audiences throughout the United States.

Many songs featured war themes. Personal sentiment meshed with government directive to depict a "good war," justifying massive sacrifice. The war was to be seen as a worthy and even noble cause. The plaintive "A Rainbow at Midnight" by country singer Ernest Tubb expressed the hope of a common "dogface" soldier looking beyond the misery and horror to the promise of a brighter tomorrow. "Till Then," recorded by the Mills Brothers, a harmonious black quartet, offered the prospect of a romantic reunion when "the world will be free." The era's best-known tune, Irving Berlin's "White Christmas," evoked a lyrical nostalgia of past celebrations with family and friends close by. On the lighter side, novelty artist Spike Jones made his name with the "razz" or "Bronx cheer," in "We're Going to Ffft in the Fuehrer's Face."

Hollywood artists meanwhile threw themselves into a perpetual round of fundraising and morale-boosting public events. Movie stars called on fans to buy war bonds and to support the troops. Combat films such as *Action in the North Atlantic* made heroes of ordinary Americans under fire, depicting GIs of different races and ethnicities discovering their common humanity. Movies with antifascist themes, such as *Tender Comrade*, promoted friendship among Russians and Americans, while films like *Since You Went Away* portrayed the loyalty and resilience of families with servicemen stationed overseas.

The wartime spirit also infected the juvenile world of comics. The climbing sales of nickel "books" spawned a proliferation of patriotic superheroes such as Flash, Hawkman, the Green Lantern, Captain Marvel, and the more comical Plastic Man. Captain America, created by the famed comic artist Jack Kirby, was a frail soldier who, when injected with a wonder drug, began delivering punches at Adolf Hitler even before the United States entered the war. Kirby went on to create "boy Commandos," intensifying juvenile identification with battlefield action. Even Bugs Bunny put on a uniform and fought sinister-looking enemies.

Fashion designers did their part. Padded shoulders and straight lines became popular for both men and women; BVD, a leading manufacturer of underwear, designed civilian clothing to resemble military attire. Patriotic Americans, such as civil defense volunteers and Red Cross workers, fancied uniforms, and women employed in defense plants wore pants, often for the first time. Restrictions on materials also influenced fashion. Production of nylon stockings was halted because the material was needed for parachutes. To save material, women's skirts were shortened, while the War Production Board encouraged cuffless "Victory Suits" for men. Executive Order M-217 restricted the colors of shoes manufactured during the war to "black, white, navy blue, and three shades of brown."

Never to see a single battle, safeguarded by two oceans, many Americans nevertheless experienced the war years as the most intense of their entire lives. Popular music, Hollywood movies, radio programs, and advertisements—all screened by the Office of War Information—encouraged a sense of personal involvement in a collective effort to preserve democracy at home and to save the world from fascism. No one was excluded, no action considered insignificant. Even casual conversation came under the purview of the government, which warned that "Loose Lips Sink Ships."

MEN AND WOMEN IN UNIFORM

During World War I, American soldiers served for a relatively brief period and in small numbers. A quarter-century later, World War II mobilized 16.4 million Americans into the armed forces. Although only 34 percent of men who served in the army saw combat—the majority during the final year of the war—the experience had a powerful impact on nearly everyone. Whether working in the steno pool at Great Lakes Naval Training Center in northern Illinois or slogging through mud with rifle in hand in the Philippines, many men and women saw their lives reshaped in unpredictable ways. Uprooted from their communities, they suddenly found themselves among strangers, in an unfamiliar geographical setting, and under a severe military regimen. For those who survived, World War II often proved to be the defining experience of their lives.

Creating the Armed Forces

Before the European war broke out in 1939, the majority of the 200,000 men in the U.S. armed forces were employed as military police, engaging in such tasks as patrolling the Mexican border or occupying colonial possessions, such as the Philippines. Neither the army nor the navy was prepared for the scale of combat World War II entailed. Only the U.S. Marine Corps, which had been planning since the 1920s to wrest control of the western Pacific from Japan, was poised to fight. Once mobilized for war, however, the United States became a first-rank military power.

On October 16, 1940, National Registration Day, all men between the ages of twenty-one and thirty-six were legally obligated to register for military service.

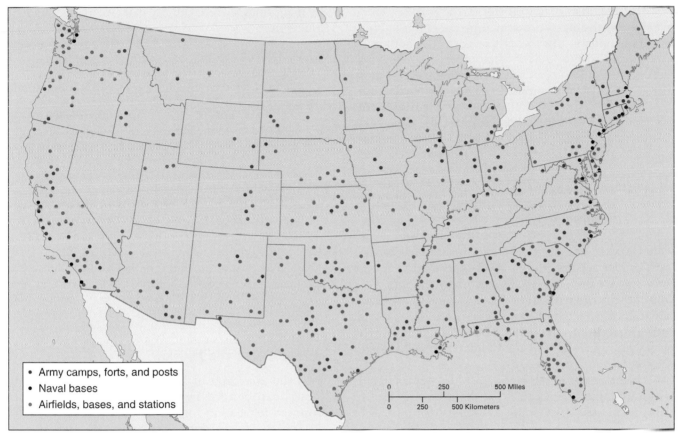

Wartime Army Camps, Naval Bases, and Airfields   Their locations chosen for political as well as defense reasons, military facilities were rapidly constructed in every state. The many facilities located in the South and West helped open these areas to economic development and an influx of new migrants.

SOURCE: Clifford L. Lord and Elizabeth H. Lord, *Lord & Lord Historical Atlas of the United States*, rev. ed. (New York: Holt, 1953), p. 309.

Just two weeks later more than 5,000 local draft boards began to draw the first numbers to send men off to camps for one year of training. After the United States entered the war, the draft age was lowered to eighteen, and local boards were instructed to choose first from the youngest.

One-third of the men examined by the Selective Service were rejected. Surprising numbers were refused induction because they were physically unfit for military service. For the first time, men were screened for "neuropsychiatric disorders or emotional problems," and approximately 1.6 million were rejected on this reason. At a time when only one American in four graduated from high school, induction centers turned away many conscripts because they were functionally illiterate.

But those who passed the screening tests joined the best-educated army in history: nearly half of white draftees had graduated from high school and 10 percent had attended college. Once inducted, a soldier went off

to one of 242 training centers. At Fort Benning, near Columbus, Georgia, up to 100,000 inductees at a time learned basic military skills such as shooting a rifle, pitching a tent, digging a foxhole, and saluting an officer before advancing to specialized training.

The officer corps, whose top-ranking members were from the Command and General Staff School at Fort Leavenworth, tended to be highly professional, politically conservative, and personally autocratic. General Douglas MacArthur, supreme commander in the Pacific theater, was said to admire the discipline of the German army and to disparage political democracy. General Dwight D. Eisenhower, however, supreme commander of the Allied forces in Europe, projected a new and contrasting spirit. Distrusted by MacArthur and many of the older brass, Eisenhower appeared to his troops a model of leadership. "The idea is to get people working together," he wrote, "because they instinctively want to do it for you. . . . [E]ssentially, you must be devoted to duty, sincere, fair and cheerful."

The democratic rhetoric of the war and the sudden massive expansion of the armed forces contributed to this transformation of the officer corps. A shortage of officers during World War I had prompted a huge expansion of the Reserve Officer Training Corps, but its drilling and discipline alone could not create good officers, and it was still insufficient to meet the demand for trained officers. Racing to make up for the deficiency, Army Chief of Staff George Marshall opened schools for officer candidates. In 1942, in seventeen-week training periods, these schools produced more than 54,000 platoon leaders. Closer in sensibility to the civilian population, these new officers were the kind of leaders Eisenhower sought.

Most GIs (short for "government issue"), who were the vast majority of draftees, had limited contact with officers at the higher levels and instead forged bonds with their company commanders and men within their own combat units. "Everyone wants someone to look up to when he's scared," one GI explained. Most of all, soldiers depended on the solidarity of the group and the loyalty of their buddies to pull through the war.

The majority of these citizen-soldiers endured military discipline "to get the task done," as revealed in numerous polls. They longed foremost for peace. "In the magazines," wrote the popular war correspondent Ernie Pyle,

> war seemed romantic and exciting, full of heroics and vitality. . . . Certainly there were great tragedies, unbelievable heroism, even a constant undertone of comedy. But when I sat down to write, I saw instead men . . . suffering and wishing they were somewhere else . . . all of them desperately hungry for somebody to talk to besides themselves, no women to be heroes in front of, damned little wine to drink, precious little song, cold and fairly dirty, just toiling from day to day in a world full of insecurity, discomfort, homesickness and a dulled sense of danger.

Pledged to fight for democracy, most GIs hoped foremost to return soon to their families and communities. The majority were nevertheless proud to serve in "the best-dressed, best-fed, best-equipped army in the world."

Women Enter the Military

With the approach of World War II, Massachusetts Republican congresswoman Edith Nourse Rogers proposed legislation for the formation of a women's corps. The army instead drafted its own bill, which both Rogers and Eleanor Roosevelt supported, creating in May 1942 the Women's Army Auxiliary Corps (WAAC), later changed to Women's Army Corps (WAC). In 1942–43 other bills established a women's division of the navy (WAVES), the Women's Airforce Service Pilots, and the Marine Corps Women's Reserve. Overall, more than 350,000 women served in World War II, two-thirds of them in the WACS and WAVES. As a group, they were better educated and more skilled—although paid less—than the average soldier.

Although barred from combat, women were not necessarily protected from danger. Nurses accompanied the troops into combat in Africa, Italy, and France, treated men under fire, and dug and lived in their own foxholes. More than 1,000 women flew planes, although not in combat missions. Others worked as photographers and cryptoanalysts.

New recruits to the Women's Army Corps (WAC) pick up their clothing "issue" (allotment). These volunteers served in many capacities, from nursing men in combat to performing clerical and communications duties "state-side" (within the United States). Approximately 140,000 women served in the WACS during World War II.

SOURCE: National Archives and Records Administration.

The vast majority remained far from battlefronts, however, stationed mainly within the United States, where they served in administration, communications, clerical, or health-care facilities.

The WACS and WAVES were both subject to hostile commentary and bad publicity. The overwhelming majority of soliders believed that most WACS were prostitutes, and the War Department itself, fearing "immorality" among women in the armed forces, closely monitored their conduct and established much stricter rules for women than for men. The U.S. Marine Corps even used intelligence officers to ferret out suspected lesbians or women who showed "homosexual tendencies" (as opposed to homosexual acts), both causes for dishonorable discharge.

Eventually some of these discriminatory practices eased, but only after women demanded fair treatment. High-ranking female officers, for example, argued for a repeal of a military policy prohibiting women from supervising male workers, even in offices. The armed forces did not, however, lift its ban on women with children.

Like the armed forces in general, the women's services were marked by racial segregation, despite government declarations of egalitarianism. Black women and white women ate in separate mess halls and slept in separate barracks. At the beginning of the war, black nurses were admitted to serve only black soldiers, and the WAVES refused all black women on the ground that the navy had no black airmen to attend. Only in 1944 did Roosevelt order the navy to incorporate black WAVES, and fewer than 100 served.

Old Practices and New Horizons

The Selective Service Act, in response to the demands of African American leaders, specified that "there shall be no discrimination against any person on account of race or color." The draft brought hundreds of thousands of young black men into the army, and African Americans enlisted at a rate 60 percent above their proportion of the general population. By 1944 black soliders represented 10 percent of the army's troops, and overall approximately 1 million African Americans served in the armed forces during World War II. The army, however, channeled black recruits into segregated, poorly equipped units, which were commanded by white officers. Secretary of War Henry Stimson refused to challenge this policy, saying that the army could not operate effectively as "a sociological laboratory." The majority served in the Signal, Engineer, and Quartermaster Corps, mainly in construction or stevedore work. Only toward the end of the war, when the shortage of infantry neared a crisis, were African Americans permitted to rise to combat status. The all-black 761st Tank Battalion,

the first African American unit in combat, won a Medal of Honor after 183 days in action. And despite the very small number of African Americans admitted to the Air Force, the 99th Pursuit Squadron earned high marks in action against the feared German air force, the Luftwaffe. Even the Marine Corps and the Coast Guard agreed to end their historic exclusion of African Americans, although they recruited and promoted only a small number.

The ordinary black soldier, sailor, or marine experienced few benefits from the late-in-the-war gains of a few. They encountered discrimination everywhere, from the army canteen to the religious chapels. Even the blood banks kept blood segregated by race (although a black physician, Dr. Charles Drew, had invented the process for storing plasma). The year 1943 marked the peak of unrest, with violent confrontations between blacks and whites breaking out at military installations, especially in the South where the majority of African American soliders were stationed. Toward the end of the war, to improve morale among black servicemen, the army relaxed its policy of segregation, mainly in recreational facilities. Although enforcement was uneven and haphazard, the new policy paved the way for integration within a decade of the war's end.

The army also grouped Japanese Americans into segregated units, sending most to fight far from the Pacific theater. Better educated than the average soldier, many Nisei soldiers who knew Japanese served state-side as interpreters and translators. When the army decided to create a Nisei regiment, more than 10,000 volunteers stepped forward, only one in five of whom was accepted. The Nisei 442nd fought heroically in Italy and France and became the most decorated regiment in the war.

Despite segregation, the armed forces ultimately pulled Americans of all varieties out of their communities. Many Jews and other second-generation European immigrants, for example, described their stint in the military as an "Americanizing" experience. Many Indian peoples left reservations for the first time, approximately 25,000 serving in the armed forces. Many Navajo "code talkers," for example, who used a special code based on their native language to transmit information among military units, learned English in special classes established by the marines. For many African Americans, military service provided a bridge to postwar civil rights agitation. Amzie Moore, who later helped to organize the Mississippi Freedom Democratic Party, traced his understanding that "people are just people" to his experiences in the armed forces during World War II.

Many homosexuals also discovered a wider world. Despite a policy barring them from military service, most slipped through mass screening at induction centers.

Moreover, the emotional pressures of wartime, especially the fear of death, encouraged close friendships, and homosexuals in the military often found more room than in civilian life to express their sexual orientation openly. In army canteens, for example, men often danced with one another, whereas in civilian settings they would have been subject to ridicule or even arrest for such activity. "The war is a tragedy to my mind and soul," one gay soldier confided, "but to my physical being, it's a memorable experience." Lesbian WACS and WAVES had similar tales.

Most soldiers looked back at the war, with all its dangers and discomforts, as the greatest experience they would ever know. As the *New Republic* predicted in 1943, they met fellow Americans from every part of the country and recognized for the first time in their lives "the bigness and wholeness of the United States." "Hughie was a Georgia cracker, so he knew something about moonshine," remembered one soldier. Another fondly recalled "this fellow from Wisconsin we called 'Moose.'" The army itself promoted these expectations of new experience. *Twenty-Seven Soldiers* (1944), a government-produced film for the troops, showed Allied soldiers of several nationalities all working together in harmony.

The Medical Corps

The chance of being killed in combat was surprisingly small, estimated at less than 1 in 50, but the risk of injury was much higher. By the time the war ended, the army reported 949,000 casualties, including 175,000 who had been killed in action. Although the European Theater produced the greatest number of casualties, the Pacific held grave dangers in addition to artillery fire. For the soliders fighting in hot, humid jungles, malaria, typhus, diarrhea, or dengue fever posed the most common threat to their lives. For the 25th Infantry Division, which landed in Guadalcanal in 1943, the malaria-carrying mosquito proved a more formidable enemy than Japanese forces.

The prolonged stress of combat also took a toll in the form of "battle fatigue." Despite the rigorous screening of recruits, more than 1 million soldiers suffered at one time or another from debilitating psychiatric symptoms, and the number of men discharged for neuropsychiatric reasons was 2.5 times greater than in previous wars. The cause, psychiatrists concluded, was not individual weakness but long stints in the front lines. In France, for example, where soldiers spent up to 200 days in the field without a break from fighting, thousands cracked, occasionally inflicting wounds on themselves in order to be sent home. One who simply fled the battlefront, Private Eddie Slovik, was tried and executed for desertion—the first such execution since the Civil War. In 1944 the army concluded that eight months in combat was the maximum and instituted,

when replacements were available, a rotation system to relieve exhausted soldiers.

To care for sick and wounded soldiers, the army depended on a variety of medical personnel. Soldiers received first aid training as part of basic training, and they went into battle equipped with bandages to treat minor wounds. For the most part, however, they relied on the talents of trained physicians and medics. The Army Medical Corps sent doctors to the front lines. Working in make-shift tent hospitals, these physicians advanced surgical techniques and, with the use of new "wonder" drugs such as penicillin, saved the lives of many wounded soldiers. Of the soldiers who underwent emergency surgery on the field, more than 85 percent survived. Over all, less than 4 percent of all soldiers who received medical care died as a result of their injuries. Much of the success in treatment came from the use of blood plasma, which reduced the often lethal effect of shock from severe bleeding. By 1945, the American Red Cross Blood Bank, which was formed four years earlier, had collected more than 13 million units of blood from volunteers, converted most of it into dried plasma, and made it readily available throughout the European Theater.

Grateful for the care of skilled surgeons, many soldiers nevertheless named medics the true heroes of the battlefront. Between thirty to forty medics were attached to each infantry battalion, and they were responsible for emergency first-aid and for transporting the wounded to the aid station and if necessary on to the field hospital. Many medics were recruited from the approximately 35,000 conscientious objectors, who were defined by the Selective Service as a person "who, by reason of religious training and belief, is conscientiously opposed to participation in war in any form."

In the military hospitals, American nurses supplied the bulk of care to recovering soldiers. Before World War II, the Army Nurse Corps, created in 1901, was scarcely a military organization, with recruits earning neither military pay nor rank. To overcome the short supply of nurses, Congress extended military rank to nurses in 1944, although only for the duration and for six months after the war ended. In 1945 Congress came close to passing a bill to draft nurses. Like medics, army nurses went first to training centers in the United States, learning how to dig foxholes and dodge bullets before being sent overseas. By 1945, approximately 56,000 women, including 500 African American women, were on active duty in the Army Nurse Corps, staffing medical facilities in every theater of the war.

Prisoners of War

Approximately 120,000 Americans became prisoners of war (POWs). Those captured by the Germans were taken back to camps—*Olfags* for officers or *Stalags* for enlisted men—where they sat out the remainder of the

A painting by Sidney Simon of American POWs freed from Japanese captors at Bilibid prison, in Manila, 1945, after the U.S. reconquest of the Philippines. The battle of the Philippine Sea and the battle of Leyte Gulf during the previous year had nearly broken Japanese resistance in the area, but the clean-up process revealed the awful price that Americans and their Filipino allies had paid. As prisoners of war, they had suffered terribly from malnutrition and improperly attended wounds and from an unsparing and inhumane Japanese military code of behavior.

SOURCE: Sidney Simon, *P.O.W.s at Bilibid Prison*, 1945. Oil on canvas, 25″ × 30″. Center of Military History, U.S. Army (CC/103010).

war, mainly fighting boredom. Registered by the Swiss Red Cross, they could receive packages of supplies and occasionally join work brigades. By contrast, Russian POWs were starved and occasionally murdered in German camps.

Conditions for POWs in the Pacific were, however, worse than abysmal. Of the 20,000 Americans captured in the Philippines early in the war, only 40 percent survived to return home in 1945. At least 6,000 American and Filipino prisoners, beaten and denied food and water, died on the notorious eighty-mile "Death March" through the jungles on the Bataan Peninsula in 1942.

After the survivors reached the former U.S. airbase Camp O'Donnell, hundreds died weekly in a cesspool of disease and squalor.

The Japanese army felt only contempt for POWs; its own soldiers evaded capture by killing themselves. The Imperial Army assigned its most brutal troops to guard prisoners and imposed strict and brutal discipline in the camps. In a postwar survey, 90 percent of former POWs from the Pacific reported that they had been beaten. A desire for retribution, as well as racist attitudes, prompted GIs to treat Japanese prisoners far more brutally than enemy soldiers captured in Europe or Africa.

THE WORLD AT WAR

During the first year of declared war, the Allies remained on the defensive. Hitler's forces held the European Continent and pounded England with aerial bombardments while driving deep into Russia and across northern Africa to take the Suez Canal. The situation in the Pacific was scarcely better. Just two hours after the attack on Pearl Harbor, Japanese planes struck the main U.S. base in the Philippines and demolished half the air force commanded by General Douglas MacArthur. Within a short time, MacArthur was forced to withdraw his troops to the Bataan Peninsula, admitting that Japan had practically seized the Pacific. Roosevelt called the news "all bad," and his military advisers predicted a long fight to victory.

But the Allies enjoyed several important advantages: vast natural resources and a skilled workforce with sufficient reserves to accelerate the production of weapons and ammunitions; the determination of millions of antifascists throughout Europe and Asia; and the capacity of the Soviet Union to endure immense losses. Slowly at first, but then with quickening speed, these advantages made themselves felt.

Soviets Halt Nazi Drive

The weapons and tactics of World War II were radically different from those of World War I. Unlike World War I, which was fought by immobile armies kept in trenches by bursts of machine-gun fire, World War II was a war of offensive maneuvers punctuated by surprise attacks. Its chief weapons were tanks and airplanes, combining mobility and concentrated firepower. Also of major importance were artillery and explosives, which according to some estimates accounted for over 30 percent of the casualties. Major improvements in communication systems, mainly two-way radio transmission and radiotelephony that permitted commanders to stay in contact with division leaders, also played a decisive role from the beginning of the war.

Early on, Hitler had used these methods to seize the advantage, purposefully creating terror among the stricken populations of western Europe as he routed their armies. The Royal Air Force, however, fought the Luftwaffe to a standstill in the Battle of Britain, frustrating Hitler's hopes of invading England. In the summer of 1941, he turned his attention to the east, hoping to invade and conquer the Soviet Union before the United States entered the war. But he had to delay the invasion in order to support Mussolini, whose weak army had been pushed back in North Africa and Greece. The attack on Russia did not come until June 22, six weeks later than planned and too late to achieve its goals before the brutal Russian winter began.

The burden of the war now fell on the Soviet Union. From June to September, Hitler's forces overran the Red Army, killing or capturing nearly 3 million soldiers and leaving thousands to die from exposure or starvation. But Nazi commanders did not count on civilian resistance. The Soviets rallied, cutting German supply lines and sending every available resource to Soviet troops concentrated just outside Moscow. After furious fighting and the onset of severe winter weather, the Red Army launched a massive counterattack, catching the freezing German troops off guard. For the first time, the Nazi war machine suffered a major setback.

Turning strategically away from Moscow, during the summer of 1942 German troops headed toward Crimea and the rich oil fields of the Caucasus. Still set on conquering the Soviet Union and turning its vast resources to his own use, Hitler decided to attack Stalingrad, a major industrial city on the Volga River. The Soviets suffered more casualties during the following battles than Americans did during the entire war. But intense house-to-house and street fighting and a massive Soviet counteroffensive took an even greater toll on the Nazi fighting machine. By February 1943, the German Sixth Army had met defeat, overpowered by Soviet troops and weapons. More than 100,000 German soldiers surrendered.

Already in retreat but plotting one last desperate attempt to halt the Red Army, the Germans threw most of their remaining armored vehicles into action at Kursk, in the Ukraine, in July 1943. The clash quickly developed into the greatest land battle in history. More than 2 million troops and 6,000 tanks went into action. After another stunning defeat, the Germans had decisively lost the initiative. Their only option was to delay the advance of the Red Army against their homeland.

Meanwhile, the Soviet Union had begun to recover from its early losses, even as tens of millions of its own people remained homeless and near starvation. Assisted by the U.S. Lend-Lease program, by 1942 the Soviets were outproducing Germany in many types of weapons and other supplies. Nazi officers and German civilians alike began to doubt that Hitler could win the war. The Soviet victories had turned the tide of the war.

The Allied Offensive

In the spring of 1942, Germany, Italy, and Japan commanded a territory extending from France to the Pacific Ocean. They controlled central Europe and a large section of the Soviet Union as well as considerable parts of China and the southwestern Pacific. But their momentum was flagging. American shipbuilding outpaced the punishment Nazi submarines inflicted on Allied shipping, and sub-sinking destroyers greatly reduced the submarines' threat. The United States

Web Exploration Examine the strategies of the Axis and the Allies. What were the key turning points of the war in Europe?
www.prenhall.com/faragher/map25.1

The War in Europe The Allies remained on the defensive during the first years of the war, but by 1943 the British and Americans, with an almost endless supply of resources, had turned the tide.

far outstripped Germany in the production of landing craft and amphibious vehicles, two of the most important innovations of the war. Also outnumbered by the Allies, the German air force was limited to defensive action. On land, the United States and Great Britain had the trucks and jeeps to field fully mobile armies, while German troops marched in and out of Russia with packhorses.

Still, German forces represented a mighty opponent on the European Continent. Fighting the Nazis almost alone, the Soviets repeatedly appealed for the creation of a Second Front, an Allied offensive against Germany from the west. The Allies focused instead on securing North Africa and then on an invasion of Italy, hoping to move from there into central Europe.

On the night of October 23–24, 1942, near El Alamein in the desert of western Egypt, the British Eighth Army halted a major offensive by the German Afrika Korps, headed by General Erwin Rommel, the famed "Desert Fox." Although suffering heavy losses—approximately 13,000 men and more than 500 tanks—British forces destroyed the Italian North African Army and much of Germany's Afrika Korps. Americans entered the war in Europe as part of Operation Torch, the landing of British and American troops on the coast of Morocco and Algeria in November 1942, the largest amphibious military landing to that date. The Allies then fought their way along the coast, entering Tunis in triumph six months later. With the surrender of a quarter-million Germans and Italians in Tunisia in May 1943, the Allies controlled North Africa and had a secure position in the Mediterranean. During the North African campaign, the Allies announced that they would accept nothing less than the unconditional surrender of their enemies. In January 1943, Roosevelt and Churchill had met in Casablanca in Morocco and ruled out any possibility of negotiation with the Axis powers. Roosevelt's supporters hailed the policy as a clear statement of goals, a promise to the world that the scourge of fascism would be completely banished. Stalin, who did not attend the meeting, criticized the policy, fearing that it would only increase the enemy's determination to fight to the end. Other critics similarly charged that the demand for total capitulation would serve to prolong the war and lengthen the casualty list.

Allied aerial bombing further increased pressure on Germany. Many U.S. leaders believed that in the B-17 Flying Fortress, the air force possessed the ultimate weapon, "the mightiest bomber ever built." The U.S. Army Air Corps described this bomber as a "humane" weapon, capable of hitting specific military targets and sparing the lives of civilians. But when weather or darkness required pilots to depend on radar for sightings, they couldn't distinguish clearly between factories and schools or between military barracks and private homes, and bombs might fall within a range of nearly two miles from the intended target. American pilots preferred to bomb during daylight hours, while the British bombed during the night. Bombing missions over the Rhineland and the Ruhr successfully took out many German factories. But the Germans responded by relocating their plants, often dispersing light industry to the countryside.

Determined to break German resistance, the Royal Air Force redirected its main attack away from military sites to cities, including fuel dumps and public transportation. Hamburg was practically leveled. Between 60,000 and 100,000 people were killed, and 300,000 buildings were destroyed. Sixty other cities were hit hard, leaving 20 percent of Germany's total residential area in ruins. The very worst air raid of the war—650,000 incendiary bombs dropped on the city of Dresden, destroying 8 square miles and killing 135,000 civilians—had no military value.

The Allied strategic air offensive weakened the German economy and undermined civilian morale. Moreover, in trying to defend German cities and factories, the Luftwaffe sacrificed many of its fighter planes. When the Allies

As part of the air war on Germany, Allied bombers launched a devastating attack on Dresden, a major economic center, in February 1945. Of the civilians who died, most from burns or smoke inhalation during the firestorm, a large number were women and children, refugees from the Eastern Front. The city was left in ruins.

SOURCE: Commuters boarding a tram. Getty Images, Inc. Photo by Fred Ramage (97K/HATY/7781/08).

finally invaded western Europe in the summer and fall of 1944, they would enjoy superiority in the air.

The Allied Invasion of Europe

During the summer of 1943, the Allies began to advance on southern Italy. On July 10, British and American troops stormed Sicily from two directions and conquered the island in mid-August. King Vittorio Emmanuel dismissed Mussolini, calling him "the most despised man in Italy," and Italians, by now disgusted with the Fascist government, celebrated in the streets. Italy surrendered to the Allies on September 8, and Allied troops landed on the southern Italian peninsula. But Hitler sent new divisions into Italy, occupied the northern peninsula, and effectively stalled the Allied campaign. When the European war ended, the German and Allied armies were still battling on Italy's rugged terrain.

Elsewhere in occupied Europe, armed uprisings against the Nazis spread. The brutalized inhabitants of Warsaw's Jewish ghetto repeatedly rose up against their tormentors during the winter and spring of 1943. Realizing that they could not hope to defeat superior forces, they finally sealed off their quarter, executed collaborators, and fought invaders, street by street and house by house. Scattered revolts followed in the Nazi labor camps, where military prisoners of war and civilians were being worked to death on starvation rations.

Partisans were active in many sections of Europe, from Norway to Greece and from Poland to France. Untrained and unarmed by any military standard, organized groups of men, women, and children risked their lives to distribute antifascist propaganda, taking action against rich and powerful Nazi collaborators. They smuggled food and weapons to clandestine resistance groups and prepared the way for Allied offensives. As Axis forces grew weaker and partially withdrew, the partisans worked more and more openly, arming citizens to fight for their own freedom.

Meanwhile, Stalin continued to push for a second front. Stalled in Italy, the Allies prepared in early 1944 for Operation Overlord, a campaign to retake the Continent with a decisive counterattack through France. American

and British forces began by filling the southern half of England with military camps. All leaves were canceled. New weapons, such as amphibious armored vehicles, were carefully camouflaged. Fortunately, Hitler had few planes or ships left, so the Germans could defend the coast only with fixed bunkers whose location the Allies ascertained. Operation Overlord began with a preinvasion air assault that dropped 76,000 tons of bombs on Nazi targets.

The Allied invasion finally began on "D-Day," June 6, 1944. Under steady German fire the Allied fleet brought to the shores of Normandy more than 175,000 troops and more than 20,000 vehicles—an accomplishment unimaginable in any previous war. Although the Germans had responded slowly, anticipating an Allied strike at Calais instead of Normandy, at Omaha Beach they had prepared their defense almost perfectly. Wave after wave of Allied landings met machine-gun and mortar fire, and the tides filled with corpses and those pretending to be dead. Some 2,500 troops died, many before they could fire a shot. Nevertheless, in the next six weeks, nearly 1 million more Allied soldiers came ashore, broke out of Normandy, and prepared to march inland.

As the fighting continued, all eyes turned to Paris, the premier city of Europe. Allied bombers pounded factories producing German munitions on the outskirts of the French capital. As dispirited German soldiers

D-Day landing, June 6, 1944, marked the greatest amphibious maneuver in military history. Troop ships ferried Allied soldiers from England to Normandy beaches. Within a month, nearly 1 million men had assembled in France, ready to retake western and central Europe from German forces.

SOURCE: Photo by Robert Capa. CORBIS.

retreated, many now hoping only to survive, the French Resistance unfurled the French flag at impromptu demonstrations on Bastille Day, July 14. On August 10, railway workers staged one of the first successful strikes against Nazi occupiers, and three days later the Paris police defected to the Resistance, which proclaimed in leaflets that "the hour of liberation has come." General Charles de Gaulle, accompanied by Allied troops, arrived in Paris on August 25 to become president of the reestablished French Republic.

One occupied European nation after another now swiftly fell to the Allied armies. But the Allied troops had only reached a resting place between bloody battles.

The High Cost of European Victory

In September 1944 Allied commanders searched for a strategy to end the war quickly. Missing a spectacular chance to move through largely undefended territory and on to Berlin, they turned north instead, intending to open the Netherlands for Allied armies on their way to Germany's industrial heartland. Faulty intelligence reports overlooked a well-armed German division at Arnhem, Holland, waiting to cut Allied paratroopers to pieces. By the end of the battle, the Germans had captured 6,000 Americans.

In a final, desperate effort to reverse the Allied momentum, Hitler directed his last reserves, a quarter-million men, at Allied lines in the Belgian forest of the Ardennes. In what is known as the Battle of the Bulge, the Germans took the Allies by surprise, driving them back 50 miles before they were stopped. This last effort—the bloodiest single campaign Americans had been involved in since the battle of Gettysburg—exhausted the German capacity for counterattack. After Christmas day 1944, the Germans fell back, retreating into their own territory.

The end was now in sight. In March 1945 the Allies rolled across the Rhine and took the Ruhr Valley with its precious industrial resources. The defense of Germany, now hopeless, had fallen into the hands of young teenagers and elderly men. By the time of the German surrender, May 8, Hitler had committed suicide in a Berlin bunker and high Nazi officials were planning their escape routes. The casualties of the Allied European campaign had been enormous, if still small compared to those of the Eastern Front: more than 200,000 killed and almost 800,000 wounded, missing, or dead in nonbattle accidents and unrelated illness.

The War in Asia and the Pacific

The war that had begun with Pearl Harbor rapidly escalated into scattered fighting across a region of the world far larger than all of Europe, stretching from Southeast Asia to the Aleutian Islands. Japan followed up its early advantage by cutting the supply routes between Burma and China, crushing the British navy, and seizing the Philippines, Hong Kong, Wake Island, British Malaya, and Thailand. Although China offically joined the Allies on December 9, 1941, and General Stillwell arrived in March as commander of the China-Burma-India theater, the military mission there remained on the defensive. Meanwhile, after tenacious fighting on the Bataan Peninsula and on the island of Corregidor, the U.S. troops not captured or killed retreated to Australia.

At first, nationalist and anticolonial sentiment played into Japanese hands. Japan succeeded with only 200,000 men because so few inhabitants of the imperial colonies of Britain and France would fight to defend them. Japan installed puppet "independent" governments in Burma and the Philippines. But the new Japanese empire proved terrifyingly cruel. A panicky exodus of refugees precipitated a famine in Bengal, India, which took nearly 3,500,000 lives in 1943. Nationalists from Indochina to the Philippines turned against the Japanese, establishing guerrilla armies that cut Japanese supply lines and prepared the way for Allied victory.

Six months after the disaster at Pearl Harbor, the United States began to regain naval superiority in the central Pacific and halt Japanese expansion. In an aircraft carrier duel with spectacular aerial battles during the Battle of the Coral Sea on May 7 and 8, the United States blocked a Japanese threat to Australia. A month later, the Japanese fleet converged on Midway Island, which was strategically vital to American communications and the defense of Hawai'i. American strategists, however, thanks to specialists who had broken Japanese codes, knew when and where the Japanese planned to attack. The two carrier fleets, separated by hundreds of miles, clashed at the Battle of Midway on June 4. American planes sank four of Japan's vital aircraft carriers and destroyed hundreds of planes, ending Japan's offensive threat to Hawai'i and the west coast of the United States.

But the war for the Pacific was far from over. By pulling back their offensive perimeter, the Japanese concentrated their remaining forces. Their commanders calculated that bitter fighting, with high casualties on both sides, would wear down the American troops. The U.S. command, divided between General Douglas MacArthur in the southwest Pacific and Admiral Chester Nimitz in the central Pacific, needed to develop a counterstrategy to strangle the Japanese import-based economy and to retake strategic islands closer to the homeland.

The Allies launched their counteroffensive campaign on the Solomon Islands and Papua, near New Guinea. American and Australian ground forces fought together through the jungles of Papua, while the marines prepared to attack the Japanese stronghold of

Web Exploration   Consider the war in the Pacific in more detail. How did strategies in this theater differ from those in Europe?
www.prenhall.com/faragher/map25.2

War in the Pacific   Across an ocean battlefield utterly unlike the European theater, Allies battled Japanese troops near their homeland.

Guadalcanal. American forces ran low on food and ammunition during the fierce six-month struggle on Guadalcanal, while the Japanese were reduced to eating roots and berries. American logistics were not always well planned: a week before Christmas in the subtropical climate, a shipment of winter coats arrived! But with strong supply lines secured in a series of costly naval battles, the Americans were finally victorious in February 1943, proving that they could defeat Japanese forces in brutal jungle combat.

For the next two years, the U.S. Navy and Marine Corps, in a strategy known as "island hopping," pushed to capture a series of important atolls from their well-armed Japanese defenders and open a path to Japan. The first of these assaults, which cost more than 1,000 marines their lives, was on Tarawa, in November 1943, in the Gilbert Islands. In subsequent battles in 1944, American forces occupied Guam, Saipan, and Tinian in the Marianas Islands, within air range of the Japanese home islands. In another decisive naval engagement, the Battle of the Philippine Sea, fought in June 1944, the Japanese fleet suffered a crippling loss.

In October 1944, General MacArthur led a force of 250,000 to retake the Philippines. In a bid to defend the islands, practically all that remained of the Japanese navy threw itself at the American invaders in the Battle of Leyte Gulf, the largest naval battle in history. The Japanese lost eighteen ships, leaving the United States in control of the Pacific. While MacArthur continued to advance toward Luzon, the marines waged a successful battle on the small but important island of Iwo Jima. The death toll, however, was high, with casualties estimated at nearly 27,000. The ground fighting in the Philippines, meanwhile, cost 100,000 Filipino civilians their lives and left Manila devastated.

The struggle for the island of Okinawa, 350 miles southwest of the home islands of Japan, proved even more bloody. The invasion of the island, which began on Easter Sunday, April 1, 1945, was the largest amphibious operation mounted by Americans in the Pacific war. It was met by waves of Japanese *kamikaze* ("divine wind") pilots flying suicide missions in planes with a 500-pound bomb and only enough fuel for a one-way flight. On the ground, U.S. troops used flame-throwers, each with three hundred gallons of napalm, against the dug-in Japanese. More Americans died or were wounded here than at Normandy. By the end of June, the fighting had killed more than 200,000 people, with the civilian death toll ranging between 80,000 and 160,000 or more.

With the war over in Europe, the Allies concentrated on Japan, and their air and sea attacks on mainland Japan began to take their toll. U.S. submarines drastically reduced the ability of ships to reach Japan with supplies. Since the taking of Guam, American bombers had been able to reach Tokyo and other Japanese cities, with devastating results. Massive fire bombings burned thousands of civilians alive in their mostly wood or bamboo homes and apartments and left hundreds of thousands homeless.

Japan could not hold out forever. Without a navy or air force, the government could not transport the oil, tin, rubber, and grain needed to maintain its soldiers. Great Britain and particularly the United States, however, pressed for quick unconditional surrender. They had special reasons to hurry. Earlier they had sought a commitment from the Soviet Union to invade Japan, but now they looked beyond the war, determined to prevent the Red Army from taking any territories held by the Japanese. These calculations and the anticipation that an invasion would be extremely bloody set the stage for the use of a secret weapon that American scientists had been preparing: the atomic bomb.

THE LAST STAGES OF WAR

From the attack on Pearl Harbor until mid-1943, President Roosevelt and his advisers had focused on military strategy rather than on plans for peace. But once the defeat of Nazi Germany appeared in sight, high government officials began to reconsider their diplomatic objectives. Roosevelt wanted both to crush the Axis powers and to establish a system of collective security to prevent another world war. He knew he could not succeed without the cooperation of the other key leaders, Stalin and Churchill.

During 1944 and 1945, the "Big Three" met to hammer out the shape of the postwar world. Although none of these nations expected to reach a final agreement, neither did they anticipate how quickly they would be confronted with momentous global events. It soon became clear that the only thing holding the Allies together was the mission of destroying the Axis.

The Holocaust

Not until the last stages of the war did Americans learn the extent of Hitler's atrocities. As part of his "final solution to the Jewish question," Hitler had ordered the systematic extermination of not only Jews, but Gypsies, other "inferior races," homosexuals, and anyone deemed an enemy of the Reich. Beginning in 1933, and accelerating after 1941, the Nazis murdered millions of people from Germany and the European nations they conquered.

During the war the U.S. government released little information on what came to be known as the Holocaust. Although liberal magazines such as the *Nation* and small committees of intellectuals tried to call attention to what was happening in German concentration camps, major news media like the *New York Times* and *Time* magazine treated reports of the camps and killings as minor news items. The experience of World War I, during which the press had published stories of German atrocities that proved in most cases to have been fabricated by the British, had bred a skeptical attitude in the American public. As late as 1943, only 43 percent of Americans polled believed that Hitler was systematically murdering European Jews.

Roosevelt and his advisers maintained that the liberation of European Jews depended primarily on a speedy and total Allied victory. When American Jews pleaded for a military strike against the rail lines leading to the notorious extermination camp in Auschwitz, Poland, the War Department replied that Allied armed forces would not be employed "for the purpose of rescuing victims of enemy oppression unless such rescues are the direct result of military operations conducted with the objective

Belsen Camp: The Compound for Women, painted by American artist Leslie Cole, depicts Belsen as the Allied troops found it when they invaded Germany in 1945.

SOURCE: Leslie Cole, *Belsen Camp. The Compound for Women.* Imperial War Museum, London.

of economic opportunities, freedom of the seas, disarmament, and "freedom from fear and want." Now, four years later, Roosevelt—ill and exhausted—realized that neither Great Britain nor the Soviet Union intended to abide by any code of conduct that compromised its national security or conflicted with its economic interests in other nations or in colonial territories. Stalin and Churchill soon reached a new agreement, one that projected their respective "spheres of influence" over the future of central Europe.

In early February 1945, Roosevelt held his last meeting with Churchill and Stalin at Yalta, a Crimean resort on the Black Sea. Seeking their cooperation, the president recognized that prospects for postwar peace also depended on compromise. Although diplomats avoided the touchy phrase "spheres of influence"—the principle according to which the great powers of the nineteenth century had described their claims to dominance over other nations—it was clear that this principle guided all negotiations. Neither the United States nor Great Britain did more than object to the Soviet Union's plan to retain the Baltic states and part of Poland as a buffer zone to protect it against any future German aggression. In return, Britain planned to reclaim its empire in Asia, and the United States hoped to hold several Pacific islands in order to monitor any military resurgence in Japan. The delegates also negotiated the terms of membership in the United Nations, which had been outlined at a meeting several months earlier.

The biggest and most controversial item on the agenda at Yalta was the Soviet entry into the Pacific war, which Roosevelt believed necessary for a timely Allied victory. After driving a hard bargain involving rights to territory in China, Stalin agreed to declare war against Japan within two or three months of Germany's surrender.

Roosevelt announced to Congress that the Yalta meeting had been a "great success," proof that the wartime alliance remained intact. Privately, however, the president concluded that the outcome of the conference revealed that the Atlantic Charter had been nothing more than "a beautiful idea."

of defeating the armed forces of the enemy." In short, the government viewed civilian rescue as a diversion of precious resources.

Allied troops discovered the death camps when they invaded Germany and liberated Poland. When Eisenhower and General George S. Patton visited the Ohrdruf concentration camp in April 1945, they found barracks crowded with corpses and crematories still reeking of burned flesh. "I want every American unit not actually in the front lines to see this place," Eisenhower declared. "We are told that the American soldier does not know what he is fighting for. Now, at least, he will know what he is fighting against." At Buchenwald in the first three months of 1944, more than 14,000 prisoners were murdered. In all, the Holocaust claimed the lives of as many as 6 million Jews, 250,000 Gypsies, and 60,000 homosexuals, among others.

The Yalta Conference

In preparing for the end of the war, Allied leaders began to reassess their goals. The Atlantic Charter, drawn up before the United States had entered the war, stated noble objectives for the world after the defeat of fascism: national self-determination, no territorial aggrandizement, equal access of all peoples to raw materials and collaboration for the improvement

The death of Franklin Roosevelt of a stroke on April 12, 1945, cast a dark shadow over all hopes for long-term, peaceful solutions to global problems. Stung by a Republican congressional comeback in 1942, Roosevelt had rebounded in 1944 to win an unprecedented fourth term as president. In an overwhelming electoral college victory (432 to 99), he had defeated Republican New York governor Thomas E. Dewey. Loyal Democrats continued to link their hopes for peace to Roosevelt's leadership, but the president did not live to witness the surrender of Germany on May 8, 1945. And now, as new and still greater challenges were appearing, the nation's great pragmatic idealist was gone.

The Atomic Bomb

Roosevelt's death made cooperation among the Allied nations much more difficult. His successor, Harry Truman, who had been a Kansas City machine politician, a Missouri judge, and a U.S. senator, lacked diplomatic experience as well as Roosevelt's personal finesse. As a result, negotiations at the Potsdam Conference, held just outside Berlin from July 17 to August 2, 1945, lacked the spirited cooperation characteristic of the wartime meetings of Allied leaders that Roosevelt had attended. The American, British, and Soviet delegations had a huge agenda, including reparations, the future of Germany, and the status of other Axis powers such as Italy. Although they divided sharply over most issues, they held fast to the demand of Japan's unconditional surrender.

It was during the Potsdam meetings that Truman first learned about the successful testing of an atomic bomb in New Mexico. Until this time, the United States had been pushing the Soviet Union to enter the Pacific war as a means to avoid a costly U.S. land invasion, and at Potsdam Truman secured Stalin's promise to be in the war against Japan by August 15. But after Secretary of War Stimson received a cable reading "Babies satisfactorily born," U.S. diplomats concluded that Soviet assistance was no longer needed to bring the war to an end.

On August 3, 1945, Japan wired its refusal to surrender. Three days later, the Army Air Force B-29 bomber *Enola Gay* dropped the bomb that destroyed the Japanese city of Hiroshima. As estimated 40,000 people died instantly; in the following weeks 100,000 more died from radiation poisoning or burns; by 1950 the death toll reached 200,000.

An editorialist wrote in the Japanese *Nippon Times*, "This is not war, this is not even murder; this is pure nihilism . . . a crime against God which strikes at the very basis of moral existence." In the United States,

several leading religious publications echoed this view. The *Christian Century* interpreted the use of the bomb as a "moral earthquake" that made the long-denounced use of poison gas by Germany in World War I utterly insignificant by comparison. Albert Einstein, whose theories about the atom provided the foundation for Manhattan Project, observed, that the atomic bomb had changed everything except the nature of man.

Most Americans learned about the atomic bomb for the first time on August 7, when the news media reported the destruction and death it had wrought in Hiroshima. But concerns about the implications of this new weapon were soon overwhelmed by an outpouring of relief when Japan surrendered on August 14 after a second bomb destroyed Nagasaki, killing another 70,000 people.

The Allied insistence on unconditional surrender and the decision to use the atomic bomb against Japan remain two of the most controversial aspects of the war. Although Truman stated in his memoirs, written much later, that he gave the order with the expectation of saving "a half a million American lives" in ground combat, no such official estimate exists. An intelligence document of April 30, 1946, states, "The dropping of the bomb was the pretext seized upon by all leaders as the reason for ending the war, but . . . [even if the bomb had not been used] the Japanese would have capitulated upon the entry of Russia into the war." There is no question, however, that the use of nuclear force did strengthen the U.S. diplomatic mission. It certainly intimidated the Soviet Union, which would soon regain its status as a major enemy of the United States. Truman and his advisers in the State Department knew that their atomic monopoly could not last, but they hoped that in the meantime the United States could play the leading role in building the postwar world.

CONCLUSION

The new tactics and weapons of the Second World War, such as massive air raids and the atomic bomb, made warfare incomparably more deadly than before to both military and civilian populations. Between 40 and 50 million people died in World War II—four times the number in World War I—and half the casualties were women and children. More than 405,000 Americans died, and more than 670,000 were wounded. Although slight compared to the casualties suffered by other Allied nations—more than 20 million Soviets died during the war—the human cost of World War II for Americans was second only to that of the Civil War.

CHRONOLOGY

1931	September: Japan occupies Manchuria
1933	March: Adolf Hitler seizes power
	May: Japan quits League of Nations
1935	October: Italy invades Ethiopia
1935–1937	Neutrality Acts authorize the president to block the sale of munitions to belligerent nations
1937	August: Japan invades China
	October: Franklin D. Roosevelt calls for international cooperation against aggression
1938	March: Germany annexes Austria
	September: Munich Agreement lets Germany annex Sudetenland of Czechoslovakia
	November: *Kristallnacht*, Nazis attack Jews and destroy Jewish property
1939	March: Germany annexes remainder of Czechoslovakia
	August: Germany and the Soviet Union sign nonaggression pact
	September: Germany invades Poland; World War II begins
	November: Soviet Union invades Finland
1940	April–June: Germany's *Bliztkrieg* sweeps over Western Europe
	September: Germany, Italy, and Japan—the Axis powers—conclude a military alliance
	First peacetime military draft in American history
	November: Roosevelt is elected to an unprecedented third term
1941	March: Lend-Lease Act extends aid to Great Britain
	May: German troops secure the Balkans
	A. Philip Randolph plans March on Washington movement for July
	June: Germany invades Soviet Union

	Fair Employment Practices Committee formed
	August: The United States and Great Britain agree to the Atlantic Charter
	December: Japanese attack Pearl Harbor; United States enters the war
1942	January: War mobilization begins
	February: Executive order mandates internment of Japanese Americans
	May–June: Battles of Coral Sea and Midway give the United States naval superiority in the Pacific
	August: Manhattan Project begins
	November: United States stages amphibious landing in North Africa; Operation Torch begins
1943	January: Casablanca Conference announces unconditional surrender policy
	February: Soviet victory over Germans at Stalingrad
	April–May: Coal miners strike
	May: German Afrika Korps troops surrender in Tunis
	July: Allied invasion of Italy
	Summer: Race riots break out in nearly fifty cities
1944	June–August: Operation Overlord and liberation of Paris
	November: Roosevelt elected to fourth term
1945	February: Yalta Conference renews American-Soviet alliance
	February–June: United States captures Iwo Jima and Okinawa in Pacific
	April: Roosevelt dies in office; Harry Truman becomes president
	May: Germany surrenders
	July–August: Potsdam Conference
	August: United States drops atomic bombs on Hiroshima and Nagasaki; Japan surrenders

Coming at the end of two decades of resolutions to avoid military entanglements, the war pushed the nation's leaders to the center of global politics and into risky military and political alliances that would not outlive the war. The United States emerged the strongest nation in the world, but in a world where the prospects for lasting peace appeared increasingly remote. If World War II raised the nation's international commitments to a new height, its impact on ordinary Americans was not so easy to gauge. Many new communities formed as Americans migrated in mass numbers to new regions that were booming as a result of the wartime economy. Enjoying a rare moment of full employment, many workers new to well-paying industrial jobs anticipated further advances against discrimination. Exuberant at the Allies' victory over fascism and the return of the troops, the majority were optimistic as they looked ahead.

REVIEW QUESTIONS

1. Describe the response of Americans to the rise of nationalism in Japan, Italy, and Germany during the 1930s. How did President Franklin D. Roosevelt ready the nation for war?
2. What role did the federal government play in gearing up the economy for wartime production?
3. How did the war affect the lives of American women?
4. Discuss the causes and consequences of the Japanese American internment program.
5. Describe the role of popular culture in promoting the war effort at home.
6. How did military service affect the lives of those who served in World War II?
7. What were the main points of Allied military strategy in both Europe and Asia?
8. How successful were diplomatic efforts in ending the war and in establishing the terms of peace?

RECOMMENDED READING

Stephen E. Ambrose, *D-Day, June 6, 1944: The Climactic Battle of World War II* (1994). A vivid reconstruction of the preparation and battle.

Philip D. Beidler, *The Good War's Greatest Hits: World War II and American Remembering* (1998). Examines the popular culture produced about World War II.

Amy Bentley, *Eating for Victory: Food Rationing and the Politics of Domesticity* (1998). Brings together food, women's history, rationing programs, and Victory Gardens during World War II.

Allan Berube, *Coming Out under Fire: The History of Gay Men and Women in World War Two* (1991). A study of government policy toward homosexuals and the formation of a gay community.

Paul Boyer, *By the Bomb's Early Light: American Thought and Culture at the Dawn of the Atomic Age* (1985). An analysis of the intellectual and cultural assumptions in relation to atomic weaponry.

Wayne S. Cole, *Roosevelt and the Isolationists, 1932–45* (1983). Shows the president and his critics sparring over foreign policy issues.

Richard M. Dalfiume, *Desegregation of the U.S. Armed Forces: Fighting on Two Fronts, 1939–1953* (1969). Analyzes wartime race relations in the military.

Roger Daniels, *Concentration Camps USA: Japanese Americans and World War II* (1981). Perhaps the best account of Japanese American internment.

Sherna Berger Gluck, *Rosie the Riveter Revisited: Women, the War, and Social Change* (1987). An oral history-based study of women workers during World War II.

Laura Hein and Mark Selden, eds., *Living With the Bomb: American and Japanese Cultural Conflict in the Nuclear Age* (1997). Essays dealing with the ambiguous legacy of the atomic bomb in both the United States and Japan.

John W. Jeffries, *Wartime America: The World War II Homefront* (1996). A useful synthesis of scholarship.

Gerald F. Linderman, *The World within War: America's Combat Experience in World War II* (1997). Emphasizes the less glamorous aspects of war, mainly the strains placed on the combat soldiers on the front lines.

Katrina R. Mason, *Children of Los Alamos: An Oral History of the Town Where the Atomic Age Began* (1995). Recollections of those who spent their childhood in Los Alamos.

Neil R. McMillan, ed., *Remaking Dixie: The Impact of World War II on the American South* (1997). A collection of essays on the impact of World War II on the South.

Robert J. Moskin, *Mr. Truman's War: The Final Victories of World War II and the Birth of the Postwar World* (1996). A lively history of the final stages of World War II.

William M. Tuttle, Jr., *"Daddy's Gone to War": The Second World War in the Lives of America's Children* (1993). Draws from 2,500 letters that the author solicited about wartime childhood memories.

David S. Wyman, *The Abandonment of the Jews: America and the Holocaust, 1941–1945* (1984). A detailed examination of U.S. immigration policy and response to Hitler's program of genocide.

MEDIA RESOURCES

U.S. HISTORY DOCUMENTS CD-ROM
World War Two
25-1   Albert Einstein, Letter to President Roosevelt (1939)
25-2   Charles Lindbergh, Radio Address (1941)
25-3   Franklin D. Roosevelt, The Four Freedoms (1941)
25-4   Franklin Delano Roosevelt, Annual Message to Congress (1941)
25-5   A. Philip Randolph, "Why Should We March?" (1942)
25-6   Japanese Relocation Order, February 19, 1942
25-7   Sterling A. Brown, "Out of Their Mouths" (1942)

COMPANION WEBSITE HIGHLIGHTS
To view an exploration, enter one of the URLs below in your browser.

Web Explorations
The War in Europe
http://www.prenhall.com/faragher/map25.1
War in the Pacific
http://www.prenhall.com/faragher/map25.2

Additional Interactive Maps
To access the map, go to this chapter's resources at
http://www.prenhall.com/faragher

Wartime Army Camps, Naval Bases, and Airfields, page 787

 HISTORY RESOURCE CENTER
To find the resources listed below, go to
http://www.prenhall.com/historyresourcecenter

Images
"Buy Victory Bonds" Poster
"Loose Talk Can Cost Lives" Poster
African American Fighter Pilots
African American Soldiers of the 369th Infantry, 93rd Division
African American Women Open a Club for Enlisted Men
America Participates in the "Great Effort"
A Soldier of the Homefront
A Young Nisei and Her Family's Belongings
Japanese Americans at Santa Anita Race Track in 1942
Joe Louis
Navaho Indians Aiding the U.S War Effort
Wartime Price Controls
"White" and "Black" Work Side by Side
Women Factory Workers Build Bombers
Women Welders—The Real "Rosie the Riveters"

Turn to the next page for the *Exploring America* activity for this chapter.

EXPLORING AMERICA
PROPAGANDA
http://www.prenhall.com/faragher/propaganda

During World War II, the federal government used propaganda to generate support for the war effort. What were the goals of propaganda? What were the various forms it took? What roles did Thomas Hart Benton, Ben Shahn, and Norman Rockwell play in the government's propaganda program? What role does propaganda play in wartime? How did Americans respond to government propaganda? This module answers these questions and others as it shows the use of propaganda as a complex issue that has several dimensions. Drawing upon representative examples from World War II, the module explores the motivations behind propaganda and illustrates its myriad uses. Equally important, it shows how propaganda was used to promote important social changes required by the war effort.

The module places the use of propaganda in World War II into a larger context of its past employment in social issues. The narrative explains some of the behind-the-scenes actions that influenced the use and appearance of certain propaganda pieces. One important example shows how the four freedoms that served as war aims were translated into propaganda. The module also presents numerous posters, some by famous artists that identify the various purposes this form of communication played during the war. An audio clip, interactive maps, and a chronology provide more content and also supply important context to the discussion.

Reflect and Respond

1. Choose two of Rockwell's four "Freedom" pictures. What elements of American life did he incorporate into each work? How did he transform these into symbols of American freedom?

2. Like Walt Whitman, Norman Rockwell believed that American values were universal human values. President Roosevelt was careful to associate the "Four Freedoms" with people "everywhere in the world." Did Rockwell's depiction of these freedoms in American cultural terms undermine this universal message?

3. Who are Rockwell's Americans who embody the "Four Freedoms"? Consider the social settings in which they were portrayed. Who got left out?

✓ Check it out
Four Freedoms

One method used to promote the United States' involvement in World War II was promoting it as a war for democracy against the twin evils of nazism and fascism. Presented in the audio clip, President Franklin D. Roosevelt's speech on the four freedoms served as the official pronouncement of these democratic war aims. The speech is important because it built not only the democratic ideals of the United States but also addressed the economic conditions on the 1930s. It also responded to the brutal government actions of the Axis governments.

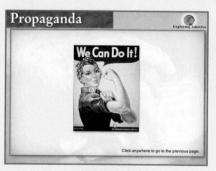

This exploration is also available on the *Exploring America* CD-ROM.

Exhibiting the *Enola Gay*

When news of the successful detonation of the atomic bomb over Hiroshima reached Los Alamos, New Mexico, horns and sirens blared in exultation. The community took pride in its achievement and, like other Americans, welcomed the prospect of Japan's surrender and the end of the devastating conflict. Chief scientist J. Robert Oppenheimer nevertheless expressed a sentiment equally common at the time, reporting that he was a "little scared of what I have made." Nearly a half-century later, Americans are no more certain about the meaning of this event.

In 1994, a major controversy erupted as the curatorial staff of the Smithsonian Institution's National Air and Space Museum (NASM) circulated their plans for an exhibition on the *Enola Gay*, the B-29 aircraft that carried "Little Boy," the weapon used on the Hiroshima mission. After reading drafts of a script that was to accompany the display, critics charged that the museum staff had crafted a message that was lop-sided at best, anti-American at worst. A writer in *Time* magazine accused the NASM curators of portraying the Japanese as "more or less innocent victims of American beastliness and lust for revenge." A columnist in the *Washington Post* expressed his opinion more bluntly, calling them a bunch of "politically correct pinheads." These judgments came as a surprise to those at the museum who had prepared the script. They had already received a positive report from a group of scholars who had reviewed the draft and judged it, in the words of a distinguished military historian, "comprehensive and dramatic" and needing only a "bit of 'tweaking.'" However, many Air Force veterans strongly disagreed, and they launched a campaign to block the proposed exhibit.

At the center of the controversy were two nagging questions. Both had been addressed by political and military leaders in August 1945 but never answered—and perhaps can never be answered—satisfactorily: was the atomic bomb necessary to end the war quickly and to save the lives of hundreds of thousands of Americans? Was the decision to deploy the bomb morally unambiguous, given the death toll of Japanese civilians?

The NASM curators had wrestled with these hard questions in preparing the original script. They decided, for example, not to use the conventional estimate of a half-million American lives saved as too high. This figure, they noted, had been projected only after the war had ended and often to rebut critics of the Hiroshima bombing. Instead, the curators relied on the actual wartime estimates by military leaders that projected perhaps tens of thousands of American casualties if a land invasion of Japan were to ensue. They also cited the U.S. Strategic Bombing Survey, which was completed soon after Japan's surrender, that concluded that even without the bomb the war would "certainly" have ended by November or December of 1945.

Many veterans who had served in the Pacific Theater objected strongly even to raising such questions. They continued to have no doubt that Truman had made the decision to drop the atomic bomb to save American lives and to shorten the war. They accused the museum staff of intentionally distorting history. Their collective memory of the battles of Guadacanal, Iwo Jima, and Okinawa, the risks posed by the ground invasion of Japan, and the torture inflicted on prisoners of war in the Japanese death camps ran directly counter to the script that read, "It is possible that there was a last opportunity to end the war without either atomic bombings or an invasion of Japan." The nation's largest veteran organization, the American Legion, issued a public letter to President Clinton calling for the cancellation of the exhibit as planned.

The controversy eventually pulled in General Paul W. Tibbets, the pilot of the *Enola Gay* (he had painted his mother's maiden name on the nose of the plane). He, too, objected to the museum staff's "second-guessing the decision to use the atomic weapons." He wanted a simple, straightforward label for the fifty-six feet of fuselage inside the museum hall: "'This airplane was the first one to drop an atomic bomb.'"

Eventually, the U.S. Congress stepped into the fray. The Senate passed a nonbinding resolution reminding the NASM staff of its "obligation to portray history in the proper context of the time." The museum, at the time averaging about 8.2 million visitors a year, more than any other museum in the world, depended mainly on government funding and therefore relied on those who controlled the federal budget, the Congress.

The NASM staff did have support for their plans, particularly among other professional historians. The Organization of American Historians condemned the intervention by members of Congress. An independent group of "historians and scholars" protested this "transparent attempt at historical cleansing."

On June 28, 1995, the exhibit finally opened, al-

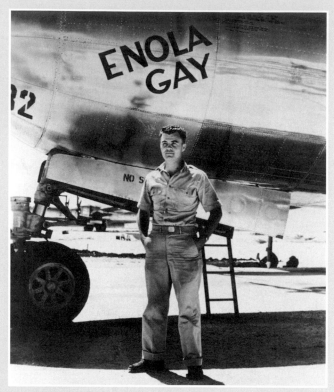

In 1937, Paul W. Tibbets, Jr., enlisted as a flying cadet in the Army Aircorps, and during World war II he became a test pilot for the B-29, the airplane that he helped to redesign to deliver the atomic bomb.

SOURCE: © Bettmann/CORBIS (BE 043411).

though in greatly reduced form. The original plans for photographs of "ground zero" in Hiroshima, for example, were scrapped, and what remained were several restored components of the B-29 aircraft, such as its fuselage, propellers, and cockpit. As to the *Enola Gay's* mission, one photograph featured the crew before take-off, another of the mushroom cloud as seen from the tail gunner's position. The wall text read simply:

> Tibbets piloted the aircraft on its mission to drop an atomic bomb on Hiroshima on Aug. 6, 1945. That bomb and the one dropped on Nagasaki three days later destroyed much of the two cities and caused tens of thousands of deaths. However, the use of the bombs led to the immediate surrender of Japan and made unnecessary the planned invasion of the Japanese home islands. Such an invasion, especially

if undertaken for both main islands, would have led to very heavy casualties among American and Allied troops and Japanese civilians and military. It was thought highly unlikely that Japan, while in a very weakened military condition, would have surrendered unconditionally without such an invasion."

"The aircraft speaks for itself in this exhibit," Smithsonian director I. Michael Heyman said, "and, 50 years after its mission, it continues to evoke strong emotions, in those who look at it."

The legacy of the atomic bomb, including the scientific research done at Los Alamos during the 1940s, remains so uncertain and contentious that an attempted explanation of the mission of the *Enola Gay* was abandoned for a celebration of the aircraft's design as an engineering marvel. Historians and military veterans seemed to speak different languages. Meanwhile, a Gallup Poll conducted at the time of the controversy surrounding the *Enola Gay* exhibit indicated that a quarter of Americans did not even know that World War II ended with the explosion of an atomic bomb over Japan. ■

Poster from 1947: *Is This Tomorrow—America under Communism!* Michael Barson (ID #002).

University of Washington, Seattle: Students and Faculty Face the Cold War

IN MAY 1948, A PHILOSOPHY PROFESSOR AT THE UNIVERSITY OF WASHington in Seattle answered a knock on his office door. Two state legislators, members of the state's Committee on Un-American Activities, entered. "Our information," they charged, "puts you in the center of a Communist conspiracy."

The accused professor, Melvin Rader, had never been a Communist. A self-described liberal, Rader drew fire because he had joined several organizations supported by Communists. During the 1930s, in response to the rise of Nazism and fascism, Rader had become a prominent political activist in his community. At one point he served as president of the University of Washington Teacher's Union, which had formed during the upsurge of labor organizing during the New Deal. When invited to join the Communist Party, Rader bluntly refused. "The experience of teaching social philosophy had clarified my concepts of freedom and democracy," he later explained. "I was an American in search of a way—but it was not the Communist way."

Despite this disavowal, Rader was caught up in a Red Scare that curtailed free speech and political activity on campuses throughout the United States. At some universities, such as Yale, the Federal Bureau of Investigation (FBI) set up camp with the consent of the college administration, spying on students and faculty, screening the credentials of job or scholarship applicants, and seeking to entice students to report on their friends or roommates. The University of Washington administration turned down the recommendation of the Physics Department to hire J. Robert Oppenheimer because the famed atomic scientist had become a vocal opponent of the arms race and the proliferation of nuclear weapons.

Although one state legislator claimed that "not less than 150 members" of the University of Washington faculty were subversives, the state's Committee on Un-American Activities turned up just six members of the Communist Party. These six were brought up before the university's Faculty Committee on Tenure and Academic Freedom, charged with violations ranging from neglect of duty to failing to inform the university administration of their party membership. Three were ultimately dismissed, while the other three were placed on probation.

What had provoked this paranoia? Instead of peace in the wake of World War II, a pattern of cold war—icy relations—prevailed between the United States and the Soviet Union. Uneasy allies during World War II, the two superpowers now viewed each other as arch-enemies, and nearly all other nations lined up with one or the other of them. Within the United States, the cold war demanded pledges of absolute loyalty from citizens in every institution, from the university to trade unions and from the mass media to government itself.

If not for the outbreak of the cold war, this era would have marked one of the most fruitful in the history of higher education. The Servicemen's Readjustment Act, popularly known as the G.I. Bill of Rights, passed by Congress in 1944, offered stipends covering tuition and living expenses to veterans attending vocational schools or college. By the 1947–48 academic year, the federal government was subsidizing nearly half of all male college students. Between 1945 and 1950, 2.3 million students benefited from the G.I. Bill, at a cost of more than $10 billion.

At the University of Washington the student population in 1946 had grown by 50 percent over its prewar peak of 10,000, and veterans represented fully two-thirds of the student body. A quickly expanded faculty taught into the evening to use classroom space efficiently. Meanwhile, the state legislature pumped in funds for the construction of new buildings, including dormitories and prefabricated units for married students.

According to many observers, a feeling of community flourished among these war-weary undergraduates. Often the first in their families to attend college, they joined fellow students in campaigns to improve the campus. Married, often fathers of young children, they expected university administrators to treat them as adults. They wanted less supervision of undergraduate social life, more affordable housing, and better cultural opportunities than had previously been the case. On some campuses, film societies and student-run cooperatives vied with fraternities and sororities as centers of undergraduate social activity.

The cold war put a damper on these community-building efforts. FBI director J. Edgar Hoover testified that the college campuses were centers of "red propaganda," full of teachers "tearing down respect for agencies of government, belittling tradition and moral custom and . . . creating doubts in the validity of the American way of life." Due to Communistic teachers and "Communist-line textbooks," a senator lamented, thousands of parents sent "their sons and daughters to college as good Americans," only to see them return home "four years later as wild-eyed radicals."

Although these extravagant charges were never substantiated, several states, including Washington, enacted or revived loyalty-security programs, obligating all state employees to swear in writing their loyalty to the United States and to disclaim membership in any subversive organization. Nationwide, approximately 200 faculty members were dismissed outright and many others were denied tenure. Thousands of students simply left school, dropped out of organizations, or changed friends after "visits" from FBI agents or interviews with administrators. The main effect on campus was the restraint of free speech generally and fear of criticizing U.S. racial, military, or diplomatic policies in particular.

This gloomy mood reversed the wave of optimism that had swept through America only a few years earlier. V-J Day, marking victory over Japan, had erupted into a two-day national holiday of wild celebrations, complete with ticker-tape parades, spontaneous dancing, and kisses for returned G.I. Americans, living in the richest and most powerful nation in the world, finally seemed to have gained the peace they had fought and sacrificed to win. But peace proved fragile and elusive. ■

GLOBAL INSECURITIES AT WAR'S END

The war that had engulfed the world from 1939 to 1945 created an international interdependence that no country could ignore. The legendary African American folk singer Leadbelly (Huddie Ledbetter) added a fresh lyric to an old spiritual melody: "We're in the same boat, brother. . . . And if you shake one end you're going to rock the other." Never before, not even at the end of World War I, had hopes been so strong for a genuine "community of nations." With Japan and Germany defeated and occupied and the European empires disintegrating, most Americans recognized, a 1945 opinion poll revealed, that prospects for a durable peace rested to a large degree on harmony between the Soviet Union and the United States.

Rivalry between these two competitors for world leadership had been placed on hold while the United States and the Soviet Union joined in the Grand Alliance to defeat fascism. This coalition, always uneasy, began to crumble during the last stages of the war. Within a year after V-J Day, the world's two most powerful nations had emerged as arch-adversaries in conceiving the shape of the postwar order. The United States viewed the Soviet Union as a ruthless, totalitarian power intent, through an aggressive policy of expansion, to bring about a global Communist revolution. In turn, the USSR considered the United States an imperialist power bent on destroying communism and committed to a capitalist world order compatible with its own economic interests. It was within a context that allowed little possibiity for accommodation or negotiation that the United States defined its national purpose with new energy as nothing less than "to lead the free world."

Financing the Future

In 1941 Henry Luce, publisher of *Time, Life,* and *Fortune* magazines, had forecast the dawn of "the American Century." Americans must, he wrote, "accept whole-heartedly our duty and our opportunity as the most powerful and vital nation in the world and in consequence to assert upon the world the full impact of our influence, for such means as we see fit." Indeed, immediately after the bombing of Hiroshima, President Truman pronounced the United States "the most powerful nation in the world—the most powerful nation, perhaps, in all history." The president and his advisors declared a definitive end to the era of isolation and pledged themselves to bring to fruition Luce's prophecy. The United States would serve not only as the model of democracy—the "City on the Hill" that John Winthrop had imagined in 1630—but the carrier of the torch of freedom throughout the world.

Americans had good reason to be confident about their prospects for setting the terms of reconstruction. Compared with Great Britain and France, reduced to second-rate powers too weak to hold their once vast empires, the United States had not only escaped the ravages of the war but had actually prospered. By June 1945, the capital assets of manufacturing had increased 65 percent over prewar levels and were equal in value to approximately half the entire world's goods and services.

Yet many Americans recognized that it was the massive government spending associated with wartime industry, rather than New Deal programs, that had ended the nightmare of the 1930s. A great question loomed: What would happen when wartime production slowed and millions of troops returned home?

"We need markets—big markets—in which to buy and sell," answered Assistant Secretary of State for Economic Affairs Will Clayton. Just to maintain the current level of growth, the United States needed an estimated $14 billion in exports—an unprecedented amount. Many business leaders even looked to the Soviet Union as a potential trading partner. With this prospect vanishing, Eastern European markets threatened, and large chunks of former colonial territories closed off, U.S. business and government leaders became determined to integrate Western Europe and Asia into a liberal international economy open to American trade and investment.

During the final stages of the war, President Roosevelt's advisers laid plans to establish U.S. primacy in the postwar global economy. In July 1944 representatives from forty-four Allied nations met at Bretton Woods, New Hampshire, and established the International Bank for Reconstruction and Development (World Bank) and the International Monetary Fund (IMF) to help rebuild war-torn Europe and to assist the nations of Asia, Latin America, and Africa. By stabilizing exchange rates to permit the expansion of international trade, the IMF would deter currency conflicts and trade wars—two maladies of the 1930s that were largely responsible for the political instability and national rivalries leading to World War II. As the principal supplier of funds for the IMF and the World Bank—more than $7 billion to each—the United States, in essence, could unilaterally shape the world economy by determining the allocation of loans. "The main prize of the victory" over the Axis powers is, a State Department document noted in 1945, a "limited and temporary power to establish the kind of world we want to live in."

The Soviet Union participated in the Bretton Woods conference but refused to ratify the agreements that, in essence, allowed the United States to rebuild the world economy along capitalist lines. By spurning both the World Bank and the IMF, Soviet Union cut off the possibility of aid to its own people as well as to its Eastern European client states and, equally important, isolated itself economically.

The Division of Europe

The Atlantic Charter of 1941 committed the Allies to recognize the right of all nations to self-determination and to renounce all claims to new territories as the spoils of war. The Allied leaders themselves, however, violated the charter's main points before the war had ended by dividing occupied Europe into spheres of influence (see Chapter 25).

So long as Franklin Roosevelt remained alive, this strategy had seemed reconcilable with world peace. The president had balanced his own international idealism with his belief that the United States was entitled to extraordinary influence in Latin America and the Philippines and that other great powers might have similar privileges or responsibilities elsewhere. Roosevelt also recognized the diplomatic consequences of the brutal ground war that had been fought largely on Soviet territory: the Soviet Union's unnegotiable demand for territorial security along its European border.

From the early days of the war, the USSR was intent on reestablishing its 1941 borders, and by the time of the Potsdam Conference in July 1945 the Soviets had not only regained but extended their territory. Much of eastern Europe, including a large portion of Poland and the little Baltic nations, was now under its control as client states. Only the Yugoslavians and Albanians, who had turned back fascist forces without the Red Army's assistance, could claim nominal independence. But the question remained: Did Stalin aim to bring all of Europe into the Communist domain?

When the Allies turned to plan the future of Germany, this question loomed over all deliberations. France, Great Britain, the Soviet Union, and the United States agreed to dismember Germany and eventually decided to divide the conquered nation into four occupation zones, each governed by one of the Allied nations. But the Allies could not agree on long-term plans. Having borne the brunt of German aggression, France and the USSR both opposed reunification. The latter, in addition, demanded heavy reparations along with a limit on postwar reindustrialization. Roosevelt appeared to agree with the Soviets. But American business leaders, envisioning a new center for U.S. commerce, shared Winston Churchill's hope of rebuilding Germany into a powerful counterforce against the Soviet Union and a strong market for U.S. and British goods.

After the war, continuing disagreements about the future Germany darkened hopes for cooperation between the Soviet Union and the United States. By July 1946, Americans had begun to withhold reparations from their zone and to institute a program of amnesty for former Nazis. Then, in December, the American and British merged their zones and extended an invitation to France and the USSR to join. Although France accepted the offer, the Soviets, fearing a resurgence of united Germany, held out.

The United States and the Soviet Union were now at loggerheads. Twice in the twentieth century, Germany had invaded Russia, and the USSR now interpreted these U.S. moves toward consolidation of Germany an act of supreme hostility. For its part, the United States envisioned a united Germany as a bulwark against Soviet expansion.

The United Nations and Hopes for Collective Security

A thin hope remained amid the gloom of disunity between the two superpowers. A month after the conference at Bretton Woods, Allied leaders met to lay plans for a system of collective security, the United Nations (UN). The dream of postwar international cooperation had been seeded earlier by President Roosevelt. In late summer and fall 1944 at the Dumbarton Oaks Conference in Washington, D.C., and again in April 1945 in

Appointed to the UN delegation by President Harry Truman in 1946, Eleanor Roosevelt (1884–1962) pressured the organization to adopt the Declaration of Human Rights in 1948. In this photograph, taken in 1946, the former First Lady is exchanging ideas with Warren Austin, also a delegate to the United Nations.

SOURCE: UPI/CORBIS–Bettmann.

San Francisco, the Allies worked to shape the United Nations as an international agency that would arbitrate disputes among members as well as impede aggressors, by military force if necessary.

The terms of membership, however, limited the UN's ability to mediate disputes. Although all member nations enjoyed representation in the General Assembly, only five members (the United States, Great Britain, the Soviet Union, France, and Nationalist China) served permanently on on the Security Council, which had the "primary responsibility for the maintenance of international peace and security," and each enjoyed absolute veto power over the decisions of the other members. By this arrangement, the Security Council could censure an act of aggression by any of its members only if that nation made the unlikely decision of abstaining from the vote.

The UN achieved its greatest success with its humanitarian programs. Its relief agency provided the war-torn countries of Europe and Asia with billions of dollars for medical supplies, food, and clothing. The UN also dedicated itself to protecting human rights, and its high standards of human dignity owed much to the lobbying of Eleanor Roosevelt, one of the first delegates from the United States.

On other issues, however, the UN operated strictly along lines dictated by the cold war. The Western nations allied with the United States held the balance of power and maintained their position by controlling the admission of new member nations. They successfully excluded Communist China, for example. Moreover,

the polarization between East and West made negotiated settlements virtually impossible.

THE POLICY OF CONTAINMENT

With the world seemingly dividing into two hostile camps, the dream of a community of nations dissolved. But perhaps it had never been more than a fantasy contrived to maintain a fragile alliance amid the urgency of World War II. In March 1946, in a speech delivered in Fulton, Missouri, Winston Churchill spoke to the new reality. With President Harry Truman at his side, the former British prime minister declared that "an iron curtain has descended across the [European] continent." He called directly upon the United States, standing "at this time at the pinnacle of world power," to recognize its "awe-inspiring accountability to the future" and to act assertively to turn back Soviet expansion.

Although Truman responded cautiously to Churchill's pronouncement, he and his administration ultimately decided to meet the challenge. Within a short time, they were wholeheartedly committed to securing U.S. leadership in the world and, equally important, preventing communism from spreading further. As a doctrine uniting military, economic, and diplomatic strategies, the "containment" of communism also fostered an ideological opposition, an "us"-versus-"them" theme that divided the world into "freedom" and "slavery," "democracy" and "autocracy," and "tolerance" and "coercive force." The Truman Doctrine laid down the first plank in a global campaign against communism.

The Truman Doctrine

Many Americans believed that Franklin D. Roosevelt, had he lived, would have been able to stem the tide of tensions between the Soviet Union and the United States. His successor sorely lacked FDR's talent for diplomacy. More comfortable with machine politicians than with polished New Dealers, the new president liked to talk tough and act defiantly. Just ten days after he took office, Truman complained that U.S.–Soviet negotiations had been a "one-way street." He vowed to "baby" them no longer.

A perceived crisis in the Mediterranean prompted President Truman to show his colors. On February 21, 1947, amid a civil war in Greece, Great Britain informed the U.S. State Department that it could no longer afford to prop up the anti-Communist government there and announced its intention to withdraw all aid. Without U.S. intervention, Truman concluded, Greece, Turkey, and perhaps the entire oil-rich Middle East would fall under Soviet control.

OVERVIEW

MAJOR COLD WAR POLICIES

Policy	Date	Provisions
Truman Doctrine	1947	Pledged the United States to the containment of communism in Europe and elsewhere. The doctrine was the foundation of Truman's foreign policy. It impelled the United States to support any nation whose stability was threatened by communism or the Soviet Union.
Federal Employees Loyalty program and Security Program	1947	Established by Executive Order 9835, this barred Communists and fascists from federal employment and outlined procedures for investigating current and prospective federal employees.
Marshall Plan	1947	U.S. program to aid war-torn Europe, also known as the European Recovery Program. The Marshall Plan was a cornerstone in the U.S. use of economic policy to contain communism.
National Security Act	1947	Established Department of Defense (to coordinate the three armed services), the National Security Council (to advise the president on security issues), and the Central Intelligence Agency (to gather and evaluate intelligence data).
Smith-Mundt Act	1948	Launches an overseas campaign of anti-Communist propaganda.
North Atlantic Treaty Organization (NATO)	1948	A military alliance of twelve nations formed to deter possible aggression of the Soviet Union against Western Europe.
NSC-68	1950	National Security Council Paper calling for an expanded and aggressive U.S. defense policy, including greater military spending and higher taxes.
Internal Security Act (also known as the McCarran Act and the Subversive Activities Control Act)	1950	Legislation providing for the registration of all Communist and totalitarian groups and authorizing the arrest of suspect persons during a national emergency.
Psychological Strategy Board created	1951	Created to coordinate anti–Communist propaganda campaigns
Immigration and Nationality Act (also known as McCarran-Walter Immigration Act)	1952	Reaffirmed the national origins quota system but tightened immigration controls, barring homosexuals and people considered subversive from entering the United States.

On March 12, 1947, the president made his argument before Congress in bold terms: "At the present moment in world history, nearly every nation must choose between alternative ways of life. . . . One way of life is based upon the will of the majority, and is distinguished by free institutions . . . and freedom from political oppression. The second way of life is based upon the will of a minority forcibly imposed on the majority . . . and the suppression of personal freedoms." Never mentioning the Soviet Union by name, he appealed for all-out resistance to a "certain ideology" wherever it appeared in the world. The preservation of peace and the freedom of all Americans depended, the president insisted, on containing communism.

Congress approved a $400 million appropriation in aid for Greece and Turkey, which helped the monarchy and right-wing military crush the rebel movement. Truman's victory buoyed his popularity for the upcoming 1948 election. It also helped to generate popular support for a campaign against communism, both at home and abroad.

The significance of what became known as the Truman Doctrine far outlasted the events in the Mediterranean: the United States had declared its right to intervene to save other nations from communism. As early as February 1946, foreign-policy adviser George F. Kennan had sent an 8,000-word "long telegram" to the State Department insisting that Soviet fanaticism made cooperation impossible. The USSR intended to extend its realm not by military means alone, he explained, but by "subversion" within "free" nations. In addition, the Truman Doctrine described the differences between the United States and the Soviet Union as absolute and irreconcilable, as an ideological breach that resonated far beyond foreign policy. It was now the responsibility of the United States, Truman insisted, to safeguard the "Free World" by diplomatic, economic, and, if necessary, military means. He had, in sum, fused anticommunism and internationalism into an aggressive foreign policy.

The Marshall Plan

The Truman Doctrine complemented the European Recovery Program, commonly known as the Marshall Plan. Introduced in a commencement speech at Harvard University on June 5, 1947, by secretary of state and former army chief of staff George C. Marshall, the plan sought to reduce "hunger, poverty, desperation, and chaos" and to restore "the confidence of the European people in the economic future of their own countries and of Europe as a whole." Although Marshall added that "our policy is directed not against any country or doctrine," the plan that bore his name additionally aimed to turn back both socialist and Communist electoral bids for power in northern and western Europe while promoting democracy through economic renewal.

Considered by many historians the most successful postwar U.S. diplomatic venture, the Marshall Plan supplemented the Bretton Woods agreements by further improving the climate for a viable capitalist economy in western Europe and, in effect, bringing recipients of aid into a bilateral agreement with the United States. In addition, the western European nations, seventeen in all, ratified the General Agreement on Tariffs and Trade (GATT), which reduced commercial barriers among member nations and opened all to U.S. trade and investment. The plan was costly to Americans, in its initial year taking 12 percent of the federal budget, but effective. Industrial production in the European nations covered by the plan rose by 200 percent between 1947 and 1952. Although deflationary programs cut wages and increased unemployment, profits soared and the standard of living improved. Supplemented by a multimedia propaganda campaign, the Marshall Plan introduced many Europeans to American consumer goods and lifestyle.

The Marshall Plan drove a deeper wedge between the United States and the Soviet Union. Although invited to participate, Stalin denounced the plan for what

it was, an American scheme to rebuild Germany and to incorporate it into an anti-Soviet bloc that encompassed all western Europe. The president readily acknowledged that the Marshall Plan and the Truman Doctrine were "two halves of the same walnut."

The Berlin Crisis and the Formation of NATO

As Stalin recognized, the Marshall Plan also sought to rebuild and integrate the western zones of Germany into unified region compatible with U.S. political and economic interests. Within a year of its introduction, the United States and Britain moved closer to this goal by introducing a common currency in the western zones. Stalin reacted to this challenge on June 24, 1948, by halting all traffic to West Berlin, formally controlled by the Western allies but situated deep within the Soviet-occupied zone.

The Berlin blockade created both a crisis and an opportunity for the Truman administration to test its mettle. In a show of strength, the president dispatched to Britain sixty B-29s, "atomic bombers" that could be carrying nuclear weapons but were not. Then, with help from the Royal Air Force, the United States began an around-the-clock airlift of historic proportions—Operation Vittles—that delivered nearly 2 million tons of supplies to West Berliners. The Soviet Union finally lifted the blockade in May 1949, clearing the way for the Western powers to merge their occupation zones into a single nation, the Federal Republic of West Germany. The USSR countered by establishing the German Democratic Republic in their sector.

The Berlin Crisis made a U.S.–led military alliance against the USSR attractive to western European nations. In April 1949 ten European nations, Canada, and the United States formed the North Atlantic Treaty Organization (NATO), a mutual defense pact in which "an armed attack against one or more of them . . . shall be considered an attack against them all." NATO complemented the Marshall Plan, strengthening economic ties among the member nations by, according to one analyst, keeping "the Russians out, the Americans in, and the Germans down." It also deepened divisions between eastern and western Europe, making a permanent military mobilization on both sides almost inevitable.

By mid-1949, Truman and his advisers were basking in the glow of these victories for containment. The U.S. Senate had ratified the first formal military treaty with a European nation since the Revolutionary War era—a giant step away from isolationism. Congress also approved $1.3 billion in military aid, which involved the creation of U.S. Army bases and the deployment of American troops abroad. Critics, such as isolationist senator Robert A. Taft, warned that the United States could not afford to police all Europe without sidetracking domestic policies and undercutting the UN.

But opinion polls revealed strong support for Truman's tough line against the Soviets.

Between 1947 and 1949, the Truman administration had defined the policies that would shape the cold war for decades to come. The Truman Doctrine explained the ideological basis of containment; the Marshall Plan put into place its economic underpinnings in western Europe; and NATO created the mechanisms for military enforcement. When NATO extended membership to a rearmed West Germany in May 1955, the Soviet Union responded by creating a counterpart, the Warsaw Pact, including East Germany. The division of East and West was complete.

Atomic Diplomacy

The policy of containment depended on the ability of the United States to back up its commitments through military means, and Truman invested his faith in the U.S. monopoly of atomic weapons. The United States began to build atomic stockpiles and to conduct tests on the Bikini Islands in the Pacific. By 1950, as a scientific adviser subsequently observed, the United States "had a stockpile capable of somewhat more than reproducing World War II in a single day."

Despite warnings to the contrary by leading scientists, U.S. military analysts estimated it would take the

WebExploration

Examine Europe during the Cold War. Which countries were aligned with the United States, and which with the Soviet Union?
www.prenhall.com/faragher/map26.1

Divided Europe During the cold war, Europe was divided into opposing military alliances, the North American Treaty Organization (NATO) and the Warsaw Pact (Communist bloc).

Soviet Union three to ten years to produce an atomic bomb. In August 1949, the Soviet Union proved them wrong by testing its own atomic bomb. "There is only one thing worse than one nation having the atomic bomb," Nobel prize-winning scientist Harold C. Urey said, "that's two nations having it."

Within a few years, both the United States and the Soviet Union had tested hydrogen bombs a thousand times more powerful than the weapons dropped on Hiroshima and Nagasaki in 1945. Both proceeded to stockpile bombs attached to missiles, inaugurating the fateful nuclear arms race that scientists had feared since 1945.

The United States and the Soviet Union were now firmly locked into the cold war. The nuclear arms race imperiled their futures, diverted their economies, and fostered fears of impending doom. Prospects for global peace had dissipated, and despite the Allied victory in World War II, the world had again divided into hostile camps.

COLD WAR LIBERALISM

Truman's aggressive, gutsy personality suited the confrontational mood of the cold war. He linked the Soviet threat in Europe to the need for a strong presidency. Pressed to establish his own political identity, "Give 'em Hell" Harry successfully portrayed himself as a fierce fighter against all challengers, yet loyal to Roosevelt's legacy.

Truman set out to enlarge the New Deal but managed mainly to consolidate FDR's bequest of a strong federal government. Social and economic justice at home went the way of peace and cooperation abroad. The compromise that Truman ultimately struck was a modest domestic agenda to promote social welfare and an antiisolationist, fiercely anti-Communist foreign policy. Fatefully, during the course of his administration, domestic and foreign policy became increasingly entangled to lay the basis of a distinctive brand of liberalism—cold war liberalism.

"To Err Is Truman"

Within a year of assuming office, Harry Truman rated lower in public approval than any twentieth-century president except Roosevelt's own predecessor, Herbert Hoover, who had been blamed for the Great Depression. The responsibilities of reestablishing peacetime conditions seemed to overwhelm the new president's administration. "To err is Truman," critics jeered.

In handling the enormous task of reconverting the economy to peacetime production, Truman appeared both inept and mean-spirited. The president faced millions of restless would-be consumers tired of rationing and eager to spend their wartime savings on shiny cars, new furniture, choice cuts of meat, and colorful clothing. The demand for consumer items rapidly outran supply, fueling inflation and creating a huge black market. When Congress proposed to extend wartime price controls, Truman vetoed the bill and prices skyrocketed.

In 1945 and 1946, the country appeared ready to explode. While homemakers protested rising prices by boycotting neighborhood stores, industrial workers struck in unprecedented numbers. Employers, fearing a rapid decline to Depression-level profits, determined to slash wages or at least hold them steady; workers wanted a bigger cut of the huge war profits they had heard about. The spectacle of nearly 4.6 million workers on picket lines alarmed the new president. In May 1946, Truman proposed to draft strikers into the army who refused to return to work under a presidential order. The usually conservative Senate killed this plan.

Congress defeated most of Truman's proposals to revive the New Deal. One week after Japan's surrender, the president introduced a twenty-one-point program that included greater unemployment compensation, higher minimum wages, and housing assistance. Later he added proposals for national health insurance and atomic energy legislation. Congress turned back the bulk of these bills, passing the Employment Act of 1946 only after substantial modification. The act created a new executive body, the Council of Economic Advisers, which would confer with the president and formulate policies for maintaining employment, production, and purchasing power. But the measure did not include funding mechanisms to guarantee full employment, thus falling far short of the bill's intent.

By 1946 Truman's popularity had dipped to 32 percent. One joke began with a reflection on what Roosevelt would do if still alive, only to end by asking "What would Truman do if he were alive?" Republicans, sensing victory in the upcoming off-year elections, asked the voters, "Had enough?" Apparently the voters had. They gave Republicans majorities in both houses of Congress and in the state capitols. And in a symbolic repudiation of Roosevelt, they passed an amendment to the Constitution establishing a two-term limit for the presidency.

The Republicans, dominant in Congress for the first time since 1931, prepared a counteroffensive against the New Deal, beginning with an attack on organized labor. Unions had by this time reached a peak in size and prestige, with membership topping 15 million and encompassing nearly 40 percent of all wage earners. Concluding that labor had gone too far, the Republican-dominated Eightieth Congress aimed to outlaw many practices approved by the Wagner Act of 1935 (see Chapter 24).

Police and strikers confront each other in Los Angeles during one of many postwar strikes in 1946. Employers wanted to cut wages, and workers refused to give up the higher living standard achieved during the war.

SOURCE: AP/Wide World Photos.

The Labor-Management Relations Act of 1947, better known as Taft-Hartley Act, brought to an end the closed shop, the secondary boycott, and the use of union dues for political activities. It also mandated an eighty-day cooling-off period in the case of strikes affecting national safety or health. Taft-Hartley furthermore required all union officials to swear under oath that they were not Communists—a cold war mandate that abridged freedoms ordinarily guaranteed by the First Amendment. Unions that refused to cooperate were denied the services of the National Labor Relations Board, which arbitrated strikes and issued credentials to unions.

Truman regained some support from organized labor when he vetoed the Taft-Hartley Act, saying it would "conflict with important principles of our democratic society." Congress, however, overrode his veto, and Truman himself went on to invoke the act against strikers.

The 1948 Election

Although lacking a strong candidate, Democrats gingerly approached the 1948 election—the first presidential contest since the inauguration of the cold war—as

an opportunity to campaign for their own post–New Deal agenda. In preparation, a group headed by Eleanor Roosevelt, labor leaders Philip Murray and Walter Reuther, and theologian Reinhold Niebuhr, among others, met in January 1947 to form Americans for Democratic Action (ADA). The most important liberal lobby of the postwar era, the ADA forged a new coalition of Democrats who wished to preserve the legacy of the New Deal and at the same time take a strong stand against communism.

The ADA identified its chief adversary in Truman's contender for the office of president, Henry A. Wallace. Truman had personally fired Wallace as secretary of commerce in 1946 for advocating a more conciliatory policy toward the Soviet Union. Wallace, however, would not retreat and made plans to run for president as candidate of the newly formed Progressive Party. Having served as Roosevelt's vice president and secretary of agriculture, he was well known as a long-time champion of the New Deal. Wallace now vowed to expand Roosevelt's programs, to move swiftly and boldly toward full employment, racial equality, and stronger trade unions, and to work in harmony with the Soviet Union. As the election neared, he remarked after a speech before 32,000 enthusiastic supporters, "We're on the march. We're really rolling now." However, the deepening cold war soon quashed Wallace's chances.

The ADA rallied around Truman and denounced Wallace and the Progressive Party for lining up "with the force of Soviet totalitarianism." Truman himself, as well as many conservatives, accused Wallace of being a tool of Communists. These timely Red-baiting attacks took a toll on the poorly organized and underfunded Wallace campaign, driving many liberals from its ranks. Moreover, Wallace, who never subscribed to communism, refused to fend off these charges, considering them a dangerous by-product of anti-Communist hysteria.

Meanwhile, Truman repositioned himself to discredit congressional Republicans. He proposed programs calling for federal funds for education and new housing and a national program of medical insurance that he knew the Republicans would oppose, and he called Congress back for a fruitless special session in 1948. He then hammered away at the Republican controlled "do-nothing Congress" to good effect in his re-election campaign.

A second tactic seemed to backfire. Pressed by ADA leaders to cut Wallace's lead on civil rights, Truman issued executive orders in July 1948 desegregating the armed forces and banning discrimination in the federal civil service. In response, some 300 southern delegates bolted from the Democratic National Convention and formed a States' Rights ("Dixiecrat") ticket, headed by Governor J. Strom Thurmond of South Carolina, known for his segregationist views. With the South as good as lost, and popular New York governor Thomas E. Dewey heading the Republican ticket, Truman appeared hopelessly far from victory.

Yet as the election neared, Truman campaigned vigorously and managed to revive the New Deal coalition. Fear of the Republicans won back the bulk of organized labor, while the recognition of the new State of Israel in May 1948 helped prevent the defection of many liberal Jewish voters from Democratic ranks. The success of the Berlin airlift also buoyed the president's popularity. By election time, Truman had deprived Henry Wallace of nearly all his liberal support. Meanwhile, Dewey, who had run a hard-hitting campaign against Roosevelt in 1944, expected to coast to victory.

"Harry Truman won the election," concluded the *New Republic*, "because Franklin Roosevelt had worked so well." Although he lost four states to Thurmond, foreshadowing the decline of Democratic strength in the South, Truman won the popular vote by a margin of 5 percent and trounced Dewey 303 to 189 in the electoral college. Moreover, Democrats again had majorities in both houses of Congress. But, as it turned out, Truman had hit the highest point of his popularity and was about to begin a steady slide downhill.

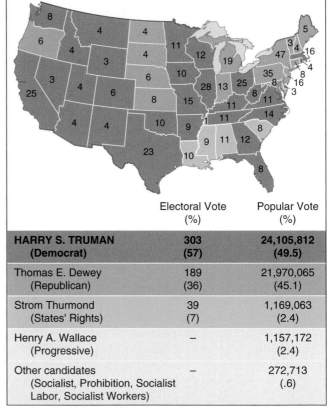

	Electoral Vote (%)	Popular Vote (%)
HARRY S. TRUMAN (Democrat)	**303 (57)**	**24,105,812 (49.5)**
Thomas E. Dewey (Republican)	189 (36)	21,970,065 (45.1)
Strom Thurmond (States' Rights)	39 (7)	1,169,063 (2.4)
Henry A. Wallace (Progressive)	–	1,157,172 (2.4)
Other candidates (Socialist, Prohibition, Socialist Labor, Socialist Workers)	–	272,713 (.6)

The Election of 1948 Harry Truman holds up a copy of the Chicago Tribune with headlines confidently and mistakenly predicting the victory of his opponent, Thomas E. Dewey. An initially unpopular candidate, Truman made a whistle-stop tour of the country by train to win 49.5 percent of the popular vote to Dewey's 45.1 percent.

SOURCE: UPI/CORBIS (U885941B).

The Fair Deal

"Every segment of our population and every individual has a right," Truman announced in January 1949, "to expect from our Government a fair deal." The return of

Democratic congressional majorities, he hoped, would enable him to translate campaign promises into concrete legislative achievements and expand the New Deal. But a powerful bloc of conservative southern Democrats and midwestern Republicans turned back his domestic agenda.

Truman broke no new ground. Congress passed a National Housing Act in 1949, promoting federally funded construction of low-income housing. It also raised the minimum wage from 40 to 75 cents per hour and expanded the Social Security program to cover an additional 10 million people. Otherwise, Truman made little headway. He and congressional liberals introduced a variety of bills to weaken southern segregationism: a federal antilynching law; outlawing the poll tax; prohibiting discrimination in interstate transportation. These measures were all defeated by southern-led filibusters. Proposals to create a national health insurance plan, provide federal aid for education, and repeal or modify Taft-Hartley remained bottled up in committees. Truman himself appeared to lose interest in the liberal agenda as his cold war foreign policy increasingly took priority over domestic issues.

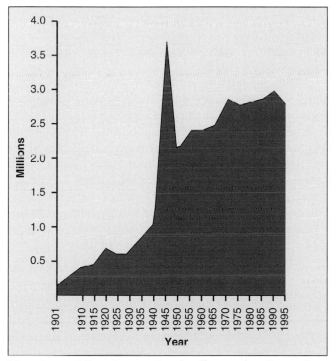

Number of Employees in the Executive Branch, 1901–1995   The federal bureaucracy, which reached a peak of nearly 4 million people during World War II, remained at unprecedentedly high levels during the cold war.

SOURCE: U.S. Bureau of the Census, *Historical Statistics of the United States, Colonial Times through 1970; Statistical Abstract of the United States, 1997.*

Truman managed best to lay out the basic principles of cold war liberalism. Toning down the rhetoric of economic equality espoused by the visionary wing of the Roosevelt coalition, his Fair Deal exalted economic growth—not the reapportionment of wealth or political power—as the proper mechanism for ensuring social harmony and national welfare. His administration insisted, therefore, on an ambitious program of expanded foreign trade, while relying on the federal government to encourage high levels of productivity at home. Equally important, Truman further tempered liberalism by making anticommunism a key element in both foreign policy and the domestic agenda.

THE COLD WAR AT HOME

"Communists . . . are everywhere—in factories, offices, butcher shops, on street corners, in private businesses," Attorney General J. Howard McGrath warned in 1949: "At this very moment [they are] busy at work—undermining your government, plotting to destroy the liberties of every citizen, and feverishly trying in whatever way they can, to aid the Soviet Union." Republican senator Joseph R. McCarthy even claimed to have in his personal possession a list of communists serving secretly in government agencies. By this time, the Communist Party, U.S.A., which had formed in 1919, was steadily losing ground since its peak of only 40,000 to 50,000 members in 1945 when the United States and the Soviet Union were wartime allies.

Nevertheless, during the earliest days of the cold war, anticommunism already occupied center stage in domestic politics. Thus FBI director J. Egar Hoover characteristically warned Americans not to be complacent in the face of low numbers of Communists because "for every party member there are ten others ready, willing, and able to do the Party's work" in infiltrating and corrupting "various spheres of American life." Hoover also helped to set the tone, using hyperbolic rhetoric to describe "the diabolic machinations of sinister figures engaged in un-American activities."

The federal government, with the help of the media, would lead the campaign, finding in the threat of communism a rationale for the massive reordering of its operation and the quieting of the voices of dissent. In this far-reaching quest for security, Americans moved toward a greater concentration of power in government, and, while promising to lead the "free world," allowed many of their own rights to be circumscribed. The United States was readying for permanent military preparedness and perpetual confrontation with its Soviet enemy.

The National Security Act of 1947

The imperative of national security destroyed old-fashioned isolation, forcing the United States into international alliances such as NATO and into the role of world leader. "If we falter in our leadership," Truman warned, "we may endanger the peace of the world–and we shall surely endanger the welfare of this nation." Such a responsibiity required a massive amount of resources. Truman went on, therefore, to argue successfully that national security demanded a substantial increase in the size of the federal government, including both military forces and surveillance agencies. Security measures were required to keep the nation in a steady state of preparedness, readily justified during wartime, now extended into the very uneasy peacetime. As a result, federal expenditures, which had dropped briefly at the end of World War II, grew to be at least seven times greater than during their New Deal peak in the 1930s.

The National Security Act of 1947, passed by Congress in July, laid the foundation for this expansion. The act established the Department of Defense and the National Security Council (NSC) to administer and coordinate defense policies and to advise the president. The Department of Defense replaced the War Department and united the armed forces—the army, navy, and air force—under the jurisdiction of a single secretary with cabinet-level status. As result, with the distinction between citizen and soldier blurred, the ties between the armed forces and the State Department grew closer, as former military officers routinely began to fill positions in the State Department and diplomatic corps. The act also created the National Security Resources Board (NSRB) to coordinate plans throughout the government "in the event of war" and, for the first time in American history, to maintain a program of military preparedness in peacetime.

The Department of Defense, together with the NSRB, became the principal sponsor of scientific research during the first ten years of the cold war. It was commonly recognized at the time that World War II had been "a physicists' war," leading to the creation of the ultimate weapon, the atom bomb, but also to major advances in military technology in areas of systems of navigation and detection, strategic targeting, and communication. Many scientists anticipated that, at the end of the war the special relationship between science and government would continue under the auspices of a new federal agency that would channel funds mainly to universities for basic research under civilian control. Indeed, in 1950, the National Science Foundation (NSF) was created for education and research. However, the NSF sponsored research with little military relevance, and its miniscule budget compared unfavor-ably to the $85 million per year that the Office of Naval Research directed toward basic research and development. Federal agencies tied to military projects meanwhile supplied well over 90 percent of funding for research in the physical sciences, a large part of the research being located in major universities.

The National Security Act added to this system of defense in 1947 by establishing the Central Intelligence Agency (CIA). With roots in the wartime Office of Strategic Services, the CIA now became a permanent operation devoted to collecting political, military, and economic information for security purposes throughout the world. Although information about the CIA was classified—that is, secret from both Congress and the public—historians have estimated that the agency soon dwarfed the State Department in number of employees and size of budget.

The national security state required a huge workforce. Before World War II, approximately 900,000 civilians worked for the federal government, with about 10 percent engaged in security work; by the beginning of the cold war, nearly 4 million people were on the government's payroll, with 75 percent working in national security agencies. The Pentagon, which had opened in 1943 as the largest office building in the world, how housed the Joint Chiefs of Staff and 35,000 military personnel. Similarly, when the State Department consolidated its various divisions in 1961, it moved into an eight-story structure covering an area the size of four city blocks.

National security took up increasingly large portions of the nation's resources and required an enormous increase in the size of the defense budget. By the end of Truman's second term, defense allocations accounted for 10 percent of the gross national product, directly or indirectly employed hundreds of thousands of well-paid workers, and subsidized some of the nation's most profitable corporations. This vast financial outlay created the rationale for permanent, large-scale military spending as a basic stimulus to economic growth. As early as 1947, Harrison Baldwin of the *New York Times* noted this ominous trend toward "militarization of [the] government and of the American state of mind."

The Loyalty-Security Program

National security also required increased surveillance at home. Within two weeks of proclamating the Truman Doctrine, the president signed Executive Order 9835 on March 21, 1947, and thereby established a loyalty program for all federal employees. The new Federal Employees Loyalty and Security Program, directed at members of the Communist Party—as well as fascists and anyone guilty of "sympathetic association" with either—in effect established a political test for federal employment. It also outlined procedures for investigating current and prospective federal employees. The loyalty review boards often asked employees about their opinions on the Soviet Union, the Marshall Plan, or NATO, or if they would report fellow workers if they found out they were Communists. Any employee could be dismissed merely on "reasonable grounds" rather than on proof of disloyalty. Later amendments added "homosexuals" as potential security risks on the grounds that they might succumb to blackmail by enemy agents. By early 1952, the FBI, which administered the program, had screened approximately 2 million federal employees.

Many state and municipal governments enacted loyalty programs and required public employees, including teachers at all levels, to sign loyalty oaths. In Detroit, the loyalty review board included city officials, FBI agents, and executives from the auto industry. Positions involving security clearances were closed off to many scientists and engineers, including several who had worked on the Manhattan Project. Only his prominence kept J. Robert Oppenheimer, who spoke critically about the atom bomb, from losing his security clearance until 1953.

Attorney General Clark aided this effort by publishing a list of hundreds of potentially subversive organizations selected by criteria so vague that any views "hostile or inimical to the American form of government" (as Clark's assistants noted in a memo) could make an organization liable for investigation and prosecution. There was, moreover, no right of appeal. Although designed primarily to screen federal employees, the attorney general's list effectively outlawed many political and social organizations, indirectly stigmatizing hundreds of thousands of individuals who had done nothing illegal. Church associations, civil rights organizations, musical groups, and even summer camps appeared on the list. Some, like the Civil Rights Congress, played important roles in defending imprisoned African Americans. Others, like the Jewish Music Alliance and Camp Kinderland, mainly served the cultural interests of Jewish Americans. The FBI compiled separate lists, and by 1960 had created files and collected information on more than 430,000 allegedly subversive individuals and groups.

Membership in a listed group provided the rationale for dismissal at nearly every level of government. Fraternal and social institutions, especially popular among aging European immigrants of various nationalities, were among the largest organizations destroyed. The state of New York, for example, legally dismantled the International Workers' Order, which had provided insurance to nearly 200,000 immigrants and their families. Only a handful of organizations had the funds to challenge the listing legally; most simply closed their doors. Even past

membership in a listed group—during the desperate 1930s many liberals had been briefly active in Communist or Communist-related movements—quickly became grounds for suspicion and likely dismissal. Many private employers also used the attorney general's list to institute similar loyalty programs.

Leaders of the labor movement, after initially resisting federal interference, carried out their own sweeping purge of Communists from their affiliated unions. Rather than cooperating with the loyalty program, several major unions withdrew from the Congress of Industrial Organizations, and nine more were expelled at the CIO's 1950 convention. The CIO, now lacking progressive leadership, narrowed its agenda by putting aside the goal of organizing women and racial minorities and foreclosed upon unionism as a social movement. At the same time, the new leaders prepared for merger with the less visionary American Federation of Labor, with George Meany as "business union" president, in 1956.

In all, some 6.6 million people underwent loyalty and security checks. An estimated 500 government workers were fired and perhaps as many as 6,000 more chose to resign. No spies or saboteurs turned up.

In 1950 Congress overrode the president's veto to pass a bill that Truman called "the greatest danger to freedom of press, speech, and assembly since the Sedition Act of 1798." The Internal Security (McCarran) Act required Communist organizations to register with the Subversive Activities Control Board and authorized the arrest of suspect persons during a national emergency. The Immigration and Nationality Act, also sponsored by Republican senator Pat McCarran of Nevada and adopted in 1952, again over Truman's veto, barred people deemed "subversive" or "homosexual" from becoming citizens or even from visiting the United States. It also empowered the attorney general to deport immigrants who were members of Communist organizations, even if they had become citizens. Challenged repeatedly on constitutional grounds, the Subversive Activities Control Board remained in place until 1973, when it was terminated.

The Red Scare in Hollywood

Anti-Communist Democratic representative Martin Dies of Texas, who had chaired a congressional committee on "un-American activities" since 1938, told reporters at a press conference in Hollywood in 1944:

> Hollywood is the greatest source of revenue in this nation for the Communists and other subversive groups. . . . Two elements stand out in . . . the making of pictures which extoll foreign ideology—propaganda for a cause which seeks

to spread its ideas to our people[,] and the "leftist" or radical screenwriters. . . . In my opinion, [motion picture executives] will do well to halt the propaganda pictures and eliminate every writer who has un-American ideas.

A few years later, Dies's successor, J. Parnell Thomas of New Jersey (later convicted and imprisoned for bribery), directed the committee to investigate supposed Communist infiltration of the movie industry.

Renamed and made a permanent standing committee in 1945, the House Un-American Activities Committee (HUAC) had the power to subpoena witnesses and to compel them to answer all questions or face contempt of Congress charges. The results were sometimes absurd. In well-publicized hearings held in Hollywood in October 1947, the mother of actress Ginger Rogers defended her daughter by saying that she had been duped into appearing in the pro-Soviet wartime film *Tender Comrade* (1943) and "had been forced" to read the subversive line "Share and share alike, that's democracy." Conservative novelist Ayn Rand added that *The Song of Russia* (1944) had intentionally deceived the American public by showing Russians smiling! HUAC encouraged such testimony by "friendly witnesses," including Ronald Reagan and Gary Cooper. The committee intimated many others who feared the loss of their careers into naming former friends and co-workers in order to be cleared for future work in Hollywood.

A small but prominent minority refused to cooperate with HUAC. By claiming the freedoms of speech and association guaranteed by the First and Sixth Amendments to the Constitution, they became known as "unfriendly witnesses." Many had worked in Hollywood films celebrating America's working people, a popular Depression-era theme but now considered indicative of subversive intentions. During World War II, many of these same screenwriters and actors had teamed up on films attacking fascism. Among the most prominent "unfriendly witnesses" were actors Orson Welles, Zero Mostel, and Charlie Chaplin, and Oscar-winning screenwriter Ring Lardner, Jr. Humphrey Bogart led a stars' delegation to "Defend the First Amendment" before Congress, but generated only headlines. A handful served prison sentences for contempt of Congress.

Hollywood studios refused to employ any writer, director, or actor who refused to cooperate with HUAC. The resulting blacklist remained in effect until the 1960s and limited the production of films dealing directly with social or political issues. Meanwhile, the privately published *Red Channels: The Report of Communist Influence in Radio and Television* (1950) persuaded advertisers to cancel their accounts with many programs considered friendly to the Soviet Union, the United Nations, or liberal causes.

Spy Cases

In August 1948, Whittaker Chambers, a *Time* magazine editor, appeared before HUAC to name Alger Hiss as a fellow Communist in the Washington underground during the 1930s. Hiss, then president of the prestigious Carnegie Endowment for International Peace and former member of FDR's State Department, denied the charges and sued his accuser for slander. Chambers then revealed his trump card, a cache of films of secret documents— hidden in and then retrieved from a hallowed-out pumpkin on his farm in Maryland—that he claimed Hiss had passed to him for transmission to the USSR. Republican representative Richard Nixon of California described the so-called "Pumpkin Papers" as proof of "the most serious series of treasonable activities . . . in the history of America." The statute of limitations for espionage having run out, a federal grand jury in January 1950 convicted Hiss of perjury (for denying he knew Chambers), and he received a five-year prison term. Hiss was released two years later, still proclaiming his innocence.

Many Democrats, including Truman himself, at first dismissed the allegations against Hiss—conveniently publicized at the start of the 1948 election campaign— as a red herring, a Republican maneuver to gain votes. Indeed, Nixon himself circulated a pamphlet entitled *The Hiss Case* to promote his own candidacy for vice president. Nevertheless, the highly publicized allegations against Hiss proved detrimental to Democrats, suggesting that both FDR and Truman had allowed Communists to infiltrate the federal government.

The most dramatic spy case of the era involved Julius Rosenberg, former government engineer, and his wife, Ethel, who were accused of stealing and plotting to convey atomic secrets to Soviet agents during World War II. The government had only a weak case against Ethel Rosenberg, hoping that her conviction would force her husband to "break." The case against Julius Rosenberg depended on documents too highly classified to present as evidence at a public trial and therefore rested on the testimony of his supposed accomplices, some of them secretly coached by the FBI. Although the Rosenbergs maintained their innocence to the end, in March 1951 a jury found them guilty of conspiring to commit espionage. The American press showed them no sympathy, but around the world the Rosenbergs were defended by citizens' committees and their convictions protested in large-scale demonstrations. Scientist Albert Einstein, the pope, and the president of France, among many prominent figures, all pleaded for clemency. Julius and Ethel Rosenberg died in the electric chair on June 19, 1953.

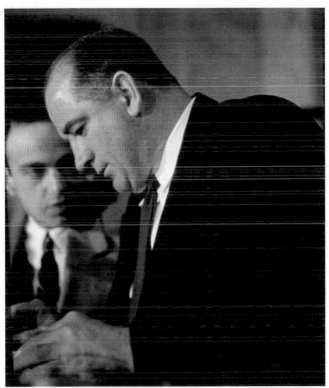

The tables turned on Senator Joseph McCarthy (1908–57) after he instigated an investigation of the U.S. Army for harboring Communists. A congressional committee then investigated McCarthy for attempting to make the army grant special privileges to his staff aide, Private David Schine. During the televised hearings, Senator McCarthy—shown here with his staff assistant Roy Cohn—discredited himself. In December 1954, the Senate voted to censure him.

SOURCE: Photo by Hank Walker. TimePix (3701).

McCarthyism

In a sensational Lincoln Day speech to the Republican Women's Club of Wheeling, West Virginia, on February 9, 1950, Republican senator Joseph R. McCarthy of Wisconsin announced that the United States had been sold out by the "traitorous actions of those who have been treated so well by the nation." These "bright young men who have been born with silver spoons in their mouths"—such as Secretary of State Dean Acheson, whom McCarthy called a "pompous diplomat in striped pants, with a phony English accent"—were part of a conspiracy, he charged, of more than 200 Communists working in the State Department.

McCarthy refused to reveal names, however, and a few days later, after a drinking bout, he told persistent reporters: "I'm not going to tell you anything. I just want you to know I've got a pailful [of dirt] . . . and I'm going to use it where it does the most good." Although investigations uncovered not a single Communist in the State Department, McCarthy launched a flamboyant offensive against New Deal Democrats and the Truman administration for failing to defend the nation's security. His name provided the label for the entire campaign to silence critics of the cold war: McCarthyism.

Behind the blitz of publicity, the previously obscure junior senator from Wisconsin had struck a chord. Communism seemed to many Americans to be much more than a military threat—indeed, nothing less than a demonic force capable of undermining basic values. It compelled patriots to proclaim themselves ready for atomic warfare: "Better Dead Than Red." McCarthy also had help from organizations such as the American Legion and the Chamber of Commerce, and prominent religious leaders and union leaders.

Civil rights organizations faced the severest persecution since the 1920s. The Civil Rights Congress and the Negro Youth Council, for instance, were destroyed after frequent charges of Communist influence. W. E. B. Du Bois, the renowned African American historian, and famed concert singer (and former All-American football hero) Paul Robeson had public appearances canceled and their right to travel abroad abridged.

In attacks on women's organizations and homosexual groups, meanwhile, anti-Communist rhetoric cloaked deep fears about changing sexual mores. HUAC published a pamphlet quoting a Columbia professor as saying that "girls' schools and women's colleges contain some of the most loyal disciples of Russia . . . often frustrated females." Republican Party chair Guy Gabrielson warned that "sexual perverts" who were possibly "as dangerous as actual Communists" had infiltrated the government. Aided by FBI reports, the federal government fired up to sixty homosexuals per month in the early 1950s. Dishonorable discharges from the U.S. armed forces for homosexuality, an administrative procedure without appeal, also increased dramatically, to 2,000 per year. Noted historian Arthur Schlesinger, Jr. suggested that critics of cold war policies were not "real" men or, perhaps, "real" women either.

Much of McCarthy's rhetoric was merely opportunistic, his campaign a ruthless attempt to gain power and fame by exploiting cold war fears. He succeeded partly because he brilliantly used the media to his own advantage. McCarthy also perfected the inquisitorial technique, asking directly, "Are you now, or have you ever been, a member of the Communist Party?"

Joseph McCarthy and his fellow Red-hunters eventually burned themselves out. During televised congressional hearings in 1954, not only did McCarthy fail to prove wild charges of Communist infiltration of the army, but in the glare of the television cameras he appeared deranged. Cowed for years, the Senate finally condemned him for "conduct unbecoming a member."

COLD WAR CULTURE

The anti-Communist campaigns and loyalty programs represented only the most palpable elements in the domestic cold war. As the Truman Doctrine clearly specified, the cold war did not necessarily depend on military confrontation; nor was it defined exclusively by a quest for economic supremacy. The cold war embodied the struggle of one "way of life" against another. It was, in short, a contest of values. The president therefore pledged the United States to "contain" communism from spreading beyond the parameters of the Soviet Union and its client states and simultaneously called for fortifications at home. If Americans were to rebuild the world based on their own values, they must rededicate themselves to the defense of their birthright: freedom and democracy. To do so required a total mobilization covering all aspects of American life, not just its formal political institutions. And to prepare Americans for this challenge, it might be necessary first—as Republican senator Arthur Vandenberg advised Truman—to "scare hell out of the country."

An Anxious Mood

At the end of World War II, while much of the world lay in rubble, the United States began the longest, steadiest period of economic growth and prosperity in its history. "We have about 50 percent of the world's wealth," George Kennan noted in 1948, "but only 3.6 percent of its population." Very large pockets of poverty remained, and not all Americans benefited from the postwar abundance. Nonetheless, millions of Americans achieved middle-class status, often through new programs subsidized by the federal government.

Prosperity did not dispel an anxious mood, fueled in part by the reality and the rhetoric of the cold war. Many Americans also feared an economic backslide. If war production had ended the hardships of the Great Depression, how would the economy fare in peacetime? No one could say. Above all, peace itself seemed precarious. President Truman himself suggested that World War III appeared inevitable, and his secretary of state, Dean Acheson, warned the nation to keep "on permanent alert." McCarthyism raised the spectre of internal as well as distant enemies.

Anxieties intensified by the cold war surfaced as major themes in popular culture. One of the most acclaimed Hollywood films of the era, the winner of nine Academy Awards, *The Best Years of Our Lives* (1946), followed the stories of three returning veterans as they tried to readjust to civilian life. The former soldiers found that the dreams of reunion with family and loved ones that had sustained them through years of fighting now seemed hollow. In some cases, their wives and children had become so self-reliant that the men had no clear function to perform in the household; in other cases, the prospect for employment appeared dim. The feeling of community shared with wartime buddies dissipated, leaving only a profound sense of loneliness.

The genre of *film noir* (French for "black") deepened this mood into an aesthetic. Movies like *Out of the Past, Detour,* and *They Live by Night* featured stories of ruthless fate and betrayal. Their protagonists were usually strangers or loners falsely accused of crimes or trapped into committing them. The high-contrast lighting of these black and white films accentuated the difficulty of distinguishing friend from foe. Feelings of frustration and loss of control came alive in tough, cynical characters played by actors such as Robert Mitchum and Robert Ryan.

Plays and novels also described alienation and anxiety in vivid terms. Playwright Arthur Miller in *Death of a Salesman* (1949) sketched an exacting portrait of self-destructive individualism. Willy Loman, the play's hero, is obsessively devoted to his career in sales but is nevertheless a miserable failure. Worse, he has trained his sons to excel in personal presentation and style—the very methods prescribed by standard American success manuals—making them both shallow and materialistic. J. D. Salinger's widely praised novel *Catcher in the Rye* (1951) explored the mental anguish of a teenage boy estranged from the crass materialism of his parents.

Cold war anxiety manifested itself in a flurry of unidentified flying object (UFO) sightings. Thousands of Americans imagined that a Communist-like invasion from outer space was already under way, or they hoped that superior creatures might arrive to show the way to world peace. The U.S. Air Force discounted the sightings of flying saucers, but dozens of private researchers and faddists claimed to have been contacted by aliens. Hollywood films fed these beliefs. The popular movie *The Day the Earth Stood Still* (1951) delivered a message of world peace in which a godlike being implores earthlings to abandon their weaponry before they destroy the planet. Other popular science fiction films carried a different message. In *The Invasion of the Body Snatchers* (1956), for example, a small town is captured by aliens who take over the minds of its inhabitants when they fall asleep, a subtle warning against apathy toward the threat of communist "subversion."

Hollywood studios played directly into the mounting fears, releasing by 1954 more than forty films with titles such as *I Married a Communist* (1950) and *The Red Menace* (1949) that sensationalized the Communist threat. The television industry sponsored the dramatic series *The Hunter*, featuring the adventures of an American businessman fighting Communist agents throughout the Free World. Few of these films or programs were popular, however.

The Family as Bulwark

Postwar prosperity helped to strengthen the ideal of domesticity, although many Americans interpreted their rush toward marriage and parenthood, as one writer put it, as a "defense—an impregnable bulwark" against the anxieties of the era. Even the ultimate symbol of postwar prosperity, the new home in the suburbs, reflected more than simple self-confidence. In 1950 the *New York Times* ran advertisements that captured a chilling quality of the boom in real estate: country properties for the Atomic Age located at least fifty miles outside major cities—the most likely targets, it was believed, of a Soviet nuclear attack. Not a few suburbanites built new additions to their homes, underground bomb shelters made of steel-reinforced concrete and outfitted with provisions to maintain a family for several weeks after an atomic explosion. Financial well-being could not in itself offset the insecurities provoked by the cold war.

Many young couples nevertheless sought security by marrying younger and producing more children than at any time in the past century. The national fertility rate had reached an all-time low during the Great Depression, bottoming out in 1933 at 75 per 1,000 women. A decade later, after wartime production had revived the economy, the birthrate climbed to nearly 109 per 1,000 women. The U.S. Census Bureau predicted that this "baby boom" would be temporary. To everyone's surprise, the birthrate continued to grow at a record pace, peaking at over 118 per 1,000 women in 1957.

The new families who enjoyed postwar prosperity inaugurated a spending spree of trailblazing proportions. "The year 1946," *Life* magazine proclaimed, "finds the U.S. on the threshold of marvels, ranging from runless stockings and shineless serge suits to jet-propelled airplanes that will flash across the country in just a little less than the speed of sound." The conversion from wartime to peacetime production took longer than many eager shoppers had hoped, but by 1950 the majority of Americans could own consumer durables, such as automatic washers, and small appliances, from do-it-yourself power tools to cameras. By the time Harry Truman left office two-thirds of all American households claimed at least one television set.

These two trends—the baby boom and high rates of consumer spending—encouraged a major change in the middle-class family. Having worked during World War II, often in occupations traditionally closed to them, many women wished to continue in full-time employment. Reconversion to peacetime production forced the majority from their factory positions, but most women quickly returned, taking jobs at a faster rate than men and providing half the total growth of the labor force. By 1952, 2 million more wives worked than during the war. Gone, however, were the high-paying unionized jobs in manufacturing. Instead, most women found minimum-wage jobs in the expanding service sector: clerical work, health care and education, and restaurant, hotel, and retail services. Older women whose children were grown might work because they had come to value a job for its own sake. Younger women often worked for reasons of "economic necessity"—that is, to maintain a middle-class standard of living that now required more than one income. Indeed, mothers of young children were the most likely to be employed.

DISTRIBUTION OF TOTAL PERSONAL INCOME AMONG VARIOUS SEGMENTS OF THE POPULATION, 1947–1970 (IN PERCENTAGES)*

Year	Poorest Fifth	Second Poorest Fifth	Middle Fifth	Second Wealthiest Fifth	Wealthiest Fifth	Wealthiest 5 Percent
1947	3.5	10.6	16.7	23.6	45.6	18.7
1950	3.1	10.5	17.3	24.1	45.0	18.2
1960	3.2	10.6	17.6	24.7	44.0	17.0
1970	3.6	10.3	17.2	24.7	44.1	16.9

Despite the general prosperity of the postwar era, the distribution of income remained essentially unchanged.

*Monetary income only.

SOURCE: Adapted from U.S. Bureau of the Census, *Historical Statistics of the United States, Colonial Times to 1970,* Bicentennial ed. (Washington, D.C.: U.S. Government Printing Office, 1975), p. 292.

This model is displaying the ideal kitchen of the 1950s. The "American way of life," defined as a high standard of living, was one of the tangible fruits of U.S. victory in World War II.

SOURCE: CORBIS (GNGN10375).

Even though most women sought employment primarily to support their families, they ran up against popular opinion and expert advice urging them to return to their homes. Public opinion registered resounding disapproval—by 86 percent of those surveyed—of a married woman's working if jobs were scarce and her husband could support her. Noting that most Soviet women worked in industry, commentators appealed to women to return home and make the family a bulwark against communism. Just as the Truman Doctrine and the Marshall Plan responded to pitfalls abroad, the American family could "contain" dangers at home—if "restored" to an imaginary "traditional" form where men alone were breadwinners and women stayed happily at home.

This campaign began on a shrill note. Ferdinand Lundberg and Marynia Farnham, in their best-selling *Modern Woman: The Lost Sex* (1947), attributed the "super-jittery age in which we live" to women's abandonment of the home to pursue careers. To counter this trend, they proposed federally funded psychotherapy to readjust women to their housewifely roles and cash subsidies to encourage them to bear more children.

Articles in popular magazines, television shows, and high-profile experts chimed in with similar messages. Talcott Parsons, the distinguished Harvard sociologist, delineated the parameters of the "democratic" family: husbands served as breadwinners while wives—"the emotional hub of the family"—stayed home to care

for their families. In the first edition of *Baby and Child Care* (1946), the child-rearing advice manual that soon outsold the Bible, Benjamin Spock similarly advised women to devote themselves full time, if financially possible, to their maternal responsibilities.

Patterns of women's higher education reflected this conservative trend. Having made slight gains during World War II when college-age men were serving in the armed forces or working in war industries, women lost ground after the G.I. Bill created a huge upsurge in male enrollment. Women represented 40 percent of all college graduates in 1940 but only 25 percent a decade later.

With a growing number of middle-class women working to help support their families, these cold war policies and prescriptions worked at cross-purposes. As early as 1947, *Life* magazine registered concern in a thirteen-page feature, "American Woman's Dilemma." How could women comfortably take part in a world beyond the home and at the same time heed the advice of FBI director J. Edgar Hoover, who exhorted the nation's women to fight

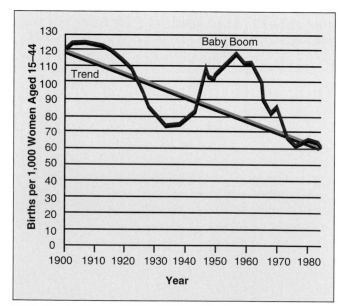

U.S. Birth Rate, 1930–1980   The bulge of the "baby boom," a leading demographic factor in the postwar economy, stands out for this fifty-year period.

"the twin enemies of freedom—crime and communism" by fulfilling their singular role as "homemakers and mothers"?

Military-Industrial Communities in the West

All regions of the United States felt the impact of the cold war but perhaps none so directly as the Trans-Mississippi West. Defense spending during World War II had stimulated the western economy and encouraged a mass migration of people eager to find employment in wartime industry. Following the war, many cities successfully converted to peacetime production, Los Angeles, for example, attracted one-eighth of all new business in the nation during the late 1940s. However, the cold war, by reviving defense funding, provided the most important boost to the western economy. The Department of Defense and private corporations and subcontractors generated billions of dollars for research and development of military equipment of various kinds.

The federal government poured so much defense money—nearly 10 percent of the entire military budget—into California that the state's rate of economic growth between 1949 and 1952 outpaced that of the nation as a whole, with nearly 40 percent coming from the manufacture of aircraft alone. Ten years later, it was estimated that one-third of all workers in Los Angeles were employed by defense industries, particularly aerospace, and that their absolute number was far greater than during the peak of production in World War II. The concentration of defense workers was even greater in the suburbs of Los Angeles. Orange County, for example, grew quickly during the cold war to become a major producer of communication equipment. The San Francisco Bay Area also benefited economically from defense spending, and cities such as Sunnyvale, Mountain View, and San Jose began their ascendance as home to the nation's budding high-technology industry.

The cold war also pumped new life into communities that had grown up during World War II. Hanford, Washington, and Los Alamos, New Mexico, both centers of the Manhattan Project, employed a greater number of people in the construction of the cold war nuclear arsenal than in the development of the atom bomb that brought an end to World War II. Los Alamos grew from its rural origins at such a fast pace that thirty years later its population density was one of the highest in the state, second only to the metropolitan region of Albuquerque. The community lost little of its secretive quality, with entry restricted to mainly well-paid workers and residents who could neither own land or homes within its boundary. Meanwhile, the federal government continued to place its distinctive stamp on the ar-

chitecture, with institutional and purely functional aesthetics governing the design of concrete structures with hospital-green interiors.

Other parts of New Mexico were virtually transformed by cold war exigencies. Three hundred miles southeast of Los Alamos, Espanola Valley, home to a population nearly 90 percent Hispanic and Native American, saw its economy grow as it became the location of Waste Isolation Pilot Project, the dump site of the laboratory's waste projects. Alamogordo, New Mexico, experienced more than a 200 percent increase in population during the first decade of the cold war because of its location next to White Sands Missile Range and Holloman Air Force Base.

New communities accompanied the growth of the U.S. military bases and training camps in the western states. Many of these installations, as well as hospitals and supply depots, not only survived but expanded during the transition from the actual warfare of World War II to the virtual warfare of the cold war. Between 1950 and 1953 approximately twenty western bases were reopened. California became at least a temporary home to more military personnel than any other state, but Texas was not far behind. The availability of public lands with areas of sparse population made western states especially attractive to military planners commissioned to design dangerous and secretive installations such as the White Sands Missile Range in the New Mexican desert.

Many older communities also benefited from such expansion. San Antonio, Texas, for example, came to depend economically on the military personnel stationed near the city in four air force bases, an army fort and hospital, the headquarters of the Fifth Army, and several Marine Corps and navy units. Fort Riley, Kansas, developed an even greater degree of interdependency with Junction City, which grew through the cold war era from a tiny town to a small city. Many Mormon communities switched from farming to manufacturing when Utah came to lead all other states in the proportion of federal military dollars making up the state's total income. Nearly equidistant from the major cold war producers of San Diego, Los Angeles, San Francisco, and Seattle, Utah emerged as a prime distribution center for military goods as well as a major storage site.

Local politicians, real estate agents, and merchants usually welcomed these projects as sources of revenue and employment for the residents of their communities. There were, however, heavy costs for speedy and unplanned federally induced growth. To accommodate the new populations, the government poured money into new highway systems and did little to bolster or build public transportation. Uncontrolled sprawl, traffic congestion, air pollution, and strains on limited water and energy resources all grew with the military-industrial communities in the West. For those populations living near nuclear weapons testing grounds, environmental degradation complemented the ultimate threat to their own physical well-being, as cancer rates soared over the next forty years.

Zeal for Democracy

World War II revitalized patriotism by rallying Americans to define themselves and their institutions against Nazi and fascist forces abroad. Pledging allegiance to the flag, for example, gained new symbolic meaning as school children were directed to avoid saluting, a gesture now perceived as disturbingly similar to the militaristic Nazi hand-raising, and were instead told to hold their right hand steadily over their heart. By 1941, the celebration of Flag Day moved even President Roosevelt, who previously showed no interest in the event, to implore Americans to show their colors "when the principles of unity and freedom symbolized by Old Glory are under attack."

Following the massive V-J Day celebrations that marked the end of World War II, Americans began to retreat from public displays of patriotism but were soon chastized for their "national apathy" by organizations like the Freedoms Foundation of Valley Forge, which aimed to mobilize a "vast articulate, creative army of ministers, teachers, professional people, students, men and women from the farm and factory" to defend "the American Way." Soon, other new groups, such as the American Heritage Foundation, founded in 1947, joined such stalwarts as the American Legion, the Chamber of Commerce, and local business and veterans groups in this endeavor.

During the tense election year of 1948, for example, the Junior Chamber of Commerce of Kansas City, Missouri, sponsored "Democracy Beats Communism" Week and prepared a small army of speakers to explain the virtues of American democracy over Soviet slavery, focusing to a large extent on superiority of free enterprise over a state-controlled economy. Students in the city's high schools thus learned that whereas one in every five Americans had a phone, only one in 188 Russians did. The week climaxed in a "Torch of Freedom" parade, a caravan of automobiles, trucks, and marching bands carrying the message to all parts of the city.

The American Legion of Mosinee, Wisconsin, utilized political theatre to inculcate the virtues of the American way, orchestrating an imaginary Communist coup of the small community. In 1950 on May Day, the traditional Communist holiday, "Communist agents," followed by more than sixty reporters, forced the mayor from his home and announced that the Council of People's Commissars had taken over the local government. The chief of police met with a similar fate,

and roadblocks were put up to prevent any of the residents from escaping to "free" territory. The restaurants served only Soviet fare: black bread, potato soup, and coffee. The local newspaper, the *Mosinee Times*, printed a special edition on pink stock under its new masthead, "Red Star." The citizens of Mosinee discovered that all private property had been confiscated by the state and that all rights guaranteed by the Constitution had been anulled. Moreover, every adult was required "to contribute to the State four extra hours of labor without compensation." That evening, after a full day of Communist indoctrination, the local residents rallied in "Red Square" where they declared an end to the Communist rule of their community. Mosinee's defenders of freedom raised the American flag and headed home to the refrain of "God Bless America." The national media, including *Life* magazine and all the radio networks, covered Mosinee's "Day Under Communism."

Meanwhile, Attorney General Tom Clark, with the support of President Truman, funding from private donors, and planning by the American Heritage Foundation, had been putting on track the "Freedom Train." Carrying documents illustrating basic American rights and liberties, such as the Bill of Rights and the Constitution, the Freedom Train traveled to various cities across the United States where local citizens got aboard to view various patriotic displays at the average rate of 8,500 people per day. The popular songwriter Irving Berlin memorialized the Freedom Train, lyrically assuring the expectant viewers who endured long lines that inside "you'll find a precious freight."

Patriotic messages also permeated public education. According to guidelines set down by the Truman administration, teachers were to "strengthen national security through education," specifically designing their lesson plans to illustrate the superiority of the American democratic system over Soviet communism. In 1947 the federal Office of Education launched the "Zeal for Democracy" program for implementation by school boards nationwide. The program veered toward propaganda, announcing its intention to "promote and strengthen democratic thinking and practice, just as the schools of totalitarian states have so effectively promoted the ideals of their respective cultures." Meanwhile, as part of a separate program in civil defense, schoolchildren were taught to "duck" under their desks and "cover" their heads to protect themselves in the event of a surprise nuclear attack by the Soviets.

Lessons in the American way also found their way into the books of the nation's leading historians, such as Samuel Eliot Morison, who shaped his interpretation of past events to highlight American values, particularly the sanctity of private property. Richard Hofstadter in his prize-winning *American Political Tradition* (1948), similarly described the uniquely American faith in "the economic virtues of capitalist culture as necessary qualities of man."

There were voices of protest to these cold war programs. The black poet Langston Hughes, for example, expressed his skepticism in verse, writing that he hoped the Freedom Train would carry no Jim Crow car. A fearless minority of scholars protested infringements on their academic freedom by refusing to sign loyalty oaths and by writing books pointing out the potential dangers of aggressively nationalistic foreign and domestic policies. But the chilling atmosphere, such as the political climate pervading the campus of the University of Washington, made many individuals reluctant to express contrary opinions or ideas.

END OF THE
DEMOCRATIC ERA

Cold war tensions festered first in Europe. Following the announcement of the Marshall Plan, the Soviet Union tightened relationships among Communist parties in Eastern Europe as well as in France and Italy by establishing the Cominform. Then, in February 1948, Communists seized power in Czechoslovakia, a move that speeded up plans by the British, French, and Americans to consolidate their occupation zones in Germany. By spring of that year, the Berlin Crisis had pushed the United States and Soviet Union to the brink of armed conflict. With so much happening in Europe, neither superpower would have predicted that events in Asia would soon transform their political and ideological competition into a war threatening to destroy the world. Yet, in 1949, Communists in China seized power in the most heavily populated nation in the world. Then, a few months later, in June 1950, Communists threatened to take over all of Korea. The precarious balance of power was seemingly shifting.

Trapped by his own tough cold war rhetoric, Truman asked Americans to sanction a limited war in Korea, and within a few years more than 1.8 millions Americans had been sent to fight a war with no victory in sight. For Truman, the "loss" of China to communism and the stalemate in Korea proved political suicide. The raging controversy that ensued ended the twenty-year Democratic lock on the presidency and the greatest era of reform in U.S. history.

The "Loss" of China

At the close of World War II, the United States acted deliberately to secure Japan firmly in its realm. General Douglas MacArthur directed an interim government in a modest reconstruction program that included land reform, the creation of independent trade unions, the abolition of contract marriages, the granting of woman suffrage, sweeping demilitarization, and, eventually, a constitutional democracy that barred Communists from all posts. American leaders worked to rebuild the nation's economy along capitalist lines and integrate Japan, like West Germany, into an anti-Soviet bloc. Japan also housed huge U.S. military bases, thus placing U.S. troops and weapons strategically close to the Soviet Union's Asian rim. The "Strategic Importance of Japan," according to a CIA report, derived from its potential to become a stabilizing force in Asia, particularly in relation to China.

The situation in China could not be handled so easily. After years of civil war, the pro-Western Nationalist government of Jiang Jeishi (Chiang Kai-shek) collapsed. Since World War II, the United States had been sending aid to the unpopular government while warning Jiang that without major reforms the Nationalists were heading for defeat. Moreover, they tried to convince him to accept a coalition government. After refusing to intervene on their behalf, the United States watched as Jiang's troops were finally forced to surrender to the Communists, led by Mao Zedong, who enjoyed the support of the Chinese countryside, where 85 percent of the population lived. Surrendering to Mao the entire China mainland, the defeated Nationalist government withdrew to the island of Formosa (Taiwan). On October 1, 1949, the People's Republic of China (PRC) was formally established.

The news of China's "fall" to communism created an uproar in the United States. The Asia First wing of the Republican Party, which envisioned the Far East rather than Europe as the prime site of U.S. trade and investment, blamed the Truman administration for the "loss" of China. In February 1950, when the USSR and the PRC joined in a formal alliance, Truman's adversaries capitalized on the growing threat of "international" communism and referred to the Democrats as a "party of treason."

The Korean War

At the end of World War II, the Allies had divided the small peninsula of Korea, ceded by Japan, at the 38th parallel. Although all parties hoped to reunite the nation under its own government, the line between North and South instead hardened. The United States backed the unpopular government of Syngman Rhee (the Republic of Korea), and the Soviet Union sponsored a rival government in North Korea under Kim Il Sung.

On June 25, 1950, the U.S. State Department received a cablegram reporting a military attack on South Korea by the Communist-controlled North. "If we are tough enough now," President Truman pledged, "if we

American soldiers fought in Korea under the command of General Douglas MacArthur until President Truman named General Matthew Ridgway as his replacement in April 1951. Nearly 1.8 million Americans served in Korea.

SOURCE: National Archives and Records Administration.

stand up to them like we did in Greece three years ago, they won't take any next steps." The Soviet Union, on the other hand, regarded the invasion as Kim Il Sung's affair. Despite Soviet disclaimers, Truman sought approval from the UN Security Council to send in troops to South Korea. Because of the absence of the Soviet delegate, who could have vetoed the decision, the Security Council agreed. Two-thirds of Americans polled approved the president's decision to send troops under the command of General Douglas MacArthur.

Military events seemed at first to justify the president's decision. Seoul, the capital of South Korea, had fallen to North Korean troops within weeks of the invasion, and Communist forces continued to push south until they had taken most of the peninsula. The situation appeared grim until Truman authorized MacArthur to carry out an amphibious landing at Inchon, which he did on September 15, 1950. With tactical brilliance and good fortune, the general orchestrated a military campaign that halted the Communist drive. By October, UN troops had retaken South Korea.

Basking in victory, the Truman administration could not resist the temptation to expand its war aims. Hoping to prove that Democrats were not "soft" on communism, the president and his advisers decided to roll back the Communists beyond the 38th parallel and ultimately to reunite Korea as a showcase for democracy. Until this point, China had not been actively involved in the war. But it now warned that any attempt to cross the dividing line would be interpreted as a threat to its own national security. Truman flew to Wake Island in the Pacific on October 15 for a conference with MacArthur, who assured the president of a speedy victory.

MacArthur had sorely miscalculated. Chinese troops massed just above the UN offensive line, at the Yalu River. Suddenly, and without any air support, the Chinese attacked in human waves. MacArthur's force was all but crushed. The Chinese drove the UN troops back into South Korea, where they regrouped along the 38th parallel. By summer 1951 a stalemate had been reached very near the old border. Negotiations for a settlement went on for the next eighteen months amid heavy fighting.

"There is no substitute for victory," MacArthur insisted as he tried without success to convince Truman to prepare for a new invasion of Communist territory. Encouraged by strong support at home, he continued to provoke the president by speaking out against official policy, calling for bombing of supply lines in China and a naval blockade of the Chinese coast—actions certain to lead to a Chinese-American war. Finally, on April 10, 1951, Truman dismissed MacArthur for insubordination and other unauthorized activities.

The Price of National Security

The Korean War had profound implications for the use of executive power. By instituting a peacetime draft in 1948 and then ordering American troops into Korea, Truman had bypassed congressional authority. Repub-

Examine the United States military campaign in Korea. How did this reflect Truman's doctrine of containment?
www.prenhall.com/faragher/map26.2

Web Exploration

The Korean War   The intensity of battles underscored the strategic importance of Korea in the cold war.

lican Senator Robert Taft called the president's actions "a complete usurpation" of democratic checks and balances and charged Truman with transforming his office into an "imperial presidency." For awhile, Truman sidestepped such criticisms and their constitutional implications by declaring a national emergency and by carefully referring to the military deployment not as a U.S. war but as a UN-sanctioned "police action."

The president derived his authority from NSC-68, a paper released to him by the National Security Council in April 1950 that reinterpreted both the basic policy of containment and decision making at the highest levels of government. Demonizing communism as "a new fanatic faith" that "seeks to impose its absolute authority over the rest of the world," NSC-68 pledged the United States not only to "contain" communism but to take a further step to drive back Communist influence wherever it appeared and to "foster the seeds of destruction within the Soviet Union." Moreover, the document designated the struggle between the United States and Soviet Union as "permanent," the era one of "total war." It specified that American citizens must be willing to make sacrifices—"to give up some of the benefits which they have come to associate with their freedom"—to defend their way of life. NSC-68 articulated the intellectual and psychological rationale behind U.S. national security policies for the next forty years.

Initially reluctant, Truman fulfilled the prescriptions of NSC-68 after the outbreak of the Korean War and agreed to its mandate for a rapid and permanent military buildup. By the time the conflict subsided, the defense budget had quadrupled, from $13.5 billion to more than $52 billion in 1953. The U.S. Army had grown to 3.6 million, or six times its size at the beginning of the conflict. At the same time, the federal government accelerated the development of both conventional and nonconventional weapons. In the first instance, it began to stockpile nuclear bombs and weapons, including the first hydrogen, or H-bomb, which was tested in November 1952. NCS-68 also proposed expensive "large-scale covert operations" for the "liberation" of Communist countries, particularly in Eastern Europe.

The Korean War also provided the rationale for the expansion of anti-Communist propaganda. At the end of World War II President Truman had taken steps to transform the Office of War Information into a peacetime program that operated on a much smaller budget. But by 1948 Congress was ready to pass with bipartisan support the Smith-Mundt Act, designed "to promote the better understanding of the United States among the peoples of the world and to strengthen cooperative international relations." Within a year, Congress doubled the budget for such programming, granting $3 million to revive the Voice of America, the short-wave international radio program that had been established in 1942. The new legislation also funded the development of film, print media, cultural exchange programs, and exhibitions, and it created a foundation to promote anti-Communist propaganda throughout the world. By mid-1950, the immediate goal was the "reorientation" of North Korea toward the Free World.

The government's vast "information programs" were designed less to "contain" communism than to "liberate" those countries already under Communist rule by causing disaffection among the people. By 1951 a massive "Campaign of Truth" was reaching 93 nations, and the Voice of America was broadcasting anti-Communist programming in 45 languages. Project Troy, which was initially designed by professors from Harvard and the Massachusetts Institute of Technology, aimed to penetrate the Iron Curtain, for example, by using air balloons

to distribute leaflets and cheap American goods, such as playing cards and plastic chess sets. Army pilots joined the effort, dropping leaflets on North Korean troops reading "ENJOY LIFE and plenty of cigarettes away from the war by coming over to the UN side. Escape. Save your life." On April 4, 1951, President Truman signed the order that created the Psychological Strategy Board to coordinate various operations aimed to roll back Soviet power. In his annual message to Congress that year, he had requested $115 million to fund these programs but, as the Korean War bogged down, he managed to get only $85 million.

By the time it ended, the Korean War had cost the United States approximately $100 billion and inaugurated an era of huge deficits in the federal budget and massive national debt but did nothing to improve the case for rolling back communism. Negotiations and fighting proceeded in tandem until the summer of 1953, when a settlement was reached in which both North Korea and South Korea occupied almost the same territory as when the war began. Approximately 54,000 Americans died in Korea; the North Koreans and Chinese lost well over 2 million people. The UN troops had employed both "carpet bombing" (an intense, destructive attack on a given area) and napalm (jellied gasoline bombs), destroying most of the housing and food supplies in both Koreas. True to the pattern of modern warfare, which emerged during World War II, the majority of civilians killed were women and children. Nearly 1 million Koreans were left homeless.

For the United States, the Korean War enlarged the geographical range of the cold war to include East Asia. The war also lined up the People's Republic of China and the United States as unwavering enemies for the next twenty years and heightened the U.S. commitment to Southeast Asia. Now, as one historian commented, the "frontiers on every continent were going to remain frontiers in the traditional American meaning of a frontier—a region to penetrate and control and police and civilize."

The Korean War, moreover, did much to establish an ominous tradition of "unwinnable" conflicts that left many Americans skeptical of official policy. Truman had initially rallied popular support for U.S. intervention by contrasting the Communist North with the "democratic" South, thus casting the conflict in the ideological terms of the cold war. MacArthur's early victories had promised the liberation of North Korea and even the eventual disintegration of the Soviet and Chinese regimes. But with the tactical stalemate came mass disillusionment.

In retrospect many Americans recognized that Truman, in fighting communism in Korea, had pledged the United States to defend a corrupt government and a brutal dictator. Decades later the Korean War inspired the dark comedy *M*A*S*H*, adapted for television from the film written by Hollywood screenwriter Ring Lardner, Jr., an "unfriendly witness" before HUAC, who was jailed during the Korean War for contempt of Congress. As late as 1990, members of Congress were still debating the terms of a Korean War memorial. "It ended on a sad note for Americans," one historian has concluded, "and the war and its memories drifted off into a void."

The Election of 1952

There was only one burning issue during the election campaign of 1952: the Korean War. Truman's popularity had wavered continually since he took office in 1945, but it sank to an all-time low in the early 1950s shortly after he dismissed MacArthur as commander of the UN troops in Korea. Congress received thousands of letters and telegrams calling for Truman's impeachment. "Oust President Truman" bumper stickers could be seen. MacArthur, meanwhile, returned home a hero, welcomed by more than 7 million fans in New York City alone.

Popular dissatisfaction with Truman increased. The Asia First lobby argued that if the president had acted more aggressively to turn back communism in China, the "limited war" in Korea would not have been necessary. Following these charges were accusations of large-scale corruption in his administration. Newspapers reported that several agencies had been dealing in 5 percent kickbacks for government contracts. Business and organized labor complained about the price and wage freezes imposed during the Korean War. A late-1951 Gallup poll showed the president's approval rating at 23 percent. In March 1952, Truman announced he would not run for reelection, a decision rare for a president eligible for another term.

In accepting political defeat and disgrace, Truman turned to the popular but uncharismatic governor of Illinois, Adlai E. Stevenson, Jr. Admired for his honesty and intelligence, Stevenson offered no solutions to the conflict in Korea, the accelerating arms race, or the cold war generally. Accepting the Democratic nomination, he candidly admitted that "the ordeal of the twentieth century is far from over," a prospect displeasing to voters aching for peace.

The Republicans made the most of the Democrats' dilemma. Without proposing any sweeping answers of their own, they pointed to all the obvious shortcomings of their opponents. Their campaign strategy, known as "K_1C_2"—Korea, Communism, and Corruption—took steady aim at the Truman administration, and when opinion polls showed that Dwight Eisenhower possessed an "unprecedented" 64 percent approval rating, they found in "Ike" the perfect candidate to head the ticket.

Eisenhower styled himself the representative of "modern Republicanism." He wisely avoided the nega-

Richard Nixon used the new medium of television to convince American voters that he had not established an illegal slush fund in his campaign for the vice presidency in 1952. Viewers responded enthusiastically to his melodramatic delivery and swamped the Republican campaign headquarters with telegrams endorsing his candidacy.

SOURCE: *Checkers* speech, September 24, 1952. AP/Wide World Photos.

tive impressions made by the unsuccessful 1948 Republican candidate, Thomas Dewey, who had seemed as aggressive as Truman on foreign policy and simultaneously eager to overturn the New Deal domestic legislation. Eisenhower knew better: voters wanted peace and a limited welfare state. He referred to New Deal reforms as "a solid floor that keeps all of us from falling into the pit of disaster." And although he did not go into specifics, he promised to end the Korean War with "an early and honorable" peace. Whenever he was tempted to address questions of finance or the economy, his advisers warned him: "The chief reason that people want to vote for you is because they think you have more ability to keep us out of another war."

Meanwhile, Eisenhower's vice presidential candidate, Richard Nixon, waged a relentless and defamatory attack on Stevenson, calling him "Adlai the Appeaser." Senator Joseph McCarthy chimed in, proclaiming that with club in hand he might be able to make "a good American" of Stevenson. A month before the election, McCarthy went on network television with his requisite "exhibits" and "documents," this time purportedly showing that the Democratic presidential candidate had promoted communism at home and

CHRONOLOGY

1941	Henry Luce forecasts the dawn of "the American Century"
1944	G.I. Bill of Rights benefits World War II veterans
	International Monetary Fund and World Bank founded
1945	Franklin D. Roosevelt dies in office; Harry S. Truman becomes president
	United Nations charter signed
	World War II ends
	Strike wave begins
	Truman proposes program of economic reforms
1946	Employment Act creates Council of Economic Advisers
	Churchill's Iron Curtain speech
	Atomic Energy Act establishes Atomic Energy Commission
	Republicans win control of Congress
	Benjamin Spock publishes *Baby and Child Care*
1947	Americans for Democratic Action founded
	Truman Doctrine announced; Congress appropriates $400 million in aid for Greece and Turkey
	Federal Employees Loyalty and Security Program established and attorney general's list of subversive organizations authorized
	Marshall Plan announced
	Taft-Hartley Act restricts union activities
	National Security Act establishes Department of Defense, the National Security Council, and the Central Intelligence Agency
	House Un-American Activities Committee hearings in Hollywood
1948	Smith-Mundt Act passed by Congress
	Ferdinand Lundberg and Marynia Farnham publish *Modern Woman: The Lost Sex*
	State of Israel founded
	Berlin blockade begins

	Henry Wallace nominated for president on Progressive Party ticket
	Truman announces peacetime draft and desegregates U.S. armed forces and civil service
	Truman wins election; Democrats sweep both houses of Congress
1949	Truman announces Fair Deal
	North Atlantic Treaty Organization (NATO) created
	Communists, led by Mao Zedong, take power in China
	Berlin blockade ends
	Soviet Union explodes atomic bomb
1950	Alger Hiss convicted of perjury
	Senator Joseph McCarthy begins anti-Communist crusade
	Soviet Union and the People's Republic of China sign an alliance
	Adoption of NSC-68 consolidates presidential war powers
	Korean War begins
	Internal Security (McCarran) Act requires registration of Communist organizations and arrest of Communists during national emergencies
1951	Truman dismisses General Douglas MacArthur
	Psychological Strategy Board created
	Armistice talks begin in Korea
1952	Immigration and Nationality Act retains quota system, lifts ban on immigration of Asian and Pacific peoples, but bans "subversives" and homosexuals
	United States explodes first hydrogen bomb
	Dwight D. Eisenhower wins presidency; Richard Nixon becomes vice president
1953	Julius and Ethel Rosenberg executed for atomic espionage
	Armistice ends fighting in Korea
1954	Army-McCarthy hearings end
1955	Warsaw Pact created

abroad. These outrageous charges kept the Stevenson campaign off balance.

The Republican campaign was itself not entirely free of scandal: Nixon had been caught accepting personal gifts from wealthy benefactors. Pleading his case on national television, he described his wife Pat's "good Republican cloth coat" and their modest style of living. He then contritely admitted that he had indeed accepted one gift, a puppy named Checkers that his daughters loved and that he refused to give back. "The Poor Richard Show," as critics called the event, defused the scandal without answering the most important charges.

Unaffected by the scandal, Eisenhower continued to enchant the voters as a peace candidate. Ten days before the election he dramatically announced, "I shall go to Korea" to settle the war. Eisenhower received 55 percent of the vote and carried thirty-nine states, in part because he brought out an unusually large number of voters in normally Democratic areas. He won the popular vote in much of the South and in the northern cities of New York, Chicago, Boston, and Cleveland. Riding his coattails, the Republicans regained narrow control of Congress. The New Deal coalition of ethnic and black voters, labor, northern liberals, and southern conservatives no longer commanded a majority.

CONCLUSION

In his farewell address, in January 1953, Harry Truman reflected: "I suppose that history will remember my term in office as the years when the 'cold war' began to overshadow our lives. I have hardly had a day in office that has not been dominated by this all-embracing struggle."

The election of Dwight Eisenhower helped to diminish the intensity of this dour mood without actually bringing a halt to the conflict. The new president pledged himself to liberate the world from communism by peaceful means rather than force. "Our aim is more subtle," he announced during his campaign, "more pervasive, more complete. We are trying to get the world, by peaceful means, to believe the truth. . . ." Increasing the budget of the CIA, Eisenhower took the cold war out of the public eye by relying to a far greater extent than Truman on psychological warfare and covert operations.

"The Eisenhower Movement," wrote journalist Walter Lippmann, was a "mission in American politics" to restore a sense of community among the American people. In a larger sense, many of the issues of the immediate post–World War II years seemed to have been settled, or put off for a distant future. The international boundaries of communism were frozen with the Chinese Revolution, the Berlin Crisis, and now the Korean War. Meanwhile, at home cold war defense spending had become a permanent part of the national budget, an undeniable drain on tax revenues but an important element in the government contribution to economic prosperity. If the nuclear arms race remained a cause for anxiety, joined by more personal worries about the changing patterns of family life, a sense of relative security nevertheless spread. Prospects for world peace had dimmed, but the worst nightmares of the 1940s had eased as well.

REVIEW QUESTIONS

1. Discuss the origins of the cold war and the sources of growing tensions between the United States and the Soviet Union at the close of World War II.
2. Describe the basic elements of President Harry Truman's policy of containment. How did the threat of atomic warfare affect this policy?
3. Compare the presidencies of Franklin D. Roosevelt and Harry S. Truman, both Democrats.
4. Describe the impact of McCarthyism on American political life. How did the anti-Communist campaigns affect the media? What were the sources of Senator Joseph McCarthy's popularity? What brought about his downfall?
5. How did the cold war affect American culture?
6. Discuss the role of the United States in Korea in the decade after World War II. How did the Korean War affect the 1952 presidential election?
7. Why did Dwight D. Eisenhower win the 1952 presidential election?

RECOMMENDED READING

Mark S. Byrnes, *The Truman Years, 1945–1953* (2000). A concise history of the Truman administration when the United States became the dominant economic power.

Warren I. Cohen, *America in the Age of Soviet Power, 1945–1991* (1993). This study examines the origins of the cold war in policies ending World War II.

Kevin J. Fernlund, ed., *The Cold War American West, 1945–1989* (1998). Ten essays illustrating the impact of the cold war on the West.

John Fousek, *To Lead the Free World: American Nationalism and the Cultural Roots of the Cold War* (2000). Examines the "public culture" of the cold war.

Richard M. Fried, *The Russians Are Coming! The Russians Are Coming!: Pageantry and Patriotism in Cold-War America* (1998). Examines, through vivid example, the creation of the fear of communism and its translation into patriotic zeal.

Margot A. Henriksen, *Dr. Strangelove's America: Society and Culture in the Atomic Age* (1997). Argues in a lively fashion that the atomic bomb played the "central, defining role" in American culture and society from 1945 into the early 1980s.

George Lipsitz, *A Rainbow at Midnight: Labor and Culture in the 1940s* (1994). Lipsitz shows how struggles for economic democracy were defeated and how popular culture arose in blue-collar communities.

Elaine Tyler May, *Homeward Bound: American Families in the Cold War Era* (1988). A lively account of the effects on family life and women's roles of the national mood of "containment."

David G. McCullough, *Truman* (1992). A heroic rendition of Truman's personal life and political career.

Patrick McGilligan and Paul Buhle, *Tender Comrades: A Backstory of the Hollywood Blacklist* (1997). A collection of interviews with thirty-five victims of the Hollywood Blacklist.

Joanne Meyerowitz, ed., *Not June Cleaver: Women and Gender in Postwar America, 1945–1960* (1994). A collection that refutes the common stereotype of women as homebound during the postwar era.

Stanley Weintraub, *MacArthur's War: Korea and the Undoing of an American Hero* (2000). Tells the story of the downfall of the commander of U.S. forces in the Far East.

▶ Media Resources

 U.S. HISTORY DOCUMENTS CD-ROM

Cold War

26-1 George F. Kennan, "Long Telegram" (1946)

26-2 Kenneth MacFarland, "The Unfinished Work" (1946)

26-3 George Marshall, The Marshall Plan (1947)

26-4 Containment (1947)

26-5 Harry S Truman, The Truman Doctrine (1947)

26-6 Ronald Reagan, Testimony Before the House Unamerican Activities Committee (1947)

26-7 Joseph R. McCarthy, from Speech Delivered to the Women's Club of Wheeling, West Virginia (1950)

26-8 National Security Council Memorandum Number 68 (1950)

26-9 Senator Joseph McCarthy's Telegram to President Truman following the "Wheeling (W. Va.) Speech," February 11, 1950

COMPANION WEBSITE HIGHLIGHTS

To view an exploration, enter one of the URLs below in your browser.

 Web Explorations

Divided Europe
http://www.prenhall.com/faragher/map26.1
The Korean War
http://www.prenhall.com/faragher/map26.2

 Additional Interactive Maps

To access the map, go to this chapter's resources at
http://www.prenhall.com/faragher
The Election of 1948, page 818

 HISTORY RESOURCE CENTER

To find the resources listed below, go to
http://www.prenhall.com/historyresourcecenter

Images

Berlin Airlift

Joseph McCarthy

Korean Conflict

Military Forces in Korea

Korean Conflict—American Prisoners of War

Korean Conflict—Invasion of Inchon

Senator Joseph McCarthy's Telegram to President Truman

Untitled Political Cartoon by Clifford K. Berryman, 1947

EXPLORING AMERICA
THE TRUMAN DOCTRINE
http://www.prenhall.com/faragher/trumandoctrine

The end of World War II saw a steady decline in relations with the Soviet Union that led to the Cold War. How did the military situation at the close of World War II influence the course of events in the immediate postwar years? Why did President Harry Truman issue the Truman Doctrine? What influenced government and public perceptions of the Soviet Union and communism? What other initiatives did the government launch in Europe to combat communism? *The Truman Doctrine* module explores the initial post World War II years that gave rise to the Cold War.

The Truman Doctrine examines the rise of the Cold War and its legacy, indicating that the development of two spheres of influence after World War II

Winston Churchill
Click anywhere to go to the previous page.

was influenced by events and, at least for the United States, by ideas based on the goals of the Soviet Union. The narrative describes the events that led to the Truman Doctrine and the Cold War, using important documents, including Truman's speech announcing his doctrine, to provide indepth analysis of issues and ideas. Interactive maps and a chronology provide important historical context to the Truman Doctrine and the Cold War.

Reflect and Respond

1 Most of Truman's speech dealt directly with Greece. What specific reasons did he offer for the United States assisting Greece?

2. What specific reasons did he offer for assistance to Turkey?

3. The Truman Doctrine asserted that "it must be the policy of the United States to support free peoples who are resisting attempted subjugation by armed minorities or by outside pressures." Truman, that is, was not merely seeking to assist Greece and Turkey, but to formulate a policy under which the United States would undertake to combat communism anywhere. How did he seek to justify the global nature of the responsibilities he urged Congress to face "squarely"?

✓ Check it out

Divided Europe

The coalition that allied to defeat the Axis in World War II broke down leading to the division into two camps. The map shows how the division reflected the

progress of the Soviets on one hand and the United States, Great Britain, and France on the other. It is also important for depicting the Allied solution to any resurgence of Germany after that nation had lost two world wars. Equally important, the map helps put the postwar reconstruction of European nations in perspective.

This exploration is also available on the *Exploring America* CD-ROM.

TWENTY-SEVEN
AMERICA AT MIDCENTURY

▶ 1952–1963

SOURCE: Photo by Willinger. Getty Images, Inc. (cat #3632)

Popular Music in Memphis

HE NINETEEN-YEAR-OLD SINGER WAS PEERING NERVOUSLY OUT OVER the large crowd. He knew that people had come to Overton Park's outdoor amphitheater that hot, sticky July day in 1954 to hear the headliner, country music star Slim Whitman. Sun Records, a local Memphis label, had just released the teenager's first record, and it had begun to receive some airplay on local radio. But the singer and his two bandmates had never played in a setting even remotely as large as this one. And their music defied categories: it wasn't black and it wasn't white; it wasn't pop and it wasn't country. But when the singer launched into his version of a black blues song called "That's All Right," the crowd went wild. "I came offstage," the singer later recalled, "and my manager told me that they was hollering because I was wiggling my legs. I went back out for an encore, and I did a little more, and the more I did, the wilder they went." Elvis Presley had arrived.

Elvis combined a hard-driving, rhythmic approach to blues and country music with a riveting performance style, inventing the new music known as rock 'n' roll. An unprecedented cultural phenomenon, rock 'n' roll was a music made largely for and by teenagers. In communities all over America, rock 'n' roll brought teens together around jukeboxes, at sock hops, in cars, and at private parties. It demonstrated the enormous consumer power of American teens. Rock 'n' roll also embodied a postwar trend accelerating the integration of white and black music. This cultural integration prefigured the social and political integration won by the civil rights movement.

Located halfway between St. Louis and New Orleans on the Mississippi River, Memphis had become a thriving commercial city by the 1850s, with an economy centered on the lucrative cotton trade of the surrounding delta region. It grew rapidly in the post–Civil War years, attracting a polyglot population of white businessmen and planters, poor rural whites and blacks, and German and Irish immigrants. By the early twentieth century Memphis also boasted a remarkable diversity of popular theater and music, including a large opera house, numerous brass bands, vaudeville and burlesque, minstrel shows, jug bands, and blues clubs.

Like most American cities, Memphis enjoyed healthy growth during World War II, with lumber mills, furniture factories, and chemical manufacturing supplementing the cotton market as sources of jobs and prosperity. And like the rest of the South, Memphis was a legally segregated city; whites and blacks lived, went to school, and worked apart. Class differences among whites were important as well. Like thousands of other poor rural whites in these years, Elvis Presley had moved from Mississippi to Memphis in 1949, where his father found work in a munitions plant. The Presleys were poor enough to qualify for an apartment in Lauderdale Courts, a Memphis public housing project. To James Conaway, who grew up in an all-white, middle-class East Memphis neighborhood, people like the Presleys were "white trash." Negroes, he recalled, were "not necessarily below the rank of a country boy like Elvis, but of another universe, and yet there was more affection for them than for some whites."

839

Gloria Wade-Gayles, who lived in the all-black Foote Homes housing project, vividly remembered that her family and neighbors "had no illusion about their lack of power, but they believed in their strength." For them, strength grew from total immersion in a black community that included ministers, teachers, insurance men, morticians, barbers, and entertainers. "Surviving meant being black, and being black meant believing in our humanity, and retaining it, in a world that denied we had it in the first place."

Yet in the cultural realm, class and racial barriers could be challenged. Elvis Presley grew up a dreamy, shy boy, who turned to music for emotional release and spiritual expression. He soaked up the wide range of music styles available in Memphis. The Assembly of God Church his family attended featured a renowned hundred-voice choir. Elvis and his friends went to marathon all-night "gospel singings" at Ellis Auditorium, where they enjoyed the tight harmonies and emotional style of white gospel quartets.

Elvis also drew from the sounds he heard on Beale Street, the main black thoroughfare of Memphis and one of the nation's most influential centers of African American music. In the postwar years, local black rhythm and blues artists like B. B. King, Junior Parker, and Muddy Waters attracted legions of black and white fans with their emotional power and exciting showmanship. At the Handy Theater on Beale Street, the teenaged Elvis Presley, like thousands of other white young people, heard black performers at the "Midnight Rambles"—late shows for white people only. Elvis himself performed along with black contestants in amateur shows at Beale Street's Palace Theater. Nat D. Williams, a prominent black Memphis disc jockey and music promoter, recalled how black audiences responded to Elvis's unique style. "He had a way of singing the blues that was distinctive. He could sing 'em not necessarily like a Negro, but he didn't sing 'em altogether like a typical white musician. . . . Always he had that certain humanness about him that Negroes like to put in their songs."

The expansion of the broadcasting and recording indus-

tries in the postwar years also contributed to the weakening of racial barriers in the musical realm. Two Memphis radio stations featured the hard-driving rhythm and blues music that was beginning to attract a strong following among young white listeners. These Memphis stations also featured spirituals by African American artists such as Mahalia Jackson and Clara Ward.

Elvis himself understood his debt to black music and black performers. "The colored folks," he told an interviewer in 1956, "been singing and playing it just like I'm doing now, man, for more years than I know. They played it like that in the shanties and in their juke joints and nobody paid it no mind until I goosed it up. I got it from them."

Dissatisfied with the cloying pop music of the day, white teenagers across the nation were increasingly turning to the rhythmic drive and emotional intensity of black rhythm and blues. They quickly adopted rock 'n' roll (the term had long been an African American slang expression for dancing and sexual intercourse) as their music. But it was more than just music: it was also an attitude, a celebration of being young, and a sense of having something that adult authority could not understand or control.

When Sun Records sold Presley's contract to RCA Records in 1956, Elvis became an international star. Records like "Heartbreak Hotel," "Don't Be Cruel," and "Jailhouse Rock" shot to the top of the charts and blurred the old boundaries between pop, country, and rhythm and blues. By helping to accustom white teenagers to the style and sound of black artists, Elvis helped establish rock 'n' roll as an interracial phenomenon. Institutional racism would continue to plague the music business—many black artists were routinely cheated out of royalties and severely underpaid—but the music of postwar Memphis at least pointed the way toward the exciting cultural possibilities that could emerge from breaking down the barriers of race. It also gave postwar American teenagers a newfound sense of community. ■

Memphis

KEY TOPICS

- Post–World War II prosperity
- Suburban life: ideal and reality
- The emergence of youth culture
- Television, mass culture, and their critics

- Foreign policy in the Eisenhower years
- John F. Kennedy and the promise of a New Frontiers

AMERICAN SOCIETY AT MIDCENTURY

With the title of his influential work, *The Affluent Society* (1958), economist John Kenneth Galbraith gave a label to postwar America. Galbraith observed that American capitalism had worked "quite brilliantly" in the years since World War II. But Americans, he argued, needed to spend less on personal consumption and devote more public funds to schools, medical care, cultural activities, and social services. For most Americans, however, strong economic growth was the defining fact of the postwar period. A fierce desire for consumer goods and the "good life" imbued American culture, and the deeply held popular belief in a continuously expanding economy and a steadily increasing standard of living—together with the tensions of the cold war—shaped American social and political life.

The Eisenhower Presidency

Dwight D. Eisenhower's landslide election victory in 1952 set the stage for the first full two-term Republican presidency since that of Ulysses S. Grant. At the core of Eisenhower's political philosophy lay a conservative vision of community. He saw America as a corporate commonwealth, similar to the "associative state" envisioned by Herbert Hoover a generation earlier (see Chapter 23). Eisenhower believed the industrial strife, high inflation, and fierce partisan politics of the Truman years could be corrected only through cooperation,

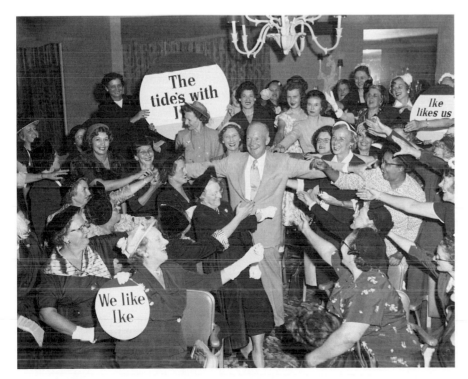

Presidential contender Dwight D. Eisenhower hosts a group of Republican National Committee women at his campaign headquarters in 1952. Ike's status as America's biggest war hero, along with his genial public persona, made him an extremely popular candidate with voters across party lines.

SOURCE: © Bettmann/CORBIS (BE036973).

self-restraint, and disinterested public service. As president, Eisenhower emphasized limiting the New Deal trends that had expanded federal power, and he encouraged a voluntary, as opposed to regulatory, relationship between government and business. Social harmony and "the good life" at home were closely linked, in his view, to maintaining a stable and American-led international order abroad.

Eisenhower viewed his leadership style as crucial for achieving the goal of a harmonious, corporate-led society. That style owed something to his roots in turn-of-the-century Kansas and his socialization in the military. In the army he had risen through the command structure by playing it safe, keeping his own counsel, and allowing his subordinates to apprise him of his options. He once described his views on leadership to a critic: "It's persuasion—and conciliation—and patience. It's long, slow, tough work. That's the only kind of leadership I know or believe in—or will practice."

Consciously, Eisenhower adopted an evasive style in public, and he was fond of the phrase "middle of the road." He told a news conference, "I feel pretty good when I'm attacked from both sides. It makes me more certain I'm on the right track." Intellectuals and liberals found it easy to satirize Eisenhower for his blandness, his frequent verbal gaffes, his vagueness, and his often contradictory pronouncements. The majority of the American public, however, evidently agreed with Eisenhower's easygoing approach to his office. He kept the conservative and liberal wings of his party united and appealed to many Democrats and independents.

Eisenhower wanted to run government in a businesslike manner while letting the states and corporate interests guide domestic policy and the economy. He appointed nine businessmen to his first cabinet, including three with ties to General Motors. Former GM chief Charles Wilson served as secretary of defense and epitomized the administration's economic views with his famous aphorism "What was good for our country was good for General Motors, and vice versa." In his appointments to the Federal Trade Commission, the Federal Communications Commission, and the Federal Power Commission, Eisenhower favored men congenial to the corporate interests they were charged with regulating. Eisenhower also secured passage of the Submerged Lands Act in 1953, which transferred $40 billion worth of disputed offshore oil lands from the federal government to the Gulf states. This transfer ensured a greater role for the states and private companies in the oil business—and cost the Treasury billions in lost revenues.

In the long run, the Eisenhower administration's lax approach to government regulation accelerated a trend toward the destruction of the natural environment. Oil exploration in Louisiana's bayous, for example, began the massive degradation of America's largest wetlands. Water diversion policies in Florida seriously damaged the biggest tropical forest in the United States. The increased use of toxic chemicals, begun during World War II and largely unregulated by law, placed warehouses of poisons in hundreds of sites, many abutting military installations. Virtually unregulated use and disposal of the pesticide DDT poisoned birds and other animals and left permanent toxic scars in the environment.

At the same time, Eisenhower accepted the New Deal legacy of greater federal responsibility for social welfare. He rejected calls from conservative Republicans, for example, to dismantle the Social Security system. His administration agreed to a modest expansion of Social Security and unemployment insurance and small increases in the minimum wage. Ike also created the Department of Health, Education and Welfare, appointing Oveta Culp Hobby as its secretary, making her the second woman to hold a cabinet post. In agriculture, Eisenhower continued the policy of parity payments designed to sustain farm prices. Between 1952 and 1960, federal spending on agriculture jumped from about $1 billion to $7 billion.

Eisenhower proved hesitant to use fiscal policy to pump up the economy, which went into recession after the Korean War ended in 1953 and again in 1958, when the unemployment rate reached 7.5 percent. The administration refused to cut taxes or increase spending to stimulate growth. Eisenhower feared starting an inflationary spiral more than he worried about unemployment or poverty. By the time he left office, he could proudly point out that real wages for an average family had risen 20 percent during his term. With low inflation and steady, if modest, growth, the Eisenhower years brought greater prosperity to most Americans. Long after he retired from public life, Ike liked to remember his major achievement as having created "an atmosphere of greater serenity and mutual confidence."

Subsidizing Prosperity

During the Eisenhower years the federal government played a crucial role in subsidizing programs that helped millions of Americans achieve middle-class status. Federal aid helped people to buy homes, attend college and technical schools, and live in newly built suburbs. Much of this assistance expanded on programs begun during the New Deal and World War II. The Federal Housing Administration (FHA), established in 1934, extended the government's role in subsidizing the housing industry. The FHA insured long-term mortgage loans made by private lenders for home building. By putting the full faith and credit of the federal government behind residential mortgages, the FHA attracted new private capital into home building and revolutionized the industry. A typical FHA mortgage required less than 10 percent for a down payment and spread low-interest monthly payments over thirty years.

Yet FHA policies also had long-range drawbacks. FHA insurance went overwhelmingly to new residential developments, usually on the fringes of urban areas, hastening the decline of older, inner-city neighborhoods. A bias toward suburban, middle-class communities manifested itself in several ways: it was FHA policy to favor the construction of single-family projects while discouraging multi-unit housing, to refuse loans for the repair of older structures and rental units, and to require for any loan guarantee an "unbiased professional estimate" rating the property, the prospective borrower, and the neighborhood. In practice, these estimates resulted in blatant discrimination against communities that were racially mixed. The FHA's Underwriting Manual bluntly warned: "If a neighborhood is to retain stability, it is necessary that properties shall continue to be occupied by the same social and racial classes." FHA policies in effect inscribed the racial and income segregation of suburbia in public policy.

The majority of suburbs were built as planned communities. One of the first was Levittown, which opened in Hempstead, Long Island, in 1947, on 1,500 acres of former potato fields. Developer William Levitt, who described his firm as "the General Motors of the housing industry," was the first entrepreneur to bring mass-production techniques to home building. All building materials were precut and prefabricated at a central factory, then assembled on-site into houses by largely unskilled, nonunion labor. In this way Levitt put up hundreds of identical houses each week. Eventually, Levittown encompassed more than 17,000 houses and 82,000 people. Yet in 1960 not one of Levittown's residents was African American, and owners who rented out their homes were told to specify that their houses would not be "used or occupied by any person other than members of the Caucasian race." Levitt himself angrily rejected any criticism of his racial policies: "As a company our position is simply this: we can solve a housing problem, or we can try to solve a racial problem, but we cannot combine the two."

The revolution in American life wrought by the 1944 Servicemen's Readjustment Act, known as the GI Bill of Rights, extended beyond its impact on higher education (see Chapter 26). In addition to educational grants, the act provided returning veterans with low-interest mortgages and business loans, thus subsidizing the growth of the suburbs as well as the postwar expansion of higher education. Through 1956, nearly 10 million veterans received tuition and training benefits under the act. Veteran's Administration–insured loans totaled more than $50 billion by 1962, providing assistance to millions of former GIs who started businesses.

The Federal Highway Act of 1956 gave another key boost to postwar growth, especially in the suburbs. It originally authorized $32 billion for the construction of a national interstate highway system. Financing was to come from new taxes on gasoline, as well as on oil, tires, buses, and trucks. Key to this ambitious program's success was that these revenues were held separately from general taxes in a Highway Trust Fund. By 1972 the program had become the single largest public works program in American history; 41,000 miles of highway were built at a cost of $76 billion. Federal subsidy of the interstate highway system stimulated both the automobile industry and suburb building. But it also accelerated the decline of American mass transit and older cities. By 1970, the nation possessed the world's best roads and one of its worst public transportation systems.

The shadow of the cold war prompted the federal government

This photo, which appeared in a 1950 issue of *Life* magazine, posed a family of pioneer suburbanites in front of their Levittown, New York, home. The prefabricated house was built in 1948.

SOURCE: Bernard Hoffman/Life Magazine/© 1950 TimePix (Set #31949).

to take new initiatives in aid for education. After the Soviet Union launched its first Sputnik satellite in the fall of 1957, American officials worried that the country might be lagging behind the Soviets in training scientists and engineers. The Eisenhower administration, with the bipartisan support of Congress, pledged to strengthen support for educating American students in mathematics, science, and technology. The National Defense Education Act (NDEA) of 1958 allocated $280 million in grants—tied to matching grants from the states—for state universities to upgrade their science facilities. The NDEA also created $300 million in low-interest loans for college students, who had to repay only half the amount if they went on to teach in elementary or secondary school after graduation. In addition, the NDEA provided fellowship support for graduate students planning to go into college and university teaching. The NDEA represented a new consensus on the importance of high-quality education to the national interest.

Suburban Life

The suburban boom strengthened the domestic ideal of the nuclear family as the model for American life. In particular, the picture of the perfect suburban wife— efficient, patient, always charming—became a dominant image in television, movies, and magazines. Suburban domesticity was usually presented as women's only path to happiness and fulfillment. This cultural image often masked a stifling existence defined by housework, child care, and boredom. In the late 1950s, Betty Friedan, a wife, mother, and journalist, began a systematic survey of her Smith College classmates. She found "a strange discrepancy between the reality of our lives as women and the image to which we were trying to conform." Friedan expanded her research and in 1963 published *The Feminine Mystique*, a landmark book that articulated the frustrations of suburban women and helped to launch a revived feminist movement.

The postwar rebirth of religious life was strongly associated with suburban living. In 1940 less than half the American population belonged to institutionalized churches; by the mid-1950s nearly three-quarters identified themselves as church members. A church-building boom was centered in the expanding suburbs. Best-selling religious authors such as Norman Vincent Peale and Bishop Fulton J. Sheen offered a shallow blend of reassurance and "the power of positive thinking." They stressed individual solutions to problems, opposing social or political activism. Their emphasis on the importance of belonging, of fitting in, meshed well with suburban social life and the ideal of family-centered domesticity.

California came to embody postwar suburban life. At the center of this lifestyle was the automobile. Cars were a necessity for commuting to work. California also led the nation in the development of drive-in facilities: motels, movies, shopping malls, fast-food restaurants, and banks. More than 500 miles of highways would be constructed around Los Angeles alone. In Orange County, southeast of Los Angeles, the "centerless city" emerged as the dominant form of community. The experience of one woman resident was typical: "I live in Garden Grove, work in Irvine, shop in Santa Ana, go to the dentist in Anaheim, my husband works in Long Beach, and I used to be the president of the League of Women Voters in Fullerton."

Contemporary journalists, novelists, and social scientists contributed to the popular image of suburban life as essentially dull, conformist, and peopled exclusively by the educated middle class. John Cheever, for example, won the National Book Award for *The Wapshot Chronicle* (1957), a novel set in fictional Remsen Park, "a community of four thousand identical homes." Psychiatrist

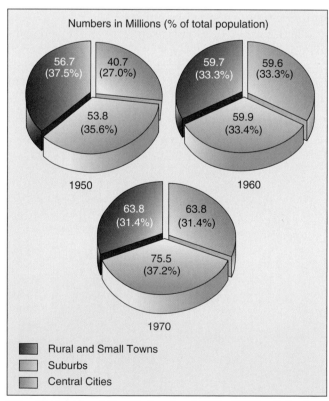

The Growth of the Suburbs, 1950–1970 Suburban growth, at the expense of older inner cities, was one of the key social trends in the twenty-five years following World War II. By 1970, more Americans lived in suburbs than in either inner cities or rural areas.

SOURCE: Adapted from U.S. Bureau of the Census, *Current Censuses, 1930–1970* (Washington, D.C.: U.S. Government Printing Office, 1975).

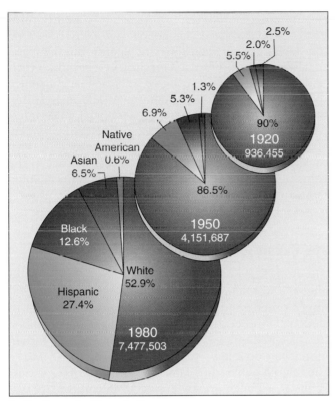

2.5%
2.0%
5.5%
1.3%
5.3%
6.9%
90%
1920
936,455

Native
American
Asian 0.6%
6.5%
86.5%
1950
4,151,687

Black
12.6%
White
52.9%
Hispanic
27.4%
1980
7,477,503

L.A. County Population

Richard Gordon's *Split Level Trap* (1960) focused on the emotional problems he observed among the suburban families of Bergen County, New Jersey. Yet these writers tended to obscure the real class and ethnic differences found among and between suburban communities. Many new suburbs had a distinctively blue-collar cast. Milpitas, California, for example, grew up around a Ford auto plant about fifty miles outside San Jose. Its residents were blue-collar assembly-line workers and their families, rather than salaried, college-educated, white-collar employees. Self-segregation and zoning ordinances gave some new suburbs distinctively Italian, Jewish, or Irish ethnic identities, similar to older urban neighborhoods. For millions of new suburbanites, architectural and psychological conformity was an acceptable price to pay for the comforts of home ownership, a small plot of land, and a sense of security and status.

Organized Labor and the AFL-CIO

By the mid-1950s American trade unions reached an historic high-point in their penetration of the labor market, reflecting the enormous gains made during the organizing drives in core mass-production industries during the New Deal and World War II. Whereas only one in eight nonagricultural workers were union members on the eve of the Great Depression, twenty-five years later the fig-

ure stood at one in three. Union influence in political life, especially within the Democratic Party, had also increased. Yet the Republican sweep to power in 1952 meant that for the first time in a generation organized labor was without an ally in the White House. New leaders in the nation's two major labor organizations, the American Federation of Labor (dominated by old line construction and craft unions) and the Congress of Industrial Organizations (centered around unions in mass-production industry), now pushed for a merger of the two rival groups as way to protect and build on the movement's recent gains.

George Meany, the gruff, cigar-chomping head of the AFL, seemed the epitome of the modern labor boss. Originally a plumber, he had worked his way through the AFL bureaucracy and had played a leading role on National War Labor Board during World War II. An outspoken anti-Communist, Meany had pushed the AFL closer to the Democratic Party, and he took pride in never having been on a strike or a picket line. Unions, he believed, must focus on improving the economic well-being of their members. Meany's counterpart in the CIO was Walter Reuther, originally a tool-and-die maker in the auto shops of Detroit. Reuther had come to prominence as a leader of the United Automobile Workers during the tumultuous organizing drives of the 1930s and 1940s. Although he had moved away from his early socialist leanings, Reuther believed strongly that American unions ought to stand for something beyond the bread and butter needs of their members. His support of a broader social vision, including racial equality, aggressive union organizing, and expansion of the welfare state, reflected the more militant tradition of CIO unions. Despite their differences, both Meany and Reuther believed a merger of their two organizations offered the best strategy for the labor movement. In 1955 the newly combined AFL-CIO brought some 12.5 million union members under one banner, with Meany as president and Reuther as director of the Industrial Union Department.

The merger marked the apex of trade union membership, and after 1955 its share of the labor market began a slow and steady decline. To be sure, union membership helped bring the trappings of middle-class prosperity to millions of workers and their families: home ownership, higher education for children, travel, and comfortable retirement. But the AFL-CIO showed little commitment to bringing unorganized workers into the fold. Scandals involving union corruption and racketeering hurt the labor movement's public image. In 1957 the AFL-CIO expelled its largest single affiliate, the International Brotherhood of Teamsters, because of its close ties to organized crime. In 1959, after highly publicized hearings into union corruption, Congress passed the Landrum Griffin Act, which widened government control over union affairs and further restricted union use of picketing and secondary boycotts during strikes. While union membership as a percentage of the total workforce declined, important growth did take place in new areas, reflecting a broader shift in the American work place from manufacturing to service jobs. During the 1950s and 1960s union membership among public sector employees, especially at the state and local level, increased dramatically. Only 400,000 government workers belonged to unions in 1955. By the early 1970s the figure reached 4 million, as civil servants, postal employees, teachers, police, and firefighters joined unions for the first time. Unions such as the American Federation of State, County, and Municipal Employees (AFSCME) and the American Federation of Teachers (AFT) would emerge as powerful players within the evolving AFL-CIO.

Lonely Crowds and Organization Men

Perhaps the most ambitious and controversial critique of postwar suburban America was sociologist David Riesman's *The Lonely Crowd* (1950). Riesman argued that modern America had given birth to a new kind of character type, the "other-directed" man. Previously the nation had cultivated "inner-directed" people— self-reliant individualists who early on in life had internalized self-discipline and moral standards. By contrast, the "other-directed" person typical of the modern era was peer-oriented. Morality and ideals came from the overarching desire to conform. Americans, Riesman thought, were now less likely to take risks or act independently. Their thinking and habits had come to be determined by cues they received from the mass media.

Similarly, William H. Whyte's *Organization Man* (1956), a study of the Chicago suburb of Park Forest, offered a picture of people obsessed with fitting into their communities and jobs. In place of the old Protestant ethic of hard work, thrift, and competitive struggle, Whyte believed, middle-class suburbanites now strove mainly for a comfortable, secure niche in the system. They held to a new social ethic, he argued: "a belief in the group as the source of creativity; a belief in 'belongingness' as the ultimate need of the individual." Sloan Wilson's *Man in the Grey Flannel Suit*, a 1955 best-seller, featured a hero who rejects the top position at his firm. His boss sympathizes with this reluctance to sacrifice, telling him, "There are plenty of good positions where it's not necessary for a man to put in an unusual amount of work."

The most radical critic of postwar society, and the one with the most enduring influence, was Texas-reared sociologist C. Wright Mills. In *White Collar* (1951), Mills analyzed the job culture that typified life for middle-class salaried employees, office workers, and bureaucrats. "When white collar people get jobs," he wrote, "they sell not only their time and energy, but their personalities as well. They sell by the week or month their smiles and their kindly gestures, and they must practice the prompt repression of resentment and aggression." In *The Power Elite* (1956), Mills argued that a small, interconnected group of corporate executives, military men, and political leaders had come to dominate American society. The arms race in particular, carried out in the name of cold war policies, had given an unprecedented degree of power to what President Eisenhower later termed the military-industrial complex.

The Expansion of Higher Education

American higher education experienced rapid growth after the war. This expansion both reflected and reinforced other trends in postwar society. The number of students enrolled in colleges and universities climbed from 2.6 million in 1950 to 3.2 million in 1960. It then more than doubled—to 7.5 million—by 1970, as the baby boom generation came of age. Most of these new students attended greatly enlarged state university systems. Main campuses at state universities in Michigan, Wisconsin, California, and other states grew bigger than ever, enrolling as many as 40,000 students. Technical colleges and "normal schools" (designed originally for the training of teachers) were upgraded and expanded into full-fledged universities, as in the branches of the State University of New York, founded in 1948.

Several factors contributed to this explosion. A variety of new federal programs, including the GI Bill and the National Defense Education Act, helped subsidize college education for millions of new students. Government spending on research and development in universities, especially for defense-related projects, pumped further resources into higher education. Much of this money supported programs in graduate work, reflecting an important postwar shift in the priorities of American universities. Graduate education and faculty research now challenged traditional undergraduate teaching as the main locus of university activity and power.

Colleges and universities by and large accepted the values of postwar corporate culture. By the mid-1950s, 20 percent of all college graduates majored in business or other commercial fields. The college degree was a gateway to the middle class. It became a requirement for a whole range of expanding white-collar occupations in banking, insurance, real estate, advertising and marketing, and other corporate enterprises. As much as educating young people, colleges trained them for careers in technical, professional, and management positions. Most administrators accommodated large business interests, which were well represented on university boards of trustees. Universities themselves were increasingly run like businesses, with administrators adopting the language of input-output, cost effectiveness, and quality control.

Researchers found college students in the 1950s generally absorbed the conventions and attitudes associated with working in a corporate environment. A typical Iowa State student told one writer, "You have to be very careful not to associate with the wrong clan of people, an introvert that isn't socially acceptable, guys who dress in the fashion of ten years ago. These people are just not accepted—and, if you associate with them, you're not accepted either."

Health and Medicine

Dramatic improvements in medical care allowed many Americans to enjoy longer and healthier lives. During the war the federal government had poured unprecedented amounts of money into medical research and the diffusion of new techniques. The armed forces had immunized and treated millions of servicemen and women for diseases ranging from syphilis to tuberculosis. New antibiotics such as penicillin were manufactured and distributed on a mass basis, and after the war they became widely available to the general population. Federal support for research continued after the war with the reorganization of the National Institutes of Health in 1948. Federal agencies, led by the National Institute of Mental Health, founded in 1949, also expanded research on and treatment of mental illness.

By 1960 many dreaded epidemic diseases, such as tuberculosis, diphtheria, whooping cough, and measles, had virtually disappeared from American life. Perhaps the most celebrated achievement of postwar medicine was the victory over poliomyelitis. Between 1947 and 1951 this disease, which usually crippled those it did not kill, struck an annual average of 39,000 Americans. In 1952, 58,000 cases, most of them children, were reported. Frightened parents warned children to stay away from crowded swimming pools and other gathering places. In 1955 Jonas Salk pioneered the first effective vaccine against the disease, using a preparation of killed virus. A nationwide program of polio vaccination, later supplemented by the oral Sabin vaccine, virtually eliminated polio by the 1960s.

Yet the benefits of "wonder drugs" and advanced medical techniques were not shared equally by all Americans. More sophisticated treatments and expensive new hospital facilities sharply increased the costs of health care. The very poor and many elderly Americans found themselves unable to afford modern medi-

Dr. Jonas E. Salk and nurse administered polio vaccine to Pauline Antloger, a student at Sunnyside School in Pittsburgh, 1955. Dr. Salk's scientific breakthrough of a killed-virus polio vaccine led to an array of viral vaccines to cure other diseases, such as hepatitis.

SOURCE: © Bettmann/CORBIS (U.1122024).

cine. Thousands of communities, especially in rural areas and small towns, lacked doctors or decent hospital facilities. Critics of the medical establishment charged that the proliferation of medical specialists and large hospital complexes had increased the number of unnecessary surgical operations, especially for women and children. The decline of the general practitioner—the family doctor—meant fewer physicians made house calls; more and more people went to hospital emergency rooms or outpatient clinics for treatment. Unreasonable faith in sophisticated medical technologies also contributed to the proliferation of iatrogenic ailments—sickness brought on by treatment for some other illness.

The American Medical Association (AMA), which certified medical schools, did nothing to increase the flow of new doctors. The number of physicians per 100,000 people actually declined between 1950 and 1960; the shortage was made up by doctors trained in other countries. The AMA also lobbied hard against efforts to expand government responsibility for the public's health. President Harry Truman had advanced a plan for national health insurance, to be run along the lines of Social Security. President Dwight Eisenhower had proposed a program that would offer government assistance to private health insurance companies. The AMA denounced both proposals as "socialized medicine." It helped block direct federal involvement in health care until the creation of Medicare (for the elderly) and Medicaid (for the poor) in 1965.

YOUTH CULTURE

The term "teenager," describing someone between thirteen and nineteen, entered standard usage only at the end of World War II. According to the *Dictionary of American Slang*, the United States is the only country with a word for this age group and the only country to consider it "a separate entity whose influence, fads, and fashions are worthy of discussion apart from the adult world." The fifteen years following World War II saw unprecedented attention to America's adolescents. Deep fears were expressed about everything from teenage sexuality and juvenile delinquency to young people's driving habits, hairstyles, and choice of clothing. At the same time, advertisers and businesses pursued the disposable income of America's affluent youth with a vengeance. Teenagers often found themselves caught between their desire to carve out their own separate sphere and the pressure to become an adult as quickly as possible.

The Youth Market

Birthrates had accelerated gradually during the late 1930s and more rapidly during the war years. The children born in those years had by the late 1950s grown into the original teenagers, the older siblings of the celebrated baby boomers of 1946–64. They came of age in a society that, compared with that of their parents and the rest of the world, was uniquely affluent. Together, the demographic growth of teens and the postwar economic expansion created a burgeoning youth market. Manufacturers and advertisers rushed to cash in on the special needs and desires of young consumers: cosmetics, clothing, radios and phonographs, and cars.

Before Elvis Presley became the ultimate teen idol, his life in Memphis mirrored the experiences of millions of American teenagers. In high school he was an average student at best, and he took part-time jobs to help out the family; after graduation he worked as a truck driver and as an electrician's helper. He enjoyed making the rounds of movies, roller rinks, and burger joints with his friends, and he dreamed of owning his own Cadillac. Like many teens, Elvis obsessed over the latest stylish clothing—which he could not afford. He could often be found haunting the shop windows at the Lansky Brothers clothing store on Beale Street in Memphis.

In 1959, *Life* summarized the new power of the youth market. "Counting only what is spent to satisfy their special teenage demands," the magazine reported, "the youngsters and their parents will shell out about $10 billion this year, a billion more than the total sales of GM." In addition, advertisers and market researchers

found that teenagers often played a critical, if hard-to-measure, role as "secret persuaders" in a family's large purchase decisions. Specialized market research organizations, such as Eugene Gilbert & Company and Teen-Age Survey Incorporated, sprang up to serve business clients eager to attract teen consumers and instill brand loyalty. Through the 1950s and into the 1960s, teenagers had a major, sometimes dominant, voice in determining America's cultural fads.

To many parents, the emerging youth culture was a dangerous threat to their authority. One mother summarized this fear in a revealing, if slightly hysterical, letter to *Modern Teen*:

> Don't you realize what you are doing? You are encouraging teenagers to write to each other, which keeps them from doing their school work and other chores. You are encouraging them to kiss and have physical contact before they're even engaged, which is morally wrong and you know it. You are encouraging them to have faith in the depraved individuals who make rock and roll records when it's common knowledge that ninety per cent of these rock and roll singers are people with no morals or sense of values.

The increasing uniformity of public school education also contributed to the public recognition of the special status of teenagers. In 1900, about one of every eight teenagers was in school; by the 1950s, the figure was six out of eight. Psychologists wrote guidebooks for parents, two prominent examples being Dorothy Baruch's *How to Live with Your Teenager* (1953) and Paul Landis's *Understanding Teenagers* (1955). Social scientists stressed the importance of peer pressure for understanding teen behavior. "The teenage group," Landis observed in *Understanding Teenagers*, "is self-sufficient now as in no previous generation." The larger point here is that traditional sources of adult authority and socialization—the marketplace, schools, child-rearing manuals, the mass media—all reinforced the notion of teenagers as a special community, united by age, rank, and status.

"Hail! Hail! Rock 'n' Roll!"

The demands of the new teen market, combined with structural changes in the postwar American mass media, reshaped the nation's popular music. As television broadcasting rapidly replaced radio as the center of family entertainment, people began using radios in new ways. The production of portable transistor radios and car radios grew rapidly in the 1950s as listeners increasingly tuned them in for diversion from or an accompaniment to other activities. Locally produced radio shows, featuring music, news, and disc jockeys,

This photo of Elvis Presley singing at a 1956 state fair in Memphis captured his dramatic stage presence. Performing with only a trio, his sound was spare but hard driving. Both the music and Presley's stage moves owed a great deal to African American rhythm and blues artists.

SOURCE: Getty Images, Inc. (C422)

replaced the old star-studded network programs. By 1956, some 2,700 AM radio stations were on the air across the United States, with about 70 percent of their broadcast time given to record shows. Most of these concentrated on popular music for the traditional white adult market: pop ballads, novelty songs, and show tunes.

In the recording industry, meanwhile, a change was in the air. Small independent record labels led the way in aggressively recording African American rhythm and blues artists. Atlantic Records, in New York, developed the most influential galaxy of artists, including Ray Charles, Ruth Brown, the Drifters, Joe Turner, LaVerne Baker, and the Clovers. Chess, in Chicago, had the blues-based, singer-songwriter-guitarists Chuck Berry and Bo Diddley, and the "doo-wop" group the Moonglows. In New Orleans, Imperial had the veteran pianist-singer Fats Domino, while Specialty unleashed the outrageous Little Richard on the world. On radio, over jukeboxes, and in record stores, all of these African American artists "crossed over," adding millions of white teenagers to their solid base of black fans.

The older, more established record companies, such as RCA, Decca, M-G-M, and Capitol, had largely ignored black music. Their response to the new trend was to offer slick, toned-down "cover" versions by white pop singers of rhythm and blues originals. Cover versions were invariably pallid imitations, artistically inferior to the originals. One has only to compare,

say, Pat Boone's covers of Fats Domino's "Ain't That a Shame" or Little Richard's "Tutti Frutti" with the originals to hear how much was lost. While African American artists began to enjoy newfound mass acceptance, there were limits to how closely white kids could identify with black performers. Racism, especially in so sexually charged an arena as musical performance, was still a powerful force in American life. Because of the superior promotional power of the major companies and the institutional racism in the music business, white cover versions almost always outsold the black originals.

Alan Freed, a popular white Cleveland disc jockey, refused to play cover versions on his "Moondog Matinee" program. He played only original rhythm and blues music, and he popularized the term "rock 'n' roll" to describe it. Freed promoted concerts around the Midwest featuring black rhythm and blues artists, and these attracted enthusiastic audiences of both black and white young people. In 1954 the music trade magazine *Billboard* noted this trend among white teenagers: "The present generation has not known the rhythmically exciting dance bands of the swing era. It therefore satisfies its hunger for 'music with a beat' in modern r&b (rhythm and blues) groups." The stage was thus set for the arrival of white rock 'n' roll artists who could exploit the new sounds and styles.

As a rock 'n' roll performer and recording artist, Elvis Presley reinvented American popular music. His success challenged the old lines separating black music from white, and pop from rhythm and blues or country. As a symbol of rebellious youth and as the embodiment of youthful sexuality, Elvis revitalized American popular culture. In his wake came a host of white rock 'n' rollers, many of them white Southerners like Elvis: Jerry Lee Lewis, Buddy Holly, the Everly Brothers, Roy Orbison. But the greatest songwriter and the most influential guitarist to emerge from this first "golden age of rock 'n' roll" was Chuck Berry, an African American from St. Louis who worked part-time as a beautician and house painter. Berry proved especially adept at capturing the teen spirit with humor, irony, and passion. He composed hits around the trials and tribulations of school ("School Days"), young love ("Memphis"), cars ("Maybellene"), and making it as a rock 'n' roller ("Johnny B. Goode"). As much as anyone, Berry created music that defined what it meant to be young in postwar America.

Almost Grown

At least some of the sense of difference, of uniqueness, associated with adolescence came from teens themselves. Teenage consumers remade the landscape of popular music into their own turf. The dollar value of annual record sales nearly tripled between 1954 and 1959, from $213 million to $603 million. New magazines aimed exclusively at teens flourished in the postwar years. *Modern Teen, Teen Digest,* and *Dig* were just a few. Most teen magazines, like rock 'n' roll music, focused on the rituals, pleasures, and sorrows surrounding teenage courtship. Paradoxically, behavior patterns among white middle-class teenagers in the 1950s and early 1960s exhibited a new kind of youth orientation and at the same time a more pronounced identification with adults.

While many parents worried about the separate world inhabited by their teenage children, many teens seemed determined to become adults as quickly as possible. Postwar affluence multiplied the number of two-car families, making it easier for sixteen-year-olds to win driving privileges formerly reserved for eighteen-year-olds. Girls began dating, wearing brassieres and nylon stockings, and using cosmetics at an earlier age than before—twelve or thirteen rather than fifteen or sixteen. Several factors contributed to this trend, including a continuing decline in the age of menarche (first menstruation), the sharp drop in the age of marriage after World War II, and the precocious social climate of junior high schools (institutions that became widespread only after 1945). The practice of going steady, derived from the college custom of fraternity and sorority pinning, became commonplace among high schoolers. By the late 1950s, eighteen had become the most common age at which American females married.

Teenagers often felt torn between their identification with youth culture and pressures to assume adult responsibilities. Many young people juggled part-time jobs with school and very active social lives. Teen-oriented magazines, music, and movies routinely dispensed advice and sympathy regarding this dilemma. Rock 'n' roll songs offered the most sympathetic treatments of the conflicts teens experienced over work ("Summertime Blues"), parental authority ("Yakety Yak"), and the desire to look adult ("Sweet Little Sixteen"). By 1960, sociologist James S. Coleman reflected a growing consensus when he noted that postwar society had given adolescents "many of the instruments which can make them a functioning community: cars, freedom in dating, continual contact with the opposite sex, money, and entertainment, like popular music and movies, designed especially for them."

Deviance and Delinquency

Many adults held rock 'n' roll responsible for the apparent decline in parental control over teens. A psychiatrist writing in the *New York Times* described rock 'n' roll as "a cannibalistic and tribalistic kind of a music" and "a communicable disease." Many clergymen and church leaders declared it "the devil's music." Much of the opposition to rock 'n' roll, particularly in the South, played on long-standing racist fears that white females might be attracted to black music and black performers. The undercurrent beneath all this opposition was a deep anxiety over the more open expression of sexual feelings by both performers and audiences.

Paralleling the rise of rock 'n' roll was a growing concern with an alleged increase in juvenile delinquency. An endless stream of magazine articles, books, and newspaper stories asserted that criminal behavior among the nation's young was chronic. Gang fights, drug and alcohol abuse, car theft, and sexual offenses received the most attention. The U.S. Senate established a special subcommittee on juvenile delinquency. Highly publicized hearings in 1955 and 1956 convinced much of the public that youthful criminals were terrorizing the country. Although crime statistics do suggest an increase in juvenile crime during the 1950s, particularly in the suburbs, the public perception of the severity of the problem was surely exaggerated.

In retrospect, the juvenile delinquency controversy tells us more about anxieties over family life and the erosion of adult authority than about crime patterns. Teenagers seemed more defined by and loyal to their peer culture than to their parents. A great deal of their music, speech, dress, and style was alien and threatening. The growing importance of the mass media in defining youth culture brought efforts to regulate or censor media forms believed to cause juvenile delinquency. In 1954, for example, psychiatrist Fredric Wertham published *Seduction of the Innocent,* arguing that crime comic books incited youngsters to criminal acts. Mass culture, he believed, could overwhelm the traditional influences of family, school, and religion. He led a highly publicized crusade that forced the comic book industry to adopt a code strictly limiting the portrayal of violence and crime.

As reactions to two of the most influential "problem youth" movies of the postwar era indicate, teens and their parents frequently interpreted depictions of youthful deviance in the mass media in very different ways. In *The Wild One* (1954), Marlon Brando played the crude, moody leader of a vicious motorcycle gang. Most adults thought of the film as a critique of mindless gang violence, but many teenagers identified with the Brando character, who, when asked, "What are you rebelling against?" coolly replied, "Whattaya got?" In *Rebel without a Cause* (1955), James Dean, Natalie Wood, and Sal Mineo played emotionally troubled youths in an affluent California suburb. The movie suggests that parents can cause delinquency when they fail to conform to conventional roles—Dean's father wears an apron and his mother is domineering. But on another level, the film suggests that young people can form their own families, without parents.

Brando and Dean, along with Elvis, were probably the most popular and widely imitated teen idols of the era. For most parents, they were vaguely threatening figures whose sexual energy and lack of discipline placed them outside the bounds of middle-class respectability. For teens, however, they offered an irresistible combination of rough exterior and sensitive core. They embodied, as well, the contradiction of individual rebellion versus the attractions of a community defined by youth.

MASS CULTURE AND ITS DISCONTENTS

No mass medium ever achieved such power and popularity as rapidly as television. The basic technology for broadcasting visual images with sound had been developed by the late 1930s, and television demonstrations were among the most popular exhibits at the 1939 New York World's Fair. But World War II and corporate competition postponed television's introduction to the public until 1946. By 1960, nearly nine in ten American families owned at least one set, which was turned on an average of more than five hours a day. Television reshaped leisure time and political life. It also helped create a new kind of national community defined by the buying and selling of consumer goods.

Important voices challenged the economic trends and cultural conformity of the postwar years. Academics, journalists, novelists, and poets offered a variety of works criticizing the overall direction of American life. These critics of what was dubbed "mass society" were troubled by the premium American culture put on conformity, status, and material consumption. Although a distinct minority, these critics were persistent. Many of their ideas and prescriptions would reverberate through the political and cultural upheavals of the 1960s and 1970s.

Television: Tube of Plenty

Television constituted a radical change from radio, and its development as a mass medium was quicker and less chaotic. The three main television networks—NBC, CBS, ABC—grew directly from radio organizations. A short-lived fourth network, Dumont, grew from a tele-

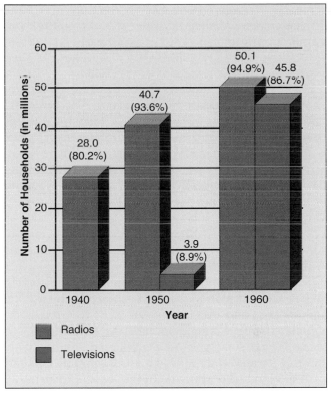

Radio and Television Ownership, 1940–1960
By 1960 nearly 90 percent of American households owned at least one television set, as TV replaced radio as the nation's dominant mass medium of entertainment. Radio ownership rose as well, but Americans increasingly listened to radio as an accompaniment to other activities, such as driving.

vision manufacturing business. The Federal Communications Commission oversaw the licensing of stations and set technical standards. The networks led the industry from the start, rather than following individual stations, as radio had done. Nearly all TV stations were affiliated with one or more of the networks; only a handful of independent stations could be found around the country.

Television not only depended on advertising, it also transformed the advertising industry. The television business, like radio, was based on the selling of time to advertisers who wanted to reach the mass audiences tuning into shows. Radio had offered entire shows produced by and for single sponsors, usually advertisers who wanted a close identification between their product and a star. But the higher costs of television production forced key changes. Sponsors left the production of programs to the networks, independent producers, and Hollywood studios.

Sponsors now bought scattered time slots for spot advertisements rather than bankrolling an entire show. Ad agencies switched their creative energy to producing slick thirty-second commercials rather than entertainment programs. A shift from broadcasting live shows to filming them opened up lucrative opportunities for reruns and foreign export. The total net revenue of the TV networks and their affiliated stations in 1947 was about $2 million; by 1957 it was nearly $1 billion. Advertisers spent $58 million on TV shows in 1949; ten years later the figure was almost $1.5 billion.

The staple of network radio, the comedy-variety show, was now produced with pictures. The first great national TV hit, *The Milton Berle Show,* followed this format when it premiered in 1948. Radio stars such as Jack Benny, Edgar Bergen, George Burns and Gracie Allen, and Eddie Cantor switched successfully to television. Boxing, wrestling, the roller derby, and other sporting events were also quite popular. For a brief time, original live drama flourished on writer-oriented shows such as *Goodyear Television Playhouse* and *Studio One.* In addition, early television featured an array of situation comedies with deep roots in radio and vaudeville.

Set largely among urban ethnic families, early shows like *I Remember Mama, The Goldbergs, The Life of Riley, Life with Luigi,* and *The Honeymooners* often featured working-class families struggling with the dilemmas posed by consumer society. Most plots turned around comic tensions created and resolved by consumption: contemplating home ownership, going out on the town, moving to the suburbs, buying on credit, purchasing a new car. Generational discord and the loss of ethnic identity were also common themes. To some degree, these early shows mirrored and spoke to the real dilemmas facing families that had survived the Great Depression and the Second World War and were now finding their place in a prosperous consumer culture.

By the late 1950s all the urban ethnic comedy shows were off the air. A new breed of situation comedies presented nonethnic white, affluent, and insular suburban middle-class families. Shows like *Father Knows Best, Leave It to Beaver, The Adventures of Ozzie and Harriet,* and *The Donna Reed Show* epitomized the ideal suburban American family of the day. Their plots focused on genial crises, usually brought on by children's mischief and resolved by kindly fathers. In retrospect, what is most striking about these shows is what is absent—politics, social issues, cities, white ethnic groups, African Americans, and Latinos were virtually unrepresented.

Television cut deeply into the filmgoing habits of Americans. The audience for movies began a steep decline from the high point of 1948. Hollywood tried desperately to compete with its new rival by pushing spectacular new techniques such as Cinerama, CinemaScope, and 3-D. By the mid-1950s, studios had begun to sell off their valuable backlog of films to the networks; old movies thus became a staple of television programming. Many TV shows were produced on the same Hollywood back lots that had churned out "B" pictures in the 1930s and 1940s. Two of the most popular genres of television in these years were old movie standbys: westerns (*Gunsmoke, Cheyenne,*

Ricky and Ozzie Nelson play piano together as David and Harriet Nelson watch, in a scene from the long-running 1950s television sit-com "Ozzie and Harriet." The show epitomized the white, suburban, middle class family ideal that dominated TV through the mid-1960s.

SOURCE: © Springer/Bettmann/CORBIS (JS-296).

The Rifleman) and crime dramas (*Dragnet, Highway Patrol, The Untouchables*).

Television also demonstrated a unique ability to create overnight fads and crazes across the nation. Elvis Presley's 1956 appearances on several network television variety shows, including those hosted by Milton Berle and Ed Sullivan, catapulted him from regional success to international stardom. Successful television advertising campaigns made household names out of previously obscure products. A memorable example of TV's influence came in 1955 when Walt Disney produced a series of three one-hour shows on the life of frontier legend Davy Crockett. The tremendous success of the series instantly created a $300 million industry of Davy Crockett shirts, dolls, toys, and coonskin caps.

Television and Politics

Prime-time entertainment shows carefully avoided any references to the political issues of the day. Network executives bowed to the conformist climate created by the domestic cold war. Any hint of political controversy could scare off sponsors, who were extremely sensitive to public protest. Anti-Communist crusaders set themselves up as private watchdogs, warning of alleged subversive influence in the broadcasting industry. In 1950 one such group published *Red Channels* (see Chapter 26), a book branding 151 of the most well-known writers, directors, and actors in radio and television as Communists or Communist dupes. Television executives responded by effectively blacklisting many talented individuals.

As in Hollywood, the cold war chill severely restricted the range of political discussion on television. Any honest treatment of the conflicts in American society threatened the consensus mentality at the heart of the television business. Even public affairs and documentary programs were largely devoid of substantial political debate. An important exception was Edward R. Murrow's *See It Now* on CBS—but that show was off the air by 1955. Television news did not come into its own until 1963, with the beginning of half-hour nightly network newscasts. Only then did television's extraordinary power to rivet the nation's attention during a crisis become clear.

Still, some of the ways that TV would alter the nation's political life emerged in the 1950s. Television made Democratic senator Estes Kefauver of Tennessee a national political figure through live coverage of his 1951 Senate investigation into organized crime. It also contributed to the political downfall of Senator Joseph McCarthy in 1954 by showing his cruel bullying tactics during Senate hearings into alleged subversive Communist influence in the army. In 1952, Republican vice presidential candidate Richard M. Nixon effectively used an emotional, direct television appeal to voters—the "Checkers" speech—to counter charges of corruption (see Chapter 26).

The 1952 election also brought the first use of TV political advertising for presidential candidates. The Republican Party hired a high-powered ad agency, Batten, Barton, Durstine & Osborn (BBD&O), to create a series of short, sophisticated advertisements touting Dwight D. Eisenhower. The Democrats were content to buy a few half-hour blocks of TV time for long speeches by their nominee, Adlai Stevenson. The BBD&O campaign saturated TV with twenty-second Eisenhower spots for two weeks before election day. Ever since then, television image-making has been the single most important element in American electoral politics.

Culture Critics

From both the left and the right, an assortment of writers expressed anger, fear, and plain disgust with the power of American mass culture. It would, they feared, overwhelm traditional standards of beauty, truth, and

quality. Indeed, the urge to denounce the mass media for degrading the quality of American life tended to unite radical and conservative critics. Thus Marxist writer Dwight Macdonald sounded an old conservative warning when he described mass culture as "a parasite, a cancerous growth on High Culture." Society's most urgent problem, Macdonald claimed, was a "a tepid, flaccid Middlebrow Culture that threatens to engulf everything in its spreading ooze."

Critics of mass culture argued that the audiences for the mass media were atomized, anonymous, and detached. The media themselves had become omnipotent, capable of manipulating the attitudes and behavior of the isolated individuals in the mass. These critics undoubtedly overestimated the power of the media. They ignored the preponderance of research suggesting that most people watched and responded to mass media in family, peer group, and other social settings. The critics also missed the genuine vitality and creative brilliance to be found within mass culture: African American music; the films of Nicholas Ray, Elia Kazan, and Howard Hawks; the experimental television of Ernie Kovacs; the satire of *Mad* magazine.

Many of these critics achieved great popularity themselves, suggesting that the public was deeply ambivalent about mass culture. One of the best-selling authors of the day was Vance Packard, whose 1957 exposé *The Hidden Persuaders* showed how advertisers exploited motivational research into the irrational side of human behavior. Paul Goodman won a wide audience for his *Growing Up Absurd* (1960), which charged that America made it very difficult for young people to find meaningful work, sexual fulfillment, or a true sense of community. Goodman was only one of the thinkers at the end of the decade whose work pointed toward the coming youth rebellion in culture and politics.

Some of the sharpest dissents from the cultural conformity of the day came from a group of writers known collectively as the Beats. Led by the novelist Jack Kerouac and the poet Allen Ginsberg, the Beats shared a distrust of the American virtues of progress, power, and material gain. The Beat sensibility celebrated spontaneity, friendship, jazz, open sexuality, drug use, and the outcasts of American society. Kerouac, born and raised in a working-class French Canadian family in Lowell, Massachusetts, coined the term "beat" in 1948. It meant for him a "weariness with all the forms of the modern industrial state"—conformity, militarism, blind faith in technological progress. Kerouac's 1957 novel *On the Road*, chronicling the tumultuous adventures of Kerouac's circle of friends as they traveled by car back and forth across America, became the Beat manifesto. Allen Ginsberg had grown up in New Jersey in an immigrant Jewish family. His father was a poet and teacher, and his mother had a history of mental problems. After being expelled from Columbia University,

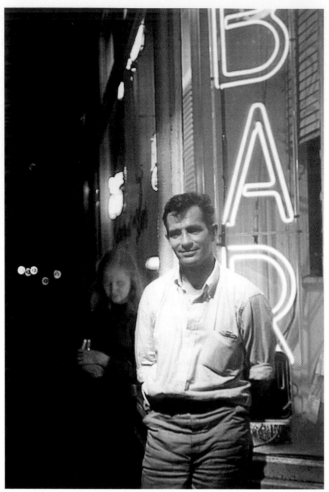

Jack Kerouac, founding voice of the Beat literary movement, in front of a neon lit bar, ca. 1950. Kerouac's public readings, often to the accompaniment of live jazz music, created a performance atmosphere underlining the connections between his writing style and the rhythms and sensibility of contemporary jazz musicians.

SOURCE: Globe Photos, Inc. (YULSMAN).

Ginsberg grew close to Kerouac and another writer, William Burroughs. At a 1955 poetry reading in San Francisco, Ginsberg introduced his epic poem *Howl* to a wildly enthusiastic audience:

> *I saw the best minds of my generation destroyed*
> *by madness, starving hysterical naked,*
> *dragging themselves through the negro streets at dawn*
> *looking for an angry fix,*
> *angelheaded hipsters burning for the ancient heavenly*
>   *connection*
> *to the starry dynamo in the machinery of night.*

Howl became one of the best-selling poetry books in the history of publishing, and it established Ginsberg as an important new voice in American literature.

Beat writers received a largely antagonistic, even virulent reception from the literary establishment. But millions of young Americans read their work and became intrigued by their alternative visions. The mass media soon managed to trivialize the Beats. A San Francisco journalist coined the term "beatnik," and by the late 1950s it had become associated with affected men and women dressed in black, wearing sunglasses and berets, and acting rebellious and alienated. But Beat writers like Kerouac, Ginsberg, Burroughs, Diane DiPrima, Gary Snyder, LeRoi Jones, and others continued to produce serious work that challenged America's official culture. They foreshadowed the mass youth rebellion and counterculture to come in the 1960s.

THE COLD WAR CONTINUED

Eisenhower's experience in foreign affairs had been one of his most attractive assets as a presidential candidate. His success as supreme commander of the Allied forces in World War II owed as much to diplomatic skill as to military prowess. As president, Eisenhower sustained the anti-Communist rhetoric of cold war diplomacy, and his administration persuaded Americans to accept the cold war stalemate as a more or less permanent fact. Eisenhower developed new strategies for containment and for the support of United States power abroad, including a greater reliance on nuclear weapons and the aggressive use of the Central Intelligence Agency (CIA) for covert action. Yet Eisenhower also resolved to do everything he could to forestall an all-out nuclear conflict. He recognized the limits of raw military power. He accepted a less than victorious end to the Korean War, and he avoided a full military involvement in Indochina. Ironically, Eisenhower's promotion of high-tech strategic weaponry fostered development of a military-industrial complex. By the time he left office in 1961, he felt compelled to warn the nation of the growing dangers posed by burgeoning military spending.

The "New Look" in Foreign Affairs

Although Eisenhower recognized that the United States was engaged in a long-term struggle with the Soviet Union, he feared that permanent mobilization for the cold war might overburden the American economy and result in a "garrison state." He therefore pursued a high-tech, capital intensive defense policy that emphasized America's qualitative advantage in strategic weaponry. The "new look" in foreign affairs promised to reduce the military budget by exploiting America's atomic and air superiority.

The emphasis on massive retaliation, the administration claimed, would also make possible cuts in the military budget. As Secretary of Defense Charles Wilson said, the goal was to "get more bang for the buck." Eisenhower largely succeeded in stabilizing the defense budget. Between 1954 and 1961 absolute spending rose only $800 million, from $46.6 billion to $47.4 billion. Military spending as an overall percentage of the federal budget fell from 66 percent to 49 percent during his two terms. Much of this saving was gained through the increased reliance on nuclear weapons and long-range delivery systems, which were relatively less expensive than conventional forces.

Secretary of State John Foster Dulles emerged as a key architect of American policy, giving shape to Eisenhower's views. Raised a devout Presbyterian and trained as a lawyer, Dulles had been involved in diplomatic affairs since World War I. He brought a strong sense of righteousness to his job, an almost missionary belief in America's responsibility to preserve the "free world" from godless, immoral communism. Dulles articulated a more assertive policy toward the Communist threat by calling not simply for containment but for a "roll-

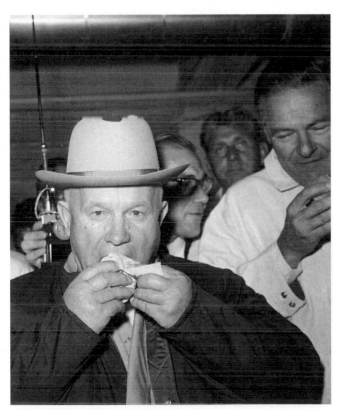

Soviet Premier Nikita Khrushchev enjoys a bite to eat during his tour of an Iowa farm in 1959. A colorful, earthy, and erratic man, Khrushchev loomed as the most visible human symbol of the USSR for Americans. On this trip he called for Soviet-American friendship, yet also boasted "We will bury you."

SOURCE: © Bettmann/CORBIS (BE031798).

back." The key would be greater reliance on America's nuclear superiority. This policy appealed to Republicans, who had been frustrated by the restriction of United Nations forces to conventional arms during the Korean War.

The "new look" conflicted, however, with Eisenhower's own sense of caution, especially during moments of crisis in Eastern Europe and potential military confrontation with the Soviet Union. The limits of a policy based on nuclear strategy became painfully clear when American leaders faced tense situations that offered no clear way to intervene without provoking full-scale war.

When East Berliners rebelled against the Soviets in 1953, cold war hard-liners thought they saw the long awaited opportunity for rollback. But precisely how could the United States respond? Public bitterness over the Korean conflict merged with Eisenhower's sense of restraint and in the end, apart from angry denunciations, the United States did nothing to prevent the Soviets from crushing the rebellion. U.S. leaders faced the same dilemma on a grander scale when Hungarians revolted against their Soviet-dominated Communist rulers in 1956, staging a general strike and taking over the streets and factories in Budapest and other cities. The United States opened its gates to thousands of Hungarian refugees, but despite urgent requests, it refused to intervene when Soviet tanks and troops crushed the revolt. Eisenhower recognized that the Soviets would defend their own borders, and all of Eastern Europe as well, by all-out military force if necessary.

The death of Josef Stalin in 1953 and the worldwide condemnation of his crimes, revealed by his successor, Nikita Khrushchev, in 1956, gave Eisenhower fresh hope for a new spirit of peaceful coexistence between the two superpowers. Khrushchev, in a gesture of goodwill, withdrew Soviet troops from Austria. The first real rollback had been achieved by negotiations and a spirit of common hope, not threats or force. In 1958 Khrushchev, probing American intentions and hoping to redirect the Soviet economy toward the production of more consumer goods, unilaterally suspended nuclear testing. Tensions rose again that year when the Soviet leader, threatened by a revived West Germany, demanded that the Western Allies leave Berlin within six months. But after Khrushchev made a twelve-day trip to America in 1959, he suspended the deadline and relations warmed. Khrushchev visited an Iowa farm, went sightseeing in Hollywood, and spent time with Eisenhower at Camp David, the presidential retreat in Maryland.

The two leaders achieved nothing concrete, but with summit diplomacy seeming to offer at least a psychological thaw in the cold war, the press began referring to the "spirit of Camp David." In early 1960

Khrushchev called for another summit in Paris, to discuss German reunification and nuclear disarmament. Eisenhower, meanwhile, planned his own friendship tour of the Soviet Union. But in May 1960 the Soviets shot down an American U-2 spy plane gathering intelligence on Soviet military installations. A deeply embarrassed Eisenhower at first denied the existence of U-2 flights, but the Soviets produced the pilot, Francis Gary Powers, who readily confessed. The summit collapsed when Eisenhower refused Khrushchev's demands for an apology and an end to the spy flights. The U-2 incident demonstrated the limits of personal diplomacy in resolving the deep structural rivalry between the superpowers.

Eisenhower often provided a moderate voice on issues of defense spending and missile development. The Soviet Union's dramatic launch of Sputnik, the first space-orbiting satellite, in October 1957 upset many Americans' precarious sense of security. In particular, this demonstration of Soviet technological prowess raised fears about Russian ability to deploy intercontinental ballistic missiles (ICBMs) against American cities. Critics attacked the Eisenhower administration for failure to keep up with the enemy. Senator Stuart Symington (D-MO) bluntly warned that, "Unless our defense policies are promptly changed, the Soviets will move from superiority to supremacy." In addition to huge increases in defense spending, some urged a massive program to build "fallout shelters" for the entire population in case of nuclear attack. But Eisenhower rejected these more radical responses. He knew from evidence provided by U-2 spy planes that the Soviet Union in fact trailed far behind the U.S. in ICBM development, but he kept this knowledge secret. Instead of panicking before Sputnik, he held to a doctrine of "sufficiency": maintaining enough military strength to survive any foreign attack and enough nuclear capability to deliver a massive counterattack. In 1958 Eisenhower did support creation of the National Aeronautics and Space Agency (NASA), to coordinate space exploration and missile development. And he also backed the National Defense Education Act that year, which funneled more federal aid into science and foreign language education. Yet, in Congress a bipartisan majority voted to increase the military budget by another $8 billion in 1958, thereby accelerating the arms race and expanding the defense sector of the economy.

Covert Action

Eisenhower combined the overt threat of massive retaliation in his "new look" approach to foreign affairs with a heavy reliance on covert interventions by the Central Intelligence Agency (CIA). He had been an enthusiastic supporter of covert operations during World War II, and during his presidency CIA-sponsored covert para-

military operations became a key facet of American foreign policy. With the American public wary of direct U.S. military interventions, the CIA promised a cheap, quick, and quiet way to depose hostile or unstable regimes. Eisenhower increasingly relied on the CIA to destabilize emerging third world governments deemed too radical or too friendly with the Soviets. Covert actions also proved vital for propping up more conservative regimes under siege by indigenous revolutionaries. These actions were particularly effective in the former colonial areas of Asia, Africa, and the Caribbean.

For CIA director, Eisenhower named Allen Dulles, brother of the secretary of state and a former leader in the CIA's World War II precursor, the Office of Strategic Services. The CIA's mandate was to collect and analyze information, but it did much more under Dulles's command. Thousands of covert agents stationed all over the world carried out a wide range of political activities. Some agents arranged large, secret financial payments to friendly political parties, such as the conservative Christian Democrats in Italy and in Latin America, or foreign trade unions opposed to socialist policies. Other agents secretly funded and guided intellectuals in, for instance, the Congress of Cultural Freedom, a prestigious group of liberal writers in Europe and the United States.

While the United States moderated its stance toward the Soviet Union and its Eastern European satellites, it hardened its policies in the third world. The need for anti-Communist tactics short of all-out military conflict pushed the Eisenhower administration to develop new means of fighting the cold war. The premise rested on encouraging confusion or rivalry within the Communist sphere and on destabilizing or destroying anticapitalist movements around the world.

The Soviet Union tried to win influence in Africa, Asia, and Latin America by appealing to a shared "anti-imperialism" and by offering modest amounts of foreign aid. In most cases, Communists played only small roles in third world independence movements. But the issue of race and the popular desire to recover national resources from foreign investors inflamed already widespread anti-European and anti-American feelings. When new nations or familiar allies threatened to interfere with U.S. regional security arrangements, or to expropriate the property of American businesses, the Eisenhower administration turned to covert action and military intervention.

Intervening around the World

The Central Intelligence Agency produced a swift, major victory in Iran in 1953. The country's popular prime minister, Mohammed Mossadegh, had nationalized Britain's Anglo-Iranian Oil Company, and the State Department

Compare American intervention in the Caribbean from 1948–1966 with intervention in this region earlier in the twentieth century (chapter 22). What are the similarities? What are the differences?
www.prenhall.com/faragher/map27.1

Web Exploration

United States and U.S. possessions
Countries influenced by U.S.-Latin American activities
Possessions of European countries
Other countries
U.S. military bases
Overt military actions
Dates shown in red indicate events as noted
Dates shown in black indicate year of independence during map period

The U.S. in the Caribbean, 1948–1966   U.S. military intervention and economic presence grew steadily in the Caribbean following World War II. After 1960, opposition to the Cuban Revolution dominated U.S. Caribbean policies.

worried that this might set a precedent throughout the oil-rich Middle East. Kermit Roosevelt, CIA chief in Iran, organized and financed an opposition to Mossadegh within the Iranian army and on the streets of Teheran. This CIA-led movement forced Mossadegh out of office and replaced him with Riza Shah Pahlavi. The shah proved his loyalty to his American sponsors by renegotiating oil contracts so as to assure American companies 40 percent of Iran's oil concessions.

The rivalry between Israel and its Arab neighbors complicated U.S. policy in the rest of the Middle East. The Arab countries launched an all-out attack on Israel in 1948 immediately after the United States and the Soviet Union had recognized its independence. Israel repulsed the attack, drove thousands of Palestinians from their homes, occupied territory that hundreds of thousands of others had fearfully fled, and seized lands far in excess of the terms of a United Nations–sponsored armistice of 1949. The Arab states refused to recognize Israel's right to exist and subjected it to a damaging economic boycott. Meanwhile, hundreds of thousands of Palestinians languished in refugee camps. Eisenhower believed that Truman had perhaps been too hasty in encouraging the Israelis. Yet most Americans supported the new Jewish state as a refuge for a people who had suffered so much persecution, especially during the Holocaust.

Israel stood as a reliable U.S. ally in an unstable region. Arab nationalism continued to vex American policymakers, culminating in the Suez crisis of 1956. Egyptian president Gamal Abdel Nasser, a leading voice of Arab nationalism, looked for American and British economic aid. He had long dreamed of building the Aswan High Dam on the Nile to create more arable land and provide cheap electric power. When negotiations broke down, Nasser announced he would nationalize the strategically sensitive Suez Canal, and he turned to the Soviet Union for aid. Eisenhower refused European appeals for U.S. help in seizing the Suez Canal and returning it to the British. When British, French, and Israeli forces attacked Egypt in October 1956, the United States sponsored a UN resolution calling for a cease-fire and a withdrawal of foreign forces. Yielding to this pressure and to Soviet threats of intervention, the British and French withdrew, and eventually so did the Israelis. Eisenhower had won a major diplomatic battle through patience and pressure, but he did not succeed in bringing lasting peace to the troubled region.

The most publicized CIA intervention of the Eisenhower years took place in Guatemala, where a fragile democracy had taken root in 1944. President Jácobo Arbenz Guzmán, elected in 1950, aggressively pursued land reform and encouraged the formation of trade unions. At the time, 2 percent of the Guatemalan population owned 72 percent of all farmland. Arbenz also challenged the long-standing dominance of the American-based United Fruit Company by threatening to expropriate hundreds of thousands of acres that United Fruit was not cultivating. The company had powerful friends in the administration (CIA director Dulles had sat on its board of trustees), and it began intensive lobbying for U.S. intervention. United Fruit linked the land-reform program to the evils of international communism, and the CIA spent $7 million training antigovernment dissidents based in Honduras.

The American navy stopped ships bound for Guatemala and seized their cargoes, and on June 14, 1954, a U.S.–sponsored military invasion began. Guatemalan citizens resisted by seizing United Fruit buildings, but U.S. Air Force bombing saved the invasion effort. Guatemalans appealed in vain to the United Nations for help. Meanwhile, President Eisenhower publicly denied any knowledge of CIA activities. The newly appointed military leader, Carlos Castillo Armas, flew to the Guatemalan capital in a U.S. embassy plane. Widespread terror followed, unions were outlawed, and thousands arrested. United Fruit circulated photos of Guatemalans murdered by

the invaders, labeling them "victims of communism." In 1957 Castillo Armas was assassinated, and a decades-long civil war ensued between military factions and peasant guerrillas.

American intervention in Guatemala increased suspicion of and resentment against American foreign policy throughout Latin America. Vice President Nixon declared that the new Guatemalan government had earned "the overwhelming support of the Guatemalan people." But in 1958, while making a "goodwill" tour of Latin America, Nixon was stoned by angry mobs in Caracas, Venezuela, suggesting that U.S. actions in the region had triggered an anti-American backlash.

In Indochina, the United States provided France with massive military aid and CIA cooperation in its desperate struggle to maintain its colonial empire. From 1950 to 1954 the United States poured $2.6 billion (about three-quarters of the total French costs) into the fight against the nationalist Vietminh movement, led by Communist Ho Chi Minh. When Vietminh forces surrounded 25,000 French troops at Dien Bien Phu in March 1954, France pleaded with the United States to intervene directly. Secretary of State Dulles and Vice President Nixon, among others, recommended the use of tactical nuclear weapons and a commitment of ground troops. But Eisenhower, recalling the difficulties of the Korean conflict, rejected this call. "I can conceive of no greater tragedy," he said, "than for the United States to become engaged in all-out war in Indochina."

At the same time, Eisenhower feared that the loss of one country to communism would inevitably lead to the loss of others. As he put it, "You have a row of dominoes set up, and you knock over the first one and what will happen to the last one is the certainty that it will go over quickly." According to this so-called domino theory, the "loss" of Vietnam would threaten other Southeast Asian nations, such as Laos, Thailand, the Philippines, and perhaps even India and Australia. After the French surrender at Dien Ben Phu, a conference in Geneva established a cease-fire and a temporary division of Vietnam along the 17th parallel into northern and southern sectors. The Geneva accord called for reunification and national elections in 1956. But the United States, although it had attended the conference along with the Soviet Union and China, refused to sign the accord. In response to the Vietnam situation the Eisenhower administration created the Southeast Asia Treaty Organization (SEATO) in 1954. This NATO-like security pact included the United States, Great Britain, France, Australia, New Zealand, Thailand, the Philippines, and Pakistan, and was dominated by the United States.

South Vietnamese leader Ngo Dinh Diem, a former Japanese collaborator and a Catholic in a country that

Venezuelan soldiers (right) tried to disperse rioters who attacked Vice President Richard M. Nixon's car in Caracas during his 1958 "goodwill tour." Demonstrations such as these revealed a reservoir of resentment in Latin America against the interventionist policies of the United States in the region.

was 90 percent Buddhist, quickly alienated many peasants with his corruption and repressive policies. American economic and military aid, along with continuing covert CIA activity, was crucial in keeping the increasingly isolated Diem in power. Both Diem and Eisenhower refused to permit the 1956 elections stipulated in Geneva because they knew popular hero Ho Chi Minh would easily win. By 1959 Diem's harsh and unpopular government in Saigon faced a civil war; thousands of peasants had joined guerrilla forces determined to drive him out. Eisenhower's commitment of military advisers and economic aid to South Vietnam, based on cold war assumptions, laid the foundation for the Vietnam War of the 1960s.

Ike's Warning: The Military-Industrial Complex

Throughout the 1950s small numbers of peace advocates in the United States had pointed to the ultimate illogic of the "new look" in foreign policy. The increasing reliance on nuclear weapons, they argued, did not strengthen national security but rather threatened the entire planet with extinction. They demonstrated at military camps, atomic-test sites, and missile-launching ranges, often getting arrested to make their point. Reports of radioactive fallout around the world rallied a larger group of scientists and prominent intellectuals against further nuclear testing. In Europe, a Ban the Bomb movement gained a wide following; an American counterpart, the National Committee for a Sane Nuclear Policy (SANE), claimed 25,000 members by 1958. The Women's International League for Peace and Freedom collected petitions calling for a test ban. The Student Peace Union, founded in 1959, established units on many campuses. Small but well-publicized actions against civil defense drills took place in several big cities: protesters marched on the streets rather than entering bomb shelters.

As he neared retirement, President Eisenhower came to share some of the protesters' anxiety and doubts about the arms race. Ironically, Eisenhower found it difficult to restrain the system he helped create. He chose to devote his Farewell Address, delivered in January 1961, to warning the nation about the dangers of what he termed the "military-industrial complex." Its total influence, he cautioned, "economic, political, even spiritual—is felt in every city, every statehouse, every office of the federal government." The conjunction of a large military establishment and a large arms industry, Eisenhower noted, was new in American history. "The potential for the disastrous rise of misplaced power exists and will persist. We must never let the weight of this combination endanger our liberties or democratic processes."

The old soldier understood perhaps better than most the dangers of raw military force. Eisenhower's public posture of restraint and caution in foreign affairs accompanied an enormous expansion of American economic, diplomatic, and military strength. Yet the Eisenhower years also demonstrated the limits of power and intervention in a world that did not always conform to the simple dualistic assumptions of cold war ideology.

JOHN F. KENNEDY AND THE NEW FRONTIER

No one could have resembled Dwight Eisenhower less in personality, temperament, and public image than John Fitzgerald Kennedy. The handsome son of a prominent, wealthy Irish American diplomat, husband of a fashionable, trend-setting heiress, forty-two-year-old JFK embodied youth, excitement, and sophistication. As only the second Catholic candidate for president—the first was Al Smith in 1928—Kennedy ran under the banner of the New Frontier. His liberalism inspired idealism and hope in millions of young people at home and abroad. In foreign affairs, Kennedy generally followed, and in some respects deepened, the cold war precepts that dominated postwar policymaking. But by the time of his assassination in 1963, he may have been veering away from the hard-line anti-Communist ideology he had earlier embraced. What a second term might have brought remains debatable, but his death ended a unique moment in American public life.

The Election of 1960

John F. Kennedy's political career began in Massachusetts, which elected him to the House in 1946 and then the Senate in 1952. Kennedy won the Democratic nomination after a bruising series of primaries in which he defeated party stalwarts Hubert Humphrey of Minnesota and Lyndon B. Johnson of Texas. Unlike Humphrey and Johnson, Kennedy had not been part of the powerful group of insiders who dominated the Senate. But he drew strength and financial support from a loyal coterie of friends and family, including

his father, Joseph P. Kennedy, and his younger brother Robert. Vice President Richard M. Nixon, the Republican nominee, had faithfully served the Eisenhower administration for eight years, and was far better known than his younger opponent. The Kennedy campaign stressed its candidate's youth and his image as a war hero. During his World War II tour of duty in the Pacific, Kennedy had bravely rescued one of his crew after their PT boat had been sunk. Kennedy's supporters also pointed to his intellectual ability. JFK had won the Pulitzer Prize in 1957 for his book *Profiles in Courage*, which in fact had been written largely by his aides.

The election featured the first televised presidential debates. Political analysts have long argued over the impact of these four encounters, but agree that they moved television to the center of presidential politics, making image and appearance more critical than ever. Nixon appeared nervous and the camera made him look unshaven. Kennedy, in contrast, benefited from a confident manner and telegenic good looks. Both candidates emphasized foreign policy. Nixon defended the Republican record and stressed his own maturity and experience. Kennedy hammered away at the alleged "missile gap" with the Soviet Union and promised more vigorous executive leadership. He also countered the anti-Catholic prejudice of evangelical Protestants with a promise to keep church and state separate.

Kennedy squeaked to victory in the closest election since 1884. He won by a little more than 100,000 votes

Presidential candidate John F. Kennedy smiles while listening to his opponent Richard M. Nixon during one of their televised debates in the 1960 election. Eighty-five million viewers watched at least one of the debates, which both reflected and increased the power of television in the electoral process.

SOURCE: AP/Wide World Photos.

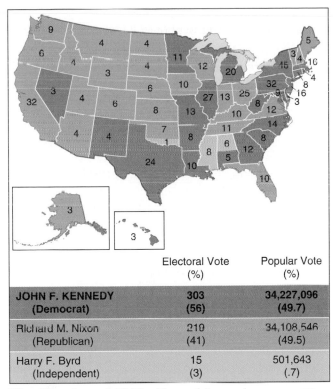

	Electoral Vote (%)	Popular Vote (%)
JOHN F. KENNEDY (Democrat)	**303** **(56)**	**34,227,096** **(49.7)**
Richard M. Nixon (Republican)	219 (41)	34,108,546 (49.5)
Harry F. Byrd (Independent)	15 (3)	501,643 (.7)

The Election of 1960   Kennedy's popular vote margin over Nixon was only a little over 100,000, making this one of the closest elections in American history.

out of nearly 69 million cast. He ran poorly in the South, but won the Catholic vote so overwhelmingly that he carried most of the Northeast and Midwest. Though the margin of victory was tiny, Kennedy was a glorious winner. Surrounding himself with prestigious Ivy League academics, Hollywood movie stars, and talented artists and writers, he imbued the presidency with an aura of celebrity. The inauguration brought out a bevy of poets, musicians, and fashionably dressed politicians from around the world. The new administration promised to be exciting and stylish, a modern-day Camelot peopled by heroic young men and beautiful women. The new president's ringing inaugural address ("Ask not what your country can do for you ask what you can do for your country") had special resonance for a whole generation of young Americans.

New Frontier Liberalism

Kennedy promised to revive the long-stalled liberal domestic agenda. His New Frontier advocated such liberal programs as a higher minimum wage, greater federal aid for education, increased Social Security benefits, medical care for the elderly, support for pub lic housing, and various antipoverty measures. Yet the thin margin of his victory and the stubborn opposition

of conservative southern Democrats in Congress made it difficult to achieve these goals. Congress refused, for example, to enact the administration's attempt to extend Social Security and unemployment benefits to millions of uncovered workers. Congress also failed to enact administration proposals for aid to public schools, mass-transit subsidies, and medical insurance for retired workers over sixty-five.

There were a few New Frontier victories. Congress did approve a modest increase in the minimum wage (to $1.25 per hour), agreed to a less ambitious improvement in Social Security, and appropriated $5 billion for public housing It also passed the Manpower Retraining Act, appropriating $435 million to train the unemployed. The Area Redevelopment Act provided federal funds for rural, depressed Appalachia. The Higher Education Act of 1963 offered aid to colleges for constructing buildings and upgrading libraries. One of the best-publicized New Frontier programs was the Peace Corps, in which thousands of mostly young men and women traveled overseas for two-year stints in under developed countries. There they provided technical and educational assistance in setting up health-care programs and improving agricultural efficiency. As a force for change, the Peace Corps produced modest results, but it epitomized Kennedy's promise to provide opportunities for service for a new generation of idealistic young people.

Kennedy helped revive the issue of women's rights with his Presidential Commission on the Status of Women, led by Eleanor Roosevelt. The commission's 1963 report was the most comprehensive study of women's lives ever produced by the federal government. It documented the ongoing discrimination faced by American women in the work place and in the legal system, as well as the inadequacy of social services such as day care. It called for federally supported day-care programs, continuing education programs for women, and an end to sex bias in Social Security and unemployment benefits. The commission also insisted that more women be appointed to policy-making positions in government. One concrete legislative result, the Equal Pay Act of 1963, made it illegal for employers to pay men and women different wages for the same job. The law did not do much to improve women's economic status, since most working women were employed in job categories, such as secretary or clerk, that included no men. But the issue of economic inequality had at least been put on the public agenda. President Kennedy also directed executive agencies to prohibit sex discrimination in hiring and promotion. The work of the commission contributed to a new generation of women's rights activism.

Taking a more aggressive stance on stimulating economic growth and creating new jobs than had Eisenhower, Kennedy relied heavily on Walter Heller, chair of the Council of Economic Advisers (CEA). Heller emphasized the goal of full employment, which he believed could be attained through deficit spending, encouragement of economic growth, and targeted tax cuts. The administration thus pushed lower business taxes through Congress, even at the cost of a higher federal deficit. The Revenue Act of 1962 encouraged new investment and plant renovation by easing tax depreciation schedules for business. Kennedy also gained approval for lower U.S. tariffs as a way to increase foreign trade. To help keep inflation down, he intervened in the steel industry in 1961 and 1962, pressuring labor to keep its wage demands low and management to curb price increases.

Kennedy also increased the federal commitment to a wholly new realm of government spending: the space program. The National Aeronautics and Space Administration (NASA) had been established under Eisenhower in response to the Soviet success with Sputnik. In 1961, driven by the cold war motivation of beating the Soviets to the moon and avoiding "another Sputnik," Kennedy won approval for a greatly expanded space program. He announced the goal of landing an American on the moon by the end of the decade. NASA eventually spent $33 billion before reaching this objective in 1969. This program of manned space flight—the Apollo missions—appealed to the public, acquiring a science fiction aura. In space, if not on earth, the New Frontier might actually be reached.

Overall, Kennedy's most long-lasting achievement as president may have been his strengthening of the

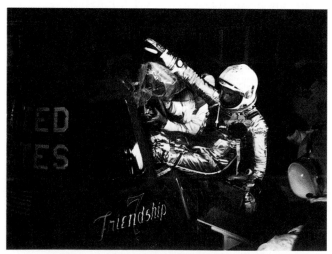

Astronaut John H. Glenn as he prepared for the first American manned space orbit of the earth. The space program of the early 1960s emphasized the technical training and courage of astronauts, consciously creating a set of public heroes as a way to ensure popular support and congressional funding.

SOURCE: NASA Headquarters.

executive branch itself. He insisted on direct presidential control of details that Eisenhower had left to advisers and appointees. Moreover, under Kennedy the White House staff assumed many of the decision-making and advisory functions previously held by cabinet members. This arrangement increased Kennedy's authority, since these appointees, unlike cabinet secretaries, escaped congressional oversight and confirmation proceedings. White House aides also lacked an independent constituency; their power and authority derived solely from their ties to the president. Kennedy's aides, "the best and the brightest," as he called them, dominated policymaking. With men such as McGeorge Bundy directing foreign affairs and Theodore Sorensen coordinating domestic issues, Kennedy began a pattern whereby American presidents increasingly operated through small groups of fiercely loyal aides, often acting in secret.

Kennedy and the Cold War

During Kennedy's three years in office his approach to foreign policy shifted from aggressive containment to efforts at easing U.S.–Soviet tensions. Certainly when he first entered office, Kennedy and his chief aides considered it their main task to confront the Communist threat. In his first State of the Union Address, in January 1961, Kennedy told Congress that America must seize the initiative in the cold war. The nation must "move outside the home fortress, and . . . challenge the enemy in fields of our own choosing." To head the State Department Kennedy chose Dean Rusk, a conservative former assistant to Truman's secretary of state, Dean Acheson. Secretary of Defense Robert McNamara, a Republican and Ford Motor Company executive, was determined to streamline military procedures and weapons buying. McNamara typified the technical, cost-efficient, superrational approach to policymaking. Allen Dulles, Eisenhower's CIA director, remained at his post. These and other officials believed with Kennedy that Eisenhower had timidly accepted stalemate when the cold war could have been won.

Kennedy built up American nuclear and conventional weapons systems. Between 1960 and 1962 defense appropriations increased by nearly a third, from $43 billion to $56 billion. JFK expanded Eisenhower's policy of covert operations, deploying the army's elite Special Forces as a supplement to CIA covert operations in counterinsurgency battles against third world guerrillas. These soldiers, fighting under the direct orders of the president, could provide "rapid response" to "brush-fire" conflicts where Soviet influence threatened American interests. The Special Forces, authorized by Kennedy to wear the green berets that gave them their unofficial name, reflected the president's desire as president to acquire greater flexibility, secrecy, and independence in the conduct of foreign policy.

The limits on the ability of covert action and the Green Berets to further American interests became apparent in Southeast Asia. In Laos, where the United States had ignored the 1954 Geneva agreement and installed a friendly military regime, the CIA-backed government could not defeat Soviet-backed Pathet Lao guerrillas. The president had to arrange with the Soviets to neutralize Laos. In neighboring Vietnam, the situation proved more difficult. When Communist Vietcong guerrillas launched a civil war in South Vietnam against the U.S.–supported government in Saigon, Kennedy began sending hundreds of Green Berets and other military advisers to support the rule of Ngo Dinh Diem. In May 1961, in response to North Vietnamese aid to the Vietcong, Kennedy ordered a covert action against Ho Chi Minh's government that included sabotage and intelligence gathering.

Kennedy's approach to Vietnam reflected an analysis of the situation in that country by two aides, General Maxwell Taylor and Walt Rostow, who saw it through purely cold war eyes. "The Communists are pursuing a clear and systematic strategy in Southeast Asia," Taylor and Rostow concluded, ignoring the inefficiency, corruption, and unpopularity of the Diem government. By 1963, with Diem's army unable to contain the Vietcong rebellion, Kennedy had sent nearly 16,000 support and combat troops to South Vietnam. By then, a wide spectrum of South Vietnamese society had joined the revolt against the hated Diem, including highly respected Buddhist monks and their students. Americans watched in horror as television news reports showed footage of Buddhists burning themselves to death on the streets of Saigon—the ultimate protest against Diem's repressive rule. American press and television also reported the mounting casualty lists of U.S. forces in Vietnam. The South Vietnamese army, bloated by U.S. aid and weakened by corruption, continued to disintegrate. In the fall of 1963, American military officers and CIA operatives stood aside with approval as a group of Vietnamese generals removed President Diem, killing him and his top advisers. It was the first of many coups that racked the South Vietnamese government over the next few years.

In Latin America, Kennedy looked for ways to forestall various revolutionary movements that were gaining ground. The erosion of peasant landholdings had accelerated rapidly after 1950. Huge expanses of fertile land long devoted to subsistence farming were converted to business-dominated agriculture that grew staple crops for export (bananas, coffee, sugar). Millions of impoverished peasants were forced to relocate to already overcrowded cities. In 1961 Kennedy unveiled the Alliance for Progress, a ten-year, $100 billion plan to spur economic development in Latin America. The United States committed $20 billion to the project, with the Latin nations responsible for the rest. The main goals included greater industrial growth and agricultural productivity, more equitable distribution of income, and improved health and housing.

Kennedy intended the Alliance for Progress as a kind of Marshall Plan that would benefit the poor and middle classes of the continent. The alliance did help raise growth rates in Latin American economies. But the expansion in export crops and in consumption by the tiny upper class did little to aid the poor or encourage democracy. The United States hesitated to challenge the power of dictators and extreme conservatives who were staunch anti-Communist allies. Thus the alliance soon degenerated into just another foreign aid program, incapable of generating genuine social change.

The Cuban Revolution and the Bay of Pigs

The direct impetus for the Alliance for Progress was the Cuban Revolution of 1959, which loomed over Latin America. The U.S. economic domination of Cuba that began with the Spanish American War (see Chapter 20) had continued through the 1950s. American-owned businesses controlled all of Cuba's oil production, 90 percent of its mines, and roughly half of its railroads and sugar and cattle industries. Havana, the island's capital, was an attractive tourist center for Americans, and U.S. crime syndicates shared control of the island's lucrative gambling, prostitution, and drug trade with dictator Fulgencio Batista.

As a response to this, in the early 1950s, a peasant-based revolutionary movement, led by Fidel Castro, began gaining strength in the rural districts and mountains outside Havana. On New Year's Day 1959, after years of guerrilla war, the rebels entered Havana and seized power amid great public rejoicing. For a brief time, Castro seemed a hero to many North Americans as well. The *New York Times* had conducted sympathetic interviews with Castro in 1958, while he was still fighting in Cuba's mountains. Many young people visited the island and returned with enthusiastic reports. Famous writers such as James Baldwin and Ernest Hemingway embraced Castro. The CIA and President Eisenhower, however, shared none of this exuberance. Castro's land-reform program, involving the seizure of acreage from the tiny minority that controlled much of the fertile land, threatened to set an example for other Latin American countries. Although Castro had not joined the Cuban Communist Party, he turned to the Soviet Union after the United States withdrew economic aid. He began to sell sugar to the Soviets and soon nationalized American owned oil companies and other enterprises. Eisenhower established an economic boycott of Cuba in 1960, then severed diplomatic relations.

Kennedy inherited from Eisenhower plans for a U.S. invasion of Cuba, including the secret arming and training of Cuban exiles. The CIA drafted the invasion plan, which was based on the assumption that a U.S.–led invasion would trigger a popular uprising of the Cuban people and bring down Castro. Kennedy went along with the plan, but at the last moment decided not to supply an Air Force cover for the operation. On April 17, 1961, a ragtag army of 1,400 counterrevolutionaries led by CIA operatives landed at the Bay of Pigs, on Cuba's south coast. Castro's efficient and loyal army easily subdued them. At the United Nations, Ambassador Adlai Stevenson, deceived by presidential aides, flatly denied any U.S. involvement, only to learn the truth later.

The debacle revealed that the CIA, blinded by cold war assumptions, had failed to understand the Cuban Revolution. There was no popular uprising against Castro. Instead, the invasion strengthened Castro's standing among the urban poor and peasants, already attracted by his programs of universal literacy and medical care. As Castro stifled internal opposition, many Cuban intellectuals and professionals fled to the United States. An embarrassed Kennedy reluctantly took the blame for the abortive invasion, and his administration was censured time and again by third world delegates to the United Nations. American liberals criticized Kennedy for plotting Castro's overthrow, while conservatives blamed him for not supporting the invasion. Despite the failure, Kennedy remained committed to getting rid of Castro and keeping up the economic boycott. The CIA continued to support anti-Castro operations and launched at least eight attempts to assassinate the Cuban leader.

The Missile Crisis

The aftermath of the Bay of Pigs led to the most serious confrontation of the cold war: the Cuban missile crisis of October 1962. Frightened by U.S. belligerency, Castro asked Soviet premier Khrushchev for military help. Khrushchev responded in the summer of 1962 by shipping to Cuba a large amount of sophisticated weaponry, including intermediate-range nuclear missiles. In early October, U.S. reconnaissance planes found camouflaged missile silos dotting the island. Several Kennedy aides demanded an immediate bombing of Cuban bases, arguing that the missiles had decisively eroded the strategic global advantage the United States had previously enjoyed. Other aides rejected this analysis, pointing out that American cities had been vulnerable to Soviet intercontinental ballistic missiles (ICBMs) since 1957.

The president and his advisers pondered their options in a series of tense meetings. Secretary of Defense McNamara was probably closest to the truth when he asserted, "I don't believe it's primarily a military prob-

lem. It's primarily a domestic political problem." Kennedy's aggressive attempts to exploit Cuba in the 1960 election now came back to haunt him, as he worried that his critics would accuse him of weakness in failing to stand up to the Soviets. The disastrous Bay of Pigs affair still rankled. Even some prominent Democrats, including Senator J. William Fulbright, chair of the Senate Foreign Relations Committee, called for an invasion of Cuba.

Kennedy went on national television on October 22. He announced the discovery of the missile sites, demanded the removal of all missiles, and ordered a strict naval blockade of all offensive military equipment shipped to Cuba. He also requested an emergency meeting of the UN Security Council and promised that any missiles launched from Cuba would bring "a full retaliatory response upon the Soviet Union." For a tense week, the American public wondered if nuclear Armageddon was imminent. Eyeball to eyeball, the two superpowers waited for each other to blink. On October 26 and 27 Khrushchev yielded, ordering twenty-five Soviet ships off their course to Cuba, thus avoiding a challenge to the American blockade.

Khrushchev offered to remove all the missiles in return for a pledge from the United States not to invade Cuba. Khrushchev later added a demand for removal of American weapons from Turkey, as close to the Soviet Union as Cuba is to the United States. Kennedy secretly assured Khrushchev that the United States would dismantle the obsolete Jupiter missiles in Turkey. On November 20, after weeks of delicate negotiations, Kennedy publicly announced the withdrawal of Soviet missiles and bombers from Cuba. He also pledged to respect Cuban sovereignty, and promised that U.S. forces would not invade the island.

The crisis had passed. The Soviets, determined not to be intimidated again, began the largest weapons buildup in their history. For his part Kennedy, perhaps chastened by this flirtation with nuclear disaster, made important gestures toward peaceful coexistence with the Soviets. In a June 1963 address at American University, Kennedy called for a rethinking of cold war diplomacy. Both sides, he said, had been "caught up in a vicious and dangerous cycle in which suspicion on one side breeds suspicion on the other, and new weapons beget counterweapons." It was important "not to see only a distorted and desperate view of the other side. . . . No government or social system is so evil that its people must be considered as lacking in virtue."

Shortly after, Washington and Moscow set up a "hot line"—a direct phone connection to permit instant communication during times of crisis. More substantial was the Limited Nuclear Test-Ban Treaty, signed in August 1963 by the United States, the Soviet Union, and Great Britain. The treaty prohibited above-ground, outer space, and underwater nuclear weapons tests. It eased international anxieties over radioactive fallout. But underground testing continued to accelerate for years. The limited test ban was perhaps more symbolic than substantive, a psychological breakthrough in East-West relations after a particularly tense three years.

The Assassination of President Kennedy

The assassination of John F. Kennedy in Dallas on November 22, 1963, sent the entire nation into shock and mourning. Just forty-six years old and president for only three years, Kennedy quickly ascended to martyrdom in the nation's consciousness. Millions had identified his strengths—intelligence, optimism, wit, charm, coolness under fire—as those of American society. In life, Kennedy had helped place television at the center of American political life. Now in the aftermath of his death, television riveted a badly shocked nation. One day after the assassination, the president's accused killer, an obscure political misfit named Lee Harvey Oswald, was himself gunned down before television cameras covering his arraignment in Dallas. Two days later tens of millions watched the televised spectacle of Kennedy's funeral, trying to make sense of the brutal murder. Although a special commission headed by Chief Justice Earl Warren found the killing to be the work of Oswald acting alone, many Americans doubted this conclusion. Kennedy's death gave rise to a host of conspiracy theories, none of which seems provable. In 1979 a House committee concluded that more than one gunman had fired on the presidential motorcade; but FBI scientists disputed this finding.

As Adlai Stevenson, one of Kennedy's longtime political rivals in the Democratic Party, noted in his eulogy to the president, "No one will ever know what this blazing political talent might have accomplished had he been permitted to live and labor long in the cause of freedom." We will never know, of course, what Kennedy might have achieved in a second term. But in his 1,000 days as president, he demonstrated a capacity to change and grow in office. Having gone to the brink during the mis-

sile crisis, he managed to launch new initiatives toward peaceful coexistence. At the time of his death, relations between the United States and the Soviet Union were more amicable than at any time since the end of World War II. Much of the domestic liberal agenda of the New Frontier would be finally implemented by Kennedy's successor, Lyndon B. Johnson, who dreamed of creating a Great Society.

CONCLUSION

America in 1963 still enjoyed the full flush of its postwar economic boom. To be sure, millions of Americans, particularly African Americans and Latinos, did not share in the good times. But millions of others had managed to achieve middle-class status since the early 1950s. An expanding economy, cheap energy, government subsidies, and a dominant position in the world marketplace had made the hallmarks of "the good life" available to more Americans than ever. The postwar "American dream" promised home ownership, college education, secure employment at decent wages, affordable appliances, and the ability to travel—for one's children if not for one's self. The nation's public culture—its schools,

Vice President Lyndon B. Johnson took the oath of office as president aboard *Air Force One* after the assassination of John F. Kennedy, November 22, 1963. Onlookers included the grief-stricken Jacqueline Kennedy (right) and Lady Bird Johnson (left). This haunting photo captured both the shock of Kennedy's assassination and the orderly succession of power that followed.

SOURCE: AP/Wide World Photos

CHRONOLOGY

1950	David Riesman publishes *The Lonely Crowd*
1952	Dwight D. Eisenhower is elected president
1953	CIA installs Riza Shah Pahlavi as leader of Iran
1954	Vietminh force French surrender at Dien Bien Phu
	CIA overthrows government of Jácobo Arbenz Guzmán in Guatemala
	United States explodes first hydrogen bomb
1955	Jonas Salk pioneers vaccine for polio
	James Dean stars in the movie *Rebel without a Cause*
1956	Federal Highway Act authorizes Interstate Highway System
	Elvis Presley signs with RCA
	Eisenhower is reelected
	Allen Ginsberg publishes *Howl*
1957	Soviet Union launches Sputnik, first space-orbiting satellite
	Jack Kerouac publishes *On the Road*

1958	National Defense Education Act authorizes grants and loans to college students
1959	Nikita Khrushchev visits the United States
1960	Soviets shoot down U-2 spy plane
	John F. Kennedy is elected president
	Almost 90 percent of American homes have television
1961	President Kennedy creates "Green Berets"
	Bay of Pigs invasion of Cuba fails
1962	Cuban missile crisis brings the world to the brink of a superpower confrontation
1963	Report by the Presidential Commission on the Status of Women documents ongoing discrimination
	Betty Friedan publishes *The Feminine Mystique*
	Limited Nuclear Test-Ban Treaty is signed
	President Kennedy is assassinated

mass media, politics, advertising—presented a powerful consensus based on the idea that the American dream was available to all who would work for it.

The presidential transition from the grandfatherly Dwight Eisenhower to the charismatic John F. Kennedy symbolized for many a generational shift as well. By 1963 young people had more influence than ever before in shaping the nation's political life, its media images, and its burgeoning consumer culture. Kennedy himself inspired millions of young Americans to pursue public service and to express their political idealism. But even by the time of Kennedy's death, the postwar consensus and the conditions that nurtured it were beginning to unravel.

REVIEW QUESTIONS

1. How did postwar economic prosperity change the lives of ordinary Americans? Which groups benefited most and which were largely excluded from "the affluent society"?
2. What role did federal programs play in expanding economic opportunities?
3. Analyze the origins of postwar youth culture. How was teenage life different in these years from previous eras? How did popular culture both reflect and distort the lives of American youth?
4. How did mass culture become even more central to American everyday life in the two decades following World War II? What problems did various cultural critics identify with this trend?
5. How did cold war politics and assumptions shape American foreign policy in these years? What were

the key interventions the United States made in Europe and the third world?

6. Evaluate the domestic and international policies associated with John F. Kennedy and the New Frontier. What continuities with Eisenhower-era politics do you find in the Kennedy administration? How did JFK break with past practices?

RECOMMENDED READING

Roslayn Fraad Baxandall and Elizabeth Ewen, *Picture Windows: How the Suburbs Happened* (2000). The best new account of postwar suburbs.

Lawrence Freedman, *Kennedy's Wars: Berlin, Cuba, Laos, and Vietnam* (2000). A comprehensive new analysis of JFK's foreign policy.

James B. Gilbert, *A Cycle of Outrage* (1986). An insightful examination of juvenile delinquency.

Kenneth T. Jackson, *Crabgrass Frontier* (1985). The most comprehensive overview of the history of American suburbs.

David E. Kaiser, *American Tragedy: Kennedy, Johnson, and the Origins of the Vietnam War* (2000). A study of how the contradictions of cold war thinking pushed policymakers toward an unnecessary and unwinnable war.

Zachary Karabell, *Architects of Intervention: The United States, the Third World, and the Cold War, 1946–1962*

(1999). A wide-ranging analysis of U.S. involvement in various Third World countries.

George Lipsitz, *Time Passages* (1990). An illuminating set of essays charting developments in American popular culture.

Elaine Tyler May, *Homeward Bound: American Families in the Cold War* (1988). A social history linking family life of the 1950s with the cold war.

Grace Palladino, *Teenagers: An American History* (1996). An account of the emergence of teenagers as a new social class.

James T. Patterson, *Grand Expectations: Postwar America, 1945–1974* (1996). A comprehensive overview of postwar life.

Mark J. White, ed., *Kennedy: The New Frontier Revisited* (1998). Essays offering a balanced view of Kennedy's presidency.

 ▶ MEDIA RESOURCES

U.S. HISTORY DOCUMENTS CD-ROM

Consensus and Conformity

27-1   The Kinsey Report (1948)
27-2   Brown v. Board of Education (1954)
27-3   Ladies Home Journal, "Young Mother" (1956)
27-4   Student Nonviolent Coordinating Committee, Statement of Purpose (1960)

The Changing Liberal State

28-1   Dwight D. Eisenhower, Decision Not to Intervene at Dien Bien Phu (1954)
28-3   John F. Kennedy, Cuban Missile Address (1962)

The Struggle for Social Change

29-1   John F. Kennedy, Inaugural Address (1961)

COMPANION WEBSITE HIGHLIGHTS

To view an exploration, enter one of the URLs below in your browser.

Web Explorations

 The U.S. in the Caribbean, 1948–1966
http://www.prenhall.com/faragher/map27.1

 Additional Interactive Maps

To access the map, go to this chapter's resources at http://www.prenhall.com/faragher
The Election of 1960, page 861

HISTORY RESOURCE CENTER

To find the resources listed below, go to http://www.prenhall.com/historyresourcecenter

Documents

Lyndon Johnson, The War on Poverty (1964)
Students for a Democratic Society, The Port Huron Statement (1962)
The Tonkin Gulf Incident (1964)
Transcript of Excomm Meeting (1962)

Images

1956 Republican National Convention
Cuban Missile Crisis
Eisenhower and Krushchev
John F. Kennedy
Missiles in Cuba
Polio Vaccine
Project Mercury

EXPLORING AMERICA
HOW TO LIE WITH STATISTICS
http://www.prenhall.com/faragher/statistics

Are statistics accurate and reliable data? What role did Darrell Huff play in promoting the idea that statistics can be manipulated for different ends? In what areas if life and society have statistics been used? How have statistics in recent years created controversies? Should Americans believe numbers and the conclusions derived from statistics? As the module's name indicates, *How to Lie with Statistics* explores the different ways and means number have been used and manipulated for different purposes. Using prominent examples, the module raises questions about our use and misuse of statistics and delves into an issue that has been debated for at least fifty years.

How to Lie with Statistics uses several methods to explore statistics and their use. Building on the ideas of a 1954 book, examples from the Red Scare of the 1950s, a scholarly study of firearms in America, and the 2000 presidential election are discussed. Graphs, an audio clip, visual images, and excerpts from primary printed sources probe the different examples while interactive maps and a chronology provide important context to the analysis.

Reflect and Respond

1. What would have been good questions to ask of Senator McCarthy or, perhaps more importantly, of the many people who were persuaded by his anticommunist campaigning? How can we reconcile the witch-hunts of the 1950s with the American political ideal of freedom of association, and the reality that Communist party membership was never illegal in the United States?

2. Do we expect always each other to understand the information provided by retailers, such as the size of a car engine? The number of megabytes or gigabytes in a computer? The odds against winning a lottery?

3. If the ideal of uniformity in the 1950s was oppressive and led to the victimization of communists or possible communists (not to mention others such as the Beats), are there lessons to be learned about the dangers of conformity? How might you, with the good vision of hindsight, alter the 1950s' approach to uniformity to avoid its abuses?

✓ Check it out
Who Votes?

The audio clip describes which groups of Americans are most likely to vote. It represents just one of the many ways numbers are used to predict, analyze, verify, and perform other functions related to increasing our knowledge and understanding. The use of statistics is an important technique that is prone to misuse either by accident or on purpose. The clip is also important for symbolizing the increasing reliance on quantitative data and analysis for such diverse purposes as assessing public opinion and the testing of students at all levels of schooling.

This exploration is also available on the *Exploring America* CD-ROM.

TWENTY-EIGHT

THE CIVIL RIGHTS MOVEMENT

▶ 1945–1966

Jacob Lawrence, *Four Students*, 1961. Photograph by Geoffrey Clements. SOURCE: CORBIS. © Geoffrey Clements/CORBIS (IE001007).

The Montgomery Bus Boycott: An African American Community Challenges Segregation

STEADY STREAM OF CARS AND PEDESTRIANS JAMMED THE STREETS around the Holt Street Baptist Church in Montgomery, Alabama. By early evening a patient, orderly, and determined crowd of more than 5,000 African Americans had packed the church and spilled over onto the sidewalks. Loudspeakers had to be set up for the thousands who could not squeeze inside. After a brief prayer and a reading from Scripture, all attention focused on the twenty-six-year-old minister who was to address the gathering. "We are here this evening," he began slowly, "for serious business. We are here in a general sense because first and foremost we are American citizens, and we are determined to apply our citizenship to the fullness of its means."

Sensing the expectant mood of the crowd, the minister got down to specifics. Rosa Parks, a seamstress and well-known activist in Montgomery's African American community, had been taken from a bus, arrested, and put in jail for refusing to give up her seat to a white passenger on December 1, 1955. Composing roughly half the city's 100,000 people, Montgomery's black community had long endured the humiliation of a strictly segregated bus system. Drivers could order a whole row of black passengers to vacate their seats for one white person. And black people had to pay their fares at the front of the bus and then step back outside and reenter through the rear door. The day of the mass meeting, more than 30,000 African Americans had answered a hastily organized call to boycott the city's buses in protest of Mrs. Parks's arrest. As the minister quickened his cadence and drew shouts of encouragement, he seemed to gather strength and confidence from the crowd. "You know, my friends, there comes a time when people get tired of being trampled over by the iron feet of oppression. There comes a time, my friends, when people get tired of being flung across the abyss of humiliation, when they experience the bleakness of nagging despair."

Even before he concluded his speech, it was clear to all present that the bus boycott would continue for more than just a day. The minister laid out the key principles that would guide the boycott—nonviolence, Christian love, unity. In his brief but stirring address the minister created a powerful sense of communion. "If we are wrong, justice is a lie," he told the clapping and shouting throng. "And we are determined here in Montgomery to work and fight until justice runs down like water and righteousness like a mighty stream." Historians would look back at Montgomery, he noted, and have to say: " 'There lived a race of people, black people, fleecy locks and black complexion, of people who had the moral courage to stand up for their rights.' And thereby they injected a new meaning into the veins of history and of civilization."

The Reverend Dr. Martin Luther King, Jr. made his way out of the church amid waves of applause and rows of hands reaching out to touch him. His prophetic speech catapulted him into leadership of the Montgomery bus boycott—but he had not started the movement. When Rosa Parks was arrested, local activists with deep roots in the black protest tradition galvanized the community with the idea of a boycott. Mrs. Parks herself had served for twelve years as secretary of the local NAACP chapter. She was a committed opponent of segregation and was thoroughly respected in the city's African American community. E. D. Nixon, president of the Alabama NAACP and head of the local Brotherhood of Sleeping Car Porters union, saw Mrs. Parks's arrest as the right case on which to make a stand. It was Nixon who brought Montgomery's black ministers together on December 5 to coordinate an extended boycott of city buses. They formed the Montgomery Improvement Association (MIA) and chose Dr. King as their leader. Significantly, Mrs. Parks' lawyer was Clifford Durr, a white liberal with a history of representing black clients. His politically active wife Virginia, for whom Mrs. Parks worked as a seamstress, had been a longtime crusader against the poll tax which prevented many blacks from voting. And two white ministers, Rev. Robert Graetz and Rev. Glenn Smiley, would offer important support to the MIA.

While Nixon organized black ministers, Jo Ann Robinson, an English teacher at Alabama State College, spread the word to the larger black community. Robinson led the Women's Political Council (WPC), an organization of black professional women founded in 1949. With her WPC allies, Robinson wrote, mimeographed, and distributed 50,000 copies of a leaflet telling the story of Mrs. Parks's arrest and urging all African Americans to stay off city buses on December 5. They did. Now the MIA faced the more difficult task of keeping the boycott going. Success depended on providing alternate transportation for the 30,000 to 40,000 maids, cooks, janitors, and other black working people who needed to get to work.

The MIA coordinated an elaborate system of car pools, using hundreds of private cars and volunteer drivers to provide as many as 20,000 rides each day. Many people walked. Local authorities, although shocked by the discipline and sense of purpose shown by Montgomery's African American community, refused to engage in serious negotiations. With the aid of the NAACP, the MIA brought suit in federal court against bus segrega-

tion in Montgomery. Police harassed boycotters with traffic tickets and arrests. White racists exploded bombs in the homes of Dr. King and E. D. Nixon. The days turned into weeks, then months, but still the boycott continued. All along, mass meetings in Montgomery's African American churches helped boost morale with singing, praying, and stories of individual sacrifice. One elderly woman, refusing all suggestions that she drop out of the boycott on account of her age, made a spontaneous remark that became a classic refrain of the movement: "My feets is tired, but my soul is rested."

The boycott reduced the bus company's revenues by two-thirds. In February 1956, city officials obtained indictments against King, Nixon, and 113 other boycotters under an old law forbidding hindrance to business without "just cause or legal excuse." A month later King went on trial. A growing contingent of newspaper reporters and TV crews from around the country watched as the judge found King guilty, fined him $1,000, and released him on bond pending appeal. But on June 4, a panel of three federal judges struck down Montgomery's bus segregation ordinances as unconstitutional. On November 13 the Supreme Court affirmed the district court ruling. After eleven hard months and against all odds, the boycotters had won.

The struggle to end legal segregation took root in scores of southern cities and towns. African American communities led these fights, developing a variety of tactics, leaders, and ideologies. With white allies, they engaged in direct-action protests such as boycotts, sit-ins, and mass civil disobedience as well as strategic legal battles in state and federal courts. The movement was not without its inner conflicts. Tensions between local movements and national civil rights organizations flared up regularly. Within African American communities, long-simmering distrust between the working classes and rural folk on the one hand and middle-class ministers, teachers, and business people on the other sometimes threatened to destroy political unity. There were generational conflicts between African American student activists and their elders. But overall, the civil rights movement created new social identities for African Americans and profoundly changed American society. ■

Montgomery

871

KEY TOPICS

- Legal and political origins of the African American civil rights struggle

- Martin Luther King's rise to leadership

- Student protesters and direct action in the South

- Civil rights and national politics

- Civil Rights Act of 1964 and Voting Rights Act of 1965

- America's other minorities

ORIGINS OF THE MOVEMENT

The experiences of African Americans during World War II and immediately after laid the foundation for the civil rights struggle of the 1950s and 1960s. Nearly 1 million black men and women had served in the armed forces. The discrepancy between fighting totalitarianism abroad while enduring segregation and other racist practices in the military embittered many combat veterans and their families. Between 1939 and 1945 nearly 2 million African Americans found work in defense plants, and another 200,000 entered the federal civil service. Black union membership doubled, reaching more than 1.2 million. But the wartime stress on national unity and consensus largely muted political protests. With the war's end, African Americans and their white allies determined to push ahead for full political and social equality.

Civil Rights after World War II

The boom in wartime production spurred a mass migration of nearly a million black Southerners to northern cities. Forty-three northern and western cities saw their black population double during the 1940s. Although racial discrimination in housing and employment was by no means absent in northern cities, greater economic opportunities and political freedom continued to attract rural African Americans after the war. With the growth of African American communities in northern cities, black people gained significant influence in local political machines in such cities as New York, Chicago, and Detroit. Within industrial unions such as the United Automobile Workers and the United Steel Workers, white and black workers learned the power of biracial unity in fighting for better wages and working conditions. Harlem congressman Adam Clayton Powell, Jr. captured the new mood of 1945 when he wrote that black people were eager "to make the dream of America become flesh and blood, bread and butter, freedom and equality."

After the war, civil rights issues returned to the national political stage for the first time since Reconstruction. Black voters had already begun to switch their allegiance from the Republicans to the Democrats during the New Deal. A series of symbolic and substantial acts by the Truman administration solidified that shift. In 1946 Truman created a President's Committee on Civil Rights. Its report, *To Secure These Rights* (1947), set out an ambitious program to end racial inequality. Recommendations included a permanent civil rights division in the Justice Department, voting rights protection, antilynching legislation, and a legal attack on segregated housing. Yet, although he publicly endorsed nearly all the proposals of the new committee, Truman introduced no legislation to make them law.

Truman and his advisers walked a political tightrope on civil rights. They understood that black voters in several key northern states would be pivotal in the 1948 election. At the same time, they worried about the loyalty of white southern Democrats adamantly opposed to changing the racial status quo. In July 1948, the president made his boldest move on behalf of civil rights, issuing an executive order barring segregation in the armed forces. When liberals forced the Democratic National Convention to adopt a strong civil rights plank that summer, a group of outraged Southerners walked out and nominated Governor Strom Thurmond of South Carolina for president on a States' Rights ticket. Thurmond carried four southern states in the election. But with the help of over 70 percent of the northern black vote, Truman barely managed to defeat Republican Thomas E. Dewey in November. The deep split over race issues would continue to rack the national Democratic Party for a generation.

Electoral politics was not the only arena for civil rights work. During the war, membership in the National Association for the Advancement of Colored People had mushroomed from 50,000 to 500,000. Working- and middle-class urban black people provided the backbone of this new membership. The NAACP conducted voter registration drives and lobbied against discrimination in housing and employment. Its Legal Defense and Education Fund, vigorously led by special counsel Thurgood Marshall, mounted several significant legal challenges to segregation laws. In *Morgan* v. *Virginia* (1946), the Supreme Court declared that segregation on interstate buses was an undue burden on interstate commerce. Other Supreme Court decisions struck down all-white election primaries, racially restrictive housing covenants, and the exclusion of blacks from law and graduate schools.

The NAACP's legal work demonstrated the potential for using federal courts in attacking segregation. Courts were one place where black people, using the constitutional language of rights, could make forceful arguments that could not be voiced in Congress or at political conventions. But federal enforcement of court decisions was often lacking. In 1947 a group of black and white activists tested compliance with the *Morgan* decision by traveling on a bus through the Upper South. This "Freedom Ride" was cosponsored by the Christian pacifist Fellowship of Reconciliation (FOR) and its recent offshoot, the Congress of Racial Equality (CORE), which was devoted to interracial, nonviolent direct action. In North Carolina, several riders were arrested and sentenced to thirty days on a chain gang for refusing to leave the bus.

Two symbolic "firsts" raised black expectations and inspired pride. In 1947 Jackie Robinson broke the color barrier in major league baseball, winning rookie of the year honors with the Brooklyn Dodgers. Robinson's courage in the face of racial epithets from fans and players paved the way for the black ballplayers who soon followed him to the big leagues. In 1950 United Nations diplomat Ralph Bunche won the Nobel Peace Prize for arranging the 1948 Arab-Israeli truce. Bunche, however, later declined an appointment as undersecretary of state because he did not want to subject his family to the humiliating segregation laws of Washington, D.C.

Cultural change could have political implications as well. In the 1940s, African American musicians created a new form of jazz that revolutionized American music and asserted a militant black consciousness. Although black musicians had pioneered the development of swing and, earlier, jazz, white bandleaders and musicians had reaped most of the recognition and money from the public. Artists such as Charlie Parker, Dizzy Gillespie, Thelonius Monk, Bud Powell, and Miles Davis revolted against the standard big-band format of swing, preferring small groups and competitive jam sessions to express their musical visions. The new music, dubbed "bebop" by critics and fans, demanded a much more sophisticated knowledge of harmony and melody and featured more complex rhythms and extended improvisation than previous jazz styles.

Charlie Parker (alto sax) and Miles Davis (trumpet) with their group in 1947, at the Three Deuces Club in New York City. Parker and Davis were two creative leaders of the "bebop" movement of the 1940s. Working in northern cities, boppers reshaped jazz music and created a distinct language and style that was widely imitated by young people. They challenged older stereotypes of African American musicians by insisting that they be treated as serious artists.

SOURCE: Frank Driggs Collection.

In urban black communities the "boppers" consciously created a music that, unlike swing, white popularizers found difficult to copy or sweeten. These black artists insisted on independence from the white-defined norms of show business. Serious about both their music and the way it was presented, they refused to cater to white expectations of grinning, easygoing black performers. Although most boppers had roots in the South, they preferred the relative freedom they found in northern urban black communities. Many northern black (and white) youths identified with the distinctive music, language, and dress of the boppers. In both their music and their public image, these musicians presented a rebellious alternative to the traditional image of the African American entertainer.

The Segregated South

In the postwar South, still home to over half the nation's 15 million African Americans, the racial situation had changed little since the Supreme Court had sanctioned "separate but equal" segregation in *Plessy* v. *Ferguson* (discussed in Chapter 20). In practice, segregation meant separate but unequal. A tight web of state and local ordinances enforced strict separation of the races in schools, restaurants, hotels, movie theaters, libraries, restrooms, hospitals, even cemeteries, and the facilities for black people were consistently inferior to those for whites. There were no black policemen in the Deep South and only a handful of black lawyers. "A white man," one scholar observed, "can steal from or maltreat a Negro in almost any way without fear of reprisal, because the Negro cannot claim the protection of the police or courts."

In the late 1940s only about 10 percent of eligible southern black people voted, most of these in urban areas. A combination of legal and extralegal measures kept all but the most determined black people disfranchised. Poll taxes, all-white primaries, and discriminatory registration procedures reinforced the belief that voting was "the white man's business." African Americans who insisted on exercising their right to vote, especially in remote rural areas, faced physical violence—beatings, shootings, lynchings. A former president of the Alabama Bar Association expressed a commonly held view when he declared, "No Negro is good enough and no Negro will ever be good enough to participate in making the law under which the white people of Alabama have to live."

Outsiders often noted that despite Jim Crow laws (see Chapter 20) contact between blacks and whites was ironically close. The mass of black Southerners worked on white-owned plantations and in white households. One black preacher neatly summarized the nation's regional differences this way: "In the South, they don't care how close you get as long as you don't get too big; in the North, they don't care how big you get as long as you don't get too close." The South's racial code forced African Americans to accept, at least outwardly, social conventions that reinforced their low standing with whites. A black person did not shake hands with a white person, or enter a white home through the front door, or address a white person except formally.

In these circumstances, survival and self-respect depended to a great degree on patience and stoicism. Black people learned to endure humiliation by keeping their thoughts and feelings hidden from white people.

 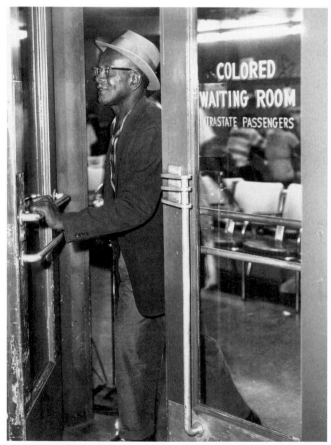

Signs designating "White" and "Colored" rest rooms, waiting rooms, entrances, benches, and even water fountains were a common sight in the segregated South. They were a constant reminder that legal separation of the races in public spaces was the law of the land.

SOURCE: (a) Photo by Dan McCoy. Black Star; (b) Segregation trailways. CORBIS.

Paul Laurence Dunbar, an African American poet, captured this bitter truth in his turn-of-the-century poem "We Wear the Mask."

> We wear the mask that grins and lies,
> It hides our cheeks and shades our eyes,
> This debt we pay to human guile;
> With torn and bleeding hearts we smile,
> And mouth with myriad subtleties.
> Why should the world be over-wise,
> In counting all our tears and sighs?
> Nay, let them only see us, while
> We wear the mask.

Brown v. Board of Education

Since the late 1930s, the NAACP had chipped away at the legal foundations of segregation. Rather than making a frontal assault on the *Plessy* separate-but-equal rule, civil rights attorneys launched a series of suits seeking complete equality in segregated facilities. The aim of this strategy was to make segregation so prohibitively expensive that the South would be forced to dismantle it. In the 1939 case *Missouri v. ex.rel. Gaines*, the Supreme Court ruled that the University of Missouri law school must either admit African Americans or build another, fully equal law school for them. NAACP lawyers pushed their arguments further, asserting that equality could not be measured simply by money or physical plant. In *McLaurin v. Oklahoma State Regents* (1950), the Court agreed with Thurgood Marshall's argument that regulations forcing a black law student to sit, eat, and study in areas apart from white students inevitably created a "badge of inferiority."

By 1951, Marshall had begun coordinating the NAACP's legal resources for a direct attack on the separate-but-equal doctrine. The goal was to overturn *Plessy* and the constitutionality of segregation itself. For a test case, Marshall combined five lawsuits challenging segregation in public schools. One of these suits argued the case of Oliver Brown of Topeka, Kansas, who sought to overturn a state law permitting cities to maintain segregated schools. The law forced Brown's eight-year-old daughter Linda to travel by bus to a black school even though she lived only three blocks from an all-white elementary school. The Supreme Court heard initial arguments on the cases, grouped together as *Brown v. Board of Education*, in December 1952.

In his argument before the Court, Thurgood Marshall tried to establish that separate facilities, by definition, denied black people their full rights as American citizens. Marshall used sociological and psychological evidence that went beyond standard legal arguments. For example, he cited the research of African American psychologist Kenneth B. Clark, who had studied the self-esteem of black children in New York City and in segregated schools in the South. Using black and white dolls and asking the children which they preferred, Clark illustrated how black children educated in segregated schools developed a negative self-image. When Chief Justice Fred Vinson died suddenly in 1953, President Dwight Eisenhower appointed California Governor Earl Warren to fill the post. After hearing further arguments, the Court remained divided on the issue of overturning *Plessy*. Warren, eager for a unanimous decision, patiently worked at convincing two holdouts. Using his political skills to persuade and achieve compromise, Warren urged his colleagues to affirm a simple principle as the basis for the decision.

On May 17, 1954, Warren read the Court's unanimous decision aloud. "Does segregation of children in public schools solely on the basis of race . . . deprive the children of the minority group of equal educational opportunities?" The chief justice paused. "We believe that it does." Warren made a point of citing several of the psychological studies of segregation's effects. He ended by directly addressing the constitutional issue. Segregation deprived the plaintiffs of the equal protection of the laws guaranteed by the Fourteenth Amendment. "We conclude that in the field of public education the doctrine of 'separate but equal' has no place. Separate educational facilities are inherently unequal." "Any language in *Plessy v. Ferguson* contrary to this finding is rejected."

African Americans and their liberal allies around the country hailed the decision and the legal genius of Thurgood Marshall. Marshall himself predicted that all segregated schools would be abolished within five years. Black newspapers were full of stories on the imminent dismantling of segregation. The *Chicago Defender* called the decision "a second emancipation proclamation." But the issue of enforcement soon dampened this enthusiasm. To gain a unanimous decision, Warren had had to agree to let the Court delay for one year its ruling on how to implement desegregation. This second *Brown* ruling, handed down in May 1955, assigned responsibility for desegregation plans to local school boards. The Court left it to federal district judges to monitor compliance, requiring only that desegregation proceed "with all deliberate speed." Thus, although the Court had made a momentous and clear constitutional ruling, the need for compromise dictated gradual enforcement by unspecified means.

Crisis in Little Rock

Resistance to *Brown* took many forms. Most affected states passed laws transferring authority for pupil assignment to local school boards. This prevented the NAACP from bringing statewide suits against segregated school

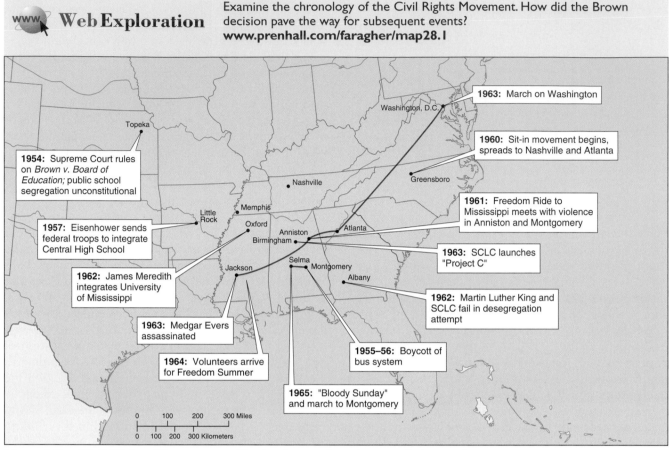

Web Exploration   Examine the chronology of the Civil Rights Movement. How did the Brown decision pave the way for subsequent events? www.prenhall.com/faragher/map28.1

1963: March on Washington

1960: Sit-in movement begins, spreads to Nashville and Atlanta

1954: Supreme Court rules on *Brown v. Board of Education;* public school segregation unconstitutional

1961: Freedom Ride to Mississippi meets with violence in Anniston and Montgomery

1957: Eisenhower sends federal troops to integrate Central High School

1963: SCLC launches "Project C"

1962: James Meredith integrates University of Mississippi

1962: Martin Luther King and SCLC fail in desegregation attempt

1963: Medgar Evers assassinated

1955–56: Boycott of bus system

1964: Volunteers arrive for Freedom Summer

1965: "Bloody Sunday" and march to Montgomery

Map of the Civil Rights Movement Key battlegrounds in the struggle for racial justice in communities across the South.

systems. Counties and towns created layers of administrative delays designed to stop implementation of *Brown.* Some school boards transferred public school property to new, all-white private "academies." State legislatures in Virginia, Alabama, Mississippi, and Georgia, resurrecting pre–Civil War doctrines, passed resolutions declaring their right to "interpose" themselves between the people and the federal government and to "nullify" federal laws. In 1956, 101 congressmen from the former Confederate states signed the Southern Manifesto, urging their states to refuse compliance with desegregation. President Dwight Eisenhower declined to publicly endorse *Brown,* contributing to the spirit of southern resistance. "I don't believe you can change the hearts of men with laws or decisions," he said. Privately, the president opposed the *Brown* decision, and he later called his appointment of Earl Warren as chief justice "the biggest damn fool mistake I ever made."

In Little Rock, Arkansas, the tense controversy over school integration became a test case of state versus federal power. A federal court ordered public schools to begin desegregation in September 1957, and the local school board made plans to comply. But Governor Orval Faubus, facing a tough reelection fight, decided to make a campaign issue out of defying the court order. He dispatched Arkansas National Guard troops to Central High School to prevent nine black students from entering. For three weeks, armed troops stood guard at the school. Screaming crowds, encouraged by Faubus, menaced the black students, beat up two black reporters, and chanted "Two, four, six, eight, we ain't going to integrate." Moderate whites, such as *Arkansas Gazette* editor Harry Ashmore, opposed Faubus, fearing that his controversial tactics would make it harder to attract new businesses and investment capital to the city.

At first, President Eisenhower tried to intervene quietly, gaining Faubus's assurance that he would protect the nine black children. But when Faubus suddenly withdrew his troops, leaving the black students at the mercy of the white mob, Eisenhower had to move. On September 24 he placed the Arkansas National Guard under federal control and ordered a thousand paratroopers of the 101st Airborne Division to Little Rock. The nine black students arrived in a U.S. Army car.

With fixed bayonets, the soldiers protected the students as they finally integrated Central High School in Little Rock. Eisenhower, the veteran military commander, justified his actions on the basis of upholding federal authority and enforcing the law. He also defended his intervention as crucial to national prestige abroad, noting the propaganda victory Faubus had handed to the Soviet bloc. "Our enemies," the President argued, "are gloating over this incident and using it everywhere to misrepresent our whole nation." But he made no endorsement of desegregation. But as the first president since Reconstruction to use armed federal troops in support of black rights, Eisenhower demonstrated that the federal government could, indeed, protect civil rights. Unfazed, Governor Faubus kept Little Rock high schools closed during the 1958–59 academic year to prevent what he called "violence and disorder."

NO EASY ROAD TO FREEDOM, 1957–62

The legal breakthrough represented by the *Brown* decision heartened opponents of segregation everywhere. Most important, *Brown* demonstrated the potential for using the federal court system as a weapon against discrimination and as a means of protecting the full rights of citizenship. Yet the widespread opposition to *Brown* and its implications showed the limits of a strictly legal strategy. In Little Rock, the ugly face of white racism received wide coverage in the mass media and quickly sobered the more optimistic champions of integration. However welcome Eisenhower's intervention, his reluctance to endorse desegregation suggested that civil rights activists could still not rely on federal help. As the Montgomery bus boycott had proved, black communities would have to help themselves first.

Martin Luther King and the SCLC

When it ended with the Supreme Court decision in November 1956, the 381-day Montgomery bus boycott had made Martin Luther King a prominent national figure. In January 1957 *Time* magazine put King on its cover. The *New York Times Magazine* published a detailed history of the bus boycott, focusing on King's role. NBC's *Meet the Press* invited him to become only the second African American ever to appear on that program. Speaking invitations poured in from universities and organizations around the country. King himself was an extraordinary and complex man. Born in 1929 in Atlanta, he enjoyed a middle-class upbringing as the son of a prominent Baptist minister. After graduating from prestigious Morehouse College, an all-black school, King earned a divinity degree at Crozer Theological Seminary in Pennsylvania and a Ph.D. in theology from Boston University.

In graduate school King explored a very diverse range of philosophers and political thinkers—the ancient Greeks, French Enlightenment thinkers, the German idealists, and Karl Marx. He was drawn to the social Christianity of American theologian Walter Rauschenbusch, who insisted on connecting religious faith with struggles for social justice. Above all, King admired Mohandas Gandhi, a lawyer turned ascetic who had led a successful nonviolent resistance movement against British colonial rule in India. Gandhi taught his followers to confront authorities with a readiness to suffer, in order to expose injustice and force those in power to end it. This tactic of nonviolent civil disobedience required discipline and sacrifice from its followers, who were sometimes called upon to lay their lives on the line against armed police and military forces. Crucially, King believed Gandhian nonviolence to be not merely a moral imperative but a potent political strategy that had "muzzled the guns of the British empire in India and freed more than three hundred and fifty million people from colonialism."

Like Gandhi and many of the Christian saints he had studied, King grappled with inner doubts about his faith and true mission. Since childhood he had suffered from extreme mood swings. He was charming and popular, but also self-restrained and dignified. Even after becoming pastor of Montgomery's Dexter Avenue Baptist Church in 1954, King often agonized over his inner emotions, including his religious faith. The rigorous discipline required by the philosophy of nonviolence helped King to master his inner turmoil. A unique blend of traditional African American folk preacher and erudite intellectual, King used his passion and intelligence to help transform a community's pain into a powerful moral force for change.

In a December 1956 address celebrating the Montgomery bus boycott victory, King laid out six key lessons from the year-long struggle: "(1) We have discovered that we can stick together for a common cause; (2) our leaders do not have to sell out; (3) threats and violence do not necessarily intimidate those who are sufficiently aroused and nonviolent; (4) our church is becoming militant, stressing a social gospel as well as a gospel of personal salvation; (5) we have gained a new sense of dignity and destiny; (6) we have discovered a new and powerful weapon—nonviolent resistance." The influence of two visiting northern pacifists, Bayard Rustin of the War Resisters' League and Glenn Smiley of the Fellowship of Reconciliation, had helped deepen King's own commitment to the Gandhian philosophy.

King recognized the need to exploit the momentum of the Montgomery movement. In early 1957, with the help of Rustin and other aides, he brought together nearly 100 black ministers to found the Southern Christian Leadership Conference (SCLC). The clergymen elected King president and his close friend, the Reverend Ralph Abernathy, treasurer. The SCLC called upon black people "to understand that nonviolence is not a symbol of weakness or cowardice, but as Jesus demonstrated, nonviolent resistance transforms weakness into strength and breeds courage in the face of danger."

But King and other black leaders also understood that the white South was no monolith. They believed white Southerners could be divided roughly into three groups: a tiny minority—often with legal training, social connections, and money—that might be counted on to help overthrow segregation; extreme segregationists who were willing and able to use violence and terror in defense of white supremacy; and a broad middle group who favored and benefited from segregation, but who were unwilling to take personal risks to prevent its destruction. In the battles to come, civil rights leaders made this nuanced view of the white South a central part of their larger political strategy. Extreme segregationists could be counted on to overreact, often violently, to civil rights campaigns, and thereby help to win sympathy and support for the cause. White moderates, especially in the business community, might be reluctant to initiate change, but they would try to distance themselves from the desperate violence of extremists and present themselves as pragmatic supporters of order and peace.

Previously, the struggle for racial equality had been dominated by a northern elite focusing on legal action. The SCLC now envisioned the southern black church, preaching massive nonviolent protest, as leading the fight. The SCLC gained support among black ministers, and King vigorously spread his message in speeches and writings. But the organization failed to generate the kind of mass, direct-action movement that had made history in Montgomery. Instead, the next great spark to light the fire of protest came from what seemed at the time a most unlikely source: black college students.

Sit-Ins: Greensboro, Nashville, Atlanta

On Monday, February 1, 1960, four black freshmen from North Carolina Agricultural and Technical College in Greensboro sat down at the whites-only lunch counter in Woolworth's. They politely ordered coffee and doughnuts. As the students had anticipated while planning the action in their dorm rooms, they were refused service. Although they could buy pencils or toothpaste, black people were not allowed to eat in Woolworth's. But the four students stayed at the counter until closing time. Word of their actions spread quickly, and the next day they returned with over two dozen supporters. On the third day, students

occupied sixty-three of the sixty-six lunch counter seats. By Thursday they had been joined by three white students from the Women's College of the University of North Carolina in Greensboro. Scores of sympathizers overflowed Woolworth's and started a sit-in down the street in S. H. Kress. On Friday hundreds of black students and a few whites jammed the lunch counters.

The week's events made Greensboro national news. City officials, looking to end the protest, offered to negotiate in exchange for an end to demonstrations. But white business leaders and politicians proved unwilling to change the racial status quo, and the sit-ins resumed on April 1. In response to the April 21 arrest of forty-five students for trespassing, an outraged African American community organized an economic boycott of targeted stores. With the boycott cutting deeply into merchants' profits, Greensboro's leaders reluctantly gave in. On July 25, 1960, the first African American ate a meal at Woolworth's.

The Greensboro sit-in sent a shock wave throughout the South. During the next eighteen months 70,000 people—most of them black students, a few of them white allies—participated in sit-ins against segregation in dozens of communities. More than 3,000 were arrested. African Americans had discovered a new form of direct-action protest, dignified and powerful, which white people could not ignore. The sit-in movement also transformed participants' self-image, empowering them psychologically and emotionally. Franklin McCain, one of the original four Greensboro students, later recalled a great feeling of soul cleansing: "I probably felt better on that day than I've ever felt in my life. Seems like a lot of feelings of guilt or what-have-you suddenly left me, and I felt as though I had gained my manhood, so to speak, and not only gained it, but had developed quite a lot of respect for it."

In Nashville, Reverend James Lawson, a northern-born black minister, had led workshops in nonviolent resistance since 1958. Lawson had served a jail term as a conscientious objector during the Korean War and had become active in the Fellowship of Reconciliation. He had also spent three years as a missionary in India, where he had learned close-up the Gandhian methods of promoting social change. Lawson gathered around him a group of deeply committed black students from Fisk, Vanderbilt, and other Nashville colleges. Young activists there talked not only of ending segregation but also of creating a "Beloved Community" based on Christian idealism and Gandhian principles.

In the spring of 1960 more than 150 Nashville students were arrested in disciplined sit-ins aimed at desegregating downtown lunch counters. Lawson, who preached the need for sacrifice in the cause of justice, found himself expelled from the divinity school

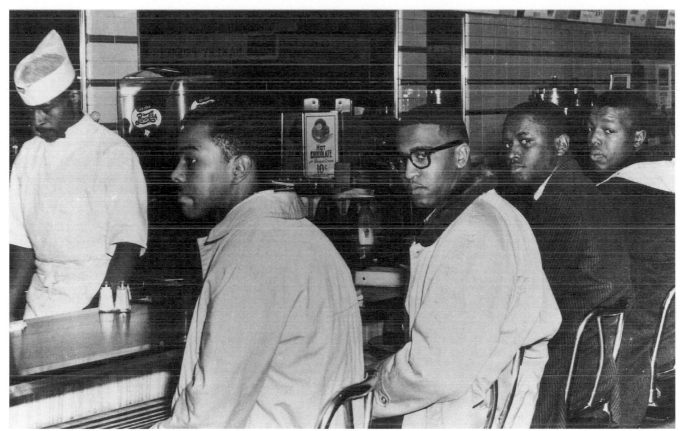

The second day of the sit-in at the Greensboro, North Carolina, Woolworth lunch counter, February 2, 1960. From left: Joseph McNeil, Franklin McCain, Billy Smith, and Clarence Henderson. The Greensboro protest sparked a wave of sit-ins across the South, mostly by college students, demanding an end to segregation in restaurants and other public places.

SOURCE: Photo by John G. Moebes. Greensboro News & Record.

at Vanderbilt. Lawson and other veterans of the Nashville sit-ins, such as John Lewis, Diane Nash, and Marion Barry, would go on to play influential roles in the national civil rights movement. The Nashville group developed rules of conduct that became a model for protesters elsewhere: "Don't strike back or curse if abused. . . . Show yourself courteous and friendly at all times. . . . Report all serious incidents to your leader in a polite manner. Remember love and nonviolence."

The most ambitious sit-in campaign developed in Atlanta, the South's largest and richest city, home to the region's most powerful and prestigious black community. Students from Morehouse, Spelman, and the other all-black schools that made up Atlanta University took the lead. On March 15, 1960, 200 young black people staged a well-coordinated sit-in at restaurants in City Hall, the State Capitol, and other government offices. Police arrested and jailed seventy-six demonstrators that day, but the experience only strengthened the activists' resolve. Led by Julian Bond and Lonnie King,

two Morehouse undergraduates, the students formed the Committee on an Appeal for Human Rights. In full-page advertisements in Atlanta newspapers, the students demanded an end to segregation and also demanded jobs, equal housing and education, and better health services for the city's black people. We will "use every legal and nonviolent means at our disposal to secure full citizenship rights as members of this great democracy of ours," the students promised. Over the summer they planned a fall campaign of large-scale sit-ins at major Atlanta department stores and a boycott of downtown merchants. Their slogan became "Close out your charge account with segregation, open up your account with freedom." In October 1960 Martin Luther King and thirty-six students were arrested when they sat down in the all-white Magnolia Room restaurant in Rich's Department Store. As in Greensboro and Montgomery, the larger African American community in Atlanta supported the continuing sit-ins, picketing, and boycotts. The campaign stretched on for months, and hundreds of protesters went to jail. The city's business leaders finally relented in September 1961, and desegregation came to Atlanta.

SNCC and the "Beloved Community"

The sit-in movement pumped new energy into the civil rights cause, creating a new generation of activists and leaders. Mass arrests, beatings, and vilification in the southern white press only strengthened the resolve of those in the movement. Students also had to deal with the fears of their families, many of whom had made great sacrifices to send them off to college. John Lewis, a seminary student in Nashville, remembered his mother in rural Alabama pleading with him to "get out of that mess, before you get hurt." Lewis wrote to his parents that he acted out of his Christian conscience: "My soul will not be satisfied until freedom, justice, and fair play become a reality for all people."

The new student militancy also caused discord within black communities. The authority of local African American elites had traditionally depended on their influence and cooperation with the white establishment. Black lawyers, schoolteachers, principals, and businessmen had to maintain regular and cordial relations with white judges, school boards, and politicians. Student calls for freedom disturbed many community leaders worried about upsetting traditional patronage networks. Some black college presidents, pressured by trustees and state legislators, sought to moderate or stop the movement altogether. The president of Southern University in Baton Rouge, the largest black college in the nation, suspended eighteen sit-in leaders in 1960 and forced the entire student body of 5,000 to reapply to the college so that agitators could be screened out.

An April 1960 conference of 120 black student activists in Raleigh, North Carolina, underlined the generational and radical aspects of the new movement. The meeting had been called by Ella Baker, executive director of the SCLC, to help the students assess their experiences and plan future actions. Fifty-five at the time, Baker had for years played an important behind-the-scenes role in the civil rights cause, serving as a community organizer and field secretary for the NAACP before heading the staff of the SCLC. She understood the psychological importance of the students' remaining independent of adult control. She counseled them to resist affiliating with any of the national civil rights organizations. Baker also encouraged the trend toward group-centered leadership among the students. She later commented that social movements needed "the development of people who are interested not in being leaders as much as in developing leadership among other people."

With Baker's encouragement, the conference voted to establish a new group, the Student Nonviolent Coordinating Committee (SNCC). The strong influence of the Nashville students, led by James Lawson, could be found in the SNCC statement of purpose:

> We affirm the philosophical or religious ideal of nonviolence as the foundation of our purpose, the presupposition of our faith, and the manner of our action. Nonviolence as it grows from Judaic-Christian tradition seeks a social order of justice permeated by love. Integration of human endeavor represents the crucial first step towards such a society.
>
> By appealing to conscience and standing on the moral nature of human existence, nonviolence nurtures the atmosphere in which reconciliation and justice become actual possibilities.

In the fall of 1960 SNCC established an organizational structure, a set of principles, and a new style of civil rights protest. The emphasis was on fighting segregation through direct confrontation, mass action, and civil disobedience. SNCC fieldworkers initiated and supported local, community-based activity. Three-quarters of the first fieldworkers were less than twenty-two years old. Leadership was vested in a nonhierarchical Coordinating Committee, but local groups were free to determine their own direction. SNCC people distrusted bureaucracy and structure; they stressed spontaneity and improvisation. Bob Moses, a former Harvard graduate student and New York City schoolteacher, best expressed the freewheeling SNCC attitude: "Go where the spirit say go and do what the spirit say do." A small but dedicated group of young white southerners, inspired by SNCC's idealism and activism, joined the cause. Groups such as the Southern Student Organizing Committee, led by Sam Shirah and Sue Thrasher, as well as SNCC activists like Bob Zellner, looked for ways to extend SNCC's radicalism to white communities. Over the next few years SNCC was at the forefront of nearly every major civil rights battle.

The Election of 1960 and Civil Rights

The issue of race relations was kept from center stage during the very close presidential campaign of 1960. As vice president, Richard Nixon had been a leading Republican voice for stronger civil rights legislation. In contrast, Democratic nominee Senator John F. Kennedy had played virtually no role in the congressional battles over civil rights during the 1950s. But during the campaign, their roles reversed. Kennedy praised the sit-in movement as part of a revival of national reform spirit. He declared, "It is in the American tradition to stand up

A Freedom Riders' bus burns after being firebombed in Anniston, Alabama, May 14, 1961. After setting the bus afire, whites attacked the passengers fleeing the smoke and flames. Violent scenes like this one received extensive publicity in the mass media and helped compel the Justice Department to enforce court rulings banning segregation on interstate bus lines.

SOURCE: UPI/CORBIS (U12 79611 < 25).

for one's rights—even if the new way is to sit down." While the Republican platform contained a strong civil rights plank, Nixon, eager to court white southern voters, minimized his own identification with the movement. In October, when Martin Luther King, Jr. was jailed after leading a demonstration in Atlanta, Kennedy telephoned King's wife, Coretta Scott King, to reassure her and express his personal support. Kennedy's brother Robert telephoned the judge in the case and angrily warned him that he had violated King's civil rights and endangered the national Democratic ticket. The judge released King soon afterward.

News of this intervention did not gain wide attention in the white South, much to the relief of the Kennedys. The race was tight, and they knew they could not afford to alienate traditional white southern Democrats. But the campaign effectively played up the story among black voters all over the country. Kennedy won 70 percent of the black vote, which helped put him over the top in such critical states as Illinois, Texas, Michigan, and Pennsylvania and secure his narrow victory over Nixon. Many civil rights activists optimistically looked forward to a new president who would have to acknowledge his political debt to the black vote.

But the very closeness of his victory constrained Kennedy on the race question. Democrats had lost ground in the House and Senate, and Kennedy had to worry about alienating conservative southern Democrats who chaired key congressional committees. Passage of major civil rights legislation would be virtually impossible. The new president told leaders such as Roy Wilkins of the NAACP that a strategy of "minimum legislation, maximum executive action" offered the best road to change. The president did appoint some forty African Americans to high federal positions, including Thurgood Marshall to the federal appellate court. He established a Committee on Equal Employment Opportunity, chaired by Vice President Lyndon B. Johnson, to fight discrimination in the federal civil service and in corporations that received government contracts.

Most significantly, the Kennedy administration sought to invigorate the Civil Rights Division of the Justice Department. That division had been created by the Civil Rights Act of 1957, which authorized the attorney general to seek court injunctions to protect people denied their right to vote. But the Eisenhower administration had made little use of this new power. Robert Kennedy, the new attorney general, began assembling a staff of brilliant and committed attorneys, headed by Washington lawyer Burke Marshall. Kennedy encouraged them to get out of Washington and get into the field wherever racial troubles arose. In early 1961, when Louisiana school officials balked at a school desegregation order, Robert Kennedy warned them that he would ask the federal court to hold them in contempt. When Burke Marshall started court proceedings, the state officials gave in. But the new, more aggressive mood at Justice could not solve the central political dilemma: how to move forward on civil rights without alienating southern Democrats. Pressure from the newly energized southern civil rights movement soon revealed the true difficulty of that problem. The movement would also provoke murderous outrage from white extremists determined to maintain the racial status quo.

Freedom Rides

In the spring of 1961 James Farmer, national director of CORE, announced plans for an interracial Freedom Ride through the South. The goal was to test compliance with court orders banning segregation in interstate travel and terminal accommodations. CORE had just recently made Farmer its leader in an effort to revitalize the organization. One of the founders of CORE in 1942, Farmer had worked for various pacifist and socialist groups and served as program director for the NAACP. He designed the Freedom Ride to induce a crisis, in the spirit of the sit-ins. "Our intention," Farmer declared, "was to provoke the southern authorities into arresting us and thereby prod the Justice Department into enforcing the law of the land." CORE received financial and tactical support from the SCLC and several NAACP branches. It also informed the Justice Department and the Federal Bureau of Investigation of its plans, but received no reply.

On May 4 seven blacks and six whites split into two interracial groups and left Washington on public buses bound for Alabama and Mississippi. At first the two buses encountered only isolated harassment and violence as they headed south. But when one bus entered Anniston, Alabama, on May 14, an angry mob surrounded it, smashing windows and slashing tires. Six miles out of town, the tires went flat. A firebomb tossed through a window forced the passengers out. The mob then beat the Freedom Riders with blackjacks, iron bars, and clubs, and the bus burst into flames. A caravan of cars organized by the Birmingham office of the SCLC rescued the wounded. Another mob attacked the second bus in Anniston, leaving one Freedom Rider close to death and permanently brain-damaged.

The violence escalated. In Birmingham, a mob of forty whites waited on the loading platform and attacked the bus that managed to get out of Anniston. Although police had been warned to expect trouble, they did nothing to stop the mob from beating the Freedom Riders with pipes and fists, nor did they make any arrests. FBI agents observed and took notes but did nothing. The remaining Freedom Riders decided to travel as a single group on the next lap, from Birmingham to Montgomery, but no bus would take them. Stranded and frightened, they reluctantly boarded a special flight to New Orleans arranged by the Justice Department. On May 17 the CORE-sponsored Freedom Ride disbanded.

But that was not the end of the Freedom Rides. SNCC leaders in Atlanta and Nashville assembled a fresh group of volunteers to continue the trip. On May 20, twenty-one Freedom Riders left Birmingham for Montgomery. The bus station in the Alabama capital was eerily quiet and deserted as they pulled in. But when the passengers left the bus a mob of several hundred whites rushed them, yelling "Get those niggers!" and clubbing people to the ground. James Zwerg, a white Freedom Rider from the University of Wisconsin, had his spinal cord severed. John Lewis, veteran of the Nashville sit-in movement, suffered a brain concussion. As he lay in a pool of blood, a policeman handed him a state court injunction forbidding interracial travel in Alabama. The mob indiscriminately beat journalists and clubbed John Siegenthaler, a Justice Department attorney sent to observe the scene. It took police more than an hour to halt the rioting. Montgomery's police commissioner later said, "We have no intention of standing guard for a bunch of troublemakers coming into our city."

The mob violence and the indifference of Alabama officials made the Freedom Ride page-one news around the country and throughout the world. Newspapers in Europe, Africa, and Asia denounced the hypocrisy of the federal government. The Kennedy administration, preparing for the president's first summit meeting with Soviet premier Nikita Khrushchev, saw the situation as a threat to its international prestige. On May 21, an angry mob threatened to invade a support rally at Montgomery's First Baptist Church. A hastily assembled group of 400 U.S. marshals, sent by Robert Kennedy, barely managed to keep the peace. The attorney general called for a cooling-off period, but Martin Luther King, Jr., James Farmer, and the SNCC leaders announced that the Freedom Ride would continue. When Robert Kennedy warned that the racial turmoil would embarrass the president in his meeting with Khrushchev, Ralph Abernathy of the SCLC replied, "Doesn't the attorney general know that we've been embarrassed all our lives?"

A bandaged but spirited group of twenty-seven Freedom Riders prepared to leave Montgomery for Jackson, Mississippi, on May 24. To avoid further violence Robert Kennedy arranged a compromise through Mississippi senator James Eastland. In exchange for a guarantee of safe passage through Mississippi, the federal government promised not to interfere with the arrest of the Freedom Riders in Jackson. This Freedom Ride and several that followed thus escaped violence. But more than 300 people were arrested that summer in Jackson on charges of traveling "for the avowed purpose of inflaming public opinion." Sticking to a policy of "jail, no bail," Freedom Riders clogged the prison, where they endured beatings and intimidation by prison guards that went largely unreported in the press. Their jail experiences turned most of them into committed core leaders of the student movement.

The Justice Department eventually petitioned the Interstate Commerce Commission to issue clear rules prohibiting segregation on interstate carriers. At the end of 1962, CORE proclaimed victory in the battle against Jim Crow interstate travel. By creating a crisis, the Freedom Rides had forced the Kennedy administration to act. But they also revealed the unwillingness of the federal government to fully enforce the law of the land. The Freedom Rides exposed the ugly face of southern racism to the world. At the same time, they reinforced white resistance to desegregation. The jailings and brutality experienced by Freedom Riders made clear to the civil rights community the limits of moral suasion alone for effecting change.

The Albany Movement: The Limits of Protest

Where the federal government chose not to enforce the constitutional rights of black people, segregationist forces tenaciously held their ground, especially in the more remote areas of the Deep South. In Albany, a small city in southwest Georgia, activists from SNCC, the NAACP, and other local groups formed a coalition known as the Albany movement. Starting in October 1961 and continuing for more than a year, thousands of Albany's black citizens marched, sat in, and boycotted as part of a citywide campaign to integrate public facilities and win voting rights. More than a thousand people spent time in jail. In December, the arrival of Martin Luther King, Jr. and the SCLC transformed Albany into a national symbol of the struggle.

But the gains at Albany proved minimal. Infighting among the various civil rights organizations hurt the cause. Local SNCC workers opposed the more cautious approach of NAACP officials, even though the more established organization paid many of the campaign's expenses. The arrival of King guaranteed national news coverage, but local activists worried that his presence might undermine the community focus and their own influence. Most important, Albany police chief Laurie Pritchett shrewdly deprived the movement of the kind of national sympathy won by the Freedom Riders. Pritchett filled the jails with black demonstrators, kept their mistreatment to a minimum, and prevented white mobs from running wild. "We met 'nonviolence' with 'nonviolence,'" he boasted.

King himself was twice arrested in the summer of 1962, but Albany officials quickly freed him to avoid negative publicity. The Kennedy administration kept clear of the developments in Albany, hoping to help the gubernatorial campaign of "moderate" Democrat Carl Sanders. By late 1962 the Albany movement had collapsed, and Pritchett proudly declared the city "as segregated as ever." One activist summed up the losing campaign: "We were naive enough to think we could fill up the jails. Pritchett was hep to the fact that we couldn't. We ran out of people before he ran out of jails." Albany showed that mass protest without violent white reaction and direct federal intervention could not end Jim Crow.

The successful battle to integrate the University of Mississippi in 1962 contrasted with the failure at Albany and reinforced the importance of federal intervention for guaranteeing civil rights to African Americans. In the fall of 1962 James Meredith, an air force veteran and a student at all-black Jackson State College, tried "to register as the first black student at the university." Governor Ross Barnett defied a federal court order and personally blocked Meredith's path at the admissions office. When Barnett refused to assure Robert Kennedy that Meredith would be protected, the attorney general dispatched 500 federal marshals to the campus. Over the radio, Barnett encouraged resistance to the "oppressive power of the United States," and an angry mob of several thousand whites, many of them armed, laid siege to the campus on September 30. A night of violence left 2 people dead and 160 marshals wounded, 28 from gunfire. President Kennedy ordered 5,000 army troops onto the campus to stop the riot. A federal guard remained to protect Meredith, who graduated the following summer.

THE MOVEMENT AT HIGH TIDE, 1963–65

The tumultuous events of 1960–62 convinced civil rights strategists that segregation could not be dismantled merely through orderly protest and moral persuasion. Only comprehensive civil rights legislation, backed by the power of the federal government, could guarantee full citizenship rights for African Americans. To build the national consensus needed for new laws, civil rights activists looked for ways to gain broader support for their cause. By 1963, their sense of urgency had led them to plan dramatic confrontations that would expose the violence and terror routinely faced by southern blacks. With the whole country—indeed, the whole world—watching, the movement reached the peak of its political and moral power.

Birmingham

At the end of 1962, Martin Luther King, Jr. and his SCLC allies decided to launch a new campaign against segregation in Birmingham, Alabama. After the failure in Albany, King and his aides looked for a way to shore up his leadership and inject new momentum into the freedom struggle. They needed a major victory. Birmingham was the most segregated big city in America, and it had a deep history of racial violence. African Americans endured total segregation in schools, restaurants, city parks, and department store dressing rooms. Although black people constituted more than 40 percent of the city's population, fewer than 10,000 of Birmingham's 80,000 registered voters were black. The city's prosperous steel industry relegated black workers to menial jobs.

Police dogs attacked a seventeen-year-old civil rights demonstrator for defying an antiparade ordinance in Birmingham, Alabama, May 3, 1963. He was part of the "children's crusade" organized by SCLC in its campaign to fill the city jails with protesters. More than 900 Birmingham schoolchildren went to jail that day.

SOURCE: Photo by Bill Hudson. AP/Wide World Photos.

Working closely with local civil rights groups led by the longtime Birmingham activist Reverend Fred Shuttlesworth, the SCLC carefully planned its campaign. The strategy was to fill the city jails with protesters, boycott downtown department stores, and enrage Public Safety Commissioner Eugene "Bull" Connor. In April, King arrived with a manifesto demanding an end to racist hiring practices and segregated public accommodations and the creation of a biracial committee to oversee desegregation. "Here in Birmingham," King told reporters, "we have reached the point of no return." Connor's police began jailing hundreds of demonstrators, including King himself, who defied a state court injunction against further protests.

Held in solitary confinement for several days, King managed to write a response to a group of Birmingham clergy who had deplored the protests. King's *Letter from Birmingham Jail* was soon widely reprinted and circulated as a pamphlet. It set out the key moral issues at stake, and scoffed at those who claimed the campaign was illegal and ill timed. King wrote:

> We know through painful experience that freedom is never voluntarily given by the oppressor; it must be demanded by the oppressed. Frankly, I have never yet engaged in a direct-action campaign that was "well timed" in the view of those who have not suffered unduly from the disease of segregation. For years now I have heard the word "Wait!" It rings in the ear of every Negro with a piercing familiarity. This "Wait" has almost always meant "Never." We must come to see, with one of our distinguished jurists, that "justice too long delayed is justice denied."

After King's release on bail, the campaign intensified. The SCLC kept up the pressure by recruiting thousands of Birmingham's young students for a "children's crusade." In early May, Bull Connor's forces began using high-powered water cannons, billy clubs, and snarling police dogs to break up demonstrations. Millions of Americans reacted with horror to the violent scenes from Birmingham shown on national television. Many younger black people, especially from the city's poor and working-class districts, began to fight back, hurling bottles and bricks at police. On May 10, mediators from the Justice Department negotiated an uneasy truce. The SCLC agreed to an immediate end to the protests. In exchange, businesses would desegregate and begin hiring African Americans over the next three months, and a biracial city committee would oversee desegregation of public facilities.

King claimed the events in Birmingham represented "the most magnificent victory for justice we've ever seen in the Deep South." But whites such as Bull Connor and Governor George Wallace denounced the agreement. A few days after the announcement, more than a thousand robed Ku Klux Klansmen burned a cross in a park on the outskirts of Birmingham. When bombs rocked SCLC headquarters and the home of King's brother, a Birmingham minister, enraged blacks took to the streets and pelted police and firefighters with stones and bottles. President Kennedy ordered 3,000 army troops into the city and prepared to nationalize the Alabama National Guard. The violence receded, and white business people and politicians began to carry out the agreed-upon pact. But in September a bomb killed four black girls in a Birmingham Baptist church, reminding the city and the world that racial harmony was still a long way off.

The Birmingham campaign and the other protests it sparked over the next seven months engaged more than 100,000 people and led to nearly 15,000 arrests. The civil rights community now drew support from millions of Americans, black and white, who were inspired by the protesters and repelled by the face of southern bigotry. At the same time, Birmingham changed the nature of black protest. The black unemployed and working poor who joined in the struggle brought a different perspective from that of the students, professionals, and members of the religious middle class who had dominated the movement before Birmingham. They cared less about the philosophy of nonviolence and more about immediate gains in employment and housing and an end to police brutality. The urgent cries for "Freedom now!" were more than simply a demand to end legal segregation, and they were a measure as well of how far the movement had traveled in the seven years since the end of the Montgomery bus boycott.

JFK and the March on Washington

The growth of black activism and white support convinced President Kennedy the moment had come to press for sweeping civil rights legislation. Continuing white resistance in the South also made clearer than ever the need for federal action. In June 1963, Alabama governor George Wallace threatened to personally block the admission of two black students to the state university. Only the deployment of National Guard troops, placed under federal control by the president, ensured the students' safety and their peaceful admission into the University of Alabama.

It was a defining moment for Kennedy. Even more than for Eisenhower at Little Rock, the realities of international cold war politics pushed Kennedy toward support for civil rights. On June 11 the president went on national television and offered his personal endorsement of the civil rights activism: "Today we are committed to a worldwide struggle to promote and protect the rights of all who wish to be free. And when Americans are sent to Vietnam or West Berlin, we do not ask for whites only . . . Are we to say to the rest of the world, and much more importantly, to each other, that this is a land of the free except for Negroes?" Reviewing the racial situation, Kennedy told his audience that "We face . . . a moral crisis as a country and a people. It cannot be met by repressive police action. It cannot be left to increased demonstrations in the streets. It cannot be quieted by token moves or talk. It is a time to act in the Congress, in your state and local legislative body, and, above all, in all our daily lives." The next week Kennedy asked Congress for a broad law that would ensure voting rights, outlaw segregation in public facilities, and bolster federal authority to deny funds for discriminatory programs. Knowing they would face a stiff fight from

As the Civil Rights movement received greater coverage in the international press, editorial cartoonists in America expressed fears that white resistance to integration provided an effective propaganda weapon to the Soviet Union and its allies. This *Oakland Tribune* cartoon appeared on September 11, 1957, in the midst of the crisis in Little Rock.

SOURCE: *Right into Their Hands.* The Oakland Tribune.

congressional conservatives, administration officials began an intense lobbying effort in support of the law. After three years of fence sitting, Kennedy finally committed his office and his political future to the civil rights cause.

Movement leaders lauded the president's initiative. Yet they understood that racial hatred still haunted the nation. Only a few hours after Kennedy's television speech, a gunman murdered Medgar Evers, leader of the Mississippi NAACP, outside his home in Jackson, Mississippi. To pressure Congress and demonstrate the urgency of their cause, a broad coalition of civil rights groups planned a massive, nonviolent March on Washington. The idea had deep roots in black protest. A. Philip Randolph, head of the Brotherhood of Sleeping Car Porters, had originally proposed such a march in 1941 to protest discrimination against blacks in the wartime defense industries. Now, more than twenty years later, Randolph, along with his aide Bayard Rustin, revived the concept and convinced leaders of the major civil rights groups to support it.

The Kennedy administration originally opposed the march, fearing it would jeopardize support for the president's civil rights bill in Congress. But as plans for the rally solidified, Kennedy reluctantly gave his approval. Leaders from the SCLC, the NAACP, SNCC, the Urban League, and CORE—the leading organizations in the civil rights community—put aside their tactical differences to forge a broad consensus for the event. John Lewis, the young head of SNCC, who had endured numerous brutal assaults, planned a speech that denounced the Kennedys as hypocrites. Lewis's speech enraged Walter Reuther, the white liberal leader of the United Auto Workers union, which had helped finance the march. Reuther threatened to turn off the loudspeakers he was paying for, believing Lewis's speech would embarrass the Kennedys. Randolph, the acknowledged elder statesman of the movement, convinced Lewis at the last moment to tone down his remarks. "We've come this far," he implored. "For the sake of unity, change it."

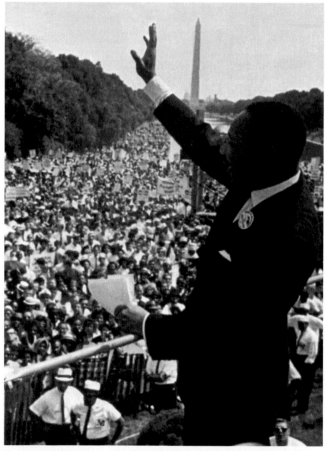

Reverend Dr. Martin Luther King, Jr., acknowledging the huge throng at the historic March on Washington for "jobs and freedom," August 28, 1963. The size of the crowd, the stirring oratory and song, and the live network television coverage produced one of the most memorable political events in the nation's history.

SOURCE: George Ballis/Take Stock.

On August 28, 1963, more than a quarter of a million people, including 50,000 whites, gathered at the Lincoln Memorial to rally for "jobs and freedom." Union members, students, teachers, clergy, professionals, musicians, actors—Americans from all walks of life joined the largest political assembly in the nation's history until then. The sight of all those people holding hands and singing "We Shall Overcome," led by the white folk singer Joan Baez, would not be easily forgotten. At the end of a long, exhilarating day of speeches and freedom songs, Martin Luther King, Jr. provided an emotional climax. Combining the democratic promise of the Declaration of Independence with the religious fervor of his Baptist heritage, King stirred the crowd with his dream for America:

> I have a dream today that one day this nation will rise up and live out the true meaning of its creed: "We hold these truths to be self-evident—that all men are created equal." . . . When we allow freedom to ring, when we let it ring from every village and every hamlet, from every state and every city, we will be able to speed up that day when all of God's children—black men and white men, Jews and Gentiles, Protestants and Catholics—will be able to join hands and sing in the words of the old Negro spiritual, "Free at last! Free at last! Thank God Almighty, we are free at last!"

LBJ and the Civil Rights Act of 1964

An extraordinary demonstration of interracial unity, the March on Washington stood as the high-water mark in the struggle for civil rights. It buoyed the spirits of movement leaders as well as the liberals pushing the new civil rights bill through Congress. But the assassination of John F. Kennedy on November 22, 1963, in Dallas threw an ominous cloud over the whole nation and the civil rights movement in particular. In the Deep South, many ardent segregationists welcomed the president's death because of his support for civil rights. Most African Americans probably shared the feelings of Coretta Scott King, who recalled her family's vigil: "We felt that President Kennedy had been a friend of the Cause and that with him as President we could continue to move forward. We watched and prayed for him."

Lyndon Baines Johnson, Kennedy's successor, had never been much of a friend to civil rights. As a senator from Texas (1948–60, including six years as majority leader), Johnson had been one of the shrewdest and most powerful Democrats in Congress. Throughout the 1950s he had worked to obstruct the passage and enforcement of civil rights laws—though as vice president he had ably chaired Kennedy's working group on equal employment. Johnson reassured a grieving nation that "the ideas and the ideals which [Kennedy] so nobly represented must and will be translated into effective action." Even so, civil rights activists looked upon Johnson warily as he took over the Oval Office.

As president, Johnson realized that he faced a new political reality, one created by the civil rights movement. Eager to unite the Democratic Party and prove himself as a national leader, he seized on civil rights as a golden political opportunity. "I knew that if I didn't get out in front on this issue," he later recalled, "they [the liberals] would get me. They'd throw up my background against me, they'd use it to prove that I was incapable of bringing unity to the land I loved so much. . . . I had to produce a civil rights bill that was even stronger than

the one they'd have gotten if Kennedy had lived." Throughout the early months of 1964, the new president let it be known publicly and privately that he would brook no compromise on civil rights.

Johnson exploited all his skills as a political insider. He cajoled, flattered, and threatened key members of the House and Senate. Working with the president, the fifteen-year-old Leadership Conference on Civil Rights coordinated a sophisticated lobbying effort in Congress. Groups such as the NAACP, the AFL-CIO, the National Council of Churches, and the American Jewish Congress made the case for a strong civil rights bill. The

OVERVIEW

LANDMARK CIVIL RIGHTS LEGISLATION, SUPREME COURT DECISIONS, AND EXECUTIVE ORDERS

Year	Decision, law, or executive order	Significance
1939	*Missouri v. ex.rel.Gaines*	Required University of Missouri Law School either to admit African Americans or build another fully equal law school
1941	Executive Order 8802 (by President Roosevelt)	Banned racial discrimination in defense industry and government offices; established Fair Employment Practices Committee to investigate violations
1946	*Morgan v. Virginia*	Ruled that segregation on interstate buses violated federal law and created an "undue burden" on interstate commerce
1948	Executive Order 9981 (by President Truman)	Desegregated the U.S. armed forces
1950	*McLaurin v. Oklahoma State Regents*	Ruled that forcing an African American student to sit, eat, and study in segregated facilities was unconstitutional because it inevitably created a "badge of inferiority"
1950	*Sweatt v. Painter*	Ruled that an inferior law school created by the University of Texas to serve African Americans violated their right to equal protection and ordered Herman Sweatt to be admitted to University of Texas Law School
1954	*Brown v. Board of Education of Topeka I*	Declared "separate educational facilities are inherently unequal," thus overturning *Plessy v. Ferguson* (1896) and the "separate but equal" doctrine as it applied to public schools
1955	*Brown v. Board of Education of Topeka II*	Ordered school desegregation to begin with "all deliberate speed," but offered no timetable
1957	Civil Rights Act	Created Civil Rights Division within the Justice Department
1964	Civil Rights Act	Prohibited discrimination in employment and most places of public accommodation on basis of race, color, religion, sex, or national origin; outlawed bias in federally assisted programs; created Equal Employment Opportunity Commission
1965	Voting Rights Act	Authorized federal supervision of voter registration in states and counties where fewer than half of voting age residents were registered; outlawed literacy and other discriminatory tests in voter registration

House passed the bill in February by a 290–130 vote. The more difficult fight would be in the Senate, where a southern filibuster promised to block the bill or weaken it. But by June, Johnson's persistence had paid off and the southern filibuster had collapsed.

On July 2, 1964, Johnson signed the Civil Rights Act of 1964. Every major provision had survived intact. This landmark law represented the most significant civil rights legislation since Reconstruction. It prohibited discrimination in most places of public accommodation; outlawed discrimination in employment on the basis of race, color, religion, sex, or national origin; outlawed bias in federally assisted programs; authorized the Justice Department to institute suits to desegregate public schools and other facilities; created the Equal Employment Opportunity Commission; and provided technical and financial aid to communities desegregating their schools.

Mississippi Freedom Summer

While President Johnson and his liberal allies won the congressional battle for the new civil rights bill, activists in Mississippi mounted a far more radical and dangerous campaign than any yet attempted in the South. In the spring of 1964, a coalition of workers led by SNCC launched the Freedom Summer project, an ambitious effort to register black voters and directly challenge the iron rule of segregation. Mississippi stood as the toughest test for the civil rights movement, racially and economically. It was the poorest, most backward state in the nation, and had remained largely untouched by the freedom struggle. African Americans constituted 42 percent of the state's population, but fewer than 5 percent could register to vote. Median black family income was under $1,500 a year, roughly one-third that of white families. A small white planter elite controlled most of the state's wealth, and a long tradition of terror against black people had maintained the racial caste system.

Bob Moses of SNCC and Dave Dennis of CORE planned Freedom Summer as a way of opening up this closed society to the glare of national publicity. The project recruited over 900 volunteers, mostly white college students, to aid in voter registration, teach in "freedom schools," and help build a "freedom party" as an alternative to Mississippi's all-white Democratic Party. Organizers expected violence, which was precisely why they wanted white volunteers. Dave Dennis later explained their reasoning: "The death of a white college student would bring on more attention to what was going on than for a black college student getting it. That's cold, but that was also in another sense speaking the language of this country." Mississippi authorities prepared for the civil rights workers as if expecting a foreign army, beefing up state highway patrols and local police forces.

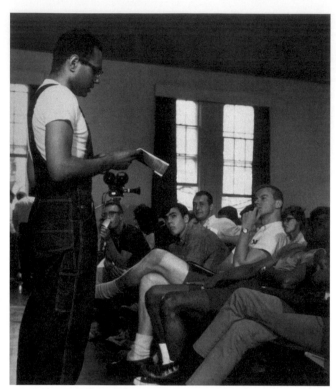

Bob Moses of the Student Nonviolent Coordinating Committee was one of the driving forces behind the 1964 Freedom Summer Project. Here he instructs student volunteers gathered in Oxford, Ohio before they leave for voter registration and other community organizing work in Mississippi. Moses, who had been working for voting rights in Mississippi since 1961, played a key role in persuading SNCC to accept white volunteers from the North.

SOURCE: Photo by Steve Shapiro. Black Star (PER 13SC HA000102).

On June 21, while most project volunteers were still undergoing training in Ohio, three activists disappeared in Neshoba County, Mississippi, when they went to investigate the burning of a black church that was supposed to serve as a freedom school. Six weeks later, after a massive search belatedly ordered by President Johnson, FBI agents discovered the bodies of the three—white activists Michael Schwerner and Andrew Goodman, and a local black activist, James Chaney—buried in an earthen dam. Goodman and Schwerner had been shot once; Chaney had been severely beaten before being shot three times. Over the summer, at least three other civil rights workers died violently. Project workers suffered 1,000 arrests, 80 beatings, 35 shooting incidents, and 30 bombings in homes, churches, and schools.

Within the project, simmering problems tested the ideal of the Beloved Community. Black veterans of SNCC resented the affluent white volunteers, many of whom had not come to terms with their own racial prejudices. White volunteers, staying only a short time in the state, often found it difficult to communicate in the southern communities with local African Americans, who were wary of breaking old codes of deference. Sexual tensions between black male and white female volunteers also strained relations. A number of both black and white women, led by Ruby Doris Robinson, Mary King, and Casey Hayden, began to raise the issue of women's equality as a companion goal to racial equality. The day-to-day reality of violent reprisals, police harassment, and constant fear took a hard toll on everyone.

The project did manage to rivet national attention on Mississippi racism, and it won enormous sympathy from northern liberals. Among their concrete accomplishments, the volunteers could point with pride to more than forty freedom schools that brought classes in reading, arithmetic, politics, and African American history to thousands of black children. Some 60,000 black voters signed up to join the Mississippi Freedom Democratic Party (MFDP). In August 1964 the MFDP sent a slate of delegates to the Democratic National Convention looking to challenge the credentials of the all-white regular state delegation.

In Atlantic City, the idealism of Freedom Summer ran into the more cynical needs of the national Democratic Party. Lyndon Johnson opposed the seating of the MFDP because he wanted to avoid a divisive floor fight. He was already concerned that Republicans might carry a number of southern states in November. But MFDP leaders and sympathizers gave dramatic testimony before the convention, detailing the racism and brutality in Mississippi politics. "Is this America," asked Fannie Lou Hamer, "the land of the free and the home of the brave, where we are threatened daily because we want to live as decent human beings?" Led by vice presidential nominee Senator Hubert Humphrey, Johnson's forces offered a compromise that would have given the MFDP a token two seats on the floor. Bitter over what they saw as a betrayal, the MFDP delegates turned the offer down. Within SNCC, the defeat of the MFDP intensified African American disillusionment with the Democratic Party and the liberal establishment.

Malcolm X and Black Consciousness

Frustrated with the limits of nonviolent protest and electoral politics, younger activists within SNCC found themselves increasingly drawn to the militant rhetoric and vision of Malcolm X, who since 1950 had been the preeminent spokesman for the black nationalist religious sect, the Nation of Islam (NOI). Founded in Depression-era Detroit by Elijah Muhammad, the NOI, like the followers of black nationalist leader Marcus Garvey in the 1920s (see Chapter 23) aspired to create a self-reliant, highly disciplined, and proud community—a separate "nation" for black people. Elijah Muhammad preached a message of racial solidarity and self-help, criticized crime and drug use, and castigated whites as "blue-eyed devils" responsible for the world's evil. During the 1950s the NOI (also called Black Muslims) successfully organized in northern black communities, appealing especially to criminals, drug addicts, and others living on the margins of urban life. It operated restaurants, retail stores, and schools as models for black economic self-sufficiency.

The man known as Malcolm X had been born Malcolm Little in 1925 and raised in Lansing, Michigan. His father, a preacher and a follower of Marcus Garvey, was killed in a racist attack by local whites. In his youth, Malcolm led a life of petty crime, eventually serving a seven-year prison term for burglary. While in jail he educated himself and converted to the Nation of Islam. He took the surname "X" to symbolize his original African family name, lost through slavery. Emerging from jail in 1952, he became a dynamic organizer, editor, and speaker for

After they were barred from the floor of the August 1964 Democratic National Convention, members of the Mississippi Freedom Democratic Party were led by Fanny Lou Hamer in a song-filled protest outside the hotel. SOURCE: Women from right: Fannie Lou Hamer, Eleanor Holmes Norton, and Ella Baker. Photo by George Ballis. Take Stock-Images of Change (0812023).

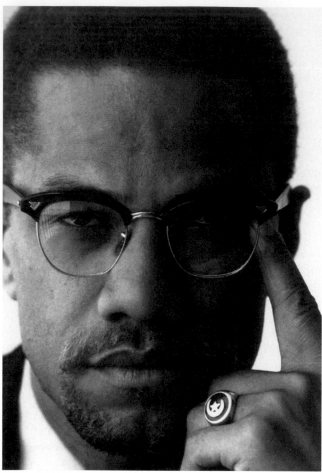

Born Malcolm Little, Malcolm X (1925–65) took the name "X" as a symbol of the stolen identity of African slaves. He emerged in the early 1960s as the foremost advocate of racial unity and black nationalism. The Black Power movement, initiated in 1966 by SNCC members, was strongly influenced by Malcolm X.

SOURCE: Malcolm X in Egypt, 1964. Photo by John Launois. Black Star.

the Nation of Islam. He spoke frequently on college campuses as well on the street corners of black neighborhoods like New York's Harlem. He encouraged his audiences to take pride in their African heritage and to consider armed self-defense rather than relying solely on nonviolence—in short, to break free of white domination "by any means necessary."

Malcolm ridiculed the integrationist goals of the civil rights movement. Black Muslims, he told audiences, do not want "to integrate into this corrupt society, but to separate from it, to a land of our own, where we can reform ourselves, lift up our moral standards, and try to be godly." In his best-selling *Autobiography of Malcolm X* (1965), he admitted that his position was extremist. "The black race here in North America is in extremely bad condition. You show me a black man who isn't an extremist," he argued, "and I'll show you one who needs psychiatric attention."

In 1964, troubled by Elijah Muhammad's personal scandals (he faced paternity suits brought by two young female employees) and eager to find a more politically effective approach to improving conditions for blacks, Malcolm X broke with the Nation of Islam. He made a pilgrimage to Mecca, the Muslim holy city, where he met Islamic peoples of all colors and underwent a "radical alteration in my whole outlook about 'white' men." He returned to the United States as El-Hajj Malik El-Shabazz, abandoned his black separatist views, and founded the Organization of Afro-American Unity. Malcolm now looked for common ground with the civil rights movement, addressing a Mississippi Freedom Democrats rally in Harlem and meeting with SNCC activists. He stressed the international links between the civil rights struggle in America and the problems facing emerging African nations. On February 21, 1965, Malcolm X was assassinated during a speech at Harlem's Audubon Ballroom. His assailants were members of a New Jersey branch of the NOI, possibly infiltrated by the FBI.

"More than any other person," remarked black author Julius Lester, "Malcolm X was responsible for the new militancy that entered The Movement in 1965." SNCC leader John Lewis thought Malcolm had been the most effective voice "to articulate the aspirations, bitterness, and frustrations of the Negro people," forming "a living link between Africa and the civil rights movement in this country." In his death he became a martyr for the idea that soon became known as Black Power. As much as anyone, Malcolm X pointed the way to a new black consciousness that celebrated black history, black culture, the African heritage, and black self-sufficiency.

Selma and the Voting Rights Act of 1965

Lyndon Johnson won reelection in 1964 by a landslide, capturing 61 percent of the popular vote. Of the 6 million black people who voted in the election, 2 million more than in 1960, an overwhelming 94 percent cast their ballots for Johnson. Republican candidate Senator Barry Goldwater managed to carry only his home state of Arizona and five Deep South states, where fewer than 45 percent of eligible black people could vote. With Democrats in firm control of both the Senate and the House, civil rights leaders believed the time was ripe for further legislative gains. Johnson and his staff began drafting a tough voting rights bill in late 1964, partly with an eye toward countering Republican gains in the Deep South with newly registered black and Democratic voters. Martin Luther King and the SCLC shared this goal of passing a strong voting rights law that would provide southern black people with direct federal protection of their right to vote.

Once again, movement leaders plotted to create a crisis that would arouse national indignation, pressure

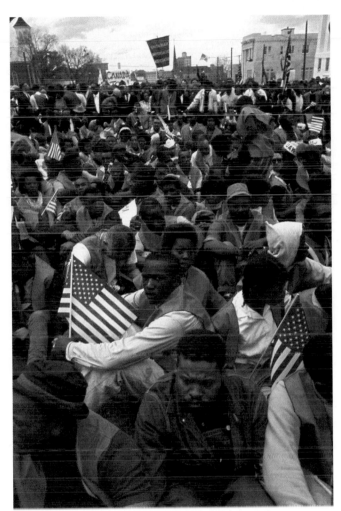

Voting rights demonstrators rallied in front of the state capitol in Montgomery, Alabama, March 25, 1965, after a four day, fifty-four mile trek from Selma. The original 3,000 marchers were joined by over 30,000 supporters by the end of their journey. SOURCE: Photo by Matt Herron. Media Image Resource Alliance (0001A030).

Congress, and force federal action. King and his aides chose Selma, Alabama, as the target of their campaign. Selma, a city of 27,000 some fifty miles west of Montgomery, had a notorious record of preventing black voting. Of the 15,000 eligible black voters in Selma's Dallas County, registered voters numbered only in the hundreds. In 1963, local activists Amelia Boynton and Reverend Fred Reese had invited SNCC workers to aid voter registration efforts in the community. But they had met a violent reception from county sheriff Jim Clark. Sensing that Clark might be another Bull Connor, King arrived in Selma in January 1965, just after accepting the Nobel Peace Prize in Oslo. "We are not asking, we are demanding the ballot," he declared. King, the SCLC staff, and SNCC workers led daily marches on the Dallas County Courthouse, where hundreds of black citizens tried to get their names added to voter lists.

By early February, Clark had imprisoned more than 3,000 protesters.

Despite the brutal beating of Reverend James Bevel, a key SCLC strategist, and the killing of Jimmy Lee Jackson, a young black demonstrator in nearby Marion, the SCLC failed to arouse the level of national indignation it sought. Consequently, in early March SCLC staffers called on black activists to march from Selma to Montgomery, where they planned to deliver a list of grievances to Governor Wallace. On Sunday, March 7, while King preached to his church in Atlanta, a group of 600 marchers crossed the Pettus Bridge on the Alabama River, on their way to Montgomery. A group of mounted, heavily armed county and state lawmen blocked their path and ordered them to turn back. When the marchers did not move, the lawmen attacked with billy clubs and tear gas, driving the protesters back over the bridge in a bloody rout. More than fifty marchers had to be treated in local hospitals.

The dramatic "Bloody Sunday" attack received extensive coverage on network television, prompting a national uproar. Demands for federal intervention poured into the White House from all over the country. King issued a public call for civil rights supporters to come to Selma for a second march on Montgomery. But a federal court temporarily enjoined the SCLC from proceeding with the march. King found himself trapped. He reluctantly accepted a face-saving compromise: in return for a promise from Alabama authorities not to harm marchers, King would lead his followers across the Pettus Bridge, stop, pray briefly, and then turn back. This plan outraged the more militant SNCC activists and sharpened their distrust of King and the SCLC.

But just when it seemed the Selma movement might die, white racist violence revived it. A gang of white toughs attacked four white Unitarian ministers who had come to Selma to participate in the march. One of them, Reverend James J. Reeb of Boston, died of multiple skull fractures. His death brought new calls for federal action. On March 15, President Johnson delivered a televised address to a joint session of Congress to request passage of a voting rights bill. In a stirring speech, the president fused the political power of his office with the moral power of the movement. "Their cause must be our cause, too. Because it is not just Negroes, but really all of us who must overcome the crippling legacy of bigotry and injustice. And," he concluded firmly, invoking the movement's slogan, "we shall overcome." Johnson also prevailed upon federal judge Frank Johnson to issue a ruling allowing the march to proceed, and he warned Governor Wallace not to interfere.

On March 21 Martin Luther King led a group of more than 3,000 black and white marchers out of Selma on the road to Montgomery, where the bus boycott that marked the beginning of his involvement had occurred nine years before. Four days later they arrived at the

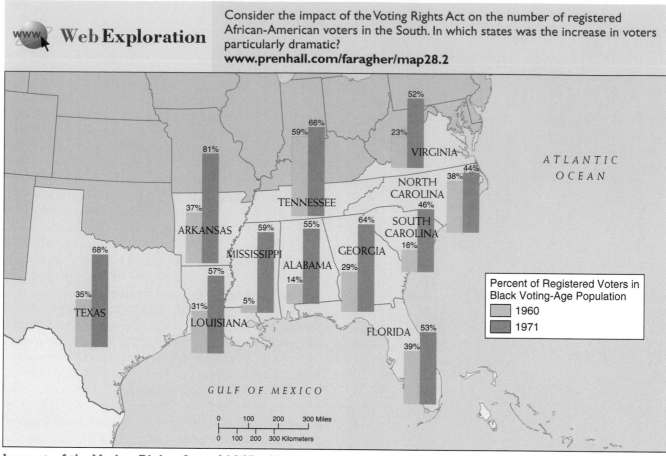

Web Exploration   Consider the impact of the Voting Rights Act on the number of registered African-American voters in the South. In which states was the increase in voters particularly dramatic?
www.prenhall.com/faragher/map28.2

Impact of the Voting Rights Act of 1965   Voter registration among African Americans in the South increased significantly between 1960 and 1971.

Alabama statehouse. Their ranks had been swelled by more than 30,000 supporters, including hundreds of prominent politicians, entertainers, and black leaders. "I know some of you are asking today," King told the crowd, "'How long will it take?'" He went on in a rousing, rhythmic cadence:

> I come to say to you this afternoon, however difficult the moment, however frustrating the hour, it will not be long because truth pressed to earth will rise again. How long? Not long, because no lie can live forever. How long? Not long, because you will reap what you sow. How long? Not long, because the arc of the moral universe is long but it bends toward justice. How long? Not long, because mine eyes have seen the glory of the coming of the Lord!

In August 1965 President Johnson signed the Voting Rights Act into law. It authorized federal supervision of registration in states and counties where fewer than half of voting-age residents were registered. It also outlawed literacy and other discriminatory tests that had been

used to prevent blacks from registering to vote. Between 1964 and 1968, black registrants in Mississippi leaped from 7 percent to 59 percent of the statewide black population; in Alabama, from 24 percent to 57 percent. In those years the number of southern black voters grew from 1 million to 3.1 million. For the first time in their lives, black Southerners in hundreds of small towns and rural communities could enjoy full participation in American politics. Ten years after the Montgomery bus boycott, the civil rights movement had reached a peak of national influence and interracial unity.

FORGOTTEN MINORITIES, 1945–65

The civil rights movement revolved around the aspirations and community strength of African Americans. The historic injustices of slavery, racism, and segregation gave a moral and political urgency to the black struggle for full citizenship rights. Yet other minorities as well had long been denied their civil rights. After World War II, Latinos, Indian peoples, and Asian Americans began making their own halting efforts to improve their political, legal, and economic status. They faced strong opposition from institutional racism and various economic interests that benefited from keeping these groups in a subordinate position. By the late 1960s, the success of the black civil rights movement had inspired these minority groups to adopt more militant strategies of their own.

Mexican Americans

The Mexican American community in the West and Southwest included both longtime U.S. citizens—who found white authorities nonetheless unwilling to recognize their rights—and noncitizen immigrants from Mexico. After World War II, several Mexican American political organizations sought to secure equal rights and equal opportunity for their community by stressing its American identity. The most important of these groups were the League of United Latin American Citizens (LULAC), founded in Texas in 1928, and the G.I. Forum, founded in Texas in 1948 by Mexican American veterans of World War II. Both emphasized the learning of English, assimilation into American society, improved education, and the promotion of

political power through voting. LULAC successfully pursued two important legal cases that anticipated *Brown* v. *Board of Education*. In *Mendez* v. *Westminster*, a 1947 California case, and in the 1948 *Delgado* case in Texas, the Supreme Court upheld lower-court rulings that declared segregation of Mexican Americans unconstitutional. Like *Brown*, these two decisions did not immediately end segregation, but they offered path-breaking legal and psychological victories to Mexican American activists. LULAC won another significant legal battle in the 1954 *Hernandez* decision, in which the Supreme Court ended the exclusion of Mexican Americans from Texas jury lists.

Mexican migration to the United States increased dramatically during and after World War II. The *bracero* program, a cooperative effort between the U.S. and Mexican governments, brought some 300,000 Mexicans to the United States during the war as temporary agricultural and railroad workers. American agribusiness came to depend on Mexicans as a key source of cheap farm labor, and the program continued after the war. Most braceros endured harsh work, poor food, and sub-standard housing in the camps in which they lived. Some migrated into the newly emerging barrio neighborhoods in cities such as San Antonio, Los Angeles, El Paso, and Denver. Many braceros and their children became American citizens, but most returned to

Delegates to the 1948 National Convention of the League of United Latin American Citizens met in Kingsville, Texas. After World War II, LULAC grew to about 15,000 members active in 200 local councils, mostly in Texas and California.

SOURCE: Benson Latin American Collection.

Mexico. Another group of postwar Mexican immigrants were the *mojados,* or "wetbacks," so called because many swam across the Rio Grande River to enter the United States illegally.

In 1954, in an effort to curb the flow of undocumented immigrants from Mexico, the Eisenhower administration launched the massive "Operation Wetback." Over the next three years Immigration Service agents rounded up some 3.7 million allegedly illegal migrants and sent them back over the border. Immigration agents made little effort to distinguish the so-called illegals from braceros and Mexican American citizens. Many families were broken up, and thousands who had lived in the United States for a decade or more found themselves deported. Many deportees were denied basic civil liberties, such as due process, and suffered physical abuse and intimidation. Most Mexican Americans had ambivalent feelings about mojados and Operation Wetback. The deportations tended to improve job opportunities and wages for those who remained. Yet the so-called illegals were considered members of *la raza,* the larger Mexican American community, and family ties between these groups were common. LULAC and the *Asociación Nacional Mexico-Americana,* founded in 1950, tried in vain to curb abuses against aliens and Mexican Americans. Among Mexican Americans, Operation Wetback left a bitter legacy of deep mistrust and estrangement from Anglo culture and politics.

Puerto Ricans

The United States took possession of the island of Puerto Rico in 1898, during the final stages of the Spanish-American War. The Jones Act of 1917 made the island an unincorporated territory of the United States and granted U.S. citizenship to all Puerto Ricans. Over the next several decades, Puerto Rico's economic base shifted from a diversified, subsistence-oriented agriculture to a single export crop—sugar. U.S. absentee owners dominated the sugar industry, claiming most of the island's arable land, previously tilled by small farmers growing crops for local consumption. Puerto Rico's sugar industry grew enormously profitable, but few island residents benefited from this expansion. By the 1930s, unemployment and poverty were widespread and the island was forced to import its foodstuffs.

Small communities of Puerto Rican migrants had begun to form in New York City during the 1920s. The largest was on the Upper East Side of Manhattan—*el barrio* in East Harlem. During World War II, labor shortages led the federal government to sponsor the recruitment of Puerto Rican workers for industrial jobs in New Jersey, Philadelphia, and Chicago. But the "great migration" took place from 1945 to 1964. During these two

decades the number of Puerto Ricans living on the mainland jumped from less than 100,000 to roughly 1 million. Economic opportunity was the chief impetus for this migration, for the island suffered from high unemployment rates and low wages.

The advent of direct air service between Puerto Rico and New York in 1945 made the city easily accessible. The Puerto Rican community in East (or Spanish) Harlem mushroomed, and new communities in the South Bronx and Brooklyn began to emerge. By 1970 there were about 800,000 Puerto Ricans in New York—more than 10 percent of the city's population. New Puerto Rican communities also took root in Connecticut, Massachusetts, New Jersey, and the Midwest. Puerto Ricans frequently circulated between the island and the mainland, often returning home when economic conditions on the mainland were less favorable.

The experience of Puerto Rican migrants both resembled and differed from that of other immigrant groups in significant ways. Like Mexican immigrants, Puerto Ricans were foreign in language, culture, and experience, yet unlike them they entered the United States as citizens. Many Puerto Ricans were also African Americans. Racial and ethnic discrimination came as a double shock, since Puerto Ricans, as citizens, entered the United States with a sense of entitlement. In New York, Puerto Ricans found themselves barred from most craft unions, excluded from certain neighborhoods, and forced to take jobs largely in the low-paying garment industry and service trades. Puerto Rican children were not well served by a public school system insensitive to language differences and too willing to track Spanish-speaking students into obsolete vocational programs.

By the early 1970s, Puerto Rican families were substantially poorer on average than the total population of the country, and they had the lowest median income of any Latino groups. The steep decline in manufacturing jobs and in the garment industry in New York during the 1960s and 1970s hit the Puerto Rican community especially hard. So did the city's fiscal crisis, which brought sharp cuts in funding for schools, health care, libraries, government jobs, and other public services traditionally available to immigrant groups. The structural shift in the U.S. economy away from manufacturing and toward service and high-technology jobs reinforced the Puerto Rican community's goal of improving educational opportunities for its members. The struggle to establish and improve bilingual education in schools became an important part of this effort. Most Puerto Ricans, especially those who had succeeded in school and achieved middle-class status, continued to identify strongly with their Puerto Rican heritage and the Spanish language.

George Gillette (left foreground), chairman of the Fort Berthold Indian Council, wept as Secretary of Interior J. A. Krug signed a contract buying 155,000 acres of the tribe's best land in North Dakota for a reservoir project, May 20, 1948. "The members of the tribal council sign this contract with heavy hearts," Gillette said.

SOURCE: CORBIS.

Indian Peoples

The postwar years also brought significant changes in the status and lives of Indian peoples. Congress reversed the policies pursued under the New Deal, which had stressed Indian sovereignty and cultural independence. Responding to a variety of pressure groups, including mining and other economic interests wishing to exploit the resources on Indian reservations, Congress adopted a policy known as "termination," designed to cancel Indian treaties and terminate sovereignty rights. In 1953, Congress passed House Concurrent Resolution 108, which allowed Congress to terminate a tribe as a political entity by passing legislation specific to that tribe. The leader of the termination forces, Senator Arthur Watkins of Utah, declared the new law meant that "the concept that the Indian people exist within the United States as independent nations has been rejected." Supporters of termination had varied motives, but the policy added up to the return of enforced assimilation for solving the "Indian problem."

Between 1954 and 1962, Congress passed twelve termination bills covering more than sixty tribes, nearly all in the West. Even when tribes consented to their own termination, they discovered that dissolution brought unforeseen problems. For example, members of the Klamaths of Oregon and the Paiutes of Utah received large cash payments from the division of tribal assets.

But after these one-time payments were spent, members had to take poorly paid, unskilled jobs to survive. Many Indian peoples became dependent on state social services and slipped into poverty and alcoholism.

Along with termination, the federal government gave greater emphasis to a relocation program aimed at speeding up assimilation. The Bureau of Indian Affairs encouraged reservation Indians to relocate to cities, where they were provided housing and jobs. For some, relocation meant assimilation, intermarriage with whites, and the loss of tribal identity. Others, homesick and unable to adjust to an alien culture and place, either returned to reservations or wound up on the margins of city life. Still others regularly traveled back and forth. In some respects, this urban migration paralleled the larger postwar shift of rural peoples to cities and suburbs.

Indians increasingly came to see termination as a policy geared mainly to exploiting resources on Indian lands. By the early 1960s, a new movement was emerging to defend Indian sovereignty. The National Congress of American Indians (NCAI) condemned termination, calling for a review of federal policies and a return to self-determination. The NCAI led a political and educational campaign that challenged the goal of assimilation and created a new awareness among white people that Indians had the right to remain Indians. When the termination policy ended in the early 1960s, it had affected only about 3 percent of federally recognized Indian peoples.

Taking their cue from the civil rights movement, Indian activists used the court system to reassert sovereign rights. Indian and white liberal lawyers, many with experience in civil rights cases, worked through the Native American Rights Fund, which became a powerful force in western politics. A series of Supreme Court decisions, culminating in *United States* v. *Wheeler* (1978), reasserted the principle of "unique and limited" sovereignty. The Court recognized tribal independence except where limited by treaty or Congress.

The Indian population had been growing since the early years of the century, but most reservations had trouble making room for a new generation. Indians suffered increased rates of poverty, chronic unemployment, alcoholism, and poor health. The average Indian family in the early 1960s earned only one-third of the average family income in the United States. Those who remained in the cities usually became "ethnic Indians," identifying themselves more as Indians than as members of specific tribes. By the late 1960s, ethnic Indians had begun emphasizing civil rights over tribal rights, making common cause with African Americans and other minorities. The National Indian Youth Council (NIYC), founded in 1960, tried to unite the two causes of equality for individual Indians and special status for tribes.

But the organization faced difficult contradictions between a common Indian identity, emphasizing Indians as a single ethnic group, and tribal identity, stressing the citizenship of Indians in separate nations.

Asian Americans

The harsh relocation program of World War II devastated the Japanese American community on the west coast (see Chapter 25). But the war against Nazism also helped weaken older notions of white superiority and racism. During the war the state of California had aggressively enforced an alien land law by confiscating property declared illegally held by Japanese. In November 1946 a proposition supporting the law appeared on the state ballot. But, thanks in part to a campaign by the Japanese American Citizens League (JACL) reminding voters of the wartime contributions of Nisei (second-generation Japanese Americans) soldiers, voters overwhelmingly rejected the referendum. One JACL leader hailed the vote as proof that "the people of California will not approve discriminatory and prejudiced treatment of persons of Japanese ancestry." Two years later the Supreme Court declared the law unconstitutional, calling it "nothing more than outright racial discrimination."

The 1952 Immigration and Nationality Act (see Chapter 26) removed the old ban against Japanese immigration, and also made Issei (first-generation Japanese Americans) eligible for naturalized citizenship. Japanese Americans, who lobbied hard for the new law, greeted it with elation. "It gave the Japanese equality with all other immigrants," said JACL leader Harry Takagi, "and that was the principle we had been struggling for from the very beginning." By 1965 some 46,000 immigrant Japanese, most of them elderly Issei, had taken their citizenship oaths. One of these wrote a poem to celebrate the achievement:

> Going steadily to study English,
> Even through the rain at night,
> I thus attain,
> Late in life,
> American citizenship.

The Immigration and Nationality Act allowed immigration from the "Asian-Pacific Triangle." It was nonetheless racially discriminatory, in that each country in Asia was permitted only 100 immigrants a year. In addition, the act continued the national-origins quotas of 1924 for European countries. The civil rights struggle helped spur a movement to reform immigration policies. "Everywhere else in our national life, we have eliminated discrimination based on national origins," Attorney General Robert Kennedy told Congress in 1964. "Yet, this system is still the foundation of our immigration law."

In 1965 Congress passed a new Immigration and Nationality Act, abolishing the national-origins quotas and providing for the admission each year of 170,000 immigrants from the Eastern Hemisphere and 120,000 from the Western Hemisphere. The new law set a limit of 20,000 per country from the Eastern Hemisphere—these immigrants to be admitted on a first-come, first-served basis—and established preference categories for professional and highly skilled immigrants.

The 1965 act would have a profound effect on Asian American communities, opening the way for a new wave of immigration. In the twenty years following the act, the number of Asian Americans soared from 1 million to 5 million. Four times as many Asians settled in the United States in this period as in the entire previous history of the nation. This new wave also brought a strikingly different group of Asian immigrants to America. In 1960 the Asian American population was 52 percent Japanese, 27 percent Chinese, and 20 percent Filipino. In 1985, the composition was 21 percent Chinese, 21 percent Filipino, 15 percent Japanese, 12 percent Vietnamese, 11 percent Korean, 10 percent Asian Indian, 4 percent Laotian, and 3 percent Cambodian. These newcomers included significant numbers of highly educated professionals and city dwellers, a sharp contrast with the farmers and rural peoples of the past.

CONCLUSION

The mass movement for civil rights was arguably the most important domestic event of the twentieth century. The struggle that began in Montgomery, Alabama, in December 1955 ultimately transformed race relations in thousands of American communities. By the early 1960s this community-based movement had placed civil rights at the very center of national political life. It achieved its greatest successes by invoking the law of the land to destroy legal segregation and win individual freedom for African Americans. The Civil Rights Act of 1964 and the Voting Rights Act of 1965 testified to the power of an African American and white liberal coalition. Yet the persistence of racism, poverty, and ghetto slums challenged a central assumption of liberalism: that equal protection of constitutional rights would give all Americans equal opportunities in life. By the mid-1960s, many black people had begun to question the core values of liberalism, the benefits of alliance with whites, and the philosophy of nonviolence. At the same time, a conservative white backlash against the gains made by African Americans further weakened the liberal political consensus.

In challenging the persistence of widespread poverty and institutional racism, the civil rights movement called

CHRONOLOGY

1941	Executive Order 8802 forbids racial discrimination in defense industries and government
1946	In *Morgan v. Virginia*, U.S. Supreme Court rules that segregation on interstate buses is unconstitutional
	President Harry Truman creates the Committee on Civil Rights
1947	Jackie Robinson becomes the first African American on a major league baseball team
1948	President Truman issues executive order desegregating the armed forces
1954	In *Brown v. Board of Education*, Supreme Court rules segregated schools inherently unequal
1955	Supreme Court rules that school desegregation must proceed "with all deliberate speed"
	Montgomery bus boycott begins
1956	Montgomery bus boycott ends in victory as the Supreme Court affirms a district court ruling that segregation on buses is unconstitutional
1957	Southern Christian Leadership Conference (SCLC) is founded
	President Dwight Eisenhower sends in federal troops to protect African American students integrating Little Rock, Arkansas, high school
1960	Sit in movement begins as four college students sit at a lunch counter in Greensboro, North Carolina, and ask to be served
	Student Nonviolent Coordinating Committee (SNCC) founded

1960	Board of Indian Commissioners is created
	Buffalo Bill, the King of the Border Men, sets off "Wild West" publishing craze
1961	Freedom Rides begin
1962	James Meredith integrates the University of Mississippi
	The Albany movement fails to end segregation in Albany, Georgia
1963	SCLC initiates campaign to desegregate Birmingham, Alabama
	Medgar Evers, leader of the Mississippi NAACP, is assassinated
	March on Washington; Martin Luther King, Jr. delivers his historic "I Have a Dream" speech
1964	Mississippi Freedom Summer project brings students to Mississippi to teach and register voters
	President Johnson signs the Civil Rights Act of 1964
	Civil rights workers Michael Schwerner, James Chaney, and Andrew Goodman are found buried in Philadelphia, Mississippi
	Mississippi Freedom Democratic Party (MFDP) is denied seats at the 1964 Democratic Presidential Convention
1965	SCLC and SNCC begin voter registration campaign in Selma, Alabama
	Malcolm X is assassinated
	Civil rights marchers walk from Selma to Montgomery
	Voting Rights Act of 1965 is signed into law

for deep structural changes in American life. By 1967, Martin Luther King, Jr. was articulating a broad and radical vision linking the struggle against racial injustice to other defects in American society. "The black revolution," he argued, "is much more than a struggle for the rights of Negroes. It is forcing America to face all its interrelated flaws—racism, poverty, militarism, and materialism. It is exposing evils that are deeply rooted in the whole structure of our society." Curing these ills would prove far more difficult than ending legal segregation.

REVIEW QUESTIONS

1. What were the key legal and political antecedents to the civil rights struggle in the 1940s and early 1950s? What organizations played the most central role?
2. How did African American communities challenge legal segregation in the South? Compare the strategies of key organizations, such as the NAACP, SNCC, SCLC, and CORE.
3. Discuss the varieties of white resistance to the civil rights movement. Which were most effective in slowing the drive for equality?
4. Analyze the civil rights movement's complex relationship with the national Democratic Party between 1948 and 1964. How was the party transformed by its association with the movement?
5. What legal and institutional impact did the movement have on American life? How did it change American culture and politics? Where did it fail?
6. What relationship did the African Americans who struggled for civil rights have with other American minorities? How—if at all—did these minorities benefit?

RECOMMENDED READING

Taylor Branch, *Parting the Waters: America in the King Years, 1954–1963* (1988); *Pillar of Fire: America in the King Years, 1963–1965* (1998).

Clayborne Carson, *In Struggle: SNCC and the Black Awakening of the 1960s* (1981).

William Chafe, *Civilities and Civil Rights: Greensboro, North Carolina, and the Black Struggle for Equality* (1980).

David Chappell, *Inside Agitators: White Southerners in the Civil Rights Movement* (1994).

Mary L. Dudziak, *Cold War Civil Rights: Race and the Image of American Democracy* (2000).

Sara Evans, *Personal Politics: The Roots of Women's Liberation in the Civil Rights Movement and the New Left* (1979).

Aldon D. Morris, *The Origins of the Civil Rights Movement: Black Communities Organizing for Change* (1984).

Howell Raines, *My Soul Is Rested: Movement Days in the Deep South Remembered* (1977).

Jo Ann Gibson Robinson, *The Montgomery Bus Boycott and the Women Who Started It.* ed. David J. Garrow (1987).

Robert Weisbrot, *Freedom Bound: A History of America's Civil Rights Movement* (1990).

▶ MEDIA RESOURCES

 U.S. HISTORY DOCUMENTS CD-ROM

The Changing Liberal State
28-2   Charles Sherrod, Student Nonviolent Coordinating Committee Memorandum (1961)
28-4   Students for a Democratic Society, The Port Huron Statement (1962)
28-5   John Lewis, Address at the March on Washington (1963)
28-6   The Civil Rights Act of 1964
28-7   The Tonkin Gulf Incident (1964)
28-8   Lyndon B. Johnson, Commencement Address at Howard University (1965)

The Struggle for Social Change
29-2   The Feminist Mystique (1963)
29-3   Lyndon Johnson, The War on Poverty (1964)

 COMPANION WEBSITE HIGHLIGHTS
To view an exploration, enter one of the URLs below in your browser.

 Web Explorations
Map of the Civil Rights Movement
http://www.prenhall.com/faragher/map28.1
Impact of the Voting Rights Act of 1965
http://www.prenhall.com/faragher/map28.2

 HISTORY RESOURCE CENTER
To find the resources listed below, go to
http://www.prenhall.com/historyresourcecenter

Documents
Student Nonviolent Coordinating Committee, Statement of Purpose (1960)

Images
1963 March on Washington for Civil Rights
Civil Rights March on Washington, D.C., 1963
Guess Who's Coming to Dinner
James Meredith Integrates Ole Miss
M.L. King Wins the Nobel Peace Prize
Malcolm X
Martin Luther King, Jr.
Martin Luther King, Jr. with His Wife Coretta and Their Children
Medgar Evers
Montgomery Bus Boycott Ends
On the Bus to the Washington March
Reverend Elijah Muhammad of the Nation of Islam
Rosa Parks' Arrest

EXPLORING AMERICA
THE AMERICAN INDIAN MOVEMENT
http://www.prenhall.com/faragher/AIM

What are the first images that come to your mind when considering American Indians? How have stereotypes of Native Americans affected their identifies and rights in the United States? What methods have American Indians used to counter these stereotypes? What role did Alcatraz play in the American Indian Movement? What are the top ten things whites say to Indians? The module answers these and other questions as it examines the rise of the Native American rights movement in the 1960s as part of centuries-long Native American resistance to white intrusion.

The American Indian Movement offers a multidimensional exploration of the question of Native Americans in United States society and culture. Focusing on the 1960s occupa-

Distribution of American Indian Populations 1990

tion of Alcatraz and other American Indian Movement activities, the module uses diverse sources to illuminate the native American situation, including print and visual sources, audio clips, and a link to the American Indian Website. Maps and a chronology combine with the narrative to place the discussion in perspective.

Reflect and Respond

1. Connecting across tribal and regional boundaries

was vital in the activism of American Indians. Yet just as not all Europeans look alike, neither do all native Americans. What stereotypes or cliches mistakenly "totalized" American Indians as one group?

2. What can you see in the present that is different because of the American Indian Movement and similar organizations that organized, educated, and agitated on behalf of oppressed people in American society in the 1960s and 1970s?

3. Do "Indian" insignias and themes belong to Native American peoples? Are such instruments as tomahawks, for example, "theirs"? Are Atlanta Braves fans or University of Florida fans misappropriating the tomahawk when they use it to support their teams? What of the name of a tribe, such as the Seminole? Or the word "brave"?

✓ Check it out

The Top Ten Things White People Say to Indians

This clip is of a Native American comedian satirizing some of the misperceptions and stereotypes of Native

Americans. The comedian's routine is important because his jokes touch upon not only the mistreatment of Indians in the past but also current public interest to Native American lineage.

This exploration is also available on the *Exploring America* CD-ROM.

COMMUNITY & MEMORY

▶ Flying the "Stars and Bars"

In 1956 African-American citizens in Montgomery, Alabama, successfully boycotted the city's segregated bus lines, thus sparking a nonviolent mass movement to end legalized segregation in the South. Nearly a century earlier, on the eve of the Civil War, Montgomery had hosted a convention which created the Confederate States of America. As both the "cradle of the Confederacy" and the birthplace of the modern Civil Rights movement, it's not surprising that Montgomery, Alabama has been the site of bitter conflict over the meaning and use of the Confederate flag. Indeed, during the 1990s, widespread controversy in the South over displays of the Confederate flag reflected both the fierce pride many white Southerners maintained for the "Lost Cause" and the enormous changes wrought by the Civil Rights movement of the 1950s and 1960s. The fight over the flag and what it represents provides a perfect example of how communities struggle over the meaning of their history. For as William Faulkner, the South's most distinguished novelist, once put it: "The past is not dead, it isn't even past."

Throughout the South, the revived use of the Confederate flag began as part of the white backlash against the campaign to end legal segregation. In 1963 Alabama Gov. George C. Wallace ordered the Confederate battle flag to fly on top of the state capitol to protest a visit by Attorney General Robert F. Kennedy, who had come to Montgomery to discuss desegregation of the state's schools. The flag, which had white stars on a blue X-shape against a red background, was the same design as the battle flag carried in the field by Confederate troops during the Civil War. The battle flag flew over the dome, along with the national and state flags, until the spring of 1992, when they were taken down during renovation work. By then, the Confederate flag had become a cultural icon of regional pride and enduring belief in white supremacy in many parts of the South. And around the nation, others adopted it as an all-purpose symbol of rebellion and resistance to authority, displayed on posters, clothing,

In March, 2000, thousands of demonstrators rallied outside the Capitol in Montgomery, calling on state officials to once again fly the Confederate flag over the building. This rally was organized by the League of the South, an organization dedicated to celebrating white Southern history and culture.

SOURCE: Alabama Department of Archives and History, Montgomery, Alabama (86.3972.1(PN10138, PN10181)).

bumper stickers, and featured in music videos.

But for most African Americans the Confederate flag meant something quite different. In the summer of 1988 fourteen black state legislators were arrested for trespassing on state property when they attempted to scale a chain-link fence and remove the flag. Rep. Alvin Holmes, one of those arrested, said, "When I walk up the Capitol steps, instead of seeing the American flag, the flag that I served under when I was in the United States Army, I see a flag that represents treason, sedition, slavery, and oppression toward my people."

In December 1992 Montgomery prepared to re-dedicate the 141-year-old state Capitol after a $28 million restoration. When Gov. Guy Hunt insisted that the "Stars and Bars" continue to fly over the building, 24 African-American legislators boycotted the ceremony in protest. Rep. Holmes filed a lawsuit asking for an injunction, claiming an 1896 state law prohibited

900

any flags other than the Alabama and U.S. flags from flying above the Capitol. Alabama citizens expressed a wide range of opinions on the subject. Most whites insisted the old symbol was about regional identity and pride, not race. John Napier, a retired Air Force colonel and leader of the Sons of Confederate veterans argued, "We celebrate our civil rights history. There are those of us who feel the earlier struggle should be commemorated historically, too. While we're running around naming streets for Rosa Parks, which I have no problem with, you're getting into removing all the symbols of the Confederacy." African Americans, for whom the flag symbolized slavery, racism, and segregation, tried to distinguish between private and public displays. "I see nothing wrong with someone flying the Confederate flag even on their front lawn or putting it on their bumper stickers," said Earl Shinhoster, an official of the NAACP. "I do, however, see something wrong when the state promotes something that many people find offensive."

As with the Montgomery bus boycott of 1956, the economic implications of the controversy were not lost on the city's the business community and political leaders. Anna Bishop, spokeswoman for the Montgomery Chamber of Commerce, noted that, "Business people are realizing that the flag contributes to a negative image for Alabama."

The Alabama State Business Council told Gov. Hunt in a letter that "the Confederate flag is detrimental to our image and is dividing our citzenry." Neal Wade of the Economic Development Partnership of Alabama asserted, "Anything that causes division within a state makes it less attractive to a potential employer, particularly from overseas."

In January 1993, just a few weeks after the dedication of the renovated Capitol, Judge William Gordon of Alabama Circuit Court in Montgomery ruled that the 1896 state law did indeed prohibit the state from flying the "Stars and Bars" over the state Capitol. The new governor, Jim Folsom, announced that he would not challenge the decision, and that the Confederate battle flag would fly instead across the street at the First White House of the Confederacy. "This has been a divisive issue in our state," he said, "and I believe it is time we put it behind us and move our state forward."

Still, in many parts of the country private and public displays of the Confederate flag have persisted—and so have the continued and deeply felt debates over the historical meanings embedded within it. ■

www.researchnavigator.com

RESOURCES FOR COLLEGE RESEARCH ASSIGNMENTS

The Community and Memory essay for this chapter deals with the controversy over the flying of the Confederate flag over public buildings. For further research on the history and use of the "Stars and Bars," use the tools available to you in Research Navigator.

As you investigate this topic, consider this question: "Why do so many African Americans object to the flying of the Confederate flag over public buildings? What arguments do supporters of the flag employ?"

ContentSelect: Search in the History database using the search term *civil rights*.

Links Library: Access the History: U.S. History database and explore the links for *civil rights movement* and *confederates*.

New York Times on the Web: To find more about the controversy over the "Stars and Bars," use the search term *Confederate flag*.

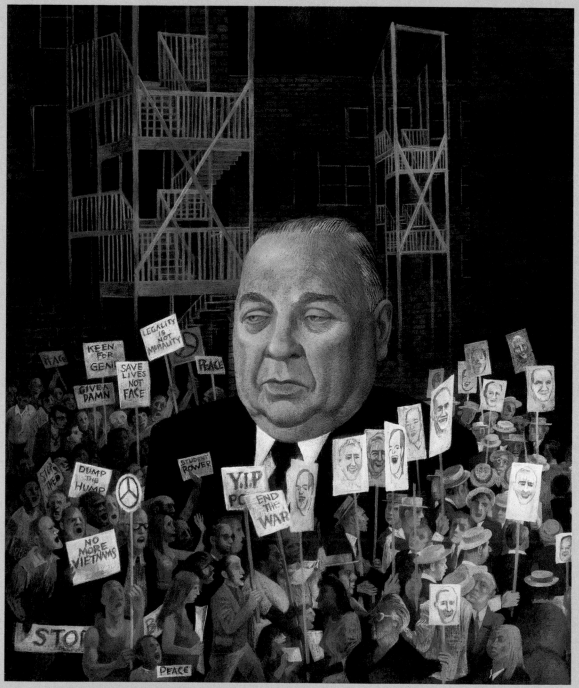

Bernard Perlin, *Mayor Richard Daley*, 1968. Collection of Philip J. and Suzanne Schiller, American Social Commentary Art, 1930–70.
SOURCE: Library of Congress.

Uptown, Chicago, Illinois

URING FREEDOM SUMMER OF 1964, WHILE TEAMS OF NORTHERN college students traveled south to join voter registration campaigns among African Americans, a small group moved to Chicago to help the city's poor people take control of their communities and to demand better city services. They targeted a neighborhood known as Uptown, a one-mile-square section five miles north of the Loop, the city center. The residents, many only recently transplanted from the poverty of the Appalachian South, lived in crowded tenements or in once-elegant mansions now subdivided into tiny, run-down apartments. Four thousand people lived on just one street running four blocks, 20 percent of them on welfare. Chicago civic authorities had also selected this neighborhood for improvement. Designating it a Conservation Area under the terms of the Urban Renewal Act, they applied for federal funds in order to upgrade the housing for middle-income families and, in effect, to clear out the current residents. In contrast, the student organizers intended to mobilize the community "so as to demand an end to poverty and the construction of a decent social order."

With the assistance of the Packinghouse Workers union, the students formed Jobs or Income Now (JOIN), opened a storefront office, and invited local residents to work with them to halt the city's plans. They spent hours and hours listening to people, drawing out their ideas and helping them develop scores of additional programs. Confronting the bureaucracy of the welfare and unemployment compensation offices stood high on their list. They also campaigned against Mayor Richard Daley's policy of "police omnipresence" that had a fleet of squad cars and paddy wagons continually patrolling the neighborhood. To curb police harassment, they demanded the creation of civilian review boards. They also helped establish new social clubs, a food-buying cooperative, a community theater, and a health clinic. Within a few years, Uptown street kids had formed the Young Patriots organization, put out a community newspaper, *Rising Up Angry*, and staffed free breakfast programs.

Chicago JOIN was one of ten similar projects sponsored by Students for a Democratic Society (SDS). Impatient with the nation's chronic poverty and cold war politics, twenty-nine students from nine universities had met in June 1960 to form a new kind of campus-based political organization. SDS soon caught the attention of liberal students, encouraging them, as part of the nation's largest college population to date, to make their voices heard. By its peak in 1968, SDS had 350 chapters and between 60,000 and 100,000 members. Its principle of participatory democracy—with its promise to give people control over the decisions affecting their lives—appealed to a wider following of more than a million students.

In June 1962, in Port Huron, Michigan, the founding members of SDS issued a declaration of principles, drafted mainly by graduate student Tom Hayden. "We are people . . . bred in at least modest comfort, housed now in universities," *The Port Huron Statement* opened, "looking uncomfortably to the world we inherit." The dire effects of poverty and social injustice, it continued, were not the only dismaying things about American society. A deeper ailment plagued American politics. Everyone, including middle-class students with few material wants, suffered from a sense of "loneliness, estrangement, and alienation." *The Port Huron Statement* defined SDS as a new kind of political movement that would bring people "out of isolation and into community." Through participatory democracy, not just the poor but all Americans could overcome their feelings of "powerlessness [and hence] resignation before the enormity of events." As one organizer explained, programs like JOIN were attempts to create a poor people's movement as well as a means for students themselves to live an "authentic life" outside the constraints of middle-class society.

SDS began with a campaign to reform the university, especially to disentangle the financial ties between campus-based research programs and the military-industrial complex. Later it expanded to the nation's cities, sending small groups of students to live and organize in the poor communities of Boston, Louisville, Cleveland, and Newark as well as Chicago. Ultimately, few of these projects succeeded in mobilizing the poor to political action. Protests against local government did little to combat unemployment, and campaigns for better garbage collection or more playgrounds rarely evolved into lasting movements. Nevertheless, organizers did succeed in bringing many neighborhood residents "out of isolation and into community." By late 1967, SDS prepared to leave JOIN in the hands of the people it had organized, which was its goal from the beginning.

Initially, even Lyndon Baines Johnson promoted the ideal of civic participation. The Great Society, as the president called his domestic program, promised more than the abolition of poverty and racial inequality. In May 1964, at the University of Michigan, the president described his goal as a society "where every child can find knowledge to enrich his mind and to enlarge his talents," where "the city of man serves not only the needs of the body and the demands of commerce but the desire for beauty and the hunger for community."

By 1967 the Vietnam War had upset the domestic agendas of both SDS and the Johnson administration. If SDSers had once believed they could work with liberal Democrats to reduce poverty in the United States, they now interpreted social injustice at home as the inevitable consequence of dangerous and destructive foreign policies pursued by liberals and conservatives alike. SDS threw its energies into the movement against the war in Vietnam. President Johnson, meanwhile, pursued a foreign policy that would swallow up the funding for his own plans for a war on poverty and would precipitate a very different war at home, Americans against Americans. As hawks and doves lined up on opposite sides, the Vietnam War created a huge and enduring rift. SDS member Richard Flacks had warned that the nation had to "choose between devoting its resources and energies to maintaining military superiority and international hegemony or rechanneling those resources and energies to meeting the desperate needs of its people." Ultimately, even President Johnson himself understood that the "bitch of a war" in Asia ruined "the woman I really loved—the Great Society." The dream of community did not vanish, but consensus appeared increasingly remote as the United States fought—and eventually lost— the longest war in its history. ■

Chicago

KEY TOPICS

- Widening U.S. involvement in the war in Vietnam

- The sixties generation" and the antiwar movement

- Poverty and urban crisis

- The election of 1968

- The rise of "liberation" movements

- The Nixon presidency and the Watergate conspiracy

VIETNAM: AMERICA'S LONGEST WAR

The Vietnam War had its roots in the Truman Doctrine and its goal of containing communism (see Chapter 26). After the defeat of the French by the Communist forces of Ho Chi Minh in 1954, Vietnam emerged as a major zone of cold war contention. President John Kennedy called it "the cornerstone of the Free World in Southeast Asia, the keystone in the arch, the finger in the dike," a barrier to the spread of communism throughout the region and perhaps the world. President Lyndon Johnson sounded the same note at the beginning of his presidency. He told the public that North Vietnam was intent on conquering South Vietnam, defeating the United States, and extending "the Asiatic dominion of communism." With American security at stake, he concluded, Americans had little choice but to fight for "the principle for which our ancestors fought in the valleys of Pennsylvania."

Vietnam was not Valley Forge, however, and the United States ultimately paid a huge price for its determination to turn back communism in Indochina. More than 50,000 Americans died in an unwinnable overseas war that only deepened divisions at home.

Johnson's War

Although President Kennedy had greatly increased the number of military advisors in South Vietnam (see Chapter 27), it was his successor, Lyndon B. Johnson, who made the decision to engage the United States in a major war there. At first, Johnson simply hoped to stay the course in Vietnam. Facing a presidential election in November 1964, he knew that a major military setback would cripple his election campaign. But he was equally determined to avoid the fate of President Truman, who had bogged down politically after "losing" China to communism and producing a stalemate in Korea. Within days of taking office, the new president said he

intended to do his utmost to help South Vietnam win its "contest against the externally directed and supported Communist conspiracy."

Throughout the winter and spring of 1964, as conditions grew steadily worse in South Vietnam, Johnson and his advisors quietly laid the groundwork for a sustained bombing campaign against North Vietnam. In early August, they found a pretext to set this plan in motion. After two U.S. destroyers in the Gulf of Tonkin, off the coast of North Vietnam, reported attacks by North Vietnamese patrol boats, Johnson retaliated by ordering air strikes against bases in North Vietnam.

Johnson now appealed to Congress to pass a resolution giving him the authority "to take all necessary measures" and "all necessary steps" to defend U.S. armed forces and to protect Southeast Asia "against aggression or subversion." This Tonkin Gulf resolution, secretly drafted six weeks before the incident for which it was named, passed the Senate on August 7 with only two dissenting votes and moved unanimously through the House. It served, in Undersecretary of State Nicholas Katzenbach's words, as the "functional equivalent" of a declaration of war.

Ironically, Johnson had campaigned for the presidency with a call for restraint in Vietnam. He assured voters that "we are not about to send American boys nine or ten thousand miles away from home to do what Asian boys ought to be doing for themselves." This strategy helped him win a landslide victory over conservative Republican Barry Goldwater of Arizona, who had proposed the deployment of nuclear weapons in Vietnam.

With the election behind him, Johnson now faced a hard decision. The limited bombing raids against North Vietnam had failed to slow the movement of the Communist Vietcong forces across the border into the South. Meanwhile, the government in Saigon, the capital city of South Vietnam, appeared near collapse. Faced with the prospect of a Communist victory, the president chose to escalate U.S. involvement in Vietnam massively.

Deeper into the Quagmire

In early February 1965, Johnson found a rationale to justify massive bombing of the North. The Vietcong had fired at the barracks of the U.S. Marine base at Pleiku in the central highlands of Vietnam, killing eight and wounding more than 100 Americans. Waving the list of casualties, the president rushed into an emergency meeting of the National Security Council to announce that the time had passed for keeping "our guns over the mantel and our shells in the cupboard." He ordered immediate reprisal bombing of North Vietnam and one week later, on February 13, authorized Operation Rolling Thunder, a campaign of gradually intensifying air attacks.

Johnson and his advisers hoped that the air strikes against North Vietnam would demonstrate U.S. resolve "both to Hanoi and to the world" and make the deployment of ground forces unnecessary. Intelligence reports, however, suggested that the bombing had little impact and noted, moreover, that North Vietnam was now sending troops into South Vietnam. With retreat his only alternative, Johnson decided to introduce ground troops for offensive operations.

Once Rolling Thunder had begun, President Johnson found it increasingly difficult to speak frankly with the American public about his policies. Initially, he announced that only two battalions of marines were being assigned to Danang to defend the airfields where bombing runs began. But six week later, 50,000 U.S. troops were in Vietnam. By November 1965 the total topped 165,000, and more troops were on the way. But even after Johnson authorized a buildup to 431,000 troops in mid-1966, victory was still nowhere in sight.

The strategy pursued by the Johnson administration and implemented by General William Westmoreland—a war of attrition—was based on the premise that continued bombing would eventually exhaust North Vietnam's resources. Meanwhile, U.S. ground forces would defeat the Vietcong in South Vietnam, forcing its soldiers to defect and supporters to scatter, thereby restoring political stability to South Vietnam's pro-Western government. As Johnson once boasted, the strongest military power in the world surely could crush a Communist rebellion in a "pissant" country of peasants.

In practice, the United States wreaked havoc in South Vietnam, tearing apart its society and bringing ecological devastation to its land. Intending to locate and eradicate the support network of the Vietcong, U.S. ground troops conducted search-and-destroy missions throughout the countryside. They attacked villagers and their homes. Seeking to ferret out Vietcong sympathizers, U.S. troops turned at any one time as many as 4 million people—approximately one-quarter of the population of South Vietnam—into refugees. By late 1968, the United States had dropped more than 3 million tons

Refugees, Binh Dinh Province, 1967. The massive bombing and ground combat broke apart the farming communities of South Vietnam, creating huge numbers of civilian casualties and driving millions into quickly constructed refugee camps or already overcrowded cities. Approximately 25 percent of the South Vietnamese population fled their native villages, many never to return.

SOURCE: Photo by Philip Jones Griffiths. Magnum Photos, Inc.

of bombs on Vietnam, and eventually delivered more than three times the tonnage dropped by the Allies on all fronts during World War II. The United States also conducted the most destructive chemical warfare in history. To deprive the Vietcong of camouflage, American troops used herbicides to defoliate forests. During Operation Ranch Hand, which ran between 1965 and 1971, 17.6 million gallons of Agent Orange were sprayed over approximately 3.6 million acres of South Vietnam.

Several advisers urged the president to inform the American people about his decisions on Vietnam, even to declare a state of national emergency. But Johnson feared he would lose momentum on domestic reform, including his antipoverty programs, if he drew attention to foreign policy. Seeking to avoid "undue excitement in the Congress and in domestic public opinion," he held to a course of intentional deceit.

The Credibility Gap

Johnson's popularity had surged at the time of the Tonkin Gulf resolution, skyrocketing in one day from 42 to 72 percent, according to a Louis Harris poll. But afterward it waned rapidly. The war dragged on. Every night network television news reported the soaring American body count, from 26 per week in 1965 to 180 in 1967. No president had worked so hard to control the news media, but by 1967 Johnson found himself badgered at press conferences by reporters who accused the president of creating a credibility gap.

Scenes of human suffering and devastation recorded by television cameras increasingly undermined the administration's moral justification of the war with claims that it was a necessary defense of freedom and democracy in South Vietnam. During the early 1960s, network news had either ignored Vietnam or had been patriotically supportive of U.S. policy. Beginning with a report on a ground operation against the South Vietnamese village of Cam Ne by Morley Safer for CBS News in August 1965, however, the tenor of news reporting changed. Although government officials described the operation as a strategic destruction of "fortified Vietcong bunkers," the *CBS Evening News* showed pictures of Marines setting fire to the thatched homes of civilians. After CBS aired Safer's report, President Johnson complained bitterly to the news director. But more critical commentary soon followed. By 1967, according to a noted media observer, "every subject tended to become Vietnam." Televised news reports now told of new varieties of American cluster bombs, which released up to 180,000 fiberglass shards, and showed the nightmarish effects of the defoliants used on forests in South Vietnam to uncover enemy strongholds.

Coverage of the war in the print media also became more skeptical of Johnson's policies. By 1967 independent news teams were probing the government's official claims. Harrison Salisbury, Pulitzer Prize–winning *New York Times* reporter, questioned the administration's claims that its bombing of the North precisely targeted military objectives, charging that U.S. planes had bombed the population center of Hanoi, capital of North Vietnam, and intentionally ravaged villages in the South. As American military deaths climbed at the rate of more than 800 per month during the first half of 1967, newspaper coverage of the war focused yet more intently on such disturbing events.

The most vocal congressional critic of Johnson's war policy was Democratic senator J. William Fulbright of Arkansas, who chaired the Senate Foreign Relations Committee and who had personally speeded the passage of the Tonkin Gulf resolution. A strong supporter of the cold war, Fulbright had decided that the war in Vietnam was unwinnable and destructive to domestic reform. In *Arrogance of Power*, a book published in 1966 that became a national bestseller, he proposed a negotiated withdrawal from a neutralized Southeast Asia. At first Fulbright stood nearly alone: in October 1966 only 15 percent of Congress favored a negotiated settlement. But he soon persuaded prominent Democrats in Congress, such as Frank Church, Mike Mansfield, and

George McGovern, to put aside their personal loyalty to Johnson and oppose his conduct of the war. In 1967 the Congress passed a nonbinding resolution appealing to the United Nations to help negotiate an end to hostilities. Meanwhile, some of the nation's most trusted European allies called for restraint in Vietnam.

The impact of the war, which cost Americans $21 billion per year, was also felt at home. Johnson convinced Congress to levy a 10 percent surcharge on individual and corporate taxes. Later adjustments in the national budget tapped the Social Security fund, heretofore safe from interference. Inflation raced upward, fed by spending on the war. Johnson replaced advisers who questioned his policy, but as casualties multiplied, more and more Americans began to question his handling of the war.

A GENERATION IN CONFLICT

As the war in Vietnam escalated, Americans from all walks of life demanded an end to U.S. involvement. Debates raged everywhere, from families to informal community meetings to the halls of Congress. Eventually the antiwar movement won over a majority. But between 1965 and 1971, its years of peak activity, it had a distinctly generational character. At the forefront were the baby boomers who were just coming of age.

This so-called sixties generation, the largest generation in American history, was also the best educated. By the late 1960s, nearly half of all young adults between the ages of 18 and 21 were enrolled in college. In 1965 there were 5 million college students; in 1973 the number had doubled to 10 million. Public universities made the largest gains; by 1970 eight had more than 30,000 students apiece. Although a small minority, groups of students began to combine protest against the war in Vietnam with a broader, penetrating critique of American society. Through music, dress, and even hairstyle, they expressed a deep estrangement from the values and aspirations of their parents' generation. As early as 1967, when opposition to the war had begun to swell, "flower children" were putting daisies in the rifle barrels of troops stationed to quash campus protests, providing a seemingly innocent counterpoint to the grim news of slaughter abroad.

Representing perhaps only one-quarter of the nation's college students, these young people had an impact far beyond their numbers. They promoted a "culture of life" against the "culture of death" symbolized by the war. Campus organizations such as SDS, which had begun in the early 1960s in an attempt to build community, now turned against the government. SDS encouraged many college students to take a militant stand against the war, calling for an immediate and unconditional withdrawal of U.S. troops from Vietnam.

Young women, dressed in hippie garb, flash the peace sign in protest against the war in Vietnam.

SOURCE: Photo by Jeffrey Blankfort. Jeroboam, Inc. (JB24-8183).

"The Times They Are A-Changin'"

The first sign of a new kind of protest was the free speech movement at the University of California at Berkeley in 1964. That fall, civil rights activists returned to the 27,000-student campus from Freedom Summer in Mississippi. They soon began to picket Bay Area stores that practiced discrimination in hiring and to recruit other students to join them. When the university administration moved to prevent them from setting up information booths on campus, eighteen groups protested, including the arch-conservative Students for Goldwater, claiming that their right to free speech had been abridged. The administration responded by sending police to break up the protest rally and arrest participants. University president Clark Kerr met with students, agreed not to press charges, and seemed set to grant them a small space on campus for political activity. Then, under pressure from conservative regents, Kerr reversed himself and announced in November that the university planned to press new charges against the free speech movement's leaders. On December 2 a crowd of 7,000 gathered to protest this decision. Joining folk singer Joan Baez in singing "We Shall Overcome," a group of 1,000 people marched toward the university's administration building, where they planned to stage a sit-in until Kerr rescinded his order. The police arrested nearly 800 protestors in the largest mass arrest in California history.

Mario Savio, a Freedom Summer volunteer and philosophy student, explained that the free speech movement wanted more than just the right to conduct political activity on campus. He spoke for many students when he complained that the university had become a faceless bureaucratic machine rather than a community of learning. Regulating the activities of students while preparing them for colorless lives as corporation clerks, the university made them "so sick at heart" that they had decided to put their "bodies upon the gears" to make it stop.

The free speech movement's social critique resonated among college students. Across the country they began to demand a say in the structuring of their education. Brown University students, for example, demanded a revamp of the curriculum that would eliminate all required courses and make grades optional. Students also protested campus rules that treated students as children instead of as adults. After a string of campus protests, most large universities, including the University of California, relinquished *in loco parentis* (in the place of parents) policies and allowed students to live off-campus and to set their own hours.

Across the bay in San Francisco, other young adults staked out a new form of community—a counterculture. In 1967, the "Summer of Love," the population of the Haight-Ashbury district swelled by 75,000 as youthful adventurers gathered for the most celebrated "be-in" of the era. Although the *San Francisco Chronicle* featured a headline reading "Mayor Warns Hippies to Stay Out of Town," masses of long-haired young men and women dressed in bell-bottoms and tie-dyed T-shirts were undeterred. They congregated in "the Haight" to listen to music, take drugs, and "be" with each other. "If you're going to San Francisco," a popular rock group sang, "be sure to wear some flowers in your hair . . . you're going to meet some gentle people there." In the fall, the majority returned to their own communities, often bringing with them a new lifestyle. *Time* magazine announced the appearance of new "hippie enclaves . . . in every major U.S. city from Boston to Seattle, from Detroit to New Orleans."

The generational rebellion took many forms, including a revolution in sexual behavior that triggered countless quarrels between parents and their maturing sons and daughters. During the 1960s more teenagers experienced premarital sex—by the decade's end three-quarters of all college seniors had engaged in sexual intercourse—and far more talked about it openly than in previous eras. With birth control widely available, including the newly developed "pill," many young women, who were no longer deterred from sex by fear of pregnancy, rejected premarital abstinence. "We've discarded the idea that the loss of virginity is related to degeneracy," one college student explained. "Premarital sex doesn't mean the downfall of society, at least not the kind of society that we're going to build." Many heterosexual couples chose to live together outside marriage, a practice few parents condoned. A much smaller but significant number formed communes—approximately 4,000 by 1970—where members could share housekeeping and child care as well as sexual partners.

Mood altering drugs played a large part in this counterculture. In the 1950s, doctors had begun to freely prescribe tranquilizers and antidepressants, and alcohol and tobacco were popular stimulants. The drug subculture that emerged in the 1960s, however, was associated primarily with illicit psychoactive substances and hallucinogenic drugs. Harvard professor Timothy Leary urged young people to "turn on, tune in, drop out" and also advocated the mass production and distribution of LSD (lysergic acid diethylamide), which was not criminalized until 1968. Hollywood movies, such as *Easy Rider*, which was released in 1969, cast Peter Fonda and Dennis Hopper as two alienated youth who indulged in both casual sex and drugs. Marijuana, illegal yet readily available, was often paired with rock music in a collective ritual of love and laughter. Singer Bob Dylan taunted adults with the lyrics of his hit single, "Everybody must get stoned."

Music played a large part in defining the counterculture. With the emergence of rock 'n' roll in the 1950s, popular music had begun to express a deliberate generational identity (see Chapter 27), a trend that gained momentum with the emergence of the British rock group The Beatles in 1964. Folk music, which had gained popularity on campuses in the early 1960s with the successful recordings of Peter, Paul, and Mary, Phil Ochs, and Judy Collins, as well as Joan Baez, continued to serve the voice of protest. Shortly after Freedom Summer, folk singer Bob Dylan issued a warning to parents:

> *Your sons and your daughters*
> *are beyond your command*
> *Your old road is*
> *rapidly agin'.*
> *Please get out of the new one*
> *If you can't lend your hand*
> *For the times they are a-changin'.*

By 1965 Dylan himself had turned to the electric guitar and rock, which triumphed as the musical emblem of a generation.

At a farm near Woodstock, New York, more than 400,000 people gathered in August 1969 for a three-day rock concert and to give witness to the ideals of the counterculture. Richie Havens opened with "Freedom," and performers including Joan Baez, Janis Joplin, Santana, and The Grateful Dead among others entertained the crowd. Thousands took drugs while security officials and local police stood by, some stripped off their clothes to dance or swim, and a few even made love in the grass. "We were exhilarated," one reveler recalled. "We felt as though we were in liberated territory."

The Woodstock Nation, as the counterculture was mythologized, did not actually represent the sentiments of most young Americans. But its attitudes and styles, especially its efforts to create a new community, did speak for the large minority seeking a peaceful alternative to the intensifying climate of war. "We used to think of ourselves as little clumps of weirdos," rock star Janis Joplin explained. "But now we're a whole new minority group." Another interpreter, Charles Reich, whose *The Greening of America* (1970) became a best-seller, defined the counterculture as a generation's attempt to create "a form of community in which love, respect, and a mutual search for wisdom replace the competition and separation of the past." The slogan "Make Love, Not War" linked generational rebellion and opposition to the U.S. invasion of Vietnam.

From Campus Protest to Mass Mobilization

Three weeks after the announcement of Operation Rolling Thunder in 1965, peace activists called for a day-long boycott of classes so that students and faculty might meet to discuss the war. At the University of Michigan in Ann Arbor, more than 3,000 students turned out for sessions held through the night because university administrators had bowed to the pressure of state legislators and had refused to cancel classes. During the following weeks, "teach-ins" spread across the United States and to Europe and Japan as well.

Students also began to protest against war-related research on their campuses. The expansion of higher education in the 1960s had depended largely on federally funded programs, including military research on counterinsurgency tactics and new chemical weapons. Student protesters demanded an end to these programs and, receiving no response from university administrators, turned to civil disobedience. In October 1967, the Dow Chemical Company, manufacturers of napalm, a form of jellied gasoline often used against civilians in Vietnam, sent job recruiters to the University of Wisconsin at Madison despite warnings that a group of students would try to prevent them from conducting interviews. A few hundred students staged a sit-in at the building where the recruitment interviews were scheduled, and 2,000 onlookers gathered outside. Ordered by university administrators to disperse the crowd, the city's police broke glass doors, dragged students through the debris, and clubbed those who refused to move. Suddenly the campus erupted. Students chanted *Sieg Heil* at the police, who attempted to disperse them with tear gas and Mace. Undergraduate students and their teaching assistants boycotted classes for a week. During the first half of 1968 alone, nearly 40,000 students staged more than 200 major demonstrations at more than 100 colleges and universities. During the next three years, the momentum grew, and demonstrations took place on campuses in every region of the country.

Many student strikes and demonstrations merged opposition to the war with other campus and community issues. At Columbia University, students struck in 1968 against the administration's plans to build a new gymnasium in a city park used by residents of neighboring Harlem. In the Southwest, Mexican American students demonstrated against the use of funds for military projects that might otherwise be allocated to antipoverty and educational programs.

By the late 1960s, the peace movement had spread well beyond the campus and commanded a diverse following. While some protesters marched, others held prayer vigils, staged art fairs, distributed leaflets door to door, or simply engaged friends and neighbors in conversation about Vietnam. In April 1967, a day-long antiwar rally at the Sheep Meadow in Manhattan's Central Park drew more than 300,000 people—more than had taken part in the civil rights movement's 1965 March on Washington. Meanwhile, 60,000 protesters turned out in San Francisco. By summer, Vietnam Veterans Against the War had begun to organize returning soldiers and sailors, encouraging them to cast off the medals and ribbons they had won in battle.

The steadily increasing size of antiwar demonstrations provoked conservatives and prowar Democrats to take a stronger stand in support of the war. On the weekend following the huge turnout in Central Park, the Veterans of Foreign Wars staged a "Loyalty Day" parade in New York City under the banner "One

Antiwar Protests on College and University Campuses, 1967–1969
Campus-based protests against the war in Vietnam, at first centered on the East Coast and in California, spread to nearly every region of the country and around the world by the decade's end.

Country, One Flag, Love It or Leave It." Although only 7,500 people participated, the event signaled a hardening of opposition to the peace movement. Several newspaper and magazine editorialists called for the arrest of antiwar leaders on charges of treason. Secretary of State Dean Rusk, appearing on NBC's *Meet the Press*, expressed his concern that "authorities in Hanoi" might conclude, incorrectly, that the majority of Americans did not back their president and that "the net effect of these demonstrations will be to prolong the war, not to shorten it."

Many demonstrators themselves concluded that mass mobilizations alone had little impact on U.S. policy. Some sought to serve as moral witnesses. Despite a congressional act of 1965 providing for a five-year jail term and a $10,000 fine for destroying a draft card, nearly 200 young men destroyed their draft cards at the April Sheep Meadow demonstration and encouraged approximately a half-million more to resist the draft or refuse induction. Two Jesuit priests, Daniel and Philip Berrigan, raided the offices of the draft board in Catonsville, Maryland, in May 1968 and poured homemade napalm over records. A few protesters even doused their clothes with gasoline and set fire to themselves, as Buddhist monks protesting the war had done in Vietnam. Other activists determined to "bring the war home." An estimated 40,000 bombing incidents or bomb threats took place from January 1969 to April 1970; more than $21 million of property was damaged, and forty-three people were killed. Most of the perpetrators were never identified.

Observers at the time noted a similarity between the violence in Vietnam and the violence in the United States. Parallel wars were now being fought, one between two systems of government in Vietnam, another between the American government and masses of its citizens. Those Americans sent to Vietnam were caught in between.

Teenage Soldiers

The Vietnam War era witnessed not only a generation gap but a fissure within the generation of young adults. Whereas the average age of the World War II soldier was twenty-six, the age of those who fought in Vietnam hovered around nineteen. Until late 1969 the Selective Service System—the draft—gave deferments to college students and to workers in selected occupations while recruiting hard in poor communities, advertising the armed forces as a provider of vocational training and social mobility. Working-class young men, disproportionately African American and Latino, signed up in large numbers under these inducements. They also bore the brunt of combat. Whereas college graduates constituted only 12 percent of all soldiers and 9 percent of those who were killed in combat, high school dropouts were the most likely to serve in Vietnam and by far the most likely to die there. The death rate for African Americans was approximately 30 percent higher than the overall death rate for U.S. forces in Southeast Asia. These disparities created a rupture that would last well past the end of the war.

Yet the soldiers were not entirely isolated from the changes affecting their generation. G.I.s in significant numbers smoked marijuana, listed to rock music, and participated in the sexual revolution. In 1968 more than 200 soldiers from Fort Hood, Texas, attended a "be-in." But most condemned antiwar protest as the expressions of their privileged peers who did not have to fight.

As the war dragged on, however, some soldiers began to show their frustration. By 1971 many G.I.s were putting peace symbols on their combat helmets, joining antiwar demonstrations, and staging their own events such as "Armed Forces Day." Sometimes entire companies refused to carry out duty assignments or even to enter battle. A smaller number took revenge by "fragging" reckless commanding officers with grenades meant for the enemy. Meanwhile African American soldiers closed ranks and often flaunted their racial

African American troops in Vietnam, 1970. Serving on the front lines in disproportionate numbers, many black soldiers echoed the growing racial militancy in the United States and increasingly chose to spend their off-duty time apart from white soldiers.

SOURCE: Mark Jury, The Vietnam Photo Book.

solidarity by weaving their bootlaces into "slave brace-lets" and carrying Black Power canes, which were ebony-colored and topped with a clenched fist. Some openly complained about being asked to fight "a white man's war" and emblazoned their helmets with slogans like "No Gook Ever Called Me Nigger." By 1971, at least fourteen organizations claimed affiliation with RITA, an acronym for "Resistance in the Army." The largest was the American Servicemen's Union, which claimed more than 10,000 members and published its own newspaper, *The Bond*.

The nature of the war fed feelings of disaffection in the armed forces. U.S. troops entering South Vietnam expected a warm welcome from the people whose home-land they had been sent to defend. Instead, they encoun-tered anti-American demonstrations and placards with slogans like "End Foreign Dominance of Our Country." Hostile Vietnamese civilians viewed the Americans as in-vaders. The enemy avoided open engagements in which the Americans could benefit from their superior arms and air power. Soldiers found themselves instead stumbling into booby traps as they chased an elusive guerrilla foe through deep, leech-infested swamps and dense jungles swarming with fire ants. They could never be sure who was friend and who was foe. Patently false U.S. govern-ment press releases that heralded glorious victories and extolled the gratitude of Vietnamese civilians deepened bitterness on the front lines.

Approximately 8.6 million men and women served in the armed forces, and many returned to civilian life quietly and without fanfare, denied the glory earned by the combat veterans of previous wars. They reen-tered a society divided over the cause for which they had risked their lives. Tens of thousands suffered debil-itating physical injuries. As many as 40 percent of them came back with drug dependencies or symptoms of post-traumatic stress disorder, haunted and de-pressed by troubling memories of atrocities. Moreover, finding and keeping a job proved to be particularly hard in the shrinking economy of the 1970s. The situ-ation was especially bleak for African American veter-ans who returned to communities with unemployment rates at least triple the national average. Many veterans felt betrayed either by members of their own genera-tion who stayed home and protested or by their politi-cal leaders who sent them to fight an unwinnable war.

WARS ON POVERTY

During the early 1960s, the civil rights movement spurred a new awareness of and concern with poverty. As poor African Americans from both the rural South and the urban North got involved in political protests, they added the issues of unemployment, low wages,

and slum housing to the demands for desegregation and voting rights. The civil rights movement also re-vealed the close link between racial discrimination and economic inequalities. What good was winning the right to sit at a lunch counter if one could not afford to buy a hamburger?

One of the most influential books of the times, Michael Harrington's *The Other America* (1962), added fuel to this fire. Harrington argued that one-fifth of the nation—as many as 40 to 50 million people—suffered from bad housing, malnutrition, poor medical care, and other deprivations of poverty. He documented the miseries of what he called the "invisible land of the other Americans," the rejects of society who simply did not exist for affluent suburbanites or the mass media. The other America, Harrington wrote, "is populated by failures, by those driven from the land and bewil-dered by the city, by old people suddenly confronted with the torments of loneliness and poverty, and by minorities facing a wall of prejudice."

These arguments motivated President Johnson to expand the antipoverty program that he had inherited from the Kennedy administration. "That's my kind of program," he told his advisers. "It will help people. I want you to move full speed ahead on it." Ironically, it was another kind of war that ultimately undercut his aspiration to wage "an unconditional war on poverty."

The Great Society

In his State of the Union message in 1964, Johnson announced his plans to build a Great Society. Over the next two years, he used the political momentum of the civil rights movement and the overwhelming Democratic majorities in the House and Senate to push through the most ambitious reform program since the New Deal. In August 1964 the Economic Opportunity Act launched the War on Poverty as a "hand up, not a handout," as the new director, Sargent Shriver, ex-plained. It established an Office of Economic Opportu-nity (OEO), which coordinated a network of federal programs designed to increase opportunities in employ-ment and education.

The programs had mixed results. The Job Corps provided vocational training mostly for urban black youth considered unemployable. Housed in dreary bar-rackslike camps far from home, trainees often found themselves learning factory skills that were already obsolete. The dropout rate was very high. The Neigh-borhood Youth Corps managed to provide work for about 2 million young people aged sixteen to twenty-one. But nearly all of these were low-paying, make-work jobs. Educational programs proved more successful. VISTA (Volunteers in Service to America) was a kind of domestic Peace Corps that brought several thousand

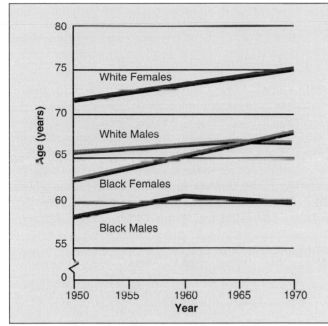

Comparative Figures on Life Expectancy at Birth by Race and Sex, 1950–1970   Shifting mortality statistics suggested that the increased longevity of females increasingly cut across race lines, but did not diminish the difference between white people and black people as a whole.

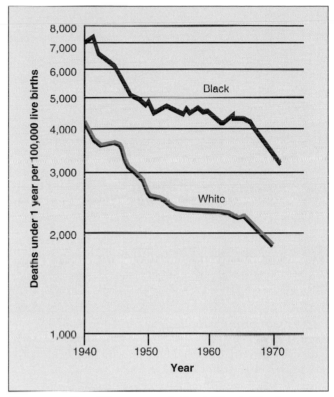

Comparative Figures on Infant Mortality by Race, 1940–1970   The causes of infant mortality such as inadequate maternal diets, prenatal care, and medical services were all rooted in poverty, both rural and urban. Despite generally falling rates of infant mortality, nonwhite people continued to suffer the effects more than white people.

idealistic volunteers into poor communities for social service work.

The most innovative and controversial element of the OEO was the Community Action Program (CAP). The program invited local communities to establish community action agencies (CAAs), to be funded through the OEO. The Economic Opportunity Act included language requiring these agencies to be "developed, conducted, and administered with the maximum feasible participation of residents of the areas and members of the groups served." In theory, as the SDS organizers had also believed, community action would empower the poor by giving them a direct say in mobilizing resources to attack poverty.

By 1966 the OEO was funding more than 1,000 CAAs, mostly in the black neighborhoods of big cities. The traditional powers in cities—mayors, business elites, and political machines—generally resisted institutional change. They looked at CAAs as merely another way to dispense services and patronage, with the federal government picking up the tab. A continual tug-of-war over who should control funding and decision making plagued the CAP in most cities, sparking intense power struggles that helped to cripple the antipoverty effort. Such was the case in Chicago, where Mayor Richard Daley demanded absolute control over the allocation of federal funds. After being challenged by OEO

activists, Daley denounced the program for "fostering class struggle."

The most successful and popular offshoots of the CAAs were the so-called national-emphasis programs, designed in Washington and administered according to federal guidelines. The Legal Services Program, staffed by attorneys, helped millions of poor people in legal battles with housing authorities, welfare departments, police, and slumlords. Head Start and Follow Through reached more than 2 million poor children and significantly improved the long-range educational achievement of participants. Comprehensive Community Health Centers—one-stop clinics—provided basic medical services to poor patients who could not afford to see doctors. Upward Bound helped low-income teenagers develop the skills and confidence needed for college. Birth control programs dispensed contraceptive supplies and information to hundreds of thousands of poor women.

But the root cause of poverty lay in unequal income distribution. The Johnson administration never committed itself to the redistribution of income or wealth.

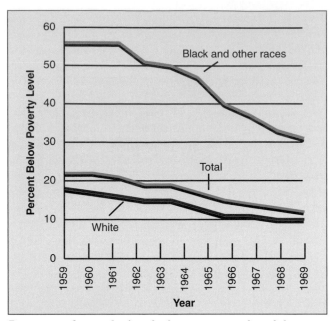

Percent of population below poverty level, by race, 1959–1969

Note: The poverty threshold for a nonfarm family of four was $3,743 in 1969 and $2,973 in 1959.

SOURCE: *Congressional Quarterly, Civil Rights: A Progress Report,* 1971, p. 46.

Spending on social welfare jumped from 7.7 percent of the gross national product in 1960 to 16 percent in 1974. But roughly three-quarters of social welfare payments went to the nonpoor. The largest sums went to Medicare, established by Congress in 1965 to provide basic health care for the aged, and to expanded Social Security payments and unemployment compensation. The major surge in federal spending on poor people resulted from the explosive growth of Aid to Families with Dependent Children (AFDC), a program begun during the New Deal. But the total cost of AFDC in the mid-1970s was only about $5 billion per year, compared with $65 billion annually for the roughly 30 million Americans receiving Social Security payments.

The War on Poverty, like the Great Society itself, became a forgotten dream. "More than five years after the passage of the Economic Opportunity Act," a 1970 study concluded, "the war on poverty has barely scratched the surface. Most poor people have had no contact with it, except perhaps to hear the promises of a better life to come." The OEO finally expired in 1974. Having made the largest commitment to federal spending on social welfare since the New Deal, Johnson could take pride in the gains scored in the War on Poverty. At the same time, he had raised expectations higher than could be reached without a more drastic redistribution of economic and political power. Even in the short run, the president could not sustain the welfare programs and simultaneously fight a lengthy and expensive war abroad.

Crisis in the Cities

As Harrington's *The Other America* pointed out, some of the nation's poorest communities were located in the Appalachian Mountains and in the Deep South. But since World War II, urban areas had suffered disproportionally from a steady process of decay. "White flight"—the exodus of white people to the suburbs—had reduced the tax base for public services of all kinds, especially schools and recreational facilities. Johnson's War on Poverty scarcely addressed the problems plaguing the nation's metropolitan areas (defined by the U.S. Census as those with populations of 250,000 people or more). On the contrary, urban conditions grew worse.

With funds for new construction limited during the Great Depression and World War II, and the postwar boom taking place in the suburbs, the housing stock in the cities diminished and deteriorated. The Federal Housing Administration had encouraged this trend by insuring loans to support the building of new homes in suburban areas (see Chapter 27). The federal government also encouraged "redlining," which left people in poor neighborhoods without access to building loans. In these areas, the supply of adequate housing declined sharply. Slumlords took advantage of this situation, collecting high rents while allowing their properties to deteriorate. City officials meanwhile appealed for federal funds under Title I of the 1949 Housing Act to upgrade housing. Designed as a program of civic revitalization, these urban renewal projects more often than not sliced apart poor neighborhoods with new highways, demolished them in favor of new office complexes, or, as in Chicago's Uptown, favored new developments for the middle class rather than the poor. In 1968 a federal survey showed that 80 percent of those residents who had been displaced under this program were nonwhite, a finding that prompted civil rights leaders to call urban renewal programs "Negro removal." As a result, the inner city became not only increasingly crowded in the 1960s but more segregated.

Urban employment opportunities declined along with the urban housing stock. The industries and corporations that had lured working men and women to the cities a century earlier either automated their plants, thus scaling back their workforces, or relocated to the suburbs or other regions, such as the South and Southwest, that promised lower corporate taxes and nonunion labor. Nationwide, military spending prompted by the escalation of the Vietnam War brought the unemployment rate down from 6 percent, where it was in 1960, to 4 percent in 1966, where it remained until the end of the decade. Black unemployment, however, was nearly twice that of white unemployment. New jobs were concentrated in the defense-related industries in the South and Southwest. In northern cities, the proportion of the workforce employed in the higher-paying manufacturing jobs declined precipitously while the proportion working in minimum-wage service industries rose at a fast rate. In short, African Americans were losing good jobs and steadily falling further behind whites.

Pollution, which had long plagued traffic-congested cities like Los Angeles and industrial cities like steel-producing Pittsburgh, became an increasingly pervasive urban problem. Cities like Phoenix that once had clean air began to issue smog alerts. Pointing to high levels of lead in the blood of urban children, scientists warned of the long-term threat of pollution to public health.

Despite deteriorating conditions, millions of Americans continued to move to the cities, mainly African Americans from the Deep South, white people from the Appalachian Mountains, and Latinos from Puerto Rico. By the mid-1960s, African Americans had become near majorities in the nation's decaying inner cities. Since World War II nearly 3 million African Americans had left the South for northern cities. In that time, New York's black population had more than doubled, and Detroit's had tripled. The vast majority of these African Americans fled rural poverty only to find themselves earning minimum wages at best and living in miserable, racially segregated neighborhoods.

Urban Uprisings

These deteriorating conditions brought urban pressures to the boiling point in the mid-1960s. In the "long, hot summers" of 1964 to 1968 the nation was rocked by more than 100 urban uprisings. As poet Imamu Amiri

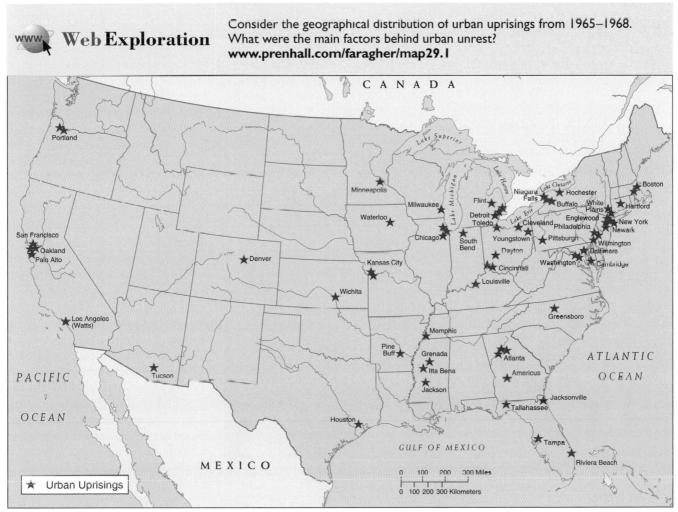

www Web Exploration   Consider the geographical distribution of urban uprisings from 1965–1968. What were the main factors behind urban unrest?
www.prenhall.com/faragher/map29.1

★ Urban Uprisings

Urban Uprisings, 1965–1968   After World War II urban uprisings precipitated by racial conflict increased in African American communities. In Watts in 1965 and in Detroit and Newark in 1967, rioters struck out at symbols of white control of their communities, such as white-owned businesses and residential properties.

Baraka (formerly LeRoi Jones) noted, these incidents were spontaneous rebellions against authority. Unlike the race riots of the 1920s and 1940s, when angry whites assaulted blacks, masses of African Americans now took revenge for the white domination of their communities and specifically for police abuse.

In 1964, waves of turbulence rippled through the black neighborhoods of Harlem, Rochester, and Philadelphia. The first major uprising erupted in August 1965 in the Watts section of Los Angeles. Here, the male unemployment rate hovered around 30 percent. Watts lacked health-care facilities—the nearest hospital was twelve miles away—and in a city with little public transportation, fewer than one-fifth of its residents owned cars. It took only a minor arrest to set off the uprising, which quickly spread outward for fifty miles. Throwing rocks and bottles through store windows, participants reportedly shouted, "This is for Selma! This is for Birmingham!" and "Burn, baby, burn!" Nearly 50,000 people turned out, and 20,000 National Guard troops were sent in. After six days, 34 people lay dead, 900 were injured, and 4,000 more had been arrested. Los Angeles chief of police William H. Parker blamed civil rights workers, the mayor accused Communists, and both feigned ignorance when the media

reported that white police assigned to "charcoal alley," their name for the Watts district, had for years referred to their nightsticks as "nigger knockers."

The following summer, large-scale uprisings occurred in San Francisco, Milwaukee, Dayton, and Cleveland. On July 12, 1967, in Newark, New Jersey, a city with severe housing shortages and the nation's highest black unemployment rate, the beating and arrest of a black taxi driver by a white police officer provoked a widespread protest. Five days of looting and burning of white-owned buildings ended with twenty-five people dead. One week later the Detroit "Great Rebellion" began. This time a vice squad of the Detroit police had raided a bar and arrested the after-hours patrons. One spectator called out, "Don't let them take our people away. . . . Let's get the bricks and bottles going." *Time* magazine later reported, "Detroit became the scene of the bloodiest uprising in a half century and the costliest in terms of property damage in U.S. history." Army tanks and paratroopers were brought in to quell the massive disturbance, which lasted a week and left 34 people dead and 7,000 under arrest.

The uprisings seemed at first to prompt badly needed reforms. After Watts, President Johnson set up a task force headed by Deputy Attorney General Ramsey Clark and allocated funds for a range of antipoverty programs. Several years later the Kerner Commission, headed by Governor Otto Kerner of Illinois, studied the riots and found that the participants in the uprisings were not the poorest or least-educated members of their communities. They suffered instead from heightened expectations sparked by the civil rights movement and Johnson's promise of a Great Society, expectations that were not to be realized. The Kerner Commission concluded its report by indicting "white racism" for creating an "explosive mixture" of poverty and police brutality and by recommending a yet more extensive program of public housing, integrated schools, 2 million new jobs, and funding for a "national system of income supplementation."

But Congress ignored both the recommendations and the commission's warning that "our nation is moving toward two societies, one black, one white—separate and unequal." Moreover, the costs of

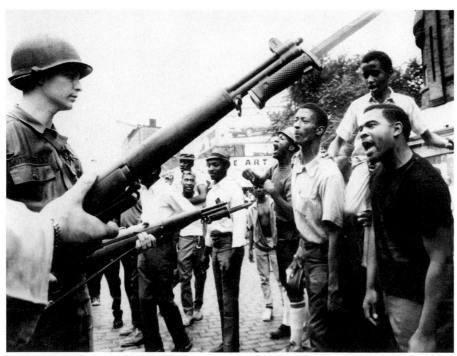

Between 1965 and 1968, racial tensions exploded into violence in more than seventy-five cities. Unlike earlier episodes of racial violence, which often took the form of clashes between black and white residents over contested neighborhoods, the riots of the 1960s were more often attacks by ghetto residents against retail establishments and property owned primarily by whites. Most deaths and injuries resulted from confrontations between police and rioters, not from fighting between black and white residents.

SOURCE: Newark, NJ, 7/14/1967. © Bettmann/CORBIS (BE 020707).

the Vietnam War left little federal money for antipoverty programs. Senator William Fulbright noted, "Each war feeds on the other, and, although the President assures us that we have the resources to win both wars, in fact we are not winning either of them."

1968

The urban uprisings of the summer of 1967 marked the most drawn-out violence in the United States since the Civil War. But, rather than offering a respite, 1968 proved to be even more turbulent. The bloodiest and most destructive fighting of the Vietnam War resulted in a hopeless stalemate that soured most Americans on the conflict and undermined their faith in U.S. invincibility in world affairs. Disillusionment deepened in the spring when two of the most revered political leaders were struck down by assassins' bullets. Once again protesters and police clashed on the nation's campuses and city streets, and millions of Americans asked what was wrong with their country. Why was it so violent? A former graduate student at Columbia University, Mike Wallace, spoke for many when he later recalled, "Nineteen sixty-eight just cracked the universe open for me."

The Tet Offensive

On January 30, 1968, the North Vietnamese and their Vietcong allies launched the Tet Offensive (named for the Vietnamese lunar new year holiday), stunning the U.S. military command in South Vietnam. The Vietcong managed to push into the major cities and provincial capitals of the South, as far as the courtyard of the U.S. embassy in Saigon. U.S. troops ultimately halted the offensive, suffering comparatively modest casualties of 1,600 dead and 8,000 wounded. The North Vietnamese and Vietcong suffered more than 40,000 deaths, about one-fifth of their total forces. Civilian casualties ran to the hundreds of thousands. As many as 1 million South Vietnamese became refugees, their villages totally ruined.

The Tet Offensive, despite the U.S. success in stopping it, shattered the credibility of American officials who had repeatedly

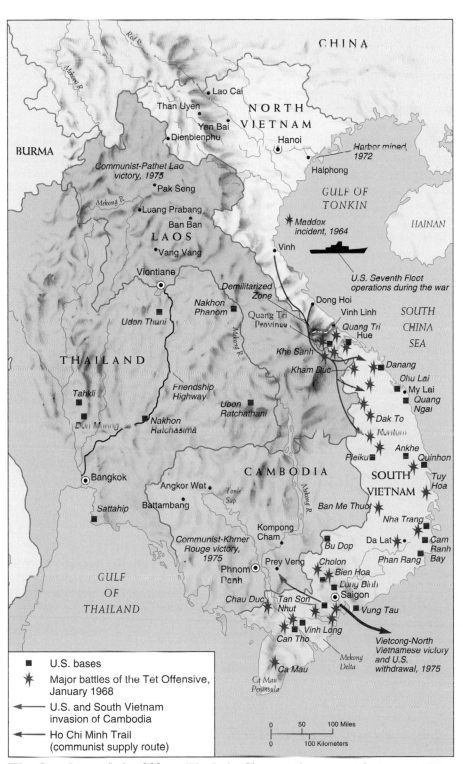

The Southeast Asian War   The Indo-Chinese subcontinent, home to long-standing regional conflict, became the center of a prolonged war with the United States.

claimed the enemy to be virtually beaten. Television and press coverage—including scenes of U.S. personnel shooting from the embassy windows in Saigon—dismayed the public. Americans saw the beautiful, ancient city of Hue devastated almost beyond recognition and heard a U.S. officer casually remark about a village in the Mekong Delta, "We had to destroy it, in order to save it." Television newscasters began to warn parents: "The following scenes might not be suitable viewing for children."

The United States had chalked up a major military victory during the Tet Offensive but lost the war at home. For the first time, polls showed strong opposition to the war, 49 percent concluding that the entire operation in Vietnam was a mistake. The majority believed that the stalemate was hopeless. Meanwhile, in Rome, Berlin, Paris, and London, students and others turned out in huge demonstrations to protest U.S. involvement in Vietnam. At home, sectors of the antiwar movement began to shift from resistance to open rebellion.

The Tet Offensive also opened a year of political drama at home. Congress resoundingly turned down a request for a general increase in troops issued by General Westmoreland. President Johnson, facing the 1968 election campaign, knew the odds were now against him. He watched as opinion polls showed his popularity plummet to an all-time low. After he squeaked to a narrow victory in the New Hampshire primary, Johnson decided to step down. On March 31 he announced

he would not seek the Democratic Party's nomination. He also declared a bombing halt over North Vietnam and called Hanoi to peace talks, which began in Paris in May. Like Truman almost thirty years earlier, and despite his determination not to repeat that bit of history, Johnson had lost his presidency in Asia.

King, the War, and the Assassination

By 1968 the civil rights leadership stood firmly in opposition to the war, and Martin Luther King, Jr. had reached a turning point in his life. The Federal Bureau of Investigation had been harassing King, tapping his telephones and spreading malicious rumors about him. Despite the threat from the FBI (Bureau Chief J. Edgar Hoover had sworn to "destroy the burrhead"), King abandoned his customary caution in criticizing U.S. policy in Vietnam. In the fall of 1965, he began to connect domestic unrest with the war abroad, calling the U.S. government the "greatest purveyor of violence in the world today." As he became more militant in opposing the war, King lost the support of liberal Democrats who remained loyal to Johnson. King refused to compromise.

In the spring of 1968 King chose Memphis, Tennessee, home of striking sanitation workers, as the place to inaugurate a Poor People's Campaign for peace and justice. Noting that the United States was "much, much sicker" than when he had begun working in 1955, he nonetheless delivered, in what was to be his final speech, a message of hope. "I have a dream this afternoon that the brotherhood of man will become a reality," King told the crowd. "With this faith, I will go out and carve a tunnel of hope from a mountain of despair." The next evening, April 4, 1968, as he stepped out on the balcony of his motel, King was shot and killed by a lone assassin, James Earl Ray.

Throughout the world crowds turned out to mourn King's death. The *New York Times* declared King's murder "a national disaster." Cheers, however, rang through the regional FBI office. President Johnson, who had ordered the investigation of King, declined to attend the funeral, sending the vice president in his place. Student Nonviolent Coordinating Committee leader Stokely Carmichael stormed, "When white America killed Dr. King, she declared war on us."

"Martin Luther King," Robert Kennedy said when he heard the news of the assassination of the civil rights leader, "dedicated his life to love and to justice for his fellow human beings, and he died because of that effort." The funeral service for King was held in the Ebenezer Baptist Church in Atlanta on April 7, 1968.

SOURCE: Walk down West Hunter Street, Atlanta. © James L. Amos/CORBIS (JA 004098).

Riots broke out in more than 100 cities. Chicago Mayor Richard Daley ordered his police to shoot to kill. In Washington, D.C., U.S. Army units set up machine guns outside the Capitol and the White House. By week's end, nearly 27,000 African Americans had been jailed. The physical scars of these riots remained for years, as banks redlined black neighborhoods and refused funds for rebuilding. The psychic scars survived even longer. With King's death, his vision of humanity as a "Beloved Community" faded.

The Democratic Campaign

The dramatic events of the first part of the year had a direct impact on the presidential campaign. For those liberals dissatisfied with Johnson's conduct of the war, and especially for African Americans suffering the loss of their greatest national leader, New York senator Robert F. Kennedy emerged as the candidate of choice. Kennedy enjoyed a strong record on civil rights, and, like King, he had begun to interpret the war as a mirror of injustice at home. Kennedy insisted during the Tet Offensive that "our nation must be told the truth about this war, in all its terrible reality." On this promise he began to build a campaign for the Democratic nomination.

Ironically, Kennedy faced an opponent who agreed with him, Minnesota senator Eugene McCarthy. The race for the Democratic nomination positioned McCarthy, the witty philosopher, against Kennedy, the charismatic campaigner. McCarthy garnered support from liberal Democrats and white suburbanites. On college campuses his popularity with idealistic students was so great that his campaign became known as the "children's crusade." Kennedy reached out successfully to African Americans and Latinos and won all but the Oregon primary.

Kennedy appeared to be the Democratic Party's strongest candidate as June 4, the day of the California primary, dawned. But as the final tabulation of his victory came in just past midnight, Robert Kennedy was struck down by the bullet of an assassin, a Jordanian national named Sirhan Sirhan.

Vice President Hubert H. Humphrey, a longtime presidential hopeful, was now the sole Democrat with the credentials to succeed Johnson. But his reputation as a cold war Democrat had become a liability. In the 1950s Humphrey had delivered stirring addresses for civil rights and antipoverty legislation; yet he also sponsored repressive cold war measures and supported huge defense appropriations that diverted needed funds from domestic programs. He fully supported the Vietnam War and had publicly scorned peace activists as cowardly and un-American. Incongruously calling his campaign the "Politics of Joy," Humphrey simultaneously courted Democrats who grimly supported the war and the King-Kennedy wing, which was sickened by it.

Humphrey skillfully cultivated the Democratic power brokers. Without entering a single state primary, he lined up delegates loyal to city bosses, labor leaders, and conservative southern Democrats. As the candidate least likely to rock the boat, he had secured his party's nomination well before delegates met in convention.

"The Whole World Is Watching!"

The events surrounding the Democratic convention in Chicago, August 21–26, demonstrated how deep the divisions within the United States had become. Antiwar activists had called for a massive demonstration at the delegates' hotel and at the convention center. The media focused, however, on the plans announced

The "police riot" in Chicago, August 1968, during the Democratic National Convention capped a spring and summer of violence. Mayor Richard Daley had prepared his city for the anticipated protest against the war by assembling more than 20,000 law enforcement officials, including police, National Guard, and U.S. Army troops carrying flame throwers and bazookas. Television cameras and photographers recorded the massive clubbing and teargassing of demonstrators as well as bystanders and news reporters.

SOURCE: Photo by Jeffrey Blankfort. Jeroboam, Inc.

by the "Yippies," or Youth International Party, a largely imaginary organization of politicized hippies led by jokester and counterculture guru Abbie Hoffman. Yippies called for a Festival of Life, including a "nude-in" on Lake Michigan beaches and the release of a greased pig—Pigasus, the Yippie candidate for president. Still reeling from the riots following King's assassination, Chicago's Mayor Richard Daley refused to issue parade permits. According to later accounts, he sent hundreds of undercover police into the crowds to encourage rock throwing and generally to incite violence so that retaliation would appear necessary and reasonable.

Daley's strategy boomeranged when his officers staged what a presidential commission later termed a "police riot," randomly assaulting demonstrators, casual passersby, and television crews filming the events. For one of the few times in American history, the media appeared to join a protest against civil authorities. Angered by the embarrassing publicity, Daley sent his agents to raid McCarthy's campaign headquarters, where Democrats opposed to the war had gathered.

Inside the convention hall, a raging debate over a peace resolution underscored the depth of the division within the party over the war. Representative Wayne Hays of Ohio lashed out at those who substituted "beards for brains . . . [and] pot [for] patriotism." When the resolution failed, McCarthy delegates put on black armbands and followed folk singer Theodore Bikel in singing "We Shall Overcome." Later, as tear gas used against the demonstrators outside turned the amphitheater air acrid, delegates heard the beaming Humphrey praise Mayor Daley and Johnson's conduct of the Vietnam War. When Senator Abraham Ribicoff of Connecticut addressed the convention and protested the "Gestapo tactics" of the police, television cameras focused on Mayor Daley saying, "You Jew son of a bitch . . . , go home!" The crowd outside chanted, "The whole world is watching! The whole world is watching!" Indeed, through satellite transmission, it was.

Protest and social strain spread worldwide. Across the United States the antiwar movement picked up steam. In Paris, students took over campuses and workers occupied factories. Young people scrawled on the walls such humorous and half-serious slogans as "Be Realistic, Demand the Impossible!" Similar protests against authority occurred in eastern Europe. In Prague, Czechoslovakia, students wearing blue jeans and singing Beatles songs threw rocks at Soviet tanks. Meanwhile, demonstrations in Japan, Italy, Ireland, Germany, and England all brought young people into the streets to demand democratic reforms in their own countries and an end to the war in Vietnam.

THE POLITICS OF IDENTITY

The tragic events of 1968 brought whole sectors of the counterculture into political activism. But, remember, hippie Tuli Kupferberg warned them, "the first revolution (but not of course the last) is in your own head." Many young Americans seemed to hear his message, intensifying their protest against the war while at the same time expressing their own political grievances and promoting their own sense of collective identity. United in their opposition to "The Establishment"—that is, the politicians and business leaders who maintained the status quo—these baby boomers sought also to empower themselves and their communities in myriad smaller but vital movements.

With great media fanfare, gay liberation and women's liberation movements emerged in the late 1960s. By the early 1970s, young Latinos, Asian Americans, and Indian peoples had pressed their own claims. In different ways, these groups drew their own lessons from the nationalist movement that formed in the wake of Malcolm X's death—Black Power. Soon, "Brown Power," "Yellow Power," and "Red Power" became the slogans of movements constituted distinctly as new communities of protest.

Black Power

In African American communities, when the Great Society programs failed to lessen poverty and black men began to die in disproportionate numbers in Vietnam, faith in the old ways lapsed. Impatient with the strategies of social change based on voting rights and integration, many younger activists spurned the tactics of civil disobedience of King's generation for direct action and militant self-defense. In 1966, Stokely Carmichael, who had helped turn SNCC into an all-black organization, began to advocate Black Power as a means for African Americans to take control of their own communities.

Derived from a century-long tradition of black nationalism, the key tenets of Black Power were self-determination and self-sufficiency. National conferences of activists, held annually beginning in 1966, adopted separatist resolutions, including a plan to partition the United States into black and white nations. Black Power also promoted self-esteem by affirming the unique history and heritage of African peoples.

The movement's boldest expression was the Black Panther Party for Self-Defense, founded in Oakland, California, in 1966 by Huey P. Newton and Bobby Seale. "We want freedom," Newton demanded. "We want power. . . . We want full employment. . . . We want all black men to be exempt from military service.

OVERVIEW

PROTEST MOVEMENTS OF THE 1960s

Year	Organization/ Movement	Description
1962	Students for a Democratic Society (SDS)	Organization of college students that became the largest national organization of left-wing white students. Calling for "participatory democracy," SDS involved students in community-based campaigns against poverty and for citizens' control of neighborhoods. SDS played a prominent role in the campaign to end the war in Vietnam.
1964	Free Speech Movement	Formed at the University of California at Berkeley to protest the banning of on-campus political fund-raising. Decried the bureaucratic character of the "multiuniversity" and advocated an expansion of student rights.
1965	Anti-Vietnam War Movement	Advocated grass-roots opposition to U.S. involvement in Southeast Asia. By 1970 a national mobilization committee organized a demonstration of a half-million protesters in Washington, D.C.
1965	*La raza*	A movement of Chicano youth to advance the cultural and political self-determination of Mexican Americans. *La raza* included the Brown Berets, which addressed community issues, and regional civil rights groups such as the Crusade for Social Justice, formed in 1965.
1966	Black Power	Militant movement that emerged from the civil rights campaigns to advocate independent institutions for African Americans and pride in black culture and African heritage. The idea of Black Power, a term coined by Stokely Carmichael, inspired the formation of the paramilitary Black Panthers.
1968	American Indian Movement (AIM)	Organization formed to advance the self-determination of Indian peoples and challenge the authority of the Bureau of Indian Affairs. Its most effective tactic was occupation. In February, 1973, AIM insurgents protesting land and treaty violations occupied Wounded Knee, South Dakota, the location of an 1890 massacre, until the FBI and BIA agents drove them out.
1968	Women's Liberation	Movement of mainly young women that took shape following a protest at the Miss America Beauty Pageant. Impatient with the legislative reforms promoted by the National Organization for Women, founded in 1966, activists developed their own agenda shaped by the slogan "The Personal Is Political." Activities included the formation of "consciousness-raising" groups and the establishment of women's studies programs.
1968	Asian American Political Alliance (AAPA)	Formed at the University of California at Berkeley, the AAPA was one of the first pan-Asian political organizations to struggle against racial oppression. The AAPA encouraged Asian Americans to claim their own cultural identity and to protest the war against Asian peoples in Vietnam.
1969	Gay Liberation	Movement to protest discrimination against homosexuals and lesbians that emerged after the Stonewall Riots in New York City. Unlike earlier organizations such as the Mattachine Society, which focused on civil rights, Gay Liberationists sought to radically change American society and government, which they believed were corrupt.

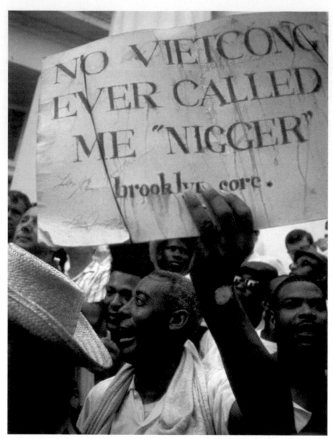

The war in Vietnam contributed to the growing racial militancy in the United States. African Americans served on the front lines in Vietnam in disproportionate numbers, and many came to view the conflict as a "white man's war." SOURCE: James Meredith march through Mississippi. Photo by Matt Herron. Media Image Resource Alliance (0001A089).

We want . . . an end to POLICE BRUTALITY. . . . We want land, bread, housing, education, clothing, and justice." Armed self-defense was the Panthers' strategy, and they adopted a paramilitary style—black leather jackets, shoes, black berets, and firearms—that infuriated local authorities. Monitoring local police, a practice Panthers termed "patrolling the pigs," was their major activity. In several communities, Panthers also ran free breakfast programs for schoolchildren, established medical clinics, and conducted educational classes. For a time the Panthers became folk heroes. A Harris poll conducted in 1970 found that a quarter of African Americans surveyed admired the Black Panthers "a great deal." Persecuted by local police and the FBI— there were more than thirty raids on Panther offices in eleven states during 1968 and 1969—the Panthers were arrested, prosecuted, and sentenced to long terms in jail that effectively destroyed the organization.

Black Power nevertheless continued to grow during the late 1960s and became a multifaceted movement. The Reverend Jesse Jackson, for example, rallied African Americans in Chicago to boycott the A&P supermarket chain until the firm hired 700 black workers. A dynamic speaker and skillful organizer, Jackson encouraged African Americans to support their own businesses and services. "We are going to see to it," he explained in 1969, "that the resources of the ghetto are not siphoned off by outside groups. . . . If a building goes up in the black community, we're going to build it." His program, Operation Breadbasket, strengthened community control. By 1970 it had spread beyond Chicago to fifteen other cities.

Cultural nationalism became the most enduring component of Black Power. In their popular book *Black Power* (1967), Stokely Carmichael and Charles V. Hamilton urged African Americans "to assert their own definitions, to reclaim their history, their culture; to create their own sense of community and togetherness." Thousands of college students responded by calling for more scholarships and for more classes on African American history and culture. At San Francisco State University, students formed the Black Student Union and, with help from the Black Panthers, demanded the creation of a black studies department. After a series of failed negotiations with the administration, the black students called for a campuswide strike and in December 1968 shut down the university. In the end, 134 school days later, the administration agreed to fund a black studies department but also fired about twenty-five faculty members and refused to drop charges against 700 arrested campus activists. Strikes for "third world studies" soon broke out on other campuses, including the Newark campus of Rutgers University, the San Diego and Berkeley campuses of the University of California, and the University of Wisconsin at Madison, where the national guard was brought in to quell the protest.

Meanwhile, trend setters put aside Western dress for African-style dashikis and hairdos, and black parents gave their children African names. Many well-known African Americans such as Imamu Amiri Baraka (formerly LeRoi Jones), Muhammad Ali (formerly Cassius Clay), and Kwame Touré (formerly Stokely Carmichael) rejected their "slave names." The African American holiday Kwanzaa began to replace Christmas as a seasonal family celebration. This deepening sense of racial pride and solidarity was summed up in the popular slogan "Black Is Beautiful."

Sisterhood Is Powerful

Betty Friedan's best-selling *Feminine Mystique* (1963) had swelled feelings of discontent among many middle-class white women who had come of age in the 1950s (see Chapter 27) and sparked the formation of the National Organization for Women (NOW) in 1966. NOW pledged itself "to take action to bring women into full participation in the mainstream of American society now." Members spearheaded campaigns for the enforcement of laws banning sex discrimination in work and in education, for maternity leaves for working mothers, and for government funding of day-care centers. NOW also came out for the Equal Rights Amendment, first introduced in Congress in 1923, and demanded the repeal of legislation that prohibited abortion or restricted birth control.

The second half of the decade produced a different kind of movement: women's liberation. Like Black Power, the women's liberation movement especially attracted women who had been active in civil rights, SDS, and campus antiwar movements. These women resented the sexist attitudes and behaviors of their fellow male activists. Women must come to understand, one angry woman wrote, that "they are not inferior—nor chicks, nor bunnies, nor quail, nor cows, nor bitches, nor ass, nor meat," but agents of their own destiny. Like Black Power, the women's liberation movement issued its own separatist plan.

In 1967 small groups of women broke off from male-led protest movements. They formed myriad all-women organizations such as the Radical Women and the Redstockings in New York, the Women's Liberation Union in Chicago, Berkeley, and Dayton, and Bread and Roses and Cell 16 in Boston. Impatient with the legislative reforms promoted by NOW, and angered by the sexism of SNCC and SDS, these women proclaimed "Sisterhood Is Powerful." "Women are an oppressed class. Our oppression is total, affecting every facet of our lives," read the Redstocking Manifesto of 1969. "We are exploited as sex objects, breeders, domestic servants, and cheap labor."

The women's liberation movement developed a scathing critique of patriarchy—that is, the power of men to dominate all institutions, from the family to business to the military to the protest movements themselves. Patriarchy, they argued, was the prime cause of exploitation, racism, and war. Outraged and sometimes outrageous, radical feminists, as they called themselves, conducted "street theater" at the 1968 Miss America Beauty Pageant in Atlantic City, crowning a live sheep as queen and "throwing implements of female torture" (bras, girdles, curlers, and copies of the *Ladies' Home Journal*) into a "freedom trash can." A few months later, the Women's International Terrorist Conspiracy from Hell (WITCH) struck in Lower Manhattan, putting a hex on the male-dominated New York Stock Exchange.

The media focused on the audacious acts and brazen pronouncements of radical feminists, but the majority involved in the women's liberation movement were less flamboyant women who were simply trying to rise above the limitations imposed on them because of their sex. Most of their activism took place outside the limelight in consciousness-raising (CR) groups. CR groups, which multiplied by the thousands in the late 1960s and early 1970s, brought women together to discuss the relationship between public events and private lives, particularly between politics and sexuality. Here women shared their most intimate feelings toward men or other women and established the constituency for the movement's most important belief, expressed in the aphorism "The personal is political." Believing that no aspect of life lacked a political dimension, women in these groups explored the power dynamics of the institutions of family and marriage as well as the workforce and government. "The small group has served as a place where thousands of us have learned to support each other," one participant reported, "where we have gained new feelings of self-respect and learned to speak about what we are thinking and to respect other women."

Participants in the women's liberation movement engaged in a wide range of activities. Some staged sit-ins at *Newsweek* to protest demeaning media depictions of women. Others established health clinics, day-care centers, rape crisis centers, and shelters for women fleeing abusive husbands or lovers. The women's liberation movement also had a significant educational impact. Feminist bookstores and publishing companies, such as the Feminist Press, reached out to eager readers. Scholarly books such as Kate Millett's *Sexual Politics* (1970) found a wide popular audience. By the early 1970s, campus activists were demanding women's studies programs and women's centers. Like black studies, women's studies programs included traditional academic goals, such as the generation of new scholarship, but also encouraged personal change and self-esteem. Between 1970 and 1975, as many as 150 women's studies programs had been established. The movement continued to grow; by 1980 nearly 30,000 women's studies courses were offered at colleges and universities throughout the United States.

The women's liberation movement remained, however, a bastion of white middle-class women. The appeal to sisterhood did not unite women across race or class or even sexual orientation. Lesbians, who charged the early leaders of NOW with homophobia, found large pockets of "heterosexism" in the women's liberation movement and broke off to form their own organizations. Although some African American women were outraged at the posturing of Black Power leaders like Stokely Carmichael, who joked that "the only position for women in SNCC is prone," the majority remained wary of white women's appeals to sisterhood. African American women formed their own "womanist" movement to address their distinct cultural and political concerns. Similarly, by 1970 a Latina feminist movement had begun to address issues uniquely relevant to women of color in an Anglo-dominated society.

Although the women's liberation movement could not dispel ethnic or racial differences, it fostered a sense of community among many women. By August 1970, hundreds of thousands of women responded to NOW's call for a Women's Strike for Equality, a mass demonstration marking the fiftieth anniversary of the woman suffrage amendment and the largest turnout for women's rights in U.S. history.

Gay Liberation

The gay community had been generations in the making but only gained visibility during World War II (see Chapter 25). By the mid-1950s, two pioneering homophile organizations, the Mattachine Society and the Daughters of Bilitis, were campaigning to reduce discrimination against homosexuals in employment, the armed forces, and all areas of social and cultural life. Other groups, such as the Society for Individual Rights, rooted themselves in New York's Greenwich Village, San Francisco's North Beach, and other centers of gay night life. But it was during the tumultuous 1960s that gay and lesbian movements encouraged many men and women to proclaim publicly their sexual identity: "Say It Loud, Gay Is Proud."

The major event prompting gays to organize grew out of repeated police raids of gay bars and the harassment of their patrons. In February 1966 New York City's popular liberal mayor John Lindsay announced a crackdown against "promenading perverts" and assigned police to patrol the bars between Times Square and Washington Square. The American Civil Liberties Union responded by pointing out that the mayor was "confusing deviant social behavior with criminal activity." Lindsay's police commissioner soon announced the end of the entrapment policy by which undercover police had been luring homosexuals into breaking the law, but various forms of individual harassment continued. Finally, on Friday, June 27, 1969, New York police raided the Stonewall Inn, a well-known gay bar in Greenwich Village, and provoked an uprising of angry homosexuals that lasted the entire night. The next day, "Gay Power" graffiti appeared on buildings and sidewalks throughout the neighborhood.

The Stonewall Riot, as it was called, sparked a new sense of collective identity among many gays and lesbians and touched off a new movement for both civil rights and liberation. Gay men and women in New York City formed the Gay Liberation Front (GLF), announcing themselves as "a revolutionary homosexual group of men and women formed with the realization that complete sexual liberation for all people cannot come about unless existing social institutions are abolished. We reject society's attempt to impose sexual roles and definitions of our nature. We are stepping outside these roles and

simplistic myths. We are going to be who we are." The GLF also took a stand against the war in Vietnam and supported the Black Panthers. It quickly adopted the forms of public protest, such as street demonstrations and sit-ins, developed by the civil rights movement and given new direction by antiwar protesters.

Changes in public opinion and policies followed. As early as 1967 a group of Episcopal priests had urged church leaders to avoid taking a moral position against same-sex relationships. The San Francisco–based Council on Religion and Homosexuality established a network for clergy sympathetic to gay and lesbian parishioners. In 1973 the American Psychiatric Association, which since World War II had viewed homosexuality as a treatable mental illness, reclassified it as a normal sexual orientation. Meanwhile, there began a slow process of decriminalization of homosexual acts between consenting adults. In 1975 the U.S. Civil Service Commission ended its ban on the employment of homosexuals.

The founders of gay liberation encouraged not only legal changes and the establishment of supporting institutions but self-pride. "Gay Is Good" (like "Black Is Beautiful" and "Sisterhood Is Powerful") expressed the aspiration of a large hidden minority (estimated at 10 million or more people) to "come out" and demand public acceptance of their sexual identity. The Gay Activist Alliance, founded in 1970, demanded "freedom of expression of our dignity and value as human beings." By the mid-1970s Gay Pride marches held simultaneously in several cities were drawing nearly 500,000 participants.

The Chicano Rebellion

By the mid-1960s young Mexican Americans had created, according to one historian, a moral community founded on collectivist principles and a determination to resist Anglo domination. Mainly high school and college students, they adopted the slang term *Chicano*, in preference to Mexican American, to express a militant ethnic nationalism. Chicano militants demanded not only equality with white people but cultural and political self-determination. Tracing their roots to the heroic Aztecs, they identified *la raza* (the race or people) as the source of a common language, religion, and heritage.

Students played a large role in shaping the Chicano movement. In East Los Angeles, high school students staged "blowouts" or strikes to demand educational reform and a curricular emphasis on the history, literature, art, and language of Mexican Americans. In 1968 President Johnson had signed the Bilingual Education Act, which reversed state laws that prohibited the teaching of classes in any language but English. Nevertheless, as Sal Castro, an East Los Angeles teacher, complained,

"If a kid speaks in Spanish, he is criticized. If a kid has a Mexican accent, he is ridiculed. If a kid talks back, in any language, he is arrested. . . . We have a gunpoint education. The school is a prison." Moreover, Chicanos had one of the highest drop-out rates in the country. Castro encouraged 15,000 students from five Los Angeles schools to strike against poor educational facilities. The police conducted a mass arrest of protesters, and within a short time students in San Antonio and Denver were conducting their own blowouts, holding placards reading "Teachers, Sí, Bigots, No!" By 1969, on September 16, Mexican Independence Day, high school students throughout the Southwest skipped classes in the First National Chicano Boycott. Meanwhile, students organized to demand Mexican American studies on their campuses. In 1969, a group staged a sit-in at the administrative offices of the University of California at Berkeley, which one commentator called "the first important public appearance of something called Brown Power."

In 1967 David Sanchez of East Los Angeles formed the Brown Berets, modeled on the Black Panthers, to address such community issues as housing and employment and generally to encourage teenagers to express *Chicanismo*, or pride in their Mexican American identity and heritage. By 1972, when the organization disbanded, the Brown Berets had organized twenty chapters, published a newspaper, *La Causa*, and run a successful health clinic. From college campuses spread a wider cultural movement that spawned literary journals in "Spanglish" (a mixture of English and Spanish), theatrical companies and music groups, and murals illustrating ethnic themes on buildings in Los Angeles and elsewhere.

Chicano nationalism inspired a variety of regional political movements in the late 1960s. One of these, Rodolfo "Corky" Gonzales's Crusade for Justice, formed in 1965 to protest the failure of the Great Society's antipoverty programs. A former boxer and popular poet, Gonzales was especially well liked by barrio youth and college students. He led important campaigns for greater job opportunities and land reform throughout the Southwest well into the 1970s. In Colorado and New Mexico, the *Alianza Federal de Mercedes*, formed in 1963 by Reies López Tijerina, fought to reclaim land fraudulently appropriated by white settlers. The Texas-based *La Raza Unida Party* (LRUP), meanwhile, increased Mexican American representation in local government and established social and cultural programs. The student-led Mexican American Youth Organization (MAYO) worked closely with the LRUP to help Mexican Americans take political power in Crystal City, Texas. The two organizations registered voters, ran candidates for office, and staged a massive boycott of Anglo-owned businesses.

Mexican American activists, even those who won local office, soon discovered that economic power remained out of community hands. Stifled by poverty, ordinary Mexican Americans had less confidence in the political process, and many fell back into apathy after early hopes of great, sudden change. Despite these setbacks, a sense of collective identity had been forged among many Mexican Americans.

The Chicano movement found vivid expression in the performing and visual arts and in literature. *Teatro*, comprising film and drama, drew creatively on Mexican and Anglo cultural forms to explore the political dimensions of Mexican American society. *La Carpa de los Rasquachis* (*The Tent of the Underdogs*), appeared in 1974 as the first full-length Chicano play and was subsequently staged in many communities. One of the most popular and visible media was the mural, often based on the works of Mexican masters such as Diego Rivera. Chicano muralists painted an estimated 1,500 murals on public buildings throughout their communities, from the exteriors of retail shops to freeway overpasses, even to large drainage pipes. Artistic expression found its way into music and dance. The rock group *Los Lobos*, for example, dedicated their first recorded album to the United Farm Workers. One of the most important writers to capture the excitement of the

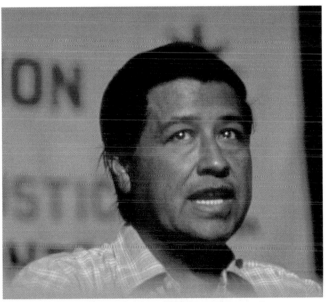

Labor activist César Chávez spearheaded the organization of Chicano agricultural workers into the United Farm Workers (UFW), the first successful union of migrant workers. In 1965, a strike of grape pickers in the fields around Delano, California, and a nationwide boycott of table grapes brought Chávez and the UFW into the media spotlight. Like Martin Luther King, Jr., he advocated nonviolent methods for achieving justice and equality. SOURCE: EPA Documercia (1927–1933) National Archives and Records Administration.

Chicano movement was Oscar Zeta Acosta, whose *Revolt of the Cockroach*, published in 1973, renders into fiction some of the major events of the era.

Red Power

The phrase "Red Power," attributed to Vine Deloria, Jr., commonly expressed a growing sense of supratribal Indian identity. At the forefront of this movement was the American Indian Movement (AIM), which was founded in 1968. Its members represented mainly urban Indian communities, and its leaders were young and militant. Like the Black Panthers and Brown Berets, AIM was initially organized to monitor law enforcement practices such as police harassment and brutality. It soon played a major role in building a network of urban Indian centers, churches, and philanthropic organizations and in establishing the "powwow circuit" that publicized news of protest activities across the country. Skillful in attracting attention from the news media,

AIM quickly inspired a plethora of new publications and local chapters. Many young Indians turned to their elders to learn tribal ways, including traditional dress and spiritual practices.

The major catalyst of Red Power was the occupation of the deserted federal prison on Alcatraz Island in San Francisco Bay on November 20, 1969. A group of eighty-nine Indians, identifying themselves as "Indians of All Tribes," claimed the island according to the terms of an 1868 Sioux treaty that gave Indians rights to unused federal property on Indian land. The group demanded federal funds for a multifaceted cultural and educational center. For the next year and a half, an occupation force averaging around 100 and a stream of visitors from a large number of tribes celebrated the occupation. Although the protestors ultimately failed to achieve their specific goals, they had an enormous impact on the Indian community. With the occupation at Alcatraz, a participant testified, "we got back our worth, our pride, our dignity, our humanity." At the

WebExploration   Examine those states with sizeable Indian reservations. How did the Civil Rights Act affect Indian identity?
www.prenhall.com/faragher/map29.2

Major Indian Reservations, 1976   Although sizable areas, designated Indian reservations represented only a small portion of territory occupied in earlier times.

same time, the occupation fostered a new identity, a multitribal ethnicity —the American Indian.

The most dramatic series of events of the Red Power movement began in 1972, when Indian activists left the cities to return to their rural roots. In November, AIM staged an event known as the "Trail of Broken Treaties " that culminated in a week-long occupation of the Bureau of Indian Affairs in Washington, D.C. Emphasizing treaty violation rather than civil rights, AIM insurgents then moved to the Pine Ridge Reservation, the site of the 1890 massacre at Wounded Knee, South Dakota, where in the spring of 1973 they began a seige that lasted ten weeks. AIM activists demanded the removal of the leader of the Oglala Lakota, whom they believed to be a corrupt puppet of the Bureau of Indian Affairs, and the restoration of treaty rights. Dozens of FBI agents then invaded under shoot-to-kill orders, leaving two Indians dead and an unknown number of casualties on both sides. AIM gained widespread support for its actions among young urban Indians but alienated many reservation Indians and their tribal leaders. In the next few years, Indian activists staged a number of occupations on reservations in New York, Wisconsin, New Mexico, South Dakota, and Washington.

The Red Power movement culminated in the "Longest Walk," a five-month protest march that began in San Francisco and ended in Washington, D.C., in July 1978. The event emphasized the history of the forced removal of Indians from their homelands and protested the U.S. government's repeated violation of treaty rights. By this time, several tribes had won in court, by legislation or by administrative fiat, small parts of what had earlier been taken from them. The sacred Blue Lake was returned to Pueblo Indians in Taos, New Mexico, and Alaskan natives were granted legal title to 40 million acres (and compensation of almost $1 billion). The Native American Rights Fund (NARF), established in 1971, gained additional thousands of acres in Atlantic coast states. But despite these victories, a rush of new legislation in Congress threatened to abrogate treaties still in place, and many tribal lands continued to suffer from industrial and government waste dumping and other commercial uses. On reservations and in urban areas with heavy Indian concentrations, alcohol abuse and ill health remained serious problems.

The 1960s also marked the beginning of an "Indian Renaissance" in literature. New books like Vine Deloria, Jr.'s *Custer Died for Your Sins* (1969)and the classic *Black Elk Speaks* (1961), reprinted from the 1930s, reached millions of readers inside and outside Indian communities. A wide variety of Indian novelists, historians, and essayists, such as Pulitzer Prize–winning N. Scott Momaday and Leslie Silko, followed up these successes, and fiction and nonfiction works about Indian life and lore continued to attract a large audience.

The Asian American Movement

Inspired by the Black Power movement, college students of Asian ancestry sought to unite fellow Asian Americans in a struggle against racial oppression "through the power of a consolidated yellow people." In 1968 students at the University of California at Berkeley founded the Asian American Political Alliance (AAPA), one of the first pan-Asian political organizations bringing together Chinese, Japanese, and Filipino American activists. Similar organizations soon appeared on campuses throughout California and spread quickly to the East Coast and Midwest.

These groups took a strong stand against the war in Vietnam, condemning it as a violation of the national sovereignty of the small Asian country. They also protested the racism directed against the peoples of Southeast Asia, particularly the practice common among American soldiers of referring to the enemy as "Gooks." This racist epithet, first used to denigrate Filipinos during the Spanish-American War, implied that Asians were something less than human and therefore proper targets for slaughter. In response, Asian American activists rallied behind the people of Vietnam and proclaimed racial solidarity with their "Asian brothers and sisters."

The antiwar movement brought many young Asian Americans into political organizations such as the AAPA that encouraged them to claim their own cultural identity. In 1968 and 1969 students at San Francisco State College and the University of California at Berkeley, for example, rallied behind the slogan "Shut It Down!" and waged prolonged campus strikes to demand the establishment of ethnic studies programs. These students sought alternatives to the goal of assimilation into mainstream society, promoting instead a unique sense of ethnic identity, a pan-Asian counterculture. Berkeley students, for example, sponsored the "Asian American Experience in America–Yellow Power" conference, inviting their peers to learn about "Asian American history and destiny, and the need to express Asian American solidarity in a predominantly white society."

Between 1968 and 1973, major universities across the country introduced courses on Asian American studies, and a few, such as the City College of New York, set up interdisciplinary departments. Meanwhile, artists, writers, documentary filmmakers, oral historians, and anthropologists worked to recover the Asian American past. Writer Frank Chin, who advocated a language that "coheres the people into a community by organizing and codifying the symbols of the people's common experience," wrote the first Asian American drama, *The Year of the Dragon*, to be produced on national television. It was, however, Maxine Hong Kingston's *Woman Warrior: A Memoir of a Girlhood among Ghosts* (1976) that became the major bestseller.

Looking to the example of the Black Panthers, young Asian Americans also took their struggle into the community. In 1968, activists presented the San Francisco municipal government with a list of grievances about conditions in Chinatown, particularly the poor housing and medical facilities, and organized a protest march down the neighborhood's main street. They led a communitywide struggle to save San Francisco's International Hotel, a low-income residential facility mainly for Filipino and Chinese men, which was ultimately leveled for a new parking lot.

Community activists ranging from college students to neighborhood artists worked in a variety of campaigns to heighten public awareness. The Redress and Reparations Movement, initiated by Sansei (third-generation Japanese Americans), for example, encouraged students to ask their parents about their wartime experiences and prompted older civil rights organizations, such as the Japanese American Citizens League, to bring forward the issue of internment. At the same time, trade union organizers renewed labor organizing among new Asian workers, mainly in service industries, such as hotel and restaurant work, and in clothing manufacturing. Other campaigns reflected the growing diversity of the Asian population. Filipinos, the fastest-growing group, organized to protest the destructive role of U.S.–backed Philippine dictator Ferdinand Marcos. Students from South Korea similarly denounced the repressive government in their homeland. Samoans sought to publicize the damage caused by nuclear testing in the Pacific Islands. Ultimately, however, in blurring intergroup differences, the Asian American movement failed to reach the growing populations of new immigrants, especially the numerous Southeast Asians fleeing their devastated homeland.

Despite its shortcomings, the politics of identity would continue to grow through the next two decades of mainly conservative rule, broadening the content of literature, film, television, popular music, and even the curricula of the nation's schools. Collectively, the various movements for social change pushed issues of race, gender, and sexual orientation to the forefront of American politics and simultaneously spotlighted the nation's cultural diversity as a major resource.

THE NIXON PRESIDENCY

The sharp divisions among Americans in 1968, mainly due to President Johnson's policies in Vietnam, paved the way for the election of Richard Milhous Nixon. The new Republican president inherited not only an increasingly unpopular war but a nation riven by internal discord. Without specifying his plans, he promised a "just and honorable peace" in Southeast Asia and the restoration of law and order at home. Yet, once in office, Nixon puzzled both friends and foes. He ordered unprecedented illegal government action against private citizens while agreeing with Congress to enhance several welfare programs and improve environmental protection. He widened and intensified the war in Vietnam, yet made stunning moves toward détente with the People's Republic of China. An architect of the cold war in the 1950s, Nixon became the first president to foresee its end. Nixon worked hard in the White House, centralizing authority and reigning defiantly as an "Imperial President"—until he brought himself down.

The Southern Strategy

In 1968, Republican presidential contender Richard Nixon deftly built on voter hostility toward youthful protesters and the counterculture. He represented, he said, the "silent majority"—those Americans who worked, paid taxes, and did not demonstrate, picket, or protest loudly, "people who are not haters, people who love their country." Recovering from defeats in elections for the presidency in 1960 and the governorship of California in 1962, Nixon declared himself the one candidate who could restore law and order to the nation.

After signing the landmark Civil Rights Act of 1964, President Johnson said privately, "I think we just delivered the South to the Republicans for a long time to come." Republican strategists moved quickly to make this prediction come true. They also recognized the growing electoral importance of the Sunbelt, where populations grew with the rise of high-tech industries and retirement communities. A powerful conservatism dominated this region, home to many military bases, defense plants, and an increasingly influential Protestant evangelism. Nixon appealed directly to these voters by promising to appoint to federal courts judges who would undercut liberal interpretations of civil rights and be tough on crime. Nixon also promised to roll back the Great Society. "I say it's time," he announced, "to quit pouring billions of dollars into programs that have failed."

Nixon selected as his running mate Maryland governor Spiro T. Agnew, known for his vitriolic oratory. Agnew treated dissent as near treason. He courted the silent majority by attacking all critics of the war as "an effete corps of impudent snobs" and blasted liberal newscasters as "nattering nabobs of negativism." Democratic nominee Hubert Humphrey chose as his running mate Maine senator Edmund Muskie.

The 1968 campaign underscored the antiliberal sentiment of the voting public. The most dramatic example was the relative success of Alabama governor George Wallace's third-party bid for the presidency. Wallace took state office in 1963 promising white

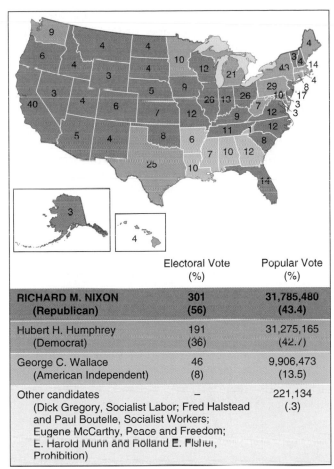

	Electoral Vote (%)	Popular Vote (%)
RICHARD M. NIXON (Republican)	**301** **(56)**	**31,785,480** **(43.4)**
Hubert H. Humphrey (Democrat)	191 (36)	31,275,165 (42.7)
George C. Wallace (American Independent)	46 (8)	9,906,473 (13.5)
Other candidates (Dick Gregory, Socialist Labor; Fred Halstead and Paul Boutelle, Socialist Workers; Eugene McCarthy, Peace and Freedom; E. Harold Munn and Rolland E. Fisher, Prohibition)	–	221,134 (.3)

The Election of 1968   Although the Republican Nixon-Agnew team won the popular vote by only a small margin, the Democrats lost in most of the northern states that had voted Democratic since the days of FDR. Segregationist Governor George Wallace of Alabama polled more than 9 million votes.

Alabamans "Segregation now! Segregation tomorrow! Segregation forever!" In 1968 he waged a national campaign around a conservative hate list that included school busing, antiwar demonstrations, and urban uprisings. His running mate in the American Independent Party, retired air force general Curtis LeMay, proposed the use of nuclear weapons to "bomb the North Vietnamese back to the Stone Age." Winning only five southern states, Wallace nevertheless captured 13.5 percent of the popular vote.

The Nixon-Agnew team squeaked to victory, capturing the popular vote by the slim margin of 43.4 percent to Humphrey and Muskie's 42.7 percent but taking nearly all the West's electoral votes. Bitterly divided by the campaign, the Democrats would remain out of presidential contention for over two decades, except when the Republicans suffered scandal and disgrace. The Republicans in 1968 had paved the way for the conservative ascendancy.

Nixon's War

Nixon promised to bring "peace with honor." Yet, despite this pledge, the Vietnam War raged for four more years before a peace settlement was reached.

Much of the responsibility for the prolonged conflict rested with Henry A. Kissinger. A dominating personality on the National Security Council, Kissinger insisted that the United States could not retain its global leadership by appearing weak to either allies or enemies. "However we got into Vietnam," he wrote in 1969, the United States "cannot accept a military defeat, or a change in the political structure of South Vietnam brought about by external military forces." Brilliant and ruthless, Kissinger helped Nixon centralize foreign policymaking in the White House. Together, they overpowered those members of the State Department who had concluded that the majority of Americans no longer supported the war.

In public Nixon followed a policy of "Vietnamization." On May 14, 1969, he announced that the time was approaching "when the South Vietnamese . . . will be able to take over some of the fighting." During the next several months, he ordered the withdrawal of 60,000 U.S. troops. Hoping to placate public opinion, Nixon also intended to "demonstrate to Hanoi that we were serious in seeking a diplomatic settlement." In private, with Kissinger's guidance, Nixon mulled over the option of a "knockout blow" to the North Vietnamese.

On April 30, 1970, Nixon made one of the most controversial decisions of his presidency. Without seeking congressional approval, Nixon added Cambodia (through which North Vietnam had been ferrying troops and supplies south) to the war zone. Although Nixon had authorized secret bombing raids of Cambodia in 1969, he now ordered U.S. troops to invade the tiny

> In view of the developments since we entered the fighting in Vietnam, do you think the United States made a mistake sending troops to fight in Vietnam?
>
> | Yes | 52% |
> | No | 39 |
> | No opinion | 9 |
>
> Interviewing Date 1/22–28/1969, Survey #774-K, Question #6/Index #45

Public Opinion on the War in Vietnam   By 1969 Americans were sharply divided in their assessments of the progress of the war and peace negotiations. The American Institute of Public Opinion, founded in 1935 by George Gallup, charted a growing dissatisfaction with the war in Vietnam.

SOURCE: *The Gallup Poll: Public Opinion, 1935–1974* (New York: Random House, 1974), p. 2189.

nation. Nixon had hoped in this way to end North Vietnamese infiltration into the South, but he had also decided to live up to what he privately called his "wild man" or "mad bomber" reputation. The enemy would be unable to anticipate the location or severity of the next U.S. strike, Nixon reasoned, and would thus feel compelled to negotiate.

Nixon could not have predicted the outpouring of protest that followed the invasion of Cambodia. The largest series of demonstrations and police-student confrontations in the nation's history took place on campuses and in city streets. At Kent State University in Ohio, twenty-eight National Guardsmen apparently panicked, shooting into an unarmed crowd of about 200 students, killing four and wounding nine. Ten days later, on May 14, at Jackson State University, a black school in Mississippi, state troopers entered a campus dormitory and began shooting wildly, killing two students and wounding twelve others. Demonstrations broke out on fifty campuses.

The nation was shocked. Thirty-seven college and university presidents signed a letter calling on the president to end the war. A few weeks later the Senate adopted a bipartisan resolution outlawing the use of funds for U.S. military operations in Cambodia, starting July 1, 1970. Although the House rejected the resolution, Nixon saw the writing on the wall. He had planned to negotiate a simultaneous withdrawal of North Vietnamese and U.S. troops, but he could no longer afford to hold out for this condition.

The president, still goaded by Kissinger, did not accept defeat easily. In February 1971 Nixon directed the South Vietnamese army to invade Laos and cut supply lines, but the demoralized invading force suffered a quick and humiliating defeat. Faced with enemy occupation of more and more territory during a major offensive in April 1972, Nixon ordered the mining of North Vietnamese harbors and directed B-52s to conduct massively destructive bombing missions in Cambodia and North Vietnam.

Nixon also sent Kissinger to Paris for secret negotiations with delegates from North Vietnam. They agreed to a cease-fire specifying the withdrawal of all U.S. troops and the return of all U.S. prisoners of war. Knowing these terms ensured defeat, South Vietnam's president refused to sign the agreement. On Christmas Day 1972, hoping for a better negotiating position, Nixon ordered one final wave of bomb attacks on North Vietnam's cities. To secure a halt to the bombing, the North Vietnamese offered to resume negotiations. But the terms of the Paris Peace Agreement, signed by North Vietnam and the United States in January 1973, differed little from the settlement Nixon could have procured in 1969, costing hundreds of thousands of deaths that might have been prevented. Beginning in March 1973, the with-

drawal of U.S. troops left the outcome of the war a foregone conclusion. By December of that year only fifty American military personnel remained, and the government of South Vietnam had no future. In April 1975 North Vietnamese troops took over Saigon, and the Communist-led Democratic Republic of Vietnam soon united the small nation. The war was finally over. It had cost the United States 58,000 lives and $150 billion. The country had not only failed to achieve its stated war goal but had lost an important post in Southeast Asia. Equally important, the policy of containment introduced by President Truman had proved impossible to sustain.

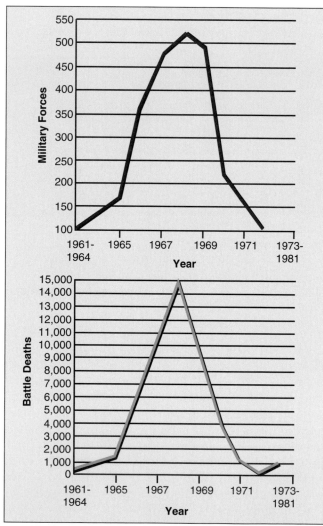

U.S. Military Forces in Vietnam and Casualties, 1961–1981   The United States government estimated battle deaths between 1969 and 1973 for South Vietnamese troops at 107,504 and North Vietnamese and Vietcong at more than a half-million. Although the United States suffered fewer deaths, the cost was enormous.

SOURCE: U.S. Department of Defense, *Selected Manpower Statistics,* annual, and unpublished data; beginning 1981, National Archives and Records Service, "Combat Area Casualty File" (3-330-80-3).

While Nixon was maneuvering to bring about "peace with honor," the chilling crimes of war had already begun to haunt Americans. In 1971 the army court-martialed a young lieutenant, William L. Calley, Jr., for the murder of "at least" twenty-two Vietnamese civilians during a 1968 search-and-destroy mission subsequently known as the My Lai Massacre. Calley's platoon had destroyed a village and slaughtered more than 350 unarmed South Vietnamese, raping and beating many of the women before killing them. "My Lai was not an isolated incident," one veteran attested, but "only a minor step beyond the standard official United States policy in Indochina." Commander of the platoon at My Lai, Calley was first sentenced to life imprisonment before being given a reduced term of ten years. The secretary of the army paroled Calley after he served three years under house arrest in his apartment.

"The China Card"

Apart from Vietnam, Nixon's foreign policy defied the expectations of liberals and conservatives alike. Actually, he followed traditions of previous Republican moderates such as Herbert Hoover and Dwight Eisenhower, who had so effectively "proved" their anticommunism that they could conciliate international foes without undermining their popularity at home. Nixon added a new page, however—a policy of détente that replaced U.S.–Soviet bipolarity with multilateral relations. Nixon could cultivate relations with the People's Republic of China, a rising world power more rigidly Communist than the Soviet Union, to form an alliance against the Soviet Union. And he could easily persuade the Soviet Union to cooperate on trade agreements, thus limiting the two nations' ruthless competition to control governments in Asia, the Middle East, and Africa. Opponents of the Vietnam War accused Nixon of double dealing, while conservatives howled at any compromise with Communist governments. But Nixon persisted in his plans, anticipating an end to the cold war on American terms.

Playing the "China card" was the most dramatic of the president's moves. Early in his political career Nixon had avidly supported the arch-conservative China lobby. But as president he considered the People's Republic of China too important to be isolated by the West and too obviously hostile to the Soviet Union to be discounted as a potential ally. "If there is anything I want to do before I die," he confided to a *Time* magazine reporter, "it is to go to China."

"Ping-pong diplomacy" began in April 1971, when the Chinese hosted a table tennis team from the United States. Henry Kissinger embarked on a secret mission a few months later. Finally, in February 1972, Richard and Pat Nixon flew to Beijing, where they were greeted by foreign minister Zhou Enlai and a band playing "The Star-Spangled Banner." It was a momentous and surprising event, one that marked a new era in East-West diplomacy. Nixon claimed that he had succeeded in bridging "16,000 miles and twenty-two years of hostility." The president's move successfully increased diplomatic pressure on the Soviet Union but simultaneously weakened the Nationalist Chinese government in Taiwan, which now slipped into virtual diplomatic obscurity.

Next the president went to Moscow to negotiate with Soviet leader Leonid Brezhnev, who was anxious about U.S. involvement with China and eager for economic assistance. Declaring, "There must be room in this world for two great nations with different systems to live together and work together," Nixon offered to sell $1 billion of grain to the Soviets. Winning the favor of American wheat farmers, this deal simultaneously relieved U.S. trade deficits and crop surpluses. Afterward, the Soviet leader became visibly more cautious about supporting revolutions in the third world. Nixon also completed negotiations of the Strategic Arms Limitation Treaty (SALT, known later as SALT I). A limited measure, SALT I represented the first success at strategic arms control since the opening of the cold war and a major public relations victory for the leaders of the two superpowers.

Nixon's last major diplomatic foray proved far less effective. The president sent Kissinger on a two-year mission of "shuttle diplomacy" to mediate Israeli-Arab disputes, to ensure the continued flow of oil, and to increase lucrative U.S. arms sales to Arab countries. The Egyptians and Israelis agreed to a cease-fire in their October 1973 Yom Kippur War, but little progress toward peace in the area was achieved.

Domestic Policy

Nixon deeply desired to restore order in American society. "We live in a deeply troubled and profoundly unsettled time," he noted. "Drugs, crime, campus revolts, racial discord, draft resistance—on every hand we find old standards violated, old values discarded." Despite his hostility to liberalism, however, Nixon had some surprises for conservatives. Determined to win reelection in 1972, he supported new Social Security benefits and subsidized housing for the poor and oversaw the creation of the Environmental Protection Agency and the Occupational Safety and Health Administration. Most notable was his support, under the guidance of Democratic adviser Daniel P. Moynihan, for the Family Assistance Plan, which proposed a minimal income for the poor in place of welfare benefits. Conservatives judged the plan too generous while liberals found it inadequate. Moreover, the plan was expensive. Bipartisan opposition ultimately killed the bill.

Nixon also embraced a policy of fiscal liberalism. Early in 1971 he accepted the idea of deficit spending. Later that year he ordered a first: he took the nation off the gold standard. Subsequently, the dollar's value would float on the world market rather than being tied to the value of gold. His ninety-day freeze on wages, rents, and prices, designed to halt the inflation caused by the massive spending on the Vietnam War, also closely resembled Democratic policies. Finally, Nixon's support of "black capitalism"—adjustments or quotas favoring minority contractors in construction projects—created an explosive precedent for "set-aside" programs later blamed on liberals.

Nixon lined up with conservatives, however, on most civil rights issues and thus enlarged southern Republican constituencies. He accepted the principle of school integration but rejected the busing programs required to implement racial balance. His nominees to the Supreme Court were far more conservative than those appointed by Eisenhower. Warren E. Burger, who replaced Chief Justice Earl Warren, steered the Court away from the liberal direction it had taken since the 1950s.

One of the most newsworthy events of Nixon's administration was a distant result of President Kennedy's determination to outshine the Soviets in outer space (see Chapter 27). On July 21, 1969, the lunar module of Apollo 11 descended to the moon's Sea of Tranquility. As millions watched on television, astronauts Neil Armstrong and Buzz Aldrin stepped out to plant an American flag and to bear the message, "We came in peace for all mankind."

WATERGATE

At times Richard Nixon expressed his yearning for approval in strange ways. A few days after the bombing of Cambodia in May 1970, he wandered out of the White House alone at 5:00 in the morning to talk to antiwar demonstrators. He tried to engage them in small talk about football and pleaded, "I know that probably most of you think I'm an SOB, but I want you to know I understand just how you feel." According to H. R. Haldeman, one of Nixon's closest advisers, the student killings at Kent State deeply troubled the president.

Yet only a few months later Nixon ordered illegal wiretaps of news professionals. He also reaffirmed his support of Central Intelligence Agency (CIA) surveillance of U.S. citizens and organizations—a policy specifically forbidden by the CIA charter—and encouraged members of his administration to spy on Democrats planning for the 1972 election campaign. When news of these illegal activities surfaced, one of the most canny politicians in American history found himself the first president since Andrew Johnson to face the likelihood of impeachment proceedings.

Foreign Policy as Conspiracy

Nixon's conduct of foreign policy offered early clues into his political character. Although he had welcomed the publicity surrounding his historic moves toward détente with the Soviet Union and normalized relations with China, Nixon generally handled the nation's foreign affairs in surreptitious fashion. But as opposition to the Vietnam War mounted in Congress, he began to face hard questions about this practice. As early as 1970, Republicans as well as Democrats had condemned covert operations in foreign countries. In response, the president, the Department of State, and the CIA developed plans to tighten security even further. Nixon issued a tough mandate against all leaks of information by government personnel, news specialists, or politicians.

At the time, apart from the highly publicized tour to China, Nixon revealed little about his policy for other parts of the globe. Unknown to most Americans, he accelerated the delivery of arms supplies to foreign dictators, including the shah of Iran, Ferdinand Marcos of the Philippines, and the regime of Pieter William Botha in South Africa. His CIA assistants trained and aided SAVAK, the Iranian secret police force notorious for torturing political dissidents. They also stood behind the South African government in its effort to curtail the activities of the antiapartheid African National Congress. In Latin America, Nixon provided financial assistance and military aid to repressive regimes such as that of Anastasio Somoza of Nicaragua, notorious for its blatant corruption and repeated violations of human rights.

Still more controversial was Nixon's plan to overthrow the legally elected socialist government of Salvador Allende in Chile. With the assistance of non-government agencies, such as the AFL-CIO's American Institute for Free Labor Development, the CIA destabilized the regime by funding right-wing parties, launching demonstrations, and preparing the Chilean army for a coup. In September 1973, a military junta killed President Allende and captured, tortured, or murdered thousands of his supporters. Nixon and Kissinger warmly welcomed the new ruler, Augusto Pinochet, granting him financial assistance to restabilize the country.

Toward the end of Nixon's term, members of Congress who had been briefed on these policies began to break silence, and reports of clandestine operations flooded the media. Several former CIA agents issued anguished confessions of their activities in other countries. More troubling to Nixon, in spite of all his efforts the United States continued to lose ground as a superpower.

The Age of Dirty Tricks

As Nixon approached the 1972 reelection campaign, he tightened his inner circle of White House staff who assisted him in withholding information from the public, discrediting critics, and engaging in assorted "dirty tricks." Circle members solicited illegal contributions for the campaign and laundered the money through Mexican bank accounts. They also formed a secret squad, "the plumbers," to halt the troublesome leaks of information. This team, headed by former CIA agent E. Howard Hunt and former FBI agent G. Gordon Liddy, assisted in conspiracy at the highest levels of government.

The first person on the squad's "hit list" was Daniel Ellsberg, a former researcher with the Department of Defense, who in 1971 had turned over to the press secret documents outlining the military history of American involvement in Vietnam. The so-called Pentagon Papers exposed the role of presidents and military leaders in deceiving the public and Congress about the conduct of the United States in Southeast Asia. Nixon sought to bar publication by the *New York Times*, but the Supreme Court ruled in favor of the newspaper on the basis of the First Amendment. Within weeks, a complete version of the Pentagon Papers became a best-selling book, and in 1972 the *New York Times* won a Pulitzer Prize for the series of articles. Frustrated in his attempt to suppress the report, Nixon directed the Department of Justice to prosecute Ellsberg on charges of conspiracy, espionage, and theft. Meanwhile, Hunt and Liddy, seeking to discredit Ellsberg, broke into the office of his former psychiatrist. They found nothing that would make their target less heroic in the eyes of an increasingly skeptical public, and by 1973 the charges against Ellsberg were dropped after the Nixon administration itself stood guilty of misconduct.

At the same time, Nixon ran a skillful negative campaign charging George McGovern, the liberal Democrat who had won his party's nomination on the first ballot, with supporting "abortion, acid [LSD], and amnesty" for those who had resisted the draft or deserted the armed forces. The Republicans also informed the news media that McGovern's running mate, Senator Thomas Eagleton, had once undergone electric shock therapy for depression, thus forcing his resignation from the Democratic team. Voter turnout fell to an all-time low, and McGovern lost every state but Massachusetts. (Later, when Nixon faced disgrace, bumper stickers appeared reading, "Don't Blame Me, I'm from Massachusetts.")

The Committee to Re-Elect the President (CREEP) enjoyed a huge war chest and spent a good portion on dirty tricks designed to divide the Democrats and discredit them in the eyes of the voting public. The most ambitious plan—wiretapping the Democratic National Committee headquarters—backfired.

On June 17, 1972, a security team had tripped up a group of intruders hired by CREEP to install listening devices in the Washington, D.C., Watergate apartment and office complex where the Democrats were headquartered. The police arrested five men, who were later found guilty of conspiracy and burglary. Although

Nixon disclaimed any knowledge of the plan, two *Washington Post* reporters, Bob Woodward and Carl Bernstein, followed a trail of evidence back to the nation's highest office.

Televised Senate hearings opened to public view more than a pattern of presidential wrongdoing: they showed an attempt to impede investigations of the Watergate case. Testifying before the committee, a former Nixon aide revealed the existence of secret tape recordings of conversations held in the Oval Office. After special prosecutor Archibald Cox refused to allow Nixon to claim executive privilege and withhold the tapes, the president ordered Cox fired. This "Saturday Night Massacre," as it came to be called, further tarnished Nixon's reputation and swelled curiosity about the tapes. On June 24, 1974, the Supreme Court voted unanimously that Nixon had to release the tapes to a new special prosecutor, Leon Jaworski.

The Fall of the Executive

The case against the president gained strength. Although incomplete, the Watergate tapes proved damning. They documented Nixon's ravings against his enemies, including anti-Semitic slurs, and his conniving efforts to harass

With impeachment a certainty in the House of Representatives, President Nixon decided to resign his office. On nation-wide television, on August 8, 1974, he said that it had become apparent that "I no longer have a strong enough political base in the Congress to justify continuing" as the President of the United States. He left Washington, D.C. the next day.

SOURCE: AP/Wide World Photos.

CHRONOLOGY

1964   President Lyndon Johnson calls for "an unconditional war on poverty" in his state of the union address

Tonkin Gulf resolution

The Economic Opportunity Act establishes the Office of Economic Opportunity

Free speech movement gets under way at University of California at Berkeley

Johnson defeats conservative Barry Goldwater for president

1965   President Johnson authorizes Operation Rolling Thunder, the bombing of North Vietnam

Teach-ins begin on college campuses

First major march on Washington for peace is organized

Watts uprising begins a wave of rebellions in black communities

1966   J. William Fulbright publishes *The Arrogance of Power*

Black Panther Party is formed

National Organization for Women (NOW) is formed

1967   Antiwar rally in New York City draws 300,000

Vietnam Veterans against the War is formed

Uprisings in Newark, Detroit, and other cities

Hippie "Summer of Love"

1968   U.S. ground troops levels in Vietnam number 500,000

Tet Offensive in Vietnam, followed by international protests against U.S. policies

Martin Luther King, Jr. is assassinated; riots break out in more than 100 cities

Vietnam peace talks begin in Paris

Robert Kennedy is assassinated

Democratic National Convention, held in Chicago, nominates Hubert Humphrey; "police riot" against protesters

Richard Nixon elected president

American Indian Movement (AIM) founded

1969   Woodstock music festival marks the high tide of the counterculture

Stonewall Riot in Greenwich Village sparks the gay liberation movement

Apollo 11 lands on the moon

1970   U.S. incursion into Cambodia sparks campus demonstrations; students killed at Kent State and Jackson State universities

Women's Strike for Equality marks the fiftieth anniversary of the woman suffrage amendment

1971   Lieutenant William Calley, Jr. court-martialed for My Lai Massacre

New York Times starts publishing the Pentagon Papers

1972   Nixon visits China and Soviet Union

SALT I limits offensive intercontinental ballistic missiles

Intruders attempting to "bug" Democratic headquarters in the Watergate complex are arrested

Nixon is reelected in a landslide

Nixon orders Christmas Day bombing of North Vietnam

1973   Paris Peace Agreement ends war in Vietnam

FBI seizes Indian occupants of Wounded Knee, South Dakota

Watergate burglars tried; congressional hearings on Watergate

CIA destabilizes elected Chilean government, which is overthrown

Vice President Spiro T. Agnew resigns

1974   House Judiciary Committee adopts articles of impeachment against Nixon

Nixon resigns the presidency

private citizens through federal agencies. The tapes also proved that Nixon had not only known about plans to cover up the Watergate break-in but had ordered it. The news media enjoyed a field day with the revelations. In July 1974, the House Judiciary Committee adopted three articles of impeachment, charging Nixon with obstructing justice.

Charges of executive criminality had clouded the Nixon administration since his vice president had resigned in disgrace. In 1972 Spiro Agnew had admitted accepting large kickbacks while serving as governor of Maryland. Pleading no contest to this and to charges of federal income tax evasion, Agnew had resigned from office in October 1973. Gerald Ford, a moderate Republican representative from Michigan, had replaced him and now stood in the wings while the president's drama unfolded.

Facing certain impeachment by the House of Representatives, Richard Nixon became, on August 9, 1974, the first U.S. president to resign from office.

CONCLUSION

The resignations of Richard Nixon and Spiro Agnew brought little to relieve the feeling of national exhaustion that attended the Vietnam War. U.S. troops had pulled out of Vietnam in 1973 and the war officially ended in 1975, but bitterness lingered over the unprecedented—and, for many, humiliating—defeat. Morover, confidence in the government's highest office was severely shaken. The passage of the War Powers Act in 1973, written to compel any future president to seek congressional approval for armed intervention abroad, dramatized both the widespread suspicion of presidential intentions and a yearning for peace. But the positive dream of community that had inspired Johnson, King, and a generaton of student activists could not be revived. No other vision took its place.

In 1968 seven prominent antiwar protesters had been brought to trial for allegedly conspiring to disrupt the Democratic National Convention in Chicago. Just a few years later, the majority of Americans had concluded that presidents Johnson and Nixon had conspired to do far worse. They had intentionally deceived the public about the nature and fortunes of the war. This moral failure signaled a collapse at the center of the American political system. Since Dwight Eisenhower left office warning of the potential danger embedded in the "military-industrial complex," no president had survived the presidency with his honor intact. Watergate, then, appeared to cap the politics of the cold war, its revelations only reinforcing futility and cynicism. The United States was left psychologically at war with itself.

REVIEW QUESTIONS

1. Discuss the events that led up to and contributed to U.S. involvement in Vietnam. How did U.S. involvement in the war affect domestic programs?

2. Discuss the reasons the protest movement against the Vietnam War started on college campuses. Describe how these movements were organized and how the opponents of the war differed from the supporters.

3. Discuss the programs sponsored by Johnson's plan for a Great Society. What was their impact on urban poverty in the late 1960s?

4. What was the impact of the assassinations of Martin Luther King, Jr. and Robert Kennedy on the election of 1968? How were various communities affected?

5. How were the "politics of identity" movements different from earlier civil rights organizations? In what ways did the various movements resemble one another?

6. Why did Richard Nixon enjoy such a huge electoral victory in 1972? Discuss his foreign and domestic policies. What led to his sudden downfall?

RECOMMENDED READING

John A. Andrew III, *Lyndon Johnson and the Great Society* (1998). An assessment of the Great Society, with special emphasis on the two major issues of civil rights and poverty.

Keith Beattie, *The Scar That Binds: American Culture and the Vietnam War* (1998). Examines memoirs, war novels, films, and the Vietnam Veterans Memorial to discuss the cultural legacy of the war.

Alexander Bloom, ed., *Long Time Gone: Sixties America Then and Now* (2001). Ten essays covering various aspects of the social and political movements of the 1960s.

Jane F. Gerhard, *Desiring Revolution. Second Wave Feminism and the Rewriting of American Sexual Thought, 1920–1982* (2001). Discusses the background of the feminist side of the sexual revolution.

Michael H. Hunt, *Lyndon Johnson's War: America's Cold War Crusade in Vietnam, 1945–1968* (1996). Tracks Johnson's decisions to wage all-out war in Vietnam.

Rebecca E. Klatch, *A Generation Divided: The New Left, the New Right, and the 1960s* (1999). Compares and contrasts the respective roles of Students for a Democratic Society and the conservative Young Americans for Freedom on college campuses.

Joan Morrison and Robert K. Morrison, eds., *From Camelot to Kent State: the Sixties Experience in the Words of Those Who Lived It* (2001). A collection of 59 oral histories with a range of people who lived through the 1960s.

Joseph Tilden Rhea, *Race Pride and the American Identity* (1997). Examines American Indians, Asian Americans, Latinos, and African Americans in their search for recognition.

Ruth Rosen, *The World Split Open: How the Modern Women's Movement Changed America* (2000). Discusses the impact of women's liberation on American politics, business, and family life.

Anthony Summers, *The Arrogance of Power: The Secret World of Richard Nixon* (2000). A popular biography of Nixon's life from his early political career in California through his presidency.

Marilyn B. Young, *The Vietnam Wars, 1945–1990* (1991). An excellent overview of the involvement of the French and the American military and diplomatic forces in Vietnam from the 1910s to 1975.

▶ MEDIA RESOURCES

U.S. HISTORY DOCUMENTS CD-ROM

The Struggle for Social Change

29-4 National Organization for Women, Statement of Purpose (1966)

29-5 The Gay Liberation Front, Come Out (1970)

29-6 Swann v. Charlotte-Mecklenburg Board of Education (1971)

29-7 Roe v. Wade (1973)

29-8 Ione Malloy, Southie Won't Go (1975)

The Changing Liberal State

28-9 Stokely Carmichael and Charles Hamilton, from Black Power (1967)

28-10 Donald Wheeldin, "The Situation in Watts Today" (1967)

28-11 Vietnamization (1969)

COMPANION WEBSITE HIGHLIGHTS

To view an exploration, enter one of the URLs below in your browser.

Web Explorations

Urban Uprisings, 1965–1968
http://www.prenhall.com/faragher/map29.1
Major Indian Reservations, 1976
http://www.prenhall.com/faragher/map29.2

Additional Interactive Maps

To access the maps, go to this chapter's resources at http://www.prenhall.com/faragher

Antiwar Protests on College and University Campuses, 1967–1969, page 910

The Southeast Asian War, page 917

The Election of 1968, page 929

HISTORY RESOURCE CENTER

To find the resources listed below, go to http://www.prenhall.com/historyresourcecenter

Documents

Lyndon B. Johnson, Commencement Address at Howard University (1965)

Lyndon B. Johnson, Remarks upon Signing the Immigration Bill (1965)

Images

Civilian Casualities in Vietnam

Environmental Worries, 1973

Job training at Cabrini Green in Chicago

Nixon's Cabinet

President Nixon Meets with China's Communist Party Leader, Mao Tse-Tung, 1971

Rand, West Virginia, 1973

Securing Deo Mang Pass

The Inauguration of Richard Nixon

Vietnam

Voter Registration Drive, Chicago, 1973

Working Women

EXPLORING AMERICA

RACHEL CARSON

http://www.prenhall.com/faragher/rachelcarson

What was killing the songbird population of the United States after World War II? Who was Rachel Carson and what was the meaning of the title of her book, *Silent Spring*? What caused the Cuyahoga River to burst into flames? What was the impact of Carson's work? *Rachel Carson* examines the rise of the environmental movement after the publication of her expose on the danger of chemical pesticides such as DDT? The module uses Carson's book as a springboard to examine environmental issues and the rise of the environmental movement over the last four decades. It also discusses the consequences of chemical warfare and past everyday practices that show the need to be aware of how business and science have sought to control the environment.

Rachel Carson uses diverse examples to depict the need for environmental awareness as it discusses various aspects of a major theme of American history, the interaction of people and the natural environment. News releases, newspaper stories, the views of former Vice

President Al Gore, an excerpt from Rachel Carson, and assorted visual images show how environmental concerns reach into almost every aspect of life, including the fitting of shoes. The content of the module is put into historical perspective by the chronology.

Reflect and Respond

1. Did the real threat of "silent springs" shock Americans into awareness? Why did such a poetic description of science have such profound effects?

2. If there are limits to humanity's power to harm itself, what might those be? What is the role of a federal government in the applications of science?

3. Did it matter for the work Carson did that she was female? How and why, or why not? What long-term consequences might there be on behalf of gender equity?

4. What would have happened had *Silent Spring* never been written?

✓ Check it out

Chronology

The chronology traces the development of the environmental movement from the publication of *Silent Spring* to the present. It shows how a combination of public activism and government legislation fueled

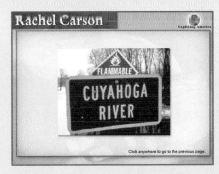

the "green revolution." The international recognition of the importance of the movement and its achievement are underscored by the winning of the Nobel Peace Prize to a major leader of the "green revolution." It also shows that environmentalism remains a major issue today.

This exploration is also available on the *Exploring America* CD-ROM.

THE CONSERVATIVE ASCENDANCY

▶ 1974–1987

Wayne Thiebaud, *Urban Freeways*, 1979–80. Oil on canvas. 44″ × 36″. Allan Stone Gallery, New York.

AMERICAN COMMUNITIES

Grass Roots Conservatism in Orange County, California

I N 1962 BEE GATHRIGHT, A BROWNIE LEADER AND MOTHER OF THREE young girls, listened to a neighbor's casual request. Would she allow the patio of her suburban Garden Grove home to be used for a meeting bringing together neighbors to hear a talk about liberalism and conservatism by a man from the nearby Knott's Berry Farm Freedom Center? Gathright agreed and found the meeting to be a revelation: "This is when I discovered that I was a conservative," she recalled three decades later. She soon arranged for the speaker to address a larger audience at the local public school. Gathright began to read widely in books and newspapers "because I began to hear that the Communists were going to bury us, were going to take over the world . . . I was afraid." She convinced her skeptical husband Neil, an aerospace engineer, to share her new-found activism. They attended study groups and soon joined the California Republican Assembly, a volunteer organization dedicated to electing conservatives to office. In 1964 the Gathrights' home served as a local headquarters for the presidential campaign of conservative Arizona Senator Barry Goldwater. After winning the Republican nomination Goldwater lost the election to President Lyndon Johnson in one of the biggest landslides in American electoral history. Most political commentators and analysts believed Goldwater's crushing defeat proved that "far Right" conservatism had little future in American politics.

Orange County in the 1960s and 1970 had thousands of "kitchen table" activists like the Gathrights, and they began a transformation of American conservatism and American politics that would culminate in the election of Ronald Reagan as president in 1980. Most of them were middle-class men and women, including large numbers of professionals and people with small businesses. Many were recent migrants to California, attracted by job opportunities in aerospace. Bee Gathright herself had arrived after World War II from Iowa, taking a job as an executive secretary at Douglas Aircraft in Santa Monica. Orange County's 800 square miles lie at the geographic center of the Southern California basin, and large lemon and orange groves dominated the economy until the 1940s. The Second World War and Cold War defense-related spending accelerated Orange County's growth as companies like Hughes Aircraft, Autonetics, and Beckman Instruments created over 30,000 new manufacturing jobs in defense and electronics between 1950 and the early 1960s. The strong demand for housing spurred a highly profitable construction boom and a roaring real estate market. By 1960, over 700,000 people lived in Orange County, an increase of nearly 400 percent since 1940, and the population doubled again to almost 1.5 million by 1970.

While Barry Goldwater's 1964 campaign had ignited great enthusiasm in Orange County, his national defeat forced conservatives to consider how they might shed the "extremism" label and put more emphasis on winning office. In 1966 they succeeded in electing Ronald Reagan as governor. A former Hollywood actor and New Deal liberal, Reagan had evolved in the 1950s into an effective conservative spokesman and a prominent Republican Party activist. His gubernatorial campaign stressed limiting state support for welfare and other social services, while expanding state power to enforce law and order.

Reagan's electoral success in California, as well as Richard Nixon's election as president in 1968, signaled an important new turn for American conservatives in the 1970s. They still championed anticommunism, but no longer engaged in the kind of loose talk about using nuclear weapons that had hurt Goldwater. They attacked the growth of "big government," but no longer spoke openly about repealing popular New Deal programs like Social Security. Instead, they responded to the concerns over "social issues" that increasingly troubled and mobilized Orange County's grass-roots activists. These issues were largely defined by a "backlash" against the antiwar movement, counterculture, feminist activism, and urban riots, and an emphasis on so-called family issues, in which opposition to sex education, obscenity, abortion rights, and gay liberation were all linked together. On the economic side, conservatives began to tap a deep well of resentment over rising property taxes and high inflation.

Two of the central themes of this new conservatism found powerful expression in Orange County, and resonated with millions of Americans well beyond it. One was the so-called tax revolt led by Howard Jarvis, a flamboyant campaigner long active in Southern California conservative circles. Saying he had been energized and inspired by local taxpayer-protest meetings, Jarvis told his supporters, "Lower taxes and less government became my holy grail. . . . The only way to cut government spending is not to give them the money in the first place." Jarvis relied on local networks to gather 1.3 million signatures to get his Proposition 13 on the ballot—a constitutional amendment that slashed the property tax rate from 3% to 1% of a home's market value, and strictly limited future tax increases. After its passage in 1978, the "tax revolt" soon spread to other states and attracted millions to the conservative message of limiting government and lowering taxes.

Orange County was a center of the second new force reshaping conservatism, the spectacular growth of "born again" evangelical Christianity. Fundamentalist sects had long been associated with the rural poor of the South. But Orange County's religious revival demonstrated how educated professionals and middle class suburbanites were also turning to "born again" Christianity in their search for spirituality and meaning, as a rejection of "permissiveness," and as a way to assert order amidst rapid cultural and social change. One of the most successful fundamentalist ministers was the Reverend Chuck Smith, who pioneered the use of Christian folk music, adopted countercultural symbols and motifs, and conducted mass ocean baptisms in Corona del Mar. By 1978 his mother church in Costa Mesa, Calvary Chapel, had 25,000 members. They found community not only in Sunday services but in a wide range of tightly organized activities: Bible study groups, summer retreats, "singles' fellowships," prayer breakfasts, and "Christian" consumer culture, which allowed people to simultaneously embrace faith, modern business techniques, and worldly goods.

The political implications of the new evangelicalism became clear by the late 1970s. Most fundamentalist preachers tied their sermons and prophesies to conservative political themes, especially fears about the decline of morality and of American power in the world. Reverend Chuck Smith warned that "the decline of the economy and government of the United States will open the doors to the rise of the anti-Christ to world power."

Newly politicized Christian voters worked diligently to elect Ronald Reagan President in 1980. In Orange County they helped Reagan get 68 percent of the vote, the most lopsided victory of any large county in the nation. For Bee Gathright, the former Goldwater supporter who by then had shifted her energies to Christian missionary work, Reagan's victory provided a national vindication of her years of grass-roots activism. For her, as for so many others in Orange County, the "Christian movement" and the conservative movement had become one and the same. ▪

Orange County

KEY TOPICS

- Structural shifts in the economy
- The Ford and Carter presidencies
- Crisis in the cities and environment
- Community politics and the rise of the New Right

- Iran hostage crisis
- The Reagan Republican presidential victory
- Reagan's domestic and foreign policies
- The growth of inequality

THE OVEREXTENDED SOCIETY

In the 1970s Americans faced an unfamiliar combination of skyrocketing prices, rising unemployment, and low economic growth. Economists termed this novel condition "stagflation." The annual rate of economic growth slowed by almost one-quarter from its robust 3.2 percent average of the 1950s. By 1975, the unemployment rate had reached nearly 9 percent, its highest level since the Great Depression, and it remained close to 7 percent for most of the rest of the decade. Inflation, meanwhile, reached double-digits.

The United States had come to a turning point in its economic history. Emerging from World War II as the most prosperous nation in the world and retaining this status through the 1960s, the country suddenly found itself falling behind western Europe and Japan. Polls conducted at the end of the 1970s revealed that a majority of Americans believed that conditions would worsen.

The gloomy economy shadowed the nation's political leaders. Republican Gerald Ford and Democrat Jimmy Carter promised little and, as far as many voters were concerned, delivered less. Neither managed to secure a second term in the White House.

A Troubled Economy

In October 1973 gasoline prices nearly doubled, jumping from 40 to nearly 70 cents per gallon. Gas lines grew up to four miles long, and fistfights broke out among frustrated motorists. Several states responded to the shortage by introducing rationing programs.

The oil crisis began suddenly, although it had been decades in the making. The United States, which used about 70 percent of all oil produced in the world, had found the domestic supply sufficient until the late 1950s. But rising demand had outstripped national re-

serves, and by 1973 the nation was importing one-third of its crude oil, mainly from the Middle East. In that year, following the Arab-Israeli War, oil prices skyrocketed. On October 17, the Organization of Petroleum Exporting Countries (OPEC), a cartel of mainly Arab oil producers, announced an embargo on oil shipments to Israel's allies, including the United States. A few weeks later, President Nixon announced, "We are heading toward the most acute shortage of energy since World War II."

The president responded to the embargo by creating an "energy czar" and paving the way for the creation of the Department of Energy in 1977. He ordered a 10 percent reduction in air travel and appealed to Congress to lower speed limits on interstate highways to 55 miles per hour (incidentally reducing highway deaths in the process), and to extend daylight-saving time into the winter months. Many state governments introduced their own programs, turning down the thermostats in public buildings to a chilly 68 degrees, reducing nonessential lighting, and restricting hours of service.

With the cost of gasoline, oil, and electricity up, many other prices also rose, from apartment rents and telephone bills to restaurant checks. As oil prices continued to rise through the 1970s, many Americans also began to look suspiciously at the pricing practices of U.S. oil companies. Whatever the causes, the oil crisis played a major role in the economic downturn, the worst since the Great Depression.

The economic downturn, according to many experts, had deeper roots in the failure of the United States to keep up with the rising industrial efficiency of Western Europe and Japan. As long as American manufacturers faced scant competition from abroad, they had little incentive to update their machinery or to establish management techniques that took full advantage of the skills of younger, more educated employees.

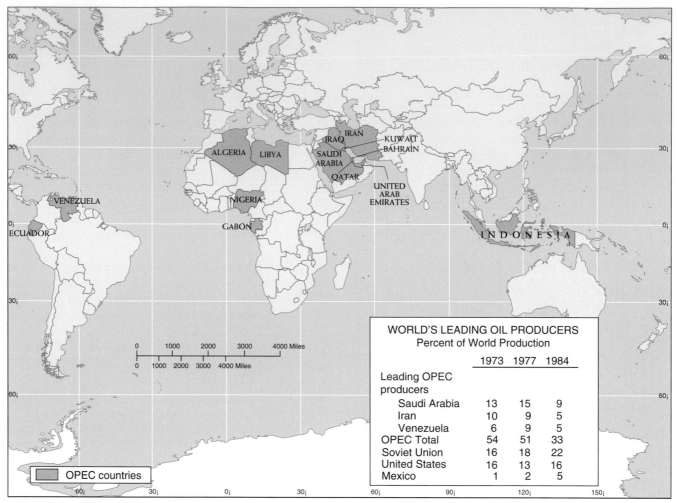

WORLD'S LEADING OIL PRODUCERS			
Percent of World Production			
	1973	1977	1984
Leading OPEC producers			
Saudi Arabia	13	15	9
Iran	10	9	5
Venezuela	6	9	5
OPEC Total	54	51	33
Soviet Union	16	18	22
United States	16	13	16
Mexico	1	2	5

World's Leading Oil Producers

Manufacturers from Asia, Latin America, and Europe now offered consumers cheaper and better products, including automobiles, long considered the monopoly of Detroit. U.S. automakers, determined to reduce costs, turned to "outsourcing"—that is, making cars and trucks from parts cheaply produced abroad and imported into the United States as semifinished materials (which were subject to a lower tariff than finished goods.) In high-tech electronics, the United States scarcely competed against Japanese-produced televisions, radios, tape players, cameras, and computers. An AFL-CIO leader complained that the United States was becoming "a nation of hamburger stands . . . a country stripped of industrial capacity and meaningful work."

The situation in agriculture was still more grim. The huge increase in oil prices translated into higher gasoline and fertilizer costs, forcing farmers to borrow heavily from banks. Soon the high interest rates on borrowed money threw many family farmers into a state of permanent indebtedness. When overseas sales declined at the end of the 1970s, tens of thousands defaulted on loans and lost their farms to banks and credit companies, ending a way of life generations old. High costs and unstable prices offered a gloomy prospect for all but the leaders in corporate-style agribusiness, the 12 percent of farmers who made 90 percent of all farm income.

Blue-Collar Blues

In past decades labor unions had typically responded to inflation by negotiating new contracts or, if necessary, striking for higher pay. But while factories closed, the National Labor Relations Board increasingly ruled in favor of management, making the organization of new union locals far more difficult. Between 1970 and 1982 the AFL-CIO lost nearly 30 percent of its membership. The only real growth took place among public employees, including teachers, civil service workers, and health professionals—all of them dependent on

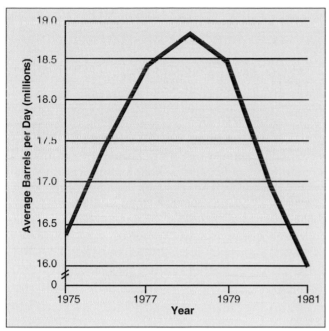

Decline of U.S. Oil Consumption, 1975–1981

SOURCE: Department of Energy, *Monthly Energy Review,* June 1982.

worked as domestics or agricultural laborers in the Southwest. Neither group earned much more than the minimum wage.

Sunbelt/Snowbelt Communities

By the 1970s the Sunbelt offered a rare showplace of American prosperity. It boasted a gross product greater than many nations and more cars, television sets, houses, and even miles of paved roads than the rest of the United States. Large influxes of immigrants from Latin America, the Caribbean, and Asia combined with the shift of Americans from the depressed Northeast to boost the region's population. From 56 million people in 1940, the Sunbelt's population more than doubled to 118 million just four decades later.

This increase had been made possible by a huge outlay of federal funds, including defense spending and the allocation of Social Security funds. The number of residents over the age of sixty-five increased by 30 percent during the 1970s, reaching 26 million by 1980.

sagging public budgets. Union-backed meaures now routinely failed in Congress, despite the Democratic majority.

Typical of hard times, women in increasing numbers sought jobs to support their families. By 1980 more than half of all married women and nearly 60 percent of mothers with children between the ages of six and seventeen were in the labor force. Yet despite these statistical changes, women had lost ground relative to men. In 1955 women earned 64 percent of the average wages paid to men; in 1980 they earned only 59 percent. The reason for this dip was that women were clustered in the clerical and service trades where the lowest wages prevailed.

African American women made some gains. Through Title VII of the Civil Rights Act, which outlawed work place discrimination by sex or race, and the establishment of the Equal Employment Opportunity Commission to enforce it, they managed to climb the lower levels of the job ladder. By 1980, northern black women's median earnings were about 95 percent of white women's earnings. Proportionately, slightly more black women than white were gainfully employed in technical, sales, and administrative jobs.

In contrast, Hispanic women, whose labor force participation leaped by 80 percent during the decade, were restricted to a very few poorly paid occupations. Puerto Ricans found jobs in the garment industry of the Northeast; Mexican Americans more typically

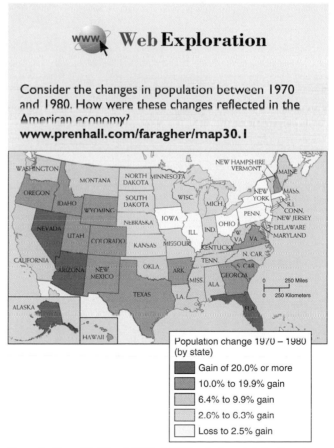

Web Exploration

Consider the changes in population between 1970 and 1980. How were these changes reflected in the American economy?
www.prenhall.com/faragher/map30.1

Population Shifts, 1970–1980   Industrial decline in the Northeast coincided with an economic boom in the Sunbelt, encouraging millions of Americans to head for warmer climates and better jobs.

Armed with retirement packages won decades earlier, huge "golden age" migrations created new communities in Florida, Arizona, and southern California.

The South witnessed a dramatic turnaround in demographic and economic trends. While manufacturing and highly subsidized agribusiness flourished, southern cities reversed the century-long trend of out-migration among African Americans. The Southwest and West changed yet more dramatically. Aided by air conditioning, water diversions, public improvements, and large-scale development, California became the nation's most populous state; Texas moved to third, behind New York. Former farms and deserts were turned almost overnight into huge metropolitan areas by the automobile and suburbs. Phoenix grew from 664,000 in 1960 to 1,509,000 in 1980, Las Vegas from 127,000 to 463,000.

Much of the Sunbelt wealth tended to be temporary or sharply cyclical, producing a boom-and-bust economy of sudden expansion and disordered sprawl. Corporate office buildings in cities such as Houston emptied almost as fast as they filled. Income was also distributed very unevenly. Older Hispanic populations made only modest gains, while recent Mexican immigrants and Indian peoples suffered from a combination of low wages and poor public services. The Sunbelt states concentrated their tax and federal dollars on strengthening police forces, building roads or sanitation systems for the expanding suburbs, and creating budget surpluses, in contrast to eastern and midwestern states that continued to spend significantly on public housing, education, and mass transit,

The "Snowbelt" (or "Rustbelt") states meanwhile suffered severe population losses accompanying the

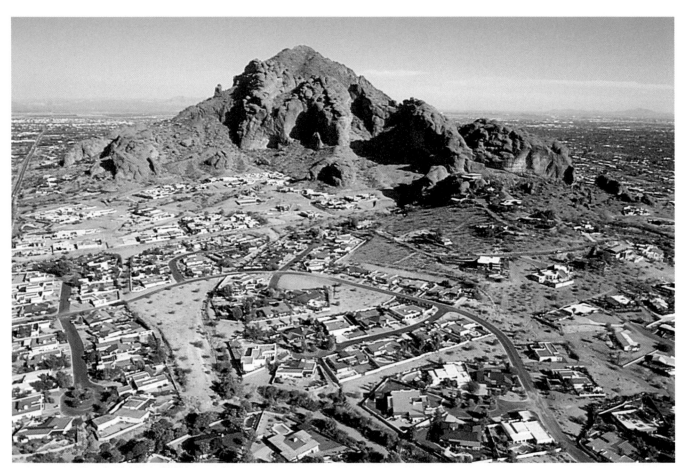

These newly built houses in Phoenix, Arizona, a popular retirement community as well as the state capital, helped accommodate a 55 percent rise in the city's population between 1970 and 1980. Like other burgeoning cities of the Mountain West, Phoenix experienced many urban tensions during this decade, including racial conflict, antagonism between affluent suburbs and the decaying downtown, air pollution, traffic congestion, and strained water supplies.

SOURCE: Aerial view. Photo by Guido Alberto Rossi. Getty Images, Inc. (233142A)

sharp decline of industry. Of the nineteen metropolitan areas that lost population during the 1970s, all were old manufacturing centers, topped by New York, Cleveland, Pittsburgh, Boston, Philadelphia, and Buffalo.

A feeling of defeat intensified in the aging industrial cities of the Monogahela River valley in western Pennsylvania. Since the late nineteenth century, "Mon Valley" had proudly stood as the steelmaking center of the nation and much of the world. With the decline of steel production, however, major firms such as U.S. Steel increased investments in overseas mining and mineral processing companies, some of which worked closely with foreign steelmakers. This policy of "disinvestment" had a devastating impact on the people and communities who for generations had helped build the nation's basic industries. During the 1980s the Mon Valley lost 30,000 people, or 10 percent of its population.

The community of Clairton epitomized these conditions. Situated on a hill about fifteen miles from Pittsburgh, Clairton was once a bustling small city, with active Slavic, Italian, and Irish communities. At the end of World War II, its coke works were the largest in the world, and its by-products division made components for thousands of different products. By the mid-1980s, however, Clairton was suffering an unemployment rate of about 35 percent and facing bankruptcy. The entire thirteen-member police force had to be laid off, and a state-appointed trustee took over the city's financial affairs.

New York City offered a still more spectacular example. A fiscal crisis in 1975 forced liberal mayor Abraham Beame to choose between wage freezes for public employees and devastating cuts and layoffs. Eventually, with the municipal government teetering on the brink of bankruptcy, he chose both. In response to cutbacks in mass transit and the deterioration of municipal services, a large sector of the middle class fled. At the same time, the proportion of poor people rose from 15 percent in 1969 to nearly 25 percent fourteen years later.

"Lean Years Presidents": Ford and Carter

Gerald R. Ford and Jimmy Carter presided over not only a depressed economy but a nation of disillusioned citizens. The revelations of the Watergate break-in and Nixon's subsequent resignation as president cast a pall over politics. Replacing Nixon in August 1974, Gerald Ford reassured the public that "our long national nightmare is over"—then quickly pardoned Nixon for all the federal crimes he may have committed. The pardon reinforced public cynicism toward government and Ford in particular. Elections later that year added fifty two Democrats to the House and four to the Senate.

Ford, who issued more vetoes of major bills than any other president in the twentieth century but saw

Congress override most of them, struck most Americans as a pleasant person of modest ability. First Lady Betty Ford was the shining star of the White House. She broke ranks with other Republicans to champion the Equal Rights Amendment. She also won praise for her courage in discussing her mastectomy for breast cancer and her voluntary entry into a substance abuse clinic for a drinking problem. In 1975 *Newsweek* magazine chose her as Woman of the Year.

Ford banked on his incumbency for the 1976 election and welcomed Senator Robert Dole of Kansas as his running mate. Democrats chose Jimmy Carter, a former one term governor of Georgia, who depicted himself as an antipolitician, an outsider, and someone who was independent of the Washington establishment. When Carter told his mother he was running for president, she reportedly asked, "President of what?"

A "born again" Christian, Carter had been born in Plains, Georgia, in 1924. After a rural childhood and service in the navy, he emerged without a career, so poor that he was the first president to have lived in government-subsidized housing. A successful Southern politician, Carter promoted regional development. In seeking the nomination, he declined to call himself a liberal, offering instead personal integrity as his chief qualification for the nation's highest office.

Carter campaigned as a moderate on domestic policy issues. Counting on support from both conservative and southern voters who would ordinarily vote Republican, he defended existing entitlement programs while opposing Senator Edward Kennedy's call for comprehensive health coverage. He capitalized on Ford's unpopular Nixon pardon and, with his running mate Senator Walter Mondale of Minnesota, won with just over 50 percent of the popular vote and a 297-to-240 margin in the Electoral College. Carter won more than 90 percent of the black vote, which provided his margin of victory in Pennsylvania, Ohio, and seven southern states. But apathy proved the next most important factor. A record 46.7 percent of eligible voters, mainly the nation's poor, did not bother to cast ballots.

In office, Carter seemed to many observers enigmatic, even uninterested in the presidency. His most successful innovation, deregulation of the airlines, brought lower fares for millions of passengers. But by freeing banks from congressional control, he inadvertently encouraged bad investments, outright fraud, and a round of disastrous bank failures. Inflation proved to be his worst enemy. As older Americans could recognize, half of all the inflation since 1940 had occurred in just ten years. Interest rates rose, driving mortgages out of reach for many would be home buyers. Rents in many locations doubles, sales of automobiles and other consumer products slumped, and many small businesses went under. Tuition costs skyrocketed along

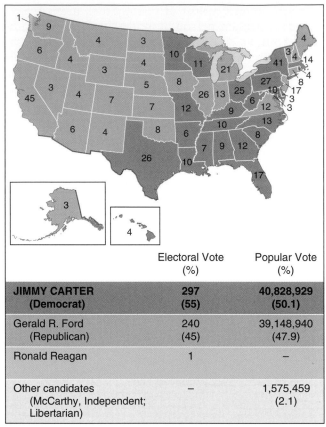

	Electoral Vote (%)	Popular Vote (%)
JIMMY CARTER (Democrat)	**297 (55)**	**40,828,929 (50.1)**
Gerald R. Ford (Republican)	240 (45)	39,148,940 (47.9)
Ronald Reagan	1	–
Other candidates (McCarthy, Independent; Libertarian)	–	1,575,459 (2.1)

The Election of 1976 Incumbent Gerald Ford could not prevail over the disgrace brought to the Republican Party by Richard Nixon. The lingering pall of the Watergate scandal, especially Ford's pardon of Nixon, worked to the advantage of Jimmy Carter, who campaigned as an outsider to national politics. Although Carter and his running mate Walter Mondale won by only a narrow margin, the Democrats gained control of both the White House and Congress.

with unemployment, and many young men and women who could neither afford to go to college nor find a job moved back home. Carter could not deliver on his promise to turn the economy around. By the time he left office in 1980, a majority of those polled agreed that "the people running the country don't really care what happens to you."

COMMUNITIES AND POLITICS

The mass demonstrations of the 1960s gave way in the 1970s to a style of political mobilization centered squarely in communities. Unlike national elections, which after 1968 registered increasing voter apathy, local campaigns brought a great many people to the voting booth and into newly organized voluntary asso-

ciations. "I didn't care so much about my neighborhood until I had children," one city dweller told a sociologist. "I wasn't aware of the various facets of the community. Then came a lot of other things that I began to do as the parent of a child in this neighborhood. We became committed to this area."

The New Urban Politics

In many cities, new groups came into political power. In several college towns, such as Berkeley, California, and Eugene, Oregon, both of which had been centers of political activism during the 1960s, student coalitions were formed to secure seats for their candidates on city councils. In 1973 labor unions, college students, and community groups in Madison, Wisconsin, elected a former student activist to the first of three terms as mayor.

African American candidates scored impressive victories during the 1970s. The newly elected African American mayor of Atlanta, Maynard Jackson, concluded that "politics is the civil rights movement of the 1970s." By 1978, 2,733 African Americans held elected offices in the South, ten times the number a decade earlier. Mississippi, a state where the civil rights movement had encountered violent opposition, had more African American elected officials by 1980 than any other state in the union. Most of these elected officials served on city councils, county commissions, school boards, and law enforcement agencies. But voters elected African American mayors in New Orleans and Atlanta. In other parts of the country, black mayors, such as Coleman Young in Detroit, Richard Hatcher in Gary, and Tom Bradley in Los Angeles, held power along with many minor black officials. Cities with black mayors spent more than other municipalities of similar size on education and social services. They worked hardest to improve community health services and to ensure equity in government employment.

Other racial or ethnic groups advanced more slowly, rarely in proportion to their actual numbers in the population. Mexican Americans had already won offices in Crystal City, Texas, and in 1978 took control of a major city council, in San Antonio, for the first time. They also scored electoral victories in other parts of Texas and in New Mexico and developed strong neighborhood or ward organizations in southern California. Puerto Ricans elected a handful of local officials in New York, mostly in the Bronx. Asian Americans advanced in similar fashion in parts of Hawai'i.

The fiscal crises of the 1970s nevertheless undercut these efforts to reform municipal government. Most new officials found themselves unable to make the sweeping changes they had promised during their campaigns. Community-based job programs could not counteract the effects of factory shutdowns and the disappearance of industrial jobs. Affirmative action programs aroused cries of "reverse discrimination" from angered whites who felt that minorities' progress had been registered at their expense. Conservatives put forward their own candidates, charging that government at all levels favored minorities, the jobless, and criminals over the law-abiding, hard-working, taxpaying majority.

The City and the Neighborhood

The nation's cities inspired a range of responses from residents who chose to resist the pull of the suburbs and from those who simply could not afford to leave. For city dwellers, the city's hospitals, public libraries, symphony orchestras, museums, and art galleries became anchoring institutions requiring public support. Changes in federal policies also encouraged local initiative. The Community Development Act of 1974, signed by President Ford, combined federal grant programs for cities into a single program and put mayors and city managers directly in charge of spending. With grants totaling $8.4 billion over three years, city governments could allocate funds as they saw fit and encourage citizens to take part in local planning. Communities Organized for Public Service (COPS) in San Antonio, Texas, and the Association of Community Organizations for Reform Now (ACORN) in Little Rock, Arkansas, were formed to advise public officials. In other cities, Save the City campaigns engaged residents in defining problems important to the community, such as traffic control, sewerage, and animal control and welfare.

Groups of preservationists organized to save historic buildings and public spaces, to form land trusts for acquiring and refurbishing old houses, and to turn vacant lots into neighborhood parks. In Rhode Island, the Providence Preservation Society worked with city planners and individual donors to restore hundreds of houses. It organized festival tours of neighborhoods to lure prospective buyers, and spurred the formation of similar societies in nearby towns.

Local and national foundations joined federal agencies in funding Community Development Corporations (CDCs) through a series of antipoverty agencies. These community groups promoted "development banks" that would facilitate "sweat equity"—that is, the granting of low-interest mortgage loans to buyers willing to rebuild or refurbish dilapidated housing. They also acted to

Geronimo, 1981, by Victor Orozco Ochoa. During the 1970s public murals appeared in many cities, often giving distinctive expression to a community's racial or ethnic identity. The murals painted in the mid-1970s on the outside of the Centro Cultural de la Raza, in San Diego, were among the most striking. After vandals ruined one section, Ochoa, whose grandmother was Yaqui, replaced it with this enormous representation of Geronimo, surrounded by figures of contemporary Chicano cultural life.

SOURCE: *Untitled*, Geronimo mural. Victor Orozco Ochoa.

prevent local banks from closing when a neighborhood became mainly black. Federal assistance proved vital to maintaining most community-based programs, especially in the late 1970s when cities faced major fiscal crises.

In 1979 President Carter's National Commission on Neighborhoods recommended the strenthening of local institutions "to reorganize our society . . . to a new democratic system of grass-roots involvement." But advocacy groups often learned to their dismay that foundations and federal agencies with money to spend resisted local decision making. While the economy worsened, mortgages moved out of reach for most buyers, and rents in many locations doubled. Local preservationists' dreams sometimes became nightmarish. "Gentrification" often accompanied restoration, with poor residents displaced by the more prosperous Americans who craved the increasingly fashionable old homes.

The Endangered Environment

On March 28, 1979, a series of mechanical problems and judgment errors at the nuclear generating facility at Three Mile Island (TMI), near Harrisburg, Pennsylvania, led to the formation of a dangerously explosive hydrogen bubble and posed the danger of a catastrophic core meltdown. After the news broke, nearly 150,000 residents fled their homes. President and First Lady Rosalynn Carter tried to reassure the stricken community by visiting the site. Ten days later, the Nuclear Regulatory Commission announced that any danger of explosion had passed, but what had seemed an isolated event in one community had already grown into a regional phenomenon with national repercussions. Elevated levels of radioactivity were found in milk supplies several hundred miles away. Massive demonstrations against nuclear power followed the accident, concluding in a rally of more than 200,000 people in New York City. Groups organized in many communites to defeat referendums to fund new nuclear power facilities or rallied around candidates who promised to shut down existing ones. Of the ninety-six under construction and the thirty more planned at the time of the TMI crisis, only a handful were completed.

Earlier in the 1970s, the discovery of high rates of cancer and birth defects in Love Canal, near Buffalo, New York, had offered compelling evidence of a growing danger to many American communities. Here toxic wastes dumped by the Hooker Chemical Laboratory had oozed into basements and backyards, and homemaker Lois Gibbs organized a vigorous publicity campaign to draw attention to the grim situation. Meanwhile, outraged Florida residents realized that the damming of the Everglades for sugar production and housing developments, undertaken by the Army

Corps of Engineers decades earlier, had degraded thousands of acres of wilderness, eliminating natural filtration systems and killing millions of birds and other species.

The roots of the modern environmentalist movement can be traced to the publication of the works of scientist Rachel Carson. In 1962 she published *Silent Spring*, which detailed the devastating effects of DDT and other pesticides. By 1970, opinion polls showed the state of the envronment outranking all other domestic issues. Senator Gaylord Nelson of Wisconsin

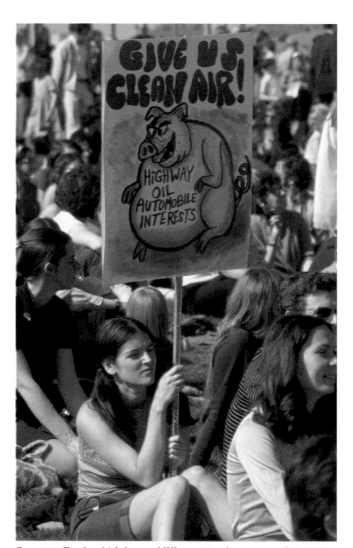

Senator Gaylord Nelson of Wisconsin, hoping to direct some of the energy of the anti–Vietnam War protests into environmental activism, organized the first Earth Day, which was celebrated on April 22, 1970. On that day, 20 million Americans demonstrated for a healthy and sustainable environment. Their protest against the deterioration of the environment led to the creation of the Environmental Protection Agency and marks the birth of the modern environmental movement.

SOURCE: Photo by Dennis Brack. Black Star (470/2584).

and Representative Paul "Pete" McCloskey of California invited Americans to devote an entire day— April 22, Earth Day—to discuss the environment. The response was overwhelming; nearly 20 million Americans gathered in local parks, high schools, and colleges, and at the nation's capital. Many wore green peace symbols and sang "All we are saying is give earth a chance," based on a Beatles' tune.

Even before the energy crisis, many Americans had begun to make changes in their own ways of living. Many families began to save glass bottles and newspapers for reuse. Some began to reduce or eliminate their consumption of beef, since beef is far more costly and uses more resources to produce than grain. Backyard vegetable gardens became popular, as did grocers who stocked organic foods. Nutritionist Frances Moore Lappe's popular *Diet for a Small Planet* (1971) sought to counter the logic of excess, while Barry Commoner's *Closing Circle* (1971) helped make the term "ecology" (the name of the branch of biology that deals with the relationship between organisms and their environment) a synonym for environmental balance (*eco* means "home" in Greek).

The environmentalist movement grew stronger in long-standing organizations, such as the Audubon Society and the Wilderness Society. The Sierra Club, formed in 1892 as a small society of western mountain hikers, grew to 100,000 members in 1970 and to 500,000 over the next decade. New groups sprang up in response to the energy crisis, often devoted to developing renewable energy sources such as solar power. Some, like Greenpeace, sponsored direct action campaigns to halt practices that caused harm to the environment.

Cutting across nearly all population groups and regions, environmentalists reached such traditionally conservative areas as the Deep South with warnings of the dangers of toxic wastes, the destruction of wetlands, and the ruin of fishing industries. Sometimes campaigns succeeded in blocking massive construction projects, such as nuclear energy plants; more often they halted small-scale destruction of a natural habitat or historic urban district. These campaigns made the public more aware of the consequences of private and government decisions about the environment.

Responding to organized pressure groups, Congress passed scores of bills designed to protect endangered species, reduce pollution caused by automobile emissions, limit and ban the use of some pesticides, and control strip-mining practices. The Environmental Protection Agency (EPA), established in 1970, grew to become the federal government's largest regulatory agency, employing more than 10,000 people by the end of the decade.

Environmentalists enjoyed only limited success in bringing about large-scale changes in policy. Cities often avoided congressional mandates for reduction in air pollution by requesting lengthy extensions of deadlines for compliance. Despite the introduction of lead-free gasoline, the air in major metropolitan areas grew no better in the long run because automobile traffic increased at a fast pace. Environmentalists lost an important campaign with the approval of the Alaskan Pipeline, 800 miles of pipe connecting oil fields with refining facilities.

Small-Town America

A host of unresolved problems, ranging from air pollution to rising crime rates to higher taxes, encouraged a massive exodus from the nation's cities. Between 1970 and 1975, for every 100 people relocating to metropolitan areas, 138 moved out. Newer residential communities in small towns and in formerly rural areas grew at a fast pace, attracting retirees and others seeking solace or security.

Government programs such as mortgage guarantees and low-interest financing on individual homes promoted these large "low-density" developments of single-family houses. In many regions, the countryside gradually disappeared into "exurbia," a trend that population experts Peter A. Morison and Judith P. Wheeler attributed to the American "wish to love one's neighbor but keep him at arm's length." Opinion poles suggested that many Americans wanted to live in a small town that was not a suburb but was still no more than thirty miles from a major city.

Soon even small towns developed their own suburbs, usually moderate-income tracts of ranch houses squeezed between older wood-frame colonial or Victorian farmhouses. Federal subsidies for the construction of sewerage and water lines, originally intended to aid rural communities, now became springboards for further development. Ironically, shopping malls on former farmland drained commercial activity from the small-town centers, channeling the benefits of development to chain stores rather than to local merchants.

Some communities organized to oppose these trends. Following the publication of E. F. Schumacher's *Small Is Beautiful* (1973), groups of people began to question the advantages of "bigness" and its toll on humanity. They principally sought to rebuild communities on a smaller scale and therefore campaigned to preserve the environment by opposing further development and the construction of new highways, nuclear energy generating plants, and toxic dumps. In Vermont, liberal "hippies" and "back-to-the-landers" joined traditionally conservative landowners to defeat a 1974 gubernatorial plan to attract developers. In other locales, such as the Berkshire Mountains of Massachusetts, community land trusts were organized to encourage common ownership of the land. "From coast to coast," the *New York Times* reported, "environmental, economic and social pressures have impelled hundreds of cities and towns to adopt limitations on the size and character of their populations." To encourage public discussion of land-use issues, President Carter created the Small Community and Rural Development Policy group. Many small towns, especially those in the Plains states, meanwhile collapsed from failing family farms and small businesses. Leaving rundown schools, inadequate medical care, and abandoned movie theaters and grocery stores. Only nursing homes and funeral parlors continued to thrive.

THE NEW CONSERVATISM

Sizable numbers of taxpayers resented the tax hikes required to fund government programs that benefited minorities, provided expanded social services for the poor, or protected the environment at the expense of economic development. In 1978 California voters staged a "taxpayers' revolt," approving Proposition 13, which cut property taxes and government revenues for social programs and education. In other economically hard-pressed urban areas, white voters who resented the gains made by African Americans and Latinos formed a powerful backlash movement. By the end of the decade, the only substantial increase in voter participation was among conservatives.

The New Right

The largest New Right constituency united behind major conservative religious and political leaders to promote what they viewed as traditional values. By the end of the 1970s, more than 50 million Americans had joined the ranks of evangelical Christians. One year after Billy Graham published his fast-selling *How to Be Born Again* (1977), 40 percent of all Americans, including the nation's president, reported that they were indeed "born again." Although not all evangelical Christians were Republicans or conservative, this expanding group became the backbone of key organizations such as the National Conservative Political Action Committee and, most especially, the Moral Majority. The Reverend Jerry Falwell formed the Moral Majority as a political lobbying group to advocate tough laws against homosexuality and pornography, to promote a reduction of government services (especially welfare payments to poor families), and to increase spending for a stronger national defense. Together these groups raised the funds to wage additional well-publicized campaigns against abortion, the ERA, and the busing of schoolchildren.

Conservative political organizations were among the first to employ direct mail campaigns. Greater success came from the work of televangelists. By the late 1960s,

televangelists such as Pat Robertson and Jim Bakker frequently mixed conservative political messages with appeals to prayer. Falwell's *Old-Time Gospel Hour* was broadcast over 200 television stations and 300 radio stations each week. Christian broadcasters generally endorsed Falwell's faith that "the free-enterprise system is clearly outlined in the Book of Proverbs of the Bible." By the end of the 1970s more than 1,400 radio stations and thirty TV stations specialized in religious broadcasts that reached an audience of perhaps 20 million weekly.

Jesse Helms was the first major politician to appeal directly to the New Right and to build his own impressive fundraising empire with its help. A North Carolina

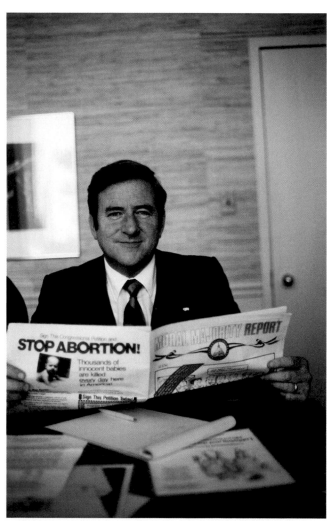

In the aftermath of the *Roe v. Wade* decision in 1973, the televangelist Jerry Falwell became increasingly political in his sermons on the *Old-Time Gospel Hour.* He declared a "war against sin" by opposing abortion, homosexual rights, pornography, and crime, and by appealing for financial contributions he generated an annual income of more than $100 million. The Reverend Falwell reached his peak in the early 1980s and was, at that time, the most visible fundamentalist preacher in the United States.

SOURCE: Photo by Eve Arnold. Magnum Photos, Inc. (PER06ARE007001)

journalist who had fought the integration of public schools and defended the Ku Klux Klan, he had often attacked Martin Luther King, Jr. as a Communist-influenced demagogue. Helms entered national politics as a Goldwater supporter in 1964 and ran for the Senate in 1972. Carried to victory with Nixon's success in North Carolina, Helms immediately promoted a host of conservative bills as well as federal support for regional tobacco interests. He introduced legislation to allow automobile owners or dealers to disconnect mandatory antipollution devices. He also defended the Watergate break-ins as necessary to offset the "traitorous conduct" of antiwar activists. By 1978 he had raised $8.1 million, the largest amount ever, for his successful reelection campaign. Helms built a powerful, loyal, and wealthy following.

The political surge rightward gained intellectual respectability from neoconservatives, former liberals who blamed the social movements of the 1960s for the demoralization of the nation. The American Enterprise Institute and the Heritage Foundation, heavily supported by major corporations, established major research centers for conservative scholars. These and other foundations also funded campus publications attacking welfare programs, affirmative action, and environmentalism.

Anti-ERA, Antiabortion

The New Right rallied support for a balanced budget amendment to the Constitution, sought unsuccessfully to return prayer to the public schools, and endorsed the Supreme Court's approval of the death penalty in 1977. Practically all the New Right's campaigns emphasized restoration of the "traditional family values" undermined, they alleged, by the women's liberation movement.

The defeat of the Equal Rights Amendment (ERA) stood at the top of the New Right agenda. Approved by Congress in March 1972, nearly fifty years after its introduction (see Chapter 22), the ERA stated: "Equality of rights under the law shall not be denied or abridged by the United States or by any State on account of sex." Endorsed by both the Democratic and Republican Parties, the amendment appeared likely to be ratified by the individual states. Nearly all mainstream women's organizations, including the Girl Scouts of America, endorsed the ERA. Even the AFL-CIO retracted its long-standing opposition and endorsed the amendment.

Cued by this groundswell of support in favor of the ERA, the New Right swung into action. Phyllis Schlafly, a self-described suburban housewife and popular conservative lecturer, headed the STOP ERA campaign, describing the amendment's supporters as "a bunch of bitter women seeking a constitutional cure for their personal problems." She warned that the ERA would deprive women of their true rights "such as the right of

a wife to be supported by her husband" and that it would lead to unisex public toilets and homosexual marriages. Hostile to "Big Government," antiratificationists believed that the ERA would allow the state to intrude further into the private domain of family by requiring massive changes in laws concerning marriage, divorce, and child custody.

The New Right mounted large, expensive campaigns in each swing state and overwhelmed pro-ERA resources. Although thirty-five states had ratified the ERA by 1979, the amendment remained three votes short of passage. Despite a three-year extension, the ERA died in 1982.

The New Right also waged a steady campaign against abortion, which the women's liberation movement had defined as a woman's right rather than a mere medical issue. In 1973 the Supreme Court had ruled in *Roe* v. *Wade* that state laws decreeing abortion a crime during the first two trimesters of pregnancy constituted a violation of a woman's right to privacy. Opponents of *Roe* rallied for a constitutional amendment defining conception as the beginning of life and arguing that the "rights of the unborn" supersede a woman's right to

---

Asked of those who said they had heard of or read about the Equal Rights Amendment: Do you favor or oppose this amendment?

Favor	58%
Oppose	24%
No opinion	18%

By Sex

Male

Favor	63%
Oppose	22%
No opinion	15%

Female

Favor	54%
Oppose	25%
No opinion	21%

Interviewing Date 3/7–10/1975, Survey #925-K

Gallup Poll on the Equal Rights Amendment, 1975 By 1973 thirty of the thirty-eight states required to ratify the ERA had done so. Although the amendment ultimately failed to achieve ratification and died in June 1982, public support was strong. In the 1976 presidential campaign, the platforms of both Democrats and Republicans included planks favoring its passage.

SOURCE: *The Gallup Poll: Public Opinion, 1935–1974* (New York: Random House, 1974).

Would you favor or oppose a law that would permit a woman to go to a doctor to end pregnancy at any time during the first three months?

Favor	40%
Oppose	50%
No opinion	10%

Interviewing Date 11/12–17/1969, Survey #793-K, Question #4, Index #54

The United States Supreme Court has ruled that a woman may go to a doctor to end pregnancy at any time during the first three months of pregnancy. Do you favor or oppose this ruling?

Favor	47%
Oppose	44%
No opinion	9%

Interviewing Date 3/8–11; 3/15–18/1974, Survey #894-K; 895 -K

Gallup Polls on Abortion: 1969, 1974 During the 1960s, numerous American women began to demand control over their own reproductive processes and the repeal of legislation in place in all fifty states rendering abortion illegal. The American Institute of Public Opinion surveyed Americans in 1969, when abortion was still illegal, and again in 1974, one year after *Roe* v. *Wade,* the Supreme Court ruling that struck down state laws prohibiting abortion during the first three months of pregnancy.

SOURCE: *The Gallup Poll: Public Opinion, 1935–1974* (New York: Random House, 1974).

control her own body. The Roman Catholic Church organized the first antiabortion demonstrations after the Supreme Court's decision and sponsored the formation of the National Right to Life Committee, which claimed 11 million members by 1980.

Antiabortion groups also picketed Planned Parenthood counseling centers, intimidating potential clients. They rallied against government-subsidized day-care centers and against sex education programs in public schools. A small minority turned to more extreme actions and bombed dozens of abortion clinics.

"The Me Decade"

The shift in the political winds of the 1970s registered not only the rise of the New Right but also the disengagement of a sizable number of Americans from politics altogether. In 1976 novelist Tom Wolfe coined the phrase the "Me Decade" to describe an era obsessed with personal well-being and emotional security. Health foods and diet crazes, a mania for physical fit-

ness, and a quest for happiness through therapy involved millions of middle-class Americans. Historian Christopher Lasch provided his own label for this enterprise in the title of his best-selling book *The Culture of Narcissism: American Life in an Age of Diminishing Expectations* (1978). "After the political turmoil of the sixties," he observed, "Americans have returned to purely personal preoccupations."

The rise of the "human potential movement" provided a vivid example of this trend. The most successful was Erhard Seminars Training (EST), a self-help program blending insights from psychology and mysticism. Founded by Werner Erhard (a former door-to-door seller of encyclopedias), the institute taught individuals to form images of themselves as successful and satisfied. Through sixty hours of intensive training involving playacting and humiliation, participants learned one major lesson: "You are the one and only source of your experience. You created it." Priced at $400 for a series of two weekend sessions, EST peaked at 6,000 participants per month, grossing $25 million in revenue in 1980.

Transcendental meditation (TM) promised a shortcut to mental tranquility and found numerous advocates among Wall Street brokers, Pentagon officials, and star athletes. Techniques of TM were taught in more than 200 special teaching centers and practiced by a reputed 350,000 devotees.

Religious cults also formed in large numbers during the 1970s. The Unification Church, founded by the Korean Reverend Sun Myung Moon, extracted intense personal loyalty from its youthful disciples, dubbed by the media as "Moonies." Moon's financial empire, which included hundreds of retail businesses and the conservative *Washington Star*, proved highly lucrative and kept his church solvent despite numerous lawsuits. By contrast, Jim Jones's People's Temple, an interracial movement organized in the California Bay Area, ended in a mass murder and suicide when Jones induced more than 900 of his followers to drink cyanide-laced Kool-Aid in a remote retreat in Guyana in 1978.

Popular music expressed and reinforced many of these trends. The songs of community and hope common in the late 1960s gave way to songs of search for more meaningful personal relationships, and to songs of nostalgia, despair, or nihilism. Bruce Springsteen, whose lyrics lamented the disappearance of the white working class, became the decade's most popular new rock artist. At the same time, heavy metal bands such as Kiss, as well as punk and new wave artists underscored themes of decadence and futility. Meanwhile country and western music hit its peak with crossover hits and numerous new all-C&W radio stations. Charismatic stars like Willie Nelson sang melodic refrains reeking of loneliness and nostalgia and appealing to older, white, working-class Americans.

ADJUSTING TO A NEW WORLD

In April 1975 the North Vietnamese struck Saigon and easily captured the city as the South Vietnamese army, now without U.S. assistance, fell apart. All fighting stopped within a few weeks, and Saigon was renamed Ho Chi Minh City. Vietnam was reunited under a government dominated by Communists. For many Americans, this outcome underscored the futility of U.S. involvement in the Vietnam War.

By the mid-1970s a new realism seemed to prevail in U.S. diplomacy. Presidents Ford and Carter, as well as their chief advisers, acknowledged that the cost of fighting the Vietnam War had been too high, speeding the decline of the United States as the world's reigning superpower. The realists shared with dissatisfied nationalists a single goal: "No More Vietnams."

A Thaw in the Cold War

The military defeat in Vietnam forced the makers of U.S. foreign policy to reassess priorities. The United States must continue to defend its "vital interests," declared Ford's secretary of state Henry Kissinger, but must also recognize that "Soviet-American relations are not designed for tests of manhood." Both nations had experienced a decline of power in world affairs. And both were suffering from the already enormous and relentlessly escalating costs of sustaining a prolonged cold war.

At the close of World War II, the United States could afford to allocate huge portions of its ample economic resources to maintaining and enlarging its global interests. Soon, however, military and defense expenses began to grow at a much faster rate than the economy itself. Whereas the Korean War had cost around $69.5 billion, the Vietnam War cost $172.2 billion. But the expenses of military conflicts accounted for only one portion of the defense budget. Clandestine operations, alliance building, and weapons production accounted for trillions of dollars more.

Military spending at this level eventually took its toll on the American economy, especially as the federal government increasingly relied on deficit spending in an attempt to cover the bill. The federal debt, which stood at $257 billion in 1950, had jumped to $908 billion by 1980, and an increasingly large part of the federal budget went to paying just the interest on this debt. At the same time, military spending diverted funds from programs that could have strengthened the economy. The results were disastrous. While the United States endured falling productivity levels and rates of personal savings, and a disappearing skilled workforce, other nations rushed ahead. When Japan and West Germany emerged in the 1970s as potent economic competitors,

Business Week noted that the American "colossus" was "clearly facing a crisis of the decay of power."

Western European nations acted to nudge U.S. foreign policy away from its cold war premises. In 1975, in Helsinki, Finland, representatives of thirty-five nations approved the national boundaries drawn in eastern and western Europe after World War II, and in return the Soviet Union agreed to enact a more liberal human rights policy, including the loosening of restrictions on the emigration of Soviet Jews. Recognizing that the Soviet Union no longer posed a military threat to their national sovereignty—if indeed it ever had—Western leaders also sought to strengthen economic relations between the two major blocs.

The Soviet Union, whose economy suffered even greater setbacks from defense spending, joined the United States in moving toward détente. The signing of SALT I, the first Strategic Arms Limitation Treaty, during Nixon's administration, followed by the U.S. withdrawal from Vietnam, encouraged new efforts to negotiate on strategic arms control. In November 1974, Ford and Soviet leader Leonid Brezhnev met in Vladivostok to set the terms of SALT II, and President Carter secured the final agreement in 1979. However, the treaty failed to win confirmation from the Senate when the Soviet Union invaded Afghanistan in December 1979.

Although repeated conflicts in the third world continued to slow the pace toward détente, leaders in both the United States and the Soviet Union usually recognized that their economic well-being depended on a reduction in defense spending. However haltingly, steps toward reconciliation had to be taken. "If you think you can run the world and then you find out you can't," the aged journalist Walter Lippmann observed, "you withdraw to what you can run."

Foreign Policy and "Moral Principles"

When he took office, President Carter presented his lack of experience in foreign affairs as an asset. "We've seen a loss of morality," he noted, "and we're ashamed." The "soul" of his policy would be an "absolute" commitment to human rights.

Carter condemned policies that allowed the United States to support "right-wing monarchs and military dictators" in the name of anticommunism. In 1976 a powerful human rights lobby pressured Congress to pass a bill that required the secretary of state to report annually on the status of human rights in all countries receiving aid from the United States and to cut off assistance to any country with a record of "gross violations." Carter's secretary of state, Cyrus R. Vance, and the assistant secretary for human rights and humanitarian affairs, Pat Derrian, worked to punish or at least to censure repressive military regimes in Brazil, Argentina, and Chile. For the first time, leading U.S. diplomats spoke out against the South African apartheid regime rather than commending or quietly supporting that government's avid anticommunism.

In line with this policy, Carter attempted to institute reforms at the Central Intelligence Agency (CIA), particularly to halt the blatant intervention in the affairs of foreign governments. He appointed Admiral Stansfield Turner, a Rhodes scholar, as director and ordered a purge of the "rogue elephants" who had pursued covert operations in Southeast Asia during the Vietnam War. "The CIA must operate within the law," Carter insisted. Under Turner, however, these reforms remained incomplete; they later proved temporary.

Carter nearly triumphed in the Middle East. Early in his administration, Carter met privately with Israeli prime minister Menachem Begin to encourage concilia-

tion with Egypt. When negotiations between the two countries stalled in 1978, Carter brought Begin together with Egyptian president Anwar el-Sadat for a thirteen-day retreat at Camp David, Maryland.

The Camp David Accords, signed in September 1978, set the formal terms for peace in the region. Egypt became the first Arab country to recognize Israel's right to exist, as the two nations established mutual diplomatic relations for the first time since the founding of Israel in 1948. In return, Egypt regained control of the Sinai Peninsula, including important oil fields and airfields. In 1979 Begin and Sadat shared the Nobel Prize for Peace.

But disappointment lay ahead. Carter staked his hopes for regional peace on the final achievement of statehood, or at least political autonomy, for Palestinians in a portion of their former lands now occupied by the Israelis. The accords specified that Israel would eventu-

President Carter signs the Middle East Peace Treaty with Egyptian President Anwar Sadat and Israeli Prime Minister Menachem Begin, in Washington, D.C., March 1979. President Carter had invited both leaders to Camp David, the presidential retreat in Maryland, where for two weeks he mediated between them on territorial rights to the West Bank and Gaza Strip. Considered Carter's greatest achievement in foreign policy, the negotiations, known as the Camp David Peace Accords, resulted in not only the historic peace treaty but the Nobel Peace Prize for Begin and Sadat.

SOURCE: CORBIS.

ally return to its approximate borders of 1967. However, although Begin agreed to dismantle some Israeli settlements in the Sinai, the Israeli government continued to sponsor more and more Jewish settlements, expropriating Palestinian holdings. The final status of the Palestinians remained in limbo, as did that of Jerusalem, which many Christians and Muslims felt should be an autonomous holy city. Meanwhile Sadat grew increasingly isolated within the Arab world. In 1981 he was assassinated by Islamic fundamentalists.

Carter scored his biggest moral victory in foreign affairs by paving the way for Panama to assume the ownership, operation, and defense of the Panama Canal Zone. Negotiations with Panama had begun during Johnson's administration, following riots by Panamanians against U.S. territorial rule in their country. Carter pressured the Senate to ratify new treaties in 1978 (by a vote of 68 to 32) that would turn the Panama Canal over to Panama by the year 2000.

But when it came to nations considered vital to U.S. interests, such as South Korea, the Philippines, and El Salvador, Carter put aside his principles to stabilize repressive regimes and dictatorships. In restoring diplomatic relations with the People's Republic of China in January 1979, Carter likewise overlooked the regular imprisonment of dissidents. "The real problem," a U.S. diplomat observed, was that human rights was "not a policy but an attitude."

(Mis)Handling the Unexpected

Mired in problems inherited from his predecessors, Carter often found himself disoriented by contradictory advice. Washington state senator Henry "Scoop" Jackson, for whom Carter had delivered a nominating speech at the 1972 Democratic National Convention, bitterly opposed Carter's appointment of moderate Paul Warnke as chief negotiator for arms' reduction talks with the Soviet Union, urging a harder line toward the Soviets. Carter's Secretary of state Cyrus Vance recommended well-planned negotiations to soothe Soviet–U.S. relations and resolve disagreements with third world nations. But national security adviser Zbigniew Brzezinski, a bitterly anti-Communist Polish exile, adhered to cold war policies and interpreted events in even remote sections of Africa or South America as plays in a zero-sum game: wherever the United States lost influence, the Soviet Union gained, and vice versa. Despite Carter's commitment to human rights, he allowed U.S. policy to resume cold war postures.

In 1979 the overthrow of the brutal Nicaraguan dictatorship of Anastasio Somoza, long-time ally of the United States, left Carter without a successor to support. When the new Sandinista revolutionary government pleaded for help, Congress turned down Carter's request for $75 million in aid to Nicaragua. Meanwhile, in El Salvador, the Carter administration continued to back a repressive government even after the assassination of Oscar Romero, a Catholic archbishop and opposition leader. Following the rape and murder of four U.S. Catholic church women, apparently by the ultraright Salvadoran armed forces trained in the United States, peace activists and other Americans pleaded with Carter to withhold further military aid. Conservatives meanwhile demanded yet more funds to bolster the repressive anti-Communist regime.

African nations vacillated between allying with the United States and courting the Soviet Union. In this tricky political territory, UN ambassador (and former civil rights leader) Andrew Young, the first major African American diplomat assigned to Africa, could not persuade Carter to recognize the antiapartheid government of Angola, which had invited 20,000 Cuban troops to help in its fight against South African–backed rebels. Nor did Carter's and Young's verbal criticisms of the South African regime, unaccompanied by economic sanctions, satisfy black Africans. After Carter fired Young for having met secretly with officials of the Palestine Liberation Organization (PLO), the president proved even less effective in negotiating with antiapartheid leaders.

The Soviet invasion of Afghanistan produced a major stalemate. In December 1979, 30,000 Soviet troops invaded their neighbor to put down a revolt by Islamic fundamentalists against the weakening Soviet-backed government. The invasion succeeded mainly in heating up the civil war, which the American press quickly labeled the "Russian Vietnam." As the war bogged down, Americans heard familiar stories, this time of Soviet soldiers using drugs and expressing disillusionment with their government.

President Carter responded to these events with his own corollary to the Monroe Doctrine. The so-called Carter Doctrine asserted the determination of the United States to protect its interests in yet another area of the world, the Persian Gulf. Carter acted on the advice of Brzezinski, who believed that the Soviet Union would soon try to secure for itself a warm-water port on the gulf, an area rich in oil and now vital to U.S. interests. The president backed up his increasingly hard-line policies by halting exports of grain and high technology to the Soviet Union, supporting Afghani resistance against the Russians, and by cancelling American participation in the 1980 Moscow Olympics.

By the end of Carter's term, conservatives had swamped liberals within the Democratic Party. With the economy still hurting from the effects of cold war spending, Carter called for ever-larger increases in the military budget. He also signed Presidential Directive 59, guaranteeing the production of weapons alleged necessary to win a prolonged nuclear war. The prospect of peace and détente dried up.

The Iran Hostage Crisis

On November 4, 1979, Iranian fundamentalists seized the U.S. embassy in Tehran and held fifty-two American employees hostage for 444 days. This event made President Carter's previous problems seem small by comparison. "I-R-A-N," Rosalynn Carter later wrote. "Those four letters had become a curse to me."

For decades, U.S. foreign policy in the Middle East had depended on a friendly government in Iran. After the CIA had helped to overthrow the reformist, constitutional government and installed the Pahlavi, royal family and the shah of Iran in 1953, millions of U.S. dollars had poured into the Iranian economy and the shah's armed forces. President Carter had toasted the shah for his "great leadership" and overlooked the rampant corruption in government and a well-organized opposition. But, by early 1979, a revolution led by Islamic fundamentalist Ayatollah Ruholla Khomeini had overthrown the shah.

After Carter had allowed Mohammad Reza Pahlavi, the deposed shah, to enter the United States to be treated for cancer in November, a group of Khomeini's followers retaliated, storming the U.S. embassy and taking the American staff as hostages.

Cyrus Vance assured Carter that only negotiations could free the Americans. Caught up in a reelection campaign and lobbied by Brzezinski for decisive action, Carter ordered U.S. military forces to stage a nighttime helicopter rescue mission. But a sandstorm caused some of the aircraft to crash and burn, leaving eight Americans dead, their burned corpses displayed by the enraged Iranians. Short of an all-out attack, which surely would have resulted in the hostages' death, Carter had used up his options.

The political and economic fallout was heavy. Cyrus Vance resigned, the first secretary of state in sixty-five years to leave office over a political difference with the president. The price of oil rose by 60 percent. Carter had failed in the one area he had proclaimed central to the future of the United States: energy. He had also violated his own human rights policy, which was intended to be his distinctive mark on American foreign affairs.

Carter's "Crisis of Confidence"

By 1979 inflation once again soared, and it was clear that Carter's program for economic recovery had failed. In July, with Vice President Walter Mondale increas-

Iranians demonstrate outside the U.S. Embassy in Tehran, raising a poster with a caricature of President Carter. The Iran hostage crisis, which began November 8, 1979, when a mob of Iranians seized the U.S. embassy in Tehran, contributed to Carter's defeat the polls the following year. Fifty-two embassy employees were held hostage for 444 days.

SOURCE: AP/WideWorld Photos.

ingly opposed to his policies and toying with the idea of resigning from office, Carter withdrew with his staff to Camp David to reassess priorities. In his first public speech after the retreat, the president announced that the nation was experiencing a "crisis of confidence," and he called upon the people to change their attitude, to stop wallowing in personal problems, and to show more faith in their leaders.

Carter's "malaise speech," as it was called—although Carter never actually used the term "malaise"—backfired. Many Americans resented the president for heaping blame on the public instead of taking responsibility for his own failures. News analysts now attacked Carter with zeal, breaking stories of minor scandals in his administration and ridiculing the president in various ways. Far from pleasing the public, Carter lost its respect. His prospects for reelection therefore appeared to rest on his conduct of international affairs. If he only could put his human rights policy on a firm ground, move toward lasting peace in the Middle East, or strike a bargain with the Soviets on arms limitation, he might restore voter confidence. If not, his presidency would end after a single term.

Ultimately, Carter's bid for renomination depended more on his incumbency than on his popularity. Until the Iranian incursion, Democrats had been expected to nominate Senator Edward Kennedy, turning aside Carter. But in the face of national humiliation, delegates at the Democratic National Convention unenthusiastically endorsed Carter along with Mondale. On the Republican side, former California governor Ronald Reagan had been building his campaign since his near nomination in 1976. Former CIA director and Texas oil executive George H. W. Bush, more moderate than Reagan, became the Republican candidate for vice president. The Moral Majority placed itself squarely in Reagan's camp, and Senator Jesse Helms's Congressional Club contributed $4.6 million to the campaign.

Reagan repeatedly asked voters, "Are you better off now than you were four years ago?" Although critics questioned Reagan's competence, the attractive, soft-spoken actor shrugged off criticisms while spotlighting the many problems besetting the country.

The Republican ticket cruised to victory. Carter won only 41.2 percent of the popular vote to Reagan's 50.9 percent, 49 votes in the Electoral College to Reagan's 489. The Republicans won control of the Senate for the first time since 1952 and with the largest majority since 1928. Still, barely half of the eligible voters turned out in the 1980 election, bringing Ronald Reagan into office with a mandate of a thin 25 percent.

THE REAGAN REVOLUTION

No other twentieth-century president except Franklin D. Roosevelt has left as deep a personal imprint on American politics as Ronald Reagan. Ironically, Reagan himself began his political life as an ardent New Deal Democrat. Even after his transformation into a conservative Republican, he regularly invoked the words and deeds of FDR and sought to avoid ideological labels. Reagan admired Roosevelt as an inspirational leader who had led the nation through depression and war. But by the time he entered the White House in 1981, Reagan had rejected the activist welfare state legacy of the New Deal era. Following his overwhelming electoral victories in 1980 and 1984, Reagan and his allies tried to reshape the political and social landscape of the nation along conservative lines.

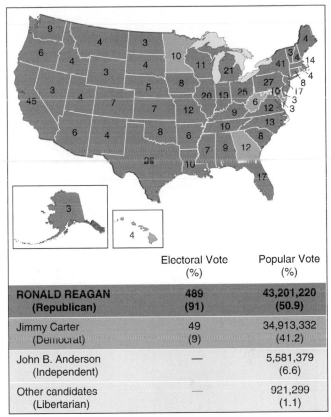

	Electoral Vote (%)	Popular Vote (%)
RONALD REAGAN (Republican)	**489** **(91)**	**43,201,220** **(50.9)**
Jimmy Carter (Democrat)	49 (9)	34,913,332 (41.2)
John B. Anderson (Independent)	—	5,581,379 (6.6)
Other candidates (Libertarian)	—	921,299 (1.1)

The Election of 1980   Ronald Reagan won a landslide victory over incumbent Jimmy Carter, who managed to carry only six states and the District of Columbia. Reagan attracted millions of traditionally Democratic voters to the Republican camp.

The Great Communicator

Ronald Reagan was born in 1911 and raised in the small town of Dixon, Illinois. His father was a salesman and an alcoholic who had a tough time holding a job. His strong-willed mother was a fundamentalist Christian who kept the family together despite frequent moves. A job with the Works Progress Administration for Reagan's father had helped the family survive the hard times of the Great Depression. As a child, Reagan learned to disconnect himself from the difficult scenes at home, taking refuge in his own world of imaginary stories and plays. Encouraged by his mother, he began acting in church plays and in productions at Eureka College, from which he graduated in 1932.

In 1937 Reagan began a Hollywood acting career that lasted for a quarter-century. Although he was never a big star, on screen he appeared tall, handsome, and affable. In later years, he credited his political success to his acting experience. He told one interviewer: "An actor knows two important things—to be honest in what he's doing and to be in touch with the audience. That's not bad advice for a politician either. My actor's

Ronald and Nancy Reagan at the Inaugural Ball, January 20, 1981. The Reagan's, supported by a circle of wealthy conservative friends from the business world and Hollywood, brought a lavish style to the White House that helped define the culture of the 1980s.

SOURCE: Photo by Dennis Brack. Black Star (1-81-8930).

instincts simply told me to speak the truth as I saw it and felt it."

While serving as president of the Screen Actors Guild from 1947 to 1952, Reagan began to distance himself from New Deal liberalism by becoming a leader of the anti-Communist forces in Hollywood. In 1954 he became the host of a new national television program, General Electric Theater, and began a long stint as a national promoter for GE. In this role he made numerous speeches celebrating the achievements of corporate America and emphasizing the dangers of big government, excessive liberalism, and radical trade unions.

Reagan switched his party affiliation to the Republicans and became a popular fundraiser and speaker for the California GOP. He took a leading role in conservative Republican Barry Goldwater's 1964 presidential campaign. A televised address on Goldwater's behalf thrust Reagan himself to national prominence. At the

core of Reagan's conservative message was an attack on big government. He lashed out at a growing bureaucracy and celebrated the achievements of entrepreneurs unfettered by government regulation or aid.

With the financial backing of a group of wealthy, conservative Californians, Reagan defeated Democratic governor Edmund G. Brown in 1966 and won reelection in 1970. As governor, he cut the state welfare rolls, placed limits on the number of state employees, and funneled a large share of state tax revenues back to local governments. He vigorously attacked student protesters and black militants, thereby tapping into the conservative backlash against the activism of the 1960s.

The conservatism that had been growing since Nixon took office now emerged as the mainstream. When Reagan entered the White House in January 1981, his supporters confidently predicted that the "Reagan revolution" would usher in a new age in American political life.

Reaganomics

During the Reagan presidency, supply-side economic theory, dubbed "Reaganomics," dominated the administration's thinking and helped redirect American economic policy. Supply-side theorists urged a sharp break with the Keynesian policies that had been dominant since the New Deal era (see Chapter 24). Keynesians traditionally favored moderate tax cuts and increases in government spending to stimulate the economy and reduce unemployment during recessions. By putting more money in people's pockets, they argued, greater consumer demand would lead to economic expansion. By contrast, supply-siders called for simultaneous tax cuts and reductions in public spending. This combination, they claimed, would give private entrepreneurs and investors greater incentives to start businesses, take risks, invest capital, and thereby create new wealth and jobs. Whatever revenues were lost in lower tax rates would be offset by revenue from new economic growth. At the same time, spending cuts would keep the federal deficit under control and thereby keep interest rates down.

George Gilder, conservative author of the bestselling *Wealth and Poverty* (1981), summarized the supply-side view: "A successful economy depends on the proliferation of the rich." On the political level, supply-siders looked to reward the most loyal Republican constituencies: the affluent and the business community. At the same time, they hoped to reduce the flow of federal dollars received by two core Democratic constituencies: the recipients and professional providers of health and welfare programs.

Reagan quickly won bipartisan approval for two key pieces of legislation based on these ideas. The Economic Recovery Tax Act of 1981 cut income and corporate taxes by $747 billion over five years. For individuals, the act cut taxes across the board. It also reduced the maximum tax on all income from 70 percent to 50 percent, lowered the maximum capital gains tax—the tax paid on profitable investments—from 28 percent to 20 percent, and eliminated the distinction between earned and unearned income. This last measure proved a boon to the small, richest fraction of the population that derives most of its income from rent, dividends, and interest instead of from wages.

With the help of conservative southern and western Democrats in the House, the administration also pushed through a comprehensive program of spending cuts, awkwardly known as the Omnibus Reconciliation Act of 1981. This bill mandated cuts of $136 billion in federal spending for the period 1982–1984, affecting more than 200 social and cultural programs. The hardest-hit areas included federal appropriations for education, the environment, health, housing, urban aid, food stamps, research on synthetic fuels, and the arts. The conservative coalition in the House allowed only one vote on the entire package of spending cuts, a strategy that allowed conservatives to slash appropriations for a wide variety of domestic programs in one fell swoop. One leading House liberal, Democrat Leon Panetta of California, lamented: "We are dealing with over 250 programs with no committee consideration, no committee hearings, no debate, and no opportunity to offer amendments."

While reducing spending on domestic programs, the Reagan administration greatly increased the defense budget. During the 1980 election campaign, Reagan's calls to "restore America's defenses" helped reinforce the public perception that President Carter had dealt ineffectively with the Iran hostage crisis. Once in office he greatly accelerated a trend already under way during the last two years of the Carter presidency: a sharp increase in defense spending. Overall, the Reagan budgets for military spending totaled $1.6 trillion over five years and indicated a significant shift in federal budget priorities under his administration. In 1980, 28 percent of federal spending went to housing, education, and urban and social services. By 1987, federal outlays for human resources totaled only 22 percent of the total. In the same period, defense spending rose from 23 percent to 28 percent of the federal budget.

Meanwhile, the Reagan administration created a chilly atmosphere for organized labor. In the summer of 1981, some 13,000 federal employees, all members of the Professional Air Traffic Controllers Organization (PATCO), went on strike. The president retaliated against the strikers by firing them, and the Federal Aviation Administration started a crash program to replace them. Conservative appointees to the National Labor Relations Board and the federal courts toughened its antiunion position. The militantly antilabor mood in Washington, combined with the continuing decline of the nation's manufacturing infrastructure, kept trade unions on the defensive. By 1990 fewer than 15 percent of American workers belonged to a labor union, the lowest proportion since before World War II.

Reagan appointed conservatives to head the Environmental Protection Agency, the Occupational Safety and Health Administration, and the Consumer Product Safety Commission. These individuals abolished or weakened hundreds of rules governing environmental protection, work-place safety, and consumer protection, all in the interest of increasing the efficiency and productivity of business. The deregulatory fever dominated cabinet departments as well. Secretary of the Interior James Watt opened up formerly protected wilderness areas and wetlands to private developers. Secretary of Transportation Andrew L. "Drew" Lewis, Jr. eliminated regulations passed in the 1970s aimed at reducing air pollution and improving fuel efficiency in cars and trucks.

Following the tenets of supply-side economics, the Reagan administration weakened the Antitrust Division of the Justice Department, the Securities and Exchange Commission, and the Federal Home Loan Bank Board. Large corporations, Wall Street stock brokerages, investment banking houses, and the savings and loan industry were all allowed to operate with a much freer hand than ever before. The appointment of Alan Greenspan in 1983, to succeed Carter appointee Paul Volker, greatly encouraged trends toward the dominance of speculation in market trading. By the late 1980s, the unfortunate consequences of this freedom would become apparent in a series of unprecedented scandals in the nation's financial and banking industries.

The Election of 1984

As the 1984 election approached, many Americans expressed doubts about the Reagan administration's defense initiatives. Polls showed that more than 70 percent of Americans favored a nuclear freeze with the Soviet Union. In June 1982, three-quarters of a million people—the largest political rally in American history—demonstrated in New York City for a halt to spending on and deployment of nuclear weapons. Many observers noted that Reagan also appeared politically vulnerable for his economic policies and cutbacks in social programs.

Hoping to win back disgruntled voters, Democrats chose Carter's vice president, Walter Mondale, as their nominee. As a former senator from Minnesota, Mondale had close ties with the party's liberal establishment and also the support of its more military-minded wing. At the Democratic National Convention, Mondale named Representative Geraldine Ferraro of New York as his running mate, a first for women in American politics. Charismatic speakers such as the Reverend Jesse Jackson, a dynamic disciple of Martin Luther King, Jr., and Governor Mario Cuomo of New York stirred the delegates and many television viewers with their appeals to compassion, fairness, and brotherhood.

Opinion polls showed Mondale running even with Reagan. But the president's enormous personal popularity, along with the booming economy, overwhelmed the Democratic ticket. While Mondale emphasized the growing deficit and called attention to Americans who were left out of prosperity, Reagan cruised above it all. It was "morning again in America," his campaign ads claimed. In one of the biggest landslides in American history, Reagan won 59 percent of the popular vote and carried every state but Minnesota and the District of Columbia. A majority of blue-collar voters cast their ballots for the president, as did 54 percent of women, despite Ferraro's presence on the Democratic ticket.

Recession, Recovery, Fiscal Crisis

Over the course of his two terms in office, Reagan's economic policies had mixed results. In 1982 a severe recession, the worst since the 1930s, gripped the nation. The official unemployment rate reached nearly 11 percent, or more than 11.5 million people. Another 3 million had been out of work so long they no longer actively looked for jobs and therefore were not counted in official statistics. But by the middle of 1983 the economy had begun to recover, and unemployment dropped to about 8 percent while inflation fell below 5 percent. The stock market boomed, pushing the Dow Jones industrial average from 776 in August 1982 to an all-time high of 2,722 in August 1987. The administration took credit for the turnaround, hailing the supply-side fiscal policies that had drastically cut taxes and domestic spending. But critics pointed to other factors: the Federal Reserve Board's tight-money policies, an energy resource glut and a consequent sharp drop in energy prices, and the billions of dollars pumped into the economy for defense spending.

Few doubted, however, that the supply-side formula intensified an ominous fiscal crisis. Although President Reagan had promised to balance the federal budget, his policies had the opposite effect. The national debt grew from $907 billion in 1980 to over $2 trillion in 1986, more than the federal government had accumulated in its entire previous history. Expenditures for paying just the interest on the national debt reached 14 percent of the annual budget in 1988, double the percentage set aside for that purpose in 1974.

In the Reagan years the fiscal crisis became a structural problem with newly distrubing and perhaps permanent implications for the American economy. Big deficits kept interest rates high, as the government drove up the cost of borrowing the money it needed to pay its own bills. Foreign investors, attracted by high interest rates on government securities, pushed up the value of the dollar in relation to foreign currencies.

The overvalued dollar made it difficult for foreigners to buy American products, while making overseas good cheaper to American consumers. Basic American industries—steel, autos, textiles—thus found it difficult to compete abroad and at home. In 1980, the United States still enjoyed a trade surplus of $166 billion. By 1987 the nation had an indebtedness to foreigners of $340 billion. Since World War I, the United States had been the world's leading creditor; in the mid-1980s it became its biggest debtor.

In late 1986, the Securities and Exchange Commission (SEC) uncovered the biggest stock scandal in history, in the process revealing the inner workings of high finance in the 1980s. Ivan Boesky, one of the nation's leading stock speculators, admitted to using confidential information about upcoming corporate takeovers to trade stocks illegally. Just two years earlier the dapper Boesky had made more than $100 million on just two deals. "Greed is all right," he told a cheering University of California Business School audience in 1985. "Everybody should be a little bit greedy. . . . You shouldn't feel guilty." Now Boesky agreed to cooperate with SEC investigators.

The biggest fish caught in their net was Michael Milken, a Boesky ally. An investment banker for Drexel Burnham Lambert, Milken perfected the art of corporate raiding through creative manipulation of debt. He showed how enormous profits could be earned from weak firms that were tempting targets for takeovers and mergers. Their debt could be used as tax write-offs; less efficient units could be sold off piecemeal; and more profitable units could be retained, merged, or sold again to form new entities. Instead of borrowing from banks, Milken financed his deals by underwriting high-yield, risky "junk bonds" for companies rated below investment grade. Investors in turn reaped huge profits by selling these junk bonds to hostile-takeover dealers.

Milken and other corporate raiders reshaped the financial world, setting off the greatest wave of buying and selling in American business history. Milken himself made a staggering $550 million in one year alone. Just before filing for bankruptcy in 1990, Drexel Burnham Lambert paid its executives $350 million in bonuses—almost as much as it owed its creditors. Milken was eventually convicted of insider trading and stock fraud and sent to prison. Too frequently, profits now depended more on debt manipulation and corporate restructuring rather than investment in research and development or the creation of new products. In 1987, the Hollywood film *Wall Street* dramatized this world of ruthless profiteering.

On Wall Street, the bull market of the 1980s ended abruptly in the fall of 1987. After reaching its new high of 2,722 at the end of August, the Dow Jones average of thirty leading industrial stocks began to slide downward and then crashed. On October 19, the Dow lost almost 23 percent of its value. The panic on

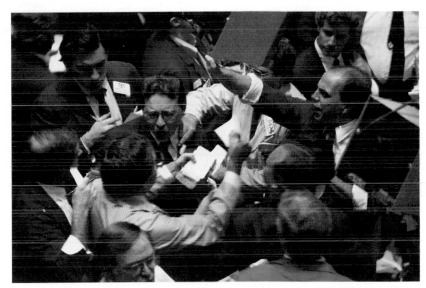

After the Dow-Jones reached an all-time high at the end of August, stocks began to slide and then crashed. On October 19, 1987—"Black Monday"—traders at the New York Stock Exchange panicked, selling off stocks at such a rate that the market lost almost twenty-three percent of its value, marking the end of a five-year "bull" market. The market soon bounced back, and by September 1989 the Dow-Jones had made up all its losses.

SOURCE: AP/Wide World Photos (025473).

the trading floors recalled the pandemonium set off by the stock market crash of 1929. Millions of Americans now feared that the 1987 crash would signal the onset of a great recession or even a depression.

BEST OF TIMES, WORST OF TIMES

The celebration of wealth, moneymaking, and entrepreneurship dominated much of popular culture, politics, and intellectual life in the 1980s. But grimmer realities lay under the surface. A variety of measures strongly suggested that the nation had moved toward greater inequality, that the middle class was shrinking, and that poverty was on the rise. Analysts disagreed over the causes of these trends. No doubt some reflected structural changes in the American economy and a rapidly changing global marketplace. After eight years of tax cuts, defense buildup, growing budget deficits, and record trade imbalances, the economic future looked uncertain at best. Two of the most cherished basic assumptions about America—that life would improve for most people and their children, and that membership in the comfortable middle-class was available to all who worked for it—looked shaky by the end of the decade.

The Celebration of Wealth

The very wealthy did extremely well during the 1980s. In 1989, the richest 1 percent of American households accounted for 37 percent of the nation's private wealth—up from 31 percent in 1983, a jump of almost 20 percent. This top 1 percent, consisting of 834,000 households with about $5.7 trillion of net worth, owned more than the bottom 90 percent of Americans, the remaining 84 million households, whose total net worth was about $4.8 trillion.

Other affluent Americans also made huge gains. In 1980 the top 5 percent of families earned 15.3 percent of the nation's total income. By 1992 their share had grown to 17.6 percent, an increase of 15 percent; their average income was $156,000 a year. In 1980 the top 20 percent of families earned 41.6 percent of the nation's total. By 1992 their share had grown to 44.6 percent, an increase of about 7 percent, with an average income of $99,000 a year. In contrast, the bottom 40 percent of families had 16.7 percent of aggregate income in 1980. By 1992 their share had declined to 14.9 percent, a drop of nearly 2 percent, with an average income of about $16,500 a year.

PERCENTAGE SHARE OF AGGRE GATE FAMILY INCOME, 1980–1992		
	1980	1992
Top 5 Percent	15.3%	17.6%
Highest Fifth	41.6	44.6
Fourth Fifth	24.3	24.0
Third Fifth	17.5	16.5
Second Fifth	11.6	10.5
First Fifth	5.1	4.4

SOURCE: U.S. Bureau of the Census, *Current Population Reports: Consumer Incomes*, Series P-60, Nos. 167 and 184, 1990, 1993. U.S. federal data compiled by Ed Royce, Rollins College.

SHARE OF TOTAL NET WORTH OF AMERICAN FAMILIES		
	1983	1989
Richest 1 percent of families	31%	37%
Next richest 9 percent	35	31
Remaining 90 percent	33	32

SOURCE: *New York Times*, April 21, 1992, from Federal Reserve Survey of Consumer Finances.

MEASURES OF AVERAGE EARNINGS, 1980–1992 (IN 1990 DOLLARS)

Year	Average Weekly Earnings	Average Hourly Earnings
1980	$373.81	$10.59
1985	363.30	10.41
1992	339.37	9.87

SOURCE: U.S. House of Representatives, Committee on Ways and Means, *Overview of Entitlement Programs* (Washington, D.C.: GPO, 1993), table 35, p. 557. U.S. federal data compiled by Ed Royce, Rollins College.

NUMBER OF POOR, RATE OF POVERTY, AND POVERTY LINE, 1979–1992

	1979	1992
Millions of poor	26.1	36.9
Rate of poverty	11.7%	14.5%
Poverty line (family of four)	$7,412	$14,335

SOURCE: U.S. Bureau of the Census, *Current Population Reports: Consumer Income*, Series P-60, Nos. 161 and 185, 1988, 1993. U.S. federal data compiled by Ed Royce, Rollins College.

The theme of money, status, and power —the values embraced by the Reagan administration—dominated popular culture. The newly elected president himself set the tone when he responded to a reporter's question asking him what was best about America. "What I want to see above all," Reagan replied, "is that this remains a country where someone can always get rich." Many thousands of Americans made fortunes in the expansive and lucrative sectors of the economy: stock trading, real estate, business services, defense contracting, and high-tech industries. A step below the new rich were the "yuppies," who were defined by their upscale consumer behavior. Yuppies ate gourmet foods, wore designer clothes, drove expensive automobiles, and lived in "gentrified" neighborhoods.

Popular culture reflected and reinforced an obsession with getting rich and living well. Once again, novelist Tom Wolfe gave a name to the cultural phenomenon— "plutography," which represented "graphic depictions of the acts of the rich." Hit TV series like *Dallas* and *Dynasty* (and their imitators) focused on the family wars and business intrigues of oil tycoons and fashion queens. Shows such as *Lifestyles of the Rich and Famous* and *Entertainment Tonight* offered vicarious pleasures by taking viewers

into the homes and on the shopping sprees of wealthy celebrities.

Tie-ins proliferated among films, television shows, advertising, newspapers and magazines, popular music, and politicians. A growing concentration of ownership among television networks, movie studios, publishers, and cable companies accelerated this trend. New media forms—the newspaper *USA Today*, the news channel Cable News Network (CNN), the weekly magazine *People*—intensified the national culture of celebrity. Demographic analysis created the most important "communities" in American life—communities of consumers, so that advertisers could define and target them to sell a product or provide a service.

A Two-Tiered Society

During the 1960s, despite the diversion of federal funds to military spending during the Vietnam War, President Johnson's Great Society had brought a higher standard of living to many Americans. By the time Carter took office in 1977, the sinking economy was undercutting these gains. Reagan's supply-side policies enlivened the economy but at the same time widened the gap between rich and poor.

NET NEW JOB CREATION BY WAGE LEVEL, 1979–1987

	Number of Net New Jobs Created	Percentage of Net New Jobs Created
Low-wage Jobs (less than $11,611)	5,955,000	50.4%
Middle-wage Jobs ($11.612 to $46,444)	4,448,000	31.7%
High-wage Jobs ($46,445 and above)	1,405,000	11.9%

SOURCE: U.S. Senate, Committee on the Budget, *Wages of American Workers in the 1980s* (Washington, D.C.: GPO, 1988). U.S. federal data compiled by Ed Royce, Rollins College.

MEDIAN FAMILY INCOME AND RATIO TO WHITE, BY RACE AND HISPANIC ORIGIN, 1980–1992 (IN 1992 DOLLARS)				
Year	All Races	White	Black	Hispanic
1980	$35,839	$37,341	$21,606 (58%)	$25,087 (67%)
1985	36,164	38,011	21,887 (58%)	25,596 (67%)
1992	36,812	38,909	21,161 (54%)	23,901 (61%)

SOURCE: U.S. Bureau of the Census, *Current Population Reports*, Series P-60, No. 184, 1993. U.S. federal data compiled by Ed Royce, Rollins College.

The number and percentage of Americans in poverty grew at an alarming rate. Since the mid-1970s, most of the new jobs clustered in low-paying service and manufacturing sectors and less than half of them paid more than the $11,611 poverty-level income for a family of four. In 1979 the government classified about 26.1 million people as poor, 11.7 percent of the total population; by 1992 the number of poor had reached 36.9 million, or 14.5 percent of the population, and nearly 22 percent of all American children under eighteen lived in poverty.

The widening gap between rich and poor was sharply defined by race. By 1992, 33 percent of all African Americans lived in poverty, as did 29 percent of Hispanics (the rate was especially high among Puerto Ricans, yet low among Cuban Americans). The gains achieved by the civil rights movement were steadily eroding. In 1954, the year of the *Brown v. Board of Education* decision, black families earned about 53 percent of the income of white families. This figure rose to 60 percent in 1969 and peaked at 62 percent in 1975. By 1979, black family income had fallen back to 57 percent and continued to slide during the next decade. Similarly, the number of African Americans attending college peaked in 1976 at 9.3 percent of the black population, a 500 percent increase over the 1960 average.

The majority of African Americans, six out of ten, lived in central cities with high unemployment rates, and the bleak prospects took a toll especially on the young. A black child was twice as likely as a white child to die before reaching the first birthday and four times more likely to be killed between the ages of one and four. Among black teenagers, the unemployment rate topped 40 percent; the few jobs available to them were among the lowest-paid in the economy. Meanwhile, the high school dropout rate skyrocketed, and the number of serious crimes, such as burglary, car theft, and murder, perpetrated by children between the ages of ten and seventeen increased at an alarming rate.

The gap between rich and poor also increased within the African American community. While the poor stayed behind in increasingly segregated urban neighborhod, nearly 45 percent of black families managed to achieve middle-class status by the mid-1970s. This trend dramatically affected the black community. Until the 1970s the majority of African Americans had held to common residential neighborhoods, institutions, and political outlooks. By the end of the decade, growing income and residential disparity, which widened faster among black people than among white people, produced sharp differences among African Americans on social, economic, and political issues.

Moreover, opportunities for advancement into the middle class were dwindling. By 1980 fewer black students attended integrated schools than in 1954, except in the South, where about half the black students did. The turnabout resulted in part from increasing opposition by white parents to court-ordered school busing, which had served since *Brown v. Board of Education* as the principal means of achieving racial balance in urban school systems. In 1975 a major clash between local white residents and black parents and their children occurred in Boston when a federally mandated busing plan was put into operation. During the 1980s the busing controversy nearly disappeared because federal judges hesitated to mandate such programs. But more important was the change in the racial composition of American cities. As a consequence of "white flight" to the suburbs, big-city school systems were serving mainly African American and Latino children, making the issue of integration moot. By this time, the dropout rate of black teenagers had reached 50 percent in inner-city schools.

New legal rulings closed off important routes to employment in the professions. A 1978 U.S. Supreme Court decision dealt a sharp blow to affirmative action. To ensure acceptance of a minimum number of minority students, the University of California at Davis Medical School had established a quota system under affirmative action guidelines. In 1973 and 1974 the school denied admission to Allan Bakke, a white student. Bakke sued the university for "reverse discrimination," claiming his academic record was better than that of the sixteen minority students who were admitted. The U.S. Supreme

Court handed down a five-to-four decision on June 18, 1978, stating that the use of an "explicit racial classification" in situations where no earlier discrimination had been demonstrated violated the equal protection clause of the Fourteenth Amendment. The Court ordered the University of California to admit Bakke to its medical school. During the 1980s, therefore, affirmative action programs could operate only when "a legacy of unequal treatment" could be proved.

The Feminization of Poverty

Despite a growing rate of labor force participation, the majority of women gainfully employed earned less than a living wage. Even if employed, women usually lost ground following a divorce, especially as new no-fault divorce laws lowered or eradicated alimony. Moreover, the majority of men defaulted on child-support payments within one year after separation. Whereas divorced men enjoyed a sizable increase in their standard of living, divorced women suffered a formidable decline. During the 1970s alone, the number of poor families headed by women increased nearly 70 percent.

A sharp rise in teenage pregnancy reinforced this pattern. Many of these mothers were too young to have gained either the education or skills to secure jobs that would pay enough to support themselves and their children. Even with Aid to Families with Dependent Children (AFDC) payments and food stamps, it was impossible for these single mothers to keep their families above the poverty line. By 1992, female-headed households, comprising 13.7 million people, accounted for 37 percent of the poor. African American and Latino women and their children had by far the highest poverty rates.

Moreover, political mobilization for protecting the rights of poor women was at a low ebb. Since its founding in 1967, the National Welfare Rights Organization (NWRO), led by African American women, had spearheaded a campaign to enable welfare recipients to have a voice in policy decisions. They demanded adequate day-care facilities and job-training programs and insisted on the legitimacy of female-headed households. NWRO activists occasionally staged sit-ins at welfare agencies to secure benefits for their members. More often, they informed poor women of their existing rights and encouraged them to apply for benefits. In 1975, NWRO, exhausted from fighting cutbacks in the federal welfare system, filed for bankruptcy.

Epidemics: Drugs, AIDS, Homelessness

Drug addiction and drug trafficking took on frightening new dimensions in the early 1980s. The arrival of "crack," a cheap, smokable, and highly addictive form of cocaine, made that drug affordable to the urban poor. As crack addiction spread, the drug trade assumed alarming new proportions both domestically and internationally. Crack ruined hundreds of thousands of lives and led to a dramatic increase in crime rates. Studies showed that over half the men arrested in the nation's largest cities tested positive for cocaine. The crack trade spawned a new generation of young drug dealers who were willing to risk jail and death for enormous profits. In city after city, drug wars over turf took the lives of dealers and innocents, both caught in the escalating violence.

By the end of the 1980s, opinion polls revealed that Americans identified drugs as the nation's number one problem. The Reagan administration declared a highly publicized "war on drugs," a multibillion-dollar campaign to bring the traffic under control. Critics charged that the war on drugs focused on supply from abroad when it needed to look at demand here at home. They urged more federal money for drug education, treatment, and rehabilitation. Drug addiction and drug use, they argued, were primarily health problems, not law enforcement issues.

In 1981 doctors in Los Angeles, San Francisco, and New York began encountering a puzzling new medical phenomenon. Young homosexual men were dying suddenly from rare types of pneumonia and cancer. The underlying cause was found to be a mysterious new viral disease that destroyed the body's natural defenses against illness, making its victims susceptible to a host of opportunistic infections. Researchers at the Centers for Disease Control (CDC) in Atlanta called the new disease acquired immune deficiency syndrome (AIDS). The virus that causes AIDS is transmitted primarily in semen and blood. Full-blown AIDS might not appear for years after initial exposure to the virus. Thus one could infect others without knowing one had the disease. Although tests emerged to determine whether one carried HIV, there was no cure. The majority of early AIDS victims were homosexual men who had been infected through sexual contact. Many Americans thus perceived AIDS as a disease of homosexuals. But other victims became infected through intravenous drug use, blood transfusions, heterosexual transmission, or birth to AIDS-carrying mothers.

AIDS provoked fear, anguish, and anger. It also brought an upsurge of organization and political involvement. In city after city, the gay community responded to the AIDS crisis with energy and determination. Most gay men changed their sexual habits, practicing "safe sex" to lessen the chances of infection. The Reagan administration, playing to antihomosexual prejudices, largely ignored the epidemic. One important exception was Surgeon General C. Everett Koop, who urged a comprehensive sex education program in the nation's schools.

Homelessness emerged as a chronic social problem during the 1980s. Often disoriented, shoeless, and forlorn, growing numbers of street people slept over

In May 1987, members of the Lesbian and Gay Community Services in Downtown Manhattan organized ACT-UP. Protesting what they perceived to be the Reagan administration's mismanagement of the AIDs crisis, they used non-violent direct action, which often took the form of dramatic acts of civil disobedience. ACT-UP grew to more than 70 chapters in the United States and the world

SOURCE: AP/Wide World Photos.

heating grates, on subways, and in parks. Homeless people wandered city sidewalks panhandling and struggling to find scraps of food. Winters proved especially difficult. In the early 1980s, the Department of Housing and Urban Development placed the number of the nation's homeless at between 250,000 and 350,000. But advocates for the homeless estimated that the number was as high as 3 million.

Who were the homeless? Analysts agreed that at least a third were mental patients who had been discharged from psychiatric hospitals amid the deinstitutionalization trend of the the 1970s. Many more were alcoholics and drug addicts unable to hold jobs. But the ranks of the homeless also included female-headed fami-

lies, battered women, Vietnam veterans, AIDS victims, and elderly people with no place to go. Some critics pointed to the decline in decent housing for poor people and the deterioration of the nation's health-care system as a cause of homelessness. Some communities made strong efforts to place their homeless residents in city run shelters, but violence and theft in the shelters scared away many people. No matter how large and what its components, the permanent class of American homeless reflected the desperate situation of America's poor

REAGAN'S FOREIGN POLICY

Throughout his presidency, Reagan campaigned to restore American leadership in world affairs. He revived cold war patriotism and championed American interventionism in the third world, especially in the Caribbean and Central America. His infusion of funds into national security programs would have enormous consequences for the domestic economy as well as for America's international stance. Yet along with its hard-line exhortations against the Soviet Union and international terrorism, the Reagan administraton also pursued a less ideological, more pragmatic approach in key foreign policy decisions. Most important, sweeping and unanticipated internal changes within the Soviet Union made the entire cold war framework of American foreign policy largely irrelevant by the late 1980s.

The Evil Empire

In the early 1980s, the Reagan administration made vigorous anti-Communist rhetoric the centerpiece of its foreign policy. In a sharp turn from President Carter's focus on human rights and President Nixon's pursuit of détente, Reagan described the Soviet Union as "an evil empire . . . the focus of evil in the modern world." The president denounced the growing movement for a nuclear freeze, arguing that "we must find peace through strength."

Administration officials argued that the nation's military strength had fallen dangerously behind that of the Soviet Union during the 1970s. Critics disputed this assertion, pointing out that the Soviet advantage in intercontinental ballistic missiles (ICBMs) was offset by American superiority in submarine-based forces and strategic aircraft. Nonetheless, the administration proceeded with plans to enlarge America's nuclear strike force.

In 1983 President Reagan introduced an unsettling new element into superpower relations when he presented his Strategic Defense Initiative (SDI), the plan for a space-based ballistic-missile defense system that journalists dubbed "Star Wars," after the popular Hollywood film series. This proposal for a five-year $26 billion program promised to give the United States the capacity to shoot down incoming missiles with laser beams and homing rockets. To critics, the plan seemed unworkable, impossibly expensive, and likely to destabilize existing arms treaties. The Reagan administration pressed ahead, spending $17 billion in research before the president left office—without achieving any convincing results. Nevertheless, the Soviets complained that the SDI carried the potential of upsetting the nuclear balance and interpreted the plan as an offensive strategy to ensure a first-strike advantage to the United States.

Attempts at meaningful arms control stalled in this atmosphere, and U.S.–Soviet relations deteriorated. In the fall of 1983, the Soviets shot down a Korean airliner that had strayed over Soviet airspace, killing 269 people. Soviet military officials, believing the plane to be on a spy mission, acted at best in a confused and incompetent manner. President Reagan immediately denounced the act as a deliberate "crime against humanity," and a wave of anti-Soviet sentiment swept the country. The Soviet Union and its Eastern European allies then boycotted the 1984 Olympic Games in Los Angeles, partly in response to the American boycott of the 1980 Moscow games. While Reagan transformed images of enthusiastic Americans chanting "USA! USA!" and "We're number one!" into an effective backdrop for his reelection campaign, the American-Soviet relationship seemed to have fallen to a new low.

The Reagan Doctrine and Central America

Declaring the "Vietnam syndrome" over, the president confidently reasserted America's right to intervene anywhere in the world to fight Communist insurgency. The Reagan Doctrine, as this declaration was later called, assumed that all political instability in the third world resulted not from indigenous factors such as poverty or corruption but from the pernicious influence of the Soviet Union. It found its most important expression in Central America, where the United States hoped to reestablish its historical control over the Caribbean basin.

On the economic front, the Caribbean Basin Initiative (CBI) promised to stimulate the Caribbean economy by encouraging the growth of business corporations and a freer flow of capital through $350 million in U.S. aid. Yet Congress refused to play by the rules of free trade, placing stiff tariffs and quotas on imports of shoes, leather goods, and sugar competing with U.S. products. Many Latin American business leaders opposed key parts of the CBI, such as generous tax breaks for foreign investors. They feared that once large multinational corporations entered their markets, the CBI would strengthen the kind of chronic economic dependency that had shaped so much of the region's past.

Throughout Central America, the Reagan administration believed, as National Security Adviser Richard Allen argued, that all problems stemmed from "Fidel Castro's Soviet directed, armed, and financed marauders" and required a military solution. Between 1980 and 1983 the United States poured more military aid into Central America than it had during the previous thirty years. In October 1983, the administration directed American marines to invade Grenada, claiming that the tiny island had become a base for the Cuban military and therefore posed a dangerous threat to the hemisphere. The easy triumph proved popular with most Grenadans and Americans. In the larger and more complicated nations of El Salvador and Nicaragua, this sort of unilateral military action proved politically and strategically more difficult to carry out.

In El Salvador, the Reagan administration continued to support the repressive regime. Military aid jumped from $6 million in 1980 to $82 million in 1982, and El Salvador received more U.S. economic assistance than any other Latin American country. By 1983 right-wing death squads, encouraged by military elements within the regime, had tortured and assassinated thousands of opposition leaders. The election in 1984 of centrist president José Napoleón Duarte failed to end the bloody civil war. Some 53,000 Salvadorans, more than one out of every hundred, lost their lives in the conflict.

In Nicaragua, the Reagan administration claimed that the revolutionary Sandinista government posed "an unusual and extraordinary threat to the national security." U.S. officials accused the Sandinistas of shipping arms to antigovernment rebels in El Salvador. In December 1981, Reagan approved a $19 million CIA plan arming and organizing Nicaraguan exiles, known as Contras, to fight against the Sandinista government. As Reagan escalated this undeclared war, the aim became not merely the cutting of Nicaraguan aid to Salvadoran rebels but the overthrow of the Sandinista regime itself.

In 1984 the CIA secretly mined Nicaraguan harbors. When Nicaragua won a judgment against the United States in the World Court over this violation of its sovereignty, the Reagan administration refused to recognize the court's jurisdiction in the case and ignored the verdict. Predictably, the U.S. covert war pushed the Sandinistas closer to Cuba and the Soviet bloc. Meanwhile, U.S. grass-roots opposition to Contra aid grew more vocal and widespread. A number of U.S. communities set up sister city projects offering humanitarian and technical assistance to Nicaraguan communities. Scores of U.S. churches offered sanctuary to political refugees from Central America.

In 1984 Congress reined in the covert war by passing the Boland Amendment, introduced by Democratic Representative Edward Boland of Massachusetts. It forbid government agencies from supporting "directly

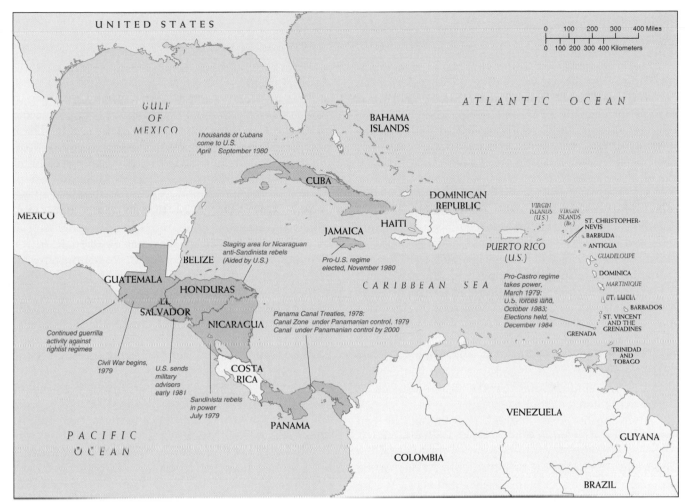

UNITED STATES

0 100 200 300 400 Miles
0 100 200 300 400 Kilometers

GULF OF MEXICO

ATLANTIC OCEAN

BAHAMA ISLANDS

Thousands of Cubans come to U.S. April–September 1980

CUBA

DOMINICAN REPUBLIC

MEXICO

HAITI

JAMAICA

VIRGIN ISLANDS (U.S.) VIRGIN ISLANDS (Br.) ST. CHRISTOPHER-NEVIS
BARBUDA
ANTIGUA

PUERTO RICO (U.S.)

GUADELOUPE
DOMINICA
MARTINIQUE

Staging area for Nicaraguan anti-Sandinista rebels (Aided by U.S.)

BELIZE

Pro-U.S. regime elected, November 1980

CARIBBEAN SEA

ST. LUCIA

GUATEMALA

HONDURAS

Pro-Castro regime takes power, March 1979; U.S. forces land, October 1983; Elections held, December 1984

BARBADOS
ST. VINCENT AND THE GRENADINES

GRENADA

EL SALVADOR

NICARAGUA

Panama Canal Treaties, 1978: Canal Zone under Panamanian control, 1979 Canal under Panamanian control by 2000

TRINIDAD AND TOBAGO

Continued guerrilla activity against rightist regimes

Civil War begins, 1979

U.S. sends military advisers early 1981

COSTA RICA

Sandinista rebels in power July 1979

VENEZUELA

PACIFIC OCEAN

PANAMA

COLOMBIA

GUYANA

BRAZIL

The United States in Central America, 1978–1990 U.S. intervention in Central America reached a new level of intensity with the so-called Reagan Doctrine. The bulk of U.S. aid came in the form of military support for the government of El Salvador and the Contra rebels in Nicaragua.

WWW

or indirectly military or paramilitary operations" in Nicaragua. Denied funding by Congress, President Reagan turned to the National Security Council to find a way to keep the Contra war going. Between 1984 and 1986, the NSC staff secretly ran the Contra assistance effort, raising $37 million in aid from foreign countries and private contributors, creating the largest mercenary army in hemispheric history. In 1987 the revelation of this unconstitutional scheme exploded before the public as part of the Iran-Contra affair, the most damaging political scandal of the Reagan years.

Glasnost and Arms Control

Meanwhile, momentous political changes within the Soviet Union led to a reduction in East-West tensions and ultimately the end of the cold war itself. Soviet premier Leonid Brezhnev, in power since 1964, died toward the end of 1982. His successors, Yuri Andropov

and Konstantin Chernenko, both died after brief terms in office. But in 1985 a new, reform-minded leader, Mikhail Gorbachev, won election as general secretary of the Soviet Communist Party. Although a lifelong Communist, Gorbachev represented a new generation of disenchanted party members. He initiated a radical new program of economic and political reform under the rubrics of *glasnost* (openness) and *perestroika* (restructuring).

Gorbachev and his advisers opened up political discussion and encouraged criticism of the Soviet economy and political culture. There was much to criticize. Inefficiency and chronic shortages plagued Soviet production of such staples as meat, grain, clothing, and housing. Even when consumer goods were available, high prices often put them beyond the means of the average Soviet family. The government released longtime dissidents like Andrei Sakharov from prison and took the first halting steps toward profit-based, private initiatives in the economy. This "new thinking" inspired an unprecedented wave of diverse, often critical perspectives in Soviet art, literature, journalism, and scholarship.

In Gorbachev's view, improving the economic performance of the Soviet system depended first on halting the arms race. Over 10 percent of the Soviet GNP (gross national product) went to defense spending, while the majority of its citizens still struggled to find even the most basic consumer items in shops. Gorbachev thus took the lead in negotiating a halt to the arms race with the United States.

The historical ironies were stunning. Reagan had made militant anticommunism the centerpiece of his administration. He staunchly resisted arms control initiatives and presided over the greatest military buildup in American history. But between 1985 and 1988 Reagan had four separate summit meetings with the new Soviet leader. In October 1986, Reagan and Gorbachev met in Reykjavík, Iceland, but this summit bogged down over the issue of SDI. Reagan refused to abandon his plan for a space-based defensive umbrella. Gorbachev insisted that the plan violated the 1972 Strategic Arms Limitation Treaty (SALT I) and that SDI might eventually allow the United States to make an all-out attack on the Soviet Union.

After another year of tough negotiating, the two sides agreed to a modest treaty that called for comprehensive, mutual, on-site inspections. It provided an important psychological breakthrough. At one of the summits a Soviet leader humorously announced, "We are going to do something terrible to you Americans—we are going to deprive you of an enemy."

The Iran-Contra Scandal

The gift of glasnost did not eliminate cold war thinking entirely, especially in the continuing covert war in Central America. Nor could it resolve long-standing and complex international disputes in regions like the Middle East. In 1987 the revelations of the Iran-Contra affair laid bare the continuing contradictions and difficulties attending America's role in world affairs. The affair also demonstrated how overzealous and secretive government officials subverted the Constitution and compromised presidential authority under the guise of patriotism.

The Middle East presented the Reagan administration with its most frustrating foreign policy dilemmas. In Afghanistan, the administration expanded military aid (begun under President Carter) to the forces resisting the Soviet-backed regime. In June 1982 Israel invaded Lebanon in an attempt to destroy the Palestine Liberation Organization (PLO). Hoping to shore up a weak Lebanese government threatened by a brutal civil war, President Reagan dispatched marines to Beirut. In Octo-

ber 1983, however, a terrorist bombing in the marine barracks killed 241 American servicemen, and the administration pulled the marines out of Lebanon, shying away from a long-term commitment of U.S. forces in the Middle East.

Terrorist acts, including the seizing of Western hostages and the bombing of commercial airplanes and cruise ships, redefined the politics of the region. These were desperate attempts by small sects, many of them splinter groups associated with the Palestinian cause or Islamic fundamentalism, to inhibit U.S. support of Israel. The Reagan administration insisted that behind international terrorism lay the sinister influence and money of the Soviet bloc, the Ayatollah Khomeini of Iran, and Libyan leader Muammar el-Qaddafi. In the spring of 1986 the president, eager to demonstrate his antiterrorist resolve, ordered the bombing of Tripoli in a failed effort to kill Qaddafi.

As a fierce war between Iran and Iraq escalated, the administration tilted publicly toward Iraq to please the Arab states around the Persian Gulf. But in 1986 Reagan's advisors began secret negotiations with the revolutionary Iranian government. They eventually offered to supply Iran with sophisticated weapons for use against Iraq in exchange for help in securing the release of Americans held hostage by radical Islamic groups in Lebanon.

Subsequent disclosures elevated the arms-for-hostages deal into a major scandal. Some of the money from the arms deal had been secretly diverted into covert aid for the Nicaraguan Contras. The American public soon learned the sordid details from investigative journalists and through televised congressional hearings held during the summer of 1987. In order to escape congressional oversight of the CIA, Reagan and CIA director William Casey had essentially turned the National Security Council, previously a policy-coordinating body, into an operational agency. Under the direction of National Security Advisers Robert McFarlane and later Admiral John Poindexter, the NSC had sold TOW and Hawk missiles to the Iranians, using Israel as a go-between. Millions of dollars from these sales were then given to the Contras in blatant and illegal disregard of the Boland Amendment.

In the televised congressional hearings, NSC staffer and marine lieutenant colonel Oliver North emerged as the figure running what he euphemistically referred to as "the Enterprise." North defiantly defended his actions in the name of patriotism. Some Americans saw the handsome and dashing North as a hero; most were appalled by his and Poindexter's blithe admissions that they had lied to Congress, shredded evidence, and refused to inform the president of details in order to guarantee his "plausible deniability." A blue-ribbon commission led by former senator John Tower

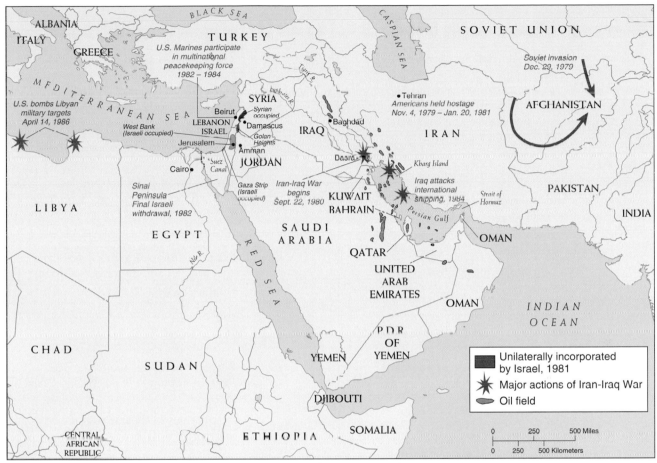

The United States in the Middle East in the 1980s   The volatile combination of ancient religious and ethnic rivalries, oil, and emerging Islamic fundamentalism made peach and stability elusive in the Middle East.

of Texas concluded that Reagan himself "did not seem to be aware" of the policy or its consequences. But the Tower Report offered a stunning portrait of a president who was at best confused and far removed from critical policy-making responsibilities. The joint congressional committee investigating the "profoundly sad" story concluded: "The common ingredients of the Iran and Contra policies were secrecy, deception, and disdain for the law. A small group of senior officials believed that they alone knew what was right."

Ultimately, the Iran-Contra investigation raised more questions than it answered. The full role of CIA director Casey, who died in 1987, particularly his relationships with North and the president, remained murky. The role of Vice President George H. W. Bush remained mysterious as well, and it would return as an issue in the 1992 presidential election. Both North and Poindexter were convicted of felonies, but their convictions were overturned by higher courts on technical grounds, although diplomatic official Elliott Abrams was convicted of lying to Congress and successfully

sentenced to public service. The scandal had mesmerized a national television audience. But Iran-Contra, unlike Watergate, produced no equivalent movement for impeachment. Reagan held fast to his plea of ignorance. When pressed on what had happened, he repeatedly claimed, "I'm still trying to find out."

In December 1992, following his reelection defeat and six years after the scandal broke, President George H. W. Bush granted pardons to six key players in the Iran-Contra affair. The Bush pardons made it unlikely that the full truth about the arms-for-hostages affair would ever be known.

CONCLUSION

The success of conservatives to halt and in some cases actually reverse key trends in American politics, from Franklin Roosevelt's New Deal to Lyndon Johnson's Great Society, was made possible by the legacy of the

CHRONOLOGY

1973	*Roe* v. *Wade* legalizes abortion
	Arab embargo sparks oil crisis in the United States
1974	Richard Nixon resigns presidency; Gerald Ford takes office
	President Ford pardons Nixon and introduces antiinflation program
1975	Unemployment rate reaches nearly 9 percent
	South Vietnamese government falls to communists
	Antibusing protests break out in Boston
1976	Percentage of African Americans attending college peaks at 9.3 percent and begins a decline
	Jimmy Carter is elected president
1977	President Carter announces human rights as major tenet in foreign policy
1978	*Bakke* v. *University of California* decision places new limits on affirmative action programs
	Camp David meeting sets terms for Middle East peace
	California passes Proposition 13, cutting taxes and government social programs
1979	Three Mile Island nuclear accident threatens a meltdown
	Nicaraguan Revolution overthrows Anastasio Somoza
	Iranian fundamentalists seize the U.S. embassy in Tehran and hold U.S. citizens hostage for 444 days
	Soviets invade Afghanistan
1980	Inflation reaches 13.5 percent
	Ronald Reagan is elected president
1981	Reagan adminisration initiates major cuts in taxes and domestic spending. Military buildup accelerates
	AIDS is recognized and named
1982	Economic recession grips the nation
1983	Reagan announces the Strategic Defense Initiative, labeled "Star Wars" by critics.
	241 marines killed in Beirut terrorist bombing
1985	Mikhail Gorbachev initates reforms—*glasnost* and *perestroika*—in the Soviet Union
1986	Iran-Contra hearings before Congress reveal arms-for-hostages deal and funds secretly and illegally diverted to Nicaraguan rebels

cold war and the trauma of defeat in Vietnam. But it also owed a great deal to a deepening anxiety of the public about cultural changes and a growing pessimism about the ability of politicians to offer solutions, especially at the national level. Those community activists struggling to extend the protest movements of the 1960s into an updated, comprehensive reformism encompassing such issues as feminism, ecology, and affirmative action readily recognized that the liberal era had ended.

President Ronald Reagan, a charismatic figure who sometimes invented his own past and seemed to believe in it, offered remedies for a weary and nostalgic nation. By insisting that the rebellious 1960s had been a terrible mistake, lowering national self-confidence along with public morals and faith in the power of economic individualism, he successfully wedded the conservatism of Christian fundamentalists, many suburbanites, and Sunbelt voters with the more traditional conservatism of corporate leaders. In many respects, the Reagan administration actually continued and added ideological fervor to the downscaling of government services and upscaling of military spending already evident under President Jimmy Carter, while offering supporters the hope of a sweeping conservative revolution.

In the end, critics suggested, supporters of Ronald Reagan and Reaganism could not go back to the 1950s—just as the erstwhile rebels of the 1960s could not go back to their favorite era. Economically, conservatives achieved many of their goals, including widespread acceptance of sharper economic divisions within society and fewer restraints on corporations and investments. But socially and culturally, their grasp was much less secure.

REVIEW QUESTIONS

1. Evaluate the significance of the major population shifts in the United States from the 1940s through the 1970s. What was their impact on local and national politics?
2. Discuss the connections between the energy crisis and the rise of the environmental movement.
3. Why was the 1970s dubbed the "Me Decade"? Interpret the decline of liberalism and the rise of conservative political groups. How did these changes affect the outcome of presidential elections?
4. Was the Iran hostage crisis a turning point in American politics or only a thorn in Carter's reelection campaign? How did Iran-Contra affect the Republicans?

5. Describe the central philosophical assumptions behind Reaganomics. What were the key policies by which it was implemented? To what extent were these policies a break with previous economic approaches?
6. Evaluate Reagan's foreign policy. How did it differ from Carter's approach to foreign affairs?
7. Analyze the key structure factors underlying recent changes in American economic and cultural life. Do you see any political solutions for the growth of poverty and inequality?

RECOMMENDED READING

Lee Edwards, *The Conservative Revolution: The Movement That Remade America* (2000). Traces the rise of modern political conservatism from its origins in cold war anticommunism.

Frances FitzGerald, *Way Out There in the Blue: Reagan, Star Wars, and the End of the Cold War* (2000). A well-documented study of the conservative mood.

Angela Howard and Sasha Ranae Addams Tarrant, eds., *Reaction to the Modern Women's Movement, 1963 to present* (1997). A collection of essays covering a wide variety of topics concerning the rise of antifeminism.

John Karaagac, *Between Promise and Policy: Ronald Reagan and Conservative Reformism* (2000). Assesses Reagan's major polities, such as increased funding for federal government and regulatory reform, in light of his professed conservative ideals.

Michael B. Katz, *Improving Poor People: The Welfare State, the "Underclass," and Urban Schools as History* (1995). Provides a broad overview of the history of urban poverty, welfare policy, and public education.

William M. LeoGrande, *Our Own Backyard: The United States in Central America, 1977–1992* (1998). Assesses the efforts of the Reagan adminstration to gain congressional approval for funding counterrevolutionary operations in El Salvador and Nicaragua.

Melani McAlister, *Epic Encounters: Culture, Media, and U.S. Interests in the Middle East, 1945–2000* (2001). A close reading of American popular culture.

Lisa McGirr, *Suburban Warriors: The Origins of the New American Right* (2001). Traces the resurgence of American conservatism.

Bruce J. Schulman, *The Seventies: The Great Shift in American Culture, Society, and Politics* (2001). Examines the move away from the public-spirited universalism that characterized the New Deal and civil rights movement.

Judith Stein, *Running Steel, Running America: Race, Economic Policy, and the Decline of Liberalism* (1998). Discusses the impact of the decline of the U.S. steel industry on its large African American labor force.

Robert A. Strong, *Working in the World: Jimmy Carter and the Making of American Foreign Policy* (2000). A collection of nine case studies of international affairs covering Carter's presidency.

Andrew Szasz, *EcoPopulism: Toxic Waste and the Movement for Environmental Justice* (1994). A careful analysis of a turning point in federal regulation of toxic waste.

Winifred D. Wandersee, *On the Move: American Women in the 1970s* (1988). A highly readable overview of the changes that brought American women into political life but also kept them at the margins of power.

▶ MEDIA RESOURCES

U.S. HISTORY DOCUMENTS CD-ROM

The Struggle for Social Change

29-9   Jimmy Carter, The "Malaise" Speech (1979)

America at the Millennium

30-1   House Judiciary Committee, Conclusion on Impeachment Resolution (1974)

30-2   Ronald Reagan, First Inaugural Address (1981)

30-3   Ronald Reagan, Speech to the House of Commons (1982)

30-4   Ronald Reagan, Address to the National Association of Evangelicals (1983)

30-5   T. Boone Pickens, "My Case for Reagan" (1984)

30-6   Paul Craig Roberts, The Supply-Side Revolution (1984)

30-7   Bill Chappell, Speech to the American Security Council Foundation (1985)

30-8   Patricia Morrisroe, "The New Class" (1985)

COMPANION WEBSITE HIGHLIGHTS

To view an exploration, enter one of the URLs below in your browser.

Web Explorations

Population Shifts, 1970–1980

http://www.prenhall.com/faragher/map30.1

Additional Interactive Maps

To access the maps, go to this chapter's resources at http://www.prenhall.com/faragher

Decline of U.S. Oil Consumption, 1975–1981, page 943

The Election of 1976, page 946

The Election of 1980, page 957

The United States in Central America, 1978–1990, page 967

United States in the Middle East in the 1980s, page 969

HISTORY RESOURCE CENTER

To find the resources listed below, go to http://www.prenhall.com/historyresourcecenter

Documents

Ione Malloy, Southie Won't Go (1975)

Images

American Hostage Crisis

Arthur Ashe

Mideast Peace Treaty

Nixon Releases Transcripts of Oval Office Tapes

Panama Canal Treaty

Shirley Chisolm

EXPLORING AMERICA

GROWING INEQUALITY

http://www.prenhall.com/faragher/inequality

Over the last 25 years, the gap between the rich and poor has substantially widened. What caused the widening of this gap? What has characterized the development of the United States economy over the last three decades? What role did the conservative philosophies and practices of Ronald Reagan play in the growing inequality? How have the changes in the economy and business contributed to the gap between the rich and poor? The module answers these and other questions, exploring the vast and deep economic changes that have occurred since 1973.

Growing Inequality surveys the various economic developments since 1973, focusing on the philosophy of Ronald Reagan in the eighties. The increasing influence of global events and trends are highlighted, as are the ways that American businesses adapted to the forces of the world market.

Equally important, the module discusses the rise of ruthless business practices and the information revolution as contributing to the shift in income distribution. Graphs, extensive excerpts from the speeches and news conferences of Ronald Reagan, and visual images illuminate the various developments while the interactive maps and chronology provide important time and space contexts.

Reflect and Respond

1. What were Walter Mondale's key criticisms of the Reagan administration's policies?
2. What were President Reagan's key arguments against Mondale's proposed tax increase?
3. How might you explain President Reagan's ability to win support from those segments of the electorate that fared the worst under his administration?

✓ Check it out

Ronald Reagan's First Inaugural Address

In 1980, Ronald Reagan's first inaugural address opened a new era in United States history. After a decade of instability and loss of pride, Reagan promised a new era of American pride and progress. The speech presents Reagan's conservative philosophy that sought to

basically roll back the liberal New Deal policies that had prevailed since 1933. It also is important because the ideas and policies Reagan described have strongly influenced government policy and practices up to the present day.

This exploration is also available on the *Exploring America* CD-ROM.

TOWARD A
TRANSNATIONAL AMERICA

▶ since 1988

Nam June Paik, *Electronic Superhighway*, 1995. Installation view at Holly Solomon Gallery. Courtesy of Nam June Paik and Holly Solomon Gallery.

AMERICAN COMMUNITIES

The World Trade Center, New York, as a Transnational Community

TELMO ALVEAR HAD QUIT HIS JOB AS A BUSBOY IN AUGUST 2001 to become a waiter at Windows on the World, a restaurant on the 106th and 107th floors of the North Tower of the World Trade Center (WTC) that was once described by *New York* magazine as "the most spectacular restaurant in the world." The posh restaurant was huge and elegant. Designed originally as part of a private club for the WTC's business clients, Windows on the World could accommodate as many as 1,000 people. In the decade after it opened in 1976, Windows was one of the most successful restaurants in the world, earning revenues that topped $20 million a year. Much of its success came from its fabulous menu, originally planned with the consultation of James Beard, one of the world's most renowned chefs. In the early 1990s, the reputation of Windows began to slip, and following a terrorist attack on the WTC in February 1993, the restaurant closed. But by the time Alvear found a job there, Windows on the World was once again thriving. Celebrity chef Michael Lomonaco was in charge, earning for the restaurant the Visitors Choice Award of "Grand Prize for Best Restaurant Overall." With views on a clear day extending for forty-five miles, and with a wine cellar and liquor stock that was modestly named "The Greatest Bar on Earth," Windows had become a prime tourist attraction and a popular dining spot for some of the most powerful international traders and merchants in the world. "It's more than a restaurant," one reviewer enthused. "It's a New York experience."

And so it was. Not just Windows on the World but the entire World Trade Center had come to represent both the best and worst of New York City, the commercial capital of the world. The twin skyscrapers, which were designed to be the tallest in the world, were audacious. Completed in 1973 at a cost of $400 million, they rose 110 stories above ground and occupied a thirteen-square-block site in Lower Manhattan, conveniently close to Wall Street and the New York Stock Exchange. When the WTC was first built, many New Yorkers, including distinguished architects, complained that the mammoth, boxy structures destroyed the city's unrivaled skyline. They stood too self-assuredly, critics charged, as tasteless monuments to commerce, wealth, and ambition. But over the years, the WTC became a preeminent symbol of the glory of New York and, by extension, the United States. The image of the twin towers was emblazoned on t-shirts and captured on postcards and sold to tourists from all over the world. The WTC provided office space to hundreds of businesses and government agencies and served as a work place for more than 50,000 people.

The people who worked in the twin towers constituted a remarkable transnational community. Although many were native New Yorkers, a large number were relative newcomers. Alvear himself was one in a huge wave of Hispanic immigration that had been transforming New York City since 1990. Immigrating from Ecuador as a teenager, he represented what census takers term "other Hispanics"—immigrants from the South and Central America, and the Caribbean who had replaced the Puerto Ricans and Cubans as the city's Hispanic majority. Alvear lived with his wife Blanca and their one-year-old son in Queens and spent his hours away from work at soccer games and dance clubs.

At his job, Alvear worked with and served people from a wide array of national backgrounds. Those who worked at Windows on the World proudly described themselves as a "little United Nations" because they represented just about every nation of the world and spoke nearly as many languages. Representing a wide range of cultures, they were well prepared to deal with the restaurant's equally diverse patrons, tourists from around the world and international traders and executives with offices in the WTC.

The Port Authority of New York and New Jersey, which owned the WTC, rented space primarily to tenants engaged in international commerce. Importers, exporters, freight handlers, steamship lines, oil traders, and insurance organizations were among the long-term renters. Many were multinational businesses, the majority with home offices in the United States, but a sizable number represented financial or commercial operations from Latin America, Asia, Africa, and Europe. American-based firms such as Verizon Communications, Morgan Stanley, and the Oppenheimer Funds occupied several floors. But Fuji Bank of Japan, Thai Farmers Bank, Zim-American Israeli Shipping Company, and the Bank of Taiwan also had offices there. To promote transnational exchanges, the World Trade Institute, on the 55th floor of the North Tower,

sponsored training courses in world trade, seminars for international businesspeople, and even language classes. Many of these firms chose to rent space in the WTC not because their businesses benefited directly from physical proximity to other international traders, but because an address at the WTC offered visibility to firms seeking a high profile in the world of commerce. The WTC offered firms the prestige of working in New York's most imposing landmark, a symbol of American wealth and power.

On September 11, 2001, two commercial jetliners hijacked by terrorists crashed into both towers of the World Trade Center and within an hour both towers had collapsed. Telmo Alvear, who usually worked the night shift, had been covering for a friend that morning. At age twenty-five he perished, along with nearly eighty members of the Hotel and Restaurant Workers Union who, like Alvear, were serving a special breakfast meeting. Nearly 3,000 people—citizens of the United States and eighty other nations—died that day. Uncounted were an unknown number of homeless New Yorkers who had sought what they believed to be a safe haven in the cavernous underground spaces of the WTC.

The WTC symbolized, if any building could, the confidence of American leadership in an era when national borders seemed to melt away. It also symbolized the transnationalism that many believed laid the foundation for a new world order based on the democratic liberalism that Americans treasured. Its vulnerability to surprise attack suggested the fragile nature of the swiftly changing society. ■

New York City

A NEW WORLD ORDER

Between 1989 and 1991, Americans watched with amazement as the Soviet empire disintegrated, and the cold war came to an end. But contrary to expectations, this dramatic event did not bring world peace. The end of the cold war let loose a multitude of furies in the form of renewed nationalism, ethnic and religious conflict, and widening divisions between the world's rich and poor. Just as dramatically, as the old geopolitical order disappeared, ideological rivalry shifted to the Middle East and other areas in the world where Islamic militants had forcefully turned against the West.

The presidential administrations of George Herbert Walker Bush (1989–1992) and Bill Clinton (1993–2000) bore the enormous responsibility of reshaping the fundamental premises that had guided the nation's foreign policy since the end of World War II. As the leader of the only surviving superpower, President George H. W. Bush faced a host of problems complicated rather than resolved by the collapse of the Soviet Union, and he brought the nation to war for the first time since Vietnam. Then, in 1992, when the Democrats recaptured the White House after twelve years of Republican control, President Clinton found himself equally entangled in foreign affairs. Threat of economic collapse in Japan and other parts of Asia, the various effects of global economic slowdown on the developing nations of Africa and Latin America, terrorism along with the continuation of localized wars and armed occupations worldwide, nuclear proliferation, and new strains on the world's natural resources—all forced reconsideration of the core principles of the nation's foreign and domestic policies.

The Collapse of Communism

The reforms initiated by Mikhail Gorbachev in the mid-1980s, known as *perestroika,* and, more immediately, the failed Soviet war in Afghanistan led to the

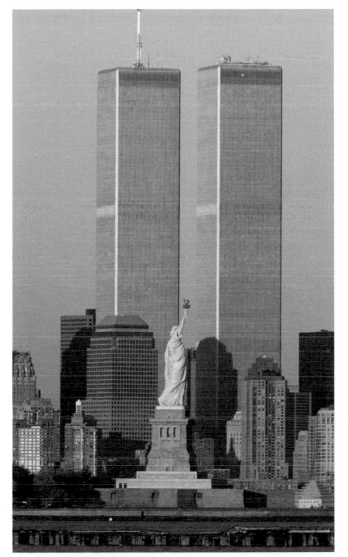

Constructed by the Port Authority of New York and New Jersey in the early 1970s, the World Trade Center provided office space to businesses from around the world. The 110-story twin towers dominated the skyline of Lower Manhattan.

SOURCE: © Joseph Sohm; Visions of America/CORBIS (JS1262341).

dissolution of the Soviet Union and to the end of Communist rule throughout Eastern Europe. Beginning in June 1989, when Poland held its first free elections since the close of World War II in 1945, prodemocracy demonstrations forced out long-time Communist leaders in Hungary, Czechoslovakia, Bulgaria, and Romania. Most dramatic of all were the events in East Germany. The Berlin Wall, which for thirty years had loomed as the ultimate symbol of cold war division, came down on November 9, 1989. Hundreds of thousands of East Germans immediately rushed into West Berlin. Popular protest intensified, paving the way for German reunification the following year.

Political changes in the Soviet Union came more slowly, accompanied by such drastically reduced living standards that successful transition to a liberal market economy and democratic political system was uncertain. In March 1989 the Soviet Union held its first open elections since 1917, and a new Congress of People's Deputies replaced the old Communist Party–dominated Supreme Soviet. In the next elections the following year, hundreds of party officials went down in defeat in key Russian cities. In August 1991 party hard-liners made a final attempt to hold on to the old order and staged a coup, placing President Gorbachev under house arrest. Although the coup quickly failed, most of the fifteen republics had meanwhile announced their withdrawal from the Soviet Union. Gorbachev found he could no longer control the government. On Christmas Day 1991 the weary and bitter president of the USSR resigned and recognized the new Commonwealth of Independent States.

The Soviet Union had dissolved, marking the end of the great superpower rivalry that had shaped American foreign policy and domestic politics for nearly a half-century. President Bush described the end of the cold war as an event of "biblical proportions." Many scholars have agreed that the changes rivaled the collapse of European empires during World War I and the rise of the cold war after World War II.

President Bush seemed both well positioned and well prepared to deal with this situation. Before serving as vice president under Ronald Reagan, he had held several major appointive offices that had involved him directly in foreign policy—UN ambassador, envoy to China, and director of the CIA. Winning election handily over Massachusetts governor George Dukakis with forty out of fifty states and 56 percent of the popular vote, he believed he could count on popular support. With the end of the cold war, Bush proclaimed, it was "time to move beyond containment to a new policy for the 1990s." But what would be that new policy?

War in the Middle East

The first great post–cold war crisis demonstrated how new kinds of conflicts—economic competition, ethnic hatreds, and regional struggles—were to redefine global politics. Events in the oil-rich Middle East, a region where both the United States and the Soviet Union had vital and often conflicting national interests, brought the two former enemies into diplomatic partnership for the first time since World War II.

On August 2, 1990, 120,000 Iraqi troops backed by 850 tanks swept into neighboring Kuwait and quickly seized control of that tiny monarchy with its rich oil fields. The motives of Saddam Hussein, Iraq's military dictator, were mixed. Like most Iraqis, Hussein believed that oil-rich Kuwait was actually an ancient province of Iraq that had been illegally carved away by British imperial agents in the 1920s as part of the dismemberment of the Ottoman Empire. Control of Kuwait would give Saddam Hussein control of its huge oil reserves, as well as Persian Gulf ports for his landlocked country.

Religion as well as economic rivalry within the Organization of Petroleum Exporting Countries (OPEC) were also major factors. Islamic militants cheered Hussein's action as a brilliant move to counter the growing influence of the United States throughout the Middle East. Just emerging from an exhausting and inconclusive eight-year war with Iran, Iraqis also bitterly resented Kuwait's production of oil beyond OPEC quotas, which had helped send the world price of oil plummeting from the highs of the 1970s and early 1980s.

The United States responded swiftly to news of the invasion. Its first concern was that Saddam Hussein also might attack Saudi Arabia, which the United States had defined as vital to its interests as far back as 1943. On August 15, President George H. W. Bush ordered U.S. forces to Saudi Arabia and the Persian Gulf, calling the action Operation Desert Shield. The president stressed the importance of oil supplies. "Our jobs, our way of life, our own freedom, and the freedom of friendly countries around the world will suffer if control of the world's great oil reserves fall in the hands of that one man, Saddam Hussein." The United States also led a broad coalition in the United Nations, including the Soviet Union, that condemned the Iraqi invasion of Kuwait and declared strict economic sanctions against Iraq if it did not withdraw. By the middle of October, some 230,000 American troops had been sent to the Persian Gulf.

In early November, President Bush announced a change in policy to what he called "an offensive military option," and the U.S. troop deployment quickly doubled and reached 580,000 by January 1991. The president also shifted to the moral high ground in justifying the biggest U.S. troop buildup since the Vietnam

War. "The fight isn't about oil," he insisted. "The fight is about naked aggression that will not stand." Administration officials now demonized Saddam Hussein as another Adolf Hitler. The UN sanctions failed to budge Hussein from Kuwait, and the drift to war now looked inevitable. In January 1991, Congress narrowly passed a joint resolution authorizing the president to use military force.

After a last-minute UN peace mission failed to break the deadlock, President Bush announced, on January 16, 1991, the start of Operation Desert Storm. U.S.–led air strikes began forty-two days of massive bombing of Iraqi positions in Kuwait, as well as Baghdad and other Iraqi cities. U.S. planes dropped 142,000 tons of bombs on Iraq and Kuwait, roughly six times the equivalent of the atomic bomb dropped on Nagasaki in World War II. The ground war, which began on February 24, took only 100 hours to force Saddam Hussein's troops out of Kuwait. Hussein's vaunted military machine—the fourth largest army in the world—turned out to be surprisingly weak. U.S. forces lost only 184 dead, compared to nearly 100,000 Iraqi deaths, mostly from the bombing.

Almost every community in the United States sent men and women to the Gulf, and the vast majority supported Operation Desert Storm. Unlike the media coverage of the Vietnam War, television new reports showed virtually no blood or death. The Pentagon required "military escorts" to accompany all reporters and carefully regulated the release of silent film footage documenting precision bombing runs. Emphasizing the technological feats, television reporters dubbed the conflict the "Nintendo" war. Air strikes looked more like video games than bombing attacks, and military officials insisted that American bombardiers never missed their targets, which were supposedly restricted to Iraqi military sites. But subsequent investigations revealed massive numbers of targeting errors and the devastation of Iraq's infrastructure, from its communications network to its water system.

Politically, the Persian Gulf War marked the high point of Bush's popularity. His approval rating with the public reached nearly 90 percent, higher than President Franklin Roosevelt's during World War II. Basking in his success, Bush proclaimed the responsibility of the United States to lead in the creation of a "new world order" that would be "freer from the threat of terror, stronger in the pursuit of justice, and more secure in the quest for peace, an era in which the nations of the world, East and West, North and South, can prosper and live in harmony."

Victory in the Gulf War rekindled national pride in many people of the United States. But for the 18 million people of Iraq, it produced the worst possible outcome. The ecological damage in the Gulf region was extensive and long-lasting. Oil fires burned out of control. The use of armor-piercing depleted uranium (DU) shells, for the first time in any war, left behind traces of radiation believed to endanger health, especially that of children and the aged. Human rights groups reported an appalling toll among civilians. Congressman Jim McDermott (D-Washington), who visited Iraq during the summer after the war, testified before a House committee on the misery he saw and posed the ethical dilemma created by the continuation of economic sanctions against the Iraqi government: "The Iraqi people did not vote for Saddam Hussein, yet hundreds of thousands of Iraqis, most of them children, are hungry, sick, and dying because of Hussein's intransigence and our commitment to oust Hussein at all cost."

The limits of military power to solve complex political and economic disputes became clear in the aftermath of victory. The Persian Gulf war failed to dislodge Saddam Hussein, who remained in power despite CIA attempts to overthrow him and repeated bombings of Iraqi military positions. Trade sanctions did little to weaken his rule, although the economic boycott, which brought increasing hardship to the civilian population, eventually divided the Western powers, leaving the United States and Great Britain isolated in their sanctions against Iraq.

U.S. Marines swept into Kuwait City, March 1991. After six weeks of intensive bombing and less than five days after the start of a massive ground offensive, U.S. and allied forces overwhelmed the Iraqi army and ended Saddam Hussein's occupation of Kuwait.

SOURCE: Photo by Patrick Downs. © Los Angeles Times. Reprinted by permission.

Moreover, regional tensions worsened in the aftermath of the war. In order to gain support from Egypt, Syria, Jordan, and Saudi Arabia to conduct military operations against Iraq, U.S. diplomats had promised to forge a just peace between the Palestinians and Israelis. President Clinton undertook secret negotiations culminating in a Declaration of Principles in Oslo, Norway, in 1993, which for the first time promised security for the Israelis and self-rule for the Palestinians. For their role in this process, Israeli prime minister Itzakh Rabin and Palestinian leader Yassar Arafat were jointly awarded a Nobel Peace Prize. But the assassination of Rabin by an Israeli religious fundamentalist, the continuing buildup of Israeli "settlements" in the occupied West Bank of the Jordan River, and the resulting violence on both sides deprived Clinton of a major diplomatic triumph.

The repercussions of the Gulf War were longlasting. The leading U.S. ally in the region, the oil-rich kingdom of Saudi Arabia, had served as the launchingpad for the invasion of Iraq, and following the war the Saudis had allowed the continuing presence of U.S. troops and weapons. This occupation of Saudi territory, which included Islamic holy sites, intensified the hatred of Americans among many Muslims and prompted appeals for revenge. Between 1980 and the turn of the twenty-first century, they bitterly observed, the United States had waged seventeen distinct military operations in the Middle East, all against Muslims.

Among those actively opposed to the U.S. role in the region was Saudi millionaire Osama bin Laden, just a few years earlier a close ally of the United States during the Russian invasion of Afghanistan. He now turned squarely against his former arms suppliers and CIA contacts. Using his own funds and a tribal network, bin Laden built his shadowy Al-Qaeda organization, training small groups in terror tactics to be used against Western interests, particularly to force American troops out of the Middle East.

Peacekeeping in the Balkans

The immediate victory in the Persian Gulf and a six-month surge of popularity did little to help President Bush when faced with a formidable candidate, William Jefferson Clinton. Unlike Bush, the last of the World War II veterans to enter the White House, Arkansas governor Clinton belonged to the Vietnam War generation and had opposed U.S. military intervention in Southeast Asia. The electorate awarded him 43 percent of the votes, compared to Bush's 38 percent, and gave the moderate Democrat a solidly Democratic House and Senate.

Despite this strong mandate, Clinton did not enjoy an easy transition. Heightened ethnic nationalism and religious fundamentalism continued to fill the vacuum left by the collapse of communism. Across the globe, from Africa to the Middle East, the Indian subcontinent, and beyond, civil wars created massive civilian casualties and new waves of refugees. Clinton, inexperienced in foreign affairs, created a team of veteran advisers including Secretary of State William Christopher and UN ambassador Madeline Albright. Together, they were compelled to grapple with a major post–cold war crisis that Bush had pushed aside—civil war in the Balkans.

With the collapse of communism, Yugoslavia had quickly fallen to pieces when four of its six states declared independence. Ethnic and religious rivalry among Serbs, Croats, and Muslims living in Bosnia erupted into a violent civil war. Bush and his foreign policy advisers, seeing no threat to American interests, opposed U.S. military intervention. But as reports of "ethnic cleansing"—forced removal and murder of Croats and Muslims by Bosnian Serbs—increased, and as the numbers of refugees grew, Clinton, with congressional support, prepared to act. By late summer 1995, U.S. and NATO fighter pilots were bombing Serbian strongholds in Bosnia. After negotiating with Yugoslavian president Slobodan Milosevic, on November 27 Clinton announced the Dayton Accords, an agreement drawn up in Dayton, Ohio, and signed in Paris that called for a federated, multiethnic state of Bosnia. An International Protection Force, one-third of whom were U.S. troops, was then installed as peacekeepers. One year later, the date Clinton had marked for withdrawal of American troops, Bosnia was still deeply divided, and American troops had settled in for a long haul.

The worst foreign crisis of Clinton's presidency erupted in Kosovo, a Serbian province about 160 miles east of Italy, across the Adriatic Sea. Milosevic, a Serb nationalist, had terminated the autonomy of the province shortly after he took office in 1989, and in response the ethnic Albanians living there organized their own government and declared their independence the following year. While preoccupied by the civil war in Bosnia, Milosevic paid comparatively little attention to Kosovo. However, in 1997, the virtual collapse of the government of neighboring Albania changed the situation dramatically. Armed Albanians poured into Kosovo and joined the rebel forces. Clashes between Serbs and Albanians intensified, and the fighting soon spread to neighboring Macedonia and to Albania itself.

President Clinton once again attempted to negotiate, but he failed to resolve the problems through diplomacy. After NATO authorized air strikes, he addressed Americans on March 24, 1999, stating that U.S. armed forces had that day joined their allies to attack Serbian forces in Kosovo. "All the ingredients for a major war are there," he explained, "ancient grievances, struggling democracies, and in the center of it all a dictator in

Serbia who has done nothing since the cold war ended but start new wars and pour gasoline on the flames of ethnic and religious division." On June 10, after a little more than two months of intensive bombing, he reported that the Serbian army was withdrawing from Kosovo and "for the first time in seventy-nine days, the skies over Yugoslavia are silent." But the bombing had destroyed many beautiful cities, the weapons deployed had left radioactive traces in the soil and water, and resentments among Muslims simmered.

His country in ruins, and voted out of office, Slobodan Miloscvic became the first head of state to be brought to trial for war crimes and crimes against humanity by the International War Crimes Tribunal in 2001. Meanwhile, in the Balkans, nationalist and ethnic conflicts continued to flare up, and U.S. peacekeepers remained.

Transnational Human Rights

The nationalist and ethnic conflicts of the post–cold war era pushed human rights to the forefront of foreign policy. This concern dated to 1947, when the UN Commission for Human Rights met for the first time to draft the Universal Declaration of Human Rights (see Chapter 26). The principle of human rights is embedded in Article 3: "Everyone has the right to life, liberty, and security of person." However, it was only in the 1970s that the United States proclaimed its international responsibility to protect and promote democracy, human rights, religious freedom, and workers rights not just as American values but as universal values. In 1976 Congress enacted legislation linking both foreign trade and monetary assistance to human rights and created a bureau within the State Department that would report annually on the status of human rights in individual countries. By the end of the century, the Bureau of Democracy, Human Rights, and Labor was surveying the status of human rights in nearly 200 countries, documenting the rise of transnational human rights networks in the public as well as private sectors, and helping to promote "an international civil society capable of promoting democracy and universal rights."

During the 1990s, with the intensification of nationalist and ethnic conflicts, the UN Commission clarified its intention to focus on the protection of vulnerable groups, including racial minorities, indigenous peoples, women, and children. The commission gave priority to the eradication of violence against women and the attainment of equal rights, and the U.S. Congress followed by creating in 1994 the position of Senior Advisor for Women's Rights.

Meanwhile, in many countries nongovernmental organizations (NGOs) were formed to cooperate with UN agencies and to provide assistance, for example, to victims of torture or religious persecution. The largest was Human Rights Watch, which had formed in 1978 to assist prodemocracy groups in Moscow, Prague, and Warsaw. In the 1990s, the organization developed into a global network of human rights advocates. It investigated and exposed war-related abuses such indiscriminate shelling of noncombatants as well as the use of rape or starvation as weapons of war. Providing assistance to refugees of civil conflict represented an enormous enterprise. In Kosovo alone, by 1999, approximately 600,000 ethnic Albanians had been driven from their homes and villages by the Serbs, and another 700,000 were living as refugees in nearby countries.

Human rights emerged as a centerpiece of President Clinton's foreign policy. Having held public office as an Arkansas governor, he was relatively inexperienced in foreign policy, and on many issues, differed little from Bush. However, like his Democratic predecessor, Jimmy Carter, he insisted that U.S. foreign policy reflect "the moral principles most American share." Now that the cold war had ended, the United States could replace the strategy of containment with humanitarian goals. Moreover, Clinton insisted, the United States, as the world's strongest nation, had a special responsibility to provide leadership to the new and emerging democracies. In 1993, Secretary of State Warren Christopher directed all American embassies to focus their programming on the advancement of human rights and democracy.

However, human rights was only one aspect of the the liberal internationalism that was the core of Clinton's foreign policy. The president insisted that the campaign for human rights depended on the expansion of democracy, which in turn depended on the simultaneous expansion of the free market throughout the world. In terms of U.S. foreign policy, Clinton therefore proposed to replace the strategy of containment with a "strategy of enlargement—enlargement of the world's free community of market democracies."

This idea drove Clinton's policy toward the People's Republic of China (PRC). The U.S. détente with China, which President Nixon had cultivated, began to fall apart during the Bush administration. During the spring of 1989, Chinese government forces brutally attacked prodemocracy demonstrators in Beijing's Tiananmen Square, resulting in the killing of some 3,000 protestors and the wounding of 10,000 more. Scenes of the massacre were broadcast live on television and provoked outrage around the world. President Bush, who had only recently extended Most Favored Nation (MFN) economic and trading status toward the PRC, hoped to maintain ties but was soon pressured by Congress to impose trade sanctions.

During his election campaign of 1992, Clinton had criticized Bush for continuing "to coddle" China in light of such gross human rights violations. Then, after taking office, he modified his position and, looking for "hopeful seeds of change," recommended restoring MFN status with the PRC. He acknowledged that serious human rights abuses continued, such as China's religious and cultural persecution in Tibet, but he pointed out that China, the world's most populous nation, had the world's fastest growing economy—as well as a nuclear arsenal and veto in the National Security Council of the UN. He defeated congressional opposition to detach human rights from MFN status and instead promoted free enterprise as a principal means to advance democracy in not only the PRC but in other nations, such as Turkey, Saudi Arabia, and Indonesia.

CHANGING AMERICAN COMMUNITIES

The dark side of the post–cold war era seemed to be offset during the 1990s by the unprecedented surge of the U.S. economy and the inclusion of millions of new immigrants, who easily found places for themselves within the rapidly expanding service sector. The patterns of growth indicated a dynamic shift toward a postindustrial economy based upon high technology, wherein today's worker with a high degree of skill and entrepreneurial initiative might be tomorrow's millionaire. After a recession, which had plagued Bush's presidency, bottomed out in 1994, Americans settled in to enjoy record profits, low unemployment rates, and unsurpassed prosperity. The business cycle, many analysts concluded, had simply disappeared, and productivity would just keep growing at a miraculous rate. In cultural as well as in economic life, in the United States and throughout the world, these changes seemed—at least for a time—revolutionary.

The Boom Years

The economy rather than foreign affairs had fueled the 1992 presidential election campaign. Republicans took credit for forcing the fall of communism and reviving America's military strength. But they had also promised to cut government spending and balance the budget. In 1985, the Republican Congress had enacted, amid great fanfare, the Balanced Budget and Emergency Deficit Reduction Act, more popularly known as Gramm-Rudman after its principal authors, senators Phil Gramm and Warren Rudman. The act mandated automatic spending cuts if the government failed to meet fixed deficit reduction goals leading to a balanced budget by 1991. But just as Bush was about to take office in 1989, many of the nation's savings and

loan institutions, which had been deregulated by Reagan, collapsed. Then, on Friday, October 13, 1989, the stock market took its worst nosedive since 1987, signaling the beginning of a major recession. With the national debt reaching an astronomical $4 trillion, the paradoxes of the Reagan-Bush years had become readily apparent.

In the Democrats' campaign headquarters a sign humorously reminded the staff: "It's the economy, stupid." Candidate Bill Clinton promised economic leadership, including deficit reduction and a tax cut for the middle class. He also effectively adopted many of the conservative themes that proved so advantageous to Republicans over the past twelve years. He called for "responsibility" on the part of recipients of social programs, spoke of the importance of stable families, promised to be tough on crime and to reduce the bureaucracy, and stressed the need for encouraging private investment to create new jobs. Economic issues also fueled the independent campaign of Texas billionaire H. Ross Perot, who with his folksy East Texas twang argued that a successful businessman such as himself was better qualified to solve the nation's economic woes than Washington insiders. Clinton interpreted Perot's

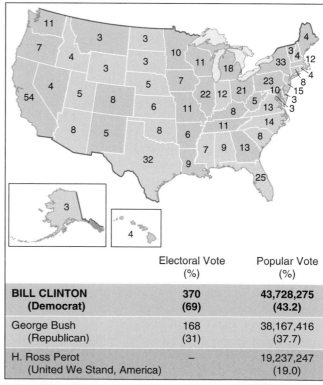

	Electoral Vote (%)	Popular Vote (%)
BILL CLINTON (Democrat)	**370** (69)	**43,728,275** (43.2)
George Bush (Republican)	168 (31)	38,167,416 (37.7)
H. Ross Perot (United We Stand, America)	–	19,237,247 (19.0)

Promising to bring about deficit reduction, Ross Perot won the largest percentage of the popular vote of any third-party candidate in U.S. history.

Republican President George Bush, Democrat Bill Clinton, and independent H. Ross Perot debated the issues on television three times during the 1992 presidential campaign. Bush emphasized the "character" issue by hammering away at Clinton's failure to serve during the Vietnam War. Clinton focused on the plight of the "forgotten middle class," many of whom had deserted the Democratic party. Perot appealed to voter frustration with the two major parties.

SOURCE: Corbis/Sygma (280232).

success at the polls to his promise to focus, as he put it, "like a laser beam on the economy."

The Clinton administration succeeded in breaking the political gridlock caused by the traditional Democratic resistance to the "economic discipline" urged by Republicans. He pursued a strategy his advisors called "triangulation," positioning himself above and between the interests of warring Democrats and Republicans. For example, despite his attacks on the Republicans as radicals, Clinton opposed his own party's efforts to block a Republican plan to dismantle the federal welfare system in place since the New Deal. The new legislation—the Welfare Reform Act—abolished the sixty-year-old Aid to Families with Dependent Children program (AFDC). Poor mothers with dependent children would now have access to aid for only a limited period and only if they were preparing for or seeking work. When Congress passed the act in August of 1996, Clinton held a public

signing ceremony and declared "an end to welfare as we know it." At the same time, he pursued this strategy to make investments at home and overseas both easier and more profitable. Clinton thus completed the economic side of the "Reagan Revolution," often with more Republican than Democratic support in Congress. Equally important, he renewed the Reagan appointment of Alan Greenspan, who chaired the Federal Reserve Board and cleverly set interest rates to check inflation and to encourage the economy to keep on growing.

President Clinton pushed two major trade agreements through Congress that built on efforts by the Reagan and Bush administrations to expand markets and encourage "free trade." Approved in November 1993, the North American Free Trade Agreement (NAFTA) eased the international flow of goods, services, and investments among the United States, Mexico, and Canada by eliminating tariffs and other trade barriers. Supplemental agreements called for cooperation on environmental and labor concerns. The stated goal of NAFTA was to improve productivity and living standards through a freer flow of commerce in North America. It created the largest free-trade zone in the world, comprising 360 million people and an annual gross national product of $6 trillion. In 1994 Congress also approved the General Agreement on Tariffs and Trade (GATT), which slashed tariffs on thousands of goods throughout the world and phased out import quotas imposed by the United States and other industrialized nations. It also established the World Trade Organization (WTO) to mediate commercial disputes among 117 nations.

Critics and supporters of NAFTA and GATT argued over whether the agreements would encourage global competition, thereby boosting American export industries and creating new high-wage jobs for American workers, or simply erode the American industrial base and accelerate environmental degradation. Cities on the U.S.–Mexican border, such as Tijuana and San Diego were clear beneficiaries, but the downside was considerable. New *maquiladoras* (factories and assembly plants) lacked pollution controls and spewed tons of toxic wastes into the air and groundwater. Despite the boost from NAFTA, the Mexican peso collapsed, and only a $20 billion bailout of the Mexican economy directed by executive order from the White House on January 31, 1995, prevented a serious depression there. From 1994 to 1997 the wages of the average Mexican worker fell from $1.45 per hour to only 78 cents. Trade did boom between the two countries, but a 1997 study conducted by the Department of Labor estimated that some 142,000 U.S. and Canadian jobs had been lost as a direct result of NAFTA.

Perhaps the greatest stimulus to Clinton's economic policy was the soaring stock market of the 1990s, with "tech stocks" leading the way. The record highs of the Bush years, when the Dow Jones index of thirty industrials approached 4,000, paled by comparison to the leap in 1999 when the Dow hit 10,000 in March and then peaked above 11,000 in May. The fastest growing sector of the market was NASDAQ, the acronym for National Association of Securities Dealers Automated Quotations, which was created in 1971 to report on the trading of domestic securities. NASDAQ grew to become the largest securities market in the United States and the prime-trading venue for technology stocks. In 1999, three companies—Intel, Cisco Systems, and Microsoft, which in terms of stock capitalization was the biggest company in the world—made up nearly a quarter of NASDAQ's total value. The market remained volatile during the decade, but profits were extraordinarily high. Annual returns on investments, generally under 6 percent during the 1970s, had risen to more than 18 percent.

Equally remarkable was the involvement "in the market" of ordinary citizens. By the end of the century, Americans had 60 percent of their investments and savings in stocks, more than double the proportion in 1982, when the market had traded at under 800. An estimated 78.7 million people held stocks, often through mutual funds or in retirement fund portfolios managed by their employers or unions. Thousands of white-collar employees working for fast-rising firms like Microsoft also acquired stock options that made them "instant millionaires" at the stocks' peak value.

The down side of the economic boom was nearly invisible. Greenspan enthusiastically announced in 1995 that the boom had solid roots: productivity had risen sharply since the 1970s while labor costs had actually declined, hoisting profits to new levels. But critics observed that while a corporate official had earned around twenty or thirty times the pay of a blue-collar worker at the same company a few decades earlier, corporate executive income was more than two hundred times greater than that of a blue-collar employee. Moreover, "downsizing" became a common strategy for increasing profits levels or defeating negative trends. By the mid-1990s, corporate leaders at IBM had laid off or fired approximately half the company workforce hired since 1980, mainly white-collar workers who usually found other jobs but often at sharply reduced pay. In the blue-collar sector, industrial jobs continued to disappear as factories closed or companies moved production of textiles, auto parts, and even electronics across borders or overseas.

Skyrocketing stock prices, while creating huge profits, inevitably raised worries of a future plunge. Anticipated returns on investments in much of Eastern Europe (especially the Soviet Union) and Latin America often did not materialize. Meanwhile, saving rates of Americans reached an all-time low, warning that a downturn could provoke massive defaults and bankruptcies sending a ripple effect through the economy. In 1998, venture capital investments reached a record $14.3 billion, an extreme example of "risk capital." By the second half of 1999, the "dot-com" internet-related stocks began to tumble, and economic analysts began to wonder if the business cycle had indeed been rendered obsolete.

Silicon Valley

Much of the growth of the 1990s was attributed to the consolidation of the "new economy," a phrased coined by economists in the 1970s to characterize the increasing importance of the service sector, corporate restructuring, and globalization. As illustrated by the successful merger of computer and communication technologies, the most important and dynamic wealth-producing activities were no longer the manufacturing and distribution of material goods but the creation, processing, and sale of information and services.

During the peak years of the new economy, a thirty-by-ten-mile strip of Santa Clara County, California, emerged as both the real and symbolic capital of the most important sector of the new economy— microelectronics. As late as 1960 this region was the major processor of fruits and vegetables in the world; forty years later one-third of the valley's workforce were employed by high-tech companies.

The nucleus for Silicon Valley dated to the early days of the cold war, when the defense industry laid the foundation for information technology. In the 1950s Stanford University began to lease unused land to electronics firms as a way to earn money, and companies such as Schockley Transitor Company, IBM, Hewlett-Packard, and Fairchild Semiconductor, seeking the advantages of proximity to a major research university, expanded to become key players in the new industry. At first, military contracts predominated, but the consumer electronics revolution of the 1970s fueled an explosive new wave of growth. Silicon Valley firms gave birth to pocket calculators, video games, home computers, cordless telephones, digital watches, and almost every other new development in electronics.

Dubbed "Silicon Valley" in 1971 after the semiconductor chip, which is made of silicon, and which became the basic building block of modern microelectronics, the region flourished thanks to its unique combination of research facilities, investment capital, attractive environment, and a large pool of highly educated people. It became home to more than 1,700 high-tech firms that specialized in gathering, processing, or distributing information or in manufacturing information technology. Companies like Atari, Apple, and Intel achieved enormous success and became household names. Silicon Valley boasted the greatest concentration of new wealth in the United States, and it attracted widespread coverage in trade magazines, business periodicals, and the popular press. Stories of millionaires made over night reinforced the powerful popular image of Silicon Valley as a place where technological innovation and great fortunes emerged from a unique culture of youth, inventiveness, and entrepreneurship.

By the end of the century, Silicon Valley had become a continuous sprawl of two dozen cities between San Francisco and San Jose and the home and work place of a diverse population. The white population stood at 44 percent, leaving no ethnic or racial majority. The managers and engineers, nearly all of whom were white males, had settled in affluent communities such as Palo Alto, Mountain View, and Sunnyvale. Manual workers on assembly lines and in low-paying service jobs clustered in San Jose and Gilroy. Most of these were Latino, African American, Vietnamese, Cambo-

dian, and Filipino men and women who constituted a cheap, nonunionized labor pool with an extremely high turnover rate. Public services in their communities— schools, welfare, police and fire protection—were poor, the glamorous lifestyle out of their reach.

The prime example of the new economy, Silicon Valley was also part of a global enterprise. Its firms were closely linked to the microelectronic industry of the greater Pacific Rim. The end of the cold war and the accompanying decline in military spending in the United States forced high-tech firms in California into greater competition on the world market and especially against similar companies in Japan, Korea, China, and Malaysia. But many American companies protected themselves against such competition by owning and managing a large share of the plants in these countries. Silicon Valley companies such as Solectron, the largest contract manufacturer of electronics in the world, Seagate Technology, Siebel Systems, and Intel, for example, all had sizable operations in Malaysia.

By the end of the century, the rate of growth showed signs of slowing, as did the infusion of new venture capital into high-tech industries. Young entrepreneurs throughout the Pacific Rim found it more difficult to start successful new companies and to make the leap from a small, start-up company to a large corporation. Then, in 2000, stocks trading on NASDAQ began to spiral downward. Within the first year of the new century, NASDAQ dropped 61 percent, a fall greater than the one caused by the oil crisis in 1973. Led by Cisco Systems, the decline inaugurated a period of retrenchment, with a slowdown in sales matched by rising unemployment throughout Silicon Valley. By this time, scarcity in housing, traffic jams, and an inflated cost of living were already leading many companies and individuals to move out of the area.

An Electronic Culture

The technological developments produced in Silicon Valley helped reconfigure cultural life in the United States and the world. Revolutions in computers and telecommunications merged telephones, televisions, computers, cable, and satellites into a global system of information exchange. The new technologies changed the way people worked and played. They made the nation's cultural life more homogeneous, played a greater role than ever in shaping politics, and ultimately created the "global village" of instant, worldwide communication that the media theorist Marshall McLuhan had predicted in the 1960s.

The twin arrivals of cable and the videocassette recorder (VCR) expanded and redefined the power of television. By the end of the 1980s pay cable services and VCRs had penetrated roughly two-thirds of American homes. Cable and satellite in the 1990s offered television viewers scores of new programming choices, especially sports events and movies. For the first time ever, the mass audience for traditional network programming declined as "narrowcasting"—the targeting of specialized audiences—competed with broadcasting. The VCR revolutionized the way people used their sets, allowing them to organize program watching around their own schedules. Hollywood studios began releasing movies on videotape, and the rental and sale of movies for home viewing quickly outstripped ticket sales at theaters as the main profit source for filmmakers. The VCR thus radically changed the economics of the entertainment business.

The intensification of television's power could be measured in many ways. In 1981, a new cable channel called MTV (for Music Television) began airing videos of popular music stars performing their work. The intent was to boost sales of the stars' audio recordings, but the music video soon became a new art form in itself. MTV redefined popular music by placing as much emphasis on image as on sound, and it revived dance as a popular performance art as well. Artists who best exploited music video, such as Madonna and Michael Jackson, achieved international superstar status. MTV also helped transform smaller, cult musical forms, such as rap and heavy metal, into giant mass-market phenomena. MTV pioneered an imaginative visual style, featuring rapid cutting, animation, and the sophisticated fusion of sound and image. Television producers, filmmakers, advertisers, and political consultants quickly adapted MTV techniques to just about every kind of image making.

More than ever, television drove the key strategies and tactics defining American political life. Politicians and their advisers focused intently on a candidate's television image. Issues, positions, and debate all paled alongside the key question: How did it look on television? In the 1992 campaign Clinton, Bush, and Perot appeared frequently on call-in television and radio talk shows in an effort to circumvent the power of professional journalists and connect more directly with voters. As the first baby-boomer candidate, the forty-six-year-old Clinton made a special effort to reach younger voters by appearing on MTV and youth-oriented programs. Fewer citizens voted or took an active role in campaigns, and most relied on television coverage to make their choices. Thus creating an effective television "character" emerged as perhaps the most crucial form of political discourse.

Perhaps no aspect of the electronics culture was more revolutionary than the creation of cyberspace, the conceptual region occupied by people linked through computers and communications networks. It began with ARPANET, the first computer network,

which was created by the Department of Defense in the early 1970s. Computer enthusiasts known as "hackers" created unexpected grass-roots spinoffs from ARPANET, including electronic mail, computer conferencing, and computer bulletin board systems. In the mid-1980s the boom in cheap personal computers capable of linking to the worldwide telecommunications network began a population explosion in cyberspace. By then, tens of thousands of researchers and scholars at universities and in private industry were linked to the Internet—the U.S. government-sponsored successor to ARPANET—through their institutions' computer centers. The establishment of the World Wide Web and easy-to-use browser software such as Netscape, introduced in 1994, made the "information highway" accessible to millions of Americans with few computer skills and created a popular communications medium with global dimensions.

By the beginning of the new century, the Census Bureau estimated that more than half of all households had at least one computer and more than 40 percent were connected to the Internet. Nearly 85 percent of classrooms in public schools were online. At work, Americans spent an average of 21 hours per week on line. At home, they spent an average of 9.5 hours per week online, gaining access to the Web from independent service providers such as America Online and Earthlink. For a flat monthly fee users could play games, send electronic mail, discuss issues in public forums, and purchase a huge array of goods and services, ranging from books and airline tickets to automobiles and psychotherapy sessions. The Web enticed millions with its advertising and spawned a new system of gambling— "day trading" on the stock market by individuals with relatively little money to spend. By 1998 there were some 320 million websites in the United States, repre-

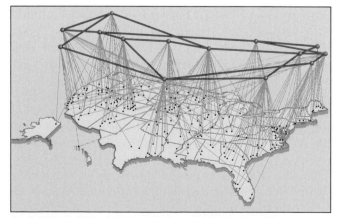

At the turn of the twenty-first century, more and more Americans were finding—and inventing—versions of community on the electronic frontier of cyberspace.

senting everything from large corporations to fringe political groups to personal "home pages."

These new information technologies gave birth to a media community that transcended national boundaries. During the 1980s, exports from Hollywood to the rest of the world doubled in value. The number of hours of television watched throughout the world nearly tripled. MTV was broadcast to an estimated 250 million households throughout the world. By the mid-1990s there were more television sets in China than in the United States. The growth of cable was phenomenal; in the Netherlands, for example, 98 percent of households received programming by cable.

Meanwhile, the ownership of media corporations became increasingly concentrated. Internationally, the News Corporation, established by the Australian Rupert Murdoch, had become a major force by the 1980s, working in nine different media on six continents. Murdoch's empire reached far into the United States. The News Corporation owned many local newspapers and broadcasting networks, such as Fox, and television stations covering more than 40 percent of TV households in the United States. Americans, however, owned a disproportionate share of the largest media corporations in the world, with Microsoft, Disney, and Time Warner in the lead. More than 40 percent of television programs in the world originated in the United States, and in Latin America the percentage of U.S.-produced programs reached 75 percent.

The New Immigrants and Their Communities

The 2000 census showed that the nation's population during the 1990s grew by 32.7 million, a number greater than that of any other decade in U.S. history. Even the 1950s, which witnessed the post–World War II baby boom, could not compete against a decade marked by a huge number of immigrants and a birthrate that surpassed the death rate. At the beginning of the new millennium, Americans numbered 281.4 million. Reflecting the economic boom of the 1990s, the data also indicated a sizable improvement in the standard of living: gains in education, housing, and mobility, and substantial increases in household income.

The 2000 census confirmed what many Americans had observed over the previous decade in their communities and work places. The face of the nation was perceptibly changing and changing on a scale that compared to the first decades of the twentieth century, when immigration from Europe peaked. At the turn of the twenty-first century, more than a third of the nation's population growth came from the influx of new immigrants. Although three-quarters of the newcomers joined many other Americans in flocking to the Sunbelt states, headed by California, Texas, and Florida, they

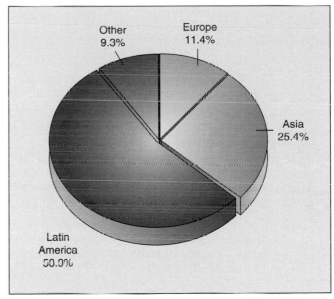

Continent of Birth for Immigrants, 1990–2000
By 2000, the number of foreign-born residents and their children —56 million according to the Census Bureau—had reached the highest level in U.S. history.

not only helped to reverse population loss in such major urban centers as New York and Chicago and slow the decline in Rustbelt cities like Cleveland, Detroit, and Milwaukee, but also for the first time in any census, they played a major role in the population increase in all fifty states. California surpassed all other states in the percent of foreign-born residents. Whereas nationally, the percentage of Americans born outside the United States was 11.2 percent, its highest point since 1930, in California the percentage of foreign born approached 26 percent.

The Immigration Act of 1965, passed almost unnoticed in the context of the egalitarian political climate created by the civil rights movement, had revolutionary consequences, some of them unintended. The act abolished the discriminatory national origins quotas that had been in place since the 1920s. It also limited immigration from the Western Hemisphere for the first time, while giving preferences to people from the nations of the Eastern Hemisphere who had specialized job skills and training. This provision created the conditions for Asian immigrants to become the fasting growing ethnic group in the United States. But in setting limits on Western Hemisphere immigration, the 1965 act tempted many thousands of people from Latin American to enter the United States illegally. By the mid-1980s, growing concern over "illegal aliens" had become a hotly debated political issue, particularly in the Southwest. The Immigration Reform and Control Act of 1986 marked a break with the past attempts to address this problem. Instead of mass deportation programs, the law offered an amnesty to all undocumented workers who had entered the country since 1982. Four years later, additional revisions of this act enlarged the quota of immigrants, once again giving priority to skilled and professional workers. Hispanics and Asians benefited from these changes in immigration law. Within the twenty fastest-growing cities, the number of Hispanics and Asians increased by approximately 70 percent. In contrast, the number of African Americans grew by less than 25 percent and whites by a mere 5 percent. In a dozen large cities, whites became a minority population for the first time.

Demographers predicted that Hispanics, who had grown from 22.4 million in 1990 to 35.3 million in 2000, according to census data, would replace African Americans as the largest minority group in the nation by the middle of the twenty-first century. By 1990 Hispanics had already formed over a third of the population of New Mexico, a quarter of the population of Texas, and over 10 percent of the populations of California, Arizona, and Colorado. Nearly a million Mexican Americans lived in Los Angeles alone.

Hispanic immigration played a large role in shifting the average age of the population. By end of the twentieth century, Americans as a group were gradually aging due to the population bulge caused by baby boomers born between 1945 and 1960. However, the population under the age of eighteen now accounted for nearly 26 percent of the total. Nearly a third of Hispanics were under age eighteen, representing the largest proportion in any major group. In areas of southern and western Texas and large parts of southern California, Hispanics made up nearly half of all the under-eighteen population.

The 2000 census showed that Mexicans were the largest Hispanic group in the United States, at 20.6 million and representing nearly 60 percent of the total Hispanic population. The boom of the U.S. economy in the 1990s, with service, agricultural, and even factory jobs readily available, had provided a significant "pull" for these newcomers. But other factors encouraged many immigrants to make an often difficult and dangerous sojourn. First, a drop in worldwide oil prices followed by the deflation of the Mexican national currency dramatically lowered living standards in Mexico in the mid-1990s. The North American Free Trade Agreement (NAFTA) and the greater integration of the U.S. and Mexican economies brought new jobs but often with increasingly expensive living conditions. Tens and perhaps hundreds of thousands of Mexicans worked in the United States temporarily while planning a permanent move north, with or without legal documentation. By 2001, the government of Mexico estimated that as many as 3 million of its citizens were living illegally in the United States.

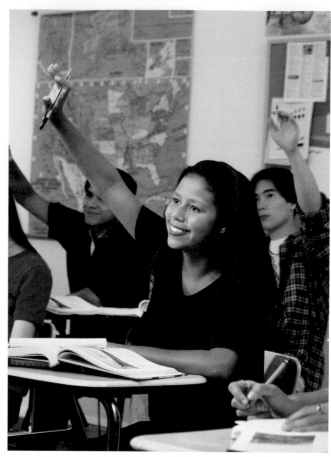

According to the 2000 Census, Hispanics were the nation's largest minority group among those 17 and younger. They represented a generation of nearly 12.3 million, the majority living in California and the Southwest.

SOURCE: Photograph by Jose L. Pelaez. Corbis/Stock Market (0-067-0130).

After settling across the border, most new Mexican Americans struggled in low-wage and often dangerous jobs such as meatpacking or construction, and they were more likely to die from work place injuries than other workers. Through education and success in business, a significant number achieved middle-class status and wealth. But almost 20 percent of Mexican Americans lived below the poverty line. They tended to live in segregated neighborhoods and were less likely than non-Hispanic whites to have health insurance or to own their own homes.

Metropolitan New York became a showcase for the new Hispanic immigration. Since the 1920s, Puerto Ricans, as the third largest group of immigrants to the U.S. mainland from the Western Hemisphere, had dominated the Spanish-speaking communities, concentrating especially in "Spanish Harlem" and in sections of the Bronx. Puerto Ricans were a special case because, as U.S. citizens since 1917, they could come and go without restrictions. Between 1945 and 1965, the Puerto

Rican–born population jumped from 100,000 to roughly 1 million. However, during the 1990s, this trend had begun to reverse, their numbers falling by 12 percent. The smaller but highly influential Cuban population declined even more, by 27 percent. Meanwhile, other Latin populations grew at an extraordinary rate of 50 percent. The Mexican-born population more than doubled, and Filipinos, who often speak Spanish as a first language, increased by 27 percent. Immigrants from the Dominican Republic, now second in population size only to Puerto Ricans, dominated sizable sections of Washington Heights and Brooklyn, while immigrants from various countries in Central and South American created new communities throughout the greater metropolitan region.

The cultural implications for all Americans, not just new New Yorkers, were far-reaching. Children born to the new immigrants of the 1980s and 1990s, despite increasing neighborhood segregation by race, played on the streets together, attended the same schools and often married outside their racial group. In the 2000 census, 6.8 million Americans nationwide listed themselves as multiracial. Identities blurred as popular entertainment created new mixes of traditions and styles. "World beat" music (heavily influenced by "Afro-Pop"), *Alterlatino* (alternative Latin music—a mixture of salsa and merengue), Tejano, Reggae, and other music in fusion mixtures became as common to Manhattan or Los Angeles as to Mexico City or Rio. By the 1990s, the West Indian carnival held annually in Brooklyn at the end of summer had become the most popular ethnic festival in Greater New York City.

Although smaller in number than Hispanics, Asians were the fasting-growing racial group in the United States. The number of Asian Americans soared from 7.3 million in 1990 to approximately 10.2 million in 2000. With a steady flow of professionals and workers skilled in technology into their communities, Chinese Americans maintained their status as the largest Asian ethnicity in the United States. However, other groups grew at faster rates, particularly Indo Americans (from the subcontinent of India), whose numbers doubled during the 1990s to 1.68 million to become the third-largest Asian group. Meanwhile Japanese Americans, once the largest and most influential members of the pan Asian community, declined. Immigration from Japan had virtually ceased during the decade, while many young Japanese Americans married someone of a different race.

Like earlier immigrant groups, new Americans from Korea, Vietnam, and the Philippines tended to cluster in their own communities and maintain a durable group identity. As a whole, Asian Americans made mobility through education a priority, along with pooling family capital and labor to support small businesses. Newcomers selected communities with job opportunities or where family members and friends had settled previously. This "chain migration" is illustrated by the large numbers of Hmongs, a tribal group from Laos, living in Minneapolis and St. Paul. The stream of Hmongs began with church-sponsored refugee programs, then gained momentum as more and more family members followed. As one of the nation's leading states in the resettlement of refugees, Minnesota saw its total Asian population triple, increasing during the 1980s from 26,000 to 78,000, and then nearly doubling in the next decade. A similar story could be told about Franklin Country, Ohio, where the Asian and Pacific Island population grew by more than 47 percent in the 1990s. Although the community was small, representing less than 3 percent of the overall

Hmong-origin immigrants were among the fastest growing Asian groups in the United States in the 1990s. In Minnesota, they were the leading Asian group coming to the state. The Hmong brought traditional clothing as well as entertainments, food, and sports and established more than 400 businesses in the Minneapolis-St. Paul region.

SOURCE: Photograph by The Merced Sun-Star. AP/Wide World Photos (6090567).

population, Asians were the fasting-growing minority group in the county. Like previous generations of immigrants, they sought opportunities, hoping to secure employment in nearby automobile factories or education at the Ohio State University in Columbus.

A NEW AGE OF ANXIETY

Despite the prosperity of the 1990s, many Americans experienced an uneasiness that resembled the anxiety of mid-twentieth century, when the world seemed on the brink of nuclear destruction. The threat of communism had expired along with the cold war, but doubts and fears about the fate of their own society had multiplied. So many changes had occurred in just the last three decades of the century that a sense of permanence had disappeared. The new economy had transformed the way Americans worked and played. The new wave of immigration had dramatically altered the demographic landscape. Even the way the nation's leaders conducted themselves appeared not only new but potentially hazardous to the moral order. In addition, many Americans had begun to fear for their personal safety, even within their own communities. Perhaps most disturbing was the lack of consensus on the meaning of these changes.

There were indications that Americans were sharply divided. The 2000 census indicated that although the poverty rate had dropped to 11.3 percent of the population, near the lowest level ever recorded, nevertheless approximately 31.1 million people still lived in poverty. Moreover, the new economy had done little to close the gap between the highest and lowest income earners, which remained at a post–World War II high. Women as a group made few gains, earning 73 cents to each dollar earned by men. And with African Americans and Latinos continuing to earn, on average, far less than non-Hispanic whites, race relations benefited little from the economic boom of the 1990s.

The Racial Divide

In the spring of 1992 an upheaval in Los Angeles offered the starkest evidence that racial tensions had not eased. The spark that ignited the worst riot of the century was outrage over police brutality. A year earlier, Rodney King, a black motorist, had been pulled from his vehicle and severely beaten by four white police officers. An amateur videotape of the incident was widely aired on television newshows. When, despite this graphic evidence, a jury acquitted the officers of all but one of eleven counts of assault, several minority communities erupted in anger. Rioters swept through South Central Los Angeles and nearby Koreatown, looting and burning businesses. Fifty-one people were killed, more

than $850 million in damage was reported, and about 500 buildings were destroyed before L.A. police and National Guard troops restored order. Approximately 12,000 people, 45 percent Latino and 41 percent African American, were arrested for looting, arson, and violations of curfew.

More than a quarter-century after the uprising in Watts, the situation in Los Angeles seemed more desperate than ever to most African Americans. The poverty rate in South Los Angeles was 30.3 percent, more than twice the national average. The unemployment rate for adult black males hovered around 40 percent, and a quarter of the population was on welfare. Los Angeles had lost 100,000 manufacturing jobs in the three years before the riot. The passage of a statewide tax cut in 1978 had led to a sharp reduction in public investment in the inner-city educational system. Drug dealing and gang warfare had escalated, reflecting the sense of despair among young people.

The events in Los Angeles exposed the deep animosity among various groups—so much so that the observers referred to the event as a "multicultural riot." Almost 2,000 Korean businesses were destroyed, and Koreans angrily accused the police of making no effort to defend their stores. The division was sharpest, though, between whites and the minority populations. "We are all quite isolated in our own communities," a resident of Westwood, a mostly white middle-class neighborhood, explained. "We don't know and don't care about the problems in the inner cities. Driving to work every day most of us don't even know where South Central is—except many of us saw the fires from that direction when we were stuck in traffic."

The situation in Los Angeles was not unique. The 2000 census showed that segregation was on the rise, and not only in cities but in their surrounding suburbs. For example, in the Atlanta region, which claimed the largest share of black suburbanites in the nation (26 percent), the percent living separately from whites had increased from 52 percent in 1990 to nearly 60 percent by 2000. Similarly, in the nation's schools, the gains from the civil rights era were diminishing and, in some communities, disappearing altogether. A report released in 2001 showed that, despite the increasing racial and ethnic diversity of nation's youth, segregation was becoming more pronounced in grades K–12. Approximately 70 percent of African American children were attending predominantly minority schools, up from 60 percent ten years earlier. The states with the most segregated schools were all in the North, with New York ranking first, followed by Michigan, Illinois, and California.

The widening racial divide also showed itself during the highly publicized trial of celebrity athlete O. J. Simpson, who was accused of brutally murdering Nicole Brown Simpson, his ex-wife, and Ronald Goldman, an acquaintance. Dubbed by the media the "Trial of the Century," the nationally televised proceedings, which lasted 133 days, provided a forum for commentary on race relations in the United States. From the beginning of the trial in January 1995 to the jury's acquittal of the ex-football star and media personality, opinions were polarized. In the end, far more blacks than whites agreed with the verdict.

The publicity generated by the arrests of Rodney King and O. J. Simpson fed several major controversies concerning the U.S. criminal justice system. In 1999 the Bureau of Justice reported that 6.3 million people were on probation, in jail or prison, or on parole, representing 3.1 percent of all adult residents. Incarceration rates, highest in the southern states of Louisiana, Texas, and Mississippi, showed a slight decline in early 2000 but nevertheless had more than tripled since 1980. Racial disparities were pronounced, with ethnic and racial minorities accounting for approximately two-thirds of state prison inmates. Based on these figures, the Bureau of Justice estimated that 28 percent of African American men would enter a state or federal prison during their lifetimes.

Various civil liberties groups reviewed these statistics and concluded that African Americans were not necessarily more prone to criminal activity but were far more likely to be stopped, searched, arrested, convicted, and given harsher penalties than white Americans. They attributed the recent rise in rates to changes in law enforcement policies dating to the Reagan administration's War on Drugs, which led to a tripling of nationwide arrests for drug offenses and accounted for one-third of all federal criminal cases by the end of the century. Critics singled out the practice of "racial profiling" whereby police disportionately stopped African Americans and Latinos as the most likely offenders. Although reports issued by the federal government at the time estimated that 80 percent of cocaine users in the United States were white and typically middle-class, the new law enforcement guidelines resulted in a significant increase in the proportion of African Americans among drug arrestees, from 25 percent in 1980 to 37 percent in 1995. By the end of the decade, in a review of various data nationwide, the National Institute of Drug Abuse estimated that although 12 percent of illegal drug users were black, they now made up 50 percent of all drug possession arrestees. By this time, "driving while black" had become a news item in all the major media, leading to the introduction of a bill into the U.S. Senate in 1999 to collect statistics on traffic stops.

The Forces of Fear

During the 1990s and first years of the new century, anxiety about terrorism and random violence escalated until the catastrophic September 11, 2001, suicide attack on the World Trade Center and the Pentagon seemed to justify all such fears. According to the CIA, incidents of international terrorism had been declining in number since the 1980s, but the drama and scale of terrorist events since then has suggested otherwise.

On December 21, 1988, Americans responded in horror to the news that a Pam Am plane en route to New York had exploded 31,000 feet over Lockerbie, Scotland, killing all 259 people aboard, including thirty-five college students returning from a Syracuse University overseas study program. This tragedy, later attributed to a bomb planted by two Libyan terrorists, became one in a series that placed Americans at risk in travel abroad.

Within their own borders, Americans were actually far safer from terrorist attacks than the citizens of many other countries. Nevertheless, two events—the attack on the World Trade Center 1993 and the destruction of the federal building in Oklahoma City in 1995—alerted Americans to danger at home.

On February 26, 1993, a small group associated with Osama bin Laden bombed the World Trade Center in New York City. The terrorists used a rented van to deliver explosives that demolished an underground parking lot, killed six people, and injured more than a thousand others. Taken in retaliation for U.S. policies in the Middle East, the attack was the most destructive act of terrorism committed within the United States to that time. It spurred the Antiterrorism and Effective Death Penalty Act of 1996, which greatly expanded the budget and powers of federal authorities to monitor likely terrorists. Despite increased surveillance of terrorist groups, bin Laden's organization struck another lethal blow. On August 7, 1998, car bombings of U.S. embassies in Nairobi, Kenya, and Dar es Salaam, Tanzania, injured more than 5,500 people and killed 225.

The bombing of the Alfred P. Murrah Federal Building in Oklahoma City raised an entirely different specter: terrorism by self-described patriotic Americans. The perpetrators represented the extremist wing of the New Right, the superpatriot movement, which included groups of people who set up "survivalist" encampments in rural areas and organized themselves into armed militias. Inspired by author William Pierce's *Turner Diaries* (1978), which predicted a revolt of "Aryans" against people of color and the federal government, the patriots found their martyrs in the Branch Davidians and their revenge in Oklahoma.

Two years earlier, on February 28, 1993, agents of the FBI and the Federal Bureau of Alcohol, Tobacco, and Firearms (ATF) had conducted a "search and arrest" operation against the Branch Davidians that turned deadly. Their object was David Koresh, the leader of the obscure religious sect who was suspected of stockpiling illegal firearms and ammunition. After a round of shots, which took the lives of four ATF agents and

Rescue workers carried an injured man from the ruble of the U.S. Embassy in Nairobi, Kenya. A terrorist bomb killed more than 100 people and injured more than 1,600 on August 8, 1998.

SOURCE: © AFP/CORBIS (FT0047338).

six Branch Davidians, Koresh's heavily armed followers barricaded themselves in their compound in Waco, Texas. Fifty-one days later, on April 19, government agents brought their siege to a fiery end. Nine Davidians managed to escape the flames engulfing their buildings, while seventy-six others, including twenty-one children, perished.

Many Americans registered their disapproval of the government's actions and their skepticism of the official accounts that assigned blame for the lethal fire to the Davidians themselves. The National Rifle Association, with 3.5 million members, likened AFT and FBI agents to Hitler's storm troopers, who squashed the rights of ordinary citizens. Right-wing paramilitarists vowed revenge. Less than a year later, at a paramilitarist demonstration near the compound, patriot Timothy McVeigh was photographed distributing bumper stickers reading, "Is Your Church AFT-Approved?"

On April 19, 1995, McVeigh and his accomplices took revenge for the tragedy in Waco. Shortly after 9:00 A.M., a bomb went off in the federal office building in Oklahoma City, killing 168 people, including 19 children, and injuring more than 500 others. People living forty miles away felt the impact of the explosion that demolished the nine-story structure in a matter of seconds. Although early news reports pointed to Islamic terrorists, the perpetrators were McVeigh, Terry Nichols, and his brother James Nichols. They had chosen April 19, the anniversary of the federal raid

at Waco, as their "Date of Doom." Arrested within hours of the bombing on a misdemeanor traffic violation, McVeigh was charged in connection with the crime just three days later. After a trial in federal court and demonstrations both for and against the death penalty, he was executed in June 2001.

Immediately after the Oklahoma City bombing, President Clinton declared a national day of mourning for the victims and their families. He addressed the nation, saying "Let us let our own children know that we will stand against the forces of fear. When there is talk of hatred, let us stand up and talk against it. When there is talk of violence, let us stand up and talk against it."

But terrorism continued, with many of the attacks politically or ideologically motivated. For example, medical clinics that provided abortion services to women became a prime target. Although the ratio of abortions to live pregnancies had been declining since 1979, groups opposed to abortion became more belligerent, emphasizing civil disobedience in addition to legal lobbying in order to promote legislation to restrict access to abortion. In 1991, Operation Rescue launched a well-publicized and illegal blockade of three abortion clinics in Wichita, Kansas. Although the "war in Wichita" ended peacefully after forty-six days, antiabortion protests became increasingly violent in its wake. Several medical providers were murdered outside their clinics, including Dr. David Gunn, who was killed by a member of the antiabortion group Rescue America in Pensacola, Florida, in March 1993. In 1994, with the support of President Clinton, Congress enacted the Freedom of Access to Clinic Entrance Act, which provides protection to any abortion clinic requesting it. Although the number of violent incidents declined since the peak of nineteen bombings in 1992 and forty-two murders in 1994, with California leading the nation in the the number of clinics torched and bombed, the attacks did not stop. In 1997, an off-duty police officer died in a bombing of an Atlanta clinic, and by the end of the century arson attacks alone reached nearly 200.

Often, the motivation for acts of domestic terror eluded even experts on the subject. Workers suspended from their jobs, fathers separated from their children, as well as individuals with grudges against the government turned to violence. One of the most highly publicized cases occurred in Littleton, Colorado, a mostly white, middle-class suburb of Denver. On April 20, 1999, two students at Columbine High School, armed with semi-automatic handguns, shotguns, and explosives, opened fire, killing one teacher and twelve of their classmates before killing themselves. Although homicides by young people age seventeen or younger declined by nearly a third in the 1990s, school killings increased. Just one month later, a teenager in Springfield, Oregon, killed his parents and then aimed fire on forty-two of his classmates, killing two.

The Culture Wars

In the 1980s and 1990s, moral and social issues, many observers noted, were replacing long-standing political markers such as religion, ethnicity, and socioeconomic class. Whereas the "New Democrats" of Clinton's administration and conservative Republicans differed little on their perception of the appropriate size and power of the federal government, they were at loggerheads over what constituted American values. Thus what one scholar described as "the struggle to define America" became hotly contested in the 1990s, with politics increasingly centered in discussions about reproductive rights and reproductive technology, homosexuality and gay rights, the curriculum in public schools, codes of speech and standards in the arts, gun control, and scientific developments such as cloning, genetic alteration, and fetal tissue research, and even the validity of Darwin's theory of evolution. With conservative radio talk-show hosts such as Rush Limbaugh and "Doctor" Laura Schlessinger firing debate on public morality, Americans became deeply divided on these and other issues.

The increasing racial and ethnic diversity of American society, as well as the expansion of rights for groups such as women and gays, had become the impetus for a broad and controversial movement known as "multiculturalism." Unlike earlier conceptions of America as a "melting pot," new metaphors such as "salad bowl" or "mosaic" became popular expressions that emphasized the unique attributes and achievements of formerly marginal groups and recent immigrants. This celebration of diversity played a big part in the campaign strategy of Bill Clinton, and he won a large share of votes by tailoring his appeals to specific groups. Like other Democrats, he received upward of 80 percent of black votes, but he won more votes from Latinos and Asian Americans than any other candidate in American history. On college campuses, multiculturalism marked the high point of the curricular reform that had been ongoing since the late 1960s and early 1970s, when specialized programs in women's studies and African American studies were launched (see Chapter 29). At the secondary level, several state legislatures and boards of education mandated instruction that would encourage students to appreciate cultural diversity.

For many conservatives, multiculturalism had replaced communism as the nation's most dangerous enemy, and they rallied to reinstate what they called universal truths and traditional moral values. University of Chicago professor Allan Bloom's best-selling *The Closing of the American Mind* (1987), for example, argued that the new lesson plans failed to prepare Americans for the responsibility of preserving their democratic legacy. In 1992, Florida conservatives contested the new legislative reforms, insisting that lessons on diversity be accompanied by instruction in the "greatness of America," including the notion that American culture is "superior to all other cultures, past and present."

The culture wars were not restricted to the academic world. Americans divided sharply over many issues, including immigration policy. In 1994, a referendum on California's ballot, Proposition 187, called for making all undocumented aliens ineligible for any welfare services, schooling, and nonemergency medical care, and it required teachers and clinic doctors to report illegal immigrants to the police. Proponents such as Republican Governor Pete Wilson argued that illegals created a crushing burden on state and local welfare agencies and school systems. They also hoped the measure would force federal action to stem the flow of illegals. A spokesman for Americans Against Illegal Immigration, a pro-Proposition 187 Southern California group, asserted, "Enough is enough. We're going broke in this state. . . . It's insanity, it doesn't make sense and the average guy in this country is not going to buy into it anymore."

Proposition 187 passed by a three to two margin, but it was immediately challenged in the streets and in the courts. In Los Angeles, more than 70,000 people marched to protest its passage and the city council voted not to enforce it. In 1998, after several years of legal wrangling, a Los Angeles federal district court judge ruled that Proposition 187 unconstitutionally usurped federal authority over immigration policy. In June 2001, the U.S. Supreme Court ruled that immigrants are entitled to same protection by the Constitution as that afforded to citizens.

But the national debate over immigration policy, in which economic issues and racial fears were deeply entangled, continued unabated in California and elsewhere. As one Stanford law professor who had worked to overturn Proposition 187 put it: "Some people genuinely worry about the problem of too many immigrants in a stagnant economy. But for most, economics is a diversion. Underneath it is race." California voters also upheld legislation enacted in 1996 that banned the consideration of race, ethnicity, and gender in college admissions and public employment, and thereby

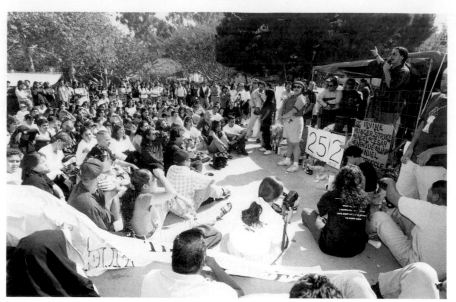

After the University of California regents voted to end the affirmative action policy governing admissions to the state-wide system, students at the University of California-Irvine protested outside the campus administrations building in October, 1995.

SOURCE: AP/Wide World Photos (000615).

abolished the affirmative-action programs established thirty years earlier.

A similar backlash gathered steam against women and gays. First Lady Hillary Rodham Clinton became the target of sustained attack for redefining and enlarging the role of the president's spouse. She led a failed campaign for reform of health care during her husband's first term, remained a vocal political adviser throughout his presidency, and became the first first lady to run for elective office. Many Americans, especially women, admired her for taking strong stands; others villified her for moving too far beyond the helpmeet role. To conservatives, Hillary Rodham Clinton symbolized the erosion of traditional American values in her support of pay equity, day-care centers, and reproductive rights.

A major controversy erupted around a push for the legal recognition of marriage for same-sex couples. Although the first law suits dated to the early 1970s, in May 1993 the Supreme Court of Hawai`i ruled that the laws barring same-sex couples from getting a marriage license were discriminatory and therefore in violation of the state constitution. This highly controversial decision prompted conservative state legislators to propose an amendment to the state constitution barring same-sex marriages, which the Hawai`ian voters overwhelmingly approved in 1998. Meanwhile, several Republicans in the U.S. Congress, fearing that if any state recognized same-sex marriages all other states would be forced to recognize these marriages as legal, sponsored legislation to deny recognition to these

unions. In 1996, President Clinton signed the Defense of Marriage Act, which specified that gay couples would be ineligible for spousal benefits provided by federal law. By the end of the century, more than thirty states had enacted similar legislation. Vermont, however, stood alone, becoming the first state to recognize civil unions, allowing same-sex couples to receive many, although not all, of the legal benefits of marriage. One year after approving "civil unions" for same-sex couples, Vermont legislators clarified the distinction between the two by banning "marriage" between members of the same sex.

In other parts of the country, local laws that prohibited bias in employment or housing on the basis of sexual orientation were overturned. In 1992, a conservative group called Colorado for Family Values pushed a referendum to enact an amendment to the state constitution that would annul all gay-rights ordinances. To the surprise of many liberal political observers, the amendment passed easily, winning a majority of votes in fifty-two of sixty-three counties in Colorado. But, in May 1996, the amendment was ruled unconstitutional by the U.S. Supreme Court.

At the end of the century, the antiabortion movement took a new turn by opposing government financing of an area of scientific research that had been growing in importance since the birth of the first test-tube baby in 1981—embryonic stem cell research. Because these microscopic clusters of cells have the potential to grow into any tissue in the body, embryonic stems cells hold promise, scientists believe, for refurbishing or replacing damaged tissues or organs and therefore might prove useful in treating or perhaps even curing diseases such as diabetes, Parkinson's, and Alzheimer's. Conservatives opposed this research because it involves the destruction of human embryos, usually derived from the excess products of *in vitro* fertilization processes and scheduled for disposal by fertility clinics. In 1995, in response to pressure from conservatives groups such as the National Right to Life Committee, Congress enacted legislation banning the use of federal funds for research that involves the destruction of human embryos. However, in his last year in office, Clinton loosened the ban and thereby generated another round of controversy. Most conservative groups remained firm in their opposition, agreeing with the United States Conference of Catholic Bishops, which insisted "that the government must not treat any living human being as research material, as a mere means for benefit to others."

Other areas of science were affected by the culture wars, including one of the most important at the end of the century: research in biological evolution. The Creation Science Movement, which had been founded in 1932 by a small group of Christians, gained widespread support for their idea that the earth was created by a deity less than 10,000 years ago and that life forms had changed little since. Evolutionists, in contrast, contended that the universe came into being 10 to 20 billion years ago, the earth about 4.5 billion year ago, and that all life forms evolved from bacteria by natural rather than divine forces. A 1997 Gallup Poll showed that 44 percent of all adults in the United States sided with the creationists, while only 5 percent of scientists did. Although the National Standards in Education adopted in 1996 specified levels of understanding of evolutionary theory among the nation's school children, many parents resisted this mandate. The Kansas Board of Education, for example, no longer required the teaching evolution in public schools.

High Crimes and Misdemeanors

Questions of private and public morality dogged Bill Clinton's political career. During the 1992 election campaign, while intending to focus on the economy, he found himself offering explanations for past behavior, such as avoiding the draft during the Vietnam War and smoking—but "not inhaling," he claimed—marijuana during his college years. However, once in office, he acted boldly on reproductive rights and put forward a controversial "don't ask, don't tell" policy for gays in the armed forces. Conservatives, including such religious groups as the Christian Coalition, the American Family Association, and the Traditional Values Coalition, as well as many Republicans, struck back.

The culture wars heated up just in time for the 1994 election campaign, making race relations, immigration, and woman's rights "hot buttons" for political candidates. With attacks on welfare, affirmative action, and federal initiatives to aid education and the inner cities, conservatives exploited a continuing white backlash against the limited economic and political gains African Americans had achieved in the previous decades. No major candidates addressed the deepening poverty and economic inequality that put one of every seven Americans, and one of every five children, below the poverty line. However, the Republicans basked in their defeat of one of Clinton's major initiatives, health-care reform, reserving as their trump card an all-out attack on Clinton's character.

During the campaign, the Republicans targeted the key item in Clinton's liberal agenda, reform of the nation's health-care system. Nearly 40 million Americans had no health insurance at all. Many simply could not afford it, and others were denied coverage by private insurers because of preexisting conditions such as AIDS and heart disease. For millions of others, health insurance was tied to the work place, and a loss or change of jobs threatened their coverage. National spending on health care had skyrocketed from roughly $200 billion in 1980 to more than $800 billion in 1992, constituting about one-seventh of the entire domestic economy. Once in office, President Clinton appointed Hillary Rodham Clinton to head a task force charged with preparing a sweeping legislative overhaul of health care. The task force sought a political middle ground between conservative approaches, which stressed fine tuning the system by making private insurance available to all, and more liberal approaches, which would have the federal government guarantee health care as a right. Powerful forces such as the Chamber of Commerce, the National Association of Manufacturers, and most Republicans immediately attacked the proposal. The Health Insurance Association of America spent millions of dollars on negative advertisements. In August, as the 1994 election campaign moved into its final phase, the president conceded that his proposal had died in Congress.

Voter turnout was light in most areas, but the majority who voted turned firmly against Clinton. Republicans gained control of both the House and Senate for the first time in forty years—a disaster of historic proportions for Clinton and the Democratic Party. Congress was now dominated by a new breed of younger, ideologically more conservative Republicans led by the new House Speaker, Newt Gingrich of Georgia.

Gingrich, first elected to Congress in 1978, had quickly won a reputation as a formidable polemicist for the Republican Party's far right. "Sixties values," Gingrich declared, "cripple human beings, weaken cities, make it difficult for us to, in fact, survive as a country." With his scathing denunciations of big government and celebration of entrepreneurship, Gingrich challenged Clinton as the key figure setting the nation's political agenda. His priorities were expressed in a set of proposals labeled the "Contract with America." Invoking the "hundred days" of Franklin D. Roosevelt's New Deal in 1933 (see Chapter 24), Gingrich promised to bring all these proposals to a vote in the House within a hundred days. The House did indeed pass much of the "Contract", including a large tax cut, an increase in military spending, cutbacks in federal regulatory power in the environment and at the work place, a tough anticrime bill, and a sharp reduction in federal welfare programs.

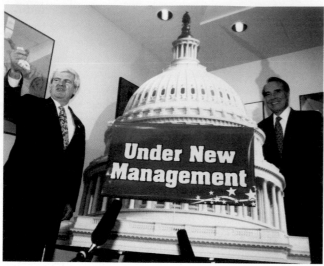

After the 1994 midterm election gave Republicans control of the House of Representatives for the first time in forty years, the new speaker, Newt Gingrich of Georgia, presented a list of legislative initiatives to be completed within the first one hundred days of the new session. On April 7, 1995, he appeared at a rally on Capitol Hill to celebrate the success of the Republican's "Contract with America."

SOURCE: Photograph by John Duricka. AP/Wide World Photos.

Differences with the Senate, however, and the threat of presidential veto ultimately thwarted Gingrich's plans and created conditions that allowed President Clinton to make a political comeback. In December of 1995 the Republican-controlled Congress forced a shutdown of the federal government rather than accede to President Clinton's demand for changes in their proposed budget. The result was a public relations disaster for the Republicans. Gingrich's reputation plummeted, and after little more than a year as Speaker he had become one of the most unpopular figures in American politics.

Meanwhile, Clinton undercut the Republicans by adapting many of their positions to his own. He endorsed the goal of a balanced federal budget and declared, in his January 1996 State of the Union message, that "the era of big government is over." With such deft maneuvers, the president set the theme for his 1996 reelection campaign, portraying himself as a reasonable conservative and the Republicans in Congress as conservative radicals.

While the Republican contender, Robert Dole of Kansas, majority leader of the Senate, waged an inept campaign for president, Clinton and his staff crafted a brilliant and well-funded one. Confounding the predictions of the political pundits who had pronounced his political death, the president won a resounding reelection victory in November of 1996. He won 49 percent of the popular vote compared to Dole's 41 percent, and carried thirty-three states. But it was a victory without coattails: the Republicans retained control of both houses of Congress. In his State of the Union address in 1997, Clinton backed yet further away from liberalism, promising a "new kind of government—not to solve all of our problems for us, but to give all our people the tools to make the most of their own lives." The era of big government may have ended, as the president proclaimed, but the era of divided government would continue.

During his second term as president, Clinton had to answer many questions about his moral conduct. Real estate deals involving both him and Hillary Rodham Clinton blew up into a major scandal known as Whitewater. More predictive of troubles ahead, a former Arkansas state employee, Paula Jones, charged Clinton with sexual assault during his gubernatorial term. Attorney General Janet Reno, under extreme pressure from conservatives, appointed an independent counsel, former judge Kenneth Starr, to investigate allegations. But in the summer of 1998, Starr delivered to the House Judiciary Committee a report focusing on an extramarital affair that the president conducted with a young White House intern, Monica Lewinsky. Starr's report outlined several potential impeachable offenses, including false testimony under oath, witness tampering, and obstruction of justice, all allegedly committed by the president to keep his relationship with Lewinsky secret.

After agreeing to testify before a grand jury empaneled by Starr—a first for an American president—Clinton made an extraordinary television address to the nation. He defended his legal position and attacked the Starr inquiry as politically motivated. The Congress and the American people at large fiercely debated the nature of the charges against the president: Were they truly impeachable—"high crimes and misdemeanors" as the Constitution put it—or merely part of a partisan political effort to overturn the election of 1996? For only the third time in history, in October 1998, the House of Representatives voted to open an inquiry into possible grounds for the impeachment.

Republicans hoping to reap a wholesale victory from the scandal in the fall elections were bitterly disappointed. Contrary to predictions and traditions in off-term elections, the president's party added seats, trimming the Republican majority in the 105th Congress.

Voters evidently had more on their minds than President Clinton's sex life. Democratic candidates benefited from continued strength in the economy, and they made effective appeals on a range of issues, from preserving Social Security and Medicare to protecting a woman's right to choose an abortion. Higher than expected turnout from such core constituencies as union members and African Americans (especially in the South) also contributed to the unexpectedly strong Democratic showing. The election also brought a shakeup in the Republican leadership. Newt Gingrich, under pressure from Republican colleagues angry about a campaign strategy that had narrowly focused on Clinton's impeachment problem, announced his resignation as Speaker of the House and from his seat in Congress. Ironically Gingrich, who had led the Republican resurgence in the 1990s, now appeared to be the first political victim of the Lewinsky scandal.

In the aftermath of the 1998 election, most politicians and analysts, and indeed most Americans, believed the impeachment inquiry to be at a dead end. But the House Judiciary Committee, after raucous televised debate, voted to bring four articles of impeachment—charging President Clinton with perjury, obstruction of justice, witness tampering, and abuse of power—to the full House. But unlike the bipartisan case the Judiciary Committee brought against Richard Nixon in 1974 (see Chapter 29), this time the votes were all along strictly party lines. Neither the 1998 election results, nor polls showing a large majority of Americans opposed to removing the president, curbed the Republican determination to push impeachment through the House and then on to the Senate for trial. On February 12, 1999, the Senate trial concluded with the president's acquittal.

ing as a persistent threat, as witnessed by yet another terrorist attack, the October 12, 2000, bombing of the USS *Cole* in Aden, Yemen, which cost the lives of seventeen American sailors. In this world of growing uncertainties, no one knew how a new Republican administration would respond to the enormous challenges accompanying the new millennium.

The Election of 2000

After a relatively dull campaign season, the 2000 election played out as high drama. Voters went to the polls as usual on election day, watched as late-night television newscasters projected a victory for the Democratic candidate, Clinton's vice president Al Gore, and then woke up the next morning to learn that perhaps the winner was not the vice president but his Republican opponent, Governor George W. Bush of Texas, son of former president George H. W. Bush. It was clear that Gore and his running mate, Connecticut Senator Joseph Lieberman, had won the popular vote, although by the closest margin since John F. Kennedy defeated Richard Nixon in 1961. In doubt was the number of votes in the Electoral College. At 2:15 A.M., the pollsters who had projected Gore as the winner changed their minds. The

THE NEW MILLENNIUM

At the beginning of the twenty-first century, citizens, politicians, and business and religious leaders had to rethink their basic assumptions about the American way of life. American society had become more stratified along lines of race and income. New immigrant groups, especially from Asia and Latin America, had changed the face of the nation's communities, schools, and work places. New media technologies had made cultural life more homogenized and caused the manipulation of image to become more crucial than ever to both politics and entertainment. The New Economy, service-oriented and high-tech, had fundamentally altered the way many Americans did business and earned a livelihood, and it depended not only on American consumers heavily burdened with debt but also on an expanding global market.

The end of the cold war had reconfigured global politics, ending the bilateralism that had dominated international affairs since the end of World War II. The United States alone held fast to its superpower status, but this achievement did not necessarily make Americans more secure or safe. The old enemy, Soviet communism, was succeeded by more fanatic, less predictable foes. It was clear that international terrorism was emerg-

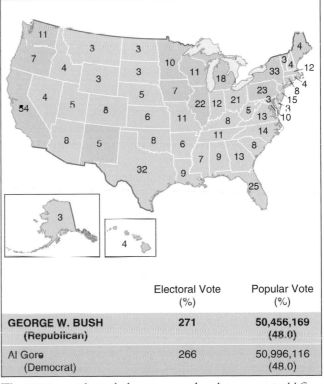

	Electoral Vote (%)	Popular Vote (%)
GEORGE W. BUSH (Republican)	**271**	**50,456,169** **(48.0)**
Al Gore (Democrat)	266	50,996,116 (48.0)

The 2000 presidential election was the closest one in U.S. history and the first one to be decided by a decision of the Supreme Court.

An election official examined a disputed punch-card ballot in the Presidential election in Florida in November 2001. He tried to figure out whether the "chad" had been dislodged or merely "dimpled."

SOURCE: © Reuters NewMedia Inc./CORBIS (UT0055362).

cliffhanger in Florida had finally ended with the state's decisive twenty-five electoral votes earmarked for the Republicans. By morning Gore had called Bush to concede. The *New York Times*, however, ran a guarded headline "Bush Appears to Defeat Gore." Only a few hundred votes in Florida gave Bush the edge, and in cases where the margin is so narrow Florida law mandates a machine recount in all sixty-seven counties. Gore soon retracted his concession, putting voters into suspense until the middle of December, when the vice president finally ended his campaign.

Such a spectacular ending to the 2000 campaign could not have been foreseen from the primaries. As the son of a former president, George W. Bush had run a low-key campaign, calling himself a "compassionate conservative" who cared about the underdog and the nation's educational system. He nevertheless did not swerve from the Republican agenda that President Reagan had shaped: tax cuts, strong military defense, and the overhaul of Social Security and Medicare. He also promised relief from environmental regulations,

new judicial appointments that would eventually limit reproductive rights, and the restoration of morality to public life. Albert Gore, Jr., also the son of a prominent politician, carried the burden of association with Bill Clinton and waged an uphill battle. More notable was his running mate, Lieberman, the first Jewish candidate for vice president. Dick Cheney, who had served prominently in the senior Bush's administration, balanced the younger Bush's relative lack of experience in federal government. The emergence of consumer advocate Ralph Nader as Green Party candidate added spice to an often dull campaign.

In November, voters themselves offered few surprises except for a round of congressional defeats for Republicans. Republicans lost ground in both the House of Representatives, where their majority fell to a dozen, and in the Senate, where Democrats and Republicans stood in equal numbers until James Jeffords of Vermont ended the stalemate by quitting the Republican Party early in the new Congress. The one major surprise was the unanticipated victory of Hillary Rodham Clinton, who beat her Republican opponent by a twelve-point margin for a seat in the U.S. Senate from the state of New York.

The 2000 campaign played out as the first disputed presidential election since 1876, when Democrat Samuel J. Tilden, who won the popular vote, charged his Republican opponent, Rutherford B. Hayes, with fraudulent vote counting. The decision went to a congressional committee which, acting strictly along party lines, gave the presidency to "Rutherfraud" B. Hayes, as he was dubbed by opponents. A similar question of legitimacy hung over the 2000 election. After Florida completed its machine recount of votes, the Democrats requested a hand tally in selected counties where the ballots were in dispute. The Republicans responded by suing in the Miami district court to prohibit the manual recounting. Meanwhile Florida election officials, mainly Republicans, set November 14 as the date to certify the election results, thereby disallowing the returns on overseas ballots which might favor Al Gore. In turn, Democrats sued to extend the deadline. Eventually, appeals by both parties reached the Florida Supreme Court and finally the U.S. Supreme Court, which voted five to four along partisan lines to halt the counting. Time had run out, and on December 12 Gore conceded defeat. With less fanfare than usual, George W. Bush took the oath of office in January 2001.

Global Warming

Bush took office without a clear agenda and for the first few months continued some of his predecessor's policies. For example, he ultimately relented on his campaign promise to prohibit federal spending on stem cell research. However, in managing the federal budget, Bush struck out on his own. Clinton, pressured by the rising deficit when he took office, did so well in curbing federal spending that he had produced a surplus. Bush immediately pushed for a new tax law that would reduce the budget surplus by $1.35 trillion over ten years with tax cuts allocated principally to wealthy Americans. With corporate profits and the economy slowing dramatically during the first months of the Bush administration, Congress approved substantial tax reductions with hope of stimulating the economy.

On policies concerning the environment, Bush acted quickly and aggressively to defer or to overturn several key programs established under Clinton. In July 2001, the Environmental Protection Agency announced a delay in asking states to draft plans to protect some 21,000 waterways severely impaired by agricultural runoff. Meanwhile, Bush's advisers reconsidered proposals that would have prohibited the development of nearly one-third of the national forests.

No issue was so important or so controversial as climate change, a challenge that most scientists and world leaders agreed required international solutions. During the late 1970s, scientists presented data indicating that the earth was warming, causing polar icecaps to melt, oceans to rise, and ultimately marine life to die, and they pointed to the emission of "greenhouse gases," the by-products of the fossil fuels burned to run factories and automobiles, as the main cause. To curb this dangerous trend, the United States, the European Economic Community, and twenty-eight other countries had ratified the Montreal Protocol on Substances that Deplete the Ozone Layer of 1987, which established a timetable for phasing out the production of greenhouse gases by the end of the century. However, a few years later, in June 1992, at the first Earth Summit sponsored by the United Nations, the U.S. delegates took a more cautious approach, demanding that limits on greenhouse gas emissions be voluntary rather than mandatory. Although responsible for the production of more greenhouse gases than any other nation, nearly 25 percent of the total worldwide, the United States now refused to make a firm commitment.

The controversy came to a head four years later at the world summit on global warming held in Kyoto, Japan. In advance of the meetings, the major U.S. automakers advised President Clinton against signing any treaty. Meanwhile Senate Republicans secured a nonbinding resolution that specified that the terms of any treaty require developing nations, including China, India, and Mexico, to control their emissions as well. Clinton sent Gore to Kyoto to find a middle ground. In the end, the Kyoto Protocol outlined targets and timetables for the reduction of greenhouse gases and required the richer, industrialized countries to take the lead, specifying an average 5.2 percent reduction from 1990s levels by 2012. Although the fifteen-member nations of the European Union endorsed the terms of the treaty, both Japan and the United States held out.

Shortly after taking office, President George W. Bush announced his opposition to the terms of the Kyoto Protocol, leaving 178 other countries to agree to mandatory reductions in greenhouse gases without the participation of the United States. Bush instead created a task force to conduct additional studies on the impact of human activity on climate change. Meanwhile, the U.S. Energy Information Administration released new data showing that carbon dioxide emissions had risen 3 percent in the United States during the previous year alone, one of the largest increases in recent times. In July 2001, 1,500 scientists affiliated with the UN Intergovernmental Panel on Climate Change, the leading authority on global warming, met in Amsterdam and confirmed, as a key member said, that "the problem of global change is real, and it is more serious than is currently perceived politically."

A Global Community?

The changing climate was only one issue tied to globalization, a term used to characterize the belief that worldwide processes were causing national economies, cultures, and borders to melt away. Beginning in the 1970s, social scientists began to study and debate the degree to which to which people throughout the world were affected by events happening far from their home lands. If nothing else, they pointed out, people in most parts of the world could keep up on these events by watching CNN or tapping into the Internet—and drink Coke while they were doing it. But the big questions concerning globalization centered on political economy. Now that communism has collapsed, they asked, would a steady expansion of free trade among nations create the basis for a global community?

There were many answers to this question. Some observers argued that the interpenetration of markets and cultural patterns—the enormous sales of Hollywood movies in China, for example—set the stage for other exchanges. President Clinton, for instance, contended that the expansion of the free market in China improved the prospects for democracy in that nation. Others argued that the global economy depended less on "interpenetration" than "domination" of the marketplace by the industrialized nations. Whereas physical occupation of territory defined the form of colonialism that prevailed before World War II, a new "colonialism" had come into existence since the 1960s that relied on a few multinational corporations controlling distant economies throughout the world. To back up this argument, they referred to a UN report that estimated that about 90 percent of the multinational corporations that did business worldwide were headquartered in the industrialized nations of North America, Europe, and Japan. Known collectively as the Triad, the consortium of these nations, home to only 15 percent of the world's population, produced nearly 75 percent of the world's goods by the late 1990s. One critic described this situation as not like a "global village" but more like "global pillage." Some traditional economists discounted the significance of these developments, insisting that trading activities date to the earliest civilizations and that well-organized transnational economies were the hallmark of the Industrial Age. The growth of international foreign trade in the last half of the twentieth century, they claimed, approximated that in the last half of the nineteenth century.

What made the current trend toward "globalization" distinctive was, therefore, not the rate of growth but the absolute volume and character of the exchange. Revenues from multinational corporations grew phenomenally at the end of the twentieth century. The 1998 total revenue of Wal-Mart Stores, Inc., with retail outlets in many parts of the world, surpassed the gross domestic product of Greece ($119.3 billion as compared to $119.1 billion). Because the member nations of the Triad were homes to the world's largest multinational corporations, they also reaped the largest share of the wealth. A UN annual human development report stated that "global inequalities in income and living standards have reached grotesque proportions." The report offered statistics showing that the gap in wealth between the upper 20 percent and the world's poorest people was at the end of the nineteenth century 30 to 1; by 1990 it reached 60 to 1; and by the end of the century it had widened to 74 to 1.

While many political observers and scholars predicted that globalization would bring both free markets and democracy to more and more of the world's people, others became increasingly skeptical. At the turn of the twenty-first century, an international protest movement emerged that targeted the most powerful organizations in the global economy: the World Trade Organization (WTO), the International Monetary Fund (IMF), and the World Bank. In November 1999, thousands of protestors converged in Seattle, Washington, site of the annual meeting of the WTO, only to be pushed back by local police. In response, the WTO formulated new procedures for its meetings, secreting delegates behind walls and banning demonstrations from the area near future sites. Nevertheless, confrontations continued, the most dramatic occurring at a meeting of delegates from the eight leading industrial nations in Genoa, Italy, in 2001, which resulted in the death of one protestor.

Experts on globalization could not agree if the trend toward a single international market challenged traditional notions of national sovereignty and laid the foundation for global democracy or if the post–cold war world order was increasingly challenged by civil wars, ethnic and religious clashes, and the breakup of nation-states.

More than 5,000 activists gathered in Seattle in November 1999 to demonstrate against the meeting of the World Trade Organization. The event, which was marked by a violent clash with police and the arrest of dozens of protestors, marked the beginning of a movement for global economic justice.

SOURCE: © AFP/CORBIS (FT0022933).

Terrorist Attack on America

On September 11, 2001, hijackers, armed only with knives and box cutters, crashed two jetliners into each of New York's World Trade Center towers, while a third jetliner slammed into the Pentagon in Virginia. A fourth plane, diverted from its terrorist mission by courageous passengers, hurtled to the ground near Pittsburgh. In all, 246 people perished in the four planes. At the sites of the attack, the damage was devastating. At the Pentagon, which had been built to withstand terrorist attacks, a huge explosion followed by fierce fires destroyed a large section of the defense complex. The death toll soon reached 184, including 59 people who had been on board the hijacked airliner. In New York, the number of lives lost was, as Mayor Rudolph W.

The United States conducted air strikes on the village of Rahesh, near the capital city Kabul, in November 2001 in a military campaign to drive the Taliban from power in Afghanistan.

SOURCE: © AP/Wide World Photos (6051224).

Guilani said, "horrendous." The collapse of the twin towers, most likely caused by the intense fires propelled by the planes' jet fuel, brought death to thousands, including hundreds of police and rescue workers who had dashed into the buildings to help. At the end of the day, the New York City Fire Department had lost 350 firefighters, nearly thirty times the number ever lost by the department in a single incident. The nation watched in horror as the events vividly unfolded in live newscoverage on TV. The stark images of the second plane hitting the WTC, the dramatic collapse of the buildings, and the fear on the faces of thousands fleeing the sites were replayed over and over again on televisions throughout the world.

While the media recalled Pearl Harbor, President Bush declared the deadly attacks an act of war and vowed to hunt down those responsible for the "evil, despicable acts of terror." Congress, with only one dissenting vote, granted him power to take whatever steps necessary. The Department of Justice began what it described as the largest and most intensive investigation ever conducted, and the president issued a blanket warning to all nations who harbor terrorists. Secretary of State Colin Powell stated clearly, "You're either with us or against us." For the first time ever, NATO invoked the mutual defense clause in its founding treaty, which in effect supported any U.S. military response.

Observers described Bush's response as the defining moment of his presidency, as it was for the lives of many Americans. A patriotic surge found flags displayed on homes and cars—even painted on the faces of children. Millions of Americans rushed to donate blood, and thousands traveled to New York to assist rescue efforts. Prayer vigils were held in churches, synagogues, and mosques, as well as in public buildings and parks. Millions of dollars were soon raised for the relief effort and to assist the families of those who perished.

Many businesses, especially those in the travel, entertainment, or hazardous materials industries, were closed in the days following the attack. Major sports events, including baseball, football, and golf, were cancelled or postponed. As a precautionary measure, skyscrapers in the largest cities, such as the Sears Tower in Chicago, the building that had surpassed the WTC as the nation's tallest, were evacuated. The stock market, after a three-day pause, reopened to the worst week in the history of Wall Street since the Great Depression. Financial analysts declared that the already faltering economy had now certainly entered a recession.

Perhaps most dramatic was the unprecedented shutdown of all airports in the United States, stranding thousands around the world. Service returned several days later at greatly reduced levels and with enhanced security. Even plastic knives were banned in airport restaurants. President Bush created a new Cabinet-level agency, Homeland Security, charged with coordinating the efforts of more than forty other agencies to protect Americans against terrorists and to respond to any such attacks. He also allocated millions of dollars to boost the budgets of the Department of Defense, the CIA, and the FBI. But fear had chilled most Americans' spirit. In the face of a $15 billion bailout of the airline industry quickly passed by the Senate, they cancelled vacations and applied for refunds for airline tickets already purchased. Two-thirds of those polled believed the worst might still come.

The day following the highly coordinated terrorist attack, President Bush identified the Saudi Arabian Osama bin Laden as the prime suspect. Administration officials linked the airline hijackers, all presumed to be Islamic fundamentalists, to his Al-Qaeda network, which apparently had dispatched them to train at American flight schools. Although a communique from bin Laden denied involvement, U.S. intelligence sources insisted that only bin Laden had the resources to carry out such a sophisticated operation and sufficient motivation. In 1998, bin Laden had issued a decree that granted religious legitimacy to all efforts to expel the United States from the lands of Islam in the Middle East. His network of terrorist cells, which reportedly operated in sixty countries, had directed rage at what they believe to be the global arrogance of the

CHRONOLOGY

1981	MTV and CNN start broadcasting as cable channels
1986	Immigration Reform and Control Act addresses concerns about illegal aliens
1987	Allan Bloom publishes *The Closing of the American Mind*
1988	Indian Gaming Regulatory Act allows Indian tribes to operate gambling establishments
	George Bush is elected president
	Terrorist attack on Pam Am plane over Lockerbie, Scotland
1989	Tiananmen Square demonstration in China
	Communist authority collapses in Eastern Europe
1990	August: Iraqi invasion of Kuwait leads to massive U.S. military presence in the Persian Gulf
1991	January–February: Operation Desert Storm forces Iraq out of Kuwait
	Operation Rescue launched in Wichita, Kansas
	Soviet Union dissolves into Commonwealth of Independent States
1992	Rodney King verdict sparks rioting in Los Angeles
	UN holds first Earth Summit
	Bill Clinton is elected president
1993	Terrorist bombing of World Trade Center kills six people
	Federal agents conduct seige of Branch Davidian compound in Waco, Texas
	Clinton administration introduces comprehensive health-care reform, but it fails to win passage in Congress
	Congress approves the North American Free Trade Agreement
1994	Republicans win control of Senate and House for first time in forty years
	Congress approves the General Agreement on Tariffs and Trade
	Congress passes the Comprehensive AIDS Revenue Emergency Act
	Congress passes "Defense of Marriage" Act
	California voters approve Proposition 187
1995	Bombing of Alfred P. Murrah Federal Building in Oklahoma City kills 168 people
	Clinton announces Dayton Accords to mediate civil war in Bosnia
1996	Congress passes Welfare Reform Act
	Congress enacts the Antiterrorism and Effective Death Penalty Act
	President Bill Clinton is reelected
1997	Kyoto Protocol endorsed by European Union but not United States
1998	U.S. embassies in Kenya and Tanzania bombed by terrorists
	House of Representatives votes to impeach President Clinton, but vote fails in Senate
1999	U.S. joins NATO forces in Kosovo
	Protesters disrupt meetings of the World Trade Organization in Seattle
2000	USS *Cole* bombed by terrorists
2001	George W. Bush becomes president after contested election
	Terrorists attack World Trade Center and Pentagon
	U.S. begins military campaign in Afghanistan

United States—its accumulation of unprecedented wealth when poverty and hopelessness extended across the Middle East.

With bin Laden presumed to be hiding in Afghanistan and supported by the ruling Taliban government, President Bush insisted that the Taliban regime hand over the terrorists "or they will share in their fate." He dispatched U.S. aircraft carriers to join the U.S. forces already assembled in the Persian Gulf region, and mobilized reservists for a possible invasion. On October

7, he ordered the first air strikes in Afghanistan, with the stated goal of destroying Al-Qaeda's terrorist training camps and bringing down the Taliban government that was shielding bin Laden.

CONCLUSION

Although the attack on the WTC and the Pentagon stunned and infuriated most Americans, it represented only the most destructive in the series of terrorist attacks that had been levied against the United States since the 1980s. In 1999, the U.S. Commission on National Security/Twenty-first Century, which has been established by Congress to evaluate the nation's defense systems, had concluded that "America will become increasingly vulnerable to hostile attack on our homeland" and that "Americans will likely die on American soil, possibly in large numbers." The security promised by the end of the cold war seemed more elusive than ever. By early 2002, the Taliban government had collapsed much sooner than anticipated by U.S. military advisors. However, the war continued. President Bush, who had asked Americans to be patient "in understanding that it will take time to achieve our goals," broadened the scope and declared a world-wide war on terrorism.

REVIEW QUESTIONS

1. Is the United States entering a "new era" in the twenty-first century? What effects have the globalized economy and the fall of the Soviet Union had on American political life?

2. How is the "new economy" different from the old economy? How has it reshaped American business and financial practices? Explain the relationship between the new economy and electronic media, such as the Internet and cable television.

3. Evaluate the presidency of Bill Clinton. Compare his domestic and foreign policies to those of the Republican presidents who preceded and followed him in office. What was the impact of the scandals that plagued his presidency?

4. Describe the major demographic trends revealed by the 2000 census. Identify the racial and ethnic groups with the greatest gains in population. How have various legislation acts since 1965 affected immigration to the United States? How have communities changed as a result of the influx of new immigrants?

5. The concept of globalization is highly controversial. Are borders between nations "melting away" as some scholars contend? How does this concept square with the description of the United States as the single superpower in the world? Does this concept apply primarily to economics, or is it useful for discussing issues related to culture, media, the environment, and population trends?

6. Earlier scholars predicted that the end of the cold war would bring peace and promote democracy throughout the world. Events, beginning with the Persian Gulf War, have instead suggested a new basis for international affairs. Describe the importance of regional and ethnic conflicts in the Middle East and Central Europe.

RECOMMENDED READING

Angus Kress Gillespie, *Twin Towers: The Life of New York City's World Trade Center* (1999). A detailed history of the buildings, including the political background and the process of design and construction. Gillespie traces the emergence of the World Trade Center as a popular symbol of New York City and center of international commerce.

Mark S. Hamm, *Apocalypse in Oklahoma: Waco and Ruby Ridge Revenge* (1997). Provides a succinct overview of the events leading to the bombing of the federal building in Oklahoma City in 1995, seeing it as an act of murderous revenge.

David Held, ed., *A Globalizing World? Culture, Economics, Politics* (2000). Four essays addressing various aspects of globalization. This slim volume offers a concise summary of the major theories of globalization and compares the contemporary situation with previous eras.

Neil Howe, *Millennials Rising: The Next Generation* (2000). An optimistic assessment of the generation of Americans who were born on or after 1982 and projections for their future. Howe surveys statistics as well as cultural trends and concludes that the rising generation shows a return to conservative family values and a respect for rules.

William G. Hyland, *Clinton's World: Remaking American Foreign Policy* (1999). Evaluates the first post–cold war president's decisions with regard to the major international events of the 1990s. Examines the developing policies toward Russia and Asia. Hyland offers a fairly negative assessment.

Robert K. Kaplan, *The Coming Anarchy: Shattering the Dreams of the Post–Cold War* (2000). Nine essays on international affairs that provide an often disturbing assessment of the prospects for peace. Kaplan discusses the rise of ethnic conflict in regions such as Sierra Leone, Russia, and India and weighs the signficance of increasing tribalistic warfare, the breakdown of central government authority in several nations, and the rise in crime in post-Communist countries.

Judith Millwer, Stephen Engelberg, and William Broad, *Germs: Biological Weapons and America's Secret War* (2001). Beginning with the use of salmonella to poison food in Oregon in 1984, this book narrates the history of biological warfare in the last half of the twentieth century. The authors, veteran reporters for the *New York Times*, argue that the United States is ill equipped to protect its citizens against a serious biological attack.

Jill Nelson, ed., *Police Brutality: An Anthology* (2000). Twelve essays written by scholars, activists, and writers that discuss, from a variety of perspectives, police presence in American communities. Several essays focus on the broad historical dimensions of this issue, tracing the roots back to the time of slavery.

New York Times staffwriters, *The Downsizing of America* (1996). A well-researched account detailing the devastating impact of corporate "downsizing" on American communities and families.

Howard Rheingold, *The Virtual Community* (1994). Very thoughtful examination of the promises and problems posed by the new computer-based technologies associated with "virtual communities."

Micah L. Sifry and Christopher Cerf, eds., *The Gulf War Reader* (1991). An excellent collection of historical essays, government documents, and political addresses that provides a comprehensive overview of the Persian Gulf War.

Janet Thomas, *The Battle in Seattle: The Story Behind and Beyond the WTO* (2000). An impassioned, eyewitness account by a participant in the 1999 demonstrations against the World Trade Organization, which the author describes as a "global tailspin at the end of the century."

▶ MEDIA RESOURCES

U.S. HISTORY DOCUMENTS CD-ROM

America at the Millennium

30-9   George Bush, Address to the Nation Announcing Allied Military Action in the Persian Gulf (1991)

HISTORY RESOURCE CENTER

To find the resources listed below, go to
http://www.prenhall.com/historyresourcecenter

Documents

George Bush, Address to the Nation Announcing Allied Military Action in the Persian Gulf (1991)

Images

A Group of Five Presidents

Chaos outside the Washington Hilton Hotel after the Assassination Attempt on President Reagan

George Bush

Kuwaiti Oil Fires

Nancy Reagan Speaking at a "Just Say No" Rally in Los Angeles

Operation Desert Storm

President Reagan Addressing the Annual Convention of the National Association of Evangelicals (the "Evil Empire" Speech)

President Ronald Reagan

Ronald Reagan and Mikhail S. Gorbachev

The Reagans at Home

William Jefferson Clinton, 43rd President of the United States

EXPLORING AMERICA
GLOBALIZATION
http://www.prenhall.com/faragher/globalization

What connections exist between the increasing globalization of recent decades and terrorism? How have various nations resisted or accommodated Western influences such as free market capitalism and republican political institutions? How have terrorists justified their actions? Against the backdrop of the attack on the World Trade Center, this module examines various aspects of globalization, indicating that recent developments are part of an ongoing course of events that date back centuries. Two examples of resistance to global trends are discussed, free market activity and terrorism.

Globalization combines an analysis of historical and contemporary developments to explore this pivotal topic in United States and world history. It also describes how nonwestern peoples have adopted such Western ideas as Marxism and republican capitalism. Union position papers, brochures, other print sources, visual images, and extensive quotes from Osama bin Laden illustrate the complex factors involved in globalization. Maps and the chronology place the discussion in historical perspective.

Reflect and Respond
1. What is bin Laden's "case" against the United States?
2. "Those who try to cover this crystal clear fact, which the entire world has admitted, are deceiving the Islamic nation. This war is fundamentally religious." What does bin Laden mean by "nation" in this statement? What does he mean by "religious"?
3. Why, according to bin Laden, should every Muslim join in the struggle?

✓ Check it out
Osama Bin Laden Transcript

Terrorist leader Osama Bin Laden presented his case for terrorism in a broadcast on Al-Jazeera. Because of the devastation caused by his followers, it is important to gain a better understanding of his rationale for terror and his beliefs. The speech is important because it shows that bin Laden views the world in stark black and white, right and wrong terms and uses his fundamentalist faith to justify his political beliefs and actions.

This exploration is also available on the *Exploring America* CD-ROM.

The World Trade Center and Ways of Remembering

The first plane hit the north tower of the World Trade Center at 8:48 am. The second plane struck the south tower at 9:03 am. The two massive, 110-story "twin towers" soon collapsed into a nightmarish rubble, as millions of disbelieving viewers watched the scene on television. By then, many Americans had already begun to speak of the event as the defining moment of their own lifetimes, declaring that they would forever remember where they were and what they were doing when reports of the tragedy reached them. While the events were still unfolding, Americans began to search for ways to place the terrorist attack on America in historical perspective. How would their memories make sense of the experience in the long run? How did the larger context of U.S. history frame the horrible events of September 11, 2001?

Newscasters, commentators, political figures, and ordinary citizens all struggled to find appropriate historical analogies for attacks on the World Trade Center and the Pentagon. They repeatedly invoked two twentieth-century events that seemed to offer at least some parallels. One was the surprise Japanese attack on the American naval fleet anchored in Pearl Harbor, Hawaii, on December 7, 1941. Both enemy attacks came from the air and lasted just over an hour. The death toll was high in both cases, with 2,403 Americans dead in Pearl Harbor. In his address the next day, President Franklin D. Roosevelt memorialized the date as one "which will live in infamy." "Always will our whole nation remember the character of the onslaught against us," he predicted while asking Congress for a declaration of war against Japan. On September 11, 2001, newscasters almost instantaneously revived President Roosevelt's descriptive phrase. This new "day of infamy," they suggested, carried as much historical weight as the event that brought the United States into World War II.

The second frequently cited historical parallel was the assassination of President John F. Kennedy on November 22, 1963. Kennedy's death and funeral underscored the new power of television to transform nation into a community witnessing momentous and shocking events as they unfolded. Indeed, millions of Americans had watched in disbelief as Kennedy's accused assassin, Lee Harvey Oswald, was gunned down in a Dallas police station the day after the President had been killed. And

just as Americans would never forget where they were and what they were doing when they heard the news about JFK, so it seemed that the WTC attack would also prove a life-long marker of memory.

These two historical analogies are far from perfect. Pearl Harbor was a military target, thousands of miles from the mainland; the attack had clearly come from a nation state that had a deep economic and diplomatic rivalry with the U.S. In contrast, the 9/11 assault came against a symbol of American economic power with no military significance, and it marked the first time that American civilians had ever suffered mass casualties at the hands of a foreign enemy. And that enemy appeared to be not a nation state but rather a shadowy international organization of radical Islamic terrorists. The JFK assassination had surely demonstrated the growing power of television to focus an entire nation's attention. But Americans would never really agree on the cause and meaning of Kennedy's tragic death. For decades, American citizens, abetted by a cottage industry of conspiracy theorists, film makers, historians, novelists, and journalists continued to argue about who was responsible, what motives were in play, and how history might have been different had Kennedy lived.

What role did the media play in shaping our understanding of the events of 9/11/01? Unlike the bombing of U.S. naval ships in Pearl Harbor, the terrorist attack on the World Trade Center occurred, virtually, before the eyes of millions of Americans. Video cameras caught the image of the second plane hitting the south tower, the panic on the faces of those fleeing the scene, the smoke billowing from the towers, and their sudden collapse. Reporters were soon on the scene to interview eyewitnesses and to pull comments from traumatized survivors. The networks immediately pre-empted regular programming and allowed millions of Americans to watch in horror as the televised images played and replayed the attack. The newscasters narrated the events, drawing out the analogy with Pearl Harbor, and giving the unfolding story a title, such as "Attack on America" or "Day of Infamy." Within a few days, programmers had edited the videotapes to enhance the drama. They added scenes, such as images of cell phones to remind viewers of the final calls many of the victims made to their loved ones. They overlaid the images of towers collapsing with

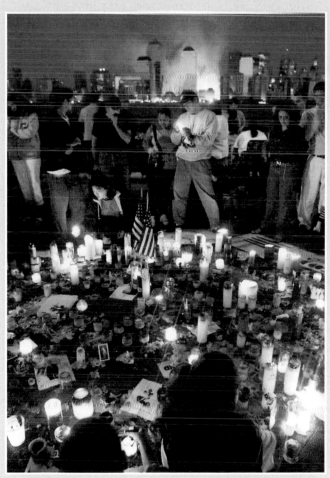

By the evening of September 11th, groups of people across the nation gathered in candlelight vigils to honor the victims of the terrorist attacks. President Bush declared September 14th a National Day of Prayer and Remembrance.

SOURCE: © Reuters New Media Inc./CORBIS.

an unfurling American flag and added patriotic music. To enhance further the emotional impact, they borrowed cinematic techniques, slowing down the pace to draw out the action. They also used jump cuts, juxtaposing in fast time an image of the burning or collapsing towers with a close-up shot of an anguished face of an observer, putting the viewer emotionally into the picture.

But the shaping of historical memory took place on other levels as well. At hundreds of funerals and memorial services held in communities throughout the Greater New York area, many thousands of strangers joined families of the victims in paying respects and trying to make

sense of it all. Makeshift memorials sprouted up in lower Manhattan with people leaving flowers, personal notes, and artwork. At the Massachusetts Institute of Technology in Cambridge, Massachusetts, faculty and students built a Reflecting Wall, consisting of a re-created fragment of the familiar World Trade Center façade.

For more long-term efforts at documenting collective memory, historians and museums looked to the Internet. Some 70 history oriented institutions came together to create a new Internet site, 911history.net, devoted to collecting oral histories and artifacts from the event. And the Library of Congress spearheaded another site, September11.archive.org, which by mid-October had already put on-line more than 500,000 pages related to the terrorist attacks, ranging from daily news reports to personal memorials. As Diane Kresh of the Library of Congress put it, "The Internet has become for many the public commons, a place where they can come together and talk." A more permanent memorial will no doubt be a part of the reconstruction of Lower Manhattan. Through all these projects, Americans will continue demonstrating how creating historical memory is an active and dynamic process. ▧

 www.researchnavigator.com

The Community and Memory essay for this chapter deals with the effort to find ways to explain and contextualize the September 11, 2001 attack on the World Trade Center. For further research on this effort, use the tools available to you in Research Navigator.

As you investigate this topic, consider this question: "What historical analogies are most often used to help explain the attack? How useful are these analogies?"

ContentSelect: Search in the General Interest database using the search terms *World Trade Center* and *Terrorism*.

Links Library: Access the History: U.S. History database and explore the links for *terrorism*.

New York Times on the Web: To find more about plans for future development of the World Trade Center site, use the search term *World Trade Center Memorial*.

APPENDIX

THE DECLARATION OF INDEPENDENCE

When in the course of human events it becomes necessary for one people to dissolve the political bands which have connected them with another and to assume, among the powers of the earth, the separate and equal station to which the laws of nature and of nature's God entitle them, a decent respect to the opinions of mankind requires that they should declare the causes which impel them to the separation.

We hold these truths to be self-evident, that all men are created equal, that they are endowed by their Creator with certain unalienable rights; that among these are life, liberty, and the pursuit of happiness. That, to secure these rights, governments are instituted among men, deriving their just powers from the consent of the governed; that, whenever any form of government becomes destructive of these ends, it is the right of the people to alter or to abolish it, and to institute a new government, laying its foundation on such principles, and organizing its powers in such form, as to them shall seem most likely to effect their safety and happiness. Prudence, indeed, will dictate that governments long established should not be changed for light and transient causes; and, accordingly, all experience hath shown that mankind are more disposed to suffer, while evils are sufferable, than to right themselves by abolishing the forms to which they are accustomed. But when a long train of abuses and usurpations, pursuing invariably the same object, evinces a design to reduce them under absolute despotism, it is their right, it is their duty, to throw off such government and to provide new guards for their future security. Such has been the patient sufferance of these colonies, and such is now the necessity which constrains them to alter their former systems of government. The history of the present King of Great Britain is a history of repeated injuries and usurpations, all having, in direct object, the establishment of an absolute tyranny over these States. To prove this, let facts be submitted to a candid world:

He has refused his assent to laws the most wholesome and necessary for the public good.

He has forbidden his governors to pass laws of immediate and pressing importance, unless suspended in their operation till his assent should be obtained; and, when so suspended, he has utterly neglected to attend to them.

He has refused to pass other laws for the accommodation of large districts of people, unless those people would relinquish the right of representation in the legislature, a right inestimable to them and formidable to tyrants only.

He has called together legislative bodies at places unusual, uncomfortable, and distant from the depository of their public records, for the sole purpose of fatiguing them into compliance with his measures.

He has dissolved representative houses, repeatedly for opposing, with manly firmness, his invasions on the rights of the people.

He has refused, for a long time after such dissolutions, to cause others to be elected; whereby the legislative powers, incapable of annihilation, have returned to the people at large for their exercise; the state remaining, in the meantime, exposed to all the danger of invasion from without and convulsions within.

He has endeavored to prevent the population of these States; for that purpose, obstructing the laws for naturalization of foreigners, refusing to pass others to encourage their migration hither, and raising the conditions of new appropriations of lands.

He has obstructed the administration of justice by refusing his assent to laws for establishing judiciary powers.

He has made judges dependent on his will alone for the tenure of their offices and the amount and payment of their salaries.

He has erected a multitude of new offices and sent hither swarms of officers to harass our people and eat out their substance.

He has kept among us, in time of peace, standing armies, without the consent of our legislatures.

He has affected to render the military independent of, and superior to, the civil power.

He has combined with others to subject us to a jurisdiction foreign to our Constitution and unacknowledged by our laws, giving his assent to their acts of pretended legislation—

For quartering large bodies of armed troops among us;

For protecting them, by mock trial, from punishment for any murders which they should commit on the inhabitants of these States;

For cutting off our trade with all parts of the world;

For imposing taxes on us without our consent;

For depriving us, in many cases, of the benefit of trial by jury;

For transporting us beyond seas to be tried for pretended offences;

For abolishing the free system of English laws in a neighboring province, establishing therein an arbitrary government, and enlarging its boundaries, so as to render it at once an example and fit instrument for introducing the same absolute rule into these colonies;

For taking away our charters, abolishing our most valuable laws, and altering, fundamentally, the powers of our governments.

For suspending our own legislatures and declaring themselves invested with power to legislate for us in all cases whatsoever.

He has abdicated government here by declaring us out of his protection and waging war against us.

He has plundered our seas, ravaged our coasts, burnt our towns, and destroyed the lives of our people.

He is, at this time, transporting large armies of foreign mercenaries to complete the works of death, desolation, and tyranny already begun with circumstances of cruelty and perfidy scarcely paralleled in the most barbarous ages, and totally unworthy the head of a civilized nation.

He has constrained our fellow citizens, taken captive on the high seas, to bear arms against their country, to become the executioners of their friends and brethren, or to fall themselves by their hands.

He has excited domestic insurrections amongst us and has endeavored to bring on the inhabitants of our frontiers, the merciless Indian savages, whose known rule of warfare is an undistinguished destruction of all ages, sexes, and conditions.

In every stage of these oppressions, we have petitioned for redress in the most humble terms; our repeated petitions have been answered only by repeated injury. A prince whose character is thus marked by every act which may define a tyrant is unfit to be the ruler of a free people.

Nor have we been wanting in attention to our British brethren. We have warned them, from time to time, of attempts made by their legislature to extend an unwarrantable jurisdiction over us. We have reminded them of the circumstances of our emigration and settlement here. We have appealed to their native justice and magnanimity, and we have conjured them, by the ties of our common kindred,

to disavow these usurpations, which would inevitably interrupt our connections and correspondence. They, too, have been deaf to the voice of justice and consanguinity. We must, therefore, acquiesce in the necessity which denounces our separation, and hold them, as we hold the rest of mankind, enemies in war, in peace, friends.

We, therefore, the representatives of the United States of America, in general Congress assembled, appealing to the Supreme Judge of the world for the rectitude of our intentions, do, in the name and by the authority of the good people of these colonies, solemnly publish and declare, that these united colonies are, and of right ought to be, free and independent states: that they are absolved from all allegiance to the British Crown, and that all political connection between them and the state of Great Britain is, and ought to be, totally dissolved; and that, as free and independent states, they have full power to levy war, conclude peace, contract alliances, establish commerce, and to do all other acts and things which independent states may of right do. And, for the support of this declaration, with a firm reliance on the protection of Divine Providence, we mutually pledge to each other our lives, our fortunes, and our sacred honor.

THE CONSTITUTION OF THE UNITED STATES OF AMERICA

We the people of the United States, in order to form a more perfect union, establish justice, insure domestic tranquillity, provide for the common defense, promote the general welfare, and secure the blessings of liberty to ourselves and our posterity, do ordain and establish this Constitution for the United States of America.

Article I

Section 1. All legislative powers herein granted shall be vested in a Congress of the United States, which shall consist of a Senate and House of Representatives.

Section 2. 1. The House of Representatives shall be composed of members chosen every second year by the people of the several States, and the electors in each State shall have the qualifications requisite for electors of the most numerous branch of the State legislature.

2. No person shall be a representative who shall not have attained to the age of twenty-five years, and been seven years a citizen of the United States, and who shall not, when elected, be an inhabitant of that State in which he shall be chosen.

3. Representatives and direct taxes[1] shall be apportioned among the several States which may be included within this Union, according to their respective numbers, which shall be determined by adding to the whole number of free persons, including those bound to service for a term of years, and excluding Indians not taxed, three fifths of all other persons.[2] The actual enumeration shall be made within three years after the first meeting of the Congress of the United States, and within every subsequent term of ten years, in such manner as they shall by law direct. The number of representatives shall not exceed one for every thirty thousand, but each State shall have at least one representative; and until such enumeration shall be made, the State of New Hampshire shall be entitled to choose three, Massachusetts eight, Rhode Island and Providence Plantations one, Connecticut five, New York six, New Jersey four, Pennsylvania eight, Delaware one, Maryland six, Virginia ten, North Carolina five, South Carolina five, and Georgia three.

4. When vacancies happen in the representation from any State, the executive authority thereof shall issue writs of election to fill such vacancies.

5. The House of Representatives shall choose their speaker and other officers; and shall have the sole power of impeachment.

Section 3. 1. The Senate of the United States shall be composed of two senators from each State, chosen by the legislature thereof,[3] for six years; and each senator shall have one vote.

2. Immediately after they shall be assembled in consequence of the first election, they shall be divided as equally as may be into three classes. The seats of the senators of the first class shall be vacated at the expiration of the second year, of the second class at the expiration of the fourth year, and of the third class at the expiration of the sixth year, so that one third may be chosen every second year; and if vacancies happen by resignation, or otherwise, during the recess of the legislature of any State, the executive thereof may make temporary appointments until the next meeting of the legislature, which shall then fill such vacancies.[4]

3. No person shall be a senator who shall not have attained to the age of thirty years, and been nine years a citizen of the United States, and who shall not, when elected, be an inhabitant of that State for which he shall be chosen.

4. The Vice President of the United States shall be President of the Senate, but shall have no vote, unless they be equally divided.

5. The Senate shall choose their other officers, and also a president pro tempore, in the absence of the Vice President, or when he shall exercise the office of the President of the United States.

6. The Senate shall have the sole power to try all impeachments. When sitting for that purpose, they shall be on oath or affirmation. When the President of the United States is tried, the chief justice shall preside: and no person shall be convicted without the concurrence of two thirds of the members present.

7. Judgment in cases of impeachment shall not extend further than to removal from office, and disqualification to hold and enjoy any office of honor, trust or profit under the United States: but the party convicted shall nevertheless be liable and subject to indictment, trial, judgment and punishment, according to law.

Section 4. 1. The times, places, and manner of holding elections for senators and representatives, shall be prescribed in each State by the legislature thereof; but the Congress may at any time by law make or alter such regulations, except as to the places of choosing senators.

2. The Congress shall assemble at least once in every year, and such meeting shall be on the first Monday in December, unless they shall by law appoint a different day.

Section 5. 1. Each House shall be the judge of the elections, returns and qualifications of its own members, and a majority of each shall constitute a quorum to do business; but a smaller number may adjourn from day to day, and may be authorized to compel the attendance of absent members, in such manner, and under such penalties as each House may provide.

2. Each House may determine the rules of its proceedings, punish its members for disorderly behavior, and, with the concurrence of two thirds, expel a member.

3. Each House shall keep a journal of its proceedings, and from time to time publish the same, excepting such parts as may in their judgment require secrecy; and the yeas and nays of the members of either House on any question

---

[1] See the Sixteenth Amendment.
[2] See the Fourteenth Amendment.
[3] See the Seventeenth Amendment.

[4] See the Seventeenth Amendment.

shall, at the desire of one fifth of those present, be entered on the journal.

4. Neither House, during the session of Congress, shall, without the consent of the other, adjourn for more than three days, nor to any other place than that in which the two Houses shall be sitting.

Section 6. 1. The senators and representatives shall receive a compensation for their services, to be ascertained by law, and paid out of the Treasury of the United States. They shall in all cases, except treason, felony, and breach of the peace, be privileged from arrest during their attendance at the session of their respective Houses, and in going to and returning from the same; and for any speech or debate in either House, they shall not be questioned in any other place.

2. No senator or representative shall, during the time for which he was elected, be appointed to any civil office under the authority of the United States, which shall have been created, or the emoluments whereof shall have been increased, during such time; and no person holding any office under the United States shall be a member of either House during his continuance in office.

Section 7. 1. All bills for raising revenue shall originate in the House of Representatives; but the Senate may propose or concur with amendments as on other bills.

2. Every bill which shall have passed the House of Representatives and the Senate, shall, before it become a law, be presented to the President of the United States; If he approves he shall sign it, but if not he shall return it, with his objections, to that House in which it shall have originated, who shall enter the objections at large on their journal, and proceed to reconsider it. If after such reconsideration two thirds of that House shall agree to pass the bill, it shall be sent, together with the objections, to the other House, by which it shall likewise be reconsidered, and if approved by two thirds of that House, it shall become a law. But in all such cases the votes of both Houses shall be determined by yeas and nays, and the names of the persons voting for and against the bill shall be entered on the journal of each House respectively. If any bill shall not be returned by the President within ten days (Sundays excepted) after it shall have been presented to him, the same shall be a law, in like manner as if he had signed it, unless the Congress by their adjournment prevent its return, in which case it shall not be a law.

3. Every order, resolution, or vote to which the concurrence of the Senate and the House of Representatives may be necessary (except on a question of adjournment) shall be presented to the President of the United States; and before the same shall take effect, shall be approved by him, or being disapproved by him, shall be repassed by two thirds of the Senate and House of Representatives, according to the rules and limitations prescribed in the case of a bill.

Section 8. The Congress shall have the power

1. To lay and collect taxes, duties, imposts, and excises, to pay the debts and provide for the common defense and general welfare of the United States; but all duties, imposts, and excises shall be uniform throughout the United States.

2. To borrow money on the credit of the United States;

3. To regulate commerce with foreign nations, and among the several States, and with the Indian tribes;

4. To establish a uniform rule of naturalization, and uniform laws on the subject of bankruptcies throughout the United States;

5. To coin money, regulate the value thereof, and of foreign coin, and fix the standard of weights and measures;

6. To provide for the punishment of counterfeiting the securities and current coin of the United States;

7. To establish post offices and post roads;

8. To promote the progress of science and useful arts, by securing for limited times to authors and inventors the exclusive right to their respective writings and discoveries;

9. To constitute tribunals inferior to the Supreme Court;

10. To define and punish piracies and felonies committed on the high seas, and offenses against the law of nations;

11. To declare war, grant letters of marque and reprisal, and make rules concerning captures on land and water;

12. To raise and support armies, but no appropriation of money to that use shall be for a longer term than two years;

13. To provide and maintain a navy;

14. To make rules for the government and regulation of the land and naval forces;

15. To provide for calling forth the militia to execute the laws of the Union, suppress insurrections and repel invasions;

16. To provide for organizing, arming, and disciplining the militia, and for governing such part of them as may be employed in the service of the United States, reserving to the States respectively, the appointment of the officers, and the authority of training the militia according to the discipline prescribed by Congress;

17. To exercise exclusive legislation in all cases whatsoever, over such district (not exceeding ten miles square) as may, by cession of particular States, and the acceptance of Congress, become the seat of the government of the United States, and to exercise like authority over all places purchased by the consent of the legislature of the State in which the same shall be, for the erection of forts, magazines, arsenals, dockyards, and other needful buildings; and

18. To make all laws which shall be necessary and proper for carrying into execution the foregoing powers, and all other powers vested by this Constitution in the government of the United States, or any department or officer thereof.

Section 9. 1. The migration or importation of such persons as any of the States now existing shall think proper to admit, shall not be prohibited by the Congress prior to the year one thousand eight hundred and eight, but a tax or duty may be imposed on such importation, not exceeding ten dollars for each person.

2. The privilege of the writ of habeas corpus shall not be suspended, unless when in cases of rebellion or invasion the public safety may require it.

3. No bill of attainder or ex post facto law shall be passed.

4. No capitation, or other direct, tax shall be laid, unless in proportion to the census or enumeration hereinbefore directed to be taken.[5]

5. No tax or duty shall be laid on articles exported from any State.

6. No preference shall be given by any regulation of commerce or revenue to the ports of one State over those of another: nor shall vessels bound to, or from, one State be obliged to enter, clear, or pay duties in another.

7. No money shall be drawn from the treasury, but in consequence of appropriations made by law; and a regular statement and account of the receipts and expenditures of all public money shall be published from time to time.

8. No title of nobility shall be granted by the United States: and no person holding any office of profit or trust under them, shall, without the consent of the Congress, accept of any present, emolument, office, or title, of any kind whatever, from any king, price, or foreign State.

Section 10. 1. No State shall enter into any treaty, alliance, or confederation; grant letters of marque and reprisal; coin money; emit bills of credit; make any thing but gold and silver coin a tender in payment of debts; pass any bill of attainder, ex post facto law, or law impairing the obligation of contracts, or grant, any title of nobility.

2. No State shall, without the consent of the Congress, lay any imposts or duties on imports or exports, except what may be absolutely necessary for executing its inspection laws: and the net produce of all duties and imposts laid by any State on imports or exports, shall be for the use of the treasury of the United States; and all such laws shall be subject to the revision and control of the Congress.

3. No State shall, without the consent of the Congress, lay any duty of tonnage, keep troops, or ships of war in time of peace, enter into any agreement or compact with another State, or with a foreign power, or engage in war, unless actually invaded, or in such imminent danger as will not admit of delay.

Article II

Section 1. 1. The executive power shall be vested in a President of the United States of America. He shall hold his office during the term of four years, and, together with the Vice President, chosen for the same term, be elected, as follows:

2. Each State shall appoint, in such manner as the legislature thereof may direct, a number of electors, equal to the whole number of senators and representatives to which the State may be entitled in the Congress: but no senator or representative, or person holding any office of trust or profit under the United States, shall be appointed an elector.

The electors shall meet in their respective States, and vote by ballot for two persons, of whom one at least shall not be an inhabitant of the same State with themselves. And they shall make a list of all the persons voted for, and of the number of votes for each; which list they shall sign and certify, and transmit sealed to the seat of the government of the United States, directed to the president of the Senate. The president of the Senate shall, in the presence of the Senate and House of Representatives, open all the certificates, and the votes shall then be counted. The person having the greatest number of votes shall be the President, if such number be a majority of the whole number of electors appointed; and if there be more than one who have such majority, and have an equal number of votes, then the House of Representatives shall immediately choose by ballot one of them for President; and if no person have a majority, then from the five highest on the list the said House shall in like manner choose the President. But in choosing the President, the votes shall be taken by States, the representation from each State having one vote; a quorum for this purpose shall consist of a member or members from two thirds of the States, and a majority of all the States shall be necessary to a choice. In every case after the choice of the President, the person having the greatest number of votes of the electors shall be the Vice President. But if there should remain two or more who have equal votes, the Senate shall choose from them by ballot the Vice President.[6]

3. The Congress may determine the time of choosing the electors, and the day on which they shall give their votes; which day shall be the same throughout the United States.

4. No person except a natural born citizen, or a citizen of the United States, at the time of the adoption of this Constitution, shall be eligible to the office of President; neither shall any person be eligible to the office who shall not have attained to the age of thirty-five years, and been fourteen years a resident within the United States.

5. In case of the removal of the President from office, or of his death, resignation, or inability to discharge the powers and duties of the said office, the same shall devolve on the Vice President, and the congress may by law provide for the case of removal, death, resignation or inability, both of the President and Vice President, declaring what officer shall then act as President, and such officer shall act accordingly until the disability be removed, or a President shall be elected.

6. The President shall, at stated times, receive for his services a compensation which shall neither be increased nor diminished during the period for which he shall have been elected, and he shall not receive within that period any other emolument from the United States, or any of them.

7. Before he enter on the execution of his office, he shall take the following oath or affirmation:—"I do

---

[5]See the Sixteenth Amendment.

[6]Superseded by the Twelfth Amendment.

solemnly swear (or affirm) that I will faithfully execute the office of President of the United States, and will to the best of my ability, preserve, protect and defend the Constitution of the United States."

Section 2. 1. The President shall be commander in chief of the army and navy of the United States, and of the militia of the several States, when called into the actual service of the United States; he may require the opinion in writing, of the principal officer in each of the executive departments, upon any subject relating to the duties of their respective offices, and he shall have power to grant reprieves and pardons for offenses against the United States, except in cases of impeachment.

2. He shall have power, by and with the advice and consent of the Senate, to make treaties, provided two thirds of the senators present concur; and he shall nominate, and by and with the advice and consent of the Senate, shall appoint ambassadors, other public ministers and consuls, judges of the Supreme Court, and all other officers of the United States, whose appointments are not herein otherwise provided for, and which shall be established by law; but the Congress may by law vest the appointment of such inferior officers, as they think proper, in the President alone, in the courts of laws, or in the heads of departments.

3. The President shall have power to fill up all vacancies that may happen during the recess of the Senate, by granting commissions which shall expire at the end of their next session.

Section 3. He shall from time to time give to the Congress information of the state of the Union, and recommend to their consideration such measures as he shall judge necessary and expedient; he may, on extraordinary occasions, convene both Houses, or either of them, and in case of disagreement between them with respect to the time of adjournment, he may adjourn them to such time as he shall think proper; he shall receive ambassadors and other public ministers; he shall take care that the laws be faithfully executed, and shall commission all the officers of the United States.

Section 4. The President, Vice President, and all civil officers of the United States, shall be removed from office on impeachment for, and conviction of, treason, bribery, or other high crimes and misdemeanors.

Article III

Section 1. The judicial power of the United States shall be vested in one Supreme Court, and in such inferior courts as the Congress may from time to time ordain and establish. The judges, both of the Supreme and inferior courts, shall hold their offices during good behavior, and shall, at stated times, receive for their services, a compensation, which shall not be diminished during their continuance in office.

Section 2. 1. The judicial power shall extend to all cases, in law and equity, arising under this Constitution, the laws of the United States, and treaties made, or which shall be made, under their authority;—to all cases of admiralty and maritime jurisdiction;—to controversies to which the United States shall be a party;[7]—to controversies between two or more States;—between a State and citizens of another State;—between citizens of different States;—between citizens of the same State claiming lands under grants of different States, and between a State, or the citizens thereof, and foreign States, citizens or subjects.

2. In all cases affecting ambassadors, other public ministers and consuls, and those in which a State shall be party, the Supreme Court shall have original jurisdiction. In all the other cases before mentioned, the Supreme Court shall have appellate jurisdiction, both as to law and fact, with such exceptions, and under such regulations as the Congress shall make.

3. The trial of all crimes, except in cases of impeachment, shall be by jury; and such trial shall be held in the State where the said crimes shall have been committed; but when not committed within any State, the trial shall be such place or places as the congress may by law have directed.

Section 3. 1. Treason against the United States shall consist only in levying war against them, or in adhering to their enemies, giving them aid and comfort. No person shall be convicted of treason unless on the testimony of two witnesses to the same overt act, or on confession in open court.

2. The Congress shall have power to declare the punishment of treason, but no attainder of treason shall work corruption of blood, or forfeiture except during the life of the person attained.

Article IV

Section 1. Full faith and credit shall be given in each State to the public acts, records, and judicial proceedings of every other State. And the Congress may by general laws prescribe the manner in which such acts, records and proceedings shall be proved, and the effect thereof.

Section 2. 1. The citizens of each State shall be entitled to all privileges and immunities of citizens in the several States.[8]

2. A person charged in any State with treason, felony, or other crime, who shall flee from justice, and be found in another State, shall on demand of the executive authority of the State from which he fled, be delivered up to be removed to the State having jurisdiction of the crime.

3. No person held to service or labor in one State under the laws thereof, escaping into another, shall, in consequence of any law or regulation therein, be discharged from such service or labor, but shall be delivered up on claim of the party to whom such service or labor may be due.[9]

Section 3. 1. New States may be admitted by the Congress into this Union; but no new State shall be formed or erected within the jurisdiction of any other State, nor any State be formed by the junction of two or more States, or parts of States, without the consent of the legislatures of the States concerned as well as of the Congress.

---

[7]See the Eleventh Amendment.
[8]See the Fourteenth Amendment, Sec. 1.
[9]See the Thirteenth Amendment.

2. The Congress shall have power to dispose of and make all needful rules and regulations respecting the territory or other property belonging to the United States; and nothing in this Constitution shall be so construed as to prejudice any claims of the United States, or of any particular State.

Section 4. The United States shall guarantee to every State in this Union a republican form of government, and shall protect each of them against invasion; and on application of the legislature, or of the executive (when the legislature cannot be convened) against domestic violence.

Article V

The Congress, whenever two thirds of both Houses shall deem it necessary, shall propose amendments to this Constitution, or, on the application of the legislatures of two thirds of the several States, shall call a convention for proposing amendments, which in either case shall be valid to all intents and purposes, as part of this Constitution, when ratified by the legislatures of three fourths of the several States, or by conventions in three fourths thereof, as the one or the other mode of ratification may be proposed by the Congress; Provided that no amendment which may be made prior to the year one thousand eight hundred and eight shall in any manner affect the first and fourth clauses in the ninth section of the first article; and that no State, without its consent, shall be deprived of its equal suffrage in the Senate.

Article VI

1. All debts contracted and engagements entered into, before the adoption of this Constitution, shall be as valid against the United States under this Constitution, as under the Confederation.[10]

2. This Constitution, and the laws of the United States which shall be made in pursuance thereof; and all treaties made, or which shall be made, under the authority of the United States, shall be the supreme law of the land; and the judges in every State shall be bound thereby, any thing in the Constitution or laws of any State to the contrary notwithstanding.

3. The senators and representatives before mentioned, and the members of the several State legislatures, and all executive and judicial officers, both of the United States and of the several States, shall be bound by oath or affirmation to support this Constitution; but no religious test shall ever be required as a qualification to any office or public trust under the United States.

Article VII

The ratification of the conventions of nine States shall be sufficient for the establishment of this Constitution between the States so ratifying the same.

Done in Convention by the unanimous consent of the States present the seventeenth day of September in the year of our Lord one thousand seven hundred and eighty-

seven, and of the independence of the United States of America the twelfth. In witness whereof we have hereunto subscribed our names.

[Names omitted]

* * *

Articles in addition to, and amendment of, the Constitution of the United States of America, proposed by Congress, and ratified by the legislatures of the several States, pursuant to the fifth article of the original Constitution.

Amendment I [*First ten amendments ratified December 15, 1791*]

Congress shall make no law respecting an establishment of religion, or prohibiting the free exercise thereof; or abridging the freedom of speech, or of the press; or the right of the people peaceably to assemble, and to petition the government for a redress of grievances.

Amendment II

A well regulated militia, being necessary to the security of a free State, the right of the people to keep and bear arms, shall not be infringed.

Amendment III

No soldier shall, in time of peace be quartered in any house, without the consent of the owner, nor in time of war, but in a manner to be prescribed by law.

Amendment IV

The right of the people to be secure in their persons, houses, papers, and effects, against unreasonable searches and seizures, shall not be violated, and no warrants shall issue, but upon probable cause, supported by oath or affirmation, and particularly describing the place to be searched, and the persons or things to be seized.

Amendment V

No person shall be held to answer for a capital or otherwise infamous crime, unless on a presentment or indictment of a grand jury, except in cases arising in the land or naval forces, or in the militia, when in actual service in time of war or public danger; nor shall any person be subject for the same offense to be twice put in jeopardy of life or limb; nor shall be compelled in any criminal case to be a witness against himself, nor be deprived of life, liberty, or property, without due process of law; nor shall private property be taken for public use, without just compensation.

Amendment VI

In all criminal prosecutions, the accused shall enjoy the right to a speedy and public trial, by an impartial jury of the State and district wherein the crime shall have been committed, which district shall have been previously ascertained by law, and to be informed of the nature and cause of the accusation; to be confronted with the witnesses against him; to have compulsory process for obtaining witnesses in his favor, and to have the assistance of counsel for his defense.

---

[10]See the Fourteenth Amendment, Sec. 4.

Amendment VII

In suits at common law, where the value in controversy shall exceed twenty dollars, the right of trial by jury shall be preserved, and no fact tried by a jury shall be otherwise reexamined in any court of the United States, than according to the rules of the common law.

Amendment VIII

Excessive bail shall not be required, nor excessive fines imposed, nor cruel and unusual punishments inflicted.

Amendment IX

The enumeration in the Constitution of certain rights shall not be construed to deny or disparage others retained by the people.

Amendment X

The powers not delegated to the United States by the Constitution, nor prohibited by it to the States, are reserved to the States respectively, or to the people.

Amendment XI [January 8, 1798]

The judicial power of the United States shall not be construed to extend to any suit in law or equity, commended or prosecuted against one of the United States by citizens of another State, or by citizens or subjects of any foreign State.

Amendment XII [September 25, 1804]

The electors shall meet in their respective States, and vote by ballot for President and Vice President, one of whom, at least, shall not be an inhabitant of the same State with themselves; they shall name in their ballots the person voted for as President, and in distinct ballots, the person voted for as Vice President, and they shall make distinct lists of all persons voted for as President and of all persons voted for as Vice President, and of the number of votes for each, which lists they shall sign and certify, and transmit sealed to the seat of the government of the United States, directed to the President of the Senate;—The President of the Senate shall, in the presence of the Senate and House of Representatives, open all the certificates and the votes shall then be counted;—The person having the greatest number of votes for President, shall be the President, if such number be a majority of the whole number of electors appointed; and if no person have such majority, then from the persons having the highest numbers not exceeding three on the list of those voted for as President, the House of Representatives shall choose immediately, by ballot, the President. But in choosing the President, the votes shall be taken by States, the representation from each State having one vote; a quorum for this purpose shall consist of a member or members from two thirds of the States, and a majority of all the States shall be necessary to a choice. And if the House of Representatives shall not choose a President whenever the right of choice shall devolve upon them, before the fourth day of March next following, then the Vice President shall act as President, as in the case of the death or other constitutional disability of the President.

The person having the greatest number of votes as Vice President shall be the Vice President, if such number be a majority of the whole number of electors appointed, and if no person have a majority, then from the two highest numbers on the list, the Senate shall choose the Vice President; a quorum for the purpose shall consist of two thirds of the whole number of Senators, and a majority of the whole number shall be necessary to a choice. But no person constitutionally ineligible to the office of President shall be eligible to that of Vice President of the United States.

Amendment XIII [December 18, 1865]

Section 1. Neither slavery nor involuntary servitude, except as a punishment for crime whereof the party shall have been duly convicted, shall exist within the United States, or any place subject to their jurisdiction.

Section 2. Congress shall have power to enforce this article by appropriate legislation.

Amendment XIV [July 28, 1868]

Section 1. All persons born or naturalized in the United States, and subject to the jurisdiction thereof, are citizens of the United States and of the State wherein they reside. No State shall make or enforce any law which shall abridge the privileges or immunities of citizens of the United States; nor shall any State deprive any person of life, liberty, or property, without due process of law; nor deny to any person within its jurisdiction the equal protection of the laws.

Section 2. Representatives shall be apportioned among the several States according to their respective numbers, counting the whole number of persons in each State, excluding Indians not taxed. But when the right to vote at any election for the choice of electors for President and Vice President of the United States, representatives in Congress, the executive and judicial officers of a State, or the members of the legislature thereof, is denied to any of the male inhabitants of such State, being twenty-one years of age, and citizens of the United States, or in any way abridged, except for participating in rebellion, or other crime, the basis of representation there shall be reduced in the proportion which the number of such male citizens shall bear to the whole number of male citizens twenty-one years of age in such State.

Section 3. No person shall be a senator or representative in Congress, or elector of President and Vice President, or hold any office, civil or military, under the United States, or under any State, who having previously taken an oath, as a member of Congress, or as an officer of the United States, or as a member of any State legislature, or as an executive or judicial officer of any State, to support the Constitution of the United States, shall have engaged in insurrection or rebellion against the same, or given aid or comfort to the enemies thereof. But Congress may by a vote of two thirds of each House, remove such disability.

Section 4. The validity of the public debt of the United States, authorized by law, including debts incurred for payment of pensions and bounties for services in suppressing insurrection or rebellion; shall not be questioned.

But neither the United States nor any State shall assume or pay any debt or obligation incurred in aid of insurrection or rebellion against the United States, or any claim for the loss or emancipation of any slave; but all such debts, obligations, and claims shall be held illegal and void.

Section 5. The Congress shall have the power to enforce, by appropriate legislation, the provisions of this article.

Amendment XV [March 30, 1870]

Section 1. The right of citizens of the United States to vote shall not be denied or abridged by the United States or by any State on account of race, color, or previous condition of servitude.

Section 2. The Congress shall have power to enforce this article by appropriate legislation.

Amendment XVI [February 25, 1913]

The Congress shall have power to lay and collect taxes on incomes, from whatever source derived, without apportionment among the several States, and without regard to any census or enumeration.

Amendment XVII [May 31, 1913]

The Senate of the United States shall be composed of two senators from each State, elected by the people thereof, for six years; and each senator shall have one vote. The electors in each State shall have the qualifications requisite for electors of the most numerous branch of the State legislature.

When vacancies happen in the representation of any State in the Senate, the executive authority of such State shall issue writs of election to fill such vacancies: *Provided,* That the legislature of any State may empower the executive thereof to make temporary appointments until the people fill the vacancies by election as the legislature may direct.

This amendment shall not be so construed as to affect the election or term of any senator chosen before it becomes valid as part of the Constitution.

Amendment XVIII'' [January 29, 1919]

After one year from the ratification of this article, the manufacture, sale, or transportation of intoxicating liquors within, the importation thereof into, or the exportation thereof from the United States and all territory subject to the jurisdiction thereof for beverage purposes is thereby prohibited.

The Congress and the several States shall have concurrent power to enforce this article by appropriate legislation.

This article shall be inoperative unless it shall have been ratified as an amendment to the Constitution by the legislatures of the several States, as provided in the constitution, within seven years from the date of the submission hereof to the States by Congress.

''Repealed by the Twenty-first Amendment.

Amendment XIX [August 26, 1920]

The right of citizens of the United States to vote shall not be denied or abridged by the United States or by any State on account of sex.

Congress shall have the power to enforce this article by appropriate legislation.

Amendment XX [January 23, 1933]

Section 1. The terms of the President and Vice President shall end at noon on the 20th day of January and the terms of Senators and Representatives at noon on the 3d day of January, of the years in which such terms would have ended if this article had not been ratified; and the terms of their successors shall then begin.

Section 2. The Congress shall assemble at least once in every year, and such meeting shall begin at noon on the 3d day of January, unless they shall by law appoint a different day.

Section 3. If, at the time fixed for the beginning of the term of President, the President-elect shall have died, the Vice President-elect shall become President. If a President shall not have been chosen before the time fixed for the beginning of his term, or if the President-elect shall have failed to qualify, then the Vice President-elect shall act as President until a President shall have qualified; and the Congress may by law provide for the case wherein neither a President-elect nor a Vice President-elect shall have qualified, declaring who shall then act as President, or the manner in which one who is to act shall be selected, and such person shall act accordingly until a President or Vice President shall have qualified.

Section 4. The Congress may by law provide for the case of the death of any of the persons from whom, the House of Representatives may choose a President whenever the right of choice shall have devolved upon them, and for the case of the death of any of the persons from whom the Senate may choose a Vice President whenever the right of choice shall have devolved upon them.

Section 5. Sections 1 and 2 shall take effect on the 15th day of October following the ratification of this article.

Section 6. This article shall be inoperative unless it shall have been ratified as an amendment to the Constitution by the legislatures of three-fourths of the several States within seven years from the date of its submission.

Amendment XXI [December 5, 1933]

Section 1. The Eighteenth Article of amendment to the Constitution of the United States is hereby repealed.

Section 2. The transportation or importation into any State, Territory, or possession of the United States for delivery or use therein of intoxicating liquors in violation of the laws thereof, is hereby prohibited.

Section 3. This article shall be inoperative unless it shall have been ratified as an amendment to the Constitution by conventions in the several States, as provided in the Constitution, within seven years from the date of the submission thereof to the States by the Congress.

Amendment XXII [March 1, 1951]

No person shall be elected to the office of the President more than twice, and no person who has held the office of President, or acted as President, for more than two years of a term to which some other person was elected President shall be elected to the office of the President more than once.

But this article shall not apply to any person holding the office of President when this article was proposed by the Congress, and shall not prevent any person who may be holding the office of President, or acting as President, during the term within which this article becomes operative from holding the office of President or acting as President during the remainder of such term.

This article shall be inoperative unless it shall have been ratified as an amendment to the Constitution by the legislatures of three-fourths of the several States within seven years from the date of its submission to the States by the Congress.

Amendment XXIII [March 29, 1961]

Section 1. The District constituting the seat of Government of the United States shall appoint in such manner as the Congress may direct.

A number of electors of President and Vice President equal to the whole number of Senators and Representatives in Congress to which the District would be entitled if it were a State, but in no event more than the least populous State; they shall be in addition to those appointed by the States, but they shall be considered, for the purposes of the election of President and Vice President, to be electors appointed by a State; and they shall meet in the District and perform such duties as provided by the twelfth article of amendment.

Section 2. The Congress shall have power to enforce this article by appropriate legislation.

Amendment XXIV [January 23, 1964]

Section 1. The right of citizens of the United States to vote in any primary or other election for President or Vice President, for electors for President or Vice President, or for Senator or Representative in Congress, shall not be denied or abridged by the United States or any State by reason of failure to pay any poll tax or other tax.

Section 2. The Congress shall have power to enforce this article by appropriate legislation.

Amendment XXV [February 10, 1967]

Section 1. In case of the removal of the President from office or of his death or resignation, the Vice President shall become President.

Section 2. Whenever there is a vacancy in the office of the Vice President, the President shall nominate a Vice President who shall take office upon confirmation by a majority of both Houses of Congress.

Section 3. Whenever the President transmits to the President pro tempore of the Senate and the Speaker of the House of Representatives his written declaration that he is unable to discharge the powers and duties of his office, and until he transmits to them a written declaration to the contrary, such powers and duties shall be discharged by the Vice President as Acting President.

Section 4. Whenever the Vice president and a majority of either the principal officers of the executive departments or of such other body as Congress may by law provide, transmit to the President pro tempore of the Senate and the Speaker of the House of Representatives their written declaration that the President is unable to discharge the powers and duties of his office, the Vice President shall immediately assume the powers and duties of the office as Acting President.

Thereafter, when the President transmits to the President pro tempore of the Senate and the Speaker of the House of Representatives his written declaration that no inability exists, he shall resume the powers and duties of his office unless the Vice President and a majority of either the principal officers of the executive departments or of such other body as Congress may by law provide, transmit within four days to the President pro tempore of the Senate and the Speaker of the House of Representatives their written declaration that the President is unable to discharge the powers and duties of his office. Thereupon Congress shall decide the issue, assembling within forty-eight hours for that purpose if not in session. If the Congress, within twenty-one days after receipt of the latter written declaration, or, if Congress is not in session, within twenty-one days after Congress is required to assemble, determines by two-thirds vote of both Houses that the President is unable to discharge the powers and duties of his office, the Vice President shall continue to discharge the same as Acting President; otherwise, the President shall resume the powers and duties of his office.

Amendment XXVI [June 30, 1971]

Section 1. The right of citizens of the United States who are eighteen years of age or older to vote shall not be denied or abridged by the United States or by any State on account of age.

Section 2. The Congress shall have power to enforce this article by appropriate legislation.

Amendment XXVII[12] [May 7, 1992]

No law, varying the compensation for services of the Senators and Representatives, shall take effect until an election of Representatives shall have intervened.

---

[12]James Madison proposed this amendment in 1789 together with the ten amendments that were adopted as the Bill of Rights, but it failed to win ratification at the time. Congress, however, had set no deadline for its ratification, and over the years—particularly in the 1980s and 1990s—many states voted to add it to the Constitution. With the ratification of Michigan in 1992 it passed the threshold of 3/4ths of the states required for adoption, but because the process took more than 200 years, its validity remains in doubt.

PRESIDENTS AND VICE PRESIDENTS

1. George Washington (1789)
   John Adams (1789)

2. John Adams (1797)
   Thomas Jefferson (1797)

3. Thomas Jefferson (1801)
   Aaron Burr (1801)
   George Clinton (1805)

4. James Madison (1809)
   George Clinton (1809)
   Elbridge Gerry (1813)

5. James Monroe (1817)
   Daniel D. Thompkins (1817)

6. John Quincy Adams (1825)
   John C. Calhoun (1825)

7. Andrew Jackson (1829)
   John C. Calhoun (1829)
   Martin Van Buren (1833)

8. Martin Van Buren (1837)
   Richard M. Johnson (1837)

9. William H. Harrison (1841)
   John Tyler (1841)

10. John Tyler (1841)

11. James K. Polk (1845)
    George M. Dallas (1845)

12. Zachary Taylor (1849)
    Millard Fillmore (1849)

13. Millard Fillmore (1850)

14. Franklin Pierce (1853)
    William R. King (1853)

15. James Buchanan (1857)
    John C. Breckinridge (1857)

16. Abraham Lincoln (1861)
    Hannibal Hamlin (1861)
    Andrew Johnson (1865)

17. Andrew Johnson (1865)

18. Ulysses S. Grant (1869)
    Schuyler Colfax (1869)
    Henry Wilson (1873)

19. Rutherford B. Hayes (1877)
    William A. Wheeler (1877)

20. James A. Garfield (1881)
    Chester A. Arthur (1881)

21. Chester A. Arthur (1881)

22. Grover Cleveland (1885)
    T. A. Hendricks (1885)

23. Benjamin Harrison (1889)
    Levi P. Morgan (1889)

24. Grover Cleveland (1893)
    Adlai E. Stevenson (1893)

25. William McKinley (1897)
    Garret A. Hobart (1897)
    Theodore Roosevelt (1901)

26. Theodore Roosevelt (1901)
    Charles Fairbanks (1905)

27. William H. Taft (1909)
    James S. Sherman (1909)

28. Woodrow Wilson (1913)
    Thomas R. Marshall (1913)

29. Warren G. Harding (1921)
    Calvin Coolidge (1921)

30. Calvin Coolidge (1923)
    Charles G. Dawes (1925)

31. Herbert C. Hoover (1929)
    Charles Curtis (1929)

32. Franklin D. Roosevelt (1933)
    John Nance Garner (1933)
    Henry A. Wallace (1941)
    Harry S. Truman (1945)

33. Harry S. Truman (1945)
    Alben W. Barkley (1949)

34. Dwight D. Eisenhower (1953)
    Richard M. Nixon (1953)

35. John F. Kennedy (1961)
    Lyndon B. Johnson (1961)

36. Lyndon B. Johnson (1963)
    Hubert H. Humphrey (1965)

37. Richard M. Nixon (1969)
    Spiro T. Agnew (1969)
    Gerald R. Ford (1973)

38. Gerald R. Ford (1974)
    Nelson A. Rockefeller (1974)

39. James E. Carter Jr. (1977)
    Walter F. Mondale (1977)

40. Ronald W. Reagan (1981)
    George H. Bush (1981)

41. George H. Bush (1989)
    James D. Quayle III (1989)

42. William J. Clinton (1993)
    Albert Gore (1993)

43. William J. Clinton (1997)
    Albert Gore (1997)

44. George W. Bush (2001)
    Richard Cheney (2001)

PRESIDENTIAL ELECTIONS

Year	Number of States	Candidates	Party	Popular Vote*	Electoral Vote[†]	Percentage of Popular Vote
1789	11	GEORGE WASHINGTON	No party designations		69	
		John Adams			34	
		Other Candidates			35	
1792	15	GEORGE WASHINGTON	No party designations		132	
		John Adams			77	
		George Clinton			50	
		Other Candidates			5	
1796	16	JOHN ADAMS	Federalist		71	
		Thomas Jefferson	Democratic-Republican		68	
		Thomas Pinckney	Federalist		59	
		Aaron Burr	Democratic-Republican		30	
		Other Candidates			48	
1800	16	THOMAS JEFFERSON	Democratic-Republican		73	
		Aaron Burr	Democratic-Republican		73	
		John Adams	Federalist		65	
		Charles C. Pinckney	Federalist		64	
		John Jay	Federalist		1	
1804	17	THOMAS JEFFERSON	Democratic-Republican		162	
		Charles C. Pinckney	Federalist		14	
1808	17	JAMES MADISON	Democratic-Republican		122	
		Charles C. Pinckney	Federalist		47	
		George Clinton	Democratic-Republican		6	
1812	18	JAMES MADISON	Democratic-Republican		128	
		DeWitt Clinton	Federalist		89	
1816	19	JAMES MONROE	Democratic-Republican		183	
		Rufus King	Federalist		34	
1820	24	JAMES MONROE	Democratic-Republican		231	
		John Quincy Adams	Democratic-Republican		1	
1824	24	JOHN QUINCY ADAMS	Democratic-Republican	108,740	84	30.5
		Andrew Jackson	Democratic-Republican	153,544	99	43.1
		William H. Crawford	Democratic-Republican	46,618	41	13.1
		Henry Clay	Democratic-Republican	47,136	37	13.2
1828	24	ANDREW JACKSON	Democrat	647,286	178	56.0
		John Quincy Adams	National-Republican	508,064	83	44.0
1832	24	ANDREW JACKSON	Democrat	687,502	219	55.0
		Henry Clay	National-Republican	530,189	49	42.4
		William Wirt	Anti-Masonic	33,108	7	2.6
		John Floyd	National-Republican		11	

*Percentage of popular vote given for any election year may not total 100 percent because candidates receiving less than 1 percent of the popular vote have been omitted.

[†]Prior to the passage of the Twelfth Amendment in 1904, the electoral college voted for two presidential candidates; the runner-up became Vice-President. Data from *Historical Statistics of the United States, Colonial Times to 1957* (1961), pp. 682–683, and *The World Almanac.*

PRESIDENTIAL ELECTIONS
(continued)

Year	Number of States	Candidates	Party	Popular Vote	Electoral Vote	Percentage of Popular Vote
1836	26	MARTIN VAN BUREN	Democrat	765,483	170	50.9
		William H. Harrison	Whig		73	
		Hugh L. White	Whig		26	
		Daniel Webster	Whig	739,795	14	49.1
		W. P. Mangum	Whig		11	
1840	26	WILLIAM H. HARRISON	Whig	1,274,624	234	53.1
		Martin Van Buren	Democrat	1,127,781	60	46.9
1844	26	JAMES K. POLK	Democrat	1,338,464	170	49.6
		Henry Clay	Whig	1,300,097	105	48.1
		James G. Birney	Liberty	62,300		2.3
1848	30	ZACHARY TAYLOR	Whig	1,360,967	163	47.4
		Lewis Cass	Democrat	1,222,342	127	42.5
		Martin Van Buren	Free-Soil	291,263		10.1
1852	31	FRANKLIN PIERCE	Democrat	1,601,117	254	50.9
		Winfield Scott	Whig	1,385,453	42	44.1
		John P. Hale	Free-Soil	155,825		5.0
1856	31	JAMES BUCHANAN	Democrat	1,832,955	174	45.3
		John C. Frémont	Republican	1,339,932	114	33.1
		Millard Fillmore	American ("Know Nothing")	871,731	8	21.6
1860	33	ABRAHAM LINCOLN	Republican	1,865,593	180	39.8
		Stephen A. Douglas	Democrat	1,382,713	12	29.5
		John C. Breckinridge	Democrat	848,356	72	18.1
		John Bell	Constitutional Union	592,906	39	12.6
1864	36	ABRAHAM LINCOLN	Republican	2,206,938	212	55.0
		George B. McClellan	Democrat	1,803,787	21	45.0
1868	37	ULYSSES S. GRANT	Republican	3,013,421	214	52.7
		Horatio Seymour	Democrat	2,706,829	80	47.3
1872	37	ULYSSES S. GRANT	Republican	3,596,745	286	55.6
		Horace Greeley	Democrat	2,843,446	*	43.9
1876	38	RUTHERFORD B. HAYES	Republican	4,036,572	185	48.0
		Samuel J. Tilden	Democrat	4,284,020	184	51.0
1880	38	JAMES A. GARFIELD	Republican	4,453,295	214	48.5
		Winfield S. Hancock	Democrat	4,414,082	155	48.1
		James B. Weaver	Greenback-Labor	308,578		3.4
1884	38	GROVER CLEVELAND	Democrat	4,879,507	219	48.5
		James G. Blaine	Republican	4,850,293	182	48.2
		Benjamin F. Butler	Greenback-Labor	175,370		1.8
		John P. St. John	Prohibition	150,369		1.5
1888	38	BENJAMIN HARRISON	Republican	5,447,129	233	47.9
		Grover Cleveland	Democrat	5,537,857	168	48.6
		Clinton B. Fisk	Prohibition	249,506		2.2
		Anson J. Streeter	Union Labor	146,935		1.3

*Because of the death of Greeley, Democratic electors scattered their votes.

PRESIDENTIAL ELECTIONS
(continued)

Year	Number of States	Candidates	Party	Popular Vote	Electoral Vote	Percentage of Popular Vote
1892	44	GROVER CLEVELAND	Democrat	5,555,426	277	46.1
		Benjamin Harrison	Republican	5,182,690	145	43.0
		James B. Weaver	People's	1,029,846	22	8.5
		John Bidwell	Prohibition	264,133		2.2
1896	45	WILLIAM MCKINLEY	Republican	7,102,246	271	51.1
		William J. Bryan	Democrat	6,492,559	176	47.7
1900	45	WILLIAM MCKINLEY	Republican	7,218,491	292	51.7
		William J. Bryan	Democrat; Populist	6,356,734	155	45.5
		John C. Woolley	Prohibition	208,914		1.5
1904	45	THEODORE ROOSEVELT	Republican	7,628,461	336	57.4
		Alton B. Parker	Democrat	5,084,223	140	37.6
		Eugene V. Debs	Socialist	402,283		3.0
		Silas C. Swallow	Prohibition	258,536		1.9
1908	46	WILLIAM H. TAFT	Republican	7,675,320	321	51.6
		William J. Bryan	Democrat	6,412,294	162	43.1
		Eugene V. Debs	Socialist	420,793		2.8
		Eugene W. Chafin	Prohibition	253,840		1.7
1912	48	WOODROW WILSON	Democrat	6,296,547	435	41.9
		Theodore Roosevelt	Progressive	4,118,571	88	27.4
		William H. Taft	Republican	3,486,720	8	23.2
		Eugene V. Debs	Socialist	900,672		6.0
		Eugene W. Chafin	Prohibition	206,275		1.4
1916	48	WOODROW WILSON	Democrat	9,127,695	277	49.4
		Charles E. Hughes	Republican	8,533,507	254	46.2
		A. L. Benson	Socialist	585,113		3.2
		J. Frank Hanly	Prohibition	220,506		1.2
1920	48	WARREN G. HARDING	Republican	16,143,407	404	60.4
		James M. Cox	Democrat	9,130,328	127	34.2
		Eugene V. Debs	Socialist	919,799		3.4
		P. P. Christensen	Farmer-Labor	265,411		1.0
1924	48	CALVIN COOLIDGE	Republican	15,718,211	382	54.0
		John W. Davis	Democrat	8,385,283	136	28.8
		Robert M. La Follette	Progressive	4,831,289	13	16.6
1928	48	HERBERT C. HOOVER	Republican	21,391,993	444	58.2
		Alfred E. Smith	Democrat	15,016,169	87	40.9
1932	48	FRANKLIN D. ROOSEVELT	Democrat	22,809,638	472	57.4
		Herbert C. Hoover	Republican	15,758,901	59	39.7
		Norman Thomas	Socialist	881,951		2.2
1936	48	FRANKLIN D. ROOSEVELT	Democrat	27,752,869	523	60.8
		Alfred M. Landon	Republican	16,674,665	8	36.5
		William Lemke	Union	882,479		1.9
1940	48	FRANKLIN D. ROOSEVELT	Democrat	27,307,819	449	54.8
		Wendell L. Willkie	Republican	22,321,018	82	44.8
1944	48	FRANKLIN D. ROOSEVELT	Democrat	25,606,585	432	53.5
		Thomas E. Dewey	Republican	22,014,745	99	46.0

PRESIDENTIAL ELECTIONS
(continued)

Year	Number of States	Candidates	Party	Popular Vote	Electoral Vote	Percentage of Popular Vote
1948	48	HARRY S. TRUMAN	Democrat	24,105,812	303	49.5
		Thomas E. Dewey	Republican	21,970,065	189	45.1
		J. Strom Thurmond	States' Rights	1,169,063	39	2.4
		Henry A. Wallace	Progressive	1,157,172		2.4
1952	48	DWIGHT D. EISENHOWER	Republican	33,936,234	442	55.1
		Adlai E. Stevenson	Democrat	27,314,992	89	44.4
1956	48	DWIGHT D. EISENHOWER	Republican	35,590,472	457[*]	57.6
		Adlai E. Stevenson	Democrat	26,022,752	73	42.1
1960	50	JOHN F. KENNEDY	Democrat	34,227,096	303[†]	49.9
		Richard M. Nixon	Republican	34,108,546	219	49.6
1964	50	LYNDON B. JOHNSON	Democrat	42,676,220	486	61.3
		Barry M. Goldwater	Republican	26,860,314	52	38.5
1968	50	RICHARD M. NIXON	Republican	31,785,480	301	43.4
		Hubert H. Humphrey	Democrat	31,275,165	191	42.7
		George C. Wallace	American Independent	9,906,473	46	13.5
1972	50	RICHARD M. NIXON[‡]	Republican	47,165,234	520	60.6
		George S. McGovern	Democrat	29,168,110	17	37.5
1976	50	JIMMY CARTER	Democrat	40,828,929	297	50.1
		Gerald R. Ford	Republican	39,148,940	240	47.9
		Eugene McCarthy	Independent	739,256		
1980	50	RONALD REAGAN	Republican	43,201,220	489	50.9
		Jimmy Carter	Democrat	34,913,332	49	41.2
		John B. Anderson	Independent	5,581,379		
1984	50	RONALD REAGAN	Republican	53,428,357	525	59.0
		Walter F. Mondale	Democrat	36,930,923	13	41.0
1988	50	GEORGE BUSH	Republican	48,901,046	426	53.4
		Michael Dukakis	Democrat	41,809,030	111	45.6
1992	50	BILL CLINTON	Democrat	43,728,275	370	43.2
		George H.W. Bush	Republican	38,167,416	168	37.7
		H. Ross Perot	United We Stand, America	19,237,247		19.0
1996	50	BILL CLINTON	Democrat	45,590,703	379	49.0
		Robert Dole	Republican	37,816,307	159	41.0
		H. Ross Perot	Reform	7,874,283		8.0
2000	50	GEORGE W. BUSH	Republican	50,456,169	271	48.0
		Albert Gore	Democrat	50,996,116	266	48.0
		Ralph Nader	Green	2,767,176	0	3.0

[*]Walter B. Jones received 1 electoral vote.

[†]Harry F. Byrd received 15 electoral votes.

[‡]Resigned August 9, 1974: Vice President Gerald R. Ford became President.

ADMISSION OF STATES INTO THE UNION

State	Date of Admission	State	Date of Admission
1. Delaware	December 7, 1787	26. Michigan	January 26, 1837
2. Pennsylvania	December 12, 1787	27. Florida	March 3, 1845
3. New Jersey	December 18, 1787	28. Texas	December 29, 1845
4. Georgia	January 2, 1788	29. Iowa	December 28, 1846
5. Connecticut	January 9, 1788	30. Wisconsin	May 29, 1848
6. Massachusetts	February 6, 1788	31. California	September 9, 1850
7. Maryland	April 28, 1788	32. Minnesota	May 11, 1858
8. South Carolina	May 23, 1788	33. Oregon	February 14, 1859
9. New Hampshire	June 21, 1788	34. Kansas	January 29, 1861
10. Virginia	June 25, 1788	35. West Virginia	June 20, 1863
11. New York	July 26, 1788	36. Nevada	October 31, 1864
12. North Carolina	November 21, 1789	37. Nebraska	March 1, 1867
13. Rhode Island	May 29, 1790	38. Colorado	August 1, 1876
14. Vermont	March 4, 1791	39. North Dakota	November 2, 1889
15. Kentucky	June 1, 1792	40. South Dakota	November 2, 1889
16. Tennessee	June 1, 1796	41. Montana	November 8, 1889
17. Ohio	March 1, 1803	42. Washington	November 11, 1889
18. Louisiana	April 30, 1812	43. Idaho	July 3, 1890
19. Indiana	December 11, 1816	44. Wyoming	July 10, 1890
20. Mississippi	December 10, 1817	45. Utah	January 4, 1896
21. Illinois	December 3, 1818	46. Oklahoma	November 16, 1907
22. Alabama	December 14, 1819	47. New Mexico	January 6, 1912
23. Maine	March 15, 1820	48. Arizona	February 14, 1912
24. Missouri	August 10, 1821	49. Alaska	January 3, 1959
25. Arkansas	June 15, 1836	50. Hawaii	August 21, 1959

DEMOGRAPHICS OF THE UNITED STATES

POPULATION GROWTH

Year	Population	Percent Increase
1630	4,600	
1640	26,600	478.3
1650	50,400	90.8
1660	75,100	49.0
1670	111,900	49.0
1680	151,500	35.4
1690	210,400	38.9
1700	250,900	19.2
1710	331,700	32.2
1720	466,200	40.5
1730	629,400	35.0
1740	905,600	43.9
1750	1,170,800	29.3
1760	1,593,600	36.1
1770	2,148,100	34.8
1780	2,780,400	29.4
1790	3,929,214	41.3
1800	5,308,483	35.1
1810	7,239,881	36.4
1820	9,638,453	33.1
1830	12,866,020	33.5
1840	17,069,453	32.7
1850	23,191,876	35.9
1860	31,443,321	35.6
1870	39,818,449	26.6
1880	50,155,783	26.0
1890	62,947,714	25.5
1900	75,994,575	20.7
1910	91,972,266	21.0
1920	105,710,620	14.9
1930	122,775,046	16.1
1940	131,669,275	7.2
1950	150,697,361	14.5
1960	179,323,175	19.0
1970	203,235,298	13.3
1980	226,545,805	11.5
1990	248,709,873	9.8
2000	281,421,906	9.0

Source: *Historical Statistics of the United States* (1975); *Statistical Abstract by the United States* (1991, 1997). Population Estimates Program, Population Division, U.S. Census Bureau, April 2001.
Note: Figures for 1630–1780 include British colonies within limits of present United States only; Native American population included only in 1930 and thereafter.

WORKFORCE

Year	Total Number Workers (1000s)	Farmers as % of Total	Women as % of Total	% Workers in Unions
1810	2,330	84	(NA)	(NA)
1840	5,660	75	(NA)	(NA)
1860	11,110	53	(NA)	(NA)
1870	12,506	53	15	(NA)
1880	17,392	52	15	(NA)
1890	23,318	43	17	(NA)
1900	29,073	40	18	3
1910	38,167	31	21	6
1920	41,614	26	21	12
1930	48,830	22	22	7
1940	53,011	17	24	27
1950	59,643	12	28	25
1960	69,877	8	32	26
1970	82,049	4	37	25
1980	108,544	3	42	23
1990	117,914	3	45	16
2000	140,900	5.5	47	10.0

Source: *Historical Statistics of the United States* (1975); *Statistical Abstract of the United States* (1991, 1996). Population Estimates Program, Population Division, U.S. Census Bureau, April 2001.

VITAL STATISTICS
(per thousands)

Year	Births	Deaths	Marriages	Divorces
1800	55	(NA)	(NA)	(NA)
1810	54.3	(NA)	(NA)	(NA)
1820	55.2	(NA)	(NA)	(NA)
1830	51.4	(NA)	(NA)	(NA)
1840	51.8	(NA)	(NA)	(NA)
1850	43.3	(NA)	(NA)	(NA)
1860	44.3	(NA)	(NA)	(NA)
1870	38.3	(NA)	9.6 (1867)	0.3 (1867)
1880	39.8	(NA)	9.1 (1875)	0.3 (1875)
1890	31.5	(NA)	9.0	0.5
1900	32.3	17.2	9.3	0.7
1910	30.1	14.7	10.3	0.9
1920	27.7	13.0	12.0	1.6
1930	21.3	11.3	9.2	1.6
1940	19.4	10.8	12.1	2.0
1950	24.1	9.6	11.1	2.6
1960	23.7	9.5	8.5	2.2
1970	18.4	9.5	10.6	3.5
1980	15.9	8.8	10.6	5.2
1990	16.7	8.6	9.8	4.7
2000	14.8	8.8	8.5	4.1

Source: *Historical Statistics of the United States* (1975); *Statistical Abstract of the United States* (1991, 1997). Population Estimates Program, Population Division, U.S. Census Bureau, January 2001.

RACIAL COMPOSITION OF THE POPULATION
(in thousands)

Year	White	Black	Indian	Hispanic	Asian
1790	3,172	757	(NA)	(NA)	(NA)
1800	4,306	1,002	(NA)	(NA)	(NA)
1820	7,867	1,772	(NA)	(NA)	(NA)
1840	14,196	2,874	(NA)	(NA)	(NA)
1860	26,923	4,442	(NA)	(NA)	(NA)
1880	43,403	6,581	(NA)	(NA)	(NA)
1900	66,809	8,834	(NA)	(NA)	(NA)
1910	81,732	9,828	(NA)	(NA)	(NA)
1920	94,821	10,463	(NA)	(NA)	(NA)
1930	110,287	11,891	(NA)	(NA)	(NA)
1940	118,215	12,866	(NA)	(NA)	(NA)
1950	134,942	15,042	(NA)	(NA)	(NA)
1960	158,832	18,872	(NA)	(NA)	(NA)
1970	178,098	22,581	(NA)	(NA)	(NA)
1980	194,713	26,683	1,420	14,609	3,729
1990	205,710	30,486	2,065	22,354	7,458
2000	226,861	35,470	2,448	31,387	11,279

Source: U.S. Bureau of the Census, *U.S. Census of Population: 1940*, vol. II, part 1, and vol. IV, part 1; *1950*, vol. II, part 1; *1960*, vol. I, part 1; *1970*, vol. I, part B; and *Current Population Reports*, P25-1095 and P25-1104; *Statistical Abstract of the United States* (1997); Population Estimates Program, Population Division, U.S. Census Bureau, January 2001.

IMMIGRATION, BY ORIGIN
(in thousands)

Period	Europe	Americas	Asia
1820–30	106	12	—
1831–40	496	33	—
1841–50	1,597	62	—
1851–60	2,453	75	42
1861–70	2,065	167	65
1871–80	2,272	404	70
1881–90	4,735	427	70
1891–1900	3,555	39	75
1901–10	8,065	362	324
1911–20	4,322	1,144	247
1921–30	2,463	1,517	112
1931–40	348	160	16
1941–50	621	355	32
1951–60	1,326	997	150
1961–70	1,123	1,716	590
1971–80	800	1,983	1,588
1981–90	762	3,616	2,738
1991–2000	1,100	3,800	2,200

Source: *Historical Statistics of the United States* (1975); *Statistical Abstract of the United States* (1991); Population Estimates Program, Population Division, U.S. Census Bureau, April 2001.

BIBLIOGRAPHY

CHAPTER 1

Settling the Continent

Larry D. Agenbroad, et al., eds., *Megafauna and Man* (1990)

John Bierhorst, ed., *The Red Swan: Myths and Tales of the American Indians* (1976)

Robson Bonnichsen and Karen L. Turnmire, *Ice Age People of North America: Environments, Origins, and Adaptations* (1999)

Michael H. Crawford, *The Origins of Native Americans: Evidence from Anthropological Genetics* (1998)

Tom D. Dillehay, *The Settling of the Americas: A New Prehistory* (2000)

E. James Dixon, *Bones, Boats, and Bison: Archaeology and the First Colonization of Western North America* (2000)

Richard Erdoes and Alfonso Ortiz, eds., *American Indian Myths and Legends* (1984)

Guy Gibbon, *Archaeology of Prehistoric Native America: An Encyclopedia* (1998)

Lee Eldridge Huddleston, *Origins of the American Indians: European Concepts, 1492–1729* (1967)

George Kubler, *Esthetic Recognition of Ancient Amerindian Art* (1991)

Hanns J. Prem, *The Ancient Americas: A Brief History and Guide to Research* (1997)

Heather Anne Pringle, *In Search of Ancient North America: An Archaeological Journey to Forgotten Cultures* (1996)

Richard F. Townsend, ed., *The Ancient Americas: Art from Sacred Landscapes* (1992)

Frederick Hadleigh West, ed., *American Beginnings: The Prehistory and Palaeoecology of Beringia* (1996)

New Ways of Living on the Land

Kenneth M. Ames and Herbert D. G. Mascher, *Peoples of the Northwest Coast: Their Archaeology and Prehistory* (2000)

David S. Brose, et al., *Ancient Art of the American Woodland Indians* (1985)

Thomas E. Emerson, et al., eds. *Late Woodland Societies: Tradition and Transformation Across the Midcontinent* (2000)

Richard I. Ford, ed., *Prehistoric Food Production in North America* (1985)

Sarah W. Neusius, *Foraging, Collecting, and Harvesting: Archaic Period Subsistence and Settlement in the Eastern Woodlands* (1986)

James L. Phillips and James A. Brown, eds., *Archaic Hunters and Gatherers in the American Midwest* (1983)

The Development of Farming

Frances R. Berdan, *The Aztecs of Central Mexico* (1982)

David S. Brose and N'omi Greber, eds., *Hopewell Archaeology* (1979)

David Carrasco, et al., eds., *Mesoamerica's Classic Heritage: From Teotihuacan to the Aztecs* (2000)

William S. Dancey and Paul J Pacheco, eds., *Ohio Hopewell Community Organization* (1997)

Emil W. Haury, *The Hohokam* (1976)

Ted Hirschfield, *Middle Mississippians: Encounters with the Prehistoric Amerindians* (1996)

Rosemary Joyce, *Gender and Power in Prehispanic Mesoamerica* (2000)

William F. Keegan, ed., *Emergent Horticultural Economies of the Eastern Woodlands* (1987)

R. Barry Lewis and Charles Stout, eds., *Mississippian Towns and Sacred Spaces* (1998)

George R. Milner, *The Cahokia Chiefdom: The Archaeology of a Mississippian Society* (1998)

Warren King Moorehead, *The Cahokia Mounds* (2000)

Barker H. Morrow and V. B. Price, eds., *Anasazi Architecture and American Design* (1997)

Timothy R. Pauketat and Thomas E. Emerson, eds., *Cahokia: Domination and Ideology in the Mississippian World* (1997)

Stephen Plog, *Ancient Peoples of the American Southwest* (1998)

Paul F. Reed, ed., *Foundations of Anasazi Culture: The Basketmaker-Pueblo Transition* (2000)

Bruce D. Smith, *The Mississippian Emergence* (1990)

David E. Stuart, *Anasazi America: Seventeen Centuries on the Road from Center Place* (2000)

Christy G. Turner, *Man Corn: Cannibalism and Violence in the Prehistoric American Southwest* (2000)

Biloine W. Young and Melvin L. Fowler, *Cahokia, The Great Native American Metropolis* (2000)

W. H. Wills, *Early Prehistoric Agriculture* (1988)

Culture Areas of North America on the Eve of Colonization

Michael A. Adler, ed., *The Prehistoric Pueblo World, a.d. 1150–1350* (1996)

Kenneth M. Ames and Herbert D. G. Mascher, *Peoples of the Northwest Coast: Their Archaeology and Prehistory* (2000)

Elizabeth M. Brumfiel and John W. Fox, *Factional Competition and Political Development in the New World* (1993)

Lyle Campbell and Marianne Mithun, eds., *The Languages of Native America* (1979)

Catherine M. Cameron, *Hopi Dwellings: Architecture at Oryi* (1999)

Paul H. Carlson, *The Plains Indians* (1999)

James Taylor Carson, *Searching for the Bright Path: The Mississippi Choctaws from Prehistory to Removal* (1999)

Cheryl Claassen and Rosemary A. Joyce, eds., *Women in Prehistory: North America and Mesoamerica* (1997)

Olive P. Dickason, *Canada's First Nations: A History of Founding Peoples* (1992)

Michelle Hegmon, ed., *The Archaeology of Regional Interaction: Religion, Warfare, and Exchange Across the American Southwest* (1999)

June Helm, *The People of Denendah: Ethnohistory of the Indians of Canada's Northwest Territories* (2000)

David LaVere, *The Caddo Chiefdoms: Caddo Economics and Politics, 700–1835* (1998)

Steven A. LeBlanc, *Prehistoric Warfare in the American Southwest* (1999)

Stephen H. Lekson, *The Chaco Meridian: Centers of Political Power in the Ancient Southwest* (1999)

Mallory McCane O'Connor, *Lost Cities of the Ancient Southeast* (1995)

Jill E. Neitzel, ed., *Great Towns and Regional Politics: In the Prehistoric American Southwest and Southeast* (1999)

Alfonso Ortiz, ed., *New Perspectives on the Pueblos* (1972)

Howard S. Russell, *Indian New England before the Mayflower* (1980)

Frank G. Speck, *Penobscot Man* (1940)

Bruce Trigger, *The Children of Aaeaentsic: A History of the Huron People to 1660* (1976)

CHAPTER 2

The Expansion of Europe

James M. Blaut, *1492: The Debate on Colonialism, Eurocentrism, and History* (1992)

Fernand Braudel, *The Mediterranean and the Mediterranean World in the Age of Philip II* (1972)

Carol Cipolla, *Before the Industrial Revolution: European Society and Economy, 1100–1700* (1976)

Patrick Collinson, *The Religion of Protestants: The Church in English Society, 1559–1625* (1982)

Andre Gunder Frank, *World Accumulation, 1492–1789* (1978)

Giancarlo Masini and Iacopo Gari, *How Florence Invented America: Vespucci, Verranzano, and Mazzei and Their Contribution to the Conception of the New World* (1998)

Douglas North, *The Rise of the Western World: A New Economic History* (1973)

José Casas Pardo, ed., *Economic Effects of the European Expansion, 1492–1824* (1992)

J. H. Parry, *The Age of Reconnaissance* (1963)

——, *Europe and a Wider World: The Establishment of the European Hegemony: Trade and Expansion in the Age of the Renaissance* (1966)

Geoffrey Vaughn Scannell, *The First Imperial Age: European Overseas Expansion c. 1400–1715* (1989)

The Spanish in the Americas

Fredi Chiapelli, ed., *First Images of America: The Impact of the New World on the Old* (1976)

Henry F. Dobyns, *Their Number Become Thinned: Native American Population Dynamics in Eastern North America* (1983)

J. H. Elliott, *The Old World and the New, 1492–1650* (1970)

Anthony Grafton, *New Worlds, Ancient Texts: The Power of Tradition and the Shock of Discovery* (1992)

John H. Hann, *A History of the Timucua Indians and Missions* (1996)

Hugh Honour, *New Golden Land: European Images of America from the Discoveries to the Present Time* (1975)

Charles Hudson and Carmen Chaves Tesser, eds., *The Forgotten Centuries: Indians and Europeans in the American South, 1521–1704* (1994)

René Jara and Nicholas Spadaccini, eds., *Amerindian Images and the Legacy of Columbus* (1992)

Elizabeth A. H. John, *Storms Brewed in Other Men's Worlds: The Confrontation of Indians, Spanish, and French in the Southwest, 1540–1795* (1975)

James Lang, *Conquest and Commerce: Spain and England in the Americas* (1975)

James Lockhart and Stuart B. Schwartz, *Early Latin America: A History of Colonial Spanish America and Brazil* (1983)

Albert Manucy, *Sixteenth-Century St. Augustine: The People and Their Homes* (1997)

Jerald T. Milanich, *Laboring in the Fields of the Lord: Spanish Missions and Southeastern Indians* (1999)

Jerald T. Milanich and Charles Hudson, *Hernando de Soto and the Indians of Florida* (1993)

James Howlett O'Donnell III, *Southeastern Frontiers: Europeans, Africans, and American Indians, 1513–1840: A Critical Bibliography* (1982)

Edmundo O'Gorman, *The Invention of America: An Inquiry into the Historical Nature of the New World and the Meaning of its History* (1961)

Irving Rouse, *The Tainos: Rise and Decline of the People Who Greeted Columbus* (1992)

Stuart B. Schwartz, *Victors and Vanquished: Spanish and Nahua Views of the Conquest of Mexico* (2000)

David M. Traboulay, *Columbus and Las Casas: The Conquest and Christianization of America, 1492–1566* (1994)

Northern Explorations and Encounters

Alfred Goldsworthy Bailey, *The Conflict of European and Eastern Algonkian Cultures, 1504–1700* (1969)

Peter T. Bradley, *British Maritime Enterprise in the New World: From the Late Fifteenth to the Mid-Eighteenth Centuries* (1999)

Carl Bridenbaugh, *Vexed and Troubled Englishmen, 1590–1642* (1968)

Susan Danforth, *Encountering the New World, 1493–1800* (1991)

G. R. Elton, *England under the Tudors* (1974)

C. H. George and Katherine George, *The Protestant Mind of the English Reformation* (1961)

John Guy, *Tudor England* (1988)

R. J. Knecht, *The French Civil Wars, 1562–1598* (2000)

Karen Ordahl Kupperman, *Indians and English: Facing Off in Early America* (2000)

Peter Laslett, *The World We Have Lost* (1965)

E. B. Leacock and N. O. Laurie, eds., *North American Indians in Historical Perspective* (1971)

Anthony McFarlane, *The British in the Americas, 1480–1815* (1994)

Lee Miller, *Roanoke: Solving the Mystery of England's Lost Colony* (2000)

David B. Quinn, *North America from Earliest Discovery to First Settlements* (1977)

——, *The Roanoke Voyages, 1584–1590*, 2 vols. (1955)

Bernard W. Sheehan, *Savagism and Civility: Indians and Englishmen in Colonial Virginia* (1980)

Russell Thornton, *American Indian Holocaust and Survival* (1987)

Margo Todd, ed., *Reformation to Revolution: Politics and Religion in Early Modern England* (1995)

Marcel Trudel, *The Beginnings of New France, 1524–1663* (1973)

Keith Wrightson, *English Society, 1580–1680* (1982)

Biography

Miles H. Davidson, *Columbus Then and Now: A Life Reexamined* (1997)

David A. Howard, *Conquistador in Chains: Cabeza de Vaca and the Indians of the Americas* (1997)

Harry Kelsey, *Sir Francis Drake: The Queen's Pirate* (1998)

Carole Levin, *The Heart and Stomach of a King: Elizabeth I and the Politics of Sex and Power* (1994)

Richard Lee Marks, *Cortés: The Great Adventurer and the Fate of Aztec Mexico* (1993)

James McDermott, *Martin Frobisher: Elizabethan Privateer* (2001)

A. L. Rowse, *Eminent Elizabethans* (1983)

P. E. Russell, *Prince Henry the Navigator: A Life* (2000)

David Starkey, *Elizabeth: The Struggle for the Throne* (2000)

Henry Raup Wagner, *The Life and Writings of Bartolomé de las Casas* (1967)

CHAPTER 3

Spain and Its Competitors in North America

Gary Clayton Anderson, *The Indian Southwest, 1580–1830: Ethnogenesis and Reinvention* (1999)

James Axtell, *The Invasion Within: The Contest of Culture in Colonial North America* (1985)

Denys Delâge, *Bitter Feast: Amerindians and Europeans in Northeastern North America, 1600–64* (1993)

W. J. Eccles, *The Canadian Frontier, 1534–1760* (1983)

Carl J. Ekberg, *French Roots in the Illinois Country: The Mississippi Frontier in Colonial Times* (1998)

J. R. Jones, *The Anglo-Dutch Wars of the Seventeenth Century* (1996)

Cathy D. Matson, *Merchants and Empire: Trading in Colonial New York* (1998)

Peter Moogk, *La Nouvelle France: The Making of French Canada, a Cultural History* (2000)

Daniel Paul, *We Were Not the Savages: A Mi'kmaq Perspective on the Collision Between European and Native American Civilizations* (2000)

Oliver Rink, *Holland on the Hudson: An Economic and Social History of Dutch New York* (1986)

Sylvia Van Kirk, *Many Tender Ties: Women in Fur-Trade Society in Western Canada, 1670–1870* (1999)

The Chesapeake

Edward L. Bond, *Damned Souls in a Tobacco Colony: Religion in Seventeenth-Century Virginia* (2000)

Kathleen M. Brown, *Good Wives, Nasty Wenches, and Anxious Patriarchs: Gender, Race, and Power in Colonial Virginia* (1996)

Wesley F. Craven, *White, Red, and Black: The Seventeenth Century Virginian* (1971)

Ronald Hoffman, *Princes of Ireland, Planters of Maryland: A Carroll Saga, 1500–1782* (2000)

Karen Ordahl Kupperman, *Settling with the Indians: The Meeting of English and Indian Cultures in America, 1580–1640* (1980)

Gloria L. Main, *Tobacco Colony: Life in Early Maryland, 1650–1720* (1982)

Michael Leroy Oberg, *Dominion and Civility: English Imperialism and Native America, 1585–1685* (1999)

New England

David Grayson Allen, *In English Ways: The Movement of Societies and the Transferal of English Local Law and Custom* (1981)

Bernard Bailyn, *The New England Merchants in the Seventeenth Century* (1955)

Carl Bridenbaugh, *Fat Mutton and Liberty of Conscience: Society in Rhode Island, 1636–1690* (1974)

David Cressy, *Coming Over: Migration and Communication between England and New England in the Seventeenth Century* (1987)

William Cronon, *Changes in the Land: Indians, Colonists, and the Ecology of New England* (1983)

Bruce Colin Daniels, *Puritans at Play: Leisure and Recreation in Colonial New England* (1995)

John Demos, *A Little Commonwealth: Family Life in Plymouth Colony* (1970)

Timothy Hall, *Separating Church and State: Roger Williams and Religious Liberty* (1998)

Francis Jennings, *The Invasion of America: Indians, Colonialism, and the Cant of Conquest* (1975)

Benjamin W. Labaree, *America and the Sea: A Maritime History* (1998)

Amy Scrager Lang, *Prophetic Women: Anne Hutchinson and the Problem of Dissent in the Literature of New England* (1987)

Elizabeth Reis, *Damned Women: Sinners and Witches in Puritan New England* (1997)

Restoration Colonies

Wesley F. Craven, *The Southern Colonies in the Seventeenth Century, 1607–1689* (1949)

Melvin B. Endy Jr., *William Penn and Early Quakerism* (1973)

Michael Kammen, *Colonial New York: A History* (1975)

Sung Bok Kim, *Landlord and Tenant in Colonial New York: Manorial Society, 1664–1775* (1978)

H. T. Merrens, *Colonial North Carolina* (1964)

Donna Merwick, *Death of a Notary: Conquest and Change in Colonial New York* (1999)

Gary B. Nash, *Quakers and Politics: Pennsylvania, 1681–1726* (1968)

Robert C. Ritchie, *The Duke's Province: A Study of New York Politics and Society, 1664–1691* (1977)

M. Eugene Sirmans, *Colonial South Carolina: A Political History, 1663–1763* (1966)

Jack M. Sosin, *English America and the Restoration Monarchy of Charles II: Transatlantic Politics, Commerce, and Kinship* (1980)

Conflict and War

Thomas J. Archdeacon, *New York City, 1664–1710* (1976)

Paul Boyer and Stephen Nissenbaum, *Salem Possessed* (1974)

Colin G. Calloway, ed., *After King Philip's War: Presence and Persistence in Indian New England* (1997)

Eveline Cruickshanks, *The Glorious Revolution* (2000)

James D. Drake, *King Philip's War: Civil War in New England, 1675–1676* (1999)

Ramón A. Gutiérrez, *When Jesus Came, the Corn Mothers Went Away: Marriage, Sexuality, and Power in New Mexico, 1500–1846* (1991)

Richard R. Johnson, *Adjustment to Empire: The New England Colonies, 1675–1715* (1981)

D. W. Jordan, *Maryland's Revolution of Government, 1689–1692* (1974)

Carol F. Karlsen, *The Devil in the Shape of a Woman: Witchcraft in Colonial New England* (1987)

Karen Ordahl Kupperman, *Indians and English: Facing Off in Early America* (2000)

Almon Wheeler Lauber, *Indian Slavery in Colonial Times within the Present Limits of the United States* (1913)

Jill Lepore, *The Name of War: King Philip's War and the Origins of American Identity* (1998)

David S. Lovejoy, *The Glorious Revolution in America* (1972)

Wilcomb E. Washburn, *The Governor and the Rebel: A History of Bacon's Rebellion in Virginia* (1957)

Stephen S. Webb, *1676: The End of American Independence* (1980)

Biography

Mary K. Geiter, *William Penn* (2000)

J. A. Leo Lemay, *The American Dream of Captain John Smith* (1991)

Edmund S. Morgan, *Puritan Dilemma: The Story of John Winthrop* (1958)

Ann Stanford, *Anne Bradstreet, the Worldly Puritan* (1974)

Marc Simmons, *The Last Conquistador: Juan de Oñate and the Settling of the Far Southwest* (1991)

Robert S. Tilton, *Pocahontas: The Evolution of an American Narrative* (1994)

Alvin Gardner Weeks, *Massasoit of the Pokanokets* (1919)

Selma R. Williams, *Divine Rebel: The Life of Anne Marbury Hutchinson* (1981)

CHAPTER 4

The African Slave Trade

Jay Coughtry, *The Notorious Triangle: Rhode Island and the African Slave Trade, 1799–1807* (1981)

Philip D. Curtin, *Economic Change in Precolonial Africa: Senegambia in the Era of the Slave Trade* (1975)

Basin Davidson, *The African Slave Trade* (1980)

Benedict G. Der, *The Slave Trade in Northern Ghana* (1998)

Elizabeth Donnan, ed., *Documents Illustrative of the History of the Slave Trade to America*, 4 vols. (1930–35)

David Eltis and David Richardson, eds., *Routes to Slavery: Direction, Ethnicity, and Mortality in the Transatlantic Slave Trade* (1997)

David Eltis, et al., eds., *The Trans-Atlantic Slave Trade: A Database on CD-ROM* (2000)

Eli Faber, *Jews, Slaves, and the Slave Trade: Setting the Record Straight* (1998)

J. E. Inikori, *Forced Migration: The Impact of the Export Slave Trade on African Societies* (1982)

Robert W. July, *A History of the African People* (1992)

Herbert S. Klein, *The Middle Passage: Comparative Studies in the Atlantic Slave Trade* (1978)

Robin Law, *The Slave Coast of West Africa, 1550–1750: The Impact of the Atlantic Slave Trade on an African Society* (1991)

Paul E. Lovejoy, ed., *Africans in Bondage: Studies in Slavery and the Slave Trade* (1986)

Daniel P. Mannix and Malcolm Crowley, *Black Cargoes: A History of the Atlantic Slave Trade* (1962)

David Northrup, ed., *The Atlantic Slave Trade* (1994)

J. A. Rawley, *The Transatlantic Slave Trade* (1981)

Edward Reynolds, *Stand the Storm: A History of the Atlantic Slave Trade* (1985)

A. C. De C. M. Saunders, *A Social History of Black Slaves and Freemen in Portugal, 1441–1555* (1982)

Jon Vogt, *Portuguese Rule on the Gold Coast, 1469–1682* (1979)

James Walvin, *Making the Black Atlantic: Britain and the African Diaspora* (2000)

The Development of North American Slave Societies

L. R. Bailey, *Indian Slave Trade in the Southwest: A Study of Slave-Taking and the Traffic in Indian Captives* (1966)

T. H. Breen and Stephen Innes, *"Myne Owne Ground": Race and Freedom on Virginia's Eastern Shore* (1980)

Verner W. Crane, *The Southern Frontier, 1670–1732* (1929)

Richard S. Dunn, *Sugar and Slaves: The Rise of the Planter Class in the English West Indies, 1624–1713* (1972)

Eltis, David, *The Rise of African Slavery in the Americas* (2000)

Laura Foner and Eugene D. Genovese, eds., *Slavery in the New World: A Reader in Comparative History* (1969)

Graham Russell Hodges, *Root and Branch: African Americans in New York and East Jersey, 1613–1863* (1999)

Thomas N. Ingersoll, *Mammon and Manon in Early New Orleans: The First Slave Society in the Deep South, 1718–1819* (1999)

Charles Joyner, *Down by the Riverside: A South Carolina Slave Community* (1984)

Alan Kulikoff, *Tobacco and Slaves: The Development of Southern Cultures in the Chesapeake, 1680–1800* (1986)

Jane Landers, *Black Society in Spanish Florida* (1999)

Daniel Littlefield, *Rice and Slaves: Ethnicity and the Slave Trade in Colonial South Carolina* (1981)

Paul E. Lovejoy, *Transformations in Slavery: A History of Slavery in Africa* (1983)

Edgar J. McManus, *Black Bondage in the North* (1973)

Gary B. Nash, *Red, White, and Black: The Peoples of Early North America* (1992)

Julia Floyd Smith, *Slavery and Rice Culture in Low Country Georgia, 1750–1860* (1985)

Brenda Stevenson, *Life in Black and White: Family and Community in the Slave South* (1996)

Peter H. Wood, *Black Majority: Negroes in Colonial South Carolina from 1670 through the Stone Rebellion* (1974)

Jeffrey Robert Young, *Domesticating Slavery: The Master Class in Georgia and South Carolina, 1607–1837* (1999)

Becoming African American

John B. Boles, *Black Southerners, 1619–1869* (1984)

Alex Bontemps, *The Punished Self: Surviving Slavery in the Colonial South* (2001)

Sylviane A. Diouf, *Servants of Allah: African Muslims Enslaved in the Americas* (1998)

John Hope Franklin and Loren Schweniger, *Runaway Slaves: Rebels in the Plantation* (1999)

Joseph E. Harris, ed., *Global Dimensions of the African Diaspora* (1982)

Michael Gomez, *Exchanging Our Country Marks: The Transformation of African Identities in the Colonial and Antebellum South* (1998)

Annette Gordon-Reed, *Thomas Jefferson and Sally Hemings: An American Controversy* (1997)

Herbert G. Gutman, *The Black Family in Slavery and Freedom, 1750–1925* (1976)

Gerald W. Mullin, *Flight and Rebellion: Slave Resistance in Eighteenth-Century Virginia* (1972)

Orlando Patterson, *Slavery and Social Death: A Comparative Study* (1982)

Mark M. Smith, *Mastered by the Clock: Time, Slavery, and Freedom in the American South* (1997)

Sterling Stuckey, *Slave Culture: Nationalist Theory and the Foundations of Black America* (1987)

V. B. Thompson, *The Making of the African Diaspora in the Americas, 1441–1900* (1984)

The Economics of Empire

Joyce O. Appleby, *Economic Thought and Ideology in Seventeenth Century England* (1978)

Heather Cateau and S. H. H. Carrington, eds., *Capitalism and Slavery Fifty Years Later: Eric Eustace Williams-A Reassessment of the Man and His Work* (2000)

Eugene Genovese and Elizabeth Fox-Genovese, *Fruits of Merchant Capital: Slavery and Bourgeois Property in the Rise and Expansion of Capitalism* (1983)

E. J. Hobsbawn, *Industry and Empire: The Making of Modern English Society, 1750 to the Present Day* (1968)

Michael Kammen, *Empire and Interest: The American Colonies and the Politics of Mercantilism* (1970)

John J. McCusker and Russell R. Menard, *The Economy of British America, 1607–1787* (1985)

Barbara L. Solow, ed., *Slavery and the Rise of the Atlantic System* (1991)

Eric Williams, *Capitalism and Slavery* (1944)

Slavery and Freedom

David Brion Davis, *The Problem of Slavery in Western Culture* (1966)

Carl N. Degler, *Neither Black nor White: Slavery and Race Relations in Brazil and the United States* (1971)

Edmund S. Morgan, *American Slavery, American Freedom: The Ordeal of Colonial Virginia* (1975)

Joel Williamson, *New People: Miscegenation and Mulattoes in the United States* (1980)

Biography

Philip D. Curtin, ed., *Africa Remembered: Narratives of West Africans from the Era of the Slave Trade* (1967)

Paul Edwards, ed., *The Interesting Narrative of the Life of Olaudah Equiano, or Gustavus Vassa, the African, written by himself* (1987)

James B. Hedges, *The Browns of Providence Plantation* (1952)

Kenneth A. Lockridge, *The Diary and Life of William Byrd II of Virginia, 1674-1744* (1987)

Phinizy Spalding, *Oglethorpe in America* (1977)

Janet Whitman, *John Woolman, American Quaker* (1942)

CHAPTER 5

North American Regions

Patricia Albers and Beatrice Medicine, eds., *The Hidden Half: Studies of Plains Indian Women* (1983)

Carole Blackburn, *Harvest of Souls: The Jesuit Missions and Colonialism in North America, 1632–1650* (2000)

Richard L. Bushman, *From Puritan to Yankee: Character and the Social Order in Connecticut, 1690–1765* (1967)

David Bussiert and Steven G. Reinhardt, eds., *Creolization in the Americas* (2000)

Edward D. Castillo, ed., *Native American Perspectives on the Hispanic Colonization of Alta California* (1992)

Andrew R. L. Cayton and Frederika J. Teute, eds., *Contact Points: American Frontiers from the Mohawk Valley to the Mississippi, 1750–1830* (1998)

Cornelia Hughes Dayton, *Women before the Bar: Gender, Law, and Society in Connecticut, 1639–1789* (1995)

Brian Leigh Dunnigan, *Frontier Metropolis: Picturing Early Detroit, 1701–1838* (2001)

John C. Ewers, *The Horse in Blackfoot Indian Culture* (1955)

David Hackett Fischer and James C. Kelly, *Bound Away: Virginia and the Westward Movement* (2000)

Joseph W. Glass, *The Pennsylvania Culture Region: A View from the Barn* (1986)

Robert F. Heizer, *The Destruction of California Indians* (1974)

Donald A. Hutslar, *The Architecture of Migration: Log Construction in the Ohio Country, 1750–1850* (1986)

Christine Leigh Hyrman, *Commerce and Culture: The Maritime Communities of Colonial Massachusetts* (1984)

Rhys Isaac, *Worlds of Experience: Communities in Colonial Virginia* (1987)

Robert H. Jackson, *Indian Population Decline: The Missions of Northwestern New Spain, 1687–1840* (1994)

Robert H. Jackson, *From Savages to Subjects: Missions in the History of the American Southwest* (2000)

Francis Jennings, *The Ambiguous Iroquois Empire* (1984)

Terry G. Jordan and Matti Kaups, *The American Backwoods Frontier: An Ethnic and Ecological Interpretation* (1988)

Lyle Kohler, *A Search for Power: "The Weaker Sex" in Seventeenth-Century New England, 1650–1750* (1982)

James T. Lemmon, *The Best Poor Man's Country: A Geographical Study of Early Southeastern Pennsylvania* (1972)

Kenneth Lockridge, *Literacy in Colonial New England* (1974)

James H. Merrell, *The Indians' New World: Catawbas and Their Neighbors from European Contact through the Era of Removal* (1989)

James H. Merrell, *Into the American Woods: Negotiators on the Pennsylvania Frontier* (1999)

Gary B. Nash, *The Urban Crucible* (1979)

Jacqueline Peterson and Jennifer S. H. Brown, eds., *The New Peoples: Being and Becoming Métis in North America* (1985)

Daniel K. Richter, *The Ordeal of the Longhouse: The Peoples of the Iroquois League in the Era of European Colonization* (1992)

Darrett B. Rutman and Anita H. Rutman, *A Place in Time: Middlesex County, Virginia, 1650–1750* (1984)

Marylynn Salmon, *Women and the Law of Property in Early America* (1986)

Sally Schwartz, *A Mixed Multitude: The Struggle for Toleration in Colonial Pennsylvania* (1987)

William S. Simmons, *Spirit of the New England Tribes: Indian History and Folklore, 1620–1984* (1986)

Daniel Blake Smith, *Inside the Great House: Planter Family Life in Eighteenth-Century Chesapeake Society* (1980)

Laurel T. Ulrich, *Good Wives: Image and Reality in the Lives of Women in Northern New England, 1650–1750* (1982)

Daniel H. Usner Jr., *Indians, Settlers, and Slaves in a Frontier Exchange Economy: The Lower Mississippi Valley before 1783* (1992)

Diverging Social and Political Patterns

Bernard Bailyn, *The Peopling of British North America: An Introduction* (1986)

Bruce C. Daniels, ed., *Power and Status: Essays on Office-holding in Colonial America* (1986)

Robert J. Dinkin, *Voting in Provincial America: A Study of Elections in the Thirteen Colonies, 1680–1776* (1977)

A. Roger Ekirch, *Bound for America: The Transportation of British Convicts to the Colonies, 1718–1775* (1987)

Jack P. Green, *The Quest for Power: The Lower Houses of Assembly in the Southern Royal Colonies, 1689–1776* (1963)

Carla Gardina Pestana and Sharon V. Salinger, eds., *Inequality in Early America* (1999)

Thomas L. Purvis, *Proprietors, Patronage, and Paper Money: Legislative Politics in New Jersey, 1703–1776* (1986)

Sharon V. Salinger, *"To Serve Well and Faithfully": Labor and Indentured Servants in Pennsylvania, 1682–1800* (1987)

The Cultural Transformation of British North America

Patricia U. Bonomi, *Under the Cope of Heaven: Religion, Society, and Politics in Colonial America* (1986)

Henry Steele Commager, *The Empire of Reason: How Europe Imagined and America Realized the Enlightenment* (1977)

Patricia Crain, *The Story of A: The Alphabetization of America from "The New England Primer" to "The Scarlet Letter"* (2000)

Ned C. Landsman, *From Colonials to Provincials: American Thought and Culture, 1680–1760* (1997)

Jackson Turner Main, *The Social Structure of Revolutionary America* (1965)

Barbara B. Oberg and Harry S. Stout, eds., *Benjamin Franklin, Jonathan Edwards, and the Representation of American Culture* (1993)

Mark A. Peterson, *The Price of Redemption: The Spiritual Economy of Puritan New England* (1997)

Nina Reid-Mahoney, *Philadelphia's Enlightenment, 1740–1800: Kingdom of Christ, Empire of Reason* (2001)

Frank Shuffelton, ed., *The American Enlightenment* (1993)

Pauline Turner Strong, *Captive Selves, Captivating Others: The Politics and Poetics of Colonial American Captivity Narratives* (1999)

Biography

Milton J. Coalter, *Gilbert Tennent, Son of Thunder* (1986)

Verner W. Crane, *Benjamin Franklin and a Rising People* (1952)

Harry Kelsey, *Juan Rodriguez Cabrillo* (1986)

Gerald R. McDermott, *Jonathan Edwards Confronts the Gods* (2000)

Robert Middlekauff, *The Mathers: Three Generations of Puritan Intellectuals, 1596–1728* (1999)

Martin J. Morgado, *Junípero Serra's Legacy* (1987)

John Edwin Smith, *Jonathan Edwards: Puritan, Preacher, Philosopher* (1992)

Harry S. Stout, *The Divine Dramatist: George Whitefield and the Rise of Modern Evangelicalism* (1991)

Laurel Ulrich, *A Midwife's Tale: The Life of Martha Ballard, Based on Her Diary, 1785–1812* (1990)

CHAPTER 6

The Seven Years' War in America

Fred Anderson, *A People's Army: Massachusetts Soldiers and Society in the Seven Years' War* (1984)

Frank W. Brecher, *Losing a Continent: France's North American Policy, 1753–1763* (1998)

Sylvia R. Frey, *The British Soldier in America: A Social History of Military Life in the Colonial Period* (1981)

Douglas E. Leach, *Roots of Conflict: British Armed Forces and Colonial Americans, 1677–1763* (1986)

Richard Middleton, *The Bells of Victory: The Pitt-Newcastle Ministry and the Conduct of the Seven Years' War, 1757–1762* (1985)

Robert C. Newbold, *The Albany Congress and Plan of Union of 1754* (1955)

Howard H. Peckham, *Pontiac and the Indian Uprising* (1947)

William Pencak, *War, Politics, and Revolution in Provincial Massachusetts* (1981)

Tom Pocock, *Battle for Empire: The Very First World War, 1756–63* (1998)

Alan Rogers, *Empire and Liberty* (1974)

David Curtis Skaggs and Larry L. Nelson, eds., *The Sixty Years' War for the Great Lakes, 1754–1814* (2001)

Noel T. St. John Williams, *Red Coats along the Hudson* (1997)

Richard White, *The Middle Ground: Indians, Empires, and Republics in the Great Lakes Region, 1650–1815* (1991)

Imperial Crisis in British North America

Stuart Andrews, *The Rediscovery of America: Transatlantic Crosscurrents in an Age of Revolution* (1998)

Thomas C. Barrow, *Trade and Empire: The British Customs Service in Colonial America* (1967)

John Brewer, *Party Ideology and Popular Politics at the Accession of George III* (1976)

Don Cook, *The Long Fuse: How England Lost the American Colonies, 1760–1785* (1995)

Theodore Draper, *A Struggle for Power: The American Revolution* (1996)

Marc Egnal, *A Mighty Empire: The Origins of the American Revolution* (1988)

Eliga H. Gould, *The Persistence of Empire: British Political Culture in the Age of the American Revolution* (2000)

Woody Holton, *Forced Founders: Indians, Debtors, Slaves, and the Making of the American Revolution in Virginia* (1999)

Alice Hanson Jones, *The Wealth of a Nation to Be* (1980)

John J. McCusker, *Rum and the American Revolution* (1989)

Philip James McFarland, *The Brave Bostonians: Hutchinson, Quincy, Franklin, and the Coming of the American Revolution* (1998)

J. G. A. Pocock, *The Machiavellian Moment: Florentine Political Thought and the Atlantic Republican Tradition* (1975)

William Lowell Putnam, *John Peter Zenger and the Fundamental Freedom* (1997)

Caroline Robbins, *The Eighteenth-Century Commonwealthman* (1959)

Arthur M. Schlesinger, *The Colonial Merchants and the American Revolution* (1917)

W. A. Speck, *Stability and Strife: England, 1714–1760* (1977)

John W. Tyler, *Smugglers and Patriots: Boston Merchants and the Advent of the American Revolution* (1986)

Carl Ubbelohde, *The Vice-Admiralty Courts and the American Revolution* (1960)

From Resistance to Rebellion

David Ammerman, *In the Common Cause: American Response to the Coercive Acts of 1774* (1974)

T. H. Breen, *Tobacco Culture: The Mentality of the Great Tidewater Planters on the Eve of Revolution* (1985)

Richard D. Brown, *Revolutionary Politics in Massachusetts: The Boston Committee of Correspondence and the Towns, 1772–1774* (1970)

Richard L. Bushman, *King and People in Provincial Massachusetts* (1985)

H. Trevor Colbourn, *The Lamp of Experience: Whig History and the Intellectual Origins of the American Revolution* (1965)

Light Townsend Cummins, *Spanish Observers and the American Revolution, 1775–1783* (1991)

Derek Davis, *Religion and the Continental Congress, 1774–1789: Contributions to Original Intent* (2000)

Bernard Donoughue, *British Politics and the American Revolution: The Path to War, 1773–1775* (1964)

Gregory T. Edgar, *Reluctant Break with Britain: From Stamp Act to Bunker Hill* (1997)

Jack P. Greene, *Understanding the American Revolution: Issues and Actors* (1995)

Dirk Hoerder, *Crowd Action in Revolutionary Massachusetts* (1977)

Benjamin W. Labaree, *The Boston Tea Party* (1974)

Pauline Maier, *From Resistance to Rebellion* (1972)

Edmund S. Morgan, *The Birth of the Republic, 1763–1789* (1956)

Jackson O'Shaughnessy, *An Empire Divided: The American Revolution and the British Caribbean* (2000)

John Shy, *Toward Lexington: The Role of the British Army in the Coming of the American Revolution* (1965)

Peter David Garner Thomas, *Tea Party to Independence: The Third Phase of the American Revolution, 1773–1776* (1991)

Morton White, *The Philosophy of the American Revolution* (1978)

Gary Wills, *Inventing America* (1978)

Biography

Bernard Bailyn, *The Ordeal of Thomas Hutchinson* (1974)

Della Gray Barthelmas, *The Signers of the Declaration of Independence* (1997)

Richard R. Beeman, *Patrick Henry: A Biography* (1974)

Jeremy Black, *Pitt the Elder* (1992)

John Brooke, *King George III* (1974)

H. W. Brands, *The First American: The Life and Times of Benjamin Franklin* (2000)

John E. Ferling, *The Loyalist Mind: Joseph Galloway and the American Revolution* (1977)

John E. Ferling, *Setting the World Ablaze: Washington, Adams, and Jefferson and the American Revolution* (2000)

Milton E. Flower, *John Dickinson: Conservative Revolutionary* (1983)

William M. Fowler, Jr., *The Baron of Beacon Hill: A Biography of John Hancock* (1979)

William M. Fowler, Jr., *Samuel Adams: Radical Puritan* (1997)

David A. McCants, *Patrick Henry, the Orator* (1990)

Peter Shaw, *The Character of John Adams* (1976)

Peter D. G. Thomas, *Lord North* (1974)

Andrew S. Walmsley, *Thomas Hutchinson and the Origins of the American Revolution* (1999)

CHAPTER 7

The War for Independence

Ian Barnes, *The Historical Atlas of the American Revolution* (2000)

Ira Berlin and Ronald Hoffman, eds., *Slavery and Freedom in the Age of the American Revolution* (1983)

Charles E. Claghorn, *Women Patriots of the American Revolution* (1991)

Lawrence D. Cress, *Citizens in Arms: The Army and the Militia in American Society to the War of 1812* (1982)

H. T. Dickinson, ed., *Britain and the American Revolution* (1998)

Paul Finkleman, ed., *Slavery, Revolutionary America, and the New Nation* (1989)

William M. Fowler, *Rebels under Sail: The American Navy during the Revolution* (1976)

Francis Fox, *Sweet Land of Liberty: The Ordeal of the American Revolution in Northampton County, Pennsylvania* (2000)

Barbara Graymont, *The Iroquois in the American Revolution* (1972)

Leslie Hall, *Land and Allegiance in Revolutionary Georgia* (2001)

Ronald Hoffman and Peter J. Albert, eds., *Arms and Independence. The Military Character of the American Revolution* (1984)

Ronald Hoffman and Peter J. Albert, eds., *Women in the Age of the American Revolution* (1989)

Ronald Hoffman and Thad W. Tate, eds., *An Uncivil War: The Southern Backcountry during the American Revolution* (1985)

Francis Jennings, *The Creation of America: Through Revolution to Empire* (2000)

Mark E. Kann, *A Republic of Men: The American Founders, Gendered Language, and Patriarchial Politics* (1998)

Cynthia A. Kierner, *Southern Women in Revolution, 1776–1800* (1998)

Arthur S. Lefkowitz, *The Long Retreat: The Calamitous American Defense of New Jersey, 1776* (1999)

Paul C. Nagel, *The Adams Women: Abigail and Louise Adams, Their Sisters and Daughters* (1987)

Gary B. Nash, *Race and Revolution* (1990)

Mary Beth Norton, *The British Americans: The Loyalist Exiles in England, 1774–1789* (1972)

James O'Donnell, *Southern Indians in the American Revolution* (1973)

Andrew Jackson O'Shaughnessy, *An Empire Divided: The American Revolution and the British Caribbean* (2000)

Howard W. Peckham, *The Toll of Independence: Engagements and Battle Casualties of the American Revolution* (1974)

Elizabeth Perkins, *Border Life: Experience and Memory in the Revolutionary Ohio Valley* (1998)

Benjamin Quarles, *The Negro in the American Revolution*, rev. ed. (1996)

David Lee Russell, *The American Revolution in the Southern Colonies* (2000)

John Shy, *A People Numerous and Armed* (1976).

Murray Smart, *The Honor of Command: General Burgoyne's Saratoga Campaign* (1998)

James W. St. G. Walker, *The Black Loyalists* (1976)

Alfred F. Young, ed., *The American Revolution: Explorations in American Radicalism* (1976).

Anthony F. C. Wallace, *The Death and Rebirth of the Seneca* (1970)

The United States in Congress Assembled

Joyce Appleby, *Inheriting the Revolution: The First Generation of Americans* (2000)

Robert A. Becker, *Revolution, Reform and the Politics of American Taxation, 1763–1783* (1980)

Richard Beeman, et al., eds., *Beyond Confederation: Origins of the Constitution and American National Identity* (1987)

E. Wayne Carp, *To Starve the Army at Pleasure: Continental Army Administration and American Political Culture, 1774–1783* (1984)

E. J. Ferguson, *The Power of the Purse: A History of American Public Finance, 1776–1790* (1960)

Calvin C. Jillson, *Congressional Dynamics: Structure, Coordination, and Choice in the First American Congress, 1774–1789* (1994)

Jackson Turner Main, *Political Parties before the Constitution* (1973)

Jack N. Rakove, *The Beginnings of National Politics: An Interpretive History of the Continental Congress* (1979)

Gerald Sourzh, *Benjamin Franklin and American Foreign Policy* (1969)

Gordon S. Wood, *The Creation of the American Republic, 1776–1787* (1969)

Revolutionary Politics in the States

Willi Paul Adams, *The First American Constitutions: Republican Ideology and the Making of the State Constitutions* (1980)

Roger H. Brown, *Redeeming the Republic: Federalists, Taxation, and the Origins of the Constitution* (1993)

Donald S. Lutz, *Popular Consent and Popular Control: Whig Political Theory in the Early State Constitutions* (1980)

Jackson Turner Main, *The Sovereign States, 1775–1789* (1973)

Biography

Silvio A. Bedini, *The Life of Benjamin Banneker* (1972)

Patricia Cleary, *Elizabeth Murray: A Woman's Pursuit of Independence in Eighteenth-Century America* (2000)

John Mack Faragher, *Daniel Boone: The Life and Legend of an American Pioneer* (1992)

Douglas Southall Freeman, *George Washington*, 7 vols. (1948–57)

Edith Belle Gelles, *Portia: The World of Abigail Adams* (1992)

Lowell Hayes Harrison, *George Rogers Clark and the War in the West* (1976)

John W. Hartmann, *The American Partisan: Henry Lee and the Struggle for Independence, 1776–1780* (2000)

Isabel Thompson Kelsay, *Joseph Brant, 1743–1807: Man of Two Worlds* (1984)

James Kirby Martin, *Benedict Arnold, Revolutionary Hero* (1997)

Gregory D. Massey, *John Laurens and the American Revolution* (2000)

Willard Sterne Randall, *George Washington: A Life* (1997)

William Henry Robinson, *Phillis Wheatley and Her Writings* (1984)

Susan Burgess Shenstone, *So Obstinately Loyal: James Moody, 1744–1809* (2000)

Barry Wilson, *Benedict Arnold: A Traitor in Our Midst* (2000)

Rosemarie Zagarri, *A Woman's Dilemma: Mercy Otis Warren and the American Revolution* (1995)

CHAPTER 8

Forming a New Government

Douglass Adair, *Fame and the Founding Fathers*, ed. Trevor Colbourn (1974)

Charles A. Beard, *An Economic Interpretation of the Constitution of the United States* (1913)

Saul Cornell, *The Other Founders: Anti-Federalism and the Dissenting Tradition in America, 1788–1828* (1999)

Max Farrand, ed., *Records of the Federal Convention of 1787*, 4 vols. (1911–37)

John P. Kaminski and Richard Leffler, eds., *Federalists and Antifederalists: The Debate Over the Ratification of the Constitution* (1998)

John P. Kaminski and Gaspare J. Saladino, eds., *The Documentary History of the Ratification of the Constitution* (1982)

Mark E. Kann, *A Republic of Men: The American Founders, Gendered Language, and Patriarchal Politics* (1998)

Leonard W. Levy, *Origins of the Bill of Rights* (1999)

Peter McNamara, ed., *The Noblest Minds: Fame, Honor, and the American Founding* (1999)

James H. Read, *Power Versus Liberty: Madison, Hamilton, Wilson, and Jefferson* (2000)

Gary Rosen, *American Compact: James Madison and the Problem of Founding* (1999)

Herbert J. Storing, ed., *The Complete Anti-Federalist*, 7 vols. (1981)

The New Nation

Kenneth R. Bowling and Donald R. Kennon, eds., *Neither Separate Nor Equal: Congress in the 1790s* (2000)

Collin G. Calloway, *Crown and Calumet: British-Indian Relations, 1783–1815* (1987)

Noble E. Cunningham, *Jefferson vs. Hamilton: Confrontations That Shaped a Nation* (2000)

Wilbur Edel, *Kekionga! The Worst Defeat in the History of the U.S. Army* (1997)

Edward S. Kaplan, *The Bank of the United States and the American Economy* (1999)

Stuart Leibiger, *Founding Friendship: George Washington, James Madison, and the Creation of the American Republic* (1999)

Peter McNamara, *Political Economy and Statesmanship: Smith, Hamilton, and the Foundation of the Commercial Republic* (1998)

Mark J. Rozell, et al., eds., *George Washington and the Origins of the American Presidency* (2000)

Garrett Ward Sheldon, *The Political Philosophy of James Madison* (2001)

Wiley Sword, *President Washington's Indian War: The Struggle for the Old Northwest, 1790–1795* (1985)

Federalists and Republicans

Doron Ben-Atar and Barbara B. Oberg, eds., *Federalists Reconsidered* (1998)

Alexander De Conde, *The Quasi-War: Politics and Diplomacy of the Undeclared War with France, 1797–1801* (1966)

Andrew Lenner, *The Federal Principle in American Politics, 1790–1833* (2001)

Forrest McDonald, *States' Rights and the Union: Imperium in Imperio, 1776–1876* (2000)

Michael A. Palmer, *Stoddert's War: Naval Operations During the Quasi-War with France, 1798–1801* (2000)

Andrew W. Robertson, *The Language of Democracy: Political Rhetoric in the United States and Britain, 1790–1900* (1995)

James Roger Sharp, *American Politics in the Early Republic: The New Nation in Crisis* (1993)

David Waldstreicher, *In the Midst of Perpetual Fetes: The Making of American Nationalism, 1776–1820* (1997)

"The Rising Glory of America"

Joyce Appleby, *Inheriting the Revolution: The First Generation of Americans* (2000)

R. A. Burchell, ed., *The End of Anglo-America: Historical Essays in the Study of Cultural Divergence* (1991)

Andrew Burstein, *Sentimental Democracy: The Evolution of America's Romantic Self-Image* (1999)

Ellen Fernandez-Sacco, *Spectacular Masculinities: The Museums of Peale, Baker, and Bowen in the Early Republic* (1998)

Linda Kerber, *Women of the Republic: Intellect and Ideology in Revolutionary America* (1980)

Biography

Robert C. Alberts, *Benjamin West: A Biography* (1978)

Gay Wilson Allen, *St. John de Crèvecoeur: The Life of an American Farmer* (1987)

Aleine Austin, *Matthew Lyon, "New Man" of the Democratic Revolution, 1749–1822* (1981)

Lance Banning, *The Sacred Fire of Liberty: James Madison and the Founding of the Federal Republic* (1995)

Richard Brookhiser, *Alexander Hamilton, American* (1999)

Harvey Lewis Carter, *The Life and Times of Little Turtle: First Sagamore of the Wabash* (1987)

Helen A. Cooper, *John Trumbull: The Hand and Spirit of a Painter* (1982)

Dorinda Evans, *The Genius of Gilbert Stuart* (1999)

E. M. Halliday, *Understanding Thomas Jefferson* (2001)

Roger G. Kennedy, *Burr, Hamilton, and Jefferson: A Study in Character* (2000)

David McCullough, *John Adams* (2001)

David Micklethwait, *Noah Webster and the American Dictionary* (2000)

Jules David Prown, *John Singleton Copley* (1966)

William M. S. Rasmussen and Robert S. Tilton, *George Washington: The Man Behind the Myths* (1999)

Sheila L. Skemp, *Judith Sargent Murray: A Brief Biography with Documents* (1998)

K. Alan Synder, *Defining Noah Webster: Mind and Morals in the Early Republic* (1990)

C. Bradley Thompson, *John Adams and the Spirit of Liberty* (1998)

Harlow G. Unger, *Noah Webster: The Life and Times of an American Patriot* (1998)

Mason Locke Weems, *The Life of Washington*. ed. Marcus Cunliffe (1962)

CHAPTER 9

North American Communities from Coast to Coast

James Gibson, *Imperial Russia in Frontier America* (1976)

Marcel Giraud, *A History of French Louisiana, 1698–1715* (1974)

Barbara Sweetland Smith and Redmond Barnett, eds., *Russian America* (1990)

David Weber, *The Spanish Frontier in North America* (1993)

The National Economy

W. Eliot Brownlee, *Dynamics of Ascent: A History of the American Economy* (1979)

Stuart Bruchey, *The Roots of American Economic Growth, 1607–1861* (1965)

Curtis P. Nettels, *The Emergence of a National Economy, 1775–1815* (1962)

Douglass C. North, *The Economic Growth of the United States, 1790–1860* (1966)

The Jefferson Presidency

Henry Adams, *The United States in 1800* (1955)

Robert Lowry Clinton, *Marbury v. Madison and Judicial Review* (1989)

Noble E. Cunningham, *The Jeffersonian Republicans and Power: Party Operations, 1801–1809* (1963)

George Drago, *Jefferson's Louisiana: Politics and the Clash of Legal Traditions* (1975)

Burton Spivak, *Jefferson's English Crisis: Commerce, Embargo, and the Republican Revolution* (1979)

Robert W. Tucker and David Hendrickson, *Empire of Liberty: The Statecraft of Thomas Jefferson* (1990)

G. Edward White, *The Marshall Court and Cultural Change, 1815–1835*, abridged ed. (1991)

James S. Young, *The Washington Community, 1800–1828* (1966)

Renewed Imperial Rivalry

Henry Warner Bowden, *American Indians and Christian Missions: Studies in Cultural Conflict* (1981)

Gregory Evans Dowd, *A Spirited Resistance: The North American Indian Struggle for Unity, 1745–1815* (1992)

Reginald Horsman, *Expansion and American Indian Policy, 1783–1812* (1967)

Drew R. McCoy, *The Last of the Fathers: James Madison and the Republican Legacy* (1989)

Francis Paul Prucha, *The Great Father: The United States Government and the American Indians*, 2 vols. (1984)

Defining the Boundaries

John Boles, *Religion in Antebellum Kentucky* (1976)

Andrew Cayton, *The Frontier Republic: Ideology and Politics in the Ohio Country, 1789–1812* (1986)

——, *Frontier Indiana* (1996)

George Dangerfield, *The Era of Good Feelings* (1952)

Anita Shafer Goodstein, *Nashville, 1780–1860: From Frontier to City* (1989)

Christine Leigh Heyrman, *Southern Cross: The Beginnings of the Bible Belt* (1997)

Walter LaFeber, ed., *John Quincy Adams and the American Continental Empire* (1965)

Malcolm J. Rohrbough, *The Land Office Business* (1968)

——, *The Trans-Appalachian Frontier: Peoples, Societies, and Institutions, 1775–1850* (1978)

Richard Slotkin, *Regeneration through Violence: The Mythology of the American Frontier* (1973)

Richard C. Wade, *The Urban Frontier: The Rise of Western Cities, 1790–1850* (1973)

CHAPTER 10

The New Democratic Politics and the Jackson Presidency

Glenn C. Altschuler and Stuart M. Blumin, *Rude Republic: Americans and Their Politics in the Nineteenth Century* (2000)

William L. Anderson, *Cherokee Removal: Before and After* (1991)

Steven C. Bullock, *Revolutionary Brotherhood: Freemasonry and the Transformation of the American Social Order, 1730–1840* (1996)

John Ehle, *Trail of Tears* (1988)

Lucy Maddox, *Removals: Nineteenth-Century American Literature and the Politics of Indian Affairs* (1991)

Arthur M. Schlesinger Jr., *The Age of Jackson* (1945)

John Ward, *Andrew Jackson: Symbol for an Age* (1955)

Chilton Williamson, *American Suffrage: From Property to Democracy, 1760–1860* (1960)

Internal Improvements

Clarence Danhof, *Changes in Agriculture: The Northern United States, 1820–1870* (1969)

E. M. Dodd, *American Business Corporations until 1860* (1954)

Albert Fishlow, *American Railroads and the Transformation of the Ante-Bellum Economy* (1965)

John Denis Haeger, *The Investment Frontier: New York Businessmen and the Economic Development of the Old Northwest* (1981)

Oscar Handlin and Mary Handlin, *Commonwealth: A Study of the Role of Government in the American Economy: Massachusetts, 1774–1861* (1947)

Morton J. Horwitz, *The Transformation of American Law, 1780–1860* (1977)

Ronald E. Shaw, *Canals for a Nation: The Canal Era in the United States, 1790–1860* (1990)

Peter Way, *Common Labour: Workers and the Digging of North American Canals, 1780–1860* (1993)

The Rise of the Whigs and the Second American Party System

Bray Hammond, *Banks and Politics in America* (1957)

Daniel W. Howe, *The Political Culture of the American Whigs* (1980)

Lawrence F. Kohl, *The Politics of Individualism: Parties and the American Character in the Jacksonian Era* (1989)

Richard P. McCormick, *The Second American Party System: Party Formation in the Jacksonian Era* (1966)

Joel H. Sibley, *The Partisan Imperative: The Dynamics of American Politics before the Civil War* (1985)

American Arts and Letters

Richard D. Brown, *Knowledge Is Power: The Diffusion of Information in Early America, 1700–1865* (1989)

Cathy N. Davidson, *Revolution and the Word: The Rise of the Novel in America* (1986)

Nathan O. Hatch, *The Democratization of American Christianity* (1989)

Barbara Novak, *Nature and Culture: American Landscape Painting 1825–1875* (1982)

Gwendolyn Wright, *Building the Dream: A Social History of Housing in America* (1981)

CHAPTER 11

King Cotton

Daniel S. Dupre, *Transforming the Cotton Frontier, Madison County, Alabama, 1800–1840* (1997)

Robert W. Fogel and Stanley Engerman, *Time on the Cross: The Economics of American Negro Slavery* (1974)

Joseph P. Reidy, *From Slavery to Agrarian Capitalism in the Cotton Plantation South:Central Georgia, 1800–1880* (1992)

Gavin Wright, *The Political Economy of the Cotton South: Households, Markets, and Wealth in the Nineteenth Century* (1978)

Slavery and African American Communities

Ira Berlin and Philip D. Morgan, eds., *Cultivation and Culture: Labor and the Shaping of Slave Life in the Americas* (1993)

John Blassingame, *The Slave Community*, rev. ed. (1979)

Randolph B. Campbell, *An Empire for Slavery: The Peculiar Institution in Texas, 1821–1865* (1989)

Charles B. Dew, *Bond of Iron: Master and Slave at Buffalo Forge* (1994)

Douglas Egerton, *Gabriel's Rebellion: The Virginia Slave Conspiracies of 1800 and 1802* (1993)

Barbara Field, *Slavery on the Middle Ground: Maryland during the Nineteenth Century* (1985)

Eugene D. Genovese, *From Rebellion to Revolution: Afro-American Slave Revolts in the Making of the Modern World* (1979)

Charles Joyner, *Down by the Riverside: A South Carolina Slave Community* (1984)

Lawrence W. Levine, *Black Culture and Black Consciousness: Afro-American Folk Thought from Slavery to Freedom* (1977)

Ann Patton Malone, *Sweet Chariot: Slave Family and Household Structure in Nineteenth-Century Louisiana* (1992)

Albert Raboteau, *Slave Religion: The "Invisible Institution" in the Antebellum South* (1978)

Kenneth Stampp, *The Peculiar Institution* (1956)

Sterling Stuckey, *Slave Culture: Nationalist Theory and the Foundation of Black America* (1987)

Richard C. Wade, *Slavery in the Cities: The South 1820–1860* (1964)

Deborah Gray White, *Arn't I a Woman?* (1985)

Yeomen, Planters, and the Defense of Slavery

David T. Bailey, *Shadow on the Church: Southwestern Evangelical Religion and the Issue of Slavery, 1783–1860* (1985)

F. N. Boney, *Southerners All* (1990)

Joan Cashin, *A Family Venture: Men and Women on the Southern Frontier* (1991)

Bill Cecil-Fronsman, *Common White: Class and Culture in Antebellum North Carolina* (1992)

William J. Cooper, *The South and the Politics of Slavery, 1829–1856* (1978)

Clement Eaton, *The Freedom of Thought Struggle in the Old South* (1964)

Drew Gilpin Faust, ed., *The Ideology of Slavery: Proslavery Thought in the Antebellum South, 1830–1860* (1981)

Elizabeth Fox-Genovese, *Within the Plantation Household* (1988)

Jean Friedman, *The Enclosed Garden: Women and Community in the Evangelical South, 1830–1900* (1985)

J. William Harris, *Plain Folk and Gentry in a Slave Society: White Liberty and Black Slavery in Augusta's Hinterlands* (1985)

Christopher Morris, *Becoming Southern: The Evolution of a Way of Life, Warren County and Vicksburg, Mississippi, 1770–1860* (1995)

James Oakes, *Slavery and Freedom: An Interpretation of the Old South* (1990)

Frank Owsley, *Plain Folk in the South* (1949)

Steven Stowe, *Intimacy and Power in the Old South: Ritual in the Lives of the Planters* (1987)

Michael Wayne, *Death of an Overseer* (2001)

Bertram Wyatt-Brown, *Southern Honor: Ethics and Behavior in the Old South* (1982)

CHAPTER 12

The Market Revolution

Thomas C. Cochran, *Frontiers of Change: Early Industrialism in America* (1981)

Robert F. Dalzell Jr., *Enterprising Elite: The Boston Associates and the World They Made* (1987)

David J. Jeremy, *Transatlantic Industrial Revolution: The Diffusion of Textile Technology between Britain and America* (1981)

Walter Licht, *Industrializing America: The Nineteenth Century* (1995)

Merritt R. Smith, *Harpers Ferry Armory and the New Technology* (1977)

Melvyn Stokes and Stephen Conway, eds., *The Market Revolution in America: Social, Political and Religious Expressions 1800–1880* (1996)

Barbara Tucker, *Samuel Slater and the Origins of the American Textile Industry, 1790–1860* (1984)

From Artisan to Worker

Mary H. Blewett, *Men, Women, and Work: Class, Gender, and Protest in the New England Shoe Industry, 1780–1910* (1988)

Paul G. Faler, *Mechanics and Manufacturers in the Early Industrial Revolution: Lynn, Massachusetts* (1981)

Michael H. Glickstein, *Concepts of Free Labor in Antebellum America* (1991)

Joan M. Jensen, *Loosening the Bonds: Mid-Atlantic Farm Women, 1750–1850* (1986)

Bruce Laurie, *Working People of Philadelphia, 1800–1850* (1980)

W. J. Rorabaugh, *The Craft Apprentice: From Franklin to the Machine Age in America* (1986)

A New Social Order

Jeanne Boydston, *Home and Work* (1990)

Stuart M. Blumin, *The Emergence of the Middle Class: Social Experience in the American City* (1989)

Janet Farrell Brodie, *Contraception and Abortion in Nineteenth-Century America* (1994)

Nancy E. Cott, *The Bonds of Womanhood: "Woman's Sphere" in New England, 1780–1835* (1977)

Anthony F. C. Wallace, *Rockdale: The Growth of an American Village in the Early Industrial Revolution* (1977)

Middle-Class Culture

Barbara A. Bardes and Suzanne Gossett, *Declarations of Independence: Women and Political Power in Nineteenth-Century American Fiction* (1990)

John F. Kasson, *Rudeness and Civility: Manners in Nineteenth-Century America* (1990)

Walter Benn Michaels and Donald E. Pease, eds., *The American Renaissance Reconsidered* (1985)

Lewis Perry, *Intellectual Life in America* (1984)

Ann Rose, *Transcendentalism as a Social Movement* (1981)

Richard Teichgraeber III, *Sublime Thoughts/Penny Wisdom: Situating Emerson and Thoreau in the American Market* (1995)

Jane Tompkins, *Sensational Designs: The Cultural World of American Fiction, 1790–1860* (1986)

CHAPTER 13

Immigration

Oscar Handlin, *The Uprooted* (1951; 2nd ed. 1973)

Noel Ignatiev, *How the Irish Became White* (1995)

Kerby A. Miller, *Emigrants and Exiles: Ireland and the Irish Exodus to North America* (1985)

Stanley Nadel, *Little Germany: Ethnicity, Religion, and Class in New York City, 1845–1880* (1990)

Dennis P. Ryan, *Beyond the Ballot Box: A Social History of the Boston Irish, 1845–1917* (1989)

Urban and Labor

Oliver E. Allen, *The Tiger: The Rise and Fall of Tammany Hall* (1995)

W. Jeffrey Bolster, *Black Jacks: African American Seamen in the Age of Sail* (1997)

John Duffy, *The Sanitarians* (1990)

Paul A. Gilje, *The Road to Mobocracy: Popular Disorder in New York City, 1763–1834* (1987)

Herbert G. Gutman, *Work, Culture, and Society in Industrializing America: Essays in American Working-Class History* (1976)

James Oliver Horton, *Free People of Color: Inside the African American Community* (1993)

Gerard T. Koeppel, *Water for Gotham* (2000)

Gary B. Nash, *Forging Freedom: Philadelphia's Black Community, 1720–1840* (1988)

Dennis C. Rousey, *Policing the Southern City, New Orleans 1805–1889* (1997)

Charles E. Rosenberg, *The Cholera Years* (1962)

Sam Bass Warner, *The Private City: Philadelphia in Three Periods of Its Growth* (1968)

Religion, Reform, and Utopianism

Lawrence Cremin, *American Education: The National Experience, 1783–1861* (1981)

Whitney R. Cross, *The Burned-Over District: The Social and Intellectual History of Enthusiastic Religion in Western New York, 1800–1850* (1950)

Barbara Epstein, *The Politics of Domesticity: Women, Evangelism, and Temperance in Nineteenth Century America* (1981)

Lori D. Ginzberg, *Women and the Work of Benevolence: Morality, Politics, and Class in the Nineteenth-Century United States* (1990)

Carl F. Kaestle, *Pillars of the Republic: Common Schools and American Society, 1780–1860* (1983)

W. J. Rorabaugh, *The Alcoholic Republic: An American Tradition* (1979)

Abolitionism

David Brion Davis, *The Problem of Slavery in the Age of Revolution, 1770–1823* (1975)

Frederick Douglass, *The Narrative of the Life of Frederick Douglass, An American Slave* (1845)

Peter P. Hinks, *To Awaken My Afflicted Brethren: David Walker and the Problem of Antebellum Slave Resistance* (1997)

Howard Jones, *Mutiny on the Amistad* (1987)

Jean Fagan Yellin, *Women and Sisters: The Antislavery Feminists in American Culture* (1989)

Women's Rights

Ellen C. Dubois, *Feminism and Suffrage: The Emergence of an Independent Women's Movement in America, 1848–1869* (1978)

Gerda Lerner, *The Grimké Sisters from South Carolina: Pioneers for Women's Rights and Abolition* (1967)

Sandra S. Weber, *Special History Study, Women's Rights National Historical Park, Seneca Falls, New York* (1985)

CHAPTER 14

Exploration, the Fur Trade, and Expansion

Jennifer S. H. Brown, *Strangers in Blood: Fur Trade Company Families in Indian Country* (1980)

William H. Goetzmann, *Army Exploration in the American West, 1803–1863* (1959)

William H. Goetzmann and William N. Goetzmann, *The West of the Imagination* (1986)

Norman A. Graebner, *Empire on the Pacific: A Study in American Continental Expansion* (1955)

LeRoy R. Hafen, ed., *The Mountain Men and the Fur Trade of the Far West*, 10 vols. (1968–72)

Sam W. Haynes, *James Polk and the Expansionist Impulse* (1997)

Thomas R. Hietala, *Manifest Design: Anxious Aggrandizement in Late Jacksonian America* (1985)

Reginald Horsman, *Race and Manifest Destiny* (1981)

Theodore J. Karaminski, *Fur Trade and Exploration: Opening of the Far Northwest, 1821–1852* (1983)

Patricia Nelson Limerick, *The Legacy of Conquest: The Unbroken Past of the Unbroken West* (1987)

Frederick Merk, *Manifest Destiny and Mission in American History: A Reinterpretation* (1963)

——, *History of the Westward Movement* (1978)

Dale Morgan, *Jedediah Smith and the Opening of the West* (1982)

Peter Nabakov, ed., *Native American Testimony: An Anthology of Indian and White Relations* (1978)

James P. Ronda, *Astoria and Empire* (1990)

Henry Nash Smith, *Virgin Land: The American West as Symbol and Myth* (1950)

Edward H. Spicer, *Cycles of Conquest: The Impact of Spain, Mexico, and the United States on the Indians of the Southwest, 1533–1960* (1981)

Robert A. Trennert, *Alternative to Extinction: Federal Indian Policy and the Beginnings of the Reservation System, 1846–1851* (1975)

Sylvia Van Kirk, *"Many Tender Ties": Women in Fur Trade Society in Western Canada, 1670–1870* (1980)

Albert K. Weinberg, *Manifest Destiny: A Study of Nationalist Expansionism in American History* (1957)

Peter Booth Wiley with Korogi Ichiro, *Yankees in the Land of the Gods: Commodore Perry and the Opening of Japan* (1990)

David J. Wishart, *The Fur Trade of the American West, 1807–1840: A Geographic Synthesis* (1979)

California and Oregon

John W. Caughey, *The California Gold Rush* (1975)

Malcolm Clark Jr., *Eden Seekers: The Settlement of Oregon, 1818–1862* (1981)

Douglas H. Daniels, *Pioneer Urbanites: A Social and Cultural History of Black San Francisco* (1980)

James R. Gibson, *Farming the Frontier: The Agricultural Opening of Oregon Country, 1786–1846* (1985)

Ramon Gutierrez and Richard J. Orsi, *Contested Eden: California Before the Gold Rush* (1998)

Albert L. Hurtado, *Indian Survival on the California Frontier* (1988)

Julie Roy Jeffrey, *Frontier Women: Civilizing The West? 1840–1860* (1998)

David Johnson, *Founding the Far West: California, Oregon, and Nevada, 1840–1890* (1992)

Alvin Josephy, *The Nez Percé and the Opening of the Northwest* (1965)

Rodman W. Paul, *California Gold: The Beginning of Mining in the Far West* (1974)

Leonard Pitt, *The Decline of the Californios: A Social History of the Spanish-Speaking Californians, 1846–1890* (1966)

James J. Rawls, *Indians of California: The Changing Image* (1984)

Brian Roberts, *American Alchemy: The California Gold Rush and Middle Class Culture* (2000)

Kevin Starr, *Americans and the California Dream, 1850–1915* (1973)

John I. Unruh Jr., *The Plains Across: Overland Emigrants and the Trans-Mississippi West, 1840–1860* (1979)

Texas and the Mexican-American War

K. Jack Bauer, *The Mexican War, 1846–1848* (1974)

William C. Binkley, *The Texas Revolution* (1952)

Gene M. Brack, *Mexico Views Manifest Destiny* (1976)

Holly Beachley Brear, *Inherit the Alamo: Myth and Ritual at an American Shrine* (1995)

Donald E. Chipman, *Spanish Texas, 1519–1821* (1992)

Seymour Conner and Odie Faulk, *North America Divided: The Mexican War, 1846–1848* (1971)

Arnoldo De Leon, *They Called Them Greasers: Anglo Attitudes toward Mexicans in Texas, 1821–1900* (1983)

John S. D. Eisenhower, *So Far from God: The U.S. War with Mexico 1846–1848* (1989)

Neil Harlow, *California Conquered: War and Peace on the Pacific, 1846–1850* (1982)

Ernest McPherson Lander Jr., *Reluctant Imperialist: Calhoun, South Carolina, and the Mexican War* (1980)

Timothy Matovina, *Tejano Religion and Ethnicity: San Antonio, 1921–1860* (1995)

Frederick Merk, *Slavery and the Annexation of Texas* (1972)

David Montejano, *Anglos and Mexicans in the Making of Texas, 1836–1986* (1987)

Chaplain W. Morrison, *Democratic Politics and Sectionalism: The Wilmot Proviso Controversy* (1967)

Stanley Noyes, *Los Comanches: The Horse People, 1751–1845* (1994)

David Pletcher, *The Diplomacy of Annexation: Texas, Oregon, and the Mexican War* (1973)

Joseph G. Raybeck, *Free Soil: The Election of 1848* (1970)

Andreas V. Reichstein, *Rise of the Lone Star: The Making of Texas* (1989)

Susan Scholwer, *Alamo Images: Changing Perceptions of a Texas Experience* (1985)

John H. Schroeder, *Mr. Polk's War: American Opposition and Dissent, 1846–1848* (1971)

Joel H. Sibley, *The Shrine of Party: Congressional Voting Behavior, 1841–1852* (1967)

Otis A. Singletary, *The Mexican War* (1960)

Jésus F. de la Teja, *San Antonio de Béxar: A Community on New Spain's Northern Frontier* (1995)

Biography

Marquis James, *The Raven: The Story of Sam Houston* (1929)

Charles G. Sellers, *James K. Polk: Jacksonian, 1795–1843* (1957)

——, *James K. Polk: Continentialist, 1843–1846* (1966)

CHAPTER 15

The Controversy over Slavery

Richard H. Abbott, *Cotton and Capital: Boston Businessmen and Antislavery Reform, 1854–1868* (1991)

Gary Collison, *Shadrach Minkins: From Fugitive Slave to Citizen* (1997)

W. Ehrlich, *They Have No Rights: Dred Scott's Struggle for Freedom* (1979)

C. C. Goen, *Broken Churches, Broken Nation* (1985)

Thomas F. Grossett, *Uncle Tom's Cabin and American Culture* (1985)

William Lee Miller, *Arguing About Slavery: The Great Battle in the United States Congress* (1996)

H. Craig Miner and William E. Unrau, *The End of Indian Kansas* (1978)

Stephen Oates, *To Purge This Land with Blood: A Biography of John Brown* (1970)

J. Rossbach, *Ambivalent Conspirators: John Brown, the Secret Six and a Theory of Black Political Violence* (1982)

Thomas P. Slaughter, *Bloody Dawn: The Christiana Riots and Racial Violence in the Antebellum North* (1991)

Gerald W. Wolff, *The Kansas-Nebraska Bill: Party, Section, and the Coming of the Civil War* (1977)

Bertram Wyatt-Brown, *Yankee Saints and Southern Sinners* (1985)

The Crisis of the National Party System

Tyler Anbinder, *Nativism and Slavery: The Northern Know-Nothings and the Politics of the 1850s* (1992)

J. H. Baker, *Affairs of Party: The Political Culture of Northern Democrats in the Mid-Nineteenth Century* (1983)

Ronald Formisano, *The Birth of Mass Political Parties: Michigan, 1827–1861* (1971)

William E. Gienapp, *The Origins of the Republican Party, 1852–1856* (1987)

Michael Holt, *The Political Crisis of the 1850s* (1978)

Robert W. Johannsen, *The Lincoln-Douglas Debates* (1965)

John Mayfield, *Rehearsal for Republicanism: Free Soil and the Politics of Antislavery* (1980)

The South Secedes

William. L. Barney, *The Road to Secession* (1972)

Charles H. Brown, *Agents of Manifest Destiny: The Lives and Times of the Filibusters* (1980)

Steven A. Channing, *Crisis of Fear: Secession in South Carolina* (1970)

William J. Cooper, *The South and the Politics of Slavery* (1978)

Avery O. Craven, *The Growth of Southern Nationalism 1848–1861* (1953)

William W. Freehling, *The Road to Disunion, vol. I: Secessionists at Bay, 1776–1854* (1991)

Michael P. Johnson, *Secession and Conservatism in the Lower South: The Social and Ideological Bases of Secession in Georgia, 1860–1861* (1983)

Robert E. May, *The Southern Dream of a Caribbean Empire, 1854–1861* (1973)

John McCardell, *The Idea of a Southern Nation: Southern Nationalists and Southern Nationalism, 1830–1861* (1979)

K. M. Stampp, *And the War Came: The North and the Secession Crisis 1860–1861* (1950)

Joe A. Stout, *The Liberators: Filibustering Expeditions into Mexico, 1848–1862, and the Last Thrust of Manifest Destiny* (1973)

Ronald L. Takaki, *A Proslavery Crusade: The Agitation to Re-open the African Slave Trade* (1971)

J. Mills Thornton, *Politics and Power in a Slavery Society* (1978)

Eric H. Walter, *The Fire-Eaters* (1992)

CHAPTER 16

The Lincoln Presidency and the Northern Home Front

Richard Franklin Bensel, *Yankee Leviathan: The Origins of Central State Authority in America, 1859–1877* (1991)

George M. Frederickson, *The Inner Civil War: Northern Intellectuals and the Crisis of the Union* (1965)

J. Matthew Gallman, *The North Fights the Civil War: The Home Front* (1994)

Ernest A. McKay, *The Civil War and New York City* (1990)

James M. McPherson, *Abraham Lincoln and the Second American Revolution* (1990)

Mark E. Neely, *The Fate of Liberty: Abraham Lincoln and Civil Liberties* (1991)

Phillip Shaw Paludan, *The Presidency of Abraham Lincoln* (1994)

Heather Cox Richardson, *The Greatest Nation of the Earth: Republican Economic Policies during the Civil War* (1997)

Anne C. Rose, *Victorian America and the Civil War* (1992)

Joel Sibley, *A Respectable Minority: The Democratic Party in the Civil War Era, 1860–1868* (1977)

Lyde Cullen Sizer, *The Political Work of Northern Women Writers and the Civil War* (2000)

Thomas H. O'Connor, *Civil War Boston: Homefront and Battlefield* (1997)

Bell I. Wiley, *The Life of Johnny Reb* (1943)

——, *The Life of Billy Yank* (1952)

The Death of Slavery

Ira Berlin, et al., eds., *Freedom, A Documentary History of Emancipation, 1861–1867*, Series 1, Volume I: *The Destruction of Slavery* (1985)

——, et al., eds. *Freedom, A Documentary History of Emancipation, 1861–1867*, Series 1, Volume II: *The Wartime Genesis of Free Labor: The Upper South* (1993)

——, et al., eds. *Freedom, A Documentary History of Emancipation, 1861–1867*, Series 1, Volume III: *The Wartime Genesis of Free Labor: The Lower South* (1990)

——, et al., eds. *Freedom, A Documentary History of Emancipation, 1861–1867*, Series 2: *The Black Military Experience* (1988)

John Hope Franklin, *The Emancipation Proclamation* (1963)

Willie Lee Rose, *Rehearsal for Reconstruction: The Port Royal Experiment* (1964)

The Confederacy and the Southern Home Front

Steven V. Ash, *When the Yankees Came: Conflict and Chaos in the Occupied South 1861–1865* (1995)

William Blair, *Virginia's Private War: Feeding Body and Soul in the Confederacy, 1861–1865* (1998)

Daniel W. Crofts, *Reluctant Confederates: Upper South Unionists in the Secession Crisis* (1989)

William C. Davis, *"A Government of Our Own": The Making of the Confederacy* (1994)

Wayne K. Durrill, *War of Another Kind: A Southern Community in the Great Rebellion* (1990)

Drew Gilpin Faust, *The Creation of Confederate Nationalism* (1988)

——, *The Confederate Republic: A Revolution against Politics* (1994)

James L. Roark, *Masters without Slaves: Southern Planters in the Civil War and Reconstruction* (1978)

William Rogers, *Confederate Home Front: Montgomery During the Civil War* (1999)

Daniel E. Sutherland, *Seasons of War: The Ordeal of a Confederate Community 1861–1865* (1995)

LeeAnn Whites, *The Civil War as a Crisis in Gender: Augusta, Georgia, 1860–1890* (1995)

The Fighting

Michael Barton, *Good Men: The Character of Civil War Soldiers* (1981)

Ken Burns, *The Civil War* (1990)

Bruce Catton, *A Stillness at Appomattox* (1953)

Shelby Foote, *The Civil War: A Narrative*, 3 vols. (1958–1974)

Joseph T. Glatthaar, *Forged in Battle: The Civil War Alliance of Black Soldiers and White Officers* (1990)

——, *The March to the Sea and Beyond: Sherman's Troops in the Savannah and Carolinas Campaign* (1985)

Mark Grimsley, *The Hard Hand of War: Union Policy toward Southern Civilians, 1861–1865* (1995)

Edward Hagerman, *The American Civil War and the Origins of Modern Warfare* (1988)

Gerald F. Linderman, *Embattled Courage: The Experience of Combat in the American Civil War* (1987)

Edwin S. Redkey, ed., *A Grand Army of Black Men: Letters from African-American Soldiers in the Union Army, 1861–1865* (1992)

Charles Royster, *The Destructive War: William Tecumseh Sherman, Stonewall Jackson, and the Americans* (1991)

CHAPTER 17

The Politics of Reconstruction

Richard H. Abbott, *The Republican Party and the South, 1855–1877* (1986)

Herman Belz, *Emancipation and Equal Rights* (1978)

Michael Les Benedict, *A Compromise of Principle: Congressional Republicans and Reconstruction* (1974)

——, *The Impeachment and Trial of Andrew Johnson* (1973)

Michael Kent Curtis, *No State Shall Abridge: The Fourteenth Amendment and the Bill of Rights* (1990)

Ellen Carol DuBois, *Feminism and Suffrage* (1978)

Eric Foner, *Politics and Ideology in the Age of the Civil War* (1980)

William C. Harris, *With Charity for All: Lincoln and the Restoration of the Union* (1997)

Robert Kaczorowski, *The Politics of Judicial Interpretation: The Federal Courts, Department of Justice, and Civil Rights, 1866–1876* (1985)

James McPherson, *Ordeal by Fire: The Civil War and Reconstruction* (1982)

Michael Perman, *Emancipation and Reconstruction, 1862–1879* (1987)

Brooks D. Simpson, *The Reconstruction Presidents* (1998)

Kenneth M. Stampp, *The Era of Reconstruction, 1865–1877* (1965)

The Meaning of Freedom

Ira Berlin et al., eds., *Freedom: A Documentary History*, 3 vols. (1985–91)

W. E. B. DuBois, *Black Reconstruction* (1935)

Barbara J. Fields, *Slavery and Freedom on the Middle Ground* (1985)

Eric Foner, *Freedom's Lawmakers: A Directory of Black Officeholders during Reconstruction* (1996)

Noralee Frankel, *Freedom's Women: Black Women and Families in Civil War Era Mississippi* (1999)

Herbert G. Gutman, *The Black Family in Slavery and Freedom* (1976)

Sharon Ann Holt, *Making Freedom Pay: North Carolina Freedpeople Working For Themselves, 1865–1900* (2000)

Thomas Holt, *Black over White: Negro Political Leadership in South Carolina during Reconstruction* (1977)

Lynda J. Morgan, *Emancipation in Virginia's Tobacco Belt* (1992)

Nell Irvin Painter, *Exodusters* (1977)

Howard N. Rabinowitz, *Race Relations in the Urban South, 1865–1890* (1978)

Roger L. Ransom and Richard Sutch, *One Kind of Freedom: The Economic Consequences of Emancipation* (1977)

Leslie A. Schwalm, *A Hard Fight For We: Women's Transition from Slavery to Freedom in South Carolina* (1997)

Southern Politics and Society

Pamela Brandwein, *Reconstructing Reconstruction: The Supreme Court and the Production of Historical Truth* (1999)

Dan T. Carter, *When the War Was Over: The Failure of Self Reconstruction in the South, 1865–1877* (1985)

Richard N. Current, *Those Terrible Carpetbaggers* (1988)

Stephen Hahn, *The Roots of Southern Populism* (1983)

William C. Harris, *The Day of the Carpetbagger: Republican Reconstruction in Mississippi* (1979)

Scott Reynolds Nelson, *Iron Confederacies: Southern Railroads, Klan Violence, and Reconstruction* (1999)

Michael S. Perman, *Reunion without Compromise: The South and Reconstruction, 1865–1868* (1973)

——, *The Road to Redemption: Southern Politics, 1868–1979* (1984)

Howard N. Rabinowitz, *The First New South, 1865–1920* (1991)

Daniel W. Stowell, *Rebuilding Zion: The Religious Reconstruction of the South, 1863–1877* (1998)

Allen W. Trelease, *White Terror: The Ku Klux Klan Conspiracy and Southern Reconstruction* (1971)

Jonathan M. Wiener, *Social Origins of the New South* (1978)

Reconstructing the North

Stephen Buechler, *The Transformation of the Woman Suffrage Movement* (1986)

Morton Keller, *Affairs of State* (1977)

James C. Mohr, ed., *Radical Republicans in the North* (1976)

David Montgomery, *Beyond Equality: Labor and the Radical Republicans, 1862–1872* (1967)

Keith I. Polakoff, *The Politics of Inertia: The Election of 1876 and the End of Reconstruction* (1973)

Amy Dru Stanley, *From Bondage to Contract: Wage Labor, Marriage, and the Market in the Age of Slave Emancipation* (1998)

Mark W. Summers, *Railroads, Reconstruction, and the Gospel of Prosperity* (1984)

——, *The Era of Good Stealings* (1993)

Xi Wang, *The Trial of Democracy: Black Suffrage and Northern Republicans, 1860–1910* (1997)

C. Vann Woodward, *Reunion and Reaction: The Compromise of 1877 and the End of Reconstruction* (1956)

Biography

David Donald, *Charles Sumner and the Rights of Man* (1970)

Russell Duncan, *Freedom's Shore: Tunis Campbell and the Georgia Freedmen* (1986)

William S. McFeely, *Frederick Douglass* (1989)

——, *Grant: A Biography* (1981)

——, *Yankee Stepfather: General O. O. Howard and the Freedmen* (1968)

Hans L. Trefousse, *Andrew Johnson* (1989)

——, *Thaddeus Stevens: Nineteenth Century Egalitarian* (1997)

CHAPTER 18

Indian Peoples and Indian-White Relations

Patricia Albers and Beatrice Medicine Albers, *The Hidden Half: Studies of Plains Indian Women* (1983)

Morris W. Foster, *Being Comanche: A Social History of an American Indian Community* (1991)

Shelley Bowen Hatfield, *Chasing Shadows: Indians Along the United States-Mexico Border, 1876–1911* (1998)

Frederick E. Hoxie, *A Final Promise: The Campaign to Assimilate the Indians, 1880–1920* (1984)

Albert L. Hurtado, *Indian Survival on the California Frontier* (1988)

Patricia Nelson Limerick, *The Legacy of Conquest: The Unbroken Past of the American West* (1987)

John D. McDermott, *A Guide to the Indian Wars of the West* (1998)

Theda Perdue, ed., *Sifters: Native American Women's Lives* (2001)

Catherine Price, *The Oglala People, 1841–1879* (1996)

Glenda Riley, *Women and Indians on the Frontier, 1825–1915* (1984)

Richard White, *The Roots of Dependency: Subsistence, Environment, and Social Change among the Choctaws, Pawnees, and Navajos* (1983)

Elliott West, *The Way to the West: Essays on the Central Plains* (1995)

Internal Empire

Armando C. Alonzo, *Tejano Legacy: Rancheros and Settlers in South Texas, 1734–1900* (1998)

Susan Armitage and Elizabeth Jameson, eds., *The Women's West* (1987)

Susan Armitage, Ruth B. Moynihan, and Christiane Fischer Dichamp, eds., *So Much to Be Done: Women Settlers on the Mining and Ranching Frontier* (1990)

Sarah Deutsch, *No Separate Refuge: Culture, Class and Gender on an Anglo-Hispanic Frontier in the American Southwest, 1880–1940* (1987)

David M. Emmons, *The Butte Irish: Class and Ethnicity in an American Mining Town, 1875–1925* (1989)

Marion S. Goldman, *Gold Diggers and Silver Miners: Prostitution and Social Life on the Comstock* (1981)

B. Carmon Hardy, *Solemn Covenant: The Mormon Polygamous Passage* (1992)

Douglas Monroy, *Thrown among Strangers: The Making of Mexican Culture in Frontier California* (1993)

Lucy E. Salyer, *Laws Harsh as Tigers: Chinese Immigrants and the Shaping of Modern Immigration Law* (1996)

Sally Zanjani, *A Mine of Her Own: Women Prospectors in the American West, 1850–1950*

Ranching and Farming

Allan G. Bogue, *From Prairie to Corn Belt: Farming on the Illinois and Iowa Prairies in the Nineteenth Century* (1963)

Mark Fiege, *The Making of an Agricultural Landscape in the American West* (1999)

Philip Durham and Everett L. Jones, *The Negro Cowboys* (1965)

Dee Garceau, *The Important Things of Life: Women, Work, and Family in Sweetwater County, Wyoming, 1880–1929* (1997)

C. Mark Hamilton, *Nineteenth-Century Mormon Architecture and City Planning* (1995)

Robert C. Haywood, *Victorian West: Class and Culture in Kansas Cattle Towns* (1991)

Stan Hoig, *The Oklahoma Land Rush of 1889* (1984)

Lawrence Jelinek, *Harvest Empire: A History of California Agriculture*, 2d ed. (1982)

Frederick C. Leubke, ed., *European Immigrants in the American West: Community Histories* (1998)

Sonya Salamon, *Prairie Patrimony: Family, Farming, and Community in the Midwest* (1992)

Paul I. Wellman, *The Trampling Herd: The Story of the Cattle Range in America* (1988)

The West, the Land, and the Imagination

Alfred L. Bush and Lee Clark Mitchell, *The Photograph and the American Indian* (1994)

Mick Gidley, *Edward S. Curtis and the North American Indian, Incorporated* (1998)

William H. Goetzmann and William N. Goetzmann, *The West of the Imagination* (1986)

Chris J. Magoc, *Yellowstone: The Creation and Selling of an American Landscape, 1870–1903* (1999)

L. G. Moses, *Wild West Shows and the Images of American Indians, 1883–1933* (1996)

Walter Nugent and Martin Ridge, eds., *The American West: The Readers* (1999)

Paul Reddin, *Wild West Shows* (1999)

Mark David Spence, *Dispossessing the Wilderness: Indian Removal and the Making of the National Parks* (1999)

Richard Slotkin, *Gunfighter Nation: The Myth of the Frontier in 20th-Century America* (1992)

Richard White and Patricia Nelson Limerick, *The Frontier in American Culture* (1994)

Richard White, *"It's Your Misfortune and None of My Own": A History of the American West* (1991)

Donald Worcester, *Rivers of Empire: Water, Aridity, and the Growth of the American West* (1985)

Biography

Matthew Baigell, *Albert Bierstadt* (1981)

Louise Barnett, *Touched by Fire: The Life, Death, and Mythic Afterlife of George Armstrong Custer* (1996)

Robert W. Larson, *Red Cloud: Warrior-Statesman of the Lakota Sioux* (1997)

Joan T. Mark, *A Stranger in Her Native Land: Alice Fletcher and the American Indians* (1988)

Sarah R. Massey, ed., *Black Cowboys of Texas* (2000)

Valerie Mathes, *Helen Hunt Jackson and Her Indian Reform Legacy* (1990)

John G. Neihardt, *Black Elk Speaks: Being the Life Story of a Holy Man of the Oglala Sioux* (1961)

Elinore Pruitt Stewart, *Letters of a Woman Homesteader* (1914; 1989)

Edwin R. Sweeny, *Cochise, Chiricahua Apache Chief* (1991)

Jerry D. Thompson, ed., *Juan Cortina and the Texas-Mexico Frontier, 1859–1877* (1994)

Benson Tong, *Susan La Flesch Picotte, M.D.: Omaha Indian Leader and Reformer* (1999)

Robert M. Utley, *The Lance and the Shield: A Life and Times of Sitting Bull* (1993)

CHAPTER 19

Science, Technology, and Industry

David A. Hounshell, *From the American System to Mass Production, 1800–1932* (1984)

Walter Licht, *Industrializing America: The Nineteenth Century* (1995)

A. J. Millard, *Edison and the Business of Innovation* (1990)

Leonard S. Reich, *The Making of American Industrial Research: Science and Business at G. E. and Bell, 1876–1926* (1985)

Business and the Economy

Wendy Gambler, *The Female Economy: The Millinery and Dressmaking Trades, 1860–1930* (1997)

Naomi R. Lamoreaux, *The Great Merger Movement in American Business, 1895–1904* (1985)

Pamela Walker Laird, *Advertising Progress: American Business and the Rise of Consumer Marketing* (1998)

Daniel Nelson, *Managers and Workers: Origins of the Factory System in the United States, 1880–1920* (1975)

Sarah Lyons Watts, *Order against Chaos: Business Culture and Labor Ideology in America, 1800–1915* (1991)

William G. Roy, *Socializing Capital: The Rise of the Large Industrial Corporation in America* (1997)

Olivier Zunz, *Making America Corporate, 1870–1920* (1990)

Working Class and Labor

Eric Arnesen, *Waterfront Workers of New Orleans: Race, Class, and Politics, 1863–1923* (1991)

John Bodnar, *Immigration and Industrialization: Ethnicity in an American Mill Town* (1977)

Lisa M. Fine, *The Souls of the Skyscraper: Female Clerical Workers in Chicago, 1870–1930* (1990)

David M. Katzman, *Seven Days a Week: Women and Domestic Service in Industrializing America* (1978)

David Montgomery, *The Fall of the House of Labor: The Workplace, the State, and American Labor Activism, 1865–1925* (1987)

Daniel T. Rodgers, *The Work Ethic in Industrial America, 1850–1920* (1978)

Robert E. Weir, *Beyond Labor's Veil: The Culture of the Knights of Labor* (1996)

The Industrial City

John S. Garner, ed., *The Midwest in American Architecture* (1991)

Dolores Hayden, *The Grand Domestic Revolution: A History of Feminist Designs for American Homes, Neighborhoods, and Cities* (1981)

Scott Molloy, *Trolley Wars: Streetcar Workers on the Line* (1996)

Mark H. Rose, *Cities of Light and Heat: Domesticating Gas and Electricity in Urban America* (1995)

Roy Rosenzweig and Elizabeth Blackmar, *The Park and the People: A History of Central Park* (1993)

John R. Stilgoe, *Borderland: Origins of the American Suburb, 1820–1939* (1988)

The New South

Edward L. Ayers, *The Promise of the New South* (1992)

Don Doyle, *New Men, New Cities, New South* (1990)

Jacquelyn D. Hall, et al., *Like a Family: The Making of a Southern Cotton Mill World* (1987)

Tara W. Hunter, *To 'Joy My Freedom: Southern Black Women's Lives and Labors after the Civil War* (1997)

Gerald D. Jaynes, *Branches without Roots: Genesis of the Black Working Class in the American South, 1862–1882* (1986)

Cathy McHugh, *Mill Family: The Labor System in the Southern Textile Industry, 1880–1915* (1988)

Karin A. Shapiro, *A New South Rebellion: The Battle Against Convict Labor in the Tennessee Coalfields, 1871–1896* (1998)

Society and Culture

Elaine S. Abelson, *When Ladies Go A-Thieving* (1989)

Stuart Blumin, *The Emergence of the Middle Class* (1989)

Sarah Burns, *Inventing the Modern Artists: Art and Culture in Gilded Age America* (1999)

Yong Chen, *Chinese San Francisco, 1850–1943* (2000)

Priscilla Ferguson Clement, *Growing Pains: Children in the Industrial Age, 1850–1890* (1997)

Steven Conn, *Museums and American Intellectual Life, 1876–1926* (1998)

Perry Duis, *Challenging Chicago: Coping with Everyday Life, 1837–1920* (1998)

Katherine C. Grier, *Culture and Comfort: Parlor Making and Middle-Class Identity, 1850–1930* (1988, 1997)

Judy Hilkey, *Character Is Capital: Success Manuals and Manhood in Gilded Age America* (1997)

John F. Kasson, *Amusing the Millions: Coney Island at the Turn of the Century* (1978)

Lawrence W. Levine, *Highbrow/Lowbrow: The Emergence of Cultural Hierarchy in America* (1988)

Patricia Marks, *Bicycles, Bangs, and Bloomers: The New Woman in the Popular Press* (1990)

Steven A. Riess, *City Games: The Evolution of American Urban Society and the Rise of Sports* (1989)

Barbara M. Solomon, *In the Company of Educated Women: A History of Women and Higher Education in America* (1985)

Biography

Robert V. Bruce, *Alexander Graham Bell and the Conquest of Solitude* (1973)

Helen Lefkowitz Horowitz, *The Power and Passion of M. Carey Thomas* (1994)

Stuart B. Kaufman, *Samuel Gompers and the Rise of the American Federation of Labor, 1884–1896* (1973)

Murray Klein, *The Life and Legend of Jay Gould* (1986)

Robert C. Twombly, *Louis Sullivan* (1986)

Michael Zuckerman, *Almost Chosen People: Oblique Biographies in the American Grain* (1993)

CHAPTER 20

The Nation and Politics

Paula C. Baker, *The Moral Frameworks of Public Life: Gender, Politics and the State in Rural New York, 1870–1930* (1991)

Rebecca Edwards, *Angels in the Machinery: Gender in American Party Politics from the Civil War to the Progressive Era* (1997)

Michael Lewis Goldberg, *An Army of Women: Gender and Politics in Gilded Age Kansas* (1997)

J. William Harris, *Deep Souths: Delta, Piedmont, and Sea Island Society in the Age of Segregation* (2001)

Gwendolyn Mink, *Old Labor and New Immigrants in American Political Development* (1986)

Douglas Steeples and David O. Whitten, *Democracy in Desperation: The Depression of 1893* (1998)

Brook Thomas, *Plessy v. Ferguson: A Brief History with Documents* (1997)

David Traxel, *1898: The Birth of the American Century* (1998)

C. Vann Woodward, *The Strange Career of Jim Crow*, 3rd rev. ed. (1974)

Populism

Lawrence Goodwyn, *Democratic Promise: The Populist Moment in America* (1976)

Steven Hahn, *The Roots of Southern Populism* (1983)

Robert C. McMath, *American Populism: A Social History* (1993)

Scott G. McNall, *The Road to Rebellion: Class Formation and Kansas Populism 1865–1900* (1988)

Norman Pollack, *The Human Economy: Populism, Capitalism and Democracy* (1990)

Protest and Reform Movements

Susan Curtis, *A Consuming Faith: The Social Gospel and Modern American Culture* (1991)

Barbara Leslie Epstein, *The Politics of Domesticity: Women, Evangelism, and Temperance in Nineteenth-Century America* (1981)

Paul Krause, *The Battle for Homestead, 1880–1892* (1992)

Ralph E. Luker, *The Social Gospel in Black and White* (1991)

Alison M. Parker, *Purifying America: Women, Cultural Reform, and Pro-Censorship Activism* (1997)

Gretchen Ritter, *Goldbugs and Greenbacks: The Antimonopoloy Tradition and the Politics of Finance in America, 1865–1896* (1997)

Richard Schneirov, Shelton Stromquist, and Nick Salvatore, eds., *The Pullman Strike and the Crisis of the 1890s: Essays on Labor and Politics* (1999)

Carlos A. Schwantes, *Coxey's Army* (1985)

Imperialism and Empire

Tunde Adeleke, *Unafrican Americans: Nineteenth-Century Black Nationalists and the Civilizing Mission* (1998)

Nupur Chauduri and Margaret Strobel, eds., *Western Women and Imperialism* (1992)

Willard B. Gatewood, Jr., *Black Americans and the White Man's Burden* (1975)

Patricia Hill, *The World Their Household: The American Women's Foreign Mission Movement and Cultural Transformation, 1870–1920* (1985)

Amy Kaplan and Donald E. Pease, eds., *Cultures of United States Imperialism* (1993)

Robert W. Rydell, *All the World's a Fair: Vision of Empire at the American International Expositions, 1876–1916* (1984)

Anders Stephanson, *Manifest Destiny: American Expansion and the Empire of Right* (1995)

Spanish-American War and the Philippines

H. W. Brands, *Bound to Empire: The United States and the Philippines* (1992)

Kristin L. Hoganson, *Fighting for American Manhood: How Gendeer Politics Provoked the Spanish-American and Philippine-American Wars* (1998)

Stuart Creighton Miller, *"Benevolent Assimilation": The American Conquest of the Philippines, 1899–1903* (1982)

Ivan Musicant, *Empire By Default: The Spanish-American War and the Dawn of the American Century* (1998)

Louis A. Perez, Jr., *The War of 1898: The United States and Cuba in History and Historiography* (1998)

Harvey Rosenfeld, *Diary of a Dirty Little War: The Spanish-American War of 1898* (2000)

Angel Smith and Emma Davila-Cox, ed., *The Crisis of 1898: Colonial Redistribution and Nationalist Mobilization* (1999)

Biography

Ruth Bordin, *Frances Willard: A Biography* (1986)

Mari Jo Buhle, Paul Buhle, and Harvey J. Kaye, eds., *The American Radical* (1995)

Edward P. Crapol, *James G. Blaine: Architect of Empire* (2000)

Jane Taylor Nelson, *A Prairie Populist: The Memoirs of Luna Kellie* (1992)

Allan Peskin, *Garfield: A Biography* (1978)

Ben Procter, *William Randolph Hearst: The Early Years, 1863–1910* (1998)

Nick Salvatore, *Eugene V. Debs* (1982)

Peggy Samuels and Harold Samuels, *Teddy Roosevelt at San Juan: The Making of a President* (1997)

Mildred Thompson, *Ida B. Wells-Barnett: An Exploratory Study of an American Black Woman* (1990)

C. Van Woodward, *Tom Watson* (1963)

CHAPTER 21

The Currents of Progressivism

Walter M. Brasch, *Forerunners of Revolution: Muckrakers and the American Social Conscience* (1990)

John D. Buenker, *Urban Liberalism and Progressive Reform* (1973)

Mina Carson, *Settlement Folk: Social Thought and the American Settlement Movement, 1885–1930* (1990)

Leon Fink, *Progressive Intellectuals and the Dilemmas of Democratic Commitment* (1997)

Richard Hofstadter, *The Age of Reform: From Bryan to FDR* (1955)

James T. Kloppenberg, *Uncertain Victory: Social Democracy and Progressivism in European and American Thought, 1870–1920* (1986)

William A. Link, *The Paradox of Southern Progressivism, 1880–1930* (1992)

Richard McCormick, *The Party Period and Public Policy* (1986)

Robert Wiebe, *The Search for Order, 1877–1920* (1967)

Social Control and Its Limits

Paul M. Boyer, *Urban Masses and Moral Order in America, 1820–1920* (1978)

Eldon J. Eisenach, *The Lost Promise of Progressivism* (1994)

Ruth Rosen, *The Lost Sisterhood: Prostitutes in America, 1900–1918* (1982)

Andrea Tone, *The Business of Benevolence: Industrial Paternalism in Progressive America* (1997)

Working-Class Communities and Protest

John Bodnar, *The Transplanted* (1985)

James R. Green, *The World of the Worker: Labor in Twentieth Century America* (1980)

Alice Kessler-Harris, *Out to Work: A History of Wage Earning Women in the United States* (1982)

David Montgomery, *The Fall of the House of Labor* (1987)

Kathy Peiss, *Cheap Amusements: Working Women and Leisure in Turn of the Century New York* (1986)

Roy Rosenzweig, *Eight Hours for What We Will* (1983)

Ronald Takaki, *Strangers from a Different Shore: A History of Asian Americans* (1989)

Women's Movements and Black Awakening

Paula Baker, *The Moral Frameworks of Public Life* (1991)

Mari Jo Buhle, *Women and American Socialism* (1983)

Rebecca Edwards, *Angels in the Machinery: Gender in American Party Politics from the Civil War to the Progressive Era* (1997)

Linda Gordon, *Woman's Body, Woman's Right: A Social History of Birth Control* (1976)

Molly Ladd-Taylor, *Mother Work: Women, Child Welfare, and the State, 1890–1930* (1994)

National Progressivism

Kendrick A. Clements, *The Presidency of Woodrow Wilson* (1992)

John M. Cooper Jr., *The Warrior and the Priest: Theodore Roosevelt and Woodrow Wilson* (1983)

Lewis L. Gould, *The Presidency of Theodore Roosevelt* (1991)

Michael McGerr, *The Decline of Popular Politics* (1986)

Biography

Ellen Chesler, *Woman of Valor: Margaret Sanger and the Birth Control Movement in America* (1992)

Allen F. Davis, *American Heroine: The Life and Legend of Jane Addams* (1973)

Louis R. Harlan, *Booker T. Washington: Wizard of Tuskegee, 1901–1915* (1983)

J. Joseph Huthmacher, *Senator Robert F. Wagner and the Rise of Urban Liberalism* (1971)

David Levering Lewis, *W. E. B. Du Bois: Biography of a Race, 1868–1919* (1993)

Nick Salvatore, *Eugene V. Debs: Citizen and Socialist* (1982)

Patricia A. Schechter, *Ida B. Wells-Barnett and American Reform, 1880–1930* (2001)

Bernard A. Weisberger, *The LaFollettes of Wisconsin* (1994)

Robert Westbrook, *John Dewey and American Democracy* (1991)

CHAPTER 22

Becoming a World Power

Richard H. Collin, *Theodore Roosevelt's Caribbean* (1990)

Friedrich Katz, *The Secret War in Mexico* (1981)

Walter LaFeber, *The Panama Canal* (1978)

Lester E. Langley, *The Banana Wars: An Inner History of American Empire, 1900–1934* (1983)

Mary A. Renda, *Taking Haiti: Military Occupation and the Culture of U.S. Imperialism, 1915–1940* (2001)

The Great War

Lloyd E. Ambrosius, *Woodrow Wilson and the American Diplomatic Tradition* (1987)

Paul Fussell, *The Great War and Modern Memory* (1973)

Martin Gilbert, *The First World War: A Complete History* (1994)

James Joll, *The Origins of the First World War* (1984)

American Mobilization

A. E. Barbeau and Florette Henri, *The Unknown Soldiers: Black American Troops in World War I* (1974)

John W. Chambers, *To Raise an Army: The Draft in Modern America* (1987)

Edward M. Coffman, *The War to End All Wars* (1968)

Stephen Vaughn, *Holding Fast the Inner Lines: Democracy, Nationalism, and the Committee on Public Information* (1980)

Over Here

Allen J. Brandt, *No Magic Bullet: A Social History of Venereal Disease in the United States since 1880* (1985)

Leslie M. DeBauche, *Reel Patriotism: The Movies and World War I* (1997)

Frances R. Early, *A World Without War: How U.S. Feminists and Pacifists Resisted World War I* (1997)

Robert H. Ferrell, *Woodrow Wilson and World War I* (1985)

Margaret Mary Finnegan, *Selling Suffrage: Consumer Culture and Votes for Women* (1999)

Maureen Greenwald, *Women, War, and Work* (1980)

Ellis W. Hawley, *The Great War and the Search for Modern Order*, 2d ed. (1992)

Jeffrey Haydu, *Making American Industries Safe for Democracy* (1997)

David M. Kennedy, *Over Here* (1980)

David Montgomery, *The Fall of the House of Labor* (1987)

Barbara Steinson, *American Women's Activism in World War I* (1982)

Repression and Reaction

James P. Grossman, *Land of Hope: Chicago, Black Southerners, and the Great Migration* (1989)

Frederick C. Luebke, *Bonds of Loyalty: German Americans and World War I* (1974)

William Preston, Jr., *Aliens and Dissenters: Federal Suppression of Radicals, 1903–1933* (1966)

William M. Tuttle, Jr., *Race Riot: Chicago in the Red Summer of 1919* (1970)

An Uneasy Peace

Dana Frank, *Purchasing Power: Consumer Organizing, Gender, and the Seattle Labor Movement, 1919–1929* (1994)

Lloyd Gardner, *Safe for Democracy: The Anglo-American Response to Revolution, 1913–1923* (1984)

Robert D. Johnson, *The Peace Progressives and American Foreign Relations* (1995)

Richard Polenberg, *Fighting Faiths: The Abrams Case, the Supreme Court, and Free Speech* (1987)

Stuart Rochester, *American Liberal Disillusionment in the Wake of World War I* (1977)

Daniel D. Stid, *The President As Statesman: Woodrow Wilson and the Constitution* (1998)

Biography

Kendrick Clements, *Woodrow Wilson: World Statesman* (1987)

Ellen Carol Dubois, *Harriot Stanton Blatch and the Winning of Woman Suffrage* (1997)

Jordan Schwarz, *The Speculator: Bernard M. Baruch in Washington, 1917–1965* (1981)

Frank E. Vandiver, *Black Jack: The Life and Times of John J. Pershing* (1977)

Jacqueline van Voris, *Carrie Chapman Catt* (1987)

CHAPTER 23

Postwar Prosperity and Its Price

David Brody, *Workers in Industrial America* (1980)

Gilbert C. Fite, *Cotton Fields No More: Southern Agriculture, 1865–1980* (1984)

Kenneth T. Jackson, *Crabgrass Frontier* (1985)

William Leuchtenberg, *The Perils of Prosperity, 1914–1932* (1958)

Clay McShane, *Down the Asphalt Path* (1994)

Gwendolyn Wright, *Building the American Dream* (1981)

Gerald Zahavi, *Workers, Managers, and Welfare Capitalism* (1988)

The New Mass Culture

Beth A. Bailey, *From Front Porch to Back Seat: Courtship in Twentieth Century America* (1988)

Daniel J. Czitrom, *Media and the American Mind* (1982)

John D'Emilio and Estelle B. Freedman, *Intimate Matters: A History of Sexuality in America* (1988)

Susan J. Douglas, *Listening In: Radio and the American Imagination* (1999)

Michele Hilmes, *Radio Voices: American Broadcasting, 1922–1952* (1997)

Pamela Walker Laird, *Advertising Progress: American Business and the Rise of Consumer Marketing* (1998)

Jackson Lears, *Fables of Abundance: A Cultural History of Advertising in America* (1994)

Steven J. Ross, *Working Class Hollywood: Silent Film and the Shaping of Class in America* (1998)

Robert Sklar, *Movie Made America*, rev. ed. (1995)

The State, the Economy, and Business

Kendrick A. Clements, *Hoover, Conservation, and Consumerism: Engineering the Good Life* (2000)

Warren I. Cohen, *Empire without Tears* (1987)

Louis Galambos and Joseph Pratt, *The Rise of the Corporate Commonwealth* (1988)

John Earl Haynes, ed., *Calvin Coolidge and the Coolidge Era* (1998)

Roland Marchand, *Creating the Corporate Soul: The Rise of Public Relations and Corporate Imagery in American Big Business* (1998)

Charles L. Mee, *The Ohio Gang: The World of Warren G. Harding* (1981)

Resistance to Modernity

Katherine M. Blee, *Women and the Klan: Racism and Gender in the 1920s* (1991)

John Higham, *Strangers in the Land: Patterns of American Nativism, 1860–1925* (1955)

Thomas R. Pegram, *Battling Demon Rum: The Struggle for a Dry America, 1800–1933* (1998)

Promises Postponed

Ruth Schwartz Cowan, *More Work for Mother* (1982)

Ann Douglas, *Terrible Honesty: Mongrel Manhattan in the 1920s* (1995)

Nathan I. Huggins, *Harlem Renaissance* (1971)

Cary D. Mintz, *Black Culture and the Harlem Renaissance* (1988)

Kathy H. Ogren, *The Jazz Revolution: Twenties America and the Meaning of Jazz* (1989)

George J. Sanchez, *Becoming Mexican American* (1993)

Judith Stein, *The World of Marcus Garvey* (1985)

Biography

Edith L. Blumhofer, *Aimee Semple McPherson* (1993)

David Burner, *Herbert Hoover: The Public Life* (1979)

Robert Creamer, *Babe: The Legend Comes to Life* (1975)

Neal Gabler, Winchell: *Gossip, Power, and the Culture of Celebrity* (1994)

David Levering Lewis, *W. E. B. DuBois: The Fight for Equality and the American Century, 1919–1963* (2000)

Fred Hobson, *Mencken: A Life* (1994)

David Nasaw, *The Chief: The Life of William Randolph Hearst* (2000)

Arnold Rampersad, *The Life of Langston Hughes*, 2 vols. (1986–88)

David Robinson, *Chaplin* (1985)

Robert A. Slayton, *Empire Statesman: The Rise and Redemption of Al Smith* (2001)

CHAPTER 24

Hard Times

Michael A. Bernstein, *The Great Depression* (1987)

Michael D. Bordo, et.al., eds., *The Defining Moment: The Great Depression and the American Economy in the Twentieth Century* (1998)

Maury Klein, *Rainbow's End: The Crash of 1929* (2001)

Robert S. McElvaine, ed., *Down and Out in the Great Depression* (1983)

Jeff Singleton, *The American Dole: Unemployment Relief and the Welfare State in the Great Depression* (2000)

Studs Terkel, *Hard Times* (1970)

T. H. Watkins, *The Hungry Years: A Narrative History of the Great Depression in America* (1999)

FDR and the First New Deal

Steve Fraser and Gary Gerstle, eds., *The Rise and Fall of the New Deal Order* (1988)

William Leuchtenberg, *The FDR Years* (1995)

George McJimsey, *The Presidency of Franklin Delano Roosevelt* (2000)

James S. Olson, *Saving Capitalism* (1988)

Theodore M. Saloutos, *The American Farmer and the New Deal* (1982)

Left Turn and the Second New Deal

Irving Bernstein, *The Turbulent Years: A History of the American Worker, 1933–1941* (1970)

Alan Brinkley, *Voices of Protest: Huey Long, Father Coughlin, and the New Deal* (1982)

Gary Gerstle, *Working Class Americanism* (1989)

Kenneth J. Heineman, *A Catholic New Deal: Religion and Reform in Depression Pittsburgh* (1999)

Robin D. G. Kelley, *Hammer and Hoe: Alabama Communists during the Great Depression* (1990)

Robert H. Zieger, *The CIO, 1935–1955* (1995)

The New Deal and the West

James M. Gregory, *American Exodus: The Dust Bowl Migration and Okie Culture in California* (1989)

Laurence Kelly, *The Assault on Assimilation: John Collier and the Origins of Indian Policy Reform, 1920–1954* (1983)

Vicki Ruiz, *Cannery Women/Cannery Lives: Mexican Women, Unionization, and the California Food Processing Industry, 1930–1950* (1987)

Charles J. Shindo, *Dust Bowl Migrants in the American Imagination* (1997)

Kevin Starr, *Endangered Dreams: The Great Depression in California* (1996)

Donald Worster, *Dust Bowl* (1979)

Depression-Era Culture

Thomas P. Doherty, *Pre-Code Hollywood: Sex, Immorality, and Insurrection in American Cinema, 1930–1934* (1999)

Lewis A. Erenberg, *Swingin' the Dream: Big Band Jazz and the Rebirth of American Culture* (1998)

Vivian Gornick, *The Romance of American Communism* (1976)

Harvey Klehr, *The Heyday of American Communism* (1984)

Anthony W. Lee, *Painting on the Left* (1999)

Richard McKinzie, *The New Deal for Artists* (1973)

Barbara Melosh, *Engendering Culture: Manhood and Womanhood in New Deal Public Art and Theater* (1991)

Thomas Schatz, *The Genius of the System: Hollywood Filmmaking in the Studio Era* (1988)

William Stott, *Documentary Expression and Thirties America* (1973)

The Limits of Reform

Francisco E. Balderrama, *Decade of Betrayal: Mexican Repatriation in the 1930's* (1995)

Suzanne Mettler, *Dividing Citizens: Gender and Federalism in New Deal Public Works* (1998)

Mark Naison, *Communists in Harlem during the Depression* (1983)

Landon R. Y. Storrs, *Civilizing Capitalism: The National Consumers' League, Women's Activism, and Labor Standards in the New Deal Era* (2000)

Patricia Sullivan, *Days of Hope: Race and Democracy in the New Deal Era* (1996)

Susan Ware, *Beyond Suffrage: Women in the New Deal* (1981)

G. Edward White, *The Constitution and the New Deal* (2000)

Biography

Blanche W. Cook, *Eleanor Roosevelt: A Life* (1992)

Kenneth S. Davis, *FDR*, 4 vols. (1972, 1975, 1986, 1992)

Steven Fraser, *Labor Will Rule: Sidney Hillman and the Rise of American Labor* (1991)

June Hopkins, *Harry Hopkins: Sudden Hero, Brash Reformer* (1999)

J. Joseph Huthmacher, *Robert F. Wagner and the Rise of Urban Liberalism* (1968)

Nelson Lichtenstein, *The Most Dangerous Man in Detroit: Walter Reuther and the Fate of American Labor* (1995)

Naomi E. Pasachoff, *Frances Perkins: Champion of the New Deal* (1999)

Lois Scharf, *Eleanor Roosevelt* (1987)

Robert Zieger, *John L. Lewis* (1988)

CHAPTER 25

Coming of World War II

Akira Iriye, *The Origins of the Second World War in Asia and the Pacific* (1988)

Deborah Lipstadt, *Beyond Belief: The American Press and the Coming of the Holocaust, 1933–1945* (1992)

Ernest Mandel, *The Meaning of the Second World War* (1986)

Frank P. Mintz, *Revisionism and the Origins of Pearl Harbor* (1985)

Geoffrey S. Smith, *To Save a Nation* (1992)

Arsenal of Democracy and the Home Front

Karen Anderson, *Wartime Women* (1981)

Alison R. Bernstein, *American Indians and World War II* (1991)

Dominic J. Capeci and Martha Wilkerson, *Layered Violence: The Detroit Rioters of 1943* (1991)

Paul D. Casdorph, *Let the Good Times Roll: Life at Home in America during World War II* (1989)

Thomas Doherty, *Hollywood, American Culture and World War II* (1993)

Lewis A. Erenberg and Susan E. Hirsch, eds., *The War in American Culture: Society and Consciousness during World War II* (1996)

Rachel Waltner Goosen, *Women Against the Good War: Conscientious Objection and Gender on the American Home Front, 1941–1947* (1997)

John W. Jeffries, *Wartime America* (1996)

Gary Y. Okihiro, *Whispered Silences: Japanese Americans and World War II* (1996)

George H. Roeder, *The Censored War: American Visual Experience during World War II* (1993)

Lawrence R. Samuel, *Pledging Allegiance: American Identity and the Bond Drive of World War II* (1997)

Bartholomew H. Sparrow, *From the Outside In: World War II and the American State* (1996)

World at War

Alison Bernstein, *American Indians and World War II* (1991)

Conrad C. Crane, *Bombs, Cities, and Civilians* (1993)

John W. Dower, *War without Mercy* (1986)

Akira Iriye, *Power and Culture: The Japanese-American War, 1941–1945* (1981)

Lee Kennett, *G.I.: The American Soldier in World War II* (1987)

Eric Markusen and David Kopf, *The Holocaust and Strategic Bombing: Genocide and Total War in the Twentieth Century* (1995)

Peter Maslowski, *Armed with Cameras: The American Military Photographers of World War II* (1996)

Murray Williamson and Allan R. Millett, *A War to be Won: Fighting the Second World War* (2000)

Brenda L. Moore, *To Serve My Country: The Story of the Only African American WACS Stationed Overseas During World War II* (1996)

Barbara Brooks Tomblin, *G.I. Nightingales: The Army Nurse Corps in World War II* (1996)

Last Stages of War

John D. Chappell, *Before the Bomb: How America Approached the End of the Pacific War* (1997)

Lloyd C. Gardner, *Spheres of Influence: The Great Powers Partition Europe, from Munich to Yalta* (1993)

Peter Schrijvers, *The Crash of Ruin: American Combat Soldiers in Europe during World War II* (1998)

Michael S. Sherry, *The Rise of American Air Power* (1987)

Atomic Bomb

Gar Alperovitz, *The Decision to Use the Atomic Bomb and the Architecture of an American Myth* (1995)

Paul Boyer, *By the Bomb's Early Light: American Thought and Culture at the Dawn of the Atomic Age* (1985)

Peter Bacon Hales, *Atomic Spaces: Living on the Manhattan Project* (1997)

Ruth H. Howes, *Their Day in the Sun: Women of the Manhattan Project* (1999)

Samuel J. Walker, *Prompt and Utter Destruction: Truman and the Use of Atomic Bombs against Japan* (1997)

Eileen Welsome, *The Plutonium Files: America's Secret Medical Experiments in the Cold War* (1999)

Biography/Memoir

Stephen E. Ambrose, *Supreme Commander: War Years of General Dwight D. Eisenhower* (1970)

Mark M. Anderson, ed., *Hitler's Exiles: Personal Stories of the Flight from Nazi Germany to America* (1998)

Carlo D'Este, *Patton: A Genius for War* (1995)

Paula F. Pfeffer, *A. Philip Randolph* (1990)

John Hubbard Preston, *Apocalypse Undone: My Survival of Japanese Imprisonment during World War II* (1990)

Robert Underhill, *FDR and Harry: Unparalleled Lives* (1996)

CHAPTER 26

Global Insecurities and the Policy of Containment

Christian G. Appy, ed., *Cold War Constructions: The Political Culture of United States Imperialism, 1945–1966* (2000)

H. W. Brands, Jr., *The Devil We Knew: Americans and the Cold War* (1993)

Robert Frazier, *Anglo-American Relations with Greece: The Coming of the Cold War, 1942–47* (1991)

John Gaddis, *We Now Know: Rethinking Cold War History* (1997)

John L. Harper, *American Visions of Europe: Franklin D. Roosevelt, George F. Kennan, and Dean G. Acheson* (1995)

Walter Hixson, *Parting the Curtain: Propaganda, Culture, and the Cold War, 1945–1961* (1997)

Townsend Hoopes and Douglas Brinkley, *FDR and the Creation of the U.N.* (1997)

Walter LeFeber, *America, Russia, and the Cold War, 1945–1992*, 7th ed. (1993)

Richard Rhodes, *Dark Sun: The Making of the Hydrogen Bomb* (1995)

Michael Schaller, *American Occupation of Japan: The Origins of the Cold War in Asia* (1985)

The Truman Presidency

Gary A. Donaldson, *Truman Defeats Dewey* (1999)

Harold I. Gullan, *The Upset That Wasn't: Harry S. Truman and the Crucial Election of 1948* (1998)

Melvyn P. Leffler, *A Preponderance of Power: National Security, the Truman Administration, and the Cold War* (1992)

Sean J. Savage, *Truman and the Democratic Party* (1997)

The Cold War at Home

Noam Chomsky, ed., *The Cold War and the University: Toward an Intellectual History of the Postwar Years* (1997)

Larry Ceplair and Steven Englund, *The Inquisition in Hollywood: Politics in the Film Community, 1930–1960* (1980)

Sigmund Diamond, *Compromised Campus: The Collaboration of Universities with the Intelligence Communities, 1945–1995* (1992)

Michael J. Hogan, *A Cross of Iron: Harry S. Truman and the Origins of the National Security States, 1945–1954* (1998)

Scott Lucas, *Freedom's War: The U.S. Crusade Against the Soviet Union, 1945–56* (1999)

Elaine McClarnand and Steve Goodson, eds., *The Impact of the Cold War on American Popular Culture* (1999)

Lisle A. Rose, *The Cold War Comes to Main Street: America in 1950* (1999)

Ellen W. Schrecker, *No Ivory Tower: McCarthyism in the Universities* (1988)

Ellen Schrecker, *Many Are the Crimes: McCarthyism in America* (1998)

Age of Anxiety

Michael Barson, *"Better Dead Than Red!" A Nostalgic Look at the Golden Years of Russiaphobia, Red-Baiting, and Other Commie Madness* (1992)

Stuart W. Leslie, *The Cold War and American Science* (1993)

J. Fred MacDonald, *Television and the Red Menace* (1985)

Lary May, ed., *Recasting America: Culture and Politics in the Age of the Cold War* (1989)

Nora Sayre, *Running Time: Films of the Cold War* (1982)

Jessica Wang, *American Science in an Age of Anxiety: Scientists, Anticommunism, and the Cold War* (1999)

Korean War

William T. Bowers, William M. Hammond, George L. MacGarrigle, *Black Solider, White Army: The 24th Infantry Regiment in Korea* (1996)

Albert E. Cowdrey, *The Medics' War* (1987)

Stephen Endicott and Edward Hagerman, *The United States and Biological Warfare: Secrets from the Early Cold War and Korea* (1998)

Paul G. Pierpaoli, Jr., *Truman and Korea: The Political Culture of the Early Cold War* (1999)

Stanley Sandler, *The Korean War: No Victors, No Vanquished* (1999)

Biography

Allida M. Black, *Casting Her Own Shadow: Eleanor Roosevelt and the Shaping of Postwar Liberalism* (1996)

Martin Bauml Duberman, *Paul Robeson* (1988)

Curt Gentry, *J. Edgar Hoover: The Man and the Secrets* (1991)

Alonzo L. Hamby, *Man of the People: A Life of Harry Truman* (1995)

Arthur Herman, *Joseph McCarthy: Reexamining the Life and Legacy of America's Most Hated Senator* (1999)

Wilson D. Miscamble, *George F. Kennan and the Making of American Foreign Policy, 1947–1950* (1992)

Geoffrey Perret, *Old Soldiers Never Die: The Life of Douglas MacArthur* (1996)

Graham White and John Maze, *Henry A. Wallace: His Search for New World Order* (1995)

CHAPTER 27

American Society at Mid-Century

Stephanie Coontz, *The Way We Never Were* (1992)

John P. Diggins, *The Proud Decades: America in War and Peace, 1941–1960* (1988)

Benita Eisler, *Private Lives: Men and Women of the Fifties* (1986)

Delores Hayden, *Redesigning the American Dream* (1984)

Kenneth W. Olson, *The GI Bill, the Veterans, and the Colleges* (1974)

Youth Culture

Wini Breines, *Young, White, and Miserable: Growing Up Female in the Fifties* (1992)

Thomas Doherty, *Teen Pics* (1994)

Nelson George, *The Death of Rhythm and Blues* (1988)

William Graebner, *Coming of Age in Buffalo* (1990)

Douglas T. Miller and Marion Novak, *The Fifties: The Way We Really Were* (1977)

Jim Miller, *Flowers in the Dustbin: The Rise of Rock and Roll, 1947–1977* (1999)

Mass Culture and Its Discontents

Erik Barnouw, *Tube of Plenty* (1982)

Nancy E. Bernhard, *U.S. Television News and Cold War Propaganda, 1947–1960* (1999)

Joel Foreman, ed., *The Other Fifties: Interrogating Midcentury American Icons* (1997)

George Lipsitz, *Class and Culture in Cold War America* (1981)

J. Fred MacDonald, *Television and the Red Menace* (1985)

David Marc, *Demographic Vistas: Television and American Culture* (1984)

Lynn Spigel, *Make Room for TV* (1992)

Stephen J. Whitfield, *The Culture of the Cold War* (1991)

The Cold War Continued

James G. Blight and Peter Kornbluh, eds., *Politics of Illusion: The of Bay Pigs Invasion Reexamined* (1999)

Robert R. Bowie, *Waging Peace: How Eisenhower Shaped An Enduring Cold War Strategy* (1998)

Nick Cullather, *Secret History: The CIA's Classified Account of its Operations in Guatemala, 1952–1954* (1999)

Paul Dickson, *Sputnik: The Shock of the Century* (2001)

Piero Gleijeses, *Shattered Hope: The Guatemalan Revolution and the United States, 1944–1954* (1991)

Richard A. Melanson and David A. Mayers, eds., *Reevaluating Eisenhower* (1986)

John F. Kennedy and the New Frontier

Michael Beschloss, *The Crisis Years* (1991)

Thomas Brown, *JFK: The History of an Image* (1988)

Trumbull Higgins, *The Perfect Failure: Kennedy, Eisenhower and the CIA at the Bay of Pigs* (1988)

Walter LaFeber, *Inevitable Revolutions* (1983)

Thomas G. Paterson, ed., *Kennedy's Quest for Victory* (1989)

Gerald L. Posner, *Case Closed: Lee Harvey Oswald and the Assassination of JFK* (1993)

Richard E. Welch, Jr., *Response to Revolution: The United States and Cuba, 1959–1961* (1985)

Garry Wills, *The Kennedy Imprisonment* (1983)

Biography

Stephen Ambrose, *Eisenhower*, 2 vols. (1983, 1984)

Chuck Berry, *The Autobiography* (1987)

David Burner, *John F. Kennedy and a New Generation* (1988)

Carol George, *God's Salesman: Norman Vincent Peale and the Power of Positive Thinking* (1993)

Peter Guralnick, *Last Train to Memphis: The Rise of Elvis Presley* (1994)

Daniel Horowitz, *Betty Friedan and the Making of the Feminine Mystique* (1998)

Barry Miles, *Allen Ginsberg* (1989)

Gerald Nicosia, *Memory Babe: A Critical Biography of Jack Kerouac* (1983)

Geoffrey Perret, *Eisenhower* (1999)

CHAPTER 28

Origins of the Movements

Michael R. Belknap, *Federal Law and Southern Order* (1987)

Scott DeVeaux, *The Birth of BeBop* (1998)

Grace Elizabeth Hale, *Making Whiteness: The Culture of Segregation in the South, 1890–1940* (1998)

Charles P. Henry, *Ralph Bunche: Model Negro or American Other* (1999)

Grace Williams O'Brien, *The Color of the Law: Race, Violence, and Justice in the Post–World War II South* (1999)

Bernard Schwartz, *The NAACP's Legal Strategy against Segregated Education* (1987)

Mark Tushnet, *Making Civil Rights Law: Thurgood Marshall and the Supreme Court, 1936–1961* (1994)

Jules Tygiel, *Baseball's Great Experiment: Jackie Robinson and His Legacy* (1983)

No Easy Road to Freedom, 1957–62

Constance Curry, et.al., *Deep In Our Hearts: Nine White Women in the Freedom Movement* (2000)

John Dittmer, *Local People: The Struggle for Civil Rights in Mississippi* (1994)

James Farmer, *Lay Bare the Heart* (1985)

James Forman, *The Making of Black Revolutionaries* (1985)

David J. Garrow, *The FBI and Martin Luther King, Jr.* (1983)

Cheryl L. Greenberg, ed., *A Circle of Trust: Remembering SNCC* (1998)

Charles M. Payne, *I've Got the Light of Freedom: The Organizing Tradition and the Mississippi Freedom Struggle* (1995)

Miles Wolff, *Lunch at the 5&10* (1990)

Howard Zinn, *SNCC: The New Abolitionists* (1965)

The Movement at High Tide, 1963–65

Seth Cagin and Philip Dray, *We Are Not Afraid* (1988)

Henry Hampton and Steve Fayer, *Voices of Freedom: An Oral History of the Civil Rights Movement* (1990)

Doug McAdam, *Freedom Summer* (1988)

Belinda Robnett, *How Long? How Long? African American Women in the Struggle for Civil Rights* (1997)

Debra L. Schultz, *Going South: Jewish Women in the Civil Rights Movement* (2001)

Clive Webb, *Fight Against Fear: Southern Jews and Black Civil Rights* (2001)

Forgotten Minorities, 1945–65

Rodolfo Acuna, *Occupied America*, 3d ed. (1981)

Larry Burt, *Tribalism in Crisis: Federal Indian Policy, 1953–1961* (1982)

Thomas W. Conger, *The National Congress of American Indians* (1999)

Donald Fixico, *Termination and Relocation: Federal Indian Policy, 1945–1960* (1986)

Manuel G. Gonzalez, *Mexicanos: A History of Mexicans in the United States* (1999)

Gary Y. Okihiro, *The Columbia Guide to Asian American History* (2001)

David Palumbo–Liu, *Asian Americans: Historical Crossings of a Racial Frontier* (1999)

Maria E. Perez y Gonzalez, *Puerto Ricans in the United States* (2000)

Kenneth R. Philip, *Termination Revisited: American Indians on the Trail to Self Determination, 1933–1953* (1999)

Cora T. Whalen, *From Puerto Rico to Philadelphia: Puerto Rican Workers and Postwar Economies* (2001)

Biography

Robert Dallek, *Flawed Giant: Lyndon B. Johnson and His Times, 1961–1973* (1998)

Michael Eric Dyson, *I May Not Get There With You: The True Martin Luther King, Jr.* (2000)

David J. Garrow, *Bearing the Cross: Martin Luther King, Jr., and the Southern Christian Leadership Conference* (1986)

Joann Grant, *Ella Baker: Freedom Bound* (1998)

Chana Kai Lee, *For Freedom's Sake: The Life of Fannie Lou Hamer* (1999)

Daniel Levine, *Bayard Rustin and the Civil Rights Movement* (2000)

John Lewis, *Walking With the Wind: A Memoir of the Movement* (1998)

Malcolm X, with Alex Haley, *The Autobiography of Malcolm X* (1965)

CHAPTER 29

Vietnam: America's Longest War

Christian G. Appy, *Working-Class War: American Combat Soldiers in Vietnam* (1993)

Larry Berman, *No Peace, No Honor: Nixon, Kissinger, and Betrayal in Vietnam* (2001)

Robert Buzzanco, *Vietnam and the Transformation of American Life* (1999)

Kenton J. Clymer, *The Vietnam War: Its History, Literature and Music* (1998)

Gerald J. DeGroot, *A Noble Cause? America and the Vietnam War* (2000)

Virginia Elwood-Akers, *Women War Correspondents in the Vietnam War, 1961–1975* (1988)

William M Hammond, *Reporting Vietnam: Media and Military at War* (1998)

George C. Herring, *America's Longest War: The United States and Vietnam, 1950–1975*, 3rd ed. (1996)

——, ed., *The Pentagon Papers*, abridged ed. (1993)

Andrew E. Hunt, *The Turning: A History of Vietnam Veterans Against the War* (1999)

Jeffrey Kimball, *Nixon's Vietnam War* (1998)

Fredrik Logevall, *Choosing War: The Lost Chance for Peace and the Escalation of War in Vietnam* (1999)

Robert Mann, *A Grand Illusion: America's Descent into Vietnam* (2001)

James S. Olson and Randy Roberts, *My Lai: A Brief History with Documents* (1998)

Randy Shilts, *Conduct Unbecoming: Lesbians and Gays in the U.S. Military, Vietnam to the Persian Gulf* (1993)

Fred Turner, *Echoes of Combat: The Vietnam War in American Memory* (1996)

James E. Westheider, *Fighting on Two Fronts: African Americans and the Vietnam War* (1997)

A Generation in Conflict

David Allyn, *Make Love, Not War: The Sexual Revolution, Unfettered History* (2000)

Beth Baily, *Sex in the Heartland* (1999)

Alexander Bloom and Wini Breines, eds., *Takin' It to the Streets: A Sixties Reader* (1996)

Aniko Bodroghkozy, *Groove Tube: Sixties Television and the Youth Rebellion* (2001)

Wini Breines, *Community and Organization in the New Left* (1982)

David Farber, *The Age of Great Dreams: America in the 1960s* (1994)

James J. Farrell, *The Spirit of the Sixties: The Making of Postwar Radicalism* (1997)

Maurice Isserman and Michael Kazin, *America Divided: The Civil War of the 1960s* (2000)

Paul Lyons, *New Left, New Right, and the Legacy of the Sixties* (1996)

John C. McWilliams, *The 1960s Cultural Revolution* (2000)

Timothy Miller, *The 60s Communes: Hippies and Beyond* (1999)

George Rising, *Clean for Gene: Eugene McCarthy's 1968 Presidential Campaign* (1997)

William L. Van Deburg, *New Day in Babylon: The Black Power Movement and American Culture, 1965–1975* (1992)

The Politics of Identity

Kathleen C. Berkeley, *The Women's Liberation Movement in America* (1999)

Dudley Clendinen and Adam Nagourney, *Out for Good: The Struggle to Build a Gay Rights Movement in America* (1999)

Susan J. Douglas, *Where the Girls Are: Growing Up Female with the Mass Media* (1994)

Martin Duberman, *Stonewall* (1993)

Gerald Horne, *Fire This Time: The Watts Uprising and the 1960s* (1996)

Blance Linden-Ward, *American Women in the 1960s* (1992)

Marguerite V. Marin, *Social Protest in an Urban Barrio: A Study of the Chicano Movement, 1966–1972* (1991)

Peter Matthiessen, *In the Spirit of Crazy Horse* (1991)

Joane Nagel, *American Indian Ethnic Renewal: Red Power and the Resurgence of Identity and Culture* (1996)

Armando Navarro, *Mexican American Youth Organization: Avant-Garde of the Chicano Movement in Texas* (1995)

Rachel Blau De Plessis and Ann Snitow, *The Feminist Memoir Project: Voices from Women's Liberation* (1998)

The Nixon Presidency and Watergate

Mary C. Brennan, *Turning Right in the Sixties: The Conservative Capture of the GOP* (1995)

Carl Bernstein and Bob Woodward, *All the President's Men* (1974)

Leonard Garment, *In Search of Deep Throat: The Greatest Political Mystery of Our Time* (2000)

Lewis L. Gould, *1968: The Election That Changed America* (1993)

Allen J. Matusow, *Nixon's Economy: Booms, Busts, Dollars and Votes* (1998)

Michael Schudson, *Watergate in American History* (1992)

Biography

David L. Anderson, ed., *The Human Tradition in the Vietnam Era* (2000)

Elaine Brown, *A Taste of Power: A Black Woman's Story* (1992)

Jody Carlson, *George C. Wallace and the Politics of Powerlessness* (1981)

Robert Dallek, *Flawed Giant: Lyndon Johnson and His Times, 1961–1973* (1998)

Robert Alan Goldberg, *Barry Goldwater* (1995)

Elliot Gorn, ed., *Muhammed Ali: The People's Champ* (1996)

Daniel Horowitz, *Betty Friedan and the Making of the Feminine Mystique: The American Left, the Cold War, and Modern Feminism* (1998)

Joan Hoff, *Nixon Reconsidered* (1994)

Jonah Raskin, *For the Hell of It: The Life and Times of Abbie Hoffman* (1996)

Kenneth S. Stern, *Loud Hawk: The United States versus the American Indian Movement* (1994)

Evan Thomas, *Robert Kennedy: His Life* (2000)

Jack Todd, *Desertion: In the Time of Vietnam* (2001)

Irwin Unger and Debi Unger, *LBJ: A Life* (1999)

CHAPTER 30

Stagflation and the Oil Crisis

Michael A. Bernstein and David E. Adler, eds., *Understanding American Economic Decline* (1994)

Gordon L. Clark, *Unions and Communities under Siege* (1989)

Claudia Goldin, *Understanding the Gender Gap: An Economic History of American Women* (1990)

Burton I. Kaufman, *The Arab Middle East and the United States: Inter-Arab Rivalry and Superpower Diplomacy* (1996)

Paul Krugman, *Peddling Prosperity: Economic Sense and Nonsense in the Age of Diminished Expectations* (1994)

Bruce J. Schulman, *From Cotton Belt to Sun Belt* (1990)

Jon Teaford, *Cities of the Heartland: The Rise and Fall of the Industrial Midwest* (1993)

"Lean Year" Presidents

George C. Edwards III, *At the Margins: Presidential Leadership of Congress* (1989)

Gary M. Fink and Hugh Davis Graham, eds., *The Carter Presidency: Policy Choices in the Post-New Deal Era* (1998)

John Robert Greene, *The Presidency of Gerald R. Ford* (1995)

Alexander P. Lamis, *The Two-Party South*, 2nd ed. (1990)

Gary Sick, *October Surprise: America's Hostages in Iran and the Election of Ronald Reagan* (1991)

Grass-Roots Politics and the New Conservatism

Henry F. Bedford, *Seabrook Station: Citizen Politics and Nuclear Power* (1990)

Nicholas Dagen Bloom, *Suburban Alchemy: 1960s New Towns and the Transformation of the American Dream* (2001)

Elinor Burkett, *The Right Woman: A Journey Through the Heart of Conservative America* (1998)

Dan T. Carter, *From George Wallace to Newt Gingrich: Race in the Conservative Counterrevolution, 1963–1994* (1996)

Craig Cox, *Storefront Revolution: Food Co-ops and the Counterculture* (1994)

Betty A. Dobratz and Stephanie L. Shanks-Meile, *"White Power, White Pride!" The White Separatist Movement in the United States* (1997)

Susan Faludi, *Backlash: The Undeclared War Against American Women* (1991)

David Frum, *How We Got Here: The 70s, The Decade That Brought You Modern Life (For Better or Worse)* (2000)

Lois Gibbs, *Love Canal: The Story Continued* (1998)

Elsebeth Hurup, ed., *The Lost Decade: America in the Seventies* (1996)

William Martin, *With God on Our Side: The Rise of the Religious Right in America* (1996)

Donald G. Mathews and Jane S. De Hart, *Sex, Gender and the Politics of ERA* (1998)

Stephen Paul Miller, *The Seventies Now: Culture as Surveillance* (1999)

Gordana Rabrenovic, *Community Builders: A Tale of Neighborhood Mobilization in Two Cities* (1996)

David Brian Robertson, ed., *Loss of Confidence: Politics and Policy in the 1970s* (1998)

Suzanne Staggenborg, *The Pro-Choice Movement: Organization and Activism in the Abortion Conflict* (1991)

Foreign Policy

William J. Broad, *Teller's War: The Top-Secret Story behind the Star Wars Deception* (1992)

Beth A. Fischer, *The Reagan Reversal: Foreign Policy and the End of the Cold War* (1997)

Christopher Hemmer, *Which Lessons Matter? American Foreign Policy Decision Making in the Middle East, 1979–1987* (2000)

Timothy P. Maga, *The World of Jimmy Carter: U.S. Foreign Policy, 1977–1981* (1994)

Morris Morley, *Washington, Somoza and the Sandinistas: State and Regime in U.S. Policy toward Nicaragua, 1969–1981* (1994)

Bob Woodward, *Veil: The Secret Wars of the CIA* (1987)

The Reagan Revolution

Matthew Dallek, *The Right Moment: Ronald Reagan's First Victory and the Decisive Turning Point in American Politics* (2000)

Rowland Evans and Robert Novak, *The Reagan Revolution* (1991)

Nicholas Laham, *Ronald Reagan and the Politics of Immigration Reform* (2000)

Michael Schaller, *Reckoning with Reagan* (1992)

John W. Sloan, *The Reagon Effect: Economics and Presidential Leadership* (1999)

Best of Times, Worst of Times

James D. Cockcroft, *Outlaws in the Promised Land: Mexican Immigrant Workers and America's Future* (1986)

Barbara Ehrenreich, *Fear of Falling: The Inner Life of the Middle Class* (1989)

Elizabeth Fee and Daniel M. Fox, eds., *AIDS: The Making of a Chronic Disease* (1992)

Jacqueline Jones, *The Dispossessed: America's Underclasses from the Civil War to the Present* (1992)

Michael B. Katz, ed., *The "Underclass" Debate* (1993)

Hilda Scott, *Working Your Way to the Bottom: The Feminization of Poverty* (1985)

Randy Shilts, *And the Band Played On: Politics, People, and the AIDS Epidemic* (1987)

Ruth Sidel, *The Plight of Poor Women in Affluent America* (1986)

Lenore J. Weitzman, *The Divorce Revolution: The Unexpected Social and Economic Consequences for Women and Children in America* (1985)

Richard White, *Rude Awakenings: What the Homeless Crisis Tells Us* (1992)

Biography

Peter G. Bourne, *Jimmy Carter: A Comprehensive Biography From Plains to Postpresidency* (1997)

Jimmy Carter, *Keeping Faith: Memoirs of a President Jimmy Carter* (1982, 1995)

Rosalynn Carter, *First Lady from Plains* (1984)

Adam Clymer, *Edward M. Kennedy: A Biography* (1999)

Jim Cullen, *Born in the U.S.A.: Bruce Springsteen and the American Tradition* (1997)

Betty Ford, with Chris Chase, *Betty, A Glad Awakening* (1987)

Marshall Frady, *Jesse: The Life and Pilgrimage of Jesse Jackson* (1996)

Ernest B. Furgurson, *The Hard Right: The Rise of Jesse Helms* (1986)

Kitty Kelley, *Nancy Reagan* (1991)

Linda J. Lear, *Rachel Carson* (1997)

Peter Meyer, *Defiant Patriot: The Life and Exploits of Lt. Colonel Oliver L. North* (1987)

Edmund Morris, *Dutch: A Memoir of Ronald Reagan* (1999)

Wilbour C. Rich, *Coleman Young and Detroit Politics* (1988)

CHAPTER 31

Foreign Policy and International Affairs

Stephen F. Cohen, *Failed Crusade: America and the Tragedy of Post-Communist Russia* (2000)

John L. Gaddis, *The United States and the End of the Cold War* (1992)

David Halberstam, *War in a Time of Peace: Bush, Clinton, and the Generals* (2001)

Avigdor Haselkorn, *The Continuing Storm: Iraq, Poisonous Weapons and Deterrence* (1999)

Richard Hallion, *Storm over Iraq* (1992)

Elaine Landau, *Osama Bin Laden: A War Against the West* (2002)

Tomas W. Lippman, *Madeleine Albright and the New American Diplomacy* (2000)

Robert Litwack, *Rogue States and U.S. Foreign Policy: Containment After the Cold War* (1999)

David Moslery and Bob Catley, *Global America: Imposing Liberalism on a Recalcitrant World* (2000)

Alvin A. Rubinstein, Albina Shayevich, and Boris Zlotnikov, eds., *The Clinton Foreign Policy Reader: Presidential Speeches with Commentary* (2000)

Jeff Wheelwright, *The Irritable Heart: The Medical Mystery of the Gulf War* (2001)

The New Economy

Paul Andrew, *How the Web Was Won* (1999)

Michael A. Bernstein and David A. Adler, eds., *Understanding American Economic Decline* (1994)

Michael Lewis, *The New New Thing: A Silicon Valley Story* (2000)

Ted G. Lewis, *Microsoft Rising and Other Tales of Silicon Valley* (1999)

Robert H. Reid, *Architects of the Web* (1997)

Bob Woodward, *Maestro: Greenspan's Fed and the American Boom* (2000)

Changing American Communities

David Brooks, *Bobos in Paradise: The New Upper Class and How They Got There* (2000)

Helen Hayes, *U.S. Immigration and the Undocumented: Ambivalent Lives, Furtive Lives* (2001)

Denis Lynn Daly Heyck, ed., *Barrios and Borderlands: Cultures of Latinos and Latinas in the United States* (1993)

Bill Ong Hing, *Making and Remaking Asian America through Immigration Policy, 1850–1990* (1993)

J. Eric Oliver, *Democracy in Suburbia* (2001)

Adam Ward Rome, *The Bulldozer in the Countryside: Suburban Sprawl and the Rise of American Environmentalism* (2001)

Reed Ueda, *Postwar Immigrant America* (1994)

New Age of Anxiety

Jewelle Taylor Gibbs, *Race and Justice: Rodney King and O. J. Simpson in a House Divided* (1996)

Chester Hartman, ed., *Double Exposure: Poverty and Race in America* (1997)

James D. Hunter, *Culture Wars: The Struggle to Define America* (1991)

Randall Kennedy, *Race, Crime, and the Law* (1997)

Lawrence Levine, *The Opening of the American Mind: Canons, Culture, and History* (1996)

Andrea McArdle and Tanya Erzen, eds., *Zero Tolerance: Quality of Life and the New Police Brutality in New York City* (2001)

Brigitte Nacos, *Terrorism and the Media* (1994)

Christian Parenti, *Lockdown America: Police and Prisons in the Age of Crisis* (1999)

David M. Reimers, *Unwelcome Strangers: American Identity and the Turn Against Immigration* (1998)

Roger Simon, *Divided We Stand: How Al Gore Beat George Bush and Lost the Presidency* (2001)

Robert C. Smith, *Racism in the Post-Civil Rights Era* (1995)

James D. Tabor and Eugene V. Gallagher, *Why Waco? Cults and the Battle for Religious Freedom in America* (1995)

The Clinton Presidency

Lauren Berlant and Lisa Duggan, eds., *Our Monica, Ourselves: The Clinton Affair and the National Interest* (2001)

Vincent Bugliosi, *The Betrayal of America: How the Supreme Court Undermined the Constitution and Chose Our President* (2001)

Colin Campbell and Bert A. Rockman, eds., *The Clinton Legacy* (1999)

James Carville, *Stickin': The Case for Loyalty* (2000)

Joe Conason and Gene Lyons, *The Hunting of the President: The Ten Year Campaign to Destroy Bill and Hillary Clinton* (2000)

Richard A. Posner, *An Affair of State: The Investigation, Impeachment, and Trial of President Clinton* (1999)

Steven E. Schier, ed., *The Postmodern Presidency: Bill Clinton's Legacy in U.S. Politics* (2000)

Susan Schmidt and Micahel Weisskopt, *Truth at Any Cost: Ken Starr and the Unmaking of Bill Clinton* (2000)

Hanes Walton, Jr., *Reelection: William Jefferson Clinton as a Native-Son Presidential Candidate* (2000)

Bob Woodward, *The Agenda: Inside the Clinton White House* (1994)

Biography

John Robert Greene, *The Presidency of George Bush* (2000)

Harry Hurt, *The Lost Tycoon: The Many Lives of Donald J. Trump* (1993)

Molly Ivins and Lou Dubose, *Shrub: The Short But Happy Political Life of George W. Bush* (2000)

Faith Karlene, *Madonna, Bawdy & Soul* (1997)

David Maraniss, *First in His Class: A Biography of Bill Clinton* (1995)

Joyce Milton, *The First Partner: Hillary Rodham Clinton* (1999)

Roger Morris, *Partners in Power: The Clintons and Their America* (1996)

Gerald L. Posner, *Citizen Perot: His Life and Times* (1996)

Richard A. Serrano, *One of Ours: Timothy McVeigh and the Oklahoma City Bombing* (1998)

Mel Steely, *The Gentleman from Georgia: The Biography of Newt Gingrich* (2000)

Globalization

Walden Bello, *The Future in the Balance* (2001)

Jeremy Brecher, Tim Costello, and Brandan Smith, *Globalization From Below* (2000)

Alexander Cockburn, Jeffrey St. Clair, and Alan Sekula, *Five Days That Shook the World: The Battle for Seattle and Beyond* (2001)

Anthony Giddens, *Runaway World* (1999)

Edward S. Herman and Robert W. McChesney, *The Global Media: The New Missionaries of Corporate Capitalism* (1997)

Joshua Karliner, *The Corporate Planet: Ecology and Politics in the Age of Globalization* (1997)

Margaret Keck and Kathryn Sikkink, *Activists Beyond Borders: Advocacy Networks in International Politics* (1998)

Amory Starr, *Naming the Enemy: Anti-Corporate Movements Confront Globalization* (2001)

John D. Wirth, *Smelter Smoke in North America: The Politics of Transborder Pollution* (2000)

Michael Hardt and Antonio Negri, *Empire* (2000)

TEXT CREDITS

INDEX

U

V

SINGLE PC LICENSE AGREEMENT AND LIMITED WARRANTY

READ THIS LICENSE CAREFULLY BEFORE OPENING THIS PACKAGE. BY OPENING THIS PACKAGE, YOU ARE AGREEING TO THE TERMS AND CONDITIONS OF THIS LICENSE. IF YOU DO NOT AGREE, DO NOT OPEN THE PACKAGE. PROMPTLY RETURN THE UNOPENED PACKAGE AND ALL ACCOMPANYING ITEMS TO THE PLACE YOU OBTAINED THEM.

1. GRANT OF LICENSE and OWNERSHIP: The enclosed computer programs ("Software") are licensed, not sold, to you by Prentice-Hall, Inc. ("We" or the "Company") and in consideration of your purchase or adoption of the accompanying Company textbooks and/or other materials, and your agreement to these terms. We reserve any rights not granted to you. You own only the disk(s) but we and/or our licensors own the Software itself. This license allows you to use and display your copy of the Software on a single computer (i.e., with a single CPU) at a single location for academic use only, so long as you comply with the terms of this Agreement. You may make one copy for back up, or transfer your copy to another CPU, provided that the Software is usable on only one computer.

2. RESTRICTIONS: You may not transfer or distribute the Software or documentation to anyone else. Except for backup, you may not copy the documentation or the Software. You may not network the Software or otherwise use it on more than one computer or computer terminal at the same time. You may not reverse engineer, disassemble, decompile, modify, adapt, translate, or create derivative works based on the Software or the Documentation. You may be held legally responsible for any copying or copyright infringement which is caused by your failure to abide by the terms of these restrictions.

3. TERMINATION: This license is effective until terminated. This license will terminate automatically without notice from the Company if you fail to comply with any provisions or limitations of this license. Upon termination, you shall destroy the Documentation and all copies of the Software. All provisions of this Agreement as to limitation and disclaimer of warranties, limitation of liability, remedies or damages, and our ownership rights shall survive termination.

4. LIMITED WARRANTY AND DISCLAIMER OF WARRANTY: Company warrants that for a period of 60 days from the date you purchase this SOFTWARE (or purchase or adopt the accompanying textbook), the Software, when properly installed and used in accordance with the Documentation, will operate in substantial conformity with the description of the Software set forth in the Documentation, and that for a period of 30 days the disk(s) on which the Software is delivered shall be free from defects in materials and workmanship under normal use. The Company does not warrant that the Software will meet your requirements or that the operation of the Software will be uninterrupted or error-free. Your only remedy and the Company's only obligation under these limited warranties is, at the Company's option, return of the disk for a refund of any amounts paid for it by you or replacement of the disk. THIS LIMITED WARRANTY IS THE ONLY WARRANTY PROVIDED BY THE COMPANY AND ITS LICENSORS, AND THE COMPANY AND ITS LICENSORS DISCLAIM ALL OTHER WARRANTIES, EXPRESS OR IMPLIED, INCLUDING WITHOUT LIMITATION, THE IMPLIED WARRANTIES OF MERCHANTABILITY AND FITNESS FOR A PARTICULAR PURPOSE. THE COMPANY DOES NOT WARRANT, GUARANTEE OR MAKE ANY REPRESENTATION REGARDING THE ACCURACY, RELIABILITY, CURRENTNESS, USE, OR RESULTS OF USE, OF THE SOFTWARE.

5. LIMITATION OF REMEDIES AND DAMAGES: IN NO EVENT, SHALL THE COMPANY OR ITS EMPLOYEES, AGENTS, LICENSORS, OR CONTRACTORS BE LIABLE FOR ANY INCIDENTAL, INDIRECT, SPECIAL, OR CONSEQUENTIAL DAMAGES ARISING OUT OF OR IN CONNECTION WITH THIS LICENSE OR THE SOFTWARE, INCLUDING FOR LOSS OF USE, LOSS OF DATA, LOSS OF INCOME OR PROFIT, OR OTHER LOSSES, SUSTAINED AS A RESULT OF INJURY TO ANY PERSON, OR LOSS OF OR DAMAGE TO PROPERTY, OR CLAIMS OF THIRD PARTIES, EVEN IF THE COMPANY OR AN AUTHORIZED REPRESENTATIVE OF THE COMPANY HAS BEEN ADVISED OF THE POSSIBILITY OF SUCH DAMAGES. IN NO EVENT SHALL THE LIABILITY OF THE COMPANY FOR DAMAGES WITH RESPECT TO THE SOFTWARE EXCEED THE AMOUNTS ACTUALLY PAID BY YOU, IF ANY, FOR THE SOFTWARE OR THE ACCOMPANYING TEXTBOOK. BECAUSE SOME JURISDICTIONS DO NOT ALLOW THE LIMITATION OF LIABILITY IN CERTAIN CIRCUMSTANCES, THE ABOVE LIMITATIONS MAY NOT ALWAYS APPLY TO YOU.

6. GENERAL: THIS AGREEMENT SHALL BE CONSTRUED IN ACCORDANCE WITH THE LAWS OF THE UNITED STATES OF AMERICA AND THE STATE OF NEW YORK, APPLICABLE TO CONTRACTS MADE IN NEW YORK, AND SHALL BENEFIT THE COMPANY, ITS AFFILIATES AND ASSIGNEES. HIS AGREEMENT IS THE COMPLETE AND EXCLUSIVE STATEMENT OF THE AGREEMENT BETWEEN YOU AND THE COMPANY AND SUPERSEDES ALL PROPOSALS OR PRIOR AGREEMENTS, ORAL, OR WRITTEN, AND ANY OTHER COMMUNICATIONS BETWEEN YOU AND THE COMPANY OR ANY REPRESENTATIVE OF THE COMPANY RELATING TO THE SUBJECT MATTER OF THIS AGREEMENT. If you are a U.S. Government user, this Software is licensed with "restricted rights" as set forth in subparagraphs (a)-(d) of the Commercial Computer-Restricted Rights clause at FAR 52.227-19 or in subparagraphs (c)(1)(ii) of the Rights in Technical Data and Computer Software clause at DFARS 252.227-7013, and similar clauses, as applicable.

Should you have any questions concerning this agreement please contact in writing: Legal Department, Prentice Hall, One Lake Street, Upper Saddle River, NJ 07458. If you need assistance with technical difficulties, call: 1-800-677-6337. If you wish to contact the Company for any reason, please contact in writing: Customer Service, Prentice Hall, One Lake Street, Upper Saddle River, NJ 07458.